FIGHTER UNITS & PILOTS OF THE 8TH AIR FORCE:
*Volume 1: Day-to-Day Operations • Fighter Group Histories*
*Volume 2: Aerial Victory Lists • Ace Data*

# FIGHTER UNITS & PILOTS OF THE 8TH AIR FORCE

*September 1942 - May 1945*

## VOLUME 1

Day-to-Day Operations • Fighter Group Histories

Kent D. Miller

**Schiffer Military History**
Atglen, PA

**Dust jacket artwork by Steve Ferguson, Colorado Springs, CO.**

**PETERSON'S PROOF**

Shown is the P-51 of Capt. Richard Peterson of the 364th Fighter Squadron, 357th Fighter Group, the "Yoxford Boys." On May 13, 1944, Peterson's squadron, along with elements of the 355th FG, escorted First Bombardment Wing B-17s into central Germany on the first leg of a strike against oil plants at distant Poznan, Poland. Heavily armed Me 410s of II./ZG 26 rose up near Grunberg and tracked the bombers briefly in order to gain altitude and the cover of the sun. The Mustangs cut them off at the onset of their attack and in the melee, Flight Leader Peterson claimed one Me 410 shot down and another heavily damaged.

**Dedication**

These volumes are dedicated to my very patient and understanding wife, Hannah, and to my children, Evan and Jenna. Thank you for giving me the time to pursue my interest. They are also dedicated to all those who served in the 8th Air Force, and especially to those who paid the ultimate price for their country. God bless.

Kent D. Miller
Hicksville, Ohio
June 2000

Book design by Robert Biondi.


Library of Congress Catalog Number: 00-106806.



Printed in China.
ISBN: 0-7643-1241-3



Published by Schiffer Publishing Ltd.
4880 Lower Valley Road
Atglen, PA 19310
Phone: (610) 593-1777
FAX: (610) 593-2002
E-mail: Schifferbk@aol.com.
Visit our web site at: www.schifferbooks.com
Please write for a free catalog.
This book may be purchased from the publisher.
Please include $3.95 postage.
Try your bookstore first.

In Europe, Schiffer books are distributed by:
Bushwood Books
6 Marksbury Ave.
Kew Gardens
Surrey TW9 4JF
England
Phone: 44 (0)208 392-8585
FAX: 44 (0)208 392-9876
E-mail: Bushwd@aol.com.
Free postage in the UK. Europe: air mail at cost.
Try your bookstore first.

# Contents

# Introduction

The American 8th Air Force was the largest and most publicized organization in the Army Air Force during World War Two. Flying from bases in England for a little over three and a half years, the 8th's heavy bombers carried out a strategic bombing campaign against Germany. The fighter groups assigned to the 8th played a three part role: first and foremost was the escort and protection of the B-17's and B-24's; secondly, they were to hunt out and destroy the Luftwaffe, whether in aerial battles or by strafing German airfields; and thirdly, to act as a long-range striking arm against enemy transportation and defensive targets. While not as deeply involved in ground attacks as their counterparts in the 9th Air Force, the 8th's fighter pilots racked up an impressive score, with approximate claims of 4,374-2,979 locomotives, 6,970-24,971 railcars, 4,738-3,603 vehicles, 42-922 vessels (barges, tugs, ships, etc.), and 314-521 flak positions/towers. In addition, numerous other targets, including hangars, buildings, and bridges, were also destroyed or damaged.

Against the Luftwaffe, the 8th's pilots claimed 5160.6 aerial and 4108.75 ground victories, while total losses to all causes was 2,145 Spitfires, Thunderbolts, Lightnings, and Mustangs. A further 204 pilots were killed in accidents from the beginning of combat until the late summer of 1945. Not included in the latter number are the pilots who died while attached to the 495th and 496th Fighter Training Groups prior to being assigned to a combat unit.

The following volumes comprise a statistical summary of all fighter operations undertaken by the 8th Air Force's fighter units from September of 1942 through May of 1945. Not included are the units assigned to the 8th in mid-1942 which were eventually sent to North Africa with the 12th Air Force. While some sorties were flown and a few claims were made, the start of operations for this book begins with the formation of the 4th Fighter Group in September of 1942.

*Volume I* is a chronological listing of day-to-day operations with the following information for each date: groups involved, a short summary of the day's missions, air and ground claims, details of losses, strafing claims, pilots killed in accidents, and crash-landings, bail-outs, etc. Also, the beginning of Volume I has a number of tables covering the 8th's fighter operations. Of note is the scoring system used; 0-0-0 air is read as destroyed-probable-damaged while 0-0 ground is destroyed-damaged. Volume I also includes a breakdown of each group into individual mini-histories. Details include a short summary of the unit, Group and Squadron CO's, aircraft markings, a statistical history, scorers, list of day-to-day scoring and losses, pilot rosters, and representative aircraft.

*Volume II* is an alphabetical listing of all aerial victory scorers with their claims. Volume II also deals with all of the 8th Air Force aces. In addition to various tables and lists, each ace has his own section with information concerning combat career.

A great number of people, veterans and non-veterans alike, have helped me in putting this story together. They are listed here, in no particular order, with my sincerest thanks for their assistance. Unfortunately, a number of the veterans have passed away since their contribution and failed to see this end result. Again, thank you all: Frank Birtciel, Wilton Johnson, Clyde Taylor, Donald McGee, Joseph Myers, Frank McCauley, Randel Murphy, Harry Corey, Vernon Rafferty, Harold Comstock, Myron Becraft, George Butler, Robert Johnson, John McGinn, Fred Alexander, Sidney Hewett, Dale Karger, Charles Elmgren, Roy Evans, Edward Kier, Robert Winks, Walter Sharbo, Vic Byers, Ray Bank, Jack Ilfrey, Frank Emory, William Allen, Clifford Armstrong, Carroll Henry, Thomas Hayes, Wayne Blickenstaff, Leslie Smith, Ed Pogue, William Beyer, George Witzel, Arthur Jeffrey, Herb Rutland, Huie Lamb, Michael Yannell, John Truluck, Ken Hansen, James Carter, Richard Conner, Donald Henley, Russell Haworth, Vincent Zettler, Edward Kulik, Richard Peterson, Andrew Evans, William Jordan, John Kirk, David Thwaites, Lowell Einhaus, Richard Gibbs, Frank Gailer, Claude Chinn, Francis Harrington, Walter Cook, Richard Hewitt, Edwin Reinhardt, Ernest Hopcroft, William Wilkerson, Billy Edens, Horace Waggoner, Donald Baccus, Robert Wright, Clifford Ashby, Robert Hatter, Jack Price, Wallace Hopkins, George Doersch, Robert Wright, John Pugh, Jerome Nagel, Robert Schimanski, William Price, William Bailey, Ray Greenwood, Verne Hooker, Robert T. Green, William Tanner, Leedom John, Melville Hightshoe, Gerald Miller, Richard Davis, Ray Friend, John Taylor, Travis Greenwood, Norbert Fisher, George Sykes, Nelson Butler, Fred McClanahan, Joseph Fulton, Edward Beaumont, Roger Mooers, Jack Mengle, Max Victor, Lloyd Lamouria, Merle Olmsted, Robert Strobell, Jerry Brasher, Harvey Mace, Richard Thieme, Burton Newmark, Ray Shewfelt, Robert Unangst, Charles Whitefield, David James, Robert Cherry, Thaddeus Buszko, Peter Randall, James Heard, Don Olander, Richard J. Davis, Anthony Chardella, Robert Clark, Joseph DeShay, Vic Plassenthal, Amos Bomberger, Vernon Davis, Richard Shults, James Frolking, Clayborn Burleson, Avery Goodrich, Alvin Walther, Richard Ozinga, Reuben Curtis, James Seibert, Carl Tucker, Stephen Kefalas, John Earnest, Milford Hater, Harmon Wheeler, Robert Pinson, Robert Jensen, Millard Easton, Earl Storer, Irving Gittin, John Warner, George Roepke, Ray Hall, Robert Krull, Clyde Bergman, Leo Lester, Jenny Blue, Al Richards, Marc Hamel, James Reid, Mark Frailey, Ron Smith, Doug and Harold Daniel, Dave Raphael, Jack Johnston, Dave McCloskey, Mike Miller, James Underwood, Joe McGorry, Mrs. William J. Sykes, Mrs. Einar A. Malmstrom, Henry Selib, James Woolnough, David Knight, Melvin Jackson, Robert Foose, Tom Ivie, James Crow, Tom Frisque, Steve Knauff, William Hess, the USAF Museum, the USAF Historical Center, and the 8th Air Force Association. Finally, a very special thank you to Ted Damick, a friend and invaluable consultant on the 8th's fighter aircraft. To any others I have forgotten to mention, excuse me, but thank you for your help as well.

## Total Days on Operations

| | |
|---|---|
| **September 1942** | 3 |
| **October** | 14 |
| **November** | 15 |
| **December** | 18 |
| **January 1943** | 19 |
| **February** | 20 |
| **March** | 28 |
| **April** | 10 |
| **May** | 21 |
| **June** | 16 |
| **July** | 15 |
| **August** | 14 |
| **September** | 15 |
| **October** | 15 |
| **November** | 12 |
| **December** | 14 |
| **January 1944** | 13 |
| **February 1944** | 20 |
| **March** | 24 |
| **April** | 23 |
| **May** | 27 |
| **June** | 28 |
| **July** | 30 |
| **August** | 26 |
| **September** | 26 |
| **October** | 19 |
| **November** | 21 |
| **December** | 21 |
| **January 1945** | 24 |
| **February** | 25 |
| **March** | 29 |
| **April** | 21 |
| **May** | 3 |
| | 629 |

**Total 1942** ............ 50
**Total 1943** .......... 199
**Total 1944** .......... 278
**Total 1945** .......... 102

**Total** .................. 629

## 8th Air Force Fighter Group Victory/Loss Percentages

| **Group** | **Air** | | **Ground** | | **Losses** | |
|---|---|---|---|---|---|---|
| 4th | 550 | (10.66%) | 461.25 | (11.22%) | 242 | (11.35%) |
| 20th | 210.6 | (4.08%) | 226.5 | (5.51%) | 145 | (6.73%) |
| 55th | 302.5 | (5.86%) | 266 | (6.47%) | 185 | (8.69%) |
| 56th | 665.5 | (12.9%) | 320.5 | (7.8%) | 139 | (6.5%) |
| 78th | 326 | (6.31%) | 342.5 | (8.32%) | 188 | (8.73%) |
| 339th | 236.5 | (4.58%) | 431 | (10.49%) | 105 | (4.9%) |
| 352nd | 502.67 | (9.74%) | 275 | (6.69%) | 115 | (5.32%) |
| 353rd | 328 | (6.36%) | 404.5 | (9.84%) | 141 | (6.59%) |
| 355th | 340 | (6.59%) | 494.5 | (12.03%) | 179 | (8.36%) |
| 356th | 200 | (3.88%) | 77 | (1.87%) | 115 | (5.37%) |
| 357th | 595.5 | (11.54%) | 107 | (2.6%) | 139 | (6.5%) |
| 358th | 1 | (0.0005%) | 0 | (0%) | 4 | (0.187%) |
| 359th | 245 | (4.74%) | 117 | (2.84%) | 127 | (5.93%) |
| 361st | 221 | (4.28%) | 111 | (2.7%) | 91 | (4.3%) |
| 364th | 262 | (5.07%) | 191 | (4.65%) | 138 | (6.16%) |
| 479th | 155 | (3.0%) | 268 | (6.52%) | 77 | (3.6%) |
| SF | 16 | (0.31%) | 5 | (0.121%) | 13 | (0.56%) |
| Ftr Wg | 3.33 | (0.06%) | 6.5 | (0.158%) | 2 | (0.093%) |
| **Total** | **5160.6** | | **4108.75** | | **2,145** | |

## Group Losses

| | 4th | 20th | 55th | 56th | 78th | 339th | 352nd | 353rd | 355th | 356th | 357th | 358th | 359th | 361st | 364th | 479th | SFs | FWs |
|---|---|---|---|---|---|---|---|---|---|---|---|---|---|---|---|---|---|---|
| **Sept.1942** | 12 | 0 | 0 | 0 | 0 | 0 | 0 | 0 | 0 | 0 | 0 | 0 | 0 | 0 | 0 | 0 | 0 | 0 |
| **Oct.** | 1 | 0 | 0 | 0 | 0 | 0 | 0 | 0 | 0 | 0 | 0 | 0 | 0 | 0 | 0 | 0 | 0 | 0 |
| **Nov.** | 1 | 0 | 0 | 0 | 0 | 0 | 0 | 0 | 0 | 0 | 0 | 0 | 0 | 0 | 0 | 0 | 0 | 0 |
| **Dec.** | 0 | 0 | 0 | 0 | 0 | 0 | 0 | 0 | 0 | 0 | 0 | 0 | 0 | 0 | 0 | 0 | 0 | 0 |
| **Jan.1943** | 2 | 0 | 0 | 0 | 0 | 0 | 0 | 0 | 0 | 0 | 0 | 0 | 0 | 0 | 0 | 0 | 0 | 0 |
| **Feb.** | 2 | 0 | 0 | 0 | 0 | 0 | 0 | 0 | 0 | 0 | 0 | 0 | 0 | 0 | 0 | 0 | 0 | 0 |
| **Mar.** | 1 | 0 | 0 | 0 | 0 | 0 | 0 | 0 | 0 | 0 | 0 | 0 | 0 | 0 | 0 | 0 | 0 | 0 |
| **Apr.** | 3 | 0 | 0 | 2 | 1 | 0 | 0 | 0 | 0 | 0 | 0 | 0 | 0 | 0 | 0 | 0 | 0 | 0 |
| **May** | 5 | 0 | 0 | 1 | 6 | 0 | 0 | 0 | 0 | 0 | 0 | 0 | 0 | 0 | 0 | 0 | 0 | 0 |
| **June** | 1 | 0 | 0 | 5 | 2 | 0 | 0 | 0 | 0 | 0 | 0 | 0 | 0 | 0 | 0 | 0 | 0 | 0 |
| **July** | 3 | 0 | 0 | 3 | 7 | 0 | 0 | 0 | 0 | 0 | 0 | 0 | 0 | 0 | 0 | 0 | 0 | 0 |
| **Aug.** | 1 | 0 | 0 | 5 | 2 | 0 | 0 | 3 | 0 | 0 | 0 | 0 | 0 | 0 | 0 | 0 | 0 | 0 |
| **Sept.** | 4 | 0 | 0 | 4 | 1 | 0 | 1 | 3 | 0 | 0 | 0 | 0 | 0 | 0 | 0 | 0 | 0 | 0 |
| **Oct.** | 2 | 0 | 1 | 1 | 1 | 0 | 1 | 4 | 2 | 0 | 0 | 0 | 0 | 0 | 0 | 0 | 0 | 0 |
| **Nov.** | 2 | 5 | 14 | 6 | 3 | 0 | 3 | 4 | 13 | 6 | 0 | 0 | 0 | 0 | 0 | 0 | 0 | 0 |
| **Dec.** | 0 | 2 | 7 | 8 | 1 | 0 | 4 | 3 | 6 | 4 | 0 | 0 | 0 | 0 | 0 | 0 | 0 | 0 |
| **Jan.1944** | 2 | 15 | 13 | 2 | 8 | 0 | 2 | 1 | 4 | 3 | 1 | 4 | 4 | 2 | 0 | 0 | 0 | 0 |
| **Feb.** | 4 | 20 | 5 | 3 | 7 | 0 | 5 | 8 | 1 | 3 | 10 | 0 | 2 | 3 | 1 | 0 | 0 | 0 |
| **Mar.** | 29 | 9 | 8 | 17 | 8 | 0 | 3 | 6 | 12 | 9 | 17 | 0 | 2 | 2 | 16 | 0 | 0 | 0 |
| **Apr.** | 24 | 11 | 11 | 5 | 6 | 0 | 10 | 7 | 19 | 12 | 15 | 0 | 6 | 6 | 17 | 0 | 0 | 2 |
| **May** | 21 | 10 | 9 | 9 | 8 | 14 | 8 | 10 | 9 | 13 | 18 | 0 | 15 | 10 | 18 | 0 | 0 | 0 |
| **June** | 24 | 14 | 16 | 10 | 17 | 14 | 17 | 16 | 17 | 11 | 10 | 0 | 17 | 15 | 3 | 12 | 0 | 0 |
| **July** | 11 | 7 | 8 | 7 | 12 | 6 | 14 | 3 | 11 | 2 | 5 | 0 | 6 | 7 | 3 | 12 | 0 | 0 |
| **Aug.** | 25 | 15 | 17 | 6 | 11 | 17 | 12 | 17 | 29 | 9 | 6 | 0 | 14 | 13 | 12 | 12 | 1 | 0 |
| **Sept.** | 12 | 1 | 12 | 16 | 21 | 11 | 10 | 8 | 9 | 9 | 15 | 0 | 18 | 9 | 12 | 6 | 0 | 0 |
| **Oct.** | 3 | 5 | 5 | 3 | 2 | 3 | 3 | 5 | 5 | 1 | 3 | 0 | 3 | 5 | 11 | 6 | 0 | 0 |
| **Nov.** | 9 | 8 | 10 | 8 | 4 | 10 | 6 | 9 | 8 | 6 | 6 | 0 | 8 | 6 | 11 | 3 | 1 | 0 |
| **Dec.** | 3 | 3 | 6 | 9 | 1 | 7 | 3 | 3 | 4 | 12 | 7 | 0 | 6 | 3 | 10 | 10 | 1 | 0 |
| **Jan.1945** | 4 | 2 | 6 | 3 | 8 | 3 | 1 | 3 | 3 | 5 | 8 | 0 | 6 | 2 | 3 | 1 | 3 | 0 |
| **Feb.** | 10 | 11 | 13 | 1 | 21 | 6 | 3 | 4 | 8 | 6 | 5 | 0 | 12 | 2 | 9 | 5 | 1 | 0 |
| **Mar.** | 9 | 3 | 12 | 2 | 17 | 10 | 5 | 19 | 5 | 3 | 7 | 0 | 5 | 4 | 5 | 3 | 1 | 0 |
| **Apr.** | 12 | 4 | 12 | 3 | 13 | 4 | 4 | 5 | 14 | 1 | 6 | 0 | 3 | 2 | 7 | 7 | 5 | 0 |

4th ............ 242
20th .......... 145
55th .......... 185
56th .......... 139
78th .......... 188
339th ........ 105
352nd ....... 115
353rd ........ 141
355th ........ 179
356th ........ 115
357th ........ 139
358th ........... 4
359th ......... 127
361st ........... 91
364th ......... 138
479th ........... 77
SF ............... 13
Ftr Wg........... 2

Total: 2,145 aircraft MIA

# Group KIAc's

| Month | Group | KIAc |
|---|---|---|
| **November 1942** | 4th: | 1 |
| **January 1943** | 78th: | 3 |
| **February** | 4th: | 1 |
| **March** | 78th: | 1 |
| **April** | 4th: | 1 |
| | 78th: | 1 |
| **June** | 4th: | 2 |
| | 56th: | 1 |
| **July** | 353rd: | 2 |
| **August** | 56th: | 2 |
| **September** | 352nd: | 1 |
| | 353rd: | 3 |
| | 355th: | 1 |
| **October** | 78th: | 1 |
| **November** | 56th: | 1 |
| **December** | 4th: | 1 |
| | 55th: | 1 |
| | 78th: | 1 |
| | 353rd: | 1 |
| | 355th: | 1 |
| **January 1944** | 20th: | 2 |
| | 55th: | 1 |
| | 352nd: | 1 |
| | 356th: | 1 |
| **February** | 4th: | 1 |
| | 56th: | 2 |
| | 356th: | 1 |
| | 359th: | 1 |
| **March** | 4th: | 1 |
| | 20th: | 1 |
| | 56th: | 1 |
| | 78th: | 1 |
| | 364th: | 1 |
| **April** | 56th: | 3 |
| | 78th: | 1 |
| | 339th: | 1 |
| | 364th: | 1 |
| **May** | 4th: | 1 |
| | 55th: | 2 |
| | 56th: | 1 |
| | 339th: | 1 |
| | 352nd: | 2 |
| | 356th: | 1 |
| | 359th: | 2 |
| | 361st: | 1 |
| | 364th: | 1 |
| | 479th: | 1 |
| | 361st: | 2 |
| **June 1944** | 4th: | 2 |
| | 55th: | 1 |
| | 78th: | 1 |
| | 339th: | 1 |
| | 352nd: | 4 |
| | 353rd: | 2 |
| | 359th: | 1 |
| | 479th: | 1 |
| **July** | 55th: | 1 |
| | 78th: | 2 |
| | 339th: | 1 |
| | 356th: | 1 |
| | 364th: | 2 |
| | 479th: | 1 |
| **August** | 55th: | 1 |
| | 352nd: | 1 |
| | 353rd: | 2 |
| | 357th: | 1 |
| | 359th: | 1 |
| | 361st: | 2 |
| | SF: | 1 |
| **September** | 20th: | 3 |
| | 56th: | 1 |
| | 353rd: | 1 |
| | 357th: | 1 |
| | 479th: | 3 |
| | SF: | 3 |
| **October** | 20th: | 1 |
| | 55th: | 1 |
| | 56th: | 1 |
| | 78th: | 1 |
| | 352nd: | 1 |
| | 353rd: | 1 |
| | 361st: | 2 |
| | 479th: | 1 |
| **November** | 4th: | 1 |
| | 20th: | 1 |
| | 78th: | 1 |
| | 339th: | 1 |
| | 361st: | 1 |
| **December** | 55th: | 1 |
| | 56th: | 2 |
| | 364th: | 2 |
| | 479th: | 3 |
| **January 1945** | 56th: | 1 |
| | 78th: | 1 |
| | 357th: | 4 |

| Month | Group | Number |
|---|---|---|
| **February 1945** | 4th: | 2 |
| | 55th: | 1 |
| | 56th: | 2 |
| | 339th: | 1 |
| | 356th: | 2 |
| | 357th: | 3 |
| | 359th: | 2 |
| | 364th: | 2 |
| | 479th: | 1 |
| **March** | 20th: | 1 |
| | 55th: | 1 |
| | 56th: | 4 |
| | 78th: | 1 |
| | 339th: | 1 |
| | 353rd: | 1 |
| | 355th: | 1 |
| | 359th: | 1 |
| | 479th: | 1 |
| **April** | 4th: | 1 |
| | 56th: | 3 |
| | 353rd: | 1 |
| | 356th: | 1 |
| | 479th: | 2 |
| | SF: | 1 |
| **May 1945** | 4th: | 3 |
| | 55th: | 2 |
| | 56th: | 2 |
| | 355th: | 1 |
| | 357th: | 3 |
| | 359th: | 1 |
| | 479th: | 1 |
| **June** | 339th: | 2 |
| | 355th: | 2 |
| | 356th: | 4 |
| | 357th: | 1 |
| | 364th: | 2 |
| **July** | 78th: | 1 |
| | 339th: | 1 |
| | 352nd: | 1 |
| | 353rd: | 2 |
| | 356th: | 2 |
| | 359th: | 1 |
| | 361st: | 2 |
| | 479th: | 1 |

4th: ................. 18
20th: ................. 9
55th: ............... 13
56th: ............... 27
78th: ............... 17
339th: ............. 10
352nd: ............ 11
353rd: ............ 15
355th: ............... 6
356th: ............ 13
357th: ............ 13
359th: ............ 10
361st: ............ 10
364th: ............ 11
479th: ............ 16
SF: ................... 5

Total: 204 pilots killed in accidents

## Losses by Aircraft Type

**MIA**

Spitfire .......................... 19
P-38 ............................ 276
P-47 ............................ 555
P-51 .......................... 1295

**2145**

**KIAc**

Spitfire .................... 1
P-38 ....................... 19
P-47 ....................... 57
P-51 ..................... 116
AT-6 ........................ 4
B-17 ........................ 2
A-35 ........................ 1
C-78 ........................ 1
Typhoon .................. 1
Non-A/C ................. 2

**204**

# General Aircraft Markings

## THEATER BANDS

### P-47's

From February of 1943, all aircraft received a 24 inch wide white cowl band, a 12 inch wide white band across the fin and rudder, and an 18 inch wide white band on the horizontal tail surfaces. These bands were in black on NMF planes which were received in early 1944. From the late summer of 1944, many P-47's had these bands removed, although some retained all or part of the tail bands.

### P-51's

From November of 1943, all aircraft carried white spinners, a 12 inch wide white cowl band, a 12 inch wide white band across the vertical tail, and a 15 inch wide white band chordwise on the horizontal tail surfaces and wings. With the introduction of nose colors in March of 1944, the nose bands were deleted and the band on the vertical tail was dropped. When NMF P-51's arrived in the spring of 1944, the wing and tail bands were now applied in black. The wing and tail bands were in use until the end of 1944 as a whole, although a few planes retained them through 1945. Many groups removed all or part of these bands during the course of the war, so from mid-1944 onwards, there was no uniform system of markings at any given time.

### P-38's

These aircraft received no theater markings due to their unique shape.

### Squadron Codes

All fifteen groups carried squadron identity codes and an individual aircraft letter on their planes. These codes were white on olive drab ships and black on NMF (except for the 56th Fighter Group in 1945). The squadron codes were usually placed forward of the national insignia with the individual letter placed aft on P-47's and P-51's. (Three groups, the 20th, 352nd, and 364th, had variations, see text of each group for particular details). On P-38's, the aircraft letter was usually on the outer coolant radiator housing with the squadron code aft on the outer boom. The individual letter was usually repeated on the inner surface of the vertical tails with the squadron symbol on the outer.

### Serial Numbers

On olive drab planes, serials were in yellow, although a very few carried them in black. On NMF planes, all serials were black. The main exception to the rule was the 56th Fighter Group, whose P-47M's carried colored serial numbers in 1945 (see text for details).

### P-38 Droop-Snoot

From April of 1944, many 20th and 55th Fighter Group planes carried special "Droop-Snoot" markings. These were intended to make normal gun carrying P-38's resemble the unarmed "droop-snoot" bomber. At the rear of the nose cone, just aft of the machine guns, there was placed an eight inch wide white band. All paint was then removed forward of this band and the metal highly polished to reflect as the plexi-glass nose piece of the real "droop-snoot".

### Invasion Stripes

Starting on June 4, 1944, all 8th Air Force fighters received special black and white invasion stripes, encompassing the entire aft fuselage on P-47's and P-51's, and the booms on P-38's. In addition, the stripes were applied to both the upper and lower wing surfaces. The stripes were banded white-black-white-black-white, and varied according to aircraft type: 20 inches wide on P-47's; 18 inches wide on P-51's; and 24 inches wide on P-38's. There were some variations in application, with some planes carrying black-white-black-white-black bands, and a few with only four bands of black-white-black-white. The stripes were ordered to be removed from the upper fuselage decking and the upper wings in July of 1944, from the lower wings in August, and to be dropped entirely by the end of 1944. A few planes, however, carried the bands well into 1945.

# PART ONE:
# Day-to-Day Operations

**September 21, 1942**
Groups Operating: Spitfire 4th
Missions: Two 335th Ftr Sqn pilots swept the Flushing-Haamstede area.
Claims: nil

*Losses-*

**4th**: Lt. John T. Slater (335th Ftr Sqn) KIA
Spitfire AV-
Hit by flak off Flushing.

**September 26, 1942**
Groups Operating: Spitfire 4th
Missions: The 336th Ftr Sqn flew an escort to the Morlaix area.
Claims: 1-0-0 air
0-0 ground

| *Group* | | *Claims* | *Location* |
|---|---|---|---|
| **4th** | | | |
| 336th: | Capt. M.E. Jackson | FW-190 dest(air) | Brest |

*Losses-*

**4th:** F/Lt. Edward G. Brettel (RAF assigned to 336th) POW(K)
Spitfire MD- BS313
Hit by flak in the Brest area. Later executed March 24, 1944.

Capt. Marion E. Jackson (336th Ftr Sqn) POW
Spitfire MD- BS279
Hit by flak and FW-190's near Brest.

Lt. Charles A. Cook (336th Ftr Sqn) POW
Spitfire MD- BR640
Ran out of fuel and hit by a FW-190 in the Brest area.

Lt. William H. Baker (336th Ftr Sqn) KIA
Spitfire MD- BS446
Last heard from reporting he was ditching.

Lt. George H. Middleton (336th Ftr Sqn) POW
Spitfire MD- BS301
Ran out of fuel and bailed out in the Brest area.

Lt. Gene P. Neville (336th Ftr Sqn) KIA
Spitfire MD- BS140
Hit by flak near Guingamp.

Lt. Leonard T. Ryerson (336th Ftr Sqn) KIA
Spitfire MD- BS275
Hit by flak in the Brest area.

Lt. Dennis D. Smith (336th Ftr Sqn) KIA
Spitfire MD- BS137
Hit by flak in the Brest area.

Lt. Robert E. Smith (336th Ftr Sqn) MIA-E
Spitfire MD- BS447
Hit by flak in the Brest area.

Lt. George B. Sperry (336th Ftr Sqn) POW
Spitfire MD- BR638
Hit by flak in the Brest area.

Lt. Gil P. Wright (336th Ftr Sqn) POW
Spitfire MD- BS138
Hit by flak in the Brest area.

**September 27, 1942**
Groups Operating: Spitfire 4th
Missions: The 334th and 335th Ftr Sqns flew a shipping recon.
Claims: nil
Losses: nil

**October 2, 1942**
Groups Operating: Spitfire 4th
Missions: Sweep of the Pas de Calais area.
Claims: 4-0-2 air
0-0 ground

| *Group* | | *Claims* | *Location* |
|---|---|---|---|
| **4th** | | | |
| HdQts: | Capt. O.H. Coen | FW-190 dest(air) | SW Dunkirk |
| | W/Cdr. R. Duke-Woolley | (.5)FW-190 dest(air) | SE Calais |
| 334th: | Lt. S.M. Anderson | FW-190 dest(air) | SW Dunkirk |
| | Lt. J.A. Clark | (.5)FW-190 dest(air) | SE Calais |
| | Lt. W.B. Morgan | FW-190 dam(air) | S/Nieuport |
| 335th: | Lt. G.B. Fetrow | FW-190 dest(air) | SW Dunkirk |
| | Maj. W.J. Daley | FW-190 dam(air) | E/Calais |

Losses: nil

**October 6, 1942**
Groups Operating: Spitfire 4th
Missions: 335th Ftr Sqn patrolled the English coast.
Claims: nil
Losses: nil

**October 9, 1942**
Groups Operating: Spitfire 4th
Missions: Escort/sweep of the Abbeville-Fecamp area.
Claims: nil
Losses: nil

**October 10, 1942**
Groups Operating: Spitfire 4th
Missions: Support for RAF bombers to Le Havre
Claims: nil
Losses: nil

**October 14, 1942**
Groups Operating: Spitfire 4th
Missions: Sweep of the Graves-The Hague area.
Claims: nil
Losses: nil

*Remarks*
4th: 0-3 ships

**October 15, 1942**
Groups Operating: Spitfire 4th
Missions: Escort for bombers to Le Havre.
Claims: nil
Losses: nil

**October 20, 1942**
Groups Operating: Spitfire 4th
Missions: Patrols carried out by pairs and flights.
Claims: nil

*Losses-*

**4th**: Lt. Anthony J. Seaman(334th Ftr Sqn) KIA
Spitfire XR-
Exploded in mid-air and crashed east of Harwich.

**October 21, 1942**
Groups Operating: Spitfire 4th
Missions: 335th Ftr Sqn flew a convoy patrol; the 335th later swept the French coast, and the 334th escorted RAF bombers to France.
Claims: nil
Losses: nil

**October 22, 1942**
Groups Operating: Spitfire 4th
Missions: Two aircraft flew a patrol.
Claims: nil
Losses: nil

**October 23, 1942**
Groups Operating: Spitfire 4th
Missions: 335th Ftr Sqn flew convoy patrols.
Claims: nil
Losses: nil

**October 24, 1942**
Groups Operating: Spitfire 4th
Missions: 334th and 335th Ftr Sqns flew patrols.
Claims: nil
Losses: nil

**October 25, 1942**
Groups Operating: Spitfire 4th
Missions: Escort/sweep to Le Havre.
Claims: nil
Losses: nil

**October 29, 1942**
Groups Operating: Spitfire 4th
Missions: Two 336th Ftr Sqn pilots flew a sweep to Belgium.
Claims: nil
Losses: nil

*Remarks*
4th: 0-2 barges

**October 31, 1942**
Groups Operating: Spitfire 4th
Missions: Two 334th Ftr Sqn aircraft swept the Berck-Sur-Mer area.
Claims: nil
Losses: nil

*Remarks*
4th: 1-0 loco

**November 6, 1942**
Groups Operating: Spitfire 4th
Missions: Support for bombers to Caen.
Claims: nil
Losses: nil

**November 8, 1942**
Groups Operating: Spitfire 4th
Missions: Escort/patrol in the Lille-Fives area.
Claims: nil
Losses: nil

**November 9, 1942**
Groups Operating: Spitfire 4th
Missions: Support of bombers to Le Havre
Claims: nil
Losses: nil

**November 10, 1942**
Groups Operating: Spitfire 4th
Missions: Support for bombers to Le Havre.
Claims: nil
Losses: nil

**November 11, 1942**
Groups Operating: Spitfire 4th
Missions: 334th Ftr Sqn flew shipping recons.
Claims: nil
Losses: nil

**November 14, 1942**
Groups Operating: Spitfire 4th
Missions: 335th Ftr Sqn flew shipping recons.
Claims: nil
Losses: nil

**November 16, 1942**
Groups Operating: Spitfire 4th
Missions: Two aircraft flew a sweep to St. Valery and two others swept the Capr d'Alprecht-Staples area.
Claims: nil
Losses: nil

**November 17, 1942**
Groups Operating: Spitfire 4th
Missions: 335th Ftr Sqn patrolled the French coast.
Claims: nil
Losses: nil

**November 18, 1942**
Groups Operating: Spitfire 4th
Missions: Two 334th Ftr Sqn pilots flew to Berck-Sur-Mer.
Claims: nil
Losses: nil

*Remarks*
4th: 1-0 loco

**November 19, 1942**
Groups Operating: Spitfire 4th
Missions: 335th Ftr Sqn swept the Flushing area.
Claims: 1-0-0 air
0-0 ground

| *Group* | | *Claims* | *Location* |
|---|---|---|---|
| **4th** | | | |
| 335th: | Lt. F.J. Smolinsky | FW-190 dest(air) | SW Flushing |

Losses: nil

**November 20, 1942**
Groups Operating: Spitfire 4th
Missions: Two 335th Ftr Sqn pilots flew a sweep to Furnes.
Claims: 1-0-0 air
0-0 ground

| *Group* | | *Claims* | *Location* |
|---|---|---|---|
| **4th** | | | |
| 335th: | Lt. R.W. Evans | Fi-156 dest(air) | SE Furnes |

*Losses-*

**4th**: Lt. Roy W. Evans (335th Ftr Sqn) ASR
Spitfire AV-
Bailed out over the North Sea after mechanical trouble.

**November 26, 1942**
Groups Operating: Spitfire 4th
Missions: Two 335th Ftr Sqn pilots swept the Dunkirk area and two 334th Ftr Sqn pilots flew a patrol.
Claims: nil
Losses: nil

KIAc's
4th: Capt. Robert S. Sprague (334th Ftr Sqn)
Spitfire XR-
Crashed near Debden on a non-operational flight.

**November 28, 1942**
Groups Operating: Spitfire 4th
Missions: Two 335th Ftr Sqn aircraft flew a sweep to Holland.
Claims: nil
Losses: nil

**November 29, 1942**
Groups Operating: Spitfire 4th
Missions: Two 335th Ftr Sqn pilots flew a patrol.
Claims: nil
Losses: nil

**November 30, 1942**
Groups Operating: Spitfire 4th
Missions: Four 335th Ftr Sqn pilots flew a patrol.
Claims: nil
Losses: nil

**December 1, 1942**
Groups Operating: Spitfire 4th
Missions: 336th Ftr Sqn flew patrols.
Claims: nil
Losses: nil

**December 4, 1942**
Groups Operating: Spitfire 4th
Missions: Sweep of the Pas de Calais area.
Claims: nil
Losses: nil

**December 5, 1942**
Groups Operating: Spitfire 4th
Missions: Two aircraft flew a patrol.
Claims: nil
Losses: nil

**December 6, 1942**
Groups Operating: Spitfire 4th
Missions: Withdrawal support from Lille plus eight pilots flew a patrol.
Claims: 0-1-0 air
0-0 ground

| *Group* | | *Claims* | *Location* |
|---|---|---|---|
| **4th** | | | |
| 335th: | Lt. G.B. Fetrow | FW-190 prob(air) | NE Gris Nez |

Losses: nil

**December 8, 1942**
Groups Operating: Spitfire 4th
Missions: Eight aircraft of the 335th Ftr Sqn flew a patrol and two of the 334th Ftr Sqn swept the Le Crotoy area.
Claims: nil
Losses: nil

*Remarks*
4th: 0-1 loco, 0-1 flak tower, 0-2 buildings

**December 9, 1942**
Groups Operating: Spitfire 4th
Missions: Two pilots of the 334th Ftr Sqn flew a patrol.
Claims: nil
Losses: nil

**December 11, 1942**
Groups Operating: Spitfire 4th
Missions: Ten aircraft flew a patrol and two 334th Ftr Sqn pilots swept the Ghent-Bruges area.
Claims: nil
Losses: nil

*Remarks*
4th: 0-1 auto

**December 12, 1942**
Groups Operating: Spitfire 4th
Missions: Sweep/escort to the Abbeville area and the 336th Ftr Sqn flew a patrol.
Claims: nil
Losses: nil

**December 13, 1942**
Groups Operating: Spitfire 4th
Missions: Two aircraft flew a patrol.
Claims: nil
Losses: nil

**December 14, 1942**
Groups Operating: Spitfire 4th
Missions: Six pilots flew patrols.
Claims: nil
Losses: nil

**December 15, 1942**
Groups Operating: Spitfire 4th
Missions: Two 334th Ftr Sqn pilots swept the Bruges-Ghent area.
Claims: 0-1-0 air
0-0 ground

| *Group* | | *Claims* | *Location* |
|---|---|---|---|
| **4th** | | | |
| 334th: | Lt. S.M. Anderson | (.5)Ju-52 prob(air) | SW Flushing |
| | Lt. R.A. Boock | (.5)Ju-52 prob(air) | SW Flushing |

Losses: nil

**December 20, 1942**
Groups Operating: Spitfire 4th
Missions: Escort/sweep to Romilly-Sur-Seine.
Claims: nil
Losses: nil

**December 21, 1942**
Groups Operating: Spitfire 4th
Missions: Two 334th Ftr Sqn pilots swept the Le Touquet area and two 336th Ftr Sqn pilots flew a Channel patrol.
Claims: nil
Losses: nil

**December 22, 1942**
Groups Operating: Spitfire 4th
Missions: Eight aircraft flew patrols.
Claims: nil
Losses: nil

**December 23, 1942**
Groups Operating: Spitfire 4th
Missions: Two aircraft flew a patrol.
Claims: nil
Losses: nil

**December 29, 1942**
Groups Operating: Spitfire 4th
Missions: Two 336th Ftr Sqn pilots swept to Nieuport and four of the 334th Ftr Sqn swept the Knocke-Dunkirk area.
Claims: nil
Losses: nil

*Remarks*
4th: 0-1 loco, 0-1 barge

**December 30, 1942**
Groups Operating: Spitfire 4th
Missions: Two 334th Ftr Sqn planes swept the Cappelle-Etaples area.
Claims: nil
Losses: nil

*Remarks*
4th: 1-0 loco

**December 31, 1942**
Groups Operating: Spitfire 4th
Missions: 336th Ftr Sqn flew convoy patrols.
Claims: nil
Losses: nil

**January 2, 1943**
Groups Operating: Spitfire 4th
Missions: 335th and 336th Ftr Sqn pilots (20) flew convoy patrols.
Claims: nil
Losses: nil

**January 3, 1943**
Groups Operating: Spitfire 4th
Missions: 334th and 335th Ftr Sqn pilots (16) flew patrols.
Claims: nil
Losses: nil

**January 4, 1943**
Groups Operating: Spitfire 4th
Missions: 334th and 335th Ftr Sqn pilots (20) flew patrols.
Claims: nil
Losses: nil

**January 8, 1943**
Groups Operating: Spitfire 4th
Missions: 335th Ftr Sqn pilots (12) flew patrols.
Claims: nil
Losses: nil

**January 9, 1943**
Groups Operating: Spitfire 4th
Missions: 334th and 336th Ftr Sqn pilots (6) flew patrols.
Claims: nil
Losses: nil

**January 11, 1943**
Groups Operating: Spitfire 4th
Missions: Two 336th Ftr Sqn pilots flew a patrol.
Claims: nil
Losses: nil

**January 12, 1943**
Groups Operating: Spitfire 4th
Missions: Two 334th Ftr Sqn pilots flew a patrol.
Claims: nil
Losses: nil

**January 13, 1943**
Groups Operating: Spitfire 4th
Missions: Two pilots flew a convoy patrol.
Claims: nil
Losses: nil

Groups Operating: Spitfire 4th
Missions: Support for bombers to St. Omer/Rouge Airfield.
Claims: nil
Losses: nil

Groups Operating: Spitfire 4th
Mission: Withdrawal support from the Lille/Fives area.
Claims: nil
Losses: nil

*Remarks*
4th: Lt. Leicester B. Bishop (336th Ftr Sqn) c/l Manston; o.k.
Spitfire MD- BL240

**January 14, 1943**
Groups Operating: Spitfire 4th
Missions: Three sweeps over Belgium; first was three 334th Ftr Sqn pilots; second was three of the 336th Ftr Sqn; third was two 336th Ftr Sqn pilots.
Claims: 2-0-0 air
0-0 ground

| *Group* | | *Claims* | *Location* |
|---|---|---|---|
| **4th** | | | |
| 334th: | Lt. S.M. Anderson | FW-190 dest(air) | W/Ostend |
| | Lt. R.A. Boock | FW-190 dest(air) | W/Ostend |

Losses: nil

*Remarks*
4th: 1-0 auto
Lt. George E. Mirsch (336th Ftr Sqn) c/l Bradwell Bay; o.k.
Spitfire MD- AD451
Lt. John Mitchellweiss (336th Ftr Sqn) c/l Bradwell Bay; o.k.
Spitfire MD- E9915

**January 15, 1943**
Groups Operating: Spitfire 4th
Missions: Two 336th Ftr Sqn pilots flew a patrol.
Claims: nil
Losses: nil

**January 17, 1943**
Groups Operating: Spitfire 4th
Missions: Four 335th Ftr Sqn pilots flew a patrol.
Claims: nil
Losses: nil

**January 20, 1943**
Groups Operating: Spitfire 4th
Missions: Two 334th Ftr Sqn pilots flew a sweep and the 335th Ftr Sqn flew a patrol.
Claims: nil
Losses: nil

*Remarks*
4th: 0-3 locos

**January 21, 1943**
Groups Operating: Spitfire 4th
Missions: Support of bombers to Caen.
Claims: nil
Losses: nil

**January 22, 1943**
Groups Operating: Spitfire 4th
Missions: Support of bombers to St. Omer.
Claims: 4-0-1 air
0-0 ground

| *Group* | | *Claims* | *Location* |
|---|---|---|---|
| **4th** | | | |
| HdQts: | Maj. O.H. Coen | FW-190 dest(air) | W/Dunkirk |
| 334th: | Lt. S.M. Anderson | FW-190 dest(air) | W/Dunkirk |
| | Lt. R.A. Boock | FW-190 dest(air) | W/Dunkirk |
| 335th: | Lt. G.B. Fetrow | FW-190 dam(air) | W/Dunkirk |
| 336th: | Lt. J.A. Matthews | FW-190 dest(air) | Mardyk/Dunkirk |

*Losses-*

**4th**: Lt. Chester P. Grimm (335th Ftr Sqn) KIA
Spitfire AV-
Hit by flak in the Dunkirk-St. Omer area.

**January 23, 1943**
Groups Operating: Spitfire 4th
Missions: Four 336th Ftr Sqn pilots flew a patrol.
Claims: nil
Losses: nil

**January 25, 1943**
Groups Operating: Spitfire 4th
Missions: Support for bombers which were recalled.
Claims: nil
Losses: nil

**January 26, 1943**
Groups Operating: Spitfire 4th
Missions: Support for RAF bombers to Bruges.
Claims: nil

*Losses-*

**4th**: Lt. Robert A. Boock (334th Ftr Sqn) ASR
Spitfire XR-
Ditched six miles off the English coast after mechanical trouble.

KIAc's
78th: Lt. Stephen L. White (82nd Ftr Sqn)
P-38F 42-12928
Collided with Lt. Perry (83rd Ftr Sqn) on a ferry flight to Ireland.

Lt. Donald S. Beals (83rd Ftr Sqn)
P-38F 41-7576
Went missiong on a ferry flight.

Lt. Henry L. Perry (83rd Ftr Sqn)
P-38F 42-12905
Collided with Lt. White (82nd Ftr Sqn) on a ferry flight to Ireland.

**January 27, 1943**
Groups Operating: Spitfire 4th
Missions: Seven 336th Ftr Sqn pilots flew an ASR patrol.
Claims: nil
Losses: nil

**January 29, 1943**
Groups Operating: Spitfire 4th
Missions: Six 335th Ftr Sqn pilots flew a coastal patrol.
Claims: nil
Losses: nil

**February 1, 1943**
Groups Operating: Spitfire 4th
Missions: 335th and 336th Ftr Sqn(20 a/c) flew convoy patrols.
Claims: nil
Losses: nil

KIAc's
4th: Lt. John Mitchellweiss (336th Ftr Sqn)
P-47C 00 41-6200
Aircraft caught fire and he bailed out northwest of Debden but his chute failed to open.

**February 2, 1943**
Groups Operating: Spitfire 4th
Missions: Support of RAF bombers to St. Omer and nine 336th Ftr Sqn pilots flew convoy patrols.
Claims: nil
Losses: nil

**February 3, 1943**
Groups Operating: Spitfire 4th
Missions: Support of RAF bombers to St. Omer and three 336th Ftr Sqn pilots flew an ASR patrol.
Claims: nil
Losses: nil

**February 4, 1943**
Groups Operating: Spitfire 4th
Missions: 335th Ftr Sqn flew two bomber supports/patrols while three 336th Ftr Sqn pilots flew an ASR patrol.
Claims: nil
Losses: nil

**February 5, 1943**
Groups Operating: Spitfire 4th
Missions: Six 335th Ftr Sqn pilots flew a sweep.
Claims: nil

*Losses-*

**4th**: Capt. William P. Kelly (335th Ftr Sqn) KIA
Spitfire AV-
Hit by flak and crashed off Walcheren.

*Remarks*
4th: 0-3 ships

**February 6, 1943**
Groups Operating: Spitfire 4th
Missions: Six 335th Ftr Sqn pilots flew patrols.
Claims: nil
Losses: nil

**February 10, 1943**
Groups Operating: Spitfire 4th
Missions: Two 336th Ftr Sqn pilots flew a patrol.
Claims: nil
Losses: nil

**February 12, 1943**
Groups Operating: Spitfire 4th
Missions: 335th and 336th Ftr Sqn (18 a/c) flew patrols.
Claims: nil
Losses: nil

**February 13, 1943**
Groups Operating: Spitfire 4th
Missions: 335th and 336th Ftr Sqn (24 a/c) flew patrols.
Claims: nil

*Losses-*

**4th**: Lt. Jap A. Powell (336th Ftr Sqn) KIA
Spitfire MD- AR341
Suffered mechanical failure and bailed out too low off the English coast.

**February 14, 1943**
Groups Operating: Spitfire 4th
Missions: 335th and 336th Ftr Sqn (18 a/c) flew patrols.
Claims: nil
Losses: nil

**February 15, 1943**
Groups Operating: Spitfire 4th
Missions: 335th and 336th Ftr Sqn (30 a/c) flew patrols.
Claims: nil
Losses: nil

**February 16, 1943**
Groups Operating: Spitfire 4th
Missions: 335th and 336th Ftr Sqn (34 a/c) flew patrols.
Claims: nil
Losses: nil

**February 17, 1943**
Groups Operating: Spitfire 4th
Missions: 335th and 336th Ftr Sqn (38 a/c) flew patrols.
Claims: nil
Losses: nil

**February 18, 1943**
Groups Operating: Spitfire 4th
Missions: 335th and 336th Ftr Sqn (26 a/c) flew patrols.
Claims: nil
Losses: nil

**February 19, 1943**
Groups Operating: Spitfire 4th
Missions: 335th and 336th Ftr Sqns swept the St. Omer area.
Claims: nil
Losses: nil

**February 20, 1943**
Groups Operating: Spitfire 4th
Missions: Two pilots flew an ASR patrol.
Claims: nil
Losses: nil

**February 24, 1943**
Groups Operating: Spitfire 4th
Missions: 335th and 336th Ftr Sqn (14 a/c) flew patrols.
Claims: nil
Losses: nil

**February 26, 1943**
Groups Operating: Spitfire 4th
Missions: 335th and 336th Ftr Sqn (6 a/c) flew patrols and both squadrons flew a support for RAF bombers to Dunkirk.
Claims: nil
Losses: nil

**February 27, 1943**
Groups Operating: Spitfire 4th
Missions: 335th and 336th Ftr Sqn (16 a/c) flew patrols and also a support for RAF bombers to Dunkirk.
Claims: nil
Losses: nil

**February 28, 1943**
Groups Operating: Spitfire 4th
Missions: 335th and 336th Ftr Sqn (12 a/c) flew patrols.
Claims: nil
Losses: nil

**March 1, 1943**
Groups Operating: Spitfire 4th
Missions: Twenty-four pilots flew patrols.
Claims: nil
Losses: nil

KIAc's
78th: F/O Robert I. Ronning (83rd Ftr Sqn)
P-47C HL-
Collided with another P-47 and crashed near Goxhill.

**March 2, 1943**
Groups Operating: Spitfire 4th
Missions: Twelve aircraft flew patrols.
Claims: nil
Losses: nil

**March 3, 1943**
Groups Operating: Spitfire 4th
Missions: Twenty-eight pilots flew patrols.
Claims: nil
Losses: nil

**March 4, 1943**
Groups Operating: Spitfire 4th
Missions: Four pilots flew patrols.
Claims: nil
Losses: nil

**March 5, 1943**
Groups Operating: Spitfire 4th
Missions: Four pilots flew a patrol.
Claims: nil
Losses: nil

**March 6, 1943**
Groups Operating: Spitfire 4th
Missions: Fourteen pilots flew patrols.
Claims: nil
Losses: nil

**March 7, 1943**
Groups Operating: Spitfire 4th
Missions: Two pilots flew a patrol.
Claims: nil
Losses: nil

**March 8, 1943**
Groups Operating: Spitfire 4th
Missions: 335th and 336th Ftr Sqns supported RAF bombers to St. Valery and eight pilots flew a patrol.
Claims: nil
Losses: nil

**March 9, 1943**
Groups Operating: Spitfire 4th
Missions: 335th and 336th Ftr Sqns swept the St. Omer area and twenty-six pilots flew patrols.
Claims: nil
Losses: nil

**March 10, 1943**
Groups Operating: Spitfire 4th
P-47 4th
Missions: 335th and 336th Ftr Sqns (Spitfires) swept the St. Omer area while fourteen pilots (334th with P-47's) swept the Blankenberghe-Ostend area.
Claims: nil
Losses: nil

**March 11, 1943**
Groups Operating: Spitfire 4th
Missions: Eighteen pilots flew patrols.
Claims: nil
Losses: nil

**March 12, 1943**
Groups Operating: Spitfire 4th
Missions: Two sweeps to St. Valery and St. Omer.
Claims: 0-0-1 air
0-0 ground

| *Group* | | *Claims* | *Location* |
|---|---|---|---|
| **4th** | | | |
| 336th: | Lt. D.S. Gentile | FW-190 dam(air) | Audruieq |

*Losses-*

**4th:** Lt. Hazen S. Anderson (336th Ftr Sqn) POW
Spitfire MD- BL240
Hit by a FW-190 northwest of St. Omer.

**March 13, 1943**
Groups Operating: Spitfire 4th
Missions: Twenty-seven pilots flew a patrol of the Dieppe area, while six others flew another patrol.
Claims: nil
Losses: nil

**March 14, 1943**
Groups Operating: Spitfire 4th
Missions: 335th and 336th Ftr Sqn (37 a/c) flew patrols.
Claims: nil
Losses: nil

**March 15, 1943**
Groups Operating: Spitfire 4th
Missions: Twenty-four pilots flew patrols.
Claims: nil
Losses: nil

**March 16, 1943**
Groups Operating: Spitfire 4th
Missions: Fourteen pilots flew patrols.
Claims: nil
Losses: nil

**March 18, 1943**
Groups Operating: Spitfire 4th
Missions: Sixteen pilots flew patrols.
Claims: nil
Losses: nil

**March 19, 1943**
Groups Operating: Spitfire 4th
Missions: Six pilots flew patrols.
Claims: nil
Losses: nil

**March 20, 1943**
Groups Operating: Spitfire 4th
Missions: Two pilots flew a patrol.
Claims: nil
Losses: nil

**March 22, 1943**
Groups Operating: Spitfire 4th
Missions: Four pilots flew a patrol.
Claims: nil
Losses: nil

**March 23, 1943**
Groups Operating: Spitfire 4th
Missions: Eight pilots flew patrols.
Claims: nil
Losses: nil

**March 24, 1943**
Groups Operating: Spitfire 4th
Missions: Twenty-six pilots flew patrols.
Claims: nil
Losses: nil

**March 25, 1943**
Groups Operating: Spitfire 4th
Missions: Twelve aircraft flew patrols.
Claims: nil
Losses: nil

**March 26, 1943**
Groups Operating: Spitfire 4th
Missions: Eight pilots flew patrols.
Claims: nil
Losses: nil

**March 28, 1943**
Groups Operating: Spitfire 4th
Missions: Thirty-three pilots flew patrols.
Claims: nil
Losses: nil

**March 29, 1943**
Groups Operating: Spitfire 4th
Missions: Eighteen pilots flew patrols.
Claims: nil
Losses: nil

**March 30, 1943**
Groups Operating: Spitfire 4th
Missions: Twenty-eight pilots flew patrols.
Claims: nil
Losses: nil

**March 31, 1943**
Groups Operating: Spitfire 4th
Missions: Thirty-one pilots flew patrols.
Claims: nil
Losses: nil

**April 1, 1943**
Groups Operating: Spitfire 4th
Missions: Fourteen aircraft of the 336th Ftr Sqn flew shipping patrols.
Claims: nil
Losses: nil

**April 3, 1943**

KIAc's
4th: Lt. Frank J. Smolinsky (335th Ftr Sqn)
P-47C WD-D 41-6181
Crashed after taking-off from Sawbridgeworth.

**April 8, 1943**
Groups Operating: P-47 4th, 56th, 78th
Missions: Sweep of the Dunkirk-Sangatte area. The 56th put up four P-47's and the 78th supplied twelve.
Claims: nil
Losses: nil

**April 10, 1943**
Groups Operating: Spitfire 4th
Missions: Two aircraft were sent on a patrol.
Claims: nil
Losses: nil

**April 11, 1943**
Groups Operating: P-47 4th
Missions: Six pilots of the 334th and 335th Ftr Sqns swept the Ostend-Dunkirk area.
Claims: nil
Losses: nil

**April 13, 1943**
Groups Operating: P-47 4th, 56th, 78th
Missions: Sweep of the St. Omer area.
Claims: nil

*Losses-*

**78th**: LtCol. Joseph E. Dickman (HdQts) ASR
P-47C WZ-M 41-6399
Blew a cylinder and bailed out off Calais.

Groups Operating: P-47 4th, 56th, 78th
Missions: Sweep of the Berck-Mardyck area.
Claims: nil
Losses: nil

*Remarks*
56th: Capt. Roger B. Dyar (63rd) c/l Deal; o.k.
P-47C UN-D 41-6395

**April 15, 1943**
Groups Operating: P-47 4th, 56th, 78th
Missions: Sweeps of the Furnes-St. Omer area.
Claims: 3-0-1 air
0-0 ground

| *Group* | | *Claims* | *Location* |
|---|---|---|---|
| **4th** | | | |
| HdQts: | LtCol. C.G. Peterson | FW-190 dest(air) | W/Ostend |
| 334th: | Lt. R.A. Boock | FW-190 dest(air) | Belgian Coast |
| | Lt. J.A. Clark | FW-190 dam(air) | Belgian Coast |
| 335th: | Maj. D.J.M. Blakeslee | FW-190 dest(air) | Knocke |

*Losses-*

**4th**: LtCol. Chesley G. Peterson (HdQts) ASR
P-47C QP-K 41-6414
Suffered mechanical failure and bailed out thirty miles off the English coast.

Capt. Stanley M. Anderson (334th Ftr Sqn) KIA
P-47C QP-E 41-6407
Hit by a FW-190 and crashed off Ostend.

Capt. Richard D. McMinn (334th Ftr Sqn) KIA
P-47C QP-M 41-6204
Hit by a FW-190 and crashed off Ostend.

KIAc's
78th: Lt. Leroy V. Dodd (83rd Ftr Sqn)
P-47C HL-W 41-6241
Killed in a training accident near Bedford.

**April 17, 1943**
Groups Operating: P-47 4th, 56th, 78th
Missions: Sweeps of the Bruges-Flushing-Blankenburghe area.
Claims: nil
Losses: nil

Groups Operating: P-47 4th, 78th
Missions: Sweep of the Walcheren-Bruges area.
Claims: nil
Losses: nil

**April 18, 1943**
Groups Operating: P-47 4th
Missions: Sixteen pilots swept the Nieuport-Dunkirk-Sangatte area.
Claims: nil
Losses: nil

**April 21, 1943**
Groups Operating: P-47 4th, 56th, 78th
Missions: Sweeps of the Westhoofd-Noordwijk-The Hague area.
Claims: nil
Losses: nil

**April 29, 1943**
Groups Operating: P-47 4th, 56th, 78th
Missions: The 4th swept the Le Crotoy-St. Omer-Ostend area, the 56th swept The Hague-Woensdrecht-Dunkirk-Calais area, and the 78th swept the Le Touquet-Hazebrouck-Dunkirk-Calais area.
Claims: nil

*Losses-*

**56th**: Capt. John C. McClure (62nd Ftr Sqn) POW
P-47C LM- 41-6394
Hit by enemy fighters near Breskens.

Lt. Winston S. Garth (62nd Ftr Sqn) POW
P-47C LM-
Hit by enemy fighters and bailed out off the Dutch coast.

**May 3, 1943**
Groups Operating: P-47 4th, 56th, 78th
Missions: Sweeps of the Walcheren-Knocke-Ostend area.
Claims: nil
Losses: nil

**May 4, 1943**
Groups Operating: P-47 4th, 56th, 78th
Missions: Support of bombers to the Antwerp area.
Claims: 0-0-1 air
0-0 ground

| *Group* | | *Claims* | *Location* |
|---|---|---|---|
| **4th** | | | |
| 335th: | Lt. G. Carpenter | FW-190 dam(air) | Walcheren |

*Losses-*

**4th**: Lt. John F. Lutz (334th Ftr Sqn) KIA
P-47C QP-P 41-6196
Suffered mechanical failure and bailed out off Flushing, but his parachute did not fully open.

**May 7, 1943**
Groups Operating: P-47 4th, 56th, 78th
Missions: Sweeps of the Flushing-Ostend-Knocke area.
Claims: nil
Losses: nil

**May 11, 1943**
Groups Operating: P-47 4th, 56th, 78th
Missions: The groups were to sweep but were recalled.
Claims: nil
Losses: nil

**May 13, 1943**
Groups Operating: P-47 4th, 56th, 78th
Missions: Support of bombers going to the St. Omer area.
Claims: nil
Losses: nil

**May 14, 1943**
Groups Operating: P-47 4th, 56th, 78th
Missions: Support for bombers to the Antwerp area.
Claims: 4-5-10 air
0-0 ground

| *Group* | | *Claims* | *Location* |
|---|---|---|---|
| **4th** | | | |
| HdQts: | LtCol. C.G. Peterson | FW-190 prob(air) | W/St. Nicholas |
| | | FW-190 dam(air) | W/St. Nicholas |
| 335th: | Maj. D.J.M. Blakeslee | FW-190 dest(air) | N/Knocke |
| | Lt. A.C. Stanhope | FW-190 dam(air) | E/Flushing |
| 336th: | Capt. L. Gover | FW-190 prob(air) | S/St. Nicholas |
| | | (2)FW-190 dam(air) | S/St. Nicholas |
| | Capt. M.L. Stepp | FW-190 dam(air) | W/Antwerp |
| **56th** | | | |
| HdQts: | Col. H. Zemke | FW-190 dam(air) | NE Antwerp |
| 61st: | Lt. A.T. Biales | FW-190 prob(air) | NW Antwerp |
| | Lt. M.A. Anderson | FW-190 dam(air) | NE Antwerp |
| | Lt. G.W. Johnson | FW-190 dam(air) | NE Antwerp |
| **78th** | | | |
| HdQts: | Col. A. Peterson | FW-190 dam(air) | E/Flushing |
| 82nd: | Capt. R.E. Adamina | FW-190 dest(air) | Antwerp |
| | Capt. J.J. Oberhansly | FW-190 prob(air) | Antwerp |
| 83rd: | Maj. J.J. Stone | FW-190 dest(air) | NE St. Nicholas |
| | Capt. E.E. McTaggart | FW-190 dest(air) | SW Antwerp |
| | Capt. C.P. London | FW-190 prob(air) | NW Antwerp |
| | Lt. W.H. Julian | FW-190 dam(air) | St. Nicholas |

*Losses-*

**78th:** Capt. Robert E. Adamina (82nd Ftr Sqn) POW
P-47C MX-D 41-6198
Hit by enemy fighters and ditched off the Belgian coast.

Capt. Elmer E. McTaggart (83rd Ftr Sqn) MIA-E
P-47C HL-C 41-6382
Hit by enemy fighters and bailed out near Knocke.

F/O Samuel R. Martinek (83rd Ftr Sqn) POW
P-47C HL-T 41-6208
Hit by fighters and bailed out northwest of Knocke.

**May 15, 1943**
Groups Operating: P-47 4th, 56th, 78th
Missions: Sweeps of the Amsterdam-Rotterdam area.
Claims: 0-0-2 air
0-0 ground

| *Group* | | *Claims* | *Location* |
|---|---|---|---|
| **56th** | | | |
| 61st: | Capt. F.S. Gabreski | FW-190 dam(air) | NE Rotterdam |
| | Lt. D.H. Mudge | FW-190 dam(air) | NE Rotterdam |

*Losses-*

**78th:** Lt. Jack R. Sandmeier (82nd Ftr Sqn) KIA
P-47C MX-
Suffered mechanical failure and bailed out over the North Sea.

**May 16, 1943**
Groups Operating: P-47 4th, 56th, 78th
Missions: Sweeps of the Walcheren-Dunkirk area.
Claims: 3-1-4 air
0-0 ground

| *Group* | | *Claims* | *Location* |
|---|---|---|---|
| **4th** | | | |
| 335th: | Lt. E.D. Beatie | FW-190 prob(air) | Walcheren |
| | Capt. G.O. Halsey | FW-190 dam(air) | Flushing |
| | Lt. A.C. Stanhope | FW-190 dam(air) | Walcheren |
| **78th** | | | |
| HdQts: | Col. A. Peterson | FW-190 dam(air) | E/Flushing |
| 84th: | F/O C.R. Brown | (2)FW-190 dest(air) | Flushing |
| | Capt. J.D. Irvin | FW-190 dest(air) | E/Sluis |
| | Lt. A.H. Downing | FW-190 dam(air) | E/Sluis |

*Losses-*

**78th:** F/O Charles R. Brown (84th Ftr Sqn) POW
P-47C WZ-D 41-6353
Hit by a FW-190 in the Eecloo area and bailed out near Walcheren.

Groups Operating: P-47 4th, 56th, 78th
Missions: Sweeps of the Cayeux-Abbeville-Gravelines area.
Claims: nil
Losses: nil

**May 17, 1943**
Groups Operating: P-47 4th, 56th, 78th
Missions: Sweeps of the Brest-Cherbourg area.
Claims: nil
Losses: nil

**May 18, 1943**
Groups Operating: P-47 4th, 56th, 78th
Missions: Sweeps of the Knocke-Blankenberghe-Nieuport area.
Claims: 2-0-0 air
0-0 ground

| *Group* | | *Claims* | *Location* |
|---|---|---|---|
| **4th** | | | |
| 334th: | Capt. T.J. Andrews | Me-109 dest(air) | Blankenberghe-Knocke |
| | Lt. D.W. Beeson | Me-109 dest(air) | Blankenberghe-Knocke |

*Losses-*

**4th:** Lt. Robert A., Boock (334th Ftr Sqn) KIA
P-47C QP-S
Hit by enemy fighters and crashed into the North Sea between Blankenberghe and Ostend.

**May 19, 1943**
Groups Operating: P-47 4th, 56th, 78th
Missions: Escort for diversion force of bombers to the Ijmuiden area.
Claims: nil
Losses: nil

**May 20, 1943**
Groups Operating: P-47 4th, 56th, 78th
Missions: Sweeps of the Haamstede-Amsterdam area.
Claims: nil

*Losses-*

**78th:** Lt. Richard A. Murray (84th Ftr Sqn) KIA
P-47C WZ-S 41-6383
Suffered mechanical failure and bailed out forty miles off the English coast.

**May 21, 1943**
Groups Operating: P-47 4th, 56th, 78th
Missions: Sweeps of the Ostend-Ghent area.
Claims: 0-0-1 air
0-0 ground

| *Group* | | *Claims* | *Location* |
|---|---|---|---|
| **4th** | | | |
| 334th: | Lt. S.N. Pissanos | FW-190 dam(air) | Ghent |

*Losses-*

**4th:** Lt. Leland L., MacFarlane (334th Ftr Sqn) KIA
P-47D QP-N 42-7920
Last seen chasing an enemy fighter near Ghent.

Lt. William B. Morgan (334th Ftr Sqn) POW
P-47D QP-U 42-8644
Hit by an enemy fighter and ditched off Ostend.

Lt. Gordon H. Whitlow (334th Ftr Sqn) KIA
P-47C QP-H 41-6406
Last seen with enemy fighters near Ghent.

**May 22, 1943**
Groups Operating: P-47 78th
Missions: Six pilots flew a coastal patrol.
Claims: nil
Losses: nil

**May 23, 1943**
Groups Operating: P-47 78th
Missions: Six pilots flew a coastal patrol.
Claims: nil
Losses: nil

**May 25, 1943**
Groups Operating: P-47 4th, 56th, 78th
Missions: Sweeps of the Ypres-Knocke area.
Claims: nil
Losses: nil

**May 26, 1943**
Groups Operating: P-47 4th, 56th, 78th
Missions: Sweeps of the Egmond-The Hague area.
Claims: nil
Losses: nil

**May 27, 1943**
Groups Operating: P-47 4th, 56th, 78th
Missions: Sweeps of the Knocke-Gravelines area.
Claims: nil
Losses: nil

**May 28, 1943**
Groups Operating: P-47 4th, 56th, 78th
Missions: Sweeps of the Walcheren-Dunkirk area.
Claims: nil
Losses: nil

**May 29, 1943**
Groups Operating: P-47 4th, 56th, 78th
Missions: Escort for bombers to the St. Nazaire area.
Claims: 0-1-0 air
0-0 ground

| *Group* | | *Claims* | *Location* |
|---|---|---|---|
| **56th** | | | |
| 61st: | Maj. L.G. McCollom | Me-109 prob(air) | SE St. Moen |

Losses: nil

**May 31, 1943**
Groups Operating: P-47 4th, 56th, 78th
Missions: Sweeps of the Knocke-Dunkirk area.
Claims: nil

*Losses-*

**56th:** Lt. Patrick M. Williams (63rd Ftr Sqn) KIA
P-47D UN-I 42-7946
Suffered oxygen failure and crashed near Courtrai.

**June 2, 1943**
Groups Operating: P-47 4th
Missions: Four pilots flew a coastal patrol.
Claims: nil
Losses: nil

**June 4, 1943**
Groups Operating: P-47 4th
Missions: Six pilots flew a coastal patrol.
Claims: nil
Losses: nil

**June 5, 1943**
<u>KIAc's</u>
56th: Lt. Richard H. Allison (61st Ftr Sqn)
P-47C HV-
Killed while on a cross-country flight.

**June 7, 1943**
Groups Operating: P-47 4th, 56th, 78th
Missions: Sweep of the Pas de Calais-Ghent area.
Claims: nil
Losses: nil

**June 10, 1943**
Groups Operating: P-47 56th, 78th
Missions: Sweep of the Dutch Islands-Ghent area.
Claims: nil
Losses: nil

**June 11, 1943**
Groups Operating: P-47 4th, 56th, 78th
Missions: Sweep of the Ostend-Eecloo area.
Claims: nil
Losses: nil

Groups Operating: P-47 4th, 56th, 78th
Missions: Sweep of the Gravelines-Ostend-Hazebrouck area.
Claims: nil
Losses: nil

**June 12, 1943**
Groups Operating: P-47 4th, 56th
Missions: Sweep of the Blankenberghe-Calais-Dunkirk area.
Claims: 1-0-0 air
0-0 ground

| *Group* | | *Claims* | *Location* |
|---|---|---|---|
| **56th** | | | |
| 62nd: | Capt. W.V. Cook | FW-190 dest(air) | Ypres |

Losses: nil

Groups Operating: P-47 78th
Missions: Sweep of the Knocke-Mordyck area.
Claims: nil
Losses: nil

**June 13, 1943**
Groups Operating: P-47 4th, 56th
Missions: Sweep of the Gravelines-Knocke-Ypres area.
Claims: 3-0-2 air
0-0 ground

| *Group* | | *Claims* | *Location* |
|---|---|---|---|
| **56th** | | | |
| HdQts: | Col. H. Zemke | (2)FW-190 dest(air) | Cassel |
| | | FW-190 dam(air) | Cassel |
| 61st: | Lt. R.S. Johnson | FW-190 dest(air) | SE Berques |
| | Lt. J.R. Curtis | FW-190 dam(air) | S/Furnes |

Losses: nil

Groups Operating: P-47 78th
Missions: Sweep of the Ypres-St. Pol area.
Claims: 0-2-0 air
0-0 ground

| *Group* | | *Claims* | *Location* |
|---|---|---|---|
| **78th** | | | |
| 82nd: | Lt. W.T. Hegman | FW-190 prob(air) | Armentieres |
| | Lt. W.D. Wien | FW-190 prob(air) | Armentieres |

*Losses-*

**78th:** Lt. Ora R. Brown (82nd Ftr Sqn) KIA
P-47C MX-
Lost for unknown reasons.

Lt. Donald M. Marshall (84th Ftr Sqn) POW
P-47C WZ-D 41-6353
Hit by enemy fighters near Lumbres.

**June 14, 1943**
KIAc's
4th: Lt. Garrett H. King (334th Ftr Sqn)
P-47C QP-T
Struck by lightning and crashed near Swaffham.

**June 15, 1943**
Groups Operating: P-47 4th
Missions: A planned escort was aborted over the Channel.
Claims: nil

*Losses-*

**4th:** Lt. Howard D. Hively (334th Ftr Sqn) ASR
P-47C QP-J 41-6576
Bailed out over the Channel after mechanical failure.

**June 17, 1943**
Groups Operating: P-47 4th, 56th, 78th
Missions: Sweep of the Westhhofd-Eecloo-Gravelines area.
Claims: nil
Losses: nil

*Remarks*
4th: Lt. Joseph L. Bennett (336th Ftr Sqn) c/l North Weald; o.k.
P-47D VF-J 42-7873

**June 19, 1943**
KIAc's
4th: Lt. Vincent R. Castle (334th Ftr Sqn)
P-47D QP-E 42-7881
Pulled up over Debden, stalled, and crashed on the field.

**June 20, 1943**
Groups Operating: P-47 4th, 78th
Missions: Sweep of the Le Touquet-St. Omer-Calais area.
Claims: nil
Losses: nil

Groups Operating: P-47 56th
Missions: Sweep of The Hague-Rotterdam area.
Claims: nil
Losses: nil

**June 22, 1943**
Groups Operating: P-47 4th, 56th, 78th
Missions: Support of bombers to the Antwerp area.
Claims: 7-0-0 air
0-0 ground

| *Group* | | *Claims* | *Location* |
|---|---|---|---|
| **4th** | | | |
| 335th: | Lt. E.D. Beatie | Me-109 dest(air) | Beveland-Walcheren |
| | | FW-190 dest(air) | Beveland-Walcheren |
| | Lt. F.D. Smith | FW-190 dest(air) | Beveland-Walcheren |
| 336th: | Lt. J.A. Goodson | FW-190 dest(air) | NW Hulst |
| **78th** | | | |
| HdQts: | Col. A. Peterson | FW-190 dest(air) | NW Walcheren |
| 83rd: | Capt. C.P. London | FW-190 dest(air) | W/Walcheren |
| | F/O H.S. Askelson | FW-190 dest(air) | Walcheren |

Losses: nil

**June 24, 1943**
Groups Operating: P-47 56th, 78th
Missions: Sweep of The Hague-St. Omer area.
Claims: 1-0-0 air
0-0 ground

| *Group* | | *Claims* | *Location* |
|---|---|---|---|
| **78th** | | | |
| 83rd: | Lt. T.W. Shepard | FW-190 dest(air) | Ostend |

Losses: nil

Groups Operating: P-47 4th
Missions: Sweep of the Hesden-Boulogne-Daillens area.
Claims: nil
Losses: nil

**June 25, 1943**
Groups Operating: P-47 4th, 56th, 78th
Missions: Support of bombers to the Wangerooge area.
Claims: nil
Losses: nil

**June 26, 1943**
Groups Operating: P-47 4th, 56th, 78th
Missions: Support of bombers to Villacoublay.
Claims: 4-1-2 air
0-0 ground

| *Group* | | *Claims* | *Location* |
|---|---|---|---|
| **4th** | | | |
| 334th: | Lt. D.W. Beeson | Me-109 dest(air) | Dieppe |
| | Lt. R.C. Care | Me-109 dest(air) | Dieppe |
| | Lt. D.B. Leaf | Me-109 dam(air) | Dieppe |
| **56th** | | | |
| 61st: | Lt. G.W. Johnson | FW-190 dest(air) | N/Dieppe |
| 62nd: | Lt. C.R. Harrison | FW-190 dest(air) | NE Rouen |
| | Capt. R. Dauphin | FW-190 dam(air) | Dieppe |
| 63rd: | Lt. D.M. Goodfleisch | FW-190 prob(air) | E/Rouen |

*Losses-*

**56th:** Capt. Robert H. Wetherbee (HdQts) KIA
P-47 HV-
Hit by enemy fighters in the Dieppe-Rouen area.

Capt. Merle C. Eby (61st Ftr Sqn) KIA
P-47 HV-
Hit by enemy fighters in the Dieppe-Rouen area.

Lt. Louis T. Barron (61st Ftr Sqn) KIA
P-47 HV-
Hit by enemy fighters in the Dieppe-Rouen area.

Lt. Ralph A. Johnson (62nd Ftr Sqn) ASR
P-47 LM-
Shot up by Me-109's and bailed out off the English coast.

Capt. Roger B. Dyar (63rd Ftr Sqn) KIA
P-47C UN-D 41-6534
Hit by enemy fighters in the Dieppe-Rouen area.

*Remarks*
56th: Lt. Justus D. Foster (61st Ftr Sqn) c/l Hawkinge; o.k.
P-47 HV-

**June 28, 1943**
Groups Operating: P-47 4th, 56th, 78th
Missions: Support of bombers to St. Nazaire.
Claims: nil
Losses: nil

*Remarks*
4th: Lt. Joseph G. Matthews (336th Ftr Sqn) c/l; o.k.
P-47C VF- 41-6573
Lt. Kenneth D. Peterson (336th Ftr Sqn) c/l; o.k.
P-47C VF- 41-6539

**June 29, 1943**
Groups Operating: P-47 4th, 56th, 78th
Missions: Support of bombers to Villacoublay.
Claims: 2-0-0 air
0-0 ground

| *Group* | | *Claims* | *Location* |
|---|---|---|---|
| **78th** | | | |
| 83rd: | Capt. C.P. London | (2)Me-109 dest(air) | Gournay |

Losses: nil

**July 1, 1943**
Groups Operating: P-47 4th, 56th, 78th
Missions: Sweeps of the Le Touquet-Abbeville-Rotterdam-Hague areas.
Claims: 3-2-2 air
0-0 ground

| *Group* | | *Claims* | *Location* |
|---|---|---|---|
| **78th** | | | |
| 83rd: | Capt. J.C. Davis | FW-190 dest(air) | Schouwen |
| | Lt. W.H. Madole | FW-190 dest(air) | Schouwen |
| | Maj. J.J. Stone | FW-190 prob(air) | W/Schouwen |
| | Capt. J.M. Cooper | FW-190 dam(air) | Schouwen |
| 84th: | Lt. J.F. Byers | FW-190 dest(air) | Brielle |
| | Maj. E.P. Roberts | FW-190 prob(air) | Goederoode Island |
| | Capt. R.T. Himes | FW-190 dam(air) | Goederoode Island |

*Losses-*

**78th:** Col. Arman Peterson (HdQts) KIA
P-47D MX-P 42-7948 "Flagari"
Last seen in a fight near Ouddorp.

**July 2, 1943**
Groups Operating: P-47 56th, 78th
Missions: Sweep of the Le Touquet area.
Claims: nil
Losses: nil

**July 4, 1943**
Groups Operating: P-47 4th, 78th
Missions: Withdrawal support from the Le Mans-Nantes-Le Treport areas.
Claims: nil
Losses: nil

**July 6, 1943**
Groups Operating: P-47 4th, 56th, 78th
Missions: Sweep of the Rotterdam-Ostend-Ghent area.
Claims: nil
Losses: nil

**July 9, 1943**
Groups Operating: P-47 4th, 56th, 78th
Missions: Sweep of the Ghent-Knocke-Ostend-Courtrai areas.
Claims: nil
Losses: nil

**July 10, 1943**
Groups Operating: P-47 4th, 56th, 78th
Missions: Support of bombers to the Caen-Abbeville area.
Claims: nil
Losses: nil

**July 28, 1943**
Groups Operating: P-47 4th, 56th, 78th
Missions: Withdrawal support from the Dutch-German border.
Claims: 9-1-6 air
0-0 ground

| *Group* | | *Claims* | *Location* |
|---|---|---|---|
| **4th** | | | |
| HdQts: | Col. E.W. Anderson | (2)Me-109 dest(air) | E/Rotterdam |
| 334th: | Lt. D.W. Beeson | Me-109 dest(air) | SE Utrecht |
| | | FW-190 dam(air) | SE Utrecht |
| | Lt. R.C. Care | FW-190 dest(air) | E/Rotterdam |
| | Lt. H.L. Mills | FW-190 dam(air) | E/Rotterdam |
| 335th: | Capt. R.W. Evans | Me-109 dest(air) | W/Arnheim |
| | | FW-190 dam(air) | W/Arnheim |
| | Lt. L.M. Blanding | FW-190 dest(air) | SE Utrecht |
| | | FW-190 dam(air) | SE Utrecht |
| | Lt. F.R. Boyles | FW 190 dest(air) | SE Utrecht |
| | Capt. G. Carpenter | FW-190 dam(air) | SE Utrecht |
| 336th: | Capt. L. Gover | FW-190 dest(air) | E/Rotterdam |
| | Capt. C.H. Miley | Me-109 dest(air) | E/Rotterdam |
| | | FW-190 prob(air) | E/Rotterdam |
| | Lt. G.F. Mirisch | FW-190 dam(air) | E/Rotterdam |

*Losses-*

**4th**: Lt. Henry L. Ayres (336th Ftr Sqn) POW
P-47C VF- 41-6238
Hit by enemy fighters near Zevenhuizen.

Groups Operating: P-47 4th, 56th, 78th
Missions: Support of bombers to the Abbeville area.
Claims: nil
Losses: nil

**July 29, 1943**
Groups Operating: P-47 4th, 56th, 78th
Missions: Sweeps over Belgium and Holland.
Claims: 0-0-1 air
0-0 ground

| *Group* | | *Claims* | *Location* |
|---|---|---|---|
| **78th** | | | |
| 83rd: | Capt. J.M. Cooper | FW-190 dam(air) | Ghent |

*Losses-*

**56th**: Lt. Robert J. Steele (62nd Ftr Sqn) POW
P-47D LM- 42-7887
Hit by a Me-109 and bailed out in the Nordwijk-Katwijk area.

Groups Operating: P-47 4th, 56th, 78th
Missions: Support for B-26's to the St. Omer area.
Claims: nil
Losses: nil

**July 30, 1943**
Groups Operating: P-47 4th, 56th, 78th
Missions: Support of bombers to Kassel.
Claims: [illegible]
0-0 ground

| *Group* | | *Claims* | *Location* |
|---|---|---|---|
| **4th** | | | |
| 335th: | Capt. D.A. Young | FW-190 dest(air) | SE Rotterdam |
| | | FW-190 dam(air) | SE Rotterdam |
| | Lt. F.R. Boyles | FW-190 dest(air) | Zaltboemel |
| | Lt. P.W. McKennon | FW-190 dest(air) | Zaltboemel |
| | Lt. A.C. Stanhope | FW-190 dest(air) | SE Arnheim |
| | | FW-190 dam(air) | SE Arnheim |
| | Lt. K.G. Smith | FW-190 dest(air) | Schouwen Island |
| **56th** | | | |
| HdQts: | Maj. L.G. McCollom | Me-109 dam(air) | Arnheim |
| 61st: | Capt. L.A. Schreiber | (2)Me-109 dest(air) | Arnheim |
| | Lt. J.H. Powers | Me-109 dest(air) | Arnheim |
| | Lt. D.F. Smith | Me-109 prob(air) | Nijmegen |
| | Lt. L.C. Smith | FW-190 dam(air) | Arnheim |

*Losses-*

**4th**: Lt. Fred D. Merritt (335th Ftr Sqn) KIA
P-47C WD- 41-6248
Last seen southeast of Rotterdam with Me-109's.

**56th**: Lt. Jack W. Horton (61st Ftr Sqn) KIA
P-47C HV-E 41-6265 "Francy Ann"
Hit by enemy fighters near Hank.

Lt. Robert E. Stover (62nd Ftr Sqn) KIA
P-47C LM- 41-6209
Hit by enemy fighters and bailed out twenty miles east of Felixstowe.

**78th**: LtCol. Melvin F. McNickle (HdQts) POW
P-47D WZ-M 42-7961
Suffered an oxygen failure, then collided with Lt. Byers near Winterswijk.

F/O Warren E. Graff (82nd Ftr Sqn) MIA-E
P-47C MX-Y 41-6391
Hit by enemy fighters and bailed out near Bakelo.

Lt. Paul H. Lehman (82nd Ftr Sqn) ASR
P-47C MX-W 41-6542
Hit by flak and bailed out over the Channel.

Lt. James F. Byers (84th Ftr Sqn) KIA
P-47D WZ-I 42-7935
Collided with LtCol. McNickle near Winterswijk.

*Remarks*
78th: 0-1 loco, 0-1 flak position
Lt. William H. Julian (83rd Ftr Sqn) c/l Wickham; o.k.
P-47C HL-R 41-6628

**August 2, 1943**
Groups Operating: P-47 4th, 56th, 78th
Missions: Planned sweeps were recalled before landfall.
Claims: nil
Losses: nil

**August 9, 1943**
Groups Operating: P-47 4th, 56th, 78th, 353rd
Missions: Sweep of the Abbeville-Poix and Rotterdam-Noordwaal areas. 16 aircraft of the 353rd flew with the 56th.
Claims: nil
Losses: nil

**August 12, 1943**
Groups Operating: P-47 4th, 56th, 78th
Missions: Support of bombers to the Bonn-Gelsenkirchen area.
Claims: 4-1-1 air
0-0 ground

| *Group* | | *Claims* | *Location* |
|---|---|---|---|
| **4th** | | | |
| 334th: | Capt. J.A. Clark | FW-190 dest(air) | Sittard |
| | Capt. W.T. O'Regan | Me-109 dest(air) | E/Sittard |
| | | Me-109 prob(air) | E/Sittard |
| | Lt. S.N. Pissanos | Me-109 dest(air) | W/Walcheren |
| 335th: | Lt. C.V. Padgett | Me-109 dest(air) | W/Duren |
| **56th** | | | |
| 62nd: | Lt. J.M. Jones | FW-190 dam(air) | W/Maastricht |

Losses: nil

Groups Operating: P-47 353rd
Missions: Sweep of the Westhoofd-Ostend-Ghent area.
Claims: nil
Losses: nil

**August 14, 1943**
Groups Operating: P-47 56th, 353rd
Missions: The 56th swept the Tessel Island area and the 353rd flew a withdrawal support from The Hague area.
Claims: nil
Losses: nil

**August 15, 1943**
Groups Operating: P-47 4th, 56th, 78th, 353rd
Missions: Sweep of the Knocke-Lille-St. Omer area.
Claims: nil
Losses: nil

Groups Operating: P-47 4th, 56th, 78th, 353rd
Missions: Support of bombers to various targets in France.
Claims: nil

*Losses-*

**78th:** Lt. Jayson M. Smith (83rd Ftr Sqn) KIA
P-47D HL-Y 42-7952
Spun-in just west of Duxford while returning as a spare.

**August 16, 1943**
Groups Operating: P-47 4th, 56th, 78th, 353rd
Missions: Support of bombers to Le Bourget and Abbeville.
Claims: 18-1-8 air
0-0 ground

| *Group* | | *Claims* | *Location* |
|---|---|---|---|
| **4th** | | | |
| 334th: | Capt. J.A. Clark | (2)FW-190 dest(air) | N/Paris |
| | Lt. H.L. Mills | (2)FW-190 dest(air) | NW Paris |
| | F/O C.D. Smith | (2)FW-190 dest(air) | SE Paris |
| | Lt. R.C. Care | FW-190 dest(air) | N/Paris |
| | | FW-190 prob(air) | N/Paris |
| | Lt. H.D. Hively | FW-190 dest(air) | NW Paris |
| 335th: | Capt. F.D. Smith | FW-190 dest(air) | SE Paris |
| | Capt. D.A. Young | FW-190 dest(air) | Paris |
| | | (2)FW-190 dam(air) | Paris |
| | Capt. R.W. Evans | Me-109 dest(air) | S/Paris |
| | Lt. J.R. Happel | FW-190 dest(air) | Paris |
| | Lt. F.M. Fink | FW-190 dest(air) | NW Paris |
| | Lt. A.C. Stanhope | Me-109 dest(air) | Melun-Paris |
| 336th: | Lt. J.A. Goodson | (2)FW-190 dest(air) | Paris |
| | | FW-190 dam(air) | Paris |
| | Maj. J.G. DuFour | Me-109 dest(air) | N/Paris |
| | | Me-109 dam(air) | N/Paris |
| | Lt. J.G. Matthews | FW-190 dest(air) | St. Denis-L'Isle Adam |
| | Lt. K.E. Carlson | FW-190 dam(air) | Paris |
| | Lt. D.S. Gentile | Me-109 dam(air) | Paris |
| **353rd** | | | |
| HdQts: | LtCol. J.A. Morris | FW-190 dam(air) | NW Paris |
| | Maj. G.E. Duncan | FW-190 dam(air) | NW Paris |

*Losses-*

**4th:** Lt. Joseph G. Matthews (336th Ftr Sqn) MIA-E
P-47D VF- 42-7949
Hit by enemy fighters near St. Denis.

**56th:** Lt. George R. Spaleny (62nd Ftr Sqn) POW
P-47D LM-
Suffered mechanical failure and bailed out near Gournay.

**353rd:** LtCol. Joseph A. Morris (HdQts) KIA
P-47D YJ-
Last seen chasing a FW-190 northwest of Paris.

*Remarks*
4th: P-47 c/l Romrey; o.k.
353rd: P-47 c/l Lewes; o.k.

**August 17, 1943**
Groups Operating: P-47 4th, 56th, 78th, 353rd
Missions: Support of bombers going to Regensburg and Schweinfurt.
Claims: 19-1-9 air
0-0 ground

| *Group* | | *Claims* | *Location* |
|---|---|---|---|
| **56th** | | | |
| HdQts: | Col. H. Zemke | Me-110 dest(air) | St. Trond |
| 61st: | Capt. G.W. Johnson | (2)Me-109 dest(air) | Hasselt-Diest |
| | | (.5)Me-110 dest(air) | N/Liege |
| | | Me-109 dam(air) | Hasselt-Diest |
| | Lt. F.E. McCauley | FW-190 dest(air) | Hasselt |
| | | (.5)Me-110 dest(air) | N/Liege |
| | | FW-190 dam(air) | Hasselt |
| | Capt. D.D. Renwick | Me-109 dest(air) | Liege |
| 62nd: | Lt. C.R. Harrison | Me-110 dest(air) | Ans |
| | Lt. C.L. Reeder | Me-110 dest(air) | Ans |
| | | Me-210 dam(air) | Ans |
| | Lt. V.H. Day | (2)Me-210 dam(air) | Ans |
| 63rd: | Lt. G.D. Schiltz | (3)FW-190 dest(air) | Ans-St. Nicholas |
| | | Me-210 dam(air) | Ans-St. Nicholas |
| | Capt. W.M. Mahurin | (2)FW-190 dest(air) | Eupen-St. Nicholas |
| | Lt. H.E. Comstock | Me-109 dest(air) | Ans |
| | Lt. J.H. Truluck | FW-190 dest(air) | Ans-St. Nicholas |
| | | Me-210 dam(air) | Ans-St. Nicholas |
| | Lt. E.D. Whitley | Me-110 dest(air) | Ans |
| | | Me-110 dam(air) | Ans |
| | Lt. G.F. Hall | Me-109 prob(air) | Eupen-St. Nicholas |
| | Lt. D.M. Goodfleisch | Me-110 dam(air) | Ans |
| **78th** | | | |
| 84th: | Maj. E.P. Roberts | Me-110 dest(air) | SE Aachen |
| | F/O P.E. Pompetti | Me-210 dest(air) | SE Aachen |
| **353rd** | | | |
| HdQts: | Maj. L.G. McCollom | Me-109 dest(air) | Diest |

*Losses-*

**56th:** Lt. Voorhis H. Day (62nd Ftr Sqn) KIA
P-47D LM-M 42-7891
Last seen chasing enemy fighters near Ans.

Lt. Robert M. Stultz (62nd Ftr Sqn) KIA
P-47C LM- 41-6398
Last seen with Lt. Day near Ans.

Lt. Arthur Sugas (63rd Ftr Sqn) KIA
P-47C UN-S 41-6372
Hit by enemy fighters near Ans.

**August 18, 1943**
Groups Operating: P-47 353rd
Missions: Sweep of the Westhoofd-Woensdrecht-Knocke area.
Claims: nil
Losses: nil

**August 19, 1943**
Groups Operating: P-47 4th, 56th, 78th, 353rd
Missions: Support for bombers to Gilze-Rijen and Woensdrecht.
Claims: 10-0-5 air
0-0 ground

| *Group* | | *Claims* | *Location* |
|---|---|---|---|
| **56th** | | | |
| HdQts: | Col. H. Zemke | FW-190 dam(air) | Numensdorp |
| 61st: | Lt. F.E. McCauley | (2)Me-109 dest(air) | Oosterhout & Schoonhoven |
| | Capt. R.A. Lamb | FW-190 dest(air) | Breda |
| | Capt. G.W. Johnson | Me-109 dest(air) | Gilze-Rijen |
| | | Me-109 dam(air) | Gilze-Rijen |
| | Lt. R.S. Johnson | Me-109 dest(air) | NE Woensdrecht |
| | Lt. J.R. Carter | Me-109 dam(air) | W/Gilze-Rijen |
| 62nd: | Lt. M.J. Quirk | FW-190 dest(air) | Gilze-Rijen |
| 63rd: | Lt. J.L. Egan | FW-190 dest(air) | Tholen Island |
| | Lt. J.W. Vogt | Me-109 dest(air) | Walcheren |
| | Lt. E.D. Whitley | Me-109 dest(air) | Walcheren |
| **78th** | | | |
| 83rd: | Lt. K.W. Dougherty | Me-109 dest(air) | Woensdrecht |
| | Lt. D. Bodenhamer | Me-109 dam(air) | Woensdrecht |
| **353rd** | | | |
| 351st: | Lt. H.J. Morris | Me-109 dam(air) | Gilze-Rijen |

*Losses-*

**56th:** Lt. Glenn E. Hodges (63rd Ftr Sqn) POW
P-47C UN-O 41-6216
Suffered mechanical failure and ditched in the North Sea.

*Remarks*
78th: Lt. Robert F. Brower (82nd Ftr Sqn) c/l Duxford; o.k.
P-47C MX-E 41-6179

**August 22, 1943**
KIAc's
56th: Lt. Conway C. Saux (62nd Ftr Sqn)
P-47C LM-X 41-6224
Collided with Lt. Tettemer and crashed near Valley Farm.

Lt. Donald Tettemer (62nd Ftr Sqn)
P-47C LM-P 41-6189
Collided with Lt. Saux and crashed near Sotherton Hall Farm.

**August 23, 1943**
Groups Operating: P-47 4th, 56th, 78th, 353rd
Missions: Sweep of the Bruges-Woensdrecht-Schipol area.
Claims: nil
Losses: nil

**August 24, 1943**
Groups Operating: P-47 4th, 56th, 78th, 353rd
Missions: Support for bombers to Villacoublay and Conches/Evreux.
Claims: 6-0-7 air
0-0 ground

| Group | | Claims | Location |
|---|---|---|---|
| **56th** | | | |
| 61st: | Capt. F.S. Gabreski | FW-190 dest(air) | Dreux |
| | Lt. R.S. Johnson | FW-190 dam(air) | Evreux |
| 62nd: | Capt. L.A. Schreiber | FW-190 dest(air) | S/Paris |
| | Lt. J.M. Jones | FW-190 dest(air) | S/Paris |
| | Capt. H.C. Craig | FW-190 dam(air) | S/Paris |
| **78th** | | | |
| 83rd: | Lt. W.H. Madole | (3)FW-190 dam(air) | Evreux |
| 84th: | Maj. E.P. Roberts | Me-109 dest(air) | Rouen-Evreux |
| | | FW-190 dest(air) | Rouen-Evreux |
| **353rd** | | | |
| 350th: | Lt. W.F. Hurst | FW-190 dest(air) | Rouen |
| | Lt. I.E. Venell | FW-190 dam(air) | Rouen |
| 351st: | Capt. W.C. Beckham | FW-190 dam(air) | N/Paris |

Losses: nil

*Remarks*
78th: 0-1 flak tower

**August 25, 1943**
Groups Operating: 56th, 353rd
Missions: Sweep of the Dunkirk-Lille-Le Treport area.
Claims: nil
Losses: nil

**August 27, 1943**
Groups Operating: P-47 4th, 56th, 78th, 353rd
Missions: Support of bombers to Watten V-1 sites.
Claims: nil
Losses: nil

KIAc's
78th: Lt. Robert F. Brower (82nd Ftr Sqn)
P-47C MX-
Spun-in near Henlow enroute to a forward base.

**August 31, 1943**
Groups Operating: P-47 4th, 56th, 78th, 353rd
Missions: Support of bombers to Amiens/Glisy Airfield.
Claims: 0-0-3 air
0-0 ground

| Group | | Claims | Location |
|---|---|---|---|
| **4th** | | | |
| 335th: | Lt. A.C. Stanhope | FW-190 dam(air) | Glisy-Montdidier |
| 336th: | Capt. C.H. Miley | (2)FW-190 dam(air) | N/Paris |

*Losses-*

**353rd**: Lt. Lester L. Dansky (352nd Ftr Sqn) KIA
P-47D SX- 42-7999
Collided with Lt. Murden north of Amiens.

Lt. Robert T. Murden (352nd Ftr Sqn) POW
P-47D SX- 42-8383
Collided with Lt. Dansky north of Amiens.

**September 2, 1943**
Groups Operating: P-47 4th, 56th, 78th, 353rd
Missions: Sweeps of France, Belgium, and Holland.
Claims: nil

*Losses-*

**4th**: Lt. Dale B. Leaf (334th Ftr Sqn) KIA
P-47D QP-I
Last seen being chased by FW-190's near Formerie.

**56th**: Lt. Walter T. Hannigan (63rd Ftr Sqn) KIA
P-47D UN-U 42-7934
Hit by enemy fighters near Ghent.

Lt. Wilfred A. Van Abel (63rd Ftr Sqn) POW
P-47C UN-Q 41-6537
Hit by enemy fighters near Hazebrouck.

*Remarks*
56th: Lt. John W. Vogt (63rd Ftr Sqn) c/l Eastchurch; o.k.
P-47C UN-T 41-6375

**September 3, 1943**
Groups Operating: P-47 4th, 56th, 78th, 353rd
Missions: Support for bombers to various targets in France.
Claims: 4-2-0 air
0-0 ground

| Group | | Claims | Location |
|---|---|---|---|
| **4th** | | | |
| 336th: | Lt. J.A. Goodson | FW-190 prob(air) | Paris |
| **56th** | | | |
| HdQts: | Col. H. Zemke | FW-190 dest(air) | NW Romilly-Sur-Seine |
| 61st: | Maj. F.S. Gabreski | FW-190 dest(air) | St. Germain |
| | Lt. H.O. Bevins | Ju-88 prob(air) | Paris |
| 63rd: | Capt. L.A. Adrianse | FW-190 dest(air) | Romilly |
| | Capt. D.M. Goodfleisch | FW-190 dest(air) | SE Paris |

*Losses-*

**56th**: Lt. Hiram O. Bevins (61st Ftr Sqn) POW
P-47C HV-B 41-6232
Hit by a FW-190 and bellied-in near Paris.

Groups Operating: P-47 56th, 78th
Missions: Sweep of the Dunkirk area.
Claims: nil
Losses: nil

**September 4, 1943**
Groups Operating: P-47 56th, 78th
Missions: Sweep of the Antwerp area.
Claims: nil
Losses: nil

**September 5, 1943**
KIAc's
353rd: Capt. Irvin E. Venell (350th Ftr Sqn)
P-47D LH-K 42-7956
Crashed in bad weather enroute to Duxford.

Lt. Harold W. Long (350th Ftr Sqn)
P-47D LH-Y 42-8475
Crashed in bad weather enroute to Duxford.

**September 6, 1943**
Groups Operating: P-47 4th, 56th, 78th, 353rd
Missions: Support of bombers to Stuttgart.
Claims: 1 0 0 air
0-0 ground

| Group | | Claims | Location |
|---|---|---|---|
| **4th** | | | |
| 335th: | Maj. R.W. Evans | FW-190 dest(air) | N/Chateau Thierry |

*Losses-*

**353rd**: F/O Earl W. Perry, Jr. (352nd Ftr Sqn) KIA
P-47D SX- 42-7901
Hit by a FW-190 and crashed near Le Chatelet.

**September 7, 1943**
Groups Operating: P-47 4th, 56th, 78th, 353rd
Missions: Support of bombers to Brussels and Bergen/Alkmaar.
Claims: 2-0-0 air
0-0 ground

| Group | | Claims | Location |
|---|---|---|---|
| **56th** | | | |
| 62nd: | Lt. A.R. Carcione | Me-109 dest(air) | Tessel Island |
| | Lt. R.A. Johnson | Me-109 dest(air) | Tessel Island |

*Losses-*

**4th**: Lt. Aubrey C. Stanhope (335th Ftr Sqn) POW
P-47C WD-X 41-6207
Was chased by a FW-190, then hit by flak near Hulst.

*Remarks*
56th: 63rd Ftr Sqn P-47 c/l; o.k.
P-47D UN-F 42-22534
353rd: 351st Ftr Sqn P-47 c/l Westleton; o.k.
P-47C YJ- 41-6585

**September 8, 1943**
Groups Operating: P-47 56th, 78th
Missions: Sweep of the Courtrai-Ghent-Haamstede area.
Claims: nil
Losses: nil

**September 9, 1943**
Groups Operating: P-47 4th, 56th, 78th, 352nd, 353rd
Missions: Support for bombers going to Paris, Beaumont Sur Oise, Beauvais/Tille, and Lille. The 352nd flew a cover patrol over off the English coast.

Claims: 1-0-1 air
0-0 ground

| *Group* | | *Claims* | *Location* |
|---|---|---|---|
| **4th** | | | |
| 334th: | Capt. J.A. Clark | FW-190 dam(air) | NE Paris |
| **56th** | | | |
| 63rd: | Capt. W.M. Mahurin | FW-190 dest(air) | S/Beauvais |

*Losses-*

**4th**: Lt. Vernon Boehle (334th Ftr Sqn) ASR
P-47C QP-O 41-6400 "Indianapolis"
Hit by enemy aircraft and bailed out forty-five miles south of Beachy Head.

Lt. Frank M. Fink (335th Ftr Sqn) POW
P-47C WD- 41-6328
Suffered mechanical failure and bailed out near Paris.

**September 13, 1943**
KIAc's
352nd: Lt. Arthur C. Eaker (328th Ftr Sqn)
P-47D PE-

**September 14, 1943**
Groups Operating: P-47 4th, 56th, 352nd, 355th
Missions: Sweep of the Dunkirk-Dutch Islands area.
Claims: nil
Losses: nil

*Remarks*
355th: Lt. Charles K. Hecht (358th Ftr Sqn) c/l Steeple Morden; o.k.
P-47D YF-Q

Groups Operating: P-47 352nd, 355th
Missions: Sweep of the Knocke-Pas de Calais area.
Claims: nil

*Losses-*

**352nd**: Lt. William H. Alm (486th Ftr Sqn) KIA
P-47D PZ- 42-22531
Suffered mechanical failure and crashed off the coast near Knocke.

**September 15, 1943**
Groups Operating: P-47 4th, 56th, 78th, 352nd, 353rd
Missions: Support for bombers to Romilly-Sur-Seine, Chartres, and Paris.
Claims: 0-0-1 air
0-0 ground

| *Group* | | *Claims* | *Location* |
|---|---|---|---|
| **4th** | | | |
| 334th: | Lt. W.M. Sobanski | FW-190 dam(air) | SW Paris |

*Losses-*

**353rd**: Lt. Walter J. Donovan (352nd Ftr Sqn) KIA
P-47D SX- 42-8494
Ran out of fuel and crashed into the Channel.

*Remarks*
353rd: Capt. Robert C. Durlin (352nd Ftr Sqn) b/o Truno; injured.
P-47D SX-

**September 16, 1943**
Groups Operating: P-47 56th, 353rd
Missions: Support for bombers to Nantes.
Claims: 2-0-0 air
0-0 ground

| *Group* | | *Claims* | *Location* |
|---|---|---|---|
| **56th** | | | |
| 62nd: | Lt. G.G. Goldstein | Me-109 dest(air) | Vitre |
| | Lt. R.B. Taylor | Me-109 dest(air) | Fougeres |

Losses: nil

**September 18, 1943**
KIAc's:
353rd: Lt. Francis J. Hajosy (352nd Ftr Sqn)
P-47D SX-
Was coming in to land at Metfield when his engine quit and he crashed near the field.

**September 22, 1943**
Groups Operating: P-47 4th, 56th, 78th, 352nd, 353rd, 355th
Missions: Sweeps of the Pas de Calais and Egmond areas.
Claims: 2-0-0 air
0-0 ground

| *Group* | | *Claims* | *Location* |
|---|---|---|---|
| **353rd** | | | |
| 352nd: | Capt. C.J. Hoey | Me-109 dest(air) | SW Utrecht |
| | Lt. J.W. Gonnam | Me-109 dest(air) | Schoonhaven |

*Losses-*

**78th**: Lt. Quentin Charlton (83rd Ftr Sqn) KIA
P-47C HL-N 41-6411
Suffered a fuel leak and bailed out over the North Sea.

*Remarks*
4th: Lt. Conrad C. Ingold (336th Ftr Sqn) c/l Debden; o.k.
P-47C VF-H 41-6579

Groups Operating: P-47 56th, 352nd, 353rd, 355th
Missions: Sweep of the Furnes-Ghent-Flushing area.
Claims: nil
Losses: nil

**September 23, 1943**
Groups Operating: P-47 4th, 56th, 78th, 353rd
Missions: Support of bombers to Nantes and Vannes.
Claims: 5-0-2 air
0-0 ground

| *Group* | | *Claims* | *Location* |
|---|---|---|---|
| **353rd** | | | |
| HdQts: | Maj. G.E. Duncan | FW-190 dest(air) | Nantes |
| 351st: | Capt. W.C. Beckham | FW-190 dest(air) | S/Nantes |
| | Lt. E.J. Albert | FW-190 dest(air) | S/Nantes |
| | Lt. V.L. Vogel | Me-109 dam(air) | S/Rennes |
| 352nd: | Lt. J.N. Poindexter | Me-109 dest(air) | NE Nantes |
| | Lt. W.F. Streit | FW-190 dest(air) | Chateaubriant |
| | | Me-109 dam(air) | Chateaubriant |

*Losses-*

**353rd**: Lt. George S. Dietz (352nd Ftr Sqn) KIA
P-47D SX- 42-7995
Hit by an enemy fighter near Nantes.

Groups Operating: P-47 352nd, 355th
Missions: Support for B-26's to Beaumont.
Claims: nil
Losses: nil

Groups Operating: P-47 4th, 56th, 353rd
Missions: Support for bombers to Nantes.
Claims: nil
Losses: nil

**September 24, 1943**
Groups Operating: P-47 78th, 352nd, 355th
Missions: Sweep of the Sangatte-Lille-Ghent-Blankenberghe area.
Claims: nil
Losses: nil

**September 25, 1943**
KIAc's:
355th: Lt. James Donovan (354th Ftr Sqn)
P-47D WR-
Spun-in enroute to Goxhill.

**September 26, 1943**
Groups Operating: P-47 4th, 56th, 78th, 352nd, 353rd, 355th
Missions: The groups were to act as escort for bombers but the formations were recalled due to the weather.

*Remarks*
353rd: P-47D c/l Metfield; o.k.

**September 27, 1943**
Groups Operating: P-47 4th, 56th, 78th, 352nd, 353rd, 355th
Missions: Support of bombers to Emden.
Claims: 22-2-4 air
0-0 ground

| *Group* | | *Claims* | *Location* |
|---|---|---|---|
| **4th** | | | |
| 336th: | Lt. W.W. Millikan | FW-190 dest(air) | Potten |
| **56th** | | | |
| 63rd: | Lt. J.H. Truluck | Me-109 dest(air) | Borkum Island |
| | | FW-190 dest(air) | Borkum Island |

| | | | |
|---|---|---|---|
| | Lt. J.E. Coenen | (2)FW-190 dest(air) | S/Juist Island |
| | Lt. W.J. O'Connor | Me-109 dest(air) | Borkum Island |
| **78th** | | | |
| 82nd: | Maj. J.J. Oberhansly | Me-109 dest(air) | Emden |
| | | Me-109 prob(air) | Emden |
| | F/O M.S. Martinez | Me-109 dest(air) | Emden |
| 83rd: | Maj. J.C. Davis | Me-109 dest(air) | Emden |
| | Lt. E.W. Powell | Me-109 dest(air) | Emden |
| 84th: | Lt. P.E. Pompetti | Me-110 dest(air) | NW Emden |
| | | Me-109 dest(air) | NW Emden |
| | Capt. J.D. Irvin | Me-109 dest(air) | NW Emden |
| | Capt. H.D. Stump | Me-109 dest(air) | NW Emden |
| | Lt. Q.L. Brown | Me-109 dest(air) | NW Emden |
| | Lt. W.W. Dougherty | Me-109 prob(air) | NW Emden |
| **353rd** | | | |
| 350th: | Maj. B. Rimerman | Me-109 dest(air) | S/Emden |
| | Lt. D.A. Fry | Me-109 dest(air) | W/Emden |
| | Lt. W.W. Odom | (1.5)Me-109 dest(air) | Emden |
| | Capt. D.E. Newhart | (.5)Me-109 dest(air) | Emden |
| | | Me-109 dam(air) | Emden |
| | Lt. J. Rosenberg | Me-109 dam(air) | Emden |
| 351st: | Capt. O.A. Kinkade | Me-109 dest(air) | SW Emden |
| | | Me-109 dam(air) | SW Emden |
| | Lt. H.F. Hunter | Me-109 dest(air) | SW Emden |
| | Lt. W.J. Maguire | Me-109 dest(air) | W/Emden |
| | | Me-109 dam(air) | W/Emden |

*Losses-*

**56th**: Capt. Harry P. Dugas (63rd Ftr Sqn) KIA
P-47C UN-W 41-6199
Last seen in a fight with enemy fighters near Juist Island.

*Remarks*
353rd: 0-3 freighters
Lt. Alan W. Lowe (350th Ftr Sqn) c/l Ludham; o.k.
P-47D LH-O

**October 2, 1943**
Groups Operating: P-47 4th, 56th, 78th, 353rd, 355th
Missions: Support of bombers to Emden.
Claims: 6-3-3 air
0-0 ground

| *Group* | | *Claims* | *Location* |
|---|---|---|---|
| **4th** | | | |
| 334th: | Lt. D.W. Beeson | FW-190 dest(air) | E/Wilhelmshaven |
| 335th: | F/O A.L. Schlegel | Me-109 dest(air) | SE Emden |
| | | Me-109 dam(air) | SE Emden |
| **56th** | | | |
| HdQts: | Maj. D.C. Schilling | Me-109 dest(air) | SE Groningen |
| | | FW-190 dest(air) | NE Emden |
| | Col. H. Zemke | FW-190 dest(air) | Groningen |
| **353rd** | | | |
| HdQts: | Maj. G.E. Duncan | Me-109 dest(air) | Emden |
| | | Me-109 prob(air) | Emden |
| 350th: | Lt. M.P. Dawson | Me-109 dam(air) | Emden |
| | Lt. R.N. Ireland | Me-109 dam(air) | Emden |
| 351st: | Capt. W.C. Beckham | FW-190 prob(air) | Emden |
| | | Me-109 prob(air) | Emden |

Losses: nil

**October 3, 1943**
Groups Operating: P-47 4th, 353rd
Missions: The 4th swept the St. Valery-Boulogne area while the 353rd covered the Dunkirk-Ghent area.
Claims: nil
Losses: nil

**October 4, 1943**
Groups Operating: P-47 4th, 56th, 353rd, 355th
Missions: Support of bombers to Frankfurt and Saarlautern.
Claims: 18-2-2 air
0-0 ground

| *Group* | | *Claims* | *Location* |
|---|---|---|---|
| **56th** | | | |
| HdQts: | Maj. D.C. Schilling | Me-110 dest(air) | E/Duren |
| 61st: | Lt. F.E. McCauley | Me-110 dest(air) | E/Aachen |
| | | Me-110 prob(air) | E/Aachen |
| | Lt. W.A. Marangello | Me-110 dest(air) | W/Aachen |
| | Lt. J.R. Carter | Me-110 prob(air) | E/Aachen |
| 63rd: | Capt. W.M. Mahurin | (3)Me-110 dest(air) | E/Duren |
| | Lt. V.P. Ludwig | (3)Me-110 dest(air) | E/Duren |
| | Capt. D.M. Goodfleisch | Me-110 dest(air) | E/Duren |
| | Lt. J.D. Brown | Me-110 dest(air) | E/Duren |
| | Lt. H.E. Comstock | Me-110 dest(air) | Bruhl |
| | Lt. G.D. Schiltz | Me-110 dest(air) | E/Duren |
| | Lt. B.R. Smith | Me-110 dest(air) | Bruhl |
| | Lt. J.W. Vogt | Me-110 dest(air) | E/Duren |
| | Lt. J.D. Wilson | Me-110 dest(air) | E/Duren |
| **353rd** | | | |
| HdQts: | Maj. G.E. Duncan | Me-109 dam(air) | Malines |
| 351st: | Capt. W.C. Beckham | Me-109 dest(air) | Malines |
| | Lt. G.B. Compton | Me-109 dam(air) | Malines |
| **355th** | | | |
| 358th: | Capt. C.F. Ekstrom | Me-109 dest(air) | Liege-Maastricht |

*Losses-*

**355th:** Lt. Ralph Dean (358th Ftr Sqn) KIA
P-47D YF-Z 42-74667
Shot-up by a FW-190 and crashed upon reaching the English coast.

**October 8, 1943**
Groups Operating: P-47 4th, 56th, 78th, 352nd, 353rd, 355th
Missions: Support of bombers to Bremen.
Claims: 12-2-11 air
0-0 ground

| *Group* | | *Claims* | *Location* |
|---|---|---|---|
| **4th** | | | |
| 334th: | Lt. D.W. Beeson | (2)Me-109 dest(air) | Meppel-Zwolle |
| | | Me-109 dam(air) | Meppel-Zwolle |
| | Maj. J.A. Clark | Me-109 dest(air) | Meppel-Zwolle |
| | F/O R.K. Hofer | Me-109 dest(air) | NE Amsterdam |
| | Lt. H.L. Mills | Me-109 prob(air) | Meppel-Zwolle |
| | Lt. R.B. Fraser | Me-109 dam(air) | Meppel-Zwolle |
| 335th: | Maj. R.W. Evans | Me-109 dest(air) | SW Oldenburg |
| | Lt. D.H. Ross | Me-210 dest(air) | Edewecht |
| **56th** | | | |
| HdQts: | Maj. D.C. Schilling | FW-190 dest(air) | Quackenbruck |
| 61st: | Lt. R.S. Johnson | FW-190 dest(air) | Lingen |
| | Capt. D.D. Renwick | FW-190 dam(air) | Lingen |
| 62nd: | Capt. L.A. Schreiber | FW-190 dest(air) | Quackenbruck |
| | Lt. H. Coronios | FW-190 dest(air) | Quackenbruck |
| | | FW-190 dam(air) | Quackenbruck |
| | Lt. M.J. Quirk | FW-190 dest(air) | Quackenbruck |
| | Capt. R. Dauphin | FW-190 prob(air) | Quackenbruck |
| | Lt. C.L. Reeder | FW-190 dam(air) | Quackenbruck |
| **353rd** | | | |
| HdQts: | Lt. W.T. Thistlethwaite | FW-190 dam(air) | Rhede |
| 350th: | Capt. D.E. Newhart | Me-210 dam(air) | Aschendorf |
| 351st: | Capt. F.H. LeFebre | (.5)Me-110 dest(air) | Friesoythe |
| | Lt. D.M. Hurlburt | (.5)Me-110 dest(air) | Friesoythe |
| | Capt. W.C. Beckham | FW-190 dam(air) | Rhede |
| | Capt. J.R. Walsh | FW-190 dam(air) | Wildeshausen |
| | Capt. O.A. Kinkade | FW-190 dam(air) | SW Emden |
| 352nd: | Capt. C.J. Hoey | Me-109 dam(air) | Garrel |

*Losses-*

**4th:** F/O Clyde D. Smith (334th Ftr Sqn) POW
P-47D QP-U 42-7915
Hit by enemy fighters and bailed out near Meppel.

Lt. Robert C. Patterson (335th Ftr Sqn) POW
P-47D WD- 42-7911
Hit by enemy fighters near Stadskannel.

**56th:** Lt. Dover C. Fleming, Jr. (63rd Ftr Sqn) KIA
P-47C UN-P 41-6268
Hit by enemy fighters near Amsterdam.

*Remarks*
4th: 0-1 ship

**October 9, 1943**
Groups Operating: P-47 78th, 352nd, 353rd, 355th
Missions: Sweep of the Leeuwarden area.
Claims: nil
Losses: nil

**October 10, 1943**
Groups Operating: P-47 4th, 56th, 78th, 352nd, 353rd
Missions: Support of bombers to Munster.
Claims: 20-2-7 air
0-0 ground

| *Group* | | *Claims* | *Location* |
|---|---|---|---|
| **4th** | | | |
| 334th: | Lt. D.W. Beeson | FW-190 dam(air) | Arnheim |
| **56th** | | | |
| HdQts: | Maj. D.C. Schilling | FW-190 dest(air) | Altenberge |
| 61st: | Capt. G.W. Johnson | Me-110 dest(air) | N/Munster |
| | | Me-210 dest(air) | N/Munster |
| | Lt. R.S. Johnson | FW-190 dest(air) | N/Munster |
| | | Me-110 dest(air) | N/Munster |
| 62nd: | Capt. W.V. Cook | Me-210 dest(air) | Altenberge |
| | Lt. A.R. Carcione | Me-109 dest(air) | Nienburg |
| | Lt. J.B. Eaves | Me-109 dest(air) | Altenberge |
| | Lt. J.M. Jones | FW-190 dest(air) | Altenberge |
| | Lt. R.B. Taylor | FW-190 dest(air) | Altenberge |
| | | FW-190 prob(air) | Altenberge |
| | Lt. W.A. Brainard | Me-210 dam(air) | Altenberge |
| 63rd: | Lt. G.D. Schiltz | FW-190 dam(air) | W/Munster |
| **78th** | | | |
| HdQts: | Maj. E.P. Roberts | Me-110 dest(air) | W/Enschede |
| | | Me-210 dest(air) | W/Enschede |
| 84th: | Lt. C.W. Silsby | Me-110 dest(air) | Ochtrup |
| | | Me-210 dest(air) | Ochtrup |
| | Lt. P.L. Larson | Me-110 dest(air) | Ochtrup |
| **353rd** | | | |
| HdQts: | LtCol. L.G. McCollom | Me-110 prob(air) | Rheine |
| 350th: | Lt. W.F. Hurst | FW-190 dest(air) | Zutphen |
| | Lt. W.F. Tanner | FW-190 dest(air) | Hengelo |
| 351st: | Capt. W.C. Beckham | (2)Me-110 dest(air) | Munster & Gransbergen |
| | | Me-210 dest(air) | Munster |
| | Lt. F.J. Mincik | Me-110 dam(air) | W/Munster |
| | F/O J.E. Wood | Me-110 dam(air) | Metelen |
| | Capt. J.R. Walsh | (.5)Me-210 dam(air) | NW Munster |
| | Lt. W.R. Burkett | (.5)Me-210 dam(air) | NW Munster |
| 352nd: | Lt. E.M. Fogarty | (.33)Me-110 dam(air) | Amersfoort |
| | Lt. W.H. Junttila | (.33)Me-110 dam(air) | Amersfoort |
| | Lt. R.V. Keywan | (.33)Me-110 dam(air) | Amersfoort |

*Losses-*

**352nd:** Lt. Fred D. Olson (328th Ftr Sqn) KIA
P-47D PE- 42-8635
Hit by enemy fighters and crashed northeast of Lowestoft.

*Remarks*
352nd: P-47 c/l Bodney; o.k.

**October 14, 1943**
Groups Operating: P-47 4th, 56th, 352nd, 353rd, 355th
Missions: Support for bombers heading to Schweinfurt.
Claims: 13-0-7 air
0-0 ground

| *Group* | | *Claims* | *Location* |
|---|---|---|---|
| **56th** | | | |
| HdQts: | Maj. J.C. Stewart | Me-110 dam(air) | W/Aachen |
| 61st: | Capt. G.W. Johnson | FW-190 dest(air) | Eupen |
| | Lt. N.E. Brooks | Me-110 dest(air) | W/Aachen |
| | Lt. F.E. McCauley | Me-110 dest(air) | W/Aachen |
| **353rd** | | | |
| 350th: | Maj. B. Rimerman | FW-190 dest(air) | Duren |
| | Lt. D.A. Fry | FW-190 dest(air) | Duren |
| | Capt. D.E. Newhart | FW-190 dam(air) | Duren |
| 351st: | Capt. W.C. Beckham | (2)FW-190 dest(air) | Aachen |
| | Capt. O.A. Kinkade | Me-109 dest(air) | Turnhout |
| | Lt. W.J. Maguire | FW-190 dest(air) | Flacher |
| | Lt. G.F. Perpente | Me-109 dam(air) | Turnhout |
| | Lt. B.E. Kraft | FW-190 dam(air) | Turnhout |
| 352nd: | Maj. W.B. Bailey | Me-109 dest(air) | Eecloo |
| | Lt. W.H. Junttila | Me-109 dest(air) | Turnhout |
| | | Me-109 dam(air) | Turnhout |
| | Lt. R.A. Newman | Me-109 dest(air) | Turnhout |
| | | Me-109 dam(air) | Turnhout |
| | Lt. W.F. Streit | Me-109 dest(air) | Turnhout |
| | Lt. R.V. Keywan | Me-109 dam(air) | Turnhout |

*Losses-*

**353rd:** Lt. Dwight A. Fry (350th Ftr Sqn) MIA-E
P-47D LH-H 42-8513
Hit by a FW-190 and bailed out near Budel.

Lt. Robert C. Peters (350th Ftr Sqn) KIA
P-47D LH-T
Crash-landed at Herongate due to battle damage.

*Remarks*
56th: Lt. Anthony S. Cavallo (63rd Ftr Sqn) c/l Breznett; o.k.
P-47D UN-K 42-8465
Lt. Russell B. Westfall (63rd Ftr Sqn) c/l Doddington; o.k.
P-47D UN-G 42-7878
353rd: Lt. Robert P. Geurtz (352nd Ftr Sqn) c/l Metfield; o.k.
P-47D SX-M 42-22482 "Stinky Poo"
355th: P-47 c/l Steeple Morden; o.k.

**October 15, 1943**
Groups Operating: P-47 356th
P-38 55th
Missions: Sweeps of the Dutch Islands-first mission for both.
Claims: nil
Losses: nil

**October 16, 1943**
Groups Operating: P-47 352nd, 355th, 356th
P-38 55th
Missions: Sweeps of the Dutch Islands.
Claims: nil
Losses: nil

**October 17, 1943**
Groups Operating: P-47 356th
P-38 55th
Missions: Sweep of the Dutch Islands.
Claims: nil
Losses: nil

**October 18, 1943**
Groups Operating: P-47 4th, 56th, 78th, 352nd, 353rd, 355th, 356th
P-38 55th
Missions: Sweeps over France, Belgium, and Holland.
Claims: 1-0-0 air
0-0 ground

| *Group* | | *Claims* | *Location* |
|---|---|---|---|
| **56th** | | | |
| HdQts: | Maj. J.C. Stewart | (.5)Me-210 dest(air) | NE Maastricht |
| 61st: | Lt. M.C. Wood | (.5)Me-210 dest(air) | NE Maastricht |

*Losses-*

**55th:** Lt. Hugh R. Gillette (38th Ftr Sqn) KIA
P-38H CG-I 42-66719
Suffered mechanical failure and crashed into the North Sea.

**78th:** Lt. Franklin B. Ressequie (84th Ftr Sqn) MIA-E
P-47C WZ-E 41-6240
Suffered mechanical failure in the Lens-St. Omer area.

**355th:** Lt. Eugene W. Maben, Jr. (358th Ftr Sqn) KIA
P-47D YF-N 42-22532
Last seen spinning down east of Cambrai.

**October 19, 1943**
Groups Operating: P-38 55th
Missions: Sweep over northern France.
Claims: nil
Losses: nil

**October 20, 1943**
Groups Operating: P-47 4th, 56th, 78th, 352nd, 353rd, 355th, 356th
P-38 55th
Missions: Support of bombers to Duren.
Claims: 4-2-6 air
0-0 ground

| *Group* | | *Claims* | *Location* |
|---|---|---|---|
| **56th** | | | |
| HdQts: | Col. H. Zemke | FW-190 dest(air) | Eindhoven |
| 63rd: | Lt. J.W. Vogt | FW-190 dest(air) | Ans |
| | Capt. D.M. Goodfleisch | FW-190 prob(air) | Dison |
| | | FW-190 dam(air) | Chateau d'Ardenne |
| | F/O A.H. Robey | FW-190 dam(air) | SW Aachen |
| **78th** | | | |
| HdQts: | LtCol. E.P. Roberts | Me-109 dest(air) | Dinant |
| 84th: | Capt. J.C. Price | Me-109 dam(air) | Dinant |
| **353rd** | | | |
| 351st: | Lt. H.J. Morris | Me-109 dam(air) | Duren |
| 352nd: | Lt. E.M. Fogarty | Me-109 prob(air) | Sittard |
| | Capt. C.J. Hoey | Me-109 dam(air) | Sittard |
| **355th** | | | |
| 358th: | Maj. R.B. Myers | FW-190 dest(air) | Ath |
| | | FW-190 dam(air) | Ath |

Losses: nil

**October 22, 1943**
Groups Operating: P-47 56th, 78th, 352nd, 353rd, 355th, 356th
P-38 55th
Missions: Support of 9th Air Force B-26's to the St. Pol-Cambrai area. Bad weather resulted in most groups not making R/V.
Claims: nil

*Losses-*

**353rd:** Lt. Alan W. Lowe (350th Ftr Sqn) KIA
P-47D LH- 42-8683
Spun-out in overcast near St. Omer.

Lt. Walter B. Stone (350th Ftr Sqn) KIA
P-47D LH- 42-7989
Spun-out in overcast near St. Omer.

*Remarks*
78th: Lt. Ernest S. Lang (84th Ftr Sqn) c/l; o.k.
P-47D WZ-
355th: P-47 c/l Steeple Morden; o.k.

**October 24, 1943**
Groups Operating: P-47 56th, 78th, 353rd, 356th
P-38 55th
Missions: General support in the Argentan-Bernay-Paris area.
Claims: 1-0-0 air
0-0 ground

| *Group* | | *Claims* | *Location* |
|---|---|---|---|
| **78th** | | | |
| 82nd: | Capt. W.E. May | (.5)Me-109 dest(air) | St. Gaillon |
| | Lt. A.W. Hill | (.5)Me-109 dest(air) | St. Gaillon |

Losses: nil

*Remarks*
78th: 0-1 loco

KIAc's
78th: Lt. Carl E. Cross (84th Ftr Sqn)
P-47 WZ-

**November 3, 1943**
Groups Operating: P-47 4th, 56th, 78th, 352nd, 353rd, 355th, 356th,
P-38 55th
Missions: Support for bombers to Wilhelmshaven.
Claims: 14-2-9 air
0-0 ground

| *Group* | | *Claims* | *Location* |
|---|---|---|---|
| **4th** | | | |
| 334th: | Lt. A. Rafalovich | Me-109 dest(air) | NE Zuider Zee |
| | Lt. R.B. Fraser | Me-109 prob(air) | Lemmer |
| **55th** | | | |
| HdQts: | LtCol. J.S. Jenkins | Me-109 dest(air) | Spiekeroog Isle |
| | | FW-190 prob(air) | Wilhelmshaven |
| 38th: | Maj. M. Joel | (.5)FW-190 dest(air) | Westerholt-Wittmund |
| | | (2)FW-190 dam(air) | N/Wilhelmshaven |
| | Lt. W.L. Kreft | (.5)FW-190 dest(air) | Westerholt-Wittmund |
| | Capt. J. Myers | FW-190 dam(air) | N/Wilhelmshaven |
| 343rd: | Lt. R.L. Buttke | (2)Me-109 dest(air) | E/Wilhelmshaven |
| | Capt. [illegible] | Me-109 dam(air) | E/Wilhelmshaven |
| | Lt. E.E. Ryan | Me-109 dam(air) | E/Wilhelmshaven |
| **56th** | | | |
| 61st: | Lt. R.S. Johnson | Me-109 dest(air) | N/Ameland Island |
| 63rd: | Capt. W.M. Mahurin | Me-110 dest(air) | N/Juist |
| | | (.5)Me-109 dest(air) | N/Essens |
| | Lt. W.J. O'Connor | (.5)Me-109 dest(air) | N/Essens |
| | Lt. A.J. Wisniewski | Me-110 dam(air) | N/Juist |
| **78th** | | | |
| 82nd: | Lt. C.B. Hahn | Me-109 dest(air) | Barzal |
| | Lt. N.D. Munson | Me-109 dam(air) | Barzal |
| | Lt. W.S. Swanson | Me-109 dam(air) | Barzal |
| **353rd** | | | |
| 351st: | Lt. H.D. Stump | Me-109 dam(air) | SW Wilhelmshaven |
| 352nd: | Lt. J.N. Poindexter | Me-110 dest(air) | Wilhelmshaven |
| | | Me-210 dest(air) | Wilhelmshaven |
| | Lt. W.H. Junttila | Me-110 dest(air) | Wilhelmshaven |
| | Lt. R.A. Newman | Me-110 dest(air) | Wilhelmshaven |
| | Lt. M. Morrison | Me-110 dest(air) | Wilhelmshaven |

*Losses-*

**4th:** F/O Frank D. Gallion (334th Ftr Sqn) KIA
P-47D QP-F 42-7924
Hit by enemy fighters near the Zuider Zee and crashed at Ijesselmeer.

Lt. Ivan R. Moon (334th Ftr Sqn) KIA
P-47C QP-M 41-6587
Downed by enemy fighters near Oosterland.

*Remarks*
4th: Lt. Lloyd W. Waterman (335th Ftr Sqn) c/l Halesworth; o.k.
P-47 WD-
356th: 0-1 barge, 0-1 vehicle, 0-1 ship, 0-1 building

**November 5, 1943**
Groups Operating: P-47 4th, 56th, 78th, 352nd, 353rd, 355th, 356th
P-38 55th
Missions: Support for bombers to Gelsenkirchen.
Claims: 19-2-17 air
0-0 ground

| *Group* | | *Claims* | *Location* |
|---|---|---|---|
| **4th** | | | |
| 335th: | Capt. F.D. Smith | FW-190 dest(air) | E/Eindhoven |
| **55th** | | | |
| 38th: | Capt. M.K. Shipman | Me-109 dest(air) | Doetinchem |
| | | (.5)Me-109 dest(air) | Nijmegen |
| | | (.5)Me-109 prob(air) | Winterswijk |
| | Maj. M. Joel | Me-109 dest(air) | W/Arnheim |
| | Capt. J. Myers | Me-109 dest(air) | Arnheim |
| | Lt. G.F. Leinweber | Me-109 dest(air) | Rotterdam |
| | Lt. C.W. Des Voignes | (.5)Me-109 dest(air) | Nijmegen |
| | | (.5)Me-109 prob(air) | Winterswijk |
| | Capt. J.H. Ayers | Do-217 prob(air) | W/Munster |
| | Lt. R.W. Forsblad | FW-190 dam(air) | E/Rotterdam |
| | Lt. D.L. Steiner | Do-217 dam(air) | Munster |
| **56th** | | | |
| HdQts: | Col. H. Zemke | FW-190 dest(air) | Enschede-Rheine |
| 61st: | Maj. F.S. Gabreski | FW-190 dest(air) | S/Rheine |
| | | FW-190 dam(air) | S/Rheine |
| | Lt. E.E. Barnum | FW-190 dest(air) | S/Rheine |
| 63rd: | Lt. G.F. Hall | Me-210 dest(air) | Enschede |
| | Lt. C.W. Reed | FW-190 dest(air) | Rheine-Munster |
| | Lt. J.D. Wilson | FW-190 dest(air) | Rheine-Munster |
| | Capt. L.A. Adrianse | FW-190 dam(air) | Rheine-Munster |
| | F/O A.H. Robey | FW-190 dam(air) | Rheine-Munster |
| **353rd** | | | |
| HdQts: | Maj. G.E. Duncan | Me-109 dam(air) | Gelsenkirchen |
| 350th: | Lt. W.J. Price | Me-210 dest(air) | Ruhr Valley |
| | Lt. R.A. Stearns | Me-210 dest(air) | Venlo |
| | Maj. B. Rimerman | (2)FW-190 dam(air) | Dusseldorf & Munchen-Gladbach |
| | Lt. W.F. Hurst | Me-109 dam(air) | W/Gelsenkirchen |
| 351st: | Capt. W.C. Beckham | Me-410 dest(air) | SW Gelsenkirchen |
| | | FW-190 dam(air) | SW Gelsenkirchen |
| | Capt. O.A. Kinkade | Me-109 dest(air) | W/Mors |
| | Lt. F.N. Emory | Me-210 dam(air) | Rheinburg |
| 352nd: | Lt. L.W. Ista | Me-109 dest(air) | Gelsenkirchen |
| | Capt. R.E. Robertson | FW-190 dam(air) | Dinslaken |
| **355th** | | | |
| 354th: | Lt. C.H. Sweat | FW-190 dest(air) | NW Gelsenkirchen |
| | Lt. P.W. Bauman | Me-109 dam(air) | NW Gelsenkirchen |
| | Lt. R.L. Vincent | Me-109 dam(air) | NW Gelsenkirchen |
| 357th: | Lt. E.L. Sluga | Me-210 dest(air) | Alben |
| | Lt. F.W. Kelley | Me-109 dam(air) | Uden |
| | Lt. C.H. Rankin | Me-210 dam(air) | Alben |
| **356th** | | | |
| 361st: | Capt. P.H. Hyde | Me-109 dam(air) | Roermond |

*Losses-*

**353rd:** Lt. Robert L. Newman (350th Ftr Sqn) KIA
P-47D LH- 42-7907
Hit by enemy fighters and crashed into the North Sea.

Capt. Orville A. Kinkade (351st Ftr Sqn) POW
P-47C YJ-K 41-6583 "Alyce"
Hit by enemy fighters and bailed out near Volkerak.

Lt. Benedict E. Kraft 351st Ftr Sqn) POW
P-47D YJ-Q 42-8428
Hit by enemy fighters and bailed out near Mulheim.

**355th**: Lt. Clark Collins (357th Ftr Sqn) KIA
P-47D OS-T 42-8406 "Eager Eve"
Hit by Me-109's west of Schouwen.

*Remarks*
352nd: P-47 c/l Bodney; o.k.

**November 7, 1943**
Groups Operating: P-47 56th, 78th, 352nd, 353rd, 355th, 356th
P-38 55th (plus 79th Ftr Sqn/20th Ftr Grp)
Missions: Support of bombers to Wesel and Duren.
Claims: 1-0-0 air
0-0 ground

| *Group* | | *Claims* | *Location* |
|---|---|---|---|
| **355th** | | | |
| 357th: | Capt. N.E. Olson | Me-210 dest(air) | Amiens |

*Losses-*

**20th**: Maj. John C. Wilkins (HdQts) KIA
P-38H LC- 42-67022
Took-off late and was never seen again.

Capt. Herbert W. Cumming (79th Ftr Sqn) KIA
P-38H MC-F 42-67039
Hit by a FW-190 and went down over the Channel.

**56th**: F/O Robert E. Sheehan (63rd Ftr Sqn) MIA-E
P-47D UN-C 42-7985
Suffered mechanical failure near Doesburg.

**355th**: Lt. Edwin O. Carlson (357th Ftr Sqn) KIA
P-47D OS-Q 42-7984 "On the Ball"
Collided with Lt. Westphal near Montdidier.

Lt. James A. Westphal (357th Ftr Sqn) POW
P-47D OS-L 42-8370 "Alabama Bound"
Collided with Lt. Carlson near Montdidier.

Capt. Walter H. Kossack (358th Ftr Sqn) POW
P-47D YF-X 42-8477
Ran out of fuel and bellied-in near the French coast.

Lt. William E. Roach (358th Ftr Sqn) POW
P-47D YF-U 42-22490 "Beetle"
Ran out of fuel and landed at Caen.

F/O Chester W. Watson (358th Ftr Sqn) KIA
P-47D YF-Z 42-8629
Ran out of fuel and bailed out over the Channel.

*Remarks*
78th: 0-1 flak tower
355th: Lt. Jack J. Woertz (358th Ftr Sqn) c/l Hastings; o.k.
P-47D YF-Y

Groups Operating: P-47 4th
P-38 55th (plus 79th Ftr Sqn/20th Ftr Grp)
Missions: Sweep of the Ostend-Lille-Pas de Calais area.
Claims: nil
Losses: nil

**November 10, 1943**
Groups Operating: P-47 4th, 78th, 355th, 356th
P-38 55th (plus 79th Ftr Sqn/20th Ftr Grp)
Missions: Sweeps over France and support for 9th Air Force B-26's.
Claims: nil
Losses: nil

**November 11, 1943**
Groups Operating: P-47 4th, 56th, 78th, 352nd, 353rd, 355th, 356th
P-38 55th (plus 79th Ftr Sqn/20th Ftr Grp)
Missions: Support of bombers to Munster.
Claims: 9-0-3 air
0-0 ground

| *Group* | | *Claims* | *Location* |
|---|---|---|---|
| **4th** | | | |
| 336th: | F/O J.L. Raphael | FW-190 dam(air) | W/Hook of Holland |
| **56th** | | | |
| 62nd: | Capt. W.V. Cook | (2)FW-190 dest(air) | Bocholt |
| | Capt. E.W. O'Neill | FW-190 dest(air) | Munster |
| | Lt. G.G. Goldstein | FW-190 dest(air) | Munster |
| | F/O J.W. Icard | FW-190 dest(air) | Munster |
| | Capt. L.A. Schreiber | FW-190 dam(air) | Munster |
| 63rd: | Capt. S.V. Burke | Me-109 dest(air) | NW Munster |
| **353rd** | | | |
| HdQts: | Maj. G.E. Duncan | Me-109 dest(air) | Numansdorp |
| | | FW-190 dest(air) | Munster |
| | | Me-109 dam(air) | Numansdorp |
| 351st: | Capt. W.C. Beckham | FW-190 dest(air) | Dulman |

*Losses-*

**56th**: Lt. Malcolm Van Meter (62nd Ftr Sqn) KIA
P-47D LM-Z 42-74626
Suffered mechanical failure and crashed into the North Sea.

Lt. Wayne J. O'Connor (63rd Ftr Sqn) KIA
P-47D UN-O 42-74722
Hit by a FW-190 near Goesfeld.

**356th**: Lt. Dolor A. Martin (360th Ftr Sqn) KIA
P-47D PI- 42-8668
Last seen in the Arnheim area, possible oxygen failure.

**November 13, 1943**
Groups Operating: P-47 4th, 56th, 78th, 352nd, 353rd, 355th, 356th
P-38 55th
Missions: Support of bombers to Bremen.
Claims: 9-4-7 air
0-0 ground

| *Group* | | *Claims* | *Location* |
|---|---|---|---|
| **55th** | | | |
| HdQts: | Capt. T.E. Beaird | FW-190 dam(air) | W/Bremen |
| 38th: | Maj. M. Joel | Ju-88 dest(air) | Bremen |
| | | Ju-88 prob(air) | Bremen |
| | | Me-109 prob(air) | Bremen |
| | | Me-109 dam(air) | Bremen |
| | Capt. J. Myers | Me-109 dest(air) | Bremen |
| | | Ju-88 dam(air) | Bremen |
| | Lt. R.F. Maloney | FW-190 dest(air) | Bremen |
| | | FW-190 dam(air) | Bremen |
| | Lt. G. Brown | Me-109 dam(air) | Bremen |
| 338th: | Lt. C.E. Beall | FW-190 dest(air) | Bremen |
| | Capt. J.P. Marsiglia | Me-210 prob(air) | Hagen |
| | Lt. K.H. Garlock | Me-210 dam(air) | Hagen |
| 343rd: | Capt. E.E. Ryan | Me-109 dest(air) | W/Bremen |
| | | FW-190 prob(air) | W/Bremen |
| | Capt. E.B. Giller | Ju-88 dest(air) | W/Bremen |
| **353rd** | | | |
| 350th: | Lt. C.W. Dinse | FW-190 dam(air) | Meppen |
| **355th** | | | |
| 354th: | Lt. T.F. Neal | Me-109 dest(air) | W/Bremen |
| | Lt. R.L. Vincent | Me-109 dest(air) | W/Meppen |
| 357th: | Capt. N.E. Olson | Me-109 dest(air) | Zwolle |

*Losses-*

**55th**: Lt. John A. Stacker (38th Ftr Sqn) KIA
P-38H CG- 42-67059
Hit by enemy fighters near Oldenburg.

Lt. Charles F. Beall (338th Ftr Sqn) KIA
P-38H CL- 42-67049
Hit by enemy fighters near Bremen.

Lt. Lynn R. Goetzman (338th Ftr Sqn) POW
P-38H CL- 42-67073
Hit by enemy fighters near Bremen.

Lt. William C. Florentine, Jr. (338th Ftr Sqn) POW
P-38H CL- 42-66732
Hit by enemy fighters near Bremen.

Lt. Robert N. Jensen (338th Ftr Sqn) POW
P-38H CL- 42-66724
Hit by enemy fighters and bailed out near Hahlemer Moor.

Lt. William W. Shank (338th Ftr Sqn) KIA
P-38H CL- 42-66727
Hit by enemy fighters near Bremen.

Lt. Gene C. Stephens (338th Ftr Sqn) KIA
P-38H CL- 42-67078
Hit by enemy fighters near Bremen.

**355th**: LtCol. Thomas H. Hubbard (HdQts) MIA-E
P-47D WR- 42-7944
Hit by flak near Bergentheim.

Lt. John Lanphier (358th Ftr Sqn) KIA
P-47D YF-W 42-8626
Last seen being chased by Me-109's near Dalfsen.

*Remarks*
55th: P-38 c/l East Wretham; o.k.
P-38 c/l Debden; o.k.
353rd: 0-1 loco

**November 15, 1943**
Groups Operating: P-47 355th
P-38 20th (77th Ftr Sqn only)
Missions: Two P-47's and one P-38 flew weather recons.
Claims: nil

*Losses-*

**355th**: Lt. Lawrence E. McGraw (357th Ftr Sqn) KIA
P-47D OS-U 42-8408 "Jean's Little Moe"
Lost for unknown reasons; possible collision with McNally.

Lt. Donald B. McNally (357th Ftr Sqn) KIA
P-47D OS-P 42-8413 "Ma Fran"
Lost for unknown reasons; possible collision with McGraw.

**November 17, 1943**
KIAc's
56th: Lt. Harry Coronios (62nd Ftr Sqn)
P-47D LM-D 42-8614
Died in a crash east of Happisburgh.

**November 19, 1943**
Groups Operating: P-47 56th, 78th, 352nd, 353rd, 355th, 356th
Missions: Support of bombers to various German and Dutch targets.
Claims: nil
Losses: nil

**November 25, 1943**
Groups Operating: P-47 56th, 78th, 352nd, 353rd, 355th
P-38 55th (plus 77th Ftr Sqn/20th Ftr Grp)
Missions: Sweep of the Lille area plus the 353rd dive-bombed St. Omer Airfield.
Claims: 4-3-2 air
0-0 ground

| *Group* | | *Claims* | *Location* |
|---|---|---|---|
| **55th** | | | |
| HdQts: | LtCol. J.S. Jenkins | FW-190 dest(air) | La Bassee |
| 38th: | Lt. R.F. Maloney | Me-109 dest(air) | Lille |
| | | Me-109 prob(air) | Hazebrouck |
| | Lt. D.L. Steiner | Me-109 dest(air) | Lille |
| | Lt. W.K. Birch | Me-109 prob(air) | NW Arras |
| 338th: | Capt. C.A. Patterson | FW-190 dest(air) | Lens |
| 343rd: | Capt. R.M. Malmstedt | Me-109 prob(air) | Lille |
| | Capt. E.E. Ryan | (2)Me-109 dam(air) | Lille |

*Losses-*

**20th**: Lt. Bill Lane (77th Ftr Sqn) KIA
P-38H LC- 42-67032
Hit by flak near St. Omer, then lost his second engine ten miles from Nuthampstead.

**55th**: Lt. Manuel J. Aldecoa (343rd Ftr Sqn) KIA
P-38H CY- 42-67061
Collided with a FW-190 near La Bassee, bailed out, but his parachute streamed.

**353rd**: LtCol. Loren G. McCollom(HdQts) POW
P-47D YJ-S 42-8395 "Cookie"
Hit by flak at St. Omer Airfield.

*Remarks*
20th: 77th Ftr Sqn P-38 c/l Bishops Stortford; o.k.
55th: P-38 c/l Duxford; o.k.

**November 26, 1943**
Groups Operating: P-47 4th, 56th, 78th, 352nd, 353rd, 355th, 356th
P-38 55th (plus 77th Ftr Sqn/20th Ftr Grp)
Missions: Support of bombers to Bremen.
Claims: 34-4-10 air
0-0 ground

| *Group* | | *Claims* | *Location* |
|---|---|---|---|
| **4th** | | | |
| 335th: | Lt. C.V. Padgett | Me-109 dest(air) | Rude |
| **20th** | | | |
| 77th: | Maj. H.E. Johnson | Do-217 dest(air) | S/Lemwerder A/F |
| **55th** | | | |
| 38th: | Lt. R.E. Erickson | FW-190 dam(air) | W/Bremen |
| 343rd: | Maj. D.W. Webb | Me-210 dest(air) | NE Bremen |
| | Capt. R.M. Malmstedt | Ju-88 dest(air) | NE Bremen |
| **56th** | | | |
| HdQts: | LtCol. D.C. Schilling | (2)FW-190 dest(air) | SE Oldenburg |
| | | Me-210 dam(air) | SE Oldenburg |
| | Maj. J.C. Stewart | Do-217 dest(air) | SE Oldenburg |
| 61st: | Maj. F.S. Gabreski | (2)Me-110 dest(air) | SE Oldenburg |
| | F/O F.W. Klibbe | Me-109 dest(air) | SE Oldenburg |
| 62nd: | Capt. W.V. Cook | (2)Me-110 dest(air) | Papenburg |
| | Capt. R.A. Johnson | (2)Me-110 dest(air) | Papenburg |
| | F/O I.E. Valenta | (2)Me-110 dest(air) | Papenburg |
| | | (2)Me-110 dam(air) | Papenburg |
| | Capt. E.W. O'Neill | FW-190 dest(air) | Papenburg |
| | | (.5)Me-110 dest(air) | Papenburg |
| | Lt. M.K. Boyle | (.5)Me-110 dest(air) | Papenburg |
| | Lt. A.R. Carcione | Me-210 dest(air) | Papenburg |
| | Lt. F.J. Christensen | Me-110 dest(air) | Papenburg |
| | Lt. S.B. Morrill | Me-109 dest(air) | Papenburg |
| | | Me-109 dam(air) | Papenburg |
| | Maj. H.C. Craig | Me-210 prob(air) | Papenburg |
| | | Me-110 prob(air) | Papenburg |
| 63rd: | Capt. W.M. Mahurin | (3)Me-110 dest(air) | S/Oldenburg |
| | | Me-110 prob(air) | S/Oldenburg |
| | Lt. H.E. Comstock | Me-110 dest(air) | Friesoythe |
| | | Me-110 dam(air) | Friesoythe |
| | | FW-190 dam(air) | Friesoythe |
| | Lt. J.H. Truluck | FW-190 dest(air) | Friesoythe |
| | | Me-110 dam(air) | Friesoythe |
| | Lt. J.D. Brown | FW-190 dam(air) | Friesoythe |
| | Lt. R.D. Petty | Me-110 dam(air) | Friesoythe |
| **78th** | | | |
| 82nd: | Lt. W.M. Wesson | FW-190 dest(air) | Beauvais |
| 83rd: | Lt. H.S. Askelson | Me-109 dest(air) | Paris |
| 84th: | Maj. J.C. Price | Me-109 dest(air) | Paris |
| | | FW-190 dest(air) | Paris |
| **352nd** | | | |
| 487th: | Maj. J.C. Meyer | Me-109 dest(air) | E/Groningen |
| | | Me-109 prob(air) | E/Groningen |
| | Capt. D.K. Dilling | Me-109 dest(air) | E/Groningen |
| | Lt. J.R. Bennett | (.5)Me-109 dest(air) | E/Groningen |
| | Lt. R.H. Berkshire | (.5)Me-109 dest(air) | E/Groningen |

*Losses-*

**56th**: Lt. Byron L. Morrill (62nd Ftr Sqn) POW
P-47D LM-C 42-7979
Ran out of fuel and bailed out near the Zuider Zee.

**78th**: Lt. John W. Herrick (82nd Ftr Sqn) MIA-E
P-47C MX-U 41-6188
Hit by enemy fighters near Beauvais and bailed out near Chantilly.

F/O Ralph E. Cormier (83rd Ftr Sqn) KIA
P-47D HL-E 42-8681
Hit by enemy aircraft near Paris.

Lt. Wayne W. Dougherty (84th Ftr Sqn) POW
P-47D WZ-L 42-8573
Hit by a Me-109 near Paris and bailed out near Moiselles.

*Remarks*
78th: 0-3 flak towers
P-47 c/l; o.k.
P-47 c/l; o.k.
P-47 c/l; o.k.

**November 29, 1943**
Groups Operating: P-47 4th, 56th, 78th, 352nd, 353rd, 355th, 356th
P-38 55th (plus 77th Ftr Sqn/20th Ftr Grp)
Missions: Support of bombers to Bremen.
Claims: 14-8-7 air
0-0 ground

| *Group* | | *Claims* | *Location* |
|---|---|---|---|
| **4th** | | | |
| 334th: | Lt. D.W. Beeson | Me-109 prob(air) | Bremen |
| 335th: | Capt. F.D. Smith | Me-109 prob(air) | Hude |
| 336th: | Lt. J.T. Godfrey | Me-109 prob(air) | Bremen |
| **55th** | | | |
| HdQts: | Capt. T.E. Beaird | Me-109 prob(air) | W/Bremen |
| 38th: | Capt. J.H. Ayers | Me-109 dest(air) | W/Bremen |
| | Lt. R.E. Erickson | Me-109 dam(air) | W/Bremen |
| 338th: | Capt. C.A. Patterson | Me-109 dest(air) | N/Bremen |
| | Capt. J.P. Marsiglia | Me-109 dam(air) | E/Bremen |

**56th**

| | | | |
|---|---|---|---|
| HdQts: | LtCol. D.C. Schilling | (.5)FW-190 dest(air) | S/Oldenburg |
| 61st: | Maj. F.S. Gabreski | (2)Me-109 dest(air) | NE Bremen |
| | Lt. J.H. Powers | Me-109 dest(air) | NE Bremen |
| | Capt. R.A. Lamb | Me-109 prob(air) | Bremen |
| 62nd: | Lt. F.D. Williamson | (.5)FW-190 dest(air) | S/Oldenburg |
| | Capt. L.A. Schreiber | (.5)Me-210 dest(air) | S/Oldenburg |
| | Lt. H.M. Pruden | (.5)Me-210 dest(air) | S/Oldenburg |
| 63rd: | Capt. W.M. Mahurin | Me-109 dest(air) | Leer-Papenburg |
| | | Me-109 dam(air) | Leer-Papenburg |
| | Lt. H.E. Comstock | Me-109 prob(air) | Papenburg |
| | Lt. B.R. Smith | Me-109 dam(air) | Lathen |

**355th**

| | | | |
|---|---|---|---|
| 358th: | Lt. J.J. Woertz | Me-109 dest(air) | W/Bremen |
| | Lt. J.C. Hull | Me-109 dam(air) | Bremen |

**356th**

| | | | |
|---|---|---|---|
| 359th: | Maj. D.A. Baccus | Me-109 dest(air) | NE Meppel |
| | Capt. E.J. White | Me-109 dest(air) | NE Meppel |
| | Lt. J.B. Smith | Me-109 dest(air) | NE Meppel |
| | | Me-109 prob(air) | NE Meppel |
| | Lt. L.F. Richason | Me-109 dam(air) | NE Meppel |
| | Lt. G.B. Peet | Me-109 dam(air) | NE Meppel |
| 360th: | Lt. R.R. Withers | Me-109 dest(air) | Meppel |
| | Capt. J.H. Bennett | Me-109 prob(air) | Meppel |
| 361st: | Lt. A.M. Metzger | Me-109 dest(air) | Meppel |

*Losses-*

**20th:** Lt. John S. Hascall (77th Ftr Sqn) POW
P-38H LC- 42-67016
Hit by enemy fighters near Aschendorf.

**55th:** Maj. Milton Joel (38th Ftr Sqn) KIA
P-38H CG- 42-67020
Hit by enemy fighters near Ijsselmeer.

Lt. Albert A. Albino (38th Ftr Sqn) KIA
P-38H CG- 42-67051
Hit by enemy fighters near Hoogeveen.

Lt. John J. Carroll (38th Ftr Sqn) POW
P-38H CG- 42-67090
Hit by enemy fighters near Zwartsluis.

Lt. James M. Garvin (38th Ftr Sqn) KIA
P-38H CG- 42-67046
Hit by enemy fighters near Oldenburg.

Lt. Fleming W. Suiter (338th Ftr Sqn) KIA
P-38H CL- 42-67069
Hit by enemy fighters near Meppel.

Lt. James W. Gilbride (343rd Ftr Sqn) KIA
P-38H CY- 42-67097
Hit by enemy fighters near Avereest.

**56th:** Lt. Fred C. Windmayer (63rd Ftr Sqn) KIA
P-47D UN-F 42-7893
Suffered mechanical failure and crashed into the North Sea.

**355th:** Lt. Alfred J. DelNegro (354th Ftr Sqn) KIA
P-47D WR-D 42-7996
Disappeared for unknown reasons.

Lt. Charles K. Hecht, Jr. (358th Ftr Sqn) POW
P-47D YF-U 42-8631
Ran out of fuel and landed near Gasselternijveen.

Lt. Richard A. Peery (358th Ftr Sqn) POW
P-47D YF-L 42-22484 "Slugger"
Hit by enemy fighters near Bremen.

**356th:** Lt. Warren H Beach (359th Ftr Sqn) POW
P-47D OC- 42-8601
Hit by B-17 fire near Aschendorf.

Lt. John D. Hull (359th Ftr Sqn) POW
P-47D OC- 42-8598
Ran out of fuel near Vreeland.

Lt. Julius B. Asbridge (360th Ftr Sqn) POW
P-47D PI-W 42-8502 "Hell's Angel"
Hit by enemy fighters near Scheveningen.

Lt. Johnnie F. Martin (361st Ftr Sqn) KIA
P-47D QI-Q 42-8692
Last seen in the overcast near Hellendoorn.

Lt. Allen M. Metzger (361st Ftr Sqn) KIA
P-47D QI-O 42-8509
Last seen in the overcast near Holdorf.

*Remarks*

56th: Lt. John D. Wilson (63rd Ftr Sqn) c/l Halesworth; o.k.
P-47C UN-E 41-6584

**November 30, 1943**

Groups Operating: P-47 4th, 56th, 78th, 352nd, 353rd, 355th, 356th
P-38 55th (plus 77th Ftr Sqn/20th Ftr Grp)
Missions: Support of bombers to Solingen.
Claims: 1-1-1 air
0-0 ground

| *Group* | | *Claims* | *Location* |
|---|---|---|---|
| **78th** | | | |
| 82nd: | Maj. J.J. Oberhansly | FW-190 dest(air) | Eupen |
| | Lt. C.G. Godard | Me-109 prob(air) | Eupen |
| | Lt. M.R. Wright | Me-109 dam(air) | Eupen |

*Losses-*

**20th:** Lt. Robert L. Thomas, Jr. (77th Ftr Sqn) POW
P-38H LC- 42-67038
Hit by a Me-109 over the Dutch Islands and bailed out over the Channel.

**56th:** Lt. William B. Grosvenor (61st Ftr Sqn) MIA-E
P-47D HV- 42-75216
Suffered mechanical failure and bailed out off the Belgian coast.

**352nd:** Lt. Robert L. Babbitt (486th Ftr Sqn) KIA
P-47D PZ- 42-22516
Hit by enemy fighters near Oirschut.

Lt. Robert M. Brown (486th Ftr Sqn) KIA
P-47D PZ- 42-8411
Hit by enemy fighters near Goirle.

Lt. David C. Kramer (486th Ftr Sqn) MIA-E
P-47D PZ- 42-8514
Hit by enemy fighters near Neerpelt.

**December 1, 1943**

Groups Operating: P-47 4th, 56th, 78th, 352nd, 353rd, 355th, 356th
P-38 55th (plus 77th Ftr Sqn, 20th Ftr Grp)
Missions: Support for bombers to Solingen and Leverkusen.
Claims: 15-7-11 air
0-0 ground

| *Group* | | *Claims* | *Location* |
|---|---|---|---|
| **4th** | | | |
| 335th: | Capt. G. Carpenter | Ju-88 dam(air) | E/Cologne |
| 336th: | Lt. J.T. Godfrey | Me-109 dest(air) | Ruhr Valley |
| | | Me-109 dam(air) | Ruhr Valley |
| **20th** | | | |
| 77th: | Lt. J.L. Gard | FW-190 dest(air) | Coblenz |
| **56th** | | | |
| 61st: | Lt. J.D. Foster | FW-190 dest(air) | Beverloo |
| | Lt. D.H. Mudge | Me-109 dest(air) | Ruhr Valley |
| 62nd: | Lt. F.J. Christensen | Me-109 dest(air) | SE Roermond |
| | Capt. R.A. Johnson | Me-109 dam(air) | SE Roermond |
| **78th** | | | |
| 82nd: | Lt. J.W. Wilkinson | Me-109 dest(air) | Eupen |
| 83rd: | Lt. H.C. Roff | Me-110 prob(air) | Duren |
| 84th: | Lt. C.N. Keppler | FW-190 dest(air) | Liege-Aachen |
| | Lt. G.H. Doyle | (2)FW-190 prob(air) | Liege-Aachen |
| | Lt. P.E. Pompetti | FW-190 dam(air) | Liege-Aachen |
| | Lt. E.E. Russell | FW-190 dam(air) | SE Aachen |
| **352nd** | | | |
| 487th: | Capt. G.E. Preddy | Me-109 dest(air) | S/Rheydt |
| | Lt. V.K. Meroney | Me-109 dest(air) | S/Rheydt |
| | | (.5)Me-210 dest(air) | S/Rheydt |
| | Lt. R.L. Grow | (.5)Me-210 dest(air) | S/Rheydt |
| **353rd** | | | |
| 350th: | Lt. R.N. Ireland | FW-190 prob(air) | Solingen |
| | Lt. W.K. Blickenstaff | Me-109 dam(air) | Solingen |
| | Lt. C.O. Durant | Me-110 dam(air) | Solingen |
| 351st: | Capt. W.C. Beckham | (2)FW-190 dest(air) | Koln |
| 352nd: | Lt. R.A. Newman | Me-210 dest(air) | Solingen |
| **355th** | | | |
| 357th: | Lt. B.D. Johnston | Me-109 dest(air) | W/Cologne |
| | | Me-109 dam(air) | W/Cologne |

| | | | |
|---|---|---|---|
| | Lt. R. Bernoske | Me-109 prob(air) | W/Cologne |
| | Capt. N.E. Olson | Me-109 dam(air) | W/Cologne |
| | Lt. W.S. Easterly | Me-109 dam(air) | W/Cologne |
| 358th: | Lt. H.M. Macurdy | Me-109 prob(air) | NW Aachen |
| | Capt. C.F. Ekstrom | Me-109 dam(air) | Duren |
| **356th** | | | |
| 361st: | Lt. J.T. Price | FW-190 dest(air) | Brussels-Louvain |
| | | FW-190 prob(air) | Brussels-Louvain |

*Losses-*

**20th**: Lt. Jack L. Gard (77th Ftr Sqn) POW
P-38H LC- 42-66723
Hit by a Me-109 near Coblenz.

**55th**: Lt. Wilton G. Erickson (38th Ftr Sqn) KIA
P-38H CG- 42-67033
Suffered mechnaical failure near Siegburg.

Lt. William C. Turner (338th Ftr Sqn) KIA
P-38J CL-
Spun-in near Gillingham.

**56th**: Lt. Cleve M. Brown, Jr. (61st Ftr Sqn) POW
P-47C HV-L 41-6211 "Jackie"
Hit by enemy fighters near Ghent.

Lt. Harry M. Pruden, Jr. (62nd Ftr Sqn) KIA
P-47D LM- 42-74631
Hit by enemy fighters near Cologne.

Lt. Vance P. Ludwig (63rd Ftr Sqn) KIA
P-47D UN-K 42-8607
Hit by enemy fighters near St. Trond.

**355th**: Lt. Jesse M. Williamson (357th Ftr Sqn) POW
P-47D OS-Z 42-22545
Hit by flak near Coblenz.

Capt. James C. Hull (358th Ftr Sqn) KIA
P-47D YF-A 42-8006
Last seen in heavy clouds near Lierre.

*Remarks*
55th: Lt. Donald E. Penn (38th Ftr Sqn) c/l; o.k.
P-38 CG-
78th: Lt. William H. Reese (83rd Ftr Sqn) c/l; o.k.
P-47D HL-C 42-8642
Lt. Robert E. Clague (84th Ftr Sqn) c/l; o.k.
P-47C WZ-H 41-6270
Lt. Ernest E. Powell (84th Ftr Sqn) c/l; o.k.
P-47D WZ-C 42-8551
353rd: Lt. Joseph Rosenberg (350th Ftr Sqn) c/l Metfield; o.k.
P-47D LH-Y 42-8697

**December 2, 1943**
KIAc's
4th: F/O John P. McNabb (334th Ftr Sqn)
P-47C QP-L 41-6484
His aircraft burst into flames and crshed near Kenton.

55th: Capt. Roland L. Malmstedt (343rd Ftr Sqn)
P-38J CY-
Lost an engine on take-off, hit the ground, and exploded.

**December 4, 1943**
Groups Operating: P-47 56th, 352nd, 353rd
Missions: The 353rd was to dive-bomb Gilze-Rijen Airfield with the 56th acting as escort and the 352nd sweeping.
Claims: 3-0-0 air
0-0 ground

| *Group* | | *Claims* | *Location* |
|---|---|---|---|
| **352nd** | | | |
| 487th: | Maj. J.C. Meyer | Me-109 dest(air) | W/Utrecht |
| | Lt. V.K. Meroney | Me-109 dest(air) | Rotterdam-Utrecht |
| | | (.5)FW-190 dest(air) | Rotterdam-Utrecht |
| | F/O J.L. Sweeney | (.5)FW-190 dest(air) | Rotterdam-Utrecht |

Losses: nil

KIAc's
355th: Lt. Roland L. Vincent (354th Ftr Sqn)
P-47D WR-S 42-8433
Tail came off in a dive near Colerne.

**December 5, 1943**
Groups Operating: P-47 4th, 56th, 78th, 352nd, 353rd, 355th, 356th
P-38 55th(plus 55th Ftr Sqn, 20th Ftr Grp)
Missions: An intended escort which was hampered by weather and most bombers did not attack their targets.
Claims: nil

*Losses-*

**56th**: Lt. George G. Goldstein (62nd Ftr Sqn) POW
P-47C LM-L 41-6242
Suffered mechanical failure and bailed out near St. Sauflieu.

**December 10, 1943**
KIAc's
78th: Lt. Melvin R. Wright (82nd Ftr Sqn)
P-47D MX-
Split-essed into the ground near Duxford.

**December 11, 1943**
Groups Operating: P-47 4th, 56th, 78th, 352nd, 353rd, 355th, 356th
P-38 55th (plus 55th Ftr Sqn, 20th Ftr Grp)
Missions: Support of bombers to Emden.
Claims: 21-0-9 air
0-0 ground

| *Group* | | *Claims* | *Location* |
|---|---|---|---|
| **4th** | | | |
| 334th: | Lt. V.J. France | Me-109 dest(air) | Leeuwarden |
| 335th: | Lt. P.W. McKennon | Me-109 dam(air) | Leeuwarden |
| | Lt. B.C. Wyman | Me-109 dam(air) | Leeuwarden |
| **56th** | | | |
| HdQts: | Col. R.B. Landry | Me-109 dest(air) | NE Emden |
| 61st: | Capt. R.A. Lamb | (3)Me-110 dest(air) | N/Langeroog Isle |
| | Lt. P.A. Conger | (2)Me-110 dest(air) | Langeroog Island |
| | | Ju-88 dest(air) | Langeroog Island |
| | | Me-110 dam(air) | Langeroog Island |
| | Lt. R.W. Roberts | Me-110 dest(air) | Langeroog Island |
| | | Ju-88 dest(air) | Langeroog Island |
| | | Ju-88 dam(air) | Langeroog Island |
| | Lt. D.F. Smith | (2)Me-110 dest(air) | Emden |
| | | (.5)FW-190 dest(air) | Emden |
| | | Me-110 dam(air) | Emden |
| | F/O W.R. Aggers | (.5)FW-190 dest(air) | Emden |
| | Lt. J.H. Powers | Me-110 dest(air) | N/Norderney Isle |
| | | FW-190 dest(air) | N/Aurich |
| | | Me-110 dam(air) | N/Aurich |
| | Maj. F.S. Gabreski | Me-110 dest(air) | Esens |
| | Lt. S.D. Hamilton | (2)Me-110 dam(air) | NW Emden |
| 62nd: | Lt. S.B. Morrill | Me-110 dest(air) | Eelde |
| 63rd: | Lt. G.D. Schiltz | Me-210 dest(air) | Emden |
| **78th** | | | |
| 84th: | Lt. G.W. Koontz | Me-109 dest(air) | SW Groningen |
| | Lt. E.F. Fleming | Me-109 dam(air) | SW Groningen |
| **352nd** | | | |
| 328th: | Lt. R.L. Cornick | Me-110 dest(air) | Drachten |
| 487th: | Capt. D.K. Dilling | Me-110 dest(air) | Leeuwarden |

*Losses-*

**56th**: Lt. Edward J. Kruer (61st Ftr Sqn) KIA
P-47D HV- 42-8606
Collided with Lt. Strand near Spiekeroog.

Lt. Larry H. Strand (61st Ftr Sqn) KIA
P-47D HV-I 42-7967
Collied with Lt. Kruer near Spiekeroog.

**355th**: Lt. Jack Woertz (358th Ftr Sqn) KIA
P-47D YF-Y 42-75045
Stalled on approach and crashed near Hastings.

*Remarks*
355th: Lt. Donald J. Laing (357th Ftr Sqn) b/o Steeple Morden; o.k.
P-47D OS-

**December 13, 1943**
Groups Operating: P-47 56th, 78th, 352nd, 353rd, 355th, 356th
P-38 55th
Missions: Support of bombers to Kiel.
Claims: 1-0-1 air
0-0 ground

| *Group* | | *Claims* | *Location* |
|---|---|---|---|
| **55th** | | | |
| 338th: | Capt. C.O. Jones | Me-109 dam(air) | N/Oldenburg |
| 343rd: | Lt. J.W. Hiner | Ju-88 dest(air) | NW Hamburg |

Losses: nil

*Remarks*
4th: Lt. Louis H. Norley (336th Ftr Sqn) c/l Debden; o.k.
P-47C VF-O 41-6183
55th: Lt. Hugh Gouldelock (343rd Ftr Sqn) c/l Ludham; o.k.
P-38H CY-L 42-67053 "Vivacious Vera"

Groups Operating: P-47 359th
Missions: Sweep of the Pas de Calais area for its first mission.
Claims: nil
Losses: nil

**December 16, 1943**
Groups Operating: P-47 4th, 355th, 356th
P-38 55th
Missions: Support of bombers to Bremen.
Claims: 1-0-0 air
0-0 ground

| *Group* | | *Claims* | *Location* |
|---|---|---|---|
| **4th** | | | |
| 336th: | Capt. D.S. Gentile | (.33)Ju-88 dest(air) | E/Zuider Zee |
| | Lt. V. Garrison | (.33)Ju-88 dest(air) | E/Zuider Zee |
| | Lt. L.H. Norley | (.33)Ju-88 dest(air) | E/Zuider Zee |

*Losses-*

**55th**: Lt. William K. Burch (38th Ftr Sqn) KIA
P-38J CG-
Spun-in near Waverly.

**356th**: Lt. James T. Price (361st Ftr Sqn) KIA
P-47D QI-K 42-74709
Spun-in northeast of Felixstowe.

*Remarks*
355th: Lt. Harold H. Macurdy (358th Ftr Sqn) c/l Rackheath; o.k.
P-47D YF-

**December 20, 1943**
Groups Operating: P-47 4th, 56th, 78th, 352nd, 353rd, 356th, 358th, 359th
P-38 55th
Missions: Support for bombers going to Bremen.
Claims: 14-2-2 air
0-0 ground

| *Group* | | *Claims* | *Location* |
|---|---|---|---|
| **4th** | | | |
| HdQts: | LtCol. D.J.M. Blakeslee | Me-110 dest(air)* | Bremen-Wilhelmshaven |
| 336th: | Lt. W.W. Millikan | Me-109 dest(air) | NW Bremen |

* - claimed while "breaking-in" the 354th Ftr Grp, a P-51 unit of the 9th Air Force.

| *Group* | | *Claims* | *Location* |
|---|---|---|---|
| **56th** | | | |
| 61st: | Capt. J.H. Bennett | Me-110 dest(air) | Falkenberg |
| | Lt. J.H. Powers | Me-109 dest(air) | NE Bremen |
| | | (.5)Me-109 dam(air) | NE Bremen |
| | | (.5)Me-210 dam(air) | NE Bremen |
| | Lt. M.C. Wood | (.5)Me-109 dam(air) | NE Bremen |
| | | (.5)Me-210 dam(air) | NE Bremen |
| 62nd: | Maj. H.C. Craig | Do-217 dest(air) | SE Bremen |
| | Capt. E.W. O'Neill | Me-109 dest(air) | Vegesack |
| | Lt. M.J. Quirk | Me-109 dest(air) | S/Bremen |
| 63rd: | Lt. C.C. Clamp | FW-190 prob(air) | Bremen |
| **78th** | | | |
| 83rd: | Lt. H.T. Barnaby | Me-109 dest(air) | SW Bremen |
| **352nd** | | | |
| 486th: | Capt. F.N. Greene | Me-109 dest(air) | SW Emden |
| 487th: | Capt. D.K. Dilling | Me-109 dest(air) | NW Oosterwalde |
| | Capt. W.E. McIntyre | Me-109 dest(air) | NW Oosterwalde |
| | Lt. D.T. Britt | Me-109 dest(air) | NW Oosterwalde |
| | Lt. H.S. Riley | FW-190 dest(air) | NW Oosterwalde |
| **353rd** | | | |
| HdQts: | LtCol. G.E. Duncan | FW-190 dest(air) | Rastede |
| 352nd: | Lt. E.G. Stiff | FW-190 prob(air) | Varel |

*Losses-*

**56th**: Lt. Robert B. Taylor (62nd Ftr Sqn) KIA
P-47D LM-H 42-22527 "Taylor Maid II"
Ran out of fuel and crashed into the North Sea.

**356th**: Capt. Paul H. Hyde, Jr. (361st Ftr Sqn) KIA
P-47D QI-L 42-8677
Collided with a B-24 near Den Helder.

*Remarks*
56th: Lt. Charles W. Reed (63rd Ftr Sqn) c/l Southwold; o.k.
P-47C UN-X 41-6367
356th: Lt. Alex S. Koczak (360th Ftr Sqn) c/l Bromeswell; o.k.
P-47D PI-

**December 21, 1943**
Groups Operating: P-47 78th, 356th, 358th, 359th
Missions: Support of 9th Air Force bombers.
Claims: nil
Losses: nil

*Remarks*
359th: Lt. Herman E. King (370th Ftr Sqn) c/l Manston; o.k.
P-47D CS-

**December 22, 1943**
Groups Operating: P-47 4th, 56th, 78th, 352nd, 353rd, 355th, 356th, 358th, 359th
P-38 55th
Missions: Support of bombers to Osnabruck and Munster.
Claims: 15-2-4 air
0-0 ground

| *Group* | | *Claims* | *Location* |
|---|---|---|---|
| **4th** | | | |
| 334th: | Lt. V.H. Wynn | (1.5)Me-109 dest(air) | Enschede |
| 336th: | Lt. J.T. Godfrey | (1.5)Me-109 dest(air) | Enschede |
| **56th** | | | |
| 61st: | Lt. R.S. Johnson | Me-109 dest(air) | N/Almelo |
| 62nd: | Lt. F.D. Williamson | Me-109 dest(air) | W/Rheims |
| 63rd: | Capt. W.M. Mahurin | (2)Me-109 dest(air) | Hesepe |
| **78th** | | | |
| 83rd: | Lt. M.D. Putnam | Me-109 dest(air) | W/Munster |
| | | Me-109 dam(air) | W/Munster |
| **352nd** | | | |
| 328th: | Lt. J.B. Coleman | Me-110 dest(air) | Zwolle |
| | Lt. F.W. Horne | Me-110 dest(air) | Zwolle |
| | Maj. E.W. Stewart | (.5)Me-110 dest(air) | Zwolle |
| | | Me-210 dam(air) | Zwolle |
| | Lt. R.H. Powell | (.5)Me-110 dest(air) | Zwolle |
| 487th: | Maj. J.C. Meyer | Me-109 dest(air) | N/Lingen |
| | Capt. G.E. Preddy | Me-210 dest(air) | E/Zuider Zee |
| | Lt. J.R. Bennett | (.5)Me-109 dest(air) | E/Zwolle |
| | | FW-190 dam(air) | E/Zwolle |
| | Lt. E.B. McMahan | (.5)Me-109 dest(air) | E/Zwolle |
| | | FW-190 dam(air) | E/Zwolle |
| | Lt. H.S. Riley | Me-109 prob(air) | E/Meppen |
| **353rd** | | | |
| 351st: | Capt. F.H. LeFebre | Me-109 dest(air) | Heerds |
| 352nd: | Lt. C.H. Sperry | Me-109 prob(air) | Canabruck |

*Losses-*

**55th**: Lt. Robert W. Brown (338th Ftr Sqn) POW
P-38H CY-F 42-67047(Note-this was a 343rd Ftr Sqn plane)
Hit by an enemy fighter and crashed near Kropswolde.

Lt. John R. Pruitt (338th Ftr Sqn) KIA
P-38H CL- 42-67021
Hit by an enemy fighter and crashed near Lotte.

**352nd**: Lt. Richard L. Grow (487th Ftr Sqn) KIA
P-47D HO-G 42-22487
Hit by an enemy fighter near Haule.

**353rd**: Lt. Leroy W. Ista (352nd Ftr Sqn) KIA
P-47D SX- 42-22458
Ran out of fuel and crashed east of Lowestoft.

**December 23, 1943**
Groups Operating: P-47 56th, 353rd
Missions: The 353rd dive-bombed Gilze-Rijen Airfield with the 56th acting as escort.
Claims: nil
Losses: nil

**December 24, 1943**
Groups Operating: P-47 4th, 56th, 78th, 352nd, 353rd, 355th, 356th, 358th, 359th
P-38 55th
Missions: Support of bombers to the Pas de Calais area.
Claims: nil
Losses: nil

*Remarks*
56th: Lt. Adam J. Wisniewski (63rd Ftr Sqn) c/l Manston; o.k.
P-47D UN-

352nd: P-47 c/l Tandridge; o.k.
359th: Lt. Charles V. Cunningham (370th Ftr Sqn) c/l Reigate; o.k.
P-47D CS-

**December 28, 1943**
Groups Operating: P-38 20th
Missions: Flew a sweep over Holland for its first full group-strength mission.
Claims: nil
Losses: nil

**December 30, 1943**
Groups Operating: P-47 4th, 56th, 78th, 352nd, 353rd, 355th, 356th, 358th, 359th
P-38 20th, 55th
Missions: Support of bombers to Ludwigshafen.
Claims: 7-3-5 air
0-0 ground

| *Group* | | *Claims* | *Location* |
|---|---|---|---|
| **56th** | | | |
| 61st: | Lt. R.S. Johnson | FW-190 dest(air) | Soissons |
| | Capt. R.A. Lamb | FW-190 dam(air) | S/Soissons |
| **78th** | | | |
| 82nd: | Lt. H.T. Hegman | Me-109 dest(air) | Reims |
| | Lt. M.S. Martinez | Me-109 dest(air) | Reims |
| | Lt. W.M. Wesson | Me-109 dest(air) | Reims |
| 83rd: | Lt. W.H. Julian | Me-109 dest(air) | Reims |
| **352nd** | | | |
| HdQts: | LtCol. E.L. Clark | (.33)Me-110 prob(air) | Chalons |
| 328th: | Lt. W.E. Hendrian | (.33)Me-110 prob(air) | Chalons |
| | Lt. D.T. Zimms | (.33)Me-110 prob(air) | Chalons |
| **353rd** | | | |
| 350th: | Lt. R.A. Stearns | Me-109 dam(air) | Charleville |
| 352nd: | Lt. W.W. Johnson | FW-190 dest(air) | Charleville |
| | Lt. J.W. Gonnam | (.5)Me-109 dest(air) | Charleville |
| | | Me-109 prob(air) | Charleville |
| | | Me-109 dam(air) | Charleville |
| | Lt. G.L. Willits | (.5)Me-109 dest(air) | Charleville |
| **355th** | | | |
| 354th: | Lt. R.F. Murdoch | Me-109 prob(air) | Soissons |
| | | Me-109 dam(air) | Soissons |
| **356th** | | | |
| 359th: | Maj. D.A. Baccus | FW-190 dam(air) | NE St. Menehould |

*Losses-*

**78th**: F/O James C.P. Eastwood (83rd Ftr Sqn) KIA
P-47C HL-A 41-6540
Suffered mechanical failure and bailed out fifty miles off Beachy Head.

**352nd**: Capt. Hayes L. Button (487th Ftr Sqn) POW
P-47D HO-B 42-8483
Hit by flak near Dunkirk.

Capt. Donald K. Dilling (487th Ftr Sqn) MIA-E
P-47D HO-S 42-8447 "Queen City Mama"
Ran out of fuel and bailed out off the enemy coast.

Capt. Winfield E. McIntyre (487th Ftr Sqn) POW
P-47D HO- 42-22551
Hit by flak and crashed near Desvres.

**353rd**: Lt. William W. Odom (350th Ftr Sqn) KIA
P-47D LH- 42-8398
Hit by a FW-190 near Charleville.

Lt. Russell E. Moriarity (352nd Ftr Sqn) POW
P-47D SX- 42-74636
Hit by enemy fighters near Charleville.

**355th**: Lt. Raymond F. Murdoch, Jr. (354th Ftr Sqn) POW
P-47D WR-K 42-8453
Hit by a Me-109 near Soissons.

Capt. Carl F. Ekstrom (358th Ftr Sqn) KIA
P-47D YF-M 42-8526
Hit by flak near St. Inglevert.

F/O Charles E. Wambier (358th Ftr Sqn) KIA
P-47D YF-U 42-75425
Hit by a Me-109 near Reims.

**356th**: F/O Everett L. Brock (360th Ftr Sqn) KIA
P-47D PI- 42-22542
Collided with Lt. Hayden near Montdidier.

Lt. William R. Hayden (361st Ftr Sqn) KIA
P-47D QI-X 42-8662
Collided with F/O Brock near Montdidier.

*Remarks*
56th: Lt. Fred J. Christensen (62nd Ftr Sqn) c/l Leiston; o.k.
P-47D LM-
Lt. Isadore T. Porowski (63rd Ftr Sqn) c/l; o.k.
P-47D UN-P 42-8609
78th: P-47 b/o England; o.k.
352nd: P-47 c/l Beachy Head; o.k.
355th: 0-1 flak position

**December 31, 1943**
Groups Operating: P-47 4th, 56th, 78th, 352nd, 353rd, 355th, 356th, 358th, 359th
P-38 20th, 55th
Missions: Support for bombers to various targets in France.
Claims: 7-0-2 air
0-0 ground

| *Group* | | *Claims* | *Location* |
|---|---|---|---|
| **20th** | | | |
| 79th: | Lt. L.F. Graham | FW-190 dam(air) | Bordeaux |
| **55th** | | | |
| HdQts: | Col. F.B. James | FW-190 dest(air) | Niort |
| 38th: | Capt. J. Myers | Me-109 dest(air) | N/Blaye et St. Luce |
| 343rd: | Lt. H.M. Bauer | FW-190 dest(air) | Niort |
| **56th** | | | |
| 61st: | Lt. R.S. Johnson | (2)FW-190 dest(air) | N/St. Giles |
| **78th** | | | |
| 83rd: | Lt. W.H. Julian | FW-190 dest(air) | NE Lorient |
| | Lt. H.C. Roff | FW-190 dest(air) | NE Lorient |
| | | FW-190 dam(air) | NE Lorient |

*Losses-*

**20th**: Lt. John W. Crago (55th Ftr Sqn) KIA
P-38J KI-L 42-67489
Crashed near Woodnewton after take-off.

**55th**: Lt. Harold M. Bauer (343rd Ftr Sqn) ASR
P-38H CY-
Ran out of fuel and ditched fifteen miles off Lizard Point.

Lt. Frank A. Larson (343rd Ftr Sqn) POW
P-38H CY- 42-67056
Hit by enemy fighters and went down in the Bay of Biscay.

**56th**: Lt. William A. Marangello (61st Ftr Sqn) KIA
P-47C HV-S 41-6337
Suffered oxygen failure and crashed into the Channel.

*Remarks*
20th: Lt. Richard C. Garrett (77th Ftr Sqn) c/l Isle of Wight; o.k.
P-38J LC-
358th: P-47 c/l Tenterden; o.k.
P-47 c/l Bexhill; o.k.
P-47 c/l Hythe; o.k.
P-47 c/l Dungeness; o.k.
P-47 c/l Gravesend; o.k.
P-47 c/l Gravesend; o.k.

**January 4, 1944**
Groups Operating: P-47 4th, 56th, 78th, 352nd, 353rd, 355th, 356th, 358th, 359th
P-38 20th, 55th
Missions: The P-38 groups supported bombers going to Kiel, while the P-47 units supported heavies attacking Munster.

Claims: 7-0-4 air
0-0 ground

| *Group* | | *Claims* | *Location* |
|---|---|---|---|
| **20th** | | | |
| 79th: | Lt. M.B. Nichols | Do-217 dam(air) | Kiel |
| **56th** | | | |
| 62nd: | Lt. M.J. Quirk | FW-190 dest(air) | Stadtlohn |
| **78th** | | | |
| 82nd: | Lt. M.S. Martinez | Me-109 dest(air) | Antwerp |
| | | Me-110 dam(air) | Antwerp |
| 83rd: | Lt. H.C. Roff | FW-190 dest(air) | Munster |
| | Lt. J.E. Stokes | FW-190 dest(air) | Munster |
| 84th: | Lt. Q.L. Brown | (2)FW-190 dest(air) | Coesfeld |
| | Lt. P.E. Pompetti | Me-109 dest(air) | Coesfeld |
| | | FW-190 dam(air) | Coesfeld |

| | | | |
|---|---|---|---|
| **353rd** | | | |
| HdQts: | LtCol. G.E. Duncan | FW-190 dam(air) | Sendenhorst |

*Losses-*

**20th**: F/O Henry M. Higginbotham (77th Ftr Sqn) KIA
P-38J LC- 42-67191
Last seen in the Neumunster area.

F/O Joseph L. Hamilton (79th Ftr Sqn) POW
P-38J MC- 42-67187
Ran out of fuel and bailed out near Cherbourg.

*Remarks*
55th: Capt. Joseph Myers(38th Ftr Sqn) c/l; o.k.
P-38 CG-
78th: 0-1 loco

**January 5, 1944**
Groups Operating: P-47 4th, 56th, 78th, 352nd, 353rd, 355th, 356th, 358th, 359th
P-38 20th, 55th
Missions: The P-38 groups supported bombers to Kiel while the P-47 units supported bombers to Bordeaux/Merignac Airfield(78th only), Tours(4th and 352nd), and Neuss, Dusseldorf, and Gelsenkirchen.
Claims: 15-3-5 air
0-0 ground

| *Group* | | *Claims* | *Location* |
|---|---|---|---|
| **4th** | | | |
| 336th: | Capt. D.S. Gentile | FW-190 dest(air) | W/Tours |
| | Lt. R.J. Messenger | FW-190 dest(air) | Tours |
| **20th** | | | |
| HdQts: | Maj. R.P. Montgomery | FW-190 dam(air) | W/Neumunster |
| **55th** | | | |
| 38th: | Capt. J.H. Hancock | FW-190 dest(air) | SW Kiel |
| | | Me-109 prob(air) | SW Kiel |
| | Lt. D.L. Steiner | FW-190 dest(air) | SW Kiel |
| | Maj. M.K. Shipman | Me-109 dam(air) | E/Meldorf |
| | Lt. R.S. Thompson | Me-109 dam(air) | SW Kiel |
| | Lt. W. Wyche | Me-109 dam(air) | SW Kiel |
| 338th: | Maj. C.O. Jones | Me-109 dest(air) | Neumunster |
| | Lt. P. Dempsey | Me-109 dest(air) | Neumunster |
| | F/O C.E. Buskirk | Me-109 dest(air) | Neumunster |
| **56th** | | | |
| HdQts: | Maj. J.C. Stewart | FW-190 dest(air) | SW Bonn |
| 61st: | Lt. R.S. Johnson | FW-190 dest(air) | N/Liege |
| 62nd: | Lt. F.J. Christensen | FW-190 dest(air) | Ans |
| | Lt. S.B. Morrill | Me-109 dest(air) | Duren |
| **78th** | | | |
| 84th: | Lt. Q.L. Brown | Me-109 dest(air) | La Rochelle |
| | Lt. P.L. Larson | Me-109 dest(air) | La Rochelle |
| | Lt. R.E. Smith | Me-109 dam(air) | La Rochelle |
| **352nd** | | | |
| 328th: | Maj. E.W. Stewart | (.33)He-177 dest(air) | Le Ferte Bernard |
| | Lt. J.B. Coleman | (.33)He-177 dest(air) | Le Ferte Bernard |
| | Lt. R.H. Powell | (.33)He-177 dest(air) | Le Ferte Bernard |
| **353rd** | | | |
| HdQts: | LtCol. G.E. Duncan | Me-109 dest(air) | Eindhoven-Gilze-Rijen |
| **356th** | | | |
| 361st: | Lt. T.F. Bailey | FW-190 prob(air) | S/Liege |
| **358th** | | | |
| 367th: | Maj. D.A. Younglas | FW-190 prob(air) | Holland-Belgium |

*Losses-*

**20th**: Lt. Arthur T. Altman, Jr. (55th Ftr Sqn) KIA
P-38J KI- 42-67194
Hit by flak near Wangerooge Island.

Lt. Robert H. French (55th Ftr Sqn) POW
P-38J KI- 42-67198
Suffered mechanical failure then hit by a FW-190 near Neumunster.

Lt. Bennie R. Carbajal (77th Ftr Sqn) KIA
P-38J LC- 42-67186
Last seen with enemy fighters near Neumunster.

**55th**: Lt. Edward F. Peters (38th Ftr Sqn) POW
P-38J CG- 42-67650
Hit by enemy fighters near Neumunster.

Lt. Herbert T. Winters (38th Ftr Sqn) KIA
P-38H CY-T 42-67060 (note he was in a 343rd Ftr Sqn a/c)
Hit by enemy fighters near Neumunster.

Lt. John Barnett (343rd Ftr Sqn) KIA
P-38H CY- 42-67045
Suffered mechanical failure and crashed into the Baltic Sea.

Lt. Robert J. Kenning (343rd Ftr Sqn) KIA
P-38H CY-R 42-67084
Hit by flak and crashed near Rendsburg.

**78th**: Lt. Arthur S. Granger (83rd Ftr Sqn) KIA
P-47D HL-N 42-8622
Ran out of fuel then hit by enemy fighters near Rennes.

Lt. Kenneth Hindersinn (83rd Ftr Sqn) POW
P-47D HL-K 42-74652
Hit by a FW-190 near Caen.

Lt. Major C. Leach (83rd Ftr Sqn) KIA
P-47C HL-L 41-6331
Hit by a FW-190 near Rennes.

Lt. Melvin D. Putnam (83rd Ftr Sqn) KIA
P-47C HL-O 41-6581
Hit by a FW-190 near Rennes.

Lt. George T. Hartman (84th Ftr Sqn) KIA
P-47D WZ-E 42-8538
Hit by a FW-190 north of La Rochelle.

*Remarks*
4th: Lt. Jack L. Raphael (336th Ftr Sqn) c/l; o.k.
P-47C VF-R 41-6354
78th: P-47 c/l Ford; o.k.

**January 7, 1944**
Groups Operating: P-47 4th, 56th, 78th, 352nd, 353rd, 355th, 356th, 358th, 359th
P-38 20th, 55th
Missions: Support of bombers to Ludwigshafen.
Claims: 7-0-3 air
0-0 ground

| *Group* | | *Claims* | *Location* |
|---|---|---|---|
| **4th** | | | |
| HdQts: | LtCol. D.J.M. Blakeslee | FW-190 dest(air) | Hosdin |
| 336th: | Capt. J.A. Goodson | (2)FW-190 dest(air) | Bethune |
| | Lt. V. Garrison | FW-190 dam(air) | La Chateau |
| **20th** | | | |
| HdQts: | Capt. C.E. Jackson | (.5)Me-109 dam(air) | Ludwigshafen |
| 55th: | Lt. W.B. Taylor | Me-109 dest(air) | Worms |
| | Lt. V.R. Stockton | (.5)Me-109 dam(air) | Ludwigshafen |
| **55th** | | | |
| 343rd: | Lt. K.J. Sorace | Me-109 dam(air) | Ludwigshafen |
| **353rd** | | | |
| 352nd: | Lt. J.E. Gonnam | (3)FW-190 dest(air) | Orleans |

*Losses-*

**55th**: Capt. Joseph P. Marsiglia (338th Ftr Sqn) POW
P-38H CL- 42-67048
Hit by enemy fighters near Krattnick.

**356th**: Lt. William F. Brown (359th Ftr Sqn) KIA
P-47D OC- 42-8639
Hit by flak near Cologne, bailed out near Aachen, and was killed on the ground.

**358th**: Lt. Mark A. Osborn (365th Ftr Sqn) KIA
P-47D CH- 42-8552
Ran out of fuel and crashed into the North Sea.

Maj. Donald A. Younglas (367th Ftr Sqn) KIA
P-47D CP- 42-75124
Hit by a FW-190 near Termonde.

Lt. Corlys A. Bedford (367th Ftr Sqn) KIA
P-47D CP- 42-75064
Hit by a FW-190 near Termonde.

Lt. Lance A. Pousette (367th Ftr Sqn) KIA
P-47D CP- 42-74678
Hit by a FW-190 near Termonde.

*Remarks*
353rd: P-47 c/l Eastchurch; o.k.

**January 8, 1944**

KIAc's

20th: F/O Martin F. Kane (77th Ftr Sqn)
P-38J LC- 42-67809
Died in a crash near Drinkstone.

**January 11, 1944**

Groups Operating: P-47 4th, 56th, 356th, 359th
Missions: Support for bombers to Oschersleben and Halberstadt.
Claims: 10-3-7 air
0-0 ground

| *Group* | | *Claims* | *Location* |
|---|---|---|---|
| **56th** | | | |
| HdQts: | LtCol. D.C. Schilling | FW-190 dest(air) | Osnabruck |
| | | FW-190 dam(air) | Osnabruck |
| 61st: | Capt. J.R. Carter | Me-109 dest(air) | N/Osnabruck |
| | | Me-109 prob(air) | N/Osnabruck |
| | | Me-109 dam(air) | N/Osnabruck |
| | Lt. J.D. Foster | Me-109 dest(air) | NE Osnabruck |
| | | Me-109 dam(air) | NE Osnabruck |
| | Capt. J.H. Bennett | (2)Me-109 dam(air) | Schwastorf |
| 62nd: | Lt. S.B. Morrill | Me-109 dest(air) | Bramsche |
| | Lt. M.J. Quirk | Me-109 prob(air) | Lingen |
| 63rd: | Lt. G.D. Schiltz | (3)Me-109 dest(air) | N/Osnabruck |
| | Maj. S.V. Burke | Me-109 dest(air) | N/Osnabruck |
| | | Me-109 dam(air) | N/Osnabruck |
| | Lt. A.H. Robey | Me-109 dest(air) | N/Osnabruck |
| | | Me-109 dam(air) | N/Osnabruck |
| | Lt. B.R. Smith | FW-190 dest(air) | N/Osnabruck |
| **356th** | | | |
| 359th: | Capt. E.J. White | Me-109 prob(air) | Lingen |

*Losses-*

**359th**: Lt. Edward J. Hyland (368th Ftr Sqn) KIA
P-47D CV- 42-8542
Hit by a Me-109 near Lingen.

Capt. James E. Buckley (370th Ftr Sqn) KIA
P-47D CS- 42-75108
Suffered oxygen failure and crashed into the North Sea.

Lt. Lynn W. Hair (370th Ftr Sqn) KIA
P-47D CS-
Killed in a crash at Chipping Warden.

Lt. William N. Tucker, Jr. (370th Ftr Sqn) KIA
P-47D CS-
Killed in a crash near Rednal, Wales.

Groups Operating: P-47 4th, 56th, 78th, 352nd, 353rd, 355th, 356th, 358th
P-38 20th, 55th
Missions: Support of bombers to Osnabruck and Brunswick.
Claims: 3-0-1 air
0-0 ground

| *Group* | | *Claims* | *Location* |
|---|---|---|---|
| **55th** | | | |
| HdQts: | LtCol. J.S. Jenkins | Me-210 dam(air) | Dummer Lake |
| **356th** | | | |
| 359th: | Lt. J.B. Smith | Ju-88 dest(air) | Steinhuder Lake |
| | Maj. D.A. Baccus | (.5)Me-110 dest(air) | Steinhuder Lake |
| | Lt. J.H. [illegible] | (.5)Me-110 dest(air) | Steinhuder Lake |
| 361st: | Lt. R.W. Racine | Me-110 dest(air) | NW Hanover |

*Losses-*

**55th**: Lt. William E. Harbert (338th Ftr Sqn) KIA
P-38H CL- 42-67100
Lost for unknown reasons.

**353rd**: Lt. Victor L. Vogel (352nd Ftr Sqn) KIA
P-47D SX-F 42-7904
Suffered mechanical failure and spun into the North Sea.

**356th**: Lt. Rolland W. Racine (361st Ftr Sqn) KIA
P-47D QI-V 42-22525
Last seen heading for enemy fighters in the Hanover area.

*Remarks*

355th: Lt. Emil L. Sluga (358th Ftr Sqn) b/o Cambridge; o.k.
P-47D YF-L

**January 14, 1944**

Groups Operating: P-47 4th, 56th, 78th, 352nd, 353rd, 355th, 356th, 358th, 359th, 361st(individual pilots only with other units)
P-38 20th, 55th
Missions: Support of bombers to Pas de Calais V-1 sites.
Claims: 12-1-10 air
0-2 ground

| *Group* | | *Claims* | *Location* |
|---|---|---|---|
| **4th** | | | |
| 334th: | Lt. E.D. Whalen | (1.5)FW-190 dest(air) | Soissons |
| | Lt. D.W. Beeson | FW-190 dest(air) | Soissons |
| | Lt. H.T. Biel | FW-190 dest(air) | Cambrai |
| | Lt. G.E. Montgomery | FW-190 dest(air) | Soissons |
| | Lt. A. Rafalovich | (.5)FW-190 dest(air) | Soissons |
| 336th: | Capt. D.S. Gentile | (2)FW-190 dest(air) | Compiegne |
| | Lt. V. Garrison | (2)FW-190 dest(air) | Compiegne |
| | F/O R.H. Richards | FW-190 dest(air) | Compiegne |
| **20th** | | | |
| HdQts: | LtCol. B.M. Russell | (.5)FW-190 dest(air) | Rouen |
| 79th: | Lt. M.B. Nichols | FW-190 dest(air) | Rouen |
| | F/O M.L. Byrd | (.5)FW-190 dest(air) | Rouen |
| | Maj. R.L. Ott | (.5)FW-190 prob(air) | S/Fecamp |
| | | FW-190 dam(air) | S/Fecamp |
| | Lt. H. Mednick | (.5)FW-190 prob(air) | S/Fecamp |
| | | FW-190 dam(air) | S/Fecamp |
| | Capt. R.J. Meyer | (2)Me-109 dam(air) | Rouen |
| | Lt. T.A. Hanzo | (2)FW-190 dam(air) | S/Fecamp |
| | Capt. L.F. Graham | Me-109 dam(air) | Rouen |
| | Lt. F.E. LeFevre | Me-109 dam(air) | S/Rouen |
| | Lt. L.S. Smutko | Me-109 dam(air) | Rouen |
| **78th** | | | |
| 84th: | Lt. P.E. Pompetti | Me-109 dam(air) | NE Lille |
| **353rd** | | | |
| HdQts: | Lt. C.L. Stafford | (.33)FW-190 dam(grd)* | Rosieres-en-Santerne |
| 351st: | Maj. W.C. Beckham | (.33)FW-190 dam(grd)* | Rosieres-en-Santerne |
| | Capt. V.L. Byers | (.5)FW-190 dam(grd) | Rosieres-en-Santerne |
| | Lt. H.D. Milligan | (.5)FW-190 dam(grd) | Rosieres-en-Santerne |
| **361st** | | | |
| 375th: | Lt. A.C. Duncan | (.33)FW-190 dam(grd)* | Rosieres-en-Santerne |

*Losses-*

**20th**: Lt. Neal J. Archer, Jr. (79th Ftr Sqn) KIA
P-38J MC- 42-67760
Hit by a Me-109 south of Rouen.

**356th**: Lt. Robert B. Conroy (359th Ftr Sqn) POW
P-47D OC-R 42-8694 "Little Texan"
Hit by a Me-109 near Arras

*Remarks*

20th: Lt. Zell M. Wyman (79th Ftr Sqn) c/l Wittering; o.k.
P-38J MC-U 42-67474

359th: Lt. Glenn C. Bach (369th Ftr Sqn) c/l East Wretham; o.k.
P-47D IV-
Lt. Homer L. Rodeheaver (369th Ftr Sqn) c/l Wormingford; o.k.
P-47D IV-

KIAc's

356th: Lt. Raymond C. Fortner (359th Ftr Sqn)
P-47D OC-S 42-22524
Died in a crash near Martlehsm Heath.

**January 21, 1944**

Groups Operating: P-47 4th, 56th, 78th, 352nd, 353rd, 355th, 356th, 358th, 359th, 361st
P-38 20th, 55th
Missions: Support of bombers to Cherbourg and Pas de Calais V-1 sites.
Claims: 7-1-5 air
1-1 ground

| *Group* | | *Claims* | *Location* |
|---|---|---|---|
| **4th** | | | |
| 336th: | F/O R.H. Richards | FW-190 dest(air) | Valenciennes-Douai |
| | | FW-190 dam(air) | Valenciennes-Douai |
| | Lt. K.D. Peterson | FW-190 dam(air) | Douai |
| **56th** | | | |
| 61st: | Lt. R.S. Johnson | FW-190 dest(air) | N/Rouen |
| | Capt. L.C. Smith | FW-190 dam(air) | NE Rouen |
| **353rd** | | | |
| HdQts: | Lt. W.T. Thistlethwaite | Me-109 dest(air) | St. Quentin |
| | LtCol. G.E. Duncan | (.33)Do-217 dest(grd) | Albert |

| | | | |
|---|---|---|---|
| 351st: | Maj. W.C. Beckham | (2)Me-109 dest(air) | St. Quentin |
| 352nd: | Lt. W.W. Johnson | (.33)Do-217 dest(grd) | Albert |
| | Lt. C.H. Sperry | (.33)Do-217 dest(grd) | Albert |
| **355th** | | | |
| 354th: | Lt. J.E. Duffy | FW-190 dest(air) | NW Dourdan |
| 357th: | Lt. A.E. Benson | FW-190 dam(air) | NW Dourdan |
| **356th** | | | |
| HdQts: | LtCol. O.H. Coen | (.5)FW-190 dam(grd) | St. Leger A/F |
| 359th: | F/O R.G. Vossler | Ju-88 prob(air) | St. Leger A/F |
| | Lt. J.D. Henry | (.5)FW-190 dam(grd) | St. Leger A/F |
| 361st: | Lt. S.H. Hewett | (.5)Ju-88 dest(air) | Cambrai |
| | Lt. D.F. Thwaites | (.5)Ju-88 dest(air) | Cambrai |
| | Maj. E.H. Montgomery | Me-109 dam(air) | NE Dunkirk |

*Losses-*

**56th:** Lt. Allen E. Dimmick (61st Ftr Sqn) KIA
P-47D HV-S 42-75658
Hit by a FW-190 near Rouen.

*Remarks*
4th: Lt. Conrad C. Ingold (336th Ftr Sqn) c/l Gravesend; o.k.
P-47D VF- 42-74663
56th: 62nd Ftr Sqn P-47 c/l Manston; o.k.
P-47D LM-R

**January 23, 1944**
Groups Operating: P-47 56th
Missions: Dive-bombing of Gilze-Rijen Airfield.
Claims: nil
Losses: nil

KIAc's
55th: Lt. Henry J. Tiedemann, Jr. (38th Ftr Sqn)
P-38 CG-

**January 24, 1944**
Groups Operating: P-47 4th, 56th, 78th, 352nd, 353rd, 355th, 356th, 358th, 359th, 361st
P-38 20th, 55th
Missions: Support of bombers to Eschweiler.
Claims: 20-1-7 air
0-0 ground

| *Group* | | *Claims* | *Location* |
|---|---|---|---|
| **20th** | | | |
| 55th: | Capt. D.H. McAuley | FW-190 dest(air) | Courtrai |
| | | FW-190 prob(air) | Courtrai |
| | Capt. M.R. McLary | FW-190 dest(air) | Courtrai |
| | | FW-190 dam(air) | Courtrai |
| | Lt. H.B. Baker | FW-190 dam(air) | Courtrai |
| **78th** | | | |
| 82nd: | Lt. J.J. Hockery | Me-110 dest(air) | Engheim |
| | Lt. C.R. Clark | Me-110 dam(air) | Engheim |
| 83rd: | Lt. R.H. Knapp | FW-190 dest(air) | Liege |
| **353rd** | | | |
| HdQts: | LtCol. G.E. Duncan | (2)Me-110 dest(air) | Tirlemont |
| 350th: | Capt. D.E. Newhart | Me-110 dest(air) | Termonde |
| | | Me-109 dest(air) | Laon-Beauvechan |
| | Lt. J.F. Furness | Me-110 dest(air) | Tirlemont |
| | Capt. C.W. Dinse | (.5)Me-110 dest(air) | Termonde |
| | Lt. R.A. Stearns | (.5)Me-110 dest(air) | Termonde |
| **356th** | | | |
| 360th: | Lt. C.A. Vitali | (3)FW-190 dest(air) | NW Lille |
| | | FW-190 dam(air) | NW Lille |
| | Maj. G.W. Johnson | FW-190 dest(air) | NE Ypres |
| | | (.5)FW-190 dam(air) | NE Ypres |
| | Capt. J.B. Stratford | FW-190 dest(air) | SW Antwerp |
| | Lt. W.E. Johnson | Me-109 dest(air) | W/Bruges |
| | Lt. L.F. Kress | Me-109 dest(air) | NE Lille |
| | Lt. W.G. Maxwell | FW-190 dest(air) | N/Lille |
| | | (.5)FW-190 dam(air) | NE Ypres |
| | Lt. A.V. Niemi | FW-190 dest(air) | N/Lille |
| | | FW-190 dam(air) | N/Lille |
| 361st: | Lt. M.F. Erickson | (.5)FW-190 dest(air) | Ghent-Bruges |
| | Lt. R.H. Gansberg | (.5)FW-190 dest(air) | Ghent-Bruges |
| | Lt. S.H. Hewett | FW-190 dam(air) | Bruges-Ostend |

*Losses-*

**20th:** Lt. John R. Frazier (55th Ftr Sqn) KIA
P-38J KI- 42-67661
Last seen with FW-190's near Ghent.

Lt. James C. Hart (77th Ftr Sqn) POW
P-38J LC- 42-67818
Hit by flak near Coblenz and crashed near Liege.

Lt. Fred M. Hartig (79th Ftr Sqn) KIA
P-38J MC-
Suffered mechanical failure and went down in the North Sea. Was picked up by ASR but had died.

**55th:** Lt. Robert S. Thompson (38th Ftr Sqn) POW
P-38J CG- 42-67520
Hit by enemy fighters near Zeebruggee.

**78th:** Lt. Clifford B. Hahn (82nd Ftr Sqn) KIA
P-47D MX-J 42-7923
Ran out of fuel over the Channel.

Lt. William F. Neel (82nd Ftr Sqn) KIA
P-47D MX-Y 42-22467
Ran out of fuel over the Channel.

**355th:** Lt. Frank L. Pipher, Jr. (357th Ftr Sqn) KIA
P-47D OS-L 42-75184
Hit by flak and spun into the Channel.

**January 25, 1944**
Groups Operating: P-47 78th, 352nd, 352nd, 353rd, 358th, 359th
Missions: All were sent out on dive-bombing assignments but only the 353rd attacked Leeuwarden.
Claims: nil
Losses: nil

**January 26, 1944**
KIAc's
20th: Lt. Esborn D. Otis (79th Ftr Sqn)
P-38J MC-E 42-67492
Crashed in The Wash on a training flight.

352nd: Lt. Lester L. Lowry (487th Ftr Sqn)
P-47D HO-Z 42-8516
Plane dove into the ground near Bodney while on a local flight.

**January 28, 1944**
Groups Operating: P-47 78th, 361st
Missions: Support for bombers to Bonnieres V-1 sites.
Claims: nil
Losses: nil

Groups Operating: P-47 352nd, 359th
Missions: Dive-bombing missions which were recalled.
Claims: nil
Losses: nil

**January 29, 1944**
Groups Operating: P-47 4th, 56th, 78th, 352nd, 353rd, 355th, 356th, 358th, 359th, 361st
P-38 20th, 55th
Missions: Support of bombers to Frankfurt.
Claims: 40-3-7 air
0-0 ground

| *Group* | | *Claims* | *Location* |
|---|---|---|---|
| **4th** | | | |
| 334th: | Capt. H.L. Mills | (2)Me-109 dest(air) | Aachen |
| | Lt. D.W. Beeson | Me-109 dest(air) | Aachen |
| | | FW-190 dest(air) | Aachen |
| | Lt. S.N. Pissanos | (2)Me-109 dest(air) | Aachen |
| | Lt. A.W. Chatterly | Me-109 dest(air) | Aachen |
| | Lt. E.D. Whalen | Me-109 dest(air) | Aachen |
| | Lt. V.J. France | FW-190 dest(air) | Hasselt |
| **20th** | | | |
| 55th: | Lt. R.D. Frey | Me-110 dest(air) | Undenheim |
| | Lt. C.A. Hallberg | Me-110 dest(air) | Undenheim |
| 77th: | Lt. W.L. Whiteside | Me-109 dest(air) | SW Frankfurt |
| | | (.5)Me-210 dest(air)[*] | SW Frankfurt |
| | Lt. E.J. Machen | Me-110 dest(air) | SW Frankfurt |
| | Lt. R.T. Bond | (.5)Me-210 dest(air)[**] | SW Frankfurt |
| | Lt. R.S. Flynn | (.5)Me-210 dest(air)[**] | SW Frankfurt |
| | Lt. R.C. Garrett | Me-110 dam(air) | W/Frankfurt |
| 79th: | Capt. L.F. Graham | (3)FW-190 dest(air) | (2) E/Lille & (1)Coblenz |
| | Maj. R.L. Ott | Me-110 dest(air) | Mainz |
| | | (.5)Me-210 dest(air)[*] | SW Frankfurt |
| | Capt. R.P. Gatterdam | FW-190 prob(air) | Coblenz |
| **55th** | | | |
| 338th: | Lt. H.E. Larsen | FW-190 dest(air) | Frankfurt |
| **56th** | | | |
| HdQts: | LtCol. F.S. Gabreski | Me-110 dest(air) | S/Coblenz |
| | LtCol. D.C. Schilling | Me-109 dest(air) | Bonn |
| 61st: | Capt. J.H. Bennett | (1.5)Me-110 dest(air) | Simmern |
| | Lt. M.C. Wood | Me-210 dest(air) | Simmern |
| | Lt. P. Neyland | (.5)Me-110 dest(air) | Simmern |
| 63rd: | Lt. A.S. Cavallo | Me-210 dest(air) | SW Coblenz |
| | | Me-210 prob(air) | SW Coblenz |
| | Lt. H.E. Comstock | FW-190 dam(air) | W/Ostend |

| | | | |
|---|---|---|---|
| **78th** | | | |
| HdQts: | LtCol. H.J. Dayhuff | (.5)FW-190 dest(air) | Coblenz |
| 82nd: | Lt. M.S. Martinez | FW-190 dest(air) | Coblenz |
| | Lt. W.S. Swanson | FW-190 dest(air) | Coblenz |
| | Lt. V.Y. Jones | (.5)FW-190 dest(air) | Coblenz |
| | | FW-190 prob(air) | Coblenz |
| **352nd** | | | |
| 328th: | Lt. J.B. Coleman | Me-109 dest(air) | Pelm |
| | Lt. D.S. Bryan | (.5)FW-190 dest(air) | Namur |
| | Lt. Q.L. Quinn | (.5)FW-190 dest(air) | Namur |
| | Capt. E.L. Abbott | FW-190 dam(air) | Pelm |
| 487th: | Capt. G.E. Preddy | FW-190 dest(air) | Malmedy |
| | Lt. C.E. Davis | FW-190 dest(air) | Malmedy |
| | Lt. V.K. Meroney | FW-190 dest(air) | Malmedy |
| | Lt. W.T. Whisner | FW-190 dest(air) | Malmedy |
| **355th** | | | |
| 357th: | Capt. J.H. Wilson | FW-190 dest(air) | W/Frankfurt |
| | Lt. R.J. DuFresne | (2)FW-190 dam(air) | W/Frankfurt |
| 358th: | Lt. H.H. Macurdy | FW-190 dest(air) | Liege |
| | | Me-109 dest(air) | Coblenz |
| **356th** | | | |
| 360th: | Lt. R.C. L'Heureux | FW-190 dest(air) | Louvain |
| **359th** | | | |
| HdQts: | Maj. R.V. Gray | (.5)Me-110 dest(air) | Dison |
| 368th: | Capt. C. Shaw | Me-110 dam(air) | Malmedy |
| 369th: | Lt. J.H. Oliphint | (.5)Me-110 dest(air) | Dison |
| | Lt. L.H. Prewitt | Me-110 dam(air) | Dison |

*Losses-*

**4th**: Lt. Burton C. Wyman (335th Ftr Sqn) KIA
P-47D WD-N 42-75119
Hit by enemy fighters near Fumay.

**20th**: Lt. Richard T. Bond (77th Ftr Sqn) KIA
P-38J LC-B 42-67228
Collided with Lt. Flynn south of Coblenz.

Lt. Robert S. Flynn (77th Ftr Sqn) KIA
P-38J LC-I 42-67735
Collided with Lt. Bond south of Coblenz.

F/O William M. Harper (79th Ftr Sqn) KIA
P-38J MC- 42-67665
Hit by a FW-190 near Coblenz.

Lt. Robert B. Moss (79th Ftr Sqn) POW
P-38J MC-D 42-67680 "Bee Pee"
Hit by a Me-210 southwest of Frankfurt.

**56th**: Lt. Kenneth K. Lewis (63rd Ftr Sqn) KIA
P-47D UN-V 42-22748
Hit by a FW-190 near Knocke and crashed into the Channel.

**78th**: F/O Milton H. Ramsey (82nd Ftr Sqn) MIA-E
P-47D MX-J 42-22463
Hit by enemy fighters near Coblenz.

**352nd**: Lt. Joel W. McPherson (HdQts) MIA-E
P-47D HO- 42-75532
Ran out of fuel and bailed out near Rouillac.

Capt. George E. Preddy (487th Ftr Sqn) ASR
P-47D HO-Y 42-8421
Hit by flak and bailed out over the Channel.

**355th**: Capt. Benjamin T. Martin (357th Ftr Sqn) MIA-E
P-47D OS-Q 42-8610
Hit by FW-190's near Limburg and bailed out near Coblenz.

Lt. Harold H. Macurdy (358th Ftr Sqn) MIA-E
P-47D YF-H 42-75455
Hit by a Me-109 near Coblenz.

Lt. Chauncey H. Rankin (358th Ftr Sqn) KIA
P-47D YF-G 42-8504
Hit by Me-109's near Coblenz.

**361st**: Lt. Charles B. Screws (374th Ftr Sqn) MIA-E
P-47D B7- 42-75417
Hit by flak and bailed out near Dunkirk.

*Remarks*

4th: Lt. David A. Van Epps (334th Ftr Sqn) c/l Lashendon; o.k.
P-47D QP-

20th: Capt. Maurice R. McLary (55th Ftr Sqn) c/l Bury St. Edmonds; o.k.
P-38J KI-Y 42-67484

356th: Lt. Robert D. Bradshaw (359th Ftr Sqn) c/l Langham; o.k.
P-47D OC-G 42-74684

**January 30, 1944**

Groups Operating: P-47 4th, 56th, 78th, 352nd, 353rd, 355th, 356th, 358th, 359th, 361st
P-38 20th, 55th

Missions: Support of bombers to Brunswick and Hanover.

Claims: 42-13-21 air
0-0 ground

| *Group* | | *Claims* | *Location* |
|---|---|---|---|
| **4th** | | | |
| 335th: | Lt. C.F. Anderson | Me-109 dest(air) | Lingen |
| | | Me-109 dam(air) | Lingen |
| | Capt. J.R. Happel | Me-109 prob(air) | Lingen |
| | Lt. E.R. Mead | Me-109 prob(air) | Gronau |
| **20th** | | | |
| 77th: | Lt. M.J. Gilbertson | Do-217 dam(air) | Osnabruck |
| 79th: | Maj. R.L. Ott | FW-190 dest(air) | Minden |
| | | Do-217 dest(air) | Minden |
| | Capt. R.P. Gatterdam | (.5)Me-210 dest(air) | Brunswick |
| | Lt. J.T. Martin | (.5)Me-210 dest(air) | Brunswick |
| | Lt. M.D. Fall | (.5)Do-217 dest(air) | Minden |
| | Lt. F.H. Roark | (.5)Do-217 dest(air) | Minden |
| **56th** | | | |
| HdQts. | LtCol. F.S. Gabreski | Me-109 dest(air) | Lingen |
| | | Me-210 dest(air) | Lingen |
| 61st: | Lt. R.S. Johnson | Me-109 dest(air) | E/Lingen |
| | | Me-210 dest(air) | E/Lingen |
| | Capt. J.R. Carter | FW-190 dest(air) | Leeuwen |
| | Lt. J.H. Powers | FW-190 dest(air) | Meppen |
| | Lt. E.E. Barnum | Me-210 dest(air) | Lingen |
| | Lt. F.W. Klibbe | Me-109 dest(air) | Lingen |
| 62nd: | Lt. M.J. Quirk | Me-109 dest(air) | Almelo |
| | | Me-109 dam(air) | Almelo |
| | Lt. A.R. Carcione | (.5)Ju-88 dest(air) | Twente |
| | Lt. S.B. Morrill | (.5)Ju-88 dest(air) | Twente |
| | | Ju-88 dam(air) | Twente |
| | Lt. M.L. Moseley | Me-210 dam(air) | Hanskamp |
| 63rd: | Lt. G.F. Hall | (2)Me-109 dest(air) | S/Quackenbruck |
| | | (2)Me-109 dam(air) | S/Quackenbruck |
| | Lt. L.M. Langdon | (2)Me-109 dest(air) | S/Quackenbruck |
| | | Me-109 dam(air) | S/Quackenbruck |
| | Capt. W.M. Mahurin | Ju-88 dest(air) | S/Quackenbruck |
| | | Ju-88 prob(air) | S/Quackenbruck |
| | Lt. J.L. Egan | Me-210 dest(air) | S/Quackenbruck |
| **78th** | | | |
| 84th: | Lt. Q.L. Brown | Me-109 dest(air) | Rheine |
| **352nd** | | | |
| HdQts: | LtCol. E.L. Clark | (2)Me-109 prob(air) | W/Zuider Zee |
| | | Me-109 dam(air) | W/Zuider Zee |
| 328th: | Lt. D.S. Bryan | FW-190 dest(air) | Emmen |
| | Lt. W.D. Schwenke | Me-109 dest(air) | Ruhlertwist |
| | Lt. J.F. Thornell | Me-109 dest(air) | Ruhlertwist |
| | | Me-109 dam(air) | Ruhlertwist |
| | Lt. J.H. Walker | Me-109 dest(air) | Ruhlertwist |
| | Lt. F.W. Horne | (.5)FW-190 dest(air) | Emmen |
| | Lt. Q.L. Quinn | (.5)FW-190 dest(air) | Emmen |
| 486th: | Capt. E.J. Gignac | (.5)Me-110 dest(air) | Nordhorn |
| | Lt. A.L. Marshall | (.5)Me-110 dest(air) | Nordhorn |
| 487th: | Lt. V.K. Meroney | Me-109 dest(air) | Zwolle |
| | | Me-109 dam(air) | Zwolle |
| | Lt. R.I. Ross | Me-109 dest(air) | Zwolle |
| **353rd** | | | |
| 350th: | Lt. W.F. Tanner | FW-190 dest(air) | Zuider Zee |
| | Lt. F.T. Walsh | Me-110 dest(air) | Vechta |
| | Lt. K. Chetwood | Me-110 prob(air) | Vechta |
| 351st: | Maj. W.C. Beckham | Me-109 dest(air) | N/Deventer |
| 352nd: | Lt. R.A. Newman | Ju-88 dest(air) | Quackenbruck |
| | Lt. W.F. Streit | Ju-88 dam(air) | Quackenbruck |
| **358th** | | | |
| 366th: | LtCol. G.L. Wertenbaker | Me-109 dam(air) | Lingen |
| 367th: | Lt. J.F. Schilke | Me-109 dest(air) | E/Zwolle |
| | Lt. G.L. Waters | Me-109 prob(air) | E/Zwolle |
| | Lt. L.L. Wilson | Me-109 prob(air) | E/Zwolle |
| | | Me-109 dam(air) | E/Zwolle |
| | Lt. L.W. Pool | Me-109 prob(air) | E/Zwolle |
| | Lt. R. Schneider | Me-109 prob(air) | E/Zwolle |
| | Lt. P.R. Ballinger | Me-109 dam(air) | E/Zwolle |
| | Lt. J.H. Pedigo | Me-109 dam(air) | E/Zwolle |

| | | | |
|---|---|---|---|
| **359th** | | | |
| HdQts: | Maj. R.V. Gray | Me-109 dest(air) | Haselunne |
| 369th: | Lt. R.J. Booth | Me-109 dest(air) | Lingen |
| | Lt. R.L. Thacker | Ju-88 dest(air) | Haselunne |
| | | Ju-88 prob(air) | Haselunne |
| | Capt. N.K. Cranfill | Me-109 dam(air) | Lingen |
| | Lt. R.L. Pherson | Ju-88 dam(air) | N/Lingen |
| | Lt. L.H. Prewitt | Ju-88 dam(air) | Haselunne |
| **361st** | | | |
| 374th: | Maj. R.A. Webb | Me-109 dest(air) | Rheine |
| | Capt. R.E. Sedman | Me-109 dest(air) | Rheine |
| | | Me-109 prob(air) | Rheine |
| | Lt. J.L. Latimer | Me-109 dest(air) | Rheine |
| | Lt. J.D. Hastin | (.5)Me-109 dest(air) | Rheine |
| | Lt. H.B. Lederer | (.5)Me-109 dest(air) | Rheine |
| | Lt. J.R. Bernert | Me-109 prob(air) | Rheine |
| | Lt. G. Lichter | Me-109 dam(air) | Rheine |
| | Lt. W.L. Moore | Me-109 dam(air) | Rheine |

*Losses-*

**4th**: Lt. Edwin R. Mead (335th Ftr Sqn) POW
P-47D WD-B 42-8506
Hit by enemy fighters east of Lingen.

**20th**: Maj. Richard L. Ott (79th Ftr Sqn) KIA
P-38J MC-L 42-67516
Lost an engine near Minden, then hit by a FW-190 near Osnabruck.

Lt. Mack D. Fall (79th Ftr Sqn) KIA
P-38J MC-A 42-67646
Hit by a FW-190 near Minden and bailed out near Hengelo.

**361st**: Lt. Ethelbert F. Amason (374th Ftr Sqn) KIA
P-47D B7- 42-75567
Hit by enemy fighters and crashed near Rijssen.

**January 31, 1944**
Groups Operating: P-47 56th, 356th
Missions: Support for bombers to St. Pol/Siracourt V-1 sites.
Claims: nil
Losses: nil

Groups Operating: P-47 4th, 78th, 355th
P-38 55th
Missions: The P-47 units dive-bombed in the Gilze-Rijen area while the 55th flew a sweep over Holland.
Claims: 13-3-1 air
0-0 ground

| *Group* | | *Claims* | *Location* |
|---|---|---|---|
| **4th** | | | |
| 334th: | Lt. D.W. Beeson | Me-109 dest(air) | Gilze-Rijen |
| | Capt. W.M. Sobanski | (.5)Me-109 dest(air) | Gilze-Rijen |
| | Lt. H.N. Moulton | (.5)Me-109 dest(air) | Gilze-Rijen |
| 335th: | Lt. R.P. Clotfelter | Me-109 dest(air) | Zevenbergen |
| | Lt. P.M. Ellington | Me-109 dest(air) | Overflakkee |
| 336th: | Lt. K.E. Carlson | Me-109 dest(air) | Gilze-Rijen |
| | Lt. V. Garrison | Me-109 dest(air) | Gilze-Rijen |
| **55th** | | | |
| 38th: | Lt. L.V. Hokinson | (2)FW-190 dest(air) | Eindhoven |
| | Lt. G. Brown | Me-109 dest(air) | Venlo |
| | Maj. M.K. Shipman | Me-109 prob(air) | N/Venlo |
| 338th: | Capt. C.A. Patterson | (2)Me-109 dest(air) | Goch & Kessel |
| | Lt. M.E. Blanchard | Me-109 dest(air) | Goch |
| | Capt. V.W. Bollwerk | Me-109 prob(air) | Geldern |
| | Lt. W.H. Burns | Me-109 prob(air) | N/Venlo |
| | Lt. G. Korinek | Me-109 dam(air) | N/Venlo |
| 343rd: | Maj. D.W. Webb | Me-109 dest(air) | NW Venlo |

*Losses-*

**55th**: Lt. David D. Fisher (38th Ftr Sqn) KIA
P-38J CG-C 42-67757
Hit by enemy fighters near Venlo.

Lt. Leroy V. Hokinson (38th Ftr Sqn) MIA-E
P-38J CG- 42-67813
Hit by enemy fighters near Venlo.

Lt. Morris (38th Ftr Sqn) KIA
P-38J CG- 42-67768
Hit by enemy fighters near Venlo.

Lt. Martin B. Miller (38th Ftr Sqn) KIA
P-38J CG- 42-67221
Hit by enemy fighters near Venlo.

Lt. Leon M. Patterson (38th Ftr Sqn) KIA
P-38J CG- 42-67301
Hit by enemy fighters and crashed into the North Sea.

Lt. Delorn L. Steiner (38th Ftr Sqn) KIA
P-38J CG- 42-67711
Hit by enemy fighters near Venlo.

*Remarks*
55th: Lt. Delbert F. Blount (338th Ftr Sqn) c/l Leiston; o.k.
P-38 CL-

**February 3, 1944**
Groups Operating: P-47 4th, 56th, 78th, 352nd, 353rd, 355th, 356th, 359th, 361st
P-38 20th, 55th
Missions: Support for bombers to Wilhelmshaven and Emden.
Claims: 6-3-2 air
0-0 ground

| *Group* | | *Claims* | *Location* |
|---|---|---|---|
| **56th** | | | |
| 63rd: | Capt. W.M. Mahurin | Me-109 dest(air) | SE Ruhlertwist |
| | Lt. C.W. Reed | Me-109 dest(air) | SE Ruhlertwist |
| | Lt. W.H. Janson | Me-109 prob(air) | SE Ruhlertwist |
| | Lt. R.B. Westfall | Me-109 dam(air) | SE Ruhlertwist |
| **352nd** | | | |
| 487th: | Lt. V.K. Meroney | FW-190 dest(air) | Groningen |
| **353rd** | | | |
| 350th: | Capt. D.E. Newhart | Me-109 prob(air) | S/Oldenburg |
| | | Me-109 dam(air) | S/Oldenburg |
| | Lt. R.N. Ireland | Me-109 prob(air) | Wilhelmshaven |
| 351st: | Maj. W.C. Beckham | Me-109 dest(air) | S/Oldenburg |
| | | FW-190 dest(air) | S/Oldenburg |
| **359th** | | | |
| 369th: | Lt. R.C. Thomson | FW-190 dest(air) | Zuider Zee |

*Losses-*

**4th**: F/O William A. Cox (334th Ftr Sqn) KIA
P-47D QP-X 42-75254
Hit by enemy aircraft near Emden.

**56th**: Lt. Lloyd M. Langdon (63rd Ftr Sqn) KIA
P-47D UN-T 42-8463
Ran out of fuel and bailed out forty miles off the English coast.

**352nd**: Lt. Ray L. Cornick (328th Ftr Sqn) KIA
P-47D PE-R 42-8563 "Ilene"
Ran out of fuel and crashed into the North Sea.

F/O Joseph L. Sweeney (487th Ftr Sqn) KIA
P-47D HO- 42-75405
Ran out of fuel and crashed into the North Sea.

**353rd**: Capt. Wilfred E. Hurst (350th Ftr Sqn) KIA
P-47D LH-M 42-7940
Had his tail chopped-off by another P-47 near Deintrop.

Lt. David C. Kenney (351st Ftr Sqn) KIA
P-47D YJ- 42-75191
Hit by enemy fighters near Wedeborn.

Lt. Lloyd A. Thornell (351st Ftr Sqn) KIA
P-47D YJ- 42-75135
Suffered mechanical failure and ditched in the Channel.

**359th**: Lt. Cecil W. Crawford (369th Ftr Sqn) KIA
P-47D IV-E 42-22791
Hit by flak near Emden and crashed into the North Sea.

*Remarks*
353rd: 0-5 ships
56th: Lt. James E. Fields (62nd Ftr Sqn) c/l near Halesworth, o.k.
P-47D LM-S 42-7938
359th: Lt. Charles W. Hipsher (370th Ftr Sqn) c/l Oulton, o.k.
P-47D CS-
352nd: P-47D c/l Wooten Park, o.k.

**February 4, 1944**
Groups Operating: P-47 4th, 56th, 78th, 352nd, 353rd, 355th, 356th, 359th, 361st
P-38 20th, 55th
Missions: Support of bombers to Frankfurt.
Claims: 8-0-5 air
0-0 ground

| Group | | Claims | Location |
|---|---|---|---|
| **56th** | | | |
| 62nd: | Capt. M.J. Quirk | FW-190 dest(air) | Charleroi |
| | | Me-110 dest(air) | St. Omer |
| | Lt. F.J. Christensen | FW-190 dest(air) | Charleroi |
| | Lt. J.E. Fields | FW-190 dest(air) | Charleroi |
| | Lt. S.B. Morrill | (2)FW-190 dam(air) | Charleroi |
| | Lt. J.M. Jones | FW-190 dam(air) | Charleroi |
| | Lt. I.E. Valenta | FW-190 dam(air) | Charleroi |
| **352nd** | | | |
| HdQts: | LtCol. E.L. Clark | FW-190 dest(air) | Hasselt |
| 328th: | Lt. F.W. Horne | FW-190 dest(air) | Brussels |
| | Lt. F.W. Miller | FW-190 dest(air) | Brussels |
| | Lt. J.H. Walker | FW-190 dest(air) | Hasselt |
| | Lt. F.A. Yochim | FW-190 dam(air) | Hasselt |

*Losses-*

**20th**: Lt. Donald L. Durand (77th Ftr Sqn) KIA
P-38J LC- 42-67407
Hit by enemy aircraft near Frankfurt and crashed near Liege.

*Remarks*
352nd: Lt. Wendell F. Parlee (328th Ftr Sqn) c/l Manston, o.k.
P-47D PE-E 42-8680

**February 5, 1944**
Groups Operating: P-47 4th, 56th, 78th, 352nd, 353rd, 355th, 356th, 359th, 361st
P-38 20th, 55th
Missions: Support of bombers to various airfields in France.
Claims: 6-0-6 air
0-0 ground

| Group | | Claims | Location |
|---|---|---|---|
| **20th** | | | |
| HdQts: | LtCol. R. Montgomery | (.33)FW-200 dest(air) | Bourges A/F |
| 77th: | Capt. P.J. Sabo | (.33)FW-200 dest(air) | Bourges A/F |
| | Lt. J.E. Davis | (.33)FW-200 dest(air) | Bourges A/F |
| | Lt. R.L. Frakes | (.33)He-111 dest(air) | Bourges A/F |
| | Lt. M.J. Gilbertson | (.33)He-111 dest(air) | Bourges A/F |
| | Lt. J.M. Morris | (.33)He-111 dest(air) | Bourges A/F |
| **55th** | | | |
| HdQts: | Capt. T.E. Beaird | Me-109 dest(air) | Chartres |
| 38th: | Lt. C.R. Watts | Me-109 dam(air) | Chartres |
| **78th** | | | |
| 84th: | Lt. L.J. Abel | FW-190 dam(air) | Bernay |
| | Lt. E.S. Laing | (.5)FW-190 dam(air) | Bernay |
| | Lt. P.E. Pompetti | (.5)FW-190 dam(air) | Bernay |
| **353rd** | | | |
| HdQts: | LtCol. G.E. Duncan | FW-190 dest(air) | Sancere |
| **355th** | | | |
| 357th: | Capt. N.E. Olson | (2)Me-109 dest(air) | W/Vendome |
| 358th: | Lt. H.J. Hoffman | (.25)Me-109 dam(air) | S/Tours |
| | Lt. J.H. McConnell | (.25)Me-109 dam(air) | S/Tours |
| | Lt. J.J. DeGeorge | (.25)Me-109 dam(air) | S/Tours |
| | Lt. J. Upchurch | (.25)Me-109 dam(air) | S/Tours |
| **357th** | | | |
| HdQts: | LtCol. D.W. Graham | FW-190 dam(air) | Romilly-Sur-Seine |

(Note - the 357th was not operational but Graham flew on TDY with the 354th Ftr Grp, 9th Air Force)

*Losses-*

**56th**: Lt. John A. Patton (61st Ftr Sqn) KIA
P-47D HV- 42-75063
Hit by a FW-190 near Forges.

**353rd**: Lt. Edgar J. Albert (351st Ftr Sqn) KIA
P-47D YJ- 42-75161
Hit by a FW-190 northwest of Orleans.

*Remarks*
55th Ftr Grp P-38 c/l Nuthampstead, o.k.

KIAc's
**56th**: Lt. Roger A. Phillips (61st Ftr Sqn)
P-47C HV-M 41-6319
Collided with Lt. Albert northeast of Wangford.

Lt. Richard A. Albert (63rd Ftr Sqn)
P-47D UN-K 42-7943
Collided with Lt. Phillips northeast of Wangford.

**February 6, 1944**
Groups Operating: P-47 4th, 56th, 78th, 352nd, 353rd, 355th, 356th, 359th, 361st
P-38 20th, 55th
Missions: Support for bombers to various airfields in France.
Claims: 11-0-3 air
1-7 ground

| Group | | Claims | Location |
|---|---|---|---|
| **4th** | | | |
| 334th: | F/O R.K. Hofer | Me-109 dest(air) | W/Paris |
| | Lt. V.J. France | Me-109 dam(air) | W/Paris |
| 335th: | Maj. G. Carpenter | FW-190 dam(air) | Versaille |
| 336th: | Lt. V. Garrison | FW-190 dest(air) | Beauvais-Marigny |
| | Lt. R.D. Hobert | FW-190 dest(air) | Beauvais-Marigny |
| **56th** | | | |
| 61st: | Capt. R.A. Lamb | Me-109 dest(air) | Beauvais |
| | Lt. J.H. Powers | Me-109 dest(air) | Beauvais |
| | Lt. S.D. Hamilton | Me-109 dest(air) | Paris |
| | Lt. R.J. Rankin | Me-109 dest(air) | Paris |
| 62nd: | Capt. E.W. O'Neill | FW-190 dest(air) | Paris |
| | Lt. J.W. Icard | FW-190 dam(air) | Albert |
| **78th** | | | |
| 82nd: | Lt. W.M. Wesson | FW-190 dest(air) | Orleans |
| | | (2)He-111 dam(grd) | Orleans |
| | Lt. J.W. Wilkinson | FW-190 dest(air) | Orleans |
| | | (.5)Ju-52 dam(grd) | Orleans |
| | | (.5)He-111 dam(grd) | Orleans |
| | F/O J.E. Brasher | (2)He-111 dam(grd) | Orleans |
| | Lt. D.E. Ludwig | (.5)Ju-52 dam(grd) | Orleans |
| | | (.5)He-111 dam(grd) | Orleans |
| 84th: | Lt. P.E. Pompetti | Hs-129 dest(grd) | Orleans/Bricy |
| | | Ju-88 dam(grd) | Orleans/Bricy |
| **356th** | | | |
| 361st: | Lt. D.J. Strait | FW-190 dest(air) | Paris-Soissons |

*Losses-*

**4th**: Lt. Hubert N. Ballew (335th Ftr Sqn) POW
P-47D WD-W 42-8495
Hit by a FW-190 near Paris.

**20th**: F/O Markrel L. Byrd (79th Ftr Sqn) POW
P-38J MC-K 42-67854
Hit by flak and bailed out near Bernay.

**55th**: Lt. William J. Ashton (343rd Ftr Sqn) KIA
P-38J CY- 42-67893
Hit by a FW-190 near Evreux.

Lt. Raymond L. Sumpter (343rd Ftr Sqn) KIA
P-38J CY-I 42-67479
Collided with another P-38 and spun-in over the Channel.

*Remarks*
78th: 0-3 locos, 0-2 tugs, 0-2 flak towers
55th: Lt. Richard G. Atchison (338th Ftr Sqn) c/l Nuthampstead; o.k.
P-38J CL-O
56th: Lt. Dick H. Thompson (61st Ftr Sqn) c/l Halesworth, o.k.
P-47D HV-
356th: Lt. Robert J. Collins (359th Ftr Sqn) c/l Manston, o.k.
P-47D OC- 42-8407

**February 8, 1944**
Groups Operating: P-47 359th
Missions: Support of bombers to Watten and Siracourt V-1 sites.
Claims: nil
Losses: nil

Groups Operating: P-47 4th, 56th, 78th, 352nd, 353rd, 355th, 356th, 361st
P-38 20th, 55th
Missions: Support of bombers to Frankfurt.
Claims: 12-1-1 air
2-5 ground

| Group | | Claims | Location |
|---|---|---|---|
| **20th** | | | |
| 77th: | Lt. J.M. Morris | (2)Me-109 dest(air) | Losheim & Denain |
| | | (2)FW-190 dest(air) | Sedan |
| **56th** | | | |
| 62nd: | Lt. J.W. Icard | Me-109 dest(air) | Cambrai |
| | Capt. L.A. Schreiber | Me-109 prob(air) | Cambrai |
| 63rd: | Maj. S.V. Burke | Me-109 dam(air) | Quesnoy |

| | | | |
|---|---|---|---|
| **78th** | | | |
| 82nd: | Lt. W.M. Wesson | He-177 dest(grd) | Paris |
| | | He-111 dest(grd) | Paris |
| | Lt. J.W. Wilkinson | (2)He-111 dam(grd) | Paris |
| | Lt. C. Webb | (2)He-111 dam(grd) | Paris |
| | Lt. P. Keller | He-111 dam(grd) | Paris |
| **353rd** | | | |
| 350th: | Capt. C.W. Dinse | FW-190 dest(air) | Luxembourg |
| 351st: | Maj. W.C. Beckham | Me-109 dest(air) | E/St. Hubert |
| | | FW-190 dest(air) | St. Hubert |
| 352nd: | Capt. R.E. Robertson | FW-190 dest(air) | St. Hubert |
| | Lt. C.F. Armstrong | FW-190 dest(air) | St. Hubert |
| | Lt. G.G. Callans | FW-190 dest(air) | St. Hubert |
| | Lt. D.J. Corrigan | FW-190 dest(air) | Libramont |

*Losses-*

**20th**: Lt. Robert L. Frakes (77th Ftr Sqn) POW
P-38J LC-A 42-67234
Hit by flak near Corry le Chateau.

Lt. William H. Rierson (79th Ftr Sqn) POW
P-38J MC- 42-67306
Suffered mechanical failure and bailed out over France.

**352nd**: Lt. James Meagher (328th Ftr Sqn) KIA
P-47D PE-M 42-8556 "Patricia Lee"
Hit by enemy fighters near St. Gobert.

Lt. Harold C. Nussman (328th Ftr Sqn) KIA
P-47D PE-X 42-8419 "Blondie"
Hit by enemy fighters near Chaug.

Lt. John H. Walker, Jr. (328th Ftr Sqn) KIA
P-47D PE-V 42-8527 "Ramblin' Rebel"
Hit by enemy fighters near Burelles.

**357th**: Capt. Lloyd M., Hubbard (363rd Ftr Sqn) KIA
P-51B FT- 43-12368
Hit by flak at Aresnes Airfield. He was on TDY to the 354th Ftr Grp, 9th Air Force.

*Remarks*
20th: 1-0 loco
78th: 0-1 hangar
361st: 0-1 loco
56th: Lt. Charles C. Clamp(63rd Ftr Sqn) c/l Manston, o.k.
P-47D UN-

**February 10, 1944**
Groups Operating: P-47 4th, 56th, 78th, 352nd, 353rd, 356th, 359th,
P-38 20th, 55th
Missions: Support of bombers to Brunswick.
Claims: 49-2-19 air
0-2 ground

| ***Group*** | | ***Claims*** | ***Location*** |
|---|---|---|---|
| **4th** | | | |
| 334th: | Lt. H.T. Biel | Me-109 dest(air) | Hengele |
| | | Me-109 dam(air) | Hengele |
| | Lt. V.J. France | FW-190 dest(air) | Lingen |
| | Lt. G.E. Montgomery | Me-109 dest(air) | Emmerich |
| 335th: | Lt. C.E. Manning | FW-190 dest(air) | SW Hanover |
| | | FW-190 dam(air) | SW Hanover |
| | Lt. C.F. Anderson | (.5)Me-109 prob(air) | SW Hanover |
| | Lt. A.L. Schlegel | (.5)Me-109 prob(air) | SW Hanover |
| 336th: | Lt. V. Garrison | Me-109 dest(air) | Dummer Lake |
| | Lt. W.W. Millikan | FW-190 dest(air) | N/Dummer Lake |
| | Lt. L.H. Norley | Me-109 dest(air) | Dummer Lake |
| **20th** | | | |
| HdQts: | LtCol. R.P. Montgomery | FW-190 dam(air) | Nienburg |
| 55th: | Capt. M.R. McLary | Me-110 dest(air) | Gifhorn |
| | | Me-410 dest(air) | Gifhorn |
| | | Me-110 dam(air) | Gifhorn |
| | | FW-190 dam(air) | Gifhorn |
| | Lt. R.D. Frey | Me-110 dest(air) | Celle |
| | Lt. W.B. Taylor | Me-109 dest(air) | NW Hanover |
| 77th: | Capt. P.J. Sabo | Me-110 dam(air) | Hanover |
| | | Me-210 dam(air) | Hanover |
| | Lt. A.L. Gese | Me-210 dam(air) | Brunswick |
| 79th: | Capt. C.E. Jackson | FW-190 dest(air) | N/Hanover |
| | Capt. R.J. Meyer | FW-190 dest(air) | N/Hanover |
| | Lt. F.E. LeFevre | Me-210 dest(air) | Lingen |
| | Lt. D.C. Cooper | FW-190 dam(air) | N/Hanover |
| **55th** | | | |
| 338th: | Capt. V.W. Bollwerk | Me-110 dest(air) | Brunswick |
| | Lt. R.K. Fruh | Me-110 dest(air) | Brunswick |
| | Lt. J.L. Odegard | Me-110 dam(air) | Brunswick |
| 343rd: | Capt. R.L. Buttke | (2)Me-210 dest(air) | NW Brunswick |
| | | Me-110 dam(air) | NW Brunswick |
| | Capt. P.E. Hoeper | Me-210 dest(air) | Brunswick |
| **78th** | | | |
| 82nd: | Lt. G.M. Turley | (2)Me-109 dest(air) | Osnabruck |
| | Lt. V.Y. Jones | Me-109 dest(air) | Rheine |
| | Lt. W.M. Wesson | FW-190 dest(air) | Osnabruck |
| 83rd: | Lt. H.T. Barnaby | Me-109 dest(air) | Lingen |
| | | FW-190 dest(air) | Lingen |
| | | Me-109 dam(air) | Lingen |
| | F/O E.J. Downey | FW-190 dest(air) | Lingen |
| | Lt. H.C. Roff | Me-109 dest(air) | Lingen |
| | Lt. W.H. Waldheim | Me-109 dest(air) | Lingen |
| 84th: | Lt. G.H. Doyle | Ju-88 dam(grd) | Soesterberg A/F |
| | Lt. R.E. Smith | Ju-88 dam(grd) | Soesterberg A/F |
| **352nd** | | | |
| 486th: | Capt. F.N. Greene | Me-109 dam(air) | Enschede |
| | Lt. C.V. Harker | Me-109 dam(air) | Enschede |
| | Lt. D.Y. Whinnem | Me-109 dam(air) | Enschede |
| 487th: | Lt. V.K. Meroney | Me-109 dest(air) | Hengelo |
| | Lt. W.E. Starck | Me-109 dest(air) | Arnheim |
| **353rd** | | | |
| 351st: | Capt. F.N. Emory | FW-190 dest(air) | Lingen |
| 352nd: | Lt. C.F. Armstrong | Me-109 dest(air) | Lingen |
| | Lt. W.J. Jordan | Me-210 prob(air) | Lingen |
| **356th** | | | |
| HdQts: | LtCol. O.H. Coen | FW-190 dam(air) | NE Lingen |
| 359th: | Maj. J.H. Thorne | FW-190 dest(air) | Meppen |
| | Capt. E.J. White | (.33)FW-190 dest(air) | Meppen |
| | Lt. R.D. Bradshaw | (.33)FW-190 dest(air) | Meppen |
| | Lt. G.W. Engel | (.33)FW-190 dest(air) | Meppen |
| | Lt. W.C. O'Barr | FW-190 dam(air) | Meppen |
| 360th: | Lt. W.E. Johnson | FW-190 dest(air) | Ruhlwertwist |
| | Lt. L.F. Kress | (.5)FW-190 dest(air) | Ruhlwertwist |
| | F/O C.W. Dunn | (.5)FW-190 dest(air) | Ruhlwertwist |
| 361st: | Capt. J.N. Wood | (1.5)FW-190 dest(air) | NE Lingen |
| | Lt. M.W. DeMerit | (.5)FW-190 dest(air) | NE Lingen |
| | F/O J.V. Jack | FW-190 dest(air) | NE Lingen |
| | Lt. R.C. McDowell | FW-190 dest(air) | NE Lingen |
| | Lt. J.P. Perrin | FW-190 dest(air) | NE Lingen |
| | | FW-190 dam(air) | NE Lingen |
| | Lt. D.J. Strait | Me-109 dest(air) | NE Lingen |
| **359th** | | | |
| 369th: | Capt. C.E. Ettlesen | Me-109 dest(air) | Dummer Lake |
| | Lt. C.E. Carter | Me-109 dam(air) | Quackenbruck |
| 370th: | Lt. W.R. Hodges | (2)Me-109 dest(air) | E/Zuider Zee |
| | Capt. C.H. Brown | Me-109 dest(air) | E/Zuider Zee |
| | Lt. R.E. Kibler | Me-109 dest(air) | E/Zuider Zee |
| | Lt. R.O. Major | Me-109 dest(air) | E/Zuider Zee |
| | Lt. R.S. Wetmore | Me-109 dest(air) | E/Zuider Zee |

*Losses-*

**20th**: Lt. Royal D. Frey (55th Ftr Sqn) POW
P-38J KI-W 42-67855
Lost an engine, then hit by flak near Ludenhausen.

Lt. John W. Lundin (55th Ftr Sqn) KIA
P-38J KI- 42-67887
Hit by a FW-190 near Hazelunne.

Lt. Jack W. Taylor (55th Ftr Sqn) KIA
P-38J KI-
Spun-in near Sutton Bridge while returning.

Capt. Robert W. Holmes (77th Ftr Sqn) POW
P-38J LC-D 42-67759
Suffered mechanical failure near Achmer.

**55th**: Lt. Jack R. Foster (338th Ftr Sqn) POW
P-38J CL-P 42-67816 "Princess Pat"
Hit by enemy fighters near Ettenbestal.

**78th**: Lt. Donald E. Ludwig (82nd Ftr Sqn) KIA
P-47C MX-H 41-6249
Hit by flak and crashed into the North Sea.

Lt. Vernon Y. Jones (82nd Ftr Sqn) KIA
P-47D MX-X 42-7883
Hit by enemy fighters near Tongeren.

**356th**: Lt. Merrill W. DeMerit (361st Ftr Sqn) POW
P-47D QI-N 42-22520
Hit by a FW-190 near Lingen.

*Remarks*
55th: 0-1 gun position
78th: 0-1 ship
4th: Lt. Robert H. Wehrman (336th Ftr Sqn) c/l High Halden; o.k.
P-47D VF-

KIAc's
359th: Lt. Alex M. Cosmos (370th Ftr Sqn)
P-47D CS-I 42-75091
Last seen flying at 800 feet in a snow storm; crashed near Somersham.

Groups Operating: P-47 355th, 361st
Missions: Support of bombers to Gilze-Rijen Airfield.
Claims: nil
Losses: nil

**February 11, 1944**
Groups Operating: P-47 356th
P-51 357th
Missions: Support of bombers to Siracourt V-1 sites.
Claims: nil
Losses: nil

Groups Operating: P-47 4th, 56th, 78th, 352nd, 353rd, 355th, 356th, 359th, 361st
P-38 20th, 55th
Missions: Support of bombers to Frankfurt.
Claims: 17-2-7 air
1-4 ground

| ***Group*** | | ***Claims*** | ***Location*** |
|---|---|---|---|
| **20th** | | | |
| 77th: | Lt. J.M. Morris | Me-109 dest(air) | Giessen |
| | Lt. B.N. Rader | Me-109 dest(air) | Giessen |
| | Maj. H.E. Johnson | Me-109 dam(air) | Chateau d'Ardenne |
| | Lt. R.G. Quinn | Me-109 dam(air) | Chateau d'Ardenne |
| 79th: | Capt. R.J. Meyer | Me-410 prob(air) | SW Frankfurt |
| | Lt. M.B. Nichols | Me-410 dam(air) | W/Frankfurt |
| **56th** | | | |
| HdQts: | Col. H. Zemke | Me-109 dest(grd) | Rheims |
| | | (2)Me-109 dam(grd) | Rheims |
| 61st: | Maj. J.C. Stewart | FW-190 dest(air) | Duren |
| | Lt. D.M. Funcheon | Me-110 dam(grd) | Rheims |
| | Lt. D.L. Altschuler | Me-110 dam(grd) | Rheims |
| 62nd: | Lt. J.W. Icard | Me-109 dest(air) | Bierset |
| | Lt. S.B. Morrill | Me-109 dest(air) | Dison |
| | Lt. F.J. Christensen | Me-109 dest(air) | Bierset |
| | Capt. L.A. Schreiber | Me-109 dam(air) | Namur |
| 63rd: | Maj. S.V. Burke | Me-109 dest(air) | Hody-Spa |
| **78th** | | | |
| 82nd: | Lt. G.M. Turley | Me-109 dest(air) | Verdun |
| | | FW-190 dest(air) | Verdun |
| | Lt. J.E. Brasher | Me-109 dest(air) | NE Luxembourg |
| | Lt. J.J. Hockery | Me-109 dest(air) | NW Luxembourg |
| | Lt. C. Webb | FW-190 dam(air) | Rouen |
| **355th** | | | |
| 357th: | Maj. E.W. Szaniawski | (2)Me-109 dest(air) | S/Koln |
| | Lt. V.A. Burroughs | FW-190 dest(air) | S/Koln |
| | | Me-109 dam(air) | S/Koln |
| **356th** | | | |
| HdQts: | LtCol. O.H. Coen | (.5)Me-109 dest(air) | NW Charleville |
| 359th: | Lt. G.B. Peet | (.5)Me-109 dest(air) | NW Charleville |
| 360th: | Lt. C.J. Garvey | FW-190 dest(air) | S/Albert |
| | Lt. P.E. McCullough | FW-190 dest(air) | Marle |
| | | FW-190 prob(air) | S/Albert |
| 361st: | Lt. J.P. Perrin | FW-190 dam(air) | Charleville |

*Losses-*

**20th**: LtCol. Robert P. Montgomery (HdQts) MIA-E
P-38J LC-M 42-68036
Hit by enemy fighters near Valenciennes.

Lt. Miles N. Keatherly (77th Ftr Sqn) POW
P-38J LC- 42-67726
Hit by enemy fighters near Chateau d'Ardenne.

Lt. Joseph O. Minton (77th Ftr Sqn) KIA
P-38J LC-C 42-67728
Hit by enemy fighters near Chateau d'Ardenne.

Lt. Donald C. Cooper (79th Ftr Sqn) KIA
P-38J MC-C 42-67718
Hit by enemy fighters near St. Aignan.

Lt. Thomas A. Hanzo (79th Ftr Sqn) POW
P-38J MC-G 42-67981
Hit by enemy fighters near Chateau d'Ardenne.

Lt. Melvin Orr (79th Ftr Sqn) MIA
P-38J MC- 42-67848
Hit by enemy fighters near Birkenfeld.

Lt. Myron R. Sands (79th Ftr Sqn) POW
P-38J MC-S 42-67830
Hit by enemy fighters near Epioux.

Lt. Leonard S. Smutko (79th Ftr Sqn) POW
P-38J MC- 42-67821
Hit by a Me-410 near Birkenfeld.

**78th**: Lt. William S. Swanson (82nd Ftr Sqn) KIA
P-47D MX-P 42-74733
Hit by a Me-109 southwest of Arras.

Lt. Donald R. Morsch (82nd Ftr Sqn) KIA
P-47D MX-D 42-22755
Hit by a Me-109 southwest of Arras.

F/O Archie F. Daniels (83rd Ftr Sqn) KIA
P-47D HL-T 42-7963
Lost a prop on take-off and crashed near Nuthampstead.

**355th**: Lt. Roland J. Dufresne (357th Ftr Sqn) MIA-E
P-47D OS-S 42-8550
Suffered mechanical failure and bailed out near Cologne.

**356th**: Capt. Byron A. Evans (360th Ftr Sqn) KIA
P-47D PI- 42-8507
Last seen chasing a Me-109 near St. Quentin.

*Remarks*
20th: 0-3 locos, 0-2 radar stations, 0-1 ship
56th: 0-4 hangars, 0-1 vehicle
353rd: 0-1 building
359th: Lt. Emer H. Cater (368th Ftr Sqn) c/l East Wretham; o.k.
P-47D CV-
Lt. Clifford E. Carter (369th Ftr Sqn) c/l East Wretham; o.k.
P-47D IV-W 42-8557 "Green Eyes"

**February 12, 1944**
Groups Operating: P-51 357th
P-47 4th
Missions: Support of bombers to St. Pol/Siracourt V-1 sites.
Claims: nil
Losses: nil

**February 13, 1944**
Groups Operating: P-51 357th
P-47 78th, 352nd, 353rd, 356th
Missions: Support of bombers to targets in the Pas de Calais area.
Claims: 6-0-4 air
0-3 ground

| ***Group*** | | ***Claims*** | ***Location*** |
|---|---|---|---|
| **78th** | | | |
| 82nd: | Capt. W.L. Boone | Ju-88 dam(grd) | Bryes-Sud A/F |
| | Lt. J.E. Brasher | Ju-88 dam(grd) | Bryes-Sud A/F |
| | Lt. W.M. Wesson | Ju-88 dam(grd) | Bryes-Sud A/F |
| **353rd** | | | |
| 351st: | Maj. W.C. Beckham | FW-190 dam(air) | Cambrai |
| **356th** | | | |
| 360th: | Lt. B.E. Ellingson | Me-109 dest(air) | Chartres |
| | Lt. W.G. Maxwell | FW-190 dest(air) | Chartres |
| | Lt. H.D. Parker | FW-190 dest(air) | Chartres |
| | Lt. A.S. Koczak | FW-190 dest(air) | Dieppe |
| | Lt. P.E. McCullough | FW-190 dam(air) | Chartres |
| 361st: | Lt. S.H. Hewett | Me-109 dest(air) | SE Paris |
| | | (2)FW-190 dam(air) | SE Paris |
| | Lt. D.F. Thwaites | Me-109 dest(air) | SW Paris |

*Losses-*

**357th**: Lt. Robert W. Brown, Jr. (362nd Ftr Sqn) ASR
P-51B G4- 43-6734
Suffered mechanical failure and bailed out over the Channel. Was rescued but was seriously injured.

*Remarks*
78th: 0-1 building
356th: Lt. James J. Meholic (359th Ftr Sqn) c/l Manston; o.k.
P-47D OC-

**February 14, 1944**
Groups Operating: P-47 353rd
Missions: Dive-bombing of Gilze-Rijen Airfield. Only a few hits were registered on dispersal areas.
Claims: nil
Losses: nil

**February 15, 1944**
Groups Operating: P-47 4th, 56th
Missions: Sent out to dive-bomb airfields in France but was recalled because of weather; the 356th did drop a few bombs on Coxyde Airfield on the way out.
Claims: nil
Losses: nil

**February 20, 1944**
Groups Operating: P-51 357th
P-47 4th, 56th, 78th, 352nd, 353rd, 355th, 356th, 359th, 361st
P-38 20th, 55th
Missions: Support of bombers to Leipzig, Brunswick, Bernburg, Gotha, Oschersleben, and other targets in Germany.
Claims: 46-3-26 air
0-7 ground

| *Group* | | *Claims* | *Location* |
|---|---|---|---|
| **4th** | | | |
| 334th: | Capt. D.W. Beeson | FW-190 dest(air) | Aachen |
| | Capt. H.L. Mills | FW-190 dest(air) | Aachen |
| 335th: | Lt. P.M. Ellington | Me-110 dest(air) | Coblenz |
| | Lt. C.A. Fiedler | Me-110 dest(air) | Coblenz |
| | | Me-110 dam(air) | Coblenz |
| | Lt. P.W. McKennon | FW-190 dest(air) | Marburg |
| | Lt. R.I. Reed | (.5)Me-110 dest(air) | Coblenz |
| | Lt. P.S. Riley | (.5)Me-110 dest(air) | Coblenz |
| | Maj. G. Carpenter | Me-110 dam(air) | W/Coblenz |
| 336th: | Lt. V. Garrison | FW-190 dam(air) | Malmedy |
| **20th** | | | |
| 55th: | Lt. C.A. Hallberg | Me-110 dam(air) | NE Coblenz |
| 77th: | Maj. H.E. Johnson | FW-190 dest(air) | Wernigeroode |
| | | FW-190 prob(air) | Wernigeroode |
| | Lt. T.M. Williams | FW-190 dest(air) | Brunswick |
| | | (.5)Me-109 dest(air) | Brunswick |
| | | FW-190 dam(air) | Brunswick |
| | Lt. C.C. Arthaud | (.5)Me-109 dest(air) | Brunswick |
| | Lt. A.L. Gese | FW-190 dam(air) | Brunswick-Gotha] |
| 79th: | Capt. L.F. Graham | (2)Me-110 dest(air) | SW Brunswick |
| | Capt. C.E. Jackson | (2)FW-190 dest(air) | SW Brunswick |
| **56th** | | | |
| HdQts: | LtCol. F.S. Gabreski | (2)Me-110 dest(air) | W/Hanover |
| | | Me-110 dam(air) | W/Hanover |
| 61st: | Lt. R.S. Johnson | (2)Me-110 dest(air) | W/Hanover |
| | | (2)Me-110 dam(air) | W/Hanover |
| | Lt. D.F. Smith | (2)Me-110 dest(air) | Steinhuder Lake |
| | | Me-110 dam(air) | Steinhuder Lake |
| | Capt. R.A. Lamb | Ju-88 dest(air) | E/Minden |
| | Capt. J.R. Carter | Me-110 dest(air) | Steinhuder Lake |
| | Lt. S.D. Hamilton | Me-110 prob(air) | Steinhuder Lake |
| | | Me-109 dam(air) | Steinhuder Lake |
| | Lt. J.D. Foster | Me-110 prob(air) | Steinhuder Lake |
| | | Me-110 dam(air) | Steinhuder Lake |
| | Lt. D.M. Funcheon | (2)Me-110 dam(air) | Steinhuder Lake |
| | Lt. C.E. Mussey | Me-110 dam(air) | Steinhuder Lake |
| | Lt. R.L. Altschuler | Me-110 dam(air) | Steinhuder Lake |
| 62nd: | Capt. L.A. Schreiber | (3)Me-109 dest(air) | Steinhuder Lake |
| | | Me-109 dam(air) | Steinhuder Lake |
| | | Do-217 dam(grd) | Steinhuder Lake |
| | Lt. F.J. Christensen | Ju-88 dest(air) | Steinhuder Lake |
| | | (.5)Do-217 dest(air) | Steinhuder Lake |
| | Lt. S.B. Morrill | Me-110 dest(air) | Steinhuder Lake |
| | | (.5)Do-217 dest(air) | Steinhuder Lake |
| | | (6)Me-110 dam(grd) | Steinhuder Lake |
| **66th**(FW) | | | |
| HdQts: | LtCol. R.W. Osborn | (1.33)Me-110 dest(air)* | Vogelsand |
| **78th** | | | |
| HdQts: | Col. J.J. Stone | FW-190 dam(air) | Coblenz |
| 82nd: | Lt. J.J. Hockery | FW-190 dest(air) | Coblenz |
| | Lt. G.M. Turley | FW-190 dest(air) | Coblenz |
| | Lt. J.W. Wilkinson | Me-109 dest(air) | Coblenz |
| **352nd** | | | |
| 328th: | Lt. L.E. McCarthy | (2)Me-110 dest(air) | Blankenheim |
| | | (2)Me-110 dam(air) | Blankenheim |
| | Capt. W.T. Halton | Me-109 dest(air) | Louvain |
| | Lt. H.L. Miller | Me-110 dest(air) | Blankenheim |
| | Lt. R.G. Phillips | Me-110 dest(air) | Blankenheim |
| | | Me-110 dam(air) | Blankenheim |
| | | FW-190 dam(air) | Blankenheim |
| | Capt. D.S. Bryan | (.33)Me-110 dest(air)* | Vogelsand |
| | Lt. D.T. Zimms | (.33)Me-110 dest(air)* | Vogelsand |
| | Lt. M.V.Long | FW-190 dam(air) | Vogelsand |
| 486th: | Maj. W.O. Jackson | Me-109 dest(air) | Charleroi |
| | | Me-109 dam(air) | Charleroi |
| | Lt. F.A. Cutler | (2)Me-109 dest(air) | Nivellers |
| | Lt. K.S. Williams | Me-109 dest(air) | Charleroi |
| **355th** | | | |
| 354th: | Lt. L.G. Mendenhall | Me-109 dam(air) | NE Bonn |
| 357th: | Capt. N.E. Olson | Me-109 dest(air) | Siegen |
| | Lt. B.D. Johnston | Me-109 dest(air) | Siegen |
| 358th: | Lt. J.B. Dickson | Me-109 dest(air) | Marienburg |
| **357th** | | | |
| 362nd: | Lt. C.L. Williams | Me-109 dest(air) | Leipzig |
| 363rd: | Lt. D.H. Ross | Me-109 dest(air) | Duben |
| | Capt. C.E. Anderson | Me-109 dam(air) | N/Dessau |

*Losses-*

**4th:** Lt. Richard I. Reed (335th Ftr Sqn) KIA
P-47D WD-R 42-75051
Hit by enemy fighters northeast of Coblenz

**20th:** Capt. Carl E. Jackson (79th Ftr Sqn) POW
P-38J MC-J 42-67988 "Jack"
Suffered Mechanical failure and bellied-in near Sassenheim.

**357th:** Lt. Donald H. Ross (363rd Ftr Sqn) POW
P-51B B6- 43-12131
Hit by a Me-109 northeast of Leipzig.

*Remarks*
4th: Lt. William P. Rawles (335th Ftr Sqn) c/l East Church; o.k.
P-47D WD-T 42-74717
356th: Lt. Herbert Weber (359th Ftr Sqn) c/l Ipswich; o.k.
P-47D OC- 42-8559

**February 21, 1944**
Groups Operating: P-51 357th
P-47 4th, 56th, 78th, 352nd, 353rd, 355th, 356th, 359th, 361st
P-38 20th, 55th
Missions: Support of bombers to various airfields, including Rheine, Quackenbruck, Diepholz, Verden, Achmer, Bramsche, Alhorn, and Hopsten, plus to Hanover and Brunswick.
Claims: 18-3-15 air
0-0 ground

| *Group* | | *Claims* | *Location* |
|---|---|---|---|
| **4th** | | | |
| 334th: | Capt. R.C. Care | FW-190 dest(air) | Dummer Lake |
| | Lt. D.W. Howe | FW-190 dest(air) | S/Dummer Lake |
| | Capt. W.M. Sobanski | FW-190 prob(air) | S/Dummer Lake |
| | Lt. A. Rafalovich | FW-190 dam(air) | Dummer Lake |
| 335th: | Lt. G.W. Barnes | Ju-88 dam(air) | Havern |
| | Lt. R.P. Clotfelter | Me-110 dam(air) | Havern |
| **55th** | | | |
| 343rd: | Lt. P.S. Dripps | Me-109 dam(air) | Ruhr Valley |
| **56th** | | | |
| 61st: | Capt. B.M. Gladych | (2)Me-109 dest(air) | Zuider Zee |
| | Lt. C.E. Mussey | Me-109 dest(air) | Zuider Zee |
| | Lt. D.M. Funcheon | Me-109 dest(air) | Zuider Zee |
| | Lt. F.W. Klibbe | Me-109 dest(air) | Zuider Zee |
| | F/O E.D. McMinn | Me-109 dest(air) | Zuider Zee |
| 62nd: | Lt. R.B. Bluhm | Me-109 dest(air) | Zwolle |
| | Lt. C.R. Harrison | Me-109 dest(air) | Soesterberg |
| | Lt. J.W. Icard | FW-190 dest(air) | Soesterberg |
| | Capt. L.A. Schreiber | FW-190 dam(air) | Osnabruck |
| 63rd: | Maj. G.W. Johnson | FW-190 dest(air) | NW Zwolle |
| | Capt. J.W. Vogt | Me-110 dest(air) | N/Munster |
| | Lt. J.L. Egan | Me-109 dest(air) | Elburg |
| | Capt. G.D. Schiltz | Me-109 dam(air) | Zuider Zee |
| **352nd** | | | |
| 487th: | Lt. R.H. Berkshire | Me-109 dam(air) | N/Osnabruck |
| **355th** | | | |
| 357th: | Capt. J.L. Elder | FW-190 dest(air) | Dummer Lake |
| | Capt. N.E. Olson | FW-190 dest(air) | Dummer Lake |
| | | FW-190 dam(air) | Dummer Lake |
| | Lt. R.L. Norman | FW-190 dam(air) | Dummer Lake |
| | Lt. V.A. Burroughs | FW-190 dam(air) | Dummer Lake |
| | Lt. C.J. Butcher | FW-190 dam(air) | Dummer Lake |
| | Lt. B.D. Johnston | FW-190 dam(air) | Dummer Lake |

| | | | |
|---|---|---|---|
| **356th** | | | |
| 359th: | Lt. W.W. Cotter | Me-109 dest(air) | Hanover |
| | Lt. W.A. Holm | Me-109 dam(air) | Hanover |
| | Capt. E.J. White | Me-109 dam(air) | Hanover |
| 360th: | Lt. H.B. McLaughlin | Me-109 prob(air) | Celle |
| | Lt. J.R. Cook | Me-109 dam(air) | Celle |
| **357th** | | | |
| 363rd: | Lt. A.R. Boyle | Me-109 dest(air) | E/Zwolle |
| | Capt. W.R. O'Brien | Me-109 prob(air) | Bussum |

*Losses-*

**356th**: Lt. Thomas Von Holzhausen (361st Ftr Sqn) KIA
P-47D QI-Z 42-74679 "China Doll"
Hit by a Me-109 near Hanover.

**357th**: Lt. Alfred R. Boyle (363rd Ftr Sqn) POW
P-51B B6-S 43-6723 "Old Crow"
Hit by a Me-109 and bailed out near Meppel.

**361st**: Lt. Floyd M. Stegall (375th Ftr Sqn) MIA-E
P-47D E2- 42-22769
Suffered mechanical failure near Edam.

*Remarks*
4th: Lt. Joseph L. Lang (334th Ftr Sqn) c/l Hardwick; o.k.
P-47D QP-P
Lt. Vermont Garrison (336th Ftr Sqn) c/l Pulham; o.k.
P-47D VF
55th: P-38 c/l Nuthampstead; o.k.
352nd: Lt. Richard C. Brookins (328th Ftr Sqn) b/o Attlebridge; o.k.
P-47D PE-

**February 22, 1944**
Groups Operating: P-51 357th
P-47 4th, 56th, 78th, 352nd, 353rd, 355th, 356th, 359th, 361st
P-38 20th, 55th
Missions: Bad weather disrupted the bombers and most failed to attack their planned targets. The fighters gave support to the formations which did hit cities in Germany and Holland.
Claims: 46-3-20 air
4.5-3 ground

| *Group* | | *Claims* | *Location* |
|---|---|---|---|
| **4th** | | | |
| 335th: | Maj. G. Carpenter | FW-190 dest(air) | Erkelenz |
| | Lt. B.L. McGrattan | FW-190 dest(air) | Erkelenz |
| | Lt. P.W. McKennon | (.5)Me-109 dest(air) | SW Ooltgersplant |
| | | (.5)FW-190 dam(air) | Erkelenz |
| | F/O J. Goetz | (.5)Me-109 dest(air) | SW Ooltgersplant |
| | | (.5)FW-190 dam(air) | Erkelenz |
| **20th** | | | |
| 55th: | Lt. E.E. Geiger | Z.506 dest(air) | Cleve |
| **56th** | | | |
| HdQts: | LtCol. F.S. Gabreski | FW-190 dest(air) | N/Lippstadt |
| | | Do-217 dest(grd) | Eindhoven |
| 61st: | Capt. L.C. Smith | (2)FW-190 dest(air) | Lippstadt |
| | Maj. J.C. Stewart | Me-109 dest(air) | SW Munster |
| | Lt. D.F. Smith | FW-190 dest(air) | Lippstadt |
| | F/O E.D. McMinn | FW-190 dest(air) | Lippstadt |
| | F/O S. Gerick | Me-110 dam(air) | E/Paderborn |
| 62nd: | Capt. M.J. Quirk | (1.5)FW-190 dest(air) | Breda |
| | Lt. J.E. Fields | (.5)FW-190 dest(air) | Breda |
| | | (.5)FW-190 dest(air) | Breda |
| | Capt. L.A. Schreiber | (.5)FW-190 dest(air) | Breda |
| | Lt. F.L. Roy | FW-190 dest(air) | Breda |
| | Lt. J.P. Bryant | FW-190 dam(air) | Breda |
| | Capt. R. Dauphin | Me-110 dam(air) | Paderborn |
| | Lt. A.R. Carcione | Me-109 dest(grd) | Eindhoven |
| | Lt. C.L. Ginn | Do-217 dam(grd) | Eindhoven |
| 63rd: | Lt. G.F. Hall | (2)Me-110 dest(air) | Paderborn |
| | Capt. J.W. Vogt | Me-110 dest(air) | Paderborn |
| | Capt. L.A. Adrianse | Me-110 dest(air) | Paderborn |
| | Lt. J.L. Egan | Me-109 dest(air) | Munster |
| | | FW-190 dam(air) | Munster |
| | Maj. G.W. Johnson | FW-190 prob(air) | SW Gutersloh |
| **78th** | | | |
| 82nd: | Maj. J.J. Oberhansly | (2)FW-190 dest(air) | Gilze Rijen & Walcheren |
| | | Me-109 dest(air) | Cologne |
| | | Me-109 dam(air) | Cologne |
| 83rd: | Capt. K.W. Dougherty | Me-109 dest(air) | Nijmegen |
| | | Me-109 prob(air) | Nijmegen |
| | Lt. J.H. Johnson | FW-190 dest(air) | Dusseldorf |
| | | FW-190 dam(air) | Dusseldorf |
| | Lt. A.M. Juchheim | Me-109 dest(air) | E/Eindhoven |
| | | FW-190 dam(air) | E/Eindhoven |
| | Lt. C.W. Hotchkiss | FW-190 dest(air) | Walcheren |
| | Lt. W.M. McDermott | FW-190 dest(air) | Nijmegen |
| | Lt. V.J. Massa | Me-109 dam(air) | Aachen |
| | Lt. H.C. Roff | FW-190 dam(air) | Nijmegen |
| | Lt. H.R. Zumwalt | Me-109 dam(air) | Aachen |
| **353rd** | | | |
| HdQts: | LtCol. G.E. Duncan | FW-190 dest(air) | Turnhout |
| | | (.5)Ju-88 dest(grd) | Bonn |
| | (shared with Maj. H.N. Holt of the 366th Ftr Grp, 9th Air Force) | | |
| 351st: | Lt. G.B. Compton | Ju-88 dest(air) | W/Diest |
| | | FW-190 dest(grd) | NE Bonn |
| | | (.25)FW-190 dam(grd) | NE Bonn |
| | | (.25)FW-190 dam(grd) | NE Bonn |
| | Maj. W.C. Beckham | (.25)FW-190 dam(grd) | NE Bonn |
| | | (.25)FW-190 dam(grd) | NE Bonn |
| | Lt. F.N. Emory | (.25)FW-190 dam(grd) | NE Bonn |
| | | (.25)FW-190 dam(grd) | NE Bonn |
| | Lt. G.F. Perpente | (.25)FW-190 dam(grd) | NE Bonn |
| | | (.25)FW-190 dam(grd) | NE Bonn |
| 352nd: | Capt. J.N. Poindexter | (2)Me-109 dest(air) | NW Koln |
| | Lt. R.A. Newman | FW-190 dest(grd) | Antwerp |
| **355th** | | | |
| 358th: | Lt. W.J. Hovde | FW-190 dest(air) | SE Munster |
| | Lt. P.H. Kenney | FW-190 dest(air) | SE Munster |
| **357th** | | | |
| HdQts: | Col. H.R. Spicer | Me-109 dest(air) | Bernburg |
| 362nd: | Lt. F.E. Adams | Me-109 dest(air) | NW Bernburg |
| | Lt. A.F. Pyeatt | Me-109 dest(air) | NW Bernburg |
| | LtCol. H.I. Egenes | FW-190 dam(air) | E/Magdeburg |
| 363rd: | Lt. E.A. Rogers | Me-109 dest(air) | NW Schoningen |
| | Lt. E.W. Hiro | Me-109 dam(air) | Leopolds Hall |
| 364th: | Capt. J.L. Medeiros | Me-109 dest(air) | Bernburg |
| | Capt. J.R. Warren | Me-109 dest(air) | Bernburg |
| | Lt. J.B. Carder | Me-109 dest(air) | Bernburg |
| | | FW-190 dam(air) | The Hague |
| **359th** | | | |
| 368th: | Lt. E.H. Cater | Me-109 dest(air) | Hamm |
| | Lt. A.T. Lemmens | Me-109 dest(air) | Hamm |
| 370th: | Lt. G.A. Doersch | FW-190 dest(air) | Ahlen |
| | Maj. J.B. Murphy | Me-109 prob(air) | Hamm |
| | Lt. A.T. Niccolai | Me-109 dam(air) | Hamm |
| **361st** | | | |
| HdQts: | Maj. J.J. Kruzel | FW-190 dam(air) | SW Nijmegen |
| 375th: | Maj. G.L. Merritt | (2)FW-190 dest(air) | NE Tilburg |
| | Lt. C.N. Keppler | FW-190 dest(air) | NE Tilburg |
| | | FW-190 dam(air) | NE Tilburg |
| 376th: | Lt. R.S. White | (2)FW-190 dam(air) | Cleve |
| | Lt. J.C. Wright | FW-190 dam(air) | S/Nijmegen |

*Losses-*

**78th**: Lt. John H. Johnson (83rd Ftr Sqn) POW
P-47C HL-A 41-6335
Hit by a FW-190 near Eindhoven.

**353rd**: Maj. Walter C. Beckham (351st Ftr Sqn) POW
P-47D YJ-X 42-75226
Hit by flak near Bonn and bailed out near Neukirchen.

Lt. Donald M. Hurlburt (351st Ftr Sqn) KIA
P-47D YJ- 42-75653
Hit by flak and crashed into the North Sea.

Lt. Joseph E. Wood (351st Ftr Sqn) KIA
P-47D YJ- 42-75647
Hit by flak and crashed into the North Sea.

Lt. Edison G. Stiff (352nd Ftr Sqn) KIA
P-47D SX-L 42-75065
Hit by flak near Eckeren.

**357th**: Lt. Albert C. Lichter (362nd Ftr Sqn) POW
P-51B G4- 43-6741
Hit by flak and bailed out east of Zwolle.

Lt. Darwin J. Carroll (364th Ftr Sqn) KIA
P-51B C5- 43-6578
Suffered mechanical failure and bailed out near Kothen.

**361st**: Lt. Danny B. Nazzarette (376th Ftr Sqn) KIA
P-47D E9- 42-75814
Downed by a FW-190 near Rosemeer.

*Remarks*
56th: 0-1 hangar
353rd: 0-2 locos, 1-2 hangars
361st: 0-4 locos

**February 23, 1944**
Groups Operating: P-38 20th
Missions: Sweep of Holland.
Claims: nil
Losses: nil

**Febrary 24, 1944**
Groups Operating: P-51 357th
P-47 4th, 56th, 78th, 352nd, 353rd, 355th, 356th, 359th, 361st
P-38 20th, 55th
Missions: Support of bombers to Schweinfurt and Gotha.
Claims: 37-4-10 air
0-5 ground

| *Group* | | *Claims* | *Location* |
|---|---|---|---|
| **4th** | | | |
| 335th: | Lt. A.L. Schlegel | FW-190 prob(air) | NE Magdeburg |
| **20th** | | | |
| 77th: | Lt. J.M. Morris | Me-110 dest(air) | Schweinfurt |
| **55th** | | | |
| 338th: | Lt. A.J. Tinto | Me-109 dest(air) | W/Gotha |
| 343rd: | Capt. E.E. Ryan | FW-190 dam(air) | E/Gotha |
| **56th** | | | |
| 61st: | Maj. J.C. Stewart | FW-190 dest(air) | Kassel |
| | Lt. G.J. Blake | FW-190 dest(air) | N/Minden |
| | Lt. D.M. Funcheon | FW-190 dest(air) | Holzminden |
| | | FW-190 prob(air) | Holzminden |
| | Lt. J.H. Powers | FW-190 dest(air) | Minden |
| | Lt. E.E. Barnum | FW-190 dam(air) | Kassel |
| 62nd: | Lt. S.B. Morrill | Me-109 dest(air) | E/Asnabruck |
| | Lt. W.P. Gordon | FW-190 dest(air) | SW Hanover |
| | Lt. I.E. Valenta | FW-190 dam(air) | SW Hanover |
| | Lt. F.J. Christensen | FW-190 dam(grd) | Quackenbruck |
| | | Me-110 dam(grd) | Quackenbruck |
| 63rd: | Maj. G.W. Johnson | FW-190 dest(air) | Minden |
| | Lt. J.H. Truluck | FW-190 dest(air) | Herford |
| | Lt. A.S. Cavallo | FW-190 dam(air) | Minden |
| | Lt. H.E. Comstock | FW-190 dam(air) | Peterhagen |
| **78th** | | | |
| 82nd: | Lt. G.M. Turley | Me-109 dest(air) | Dummer Lake |
| 83rd: | Lt. A.M. Juchheim | (2)Me-109 dest(air) | Furstenau |
| | Lt. R.E. Wise | FW-190 dest(air) | Furstenau |
| | | u/i a/c dam(grd) | Furstenau |
| | Lt. R.B. Hathway | Me-109 dest(air) | Furstenau |
| | Lt. C.M. Peal | Me-109 dest(air) | Furstenau |
| | Lt. W. Tonkin | FW-190 dest(air) | Furstenau |
| | Lt. H.C. Roff | Me-109 prob(air) | Furstenau |
| **352nd** | | | |
| HdQts: | Col. J.L. Mason | Me-109 dest(air) | Schwagstorf |
| 328th: | Capt. D.S. Bryan | Me-109 dest(air) | Dummer Lake |
| | Lt. R.H. Sharp | Me-109 dam(air) | Dummer Lake |
| 487th: | Lt. G.T. Moran | Me-109 dest(air) | Enschede |
| | | Me-109 dam(air) | Enschede |
| | Lt. R.W. Hamilton | Me-109 dam(air) | Enschede |
| **353rd** | | | |
| HdQts: | LtCol. G.E. Duncan | FW-190 dest(air) | Steinhuder Lake |
| | | Ju-88 dam(grd) | Steinhuder Lake |
| 350th: | Lt. R.A. Stearns | (2)FW-190 dest(air) | Obernkirchen |
| | Lt. C. Rowan | FW-190 dest(air) | Steinhuder Lake |
| | Lt. F.T. Walsh | FW-190 dest(air) | Steinhuder Lake |
| 352nd: | Capt. J.N. Poindexter | FW-190 dam(air) | Steinhuder Lake |
| **356th** | | | |
| 360th: | Lt. W.H. Fletcher | Me-109 dam(air) | SW Aachen |
| **357th** | | | |
| HdQts: | Col. H.R. Spicer | Me-110 dest(air) | Erfurt |
| | | Ju-88 dest(air) | Erfurt |
| 362nd: | Lt. D.R. Rice | FW-190 dest(air) | E/Linz |
| 363rd: | Lt. W.D. Michaely | FW-190 dest(air) | Gotha |
| 364th: | Capt. J.L. Medeiros | FW-190 dest(air) | Gotha |
| | Lt. R.C. Smith | Me-109 dest(air) | NW Gotha |
| | Maj. T.L. Hayes | Me-109 prob(air) | NW Gotha |
| **359th** | | | |
| 368th: | Maj. A.R. Tyrrell | (2)FW-190 dest(air) | Neuenhaus |
| | Lt. T.J. McGeever | FW-190 dest(air) | Neuenhaus |
| 370th: | Maj. J.B. Murphy | Me-109 dest(air) | Hardenbergh |
| **361st** | | | |
| 374th: | Lt. R.J. Stolzy | Me-109 dest(air) | Dummer Lake |
| | | Me-110 dam(grd) | Hesepe A/F |
| 375th: | Capt. J.W. Guckeyson | Me-109 dest(air) | N/Loningen |

*Losses-*

**4th**: Lt. Joseph W. Sullivan (335th Ftr Sqn) KIA
P-47C WD-Y 41-6369
Hit by enemy fighters northwest of Coblenz.

**20th**: Lt. Everett E. Geiger (55th Ftr Sqn) POW
P-38J KI-V 42-67860
Suffered mechanical failure near Hillgrom.

Lt. Otto A. Quiring (55th Ftr Sqn) KIA
P-38J KI-Y 42-67878
Ran out of fuel near Schluctern.

**55th**: Lt. William Turner (38th Ftr Sqn) KIA
P-38J CG- 42-67939
Hit by flak near Watten.

Capt. Wesley M. Tibbetts (338th Ftr Sqn) KIA
P-38J CL- 42-67752
Hit by enemy aircraft near Gotha.

**56th**: Lt. Wilbur N. Kelley (62nd Ftr Sqn) KIA
P-47D LM-K 42-75037 "Onny's Angel"
Hit by flak near Quackenbruck.

**357th**: Lt. Donald R. Rice (362nd Ftr Sqn) POW
P-51B G4- 43-6743
Hit by enemy fighters near Coblenz.

Lt. Charles E. McKee (363rd Ftr Sqn) POW
P-51B B6- 43-6940
Hit by B-24 fire and bailed out near Gotha.

**359th**: Lt. Albert T. Niccolai (370th Ftr Sqn) KIA
P-47D CS-F 42-8636
Hit by a Me-109 east of the Zuider Zee.

**361st**: Lt. Dennis B. Weaver (376th Ftr Sqn) KIA
P-47D E9- 42-75401
Hit by fire from an E-boat and crashed east of Southend.

*Remarks*
352nd: 0-1 E-boat
361st: 0-1 loco, 0-1 E-boat

**February 25, 1944**
Groups Operating: P-51 357th
P-47 4th, 56th, 78th, 352nd, 353rd, 355th, 356th, 359th, 361st
P-38 20th, 55th
Missions: Support of bombers to Augsburg, Regensburg, and Furth.
Claims: 19-1-9 air
1-2 ground

| *Group* | | *Claims* | *Location* |
|---|---|---|---|
| **4th** | | | |
| 334th: | Capt. D.W. Beeson | FW-190 dest(air) | Beckingen |
| 335th: | Lt. P.W. McKennon | FW-190 dest(air) | SE Luxembourg |
| 336th: | Capt. D.S. Gentile | FW-190 dest(air) | SE Luxembourg |
| | Lt. V. Garrison | FW-190 dest(air) | Luxembourg |
| | Lt. G.A. Herter | FW-190 dest(air) | SE Luxembourg |
| **55th** | | | |
| HdQts: | Maj. M.K. Shipman | Me-410 dam(air) | Augsburg |
| 38th: | Lt. N.R. Tipton | Me-410 dam(air) | Augsburg |
| 343rd: | Capt. E.B. Giller | Me-410 dest(air) | SE Augsburg |
| | Capt. E.E. Ryan | Me-410 prob(air) | Augsburg |
| **56th** | | | |
| 61st: | Capt. R.A. Lamb | Me-109 dest(air) | Landau |
| | Lt. D.M. Funcheon | Me-109 dest(air) | Landau |
| | Lt. E.E. Barnum | Me-109 dam(air) | Landau |
| 62nd: | Capt. M.J. Quirk | FW-190 dest(air) | Homburg |
| | Lt. T.S. Buszko | FW-190 dam(air) | Homburg |
| **78th** | | | |
| 83rd: | Capt. K.W. Dougherty | Me-109 dest(air) | Boekingen |
| **353rd** | | | |
| 352nd: | Lt. W.F. Streit | (.5)Me 110 dest(grd) | Luxembourg |
| | | Ju-88 dam(grd) | Charleroi |
| | Lt. W.S. Marchant | (.5)Me-110 dest(grd) | Luxembourg |
| | | Do-217 dam(grd) | Charleroi |
| **356th** | | | |
| HdQts: | Capt. H.A. Ogden | (2)Me-109 dam(air) | Metz |
| **357th** | | | |
| 362nd: | Lt. R.H. Becker | (1.5)Me-110 dest(air) | Regensburg |
| | Capt. A.M. Lingo | (.5)Me-110 dest(air) | Regensburg |

| | | | |
|---|---|---|---|
| | Capt. J.E. Broadhead | Me-109 dest(air) | Regensburg |
| | Lt. R.D. Brown | FW-190 dest(air) | Regensburg |
| | Lt. M.R. Kehrer | Ju-88 dest(air) | W/Schweinfurt |
| | Lt. A.F. Pyeatt | FW-190 dest(air) | Regensburg |
| **361st** | | | |
| HdQts: | Capt. J.M. Todd | Me-109 dam(air) | SE St. Quentin |
| 376th: | Lt. E.C. Alcorn | Me-109 dest(air) | Longuyon |
| | Lt. J.D. Duncan | Me-109 dest(air) | Courtrai |
| | Lt. H.A. Lane | FW-190 dest(air) | N/Metz |
| | Maj. R.B. Caviness | FW-190 dam(air) | NE Metz |
| | Lt. D.T. Woodward | Me-109 dam(air) | Verdun |

*Losses-*

**357th**: Lt. Thomas A. Beemer (362nd Ftr Sqn) KIA
P-51B G4- 43-6927
Hit by B-17 fire near Regensburg.

Lt. Merlin R. Kehrer (362nd Ftr Sqn) POW
P-51B G4-N 43-6625
Hit by enemy fighters near Stuttgart.

*Remarks*
78th: 0-3 locos, 0-2 buildings, 0-1 vehicle
55th: Lt. Clair E. Buskirk (338th Ftr Sqn) c/l Langford; o.k.
P-38J CL-
357th: Lt. Paul D. Fairweather (364th Ftr Sqn) c/l Leiston; o.k.
P-51B C5-

**February 26, 1944**
KIAc's
356th: Lt. William W. Cotter (359th Ftr Sqn)
P-47D OC-C 42-8492
Crashed while buzzing Martlesham Heath.

**February 28, 1944**
Groups Operating: P-47 56th
Missions: Support of bombers to V-1 sites at Ecalles Sur Burchy.
Claims: nil
Losses: nil

Groups Operating: P-51 4th
P-47 355th, 356th
P-38 20th, 55th
Missions: Support for bombers to various targets in the Pas de Calais area.
Claims: 0-0-0 air
1-0 ground

| *Group* | | *Claims* | *Location* |
|---|---|---|---|
| **4th** | | | |
| 334th: | Capt. D.W. Beeson | (.25)Ju-88 dest(grd) | Soissons |
| | Lt. N. Megura | (.25)Ju-88 dest(grd) | Soissons |
| | Lt. W.B. Smith | (.25)Ju-88 dest(grd) | Soissons |
| 336th: | Lt. V. Garrison | (.25)Ju-88 dest(grd) | Soissons |

Losses: nil

*Remarks*
20th: Lt. Willard H. Lewis (79th Ftr Sqn) c/l Kingscliffe; o.k.
P-38J MC-L 42-67962

KIAc's
4th: Lt. Robert B. Frazier (334th Ftr Sqn)
P-51B QP-N 43-6656
Turning to land at Debden when the plane stalled, flipped over, and dove into the ground.

**February 29, 1944**
Groups Operating: P-51 4th, 357th
P-47 56th, 352nd, 355th, 356th, 359th, 361st
P-38 20th, 55th
Missions: Support of bombers to Brunswick.
Claims: 1-0-0 air
0-0 ground

| *Group* | | *Claims* | *Location* |
|---|---|---|---|
| **56th** | | | |
| 63rd: | Maj. G.W. Johnson | Ju-52 dest(air) | Harderwijk |

*Losses-*

**20th**: Lt. Robert P. Johnson (77th Ftr Sqn) POW
P-38J LC- 42-67831
Suffered mechanical failure and bailed out near Amsterdam.

**364th**: Col. Fred C. Grambo (HdQts) KIA
P-38J N2- 42-67404
Suffered mechanical failure east of the Zuider Zee and crashed at Geithoorn. He was on TDY to the 20th Ftr Grp

*Remarks*
4th: 0-2 locos

Groups Operating: P-47 78th
Missions: Support of bombers to V-1 sites at Lottingham.
Claims: nil
*Losses-*

**78th**: Lt. Robert C. Orr (82nd Ftr Sqn) POW
P-47D MX-O 42-7916
Suffered mechanical failure and bailed out in the Amiens/Lille area.

**March 2, 1944**
Groups Operating: P-51 4th, 357th
P-47 56th, 352nd, 353rd, 355th, 356th, 359th, 361st
P-38 364th
Missions: Support of bombers to Frankfurt.
Claims: 10-0-3 air
0-2 ground

| *Group* | | *Claims* | *Location* |
|---|---|---|---|
| **4th** | | | |
| 334th: | Lt. V.H. Wynn | Me-109 dest(air) | S/Coblenz |
| 336th: | Lt. G.A. Herter | FW-190 dest(air) | SW Coblenz |
| | | FW-190 dam(air) | SW Coblenz |
| | Lt. J.T. Godfrey | FW-190 dam(air) | SW Coblenz |
| **56th** | | | |
| 63rd: | Maj. G.W. Johnson | Me-109 dest(air) | SE Aachen |
| **355th** | | | |
| 358th: | Lt. C.W. Blair | Me-109 dest(air) | NE Liege |
| | Lt. W.V. Gresham | FW-190 dest(air) | SE Charleroi |
| | Lt. H.J. Hoffman | Me-109 dest(air) | NE Liege |
| | Maj. R.B. Myers | (.5)Me-109 dest(air) | NE Liege |
| | F/O W.J. McGinty | (.5)Me-109 dest(air) | NE Liege |
| | Lt. R.J. Fussell | (.5)FW-190 dest(air) | SE Charleroi |
| | F/O L.M. Dudley | (.5)FW-190 dest(air) | SE Charleroi |
| **357th** | | | |
| 364th: | Maj. T.L. Hayes | Me-109 dest(air) | N/Frankfurt |
| | Lt. J.B. Carder | Me-109 dest(air) | N/Frankfurt |
| **359th** | | | |
| 370th: | Capt. D.D. McKee | FW-190 dam(air) | Neufchateau |
| **361st** | | | |
| 374th: | Lt. R.P. Lacy | Ju-88 dam(grd) | Chievres |
| | Lt. L.C. Vandiver | Ju-88 dam(grd) | Chievres |

*Losses-*

**4th**: Lt. George K. Villinger (336th Ftr Sqn) KIA
P-51B VF-C 43-6985
Hit by enemy fighters near Linburg.

**56th**: Lt. Edward N. Rogeau (62nd Ftr Sqn) POW
P-47D LM-V 42-8676
Suffered mechanical failure near Beverloo.

*Remarks*
4th: 0-2 locos, 1-0 vehicle
56th: 0-2 hangars
364th: Lt. Kenneth F. Nicholson (383rd Ftr Sqn) c/l Honington; o.k.
P-38J N2-N

Groups Operating: P-47 78th
P-38 20th, 55th
Missions: Support of bombers to Chartres.
Claims: 0-0-0 air
2-0 ground

| *Group* | | *Claims* | *Location* |
|---|---|---|---|
| **78th** | | | |
| 84th: | Lt. E.S. Lang | (.5)Hs-126 dest(grd) | Chartres |
| | | (.5)Ju-52 dest(grd) | Chartres |
| | Lt. P.E. Pompetti | (.5)Hs-126 dest(grd) | Chartres |
| | | (.5)Ju-52 dest(grd) | Chartres |

Losses: nil

*Remarks*
55th: Lt. George C. Korinek(338th Ftr Sqn) c/l; o.k.
P-38J CL-
78th: 0-2 hangars

**March 3, 1944**
Groups Operating: P-51 4th, 357th
P-47 56th, 78th, 352nd, 353rd, 355th, 356th, 359th, 361st
P-38 20th, 55th, 364th
Missions: The bombers were scheduled to go to Berlin but weather forced most to turn back or hit targets of opportunity. The fighters gave general support over a wide area.
Claims: 5-2-3 air
0-0 ground

| *Group* | | *Claims* | *Location* |
|---|---|---|---|
| **4th** | | | |
| 336th: | Capt. D.S. Gentile | (2)FW-190 dest(air) | Wittenburg |
| | | Do-217 dam(air) | Wittenburg |
| | Lt. V. Garrison | FW-190 dest(air) | NW Berlin |
| | | Me-110 prob(air) | NW Berlin |
| | | Me-110 dam(air) | NW Berlin |
| | Lt. W.W. Millikan | Me-110 dest(air) | Wittenburg |
| | Lt. K.E. Carlson | Me-110 dest(air) | E/Hanover |
| | Capt. P.H. Dunn | He-111 prob(air) | Bordeaux |
| | | Me-210 dam(air) | Wittenburg |

*Losses-*

**4th:** Lt. George W. Barnes (335th Ftr Sqn) KIA
P-51B WD-L 43-6643
Suffered mechanical failure and crashed into the Channel.

Capt. Philip H. Dunn (336th Ftr Sqn) POW
P-51B VF-Y 43-6903
Became lost and ran out of fuel eight miles from Spain.

Lt. Glenn A. Herter (336th Ftr Sqn) KIA
P-51B VF-R 43-6740
Hit by enemy fighters near Wittenburg.

Lt. Vermont Garrison (336th Ftr Sqn) POW
P-51B VF-H 43-6871
Hit by flak near Boulogne.

**20th:** Lt. Donald D. Goble (55th Ftr Sqn) KIA
P-38J KI- 42-67705
Suffered mechanical failure and crashed into the North Sea.

**357th:** Lt. Robert W. Foy (363rd Ftr Sqn) ASR
P-51B B6- 43-6998
Suffered mechanical failure and bailed out fifteen miles east of Manston.

**March 4, 1944**
Groups Operating: P-51 4th(mixed), 355th(mixed), 357th
P-47 4th, 56th, 78th, 352nd, 353rd, 355th, 356th, 359th, 361st
P-38 20th, 55th, 364th
Missions: Support of bombers to Berlin (only a few fighters made it) and Bonn.
Claims: 6-4-5 air
0-0 ground

| *Group* | | *Claims* | *Location* |
|---|---|---|---|
| **4th** | | | |
| 334th: | Lt. N. Megura | Me-109 dest(air) | NW Leipzig |
| 335th: | Lt. P.S. Riley | Me-109 prob(air) | NW Berlin |
| | Lt. H.A. Ward | Me-109 prob(air) | Berlin |
| 336th: | Lt. W.F. Sooman | Ju-52 dest(air) | Helmstedt |
| **357th** | | | |
| 362nd: | Lt. R.D. Wallen | Me-109 dest(air) | Berlin |
| 363rd: | F/O C.E. Yeager | Me-109 dest(air) | SE Kassel |
| | | He-111 dam(air) | Wittenburg |
| **359th** | | | |
| 368th: | Capt. C.E. Mosse | Me-109 dam(air) | Bonn |
| 369th: | Lt. R.H. Broach | Me-109 prob(air) | Aachen |
| 370th: | Maj. J.B. Murphy | (.5)FW-190 dest(air) | Bonn |
| | | (.25)Me-109 dest(air) | Bonn |
| | | Me-109 dam(air) | Bonn |
| | Lt. P.H. Bateman | (.5)FW-190 dest(air) | Bonn |
| | | (.25)Me-109 dest(air) | Bonn |
| | Lt. A.C. Porter | (.25)Me-109 dest(air) | Bonn |
| | Lt. R.S. Wetmore | (.25)Me-109 dest(air) | Bonn |
| | | Me-109 dam(air) | Bonn |
| | Lt. W.R. Hodges | Me-109 prob(air) | Bonn |
| | Lt. H.D. Hollis | Me-109 dam(air) | Bonn |

*Losses-*

**4th:** Lt. Paul M. Ellington (335th Ftr Sqn) POW
P-51D WD-U 43-7004
Suffered mechanical failure and bailed out over Holland.

Lt. Hugh A. Ward (335th Ftr Sqn) POW
P-51B WD-R 43-6810
Suffered mechanical failure near Berlin.

Lt. Robert H. Richards (336th Ftr Sqn) KIA
P-51B VF- 43-6786
Crashed at Framlingham upon return from the mission.

**20th:** Lt. Harry E. Bisher (55th Ftr Sqn) MIA-E
P-38J KI- 42-67923
Lost an engine and headed home; when halfway across the North Sea he turned back and was hit by a FW-190 near St. Leger.

Lt. Edward C. Pfeiffer (55th Ftr Sqn) POW
P-38J KI-O 42-68097
Suffered mechanical failure near Sonneberg.

Lt. James C. Scott (55th Ftr Sqn) KIA
P-38J KI- 42-67864
Suffered oxygen failure northwest of Amsterdam.

**55th:** Lt. Howard J. Bone (338th Ftr Sqn) KIA
P-38J CL-
Crashed near Mesden after take-off.

Lt. Robert V. Lloyd (343rd Ftr Sqn) MIA
P-38J CY- 42-68162
Suffered mechanical failure near Ijsselmer.

**56th:** Lt. Irvin E. Valenta (62nd Ftr Sqn) KIA
P-47D LM-U 42-7942
Last seen spinning down near The Hague.

**78th:** Lt. Everett W. Powell (83rd Ftr Sqn) POW
P-47C HL-U 42-6374
Suffered mechanical failure near Malines.

**353rd:** Lt. William R. Burkett (351st Ftr Sqn) KIA
P-47D YJ- 42-75850
Hit by flak and last seen near Liege.

**357th:** Capt. John L. Medeiros (364th Ftr SQn) POW
P-51B C5- 43-6853
Hit by flak west of Magdeburg.

*Remarks*
4th: 0-1 loco
Lt. Albert L. Schlegel (335th Ftr Sqn) c/l Debden; o.k.
P-51B WD-O 43-6770
20th: Lt. Albert R. Fogg (79th Ftr Sqn) c/l Spanhoe; o.k.
P-38J MC-J 42-67736
357th: 0-1 loco

**March 5, 1944**
Groups Operating: P-51 4th, 357th
P-47 78th, 356th, 361st
P-38 364th
Missions: Support for bombers to airfields in France.
Claims: 16-1-6 air
2-2 ground

| *Group* | | *Claims* | *Location* |
|---|---|---|---|
| **4th** | | | |
| 334th: | Lt. H.D. Hively | (2)Me-109 dest(air) | Mont de Marson |
| | Lt. S.N. Pissanos | (2)Me-109 dest(air) | Bordeaux |
| | Capt. D.W. Beeson | Me-109 dest(air) | S/Bordeaux |
| | | (.5)FW-200 dest(grd) | Bordeaux |
| | | (shared with an unknown 4th Ftr Grp pilot) | |
| | | FW-200 dam(grd) | Bordeaux |
| | Lt. C.D. Carr | Ju-88 dam(grd) | Fontenet A/F |
| 335th: | Lt. J.D. Dye | FW-190 dest(air) | Redon |
| | Lt. J.F. Steele | FW-200 dest(air) | Bergerac A/F |
| | Capt. K.G. Smith | (.5)FW-200 dest(air) | Bergerac A/F |
| | Lt. E.P. Freeburger | (.5)FW-200 dest(air) | Bergerac A/F |
| | Capt. J.R. Happel | FW-190 dam(air) | E/Bordeaux |
| | Lt. P.S. Riley | Me-109 dam(air) | S/Bordeaux |
| 336th: | Capt. K.D. Peterson | FW-200 dest(air) | Bordeaux |
| | | FW-200 dest(grd) | Bordeaux |
| **357th** | | | |
| HdQts: | Capt. I.H. Dregne | FW-190 dam(air) | SE Bordeaux |
| 362nd: | Lt. G.M. O'Brien | FW-190 dest(air) | Bordeaux |
| | | (.5)FW-190 dam(air) | Bordeaux |
| | Lt. A.E. Smith | (.5)FW-190 dam(air) | Bordeaux |
| 363rd: | Lt. E.A. Rogers | Me-109 dest(air) | E/Bordeaux |
| | | (.33)FW-190 dest(air) | S/Bordeaux |
| | Lt. D.H. Bochkay | (.33)FW-190 dest(air) | S/Bordeaux |
| | Lt. C.K. Peters | (.33)FW-190 dest(air) | S/Bordeaux |
| | Capt. W.R. O'Brien | FW-190 prob(air) | N/Bordeaux |
| | | FW-190 dam(air) | N/Bordeaux |

| | | | |
|---|---|---|---|
| 364th: | Capt. G.V. Davis | (2)FW-200 dest(air) | Parthenay A/F |
| | Lt. M.A. Stanley | FW-200 dest(air) | Parthenay A/F |
| | Lt. R.A. Peterson | FW-190 dest(air) | Bordeaux |
| **364th** | | | |
| 384th: | Lt. C.H. Leo | FW-190 dam(air) | N/Angouleme |

*Losses-*

**4th**: Lt. Spiros N. Pissanos (334th Ftr Sqn) MIA-E
P-51B QP-D 43-6798
Suffered mechanical failure south of Le Havre.

**357th**: Col. Henry R. Spicer (HdQts) POW
P-51B B6- 43-6880 "Tony Boy"
Hit by flak and bailed out southwest of Le Havre.

F/O Charles E. Yeager (363rd Ftr Sqn) MIA-E
P-51B B6-Y 43-6763 "Glamorous Glenn"
Hit by enemy fighters an bailed out southeast of Angouleme.

**361st**: Lt. Glenn T. Berge (374th Ftr Sqn) KIA
P-47D B7- 42-75152
Prop ran-away on take-off and crashed at Bottisham.

**364th**: Capt. Paul F. Miller (HdQts) MIA-E
P-38J N2- 42-67745
Ran out of fuel and bailed out near Poiters.

*Remarks*
4th: Lt. Robert H. Wehrman (336th Ftr Sqn) c/l Heathfield; o.k.
P-51B VF-N 43-7005
357th: Lt. Lawrence D. Wood (363rd Ftr Sqn) c/l Leiston; o.k.
P-51B B6-

**March 6, 1944**
Groups Operating: P-51 4th, 357th
P-47 56th, 78th, 352nd, 353rd, 355th, 356th, 359th, 361st
P-38 20th, 55th, 364th
Missions: Support for bombers going to Berlin and Genshagen.
Claims: 74-7-21 air
1-9 ground

| *Group* | | *Claims* | *Location* |
|---|---|---|---|
| **4th** | | | |
| HdQts: | LtCol. D.J.M. Blakeslee | Me-210 dest(air) | Berlin |
| 334th: | Lt. N. Megura | (2)Me-110 dest(air) | SW Berlin |
| | | Me-110 dam(air) | SW Berlin |
| | Maj. H.L. Mills | FW-190 dest(air) | W/Brandenburg |
| | Lt. A.W. Chatterly | Me-110 dest(air) | W/Brandenburg |
| | | Me-210 prob(air) | W/Brandenburg |
| | | (2)u/i a/c dam(grd) | W/Brandenburg |
| | | Ju-88 dam(grd) | W/Brandenburg |
| | Lt. A. Rafalovich | Me-109 dest(air) | Brandenburg |
| | Lt. E.D. Whalen | Me-110 dest(air) | Nienburg |
| | Capt. D.A. Van Epps | (.5)Me-110 dest(air) | Nienburg |
| | | Me-110 dam(air) | Nienburg |
| | | FW-190 dam(air) | Nienburg |
| | | FW-190 dam(grd) | Nienburg |
| | Lt. H.N. Moulton | (.5)Me-110 dest(air) | Nienburg |
| | | FW-190 dam(air) | Nienburg |
| 335th: | Capt. C.E. Manning | Do-217 dest(air) | SE Brandenburg |
| | | Do-217 prob(air) | SE Brandenburg |
| | Lt. C.F. Anderson | Do-217 dest(air) | SE Brandenburg |
| | Lt. J.D. Dye | Do-217 dest(air) | SW Berlin |
| | Lt. B.L. McGrattan | Me-110 dest(air) | NE Magdeburg |
| | Lt. P.W. McKennon | Me-109 dest(air) | [illegible] |
| | F/O L.W. Waterman | Me-110 dest(air) | SW Berlin |
| | | Me-110 dam(air) | SW Berlin |
| 336th: | Lt. J.T. Godfrey | Me-109 dest(air) | N/Hanover |
| | | FW-190 dam(air) | N/Hanover |
| | F/O F.W. Glover | FW-190 prob(air) | W/Berlin |
| **20th** | | | |
| 55th: | Lt. J.J. Yelton | FW-190 dest(air) | Oldenburg |
| **56th** | | | |
| HdQts: | Col. H. Zemke | (1.25)Me-109 dest(air) | Minden-Osnabruck |
| | | FW-190 dest(air) | Minden-Osnabruck |
| | | FW-190 prob(air) | Minden-Osnabruck |
| 61st: | Maj. J.C. Stewart | (2)FW-190 dest(air) | N/Dummer Lake |
| | Lt. R.S. Johnson | FW-190 dest(air) | N/Dummer Lake |
| | Lt. S.D. Hamilton | Me-109 dam(air) | NE Dummer Lake |
| | Capt. B.M. Gladych | Me-109 dest(grd) | Vechta |
| 62nd: | Lt. F.J. Christensen | FW-190 dest(air) | N/Dummer Lake |
| | Lt. J.W. Icard | FW-190 dest(air) | Dummer Lake |
| | Lt. D.A. Nordquist | FW-190 dam(air) | N/Dummer Lake |
| 63rd: | Capt. W.M. Mahurin | FW-190 dest(air) | Wenzendorf A/F |
| | | FW-190 prob(air) | Wenzendorf A/F |
| | Lt. G.F. Hall | FW-190 dest(air) | Ulzen |
| | Lt. M.H. Becker | (.25)Me-109 dest(air) | Minden-Osnabruck |
| | Lt. D.V. Peters | (.25)Me-109 dest(air) | Minden-Osnabruck |
| | Lt. C.W. Reed | (.25)Me-109 dest(air) | Minden-Osnabruck |
| | Maj. G.W. Johnson | FW-190 dam(air) | Wenzendorf A/F |
| | Lt. B.P. Casteel | Me-109 dam(air) | Steinhuder Lake |
| **78th** | | | |
| 82nd: | Lt. J.W. Wilkinson | FW-190 dest(air) | Barenburg |
| | Lt. R.P. Spaulding | FW-190 dest(air) | Barenburg |
| | Lt. R.L. Wolfe | FW-190 dam(air) | Barenburg |
| 83rd: | Lt. W. Tonkin | Me-109 dam(air) | NE Dummer Lake |
| | Lt. R.E. Wise | Me-109 dam(air) | Dummer Lake |
| **353rd** | | | |
| HdQts: | LtCol. G.E. Duncan | (2)FW-190 dest(air) | Steinhuder Lake |
| 351st: | Capt. V.L. Byers | (.5)FW-190 dest(air) | SW Nienburg |
| | Lt. J. Terzian | (.5)FW-190 dest(air) | SW Nienburg |
| **355th** | | | |
| HdQts: | LtCol. E.W. Stewart | Me-109 dest(air) | NW Hanover |
| 354th: | Capt. W.J. Koraleski | (2.33)Me-109 dest(air) | Dummer Lale |
| | Lt. N.J. Fortier | (.33)Me-109 dest(air) | Dummer Lake |
| | F/O C.R. Barger | (.33)Me-109 dest(air) | Dummer Lake |
| 357th: | Lt. B.L. Hill | FW-190 dest(air) | W/Lingen |
| | Lt. W.S. Easterly | FW-190 dest(air) | E/Dummer Lake |
| | Lt. D.D. McCasland | Me-109 dest(air) | E/Dummer Lake |
| 358th: | Lt. J.B. Dickson | Me-109 dest(air) | N/Enschede |
| **356th** | | | |
| 359th: | Lt. W.L. Farmer | Me-109 dest(air) | Nienburg |
| | Lt. J.J. Meholic | Me-109 dest(air) | Nienburg |
| | Lt. C.H. Rubner | Me-109 dest(air) | Nienburg |
| | Lt. G.H. Engel | Me-109 prob(air) | Nienburg |
| | Lt. J.D. Henry | FW-190 dam(air) | Nienburg |
| 361st: | Maj. W. Waller | (.5)Me-109 dest(air) | N/Steinhuder L. |
| | | (.5)Me-109 dam(air) | N/Steinhuder L. |
| | Lt. H.C. Leyser | (.5)Me-109 dest(air) | N/Steinhuder L. |
| | | (.5)Me-109 dam(air) | N/Steinhuder L. |
| | Capt. F.S. Porter | Me-109 dest(air) | N/Steinhuder L. |
| | Lt. S.H. Hewett | Me-109 dest(air) | NW Steinhuder L. |
| **357th** | | | |
| HdQts: | LtCol. H.I. Egenes | Me-110 dam(air) | W/Berlin |
| 362nd: | Capt. D.T. Perron | (2)FW-190 dest(air) | SW Berlin |
| | | Me-210 dest(air) | SW Berlin |
| | Capt. J.E. Broadhead | Me-110 dest(air) | E/Berlin |
| | Lt. R.M. Starkey | Me-109 dest(air) | Berlin |
| | Lt. K.E. Hagan | (.5)Me-110 dest(air)* | SW Berlin |
| | | (.5)Me-110 dest(air)** | Berlin |
| | Lt. A.J. Roberson | (.5)Me-110 dest(air)** | Berlin |
| | Lt. C.L. Williams | (.5)Me-110 dest(air)* | SW Berlin |
| | Lt. T.E. Norris | Me-109 dam(air) | NE Berlin |
| 363rd: | Lt. D.H. Bochkay | (2)Me-110 dest(air) | W/Berlin |
| | Lt. R.E. Pagels | Me-110 dest(air) | W/Berlin |
| | Lt. J.F. Pierce | Me-110 dest(air) | W/Berlin |
| | Capt. W.R. O'Brien | (.5)Me-110 dest(air)# | Berlin |
| | Lt. C.L. Jones | Me-410 dam(air) | W/Berlin |
| 364th: | Capt. G.V. Davis | Me-110 dest(air) | E/Berlin |
| | | (.5)FW-190 dest(air) | NW Berlin |
| | Lt. T.L. Harris | Me-110 dest(air) | E/Berlin |
| | | (.5)FW-190 dest(air) | NW Berlin |
| | Lt. L.A. Ruder | (1.5)Me-110 dest(air)# | Berlin |
| | Maj. T.L. Hayes | Me-109 dest(air) | E/Ulzen |
| | Lt. M.A. Stanley | Me-110 dest(air) | Brandenburg |
| | F/O T.M. McKinney | Me-110 dest(air) | Brandenburg |
| | Lt. J.B. Carder | Me-109 dest(air) | E/Bremen |
| | | Me-109 dam(grd) | Berlin |
| | Lt. R.C. Smith | (2)He-111 dam(grd) | Ulzen |
| **359th** | | | |
| 368th: | Capt. W.N. Bolefahr | Me-109 dest(air) | Dummer Lake |
| | Lt. E.H. Cater | FW-190 dam(air) | Vechta |
| | Lt. R.B. Janney | FW-190 dam(air) | Dummer Lake-Steinhuder Lake |
| 369th: | Lt. R.J. Booth | FW-190 dest(air) | Quackenbruck |
| | Lt. R.L. Pherson | Me-109 dest(air) | Vechta |
| **361st** | | | |
| 374th: | Capt. R.E. Sedman | FW-190 dest(air) | Zuider Zee |
| | Lt. W.L. Moore | FW-190 dest(air) | Zuider Zee |
| 375th: | Lt. A.B. Snyder | FW-190 dest(air) | S/Quackenbruck |
| 376th: | Lt. J.M. Bentley | FW-190 dest(air) | Lingen |
| | Lt. M.C. Williams | FW-190 dest(air) | NW Dummer Lake |
| **364th** | | | |
| 384th: | Capt. J.H. Lowell | Me-109 dest(air) | W/Hanover |
| | | Me-109 prob(air) | W/Hanover |
| | Lt. S.C. Phillips | Me-109 dam(air) | W/Hanover |

*Losses-*

**4th**: Maj. Henry L. Mills (334th Ftr Sqn) POW
P-51B QP-Q 43-6690
Suffered mechanical failure and bailed out west of Brandenburg.

Lt. Edmund D. Whalen (334th Ftr Sqn) KIA
P-51B QP-O 43-6899
Was hit by debris from a Me-110 near Nienburg.

Capt. Cecil E. Manning (335th Ftr Sqn) POW
P-51B WD-H 43-6887
Hit by a Do-217 and bailed out near Sogal.

Lt. Robert J. Messenger (336th Ftr Sqn) POW
P-51B VF-U 43-6630 "Missouri Mauler"
Hit by enemy aircraft near Dessau.

**56th**: Lt. Andrew B. Stauss (61st Ftr Sqn) KIA
P-47D HV- 42-75397
Hit by enemy fighters and bailed out near Diepholz.

**78th**: Lt. Grant M. Turley (82nd Ftr Sqn) KIA
P-47D MX-N 42-7998 "Kitty"
Hit by a FW-190 near Barenburg.

F/O Edward J. Downey (83rd Ftr Sqn) KIA
P-47D HL-W 42-7983
Hit by a FW-190 near Hasselunne.

**353rd**: Lt. Robert N. Ireland (350th Ftr Sqn) KIA
P-47D LH- 42-22771
Shot-up by enemy fighters, he spun-in while trying to land at Metfield.

**356th**: Lt. Milton F. Erickson (361st Ftr Sqn) POW
P-47D QI-N 42-75255
Hit by a Me-109 near Lingen.

**364th**: Lt. Larry N. Ferguson (384th Ftr Sqn) POW
P-38J 5Y- 42-67461
Hit by enemy aircraft northeast of Gardelegen and bailed out near Winterfeld.

*Remarks*
4th: 0-5 locos
56th: 0-2 barracks, 0-1 gun position
78th: 2-1 locos
357th: 0-1 loco, 0-1 control tower
359th: 0-1 ship
Lt. Harry L. Matthew (369th Ftr Sqn) c/l; o.k.
P-47D IV-T
361st: Lt. Leroy H. Sypher (375th Ftr Sqn) c/l Bottisham; o.k.
P-47D E2-

**March 8, 1944**
Groups operating; P-51 4th, 352nd(mixed), 355th(mixed), 357th
P-47 56th, 78th, 352nd, 353rd, 355th, 356th, 359th, 361st
P-38 20th, 55th, 364th
Missions: Support of bombers going to Berlin.
Claims: 72-9-32 air
11-12 ground

| *Group* | | *Claims* | *Location* |
|---|---|---|---|
| **4th** | | | |
| 334th: | Lt. N. Megura | FW-190 dest(air) | W/Berlin |
| | | Me-109 dest(air) | W/Berlin |
| | | FW-190 dam(air) | W/Berlin |
| | | Ju-88 dam(air) | Ruhr |
| | Maj. J.A. Clark | Me-109 dest(air) | S/Berlin |
| | Lt. A.F. Bunte | Fi-156 dest(air) | Brunswick |
| | | Me-109 dam(air) | SW Berlin |
| | Lt. V.J. France | Me-109 dest(air) | Stendal |
| | Lt. D.W. Howe | Me-109 dest(air) | S/Berlin |
| 335th: | Capt. K.G. Smith | Me-110 dest(air) | Magdeburg |
| | | Bu-181 dam(air) | Magdeburg |
| | Lt. R.P. Clotfelter | FW-190 dest(air) | Magdeburg |
| | Lt. J.D. Dye | Me-109 dest(air) | Luckenwalde |
| | | FW-190 prob(air) | Dahme |
| | Lt. A.L. Schlegel | Me-109 prob(air) | NE Magdeburg |
| | Capt. L.M. Blanding | Me-109 dam(air) | Burg-Genthin |
| | Lt. C.A. Fiedler | Me-109 dam(air) | NE Berlin |
| 336th: | Capt. D.S. Gentile | (3.5)Me-109 dest(air) | Berlin |
| | Lt. J.T. Godfrey | (2.5)Me-109 dest(air) | Berlin |
| | Lt. R.S. Tussey | Ju-88 dest(air) | Magdeburg |
| | Lt. W.F. Sooman | Me-109 dam(air) | SW Berlin |
| **56th** | | | |
| HdQts: | LtCol. D.C. Schilling | FW-190 dam(air) | Dummer Lake |
| | | Me-210 dest(grd) | Dummer Lake |
| | LtCol. F.S. Gabreski | FW-190 dest(grd) | Weinstorf A/F |
| | | (4)FW-190 dam(grd) | Weinstorf A/F |
| 61st: | Capt. J.H. Bennett | (2)Me-109 dest(air) | E/Steinhuder L. |
| | | FW-190 dest(air) | Munstorf A/F |
| | Maj. J.C. Stewart | FW-190 dest(air) | S/Steinhuder L. |
| | | Me-110 dest(air) | S/Steinhuder L. |
| | Lt. R.S. Johnson | (2)Me-109 dest(air) | NE Steinhuder L. |
| | Capt. B.M. Gladych | FW-190 dest(air) | Dummer Lake |
| | | (3)FW-190 dam(grd) | Dummer Lake |
| | Lt. C.E. Mussey | Me-109 dest(air) | E/Steinhuder L. |
| | | Ju-88 prob(air) | E/Steinhuder L. |
| | Lt. F.W. Klibbe | FW-190 dest(air) | Steinhuder Lake |
| | Lt. G.J. Blake | FW-190 dest(air) | NE Steinhuder L. |
| | Capt. L.C. Smith | FW-190 dam(air) | Steinhuder Lake |
| | Lt. N.E. Brooks | FW-190 dam(air) | Dummer Lake |
| | Lt. D.H. Mudge | FW-190 dam(air) | S/Steinhuder L. |
| 62nd: | Capt. L.A. Schreiber | Me-109 dest(air) | Steinhuder Lake |
| | | FW-190 dest(air) | Steinhuder Lake |
| | Lt. R.C. Cherry | FW-190 dest(air) | Steinhuder Lake |
| | | FW-190 prob(air) | Steinhuder Lake |
| | | FW-190 dam(air) | Steinhuder Lake |
| | Lt. J.E. Fields | FW-190 dest(air) | Steinhuder Lake |
| | | FW-190 dam(air) | Steinhuder Lake |
| | Lt. M.L. Moseley | FW-190 dest(air) | Dummer Lake-Steinhuder Lake |
| | | FW-190 dam(air) | Dummer Lake-Steinhuder Lake |
| | Lt. F.D. Williamson | FW-190 dest(air) | Minden |
| | Capt. M.J. Quirk | (.5)FW-190 dest(air) | Celle |
| | Lt. J.B. Eaves | (.5)FW-190 dest(air) | Celle |
| | Lt. C.L. Reeder | (2)FW-190 prob(air) | Hanover |
| | Lt. W.A. McClure | FW-190 dam(air) | Minden |
| 63rd: | Capt. W.M. Mahurin | (2)FW-190 dest(air) | Wesendorf A/F |
| | | Ju-88 dest(air) | Wesendorf A/F |
| | Maj. G.W. Johnson | (2)Me-109 dest(air) | Celle-Dummer L. |
| | Lt. M.H. Becker | Me-109 dest(air) | E/Dummer Lake |
| | Lt. A.H. Robey | Me-109 dest(air) | Dummer Lake |
| | Lt. B.R. Smith | Me-110 dest(air) | NW Steinhuder L. |
| | Lt. J.H. Truluck | Me-109 dest(air) | Dummer Lake |
| | Lt. J.C. Marcotte | FW-190 prob(air) | Dummer Lake |
| | Lt. S.O. Stamps | Me-109 dam(air) | S/Dummer Lake |
| **78th** | | | |
| 84th: | Lt. E.S. Lang | (.5)FW-190 dam(grd) | Bohmte |
| | Lt. P.E. Pompetti | (.5)FW-190 dam(grd) | Bohmte |
| **352nd**(all P-47) | | | |
| 486th: | Capt. E.J. Gignac | Me-109 dest(air) | Minden |
| 487th: | Capt. V.K. Meroney | Me-109 dest(air) | Meppen |
| | Lt. D.R. Donohue | Me-109 dam(air) | Meppen |
| **353rd** | | | |
| HdQts: | LtCol. B. Rimerman | FW-190 prob(air) | Hanover |
| 350th: | Lt. R.S. Hart | FW-190 dest(air) | Dummer Lake-Steinhuder Lake |
| | Lt. J. Zolner | FW-190 dest(air) | Hanover |
| 352nd: | Capt. R.E. Robertson | FW-190 dest(air) | N/Dummer Lake |
| | | FW-190 dam(air) | N/Dummer Lake |
| | Lt. J.L. Knoble | FW-190 dest(air) | N/Dummer Lake |
| | | FW-190 dam(air) | N/Dummer Lake |
| | Lt. H.H. Dustin | FW-190 dest(air) | N/Dummer Lake |
| **355th** | | | |
| HdQts: | Maj. G.J. Dix | FW-190 dest(air) | NE Brunswick |
| 354th: | Lt. H.W. Brown | (3.5)Ju-88 dest(grd) | Hesepe |
| | | Me-110 dest(grd) | Hesepe |
| | | (2)Ju-88 dam(grd) | Hesepe |
| | F/O C.R. Barger | (3)Ju-88 dest(grd) | Hesepe |
| | Capt. C.G. Johnston | (.5)Ju-88 dest(grd) | Hesepe |
| 357th: | Lt. R.L. Norman | FW-190 dest(air) | Dummer Lake |
| | (Note-Dix & 357th Ftr Sqn were P-51; 354th was P-47) | | |
| **356th** | | | |
| 359th: | Lt. J.D. Henry | Me-110 dest(grd) | Hesepe |
| | | Me-110 dam(grd) | Hesepe |
| | Lt. J.H. Wadlow | Me-110 dam(grd) | Hesepe |
| 360th: | Maj. J.R. Williams | Me-109 dest(air) | NW Lingen |
| | Lt. B. Borelli | Me-109 dest(air) | NW Lingen |
| **357th** | | | |
| HdQts: | LtCol. D.W. Graham | FW-190 dest(air) | Berlin |
| | | Me-109 dam(air) | Berlin |
| 362nd: | Lt. J.B. England | Me-109 dest(air) | Steinhuder Lake |
| 363rd: | Capt. C.E. Anderson | Me-109 dest(air) | NW Hanover |
| | Lt. F.W. Reust | FW-190 dam(air) | SW Berlin |
| 364th: | Maj. T.L. Hayes | Me-410 dest(air) | W/Berlin |
| | Capt. J.R. Warren | FW-190 dest(air) | SE Berlin |
| | Lt. J.B. Carder | FW-190 dest(air) | S/Berlin |
| | Capt. G.V. Davis | (.5)FW-190 dest(air) | Dummer Lake |
| | Lt. T.L. Harris | (.5)FW-190 dest(air) | Dummer Lake |
| | Lt. H.R. Nowlin | FW-190 dam(air) | Berlin |
| | Lt. R.A. Peterson | FW-190 dam(air) | Berlin |

**359th**

| | | | |
|---|---|---|---|
| 368th: | Lt. R.B. Janney | Me-109 dam(air) | N/Minden |
| 369th: | Lt. C.W. Staley | FW-190 dam(air) | Nuiden |

**361st**

| | | | |
|---|---|---|---|
| HdQts: | LtCol. J.J. Kruzel | (.5)FW-190 dest(air) | W/Dummer Lake |
| 375th: | Capt. J.W. Guckeyson | Me-109 dest(air) | Lemforde |
| | Lt. E.W. Kinnaird | (.5)FW-190 dest(air) | W/Dummer Lake |
| | Lt. C.N. Keppler | Me-109 dam(air) | Lemforde |

**364th**

| | | | |
|---|---|---|---|
| 383rd: | Capt. L.A. Gilliland | (2)FW-190 dest(air) | N/Rheine & N/Magdeburg |
| | | FW-190 prob(air) | N/Magdeburg |
| | | FW-190 dam(air) | N/Magdeburg |
| | Capt. G.F. Ceuleers | FW-190 dest(air) | Nienburg |
| | | FW-190 dam(air) | Nienburg |
| 384th: | Capt. J.H. Lowell | (2)FW-190 dest(air) | Stendal-Alt Ruppin |
| | Capt. J.C. Ford | FW-190 dest(air) | NE Brunswick |
| | Lt. M.C. Linn | (2)Me-109 dam(air) | E/Steinhuder L. |
| | Lt. R.E. Lacy | FW-190 dam(air) | NE Brunswick |
| 385th: | Lt. W.P. O'Connell | Me-109 dest(air) | Belzig |
| | Lt. R.E. Squillario | Me-109 dest(air) | W/Berlin |
| | Lt. C.B. Warner | Me-109 dest(air) | Gifhorn |
| | Capt. R.O. Smith | Me-109 dam(air) | Gifhorn |

*Losses-*

**4th**: Maj. Seldon R. Edner (HdQts) POW
P-51B VF- 43-6442
Hit by enemy fighters near Hegensburg.

**55th**: Lt. Joseph M. Fluty (343rd Ftr Sqn) KIA
P-38J CY-
Died in a crash near Dovercourt.

**56th**: Lt. Anthony R. Carcione (62nd Ftr Sqn) KIA
P-47D LM- 42-74697
Hit by enemy fighters near Minden.

Lt. Joseph W. Icard (62nd Ftr Sqn) KIA
P-47D LM-I 42-75040
Hit by enemy fighters near Diepholz.

Lt. Caleb L. Reeder (62nd Ftr Sqn) POW
P-47D LM-O 42-74623
Hit by flak near Fockinghausen.

Lt. Fred L. Roy (62nd Ftr Sqn) KIA
P-47D LM- 42-75697
Hit by enemy fighters near Diepholz.

Lt. John C. Marcotte (63rd Ftr Sqn) POW
P-47D UN-N 42-7885
Hit by flak and bailed out near Schmalge.

**78th**: Lt. George C. Maitland (83rd Ftr Sqn) KIA
P-47C HL-J 41-6229
Crashed at Needham Market upon mission return.

**352nd**: Lt. Earl H. Bond (486th Ftr Sqn) KIA
P-47D PZ-O 42-8652 "The Bid"
Collided after take-off and crashed near Bracon Ash.

**353rd**: Lt. John Zolner (350th Ftr Sqn) MIA-E
P-47D LH- 42-8557
Hit by flak near Hanover and bailed out near Almelo.

**355th**: Lt. Charles H. Sweat (354th Ftr Sqn) KIA
P-47D WR-R 42-8441
Hit by flak at Hesepe Airfield.

Lt. Daniel S. Rothenberg (357th Ftr Sqn) KIA
P-51B OS- 43-6989
Hit by a FW-190 near Osnabruck.

**356th**: Lt. Justus D. Henry (359th Ftr Sqn) KIA
P-47D OC-L 42-8467
Hit by flak and crashed into a hangar at Hesepe Airfield.

**357th**: Lt. William W. Gambill (363rd Ftr Sqn) POW(D)
P-51C B6-F 42-103041 "Speedball Alice"
Hit by a Me-109 west of Hanover; was later killed during an Allied bombing raid.

**364th**: Capt. Leown A. Gilliland (383rd Ftr Sqn) KIA
P-38J N2-
Ran out of fuel and ditched in the Channel.

Lt. Charles E. Brock (383rd Ftr Sqn) POW
P-38J N2- 42-67233
Hit by flak near Berlin and bailed out near Kolbitz.

Lt. Kenneth F. London (383rd Ftr Sqn) KIA
P-38J N2- 42-67223
Hit by a Me-109 near Nienburg.

*Remarks*
4th: 0-3 locos, 0-2 barges
56th: 0-1 loco, 0-1 barracks, 0-1 radar station
Capt. Bolek M. Gladych (61st Ftr Sqn) b/o Hollesley; o.k.
P-47D HV-U 42-75140
78th: 1-0 vehicle
352nd: Lt. Don W. McKibben (486th Ftr Sqn) b/o; o.k.
P-47D PZ-Y 42-76323 "Sneezy"
Lt. Henry J. Miklajcyk (486th Ftr Sqn) b/o; o.k.
P-47D LH-Y 42-75157 (borrowed 353rd Ftr Grp a/c)
353rd: 0-1 loco, 0-1 gun position
355th: 2-0 locos, 0-2 gun positions
356th: 1-0 hangar
357th: 4-0 locos
Lt. Ernest Tiede (363rd Ftr Sqn) c/l Leiston; o.k.
P-51B B6-
359th: Lt. Charles W. Hipsher (370th Ftr Sqn) c/l Bungay; o.k.
P-47D CS-H
361st: P-47 c/l Bottisham; o.k.
364th: 0-1 factory
Lt. Ray E. Squillario (385th Ftr Sqn) c/l; o.k.
P-38J 5E- 42-67272

**March 9, 1944**
Groups Operating: P-51 4th, 352nd(mixed), 355th(mixed), 357th
P-47 56th, 78th, 352nd, 353rd, 355th, 356th, 359th, 361st
P-38 20th, 55th, 364th
Missions: Support of bombers to Berlin and Hanover.
Claims: nil

*Losses-*

**355th**: Lt. William Momberger (357th Ftr Sqn) KIA
P-47D OS-E 42-22549 "Kay"
Crashed at Bassingbourne while forming-up.

**364th**: Lt. Roy D. Kunzler (384th Ftr Sqn) MIA
P-38J 5Y-R 42-67230
Suffered mechanical failure and was hit by flak in the Osnabruck area.

*Remarks*
55th: Lt. Victor J. LaBella (338th Ftr Sqn) b/o Tuddenham; o.k.
P-38J CL-

**March 11, 1944**
Groups Operating: P-51 355th
P-47 56th, 359th
Missions: Support of bombers to Munster.
Claims: nil

*Losses-*

**355th**: Lt. Lawrence F. Allard (354th Ftr Sqn) POW
P-51B WR-K 43-6849
Hit by flak and bailed out near Munster.

F/O John A. Chalot (358th Ftr Sqn) POW
P-51B YF-R 43-6554
Suffered mechanical failure and bailed out near Gladbeck.

Groups Operating: P-47 352nd, 353rd
P-38 364th
Missions: 352nd swept the St. Nazaire area while the 353rd and 364th's escort to Wizerne was recalled over the Channel.
Claims: nil

*Losses-*

**352nd**: Lt. William D. Schwenke (328th Ftr Sqn) KIA
P-47D PE-S 42-8424 "Kathie"
Hit by flak and bailed out west of the Somme Estuary.

Lt. Harold S. Riley, Jr. (487th Ftr Sqn) KIA
P-47D HO-R 42-22530 "The Kid"
Hit by flak near Oisemont.

*Remarks*
352nd: 0-14 flak towers, 0-8 gun positions, 0-1 vehicle, 0-1 E-boat
Lt. Robert H. Berkshire (487th Ftr Sqn) c/l; o.k.
P-47D HO-U 42-22515 "Brutal Lulu"

**March 13, 1944**
Groups Operating: P-47 352nd, 353rd, 356th, 359th, 361st
Missions: Support for bombers to Pas de Calais V-1 sites.
Claims: nil
Losses: nil

KIAc's

78th: Lt. Roy E. Wendell (84th Ftr Sqn)
P-47D WZ-L 41-6223 "Isabel"
Shot down by another P-47 on a practice gunnery flight.

**March 15, 1944**

Groups Operating: P-47 56th, 78th, 352nd, 353rd, 356th, 359th, 361st
P-38 20th, 55th, 364th
Missions: Support for bombers to Brunswick.
Claims: 35-4-12 air
0-0 ground

| *Group* | | *Claims* | *Location* |
|---|---|---|---|
| **56th** | | | |
| 61st: | Lt. R.S. Johnson | (2)FW-190 dest(air) | Dummer Lake |
| | | Me-109 dest(air) | Dummer Lake |
| | Lt. R.J. Rankin | (2)Me-109 dest(air) | Dummer Lake |
| | | Me-109 prob(air) | Dummer Lake |
| | | FW-190 dam(air) | Dummer Lake |
| | Lt. J.H. Powers | FW-190 dest(air) | Dummer Lake |
| | | Me-109 dest(air) | Dummer Lake |
| | | FW-190 dam(air) | Dummer Lake |
| | Capt. L.C. Smith | Me-109 dest(air) | Dummer Lake-Solingen |
| | Lt. F.W. Klibbe | FW-190 dest(air) | S/Barenburg |
| | F/O S. Gerick | Me-109 dest(air) | Dummer Lake |
| | | Me-109 dam(air) | Dummer Lake |
| | Maj. J.C. Stewart | Me-109 dam(air) | Dummer Lake |
| | F/O E.D. McMinn | Me-109 dam(air) | NE Dummer Lake |
| 62nd: | Lt. F.J. Christensen | (2)FW-190 dest(air) | Dummer Lake |
| | | (2)FW-190 dam(air) | Dummer Lake |
| | Capt. M.J. Quirk | FW-190 dest(air) | Dummer Lake |
| | Lt. J.P. Bryant | FW-190 dest(air) | Dummer Lake |
| | Lt. J.E. Fields | FW-190 dest(air) | Dummer Lake |
| | Lt. J.M. Jones | FW-190 dest(air) | Dummer Lake |
| | | FW-190 dam(air) | Dummer Lake |
| | Lt. M.L. Moseley | FW-190 dest(air) | Dummer Lake |
| 63rd: | Maj. G.W. Johnson | (2)Me-109 dest(air) | Nienburg |
| | Lt. A.H. Robey | (2)FW-190 dest(air) | Vechta |
| | Lt. J.L. Egan | FW-190 dest(air) | Nienburg |
| | Lt. D.V. Peters | Me-109 dest(air) | Hanover |
| | Lt. J.H. Truluck | FW-190 dest(air) | Hanover |
| | | Me-109 dam(air) | Hanover |
| | Lt. M.H. Becker | FW-190 dam(air) | Hanover |
| **78th** | | | |
| 84th: | Lt. Q.L. Brown | Me-109 dest(air) | W/Munster |
| | Lt. R.E. Smith | Me-109 dest(air) | W/Munster |
| **352nd** | | | |
| 328th: | Lt. J.F. Thornell | (2)Me-109 dest(air) | Heusden |
| | Capt. D.S. Bryan | Me-109 dest(air) | Heusden |
| | Lt. F.W. Miller | Me-109 dest(air) | Heusden |
| | Lt. F.A. Yochim | Me-109 prob(air) | Heusden |
| 486th: | Capt. S.W. Andrew | Me-109 dest(air) | Aldensaal |
| **356th** | | | |
| 359th: | Lt. J.J. Meholic | (.5)Me-109 dest(air) | SE Nijmegen |
| | Lt. H. Weber | (.5)Me-109 dest(air) | SE Nijmegen |
| **359th** | | | |
| 368th: | Lt. T.J. McGeever | Me-109 prob(air) | Steinhuder Lake |
| | | (2)FW-190 dam(air) | Steinhuder Lake |
| 369th: | Lt. C.H. Kruger | Me-109 dest(air) | SW Hanover |
| | | Me-109 prob(air) | SW Hanover |
| **364th** | | | |
| 385th: | Capt. R.M. Scott | (.5)FW-190 dest(air) | Dummer Lake |
| | | (.5)Me-109 dest(air) | Dummer Lake |
| | Lt. J.C. Tallman | (.5)FW-190 dest(air) | Dummer Lake |
| | Lt. J.D. Turner | (.5)Me-109 dest(air) | Dummer Lake |

*Losses-*

**55th:** Lt. Ben H. Gourley (343rd Ftr Sqn) KIA
P-38J CY- 42-67228
Hit by flak and ditched sixty miles east of Lowestoft.

**56th:** Lt. John Kozey, Jr. (61st Ftr Sqn) KIA
P-47D HV-N 42-22456
Hit by enemy fighters near Quackenbruck.

**364th:** Capt. Richard M. Scott (385th Ftr Sqn) POW
P-38J 5E-S 42-68062
Hit by enemy fighters near Rheine.

Lt. John C. Tallman (385th Ftr Sqn) POW
P-38J 5E-K 42-68178
Hit by enemy fighters near Rheine.

Lt. James D. Turner (385th Ftr Sqn) POW
P-38J 5E-Q 42-67205
Hit by enemy fighters near Rheine.

*Remarks*

55th: P-38 c/l; o.k.
56th: 0-5 locos, 0-2 boats, 0-1 barge
352nd: 0-1 hangar, 0-1 barracks
356th: 4-0 locos, 0-4 railcars, 1-0 vehicle, 0-1 flak tower
359th: 0-2 locos

Groups Operating: P-47 353rd
Missions: Eight aircraft (two with bombs) dive-bombed barges in the Zuider Zee.
Claims: nil
Losses: nil

*Remarks*

353rd: 0-1 barge

**March 16, 1944**

Groups Operating: P-51 4th, 355th, 357th
P-47 56th, 78th, 352nd, 353rd, 356th, 359th, 361st
P-38 20th, 55th, 364th
Missions: Support of bombers going to Augsburg and Friedrichshafen.
Claims: 63-5-25 air
2-14 ground

| *Group* | | *Claims* | *Location* |
|---|---|---|---|
| **4th** | | | |
| HdQts: | Col. D.J.M. Blakeslee | Me-110 dam(air) | SW Munich |
| 334th: | Lt. A.W. Chatterly | Me-110 dest(air) | Munich |
| | F/O R.K. Hofer | Me-110 dest(air) | Munich |
| 335th: | Maj. G. Carpenter | (2)Me-110 dest(air) | SW Munich |
| | | FW-190 dam(grd) | SW Munich |
| | Capt. K.G. Smith | Me-110 dest(air) | Wurm Lake |
| | Lt. P.S. Riley | Me-110 dest(air) | SW Munich |
| | | Me-110 dam(air) | SW Munich |
| 336th: | Maj. J.A. Goodson | (2)Me-110 dest(air) | Kaufburen |
| | Lt. K.E. Carlson | (2)Me-110 dest(air) | Kaufburen |
| | F/O F.W. Glover | (2)Me-110 dest(air) | Kaufburen |
| | Lt. J.T. Godfrey | Me-110 dest(air) | Kaufburen |
| **56th** | | | |
| HdQts: | LtCol. F.S. Gabreski | (2)FW-190 dest(air) | Nancy |
| | Col. H. Zemke | Me-109 dam(air) | Chalons |
| 61st: | Lt. J.H. Powers | Me-109 dest(air) | St. Dizier |
| | | FW-190 dam(air) | St. Dizier |
| | F/O E.D. McMinn | FW-190 dest(air) | St. Dizier |
| 62nd: | Lt. F.J. Christensen | (2)FW-190 dest(air) | St. Dizier |
| | Capt. L.A. Schreiber | Me-109 dest(air) | St. Dizier |
| | | (.5)FW-190 dest(air) | St. Dizier |
| | Lt. A.W. Canizares | (.5)FW-190 dest(air) | St. Dizier |
| | | Me-109 dam(air) | St. Dizier |
| | Lt. T.S. Buszko | FW-190 dest(air) | St. Dizier |
| | Lt. S.B. Morrill | FW-190 dest(air) | St. Dizier |
| | Lt. F.D. Williamson | FW-190 dest(air) | St. Dizier |
| | Lt. M.K. Boyle | FW-190 prob(air) | St. Dizier |
| | Lt. J.M. Jones | FW-190 dam(air) | St. Dizier |
| | Lt. C.L. Ginn | FW-190 dam(grd) | Burvinnes A/F |
| 63rd: | Lt. A.S. Cavallo | Me-109 dam(air) | Vitry |
| **78th** | | | |
| 82nd: | Lt. R.A. Hewitt | Me-109 dest(air) | Strasbourg |
| | | Me-109 dam(air) | Strasbourg |
| 83rd: | Lt. A.B. Werder | FW-190 dam(air) | Chievres |
| 84th: | Lt. Q.L. Brown | (2)Me-109 dest(air) | St. Dizier |
| | | FW-190 dest(air) | St. Dizier |
| | | Ju-88 dest(grd) | St. Dizier |
| | | (2)u/i a/c dam(grd) | St. Dizier |
| | Lt. J.P. Maxwell | Me-109 dest(air) | St. Dizier |
| | | Me-109 dam(air) | St. Dizier |
| | Lt. E.E. Russell | Me-110 dest(grd) | St. Dizier |
| | Lt. E.S. Lang | Me-110 dam(grd) | S/Nancy |
| | | Me-109 dam(grd) | S/Nancy |
| | Lt. P.E. Pompetti | Me-109 dam(grd) | S/Nancy |
| **352nd** | | | |
| 328th: | Capt. W.F. Parlee | Me-109 dest(air) | Saulx |
| 487th: | Capt. V.K. Meroney | Me-109 dest(air) | S/Bar de Luc |
| **353rd** | | | |
| HdQts: | Col. G.E. Duncan | (1.5)u/i a/c dam(grd) | Laon |
| 351st: | Lt. J. Terzian | (1.5)u/i a/c dam(grd) | Laon |
| 352nd: | Lt. J.W. Gonnam | (.5)Me-110 dam(grd) | Laon |
| | | (.5)Me-110 dam(grd) | Laon |
| | | (.5)He-111 dam(grd) | Laon |
| | Lt. H. Herfurth | (.5)Me-110 dam(grd) | Laon |
| | | (.5)Me-110 dam(grd) | Laon |
| | | (.5)He-111 dam(grd) | Laon |

| | | | |
|---|---|---|---|
| **355th** | | | |
| HdQts: | LtCol. E.W. Stewart | Me-109 dest(air) | Augsburg-Luneville |
| | | Me-109 prob(air) | Augsburg-Lune. |
| | | Me-109 dam(air) | Augsburg-Lune. |
| 354th: | Lt. T.F. Neal | (2.5)Me-109 dest(air) | NW Ulm |
| | Lt. C.W. Lenfest | (1.5)Me-109 dest(air) | NW Ulm |
| | Capt. W.J. Koraleski | Me-109 dest(air) | Ulm |
| | Lt. R.S. Morris | Me-109 dest(air) | NW Ulm |
| | Lt. J.E. Duffy | Me-109 dest(air) | W/Ulm |
| 357th: | Lt. V.A. Burroughs | Me-109 dest(air) | S/Reutlingen |
| | Lt. C.C. Colson | Me-109 dest(air) | S/Reutlingen |
| | Lt. H.S. Bille | Me-109 dam(air) | S/Reutlingen |
| | Lt. D.E. Schoenfeldt | Me-109 dam(air) | S/Reutlingen |
| | Lt. H.H. Kirby | Me-109 dam(air) | W/Augsburg |
| | Lt. W.E. MacFarlane | Me-109 dam(air) | W/Augsburg |
| 358th: | Maj. C.J. Rosenblatt | Me-109 dest(air) | NW Augsburg |
| | Lt. J.B. Dickson | Me-109 dest(air) | W/Augsburg |
| | | Me-109 prob(air) | W/Augsburg |
| | Lt. J.J. DeGeorge | Me-109 dest(air) | W/Augsburg |
| | | (2)Me-109 dam(air) | W/Augsburg |
| | Lt. W.V. Gresham | Me-109 dest(air) | W/Augsburg |
| | Lt. P.H. Kenney | Me-109 dest(air) | W/Augsburg |
| | | (3)Me-109 dam(air) | W/Augsburg |
| | Lt. J.E. Reed | (2)Me-109 dam(air) | W/Augsburg |
| **356th** | | | |
| 359th: | Lt. W.C. O'Barr | (.5)Me-109 dest(air) | SE St. Dizier |
| | Lt. R.B. Warren | (.5)Me-109 dest(air) | SE St. Dizier |
| | Lt. R.D. Bradshaw | u/i a/c dam(grd) | S/Dummer Lake |
| **357th** | | | |
| HdQts: | LtCol. H.I. Egenes | (2)Me-109 dest(air) | SW Stuttgart |
| | Maj. I.H. Dregne | Me-109 dest(air) | SW Munich |
| 362nd: | Lt. J.B. England | Me-110 dest(air) | S/Stuttgart |
| | Lt. A.J. Roberson | FW-190 prob(air) | SE Stuttgart |
| | Capt. J.E. Broadhead | Me-410 dam(air) | S/Stuttgart |
| 363rd: | Capt. M.H. Throop | Me-110 dest(air) | N/Lake Constance |
| | Lt. W.R. McGinley | Me-109 prob(air) | S/Stuttgart |
| | Lt. H.S. Hinman | Ju-88 dam(air) | Ludwigshafen |
| 364th: | Capt. J.R. Warren | (2)Me-110 dest(air) | Augsburg |
| | | FW-190 dest(air) | Augsburg |
| | Lt. W.C. Reese | Me-110 dest(air) | Augsburg |
| | | Do-217 dest(air) | Augsburg |
| | Capt. G.V. Davis | Me-109 dest(air) | Ulm |
| | | (.5)Me-110 dest(air) | Ulm |
| | Maj. T.L. Hayes | Me-110 dest(air) | SE Stuttgart |
| | Lt. R.A. Peterson | (.5)Me-110 dest(air) | Ulm |
| | Lt. G.A. Hubbard | Me-109 dam(air) | S/Stuttgart |
| **359th** | | | |
| 369th: | Lt. H.A. Linderer | Me-109 dest(air) | St. Dizier |
| 370th: | Lt. R.S. Wetmore | (2)FW-190 dest(air) | Sommesous |

*Losses-*

**4th**: Lt. Ernest K. Skilton (336th Ftr Sqn) KIA
P-51B VF- 43-6652
Hit by flak near Gussenstadt.

**20th**: Lt. Robert A. Matyasz (55th Ftr Sqn) KIA
P-38J KI-U 42-67907
Hit by flak near Liege.

**78th**: Lt. Walter Tonkin (83rd Ftr Sqn) KIA
P-47D HL-U 42-8543
Hit the ground while chasing an enemy fighter near Chievres.

**353rd**: Lt. Harry H. Dustin (352nd Ftr Sqn) MIA
P-47D SX-Q 42-75544
Hit by flak near Clastres.

Lt. Robert A. Newman (352nd Ftr Sqn) KIA
P-47D SX-N 42-75530 "Wham Bam"
Hit by flak near Laon.

**355th**: Capt. Donald H. Wright (358th Ftr Sqn) POW
P-51B YF-S 43-6842 "Mona Lou"
Last seen chasing a Me-109 east of Augsburg.

Lt. Harold I. Carver (358th Ftr Sqn) POW
P-51B YF-J 43-6527 "Indiana Clipper"
Hit by a Me-109 near Gunzburg.

**357th**: Lt. Robert A. Meyer (362nd Ftr Sqn) POW
P-51B G4- 43-6956
Hit by enemy fighters near Stuttgart and bailed out in the Reutlingen area.

Lt. Alvin F. Pyeatt, III (362nd Ftr Sqn) POW(D)
P-51B G4-S 43-7960 "Scrappy"
Hit by enemy fighters near Stuttgart and crashed near Reutlingen; died of injuries shortly after.

*Remarks*

56th: 0-1 loco, 0-1 gun position
78th: 0-3 hangars, 0-1 gun position
355th: 0-1 loco
P-51 c/l Steeple Morden; o.k.
356th: 0-1 loco, 0-2 buildings, 0-1 flak tower
357th: P-51 c/l Leiston; o.k.

**March 17, 1944**

Groups Operating: P-47 78th, 353rd, 359th, 361st
Missions: Strafing sweeps to airfields in France.
Claims: 0-0-0 air
3-11 ground

| *Group* | | *Claims* | *Location* |
|---|---|---|---|
| **78th** | | | |
| 83rd: | Lt. B.W. Sorenson | (.5)Do-217 dest(grd) | N/Reims |
| | Lt. W.H. Waldheim | (.5)Do-217 dest(grd) | N/Reims |
| | | (4)Bu-133 dam(grd) | N/Reims |
| | | Do-217 dam(grd) | N/Reims |
| | Lt. R.B. Hathway | u/i a/c dam(grd) | N/Reims |
| 84th: | Lt. E.S. Lang | (.5)He-111 dam(grd) | Beauvais |
| | Lt. P.E. Pompetti | (.5)He-111 dam(grd) | Beauvais |
| **361st** | | | |
| HdQts: | Col. T.J.J. Christian | (.5)u/i a/c dam(grd) | Chartres |
| | Capt. J.M. Todd | Me-109 dam(grd) | Chartres |
| 375th: | Maj. G.L. Merritt | Me-109 dest(grd) | Chartres |
| | | Me-109 dam(grd) | Chartres |
| 376th: | Maj. R.B. Caviness | u/i a/c dest(grd) | Chartres |
| | Lt. R.G. Van Stryland | Ju-88 dam(grd) | Chartres |
| | Lt. C.A. Laxton | (.5)u/i a/c dam(grd) | Chartres |

*Losses-*

**78th**: Lt. Courtlyn W. Hotchkiss (83rd Ftr Sqn) MIA-E
P-47D HL-B 42-8688
Hit by flak near Reims.

Lt. Peter E. Pompetti (84th Ftr Sqn) POW
P-47D WZ-Z 42-74641
Hit by flak at Beauvais and bailed out near Villeteneuse.

*Remarks*

78th: 0-1 hangar, 0-2 gun positions
361st: 0-2 flak towers, 0-2 hangars, 0-1 vehicle
Maj. Roy B. Caviness (376th Ftr Sqn) c/l Bottisham; o.k.
P-47D E9-C 42-22794

**March 18, 1944**

Groups Operating: P-51 4th, 355th, 357th
P-47 56th, 78th, 352nd, 353rd, 356th, 359th, 361st
P-38 20th, 55th, 364th
Missions: Support of bombers to Oberpfaffenhofen, Friedrichshafen, and Munich.
Claims: 32-4-9 air
2-4 ground

| *Group* | | *Claims* | *Location* |
|---|---|---|---|
| **4th** | | | |
| HdQts: | Col. D.J.M. Blakeslee | FW-190 dest(air) | S/Augsburg |
| 334th: | F/O R.K. Hofer | (2)Me-109 dest(air) | SE Mannheim |
| | Capt. D.W. Beeson | Me-109 dest(air) | E/Mannheim |
| | Lt. A.W. Chatterly | Me-109 dest(air) | SE Mannheim |
| | Lt. N. Megura | Me-109 dest(air) | SE Mannheim |
| | Lt. H.T. Biel | Me-109 dam(air) | SE Mannheim |
| 335th: | Maj. G. Carpenter | Me-109 dest(air) | SE Saarbrucken |
| | | Me-109 prob(air) | SE Saarbrucken |
| | Capt. K.G. Smith | FW-190 dest(air) | Gunzburg |
| | Lt. B.L. McGrattan | He-111 dest(air) | NE Augsburg |
| 336th: | Capt. D.S. Gentile | FW-190 dest(air) | Augsburg |
| | Maj. J.A. Goodson | (2)He-111 dest(grd) | Mannheim |
| | Lt. K.E. Carlson | (2)He-111 dam(grd) | Ludwigshafen |
| **20th** | | | |
| HdQts: | LtCol. M.E. Hubbard | (2.5)Me-109 dest(air) | Memmingen |
| | | Me-109 prob(air) | Memmingen |
| 55th: | Maj. D.H. McAuley | Me-109 dest(air) | Erding |
| | Capt. J.C. Serros | (.5)Me-110 dest(air) | Memmingen |
| | Lt. C.A. Hallberg | (.5)Me-110 dest(air) | Memmingen |
| 77th: | Lt. A.F. Clark | (1.5)Me-109 dest(air) | Memmingen |
| 79th: | Maj. R.C. Franklin | Me-110 dest(air) | Ulm |
| | Capt. M.B. Nichols | Me-110 dest(air) | Ulm |
| | Capt. L.F. Graham | (.5)Me-110 dest(air) | Ulm |
| | Lt. A.W. Heiden | (.5)Me-110 dest(air) | Ulm |
| **55th** | | | |
| 38th: | Lt. G. Brown | FW-190 dest(air) | Nancy |
| 338th: | Lt. R.K. Fruh | Me-109 dest(air) | E/French border |
| | | (2)Me-109 prob(air) | E/French border |

| | | | |
|---|---|---|---|
| | Lt. G. Korinek | Me-109 dest(air) | E/Frieburg |
| | Capt. V.W. Bollwerk | (3)Me-109 dam(air) | SE Strasbourg |
| 343rd: | Lt. F.J. Leone | FW-190 dam(air) | SE Strasbourg |
| **56th** | | | |
| 61st: | Lt. J.H. Powers | FW-190 dest(air) | Cambrai-Givet |
| | Lt. D.E. Stream | FW-190 dest(air) | Cambrai-Givet |
| | Lt. S.D. Hamilton | FW-190 dam(air) | Cambrai-Givet |
| **355th** | | | |
| HdQts: | LtCol. E.W. Stewart | Me-109 dest(air) | SW Munich |
| 354th: | Lt. T.F. Neal | Me-109 dest(air) | NE Munich |
| | Lt. H.W. Brown | Me-109 dest(air) | Nancy |
| | | Me-110 dam(air) | W/Munich |
| | Lt. C.W. Lenfest | (.5)Me-109 dest(air) | NE Munich |
| | | Me-109 dam(air) | NE Munich |
| | Lt. L.G. Mendenhall | (.5)Me-109 dest(air) | NE Munich |
| 358th: | Lt. W.J. Hovde | (2)FW-190 dest(air) | Gunzburg-Augsburg |
| | | FW-190 dam(air) | Gunzburg-Augsburg |
| **356th** | | | |
| 359th: | Lt. W.C. O'Barr | glider dam(grd) | W/Nancy |
| | | (.25)Do-217 dam(grd) | W/Nancy |
| | Maj. D.A. Baccus | (.25)Do-217 dam(grd) | W/Nancy |
| | Lt. R.K. Holtz | (.25)Do-217 dam(grd) | W/Nancy |
| | Lt. G.B. Peet | (.25)Do-217 dam(grd) | W/Nancy |
| **357th** | | | |
| 362nd: | Lt. F.E. Adams | Me-109 dest(air) | NW Paris |
| 364th: | Lt. R.A. Peterson | Me-109 dest(air) | Augsburg |

*Losses-*

**4th**: Lt. Edward P. Freeburger (335th Ftr Sqn) KIA
P-51B WD-F 43-6460
Hit by enemy fighters near Ulm and crashed near Nancy.

Lt. Woodrow F. Sooman (336th Ftr Sqn) POW
P-51B VF-D 43-6936
Suffered mechanical failure near Frankfurt.

**20th**: LtCol. Mark E. Hubbard (HdQts) POW
P-38J LC-T 42-67708
Hit by flak near Augsburg.

Lt. Allen D. Singleton (55th Ftr Sqn) ASR
P-38J KI- 42-67883
Suffered mechanical failure and bailed out over the Channel.

Lt. Ival E. Butler (77th Ftr Sqn) KIA
P-38J LC- 42-67525
Suffered mechanical failure and bailed out off Texel Island.

Capt. Lindol F. Graham (79th Ftr Sqn) KIA
P-38J MC-L 42-67926 "Susie"
Hit the ground while shooting-up a crashed Me-110 near Ulm.

**55th**: Lt. Bradford R. Wikholm (338th Ftr Sqn) KIA
P-38J CL- 42-67989
Hit by enemy fighters near Ettenheim.

**356th**: Lt. Blefterios A. Vangos (361st Ftr Sqn) POW
P-47D QI-Y 42-74715 "The Vangoose"
Hit by flak near Lille and bellied-in southeast of Cambrai.

**357th**: Lt. Konstantin J. Vogel (362nd Ftr Sqn) KIA
P-51B G4-H 43-12442
Hit by enemy aircraft near Gunzburg.

Capt. Jack R. Warren (364th Ftr Sqn) KIA
P-51B C5-F 43-12124
Last seen near Ostend in heavy overcast.

**359th**: Capt. Benjamin H. Albertson (370th Ftr Sqn) POW
P-47D CS-N 42-75136
Hit by flak and bailed out near Abbeville.

*Remarks*
352nd: 0-1 hangar, 1-0 ammo dump
355th: Lt. Henry H. Kirby(357th Ftr Sqn) c/l; o.k.
P-51B OS-N 43-12422
357th: 0-3 locos

**March 19, 1944**
Groups Operating: P-47 359th, 361st
Missions: Support of bombers to V-1 sites at Wizerne, Watten, and Marquise/Mimoyeques.
Claims: nil
Losses: nil

Groups Operating: P-51 4th
P-47 78th
Missions: The 78th dive-bombed Gilze-Rijen Airfield with the 4th providing cover.
Claims: nil
Losses: nil

KIAc's
364th: Lt. Creyaton Carlson (383rd Ftr Sqn)
P-38J N2-
Spun-out at low altitude while on a practice flight near Honington.

**March 20, 1944**
Groups Operating: P-51 4th, 355th, 357th
P-47 56th, 78th, 352nd, 353rd, 356th, 359th, 361st
P-38 364th
Missions: Support of bombers to Frankfurt (most were recalled)
Claims: 3-1-2 air
1-1 ground

| ***Group*** | | ***Claims*** | ***Location*** |
|---|---|---|---|
| **56th** | | | |
| 61st: | Maj. J.C. Stewart | (2)Me-109 dest(air) | S/Charleville |
| | | Me-109 prob(air) | S/Charleville |
| | Lt. D.E. Stream | u/i a/c dest(grd) | Charleville |
| **355th** | | | |
| 354th: | Lt. H.W. Brown | FW-190 dam(air) | Coxyde |
| | Lt. B.C. Williamson | FW-190 dam(air) | Coxyde |
| **356th** | | | |
| HdQts: | LtCol. E.A. Malmstrom | Me-109 dest(air) | Charleville |
| 361st: | Capt. F.S. Porter | Me-110 dam(grd) | N/Brussels |

*Losses-*

**356th**: Lt. Charles J. Garvey, Jr. (360th Ftr Sqn) POW
P-47D PI-D 42-74638 "Nashville Belle"
Lost in bad weather near Loxbergen.

Lt. Philip E. McCullough (360th Ftr Sqn) POW
P-47D PI- 42-74622
Hit by flak near Beauvechin.

F/O Howard P. Maupin (360th Ftr Sqn) MIA-E
P-47D PI-N 42-22535 "Kathleen Ann"
Lost in bad weather near Neerwinden.

Capt. Fred S. Porter, Jr. (361st Ftr Sqn) POW
P-47D QI-I 42-74646
Hit by flak strafing an airfield north of Brussels.

Lt. DeWitt T. Bell (361st Ftr Sqn) KIA
P-47D QI-Z 42-75553
Hit by flak strafing an airfield north of Brussels.

Lt. Bernard A. Tuckey (361st Ftr Sqn) KIA
P-47D QI-P 42-8440
Spun-out in heavy overcast off Orfordness.

*Remarks*
4th: 0-1 loco, 0-1 gun position
56th: 0-1 gun position
355th: 2-0 locos
356th: 0-2 flak towers

**March 21, 1944**
Groups Operating: P-51 4th
P-47 78th
Missions: The 78th supported bombers to Watten V-1 sites and the 4th swept the Bordeaux area.
Claims: 10-1-0 air
11-2 ground

| ***Group*** | | ***Claims*** | ***Location*** |
|---|---|---|---|
| **4th** | | | |
| HdQts: | Maj. J.A. Clark | FW-190 dest(air) | Bordeaux |
| | | FW-190 dest(grd) | Bordeaux |
| 334th: | Lt. A.W. Chatterly | (.5)FW-190 dest(air) | NE Bordeaux |
| | Lt. N. Megura | (.5)FW-190 dest(air) | NE Bordeaux |
| | | He-177 dest(grd) | NE Bordeaux |
| | Lt. V.J. France | (2)FW-190 dest(grd) | Bordeaux |
| | F/O R.K. Hofer | He-177 dest(grd) | Langen A/F |
| | Capt. H.D. Hively | (.5)Ju-88 dest(grd)* | Langen A/F |
| | Lt. A. Rafalovich | (.5)Do-217 dest(grd) | E/Bordeaux |
| | Capt. D.A. Van Epps | (.5)Do-217 dest(grd) | E/Bordeaux |
| | Lt. L.R. Pierce | Me-110 dam(grd) | Langen A/F |
| 335th: | Maj. G. Carpenter | (1.5)FW-190 dest(air) | NE Bordeaux |
| | | (.5)FW-190 dest(grd) | NE Bordeaux |
| | | (.5)Ju-52 dest(grd) | NE Bordeaux |

| | | | |
|---|---|---|---|
| | Lt. C.F. Anderson | (1.5)FW-190 dest(air) | NE Bordeaux |
| | | (.5)FW-190 dest(grd) | NE Bordeaux |
| | | (.5)Ju-52 dest(grd) | NE Bordeaux |
| | Capt. K.G. Smith | (.5)Fi-156 dest(air) | NE Bordeaux |
| | Lt. J.H. Brandenburg | (.5)Fi-156 dest(air) | NE Bordeaux |
| | Lt. A.L. Schlegel | He-111 dest(air) | Saintes |
| | Lt. W.C. Hawkins | Me-110 dest(air) | Cozes |
| | Lt. P.W. McKennon | FW-190 dest(air) | W/Lans de Bussac |
| | Lt. C.A. Fiedler | FW-190 dest(grd) | Lans de Bussac |
| | Lt. J.W. Goodwyn | (.5)Ju-88 dest(grd)* | Langen A/F |
| | Lt. R.C. Church | FW-190 dam(grd) | NE Bordeaux |
| 336th: | Capt. R.D. Hobert | FW-190 dest(air) | SW Evreux |
| | Lt. D.R. Emerson | FW-190 prob(air) | SW Evreux |
| | Maj. J.A. Goodson | Me-410 dest(grd) | Langen A/F |

*Losses-*

**4th:** Lt. Alex Rafalovich (334th Ftr Sqn) POW
P-51B QP-N 43-6839
Hit by flak and bailed out north of Bordeaux.

Lt. Robert G. Williams (334th Ftr Sqn) POW
P-51B QP-U 43-6869
Hit by flak near Angars.

Capt. Earle W. Carlowe (335th Ftr Sqn) POW
P-51B WD-P 43-6639
Hit by flak and bailed out north of Bordeaux.

Capt. Kenneth G. Smith (335th Ftr Sqn) POW
P-51B WD-K 43-6803
Hit by flak at Bordeaux and crashed near Caen.

Lt. James H. Brandenburg (335th Ftr Sqn) KIA
P-51B WD-E 43-6641
Hit by flak north of Bordeaux and bailed out too low.

F/O Joseph Goetz (335th Ftr Sqn) KIA
P-51B WD-L 43-12469
Hit by flak north of Bordeaux.

Lt. William C. Hawkins (335th Ftr Sqn) MIA-E
P-51B WD-H 43-6316
Hit by flak north of Bordeaux.

*Remarks*
4th: 0-1 hangar

**March 22, 1944**
Groups Operating: P-51 4th, 355th, 357th
P-47 56th, 78th, 352nd, 353rd, 356th, 359th, 361st
P-38 20th, 55th, 364th
Missions: Support of bombers going to Berlin.
Claims: 2-0-0 air
0-0 ground

| Group | | Claims | Location |
|---|---|---|---|
| **352nd** | | | |
| 328th: | Capt. E.L. Abbott | (.25)FW-200 dest(air) | Hesepe |
| | Lt. R.C. Brookins | (.25)FW-200 dest(air) | Hesepe |
| | Lt. J.F. Thornell | (.25)FW-200 dest(air) | Hesepe |
| | Lt. E. Zellner | (.25)FW-200 dest(air) | Hesepe |
| **357th** | | | |
| 363rd: | Lt. C.L. Jones | Me-109 dest(air) | Munster |

*Losses-*

**55th:** Lt. Victor J. LaBella (338th Ftr Sqn) POW
P-38J CL- 42-67919
Suffered mechanical failure near Langenhorst.

**56th:** Lt. Donald M. Funcheon (61st Ftr Sqn) KIA
P-47D HV-F 42-75126
Crashed into the Channel in bad weather.

Lt. Claude E. Mussey (61st Ftr Sqn) KIA
P-47D HV-Y 42-8579
Crashed into the Channel in bad weather.

Lt. Dale E. Stream (61st Ftr Sqn) KIA
P-47D HV-P 42-8461 "Lucky"
Crashed into the Channel in bad weather.

Lt. Melvin C. Wood (61st Ftr Sqn) POW
P-47D HV- 42-75446
Hit by flak near Egmond.

**357th:** Lt. Carter L. Jones (363rd Ftr Sqn) POW
P-51B B6- 43-12315
Hit by flak near Bremen.

**361st:** Lt. James A. Rogers (375th Ftr Sqn) KIA
P-47D E2- 42-8512
Hit by flak and ditched thirty-five miles off Southwold.

**364th:** Capt. Roy O. Smith, Jr. (385th Ftr Sqn) POW
P-38J 5E-G 42-67934
Hit by flak near Kortgene.

Lt. William R. Jackson (385th Ftr Sqn) POW
P-38J 5E- 42-68069
Hit by flak and crashed into the North Sea.

*Remarks*
56th: 0-10 locos, 0-1 hangar, 0-2 railcars, 0-1 trawler, 0-1 flak tower
78th: 0-6 boats
F/O Charles W. DeWitt(82nd Ftr Sqn) c/l Duxford; o.k.
P-47D MX-E 42-8530
352nd: 0-3 locos
355th: 1-2 locos
357th: (2)P-51 c/l; o.k.
361st: 0-1 vehicle, 0-1 hangar, 0-1 building, 0-1 gun position

**March 23, 1944**
Groups Operating: P-51 4th, 355th, 357th
P-47 56th, 78th, 352nd, 353rd, 356th, 359th, 361st
P-38 20th, 55th, 364th
Missions. Support of bombers to Brunswick, Munster, and other targets of opportunity.
Claims: 14-1-5 air
1-4 ground

| Group | | Claims | Location |
|---|---|---|---|
| **4th** | | | |
| HdQts: | Col. D.J.M. Blakeslee | FW-190 dam(air) | Osnabruck |
| | Maj. J.A. Clark | Me-109 dest(air) | SE Steinhuder L. |
| | | FW-190 dest(air) | SE Steinhuder L. |
| 334th: | Capt. D.W. Beeson | (2)Me-109 dest(air) | E/Munster |
| | Lt. A.F. Bunte | Me-109 dest(air) | Osnabruck-Herford |
| | | Me-109 dam(air) | Osnabruck-Herford |
| | F/O R.K. Hofer | FW-190 dest(air) | E/Hamm |
| | | Me-109 dam(air) | E/Hamm |
| | Lt. N. Megura | FW-190 dest(air) | Munster |
| | Lt. L.R. Pierce | Me-109 dest(air) | Munster-Hamm |
| | Capt. H.D. Hively | FW-190 dam(air) | Herford |
| 335th: | Lt. F.E. Hupe | Me-109 dam(air) | E/Hanover |
| 336th: | Maj. J.A. Goodson | (2)Me-109 dest(air) | Munster |
| | Capt. D.S. Gentile | (2)Me-109 dest(air) | Munster |
| | Lt. J.T. Godfrey | Me-109 dest(air) | Munster |
| **78th** | | | |
| 84th: | Lt. O.L. Brown | FW-190 dest(air) | Goch |
| | Lt. L.J. Abel | Me-410 dest(grd) | Brussels |
| | | (3)Me-410 dam(grd) | Brussels |
| **356th** | | | |
| 359th: | Lt. J.B. Smith | Me-110 dam(grd) | W/Duren |
| **357th** | | | |
| 364th: | Lt. R.A. Peterson | Me-109 prob(air) | E/Brunswick |

*Losses-*

**357th:** Lt. Robert P. Humphrey (HdQts) POW
P-51B B6- 43-7019
Hit by enemy aircraft west of Brunswick

*Remarks*
4th: 0-1 loco
356th: 1-0 loco, 0-1 E-boat
357th: 1-0 loco

**March 24, 1944**
Groups Operating: P-51 4th, 355th
P-47 56th, 78th, 356th, 361st
P-38 55th, 364th
Missions: Support of bombers to Schweinfurt, Frankfurt, and St. Dizier.
Claims: 1-0-0 air
2-3 ground

| Group | | Claims | Location |
|---|---|---|---|
| **78th** | | | |
| 82nd: | Lt. J.J. Hockery | Ju-188 dest(air) | Paris |
| 84th: | Capt. G.H. Doyle | Ju-52 dest(grd) | Beaumont-Sur-Oise |
| | | Ju-52 dam(grd) | Beaumont-Sur-Oise |
| | Lt. J.F. Casey | u/i a/c dest(grd) | St. Dizier |
| | Lt. R.E. Belliveau | Ju-52 dam(grd) | Beaumont-Sur-Oise |
| | F/O J.W. Mundy | Ju-52 dam(grd) | Beaumont-Sur-Oise |

*Losses-*

**55th**: Lt. Ernest W. George (338th Ftr Sqn) POW
P-38J CL- 42-67467
Collided with Lt. West near Delouze.

Lt. Fred W. West (338th Ftr Sqn) MIA-E
P-38J CL- 42-67738
Collided with Lt. George near Delouze.

*Remarks*
78th: 2-0 hangars
355th: 0-3 locos

KIAc's
20th: Lt. Lauren J. Taylor (55th Ftr Sqn)
P-38J LC-

**March 26, 1944**
Groups Operating: P-47 56th, 78th, 352nd, 353rd, 353rd"C", 359th, 361st
Missions: Support for bombers to V-1 sites in the Cherbourg and Pas de Calais area. Also, this was the first mission for the 353rd"C" group, the "Bill's Buzz Boy" unit put together to practice ground attack concepts.
Claims: 0-0-0 air
2-4 ground

| *Group* | | *Claims* | *Location* |
|---|---|---|---|
| **353rd "C"** | | | |
| 350th: | Lt. C.O. Durant | FW-190 dam(grd) | Chartres |
| 351st: | Lt. J.A. Sullivan | Me-109 dam(grd) | Chartres |
| 354th: | Capt. A.B. Starr | u/i a/c dest(grd) | Chateaudun |
| 369th: | Lt. J.H. Oliphint | Me-110 dest(grd) | Chateaudun |
| | | He-177 dam(grd) | Chateaudun |
| | Lt. C.E. Carter | He-111 dam(grd) | Chateaudun |

*Losses-*

**353rd "C"**: Lt. Kenneth D. Williams (354th Ftr Sqn/355th Ftr Grp) MIA-E
P-47D YF-K 42-8443 "Miss Clean Sweep"
Hit by flak at Chateaudun.

*Remarks*
353rd "C": 1-3 hangars, 0-2 buildings, 0-1 flak tower

**March 27, 1944**
Groups Operating: P-51 4th, 355th, 357th
P-47 56th, 78th, 352nd, 353rd, 353rd"C", 356th, 359th, 361st
P-38 20th, 55th, 364th
Missions: Support for bombers to various airfields in France.
Claims: 11-1-3 air
24-14 ground

| *Group* | | *Claims* | *Location* |
|---|---|---|---|
| **4th** | | | |
| HdQts: | Maj. J.A. Clark | (1.5)Ju-88 dest(grd)[*] | Cazaux A/F |
| 334th: | Lt. W.B. Smith | Me-109 dest(air) | Lake Biscarosse |
| | | Me-109 dest(grd) | Angouleme |
| | Lt. A.W. Chatterly | Me-109 dest(air) | Angouleme |
| | Lt. N. Megura | Me-109 dam(air) | Angars |
| | | (.5)Ju-88 dest(grd)[**] | Cazaux A/F |
| | | FW-190 dam(grd) | Cazaux A/F |
| | Lt. E.H. Markel | (.5)Ju-88 dest(grd)[**] | Cazaux A/F |
| | Capt. D.W. Beeson | (1.5)Ju-88 dest(grd)[#] | Cazaux A/F |
| | | Hs-126 dest(grd) | Cazaux A/F |
| | Lt. H.T. Biel | (1.5)Ju-88 dest(grd)[#] | Cazaux A/F |
| | | Me-410 dest(grd) | Cazaux A/F |
| | | FW-190 dam(grd) | Cazaux A/F |
| | Lt. G.E. Montgomery | (2)Ju-88 dest(grd) | Cazaux A/F |
| | | FW-190 dest(grd) | Cazaux A/F |
| | | Ju-52 dest(grd) | Cazaux A/F |
| | | Ju-88 dam(grd) | Cazaux A/F |
| | Lt. V.H. Wynn | Do-217 dest(grd) | Cazaux A/F |
| | | Ju-88 dest(grd) | Cazaux A/F |
| | Lt. V.J. France | Ju-88 dest(grd) | Cazaux A/F |
| | | Ju-52 dest(grd) | Cazaux A/F |
| | | Ju-88 dam(grd) | Cazaux A/F |
| | Capt. H.D. Hively | Ju-88 dest(grd) | Cazaux A/F |
| | Lt. S.W. Monroe | Me-410 dest(grd) | Cazaux A/F |
| | Lt. R.P. Kenyon | Do-217 dam(grd) | Cazaux A/F |
| | | Ju-88 dam(grd) | Cazaux A/F |
| | Lt. R.P. Claus | Ju-88 dam(grd) | Cazaux A/F |
| 335th: | Maj. G. Carpenter | FW-190 dest(air) | SW Bordeaux |
| | Lt. C.F. Anderson | FW-190 dest(air) | W/Bordeaux |
| | Capt. J.R. Happel | (.5)FW-190 dam(air) | Libourne |
| | Lt. A.L. Schlegel | (.5)FW-190 dam(air) | Libourne |
| 336th: | Capt. D.S. Gentile | (2)Me-110 dest(grd) | Cazaux A/F |
| | Lt. W.W. Millikan | He-177 dest(grd) | Cazaux A/F |
| | Lt. L.H. Norley | Ju-88 dest(grd) | Cazaux A/F |
| | Lt. D.R. Emerson | (.5)Ju-88 dest(grd)[*] | Cazaux A/F |
| | Capt. R.D. Hobert | Ju-88 dam(grd) | Cazaux A/F |
| **56th** | | | |
| HdQts: | LtCol. F.S. Gabreski | (2)Me-109 dest(air) | NE Nantes |
| | LtCol. D.C. Schilling | Ju-52 dest(grd) | Chateaudun |
| 61st: | Capt. B.M. Gladych | Me-109 dest(air) | S/Angars |
| | Capt. L.C. Smith | u/i a/c dam(grd) | Gael A/F |
| 63rd: | Maj. W.M. Mahurin | (.25)Do-217 dest(air) | S/Chartres |
| | Lt. W.D. Johnson | (.25)Do-217 dest(air) | S/Chartres |
| | Lt. I.T. Porowski | (.25)Do-217 dest(air) | S/Chartres |
| | F/O S.J. Lowman | (.25)Do-217 dest(air) | S/Chartres |
| **355th** | | | |
| 357th: | Capt. J.H. Wilson | (.5)Me-109 dest(air) | Biscarosse |
| | Lt. I. Reedy | (.5)Me-109 dest(air) | Biscarosse |
| | Lt. C.J. Butcher | (2)Ju-88 dam(grd) | Biscarosse |
| | Capt. J.L. Elder | Ju-88 dam(grd) | Biscarosse |
| | Lt. C.C. Colson | Ju-88 dam(grd) | Biscarosse |
| | Lt. C.M. Lee | Ju-88 dam(grd) | Biscarosse |
| **359th** | | | |
| 369th: | Lt. F.S. Fong | FW-190 dest(air) | Gallardson |
| | Lt. R.L. Pherson | Me-109 dest(air) | Gallardson |
| 370th: | Capt. D.D. McKee | FW-190 prob(air) | Chartres |
| | | Me-109 dam(air) | Chartres |

*Losses-*

**4th**: Lt. Archie W. Chatterly (334th Ftr Sqn) POW
P-51B QP-G 43-6860
Hit by flak at Lake Biscarosse.

**56th**: Lt. James E. Fields (62nd Ftr Sqn) POW
P-47D LM-L 42-75213
Hit by flak in the Chartres area.

Maj. Gerald W. Johnson (63rd Ftr Sqn) POW
P-47D UN-V 42-76249
Hit by flak and bailed out near Cheux.

Maj. Walker M. Mahurin (63rd Ftr Sqn) MIA-E
P-47D UN-M 42-8487
Hit by a Do-217 gunner south of Chartres.

Lt. Evert G. Everett (63rd Ftr Sqn) KIA
P-47D UN- 42-75234
Hit by flak and later crashed into the Channel.

**355th**: Lt. Chester J. Butcher (357th Ftr Sqn) POW
P-51B OS-F 43-6777 "The Butcher"
Hit by flak and crashed near Biscarosse.

**357th**: Lt. James E. Strode (364th Ftr Sqn) KIA
P-51B C5- 43-6978
Last seen in the overcast and crashed off Clacton.

**359th**: Lt. John E. Kerns (370th Ftr Sqn) KIA
P-47D CS-I 42-7891
Last seen chasing an enemy fighter near Gallardson.

**364th**: Lt. William G. Coltman (384th Ftr Sqn) POW
P-38J 5Y- 42-67416
Collided with Lt. Westmore near Mayenne.

Lt. Harry W. Westmore (384th Ftr Sqn) POW
P-38J 5Y- 42-67428
Collided with Lt. Coltman near Mayenne.

*Remarks*
4th: 0-1 ship, 0-1 building
56th: 5-1 vehicles, 0-1 building, 0-1 flak tower
352nd: 0-1 hangar
355th: 0-1 hangar, 0-1 barracks, 0-1 control tower
356th: Capt. Roland J. Halverson (360th Ftr Sqn) c/l; o.k.
P-47D PI-

**March 28, 1944**
Groups Operating: P-51 4th, 355th, 357th
P-47 56th, 78th, 352nd, 353rd, 359th, 361st
P-38 20th
Missions: Support for bombers to various French airfields.
Claims: 0-0-0 air
28-36 ground

| *Group* | | *Claims* | *Location* |
|---|---|---|---|
| **4th** | | | |
| 334th: | Lt. A.H. Markel | Me-109 dam(grd) | W/Dreux |
| 335th: | Lt. C.F. Anderson | u/i a/c dest(grd) | S/Dreux |
| | Lt. P.W. McKennon | Ju-88 dam(grd) | S/Dreux |

| | Pilot | Claims | Location |
|---|---|---|---|
| **355th** | | | |
| HdQts: | LtCol. G.J. Dix | (.5)Ju-88 dest(grd) | Dijon |
| | Lt. L.D. Minchew | (.5)He-111 dest(grd) | Dijon |
| 354th: | Capt. C.G. Johnston | Me-110 dest(grd) | Dijon |
| | Lt. R.S. Morris | He-111 dest(grd) | Dijon |
| | Lt. H.E. Culp | (.5)Ju-88 dest(grd) | Dijon |
| | Lt. T.F. Neal | (.5)He-111 dest(grd) | Dijon |
| | Lt. B.C. Williamson | u/i a/c dam(grd) | Dijon |
| 357th: | Maj. E.W. Szaniawski | Me-110 dest(grd) | Dijon |
| | | Me-410 dest(grd) | Dijon |
| | | Ju-88 dest(grd) | Dijon |
| | | (3)Ju-88 dam(grd) | Dijon |
| | | Me-210 dam(grd) | Dijon |
| | Lt. R.B. Butler | (2)Ju-88 dest(grd) | Dijon |
| | | (2)Ju-88 dam(grd) | Dijon |
| | | Go-242 dam(grd) | Dijon |
| | Lt. B.D. Johnston | (2)Me-210 dest(grd) | Dijon |
| | | Ju-88 dest(grd) | Dijon |
| | | Me-210 dam(grd) | Dijon |
| | | Me-109 dam(grd) | Dijon |
| | | Ju-88 dam(grd) | Dijon |
| | F/O J.D. Sturm | He-111 dest(grd) | Dijon |
| | | Ju-88 dest(grd) | Dijon |
| | | (2)Ju-88 dam(grd) | Dijon |
| | | He-111 dam(grd) | Dijon |
| | Lt. B.L. Hill | Do-217 dest(grd) | Dijon |
| | | He-111 dest(grd) | Dijon |
| | | (2)Ju-88 dam(grd) | Dijon |
| | | He-111 dam(grd) | Dijon |
| | | Me-110 dam(grd) | Dijon |
| | | u/i a/c dam(grd) | Dijon |
| | Capt. N.E. Olson | He-111 dest(grd) | Dijon |
| | | FW-190 dam(grd) | Dijon |
| | Lt. V.A. Burroughs | Fi-156 dest(grd) | Dijon |
| | | Ju-88 dam(grd) | Dijon |
| | Lt. R.F. DeMers | He-111 dest(grd) | Dijon |
| | | (2)He-111 dam(grd) | Dijon |
| | | Ju-88 dam(grd) | Dijon |
| | Lt. D.E. Schoenfeldt | Ju-88 dest(grd) | Dijon |
| | | (2)Ju-88 dam(grd) | Dijon |
| | Lt. H.K. Hillman | Ju-88 dest(grd) | Dijon |
| | | Me-109 dam(grd) | Dijon |
| | | Me-210 dam(grd) | Dijon |
| | | Ju-88 dam(grd) | Dijon |
| | Lt. H.F. Packard | Ju-88 dest(grd) | Dijon |
| | | (3)Ju-88 dam(grd) | Dijon |
| | Lt. R.B. Kaminski | Ju-88 dam(grd) | Dijon |
| 358th: | Lt. W.J. Hovde | He-111 dam(grd) | Marigny |
| **357th** | | | |
| 362nd: | Lt. A.E. Smith | (2.5)Ju-88 dest(grd) | S/Paris |
| | Lt. A.J. Roberson | Ju-88 dest(grd) | S/Paris |
| | Lt. R.M. Starkey | Ju-88 dest(grd) | S/Paris |
| | Lt. L.K. Carson | (.5)Ju-88 dest(grd) | S/Paris |

*Losses-*

**4th:** Lt. Raymond P. Clotfelter (335th Ftr Sqn) POW
P-51B WD-B 43-6843
Suffered mechanical failure near Dreux.

**357th:** LtCol. Hubert I. Egenes (HdQts) KIA
P-51B G4- 43-6794
Hit by flak south of Paris.

Lt. Lynn H. Drollinger (362nd Ftr Sqn) MIA-E
P-51B G4- 43-6729
Suffered mechanical failure and bailed out northeast of Dijon.

*Remarks*
352nd: 0-3 hangars, 0-1 barracks
355th: 1-0 loco, 0-1 hangar, 0-1 flak tower, 0-1 vehicle

**March 29, 1944**
Groups Operating: P-51 4th, 355th, 357th
P-47 56th, 78th, 352nd, 353rd, 353rd"C", 356th, 359th
P-38 364th
Missions: Support of bombers to Brunswick.
Claims: 43.5-6-12 air
16-25 ground

| *Group* | | *Claims* | *Location* |
|---|---|---|---|
| **4th** | | | |
| HdQts: | LtCol. J.A. Clark | FW-190 dest(air) | Gifhorn |
| 334th: | Lt. A.F. Bunte | FW-190 dest(air) | Magdeburg |
| | Lt. H.T. Biel | FW-190 dest(air) | Gifhorn |
| | Lt. D.W. Howe | FW-190 dest(air) | NW Brunswick |
| | Capt. W.M. Sobanski | FW-190 dam(air) | Hanover |
| | | Ju-52 dest(grd) | Steinhuder Lake |
| | Capt. D.A. Van Epps | FW-190 dam(air) | Brunswick |
| 335th: | Maj. G. Carpenter | Me-109 dest(air) | Gifhorn |
| | | (.33)He-111 dest(air) | Brunswick |
| | | Me-109 dam(air) | Gifhorn |
| | Lt. C.F. Anderson | (2.5)FW-190 dest(air) | Gifhorn |
| | | (shared with an unknown pilot) | |
| | Lt. R.C. Church | Me-109 dest(air) | NE Gifhorn |
| | Lt. C.A. Fiedler | Me-109 dest(air) | N/Brunswick |
| | Lt. P.W. McKennon | Me-109 dest(air) | NE Brunswick |
| | Lt. P.S. Riley | Me-109 dest(air) | E/Ulzen |
| | Lt. R.W. Saunders | Me-109 dest(air) | Lingen |
| | Lt. W.E. Newell | FW-190 prob(air) | Brunswick |
| 336th: | Capt. D.S. Gentile | (2)FW-190 dest(air) | Brunswick |
| | | Me-109 dest(air) | Brunswick |
| | Capt. K.D. Peterson | (2)FW-190 dest(air) | SW Brunwick |
| | Lt. J.T. Godfrey | FW-190 dest(air) | Brunswick |
| | | (.33)He-111 dest(air) | Brunswick |
| | F/O F.W. Glover | FW-190 dest(air) | Brunswick |
| | | (.33)He-111 dest(air) | Brunswick |
| | Lt. R.S. Tussey | FW-190 prob(air) | SE Brunswick |
| | Lt. O.F. LaJeunesse | Ju-88 dam(air) | E/Hanover |
| | | Ju-88 dest(grd) | E/Hanover |
| | Maj. J.A. Goodson | Ju-88 dest(grd) | NE Brunswick |
| | | (2)Ju-88 dam(grd) | NE Brunswick |
| **56th** | | | |
| HdQts: | LtCol. D.C. Schilling | Me-109 dest(air) | NE Dummer Lake |
| | | Me-109 dam(air) | NE Dummer Lake |
| 61st: | Lt. R.J. Rankin | Me-109 dest(air) | NE Dummer Lake |
| **353rd** | | | |
| 351st: | Capt. V.L. Byers | Ju-88 dam(grd) | SE Steinhuder L. |
| | Lt. J. Terzian | u/i a/c dam(grd) | SE Steinhuder L. |
| 352nd: | Capt. T.J. Forkin | (2)Me-109 dest(air) | SW Bremen |
| | | Me-109 dam(air) | SW Bremen |
| | Lt. G.G. Callans | Me-109 dest(air) | SW Bremen |
| | Lt. W.J. Jordan | Me-109 dest(air) | SW Bremen |
| | Lt. W.F. Streit | Me-109 dest(air) | SW Bremen |
| **353rd "C"** | | | |
| HdQts: | Col. G.E. Duncan | Me-110 dest(grd) | Dummer Lake |
| | | B-17 dest(grd) | Dummer Lake |
| | | (6)u/i a/c dam(grd) | Dummer Lake |
| | | Me-210 dam(grd) | Dummer Lake |
| 354th: | Lt. N.J. Fortier | u/i a/c dest(grd) | Dummer Lake |
| 369th: | Lt. C.E. Carter | (2)Me-410 dest(grd) | Dummer Lake |
| | Capt. C.C. Ettlesen | u/i a/c dam(grd) | Dummer Lake |
| 375th: | Lt. M.H. Johnson | FW-190 dest(grd) | Rheine |
| | | Ju-88 dest(grd) | Rheine |
| | Lt. E.W. Kinnaird | (2)FW-190 dam(grd) | Dummer Lake |
| 376th: | Lt. J.C. Wright | Ju-88 dest(grd) | Dummer Lake |
| | | (2)u/i a/c dam(grd) | Dummer Lake |
| | Lt. J.D. Kelly | Ju-88 dam(grd) | Dummer Lake |
| **355th** | | | |
| HdQts: | LtCol. E.W. Stewart | (2)Me-108 dest(air) | E/Goslar A/F |
| | | FW-190 dam(air) | S/Brunswick |
| | | (2)Me-108 dam(grd) | Goslar A/F |
| 354th: | Maj. C.H. Kinnard | FW-190 dest(air) | SW Brunswick |
| | Capt. W.J. Koraleski | FW-190 dest(air) | Brunswick |
| | Lt. H.W. Brown | FW-190 dest(air) | Brunswick |
| | Lt. C.W. Lenfest | Me-108 dest(air) | Goslar A/F |
| | | u/i a/c dest(grd) | Goslar A/F |
| | Lt. R.A. Browning | (.5)u/i a/c dam(grd) | NE Brunswick |
| | | (.5)u/i a/c dam(grd) | NE Brunswick |
| 357th: | Capt. B.D. Johnston | (2)FW-190 dest(air) | Brunswick |
| | | FW-190 dam(air) | Brunswick |
| | Capt. F.L. Ramsdell | FW-190 dest(air) | NE Brunswick |
| | Capt. J.J. Elder | FW-190 dest(air) | NE Brunswick |
| | | FW-190 dam(air) | NE Brunswick |
| | Lt. V.A. Burroughs | FW-190 dest(air) | NE Brunswick |
| | | FW-190 prob(air) | NE Brunswick |
| | | (2)FW-190 dam(air) | NE Brunswick |
| | Lt. D.D. McCasland | FW-190 dest(air) | Brunswick |
| | | FW-190 prob(air) | Brunswick |
| | Lt. R.B. Kaminski | FW-190 dest(air) | NE Brunswick |
| | | (2)u/i a/c dam(grd) | NE Brunswick |
| | | (.5)u/i a/c dam(grd) | NE Brunswick |
| | | (.5)u/i a/c dam(grd) | NE Brunswick |
| | Lt. C.M. Lee | FW-190 prob(air) | NE Brunswick |
| | Lt. H.K. Hillman | FW-190 dam(air) | NE Brunswick |
| **356th** | | | |
| HdQts: | Maj. J.H. Thorne | Me-109 dest(air) | Steinhuder Lake |
| 359th: | Lt. C.H. Rubner | Me-109 dest(air) | Steinhuder Lake |
| | Lt. J.B. Smith | Me-109 prob(air) | Steinhuder Lake |
| 360th: | Lt. W.E. Johnson | (2)Me-410 dest(grd) | Cloppenberg A/F |
| | Lt. H.B. McLaughlin | Me-410 dest(grd) | Cloppenberg A/F |
| | Lt. B. Borelli | Me-410 dam(grd) | Cloppenberg A/F |
| **357th** | | | |
| 362nd: | Capt. J.E. Broadhead | Me-109 dest(air) | Brunswick |

**364th**

| | | | |
|---|---|---|---|
| 384th: | Maj. J.H. Lowell | Ju-52 dest(grd) | Osnabruck |
| | | FW-190 dam(grd) | Osnabruck |
| | Capt. J.C. Ford | Me-109 dest(air) | Rheine/Enschede |

*Losses-*

**4th**: Lt. William E. Newell (335th Ftr Sqn) POW
P-51B WD-P 43-6759
Hit by enemy fighters near Lingen.

Lt. Glenn J. Smart (335th Ftr Sqn) ASR
P-51B WD-W 43-6973
Hit by enemy fighters and bailed out over the Channel.

Capt. Kenneth D. Peterson (336th Ftr Sqn) POW
P-51B VF-F 43-6696
Hit by enemy fighters near Braunschwig.

**353rd**: Lt. Francis L. Edwards (351st Ftr Sqn) ASR
P-47D YJ-
Hit by flak at Twente/Enschede and bailed out over the Channel.

**355th**: Capt. Howard L. Lambert, Jr. (357th Ftr Sqn) KIA
P-51B OS-O 43-6508
Ran out of fuel and ditched in the Channel.

Capt. Ben D. Johnston, Jr. (357th Ftr Sqn) POW
P-51B OS-I 43-12452
Suffered mechanical failure near Brussels.

Lt. James C. McConnell (358th Ftr Sqn) POW
P-51B YF-C 43-6317 "Duel Purpose"
Hit by flak near Arnheim and bailed out near Rotterdam.

**357th**: Lt. Santiago R. Gutierrez (363rd Ftr Sqn) KIA
P-51B B6- 43-7052
Collided with Lt. McGinley over the North Sea.

Lt. William R. McGinley (363rd Ftr Sqn) KIA
P-51B B6-K 43-6628 "Typhoon McGoon"
Collided with Lt. Gutierrez over the North Sea.

Lt. Edward R. Sutton (364th Ftr Sqn) KIA
P-51B C5- 43-6454
Hit by enemy fighters north of Brunswick.

**364th**: Capt. Leown A. Gilliland (383rd Ftr Sqn) KIA
P-38J N2- 42-67416
Suffered mechanical failure and crashed off Lowestoft.

Lt. Norman L. MacLean (384th Ftr Sqn) KIA
P-38J 5Y- 42-67984
Hit by flak and bellied-in near Rheine.

Lt. Curtis A. Smith (385th Ftr Sqn) KIA
P-38J 5E- 42-67895
Crashed at Tibbenham upon returning from the mission.

*Remarks*
4th: 0-2 locos
56th: 1-3 locos, 0-1 building
78th: 1-3 locos
353rd: 0-2 locos
353rd "C": 9-3 locos, 0-3 hangars, 0-6 flak towers, 0-2 vehicles, 0-1 barge, 0-1 building
355th: 5-1 locos
356th: 3-8 locos, 0-1 tug
Lt. Edward P. Lee (361st Ftr Sqn) c/l Leiston; o.k.
P-47D QI-
364th: 0-8 locos, 0-7 barges, 0-14 barracks, 0-6 buildings, 0-1 boat, 0-1 flak tower
Lt. Kenneth M. Shaffer (384th Ftr Sqn) b/o Honington; o.k.
P-38J 5Y-
Lt. James F. Vann (385th Ftr Sqn) c/l Knettishall; o.k.
P-38J 5E-

Groups Operating: P-47 361st
Missions: Support for bombers to Watten V-1 sites.
Claims: nil
Losses: nil

KIAc's
56th: Capt. Stanley B. Morrill (62nd Ftr Sqn)
Died in the explosion of a B-24's bomb load near Halesworth. He was helping to get crew men to safety when killed.

**March 30, 1944**
Groups Operating: P-47 359th, 361st
Missions: 359th dive-bombed Soesterburg and 361st attacked Eindhoven.
Claims: nil
Losses: nil

*Remarks*
359th: Lt. John B. Hunter (368th Ftr Sqn) c/l East Wretham; o.k.
P-47D CV-
361st: 0-1 loco, 0-1 building

Groups Operating: P-47 78th
Missions: Strafing sweep to Venlo, Twente/Enschede, and Deelan.
Claims: 1-0-0 air
1-4 ground

| ***Group*** | | ***Claims*** | ***Location*** |
|---|---|---|---|
| **78th** | | | |
| 82nd: | Lt. J.J. Bernhard | glider dam(grd) | Wesel |
| | Lt. J.W. Wilkinson | glider dam(grd) | Wesel |
| 83rd: | Lt. P.C. Holden | Me-109 dest(grd) | N/Venlo |
| | Lt. C.M. Peal | Me-410 dam(grd) | N/Venlo |
| 84th: | Lt. Q.L. Brown | (.33)Do-217 dest(air) | Twente/Enschede |
| | Lt. L.J. Abel | (.33)Do-217 dest(air) | Twente/Enschede |
| | Lt. E.S. Lang | (.33)Do-217 dest(air) | Twente/Enschede |
| | Lt. H.H. Just | Me-323 dam(grd) | Deelan A/F |

*Losses-*

**78th**: Lt. Albert B. Werder (83rd Ftr Sqn) KIA
P-47D HL-R 42-7906
Hit by flak and bailed out near Venlo.

*Remarks*
78th: 7-13 locos, 1-2 tugs, 1-2 barges

**March 31, 1944**
KIAc's
4th: Lt. Peter G. Lehman (336th Ftr Sqn)
P-51B VF-S 43-6844
Crashed while involved in dog-fighting near Duxford.

**April 1, 1944**
Groups Operating: P-51 4th, 352nd(mixed), 355th, 357th
P-47 56th, 78th, 352nd, 353rd, 353rd"C", 356th, 361st
Missions: Support of bombers to Ludwigshafen and Pfozheim.
Claims: 3-0-4 air
14-11 ground

| ***Group*** | | ***Claims*** | ***Location*** |
|---|---|---|---|
| **4th** | | | |
| 334th: | Capt. D.W. Beeson | Me-109 dest(air) | N/Lake Constance |
| | F/O R.K. Hofer | Me-109 dest(air) | NW Lake Constance |
| | Lt. N. Megura | Me-109 dam(air) | NW Lake Constance |
| 335th: | Maj. G. Carpenter | Me-109 dam(air) | Antwerp |
| | Lt. C.F. Anderson | Me-109 dam(air) | Antwerp |
| 336th: | Capt. D.S. Gentile | Me-109 dest(air) | SW Stuttgart |
| | Lt. R.F. Nelson | Ju-88 dam(grd) | Belgium |
| **78th** | | | |
| 82nd: | Capt. W.L. Boone | (.33)u/i a/c dest(grd) | Verdun |
| | | (.33)u/i a/c dest(grd) | Verdun |
| | | (.125)Do-217 dest(grd) | Verdun |
| | | Me-410 dam(grd) | Verdun |
| | | Ju-52 dam(grd) | Verdun |
| | Lt. B.M. Watkins | (.33)u/i a/c dest(grd) | Verdun |
| | | (.33)u/i a/c dest(grd) | Verdun |
| | | (.125)Do-217 dest(grd) | Verdun |
| | | (2)u/i a/c dam(grd) | Verdun |
| | Lt. P.H. Hazelett | Ju-87 dest(grd) | Verdun |
| | | u/i a/c dest(grd) | Verdun |
| | Lt. K.R. Wagner | He-111 dest(grd) | Verdun |
| | Lt. C. Webb | (.33)u/i a/c dest(grd) | Verdun |
| | | (.33)u/i a/c dest(grd) | Verdun |
| | Capt. W.E. May | (.125)Do-217 dest(grd) | Verdun |
| | Lt. C.R. Clark | (.125)Do-217 dest(grd) | Verdun |
| | Lt. H.L. Eakes | (.125)Do-217 dest(grd) | Verdun |
| | Lt. J.J. Hockery | (.125)Do-217 dest(grd) | Verdun |
| | Lt. R.V. Hearn | (.125)Do-217 dest(grd) | Verdun |
| | F/O C.W. DeWitt | (.125)Do-217 dest(grd) | Verdun |
| | | He-111 dam(grd) | Verdun |
| | Lt. D.D. Hagarty | (2)Do-217 dam(grd) | Verdun |
| | Lt. C.G. Godard | Ju-88 dam(grd) | Verdun |
| **353rd "C"** | | | |
| 369th: | Lt. C.E. Carter | Me-109 dam(air) | Dummer Lake |
| 375th: | Lt. E.W. Kinnaird | Ju-88 dest(grd) | Gutersloh |
| 376th: | Lt. J.D. Kelly | (2)Ju-88 dest(grd) | Gutersloh |
| | Lt. J.C. Wright | Ju-88 dest(grd) | Gutersloh |
| **356th** | | | |
| HdQts: | Capt. H.A. Ogden | Me-410 dest(grd) | Dummer Lake |
| 359th: | Lt. R.B. Warren | (2)Me-410 dest(grd) | Dummer Lake |
| | LtCol. D.A. Baccus | Me-410 dest(grd) | Dummer Lake |

| | | | |
|---|---|---|---|
| | Lt. J.J. Meholic | (.5)Me-410 dam(grd) | Dummer Lake |
| | | (.5)Me-410 dam(grd) | Dummer Lake |
| | Lt. H. Weber | (.5)Me-410 dam(grd) | Dummer Lake |
| | | (.5)Me-410 dam(grd) | Dummer Lake |

*Losses-*

**56th**: Lt. Thomas P. Owens, Jr. (61st Ftr Sqn) KIA
P-47D HV- 42-75839
Hit by flak near Lille and crashed near Neuville/St. Vaast.

**78th**: Lt. Calvin Webb (82nd Ftr Sqn) KIA
P-47C MX-I 42-6535
Hit by flak near Armentieres.

**357th**: Capt. Davis T. Perron (362nd Ftr Sqn) KIA
P-51B G4- 43-6782
Crashed near Doullens in bad weather.

Lt. Elmer D. Rydberg (362nd Ftr Sqn) KIA
P-51B G4- 43-6629
Crashed near Erevent in bad weather.

*Remarks*
78th: 0-1 hangar, 0-1 flak tower, 0-1 gun position
353rd "C": 0-13 locos, 0-3 tugs, 0-2 hangars
355th: 1-2 locos
356th: 8-10 locos, 2-3 tugs, 0-8 barges, 0-3 flak towers

**April 5, 1944**
Groups Operating: P-47 361st
Missions: Support for bombers to St. Pol/Siracourt V-1 sites.
Claims: nil
Losses: nil

Groups Operating: P-51 4th, 352nd(mixed), 355th
P-47 56th, 78th, 352nd, 353rd, 353rd"C", 356th, 359th
P-38 20th, 364th
Missions: Strafing sweeps to Germany.
Claims: 12-0-2 air
85.5-128 ground

| ***Group*** | | ***Claims*** | ***Location*** |
|---|---|---|---|
| **4th** | | | |
| HdQts: | Col. D.J.M. Blakeslee | (2)Ju-88 dam(grd) | Brandenburg-Briest |
| | | u/i a/c dam(grd) | Brandenburg-Briest |
| 334th: | Capt. D.W. Beeson | (.33)Ju-88 dest(air)[*] | Plaue A/F |
| | | (1.5)Ju-88 dest(grd) | Weissewarte/Busch |
| | | (shared with an unknown pilot) | |
| | | Me-323 dam(grd) | Brandenburg-Briest |
| | | Me-109 dam(grd) | Brandenburg-Briest |
| | | (.25) of(5)Ju-52 dam(grd) | Brandenburg-Briest |
| | Lt. H.T. Biel | (.33)Ju-88 dest(air)[*] | Plaue A/F |
| | | He-111 dest(grd) | Brandenburg-Briest |
| | | Ju-88 dam(grd) | Brandenburg-Briest |
| | | (.25) of(5)Ju-52 dam(grd) | Brandenburg-Briest |
| | Lt. H.J. Blanchfield | (2)Do-217 dest(grd) | Brandenburg-Briest |
| | | (.33)He-111 dest(grd) | Brandenburg-Briest |
| | | (2)Ju-52 dam(grd) | Brandenburg-Briest |
| | Lt. G.E. Montgomery | (2)Ju-88 dest(grd) | Brandenburg-Briest |
| | Lt. V.J. France | (.33)He-111 dest(grd) | Brandenburg-Briest |
| | | FW-190 dam(grd) | Brandenburg-Briest |
| | | Ju-52 dam(grd) | Brandenburg-Briest |
| | Lt. L.R. Pierce | Ju-88 dest(grd) | Brandenburg-Briest |
| | | (.33)He-111 dest(grd) | Brandenburg-Briest |
| | Lt. C.D. Carr | Ju-52 dest(grd) | Brandenburg-Briest |
| | | Ju-88 dam(grd) | Brandenburg-Briest |
| | | (.25) of(5)Ju-52 dam(grd) | Brandenburg-Briest |
| 335th: | Lt. C.A. Fiedler | (.33)Ju-88 dest(air)[*] | Plaue A/F |
| | | (2)Ju-88 dam(grd) | Plaue A/F |
| | | u/i a/c dam(grd) | Plaue A/F |
| | Lt. C.F. Anderson | (2)Si-204 dest(grd) | Brandenburg |
| | Lt. F.C. Jones | (2)u/i a/c dest(grd) | SE Berlin |
| | Lt. J.W. Goodwyn | (.5)He-111 dest(air) | N/Brandenburg |
| | | (2)Ju-88 dam(grd) | Brandenburg |
| | Lt. P.S. Riley | (.5)He-111 dest(air) | N/Brandenburg |
| | | (2)He-111 dest(grd) | Brandenburg |
| | Lt. A.L. Schlegel | He-111 dest(grd) | Brandenburg |
| | | Ju-88 dest(grd) | Brandenburg |
| | | Ju-52 dam(grd) | Brandenburg |
| | | u/i a/c dam(grd) | Brandenburg |
| | Maj. G. Carpenter | u/i a/c dest(grd) | Berlin |
| | Lt. R.W. Saunders | Ju-52 dest(grd) | W/Brandenburg |
| | | Me-110 dam(grd) | W/Brandenburg |
| | | Ju-88 dam(grd) | W/Brandenburg |
| | Lt. G.I. Stanford | (3)Ju-88 dam(grd) | Brandenburg |
| 336th: | Capt. R.D. Hobert | (3)Ju-88 dest(grd) | Stendal |
| | | Ju-88 dam(grd) | Stendal |
| | Maj. J.A. Goodson | Ju-88 dest(grd) | Stendal |
| | | FW-190 dest(grd) | Stendal |
| | | Ju-52 dest(grd) | Stendal |
| | | (.5)Ju-88 dest(grd)[**] | Stendal |
| | | (.5)Ju-88 dest(grd)[@] | Stendal |
| | | (.5)Ju-88 dest(grd) | Stendal |
| | | (shared with an unknown pilot) | |
| | Capt. D.S. Gentile | (3)Ju-88 dest(grd) | Stendal |
| | | (.5)Ju-88 dest(grd)[@] | Stendal |
| | | (.5)Ju-88 dest(grd)[@@] | Stendal |
| | Lt. J.T. Godfrey | (1.5)Ju-88 dest(grd)[@@] | Stendal |
| | | Me-110 dest(grd) | Stendal |
| | | (2)Me-110 dam(grd) | Stendal |
| | | (2)Ju-88 dam(grd) | Stendal |
| | | Ju-52 dam(grd) | Stendal |
| | Lt. D.R. Emerson | (.5)Ju-88 dest(grd)[**] | Stendal |
| | | (.5)Ju-88 dest(grd) | Stendal |
| | | (shared with an unknown pilot) | |
| | | Ju-88 dam(grd) | Stendal |
| | Lt. D.J. Patchen | (2.5)Ju-88 dest(grd) | Stendal |
| | | (shared with an unknown pilot) | |
| | F/O F.W. Glover | (2)Ju-52 dest(grd) | Stendal |
| | | (2)Ju-88 dam(grd) | Stendal |
| | Lt. R. Simon | (2)u/i a/c dest(grd) | W/Brandenburg |
| | Lt. K.E. Carlson | Ju-88 dest(grd) | Stendal |
| | Lt. R.S. Tussey | Me-110 dest(grd) | Stendal |
| | | Ju-88 dam(grd) | Stendal |
| | | (.25) of(5)Ju-52 dam(grd) | Brandenburg-Briest |
| | Lt. R.F. Nelson | Ju-88 dest(grd) | Brandenburg |
| | | He-177 dam(grd) | Brandenburg |
| | | Ju-88 dam(grd) | Brandenburg |
| | Lt. W.E. Johnson | (1.5)Ju-88 dest(grd) | Stendal |
| | | (shared with an unknown pilot) | |
| | | Ju-88 dam(grd) | Stendal |
| | Lt. R.E. Hughes | u/i a/c dam(grd) | Stendal |
| **20th** | | | |
| 55th: | Lt. J.J. Yelton | FW-190 dest(air) | SW Hanover |
| | | FW-200 dest(air) | SW Hanover |
| **78th** | | | |
| 82nd: | Lt. H.L. Eakes | (.33)Go-242 dest(grd) | Ruwer |
| | | (.33)DFS-230 dest(grd) | Ruwer |
| | Lt. J.J. Hockery | (.33)Go-242 dest(grd) | Ruwer |
| | | (.33)DFS-230 dest(grd) | Ruwer |
| | F/O C.W. DeWitt | (.33)Go-242 dest(grd) | Ruwer |
| | | (.33)DFS-230 dest(grd) | Ruwer |
| | Lt. M.K. Woller | Go-242 dam(grd) | Ruwer |
| | | DFS-230 dam(grd) | Ruwer |
| | Capt. W.E. May | Go-242 dam(grd) | Ruwer |
| | Lt. J.E. Brasher | Go-242 dam(grd) | Ruwer |
| | Lt. P.H. Hazelett | Go-242 dam(grd) | Ruwer |
| | Lt. R.A. Hewitt | Go-242 dam(grd) | Ruwer |
| | Lt. J.W. Wilkinson | Ju-188 dam(grd) | Ruwer |
| **355th** | | | |
| HdQts: | Col. W.J. Cummings | (2)Do-217 dest(grd) | Munich |
| | | Do-217 dam(grd) | Munich |
| 354th: | Maj. C.H. Kinnard | W-34 dest(air) | Landsberg |
| | | (2)Do-217 dest(grd) | Landsberg |
| | | Me-110 dest(grd) | Landsberg |
| | | (3)Do-217 dam(grd) | Landsberg |
| | Lt. H.W. Brown | (.5)Me-108 dest(air) | Landsberg |
| | | (.2)Do-217 dest(air) | Landsberg |
| | Capt. C.G. Johnston | (.2)Do-217 dest(air) | Landsberg |
| | Capt. W.J. Koraleski | (.5)Me-109 dest(air) | Landsberg |
| | | (.5)FW-44 dest(air)[*] | Landsberg |
| | | (.2)Do-217 dest(air) | Landsberg |
| | | Do-217 dam(grd) | Landsberg |
| | | Me-110 dam(grd) | Landsberg |
| | Lt. B.C. Williamson | W-34 dest(air) | Landsberg |
| | | (.5)FW-44 dest(air)[**] | Landsberg |
| | | (.2)Do-217 dest(air) | Landsberg |
| | | Do-217 dam(grd) | Landsberg |
| | | FW-44 dam(grd) | Landsberg |
| | Lt. C.W. Lenfest | (.5)Me-108 dest(air) | Landsberg |
| | Lt. J.E. Duffy | (.2)Do-217 dest(air) | Landsberg |
| | | (5)Do-217 dam(grd) | Landsberg |
| | | FW-44 dam(grd) | Landsberg |
| | Lt. R.E. Woody | (.5)Me-109 dest(air) | Landsberg |
| | | (.5)FW-44 dest(air)[*] | Landsberg |
| | | (.5)FW-44 dest(air)[**] | Landsberg |
| | | Do-217 dam(grd) | Landsberg |
| | | Me-110 dam(grd) | Landsberg |
| | Lt. B.G. Houston | Me-108 dam(air) | Landsberg |
| | | (4)Do-217 dam(grd) | Landsberg |
| | | Me-110 dam(grd) | Landsberg |
| | Lt. L.G. Mendenhall | (3)Ju-88 dest(grd) | Landsberg |
| | | (3)Ju-88 dam(grd) | Landsberg |
| | Lt. W.P. Boulet | FW-200 dest(grd) | Landsberg |
| | | Do-217 dest(grd) | Landsberg |

| | | | |
|---|---|---|---|
| | | (2)Do-217 dam(grd) | Landsberg |
| | Lt. R.G. Kurtz | Do-217 dest(grd) | Landsberg |
| | | (2)Do-217 dam(grd) | Landsberg |
| | Lt. R.S. Morris | Me-110 dest(grd) | Landsberg |
| | | He-111 dest(grd) | Landsberg |
| | | He-111 dam(grd) | Landsberg |
| 357th: | Lt. I. Reedy | Ju-88 dest(grd) | Ottingen |
| | | Me-109 dam(grd) | Ottingen |
| | | Ju-88 dam(grd) | Ottingen |
| | Lt. R.B. Butler | Ju-88 dest(grd) | Ottingen |
| | Lt. R.B. Kaminski | Me-110 dest(grd) | Deiningen |
| | Lt. H.L. Packard | Me-110 dest(grd) | Deiningen |
| | | Me-110 dam(grd) | Deiningen |
| | Lt. C.M. Lee | (3)Me-110 dam(grd) | Ottingen |
| | Lt. J.F. Kerch | (2)Me-110 dam(grd) | Ottingen |
| | Lt. J.D. Sturm | FW-200 dam(grd) | Ottingen |
| | | Me-110 dam(grd) | Ottingen |
| | | Ju-88 dam(grd) | Ottingen |
| | | Ju-52 dam(grd) | Ottingen |
| | Lt. A.E. Benson | (2)Do-217 dam(grd) | Landsberg |
| 358th: | F/O L.M. Dudley | FW-44 dest(air) | Oberpfaffenhofen |
| | | Me-110 dest(grd) | Landsberg |
| | F/O J.M. Beckman | Me-109 dam(air) | Landsberg |
| | | Do-217 dest(grd) | Landsberg |
| | | Ju-88 dest(grd) | Landsberg |
| | | (5)Do-217 dam(grd) | Landsberg |
| | Maj. R.B. Myers | (2)Do-217 dest(grd) | Munich |
| | | DFS-230 dest(grd) | Munich |
| | | (6)Do-217 dam(grd) | Munich |
| | F/O J.S. MacConkey | (2)Do-217 dest(grd) | Munich |
| | | (3)Do-217 dam(grd) | Munich |
| | | Me-110 dam(grd) | Munich |
| | Lt. H.J. Hoffman | Me-110 dest(grd) | Munich |
| | | u/i a/c dest(grd) | Munich |
| | | (2)Do-217 dam(grd) | Munich |
| | | (2)u/i a/c dam(grd) | Munich |
| | Lt. L.J. Dissette | (2)Me-110 dest(grd) | Munich |
| | | Me-110 dam(grd) | Landsberg |
| | | DFS-230 dam(grd) | Landsberg |
| | Lt. W.V. Gresham | (2)He-111 dest(grd) | Munich |
| | Lt. J.C. Harrington | (2)Me-110 dest(grd) | Munich |
| | | (6)Me-110 dam(grd) | Munich |
| | Lt. J.E. Reed | Me-109 dest(grd) | Munich |
| | | Do-217 dest(grd) | Munich |
| | Maj. C.J. Rosenblatt | Do-217 dest(grd) | Landsberg |
| | | (4)Do-217 dam(grd) | Landsberg |
| | Lt. J.N. McElroy | Me-110 dest(grd) | Munich |
| | | Me-110 dam(grd) | Munich |
| | Lt. N.E. Peterson | Ju-88 dest(grd) | Munich |
| | | (3)Ju-88 dam(grd) | Munich |
| | Lt. A.T. Robinson | (2)Do-217 dam(grd) | E/Schwerin |

*Losses-*

**4th:** Capt. Duane W. Beeson (334th Ftr Sqn) POW
P-51B QP-B 43-6819 "Bee"
Hit by flak near Brandenburg and bailed out near Stendal.

Lt. Allan F. Bunte (334th Ftr Sqn) POW
P-51B QP-L 43-6946
Hit wires near Gardelegen and crashed into a lake at Potsdam.

Lt. Charles D. Carr (334th Ftr Sqn) POW
P-51B QP-I 43-6837
Hit by flak near Brandenburg.

Capt. Robert D. Hobert (336th Ftr Sqn) KIA
P-51B VF- 43-6836
Bailed out over the Channel and died of exposure.

**20th:** Lt. Jack J. Yelton (55th Ftr Sqn) POW
P-38J KI-T 42-67753 "Cactus Jack"
Hit by flak near Lippstadt.

**78th:** Lt. Harvey L. Eakes (82nd Ftr Sqn) KIA
P-47D MX-E 42-75602
Hit by flak near St. Valery.

**355th:** Lt. Harold F. Culp (354th Ftr Sqn) KIA
P-51B WR-P 43-7076
Hit power lines near Landsberg.

Lt. Byron L. Hill (357th Ftr Sqn) KIA
P-51B OS-C 43-6890
Hit by flak at Deiningen Airfield.

Lt. Edward Ondris (358th Ftr Sqn) KIA
P-51B YF-M 43-6937
Hit by a Me-109 near Landsberg.

*Remarks*
4th: 0-1 loco, 0-4 barges, 0-1 tug, 0-2 buildings
20th: 0-1 barge, 0-1 bridge
78th: 3-1 locos, 0-2 vehicles
355th: 0-7 locos, 0-3 vehicles, 0-1 gun position

**April 6, 1944**
Groups Operating: P-47 352nd
Missions: Support for bombers to Watten V-1 sites.
Claims: nil
Losses: nil

**April 8, 1944**
Groups Operating: P-51 4th, 352nd(mixed), 355th, 357th
P-47 56th, 78th, 352nd, 353rd, 353rd"C", 356th, 359th, 361st
P-38 20th, 55th, 364th
Missions: Support of bombers to Quackenbruck, Brunswick, Achmer, Rheine, and Oldenburg. The 20th also flew an afternoon sweep (they did not participate in the escort operations).
Claims: 57.6-3-10 air
53.5-47 ground

| ***Group*** | | ***Claims*** | ***Location*** |
|---|---|---|---|
| **4th** | | | |
| 334th: | Lt. S.W. Monroe | (1.5)FW-190 dest(air)* | Celle |
| | | (.5)Me-109 dest(air)* | Celle |
| | Capt. R.C. Care | Me-109 dest(air) | Ulzen |
| | Capt. H.N. Moulton | Me-109 dest(air) | Celle |
| | Lt. A.H. Markel | FW-190 dest(air) | Celle |
| | | Me-109 dam(air) | Celle |
| | Lt. W.B. Smith | FW-190 dest(air) | Celle |
| | | FW-190 dam(air) | Celle |
| | F/O R.K. Hofer | Me-109 dest(air) | Celle |
| | Capt. W.M. Sobanski | Me-109 dam(air) | Celle |
| | | FW-190 dam(grd) | Celle |
| | Lt. H.T. Biel | Ju-52 dest(grd) | Celle |
| | | Me-109 dam(grd) | Celle |
| | | Ju-88 dam(grd) | Celle |
| | Lt. M.H. Kolter | (2)FW-190 dam(grd) | Celle |
| 335th: | Maj. G. Carpenter | (2)FW-190 dest(air) | Celle |
| | Lt. C.A. Fiedler | (2)Me-109 dest(air) | Wolfenbuttel |
| | Lt. A.L. Schlegel | (1.5)FW-190 dest(air)* | Celle |
| | | (.5)Me-109 dest(air)* | Celle |
| | | FW-190 dest(grd) | Brunswick |
| | | FW-190 dam(grd) | Brunswick |
| | Capt. J.R. Happel | He-111 dest(air) | S/Ulzen |
| | Lt. B.L. McGrattan | Me-109 dest(air) | Wolfenbuttel |
| | Lt. P.S. Riley | FW-190 dest(air) | N/Brunswick |
| | Lt. P.W. McKennon | FW-190 dest(air) | NW Brunswick |
| | | FW-190 dam(air) | NW Brunswick |
| | Lt. C.F. Anderson | FW-190 dest(air) | Gifhorn |
| | Lt. G.I. Stanford | Me-109 dest(air) | Gifhorn |
| | Lt. F.C. Jones | Me-109 dam(air) | Wolfenbuttel |
| 336th: | Capt. D.S. Gentile | (3)FW-190 dest(air) | Ruhrburg |
| | Lt. W.W. Millikan | (3)Me-109 dest(air) | Ulzen |
| | Lt. L.H. Norley | (3)FW-190 dest(air) | Ulzen |
| | Capt. J.H. Bennett | Me-109 dest(air) | Huden |
| | F/O F.W. Glover | FW-190 dest(air) | Ulzen |
| | Lt. R. Simon | FW-190 dest(air) | Brunswick |
| | Lt. R.E. Hughes | FW-190 prob(air) | Ulzen |
| | | Me-109 dam(air) | Ulzen |
| **20th** | | | |
| HdQts: | LtCol. H.J. Rau | Me-109 dest(air) | Salzwedel |
| | | (3)Ju-88 dest(grd) | Salzwedel |
| | | Ju-52 dest(grd) | Salzwedel |
| 77th: | Maj. H.E. Johnson | He-177 dest(air) | Salzwedel |
| | | u/i a/c dest(grd) | Salzwedel |
| | | Me-110 dam(grd) | Salzwedel |
| | | u/i a/c dam(grd) | Salzwedel |
| | Capt. E.J. Machen | (2)Ju-88 dest(grd) | Salzwedel |
| | | (2)Ju-88 dam(grd) | Salzwedel |
| | Lt. C.G. Horne | FW-190 dest(air) | Salzwedel |
| | | (3)u/i a/c dam(grd) | Salzwedel |
| | | Ju-88 dam(grd) | Salzwedel |
| | Capt. J.M. Morris | Me-410 dest(grd) | Salzwedel |
| | | (.5)Ju-88 dest(grd) | Salzwedel |
| | | (.33)u/i a/c dest(grd) | Salzwedel |
| | Lt. I.W. Fernandes | Do-217 dest(grd) | Salzwedel |
| | | (.33)u/i a/c dest(grd) | Salzwedel |
| | | (.5)Ju-52 dam(grd) | Salzwedel |
| | Lt. E.C. Fiebelkorn | u/i a/c dest(grd) | Salzwedel |
| | | (2)u/i a/c dam(grd) | Salzwedel |
| | Lt. W.F. Kuemmerle | (.33)u/i a/c dest(grd) | Salzwedel |
| | Lt. B.N. Rader | (.5)Ju-88 dest(grd) | Salzwedel |
| | | (.5)Ju-52 dam(grd) | Salzwedel |
| | Lt. W.L. Whiteside | (4)Ju-88 dam(grd) | Salzwedel |
| | Lt. P. Chubin | (3)Ju-88 dam(grd) | Salzwedel |
| | Lt. H.F. Hendricks | (2)Ju-88 dam(grd) | Salzwedel |
| | Lt. J.W. Fagg | Ju-88 dam(grd) | Salzwedel |

| Sqn | Pilot | Claim | Location |
|---|---|---|---|
| 79th: | Maj. R.C. Franklin | Me-109 dest(air) | Salzwedel |
| | | (.2)He-177 dest(air)[@] | Salzwedel |
| | Lt. F.E. Lefevre | Me-109 dest(air) | Salzwedel |
| | | (2)Ju-88 dest(grd) | Salzwedel |
| | Lt. M.P. Snow | Me-109 dest(air) | Hermansburg |
| | Capt. D.E. Anderson | (.2)He-177 dest(air)[@] | Salzwedel |
| | | (2)He-177 dest(grd) | Salzwedel |
| | Capt. R.P. Gatterdam | (.2)He-177 dest(air)[@] | Salzwedel |
| | Lt. R.H. Black | Ju-88 dest(grd) | Salzwedel |
| | | u/i a/c dest(grd) | Salzwedel |
| | Lt. A.W. Heiden | (.5)He-111 dest(grd)[@@] | Salzwedel |
| | | Ju-88 dam(grd) | Salzwedel |

(Note - Two 474th Ftr Grp pilots on D.S. from the 9th Air Force flew with the 20th and shared in the He-177 and He-111 above. Capt. E.C. Hedlund shared in both while Lt. R.H. Dettre shared in only the He-177)

**55th**

| Sqn | Pilot | Claim | Location |
|---|---|---|---|
| 38th: | Capt. G. Brown | Me-109 dest(air) | Lingen |

**56th**

| Sqn | Pilot | Claim | Location |
|---|---|---|---|
| 62nd: | Capt. J.M. Jones | Ju-88 dest(grd) | Quackenbruck |
| | Maj. L.A. Schreiber | (.5)Me-109 dest(grd) | Quackenbruck |
| | | (.5)Me-410 dest(grd) | Quackenbruck |
| | Lt. A.W. Canizares | (.5)Me-109 dest(grd) | Quackenbruck |
| | | (.5)Me-410 dest(grd) | Quackenbruck |

**78th**

| Sqn | Pilot | Claim | Location |
|---|---|---|---|
| 82nd: | Maj. J.J. Oberhansly | Me-109 dest(grd) | Trier |
| | | (.2) of(3)Me-110 dest(grd) | Trier |
| | | Ju-52 dam(grd) | Trier |
| | Capt. N.D. Munson | Me-110 dest(grd) | Trier |
| | | (.2) of(3)Me-110 dest(grd) | Trier |
| | | (.33)Ar-196 dest(grd) | Trier |
| | Lt. J.E. Brasher | (.33)Ar-196 dest(grd) | Trier |
| | | (.2) of(3)Me-110 dest(grd) | Trier |
| | | Ju-52 dam(grd) | Trier |
| | Lt. R.A. Hewitt | Ju-52 dest(grd) | Trier |
| | | (.33)Ar-196 dest(grd) | Trier |
| | Lt. M.K. Woller | (.2) of(3)Me-110 dest(grd) | Trier |
| | | Ju-52 dam(grd) | Trier |
| | F/O C.W. DeWit | t(.2) of(3)Me-110 dest(grd) | Trier |
| 83rd: | F/O J.W. Mundy | FW-190 dam(air) | Antwerp |
| | Lt. W.E. Hunt | (3)glider dam(grd) | NE Frankfurt |
| | Lt. M.H. Smith | (2)glider dam(grd) | NE Frankfurt |
| | Lt. J.O. Patton | u/i a/c dam(grd) | NE Frankfurt |
| | Lt. R.E. Smith | glider dam(grd) | NE Frankfurt |

**352nd**(P-47)

| Sqn | Pilot | Claim | Location |
|---|---|---|---|
| HdQts: | LtCol. E.L. Clark | (2)Me-210 dest(grd) | Quackenbruck |
| 328th: | Capt. J.B. Coleman | (2)Me-110 dest(grd) | Quackenbruck |
| | | u/i a/c dam(grd) | Quackenbruck |
| | Capt. W.E. Hendrian | (2)Me-210 dest(grd) | Quackenbruck |
| | | Me-210 dam(grd) | Quackenbruck |
| | Lt. C.J. Bennette | u/i a/c dest(grd) | Quackenbruck |
| | | (.5)Me-110 dest(grd) | Quackenbruck |
| | Lt. W.W. Furr | Me-210 dest(grd) | Quackenbruck |
| | Lt. F.W. Miller | Me-210 dest(grd) | Quackenbruck |
| | Lt. R.H. Powell | Me-210 dest(grd) | Quackenbruck |
| | | Me-210 dam(grd) | Quackenbruck |
| | Lt. D.T. Zimms | Me-110 dest(grd) | Quackenbruck |
| | Lt. R.C. Brookins | (.5)Me-210 dest(grd) | Quackenbruck |
| | | (.5)u/i a/c dest(grd) | Quackenbruck |
| | Lt. F.A. Yochim | (.5)Me-210 dest(grd) | Quackenbruck |
| | | (.5)u/i a/c dest(grd) | Quackenbruck |
| | Lt. M.V. Long | (.5)Me-110 dest(grd) | Quackenbruck |
| | | Me-110 dam(grd) | Quackenbruck |

**353rd**

| Sqn | Pilot | Claim | Location |
|---|---|---|---|
| 350th: | Maj. S.R. Pidduck | Me-109 dam(grd) | Hoperhofen |
| | Lt. R.S. Hart | u/i a/c dam(grd) | Hoperhofen |
| | Lt. T. Lorance | FW-190 dam(grd) | Hoperhofen |
| | Lt. C.W. Mueller | u/i a/c dam(grd) | Hoperhofen |

**355th**

| Sqn | Pilot | Claim | Location |
|---|---|---|---|
| 354th: | Capt. R.G. Kurtz | (.5)Me-109 dest(air) | Sachau A/F |
| | Lt. H.W. Brown | (.5)Me-109 dest(air) | Sachau A/F |
| | Lt. B.G. Houston | Me-109 dam(air) | Brunswick |
| 357th: | Maj. E.W. Szaniawski | Me-109 dest(air) | Meppen |
| | | Me-109 dam(air) | Meppen |
| | Lt. L.D. Minchew | Me-109 dest(air) | W/Brunswick |
| | Lt. E.P. McNeff | Me-109 dam(air) | Gifhorn |
| | Capt. J.L. Elder | (2)Ju-88 dest(grd) | Gifhorn |
| | Lt. H.H. Kirby | Do-217 dest(grd) | Gifhorn |
| | | Ju-88 dest(grd) | Gifhorn |
| | Capt. N.E. Olson | Ju-88 dest(grd) | Gifhorn |
| | Capt. J.H. Wilson | Me-210 dest(grd) | Gifhorn |
| | Lt. D.D. McCasland | Ju-88 dest(grd) | Gifhorn |
| 358th: | Capt. E.L. Sluga | (1.5)Me-109 dest(air) | E/Brunswick |
| | Capt. W.J. Hovde | Me-109 dest(air) | E/Brunswick |
| | Lt. J.C. Harrington | (.5)Me-109 dest(air) | E/Brunswick |

**356th**

| Sqn | Pilot | Claim | Location |
|---|---|---|---|
| 359th: | Lt. J.B. Smith | Do-217 dam(grd) | Salzbergen A/F |

**357th**

| Sqn | Pilot | Claim | Location |
|---|---|---|---|
| 362nd: | Capt. A.M. Lingo | Me-109 dest(air) | W/Brunswick |
| | Lt. H.R. Ankeny | Me-109 dest(air) | W/Brunswick |
| | Lt. J.F. Pugh | Me-109 dest(air) | S/Brunswick |
| | Lt. L.K. Carson | (.5)Me-109 dest(air) | SW Brunswick |
| | Lt. J.S. Coon | (.5)Me-109 dest(air) | SW Brunswick |
| 363rd: | Lt. D.H. Bochkay | Me-109 dest(air) | NW Braunsweig |

**361st**

| Sqn | Pilot | Claim | Location |
|---|---|---|---|
| HdQts: | Lt. S.L. Naedle | Me-109 dest(air) | W/Dummer Lake |
| 374th: | Capt. R.E. Sedman | Me-109 dest(air) | N/Dummer Lake |
| | Lt. R.T. Eckfeldt | Me-109 dest(air) | N/Dummer Lake |
| | Lt. R.P. Lacy | Me-109 dest(air) | N/Dummer Lake |
| | Lt. L.C. Vandiver | Me-109 dest(air) | N/Dummer Lake |
| 375th: | Lt. A.B. Snyder | Me-109 dest(air) | SW Dummer Lake |
| | | FW-190 dest(air) | N/Zwolle |
| | Lt. E. Cole | Me-109 dest(air) | Diepholz |
| | | FW-190 prob(air) | N/Zwolle |
| | Lt. C.N. Keppler | FW-190 dest(air) | NW Dummer Lake |
| | Lt. R.J. Sobieski | FW-190 prob(air) | N/Zwolle |

*Losses-*

**4th**: Capt. Howard N. Moulton, Jr. (334th Ftr Sqn) POW
P-51B QP-D 43-6967
Hit by a FW-190 near Celle and bailed out near Wittengen.

Lt. Robert P. Claus (334th Ftr Sqn) KIA
P-51B QP-U 43-7029
Hit by enemy fighters near Celle.

Lt. Robert E. Hughes (336th Ftr Sqn) POW
P-51B VF- 43-6866
Hit by enemy fighters near Celle.

**20th**: Lt. Allen D. Singleton, Jr. (55th Ftr Sqn) POW
P-38J KI- 42-67719
Hit by flak near Ulzen.

Capt. Evan J. Machen (77th Ftr Sqn) KIA
P-38J LC-J 42-68181
Hit by flak near Salzwedel and crashed into a woods.

Lt. John F. Esau (79th Ftr Sqn) POW
P-38J MC- 42-68084
Hit by a Me-109 near Salzwedel and bailed out north of Celle.

Lt. Mitchell P. Snow (79th Ftr Sqn) KIA
P-38J MC-D 42-68012
Collided with a Me-109 which had been shot down by another pilot near Salzwedel.

**55th**: Lt. Thomas F. Knudson (338th Ftr Sqn) MIA
P-38J CL- 42-67721
Hit by a Me-109 east of Minden.

**65th(FW)**: Capt. Frank R. Boyles (HdQts) KIA
P-51B WD-F 43-7098
Hit by enemy fighters near Celle. He was flying with the 4th Ftr Grp on the mission.

**352nd**: Capt. Virgil K. Meroney (487th Ftr Sqn) POW
P-51B HO-V 43-7166 "Sweet Louise II"
Hit by flak at Bramsche Airfield.

**353rd**: Lt. Gordon L. Willits (352nd Ftr Sqn) KIA
P-47D SX-X 42-22708
Hit a tree near Zwischenachmer and crashed near Ijsselneer.

**353rd "C"**: Lt. Clifford E. Carter (369th Ftr Sqn/359th Ftr Grp) KIA
P-47D IV- 42-22464
Hit a house and crashed near Herringhausen.

**355th**: Capt. Norman E. Olson (357th Ftr Sqn) KIA
P-51B OS-X 43-6589
Hit by flak near Celle and crashed near Hoefen.

Lt. Irving Reedy (357th Ftr Sqn) POW
P-51B OS-U 42-106463
Hit by enemy fighters west of Brunswick.

Lt. James B. Dickson (358th Ftr Sqn) KIA
P-51B YF-X 43-7147
Hit by enemy fighters near Emden.

**361st**: Lt. Albert C. Duncan (375th Ftr Sqn) KIA
P-47D E2- 42-75424
Hit by enemy fighters near Lembauch.

*Remarks*
4th: 0-1 loco
20th: 11-3 locos, 37-2 railcars, 0-13 flak positions, 0-4 barracks, 1-5 buildings, 0-2 hangars, 0-2 bridges
56th: 0-6 locos, 0-1 hangar, 1-0 ammo dump
78th: 15-21 locos, 0-6 railcars, 3-5 vehicles, 0-1 flak tower, 0-4 buildings, 0-1 gun position.
P-47 c/l Wattisham; o.k.
352nd: 1-1 locos, 0-6 hangars, 0-3 buildings, 0-2 flak positions
353rd: 1-2 locos, 1-0 gun positions
353rd "C": 2-2 locos, 1-0 tug, 0-2 barges, 0-1 launch
356th: 0-1 vehicle, 0-2 gun positions, 0-1 launch

**April 9, 1944**
Groups Operating: P-51 4th, 352nd(mixed), 355th, 357th
P-47 56th, 78th, 352nd, 353rd, 356th, 359th, 361st
P-38 20th, 55th, 364th
Missions: Support of bombers to Marienburg, Tutow, Posen, and Warnemunde but many were recalled or hit other targets.
Claims: 11-1-8 air
19-7 ground

| *Group* | | *Claims* | *Location* |
|---|---|---|---|
| **4th** | | | |
| 334th: | Lt. A.H. Markel | u/i a/c dam(grd) | S/Osnabruck |
| 335th: | Capt. J.R. Happel | (.33)Ju-88 dest(grd) | Lingen-Plantlunne |
| | | (.33)Ju-88 dest(grd) | Lingen-Plantlunne |
| | Lt. P.W. McKennon | (.33)Ju-88 dest(grd) | Lingen-Plantlunne |
| | | (.33)Ju-88 dest(grd) | Lingen-Plantlunne |
| 336th: | Lt. J.T. Godfrey | Me-410 dest(grd) | Lingen-Plantlunne |
| | | (.33)Ju-88 dest(grd) | Lingen-Plantlunne |
| | | (.33)Ju-88 dest(grd) | Lingen-Plantlunne |
| **56th** | | | |
| HdQts: | LtCol. D.C. Schilling | (2)FW-190 dest(air) | NE Schleswig |
| | | FW-190 dam(air) | NE Schleswig |
| | | W-34 dam(air) | Schleswig |
| | | Ar-196 dest(grd) | Schleswig |
| | LtCol. F.S. Gabreski | (.5)u/i a/c dest(grd)* | Schleswig |
| 61st: | Capt. R.S. Johnson | FW-190 dest(air) | NW Kiel |
| | Capt. L.C. Smith | Me-109 dest(air) | E/Neumunster |
| | Capt. T. Anderz | Me-109 dest(air) | SE Kiel |
| | Lt. S.D. Hamilton | FW-190 dest(air) | NW Kiel |
| | | (2)FW-190 dam(air) | NW Kiel |
| 62nd: | Capt. J.H. Powers | Me-109 dest(air) | S/Kiel |
| | Maj. L.A. Schreiber | (.5)Me-109 dest(air) | Lubeck |
| | | (3)Me-109 dam(grd) | Lubeck |
| | Lt. A.W. Canizares | (.5)Me-109 dest(air) | Lubeck |
| | Lt. W.A. McClure | (2)FW-190 dam(air) | Lubeck |
| | Capt. C.R. Harrison | Me-109 dam(air) | Lubeck |
| 63rd: | Lt. H.L. Matthew | Me-109 dest(grd) | Jagel A/F |
| | | (.5)u/i a/c dest(grd)* | Schleswig |
| | F/O W.R. Frederick | He-115 dest(grd) | Schleswig |
| | | He-115 dam(grd) | Schleswig |
| | Lt. W.E. Kerr | Ar-196 dest(grd) | Schleswig |
| **78th** | | | |
| 82nd: | Capt. W.E. May | FW-190 dest(air) | Dummer Lake |
| **352nd** | | | |
| 328th: | Lt. M.V. Long | FW-190 dest(air) | Osnabruck |
| | Lt. F.A. Yochim | FW-190 dest(air) | Dummer Lake |
| | Maj. W.O. Jackson | FW-190 prob(air) | Dummer Lake |
| 487th: | Lt. C.J. Luksic | (3)Ju-88 dest(grd) | W/Dummer Lake |
| | Capt. C.E. Davis | (2)Ju-88 dest(grd) | Vechta |
| | Lt. W.T. Whisner | (2)Ju-88 dest(grd) | Vechta |
| | Lt. R.H. Berkshire | Ju-88 dest(grd) | Vechta |
| | Lt. E.B. McMahan | Ju-88 dest(grd) | Vechta |
| | Lt. C.J. Palmer | Ju-88 dest(grd) | Vechta |
| **353rd** | | | |
| 350th: | Lt. W.F. Tanner | He-115 dam(grd) | Eckenforder Bay |
| **361st** | | | |
| 375th: | Lt. D.R. Morehouse | FW-190 dam(air) | NW Dummer Lake |
| **364th** | | | |
| 384th: | Maj. J.H. Lowell | FW-190 dest(grd) | Bramsche/Rheine |
| | | FW-190 dam(grd) | Bramsche/Rheine |

*Losses-*

**4th:** Capt. David A. Van Epps (334th Ftr Sqn) POW
P-51B QP-T 43-6941
Hit by flak near Tutrow.

**55th:** Lt. Newell Anderson (338th Ftr Sqn) KIA
P-38J CL-
Crashed on take-off from Nuthampstead.

**56th:** Lt. Arlington W. Canizares (62nd Ftr Sqn) KIA
P-47D LM-D
Ran out of fuel and bailed out over the North Sea; he was picked-up but died of injuries.

**352nd:** Lt. Fred A. Yochim (328th Ftr Sqn) POW
P-47D PE-V 42-8434 "Desiree Y"
Hit by enemy fighters near Osnabruck.

Lt. Ralph I. Williamson (487th Ftr Sqn) KIA
P-47D HO-
He was radio relay and his aircraft exploded for unknown reasons near Harwick.

**353rd:** Lt. Richard A. Stearns (350th Ftr Sqn) POW
P-47D LH- 42-8499
Hit by flak at Wittensee Airfield.

Lt. Jack Terzian (351st Ftr Sqn) ASR
P-47D YJ-
Bailed out seventy miles off Great Yarmouth.

**356th:** Lt. Carl W. Dunn (360th Ftr Sqn) KIA
P-47D PI- 42-76147
He was spotter and crashed in bad weather near Gissing.

**364th:** Lt. Eugene J. Zakovec (385th Ftr Sqn) KIA
P-38J 5E- 42-67957
Hit by flak at Rheine Airfield.

*Remarks*
4th: 0-1 loco
56th: 1-3 locos, 0-2 ships
352nd: 6-2 locos, 0-3 buildings, 0-1 gun position
353rd: 0-2 locos, 0-1 E-boat, 1-0 building
Lt. Carl F. Mueller (350th Ftr Sqn) c/l; o.k.
P-47D LH-X 42-25506 "Dove of Peace"
356th: 0-1 loco, 1-0 railcar, 0-10 barges, 0-2 buildings
364th: 0-21 buildings, 0-6 flak towers, 0-2 gun positions
P-38 c/l; o.k.

**April 10, 1944**

Groups Operating: P-51 4th, 352nd(mixed), 355th, 357th
P-47 56th, 78th, 352nd, 353rd, 356th, 359th, 361st
P-38 364th
Missions: The 364th supported bombers to Marquise/Mimoytecques V-1 sites while the other groups provided escort to bombers hitting numerous airfields in France and Belgium.
Claims: 8-0-0 air
42-24 ground

| *Group* | | *Claims* | *Location* |
|---|---|---|---|
| **4th** | | | |
| HdQts: | LtCol. J.A. Clark | (2)u/i a/c dest(grd) | Romorantin A/F |
| 334th: | Lt. G.E. Montgomery | (1.5)Bu-131 dest(grd)* | Romorantin A/F |
| | Lt. H.T. Biel | u/i a/c dest(grd) | Romorantin A/F |
| | Lt. H.J. Blanchfield | Hs-126 dest(grd) | Romorantin A/F |
| | Lt. R.L. Hills | u/i a/c dest(grd) | Romorantin A/F |
| | Lt. G.C. Siems | (.5)Bu-131 dest(grd)* | Romorantin A/F |
| | Lt. D.W. Howe | (.5)u/i a/c dest(grd) | Romorantin A/F |
| | | (shared with an unknown pilot) | |
| | Lt. D.M. Malmsten | u/i a/c dam(grd) | Romorantin A/F |
| 335th: | Capt. J.R. Happel | (2)Bu-131 dest(grd) | Romorantin A/F |
| | | (2)u/i a/c dest(grd) | Romorantin A/F |
| | Lt. P.S. Riley | Bu-131 dest(air) | Romorantin A/F |
| | | Bu-131 dest(grd) | Romorantin A/F |
| | Lt. J.W. Russell | u/i a/c dest(grd) | Romorantin A/F |
| | | u/i a/c dam(grd) | Romorantin A/F |
| | Lt. A.L. Schlegel | u/i a/c dest(grd) | Romorantin A/F |
| | Lt. G.I. Stanford | u/i a/c dest(grd) | Romorantin A/F |
| | | u/i a/c dam(grd) | Romorantin A/F |
| | Lt. C.F. Anderson | (.5)Bu-131 dest(grd) | Romorantin A/F |
| | | (shared with an unknown pilot) | |
| | Lt. F.C. Jones | (2)u/i a/c dam(grd) | Romorantin A/F |
| | Lt. P.W. McKennon | u/i a/c dam(grd) | Romorantin A/F |
| | Lt. Z.S. Sensibaugh | u/i a/c dam(grd) | Romorantin A/F |
| | Lt. M.G. Scarbrough | u/i a/c dam(grd) | Romorantin A/F |
| 336th: | Maj. J.A. Goodson | (4.5)u/i a/c dest(grd) | Romorantin A/F |
| | | Hs-126 dest(grd) | Romorantin A/F |
| | Lt. R.F. Nelson | u/i a/c dest(grd) | Romorantin A/F |
| | Lt. C.H. Schilke | (.5)u/i a/c dest(grd) | Romorantin A/F |
| | Lt. N. Van Wyk | (4)u/i a/c dam(grd) | Romorantin A/F |
| **78th** | | | |
| 83rd: | Lt. A.M. Juchheim | (3)FW-190 dest(grd) | Romorantin A/F |
| | | Hs-123 dest(grd) | Romorantin A/F |
| | Lt. C.M. Peal | (3)Bu-133 dest(grd) | Romorantin A/F |
| | | Me-109 dest(grd) | Romorantin A/F |
| | | Bu-133 dam(grd) | Romorantin A/F |
| | Lt. H.L. Blystone | (2)u/i a/c dest(grd) | Romorantin A/F |

| | Pilot | Claims | Location |
|---|---|---|---|
| | Lt. K.C. Allstaedt | FW-190 dest(grd) | Romorantin A/F |
| | | u/i a/c dest(grd) | Romorantin A/F |
| | | u/i a/c dam(grd) | Romorantin A/F |
| | Lt. P.C. Holden | FW-190 dest(grd) | Romorantin A/F |
| | | u/i a/c dam(grd) | Romorantin A/F |
| **352nd** | | | |
| 328th: | Lt. J.F. Thornell | FW-190 dest(air) | Dormans |
| | Lt. F.W. Miller | FW-190 dest(air) | Dormans |
| | Capt. D.S. Bryan | (.5)FW-190 dest(air) | Dormans |
| | Lt. J.L. Laing | (.5)FW-190 dest(air) | Dormans |
| 487th: | Maj. J.C. Meyer | Me-109 dest(air) | SW Rheims |
| | | (.5)FW-190 dest(air) | SW Rheims |
| | Lt. R.G. O'Nan | FW-190 dest(air) | SW Rheims |
| | Capt. C.E. Davis | (.5)Me-109 dest(air) | SW Rheims |
| | Lt. E.B. McMahan | (.5)Me-109 dest(air) | SW Rheims |
| | Lt. C.J. Luksic | (.5)FW-190 dest(air) | SW Rheims |

(Note - the 328th flew P-47's, the 487th flew P-51's)

| | Pilot | Claims | Location |
|---|---|---|---|
| **355th** | | | |
| 354th: | Maj. C.H. Kinnard | Ju-88 dest(grd) | Bourges A/F |
| | | u/i a/c dam(grd) | Bourges A/F |
| | Capt. R.G. Kurtz | Do-217 dest(grd) | Bourges A/F |
| | | FW-190 dest(grd) | Bourges A/F |
| | Capt. R.E. Woody | He-111 dest(grd) | Bourges A/F |
| | | He-111 dam(grd) | Bourges A/F |
| | Lt. J.P. Austin | Me-109 dest(grd) | Bourges A/F |
| | | u/i a/c dam(grd) | Bourges A/F |
| | Lt. J.E. Duffy | He-111 dest(grd) | Bourges A/F |
| | | W-34 dam(grd) | Bourges A/F |
| | Lt. R.C. Schutt | (2)Do-217 dam(grd) | Bourges A/F |
| | | u/i a/c dam(grd) | Bourges A/F |
| | Lt. W.P. Boulet | He-111 dam(grd) | Bourges A/F |
| | Lt. T.F. Neal | u/i a/c dam(grd) | Bourges A/F |

*Losses-*

**4th**: Lt. Clemmons A. Fiedler (335th Ftr Sqn) KIA
P-51B WD-W 43-7190
Hit by flak at Romorantin Airfield.

**356th**: Lt. William E. Johnson, Jr. (360th Ftr Sqn) KIA
P-47D PI- 42-74639
Last seen chasing enemy fighters through the bomber formation near Argentan.

*Remarks*
4th: 0-3 flak owers, 0-1 hangar, 3-0 oil tanks
78th: 0-3 hangars, 0-1 gun position
355th: 0-2 oil tanks

Groups Operating: P-47 353rd "C"
P-38 20th, 55th
Missions: The 55th dive-bombed Coulommiers Airfield, the 20th was to hit Florennes/Juzaine but weather prevented attacks, and the "Buzz Boys" provided area support and strafed Villaroche Airfield.
Claims: 1-0-0 air
2-1 ground

| *Group* | | *Claims* | *Location* |
|---|---|---|---|
| **67th(FW)** | | | |
| HdQts: | Maj. D.K. Willis (he flew with the 20th Ftr Grp) | u/i a/c dest(air) | Rotterdam |
| **353rd "C"** | | | |
| 350th: | Lt. C.O. Durant | Me-110 dest(grd) | Villaroche |
| 376th: | Lt. J.C. Wright | Me-110 dest(grd) | Villaroche |
| | | Me-110 dam(grd) | Villaroche |

*Losses-*

**55th**: LtCol. Jack S. Jenkins (HdQts) POW
P-38J CG-J 42-67825 "Texas Ranger IV"
Bellied-in after flak hits at Coulommiers Airfield.

Lt. Anthony Piscitelli (343rd Ftr Sqn) KIA
P-38J CY- 42-67866
Hit by flak at Coulommiers Airfield.

*Remarks*
55th: 0-2 hangars, 0-2 gun positions
353rd "C": 0-2 hangars, 0-1 flak tower, 0-1 building, 0-1 control tower

Groups Operating: P-47 359th
P-38 20th
Missions: The 20th attacked Gutersloh Airfield with the 359th providing support.
Claims: nil

*Losses-*

**67th(FW)**: Maj. Donald K. Willis (HdQts) POW
P-38J KI-X 42-68077
Suffered mechanical failure and bellied-in north of Rotterdam. He was flying with the 20th Ftr Grp.

**April 11, 1944**
Groups Operating: P-51 4th, 352nd(mixed), 355th, 357th
P-47 56th, 78th, 352nd, 353rd, 356th, 359th, 361st
P-38 20th, 55th, 364th
Missions: Support of bombers to Oschersleben, Sorau, Stettin, and Rostock.
Claims: 42.5-4-18 air
64-58 ground

| *Group* | | *Claims* | *Location* |
|---|---|---|---|
| **4th** | | | |
| 334th: | Capt. R.C. Care | Me-110 dest(air) | SE Stettin |
| | F/O R.K. Hofer | Me-110 dest(air) | SE Stettin |
| | Lt. W.B. Smith | (.5)Do-217 dest(air) (shared with an unknown pilot) | SE Stettin |
| | | (2)FW-190 dest(grd) | SE Stettin |
| | | Me-410 dam(grd) | SE Stettin |
| | Capt. W.M. Sobanski | Me-110 dam(air) | SE Stettin |
| | Lt. H.T. Biel | Me-410 dest(grd) | SE Stettin |
| | | Me-110 dest(grd) | SE Stettin |
| | Lt. R.L. Hills | FW-190 dest(grd) | SE Stettin |
| | | Ju-88 dest(grd) | SE Stettin |
| | | FW-190 dam(grd) | SE Stettin |
| **56th** | | | |
| 62nd: | Lt. M.K. Boyle | u/i a/c dam(air) | Schleswig |
| | | He-115 dest(grd) | Schleswig |
| | Lt. R.B. Bluhm | u/i a/c dam(grd) | Schleswig |
| **78th** | | | |
| 82nd: | Lt. J.W. Wilkinson | Ju-88 dest(grd) | Rheine |
| | | (2)Ju-88 dam(grd) | Rheine |
| | Lt. B.M. Watkins | u/i a/c dam(grd) | Osnabruck |
| 83rd: | Lt. A.M. Juchheim | FW-190 dest(air) | Luneburg |
| | | FW-190 prob(air) | Luneburg |
| 84th: | Capt. G.H. Doyle | Me-109 dam(air) | Hanover |
| **352nd**(all P-51) | | | |
| 486th: | Lt. F.A. Cutler | (2)FW-190 dest(air) | W/Torgau |
| | | (.5)Ju-52 dest(air) | W/Torgau |
| | | Ju-88 dest(grd) | Lonnewitz |
| | | Ju-52 dam(grd) | Lonnewitz |
| | Lt. W.W. Anderson | (.5)Ju-52 dest(air) | W/Torgau |
| | | Ju-88 dest(grd) | Lonnewitz |
| | | Ju-88 dam(grd) | Lonnewitz |
| | Capt. S.W. Andrew | (2)Ju-86 dest(grd) | Finsterwalde |
| | Lt. M.E. Corcoran | Ju-88 dest(grd) | Lonnewitz |
| | | Me-109 dam(grd) | Lonnewitz |
| | | u/i a/c dam(grd) | Lonnewitz |
| | Lt. T.W. Colby | Ju-86 dest(grd) | SE Berlin |
| | | (2)Ju-86 dam(grd) | SE Berlin |
| | Lt. S.G. Miles | Ju-88 dest(grd) | SE Berlin |
| | Lt. A.L. Marshall | Ju-88 dam(grd) | Nehesdorf |
| | | u/i a/c dam(grd) | Nehesdorf |
| 487th: | Maj. J.C. Meyer | (2)u/i a/c dest(grd) | SE Berlin |
| | | FW-200 dam(grd) | SE Berlin |
| | | Ju-290 dam(grd) | SE Berlin |
| | Lt. C.J. Luksic | (2)Ju-88 dest(grd) | W/Berlin |
| | | Me-110 dest(grd) | W/Berlin |
| | | He-111 dest(grd) | W/Berlin |
| | | (3)Ju-88 dam(grd) | W/Berlin |
| | Maj. G.E. Preddy | He-111 dest(grd) | SE Berlin |
| | | He-111 dam(grd) | SE Berlin |
| | Capt. C.E. Davis | Ju-52 dest(grd) | W/Berlin |
| | Lt. F.M. Allison | Ju-88 dest(grd) | SW Berlin |
| | | Ju-88 dam(grd) | SW Berlin |
| | Lt. J.P. Kessler | FW-200 dest(grd) | SW Berlin |
| | | Ju-52 dam(grd) | SW Berlin |
| | Lt. G.T. Moran | Ju-88 dest(grd) | SE Berlin |
| | | Ar-196 dam(grd) | SE Berlin |
| | | u/i a/c dam(grd) | SE Berlin |
| | | Caudron dam(grd) | SE Berlin |
| | Lt. R.I. Ross | FW-189 dest(grd) | SW Berlin |
| | | Ju-88 dam(grd) | SW Berlin |
| | | Ju-52 dam(grd) | SW Berlin |
| | Lt. W.E. Fowler | Me-110 dam(grd) | Stendal |
| | Lt. D.W. McIntire | Ju-290 dam(grd) | SE Berlin |
| **355th** | | | |
| HdQts: | LtCol. E.W. Stewart | Me-410 dest(air) | NW Pyritz |
| | | Ju-188 dest(air) | Schau |
| | | (2)Ar-196 dam(grd) | Schau |
| 354th: | Lt. H.W. Brown | FW-190 dest(air) | E/Berlin |
| | | Ju-52 dest(grd) | Strasbourg |
| | | Ju-88 dam(grd) | Strasbourg |

| | Pilot | Claim | Location |
|---|---|---|---|
| | Capt. R.E. Woody | Ju-188 prob(air) | S/Madu Lake |
| | | Ju-87 dam(grd) | S/Madu Lake |
| | Capt. C.G. Johnston | (2)Ju-88 dest(grd) | Strasbourg |
| | | He-111 dest(grd) | Strasbourg |
| | Lt. D.J. Jacobson | (2)Ju-88 dest(grd) | Strasbourg |
| | | FW-190 dam(grd) | Strasbourg |
| | | Ju-88 dam(grd) | Strasbourg |
| | Lt. R.C. Brown | Ju-52 dest(grd) | Strasbourg |
| | | He-111 dam(grd) | Strasbourg |
| | Lt. R.C. Schutt | Me-109 dest(grd) | S/Madu Lake |
| | Capt. R.G. Kurtz | Ju-88 dam(grd) | Madu Lake |
| | Lt. J.P. Austin | u/i a/c dam(grd) | Pyritz |
| | Lt. W.P. Boulet | FW-44 dam(grd) | S/Madu Lake |
| 357th: | Lt. D.D. McCasland | (2)Ju-88 dest(grd) | Wensdorf A/F |
| | | FW-190 dam(grd) | Wensdorf A/F |
| | Capt. W.S. Easterly | Ju-88 dest(grd) | Wensdorf A/F |
| | Lt. D.E. Schoenfeldt | Ju-88 dest(grd) | Wensdorf A/F |
| | | (2)Ju-88 dam(grd) | Wensdorf A/F |
| 358th: | Maj. R.B. Myers | Me-410 dest(air) | W/Berlin |
| | Capt. E.L. Sluga | Me-109 dest(air) | NE Berlin |
| | | Me-109 dam(air) | NE Berlin |
| | Lt. J.E. Reed | Me-109 dest(air) | N/Berlin |
| | F/O L.M. Dudley | (1.25)Me-410 dest(air) | NE Berlin |
| | | (.25)Ju-88 dest(air) | NE Berlin |
| | Lt. D.M. Martyn | (.25)Me-410 dest(air) | NE Berlin |
| | | (.25)Ju-88 dest(air) | NE Berlin |
| | Lt. R.J. Fussell | (.5)Me-410 dest(air) | NE Berlin |
| | | (.25)Me-410 dest(air) | NE Berlin |
| | | (.25)Ju-88 dest(air) | NE Berlin |
| | Lt. W.V. Gresham | (.5)Me-410 dest(air) | NE Berlin |
| | | (.25)Me-410 dest(air) | NE Berlin |
| | | (.25)Ju-88 dest(air) | NE Berlin |

**356th**

| | Pilot | Claim | Location |
|---|---|---|---|
| HdQts: | Col. E.A. Malmstrom | (2)Me-110 dest(grd) | Gifhorn |
| | | (.25)Me-109 dest(grd) | Gifhorn |
| | | (.25)Ju-88 dest(grd) | Gifhorn |
| 361st: | Lt. R.H. Gansberg | (2)Me-110 dest(grd) | Gifhorn |
| | | (2)Ju-88 dest(grd) | Gifhorn |
| | Lt. S.H. Hewett | (2)Ju-88 dest(grd) | Gifhorn |
| | | (.5)FW-190 dest(grd) | Gifhorn |
| | | Ju-52 dam(grd) | Gifhorn |
| | Lt. E.M. Parham | Ju-88 dest(grd) | Gifhorn |
| | | (.5)FW-190 dest(grd) | Gifhorn |
| | Lt. W.W. Burns | Ju-88 dest(grd) | Gifhorn |
| | | u/i a/c dam(grd) | Gifhorn |
| | F/O E.L. Decker | (.25)Me-109 dest(grd) | Gifhorn |
| | | (.25)Ju-88 dest(grd) | Gifhorn |
| | Lt. R. Gibson | (.25)Me-109 dest(grd) | Gifhorn |
| | | (.25)Ju-88 dest(grd) | Gifhorn |
| | Lt. J.V. Jack | (.25)Me-109 dest(grd) | Gifhorn |
| | | (.25)Ju-88 dest(grd) | Gifhorn |
| | Lt. H.C. Leyser | u/i a/c dam(grd) | Gifhorn |

**357th**

| | Pilot | Claim | Location |
|---|---|---|---|
| 362nd: | Lt. F.E. Adams | (2)Me-109 dest(air) | N/Magdeburg |
| | Lt. G.M. O'Brien | Me-109 dest(air) | Magdeburg |
| | | (2)Me-109 dam(air) | Magdeburg |
| | Lt. J.F. Pugh | Me-109 dest(air) | Magdeburg |
| | Lt. A.J. Roberson | Me-109 dest(air) | E/Magdeburg |
| | Lt. H.R. Ankeny | (.5)Me-109 dest(air) | NE Magdeburg |
| | Lt. J.B. England | (.5)Me-109 dest(air) | NE Magdeburg |
| | Capt. C.L. Williams | FW-190 dam(air) | N/Magdeburg |
| | Lt. J.E. Roughgarden | FW-190 dam(air) | NE Magdeburg |
| 363rd: | Capt. C.E. Anderson | Me-109 dest(air) | W/Hanover |
| | | (.25)He-111 dest(air) | W/Hanover |
| | | Me-109 dam(air) | W/Hanover |
| | Lt. H.R. Kayser | Me-109 dest(air) | W/Hanover |
| | | (.25)He-111 dest(air) | W/Hanover |
| | Lt. E.K. Simpson | Me-109 dest(air) | W/Hanover |
| | | (.25)He-111 dest(air) | W/Hanover |
| | Capt. P.K. DeVries | Me-109 dest(air) | W/Magdeburg |
| | Capt. M.H. Throop | FW-190 dest(air) | N/Hanover |
| | Lt. H.M. Kenney | FW-190 dest(air) | Steinhuder Lake |
| | | FW-190 dam(air) | Steinhuder Lake |
| | Lt. C.K. Peters | Me-109 dest(air) | Magdeburg |
| | Lt. W.B. Overstreet | (.25)He-111 dest(air) | W/Hanover |
| | | (3)Me-109 dam(air) | W/Hanover |
| | Lt. D.H. Bochkay | (.5)Me-109 dest(air)* | Magdeburg |
| 364th: | Lt. J.B. Carder | Me-109 dest(air) | NE Leipzig |
| | Lt. H.R. Nowlin | Me-109 dest(air) | Hanover |
| | Lt. R.A. Peterson | Me-109 dest(air) | Magdeburg |
| | Lt. W.C. Reese | Me-109 dest(air) | E/Hanover |
| | Lt. R.M. Shaw | Me-109 dest(air) | NE Brunswick |
| | Lt. Rob C. Smith | Me-109 dest(air) | NE Magdeburg |
| | Lt. L.A. Ruder | FW-190 dest(air) | NE Brunswick |
| | Lt. M.A. Postle | (.5)Me-109 dest(air)* | Magdeburg |
| | Lt. M.H. Stepelton | (.5)FW-190 dest(air) | Leipzig |
| | Lt. C.D. Sumner | (.5)FW-190 dest(air) | Leipzig |
| | Lt. H.H. Hermanson | Me-109 dam(air) | NW Hanover |

**359th**

| | Pilot | Claim | Location |
|---|---|---|---|
| 370th: | Lt. G.A. Doersch | FW-190 dest(air) | Brunswick |
| | Lt. E.N. Dunlap | FW-190 dest(air) | Fallersleben |
| | | FW-190 dam(air) | Fallersleben |
| | Capt. S.R. Smith | FW-190 prob(air) | Gutersloh |
| | | (2)FW-190 dest(grd) | Gutersloh |
| | | FW-190 dam(grd) | Gutersloh |
| | Lt. R.E. Kibler | Me-109 dam(air) | Fallersleben |
| | Lt. W.D. Burgsteiner | (4)FW-190 dest(grd) | Gutersloh |
| | | FW-190 dam(grd) | Gutersloh |
| | Lt. R.S. Wetmore | (2)Ju-88 dest(grd) | Volkenrod |
| | | Ju-88 dam(grd) | Volkenrod |
| | Capt. D.D. McKee | Ju-88 dest(grd) | Volkenrod |
| | | (2)Ju-88 dam(grd) | Volkenrod |
| | Lt. V.W. Ambrose | Ju-88 dest(grd) | Gutersloh |
| | Lt. J.E. Shupe | Ju-88 dest(grd) | Volkenrod |
| | | Ju-88 dam(grd) | Volkenrod |
| | Lt. H.D. Hollis | Ju-88 dest(grd) | Volkenrod |
| | Lt. R.M. Callahan | (5)FW-190 dam(grd) | Gutersloh |
| | Lt. R.M. Borg | (2)u/i a/c dam(grd) | Volkenrod |
| | Lt. A.C. Porter | Ju-88 dam(grd) | Volkenrod |

**364th**

| | Pilot | Claim | Location |
|---|---|---|---|
| 383rd: | Lt. E.E. Bankey | Me-109 dest(air) | Halberstadt |
| | Lt. N.F. Bettin | Me-109 prob(air) | Halberstadt |
| | Lt. B.B. Wilson | Me-109 dam(air) | Halberstadt |

*Losses-*

**78th:** F/O William H. Reese (83rd Ftr Sqn) KIA
P-47C HL-A 41-6210
Hit by flak near Lingen.

**352nd:** Lt. Alfred L. Marshall (486th Ftr Sqn) KIA
P-51B PZ-Q 43-7031 "Sweet Chariot"
Hit by flak and bailed out south of Hanover.

**355th:** Capt. Curtis G. Johnston (354th Ftr Sqn) POW
P-51B WR-O 43-6944
Hit by flak near Sorau.

Capt. William S. Easterly (357th Ftr Sqn) POW
P-51B OS-J 43-6627 "Brenda"
Hit by flak at Wensdorf Airfield.

**356th:** Capt. Hunter D. Parker (360th Ftr Sqn) POW
P-47D PI-G 42-76449
Hit by flak southeast of Dummer Lake.

Lt. Ernest M. Parham (361st Ftr Sqn) KIA
P-47D QI-O 42-76126
Hit by flak at Gifhorn Airfield.

**357th:** Capt. Arthur M. Lingo (362nd Ftr Sqn) KIA
P-51B G4-M 43-12122
Hit by enemy fighters northeast of Magdeburg.

Capt. George D. Currie (364th Ftr Sqn) POW
P-51B C5- 43-6773
Hit by enemy fighters near Brunswick.

Lt. William A. Gray (364th Ftr Sqn) POW
P-51B C5- 43-6515
Suffered mechanical failure and bailed out north of Hanover.

**359th:** Lt. James R. Pino (368th Ftr Sqn) POW
P-47D CV-I 42-75141
Engine froze and bellied-in near Volkenrod.

Lt. Elmer N. Dunlap (370th Ftr Sqn) POW
P-47D CS- 42-75079
Hit by a Me-109 near Fallersleben.

Lt. Thomas P. Smith (370th Ftr Sqn) MIA-E
P-47D CS-P 42-74737
Ran out of fuel and bailed out near Bielefeld.

*Remarks*

56th: 2-4 locos, 2-3 boats, 0-4 buildings
78th: 8-3 locos, 0-4 flak towers, 0-4 buildings, 0-2 barracks
352nd: 5-4 locos, 0-2 hangars, 0-3 buildings
355th: 0-5 locos, 0-1 hangar
P-51 c/l; o.k.
356th: 2-6 locos, 4-6 railcars, 0-2 hangars
357th: 2-2 locos, 0-1 barge, 0-1 factory
364th: 0-1 flak tower, 0-1 barracks, 0-2 buildings

**April 12, 1944**

Groups Operating: P-51 4th, 352nd, 355th, 357th
P-47 56th, 78th, 353rd, 353rd"C", 356th, 359th, 361st
P-38 20th, 55th, 364th

Missions: Support of bombers to Zwickau, Oschersleben, Halle, and Leipzig, plus eight pilots of the 357th flew a PRU escort to Munich.
Claims: 11-1-2 air
0-8 ground

| Group | | Claims | Location |
|---|---|---|---|
| **4th** | | | |
| 335th: | Lt. C.F. Anderson | (2)Me-109 dest(air) | NW Brunswick |
| | | Ju-88 dam(grd) | NW Brunswick |
| | Maj. G. Carpenter | Me-109 dest(air) | NW Brunswick |
| | | Ju-88 dam(grd) | NW Brunswick |
| | Lt. F.C. Jones | Me-109 dest(air) | Brunswick |
| **78th** | | | |
| 82nd: | Capt. J.J. Hockery | Ju-87 dest(air) | Sedan |
| | Lt. D.D. Hagarty | Ju-87 dest(air) | Sedan |
| | | Ju-87 dam(air) | Sedan |
| | Lt. J.T. Lamb | Ju-87 dest(air) | Sedan |
| | | Ju-87 dam(grd) | Sedan |
| | Lt. K.R. Wagner | FW-190 dest(air) | Malmedy |
| | Lt. B.M. Watkins | Ju-87 dest(air) | Sedan |
| | | (3)Ju-87 dam(grd) | Sedan |
| | Maj. L.P. Marshall | (.33)FW-190 dest(air) | Malmedy |
| | Lt. R.L. Baker | (.33)FW-190 dest(air) | Malmedy |
| | Lt. G.J. Lundigan | (.33)FW-190 dest(air) | Malmedy |
| | Lt. J.W. Wilkinson | (2)Me-109 dam(grd) | Florennes |
| 84th: | Capt. Q.L. Brown | FW-190 dest(air) | Duren |
| **364th** | | | |
| 383rd: | Lt. M.W. Glascow | FW-190 prob(air) | E/Frankfurt |
| | Lt. C.A. Barnes | Me-109 dam(air) | N/Frankfurt |

*Losses-*

**20th**: Lt. James H. Corbet (79th Ftr Sqn) KIA
P-38J MC- 42-67862
Went down over Holland; was apparently flying with a 9th Air Force unit as 20th records make no mention of him on their mission.

**55th**: Lt. Elton S. Walters (38th Ftr Sqn) KIA
P-38J CG- 42-67730
Hit by flak and exploded off Ostend.

**357th**: Lt. Fred W. Reust (363rd Ftr Sqn) POW
P-51B B6- 43-6720
Suffered mechanical failure near Saalfield.

**364th**: Lt. Edmund Brennan (383rd Ftr Sqn) POW
P-38J N2- 42-67445
Hit by enemy fighters east of Frankfurt.

Lt. Theodore G. Bushnell (383rd Ftr Sqn) POW
P-38J N2- 42-104170
Hit by enemy fighters east of Frankfurt.

*Remarks*
56th: 2-0 locos, 0-17 barges, 3-3 tugs, 0-2 boats, 0-2 buildings, 2-13 barracks, 2-0 flak towers
353rd "C": 7-0 locos, 2-0 railcars
356th: 0-2 buildings
357th: 2-0 locos
361st: 0-6 locos, 0-12 barges, 0-2 tugs

**April 13, 1944**
Groups Operating: P-51 4th, 352nd(mixed), 355th, 357th
P-47 56th, 78th, 352nd, 353rd, 356th, 359th, 361st
P-38 20th, 55th, 364th
Missions: Support of bombers to Schweinfurt, Oberpfaffenhofen, and Augsburg.
Claims: 27-3-5 air
38-23 ground

| Group | | Claims | Location |
|---|---|---|---|
| **4th** | | | |
| 334th: | Capt. W.M. Sobanski | FW-190 dest(air) | Ludwigshafen |
| | Lt. N. Megura | FW-190 dest(air) | SE Mannheim |
| 335th: | Maj. G. Carpenter | FW-190 dest(air) | SW Schweinfurt |
| | Lt. P.W. McKennon | FW-190 dest(air) | SW Schweinfurt |
| 336th: | Lt. L.H. Norley | FW-190 dest(air) | Schweinfurt |
| **55th** | | | |
| 343rd: | Maj. D.W. Webb | Me-109 dam(air) | Donauworth |
| **56th** | | | |
| HdQts: | LtCol. D.C. Schilling | Me-109 dest(air) | Ludwigshafen |
| 61st: | Lt. R.S. Johnson | (2)FW-190 dest(air) | Kaiserlautern |
| 62nd: | Lt. M.K. Boyle | Me-109 dest(air) | Ludwigshafen |
| | Capt. J.H. Powers | Me-109 dam(air) | Ludwigshafen |
| **78th** | | | |
| 83rd: | Lt. A.M. Juchheim | FW-190 dest(air) | Beuchenbeuren |
| | | FW-190 dest(grd) | Beuchenbeuren |
| | Lt. C.M. Peal | FW-190 dest(air) | Beuchenbeuren |
| | Lt. G. Riccardo | FW-190 dam(air) | Korbach |
| | Lt. H.R. Zumwalt | FW-190 dam(air) | NE Trier |
| **352nd**(all P-51) | | | |
| 486th: | Lt. R.C. Frascotti | Me-110 dest(grd) | S/Stuttgart |
| | | FW-190 dest(grd) | S/Stuttgart |
| | Lt. W.W. Anderson | Hs-123 dest(grd) | S/Stuttgart |
| | Lt. F.A. Cutler | Me-109 dest(grd) | S/Stuttgart |
| | Lt. D.Y. Whinnem | He-111 dest(grd) | S/Stuttgart |
| | Capt. S.W. Andrew | (.5)He-111 dest(grd) | S/Stuttgart |
| | Lt. M.R. Cunningham | (.5)He-111 dest(grd) | S/Stuttgart |
| | Lt. K.S. Williams | He-111 dam(grd) | S/Stuttgart |
| 487th: | Lt. R.I. Ross | u/i a/c dest(air) | SE Stuttgart |
| | | u/i a/c dest(grd) | SE Stuttgart |
| | Maj. J.C. Meyer | (2)He-111 dest(grd) | SE Stuttgart |
| | | Ju-52 dest(grd) | SE Stuttgart |
| | Maj. G.E. Preddy | Bu-133 dest(grd) | SE Stuttgart |
| | Lt. G.T. Moran | Ju-88 dest(grd) | SE Stuttgart |
| | | FW-190 dam(grd) | SE Stuttgart |
| | Capt. J.R. Bennett | u/i a/c dam(grd) | SE Stuttgart |
| **355th** | | | |
| 354th: | Maj. C.H. Kinnard | (3)Ju-88 dest(grd) | Oberpfaffenhofen |
| | | Do-217 dest(grd) | Oberpfaffenhofen |
| | | Do-217 dam(grd) | Oberpfaffenhofen |
| | Lt. R.C. Brown | (2)Ju-88 dest(grd) | Oberpfaffenhofen |
| | Lt. H.W. Brown | (2)Ju-88 dest(grd) | Oberpfaffenhofen |
| | Lt. R.S. Morris | (2)Do-217 dest(grd) | Oberpfaffenhofen |
| | | Do-217 dam(grd) | Oberpfaffenhofen |
| | F/O C.R. Barger | Do-217 dest(grd) | Oberpfaffenhofen |
| | | Ju-88 dest(grd) | Oberpfaffenhofen |
| | | Do-217 dam(grd) | Oberpfaffenhofen |
| | | Ju-88 dam(grd) | Oberpfaffenhofen |
| | Lt. R.A. Browning | (2)Do-217 dest(grd) | Oberpfaffenhofen |
| | Lt. J.E. Duffy | Me-110 dest(grd) | Oberpfaffenhofen |
| | | Do-217 dest(grd) | Oberpfaffenhofen |
| | | (2)Me-210 dam(grd) | Oberpfaffenhofen |
| | | He-111 dam(grd) | Oberpfaffenhofen |
| | | Do-217 dam(grd) | Oberpfaffenhofen |
| | Lt. B.C. Williamson | (2)Do-217 dest(grd) | Oberpfaffenhofen |
| | | Do-217 dam(grd) | Oberpfaffenhofen |
| | | u/i a/c dam(grd) | Oberpfaffenhofen |
| | Capt. R.E. Woody | Me-110 dest(grd) | Oberpfaffenhofen |
| | | Me-110 dam(grd) | Oberpfaffenhofen |
| | Lt. W.P. Boulet | He-177 dest(grd) | Oberpfaffenhofen |
| | | Me-110 dam(grd) | Oberpfaffenhofen |
| 357th: | Maj. E.W. Szaniawski | Me-109 dest(air) | Augsburg |
| | | Me-109 prob(air) | Augsburg |
| | | Me-109 dam(air) | Augsburg |
| | | (.33)Me-110 dest(grd) | Crailsheim |
| | | (.33)Me-323 dest(grd) | Crailsheim |
| | Capt. H.S. Bille | Me-109 dest(air) | Augsburg |
| | | Me-323 dam(grd) | Crailsheim |
| | Capt. J.H. Wilson | Me-109 dest(air) | Augsburg |
| | | (.5)Me-323 dest(grd) | Crailsheim |
| | | Me-323 dam(grd) | Crailsheim |
| | Lt. H.K. Hillman | Me-109 dest(air) | Augsburg |
| | Lt. J.D. Sturm | Me-109 dest(air) | Augsburg |
| | | (.5)Me-323 dest(grd) | Crailsheim |
| | Capt. J.F. Kerch | Me-109 prob(air) | Augsburg |
| | | (.33)Me-323 dest(grd) | Crailsheim |
| | Lt. R.L. Norman | (.33)Me-110 dest(grd) | Crailsheim |
| | | (.33)Me-323 dest(grd) | Crailsheim |
| | Lt. R.T. DeMers | (.33)Me-110 dest(grd) | Crailsheim |
| 358th: | Maj. R.B. Myers | FW-190 dest(air) | Nordlingen |
| **356th** | | | |
| HdQts: | Capt. H.A. Ogden | Me-110 dest(grd) | Bischwiller A/F |
| | | (2)Me-110 dam(grd) | Bischwiller A/F |
| 361st: | Maj. E.H. Montgomery | (2)FW-190 dest(air) | Huy |
| | F/O E.L. Decker | Me-110 dest(grd) | Bischwiller A/F |
| | Lt. E.P. Lee | (4)He-111 dam(grd) | Hagenau |
| **357th** | | | |
| 362nd: | Lt. R.H. Becker | FW-190 dest(air) | S/Mannheim |
| | Lt. L.K. Carson | FW-190 dest(air) | NW Mannheim |
| | Lt. J.B. England | FW-190 dest(air) | W/Mannheim |
| 364th: | Capt. G.V. Davis | Me-109 dest(air) | Frankfurt |
| | Lt. M.A. Postle | Me-109 dest(air) | Luxembourg |
| | Lt. R.M. Shaw | Me-109 dest(air) | Frankfurt |
| | Lt. P.D. Fairweather | (.5)Me-109 dest(air) | Donauworth |
| | Lt. R.C. Smith | (.5)Me-109 dest(air) | Donauworth |
| | | Me-109 prob(air) | Frankfurt |

*Losses-*

**4th**: Capt. Vasseure F. Wynn (334th Ftr Sqn) POW
P-51B QP-X 43-7035
Hit by a FW-190 near Aschaffenburg.

Lt. Ralph W. Saunders (335th Ftr Sqn) KIA
P-51B WD-Z 43-6325
Hit by enemy fighters near Schweinfurt.

**55th**: Lt. Melvin A. Hawes (38th Ftr Sqn) ASR
P-38J CG-
Ditched in the Channel after mechanical failure.

**78th**: Lt. Donald R. Roberts (82nd Ftr Sqn) POW
P-47D MX-H 42-76074
Hit by a FW-190 north of Saarbrucken.

**359th**: Lt. Cecil R. Brown (368th Ftr Sqn) KIA
P-47D CV- 42-75104
Suffered mechanical failure and bailed out over the Channel.

**364th**: Lt. Walter F. Pogue (384th Ftr Sqn) KIA
P-38J 5Y-F 42-104195
Suffered mechanical failure near Liege.

*Remarks*
4th: Capt. Don S. Gentile (336th Ftr Sqn) c/l Debden; o.k.
P-51B VF-T 43-6913 "Shangri-La"
55th: Lt. Anthony Tinto (338th Ftr Sqn) c/l; o.k.
P-38J CL-
78th: 9-0 locos, 0-2 buildings
352nd: 0-3 locos, 1-1 hangars, 0-1 barracks, 0-1 flak tower
355th: 0-1 hangar, 0-1 barracks, 0-1 radar tower
356th: 2-1 tugs, 0-8 barges, 1-0 paddle-wheeler
357th: 0-1 tug

**April 15, 1944**
Groups Operating: P-51 4th, 352nd(mixed), 355th, 357th
P-47 56th, 78th, 352nd, 353rd, 356th, 359th, 361st
P-38 20th, 55th, 364th
Missions: Sweeps over Germany and Denmark.
Claims: 17-1-9 air
40-23 ground

| *Group* | | *Claims* | *Location* |
|---|---|---|---|
| **4th** | | | |
| 334th: | Lt. G.E. Montgomery | He-177 dest(grd) | Hagenow |
| | | Ju-88 dest(grd) | Hagenow |
| | Lt. H.J. Blanchfield | Ju-88 dest(grd) | Hagenow |
| | Capt. R.C. Care | (.5)Ju-88 dest(grd) | Magdeburg |
| | Lt. H.T. Biel | (.5)Ju-88 dest(grd) | Magdeburg |
| 335th: | Lt. C.F. Anderson | He-177 dest(grd) | Hagenow |
| | | He-177 dam(grd) | Hagenow |
| | Lt. F.C. Jones | He-177 dest(grd) | Hagenow |
| | Lt. A.L. Schlegel | He-177 dest(grd) | Hagenow |
| | Lt. M.G. Scarbrough | He-177 dam(grd) | Hagenow |
| 336th: | Lt. R.F. Nelson | Fi-156 dest(air) | Fassberg A/F |
| | | (2)He-177 dest(grd) | Fassberg A/F |
| | F/O F.W. Glover | Me-110 dest(grd) | Hagenow |
| | | u/i a/c dam(grd) | Hagenow |
| | Lt. W.W. Millikan | He-177 dest(grd) | Hagenow |
| | Lt. O.F. Lajeunesse | He-177 dam(grd) | NE Hanover |
| **55th** | | | |
| 38th: | Capt. G. Brown | FW-190 dest(air) | Munster |
| | | He-111 dest(air) | Munster |
| | Lt. D.E. Penn | Ju-88 dest(grd) | Osnabruck |
| **56th** | | | |
| HdQts: | Col. H. Zemke | (3)He-111 dest(grd) | Flensburg |
| | | (3)He-111 dam(grd) | Flensburg |
| 61st: | Capt. P.A. Conger | FW-190 dest(air) | Elmshorn |
| | F/O E.D. McMinn | He-111 dest(grd) | Flensburg |
| | | Me-210 dest(grd) | Flensburg |
| | | He-111 dam(grd) | Flensburg |
| | | Me-210 dam(grd) | Flensburg |
| | Capt. L.C. Smith | He-111 dest(grd) | Flensburg |
| | | He-111 dam(grd) | Flensburg |
| | Lt. E.A. Sisson | He-111 dest(grd) | Flensburg |
| | | (2)Me-410 dam(grd) | Flensburg |
| | Lt. H.R. Holtmeier | Ju-88 dam(grd) | Flensburg |
| 62nd: | Capt. F.J. Christensen | (2)Me-109 dest(air) | Altona |
| | Lt. W.P. Chattaway | FW-190 dest(air) | Altona |
| | | (2)FW-190 dam(air) | Altona |
| | Lt. J.E. Greene | (3)FW-190 dam(air) | N/Hamburg |
| | Lt. H.E. Gallagher | FW-190 dam(air) | Altona |
| | Lt. W.H. Merrill | FW-190 dam(air) | Altona |
| | Maj. L.A. Schreiber | He-111 dest(grd) | Schleswig |
| 63rd: | Lt. W.D. Johnson | (.5)FW-190 dest(air) | Flensburg-Husum |
| | | He-111 dam(grd) | Flensburg |
| | Lt. S.O. Stamps | (.5)FW-190 dest(air) | Flensburg-Husum |
| | | He-111 dam(grd) | Flensburg |
| | Lt. M.H. Becker | He-111 dest(grd) | Flensburg |
| | F/O S.J. Lowman | He-111 dest(grd) | Flensburg |
| | Lt. C.W. Reed | He-111 dest(grd) | Flensburg |
| **352nd** | | | |
| 328th: | Lt. W.W. Furr | Me-110 dest(grd) | Diepholz |
| 486th: | Lt. M.E. Corcoran | (2)FW-190 dest(air) | NE Vechta |
| | Lt. A.J. Wallace | (2)FW-190 dest(air) | NE Vechta |
| | LtCol. L.H. Richmond | FW-190 dest(air) | E/Vechta |
| | Lt. M.R. Cunningham | FW-190 dest(air) | NE Vechta |
| | Lt. H.J. Miklajcyck | FW-190 dest(air) | SE Vechta |
| | (Note - 328th Ftr Sqn flew P-47's, 486th Ftr Sqn flew P-51's) | | |
| **355th** | | | |
| 357th: | Capt. J.L. Elder | Me-109 dest(air) | E/Celle |
| | Lt. W.E. MacFarlane | u/i a/c dest(grd) | E/Celle |
| 358th: | Lt. J.N. McElroy | (5)Do-217 dest(grd) | Glienicke |
| | Maj. R.B. Myers | Do-217 dest(grd) | Glienicke |
| | Capt. L.J. Dissette | Do-217 dest(grd) | Glienicke |
| | | u/i a/c dam(grd) | Glienicke |
| | F/O J.M. Beckman | Do-217 dest(grd) | Glienicke |
| | | Do-217 dam(grd) | Glienicke |
| | Lt. P.H. Kenney | Do-217 dest(grd) | Glienicke |
| | F/O J.S. MacConkey | Do-217 dest(grd) | Glienicke |
| | | Do-217 dam(grd) | Glienicke |
| | Lt. T.H. Worth | Me-110 dam(grd) | Glienicke |
| **359th** | | | |
| 370th: | Lt. G.A. Doersch | Ju-88 dam(air) | Varel |
| | Lt. R.M. Callahan | Ju-88 dest(grd) | Oldenburg |
| | Lt. H.D. Hollis | Ju-88 dest(grd) | Oldenburg |
| | Capt. D.D. McKee | (2)Ju-88 dam(grd) | Oldenburg |
| **361st** | | | |
| 375th: | Lt. W.A. Rautenbush | u/i a/c dest(grd) | Fritzlar A/F |
| | | (.33)Ju-52 dest(grd) | Fritzlar A/F |
| | Capt. J.W. Guckeyson | (.33)Ju-52 dest(grd) | Fritzlar A/F |
| | Lt. S.D. Rames | (.33)Ju-52 dest(grd) | Fritzlar A/F |
| **364th** | | | |
| 383rd: | Maj. G.F. Ceuleers | (.5)Me-109 dest(air) | SE Bremen |
| | Lt. L.S. Ayoub | (.5)Me-109 dest(air) | SE Bremen |
| | Lt. H.B. Saylor | Me-109 prob(air) | W/Hamburg |
| 384th: | Capt. R.E. Lacy | (.33)BV-138 dest(grd) | Elbe Estuary |
| | Capt. C.W. Stapleton | (.33)BV-138 dest(grd) | Elbe Estuary |
| | Lt. D.J. Pick | (.33)BV-138 dest(grd) | Elbe Estuary |
| | Lt. F.J. Hoenselaar | Do-217 dam(grd) | Basbeck |
| | | Ju-52 dam(grd) | Basbeck |
| 385th: | Lt. W.L. Poore | Me-109 dam(air) | Vechta |

*Losses-*

**4th**: Capt. Raymond C. Care (334th Ftr Sqn) POW
P-51B QP-R 43-7183
Hit by flak near Celle.

Lt. Robert H. Seifert (336th Ftr Sqn) KIA
P-51B VF- 43-6818
Suffered mechanical failure and bailed out over the Channel.

**55th**: Lt. Julius M. Hummel (38th Ftr Sqn) POW
P-38J CG- 42-68157
Hit by flak near Osnabruck.

Lt. William Laubner (38th Ftr Sqn) KIA
P-38J CG- 42-68079
Hit by flak near Osnabruck.

Lt. Tunis J. Lyon (338th Ftr Sqn) KIA
P-38J CL- 42-67413
Hit by flak and bellied-in near Herford.

**56th**: Capt. Dick H. Mudge (61st Ftr Sqn) POW
P-47D HV-X 42-8691
Hit by flak south of Eggebeck.

Maj. Leroy A. Schreiber (62nd Ftr Sqn) KIA
P-47D LM-T 42-25577
Hit by flak at Flensburg Airfield.

Capt. Charles R. Harrison (62nd Ftr Sqn) KIA
P-47D LM-H 42-75388
Hit by a FW-190 west of Hamburg.

**78th**: Capt. Charles W. Silsby (84th Ftr Sqn) KIA
P-47D WZ-A 42-25537
Last seen in heavy overcast over the North Sea.

F/O Joseph W. Mundy (84th Ftr Sqn) KIA
P-47D WZ-V 42-76412
Last seen in heavy overcast over the North Sea.

**352nd**: Lt. Fremont W. Miller (328th Ftr Sqn) ASR
P-47D PE-W 42-8511 "Red Raider"
Hit by flak and bailed out over the Channel; was rescued on April 18.

LtCol. Luther H. Richmond (486th Ftr Sqn) POW
P-51B PZ-R 43-7196 "Sweetie II"
Hit by flak near Vechta.

Lt. Robert I. Ross (487th Ftr Sqn) KIA
P-51B HO-R 43-7192
Hit by flak in the Diepholz-Vechta area and spun-into the North Sea.

**355th**: Capt. Walter J. Koraleski (354th Ftr Sqn) POW
P-51B WR-L 43-6968 "Miss Thunder"
Lost coolant and bailed out near Utrecht.

Capt. Joseph F. Kerch (357th Ftr Sqn) POW
P-51B OS-U 42-106698 "Bea"
Hit by flak near Wagonhof Airfield.

Lt. Darwin D. McCasland (357th Ftr Sqn) POW
P-51B OS-M 43-6525
Hit by flak near Wagonhof Airfield.

Lt. Paul H. Kenney (358th Ftr Sqn) POW
P-51B YF-P 43-6925
Hit by flak near Wittstock.

**357th**: Lt. Maurice A. Postle (364th Ftr Sqn) POW
P-51B C5- 43-6413
Suffered mechanical failure near The Hague.

**361st**: Lt. John M. Bentley (376th Ftr Sqn) POW
P-47D E9- 42-22756
Collided with a P-47 near Rhenen.

**364th**: Capt. Orvil E. Myers (384th Ftr Sqn) KIA
P-38J 5Y-M 42-67737
Last seen in the Diepholz area.

Lt. Edward L. Henkle (384th Ftr Sqn) POW
P-38J 5Y- 42-104214
Last seen near Virden.

Lt. Fred F. Kingsbury (384th Ftr Sqn) KIA
P-38J 5Y- 42-67240
Last seen near Virden.

Lt. Willard E. Moore (384th Ftr Sqn) POW
P-38J 5Y- 42-68148
Hit by flak at Stade Airfield.

Capt. Reed H. Dominy (385th Ftr Sqn) KIA
P-38J 5E- 42-67938
Hit by flak north of Dummer Lake and crashed near Vechta.

Capt. Robert B. Reynolds (385th Ftr Sqn) KIA
P-38J 5E- 42-68041
Hit by flak southeast of Bremen.

Lt. William J. Sims (385th Ftr Sqn) POW
P-38J 5E- 42-67851
Hit by flak north of Dummer Lake and crashed near Vechta.

Lt. Clyde M. Street (385th Ftr Sqn) KIA
P-38J 5E- 42-67302
Bailed out forty miles southeast of Great Yarmouth.

*Remarks*
4th: 1-2 locos, 0-2 gun positions
55th: 10-4 locos, 1-2 vehicles, 2-2 barges, 0-6 buildings, 0-1 flak tower
56th: 1-7 locos, 0-4 hangars, 0-5 buildings, 0-3 flak towers
352nd: 2-5 locos, 0-3 hangars, 0-1 boat
355th: 0-6 locos, 0-5 gun positions, 0-1 hangar, 0-1 building
359th: 1-0 loco, 0-3 barracks, 0-2 flak towers, 0-3 radar stations
361st: 0-19 vehicles, 0-10 huts, 0-1 hangar
364th: 4-11 locos, 0-7 buildings, 0-4 flak towers, 0-1 vehicle, 0-4 radar stations

KIAc's
78th: Lt. Martin G. O'Connell, Jr. (83rd Ftr Sqn)
P-47D HL-O 42-76474
Died in a crash near Duxford.

**April 17, 1944**
Groups Operating: P-47 353rd
Missions: Support of bombers to Wizernes V-1 sites.
Claims: nil
Losses: nil

**April 18, 1944**
Groups Operating: P-51 4th, 352nd, 355th, 357th
P-47 56th, 78th, 353rd, 356th, 359th, 361st
P-38 20th, 55th, 364th
Missions: Support of bombers to Oranienburg, Brandenburg, and Rathenow.
Claims: 5-0-0 air
16-13 ground

| *Group* | | *Claims* | *Location* |
|---|---|---|---|
| **4th** | | | |
| HdQts: | Col. D.J.M. Blakeslee | He-177 dest(grd) | Fassberg A/F |
| | | u/i a/c dam(grd) | Fassberg A/F |
| 334th: | Capt. V.J. France | (.33)Me-109 dest(air) | Fassberg A/F |
| | Lt. N. Megura | (.33)Me-109 dest(air) | Fassberg A/F |
| | | Ju-88 dam(grd) | Brandenburg |
| | | u/i a/c dam(grd) | Brandenburg |
| | Lt. G.C. Siems | (.33)Me-109 dest(air) | Fassberg A/F |
| | | u/i a/c dam(grd) | Fassberg A/F |
| | F/O R.K. Hofer | (2)He-177 dest(grd) | Fassberg A/F |
| | Lt. R.P. Kenyon | He-111 dest(grd) | Fassberg A/F |
| | Lt. D.W. Howe | (2)Ju-52 dest(grd) | Juterbog A/F |
| | | (.25) of(6)Ju-52 dam(grd) | Juterbog A/F |
| | Lt. J.L. Lang | (3)Ju-52 dest(grd) | Juterbog A/F |
| | | (.25) of(6)Ju-52 dam(grd) | Juterbog A/F |
| | Lt. S.W. Monroe | (2)Ju-52 dest(grd) | Juterbog A/F |
| | | (.25) of(6)Ju-52 dam(grd) | Juterbog A/F |
| | Lt. D.M. Malmsten | Ju-52 dest(grd) | Juterbog A/F |
| | | (.25) of(6)Ju-52 dam(grd) | Juterbog A/F |
| 335th: | Maj. G. Carpenter | Me 109 dest(air) | Rathenow-Nauen |
| | | FW-190 dest(air) | Rathenow-Nauen |
| | Lt. P.W. McKennon | FW-190 dest(air) | Rathenow |
| 336th: | Lt. D.R. Emerson | Me-109 dest(air) | Wenzendorf A/F |
| | Lt. R.F. Nelson | Me-109 dest(grd) | Genthin A/F |
| | | Me-109 dam(grd) | Genthin A/F |
| | | Ju-88 dam(grd) | Genthin A/F |
| | | u/i a/c dam(grd) | Genthin A/F |
| | Lt. G.H. Logan | (.5)FW-190 dest(grd) | Wenzendorf A/F |
| | Lt. N. Van Wyk | (.5)FW-190 dest(grd) | Wenzendorf A/F |
| **361st** | | | |
| 375th: | Maj. G.L. Merritt | Ju-88 dest(air) | Zwischenaschmer |
| | Lt. M.H. Johnson | Ar-196 dest(grd) | Zwischenaschmer |

*Losses-*

**4th**: Capt. Victor J. France (334th Ftr Sqn) KIA
P-51B QP-K 43-6832 "Miss Dallas"
Hit the ground while chasing a Me-109 near Stendal.

Maj. George Carpenter (335th Ftr Sqn) POW
P-51B WD-I 42-106675
Hit by a Me-109 near Rathenow.

Lt. Lloyd F. Henry (335th Ftr Sqn) KIA
P-51B WD-S 43-6579 "Snafu"
Hit by enemy fighters near Berlin.

**20th**: Lt. Leland K. Henslee (55th Ftr Sqn) KIA
P-38J KI-U 42-68126
An engine blew up and he bailed out twenty-five miles off the Belgian coast.

**361st**: Lt. Scott L. Naedle (HdQts) POW
P-47D E2- 42-75122
Hit by flak near Zwischenahn Airfield.

*Remarks*
[illegible]: [illegible] locos, [illegible] railcars, 0-1 flak tower
20th: Lt. John F. Dyer (55th Ftr Sqn) b/o; injured
P-38J KI- 42-104312
55th: P-38 c/l Southwold; o.k.
P-38 c/l Nuthampstead; o.k.
353rd: 0-2 locos
355th: 0-1 loco
361st: 2-2 locos, 0-1 control tower

**April 19, 1944**
Groups Operating: P-51 4th, 352nd(mixed), 355th, 357th
P-47 56th, 78th, 352nd, 353rd, 356th, 359th, 361st
P-38 20th, 55th, 364th
Missions: Support of bombers to Kassel, Lippstadt, and Paderborn.
Claims: 16-1-2 air
0-0 ground

| *Group* | | *Claims* | *Location* |
|---|---|---|---|
| **4th** | | | |
| 334th: | Lt. R.P. Kenyon | Me-109 dest(air) | Eschwege |
| | Lt. N. Megura | (.5)FW-190 dest(air) | Eschwege |
| | Lt. M.H. Kolter | Me-109 prob(air) | Eschwege-Kassel |

| | | | |
|---|---|---|---|
| 335th: | Lt. B.L. McGrattan | Me-109 dest(air) | Eschwege |
| | | (.5)FW-190 dest(air) | Eschwege |
| | Lt. P.W. McKennon | Me-109 dest(air) | Eschwege |
| 336th: | Lt. W.W. Millikan | Me-109 dest(air) | NE Eschwege |
| **352nd**(all P-51) | | | |
| 328th: | Lt. J.F. Thornell | (2)FW-190 dest(air) | SW Kassel |
| | | FW-190 dam(air) | SW Kassel |
| 486th: | Lt. D.W. McKibben | Me-109 dest(air) | SE Kassel |
| **355th** | | | |
| 354th: | Capt. R.E. Woody | Me-109 dest(air) | Nordhausen |
| 358th: | Lt. R.J. Fussell | FW-190 dest(air) | SW Brunswick |
| | Lt. T.O. Meteyer | Me-109 dest(air) | SW Brunswick |
| | Lt. J.N. McElroy | Me-109 dam(air) | SW Brunswick |
| **357th** | | | |
| HdQts: | Maj. T.L. Hayes | Me-109 dest(air) | S/Kassel |
| 364th: | Capt. G.V. Davis | FW-190 dest(air) | S/Bleicherode |
| | Lt. J.B. Carder | Me-109 dest(air) | SE Kassel |
| | Lt. T.L. Harris | FW-190 dest(air) | S/Bliecherode |
| | Lt. M.A. Stanley | FW-190 dest(air) | S/Bliecherode |

*Losses-*

**4th**: Capt. Charles F. Anderson (335th Ftr Sqn) KIA
P-51B WD-L 43-7181
Suffered mechanical failure and was last seen over Belgium.

**355th**: F/O Jack S. MacConkey (358th Ftr Sqn) KIA
P-51B YF-L 43-7156 "Slugger"
Hit by a Me-109 near Gottingen.

*Remarks*
353rd: 1-0 loco
359th: 1-4 locos, 1-0 flak tower
361st: 0-1 loco

**April 20, 1944**
Groups Operating: P-51 4th, 352nd, 355th
P-47 56th, 353rd, 356th, 359th, 361st
P-38 20th, 364th
Missions: Support for bombers hitting V-1 sites in the Pas de Calais area.
Claims: 4-0-1 air
3-1 ground

| ***Group*** | | ***Claims*** | ***Location*** |
|---|---|---|---|
| **56th** | | | |
| 62nd: | Capt. F.D. Williamson | (.5)Ju-88 dest(air) | NE Paris |
| | Lt. W.A. McClure | (.5)Ju-88 dest(air) | NE Paris |
| **352nd** | | | |
| 486th: | Capt. S.W. Andrew | Me-109 dest(air) | E/Paris |
| 487th: | Lt. C.J. Luksic | (1.5)Me-109 dest(air) | SE Paris |
| | Lt. A. Bielok | (.5)Me-109 dest(air) | SE Paris |
| | Maj. G.E. Preddy | Me-109 dam(air) | Beauvais-Chartres |
| **355th** | | | |
| 354th: | Capt. R.G. Kurtz | He-111 dest(grd) | Blois A/F |
| | | Ju-52 dest(grd) | Blois A/F |
| | Lt. B.G. Houston | FW-190 dest(grd) | Blois A/F |
| | Lt. R.A. Browning | Ju-88 dam(grd) | Blois A/F |

Losses: nil

*Remarks*
4th: Lt. Robert H. Homuth (335th Ftr Sqn) c/l; o.k.
P-51B WD-R
352nd: 0-1 flak position

Groups Operating: P-51 357th
P-47 78th
Missions: The 357th dive-bombed Cambrai/Epinoy and Vitry Airfields with the 78th giving area cover.
Claims: nil
Losses: nil

Groups Operating: P-47 78th
P-38 55th
Missions: The 55th was to attack St. Trond Airfield but was recalled.
Claims: nil
Losses: nil

**April 22, 1944**
Groups Operating: P-51 4th, 352nd(mixed), 355th, 357th
P-47 56th, 78th, 352nd, 353rd, 356th, 359th, 361st
P-38 20th, 55th, 364th
Missions: Support of bombers to Hamm plus eight pilots from the 20th flew an ASR search.
Claims: 32-1-3 air
6-7 ground

| ***Group*** | | ***Claims*** | ***Location*** |
|---|---|---|---|
| **4th** | | | |
| HdQts: | Col. D.J.M. Blakeslee | (2)Me-109 dest(air) | Kassel |
| 334th: | Lt. W.B. Smith | (.5)Me-109 dest(air)* | SW Kassel |
| 335th: | Capt. A.L. Schlegel | (2)Me-109 dest(air) | SW Kassel |
| | Lt. F.C. Jones | Me-109 dest(air) | Kassel |
| | Lt. P.S. Riley | (.5)Me-109 dest(air)* | SW Kassel |
| 336th: | Lt. W.W. Millikan | (4)Me-109 dest(air) | SW Kassel |
| | Lt. J.T. Godfrey | (3)Me-109 dest(air) | SW Kassel |
| | Lt. L.H. Norley | (2)Me-109 dest(air) | SW Kassel |
| | Lt. K.E. Carlson | (1.5)Me-109 dest(air)** | SW Kassel |
| | Lt. R. Simon | Me-109 dest(air) | SW Kassel |
| | Lt. D.R. Emerson | (.5)Me-109 dest(air)** | SW Kassel |
| **55th** | | | |
| 343rd: | Capt. R.L. Buttke | Me-109 dest(air) | W/Hamm |
| | | Me-109 dam(air) | W/Hamm |
| | Capt. E.E. Ryan | FW-190 dest(air) | W/Hamm |
| | Lt. G.R. Fair | Me-109 dest(air) | W/Hamm |
| **352nd**(all P-51) | | | |
| 328th: | Capt. J.B. Coleman | (.5)Me-210 dest(grd) | Dummer Lake |
| | Lt. Q.L. Quinn | (.5)Me-210 dest(grd) | Dummer Lake |
| | Capt. W.T. Halton | Ju-188 dam(grd) | Dummer Lake |
| 487th: | Maj. G.E. Preddy | (.33)Ju-88 dest(air) | Stade A/F |
| | | Ju-52 dest(grd) | Salzwedel |
| | Lt. D.R. Donohue | (.33)Ju-88 dest(air) | Stade A/F |
| | Lt. J.P. Kessler | (.33)Ju-88 dest(air) | Stade A/F |
| | LtCol. J.C. Meyer | Me-210 dest(grd) | Stade A/F |
| | | (2)He-111 dam(grd) | Stade A/F |
| | Capt. E.B. McMahan | Ju-88 dest(grd) | Stade A/F |
| | Capt. C.E. Davis | Ju-88 dest(grd) | N/Hanover |
| | | Ju-88 dam(grd) | N/Hanover |
| | Lt. W.E. Fowler | Me-110 dest(grd) | Hanover |
| | Capt. R.W. Hamilton | (3)He-111 dam(grd) | Salzwedel |
| **353rd** | | | |
| 351st: | Lt. H.K. Field | FW-190 dest(air) | N/Hamm |
| | Lt. H.F. Hunter | FW-190 prob(air) | N/Hamm |
| **357th** | | | |
| 362nd: | Capt. J.E. Broadhead | FW-190 dest(air) | N/Dummer Lake |
| | | FW-190 dam(air) | N/Dummer Lake |
| | Lt. G.M. O'Brien | FW-190 dest(air) | N/Dummer Lake |
| **359th** | | | |
| 369th: | Lt. R.J. Booth | FW-190 dest(air) | Hamm |
| | Lt. H.L. Matthew | FW-190 dest(air) | Ostbeuren |
| 370th: | Lt. R.E. Kibler | (2)FW-190 dest(air) | Hamm |
| | Lt. H.D. Hollis | FW-190 dest(air) | Hamm |
| | Lt. R.B. Lancaster | FW-190 dest(air) | Hamm |
| | | FW-190 dam(air) | Hamm |
| | Lt. R.S. Wetmore | FW-190 dest(air) | Hamm |

*Losses-*

**4th**: Lt. Robert F. Nelson (336th Ftr Sqn) POW
P-51B VF-Y 43-6802
Suffered mechanical failure southeast of Kassel.

**55th**: Capt. Bernie V. Guthrie (HdQts) KIA
P-38J CY-J 42-68048
Hit by a Me-109 near Waldbrol.

Lt. Clair A. Penners (343rd Ftr Sqn) POW
P-38J CY-Q 42-67966 "Little Man"
Hit by enemy fighters near Kirchunden.

**352nd**: Lt. Marion V. Long (328th Ftr Sqn) POW
P-51B PE-Y 42-106624 "Helen"
Hit by flak west of Lingen.

**353rd**: Lt. Paul J. Trudeau (351st Ftr Sqn) ASR
P-47D YJ-M 42-75114 "Boston Bull"
Bailed out over the North Sea and was rescued the next day.

**359th**: Lt. Earl W. Thomas, Jr. (370th Ftr Sqn) KIA
P-47D CS- 42-75263
Hit by enemy fighters near Hamm.

**361st**: Lt. James M. Norman, Jr. (374th Ftr Sqn) KIA
P-47D B7- 42-75521
Hit by flak and crashed off Zeebruggee Mole.

*Remarks*
20th: 2-0 locos, 0-2 steamers, 0-2 buildings
352nd: 11-7 locos, 1-1 railcars, 0-2 buildings, 0-1 flak position
353rd: 6-6 locos, 0-3 buildings
Lt. Robert P. Geurtz (352nd Ftr Sq) c/l; o.k.
P-47D SX-I 42-8390

355th: 0-7 locos, 0-17 railcars, 0-10 barges
356th: 1-12 locos, 0-16 barges, 1-1 tugs, 0-3 buildings
357th: 6-0 locos, 0-4 barges, 0-2 tugs
359th: 7-6 locos, 0-3 buildings, 0-1 barge, 0-1 tanker
361st: 1-0 loco
364th: 0-3 barges
Col. Roy W. Osborn (HdQts) b/o Honington; o.k.
P-38J N2- 42-104176

KIAc's
56th: Lt. George M. Bracken (61st Ftr Sqn)
P-47D HV- 42-75540

Lt. Archie H. Robey (63rd Ftr Sqn)
P-47D UN-P 42-8426
Crashed twenty miles off Orfordness while practicing dive-bombing.

**April 23, 1944**
Groups Operating: P-51 352nd, 357th
P-47 78th, 353rd, 356th, 359th, 361st
P-38 20th, 55th, 364th
Missions: Fighter-bomber operations in France, Belgium, and Germany. The 20th went to Tours and Chateaudun with the 352nd as escort; the 55th went to Laon Airfield with the 78th as escort; the 357th hit Leningen Airfield; the 359th went to Le Culot; the 361st hit Chievres and Denain/Prouvy; the 356th went to Hagenau; the 353rd went to Achmer/Bramsche; and the 364th provided three sections for PRU escort which were recalled before completing the missions.
Claims: 2-0-0 air
11-28 ground

| *Group* | | *Claims* | *Location* |
|---|---|---|---|
| **4th** | | | |
| 336th: | Maj. J.A. Goodson | (2)Me-109 dest(air) | Wienar Neustadt[*] |

[*] - was in Italy with the 15th Air Force breaking-in a P-51 unit.

| | | | |
|---|---|---|---|
| **20th** | | | |
| 55th: | Capt. R.M. Scrutchfield | He-111 dest(grd) | Chateaudun |
| | | (2)u/i a/c dam(grd) | Chateaudun |
| | | Ju-87 dam(grd) | Chateaudun |
| 79th: | Maj. R.C. Franklin | He-111 dest(grd) | Chateaudun |
| **352nd** | | | |
| 486th: | Lt. E.J. Meyer | Ju-88 dest(grd) | SE Paris |
| | | Me-110 dam(grd) | SE Paris |
| | Lt. D.W. McKibben | Ju-88 dest(grd) | SE Paris |
| | Lt. E.L. Heller | (.5)Ju-52 dest(grd) | SE Paris |
| | Lt. H.J. Miklajcyk | (.5)Ju-52 dest(grd) | SE Paris |
| **356th** | | | |
| HdQts: | Col. E.A. Malmstrom | (3)He-111 dest(grd) | Hagenau |
| | Capt. H.A. Ogden | He-111 dest(grd) | Hagenau |
| | | (.5)Go-242 dam(grd)[*] | Hagenau |
| | Maj. J.H. Thorne | (.5)He-111 dam(grd)[**] | Hagenau |
| 359th: | Lt. W.C. Brearley | Go-242 dam(grd) | Hagenau |
| | Lt. M.M. Clayborne | (.5)Go-242 dam(grd)[***] | Hagenau |
| | | (.5)He-111 dam(grd)[@] | Hagenau |
| | Lt. C.F. Krowiak | He-111 dam(grd) | Hagenau |
| | | (.5)Go-242 dam(grd)[@@] | Hagenau |
| | F/O F.A. Forsyth | (.5)Go-242 dam(grd)[*] | Hagenau |
| | Lt. R.B. Warren | (.5)He-111 dam(grd)[@] | Hagenau |
| | | (.5)Go-242 dam(grd)[***] | Hagenau |
| | Lt. R.J. Collins | (.5)He-111 dam(grd)[**] | Hagenau |
| | Lt. W.L. Farmer | (.5)Go-242 dam(grd)[@@] | Hagenau |
| 360th: | Lt. L.H. Knapp | He-111 dest(grd) | Hagenau |
| | | (1.5)Go-242 dam(grd)[#] | Hagenau |
| | Capt. L.F. Kress | (1.5)Go-242 dam(grd)[#] | Hagenau |
| | Lt. C.W. Adams | (.5)Go-242 dam(grd)[##] | Hagenau |
| | Lt. R.C. L'Heureux | (.5)Go-242 dam(grd)[##] | Hagenau |
| | Lt. V. Hockmeyer | (1.5)Go-242 dam(grd)[###] | Hagenau |
| | Lt. R.R. Withers | (1.5)Go-242 dam(grd)[###] | Hagenau |
| 361st: | F/O J.H. Culp | Me-109 dest(grd) | Hagenau |
| | Capt. J.P. Perrin | He-111 dam(grd) | Hagenau |
| | Lt. G.L. Yoakum | (2)Go-242 dam(grd) | Hagenau |
| | | Me-109 dam(grd) | Hagenau |
| | Lt. H.J. Kaczynski | (2)He-111 dam(grd) | Hagenau |
| | Lt. J.L. Bruce | Go-242 dam(grd) | Hagenau |
| | Lt. R.L. Campbell | He-111 dam(grd) | Hagenau |
| | Lt. E.C. Fremaux | He-111 dam(grd) | Hagenau |
| | Lt. R.H. Gansberg | He-111 dam(grd) | Hagenau |

*Losses-*

**20th**: Maj. Donald H. McAuley (55th Ftr Sqn) KIA
P-38J KI-A 42-67949 "Lil Henry"
Hit by flak at Chateaudun.

Lt. Robert W. Ahern (55th Ftr Sqn) KIA
P-38J KI-L 42-67885
Hit by flak near Valmeray.

**353rd**: Lt. Cletus W. Peterson (351st Ftr Sqn) POW
P-47D YJ-P 42-75149 "Double S"
Hit by ground fire and bailed out southeast of Lingen.

Capt. Jesse W. Gonnam (352nd Ftr Sqn) POW
P-47D SX-U 42-76394
Hit by flak at Achmer/Bramsche Airfield.

**356th**: Col. Einar A. Malmstrom (HdQts) POW
P-47D QI-R 42-25513 "Kay-J"
Hit by flak at Hagenau Airfield.

Lt. Daughtry L. Hall (360th Ftr Sqn) POW
P-47D PI- 42-75134
Hit by flak at Hagenau Airfield.

Lt. Henry J. Kaczynski (361st Ftr Sqn) POW
P-47D QI-Z 42-76570
Hit by flak at Hagenau Airfield.

*Remarks*
20th: 0-7 gun positions, 0-3 flak towers, 0-3 hangars, 0-1 barracks
Lt. Vernon M. Beesley (79th Ftr Sqn) c/l Poddington; o.k.
P-38J MC-H 42-67427
353rd: 2-0 locos, 0-1 railcar, 0-4 boats, 2-39 barges, 0-8 control towers
364th: P-38 c/l; o.k.

**April 24, 1944**
Groups Operating: P-51 4th, 352nd, 355th, 357th
P-47 56th, 78th, 353rd, 356th, 359th, 361st
P-38 20th, 55th, 364th
Missions: Support of bombers to various airfields and aviation industry targets in Germany.
Claims: 60-5-21 air
56-42 ground

| *Group* | | *Claims* | *Location* |
|---|---|---|---|
| **4th** | | | |
| HdQts: | Col. D.J.M. Blakeslee | (1.5)FW-190 dest(air) | N/Worms |
| | | FW-190 dam(air) | N/Worms |
| 334th: | Lt. N. Megura | (2)FW-190 dest(air) | S/Frankfurt |
| | | FW-190 dam(air) | S/Frankfurt |
| | Lt. D.W. Howe | Me-109 dest(air) | Darmstadt |
| | Lt. L.R. Pierce | FW-190 dam(air) | N/Frankfurt |
| 335th: | Capt. A.L. Schlegel | (2.5)FW-190 dest(air) | N/Worms |
| | Capt. J.R. Happel | FW-190 dest(air) | NE Worms |
| | Lt. P.S. Riley | FW-190 dest(air) | N/Mannheim |
| | | FW-190 prob(air) | N/Mannheim |
| | Lt. B.L. McGrattan | FW-190 dest(air) | Knocke |
| | Lt. L. Read | FW-190 dest(air) | N/Worms |
| | Lt. M.G. Scarbrough | FW-190 prob(air) | S/Mannheim |
| 336th: | Lt. J.T. Godfrey | FW-190 dest(air) | NW Ludwigshafen |
| | | FW-190 dam(air) | NW Ludwigshafen |
| | Lt. T.K. McDill | FW-190 dam(air) | NW Ludwigshafen |
| | Lt. C.J. Netting | FW-190 dam(air) | NW Ludwigshafen |
| **20th** | | | |
| 55th: | Capt. W.B. Taylor | Me-109 dest(air) | W/Worms |
| | Lt. W.G. Schultz | (1.5)Me-109 dest(air) | Worms |
| | Lt. R.P. Watson | Me-109 dest(air) | W/Worms |
| 77th: | Capt. D.A. Reihmer | (.5)Me-109 dest(air) | Worms |
| **55th** | | | |
| 343rd: | Lt. C.D. Porter | Me-109 dest(air) | NW Lake Constance |
| | Lt. A.A. DeYoung | Me-109 dam(air) | NW Lake Constance |
| **56th** | | | |
| HdQts: | Maj. J.C. Stewart | Ju-87 dest(grd) | Thronville A/F |
| | | Ju-87 dam(grd) | Thronville A/F |
| | | u/i a/c dam(grd) | Thronville A/F |
| 61st: | LtCol. F.S. Gabreski | He-111 dam(grd) | Frieburg A/F |
| 63rd: | Lt. W.E. Kerr | (2)Me-109 dest(grd) | Thalheim A/F |
| | | Me-110 dest(grd) | Thalheim A/F |
| | | Me-110 dam(grd) | Thalheim A/F |
| | Lt. J.A. Aranyos | Do-217 dest(grd) | Thalheim A/F |
| | | Me-109 dest(grd) | Thalheim A/F |
| | | Me-210 dam(grd) | Thalheim A/F |
| | | Do-217 dam(grd) | Thalheim A/F |
| | Lt. S.B. Dale | Me-109 dest(grd) | Thalheim A/F |
| | | FW-190 dest(grd) | Thalheim A/F |
| | | (.25)u/i a/c dam(grd) | Thalheim A/F |
| | Lt. D.V. Peters | Me-109 dest(grd) | Thalheim A/F |
| | | Me-210 dest(grd) | Thalheim A/F |
| | | (2)Me-109 dam(grd) | Thalheim A/F |
| | Capt. J.H. Truluck | Do-217 dest(grd) | Thalheim A/F |
| | | (3)Do-217 dam(grd) | Thalheim A/F |
| | Lt. H.F. Warner | Ju-87 dest(grd) | Thalheim A/F |
| | | (.25)u/i a/c dam(grd) | Thalheim A/F |
| | Lt. D.W. Marshall | (.5)Me-210 dest(grd) | Thalheim A/F |
| | | (1.25)u/i a/c dam(grd) | Thalheim A/F |
| | | Me-109 dam(grd) | Thalheim A/F |

| | | | |
|---|---|---|---|
| | Lt. A.J. Wisniewski | (.5)Me-210 dest(grd) | Thalheim A/F |
| | | Ju-87 dam(grd) | Thalheim A/F |
| | | (.25)u/i a/c dam(grd) | Thalheim A/F |
| **78th** | | | |
| 82nd: | Lt. J.E. Brasher | Do-217 dest(grd) | Diest |
| 83rd: | Lt. A.M. Juchheim | (.5)Me-110 dest(grd) | Trier |
| | | Me-110 dam(grd) | Trier |
| | Lt. V.J. Massa | (.5)Me-110 dest(grd) | Trier |
| | Lt. C.P. Hurst | Do-217 dam(grd) | Diest |
| | | u/i a/c dam(grd) | Diest |
| **352nd** | | | |
| 486th: | Lt. H.J. Miklajcyk | Ju-52 dest(air) | E/Neuburg |
| | | (3)Ju-88 dest(grd) | E/Neuburg |
| | Lt. E.L. Heller | (3)Me-110 dest(grd) | Crailsheim-Bokingen |
| | | (2)Ju-88 dest(grd) | Crail.-Bokingen |
| | | Ju-52 dest(grd) | Crail.-Bokingen |
| | | u/i a/c dest(grd) | Crail.-Bokingen |
| | | (4)Me-110 dam(grd) | Crail.-Bokingen |
| | | Ju-52 dam(grd) | Crail.-Bokingen |
| | Capt. R.G. McKean | (3)He-111 dest(grd) | Ingolstadt |
| | | (2)Ju-88 dest(grd) | Ingolstadt |
| | Lt. W.W. Anderson | (2)Ju-88 dest(grd) | Ingolstadt |
| | | Do-217 dest(grd) | Ingolstadt |
| | | He-111 dest(grd) | Neuburg |
| | Lt. T.W. Colby | (2)He-177 dest(grd) | Ingolstadt |
| | | u/i a/c dam(grd) | Ingolstadt |
| | Lt. C.V. Harker | Do-217 dest(grd) | Ingolstadt |
| | | Me-410 dest(grd) | Neuburg |
| | | Ju-88 dam(grd) | Neuburg |
| | Lt. A.J. Wallace | Do-217 dest(grd) | Neuburg |
| | | Ju-88 dest(grd) | Ingolstadt |
| | | (4)Ju-88 dam(grd) | Ingolstadt |
| | Lt. D.Y. Whinnem | (2)Ju-88 dest(grd) | Ingolstadt |
| | | (6)Ju-88 dam(grd) | Ingolstadt |
| | Capt. S.W. Andrew | u/i a/c dest(grd) | Neuburg |
| | | Ju-88 dam(grd) | Ingolstadt |
| | Lt. S.G. Miles | Me-110 dest(grd) | Ingolstadt |
| | | (3)u/i a/c dam(grd) | Ingolstadt |
| **353rd** | | | |
| 351st: | Capt. V.A. Leatherman | FW-190 prob(air) | Mannheim |
| | F/O R.M. Tumlin | FW-190 dam(air) | Mannheim |
| **355th** | | | |
| HdQts: | LtCol. G.J. Dix | FW-190 dest(air) | NE Augsburg |
| | | Me-109 dam(air) | NE Augsburg |
| 354th: | Capt. R.E. Woody | (4.5)Me-109 dest(air)* | SE Munich |
| | | Me-109 dam(air) | SE Munich |
| | Capt. H.B. Kucheman | (3)Me-109 dest(air) | NW Munich |
| | Lt. W.P. Boulet | (2.5)Me-109 dest(air)* | SE Munich |
| | | (.5)Me-109 dest(air)** | SE Munich |
| | | Me-109 dam(air) | SE Munich |
| | Lt. N.J. Fortier | (1.5)Me-109 dest(air)** | SE Munich |
| | | Me-109 dam(air) | SE Munich |
| | Lt. H.W. Brown | (2)Me-109 dest(air) | S/Munich |
| 357th: | Lt. R.F. DeMers | (2)Me-109 dest(air) | NE Munich |
| | Capt. H.S. Bille | FW-190 dest(air) | NW Munich |
| | Capt. J.H. Wilson | Me-109 dest(air) | NW Munich |
| | | Me-109 dam(air) | NW Munich |
| | Lt. R.B. Butler | (.5)Me-109 dest(air) | NE Munich |
| | Lt. E.P. McNeff | (.5)Me-109 dest(air) | NE Munich |
| | F/O M.A. King | Me-109 dam(air) | SW Munich |
| | Lt. L.D. Minchew | Me-109 dam(air) | SW Munich |
| **357th** | | | |
| 362nd: | Lt. F.E. Adams | (3)Me-110 dest(air) | Munich |
| | Lt. J.B. England | (3)Me-110 dest(air) | S/Munich |
| | Lt. H.E. Beal | (2)Me-110 dest(air) | E/Munich |
| | | Me-110 dam(air) | E/Munich |
| | Capt. F.C. Smith | Me-109 dest(air) | S/Munich |
| | Capt. C.L. Williams | Me-109 dest(air) | NW Munich |
| | Lt. F.J. Connaghan | Me-110 dest(air) | Munich |
| | Lt. A.E. Smith | Me-110 prob(air) | Munich |
| | | Me-110 dam(air) | Munich |
| | Lt. J.E. Roughgarden | (2)Me-110 dam(air) | E/Munich |
| | Lt. J.S. Coon | Me-110 dam(air) | E/Munich |
| | Lt. O.E. Harris | Me-110 dam(air) | E/Munich |
| 363rd: | Lt. J.F. Pierce | Me-109 dest(air) | W/Munich |
| | | Ju-88 dest(air) | W/Munich |
| | Capt. E.W. Hiro | Me-109 dest(air) | SE Munich |
| | Capt. M.H. Throop | Me-109 dest(air) | N/Munich |
| | Lt. D.H. Bochkay | Me-109 dest(air) | NE Munich |
| | Lt. J.W. Browning | Me-109 dest(air) | N/Augsburg |
| 364th: | Lt. J.B. Carder | Me-109 dest(air) | S/Munich |
| | Lt. T.M. McKinney | Me-109 dest(air) | N/Augsburg |
| | Lt. R.A. Peterson | Me-109 dest(air) | Munich |
| | Lt. W.C. Reese | Me-109 dest(air) | Munich |
| | Lt. C.D. Sumner | Me-109 dest(air) | Munich |
| | Lt. R.M. Shaw | Me-109 prob(air) | SE Munich |
| **359th** | | | |
| HdQts: | Capt. S.R. Smith | (1.33)u/i a/c dest(grd) | St. Dizier |
| 368th: | Capt. C.E. Mosse | (.5)u/i a/c dest(grd)* | St. Dizier |
| | Lt. R.E. Burton | (.5)u/i a/c dest(grd)** | St. Dizier |
| | Lt. R.B. Janney | (.5)u/i a/c dest(grd)** | St. Dizier |
| | Lt. A.T. Lemmens | (.5)u/i a/c dest(grd)* | St. Dizier |
| 370th: | Lt. P.H. Bateman | Me-109 dest(grd) | St. Dizier |
| | | (.33)u/i a/c dest(grd) | St. Dizier |
| | Lt. R.S. Wetmore | Me-109 dest(grd) | St. Dizier |
| | | (.33)u/i a/c dest(grd) | St. Dizier |
| | | Me-109 dam(grd) | St. Dizier |
| | Lt. A.C. Porter | Me-109 dest(grd) | St. Dizier |
| **361st** | | | |
| 375th: | Lt. M.H. Johnson | Me-109 dest(grd) | Metz |
| | | Me-110 dest(grd) | Metz |
| | | FW-190 dest(grd) | Metz |
| | Capt. D.C. Casto | Me-109 dest(grd) | Metz |
| | Lt. W.A. Rautenbush | Ju-88 dest(grd) | Metz |
| | Lt. D.R. Morehouse | He-111 dam(grd) | Metz |

*Losses-*

**4th:** Lt. Hipolitus T. Biel (334th Ftr Sqn) KIA
P-51B QP-X 42-106636
Hit by enemy fighters south of Darmstadt.

Lt. Paul S. Riley (335th Ftr Sqn) POW
P-51B WD-Y 43-6922
Collided with a FW-190 near Worms.

Lt. Milton G. Scarbrough (335th Ftr Sqn) POW
P-51B WD-F 43-6767
Hit by enemy fighters near Worms.

**352nd:** Capt. Robert G. MacKean (486th Ftr Sqn) KIA
P-51B PZ-Z 43-7198
Hit by flak and crashed near Lenting.

**353rd:** Lt. William C. Crampton (351st Ftr Sqn) POW
P-47D YJ- 42-75804
Hit by enemy fighters near Neustadt.

**355th:** Lt. Raymond F. DeMers (357th Ftr Sqn) KIA
P-51B OS-G 42-106723
Hit by flak near Bingen.

Lt. Howard K. Hillman (357th Ftr Sqn) KIA
P-51B OS-O 43-7103 "Miss Doris"
Hit by enemy fighters near Munich.

Lt. Robert L. Norman (357th Ftr Sqn) KIA
P-51B OS-R 42-106433
Hit by enemy fighters near Munich.

Lt. Jack D. Sturm (357th Ftr Sqn) POW
P-51B OS-N 43-7140
Hit by enemy fighters near Knocke.

**356th:** Lt. William B. Ingram (361st Ftr Sqn) POW
P-47D QI-H 43-25271
Ran out of fuel northwest of Lille.

**357th:** Lt. Frank J. Connaghan (362nd Ftr Sqn) KIA
P-51B G4-I 43-7176
Collided with a Me-110 near Munich.

Lt. Ralph H. Donnell (363rd Ftr Sqn) POW
P-51B B6- 43-6986
Collided with a Me-110 near Munich.

Lt. Howard S. Hinman (363rd Ftr Sqn) POW
P-51B B6- 43-6624
Hit by enemy fighters east of Munich.

Lt. Joseph F. Stager (364th Ftr Sqn) POW
P-51B C5- 42-106740
Hit by flak near Ludwigshafen and bailed out southeast of Strasbourg.

**364th:** Lt. Walter J. Shea (385th Ftr Sqn) KIA
P-38J 5E-
Suffered mechanical failure and crashed southeast of Risby.

*Remarks*

20th: 3-4 locos, 2-1 flak positions
55th: Lt. William R. Monty (38th Ftr Sqn) c/l Manston; o.k.
P-38J CG-
355th: 0-2 barges
359th: 2-0 hangars
361st: 0-2 hangars, 0-1 fuel dump
364th: 1-1 locos, 1-0 barge

**April 25, 1944**
Groups Operating: P-51 4th, 352nd, 355th, 357th
P-47 56th, 78th, 353rd, 356th, 359th, 361st
P-38 20th, 55th, 364th
Missions: Support of bombers to Dijon/Longvic and Metz/Frascaty Airfields, Mannheim, and Landau. The 55th also bombed Amiens/Glisy Airfield.
Claims: 3-0-0 air
13-5 ground

| *Group* | | *Claims* | *Location* |
|---|---|---|---|
| **56th** | | | |
| HdQts: | Col. H. Zemke | (2)Ju-88 dest(grd) | Metz |
| 61st: | F/O S. Gerick | Me-109 dest(grd) | Metz |
| | Capt. B.M. Gladych | FW-190 dam(grd) | Metz |
| | | Ju-88 dam(grd) | Metz |
| | | u/i a/c dam(grd) | Metz |
| | Lt. R.M. Heineman | Me-109 dam(grd) | Metz |
| **78th** | | | |
| 83rd: | Lt. K.C. Allstaedt | FW-190 dest(air) | S/Verdun |
| | Lt. H.J. Morris | (.5)FW-190 dest(air) | S/Verdun |
| | Lt. B.W. Sorenson | (.5)FW-190 dest(air) | S/Verdun |
| **352nd** | | | |
| 486th: | Capt. S.W. Andrew | Ju-88 dest(grd) | Metz |
| | Lt. M.R. Cunningham | Hs-129 dest(grd) | Metz |
| | Lt. C.V. Harker | Me-110 dest(grd) | Metz |
| | Lt. H.J. Miklajcyk | Hs-129 dest(grd) | Metz |
| | Lt. S.G. Miles | FW-190 dest(grd) | Metz |
| | Lt. A.J. Wallace | Hs-129 dest(grd) | Metz |
| **359th** | | | |
| 369th: | Lt. R.J. Booth | Me-109 dest(air) | Salmagne |
| 370th: | Lt. R.M. Callahan | FW-190 dest(grd) | Bar Le Duc |
| **361st** | | | |
| 375th: | Capt. J.W. Guckeyson | Fi-156 dest(grd) | Nancy |
| | | Ju-52 dest(grd) | Nancy |
| | Lt. E. Cole | FW-190 dest(grd) | Nancy |
| | | u/i a/c dam(grd) | Nancy |

Losses: nil

*Remarks*
56th: 0-1 loco, 0-2 hangars, 0-1 flak position
355th: 0-2 hangars
359th: 1-0 vehicle, 0-1 hangar, 0-1 flak position, 0-1 barracks
361st: 0-3 hangars, 0-1 radar station
364th: Lt. Donald S. Chaplin (385th Ftr Sqn) c/l Grisby; o.k.
P-38J 5E-

Groups Operating: P-47 359th
Missions: Support of bombers to Wizernes V-1 sites.
Claims: nil
Losses: nil

**April 26, 1944**
Groups Operating: P-51 4th, 352nd, 355th
P-47 56th, 78th, 353rd, 356th, 359th
P-38 20th, 364th
Missions: Support of bombers to Brunswick.
Claims: nil

*Losses-*

**355th**: Lt. William P. Boulet (354th Ftr Sqn) POW
P-51B WR-P 43-6948 Lottie II
Hit by fire from a B-17 near Clausthal.

**356th**: Lt. Richard B. Warren (359th Ftr Sqn) KIA
P-47D OC-S 42-75159
Collided with a P-47 near Bromeswell while preparing to land.

**364th**: Lt. Ira A. Whipple (385th Ftr Sqn) KIA
P-38J 5E- 42-68141
Suffered mechanical failure and crashed forty-five miles northeast of Manston.

Groups Operating: P-51 357th
P-47 361st
Missions: Sweeps and support fo bombers to Cologne.
Claims: 0-0-0 air
1-1 ground

| *Group* | | *Claims* | *Location* |
|---|---|---|---|
| **361st** | | | |
| 376th: | Capt. W.B. Frank | Ju-88 dest(grd) | Montdidier |
| | Lt. J.C. Stewart | Ju-88 dam(grd) | Montdidier |

Losses: nil

*Remarks*
361st: 0-1 vehicle, 0-1 barracks, 0-2 gun positions

Groups Operating: P-38 55th
Missions: Dive-bombing of Le Mans Airfield.
Claims: nil
Losses: nil

Groups Operating: P-51 352nd
Missions: Dive-bombing of the Cormeilles-en-Vixen area.
Claims: nil
Losses: nil

**April 27, 1944**
Groups Operating: P-51 357th
P-47 56th, 78th, 353rd, 359th, 361st
P-38 364th
Missions: Support of bombers to Pas de Calais and Cherbourg V-1 sites.
Claims: 0-0-0 air
0-3 ground

| *Group* | | *Claims* | *Location* |
|---|---|---|---|
| **361st** | | | |
| 375th: | Capt. J.W. Guckeyson | (2)He-111 dam(grd) | Etampes |
| | Capt. C.N. Keppler | He-111 dam(grd) | Etampes |

*Losses-*

**357th**: Lt. Ben F. Elliott, Jr. (364th Ftr Sqn) POW
P-51B C5- 42-106790
Suffered mechanical failure and bailed out north of Courtrai.

**361st**: Lt. Jack D. Cornett (375th Ftr Sqn) MIA-E
P-47D E2- 42-75219
Hit by flak southeast of Etampes/Montdidier Airfield.

*Remarks*
361st: 0-4 hangars, 0-1 building

Groups Operating: P-38 55th
Missions: Dive-bombing of Roye/Amy Airfield.
Claims: nil
Losses: nil

Groups Operating: P-38 20th
Missions: Dive-bombing of Albert/Meaulte Airfield.
Claims: nil
Losses: nil

*Remarks*
20th: 1-0 loco, 0-6 railcars, 0-3 buildings, 0-9 gun positions,
0-1 hangar, 0-1 flak position

Groups Operating: P-51 352nd
Missions: Dive-bombing of Cormeilles-en-Vixen Airfield.
Claims: nil
Losses: nil

Groups Operating: P-51 4th, 352nd, 355th, 357th
P-47 56th, 78th, 353rd, 356th, 359th, 361st
P-38 20th, 55th, 364th
Missions: Support of bombers to marshalling yards and airfields in France.
Claims: 4-0-1 air
3-1 ground

| *Group* | | *Claims* | *Location* |
|---|---|---|---|
| **4th** | | | |
| 335th: | Lt. L. Read | u/i a/c dest(grd) | Toul |
| **356th** | | | |
| HdQts: | Capt. H.A. Ogden | (.5)FW-190 dest(air) | Reims-Chateau Thierry |
| 359th: | Lt. R.K. Holtz | FW-190 dest(air) | Reims-Chateau Thierry |
| | Lt. R.J. Collins | (.5)FW-190 dest(air) | Reims-Chateau Thierry |
| 360th: | Lt. W.E. Leathers | FW-190 dest(air) | Laon |
| | Lt. D.B. Mercer | FW-190 dest(air) | Laon |
| | | FW-190 dam(air) | Laon |
| **361st** | | | |
| 375th: | Maj. G.L. Merritt | He-111 dest(grd) | Etampes |
| | Lt. J.S. Crandell | (.5)He-111 dest(grd) | Etampes |
| | Lt. S.D. Rames | (.5)He-111 dest(grd) | Etampes |
| | Capt. C.H. Feller | He-111 dam(grd) | Etampes |

*Losses-*

**356th**: Lt. Raymond K. Holtz (359th Ftr Sqn) MIA-E
P-47D OC-B 43-25557
Hit by a FW-190 near Laon.

Lt. Casimir F. Krowiak (359th Ftr Sqn) KIA
P-47D OC- 42-76220
Hit by a FW-190 northwest of Reims.

Capt. John B. Stratford, Jr. (360th Ftr Sqn) KIA
P-47D PI- 42-76135
Hit by a FW-190 northwest of Reims.

**361st**: Capt. Charles H. Feller (375th Ftr Sqn) KIA
P-47D E2-Q 42-75447
Hit by flak northwest of Etampes.

*Remarks*
353rd: P-47 c/l; o.k.
361st: 0-2 hangars, 0-1 vehicle, 0-2 gun positions

**April 28, 1944**
Groups Operating: P-51 352nd, 357th
P-47 56th, 78th
Missions: Support of bombers to Avord Airfield.
Claims: 0-0-0 air
2-12 ground

| *Group* | | *Claims* | *Location* |
|---|---|---|---|
| **78th** | | | |
| 82nd: | Lt. J.J. Bernhard | (2)He-111 dam(grd) | Chateaudun |
| | Lt. R.L. Wolfe | He-111 dam(grd) | Chateaudun |
| **352nd** | | | |
| 328th: | Lt. R.H. Powell | Ju-88 dest(grd) | Herbeuville |
| | | (.5)Ju-88 dam(grd) | Avord A/F |
| | Capt. R.H. Sharp | (.5)Ju-88 dam(grd) | Avord A/F |
| 486th: | Capt. S.W. Andrew | FW-200 dest(grd) | Chateaudun |
| | Lt. E.J. Meyer | Ju-88 dam(grd) | Orleans-Bricy |
| 487th: | Capt. R.W. Hamilton | He-111 dam(grd) | Bourges |
| | | Ju-88 dam(grd) | Bourges |
| | Lt. F.M. Allison | He-111 dam(grd) | Bourges |
| | | u/i a/c dam(grd) | Bourges |
| | Lt. M.C. Pickering | He-111 dam(grd) | Bourges |
| | | Ju-88 dam(grd) | Bourges |
| | Maj. G.E. Preddy | He-111 dam(grd) | Bourges |

*Losses-*

**352nd**: Lt. James L. Laing (328th Ftr Sqn) POW
P-51C PE- 42-103290
Hit by flak near Herbeuville and bailed out near Chateaudun.

**357th**: Capt. Glendon V. Davis (364th Ftr Sqn) MIA-E
P-51B C5-O 43-6867 "Pregnant Polecat"
Suffered mechanical failure and bailed out west of Bourges.

*Remarks*
352nd: 0-2 hangars, 0-2 buildings

Groups Operating: P-47 356th
Missions: Support of bombers to Sottevast V-1 sites.
Claims: nil
Losses: nil

Groups Operating: P-38 20th
Missions: Dive-bombing of Tours Airfield.
Claims: nil

*Losses-*

**20th**: Lt. Ferdinand E. LeFevre (79th Ftr Sqn) KIA
P-38J MC-U 42-68035
Hit by flak in the Calais area and bailed out over the Channel.

Groups Operating: P-47 353rd
P-38 55th
Missions: Dive-bombing of Chateaudun Airfield.
Claims: 0-0-0 air
1-1 ground

| *Group* | | *Claims* | *Location* |
|---|---|---|---|
| **353rd** | | | |
| HdQts: | Col. G.E. Duncan | u/i a/c dest(grd) | Chateaudun |
| | | u/i a/c dam(grd) | Chateaudun |

Losses: nil

Groups Operating: P-47 361st
Missions: Support of bombers to Marquise/Mimoyecques V-1 sites.
Claims: nil
Losses: nil

Groups Operating: P-47 56th
Missions: Dive-bombing of an airfield near Paris.
Claims: nil
Losses: nil

KIAc's
364th: Lt. William P. O'Connell (385th Ftr Sqn)
P-38J 5E-
Died in a crash near Rushdon.

**April 29, 1944**
Groups Operating: P-51 4th, 352nd, 355th, 357th
P-47 56th, 78th, 353rd, 356th, 359th, 361st
P-38 20th, 55th, 364th
Missions: Support of bombers to Berlin.
Claims: 5-5-7 air
7-3 ground

| *Group* | | *Claims* | *Location* |
|---|---|---|---|
| **4th** | | | |
| 334th: | Lt. N. Megura | Ju-52 dest(grd) | Nordhausen |
| | | (.5)Ju-52 dest(grd)[*] | Nordhausen |
| | | (.5)Ju-52 dest(grd)[**] | Nordhausen |
| | Lt. S.W. Monroe | (1.5)Ju-52 dest(grd)[*] | Nordhausen |
| | Lt. J.L. Barden | (.5)Ju-52 dest(grd)[**] | Nordhausen |
| 336th: | Lt. J.T. Godfrey | Do-217 dest(grd) | Nordhausen |
| | | (.5)Ju-52 dest(grd)[@] | Nordhausen |
| | | (.5)Ju-52 dest(grd)[@@] | Nordhausen |
| | | Do-217 dam(grd) | Nordhausen |
| | Lt. I.E. Grounds | (.5)Ju-52 dest(grd)[@] | Nordhausen |
| | Lt. J.A. Patteeuw | (.5)Ju-52 dest(grd)[@@] | Nordhausen |
| **20th** | | | |
| 77th: | Capt. D.A. Reihmer | (2)Me-109 dam(air) | Wittenburg |
| **56th** | | | |
| HdQts: | Maj. J.C. Stewart | Me-109 dam(air) | W/Steinhuder Lake |
| **352nd** | | | |
| 328th: | Capt. E.L. Abbott | Me-109 dest(air) | Neuhaldensleben |
| | | glider dam(grd) | Burg |
| | Lt. S.E. Dyke | (.5)FW-190 dest(air) | Calvorde |
| | Lt. F.W. Horne | (.5)FW-190 dest(air) | Calvorde |
| | Lt. L. Fieg | u/i a/c dam(grd) | Burg |
| **355th** | | | |
| 354th: | Lt. H.W. Brown | Me-109 dest(air) | Brunswick |
| **357th** | | | |
| 363rd: | Lt. J.F. Pierce | Me-109 dam(air) | Berlin |
| **359th** | | | |
| 370th: | Lt. C.V. Cunningham | FW-190 prob(air) | Gehrden |
| **361st** | | | |
| HdQts: | LtCol. J.J. Kruzel | Me-109 dest(air) | Steinhuder Lake |
| 375th: | Lt. S.D. Rames | Me-109 dest(air) | Steinhuder Lake |
| **364th** | | | |
| HdQts: | Maj. A.L. Chilton | Me-109 prob(air) | Stendal |
| 383rd: | Maj. J.B. McManus | FW-190 prob(air) | Stendal |
| | Lt. E.E. Bankey | FW-190 prob(air) | Stendal |
| 384th: | Capt. R.M. Spradlin | Me-109 prob(air) | Brandenburg |
| | Capt. R.E. Lacy | Me-109 dam(air) | N/Brandenburg |
| | Lt. F.J. Hoenselaar | Me-109 dam(air) | Steinhuder Lake-Berlin |
| | Lt. D.J. Pick | FW-190 dam(air) | N/Brunswick |

*Losses-*

**4th**: Lt. John L. Barden (334th Ftr Sqn) POW
P-51B QP-B 42-106682
Hit by fire from another P-51 while strafing Nordhausen Airfield.

Lt. Peter R. Kennedy (334th Ftr Sqn) POW
P-51B QP-L 43-6646
Hit by flak and bailed out near Fuechtof.

**355th**: Capt. Thomas F. Neal, Jr. (354th Ftr Sqn) KIA
P-51B WR-J 43-6577
Last seen chasing FW-190's near Rathenow.

**364th**: Lt. Shornden D. McCloud (384th Ftr Sqn) POW
P-38J 5Y-D 42-67417
Collided with Lt. Smith north of Brunswick.

Lt. Kenneth M. Shaffer (384th Ftr Sqn) POW
P-38J 5Y-I 42-67438
Hit by a Me-109 near Brandenburg.

Lt. Eugene L. Smith (384th Ftr Sqn) POW
P-38J 5Y- 42-67447
Collided with Lt. McCloud north of Brunswick.

*Remarks*
4th: 0-3 locos, 1-0 railcar, 0-1 hangar
P-51 c/l; o.k.
355th: 0-1 loco
359th: 14-7 locos
Capt. Daniel D. McKee (370th Ftr Sqn) c/l Framlingham; o.k.
P-47D CS-

KIAc's
339th: Lt. Ralph M. Degner (504th Ftr Sqn)
P-51B 5Q-

**April 30, 1944**
Groups Operating: P-51 4th, 352nd, 355th, 357th
P-47 56th, 78th, 353rd, 356th, 359th, 361st
P-38 20th, 55th, 364th
Missions: Support to Lyon/Bron and Clermont Airfields; dive-bombing operations by some P-47 units, and the 364th supported bombers to Siracourt V-1 sites.
Claims: 17-1-4 air
10-11 ground

| Group | | Claims | Location |
|---|---|---|---|
| **4th** | | | |
| HdQts: | Col. D.J.M. Blakeslee | (.5)Do-24 dest(grd)[*] | Lyon Anchorage |
| 334th: | Capt. W.M. Sobanski | (.33)Me-110 dest(air) | N/Lyon |
| | Lt. J.L. Lang | (.33)Me-110 dest(air) | N/Lyon |
| | | Me-110 dest(grd) | Lyon |
| | | (2)Me-110 dam(grd) | Lyon |
| | | He-111 dam(grd) | Lyon |
| | Lt. S.W. Monroe | (.33)Me-110 dest(air) | N/Lyon |
| | | Me-110 dam(grd) | Lyon/Bron |
| 336th: | Lt. F.W. Glover | (1.5)u/i a/c dest(grd) | Valence A/F |
| | Capt. J.T. Godfrey | (.5)Do-24 dest(grd)[**] | Lyon Anchorage |
| | Lt. T.K. McDill | (.5)Do-24 dest(grd)[**] | Lyon Anchorage |
| | Lt. H.H. Frederick | (.5)u/i a/c dest(grd) | Valence A/F |
| | Lt. J.A. Patteeuw | (.5)Do-24 dest(grd)[*] | Lyon Anchorage |
| | Lt. F.S. Harris | (.5)Do-24 dest(grd)[@] | Lyon Anchorage |
| | Lt. W.E. Johnson | (.5)Do-24 dest(grd)[@] | Lyon Anchorage |
| | Lt. W.W. Millikan | Do-24 dam(grd) | Lyon Anchorage |
| **78th** | | | |
| 83rd: | Lt. A.M. Juchheim | (2)FW-190 dest(air) | Dreux |
| | | FW-190 prob(air) | Dreux |
| | | FW-190 dam(air) | Dreux |
| | Maj. O.E. Gilbert | FW-190 dest(air) | SW Paris |
| | Lt. W.M. McDermott | (.5)FW-190 dest(air) | Dreux |
| | Lt. F. White | (.5)FW-190 dest(air) | Dreux |
| | Lt. E.T. Kitley | (2)FW-190 dam(air) | Dreux |
| | Lt. L.R. Casey | FW-190 dam(air) | Dreux |
| **352nd** | | | |
| 486th: | Capt. S.W. Andrew | FW-190 dest(air) | Clermont-Berrand |
| | Lt. W.W. Anderson | FW-190 dest(air) | Clermont-Berrand |
| | | (2)Me-110 dest(grd) | Clermont-Berrand |
| 487th: | Lt. W.T. Whisner | FW-190 dest(air) | Clermont-Berrand |
| | Capt. C.E. Davis | (3)u/i a/c dam(grd) | Clermont-Berrand |
| | Lt. R.L. Hall | (2)u/i a/c dam(grd) | Clermont-Berrand |
| **357th** | | | |
| 362nd: | Capt. J.E. Broadhead | Me-109 dest(air) | S/Paris |
| | Lt. R.H. Becker | Me-109 dest(air) | S/Paris |
| | Lt. R.D. Brown | Me-109 dest(air) | S/Paris |
| | Lt. G.M. O'Brien | (.5)Me-109 dest(air) | S/Paris |
| 363rd: | Lt. J.F. Pierce | (2)FW-190 dest(air) | NE Orleans |
| | Capt. C.E. Anderson | FW-190 dest(air) | SE Orleans |
| 364th: | Lt. R.A. Peterson | (2)FW-190 dest(air) | Auxerre |
| | Lt. T.M. McKinney | (.5)Me-109 dest(air) | S/Paris |
| **359th** | | | |
| 368th: | Capt. C.E. Mosse | Me-410 dest(grd) | Bricy A/F |
| | Lt. R.B. Janney | Me-410 dest(grd) | Bricy A/F |
| | | Me-410 dam(grd) | Bricy A/F |

*Losses-*

**4th**: Lt. Fred W. Glover (336th Ftr Sqn) MIA-E
P-51B VF- 42-106856
Hit by flak at Valence Airfield and bailed out north of Tain.

**20th**: Lt. Albert R. Fogg (79th Ftr Sqn) POW
P-38J MC-G 42-68140 "Puddin"
Hit by flak near Tours.

**357th**: Lt. Cordell L. Summers (364th Ftr Sqn) MIA-E
P-51B C5- 43-6701
Hit by flak and bailed out near Auxerre.

Lt. Charles J. Schreiber (364th Ftr Sqn) ASR
P-51B C5- 43-6856
Hit by enemy fighters and bailed out ten miles off Calais.

*Remarks*
4th: Lt. Harold H. Frederick (336th Ftr Sqn) c/l Manston; o.k.
P-51B VF- 43-6362
20th: 0-1 hangar, 0-1 flak position, 0-1 control tower
352nd: 0-2 barracks, 0-1 hangar
359th: 0-2 hangars, 1-0 ammo dump
Lt. Robert V. Beaupre (368th Ftr Sqn) c/l; o.k.
P-47D CV-

Groups Operating: P-51 339th
P-47 353rd
P-38 20th, 364th
Missions: The 20th and 353rd dive-bombed Orleans/Bricy Airfield with the 364th covering while the 339th flew a sweep.
Claims: nil
Losses: nil

*Remarks*
20th: 1-13 flak positions, 0-1 building, 0-1 ammo dump

KIAc's
56th: Lt. George H. Lovett (63rd Ftr Sqn)
P-47D UN-T 42-75137
Spun-in near Stansted.

**May 1, 1944**
Groups Operating: P-51 339th, 352nd, 357th
P-47 356th, 359th, 361st
Missions: Support for bombers to targets in the Pas de Calais area while the 339th swept the Belgian coast.
Claims: nil
Losses: nil

Groups Operating: P-51 4th, 352nd, 355th, 357th
P-47 56th, 78th, 353rd, 356th, 359th, 361st
P-38 20th, 55th, 364th
Missions: Support for bombers going to marshalling yards in France and Belgium.
Claims: 6-0-3 air
0-0 ground

| Group | | Claims | Location |
|---|---|---|---|
| **4th** | | | |
| 334th: | Lt. R.K. Hofer | Me-109 dest(air) | Koln |
| 335th: | Lt. F.C. Jones | Me-109 dest(air) | Zweibricken |
| | | Me-109 dam(air) | Zweibricken |
| | Lt. B.L. McGrattan | Me-109 dest(air) | Losheim |
| | Lt. J.W. Goodwyn | Me-109 dam(air) | Losheim |
| 336th: | Capt. J.T. Godfrey | Me-109 dest(air) | NW Saarbrucken |
| **355th** | | | |
| 354th: | Lt. N.J. Fortier | FW-190 dam(air) | Trier |
| 358th: | Capt. L.J. Dissette | Me-109 dest(air) | Traben-Trarbach |
| **361st** | | | |
| 375th: | Capt. J.W. Guckeyson | (.5)Ju-188 dest(air) | W/Verdun |
| | Lt. W.A. Rautenbush | (.5)Ju-188 dest(air) | W/Verdun |

Losses:

**20th**: Lt. Philip E. Pearson (55th Ftr Sqn) KIA
P-38J KI-I 42-67763
Hit by flak south of Liege.

Lt. William G. Schultz (55th Ftr Sqn) KIA
P-38J KI-P 42-104314
Hit by flak south of Liege.

**355th**: Lt. Rudolph B. Kaminski (357th Ftr Sqn) KIA
P-51B OS-B 43-6648
Hit by a Me-109 near Metz.

*Remarks*
20th: 1-3 locos, 0-25 railcars, 0-1 flak position, 0-4 signal towers
339th: Lt. Valdee Wyatt (503rd Ftr Sqn) c/l Fowlmere; o.k.
P-51 D7-

KIAc's
359th: Capt. Carey H. Brown (370th Ftr Sqn)
P-51C CS-Q 42-103294
Died in a crash near East Wretham.

**May 2, 1944**
Groups Operating: P-51 339th
P-47 361st
Missions: Support of bombers to Pas de Calais V-1 sites.
Claims: nil
Losses: nil

KIAc's
359th: Lt. Raymond L. Botsford (368th Ftr Sqn)
P-51B CV- 43-6430
Died in a crash near Thetford.

**May 3, 1944**
Groups Operating: P-51 339th
P-47 78th
Missions: Support of bombers to Pas de Calais V-1 sites.
Claims: nil
Losses: nil

KIAc's
364th: Capt. Marcus C. Linn (385th Ftr Sqn)
P-38J 5E- 42-68187
Hit the water while practicing skip-bombing southeast of Clacton.

**May 4, 1944**
Groups Operating: P-51 4th, 339th, 352nd, 355th, 359th(mixed)
P-47 56th, 356th, 359th, 361st
P-38 20th
Missions: Support of bombers going to Bergen/Alkmaar.
Claims: 10-2-7 air
0-0 ground

| *Group* | | *Claims* | *Location* |
|---|---|---|---|
| **56th** | | | |
| 62nd: | Lt. R.C. Cherry | Me-410 dest(air) | Nordhausen |
| | | (.5)FW-190 dest(air) | Nordhausen |
| | Capt. J.H. Powers | Me-109 dest(air) | Quackenbruck |
| | Lt. E.E. Bennett | (.5)FW-190 dest(air) | Nordhausen |
| | Lt. R.B. Bluhm | Me-109 dam(air) | Dummer Lake |
| **355th** | | | |
| 358th: | Lt. D.M. Martyn | Me-109 dest(air) | SW Hanover |
| | | Me-109 dam(air) | SW Hanover |
| | Capt. W.V. Gresham | Me-109 prob(air) | SW Hanover |
| | | Me-109 dam(air) | SW Hanover |
| | Lt. A.T. Robinson | Me-109 prob(air) | SW Hanover |
| | | Me-109 dam(air) | SW Hanover |
| | Lt. C.W. Blair | Me-109 dam(air) | SW Hanover |
| | Lt. R.L. Coleman | Me-109 dam(air) | SW Hanover |
| **356th** | | | |
| 361st: | Capt. J.N. Wood | (3)FW-190 dest(air) | N/Steinhuder L. |
| | Lt. J.H. Culp | (2)FW-190 dest(air) | N/Steinhuder L. |
| | Capt. J.P. Perrin | FW-190 dest(air) | N/Steinhuder L. |
| | Lt. J.K. Johnson | FW-190 dam(air) | N/Steinhuder L. |

*Losses-*

**355th:** Lt. Donald M. Martyn (358th Ftr Sqn) KIA
P-51B YF-V 43-6873
Hit by a Me-109 in the Hanover area.

**356th:** Capt. Sidney H. Hewett (361st Ftr Sqn) POW
P-47D QI-F 42-76397 "Clarkie"
Downed by a FW-190 in the Steinhuder Lake area.

Lt. Jack H. Culp (361st Ftr Sqn) POW
P-47D QI-N 42-22766
Hit by a FW-190 in the Steinhuder Lake area.

Lt. John L. Bruce (361st Ftr Sqn) KIA
P-47D QI-B 43-25516
Acted as relay; turned too tight while landing at Martlesham Heath.

*Remarks*
56th: 7-11 locos
P-47 c/l Beaumont; o.k.
P-47 c/l Orford; o.k.
355th: 0-1 loco
356th: 0-3 locos
357th: P-51 c/l; o.k.
359th: 0-5 barracks, 0-1 hangar

**May 5, 1944**
Groups Operating: P-51 339th
Missions: Support of bombers to Sottevast V-1 sites.
Claims: nil
Losses: nil

**May 6, 1944**
Groups Operating: P-51 339th, 359th
P-47 56th
Missions: Support of bombers to Pas de Calais and Siracourt V-1 sites.
Claims: nil
Losses: nil

KIAc's
4th: Lt. Ralph G. Boyce (335th Ftr Sqn)
P-51B WD-
Crashed while landing at Ridgewell.

**May 7, 1944**
Groups Operating: P-51 4th, 339th, 352nd, 355th, 357th
P-47 56th, 78th, 356th, 361st
P-38 20th, 55th, 364th
Missions: Support of bombers to Berlin, Osnabruck, and Munster.
Claims: nil

*Losses-*

**55th:** Lt. Russell W. Erb (343rd Ftr Sqn) ASR
P-38J CY-
Ditched in the Channel after mechanical failure.

**339th:** Lt. Arch B. Luper (505th Ftr Sqn) KIA
P-51B 6N- 42-106807
Hit by flak near Gees and bailed out near Solingen.

**356th:** Lt. William H. Wood (359th Ftr Sqn) POW
P-47D OC-A 42-8417 "Ich Brauche Du"
Lost oil pressure and bailed out north of Lingen.

**364th:** Lt. Alfred C. Stepman (385th Ftr Sqn) KIA
P-38J 5E- 42-67248
Suffered mechanical failure and ditched ten miles west of Tessel Island.

*Remarks*
339th: F/O Arthur R. Steier (503rd Ftr Sqn) b/o Fowlmere; o.k.
P-51 D7-

Groups Operating: P-51 339th
P-47 56th
Missions: Support of bombers to Liege.
Claims: nil
Losses: nil

**May 8, 1944**
Groups Operating: P-51 4th, 339th, 352nd, 355th, 357th, 359th
P-47 56th, 78th, 353rd, 356th, 361st
P-38 20th, 55th, 364th
Missions: Support of bombers to Berlin and Brunswick.
Claims: 52-6-14 air
1-0 ground

| *Group* | | *Claims* | *Location* |
|---|---|---|---|
| **56th** | | | |
| 61st: | Lt. F.W. Klibbe | Me-109 dest(air) | W/Celle |
| | | FW-190 dest(air) | W/Celle |
| | LtCol. F.S. Gabreski | Me-109 dest(air) | Celle |
| | Lt. J.H. Perry | FW-190 prob(air) | W/Celle |
| 62nd: | Capt. R.S. Johnson | Me-109 dest(air) | Brunswick-Hanover |
| | | FW-190 dest(air) | Brunswick-Hanover |
| | Lt. G.H. Lewis | FW-190 dest(air) | Oschersleben |
| | Lt. H.E. Hartney | FW-190 dam(air) | Celle |
| **78th** | | | |
| 83rd: | Lt. P.A. Caulfield | Me-109 dam(air) | Verdun |
| | Lt. P.C. Holden | Me-109 dam(air) | Verdun |
| **352nd** | | | |
| HdQts: | Col. J.L. Mason | FW-190 dest(air) | N/Nienburg |
| | | FW-190 dam(air) | N/Nienburg |
| | LtCol. J.C. Edwards | FW-190 dam(air) | Nienburg |
| 328th: | Lt. J.F. Thornell | (3)Me-109 dest(air) | Nienburg |
| | Lt. Q.L. Quinn | Me-109 dest(air) | NW Bremen |
| | | FW-190 prob(air) | E/Bremen |
| | Lt. R.G. Phillips | Me-109 dest(air) | SE Nienburg |
| | Lt. E.J. Whiting | Me-109 prob(air) | Unterlusz |
| | Lt. F.W. Horne | FW-190 prob(air) | E/Bremen |
| | Lt. J.W. Galiga | FW-190 prob(air) | Nienburg |
| | Lt. H.L. Miller | Me-109 dam(air) | NE Bremen |
| 486th: | Capt. F.A. Cutler | (2)Me-109 dest(air) | Gifhorn |
| | | u/i a/c dest(grd) | Gifhorn |
| | Lt. E.L. Heller | (2)Me-109 dest(air) | Gifhorn |
| | Maj. S.W. Andrew | FW-190 dest(air) | NE Hanover |
| 487th: | Lt. C.J. Luksic | (3)FW-190 dest(air) | Brunswick |
| | | (2)Me-109 dest(air) | Brunswick |
| | LtCol. J.C. Meyer | (3)Me-109 dest(air) | Hanover-Brunswick-Bremen |
| | Capt. C.E. Davis | (3)Me-109 dest(air) | Brunswick |
| | | (.5)FW-190 dest(air) | Brunswick |
| | Lt. W.E. Fowler | (.5)FW-190 dest(air) | Brunswick |
| | Lt. R.G. O'Nan | Me-109 dest(air) | NE Brunswick |
| | Lt. M.C. Pickering | FW-190 dest(air) | Nienburg |

| | | | |
|---|---|---|---|
| **357th** | | | |
| HdQts: | Maj. I.H. Dregne | FW-190 dam(air) | N/Hanover |
| 363rd: | Capt. C.E. Anderson | FW-190 dest(air) | Soltau |
| | Lt. J.F. Pierce | FW-190 dest(air) | Soltau |
| 364th: | Lt. Rob. C. Smith | FW-190 dam(air) | S/Hanover |
| **359th** | | | |
| 368th: | Capt. W.N. Bolefahr | Me-109 dest(air) | SE Bremen |
| | | Me-109 dam(air) | SE Bremen |
| | Lt. B.M. Hagan | (.5)Me-109 prob(air) | SW Brunswick |
| | Lt. A.G. Homeyer | Me-109 dam(air) | SE Bremen |
| 369th: | Lt. R.J. Booth | (2)Me-109 dest(air) | Mellendorf-Drakenburg |
| | | FW-190 dest(air) | Mellendorf-Drakenburg |
| | Capt. C.C. Ettlesen | Me-109 dest(air) | Hermansburg |
| | Lt. H.C. Burton | Me-109 dest(air) | Hermansburg |
| | Capt. N.K. Cranfill | (.5)Me-109 prob(air) | SW Brunswick |
| 370th: | Lt. G.A. Doersch | FW-190 dest(air) | Enschede |
| | | Me-109 dest(air) | Enschede |
| | | FW-190 dam(air) | Enschede |
| | Lt. J.E. Shupe | (2)FW-190 dest(air) | Enschede |
| **361st** | | | |
| 375th: | Maj. G.L. Merritt | FW-190 dest(air) | N/Nienburg |
| | Lt. L.H. Sypher | Me-109 dest(air) | NE Steinhuder L. |
| | | Me-109 dam(air) | NE Steinhuder L. |
| 376th: | Lt. H.D. Chapman | Me-109 dest(air) | Nienburg |
| | Capt. W.B. Frank | FW-190 dam(air) | Nienburg |
| **364th** | | | |
| HdQts: | Col. R.W. Osborn | Me-109 dest(air) | Steinhuder Lake |
| | | Me-109 dam(air) | Steinhuder Lake |
| 383rd: | Lt. M.W. Glascow | Me-109 dam(air) | NE Dummer Lake |
| 384th: | Capt. R.M. Spradlin | (2)Me-109 dest(air) | Steinhuder Lake |
| | Lt. R.M. Heyman | Me-109 dest(air) | Steinhuder Lake |
| | | Me-109 dam(air) | Steinhuder Lake |
| | Lt. A.D. Parsley | Me-109 dest(air) | Steinhuder Lake-Gifhorn |

*Losses-*

**20th**: Lt. John J. Connor, Jr. (55th Ftr Sqn) MIA
P-38J KI-C 42-67901
Suffered mechanical failure near Ostenholz.

**56th**: Lt. Gordon H. Lewis (62nd Ftr Sqn) POW
P-47D LM-N 42-76503
Hit by enemy fighters near Versbeck and bailed out near Oschersleben.

**78th**: Lt. John D. Motsenbocker (83rd Ftr Sqn) POW
P-47D HL-P 42-76227
Hit by a Me-109 near Verdun.

**352nd**: Lt. George Kopecky (487th Ftr Sqn) POW
P-51B HO-G 43-7105
Hit by enemy fighters near Nienburg.

**357th**: Capt. Ellis A. Rogers (363rd Ftr Sqn) KIA
P-51B B6- 42-106793
Hit by flak and lost a wing near Soltau.

Lt. Ray Sparks, Jr. (364th Ftr Sqn) POW
P-51B C5-C 43-6801 "Boiler Maker"
Hit by flak southwest of Ulzen.

**359th**: Lt. Stanley E. Sackett (369th Ftr Sqn) KIA
P-51B IV-S 42-106904
Hit by enemy fighters near Wunstorf.

Lt. Alan C. Porter (370th Ftr Sqn) KIA
P-51B CS-R 43-7179
Hit by enemy fighters near Enschede.

**361st**: Lt. William A. Rautenbush (375th Ftr Sqn) KIA
P-47D E2-Y 42-75555
Hit by enemy fighters near Bruchhausen.

Lt. Collier W. Todd, Jr. (375th Ftr Sqn) KIA
P-47D E2-J 42-75249
Hit the ground near Lohne and crashed shortly after.

**364th**: Lt. Walter C. Bosworth (383rd Ftr Sqn) POW
P-38J N2- 42-104198
Hit by a Me-109 near Barver.

Capt. Roy M. Spradlin (384th Ftr Sqn) POW
P-38J 5Y-D 42-68070
Hit by a Me-109 northeast of Hanover.

Lt. Lynn Steincamp (385th Ftr Sqn) POW
P-38J 5E- 42-104326
Suffered mechanical failure and bailed out southeast of Brunswick.

*Remarks*
20th: Lt. Ben E. McCarty (79th Ftr Sqn) c/l Wittering; o.k.
P-38J MC-
339th: 1-0 loco, 0-3 barges
352nd: 6-5 locos, 0-5 railcars
357th: 0-1 loco, 0-2 tugs
359th: 2-0 locos
361st: 2-2 locos, 1-0 oil tank
364th: 2-1 locos

Groups Operating: P-47 78th, 353rd
Missions: Support of bombers to the Brussels area and to V-1 sites at Glacerie/Sottevast.
Claims: nil
Losses: nil

KIAc's
352nd: Lt. John B. Worcester (486th Ftr Sqn)
P-51B PZ-F 43-6850 "The Joker"

**May 9, 1944**
Groups Operating: P-51 4th, 339th, 352nd, 355th, 357th, 359th
P-47 56th, 78th, 353rd, 356th, 361st
P-38 20th, 55th, 364th
Missions: Support for bombers to various airfields and marshalling yards in France, Belgium, and Luxembourg.
Claims: 3-0-1 air
1-3 ground

| ***Group*** | | ***Claims*** | ***Location*** |
|---|---|---|---|
| **4th** | | | |
| 334th: | Lt. G.C. Siems | Ju-88 dest(grd) | Reims-Champiegne |
| | Capt. H.D. Hively | (2)Ju-88 dam(grd) | Reims-Champiegne |
| **339th** | | | |
| 505th: | Lt. H.E. Everett | Me-109 dest(air) | Vouziers |
| | | Me-109 dam(air) | Vouziers |
| | Lt. W.A. Jones | Me-109 dest(air) | Vouziers |
| **357th** | | | |
| 363rd: | Lt. L.D. Wood | FW-190 dest(air) | Herenthals |
| **361st** | | | |
| 375th: | Lt. F.T. Glankler | Me-109 dam(grd) | Juvincourt |

*Losses-*

**4th**: Capt. Herbert J. Blanchfield (334th Ftr Sqn) POW
P-51B QP-E 42-106767
Hit by flak and bailed out southwest of St. Dizier.

Lt. Vernon A. Burroughs (334th Ftr Sqn) POW
P-51B QP-N 43-6636 "Ill Wind?"
Hit by enemy fighters southwest of St. Dizier.

Lt. Robert S. Sherman (334th Ftr Sqn) POW
P-51B QP-D 43-7002
Prop hit the ground near Thrablemont.

Lt. Lloyd W. Waterman (335th Ftr Sqn) POW
P-51B WD-A 42-106911 "Yippee Joe!!"
Suffered mechnical failure near Pont a Binson.

**20th**: Lt. Benjamin E. McCarty (79th Ftr Sqn) POW
P-38J MC- 42-104289
Hit by enemy fighters and bailed out near Nancy.

**357th**: Lt. [illegible] (363rd Ftr Sqn) POW
P-51B B6- 43-7011
Hit by a FW-190 near Herenthals.

Lt. Donovan D. Siverts (363rd Ftr Sqn) KIA
P-51B B6- 43-6427
Hit by a FW-190 near Herenthals.

*Remarks*
55th: P-38 c/l; o.k.
361st: 0-1 radio tower, 0-1 shack

KIAc's
352nd: Capt. Ernest B. McMahon (487th Ftr Sqn)
P-51C HO-B 42-103310
Crashed while practicing dive-bombing at Mersa Flats.

**May 10, 1944**
Groups Operating: P-38 364th
Missions: Sweep of the Brussels-Calais area.
Claims: nil
Losses: nil

**May 11, 1944**

Groups Operating: P-51 339th, 352nd, 357th, 359th
P-47 56th, 78th, 353rd, 356th
P-38 20th, 55th, 364th

Missions: Support of bombers to various marshalling yards in France.

Claims: 3-0-2 air
6-10 ground

| *Group* | | *Claims* | *Location* |
|---|---|---|---|
| **20th** | | | |
| 77th: | Capt. D.A. Reihmer | Ju-88 dest(grd) | Bretigny A/F |
| | Lt. J.D. McArthur | Ju-88 dest(grd) | Bretigny A/F |
| **78th** | | | |
| 82nd: | Lt. C.W. DeWitt | u/i a/c dest(grd) | Dijon |
| | | (3)u/i a/c dam(grd) | Dijon |
| | Capt. J.W. Wilkinson | (.5)He-111 dest(grd) | Dijon |
| | | (2)u/i a/c dam(grd) | Dijon |
| | | Go-242 dam(grd) | Dijon |
| | Lt. W.V. Van Dyk | (.5)He-111 dest(grd) | Dijon |
| | | (.5)Ju-52 dest(grd) | Dijon |
| | Lt. B.M. Watkins | (.5)Ju-52 dest(grd) | Dijon |
| | | (3)u/i a/c dam(grd) | Dijon |
| | Lt. P.H. Hazelett | Go-242 dam(grd) | Dijon |
| 83rd: | Lt. F.R. Pursell | FW-190 dest(air) | Montargis |
| | Lt. W.M. McDermott | FW-190 dam(air) | Montargis |
| 84th: | Lt. R.J. McIntosh | FW-190 dest(air) | W/Orleans |
| | | FW-190 dam(air) | W/Orleans |
| | Lt. J.B. Putnam | FW-190 dest(air) | Orleans |
| **359th** | | | |
| 370th: | Lt. H.D. Hollis | Me-410 dest(grd) | Reims-Champagne |

*Losses-*

**78th**: Lt. Anthony I. Kosinski (82nd Ftr Sqn) MIA-E
P-47D MX-O 42-25994
Hit by flak at Dijon Airfield.

Lt. Richard D. Steele (82nd Ftr Sqn) INT
P-47D MX-Q 42-76131
Hit by flak at Dijon Airfield and made his way to Switzerland.

**359th**: Lt. William R. Hodges (370th Ftr Sqn) MIA-E
P-51B CS-Q 43-24833
Hit by flak at Reims-Champagne Airfield.

Lt. Ralph E. Kibler (370th Ftr Sqn) KIA
P-51B CS-M 42-106865
Hit by flak at Reims-Champagne Airfield.

Lt. Edward J. Maslow (370th Ftr Sqn) POW
P-51C CS-D 42-103343
Hit by flak at Reims-Champagne Airfield.

*Remarks*

359th: Lt. Daniel R. Tuchsherer (370th Ftr Sqn) c/l Manston; o.k.
P-51 CS-

Groups Operating: P-51 4th, 355th, 361st(mixed)
P-47 78th, 353rd, 361st

Missions: Support for bombers to marshalling yards in Belgium and Luxembourg.

Claims: nil

*Losses-*

**4th**: Lt. Robert S. Tussey (336th Ftr Sqn) KIA
P-51B VF- 43-24771
Suffered mechanical failure and bailed out over the North Sea. Was rescued but died of injuries.

**May 12, 1944**

Groups Operating: P-51 4th, 339th, 352nd, 355th, 357th, 359th, 361st
P-47 56th, 78th, 353rd, 356th, 361st(mixed)
P-38 20th, 55th, 364th

Missions: Support to bombers hitting oil targets, primarily Merseburg, Zwickau, Zeitz, and Brux.

Claims: 60-0-7 air
6-4 ground

| *Group* | | *Claims* | *Location* |
|---|---|---|---|
| **4th** | | | |
| 334th: | Capt. H.D. Hively | Me-109 dest(air) | Plauen |
| | Lt. G.C. Siems | Me-109 dest(air) | Coburg |
| | Lt. R.K. Hofer | (.5)Me-109 dest(air) | N/Coburg |
| | Lt. L.R. Pierce | (.5)Me-109 dest(air) | N/Coburg |
| 335th: | Capt. J.R. Happel | Me-109 dest(air) | Giessen |
| | Lt. E.H. Shapleigh | (1.5)Me-109 dest(air) | Giessen-Marburg |
| | Lt. R.H. Homuth | Me-109 dest(air) | E/Giessen |
| | Lt. T.E. Lines | Me-109 dest(air) | E/Frankfurt |
| | Lt. G.I. Stanford | (.5)Me-109 dest(air) | Giessen-Marburg |
| 336th: | Maj. J.A. Goodson | Me-109 dest(air) | Kassel |
| | Lt. T.K. McDill | Me-109 dest(air) | Kassel |
| **20th** | | | |
| 77th: | Lt. I.C. Baker | Me-109 dest(air) | SW Kassel |
| **55th** | | | |
| 38th: | Lt. N.R. Tipton | FW-190 dest(air) | Wiesbaden |
| **56th** | | | |
| HdQts: | Col. H. Zemke | Me-109 dest(air) | SW Coblenz |
| 61st: | Lt. R.J. Rankin | (5)Me-109 dest(air) | NW Marburg |
| | Capt. P.A. Conger | (2)FW-190 dest(air) | N/Marburg |
| | | FW-190 dam(air) | N/Marburg |
| | Lt. A.C. Maul | Me-109 dest(air) | N/Marburg |
| | Lt. C.C. Thomton | Me-109 dest(air) | Marburg |
| | F/O S. Gerick | FW-190 dest(air) | NW Marburg |
| | | Me-109 dam(air) | NW Marburg |
| | Lt. P. Neyland | Me-109 dam(air) | N/Marburg |
| 62nd: | Lt. J.E. Greene | Me-109 dest(air) | Frankfurt |
| | Lt. H.E. King | Me-109 dest(air) | Frankfurt |
| | Capt. J.H. Powers | (.5)Me-109 dest(air) | Frankfurt |
| | F/O J. Vitale | (.5)Me-109 dest(air) | Frankfurt |
| 63rd: | Lt. J.C. Wakefield | (3)Me-109 dest(air) | NW Frankfurt |
| | Lt. A.S. Cavallo | (2)FW-190 dest(air) | Coblenz |
| **78th** | | | |
| 82nd: | Lt. D.D. Hagarty | (2)FW-190 dest(air) | Trier |
| | Capt. J.W. Wilkinson | FW-190 dest(air) | Coblenz |
| | Lt. M.R. Capp | FW-190 dest(air) | Coblenz |
| | Lt. R.L. Baker | FW-190 dest(air) | Coblenz |
| | Lt. B.M. Watkins | FW-190 dest(air) | Mannheim |
| **352nd** | | | |
| 328th: | Lt. G.R. Clark | Me-109 dest(air) | Coburg |
| | Lt. J.W. Galiga | (.5)Me-109 dest(air)* | Coburg |
| 486th: | Maj. S.W. Andrew | FW-190 dest(air) | Gotha |
| 487th: | LtCol. J.C. Meyer | Me-109 dest(air) | SW Frankfurt |
| | | He-177 dest(grd) | SW Frankfurt |
| | Capt. F.M. Allison | (1.5)Me-109 dest(air)** | SE Coblenz |
| | | Me-109 dam(air) | SE Coblenz |
| | Lt. D.W. McEntire | Me-109 dest(air) | SE Coblenz |
| | Lt. R.K. Butler | (.5)Me-109 dest(air)** | SE Coblenz |
| | Lt. H.H. Barnes | (.5)Me-109 dest(air)* | Coburg |
| | Lt. W.T. Whisner | Ju-52 dest(grd) | Frankenhausen |
| | Maj. G.E. Preddy | (3)u/i a/c dam(grd) | Frankenhausen |
| **353rd** | | | |
| HdQts: | Col. G.E. Duncan | FW-190 dest(air) | Wiesbaden |
| | | (2)FW-190 dam(air) | Wiesbaden |
| 350th: | Lt. K. Chetwood | (.5)Me-109 dest(air) | Selters |
| | Lt. W.F. Tanner | (.5)Me-109 dest(air) | Selters |
| **357th** | | | |
| HdQts: | Maj. I.H. Dregne | Me-109 dest(air) | NE Frankfurt |
| 362nd: | Lt. T.E. Norris | (1.5)Me-109 dest(air) | SE Frankfurt |
| | Capt. M.F. Baker | Me-109 dest(air) | N/Wurzburg |
| | Lt. A.O. Hood | (.5)Me-109 dest(air) | SE Frankfurt |
| 363rd: | Capt. C.E. Anderson | Me-109 dest(air) | NE Frankfurt |
| | | Me-109 dest(grd) | NE Frankfurt |
| | Capt. P.K. DeVries | FW-190 dest(air) | NE Frankfurt |
| | Capt. W.R. O'Brien | Me-109 dest(air) | N/Frankfurt |
| | Lt. J.F. Pierce | Me-109 dest(air) | NE Frankfurt |
| | Maj. M.H. Throop | FW-190 dam(air) | NE Frankfurt |
| | Lt. W.B. Overstreet | Ju-52 dest(grd) | NE Frankfurt |
| 364th: | Lt. T.M. McKinney | Me-109 dest(air) | NE Frankfurt |
| | Lt. Ric. C. Smith | FW-190 dest(air) | N/Frankfurt |
| | Lt. Rob. C. Smith | FW-190 dest(air) | N/Frankfurt |
| | Lt. W.C. Reese | Me-109 dest(air) | N/Schweinfurt |
| | Lt. C.D. Sumner | Me-109 dest(air) | NE Frankfurt |
| | Capt. R.A. Peterson | (.5)FW-190 dest(air) | NE Frankfurt |
| | Capt. J.A. Storch | (.5)FW-190 dest(air) | NE Frankfurt |
| **359th** | | | |
| 369th: | Capt. C.C. Ettlesen | (.5)u/i a/c dest(grd) | Thamsbruck A/F |
| | | u/i a/c dam(grd) | Thamsbruck A/F |
| | Lt. D.H. Laing | u/i a/c dest(grd) | Thamsbruck A/F |
| | Lt. R.L. Thacker | (.5)u/i a/c dest(grd) | Thamsbruck A/F |

*Losses-*

**56th**: LtCol. Preston Piper (HdQts) POW
P-47D UN-L 42-74750 "Lady Jane"
Hit by a Me-109 near Coblenz.

Lt. Jack E. Greene (62nd Ftr Sqn) POW
P-47D LM-H 42-75162
Hit by enemy fighters near Frankfurt.

Lt. Willard D. Johnson (63rd Ftr Sqn) POW
P-47D UN-W 42-75109 "Louisiana Pirate"
Hit by a Me-109 near Coblenz.

**78th**: Lt. Daniel D. Hagarty (82nd Ftr Sqn) POW
P-47D MX-R 42-26025
Hit by enemy fighters near Trier.

**352nd**: Lt. Alfred P. Howard, Jr. (487th Ftr Sqn) KIA
P-51B HO-Y 43-6929
Hit by enemy fighters near Rainrod.

**353rd**: Lt. William T. Thistlethwaite (351st Ftr Sqn) KIA
P-47D YJ-Q 42-76352
Hit by flak and bailed out twenty miles off the enemy coast.

**357th**: Lt. Roger A. Hilsted (362nd Ftr Sqn) KIA
P-51B G4-C 43-6634 "Nooky Booky"
Hit by enemy fighters near Wurzburg.

Capt. John B. Carder (364th Ftr Sqn) POW
P-51B C5-J 42-106777 "Taxpayer's Delight"
Hit by enemy fighters near Bischoffen.

*Remarks*
78th: 0-2 locos
339th: Lt. William Jaaskelainen (505th Ftr Sqn) c/l Fowlmere; o.k.
P-51C 6N-U 42-103305
357th: 1-0 loco

**May 13, 1944**
Groups Operating: P-51 4th, 339th, 352nd, 355th, 357th, 359th, 361st
P-47 56th, 78th, 353rd, 356th
P-38 20th, 55th, 364th
Missions: Support for bombers to Stettin, Tutow, and Osnabruck.
Claims: 41-8-8 air
1-0 ground

| *Group* | | *Claims* | *Location* |
|---|---|---|---|
| **4th** | | | |
| 336th: | Lt. H.H. Fredericks | Me-109 prob(air) | SE Canabruck |
| **56th** | | | |
| 61st: | Lt. R.J. Keen | (3)FW-190 dest(air) | W/Hagenow |
| | | FW-190 prob(air) | W/Hagenow |
| | Lt. J.M. Jure | FW-190 dest(air) | NE Hamburg |
| 62nd: | Maj. L.A. Dade | FW-190 dest(air) | Lubeck |
| **339th** | | | |
| 505th: | Capt. D.A. Larson | FW-190 prob(air) | SE Lubeck |
| **352nd** | | | |
| HdQts: | Col. J.L. Mason | (2)Me-109 dest(air) | Demmin-Friedland |
| | | FW-190 dest(air) | Demmin-Friedland |
| | | Me-109 dam(air) | Demmin-Friedland |
| 328th: | Capt. J.B. Coleman | (2)Me-109 dest(air) | Demmin |
| | Lt. F.W. Horne | (2)FW-190 dest(air) | Demmin |
| 486th: | Capt. W.W. Anderson | Me-109 dest(air) | Tribsees |
| | | u/i a/c dest(grd) | Wangerooge |
| | Capt. F.A. Cutler | Me-109 dest(air) | Neubrandenburg |
| | Capt. F.N. Greene | Me-109 dest(air) | Tribsees |
| | Capt. D.H. Higgins | Me-109 dest(air) | Tribsees |
| | Lt. S.G. Miles | Me-109 dest(air) | Tribsees |
| 487th: | Maj. G.E. Preddy | (2)Me-109 dest(air) | Neubrandenburg |
| | Lt. M.J. Nutter | Me-109 dest(air) | Neubrandenburg |
| | Lt. C.J. Luksic | (.5)Ju-88 dest(air) | E/Neubrandenburg |
| | Lt. [illegible] | (.5)Ju-88 dest(air) | E/Neubrandenburg |
| **355th** | | | |
| HdQts: | LtCol. G.J. Dix | (2)Me-410 dest(air) | SE Landsberg |
| 354th: | Lt. R.S. Morris | (2)Me-410 dest(air) | E/Berlin |
| | Lt. N.J. Fortier | FW-190 dest(air) | NE Bremen |
| | | Ju-88 dest(air) | N/Landsberg |
| | Lt. H.W. Brown | Me-210 dest(air) | Landsberg |
| | Lt. W.D. Martin | Hs-129 dest(air) | Landsberg |
| | Lt. E.F. Perry | FW-190 dest(air) | NE Bremen |
| | | FW-190 prob(air) | NE Bremen |
| | | FW-190 dam(air) | NE Bremen |
| | Lt. D.J. Jacobson | Me-410 dam(air) | Landsberg |
| **356th** | | | |
| HdQts: | LtCol. D.A. Baccus | (.5)FW-190 dest(air) | Kiel-Lubeck |
| | | FW-190 dam(air) | Kiel-Lubeck |
| 359th: | Lt. W.L. Farmer | FW-190 dest(air) | Kiel-Lubeck |
| | Lt. R.A. Coughenour | (.5)FW-190 dest(air) | Kiel-Lubeck |
| | Capt. W.A. Holm | FW-190 prob(air) | Kiel-Lubeck |
| | Lt. J.A. Wyatt | FW-190 prob(air) | Kiel-Lubeck |
| | | FW-190 dam(air) | Kiel-Lubeck |
| 360th: | Lt. R.R. Withers | FW-190 dest(air) | Kiel |
| | Lt. C.W. Adams | FW-190 prob(air) | Kiel |
| | Lt. A.A. Perryman | FW-190 dam(air) | Kiel |
| 361st: | Capt. T.F. Bailey | FW-190 dest(air) | SE Lubeck |
| | Lt. B.A. Swift | FW-190 dest(air) | S/Kiel |
| | Lt. D.F. Thwaites | FW-190 dest(air) | Hamburg |
| | Lt. E.L. Faison | FW-190 prob(air) | SE Lubeck |
| **357th** | | | |
| 363rd: | Lt. R.N. Moore | Me-109 dest(air) | W/Hamburg |
| | | Me-109 dam(air) | W/Hamburg |
| 364th: | Lt. J.G. Sullivan | FW-44 dest(air) | E/Grunberg |
| | | (.5)Me-410 dest(air)* | E/Grunberg |
| | | Me-410 dam(air) | E/Grunberg |
| | Capt. R.A.. Peterson | (1.5)Me-410 dest(air)* | E/Grunberg |
| | Lt. C.H. Dooley | (.5)Me-410 dest(air)** | E/Grunberg |
| | Lt. R.M. Shaw | (.5)Me-410 dest(air)** | E/Grunberg |

*Losses-*

**4th**: Lt. Leonard R. Pierce (334th Ftr Sqn) KIA
P-51B QP-G 42-106441
Suffered mechanical failure and bailed out east of Southwold.

**20th**: Lt. Hal W. Everett (77th Ftr Sqn) POW
P-38J LC-K 42-68026
Hit by flak near Leck Airfield.

**56th**: Lt. Harold E. Hartney, Jr. (62nd Ftr Sqn) KIA
P-47D LM-Z 42-75444
Hit by enemy fighters near Brockenlomde.

**352nd**: Capt. Frank A. Cutler (486th Ftr Sqn) KIA
P-51B PZ-Y 42-106483 "Miss Lace"
Collided with a Me-109 near Zarneka.

**356th**: Capt. Willis A. Holm (359th Ftr Sqn) KIA
P-47D OC-M 42-74689 "Lady Jane"
Downed by a FW-190 near Hamburg.

*Remarks*
20th: 0-1 tug, 0-1 barge, 0-1 boat, 0-1 barracks, 0-1 hangar, 0-3 buildings, 0-2 gun positions
55th: Lt. Melvin A. Hawes (38th Ftr Sqn) b/o; injured
P-38J CG-
352nd: 0-1 loco, 0-2 flak towers, 0-1 vehicle, 0-1 boat
356th: 0-8 buildings
Lt. Charles W. Adams (360th Ftr Sqn) c/l Beccles; o.k.
P-47D PI-

**May 15, 1944**
Groups Operating: P-51 339th, 357th
Missions: Support of bombers to Siracourt and Marquis/Mimoyecques V-1 sites.
Claims: nil

*Losses-*

**339th**: Lt. Albert L. Wyer (503rd Ftr Sqn) POW
P-51C D7- 42-103393
Lost coolant and bailed out near St. Pol.

**May 16, 1944**
<u>KIAc's</u>
361st: Lt. Eugene W. Kinnaird (375th Ftr Sqn)
P-51B E2-X 43-24790
Died in a crash near Water Beach.

**May 17, 1944**
<u>KIAc's</u>
56th: Lt. James E. Elliott (62nd Ftr Sqn)
P-47D UN-<u>B</u> (note this was a 63rd Ftr Sqn a/c)
Collided with an A-20.

**May 18, 1944**
<u>KIAc's</u>
55th: Lt. Kenneth H. Underwood (38th Ftr Sqn)
P-38J CG-K 42-104334
Crashed near Bury St. Edmunds while practicing at low-level.

**May 19, 1944**
Groups Operating: P-51 4th, 339th, 352nd, 355th, 357th, 359th, 361st
P-47 56th, 78th, 353rd, 356th
P-38 20th, 55th, 364th
Missions: Support of bombers to Berlin and Brunswick.
Claims: 66-2-21 air
6-12 ground

| *Group* | | *Claims* | *Location* |
|---|---|---|---|
| **4th** | | | |
| 334th: | Capt. H.D. Hively | (3)Me-109 dest(air) | Lubeck-Schwerin |

| Sqn | Pilot | Claim | Location |
|---|---|---|---|
| | Lt. J.L. Lang | Me-109 dest(air) | Weismar |
| | | u/i a/c dest(air) | Weismar |
| | | Me-109 dam(air) | Weismar |
| | Lt. D.W. Howe | Me-109 dest(air) | Neustadt Bay |
| | Lt. J.F. Scott | (.5)Me-109 dest(air)[*] | Lubeck-Schwerin |
| **56th** | | | |
| 61st: | Maj. L.C. Smith | (2)FW-190 dest(air) | N/Wernigerode |
| | Lt. R.M. Heineman | FW-190 dest(air) | Halberstadt |
| 62nd: | Capt. J.B. Eaves | (2)FW-190 dest(air) | N/Hanover |
| **78th** | | | |
| 82nd: | Lt. M.K. Woller | (2)Me-109 dest(air) | Dummer Lake |
| | Capt. J.W. Wilkinson | FW-190 dest(air) | Dummer Lake |
| | | FW-190 dam(air) | Dummer Lake |
| | Lt. M.R. Capp | Me-109 dest(air) | Dummer Lake |
| | Lt. R.L. Baker | Me-109 dam(air) | Dummer Lake |
| | | (2)Me-110 dest(grd) | Dummer Lake & Plantlunne |
| | Lt. C.W. DeWitt | FW-190 dam(air) | Dummer Lake |
| | Lt. H.B. Slater | Me-109 dam(air) | Dummer Lake |
| | Lt. K.R. Wagner | Me-109 dam(air) | Dummer Lake |
| | Lt. P.H. Hazelett | Me-110 dest(grd) | Plantlunne |
| | Capt. W.A. Guilfoyle | (.5)He-111 dam(grd) | Plantlunne |
| | Lt. L.H. Hosford | (.5)He-111 dam(grd) | Plantlunne |
| 83rd: | Capt. R.E. Ealey | Me-109 dest(air) | Lingen |
| | Lt. P.C. Holden | Me-109 dest(air) | Lingen |
| | Lt. F. White | Me-109 dest(air) | Lingen |
| 84th: | Capt. W.F. Hunt | Me-109 dest(air) | E/Nienburg |
| | Lt. H.L. Boyle | FW-190 dest(air) | Quackenbruck |
| | Lt. L.K. Covelle | Me-109 dest(air) | Nienburg |
| | Lt. R.M. Holly | Me-109 dest(air) | Nienburg |
| | Lt. W.J. Luckey | Me-109 dest(air) | Nienburg |
| **339th** | | | |
| HdQts: | Maj. M.G.H. McPharlin | (.5)Me-109 dest(air)[*] | Lubeck-Schwerin |
| | | Me-109 dam(air) | Lubeck-Schwerin |
| 503rd: | Lt. J.R. Crockett | (2)Ju-52 dest(grd) | Ludwigslust |
| | Lt. J. Wolfort | u/i a/c dest(grd) | Ludwigslust |
| | Capt. W.T. Carter | (3)u/i a/c dam(grd) | Steinhuder Lake |
| | Lt. N.T. Folwell | (3)Me-109 dam(grd) | Pritzwalk |
| | | u/i a/c dam(grd) | Pritzwalk |
| | Lt. R.S. Whitelaw | (3)u/i a/c dam(grd) | Steinhuder Lake |
| 504th: | Lt. W.R. O'Sullivan | FW-190 dest(air) | Berlin |
| 505th: | Lt. E.M. Johnson | (1.5)FW-190 dest(air) | Gustrow |
| | Lt. J.R. Starnes | (.5)FW-190 dest(air) | Gustrow |
| **352nd** | | | |
| HdQts: | LtCol. E.L. Clark | Me-109 dest(air) | NW Wittenburg |
| 328th: | Lt. R.C. Brookins | Me-109 dest(air) | Wittenburg-Havelburg |
| | Capt. R.H. Sharp | (.5)Me-109 dest(air)[#] | Wittenburg |
| | Lt. M.M. Carlone | (.5)Me-109 dest(air)[#] | Wittenburg |
| | Lt. E. Zellner | (.5)Me-109 dest(air)[**] | Wittenburg-Havelburg |
| | | Me-109 prob(air) | Wittenburg-Havelburg |
| 486th: | Maj. S.W. Andrew | Me-109 dest(air) | Rathenow |
| | Lt. T.W. Colby | Me-109 dest(air) | Rathenow |
| 487th: | Lt. C.J. Luksic | Me-109 dest(air) | Ludwigslust |
| | Lt. G.T. Moran | Me-109 dest(air) | Ludwigslust |
| | Lt. J.P. Kessler | Me-109 prob(air) | Ludwigslust |
| | | Me-109 dam(air) | Ludwigslust |
| **353rd** | | | |
| 352nd: | Lt. W.W. Johnson | Me-109 dam(air) | SW Brunswick |
| | Lt. W.S. Marchant | Me-109 dam(air) | SW Brunswick |
| **356th** | | | |
| 359th: | Lt. H. Weber | Me-109 dest(air) | Steinhuder Lake |
| 360th: | Capt. J.W. Vogt | FW-190 dest(air) | SW Celle |
| | Lt. W.G. Maxwell | Me-109 dest(air) | Nienburg |
| | Lt. A.A. Perryman | FW-190 dest(air) | SW Celle |
| | Lt. F.M. Russell | FW-190 dest(air) | Hanover |
| | Lt. C.A. Vitali | Me-109 dest(air) | Steinhuder Lake |
| | Lt. R.R. Withers | Me-109 dest(air) | Hanover |
| | | Me-109 dam(air) | Hanover |
| | Lt. R.C. L'Heureux | Me-109 dam(air) | Hanover |
| 361st: | Capt. D.J. Strait | Me-109 dest(air) | Quackenbruck |
| | Lt. H.M. Engelhorn | Me-109 dest(air) | Quackenbruck |
| | Lt. R.H. Gansberg | Me-109 dest(air) | Quackenbruck |
| | Lt. D.F. Thwaites | FW-190 dest(air) | Quackenbruck |
| | | (3)FW-190 dam(air) | Quackenbruck |
| | LtCol. W. Waller | Me-109 dam(air) | NE Dummer Lake-Minden |
| **357th** | | | |
| HdQts: | Maj. I.H. Dregne | Me-109 dest(air) | Wittenburg |
| 362nd: | Capt. F.E. Adams | (.5)Me-109 dest(air) | Hagenow |
| | Lt. A.J. Roberson | (.5)Me-109 dest(air) | Hagenow |
| 363rd: | Lt. R.W. Foy | (3)Me-109 dest(air) | NW Brandenburg |
| | Capt. E.W. Hiro | (2)Me-109 dest(air) | NW Brandenburg |
| | | Me-109 dam(air) | NW Brandenburg |
| | Lt. C.K. Peters | Me-109 dest(air) | NW Brandenburg |
| | | Me-109 dam(air) | NW Brandenburg |
| 364th: | Capt. J.A. Storch | Me-109 dest(air) | NE Salzwedel |
| | Lt. L.A. Ruder | FW-190 dest(air) | N/Berlin |
| **359th** | | | |
| 368th: | Capt. C.E. Mosse | Me-109 dest(air) | NW Berlin |
| | Lt. R.B. Janney | Me-109 dest(air) | Neuruppin |
| 369th: | Lt. H.C. Burton | (2)Me-109 dest(air) | Rathenow |
| | Capt. C.C. Ettlesen | (.5)Me-109 dest(air)[**] | NW Berlin |
| | Lt. C.H. Kruger | Me-109 dest(air) | Rathenow |
| | Lt. J.H. Oliphint | Me-109 dest(air) | Wittengen |
| | Lt. R.C. Thomson | Me-109 dest(air) | Wittengen |
| 370th: | Lt. R.S. Wetmore | (2)Me-109 dest(air) | Stendal |
| | Lt. P.H. Bateman | FW-190 dest(air) | Stendal |
| | Lt. C.W. Hipsher | Me-109 dam(air) | Stendal |
| **364th** | | | |
| 383rd: | Lt. J. Kerr | FW-190 dam(air) | Trenemunde A/F |
| | Lt. K.F. Nicholson | FW-190 dam(air) | Lubeck Bay |
| 384th: | Capt. R.E. Lacy | He-111 dam(grd) | NW Schleswig |

*Losses-*

**4th**: Lt. Donald J. Patchen (336th Ftr Sqn) POW
P-51B VF-A 43-6584
Hit by flak near Hanover.

**56th**: Lt. Anthony S. Cavallo (63rd Ftr Sqn) ASR
P-47D UN-G 42-22772 "El Diablo II"
Suffered mechanical failure and bailed out over the North Sea.

**339th**: Lt. James R. Crockett (503rd Ftr Sqn) KIA
P-51B D7-Q 42-106785
Caught in the explosion of a loco near Messdorf.

Lt. Walter R. O'Sullivan (504th Ftr Sqn) POW
P-51C 5Q- 42-103342
Hit by a Me-109 near Lubeck.

**352nd**: Lt. Michele M. Carlone (328th Ftr Sqn) KIA
P-51B PE-N 42-106668
Hit by enemy fighters near Wittenburg.

**355th**: LtCol. Edward W. Szaniawski (357th Ftr Sqn) POW
P-51B OS-A 43-7142 "Available Jones 5th"
Hit by flak while strafing near Diepholz.

Lt. Hudson F. Packard (357th Ftr Sqn) KIA
P-51B OS-I 42-106762
Collided with a Do-217 near Kolonie Breiteich.

**356th**: Lt. Edwin D. Cook (360th Ftr Sqn) POW
P-47D PI- 42-25294
Hit by enemy fighters near Hanover.

Lt. Allen A. Perryman, Jr. (360th Ftr Sqn) POW
P-47D PI- 43-25302
Hit by a Me-109 near Celle.

Lt. James K. Johnson (361st Ftr Sqn) POW
P-47D QI-Y 42-75505
Hit by enemy fighters near Quackenbruck.

**357th**: Lt. Archie F. Bridges (364th Ftr Sqn) POW
P-51B C5- 42-106648
Suffered mechanical failure east of Brandenburg.

**359th**: Capt. Charles E. Mosse (368th Ftr Sqn) POW
P-51B CV-B 42-106890
Hit by a Me-109 northwest of Berlin.

Lt. James B. Smith (368th Ftr Sqn) POW
P-51B CV-S 42-106804
Hit by enemy fighters near Krummbeck.

Lt. D.H. Laing (369th Ftr Sqn) POW
P-51B IV-E 42-106893
Suffered mechanical failure near Klietz.

**361st**: Lt. Dennis P. Noble (376th Ftr Sqn) ASR
P-51B E9-
Bailed out over the Channel.

**364th**: Lt. Nick W. Cruger (383rd Ftr Sqn) MIA
P-38J N2- 43-28360
Hit by flak and crashed northeast of Cromer.

Lt. John Kerr (383rd Ftr Sqn) MIA
P-38J N2-A 42-68013
Hit by flak and bailed out near Juist.

Lt. Marvin H. Brown (384th Ftr Sqn) POW
P-38J 5Y-T 42-104402
Hit by flak near Husum and bellied-in near Nordstrand.

Lt. Edwin F. Gaines (384th Ftr Sqn) POW
P-38J 5Y- 42-67882
Hit by flak near Husum and bellied-in near Nordstrand.

*Remarks*
56th: 0-1 loco
78th: 0-2 locos
339th: 3-0 locos, 0-4 barges
355th: 0-1 vehicle
356th: 0-1 flak position
359th: 2-0 locos, 1-0 railcar, 1-3 barges, 1-1 tugs, 0-4 flak positions
361st: 1-0 loco

**May 20, 1944**
Groups Operating: P-51 4th, 339th, 352nd, 355th, 357th, 359th, 361st
P-47 56th, 78th, 353rd, 356th
P-38 20th, 55th, 364th
Missions: Support for bombers to Orly, Villacoublay, Reims, Leige, and Brussels.
Claims: 2-0-1 air
1-1 ground

| *Group* | | *Claims* | *Location* |
|---|---|---|---|
| **55th** | | | |
| 38th: | Lt. A.L. Thorsen | FW-190 dam(air) | Troyes |
| 338th: | Lt. J.K. Garnett | FW-190 dest(air) | Sens |
| | Lt. H.E. Larsen | FW-190 dest(air) | Sens |
| **364th** | | | |
| 385th: | Capt. C.W. Stapleton | Ju-88 dest(grd) | Soissons |
| | Lt. E.W. Bankey | Ju-88 dam(grd) | Soissons |

*Losses-*

**55th**: Lt. John W. Thomas (338th Ftr Sqn) KIA
P-38J CL- 42-67715
Last seen near Sens; possibly hit by enemy fighters.

**355th**: Lt. Clarence Donaldson (354th Ftr Sqn) KIA
P-51B WR-B 43-6574
Hit by a Me-109 near Erkelenz.

Lt. Donald J. Jacobson (354th Ftr Sqn) KIA
P-51B WR-D 43-6857
Hit by a Me-109 near Erkelenz.

**356th**: Lt. Alex S. Koczak (360th Ftr Sqn) POW
P-47D PI- 42-8533
Suffered mechanical failure and bailed out near Valenciennes.

**May 21, 1944**
Groups Operating: P-47 56th
Missions: Support of bombers to Marquise/Mimoyecques and Siracourt V-1 sites.
Claims: nil
Losses: nil

Groups Operating: P-51 4th, 339th, 352nd, 355th, 357th, 359th, 361st
P-47 78th, 353rd, 356th
P-38 20th, 55th, 364th
Missions: "Chattanooga Choo-Choo"-attacks against rail and transportation targets.
Claims: 21-0-2 air
97-83 ground

| *Group* | | *Claims* | *Location* |
|---|---|---|---|
| **4th** | | | |
| 334th: | Lt. R.K. Hofer | (.5)Bu-131 dest(air) | Rathenow |
| | | Bu-131 dest(grd) | Rathenow |
| | Lt. A.C. Hewatt | (.5)Bu-131 dest(air) | Rathenow |
| | Lt. G.C. Siems | (2)Me-210 dest(grd) | Rathenow |
| | | (2)Me-210 dam(grd) | Rathenow |
| | Lt. F.E. Speer | Ju-52 dest(grd) | Rathenow |
| | | Ju-88 dest(grd) | Rathenow |
| | Lt. T.E. Fraser | (2)Ju-88 dam(grd) | Buch A/F |
| | | u/i a/c dam(grd) | Buch A/F |
| **55th** | | | |
| 38th: | Lt. D.E. Penn | Hs-129 dest(air) | Brunswick |
| | Capt. J.D. Landers | (.5)u/i a/c dest(grd) | E/Helmstedt |
| | | (.5)u/i a/c dest(grd) | E/Helmstedt |
| | Lt. N.R. Tipton | (.5)u/i a/c dest(grd) | E/Helmstedt |
| | | (.5)u/i a/c dest(grd) | E/Helmstedt |
| | Lt. V.H. Soule | (2)u/i a/c dam(grd) | E/Helmstedt |
| 338th: | Lt. P. Dempsey | (2)Me-109 dest(grd) | Helmstedt |
| | | (3)FW-190 dam(grd) | Helmstedt |
| | Maj. V.W. Bollwerk | Hs-129 dest(grd) | Helmstedt |
| | Lt. S.E. Hansard | Ju-88 dest(grd) | Magdeburg |
| **339th** | | | |
| 503rd: | Lt. L.M. Wright | He-111 dest(air) | Riesa A/F |
| | | Ju-88 dam(grd) | Riesa A/F |
| | Lt. W.E. Bryan | (2)u/i a/c dest(grd) | Pelenz-Meckau |
| | Lt. R.H. Deary | u/i a/c dest(grd) | Pelenz-Meckau |
| | | (2)u/i a/c dam(grd) | Pelenz-Meckau |
| | Lt. E.E. Erickson | u/i a/c dest(grd) | Pelenz-Meckau |
| | Lt. L.J. Fiorito | Me-109 dest(grd) | Pelenz-Meckau |
| | | Ju-88 dam(grd) | Pelenz-Meckau |
| | Lt. A.L. Lowery | u/i a/c dest(grd) | Pelenz-Meckau |
| | Lt. G.H. Reynolds | u/i a/c dest(grd) | Pelenz-Meckau |
| | Lt. A.S. Harte | (2)Ju-88 dam(grd) | Riesa A/F |
| | Lt. J.B. Price | (2)Ju-88 dam(grd) | Pelenz A/F |
| | Lt. E.B. Stephenson | Ju-88 dam(grd) | Riesa A/F |
| | Lt. R.S. Whitelaw | u/i a/c dam(grd) | Pelenz A/F |
| 504th: | Capt. B.C. Routt | (2)Me-109 dest(air) | Dobeln |
| | Lt. G.P. Harry | Me-109 dam(air) | Leipzig |
| | | Ju-87 dam(grd) | Leipzig |
| | Lt. L.D. Eisenhart | FW-190 dest(grd) | W/Leipzig |
| 505th: | Lt. J.L. Lynch | (1.5)Do-217 dest(air) | Riesa |
| | | u/i a/c dest(air) | Riesa |
| | Lt. G.F. Perry | (.5)Do-217 dest(air) | Riesa |
| | Lt. J.R. Hanson | (1.5)u/i a/c dest(air) | Leipzig-Dresden |
| | Lt. J.R. Starnes | (.5)u/i a/c dest(air) | Leipzig-Dresden |
| | Lt. L. Reid | (1.5)Ju-88 dest(air)* | W/Dresden |
| | Lt. C.J. Hanseman | (2)u/i a/c dest(air) | W/Dresden |
| | | (.5)Ju-88 dest(air)* | W/Dresden |
| | Lt. H.M. Everett | (.5)Ju-88 dest(air)** | Schwepnitz |
| | Lt. W.F. Mudge | (.5)Ju-88 dest(air)** | Schwepnitz |
| | Lt. R.W. Strong | u/i a/c dest(air) | Dresden |
| | Lt. O.P. Farmer | u/i a/c dam(air) | Oschatz |
| **352nd** | | | |
| 328th: | Capt. E.L. Abbott | u/i a/c dest(grd) | Alt Ruppin |
| | | (2)u/i a/c dam(grd) | Alt Ruppin |
| | Capt. R.H. Sharp | (2)Ju-88 dest(grd) | Alt Ruppin |
| | | He-111 dam(grd) | Alt Ruppin |
| | | u/i a/c dam(grd) | Alt Ruppin |
| | Lt. R.G. Phillips | FW-190 dest(grd) | Alt Ruppin |
| | | Ju-52 dest(grd) | Alt Ruppin |
| | | u/i a/c dest(grd) | Alt Ruppin |
| | Lt. C.J. Bennette | He-111 dest(grd) | Alt Ruppin |
| | | u/i a/c dest(grd) | Alt Ruppin |
| | Lt. R.H. Powell | (2)He-111 dest(grd) | Alt Ruppin |
| | | (2)He-111 dam(grd) | Alt Ruppin |
| | Lt. S.E. Dyke | (2)He-111 dest(grd) | Alt Ruppin |
| | Lt. J.F. Thornell | (2)He-111 dest(grd) | Alt Ruppin |
| | | He-177 dam(grd) | Alt Ruppin |
| | Lt. E. Zellner | (2)Ju-86 dest(grd) | Alt Ruppin |
| | Lt. G. Rayborn | (2)He-111 dest(grd) | Alt Ruppin |
| | Lt. W.W. Furr | Ju-52 dest(grd) | Alt Ruppin |
| | Lt. E.L. Smith | He-111 dest(grd) | Alt Ruppin |
| | | u/i a/c dam(grd) | Alt Ruppin |
| | Lt. F.W. Horne | u/i a/c dest(grd) | Alt Ruppin |
| | | He-111 dam(grd) | Alt Ruppin |
| | Lt. J. Campbell | He-111 dest(grd) | Alt Ruppin |
| | | Do-217 dam(grd) | Alt Ruppin |
| | Lt. L. Fieg | (3)u/i a/c dam(grd) | Alt Ruppin |
| **355th** | | | |
| 357th: | Lt. J.C. Engelbreit | (.5)Me-108 dest(air) | W/Schwerin |
| | | Do-217 dest(grd) | SE Schwerin |
| | | (2)Do-217 dam(grd) | SE Schwerin |
| | Lt. W.E. MacFarlane | (.5)Me-108 dest(air) | W/Schwerin |
| | | Do-217 dest(grd) | Schwerin |
| | | (5)Do-217 dam(grd) | Schwerin |
| | Lt. M.A. King | (2)Do-217 dest(grd) | SE Schwerin |
| | | Do-217 dam(grd) | SE Schwerin |
| **356th** | | | |
| 360th: | Capt. N.D. Cota | He-177 dest(air) | Stade |
| **357th** | | | |
| HdQts: | Maj. I.H. Dregne | (1.5)Me-109 dest(grd)* | S/Eichhof |
| 362nd: | Lt. R.M. Starkey | Me-110 dam(grd) | Tarnewitz |
| | | Ju-52 dam(grd) | Tarnewitz |
| | Lt. H.R. Ankeny | Me-110 dam(grd) | Tarnewitz |
| 364th: | Lt. R.C. Smith | (3)Me-109 dest(grd) | S/Eichhof |
| | Capt. J.A. Storch | Me-109 dest(grd) | S/Eichhof |
| | | (.5)FW-44 dest(grd) | S/Eichhof |
| | Lt. C.H. Dooley | Me-109 dest(grd) | S/Eichhof |
| | | (.5)FW-44 dest(grd) | S/Eichhof |
| | Lt. C.D. Conklin | (1.5)Me-109 dest(grd)** | S/Eichhof |
| | Lt. H.R. Nowlin | (1.5)Me-109 dest(grd)** | S/Eichhof |
| | Lt. M.A. Stanley | (1.5)Me-109 dest(grd)* | S/Eichhof |
| | Lt. M.H. Stepelton | Me-109 dest(grd) | S/Eichhof |
| **359th** | | | |
| 368th: | Lt. R.B. Hatter | (6)u/i a/c dest(grd) | N/Grevesmuhlen |
| | | (3)u/i a/c dam(grd) | N/Grevesmuhlen |

| | | | |
|---|---|---|---|
| | Lt. T.J. McGeever | Ju-52 dest(air) | Gadebusch |
| | | u/i a/c dest(grd) | Gadebusch |
| | Lt. G.C. Bach | (2)FW-190 dest(grd) | N/Grevesmuhlen |
| | | (4)u/i a/c dam(grd) | N/Grevesmuhlen |
| | Lt. T.S. Lane | (2)u/i a/c dest(grd) | N/Grevesmuhlen |
| | | (3)u/i a/c dam(grd) | N/Grevesmuhlen |
| | Lt. A.G. Homeyer | FW-190 dest(grd) | N/Grevesmuhlen |
| | | FW-190 dam(grd) | N/Grevesmuhlen |
| | | Ju-52 dam(grd) | N/Grevesmuhlen |
| | Lt. B.M. Hagan | u/i a/c dest(grd) | Carlowe |
| | | (2)u/i a/c dam(grd) | Carlowe |
| | Lt. G.M. Randolph | (3)u/i a/c dam(grd) | Gadebusch |
| | Lt. O.P. Drake | He-111 dam(grd) | Wismar-Rostock |
| | | Go-242 dam(grd) | Wismar-Rostock |
| 369th: | Capt. R.H. Broach | (.5)u/i a/c dest(air) | NW Klutz |
| | Lt. R.B. Sander | (.5)u/i a/c dest(air) | NW Klutz |
| | Lt. E.R. Orwig | u/i a/c dest(grd) | Lubeck-Schwerin |
| | | u/i a/c dam(grd) | Lubeck-Schwerin |
| 370th: | Lt. J.E. Shupe | (4)Ju-88 dest(grd) | Schwerin |
| | | (3)Ju-88 dam(grd) | Schwerin |
| | Lt. R.M. Callahan | Ju-88 dest(grd) | Schwerin |
| | | Ju-88 dam(grd) | Schwerin |
| | Lt. W.R. Newberg | (2)Ju-88 dam(grd) | Schwerin |
| | Lt. G.A. Doersch | u/i a/c dam(grd) | Bruel |
| **361st** | | | |
| 374th: | Capt. R.E. Sedman | u/i a/c dest(grd) | Grossenheim A/F |
| | | (2)u/i a/c dam(grd) | Grossenheim A/F |
| **364th** | | | |
| HdQts: | Maj. A.L. Chilton | Ju-88 dest(grd) | Hagenow |
| | | Ju-52 dest(grd) | Hagenow |
| 383rd: | Lt. M.W. Glascow | FW-190 dest(grd) | Rechlin |
| | | Ju-88 dest(grd) | Rechlin |
| | | (2)Ju-88 dam(grd) | Rechlin |
| | Lt. B.B. Wilson | (2)Ju-88 dest(grd) | Rechlin |
| | | Ju-88 dam(grd) | Rechlin |
| | Maj. J.B. McManus | Me-410 dest(grd) | NW Renow |
| | Lt. C.A. Barnes | Ju-88 dest(grd) | NW Renow |
| | Lt. L.R. Wilson | Me-323 dest(grd) | NW Renow |
| | | Do-217 dam(grd) | NW Renow |
| | Lt. J.J. Bannister | (2)Ju-88 dam(grd) | Rechlin |
| | Lt. L.J. Miller | Me-410 dam(grd) | NW Renwo |
| 384th: | Maj. J.H. Lowell | (2)Ju-52 dest(grd) | Prachim-Ludwigslust-Hagenow |
| | | He-111 dest(grd) | Par-Lud-Hagenow |
| | | Ju-88 dest(grd) | Par-Lud-Hagenow |
| | | FW-190 dam(grd) | Par-Lud-Hagenow |
| | Capt. J.C. Ford | Ju-88 dest(grd) | Par-Lud-Hagenow |
| | Lt. S.C. Phillips | He-111 dest(grd) | Par-Lud-Hagenow |
| | | Ju-88 dam(grd) | Par-Lud-Hagenow |
| | Lt. B.P. Yost | Ju-52 dest(grd) | Par-Lud-Hagenow |
| 385th: | Lt. C.S. Hill | (.5)He-111 dest(air) | SE Luneburg |
| | Lt. E.F. Izor | (.5)He-111 dest(air) | SE Luneburg |
| | Lt. R. Visconte | Ju-88 dest(grd) | Schwerin-Ludwigslust-Luneburg |
| | Lt. E.A. Taylor | Me-210 dest(grd) | Schw-Lud-Lune. |
| | Lt. S.J. Walsh | Ju-88 dest(grd) | Schw-Lud-Lune. |

*Losses-*

**4th:** Lt. William W. Hunt (335th Ftr Sqn) KIA
P-51B WD-F 43-6901
Hit by flak near Zossen.

**55th:** Lt. Noah R. Tipton (38th Ftr Sqn) POW
P-38J CG- 42-68076
Hit by flak and bellied-in near Kampen.

Lt. Burt R. Shepard (38th Ftr Sqn) POW
P-38J CG- 42-67713
Hit by flak and bellied-in near Helmstedt.

Capt. Karl H. Garlock (338th Ftr Sqn) POW
P-38J CL- 42-67771
Hit by flak near Brunswick.

Lt. Horace K. Walter (338th Ftr Sqn) KIA
P-38J CL- 42-104280
Last seen near Flensburg with an engine out.

Lt. James H. Weisel (343rd Ftr Sqn) POW
P-38J CY- 42-68086
Hit by flak and bellied-in near Celle.

Lt. Henry K. Warwick (343rd Ftr Sqn) MIA
P-38J CY- 42-104250
Hit by flak and disappeared near Celle.

**339th:** Capt. Walter T. Carter (503rd Ftr Sqn) POW
P-51B D7-B 42-106863 "Mon Petite"
Hit by flak near Leipzig.

Lt. Robert F. Mulvey (503rd Ftr Sqn) KIA
P-51C D7- 42-103295
Ran out of fuel near Willesbord.

Lt. Arthur R. Steier (503rd Ftr Sqn) KIA
P-51B D7- 42-106674
Hit by flak near Eilenberg.

Lt. Floyd P. Heneghan (505th Ftr Sqn) KIA
P-51B 6N- 42-106678
Hit by flak at Riesa Airfield.

**352nd:** LtCol. Eugene L. Clark (HdQts) POW
P-51C PE-L 42-103316 "Panama Mamita"
Hit by flak near Diepholz and bailed out west of Dummer Lake.

**353rd:** Lt. Chauncey Rowan (350th Ftr Sqn) POW
P-47D LH-D 42-76280
Hit by flak near Bremen.

Lt. Raymond Eluhow (352nd Ftr Sqn) ASR
P-47D SX-P
Hit by flak and bailed out east of Woodbridge.

**356th:** Lt. Edwin E. Anderson (360th Ftr Sqn) POW
P-47D PI- 42-76396
Hit by flak near Oldenburg.

Lt. Wallace G. Maxwell (360th Ftr Sqn) KIA
P-47D PI-Q 42-76499
Hit by flak and bailed out over the North Sea off Wilhelmshaven.

**357th:** Lt. William D. Michaely (363rd Ftr Sqn) POW
P-51C B6- 42-103286
Hit by flak near Anklam.

Lt. Joseph F. Pierce (363rd Ftr Sqn) KIA
P-51B B6-Z 43-6429
Hit by flak northwest of Anklam.

Lt. William C. Reese (364th Ftr Sqn) KIA
P-51B C5-F 43-12313 "Bear River Betsy"
Hit by flak near Strasbourg.

**359th:** Lt. Arlen R. Baldridge (368th Ftr Sqn) POW(D)
P-51B CV-Y 43-6962
Hit by flak northeast of Wismar and bellied-in near Barenhorst; was captured then shot and killed.

Lt. Clyde M. Huddleston (368th Ftr Sqn) KIA
P-51B CV-G 42-106620
Hit by flak near Wismar.

Lt. Homer L. Rodeheaver (369th Ftr Sqn) KIA
P-51B IV-U 42-106818
Hit by flak near Reinfeld/Mecklenburg.

Lt. Joseph E. Shupe (370th Ftr Sqn) KIA
P-51B CS-G 42-106921
Hit by flak near Schwerin.

**361st:** Capt. John W. Guckeyson (375th Ftr Sqn) KIA
P-51C E2-W 42-103349
Hit by flak while strafing a train south of Stendal.

F/O Cornelius G. Hogelin (375th Ftr Sqn) KIA
P-51B E2-B 43-24783
Hit by flak and bailed out off Noordwal.

**364th:** Maj. Andrew L. Chilton (HdQts) KIA
P-38J 5Y-A 43-28734
Hit by flak at Hagenow and crashed into a house.

Lt. Lamarr J. Miller (383rd Ftr Sqn) POW
P-38J N2-I 43-28272
Hit by flak at Rechlin/Larz and bellied-in near the field.

*Remarks*

4th: 0-28 locos, 0-5 railcars, 3-11 vehicles, 0-7 barges, 0-3 tugs, 2-6 buildings
55th: 23-15 locos, 11-2 railcars, 5-0 vehicles, 1-3 steamers, 6-3 barges, 0-11 tugs, 0-3 hangars, 1-8 buildings, 1-3 flak towers
P-38 c/l Old Buckenham; o.k.
P-38 c/l Nuthampstead; o.k.
78th: 1-16 locos, 0-7 railcars, 0-2 barges, 0-1 tug
339th: 7-14 locos, 6-0 flak towers, 2-0 barracks, 0-5 buildings, 0-1 hangar, 2-2 storage tanks.
352nd: 12-13 locos, 6-1 railcars, 0-1 vehicle, 0-2 buildings
P-51 c/l; o.k.

353rd: 7-3 locos, 10-2 railcars, 0-1 barge, 0-2 buildings
355th: 0-5 locos, 0-4 vehicles, 0-1 flak tower
356th: 4-2 locos, 0-1 flak tower
357th: 6-4 locos, 1-1 hangars, 1-0 vehicle
359th: 5-24 locos, 1-0 tug, 1-6 buildings, 0-5 signal towers, 0-1 gun position
361st: 22-4 locos, 0-2 railcars, 2-6 vehicles, 0-13 barges, 0-9 buildings, 0-4 flak towers
364th: 7-9 locos, 1-0 railcar, 1-0 vehicle, 0-7 tugs, 0-2 barges, 0-2 steamers, 0-5 flak towers, 0-1 hangar, 0-2 switch-towers
Lt. James W. Purvis(384th Ftr Sqn) c/l; o.k.
P-38J 5Y-

**May 22, 1944**
Groups Operating: P-51 4th, 339th, 352nd, 355th, 357th, 359th, 361st
P-47 56th, 356th
P-38 20th, 55th, 364th
Missions: Support of bombers to Siracourt V-1 sites and Kiel.
Claims: 22.5-4-8 air
0-0 ground

| ***Group*** | | ***Claims*** | ***Location*** |
|---|---|---|---|
| **4th** | | | |
| 334th: | Lt. R.K. Hofer | Me-109 dest(air) | Hamburg |
| | Capt. N. Megura | (.5)Me-109 dest(air) | SW Kiel |
| | | (shared with an unknown P-38 pilot) | |
| 336th: | Capt. W.W. Millikan | Me-109 dest(air) | NW Kiel |
| | Capt. J.H. Bennett | Me-109 prob(air) | Lubeck |
| **20th** | | | |
| 77th: | Maj. R.F. Gustke | FW-190 dest(air) | NW Kiel |
| **55th** | | | |
| 38th: | Maj. J.H. Hancock | FW-190 dest(air) | SW Kiel |
| | Lt. C.W. Des Voignes | FW-190 dest(air) | SW Neumunster |
| 338th: | Lt. M.E. Blanchard | FW-190 dest(air) | Neumunster |
| **56th** | | | |
| 61st: | LtCol. F.S. Gabreski | (3)FW-190 dest(air) | Hoperhofen A/F |
| | | FW-190 prob(air) | Hoperhofen A/F |
| | Lt. R.M. Heineman | (2)FW-190 dest(air) | Hoperhofen A/F |
| | F/O E.D. McMinn | (2)FW-190 dest(air) | Rotenburg |
| | | FW-190 dam(air) | Rotenburg |
| | Capt. J.R. Carter | FW-190 dest(air) | Hoperhofen A/F |
| | | FW-190 prob(air) | Hoperhofen A/F |
| | | FW-190 dam(air) | Hoperhofen A/F |
| | Lt. R.A. Herin | FW-190 dest(air) | Hoperhofen A/F |
| | Lt. P. Neyland | FW-190 dest(air) | Hoperhofen A/F |
| | Lt. J.J. Clark | FW-190 dest(air) | Hoperhofen A/F |
| | | FW-190 dam(air) | Hoperhofen A/F |
| | P/O W.A. Lanowski | FW-190 dest(air) | Hoperhofen A/F |
| **355th** | | | |
| HdQts: | LtCol. G.J. Dix | Me-109 prob(air) | SW Kiel |
| 357th: | Lt. J. Guerrant | Me-109 dam(air) | Kiel |
| **364th** | | | |
| 383rd: | Capt. S.J. Wicker | (2)FW-190 dest(air) | SW Kiel |
| | Lt. J.B. MacDermott | FW-190 dest(air) | Kiel |
| | | FW-190 dam(air) | Kiel |
| | Lt. K.F. Nicholson | FW-190 dest(air) | SE Kiel |
| | Lt. N.F. Bettin | FW-190 dam(air) | SW Kiel |
| 384th: | Lt. V.L. Kercher | FW-190 dam(air) | SW Kiel |
| 385th: | Lt. F.C. McClanahan | (.5)FW-190 dam(air) | Neumunster |
| | Lt. H.H. Stubblefield | (.5)FW-190 dam(air) | Neumunster |

*Losses-*

**4th**: Capt. Nicholas Megura (334th Ftr Sqn) INT
P-51B QP-F 43-7158
Shot-up by a P-38 and landed in Sweden.

**20th**: Capt. William K. Coon (77th Ftr Sqn) POW
P-38J LC- 43-28270
Hit by a FW-190 northwest of Kiel.

**56th**: Lt. Cletus B. Nale (61st Ftr Sqn) KIA
P-47D HV- 42-74752
Hit by a FW-190 near Suederwalsede.

Lt. Richard M. Heineman (61st Ftr Sqn) KIA
P-47D HV-W 42-76509
Hit by a FW-190 near Hoperhofen Airfield.

Lt. Eugene E. Bennett (62nd Ftr Sqn) ASR
P-47D LM-
Bailed out over the Channel.

**364th**: Lt. Milton S. Damron (384th Ftr Sqn) POW
P-38J 5Y- 42-68125
Last seen chasing a FW-190 near Kiel.

Lt. Howard V. Kilpatrick (384th Ftr Sqn) KIA
P-38J 5Y-M 43-28470
Last seen in a fight near Kiel with one engine on fire.

*Remarks*
56th: 6-7 locos, 0-16 barges
P-47 c/l; o.k.
P-47 c/l; o.k.
78th: 10-3 locos
352nd: 2-1 locos, 0-1 vehicle, 0-1 building

Groups Operating: P-47 56th, 78th, 353rd, 356th
Missions: Dive-bombing of rail bridges near Hasselt and Liege.
Claims: nil

*Losses-*

**353rd**: Lt. Jack Terzian (351st Ftr Sqn) POW
P-47D YJ- 42-25730
Hit by flak and bellied-in near Letterhouten.

*Remarks*
356th: 0-2 bridges

**May 23, 1944**
Groups Operating: P-51 4th, 339th, 352nd, 355th, 357th, 359th, 361st
P-47 56th, 78th, 353rd, 356th
P-38 20th, 55th, 364th
Missions: Support of bombers to airfields and marshalling yards in France.
Claims: nil
Losses: nil

*Remarks*
353rd: Lt. Horace Q. Waggoner (352nd Ftr Sqn) c/l Raydon; o.k.
P-47D SX-D
356th: Lt. Joseph B. Hepfer (360th Ftr Sqn) c/l Hawkinge; o.k.
P-47D PI-H 42-22780

Groups Operating: P-51 359th, 361st
Missions: Dive-bombing the Hasselt rail bridge (it was destroyed).
Claims: nil

*Losses-*

**361st**: Lt. Joseph D. Kelly (376th Ftr Sqn) POW
P-51B E9-L 42-106739
Hit by flak near Hulsthout and bailed out east of Lierre.

KIAc's
356th: Lt. Grant F. Moyer (360th Ftr Sqn)
P-47D QI-V 42-22479 (this was a 361st Ftr Sqn a/c)
Crashed into Bradwell Bay while on a practice flight.

**May 24, 1944**
Groups Operating: P-51 4th, 339th, 352nd, 355th, 357th, 359th, 361st
P-47 56th, 78th, 353rd, 356th
P-38 20th, 55th, 364th
Missions: Support for bombers to Berlin and to airfields in the Paris area.
Claims: 31-4-13 air
2-1 ground

| ***Group*** | | ***Claims*** | ***Location*** |
|---|---|---|---|
| **4th** | | | |
| 334th: | Lt. R.K. Hofer | (2)Me-109 dest(air) | E/Hamburg |
| | Capt. H.D. Hively | Me-109 dest(air) | Hamburg |
| | Lt. T.E. Fraser | FW-190 dest(air) | E/Hamburg |
| | Lt. W.G. Gillette | Me-109 dest(air) | NE Hamburg |
| | Lt. J.L. Lang | Me-109 dest(air) | N/Hamburg |
| | Lt. F.E. Speer | Me-109 dest(air) | E/Hamburg |
| 335th: | Lt. J.W. Russell | Me-109 dest(air) | Hamburg-Lubeck |
| | Lt. J.W. Goodwyn | Me-109 prob(air) | N/Hamburg |
| | Lt. F.C. Jones | Me-109 prob(air) | Hamburg |
| **20th** | | | |
| 79th: | Capt. J.M. Ilfrey | (2)Me-109 dest(air) | Eberswalde |
| | Maj. D.E. Anderson | Me-109 dam(air) | Eberswalde |
| | Lt. K.H. Stevens | Me-109 dam(air) | Eberswalde |
| | Lt. H.J. Watson | Me-109 dam(air) | Eberswalde |
| **339th** | | | |
| 503rd: | Lt. W.E. Bryan | (.5)FW-190 dest(air)* | Dannenberg |
| | Lt. E.H. Graham | (.5)FW-190 dest(air)* | Dannenberg |
| | Lt. R.B. Brown | (.5)Me-109 dest(air) | SW Berlin |
| | | (2)Me-109 dam(air) | SW Berlin |
| | Lt. J. Wolfort | (.5)Me-109 dest(air) | SW Berlin |
| | | Me-109 dam(air) | SW Berlin |
| | Maj. H.W. Scruggs | (.5)FW-190 dest(air)** | NW Berlin |
| | Lt. R.S. Whitelaw | (.5)FW-190 dest(air)** | NW Berlin |
| 504th: | Lt. W.B. Griffith | Me-109 dest(air) | Berlin |

| | | | |
|---|---|---|---|
| | Lt. B.V. Stevens | Me-109 prob(air) | Berlin |
| | | (2)Me-109 dam(air) | Berlin |
| | Lt. M.R. Ball | Me-109 dam(air) | Berlin |
| 505th: | Maj. D.A. Larson | (2)Me-109 dest(air) | Berlin |
| | | FW-190 dest(air) | Berlin |
| | | FW-190 dam(air) | Berlin |
| | Lt. E.M. Johnson | FW-190 dest(air) | Berlin |
| | Lt. J.L. Lynch | Me-109 dest(grd) | Gifhorn |
| **352nd** | | | |
| 328th: | Lt. W.W. Furr | Me-109 dest(air) | W/Perleberg |
| | Lt. E. Zellner | Me-109 dest(air) | W/Perleberg |
| 486th: | Capt. W.W. Anderson | Me-109 dest(air) | NW Berlin |
| | Lt. J.L. Gerst | Me-109 dest(air) | N/Berlin |
| **355th** | | | |
| 357th: | Lt. T.J. Foster | Me-109 dest(air) | Kyritz |
| 358th: | LtCol. R.B. Myers | Me-109 dest(air) | Berlin |
| | | Me-109 dam(air) | Berlin |
| **357th** | | | |
| 363rd: | Capt. W.R. O'Brien | Me-109 dest(air) | E/Berlin |
| | Capt. E.W. Hiro | FW-190 prob(air) | SE Berlin |
| **359th** | | | |
| 368th: | Lt. J.B. Hunter | (.5)Me-109 dest(air) | NW Berlin |
| 369th: | Lt. V.E. Sansing | (1.5)Me-109 dest(air) | NW Berlin |
| **361st** | | | |
| 374th: | Lt. P.C. Holter | Me-109 dam(air) | NE Berlin |
| 375th: | Maj. G.L. Merritt | Me-109 dest(air) | Berlin |
| | Capt. C.N. Keppler | Me-109 dam(air) | N/Berlin |
| 376th: | Lt. M.C. Williams | Me-109 dest(air) | Berlin |
| **364th** | | | |
| 383rd: | Lt. W.D. Boyd | (.5)Do-217 dest(grd) | SW Berlin |
| | Lt. K.F. Nicholson | (.5)Do-217 dest(grd) | SW Berlin |
| 385th: | Lt. H.D. Burkhard | (.5)Do-217 dest(air)* | Gifhorn |
| | | Go-242 dam(grd) | Gifhorn |
| | Lt. R.C. Scott | (.5)Do-217 dest(air)* | Gifhorn |
| | Lt. C.S. Hill | (.5)Do-217 dest(air)** | Gifhorn |
| | Lt. J.J. Pascoe | (.5)Do-217 dest(air)** | Gifhorn |

*Losses-*

**4th**: Lt. Harry E. Jennings (335th Ftr Sqn) KIA
P-51B WD-W 42-106429 "Judy IV"
Hit by enemy fighters near Hamburg.

**20th**: Lt. Raymond E. Huarte (79th Ftr Sqn) POW
P-38J MC- 42-67858
Hit by enemy fighters north of Hamburg.

**78th**: Lt. William H. Genge (82nd Ftr Sqn) POW
P-47D MX-F 42-76585
Suffered mechanical failure south of Alkmaar.

**339th**: Lt. Joseph Wolfort (503rd Ftr Sqn) KIA
P-51B D7-T 42-106755
Hit by flak near Roxel.

**352nd**: Lt. James D. Hannon (487th Ftr Sqn) POW
P-51B HO-C 43-6805 "Marjorie II"
Hit by flak near Stendal and bellied-in near Celle.

Lt. Carl J. Luksic (487th Ftr Sqn) POW
P-51B HO-Z 42-106788
Hit by flak near Stendal and bailed out near Celle.

**355th**: Lt. Herbert F. Fritts (354th Ftr Sqn) KIA
P-51B WR-F 42-106874 "Lorie II!"
Crashed into a train while strafing near Hamburgen.

**361st**: Lt. Stanley D. Rames (375th Ftr Sqn) POW
P-51B E2-W 42-106792
Suffered mechanical failure near Altslandberg.

Lt. Warren D. Wherry (375th Ftr Sqn) KIA
P-51B E2-B 42-106912
Hit by enemy fighters near Alt Lewin.

Lt. Morris C. Williams (376th Ftr Sqn) POW
P-51B E9-X 42-106660
Hit by enemy fighters near Alstaette.

*Remarks*
56th: 1-8 locos, 0-2 buildings
339th: 1-2 locos
352nd: 18-9 locos, 0-6 railcars, 0-2 flak towers, 0-1 tug, 0-1 building
355th: 0-11 locos
356th: LtCol. Donald A. Baccus(HdQts) c/l Manston; o.k.
P-47D OC-G 42-76583
359th: 8-0 locos, 6-0 railcars, 2-0 vehicles, 0-3 tugs, 0-3 barges
Lt. Charles H. Kruger(369th Ftr Sqn) c/l East Wretham; o.k.
P-51B IV-K 42-106629 "Nancy June 2nd"
361st: 0-3 locos, 0-1 vehicle
364th: 21-6 locos, 5-20 railcars, 5-0 vehicles, 0-3 hangars, 0-2 flak towers

Groups Operating: P-51 4th, 339th, 355th, 357th
Missions: Fighter-bomber operations in France.
Claims: 5.5-0-0 air
3-1 ground

| *Group* | | *Claims* | *Location* |
|---|---|---|---|
| **339th** | | | |
| 503rd: | Lt. C.W. Knott | (.5)Me-109 dest(air) | SW Soissons |
| | | (.5)Me-109 dest(grd) | SW Soissons |
| | Lt. C.E. Shake | (.5)Me-109 dest(air) | SW Soissons |
| | | (.5)Me-109 dest(grd) | SW Soissons |
| 505th: | Lt. H.M. Everett | (2)FW-190 dest(air) | St. Quentin |
| | Lt. C.J. Hanseman | (1.5)Me-109 dest(air) | St. Gobain-Laon |
| | | (shared with an unknown pilot) | |
| **355th** | | | |
| 354th: | Lt. E.F. Perry | FW-190 dest(grd) | Cormeilles-en-Vixen |
| | | FW-190 dam(grd) | Cormeilles-en-Vixen |
| **357th** | | | |
| 364th: | Capt. R.A. Peterson | (.5)u/i a/c dest(grd) | St. Leger |
| | Lt. N.J. Frederick | (.5)u/i a/c dest(grd) | St. Leger |

*Losses-*

**339th**: Lt. Harold M. Everett (505th Ftr Sqn) POW-E
P-51B 6N- 42-106646
Hit by a FW-190 near Grougis.

**357th**: Lt. Joseph M. Jenkins (364th Ftr Sqn) KIA
P-51C C5- 42-103389
Hit by flak near Albert.

Lt. Joseph G. Sullivan (364th Ftr Sqn) MIA-E
P-51B C5- 42-106884
Hit by flak near Laon.

*Remarks*
56th: 6-2 locos, 0-20 railcars, 2-0 barges
339th: 4-8 locos, 9-30 railcars, 0-5 buildings, 0-1 barracks
355th: 1-0 loco
357th: 2-4 locos, 0-2 hangars

**May 25, 1944**
Groups Operating: P-51 4th, 339th, 352nd, 355th, 357th, 359th, 361st
P-47 56th, 78th, 353rd, 356th
P-38 20th, 55th, 364th
Missions: Support for bombers to various marshalling yards in France and Belgium.
Claims: 12-2-4 air
3-4 ground

| *Group* | | *Claims* | *Location* |
|---|---|---|---|
| **4th** | | | |
| 336th: | Capt. J.H. Bennett | (2)Me-109 dest(air) | Strasbourg |
| | | (2)FW-190 prob(air) | Strasbourg |
| | | FW-190 dam(air) | Strasbourg |
| | Maj. J.A. Goodson | FW-190 dest(air) | Strasbourg |
| | Lt. T.K. McDill | Me-109 dest(air) | Strasbourg |
| | Lt. I.E. Grounds | FW-190 dam(air) | Strasbourg |
| **78th** | | | |
| 82nd: | Capt. J.W. Wilkinson | (.5)FW-190 dest(grd) | Metz |
| | Lt. R.E. Wilkinson | (.5)FW-190 dest(grd) | Metz |
| 83rd: | Capt. A.M. Juchheim | Me-109 dest(air) | SE St. Dizier |
| | | (.5)He-111 dest(grd) | St. Dizier |
| | Lt. W.M. McDermott | Me-109 dest(air) | St. Dizier |
| | Lt. L.R. Casey | (.5)He-111 dest(grd) | St. Dizier |
| 84th: | Lt. R.E. Belliveau | FW-190 dam(air) | Chaumont |
| | F/O H.W. Kramer | FW-190 dam(grd) | Paris |
| **339th** | | | |
| 505th: | Lt. G.J. Hrico | (.5)FW-190 dest(air) | Paris |
| | Lt. W.F. Mudge | (.5)FW-190 dest(air) | Paris |
| **353rd** | | | |
| 352nd: | Lt. W.S. Marchant | u/i a/c dest(grd) | N/Reims |
| | | (3)Me-109 dam(grd) | N/Reims |
| **356th** | | | |
| 360th: | Lt. R.M. Leidy | Me-109 dest(air) | W/Neufchateau |
| 361st: | Lt. D.F. Thwaites | Me-109 dest(air) | W/Neufchateau |

| | | | |
|---|---|---|---|
| **364th** | | | |
| 383rd: | Lt. L.S. Ayoub | FW-190 dest(air) | Paris |
| | Lt. K.F. Nicholson | FW-190 dest(air) | Paris |
| | Lt. J.F. Potochnik | FW-190 dest(air) | SW Paris |
| | Capt. J.A. Kerig | FW-190 dam(air) | Dreux |

*Losses-*

**4th**: Capt. Joseph H. Bennett (336th Ftr Sqn) POW
P-51B VF-N 43-6572
Hit byb enemy fighters near Strasbourg.

Lt. Thomas K. McDill (336th Ftr Sqn) POW
P-51B VF-Q 43-6633
Hit by enemy fighters near Strasbourg.

**20th**: Lt. Peter A. Boele (55th Ftr Sqn) KIA
P-38J KI-T 42-104395
Hit by flak near Flushing and crashed into the North Sea.

Lt. Marvin F. Bench, Jr. (79th Ftr Sqn) KIA
P-38J MC- 42-68094
Hit by flak over the Dutch Islands.

Lt. Harry J. Watson, Jr. (79th Ftr Sqn) POW
P-38J MC-M 42-67929 "Bob Cat II"
Hit by flak near Nuiewlande.

**359th**: Capt. Charles C. Ettlesen (369th Ftr Sqn) MIA-E
P-51C IV-D 42-103354
Hit by flak at Saarbrucken and bailed out near Sarrebourg.

**364th**: Lt. Vaude V. Ames (383rd Ftr Sqn) POW
P-38J N2- 42-67222
Hit by a FW-190 in the Chartres area.

Lt. Leroy Q. Olson (383rd Ftr Sqn) POW
P-38J N2-S 42-68034
Hit by a FW-190 near Chartres.

Lt. Clarence F. Scrivner (383rd Ftr Sqn) POW
P-38J N2-Z 43-28425
Hit by a FW-190 near Chartres.

Lt. Donald S. Chaplin (385th Ftr Sqn) POW
P-38J 5E- 42-68158
Hit by flak southeast of Paris.

Lt. John W. Wittgreve (385th Ftr Sqn) POW
P-38J 5E-N 42-67258
Hit by flak southeast of Paris.

Lt. Clarence B. Warner (385th Ftr Sqn) KIA
P-38J 5E- 43-28760
Hit by flak southeast of Paris.

*Remarks*

| | |
|---|---|
| 20th: | 5-9 locos, 1-55 railcars, 0-10 barges, 0-1 tug, 0-1 bridge, 0-8 gun emplacements, 0-2 buildings |
| 55th: | 0-1 loco |
| 56th: | 1-5 locos |
| 78th: | 14-9 locos |
| 339th: | 8-4 locos |
| 353rd: | 6-3 locos |
| 355th: | 1-1 locos |
| 364th: | 5-0 locos, 0-42 railcars, 0-2 buildings |

KIAc's

479th: Capt. William A. Walker (436th Ftr Sqn)
P-38J 9B-A 42-104318

**May 26, 1944**
Groups Operating: P-38 479th
Missions: Flew two sweeps of the Dutch coast for its first missions in the ETO.
Claims: nil
Losses: nil

**May 27, 1944**
Groups Operating: P-51 4th, 339th, 352nd, 355th, 357th, 359th, 361st
P-47 56th, 78th, 353rd, 356th
P-38 20th, 55th, 364th, 479th
Missions: Support of bombers to Ludwigshafen, Karlsruhe, Saarbrucken, and other rail targets.
Claims: 38-3-6 air
9-2 ground

| *Group* | | *Claims* | *Location* |
|---|---|---|---|
| **78th** | | | |
| 83rd: | Capt. A.M. Juchheim | Me-109 dest(air) | Frieburg |
| **339th** | | | |
| 505th: | Capt. J.L. Thury | Fi-156 dest(grd) | Frankfurt |
| | | He-111 dest(grd) | Frankfurt |
| | | Fi-156 dam(grd) | Frankfurt |
| | | u/i a/c dam(grd) | Frankfurt |
| | Lt. P.H. Ewing | Fi-156 dest(grd) | Frankfurt |
| | | u/i a/c dest(grd) | Frankfurt |
| | Lt. R.B. Olander | Me-109 dest(grd) | Reims |
| | Lt. R.A. Rohm | Fi-156 dest(grd) | Frankfurt |
| | Lt. J.F. Sawicki | Fi-156 dest(grd) | Frankfurt |
| **352nd** | | | |
| HdQts: | LtCol. J.C. Edwards | Me-109 dest(air) | Karlsruhe |
| 328th: | Lt. J.F. Thornell | (2)Me-109 dest(air) | S/Strasbourg |
| | Lt. W.W. Furr | Me-109 dest(air) | S/Strasbourg |
| | | Me-109 dam(air) | S/Strasbourg |
| | Lt. E. Zellner | Me-109 dest(air) | S/Strasbourg |
| | | (.5)FW-190 dest(air)* | S/Strasbourg |
| | Lt. D.T. Zimms | Me-109 dest(air) | S/Strasbourg |
| 487th: | Lt. R.H. Berkshire | (2)Me-109 dest(air) | Strasbourg |
| | Lt. G.T. Moran | (2)Me-109 dest(air) | Strasbourg |
| | Capt. R.W. Hamilton | FW-190 dest(air) | Strasbourg |
| | | FW-190 prob(air) | Strasbourg |
| | Capt. W.E. Starck | Me-109 dest(air) | Strasbourg |
| **353rd** | | | |
| 352nd: | Lt. L.P. Cles | Me-109 dest(grd) | Saverne |
| | Lt. H.Q. Waggoner | Do-217 dest(grd) | Saverne |
| | F/O J.R. Hicks | Me-109 dam(air) | Saverne |
| **357th** | | | |
| 362nd: | Capt. F.E. Adams | FW-190 dest(air) | N/Strasbourg |
| | Capt. J.B. England | Me-109 dest(air) | N/Strasbourg |
| | Lt. H.L. Hill | Me-109 dest(air) | N/Strasbourg |
| | Lt. G.M. O'Brien | FW-190 dest(air) | N/Strasbourg |
| | Lt. J.F. Pugh | FW-190 dest(air) | N/Strasbourg |
| | Lt. A.E. Smith | Me-109 dest(air) | N/Strasbourg |
| | Capt. C.L. Williams | FW-190 dam(air) | N/Strasbourg |
| | Capt. R.D. Brown | Me-109 dam(air) | Strasbourg |
| | Lt. J.B. Badger | Me-109 dam(air) | N/Strasbourg |
| 363rd: | Capt. C.E. Anderson | (2)Me-109 dest(air) | N/Strasbourg |
| | Capt. J.W. Browning | Me-109 dest(air) | Strasbourg |
| | Capt. W.R. O'Brien | Me-109 dest(air) | Strasbourg |
| | Lt. E.K. Simpson | Me-109 dest(air) | Strasbourg |
| | Lt. R.C. Gangwish | Me-109 prob(air) | SE Baden Baden |
| 364th: | Maj. J.A. Storch | (2)Me-109 dest(air) | Strasbourg |
| | | (.5)FW-190 dest(air)* | S/Strasbourg |
| | Capt. T.L. Harris | (2)Me-109 dest(air) | Colmar |
| | | Me-109 prob(air) | Colmar |
| | Lt. C.D. Conklin | (2)Me-109 dest(air) | Mulhausen |
| | Lt. M.A. Stanley | (2)FW-190 dest(air) | Strasbourg |
| | Lt. P.D. Fairweather | Me-109 dest(air) | Strasbourg |
| | Lt. L.A. Ruder | Me-109 dest(air) | Strasbourg |
| | Lt. R.M. Shaw | Me-109 dest(air) | SW Strasbourg |
| | | Me-109 dam(air) | SW Strasbourg |
| | Lt. M.H. Stepelton | Me-109 dest(air) | Strasbourg |
| **361st** | | | |
| 375th: | Maj. G.L. Merritt | FW-190 dest(air) | W/Lille |

*Losses-*

**4th**: Lt. Elliott H. Shapleigh (335th Ftr Sqn) MIA-E
P-51B WD-O 42-106464
Suffered mechanical failure and bailed out near Laon.

**55th**: Lt. Clifford O. Williams (343rd Ftr Sqn) MIA-E
P-38J CY- 42-67876
Hit by flak near Legers.

**357th**: Capt. Robert D. Brown (362nd Ftr Sqn) INT
P-51B G4-B 43-6556 "Chicago Gun Moll"
Shot-up by enemy fighters and came down in Switzerland.

Capt. Thomas L. Harris (364th Ftr Sqn) POW
P-51B C5-S 43-6653 "Lil Red's Rocket"
Collided with Lt. Post near Strasbourg.

Lt. Cyril D. Conklin (364th Ftr Sqn) POW
P-51B C5- 42-106640
Hit by enemy fighters near Strasbourg.

Lt. Dean N. Post, Jr. (364th Ftr Sqn) KIA
P-51B C5- 42-106632
Collided with Capt. Harris near Strasbourg.

*Remarks*

| | |
|---|---|
| 20th: | 2-1 locos, 0-1 flak tower |
| 55th: | 20-2 locos, 2-0 railcars, 6-0 barges, 2-0 vehicles, 2-0 tugs, 1-1 flak towers, |
| 56th: | 0-1 loco |

339th: 7-5 locos, 1-3 flak towers, 0-1 vehicle, 0-1 building
352nd: 1-0 vehicle
353rd: 10-6 locos, 2-14 railcars, 0-1 barge, 0-1 gun position
361st: 1-2 locos, 1-2 vehicles
Lt. Donald T. Woodward (376th Ftr Sqn) c/l; o.k.
P-51B E9-M 42-106754

Groups Operating: P-47 56th
Missions: Fighter-bomber operations in the Willenstadt-Meerije area.
Claims: nil
Losses: nil

*Remarks*
56th: 2-0 barges

KIAc's
55th: Lt. Victor T. McConnell (343rd Ftr Sqn)
P-38J CY-
Crashed four miles from Nuthampstead.

339th: Lt. Robert L. Dickens, Jr. (503rd Ftr Sqn)
P-51B D7-U 42-106907
Collided with an A-20 at Little Walden.

**May 28, 1944**
Groups Operating: P-51 4th, 339th, 352nd, 355th, 357th, 359th, 361st
P-47 56th, 78th, 353rd, 356th
P-38 20th, 55th, 364th, 479th
Missions: Support of bombers to numerous oil targets, including Magdeburg, Konigsburg, Merseburg, Lutzkendorf, Dessau, Cologne, and Zeitz.
Claims: 26-1-4 air
0-1 ground

| *Group* | | *Claims* | *Location* |
|---|---|---|---|
| **4th** | | | |
| 334th: | Lt. J.L. Lang | (1.5)Me-109 dest(air)* | Magdeburg |
| | Capt. W.M. Sobanski | Me-109 dest(air) | Wittenburg-Magdeburg |
| | Lt. R.K. Hofer | Me-109 dest(air) | Magdeburg |
| | Lt. R.P. Kenyon | Me-109 dest(air) | Magdeburg |
| | Lt. M.H. Kolter | Me-109 dest(air) | Magdeburg |
| | Lt. G.C. Siems | FW-190 dest(air) | Magdeburg |
| **78th** | | | |
| 82nd: | Lt. C.W. DeWitt | Ju-52 dam(grd) | Hanover |
| 83rd: | Lt. W.M. McDermott | (.5)Me-109 dest(air) | Gardelegen |
| | Lt. F. White | (.5)Me-109 dest(air) | Gardelegen |
| **339th** | | | |
| HdQts: | Maj. M.G.H. McPharlin | Me-109 dest(air) | Magdeburg |
| | | Me-109 dam(air) | Magdeburg |
| **352nd** | | | |
| 328th: | Capt. H.W. White | FW-190 dest(air) | W/Magdeburg |
| | Lt. J.F. Thornell | Me-109 dest(air) | W/Magdeburg |
| | Lt. R.G. Phillips | Me-109 dam(air) | W/Magdeburg |
| 486th: | Lt. E.L. Heller | (1.5)Me-109 dest(air)* | Dessau & 1/2 Magdeburg |
| | Maj. S.W. Andrew | Me-109 dest(air) | NE Dessau |
| | Capt. W.W. Anderson | Me-109 dest(air) | Dessau |
| | Lt. L.L. Howell | Me-109 dest(air) | Dessau |
| 487th: | Lt. H.H. Barnes | Me-109 dest(air) | W/Leipzig |
| | | Me-109 dam(air) | W/Leipzig |
| **353rd** | | | |
| HdQts: | Maj. K.W. Gallup | Me-109 dest(air) | Gutersloh |
| **355th** | | | |
| 357th: | Lt. F.L. Eshelman | Me-109 dest(air) | N/Limburg |
| | Lt. W.E. MacFarlane | Me-109 dest(air) | N/Limburg |
| **357th** | | | |
| HdQts: | Maj. T.L. Hayes | Me-109 dest(air) | NW Magdeburg |
| 362nd: | Maj. J.E. Broadhead | FW-190 dest(air) | NW Magdeburg |
| | Lt. L.K. Carson | FW-190 dest(air) | N/Magdeburg |
| | Capt. K.E. Hagan | Me-410 dam(air) | N/Magdeburg |
| 363rd: | Lt. C.K. Peters | Me-109 dest(air) | N/Magdeburg |
| | Capt. E.W. Hiro | Me-109 prob(air) | N/Magdeburg |
| 364th: | Capt. R.A. Peterson | Me-109 dest(air) | NW Magdeburg |
| | Lt. J.C. Howell | Me-109 dest(air) | NW Magdeburg |
| | Lt. L.A. Ruder | Me-109 dest(air) | NW Magdeburg |

*Losses-*

**4th:** Lt. Richard L. Bopp (334th Ftr Sqn) POW
P-51B QP-H 42-106846
Ran out of fuel near Ruhland.

Lt. Aubrey E. Hewatt (334th Ftr Sqn) POW
P-51B QP-Y 43-6933
Hit by a Me-109 east of Magdeburg.

**78th:** Lt. Philip H. Hazelett (82nd Ftr Sqn) KIA
P-47D MX-Y 42-26064
Hit by flak near Osnabruck.

Lt. William S. Orvis, Jr. (82nd Ftr Sqn) KIA
P-47D MX-W 42-76318
Hit by flak near Erlberben.

Capt. Alwin M. Juchheim (83rd Ftr Sqn) POW
P-47D HL-A 42-26016
Collided with a P-51 near Gardelegen.

**352nd:** Capt. Woodrow W. Anderson (486th Ftr Sqn) KIA
P-51B PZ-A 42-106635 "Texas Blue Bonnet"
Hit by enemy aircraft near Quedlinburg.

**353rd:** Lt. Joseph R. Farley (351st Ftr Sqn) KIA
P-47D YJ- 42-75457
Hit by flak near Loddenherde.

**355th:** Lt. Clarence R. Barger (354th Ftr Sqn) KIA
P-51B WR-T 43-6631
Hit by a Me-109 near Zerbst.

Lt. Walter N. Christensen (354th Ftr Sqn) KIA
P-51B WR-O 43-6893
Hit by a Me-109 near Buhlendorf.

*Remarks*
4th: Lt. Francis M. Grove (336th Ftr Sqn) c/l North Weald; o.k.
P-51B VF- 43-24769
20th: 3-0 locos, 0-26 railcars, 0-12 vehicles, 0-3 buildings
55th: 1-3 locos, 1-1 vehicles, 1-0 barge, 0-1 boat, 0-3 buildings
56th: 0-20 barges
78th: 0-1 loco, 0-1 barge
339th: 1-0 loco
352nd: 0-1 loco
353rd: 15-4 locos, 0-1 railcar
355th: 0-1 loco
356th: Lt. William C. Craig (359th Ftr Sqn) c/l Martlesham Heath; o.k.
P-47D OC-I 42-8568
0-12 barges, 0-1 gun position
361st: Lt. Vernon R. Richards (374th Ftr Sqn) c/l Fowlmere; o.k.
P-51B B7-

**May 29, 1944**
Groups Operating: P-51 4th, 339th, 352nd, 355th, 357th, 359th, 361st
P-47 56th, 78th, 353rd, 356th
P-38 20th, 55th, 364th, 479th
Missions: Support for bombers to Politz, Leipzig, Tutow, and various aircraft plants.
Claims: 40-2-6 air
16-15 ground

| *Group* | | *Claims* | *Location* |
|---|---|---|---|
| **4th** | | | |
| HdQts: | Col. D.J.M. Blakeslee | Me-410 dest(air) | N/Falkenburg |
| | | (2)Do-18 dam(grd) | Dievenow |
| 334th: | Lt. O.C. Snell | Me-109 dest(air) | Cammin |
| | Lt. R.K. Hofer | (4)He-177 dest(grd) | Mackfitz A/F |
| | Lt. F.E. Speer | (3)He-177 dest(grd) | Mackfitz A/F |
| | Lt. M.H. Kolter | Ar-196 dest(grd) | Dievenow |
| | | (.5)Do-18 dam(grd)* | Dievenow |
| | Capt. T.E. Joyce | (.5)Do-18 dam(grd)* | Dievenow |
| | Lt. J.F. Scott | Do-18 dam(grd) | Dievenow |
| | Lt. E.J. Steppe | Do-18 dam(grd) | Dievenow |
| | Capt. W.M. Sobanski | (.5)Do-18 dam(grd)** | Dievenow |
| | | (.5)Do-18 dam(grd)@ | Dievenow |
| | Lt. J.P. Fernandez | (.5)Do-18 dam(grd)** | Dievenow |
| | | (.5)Do-18 dam(grd)@ | Dievenow |
| | Lt. T.S. Sharp | Do-18 dam(grd) | Dievenow |
| 335th: | Capt. B.L. McGrattan | FW-190 dest(air) | Laaland Island |
| | Lt. R.C. Church | Me-109 dest(air) | Elmarn Belt |
| 336th: | Lt. D.R. Emerson | (.5)Me-110 dest(air) | N/Falkenburg |
| | | Do-18 dam(grd) | N/Falkenberg |
| | Lt. C.J. Netting | (.5)Me-110 dest(air) | N/Falkenberg |
| | | (2)Do-18 dam(grd) | N/Falkenberg |
| **78th** | | | |
| 82nd: | Capt. J.W. Wilkinson | FW-190 dam(grd) | Twente-Enschede |
| **339th** | | | |
| HdQts: | Maj. M.G.H. McPharlin | Do-18 dest(grd) | Dievenow |
| 505th: | Capt. J.L. Thury | FW-190 dest(air) | NE Stettin |
| | Lt. J.R. Starnes | FW-190 dest(air) | NE Stettin |
| **352nd** | | | |
| 328th: | Lt. J.F. Thornell | (2)Me-109 dest(air) | N/Neubrandenburg |
| | Capt. E.L. Abbott | Me-109 dest(air) | N/Neubrandenburg |
| 487th: | Lt. G.T. Moran | (1.5)Me-109 dest(air) | Gustrow & 1/2 Wolgast |
| | | FW-190 dam(air) | Gustrow |

| | | | |
|---|---|---|---|
| | Lt. W.T. Whisner | FW-190 dest(air) | Gustrow |
| | Lt. J.V. Conard | (.5)Me-109 dest(air) | Wolgast |
| | Lt. R.K. Butler | Me-109 dam(air) | Gustrow |
| | Capt. R.W. Hamilton | (2)u/i a/c dam(grd) | Jasmunder Bay |
| **359th** | | | |
| 368th: | Lt. B.M. Hagan | Me-109 dest(air) | Ratzeburg |
| | Lt. R.B. Hatter | Me-109 dest(air) | Plau |
| 369th: | Lt. R.J. Booth | FW-190 dest(air) | Stettnerhaven |
| | Lt. R.L. Thacker | FW-190 dest(air) | Malchin |
| 370th: | Lt. H.F. Grimes | (2)FW-190 dest(air) | Stettin |
| | Lt. R.S. Wetmore | (2)FW-190 dest(air) | Stettin |
| | Maj. J.B. Murphy | (1.5)FW-190 dest(air) | Stettin |
| | Lt. G.A. Doersch | (.5)FW-190 dest(air) | Stettin |
| | | (.5)FW-190 dest(air) | Stettin |
| | Lt. R.W. Siltamaki | (.5)FW-190 dest(air) | Stettin |
| | Capt. R.B. Lancaster | Me-109 dest(air) | Stettin |
| | | Me-109 prob(air) | Stettin |
| **361st** | | | |
| HdQts: | Maj. W.E. Hopkins | (2)FW-190 dest(air) | Pitka |
| 374th: | Lt. E.B. Murdy | (1.5)FW-190 dest(air)* | E/Schwerin |
| | Maj. R.A. Webb | FW-190 dest(air) | Pitka |
| | Lt. G. Lichter | FW-190 dest(air) | Pitka |
| | | FW-190 prob(air) | Pitka |
| | | FW-190 dam(air) | Pitka |
| | Lt. D.L. Calloway | FW-190 dest(air) | Pitka |
| | | FW-190 dam(air) | Pitka |
| | Lt. L.E. Downey | FW-190 dest(air) | Pitka |
| | | FW 190 dam(air) | Pitka |
| | Lt. R.T. Eckfeldt | FW-190 dest(air) | Pitka |
| 375th: | Maj. G.L. Merritt | (2)He-111 dest(grd) | Lackau-Juterbog |
| | Lt. R.C. Wright | (2)Ju-52 dest(grd) | Lackau-Juterbog |
| | | He-111 dest(grd) | Lackau-Juterbog |
| | | Ju-88 dest(grd) | Lackau-Juterbog |
| | | Ju-88 dam(grd) | Lackau-Juterbog |
| | Lt. D.R. Morehouse | u/i a/c dest(grd) | Lackau-Juterbog |
| 376th: | Lt. D.F. Spencer | (4)Me-410 dest(air) | E/Schwerin |
| | Capt. J.B. Cheney | (.5)FW-190 dest(air)* | E/Schwerin |
| | Capt. W.B. Frank | (.5)FW-190 dest(air)** | Schwerin |
| | | FW-190 dam(air) | Schwerin |
| | Lt. W.T. Butts | (.5)FW-190 dest(air)** | Schwerin |
| | Lt. W.J. Kozicki | FW-190 dam(air) | Schwerin |

*Losses-*

**4th:** Lt. Frank E. Speer (334th Ftr Sqn) POW
P-51B QP-W 43-6560
Hit by flak at Mackfitz and bellied-in northeast of Stargard.

**339th:** Lt. James L. Lynch (505th Ftr Sqn) KIA
P-51B 6N-C 42-106626 "Butch"
Last heard from south of the Isle of Wight reporting he was low on fuel.

Lt. Gordon F. Perry (505th Ftr Sqn) KIA
P-51B 6N- 42-106745
Ran out of fuel and crashed into the Channel.

**353rd:** Lt. Arthur C. Bergeron (350th Ftr Sqn) KIA
P-47D LH- 42-26109
Hit by flak near Quackenbruck.

Lt. Joseph C. McDonald (350th Ftr Sqn) KIA
P-47D LH-U 42-76320
Hit by flak near Quackenbruck and bellied-in near Meppel.

Lt. Albert W. Barlow (351st Ftr Sqn) ASR
P-47D [illegible]
Bailed out sixteen miles east of Orfordness.

**356th:** Lt. William C. O'Barr (359th Ftr Sqn) POW
P-47D OC-E 42-76372
Suffered mechanical failure and bailed out southwest of the Northeast Polder.

**359th:** Lt. Lowell W. Brundage (369th Ftr Sqn) KIA
P-51B IV-H 42-106691
Hit by enemy fighters near Malchin.

Lt. Myron C. Morrill(369th Ftr Sqn) KIA
P-51B IV-J 42-106913
Hit by enemy fighters near Malchin.

**361st:** Lt. Abe P. Rosenberger (375th Ftr Sqn) ASR
P-51B E2-
Bailed out over the Channel after mechanical failure.

*Remarks*
55th: 4-6 locos, 1-12 railcars, 1-7 barges, 0-1 building
56th: 3-1 locos, 0-30 railcars
78th: 1-0 loco
339th: 0-2 locos
Capt. Bill C. Rout (504th Ftr Sqn) c/l Woodbridge; o.k.
P-51B 5Q-A 42-106838 "Fabasca IV"
Lt. Melville R. Ball (504th Ftr Sqn) c/l Woodbridge; o.k.
P-51 5Q-
353rd: 5-3 locos, 0-2 railcars

**May 30, 1944**

Groups Operating: P-51 4th, 339th, 352nd, 355th, 357th, 359th, 361st
P-47 56th, 78th, 353rd, 356th
P-38 20th, 55th, 364th, 479th

Missions: Support for bombers to various targets in Germany and to marshalling yards in France and Belgium.

Claims: 52.5-2-6 air
3-2 ground

| *Group* | | *Claims* | *Location* |
|---|---|---|---|
| **4th** | | | |
| 334th: | Lt. R.K. Hofer | (2.5)FW-190 dest(air) | Oschersleben |
| | Lt. J.F. Scott | Me-109 dest(air) | Dessau-Bernburg |
| | Lt. T.S. Sharp | FW-190 dam(air) | W/Brandenburg |
| | | (2)FW-190 dest(grd) | Oschersleben |
| 335th: | Lt. F.C. Jones | (1.5)FW-190 dest(air) | Oschersleben |
| | | FW-190 dam(air) | Oschersleben |
| 336th: | Lt. O.F. Lajeunesse | Me-109 dest(air) | Magdeburg |
| **339th** | | | |
| 503rd: | Lt. W.E. Bryan | (2)FW-190 dest(air) | Magdeburg |
| 504th: | Lt. B.V. Stevens | (2)FW-190 dest(air) | SE Brunswick |
| | Maj. E.B. Gravette | FW-190 dest(air) | Magdeburg |
| | | FW-190 dam(air) | Magdeburg |
| | Capt. L.S. Peter | FW-190 prob(air) | Magdeburg |
| **352nd** | | | |
| 328th: | Lt. W.W. Furr | (1.5)FW-190 dest(air) (shared with an unknown pilot) | Schoningen |
| | Lt. R.C. Brookins | Me-109 dest(air) | Halberstadt |
| 486th: | Maj. S.W. Andrew | FW-190 dest(air) | Magdeburg |
| 487th: | Maj. G.E. Preddy | (2.5)Me-109 dest(air) | Magdeburg |
| | Lt. W.T. Whisner | (.5)Me-109 dest(air) | Magdeburg |
| | Lt. R.H. Berkshire | Me-109 dest(air) | Magdeburg |
| | | FW 190 dest(air) | Ulzen |
| | Lt. G.T. Moran | Me-109 dest(air) | Ulzen |
| | | FW-190 dest(air) | Ulzen |
| | | FW-190 dam(air) | Ulzen |
| | Capt. J.P. Kessler | Me-109 dest(air) | Halberstadt |
| | | Me-109 prob(air) | Halberstadt |
| | Capt. C.J. Palmer | FW-190 dest(air) | Halberstadt |
| | Lt. H.H. Barnes | Me-109 dest(air) | N/Halberstadt |
| | Lt. M.C. Pickering | FW-190 dest(air) | Halberstadt |
| **353rd** | | | |
| 352nd: | Capt. J.N. Poindexter | (2)FW-190 dest(air) | Peine |
| **355th** | | | |
| 358th: | Lt. A.R. Santos | (2)FW-190 dest(air) | SE Brunswick |
| | Lt. D.A. Donovan | Me-109 dest(air) | SE Brunswick |
| | | (.5)FW-190 dest(air) (shared with an unknown pilot) | SE Brunswick |
| | Lt. A.T. Robinson | FW-190 dest(air) | SE Hanover |
| | | FW-190 dam(air) | SE Hanover |
| **357th** | | | |
| 362nd: | Capt. R.H. Becker | (3)Me-109 dest(air) | Bernburg |
| | Lt. A.J. Roberson | (2)Me-109 dest(air) | NE Bernburg |
| | Lt. L.K. Carson | Me-410 dest(air) | W/Bernburg |
| | Lt. O.E. Homrig | Me-410 dest(air) | E/Bernburg |
| | Lt. L.W. Mitchell | Me-109 dest(air) | W/Bernburg |
| | Lt. G.M. O'Brien | Me-109 dest(air) | Celle |
| | | (.5)Me-410 dest(air) | W/Bernburg |
| | Capt. F.E. Adams | (.5)Me-410 dest(air) | W/Bernburg |
| | Lt. D.W. Vogel | FW-190 dest(air) | Magdeburg |
| | Lt. T.E. Norris | Me-109 dam(air) | N/Celle |
| | Lt. R.D. Wallen | FW-190 dest(grd) | W/Bernburg |
| 363rd: | Capt. W.R. O'Brien | (2)Me-109 dest(air) | NE Schonebeck |
| | Capt. C.E. Anderson | Me-109 dest(air) | E/Schonebeck |
| | Capt. J.W. Browning | Me-109 dest(air) | NE Schonebeck |
| | Lt. R.N. Moore | Me-109 dest(air) | NE Schonebeck |
| 364th: | Lt. J.C. Howell | (.5)Me-410 dest(air) | NW Bernburg |
| | Lt. R.M. Shaw | (.5)Me-410 dest(air) | NW Bernburg |
| **359th** | | | |
| HdQts: | Col. A.P. Tacon | FW-190 dam(grd) | Paderborn |
| 368th: | Capt. W.C. Forehand | Me-109 dest(air) | Dessau |
| | Lt. J.B. Hunter | (.5)Me-109 dest(air) | W/Dessau |
| | Lt. R.W. Hawkinson | (.5)Me-109 dest(air) | W/Dessau |
| 369th: | Lt. R.J. Booth | Ju-88 dam(grd) | Harsleben |
| 370th: | Lt. C.W. Hipsher | (.5)Me-109 dest(air)* | Dessau |
| | Lt. R.W. Siltamaki | (.5)Me-109 dest(air)* | Dessau |
| | Lt. H.E. Grimes | (.5)Me-109 dest(air) (shared with an unknown pilot) | Dessau |

*Losses-*

**4th:** Lt. Mark H. Kolter (334th Ftr Sqn) KIA
P-51B QP-Q 43-7178
Hit by flak southwest of Brandenburg.

Capt. Willard W. Millikan (336th Ftr Sqn) POW
P-51B VF-U 43-24769 "Missouri Mauler"
Collided with Lt. Young near Wittenburg.

Lt. Samuel H. Young (336th Ftr Sqn) POW
P-51B VF- 43-24787
Collided with Capt. Millikan near Wittenburg.

**339th:** Lt. Paul M. Meyer (504th Ftr Sqn) KIA
P-51B 5Q-A 42-106601
Hit by a FW-190 near Eggersdorf.

Lt. Edward A. Thistlethwaite (504th Ftr Sqn) POW
P-51B 5Q-T 42-106908 "Cajun"
Hit by a FW-190 near Kleinmuehlingen.

**353rd:** Lt. Francis L. Edwards (352nd Ftr Sqn) KIA
P-47D SX-Z 42-75683 "Big Totsy"
Hit by enemy fighters near Peine.

**357th:** Capt. Fletcher E. Adams (362nd Ftr Sqn) KIA
P-51B G4-L 43-12468 "Southern Belle"
Hit by a Me-109 in the Wessendorf-Celle area.

Lt. Robert W. Foy (363rd Ftr Sqn) ASR
P-51B B6-
Suffered mechanical failure and bailed out fifty miles off the English coast.

*Remarks*
20th: 9-3 locos, 0-34 railcars, 5-4 tugs, 4-3 barges, 1-0 vehicle, 1-0 flak tower, 0-3 buildings
56th: 0-4 locos
353rd: 1-1 loco
355th: 2-0 locos, 0-2 tugs, 0-2 barges
356th: 0-2 boats
359th: 0-1 loco, 0-1 railcar, 0-1 vehicle, 0-1 barge
Lt. Andrew T. Lemmens (370th Ftr Sqn) c/l; o.k.
P-51B CS-C 43-12294 "Shrimp"
361st: Lt. George Lichter(374th Ftr Sqn) c/l; o.k.
P-51C B7-J 42-103301
364th: Lt. Byron P. Yost (384th Ftr Sqn) c/l; o.k.
P-38J 5Y-

Groups Operating: P-47 56th, 78th, 353rd, 356th
Missions: Dive-bombing of rail bridges in northern France.
Claims: nil

*Losses-*

**353rd:** Lt. Harry F. Hunter (351st Ftr Sqn) POW
P-47D YJ- 42-75688
Hit by flak near Montdidier.

*Remarks*
56th: 2-0 bridges
78th: 0-2 locos, 0-1 bridge
353rd: 2-4 locos, 2-3 barges, 0-10 railcars, 0-1 bridge

**May 31, 1944**
Groups Operating: P-51 4th, 339th, 352nd, 355th, 357th, 359th, 361st
P-47 56th, 78th, 353rd, 356th
P-38 20th, 55th, 364th, 479th
Missions: Support for bombers to marshalling yards and other targets in France, Belgium, and Germany.
Claims: 0-0-0 air
3-0 ground

| *Group* | | *Claims* | *Location* |
|---|---|---|---|
| **4th** | | | |
| 334th: | Lt. R.K. Hofer | (3)Bu-131 dest(grd) | Luxeuil A/F |

*Losses-*

**4th:** Capt. Carroll B. McElroy (335th Ftr Sqn) POW
P-51C WD-G 42-103609
Lost in bad weather near Sandbergen.

Lt. Robert H. Homuth (335th Ftr Sqn) KIA
P-51B WD-S 43-7032
Lost in bad weather near Onkerzele.

**356th:** Lt. Lawrence L. Goldwasser (360th Ftr Sqn) POW
P-47D PI- 43-25590
Suffered mechanical failure and bailed out near Zevenburgen.

*Remarks*
20th: 29-4 locos, 0-7 railcars, 0-1 building
56th: 0-4 locos

Groups Operating: P-47 56th, 353rd
P-38 20th
Missions: The P-47's dive-bombed Gutersloh Airfield while the 20th hit Rheine/Hopsten.
Claims: 5-1-3 air
0-1 ground

| *Group* | | *Claims* | *Location* |
|---|---|---|---|
| **56th** | | | |
| HdQts: | Col. H. Zemke | (2)FW-190 dest(air) | Gutersloh-Detmold |
| | | FW-190 prob(air) | Gutersloh-Detmold |
| | | FW-190 dam(air) | Gutersloh-Detmold |
| 62nd: | Capt. C.E. Tucker | FW-190 dest(air) | Meldorf |
| | | FW-190 dam(air) | Meldorf |
| | Lt. W.A. McClure | FW-190 dest(air) | Meldorf |
| 63rd: | Lt. D.V. Peters | FW-190 dest(air) | NW Kassel |
| | Lt. R.D. Campbell | FW-190 dam(air) | NW Kassel |
| **353rd** | | | |
| 352nd: | Lt. H. Herfurth | Me-410 dam(grd) | Gutersloh A/F |

Losses: nil

*Remarks*
20th: 12-4 locos, 0-1 flak tower
56th: 0-3 hangars
353rd: 0-6 hangars

**June 2, 1944**
Groups Operating: P-51 4th, 339th, 352nd, 355th, 357th, 359th, 361st
P-47 56th, 78th, 353rd, 356th
P-38 20th, 55th, 364th, 479th
Missions: Support for bombers to Pas de Calais V-1 sites and to airfields and rail targets in France.
Claims: nil
Losses: nil

*Remarks*
479th: 0-1 loco

**June 3, 1944**
Groups Operating: P-51 339th, 355th, 357th, 361st
P-47 56th, 78th, 353rd, 356th
P-38 20th, 55th, 364th, 479th
Missions: Support for bombers to Pas de Calais V-1 sites.
Claims: nil

*Losses-*

**355th:** Lt. Robert A. Browning (354th Ftr Sqn) POW
P-51B WR-K 42-106708
Lost coolant west of Paris and bellied-in near Abbeville.

**June 4, 1944**
Groups Operating: P-51 4th, 339th, 352nd, 355th, 359th, 361st
P-47 56th, 78th, 353rd
Missions: Support of bombers to the Pas de Calais area.
Claims: nil

*Losses-*

**355th:** F/O Henry W. Davis (354th Ftr Sqn) MIA
P-51B WR-W 43-6520
Lost coolant then hit by flak near St. Quentin.

**359th:** Lt. Emer H. Cater (368th Ftr Sqn) KIA
P-51B CV-E 43-6491 "Wanna Honey"
Suffered mechanical failure and bailed out twenty miles off Felixstowe.

Groups Operating: P-51 4th, 339th, 352nd, 355th, 357th, 359th, 361st
P-47 56th, 78th, 353rd
Missions: Support for bombers hitting rail bridges and airfields in the Paris area.
Claims: 1-0-1 air
0-0 ground

| *Group* | | *Claims* | *Location* |
|---|---|---|---|
| **361st** | | | |
| 374th: | Capt. C.H. Bergmann | (.5)Me-109 dest(air) | SE Melun |
| | Lt. J.K. Wood | (.5)Me-109 dest(air) | SE Melun |
| | Lt. E.B. Murdy | Me-109 dam(air) | SE Melun |

*Losses-*

**361st:** Lt. Walter J. Kozicki (376th Ftr Sqn) MIA-E
P-51B E9-K 43-6498
Hit by a Me-109 and bailed out northeast of Melun.

KIAc's

4th: Lt. Robert L. Kackerback (336th Ftr Sqn)
P-51B VF- 43-7059
Died in a crash near Steeple Bumpstead.

78th: Capt. James W. Wilkinson (82nd Ftr Sqn)
P-47D MX-G 42-26526
Crashed into a mountain near Llandovery, Wales.

**June 5, 1944**
Groups Operating: P-51 4th, 339th, 352nd, 355th, 357th, 361st
P-47 56th, 78th, 353rd
Missions: Support of bombers in the Cherbourg and Pas de Calais areas.
Claims: nil

*Losses-*

**78th**: Lt. John C.E. Steinwedel (82nd Ftr Sqn) KIA
P-47D MX-Y 42-76473
Crashed after icing-up near Amiens.

**352nd**: Lt. William W. Furr (328th Ftr Sqn) POW
P-51B PE-T 42-106717
Suffered mechanical failure near Merville.

*Remarks*
56th: Lt. James M. Jure (61st Ftr Sqn) c/l Ardeleigh; o.k.
P-47D HV-
78th: Lt. Tom E. Hughes (83rd Ftr Sqn) c/l, o.k.
P-47D HL-K 42-75182

Groups Operating: P-51 4th
Missions: Strafing sweep of the Lille area.
Claims: nil
Losses: nil

*Remarks*
4th: 2-0 vehicles

**June 6, 1944**
Groups Operating: P-51 4th, 339th, 352nd, 355th, 357th, 359th, 361st
P-47 56th, 78th, 353rd, 356th
P-38 20th, 55th, 364th, 479th
Missions: Support of bombers to Argentan and the invasion area, plus constant patrols and sweeps. Most groups flew at least three missions with many flying six to eight.
Claims: 23-1-8 air
5-0 ground

| *Group* | | *Claims* | *Location* |
|---|---|---|---|
| **4th** | | | |
| 334th: | Lt. S.W. Monroe | FW-190 dest(air) | Evreux |
| | Lt. J.F. Scott | FW-190 dest(air) | Evreux |
| | Lt. G.C. Siems | FW-190 dest(air) | Evreux |
| | Lt. J.P. Fernandez | (.5)FW-190 dest(air) | Evreux |
| | Lt. J.T. Simon | (.5)FW-190 dest(air) | Evreux |
| **56th**(#5) | | | |
| 62nd: | Lt. W.W. McElhare | FW-190 dest(air) | Rambouillet |
| (#7) | | | |
| HdQts: | Col. H. Zemke | FW-190 dest(air) | NE Bernay |
| 61st: | Capt. B.M. Gladych | Me-109 dest(air) | Croisy |
| **78th** | | | |
| HdQts: | Col. F.C. Gray | (.5)FW-190 dest(air) | Mayenne |
| 83rd: | Lt. P.A. Caulfield | FW-190 dest(air) | Mayenne |
| | Lt. V.J. Massa | (.5)FW-190 dest(air) | Mayenne |
| **339th** | | | |
| HdQts: | Maj. M.G.H. McPharlin | FW-190 dam(air) | Evreux |
| 505th: | Lt. P.J. McMahon | (2)Ju-87 dest(air) | Orleans |
| | Lt. W.F. Mudge | Ju-87 dest(air) | Orleans |
| **352nd** | | | |
| 328th: | Lt. R.C. Brookins | FW-190 dest(air) | SE Rouen |
| | | FW-190 dam(air) | SE Rouen |
| | Lt. L.J. Allain | (.5)FW-190 dest(air) | SE Rouen |
| | Lt. F.W. Horne | (.5)FW-190 dest(air) | SE Rouen |
| **355th** | | | |
| HdQts: | LtCol. G.J. Dix | Ju-87 dam(air) | Chartres |
| | | Ju-87 dest(grd) | Chartres |
| 354th: | Capt. B.W. Marshall | Ju-87 dest(air) | Chartres-Dire |
| | Lt. N.J. Fortier | Ju-87 dest(air) | Chartres |
| | Lt. R.S. Morris | (.5)Ju-87 dest(air) | Chartres-Dire |
| | Lt. F.K. Taylor | (.5)Ju-87 dest(air) | Chartres-Dire |
| | Lt. C.H. Graham | Ju-87 dest(grd) | Chartres |
| 357th: | Capt. F.W. Kelley | (2)Ju-87 dest(air) | NE Janville |
| | Lt. R. Bernoske | Ju-87 dest(air) | NE Janville |
| | Lt. J.A. Cotter | Ju-87 dest(air) | NE Janville |
| | Lt. L.B. Fuller | Ju-87 dest(air) | NE Janville |
| | | Ju-87 prob(air) | NE Janville |
| | | Ju-87 dam(air) | NE Janville |
| | Lt. W.W. James | Ju-87 dest(air) | NE Janville |
| | | (2)Ju-87 dam(air) | NE Janville |
| | | Ju-87 dest(grd) | NE Janville |
| | Capt. J.H. Wilson | Ju-87 dam(air) | NE Janville |
| | Lt. L.D. Minchew | Ju-87 dam(air) | NE Janville |
| **361st** | | | |
| 374th: | Capt. G.R. Rew | (.5)Me-109 dest(grd) | Vendome |
| | Lt. V.R. Richards | (.5)Me-109 dest(grd) | Vendome |
| 375th: | Maj. G.L. Merritt | Ju-88 dest(grd) | Tours |

*Losses-*

**4th**: Maj. Winslow M. Sobanski (334th Ftr Sqn) KIA
P-51B QP-J 43-6898 "Deacon"
Hit wires then bounced by enemy fighters near Dreux.

Lt. Thomas E. Fraser (334th Ftr Sqn) POW
P-51B QP-G 43-24825 "Jerry"
Hit by enemy fighters near Rouen.

Lt. Edward J. Steppe (334th Ftr Sqn) KIA
P-51B QP-M 43-6957 "Turnip Termite"
Hit by enemy fighters near Dreux.

Capt. Bernard L. McGrattan (335th Ftr Sqn) KIA
P-51B WD-D 42-106576
Hit by enemy fighters near Rouen.

Lt. Cecil E. Garbey (335th Ftr Sqn) KIA
P-51B WD-E 43-6575
Hit by enemy fighters near Rouen.

Lt. Harold L. Ross (335th Ftr Sqn) KIA
P-51B WD-K 42-106786
Hit by enemy fighters near Rouen.

F/O Walter Smith (335th Ftr Sqn) KIA
P-51B WD-H 43-7172 "Three Jokers"
Hit by enemy fighters near Rouen.

Lt. Harold H. Frederick (336th Ftr Sqn) MIA-E
P-51C VF- 42-103287
Hit by flak and bellied-in near Evreux.

Lt. Oscar F. Lajeunesse (336th Ftr Sqn) POW
P-51C VF- 42-103332
Hit by flak and bailed out near Lyons.

**56th**: Lt. Evan D. McMinn (61st Ftr Sqn) KIA
P-47D HV- 42-25963
Hit by flak while strafing near Bernay.

**78th**: Lt. Wallace R. Haily (84th Ftr Sqn) ASR
P-47D WZ-F 43-25578
Hit by flak and bailed out over the Channel.

**339th**: Maj. Michael G.H. McPharlin (HdQts) KIA
P-51B 6N-Z 42-106909 "Wee Ginny"
Last heard from with mechanical failure near Evreux. He was flying with the 334th Ftr Sqn, 4th Ftr Grp on this date.

Lt. Elton J. Brownshadel (504th Ftr Sqn) KIA
P-51 5Q-
Crashed after take-off from Fowlmere.

**352nd**: Lt. Robert C. Frascotti (486th Ftr Sqn) KIA
P-51B PZ-F 43-6685 "Umbriago"
Crashed on take-off from Bodney.

Lt. Robert K. Butler (487th Ftr Sqn) POW
P-51B HO-W 42-106449 "Princess Elizabeth"
Hit by flak near Epaignes.

Lt. Robert G. O'Nan (487th Ftr Sqn) POW
P-51B HO-E 43-7096 "Barbara M"
Hit by flak near Evreux.

**353rd**: F/O Earl W. Green (352nd Ftr Sqn) MIA-E
P-47D SX-R 42-75552 "Highlander"
Hit by flak near Mortain.

**355th**: Lt. Walter A. Douglas (357th Ftr Sqn) POW
P-51B OS- 42-106862
Hit by flak over Calais and bailed out off the coast.

Lt. George W. Phillips (357th Ftr Sqn) KIA
P-51B OS-H 43-6640
Hit by flak near La Maileraye and hit the tail of his P-51 when bailing out.

**356th**: Lt. George C. Kariva (360th Ftr Sqn) POW
P-47D PI- 42-75625
Suffered mechanical failure and bailed out off Dunkirk.

F/O Emil F. Sova (360th Ftr Sqn) POW
P-47D PI- 42-25997
Hit by flak and bailed out near Angars.

**357th**: Lt. Roger E. Pagels (363rd Ftr Sqn) MIA-E
P-51B B6- 43-6397
Hit by flak and bailed out over the North Sea.

Lt. Irving A. Smith (363rd Ftr Sqn) KIA
P-51B B6- 43-6947
Hit by flak while bombing near La Fleche.

Capt. Leroy A. Ruder (364th Ftr Sqn) KIA
P-51B C5-X 42-106768 "Linda Lu"
Suffered mechanical failure southeast of Cherbourg. Possibly killed after reaching the ground.

**361st**: Lt. James R. Golden (374th Ftr Sqn) POW
P-51B B7-A 43-6977
Oil line broke and he bailed out near Forges.

Lt. Lawrence B. Perry (375th Ftr Sqn) KIA
P-51C E2-A 42-103347
Hit by flak near Dreux.

Lt. William D. Willet (376th Ftr Sqn) POW
P-51B E9-G 42-106651
Hit by flak near Mondenbleau.

*Remarks*
4th: 0-3 locos, 0-1 bridge
20th: Maj. George S. Wemyss (HdQts) c/l; o.k.
P-38J LC-
56th: 23-0 locos, 7-0 vehicles
78th: 2-0 locos
352nd: 3-7 locos, 16-7 vehicles
353rd: 3-0 locos, 22-0 vehicles
355th: 2-7 locos, 4-0 barges, 2-0 tugs
356th: 2-0 locos, 16-21 vehicles, 4-35 railcars, 0-1 bridge
359th: 6-1 locos, 38-76 railcars, 2-1 vehicles
361st: 5-12 locos, 27-0 railcars, 10-11 vehicles

**June 7, 1944**
Groups Operating: P-51 4th, 339th, 352nd, 355th, 357th, 359th, 361st
P-47 56th, 78th, 353rd, 356th
P-38 20th, 55th, 364th, 479th
Missions: Support of bombers to targets in France, strafing sweeps, and patrols of the invasion area.
Claims: 32-1-12 air
23-9 ground

| ***Group*** | | ***Claims*** | ***Location*** |
|---|---|---|---|
| **56th**(#3) | | | |
| 63rd: | Lt. J.R. Curtis | FW-190 dest(air) | Lyones la Foret |
| (#4) | | | |
| 61st: | LtCol. F.S. Gabreski | Me-109 dest(air) | E/Dreux |
| | | FW-190 dest(air) | E/Dreux |
| | Capt. B.M. Gladych | Me-109 dest(air) | SE Houdan |
| | F/O S. Gerick | Me-109 dest(air) | SE Houdan |
| | | Me-109 dam(air) | SE Houdan |
| | Lt. J.I. Popplewell | Me-109 dest(air) | SE Houdan |
| (#5) | | | |
| 62nd: | Lt. G.E. Bostwick | Me-109 dest(air) | Grandvillers A/F |
| | Lt. M.L. Moseley | (.5)Ju-88 dest(air) | St. Andre de L'Eure |
| | Lt. J.W. Pierce | (.5)Ju-88 dest(air) | St. Andre de L'Eure |
| (#7) | | | |
| HdQts: | Col. H. Zemke | (2)FW-190 dest(air) | Chartres/Etampes |
| | | FW-190 dam(air) | Chartres/Etampes |
| 61st: | Lt. R.J. Rankin | Me-109 dest(air) | SE Senlis |
| | | Me-109 dam(air) | SE Senlis |
| | F/Lt. Z. Janicki | FW-190 prob(air) | S/Rouen |
| | | FW-190 dam(air) | S/Rouen |
| (#8) | | | |
| 63rd: | Lt. M.H. Becker | (.5)FW-190 dest(air) | Les Andelys Craches |
| | Lt. S.B. Dale | (.5)FW-190 dest(air) | Les Andelys Craches |
| **78th** | | | |
| 84th: | Capt. B.I. Mayo | Me-109 dest(air) | S/Montdidier |
| | Lt. L.K. Covelle | Me-109 dest(air) | Montdidier |
| | Lt. D. Ledington | Me-109 dest(air) | Montdidier |
| | Lt. D.T. Loyd | Me-109 dest(air) | Montdidier |
| | Lt. W.J. Hardin | Me-109 dam(air) | Montdidier |
| **339th** | | | |
| 504th: | Lt. R.N. Attebury | FW-190 dest(air) | Laval |
| | | FW-190 dest(grd) | Laval |
| | Capt. L.S. Peter | FW-190 dest(air) | Laval |
| | Lt. M.F. Caldwell | FW-190 dest(grd) | Laval |
| | Lt. L.L. Corbin | FW-190 dest(grd) | Laval |
| | Lt. B.V. Stevens | FW-190 dest(grd) | Laval |
| | Lt. F.T. Waters | FW-190 dest(grd) | Laval |
| **353rd**(#3) | | | |
| 352nd: | Capt. J.N. Poindexter | Me-109 dest(grd) | Compiegne |
| | | (1.5)Me-109 dam(grd) | Compiegne |
| | Lt. R.P. Greenwood | Me-109 dest(grd) | Compiegne |
| | Lt. E.D. Reinhardt | Me-109 dest(grd) | Compiegne |
| | Lt. R.V. Keywan | (1.5)Me-109 dam(grd) | Compiegne |
| (#5) | | | |
| 351st: | Lt. G.H. McLaughlin | (2)Me-109 dest(air) | Beauvais/Tille |
| | | Me-109 dest(grd) | Beauvais/Tille |
| | | (3)Me-109 dam(grd) | Beauvais/Tille |
| | Lt. W.J. Maguire | (2)Me-109 dest(air) | Beauvais/Tille |
| | | Me-109 dam(air) | Beauvais/Tille |
| | Lt. W.G. Cobb | Me-109 dest(air) | Beauvais/Tille |
| | Lt. H.K. Field | Me-109 dest(air) | Beauvais/Tille |
| | Lt. A.S. Hartley | Me-109 dest(air) | Beauvais/Tille |
| | | (2)Me-109 dam(air) | Beauvais/Tille |
| | Lt. M.B. Hungate | Me-109 dest(air) | Beauvais/Tille |
| | Lt. G.W. Franklin | Me-109 dest(air) | Beauvais/Tille |
| | | (2)Me-109 dam(grd) | Beauvais/Tille |
| | Lt. J.P. Mitchell | Me-109 dam(air) | Beauvais/Tille |
| (#6) | | | |
| 352nd: | F/O J.R. Hicks | (2)FW-190 dest(grd) | Angars |
| | | Ju-88 dest(grd) | Angars |
| | Lt. L.P. Cles | Me-110 dest(grd) | Cormeilles-en-Vixen |
| | | Me-109 dest(grd) | Cormeilles-en-Vixen |
| | Lt. H.Q. Waggoner | FW-190 dest(grd) | Cormeilles-en-Vixen |
| | Lt. B.B. Mayhew | FW-190 dam(grd) | Cormeilles-en-Vixen |
| | Lt. W.T. McGarry | FW-190 dam(grd) | Cormeilles-en-Vixen |
| (#8) | | | |
| HdQts: | Col. G.E. Duncan | Ju-52 dest(air) | E/Ribecourt |
| | | (.5)Me-109 dest(air) | E/Ribecourt |
| 351st: | Capt. G.B. Compton | (.5)Me-109 dest(air) | E/Ribecourt |
| **356th** | | | |
| HdQts: | LtCol. D.A. Baccus | Me-323 dest(grd) | Laval |
| 359th: | Lt. L.F. Richason | Me-109 dest(grd) | Laval |
| | | Ju-52 dest(grd) | Laval |
| | | Me-109 dam(grd) | Laval |
| | Capt. G.W. Engel | Ju-52 dest(grd) | Laval |
| | Lt. A.E. Bergstrom | Me-109 dest(grd) | Laval |
| 361st: | F/O E.L. Decker | FW-190 dest(air) | SE Laval |
| | Lt. D.F. Thwaites | Ju-52 dest(grd) | Laval |
| **361st** | | | |
| 374th: | Lt. W.H. Sargent | Ju-52 dest(grd) | Orleans/Bricy |
| | Lt. R.J. Stolzy | Ju-52 dest(grd) | Orleans/Bricy |
| 375th: | Capt. D.C. Casto | Me-109 dam(air) | Chartres |
| 376th: | Capt. J.B. Cheney | FW-190 dest(air) | N/Chateaudun |
| | Lt. S.C. Wilkerson | He-177 dest(air) | NE Vendome |

*Losses-*

**4th**: Lt. Osce R. Jones (335th Ftr Sqn) POW
P-51B WD-J 43-7042
Hit by flak in the Dol-Deb/Medard area.

Lt. Kenneth D. Smith (336th Ftr Sqn) KIA
P-51B VF- 43-6673
Collided on take-off and crashed near Debden.

**56th**: Lt. Eugene Bennett (62nd Ftr Sqn) MIA-E
P-47D LM- 42-76254
Hit by flak and bailed out near Orbec.

Lt. Alfred D. Evans, Jr. (62nd Ftr Sqn) KIA
P-47D LM- 42-76118
Hit by flak and bellied-in near Argeuil.

Lt. Donald J. Furlong (62nd Ftr Sqn) KIA
P-47D LM- 42-26274
Hit by flak near Argeuil.

Lt. Wendel A. McClure (62nd Ftr Sqn) MIA-E
P-47D LM-S 42-26342
Hit by enemy fighters near Beauvais.

Lt. Harry F. Warner (63rd Ftr Sqn) KIA
P-47D UN- 43-25286
Damaged by bomb blast near Liancourt.

**78th**: Lt. Harry H. Just, Jr. (84th Ftr Sqn) KIA
P-47D WZ-T 42-25712
Hit by a Me-109 near Montdidier.

Lt. Harold H. Rice (84th Ftr Sqn) POW
P-47D WZ-K 42-76184
Hit by a Me-109 near Montdidier.

**352nd**: Maj. Edward J. Gignac (HdQts) KIA
P-51B PZ-J 42-106661 "Hot Stuff"
Hit by flak near Le Merlerault.

Lt. Robert L. Hall (487th Ftr Sqn) KIA
P-51B HO-R 43-24845
Hit by flak near Argentan.

Lt. Clifford P. Garney (487th Ftr Sqn) KIA
P-51B HO-M 42-106471 "Lambie II"
Spun-in over England upon returning from a mission.

**353rd**: Capt. Francis T. Walsh (350th Ftr Sqn) KIA
P-47D LH- 42-8515
Hit by flak and crashed into the Channel.

Lt. Herbert K. Field (351st Ftr Sqn) KIA
P-47D YJ-F 42-75570
Hit by a Me-109 and bailed out over the Channel.

Lt. Luther Avakian (352nd Ftr Sqn) KIA
P-47D SX-Y 42-76195 "The Mole"
Hit by flak near Meulers.

**355th**: Lt. Robert D. Couture (354th Ftr Sqn) MIA-E
P-51B WR-P 43-6895
Hit by flak in the Nogent area.

Lt. Thomas J. Foster (357th Ftr Sqn) KIA
P-51B OS-G 42-106742
Downed by bomb blast near Aunay Sous Auneau.

Lt. John Guerrant, Jr. (357th Ftr Sqn) KIA
P-51B OS-N 42-106810
Hit by a Me-109 near Aquigny.

Lt. Harwood H. Harrell (357th Ftr Sqn) MIA-E
P-51B OS-E 43-6886 "Kay"
Hit by flak and bellied-in near Chateaudun.

Lt. Nils E. Holman, Jr. (357th Ftr Sqn) KIA
P-51B OS-E 43-6916
Hit by a Me-109 near Aquigny.

Lt. Walter E. MacFarlane (357th Ftr Sqn) POW
P-51B OS-S 43-7039 "Red Eye"
Hit by a Me-109 near Aquigny.

**357th**: Lt. John N. Denesha (364th Ftr Sqn) KIA
P-51B C5- 42-106652
Hit by flak near Plancoet.

**359th**: Lt. John S. Marcinkiewicz (370th Ftr Sqn) POW
P-51B CS-L 42-106667 "Sweet Sue"
Hit by debris from an exploding truck and bailed out near Fecamp.

**361st**: Maj. George L. Merritt, Jr. (375th Ftr Sqn) KIA
P-51B E2- 42-106835
Hit a pole while strafing near Roiffe.

*Remarks*

4th: Maj. James A. Goodson (336th Ftr Sqn) c/l Merston; o.k.
P-51D VF-B 44-13300
56th: 7-9 locos, 30-99 railcars, 1-5 vehicles, 0-1 bridge
78th: 1-1 locos
339th: Lt. Nathan T. Folwell (503rd Ftr Sqn) c/l Fowlmere; o.k.
P-51B D7-
352nd: 1-4 locos
353rd: 9-2 locos, 0-11 railcars, 7-1 vehicles, 0-1 bridge, 0-1 flak position
P-47 c/l Wattisham; o.k.
355th: 1-0 loco, 3-0 vehicles
Lt. Charles C. Colson (357th Ftr Sqn) c/l Manston; o.k.
P-51B OS-
356th: 3-4 locos, 2-43 railcars, 55-54 vehicles, 0-1 bridge
357th: 3-1 locos, 0-12 railcars, 0-2 flak towers
359th: 13-15 vehicles
361st: 0-3 locos, 7-60 railcars, 12-8 vehicles

KIAc's
352nd: Lt. William C. Mulvey (487th Ftr Sqn)
P-51B HO-
Crashed shortly after take-off.

**June 8, 1944**
Groups Operating: P-51 4th, 339th, 352nd, 355th, 357th, 359th, 361st
P-47 56th, 78th, 353rd, 356th
P-38 20th, 55th, 364th, 479th
Missions: Fighter-bomber operations in France, sweeps and patrols of the invasion area, and support for bombers to targets in northern France.
Claims: 29-2-5 air
12-8 ground

| *Group* | | *Claims* | *Location* |
|---|---|---|---|
| **56th** | | | |
| 62nd: | Lt. B.G. Edens | (2)Me-109 dest(air) | St. Andre de L'Eure |
| | | FW-190 dest(air) | St. Andre de L'Eure |
| | Lt. M.L. Moseley | (2)FW-190 dest(air) | St. Andre de L'Eure |
| | Lt. G.H. Butler | Me-109 dest(air) | St. Andre de L'Eure |
| | Lt. G.H. Van Noy | Me-109 dest(air) | St. Andre de L'Eure |
| **78th** | | | |
| 84th: | Lt. J.F. Casey | Me-109 dam(air) | W/Gourey |
| **339th** | | | |
| 503rd: | Lt. R.H. Ammon | FW-190 dest(air) | Fourgeres |
| | | Me-109 dam(air) | Rennes |
| | Lt. R.S. Whitelaw | FW-190 dest(air) | Rennes |
| 504th: | Lt. M.R. Ball | FW-190 dest(air) | Rennes |
| 505th: | Lt. A.A. Tower | FW-190 dest(air) | Laigle |
| | | (.5)Do-217 dest(air) | Laigle |
| | Lt. W.R. Opitz | (.5)Do-217 dest(air) | Laigle |
| | Lt. J.R. Starnes | Me-109 dest(air) | Fourgeres |
| | | (.5)FW-190 dest(air)* | Rennes |
| | Lt. P.J. McMahon | (1.5)FW-190 dest(air)* | Rennes |
| | Lt. W. Jaaskelainen | FW-190 dest(air) | Rennes |
| | Lt. W.A. Jones | FW-190 dest(air) | Rennes |
| | Lt. R.B. Olander | (.5)FW-190 dest(air)** | Rennes |
| | Lt. A. Sirochman | (.5)FW-190 dest(air)** | Rennes |
| **352nd** | | | |
| 486th: | Lt. D.Y. Whinnem | (2)FW-190 dest(grd) | Le Mans |
| | Maj. S.W. Andrew | FW-190 dam(grd) | Le Mans |
| **353rd**(#1) | | | |
| HdQts: | Maj. K.W. Gallup | FW-190 dest(grd) | Le Mans |
| | | FW-190 dam(grd) | Le Mans |
| 350th: | Lt. A.B. Starr | He-111 dest(grd) | Breteuil |
| | | (2)Me-109 dam(grd) | Breteuil |
| | F/O D.L. Yocum | Me-110 dest(grd) | Breteuil |
| | | Me-110 dam(grd) | Breteuil |
| 351st: | Capt. G.B. Compton | FW-190 dest(air) | SW Angars |
| | Capt. F.N. Emory | FW-190 dest(air) | SW Angars |
| | Lt. J.J. Hatch | FW-190 dest(air) | SW Angars |
| | Lt. W.J. Weaver | FW-190 dest(air) | SW Angars |
| | | FW-190 dam(air) | SW Angars |
| | Lt. J.R. Mitchell | Me-109 dest(grd) | Angars |
| | | He-111 dam(grd) | Breteuil |
| 352nd: | Lt. C.F. Armstrong | (1.5)FW-190 dest(grd) | Angars |
| | | (.5)Ju-88 dest(grd) | Angars |
| | Lt. H.O. Miller | FW-190 dest(grd) | Angars |
| | | (.5)Ju-88 dest(grd) | Angars |
| | Lt. H.Q. Waggoner | (1.5)FW-190 dest(grd) | Angars |
| | | (2)FW-190 dam(grd) | Angars |
| (#2) | | | |
| 351st: | Lt. H.J. Carbonneau | Me-109 dest(air) | Domfort |
| | Lt. G.H. McLaughlin | FW-190 prob(air) | Domfort |
| | Lt. R.C. Strobell | FW-190 prob(air) | Domfort |
| | Lt. G.N. Ahles | FW-190 dam(air) | Domfort |
| **355th** | | | |
| 358th: | Lt. W.J. McGinty | (.5)He-177 dest(air) | N/Angoulieme |
| | Lt. C.J. Brien | (.5)He-177 dest(air) | N/Angoulieme |
| **356th** | | | |
| 359th: | Lt. M.M. Clayborne | FW-190 dest(air) | Beauvais-Nivillers |
| 361st: | Lt. H.E. Wiggins | (.5)FW-190 dest(air) | Beauvais-Nivillers |
| | | (.5)FW-190 dest(grd) | Beauvais-Nivillers |
| | Lt. G.L. Yoakum | (.5)FW-190 dest(air) | Beauvais-Nivillers |
| | Capt. D.B. Clayton | (.5)FW-190 dest(grd) | Beauvais-Nivillers |
| **361st** | | | |
| 374th: | Capt. C.H. Bergmann | Me-109 dest(air) | St. Pierre |
| | Lt. J.O. Adkins | Me-109 dest(air) | St. Pierre |
| | Lt. R.T. Eckfeldt | Me-109 dest(air) | St. Pierre |
| | Lt. P.C. Holter | Me-109 dam(air) | St. Pierre |

*Losses-*

**4th**: Lt. Eacott G. Allen (334th Ftr Sqn) MIA-E
P-51B QP-K 42-106823
Collided with Lt. Scott near Le Mans.

Lt. James F. Scott (334th Ftr Sqn) KIA
P-51B QP-P 43-7150
Collided with Lt. Allen near Le Mans.

**339th**: Lt. Robert C. Smith (503rd Ftr Sqn) KIA
P-51C D7- 42-103299
Hit by FW-190's near Fourgeres.

Lt. Philip H. Ewing (505th Ftr Sqn) MIA-E
P-51B 6N- 42-106699
Damaged by a bomb blast near Lisieux.

Lt. Joseph F. Sawicki, Jr. (505th Ftr Sqn) KIA
P-51B 6N-F 42-106653
Hit by a FW-190 near Rennes.

**352nd**: Lt. John Campbell (328th Ftr Sqn) KIA
P-51B PE-J 43-24801
Hit by flak near Chartres.

Lt. Harry L. Miller, Jr. (328th Ftr Sqn) MIA
P-51B PE-Q 43-6988 "Denali"
Last seen over France in heavy overcast.

Lt. Ted P. Fahrenwald (486th Ftr Sqn) MIA-E
P-51C PZ-F 42-103336
Hit by flak near Elbeuf.

**355th**: LtCol. Gerald J. Dix (HdQts) POW
P-51B YF-D 43-7164
Hit by flak near Niort.

Lt. David A. Donovan (358th Ftr Sqn) MIA-E
P-51B YF-K 43-6879 "Mary Joyce"
Hit by flak near Montboyen.

F/O Edward R. Williams (358th Ftr Sqn) KIA
P-51B YF-N
Damaged by flak and crashed near Eyeworth.

**356th**: Lt. Robert A. Coughenour (359th Ftr Sqn) KIA
P-47D OC- 42-26253
Lost oil pressure and crashed off Orfordness.

Lt. James B. Smith (359th Ftr Sqn) MIA-E
P-47D OC-R 42-76168
Hit by a Me-109 east of Amiens.

Lt. Joseph Obosla (360th Ftr Sqn) KIA
P-47D PI- 42-76431
Damaged by a bomb blast near Rouen.

F/O Edmund L. Decker (361st Ftr Sqn) KIA
P-47D QI-K 42-75556
Hit the ground while strafing near Bouconvillers.

Lt. Raymond F. Engle (361st Ftr Sqn) KIA
P-47D QI-O 42-8427
Reported he was low on fuel near Abbeville.

Lt. Edward P. Lee, Jr. (361st Ftr Sqn) KIA
P-47D QI-S 42-76422
Hit by flak near Montdidier.

**357th**: Lt. Ollie E. Harris (362nd Ftr Sqn) ASR
P-51B G4-
Bailed out off New Haven.

**359th**: Lt. Benjamin M. Hagan, III (368th Ftr Sqn) POW
P-51B CV-D 42-106898 "Boots"
Hit by flak near Chartres.

Lt. Robert J. Booth (369th Ftr Sqn) POW
P-51B IV-F 43-7199
Hit by flak near La Fleche.

Lt. John H. Oliphint (369th Ftr Sqn) POW(E)
P-51B IV-O 42-106679 "The Mad Rebel"
Hit by flak near La Fleche.

Lt. Robert B. Sander (369th Ftr Sqn) KIA
P-51B IV-L 42-106906 "Mary"
Hit by flak in the Orleans-Tours area.

**361st**: Lt. James D. Hastin (374th Ftr Sqn) POW
P-51B B7- 43-6982
Damaged by a bomb blast near Anet.

**364th**: Lt. Loren R. Wilson (383rd Ftr Sqn) KIA
P-38J N2-K 42-104417
Spun-in near Funting upon return from a mission.

*Remarks*
56th: 10-0 vehicles, 1-0 gun position, 0-1 building
339th: Lt. William A. Jones (505thFtr Sqn) b/o Friston; o.k.
P-51B 6N-
Lt. Donald A. Zeine (504th Ftr Sqn) c/l t/o; o.k.
P-51B 5Q-
352nd: 0-2 locos
353rd: 3-0 locos, 42-0 vehicles, 2-0 hangars
355th: 0-3 locos, 0-8 vehicles, 50-1 railcars
356th: 4-2 locos, 26-95 railcars, 0-2 barges, 1-0 vehicle
357th: 3-2 locos, 26-35 railcars, 6-0 vehicles
359th: 1-0 loco, 11-4 railcars, 5-14 vehicles
361st: 0-2 locos, 15-6 railcars, 26-7 vehicles

KIAc's
4th: Lt. James T. Byrd, Jr. (334th Ftr Sqn)
P-51B QP-D 43-6433
Dove into the ground near Leiston.

**June 9, 1944**
KIAc's
352nd: Lt. Robert H. Sharp (328th Ftr Sqn)
P-51B PE-I 43-7174

Lt. Richard A. Pratt (328th Ftr Sqn)
P-51B PE-P 42-106868 "Hildegarde"

479th: Lt. Edward J. Spillane (436th Ftr Sqn)
P-38J 9B-Q

**June 10, 1944**
Groups Operating: P-51 4th, 339th, 352nd, 355th, 357th, 359th, 361st
P-47 56th, 78th, 353rd, 356th
P-38 20th, 55th, 364th, 479th
Missions: Support of bombers to targets in France plus dive-bombing and sweeps of the invasion area.
Claims: 16-1-8 air
1-2 ground

| *Group* | | *Claims* | *Location* |
|---|---|---|---|
| **78th** | | | |
| 83rd: | Maj. D.W. McLeod | (2)Me-109 dest(air) | S/Lisieux |
| | | (2)Me-109 dam(air) | S/Lisieux |
| | Capt. R.E. Ealey | Me-109 dest(air) | Argentan |
| | Lt. F.R. Pursell | FW-190 dest(air) | Argentan |
| | | FW-190 dam(air) | Argentan |
| | Lt. R.B. Hathway | FW-190 dam(air) | Argentan |
| 84th: | Lt. L.J. Abel | Me-109 dest(air) | La Ferte Mace |
| | Lt. D. Ledington | Me-109 dest(air) | La Ferte Mace |
| | Lt. R.J. McIntosh | FW-190 dest(air) | La Ferte Mace |
| **339th** | | | |
| 504th: | Lt. H.S. Stockman | Me-109 prob(air) | SE Le Havre |
| | Lt. M.R. Ball | Me-109 dam(air) | SE Le Havre |
| 505th: | Lt. C.J. Hanseman | Me-109 dest(air) | Laigle |
| | | Ju-88 dam(grd) | Laigle |
| | Capt. L. Reid | (.5)Ju-52 dest(air) | Laigle |
| | Lt. E.M. Johnson | (.5)Ju-52 dest(air) | Laigle |
| **352nd** | | | |
| 328th: | Lt. J.F. Thornell | (2)Me-109 dest(air) | Bayeux |
| | Lt. C.J. Bennette | Me-109 dest(air) | Bayeux |
| | | Me-109 dam(air) | Bayeux |
| 487th: | Lt. H.H. Barnes | Me-109 dam(air) | NW Mortain |
| **353rd** | | | |
| 352nd: | Lt. C.F. Armstrong | FW-190 dest(air) | SW Nantes-Gassicourt |
| **356th** | | | |
| 359th: | Lt. L.F. Richason | FW-190 dest(grd) | SE Dreux |
| | | FW-190 dam(grd) | SE Dreux |
| **359th** | | | |
| 368th: | Lt. O.P. Drake | (2)Me-109 dest(air) | Evreux |
| | Lt. G.A. Doersch | Me-109 dest(air) | Evreux |
| | Lt. V.W. Ambrose | Me-109 dam(air) | Evreux |

*Losses-*

**4th**: Capt. Frank D. Caple (336th Ftr Sqn) POW
P-51B VF- 43-6889
Hit by flak near Dieppe.

Lt. Conrad J. Netting (336th Ftr Sqn) KIA
P-51B VF- 42-106669 "Coujon IV"
Hit by flak near St. Michel.

**56th**: Lt. Joseph Vitale (62nd Ftr Sqn) MIA-E
P-47D LM- 43-25523
Hit by flak near Mayenne.

**78th**: Lt. Robert L. Baker (82nd Ftr Sqn) KIA
P-47D MX-X 42-76547
Hit by flak near Beaumont.

Lt. Richard S. Kuehner (82nd Ftr Sqn) KIA
P-47D MX-U 42-26317
Hit a tree while strafing near Beaumont.

Maj. Donald W. McLeod (83rd Ftr Sqn) MIA-E
P-47D HL-V 42-76505
Hit by a Me-109 near Argentan.

Lt. Vincent J. Massa (83rd Ftr Sqn) KIA
P-47D HL-S 43-25319
Hit by enemy fighters near Argentan.

Lt. William M. McDermott (83rd Ftr Sqn) KIA
P-47D HL-E 42-26053
Collided with a P-47 and crashed near Southminster.

Maj. Harold E. Stump (84th Ftr Sqn) KIA
P-47D WZ-X 42-25736
Hit by a Me-109 near Argentan.

Capt. William F. Hunt (84th Ftr Sqn) KIA
P-47D WZ-W 42-26031
Hit by a Me-109 near Argentan.

Lt. James F. Casey (84th Ftr Sqn) MIA-E
P-47D WZ-M 42-26149
Hit by enemy fighters near Argentan.

Lt. Daniel T. Loyd (84th Ftr Sqn) KIA
P-47D WZ-Z 42-25981
Hit by a Me-109 near Argentan.

Lt. Robert J. McIntosh (84th Ftr Sqn) MIA-E
P-47D WZ-Q 42-76506
Hit by a FW-190 near Argentan.

**339th**: Lt. Hetzel K. Boden (504th Ftr Sqn) POW
P-51B 5Q- 42-106700
Hit by flak and bailed out over the Channel.

**352nd**: Lt. Raymond G. Phillips (328th Ftr Sqn) KIA
P-51B PE-W 42-106756
Hit trees near Bayeux and bailed out near Le Havre.

Lt. Lincoln C. Bundy (486th Ftr Sqn) KIA
P-51B PZ-R 43-7153 "Rustler"
Hit by flak near La Mailleraue.

Lt. Donald J. Markle (486th Ftr Sqn) KIA
P-51B PZ-M 43-6776
Hit trees while strafing near St. Lo.

**353rd**: Lt. Martin D. Coffey (350th Ftr Sqn) KIA
P-47D LH- 43-25581
Hit by flak near Gace.

F/O James R. Hicks (352nd Ftr Sqn) KIA
P-47D SX-W 42-8630 "Bobbie Baby"
Hit by flak in the Pas de Calais area.

Lt. Virgil C. Johnston (352nd Ftr Sqn) KIA
P-47D SX-I 42-25771
Hit by flak near Rennes.

Lt. William S. Marchant (352nd Ftr Sqn) KIA
P-47D SX-O 42-76501
Hit by flak near Rennes.

**356th**: Lt. Elijah P. Harris, Jr. (361st Ftr Sqn) KIA
P-47D QI-Z 42-7886
Hit by flak near Gassicourt.

**357th**: Lt. John K. Childs (363rd Ftr Sqn) KIA
P-51B B6-P 43-6563 "Gentleman Jim"
Hit by P-51 fire while strafing near Mortagne.

**359th**: Capt. Wayne N. Bolefahr (368th Ftr Sqn) KIA
P-51B CV- 43-24786
Hit by flak near Wildert.

Lt. Olin P. Drake (368th Ftr Sqn) MIA-E
P-51C CV-Z 42-103329
Hit by a Me-109 near Evreux.

**361st**: Capt. Wallace B. Frank (374th Ftr Sqn) POW
P-51B E9-F 43-24759
Hit by flak near Gace.

*Remarks*
4th: 0-4 locos, 0-40 railcars
20th: 28-5 vehicles
56th: 6-1 vehicles, 1-0 gun position
Lt. James J. Clark (61st Ftr Sqn) c/l; o.k.
P-47D HV-
78th: Lt. Herbert L. Boyle (84th Ftr Sqn) c/l; o.k.
P-47D WZ-
Lt. Daniel T. Loyd (84th Ftr Sqn) c/l; o.k.
P-47D WZ-
(Note - Loyd was KIA later in day)
353rd: 1-0 loco, 43-0 vehicles
Lt. Edwin D. Reinhardt (352nd Ftr Sqn) c/l Wattisham; o.k.
P-47D SX-B
355th: 0-20 railcars, 10-12 vehicles
356th: 0-2 locos, 4-104 railcars, 4-50 vehicles, 0-2 hangars
357th: Lt. James B. Badger (362nd Ftr Sqn) c/l; o.k.
P-51B G4-
359th: 1-0 loco, 1-4 railcars, 8-2 vehicles
Lt. D.R. Tuchscherer (370th Ftr Sqn) c/l Exeter; o.k.
P-51B CS-O 42-106926
361st: 2-7 locos, 32-14 vehicles, 0-2 bridges

**June 11, 1944**
Groups Operating: P-51 4th, 339th, 352nd, 355th, 357th, 359th, 361st
P-47 56th, 78th, 353rd, 356th
P-38 20th, 55th, 364th, 479th
Missions: Support of bombers to targets in the Paris and Brittany areas, plus fighter-bomber operations and sweeps/patrols in the invasion area.
Claims: 10-1-2 air
0-0 ground

| *Group* | | *Claims* | *Location* |
|---|---|---|---|
| **55th** | | | |
| 338th: | Maj. V.W. Bollwerk | Me-109 dest(air) | Beauvais |
| | Lt. S.P. Richardson | Me-109 dest(air) | Beauvais |
| | Lt. T.D. Schank | Me-109 dest(air) | Beauvais |
| | Lt. A.J. Tinto | Me-109 dest(air) | Beauvais |
| | Capt. M.E. Blanchard | Me-109 dam(air) | Amiens |
| 343rd: | Lt. R.P. Hjelm | (2)FW-190 dest(air) | Clermont |
| | Lt. C.D. Porter | FW-190 dest(air) | Clermont |
| | | Me-109 dam(air) | Clermont |
| | Lt. R.S. Seely | Me-109 dest(air) | W/Beauvais |
| | Lt. F.J. Leone | Me-109 prob(air) | Clermont |
| **356th** | | | |
| 361st: | Lt. R.H. Gansberg | Me-109 dest(air) | SW Bernay |
| | Lt. D. Kahle | Me-109 dest(air) | SW Bernay |

*Losses-*

**4th**: Lt. Leon J. Cole, Jr. (334th Ftr Sqn) KIA
P-51C QP-B 42-103292
Hit the ground while strafing near Villedieu.

Lt. Harry B. Noon (334th Ftr Sqn) KIA
P-51B QP-U 43-6586
Hit trees while dive-bombing near Villedieu.

**55th**: Maj. Val W. Bollwerk (338th Ftr Sqn) POW
P-38J CL- 42-104396
Hit by a FW-190 near Amiens.

Lt. Karl J. Goethel (343rd Ftr Sqn) MIA-E
P-38J CY- 43-28388
Hit by a FW-190 near Estrees.

Lt. Rex P. Hjelm (343rd Ftr Sqn) MIA-E
P-38J CY- 42-68102
Hit by a FW-190 near Clermont.

**78th**: Lt. Lawrence R. Casey (83rd Ftr Sqn) POW
P-47D HL-N 42-75610
Suffered mechanical failure near Bernay.

**359th**: Lt. William R. Simmons (368th Ftr Sqn) KIA
P-51B CV- 43-6775
Hit by flak near Bretteville.

Lt. Gilbert R. Ralston (369th Ftr Sqn) ASR
P-51B IV-R 43-6620
Damaged by flak and bailed out over the Channel.

*Remarks*
4th: 32-2 vehicles, 0-1 bridge
55th: 5-0 locos, 0-3 railcars
56th: 100-20 railcars, 3-7 vehicles
353rd: 1-1 locos, 1-2 vehicles
355th: 0-20 railcars, 7-0 vehicles, 0-2 bridges
356th: 1-0 loco, 5-0 railcars

357th: 4-0 railcars, 0-3 tanks
359th: 4-4 railcars, 8-12 vehicles, 0-1 bridge
361st: 0-8 locos, 35-7 railcars, 0-5 vehicles

**June 12, 1944**
Groups Operating: P-51 339th, 352nd, 355th, 357th, 359th, 361st
P-47 56th, 78th, 353rd, 356th
P-38 20th, 55th, 364th, 479th
Missions: Support for bombers to targets in France plus patrols and fighter-bomber operations.
Claims: 25-1-14 air
1-1 ground

| *Group* | | *Claims* | *Location* |
|---|---|---|---|
| **56th** | | | |
| 61st: | LtCol. F.S. Gabreski | (2)Me-109 dest(air) | Evreux |
| | F/O S. Gerick | (2)Me-109 dest(air) | Evreux |
| | | (4)Me-109 dam(air) | Evreux |
| | Lt. O.M. Belk | Me-109 dest(air) | Quittlebeuf |
| | Lt. A.C. Maul | Me-109 dam(air) | Evreux |
| | Lt. C.A. Dudley | Me-109 dam(air) | Evreux |
| | Lt. W.S. Patterson | Me-109 dam(air) | Evreux |
| **352nd** | | | |
| 328th: | Lt. L.E. McCarthy | (.5)Me-109 dest(air) | S/St. Malo |
| | Lt. J.F. Thornell | (.5)Me-109 dest(air) | S/St. Malo |
| 487th: | Maj. G.E. Preddy | Me-109 dest(air) | SW Rennes |
| | Lt. G.T. Moran | Me-109 dest(air) | SW Rennes |
| **353rd**(#1) | | | |
| HdQts: | Col. G.E. Duncan | (3)Me-109 dest(air) | Evreux-Dreux |
| 350th: | Lt. J.O. Ruscitto | Me-109 dest(air) | Dreux |
| | | Me-109 dam(air) | Dreux |
| | Lt. S.T. Benjamin | Me-109 dam(air) | Dreux |
| 352nd: | Lt. R.V. Keywan | Me-109 dest(air) | Evreux-Dreux |
| | | (2)Me-109 dam(air) | Evreux-Dreux |
| | Lt. H.O. Miller | Me-109 dest(air) | Dreux |
| | Lt. C.H. Sperry | Me-109 prob(air) | Dreux |
| (#2) | | | |
| HdQts: | Maj. K.W. Gallup | (2)Me-109 dest(air) | SW Paris |
| | LtCol. B. Rimerman | (1.5)Me-109 dest(air) | S/Paris |
| 350th: | Lt. J.F. Furness | (2)Me-109 dest(air) | SW Paris |
| | Lt. W.F. Tanner | (2)Me-109 dest(air) | SW Paris |
| | Lt. J.F. Starr | Me-109 dam(air) | SW Paris |
| 351st: | Lt. R.M. Tumlin | Me-109 dest(air) | SW Paris |
| | | Me-109 dam(air) | SW Paris |
| | Lt. W.J. Frank | (.5)Me-109 dest(air) | S/Paris |
| | Lt. N.T. Ott | Me-109 dam(air) | SW Paris |
| **359th** | | | |
| 369th: | Lt. L.D. Hess | (2)FW-190 dest(air) | W/Paris |
| | Maj. C.S. Irvine | Me-109 dam(grd) | W/Paris |
| **361st** | | | |
| 374th: | Capt. G.R. Rew | FW-190 dest(grd) | Chateau DuLoir |

*Losses-*

**20th:** Lt. Alert L. Gese (77th Ftr Sqn) KIA
P-38J LC-X 42-67462
Hit by flak north of Flers.

Lt. Hugh L. Jacobson (77th Ftr Sqn) KIA
P-38J LC- 42-68111
Last seen strafing a convoy near Brest.

Lt. Dixon V. Kendrick (77th Ftr Sqn) POW
P-38J LC-M 42-67478
Hit by flak near Caen.

Lt. Benjamin N. Rader (77th Ftr Sqn) ASR
P-38J LC-Z 42-68045
Suffered mechanical failure and bailed out twelve miles off the Normandy coast.

**78th:** Capt. John C. Ramsey (82nd Ftr Sqn) KIA
P-47D MX-C 42-75591
Hit by flak near Chartrettes.

**353rd:** Capt. Dewey E. Newhart (350th Ftr Sqn) KIA
P-47D LH-U 42-26402
Hit by a Me-109 near Dreux.

Lt. Richard L. Bedford (350th Ftr Sqn) POW
P-47D LH- 42-25768
Hit by a Me-109 near Dreux.

Lt. Earl C. Main (350th Ftr Sqn) POW
P-47D LH- 42-26313
Hit by a Me-109 near Dreux.

Lt. Goffred R. Moretto (350th Ftr Sqn) MIA-E
P-47D LH- 43-25541
Hit by a Me-109 near Dreux.

Lt. Edwin H. Peters (350th Ftr Sqn) ASR
P-47D LH-
Damaged by a Me-109 and bailed out over the Channel.

F/O John J. Phelan (350th Ftr Sqn) KIA
P-47D LH- 42-22779
Hit by a Me-109 near Evreux.

Lt. John R. Gabriel, Jr. (352nd Ftr Sqn) MIA-E
P-47D SX-D 42-26011
Hit by a Me-109 near Evreux.

Lt. Richard V. Keywan (352nd Ftr Sqn) KIA
P-47D SX-A 42-75707 "Little Hotsy"
Hit by a Me-109 near St. Andre de'Lure.

**359th:** Capt. Robert L. Pherson (369th Ftr Sqn) KIA
P-51B IV-N 42-106848 "Deviless 2nd"
Hit by a FW-190 west of Paris.

Lt. Leroy D. Hess (369th Ftr Sqn) POW
P-51B IV-Q 42-106841
Hit by a FW-190 west of Paris.

Lt. Howard A. Linderer (369th Ftr Sqn) POW
P-51B IV-G 42-106649
Hit by flak, then flew through power lines and bellied-in near Pallseaux.

*Remarks*
20th: 2-7 locos, 1-13 railcars, 51-23 vehicles
Capt. Maurice McLary (55th Ftr Sqn) c/l; o.k.
P-38J KI-P 42-104239
Lt. Walter F. Kuemmerle (77th Ftr Sqn) c/l beach-head; o.k.
P-38J LC-
55th: 0-1 bridge
56th: 30-0 railcars, 1-0 vehicle
Lt. Earl Hertel (61st Ftr Sqn) c/l beach-head; o.k.
P-47D HV-
356th: 0-2 locos, 0-20 railcars
359th: 0-2 locos, 0-2 railcars, 1-3 vehicles
361st: 0-1 loco, 0-2 railcars, 15-2 vehicles

**June 13, 1944**
Groups Operating: P-51 4th, 339th, 352nd, 355th, 357th, 359th, 361st
P-47 56th, 78th, 353rd, 356th
P-38 20th, 55th, 364th, 479th
Missions: Support of bombers to airfields and bridges in France plus fighter-bomber operations.
Claims: 6-0-0 air
0-0 ground

| *Group* | | *Claims* | *Location* |
|---|---|---|---|
| **78th** | | | |
| 83rd: | Maj. O.E. Gilbert | FW-190 dest(air) | Orleans |
| | Lt. P.C. Holden | Me-109 dest(air) | Orleans |
| **361st** | | | |
| HdQts: | LtCol. J.J. Kruzel | Me-109 dest(air) | St. Brieuc |
| 374th: | Maj. R.A. Webb | Me-109 dest(air) | St. Brieuc |
| | Lt. R.E. Downey | Me-109 dest(air) | St. Brieuc |
| | Lt. R.P. Lacy | Me-109 dest(air) | St. Brieuc |

*Losses-*

**20th:** Lt. Russell G. Quinn (77th Ftr Sqn) KIA
P-38J LC- 44-23174
Hit by flak in the Domfort area.

Maj. Jack M. Ilfrey (79th Ftr Sqn) MIA-E
P-38J MC-O 43-28431 "Happy Jack's Go Buggy"
Hit by flak and bailed out north of Angars.

**56th:** Capt. Zbigniew Janicki (61st Ftr Sqn) KIA
P-47D HV-
Suffered mechanical failure and reported he was landing near Saumur.

**339th:** Lt. Jack E. Shively (504th Ftr Sqn) KIA
P-51B 5Q- 42-106847
Hit by flak near Saumur.

*Remarks*
4th: 9-0 vehicles
20th: 3-6 locos, 9-5 vehicles
55th: 1-3 locos, 0-22 railcars
339th: Lt. William R. Opitz (505th Ftr Sqn) b/o Epping; injured
353rd: 0-1 bridge
Lt. Thomas W. Jones (352nd Ftr Sqn) c/l beach-head; injured
P-47D SX-L

**June 14, 1944**
Groups Operating: P-51 339th, 352nd, 355th, 357th, 359th, 361st
P-47 56th, 78th, 353rd, 356th
P-38 20th, 55th, 364th, 479th
Missions: Support of bombers to airfields in France and Belgium plus fighter-bomber operations.
Claims: 5-0-6 air
0-0 ground

| *Group* | | *Claims* | *Location* |
|---|---|---|---|
| **55th** | | | |
| 38th: | Lt. D.H. Snell | FW-190 dest(air) | Paris |
| | Lt. C.R. Watts | Me-109 dest(air) | Paris |
| | Capt. D.E. Penn | Me-109 dam(air) | S/Paris |
| 338th: | Lt. L.J. Berry | Me-109 dest(air) | Paris |
| | Lt. T.A. Parker | Me-109 dam(air) | Paris |
| **56th** | | | |
| 63rd: | Lt. W.R. Frederick | (3)Me-109 dam(air) | S/Soissons |
| **357th** | | | |
| 364th: | Lt. R.M. Shaw | FW-190 dest(air) | E/Paris |
| | | FW-190 dam(air) | E/Paris |
| | Lt. J.E. Colburn | FW-190 dest(air) | E/Paris |

*Losses-*

**20th:** Lt. Stanley P. Spencer (55th Ftr Sqn) KIA
P-38J KI-M 42-68170
Hit by flak near Hengelo.

Capt. Terrence M. Williams (77th Ftr Sqn) POW
P-38J LC-K 42-68066
Hit by flak near Zwolle.

**55th:** Lt. Arthur Baranick (338th Ftr Sqn) MIA
P-38J CL- 42-68130
Hit by a Me-109 north of Paris.

Capt. Kenneth J. Sorace (343rd Ftr Sqn) MIA-E
P-38J CY-S 43-28666
Hit by a Me-109 north of Paris.

Lt. Louis J. Sturdivan (343rd Ftr Sqn) MIA
P-38J CY- 42-67964
Hit by a Me-109 north of Paris.

**356th:** Lt. Fred C. Phillips (360th Ftr Sqn) POW
P-47D PI-P 42-75273 "Hard Luck"
Suffered mechanical failure near Hertogenbosch.

**357th:** Lt. James E. Colburn (364th Ftr Sqn) KIA
P-51B C5- 43-24763
Hit by a Me-109 east of Paris.

*Remarks*
20th: 13-0 locos, 0-2 railcars
55th: 0-1 loco, 0-3 railcars, 0-3 vehicles, 8-0 flak towers, 0-2 buildings
353rd: 0-3 vehicles
355th: 2-0 locos
356th: 0-30 railcars
364th: P-38 c/l beach-head; o.k.

**June 15, 1944**
Groups Operating: P-51 4th, 339th, 352nd, 355th, 357th, 359th
P-47 56th, 78th, 353rd, 356th
P-38 20th, 55th, 364th, 479th
Missions: Support for bombers to [illegible] airfields and marshalling yards in France, plus fighter-bomber operations.
Claims: 5-0-3 air
0-0 ground

| *Group* | | *Claims* | *Location* |
|---|---|---|---|
| **339th** | | | |
| 503rd: | Capt. V. Wyatt | FW-190 dest(air) | Montiers |
| | Lt. L.J. Fiorito | Me-109 dest(air) | Montiers |
| | Lt. V.W. Meyer | FW-190 dest(air) | Montiers |
| 504th: | Lt. H.R. Waymire | Me-109 dest(air) | Chateuadun |
| **352nd** | | | |
| 328th: | Lt. G.A. Middleton | FW-190 dam(air) | Laigle |
| **356th** | | | |
| 361st: | Capt. W.R. Scheible | Me-109 dest(air) | SE Rouen |
| | Capt. E. Korhorn | Me-109 dam(air) | SE Rouen |
| | Lt. D. Kahle | Me-109 dam(air) | SE Rouen |

*Losses-*

**20th:** Lt. Walter F. Perra (77th Ftr Sqn) KIA
P-38J LC-V 42-104067 "Little Bug"
Hit by flak in the Dreux area.

**55th:** Lt. Edwin C. Wheeler (338th Ftr Sqn) POW
P-38J CL- 42-67867
Collided with a P-38 northwest of Hanover.

**339th:** Lt. Richard W. Montell, Jr. (504th Ftr Sqn) KIA
P-51B 5Q- 43-24772
Hit by enemy fighters near Quillebeuf.

*Remarks*
20th: 1-1 locos, 0-4 railcars, 5-6 vehicles, 0-1 barracks
357th: Lt. Erle A. Taylor (362nd Ftr Sqn) c/l; o.k.
P-51B G4-

**June 16, 1944**
Groups Operating: P-51 339th, 352nd, 355th, 357th, 359th, 361st
P-47 56th, 78th, 353rd, 356th
P-38 20th, 55th, 364th, 479th
Missions: Support of bombers to airfields and V-1 sites in France, plus fighter-bomber operations.
Claims: 1-0-0 air
3-0 ground

| *Group* | | *Claims* | *Location* |
|---|---|---|---|
| **56th** | | | |
| 61st: | Lt. E.A. Sisson | Me-109 dest(air) | Rouen |
| **361st** | | | |
| 375th: | Lt. J.S. Crandell | Ju-52 dest(grd) | Toussus/Le Noble |
| | Lt. U.L. Drew | Ju-52 dest(grd) | Toussus/Le Noble |
| | Lt. M.H. Johnson | Ju-52 dest(grd) | Toussus/Le Noble |

*Losses-*

**20th:** Maj. Paul A. Lobinger (HdQts) KIA
P-38J LC- 43-28430
Crashed near Purleigh after returning from the mission.

**55th:** Lt. Vernie B. Greenamyre (38th Ftr Sqn) POW
P-38J CG- 43-28423
Hit by flak near Amiens.

Lt. George W. Peterson (338th Ftr Sqn) POW
P-38J CL- 43-28273
Hit by flak near Abbeville.

Lt. Clair D. Porter (343rd Ftr Sqn) KIA
P-38J CY- 43-28713
Hit by flak near Oisement.

*Remarks*
55th: 2-0 locos, 0-10 railcars, 1-30 vehicles
Lt. Robert K. Fruh (338th Ftr Sqn) b/o Lympth; o.k.
353rd: 2-0 locos, 0-1 flak tower
355th: 0-2 locos
356th: 0-1 loco, 0-72 railcars, 0-6 vehicles, 0-13 barges
357th: 0-20 railcars

**June 17, 1944**
Groups Operating: P-51 339th, 352nd, 355th, 357th, 359th, 361st
P-47 56th, 78th, 353rd, 356th
P-38 20th, 55th, 364th, 479th
Missions: Support of bombers to airfields in France, plus fighter-bomber operations.
Claims: 3-0-0 air
0-0 ground

| *Group* | | *Claims* | *Location* |
|---|---|---|---|
| **78th** | | | |
| 83rd: | Lt. E.T. Kitley | FW-190 dest(air) | S/Laigle |
| | Lt. K.C. Allstaedt | (.5)FW-190 dest(air) | S/Laigle |
| | Lt. R.W. Oxley | (.5)FW-190 dest(air) | S/Laigle |
| **353rd** | | | |
| 351st: | Lt. J.J. Hatch | FW-190 dest(air) | Falaise |

*Losses-*

**20th:** Lt. Richard M. Hairston (77th Ftr Sqn) POW
P-38J LC- 43-28684
Hit by flak and bailed out near Amiens.

Lt. Earl O. Smith, Jr. (79th Ftr Sqn) KIA
P-38J MC-W 42-67905
Hit by flak and bailed out near Le Treport.

Lt. Emery K. Ryan (79th Ftr Sqn) KIA
P-38J MC-R 42-104308
Hit by flak near Amiens and bailed out but his chute failed.

**55th**: Lt. William C. DuRose (38th Ftr Sqn) MIA-E
P-38J CG- 43-28724
Hit by flak near Chaulnes.

**339th**: Lt. Walter M. Armistead (505th Ftr Sqn) POW
P-51B 6N-T 42-106720
Suffered mechanical failure near Chateaudun.

**357th**: Capt. Kenneth E. Hagan (362nd Ftr Sqn) MIA-E
P-51B G4-G 42-106831
Suffered mechanical failure southwest of Caen.

**479th**: Lt. James K. Ohligschlager (434th Ftr Sqn) KIA
P-38J L2-Q 43-28729
Collided with a P-38 near Rennes.

Capt. Calvin J. Butler (435th Ftr Sqn) MIA
P-38J J2- 44-23168
Hit by flak near Paris

*Remarks*
20th: 7-6 vehicles
55th: 2-2 locos, 4-18 railcars, 1-0 flak tower, 0-2 buildings
Lt. William Monty (38th Ftr Sqn) c/l; injured
P-38J CG-

KIAc's
359th: Maj. Wayne W. Brown (368th Ftr Sqn)
P-51B CV-

**June 18, 1944**
Groups Operating: P-51 4th, 339th, 352nd, 355th, 357th, 359th, 361st
P-47 56th, 78th, 353rd, 356th
P-38 20th, 55th, 364th, 479th
Missions: Support of bombers to various targets (mainly Hamburg), plus fighter-bomber operations.
Claims: nil

*Losses-*

**4th**: Lt. James H. Glynn (335th Ftr Sqn) MIA-E
P-51B WD-B 43-7187
Hit by flak and bailed out near Avranches.

Lt. Robert W. Little (335th Ftr Sqn) POW
P-51B WD-G 43-6770
Hit by flak and bailed out near Del-Deb.

Lt. Harvie J. Arnold (336th Ftr Sqn) KIA
P-51D VF-J 44-13307
Hit by flak near Combourg.

*Remarks*
4th: Lt. Henry A. Ingalls (336th Ftr Sqn) c/l Debden; o.k.
P-51B VF-U 43-6997
55th: 2-0 locos, 4-0 vehicles
56th: 1-0 loco, 0-2 vehicles
353rd: 0-2 locos

KIAc's
352nd: Lt. Robert S. Daugherty (487th Ftr Sqn)
P-51B HO-N 43-7160

**June 19, 1944**
Groups Operating: P-51 4th, 339th, 352nd, 355th, 357th, 359th, 361st
P-47 78th, 353rd
P-38 20th, 55th, 364th, 479th
Missions: Support of bombers to airfields in Bordeaux and to V-1 sites in the Pas de Calais area.
Claims: nil

*Losses-*

**4th**: Lt. Dean J. Hill (335th Ftr Sqn) KIA
P-51B WD-F 43-6896
Crashed into the Channel in bad weather.

**339th**: Capt. Nathan T. Folwell (503rd Ftr Sqn) KIA
P-51B D7- 42-106905
Crashed near Le Mans in bad weather.

Lt. Robert B. Brown (503rd Ftr Sqn) KIA
P-51B D7-P 42-106889
Crashed near Le Mans in bad weather.

Lt. Ralph H. Dearey (503rd Ftr Sqn) KIA
P-51B D7-R 42-106615
Crashed near Le Mans in bad weather.

**355th**: Lt. Ralph L. Coleman (358th Ftr Sqn) KIA
P-51B YF-Q 42-106858
Spun-out in the overcast near Bordeaux.

Lt. Willis W. Reeves (358th Ftr Sqn) KIA
P-51B YF-E 43-6523 "Leakin' Liz"
Spun-out in the overcast near Bordeaux.

**361st**: Capt. Joseph L. Latimer (374th Ftr Sqn) KIA
P-51B B7- 42-106735
Crashed near Vire in bad weather.

Lt. David L. Calloway (374th Ftr Sqn) KIA
P-51B B7-C 42-106713
Crashed near Vire in bad weather.

Lt. Lawrence J. Downey (374th Ftr Sqn) KIA
P-51B B7-D 43-24830
Crashed near Vire in bad weather.

Lt. Merrill E. Roberts (374th Ftr Sqn) MIA-E
P-51B B7- 43-24785
Crashed near Vire in bad weather.

Lt. Walter H. Sargent (374th Ftr Sqn) KIA
P-51B B7-B 42-106871
Crashed near Vire in bad weather.

Lt. Robert J. Stolzy (374th Ftr Sqn) KIA
P-51C B7- 42-103724
Crashed near Vire in bad weather.

**479th**: Lt. Frank Grdenich (434th Ftr Sqn) MIA-E
P-38J L2-T 43-28456
Collided with Lt. Kuentzal near Rennes.

Lt. Ward A. Kuentzal (434th Ftr Sqn) KIA
P-38J L2- 42-104427
Collided with Lt. Grdenich near Rennes.

Lt. Leland K. Horne (435th Ftr Sqn) MIA
P-38J J2- 42-68161
Collided with Lt. McClure near Murau.

Lt. Donald D. McClure (435th Ftr Sqn) MIA
P-38J J2- 42-68189
Collided with Lt. Horne near Murau.

*Remarks*
20th: Lt. Roger S. Peterson (79th Ftr Sqn) c/l; o.k.
P-38J MC-B 43-28433
364th: 1-0 loco

**June 20, 1944**
Groups Operating: P-51 4th, 339th, 352nd, 355th, 357th, 359th, 361st
P-47 56th, 78th, 353rd, 356th
P-38 20th, 55th, 364th, 479th
Missions: Support of bombers to Politz, Magdeburg, Harburg, Hamburg, Fallersleben, and V-1 sites in the Pas de Calais area, plus fighter-bomber operations.
Claims: 37-1-8 air
20-24 ground

| *Group* | | *Claims* | *Location* |
|---|---|---|---|
| **4th** | | | |
| HdQts: | LtCol. J.A. Clark | Me-410 dest(air) | SW Anklam |
| 334th: | Lt. W.G. Gillette | Ju-88 dest(air) | E/Pasewalk |
| | | Do-217 dest(grd) | Neubrandenburg |
| | | (.5)Ju-88 dest(grd)* | Neubrandenburg |
| | Lt. R.A. Dickmeyer | Me-109 dest(air) | E/Pasewalk |
| | Lt. D.M. Malmsten | Ju-88 dest(air) | Pasewalk |
| | Lt. S.W. Monroe | Me-109 dest(air) | E/Pasewalk |
| | Capt. T.E. Joyce | (.5)Me-109 dest(air) | E/Pasewalk |
| | Lt. A.C. Cwiklinski | (.5)Me-109 dest(air) | E/Pasewalk |
| | | Me-109 dam(air) | E/Pasewalk |
| 335th: | Capt. F.C. Jones | Me-109 dest(air) | Stettin |
| | Lt. G.W. Cooley | Me-109 dest(air) | Politz |
| | | Me-109 dam(air) | Politz |
| | Lt. G.I. Stanford | (.5)Me-210 dest(air) | Ratzeburger Lake |
| | F/O L.B. Godwin | (.5)Me-210 dest(air) | Ratzeburger Lake |
| 336th: | Capt. O.M. Glass | Me-109 dest(air) | S/Anklam |
| | Lt. D.R. Emerson | FW-190 dest(air) | S/Anklam |
| | Lt. C.H. Shilke | Do-217 dest(grd) | Neubrandenburg |
| | | (.5)Ju-88 dest(grd)* | Neubrandenburg |
| | Lt. F.S. Harris | Do-217 dest(grd) | Neubrandenburg |
| | | Do-217 dam(grd) | Neubrandenburg |
| **78th** | | | |
| 82nd: | Capt. B.I. Mayo | Me-109 dest(air) | Montdidier |
| 83rd: | Lt. G.G. Boteler | (.5)Me-109 dest(air) | Amiens |

| | | | |
|---|---|---|---|
| | Lt. P.C. Holden | (.5)Me-109 dest(air) | Amiens |
| 84th: | Lt. W.K. Dacci | Me-109 dest(air) | Montdidier |
| **352nd** | | | |
| 486th: | Lt. L.L. Howell | Me-109 dest(air) | Magdeburg |
| | | He-177 dam(grd) | N/Burg |
| | Lt. W.C. Raub | Me-109 dest(air) | Magdeburg |
| | Maj. S.W. Andrew | Ju-52 dest(grd) | N/Burg |
| | Lt. W.H. Brashear | Ju-88 dest(grd) | N/Burg |
| 487th: | Maj. G.E. Preddy | FW-190 dest(air) | E/Bernburg |
| | | (.5)Me-410 dest(air) | E/Bernburg |
| | Lt. J.N. Wood | (.5)Me-410 dest(air) | E/Bernburg |
| | Capt. W.E. Starck | FW-190 prob(air) | NW Magdeburg |
| | Lt. R.H. Berkshire | Me-410 dam(air) | Magdeburg |
| **353rd**(#1) | | | |
| HdQts: | Col. G.E. Duncan | (2)He-111 dest(grd) | Plantlunne |
| 352nd: | Capt. J.N. Poindexter | He-111 dest(grd) | Plantlunne |
| | Capt. V.N. Curtis | He-111 dest(grd) | Plantlunne |
| | Lt. R.P. Greenwood | He-111 dest(grd) | Plantlunne |
| | Lt. D.E. Harris | u/i a/c dam(grd) | Plantlunne |
| | Lt. H.Q. Waggoner | Ju-88 dam(grd) | Plantlunne |
| (#2) | | | |
| HdQts: | LtCol. B. Rimerman | (.5)He-111 dest(grd) | Plantlunne |
| | | (2)u/i a/c dam(grd) | Plantlunne |
| 350th: | Lt. J.B. Brooks | Me-110 dest(grd) | Plantlunne |
| | Lt. R.F. Unangst | Ju-88 dest(grd) | Plantlunne |
| | Lt. V.G. Rafferty | (.5)He-111 dest(grd) | Plantlunne |
| 351st: | Capt. G.B. Compton | Ju-88 dest(grd) | Plantlunne |
| | | (.5)He-111 dam(grd) | Plantlunne |
| | Lt. J.L. Dwyer | (.5)He-111 dam(grd) | Plantlunne |
| 352nd: | Capt. L.P. Cles | Me-110 dest(grd) | Twente/Enschede |
| | | Hs-129 dam(grd) | Twente/Enschede |
| | Lt. E.D. Reinhardt | He-111 dest(grd) | Twente/Enschede |
| | Lt. H.Q. Waggoner | Hs-129 dam(grd) | Twente/Enschede |
| **355th** | | | |
| 354th: | Capt. B.W. Marshall | (2)Me-109 dest(air) | Bergen |
| | Lt. W.D. Martin | (2)Me-109 dest(air) | Rugen |
| | Lt. G.S. Wright | (2)Me-109 dest(air) | Bergen |
| | Maj. H.B. Kucheman | Me-410 dest(air) | NW Stettin |
| | | Me-410 dam(air) | NW Stettin |
| | Lt. C.H. Graham | Me-410 dest(air) | NW Stettin |
| | Lt. G.C. Hoffman | Me-109 dest(air) | Rugen |
| | Lt. R.G. Taylor | Me-410 dest(air) | Rugen |
| | Lt. H.M. Huish | (.5)Me-410 dest(air) | Rugen |
| | Lt. S.C. Williams | (.5)Me-410 dest(air) | Rugen |
| | Lt. R.E. Hulderman | Me-410 dam(air) | Bergen |
| | Lt. A.S. White | Me-410 dam(air) | Bergen |
| 357th: | Capt. L.D. Minchew | Me-109 dest(air) | Pomeranian Bay |
| | Lt. C.R. Buckles | (.5)Me-410 dest(air) | Pomeranian Bay |
| | Lt. L.B. Fuller | (.5)Me-410 dest(air) | Pomeranian Bay |
| **357th** | | | |
| 362nd: | Lt. L.K. Carson | (.5)Me-110 dam(grd) | Neumunster |
| | Lt. T.W. Martinek | (.5)Me-110 dam(grd) | Neumunster |
| 364th: | Capt. R.C. Smith | Me-109 dest(air) | E/Eberswalde |
| | Lt. N.J. Frederick | Me-109 dest(air) | Pasewalk |
| | | (.5)Fi-156 dest(air) | Pasewalk |
| | Lt. J.J. Salsman | Me-109 dest(air) | Pasewalk |
| | Maj. J.A. Storch | (.5)Me-109 dest(air) | Pasewalk |
| | Lt. L.A. Fecher | (.5)Me-109 dest(air) | Pasewalk |
| | Lt. M.F. Allen | (.5)Fi-156 dest(air) | Pasewalk |
| | Lt. D.L. Finley | Me-109 dam(air) | Pasewalk |
| | Lt. H.E. Redd | Me-109 dam(air) | Pasewalk |
| **359th** | | | |
| 369th: | Lt. H.C. Burton | (.5)Me-410 dest(air) | NW Putbus |
| | Lt. G.M. Perrin | (.5)Me-410 dest(air) | NW Putbus |
| **361st** | | | |
| HdQts: | Col. T.J.J. Christian | He-115 dest(grd) | Putnitz |
| 375th: | Capt. C.N. Keppler | (1.5)glider dam(grd)[*] | Putnitz |
| | | (.5)Me-110 dam(grd) | Putnitz |
| | Lt. E.E. Neeley | (1.5)glider dam(grd)[*] | Putnitz |
| | | (.5)Me-110 dam(grd) | Putnitz |
| | Lt. D.R. Morgan | (2)Me-110 dam(grd) | Putnitz |
| | Lt. S. Armsby | (.5)glider dam(grd)[**] | Putnitz |
| | | (.5)BV-138 dam(grd)[@] | Putnitz |
| | Lt. J.T. Thomas | (.5)glider dam(grd)[**] | Putnitz |
| | | (.5)BV-138 dam(grd)[@] | Putnitz |
| | Lt. D.R. Morehouse | (2)glider dam(grd) | Putnitz |
| | | Me-210 dam(grd) | Putnitz |
| | Lt. M.E. Elliott | (.5)BV-138 dam(grd)[@@] | Putnitz |
| | Lt. W.D. Rogers | (.5)BV-138 dam(grd)[@@] | Putnitz |
| | | (.5)FW-189 dam(grd) | Putnitz |
| | Lt. H.A. Spaulding | (.5)FW-189 dam(grd) | Putnitz |
| 376th: | Lt. S.C. Wilkerson | He-111 dest(grd) | Putnitz |
| | Lt. D.F. Spencer | (.5)BV-138 dest(grd) | Putnitz |
| | Lt. B.D. Welsh | (.5)BV-138 dest(grd) | Putnitz |
| | Lt. C.E. Sullivan | Do-24 dam(grd) | Putnitz |

*Losses-*

**4th**: Lt. Vol R. Harris, Jr. (335th Ftr Sqn) POW
P-51B WD-R 42-106706
Hit by enemy fighters near Stettin.

Maj. James A. Goodson (336th Ftr Sqn) POW
P-51D VF-B 44-13303
Hit by flak near Neubrandenburg.

**78th**: Lt. Ben H. Hodges (82nd Ftr Sqn) KIA
P-47D MX-I 42-26446
Hit by a Me-109 near Montdidier.

**352nd**: Lt. Waldo C. Raub (486th Ftr Sqn) KIA
P-51B PZ-R 42-106609
Collided with an enemy plane near Burg.

**357th**: Lt. Heyward C. Spinks (364th Ftr Sqn) MIA-E
P-51B C5-T 43-6935 "Hurry Home Honey"
Hit by flak north of Paris.

**359th**: Lt. Virgal E. Sansing (369th Ftr Sqn) MIA-E
P-51B IV-C 42-106670
Hit by flak northeast of Paris and bailed out near Compiegne.

**361st**: Lt. Miles E. Elliott (375th Ftr Sqn) KIA
P-51B E2- 42-106861
Hit by flak and bailed out southwest of Ribnitz.

**479th**: Lt. Lewis K. Nesselbush (436th Ftr Sqn) POW
P-38J 9B-N 42-67452 "Rabble Rouser"
Suffered mechanical failure and bailed out near Ottersberg.

*Remarks*

352nd: 0-9 vehicles, 0-1 barge
353rd: 2-2 locos
355th: 2-0 locos, 0-20 railcars, 0-32 barges, 0-2 vehicles
357th: 0-16 locos, 8-85 railcars, 5-0 vehicles
359th: 3-9 locos, 10-25 railcars, 3-0 vehicles
361st: 3-12 locos, 3-22 railcars, 2-11 vehicles, 0-4 barges
P-51 c/l; o.k.

**June 21, 1944**

Groups Operating: P-51 4th, 339th, 352nd, 355th, 357th, 359th, 361st
P-47 56th, 78th, 353rd, 355th
P-38 20th, 55th, 364th, 479th

Missions: Support of bombers to Pas de Calais V-1 sites, Berlin, Ruhland, and Basdorf. Also, the 4th Ftr Grp and the 486th Ftr Sqn/352nd Ftr Grp escorted "Frantic I" bombers to their targets then on to Russia on the first shuttle mission.

Claims: 16-1-7 air
4-2 ground

| ***Group*** | | ***Claims*** | ***Location*** |
|---|---|---|---|
| **4th** | | | |
| 334th: | Lt. J.L. Lang | Me-109 dest(air) | SE Warsaw |
| | Lt. R.K. Hofer | Me-109 dam(air) | Siedlce |
| 335th: | Capt. F.C. Jones | Me-109 dest(air) | Kobryn |
| | | Me-109 dam(air) | Kobryn |
| **339th** | | | |
| 503rd: | Capt. W.E. Bryan | Me-410 dest(air) | Stettin |
| | | (.5)Me-410 prob(air) | Stettin |
| | Lt. R.C. Wort | Me-410 dest(air) | Stettin |
| | Lt. F.D. Talcott | (.5)Me-410 prob(air) | Stettin |
| 504th: | Lt. H.G. Thibert | Me-109 dest(air) | Soldin |
| 505th: | Lt. E.C. Ball | Me-410 dam(air) | N/Berlin |
| **352nd** | | | |
| 328th: | Lt. S.E. Dyke | (.5)Me-410 dest(air)[*] | Dahmsdorf |
| | Lt. J.F. Thornell | (.5)Me-410 dest(air)[*] | Dahmsdorf |
| | Lt. J.W. Galiga | (.5)Me-410 dest(air)[**] | Dahmsdorf |
| | Lt. E.L. Smith | (.5)Me-410 dest(air)[**] | Dahmsdorf |
| | Lt. E.W. Briggs | Me-410 dam(air) | Dahmsdorf |
| | Lt. D.J. Maxwell | Me-410 dam(air) | Dahmsdorf |
| | Lt. R.H. Powell | Me-410 dam(air) | Dahmsdorf |
| 486th: | Lt. L.W. Northrop | (2)Me-109 dest(air) | E/Warsaw |
| | Lt. E.L. Heller | Me-109 dest(air) | Brest-Litovsk |
| | Lt. D.Y. Whinnem | Me-109 dest(air) | E/Warsaw |
| 487th: | Maj. G.E. Preddy | Me-109 dest(air) | E/Magdeburg |
| | Lt. G.T. Moran | Me-109 dest(air) | E/Magdeburg |
| | Lt. C.M. Greer | Me-109 dam(air) | E/Magdeburg |
| **355th** | | | |
| 357th: | Capt. F.R. Haviland | Me-109 dest(air) | N/Magdeburg |
| | Lt. C.J. Salinsky | Me-109 dest(air) | N/Magdeburg |
| | Lt. J.M. Chapman | Me-109 dest(air) | Juterbog |

| | | | |
|---|---|---|---|
| **359th** | | | |
| 368th: | LtCol. A.R. Tyrrell | Me-110 dest(grd) | Wittstock |
| | | Me-410 dest(grd) | Wittstock |
| | | FW-189 dest(grd) | Wittstock |
| | Lt. J.J. Lubien | (2)u/i a/c dam(grd) | E/Plau |
| **361st** | | | |
| 375th: | Lt. M.H. Johnson | u/i a/c dest(grd) | Zwischenaschmer |

*Losses-*

**4th**: Lt. Frank T. Sibbett (335th Ftr Sqn) KIA
P-51B WD-X 43-6784
Hit by a Me-109 near Siedlce.

**55th**: Lt. Malcolm G. Armstrong (338th Ftr Sqn) MIA
P-38J CL- 42-68127
Hit by flak and bailed out west of Borkum.

**56th**: Lt. Harold L. Matthews (63rd Ftr Sqn) KIA
P-47D UN- 42-26305
Crashed while strafing a train near Paderborn.

**359th**: LtCol. Albert R. Tyrrell (368th Ftr Sqn) POW
P-51D CV-A 44-13387
Hit by flak at Wittstock and bailed out near Parchim.

*Remarks*
20th: Lt. Harold Horst (79th Ftr Sqn) c/l; o.k.
P-38J MC-
56th: 0-6 locos
78th: 0-2 locos, 0-75 railcars, 1-25 barges, 0-3 launches
339th: 1-0 loco, 4-0 railcars
352nd: 0-9 locos
353rd: 1-0 loco
355th: 0-5 locos, 0-4 barges, 0-2 launches, 0-1 vehicle
359th: 0-1 loco, 0-5 railcars

**June 22, 1944**
Groups Operating: P-51 339th, 352nd, 355th, 357th, 359th, 361st
P-47 56th, 78th, 353rd, 356th
P-38 20th, 55th, 364th, 479th
Missions: Support of bombers to targets in France plus fighter-bomber operations.
Claims: 3-0-0 air
0-0 ground

| *Group* | | *Claims* | *Location* |
|---|---|---|---|
| **353rd** | | | |
| 352nd: | Lt. H.O. Miller | Me-109 dest(air) | S/Rouen |
| **356th** | | | |
| 361st: | Lt. W.S. Hurley | (.5)Me-109 dest(air) | Evreux |
| | Lt. G.L. Yoakum | (.5)Me-109 dest(air) | Evreux |
| **479th** | | | |
| 436th: | Lt. C.O. Johnson | Fi-156 dest(air) | Reims |

*Losses-*

**20th**: Lt. John A. Pierson (55th Ftr Sqn) KIA
P-38J KI-V 42-68131 "Murph III"
Hit by flak near Jussy.

**56th**: Capt. Charles E. Tucker (62nd Ftr Sqn) KIA
P-47D LM-J 42-75282 "Eradicator"
Was in landing pattern when he collided with a P-47.

**78th**: Lt. Ollie E. Gibbs (83rd) KIA
P-47D HL-E 42-26623
Suffered mechanical failure on take-off from Duxford.

**339th**: Lt. Arthur L. Lowery (503rd Ftr Sqn) KIA
P-51C D7-W 42-103346
Hit the ground while strafing near Denain.

**355th**: Lt. Myles A. King (357th Ftr Sqn) POW
P-51C OS-U 42-103282
Lost coolant and bailed out near Albert.

**359th**: Lt. Howard E. Grimes (370th Ftr Sqn) KIA
P-51B CS-D 43-24791
Hit by flak near Nanteuil-Sur-Marne.

Lt. Harold D. Hollis (370th) KIA
P-51B CS- 42-106808
Hit by flak near Nanteuil-Sur-Marne

**479th**: Lt. Keith E. Canella (434th Ftr Sqn) KIA
P-38J L2-K 43-28731 "Sweet Mary"
Hit by flak southeast of La Fere.

Lt. Dwight F. Ilsley (434th Ftr Sqn) KIA
P-38J L2-G 42-104258
Hit by flak near La Fere.

Lt. Leroy Lutz (434th Ftr Sqn) KIA
P-38J L2-L 43-28714 "Lucky Lady"
Hit by flak near La Fere.

Lt. Albert S.J. Tucker, Jr. (434th Ftr Sqn) MIA
P-38J L2-B 43-28349
Hit by flak near Cambrai.

*Remarks*
20th: 1-0 loco, 10-2 vehicles
P-38 c/l Sudbury; o.k.
55th: 2-0 locos, 1-0 vehicle
56th: 1-0 loco, 1-0 vehicle, 0-25 barges, 0-1 building
78th: 3-0 locos, 6-35 railcars, 6-0 vehicles
353rd: 2-16 railcars, 3-0 vehicles, 0-5 barges, 0-1 building
355th: 1-2 locos, 6-20 railcars, 0-1 hangar
356th: 0-2 vehicles
359th: 0-1 bridge
364th: Lt. Grant L. Jones (385th Ftr Sqn) c/l Honington; o.k.
P-38J 5E-
479th: 1-0 loco, 23-0 railcars, 9-0 vehicles, 1-0 barge, 1-0 bridge, 0-4 buildings
Lt. Harold E. Matthews (434th Ftr Sqn) c/l Sudbury; o.k.
P-38J L2-

**June 23, 1944**
Groups Operating: P-51 339th, 352nd, 355th, 357th, 359th, 361st
P-47 56th, 78th, 353rd, 356th
P-38 20th, 55th, 364th, 479th
Missions: Support of bombers to Pas de Calais V-1 sites and to airfields and rail targets in France, plus fighter-bomber operations.
Claims: nil

*Losses-*

**55th**: Lt. Grant H. Corey (38th Ftr Sqn) MIA
P-38J CG- 42-104284
Hit by a Me-109 near Dreux.

Lt. Robert B. Hoffman (38th Ftr Sqn) MIA
P-38J CG- 42-67578
Hit by a Me-109 near Dreux.

**361st**: F/O George T. Davis (374th Ftr Sqn) POW
P-51B B7- 43-24835
Damaged by a train exploding near Troyes.

*Remarks*
20th: 3-0 locos, 0-3 railcars, 3-5 vehicles, 2-5 bridges, 0-11 barges, 1-1 flak positions, 0-2 buildings
55th: 2-3 locos, 1-1 vehicles
78th: 1-0 loco, 0-20 railcars, 4-0 vehicles, 0-1 building
339th: 0-15 railcars
352nd: 2-0 locos, 7-3 vehicles
357th: 0-3 locos, 3-46 railcars, 6-4 vehicles
361st: 3-4 locos, 125-6 railcars, 8-0 vehicles
364th: 1-3 locos
479th: 0-1 bridge

**June 24, 1944**
Groups Operating: P-51 339th, 352nd, 355th, 357th, 359th, 361st
P-47 56th, 78th, 353rd, 356th
P-38 20th, 55th, 364th, 479th
Missions: Support for bombers to Bremen and to airfields and bridges in France.
Claims: 0-0-0 air
32-8 ground

| *Group* | | *Claims* | *Location* |
|---|---|---|---|
| **56th** | | | |
| HdQts: | Col. H. Zemke | Ju-88 dest(grd) | Sailly-Laurette |
| **353rd** | | | |
| 351st: | Capt. L.G. Hally | He-111 dest(grd) | Deelan |
| | | (.5)Me-109 dest(grd) | Deelan |
| | Capt. G.B. Compton | Ju-52 dest(grd) | Deelan |
| | Lt. D.L. Claiville | (.5)Me-109 dest(grd) | Deelan |
| **355th** | | | |
| 354th: | LtCol. C.H. Kinnard | (3)Me-109 dest(grd) | Seiches |
| | Lt. R.S. Morris | (3)Me-109 dest(grd) | Seiches |
| | Lt. J.C. Ellison | (2)Me-109 dest(grd) | Seiches |
| | Lt. W.D. Martin | (2)Me-109 dest(grd) | Angars |
| | Lt. E.F. Perry | (2)Me-109 dest(grd) | Seiches |
| | Lt. R.G. Cross | Me-109 dest(grd) | Seiches |
| | Lt. R.E. Hulderman | Me-109 dest(grd) | Seiches |
| | Lt. F.W. Trembarth | Me-109 dest(grd) | Seiches |
| | Maj. H.B. Kucheman | (2)Me-109 dam(grd) | Seiches |

| | | | |
|---|---|---|---|
| | Lt. G.S. Wright | Me-109 dam(grd) | Seiches |
| 357th: | Capt. F.R. Haviland | (3)Me-109 dest(grd) | E/Angars |
| | Lt. C.J. Salinsky | (3)Me-109 dest(grd) | NE Angars |
| | | (2)Me-109 dam(grd) | NE Angars |
| | Lt. J.L. Crandell | (2)Me-109 dest(grd) | E/Angars |
| | | (3)Me-109 dam(grd) | E/Angars |
| | Lt. H.W. Spencer | (2)Me-109 dest(grd) | E/Angars |
| | Lt. G.W. Forker | Me-109 dest(grd) | NE Angars |
| | Lt. P.M.N. McHugh | Me-109 dest(grd) | E/Angars |
| | Lt. E.P. McNeff | Me-109 dest(grd) | E/Angars |

*Losses-*

**55th**: Lt. George Korinek (338th Ftr Sqn) POW
P-38J CL- 42-68083
Hit by flak near Acquigny.

*Remarks*
55th: 2-0 locos, 0-14 railcars
56th: 1-0 loco, 0-3 railcars, 1-0 vehicle
78th: 1-1 vehicles, 0-7 railcars
339th: 0-50 railcars
353rd: 9-0 locos
355th: 1-5 locos, 0-23 railcars, 0-2 vehicles, 0-2 gun positions
357th: 1-?? railcars
359th: 0-1 loco, 0-30 railcars
361st: 2-2 locos, 6-15 railcars, 1-3 vehicles

KIAc's
339th: Lt. Rodney C. West (503rd Ftr Sqn)
Died in a jeep accident at Fowlmere.

**June 25, 1944**
Groups Operating: P-51 339th, 352nd, 355th, 357th, 359th, 361st
P-47 56th, 78th, 353rd, 356th
P-38 20th, 55th, 364th, 479th
Missions: Support for bombers hitting various airfields and bridges in France plus fighter-bomber operations.
Claims: 23-1-6.5 air
3-2 ground

| *Group* | | *Claims* | *Location* |
|---|---|---|---|
| **20th** | | | |
| HdQts: | LtCol. C. Wilson | Me-109 dest(air) | S/Paris |
| **55th** | | | |
| 38th: | Maj. J.D. Landers | FW-190 dest(air) | SW Paris |
| | | Me-109 dam(air) | SW Paris |
| | Lt. W.J. Reilly | FW-190 dest(air) | SW Paris |
| | Lt. H.W. Rhodes | Me-109 dest(air) | SW Paris |
| | Lt. R.P. Tibor | Me-109 dest(air) | SW Paris |
| **352nd** | | | |
| 487th: | Lt. G.T. Moran | Me-109 dest(air) | Soissons |
| | | Me-109 dam(air) | Soissons |
| **353rd** | | | |
| 351st: | Capt. W.J. Maguire | Me-410 dest(grd) | Bourges |
| | Lt. G.W. Franklin | Me-410 dest(grd) | Bourges |
| | Lt. J.W. Furneaux | Me-410 dest(grd) | Bourges |
| | Lt. N.T. Ott | Me-410 dam(grd) | Bourges |
| **361st** | | | |
| HdQts: | LtCol. J.J. Kruzel | FW-190 dest(air) | N/Lisieux |
| 374th: | Lt. V.R. Richards | Me-109 dest(air) | S/Caen |
| | | FW-190 dest(air) | S/Caen |
| | LtCol. R.A. Webb | FW-190 dest(air) | S/Caen |
| 375th: | Lt. J.S. Crandell | (2)Me-109 dest(air) | N/Rouen |
| | Capt. C.R. Cummins | Me-109 dest(air) | N/Lisieux |
| | Lt. U.L. Drew | Me-109 dest(air) | N/Lisieux |
| 376th: | Capt. R.M. Durbin | Me-109 dest(air) | S/Le Havre |
| | Lt. H.D. Chapman | Me-109 dest(air) | Bernay |
| | | (.5)Me-109 dam(air) | Bernay |
| | | (shared with an unknown pilot) | |
| **364th**(#1) | | | |
| 383rd: | Lt. C. Hatfield | (.5)Me-109 dest(air) | E/Blois |
| 384th: | Lt. V.L. Kercher | (2)Me-109 dest(air) | E/Blois |
| | Lt. W.E. Bristow | Me-109 dest(air) | E/Blois |
| | | Me-109 dam(air) | E/Blois |
| | Lt. R.S. Hunt | Me-109 dest(air) | E/Blois |
| | Lt. J.R. Korecky | Me-109 dest(air) | E/Blois |
| | | Me-109 dam(air) | E/Blois |
| | Lt. J.M. Stuckrath | FW-190 dest(air) | E/Blois |
| | | FW-190 dam(air) | E/Blois |
| | Capt. J.C. Ford | (.5)Me-109 dest(air) | E/Blois |
| | Lt. D.W. Williams | Me-109 prob(air) | E/Blois |
| | Lt. C.J. Pushcar | Me-109 dam(air) | E/Blois |
| (#2) | | | |
| 383rd: | Lt. H.A. Chesney | (.5)Me-109 dam(grd) | Angars |
| | Lt. M.E. Coates | (.5)Me-109 dam(grd) | Angars |

*Losses-*

**352nd**: F/O William W. Drisko (487th Ftr Sqn) POW
P-51B HO-A 43-6902
Hit by a Me-109 near Soissons.

*Remarks*
56th: 0-10 locos, 0-100 railcars, 1-0 vehicle
78th: 2-2 locos, 12-35 railcars, 0-9 vehicles
352nd: 0-5 locos
353rd: Lt. Kenneth Chetwood (350th Ftr Sqn) c/l Etrepagny; o.k.
P-47D LH-
357th: 3-0 locos, 9-15 railcars
364th: 0-8 railcars, 2-0 vehicles

**June 26, 1944**
Groups Operating: P-51 4th, 352nd (486th Ftr Sqn only)
Missions: Support for "Frantic I" bombers from Russia to Drohobycz, Poland, then on to Italy.
Claims: nil
Losses: nil

**June 27, 1944**
Groups Operating: P-51 339th, 352nd, 355th, 357th, 359th, 361st
P-47 56th, 78th, 353rd, 356th
P-38 20th, 55th, 364th, 479th
Missions: Support for bombers to Pas de Calais area V-1 sites and targets in the Creil area, plus fighter-bomber operations.
Claims: 14-1-6 air
1-1 ground

| *Group* | | *Claims* | *Location* |
|---|---|---|---|
| **56th** | | | |
| 61st: | LtCol. F.S. Gabreski | Me-109 dest(air) | La Perth A/F |
| | Lt. J.M. Jure | Me-109 dest(air) | Esternay |
| | | Me-109 prob(air) | Esternay |
| | F/Lt. W.A. Lanowski | Me-109 dest(air) | La Perth A/F |
| | Lt. W.S. Patterson | Me-109 dest(air) | Connentre |
| | Lt. S. Gerick | Me-109 dam(air) | Esternay |
| 62nd: | Capt. F.J. Christensen | Me-109 dest(air) | Cambrai-Lens |
| | Lt. R.C. Cherry | Me-109 dest(air) | La Perth A/F |
| | Lt. W.W. McElhare | Me-109 dam(air) | La Perth A/F |
| **339th** | | | |
| 505th: | Capt. J.L. Thury | FW-190 dest(air) | SE Paris |
| | Lt. O.P. Farmer | (.5)FW-190 dest(air) | Paris |
| | Lt. W.G. Fish | (.5)FW-190 dest(air) | Paris |
| **352nd** | | | |
| 487th: | Lt. J.V. Conard | (2)FW-190 dest(air) | N/Noyon |
| | Lt. C.O. Corson | FW-190 dest(air) | Noyon |
| | Lt. A.F. Sears | FW-190 dest(air) | Noyon |
| **353rd** | | | |
| 350th: | Maj. K.W. Gallup | Me-109 dest(air) | Epernay |
| | Lt. S.T. Benjamin | (.5)Me-109 dest(grd) | Chalons |
| | Lt. M.V. Bledsoe | (.5)Me-109 dest(grd) | Chalons |
| | Lt. V.G. Rafferty | Me-109 dam(grd) | Chalons |
| 351st: | Lt. A.S. Hartley | Me-109 dest(air) | S/Chalons |
| | Lt. M.B. Hungate | Me-109 dam(air) | SE Epernay |
| | Lt. G.H. McLaughlin | Me-109 dam(air) | S/Chalons |
| 352nd: | Lt. H.O. Miller | (2)Me-109 dam(air) | N/Troyes |

*Losses-*

**352nd**: Lt. Robert H. Berkshire (487th Ftr Sqn) MIA-E
P-51B HO-G 43-7167 "Brutal Lulu"
Hit by flak near Noyon.

**355th**: Lt. Thomas W. Ruark (354th Ftr Sqn) MIA-E
P-51C WR-K 42-103802
Hit by a Me-109 near Chateau Thierry.

**364th**: Lt. Jarrette L. Bowen (384th Ftr Sqn) POW
P-38J 5Y- 42-68063
Hit by flak northeast of Verdun.

Lt. Max J. Woolley (384th Ftr Sqn) MIA-E
P-38J 5Y- 42-67979
Hit by flak north of Charleroi.

**479th**: Lt. Burton S. Cross (435th Ftr Sqn) KIA
P-38J J2- 42-104416
Hit by flak near Creney.

*Remarks*

20th: 12-8 locos, 4-41 railcars, 0-5 vehicles, 0-3 barges
LtCol. Herbert E. Johnson (HdQts) c/l Wittering; o.k.
P-38J
Lt. Rex E. Moncrieff (77th Ftr Sqn) c/l Kingscliffe; o.k.
P-38J LC-
55th: 6-16 locos, 42-226 railcars, 22-22 vehicles, 1-10 barges, 0-2 flak towers, 0-3 barracks
P-38 c/l; o.k.
78th: 0-1 loco, 0-15 railcars
339th: 1-0 loco, 5-0 railcars
352nd: 1-3 locos, 8-35 railcars, 0-1 vehicle
353rd: 1-0 loco
355th: Lt. Edward P. Ludeke (357th Ftr Sqn) c/l Matching; o.k.
P-51B OS-
357th: 2-0 locos, 20-20 railcars, 20-6 vehicles
361st: 2-2 locos, 6-120 railcars, 20-0 vehicles
364th: 13-4 locos, 25-10 railcars, 1-0 flak tower, 0-1 bridge

**June 28, 1944**

Groups Operating: P-51 4th, 339th, 352nd, 355th, 357th, 359th, 361st
P-47 56th, 78th, 353rd, 356th
P-38 20th, 55th, 364th, 479th

Missions: Support for bombers to Saarbrucken and various targets in the Paris area plus fighter-bomber operations.

Claims: 2-0-0 air
0-0 ground

| *Group* | | *Claims* | *Location* |
|---|---|---|---|
| **20th** | | | |
| 55th: | Lt. R.E. Miles | Me-109 dest(air) | Nivelles |
| 79th: | Lt. R.W. Bebout | FW-190 dest(air) | Beaumont |

*Losses-*

**352nd:** Lt. Adolph Bielok (487th Ftr Sqn) KIA
P-51B HO-L 43-6868
Hit by flak near St. Omer.

**356th:** Lt. Charles B. Earnhart (359th Ftr Sqn) MIA-E
P-47D OC-O 42-25508
Hit a pole while strafing in the Brussels-Ghent area.

*Remarks*

56th: 0-2 locos, 1-15 railcars, 0-1 vehicle
339th: 1-1 locos, 0-40 railcars, 0-1 building
352nd: 0-1 loco
Lt. George C. Arnold (487th Ftr Sqn) c/l SW Manston; o.k.
P-51B HO-
356th: 2-0 locos, 0-8 railcars, 0-5 vehicles
364th: 2-3 locos, 1-0 vehicle, 1-0 flak tower
479th: 0-1 railcar

KIAc's

55th: Lt. Arthur Carmel (38th Ftr Sqn)
P-38J

353rd: Lt. John F. Starr (350th Ftr Sqn)
P-47D LH-
Crashed near Raydon while on a test hop with new pilots.

**June 29, 1944**

Groups Operating: P-51 4th, 339th, 352nd, 355th, 357th, 361st
P-47 56th, 78th, 353rd, 356th
P-38 20th, 55th, 364th, 479th

Missions: Support for bombers hitting targets in the Leipzig area.

Claims: 33-0-7 air
20-12 ground

| *Group* | | *Claims* | *Location* |
|---|---|---|---|
| **339th** | | | |
| HdQts: | LtCol. H.W. Scruggs | (2)FW-190 dest(air) | Eisleben |
| | | (2)FW-190 dam(air) | Eisleben |
| 503rd: | Lt. V.W. Meyer | FW-190 dest(air) | Eisleben |
| | | (.5)Me-410 dest(air) | Eisleben |
| | | Me-109 dam(air) | Eisleben |
| | | (shared with an unknown 505th Ftr Sqn pilot) | |
| | Lt. C.W. Knott | FW-190 dest(air) | Eisleben |
| | Lt. L.M. Wright | Me-109 dam(air) | Leipzig |
| | | Ju-88 dam(grd) | Leipzig |
| 504th: | Lt. L.D. Eisenhart | FW-190 dest(air) | Nordhausen |
| 505th: | Lt. E.M. Johnson | (.5)Me-109 dest(air) | Halle/Magdeburg |
| | | (.5)Me-410 dest(air)* | Halle/Magdeburg |
| | Lt. G.E. Graham | (.5)Me-410 dest(air)* | Halle/Magdeburg |
| | Lt. A. Sirochman | (.5)Me-109 dest(air) | Halle/Magdeburg |
| **352nd** | | | |
| 487th: | Maj. G.E. Preddy | Ju-52 dest(grd) | Burg A/F |
| | Lt. G.T. Moran | Ju-52 dest(grd) | Burg A/F |
| | Lt. M.C. Pickering | He-111 dest(grd) | Burg A/F |
| | | Me-110 dam(grd) | Burg A/F |
| | Lt. J.N. Wood | He-111 dest(grd) | Burg A/F |
| **353rd** | | | |
| 352nd: | Capt. V.N. Curtis | (.5)He-111 dam(grd) | Plantlunne |
| | Lt. L. Hunt | (.5)He-111 dam(grd) | Plantlunne |
| **357th** | | | |
| HdQts: | LtCol. T.L. Hayes | Me-109 dest(air) | W/Leipzig |
| | | (.5)Me-410 dest(air)* | NW Leipzig |
| 362nd: | Capt. F.C. Smith | FW-190 dest(air) | Naumberg |
| | Lt. T.E. Norris | Me-410 dest(air) | Naumberg |
| | Lt. J.F. Pugh | Me-109 dest(air) | Naumberg |
| 363rd: | Capt. C.E. Anderson | (3)FW-190 dest(air) | SW Leipzig |
| | Capt. R.W. Foy | (2)Me-109 dest(air) | SW Leipzig |
| | | FW-190 dest(air) | SW Leipzig |
| | Capt. R.W. Browning | (1.5)Me-410 dest(air)** | SW Leipzig |
| | | (.5)FW-190 dest(air) | SW Leipzig |
| | Capt. D.H. Bochkay | Me-109 dest(air) | Schoningen |
| | Lt. W.B. Overstreet | FW-190 dest(air) | SW Leipzig |
| | Lt. W.S. Fennell | (.5)Me-410 dest(air)** | SW Leipzig |
| | Lt. R.W. Staudte | (.5)FW-190 dest(air) | SW Leipzig |
| 364th: | Capt. C.D. Sumner | Me-109 dest(air) | SW Leipzig |
| | | FW-190 dest(air) | SW Leipzig |
| | Capt. M.H. Stepelton | FW-190 dest(air) | W/Leipzig |
| | Capt. J.C. Howell | Me-109 dest(air) | SW Leipzig |
| | | FW-190 dam(air) | SW Leipzig |
| | Lt. G.E. Tyler | Me-109 dest(air) | SW Leipzig |
| | Lt. M.F. Allen | (.5)Me-410 dest(air)* | NW Leipzig |
| | | FW-190 dam(air) | SW Leipzig |
| | Capt. B.W. McIntyre | He-177 dam(grd) | Leipzig |
| **361st** | | | |
| HdQts: | LtCol. W.E. Hopkins | (4)FW-190 dest(grd) | Oschersleben |
| | | (1.5)FW-190 dam(grd)* | Oschersleben |
| 374th: | LtCol. R.A. Webb | (5)FW-190 dest(grd) | Oschersleben |
| | | FW-190 dam(grd) | Oschersleben |
| | Lt. R.T. Eckfeldt | (4)FW-190 dest(grd) | Oschersleben |
| | | (2.5)FW-190 dam(grd)** | Oschersleben |
| | Lt. V.R. Richards | (3)FW-190 dest(grd) | Oschersleben |
| | | (.5)FW-190 dam(grd)* | Oschersleben |
| | | (.5)FW-190 dam(grd)** | Oschersleben |
| 375th: | Lt. R.C. Wright | (1.5)Me-109 dest(air) | SW Kothen |
| | Capt. E. Cole | Me-109 dest(air) | SE Kothen |
| | Lt. T.F. Brubaker | Me-109 dest(air) | SE Kothen |
| | Lt. S. Armsby | (.5)Me-109 dest(air) | SW Kothen |
| | Lt. E.E. Neely | Me-109 dam(air) | SE Kothen |

*Losses-*

**339th:** Capt. Richard S. Whitelaw (503rd Ftr Sqn) KIA
P-51B D7-C 42-106821
Hit by enemy fighters near Kalbsrieth.

**357th:** Capt. Richard C. Smith (364th Ftr Sqn) MIA
P-51B C5-K 43-6974 "Mr. Period"
Hit by enemy fighters near Leipzig.

*Remarks*

4th: Lt. Joseph Callahan (334th Ftr Sqn) c/l Sampieri; o.k.
P-51B QP-R
20th: 1-2 vehicles
56th: 1-0 loco, 2-6 vehicles, 0-1 tug, 0-1 barge
78th: 4-3 locos, 1-50 railcars, 2-0 vehicles
339th: 2-0 locos, 0-50 railcars
352nd: 1-0 loco
353rd: 4-2 locos, 0-17 railcars
355th: P-51 c/l Lavenham; o.k.
356th: 1-1 locos, 0-4 railcars
357th: 1-1 locos
361st: 1-1 locos, 0-1 steam roller
364th: 1-2 tugs, 0-9 barges

**June 30, 1944**

Groups Operating: P-51 339th, 352nd, 355th, 357th, 359th
P-47 56th, 78th, 353rd, 356th
P-38 20th, 55th, 364th, 479th

Missions: Support for bombers to airfields in France and Belgium plus fighter-bomber operations.

Claims: 3-2-3 air
1-0 ground

| *Group* | | *Claims* | *Location* |
|---|---|---|---|
| **20th** | | | |
| 55th: | Capt. H.B. Baker | Me-109 dest(air) | Dreux |
| | Lt. D.H. Larrabee | Me-109 dest(air) | Dreux |
| **56th** | | | |
| 63rd: | Lt. M.H. Becker | Ju-88 dest(air) | S/Noyon |

| | | | |
|---|---|---|---|
| **78th** | | | |
| 82nd: | Lt. H.K. Shope | Me-109 dest(grd) | Meilleray |
| **353rd** | | | |
| 350th: | Capt. W.K. Blickenstaff | Me-109 prob(air) | W/Chalons |
| | | Me-109 dam(air) | W/Chalons |
| | Lt. J.O. Ruscitto | Me-109 prob(air) | W/Chalons |
| | F/O D.L. Yocum | (2)Me-109 dam(air) | W/Chalons |

*Losses-*

**55th**: Lt. Warren E. Loring (343rd Ftr Sqn) MIA-E
P-38J CY- 42-67876
Hit by flak and bailed out west of Nevers.

*Remarks*
20th: 7-4 locos, 75-4 railcars, 8-1 vehicles, 0-2 bridges, 0-1 building
55th: 7-0 locos, 2-0 railcars
56th: 4-0 locos,[@] 100-0 railcars
78th: 0-1 loco, 2-15 railcars, 0-2 bridges
339th: 0-1 flak tower
353rd: 5-2 locos, 6-27 railcars, 20-3 vehicles
355th: 0-2 barges
356th: 3-1 locos, 3-2 railcars, 0-5 barges, 0-1 bridge
Lt. Millard M. Clayborne (359th Ftr Sqn) c/l Manston; o.k.
P-47D OC-
357th: 2-3 locos, 10-35 railcars, 1-1 vehicles, 0-3 buildings
364th: 9-2 locos, 75-24 railcars, 1-2 buildings
479th: 3-0 locos, 6-51 railcars, 2-0 vehicles, 3-5 flak towers, 1-1 buildings

KIAc
353rd: Lt. Robert W. Larson (351st)
P-47D YJ-K 42-8511
Collided with a P-47 and crashed near Tibenham.

**July 1, 1944**
Groups Operating: P-51 352nd, 357th, 361st
P-47 78th, 353rd
P-38 20th, 364th
Missions: Support of bombers to Mont Louis Ferme plus fighter-bomber operations.
Claims: 8-0-7 air
0-0 ground

| ***Group*** | | ***Claims*** | ***Location*** |
|---|---|---|---|
| **78th** | | | |
| 82nd: | Lt. H.F. Scholz | FW-190 dest(air) | Reims |
| | Capt. B.I. Mayo | FW-190 dam(air) | St. Quentin |
| 83rd: | Lt. R.E. Mullins | Me-109 dam(air) | Cambrai |
| 84th: | Capt. H.T. Lay | Me-109 dest(air) | St. Quentin |
| | Lt. W.J. Luckey | Me-109 dest(air) | St. Quentin |
| | Capt. A.F. Eaton | Me-109 dam(air) | St. Quentin |
| **352nd** | | | |
| 328th: | Lt. R.H. Powell | Me-109 dam(air) | Bethune |
| 487th: | Capt. W.E. Starck | Me-109 dest(air) | St. Quentin |
| | | Me-109 dam(air) | St. Quentin |
| | Lt. C.M. Greer | Me-109 dam(air) | St. Quentin |
| **357th** | | | |
| 362nd: | Capt. C.L. Williams | Me-109 dest(air) | E/St. Quentin |
| | Lt. P.E. Holmberg | Me-109 dest(air) | E/St. Quentin |
| | Lt. A.E. Smith | Me-109 dam(air) | E/St. Quentin |
| 364th: | Capt. R.A. Peterson | (2)Me-109 dest(air) | E/St. Quentin |

*Losses-*

**78th**: Lt. Edward I. Kitley (83rd Ftr Sqn) KIA
P-47D HL-R 43-25513
Collided with Lt. Raese on take-off at Duxford.

Lt. Cleon W. Raese, Jr. (83rd Ftr Sqn) KIA
P-47D HL-F 43-25588
Collided with Lt. Kitley on take-off at Duxford.

Lt. Ross Orr (84th Ftr Sqn) KIA
P-47D WZ-X 42-26640
Hit by a Me-109 near St. Quentin.

**357th**: Lt. Donald W. Vogel (362nd Ftr Sqn) MIA-E
P-51B G4-A 43-12455 "Blythe Spirit"
Hit by enemy fighters near St. Quentin.

**361st**: Lt. John T. Thomas (375th Ftr Sqn) ASR
P-51B E2-M 42-106880
Bailed out over the Channel after mechanical failure.

*Remarks*
352nd: 0-1 barge

**July 2, 1944**
Groups Operating: P-51 339th, 355th, 359th, 361st
Missions: Support of bombers hitting V-1 sites in the Pas de Calais area.
Claims: nil
Losses: nil

Groups Operating: P-51 4th, 352nd (486th Ftr Sqn only)
Missions: These Shuttle Force fighters swept the Budapest area.
Claims: 8-0-1 air
0-0 ground

| ***Group*** | | ***Claims*** | ***Location*** |
|---|---|---|---|
| **4th** | | | |
| HdQts: | Col. D.J.M. Blakeslee | Me-109 dest(air) | Budapest |
| 334th: | Capt. H.D. Hively | (3)Me-109 dest(air) | Budapest |
| | Capt. W.F. Hedrick | Me-109 dest(air) | Budapest |
| | | Me-109 dam(air) | Budapest |
| | Lt. G.C. Siems | Me-109 dest(air) | Budapest |
| 336th: | Lt. D.R. Emerson | (.5)Me-109 dest(air)* | W/Budapest |
| **352nd** | | | |
| 486th: | Capt. D.H. Higgins | FW-190 dest(air) | Budapest |
| | | (.5)Me-109 dest(air)* | W/Budapest |

*Losses-*

**4th**: Lt. Ralph K. Hofer (334th Ftr Sqn) KIA
P-51B QP-X 43-6746
Hit by a Me-109 near Budapest and crashed near Mostar.

Lt. Thomas S. Sharp (334th Ftr Sqn) KIA
P-51B QP-D 42-106650
Hit by enemy fighters near Budapest.

Lt. George I. Stanford, Jr. (335th Ftr Sqn) POW
P-51D WD-K 44-13402
Hit by enemy fighters near Budapest.

Lt. J.C. Norris (336th Ftr Sqn) POW
P-51B VF- 43-6650
Hit by enemy fighters near Budapest.

**352nd**: Maj. Stephen W. Andrew (486th Ftr Sqn) POW
P-51B PZ-A 42-106467
Suffered mechanical failure near Adony.

Lt. Lester L. Howell (486th Ftr Sqn) KIA
P-51B PZ-V 42-106857 "Texas Knight"
Hit by enemy fighters near Budapest.

**July 3, 1944**
Groups Operating: P-51 4th, 352nd (486th Ftr Sqn only)
Missions: Support of bombers from Italy to Arad, Rumania, and back to Italy.
Claims: nil
Losses: nil

**July 4, 1944**
Groups Operating: P-51 4th, 339th, 352nd, 355th, 357th, 361st
P-47 56th, 78th, 353rd, 356th
P-38 20th, 55th, 364th, 479th
Missions: Support of bombers to various airfields and bridges in France, plus fighter-bomber operations. The 4th and 352nd contingents in Italy did not operate.
Claims: 19-0-12 air
1-0 ground

| ***Group*** | | ***Claims*** | ***Location*** |
|---|---|---|---|
| **20th** | | | |
| 77th: | Lt. R.E. Moncrieff | Me-109 dest(grd) | Tours |
| **56th** | | | |
| HdQts: | Col. H. Zemke | Me-109 dam(air) | N/Conches A/F |
| 61st: | Capt. J.R. Carter | Me-109 dest(air) | W/Louviers |
| 62nd: | Lt. G.E. Bostwick | (3)Me-109 dest(air) | Conches |
| | | Me-109 dam(air) | Conches |
| | Maj. L.A. Dade | (2)Me-109 dest(air) | Conches |
| | | (2)Me-109 dam(air) | Conches |
| | Lt. W.H. Merrill | (2)Me-109 dest(air) | Conches |
| | | Me-109 dam(air) | Conches |
| | Maj. G.E. Baker | Me-109 dest(air) | Conches |
| | | Me-109 dam(air) | Conches |
| | Capt. M.L. Moseley | Me-109 dest(air) | Conches |
| | Capt. M.J. Jackson | Me-109 dest(air) | Conches |
| | Lt. A.P. Knafelz | Me-109 dest(air) | Conches |
| | | Me-109 dam(air) | Conches |
| | Lt. B.M. Knox | Me-109 dest(air) | Conches |
| | | Me-109 dam(air) | Conches |
| | Lt. W.W. McElhare | Me-109 dest(air) | Conches |
| | | (3)Me-109 dam(air) | Conches |

| | | | |
|---|---|---|---|
| | Lt. D.C. Sheridan | Me-109 dest(air) | Conches |
| | Lt. F.C. Newell | (.5)Me-109 dest(air) | Conches |
| | Lt. D.E. McMahan | (.5)Me-109 dest(air) | Conches |
| 63rd: | Lt. J.R. Curtis | Me-109 dest(air) | Bernay-Evreux |
| | | (.5)Me-109 dest(air) | Conches |
| | Lt. W.R. Frederick | (.5)Me-109 dest(air) | Conches |
| | | FW-190 dam(air) | N/Chateaudun |
| | F/O R.W. Magel | Me-109 dam(air) | SW Evreux |

*Losses-*

**20th**: Lt. Ernest S. Riddle (77th Ftr Sqn) KIA
P-38J LC-
Damaged by flak and crashed near Peteworth upon return.

**56th**: Lt. Sam B. Dale, Jr. (63rd Ftr Sqn) KIA
P-47D UN-C 42-75859
Hit by enemy fighters near Evreux.

**78th**: Lt. Lonnie L. Moseley (84th Ftr Sqn) MIA-E
P-47D WZ-L 42-25529
Lost oil and bailed out near Routot.

**339th**: Lt. Carl H. Bundgaard (505th Ftr Sqn) MIA-E
P-51C 6N- 42-103314
Suffered mechanical failure and bailed out near Buzancais.

**353rd**: Lt. Lloyd Hunt (352nd Ftr Sqn) MIA-E
P-47D SX-W 42-26667
Hit by flak and bellied-in southwest of Troyes.

**479th**: Capt. Robert D. Green (HdQts) MIA
P-38J J2- 43-28467
Hit by flak and spun-in near Laval.

Lt. Jack S. Denny (434th Ftr Sqn) MIA
P-38J L2-A 43-28367
Hit by flak and crashed near Cande.

Lt. Rayne B. Fairchild (435th Ftr Sqn) MIA
P-38J J2- 44-23484
Hit by flak and bellied-in near Laval.

*Remarks*

| | |
|---|---|
| 20th: | 36-0 locos, 2-171 railcars, 15-40 vehicles. |
| | Maj. Martin Low (55th Ftr Sqn) c/l; o.k. |
| | P-38J KI- |
| 55th: | 13-28 locos, 94-232 railcars, 3-7 buildings, 1-0 flak tower |
| 56th: | 3-0 vehicles |
| 78th: | 0-3 locos, 50-142 railcars |
| | P-47 c/l; o.k. |
| 353rd: | 16-0 locos, 25-92 railcars, 2-1 vehicles |
| 356th: | 4-4 locos, 0-6 railcars, 2-5 barges, 0-6 vehicles, 0-1 flak tower |
| 361st: | 0-1 loco, 0-15 railcars, 1-0 vehicle |
| 364th: | 0-1 loco, 0-30 railcars |
| 479th: | 4-4 locos, 14-62 railcars, 10-10 flak towers, 0-13 buildings, 1-4 vehicles |

**July 5, 1944**

Groups Operating: P-51 4th, 339th, 352nd, 355th, 357th, 359th, 361st
P-47 56th, 78th, 353rd, 356th
P-38 20th, 55th, 364th, 479th

Missions: Support of bombers to airfields in Holland and Belgium; to marshalling yards and V-1 sites in France; and some P-47 units flew fighter-bomber sorties. Also, the 4th Ftr Grp and 486th Ftr Sqn supported the "Frantic" force from Italy to Beziers and then back to England.

Claims: 24-1-10 air
3-2 ground

| ***Group*** | | ***Claims*** | ***Location*** |
|---|---|---|---|
| **20th** | | | |
| HdQts: | LtCol. H.E. Johnson | (.5)He-177 dest(air) | Cognac |
| 55th: | Lt. J.S. Reynolds | (.5)He-177 dest(air) | Cognac |
| **56th** | | | |
| 61st: | Lt. R.J. Keen | (3)Me-109 dest(air) | Evreux |
| | | Me-109 dam(air) | Evreux |
| | LtCol. F.S. Gabreski | Me-109 dest(air) | Evreux |
| | Maj. B.M. Gladych | Me-109 dest(air) | Evreux |
| | F/Lt. W.A. Lanowski | Me-109 dest(air) | Conches A/F |
| 62nd: | Capt. F.J. Christensen | FW-190 dest(air) | N/Evreux |
| | Lt. G.H. Butler | FW-190 dest(air) | N/Evreux |
| | Lt. R.C. Cherry | FW-190 dest(air) | W/Paris |
| | Lt. B.G. Edens | FW-190 dest(air) | N/Evreux |
| | Lt. J.W. Pierce | FW-190 dest(air) | N/Evreux |
| | Capt. M.J. Jackson | FW-190 dam(air) | N/Evreux |
| | Lt. H.E. King | FW-190 dam(air) | N/Evreux |
| 63rd: | Lt. W.L. Flagg | Me-109 dest(air) | Evreux |
| | | Me-109 dam(air) | Evreux |
| **78th** | | | |
| 83rd: | Maj. W.H. Julian | FW-190 dest(air) | Evreux |
| | Lt. G. Riccardo | FW-190 prob(air) | Evreux |
| | Capt. D.A. Lawhead | (2)FW-190 dam(air) | Evreux |
| | Lt. R.R. Bonebrake | FW-190 dam(air) | Evreux |
| **353rd** | | | |
| HdQts: | Col. G.E. Duncan | Me-109 dest(air) | Pont Audemer |
| **355th** | | | |
| HdQts: | LtCol. C.H. Kinnard | (.5)Ju-88 dest(grd) | Chateauroux |
| 354th: | Lt. W.A. Schwab | Ju-88 dest(grd) | Chateauroux |
| | Lt. R.E. Hulderman | (.5)Ju-88 dest(grd) | Chateauroux |
| **357th** | | | |
| 363rd: | Capt. D.H. Bochkay | Me-109 dest(air) | SE Rouen |
| | | FW-190 dest(air) | SE Rouen |
| 364th: | Lt. R.M. Shaw | FW-190 dest(air) | SE Rouen |
| | Lt. G.E. Tyler | FW-190 dest(air) | SE Rouen |
| | Capt. C.D. Sumner | FW-190 dam(air) | SE Rouen |
| **361st** | | | |
| 374th: | Lt. J.R. Mau | Me-109 dest(air) | Amiens |
| | | Me-109 dam(air) | Amiens |
| | Lt. J.K. Wood | Me-109 dest(air) | Amiens |
| | Capt. S.J. Harris | Ju-88 dest(grd) | Chateau Thierry |
| | Lt. G. Lichter | Ju-88 dam(grd) | Chateau Thierry |
| 376th: | Lt. D.F. Spencer | (2)Me-109 dest(air) | Rouen-Evreux |
| | | Me-109 dam(air) | Rouen-Evreux |
| **479th** | | | |
| 434th: | Capt. A.F. Jeffrey | FW-200 dest(air) | Cognac/Chateaubernard A/F |
| | Lt. B.A. Williams | Ju-88 dam(grd) | Cognac/Chateaubernard A/F |

*Losses-*

**55th**: Lt. Lawrence J. Berry (338th Ftr Sqn) KIA
P-38J CL- 43-28471
Hit by flak near Houdon.

**56th**: Lt. Timothy J. Sullivan (61st Ftr Sqn) KIA
P-47D HV- 42-75578
Hit by enemy fighters near St. Martin.

**78th**: Lt. William Newton, III (84th Ftr Sqn) KIA
P-47D WZ-T 42-26583
Shot down by a Spitfire near Breteuil.

**353rd**: Lt. Daniel L. Claiville (351st Ftr Sqn) KIA
P-47D YJ-B 42-26047
Hit by a Me-109 near Pont Audemer.

**355th**: Lt. Victor E. Denti (354th Ftr Sqn) KIA
P-51B WR-N 42-106870
Hit by flak at Chateauroux Airfield.

**361st**: Capt. Shelby J. Harris (374th Ftr Sqn) POW
P-51D B7-H 44-13333
Hit by flak south of Beauvais.

Lt. John R. Bernert (374th Ftr Sqn) KIA
P-51D B7- 44-13538
Hit by enemy fighters near Amiens.

**479th**: Lt. Clayton F. Proctor (434th Ftr Sqn) KIA
P-38J L2-X 42-68029
Hit by flak near Montignac.

*Remarks*

| | |
|---|---|
| 20th: | 7-4 locos, 22-50 railcars, 1-35 vehicles |
| 55th: | 3-8 locos, 15-131 railcars, 26-2 vehicles, 0-13 flak towers, 0-1 gun position, 2-3 tugs, |
| | Lt. William Caldwell (38th Ftr Sqn) c/l; o.k. |
| | P-38J CG- |
| 56th: | 0-8 railcars, 3-0 vehicles |
| 339th: | 1-0 loco, 0-25 railcars |
| 353rd: | 1-0 loco, 3-25 railcars, 7-0 vehicles |
| 356th: | 0-2 locos, 0-50 railcars, 0-1 barge |
| 361st: | 0-1 loco |
| 364th: | 7-0 locos, 0 10 railcars, 2-5 barges |
| 479th: | 2-0 locos, 0-31 railcars, 1-1 hangars, 0-5 flak towers, 0-2 buildings, 0-1 gun position |
| | Lt. Carl L. Peterson (434th Ftr Sqn) c/l; o.k. |
| | P-38J L2- 42-28707 |

**July 6, 1944**

Groups Operating: P-51 4th, 339th, 352nd, 355th, 357th, 359th, 361st
P-47 56th, 78th, 353rd, 356th
P-38 20th, 55th, 364th, 479th

Missions: Support of bombers to Kiel, V-1 sites in the Pas de Calais, area, and bridges in the Paris area, plus fighter-bomber operations.

Claims: 18-3-7 air
0-0 ground

| *Group* | | *Claims* | *Location* |
|---|---|---|---|
| **55th** | | | |
| 338th: | Capt. O.E. Goodman | Me-109 dest(air) | Laon |
| | Lt. J.K. Garrett | Me-109 dest(air) | Laon |
| | Lt. K.M. Glasser | Me-109 dest(air) | Laon |
| | Capt. M.E. Blanchard | Me-109 dam(air) | Laon |
| **56th** | | | |
| 62nd: | Capt. M.L. Moseley | Me-109 dest(air) | Beaumont |
| | Lt. G.E. Bostwick | Me-109 dest(air) | Beaumont |
| 63rd: | Lt. B.P. Casteel | FW-190 dest(air) | E/Chartres |
| | Lt. J.R. Curtis | Me-109 dest(air) | N/Evreux |
| | Lt. T. Guerrero | FW-190 dest(air) | E/Chartres |
| **78th** | | | |
| 83rd: | Lt. F.E. Higginbottom | FW-190 dest(air) | Rambouillet |
| | Lt. F.R. Pursell | FW-190 dest(air) | Rambouillet |
| | Capt. D.A. Lawhead | FW-190 prob(air) | Rambouillet |
| | Lt. H.L. Blystone | FW-190 dam(air) | Rambouillet |
| 84th: | Capt. H.T. Lay | FW-190 dest(air) | NW Paris |
| | Lt. C.E. Parmelee | FW-190 dest(air) | NW Paris |
| | Lt. J.B. Putnam | FW-190 dest(air) | NW Paris |
| **353rd** | | | |
| 350th: | Maj. K.W. Gallup | Me-109 dest(air) | SW Limay |
| 352nd: | Lt. D.L. Barber | FW 190 dest(air) | Evreux-Paris |
| **356th** | | | |
| 361st: | Lt. E.L. Thompson | Me-109 dest(air) | S/Fontainbleau |
| **357th** | | | |
| 363rd: | Lt. E.K. Simpson | Ju-88 dest(air) | N/Nordernay Isle |

(Note - this Ju-88 was actually destroyed by C.E. Yeager, but since Yeager was not to be on ops, the kill was given to Simpson.)

| *Group* | | *Claims* | *Location* |
|---|---|---|---|
| **364th** | | | |
| 385th: | Lt. J.J. Pascoe | FW-190 prob(air) | S/Chalons |
| | Capt. F.C. McClanahan | (2)FW-190 dam(air) | Chalons |
| | Lt. W.G. Erfkamp | FW-190 dam(air) | Chalons |
| | Lt. D.K. Hustead | FW-190 dam(air) | Chalons |
| | Lt. E.K. Tazzia | Me-109 dam(air) | Chalons |
| **479th** | | | |
| 434th: | Lt. J.T. Tipps | Me-109 dest(air) | Valenciennes |
| | Lt. J.A. Haas | FW-190 prob(air) | Cambrai |

*Losses-*

**56th**: Lt. Samuel J. Lowman, Jr. (63rd Ftr Sqn) KIA
P-47D UN-P 42-25701
Hit by enemy fighters near Bernay.

**78th**: Lt. Robert E. Mullins (83rd Ftr Sqn) KIA
P-47D HL-M 42-26536
Hit by a FW-190 near Rambouillet.

**355th**: Lt. Norman E. Dixon (357th Ftr Sqn) POW
P-51B OS-K 42-106634
Hit by flak near Schwerin.

**479th**: Lt. Jene A. Haas (434th Ftr Sqn) POW
P-38J L2-P 42-67732
Hit by a FW-190 near Favril.

*Remarks*
78th: 0-1 loco, 0-25 railcars
339th: 1-0 loco, 0-25 railcars
353rd: 8-0 locos, 0-13 railcars, 1-0 vehicle
Lt. Harold O. Miller (352nd Ftr Sqn) c/l beach-head; o.k.
P-47D SX-L
356th: 2-5 locos, 3-60 railcars, 1-0 vehicle
364th: 11-4 locos, 6-128 railcars, 1-0 flak tower, 1-1 control towers
479th: 3-1 locos, 2-7 railcars, 4-4 vehicles, 0-1 flak tower

**July 7, 1944**

Groups Operating: P-51 4th, 339th, 352nd, 355th, 357th, 359th, 361st
P-47 56th, 78th, 353rd, 356th
P-38 20th, 55th, 364th, 479th

Missions: Support of bombers to Lutzkendorf, Merseburg, Kolleda, Halle, Aschersleben, Leipzig, and Bernburg.

Claims: 75.5-3-21 air
4-0 ground

| *Group* | | *Claims* | *Location* |
|---|---|---|---|
| **4th** | | | |
| 334th: | Capt. T.E. Joyce | (2)Me-109 dest(air) | Aschersleben |
| | Lt. W.G. Gillette | Me-109 dest(air) | Sangerhausen |
| | | Me-109 prob(air) | Sangerhausen |
| | | (2)Me-109 dam(air) | Sangerhausen |
| | Lt. P.B. Hardy | Me-109 dest(air) | Blankenberg |
| | | Me-109 prob(air) | Blankenberg |
| | | (2)Me-109 dam(air) | Blankenberg |
| | Lt. J.J. Scally | Me-410 dest(air) | Sangerhausen |
| | Lt. J.D. McFadden | Me-109 dam(air) | Aschersleben |
| | Lt. S.W. Monroe | FW-190 dam(air) | E/Pasewalk |
| | Lt. E.C. Walsh | Me-109 dam(air) | Eisleben |
| 335th: | Lt. J.W. Goodwyn | Me-109 dest(air) | Bad Frankenhausen |
| 336th: | Lt. G.C. Chapman | FW-190 dest(air) | Bernburg |
| **20th** | | | |
| 55th: | Lt. R.O. Loehnert | (2)Me-109 dest(air) | Halle |
| | Lt. C.A. Hallberg | Me-109 dest(air) | Halle |
| 77th: | Capt. J.M. Morris | Me-410 dest(air) | Leipzig-Halle |
| | Lt. I.W. Fernandes | FW-190 dest(air) | Halle |
| | | FW-190 dam(air) | Halle |
| | Lt. A.F. Clark | FW-190 dest(air) | Halle |
| | Lt. L.W. Adams | Me-410 dest(air) | Oschersleben |
| | | FW-190 dam(air) | Halle |
| | Lt. A.D. Payne | FW-190 dam(air) | Halle |
| | Lt. P. Chubin | FW-190 dam(air) | Halle |
| **55th** | | | |
| 38th: | Maj. J.D. Landers | (3)Me-410 dest(air) | Bernburg |
| | Lt. E.M. Holderman | (2)Me-410 dest(air) | Bernburg |
| | | Me-410 dam(air) | Bernburg |
| | Lt. R.E. Callahan | Me-410 dest(air) | Bernburg |
| | Lt. W.J. Reilly | FW-190 dest(air) | Bernburg |
| 338th: | Capt. L.D. Anderson | (2)Me-109 dest(air) | Bernburg |
| | Lt. T.A. Parker | Me-109 dest(air) | SW Magdeburg |
| | | FW-190 dest(air) | SW Magdeburg |
| | Capt. O.E. Goodman | FW-190 dest(air) | W/Bernburg |
| | | (.5)Me-109 dest(air) | W/Bernburg |
| | Lt. C.A. Biedul | FW-190 dest(air) | W/Bernburg |
| | Lt. W.H. Earnest | FW-190 dest(air) | W/Bernburg |
| | Lt. J.K. Garnett | FW-190 dest(air) | W/Bernburg |
| | Lt. J.L. Gerry | FW-190 dest(air) | W/Bernburg |
| | Lt. D.R. Hailey | FW-190 dest(air) | W/Bernburg |
| | | Me-109 dam(air) | W/Bernburg |
| | Lt. J.E. McKee | FW-190 dest(air) | W/Bernburg |
| | | Me-109 prob(air) | W/Bernburg |
| | Lt. J.M. Wakeland | FW-190 dam(air) | W/Bernburg |
| | Lt. G.E. Funk | (.5)Me-109 dest(air) | W/Bernburg |
| **56th** | | | |
| 61st: | Lt. S. Gerick | u/i a/c dest(grd) | Peine A/F |
| 62nd: | Capt. F.J. Christensen | (6)Ju-52 dest(air) | Gardelegen A/F |
| | Lt. B.G. Edens | (3)Ju-52 dest(air) | Gardelegen A/F |
| | Capt. M.J. Jackson | Ju-52 dest(air) | Gardelegen A/F |
| **339th** | | | |
| 503rd: | Capt. V. Wyatt | (.5)Me 109 dest(air) | Leipzig |
| | Lt. J.P. Bush | (.5)Me-109 dest(air) | Leipzig |
| | Lt. R.H. Ammon | Me-109 dam(air) | Leipzig |
| 504th: | Lt. M.F. Caldwell | (2)Me-109 dest(air) | Eisleben |
| | Lt. R.H. Wilcox | (2)Me-109 dest(air) | Eisleben |
| | Maj. B.C. Routt | Me-109 dest(air) | Eisleben |
| **353rd** | | | |
| HdQts: | Col. G.E. Duncan | He-111 dest(grd) | Wesendorf |
| 351st: | Lt. G.W. Franklin | FW-190 dest(grd) | Wesendorf |
| | Lt. R.M. Tumlin | He-111 dest(grd) | Wesendorf |
| **355th** | | | |
| HdQts: | LtCol. C.H. Kinnard | (2)Me-410 dest(air) | Lingen |
| | | Me-109 dest(air) | Lingen |
| 354th: | Lt. R.G. Cross | (2)Me-410 dest(air) | Lingen |
| | Lt. E.F. Perry | Me-410 dest(air) | Lingen |
| | Lt. S.G. Betounes | (.5)Ju-88 dest(air) | Lingen |
| | Lt. R.G. Taylor | (.5)Ju-88 dest(air) | Lingen |
| 357th: | Capt. L.D. Minchew | (2.5)Me-410 dest(air) | Nordhausen |
| | | (2)Me-410 dam(air) | Nordhausen |
| | | (shared with an unknown P-38 pilot) | |
| | Capt. F.R. Haviland | (2)Me-410 dest(air) | Halle |
| | | Me-410 dam(air) | Halle |
| | Lt. J.A. Cotter | Me-410 dest(air) | S/Halle |
| | Lt. E.P. McNeff | Me-109 dest(air) | Nordhausen |
| | Lt. L.B. Fuller | Me-410 dest(air) | Halle-Nordhausen |
| | Lt. F.L. Eshelman | Me-109 dam(air) | Nordhausen |
| **357th** | | | |
| 363rd: | Capt. C.E. Anderson | Me-109 dest(air) | N/Leipzig |
| | Lt. W.S. Fennell | Me-109 dest(air) | N/Leipzig |
| | Lt. E.K. Simpson | Me-109 dest(air) | N/Leipzig |
| **361st** | | | |
| 375th: | Lt. R.C. Wright | (2)Me-109 dest(air) | N/Leipzig |

| | | | |
|---|---|---|---|
| | Lt. R.J. Sobieski | Me-410 dest(air) | NW Leipzig |
| | | (.5)Me-109 dest(air) | NW Leipzig |
| | Lt. D.R. Morehouse | Me-109 dest(air) | N/Leipzig |
| | Lt. D.R. Morgan | (.5)Me-109 dest(air) | NW Leipzig |
| | Capt. W.G. Shackleford | Me-109 dam(air) | N/Leipzig |
| 376th: | Lt. D.F. Spencer | (2)Me-109 dest(air) | Wittenberg |
| | Lt. R.S. White | Me-109 dest(air) | Wittenberg |
| | | FW-190 dest(air) | Wittenberg |
| | Capt. R.M. Durbin | FW-190 dam(air) | Halle |

*Losses-*

**4th**: Lt. John J. Scally (334th Ftr Sqn) POW
P-51B QP-E 43-6567
Collided with a Me-410 near Nordhausen.

**20th**: Capt. James M. Morris (77th Ftr Sqn) POW
P-38J LC-O 43-28397
Hit by a Me-410 in the Leipzig-Halle area.

**353rd**: Col. Glenn E. Duncan (HdQts) MIA-E
P-47D LH-X 42-25971 "Dove of Peace"
Hit by flak at Wesendorf and bellied-in near Nienburg.

**355th**: Lt. Heber M. Huish (354th Ftr Sqn) KIA
P-51B WR-T 43-6915
Hit by debris from a Me-410 near Halle.

Lt. Leonard B. Fuller (357th Ftr Sqn) KIA
P-51D OS-E 44-13526
Hit by flak near Naumburg.

**357th**: Lt. Frank Koka (363rd Ftr Sqn) KIA
P-51B B6- 43-6858
Hit by enemy fighters north of Leipzig and bailed out north-west of Bernburg.

*Remarks*
20th: 4-0 locos, 5-26 railcars
78th: 2-4 locos, 0-10 railcars
356th: 1-0 loco
361st: Lt. Albert C. Wilson (376th Ftr Sqn) c/l; o.k.
P-51 E9-

**July 8, 1944**
Groups Operating: P-51 339th, 352nd, 355th, 357th, 359th, 361st
P-47 56th, 78th, 353rd, 356th
P-38 20th, 55th, 364th, 479th
Missions: Support for bombers hitting bridges, rail targets, and V-1 sites in France, plus fighter-bomber activities.
Claims: 0-0-0 air
20-19 ground

| *Group* | | *Claims* | *Location* |
|---|---|---|---|
| **355th** | | | |
| 354th: | Maj. H.B. Kucheman | (2)Me-410 dest(grd) | SW Chalons |
| | | Me-109 dam(grd) | SW Chalons |
| | Lt. R.S. Morris | Me-410 dest(grd) | SW Chalons |
| | | Me-109 dest(grd) | SW Chalons |
| | Lt. S.C. Williams | Me-410 dest(grd) | SW Chalons |
| | | Me-109 dest(grd) | SW Chalons |
| | | Me-410 dam(grd) | SW Chalons |
| | Lt. R.T. Bradley | Me-109 dest(grd) | SW Chalons |
| | Lt. N.P. Jackson | Me-109 dest(grd) | SW Chalons |
| | Lt. C.H. Graham | Me-109 dest(grd) | SW Chalons |
| | | Me-109 dam(grd) | SW Chalons |
| | Lt. W.D. Martin | Me-109 dest(grd) | SW Chalons |
| | | (2)Me-109 dam(grd) | SW Chalons |
| | Capt. N.J. Fortier | (.5)Me-109 dest(grd) | SW Chalons |
| | Lt. R.G. Cross | (.5)Me-109 dest(grd) | SW Chalons |
| | | Me-410 dam(grd) | SW Chalons |
| 357th: | Lt. P.M.N. McHugh | (2)Me-410 dest(grd) | SW Chalons |
| | | (3)Me-410 dam(grd) | SW Chalons |
| | Lt. G.W. Forker | Me-109 dest(grd) | SW Chalons |
| | Lt. R.W. Strachan | Me-109 dest(grd) | SW Chalons |
| | Lt. W.A. Cox | Me-410 dam(grd) | SW Chalons |
| | Lt. W.L. Reiff | Me-109 dam(grd) | SW Chalons |
| 358th: | Lt. W.J. McGinley | FW-190 dest(grd) | SW Chalons |
| | | (2)FW-190 dam(grd) | SW Chalons |
| | Lt. V.W. Covault | FW-190 dest(grd) | SW Chalons |
| | | FW-190 dam(grd) | SW Chalons |
| | Lt. R.L. Michelena | FW-190 dest(grd) | SW Chalons |
| | | FW-190 dam(grd) | SW Chalons |
| | Lt. R.I. McNally | FW-190 dest(grd) | SW Chalons |
| | Lt. H.W. Pardee | FW-190 dest(grd) | SW Chalons |
| | | (3)Me-109 dam(grd) | SW Chalons |
| | Lt. W. Winn | Me-109 dam(grd) | SW Chalons |

*Losses-*

**355th**: Lt. James P. Lowder, Jr. (358th Ftr Sqn) KIA
P-51B YF-R 43-6945 "Wizard Kite"
Hit by flak and crashed into trees near Montmiral.

*Remarks*
20th: 1-1 locos
56th: 1-0 vehicle, 0-1 building
339th: Capt. Evan M. Johnson (505th Ftr Sqn) b/o Fowlmere; o.k.
P-51D 6N-J 44-13471
355th: 2-2 locos, 1-2 vehicles
356th: 1-2 locos, 0-58 railcars, 2-0 vehicles
364th: 11-0 locos, 8-50 railcars, 1-0 flak tower
479th: 1-0 loco, 4-0 railcars

**July 9, 1944**
Groups Operating: P-51 4th, 339th, 352nd, 355th, 359th, 361st
P-47 78th, 353rd, 356th
P-38 20th, 55th
Missions: Support for bombers to bridges and V-1 sites in France.
Claims: 6-0-3 air
0-0 ground

| *Group* | | *Claims* | *Location* |
|---|---|---|---|
| **20th** | | | |
| 79th: | Lt. J.E. Carpenter | Ju-290 dest(air) | Moulins |
| **353rd** | | | |
| 350th: | Capt. E.S. Middleton | Me-109 dam(air) | Argentan |
| | Lt. B.C. Auchincloss | Me-109 dam(air) | E/Evreux |
| 351st: | Lt. J.J. Hatch | (2)Me-109 dest(air) | Argentan |
| | Capt. W.J. Maguire | Me-109 dest(air) | Argentan |
| | Lt. J.W. Furneaux | Me-109 dest(air) | Argentan |
| | Lt. R.C. Strobell | Me-109 dest(air) | Argentan |
| | Capt. V.L. Byers | Me-109 dam(air) | Argentan |

*Losses-*

**55th**: Lt. John E. Walker (343rd Ftr Sqn) POW
P-38J CY-Q 42-68014
Hit by flak near Angars.

**78th**: Lt. Jack B. Miller (83rd Ftr Sqn) ASR
P-47D HL-P 42-76232
Lost oil pressure, then shot up by Spitfires and bailed out over the Channel.

**361st**: Lt. Leroy H. Sypher (375th Ftr Sqn) POW
P-51D E2- 44-13576
Hit by flak near Louviers.

*Remarks*
20th: 9-4 locos, 114-144 railcars, 52-90 vehicles, 1-2 flak towers
55th: 21-28 locos, 12-249 railcars, 2-0 vehicles, 0-5 buildings
356th: Maj. Ernest J. White (359th Ftr Sqn) c/l Woodbridge; o.k.
P-47D OC-

**July 11, 1944**
Groups Operating: P-51 4th, 339th, 352nd, 355th, 357th, 359th, 361st
P-47 56th, 78th, 353rd, 356th
P-38 20th, 55th, 364th, 479th
Missions: Support for bombers to Munich.
Claims: 0-0-1 air
1-0 ground

| *Group* | | *Claims* | *Location* |
|---|---|---|---|
| **339th** | | | |
| 503rd: | Capt. E.B. Stephenson | Me-110 dam(air) | Landsberg |
| 505th: | Lt. James R. Starnes | u/i a/c dest(grd) | NE Lake Constance |

*Losses-*

**4th**: Lt. James S. Hanrahan (335th Ftr Sqn) MIA-E
P-51B WD-N 43-6562
Suffered mechanical failure near Bonniques.

**78th**: Lt. Lester E. Ford (84th Ftr Sqn) KIA
P-47D WZ-N 43-25313
Hit by a Me-109 near Etables.

**339th**: Lt. Peter J. McMahan (505th Ftr Sqn) KIA
P-51C 6N- 42-103559
Hit the ground while strafing near Busigny.

**359th**: Lt. Bennie F. White (370th Ftr Sqn) KIA
P-51B CS-J 43-24810
Last seen over the North Sea.

*Remarks*

355th: Lt. Floyd W. Trembarth (354th Ftr Sqn) b/o; o.k.
P-51 WR-

359th: 1-3 locos

**July 12, 1944**

Groups Operating: P-51 4th, 339th, 352nd, 355th, 357th, 359th, 361st
P-47 56th, 78th, 353rd, 356th
P-38 20th, 55th, 364th, 479th

Missions: Support of bombers to Munich.

Claims: nil

Losses: nil

*Remarks*

20th: Lt. Richard Robbins (77th Ftr Sqn) c/l; o.k.
P-38J LC-I 42-68176

**July 13, 1944**

Groups Operating: P-51 4th, 339th, 352nd, 355th, 359th, 361st
P-47 56th, 78th, 353rd
P-38 20th, 55th, 364th, 479th

Missions: Support of bombers to Munich and Saarbrucken.

Claims: 2-1-2 air
0-0 ground

| *Group* | | *Claims* | *Location* |
|---|---|---|---|
| **352nd** | | | |
| HdQts: | LtCol. J.C. Edwards | Me-109 dest(air) | SE Strasbourg |
| 487th: | Lt. C.M. Greer | Me-109 dam(air) | E/Schweighausen |
| **355th** | | | |
| 357th: | Lt. E.M. Hendrickson | Me-109 dest(air) | Sarreburg |
| | | Me-109 prob(air) | Sarreburg |
| | Lt. P.M.N. McHugh | Me-109 dam(air) | Sarreburg |

*Losses-*

**4th**: Maj. Wilson V. Edwards (HdQts) POW
P-51D VF- 44-13608
Hit by flak near Mannheim and bailed out near Metz.

**20th**: Lt. Charles W. Dungan (77th Ftr Sqn) ASR
P-38J LC-M 42-68156
Suffered mechanical failure and bailed out near the Thames Estuary.

**55th**: Capt. Clair W. Des Voignes (38th Ftr Sqn) KIA
P-38J CG- 43-28279
Collided with Lt. Palmer (56th Ftr Grp) near St. Denis.

**56th**: Lt. James A. Palmer (62nd Ftr Sqn) KIA
P-47D LM-M 42-25713
Collided with Capt. Des Voignes(55th Ftr Grp) near St. Denis.

**359th**: Lt. Thomas S. Lane (368th Ftr Sqn) ASR
P-51 CV-
Suffered mechanical failure and bailed out twenty miles southeast of Bradwell Bay.

*Remarks*

78th: 4-6 locos, 0-18 railcars, 0-1 building

**July 14, 1944**

Groups Operating: P-51 4th, 339th, 352nd, 355th, 357th, 359th, 361st
P-47 56th, 78th, 353rd, 356th
P-38 20th, 55th, 479th

Missions: Support for bombers to Southern France (dropping supplies to Maquis forces) and to Peronne and Montdidier Airfields.

Claims: 6-0-0 air
0-0 ground

| *Group* | | *Claims* | *Location* |
|---|---|---|---|
| **20th** | | | |
| 55th: | Lt. W. Mullins | FW-190 dest(air) | S/Nogent |
| 77th: | Lt. C.C. Arthaud | (.5)FW-190 dest(air) | SW Reims |
| | Lt. E.C. Fiebelkorn | (.5)FW-190 dest(air) | SW Reims |
| **357th** | | | |
| HdQts: | LtCol. T.L. Hayes | Me-109 dest(air) | Valence |
| 364th: | Capt. M.H. Stepelton | FW-190 dest(air) | Valence |
| | Lt. D.L. Finley | Me-109 dest(air) | Valence |
| | Lt. N.J. Frederick | Me-109 dest(air) | Valence |

*Losses-*

**20th**: Lt. Adam L. Hunt, Jr. (55th Ftr Sqn) MIA
P-38J KI-L 43-28354
Hit by flak near Menehould.

*Remarks*

20th: 16-2 locos, 62-41 railcars, 1-0 flak tower, 0-3 vehicles
Maj. Martin Low (55th Ftr Sqn) c/l Sibson; o.k.
P-38J KI-N 43-28404
Lt. Keith C. Price (79th Ftr Sqn) c/l Kingscliffe; o.k.
P-38J MC-

56th: 2-0 vehicles

339th: 0-2 flak towers

364th: 5-0 railcars, 0-2 vehicles, 0-4 buildings

**July 15, 1944**

Groups Operating: P-47 56th, 356th
P-38 364th, 479th

Missions: Fighter-bomber operations southeast of Paris.

Claims: nil

*Losses-*

**56th**: Lt. Robert E. Jenkins (63rd Ftr Sqn) KIA
P-47D UN-O 42-76578
Hit by flak near Molineuf.

**364th**: Capt. Victor L. Kercher (384th Ftr Sqn) KIA
P-38J 5Y-K 42-104421 "Daddy's Baby"
Collided with Lt. Yost near La Charite.

Lt. Byron P. Yost (384th Ftr Sqn) KIA
P-38J 5Y-F 42-67980
Collided with Capt. Kercher near La Charite.

**479th**: Lt. Flamm D. Harper (434th Ftr Sqn) MIA-E
P-38J L2-V 42-68147
Hit by debris of an exploding ammo dump near Montmorillion.

*Remarks*

56th: 0-16 railcars, 0-9 vehicles

364th: 4-0 locos, 150-100 railcars, 0-1 vehicle, 0-1 building

479th: 0-2 locos, 0-11 railcars, 1-4 bridges, 0-6 buildings,
0-2 flak towers
Lt. Fred M. Mead (436th Ftr Sqn) c/l Canterbury; o.k.
P-38J 9B-

**July 16, 1944**

Groups Operating: P-51 4th, 339th, 352nd, 355th, 357th, 359th, 361st
P-47 56th, 78th, 353rd, 356th
P-38 20th, 55th, 364th, 479th

Missions: Support of bombers to Munich, Stuttgart, and Saarbrucken.

Claims: nil

*Losses-*

**20th**: Lt. John E. Klink (55th Ftr Sqn) ASR
P-38J KI-N 42-104207
Damaged by flak and bailed out off Margate.

**339th**: Lt. Wesley G. Fish (505th Ftr Sqn) POW
P-51D 6N- 44-13413
Hit by flak near Nancy and bailed out near Verdun.

**352nd**: Lt. Jule V. Conard (487th Ftr Sqn) POW
P-51B HO-P 42-106451 "Cripes A'Mighty"
Suffered mechanical failure near Munich and was last seen near Aalen.

*Remarks*

56th: 3-4 locos, 1-42 railcars

357th: 0-1 hangar, 0-1 flak tower

**July 17, 1944**

Groups Operating: P-51 4th, 339th, 352nd, 355th, 357th, 359th, 361st
P-47 78th
P-38 20th, 364th, 479th

Missions: Escort to various targets in France and V-1 sites in the Pas de Calais area.

Claims: 0-0-1 air
0-0 ground

| *Group* | | *Claims* | *Location* |
|---|---|---|---|
| **4th** | | | |
| 335th: | Maj. L.M. Blanding | Me-109 dam(air) | NE Munich |

*Losses-*

**78th**: Capt. Harry T. Lay (84th Ftr Sqn) KIA
P-47D WZ-Z 42-26652
Hit by flak and bailed out near Liffel-LeGrand.

*Remarks*

4th: 0-3 locos, 12-27 railcars, 18-10 vehicles

20th: 17-1 locs, 15-55 railcars, 0-15 vehicles

78th: 5-0 locos, 0-65 railcars

359th: 1-8 locos, 15-22 railcars, 14-11 vehicles

**July 18, 1944**
Groups Operating: P-51 4th, 339th, 352nd, 355th, 357th, 359th, 361st
P-47 356th
P-38 20th, 364th, 479th
Missions: Support of bombers to Kiel, Peenemunde, Solier, Troarns, and Frenouville.
Claims: 19-2-15 air
0-0 ground

| *Group* | | *Claims* | *Location* |
|---|---|---|---|
| **352nd** | | | |
| 328th: | Capt. H.W. White | Me-109 dest(air) | Wismar |
| | Lt. F.L. Kebelman | Me-109 dest(air) | Wismar |
| | Lt. E.L. Smith | Me-109 dest(air) | Wismar |
| | Lt. J.W. Galiga | (2)Ju-88 dam(air) | Wismar |
| | Lt. W.D. Wilson | Me-109 dam(air) | Wismar |
| | F/O W.E. Montgomery | Ju-88 dam(air) | Wismar |
| 486th: | Maj. W.O. Jackson | Me-109 dest(air) | N/Warnemunde |
| | | Ju-88 dest(air) | N/Warnemunde |
| | Lt. D.J. French | Me-410 dest(air) | NE Berlin |
| | | (3)Me-410 dam(air) | NE Berlin |
| | Lt. R.J. Miller | Me-410 dest(air) | S/Rostock |
| | | Me-410 dam(air) | S/Rostock |
| | Lt. D.M. Reichman | Ju-88 dest(air) | S/Rostock |
| | Lt. E.O. Bostrom | Ju-88 dest(air) | SE Warnemunde |
| | Lt. M.B. Stoll | Ju-88 dest(air) | N/Warnemunde |
| | Lt. D.W. McKibben | Me-109 prob(air) | N/Warnemunde |
| | Lt. M.J. Stover | Me-109 dam(air) | NE Berlin |
| 487th: | Maj. G.E. Preddy | (2)Ju-88 dest(air) | NE Rostock |
| | | Me-109 dest(air) | NE Rostock |
| | | Ju-88 prob(air) | NE Rostock |
| | | (2)Ju-88 dam(air) | NE Rostock |
| | Lt. C.E. Ellison | (3)Ju-88 dest(air) | SE Rostock |
| | Lt. W.E. Fowler | (2)Me-109 dest(air) | Demnin |
| | Lt. S.K. Moats | Me-109 dest(air) | SE Rostock |
| | Lt. J.P. Vickery | (2)Ju-88 dam(air) | NE Rostock |
| | Capt. J.P. Kessler | Me-109 dam(air) | NE Rostock |
| **357th** | | | |
| 364th: | Lt. R.M. Shaw | Me-109 dam(air) | NW Rostock |

*Losses-*

**352nd**: Lt. James A. Burr (328th Ftr Sqn) MIA
P-51D PE- 44-13320
Last seen chasing enemy fighters near Warnemunde.

Lt. John W. Galiga (328th Ftr Sqn) MIA
P-51B PE-K 43-7165 "Lady Lynn"
Last seen chasing enemy planes near Parchim.

**355th**: Lt. Fred W. Johnson (354th Ftr Sqn) ASR
P-51 WR-
Bailed out thirty miles off Great Yarmouth.

*Remarks*
352nd: Lt. Robert H. Powell (328th Ftr Sqn) c/l Bodney; o.k.
P-51B PE-P 42-106914 "The West, By Gawd, Virginian"

KIAc's
356th: Lt. Shirley J. Green (360th Ftr Sqn)
P-47D PI-
Collided with another P-47 and crashed near Woodbridge.

364th: Capt. John C. Ford (384th Ftr Sqn)
P-38J 5Y-O 42-68101
Lost an engine on take-off and spun-in south of Honington.

**July 19, 1944**
Groups Operating: P-51 4th, 55th(mixed), 339th, 352nd, 355th, 357th, 359th, 361st
P-47 56th, 78th, 353rd, 356th
P-38 20th, 55th, 364th, 479th
Missions: Support for bombers to Augsburg, Schweinfurt, Coblenz, Saarbrucken, Lechfeld, Boblingen, and various other targets in southwestern Germany.
Claims: 15-2-2 air
34-13 ground

| *Group* | | *Claims* | *Location* |
|---|---|---|---|
| **4th** | | | |
| 336th: | Lt. I.E. Grounds | (2)Me-109 dest(air) | E/Munchen |
| | Lt. F.M. Grove | Me-109 dest(air) | E/Munchen |
| **78th** | | | |
| 82nd: | Maj. N.D. Munson | (2.5)u/i a/c dest(grd) | Stuttgart |
| | Lt. J.R. Kinsolving | Ju-52 dest(grd) | Stuttgart |
| | | (.5)u/i a/c dest(grd) | Stuttgart |
| 83rd: | Lt. E.H. Miller | (2)Ju-188 dest(grd) | Linburg-Coblenz |
| | Lt. B.W. Sorenson | (2)Ju-188 dest(grd) | Linburg-Coblenz |
| | | Ju-188 dam(grd) | Linburg-Coblenz |
| | Capt. R.W. Smith | Ju-188 dest(grd) | Linburg-Coblenz |
| | | (2)Ju-188 dam(grd) | Linburg-Coblenz |
| | Capt. R.R. Bonebrake | Do-217 dest(grd) | Linburg-Coblenz |
| | Lt. G. Riccardo | Ju-188 dest(grd) | Linburg-Coblenz |
| | | Ju-188 dam(grd) | Linburg-Coblenz |
| | Lt. J.B. Miller | Ju-188 dest(grd) | Linburg-Coblenz |
| | Lt. F.E. Higginbottom | (2)Ju-188 dam(grd) | Linburg-Coblenz |
| | Lt. R.W. Oxley | Ju-188 dam(grd) | Linburg-Coblenz |
| 84th: | Maj. B.I. Mayo | (1.5)Do-217 dest(grd) | Eutingen |
| | | u/i a/c dest(grd) | Eutingen |
| | Capt. A.F. Eaton | (1.5)Do-217 dest(grd) | Eutingen |
| | | Me-410 dest(grd) | Eutingen |
| | Lt. C.E. Parmelee | Do-217 dest(grd) | Eutingen |
| | Lt. J.B. Putnam | Ju-188 dest(grd) | Eutingen |
| | F/O A.G. McGuire | Me-110 dest(grd) | Eutingen |
| | | Do-217 dam(grd) | Eutingen |
| | Lt. S.B. Calderon | Do-217 dam(grd) | Eutingen |
| | | Ju-87 dam(grd) | Eutingen |
| **339th** | | | |
| 505th: | Maj. J.L. Thury | Me-109 dest(grd) | SW Augsburg |
| | | u/i a/c dest(grd) | SW Augsburg |
| | Lt. W.F. Mudge | FW-190 dest(grd) | SW Augsburg |
| | | Ju-188 dest(grd) | SW Augsburg |
| | Lt. C.J. Hanseman | Ju-188 dest(grd) | SW Augsburg |
| | | u/i a/c dest(grd) | SW Augsburg |
| | Lt. R.B. Olander | Ju-188 dest(grd) | SW Augsburg |
| | Lt. J.R. Starnes | Ju-188 dest(grd) | SW Augsburg |
| | Lt. A.A. Tower | Ju-188 dest(grd) | SW Augsburg |
| | Lt. J.R. Hanson | Ju-188 dest(grd) | SW Augsburg |
| | Lt. G. Knight | (.5)Ju-188 dest(grd)[*] | SW Augsburg |
| | Lt. W.H. Krauss | (.5)Ju-188 dest(grd)[*] | SW Augsburg |
| | Lt. A. Sirochman | (.5)Ju-188 dest(grd)[**] | SW Augsburg |
| | Lt. R.H. Tannous | (.5)Ju-188 dest(grd)[**] | SW Augsburg |
| **352nd** | | | |
| 486th: | Capt. L.A. Rauk | (2)Me-109 dest(air) | E/Munich |
| | Lt. E.L. Mundell | (2)Me-109 dest(air) | E/Munich |
| | Lt. L.J. Vitek | (2)Me-109 dest(air) | Munich |
| | | Me-109 dam(air) | Munich |
| | Maj. W.O. Jackson | Me-109 dest(air) | E/Munich |
| | Lt. E.R. Lazear | Me-109 prob(air) | NE Munich |
| 487th: | Lt. R.C. Draftz | Me-109 dest(air) | Wolfratshausen |
| **355th** | | | |
| 354th: | Lt. J.M. Folger | FW-190 dest(air) | Biberach |
| 358th: | Capt. W.J. Hovde | Me-109 dest(air) | Augsburg |
| | Lt. J.N. McElroy | FW-190 dest(air) | Augsburg |
| | | FW-190 dam(air) | Augsburg |
| | Lt. R.M. Thompson | Me-109 dest(air) | Augsburg |
| | Lt. V.W. Covault | FW-190 prob(air) | Augsburg |
| | F/O A.G. Duppstadt | Ju-88 dest(grd) | Munich |
| | | glider dest(grd) | Munich |
| | | Ju-88 dam(grd) | Munich |
| **356th** | | | |
| 359th: | Capt. H. Weber | Me-410 dam(grd) | Le Culot |
| | Lt. H.F. LeMoyne | Me-410 dam(grd) | Le Culot |

*Losses-*

**4th**: Lt. Kermit O. Dahlen (335th Ftr Sqn) KIA
P-51B WD- 43-6463
Hit by a Me-109 near Munich.

Lt. Curtis Simpson (335th Ftr Sqn) INT
P-51B WD-U 42-106438
Suffered mechanical failure and landed in Switzerland.

**20th**: Lt. Owen T. Hillyard (79th Ftr Sqn) KIA
P-38J MC-X 42-67251
Suffered mechanical failure and crashed into the North Sea.

**56th**: Capt. Joseph L. Egan, Jr. (63rd Ftr Sqn) KIA
P-47D UN-G 42-26524 "Lil Goody"
Hit by flak near St. Avolt.

**78th**: Maj. Norman D. Munson (82nd Ftr Sqn) KIA
P-47D MX-X 42-26671 "No Guts, No Glory!"
Hit by flak at Freundenstadt Airfield.

**352nd**: Lt. William D. Wilson (328th Ftr Sqn) POW
P-51B PE-V 43-7146
Ran out of fuel and bailed out near Lille.

**355th**: Lt. Warren A. Schwab (354th Ftr Sqn) POW
P-51B WR-V 43-6938
Suffered mechanical failure and bailed out near Biberach.

*Remarks*
56th: 9-8 locos, 0-15 railcars, 8-1 vehicles
78th: 0-4 locos
339th: 1-1 locos, 0-1 hangar, 0-1 barracks
356th: 3-0 locos, 0-5 railcars, 0-1 vehicle
Lt. Harry F. LeMoyne(359th Ftr Sqn) c/l Manston; o.k.
P-47D OC-
359th: 0-1 loco
364th: 2-2 locos, 2-0 vehicles
P-38 c/l Honington; o.k.

KIAc's
78th: Lt. John B. Putnam(84th Ftr Sqn)
Lt. Martin H. Smith(84th Ftr Sqn)
Died when the B-17 they were riding in crashed at Duxford.

**July 20, 1944**
Groups Operating: P-51 4th, 20th(mixed), 55th(mixed), 339th, 352nd, 355th, 357th, 359th, 361st
P-47 56th, 78th, 353rd, 356th
P-38 20th, 55th, 364th, 479th
Missions: Support to various oil and industrial targets in Germany.
Claims: 11-1-4 air
11-12 ground

| *Group* | | *Claims* | *Location* |
|---|---|---|---|
| **56th** | | | |
| 61st: | Lt. W.H. Barnes | (3)He-111 dest(grd) | Bassenheim A/F |
| | | He-111 dam(grd) | Bassenheim A/F |
| | Lt. S.H. Getz | (2)He-111 dest(grd) | Bassenheim A/F |
| | | (2)He-111 dam(grd) | Bassenheim A/F |
| | LtCol. F.S. Gabreski | He-111 dest(grd) | Bassenheim A/F |
| | Capt. D.F. Smith | He-111 dest(grd) | Bassenheim A/F |
| | | He-111 dam(grd) | Bassenheim A/F |
| | Lt. W.S. Patterson | He-111 dest(grd) | Bassenheim A/F |
| | | He-111 dam(grd) | Bassenheim A/F |
| | Lt. P. Neyland | He-111 dam(grd) | Bassenheim A/F |
| | Lt. C.C. Thomton | He-111 dam(grd) | Bassenheim A/F |
| | Lt. C.E. Westman | He-111 dam(grd) | Bassenheim A/F |
| **352nd** | | | |
| 487th: | Maj. G.E. Preddy | Me-410 dest(grd) | Nordhausen |
| | | He-111 dam(grd) | Nordhausen |
| | Lt. C.M. Greer | (2)He-111 dam(grd) | Nordhausen |
| | Lt. R.W. Graham | He-111 dam(grd) | Nordhausen |
| **355th** | | | |
| 354th: | Capt. N.J. Fortier | Me-109 dest(air) | W/Oschatz |
| | Lt. J.M. Folger | Me-109 dam(air) | W/Oschatz |
| 357th: | Lt. W.O. Costello | Me-109 prob(air) | W/Leipzig |
| 358th: | Lt. R.O. Peters | (2)FW-190 dest(air) | E/Leipzig |
| | | Do-217 dest(air) | E/Leipzig |
| | | He-111 dest(grd) | E/Leipzig |
| | | Ju-88 dest(grd) | E/Leipzig |
| | Lt. N.E. Peterson | Me-109 dest(air) | Dresden |
| | | Me-109 dam(air) | Dresden |
| **359th** | | | |
| 370th: | Lt. W.K. Baker | Me-109 dest(air) | Zeitz |
| | | FW-190 dam(air) | Zeitz |
| | F/O L.C. Reese | Me-109 dam(air) | Zeitz |
| **361st** | | | |
| 375th: | Lt. S. Armsby | (3)Me-109 dest(air) | N/Leipzig |
| | Lt. W.T. Kemp | Me-109 dest(air) | N/Leipzig |
| | | FW-190 dest(air) | N/Leipzig |

*Losses-*

**4th**: Lt. Lester B. Godwin (335th Ftr Sqn) MIA-E
P-51C WD-H 42-103561
Hit by flak near Aachen and bailed out near Antwerp.

**55th**: Lt. Wallace H. Earnest (338th Ftr Sqn) KIA
P-51C CL- 43-25069
Suffered mechanical failure and crashed into the Channel.

**56th**: LtCol. Francis S. Gabreski (61st Ftr Sqn) POW
P-47D HV-A 42-26418
Hit the ground while strafing Bassenheim Airfield.

**355th**: Lt. Walter O. Costello (357th Ftr Sqn) MIA-E
P-51B OS-N 43-24795 "Arkansas Traveler"
Hit by flak near Oschatz and bailed out near Avranches.

Lt. Robert W. Strachan (357th Ftr Sqn) ASR
P-51 OS-
Bailed out northeast of Margate.

**356th**: Capt. Carmen F. Rhodes (360th Ftr Sqn) POW
P-47D PI-M 42-25751 "Joker"
Collided with Lt. Robinson near Hisenden.

Lt. Robert A. Robinson (360th Ftr Sqn) POW
P-47D PI- 42-76493
Collided with Capt. Rhodes near Hisenden.

**359th**: Lt. Gordon M. Shortness (370th Ftr Sqn) KIA
P-51B CS-M 42-106474
Last seen chasing a Me-109 near Niedermuelsen.

*Remarks*
56th: 0-6 locos, 0-17 railcars
353rd: 2-0 locos, 0-15 railcars
357th: Lt. Howlis R. Nowlin (364th Ftr Sqn) c/l; o.k.
P-51C C5-M 42-103348
Lt. Dwaine A. Sandborn (364th Ftr Sqn) c/l; injured
P-51 C5-

**July 21, 1944**
Groups Operating: P-51 4th, 20th(mixed), 55th, 339th, 352nd, 355th, 357th, 359th, 361st
P-47 56th, 78th, 353rd, 356th
P-38 20th, 364th, 479th
Missions: Support of bombers to targets in southwestern Germany.
Claims: 7-1-1 air
3-15 ground

| *Group* | | *Claims* | *Location* |
|---|---|---|---|
| **55th** | | | |
| 38th: | Capt. R.W. Forsblad | Me-109 dest(air) | Munich |
| 338th: | Lt. D.F. Blount | (2)Me-109 dest(air) | NE Kempton |
| | | Me-109 dam(air) | NE Kempton |
| **352nd** | | | |
| 487th: | Capt. W.E. Starck | Me-109 dest(air) | E/Munich |
| | Lt. M.C. Pickering | Me-109 dest(air) | E/Munich |
| | Maj. G.E. Preddy | (.5)Me-109 dest(air) | E/Munich |
| | Lt. S.K. Moats | (.5)Me-109 dest(air) | E/Munich |
| **355th** | | | |
| 358th: | Lt. R.M. Thompson | Me-109 prob(air) | Munich |
| **359th** | | | |
| 370th: | LtCol. J.B. Murphy | Me-109 dest(air) | Ammer Lake |
| | Lt. R.W. Siltamaki | Ju-88 dest(grd) | N/Landsberg |
| | | (3)He-111 dam(grd) | W/Munich |
| | | (2)u/i a/c dam(grd) | W/Munich |
| | F/O W.W. Wiley | Ju-88 dest(grd) | N/Landsberg |
| | | (10)Ju 88 dam(grd) | N/Landsberg |
| | Lt. L.C. Reese | Ju-88 dest(grd) | N/Landsberg |

*Losses-*

**55th**: Lt. Delbert F. Blount (338th Ftr Sqn) POW
P-51D CL-H 44-13807
Suffered mechanical failure near Kempton.

**352nd**: Lt. Richard H. Casper (328th Ftr Sqn) KIA
P-51B PE-M 43-6906 "Patty III"
Ran out of fuel and crashed into the North Sea.

Lt. Elmo B. Dubay (328th Ftr Sqn) ASR
P-51D PE-H 44-13582
Ran out of fuel and bailed out northeast of Cromer.

Lt. James C. Lanter (328th Ftr Sqn) KIA
P-51B PE-I 43-24788
Ran out of fuel and crashed into the North Sea.

Lt. David T. Zimms (328th Ftr Sqn) ASR
P-51B PE-C 42-106694 "Stinky"
Ran out of fuel and bailed out northeast of Cromer.

Lt. Robert R. Lampman (328th Ftr Sqn) KIA
P-51B PE-Z 42-106459 "La Riena Peg"
Ran out of fuel and crashed into the North Sea.

**359th**: Lt. Luther C. Reese (370th Ftr Sqn) KIA
P-51B CS-E 43-7013
Hit by flak and crashed near Aalen.

Lt. Robert W. Siltamaki (370th Ftr Sqn) POW
P-51B CS-W 43-12147
Hit by flak near Aalen.

**361st**: Lt. Warren L. Ewert (375th Ftr Sqn) POW
P-51B E2-P 43-24768
Hit by flak near Biblis and bellied-in southwest of Darmstadt.

**479th**: Capt. Jack G. Grossenbacher (434th Ftr Sqn) KIA
P-38J L2-G 43-28647
Hit by flak northwest of Frankfurt and crashed near Kindsbach.

*Remarks*
352nd: Lt. Glenn R. Clark (328th Ftr Sqn) c/l; o.k.
P-51 PE-
Lt. Charles E. Rogers (328th Ftr Sqn) c/l; o.k.
P-51 PE-
353rd: 2-0 locos
356th: 1-0 loco, 1-5 vehicles
359th: 0-1 loco, 0-2 oil tanks
Lt. Chester R. Gilmore (368th Ftr Sqn) b/o Knollthen Park; o.k.
P-51B CV-Q 43-6935
361st: Lt. Barry H. Hicks (374th Ftr Sqn) c/l; o.k.
P-51B B7-H 42-106655 "Ferocious Frankie"
364th: 2-0 locos, 0-18 railcars

**July 22, 1944**
Groups Operating: P-51 4th
Missions: Support for bombers dropping leaflets on Bremen, Hamburg, and Kiel.
Claims: nil

*Losses-*

**4th**: Lt. Lloyd G. Kingham (335th Ftr Sqn) KIA
P-51D WD-R 44-13641
Suffered mechanical failure on take-off and spun-in near Audley End.

*Remarks*
4th: Lt. James W. Ayers (334th Ftr Sqn) c/l Carlton Hawthorne; o.k.
P-51B QP-Y
Lt. Maurice W. Miller (336th Ftr Sqn) c/l; o.k.
P-51D VF- 44-13649

**July 23, 1944**
Groups Operating: P-51 352nd, 359th, 361st
P-38 364th
Missions: Support for bombers to Creil, Juvincourt, Laon/Athies, and Laon/Couvron Airfields.
Claims: nil
Losses: nil

*Remarks*
361st: 6-0 locos, 7-20 railcars, 1-0 vehicle

**July 24, 1944**
Groups Operating: P-51 4th, 20th, 55th, 339th, 352nd, 355th, 357th, 359th
P-47 56th, 78th, 353rd, 356th
P-38 364th, 479th
Missions: Support for bombers to the Periers/St. Lo area and several P-51 groups swept the Lechfeld-Leipheim area.
Claims: 4-0-1 air
13-16 ground

| *Group* | | *Claims* | *Location* |
|---|---|---|---|
| **56th** | | | |
| HdQts: | LtCol. D.C. Schilling | (.5)Me-210 dest(grd) | Villaroche A/F |
| | | (.5)Me-210 dam(grd) | Villaroche A/F |
| 61st: | Lt. A.J. Bux | (.5)Me-210 dest(grd) | Villaroche A/F |
| | | (.5)Me-210 dam(grd) | Villaroche A/F |
| **355th** | | | |
| 354th: | Lt. G.C. Hoffman | He-280 dest(grd) | Lechfeld |
| | Lt. G.T. Patterson | He-280 dest(grd) | Lechfeld |
| | Capt. N.J. Fortier | Me-262 dam(grd) | Lechfeld |
| 357th: | Lt. J.A. Cotter | u/i a/c dest(grd) | Lechfeld |
| | | Me-109 dam(grd) | Lechfeld |
| | Lt. A.G. Gilleland | Do-217 dest(grd) | Lechfeld |
| | | Do-217 dam(grd) | Lechfeld |
| | | FW-190 dam(grd) | Lechfeld |
| | | Me-109 dam(grd) | Lechfeld |
| | Lt. C.J. Salinsky | Me-109 dam(grd) | Lechfeld |
| | | u/i a/c dam(grd) | Lechfeld |
| 358th: | Capt. W.J. Hovde | Do-217 dest(grd) | Augsburg |
| | | Ju-88 dest(grd) | Augsburg |
| | Lt. D.C. Blaylock | Do-217 dest(grd) | Augsburg |
| | | (3)Do-217 dam(grd) | Augsburg |
| | Lt. W.H. Douglas | FW-190 dest(grd) | Augsburg |
| | Lt. R.M. Dillon | Ju-88 dest(grd) | Augsburg |
| | | u/i a/c dam(grd) | Augsburg |
| | Lt. J.J. Maisch | Do-217 dest(grd) | Augsburg |
| | Lt. R.I. McNally | Ju-88 dest(grd) | Augsburg |
| | Lt. N.E. Peterson | Ju-88 dest(grd) | Augsburg |
| | Lt. H.W. Pardee | Do-217 dam(grd) | Augsburg |
| **359th** | | | |
| HdQts: | Col. A.P. Tacon | u/i a/c dam(grd) | Ulm |
| 368th: | Lt. D.W. Chatfield | (2)u/i a/c dam(grd) | Ulm |
| | Lt. J.P. Kelsey | u/i a/c dam(grd) | Ulm |
| 370th: | Lt. R.M. Callahan | Fi-156 dest(air) | Neu Ulm |
| | Lt. W.R. Newberg | Fi-156 dest(air) | Neu Ulm |
| | Lt. E.W. Tilton | Fi-156 dest(air) | Neu Ulm |
| **479th** | | | |
| 435th: | Capt. J.A. Sullivan | Me-109 dam(air) | SW Evreux |
| 436th: | Lt. H.J. Grasshoff | (.5)Me-109 dest(air) | Evreux |
| | Lt. H.P. Plunk | (.5)Me-109 dest(air) | Evreux |

*Losses-*

**355th**: Lt. Peter N. Sawchuck (354th Ftr Sqn) KIA
P-51C WR-J 42-103334 "Martin's Gloria"
Hit by flak at Lechfeld Airfield.

Lt. Wayne E. Walburn (358th Ftr Sqn) POW
P-51B YF-C 42-106780
Hit by flak at Lechfeld Airfield and bellied-in near Mindelheim.

**479th**: Lt. Alex Evanenko (435th Ftr Sqn) KIA
P-38J J2- 43-28716
Hit by flak and crashed five miles south of Dungeness.

Capt. Thomas T. Galloway (436th Ftr Sqn) KIA
P-38J 9B- 43-28419
Collided with Lt. Kemper southwest of Evreux.

Lt. Neil W. Kemper (436th Ftr Sqn) MIA-E
P-38J 9B- 44-23172
Collided with Capt. Galloway southwest of Evreux.

*Remarks*
4th: 0-28 locos, 8-210 railcars, 2-0 buildings, 0-3 boats
78th: 0-20 railcars
Lt. George G. Boteler (83rd Ftr Sqn) c/l Wattisham; o.k.
P-47D HL-
353rd: 8-0 locos, 3-2 vehicles
355th: 0-3 locos, 0-2 tugs
359th: 0-1 loco, 0-1 hangar

**July 25, 1944**
Groups Operating: P-51 4th, 20th, 55th, 339th, 355th, 357th, 361st
P-47 56th, 78th, 353rd, 356th
P-38 364th, 479th
Missions: Support for bombers to Periers/St. Lo and Brussels, plus fighter-bomber operations.
Claims: 11-0-5 air
2-0 ground

| *Group* | | *Claims* | *Location* |
|---|---|---|---|
| **55th** | | | |
| 338th: | Lt. T.D. Schank | (2)Me-109 dest(air) | Dreux A/F |
| | | (3)Me-109 dam(air) | Dreux A/F |
| **339th** | | | |
| HdQts: | Maj. J.R. Reynolds | FW-190 dest(air) | Etrepagny |
| 503rd: | Capt. E.B. Stephenson | Me-109 dest(air) | Etrepagny |
| | Capt. V. Wyatt | Me-109 dest(air) | Etrepagny |
| | Lt. E.H. Beavers | FW-190 dest(air) | Etrepagny |
| 505th: | Lt. J.G. Holloway | Me-109 dest(air) | Beauvais |
| **356th** | | | |
| 360th: | Capt. N.D. Cota | (.5)Me-109 dam(air) | NW Paris |
| | Lt. C.M. Taylor | (.5)Me-109 dam(air) | NW Paris |
| **357th** | | | |
| 362nd: | Capt. L.K. Carson | FW-190 dest(air) | Paris |
| | Capt. J.F. Pugh | Me-109 dest(air) | Versailles |
| 363rd: | Capt. D.H. Bochkay | Me-109 dest(air) | Paris |
| | | Me-109 dam(air) | Paris |
| | Capt. R.W. Foy | FW-190 dest(air) | SE Paris |
| **361st** | | | |
| 374th: | Capt. R.E. Locke | (.5)Me-109 dest(grd)* | N/Alencon |
| | Lt. J.O. Adkins | (.5)Me-109 dest(grd)* | N/Alencon |
| | Lt. H.B. Lederer | (.5)Me-109 dest(grd)** | N/Alencon |
| | Lt. M.L. Bryant | (.5)Me-109 dest(grd)** | N/Alencon |

*Losses-*

**55th**: Lt. Stoddard B. Gerald (338th Ftr Sqn) POW
P-51D CL- 44-13703
Hit by flak near Lisieux.

**361st**: Lt. Robert O. Comstock (376th Ftr Sqn) POW
P-51D E9- 44-13566
Took off late and was last seen trying to catch up with the rest of the group.

*Remarks*
56th: 3-0 vehicles
78th: 0-10 railcars, 1-1 vehicles

353rd: 0-1 loco, 1-2 vehicles
361st: 0-1 radio tower

KIAc's
339th: Lt. John W. Cozad (503rd Ftr Sqn)
P-51D D7-B 44-13662

**July 26, 1944**
Groups Operating: P-47 56th, 78th, 353rd, 356th
Missions: Fighter-bomber operations in the Givet-St. Just area.
Claims: 0-0-0 air
1-0 ground

| *Group* | | *Claims* | *Location* |
|---|---|---|---|
| **356th** | | | |
| HdQts: | LtCol. D.A. Baccus | He-111 dest(grd) | Cormeilles-en-Vixen |

*Losses-*

**78th**: Lt. Harold J. Morris (82nd Ftr Sqn) KIA
P-47D MX-V 42-26461
Hit trees while strafing west of Laval.

*Remarks*
56th: 0-4 locos, 0-185 railcars
78th: 0-1 loco, 0-20 railcars, 2-3 vehicles
353rd: 9-5 locos, 1-7 vehicles
356th: 7-60 railcars, 2-0 vehicles

**July 27, 1944**
Groups Operating: P-51 20th, 364th(mixed)
P-47 56th, 78th, 353rd, 356th
P-38 364th, 479th
Missions: Support for bombers to Brussels, Ostend, and the Pas de Calais area.
Claims: 0-0-0 air
0-1 ground

| *Group* | | *Claims* | *Location* |
|---|---|---|---|
| **479th** | | | |
| 434th: | Lt. Q.S. Pavlock | (.5)Ju-88 dam(grd) | Romilly |
| | Lt. W.H. Rodgers | (.5)Ju-88 dam(grd) | Romilly |

*Losses-*

**364th**: Lt. James B. MacDermott (383rd Ftr Sqn) POW
P-51D N2- 44-13878
Suffered mechanical failure and bailed out southeast of Arras.

**479th**: Lt. Marden L. McArthur (434th Ftr Sqn) KIA
P-38J L2-U 42-67865
Hit by flak near Chartres.

Lt. William B. McKay (435th Ftr Sqn) KIA
P-38J J2- 44-23160
Hit by flak near Jaulgonne.

*Remarks*
20th: Lt. Woodrow W. Williams (79th Ftr Sqn) b/o Bedford; o.k.
P-51 MC-
56th: 0-100 railcars
78th: 1-0 loco, 0-80 railcars, 26-48 vehicles
353rd: 1-0 loco, 0-10 railcars
356th: 2-0 vehicles, 0-2 buildings
364th: 1-0 loco
479th: 7-0 locos, 22-0 railcars, 0-12 flak towers, 0-4 buildings, 0-1 bridge.

**July 28, 1944**
Groups Operating: P-51 4th, 20th, 55th, 339th, 352nd, 355th, 357th, 359th, 361st, 364th(mixed)
P-47 56th, 78th, 353rd, 356th
P-38 364th, 479th
Missions: Support for bombers to Merseburg, Leipzig, Brussels, and V-1 sites in France.
Claims: 4-1-1 air
0-0 ground

| *Group* | | *Claims* | *Location* |
|---|---|---|---|
| **4th** | | | |
| 334th: | Capt. H.D. Hively | Me-109 prob(air) | Nordhausen |
| **339th** | | | |
| 505th: | Maj. D.A. Larson | Ju-52 dest(air) | Ansbach |
| **355th** | | | |
| 354th: | Capt. B.W. Marshall | Me-109 dest(air) | Mulhausen |
| 358th: | Lt. J.N. McElroy | Me-109 dest(air) | S/Merseburg |
| | | FW-190 dest(air) | S/Merseburg |
| | Lt. R.N. Watkins | Me-109 dam(air) | S/Merseburg |

*Losses-*

**55th**: Lt. Howard W. Rhodes (38th Ftr Sqn) MIA
P-51D CG-L 44-13609
Suffered mechanical failure near Naumburg and bailed out west of Merseburg.

**359th**: F/O Walter W. Wiley (370th Ftr Sqn) POW
P-51B CS-L 43-6961
Ran out of fuel and bailed out south of Rotterdam.

*Remarks*
4th: 0-3 locos, 0-30 railcars
78th: 1-2 locos, 3-0 vehicles
355th: 2-0 locos
356th: 1-2 locos, 13-0 vehicles
359th: 11-1 locos, 2-0 railcars, 4-0 vehicles
361st: 1-0 loco, 0-12 railcars, 1-0 vehicle

KIAc's
55th: Lt. Joseph K. Garnett (338th Ftr Sqn)
P-51 CL-
Died in a crash south of Boxted.

479th: Lt. Robert R. Teetor (436th Ftr Sqn)
P-38J 9B-

**July 29, 1944**
Groups Operating: P-51 4th, 20th, 55th, 339th, 352nd, 355th, 357th, 359th, 361st, 364th(mixed)
P-47 56th, 78th, 353rd, 356th
P-38 479th
Missions: Support for bombers to Merseburg, Bremen, Juvincourt Airfield and Laon/Couvron Airfield.
Claims: 23-2-4 air
3-3 ground

| *Group* | | *Claims* | *Location* |
|---|---|---|---|
| **20th** | | | |
| 77th: | Lt. L.W. Adams | (2)Me-109 dest(air) | Gutersloh |
| | Lt. R.E. Moncrieff | Me-109 dest(air) | Gutersloh |
| | | Me-109 dam(air) | Gutersloh |
| **339th** | | | |
| 504th: | Lt. F.S. Rutan | (2)Me-109 dest(air) | Naumburg |
| | Lt. H.S. Stockman | Me-109 dest(air) | Merseburg-Naumburg |
| | | Me-109 prob(air) | Merseburg-Naumburg |
| | | Me-109 dam(air) | Merseburg-Naumburg |
| | Lt. R.N. Attebury | FW-190 dest(air) | Naumburg |
| | Lt. J.R. Trester | Me-109 prob(air) | Merseburg-Naumburg |
| 505th: | Lt. W.H. Krauss | (.5)Me-109 dest(air) | NW Naumburg |
| | Lt. J.R. Starnes | (.5)Me-109 dest(air) | NW Naumburg |
| | Lt. W.F. Mudge | Ju-52 dest(grd) | NW Naumburg |
| | Lt. G.J. Hrico | (.5)Ju-52 dest(grd) | NW Naumburg |
| | Lt. W.A. Jones | (.5)Ju-52 dest(grd) | NW Naumburg |
| **352nd** | | | |
| 328th: | Lt. C.J. Bennette | Me-109 dest(air) | Merseburg |
| | | Me-109 dam(air) | Merseburg |
| | Lt. C.J. Cesky | FW-190 dest(air) | Merseburg |
| 486th: | Maj. G.E. Lundquist | (2)Me-109 dest(air) | Magdeburg |
| 487th: | Maj. G.E. Preddy | Me-109 dest(air) | Naumburg |
| | Capt. C.J. Palmer | Me-109 dest(air) | Merseburg |
| | Lt. A.F. Sears | Me-109 dest(air) | W/Naumburg |
| | Lt. S.K. Moats | Me-109 dest(air) | Merseburg |
| **356th** | | | |
| 359th: | Capt. G.B. Peet | He-111 dam(grd) | St. Andre de L'Eure |
| **357th** | | | |
| 362nd: | Capt. L.K. Carson | Me-109 dest(air) | W/Merseburg |
| | Lt. H.F. Mace | Me-109 dest(air) | W/Merseburg |
| | Lt. G.M. O'Brien | Me-109 dest(air) | W/Merseburg |
| | Capt. R.H. Becker | (.5)Me-109 dest(air) | W/Merseburg |
| | Lt. T.W. Martinek | (.5)Me-109 dest(air) | W/Merseburg |
| 363rd: | Capt. D.H. Bochkay | FW-190 dest(air) | SW Merseburg |
| | Lt. W.B. Overstreet | Me-109 dest(air) | W/Merseburg |
| | | FW-190 dest(grd) | W/Merseburg |
| | | FW-190 dam(grd) | W/Merseburg |
| | | Do-217 dam(grd) | W/Merseburg |
| 364th: | Lt. J.J. Salsman | FW-190 dam(air) | Merseburg |
| **479th** | | | |
| 434th: | Capt. A.F. Jeffrey | Me-163 dest(air) | Wilhelmshaven |

*Losses-*

**339th**: Lt. Ray N. Attebury (504th Ftr Sqn) POW
P-51B 5Q- 42-106642
Hit by enemy fighters near Rosslaben.

Lt. Fred S. Rutan, Jr. (504th Ftr Sqn) POW
P-51C 5Q- 42-103394 "Whistler's Wings"
Hit by a FW-190 near Naumburg and bailed out near Bad Frankenhausen.

Lt. Chris J. Hanseman (505th Ftr Sqn) KIA
P-51D 6N-H 44-13556 "Eleanor IV"
Wing hit the ground while strafing northwest of Naumburg.

**352nd**: Maj. Gustav E. Lundquist (486th Ftr Sqn) POW
P-51D PZ-M 44-13395
Hit by enemy fighters near Sanderhausen.

**357th**: Lt. Rollin L. Carter (362nd Ftr Sqn) POW
P-51B G4-Y 43-7143 "Miss Florida"
Suffered mechanical failure near Gelnhausen and bailed out south of Nordhausen.

Lt. Paul E. Holmberg (362nd Ftr Sqn) KIA
P-51B G4-I 43-6727
Aircraft exploded west of Merseburg.

Lt. Daniel L. Finley (364th Ftr Sqn) POW(D)
P-51B C5-A 42-106843 "Round Trip Jr."
Suffered mechanical failure near Bad Oeynhausen; later died in prison camp.

*Remarks*
55th: 5-1 locos
353rd: 33-8 locos, 2-25 railcars, 7-0 vehicles
361st: 4-1 locos, 1-2 barges

**July 30, 1944**
Groups Operating: P-51 55th, 339th, 357th
P-47 78th, 353rd
Missions: Sweeps of the Evreux-St. Quentin-Paris-Orleans area.
Claims: 3-0-1 air
9-0 ground

| *Group* | | *Claims* | *Location* |
|---|---|---|---|
| **353rd** | | | |
| 352nd: | Capt. L.P. Cles | (2.5)u/i a/c dest(grd) | Orleans/Bricy |
| | Lt. W.J. Jordan | (2.5)u/i a/c dest(grd) | Orleans/Bricy |
| | Lt. R. Eluhow | (2)u/i a/c dest(grd) | Orleans/Bricy |
| | Capt. V.N. Curtis | u/i a/c dest(grd) | Orleans/Bricy |
| | Lt. T.W. Jones | u/i a/c dest(grd) | Orleans/Bricy |
| **357th** | | | |
| 362nd: | Maj. T.L. Gates | Me-109 dest(air) | NW Paris |
| | | Me-109 dam(air) | NW Paris |
| | Lt. A.E. Smith | Me-109 dest(air) | NW Paris |
| 363rd: | Maj. E.W. Hiro | Me-109 dest(air) | W/Paris |

*Losses-*

**55th**: Lt. James D. Brokaw (343rd Ftr Sqn) MIA
P-51D CY- 44-13665
Suffered mechanical failure and bailed out near Brumetz.

KIAc's
364th: Lt. James R. Korecky (384th Ftr Sqn)
P-51D 5Y-D 44-14034
Stalled on take-off, clipped a parked B-17, and crashed at the end of the field at Honington.

**July 31, 1944**
Groups Operating: P-51 4th, 20th, 339th, 352nd, 355th, 357th, 359th, 361st, 364th
P-47 56th, 78th, 353rd, 356th
P-38 479th
Missions: Support of bombers to Munich, Ludwigshafen, and Creil and Laon/Athies Airfields.
Claims: 0-0-0 air
18-12 ground

| *Group* | | *Claims* | *Location* |
|---|---|---|---|
| **78th** | | | |
| 83rd: | Lt. W.E. Bennett | u/i a/c dest(grd) | Neustadt A/F |
| | Lt. W.J. Korsmeyer | u/i a/c dest(grd) | Neustadt A/F |
| | Lt. J.S. Reems | u/i a/c dest(grd) | Neustadt A/F |
| **339th** | | | |
| 505th: | Maj. J.L. Thury | (2)u/i a/c dest(grd) | Holzkirchen |
| | | (.5)Me-410 dest(grd) | Holzkirchen |
| | | u/i a/c dam(grd) | Holzkirchen |
| | Lt. W.F. Mudge | FW-190 dest(grd) | Holzkirchen |
| | | Me-110 dest(grd) | Holzkirchen |
| | | Ju-88 dest(grd) | Holzkirchen |
| | | (2)u/i a/c dam(grd) | Holzkirchen |
| | Lt. R.B. Olander | Ju-87 dest(grd) | Holzkirchen |
| | | u/i a/c dest(grd) | Holzkirchen |
| | | u/i a/c dam(grd) | Holzkirchen |
| | Lt. J.R. Starnes | FW-190 dest(grd) | Holzkirchen |
| | | u/i a/c dest(grd) | Holzkirchen |
| | | FW-190 dam(grd) | Holzkirchen |
| | Lt. T.B. Staggers | FW-190 dest(grd) | Holzkirchen |
| | | u/i a/c dest(grd) | Holzkirchen |
| | Lt. B.O. Jackson | FW-190 dest(grd) | Holzkirchen |
| | Lt. L.J. Powell | Me-410 dest(grd) | Holzkirchen |
| | | u/i a/c dam(grd) | Holzkirchen |
| | Lt. C.R. Stewart | u/i a/c dest(grd) | Holzkirchen |
| | | u/i a/c dam(grd) | Holzkirchen |
| | Lt. G.E. Graham | (.5)Me-410 dest(grd) | Holzkirchen |
| | | u/i a/c dam(grd) | Holzkirchen |
| | Lt. O.P. Farmer | (3)u/i a/c dam(grd) | Holzkirchen |
| | Lt. M.N. Nay | u/i a/c dam(grd) | Holzkirchen |

*Losses-*

**5th**: Lt. John W. Clark (ERS) KIA
P-47D 5F- 43-25711
Crashed into the Channel in bad weather.

**20th**: Lt. Leonard L. Richter (79th Ftr Sqn) KIA
P-51 MC-
Killed in a crash upon return.

**78th**: Lt. Willard J. Korsmeyer (83rd Ftr Sqn) POW
P-47D HL-V 42-26672
Hit by flak at Neustadt Airfield.

**352nd**: Lt. McDonald Godfrey (328th Ftr Sqn) POW
P-51B PE-G 42-106827 "Candy Lamb"
Spun-out in overcast near Brussels.

Lt. Edmond Zellner (328th Ftr Sqn) MIA-E
P-51D PE- 44-13910
Hit by flak near Charleroi and bailed out southwest of Brussels.

**361st**: Lt. William V. Staples (374th Ftr Sqn) KIA
P-51B B7-G 43-24840
Died in a crash at Cowlinge.

*Remarks*
56th: 0-3 locos, 3-2 vehicles

**August 1, 1944**
Groups Operating: P-51 4th, 20th, 55th, 339th, 352nd, 355th, 357th, 359th, 361st, 364th
P-47 56th, 353rd, 356th
P-38 479th
Missions: Support for bombers to airfields and bridges in France.
Claims: 1-0-0 air
3-0 ground

| *Group* | | *Claims* | *Location* |
|---|---|---|---|
| **353rd** | | | |
| 352nd: | Capt. J.N. Poindexter | Me-410 dest(grd) | Laon/Couvron |
| | Lt. R.P. Greenwood | Me-410 dest(grd) | Laon/Couvron |
| | F/O K. Ames | Me-410 dest(grd) | Laon/Couvron |
| **355th** | | | |
| 358th: | Lt. R.M. Dillon | Me-109 dest(air) | Chateaudun |

*Losses-*

**SF**: Capt. Vincent G. Dressendorfer (2nd) KIA
P-51D YF-C 44-13533
Hit by enemy fighters near La Loupe.

**353rd**: Lt. Delbert E. Harris (352nd Ftr Sqn) POW
P-47D SX-P 42-26036
Hit by flak south of Bourgtherovde.

F/O Kenneth Ames (352nd Ftr Sqn) KIA
P-47D SX-D 42-26533
Hit by flak at Laon/Couvron Airfield.

**355th**: Lt. Albert H. Debacker (357th Ftr Sqn) ASR
P-51C OS- 42-103009
Suffered mechanical failure and bailed out over the Channel.

**364th**: Lt. Niel T. Baker (384th Ftr Sqn) KIA
P-51C 5Y-F 43-25040
Collided with a P-51 on take-off from Honington and crashed at Tuddenham.

*Remarks*
4th: 2-0 vehicles
Lt. George D. Green (335th Ftr Sqn) b/o Bishop's Stortford; o.k.
P-51B WD-H
56th: 0-3 vehicles
339th: 0-8 locos, 0-120 railcars, 0-2 barges
P-51 c/l Manston; o.k.
P-51 c/l Ford; o.k.
353rd: 20-7 locos, 41-42 railcars, 2-1 vehicles

359th: Lt. Cornelius J. Cavanaugh (368th Ftr Sqn) b/o Hunsdon; o.k.
P-51 CV-
364th: Lt. Carl J. Pushcar (384th Ftr Sqn) b/o Tuddenham; o.k.
P-51D 5Y-W 44-13975

**August 2, 1944**
Groups Operating: P-51 4th, 20th, 339th, 352nd, 355th, 357th, 359th, 361st, 364th
P-47 56th, 78th, 353rd, 356th
P-38 479th
Missions: Support for bombers to bridges and tactical targets in France plus fighter-bomber operations.
Claims: 1-0-0 air
0-0 ground

| *Group* | | *Claims* | *Location* |
|---|---|---|---|
| **353rd** | | | |
| HdQts: | LtCol. B. Rimerman | Me-109 dest(air) | S/Compiegne |

*Losses-*

**4th:** Lt. Gerald C. Chapman (336th Ftr Sqn) KIA
P-51B VF- 43-6846
Hit by flak near Beauvais.

**20th:** Lt. Stephen J. Nelson (55th Ftr Sqn) KIA
P-51B KI-
Crashed at Werrington on take-off.

**78th:** Capt. Charles R. Clark (82nd Ftr Sqn) POW
P-47D MX-F 42-26314
Hit by flak and bailed out near Euverman.

**339th:** Lt. Lewis H. Schneider (504th Ftr Sqn) KIA
P-51B 5Q-U 42-106641
Hit by flak near Lassigny.

**355th:** Maj. John L. Elder (357th Ftr Sqn) ASR
P-51 OS-
Hit by flak near Albert and ditched in the Channel.

Lt. Franklin R. Gowing (357th Ftr Sqn) MIA-E
P-51B OS-R 42-106733
Hit by flak near St. Pol and bailed out near Concour.

Lt. Benjamin F. Orr, Jr. (358th Ftr Sqn) KIA
P-51B YF-C 43-6820
Hit by flak near Londimiernes.

**359th:** Capt. Robert W. Hawkinson (368th Ftr Sqn) MIA-E
P-51D CV-N 44-13386 "Miss Janet"
Hit by flak and bailed out near Rouen.

**364th:** Lt. Houston L. Braley (383rd Ftr Sqn) KIA
P-51D N2- 44-13797
Downed by bomb blast southwest of Compiegne.

**479th:** Lt. Fred A. Moser, Jr. (436th Ftr Sqn) POW
P-38J 9B- 42-104397
Hit by flak near Compenhout and bailed out near Brussels.

*Remarks*
4th: 0-3 locos, 0-32 railcars, 4-10 vehicles
20th: 0-7 locos, 0-3 railcars, 5-2 vehicles
56th: 0-2 buildings
78th: 1-1 locos, 13-45 railcars, 7-7 vehicles
339th: 3-0 locos, 0-15 railcars, 0-1 flak position
353rd: 23-5 locos, 118-117 railcars, 6-16 vehicles
355th: 0-12 locos, 0-63 railcars, 0-2 flak positions, 1-0 vehicle
Lt. John J. Gilmore(358th Ftr Sqn) c/l; o.k.
P-51B YF-T 43-6592
356th: 0-1 loco, 0-15 railcars, 0-2 bridges
359th: 0-2 vehicles
364th: 3-0 locos, 60-25 railcars, 4-0 vehicles
479th: 3-1 locos, 0-25 railcars, 0-11 buildings
P-38 c/l Debden; o.k.

**August 3, 1944**
Groups Operating: P-51 4th, 20th, 55th, 339th, 352nd, 355th, 357th, 359th, 361st, 364th
P-47 56th, 78th, 353rd, 356th
P-38 479th
Missions: Support for bombers to Pas de Calais V-1 sites, rail targets in France and Germany, oil targets in France and Belgium, and fighter-bomber operations.
Claims: 7-0-1 air
5-2 ground

| *Group* | | *Claims* | *Location* |
|---|---|---|---|
| **56th** | | | |
| 63rd: | Lt. R.B. Anderson | FW-190 dest(air) | SW Sarreburg |
| **339th** | | | |
| 505th: | Maj. D.A. Larson | Do-217 dest(grd) | Benestroff |
| | | FW-190 dest(grd) | Benestroff |
| | Lt. G.E. Graham | Do-217 dest(grd) | Benestroff |
| | Lt. A. Sirochman | u/i a/c dest(grd) | Benestroff |
| | | u/i a/c dam(grd) | Benestroff |
| | Lt. B.V. Shaw | FW-190 dam(grd) | Benestroff |
| **355th** | | | |
| 354th: | Capt. C.W. Lenfest | Me-109 dest(air) | E/Mannheim |
| | F/Lt. W.B. Peglar | Me-109 dest(air) | E/Mannheim |
| | | FW-190 dest(air) | E/Mannheim |
| 357th: | Capt. F.R. Haviland | FW-190 dest(air) | Sarreburg |
| | | Me-109 dam(air) | Sarreburg |
| | Capt. L.D. Minchew | Me-109 dest(air) | Baden Baden |
| | Lt. J.A. Cotter | Me-109 dest(air) | Baden Baden |
| **479th** | | | |
| 435th: | Capt. W.N. Gates | B-24 dest(grd) | Ensisheim |

*Losses-*

**4th:** Maj. Fonzo D. Smith (HdQts) POW
P-51D VF- 44-13934
Suffered mechanical failure near Athis.

**56th:** Lt. Roach S. Stewart (63rd Ftr Sqn) KIA
P-47D UN-S 42-25969
Hit by flak southwest of Sarreburg.

**355th:** Capt. Robert G. Kurtz (354th Ftr Sqn) POW
P-51D WR-A 44-14001
Hit by a Me-109 near Gompelscheuer.

Lt. Garlyn O. Hoffman (354th Ftr Sqn) POW
P-51B WR-H 43-24824 "Sophia S"
Collided with Lt. Patterson near Neuweiler.

Lt. Gilbert T. Patterson (354th Ftr Sqn) KIA
P-51B WR-X 43-6885 "Texas Terror III"
Collided with Lt. Hoffman near Neuweiler.

Lt. Floyd K. Taylor (354th Ftr Sqn) MIA-E
P-51D WR-K 44-13912
Suffered mechanical failure and bellied-in in Switzerland.

Lt. John A. Cotter (357th Ftr Sqn) POW
P-51D OS- 44-13654
Hit by flak while chasing a Me-109 near Mannheim.

*Remarks*
20th: 1-0 loco, 3-0 vehicles
55th: 1-0 loco, 0-25 railcars
56th: 17-14 locos, 1-114 railcars, 1-3 vehicles
78th: 10-3 locos, 21-80 railcars, 0-4 vehicles
339th: 2-10 railcars, 1-0 hangar, 1-0 gun position
355th: Lt. Edwin M. Hendrickson (357th Ftr Sqn) c/l; o.k.
P-51D OS-U 44-13353 "Gin Rummy"
479th: 6-6 locos, 2-8 railcars, 2-2 vehicles, 0-5 buildings

**August 4, 1944**
Groups Operating: P-51 4th, 20th, 55th, 339th, 352nd, 355th, 357th, 359th, 351st, 364th(mixed)
P-47 56th, 78th, 353rd, 356th
P-38 364th, 479th
Missions: Support of bombers to Hamburg, Kiel, Peenemunde, and other targets plus fighter-bomber operations.
Claims: 38-3-4 air
43-12 ground

| *Group* | | *Claims* | *Location* |
|---|---|---|---|
| **20th** | | | |
| 77th: | Lt. F.H. Alexander | He-111 dest(grd) | Putnitz |
| | Lt. G.R. Brucks | Ju-88 dam(grd) | Barth |
| | Lt. B.N. Rader | Ju-88 dam(grd) | Barth |
| **56th**(#1) | | | |
| 61st: | Lt. A.C. Maul | Me-109 dest(air) | S/Hamburg |
| | Maj. G.E. Baker | (.5)u/i a/c dest(grd)* | Salenter Lake |
| | Lt. C.E. Westman | (.5)u/i a/c dest(grd)* | Salenter Lake |
| | Lt. S.H. Getz | (.5)u/i a/c dest(grd)** | Salenter Lake |
| | Lt. J.M. Jure | (.5)u/i a/c dest(grd)** | Salenter Lake |
| (#2) | | | |
| HdQts: | Col. H. Zemke | (1.5)He-111 dest(grd) | Plantlunne |
| | | (2)He-111 dam(grd) | Plantlunne |
| 62nd: | Lt. B.G. Edens | (2)He-111 dest(grd) | Plantlunne |
| | | (2)He-111 dam(grd) | Plantlunne |
| | Lt. J.W. Ferguson | (.5)He-111 dest(grd) | Plantlunne |
| | Capt. M.J. Quirk | (3)He-111 dam(grd) | Plantlunne |

| | | | |
|---|---|---|---|
| **339th** | | | |
| 503rd: | Lt. L.J. Fiorito | FW-190 dest(air) | SW Hamburg |
| 505th: | Maj. D.A. Larson | (2)Me-109 dest(air) | Ulzen-Celle |
| | | Me-410 dest(grd) | E/Celle |
| | Lt. J.G. Holloway | Me-109 dest(air) | S/Hamburg |
| | Lt. A.E. Tongue | Me-109 dest(air) | Ulzen-Celle |
| | | (.5)Me-109 dest(air)* | Ulzen |
| | | (.5)Me-109 dest(air)** | S/Hamburg |
| | Lt. J.R. Starnes | Me-109 dest(air) | S/Hamburg |
| | Lt. L.J. Powell | FW-190 dest(air) | S/Hamburg |
| | | (.5)Me-109 dest(air)* | S/Hamburg |
| | Lt. J.B. Muller | (.5)Me-109 dest(air)** | Ulzen |
| | | Me-410 dest(grd) | E/Celle |
| | Lt. R.A. Rohm | Ju-88 dest(grd) | E/Celle |
| | Lt. B.V. Shaw | Ju-88 dest(grd) | E/Celle |
| | Lt. A. Sirochman | Ju-88 dest(grd) | E/Celle |
| | Lt. R.W. Strong | Ju-88 dest(grd) | E/Celle |
| | Lt. W.R. Slovak | Ju-88 dam(grd) | E/Celle |
| **353rd**(#1) | | | |
| HdQts: | Capt. C.L. Stafford | Me-109 dest(air) | SE Bremen |
| | | Me-109 dam(air) | SE Bremen |
| 350th: | Maj. K.W. Gallup | Me-109 dest(air) | Neunkirchen |
| | | Me-109 prob(air) | Neunkirchen |
| | Capt. E.S. Middleton | Me-109 dest(air) | NE Soltau |
| | Lt. O.I. Aal | Me-109 dest(air) | NE Hanover |
| | Lt. T.C. Creekmur | Me-109 dest(air) | E/Verdun |
| | Lt. J.O. Ruscitto | Me-109 dam(air) | Wenzendorf |
| 351st: | Lt. A.S. Hartley | (2)Me-109 dest(air) | Steinhuder Lake-Dummer Lake |
| | Lt. A.W. Barlow | Me-109 dest(air) | S/Bremen |
| | Lt. H. Moretz | Me-109 dest(air) | S/Bremen |
| | Lt. C.W. Craft | (2)Me-109 prob(air) | NE Bremen |
| | Lt. J.F. Hinchey | Me-109 dam(air) | S/Bremen |
| 352nd: | Lt. H.B. Tordoff | (2)Me-109 dest(air) | E/Bremen |
| | Lt. D.L. Barber | Me-109 dest(air) | E/Bremen |
| | Lt. H.O. Miller | (2)He-111 dest(grd) | Plantlunne |
| | Lt. R.P. Greenwood | He-111 dest(grd) | Plantlunne |
| (#2) | | | |
| HdQts: | LtCol. W.B. Bailey | (2)He-111 dest(grd) | Plantlunne |
| | | Ju-88 dest(grd) | Plantlunne |
| 350th: | Lt. V.G. Rafferty | (3)He-111 dest(grd) | Plantlunne |
| 351st: | Capt. L.G. Hally | He-111 dest(grd) | Plantlunne |
| | | Ju-88 dest(grd) | Plantlunne |
| | Capt. V.L. Byers | Ju-88 dest(grd) | Plantlunne |
| 352nd: | Lt. T.W. Jones | (2)He-111 dest(grd) | Plantlunne |
| | | u/i a/c dest(grd) | Plantlunne |
| | Capt. F.L. Uttwenweiler | (2)He-111 dest(grd) | Plantlunne |
| | Lt. E.D. Reinhardt | He-111 dest(grd) | Plantlunne |
| | | Me-410 dest(grd) | Plantlunne |
| | F/O J.J. Swanezy | He-111 dest(grd) | Plantlunne |
| | | Me-410 dest(grd) | Plantlunne |
| | Lt. H.B. Tordoff | He-111 dest(grd) | Plantlunne |
| | | u/i a/c dest(grd) | Plantlunne |
| | Lt. J.M. Tuttle | (2)u/i a/c dest(grd) | Plantlunne |
| | Lt. R.P. Greenwood | He-111 dest(grd) | Plantlunne |
| | Lt. W.J. Jordan | (.5)u/i a/c dest(grd) | Plantlunne |
| | Lt. G.N. Porterfield | (.5)u/i a/c dest(grd) | Plantlunne |
| **356th** | | | |
| 359th: | Capt. G.B. Peet | Me-109 dest(air) | NE Bremen |
| | Lt. L.G. Alphonse | Me-109 dest(air) | Selseigen-Ottersberg |
| | Lt. M.M. Clayborne | Me-109 dest(air) | Selseigen-Ottersberg |
| 360th: | Maj. J.W. Vogt | (2)Me-109 dest(air) | SW Hamburg |
| | Lt. W.H. Fletcher | (2)Me-109 dest(air) | SW Hamburg |
| | Lt. R.S. Gleason | Me-109 dest(air) | SW Hamburg |
| | Lt. T.D. Teel | Me-109 dest(air) | SW Hamburg |
| | Lt. J.H. Williams | Me-109 dest(air) | S/Hamburg |
| 361st: | Lt. H.E. Wiggins | (2)Me-109 dest(air) | Bremen-Hamburg |
| | Lt. E.L. Faison | Me-109 dest(air) | Bremen-Hamburg |
| | Lt. W.S. Hurley | Me-109 dest(air) | Bremen-Hamburg |
| | Lt. D.F. Thwaites | Me-109 dest(air) | Bremen-Hamburg |
| | Lt. R.E. Rodgers | Me-109 dam(air) | Bremen-Hamburg |
| **359th** | | | |
| 370th: | Lt. W.K. Baker | Me-110 dest(air) | Denmark |
| **361st** | | | |
| 376th: | Capt. S.C. Wilkerson | (2)Ju-88 dest(grd) | Anklam |
| | Lt. V.E. Bocquin | Ju-88 dest(grd) | Anklam |
| | | Ju-88 dam(grd) | Anklam |
| | Lt. R.R. Volkman | Ju-88 dam(grd) | Anklam |

*Losses-*

**20th**: Capt. Donald A. Reihmer (HdQts) MIA-E
P-51D LC-R 44-13696
Hit by flak west of Peenemunde.

Capt. Harry B. Baker (55th Ftr Sqn) KIA
P-51D KI-
Crashed on take-off from Kingscliffe.

**339th**: Maj. Donald A. Larson (505th Ftr Sqn) KIA
P-51D 6N-B 44-13881
Collided with Lt. Burns northwest of Ulzen.

Lt. Robert F. Burns (505th Ftr Sqn) POW
P-51D 6N- 44-13897
Collided with Maj. Larson northwest of Ulzen.

Lt. Roland W. Strong (505th Ftr Sqn) POW
P-51B 6N- 43-24773
Hit by flak near Wilhelmshaven.

**353rd**: Lt. Harry V. Aldridge (350th Ftr Sqn) KIA
P-47D LH- 42-76268
Hit by flak near Oldenzaal.

Lt. Denny L. Yocum (350th Ftr Sqn) KIA
P-47D LH-Z 42-26663
Hit by enemy fighters near Bremen.

**356th**: Lt. Joseph W. Mills (361st Ftr Sqn) KIA
P-47D QI-S 42-25842
Last seen with Me-109's near Hamburg.

**357th**: Lt. Wallace J. Reid (364th Ftr Sqn) POW
P-51B C5- 42-106978
Lost coolant and bailed out northeast of Kiel.

**359th**: Capt. Raymond B. Lancaster (370th Ftr Sqn) INT
P-51D CS-W 44-13939
Lost oil pressure and landed in Sweden.

Lt. Wilson K. Baker, Jr. (370th Ftr Sqn) INT
P-51B CS-Q 43-6461 "Hot Pants"
Escorted Capt. Lancaster to Sweden.

Lt. Richard O. Rabb (370th Ftr Sqn) INT
P-51B CS-F 43-12463
Escorted Capt. Lancaster to Sweden.

**361st**: Lt. Pernin G. Potts (374th Ftr Sqn) POW
P-51B B7-M 42-106820
Suffered mechanical failure and bailed out near Heligoland.

Lt. Joseph V. Kapr (375th Ftr Sqn) KIA
P-51B E2-R 42-106741
Hit by flak and bailed out northeast of Stralsund.

Capt. Samuel C. Wilkerson (376th Ftr Sqn) POW
P-51D E9-O 44-13673
Hit by flak and bailed out southeast of Griefswald.

**364th**: Lt. Clyde W. Diffenbach (383rd Ftr Sqn) POW
P-51D N2- 44-13922
Last seen near Roeby Haun with mechanical problems.

Lt. John F. Potochnik (383rd Ftr Sqn) POW
P-51D N2- 44-13920
Hit by flak and bailed out north of Zingst.

**479th**: Capt. Elmer Hartman (436th Ftr Sqn) KIA
P-38J 9B-
Crashed on take-off from Wattisham.

*Remarks*

4th: 0-8 locos
56th: 2-0 locos, 0-25 railcars, 0-8 barracks, 0-2 hangars, 0-1 barge
353rd: 5-3 locos, 3-0 vehicles, 7-5 flak positions, 2-2 hangars, 2-2 buildings
P-47 c/l Wattisham; o.k.
359th: 0-1 boat
361st: 0-1 loco
364th: 0-10 railcars

**August 5, 1944**

Groups Operating: P-51 4th, 20th, 55th, 339th, 352nd, 355th, 359th, 361st, 364th(mixed)
P-47 56th, 78th, 353rd, 356th
P-38 364th, 479th

Missions: Support of bombers to Magdeburg, Halberstadt, Nienburg, Brunswick, Hanover, and V-1 sites in the Calais area.

Claims: 29-3-9 air
4-5 ground

| *Group* | | *Claims* | *Location* |
|---|---|---|---|
| **4th** | | | |
| 336th: | Capt. J.T. Godfrey | Me-109 dest(air) | N/Osnabruck |
| | | (3)Ju-52 dest(grd) | SE Munden |
| | | (3)Ju-52 dam(grd) | SE Munden |

*Formation of 62nd Fighter Squadron P-47's in July 1943. First three planes are LM-R 42-7870 "Pappy" of Horace Craig, LM-X 41-6224 "Two Roll Charlie", and LM-O 41-6347 "Lil Abner" of Eugene O'Neill.*

*Dave Schilling's 62nd Fighter Squadron P-47, LM-S 42-7938.*

*354th Fighter Squadron P-47 of Robert Woody, WR-W 42-8493.*

*Robert Johnson's second P-47 of the 61st Fighter Squadron, HV-P 42-8461 "Lucky."*

*63rd Fighter Squadron P-47 of Walker Mahurin, UN-M 42-8487.*

*Another view of Eugene O'Neill's P-47C "Lil Abner."*

*YJ-N 42-74706 "Babe" of the 351st Fighter Squadron.*

*Joe Egan with his 63rd Thunderbolt UN-E 41-6230 "Holy Joe."*

*358th Fighter Squadron P-47 of Walter Kossack after a force- landing on September 14, 1943. YF-X 42-8455.*

*The mount of 359th Fighter Squadron CO Donald Baccus, OC-I 42-8568 "The Bloody Shaft..."*

*CV-S 42-22766 of the 368th Fighter Squadron*

*Virgil Meroney's 487th Fighter Squadron P-47, HO-V 42-8473 "Sweet Louise"*

*A 55th Fighter Group P-38 which crash-landed on November 13, 1943.*

*Wayne O'Connor with his P-47C of the 63rd Fighter Squadron, UN-O 41-6216.*

*Walter Kossack's later 358th Fighter Squadron plane after he was captured on November 7, 1943. YF-X 42-8477.*

*Ace Jack Price, who flew with both the 78th and 20th Fighter Groups.*

*Another two group ace, Jack Oberhansly, who served with the 78th and 4th Fighter Groups.*

*Right: Phil Tukey while CO of the 63rd Fighter Squadron. After service with the 56th, Tukey would fly two more tours as CO of the 356th Fighter Group.*

*Don Baccus, seen here with his 356th Fighter Group P-47, would end the war as CO of the 359th Fighter Group.*

*Harold Rau came overseas as CO of the 356th Fighter Group, moved to 8th Air Force Headquarters, then served as CO of the 20th Fighter Group two times. The plane here is his first "Gentle Annie", QI-R 42-8425.*

*Future ace Frank Emory and his 351st Fighter Squadron Thunderbolt, YJ-E 42-8602 "Sis."*

The 8th Air Force's first ace, Charles London of the 83rd Fighter Squadron.

*Joe Myers of the 38th Fighter Squadron with his crew of "Journey's End". Myers would fly tours with the 55th and 78th Fighter Groups before flying yet another with the 55th late in the war.*

*Another early ace for the 8th was Frank McCauley of the 61st Fighter Squadron seen here in HV-Z 41-6271 "Rat Racer."*

*Legendary ace Glenn Duncan of the 353rd Fighter Group. The P-47 shown here was LH-X 42-8634 "Dove of Peace IV."*

*Leading Thunderbolt scorer of the 4th Fighter Group was Duane Beeson of the 334th Fighter Squadron.*

*Eugene Roberts of the 78th Fighter Group was the 8th's second ace and ended the war as CO of the 364th Fighter Group.*

*Right: Ray Withers of the 360th Fighter Squadron with his PI-N "Kathleen Ann."*

*Leroy Schreiber who flew with the 61st and 62nd Fighter Squadrons before his death in April 1944.*

*343rd Fighter Squadron ace Frank Birtciel.*

*Joe Powers who also flew with the 61st and 62nd Fighter Squadrons.*

*Early photo of 350th Fighter Squadron ace Wayne Blickenstaff.*

*Trio of 56th Fighter Group aces with Bob Johnson's "Lucky" L-R Johnson, Hubert Zemke, Bud Mahurin.*

Henry Brown, top scorer of the 355th Fighter Group.

Ralph Hofer of the 334th Fighter Squadron who claimed a kill on his first mission in October 1943.

Mike Quirk of the 62nd Fighter Squadron.

George Carpenter, 335th Fighter Squadron ace.

*Operations Officer and later CO of the 63rd Fighter Squadron, Sylvester Burke.*

*Publicity shot of 56th Fighter Group pilots; L-R on wing: Walt Cook and Dave Schilling, standing: Francis Gabreski, Bob Johnson, Bud Mahurin, Robert Landry (non-ace and 56th CO).*

*369th Fighter Squadron armorer Anthony Chardella with P-47D IV-E 42-74645.*

*P-47's of the 370th Fighter Squadron showing the early code letters. Second from left is CR-P 42-74737.*

*E9-Z 42-75105 of the 376th Fighter Squadron.*

*Well worn P 51B of the 335th Fighter Squadron, WD-Q 43-6770.*

*363rd Fighter Squadron P-51B in early February 1944, B6-K 43-6628 "Typhoon McGoon."*

*Mike Quirk's LM-K 42-75242 of the 62nd Fighter Squadron.*

*P-47's of the 361st Fighter Squadron ready to roll. In foreground is William Waller's QI-A 42-8482 "Skeeter, Kiss O'Death" with James Johnson's QI-G 42-8436 in back.*

*P-47 of 370th Fighter Squadron ace Ray Wetmore, CS-P 42-75068.*

| | | | |
|---|---|---|---|
| | Lt. F.W. Glover | Me-109 dest(air) | Gardelegen |
| **20th** | | | |
| 77th: | Capt. M.J. Gilbertson | Me-109 dest(air) | NW Hamburg |
| | Lt. E.C. Fiebelkorn | Me-109 dest(air) | S/Hamburg |
| | Lt. L.E. Rowlett | Me-109 dam(air) | S/Hamburg |
| 79th: | Lt. H.O. Binkley | Me-109 dest(air) | Hamburg-Bremen |
| | Lt. R.E. Campbell | Me-109 dest(air) | Hamburg-Bremen |
| | | Me-109 dam(air) | Hamburg-Bremen |
| | Lt. G.M. Webb | Me-109 dam(air) | Hamburg-Bremen |
| **339th** | | | |
| 503rd: | Maj. J. Aitken | (2)FW-190 dest(air) | S/Hameln |
| | Capt. W.E. Bryan | FW-190 dest(air) | S/Hameln |
| | Lt. E.H. Graham | Me-109 dam(air) | S/Hameln |
| **352nd** | | | |
| 486th: | Lt. D.J. French | (2)Me-109 dest(air) | Wilhelmshaven |
| | | Me-109 dam(air) | Wilhelmshaven |
| | Lt. D.Y. Whinnem | Me-109 prob(air) | S/Hamburg |
| | | Me-109 dam(air) | S/Hamburg |
| 487th: | Maj. G.E. Preddy | Me-109 dest(air) | S/Hamburg |
| | | Me-109 prob(air) | S/Hamburg |
| | Lt. G.T. Moran | Me-109 dest(air) | S/Hamburg |
| | Lt. A.F. Sears | Me-109 dest(air) | S/Hamburg |
| | Lt. G.P. Taylor | Me-109 dest(air) | S/Hamburg |
| **353rd** | | | |
| 350th: | Maj. K.W. Gallup | Me-109 dest(air) | Rheine |
| **359th** | | | |
| 369th: | Capt. E.F. Pezda | Me-109 dest(air) | Tarmstedt |
| | Capt. L.G. Taylor | FW-190 dest(air) | Tarmstedt |
| | Lt. H.R. Burt | Me-109 dest(air) | Tarmstedt |
| | Lt. E.L. Sjoblad | Me-109 dest(air) | Bremen |
| | Lt. F.W. Holliday | Me-109 dam(air) | Bremen-Hamburg |
| **361st** | | | |
| 374th: | Lt. H.B. Lederer | Me-109 dest(air) | Hoperhofen |
| | | Me-109 dam(air) | Hoperhofen |
| | Lt. P.C. Holter | Me-109 dest(air) | Hoperhofen |
| | Lt. G. Lichter | Me-109 dest(air) | Hoperhofen |
| 375th: | Lt. S. Armsby | Me-109 dest(air) | N/Nienburg |
| | Lt. D.W. Edwards | Me-109 dest(air) | S/Bremen |
| | Capt. W.G. Shackleford | Do-217 dest(grd) | Alhorn |
| | | (2)Me-163 dam(grd) | Alhorn |
| **479th** | | | |
| 435th: | Capt. R.S. Carter | Me-109 dest(air) | S/Hamburg |
| | | Me-109 prob(air) | S/Hamburg |
| | Capt. G.K. Sykes | Me-109 dest(air) | S/Hamburg |
| | | Me-109 dam(air) | S/Hamburg |
| 436th: | Capt. C.J. Moore | Me-109 dest(air) | NE Stendal |
| | Lt. M.S. Mickey | Me-109 dest(air) | NE Stendal |

*Losses-*

**20th**: Lt. Irwin W. Fernandes (77th Ftr Sqn) KIA
P-51D LC-Y 44-13713
Hit by enemy fighters near Zoven.

**78th**: Lt. John J. Myler (84th Ftr Sqn) KIA
P-47D WZ-P 42-74723
Hit by flak east of Bremen.

**339th**: Lt. Edward C. Flaherty (503rd Ftr Sqn) KIA
P-51 D7-
Collided with a P-51 on take-off and crashed near Thriplow.

**352nd**: Lt. David J. French (486th Ftr Sqn) POW
P-51B PZ-F 43-6864
Hit by enemy fighters near Appeln.

Lt. Clifford R. Wilcox (487th Ftr Sqn) POW
P-51C HO-C 42-103312 "Channel Belle"
Hit by enemy fighters near Ziesar.

**353rd**: Lt. John J. Hatch (351st Ftr Sqn) KIA
P-47D YJ-D 42-26027 "Georgie Fay"
Suffered mechanical failure and bailed out east of Felixstowe.

**479th**: Lt. Carl W. Moore (435th Ftr Sqn) KIA
P-38J J2- 43-28472
Suffered mechanical failure near Ottensen.

*Remarks*

4th: 0-9 locos, 0-10 railcars, 0-2 oil tanks
20th: 6-26 railcars
55th: 0-1 loco, 1-0 vehicle
56th: 4-4 locos, 22-26 railcars, 18-3 vehicles
78th: 2-1 locos, 0-1 railcar
339th: 0-1 radar tower
Lt. Frank M. Stillwell (503rd Ftr Sqn) b/o; o.k.
P-51 D7-
353rd: 0-2 locos
356th: 2-0 locos
359th: 1-0 loco

**August 6, 1944**

Groups Operating: P-51 4th, 20th, 55th, 339th, 352nd, 355th, 357th, 359th, 361st, 364th(mixed)
P-47 56th, 78th, 353rd, 356th
P-38 364th, 479th

Missions: Support of bombers to Berlin, Brandenburg, Hamburg, and Pas de Calais V-1 sites. The 357th also took "Frantic II" bombers to Russia with a small contingent remaining in England to continue operations from there.

Claims: 33-0-6 air
4-3 ground

| *Group* | | *Claims* | *Location* |
|---|---|---|---|
| **4th** | | | |
| 336th: | Capt. J.T. Godfrey | Me-410 dest(air) | NE Berlin |
| | | Me-109 dam(grd) | SE Berlin |
| | Capt. O.M. Glass | (2)Ju-52 dest(grd) | SE Berlin |
| | | Me-109 dam(grd) | SE Berlin |
| | | Ju-52 dam(grd) | SE Berlin |
| | Lt. F.W. Glover | Me-109 dest(grd) | SE Berlin |
| | Lt. J.A. Patteeuw | Me-410 dest(grd) | SE Berlin |
| **20th** | | | |
| HdQts: | LtCol. C. Wilson | FW-190 dam(air) | Potsdam |
| 55th: | Lt. J.E. Klink | Do-217 dest(air) | Strausburg A/F |
| | Lt. J.L. Mansker | FW-190 dest(air) | S/Brandenburg |
| | Lt. K.C. Smeltz | FW-190 dest(air) | Schonfeld A/F |
| 77th: | Lt. F.H. Alexander | (2)Me-109 dest(air) | Belzig |
| | Lt. B.N. Rader | Me-109 dest(air) | Potsdam |
| 79th: | Lt. W.H. Lewis | Me-109 dest(air) | SW Berlin |
| | | Me-109 dam(air) | SW Berlin |
| **78th** | | | |
| 82nd: | Capt. R.E. Conner | (.5)Me-109 dest(air) | Hamburg |
| | Lt. J.B. Stallings | (.5)Me-109 dest(air) | Hamburg |
| | F/O R.I. Miller | Me-109 dam(air) | Hamburg |
| | Lt. H.K. Shope | Me-109 dam(air) | Hamburg |
| **339th** | | | |
| 503rd: | Capt. E.B. Stephenson | Me-109 dest(air) | S/Schweriner Lake |
| | Lt. W.W. Behrend | Me-109 dest(air) | S/Schweriner Lake |
| | Lt. P.D. Fickel | Me-109 dest(air) | S/Schweriner Lake |
| 504th: | Lt. D.E. Penny | Me-109 dest(air) | Havelburg |
| | Lt. M.R. Winkelman | Me-109 dest(air) | Havelburg |
| | Lt. R.T. Wood | Me-109 dest(air) | Havelburg-Pritzwalk |
| | Lt. D.A. Zeine | Me-109 dest(air) | Havelburg |
| **352nd** | | | |
| 328th: | Lt. C.J. Cesky | (2)Me-109 dest(air) | E/Luneburg |
| 486th: | Capt. H.J. Miklajcyck | (2)Me-109 dest(air) | SE Hamburg |
| 487th: | Maj. G.E. Preddy | (6)Me-109 dest(air) | Luneburg-Havelburg |
| | F/O C.B. Doleac | Me-109 dest(air) | Hamburg |
| | Lt. S.L. Heyer | Me-109 dest(air) | Hamburg |
| **355th** | | | |
| 354th: | Capt. C.W. Lenfest | Me-109 dest(air) | S/Hamburg |
| | Capt. B.W. Marshall | Me-109 dest(air) | S/Hamburg |
| | Lt. W.D. Martin | Me-109 dest(air) | S/Hamburg |
| **357th** | | | |
| 364th: | Lt. R.M. Shaw | Me-109 dest(air) | N/Warsaw |
| | Lt. K.M. Brown | (.5)Ju-88 dest(air) | NE Warsaw |
| | Lt. N.J. Frederick | (.5)Ju-88 dest(air) | NE Warsaw |
| | Maj. J.A. Storch | FW-190 dam(air) | Danzig |
| | Lt. H.R. Nowlin | Me-109 dam(air) | NE Warsaw |

*Losses-*

**20th**: Lt. Walker L. Whiteside (77th Ftr Sqn) KIA
P-51D LC-J 44-13792
Hit by enemy fighters near Hennickendorf.

**78th**: F/O Gene T. Cumming (84th Ftr Sqn) POW
P-47D WZ-H 42-76584
Suffered mechanical failure and bailed out near Bissel.

**339th**: Lt. Victor W. Meyer (503rd Ftr Sqn) KIA
P-51D D7-J 44-13601
Hit by a Me-109 and bailed out north of Hamburg.

Lt. Franklin D. Talcott (503rd Ftr Sqn) INT
P-51D D7-L 44-13917 "You've Had It"
Suffered a coolant leak and landed in Sweden.

Lt. Arthur E. Tongue, Jr. (505th Ftr Sqn) KIA
P-51B 6N- 42-106842
Spun-in five miles east of Cambridge.

**352nd**: Lt. Walter Gehrke (328th Ftr Sqn) KIA
P-51C PE-J 42-103787
Lost a wing east of Luneburg.

**355th**: Lt. John M. Folger (354th Ftr Sqn) KIA
P-51B WR-Q 43-7127
Hit by a Me-109 near Bremervoerde.

*Remarks*
4th: 0-4 locos, 10-3 railcars
20th: 1-0 loco, 2-2 railcars, 1-0 hangar
56th: 4-2 locos, 0-6 railcars, 3-1 vehicles, 1-0 building
352nd: 0-3 locos
355th: 5-10 railcars
359th: 2-0 locos, 55-6 railcars

KIAc's
352nd: Capt. Quentin L. Quinn (328th Ftr Sqn)
P-51 PE-
Died in a crash near Thetford.

353rd: Lt. Thomas C, Creekmur (350th Ftr Sqn)
P-47D LH-R
Died in a crash near Weeping Hill.

**August 7, 1944**
Groups Operating: P-51 4th, 20th, 55th, 339th, 352nd, 355th, 357th, 359th, 361st, 364th
P-47 56th, 78th, 353rd, 356th
P-38 479th
Missions: Support for bombers hitting bridges and fuel dumps in France along with ground attacks in the Paris area. The 357th Group also escorted their Russia based bombers to Trzebinia and landed back in Russia.
Claims: 4-0-2 air
3-3 ground

| *Group* | | *Claims* | *Location* |
|---|---|---|---|
| **353rd** | | | |
| 350th: | Lt. S.T. Benjamin | Me-410 dest(grd) | SE Amiens |
| | Lt. M.V. Bledsoe | Me-410 dest(grd) | SE Amiens |
| | Lt. W.P. Knowling | Me-410 dest(grd) | SE Amiens |
| | Lt. M.W. Hightshoe | Me-410 dam(grd) | SE Amiens |
| | | Me-109 dam(grd) | SE Amiens |
| **357th** | | | |
| 362nd: | Capt. J.F. Pugh | FW-190 dest(air) | Cracow |
| 364th: | Lt. H.R. Nowlin | (1.5)Me-109 dest(air) | Oswiecim |
| | Maj. J.A. Storch | (.5)Me-109 dest(air) | Oswiecim |
| **361st** | | | |
| 375th: | Lt. W.T. Kemp | FW-190 dest(air) | Chartres |
| | | FW-190 dam(air) | Chartres |
| | | (.5)Me-109 dam(grd) | Chartres |
| | Lt. U.L. Drew | Me-109 dam(air) | Chartres |
| | Lt. L.A. Wood | (.5)Me-109 dam(grd) | Chartres |

*Losses-*

**4th**: Lt. Donald M. Malmsten (334th Ftr Sqn) MIA-E
P-51B QP-U 43-24979
Bellied-in after a flak hit near Dijon.

Lt. Sidney V. Wadsworth (335th Ftr Sqn) POW
P-51B WD-V 43-6437
Hit by flak near Pont de Pany.

**56th**: Lt. Arthur C. Maul (61st Ftr Sqn) KIA
P-47D HV-M 42-25836 "Pengie III"
Collided with a P-47 near Marlers.

F/O Robert W. Magel (63rd Ftr Sqn) POW
P-47D UN-G 42-75206
Hit by flak at a marshalling yard near Peronne.

**353rd**: Lt. Richard Daines (352nd Ftr Sqn) KIA
P-47D SX-I 42-26631
Hit by flak near Dernancourt.

*Remarks*
4th: 1-86 locos, 0-199 railcars, 2-6 vehicles, 0-2 buildings
56th: 1-6 locos, 14-66 railcars, 6-5 vehicles
353rd: 19-2 locos, 85-86 railcars, 55-66 vehicles, 0-3 flak positions
Lt. George N. Porterfield (352nd Ftr Sqn) c/l; o.k.
P-47D SX-N
355th: 0-1 loco, 2-34 railcars, 0-3 flak positions
357th: 5-28 railcars
359th: 0-1 vehicle
361st: 3-0 vehicles, 0-25 railcars, 0-3 flak towers
364th: 4-3 locos, 0-15 railcars
479th: 2-2 locos, 0-172 railcars, 0-3 barges, 2-1 vehicles, 0-2 flak towers, 0-2 buildings

**August 8, 1944**
Groups Operating: P-51 4th, 55th, 339th, 352nd, 355th, 357th, 359th, 361st, 364th
P-47 56th, 78th, 353rd, 356th
P-38 479th
Missions: Support for bombers to V-1 sites in the Pas de Calais area and airfields in France; he 4th escorted RAF Beaufighters, to Norway; the 357th escorted their "Frantic" bombers to targets in Romania then landed in Italy; and fighter-bomber operations.
Claims: 5-0-7 air
1-0 ground

| *Group* | | *Claims* | *Location* |
|---|---|---|---|
| **4th** | | | |
| 335th: | Capt. F.C. Jones | Ju-88 dest(grd) | Stravanger/Sola |
| **357th** | | | |
| 363rd: | Capt. R.N. Moore | Me-109 dest(air) | Crocil(Romania) |
| **359th** | | | |
| 368th: | Lt. J.S. Keesey | FW-190 dest(air) | Dreux |
| | | (3)FW-190 dam(air) | Dreux |
| | Lt. C.J. Cavanaugh | FW-190 dam(air) | Dreux |
| **361st** | | | |
| HdQts: | LtCol. W.E. Hopkins | (2)FW-190 dest(air) | Evreux |
| 374th: | Lt. E.W. Kepplinger | FW-190 dest(air) | Evreux |
| | | FW-190 dam(air) | Evreux |
| | Lt. J.O. Adkins | FW-190 dam(air) | Evreux |
| **479th** | | | |
| 436th: | Lt. H.J. Grasshoff | Me-109 dam(air) | S/Paris |

*Losses-*

**4th**: Lt. Thomas A. Underwood (334th Ftr Sqn) POW
P-51B QP-C 43-24793
Hit by flak and bailed out near Varnaug.

Capt. Frank C. Jones (335th Ftr Sqn) KIA
P-51D WD-P 44-14027
Hit by flak leaving Norway and crashed into the North Sea.

Lt. Robert G. Fischer (335th Ftr Sqn) KIA
P-51B WD-N 42-106940
Hit by flak near Stravanger/Sola Airfield.

**78th**: Lt. James T. Fitzgerald, Jr. (82nd Ftr Sqn) POW
P-47D MX-J 43-25536
Hit by flak east of Brias.

**339th**: Lt. Edwin C. Ball (505th Ftr Sqn) KIA
P-51B 6N- 42-106937
Hit by flak near Roulers.

**353rd**: Lt. Robert S. Hart (350th Ftr Sqn) KIA
P-47D LH- 42-26454
Caught by a bomb blast near Gaudechard.

**355th**: Lt. Robert Bernoske (357th Ftr Sqn) MIA-E
P-51B OS-Z 42-106815
Hit by flak northeast of Vitry.

Lt. Charles M. Lee (357th Ftr Sqn) KIA
P-51B OS-V 43-6835
Hit by flak near St. Dizier.

**359th**: Lt. John C. Allen (368th Ftr Sqn) KIA
P-51B CV-I 42-106867
Hit by flak near Dreux.

Lt. Willis J. Cherry (368th Ftr Sqn) KIA
P-51B CV-X 42-106577 "Pegelin"
Hit by enemy fighters near Poix and bailed out near Sommery.

**361st**: Lt. Jacob L. Rawls (374th Ftr Sqn) MIA-E
P-51B B7-X 42-106586
Lost for unknown reasons near Dreux.

**364th**: Lt. William P. Dean (385th Ftr Sqn) KIA
P-51D 5E- 44-14008
Hit by flak near Fresquienne.

**479th**: Capt. John J. Courtney, Jr. (435th Ftr Sqn) MIA-E
P-38J J2- 43-28426
Hit trees while strafing near Rauieres.

*Remarks*
4th: 0-2 locos, 3-15 railcars, 3-17 vehicles
56th: 13-57 railcars, 2-0 vehicles
78th: 2-1 locos, 1-71 railcars, 10-4 vehicles, 1-1 building
339th: 2-1 locos, 4-516 railcars, 0-2 vehicles
352nd: 0-1 loco, 0-1 vehicle
353rd: 3-4 locos, 42-94 railcars, 10-7 vehicles, 1-0 flak position
355th: 0-10 locos, 16-215 railcars, 0-48 vehicles, 0-2 barges, 0-2 flak towers
356th: 7-11 locos, 6-113 railcars, 2-6 vehicles, 0-5 flak towers
357th: Lt. Howard Egeland (362nd Ftr Sqn) c/l Russia; o.k.
P-51B G4-W 43-6721
359th: 0-34 railcars, 8-3 vehicles, 0-2 flak towers
361st: 16-17 locos, 156-520 railcars, 23-92 vehicles, 1-2 bridges, 0-1 barge, 0-1 boat
479th: 9-7 locos, 17-19 railcars, 5-1 vehicle, 0-2 buildings

**August 9, 1944**
Groups Operating: P-51 4th, 20th, 55th, 339th, 352nd, 355th, 357th, 359th, 361st, 364th
P-47 56th, 78th, 353rd, 356th
P-38 479th
Missions: Support for bombers to various targets in southeastern Germany; many of the heavies were recalled.
Claims: 31-2-10 air
29-24 ground

| *Group* | | *Claims* | *Location* |
|---|---|---|---|
| **20th** | | | |
| HdQts: | LtCol. J.P. Randolph | Me-109 dest(air) | S/Augsburg |
| 55th: | Lt. R.I. Brown | Me-109 dest(air) | S/Augsburg |
| | Lt. D.R. Franklin | Me-109 dest(air) | S/Augsburg |
| 79th: | Lt. Q. Klatt | (2.5)Me-109 dest(air) | SW Ulm |
| | Capt. R.J. Meyer | (2)FW-190 dest(air) | SW Ulm |
| | | FW-190 dam(air) | SW Ulm |
| | Capt. W.W. Smith | (2)FW-190 dest(air) | SW Ulm |
| | | FW-190 dam(air) | SW Ulm |
| | Lt. R.W. Bebout | (2)FW-190 dest(air) | SW Ulm |
| | Capt. J.O. Yaryan | FW-190 dest(air) | SW Ulm |
| | Lt. H.O. Binkley | FW-190 dest(air) | SW Ulm |
| | | FW-190 dam(air) | SW Ulm |
| | Lt. J.E. Carpenter | FW-190 dest(air) | SW Ulm |
| | Lt. K.C. Price | FW-190 dest(air) | SW Ulm |
| | | FW-190 dam(air) | SW Ulm |
| | Lt. F.H. Roark | FW-190 dest(air) | SW Ulm |
| | Lt. J.N. Reichard | (.5)FW-190 dest(air) | SW Ulm |
| | Lt. J.L. Armstrong | FW-190 dam(air) | SW Ulm |
| **359th** | | | |
| 368th: | Lt. J.S. Keesey | FW-190 prob(air) | Munich |
| | F/O E.C. Cook | Me-109 dam(air) | Munich |
| 370th: | LtCol. J.B. Murphy | FW 190 dest(air) | Gunzburg |
| | Lt. C.W. Jones | Me-109 dest(air) | Gunzburg |
| | | Me-109 dam(air) | Gunzburg |
| | Lt. F.O. Lux | Me-109 dest(air) | Gunzburg |
| | Lt. E.W. Tilton | Me-109 dest(air) | Gunzburg |
| | Lt. R.M. York | Me-109 dest(air) | Gunzburg |
| | Lt. J.W. Wilson | Me-109 prob(air) | Gunzburg |
| **364th** | | | |
| 383rd: | Maj. G.F. Ceuleers | FW-190 dest(air) | Munich |
| | | (2)FW-190 dam(air) | Munich |
| | Lt. E.C. Beaumont | FW-190 dest(air) | Munich |
| | Lt. R.P. Davis | FW-190 dest(air) | Munich |
| | Lt. C.K. Voss | FW-190 dest(air) | Munich |
| | Capt. M.W. Glascow | (2)Ju-88 dest(grd) | W/Munich |
| | | (.5)u/i a/c dest(grd) | W/Munich |
| | Lt. P.J. Goldberg | (1.5)u/i a/c dest(grd) | W/Munich |
| | | u/i a/c dam(grd) | W/Munich |
| | Lt. M.E. Coates | FW-190 dest(grd) | W/Munich |
| | | Ju-88 dest(grd) | W/Munich |
| | | Me-109 dam(grd) | W/Munich |
| | Lt. T.H. Hall | (2)Ju-88 dest(grd) | W/Munich |
| | Lt. A.J. Acosta | u/i a/c dest(grd) | W/Munich |
| | | Ju-88 dam(grd) | W/Munich |
| | | u/i a/c dam(grd) | W/Munich |
| 384th: | Capt.C.H. Leo | FW-190 dest(air) | Kaufburen |
| | Capt. J.R. Steinbacher | FW-190 dest(air) | Kaufburen |
| | Capt. J.M. Stuckrath | FW-190 dest(air) | Kaufburen |
| | Lt. J.J. Gawienowski | (.5)FW-190 dest(air)[*] | Kaufburen |
| | | (.5)u/i a/c dest(air) | Kaufburen |
| | | Me-109 dam(grd) | Schongen |
| | Lt. F.T. Kozloski | (.5)FW-190 dest(air)[*] | Kaufburen |
| | | (.5)u/i a/c dest(air) | Kaufburen |
| | | FW-190 dam(grd) | Schongen |
| | Lt. W.N. Champion | (.5)FW-190 dest(air)[**] | Kaufburen |
| | Lt. J.E. Wilson | (.5)FW-190 dest(air)[**] | Kaufburen |
| | Lt. W.P. Derr | FW-190 dam(grd) | Kaufburen |
| | Lt. J.L. Grimshaw | Me-410 dam(grd) | Schongen |
| 385th: | Lt. R. Visconte | (3)Me-109 dest(grd) | Gaukonigshafen |
| | | Me-110 dest(grd) | Gaukonigshafen |
| | | Me-110 dam(grd) | Gaukonigshafen |
| | | (.5)FW-200 dam(grd) | Gaukonigshafen |
| | Capt. F.C. McClanahan | Me-109 dest(grd) | Gaukonigshafen |
| | | Me-210 dest(grd) | Gaukonigshafen |
| | Lt. R.A. Crouch | Me-109 dest(grd) | Gaukonigshafen |
| | | Me-210 dest(grd) | Gaukonigshafen |
| | Lt. D.J. Hustead | (2)Me-110 dest(grd) | Gaukonigshafen |
| | | (3)Me-110 dam(grd) | Gaukonigshafen |
| | | (.5)FW-200 dam(grd) | Gaukonigshafen |
| | Lt. E.L. Wilson | Me-110 dest(grd) | Gaukonigshefen |
| | | Me-210 dest(grd) | Gaukonigshafen |
| | | (2)Me-110 dam(grd) | Gaukonigshafen |
| | Lt. W.G. Erfkamp | Me-210 dest(grd) | Gaukonigshafen |
| | | Me-210 dam(grd) | Gaukonigshafen |
| | Lt. H.H. Stubblefield | Me-110 dest(grd) | Gaukonigshafen |
| | | (4)Me-110 dam(grd) | Gaukonigshafen |
| **479th** | | | |
| 434th: | Lt. W.H. Hehn | (2)He-111 dest(grd) | Nuneburg |
| | | Ju-52 dam(grd) | Nuneburg |
| | Maj. F.J. Keller | FW-200 dest(grd) | Nuneburg |
| | | (.5)He-111 dam(grd) | Nuneburg |
| | Lt. G.D. Hendrix | Ju-88 dest(grd) | Nuneburg |
| | Lt. H.E. Mathews | FW-200 dest(grd) | Nuneburg |
| | Lt. T.D. Neely | He-111 dest(grd) | Nuneburg |
| | | (.5)He-111 dam(grd) | Nuneburg |

*Losses-*

**356th**: Lt. Robert E. Rodgers (361st Ftr Sqn) POW
P-47D QI-M 42-26272 "Angel Eyes"
Hit by flak in the Trier-Liege area.

**364th**: Lt. Theodore J. Nielson (384th Ftr Sqn) MIA
P-51D 5Y-N 44-13766
Hit by flak at Kitzingen and bailed out southeast of Rottenberg

**479th**: Maj. Frank J. Keller (434th Ftr Sqn) POW
P-38J L2-I 43-28377 "Hilo Hattie"
Hit by flak and bailed out west of Furth.

*Remarks*
4th: 1-18 locos, 17-176 railcars, 0-1 flak tower
56th: 9-17 locos, 32-297 railcars, 5-1 vehicles
78th: 21-2 locos, 0-13 railcars, 2-2 vehicles
339th: 0-1 boat
353rd: 7-3 locos, 37-127 railcars, 14-33 vehicles, 2-0 flak positions
356th: 11-2 locos, 0-50 railcars, 2-0 vehicles, 1-0 building, 0-1 flak position
359th: 2-0 locos
364th: 1-0 loco, 2-0 barracks, 1-0 vehicle, 0-1 gun position

KIAc's
361st: Lt. Donald D. Dellinger (375th Ftr Sqn)
P-51D E2-S 44-13926
Died in a crash near Stalham.

**August 10, 1944**
Groups Operating: P-51 4th, 20th, 55th, 352nd, 355th, 357th, 359th, 361st, 364th
P-47 56th, 78th, 356th
P-38 479th
Missions: Support of bombers to targets around Paris and fighter-bomber operations. The 357th also escorted some C-47's in Italy.
Claims: 8-0-0 air
19-5 ground

| *Group* | | *Claims* | *Location* |
|---|---|---|---|
| **55th** | | | |
| 338th: | Capt. L.D. Anderson | Me-109 dest(air) | Damville |
| | Lt. J.R. Eskridge | Me-109 dest(air) | Damville |
| | Lt. S.E. Hansard | Me-109 dest(air) | Damville |
| | Lt. W.J. Ingram | Me-109 dest(air) | Damville |
| **78th** | | | |
| 82nd: | Lt. R.R. Bosworth | Ju-88 dest(grd) | Verdun |
| | Lt. R.W. Dunham | Ju-88 dam(grd) | Verdun |
| 83rd: | Capt. C.M. Peal | (2.5)Ju-52 dest(grd)[*] | Chateau-Salines |
| | | (1.5)He-111 dest(grd)[**] | Chateau-Salines |
| | LtCol. O.E. Gilbert | He-111 dest(grd) | Chateau-Salines |
| | | u/i a/c dest(grd) | Chateau-Salines |
| | Capt. R.R. Bonebrake | He-111 dest(grd) | Chateau-Salines |
| | | Ju-52 dest(grd) | Chateau-Salines |
| | Lt. R.T. Green | (1.5)He-111 dest(grd)[**] | Chateau-Salines |
| | | (.5)Ju-52 dest(grd)[*] | Chateau-Salines |
| | Lt. R.L. Burgher | He-111 dest(grd) | Chateau-Salines |
| | | (.5)Ju-52 dest(grd)[@] | Chateau-Salines |
| | Lt. J.S. Reems | He-111 dest(grd) | Chateau-Salines |
| | | (.5)Ju-52 dest(grd)[@] | Chateau-Salines |
| | Lt. D.J. DeVilliers | He-111 dest(grd) | Chateau-Salines |
| | Lt. G. Riccardo | (.5)He-111 dest(grd)[@@] | Chateau-Salines |
| | | u/i a/c dam(grd) | Chateau-Salines |
| | F/O J.A. Moothart | (.5)He-111 dest(grd)[@@] | Chateau-Salines |

| | | | |
|---|---|---|---|
| | Lt. K.P. Dunaway | He-111 dam(grd) | Chateau-Salines |
| | | Ju-52 dam(grd) | Chateau-Salines |
| | Lt. J.B. Miller | u/i a/c dam(grd) | Chateau-Salines |
| 84th: | Lt. H.F. Beck | (1.5)Ju-88 dest(grd) | Conflans |
| | Lt. W.K. Grimes | Me-109 dest(grd) | Conflans |
| | | (.5)Ju-88 dest(grd) | Conflans |
| **364th** | | | |
| 383rd: | Maj. G.F. Ceuleers | Me-109 dest(air) | NW Paris |
| | Lt. C.K. Voss | Me-109 dest(air) | W/Paris |
| 384th: | Capt. D.J. Pick | Me-109 dest(air) | SW Paris |
| | Lt. L.A. Johnson | Me-109 dest(air) | SW Paris |

*Losses-*

**20th:** Lt. Lee W. Anderson (55th Ftr Sqn) MIA
P-51D KI- 44-13679
Hit by flak at Epioux.

Lt. William D. Rollins (77th Ftr Sqn) KIA
P-51D LC-J 44-13811
Hit by flak near Heispelt.

**55th:** Lt. David G. Elliott (38th Ftr Sqn) POW(E)
P-51D CG-K 44-13623
Damaged by ground explosion near Sommesous.

Lt. William H. Lewis (38th Ftr Sqn) MIA
P-51D CG-O 44-13973
Hit by flak near Montmirail.

Lt. Lester E. Jaklish (38th Ftr Sqn) MIA
P-51D CG-W 44-13888
Hit by flak in the Fere-Champenoise area.

Lt. Arthur M. McFarland (338th Ftr Sqn) KIA
P-51D CL-J 44-14007
Hit trees while strafing near Chalons.

**78th:** Lt. Louis A. Dicks (82nd Ftr Sqn) KIA
P-47D MX-Q 42-26333
Hit by flak north of Epernay.

**357th:** Capt. Edward K. Simpson, Jr. (363rd Ftr Sqn) KIA
P-51D B6-V 44-13712 "Reluctant Rebel"
Collided with Lt. Ferron west of Sens.

Lt. Donald J. Ferron (363rd Ftr Sqn) KIA
P-51B B6- 42-106696
Collided with Capt. Simpson west of Sens.

**359th:** Lt. Lester W. Hovden (368th Ftr Sqn) KIA
P-51B CV-X 42-106702
Lost a wing while dive-bombing near Bishwiller.

Lt. Paul E. McCluskey (369th Ftr Sqn) KIA
P-51C IV-M 42-103743
Hit by flak near Wingen.

**364th:** Lt. Paul J. Goldberg (383rd Ftr Sqn) MIA-E
P-51C N2-B 43-25058
Hit by a Me-109 near Dreux.

**479th:** LtCol. Kyle L. Riddle (HdQts) MIA-E
P-38J J2-Q 44-23171
Hit by flak near Meaux.

Lt. James E. Fleming, Jr. (434th Ftr Sqn) KIA
P-38J L2-W 43-28341 "Scat"
Hit by flak near Romery.

*Remarks*

4th: 0-14 locos, 1-7 railcars, 0-1 flak ower
20th: 37-21 locos, 15-235 railcars, 2-3 vehicles, 3-2 buildings
55th: 28-5 locos, 90-122 railcars, 19-12 vehicles, 6-3 barges, 6-1 flak towers
56th: 0-23 locos, 38-17 railcars, 22-2 vehicles
78th: 12-9 locos, 110-245 railcars, 2-1 vehicles, 0-2 flak towers
352nd: 0-3 locos, 4-61 railcars, 2-3 vehicles, 0-3 buildings
356th: 8-4 locos, 87-217 railcars, 22-27 vehicles, 1-0 barge
359th: 5-12 locos, 3-30 railcars, 1-0 vehicle, 1-0 bridge, 1-0 building
361st: 1-20 locos, 0-12 railcars, 5-3 vehicles
364th: 0-20 railcars
479th: 9-4 locos, 18-112 railcars, 6-0 vehicles, 0-18 flak positions

KIAc's

359th: Lt. Lawrence A. Bearden (369th Ftr Sqn)
P-51 IV-
Flipped over and spun-in at East Wretham.

**August 11, 1944**

Groups Operating: P-51 4th, 20th, 55th, 339th, 352nd, 355th, 357th, 361st
P-47 56th, 78th, 353rd, 356th
P-38 479th

Missions: Support of bombers hitting targets on the Brest Peninsula plus fighter-bomber operations.

Claims: 4-0-0 air
3-0 ground

| ***Group*** | | ***Claims*** | ***Location*** |
|---|---|---|---|
| **78th** | | | |
| 84th: | Lt. C.E. Parmelee | (2)Me-109 dest(air) | NW Paris |
| **353rd**(#1) | | | |
| 350th: | LtCol. K.W. Gallup | u/i a/c dest(grd) | Maraville |
| | Lt. J.O. Ruscitto | Me-109 dest(grd) | Maraville |
| (#2) | | | |
| 351st: | Capt. V.L. Byers | Me-109 dest(air) | S/Paris |
| | Lt. M.B. Hungate | Me-109 dest(air) | S/Paris |
| **355th** | | | |
| 354th: | F/Lt. W.B. Peglar | Ju-52 dest(grd) | Saarbrucken |

*Losses-*

**355th:** Lt. Frank Michela (358th Ftr Sqn) KIA
P-51B YF-H 43-6649
Hit by flak near Metz.

*Remarks*

4th: 1-2 locos, 1-8 railcars
Lt. Willard G. Gillette (334th Ftr Sqn) b/o Haverhill; o.k.
P-51D QP-B 44-13372
20th: 1-4 locos
55th: 22-0 locos, 7-0 vehicles, 1-0 flak tower
339th: Lt. Ely N. Van Cleave (504th Ftr Sqn) c/l Luton; o.k.
P-51 5Q-
353rd: 6-4 gun positions
355th: 0-9 locos
361st: 1-0 loco, 3-12 vehicles

KIAc's

353rd: Lt. Robert A. Metz (350th Ftr Sqn)
P-47D LH-R
Crashed while trying to land at Raydon after a test hop.

**August 12, 1944**

Groups Operating: P-51 4th, 20th, 55th, 339th, 352nd, 355th, 357th, 359th, 361st, 364th
P-47 56th, 78th, 353rd, 356th
P-38 479th

Missions: Support for bombers hitting airfields and marshalling yards in Belgium and France, fighter-bomber operations, and the 357th flew home from Italy.

Claims: 5-1-0 air
11-1 ground

| ***Group*** | | ***Claims*** | ***Location*** |
|---|---|---|---|
| **56th**(#1) | | | |
| 61st: | Maj. B.M. Gladych | Ju-88 dest(air) | Cambrai |
| (#2) | | | |
| 63rd: | Capt. R.T. Fling | Me-109 dest(air) | Maubeuge |
| **353rd** | | | |
| HdQts: | LtCol. B. Rimerman | Ju-88 dest(grd) | SW Coulommiers |
| 351st: | Lt. J.F. Hinchey | Ju-88 dest(grd) | SW Coulommiers |
| | Lt. W.K. Lahke | Me-109 dest(grd) | SW Coulommiers |
| | Lt. C.W. Craft | (.5)Ju-88 dam(grd) | SW Coulommiers |
| | Lt. H. Moretz | (.5)Ju-88 dam(grd) | SW Coulommiers |
| 352nd: | Lt. R.P. Greenwood | (2)u/i a/c dest(grd) | E/Paris |
| | | FW-190 dest(grd) | E/Paris |
| | Lt. T.W. Jones | (2)He-111 dest(grd) | E/Paris |
| | Lt. R.R. Akard | FW-190 dest(grd) | S/Tournan |
| | Lt. E.D. Reinhardt | FW-190 dest(grd) | S/Tournan |
| | Lt. R. Eluhow | (.5)u/i a/c dest(grd) | E/Paris |
| | Lt. W.J. Jordan | (.5)u/i a/c dest(grd) | E/Paris |
| **356th** | | | |
| 361st: | Lt. E.C. Fremaux | (.5)Ju-88 dest(air) | Guise-Avesnes |
| | | (.5)Ju-88 dest(air) | Guise-Avesnes |
| | Capt. D.B. Clayton | (.5)Ju-88 dest(air) | Guise-Avesnes |
| | Lt. R.W. Gillette | (.5)Ju-88 dest(air) | Guise-Avesnes |
| **357th** | | | |
| 364th: | Lt. M.F. Allen | Ju-188 prob(air) | W/Toulosse |
| | (Note-this was later proven to actually be an Allied Mosquito) | | |
| **479th** | | | |
| 434th: | Lt. G.D. Hendrix | Ju-88 dest(air) | Compiegne |

*Losses-*

**20th**: Lt. Alvin F. Clark (77th Ftr Sqn) MIA-E
P-51D LC-B 44-13775
Hit by debris from an exploding train and bailed out near Reims.

Lt. Paul Denbo (79th Ftr Sqn) MIA
P-51D MC-H 44-13620
Hit by flak near Peche.

**55th**: Lt. Richard J. Keogh (338th Ftr Sqn) POW
P-51D CL- 44-14028
Damaged by an ground explosion near Boult.

Lt. James R. McCutcheon (338th Ftr Sqn) KIA
P-51D CL-A 44-13744
Hit by flak near Revigny.

Lt. William E. McMillan (338th Ftr Sqn) KIA
P-51D CL-S 44-13739
Hit the ground while strafing near Prunay.

**56th**: Lt. William H. Barnes (61st Ftr Sqn) MIA-E
P-47D HV- 42-75704
Suffered mechanical failure near Landries.

**352nd**: Lt. Gerald D. Thurman (486th Ftr Sqn) MIA
P-51D PZ-I 44-13736 "Dotty"
Suffered mechanical failure and crashed into the Channel.

Lt. Robert W. Graham (487th Ftr Sqn) POW
P-51D HO-B 44-13619 "William's Villian"
Hit by flak near Marest.

**353rd**: Lt. Raymond P. Greenwood (352nd Ftr Sqn) MIA-E
P-47D SX-O 42-26570
Hit by flak near Paris.

Lt. James M. Tuttle (352nd Ftr Sqn) MIA-E
P-47D SX-J 42-22466
Damaged by a bomb blast near Melun.

**355th**: Lt. Francis L. Eshelman (357th Ftr Sqn) MIA-E
P-51B OS-I 43-6626 "Terry Fran"
Lost coolant and bailed out near Meaux.

**356th**: Lt. Herbert P. Causer (360th Ftr Sqn) MIA-E
P-47D PI-Y 42-26271
Hit by flak in the Paris area.

Lt. Lester H. Knapp (360th Ftr Sqn) KIA
P-47D PI- 42-26563
Hit by flak near Montcornet.

**361st**: Col. Thomas J.J. Christian, Jr. (HdQts) KIA
P-51D E2-C 44-13410 "Lou IV"
Hit by flak near Arras.

Lt. Clarence Zieske (374th Ftr Sqn) KIA
P-51B B7-A 42-106942
Hit by flak near Dernancourt.

Lt. John E. Engstrom (375th Ftr Sqn) MIA-E
P-51B E2-G 42-106778
Hit by flak near Salmagne.

Lt. Merle C. Rainey (375th Ftr Sqn) POW
P-51B E2-C 42-106787
Hit by flak near Tournai.

*Remarks*
4th: Lt. Jerome E. Jahnke (334th Ftr Sqn) b/o Bradwell Bay; o.k.
P-51 QP-T
20th: 17-3 locos, 8-75 railcars, 40-19 vehicles, 2-13 barges
55th: 48-13 locos, 112-187 railcars, 6-0 vehicles, 1-0 barge
56th: 27-23 locos, 90-163 railcars, 36-23 vehicles
78th: 8-0 locos, 55-0 railcars
352nd: 0-5 locos, 61-21 railcars, 0-3 vehicles, 0-16 barges
353rd: 13-13 locos, 88-107 railcars, 39-8 vehicles, 6-0 buildings
355th: 0-4 locos, 6-20 railcars, 30-2 vehicles
356th: 15-12 locos, 65-349 railcars, 13-4 vehicles
357th: Capt. Maurice F. Baker (362nd Ftr Sqn) c/l Italy;
P-51D G4-O 44-13517 "Sebastian Jr."
359th: 0-1 loco, 3-35 railcars, 2-2 vehicles
Lt. John T. Gordon (368th Ftr Sqn) c/l East Wretham; o.k.
P-51 CV-
361st: 5-2 locos, 9-97 railcars, 7-2 vehicles
364th: Capt. Adrian D. Parsley (384th Ftr Sqn) c/l Eastbourne; o.k.
P-51D 5Y-H 44-13750

**August 13, 1944**
Groups Operating: P-51 4th, 55th, 339th, 352nd, 355th, 359th, 361st 364th
P-47 56th, 78th, 353rd, 356th
P-38 479th
Missions: Support of bombers hitting targets from Le Havre to Paris plus fighter-bomber operations.
Claims: nil

*Losses-*

**4th**: Lt. Stephen R. Boren (335th Ftr Sqn) KIA
P-51D WD-W 44-13997
Hit trees while strafing near Troesnes.

**55th**: Lt. Robert M. Littlefield (38th Ftr Sqn) MIA-E
P-51D CG-V 44-13577
Hit by flak near Rouen.

Lt. Donald D. Gilmore (338th Ftr Sqn) KIA
P-51D CL-B 44-13360
Hit by flak near Serans.

**78th**: Lt. Billy V. Smith (82nd Ftr Sqn) KIA
P-47D MX- 42-26512
Control wire broke while landing and crashed at Duxford.

**339th**: Lt. Myer R. Winkelman (504th Ftr Sqn) KIA
P-51D 5Q-B 44-13521
Hit by a bomb blast near St. Just.

Lt. Andrew Sirochman (505th Ftr Sqn) MIA-E
P-51B 6N-Q 42-106918
Damaged by an explosion near St. Omer.

**352nd**: Lt. Leroy J. Allain, Jr. (328th Ftr Sqn) POW
P-51B PE-R 42-106460 "Lois"
Hit by flak near Royville.

Lt. Harry H. Barnes (487th Ftr Sqn) POW
P-51D HO-V 44-13588
Hit by flak near Fauville.

**353rd**: Lt. Max K. Graham (350th Ftr Sqn) KIA
P-47D LH- 42-26269
Hit by flak near Gambais.

Lt. George W. McInis (350th Ftr Sqn) KIA
P-47D LH- 42-8404
Hit by flak near Gambais.

Capt. Victor N. Curtis (352nd Ftr Sqn) MIA-E
P-47D SX-Y
Hit by flak and bellied-in somewhere in France.

**356th**: Lt. Henry L. Lewis (361st Ftr Sqn) KIA
P-47D QI-X 42-75230
Hit by British ground fire while crossing the English coast.

**361st**: Lt. Robert H. Magnuson (374th Ftr Sqn) POW
P-51B B7-E 42-106839
Lost for unknown reasons northeast of Orleans.

Lt. Loren L. Montgomery (374th Ftr Sqn) POW
P-51D B7-O 44-13857
Hit by flak near Orleans.

*Remarks*
4th: 1-30 locos, 33-135 railcars, 11-6 vehicles
55th: 9-1 locos, 9-147 railcars, 3-0 vehicles
56th: 3-9 locos, 24-112 railcars, 14-5 vehicles
352nd: 2-0 vehicles
353rd: 10-1 locos, 51-41 railcars, 150-92 vehicles, 1-1 bridge, 0-2 flak positions
355th: 28-2 vehicles, 6-0 railcars, 0-2 flak towers
356th: 9-8 locos, 38-108 railcars, 9-2 vehicles, 2-1 flak towers, 1-0 bridge
359th: 10-0 railcars, 2-4 vehicles, 0-2 bridges, 0-1 gun position
Lt. Don W. Chatfield (368th Ftr Sqn) b/o; o.k.
P-51 CV-
361st: 31-50 railcars, 3-4 vehicles
364th: 14-10 railcars, 0-1 bridge

**August 14, 1944**
Groups Operating: P-51 4th, 20th, 55th, 339th, 352nd, 355th, 357th, 359th, 361st, 364th
P-47 56th, 78th, 353rd, 356th
P-38 479th
Missions: Support of bombers to Mannheim, Stuttgart, Kaiserlautern, and various airfields and rail targets in France plus the P-47 and P-38 units carried out fighter-bomber operations.
Claims: 3-0-0 air
7-10 ground

| *Group* | | *Claims* | *Location* |
|---|---|---|---|
| **353rd** | | | |
| 350th: | Lt. R.F. Unangst | Ju-88 dest(air) | Chateau Thierry |
| **364th** | | | |
| 383rd: | Lt. M.L. Casagrande | (2)He-111 dest(grd) | Memmingen |
| | | Ju-88 dest(grd) | Memmingen |
| | | (2)He-111 dam(grd) | Memmingen |
| | Lt. E. Levin | (2)He-111 dest(grd) | Memmingen |
| | | (3)He-111 dam(grd) | Memmingen |
| | Maj. J.B. McManus | He-111 dest(grd) | Memmingen |
| | | He-111 dam(grd) | Memmingen |
| | Lt. W.T. Dalton | Me-410 dest(grd) | Memmingen |
| | | He-111 dam(grd) | Memmingen |
| | Lt. A.J. Acosta | (2)Me-410 dam(grd) | Memmingen |
| | Lt. N.M. Staranick | He-111 dam(grd) | Memmingen |
| **479th** | | | |
| 434th: | Capt. R. Olds | (2)FW-190 dest(air) | Montmirail |

*Losses-*

**78th**: Capt. Charles M. Peal (83rd Ftr Sqn) KIA
P-47D HL-X 42-26449
Hit by flak near Noyon.

**355th**: Lt. William A. Shade (357th Ftr Sqn) MIA-E
P-51D OS-S 44-13734
Hit by flak near Saarebourg.

**356th**: Lt. Louis G. Alphonse (359th Ftr Sqn) KIA
P-47D OC-C 42-8491
Was chasing a Me-109 near Laval when Allied ground fire shot him down.

**479th**: Lt. Thomas J. O'Holleran (436th Ftr Sqn) POW
P-38J 9B- 43-28432
Hit by flak near Rheims.

*Remarks*

55th: 17-0 locos, 10-78 railcars, 0-1 building
56th: 3-3 locos, 30-68 railcars, 10-2 vehicles, 2-11 barges
78th: 1-0 loco, 30-74 railcars
Capt. Wallace E. Bennett (83rd Ftr Sqn) c/l Duxford; o.k.
P-47D HL-O 42-75196
353rd: 8-11 locos, 21-81 railcars, 4-0 vehicles, 0-2 buildings
355th: 1-27 locos, 3-65 railcars, 0-80 vehicles, 1-3 buildings
356th: 1-0 loco, 2-11 railcars, 0-3 vehicles
359th: 1-1 locos, 0-24 railcars, 1-1 vehicles
479th: 1-1 locos, 0-65 railcars, 4-0 vehicles, 0-4 bridges

**August 15, 1944**

Groups Operating: P-51 4th, 20th, 55th, 339th, 352nd, 355th, 357th, 359th, 361st, 364th
P-47 56th, 78th, 353rd, 356th
P-38 479th

Missions: Support of bombers to numerous airfields in Germany, Belgium, and Holland plus fighter-bomber operations.

Claims: 14-0-1 air
9-11 ground

| *Group* | | *Claims* | *Location* |
|---|---|---|---|
| **56th** | | | |
| 63rd: | Capt. R.D. Campbell | Me-109 dest(grd) | St. Trond |
| | Lt. C.M. Rotzler | Me-109 dam(grd) | St. Trond |
| **355th** | | | |
| 358th: | Capt. W.V. Gresham | Me-109 dest(air) | NW Zwolle |
| **361st** | | | |
| 375th: | Capt. M.H. Johnson | Ju-88 dest(grd) | Wittmunhafen |
| | Lt. S. Armsby | u/i a/c dest(grd) | Wittmunhafen |
| | | (2)Me-110 dam(grd) | Wittmunhafen |
| | Lt. J.T. Thomas | Ju-88 dest(grd) | Wittmunhafen |
| | | Ju-88 dam(grd) | Wittmunhafen |
| | Lt. M.J. Moore | Me-110 dam(grd) | Wittmunhafen |
| | Lt. W.D. Rogers | Ju-88 dam(grd) | Wittmunhafen |
| **364th** | | | |
| HdQts: | LtCol. J.D. Dale | FW-190 dest(air) | W/Frankfurt |
| 383rd: | Lt. T.H. Hall | (2)Me-109 dest(air) | Mannheim |
| | Capt. H.A. Chesney | Me-109 dest(air) | Mannheim |
| | Capt. S.J. Wicker | Me-109 dest(air) | Frankfurt |
| | Lt. M.L. Casagrande | Me-109 dest(air) | Mannheim |
| | Lt. R.H. Dwyer | Me-109 dest(air) | Frankfurt |
| | Lt. G.A. McCoy | Me-109 dest(air) | Frankfurt |
| 384th: | Lt. W.N. Champion | (.5)FW-190 dest(air) | W/Weichaden |
| | | (.5)FW-190 dam(air) | W/Weichaden |
| | Lt. L.A. Johnson | (.5)FW-190 dest(air) | W/Weichaden |
| | | (.5)FW-190 dam(air) | W/Weichaden |
| 385th: | Lt. J.O. Eubanks | Me-109 dest(air) | Frankfurt |
| **479th** | | | |
| 434th: | Capt. A.F. Jeffrey | Me-109 dest(air) | Steenwijk A/F |
| | Lt. J.W. Hanson | Me-109 dest(air) | Steenwijk A/F |
| | | (2)Me-109 dest(grd) | Steenwijk A/F |
| | | Me-109 dam(grd) | Steenwijk A/F |
| | | u/i a/c dam(grd) | Steenwijk A/F |
| | Lt. Q.S. Pavlock | Me-109 dest(air) | Steenwijk A/F |
| | Lt. G.D. Hendrix | Me-109 dest(grd) | Steenwijk A/F |
| | | (2)Me-109 dam(grd) | Steenwijk A/F |
| | Lt. C.J. Murphy | Me-109 dest(grd) | Steenwijk A/F |
| | | Me-109 dam(grd) | Steenwijk A/F |
| 436th: | Lt. G.M. Mulvaney | (.5)B-24 dest(grd) | N/Mulhouse |
| | Lt. T.E. Myers | (.5)B-24 dest(grd) | N/Mulhouse |

*Losses-*

**4th**: Lt. Norman W. Achen (334th Ftr Sqn) POW
P-51B QP-A 43-6882
Hit by flak at Bad Zwischenachmer.

**56th**: Capt. Robert D. Campbell, Jr. (63rd Ftr Sqn) KIA
P-47D UN- 42-75870
Hit by flak near St. Trond.

**355th**: Lt. Michael E. Graczyk (358th Ftr Sqn) POW
P-51B YF-C 43-6834
Hit by flak at a marshalling yard near Fulda.

**359th**: Lt. Frank A. Westall, Jr. (370th Ftr Sqn) KIA
P-51B CS-Y 42-106799
Suffered mechanical failure and went down south of Dunkirk.

**479th**: Capt. Hiram G. Turner, Jr. (434th Ftr Sqn) POW
P-38J L2-U 43-28376
Hit by flak near Veeningen.

Lt. James L. Wallace (434th Ftr Sqn) KIA
P-38J L2-Z 44-23169 "Sleepytime Gal"
Hit by flak and crashed near Uffelte.

*Remarks*

4th: 1-9 locos, 0-6 railcars, 1-3 vehicles, 0-1 building
20th: 1-0 loco, 1-0 vehicle
55th: 1-0 loco, 0-12 railcars, 0-10 barges
56th: 11-7 locos, 1-75 railcars, 0-1 radar station
355th: 6-10 locos, 35-37 railcars, 0-53 vehicles, 1-2 barges, 1-1 building
356th: 6-2 locos, 0-15 railcars, 1-0 radar station
361st: 3-5 locos, 0-18 railcars, 1-0 vehicle
479th: 0-1 flak position

**August 16, 1944**

Groups Operating: P-51 4th, 20th, 55th, 339th, 352nd, 355th, 357th, 359th, 361st, 364th
P-47 56th, 78th, 353rd, 356th
P-38 479th

Missions: Support of bombers to Zeitz, Delitzsch, Halberstadt, Halle, Magdeburg, Dessau, Bohlen, and Rositz.

Claims: 32-1-3 air
0-0 ground

| *Group* | | *Claims* | *Location* |
|---|---|---|---|
| **4th** | | | |
| 336th: | Lt. I.E. Grounds | Me-109 dest(air) | Magdeburg |
| **20th** | | | |
| HdQts: | LtCol. C. Wilson | FW-190 dest(air) | Eisenach |
| | | Me-109 dest(air) | Eisenach |
| 77th: | Capt. J.T. McKeon | Me-109 dest(air) | Mulhausen |
| | | FW-190 dam(air) | Mulhausen |
| | Capt. M.J. Gilbertson | Me-109 dest(air) | Mulhausen |
| | Lt. L.W. Adams | Me-109 dest(air) | Northeim |
| | Lt. C.C. Arthaud | FW-190 dest(air) | Eisenach |
| | Lt. L.E. Rowlett | Me-109 dest(air) | Mulhausen |
| | Lt. L.J. Robertson | Me-109 prob(air) | Altenburg |
| 79th: | Lt. R.E. Campbell | Me-109 dest(air) | S/Hanover |
| **339th** | | | |
| 503rd: | Lt. F.R. Gerard | Me-109 dest(air) | Gotha |
| 504th: | Maj. B.C. Routt | Me-109 dest(air) | Mulhausen |
| | | Me-109 dam(air) | Mulhausen |
| | Lt. C.M. Hunter | Me-109 dest(air) | Mulhausen |
| | Lt. R.C. Penrose | Me-109 dest(air) | Mulhausen |
| | Lt. H.S. Stockman | Me-109 dest(air) | Mulhausen |
| **352nd** | | | |
| 328th: | Capt. W.E. Hendrain | (.5)Me-109 dest(air) | W/Mehlis |
| | Lt. C.J. Cesky | (.5)Me-109 dest(air) | W/Mehlis |
| 486th: | Capt. A.J. Wallace | Me-109 dest(air) | Eisenach |
| 487th: | Lt. M.C. Pickering | FW-190 dest(air) | Plauen |

| Group | | Claims | Location |
|---|---|---|---|
| **355th** | | | |
| 357th: | Maj. J.L. Elder | (2)Me-109 dest(air) | SE Hildesheim |
| | Capt. H.S. Bille | (2)Me-109 dest(air) | SE Hildesheim |
| | Lt. W.J. Cullerton | (2)Me-109 dest(air) | SE Hildehseim |
| | Lt. H.W. Spencer | (2)Me-109 dest(air) | SE Hildesheim |
| | Capt. C.W. Lamer | Me-109 dest(air) | SE Hildesheim |
| | Lt. J.L. Crandell | Me-109 dest(air) | SE Hildesheim |
| | Lt. K.M. Michels | Me-109 dest(air) | S/Hildesheim |
| **359th** | | | |
| HdQts: | Maj. N.K. Cranfill | Me-109 dest(air) | Einbeck |
| 370th: | LtCol. J.B. Murphy | Me-163 dest(air) | SE Leipzig |
| | Lt. C.W. Jones | Me-163 dest(air) | SE Leipzig |
| | Lt. F.O. Lux | Me-109 dest(air) | Erfurt |
| | Lt. J.C. Shoffitt | Me-163 dam(air) | Bohlen |

*Losses-*

**55th**: Lt. Joseph B. Jiorles (343rd Ftr Sqn) POW
P-51D CY- 44-14051
Suffered mechanical failure near Borringhausen.

**339th**: Lt. Charles M. Hunter (504th Ftr Sqn) KIA
P-51D 5Q-T 44-13584
Last seen chasing a Me-109 near Mulhausen.

**355th**: Lt. John D. Riggs, Jr. (357th Ftr Sqn) KIA
P-51B OS-W 43-7101
Hit by a Me-109 near Hildesheim.

*Remarks*
4th: 0-2 locos, 0-45 railcars
20th: 1-0 barge
55th: 9-2 locos, 0-30 railcars
56th: 1-2 locos, 4-50 railcars, 2-1 vehicles
356th: 2-0 locos, 0-3 railcars
361st: 0-12 barges, 0-1 tug
364th: 1-0 loco, 0-7 railcars, 0-1 vehicle
Lt. Ernest L. Wilson (385th Ftr Sqn) c/l Honington; o.k.
P-51D 5E-G 44-13940

**August 17, 1944**
Groups Operating: P-51 4th, 55th, 339th, 352nd, 355th, 357th, 359th, 364th
P-47 56th, 78th, 353rd, 356th
P-38 479th
Missions: Fighter-bomber operations in the Paris-Brussels area plus eleven pilots of the 339th escorted a B-17 to La Pallice.
Claims: 0-0-0 air
2-3 ground

| *Group* | | *Claims* | *Location* |
|---|---|---|---|
| **78th** | | | |
| 84th: | Capt. R.E. Smith | (.5)Me-109 dest(grd) | W/Chaudun |
| | | (.5)Me-109 dam(grd) | W/Chaudun |
| | Lt. R.L. Baron | (.5)Me-109 dest(grd) | W/Chaudun |
| | | Me-109 dam(grd) | W/Chaudun |
| | Lt. M.R. Capp | (.5)Me-109 dest(grd) | S/Hamm |
| | Lt. E.H. Schneider | (.5)Me-109 dest(grd) | S/Hamm |
| | Lt. P.H. McKenney | (1.5)Me-109 dam(grd) | W/Chaudun |

*Losses-*

**55th**: Lt. James W. Roberts (343rd Ftr Sqn) KIA
P-51D CY- 44-13612 "Oh Murder!"
Hit by flak near Virelles.

**339th**: Lt. William J. Pastor (504th Ftr Sqn) KIA
P-51B 5Q-I 42-106649
Hit by flak near Ghent.

**352nd**: Lt. William H. Reese (486th Ftr Sqn) MIA-E
P-51D PZ-R 44-13398
Hit by flak near Chalons.

Capt. Clayton E. Davis (487th Ftr Sqn) MIA-E
P-51D HO-C 44-13651
Hit by flak near Noyon.

**357th**: Lt. Harold M. Kenney (363rd Ftr Sqn) MIA-E
P-51D B6-G 44-13522 "Billy's Bitch"
Hit by flak and bailed out near Charleroi.

**359th**: Lt. Theophalus A. Williams (370th Ftr Sqn) KIA
P-51B CS-A 42-106878
Hit by a FW-190 near Rouen.

**364th**: Lt. Harold D. Burkhard (385th Ftr Sqn) MIA-E
P-51D 5Y- 44-13700
Hit by flak at Ervillers and bailed out near Bourbourville.

*Remarks*
55th: 3-2 locos, 0-25 railcars
56th: 14-19 locos, 7-78 railcars, 23-25 vehicles, 0-6 barges
78th: 3-2 locos, 8-4 railcars, 2-8 barges, 1-0 vehicle, 0-2 buildings
339th: 1-0 loco, 6-45 railcars, 1-2 vehicles
Lt. Ray D. Mayer (503rd Ftr Sqn) c/l Boxted; o.k.
P-51B D7-V 42-106791
352nd: 2-0 locos, 72-163 railcars, 5-17 vehicles
353rd: 1-5 locos, 7-28 railcars, 11-2 vehicles, 3-1 buildings
357th: 15-35 railcars, 7-3 vehicles, 2-1 buildings
359th: 1-14 locos, 3-28 railcars, 16-9 vehicles, 2-1 bridges, 1-0 flak position
364th: 1-0 loco, 50-5 railcars, 0-2 flak positions
479th: 4-0 locos, 8-199 railcars

KIAc's
357th: Lt. Charles O. Campbell (363rd Ftr Sqn)
P-51B B6-B 43-6999

**August 18, 1944**
Groups Operating: P-51 4th, 20th, 55th, 339th, 352nd, 355th, 357th, 359th, 361st, 364th
P-47 56th, 78th, 353rd, 356th
P-38 479th
Missions: Support of bombers to various targets in France and Belgium plus fighter-bomber operations.
Claims: 14-1-7 air
52-37 ground

| *Group* | | *Claims* | *Location* |
|---|---|---|---|
| **4th** | | | |
| 334th: | Lt. A.C. Cwiklinski | (2)Me-109 dest(air) | SW Beauvais |
| | | Me-109 dam(air) | SW Beauvais |
| | Lt. P.B. Hardy | Me-109 dest(air) | SW Beauvais |
| | | Me-109 dam(air) | SW Beauvais |
| | Lt. W.E. Whalen | Me-109 dest(air) | Beauvais |
| 335th: | Lt. B. Diamond | Me-109 dest(air) | NE Paris |
| | Lt. P.S. Iden | Me-109 dest(air) | NE Paris |
| | Lt. D.D. Perkins | Me-109 dest(air) | Beaumont-Sur-Oise |
| **356th** | | | |
| 359th: | Lt. F.A. Forsyth | FW-190 dest(air) | Beauvais |
| | Lt. R.G. Vossler | FW-190 dest(air) | Beauvais |
| | | FW-190 dam(air) | Beauvais |
| | Capt. J.D. Tarbutton | (.5)FW-190 dam(air) | Beauvais |
| | Lt. L.F. Richason | (.5)FW-190 dam(air) | Beauvais |
| 361st: | Lt. J.A. Hargreaves | FW-190 dest(air) | Beauvais |
| | | FW-190 prob(air) | Beauvais |
| | Lt. E.A. Kovacs | FW-190 dest(air) | Beauvais |
| | Lt. E.L. Thompson | FW-190 dest(air) | Beauvais |
| | | (2)FW-190 dam(air) | Beauvais |
| **357th** | | | |
| 362nd: | Lt. C. Anderson | Me-109 dest(air) | NE Paris |
| | Capt. J.B. England | (.5)Me-109 dest(air) | NE Paris |
| | Lt. W.N. Perry | (.5)Me-109 dest(air) | NE Paris |
| | Lt. W.T. Gilbert | (.5)FW-190 dam(grd) | Rosieres A/F |
| | F/Lt. E.B.H. Woolley | (.5)FW-190 dam(grd) | Rosieres A/F |
| **359th** | | | |
| 369th: | Lt. R.L. Burtner | (3)Me-109 dest(grd) | St. Dizier |
| | | Ju-52 dam(grd) | St. Dizier |
| | | Ju-88 dam(grd) | St. Dizier |
| | Lt. C.J. Crenshaw | Ju-52 dest(grd) | St. Dizier |
| | | Ju-88 dest(grd) | St. Dizier |
| | | Ju-88 dam(grd) | St. Dizier |
| | Capt. E.F. Pezda | (2)Ju-88 dam(grd) | St. Dizier |
| **361st** | | | |
| 376th: | LtCol. R.B. Caviness | Ju-52 dest(grd) | Romilly-Sur-Seine |
| | Lt. E.L. Czapla | Ju-52 dest(grd) | Romilly-Sur-Seine |
| | Lt. J.D. Smith | Ju-88 dest(grd) | Romilly-Sur-Seine |
| **479th** | | | |
| 434th: | Capt. R. Olds | (2)Ju-88 dest(grd) | Nancy/Essey |
| | | He-111 dest(grd) | Nancy/Essey |
| | Lt. T.C. Olson | (1.5)He-111 dest(grd)* | Nancy/Essey |
| | | Me-109 dest(grd) | Nancy/Essey |
| | | Ju-88 dest(grd) | Nancy/Essey |
| | | (.5)FW-190 dest(grd)** | Nancy/Essey |
| | | He-111 dam(grd) | Nancy/Essey |
| | LtCol. J.M. Herren | He-111 dest(grd) | Nancy/Essey |
| | | Ju-52 dest(grd) | Nancy/Essey |
| | Lt. W.M. Drake | (2)Ju-88 dest(grd) | Nancy/Essey |
| | | FW-190 dest(grd) | Nancy/Essey |
| | Lt. R.H. Hendrickson | (2)Ju-88 dest(grd) | Nancy/Essey |
| | | Ju-88 dam(grd) | Nancy/Essey |
| | Lt. H.F. Grenning | He-111 dest(grd) | Nancy/Essey |
| | | Ju-88 dest(grd) | Nancy/Essey |
| | | (2)Ju-88 dam(grd) | Nancy/Essey |
| | Lt. J.W. Hansen | He-111 dest(grd) | Nancy/Essey |
| | | Ju-88 dest(grd) | Nancy/Essey |
| | | He-111 dam(grd) | Nancy/Essey |

| | | | |
|---|---|---|---|
| | Lt. G.W. Gleason | FW-190 dest(grd) | Nancy/Essey |
| | | (.5)Ju-88 dest(grd)[@@@] | Nancy/Essey |
| | | (.5)He-111 dest(grd)[&] | Nancy/Essey |
| | | (.5)He-111 dest(grd)[&] | Nancy/Essey |
| | | FW-190 dam(grd) | Nancy/Essey |
| | Capt. C.A.P. Duffie | (1.5)Ju-88 dest(grd)[@] | Nancy/Essey |
| | Lt. H.C. Little | Ju-88 dest(grd) | Nancy/Essey |
| | | (.5)He-111 dest(grd)[@@] | Nancy/Essey |
| | | (2)He-111 dam(grd) | Nancy/Essey |
| | Lt. C.J. Murphy | FW-190 dest(grd) | Nancy/Essey |
| | | Ju-88 dam(grd) | Nancy/Essey |
| | Lt. C.L. Peterson | Ju-52 dest(grd) | Nancy/Essey |
| | Lt. W.H. Rodgers | (4)Ju-88 dam(grd) | Nancy/Essey |
| | Lt. D.L. Maley | (2)He-111 dam(grd) | Nancy/Essey |
| | | FW-190 dam(grd) | Nancy/Essey |
| | Lt. G.W. Hendrix | Ju-88 dam(grd) | Nancy/Essey |
| 435th: | Lt. H.C. Smith | (4)He-111 dest(grd) | Nancy/Essey |
| | Lt. C.W. Granville | He-111 dest(grd) | Nancy/Essey |
| | | Ju-88 dest(grd) | Nancy/Essey |
| | Lt. R.S. Pigg | He-111 dest(grd) | Nancy/Essey |
| | | Ju-88 dest(grd) | Nancy/Essey |
| | | (4)He-111 dam(grd) | Nancy/Essey |
| | | Ju-88 dam(grd) | Nancy/Essey |
| | Capt. G.K. Sykes | (1.5)He-111 dest(grd)[@@] | Nancy/Essey |
| | Lt. T.J. Sowerby | Ju-88 dest(grd) | Nancy/Essey |
| | | (.5)FW-190 dest(grd)[**] | Nancy/Essey |
| | | (2)He-111 dam(grd) | Nancy/Essey |
| | | Ju-88 dam(grd) | Nancy/Essey |
| | Lt. P.D. Gossard | He-111 dest(grd) | Nancy/Essey |
| | Lt. V.E. Hooker | (.5)He-111 dest(grd)[#] | Nancy/Essey |
| | | (.5)He-111 dest(grd)[##] | Nancy/Essey |
| | | Ju-88 dam(grd) | Nancy/Essey |
| | Lt. D.L. Naule | He-111 dest(grd) | Nancy/Essey |
| | Lt. C.F. Monsell | (.5)He-111 dest(grd)[&] | Nancy/Essey |
| | | (.5)He-111 dest(grd)[&] | Nancy/Essey |
| | | (.5)He-111 dest(grd)[#] | Nancy/Essey |
| | Lt. N.W. Butler | (.5)He-111 dest(grd)[*] | Nancy/Essey |
| | | (.5)He-111 dest(grd)[##] | Nancy/Essey |
| | Lt. R.K. Friend | (.5)Ju-88 dest(grd)[@] | Nancy/Essey |
| | | (3)He-111 dam(grd) | Nancy/Essey |
| | Lt. H.W. Detlefson | (.5)Ju-88 dest(grd)[@@@] | Nancy/Essey |
| | | He-111 dam(grd) | Nancy/Essey |
| | Lt. W. Muller | (2)Ju-88 dam(grd) | Nancy/Essey |

*Losses-*

**4th**: Lt. Arthur C. Cwiklinski (334th Ftr Sqn) MIA-E
P-51D QP-X 44-13314
Hit by a Me-109 south of Beauvais.

Lt. C.G. Howard (334th Ftr Sqn) KIA
P-51B QP-D 43-24841
Hit by a Me-109 near Beauvais.

Lt. Dean C. Lange (334th Ftr Sqn) POW
P-51C QP-N 42-103791
Hit by a Me-109 southwest of Beauvais.

Lt. John T. Conley (335th Ftr Sqn) KIA
P-51B WD-N 43-24813
Hit by a Me-109 near Les Andelys.

Lt. Robert J. Cooper (335th Ftr Sqn) KIA
P-51B WD-Z 42-106855
Hit by a Me-109 near Les Andelys.

Lt. Leo Dailey (335th Ftr Sqn) KIA
P-51B WD-M 42-106555
Hit by a Me-109 near La Ferte.

Lt. Bernard J. Rosenson (335th Ftr Sqn) KIA
P-51D WD-O 44-13567
Hit by a Me-109 near Les Andelys.

Lt. Donald E. Smith (335th Ftr Sqn) KIA
P-51D WD-R 44-13563
Hit by a Me-109 near Les Andelys.

Capt. Otey M. Glass, Jr. (336th Ftr Sqn) MIA-E
P-51B VF-G 42-106797
Hit by enemy fighters near Gisors.

**78th**: Lt. Jack B. Miller (83rd Ftr Sqn) KIA
P-47D HL-S 42-26458
Collided with Lt. Dahl (361st Ftr Grp) near Bottisham.

**353rd**: Lt. Dwight W. Johnson (351st Ftr Sqn) POW
P-47D YJ-U 42-75863
Hit by flak and bailed out near Bethunne.

F/O John J. Swanezy, Jr. (352nd Ftr Sqn) MIA-E
P-47D SX-F 42-75622 "Hun Buster"
Hit the ground while strafing near Paris.

**355th**: Capt. Bert Marshall, Jr. (354th Ftr Sqn) MIA-E
P-51D WR-
Hit by flak east of Paris; bellied-in and was rescued when Lt. Royce W. Priest landed and picked him up.

Capt. Emil L. Sluga (358th Ftr Sqn) ASR
P-51D YF-R 44-13625
Damaged by flak and bailed out over the Channel.

Lt. Cleveland J. Brien, Jr. (358th Ftr Sqn) MIA-E
P-51B YF-A 42-106860
Hit by flak near Soissons.

**356th**: Lt. John R. Tillman (361st Ftr Sqn) KIA
P-47D QI-D 42-75549
Hit by a FW-190 near Beauvais.

**359th**: Lt. Rene L. Burtner (369th Ftr Sqn) MIA-E
P-51B IV-R 43-12186
Hit by flak at St. Dizier and bailed out west of the field.

Lt. Donald S. Melrose (369th Ftr Sqn) KIA
P-51B IV-D 42-106916 "Loretta"
Hit by flak near St. Dizier.

**361st**: Lt. Milton A. Dahl (376th Ftr Sqn) KIA
P-51B E9-A 42-106759
Collided with Lt. Miller (78th Ftr Grp) near Bottisham.

**479th**: Lt. Philip W. Manning (434th Ftr Sqn) KIA
P-38J L2-R 42-67296
Hit by flak at Nancy/Essey Airfield and crashed in Nancy.

*Remarks*

| | |
|---|---|
| 4th: | 42-62 railcars, 4-12 vehicles |
| 55th: | 30-0 railcars, 0-1 vehicle |
| 56th: | 0-4 locos, 9-23 railcars, 2-5 vehicles |
| 78th: | 1-0 loco, 10-98 railcars, 10-22 vehicles |
| 339th: | 6-3 locos, 81-173 railcars, 2-3 barges, 1-0 vehicle |
| 352nd: | P-51 c/l Manston; o.k. |
| 353rd: | 7-4 locos, 14-18 railcars, 61-27 vehicles, 1-0 building |
| 355th: | 0-1 loco, 15-15 railcars, 18-4 vehicles |
| | 358th Ftr Sqn P-51 c/l; o.k. |
| | P-51 YF- |
| 356th: | 1-0 loco, 15-13 railcars, 1-0 vehicle |
| 357th: | 5-3 locos, 8-74 railcars, 37-21 vehicles, 2-1 buildings |
| 364th: | 2-1 locos, 64-36 railcars, 6-1 vehicles |

**August 23, 1944**
Groups Operating: P-47 56th, 78th, 353rd, 356th
Missions: Fighter-bomber operations in the St. Omer-Reims-Hamm area.
Claims: nil
Losses: nil

*Remarks*

| | |
|---|---|
| 56th: | 2-19 locos, 21-90 railcars, 1-2 vehicles |
| 78th: | 2-0 locos, 3-15 railcars, 9-10 vehicles, 1-11 barges |
| 353rd: | 30-18 railcars, 25-6 vehicles, 2-0 buildings |

KIAc's

SF: LtCol. Gerald C. Price (1st)
P-51D YF-B 44-13636

55th: Lt. Bill Chambliss (338th Ftr Sqn)
P-51 CL-
Died in a crash at Little Horkesley.

**August 24, 1944**
Groups Operating: P-51 4th, 20th, 55th, 339th, 352nd, 355th, 357th, 359th, 361st, 364th
P-47 56th, 78th, 353rd, 356th
P-38 479th
Missions: Support of bombers to airfields and oil targets in Germany.
Claims: 10-0-1 air
14-0 ground

| *Group* | | *Claims* | *Location* |
|---|---|---|---|
| **4th** | | | |
| 335th: | Lt. T.E. Lines | (2)Me-109 dest(air) | SE Emden |
| 336th: | Capt. J.T. Godfrey | (4)Ju-52 dest(grd) | Nordhausen |
| | Lt. M.N. Dickey | (3)Ju-52 dest(grd) | Nordhausen |
| | Capt. P.L. Wiggin | Ju-52 dest(grd) | Nordhausen |
| **55th** | | | |
| 38th: | Maj. J.D. Landers | (2)Ju-88 dest(grd) | Burg A/F |

| Group | | Claims | Location |
|---|---|---|---|
| | Lt. K.I. Crawford | Ju-88 dest(grd) | Burg A/F |
| | Lt. E.R. Fryer | Ju-88 dest(grd) | Burg A/F |
| | Lt. T.B. Luckett | Ju-88 dest(grd) | Burg A/F |
| | Lt. C.R. Watts | Ju-88 dest(grd) | Burg A/F |
| **353rd** | | | |
| 350th: | Lt. H.E. Asper | Me-109 dest(air) | S/Hanover |
| | Lt. B.C. Auchincloss | Me-109 dest(air) | S/Hanover |
| **357th** | | | |
| 364th: | Lt. H.H. Hermanson | Me-109 dest(air) | S/Brunswick |
| | Lt. G.E. Tyler | Me-109 dest(air) | S/Brunswick |
| **364th** | | | |
| 383rd: | Lt. A.J. Acosta | Me-109 dest(air) | Seyda |
| | Lt. E.C. Beaumont | Me-109 dest(air) | Seyda |
| | | Me-109 dam(air) | Seyda |
| 384th: | Lt. J.J. Gawienowski | Me-109 dest(air) | S/Hamburg |
| 385th: | Lt. G.L. Jones | (.5)Me-109 dest(air) | Hamburg |
| | Lt. E.A. Taylor | (.5)Me-109 dest(air) | Hamburg |

*Losses-*

**4th**: (335th Ftr Sqn) ASR
P-51C WD- 43-25061
Bailed out east of Great Yarmouth.

Capt. John T. Godfrey (336th Ftr Sqn) POW
P-51D VF-F 44-13412
Shot down by his wingman while strafing Nordhausen Airfield.

**55th**: Lt. Thomas B. Luckett (38th Ftr Sqn) KIA
P-51D CG-X 44-13749 "Jeanne"
Hit by flak at Burg Airfield.

**339th**: Lt. Bernell V. Shaw (505th Ftr Sqn) POW
P-51D 6N- 44-13385
Hit by flak near Gerville.

*Remarks*
4th: 0-1 flak position
56th: 2-0 locos, 0-6 railcars, 2-0 vehicles, 2-0 ships
339th: 0-1 loco, 0-1 vehicle
Lt. Ermy L. Beadle (504th Ftr Sqn) c/l Fowlmere; injured
359th: 1-0 loco, 0-1 trawler

**August 25, 1944**
Groups Operating: P-51 4th, 20th, 55th, 339th, 352nd, 355th, 357th, 359th, 361st, 364th
P-47 56th, 78th, 353rd, 356th
P-38 479th
Missions: Support of bombers to Rostock, Schwerin, Lubeck, Wismar, Rechlin, Neubrandenburg, Politz, Peenemunde, and half a dozen targets in Belgium and northern France.
Claims: 12-1-2 air
42-31 ground

| *Group* | | *Claims* | *Location* |
|---|---|---|---|
| **4th** | | | |
| 336th: | Lt. H.N. Hagan | Me-109 dest(air) | SW Rostock |
| | Lt. G.H. Logan | Me-109 dest(air) | E/Schwerin |
| | Lt. I.E. Grounds | Me-109 prob(air) | SW Rostock |
| | | (2)Me-109 dam(air) | SW Rostock |
| **20th** | | | |
| HdQts: | LtCol. J.P. Randolph | BV-140 dest(grd) | Parow A/F |
| | | Ju-88 dest(grd) | Parow A/F |
| | | (2)Ju-88 dam(grd) | Parow A/F |
| 55th: | Lt. J.L. Mansker | (.5)Ju-88 dest(grd) | Parow A/F |
| | | BV-140 dest(grd) | Parow A/F |
| | | (3)Ju-88 dam(grd) | Parow A/F |
| | Lt. K.C. Smeltz | (3)Ju-88 dest(grd) | Parow A/F |
| | | (2)Ju-88 dam(grd) | Parow A/F |
| | | BV-140 dam(grd) | Parow A/F |
| | Lt. J.E. Burford | BV-140 dest(grd) | Parow A/F |
| | | Hs-126 dest(grd) | Parow A/F |
| | | (2)Ju-88 dam(grd) | Parow A/F |
| | | Ju-52 dam(grd) | Parow A/F |
| | Lt. H.B. Bynum | Ju-88 dest(grd) | Parow A/F |
| | | Ju-52 dest(grd) | Parow A/F |
| | Lt. J.S. Ford | Ju-88 dest(grd) | Parow A/F |
| | | Ju-52 dest(grd) | Parow A/F |
| | | Ju-88 dam(grd) | Parow A/F |
| | Lt. E.E. Wasil | (2)Do-18 dest(grd) | Parow A/F |
| | Lt. W.W. Wells | Me-410 dest(grd) | Parow A/F |
| | | u/i a/c dest(grd) | Parow A/F |
| | | (2)Ju-88 dam(grd) | Parow A/F |
| | | u/i a/c dam(grd) | Parow A/F |
| | Lt. R.H. Riemensnider | (1.5)Do-18 dest(grd) | Parow A/F |
| | | u/i a/c dest(grd) | Parow A/F |
| | | Do-18 dam(grd) | Parow A/F |
| | Capt. E.W. Hower | BV-140 dest(grd) | Parow A/F |
| | | Ju-88 dam(grd) | Parow A/F |
| | Lt. H.M. Anderson | Ju-88 dest(grd) | Parow A/F |
| | Lt. C.F. Bain | Ju-88 dest(grd) | Parow A/F |
| | | Ju-88 dam(grd) | Parow A/F |
| | Lt. R.M. Howard | BV-140 dest(grd) | Parow A/F |
| | | BV-140 dam(grd) | Parow A/F |
| | Lt. D.D. Oxley | FW-190 dest(grd) | Parow A/F |
| | | Ju-88 dam(grd) | Parow A/F |
| | Lt. K.D. McNeel | (.5)Do-18 dest(grd) | Parow A/F |
| | Lt. H.L. Brown | Ju-88 dam(grd) | Parow A/F |
| **352nd** | | | |
| 487th: | LtCol. J.C. Meyer | He-177 dest(grd) | Neubrandenburg |
| | | Ju-52 dest(grd) | Neubrandenburg |
| | | (2)u/i a/c dam(grd) | Neubrandenburg |
| | Lt. R.H. Littge | (2)Me-210 dest(grd) | Neubrandenburg |
| | | Me-109 dam(grd) | Neubrandenburg |
| | Capt. C.O. Johnson | He-177 dest(grd) | Neubrandenburg |
| | | Hs-129 dam(grd) | Neubrandenburg |
| | Lt. J.H. Forga | Me-109 dest(grd) | Neubrandenburg |
| | Lt. C.E. Ellison | Me-110 dam(grd) | Neubrandenburg |
| | Lt. G.T. Moran | Me-210 dam(grd) | Neubrandenburg |
| | | Caudron dam(grd) | Neubrandenburg |
| | F/Lt. E.H. King | Me-109 dam(grd) | Neubrandenburg |
| **359th** | | | |
| 368th: | Lt. D.B. Archibald | u/i a/c dest(grd) | Gustrow |
| **361st** | | | |
| 375th: | Capt. M.H. Johnson | Me-109 dest(air) | SW Rostock |
| | Lt. U.L. Drew | Me-109 dest(air) | SW Rostock |
| | Lt. D.R. Morgan | Me-109 dest(air) | E/Wismar |
| **364th** | | | |
| 385th: | LtCol. R.D. Neece | (2)Ju-88 dest(grd) | Anklam |
| | Lt. E.F. Izor | Me-210 dest(grd) | Anklam |
| | | (2)Me-210 dam(grd) | Anklam |
| | Lt. J.O. Eubanks | Ju-88 dest(grd) | Anklam |
| | Lt. E.K. Tazzia | Ju-88 dest(grd) | Anklam |
| **479th** | | | |
| 434th: | Capt. R. Olds | (3)Me-109 dest(air) | Rostock |
| | Capt. C.A.P. Duffie | (2)Me-109 dest(air) | Rostock |
| | Lt. B.E. Hollister | (2)Me-109 dest(air) | Rostock |

*Losses-*

**4th**: Lt. Kenneth J. Rudkin (334th Ftr Sqn) POW
P-51D QP-R 44-13732
Hit by flak in the Lubeck area.

**20th**: Lt. Charles F. Bain (55th Ftr Sqn) KIA
P-51C KI-D 43-25033
Hit by flak at Parow Airfield and bailed out over the Baltic.

**352nd**: Lt. Richard F. Semon (328th Ftr Sqn) ASR
P-51C PE-X 42-103789
Suffered mechanical failure and bailed out northeast of Great Yarmouth.

**357th**: Lt. Walter Baron (364th Ftr Sqn) INT
P-51B C5-B 42-106854 "Peabody's Pet"
Suffered mechanical failure and landed in Sweden.

Lt. Charles E. Burtner (364th Ftr Sqn) INT
P-51D C5-I 44-13345 "Mary Ann"
Escorted Lt. Baron to Sweden.

**364th**: Lt. Duane D. Owens (385th Ftr Sqn) POW
P-51C 5E-O 42-103593
Hit by flak at Anklam.

Lt. Edward K. Tazzia (385th Ftr Sqn) POW
P-51C 5E-Y 43-25030 "Lucky II"
Hit by flak at Anklam.

*Remarks*
56th: 0-1 loco, 0-8 railcars
339th: 1-0 loco
352nd: 1-0 railcar
359th: 0-1 loco, 0-1 ship

**August 26, 1944**
Groups Operating: P-51 4th, 20th, 55th, 339th, 352nd, 355th, 357th, 359th, 361st, 364th
P-47 56th, 78th, 364th, 479th
P-38 479th
Missions: Support of bombers to the Brest area, Ludwigshafen, Gelsenkirchen, and oil targets plus fighter-bomber operations.
Claims: 1-0-0 air
1-0 ground

| Group | | Claims | Location |
|---|---|---|---|
| **353rd** | | | |
| 352nd: | Lt. W.M. Newton | FW-190 dest(air) | S/Charleroi |
| **355th** | | | |
| 357th: | Lt. W.J. Cullerton | FW-200 dest(grd) | Speyer |

*Losses-*

**55th:** Lt. John R. Eskridge (338th Ftr Sqn) POW
P-51D CL- 44-14014
Suffered mechanical failure near Soerten.

Lt. Samuel D. Gevorkian (338th Ftr Sqn) MIA-E
P-51D CL-P 44-13954 "DaQuake"
Ran out of fuel and bellied-in near Truc Vert.

Lt. Samuel E. Hansard (338th Ftr Sqn) KIA
P-51D CL- 44-14094
Ran out of fuel and crashed into the Channel.

Lt. John E. Kester (338th Ftr Sqn) MIA-E
P-51D CL- 44-13663
Ran out of fuel and bellied-in near Truc Vert.

Lt. James W. Hiner (343rd Ftr Sqn) KIA
P-51D CY-Y 44-13904
Lost coolant due to a ground explosion near St. Michel and bailed out west of Nancy.

**78th:** Capt. Wilbur J. Coss, Jr. (82nd Ftr Sqn) MIA-E
P-47D MX-K 42-26585
Hit by flak and bailed out near Peruwels.

**339th:** Lt. Ely N. Van Cleave (504th Ftr Sqn) ASR
P-51 5Q-
Suffered mechanical failure and bailed out northwest of Guernsey Island.

**353rd:** Lt. Alex S. Hartley (351st Ftr Sqn) ASR
P-47D YJ-M 42-26126 "Lil Boston Bull"
Damaged by flak and bailed out southeast of Manston.

**355th:** Lt. Richard G. Daves (358th Ftr Sqn) KIA
P-51B YF-Z 43-7036 "Jackie II"
Dove into the Channel for unknown reasons.

**361st:** Lt. Sherman Armsby (375th Ftr Sqn) KIA
P-51B E2-I 43-24761 "Jacquline"
Damaged by ground explosion near Longoyon.

Lt. Jack S. Crandell (375th Ftr Sqn) KIA
P-51B E2-K 42-106917 "Nita-Bottom's Up"
Hit by flak near Konach.

*Remarks*
55th: 7-1 locos, 0-67 railcars, 1-0 vehicle
56th: 5-2 locos, 3-4 railcars, 7-0 vehicles
78th: 18-12 locos, 92-230 railcars, 25-8 vehicles, 0-4 barges
353rd: 14-61 locos, 62-49 railcars, 14-39 vehicles, 3-2 buildings
355th: 0-4 locos
357th: 7-2 locos, 25-21 railcars, 97-81 vehicles, 0-1 flak tower
361st: 1-2 locos, 60-27 railcars
364th: Capt. Gerald W. Rooney (385th Ftr Sqn) c/l Honington; o.k.
P-51D 5E-P 44-13993

**August 27, 1944**
Groups Operating: P-51 4th, 20th, 55th, 339th, 352nd, 355th, 357th, 359th, 361st, 364th
P-47 56th, 78th, 353rd, 356th
P-38 479th
Missions: Fighter-bomber operations while the planned support for the bombers to the Berlin area ran into bad weather and most of the aircraft were recalled.
Claims: 1-0-0 air
13-5 ground

| Group | | Claims | Location |
|---|---|---|---|
| **20th** | | | |
| 55th: | Lt. K.C. Smeltz | Ju-88 dest(grd) | Habjeerg A/F |
| **78th** | | | |
| 82nd: | Capt. R.E. Conner | Me-110 dest(grd) | Thionville |
| | Lt. R.C. Boeckman | He-111 dest(grd) | Chatel-Cherary |
| | Lt. T.L. Eggleston | (.5)He-111 dest(grd) | Chatel-Cherary |
| | Lt. R.L. Wolfe | (.5)He-111 dest(grd) | Chatel-Cherary |
| **353rd** | | | |
| HdQts: | LtCol. B. Rimerman | (.5)FW-190 dest(grd)* | Metz |
| | | (.5)Me-109 dam(grd) | Metz |
| 350th: | Lt. L.M. Davis | (2)FW-190 dest(grd) | Verdun |
| | | FW-190 dam(grd) | Verdun |
| | Lt. B.C. Auchincloss | (1.5)FW-190 dest(grd)** | Verdun |
| | | FW-190 dam(grd) | Verdun |
| | Lt. J.L. Schilt | (1.5)FW-190 dest(grd)** | Verdun |
| | | FW-190 dam(grd) | Verdun |
| 351st: | Capt. L.G. Hally | Ju-88 dest(grd) | NE Metz |
| | Lt. M.Q. Williams | Me-109 dest(grd) | W/Metz |
| 352nd: | Lt. J.L. Motley | Me-109 dest(grd) | Metz |
| | Lt. T.J. Forkin | (.5)FW-190 dest(grd)* | Metz |
| | | Ju-88 dam(grd) | Metz |
| | | (.5)Me-109 dam(grd) | Metz |
| **359th** | | | |
| 370th: | Lt. L.A. Ziska | u/i a/c dest(air) | Munster |

*Losses-*

**20th:** LtCol. Cy Wilson (HdQts) POW
P-51D KI-W 44-13951 "Wrangler Jr."
Hit by flak over Denmark and bailed out off the coast.

Lt. Harry M. Anderson (55th Ftr Sqn) KIA
P-51D KI-F 44-13733
Hit by flak near Kallingen.

Lt. Alphonso H. Kent, Jr. (55th Ftr Sqn) POW
P-51C KI- 43-25049
Hit by flak over Denmark and bailed out off the coast.

Lt. Edward W. Doering (77th Ftr Sqn) POW
P-51D LC-A 44-13991
Hit by flak over Denmark and bailed out off the coast.

**56th:** Lt. Thomas J. Price (62nd Ftr Sqn) KIA
P-47D LM-F 42-75093
Hit the ground while strafing near Heestert.

**339th:** Lt. John M. Carothers (503rd Ftr Sqn) KIA
P-51C D7-N 42-103325 "Reddy Teddy"
Suffered mechanical failure and crashed into the North Sea.

**352nd:** Lt. Charles E. Ferris (486th Ftr Sqn) KIA
P-51D PZ-N 44-13688 "Donna Dae VI"
Suffered mechanical failure and bailed out off Heligoland.

Lt. Carl J. Fuenpstueck (486th Ftr Sqn) POW
P-51B PZ-A 42-106480
Hit by enemy fighters near Kiel.

**359th:** Lt. Paul E. Sundheim (370th Ftr Sqn) POW
P-51B CS-I 42-106580
Last seen in the Munster area and crashed near Lochtenburg.

**364th:** Lt. Argent J. Acosta, Jr. (383rd Ftr Sqn) POW
P-51D N2-W 44-13936 "Carolina Moon"
Hit by flak in the Kiel area.

Lt. Charles A. King (385th Ftr Sqn) POW
P-51D 5E-I 44-14024
Lost in bad weather near Kiel.

*Remarks*
20th: 6-0 locos, 4-35 railcars, 8-2 vehicles, 0-2 ships, 0-1 gun position
55th: Lt. John W. Silk (38th Ftr Sqn) c/l; o.k.
P-51 CG-
56th: 17-16 locos, 50-243 railcars, 0-1 vehicle, 0-2 buildings
78th: 17-12 locos, 75-152 railcars, 2-2 vehicles, 0-12 gun positions
353rd: 38-5 locos, 37-172 railcars, 11-0 vehicles, 1-0 bridge
356th: 9-12 locos, 22-122 railcars, 0-6 vehicles
359th: 18-12 locos, 0-119 railcars, 2-0 vehicles, 1-3 tugs, 3-13 barges
364th: 1-0 loco, 0-5 barges, 0-1 steamer
Lt. Rodney E. Simcoke (384th Ftr Sqn) c/l Huntington; o.k.
P-51D 5Y-T 44-13342

**August 28, 1944**
Groups Operating: P-51 4th, 20th, 55th, 339th, 352nd, 355th, 357th, 359th, 364th
P-47 56th, 78th, 353rd, 356th
P-38 479th
Missions: Fighter-bomber operations in France-Belgium, Holland, and Germany.
Claims: 22-0-0 air
11-7 ground

| Group | | Claims | Location |
|---|---|---|---|
| **55th** | | | |
| 338th: | Lt. W.J. Lanham | Do-217 dest(air) | Dromersheim |
| | Lt. R.C. Haworth | (.5)DFS-230 dest(air) | Dromersheim |
| | Lt. A.J. Ramm | (.5)DFS-230 dest(air) | Dromersheim |
| 343rd: | Lt. D.L. Mercier | He-111 dest(air) | SW Coblenz |

| | | | |
|---|---|---|---|
| **56th** | | | |
| HdQts: | LtCol. D.C. Schilling | He-111 dest(air) | S/Trier |
| 61st: | Capt. P.A. Conger | (.5)He-111 dest(air) | S/Saarbrucken |
| | Lt. J.M. Jure | (.5)He-111 dest(air) | S/Saarbrucken |
| | Maj. G.E. Baker | Ju-88 dest(grd) | Wach |
| 62nd: | Capt. M.J. Jackson | Ju-88 dest(air) | Irsch |
| | Lt. B.M. Knox | He-111 dam(grd) | Jerny |
| 63rd: | Lt. E.M. Albright | He-111 dest(air) | N/Saarbrucken |
| | Lt. W.L. Flagg | Me-109 dest(air) | Charleroi |
| | Lt. W.R. Groce | He-111 dest(air) | N/Kaiserlautern |
| | Lt. T.W. Queen | Ju-88 dam(grd) | Bad Brommach |
| **78th** | | | |
| HdQts: | LtCol. J.J. Oberhansly | Ju-88 dest(air) | Charleroi |
| 82nd: | Maj. J. Myers | (.5)Me-262 dest(air) | Termonde |
| | Lt. M.O. Croy | (.5)Me-262 dest(air) | Termonde |
| **339th** | | | |
| HdQts: | Maj. J.R. Reynolds | (.5)Ju-88 dest(grd) | Saverne |
| 503rd: | Lt. J.P. Bush | Ju-88 dest(grd) | Saverne |
| 505th: | Lt. J.F. Marts | Ju-88 dest(grd) | Saverne |
| | Lt. A.D. Young | (.5)Ju-88 dest(grd) | Saverne |
| **353rd**(#1) | | | |
| 350th: | LtCol. K.W. Gallup | (1.5)Fi-156 dest(air) | Verdun |
| | | (.5)He-111 dest(air) | SE Arlon |
| | Lt. R.W. Hedler | He-111 dest(air) | SE Arlon |
| | Lt. J.B. Brooks | (.5)Fi-156 dest(air) | Verdun |
| | Lt. J.L. Schilt | (.5)He-111 dest(air) | SE Arlon |
| | Capt. W.D. Smith | He-111 dest(grd) | Verdun |
| 352nd: | Lt. T.W. Jones | (.5)Ju-88 dest(air) | SE Luxembourg |
| | Lt. B. Parker | (.5)Ju-88 dest(air) | SE Luxembourg |
| (#2) | | | |
| 350th: | Capt. J.O. Ruscitto | (2)Me-110 dest(air) | Wavre |
| | Capt. W.J. Price | Me-410 dest(grd) | Wavre |
| | | (2)Me-410 dam(grd) | Wavre |
| | Lt. R.T. Allison | Me-410 dest(grd) | Wavre |
| 351st: | Lt. W.K. Lahke | Me-109 dest(air) | Dinan |
| 352nd: | Lt. F.H. Bouldin | Me-110 dest(air) | SE Brussels |
| **357th** | | | |
| 362nd: | Capt. C.L. Williams | Ju-52 dest(grd) | Trier |
| | Capt. H.E. Beal | (.5)Ju-52 dest(grd) | Trier |
| | Lt. J.H. Sehl | (.5)Ju-52 dest(grd) | Trier |
| | Lt. A.E. Smith | FW-190 dam(grd) | Trier |
| | | Ju-52 dam(grd) | Trier |
| **359th** | | | |
| 368th: | Lt. O.R. Fladmark | Ju-88 dest(grd) | Saarbrucken |
| **479th** | | | |
| 434th: | Capt. A.F. Jeffrey | Ju-52 dest(air) | Sedan/Douzy A/F |
| | Lt. T.C. Olson | FW-190 dest(air) | Sedan/Douzy A/F |
| | | u/i a/c dam(grd) | Sedan/Douzy |
| | Capt. J.M. Hollingsworth | Do-217 dest(grd) | Sedan/Douzy |

*Losses-*

**4th:** Lt. Herbert Vandervate, Jr. (334th Ftr Sqn) KIA
P-51D QP-K 44-14310
Hit by flak near Strasbourg.

Maj. Archibald M. Thomson, Jr. (335th Ftr Sqn) MIA-E
P-51D WD-F 44-13534
Hit by flak near Strasbourg.

Capt. Pierce W. McKennon (335th Ftr Sqn) MIA-E
P-51D WD-A 44-13883 "Ridge Runner"
Hit by flak near Niederbronn.

Capt. Albert L. Schlegel (335th Ftr Sqn) KIA
P-51D WD-O 44-14066
Hit by flak near Strasbourg.

Lt. Ferris S. Harris (336th Ftr Sqn) KIA
P-51C VF- 42-103796
Hit by flak near Strasbourg.

**20th:** Lt. John L. Armstrong (79th Ftr Sqn) POW
P-51D MC-S 44-13791 "Guardian Angel"
Suffered mechanical failure near Bad Kreuznach.

**78th:** LtCol. Olin E. Gilbert (HdQts) MIA-E
P-47D HL-X 42-28408
Hit by flak and bailled-in near Charleroi.

Lt. John F. Lacy (84th Ftr Sqn) POW
P-47D WZ-O 42-8650
Damaged by ground explosion near Beaumont.

**339th:** Lt. Russell W. Wilcox (505th Ftr Sqn) KIA
P-51 6N-
Damaged by flak and bailed out off Margate.

**355th:** Lt. Bert Smith (354th Ftr Sqn) MIA-E
P-51B WR-O 43-6431
Hit by flak near Metz.

Lt. John T. Hurley (357th Ftr Sqn) MIA-E
P-51D OS-M 44-14201 "Mustang"
Hit by flak near Metz.

Lt. Lawrence A. Phillips (357th Ftr Sqn) MIA-E
P-51D OS-K 44-13945
Hit by flak near Metz.

Lt. Arthur C. Duppstadt (358th Ftr Sqn) MIA-E
P-51D YF-E 44-13302 "Raunchy Runt"
Hit by flak near Metz.

Lt. John J. Gilmore, Jr. (358th Ftr Sqn) KIA
P-51B YF-B 43-6385 "Shanghai Lil"
Hit by flak near Metz.

Lt. Kenneth Hughes (358th Ftr Sqn) MIA-E
P-51B YF-C 42-106932 "Jo-Jo"
Hit by flak near Metz.

Lt. William W. Tolby (358th Ftr Sqn) MIA-E
P-51B YF-W 42-106452 "Buzz Boy"
Landed to pick up Lt. Duppstadt near Metz and failed.

Lt. William B. Weber (358th Ftr Sqn) KIA
P-51D YF-N 44-13565 "Baltimore Jo-Jo"
Hit by flak near Metz; bailed out but his chute failed.

**356th:** Lt. James H. Perry (359th Ftr Sqn) ASR
P-47D OC-
Suffered mechanical failure and bailed out over the Channel.

**359th:** Lt. Ferris C. Suttle (369th Ftr Sqn) KIA
P-51B IV-V 43-24756
Last seen near Nancy and crashed near Luneville.

**479th:** Lt. William N. Howard (436th Ftr Sqn) MIA-E
P-38J 9B- 42-104407 "Marion"
Hit by flak near Dijon.

*Remarks*

4th: 2-25 locos, 8-99 railcars, 5-0 vehicles, 0-2 barges, 0-4 buildings
20th: 25-24 locos, 0-16 railcars, 4-2 vehicles, 0-7 buildings
55th: 36-12 locos, 0-90 railcars, 1-18 vehicles
56th: 8-18 locos, 10-132 railcars, 0-20 barges, 0-3 vehicles
78th: 12-12 locos, 45-188 railcars, 21-8 vehicles, 1-1 buildings
339th: 23-24 locos, 99-240 railcars, 0-3 barges, 1-1 barracks, 0-1 flak position
352nd: 2-9 locos, 22-155 railcars, 11-6 vehicles
353rd: 54-14 locos, 83-80 railcars, 42-19 vehicles, 0-1 building
355th: 0-11 locos, 0-95 railcars, 66-7 vehicles, 0-2 flak positions
Capt. Bert W. Marshall (354th Ftr Sqn) c/l; o.k.
P-51 WR-
Lt. John M. Chapman (357th Ftr Sqn) c/l; o.k.
P-51C OS-N 42-103753
356th: 10-6 locos, 4-52 railcars, 3-0 vehicles, 0-1 barge
357th: 11-0 locos, 7-56 railcars, 10-1 vehicles, 2-0 barracks
359th: 30-8 locos, 29-208 railcars, 20-20 vehicles, 0-6 barges, 1-2 flak positions
Lt. Frank O. Lux (370th Ftr Sqn) c/l; o.k.
P-51D CS-W 44-14122
Lt. John W. McWilliams (370th Ftr Sqn) c/l; o.k.
P-51D CS-G 44-14038
364th: 9-3 locos, 1-63 railcars, 5-7 barges, 3-0 vehicles
479th: 8-6 locos, 32-70 railcars, 0-3 buildings, 0-1 bridge
Lt. William M. Gates (435th Ftr Sqn) c/l; o.k.
P-38J J2-
Lt. Charles F. Monsell(435th Ftr Sqn) c/l Friston; o.k.
P-38J J2-
Lt. Stephen H. Zuchowski (435th Ftr Sqn) c/l; o.k.
P-38J J2-

**August 29, 1944**
Groups Operating: P-47 56th, 78th, 353rd, 356th
P-38 479th
Missions: Fighter-bomber operations in France, Belgium, and Germany.
Claims: 0-0-0 air
19-11 ground

| *Group* | | *Claims* | *Location* |
|---|---|---|---|
| **353rd** | | | |
| 350th: | Lt. S.T. Benjamin | (3)Me-109 dest(grd) | Diest |
| | | (2)Me-410 dest(grd) | Diest |
| | | (4)Me-109 dam(grd) | Diest |

| | | | |
|---|---|---|---|
| | Lt. M.V. Bledsoe | (2)Me-110 dest(grd) | Diest |
| | | (2)Me-109 dest(grd) | Diest |
| | | (2)Me-110 dam(grd) | Diest |
| | | (2)Me-109 dam(grd) | Diest |
| | Capt. W.J. Price | (3)Me-109 dest(grd) | Diest |
| | | Me-109 dam(grd) | Diest |
| | Lt. M.W. Hightshoe | (2)Me-109 dest(grd) | Diest |
| | | Me-410 dest(grd) | Diest |
| | | (2)Me-109 dam(grd) | Diest |
| | Lt. O.I. Aal | (2)Me-110 dest(grd) | Diest |
| | Capt. W.D. Smith | u/i a/c dest(grd) | Wavre |
| 351st: | Lt. D.F. Kohler | u/i a/c dest(grd) | Chievres |

*Losses-*

**353rd**: Capt. William D. Smith (350th Ftr Sqn) KIA
P-47D LH-H 42-26668 "Skipper"
Hit by flak near Chievres.

Lt. Olger I. Aal (350th Ftr Sqn) KIA
P-47D LH-O 44-19580
Damaged by an aircraft exploding at Diest.

**356th**: Lt. Thomas D. Teel (360th Ftr Sqn) KIA
P-47D PI- 42-25524 "Grace"
Hit by flak near Lille and was seen to bail out in the overcast.

*Remarks*
56th: 3-7 locos, 45-10 railcars, 107-51 vehicles, 45-9 horse-drawn carts
78th: 25-12 locos, 72-14 railcars, 26-5 vehicles, 3-1 buildings
353rd: 24-7 locos, 9-7 railcars, 59-3 vehicles
356th: 10-2 locos, 0-71 railcars, 4-2 vehicles
479th: 30-0 railcars, 0-1 building

KIAc's
361st: Lt. Harry G. Bosyk (374th)
P-51B B7-

**August 30, 1944**
Groups Operating: P-51 4th, 20th, 55th, 339th, 352nd, 357th, 359th
Missions: Support for bombers to Pas de Calais V-1 sites,(4th Ftr Grp only) and to Kiel and Bremen.
Claims: nil
Losses: nil

**September 1, 1944**
Groups Operating: P-51 4th, 20th, 55th, 339th, 352nd, 355th, 357th, 359th, 361st, 364th
P-47 56th, 78th, 353rd, 356th
P-38 479th
Missions: The P-47 groups carried out fighter-bomber sorties in France and Belgium while the other units were to support the bombers but the heavies were recalled.
Claims: 5-0-2 air
6-3 ground

| ***Group*** | | ***Claims*** | ***Location*** |
|---|---|---|---|
| **78th** | | | |
| 83rd: | Lt. G.G. Boteler | Me-110 dest(air) | Gilze-Rijen |
| | Lt. C.E. Kuykendall | Me-110 dest(air) | Gilze-Rijen |
| | | Me-110 dam(air) | Gilze-Rijen |
| | Lt. J. LaGrange | (.5)Me-110 dest(air) | Gilze-Rijen |
| | | (.5)Me-110 dest(air) | Gilze-Rijen |
| | Lt. P. Bingham | (.5)Me-110 dest(air) | Gilze-Rijen |
| | F/O J.A. Moothart | (.5)Me-110 dest(air) | Gilze-Rijen |
| | | Me-110 dam(air) | Gilze-Rijen |
| 84th: | Maj. Q.L. Brown | Me-109 dest(air) | Liege-Trier |
| | Lt. C.E. Parmelee | FW-190 dest(grd) | SW Antwerp |
| | Lt. H.W. Elin | FW-190 dam(grd) | SW Antwerp |
| **356th**(#1) | | | |
| 360th: | Lt. R.M. Leidy | Me-109 dest(grd) | Le Culot |
| | | Me-109 dam(grd) | Le Culot |
| (#2) | | | |
| 360th: | Lt. E.W. Pleasant | Ju-52 dest(grd) | SE Nancy |
| | Lt. W.H. Fletcher | (.5)Ju-52 dest(grd)[*] | SE Nancy |
| | Lt. E.M. Nebinger | (.5)Ju-52 dest(grd)[**] | SE Nancy |
| | | (.5)Ju-52 dam(grd) | SE Nancy |
| | Lt. J.T. Romine | (.5)Ju-52 dest(grd)[*] | SE Nancy |
| | | (.5)Ju-52 dam(grd) | SE Nancy |
| | Lt. H.S. Olive | (.5)Ju-52 dest(grd)[**] | SE Nancy |
| | Lt. F.W. Peacock | (.5)Ju-52 dest(grd)[@] | SE Nancy |
| | Lt. C.M. Taylor | (.5)Ju-52 dest(grd)[@] | SE Nancy |

*Losses-*

**55th**: Lt. John E. Bauer (338th Ftr Sqn) POW
P-51D CL- 44-13625 "Georgetta"
Lost for unknown reasons west of Paris.

**78th**: Lt. Kenneth P. Dunnaway (83rd Ftr Sqn) MIA-E
P-47D HL-U 42-22776
Hit by flak near Gilze-Rijen and bailed out near Brussels.

Lt. Robert N. Jones (83rd Ftr Sqn) POW
P-47D HL-K 42-26543
Damaged by an exploding loco and bailed out near Mahnes.

**356th**: Lt. Frank A. Forsyth (359th Ftr Sqn) MIA-E
P-47D OC-I 42-26141 "Fearless Fosdick"
Damaged by an exploding loco and bellied-in southwest of Brussels.

**359th**: Lt. Edward C. Kasloski (368th Ftr Sqn) KIA
P-51C CV-U 42-103318
Lost oil pressure and bailed out over the Channel.

**364th**: Lt. Richard P. Davis (383rd Ftr Sqn) ASR
P-51D N2-A 44-13757
Suffered mechanical failure and bailed out over the Channel.

*Remarks*
56th: 3-8 locos, 48-47 railcars, 70-36 vehicles, 0-1 barge, 0-1 tug
78th: 15-4 locos, 35-53 railcars, 92-65 vehicles
353rd: 67-8 locos, 39-141 railcars, 70-45 vehicles, 1-0 bridge
356th: 6-1 locos, 3-36 railcars, 35-6 vehicles

KIAc's
SF: Lt. Teleschor Lojewski (1st)
AT-6
Lt. Charles E. Wright (1st)
AT-6

56th: Lt. John R. Allen (62nd Ftr Sqn)
P-47D LM-

**September 2, 1944**
Groups Operating: P-51 359th
P-47 56th
Missions: The 56th flew a strafing sweep to Belgium while four pilots of the 359th flew an ASR search for Lt. Kasloski.
Claims: nil
Losses: nil

*Remarks*
56th: 0-3 locos, 0-16 railcars, 35-11 vehicles, 5-0 gun positions,
2-0 buildings
P-47 c/l; o.k.
P-47 c/l; o.k.

**September 3, 1944**
Groups Operating: P-51 20th, 55th, 352nd, 357th, 359th, 364th
P-47 78th, 353rd, 356th
P-38 479th
Missions: Support of bombers to the Brest area and Ludwigshafen, plus the 479th conducted fighter-bomber operations in the Brest area and the P-47 groups carried them out in Belgium.
Claims: 7-0-1 air
0-1 ground

| ***Group*** | | ***Claims*** | ***Location*** |
|---|---|---|---|
| **55th** | | | |
| HdQts: | LtCol. W.J. Kelley | FW-190 dest(air) | Antwerp |
| 38th: | Capt. M. Clark | FW-190 dest(air) | Antwerp |
| | Lt. B. Clemmons | FW-190 dest(air) | Antwerp |
| | | FW-190 dam(air) | Antwerp |
| | | Me-109 dam(grd) | Antwerp |
| | Lt. C.C. Sherman | FW-190 dest(air) | Antwerp |
| 338th: | Maj. J.L. McGinn | FW-190 dest(air) | Brussels |
| | Lt. D.S. Cramer | FW-190 dest(air) | Brussels |
| | Lt. H.J. Schonenberg | FW-190 dest(air) | Brussels |

*Losses-*

**78th**: Lt. Richard D. Stark (82nd Ftr Sqn) POW
P-47D MX-G 42-27607
Hit by flak near Maastricht and bellied-in near Roermond.

**355th**: Lt. Sumner C. Williams (354th Ftr Sqn) MIA-E
P-51D WR-W 44-13349
Was flying with the Scouting Force when his aircraft suffered mechanical failure and he bellied-in near Nantes.

*Remarks*
78th: 23-5 locos, 8-47 railcars, 28-0 vehicles, 0-2 barges, 0-1 tug
Capt. Robert R. Bonebrake (83rd Ftr Sqn) b/o Manston; o.k.
P-47D HL-E 42-25724
353rd: 1-0 loco, 90-46 vehicles
356th: 18-9 locos, 0-24 railcars, 19-18 vehicles

**September 5, 1944**
Groups Operating: P-51 4th, 20th, 55th, 339th, 352nd, 355th, 357th, 359th, 361st, 364th
P-47 56th, 78th, 353rd, 356th
P-38 479th
Missions: Support for bombers to Stuttgart, Ludwigshafen, Karlsruhe, and the Brest area plus fighter-bomber operations.
Claims: 27-1-2 air
119-82 ground

| *Group* | | *Claims* | *Location* |
|---|---|---|---|
| **55th** | | | |
| 38th: | Maj. J.D. Landers | Ju-88 dest(grd) | Stuttagrt-Boblingen |
| | | u/i a/c dam(grd) | Stuttgart-Boblingen |
| | Maj. A.B. Parsons | He-111 dest(grd) | Stuttgart-Boblingen |
| | Lt. R.F. Maloney | Ju-88 dest(grd) | Stuttgart-Boblingen |
| | Lt. F.M. Matney | FW-190 dest(grd) | Stuttgart-Boblingen |
| | Capt. M. Clark | Me-109 dam(grd) | Stuttgart-Boblingen |
| | | Ju-87 dam(grd) | Stuttgart-Boblingen |
| | Lt. D.H. Courtney | Ju-87 dam(grd) | Stuttgart-Boblingen |
| | Lt. A.M. Koenig | u/i a/c dam(grd) | Stuttgart-Boblingen |
| | Lt. F.J. Waice | FW-190 dam(grd) | Stuttgart-Boblingen |
| 343rd: | Lt. W.H. Allen | (5)Trainer dest(air) | N/Goppingen A/F |
| | Lt. W.H. Lewis | (5)Trainer dest(air) | N/Goppingen A/F |
| | Lt. T.E. Hoffman | (4)Trainer dest(air) | N/Goppingen A/F |
| | Lt. W.R. Perez | Trainer dest(air) | N/Goppingen A/F |
| | Lt. R.D. Bartlett | (2)He-111 dest(grd) | Stuttgart-Echterdingen |
| | | Me-110 dest(grd) | Stut/Echterdingen |
| | | Me-109 dam(grd) | Stut/Echterdingen |
| | | (.5)glider dam(grd) | Stut/Echterdingen |
| | Lt. F.D. Blair | He-177 dest(grd) | Stut/Echterdingen |
| | | u/i a/c dam(grd) | Stut/Echterdingen |
| | | (.5)Ju-52 dam(grd) | Stut/Echterdingen |
| | Lt. P.S. Dripps | He-111 dest(grd) | Stut/Echterdingen |
| | | (2)He-111 dam(grd) | Stut/Echterdingen |
| | Lt. F.C. Lawrence | He-111 dest(grd) | Stut/Echterdingen |
| | Lt. G.D. Leslie | Ju-52 dest(grd) | Stut/Echterdingen |
| | Lt. W.E. Rosenhoff | He-111 dest(grd) | Stut/Echterdingen |
| | | He-111 dam(grd) | Stut/Echterdingen |
| | | Me-410 dam(grd) | Stut/Echterdingen |
| | Lt. M.R. King | Ju-87 dest(grd) | Goppingen |
| | | Me-110 dam(grd) | Goppingen |
| | Capt. D.A. Parker | (.5)Ju-52 dam(grd) | Stut/Echterdingen |
| | | (.5)glider dam(grd) | Stut/Echterdingen |
| | Lt. P.P. Porter | (2)He-111 dam(grd) | Stut/Echterdingen |
| | Lt. W.K. Pope | (2)He-177 dam(grd) | Goppingen |
| **56th**(#1) | | | |
| HdQts: | Maj. L.A. Dade | (2)Me-210 dest(grd) | Gelnhausen |
| | | He-111 dest(grd) | Gelnhausen |
| 61st: | Lt. W.D. Clark | Me-110 dest(grd) | Merzhausen |
| | | Me-410 dest(grd) | Merzhausen |
| | | u/i a/c dam(grd) | Merzhausen |
| | Capt. B.E. Cathers | Ju-88 dest(grd) | Merzhausen |
| | | u/i a/c dam(grd) | Merzhausen |
| | Lt. J.M. Jure | He-111 dest(grd) | Merzhausen |
| | | Ju-88 dam(grd) | Merzhausen |
| | | u/i a/c dam(grd) | Merzhausen |
| | Lt. C.C. Thomton | (.5)Me-110 dest(grd) | Merzhausen |
| | | u/i a/c dam(grd) | Merzhausen |
| | Lt. J.J. Clark | (.5)Me-110 dest(grd) | Merzhausen |
| | | FW-190 dam(grd) | Merzhausen |
| | Lt. W.E. Bour | He-111 dam(grd) | Merzhausen |
| 62nd: | Capt. M.J. Jackson | (2)Ju-88 dest(grd) | Limburg |
| | | (1.5)Me-210 dest(grd) | Limburg |
| | | Me-109 dest(grd) | Limburg |
| | | (2)Ju-88 dam(grd) | Limburg |
| | Lt. S.T. Murray | (2)Fi-156 dest(grd) | Limburg |
| | | (2)Ju-88 dest(grd) | Limburg |
| | | (.5)Me-210 dest(grd) | Limburg |
| | | Me-109 dam(grd) | Limburg |
| | Capt. H.E. King | He-111 dest(grd) | Merzhausen |
| | | Me-110 dest(grd) | Merzhausen |
| | | Ju-88 dest(grd) | Merzhausen |
| | Lt. F.B. McIntosh | Me-110 dest(grd) | Limburg |
| | | Me-210 dest(grd) | Limburg |
| | | (2)Me-210 dam(grd) | Limburg |
| | | (2)Ju-88 dam(grd) | Limburg |
| | | Me-110 dam(grd) | Limburg |
| | Capt. W.F. Wilkerson | He-111 dest(grd) | Limburg |
| | Lt. H.O. Womack | Me-210 dest(grd) | Merzhausen |
| | | Me-109 dam(grd) | Limburg |
| | | Ju-88 dam(grd) | Limburg |
| 63rd: | Lt. R.B. Anderson | (2)Me-109 dest(air) | NE Coblenz |
| | Lt. C.M. Hart | Me-109 dest(air) | NE Coblenz |
| | | Me-109 prob(air) | NE Coblenz |
| | | Me-109 dam(air) | NE Coblenz |
| | Lt. R.J. Daniel | Me-109 dest(air) | NE Coblenz |
| | Lt. J.A. Kyle | Me-109 dest(air) | NE Coblenz |
| | Lt. R.T. Warboys | Me-109 dest(air) | NE Coblenz |
| | Lt. T.W. Queen | Me-109 dam(air) | NE Coblenz |
| (#2) | | | |
| HdQts: | LtCol. D.C. Schilling | (2)FW-190 dest(grd) | Gelnhausen |
| | | (2)u/i a/c dest(grd) | Gelnhausen |
| | | FW-190 dam(grd) | Gelnhausen |
| 61st: | Capt. R.J. Keen | (3)FW-190 dest(grd) | Gelnhausen |
| | | (3)FW-190 dam(grd) | Gelnhausen |
| | Capt. P.A. Conger | (1.5)Me-210 dam(grd) | Gelnhausen |
| | Lt. F.H. Barrett | (1.5)Me-210 dam(grd) | Gelnhausen |
| | Lt. W.M. Hartshorn | FW-190 dam(grd) | Gelnhausen |
| 62nd: | Lt. G.H. Butler | FW-44 dest(air) | NE Gelnhausen |
| | | (2)Me-109 dest(grd) | Gelnhausen |
| | | FW-190 dest(grd) | Gelnhausen |
| | Capt. M.J. Quirk | (4)FW-190 dest(grd) | Gelnhausen |
| | | (4)FW-190 dam(grd) | Gelnhausen |
| | Lt. D.E. McMahan | (4)FW-190 dest(grd) | Gelnhausen |
| | Lt. R.L. Patterson | (2)FW-190 dest(grd) | Gelnhausen |
| | | u/i a/c dam(grd) | Gelnhausen |
| | Lt. E.M. Beason | FW-190 dest(grd) | Gelnhausen |
| | | u/i a/c dam(grd) | Gelnhausen |
| | Lt. T.A. Edwards | FW-190 dest(grd) | Gelnhausen |
| | | FW-190 dam(grd) | Gelnhausen |
| | Lt. F.B. McIntosh | FW-190 dest(grd) | Gelnhausen |
| | | FW-190 dam(grd) | Gelnhausen |
| | Lt. J.W. Pierce | FW-190 dest(grd) | Gelnhausen |
| | | FW-190 dam(grd) | Gelnhausen |
| | Lt. R.E. Winters | FW-190 dest(grd) | Gelnhausen |
| 63rd: | Lt. E.J. Timony | FW-190 dest(air) | S/Coblenz |
| | | (2)Bu-131 dest(grd) | Gelnhausen |
| | | FW-190 dest(grd) | Gelnhausen |
| | Lt. E.M. Albright | FW-190 dest(grd) | Gelnhausen |
| | | Ju-52 dest(grd) | Gelnhausen |
| | Lt. C.M. Rotzler | (2)FW-190 dest(grd) | Gelnhausen |
| | | (2)FW-190 dam(grd) | Gelnhausen |
| | | Me-109 dam(grd) | Gelnhausen |
| | Lt. C.A. Chinn | u/i a/c dest(grd) | Gelnhausen |
| | Lt. R.J. Daniel | FW-190 dest(grd) | Gelnhausen |
| | Lt. E.A. Henderson | FW-190 dest(grd) | Gelnhausen |
| | Lt. T.W. Queen | FW-190 dest(grd) | Gelnhausen |
| | | FW-190 dam(grd) | Gelnhausen |
| | Lt. R.T. Warboys | Me-109 dest(grd) | Gelnhausen |
| **339th** | | | |
| 503rd: | Lt. N. Ostrow | (1.5)Me-109 dest(air) | Schaffhausen |
| | Lt. E.E. Erickson | (.5)Me-109 dest(air) | Schaffhausen |
| 505th: | Capt. E.M. Johnson | Me-410 dam(grd) | Sinsheim |
| | Lt. C.H. Bundgaard | Me-410 dam(grd) | Sinsheim |
| | Lt. G.E. Graham | Me-410 dam(grd) | Sinsheim |
| **353rd** | | | |
| 352nd: | Capt. G.S. Burlingame | Do-217 dest(air) | Apeldoorn |
| **356th** | | | |
| 361st: | Capt. D.F. Thwaites | (.5)He-111 dest(air) | Twente/Enschede |
| | Lt. F.A. Morgan | (.5)He-111 dest(air) | Twente/Enschede |
| **479th**(#1) | | | |
| 435th: | Lt. V.E. Hooker | He-111 dam(grd) | Hoehst Oberau |
| 436th: | Lt. H.J. Grasshoff | (4)FW-190 dest(grd) | Bad Nauheim |
| | | FW-190 dam(grd) | Bad Nauheim |
| | Lt. E.C. Lewin | (2)FW-190 dest(grd) | Bad Nauheim |
| | | Fi-156 dest(grd) | Bad Nauheim |
| | | u/i a/c dam(grd) | Bad Nauheim |
| | Lt. G.M. Mulvaney | (2)FW-190 dest(grd) | Bad Nauheim |
| | | FW-190 dam(grd) | Bad Nauheim |
| | Lt. V.G. Hartnett | (2)FW-190 dest(grd) | Bad Nauheim |
| | | FW-190 dam(grd) | Bad Nauheim |
| | Lt. V. Wolski | (2)FW-190 dest(grd) | Bad Nauheim |
| | | FW-190 dam(grd) | Bad Nauheim |
| | Capt. C.J. Moore | u/i a/c dest(grd) | Bad Nauheim |
| | | (2)FW-190 dam(grd) | Bad Nauheim |
| | Lt. J.E. Frolking | FW-190 dest(grd) | Bad Nauheim |
| | | FW-190 dam(grd) | Bad Nauheim |
| | Lt. J.W. Hedenburg | u/i a/c dest(grd) | Hoehst Oberau |
| | | u/i a/c dam(grd) | Hoehst Oberau |
| | Lt. A.E. Huycke | He-111 dest(grd) | Merzhausen |
| | | He-111 dam(grd) | Merzhausen |
| | | Do-217 dam(grd) | Merzhausen |
| | Maj. J.A. Sullivan | (2)Do-217 dam(grd) | Hoehst Oberau |
| | | He-111 dam(grd) | Bad Nauheim |
| | Lt. Z. Ogrom | (3)FW-190 dam(grd) | Bad Nauheim |
| | Lt. E.J. Fillipaw | (2)FW-190 dam(grd) | Bad Nauheim |
| | Capt. J.M. Rosness | He-111 dam(grd) | Hoehst Oberau |
| (#2) | | | |
| HdQts: | LtCol. S.S. Woods | Ju-88 dest(grd) | Ettinghausen |
| 434th: | Capt. J.M. Hollingsworth | (4)Me-410 dest(grd) | Ettinghausen |
| | | (2)Do-217 dest(grd) | Ettinghausen |
| | Lt. T.C. Olson | (4)Do-217 dest(grd) | Ettinghausen |
| | | Me-110 dest(grd) | Ettinghausen |
| | Lt. T.D. Neely | (2)Me-110 dest(grd) | Ettinghausen |
| | | Ju-88 dest(grd) | Ettinghausen |

| | | | |
|---|---|---|---|
| | Lt. J.N. Murr | (3)Me-110 dest(grd) | Ettinghausen |
| | Lt. R.H. Hendrickson | (2)Do-217 dest(grd) | Ettinghausen |
| | Lt. B.E. Hollister | (2)Ju-88 dest(grd) | Ettinghausen |
| | Lt. B.A. Williams | (2)Do-217 dest(grd) | Ettinghausen |
| | Lt. H.E. Mathews | Ju-88 dest(grd) | Ettinghausen |
| | Lt. J.W. Morrow | Me-109 dest(grd) | Ettinghausen |
| | Lt. C.J. Murphy | Me-410 dest(grd) | Ettinghausen |
| | Lt. J.T. Tipps | Do-217 dest(grd) | Ettinghausen |

*Losses-*

**55th**: Lt. William C. Cole (343rd Ftr Sqn) KIA
P-51C CY- 42-103507 "Gremlin Leader"
Hit by flak and crashed into the North Sea.

**56th**: Lt. William M. Heaton (61st Ftr Sqn) KIA
P-47D HV- 42-26468
Hit by flak near Altenkirchen and crashed near Limburg.

Lt. Earl Hertel (61st Ftr Sqn) POW
P-47D HV-S 42-75237
Hit by flak in the Koln area.

Lt. Chester E. Frye (63rd Ftr Sqn) POW
P-47D UN-T 42-26258 "Mop Top's Pride"
Hit by flak near Eupen.

**78th**: Capt. Gray H. Doyle (HdQts) KIA
P-47D HL-P 44-19573
Hit by flak near Metelen.

Lt. Charles E. Kuykendall (83rd Ftr Sqn) MIA-E
P-47D HL-B 42-76563 "Jeri"
Hit by flak near Hooksbergen.

**339th**: Lt. Martin F. Nay (505th Ftr Sqn) MIA-E
P-51D 6N- 44-13828
Hit by flak near Rastadt and bellied-in near Kemplich.

**353rd**: Lt. John W. Furneaux (351st Ftr Sqn) POW
P-47D YJ-T 42-8678 "Jose"
Hit by flak near Nijverdal.

**364th**: Lt. John R. Vickers (385th Ftr Sqn) KIA
P-51D 5E- 44-14236
Suffered mechanical failure southwest of Luxembourg.

**479th**: Maj. Raymond S. Carter (435th Ftr Sqn) KIA
P-38J J2-N 44-23177
Hit by flak near Altenstadt.

*Remarks*
4th: Capt. Gerald Brown (334th Ftr Sqn) b/o S/Brequoy; o.k.
P-51D QP-T 44-14056
55th: 1-0 hangar, 0-1 building
56th: 1-1 locos, 12-4 vehicles, 3-0 flak positions, 2-0 hangars
Lt. James J. Clark (61st Ftr Sqn) c/l Amiens; o.k.
P-47D HV-
Lt. James M. Jure (61st Ftr Sqn) c/l; o.k.
P-47D HV-
Lt. Claude A. Chinn (63rd Ftr Sqn) c/l Lantages; o.k.
P-47D UN-
78th: 25-9 locos, 13-132 railcars, 36-10 vehicles, 0-1 barge
Lt. Peter W. Klassen (83rd Ftr Sqn) c/l Duxford; o.k.
P-47D HL-H 43-25528
353rd: 25-3 locos, 25-0 railcars, 114-48 vehicles, 0-2 barges, 0-2 gun positions
356th: 1-1 locos, 0-18 railcars, 16-11 vehicles, 2-3 barges
479th: 1-0 gun position

**September 6, 1944**
Groups Operating: P-51 4th
P-47 56th, 78th, 353rd, 356th
P-38 479th
Missions: The P-47 and P-38 groups carried out strafing sweeps over Holland and western Germany, while the 4th had six P-51's escort some C-47's to Amiens.
Claims: nil

*Losses-*

**78th**: Lt. Percy Bingham (83rd Ftr Sqn) POW
P-47D HL-T 42-76512
Hit by flak near Namur.

Lt. George Rich, III (83rd Ftr Sqn) POW
P-47D HL-J 42-76486
Hit by flak and bailed out near Heuzer.

Maj. Quince L. Brown (84th Ftr Sqn) KIA
P-47D WZ-Z 44-19569 "Okie II"
Hit by flak at Vogelsand Airfield and bailed out near Schleiden. Once upon the ground he was shot by a civilian.

**479th**: Lt. Calvin J. Murphy, Jr. (434th Ftr Sqn) KIA
P-38J L2-O 42-104425 "Boomerang"
Hit by flak near Darmstadt.

*Remarks*
56th: 0-1 loco, 43-20 vehicles, 2-12 horse-drawn vehicles, 2-0 gun positions.
78th: 4-0 locos, 0-10 railcars, 60-27 vehicles
353rd: 29-1 locos, 45-108 railcars, 20-9 vehicles, 0-1 gun position
356th: 17-0 locos, 2-70 railcars, 11-9 vehicles

**September 8, 1944**
Groups Operating: P-51 4th, 20th, 55th, 339th, 352nd, 355th, 357th, 359th, 361st
P-47 56th, 78th, 353rd, 356th
P-38 479th
Missions: Support for bombers to Ludwigshafen, Karlsruhe, Kassel, and Gustavsburg, plus some fighter-bomber activities.
Claims: 0-0-0 air
11-7 ground

| *Group* | | *Claims* | *Location* |
|---|---|---|---|
| **56th** | | | |
| 61st: | Maj. G.E. Baker | u/i a/c dest(grd) | Euskirchen |
| 62nd: | Lt. G.E. Bostwick | (3)FW-190 dest(grd) | Coblenz |
| | Lt. L.R. Brown | u/i a/c dest(grd) | Coblenz |
| | Lt. J.L. Carwell | Me-109 dest(grd) | Coblenz |
| | Lt. B.G. Edens | u/i a/c dest(grd) | Coblenz |
| 63rd: | Lt. E.J. Timony | Ju-88 dest(grd) | Euskirchen |
| | Lt. J.E. Lister | (3)Ju-88 dam(grd) | Euskirchen |
| | Lt. E.M. Albright | u/i a/c dam(grd) | Euskirchen |
| | Lt. R. Frederickson | Me-110 dam(grd) | Euskirchen |
| | Lt. W.R. Groce | Me-109 dam(grd) | Euskirchen |
| **359th** | | | |
| 368th: | Lt. J.M. Aschenmacher | Ju-52 dest(grd) | Cronberg |
| | | Ju-52 dam(grd) | Cronberg |
| | Lt. C.R. Gilmore | Ju-52 dest(grd) | Cronberg |
| | Lt. G.F. Baker | (.5)Ju-52 dest(grd) | Cronberg |
| | Lt. R.E. Benefiel | (.5)Ju-52 dest(grd) | Cronberg |

*Losses-*

**352nd**: Capt. Duncan R. Donahue (487th Ftr Sqn) KIA
P-51D HO-L 44-14109
Damaged by a ground explosion and crashed near Keilbach.

**353rd**: Lt. Albert W. Barlow, Jr. (351st Ftr Sqn) MIA-E
P-47D YJ-J 42-22579 "Jeannie"
Hit by flak and bailed out near Aachen.

*Remarks*
56th: 25-10 vehicles, 3-4 gun positions
352nd: 4-9 locos, 17-14 railcars, 8-2 vehicles
353rd: 16-0 locos, 16-50 railcars, 62-19 vehicles
355th: Capt. William J. Hovde (358th Ftr Sqn) c/l; o.k.
P-51D YF-I 44-13531 "Ole III"
359th: 31-21 locos, 11-21 railcars, 17-9 vehicles, 0-1 ship
361st: P-51 b/o; o.k.

**September 9, 1944**

Groups Operating: P-51 4th, 20th, 55th, 339th, 352nd, 357th, 359th, 361st, 364th
P-47 56th, 78th, 353rd, 356th
Missions: Support of bombers to Mannheim, Mainz, and Dusseldorf, plus fighter-bomber operations.
Claims: 9-0-4 air
4-1 ground

| *Group* | | *Claims* | *Location* |
|---|---|---|---|
| **78th** | | | |
| 82nd: | Lt. W.L. Coleman | (3)FW-190 dest(air) | Hersfeld |
| | Lt. H.F. Scholz | (2)FW-190 dest(air) | Giessen |
| | | FW-190 dam(air) | Giessen |
| | | Ju-88 dest(grd) | Munster |
| | Lt. J.L. Mattern | FW-190 dam(air) | Coblenz |
| | Lt. R.W. Dunham | (.5)FW-190 dam(air)* | Giessen |
| | Lt. H.K. Shope | Ju-88 dest(grd) | Giessen |
| | Capt. R.E. Conner | (.5)Me-109 dest(grd) | Giessen |
| | Lt. D.C. Hart | (.5)Me-109 dest(grd) | Giessen |
| 84th: | Maj. B.I. Mayo | (2)FW-190 dest(air) | Giessen |
| | Lt. W.K. Grimes | FW-190 dest(air) | Giessen |
| | | (.5)FW-190 dam(air)* | Giessen |
| **353rd** | | | |
| 350th: | Lt. S.T. Benjamin | Do-217 dest(air) | Hesepe A/F |
| | Lt. M.W. Hightshoe | Do-217 dam(grd) | Hesepe A/F |
| **356th** | | | |
| 359th: | Lt. D.F. Tucker | He-111 dest(grd) | W/Bad Nauheim |
| 360th: | Lt. J.T. Romine | FW-190 dam(air) | W/Giessen |

*Losses-*

**4th**: Lt. Earl C. Walsh (334th Ftr Sqn) ASR
P-51D QP-V 44-13352
Bailed out thirty miles west of Schouwen Island.

**55th**: Lt. Raymond L. Mull (343rd Ftr Sqn) MIA-E
P-51D CY- 44-11158
Suffered mechanical failure northeast of Turnhout.

**56th**: Capt. Roy T. Fling (63rd Ftr Sqn) KIA
P-47D UN-V 42-28543 "Pat"
Hit by flak near Etten.

Lt. Everett A. Henderson (63rd Ftr Sqn) KIA
P-47D UN- 42-8575
Hit the ground while strafing near Etten.

**78th**: Lt. Kenneth L. Moore (82nd Ftr Sqn) POW
P-47D MX-O 42-76351
Hit by a FW-190 near Dellhofen.

**356th**: Lt. John H. Garlent (360th Ftr Sqn) KIA
P-47D PI- 42-22469 "Old Master"
Hit by a FW-190 near Wetzlar.

Lt. Robert N. Leidy (360th Ftr Sqn) KIA
P-47D PI-C 42-26683 "Mugsy"
Last seen being chased by FW-190's near Eichelhardt.

Lt. Harry F. Rideout (360th Ftr Sqn) KIA
P-47D PI- 42-25861
Hit by FW-190's near Illerach.

*Remarks*
4th: 0-3 tugs, 0-4 ships
56th: 1-1 locos, 28-5 railcars, 31-13 vehicles, 31-9 horse-drawn vehicles, 1-1 gun positions
78th: 14-16 locos, 4-13 railcars, 8-0 vehicles, 2-0 barracks, 0-1 hangar
356th: 10-4 locos, 0-63 railcars
Lt. Howell L. Broxton (359th Ftr Sqn) c/l; o.k.
P-47D OC-R 42-8549 "Elsie"

KIAc's
479th: Lt. Everett P. Ford (435th Ftr Sqn)
P-38J J2-

**September 10, 1944**
Groups Operating: P-51 4th, 20th, 55th, 339th, 352nd, 355th, 357th, 359th, 361st, 364th
P-47 56th, 78th, 353rd, 356th
P-38 479th
Missions: Support of bombers to Ulm, Heilbronn, Nurnberg, Stuttgart, Giebelstadt, Zuffenhausen, and Gaggenau.
Claims: 6-0-1 air
112-71 ground

| *Group* | | *Claims* | *Location* |
|---|---|---|---|
| **4th** | | | |
| 335th: | Lt. T.E. Lines | (3)Me-109 dest(air) | Strasbourg |
| | | Ju-88 dest(air) | S/Kaiserlautern |
| **20th** | | | |
| 79th: | Lt. E.H. Coughran | (3)u/i a/c dest(grd) | SW Stuttgart |
| | Lt. H.O. Binkley | Me-110 dest(grd) | SW Stuttgart |
| | | u/i a/c dest(grd) | SW Stuttgart |
| | Lt. C.J. Dixon | u/i a/c dam(grd) | SW Stuttgart |
| **55th** | | | |
| 38th: | Lt. O.B. Clifton | Ju-88 dest(grd) | Kitzingen |
| | Lt. R.F. Maloney | Ju-88 dest(grd) | Kitzingen |
| | Lt. G.V. Wegner | Ju-88 dam(grd) | Kitzingen |
| 343rd: | Lt. E.J. Dvorak | (.5)Hs-126 dest(air) | Schwasbmunchen |
| | Lt. G.D. Leslie | (.5)Hs-126 dest(air) | Schwasbmunchen |
| | Capt. D.A. Parker | He-111 dest(grd) | Illesheim |
| | | Ju-88 dest(grd) | Illesheim |
| | Lt. F.C. Lawrence | (2)Me-210 dest(grd) | Illesheim |
| | | (4)Me-210 dam(grd) | Illesheim |
| | Lt. K.T. Williams | He-111 dest(grd) | NE Augsburg |
| | | Ju-88 dest(grd) | NE Augsburg |
| | Capt. R.D. Brown | He-111 dest(grd) | NE Augsburg |
| | Lt. F.A. Blair | u/i a/c dest(grd) | Illesheim |
| | Lt. G.H. Cole | Me-109 dest(grd) | S/Augsburg |
| | Lt. D.M. Fry | He-111 dest(grd) | NE Augsburg |
| | | He-111 dam(grd) | NE Augsburg |
| | Lt. D.L. Mercier | Me-109 dest(grd) | NE Augsburg |
| **56th** | | | |
| 62nd: | Capt. M.J. Quirk | He-111 dest(grd) | Seligenstadt |
| | Lt. J.W. Pierce | He-111 dest(grd) | Seligenstadt |
| | Lt. G.H. Butler | u/i a/c dam(grd) | Seligenstadt |
| | Lt. G.H. Van Noy | Ju-88 dam(grd) | Seligenstadt |
| **78th** | | | |
| 82nd: | Lt. R.R. Bosworth | (4)Ju-88 dest(grd) | Meinbullen |
| | Maj. J. Myers | (3)He-111 dest(grd) | Meinbullen |
| | | He-111 dam(grd) | Meinbullen |
| | Lt. T.L. Eggleston | (3)He-111 dest(grd) | Meinbullen |
| | Capt. R.A. Hewitt | (2)Ju-88 dest(grd) | Meinbullen |
| | Lt. W.O. Lacy | (2)Ju-88 dest(grd) | Meinbullen |
| | | (2)Ju-88 dam(grd) | Meinbullen |
| | Lt. W.B. Slater | (2)He-111 dest(grd) | Meinbullen |
| | | He-111 dam(grd) | Meinbullen |
| | F/O W.I. Warren | Ju-88 dest(grd) | Meinbullen |
| | Lt. I.H. Keatley | He-111 dam(grd) | Meinbullen |
| 83rd: | Lt. W.B. Sommer | Me-410 dest(grd) | Germsheim |
| | | FW-190 dest(grd) | Germsheim |
| | Lt. W.E. Bennett | (.5)He-111 dest(grd) | Germsheim |
| | Lt. D.D. Hartley | (.5)He-111 dest(grd) | Germsheim |
| | Lt. F.E. Harrington | Me-410 dam(grd) | Germsheim |
| | | Ju-87 dam(grd) | Germsheim |
| 84th: | Capt. R.E. Smith | (4.5)He-111 dest(grd)[*] | Meinbullen |
| | | He-111 dam(grd) | Meinbullen |
| | Lt. E.W. Wood | (2)He-111 dest(grd) | Meinbullen |
| | | Fi-156 dest(grd) | Meinbullen |
| | | (2)He-111 dam(grd) | Meinbullen |
| | Lt. A.P. Manning | (2.5)He-111 dest(grd)[*] | Meinbullen |
| | | He-111 dam(grd) | Meinbullen |
| | Lt. M.R. Capp | (3)He-111 dest(grd) | Meinbullen |
| | | He-111 dam(grd) | Meinbullen |
| | Lt. A.G. McGuire | (2)He-111 dest(grd) | Meinbullen |
| | | (4)He-111 dam(grd) | Meinbullen |
| | Lt. R.L. Baron | He-111 dest(grd) | Meinbullen |
| | | He-111 dam(grd) | Meinbullen |
| | Lt. A.A. Garback | He-111 dest(grd) | Meinbullen |
| | | He-111 dam(grd) | Meinbullen |
| | Lt. R.E. Clague | (.5)He-111 dest(grd)[**] | Meinbullen |
| | Lt. M.T. Wilson | (.5)He-111 dest(grd)[**] | Meinbullen |
| | Lt. S.B. Calderon | (2)He-111 dam(grd) | Meinbullen |
| **339th** | | | |
| 505th: | Maj. J.L. Thury | Ju-52 dest(grd) | Weizenburg |
| | | Ju-88 dest(grd) | Weizenburg |
| | Lt. A.D. Young | (3)u/i a/c dest(grd) | Weizenburg |
| | Lt. C. Malarz | (2)Ju-88 dest(grd) | Weizenburg |
| | | Me-410 dest(grd) | Weizenburg |
| | | (3)He-111 dam(grd) | Weizenburg |
| | | Ju-88 dam(grd) | Weizenburg |
| | Lt. B.O. Jackson | (2)u/i a/c dest(grd) | Weizenburg |
| | | Ju-88 dest(grd) | Weizenburg |
| | Lt. W.A. Jones | Ju-87 dest(grd) | Weizenburg |
| | | u/i a/c dest(grd) | Weizenburg |
| | | (.5)Me-109 dest(grd) | Weizenburg |
| | | (2)He-111 dam(grd) | Weizenburg |
| | Lt. L.J. Powell | Me-410 dest(grd) | Weizenburg |
| | | Do-217 dest(grd) | Weizenburg |
| | | (4)u/i a/c dam(grd) | Weizenburg |
| | Lt. J.F. Marts | (2)Me-410 dest(grd) | Weizenburg |
| | | (2)He-111 dam(grd) | Weizenburg |
| | | Ju-88 dam(grd) | Weizenburg |
| | | u/i a/c dam(grd) | Weizenburg |
| | Lt. C.R. Stewart | (2)Ju-88 dest(grd) | Munich |
| | | (.5)Me-109 dest(grd) | Weizenburg |
| | | (3)Ju-88 dam(grd) | Munich |
| | Capt. A.A. Tower | Ju-88 dest(grd) | Munich |
| | | Ju-52 dest(grd) | Munich |
| | | (2)He-111 dam(grd) | Munich |
| | | Ju-88 dam(grd) | Munich |
| | Lt. R.H. Tannous | Me-410 dest(grd) | Weizenburg |
| | | u/i a/c dest(grd) | Weizenburg |
| | | (6)u/i a/c dam(grd) | Weizenburg |
| | Lt. O.P. Farmer | u/i a/c dest(grd) | Weizenburg |
| | Lt. W.R. Moore | Ju-88 dest(grd) | Munich |
| | Lt. J.B. Muller | Ju-88 dest(grd) | Weizenburg |
| | Lt. G.T. Rich | FW-190 dest(grd) | Weizenburg |
| | Capt. R.M. Mitchell | Ju-88 dam(grd) | Weizenburg |
| | Lt. W.H. Krauss | Ju-88 dam(grd) | Weizenburg |
| **352nd** | | | |
| 487th: | LtCol. J.C. Meyer | (3)Ju-52 dest(grd) | Wertheim |
| | | u/i a/c dest(grd) | Wertheim |
| | Capt. C.O. Johnson | (5)Ju-52 dest(grd) | Wertheim |
| | Lt. J.B. Ayers | Ju-52 dest(grd) | Wertheim |
| | | u/i a/c dest(grd) | Wertheim |
| | Lt. M.C. Pickering | (2)u/i a/c dest(grd) | Wertheim |
| | Lt. P.B. Waters | (2)Ju-52 dest(grd) | Wertheim |
| | Capt. J.R. Bennett | Ju-52 dest(grd) | Wertheim |
| | Lt. G.L. Bowers | Ju-52 dest(grd) | Wertheim |
| | Lt. D.M. Huston | Ju-52 dest(grd) | Wertheim |
| | Lt. J.C. Landrum | Ju-52 dest(grd) | Wertheim |
| | Lt. A.P. Rigby | u/i a/c dest(grd) | Wertheim |

| | | | |
|---|---|---|---|
| **355th** | | | |
| 354th: | Lt. H.W. Brown | (6)He-60 dest(grd) | Frankfurt |
| | Lt. S.G. Betounes | (4)He-60 dam(grd) | Frankfurt |
| **359th** | | | |
| 369th: | Lt. K.L. Hobson | u/i a/c dest(air) | NW Stuttgart |
| | | u/i a/c dam(air) | NW Stuttgart |
| **479th** | | | |
| 434th: | Lt. R.L. Maley | He-111 dam(grd) | Malmsheim |
| | Lt. H.E. Mathews | He-111 dam(grd) | Malmsheim |

*Losses-*

**4th:** Lt. Robert W. White (336th Ftr Sqn) KIA
P-51B VF- 43-6891
Crashed at Boxted on return from the mission.

**55th:** Lt. Maynard R. King (343rd Ftr Sqn) KIA
P-51D CY- 44-13843
Hit by flak and crashed into a hangar at Herzogenaurach.

**56th:** Capt. Michael J. Quirk (62nd Ftr Sqn) POW
P-47D LM-K 42-27382
Hit by flak at Seligenstadt Airfield.

Lt. Billy G. Edens (62nd Ftr Sqn) POW
P-47D LM-H 42-25522
Hit by flak near Trier.

**78th:** Lt. William O. Lacy (82nd Ftr Sqn) KIA
P-47D MX-B 42-75243
Hit by flak at Meinbullen.

Lt. Lawton E. Clark (84th Ftr Sqn) KIA
P-47D WZ-E 42-26590
Flew into the ground while strafing near Heilbronn.

Lt. Robert E. Clague (84th Ftr Sqn) POW
P-47D WZ-F 42-25698
Hit by flak near Graefenhausen.

Lt. Paul H. McKinny (84th Ftr Sqn) POW
P-47D WZ-J 43-25303
Hit by flak near Aschaffenburg.

Lt. Charles E. Parmelee (84th Ftr Sqn) KIA
P-47D WZ-L 43-25593
Hit by flak and crashed into a wall while belly-landing near Wiesbaden.

**339th:** Maj. John R. Reynolds (HdQts) KIA
P-51D D7- 44-14069
Hit by flak near Weizenburg.

Lt. Raymond F. Reuter (503rd Ftr Sqn) MIA-E
P-51B D7-G 42-106614
Suffered mechanical failure near Saarburg.

**359th:** Lt. Benjamin J. Vos, Jr. (370th Ftr Sqn) KIA
P-51D CS- 44-14240
Hit by flak southeast of Wurzburg.

*Remarks*
55th: 9-0 locos, 0-22 railcars, 4-0 vehicles, 0-1 barracks
78th: 0-1 loco,
P-47 c/l Belgium; o.k.
352nd: 0-1 loco, 0-8 gun positions
353rd: 10-0 locos, 0-16 railcars
355th: Lt. Clarence H. Kouche (358th Ftr Sqn) c/l Liege; o.k.
P-51B YF-O 43-6815
356th: 7-4 locos, 4-2 vehicles
359th: 3-1 locos, 2-1 vehicles
361st: Lt. Norman L. Smith (376th Ftr Sqn) c/l Montdidier; o.k.
P-51B E9-C 42-106688

**September 11, 1944**
Groups Operating: P-51 4th, 20th, 55th, 339th, 352nd, 355th, 357th, 359th, 361st, 364th
P-47 56th, 78th, 353rd, 356th
P-38 479th
Missions: Support for bombers to Merseburg, Lutzkendorf, Misburg, Magdeburg, Chemnitz, Bohlen, and other oil targets, plus the 20th escorted "Frantic III" bombers to Russia.
Claims: 114-10-23 air
49-48 ground

| *Group* | | *Claims* | *Location* |
|---|---|---|---|
| **4th** | | | |
| HdQts: | LtCol. C.H. Kinnard | Me-109 dest(air) | Halle |
| | | Me-410 dest(grd) | Halle |
| 334th: | Capt. G.E. Montgomery | Me-109 dest(air) | Aschersleben |
| | Lt. L.R. Werner | Me-109 dest(air) | Eisenach-Gotha |
| | | FW-190 dam(air) | Eisenach-Gotha |
| | Lt. H.E. Clifton | FW-190 dam(air) | Aschersleben |
| 335th: | Lt. G.W. Cooley | (2)FW-190 dest(air) | NW Naumburg |
| | Lt. R.J. Rinebolt | FW-190 dest(air) | NW Naumburg |
| | Lt. J.W. Russell | Me-109 dest(air) | Erfurt |
| | | Me-109 prob(air) | Erfurt |
| | | FW-190 prob(air) | Erfurt |
| | Lt. J.N. Peters | Me-109 prob(air) | NW Naumburg |
| 336th: | Lt. H.E. Dugan | Me-109 dest(air) | Korbach |
| | Lt. J.H. Joiner | Me-109 dest(air) | Korbach |
| | Lt. C.W. Dupree | (2)FW-190 dest(grd) | Langensalza |
| | F/O D.J. Pierni | (2)FW-190 dest(grd) | Langensalza |
| | Lt. F.M. Grove | FW-190 dest(grd) | Langensalza |
| | | (2)FW-190 dam(grd) | Langensalza |
| | | Ju-188 dam(grd) | Langensalza |
| | Lt. H.A. Ingalls | FW-190 dest(grd) | Langensalza |
| | Lt. C.H. Patterson | FW-190 dest(grd) | Langensalza |
| **55th** | | | |
| 38th: | Lt. E.R. Fryer | (2)Me-109 dest(air) | S/Erfurt |
| | Lt. F.M. Matney | (2)Me-109 dest(air) | Erfurt |
| | Lt. M.M. Coons | Me-109 dest(air) | Erfurt |
| | | Me-109 prob(air) | Erfurt |
| | Lt. K.I. Crawford | Me-109 dest(air) | S/Erfurt |
| | Lt. T.H. Holleman | Me-109 dest(air) | E/Meiningen |
| | Lt. C.C. Sherman | Me-109 dest(air) | Erfurt |
| | Lt. A.L. Thorsen | Me-109 dest(air) | SE Erfurt |
| 338th: | Lt. W.J. Ingram | (2.5)Me-109 dest(air) | S/Meiningen |
| | | (shared with an unknown pilot) | |
| | | Me-109 dam(air) | S/Meiningen |
| | Lt. R.C. Haworth | (2)Me-109 dest(air) | S/Meiningen |
| | | Me-109 dam(air) | S/Meiningen |
| | Lt. J.M. Wakeland | (2)Me-109 dest(air) | S/Meiningen |
| | | Me-109 dam(air) | S/Meiningen |
| | Lt. D.S. Cramer | (1.5)Me-109 dest(air) | S/Meiningen |
| | | (shared with an unknown pilot) | |
| | LtCol. J.L. McGinn | Me-109 dest(air) | S/Meiningen |
| | | (2)Me-109 dam(air) | S/Meiningen |
| | Lt. R.I. Barrett | Me-109 dest(air) | S/Meiningen |
| | Lt. R.K. Fruh | Me-109 dest(air) | S/Meiningen |
| | Lt. W.J. Konantz | Me-109 dest(air) | S/Meiningen |
| | Lt. W.J. Leonard | Me-109 dest(air) | S/Meiningen |
| | | Me-109 dam(air) | S/Meiningen |
| 343rd: | Lt. R.D. Bishop | FW-190 dest(air) | Saalfeld |
| | | FW-190 dam(air) | Saalfeld |
| | | FW-190 dest(grd) | Saalfeld |
| | Lt. R.H. Yee Litt | FW-190 dest(air) | Sonneburg |
| | Lt. F.L. Tischer | Me-109 prob(air) | Sonneburg |
| **339th** | | | |
| 503rd: | Lt. F.R. Gerard | (3)Me-109 dest(air) | Annaburg |
| | | FW-190 dest(air) | Annaburg |
| | | Me-109 dam(air) | Annaburg |
| | Lt. R.D. Mayer | (2)Me-109 dest(air) | Annaburg |
| | Maj. J. Aitken | Me-109 dest(air) | Annaburg |
| | | FW-190 dam(air) | Annaburg |
| | Capt. C.E. Cloud | Me-109 dest(air) | Annaburg |
| | Lt. E.E. Erickson | FW-190 dest(air) | Annaburg |
| | | FW-190 prob(air) | Annaburg |
| | Lt. J.B. Price | FW-190 dest(air) | Annaburg |
| | Lt. C.S. Coe | FW-190 dest(air) | Annaburg |
| | | (.5)FW-190 dest(air)* | Annaburg |
| | Lt. E.H. Graham | (.5)FW-190 dest(air)* | Annaburg |
| | | (.5)Me-109 dest(air) | Annaburg |
| | Lt. D.E. McClish | (.5)Me-109 dest(air) | Annaburg |
| | | (.5)FW-190 dest(air)** | Annaburg |
| | | FW-190 prob(air) | Annaburg |
| | Capt. J.G. Robinson | (.5)FW-190 dest(air)** | Annaburg |
| | Lt. W.D. Stockton | FW-190 dam(air) | Annaburg |
| 505th: | Capt. A.A. Tower | (2)Ju-88 dest(grd) | Munich |
| | | He-111 dest(grd) | Munich |
| | | Me-410 dest(grd) | Munich |
| | | Ju-87 dest(grd) | Munich |
| | | (2)Ju-88 dam(grd) | Munich |
| | Lt. W.H. Krauss | (2)Me-410 dest(grd) | Munich |
| | | Me-110 dest(grd) | Munich |
| | | Ju-88 dest(grd) | Munich |
| | | (3)Me-410 dam(grd) | Munich |
| | Maj. J.L. Thury | (2)Ju-88 dest(grd) | Munich |
| | | He-111 dam(grd) | Munich |
| | | Me-109 dam(grd) | Munich |
| | | Me-410 dam(grd) | Munich |
| | | Ju-88 dam(grd) | Munich |
| | Lt. C.H. Bundgaard | (2)Ju-88 dest(grd) | Munich |
| | | (3)Ju-52 dam(grd) | Munich |
| | Lt. G.T. Rich | (2)u/i a/c dest(grd) | Munich |
| | | Me-410 dest(grd) | Munich |
| | | Me-410 dam(grd) | Munich |
| | Lt. W.R. Slovak | Me-410 dest(grd) | Munich |
| | | u/i a/c dest(grd) | Munich |
| | | (2)Me-410 dam(grd) | Munich |

| Unit | Pilot | Claim | Location |
|---|---|---|---|
| | Lt. T.R. Staggers | Me-110 dest(grd) | Munich |
| | | Ju-88 dest(grd) | Munich |
| | | Me-110 dam(grd) | Munich |
| | | He-111 dam(grd) | Munich |
| | | Ju-88 dam(grd) | Munich |
| | Lt. W.A. Jones | Ju-88 dest(grd) | Munich |
| | | Ju-52 dest(grd) | Munich |
| | | Ju-88 dam(grd) | Munich |
| | Capt. R.B. Olander | u/i a/c dest(grd) | Munich |
| | | (2)u/i a/c dam(grd) | Munich |
| | Lt. G.E. Graham | Me-410 dest(grd) | Munich |
| | | Me-410 dam(grd) | Munich |
| | | Do-217 dam(grd) | Munich |
| | | Ju-88 dam(grd) | Munich |
| | Lt. W. Jaaskelainen | Ju-88 dest(grd) | Munich |
| | | He-111 dam(grd) | Munich |
| **352nd** | | | |
| 328th: | Capt. W.E. Hendrian | FW-190 dest(air) | E/Meiningen |
| | Lt. R.F. Semon | FW-190 dest(air) | E/Meiningen |
| 487th: | LtCol. J.C. Meyer | (3)Me-109 dest(air) | Gottingen-Nordhausen-Mulhausen |
| | | FW-190 dest(air) | Gott-Nord-Muhl. |
| | Capt. C.O. Johnson | (2)Me-109 dest(air) | Gottingen |
| | Lt. J.H. Forga | (2)FW-190 dest(air) | Gottingen |
| | | Me-109 dest(air) | Gottingen |
| | Capt. J.R. Bennett | FW-190 dest(air) | Gott-Nord-Muhl. |
| | | (2)Me-109 dam(air) | Gott-Nord-Muhl. |
| | Lt. D.H. Schuh | Me-109 dest(air) | Einbeck-Gottingen |
| | Lt. P.B. Waters | FW-190 dest(air) | Gottingen |
| | Lt. R.H. Littge | (2)Ju-88 dest(grd) | Gotha |
| | | (2)Ju-88 dam(grd) | Gotha |
| | Lt. A.F. Sears | u/i a/c dest(grd) | Langensalza |
| | Lt. H.M. Stewart | Ju-88 dest(grd) | Gotha |
| | | (2)Ju-88 dam(grd) | Gotha |
| **355th** | | | |
| 354th: | Lt. H.W. Brown | (3)Me-109 dest(air) | S/Kassel |
| | Capt. B.W. Marshall | (2)Me-109 dest(air) | S/Kassel |
| | | Me-109 dam(air) | S/Kassel |
| | F/Lt. W.B. Peglar | (2)Me-109 dest(air) | S/Kassel |
| | Lt. R.W. Priest | Me-109 dest(air) | S/Kassel |
| | Lt. F.W. Schultz | Me-109 dest(air) | S/Kassel |
| | | (.5)Me-109 dest(grd) | Marburg |
| | Capt. B.C. Williamson | FW-190 dest(grd) | S/Kassel |
| | Lt. R.M. White | (1.5)Me-109 dest(grd) | Marburg |
| | Lt. C.R. McCurry | Ju-52 dest(grd) | S/Kassel |
| 358th: | Lt. J.J. Maisch | (2)Me-109 dest(air) | Marburg |
| | F/Lt. L.S. Frost | Me-109 dest(air) | S/Kassel |
| | | Me-109 dam(air) | S/Kassel |
| | | (2)Do-217 dam(grd) | S/Kassel |
| **359th** | | | |
| 368th: | Capt. B.H. King | (2)FW-190 dest(air) | Eisleben |
| | | Me-109 dest(air) | Eisleben |
| | Lt. G.F. Baker | (2)FW-190 dest(air) | Halberstadt |
| | Lt. L.E. Barnett | (2)FW-190 dest(air) | Eisleben |
| | | FW-190 prob(air) | Eisleben |
| | Lt. C.R. Gilmore | FW-190 dest(air) | Eisleben |
| | Lt. J.D. Flack | (.5)Me-109 dest(air) | Eisenach |
| | Lt. C.M. Lambright | (.5)Me-109 dest(air) | Eisenach |
| | Lt. R.E. Benefiel | (2)Me-109 dam(air) | Eisenach |
| | Lt. A.F. Kysely | FW-190 dam(air) | Weimar |
| | Lt. W.H. Lewis | Me-109 dam(air) | Eisenach |
| 369th: | Lt. C.J. Crenshaw | (2)Me-109 dest(air) | Kolleda |
| | | u/i a/c dest(grd) | Kolleda |
| | Lt. G.M. Perrin | (2)FW-190 dest(air) | Kolleda |
| | | Me-109 prob(air) | Kolleda |
| | Lt. G.R. Ralston | Me-109 dest(air) | Kolleda |
| | | FW-190 dest(air) | Kolleda |
| | Capt. J.W. Parsons | Me-109 dest(air) | Kolleda |
| | Lt. F.W. Holliday | Me-109 dest(air) | N/Erfurt |
| | Lt. J.E. Keur | Me-109 dest(air) | N/Erfurt |
| | Lt. R.S. Gaines | Me-109 prob(air) | Weimar |
| | Lt. T.J. Klem | Me-109 dam(air) | N/Leipzig |
| | Lt. J.R. Parsons | (2)Ju-88 dest(grd) | S/Merseburg |
| | | (3)Ju-88 dam(grd) | S/Merseburg |
| | Lt. J.W. Mejaski | (2)Ju-88 dest(grd) | S/Merseburg |
| | | (3)Ju-88 dam(grd) | S/Merseburg |
| 370th: | Lt. C.W. Jones | (4)Me-109 dest(air) | Gotha |
| | | He-177 dest(grd) | Gotha |
| | | Ju-88 dest(grd) | Gotha |
| | | (2)Me-410 dam(grd) | Gotha |
| | | (2)Ju-88 dam(grd) | Gotha |
| | | (.5)He-177 dam(grd) | Gotha |
| | Lt. W.E. Buchanan | Me-109 dest(air) | Gotha |
| | | Ju-88 dam(grd) | Gotha |
| | Lt. W.C. Murray | Me-109 dest(air) | Gotha |
| | | (2)Ju-88 dam(grd) | Gotha |
| | | (.5)He-177 dam(grd) | Gotha |
| | Lt. J.H. O'Shea | FW-190 dest(air) | Mulhausen |
| | Lt. J.W. Wilson | Me-109 dest(air) | Mulhausen |
| | | FW-190 dam(air) | Mulhausen |
| **361st** | | | |
| 375th: | Lt. U.L. Drew | Me-109 dest(air) | S/Gottingen |
| **364th** | | | |
| 383rd: | Capt. C.A. Barnes | Me-109 dam(air) | Sangerhausen |
| 384th: | Lt. W.E. Bristow | Me-109 dest(air) | Nordhausen |
| | | FW-190 dest(air) | Nordhausen |
| 385th: | Capt. C.S. Hill | Me-109 dest(air) | Sangerhausen |
| | | FW-190 dest(air) | Sangerhausen |
| | Lt. W.F. Wilson | (2)FW-190 dest(air) | W/Leipzig |
| | | Me-109 dest(air) | W/Leipzig |
| | Lt. G.L. Jamison | (2)FW-190 dest(air) | SW Leipzig |
| | Lt. J.J. Pascoe | (2)FW-190 dest(air) | SW Leipzig |
| | Lt. A.J. Trybuszewski | (2)Me-109 dest(air) | W/Leipzig |

*Losses-*

**4th**: Lt. William R. Groseclose (335th Ftr Sqn) POW
P-51D WD-Q 44-14431
Hit by a Me-109 near Naumburg.

Lt. Paul S. Iden (335th Ftr Sqn) KIA
P-51B WD-Z 43-6959
Hit by a Me-109 near Naumburg.

Lt. James W. Russell, Jr. (335th Ftr Sqn) POW
P-51D WD-R 44-14158
Hit by enemy fighters near Fulda.

Lt. Henry A. Ingalls (336th Ftr Sqn) POW
P-51B VF-P 43-6573
Hit by flak near Langensalza.

Lt. Rufus L. Patterson (336th Ftr Sqn) KIA
P-51D VF- 44-14266
Hit by flak near Lutsendorf.

**55th**: Lt. Kenneth I. Crawford (38th Ftr Sqn) KIA
P-51D CG-T 44-13723 "One Mustang"
Hit by enemy fighters near Oberhof.

Lt. William M. Lewis, Jr. (38th Ftr Sqn) KIA
P-51D CG- 44-14176
Hit by enemy fighters near Gera.

Lt. Wayne E. Rosenhoff (343rd Ftr Sqn) POW
P-51D CY- 44-13724
Damaged by an exploding aircraft near Sonneburg.

Lt. Kenneth T. Williams (343rd Ftr Sqn) KIA
P-51D CY- 44-13850
Suffered mechanical failure near Chemnitz.

**339th**: Lt. William A. Jones (505th Ftr Sqn) POW
P-51C 6N- 42-103742 "Man O'War"
Mechanical failure, then hit by a Me-262 near Eberach.

Lt. Ted B. Staggers (505th Ftr Sqn) POW
P-51D 6N-U 44-13616 "Baggy Pants"
Hit by flak southeast of Munich.

**352nd**: Lt. Garland Rayborn (328th Ftr Sqn) KIA
P-51D PE-Z 44-13785 "La Riena Peg II"
Hit by enemy fighters south of Gotha.

Lt. Howard R. Combs, Jr. (486th Ftr Sqn) KIA
P-51D PZ-T 44-14043 "Lil Evey"
Hit by flak near Herzberg.

**355th**: Capt. Kevin G. Rafferty (354th Ftr Sqn) KIA
P-51B WR-P 42-106950 "The Iowa Beaut"
Hit by flak near Marburg.

Lt. Charles R. McCurry (354th Ftr Sqn) KIA
P-51B WR-R 43-6943 "Patricia"
Hit by flak near Marburg; bailed out but his chute failed.

Capt. Walter L. Morgan (358th Ftr Sqn) KIA
P-51B YF-S 43-7023 "Big Stoop"
Hit by flak at Kirchain Airfield.

**359th**: F/O Charles R. Bruening (369th Ftr Sqn) KIA
P-51D IV- 44-14399
Hit by enemy fighters near Diemerode.

Lt. Frank W. Holliday (369th Ftr Sqn) KIA
P-51D IV-P 44-14307
Hit by enemy fighters near Meiches.

Lt. James F. Hutton (369th Ftr Sqn) KIA
P-51D IV- 44-14108
Hit by enemy fighters near Hemleben.

Lt. Ivan B. Holloman (369th Ftr Sqn) MIA-E
P-51D IV-H 44-13689
Hit by enemy fighters near Kolleda.

F/O James J. O'Shea (370th Ftr Sqn) KIA
P-51D CS-D 44-13529 "Pandemonium"
Hit by enemy fighters near Mulhausen.

**361st**: Lt. John H. Lougheed (375th Ftr Sqn) KIA
P-51C E2-X 42-103749 "Betty Lou"
Collided with a B-24 near Eerde.

**364th**: Lt. Alfred A. Albrecht (384th Ftr Sqn) MIA
P-51D 5Y- 44-14174
Hit by enemy fighters near Giessen.

Lt. Daniel W. Davis (385th Ftr Sqn) POW
P-51D 5E-M 44-14033 "Doodlebug"
Hit by enemy fighters near Sangerhausen.

*Remarks*

4th: Lt. George W. Cooley (335th Ftr Sqn) c/l Liege; o.k.
P-51C WD-X 42-103291
Lt. Brack Diamond (335th Ftr Sqn) c/l; o.k.
P-51D WD-T
Lt. Paul M. Morgan (336th Ftr Sqn) c/l; o.k.
P-51 VF-
20th: Lt. John H. Tennant (55th Ftr Sqn) c/l Russia; o.k.
P-51D KI-Z 44-13695
55th: 4-0 locos
56th: 2-0 locos, 6-0 railcars
352nd: 3-14 locos, 24-12 railcars
355th: 1-9 locos, 0-10 railcars
Lt. Albert A. Zimmerman (354th Ftr Sqn) c/l France; o.k.
P-51 WR-
356th: 2-2 locos, 1-7 railcars
357th: 2-0 locos, 4-6 railcars, 1-1 vehicles
359th: 7-1 locos, 0-3 railcars
361st: 4-3 locos
364th: 2-8 locos, 0-10 railcars
P-51 c/l Honington; o.k.

KIAc's

SF: Lt. Robert Bertleson (2nd)
At-6
Died in a crash near Steeple Morden.

**September 12, 1944**

Groups Operating: P-51 4th, 55th, 339th, 352nd, 355th, 357th, 359th, 361st, 364th
P-47 56th, 78th, 353rd, 356th
P-38 479th

Missions: Support of bombers to numerous oil targets, including Magdeburg, Ruhland, Brux, Plauen, and Hemmingstedt.

Claims: 61-4-9 air
27-23 ground

| ***Group*** | | ***Claims*** | ***Location*** |
|---|---|---|---|
| **4th** | | | |
| 334th: | Lt. R.A. Dickmeyer | (1.5)FW-190 dest(air) | Wiesbaden |
| 335th: | Lt. A.J. Davis | Me-109 dest(air) | NE Frankfurt |
| 336th: | Lt. E.F. Hustwit | (1.5)FW-190 dest(air) | Wiesbaden |
| | Lt. V.E. Chandler | FW-190 dest(air) | Wiesbaden |
| | | FW-190 dam(air) | Wiesbaden |
| | Lt. G.W. Hunt | Me-109 dest(air) | NW Frankfurt |
| | Lt. J.C. Lane | Me-109 dest(air) | Trier |
| | | Me-109 dam(air) | Trier |
| | Lt. E.A. Quist | Me-109 prob(air) | NW Frankfurt |
| **55th** | | | |
| 38th: | Lt. C.C. Sherman | (1.5)Me-109 dest(air)* | Frankfurt |
| | Capt. M. Clark | (.5)Me-109 dest(air)** | N/Frankfurt |
| | | Me-410 dam(grd) | Herzogenaurach |
| | Lt. E.B. Lawrence | Me-109 dest(air) | Frankfurt |
| | Lt. J.W. Silk | Me-109 dest(air) | Frankfurt |
| | | (.5)He-177 dam(grd) | Herzogenaurach |
| | F/O D.M. Amoss | u/i a/c dest(grd) | Herzogenaurach |
| | | (.5)Ju-52 dest(grd) | Herzogenaurach |
| | Lt. W.J. Reilly | (.5)Ju-52 dest(grd) | Herzogenaurach |
| | Maj. A.B. Parsons | (.5)u/i a/c dest(grd) | Herzogenaurach |
| | | Me-410 dam(grd) | Herzogenaurach |
| | | Ju-87 dam(grd) | Herzogenaurach |
| | Lt. D.F. Jewell | (.5)u/i a/c dest(grd) | Herzogenaurach |
| | Capt. E.M. Holderman | (2)Ju-88 dam(grd) | Herzogenaurach |
| | Lt. R.E. Callahan | Ju-88 dam(grd) | Herzogenaurach |
| | Lt. F.J. Waice | Ju-88 dam(grd) | Herzogenaurach |
| | Capt. C.L. Peterson | (.5)He-177 dam(grd) | Herzogenaurach |
| 338th: | Capt. W.H. Burns | (.5)Me-109 dest(air)** | N/Frankfurt |
| | Lt. R.C. Haworth | (.5)Me-109 dest(air)* | Frankfurt |
| | Lt. M. Alba | He-111 dest(grd) | Giessen |
| **56th** | | | |
| 61st: | Lt. J.J. Clark | Me-109 dest(air) | N/Brandenburg |
| | Lt. J.M. Jure | Me-109 dest(air) | N/Brandenburg |
| | Lt. S.H. Getz | Me-109 dam(air) | N/Brandenburg |
| 62nd: | Lt. D.E. McMahan | Me-109 dest(air) | Sachau A/F |
| **339th** | | | |
| 503rd: | Capt. A.S. Harte | Me-109 dest(air) | Magdeburg |
| 504th: | Capt. B.V. Stevens | Me-109 dest(air) | Halbustalt |
| 505th: | Capt. R.B. Olander | Me-109 dest(air) | Goslar |
| **352nd** | | | |
| 328th: | Lt. C.J. Cesky | FW-190 dest(air) | N/Pritzwalk |
| | Lt. J.W. Stott | FW-190 dest(air) | N/Pritzwalk |
| 486th: | Lt. E.R. Lazear | (3)Me-109 dest(air) | Kyritz |
| | Lt. W.T. Gerbe | (2)Me-109 dest(air) | Kyritz |
| | Capt. H.J. Miklajcyk | (1.5)FW-190 dest(air) | Kustrin |
| | | Ju-52 dest(grd) | Kustrin |
| | Lt. E.O. Bostrom | FW-190 dest(air) | Berlin |
| | Lt. C.M. Freeman | Me-109 dest(air) | Kyritz |
| | Lt. J.D. Stearns | FW-190 dest(air) | S/Havelburg |
| | Lt. G.W. Wensch | Me-109 dest(air) | Kyritz |
| | Lt. J.D. Carter | (.5)FW-190 dest(air) | Kustrin |
| | Lt. T.R. Kyle | Me-109 dam(air) | NW Berlin |
| | Lt. M.B. Stoll | Me-109 dam(air) | Havelburg |
| **355th** | | | |
| 357th: | Lt. P.M.N. McHugh | (2)FW-190 dest(air) | E/Muritz Lake |
| | Lt. H.L. Monahan | FW-190 dest(air) | E/Muritz Lake |
| | Capt. H.S. Bille | FW-190 dam(air) | NE Berlin |
| | Lt. J.E. Erickson | FW-190 dam(air) | E/Muritz Lake |
| | Lt. W.J. Cullerton | (3)u/i a/c dest(grd) | Schwartz A/F |
| | | (2)Me-110 dest(grd) | Schwartz A/F |
| | | (2)Ju-88 dest(grd) | Schwartz A/F |
| | | Me-110 dam(grd) | Schwartz A/F |
| | | Ju-88 dam(grd) | Schwartz A/F |
| | Lt. J.O. Juntilla | (2)Ju-88 dest(grd) | Schwartz A/F |
| | | Ju-52 dest(grd) | Schwartz A/F |
| | | u/i a/c dest(grd) | Schwartz A/F |
| | | (2)Ju-88 dam(grd) | Schwartz A/F |
| | | (2)u/i a/c dam(grd) | Schwartz A/F |
| | Capt. F.R. Haviland | (3)Ju-88 dest(grd) | Schwartz A/F |
| | | Me-110 dam(grd) | Schwartz A/F |
| | | Do-217 dam(grd) | Schwartz A/F |
| | Lt. J.M. Chapman | (2)Me-410 dam(grd) | Wittstock |
| | | Do-217 dam(grd) | Wittstock |
| 358th: | Lt. R.M. Thompson | Me-109 dest(air) | Hanover |
| | Lt. J.J. Vigna | FW-190 dam(air) | E/Berlin |
| **359th** | | | |
| 368th: | Lt. R.B. Hatter | (2)FW-190 dest(air) | Liebenwalde |
| | Capt. B.H. King | Me-109 dest(air) | Gransee |
| | Lt. M.B. Barth | Me-109 dest(air) | NW Wittenburg |
| | Lt. E.J. Beal | Me-109 dest(air) | Gransee |
| | Lt. L.D. Carter | FW-190 dest(air) | N/Berlin |
| | | FW-190 dam(air) | N/Berlin |
| | Lt. J.H. Haas | FW-190 dest(air) | Pritzwalk |
| 369th: | Lt. H.R. Burt | FW-190 dest(air) | NE Berlin |
| | Lt. G.C. Deen | FW-190 dest(air) | NE Berlin |
| 370th: | Lt. D.D. Connelly | Me-109 dest(air) | S/Berlin |
| | | FW-190 dest(air) | Magdeburg |
| | Lt. C.W. Jones | (3)u/i a/c dest(grd) | S/Memmingen |
| | Lt. R.L. McInnes | (2)u/i a/c dest(grd) | S/Memmingen |
| | | Ju-52 dest(grd) | S/Memmingen |
| | | (4)u/i a/c dam(grd) | S/Memmingen |
| | Lt. J.W. Lamont | (2)u/i a/c dest(grd) | S/Memmingen |
| **361st** | | | |
| 375th: | Lt. W.T. Kemp | (3)Me-109 dest(air) | NE Magdeburg |
| | Maj. C.R. Cummins | Me-109 dest(air) | NE Magdeburg |
| | Lt. D.F. Knupp | Me-109 dest(air) | NE Magdeburg |
| | Lt. C.W. Narvis | Me-109 dest(air) | NE Magdeburg |
| 376th: | Lt. D.F. Spencer | (1.5)Me-109 dest(air) | W/Magdeburg |
| | Lt. V.E. Bocquin | Me-109 dest(air) | W/Magdeburg |
| | Lt. W.T. Butts | Me-109 dest(air) | W/Magdeburg |
| | Lt. C.P. Chennault | Me-109 dest(air) | W/Magdeburg |
| | Lt. D.P. Overholt | Me-109 dest(air) | W/Magdeburg |
| | Lt. D.P. Vulgamore | Me-109 dest(air) | W/Magdeburg |
| | Lt. R.W. Ward | (.5)Me-109 dest(air) | W/Magdeburg |
| | F/O W.F. Chapin | Me-109 prob(air) | W/Magdeburg |

| | | | |
|---|---|---|---|
| **364th** | | | |
| 383rd: | Capt. B.B. Wilson | FW-190 dest(air) | N/Berlin |
| | Lt. C.K. Voss | FW-190 dest(air) | NE Berlin |
| | Capt. M.W. Glascow | (2)FW-190 prob(air) | N/Berlin |

*Losses-*

**4th:** Capt. Thomas E. Joyce (334th Ftr Sqn) POW
P-51D QP-K 44-14271
Hit by flak and bellied-in near Darmstadt.

Lt. James C. Lane (336th Ftr Sqn) POW
P-51D VF-J 44-13260
Suffered mechanical failure and bailed out northeast of Trier.

**55th:** Lt. Douglas E. Mayer (38th Ftr Sqn) KIA
P-51D CG-Y 44-13909 "Mom's Pride"
Hit by flak near Rheine.

**352nd:** Lt. Joseph A. Broadwater (328th Ftr Sqn) KIA
P-51B PE-T 42-106872 "Pattie Ann II"
Hit by enemy fighters near Muncheberg.

**355th:** Lt. James C. Ellison (354th Ftr Sqn) MIA
P-51B WR-Y 43-7182
Hit by a FW-190 near Eberswalde.

Lt. John M. Chapman (357th Ftr Sqn) POW
P-51D OS-N 44-13796
Hit by flak at Schwartz Airfield.

Lt. Roddy W. Reed (358th Ftr Sqn) KIA
P-51D YF-E 44-14077 "Raunchy Runt II"
Hit by flak and last seen flying on the deck.

**359th:** Lt. Louis E. Barnett (368th Ftr Sqn) KIA
P-51D CV-Z 44-13404
Hit by enemy fighters near Wittenburg.

Lt. James H. Haas (368th Ftr Sqn) POW
P-51D CV-E 44-14081 "Tootsie"
Lost a wing while chasing a fighter and bailed out in the Pritzwalk area.

Lt. Kenneth L. Hobson (369th Ftr Sqn) POW
P-51D IV-Z 44-14216
Suffered mechanical failure and bailed out near Berlin.

Lt. John E. Hughes (369th Ftr Sqn) KIA
P-51D IV- 44-14188
Last seen strafing a train near Wittenburg.

Lt. Cyril W. Jones (370th Ftr Sqn) KIA
P-51D CS-W 44-14071 "Dora De"
Hit by flak and crashed into a woods near Coburg.

**361st:** Lt. Robert E. Geck (375th Ftr Sqn) KIA
P-51B E2-S 42-106677
Hit by enemy fighters near Ondrup.

*Remarks*
355th: 0-2 flak towers
359th: 3-0 locos
Lt. David B. Archibald (368th Ftr Sqn) c/l; o.k.
P-51D CV-Q 44-13549
Lt. Robert E. Benefiel (368th Ftr Sqn) c/l; o.k.
P-51B CV-B 43-24764
Lt. Eugene F. Britton (368th Ftr Sqn) c/l; o.k.
P-51B CV-K 42-106611

**September 13, 1944**
Groups Operating: P-51 4th, 20th, 55th, 339th, 352nd, 357th, 359th, 361st, 364th, 479th(mixed)
P-47 56th, 78th, 353rd, 356th
P-38 479th
Missions: Support for bombers to oil and other targets in southern Germany. The 20th took their "Frantic" bombers from Russia to Diosgyor then landed in Italy.
Claims: 33-0-5 air
25-11 ground

| *Group* | | *Claims* | *Location* |
|---|---|---|---|
| **4th** | | | |
| HdQts: | LtCol. C.H. Kinnard | (2)Hs-123 dest(grd) | Gelcheim |
| 334th: | Capt. W.B. Smith | u/i a/c dest(grd) | Schwabisch Hall |
| | Lt. W.G. Gillette | FW-200 dam(grd) | Halle |
| 335th: | Lt. B. Diamond | (3)Hs-123 dest(grd) | Gelchiem |
| | F/O C.E. Poage | (3)Hs-123 dest(grd) | Gelcheim |
| | Lt. G.W. Ceglareski | (2)u/i a/c dest(grd) | Gelcheim |
| | | u/i a/c dam(grd) | Gelcheim |
| | Lt. W.B. Eaton | Hs-123 dest(grd) | Gelcheim |
| **55th** | | | |
| 38th: | Capt. M. Clark | Me-109 dest(air) | Erfurt |
| | Capt. E.M. Holderman | Me-109 dest(air) | Erfurt |
| | Lt. D.L. Castle | Me-109 dest(air) | Erfurt |
| | | Me-109 dam(air) | Erfurt |
| | Lt. B. Clemmons | Me-109 dest(air) | Erfurt |
| | Lt. J.F. Coonan | Me-109 dest(air) | Erfurt |
| | Lt. M.M. Coons | Me-109 dest(air) | Erfurt |
| | Lt. R.L. Lapham | Me-109 dest(air) | Erfurt |
| 338th: | Lt. D.S. Cramer | (1.5)Me-109 dest(air) | Eisenach-Gotha |
| | Lt. M. Alba | Me-109 dest(air) | Eisenach-Gotha |
| | Lt. R.D. Miller | Me-109 dest(air) | Eisenach-Gotha |
| | Lt. T.D. Schank | Me-109 dest(air) | Eisenach-Gotha |
| | Lt. J.M. Wakefield | Me-109 dest(air) | Eisenach-Gotha |
| | Capt. E.S. Gregg | (.5)Me-109 dest(air) | Eisenach-Gotha |
| 343rd: | Lt. G.H. Cole | Me-109 dest(air) | Eisenach-Gotha |
| | Lt. W.H. Lewis | Me-109 dest(air) | Eisenach-Gotha |
| | | Me-109 dam(air) | Eisenach-Gotha |
| | Lt. R.E. Welch | Me-109 dest(air) | Eisenach-Gotha |
| | | Me-109 dam(air) | Eisenach-Gotha |
| **339th** | | | |
| 503rd: | Maj. J. Aitken | Ju-88 dest(grd) | Holzkirchen |
| | Lt. W.D. Stockton | Ju-88 dest(grd) | Holzkirchen |
| 504th: | Lt. M.F. Caldwell | FW-190 dest(grd) | Munich |
| | | u/i a/c dest(grd) | Munich |
| 505th: | Capt. R.M. Mitchell | Do-217 dest(grd) | SE Munich |
| | Lt. L.J. Powell | (.5)Ju-88 dest(grd) | SE Munich |
| | Lt. W.R. Moore | (.5)Ju-88 dest(grd) | SE Munich |
| | Lt. G.J. Hrico | (2)u/i a/c dam(grd) | SE Munich |
| **353rd** | | | |
| HdQts: | Capt. C.L. Stafford | (3)Me-109 dam(grd) | SW Stuttgart |
| 351st: | Lt. C.L. McGraw | Do-217 dest(grd) | NW Stuttgart |
| | Lt. H.P. Maree | (.5)FW-200 dest(grd) | Hellingen |
| | Lt. H.D. Milligan | (.5)FW-200 dest(grd) | Hellingen |
| **356th** | | | |
| 360th: | Capt. W.H. Fletcher | FW-190 dest(grd) | NW Stuttgart |
| | | Me-410 dam(grd) | NW Stuttgart |
| | Lt. O.L. Burwell | Me-410 dest(grd) | NW Stuttgart |
| | | FW-190 dam(grd) | NW Stuttgart |
| | Lt. E.W. Pleasant | Me-410 dam(grd) | NW Stuttgart |
| **357th** | | | |
| 362nd: | Capt. J.B. England | (2.5)Me-109 dest(air)* | S/Nordhausen |
| | Lt. S.G. Fuller | (.5)Me-109 dest(air)* | S/Nordhausen |
| | F/O O.D. Jenkins | (1.5)Me-109 dest(air)** | S/Nordhausen |
| | Lt. J.A. Kirla | (1.5)Me-109 dest(air)** | S/Nordhausen |
| | Lt. F.A. Taylor | Me-109 dest(air) | S/Nordhausen |
| | Lt. J.S. Templin | Me-109 dest(air) | S/Nordhausen |
| | Lt. J.W. Kenney | Me-109 dam(air) | S/Nordhausen |
| 363rd: | Lt. H.O. Hand | Me-109 dest(air) | E/Kassel |
| | Lt. F.L. Gailer | (.5)Me-109 dest(air)@ | S/Kassel |
| | Lt. C.E. Yeager | (.5)Me-109 dest(air)@ | S/Kassel |
| 364th: | Lt. H.P. Howell | (2)Me-109 dest(air) | E/Bad Frankenhausen |
| | Maj. J.A. Storch | (1.5)Me-109 dest(air)# | E/Bad Franken. |
| | Lt. M.F. Allen | Me-109 dest(air) | E/Bad Franken. |
| | Lt. R.G. Schimanski | (.5)Me-109 dest(air)# | E/Bad Franken. |
| **361st** | | | |
| 375th: | Capt. T.F. Brubaker | u/i a/c dest(grd) | Schwabisch Hall |
| | Lt. E.J. Marevka | u/i a/c dest(grd) | Schwabisch Hall |
| | Lt. C.W. Narvis | u/i a/c dest(grd) | Schwabisch Hall |
| | | u/i a/c dam(grd) | Schwabisch Hall |
| **364th** | | | |
| 384th: | Lt. J.A. Walker | Me-262 dam(air) | S/Stralsund |
| 385th: | Lt. G.L. Jamison | Me-109 dest(air) | SE Kassel |
| | Lt. J.F. Vann | Me-109 dest(air) | SE Kassel |

*Losses-*

**4th:** Capt. William B. Smith (334th Ftr Sqn) KIA
P-51D QP-Y 44-14281
Hit by flak at Schwabisch Hall.

**55th:** Lt. Durward D. Carson (338th Ftr Sqn) POW
P-51D CL-H 44-13607 "Marybelle III"
Suffered mechanical failure near Oberof.

Lt. David M. Fry (343rd Ftr Sqn) POW
P-51D CY-D 44-13374 "Julia"
Suffered mechanical failure near Homburg.

**339th:** Lt. William R. Moore (505th Ftr Sqn) POW
P-51C 6N-F 42-103756
Hit by flak near Katzenburg.

Lt. William R. Slovak (505th Ftr Sqn) KIA
P-51D 6N- 44-13847
Hit by flak near Saverlach.

**357th:** Lt. Howard L. Johnson (362nd Ftr Sqn) POW
P-51B G4-M 42-106654 "Jersey Bounce"
Suffered mechanical failure near Gembloux.

Lt. James A. Valkwitch (362nd Ftr Sqn) KIA
P-51B G4-N 42-106473 "Geronimo"
Suffered mechanical failure near Halle.

Lt. Marion E. Burnett (363rd Ftr Sqn) KIA
P-51D B6-C 44-13745 "Hi Phyl"
Hit by enemy fighters east of Kassel.

Lt. Kirby N. Brown (364th Ftr Sqn) KIA
P-51D C5-J 44-13698 "Shady Lady"
Hit by flak near Bad Frankenhausen.

Lt. Robert C. Goldsworthy (364th Ftr Sqn) ASR
P-51D C5- 44-13648
Bailed out fifty-five miles off Clacton.

**361st:** Lt. Edward J. Marevka (375th Ftr Sqn) POW
P-51B E2-M 42-106796
Hit by flak north of Goppingen and bailed out near Altenhausen.

*Remarks*
4th: 0-1 loco
56th: 1-0 loco, 0-10 railcars
361st: 1-1 loco, 0-14 railcars

**September 14, 1944**
Groups Operating: P-47 78th, 353rd
Missions: Support of bombers to Hemmingstadt.
Claims: nil
Losses: nil

KIAc's
479th: Lt. Ivan E. Ervin (435th Ftr Sqn)
P-51 J2-
Lt. Chester W. Granville (435th Ftr Sqn)
P-51D J2- 44-14437

**September 15, 1944**
Groups Operating: P-51 4th, 355th, 357th
Missions: Support for bombers going to Warsaw but were recalled shortly after crossing-in.
Claims: 0-0-0 air
0-1 ground

| *Group* | | *Claims* | *Location* |
|---|---|---|---|
| **357th** | | | |
| 363rd: | Lt. W.R. Dunlop | Do-24 dam(grd) | Cristianmund |

*Losses-*

**357th:** Lt. Louis E. Nowlin (362nd Ftr Sqn) KIA
P-51B G4-O 42-106783 "Flying Panther"
Collided with Lt. Graeff over the North Sea.

Lt. Kenneth F. Graeff (363rd Ftr Sqn) KIA
P-51B B6-E 43-24842 "$ Blackpool Bat"
Collided with Lt. Nowlin over the North Sea.

**September 16, 1944**
Groups Operating: P-51 20th, 352nd, 355th, 359th, 361st, 364th, 479th
P-47 56th, 78th, 353rd, 356th
Missions: Fighter-bomber operations in the Mannheim-Kaiserlautern area and the 20th flew from Foggia, Italy, back to England.
Claims: 0-0-0 air
3-1 ground

| *Group* | | *Claims* | *Location* |
|---|---|---|---|
| **56th** | | | |
| 61st: | Capt. R.J. Keen | Ju-88 dest(grd) | Dummer Lake |
| | Capt. D.F. Smith | He-177 dest(grd) | Alhorn A/F |
| 62nd: | Lt. F.A. Nolan | He-111 dam(grd) | Dummer Lake |
| 63rd: | Capt. H.E. Comstock | He-177 dest(grd) | Alhorn A/F |

*Losses-*

**364th:** Lt. Grant L. Jones (385th Ftr Sqn) KIA
P-51D 5E-B 44-13964
Hit by flak near Nienburg and bailed out east of the city.

*Remarks*
352nd: 10-14 locos, 6-57 railcars, 11-10 vehicles, 1-2 barges, 0-1 tug
353rd: 15-1 locos, 14-90 railcars, 16-4 vehicles
356th: 9-3 locos, 2-53 railcars, 0-4 barges, 0-1 tug
364th: 4-0 locos, 16-8 railcars, 1-0 vehicle

**September 17, 1944**
Groups Operating: P-51 4th, 20th, 55th, 339th, 352nd, 355th, 357th, 359th, 361st, 364th, 479th(mixed)
P-47 56th, 78th, 353rd, 356th
P-38 479th
Missions: Fighter-bomber operations and general support of the airborne invasion of Holland. The P-47 groups were also assigned to flak-busting duties.
Claims: 7-0-0 air
1-0 ground

| *Group* | | *Claims* | *Location* |
|---|---|---|---|
| **4th** | | | |
| 335th: | Lt. T.E. Lines | (3)FW-190 dest(air) | Bocholt |
| | Lt. A.J. Davis | (2)FW-190 dest(air) | Bocholt |
| | Capt. L.H. Norley | FW-190 dest(air) | Bocholt |
| **78th** | | | |
| 82nd: | Lt. H.K. Shope | Me-109 dest(grd) | Gilze-Rijen A/F |
| **361st** | | | |
| 376th: | Lt. W.R. Beyer | Me-109 dest(air) | Hasselt-Wesel |

*Losses-*

**4th:** Lt. Clifford F. Holske (335th Ftr Sqn) KIA
P-51D WD-I 44-14054
Hit by enemy fighters near Bocholt.

Lt. Nicholas W. Vozzy (335th Ftr Sqn) KIA
P-51B WD-J 43-6841
Hit by enemy fighters near Bocholt.

**55th:** Lt. Paul R. Porter (343rd Ftr Sqn) ASR
P-51D CY-S 44-13907
Suffered mechanical failure and bailed out over the Channel.

**56th:** Lt. Edward M. Albright, Jr. (63rd Ftr Sqn) KIA
P-47D UN-A 44-19786
Hit by flak near Zoelen.

**78th:** Lt. Donald C. Hart (82nd Ftr Sqn) ASR
P-47D MX-H 42-26330
Hit by flak and bailed out over the Channel.

**353rd:** Lt. Robert N. Greene (351st Ftr Sqn) MIA-E
P-47D YJ-E 42-75815 "Patricia Baby"
Hit by a bomb blast near Wekeron.

**356th:** Lt. Howell L. Broxton (359th Ftr Sqn) MIA-E
P-47D OC-Y 42-74658 "Little Fi-Fi"
Hit by flak and bellied-in near Groesbeek.

Capt. Westwood H. Fletcher, Jr. (360th Ftr Sqn) MIA-E
P-47D PI-D 42-28472 "Podunk III"
Hit by flak near Nijmegen and bellied-in near Amersfoort.

F/O John P. Tucker (360th Ftr Sqn) KIA
P-47D PI- 42-76353 "Naughty Patricia"
Hit by flak near Nijmegen.

**359th:** Lt. Harold R. Burt (369th Ftr Sqn) KIA
P-51C IV-K 42-103785 "Nancy June 3rd"
Suffered mechanical failure northwest of Antwerp.

**361st:** Lt. Woodrow W. Glover (376th Ftr Sqn) KIA
P-51B E9-A 42-106944 "Mary Jane"
Hit by a Me-109 near Geldern.

**364th:** Lt. Harry H. Johnson, Jr. (383rd Ftr Sqn) MIA
P-51D N2-V 44-13866 "Rosey Doates"
Hit by flak near Arnheim.

Lt. Douglas R. Drysdale (385th Ftr Sqn) MIA-E
P-51D 5E-T 44-14025 "Lovin' Aline"
Hit by flak near Nijmegen and bailed out southwest of Zeeland.

**479th:** Capt. George K. Sykes (435th Ftr Sqn) MIA-E
P-51D J2- 44-14424 "Sugar Kane"
Hit by flak near Ede.

*Remarks*
56th: 0-4 locos, 18-25 railcars, 10-8 vehicles, 20-3 flak positions, 0-10 barracks, 0-1 barge
Lt. Carl E. Westman (61st Ftr Sqn) b/o Wattisham; o.k.
P-47D HV-
P-47 c/l Southwold; o.k.
78th: 16-37 gun positions, 0-1 barracks

352nd: 12-2 vehicles
P-51 c/l Brussels; o.k.
353rd: 2-0 locos, 80-36 railcars, 6-0 vehicles, 31-18 gun positions, 0-3 barracks, 0-2 bridges
355th: 1-0 loco
356th: 36-0 flak positions, 12-0 machine-gun positions
357th: P-51 c/l Leiston; o.k.
364th: 0-2 gun positions

KIAc's
20th: Lt. David E. Cruickshank (55th Ftr Sqn)
P-51 KI-
Lt. William R. Taylor (55th Ftr Sqn)
P-51 KI-

**September 18, 1944**
Groups Operating: P-51 4th, 20th, 55th, 339th, 352nd, 355th, 357th, 359th, 361st, 364th, 479th(mixed)
P-47 56th, 78th, 353rd, 356th
P-38 479th
Missions: Support of the airborne invasion of Holland, including fighter-bomber and flak-busting operations, plus the 355th took "Frantic IV" heavies to Russia.
Claims: 38-0-4 air
3-7 ground

| Group | | Claims | Location |
|---|---|---|---|
| **355th** | | | |
| HdQts: | Capt. H.H. Kirby | Me-109 dest(air) | NW Warsaw |
| 354th: | Capt. H.W. Brown | Me-109 dest(air) | Warsaw |
| | | Me-109 dam(air) | Warsaw |
| | | Ju-87 dam(grd) | Warsaw |
| 357th: | Maj. J.L. Elder | Me-109 dest(air) | NW Warsaw |
| 358th: | Lt. R.L. Michelena | Me-109 dest(air) | Warsaw |
| | | Me-109 dam(air) | Warsaw |
| | Lt. M.E. Webb | Me-109 dam(air) | Warsaw |
| **357th** | | | |
| 362nd: | Maj. T.L. Gates | Me-109 dest(air) | Nijmegen |
| | Capt. F.C. Smith | Me-109 dest(air) | Nijmegen |
| | Lt. J.L. Blanchard | Me-109 dest(air) | Nijmegen |
| | Lt. H.B. Egeland | Me-109 dest(air) | Nijmegen |
| | Lt. H.F. Mace | Me-109 dest(air) | Nijmegen |
| | Lt. W.N. Perry | Me-109 dest(air) | Nijmegen |
| | Lt. J.S. Templin | Me-109 dest(air) | Nijmegen |
| 363rd: | Lt. W.R. Dunlop | Me-109 dest(air) | Apeldoorn |
| | Lt. K. Landis | Me-109 dest(air) | W/Arnheim |
| | Lt. H.T. Pascoe | Me-109 dest(air) | Arnheim |
| | Capt. T.E. Hughes | (.5)FW-190 dest(air) | Arnheim |
| | Lt. F.L. Gailer | (.5)FW-190 dest(air) | Arnheim |
| | Lt. W.S. Fennell | (.5)Me-109 dest(air) | W/Arnheim |
| | Lt. R.S. Fifield | (.5)Me-109 dest(air) | W/Arnheim |
| 364th: | Lt. G.E. Tyler | (2)Me-109 dest(air) | N/Maastricht |
| | | FW-190 dest(air) | N/Maastricht |
| | Lt. R.L. Smith | (2)Me-109 dest(air) | N/Maastricht |
| | Lt. J. Jacobs | Me-109 dest(air) | N/Maastricht |
| | | FW-190 dest(air) | N/Maastricht |
| | Capt. B.K. Seitzinger | Me-109 dest(air) | N/Maastricht |
| | | Me-109 dam(air) | N/Maastricht |
| | Lt. B.K. Braley | FW-190 dest(air) | N/Maastricht |
| | Lt. I.L. McGuire | FW-190 dest(air) | N/Maastricht |
| | Lt. H.E. Moebius | FW-190 dest(air) | N/Maastricht |
| | Lt. H.J. Moorhouse | FW-190 dest(air) | N/Maastricht |
| | Lt. G.W. Morris | FW-190 dest(air) | N/Maastricht |
| | Lt. R.M. Shaw | Me-109 dest(air) | N/Maastricht |
| **359th** | | | |
| 369th: | Lt. C.J. Crenshaw | Me-109 dest(air) | Dusseldorf |
| | Lt. G.C. Deen | FW-190 dest(air) | Krefeld |
| | Lt. J.R. Parsons | FW-190 dest(air) | Diernen |
| | Lt. J.E. Keur | (.5)Me-109 dest(air) | SE Munster |
| | F/O T.G. Bur | (.5)Me-109 dest(air) | SE Munster |
| **361st** | | | |
| 374th: | Lt. M.L. Bryant | Me-109 dest(air) | SE Jagel A/F |
| | Lt. A.B. MaClay | Me-109 dest(grd) | Jagel A/F |
| | | (4)Me-109 dam(grd) | Jagel A/F |
| | Lt. A.B. Cook | Me-109 dest(grd) | Jagel A/F |
| | | Me-109 dam(grd) | Jagel A/F |
| | Lt. T.J. Moore | Me-109 dam(grd) | Jagel A/F |
| 375th: | Lt. U.L. Drew | He-111 dest(grd) | Fehrman Belt |
| | Lt. W.D. Rogers | (.5)BV-138 dest(grd) | Bug S/P Base |
| | Lt. L.C. Travis | (.5)BV-138 dest(grd) | Bug S/P Base |
| 376th: | Lt. J.B. Bricker | Me-109 dest(air) | N/Schleswig |
| | Lt. W.T. Butts | (.5)Me-109 dest(air) | N/Schleswig |
| | Lt. C.W. Hanley | (.5)Me-109 dest(air) | N/Schleswig |

*Losses-*

**56th:** Lt. Trevor A. Edwards (62nd Ftr Sqn) POW
P-47D LM-G 42-26337
Hit by flak near Eindhoven.

Lt. William W. McElhare (62nd Ftr Sqn) POW
P-47D LM-X 42-26636
Hit by flak near Effern.

Capt. Gordon S. Stevens (63rd Ftr Sqn) KIA
P-47D UN- 44-19730
Hit by flak near Thuernich.

Lt. Robert G. Kelly (63rd Ftr Sqn) POW
P-47D UN-A 42-25531
Hit by flak near Erkelentz.

Lt. Elwood D. Raymond (63rd Ftr Sqn) KIA
P-47D UN-F 42-26057
Hit by flak and crashed into the North Sea.

**78th:** Lt. Richard C. Snyder (82nd Ftr Sqn) POW
P-47D MX-M 42-75551
Hit by flak and bellied-in near Rotterdam.

Lt. John R. Loegering (83rd Ftr Sqn) POW
P-47D HL-Q 42-76587 "Thrunny Bit"
Hit by flak and bellied-in near Goch.

Lt. Russell C. MacDuffie (83rd Ftr Sqn) POW
P-47D HL-M 42-26020 "Duffie's Special"
Hit by flak and bailed out near Turnhout.

Lt. John R. Fees (84th Ftr Sqn) POW
P-47D WZ-C 42-25985
Hit by flak and bailed out near Nijmegen.

Lt. Eugene W. Wood (84th Ftr Sqn) KIA
P-47D WZ-D 43-25297
Hit by flak near Nijmegen.

**353rd:** Capt. James O. Ruscitto (350th Ftr Sqn) MIA-E
P-47D LH-R 42-28357 "Natalie Ann II"
Hit by flak and bellied-in near Tilburg.

**355th:** Lt. Robert O. Peters (358th Ftr Sqn) KIA
P-51D YF-X 44-13675
Shot down by a P-51 near Warsaw.

Lt. Joseph J. Vigna (358th Ftr Sqn) KIA
P-51C YF-M 42-103317 "Dakota Kid"
Hit by a Me-109 near Warsaw.

**356th:** Lt. James H. Perry (359th Ftr Sqn) KIA
P-47D OC-W 43-25530 "We Four II"
Hit by flak near Nijmegen.

Capt. Reginald C. McDowell (361st Ftr Sqn) MIA-E
P-47D QI-M 42-26534
Hit by flak and bellied-in near Groesbeek.

**357th:** Capt. Bernard K. Seitzinger (364th Ftr Sqn) MIA-E
P-51B C5-S 42-106923 "Almost"
Hit by a Me-109 northeast of Maastricht.

Lt. Robert J. Fandry (364th Ftr Sqn) KIA
P-51D C5-A 44-13543 "Just Right"
Hit by enemy fighters northeast of Maastricht.

**359th:** Lt. Grover C. Deen (369th Ftr Sqn) POW
P-51C IV-F 42-103799
Hit by enemy fighters near Hengelo.

Lt. Edwin L. Sjoblad (369th Ftr Sqn) POW
P-51D IV- 44-14545
Hit by a FW-190 near Hengelo.

**361st:** Lt. Clyde A. Arrants (374th Ftr Sqn) KIA
P-51D B7-G 44-13949
Hit by flak near Vioel.

*Remarks*
56th: 4-0 locos, 17-0 vehicles, 5-0 gun positions
Lt. William G. Bartle (61st Ftr Sqn) b/o Tilburg; o.k.
P-47D HV-
Lt. William M. Hartshorn (61st Ftr Sqn) b/o Schjudel; o.k.
P-47D HV- 44-19719
Lt. Philip E. Fleming (62nd Ftr Sqn) c/l St. Quentin; o.k.
P-47D LM-
Lt. James P. Hodges (62nd Ftr Sqn) c/l Belgium; injured
P-47D LM-
Lt. George H. Van Noy (62nd Ftr Sqn) c/l Charleroi; o.k.
P-47D LM-
Lt. William F. Wilkerson (62nd Ftr Sqn) b/o Aachen; o.k.
P-47D LM-

Lt. Thomas Guerrero (63rd Ftr Sqn) c/l Belgium; injured
P-47D UN-
Lt. David P. Kling (63rd Ftr Sqn) c/l Turnhout; o.k.
P-47D UN-
Lt. Charles M. Rotzler (63rd Ftr Sqn) c/l Brussels; o.k.
P-47D UN-

78th: 0-4 railcars, 12-3 vehicles, 1-11 gun positions
Lt. Allen A. Rosenblum (82nd Ftr Sqn) c/l; o.k.
P-47D MX-I 42-25300
353rd: 33-4 gun positions, 41-9 vehicles, 5-4 buildings, 0-1 barge
355th: Capt. Brady C. Williamson (354th Ftr Sqn) c/l; o.k.
P-51D WR-H 44-14252 "Palma"
356th: 35-0 gun positions
359th: Lt. John F. Lausen (368th Ftr Sqn) c/l Forsfeld; o.k.
P-51 CV-

**September 19, 1944**

Groups Operating: P-51 4th, 339t, 352nd, 355th, 357th, 359th, 361st, 364th
P-47 56th, 356th
Missions: Support for bombers to marshalling yards in western Germany and patrols over Holland. Also, the 355th supported "Frantic IV" bombers to Szolnok, Hungary, then landed in Italy.
Claims: 32-2-5 air
0-0 ground

| *Group* | | *Claims* | *Location* |
|---|---|---|---|
| **55th** | | | |
| 338th: | Lt. W.P. Gebhardt | Me-109 dest(air) | Dusseldorf |
| | Lt. J.L. Gerry | Me-109 dest(air) | Cologne |
| | Lt. T.D. Schank | Me-109 dest(air) | Cologne |
| | Lt. G.E. Funk | Me-109 dam(air) | S/Dusseldorf |
| **357th** | | | |
| 362nd: | Lt. A.J. Roberson | (2)Me-109 dest(air) | Ijsselstein |
| | F/O O.D. Jenkins | Me-109 dest(air) | SE Ijsselstein |
| | | FW-190 dest(air) | Ijsselstein |
| | Lt. J.A. Kirla | Me-109 dest(air) | Ijsselstein |
| | Lt. W.N. Perry | Me-109 dest(air) | Ijsselstein |
| | Lt. J.H. Sehl | Me-109 dest(air) | Ijsselstein |
| | Lt. C.E. Weaver | Me-109 dest(air) | S/Zuider Zee |
| | Capt. C.L. Williams | Me-109 prob(air) | Ijsselstein |
| | Capt. H.E. Beal | Me-109 dam(air) | Ijsselstein |
| 363rd: | Lt. D.J. Pasaka | (2)Me-109 dest(air) | Anklam |
| | Lt. R.C. Roper | (2)Me-109 dest(air) | W/Arnheim |
| | Maj. E.W. Hiro | Me-109 dest(air) | W/Arnheim |
| | Lt. W.R. Dunlop | Me-109 dest(air) | W/Arnheim |
| | Lt. F.L. Gailer | (.5)Me-109 dest(air) | W/Arnheim |
| | Lt. H.O. Hand | (.5)Me-109 dest(air) | W/Arnheim |
| 364th: | Capt. B.W. McIntyre | Me-109 dest(air) | Emmerich |
| | | FW-190 dest(air) | Emmerich |
| | Lt. H.E. Moebius | (2)FW-190 dest(air) | SE Arnheim |
| | Lt. C.K. Maxwell | Me-109 dest(air) | SW Arnheim |
| | | FW-190 dest(air) | SW Arnheim |
| | Lt. B.K. Braley | Me-109 dest(air) | E/Arnheim |
| | Lt. J. Jacobs | Me-109 dest(air) | SE Arnheim |
| | Lt. D.A. Sandborn | Me-109 dest(air) | E/Arnheim |
| | Lt. G.E. Tyler | Me-109 dest(air) | E/Arnheim |
| **364th** | | | |
| 384th: | Lt. E.O. Bowers | (1.5)Me-109 dest(air)[*] | Duisenburg |
| | F/O W.E. Randolph | (.5)Me-109 dest(air)[*] | Duisenburg |
| | | (2)Me-109 dam(air) | Duisenburg |
| | Lt. R.L. Stiefvater | (.5)Me-109 dest(air)[**] | Duisenburg |
| | Lt. B.W. Ward | (.5)Me-109 dest(air)[**] | Duisenburg |
| | | Me-109 prob(air) | Duisenburg |
| | | Me-109 dam(air) | Duisenburg |
| 385th: | Lt. J.J. Pascoe | FW-190 dest(air) | Arnheim |

*Losses-*

**357th:** Lt. James L. Blanchard (362nd Ftr Sqn) KIA
P-51D G4-G 44-13741 "Buddy Boy"
Hit by a Me-109 in the Arnheim-Deventer area.

Maj. Edwin W. Hiro (363rd Ftr Sqn) KIA
P-51D B6-D 44-13518 "Horse's Itch"
Hit by a Me-109 near Vreden.

Capt. Bryce W. McIntyre (364th Ftr Sqn) POW
P-51D C5-E 44-14429 "Tangerine"
Shot down by a Spitfire near Emmerich.

Lt. Jerome Jacobs (364th Ftr Sqn) POW
P-51B C5-E 43-6813 "Evelyn"
Hit by a Me-109 southeast of Arnheim.

Lt. Howard E. Moebius (364th Ftr Sqn) MIA-E
P-51D C5-M 44-13801
Hit by enemy fighters near Arnheim.

**361st:** Lt. Robert C. Clement (376th Ftr Sqn) KIA
P-51D E9-J 44-13872
Crashed while landing at Little Walden.

**364th:** Lt. Elmer O. Bowers (384th Ftr Sqn) MIA
P-51D 5Y-B 44-13822
Hit by a Me-109 in the Wesel-Duisenburg area.

*Remarks*

4th: Lt. Van E. Chandler (336th Ftr Sqn) b/o Willebroeck; o.k.
P-51B VF-H 43-24877

**September 20, 1944**

Groups Operating: P-51 4th, 20th, 55th, 339th, 352nd, 357th, 359th, 361st, 364th
P-47 56th, 78th, 353rd, 356th
P-38 479th
Missions: General support over Holland.
Claims: nil

*Losses-*

**359th:** Lt. John E. Keur (369th Ftr Sqn) ASR
P-51D IV-Q 44-14432
Bailed out three miles off Lowestoft.

*Remarks*

56th: 1-0 gun position, 0-1 railcar
P-47 c/l; o.k.
78th: 4-0 vehicles, 2-0 horse-drawn vehicles, 0-1 flak position
361st: Lt. Edward T. Knickman (374th Ftr Sqn) c/l; o.k.
P-51B B7-H 42-106817
479th: Lt. Theodore J. Sowerby (435th Ftr Sqn) c/l; o.k.
P-38J J2-

**September 21, 1944**

Groups Operating: P-51 55th, 357th, 359th, 479th(mixed)
P-47 56th, 353rd
P-38 479th
Missions: Support of bombers to Ludwigshafen, Mainz, and Coblenz, plus some patrols over Holland.
Claims: 19-1-2 air
0-0 ground

| *Group* | | *Claims* | *Location* |
|---|---|---|---|
| **56th** | | | |
| HdQts: | LtCol. D.C. Schilling | (3)FW-190 dest(air) | Lochem |
| 61st: | Maj. B.M. Gladych | (2)FW-190 dest(air) | E/Arnheim |
| | Lt. R.S. Kyler | FW-190 dest(air) | Deventer |
| | Lt. S.H. Getz | (.5)FW-190 dest(air) | Deventer |
| | Lt. W.J. Osborne | (.5)FW-190 dest(air) | Deventer |
| 62nd: | Capt. M.J. Jackson | FW-190 dest(air) | NE Arnheim |
| | Lt. L.R. Brown | FW-190 dest(air) | Arnheim |
| | Lt. D. Henley | FW-190 dest(air) | Arnheim |
| | Lt. R.L. Patterson | FW-190 dest(air) | Arnheim |
| | Lt. R.E. Winters | FW-190 dest(air) | NE Arnheim |
| 63rd: | Lt. W.H. Pitts | (2)FW-190 dest(air) | NE Arnheim |
| | Lt. W.R. Groce | FW-190 dest(air) | NE Arnheim |
| | Lt. J.A. Kyle | FW-190 dam(air) | NE Arnheim |
| **353rd** | | | |
| 350th: | Lt. R.W. Hedler | (1.5)FW-190 dest(air) | SE Arnheim |
| | Lt. J.L. Schilt | FW-190 dest(air) | S/Arnheim |
| | Lt. V.G. Rafferty | (.5)FW-190 dest(air) | SE Arnheim |
| | Lt. R.T. Allison | FW-190 prob(air) | SW Nijmegen |
| | Lt. B.C. Auchincloss | FW-190 dam(air) | SE Arnheim |
| 351st: | Lt. R.F. Vomaske | Me-109 dest(air) | Arnheim-Nijmegen |

*Losses-*

**56th:** Lt. Oscar L. Cagle, Jr. (63rd Ftr Sqn) KIA
P-47D UN-C 42-26316
Last seen with enemy fighters near Lochem.

Lt. Harold E. Spicer (63rd Ftr Sqn) KIA
P-47D UN-T 42-25515 "Ann K"
Last seen chasing a FW-190 near Devekamp.

**353rd:** Capt. Lloyd G. Hally (351st Ftr Sqn) KIA
P-47D YJ-D 42-22523 "Angel of Mercy"
Chased a FW-190 then hit by flak near Nijmegen.

**479th:** Lt. Thomas A. Gayrys (434th Ftr Sqn) KIA
P-51D L2-G 44-14138 "Miss Fortune"
Lost for unknown reasons; possibly mechanical failure.

*Remarks*

56th: Lt. Andrew Chasko (62nd Ftr Sqn) c/l Brussels; o.k.
P-47D LM-

**September 22, 1944**
Groups Operating: P-51 339th, 355th, 357th, 359th, 361st, 364th
P-47 56th, 78th, 353rd
Missions: Support of bombers to Kassel plus the 355th brought the "Frantic IV" bombers back to England from Italy.
Claims: nil
Losses: nil

*Remarks*
339th: Lt. Charles S. Coe (503rd Ftr Sqn) c/l Fowlmere; o.k.
P-51B D7-O 43-24800
359th: Lt. Ray E. McGee (369th Ftr Sqn) c/l East Wretham; o.k.
P-51 IV-
364th: P-51 c/l Liege; o.k.

**September 23, 1944**
Groups Operating: P-51 4th, 20th, 55th, 339th, 352nd, 357th, 361st, 364th
P-47 78th, 353rd, 356th
Missions: Area support in the Nijmegen area.
Claims: 24-3-6 air
0-0 ground

| *Group* | | *Claims* | *Location* |
|---|---|---|---|
| **339th** | | | |
| 503rd: | Lt. R.H. Ammon | (2)FW-190 dest(air) | SW Wesel |
| | Lt. E.H. Beavers | FW-190 dest(air) | SW Wesel |
| | Lt. L.C. Marsh | FW-190 dest(air) | SW Wesel |
| | Lt. R.D. Mayer | FW-190 dest(air) | SW Wesel |
| 504th: | Lt. M.L. Cernicky | FW-190 prob(air) | Venlo |
| 505th: | Lt. L.J. Powell | FW-190 dest(air) | Geldern-Weeze |
| | Lt. R.H. Tannous | FW-190 dest(air) | Geldern-Weeze |
| | | FW-190 dam(air) | Geldern-Weeze |
| **353rd** | | | |
| HdQts: | Capt. J.W. Eanes | FW-190 dest(air) | SE Arnheim |
| 350th: | Lt. B.C. Auchincloss | Me-109 dest(air) | SE Arnheim |
| | | FW-190 dest(air) | SE Arnheim |
| | | FW-190 prob(air) | SE Arnheim |
| | Lt. V.G. Rafferty | Me-109 dest(air) | SE Arnheim |
| | | FW-190 dest(air) | SE Arnheim |
| | Capt. E.S. Middleton | FW-190 dest(air) | SE Arnheim |
| | Capt. W.J. Price | FW-190 dest(air) | SE Arnheim |
| | Lt. R.W. Abernathy | Me-109 dest(air) | SE Arnheim |
| | Lt. H.E. Asper | FW-190 dest(air) | SE Arnheim |
| | Lt. G.P. Devine | FW-190 dest(air) | SE Arnheim |
| | | FW-190 dam(air) | SE Arnheim |
| | Lt. H.E. Haynes | Me-109 dest(air) | SE Arnheim |
| | Lt. G.P. Province | FW-190 dest(air) | SE Arnheim |
| | Lt. W.P. Knowling | Me-109 prob(air) | SE Arnheim |
| | Lt. L.M. Davis | Me-109 dam(air) | SE Arnheim |
| | Lt. L.M. Grainger | FW-190 dam(air) | SE Arnheim |
| 352nd: | Lt. J.F. Cross | FW-190 dest(air) | SE Arnheim |
| | Lt. G.N. Porterfield | FW-190 dest(air) | SE Arnheim |
| | Lt. C.N. Sladek | FW-190 dest(air) | SE Arnheim |
| **364th** | | | |
| 385th: | Lt. R. Visconte | Me-109 dest(air) | Emmerich |
| | | FW-190 dest(air) | Emmerich |
| | Lt. W.T. Housholder | FW-190 dest(air) | E/Arnheim |
| | | Me-109 dam(air) | E/Arnheim |

*Losses-*

**78th**: Lt. Dunston D. Hartley (83rd Ftr Sqn) KIA
P-47D HL-X 42-28365
Hit by flak near Heteren.

**339th**: Lt. Alfred O. Manke (503rd Ftr Sqn) POW
P-51D D7- 44-14247
Hit by a FW-190 near Wesel.

Capt. Raymond M. Mitchell, Jr. (505th Ftr Sqn) POW
P-51D 6N- 44-14542
Hit by flak near Jagen.

Lt. James B. Muller (505th Ftr Sqn) POW
P-51D 6N-A 44-13624 "Sniffles"
Hit by a FW-190 near Haltern.

**352nd**: Maj. Jack D. Blanchard (328th Ftr Sqn) MIA-E
P-51D PE-T 44-13996 "Slender, Tender, & Tall"
Hit by flak near Bergharen.

Capt. Clarence O. Johnson (487th Ftr Sqn) KIA
P-51D HO- 44-14078
Hit by a Me-109 near Lusiendorf.

Lt. Joseph B. Ayers (487th Ftr Sqn) KIA
P-51B HO-J 42-106901 "Helen of Troy III"
Hit by a Me-109 near Lusiendorf.

Lt. John F. Clark (487th Ftr Sqn) POW
P-51B HO-O 42-106454 "Louisiana Lady"
Hit by a Me-109 near Heidkamp.

Lt. Phanor B. Waters (487th Ftr Sqn) KIA
P-51B HO-S 43-7094 "Gracie"
Hit by a Me-109 near Almelo.

**353rd**: Capt. Ellis S. Middleton (350th Ftr Sqn) KIA
P-47D LH-V 42-26525
Hit by enemy fighters southeast of Arnheim.

Lt. John G. Edwards (350th Ftr Sqn) KIA
P-47D LH-S 42-26642
Hit by enemy fighters southeast of Arnheim.

Lt. Gerald F. Province (350th Ftr Sqn) KIA
P-47D LH-Z 44-19577
Hit by enemy fighters southeast of Arnheim.

**364th**: Lt. Norman F. Bettin (383rd Ftr Sqn) KIA
P-51D N2-
Hit by flak near Arnheim.

Lt. Clyde K. Voss (383rd Ftr Sqn) MIA-E
P-51D N2-D 44-13971 "Priss IV"
Hit by flak near Apeldoorn.

*Remarks*
55th: Lt. Claude L. Chamberlain (38th Ftr Sqn) b/o Holland; o.k.
P-51D CG- 44-13260
78th: 3-0 vehicles, 1-7 flak positions
339th: P-51 c/l Belgium; o.k.
353rd: 2-0 flak positions
356th: 4-0 flak positions
Maj. James N. Wood (361st Ftr Sqn) c/l Diest; o.k.
P-47D QI-S 44-19764
364th: 16-1 vehicles

**September 25, 1944**
Groups Operating: P-51 4th, 20th, 55th, 339th, 352nd, 355th, 357th, 359th, 361st, 364th, 479th(mixed)
P-47 356th
P-38 479th
Missions: Support of bombers to Ludwigshafen, Frankfurt, and Coblenz.
Claims: 0-0-0 air
1-0 ground

| *Group* | | *Claims* | *Location* |
|---|---|---|---|
| **4th** | | | |
| 336th: | Lt. W.H. Williams | Ju-88 dest(grd) | Lippsringe |

*Losses-*

**352nd**: Lt. Evan J. Evans (487th Ftr Sqn) POW
P-51B HO-I 43-6707 "Peanuts"
Hit by flak near Biblis.

**359th**: Lt. John F. Lausen (368th Ftr Sqn) KIA
P-51B CV- 43-24100
Hit by flak near Wiesbaden.

*Remarks*
4th: 0-4 locos, 0-6 railcars, 4-0 vehicles

**September 26, 1944**
Groups Operating: P-51 4th, 20th, 55th, 339th, 352nd, 355th, 357th, 359th, 361st, 364th, 479th(mixed)
P-47 56th, 78th, 353rd, 356th
P-38 479th
Missions: Cover for operations in Holland and support for bombers to Osnabruck, Hamm, and Bremen.
Claims: 29-0-7 air
2-3 ground

| *Group* | | *Claims* | *Location* |
|---|---|---|---|
| **361st** | | | |
| 375th: | Lt. B.W. Rowlett | FW-190 dest(grd) | Achmer |
| | | He-177 dest(grd) | Achmer |
| | | (2)FW-190 dam(grd) | Achmer |
| | Lt. L.H. Mottis | u/i a/c dam(grd) | Achmer |
| **479th** | | | |
| HdQts: | Col. H. Zemke | (2)Me-109 dest(air) | Haltern |
| | | Me-109 dam(air) | Haltern |
| 434th: | LtCol. J.M. Herren | (3)Me-109 dest(air) | SW Munster |
| | Lt. G.W. Gleason | (3)Me-109 dest(air) | SW Munster |
| | | Me-109 dam(air) | SW Munster |
| | Lt. Q.S. Pavlock | (2)Me-109 dest(air) | SW Munster |
| | | FW-190 dest(air) | SW Munster |
| | Capt. C.A.P. Duffie | Me-109 dest(air) | SW Munster |
| | | (2)Me-109 dam(air) | SW Munster |

| | | | |
|---|---|---|---|
| | Lt. W.M. Drake | Me-109 dest(air) | SW Munster |
| | Lt. H.F. Grenning | Me-109 dest(air) | SW Munster |
| | Lt. J.W. Hansen | Me-109 dest(air) | SW Munster |
| | | Me-109 dam(air) | SW Munster |
| | Lt. R.L. Maley | Me-109 dest(air) | SW Munster |
| | Lt. R.G. McChrystal | Me-109 dest(air) | SW Munster |
| | | Me-109 dam(air) | SW Munster |
| | Lt. J.W. Morrow | Me-109 dest(air) | SW Munster |
| | Lt. J.N. Murr | Me-109 dest(air) | SW Munster |
| 435th: | Lt. N.W. Butler | (2)Me-109 dest(air) | SW Munster |
| | Lt. W.H. Pickering | (2)Me-109 dest(air) | SW Munster |
| | Capt. R.R. Coursey | Me-109 dest(air) | SW Munster |
| | Lt. R.K. Friend | Me-109 dest(air) | SW Munster |
| | | Me-109 dam(air) | SW Munster |
| | Lt. M.G. Gorian | Me-109 dest(air) | SW Munster |
| | Lt. C.F. Monsell | Me-109 dest(air) | SW Munster |
| 436th: | Lt. H.J. Grasshoff | (.5)Me-109 dest(air) | S/Munster |
| | Lt. G.W. Mulvany | (.5)Me-109 dest(air) | S/Munster |

NOTE - HdQts and 435th Ftr Sqn flew P-51's. 434th and 436th Ftr Sqns flew P-38's.

*Losses-*

**339th**: Lt. Paul D. Fickel (503rd Ftr Sqn) POW
P-51D D7-Z 44-13980 "Shy Ann"
Lost coolant and bailed out near Altgoedens.

**361st**: Lt. Daniel F. Knupp (375th Ftr Sqn) KIA
P-51B E2- 42-106738
Hit by flak near Havenhorst.

**479th**: Lt. Harry E. Little (434th Ftr Sqn) POW
P-38J L2-N 42-67264
Hit by enemy fighters near Munster.

*Remarks*
479th: Lt. John N. Murr (434th Ftr Sqn) c/l; o.k.
P-38J L2-C

**September 27, 1944**
Groups Operating: P-51 4th, 20th, 55th, 339th, 352nd, 355th, 357th, 359th, 361st, 364th, 479th(mixed)
P-47 56th, 78th, 353rd, 356th
P-38 479th
Missions: Support of bombers to Cologne, Ludwigshafen, Mainz, and Kassel.
Claims: 31-0-9 air
5-1 ground

| ***Group*** | | ***Claims*** | ***Location*** |
|---|---|---|---|
| **4th** | | | |
| 334th: | Lt. A.J. Senecal | Me-109 dest(air) | Giessen |
| 335th: | Lt. R.J. Anderson | FW-190 dam(air) | S/Kassel |
| 336th: | Lt. G.C. Smith | Me-109 dest(air) | S/Kassel |
| | | FW-190 dest(air) | S/Kassel |
| | Capt. J.D. McFarlane | FW-190 dest(air) | SE Kassel |
| | Lt. C.W. Dupree | FW-190 dest(air) | SW Kassel |
| **352nd** | | | |
| 328th: | Capt. D.S. Bryan | (2)Me-109 dest(air) | NW Frankfurt |
| | | Me-109 dam(air) | NW Frankfurt |
| | Lt. R.C. Brookins | FW-190 dest(air) | NW Frankfurt |
| | F/O W.E. Montgomery | Me-109 dest(air) | NW Frankfurt |
| **353rd** | | | |
| 352nd: | Lt. H.B. Tordoff | Me-109 dest(air) | Hanau |
| **355th** | | | |
| HdQts: | LtCol. E.W. Stewart | (.5)Ju-88 dest(grd) | Eschwege |
| 354th: | Capt. H.W. Brown | (2)FW-190 dest(air) | Eschwege |
| | Lt. R.W. Priest | FW-190 dest(air) | Eschwege |
| | Capt. B.C. Williamson | FW-190 dest(grd) | Eschwege |
| | Lt. H.R. Mann | (.5)Ju-88 dest(grd) | Eschwege |
| **361st** | | | |
| 376th: | Lt. W.R. Beyer | (5)FW-190 dest(air) | Eisenach |
| | Lt. V.E. Bocquin | (3)FW-190 dest(air) | Eisenach |
| | Lt. H.G. Powell | (2)FW-190 dest(air) | Eisenach |
| | F/O W.F. Chapin | (2)FW-190 dest(air) | Eisenach |
| | Lt. W.J. Sykes | FW-190 dest(air) | Eisenach |
| | | (2)Me-410 dest(grd) | Eisenach |
| | Lt. D.P. Vulgamore | FW-190 dest(air) | Eisenach |
| | | Me-410 dest(grd) | Eisenach |
| | | Me-410 dam(grd) | Eisenach |
| | Lt. J.B. Bricker | FW-190 dest(air) | Eisenach |
| | | FW-190 dam(air) | Eisenach |
| | Lt. C.W. Hanley | FW-190 dest(air) | Eisenach |
| | Lt. R.W. Myers | FW-190 dest(air) | Eisenach |
| | | FW-190 dam(air) | Eisenach |
| | Lt. R.R. Volkman | FW-190 dest(air) | Eisenach |
| | Lt. R.J. Bain | (2)FW-190 dam(air) | Eisenach |
| | | Me-109 dam(air) | Eisenach |
| | Lt. B.L. Dennehy | FW-190 dam(air) | Eisenach |
| | Lt. R.W. Ward | FW-190 dam(air) | Eisenach |

*Losses-*

**361st**: Lt. Leo H. Lamb (376th Ftr Sqn) KIA
P-51B E9-W 42-106627
Collided with a FW-190 near Eisenach.

**479th**: Lt. William H. Rodgers (434th Ftr Sqn) MIA
P-51D L2-L 44-14324
Suffered mechanical failure and crashed into the Channel.

*Remarks*
353rd: 3-0 locos, 2-0 railcars
361st: 3-2 locos
479th: Capt. Claire A.P. Duffie (434th Ftr Sqn) c/l Kirton; o.k.
P-51D L2-A 44-14355
Lt. George D. Hendrix (434th Ftr Sqn) c/l; o.k.
P-38J L2- 42-68075

KIAc's
20th: Lt. Harry L. Knapp (77th Ftr Sqn)
P-51D LC-C 44-13992
Died in a crash southeast of Yaxley.

**September 28, 1944**
Groups Operating: P-51 4th, 20th, 55th, 339th, 352nd, 355th, 357th, 359th, 361st, 364th, 479th(mixed)
P-47 56th, 78th, 353rd, 356th
P-38 479th
Missions: Support of bombers to Magdeburg, Merseburg, and Kassel.
Claims: 26-0-14 air
1-0 ground

| ***Group*** | | ***Claims*** | ***Location*** |
|---|---|---|---|
| **4th** | | | |
| 334th: | Lt. D.W. Howe | FW-190 dest(air) | NE Kassel |
| **20th** | | | |
| 77th: | Lt. E.C. Fiebelkorn | (3)Me-109 dest(air) | S/Magdeburg |
| | | FW-190 dest(air) | S/Magdeburg |
| | | Me-109 dam(air) | S/Magdeburg |
| | Lt. L.J. Robertson | (2)FW-190 dest(air) | Aschersleben |
| | Lt. T.E. Slanker | FW-190 dest(air) | S/Magdeburg |
| | | FW-190 dam(air) | S/Magdeburg |
| | | Me-210 dest(grd) | S/Magdeburg |
| | Lt. P.J. McCully | Me-109 dam(air) | S/Magdeburg |
| | Lt. R.L. Van Woert | Me-109 dam(air) | S/Magdeburg |
| **339th** | | | |
| 503rd: | Lt. R.H. Ammon | (2)FW-190 dest(air) | SE Brunswick |
| **364th** | | | |
| 383rd: | Lt. W.D. Boyd | FW-190 dest(air) | S/Magdeburg |
| | | FW-190 dam(air) | S/Magdeburg |
| | Lt. F.L. Sorrells | FW-190 dam(air) | S/Magdeburg |
| 385th: | LtCol. R.D. Neece | FW-190 dest(air) | W/Magdeburg |
| | Lt. E.F. Izor | FW-190 dest(air) | SW Magdeburg |
| | Capt. E.A. Taylor | FW-190 dam(air) | W/Magdeburg |
| | Lt. J.J. Pascoe | FW-190 dam(air) | W/Magdeburg |
| **479th** | | | |
| 434th: | Lt. G.W. Gleason | Me-109 dest(air) | W/Halberstadt |
| | | FW-190 dest(air) | W/Halberstadt |
| | LtCol. J.M. Herren | Me-109 dest(air) | W/Halberstadt |
| | Lt. R.M. Lunstrum | FW-190 dest(air) | Halberstadt |
| | Lt. R.B. Kline | Me-109 dam(air) | W/Halberstadt |
| | Lt. E.H. Wendt | FW-190 dam(air) | W/Halberstadt |
| 436th: | Lt. D.A. Dunn | (3)FW-190 dest(air) | W/Magdeburg |
| | Lt. V. Wolski | (3)FW-190 dest(air) | W/Magdeburg |
| | | FW-190 dam(air) | W/Magdeburg |
| | Maj. J.D. Biscayart | (2)FW-190 dest(air) | W/Magdeburg |
| | Lt. G. Straub | FW-190 dest(air) | W/Magdeburg |
| | | FW-190 dam(air) | W/Magdeburg |
| | Lt. J.E. Frolking | FW-190 dam(air) | W/Magdeburg |
| | Lt. H.G. Hightower | FW-190 dam(air) | W/Magdeburg |

NOTE - 436th and Wendt of 434th flew P-38's. Rest of 434th flew P-51's.

*Losses-*

**20th**: Lt. Kenneth M. Geiger (77th Ftr Sqn) POW
P-51D LC-Y 44-14269 "Flamme De Pouseuite"
Hit by enemy fighters near Magdeburg.

**56th**: Lt. Walter H. Pitts (63rd Ftr Sqn) KIA
P-47D UN-
Flew into the ground while strafing southwest of Coblenz.

**357th**: Lt. John S. Templin (362nd Ftr Sqn) POW
P-51B G4-S 43-6698 "Bow-Legs"
Suffered mechanical failure southwest of Bad Faulkenhausen.

**359th**: Lt. Howard E. Steussey (370th Ftr Sqn) KIA
P-51D CS-R 44-13633 "Satan's Lady"
Lost in bad weather near Coblenz.

**361st**: Lt. John R. Ryan (375th Ftr Sqn) POW
P-51B E2-L 43-24774 "Slick Chick"
Hit by flak near Belgershain.

**364th**: Lt. John W. Dupont (383rd Ftr Sqn) KIA
P-51D N2-X 44-13932 "Copperhead"
Hit by enemy fighters west of Magdeburg.

Lt. Glenn W. Loucks (385th Ftr Sqn) KIA
P-51D 5E-S 44-13962 "Bloody Rebel"
Suffered mechanical failure west of Magdeburg.

*Remarks*
20th: 1-1 locos
364th: 10-1 locos, 0-25 railcars, 1-2 vehicles
Lt. William N. Champion (384th Ftr Sqn) c/l Brussels; o.k.
P-51D 5Y- 44-13986

KIAc's
353rd: Lt. Charles E. Sladek (352nd Ftr Sqn)
P-51D SX-P
Spun-in near Woolpit on a test hop.

357th: Lt. James W. Leek (364th Ftr Sqn)
P-51B C5-U 43-6971

**September 30, 1944**
Groups Operating: P-51 4th, 20th, 55th, 339th, 352nd, 355th, 357th, 359th, 361st, 364th, 479th(mixed)
P-47 56th, 78th, 353rd, 356th
P-38 479th
Missions: Support of bombers to Bielefeld, Munster, and Hamm.
Claims: nil
Losses: nil

*Remarks*
359th: Lt. Galen E. Ramser (370th Ftr Sqn) c/l East Wretham; o.k.
P-51B CS-H 43-24778 "Zombie"
364th: P-51 c/l Honington

**October 1, 1944**
KIAc's
78th: Lt. Dwight G. Belt (84th Ftr Sqn)
P-47D WZ-U 42-25690
Collided with a B-17 and crashed near Greenstead Green.

**October 2, 1944**
Groups Operating: P-51 4th, 20th, 55th, 339th, 352nd, 353rd(mixed), 355th, 357th, 359th, 361st, 364th, 479th(mixed)
P-47 56th, 78th, 353rd, 356th
P-38 479th
Missions: Support of bombers to Kassel, Cologne, and Hamm.
Claims: nil

*Losses-*

**4th**: Lt. George H. Logan, Jr. (336th Ftr Sqn) KIA
P-51D VF- 44-14172
Suffered mechanical failure northeast of Apeldoorn.

**479th**: Lt. Quentin S. Pavlock (434th Ftr Sqn) KIA
P-51D L2-
Crashed on take-off from Wattisham.

*Remarks*
78th: LtCol. Jack J. Oberhansly (HdQts) c/l Lille; o.k.
P-47D MX-X 44-19566
359th: 12-0 locos, 50-0 railcars
Lt. Don E. Cannon (369th Ftr Sqn) b/o East Wretham; o.k.
P-51B IV-S 42-106689 "Briney Marlin"
Lt. Lawrence A. Ziska (370th Ftr Sqn) c/l France; o.k.
P-51D CS- 44-14265
361st: Capt. James D. Smith (376th Ftr Sqn) c/l; o.k.
P-51D E9-Y 44-14042

**October 3, 1944**
Groups Operating: P-51 4th, 20th, 55th, 339th, 352nd, 353rd(mixed), 355th, 357th, 359th, 361st, 364th
P-47 56th, 78th, 353rd, 356th
P-38 479th
Missions: Support of bombers to airfields and other targets in Germany.
Claims: 0-0-0 air
2-0 ground

| Group | | Claims | Location |
|---|---|---|---|
| **355th** | | | |
| 354th: | Maj. C.W. Lenfest | FW-190 dest(grd) | Nordlingen |
| | Capt. H.W. Brown | Me-110 dest(grd) | Nordlingen |

*Losses-*

**55th**: Lt. Alfred E. Carr (38th Ftr Sqn) ASR
P-51D CG- 44-14097
Suffered mechanical failure and bailed out over the North Sea.

**353rd**: Capt. Harold E. Daniel (351st Ftr Sqn) POW
P-51D YJ- 44-14505
Suffered mechanical failure and bailed out over France.

**355th**: Maj. Charles W. Lenfest (354th Ftr Sqn) POW
P-51D WR-F 44-14409 "Lorie IV"
Landed near Deiningen to pick-up Capt. Brown but became stuck in the mud.

Capt. Henry W. Brown (354th Ftr Sqn) POW
P-51D WR-Z 44-13305 "Hun Hunter From Texas"
Hit by flak at Nordlingen and bellied-in near Deiningen.

*Remarks*
353rd: Lt. Gerald P. Devine (350th Ftr Sqn) c/l Brussels; o.k.
P-51D LH-
359th: Lt. Don W. Chatfield (368th Ftr Sqn) c/l Continent; o.k.
P-51D CV

KIAc's
361st: Lt. Charles C. McKivett (374th Ftr Sqn)
P-51D B7-
Crashed after taking-off for a practice mission.

**October 5, 1944**
Groups Operating: P-51 4th, 20th, 55th, 339th, 352nd, 353rd, 355th, 357th, 359th, 361st, 364th, 479th
P-47 56th, 78th, 356th
Missions: Support of bombers to Cologne, Lippstadt, Munster, Rheine, and targets of opportunity.
Claims: 0-0-1 air
13-7 ground

| Group | | Claims | Location |
|---|---|---|---|
| **56th** | | | |
| HdQts: | LtCol. D.C. Schilling | (3)Me-210 dest(grd) | S/Geseke |
| | | (3)Me-210 dam(grd) | S/Geseke |
| 62nd: | Lt. R.L. Patterson | Me-109 dest(grd) | S/Geseke |
| | | Ju-88 dest(grd) | S/Geseke |
| | Lt. R.W. Davis | Me-109 dest(grd) | S/Geseke |
| | | Ju-88 dest(grd) | S/Geseke |
| | | Me-109 dam(grd) | S/Geseke |
| | Capt. J.B. Eaves | FW-190 dest(grd) | S/Geseke |
| | Lt. E.M. Beason | Me-110 dest(grd) | S/Geseke |
| | Lt. G.R. Choate | Me-110 dest(grd) | S/Geseke |
| | Lt. F.A. Nolan | Ju-88 dest(grd) | S/Geseke |
| | Lt. R.E. Winters | Me-109 dest(grd) | S/Geseke |
| | Capt. W.F. Wilkerson | (2)He-111 dam(grd) | S/Geseke |
| | | Me-109 dam(grd) | S/Geseke |
| 63rd: | Lt. J.E. Lister | Me-109 dam(air) | S/Geseke |
| | Lt. W.E. Kerr | Me-110 dest(grd) | S/Geseke |

*Losses-*

**339th**: Lt. Stephen C. Ananian (505th Ftr Sqn) ASR
P-51B 6N-M 42-106946 "Bison Bull"
Hit by flak over the Zuider Zee and bailed out forty miles off Aldeburgh.

**352nd**: Capt. John B. Coleman, Jr. (328th Ftr Sqn) MIA-E
P-51D PE-M 44-13983 "Patty IV"
Suffered mechanical failure and bellied-in northwest of Tilburg.

**355th**: Lt. James O. Juntilla (357th Ftr Sqn) POW
P-51C OS-F 42-103735 "Gooch's Revenge"
Suffered mechanical failure and bailed out near Aartwood.

**359th**: Lt. Clifford L. Bartlett (368th Ftr Sqn) KIA
P-51D CV-I 44-13669
Spun-out in overcast near Tirlemomt.

**364th**: Lt. Joseph R. Gonder (385th Ftr Sqn) KIA
P-51D 5E-K 44-13942 "Pinnochio"
Suffered mechanical failure and ditched west of Schouwen.

*Remarks*
4th: 0-5 locos, 0-10 railcars
56th: 1-0 loco, 4-0 flak positions
357th: Lt. Ray T. Conlin (362nd Ftr Sqn) c/l Brussels; o.k.
P-51B G4- 43-6710
Lt. John J. Breunig (362nd Ftr Sqn) b/o Nijmegen; o.k.
P-51D G4-

**October 6, 1944**
Groups Operating: P-51 4th, 20th, 55th, 339th, 352nd, 353rd(mixed), 355th, 357th, 359th, 361st, 364th, 479th
P-47 56th, 78th, 353rd, 356th
Missions: Support of bombers to Berlin, Stralsund, Harburg, Hamburg, Wenzendorf, and other targets of opportunity.
Claims: 18-1-8 air
40-12 ground

| *Group* | | *Claims* | *Location* |
|---|---|---|---|
| **4th** | | | |
| 334th: | Lt. L.R. Werner | Me-109 dest(air) | Neven |
| | | FW-190 dam(air) | Neven |
| 335th: | Lt. R.E. Lewis | (.5)Me-410 dest(air) | NW Heligoland |
| | Lt. E.N. McCall | (.5)Me-410 dest(grd) | NW Heligoland |
| 336th: | Lt. J.H. Joiner | Me-109 dest(air) | Korbach |
| **20th** | | | |
| HdQts: | LtCol. J.P. Randolph | (2)Do-24 dest(grd) | Kubitzer Bay |
| 55th: | Capt. J.T. McKeon | (2)Do-24 dest(grd) | Kubitzer Bay |
| | Capt. W.B. Taylor | Do-24 dest(grd) | Kubitzer Bay |
| | | u/i a/c dest(grd) | Kubitzer Bay |
| | Lt. W.M. Hurst | (2)Do-24 dest(grd) | Kubitzer Bay |
| | Lt. R.M. Howard | BV-140 dest(grd) | Kubitzer Bay |
| | | Do-24 dest(grd) | Kubitzer Bay |
| | | (3)BV-140 dam(grd) | Kubitzer Bay |
| | Lt. D.D. Oxley | (2)Do-24 dest(grd) | Kubitzer Bay |
| | Lt. J.L. Mansker | u/i a/c dest(grd) | Kubitzer Bay |
| | Lt. K.D. McNeel | u/i a/c dest(grd) | Kubitzer Bay |
| | Lt. E.W. Cavell | Do-24 dest(grd) | Kubitzer Bay |
| | | Do-24 dam(grd) | Kubitzer Bay |
| | Lt. R.I. Bowman | Do-24 dest(grd) | Kubitzer Bay |
| | | Do-24 dam(grd) | Kubitzer Bay |
| | Lt. D.B. Benedict | Do-24 dest(grd) | Kubitzer Bay |
| | Lt. T.C. Barnes | Do-24 dest(grd) | Kubitzer Bay |
| | | Do-24 dam(grd) | Kubitzer Bay |
| | Lt. M. Maldanado | Do-24 dest(grd) | Kubitzer Bay |
| | | Do-24 dam(grd) | Kubitzer Bay |
| | F/O J.D. Leon | Do-24 dest(grd) | Kubitzer Bay |
| | | Do-24 dam(grd) | Kubitzer Bay |
| 77th: | Lt. F.H. Alexander | (3)He-111 dest(grd) | Bad Berg-Dievenow |
| | | He-115 dest(grd) | Bad Berg-Dievenow |
| | | Do-18 dest(grd) | Bad Berg-Dievenow |
| | Lt. R.R. Flowers | (2.5)Do-18 dest(grd)* | Bad Berg-Dievenow |
| | Lt. L.W. Adams | Ar-196 dest(grd) | Bad Berg-Dievenow |
| | | Do-18 dest(grd) | Bad Berg-Dievenow |
| | Capt. J.H. Herbert | Ar-196 dest(grd) | Bad Berg-Dievenow |
| | Lt. J.M. Garner | (1.5)Do-18 dest(grd)* | Bad Berg-Dievenow |
| | | Do-18 dam(grd) | Bad Berg-Dievenow |
| | Lt. D.W. Van Sickle | (.5)Do-18 dest(grd)** | Bad Berg-Dievenow |
| | | Do-18 dam(grd) | Bad Berg-Dievenow |
| | Lt. F.E. Snodgrass | (.5)Do-18 dest(grd)** | Bad Berg-Dievenow |
| | | Do-18 dam(grd) | Bad Berg-Dievenow |
| 79th: | Capt. R.P. Gatterdam | (2.5)He-115 dest(grd) | Bad Berg-Dievenow |
| | Lt. M.G. Ingebrigsten | (1.5)He-115 dest(grd) | Bad Berg-Dievenow |
| | Lt. W.E. Bullers | He-115 dest(grd) | Bad Berg-Dievenow |
| | Lt. J.E. Carpenter | He-115 dest(grd) | Bad Berg-Dievenow |
| | Lt. Z.M. Wyman | u/i a/c dest(grd) | Bad Berg-Dievenow |
| | Lt. R.H. Pollock | u/i a/c dam(grd) | Bad Berg-Dievenow |
| **355th** | | | |
| 357th: | Capt. C.W. Lamer | (2)FW-190 dest(air) | W/Berlin |
| | Capt. C.C. Colson | Me-109 dam(air) | W/Berlin |
| **357th** | | | |
| 362nd: | Capt. J.B. England | (2)Me-109 dest(air) | NW Berlin |
| | | Me-109 dam(air) | NW Berlin |
| | Lt. W.T. Gilbert | FW-190 dest(air) | NW Berlin |
| | F/O O.D. Jenkins | FW-190 dest(air) | NW Berlin |
| | Lt. T.W. Martinek | FW-190 dest(air) | NW Berlin |
| | | FW-190 prob(air) | NW Berlin |
| | Lt. W.H. Mooney | FW-190 dam(air) | NW Berlin |
| | Lt. W.N. Perry | FW-190 dam(air) | NW Berlin |
| 364th: | Capt. R.A. Peterson | FW-190 dest(air) | W/Berlin |
| **359th** | | | |
| 370th: | Capt. G.A. Doersch | (2)FW-190 dest(air) | S/Stettin |
| | | FW-190 dam(air) | S/Stettin |
| | Lt. R.L. McInnes | FW-190 dest(air) | S/Stettin |
| | | FW-190 dam(air) | S/Stettin |
| | F/O J.E. McCoskey | FW-190 dest(air) | S/Stettin |
| **361st** | | | |
| 375th: | Capt. T.F. Brubaker | Me-109 dest(air) | NW Berlin |
| **479th** | | | |
| 434th: | Capt. R. Olds | FW-190 dest(air) | W/Berlin |
| | Lt. G.D. Hendrix | FW-190 dam(air) | W/Berlin |
| 436th: | Lt. T.E. Myers | Me-109 dest(air) | E/Berlin |

*Losses-*

**55th:** Lt. Warren E. Lewis (343rd Ftr Sqn) POW
P-51D CY-N 44-14442
Ran out of fuel near Rheurt.

**352nd:** Lt. James H. Forga, Jr. (487th Ftr Sqn) MIA
P-51B HO-G 43-7139 "Lili Marlene"
Lost coolant and crashed west of Wangerooge.

**361st:** Capt. Thomas F. Brubaker (375th Ftr Sqn) POW
P-51D E2-A 44-14132
Collided with a Me-109 north of Berlin.

Lt. David R. Morgan (375th Ftr Sqn) POW
P-51D E2- 44-14516
Suffered mechanical failure near Erringen.

*Remarks*
56th: 0-1 E-boat
353rd: 5-0 locos
364th: 2-0 locos
Lt. Lawrence E. Muscavitch (384th Ftr Sqn) c/l Halvergate; o.k.
P-51D 5Y-

**October 7, 1944**
Groups Operating: P-51 4th, 20th, 55th, 339th, 352nd, 353rd(mixed), 355th, 357th, 359th, 361st, 364th
P-47 56th, 78th, 353rd, 356th
P-38 479th
Missions: Support of bombers to Merseburg, Politz, Kassel, Brux, Bohlen, Zwickau, Lutzkenforf, and targets of opportunity.
Claims: 22-0-1 air
15-24 ground

| *Group* | | *Claims* | *Location* |
|---|---|---|---|
| **20th** | | | |
| 55th: | Capt. R.M. Scrutchfield | Do-18 dest(grd) | Ribnitz A/F |
| 77th: | Capt. R.T. Stovall | Ju-88 dest(grd) | Peenemunde |
| | Lt. C.W. Dungan | Ju-88 dest(grd) | Peenemunde |
| | Lt. T.P. Hambelton | Ju-88 dam(grd) | Peenemunde |
| | Lt. D.W. Van Sickle | u/i a/c dam(grd) | Peenemunde |
| 79th: | Capt. R.J. Meyer | (.5)He-115 dest(grd) | Bad Berg-Dievenow |
| | Lt. Z.M. Wyman | (.5)He-115 dest(grd) | Bad Berg-Dievenow |
| **55th** | | | |
| 38th: | Lt. C.C. Sherman | Me-109 dest(air) | Leipzig |
| 338th: | Lt. D.S. Cramer | Me-109 dest(air) | Leipzig |
| **78th** | | | |
| 82nd: | Maj. R.E. Conner | Me-262 dest(air) | Osnabruck |
| | Maj. J. Myers | Me-109 dest(air) | Leipzig |
| | Lt. R.R. Bosworth | Me-109 dest(air) | Leipzig |
| | Lt. A.S. Miller | Me-109 dam(air) | Leipzig |
| **355th** | | | |
| 357th: | Lt. H.L. Monahan | FW-190 dest(air) | SW Leipzig |
| | | Me-109 dest(air) | SW Leipzig |
| | | Ju-88 dam(grd) | SW Leipzig |
| **356th** | | | |
| 361st: | Capt. W.R. Scheible | (2)Me-110 dest(grd) | Fritzlar |
| | | Ju-88 dest(grd) | Fritzlar |
| | | (4)Ju-88 dam(grd) | Fritzlar |
| | Lt. E.L. Thompson | Ju-88 dest(grd) | Fritzlar |
| | | u/i a/c dest(grd) | Fritzlar |
| | | Me-110 dam(grd) | Fritzlar |
| | | Hs-123 dam(grd) | Fritzlar |
| | | Ju-88 dam(grd) | Fritzlar |
| | Lt. H.E. Whitmore | Ju-88 dest(grd) | Fritzlar |
| | | (2.5)Ju-88 dam(grd) | Fritzlar |
| | Lt. F.F. Hooker | Me-110 dest(grd) | Fritzlar |
| | | Me-110 dam(grd) | Fritzlar |
| | | Me-410 dam(grd) | Fritzlar |
| | Lt. D. Kahle | Me-110 dest(grd) | Fritzlar |
| | | (2)Me-110 dam(grd) | Fritzlar |
| | Lt. P.J. Roberts | Me-110 dest(grd) | Fritzlar |
| | Capt. R.J. Upp | (3.5)Ju-88 dam(grd) | Fritzlar |
| | Capt. J.M. Hallmark | (3)Me-110 dam(grd) | Fritzlar |
| **357th** | | | |
| 362nd: | Lt. T.W. Martinek | (2)FW-190 dest(air) | SW Leipzig |
| 363rd: | Lt. F.L. Gailer | FW-190 dest(air) | SW Zeitz |
| 364th: | Capt. R.A. Peterson | Me-109 dest(air) | Jena |
| | Lt. J.J. Salsman | Me-109 dest(air) | SW Leipzig |
| **359th** | | | |
| 370th: | Capt. G.A. Doersch | (.5)BV-140 dest(grd) | Dievenow |
| | F/O J.E. McCoskey | (.5)BV-140 dest(grd) | Dievenow |
| | Lt. E.G. Johnson | (.5)Ar-196 dam(grd) | Dievenow |
| | Lt. R.M. York | (.5)Ar-196 dam(grd) | Dievenow |

**361st**

| | | | |
|---|---|---|---|
| 374th: | Lt. P.B. Collins | Me-109 dest(air) | Naumburg |
| | Lt. A.E. Davis | Me-109 dest(air) | Naumburg |
| | Lt. W.J. Quinn | Me-109 dest(air) | Naumburg |
| 375th: | Lt. U.L. Drew | (2)Me-262 dest(air) | Achmer A/F |
| 376th: | Lt. W.T. Butts | Me-109 dest(air) | Merseburg |
| | Lt. H.D. Mitchell | Me-109 dest(air) | Merseburg |
| | Lt. W.R. Young | Me-109 dest(air) | Merseburg |

**364th**

| | | | |
|---|---|---|---|
| 385th: | Capt. E.A. Taylor | (.5)Me-163 dest(air) | Brux |
| | Lt. W.G. Erfkamp | (.5)Me-163 dest(air) | Brux |

**479th**

| | | | |
|---|---|---|---|
| HdQts: | Col. H. Zemke | (.5)Me-109 dest(air) | W/Chemnitz |
| 434th: | Maj. A.F. Jeffrey | Me-109 dest(air) | S/Leipzig |
| 435th: | Lt. N.R. Benoit | (.5)Me-109 dest(air) | W/Chemnitz |

*Losses-*

**4th**: F/O Kenneth E. Foster (334th Ftr Sqn) ASR
P-51B QP-T 43-6719
Suffered mechanical failure and bailed out over the Channel.

**20th**: Capt. Joseph T. McKeon (55th Ftr Sqn) POW
P-51D KI-N 44-13541 "Olivia De"
Collided with Lt. Brown near Stettin.

Lt. Robert C. Brown (55th Ftr Sqn) POW
P-51D KI-A 44-14331
Collided with Capt. McKeon near Stettin.

Lt. Charles W. Dungan (77th Ftr Sqn) MIA-E
P-51C LC-Q 43-25046
Hit by flak at Peenemunde and bailed out over Denmark.

**55th**: Capt. Peter Dempsey (338th Ftr Sqn) POW
P-51D CL-P 44-14291 "DaQuake"
Hit by flak near Almenhausen.

**78th**: Lt. Robert D. Smith (84th Ftr Sqn) KIA
P-47D WZ-I 43-25305
Crashed into trees while strafing near Neustadt.

**356th**: Lt. Paul J. Roberts (361st Ftr Sqn) KIA
P-47D QI-P 42-76177 "Mad Wolves"
Hit by flak at Fritzlar and bailed out northwest of Marburg.
He was killed on the ground by civilians.

**359th**: Lt. Wallace C. Murray (370th Ftr Sqn) KIA
P-51C CS- 43-25067 "Sandra Lynn"
Hit by flak near Dievenow.

**361st**: Lt. Robert K. McCandliss (375th Ftr Sqn) POW
P-51B E2-H 42-106830 "Ted's Reply"
Hit by flak near Wettringen.

**479th**: Lt. James E. Frolking (436th Ftr Sqn) MIA-E
P-51D 9B-N 44-14577
Hit by flak near Scheldt and bailed out off the Dutch coast.

Lt. Victor Wolski (436th Ftr Sqn) ASR
P-51D 9B- 44-14553
Suffered mechanical failure and bailed out over the Channel.

*Remarks*
20th: 0-2 gun positions, 0-1 control tower
78th: 3-0 locos
364th: 2-0 locos

**October 9, 1944**
Groups Operating: P-51 4th, 20th, 55th, 339th, 352nd, 353rd(mixed), 355th, 357th, 359th, 361st, 364th, 479th(mixed)
P-47 56th, 78th, 353rd, 356th
P-38 479th
Missions: Support of bombers to Schweinfurt, Mainz, and Gustavsburg.
Claims: nil
Losses: nil

*Remarks*
20th: Lt. Robert E. Murrell (77th Ftr Sqn) c/l; o.k.
P-51 LC-
353rd: 1-0 loco, 6-9 railcars
357th: F/O Otto D. Jenkins (362nd Ftr Sqn) c/l Belgium; o.k.
P-51B G4-P 42-106829 "Floogie"

KIAc's
55th: Lt. Francis R. Sharp (338th Ftr Sqn)
P-51D CL-I 44-13668

**October 10, 1944**
KIAc's
56th: Capt. John B. Eaves (62nd Ftr Sqn)
P-47D LM-
Suffered mechanical failure and hit an embankment while trying to force-land.

**October 11, 1944**
Groups Operating: P-51 4th
P-47 56th, 78th, 356th
Missions: The Thunderbolt groups supported bombers to Wessling and Coblenz while eight P-51's flew an ASR patrol.
Claims: nil

*Losses-*

**56th**: Lt. Julius DeMayo (63rd Ftr Sqn) KIA
P-47D UN-L 42-27322
Hit by flak near Euskirchen.

*Remarks*
4th: 0-8 barges

**October 12, 1944**
Groups Operating: P-51 4th, 55th, 339th, 352nd, 353rd, 355th, 357th, 361st, 364th, 479th
P-47 56th, 78th
Missions: Support of bombers to Osnabruck and Bremen.
Claims: 19-2-1 air
0-0 ground

| *Group* | | *Claims* | *Location* |
|---|---|---|---|
| **56th** | | | |
| 63rd: | Lt. J.E. Lister | FW-190 dest(air) | Dummer Lake |
| | F/O E.W. Andermatt | Me-109 prob(air) | Dummer Lake |
| **78th** | | | |
| 82nd: | Maj. R.E. Conner | FW-190 dest(air) | Hamburg |
| | Lt. H.H. Lamb | Me-109 dest(air) | Hamburg |
| **357th** | | | |
| 363rd: | Lt. C.E. Yeager | (5)Me-109 dest(air) | Steinhuder Lake-Hanover |
| | Lt. R.C. Roper | (2)Me-109 dest(air) | Hanover |
| | Lt. F.L. Gailer | Me-109 dest(air) | Hanover |
| **364th** | | | |
| 384th: | Capt. E.B. Shepard | Me-109 dest(air) | N/Bremen |
| | Lt. R.L. Stiefvater | FW-190 dest(air) | N/Bremen |
| 385th: | Lt. A.R. Jones | (3)FW-190 dest(air) | N/Bremen |
| | | FW-190 dam(air) | N/Bremen |
| | Capt. W.S. Crombie | Me-109 dest(air) | W/Bremen |
| | Lt. G.L. Jamison | FW-190 dest(air) | NE Bremen |
| | Lt. R. Visconte | FW-190 dest(air) | NE Bremen |
| | Lt. W.A. Sullivan | FW-190 prob(air) | NE Bremen |

*Losses-*

**357th**: Capt. Herschel T. Pascoe (363rd Ftr Sqn) POW
P-51D B6-B 44-13714 "Desert Rat"
Hit by a FW-190 near Wunstorf.

**364th**: Lt. Frank T. Kozloski (384th Ftr Sqn) POW
P-51D 5Y-F 44-14074 "Kay"
Hit by flak at Jener Airfield.

Lt. Roy A. Crouch, Jr. (385th Ftr Sqn) POW
P-51D 5E- 44-14708
Hit by enemy fighters near Bremen.

Lt. Harold J. Joy (385th Ftr Sqn) MIA
P-51D 5E-E 44-13899
Hit by enemy fighters near Bremen.

Lt. Wilfred A. Pohmer (385th Ftr Sqn) MIA
P-51D 5E- 44-13347
Hit by enemy fighters near Bremen.

*Remarks*
4th: 0-3 locos, 0-5 railcars, 0-2 vehicles
56th: 1-0 loco, 0-4 railcars, 0-1 flak tower
78th: 0-2 locos

**October 14, 1944**

Groups Operating: P-51 4th, 20th, 55th, 339th, 352nd, 353rd, 355th, 357th, 359th, 361st, 364th, 479th
P-47 56th, 78th, 356th
Missions: Support of bombers to Cologne, Saarbrucken, and Kaiserlautern.
Claims: 2-0-0 air
0-0 ground

| Group | | Claims | Location |
|---|---|---|---|
| **4th** | | | |
| 334th: | Capt. J.L. Lang | (2)Me-109 dest(air) | Nancy/St. Dizier |

*Losses-*

**4th:** Capt. Joseph L. Lang (334th Ftr Sqn) KIA
P-51D QP-Z 44-14123
Hit by a Me-109 near Kaiserlautern and crashed near Eurville.

**55th:** Lt. Edwin D. Lawrence (38th Ftr Sqn) KIA
P-51D CG-D 44-13701
Killed in a crash near Wormingford.

*Remarks*
479th: P-51 c/l Charleroi; o.k.

KIAc's
361st: F/O Walter F. Chapin (376th Ftr Sqn)
P-51B E9-E 42-106802 "Blue Eyes"

**October 15, 1944**
Groups Operating: P-51 4th, 20th, 55th, 339th, 352nd, 353rd, 355th, 357th, 359th, 361st, 364th, 479th
P-47 56th, 78th, 356th
Missions: Support of bombers to Cologne and various targets of opportunity. Also provided escort for two "Aphrodite" missions to Heligoland.
Claims: 7-0-2 air
2-2 ground

| Group | | Claims | Location |
|---|---|---|---|
| **56th** | | | |
| 62nd: | Lt. L.R. Brown | Me-109 dest(grd) | Rheine A/F |
| 63rd: | Lt. J.A. Kyle | (.5)Me-109 dest(grd) | Rheine A/F |
| | Lt. T.W. Saling | (.5)Me-109 dest(grd) | Rheine A/F |
| **78th** | | | |
| 82nd: | Lt. H.H. Lamb | Me-262 dest(air) | Bohmte |
| 83rd: | Lt. R.T. Green | (3.5)FW-190 dest(air) | Bohmte |
| | Lt. J.S. Reems | (1.5)FW-190 dest(air) | Bohmte |
| | F/O L.L. Eadline | FW-190 dest(air) | Bohmte |
| | Lt. H.O. Foster | Me-262 dam(air) | Bohmte |
| | Lt. F.E. Harrington | FW-190 dam(air) | Bohmte |
| | Lt. W.E. Sonner | Me-109 dest(grd) | Fassberg A/F |
| | Lt. F.E. Higginbottom | Do-217 dam(grd) | Munster |

*Losses-*

**55th:** Lt. John T. Kibler, Jr. (343rd Ftr Sqn) MIA
P-51D CY-X 44-14632
Suffered mechanical failure near St. Nicholas.

**78th:** Lt. Jack LaGrange, Jr. (83rd Ftr Sqn) POW
P-47D HL-K 42-28544 "Fast Action Jackson"
Hit by flak and bailed out near Heber.

**361st:** Maj. James B. Cheney (376th Ftr Sqn) POW
P-51D E9-H 44-14219 "Scat Cat"
Suffered mechanical failure near Dorsten.

*Remarks*
56th: 8-3 locos, 0-180 railcars
Lt. David M. Magel (63rd Ftr Sqn) c/l Woodbridge; o.k.
P-47D UN-
78th: 14-18 locos, 41-165 railcars, 0-14 vehicles, 0-2 buildings
355th: P-51 c/l; o.k.
356th: 3-1 locos, @50-0 railcars
359th: Lt. Carl M. Anderson (368th Ftr Sqn) c/l East Wretham; o.k.
P-51 CV-
361st: 3-0 vehicles
364th: Lt. Jack V. Johnson (384th Ftr Sqn) c/l SE Liege; o.k.
P-51D 5Y- 44-14031

**October 17, 1944**
Groups Operating: P-51 4th, 20th, 55th, 339th, 352nd, 353rd, 355th, 357th, 359th, 361st, 364th, 479th
P-47 56th, 78th, 356th
Missions: Support of bombers to Cologne.
Claims: nil

*Losses-*

**364th:** Lt. Vernon C. Prickett (383rd Ftr Sqn) POW
P-51D N2- 44-14242
Hit by flak near Cologne and bailed out near Duren.

**October 18, 1944**
Groups Operating: P-51 4th, 55th, 339th, 352nd, 353rd, 355th, 357th, 361st, 364th, 479th
P-47 56th, 78th, 356th
Missions: Support of bombers to Kassel and Cologne.
Claims: nil

*Losses-*

**339th:** Lt. Raymond D. Mayer (503rd Ftr Sqn) KIA
P-51D D7-X 44-13955
Hit wires and crashed near Rotenkirchen.

Lt. William D. Stockton (503rd Ftr Sqn) KIA
P-51 D7-
Died in a crash near Ghent.

**353rd:** Lt. Robert D. Corgan (352nd Ftr Sqn) POW
P-51D SX-D 44-11188
Lost coolant and bailed out near Coblenz.

**355th:** Lt. William Lonkausky (357th Ftr Sqn) KIA
P-51D OS-E 44-14186
Hit by flak near Cologne.

**357th:** Lt. Horace M. Roycroft (363rd Ftr Sqn) KIA
P-51D B6-Y 44-13897
Spun-in near Ghent.

*Remarks*
339th: Capt. Valdee Wyatt (503rd Ftr Sqn) b/o Continent; injured
P-51D D7-
364th: 9-0 locos, 20-25 railcars

KIAc's
20th: Lt. Walter H. Mullins (55th Ftr Sqn)
P-51D KI-S 44-13859

**October 19, 1944**
Groups Operating: P-51 4th, 20th, 55th, 339th, 352nd, 353rd, 355th, 357th, 359th, 361st, 364th, 479th
P-47 56th, 78th, 356th
Missions: Support of bombers to Mainz, Mannheim, and Gustavsburg.
Claims: nil

*Losses-*

**20th:** Capt. Willis B. Taylor (55th Ftr Sqn) POW
P-51D KI-K 44-13892 "Idiot's Delight"
Suffered mechanical failure and bailed out near Boppard.

**357th:** Lt. Charles G. Goss (362nd Ftr Sqn) MIA-E
P-51D G4-Z 44-13963 "Morning Star"
Suffered mechanical failure east of Neustadt.

*Remarks*
78th: P-47 c/l Duxford; o.k.
479th: Lt. George W. Gleason (434th Ftr Sqn) b/o Calais; o.k.
P-51D L2-

**October 22, 1944**
Groups Operating: P-51 4th, 20th, 55th, 339th, 352nd, 353rd, 355th, 357th, 359th, 361st, 364th, 479th
P-47 56th, 78th, 356th
Missions: Support of bombers to Brunswick, Hamm, Hanover, and Munster.
Claims: nil

*Losses-*

**355th:** Capt. Norman B. McDonald (354th Ftr Sqn) KIA
P-51D WR-T 44-14760
Died when a P-51 collided with his aircraft while taxi-ing at Steeple Morden.

**364th:** Lt. Frank J. Hoder (383rd Ftr Sqn) POW
P-51D N2- 44-13532 "Betty Joyce"
Suffered mechanical failure near Haarlem.

*Remarks*
4th: 0-13 locos, 0-5 barges, 0-5 tugs, 0-2 boats
355th: P-51 c/l Continent; o.k.
357th: P-51 c/l Leiston; o.k.
359th: Lt. James H. O'Shea (370th Ftr Sqn) c/l East Wretham; o.k.
P-51D CS- 44-14422

**October 24, 1944**
Groups Operating: P-51 20th, 339th, 352nd, 353rd, 357th, 359th, 364th
P-47 56th, 356th
Missions: Sweeps of the Kassel-Hanover area.
Claims: 2-0-0 air
4-3 ground

| Group | | Claims | Location |
|---|---|---|---|
| **353rd** | | | |
| 352nd: | Capt. F.L. Uttwenweiler | (4)He-111 dest(grd) | N/Luxembourg |
| | | (3)He-111 dam(grd) | N/Luxembourg |
| **359th** | | | |
| 368th: | Lt. M.B. Barth | FW-190 dest(air) | Nordhausen |
| | F/O B.N. Adkins | FW-190 dest(air) | Nordhausen |

*Losses-*

**56th:** Lt. William J. Osborne (61st Ftr Sqn) KIA
P-47D HV-U 42-26646 "Pockey Doc"
Hit by flak near Marken Island and crashed into the Zuider Zee.

Lt. George R. Choate, Jr. (62nd Ftr Sqn) KIA
P-47D LM- 44-19929
Hit by flak and crashed southeast of Elburg.

**352nd:** Lt. Thompson R. Kyle (486th Ftr Sqn) POW
P-51B PZ-B 42-106613 "Ellie"
Hit by flak near Engelhern.

**353rd:** Capt. Carl F. Mueller (350th Ftr Sqn) POW
P-51D LH-M 44-14770 "Fern Marie III"
Suffered mechanical failure and bellied-in southeast of Hamburg.

Lt. Robert W. Hedler (350th Ftr Sqn) KIA
P-51D LH-S 44-14654 "Molly M"
Hit by flak in the Bremen area.

**364th:** Lt. Howard M. Laity (385th Ftr Sqn) MIA
P-51D 5E- 44-13985 "Joker III"
Hit the ground while strafing near Rengershausen.

Lt. Walter A. Sullivan (385th Ftr Sqn) POW
P-51D 5E-D 44-13830
Hit by flak near Friedland.

*Remarks*
20th: 2-0 locos, 0-1 building
56th: 1-2 locos, 0-82 railcars
352nd: 7-8 locos, 4-23 railcars, 6-0 vehicles, 0-5 flak towers
353rd: 30-9 locos, 69-91 railcars, 3-5 vehicles, 0-5 barges, 1-0 ship
356th: 7-1 locos, 0-55 railcars
Maj. Maurice A. Cristadoro (HdQts) c/l Martlesham Heath; o.k.
P-47D QI-D 42-28816
Lt. Robert M. Tomlinson (361st Ftr Sqn) b/o Chedburch; o.k.
P-47D QI-T 42-25844 "Jersey Jerk"
359th: 52-2 locos, 5-78 railcars, 16-55 vehicles, 0-14 tanks, 0-1 barge
364th: 29-6 locos, 165-109 railcars, 1-22 vehicles, 0-4 barges, 1-4 buildings, 0-1 boat

KIAc's
352nd: Lt. Jack C. Landrum (487th Ftr Sqn)
P-51D HO-F 44-13597 "Stardust"

**October 25, 1944**
Groups Operating: P-51 4th, 20th, 55th, 352nd, 353rd, 357th, 359th, 364th, 479th
P-47 56th, 356th
Missions: Support of bombers to Hamburg, Neumunster, Harburg, Hamm, and Scholven/Buer.
Claims: nil

*Losses-*

**353rd:** Lt. Bernard J. French (351st Ftr Sqn) KIA
P-51D YJ-K 44-14558 "Jean III"
Hit by fire from a B-24 and bailed out off Terschelling Island.

*Remarks*
353rd: 8-1 locos, 10-30 railcars, 1-0 barge, 1-0 gun position
364th: 384th Ftr Sqn P-51 c/l; o.k.
P-51D 5Y- 44-14021

**October 26, 1944**
Groups Operating: P-51 4th, 20th, 55th, 339th, 352nd, 353rd, 355th, 357th, 359th, 361st
P-47 56th, 78th, 356th
Missions: Support of bombers to Bielefeld, Munster, Hanover, Minden, and Bottrop.
Claims: nil

*Losses-*

**20th:** Lt. Kenneth Kautz, Jr. (79th Ftr Sqn) POW
P-51D MC-K 44-13580 "Little Ronnie"
Suffered mechanical failure and bailed out east of the Zuider Zee.

*Remarks*
78th: Lt. Edwin Milliron (83rd Ftr Sqn) c/l; o.k.
P-47D HL-T 44-19884
361st: Lt. Joseph B. Wolfe (375th Ftr Sqn) c/l; o.k.
P-51D E2-X 44-14270

**October 27, 1944**
KIAc's
353rd: Lt. Marvin E. Albertson (350th Ftr Sqn)
P-51D LH-
Collided with another P-51 and crashed south of Little Staughton.

**October 28, 1944**
Groups Operating: P-51 20th, 339th, 357th, 364th
Missions: Support of bombers to Hamm and Munster.
Claims: nil

*Losses-*

**364th:** Lt. Robert F. Brown (385th Ftr Sqn) MIA-E
P-51D 5E-I 44-14241
Suffered mechanical failure and bailed out southwest of Munster.

Lt. Joseph F. Davis (385th Ftr Sqn) POW
P-51D 5E-H 44-14835
Suffered mechanical failure and bailed out southeast of Emmerich.

**October 30, 1944**
Groups Operating: P-51 4th, 55th, 339th, 352nd, 353rd(mixed), 355th, 357th, 359th, 361st, 364th, 479th
P-47 56th, 78th, 353rd, 356th
Missions: Support of bombers to Hamburg and Hamm, plus two sections of P-47's escorted two "Aphrodite" missions to Heligoland.
Claims: nil

*Losses-*

**359th:** Lt. Russell H. Jenner (369th Ftr Sqn) KIA
P-51D IV-Y 44-13336 "Yankee Clipper"
Suffered mechanical failure and crashed near St. Trond.

**361st:** Lt. Francis Christensen (374th Ftr Sqn) KIA
P-51C B7-L 43-25032
Hit by flak near Tarnewitz.

**479th:** Col. Hubert Zemke (HdQts) POW
P-51D 9B-Z 44-14351
Encountered bad weather southeast of Hamburg and bailed out near Niendorf.

LtCol. James M. Herren, Jr. (434th Ftr Sqn) KIA
P-51D L2-A 44-14396 "Touche'"
Collided with a P-51 in bad weather near Hassel.

Lt. Douglas I. Holmes (434th Ftr Sqn) POW
P-51D L2-S 44-14627 "Pauline"
Collided with a P-51 in bad weather near Hassel.

KIAc's
479th: Lt. Douglas T. Thomas (434th Ftr Sqn)
P-51D L2-O 44-14225

**November 1, 1944**
Groups Operating: P-51 4th, 20th, 352nd, 355th, 357th, 359th, 361st
P-47 56th, 356th
Missions: Support of bombers to Gelsenkirchen.
Claims: 1-0-0 air
0-0 ground

| Group | | Claims | Location |
|---|---|---|---|
| **56th** | | | |
| 63rd: | Lt. W.R. Groce | (.5)Me-262 dest(air) | E/Arnheim-Hengelo |
| **352nd** | | | |
| 486th: | Lt. W.T. Gerbe | (.5)Me-262 dest(air) | E/Arnheim/Hengelo |

*Losses-*

**20th:** Lt. Dennis J. Alison (77th Ftr Sqn) KIA
P-51D LC-A 44-14378 "Hookin' Bull"
Hit by a Me-262 in the Hengelo area.

**361st:** Lt. James A. Eason (375th Ftr Sqn) KIA
P-51B E2- 42-106688
Killed in a crash near Beechamwell upon return.

*Remarks*
356th: 1-0 vehicle, 0-3 barges, 0-1 tank
359th: Lt. David B. Archibald (368th Ftr Sqn) b/o northeast of Norwich.
P-51D CV-Q 44-14854

**November 2, 1944**
Groups Operating: P-51 4th, 20th, 55th, 339th, 352nd, 353rd(mixed), 355th, 357th, 359th, 361st, 364th, 479th
P-47 56th, 78th, 353rd, 356th
Missions: Support of bombers to Merseburg, Bielefeld, Sterkrade, and Castrop/Rauxel.
Claims: 136-7-20 air
26-0 ground

| Group | | Claims | Location |
|---|---|---|---|
| **4th** | | | |
| 335th: | Capt. L.H. Norley | Me-163 dest(air) | SE Leipzig |
| | Lt. C.L. Brock | Me-109 dest(air) | Merseburg |
| | Lt. J.E. Kolbe | Me-109 dest(air) | Leipzig |

| | | | |
|---|---|---|---|
| 336th: | Capt. F.W. Glover | Me-163 dest(air) | E/Leipzig |

**20th**

| | | | |
|---|---|---|---|
| HdQts: | LtCol. R.P. Montgomery | (2)Me-109 dest(air) | Halle-Merseburg |
| | | FW-190 dest(air) | Halle-Merseburg |
| 55th: | Capt. J.H. Tennant | (2)FW-190 dest(air) | Halle-Merseburg |
| | | Me-109 dest(air) | Halle-Merseburg |
| | Lt. H.L. Brown | (2)FW-190 dest(air) | Halle-Merseburg |
| | | Me-109 dest(air) | Halle-Merseburg |
| | | Me-109 dam(air) | Halle-Merseburg |
| | Lt. J.L. Mansker | (2)Me-109 dest(air) | Halle-Merseburg |
| | | Me-109 prob(air) | Halle-Merseburg |
| | Lt. D.E. Chrissinger | Me-109 dest(air) | Halle |
| | Lt. D.I. Freedman | Me-109 dest(air) | Halle |
| | | Me-109 dam(air) | Halle |
| | Lt. W.M. Hurst | Me-109 dest(air) | Halle |
| | F/O J.D. Leon | Me-109 dest(air) | SW Merseburg |
| | | Me-109 prob(air) | SW Merseburg |
| 77th: | Lt. E.C. Fiebelkorn | (3)Me-109 dest(air) | N/Leipzig |
| | Lt. J.M. Garner | (2)Me-109 dest(air) | N/Leipzig |
| | Lt. L.E. Rowlett | (2)Me-109 dest(air) | Merseburg |
| | Lt. R.D. Jones | Me-109 dest(air) | Merseburg |
| | | Me-109 prob(air) | Merseburg |
| | Lt. G.L. Reynolds | Me-109 dest(air) | Merseburg |
| | Lt. P.L. Schallo | Me-109 dam(air) | N/Leipzig |
| 79th: | Capt. R.P. Gatterdam | Me-109 dest(air) | SW Merseburg |
| | Capt. G.M. Webb | Me-109 dest(air) | SW Merseburg |
| | Lt. R.L. Pubentz | Me-109 dest(air) | SW Merseburg |

**55th**

| | | | |
|---|---|---|---|
| 38th: | Capt. M.M. Coons | FW-190 dest(air) | W/Merseburg |
| | Capt. E.R. Fryer | FW-190 dest(air) | Merseburg |
| | Lt. C.C. Gould | Me-109 dest(air) | S/Merseburg |
| | Lt. N.L. Larson | Me-109 dest(air) | W/Merseburg |
| | Lt. T.H. Holleman | FW-190 dest(air) | Merseburg |
| | Capt. J.F. Coonan | (.5)FW-190 dest(air) | W/Merseburg |
| | Lt. D.H. Courtney | (.5)FW-190 dest(air) | W/Merseburg |
| | Lt. D.F. Jewell | (.5)Me-109 dest(air) | W/Merseburg |
| | Lt. F.M. Matney | (.5)Me-109 dest(air) | W/Merseburg |
| 338th: | Lt. M. Alba | Me-109 dest(air) | Merseburg |
| | | Me-109 dam(air) | Merseburg |
| | Lt. S.D. Gevorkian | Me-109 dest(air) | NW Leipzig |
| | Lt. R.C. Haworth | Me-109 dest(air) | Merseburg |
| | Lt. J.E. Kester | FW-190 dest(air) | W/Leipzig |
| | LtCol. E.G. Rightetti | (.5)Me-109 dest(air) | SW Leipzig |
| | Capt. D.S. Cramer | (.5)Me-109 dest(air) | SW Leipzig |
| 343rd: | Capt. R.D. Brown | Me-109 dest(air) | SE Leipzig |
| | Capt. D.A. Parker | Me-109 dest(air) | Weimar |
| | Lt. N.P. Babaeff | Me-109 dest(air) | Naumburg |
| | Lt. R.W. Erb | Me-109 dest(air) | W/Merseburg |
| | Lt. R.E. Welch | Me-109 dest(air) | Naumburg |
| | Lt. R.D. Bartlett | (.5)Me-109 dest(air)* | SW Leipzig |
| | Lt. J. Eliades | (.5)Me-109 dest(air)* | SW Leipzig |
| | Lt. D.L. Mercier | (.5)Me-109 dest(air)** | Erfurt-Weimar |
| | Lt. G.D. Leslie | Me-109 dam(air) | Naumburg |

**339th**

| | | | |
|---|---|---|---|
| 504th: | Lt. R.F. Herrmann | FW-190 dest(air) | Mulhausen |
| | Lt. D.E. Penny | Me-109 dest(air) | Naumburg |

**352nd**

| | | | |
|---|---|---|---|
| HdQts: | LtCol. J.D. Mayden | Me-109 dest(air) | Merseburg |
| 328th: | Capt. D.S. Bryan | (5)Me-109 dest(air) | Merseburg |
| | | (2)Me-109 dam(air) | Merseburg |
| | Lt. A.E. Hudson | (4)Me-109 dest(air) | Merseburg |
| | Lt. C.E. Goodman | (3)Me-109 dest(air) | Merseburg |
| | Capt. W.J. Stangel | (2)Me-109 dest(air) | Merseburg |
| | | (.5)Me-109 dest(air) | Merseburg |
| | | (.5)Me-109 dest(air) | Merseburg |
| | Lt. E.W. James | (.5)Me-109 dest(air) | Merseburg |
| | | (.5)Me-109 dest(air) | Merseburg |
| | Maj. E.L. Abbott | (2)Me-109 dest(air) | Merseburg |
| | Lt. G.R. Clark | (2)Me-109 dest(air) | Merseburg |
| | Lt. C.E. Rogers | (2)Me-109 dest(air) | Merseburg |
| | Maj. G.E. Preddy | Me-109 dest(air) | Merseburg |
| | Lt. F.R. Hill | Me-109 dest(air) | Merseburg |
| | Lt. D.J. Maxwell | Me-109 dest(air) | Merseburg |
| | Lt. E.W. Briggs | Me-109 prob(air) | Merseburg |
| 486th: | Capt. H.J. Miklajcyk | Me-109 dest(air) | Merseburg |
| | | FW-190 dest(air) | Merseburg |
| | Lt. E.O. Bostrom | (2)Me-109 dest(air) | W/Halle |
| | Lt. H.L. Edwards | Me-109 dest(air) | Merseburg |
| | Lt. L.J. Vitek | Me-109 dest(air) | SW Merseburg |
| | LtCol. W.O. Jackson | Me-109 dam(air) | N/Merseburg |
| | | FW-190 dam(air) | N/Merseburg |
| 487th: | Lt. J.P. Vickery | (2)Me-109 dest(air) | Merseburg |
| | Capt. W.T. Halton | Me-109 dest(air) | E/Merseburg |
| | Capt. W.T. Whisner | Me-109 dest(air) | Merseburg |
| | Lt. J.N. Wood | Me-109 dest(air) | E/Merseburg |
| | Lt. D.H. Schuh | Me-109 dest(air) | Merseburg |
| | Lt. K.M. Waldron | Me-109 dest(air) | Merseburg |
| | Lt. N.R. Jessup | FW-190 dest(air) | Merseburg |

**353rd** (all were with P-51)

| | | | |
|---|---|---|---|
| 350th: | Lt. L.M. Grainger | (2)Me-109 dest(air) | Merseburg |
| | Lt. R.W. Abernathy | Me-109 dest(air) | Merseburg |
| | Capt. H.G. Kolb | FW-190 dam(air) | NW Merseburg |
| 352nd: | Capt. L.P. Cles | FW-190 prob(air) | Naumburg |
| | Lt. H.E. Tear | Me-109 prob(air) | Naumburg |

**355th**

| | | | |
|---|---|---|---|
| 354th: | Lt. R.W. Priest | Me-109 dest(air) | W/Naumburg |
| | Lt. M.L. Woolard | Me-109 dest(air) | W/Naumburg |
| 357th: | Lt. W.J. Cullerton | Me-109 dest(air) | Wernigerode |
| | | FW-190 dest(air) | Wernigerode |
| | | (6)u/i a/c dest(grd) | Wernigerode |
| | Maj. J.L. Elder | Me-109 dest(air) | Wernigerode |
| | | (5)u/i a/c dest(grd) | Wernigerode |
| | Lt. E.J. Moroney | Me-109 dest(air) | Wernigerode |
| | | (2)u/i a/c dest(grd) | Wernigerode |
| | Lt. H.O. Wilkes | FW-190 dest(air) | S/Wernigerode |
| | Lt. J.E. Erickson | (4)u/i a/c dest(grd) | Wernigerode |
| | Capt. R.J. DuFresne | (2)u/i a/c dest(grd) | Wernigerode |
| | Lt. K.J. Miller | (2)u/i a/c dest(grd) | Wernigerode |
| | Lt. B.G. Williams | (2)u/i a/c dest(grd) | Wernigerode |
| | Capt. J.C. Engelbreit | u/i a/c dest(grd) | Wernigerode |
| | Lt. J.V. Cavender | u/i a/c dest(grd) | Wernigerode |
| | F/O E.H. Riffle | u/i a/c dest(grd) | Wernigerode |
| 358th: | Lt. K.E. Mikalauskas | FW-190 dest(air) | Merseburg |
| | Lt. J.N. McElroy | Me-109 dam(air) | Merseburg |

**357th**

| | | | |
|---|---|---|---|
| 362nd: | Capt. L.K. Carson | Me-109 dest(air) | Naumburg |
| 363rd: | Capt. T.E. Hughes | FW-190 dest(air) | E/Leipzig |
| | | (2)FW-190 dam(air) | E/Leipzig |
| | Lt. H.O. Hand | Me-109 dest(air) | E/Leipzig |
| | | Me-109 dam(air) | E/Leipzig |
| 364th: | Capt. R.A. Peterson | FW-190 dest(air) | NW Merseburg |
| | Lt. G.L. Weber | FW-190 dam(air) | NW Merseburg |

**359th**

| | | | |
|---|---|---|---|
| 368th: | Capt. G.F. Baker | (.5)Me-109 dest(air) | Quedlinburg |
| | | Me-109 dam(air) | Quedlinburg |
| | Lt. O.R. Fladmark | (.5)Me-109 dest(air) | Quedlinburg |
| 370th: | Capt. R.S. Wetmore | (2)Me-109 dest(air) | Erfurt-Weimar |
| | Capt. R.L. Cox | Me-109 dest(air) | Erfurt-Weimar |
| | Lt. D.D. Connelly | Me-109 dest(air) | Erfurt-Weimar |
| | Capt. S.J. Huskins | (.5)Me-109 dest(air)** | Erfurt-Weimar |

**361st**

| | | | |
|---|---|---|---|
| 374th: | Lt. J.G. Vear | Me-109 dest(air) | N/Erfurt |
| 375th: | Lt. L.A. Wood | Me-109 dest(air) | S/Weiszenfels |
| 376th: | Lt. W.J. Sykes | Me-109 dest(air) | N/Erfurt |
| | | FW-190 dest(air) | N/Erfurt |
| | Lt. W.R. Beyer | FW-190 dest(air) | N/Erfurt |
| | Lt. J.B. Bricker | FW-190 dest(air) | N/Erfurt |
| | Lt. H.D. Mitchell | FW-190 dest(air) | N/Erfurt |
| | Lt. J.J. Sadinski | FW-190 dest(air) | N/Erfurt |
| | Lt. G.R. Vanden Heuval | FW-190 dest(air) | N/Erfurt |

**364th**

| | | | |
|---|---|---|---|
| 383rd: | Lt. E.C. Beaumont | Me-109 dest(air) | Merseburg |
| | | FW-190 dam(air) | Merseburg |
| | Lt. T.H. Hall | FW-190 dest(air) | Merseburg |
| 384th: | Lt. J.M. Fowle | Me-109 dest(air) | S/Merseburg |
| 385th: | Capt. E.F. Izor | (3)Me-109 dest(air) | Halle |
| | Lt. J.J. Pascoe | (2)Me-109 dest(air) | Halle |
| | Capt. W.S. Crombie | Me-109 dest(air) | Halle |
| | Lt. E.N. Farrell | Me-109 dest(air) | N/Merseburg |
| | Lt. J.E. Hargrove | Me-109 dest(air) | Halle |
| | Lt. W.T. Housholder | Me-109 dest(air) | Halle |
| | | Me-109 prob(air) | Halle |
| | Lt. A.B. McCormick | Me-109 dest(air) | Halle |
| | | Me-109 dam(air) | Halle |
| | Lt. H.W. Head | Me-109 dam(air) | Merseburg |
| | Lt. E.H. Rivers | FW-190 dam(air) | Merseburg |

**479th**

| | | | |
|---|---|---|---|
| 434th: | Maj. A.F. Jeffrey | Me-109 dest(air) | Zeitz |
| | Lt. J.C. Donnell | Me-109 dest(air) | SW Leipzig |

*Losses-*

**20th:** Capt. Jerome C. Serros (55th Ftr Sqn) KIA
P-51D KI-G 44-13838 "Okie Blokie"
Suffered mechanical failure and bailed out east of the Zuider Zee.

Lt. Jack W. Kennedy (77th Ftr Sqn) KIA
P-51D LC-M 44-13746 "Little Sister"
Suffered mechanical failure and bailed out off Ostend.

Lt. Richard L. Van Woert (77th Ftr Sqn) KIA
P-51D LC-U 44-13840 "Van's Can"
Hit by enemy fighters near Merseburg.

**55th**: Lt. Fred L. Sturgess (38th Ftr Sqn) POW
P-51D CG-I 44-13747 "Six-Gun Pete"
Hit by enemy fighters near Leipzig.

**352nd**: Lt. Glenn R. Clark (328th Ftr Sqn) POW
P-51D PE-D 44-11153 "Mom and Dad"
Hit by enemy fighters near Halberstadt.

Capt. Henry J. Miklajcyk (486th Ftr Sqn) KIA
P-51D PZ-K 44-13690 "The Syracusan 3rd"
Hit by enemy fighters near Halle.

**353rd**: Lt. Lester M. Grainger (350th Ftr Sqn) ASR
P-51D LH-G
Ran out of gas and bailed out over the Channel.

**355th**: Lt. Albert A. Zimmerman (354th Ftr Sqn) KIA
P-51D WR-M 44-13630
Suffered mechanical failure and bellied-in near Voorthoszen.

Capt. Joseph C. Engelbreit (357th Ftr Sqn) POW
P-51D OS-C 44-14203 "Spook III"
Hit by flak while strafing near Wernigerode.

**357th**: Maj. Lawrence P. Giarrizzo (362nd Ftr Sqn) KIA
P-51D G4-H 44-13735
Lost a wing while chasing enemy fighters near Naumberg.

**361st**: Lt. Charles E. Moore (375th Ftr Sqn) KIA
P-51B E2- 42-106900
Hit by enemy fighters near Naumburg.

Lt. Charles W. Narvis (375th Ftr Sqn) KIA
P-51D E2-G 44-14226 "Babe Schomarrech"
Suffered mechanical failure near Roedgen.

**364th**: Lt. William T. Housholder (385th Ftr Sqn) KIA
P-51D 5E-H 44-14006
Hit by a Me-109 near Merseburg.

*Remarks*
4th: 0-4 locos
55th: 4-1 locos, 3-2 vehicles
353rd: 1-0 loco
355th: 1-2 locos
357th: 2-1 locos
78th: Lt. Foy E. Higginbottam (83rd Ftr Sqn) c/l France; o.k.
P-47D HL-R 42-27370

**November 4, 1944**
Groups Operating: P-51 4th, 20th, 55th, 339th, 352nd, 353rd, 355th, 357th, 359th, 361st, 364th, 479th
P-47 56th, 78th, 356th
Missions: Support of bombers to Neunkirchen, Hanover, Hamburg, Bottrop, and Gelsenkirchen.
Claims: 0-0-1 air
0-2 ground

| *Group* | | *Claims* | *Location* |
|---|---|---|---|
| **20th** | | | |
| 77th: | Maj. R.F. Gustke | He-177 dam(grd) | SW Dummer Lake |
| | Lt. T.E. Slanker | FW-190 dam(grd) | W/Munster |
| **356th** | | | |
| 359th: | Capt. R.A. Rann | Me-262 dam(air) | Lingen-Enschede |

*Losses-*

**356th**: F/O Willard W. Royer (360th Ftr Sqn) KIA
P-47D PI-N 42-26289 "Georgia's Best"
Hit by a Me-262 near Enschede.

**359th**: Lt. Edward J. Thorne (369th Ftr Sqn) POW
P-51C IV-F 42-103339 "Princess Pat"
Hit by flak and bailed out near Quackenbruck.

*Remarks*
55th: 9-0 locos
352nd: 1-0 loco
355th: 0-3 barges
356th: 1-0 loco
359th: 2-0 locos, 0-2 railcars
339th: Lt. Leo H. Becker (505th Ftr Sqn) c/l Kessingland; o.k.
P-51D 6N-

**November 5, 1944**
Groups Operating: P-51 4th, 20th, 55th, 339th, 352nd, 353rd, 355th, 357th, 359th, 361st, 364th, 479th
P-47 56th, 78th, 356th
Missions: Support of bombers to Frankfurt, Ludwigshafen, and Karlsruhe.
Claims: nil

*Losses-*

**4th**: Lt. Russell J. Anderson (335th Ftr Sqn) POW
P-51D WD-U 44-14339
Hit by flak near Baden Baden.

**55th**: Lt. Gus D. Leslie (343rd Ftr Sqn) MIA
P-51D CY-A 44-13363 "Bama Blitz"
Hit by flak near Eberbach.

**56th**: Lt. Robert F. Healey (63rd Ftr Sqn) KIA
P-47D UN-R 42-76530
Ran out of fuel and bailed out over the Channel.

Lt. Albert L. Henry (63rd Ftr Sqn) KIA
P-47D UN-X 42-76471
Hit by flak near Neuhuetten.

**359th**: Lt. Maurice N. Haines (369th Ftr Sqn) POW
P-51D IV- 44-14857 "Brooklyn Devil"
Hit by flak and bailed out southwest of Darmstadt.

*Remarks*
4th: 0-9 locos, 0-34 railcars, 0-3 vehicles
20th: 0-2 barges, 0-1 building
55th: 21-2 locos, 0-65 railcars, 0-5 vehicles, 0-3 barges
56th: 4-2 locos, 3-39 railcars, 10-4 vehicles
359th: 2-0 locos, 5-0 vehicles
Capt. Ralph L. Brown (368th Ftr Sqn) c/l East Wretham; o.k.
P-51D CV-

**November 6, 1944**
Groups Operating: P-51 4th, 20th, 55th, 339th, 352nd, 353rd, 355th, 357th, 359th, 361st, 364th, 479th
P-47 56th, 78th, 356th
Missions: Support of bombers to Hamburg, Neumunster, Minden, Bottrop, Sterkrade, and Duisburg.
Claims: 4-1-6 air
1-0 ground

| *Group* | | *Claims* | *Location* |
|---|---|---|---|
| **4th** | | | |
| 334th: | Lt. J.D. McFadden | Me-109 dest(air) | Rheine |
| | Lt. R.A. Dickmeyer | Me-109 dam(air) | Rheine |
| | Lt. E.C. Walsh | Me-109 prob(air) | Rheine |
| | | Me-109 dam(air) | Rheine |
| 336th: | Lt. V.E. Chandler | FW-190 dest(air) | Minden |
| **56th** | | | |
| 62nd: | Capt. M.J. Jackson | Me-410 dam(air) | Deventer |
| **357th** | | | |
| 363rd: | Capt. C.E. Yeager | Me-262 dest(air) | E/Assen |
| | | (2)Me-262 dam(air) | E/Assen |
| **361st** | | | |
| 374th: | Lt. W.J. Quinn | Me-262 dest(air) | Bessum |
| | F/O J.R. Voss | Me-262 dam(air) | Rehburg |
| **479th** | | | |
| 434th: | Lt. W.H. Marlowe | (.5)FW-190 dest(grd) | Hesepe |
| | Lt. T.C. Olson | (.5)FW-190 dest(grd) | Hesepe |

*Losses-*

**4th**: Lt. John L. Childs (334th Ftr Sqn) KIA
P-51D QP-Z 44-14772
Hit by a FW-190 near Rheine.

Lt. Earl C. Walsh (334th Ftr Sqn) POW
P-51D QP-N 44-14229
Hit by a Me-109 near Rheine.

**55th**: Lt. Paul R. Porter (343rd Ftr Sqn) KIA
P-51D CY-K 44-13874 "Junie Bug II"
Suffered mechanical failure and bailed out over the Channel.

**364th**: Lt. Stanley M. Pettengill (383rd Ftr Sqn) POW
P-51D N2-B 44-13906 "Doc"
Suffered mechanical failure and bailed out north of Amsterdam.

**479th**: Lt. Marion W. Steele (436th Ftr Sqn) KIA
P-51D 9B- 44-11201
Suffered mechanical failure and crashed into the North Sea.

*Remarks*
4th: 0-2 locos
20th: 0-2 barges, 0-1 building

355th: 0-1 loco
Lt. James N. McElroy (358th Ftr Sqn) c/l Steeple Morden; o.k.
P-51D YF-S 44-14498 "Big Stoop II"
353rd: Lt. George N. Porterfield (352nd Ftr Sqn) c/l; o.k.
P-51D SX-Q
479th: 0-2 locos, 0-11 railcars, 2-0 vehicles

KIAc's
4th: Lt. Charles Y. Mead (336th Ftr Sqn)
P-51C VF- 42-103794
Bailed out too low near Little Walden after mechanical trouble.

**November 8, 1944**
Groups Operating: P-51 4th, 20th, 55th, 339th, 352nd, 353rd(mixed), 355th, 357th, 359th, 361st, 364th, 479th
P-47 56th, 78th, 353rd, 356th
Missions: Support for bombers to Merseburg and Rheine.
Claims: 4-0-0 air
0-1 ground

| ***Group*** | | ***Claims*** | ***Location*** |
|---|---|---|---|
| **20th** | | | |
| 77th: | Lt. E.C. Fiebelkorn | (.5)Me-262 dest(air)* | Dummer Lake |
| **353rd** (made with P-51) | | | |
| 352nd: | Capt. L.P. Cless | (.5)Ju-88 dam(grd) | Plantlunne |
| | Lt. J.R. Evans | (.5)Ju-88 dam(grd) | Plantlunne |
| **357th** | | | |
| 362nd: | Lt. J.W. Kenney | Me-262 dest(air) | Quackenbruck |
| 364th: | Lt. E.R. Haydon | (.5)Me-262 dest(air)* | Dummer Lake |
| **361st** | | | |
| 375th: | Lt. A. Maurice | Me-262 dest(air) | W/Meppel |
| **364th** | | | |
| 384th: | Lt.R.W. Stevens | Me-262 dest(air) | Dummer Lake |

*Losses-*

**4th**: Lt. Earl A. Quist (336th Ftr Sqn) POW
P-51D VF-L 44-13961
Last heard from near the German border.

**20th**: Lt. Elmer H. Coughran (77th Ftr Sqn) KIA
P-51D LC-
Suffered mechanical failure and came down near Allied lines.

**55th**: Capt. Earl R. Fryer (38th Ftr Sqn) KIA
P-51D CG-Z 44-13804 "Spunktown"
Hit by flak near Hilversum.

Capt. Eugene S. Gregg, Jr. (38th Ftr Sqn) POW
P-51D CG- 44-14026
Hit by flak near Boenninghardt.

**353rd**: Capt. Leslie P. Cles (352nd Ftr Sqn) POW
P-51D SX-U 44-14831 "Pregnant Patty"
Hit by flak near Plantlunne and bellied-in near Hohenkoerben.

**356th**: Lt. William L. Hoffert (359th Ftr Sqn) POW
P-47D OC- 42-28845
Hit by a Me-262 near Osnabruck.

Lt. Charles C. McKelvy (359th Ftr Sqn) POW
P-47D OC-J 42-76208"Dodie Darlin"
Hit by a Me-262 near Osnabruck.

**357th**: Lt. Warren B. Corwin (362nd Ftr Sqn) KIA
P-51B G4-V 43-12227
Damaged by a Me-262 and bellied-in near Termonde.

Lt. Warren J. Doransky (363rd Ftr Sqn) KIA
P-51D B6-
Suffered mechanical failure and bailed out over the North Sea but his chute failed to open.

**359th**: Maj. James A. Howard (369th Ftr Sqn) KIA
P-51D IV- 44-14286
Hit by flak while strafing near Meppen.

**479th**: Lt. Heinz W. Detlefson (435th Ftr Sqn) KIA
P-51D J2- 44-14294
Collided with Lt. Smith near Minden.

Lt. Thomas V. Smith (435th Ftr Sqn) POW
P-51D J2- 44-14589
Collided with Lt. Detlefson near Minden.

*Remarks*
4th: 0-9 locos, 0-3 barges, 0-2 vehicles
20th: 1-0 loco, 0-1 flak position
Lt. Irving T. Bradford (79th Ftr Sqn) c/l Little Snoring; o.k.
P-51D MC-
55th: 20-2 locos, 3-30 railcars, 9-2 vehicles
56th: 1-0 loco, 0-4 railcars, 2-0 vehicles
78th: 3-1 locos, 0-12 railcars, 0-4 vehicles
355th: 0-10 locos, 0-68 railcars
357th: 7-0 locos, 2-0 vehicles, 1-0 flak position
359th: 1-0 loco, 0-15 railcars
364th: Lt. Charles G. Goodner (384th Ftr Sqn) c/l Manston; o.k.
P-51D 5Y- 44-14703 "G.I. Buzz Buggy"

**November 9, 1944**
Groups Operating: P-51 4th, 20th, 55th, 339th, 352nd, 353rd, 355th, 357th, 359th, 361st, 364th, 479th
P-47 56th, 78th, 356th
Missions: Support for bombers to Saarbrucken and the Thionville-Metz area.
Claims: 0-0-0 air
1-4 ground

| ***Group*** | | ***Claims*** | ***Location*** |
|---|---|---|---|
| **78th** | | | |
| 84th: | Lt. J.M. Farmer | Fi-156 dest(grd) | Hanover |
| | Capt. L.P. Marshall | (2)He-111 dam(grd) | Schenfheim A/F |
| | Lt. R.O. Laho | Ju-88 dam(grd) | Schenfheim A/F |
| | Lt. R.H. Spooner | Ju-88 dam(grd) | Schenfheim A/F |

*Losses-*

**20th**: Lt. Edward A. Loetscher (55th Ftr Sqn) KIA
P-51D KI-K 44-13715
Lost control while strafing near Saarbrucken and crashed.

Lt. John R. Wilson (77th Ftr Sqn) KIA
P-51D LC-S 44-13670
Wing came off while dive-bombing near Saarbrucken.

**78th**: Lt. Alan R. Jacobson (83rd Ftr Sqn) KIA
P-47D HL-B 44-19932
Hit by flak and bailed out too low near Eisenberg.

**352nd**: Lt. Charles E. Rogers (328th Ftr Sqn) MIA
P-51D PE-S 44-14273 "Georgia Peach II"
Suffered mechanical failure northeast of Lille.

**355th**: Lt. Carl V. Hull, Jr. (354th Ftr Sqn) POW
P-51D WR-V 44-14536
Hit by flak and bellied-in near Miltenberg.

**361st**: Capt. Richard M. Durbin (HdQts) KIA
P-51D B7-H 44-13704
Crashed while landing at Little Walden.

*Remarks*
4th: 0-18 locos, 0-78 railcars, 0-11 barges, 0-1 vehicle
20th: 1-0 loco, 0-3 railcars, 1-0 vehicle, 0-2 buildings, 0-1 bridge
56th: 16-9 locos, 1-52 railcars, 3-60 vehicles, 1-0 barracks
78th: 12-0 locos, 0-65 railcars, 1-0 vehicle, 0-1 hangar, 0-1 flak tower
339th: P-51 c/l Charleville; o.k.
364th: 385th Ftr Sqn P-51 c/l Honington; o.k.
P-51D 5E- 44-13657

KIAc's
78th: Lt. William G. Kelly (84th Ftr Sqn)
P-47D WZ-
Crashed for unknown reasons on a training hop.

**November 10, 1944**
Groups Operating: P-51 4th, 20th, 55th, 339th, 352nd, 353rd(mixed), 355th, 357th, 359th, 361st, 364th, 479th
P-47 56th, 78th, 353rd, 356th
Missions: Support of bombers to Hanau, Wiesbaden, and Cologne, plus some P-47 units flew fighter-bomber operations.
Claims: 0-0-0 air
4-0 ground

| ***Group*** | | ***Claims*** | ***Location*** |
|---|---|---|---|
| **353rd**(with P-51) | | | |
| 350th: | Lt. J.M. Ard | Bu-133 dest(grd) | Fulda |
| | Lt. H.E. Caton | Bu-133 dest(grd) | Fulda |
| | Lt. A.L. Deeds | Bu-133 dest(grd) | Fulda |
| | Lt. H.E. Haynes | Bu-133 dest(grd) | Fulda |

*Losses-*

**56th**: Lt. Thomas W. Saling, III (63rd Ftr Sqn) KIA
P-47D UN- 44-19887
Hit by flak near Ulzen.

*Remarks*

55th: Lt. Jordan Eliades (343rd Ftr Sqn) c/l Rouen; o.k.
P-51D CY-J 44-14049

56th: 10-1 locos, 66-5 vehicles

78th: 5-2 locos, 0-36 railcars, 0-1 vehicle, 0-1 barge, 0-2 buildings

352nd: 3-3 locos, 0-25 railcars, 0-15 barges

353rd: 9-1 locos, 0-15 railcars, 5-0 vehicles, 0-1 hangar

364th: 2-0 locos, 0-35 railcars, 68-13 vehicles, 0-1 barge, 0-1 boat

479th: Lt. Jack S. Denny (434th Ftr Sqn) c/l; o.k.
P-51D L2-

**November 11, 1944**

Groups Operating: P-51 4th, 55th, 339th, 352nd, 353rd, 355th, 357th, 361st, 364th, 479th
P-47 56th, 78th

Missions: Support of bombers to Oberlahnstein, Gelsenkirchen, and Bottrop.

Claims: nil

*Losses-*

**364th**: Lt. James S. Massey (383rd Ftr Sqn) MIA
P-51D N2- 44-15064
Last seen near Dorsten; possible oxygen failure.

**November 14, 1944**

Groups Operating: P-51 55th

Missions: Eight pilots flew a PRU escort to Bohlen.

Claims: nil

Losses: nil

KIAc

361st: Lt. John J. Sadinski (376th Ftr Sqn)
C-78
Crashed into a mountain flying in thick fog.

**November 16, 1944**

Groups Operating: P-51 20th, 55th, 339th, 355th, 357th, 361st
P-47 56th, 78th, 353rd

Missions: Support for bombers to Duren and Eschweiler.

Claims: nil

*Losses-*

**355th**: Lt. Marion L. Woolard (354th Ftr Sqn) POW(D)
P-51B WR-W 42-106896
Hit by flak and bailed out near Barleburg. Was later killed in April of 1945 by an artillery barrage after escaping.

**357th**: Lt. Robert Wiser (364th Ftr Sqn) KIA
P-51D C5-Y 44-14549 "Marie"
Hit trees while landing at Leiston.

**361st**: Lt. Alfred B. Cook (374th Ftr Sqn) KIA
P-51D B7-R 44-13357
Killed in a crash near Baldock.

*Remarks*

55th: 343rd Ftr Sqn P-51 c/l Manston; o.k.
P-51D CY-

339th: Lt. Ralph S. Hill (503rd) c/l Fowlmere; o.k.
P-51C D7-M 42-103600 "Sally"
Lt. Elmer E. Haidle (503rd Ftr Sqn) c/l Fowlmere; o.k.
P-51 D7-B 44-14012

355th: 7-3 locos, 0-43 railcars

**November 18, 1944**

Groups Operating: P-51 4th, 339th, 353rd, 355th, 357th, 361st, 479th
P-47 56th

Missions: Strafing sweeps of the Langenseebold-Weissenborn-Freiham-Neuburg area.

Claims: 24-4-7 air
57-71 ground

| *Group* | | *Claims* | *Location* |
|---|---|---|---|
| **4th** | | | |
| HdQts: | Maj. R.A. Ackerly | Me-262 dest(grd) | Leipheim |
| 334th: | Lt. C.F. Brown | (2)Me-262 dest(grd) | Leipheim |
| | | Me-262 dam(grd) | Leipheim |
| | F/O C.W. Harre | (2)Me-262 dest(grd) | Leipheim |
| | | (2)Me-262 dam(grd) | Leipheim |
| | Maj. H.D. Hively | Me-262 dest(grd) | Leipheim |
| | Capt. G.E. Montgomery | Me-262 dest(grd) | Leipheim |
| | | (4)Me-262 dam(grd) | Leipheim |
| | Lt. C.G. Payne | Me-262 dest(grd) | Leipheim |
| | | Me-262 dam(grd) | Leipheim |
| | Lt. R.A. Dyer | (4)Me-262 dam(grd) | Leipheim |
| | Lt. J.D. McFadden | (2)Me-262 dam(grd) | Leipheim |
| | Lt. A.J. Senecal | (2)Me-262 dam(grd) | Leipheim |
| | Lt. W.J. Dvorak | Me-262 dam(grd) | Leipheim |
| | F/O K.E. Foster | Me-262 dam(grd) | Leipheim |
| | Lt. W.B. Hoelscher | Me-262 dam(grd) | Leipheim |
| 335th: | Capt. J.C. Fitch | (.5)Me-262 dest(air) | S/Leipheim |
| | | Me-109 dest(grd) | Leipheim |
| | Lt. J.N. Creamer | (.5)Me-262 dest(air) | S/Leipheim |
| | Capt. W.C. Anderson | Me-262 dest(grd) | Leipheim |
| | | Me-262 dam(grd) | Leipheim |
| | Lt. W.B. Eaton | Me-262 dest(grd) | Leipheim |
| | | Me-262 dam(grd) | Leipheim |
| | Lt. J.E. Kolbe | Me-262 dest(grd) | Leipheim |
| | Lt. R.J. Mabie | (2)Me-262 dam(grd) | Leipheim |
| | Lt. E.N. McCall | Me-262 dam(grd) | Leipheim |
| | | Me-109 dam(grd) | Leipheim |
| | Lt. E. Jungling | Me-262 dam(grd) | Leipheim |
| | Lt. R.L. Stallings | Me-109 dam(grd) | Leipheim |
| 336th: | Lt. F.M. Grove | (2)Me-262 dam(grd) | Leipheim |
| | Capt. D.R. Emerson | Me-262 dam(grd) | Leipheim |
| | Lt. D.J. Pierni | Me-262 dam(grd) | Leipheim |
| | Lt. J.H. Joiner | (.5)Me-262 dam(grd) | Leipheim |
| | | (.5)Me-262 dam(grd) | Leipheim |
| | | (.5)Me-262 dam(grd) | Leipheim |
| | Lt. H.A. Kaul | (.5)Me-262 dam(grd) | Leipheim |
| | | (.5)Me-262 dam(grd) | Leipheim |
| | | (.5)Me-262 dam(grd) | Leipheim |
| **56th** | | | |
| 61st: | Capt. J.R. Carter | Me-109 dest(air) | E/Hanau |
| | Capt. W.A. Lanowski | FW-190 dest(air) | E/Hanau |
| | Lt. R.A. Baughman | FW-190 dest(air) | E/Hanau |
| | Lt. A.H. Gerow | FW-190 dest(air) | E/Hanau |
| | | FW-190 prob(air) | E/Hanau |
| | Lt. R.S. Kyler | FW-190 dest(air) | E/Hanau |
| | Lt. C.J. Raymond | FW-190 dest(air) | E/Hanau |
| | Capt. B.E. Cathers | FW-190 prob(air) | E/Hanau |
| | Lt. W.D. Clark | FW-190 prob(air) | E/Hanau |
| | | FW-190 dam(air) | E/Hanau |
| | Lt. L.P. Hines | FW-190 dam(air) | E/Hanau |
| | Lt. R.E. Walker | FW-190 dam(air) | E/Hanau |
| 62nd: | Capt. M.J. Jackson | FW-190 dest(air) | E/Hanau |
| | Capt. W.F. Wilkerson | FW-190 dest(air) | E/Hanau |
| | Lt. J.W. Ferguson | FW-190 dest(air) | E/Hanau |
| | Lt. N.D. Gould | Me-109 dest(air) | E/Hanau |
| 63rd: | Lt. R.R. Davis | FW-190 dest(air) | E/Hanau |
| | Lt. W.C. Scherz | FW-190 dam(air) | E/Hanau |
| | Lt. C.A. Chinn | (3)Me-109 dest(grd) | Gross Ostheim |
| | Maj. H.E. Comstock | He-111 dest(grd) | Gross Ostheim |
| | Lt. R.L. Murphy | FW-190 dest(grd) | Gross Ostheim |
| | Lt. R.J. Daniel | (.5)u/i a/c dam(grd) | Gross Ostheim |
| | Lt. R. Frederickson | (.5)u/i a/c dam(grd) | Gross Ostheim |
| **339th** | | | |
| 503rd: | Capt. E.H. Beavers | Me-109 dest(air) | Mannheim |
| | Capt. D.E. Shafer | Me-109 dest(air) | Mannheim |
| | Lt. L.C. Marsh | Me-109 dest(air) | Mannheim |
| | Lt. F.M. Stillwell | Me-109 prob(air) | Mannheim |
| 504th: | Lt. C.M. Mead | Me-109 dest(air) | Dachau |
| 505th: | Capt. E.M. Johnson | Me-109 dest(air) | Heilbronn |
| | | Me-109 dam(air) | Heilbronn |
| | Lt. C.H. Bundgaard | Me-109 dest(air) | Neustadt |
| | Lt. C. Malarz | (.5)Me-109 dest(air) | Neustadt |
| | Lt. G.T. Rich | (.5)Me-109 dest(air) | Neustadt |
| **353rd** | | | |
| 350th: | Capt. W.J. Price | u/i a/c dest(air) | Lechfeld |
| | | (.5)u/i a/c dam(grd) | Lechfeld |
| | Lt. M.W. Hightshoe | (2)He-177 dest(grd) | Lechfeld |
| | | u/i a/c dest(grd) | Lechfeld |
| | Capt. W.F. Tanner | He-177 dest(grd) | Lechfeld |
| | Lt. J.E. Jessup | Me-110 dest(grd) | Lechfeld |
| | Lt. C.A. Larson | He-111 dest(grd) | Lechfeld |
| | | He-111 dam(grd) | Lechfeld |
| | Lt. A.K. Ferrell | He-111 dest(grd) | Lechfeld |
| | | He-111 dam(grd) | Lechfeld |
| | Lt. A.L. Deeds | FW-190 dam(grd) | Lechfeld |
| | Lt. R.W. Abernathy | (.5)u/i a/c dam(grd) | Lechfeld |
| 351st: | Lt. G.E. Markham | Me-262 dest(air) | S/Augsburg |
| | Capt. G.B. Compton | (2)Ju-88 dest(grd) | Lechfeld |
| | | u/i a/c dam(grd) | Lechfeld |
| | Capt. A.C. Carroll | He-111 dest(grd) | Lechfeld |
| | | He-111 dam(grd) | Lechfeld |
| | Lt. T.R. Drybrough | FW-190 dest(grd) | Landsberg |
| | F/O T.C. Brock | Ju-88 dam(grd) | Prittrishing |
| 352nd: | Lt. W.C. Davis | (2)He-111 dest(grd) | Lechfeld |
| | Capt. W.J. Jordan | FW-190 dest(grd) | Lechfeld |
| | Capt. J.N. Poindexter | He-177 dest(grd) | Lechfeld |
| | | He-177 dam(grd) | Lechfeld |
| | Lt. V.M. Hernandez | Ju-88 dest(grd) | Lechfeld |
| | Lt. M. Morrison | Me-163 dest(grd) | Lechfeld |
| | | He-177 dam(grd) | Lechfeld |
| | Lt. E.D. Thomas | Ju-88 dest(grd) | Lechfeld |
| | | Me-163 dam(grd) | Lechfeld |
| | | u/i a/c dam(grd) | Lechfeld |
| | Lt. S.J. Kritz | FW-190 dam(grd) | Lechfeld |

| | | | |
|---|---|---|---|
| **355th** | | | |
| 354th: | Capt. N.J. Fortier | (2)Me-262 dest(grd) | Leipheim |
| | | u/i a/c dam(grd) | Leipheim |
| | Capt. J.E. Duffy | Me-262 dest(grd) | Leipheim |
| | Lt. T.P. Todd | Me-262 dam(grd) | Leipheim |
| 357th: | Lt. T.C. Long | (2)Me-262 dest(grd) | Leipheim |
| | | (2)Me-262 dam(grd) | Leipheim |
| | Maj. J.H. Wilson | Me-262 dest(grd) | Leipheim |
| | | Me-262 dam(grd) | Leipheim |
| | Lt. T.L. Wood | Me-262 dest(grd) | Leipheim |
| | Capt. F.R. Haviland | (4)Me-262 dam(grd) | Leipheim |
| | Capt. C.C. Colson | (4)Me-262 dam(grd) | Leipheim |
| | Lt. E.J. Moroney | (3)Me-262 dam(grd) | Leipheim |
| | Lt. J.H. Max | (2)Me-262 dam(grd) | Leipheim |
| | Lt. J.E. Nelson | Me-262 dam(grd) | Leipheim |
| | Lt. R.M. White | Me-262 dam(grd) | Leipheim |
| 358th: | Lt. W.W. Beaty | Me-262 dest(grd) | Leipheim |
| **357th** | | | |
| HdQts: | LtCol. J.D. Landers | Me-109 dest(air) | Villingen A/F |
| | | Me-109 dest(grd) | Villingen A/F |
| 362nd: | Capt. A.C. Murphy | (2)Me-109 dest(grd) | Mengen A/F |
| | Lt. O.D. Jenkins | (2)Me-109 dest(grd) | Mengen A/F |
| | Lt. C.E. Weaver | (2)Me-109 dest(grd) | Mengen A/F |
| | Capt. L.K. Carson | Me-109 dest(grd) | Mengen A/F |
| | Capt. J.B. England | Me-109 dest(grd) | Mengen A/F |
| | F/O D.W. Cheever | Me-109 dest(grd) | Mengen A/F |
| | Lt. W.T. Gilbert | (.5)He-111 dest(grd) | Mengen A/F |
| | Lt. J.A. Kirla | (.5)He-111 dest(grd) | Mengen A/F |
| | Lt. H.D. Chandler | Me-109 dam(grd) | Mengen A/F |
| 363rd: | Capt. R.W. Foy | Me-109 dest(air) | Villingen A/F |
| | | Me-109 dest(grd) | Villingen A/F |
| | | Me-109 dam(air) | Villingen A/F |
| | | (3)Me-109 dam(grd) | Villingen A/F |
| | Lt. F.L. Gailer | Me-109 dest(grd) | Mengen A/F |
| 364th: | Capt. R.A. Peterson | Me-109 dest(air) | Neuhausen A/F |
| | Lt. R.P. Winks | Me-109 dest(air) | Neuhausen A/F |
| | Lt. E.R. Haydon | FW-190 dest(grd) | Neuhausen A/F |

*Losses-*

**4th:** Lt. Ralph E. Lewis (335th Ftr Sqn) KIA
P-51D WD-X 44-14529
Hit by flak near Gunzburg.

**56th:** Capt. Gordon J. Blake (61st Ftr Sqn) POW
P-47D HV-N 42-28623
Hit by enemy fighters east of Hanau.

Lt. Jack D. DeMars (61st Ftr Sqn) POW
P-47D HV- 42-26831
Hit by a FW-190 east of Hanau.

**339th:** Lt. Vincent J. Spaziano (503rd Ftr Sqn) KIA
P-51D D7- 44-14829
Hit by Allied flak and crashed near Metz.

Lt. Laird D. Travis (505th Ftr Sqn) KIA
P-51D 6N- 44-15368 "Nornie"
Hit by flak near Kaiserlautern.

Lt. Allen D. Young (505th Ftr Sqn) POW
P-51D 6N- 44-14729 "Betty Lou"
Hit by flak near Trier.

**357th:** Lt. Sam G. Fuller (362nd Ftr Sqn) KIA
P-51D G4-S 44-13596 "Screamin' Demon"
Hit by flak at Mengen Airfield.

*Remarks*
56th: 2-0 locos, 3-0 railcars, 1-0 vehicle, 0-1 flak position
339th: 0-2 locos
P-51 c/l; o.k.
353rd: 1-0 loco, 0-10 railcars, 2-0 flak positions
355th: 6-2 locos, 5-66 railcars
357th: 3-0 locos, 2-0 railcars, 1-0 hangar
361st: 8-1 railcars, 1-0 gun position, 1-1 building
479th: P-51 c/l Grave; o.k.

KIAc's
20th: Lt. Donald E. Chrissinger (55th Ftr Sqn)
P-51D KI-E 44-13702
Crashed while landing at Kingscliffe after a test hop.

339th: Lt. Alan F. Crump (503rd Ftr Sqn)
P-51D D7-A 44-14004
Crashed while on a practice flight near Fowlmere.

**November 19, 1944**
Groups Operating: P-51 4th, 20th
Missions: Twenty-four aircraft flew PRU escorts to Germany.
Claims: nil
Losses: nil

**November 20, 1944**
Groups Operating: P-51 4th, 20th, 55th, 339th, 353rd, 355th, 356th(mixed), 357th, 359th, 361st, 479th
P-47 56th, 356th
Missions: Support of bombers to Gelsenkirchen and Munster plus fighter-bomber operations over western Germany.
Claims: nil

*Losses-*

**4th:** Lt. Donald L. Bennett (334th Ftr Sqn) POW
P-51D QP-R 44-13615
Suffered mechanical failure southeast of the Zuider Zee.

Lt. Leonard R. Werner (335th Ftr Sqn) KIA
P-51D WD-Q 44-13411
Suffered mechanical failure southeast of the Zuider Zee.

**55th:** Lt. Richard L. Lapham (38th Ftr Sqn) MIA
P-51D CG- 44-14586 "Phyllis Jean"
Hit by flak near Werkenden.

Lt. Jordan Eliades (343rd Ftr Sqn) POW
P-51D CY-C 44-14535
Hit by flak near Haaten.

**56th:** Capt. Robert J. Bradford (63rd Ftr Sqn) KIA
P-47D UN- 42-75670
Hit by flak east of Aachen.

**355th:** Lt. Robert White (357th Ftr Sqn) KIA
P-51D OS-
Suffered mechanical failure and ditched in the North Sea.

Lt. Edward F. Baraburda (358th Ftr Sqn) KIA
P-51D YF-C 44-13564 "Little Nobody"
Hit by flak near Zulpich.

**356th:** Lt. Louis B. Runyan (361st Ftr Sqn) KIA
P-51D QI-V 44-15098
Last seen heading southwest from Martlesham Heath after take-off.

**359th:** Lt. Merle B. Barth (368th Ftr Sqn) KIA
P-51D CV-C 44-14062
Suffered mechanical failure and bailed out over the Channel.

*Remarks*
56th: 2-0 locos, 3-8 railcars, 9-32 vehicles, 4-30 flak positions

**November 21, 1944**
Groups Operating: P-51 4th, 20th, 55th, 339th, 352nd, 353rd, 355th, 356th(mixed), 357th, 359th, 361st, 364th, 479th
P-47 56th, 78th, 356th
Missions: Support of bombers to Merseburg, Osnabruck, and Hamburg.
Claims: 68.5-10-23 air
6-3 ground

| *Group* | | *Claims* | *Location* |
|---|---|---|---|
| **4th** | | | |
| 335th: | Lt. J.E. Kolbe | Me-109 dest(air) | NW Merseburg |
| 336th: | Capt. F.W. Glover | (3)Me-109 dest(air) | W/Merseburg |
| | Lt. D.N. Groshong | (2)Me-109 dest(air) | W/Merseburg |
| | Lt. J.E. Hileman | Me-109 prob(air) | W/Merseburg |
| | | Me-109 dam(air) | W/Merseburg |
| **20th** | | | |
| 77th: | Lt. B.C. Halpin | Me-109 dest(air) | Munster |
| **78th** | | | |
| HdQts: | Capt. R.B. Holmes | Me-109 dest(air) | Hanover |
| 82nd: | Maj. R.E. Conner | (2)Me-109 dest(air) | Hanover |
| | | Ju-88 dest(grd) | Gutersloh |
| | Capt. R.A. Hewitt | Me-109 dest(air) | Hanover |
| | Lt. A.A. Rosenblum | Me-109 dest(air) | Hanover |
| | F/O G.L. Weston | Me-109 prob(air) | Hanover |
| | Lt. W.E. Hydorn | FW-190 dam(air) | Hanover |
| | Lt. D.C. Hart | Me-109 dam(air) | Hanover |
| | | (.5)Ju-88 dest(grd) | Gutersloh |
| | F/O H.R. Liebenrood | (.5)Ju-88 dest(grd) | Gutersloh |
| | Lt. D.C. Zboinski | Ju-88 dam(grd) | Gutersloh |
| **339th** | | | |
| HdQts: | Capt. C.W. Dowell | (.5)Me-109 dest(air) | Munster |
| 505th: | Lt. G.T. Rich | Me-109 dest(air) | Warburg |

| | | | |
|---|---|---|---|
| | F/O G.W. Palmer | (.5)Me-109 dest(air) | Munster |
| | Lt. B.O. Jackson | Ju-88 dest(grd) | NE Munster |
| **352nd** | | | |
| HdQts: | LtCol. J.C. Meyer | (3)FW-190 dest(air) | SW Merseburg |
| 328th: | Lt. F.L. Kebelman | (2)Me-109 dest(air) | Merseburg |
| | Maj. G.E. Preddy | FW-190 dest(air) | Merseburg |
| | | FW-190 prob(air) | Merseburg |
| | | FW-190 dam(air) | Merseburg |
| | Lt. D.J. Maxwell | FW-190 dest(air) | Merseburg |
| | | FW-190 dam(air) | Merseburg |
| | Lt. L.V. Intravartola | Me-109 dest(air) | W/Merseburg |
| | | FW-190 dam(air) | W/Merseburg |
| | Maj. E.L. Abbott | (.5)FW-190 dest(air) (shared with an unknown pilot) | Merseburg |
| | Capt. W.E. Hendrian | (.5)FW-190 dest(air)* | Merseburg |
| | Lt. J.F. Lambright | (.5)FW-190 dest(air)* | Merseburg |
| | | FW-190 dam(air) | Merseburg |
| | Lt. L. Fieg | Me-109 prob(air) | W/Merseburg |
| | Lt. E.W. Briggs | FW-190 prob(air) | W/Merseburg |
| 487th: | Capt. W.T. Whisner | (5)FW-190 dest(air) | SW Merseburg |
| | | (2)FW-190 prob(air) | SW Merseburg |
| | Lt. K.M. Waldron | (2)FW-190 dest(air) | SW Merseburg |
| | Lt. N.R. Jessup | (2)FW-190 dest(air) | SW Merseburg |
| | Capt. W.E. Starck | FW-190 dam(air) | SW Merseburg |
| | Lt. W.C. Miller | FW-190 dam(air) | SW Merseburg |
| **359th** | | | |
| 368th: | Capt. T.J. McGeever | FW-190 dest(grd) | Gotha |
| | Lt. J.S. Keesey | FW-190 dam(air) | Erfurt |
| 369th: | Lt. C.J. Crenshaw | (4)FW-190 dest(air) | Merseburg |
| | | FW-190 prob(air) | Merseburg |
| | Lt. H. Tenenbaum | FW-190 dest(air) | Merseburg |
| 370th: | Capt. R.L. Cox | (3)FW-190 dest(air) | SW Merseburg |
| | Capt. W.R. Hodges | (2)FW-190 dest(air) | SE Kassel |
| | | FW-190 prob(air) | SE Kassel |
| | | FW-190 dam(air) | SE Kassel |
| | Lt. V.L. Caid | (2)FW-190 dest(air) | SW Merseburg |
| | | FW-190 dam(air) | SW Merseburg |
| | Lt. T.P. Smith | (2)FW-190 dest(air) | SW Merseburg |
| | | (2)FW-190 dam(air) | SW Merseburg |
| | Lt. H.A. Staup | (2)FW-190 dest(air) | SW Merseburg |
| | Maj. D.D. McKee | FW-190 dest(air) | SW Merseburg |
| | Capt. W.D. Burgsteiner | FW-190 prob(air) | SW Merseburg |
| | Lt. J.W. Lamont | FW-190 dam(air) | SW Merseburg |
| **361st** | | | |
| 374th: | Capt. L.G. LaCroix | FW-190 dest(air) | Jena |
| **364th** | | | |
| HdQts: | Col. R.W. Osborn | FW-190 dest(air) | S/Merseburg |
| | LtCol. J.H. Lowell | FW-190 dest(air) | E/Leipzig |
| 383rd: | Lt. M.E. Coates | (2)FW-190 dest(air) | S/Nordhausen |
| | | FW-190 dam(air) | S/Nordhausen |
| | Lt. R.H. Farley | (2)FW-190 dest(air) | Meiningen |
| | Lt. J.C. Hunter | (2)FW-190 dest(air) | S/Nordhausen |
| | | FW-190 dam(air) | S/Nordhausen |
| | Lt. E.H. Harman | FW-190 dest(air) | S/Nordhausen |
| | Lt. M.L. Murphy | FW-190 dam(air) | S/Nordhausen |
| 384th: | Lt. J.L. Grimshaw | FW-190 dest(air) | SW Merseburg |
| | | Me-109 dam(air) | SW Merseburg |
| | Lt. E.H. Miller | FW-190 dest(air) | NE Nordhausen |
| | Lt. L. Visconti | FW-190 dest(air) | SW Merseburg |
| | Lt. E.H. Duderstadt | (.5)FW-190 dest(air) | Mulhausen |
| | Lt. E.W. Farnsworth | (.5)FW-190 dest(air) | Mulhausen |
| | Capt. J.R. Steinbacher | (2)FW-190 dam(air) | SW Halle |
| | Capt. W.E. Bristow | FW-190 dam(air) | SW Halle |
| 385th: | Lt. R.F. Edwards | FW-190 dest(air) | Eisleben |
| | Lt. R.M. McKibben | FW-190 dest(air) | W/Merseburg |
| | Lt. E.N. Farrell | FW-190 dest(air) | S/Merseburg |
| | Lt. N.L. Box | (.5)FW-190 dest(air)* | SW Merseburg |
| | | FW-190 dam(air) | SW Merseburg |
| | Lt. H.W. Head | (.5)FW-190 dest(air)* | SW Merseburg |
| | Capt. T.P. Farrell | (.5)FW-190 dest(air)** | Erfurt |
| | Lt. S.L. Lett | (.5)FW-190 dest(air)** | Erfurt |
| | Lt. J.L. McCubbin | u/i a/c dest(grd) | SE Eisleben |
| | | u/i a/c dam(grd) | SE Eisleben |
| | Lt. A.B. McCormick | u/i a/c dest(grd) | SE Eisleben |
| | Lt. C.S. Hogan | u/i a/c dam(grd) | SE Eisleben |

*Losses-*

**4th**: Lt. Carmen J. Delnero (334th Ftr Sqn) KIA
P-51D QP-H 44-14119 "Sizzlin' Liz"
Hit by a Me-109 near Meerane.

Lt. George L. Klaus (336th Ftr Sqn) POW
P-51B VF-D 43-6942 "Meiner Kleiner"
Hit by flak northeast of Halle.

**20th**: Lt. Bernard C. Halpin (77th Ftr Sqn) POW
P-51D LC-L 44-14063
Hit by a Me-109 near Munster.

**78th**: Lt. Harry A. Thompson (82nd Ftr Sqn) POW
P-47D MX-B 44-19908
Hit by flak and bellied-in southeast of Munster.

**339th**: Capt. Charles W. Dowell (HdQts) KIA
P-51D 6N- 44-14092
Hit by flak near Meckenheim.

Lt. Leland M. Stoudt (505th Ftr Sqn) KIA
P-51D 6N- 44-14115
Hit by flak near Handorf.

Lt. Boyd O. Jackson (505th Ftr Sqn) KIA
P-51D 6N- 44-15306
Hit by flak near Handorf.

**356th**: Lt. Walter O. Hedrick (360th Ftr Sqn) MIA-E
P-51D PI-
Became lost and bellied-in near Haro, Spain.

**359th**: Capt. Thomas J. McGeever (368th Ftr Sqn) KIA
P-51D CV-F 44-14670
Hit by flak near Gotha.

Lt. Carl M. Anderson (368th Ftr Sqn) KIA
P-51D CV-J 44-14444 "Supermouse"
Suffered mechanical failure near Sanderhausen.

Lt. Stanley F. Stegnerski (370th Ftr Sqn) KIA
P-51D CS-Q 44-14185
Hit by enemy fighters southwest of Merseburg.

**364th**: Lt. Cidney B. Fairrington (384th Ftr Sqn) POW
P-51D 5Y-V 44-14328
Hit by flak near Nordhausen.

Lt. Rodney E. Simcoke (384th Ftr Sqn) KIA
P-51D 5Y- 44-13976 "Marcy III"
Hit by enemy fighters near Merseburg.

Lt. Henry J. Lysowski (384th Ftr Sqn) KIA
P-51D 5Y- 44-15176
Hit by flak southeast of Merseburg.

*Remarks*

4th: 0-12 locos, 5-0 vehicles
78th: 7-1 locos, 0-34 railcars, 1-0 vehicle
352nd: 1-0 loco, 2-0 railcars
Lt. Francis J. McCarty (328th Ftr Sqn) c/l; o.k.
P-51D PE-
Lt. William H. Sanford (328th Ftr Sqn) c/l; o.k.
P-51D PE-
355th: 1-4 locos, 0-8 railcars
364th: 6-1 locos, 0-5 railcars, 0-2 vehicles

**November 23, 1944**
Groups Operating: P-51 20th, 352nd
Missions: Support of bombers to Gelsenkirchen.
Claims: nil
Losses: nil

*Remarks*

20th: Lt. Robert E. Murrell (77th Ftr Sqn) c/l; o.k.
P-51D LC-

**November 25, 1944**
Groups Operating: P-51 4th, 20th, 55th, 339th, 352nd, 353rd, 355th, 356th, 357th, 359th, 361st, 364th, 479th
P-47 56th, 78th
Missions: Support of bombers to Merseburg/Leuna and Bingen.
Claims: 0-0-0 air
7-11 ground

| *Group* | | *Claims* | *Location* |
|---|---|---|---|
| **356th** | | | |
| 359th: | Lt. J.B. Cornett | Ju-88 dam(grd) | Ettinghausen |
| | Lt. R.C. Scharnberg | Ju-88 dam(grd) | Ettinghausen |
| 361st: | Lt. C.T. Ashby | (2)FW-190 dest(grd) | Zwickau |
| | | FW-190 dam(grd) | Zwickau |
| | Lt. C.D. Burdick | FW-190 dest(grd) | Zwickau |
| | Lt. W.S. Hurley | FW-190 dest(grd) | Zwickau |
| | | (2)FW-190 dam(grd) | Zwickau |
| | Lt. H.E. Wiggins | FW-190 dest(grd) | Zwickau |
| | | (3)FW-190 dam(grd) | Zwickau |
| | Lt. S.N. Jett | FW-190 dam(grd) | Zwickau |

| Group | Pilot | Claims | Location |
|---|---|---|---|
| **357th** | | | |
| 362nd: | Capt. L.K. Carson | FW-44 dest(grd) | Maraburg |
| | Lt. J.L. Sublett | FW-44 dest(grd) | Maraburg |
| **364th** | | | |
| 385th: | Lt. H.W. Head | FW-190 dam(grd) | Fulda |
| | Lt. G.L. Jamison | Me-109 dam(grd) | Fulda |

*Losses-*

**353rd:** Lt. Frank Elkins (350th Ftr Sqn) POW
P-51D LH-X 44-11167 "Danny Boy"
Hit by flak and bailed out near Hanau.

Lt. William L. Miller (350th Ftr Sqn) POW
P-51D LH-G 44-14969 "Lady Grace"
Ran out of fuel and bailed out near Texel Island.

Lt. Clarence G. Bevington (351st Ftr Sqn) KIA
P-51D YJ-B 44-11216
Lost a wing while strafing near Zell.

Lt. James W. Jeter (351st Ftr Sqn) KIA
P-51D YJ-G 44-14972
Suffered mechanical failure and crashed in Belgium.

**356th:** Lt. James A. Des Jardins (360th Ftr Sqn) KIA
P-51D PI- 44-15133
Hit by flak at a marshalling yard near Fulda.

*Remarks*
4th: 0-2 locos
353rd: 5-0 locos, 0-9 railcars, 3-0 vehicles
355th: Lt. John H. Lanius (358th Ftr Sqn) c/l; o.k.
P-51D YF-B 44-14252
356th: 9-7 locos, 2-23 railcars, 0-14 vehicles
Lt. Ernest W. Corner (360th Ftr Sqn) c/l Ghent; o.k.
P-51D PI-
357th: 8-1 locos, 5-0 railcars
364th: 6-0 locos, 10-7 railcars, 0-1 building
479th: 0-3 locos

**November 26, 1944**
Groups Operating: P-51 4th, 20th, 55th, 339th, 352nd, 353rd, 355th, 356th, 357th, 359th, 361st, 364th, 479th
P-47 56th, 78th
Missions: Support of bombers to Misburg, Bielefeld, and Hamm.
Claims: 121-10-34 air
12-8 ground

| *Group* | | *Claims* | *Location* |
|---|---|---|---|
| **SF** | | | |
| 2nd: | Lt. W.E. Whalen | (3)FW-190 dest(air) | S/Hanover |
| | Capt. R.V. Whitlow | FW-190 dest(air) | S/Hanover |
| | | FW-190 prob(air) | S/Hanover |
| | Lt. G.W. Ceglarski | FW-190 dest(air) | S/Hanover |
| | Lt. J.H. Miller | FW-190 prob(air) | S/Hanover |
| | | FW-190 dam(air) | S/Hanover |
| | Lt. L.H. Marmon | FW-190 dam(air) | S/Hanover |
| **55th** | | | |
| 338th: | Capt. D.S. Cramer | (2)FW-190 dest(grd) | Vorden A/F |
| | | Me-109 dam(grd) | Vorden A/F |
| | Lt. R.I. Barrett | FW-190 dest(grd) | Vorden A/F |
| | Lt. A.J. Ramm | FW-190 dest(grd) | Vorden A/F |
| | Lt. M.J. Wiens | FW-190 dest(grd) | Vorden A/F |
| | | (2)FW-190 dam(grd) | Vorden A/F |
| | Lt. P. Brooks | FW-190 dam(grd) | Vorden A/F |
| | Lt. C.D. Henry | FW-190 dam(grd) | Vorden A/F |
| | Lt. J.L. Gerry | FW-190 dam(grd) | Vorden A/F |
| | Lt. A.E. Wright | FW-190 dam(grd) | Vorden A/F |
| | Capt. C.E. Buskirk | (.5)FW-190 dam(grd) | Vorden A/F |
| | Lt. R.C. Herbst | (.5)FW-190 dam(grd) | Vorden A/F |
| **78th** | | | |
| 82nd: | Capt. J.J. Hockery | (2)Me-109 dest(air) | Rheine |
| | | FW-190 prob(air) | Rheine |
| | Lt. M.O. Croy | (2)Me-109 dest(air) | Rheine |
| | Lt. D.C. Hart | Me-109 dest(air) | Rheine |
| | F/O H.R. Liebenrood | Me-109 dest(air) | Rheine |
| | Lt. I.H. Keatley | Me-109 dam(air) | Rheine |
| 83rd: | Capt. R.R. Bonebrake | Me-109 dest(air) | S/Dummer Lake |
| | Capt. H.T. Barnaby | u/i a/c dest(grd) | Weisswarte A/F |
| 84th: | Capt. P.L. Larson | FW-190 dest(air) | Vorden A/F |
| | Lt. W.H. Lutz | FW-190 dest(grd) | Vorden A/F |
| **339th** | | | |
| 503rd: | LtCol. H.E. Henderson | (2)FW-190 dest(air) | SE Dummer Lake |
| | Capt. D.W. Johnson | (3)FW-190 dest(air) | SE Dummer Lake |
| | Lt. L.C. Marsh | (3)FW-190 dest(air) | SE Dummer Lake |
| | | FW-190 prob(air) | SE Dummer Lake |
| | | FW-190 dam(air) | SE Dummer Lake |
| | Capt. E.H. Beavers | (2)FW-190 dest(air) | SE Dummer Lake |
| | Capt. M.B. Edens | (2)FW-190 dest(air) | SE Dummer Lake |
| | Lt. J.P. Wilson | (2)FW-190 dest(air) | SE Dummer Lake |
| | Lt. C.S. Coe | FW-190 dest(air) | SE Dummer Lake |
| | Lt. L.J. French | FW-190 dest(air) | SE Dummer Lake |
| | Lt. P.E. Petitt | FW-190 dest(air) | SE Dummer Lake |
| | Lt. F.M. Stillwell | FW-190 dest(air) | SE Dummer Lake |
| | Lt. B.A. Allen | FW-190 dam(air) | SE Dummer Lake |
| | Lt. J.W. Gokey | FW-190 dam(air) | SE Dummer Lake |
| 504th: | Lt. A.W. Bates | FW-190 dest(air) | S/Dummer Lake |
| 505th: | Lt. J.S. Daniell | (5)FW-190 dest(air) | S/Dummer Lake |
| | Lt. W.R. Phillippi | (1.5)FW-190 dest(air) | S/Dummer Lake |
| | Lt. P.M. Loveless | (.5)FW-190 dest(air) | S/Dummer Lake |
| | Lt. C.H. Bundgaard | FW-190 dest(air) | S/Hanover |
| | | FW-190 dam(air) | S/Hanover |
| | Lt. H.E. Girzi | FW-190 dest(air) | S/Hanover |
| | Lt. B. Stiles | FW-190 dest(air) | S/Hanover |
| **353rd** | | | |
| 350th: | Capt. J.H. Winder | FW-190 dest(air) | Dummer Lake |
| | Capt. W.L. Boone | FW-190 dest(air) | Minden |
| | F/O F.J. Orzelek | FW-190 dest(air) | SE Dummer Lake |
| **355th** | | | |
| 354th: | Lt. C.D. Hauver | (2)FW-190 dest(air) | W/Hanover |
| | Lt. R.M. McLean | (2)Me-109 dest(air) | Gifhorn-W/Hanover |
| | Lt. R.W. Priest | (2)FW-190 dest(air) | Misburg |
| | Capt. J.E. Duffy | FW-190 dest(air) | Gifhorn-W/Hanover |
| | Lt. J.E. Mellen | FW-190 dest(air) | S/Misburg |
| | F/O J.E. Molnar | FW-190 dest(air) | Misburg |
| | | FW-190 dam(air) | Misburg |
| | Lt. F.W. Schultz | Me-109 dam(air) | Gifhorn-W/Hanover |
| | | FW-190 dam(air) | Gifhorn-W/Hanover |
| | Lt. N.P. Jackson | FW-190 dam(air) | S/Misburg |
| | F/O H.W. Falvey | FW-190 dam(air) | Gifhorn |
| 357th: | Lt. E.J. Moroney | (2)FW-190 dest(air) | W/Gardelegen |
| | Lt. J.H. Max | (2)FW-190 dest(air) | W/Gardelegen |
| | Capt. F.R. Haviland | FW-190 dest(air) | W/Gardelegen |
| | | Me-109 dest(air) | W/Gardelegen |
| | Lt. B.R. Barab | Me-109 dest(air) | W/Gardelegen |
| | Lt. W.S. Lyons | Me-109 dest(air) | W/Gardelegen |
| | Capt. H.S. Bille | Me-109 prob(air) | W/Gardelegen |
| 358th: | F/O F.R. Masters | (3)FW-190 dest(air) | Hanover |
| | Lt. J.M. Beckman | FW-190 dest(air) | Hanover-Berlin |
| | Maj. E.L. Sluga | FW-190 dam(air) | Hanover |
| | Lt. N.B. Woodson | FW-190 dam(air) | W/Hanover |
| **356th** | | | |
| HdQts: | LtCol. D.A. Baccus | (2)Me-109 dest(air) | Dummer Lake |
| 359th: | Capt. R.A. Rann | (2)Me-109 dest(air) | NW Dummer Lake |
| | Lt. W.C. Cooley | (2)Me-109 dest(air) | NW Dummer Lake |
| | Capt. D.F. Tucker | Me-109 dest(air) | NW Dummer Lake |
| | | Me-109 dam(air) | NW Dummer Lake |
| | Lt. H.R. Gohsler | Me-109 dest(air) | NW Dummer Lake |
| | Lt. A.R. Hale | FW-190 dest(air) | NW Dummer Lake |
| 360th: | Capt. M.P. Yannell | (2)Me-109 dest(air) | Dummer Lake |
| | | (2)Me-109 dam(air) | Dummer Lake |
| | Lt. T.J. Urban | Me-109 dest(air) | Dummer Lake |
| | Capt. B. Borelli | Me-109 dam(air) | Dummer Lake |
| | Lt. R.E. Barnhart | Me-109 dam(air) | Dummer Lake |
| | Lt. N.B. Ceraolo | Me-109 dam(air) | Dummer Lake |
| | Lt. W.K. Dunn | Me-109 dam(air) | Dummer Lake |
| 361st: | Capt. W.R. Scheible | (3)Me-109 dest(air) | Osnabruck-Dummer L |
| | | (2)Me-109 dam(air) | Osnabruck-Dummer L |
| | Lt. H.E. Wiggins | (2)Me-109 dest(air) | Osnabruck-Dummer L |
| | Capt. D.J. Strait | (1.5)Me-109 dest(air) | Osnabruck-Dummer L |
| | Lt. S.N. Jett | (.5)Me-109 dest(air) | Osmabruck-Dummer L |
| | Lt. C.E. Beck | Me-109 dest(air) | Osnabruck-Dummer L |
| | Lt. J.A. Bowers | Me-109 dest(air) | Osnabruck-Dummer L |
| | Lt. R.R. Burden | FW-190 dest(air) | Osnabruck-Dummer L |
| | Lt. W.C. Jarvis | Me-109 dest(air) | Osnabruck-Dummer L |
| | | FW-190 dam(air) | Osnabruck-Dummer L |
| | Lt. H.E. Whitmore | Me-109 dest(air) | Osnabruck-Dummer L |
| | Lt. B.B. Barnes | FW-190 dam(air) | Osnabruck-Dummer L |
| **359th** | | | |
| HdQts: | Maj. R.W. Evans | Me-109 dest(air) | Kassel |
| | | Me-109 dam(air) | Kassel |
| **361st** | | | |
| 374th: | Maj. M.F. Glessner | FW-190 dest(air) | Wittingen |
| | Lt. R.E. Chandler | FW-190 dest(air) | Wittingen |
| | Lt. B.R. Hicks | FW-190 dest(air) | Wittingen |
| | Lt. J.G. Vear | FW-190 dest(air) | Wittingen |
| | | FW-190 dam(air) | Wittingen |
| | Lt. J.C. Wilkinson | FW-190 dest(air) | Wittingen |
| | | FW-190 dam(air) | Wittingen |

| | | | |
|---|---|---|---|
| | Capt. L.G. LaCroix | FW-190 dam(air) | Wittingen |
| 375th: | Capt. E.E. Neely | (2)FW-190 dest(air) | S/Hanover |
| | | FW-190 dam(air) | NE Brunswick |
| | Lt. P.H. Klees | Me-109 dest(air) | Celle-Gifhorn |
| | | FW-190 dest(air) | Celle-Gifhorn |
| | Lt. R.G. Adams | FW-190 dest(air) | Celle-Gifhorn |
| | Lt. W.R. Stevens | FW-190 dest(air) | Celle-Gifhorn |
| | Lt. J.J. Sullivan | Me-109 dest(air) | Celle-Gifhorn |
| | Lt. W.E. McCoppin | Me-109 dest(air) | NE Brunswick |
| | Lt. R.J. Farney | FW-190 dest(air) | S/Steinhuder Lake |
| | Lt. L.A. Wood | FW-190 dest(air) | S/Steinhuder Lake |
| | Lt. L.C. Travis | FW-190 dest(air) | NE Misburg |
| | Lt. H.A. Spaulding | (2)FW-190 dam(air) | Celle-Gifhorn |
| | Lt. W.B. Farnum | FW-190 dam(air) | NE Steinhuder L. |
| 376th: | Capt. W.R. Beyer | Me-109 dest(air) | S/Ulzen |
| | | FW-190 dest(air) | S/Ulzen |
| | Lt. G.R. Vanden Heuval | (2)FW-190 dest(air) | S/Ulzen |
| | Lt. D.R. Ford | FW-190 dest(air) | S/Ulzen |
| | Lt. C.W. Hanley | FW-190 dest(air) | S/Ulzen |
| | Lt. K.J. Scott | FW-190 prob(air) | S/Ulzen |
| | | FW-190 dam(air) | S/Ulzen |
| | Lt. W.J. Kozicki | FW-190 prob(air) | S/Ulzen |
| | Lt. L.P. Chadwick | FW-190 prob(air) | E/Ulzen |
| **364th** | | | |
| 383rd: | Lt. J.T. Gaston | (.5)Me-109 dest(air) | Dummer Lake |
| | Lt. G.E. Smith | (.5)Me-109 dest(air) | Dummer Lake |
| 384th: | Lt. J.V. Johnson | Me-109 dest(air) | W/Steinhuder Lake |
| | | FW-190 dest(air) | W/Steinhuder Lake |
| | Lt. J.M. Fowle | FW 190 dest(air) | SE Dummer Lake |
| 385th: | Maj. J.D. Monahan | FW-190 dest(air) | Uchte |
| | Capt. E.E. Bankey | Me-109 dest(air) | NE Dummer Lake |
| | | Me-109 prob(air) | NE Dummer Lake |
| | Capt. R. Visconte | Me-109 dest(air) | Hoyde |
| | Lt. T.L. Allinder | Me-109 prob(air) | Dummer Lake |
| | Lt. A.B. McCormick | (4)Ju-88 dest(grd) | SE Jade Bay |
| | Lt. R.A. Auguste | Ju-88 dest(grd) | SE Jade Bay |
| **479th** | | | |
| 435th: | Lt. T.J. Sowerby | FW-190 dest(air) | Minden |

*Losses-*

**SF**: Capt. James B. Stauder (2nd) KIA
P-51D YF- 44-14439
Suffered mechanical failure and crashed into the North Sea.

**55th**: Lt. Huey R. Coward (38th Ftr Sqn) KIA
P-51D CG- 44-15022
Hit by enemy aircraft near Emlichheim.

Lt. Richard I. Barrett (338th Ftr Sqn) POW
P-51D CL- 44-14167 "Purple Shaft"
Hit by flak at Vorden Airfield and again at Achmer, then went down near Soesterberg.

**78th**: Capt. John J. Hockery (82nd Ftr Sqn) POW
P-47D MX-L 44-19950
Hit by flak near Rheine.

Lt. Troy L. Eggleston (82nd Ftr Sqn) KIA
P-47D MX-V 42-27297
Hit by enemy fighters near Rheine.

**339th**: Lt. Ely Van Cleave (504th Ftr Sqn) KIA
P-51D 5Q-S 44-13938
Hit by a FW-190 near Hassell.

Lt. Bert Stiles (505th Ftr Sqn) KIA
P-51D 6N-X 44-14113 "Tarheel"
Followed a FW-190 into the ground south of Hanover.

**353rd**: Lt. Stepehn J. Kritz (352nd Ftr Sqn) KIA
P-51D SX-Z 44-14259
Crashed on take-off from Raydon.

**355th**: Lt. Bernard R. Barab (357th Ftr Sqn) KIA
P-51D OS- 44-13574
Collided with Lt. Kelly west of Dummer Lake.

Lt. Charles W. Kelly (357th Ftr Sqn) KIA
P-51B OS- 42-106910
Collided with Lt. Barab west of Dummer Lake.

**364th**: Lt. Jack T. Gaston (383rd Ftr Sqn) POW
P-51D N2-A 44-13707 "Lady Dorothy IV"
Hit by a Me-109 near Groenlo.

*Remarks*
4th: 0-8 barges, 0-1 tug
56th: 63rd Ftr Sqn P-47 c/l Boxted; o.k.
P-47D UN-
355th: Lt. Clarence H. Kouche (358th Ftr Sqn) c/l; o.k.
P-51D YF-H 44-14342
361st: Capt. Lucius G. LaCroix (374th Ftr Sqn) c/l; o.k.
P-51D B7-V 44-13676
Lt. Herman R. Auth (375th Ftr Sqn) b/o Holland; o.k.
P-51D E2-
Lt. Walter R. Stevens (375th Ftr Sqn) c/l Continent; o.k.
P-51D E2-X 44-15076 "Betty Lee III"
364th: 2-0 locos, 1-0 vehicle

**November 27, 1944**
Groups Operating: P-51 4th, 20th, 55th, 339th, 352nd, 353rd, 355th, 356th, 357th, 359th, 361st, 364th, 479th
P-47 56th, 78th
Missions: Support for bombers to Bingen and Offenberg, plus some fighter-bomber operations.
Claims: 93-11-13 air
3-1 ground

| *Group* | | *Claims* | *Location* |
|---|---|---|---|
| **56th** | | | |
| 63rd: | Lt. R. Frederickson | (2)Me-109 dest(air) | SE Dummer Lake |
| | Lt. J.E. Lister | Me-109 dest(air) | SE Dummer Lake |
| **352nd** | | | |
| HdQts: | LtCol. J.C. Meyer | Me-109 dest(air) | E/Munster |
| 328th: | Capt. C.J. Cesky | Me-109 dest(air) | Hanover |
| | Lt. E.B. Dubay | Me-109 dest(air) | Hanover |
| 487th: | Capt. W.E. Starck | (3)Me-109 dest(air) | Osnabruck-Hameln |
| | Capt. R.W. Hamilton | (2)Me-109 dest(air) | Hameln |
| | Capt. W.T. Whisner | (2)Me-109 dest(air) | Hameln |
| | Lt. R.H. Littge | (2)Me-109 dest(air) | Hameln |
| | Maj. E.D. Duncan | Me-109 dest(air) | Hameln |
| | Capt. W.T. Halton | Me-109 dest(air) | Hameln |
| | Capt. W.S. Smith | Me-109 dest(air) | Munster |
| | Lt. K.K. Dittmer | Me-109 dest(air) | N/Hanover |
| | Lt. H.M. Stewart | Me-109 dest(air) | Hameln |
| | Lt. A.P. Rigby | Me-109 dest(air) | Minden |
| | Lt. S.K. Moats | Me-109 dest(air) | Munster |
| | | Me-109 dam(air) | Munster |
| | Lt. D.M. Huston | Me-109 dest(air) | Munster |
| **353rd** | | | |
| 350th: | Maj. W.K. Blickenstaff | (4)FW-190 dest(air) | Steinhuder Lake-Brunswick |
| | Capt. W.L. Boone | FW-190 dest(air) | Brunswick |
| | | FW-190 prob(air) | Brunswick |
| | Capt. J.H. Winder | FW-190 dest(air) | Brunswick |
| | Lt. J.E. Jessup | FW-190 prob(air) | Brunswick |
| | Lt. R.W. Abernathy | FW-190 dam(air) | Brunswick |
| 351st: | Capt. A.C. Carroll | FW-190 dest(air) | NE Steinhuder L. |
| | | FW-190 dam(air) | NE Steinhuder L. |
| | Capt. G.B. Compton | FW-190 dest(air) | NE Steinhuder L. |
| | Lt. H.W. Chase | Me-109 dest(air) | NE Steinhuder L. |
| | | Me-109 dam(air) | NE Steinhuder L. |
| | Lt. T.R. Drybrough | FW-190 dest(air) | NE Steinhuder L. |
| | | FW-190 prob(air) | NE Steinhuder L. |
| | Lt. G.E. Markham | FW-190 dest(air) | NE Steinhuder L. |
| | Lt. J.M. Nicklebur | FW-190 dest(air) | NE Steinhuder L. |
| | | Me-109 dam(air) | NE Steinhuder L. |
| | Lt. R.K. Wiehe | Me-109 dest(air) | NE Steinhuder L. |
| | Lt. G.S. Montgomery | (.5)Me-109 dest(air) | N/Dummer Lake |
| | Lt. R. Hilgenburg | (.5)Me-109 dest(air) | N/Dummer Lake |
| 352nd: | Capt. J.L. Knoble | Me-109 dest(air) | Magdeburg |
| | Lt. A.C. Cundy | Me-109 dest(air) | Magdeburg |
| | Lt. F.H. Bouldin | Me-109 dest(air) | Magdeburg |
| | Lt. J.R. Evans | Me-109 dest(air) | Magdeburg |
| | Lt. J.E. Davenport | (2)Me-109 dam(air) | Magdeburg |
| | Maj. W.H. Junttila | Me-109 dam(air) | Magdeburg |
| **356th** | | | |
| 359th: | Capt. D.F. Tucker | FW-190 dest(air) | N/Munster |
| | Capt. R.R. Withers | Me-109 dest(air) | N/Munster |
| | Lt. R.E. Carr | FW-190 prob(air) | N/Munster |
| | Lt. J.E. Blewett | Me-109 prob(air) | N/Munster |
| | Lt. G. Crum | Me-109 dam(air) | N/Munster |
| **357th** | | | |
| HdQts: | Maj. A.J. Evans | FW-190 dest(air) | S/Magdeburg |
| 362nd: | Capt. L.K. Carson | (5)FW-190 dest(air) | S/Magdeburg |
| | Capt. J.B. England | (4)FW-190 dest(air) | S/Magdeburg |
| | Lt. J.L. Sublett | (3)FW-190 dest(air) | S/Magdeburg |
| | Lt. C.E. Weaver | (2)FW-190 dest(air) | S/Magdeburg |
| | | FW-190 prob(air) | S/Magdeburg |
| | | FW-190 dam(air) | S/Magdeburg |
| | Capt. A.C. Murphy | Me-109 dest(air) | S/Magdeburg |
| | | FW-190 dest(air) | S/Magdeburg |
| | Lt. C. Anderson | FW-190 dest(air) | S/Magdeburg |
| | Lt. H.H. Delager | Me-109 dest(air) | S/Magdeburg |
| | Lt. W.T. Gilbert | FW-190 dest(air) | S/Magdeburg |

| | | | |
|---|---|---|---|
| 363rd: | Capt. C.E. Yeager | (4)FW-190 dest(air) | SW Magdeburg |
| | Capt. C.E. Anderson | (2)FW-190 dest(air) | Noyehausen & Magdeburg |
| | | FW-190 prob(air) | Magdeburg |
| | Lt. F.L. Gailer | (2)FW-190 dest(air) | SE Magdeburg |
| | Lt. J.R. Sloan | FW-190 dest(air) | SW Magdeburg |
| | Lt. R.E. Wolf | FW-190 dest(air) | Noyehausen |
| 364th: | Lt. R.G. Schimanski | Me-109 dest(air) | S/Brandenburg |
| **359th** | | | |
| 368th: | Maj. N.K. Cranfill | (2)Me-109 dest(air) | W/Merseburg |
| | | FW-190 dest(air) | W/Merseburg |
| | Lt. R.H. Daniels | FW-190 prob(air) | SE Hanover |
| 369th: | Lt. R.T. Lancaster | Me-109 prob(air) | S/Hanover |
| 370th: | Capt. R.S. Wetmore | (3)Me-109 dest(air) | SE Hanover |
| | Lt. R.M. York | (3)Me-109 dest(air) | SE Hanover |
| | | Me-109 dest(air) | SE Hanover |
| | Lt. D.L. Windmiller | (2)Me-109 dest(air) | Hameln |
| | Lt. F.R. Marshall | Me-109 dest(air) | Hanover |
| **361st** | | | |
| 374th: | Lt. S.M. Popy | Me-109 dest(air) | Dummer Lake |
| | Lt. E.L. Wilsey | Me-109 dest(air) | Dummer Lake |
| 375th: | Maj. C.N. Keppler | Me-109 dam(air) | Dummer Lake |
| | Lt. R.G. Adams | Me-109 dam(air) | N/Munster |
| 376th: | Lt. W.J. Sykes | Me-109 dest(air) | S/Munster |
| | | Me-109 prob(air) | S/Munster |
| | | (2)Me-410 dest(grd) | Munster |
| | | Me-110 dest(grd) | Munster |
| | Lt. K.G. Scott | Me-109 dest(air) | S/Munster |
| | Lt. R.W. Ward | Me-109 dest(air) | W/Munster |
| **479th** | | | |
| 434th: | Lt. T.C. Olson | Me-410 dam(grd) | Vechta |
| 435th: | Lt. L.P. Petterson | FW-190 dest(air) | NE Dummer Lake |
| | Capt. J.W. Harrell | FW-190 dam(air) | SE Dummer Lake |
| 436th: | Lt. H.J. Grasshoff | FW-190 dest(air) | Osnabruck |

*Losses-*

**55th**: Lt. Robert K. Harbeck (338th Ftr Sqn) KIA
P-51D CL- 44-14204 "Skylark"
Suffered mechanical failure and crashed into the North Sea.

**56th**: Lt. Leo J. Czarnota (63rd Ftr Sqn) POW
P-47D UN- 42-25957
Suffered mechanical failure near Engden.

**339th**: Capt. Edward H. Beavers, Jr. (503rd Ftr Sqn) KIA
P-51D D7-Z 44-14525 "Joanie"
Hit by flak at an airfield near Cologne.

Lt. Felix J. Girone (503rd Ftr Sqn) KIA
P-51D D7-A 44-14587 "PeeWee Peckerwood"
Hit by enemy fighters near Rengershausen.

**352nd**: Lt. Arthur E. Hudson (328th Ftr Sqn) KIA
P-51D PE-Z 44-15012"Jeanie Boy"
Hit by enemy fighters near Aulendorf.

Capt. Walter E. Starck (487th Ftr Sqn) POW
P-51D HO-F 44-14794 "Buzz Boy"
Hit by enemy fighters near Hameln.

Capt. Walter S. Smith (487th Ftr Sqn) POW
P-51D HO- 44-14638 "Sweet Sue"
Hit by enemy fighters near Munster.

**353rd**: Lt. George C. Moran (350th Ftr Sqn) KIA
P-51D LH-L 44-14666 "Zelma"
Hit by enemy fighters near Winzenburg.

Lt. James F. Cross (352nd Ftr Sqn) KIA
P-51D SX-U 44-15388 "Stasia"
Hit by enemy fighters near Altenau.

**357th**: Lt. Frank L. Gailer, Jr. (363rd Ftr Sqn) POW
P-51D B6-A 44-11331 "Expectant"
Hit by a P-51 and bailed out near Groningen.

**359th**: Lt. Dick D. Connelly (370th Ftr Sqn) KIA
P-51D CS-V 44-14096 "De De III"
Hit by enemy fighters north of Kassel.

**361st**: Lt. Lewis P. Chadwick (376th Ftr Sqn) MIA-E
P-51C E9-I 42-103350
Suffered mechanical failure and bailed out near Nijmegen.

**364th**: Lt. John L. Bassan (385th Ftr Sqn) KIA
P-51D 5E-U 44-14336
Suffered mechanical failure near St. Dizier.

Lt. Robert F. Edwards (385th Ftr Sqn) KIA
P-51D 5E-X 44-14456
Hit by flak and exploded near Giessen.

*Remarks*
55th: 4-1 locos, 0-20 railcars
78th: 19-2 locos, 3-126 railcars, 0-14 vehicles
339th: 1-0 loco, 1-0 railcar
352nd: 16-15 locos, 7-33 railcars, 0-17 barges, 5-16 vehicles
353rd: Lt. Ralph B. Snyder (352nd Ftr Sqn) c/l; o.k.
P-51D SX-V
356th: Lt. Ralph E. Odenwald (359th Ftr Sqn) c/l; o.k.
P-51D OC-
Lt. Thomas A. Cook (360th Ftr Sqn) b/o; injured(broken arm)
P-51D PI-
357th: 6-0 locos
479th: 2-0 locos, 0-5 railcars

**November 29, 1944**
Groups Operating: P-51 4th, 20th, 55th, 339th, 352nd, 353rd, 355th, 356th, 357th, 359th, 361st, 364th, 479th
P-47 56th, 78th
Missions: Support of bombers to Misburg, Altenbeken, Bielefeld, and Hamm.
Claims: nil
Losses: nil

*Remarks*
56th: Lt. William H. Stovall (62nd Ftr Sqn) c/l Halesworth; o.k.
P-47D LM-
78th: 1-0 loco, 0-8 railcars
353rd: 3-0 locos, 0-9 vehicles, 0-2 barges, 0-1 boat
355th: 0-1 loco
LtCol. Bert W. Marshall (HdQts) c/l; o.k.
P-51D WR-B 44-14799 "Jane IV"

**November 30, 1944**
Groups Operating: P-51 4th, 20th, 55th, 339th, 352nd, 353rd, 355th, 356th, 357th, 359th, 361st, 364th, 479th
P-47 56th, 78th
Missions: Support of bombers to Merseburg, Zeitz, Lutzkenfdorf, Neunkirchen, Bohlen, and Homburg.
Claims: 4-0-0 air
0-3 ground

| *Group* | | *Claims* | *Location* |
|---|---|---|---|
| **352nd** | | | |
| 486th: | LtCol. W.O. Jackson | Me-109 dest(air) | W/Chemnitz |
| | Capt. C.E. Griffiths | Me-109 dest(air) | Glauchau |
| | Lt. E.R. Lazear | Me-109 dest(air) | S/Merseburg |
| | Lt. B.J. Grabovski | (2)FW-190 dam(grd) | W/Leipzig |
| | | He-111 dam(grd) | W/Leipzig |
| **364th** | | | |
| 384th: | Lt. E.W. Farnsworth | Me-109 dest(air) | SE Zeitz |

*Losses-*

**56th**: F/O Alben G. Calmes (62nd Ftr Sqn) KIA
P-47D LM-C 42-28806
Hit by flak near Westerburg.

**364th**: Lt. Richard J. O'Connor (384th Ftr Sqn) KIA
P-51D 5Y-B 44-13999
Suffered mechanical failure and bailed out southwest of Giessen.

Lt. Erskin H. Rivers (385th Ftr Sqn) POW
P-51D 5E-J 44-13947
Suffered mechanical failure and bailed out east of Frankfurt.

*Remarks*
56th: 4-0 locos, 0-85 railcars
Lt. David L. Mauldin (61st Ftr Sqn) c/l Continent; o.k.
P-47D HV-
352nd: 0-7 locos, 0-20 railcars
357th: Lt. Richard E. Ecker (362nd Ftr Sqn) c/l Leiston; o.k.
P-51D G4-
Lt. Peter Pielich (363rd Ftr Sqn) c/l Boreham; o.k.
P-51D B6-

**December 2, 1944**
Groups Operating: P-51 4th, 20th, 55th, 352nd, 353rd, 355th, 357th, 361st, 364th
P-47 56th
Missions: Support of bombers to Bingen and Oberlahnstein plus the 56th and some P-51 units carried out sweeps.
Claims: 31-1-5 air
0-0 ground

| Group | | Claims | Location |
|---|---|---|---|
| **4th** | | | |
| 334th: | Lt. C.F. Brown | FW-190 dest(air) | Hottenbach |
| | Lt. J.D. McFadden | FW-190 dest(air) | Hottenbach |
| | Lt. A.C. Lacy | FW-190 dam(air) | Hottenbach |
| | Lt. M.R. Savage | Me-109 dam(air) | SE Bingen |
| **20th** | | | |
| 55th: | Lt. E. Planchak | (2)Me-109 dest(air) | Coblenz-St. Goar |
| | Lt. H.L. Brown | FW-190 dest(air) | Coblenz-St. Goar |
| 77th: | LtCol. R.F. Gustke | Me-109 dest(air) | Coblenz |
| | Lt. J.M. Garner | FW-190 dest(air) | Coblenz |
| | Lt. R.E. Murrell | FW-190 dest(air) | Coblenz |
| **56th** | | | |
| 62nd: | Capt. R.W. Davis | (2)Me-109 dest(air) | E/Coblenz |
| 63rd: | Maj. P.A. Conger | (2)Me-109 dest(air) | S/Marburg |
| | Capt. J.C. Fahringer | (2)Me-109 dest(air) | S/Marburg |
| | Lt. R.B. Anderson | Me-109 dest(air) | S/Marburg |
| | Lt. S.K. Batson | Me-109 dest(air) | S/Marburg |
| | Lt. R. Frederickson | Me-109 dest(air) | S/Marburg |
| | | Me-109 prob(air) | S/Marburg |
| | Lt. W.R. Groce | Me-109 dest(air) | S/Marburg |
| | | Me-109 dam(air) | S/Marburg |
| | Lt. P.B. Trumble | Me-109 dest(air) | S/Marburg |
| | Lt. D.M. Magel | Me-109 dam(air) | S/Marburg |
| **357th** | | | |
| HdQts: | Capt. R.W. Foy | Ju-88 dest(air) | NE Coblenz |
| 362nd: | Capt. L.K. Carson | (2)Me-109 dest(air) | Bingen |
| | Capt. A.C. Murohy | (2)Me-109 dest(air) | Bingen |
| | Lt. H.H. Delager | Me-109 dest(air) | Bingen |
| | Lt. R.L. Schlieker | Me-109 dest(air) | Bingen |
| **361st** | | | |
| 374th: | Capt. J.R. Mau | (2)FW-190 dest(air) | Meinsenheim |
| | Lt. E.W. Keplinger | FW-190 dam(air) | Meinsenheim |
| 376th: | Lt. H.D. Mitchell | FW-190 dest(air) | Bingen |
| **364th** | | | |
| 385th: | Capt. R. Visconte | FW-190 dest(air) | NW Ludwigshafen |
| | Lt. J.L. McCubbin | Me-109 dest(air) | Mannheim |

*Losses-*

**20th**: Lt. Merle P. Joseph (77th Ftr Sqn) KIA
P-51D LC-Z 44-13824
Last seen in heavy overcast near Brussels.

**56th**: Capt. Eugene E. Barnum (61st Ftr Sqn) KIA
P-47D HV- 44-19739
Collided with Lt. Baker near Guell.

Lt. Donald Allayaud (62nd Ftr Sqn) KIA
P-47D LM- 42-28683
Hit by enemy fighters near Valenciennes.

Lt. Wyman A. Baker (63rd Ftr Sqn) KIA
P-47D UN-C 42-28741
Collided with Capt. Barnum near Guell.

*Remarks*

20th: Lt. Glen R. Hall (77th Ftr Sqn) c/l Brussels; o.k.
P-51D LC-

364th: Lt. George Z. Schroeder (384th Ftr Sqn) c/l Lowestoft.; o.k.
P-51D 5Y- 44-14032

**December 4, 1944**

Groups Operating: P-51 4th, 20th, 55th, 339th, 352nd, 353rd, 355th, 356th, 357th, 359th, 361st, 364th, 479th
P-47 56th, 78th

Missions: Support of bombers to Kassel, Soest, Bebra, Coblenz, Giessen, Mainz, and Friedburg.

Claims: 0-0-0 air
11-14 ground

| Group | | Claims | Location |
|---|---|---|---|
| **56th** | | | |
| 61st: | Lt. C.R. Woock | u/i a/c dest(grd) | Neuburg |
| | Lt. C.R. Bond | (2)u/i a/c dam(grd) | Ingolstadt |
| 62nd: | Capt. M.J. Jackson | Me-262 dest(grd) | Neuburg |
| | | Me-262 dam(grd) | Neuburg |
| | | FW-200 dam(grd) | Neuburg |
| | Capt. F.A. Nolan | FW-200 dest(grd) | Neuburg |
| | | Me-262 dam(grd) | Neuburg |
| | Lt. E.M. Beason | He-177 dest(grd) | Neuburg |
| | | FW-190 dest(grd) | Neuburg |
| | Capt. W.F. Wilkerson | He-111 dest(grd) | Neuburg |
| | Lt. N.D. Gould | Me-262 dest(grd) | Neuburg |
| | | Me-262 dam(grd) | Neuburg |
| | Lt. S.N. Ball | (.5)u/i a/c dest(grd) | Neuburg |
| | Lt. D. Henley | (.5)u/i a/c dest(grd) | Neuburg |
| | Lt. A. Chasko | (.5)He-177 dest(grd) | Neuburg |
| | | (4)Me-262 dam(grd) | Neuburg |
| | Lt. W.C. Daley | (.5)He-177 dest(grd) | Neuburg |
| | | Me-262 dam(grd) | Neuburg |
| 63rd: | Lt. C.A. Chinn | (2)Me-262 dest(grd) | Neuburg |
| | | Me-262 dam(grd) | Neuburg |
| | Lt. W.R. Groce | u/i a/c dam(grd) | Neuburg |
| | Lt. R.L. Murphy | FW-200 dam(grd) | Neuburg |

*Losses-*

**339th**: Lt. Richard C. Cain (505th Ftr Sqn) POW
P-51D 6N- 44-14072
Suffered mechanical failure near Trier.

**353rd**: Lt. Victor N. Hernandez (352nd Ftr Sqn) MIA
P-51D SX-Q
Suffered mechanical failure northwest of Wiesbaden.

*Remarks*

56th: 3-1 locos, 3-12 railcars, 1-0 flak position
F/O Longfin M. Winski (61st Ftr Sqn) c/l Yvetet; o.k.
P-47D HV-
Maj. Robert W. Hall (62nd Ftr Sqn) b/o Brittany; injured
P-47D LM-
Lt. Frank R. Aheron (62nd Ftr Sqn) c/l St. Trond; o.k.
P-47D LM-
Lt. Charles E. Carlson (62nd Ftr Sqn) c/l Abbeville; o.k.
P-47D LM-
F/O Virgil E. Elliott (62nd Ftr Sqn) b/o Brittany; o.k.
P-47D LM-
Lt. Norman D. Gould (62nd Ftr Sqn) c/l Brittany; o.k.
P-47D LM-
Lt. Russell W. Campbell (63rd Ftr Sqn) c/l Chaumont; o.k.
P-47D UN-
Lt. Charles R. Clark (63rd Ftr Sqn) c/l Chaumont; o.k.
P-47D UN-

339th: Capt. William H. Krauss (505th Ftr Sqn) b/o Trier; o.k.
P-51D 6N-

KIAc's

364th: Lt. Gerald C. Reidenbach (384th Ftr Sqn)
P-51B 5Y- 42-106659
Aircraft exploded and crashed south of Bury St. Edmonds.

**December 5, 1944**

Groups Operating: P-51 4th, 20th, 55th, 339th, 352nd, 353rd, 355th, 356th, 357th, 359th, 361st, 364th, 479th
P-47 56th, 78th

Missions: Support of bombers to Berlin and Munster.

Claims: 89-13-20 air
0-2 ground

| Group | | Claims | Location |
|---|---|---|---|
| **4th** | | | |
| 334th: | Maj. H.D. Hively | FW-190 dest(air) | NW Nordhorn |
| **55th** | | | |
| 38th: | Capt. M.M. Coons | Me-109 dest(air) | N/Berlin |
| | | FW-190 dest(air) | N/Berlin |
| | Capt. M. Clark | FW-190 dest(air) | NE Berlin |
| | Lt. D.F. Jewell | FW-190 dest(air) | NE Berlin |
| | Lt. J.W. Kavanaugh | FW-190 dest(air) | NE Berlin |
| | Lt. F.M. Matney | FW-190 dest(air) | NE Berlin |
| **339th** | | | |
| 503rd: | Capt. D.E. Shafer | FW-190 dam(air) | S/Wittstock |
| **352nd** | | | |
| 486th: | Lt. B.J. Grabovski | Me-262 dam(air) | Osnabruck |
| **353rd** | | | |
| 350th: | Capt. W.F. Tanner | FW-190 dest(air) | S/Steinhuder L. |
| | | FW-190 dam(air) | S/Steinhuder L. |
| | Lt. N.N. Cowen | FW-190 dest(air) | S/Steinhuder L. |
| | Lt. A.L. Deeds | FW-190 dest(air) | S/Steinhuder L. |
| 351st: | Maj. F.H. LeFebre | FW-190 dest(air) | N/Berlin |
| | | Me-109 dam(air) | N/Berlin |
| 352nd: | Lt. J.R. Evans | (2)FW-190 dest(air) | NE Berlin |
| | | FW-190 prob(air) | NE Berlin |
| | Capt. W.W. Johnson | FW-190 dest(air) | NE Berlin |
| | Capt. J.L. Knoble | FW-190 dest(air) | NE Berlin |
| | Lt. F.H. Bouldin | FW-190 dest(air) | NE Berlin |
| | Lt. W.R. Curry | FW-190 prob(air) | NE Berlin |

**355th**

| | | | |
|---|---|---|---|
| 354th: | Capt. J.E. Duffy | FW-190 dest(air) | N/Berlin |
| | Lt. S.E. Silva | FW-190 dest(air) | N/Berlin |
| 358th: | Maj. W.J. Hovde | (4.5)FW-190 dest(air) | Berlin |
| | | Me-109 dest(air) | Berlin |
| | Lt. R.G. Baker | (2)FW-190 dest(air) | Berlin |
| | | FW-190 dam(air) | Berlin |
| | Lt. A.K. Alexander | (1.5)FW-190 dest(air) | Berlin |
| | Lt. R.H. Brown | FW-190 dest(air) | Berlin |
| | Lt. J.N. McElroy | FW-190 dest(air) | Berlin |
| | | (3)FW-190 dam(air) | Berlin |

**356th**

| | | | |
|---|---|---|---|
| 359th: | Capt. J.D. Tarbutton | (2)FW-190 dest(air) | NW Berlin |
| | Capt. C.J. Hackney | FW-190 dest(air) | Muritz Lake-Berlin |
| | Lt. F.A. Forsythe | FW-190 dest(air) | Muritz L.-Berlin |
| | | FW-190 prob(air) | Muritz L.-Berlin |
| | Lt. L. Oliver | FW-190 dest(air) | Muritz L.-Berlin |
| | Capt. L.L. Robertson | FW-190 prob(air) | N/Berlin |
| | Lt. A.R. Hale | FW-190 dam(air) | Muritz L.-Berlin |
| 361st: | Capt. W.R. Scheible | (2)FW-190 dest(air) | Eberswalde |
| | Capt. D.J. Strait | (2)FW-190 dest(air) | Eberswalde |
| | Lt. R.H. Campbell | (2)FW-190 dest(air) | Eberswalde |
| | Lt. C.T. Ashby | FW-190 dest(air) | Eberswalde |
| | | FW-190 prob(air) | Eberswalde |
| | Lt. C.D. Burdick | FW-190 dest(air) | Eberswalde |
| | | FW-190 dam(air) | Eberswalde |

**357th**

| | | | |
|---|---|---|---|
| 362nd: | Lt. J.A. Kirla | Me-109 dest(air) | Berlin |
| | | FW-190 dest(air) | Berlin |
| | Maj. J.E. Broadhead | FW-190 dest(air) | Berlin |
| | Capt. L.K. Carson | Me-109 dest(air) | Berlin |
| | Lt. W.T. Gilbert | Me-410 dam(grd) | Berlin |
| 363rd: | Capt. C.E. Anderson | (2)FW-190 dest(air) | W/Berlin |
| | | FW-190 prob(air) | W/Berlin |
| | Capt. D.H. Bochkay | (2)FW-190 dest(air) | NE Berlin |
| | Capt. J.W. Browning | Me-109 dest(air) | N/Berlin |
| | Lt. J.L. Carter | FW-190 dest(air) | N/Berlin |
| | Lt. J.R. Stern | FW-190 dest(air) | N/Berlin |
| | Lt. G.J. Rice | FW-190 dest(air) | N/Berlin |
| | Lt. J.T. Crump | FW-190 prob(air) | N/Berlin |
| | Capt. A.G. Manthos | FW-190 dam(air) | N/Berlin |
| 364th: | Lt. D.E. Karger | (2)FW-190 dest(air) | Berlin |
| | Lt. F.C. McCall | (2)FW-190 dest(air) | NW Berlin |
| | Capt. H.R. Zetterquist | FW-190 dest(air) | N/Berlin |
| | Lt. T.H. Adams | FW-190 dest(air) | NW Berlin |
| | Lt. M.E. Gallant | FW-190 dest(air) | NW Berlin |
| | Lt. P.R. Hatala | Me-109 dest(air) | NW Berlin |
| | Lt. E.J. Juszczyk | FW-190 dest(air) | N/Berlin |
| | Lt. R.G. Schimanski | FW-190 dest(air) | N/Berlin |

**364th**

| | | | |
|---|---|---|---|
| HdQts: | LtCol. J.H. Lowell | (3)FW-190 dest(air) | N/Berlin |
| | | FW-190 dam(air) | N/Berlin |
| 384th: | Lt. E.W. Farnsworth | FW-190 dest(air) | NW Berlin |
| | Lt. W.E. Flynt | (.5)FW-190 dest(air) | NW Berlin |
| | Lt. D.L. Leftwich | (.5)FW-190 dest(air) | NW Berlin |
| 385th: | Capt. W.F. Wilson | (2)FW-190 dest(air) | N/Berlin |
| | | FW-190 dam(air) | N/Berlin |
| | Lt. J.L. McCubbin | (2)FW-190 dest(air) | N/Berlin |
| | | (2)FW-190 prob(air) | N/Berlin |
| | Maj. C.W. Stapleton | FW-190 dest(air) | N/Berlin |
| | Capt. T.P. Farrell | FW-190 dest(air) | N/Berlin |
| | Lt. E.N. Farrell | (2)FW-190 dam(air) | N/Berlin |

**479th**

| | | | |
|---|---|---|---|
| HdQts: | LtCol. K.L. Riddle | FW-190 dest(air) | NW Berlin |
| | | FW-190 dam(air) | NW Berlin |
| 434th: | Maj. A.F. Jeffrey | (3)FW-190 dest(air) | Neuruppin |
| | | FW-190 dam(air) | Neuruppin |
| | Lt. G.E. Jacobson | (2)FW-190 dest(air) | Neuruppin |
| | Lt. H.E. Mathews | FW-190 dest(air) | Neuruppin |
| | Lt. R.G. McChrystal | Me-109 dest(air) | Neuruppin |
| | | Me-109 dam(air) | Neuruppin |
| | Lt. B.E. Hollister | FW-190 prob(air) | Neuruppin |
| | Lt. R.L. Maley | FW-190 prob(air) | Neuruppin |
| 435th: | Lt. R.G. Candelaria | (2)FW-190 dest(air) | NW Berlin |
| | Lt. G.L. Doolittle | FW-190 dest(air) | NW Berlin |
| | | FW-190 prob(air) | NW Berlin |
| | | FW-190 dam(air) | NW Berlin |
| | Lt. P.D. Gossard | FW-190 dest(air) | NW Berlin |
| | Lt. B.C. Means | Me-109 dest(air) | NW Berlin |
| | Lt. F.L. Hart | FW-190 prob(air) | NW Berlin |
| | Lt. N.R. Benoit | Me-262 dam(grd) | Bremen |
| 436th: | Lt. T.E. Myers | (.5)FW-190 dest(air) | N/Berlin |
| | | Me-109 dam(air) | N/Berlin |
| | Lt. P.C. Vasseur | (.5)FW-190 dest(air) | N/Berlin |

*Losses-*

**339th:** LtCol. Harvey E. Henderson (503rd Ftr Sqn) POW
P-51D D7- 44-15520
Hit by a FW-190 near Rechlin.

Lt. James A. Baker (505th Ftr Sqn) KIA
P-51D 6N- 44-13370
Suffered mechanical failure near Giessen.

**353rd:** Lt. Noah N. Cowen (350th Ftr Sqn) KIA
P-51D LH-E 44-14538 "Margaret Too"
Hit by a FW-190 near Wunstorf.

Lt. Alvin L. Deeds (350th Ftr Sqn) KIA
P-51D LH-P 44-14727 "Bee-Jay"
Hit by a FW-190 near Hohnhorst.

**355th:** Lt. Ben C. Williams (357th Ftr Sqn) POW
P-51D OS-D 44-15013
Suffered mechanical failure and bailed out north of Berlin.

**356th:** Capt. Jean D. Tarbutton (359th Ftr Sqn) POW
P-51D OC-B 44-15219
Hit by a FW-190 northwest of Berlin.

Lt. Russell C. Scharnberg (359th Ftr Sqn) KIA
P-51K OC- 44-11326
Hit by a FW-190 near Eberswalde and carshed near Neuruppin.

Capt. Raymond H. Gansberg (361st Ftr Sqn) KIA
P-51D QI-D 44-15118
Hit by a FW-190 near Eberswalde.

Lt. Ben B. Barnes (361st Ftr Sqn) KIA
P-51D QI-R 44-15169
Hit by a FW-190 near Eberswalde.

Lt. Jack T. Smith (361st Ftr Sqn) KIA
P-51D QI-N 44-15079
Hit by a FW-190 near Eberswalde.

**357th:** Lt. Matthew S. Martin (362nd Ftr Sqn) POW
P-51D G4-N 44-14722 "Temptation"
Suffered mechanical failure west of Brandenburg.

Capt. Herman R. Zetterquist (364th Ftr Sqn) POW
P-51D C5-R 44-13546 "The Shillelagh"
Hit by enemy fighters near Eberswalde.

**361st:** Lt. Denver J. Wood (374th Ftr Sqn) POW
P-51B B7-V 42-106695
Suffered mechanical failure near Leiden.

**364th:** Capt. Romildo Visconte (385th Ftr Sqn) KIA
P-51D 5E-O 44-14322 "Coffin Wit Wings"
Crashed while trying to land at Liege.

**479th:** Lt. Walter A. Neuman (434th Ftr Sqn) KIA
P-51D L2-U 44-14592 "Buzzin' Texan"
Hit by enemy fighters near Neuruppin.

Lt. Ronald L. Maley (434th Ftr Sqn) POW
P-51D L2-T 44-11214 "Tommy Trojan"
Hit by flak near Scharfenberg.

Maj. John A. Sullivan (436th Ftr Sqn) KIA
P-51D 9B-A 44-14636 "Carol II & III"
Suffered mechanical failure and crashed into the North Sea.

Lt. Barrett B. Eskell (436th Ftr Sqn) POW
P-51B 9B- 44-14517 "Lil Exterminator"
Collided with a P-51 near Muenschehagen.

*Remarks*

4th: 0-9 locos, 0-3 vehicles, 0-3 barges
56th: Lt. Bernard S. Miller (61st Ftr Sqn) c/l; injured
P-47D HV-
352nd: 0-2 railcars
353rd: 0-1 loco
355th: 0-4 locos, 0-12 railcars
Lt. Grant Seely (358th Ftr Sqn) c/l; o.k.
P-51D YF-M 44-14126
357th: 1-0 loco, 12-0 railcars
364th: 1-0 loco, 0-6 railcars

**December 6, 1944**

Groups Operating: P-51 4th, 20th, 55th, 339th, 352nd, 353rd, 355th, 356th, 357th, 359th, 361st, 364th, 479th
P-47 78th

Missions: Support of bombers to Merseburg, Bielefeld, and Minden.
Claims: 0-0-0 air
0-1 ground

| Group | Claims | Location |
|---|---|---|
| **479th** | | |
| 435th: Lt. N.R. Benoit | He-111 dam(grd) | W/Dummer Lake |

*Losses-*

**20th**: Lt. Calvin Katz (77th Ftr Sqn) KIA
P-51D LC-
Aborted the mission and crashed near Ipswich.

**364th**: Lt. Donald P. Voelker (383rd Ftr Sqn) MIA
P-51D N2-S 44-14088
Suffered mechanical failure and bailed out near Eisleben.

*Remarks*
479th: 1-0 loco, 0-3 barges

**December 9, 1944**
Groups Operating: P-51 4th, 20th, 339th, 352nd, 355th, 361st
P-47 78th
Missions: Support of bombers to Stuttgart.
Claims: 1-0-0 air
0-0 ground

| Group | Claims | Location |
|---|---|---|
| **352nd** | | |
| 486th: Lt. H.L. Edwards | Me-262 dest(air) | Kirchem |

Losses: nil

*Remarks*
352nd: 6-0 locos, 0-27 railcars
355th: Lt. Victor D. Iglesias (357th Ftr Sqn) c/l Steeple Morden; o.k.
P-51D OS-S

KIAc's
364th: Capt. John R. Steinbacher (384th Ftr Sqn)
P-51D 5Y- 44-13709
Turned too-tight and spun-in near Honington.

**December 10, 1944**
Groups Operating: P-51 4th, 20th, 339th, 352nd, 353rd, 355th, 357th, 359th, 479th
P-47 56th, 78th
Missions: Support of bombers to Bingen and Coblenz.
Claims: nil

*Losses-*

**20th**: Lt. Everett T. Urbanski (55th Ftr Sqn) KIA
P-51D KI-N 44-14870
Suffered mechanical failure near Frankfurt.

**355th**: Lt. Maurice H. Ivey (354th Ftr Sqn) POW
P-51D WR-B 44-14293 "Lackin' Shackin"
Suffered mechanical failure west of Bingen.

*Remarks*
55th: 3-0 locos

KIAc's
479th: Lt. William D. Clark(435th Ftr Sqn)
P-51 J2-

**December 11, 1944**
Groups Operating: P-51 4th, 20th, 55th, 339th, 352nd, 353rd, 355th, 356th, 357th, 359th, 361st, 364th, 479th
P-47 56th, 78th
Missions: Support of bombers to Frankfurt, Hanau, Coblenz, Giessen, and Mannheim.
Claims: 0-0-0 air
0-1 ground

| Group | Claims | Location |
|---|---|---|
| **55th** | | |
| 343rd: Capt. D.A. Parker | Me-410 dam(grd) | SE Kassel |

*Losses-*

**55th**: Capt. Harry E. Larsen (338th Ftr Sqn) KIA
P-51D CL- 44-14211 "Harvest Moon"
Hit by flak near Padberg.

*Remarks*
4th: Lt. Paul M. Morgan (336th Ftr Sqn) b/o France; o.k.
P-51D VF- 44-15350
55th: 14-3 locos, 3-1 vehicles
56th: P-47 b/o; o.k.
P-47 b/o; o.k.
339th: Lt. John W. Gokey (503rd Ftr Sqn) b/o Frinton By Sea; o.k.
P-51D D7-

**December 12, 1944**
Groups Operating: P-51 4th, 20th, 55th, 339th, 352nd, 353rd, 355th, 356th, 357th, 359th, 361st, 364th, 479th
P-47 56th, 78th
Missions: Support of bombers to Merseburg, Hanau, and Darmstadt.
Claims: 0-0-0 air
1-0 ground

| Group | Claims | Location |
|---|---|---|
| **355th** | | |
| 358th: Lt. A.R. Curran | u/i a/c dest(grd) | Gotha |

*Losses-*

**339th**: Lt. Harry G. Loskill (504th Ftr Sqn) POW
P-51D 5Q-F 44-13378 "Ollie"
Suffered mechanical failure near Kuels.

**356th**: Lt. Percy C. O'Quinn (359th Ftr Sqn) ASR
P-51D OC-
Suffered mechanical failure and bailed out off Margate.

**364th**: Capt. Jack V. Johnson (384th Ftr Sqn) KIA
P-51D 5Y-L 44-14992 "Penny III"
Hit by flak near Limburg.

Lt. Everett N. Farnsworth (384th Ftr Sqn) KIA
P-51D 5Y-Y 44-14018 "Six Gun Pete"
Hit by flak near Limburg.

Lt. George C. Kuhn (384th Ftr Sqn) KIA
P-51D 5Y- 44-15580
Hit by flak near Ziegenheim.

Lt. Lawrence Visconti (384th Ftr Sqn) KIA
P-51D 5Y-B 44-14148 "Laurie's Eleanor"
Hit by enemy fighters near Beienbach.

**479th**: Lt. Robert N. Pigg (435th Ftr Sqn) KIA
P-51D J2- 44-14344
Suffered mechanical failure and bailed out over Belgium; while descending in his chute he was hit by a B-26.

*Remarks*
4th: 0-1 loco, 3-0 railcars
20th: Lt. Vincent J. Rudnick (79th Ftr Sqn) c/l Antwerp; o.k.
P-51D MC-J
355th: 2-0 locos, 0-17 railcars
361st: Lt. Joseph E. Wolfe (375th Ftr Sqn) c/l; o.k.
P-51D E2-
364th: 0-1 vehicle

KIAc's
479th: Lt. Robert B. Hymans (435th Ftr Sqn)
P-51B J2-7 43-7157
Crashed into the North Sea on a training flight.

**December 13, 1944**
KIAc's
479th: Lt. Dewey H. Hollis (434th Ftr Sqn)
P-51 L2-

**December 14, 1944**
KIAc's
56th: Lt. Lowell C. Buchmiller (62nd Ftr Sqn)
P-47D LM-
Crashed into the North Sea on a training flight.

**December 15, 1944**
Groups Operating: P-51 4th, 339th, 353rd, 355th, 356th, 357th, 359th, 364th
P-47 56th, 78th
Missions: Support of bombers to Kassel and Hanover.
Claims: nil

*Losses-*

**355th**: Lt. Arthur K. Alexander (358th Ftr Sqn) POW
P-51D YF-J 44-15014
Suffered mechanical failure and bailed out north of Munster.

**364th**: Lt. Lee P. Russell (384th Ftr Sqn) KIA
P-51D 5Y- 44-15557
Suffered mechanical failure and bailed out forty-five miles east of Clacton.

**December 16, 1944**
Groups Operating: P-51 55th, 339th, 353rd
Missions: Support for bombers to Stuttgart and Bietingheim.
Claims: nil
Losses: nil

*Remarks*
55th: 7-0 locos, 0-30 railcars, 0-2 buildings

**December 18, 1944**
Groups Operating: P-51 4th, 20th, 55th, 339th, 352nd, 353rd, 355th, 356th, 357th, 359th, 361st, 364th, 479th
P-47 56th
Missions: Support of bombers to Cologne, Mainz, Kaiserlautern, and Coblenz.
Claims: 3-0-0 air
0-0 ground

| *Group* | | *Claims* | *Location* |
|---|---|---|---|
| **4th** | | | |
| 334th: | Lt. H.E. Clifton | Me-109 dest(air) | E/Dortmund |
| 335th: | Capt. W.J. O'Donnell | Me-109 dest(air) | NE Frankfurt |
| | Lt. R.L. Stallings | FW-190 dest(air) | NE Frankfurt |

*Losses-*

**4th**: Capt. Charles D. Hewes (335th Ftr Sqn) KIA
P-51D WD- 44-15455
Hit by flak in the Giessen area.

**56th**: Lt. Wilburn A. Haggard (62nd Ftr Sqn) POW
P-47D LM-A 42-28688
Hit by flak near Neuschierholz.

**356th**: Lt. Donald L. Turnidge (360th Ftr Sqn) POW
P-51D PI- 44-15033
Suffered mechanical failure near Dusseldorf.

**359th**: Lt. David B. Archibald (368th Ftr Sqn) POW
P-51D CV-L 44-15555
Hit by fighters and flak in the Aachen-Koln area.

Lt. Paul E. Olson (368th Ftr Sqn) POW
P-51D CV-T 44-14131
Hit by enemy fighters in the Aachen-Koln area.

*Remarks*
4th: 2-0 vehicles
Capt. Shelton W. Monroe (334th Ftr Sqn) c/l Grutrode; o.k.
P-51D QP-N 44-15312
20th: Capt. Robert L. Pubentz (79th Ftr Sqn) c/l; o.k.
P-51D MC-H
359th: P-51 c/l Continent; o.k.

**December 19, 1944**
Groups Operating: P-47 78th
Missions: Support of bombers/sweep of the Trier-Coblenz area.
Claims: 7-0-1 air
0-0 ground

| *Group* | | *Claims* | *Location* |
|---|---|---|---|
| **78th** | | | |
| 83rd: | Capt. R.R. Bonebrake | Me-109 dest(air) | S/Coblenz |
| | | FW-190 dest(air) | S/Coblenz |
| | Lt. F.E. Harrington | Me-109 dest(air) | S/Coblenz |
| | | FW-190 dest(air) | S/Coblenz |
| | Lt. J.A. Kirk | Me-109 dest(air) | S/Coblenz |
| | | FW-190 dest(air) | S/Coblenz |
| | Lt. F.A. Fish | Me-109 dest(air) | S/Coblenz |
| | Maj. S.R. Beckley | Me-109 dam(air) | S/Coblenz |

Losses: nil

*Remarks*
78th: 15-0 vehicles
Lt. John B. Wade (83rd Ftr Sqn) c/l Duxford; o.k.
P-47D MX-L 42-28455 (note this was an 82nd Ftr Sqn a/c)
F/O Marquis D. Hilbert (83rd Ftr Sqn) c/l St. Trond; o.k.
P-47D HL-J 44-19875

**December 23, 1944**
Groups Operating: P-51 4th, 55th, 352nd, 353rd, 355th, 356th, 357th 359th, 361st, 364th, 479th
P-47 56th
Missions: Support of bombers to numerous communication and transportation targets in Germany.
Claims: 77-6-20 air
0-0 ground

| *Group* | | *Claims* | *Location* |
|---|---|---|---|
| **56th** | | | |
| HdQts: | Col. D.C. Schilling | (3)Me-109 dest(air) | Euskirchen-Bonn |
| | | (2)FW-190 dest(air) | Euskirchen-Bonn |
| 61st: | Capt. J.H. Perry | (2)FW-190 dest(air) | Coblenz |
| | Lt. J.F. Frazier | (2)FW-190 dest(air) | Coblenz |
| | Lt. V.E. Bast | FW-190 dest(air) | Coblenz |
| | Lt. C.R. Woock | FW-190 prob(air) | E/Bonn |
| | | (2)FW-190 dam(air) | E/Bonn |
| | Lt. J.T. Allen | FW-190 dam(air) | E/Bonn |
| 62nd: | Capt. F.D. Williamson | Me-109 dest(air) | Euskirchen |
| | | FW-190 dest(air) | Euskirchen |
| | Lt. A.O. Perry | (2)FW-190 dest(air) | Bonn-Coblenz |
| | Lt. A. Chasko | Me-109 dest(air) | Euskirchen-Bonn |
| | | FW-190 dam(air) | Euskirchen-Bonn |
| | Lt. S.N. Ball | FW-190 dest(air) | Euskirchen |
| | Lt. E.M. Beason | Me-109 dest(air) | Euskirchen-Bonn |
| | Lt. C.E. Carlson | FW-190 dest(air) | Euskirchen-Bonn |
| | Lt. W.C. Daley | Me-109 dest(air) | Bonn-Coblenz |
| | Lt. N.D. Gould | FW-190 dest(air) | Euskirchen |
| | Lt. W.S. Lear | FW-190 dest(air) | Euskirchen |
| | Lt. D.A. Westover | (.5)FW-190 dest(air) | Euskirchen-Bonn |
| | | (2)FW-190 dam(air) | Euskirchen-Bonn |
| | Lt. L.F. Geron | (.5)FW-190 dest(air) | Euskirchen-Bonn |
| | Lt. L.R. Brown | (3)FW-190 prob(air) | Coblenz |
| | | FW-190 dam(air) | Coblenz |
| | Lt. R.E. Winters | Me-109 prob(air) | Euskirchen-Bonn |
| | | FW-190 dam(air) | Euskirchen-Bonn |
| 63rd: | Maj. H.E. Comstock | (2)FW-190 dest(air) | SW Bonn |
| | | (2)FW-190 dam(air) | SW Bonn |
| | Capt. C.M. Hart | (2)FW-190 dest(air) | NW Coblenz |
| | | FW-190 dam(air) | NW Coblenz |
| | Lt. R.L. Murphy | (2)FW-190 dest(air) | NW Coblenz |
| | Lt. S.K. Batson | FW-190 dest(air) | NW Coblenz |
| | Lt. W.C. Scherz | FW-190 dest(air) | NW Coblenz |
| | | FW-190 prob(air) | NW Coblenz |
| | | FW-190 dam(air) | NW Coblenz |
| | F/O M.J. Hughes | FW-190 dest(air) | NW Coblenz |
| | | FW-190 dam(air) | NW Coblenz |
| | Lt. R.J. Daniel | FW-190 dest(air) | NW Coblenz |
| | Lt. C.R. Clark | FW-190 dest(air) | NW Coblenz |
| | Lt. W.R. Hoffman | FW-190 dest(air) | NW Coblenz |
| | Lt. P.B. Trumble | FW-190 dam(air) | NW Coblenz |
| **352nd** | | | |
| 328th: | Capt. D.S. Bryan | FW-190 dest(air) | S/Liege |
| | Lt. W.H. Sanford | FW-190 dest(air) | S/Liege |
| **353rd** | | | |
| 351st: | Capt. H.D. Stump | Me-262 dam(air) | Magdeburg-SE Hanover |
| 352nd: | Lt. S.E. Stephenson | Me-262 dam(air) | W/Magdeburg |
| **357th**(#1) | | | |
| HdQts: | Capt. R.W. Foy | Me-109 dest(air) | Wetzlar A/F |
| | | Ju-88 dest(air) | Wetzlar A/F |
| (#2) | | | |
| 362nd: | Lt. C.E. Weaver | Me-109 dest(air) | N/Donauworth |
| 363rd: | F/O S. Sitzer | Me-109 dest(air) | S/Ludwigshafen |
| **359th** | | | |
| 368th: | Lt. R.E. Benefiel | Me-109 dest(air) | Coblenz |
| | Lt. E.C. Cook | Me-109 dest(air) | Coblenz |
| **361st** | | | |
| 375th: | Lt. C.J. Layton | (2)FW-190 dest(air) | SE Bonn |
| | Lt. W.H. Street | Me-109 dest(air) | SE Bonn |
| **364th** | | | |
| 383rd: | Maj. G.F. Ceuleers | (4)Me-109 dest(air) | NW Trier |
| | Lt. R.W. Orndorff | (2)FW-190 dest(air) | NW Trier |
| | Lt. R.M. Baughn | FW-190 dest(air) | NW Trier |
| | Lt. C.E. Hammett | FW-190 dest(air) | NW Trier |
| | Lt. J.D. Woodside | Me-109 dest(air) | NW Trier |
| | | Me-109 dam(air) | NW Trier |
| | Lt. E.F. Heyn | Me-109 dam(air) | NW Trier |
| 384th: | Lt. J.M. Fowle | (4)Me-109 dest(air) | NW Trier |
| | Lt. W.F. Flynt | Me-109 dest(air) | Luxembourg |
| | Lt. T.H. Wells | Me-109 dest(air) | Luxembourg |
| 385th: | Capt. T.P. Farrell | (2)FW-190 dest(air) | W/Trier |
| | Lt. W.G. Erfkamp | (2)Me-109 dest(air) | Luxembourg |
| | Lt. S.L. Lett | FW-190 dest(air) | NW Trier |
| | Lt. C.R. Roesch | FW-190 dam(air) | Luxembourg |
| **479th** | | | |
| 434th: | Maj. A.F. Jeffrey | (3)Me-109 dest(air) | SE Bonn |
| | Lt. G.W. Gleason | (2)FW-190 dest(air) | SE Bonn |
| | | FW-190 dam(air) | SE Bonn |
| | Lt. T.D. Neely | (2)FW-190 dest(air) | SE Bonn |

| | | | |
|---|---|---|---|
| | Lt. G.E. Jacobson | FW-190 dest(air) | SE Bonn |
| 436th: | Capt. C.V. Ernst | Me-109 dest(air) | Cologne |
| | Capt. A.E. Huycke | FW-190 dest(air) | Cologne |
| | Capt. E.C. Lewin | Me-109 dest(air) | NW Cologne |
| | Capt. J.R. Struby | FW-190 dest(air) | E/Cologne |

*Losses-*

**55th**: Lt. John E. McDonnell (343rd Ftr Sqn) KIA
P-51D CY-L 44-13643 "Sweet Pootie"
Hit by flak near Ober-Raden.

**56th**: Lt. Lewis R. Brown (62nd Ftr Sqn) POW
P-47D LM-B 44-20615
Hit by enemy fighters in the Euskirchen-Bonn area.

Lt. Charles E. Carlson (62nd Ftr Sqn) KIA
P-47D LM-M 44-19767
Hit by enemy fighters near Euskirchen.

F/O John E. Lewis (63rd Ftr Sqn) KIA
P-47D UN- 44-19911
Hit by enemy fighters near Queekenburg.

**357th**: Capt. Walter N. Perry, Jr. (362nd Ftr Sqn) KIA
P-51K G4-X 44-11689 "Toolin' Fool"
Lost a wing in a dive near Fulda.

**361st**: Lt. Caleb J. Layton (375th Ftr Sqn) KIA
P-51D E2-E 44-14064 "Suzy Anne"
Hit by enemy fighters near Bonn.

**479th**: Lt. Thomas D. Neely (434th Ftr Sqn) POW
P-51D L2-X 44-14596 "Rumboogie Jr."
Hit by flak near Ecuwied.

*Remarks*
56th: Lt. Robert J. Daniel (63rd Ftr Sqn) b/o S/Paris; o.k.
P-47D UN-F 44-20543
355th: Lt. Robert A. Goth (354th Ftr Sqn) c/l; o.k.
P-51D WR-
Lt. Robert L. Heaton (354th Ftr Sqn) c/l; o.k.
P-51D WR-
Lt. George W. Schmidt (357th Ftr Sqn) c/l; o.k.
P-51D OS-D
479th: 1-0 loco

**December 24, 1944**

Groups Operating: P-51 4th, 20th, 55th, 352nd, 353rd, 355th, 356th, 357th, 359th, 361st, 364th, 479th
P-47 56th
Missions: Support for bombers to numerous airfields and marshalling yards in Germany.
Claims: 73-3-9 air
0-0 ground

| ***Group*** | | ***Claims*** | ***Location*** |
|---|---|---|---|
| **SF** | | | |
| 3rd: | Capt. H.B. Howard | (2)Me-109 dest(air) | Frankfurt-Darmstadt |
| | Lt. W.C. Klank | Me-109 dest(air) | Frankfurt-Darmstadt |
| **4th** | | | |
| 335th: | Lt. C.W. Willruth | Me-109 dest(air) | W/Giessen |
| | Lt. G.D. Green | Me-109 prob(air) | W/Giessen |
| **55th** | | | |
| 38th: | Lt. M.O. Anderson | Me-109 dest(air) | W/St. Vith |
| | Lt. C.E. Breathwit | Me-109 dest(air) | W/St. Vith |
| | Lt. D.G. Jackson | FW-190 dest(air) | Coblenz |
| | Lt. R.F. Malnoey | (.5)FW-190 dest(air) | S/Coblenz |
| | Lt. W.B. Staggs | (.5)FW-190 dest(air) | S/Coblenz |
| | Capt. D.E. Penn | (2)Me-109 dam(air) | W/St. Vith |
| 338th: | LtCol. E.G. Righetti | (3)FW-190 dest(air) | SE Munster |
| | | (2)FW-190 dam(air) | SE Munster |
| | Lt. F.D. Bradford | FW-190 dest(air) | E/Frankfurt |
| | | FW-190 dam(air) | E/Frankfurt |
| | Lt. R.C. Haworth | Me-109 dest(air) | Vogelsburg |
| | Lt. J.R. McDonald | Me-109 dest(air) | S/Coblenz |
| | Lt. S.D. Gevorkian | (.5)Me-109 dest(air) | Friedburg |
| | | (.5)FW-190 dest(air) | Friedburg |
| | Lt. K.A. Lashbrook | (.5)Me-109 dest(air) | Friedburg |
| | | (.5)FW-190 dest(air) | Friedburg |
| 343rd: | Lt. J.C. McVay | FW-190 dest(air) | S/Frankfurt |
| | Lt. G. Morris | FW-190 dest(air) | S/Frankfurt |
| | Lt. R.E. Welch | Me-109 dest(air) | S/Duren |
| **353rd**(#1) | | | |
| 350th: | Capt. J.H. Winder | (2)Me-109 dest(air) | Coblenz-Limburg |
| | Lt. R.W. Abernathy | (2)Me-109 dest(air) | Coblenz-Limburg |
| | Lt. G.S.H. Lee | Me-109 dest(air) | Coblenz |
| 352nd: | Lt. A.C. Cundy | Me-109 dest(air) | Laacher Lake |
| | Lt. H.Q. Waggoner | Me-109 dest(air) | SW Euskirchen |
| (#2) | | | |
| 352nd: | Lt. J.E. Jessup | Me-109 dest(air) | Leipzig |
| **357th** | | | |
| HdQts: | LtCol. I.H. Dregne | Me-109 dest(air) | Coblenz |
| 362nd: | Lt. O.D. Jenkins | (4)FW-190 dest(air) | Fulda |
| | Lt. J.A. Kirla | (3)FW-190 dest(air) | Fulda |
| | Lt. W.T. Gilbert | (2)FW-190 dest(air) | Fulda |
| | Lt. E.D. Hyman | (2)FW-190 dest(air) | Fulda |
| | Lt. P.A. Pelon | (2)FW-190 dest(air) | Fulda |
| | Capt. L.K. Carson | FW-190 dest(air) | Fulda |
| | Lt. G.A. Behling | FW-190 dest(air) | Fulda |
| | Lt. J.R. Frey | FW-190 dest(air) | Fulda |
| 363rd: | Lt. J.L. Carter | Me-109 dest(air) | W/Coblenz |
| | | FW-190 dest(air) | W/Coblenz |
| | Maj. G.I. Carlisle | Me-109 dest(air) | W/Coblenz |
| | Lt. J.T. Crump | Me-109 dest(air) | W/Coblenz |
| | Lt. W.R. Dunlop | Me-109 dest(air) | W/Coblenz |
| | Lt. W.P. Roberts | Me-109 dest(air) | W/Coblenz |
| | Lt. J.R. Sloan | Me-109 dest(air) | W/Coblenz |
| 364th: | Lt. R.M. Bank | Me-109 dest(air) | S/Kassel |
| | Lt. B.K. Braley | FW-190 dest(air) | S/Kassel |
| | Lt. D.E. Karger | Me-109 dest(air) | S/Kassel |
| | Lt. F.C. McCall | Me-109 dest(air) | E/Fulda |
| | Lt. I.L. McGuire | FW-190 dest(air) | S/Kassel |
| | Lt. R.G. Schimanski | Me-109 dest(air) | Kassel |
| | Lt. R.P. Winks | FW-190 dest(air) | Fulda |
| **359th** | | | |
| 368th: | Lt. E.J. Beal | (2)FW-190 dest(air) | Cologne |
| | | FW-190 prob(air) | Cologne |
| | Lt. R.A. Boyd | FW-190 dam(air) | Cologne |
| 369th: | Lt. J.J. Kelly | Me-109 dest(air) | Vogelsand |
| | Lt. B.H. Thomson | Me-109 dest(air) | Vogelsand |
| | Lt. J.E. Keur | Me-109 dam(air) | Vogelsand |
| 370th: | Lt. E.G. Johnson | (2)FW-190 dest(air) | Bonn |
| | | (2)FW-190 dam(air) | Bonn |
| | Capt. W.R. Hodges | FW-190 dest(air) | Bonn |
| | Capt. A.T. Lemmens | FW-190 dest(air) | Bonn |
| | Lt. R.G. Oakley | FW-190 dest(air) | Bonn |
| | Lt. J.W. Wilson | FW-190 dest(air) | Bonn |
| **361st** | | | |
| 376th: | Lt. W.J. Sykes | Me-109 dest(air) | Wengerohr |
| | | Me-109 prob(air) | Wengerohr |
| | Lt. J.B. Bricker | Me-109 dest(air) | Wengerohr |
| | Lt. C.E. Sullivan | Me-109 dest(air) | Wengerohr |
| | Lt. G.R. Vanden Heuval | Me-109 dest(air) | Wengerohr |
| **479th** | | | |
| 435th: | Lt. N.W. Butler | FW-190 dest(air) | NE Liege |

*Losses-*

**SF**: Lt. Walter C. Klank, Jr. (3rd) POW
P-51D CL- 44-13886 "Miss Jane I"
Hit by a Me-109 near Floersheim.

**55th**: Lt. Kenneth W. Griffith (338th Ftr Sqn) KIA
P-51D CL- 44-13767
Hit by enemy fighters near Lippstadt.

Lt. Kenneth J. Mix (343rd Ftr Sqn) KIA
P-51D CY-M 44-13837 "Miss Marilyn"
Collided with Lt. Helwig(357th Ftr Grp) near Daun.

**356th**: Lt. Arthur Wong, Jr. (359th Ftr Sqn) POW
P-51D OC- 44-15193
Suffered mechanical failure and bailed out near Laacher See.

**357th**: Lt. William T. Gilbert, Jr. (362nd Ftr Sqn) KIA
P-51D G4-A 44-15620
Hit by a FW-190 near Fulda.

Capt. William H. Mooney, Jr. (362nd Ftr Sqn) KIA
P-51D G4-X 44-11198 "Libby B"
Hit by a FW-190 near Fulda.

Lt. Wendell T. Helwig (363rd Ftr Sqn) KIA
P-51D B6- 44-13923 "Big Beautiful Doll"
Collided with Lt. Mix(55th Ftr Grp) near Daun.

**359th**: Lt. Raymond A. Boyd, Jr. (368th Ftr Sqn) POW
P-51D CV-X 44-14329
Hit by a FW-190 near Cologne.

**361st**: Lt. William J. Sykes (376th Ftr Sqn) POW
P-51D E9-F 44-11203 "Hiya Honey"
Hit by a Me-109 near Wengerohr.

*Remarks*
55th: 5-0 locos, 30-0 railcars
357th: P-51 c/l Continent; o.k.
359th: Lt. Bryce H. Thomson (369th Ftr Sqn) b/o Continent; o.k.
P-51D IV-I 44-15016
479th: P-51 c/l Bruges; o.k.

**December 25, 1944**
Groups Operating: P-51 4th, 20th, 55th, 352nd, 353rd, 355th, 356th, 357th, 361st, 364th, 479th
P-47 56th
Missions: Support of bombers to various communication targets and bridges in Germany.
Claims: 59-7-11 air
0-0 ground

| *Group* | | *Claims* | *Location* |
|---|---|---|---|
| **4th** | | | |
| 334th: | Lt. T.J. Cronin | (1.5)FW-190 dest(air)* | S/Bonn |
| | Lt. W.B. Hoelscher | FW-190 dest(air) | NE Trier |
| | | (.5)Me-109 dest(air) | NE Trier |
| | | FW-190 dam(air) | NE Trier |
| | Lt. V.R.T. Rentschler | FW-190 dest(air) | NE Trier |
| | | (.5)Me-109 dest(air) | NE Trier |
| | | FW-190 dam(air) | NE Trier |
| 335th: | Maj. P.W. McKennon | (.5)FW-190 dest(air)* | S/Bonn |
| | Lt. C.E. Poage | (2)FW-190 prob(air) | SE Duren |
| 336th: | Capt. D.R. Emerson | (2)FW-190 dest(air) | SW Coblenz |
| | Lt. V.E. Chandler | Me-109 dest(air) | SW Coblenz |
| | | FW-190 dest(air) | SW Coblenz |
| | Maj. F.W. Glover | FW-190 dest(air) | SW Coblenz |
| **55th** | | | |
| 343rd: | Lt. B.H. Howes | (2)Me-109 dest(air) | SW Frankfurt |
| | Lt. R.E. Welch | (2)Me-109 dest(air) | W/Coblenz |
| | Lt. R.A. Maxwell | Me-109 dest(air) | W/Coblenz |
| **56th** | | | |
| 61st: | Lt. W.D. Clark | FW-190 dest(air) | Cologne |
| 62nd: | Lt. W.C. Daley | (2)Me-109 dest(air) | Bonn-Coblenz |
| | F/O W.J. Sharbo | (2)Me-109 dest(air) | Bonn-Coblenz |
| | Capt. M.J. Jackson | Me-109 dest(air) | Bonn-Coblenz |
| 63rd: | Capt. C.M. Hart | Me-109 dest(air) | SE Cologne |
| | Lt. S.K. Batson | Me-109 dam(air) | SE Cologne |
| **352nd** | | | |
| 328th: | Capt. C.J. Cesky | (3)FW-190 dest(air) | Maastricht |
| | Maj. G.E. Preddy | (2)Me-109 dest(air) | SW Coblenz |
| | Capt. W.J. Stangel | (2)Me-109 dest(air) | SW Coblenz |
| | Lt. A.J. Chesser | FW-190 dest(air) | Maastricht |
| | Lt. C.E. Goodman | Me-109 dest(air) | SW Coblenz |
| | Lt. J.F. Lambright | Me-109 dest(air) | SW Coblenz |
| | | Me-109 dam(air) | SW Coblenz |
| | Lt. R.R. Mitchell | Me-109 dest(air) | SW Coblenz |
| **353rd** | | | |
| 352nd: | Lt. H.Q. Waggoner | Me-109 dest(air) | NE St. Vith |
| **355th** | | | |
| 354th: | Lt. C.D. Hauver | Me-109 dest(air) | NW Trier |
| | | FW-190 dest(air) | NW Trier |
| | Maj. G.M. Graham | FW-190 dest(air) | NW Trier |
| | | FW-190 prob(air) | NW Trier |
| 357th: | Lt. V.D. Iglesias | FW-190 dest(air) | W/Coblenz |
| **356th** | | | |
| HdQts: | LtCol. D.A. Baccus | Me-109 dest(air) | Bonn |
| 359th: | Lt. E.F. Troge | FW-190 dest(air) | Bonn |
| | Lt. A.L. Brown | FW-190 dam(air) | Bonn |
| 360th: | Capt. B.E. Ellingson | Me-109 dest(air) | S/Bonn |
| | | FW-190 dest(air) | S/Bonn |
| | Capt. E.W. Pleasant | FW-190 dest(air) | Bonn |
| | | FW-190 dam(air) | Bonn |
| | Lt. D.F. Jones | FW-190 dam(air) | S/Bonn |
| | Lt. T.J. Urban | FW-190 dam(air) | Bonn |
| 361st: | Capt. D.J. Strait | Me-109 dest(air) | SW Coblenz |
| **479th** | | | |
| 434th: | Lt. G.W. Gleason | (3)FW-190 dest(air) | SW Bonn |
| | Maj. A.F. Jeffrey | Me-109 dest(air) | SW Bonn |
| | Lt. P.A. Brown | FW-190 dest(air) | SW Bonn |
| | | FW-190 prob(air) | SW Bonn |
| | Lt. R.D. Creighton | FW-190 dest(air) | SW Bonn |
| | Lt. A.G. Helding | FW-190 dest(air) | SW Bonn |
| | Lt. H.M. Jenkins | FW-190 dest(air) | SW Bonn |
| | Lt. J.N. Murr | FW-190 dest(air) | SW Bonn |
| | | FW-190 prob(air) | SW Bonn |
| | | FW-190 dam(air) | SW Bonn |
| | Lt. E.E. Sears | Me-109 dest(air) | SW Bonn |
| | Capt. J.M. Hollingsworth | Me-109 prob(air) | SW Bonn |
| | | Me-109 dam(air) | SW Bonn |
| | Lt. G.E. Jacobson | FW-190 prob(air) | SW Bonn |
| 435th: | Capt. J.W. Harrell | Me-109 dest(air) | SW Aachen |
| | Lt. N.R. Benoit | Me-109 dest(air) | SW Cologne |
| | | Me-109 dam(air) | SW Cologne |
| | Lt. T.J. Sowerby | FW-190 dest(air) | Bonn |
| 436th: | Capt. R.S. Spencer | (2)FW-190 dest(air) | SE Malmedy |

*Losses-*

**4th:** Lt. Charles E. Poage (335th Ftr Sqn) POW
P-51D WD- 44-14540 "Ascend Charlie"
Hit by a FW-190 northwest of Laacher See.

Capt. Donald R. Emerson (336th Ftr Sqn) KIA
P-51D VF-D 44-15054
Hit by Allied ground-fire in Belgium.

**55th:** Lt. Robert A. Maxwell (343rd Ftr Sqn) POW
P-51D CY-B 44-14384 "Lil Pearl"
Hit by enemy fighters near Mayenne.

**352nd:** Maj. George E. Preddy (328th Ftr Sqn) KIA
P-51D PE-P 44-14906 "Cripes A'Mighty"
Was chasing a FW-190 when American ground-fire knocked him down near Liege.

**355th:** Lt. Harold L. Monahan (357th Ftr Sqn) KIA
P-51D OS- 44-15304
Hit by a FW-190 south of Coblenz.

**356th:** Lt. Richard J. Andrino (360th Ftr Sqn) KIA
P-51D PI- 44-15307
Hit by a FW-190 near Bonn.

Lt. Milton H. Huebner (360th Ftr Sqn) KIA
P-51D PI- 44-15364
Hit by a FW-190 near Bonn.

**479th:** Capt. James M. Hollingsworth (434th Ftr Sqn) POW
P-51D L2-A 44-14892
Hit by enemy fighters near Bonn.

Lt. Wendell H. Marlowe (434th Ftr Sqn) MIA
P-51D L2-I 44-15325 "Swanee Jr."
Hit by enemy fighters near Bonn.

Lt. Edward L. Hurtig (434th Ftr Sqn) KIA
P-51D L2-M 44-14416
Hit by enemy fighters near Bonn.

Lt. Douglas L. Red (436th Ftr Sqn) KIA
P-51D 9B- 44-14559 "Daisy Mae"
Hit by enemy fighters near Grossenheim.

*Remarks*
479th: Lt. James E. Bouchier (434th Ftr Sqn) b/o Liege; o.k.
P-51D L2-

**December 26, 1944**
Groups Operating: P-51 55th, 352nd, 356th, 357th, 359th, 361st, 364th, 479th
P-47 56th
Missions: Support of bombers to rail targets and bridges in Germany. Bad weather limited bomber operations.
Claims: 26.5-0-2 air
0-0 ground

| *Group* | | *Claims* | *Location* |
|---|---|---|---|
| **56th** | | | |
| 62nd: | Lt. A.O. Perry | (2)FW-190 dest(air) | Coblenz |
| | | FW-190 dam(air) | Coblenz |
| | Maj. L.C. Smith | FW-190 dest(air) | Coblenz |
| **352nd**(#1) | | | |
| HdQts: | LtCol. J.C. Meyer | (1.5)Me-109 dest(air) (shared with an unknown pilot) | Ollheim |
| 487th: | Maj. W.T. Halton | Me-109 dest(air) | SW Bonn |
| | Capt. R.W. Hamilton | Me-109 dest(air) | SW Bonn |
| | Capt. M.J. Nutter | Me-109 dest(air) | SW Bonn |
| | Lt. W.G. Diamond | Me-109 dest(air) | Ollheim |
| | Lt. R.H. Littge | Me-109 dest(air) | Ollheim |
| | Lt. A.F. Sears | Me-109 dest(air) | Ollheim |
| (#2) | | | |
| HdQts: | LtCol. J.C. Meyer | Me-109 dest(air) | Uxheim |
| 487th: | Lt. D.H. Schuh | (3)Me-109 dest(air) | Veldenbor |
| | Lt. W.C. Miller | Me-109 dest(air) | Veldenbor |
| | | Me-109 dam(air) | Veldenbor |
| | Lt. J.A. Bateman | Me-109 dest(air) | SE St. Vith |

| | | | |
|---|---|---|---|
| **356th** | | | |
| 359th: | Lt. W.C. Cooley | (2)FW-190 dest(air) | NE Bonn |
| | Capt. C.J. Hackney | FW-190 dest(air) | NE Bonn |
| | Lt. J.W. Meade | FW-190 dest(air) | NE Bonn |
| **361st** | | | |
| 376th: | Lt. G.R. Vanden Heuval | (1.5)FW-190 dest(air) | Merzig |
| | Lt. C.P. Chennault | FW-190 dest(air) | Merzig |
| | Lt. B.L. Dennehy | FW-190 dest(air) | Merzig |
| | Lt. D.P. Overholt | FW-190 dest(air) | NW Merzig |
| | Lt. H.G. Powell | FW-190 dest(air) | N/Merzig |
| | Capt. J.W. Ruch | (.5)FW-190 dest(air) | Merzig |

*Losses-*

**352nd**: Lt. Carl G. Tafel, Jr. (487th Ftr Sqn) KIA
P-51D HO-C 44-13953 "Nancy M"
Hit by enemy fighters near Heimerzheim.

**356th**: Capt. Claude J. Hackney, Jr. (359th Ftr Sqn) KIA
P-51D OC- 44-15609
Hit by a FW-190 east of Bonn.

Lt. Warren C. Cooley (359th Ftr Sqn) POW
P-51D OC- 44-15029 "Pottsville Express"
Hit by flak northeast of Bonn.

*Remarks*
357th: Maj. John B. England (362nd Ftr Sqn) c/l; o.k.
P-51D G4-W 44-14152

**December 27, 1944**
Groups Operating: P-51 4th, 20th, 352nd, 353rd, 356th, 357th, 359th, 361st, 364th, 479th
P-47 56th
Missions: Support of bombers to rail targets in Germany.
Claims: 51-1-10 air
0-0 ground

| ***Group*** | | ***Claims*** | ***Location*** |
|---|---|---|---|
| **352nd** | | | |
| HdQts: | LtCol. J.C. Meyer | (2)FW-190 dest(air) | SW Bonn |
| | | (2)FW-190 dam(air) | SW Bonn |
| 486th: | Lt. R.L. Henderson | (2)Me-109 dest(air) | W/Bonn |
| | Lt. W.H. Reese | (2)Me-109 dest(air) | SW Bonn |
| | LtCol. W.O. Jackson | Me-109 dest(air) | SW Bonn |
| | Maj. F.N. Greene | Me-109 dest(air) | SE Liege |
| | Lt. E.R. Lazear | Me-109 dest(air) | SW Bonn |
| 487th: | Maj. W.T. Halton | (3.5)Me-109 dest(air)[*] | SW Bonn |
| | Lt. R.H. Littge | (3)FW-190 dest(air) | Mauen |
| | Capt. M.J. Nutter | (2)Me-109 dest(air) | SW Bonn |
| | Lt. J.A. Bateman | Me-109 dest(air) | SW Bonn |
| | Lt. S.K. Moats | FW-190 dest(air) | SW Bonn |
| | Lt. R.H. Ross | FW-190 dest(air) | Mauen |
| | Lt. J.N. Wood | FW-190 dest(air) | W/Mauen |
| | F/O E.H. Goebel | (.5)Me-109 dest(air)[*] | SW Bonn |
| | | (.5)Me-109 dest(air)[**] | Bonn |
| **364th** | | | |
| HdQts: | Capt. E.E. Bankey | (4)FW-190 dest(air) | Bonn |
| | | (1.5)FW-190 dest(air)[**] | Bonn |
| | LtCol. J.H. Lowell | (.5)Me-109 dest(air)[@] | W/Coblenz |
| | | Me-109 dam(air) | W/Coblenz |
| 383rd: | Capt. E.N. Fiery | (2)FW-190 dest(air) | Frankfurt |
| | | FW-190 dam(air) | Frankfurt |
| | Lt. H.D. Sandkaut | FW-190 dest(air) | NW Frankfurt |
| | Lt. G.E. Smith | FW-190 dam(air) | SW Frankfurt |
| 384th: | Lt. R.K. Allen | (2.5)Me-109 dest(air)[@@] | SW Coblenz |
| | | FW-190 dam(air) | SW Coblenz |
| | Lt. E.H. Duderstadt | (2)FW-190 dest(air) | W/Coblenz |
| | | Me-109 dest(air) | W/Coblenz |
| | Lt. D.L. Leftwich | (2)FW-190 dest(air) | W/Coblenz |
| | Lt. R.S. Faulkner | FW-190 dest(air) | S/Coblenz |
| | Lt. S.J. Price | (.5)Me-109 dest(air)[@] | W/Coblenz |
| | Lt. H.M. James | Me-109 dam(air) | Bonn |
| | Lt. R.W. Stevens | Me-109 dam(air) | Bonn |
| 385th: | Capt. G.L. Jamison | (3)FW-190 dest(air) | SW Bonn |
| | | Me-109 dam(air) | E/Liege |
| | Lt. E.N. Farrell | Me-109 dest(air) | SE Bonn |
| | | FW-190 dest(air) | SE Bonn |
| | Lt. W.S. Sagar | FW-190 dest(air) | W/Coblenz |
| | | (.5)Me-109 dest(air)[@@] | SW Coblenz |
| | | Me-109 dam(air) | W/Coblenz |
| | Lt. J.T. Barrie | Me-109 dest(air) | SW Bonn |
| | Lt. D.L. Bloodgood | FW-190 dest(air) | SE Bonn |
| | Lt. H.W. Head | FW-190 dest(air) | NW Bonn |
| | Lt. C.S. Hogan | FW-190 dest(air) | Laachen Lake |
| | | FW-190 prob(air) | Laachen Lake |

*Losses-*

**359th**: Lt. George M. Givan (369th Ftr Sqn) KIA
P-51D IV- 44-14964
He and Lt. Parsons landed at Reims and headed back for England later in the day; both were last seen near the Thames River.

Lt. James R. Parsons, Jr. (369th Ftr Sqn) KIA
P-51K IV-G 44-11659 "San'Tone Sweetheart"
See Givan above.

**364th**: Lt. Ralph L. Hubley (383rd) KIA
P-51D N2-F 44-14528
Hit by fighters near Roetz.

*Remarks*
4th: 0-4 locos, 0-9 railcars, 0-1 vehicles
357th: 2-1 locos, 6-0 vehicles
361st: 1-1 locos

**December 28, 1944**
Groups Operating: P-51 4th, 20th, 55th, 339th, 352nd, 353rd, 355th, 356th, 357th, 359th, 361st, 364th, 479th
P-47 56th, 78th
Missions: Support of bombers to rail targets and bridges in western Germany.
Claims: nil
Losses: nil

*Remarks*
355th: Lt. O.N. Stanton(354th Ftr Sqn) c/l Brussels; o.k.
P-51D WR-
364th: Lt. Sterling J. Price(384th Ftr Sqn) b/o Honington; o.k.
P-51D 5Y-

**December 29, 1944**
Groups Operating: P-51 4th, 20th, 55th, 78th(mixed), 339th, 352nd, 353rd, 355th, 357th, 361st, 364th, 479th
P-47 56th, 78th
Missions: Support of bombers to rail and communication targets in Germany.
Claims: nil

*Losses-*

**78th**: Lt. Huie H. Lamb (82nd Ftr Sqn) ASR
P-51D MX-V 44-63286 "Etta Jeanne"
Lost coolant and ditched in the North Sea.

**339th**: Lt. Charles M. Meade (504th Ftr Sqn) KIA
P-51D 5Q- 44-14287 "Pin-Up Girl"
Suffered mechanical failure near Coblenz.

**364th**: Lt. William F. Flynt (384th Ftr Sqn) POW
P-51D 5Y-U 44-63161 "Good Priss"
Suffered mechanical failure southwest of Giessen.

*Remarks*
78th: P-51 c/l Duxford; o.k.
355th: 3-3 locos, 0-40 railcars, 0-11 vehicles
479th: P-51 c/l Wattisham; o.k.
P-51 c/l Wattisham; o.k.

**December 30, 1944**
Groups Operating: P-51 4th, 20th, 55th, 78th(mixed), 339th, 352nd, 353rd, 355th, 356th, 357th, 359th, 361st, 479th
P-47 56th, 78th
Missions: Support of bombers to rail and communication targets in Germany.
Claims: nil

*Losses-*

**55th**: Lt. Harold B. Metcalf (338th Ftr Sqn) KIA
P-51D CL- 44-13867
Suffered mechanical failure near Fellen.

**357th**: Lt. Harold D. Chandler (362nd Ftr Sqn) MIA
P-51D G4-G 44-13719 "Pitter Pat"
Hit by flak east of Coblenz.

*Remarks*
357th: 0-25 railcars

KIAc's
56th: Lt. Samuel K. Batson (63rd Ftr Sqn)
P-47D UN-
Engine failed on take-off and crashed short of the runway.

**December 31, 1944**
Groups Operating: P-51 4th, 20th, 55th, 78th(mixed), 339th, 352nd, 353rd, 355th, 356th, 357th, 359th, 361st, 364th, 479th
P-47 56th, 78th

Missions: Support of bombers to Hamburg, Wenzendorf, Neuss, Coblenz, and other rail and communication targets plus PRU escorts.
Claims: 54.5-3-7 air
1-0 ground

| Group | | Claims | Location |
|---|---|---|---|
| **SF** | | | |
| 3rd: | Capt. H.B. Howard | FW-190 dest(air) | N/Steinhuder Lake |
| **56th** | | | |
| 62nd: | Capt. F.A. Nolan | (2)FW-190 dest(air) | Quackenbruck |
| | Lt. W.H. Stovall | (2)FW-190 dest(air) | Burgsteinfort |
| | F/O L.F. Butiste | FW-190 dest(air) | Quackenbruck |
| | | FW-190 dam(air) | Quackenbruck |
| | | Me-109 dam(air) | Quackenbruck |
| **78th**(P-47) | | | |
| 84th: | Capt. J.P. Maxwell | FW-190 dest(air) | Solingen |
| **339th** | | | |
| 503rd: | Capt. W.E. Bryan | FW-190 dest(air) | S/Hamburg |
| | Capt. A.G. Hawkins | FW-190 dest(air) | S/Hamburg |
| | | Me-262 dam(air) | S/Hamburg |
| | Lt. B.A. Allen | FW-190 dest(air) | S/Hamburg |
| 504th: | Lt. R.F. Herrmann | (2)FW-190 dest(air) | Hamburg |
| | Lt. L.W. Allers | FW-190 dest(air) | Hamburg |
| | Lt. V.N. Barto | FW-190 dam(air) | Hamburg |
| **352nd** | | | |
| HdQts: | LtCol. J.C. Meyer | Ar-234 dest(air) | Euskirchen |
| 328th: | Capt. D.S. Bryan | Ar-234 dam(air) | S/Verviers |
| **353rd** | | | |
| 352nd: | Lt. G.N. Porterfield | FW-190 dest(air) | W/Coblenz |
| **355th** | | | |
| 354th: | Maj. G.M. Graham | (2)FW-190 dest(air) | SW Hamburg |
| | Lt. C.D. Hauver | FW-190 dest(air) | SW Hamburg |
| | | FW-190 dam(air) | SW Hamburg |
| **359th** | | | |
| 368th: | Capt. G.F. Baker | (2)FW-190 dest(air) | SE Stade |
| 369th: | Lt. W.F. Collins | (1.5)FW-190 dest(air) | SW Hamburg |
| | | (.5)FW-190 dest(air) | SW Hamburg |
| | Lt. A.B. Morris | (1.5)FW-190 dest(air) | SW Hamburg |
| | | (.5)FW-190 dest(air) | SW Hamburg |
| 370th: | Capt. R.S. Wetmore | (1.5)Me-109 dest(air)* | Hanover |
| | Lt. F.O. Lux | (1.5)Me-109 dest(air)** | Hanover |
| | Capt. A.T. Lemmens | Me-109 dest(air) | Hanover |
| | Lt. W.J. Rueschenberg | (.5)Me-109 dest(air)* | Hanover |
| | Lt. E.G. Johnson | (.5)Me-109 dest(air) | Hanover |
| | | (shared with an unknown pilot) | |
| | Lt. L.A. Ziska | (.5)Me-109 dest(air)** | Hanover |
| | Lt. G.E. Ramser | Me-109 prob(air) | Hanover |
| | Lt. J.E. McCoskey | Me-109 dam(air) | Hanover |
| **364th** | | | |
| 383rd: | Maj. S.J. Wicker | (4)FW-190 dest(air) | SW Hamburg |
| | Lt. D.C. Fisher | FW-190 dest(air) | SW Hamburg |
| | Lt. R.W. Orndorff | FW-190 dest(air) | SW Hamburg |
| 384th: | Lt. W.P. Hess | (3)FW-190 dest(air) | SE Hamburg |
| | | Ju-87 dest(grd) | SE Hamburg |
| | Lt. J.M. Fowle | (2)FW-190 dest(air) | SW Hamburg |
| | Lt. E.H. Miller | (2)FW-190 dest(air) | Hamburg |
| | Lt. W.E. Randolph | (2)FW-190 dest(air) | S/Hamburg |
| | Lt. T.H. Wells | (2)FW-190 dest(air) | Hamburg |
| | Lt. H.M. James | FW-190 dest(air) | SE Hamburg |
| | Lt. G.Z. Schroeder | FW-190 dest(air) | Hamburg |
| | Lt. R.S. Faulkner | (.5)FW-190 dest(air) | SW Hamburg |
| | Lt. D.L. Leftwich | (.5)FW-190 dest(air) | SW Hamburg |
| | Lt. L.L. Lefforge | FW-190 prob(air) | SW Hamburg |
| 385th: | Capt. W.S. Crombie | FW-190 dest(air) | Hamburg |
| | Lt. H.W. Head | FW-190 dest(air) | SE Hamburg |
| | Lt. R.M. McKibben | FW-190 dest(air) | SE Hamburg |
| | Lt. E. Murphy | FW-190 dest(air) | Hamburg |
| | Lt. T.L. Allinder | (.5)FW-190 dest(air) | SW Hamburg |
| | F/O C.L. Smart | (.5)FW-190 dest(air) | SW Hamburg |
| | Lt. F.X. Radley | FW-190 prob(air) | Hamburg |

*Losses-*

**56th**: Lt. Andrew Chasko (62nd Ftr Sqn) POW
P-47D LM- 44-19930
Hit by flak near Mesum.

Lt. William H. Stovall, Jr. (62nd Ftr Sqn) KIA
P-47D LM-K 44-19792
Shot down by a P-47 near Burgsteinfort.

**339th**: Capt. Anthony G. Hawkins (503rd Ftr Sqn) KIA
P-51D D7-O 44-14626 "Sweet Sue"
Last seen chasing a Me-262 near Soltau.

Lt. James A. Mankie (503rd Ftr Sqn) POW
P-51D D7-Q 44-15700 "Sweet Jeanne"
Hit by a Me-262 near Westertimke.

**352nd**: F/O Hugh A. Howard, Jr. (328th Ftr Sqn) KIA
P-51D PE-K 44-13759 "Lonesome Polecat"
Crashed into the Channel in bad weather.

**359th**: Lt. Donald L. Murphy (368th Ftr Sqn) KIA
P-51D CV-B 44-13786 "Adabelle"
Last seen near Stade and crashed near Grossenheim.

**364th**: Lt. William S. Sagar, Jr. (385th Ftr Sqn) POW
P-51D 5E-K 44-14584
Hit by enemy fighters southwest of Wenzendorf.

*Remarks*
4th: Lt. Michael J. Kennedy (334th Ftr Sqn) c/l La Rochelle; o.k.
P-51D QP-I
78th: 2-0 locos
352nd: Capt. Charles J. Cesky (328th Ftr Sqn) c/l Continent; o.k.
P-51D PE-
357th: Lt. Michael R. Emery (363rd Ftr Sqn) c/l Leiston; o.k.
P-51D B6-M 44-13681

KIAc's
55th: Lt. Richard L. Engel (343rd Ftr Sqn)
P-51D CY- 44-14171 "Daisy Jr."
Crashed into the Channel on a training flight.

**January 1, 1945**
Groups Operating: P-51 4th, 20th, 55th, 78th, 339th, 352nd, 353rd, 355th, 356th, 357th, 359th, 361st, 364th, 479th
P-47 56th
Missions: Support for bombers to numerous oil and transportation targets in Germany plus some PRU escorts.
Claims: 41-0-4 air
0-0 ground

| Group | | Claims | Location |
|---|---|---|---|
| **4th** | | | |
| 336th: | Lt. F.W. Young | Me-262 dest(air) | Ulzen |
| | | Me-109 dest(air) | Ulzen |
| | Lt. V.E. Chandler | Me-109 dest(air) | Ulzen |
| | Lt. D.J. Pierni | Me-109 dest(air) | Ulzen |
| | Lt. G.L. Kesler | (.5)Me-109 dest(air) | Ulzen |
| | Lt. A.O. Wallace | (.5)Me-109 dest(air) | Ulzen |
| **20th** | | | |
| 55th: | Capt. W.M. Hurst | Me-262 dam(air) | Magdeburg |
| **352nd** | | | |
| HdQts: | LtCol. J.C. Meyer | (2)FW-190 dest(air) | N/Liege |
| 487th: | Capt. W.T. Whisner | (2)Me-109 dest(air) | N/Liege |
| | | (2)FW-190 dest(air) | N/Liege |
| | Lt. S.K. Moats | (4)FW-190 dest(air) | N/Liege |
| | Capt. H.M. Stewart | (3)Me-109 dest(air) | N/Liege |
| | Lt. A.P. Rigby | (2)FW-190 dest(air) | N/Liege |
| | | (.5)Me-109 dest(air)* | N/Liege |
| | | (.5)Me-109 dest(air)* | N/Liege |
| | | (*- shared with an unknown pilot) | |
| | Lt. R.H. Littge | (2)FW-190 dest(air) | N/Liege |
| | Maj. W.T. Halton | FW-190 dest(air) | N/Liege |
| | Lt. W.G. Diamond | FW-190 dest(air) | N/Liege |
| | | FW-190 dam(air) | N/Liege |
| | Lt. A.F. Sears | Me-109 dest(air) | N/Liege |
| | Lt. D.M. Huston | FW-190 dest(air) | N/Liege |
| | Lt. N.R. Jesup | FW-190 dest(air) | N/Liege |
| **359th** | | | |
| 368th: | Lt. B.D. Kasper | Me-109 dest(air) | Stendal |
| | F/O B.N. Adkins | FW-190 dest(air) | Havelburg |
| | Lt. L.D. Carter | FW-190 dam(air) | Havelburg |
| 370th: | Capt. R.S. Wetmore | Me-109 dest(air) | Luneburg |
| | Lt. R.M. York | FW-190 dest(air) | Luneburg |
| **364th** | | | |
| 383rd: | Maj. G.F. Ceuleers | (2)Me-109 dest(air) | Hamburg |
| | Lt. F.L. Sorrells | Me-109 dest(air) | W/Stendal |
| | Lt. J.D. Woodside | Me-109 dest(air) | Hamburg |
| 385th: | Capt. W.S. Crombie | FW-190 dest(air) | SE Hamburg |
| | Lt. H.W. Head | FW-190 dest(air) | SE Hamburg |
| | Lt. J.L. McCubbin | Me-109 dest(air) | SE Hamburg |
| | Lt. J.E. Hargrove | (.5)FW-190 dest(air) | Hamburg |
| | Lt. F.X. Radley | (.5)FW-190 dest(air) | Hamburg |

**479th**

| | | | |
|---|---|---|---|
| HdQts: | LtCol. K.L. Riddle | (.5)FW-190 dest(air) | Nienburg |
| 434th: | Lt. C.W. Bowers | (.5)FW-190 dest(air) | Nienburg |
| | Lt. R.I. Bromschwig | FW-190 dam(air) | Nienburg |

*Losses-*

**364th**: Lt. John M. Geary (384th Ftr Sqn) MIA-E
P-51D 5Y-H 44-15202
Suffered mechanical failure north of the Frisian Islands.

Lt. James A. Porter (384th Ftr Sqn) KIA
P-51D 5Y- 44-14881
Hit by enemy aircraft near Oldendorf.

*Remarks*
55th: Lt. Hugh Bodiford (338th Ftr Sqn) b/o Charleville; o.k.
P-51D CL-
78th: Lt. Alvin M. Rosenberg (82nd Ftr Sqn) c/l Duxford; o.k.
P-51D MX-W 44-15722
357th: 11-0 locos, 3-0 barges, 1-0 tug

**January 2, 1945**
Groups Operating: P-51 4th, 20th, 55th, 78th, 339th, 352nd, 353rd, 355th, 356th, 357th, 359th, 361st, 364th, 479th
P-47 56th
Missions: Support for bombers to communication and transportation targets in Germany plus PRU escorts.
Claims: 7-0-0 air
0-0 ground

| *Group* | | *Claims* | *Location* |
|---|---|---|---|
| **4th** | | | |
| 334th: | Lt. C.G. Payne | (.5)Me-109 dest(air) | Westerburg |
| | | (.5)Me-109 dest(air) | Westerburg |
| | Lt. V.R.T. Rentschler | (.5)Me-109 dest(air) | Westerburg |
| | Lt. A.J. Senecal | (.5)Me-109 dest(air) | Westerburg |
| **361st** | | | |
| 375th: | Lt. R.J. Farney | Me-109 dest(air) | N/Stuttgart |
| | Lt. D.L. Farrar | Me-109 dest(air) | N/Stuttgart |
| | Lt. W.H. Street | Me-109 dest(air) | N/Stuttgart |
| | Lt. J.J. Sullivan | Me-109 dest(air) | N/Stuttgart |
| | Lt. A. Maurice | (.5)Me-109 dest(air) | N/Stuttgart |
| | Lt. G.R. Stockmeier | (.5)Me-109 dest(air) | N/Stuttgart |

*Losses-*

**4th**: Lt. Arthur J. Senecal (334th Ftr Sqn) KIA
P-51B QP-Z 43-6587
Hit by flak near Koningsfeld and bailed out too low.

**78th**: F/O George W. Morrison (82nd Ftr Sqn) POW
P-51K MX-D 44-11657
Suffered mechanical failure north of Saarbrucken.

**357th**: F/O Saul Sitzer (363rd Ftr Sqn) POW
P-51D B6- 44-14490
Hit by flak near Cologne.

*Remarks*
78th: Lt. Donald C. Hart (82nd Ftr Sqn) c/l Duxford; o.k.
P-51D WZ-S 44-15505
353rd: Capt. Ralph T. Allison (350th Ftr Sqn) c/l Antwerp; o.k.
P-51D LH-
357th: 12-6 locos, 0-25 railcars, 4-2 vehicles
479th: b/o Merville; o.k.
P-51

**January 3, 1945**
Groups Operating: P-51 4th, 20th, 55th, 78th, 339th, 353rd, 355th, 356th, 357th, 359th, 364th, 479th
Missions: Support of bombers hitting rail and communication targets in western Germany, plus PRU escorts.
Claims: 4-0-0 air
0-0 ground

| *Group* | | *Claims* | *Location* |
|---|---|---|---|
| **55th** | | | |
| 38th: | Lt. J.W. Kavanaugh | (1.5)Ar-196 dest(air) | SE Ulm |
| | Capt. J.F. Coonan | Ar-196 dest(air) | SE Ulm |
| | Lt. R.K. Jones | Ar-196 dest(air) | SE Ulm |
| | Lt. D.H. Courtney | (.5)Ar-196 dest(air) | SE Ulm |

*Losses-*

**20th**: F/O Charles E. Sheffield, Jr. (77th Ftr Sqn) KIA
P-51D LC-K 44-13748
Lost coolant and bailed out eighteen miles northwest of Ostend.

**55th**: Capt. John F. Coonan (38th Ftr Sqn) POW
P-51D CG-P 44-14358
Hit by flak near Gutenzell.

**353rd**: Maj. James N. Poindexter (352nd Ftr Sqn) KIA
P-51D SX-G 44-14589 "Honey IV"
Aborted with mechanical failure and crashed at Capel St. Mary.

**364th**: Lt. Charles E. Kearney (383rd Ftr Sqn) MIA
P-51D N2-N 44-13916
Suffered mechanical failure and bailed out northeast of Manston.

*Remarks*
78th: Lt. Jack D. Hodge (83rd Ftr Sqn) c/l; o.k.
P-51D HL-E 44-15499
339th: Lt. Vernon D. Carr (505th Ftr Sqn) c/l Fowlmere; o.k.
P-51 6N-
Lt. Waldon E. Howard (505th Ftr Sqn) c/l Fowlmere; o.k.
P-51 6N-
355th: Lt. George W. Schmidt (357th Ftr Sqn) b/o Charleville; o.k.
P-51D OS-
Capt. Grant A. Seeley (358th Ftr Sqn) c/l Steeple Morden; o.k.
P-51D YF-
479th: Lt. Jerome K. Nagel (434th Ftr Sqn) c/l Ipswich; o.k.
P-51D L2-F

**January 4, 1945**
KIAc's
361st: Lt. John R. Wilson (374th Ftr Sqn)
P-51D B7

Lt. Robert M. Zelinsky (374th Ftr Sqn)
P-51D B7-

**January 5, 1945**
Groups Operating: P-51 4th, 20th, 55th, 78th, 339th, 352nd, 353rd, 355th, 356th, 357th, 361st, 479th
Missions: Support of bombers to numerous rail targets and airfields in Germany, plus PRU escorts.
Claims: 1-0-0 air
4-0 ground

| *Group* | | *Claims* | *Location* |
|---|---|---|---|
| **357th** | | | |
| 364th: | Lt. T.H. Adams | (.5)FW-190 dest(air) | N/Hanau |
| | Lt. I.E. Snedeker | (.5)FW-190 dest(air) | N/Hanau |
| | Maj. R.A. Peterson | (2)Ju-88 dest(grd) | Altenstadt A/F |
| | | Me-109 dest(grd) | Altenstadt A/F |
| | Lt. B.K. Braley | Me-109 dest(grd) | Altenstadt A/F |

Losses: nil

*Remarks*
20th: Lt. Walter H. Skroback (55th Ftr Sqn) c/l Leiston; o.k.
P-51D KI-C 44-13794
Lt. Wallace E. Lowman (55th Ftr Sqn) c/l Kingscliffe; o.k.
P-51D KI-
55th: 11-3 locos, 0-23 railcars, 1-0 radar station

**January 6, 1945**
Groups Operating: P-51 4th, 20th, 55th, 353rd, 355th, 356th, 359th, 364th, 479th
P-47 56th
Missions: Support of bombers to Cologne, Coblenz, Bonn, and other rail and communication targets in Germany, a few PRU escorts, and the 56th flew a fighter-bomber operation in the Siegen area.
Claims: 0-0-0 air
14-0 ground

| *Group* | | *Claims* | *Location* |
|---|---|---|---|
| **55th** | | | |
| 338th: | LtCol. E.G. Righetti | (3)Ju-88 dest(grd) | Giebelstadt |
| | Lt. A.J. Ramm | (2)Ju-88 dest(grd) | Giebelstadt |
| | | (2)u/i a/c dest(grd) | Giebelstadt |
| | Lt. D.J. Meade | Ju-88 dest(grd) | Giebelstadt |
| | | u/i a/c dest(grd) | Giebelstadt |
| | Capt. B. McDowell | Ju-88 dest(grd) | Giebelstadt |
| | Capt. C.E. Buskirk | Ju-88 dest(grd) | Giebelstadt |
| | Lt. P. Brooks | Do-217 dest(grd) | Giebelstadt |
| | Lt. W.J. Konantz | Ju-88 dest(grd) | Giebelstadt |
| | Lt. R.D. Miller | Do-217 dest(grd) | Giebelstadt |

*Losses-*

**55th**: Capt. Clair E. Buskirk (338th Ftr Sqn) POW
P-51D CL- 44-14901
Hit by flak at Giebelstadt and bailed out near Schluchtern.

**78th**: F/O Gordon L. Weston (82nd Ftr Sqn) KIA
P-51K MX-L 44-11672
Hit a smokestack while flying in heavy fog on the way back to Duxford.

Capt. Wilbur K. Grimes (84th Ftr Sqn) MIA-E
P-51K WZ-F 44-11691
Hit by flak near Speyer and bailed out near Marche.

**359th**: Capt. Robert V. Beaupre (368th Ftr Sqn) KIA
P-51D CV-X 44-14509
Crashed on take-off from East Wretham.

*Remarks*
55th: 27-0 locos, 0-6 railcars, 1-12 vehicles
Lt. Albert J. Ramm (338th) c/l Wormingford; o.k.
P-51D CL-
78th: Capt. Ray E. Smith (84th Ftr Sqn) c/l; o.k.
P-51K WZ-B 44-11693
Lt. Thomas M. Reeves (84th Ftr Sqn) c/l; o.k.
P-51K WZ-W 44-11578
359th: Lt. John F. Collins (368th Ftr Sqn) c/l Merville; o.k.
P-51K CV- 44-11671

**January 7, 1945**
Groups Operating: P-51 4th, 20th, 55th, 78th, 339th, 353rd, 355th, 356th, 357th, 359th, 364th, 479th
P-47 56th
Missions: Support of bombers to rail and communication targets and bridges in Germany plus PRU escorts.
Claims: nil

*Losses-*

**55th**: F/O Frank R. Russell (38th Ftr Sqn) MIA
P-51D CG- 44-14274
Ran out of fuel and was last seen over Holland.

*Remarks*
55th: 11-0 locos, 0-54 railcars

**January 8, 1945**
Groups Operating: P-51 4th, 20th, 78th, 339th, 355th, 479th
Missions: Support of bombers to rail and communication targets and bridges in Germany plus PRU escorts.
Claims: nil
Losses: nil

**January 10, 1945**
Groups Operating: P-51 20th, 78th, 339th, 352nd, 353rd, 357th, 361st
P-47 56th
Missions: Support of bombers to rail and communication targets and airfields in Germany, plus PRU escorts.
Claims: 1-0-0 air
2-0 ground

| *Group* | | *Claims* | *Location* |
|---|---|---|---|
| **357th** | | | |
| 364th: | Lt. T.H. Adams | Me-109 dest(air) | Paderborn A/F |
| | | He-111 dest(grd) | Paderborn A/F |
| | Lt. F.C. McCall | He-111 dest(grd) | Paderborn A/F |

*Losses-*

**SF**: Lt. William J. Doherty (1st SF) MIA
P-51D 5E- 44-13283 "Caroline Ann"
Was last seen flying near Vielselm.

**357th**: Lt. Fred C. McCall (364th Ftr Sqn) KIA
P-51D C5-U 44-15026 "Cathy Mae"
Hit by flak near Paderborn.

*Remarks*
56th: F/O Walter J. Sharbo (62nd Ftr Sqn) c/l; o.k.
P-47D LM-
78th: Lt. William J. DeGain (84th Ftr Sqn) c/l; o.k.
P-51D WZ-H 44-15692
339th: Lt. Robert V.E. Blizzard (504th Ftr Sqn) c/l Chrisall Grange; o.k.
P-51B 5Q-O 42-106886 "Punkie"
353rd: Capt. Thomas J. Forkin (352nd Ftr Sqn) c/l; o.k.
P-51D SX-W 44-14486
357th: Lt. Roscoe R. Lepore (364th Ftr Sqn) c/l Leiston; o.k.
P-51D C5-C 44-11224 "Pretty Pat"
361st: 20-0 railcars

**January 13, 1945**
Groups Operating: P-51 4th, 55th, 78th, 339th, 352nd, 353rd, 355th, 356th, 357th, 359th, 361st, 479th
P-47 56th
Missions: Support of bombers to marshalling yards in Germany and Rhine bridges plus PRU escorts.
Claims: 3-0-0 air
3-1 ground

| *Group* | | *Claims* | *Location* |
|---|---|---|---|
| **55th** | | | |
| 338th: | LtCol. E.G. Righetti | Me-109 dest(air) | W/Wurzburg |
| | | Ju-88 dest(grd) | Giebelstadt A/F |
| | Lt. C.D. Henry | Me-109 dest(air) | W/Giebelstadt |
| | Lt. W.J. Konantz | Me-262 dest(air) | Giebelstadt A/F |
| | Lt. R.D. Miller | Me-262 dest(grd) | Giebelstadt A/F |
| | | Ju-88 dam(grd) | Giebelstadt A/F |
| | Lt. P. Brooks | (.5)Do-217 dest(grd) | Giebelstadt A/F |
| | Lt. F.R. Sharp | (.5)Do-217 dest(grd) | Giebelstadt A/F |

*Losses-*

**55th**: Lt. Philip Eastman, Jr. (338th Ftr Sqn) POW
P-51D CL- 44-63245
Hit by flak near Stettin.

**78th**: Lt. Herbert W. Elin (84th Ftr Sqn) KIA
P-51D WZ-C 44-63181
Spun-in near Bassingbourne in bad weather.

**353rd**: Lt. George S.H. Lee (350th Ftr Sqn) KIA
P-51D LH-
Crashed near Sudbury after take-off in bad weather.

**355th**: Lt. Thomas A. Ksanzak (358th Ftr Sqn) KIA
P-51D YF-O 44-13319
Spun-in near Melbourne after take-off in bad weather.

**356th**: Lt. Wendell J.A. Nelson (360th Ftr Sqn) KIA
P-51D PI-N 44-15305
Spun-in near Grundisburgh in bad weather.

**357th**: Lt. Robert L. Schliecker (362nd Ftr Sqn) KIA
P-51D G4-P 44-14245
Crashed east of Woodbridge upon returning from the mission.

**359th**: Capt. Karl K. Shearer (369th Ftr Sqn) KIA
P-51K IV-N 44-11686
Spun-in near Ashill upon return from the mission.

**479th**: Lt. Raymond E. King (436th Ftr Sqn) KIA
P-51D 9B-J 44-14754
Suffered mechanical failure and ditched off Clacton; was rescued but died from exposure.

*Remarks*
55th: 3-4 locos, 0-15 railcars
359th: Maj. Niven K. Cranfill (368th Ftr Sqn) c/l; o.k.
P-51D CV-
361st: 0-36 railcars, 3-4 vehicles, 0-1 building

KIAc's
357th: Lt. Richard A. Anderson (362nd Ftr Sqn)
P-51B G4-Z 43-6987
Died in a crash near Horham.

**January 14, 1945**
Groups Operating: P-51 4th, 20th, 55th, 78th, 339th, 352nd, 353rd, 355th, 356th, 357th, 359th, 361st, 364th, 479th
P-47 56th
Missions: Support for bombers to oil targets in central Germany and bridges near Cologne.
Claims: 157.5-6-25 air
3-5 ground

| *Group* | | *Claims* | *Location* |
|---|---|---|---|
| **20th** | | | |
| 55th: | Maj. R.P. Gatterdam | (2)FW-190 dest(air) | Perleberg |
| | Lt. H.L. Brown | (2)Me-109 dest(air) | Perleberg |
| | Lt. J.D. Leon | (2)FW-190 dest(air) | Perleberg |
| | Lt. J.K. Brown | (2)FW-190 dest(air) | Perleberg |
| | Lt. S.A. Baker | (1.5)FW-190 dest(air) | Perleberg |
| | | (shared with an unknown pilot) | |
| | Lt. S.G. Stitzer | FW-190 dest(air) | Perleberg |
| | Lt. R.W. Fruechtenicht | FW-190 dam(air) | Perleberg |
| | Lt. K.D. McNeel | Me-262 dam(air) | Perleberg |
| 77th: | Capt. C.H. Cole | Me-109 dest(air) | Perleberg |
| | Lt. R.D. Jones | FW-190 dest(air) | Perleberg |
| | Capt. M.J. Gilbertson | (.5)Me-109 dest(air) | Perleberg |
| | Lt. J.P. Starke | (.5)Me-109 dest(air) | Perleberg |
| | Lt. D.W. Van Sickle | Me-109 prob(air) | Perleberg |
| 79th: | Maj. M.B. Nichols | Me-109 dest(air) | Perleberg |
| | Lt. R.H. Black | Me-109 dest(air) | E/Wittenburg |
| | | Me-109 dam(air) | E/Wittenburg |
| | Lt. D.N. Jones | Me-109 dest(air) | E/Wittenberg |
| | Lt. D.F. Kelso | Me-109 dest(air) | E/Wittenberg |
| | | Me-109 dam(air) | E/Wittenberg |
| | Lt. D.A. Beschen | Me-109 dest(air) | E/Wittenberg |
| | F/O A.L. Shaffer | Me-109 dest(air) | NW Berlin |
| | Lt. R.M. Scott | Me-109 dam(air) | E/Wittenburg |
| **55th** | | | |
| 38th: | Capt. D.M. Cummings | Me-109 dest(air) | E/Wittenburg |
| | Capt. M. Clark | FW-190 dam(air) | NW Osnabruck |
| | Lt. H.B. Mooers | FW-190 dam(air) | NW Osnabruck |

| | | | |
|---|---|---|---|
| 338th: | Capt. D.S. Cramer | Me-262 dam(air) | Parchim A/F |
| | | Me-110 dam(grd) | SE Salzwedel |
| | Lt. J.R. McDonald | Me-262 dest(grd) | Parchim A/F |
| | Lt. F.R. Sharp | Me-110 dest(grd) | SE Salzwedel |
| | Lt. H. Bodiford | Do-217 dam(grd) | SE Salzwedel |
| 343rd: | Lt. B.J. Liles | FW-190 dest(air) | W/Salzwedel |

**56th**

| | | | |
|---|---|---|---|
| 61st: | Lt. R.S. Kyler | Me-109 dest(air) | E/Rheine |
| | Lt. R.E. Walker | Me-109 dest(air) | E/Rheine |
| 62nd: | Capt. F.D. Williamson | (4)Me-109 dest(air) | N/Burg |
| | | FW-190 dest(air) | N/Burg |
| | Maj. M.J. Jackson | Me-109 dest(air) | Rheine |
| | | FW-190 dest(air) | Rheine |
| | Lt. D. Henley | (1.5)Me-109 dest(air) | Magdeburg |
| | Lt. H.O. Womack | (.5)Me-109 dest(air) | Magdeburg |
| | Lt. K.L. Smith | Me-109 dest(air) | Rheine |
| | Lt. W.C. Daley | Me-109 dest(air) | Rheine |
| | Lt. F.R. Aheron | Me-109 prob(air) | Magdeburg |
| 63rd: | Lt. C.T. McBath | (2)Me-109 dest(air) | Munster |
| | Maj. P.A. Conger | Me-109 dest(air) | Stendal |
| | | Me-109 dam(air) | Stendal |
| | Lt. R.R. Davis | Me-109 dest(air) | Munster |
| | Lt. C.R. Rotzler | Me-109 dest(air) | Munster |
| | Lt. P.B. Trumble | Me-109 dest(air) | Stendal |
| | | Me-109 prob(air) | Stendal |

**66th(FW)**

| | | | |
|---|---|---|---|
| HdQts: | LtCol. W.C. Clark | FW-190 dest(air) | S/Schwerin |
| | (was flying with the 357th Ftr Grp) | | |

**78th**

| | | | |
|---|---|---|---|
| 82nd: | Lt. W. Warren | (2)FW-190 dest(air) | Cologne |
| | Lt. R.E. Smith | FW-190 dest(air) | Cologne |
| | Capt. J.I. Brown | Me-109 dam(air) | Cologne |
| | Lt. R.J. Blossom | FW-190 dam(air) | Cologne |
| 83rd: | Capt. P.A. Caulfield | FW-190 dest(air) | N/Diephals |
| 84th: | Lt. W.H. Lutz | Me-109 dest(air) | SW Cologne |
| | | FW-190 dest(air) | SW Cologne |
| | | (2)FW-190 dam(air) | SW Cologne |
| | Lt. R.H. Spooner | Me-109 dest(air) | SW Cologne |
| | | FW-190 dest(air) | SW Cologne |
| | Maj. L.P. Marshall | Me-109 dest(air) | S/Cologne |
| | Lt. W.J. DeGain | Me-109 dest(air) | E/Cologne |
| | Lt. C.R. Hereford | Me-109 dest(air) | SW Cologne |
| | Lt. F.E. Oiler | FW-190 dest(air) | Cologne |
| | | Me-109 dam(air) | Cologne |
| | Lt. E.L. Stier | Me-109 dest(air) | SW Cologne |
| | | Me-109 dam(air) | SW Cologne |
| | Lt. M.T. Wilson | Me-109 dest(air) | SE Cologne |

**352nd**

| | | | |
|---|---|---|---|
| 486th: | Lt. W.H. Reese | (2)FW-190 dest(air) | Almello |
| | Lt. F.O. Bostrom | FW-190 dest(air) | Almello |
| | Lt. E.L. Mundell | FW-190 dest(air) | Almello |
| | Lt. G.G. Contos | (.5)FW-190 dest(air) | Almello |
| | | (.5)FW-190 dest(air) | Almello |
| | | (one was shared with an unknown pilot) | |
| | Lt. J.D. Stearns | (.5)FW-190 dest(air) | Almello |

**353rd**

| | | | |
|---|---|---|---|
| 351st: | Lt. J.F. Hinchey | (2)FW-190 dest(air) | NE Hanover |
| | | Me-109 dest(air) | NE Hanover |
| | Lt. H.P. Maree | Me-109 dest(air) | SE Hamburg |
| | | FW-190 dest(air) | SE Hamburg |
| | Lt. J.E. Frye | Me-109 dest(air) | NE Hanover |
| | Lt. B.J. Murray | Me-262 dest(air) | Wittenburg |
| | Lt. J.W. Rohrs | (.5)Me-262 dest(air) | E/Wittenburg |
| | Lt. G.J. Rosen | (.5)Me-262 dest(air) | E/Wittenburg |
| | Lt. M.A. Arnold | (.5)Me-262 dam(air) | E/Hanover |
| | Lt. G.E. Markham | (.5)Me-262 dam(air) | E/Hanover |
| 352nd: | Lt. A.C. Cundy | FW-190 dest(air) | SW Dummer Lake |
| | Lt. J.R. Evans | (.5)u/i a/c dam(grd) | Brandenburg-Briest |
| | | (.5)u/i a/c dam(grd) | Brandenburg-Briest |
| | F/O R.C. Hassell | (.5)u/i a/c dam(grd) | Brandenburg-Briest |
| | | (.5)u/i a/c dam(grd) | Brandenburg-Briest |

**355th**

| | | | |
|---|---|---|---|
| 354th: | Lt. N.F. Mills | (2)Me-109 dest(air) | E/Meppen |
| | | FW-190 dest(air) | E/Meppen |
| | Maj. G.M. Graham | (2)FW-190 dest(air) | E/Meppen |
| | | FW-190 dam(air) | E/Meppen |
| | Lt. G.A. Kemper | (2)FW-190 dest(air) | E/Meppen & SW Dummer Lake |
| | Lt. C.E. Decklar | Me-109 dest(air) | E/Meppen |
| | | FW-190 dest(air) | E/Meppen |
| | Lt. T.L. Wood | Me-109 dest(air) | E/Meppen |
| 357th: | Maj. J.L. Elder | Me-109 dest(air) | Munster |

**356th**

| | | | |
|---|---|---|---|
| 360th: | Lt. R.E. Barnhart | FW-190 dest(air) | S/Osnabruck |
| | Lt. T.J. Urban | FW-190 dest(air) | S/Osnabruck |
| 361st: | Lt. C.T. Ashby | (2.5)FW-190 dest(air) | SW Dummer Lake |
| | Lt. W.M. Baskin | (1.5)FW-190 dest(air) | SW Dummer Lake |
| | Lt. C.D. Burdick | (2)FW-190 dest(air) | SW Dummer Lake |
| | | (2)FW-190 dam(air) | SW Dummer Lake |
| | Lt. F.F. Hooker | (2)FW-190 dest(air) | SW Dummer Lake |
| | | Me-262 dam(grd) | Hesepe |
| | Maj. D.J. Strait | FW-190 dest(air) | SW Dummer Lake |
| | Lt. M.W. Baylor | FW-190 dest(air) | SW Dummer Lake |
| | | FW-190 dam(air) | SW Dummer Lake |
| | Lt. W.C. Jarvis | FW-190 dest(air) | SW Dummer Lake |
| | Lt. J.A. Bowers | FW-190 dam(air) | SW Dummer Lake |
| | Lt. R.N. Whitson | FW-190 dam(air) | SW Dummer Lake |

**357th**

| | | | |
|---|---|---|---|
| HdQts: | LtCol. A.J. Evans | (2)FW-190 dest(air) | NW Brandenburg |
| | | (2)Me-109 dest(air) | NW Brandenburg |
| | Capt. R.W. Foy | (2)FW-190 dest(air) | NW Berlin |
| | | FW-190 dest(grd) | Berlin |
| | LtCol. I.H. Dregne | Me-109 dest(air) | NW Brandenburg |
| | | FW-190 dam(air) | NW Brandenburg |
| 362nd: | Lt. J.A. Kirla | (2)FW-190 dest(air) | NW Berlin |
| | | (2)Me-109 dest(air) | NW Berlin |
| | Capt. L.K. Carson | (2)FW-190 dest(air) | NW Berlin |
| | | Me-109 dest(air) | NW Berlin |
| | Lt. J.L. Sublett | (2)Me-109 dest(air) | NW Berlin |
| | Lt. J.F. Duncan | (2)FW-190 dest(air) | NW Berlin |
| | Lt. C.F. Weaver | Me-109 dest(air) | NW Berlin |
| | | FW-190 dest(air) | NW Berlin |
| | Maj. J.E. Broadhead | Me-109 dest(air) | NW Berlin |
| | Maj. J.B. England | Me-109 dest(air) | NW Berlin |
| | Lt. D.W. Chhever | FW-190 dest(air) | NW Berlin |
| | Lt. J.R. Frey | Me-109 dest(air) | NW Berlin |
| | Lt. J.A. Gasser | FW-190 dest(air) | NW Berlin |
| | Lt. H.A. Wyatt | FW-190 dest(air) | NW Berlin |
| 363rd: | Lt. J.R. Stern | (3)Me-109 dest(air) | N/Brandenburg |
| | Capt. J.W. Browning | Me-109 dest(air) | N/Brandenburg |
| | | (2)Me-109 prob(air) | N/Brandenburg |
| | | Me-109 dam(air) | N/Brandenburg |
| | Lt. W.R. Dunlop | Me-109 dest(air) | N/Brandenburg |
| | Lt. G.J. Rice | Me-109 dest(air) | N/Brandenburg |
| | Lt. J.R. Sloan | Me-109 dest(air) | N/Brandenburg |
| | Lt. J.E. Taylor | Me-109 dest(air) | N/Brandenburg |
| | Lt. R.E. Wolfe | Me-109 dest(air) | N/Brandenburg |
| | | Me-109 dam(air) | N/Brandenburg |
| | Lt. J.T. Windham | (.5)Me-109 dest(air) | N/Brandenburg |
| | Lt. G.A. Zarnke | (.5)Me-109 dest(air) | N/Brandenburg |
| 364th: | Capt. C.K. Maxwell | (3)FW-190 dest(air) | W/Berlin |
| | Maj. J.A. Storch | (2)FW-190 dest(air) | S/Schwerin |
| | | Me-109 dest(air) | S/Schwerin |
| | Lt. R.M. Bank | (3)FW-190 dest(air) | S/Schwerin |
| | Lt. R.P. Winks | (2)FW-190 dest(air) | SW Ludwigslust |
| | | (.5)Me-109 dest(air) | SW Ludwigslust |
| | | (shared with an unknown pilot) | |
| | Capt. T.H. Adams | (2)FW-190 dest(air) | Ludwigslust |
| | Lt. P.R. Hatala | (2)FW-190 dest(air) | W/Berlin |
| | Lt. E.W. Johnson | FW-190 dest(air) | NE Berlin |
| | Lt. D.E. Karger | Me-109 dest(air) | NW Berlin |
| | Lt. I.E. Snedeker | FW-190 dest(air) | NW Berlin |
| | Lt. D.R. Williams | FW-190 dest(air) | W/Berlin |
| | Lt. V.V. Zettler | FW-190 dam(air) | W/Berlin |

**359th**

| | | | |
|---|---|---|---|
| 370th: | Capt. R.S. Wetmore | (4.5)FW-190 dest(air) | Vorden A/F |
| | Capt. G.A. Doersch | (2)FW-190 dest(air) | Vorden A/F |
| | Lt. W.J. Rueschenberg | (.5)FW-190 dest(air) | Vorden A/F |

**479th**

| | | | |
|---|---|---|---|
| 435th: | Maj. H.H. Jordan | Me-109 dest(air) | NW Wesel |

*Losses-*

**55th:** Lt. John E. Kester (338th Ftr Sqn) KIA
P-51D CL-N 44-15045 "Sunday Morning"
Hit by flak near Parchim.

**56th:** Lt. Jack D. Hedke (61st Ftr Sqn) KIA
P-47D HV-
Damaged by a FW-190 and crashed twenty-five miles off Clacton.

Lt. James S. Wither (62nd Ftr Sqn) KIA
P-47D LM- 44-19964
Hit by a FW-190 near Burg.

**339th:** Lt. Lawrence J. Powell, Jr. (505th Ftr Sqn) POW
P-51D 6N- 44-14731 "St. Louis Blues"
Hit wires while strafing and bailed out near Ibbenburen.

**356th**: Lt. Freeman F. Hooker (361st Ftr Sqn) POW
P-51K QI-Y 44-11329
Hit by flak at Hesepe Airfield and bellied-in near the field.

**357th**: Lt. George A. Behling (362nd Ftr Sqn) POW
P-51D G4-J 44-15527 "Chi-Lassie"
Engine quit while being chased by a FW-190 northwest of Brandenburg.

Lt. William R. Dunlop, Jr. (363rd Ftr Sqn) POW
P-51D B6- 44-15370
Hit by enemy fighters northwest of Brandenburg.

Lt. James R. Sloan (363rd Ftr Sqn) POW
P-51D B6-Q 44-14784 "Q-Pee"
Hit by a Me-109 northwest of Brandenburg.

**359th**: Lt. Jack E. McCoskey (370th Ftr Sqn) POW
P-51D CS-X 44-15543 "Lydia May"
Overshot a FW-190 and crashed near Vorden Airfield.

*Remarks*
20th: 1-1 loco
55th: 34-0 locos, 3-14 railcars, 0-1 vehicle, 1-0 flak position
78th: Lt. Louis R. Hereford (84th Ftr Sqn) c/l Merville; o.k.
P-51K WZ-O 44-11666
Lt. Willis H. Lutz (84th Ftr Sqn) b/o Hauset; o.k.
P-51D WZ-T 44-63174
339th: Lt. Leonard A. Kunz (504th Ftr Sqn) c/l Arrington; o.k.
P-51 5Q-
353rd: 7-2 locos, 0-20 railcars, 0-3 barges
355th: 2-2 locos
357th: Capt. Chester K. Maxwell (364th Ftr Sqn) c/l Antwerp; o.k.
P-51D C5-
364th: Lt. Jackie D. Woodside (383rd Ftr Sqn) c/l; o.k.
P-51D N2- 44-14013

**January 15, 1945**
Groups Operating: P-51 4th, 20th, 55th, 78th, 339th, 353rd, 355th, 356th, 357th, 359th, 361st, 364th, 479th
P-47 56th
Missions: Support of bombers to marshalling yards in Germany, some fighter-bomber operations, and PRU escorts.
Claims: 2-0-0 air
11-12 ground

| *Group* | | *Claims* | *Location* |
|---|---|---|---|
| **55th** | | | |
| 38th: | Lt. B. Clemmons | (.5)Ju-188 dest(air) | SW Stuttgart |
| | Lt. D.H. Courtney | (.5)Ju-188 dest(air) | SW Stuttgart |
| **355th** | | | |
| 354th: | Maj. G.M. Graham | Ju-188 dest(grd) | Kotha |
| | | (2)u/i a/c dam(grd) | Oberpfaffenhofen |
| | Capt. N.J. Fortier | Ju-52 dest(grd) | Oberpfaffenhofen |
| | | Ju-52 dam(grd) | Oberpfaffenhofen |
| | F/O H.W. Falvey | FW-190 dest(grd) | Landsberg |
| | | u/i a/c dest(grd) | Landsberg |
| | | u/i a/c dam(grd) | Landsberg |
| 357th: | Lt. R.W. Delhamer | (2)Me-110 dest(grd) | Landsberg |
| | | u/i a/c dest(grd) | Landsberg |
| | Maj. J.H. Wilson | u/i a/c dest(grd) | Landsberg |
| | Lt. J.V. Cavender | (2)Me-110 dam(grd) | Landsberg |
| | Lt. R.L. Garlich | u/i a/c dam(grd) | Landsberg |
| | Lt. J.E. Lake | u/i a/c dam(grd) | Landsberg |
| 358th: | Lt. R. Allen | Me-110 dest(grd) | Landsberg |
| | Lt. R.J. Fussell | u/i a/c dest(grd) | Landsberg |
| | | (2)u/i a/c dam(grd) | Landsberg |
| | Lt. V.E. Gore | u/i a/c dest(grd) | Landsberg |
| | | (2)u/i a/c dam(grd) | Landsberg |
| **357th** | | | |
| 364th: | Lt. R.P. Winks | Me-262 dest(air) | Shongau |

*Losses-*

**SF**: Lt. William W. Patton, Jr. (3rd SF) MIA
P-51D CL- 44-15331
Lost for unknown reasons.

**78th**: Lt. Richard H. Spooner (84th Ftr Sqn) POW
P-51D WZ-I 44-15720
Hit by flak east of Bruchstadt.

*Remarks*
55th: 45-0 locos, 15-54 railcars, 3-0 vehicles
78th: Lt. Richard W. Taylor (84th Ftr Sqn) c/l Fowlmere; o.k.
P-51K WZ-L 44-11747
355th: 2-1 locos, 0-6 railcars
361st: 2-10 railcars, 0-2 barges
364th: 384th Ftr Sqn P-51 c/l; o.k.
P-51K 5Y-P 44-11567 "Dana Kay"

**January 16, 1945**
Groups Operating: P-51 4th, 55th, 339th, 352nd, 353rd, 355th, 356th, 357th, 359th, 361st, 364th, 479th
P-47 56th
Missions: Due to weather conditions, most bombers were recalled or hit targets of opportunity; the fighters gave general cover.
Claims: 0-0-0 air
33-3 ground

| *Group* | | *Claims* | *Location* |
|---|---|---|---|
| **4th** | | | |
| 334th: | Lt. J.W. Ayers | (.5)He-177 dest(grd) | Neuburg |
| | Lt. M.J. Kennedy | (.5)He-177 dest(grd) | Neuburg |
| | Lt. C.F. Brown | (.5)Me-262 dest(grd) | Neuburg |
| | Lt. J.E. Jahnke | (.5)Me-262 dest(grd) | Neuburg |
| 336th: | Capt. J.H. Joiner | (4)FW-190 dest(grd) | Neuhausen |
| | Lt. V.E. Chandler | (2)FW-190 dest(grd) | Neuhausen |
| | | (2)Ju-52 dest(grd) | Neuhausen |
| | Maj. F.W. Glover | (2)Ju-87 dest(grd) | Neuhausen |
| | | FW-190 dest(grd) | Neuhausen |
| | Lt. R.J. Corbett | (2)Ju-87 dest(grd) | Neuhausen |
| | | FW-190 dest(grd) | Neuhausen |
| | Capt. C.R. Alfred | (2)FW-190 dest(grd) | Neuhausen |
| | Lt. H.N. Hagen | FW-190 dest(grd) | Neuhausen |
| | | He-177 dest(grd) | Neuhausen |
| | Lt. G.L. Kesler | FW-190 dest(grd) | Neuhausen |
| | | He-177 dest(grd) | Neuhausen |
| | Lt. T.A. McCord | FW-190 dest(grd) | Neuhausen |
| | | Ju-87 dest(grd) | Neuhausen |
| | Capt. L.A. Carpenter | FW-190 dest(grd) | Neuhausen |
| | Lt. D.N. Groshong | FW-190 dest(grd) | Neuhausen |
| | Lt. H.A. Kaul | FW-190 dest(grd) | Neuhausen |
| | Lt. W.D. Riedel | FW-190 dest(grd) | Neuhausen |
| | Lt. A.O. Wallace | FW-190 dest(grd) | Neuhausen |
| **353rd** | | | |
| 352nd: | Capt. G.G. Callans | Me-163 dest(grd) | Deiningen |
| | | Ju-88 dam(grd) | Deiningen |
| | Lt. L.W. Grove | FW-190 dest(grd) | Deiningen |
| | | Ju-88 dam(grd) | Deiningen |
| | Lt. H.R. Lammie | Ju-88 dam(grd) | Deiningen |

*Losses-*

**4th**: Lt. Victor R.T. Rentschler (334th Ftr Sqn) POW
P-51D QP-M 44-15324
Hit by flak at Neuburg and bailed out near Reutlingen.

Lt. Fred D. Hall (336th Ftr Sqn) KIA
P-51D VF- 44-14533
Crashed at Folkstone upon return from the mission.

**356th**: Lt. Vance C. Harney (359th Ftr Sqn) KIA
P-51D OC- 44-15528
Suffered mechanical failure and crashed near Biggleswade.

**357th**: Lt. William B. Thompson (363rd Ftr Sqn) KIA
P-51D B6- 44-63220
Crashed near Framlingham after take-off.

**359th**: Lt. Graham Lupton (368th Ftr Sqn) KIA
P-51B CV-M 42-106693
Suffered mechanical failure near Amersfoort.

Lt. Douglas A. Maclean (368th Ftr Sqn) KIA
P-51D CV-Y 44-63776
Crashed on take-off from East Wretham.

*Remarks*
4th: Lt. Thomas R. Bell (334th Ftr Sqn) c/l Laon; o.k.
P-51D QP-S
55th: 12-0 locos, 2-50 railcars, 7-0 vehicles
56th: Lt. John A. Arnold (63rd Ftr Sqn) b/o Clacton; o.k.
P-47D UN-
Lt. Walter R. Groce (63rd Ftr Sqn) b/o Boxted; o.k.
P-47D UN-
339th: Lt. Lorne W. Allers (504th Ftr Sqn) c/l St. Trond; o.k.
P-51 5Q-
353rd: Capt. Glenn G. Callans (352nd Ftr Sqn) b/o ; o.k.
P-51D SX-V
Capt. William J. Maguire (351st Ftr Sqn) b/o Strasbourg; o.k.
P-51D YJ-
355th: Lt. James V. Cavender (357th Ftr Sqn) b/o; o.k.
P-51D OS-
Lt. Sam Sitton (357th Ftr Sqn) b/o; o.k.
P-51D OS-

Maj. William J. Hovde (358th Ftr Sqn) c/l; o.k.
P-51D YF-I "Ole IV"
356th: Lt. Vincent S. Ray (361st Ftr Sqn) c/l Continent; o.k.
P-51D QI-I 44-15101
359th: F/O Boyd N. Adkins (368th Ftr Sqn) c/l Merville, o.k.
P-51D CV-

**January 17, 1945**
Groups Operating: P-51 4th, 20th, 78th, 339th, 353rd, 355th, 356th, 357th, 364th, 479th
P-47 56th
Missions: Support of bombers to Hamburg, Harburg, and Paderborn.
Claims: nil

*Losses-*

**SF**: Lt. William E. Hornickel (2nd SF) MIA
P-51D YF-W 44-14581
Suffered mechanical failure and crashed near Wangerooge.

**4th**: Lt. Robert L. Stallings (335th Ftr Sqn) KIA
P-51K WD-J 44-11339
Suffered mechanical failure near Den Helder and crashed off Lowestoft.

**20th**: Lt. Eugene L. Planchak (55th Ftr Sqn) POW
P-51D KI-K 44-15591 "Dragon Wagon IV"
Hit by flak north of Munster and bailed out north of Dusseldorf.

**78th**: Lt. Gerald F. Boner (83rd Ftr Sqn) KIA
P-51D HL-G 44-15506 "Miss Debbie"
Suffered mechanical failure and bailed out east of Great Yarmouth.

Lt. Allen R. Packer (84th Ftr Sqn) POW
P-51D WZ-J 44-63188
Hit by flak and bailed out northwest of Hamburg.

**339th**: Capt. Richard B. Olander (505th Ftr Sqn) KIA
P-51D 6N-C 44-15616 "Pauline"
Hit by flak near Gladbeck.

Lt. Walden E. Howard (505th Ftr Sqn) KIA
P-51B 6N- 42-106676 "Princess Marie"
Hit by flak and crashed near Stadthagen.

**356th**: Lt. Robert E. Carr (359th Ftr Sqn) KIA
P-51D OC-M 44-15331 "Junie"
Crashed on take-off from Beauvais/Tille Airfield.

*Remarks*
4th: Lt. Harry N. Hagen (336th Ftr Sqn) b/o Folkstone; o.k.
P-51D VF-Y 44-14317 "Duke"
20th: 3-0 locos, 0-8 railcars, 0-5 switch-towers, 0-1 building
78th: P-51 c/l; o.k.
355th: 11-0 locos, 43-0 railcars

**January 18, 1945**
Groups Operating: P-51 55th, 353rd, 355th, 356th
Missions: Support of bombers to Kaiserlautern.
Claims: nil

*Losses-*

**55th**: Lt. John E. Finlayson (38th Ftr Sqn) MIA
P-51D CG-A 44-14580 "Ellie, My Little Six"
Crashed into the Channel due to bad weather.

**353rd**: Lt. Anthony R. Rosatone (352nd Ftr Sqn) KIA
P-51D SX-U 44-15587 "Stasia II"
Suffered mechanical failure and was last seen south of Brussels.

**356th**: Lt. Chester W. Lawrence (359th Ftr Sqn) KIA
P-51D OC- 44-63268 "Little Mary"
Took off from Laon/Couvron and spun-in off Felixstowe.

*Remarks*
55th: 6-5 locos

**January 19, 1945**
KIAc's
357th: Lt. Herman H. Delager (362nd Ftr Sqn) Vanished while on a ferry flight from Stamstead.
P-51D G4-T 44-63658

Lt. Morris E. Gallant (364th Ftr Sqn) Crashed in bad weather while on a local test flight.
P-51B C5-G 42-106721 "Seregent"

**January 20, 1945**
Groups Operating: P-51 4th, 78th, 339th, 353rd, 355th, 357th, 359th, 364th
Missions: Support of bombers to Mannheim, Heilbronn, Rheine, and Sterkrade.
Claims: 2-0-0 air
0-0 ground

| Group | | Claims | Location |
|---|---|---|---|
| **357th** | | | |
| 364th: | Lt. D.E. Karger | Me-262 dest(air) | N/Munich |
| | Lt. R.R. Wright | Me-262 dest(air) | Lechfeld A/F |

*Losses-*

**78th**: Lt. Kenneth J. DeMaagd (84th Ftr Sqn) POW
P-51K WZ-J 44-11682
Suffered mechanical failure and bellied-in near Wesel.

**355th**: Lt. Frank R. Masters (358th Ftr Sqn) POW
P-51D YF-V 44-63162
Hit by flak and bellied-in near Minden.

**357th**: Lt. Edward R. Haydon (364th Ftr Sqn) POW
P-51D C5-J 44-11165 "Lady Nelda"
Hit by flak at Lechfeld and bailed out near Kaufburen.

*Remarks*
355th: 4-0 locos, 12-28 railcars, 0-1 barge
357th: 1-0 loco, 0-10 railcars, 1-0 vehicle

KIAc's
78th: F/O William E. Bradley (83rd Ftr Sqn)
P-51K HL- 44-11679
Spun-out and crashed near Isle of Grange.

**January 21, 1945**
Groups Operating: P-51 4th, 20th, 55th, 78th, 339th, 352nd, 355th, 356th, 357th, 479th
P-47 56th
Missions: Support of bombers to Aschaffenburg, Mannheim, and Heilbronn, plus PRU escorts.
Claims: 0-0-0 air
6-3 ground

| Group | | Claims | Location |
|---|---|---|---|
| **55th** | | | |
| 38th: | Lt. M.O. Anderson | (.5)u/i a/c dest(grd)* | Stuttgart-Boblingen |
| | Lt. A.E. Carr | (.5)u/i a/c dest(grd)* | Stuttgart-Boblingen |
| | Lt. B. Clemmons | (.5)u/i a/c dest(grd)** | Stuttgart-Boblingen |
| | F/O W.V. Totten | (.5)u/i a/c dest(grd)** | Stuttgart-Boblingen |
| **56th** | | | |
| 62nd: | LtCol. L.C. Smith | Ju-88 dest(grd) | Thalheim |
| | | (.5)Ju-52 dest(grd) | Huntingen |
| | Lt. N.D. Gould | (.5)Ju-52 dest(grd) | Huntingen |
| **479th** | | | |
| 435th: | Lt. T.J. Sowerby | Ju-52 dest(grd) | Leipheim |
| | | Ju-88 dest(grd) | Leipheim |
| | Lt. N.R. Benoit | Me-262 dam(grd) | Leipheim |
| | | Ju-88 dam(grd) | Leipheim |
| | Lt. E.H. Sims | Ju-52 dam(grd) | Leipheim |

*Losses-*

**56th**: Lt. Robert S. Hall (63rd Ftr Sqn) KIA
P-47D UN-
Stopped while taking-off at Boxted and was rammed by another P-47.

*Remarks*
4th: 0-2 locos, 2-10 railcars, 1-1 vehicles, 0-1 building
56th: 0-1 loco, 0-20 railcars, 0-1 hangar, 0-1 gun position

KIAc's
56th: Lt. Max H. Dahl (62nd Ftr Sqn)
P-47D LM-
Collided with another P-47 and crashed near Romford.

**January 22, 1945**
Groups Operating: P-51 55th, 78th, 352nd, 361st
P-47 56th
Missions: The 56th supported bombers to Sterkrade while the P-51 units swept the Karlsruhe-Coblenz area.
Claims: 0-0-0 air
3-1 ground

| Group | | Claims | Location |
|---|---|---|---|
| **55th** | | | |
| 38th: | F/O W.V. Totten | (2)Ju-88 dest(grd) | Hanover-Langenhagen |
| | Lt. A.E. Carr | Ju-88 dest(grd) | Hanover-Langenhagen |
| | | Ju-88 dam(grd) | Hanover-Langenhagen |

*Losses-*

**361st**: Capt. Alton B. Snyder (375th Ftr Sqn) POW
P-51D E2-S 44-14803 "Snitz"
Hit by flak and bellied-in near Kenn.

*Remarks*
55th: 6-0 locos, 3-6 railcars, 3-0 vehicles
361st: 3-5 railcars, 0-12 vehicles, 0-1 horse-drawn vehicle

**January 23, 1945**
Groups Operating: P-51 352nd, 353rd, 355th, 356th
Missions: Support of bombers to Neuss.
Claims: 1-0-0 air
0-0 ground

| *Group* | | *Claims* | *Location* |
|---|---|---|---|
| **352nd** | | | |
| 486th: | Capt. L.J. Vitek | (.5)Me-109 dest(air) | SW Dusseldorf |
| | Lt. G.G. Contos | (.5)Me-109 dest(air) | SW Dusseldorf |

Losses: nil

*Remarks*
353rd: Lt. John M. Nickelbur (351st Ftr Sqn) c/l Antwerp; o.k.
P-51D YJ-N
355th: P-51 c/l Steeple Morden; o.k.

**January 24, 1945**
Groups Operating: P-51 352nd, 361st
Missions: Sweep of the Bonn-Cologne area.
Claims: 3-0-0 air
0-0 ground

| *Group* | | *Claims* | *Location* |
|---|---|---|---|
| **352nd** | | | |
| 328th: | Lt. C.E. Goodman | (.5)Me-109 dest(air) | Duren |
| | Lt. E.B. Dubay | (.5)Me-109 dest(air) | Duren |
| 487th: | Maj. W.T. Halton | Me-109 dest(air) | Cologne |
| | Lt. R.H. Littge | Me-109 dest(air) | Bonn |

*Losses-*

**352nd**: Maj. Earl L. Abbott (328th Ftr Sqn) KIA
P-51D PE-A 44-14710 "Flossie"
Hit by enemy aircraft near Aachen.

**January 25, 1945**
Groups Operating: P-51 352nd, 361st
Missions: Sweep of the Mannheim-Karlsruhe area.
Claims: 2-0-0 air
0-0 ground

| *Group* | | *Claims* | *Location* |
|---|---|---|---|
| **361st** | | | |
| 375th: | Lt. R.J. Farney | Me-109 dest(air) | SE Speyer |
| | Lt. P.A. Dougherty | (.5)Me-110 dest(air) | NE Mannheim |
| | F/O W.M. Hart | (.5)Me-110 dest(air) | NE Mannheim |

*Losses-*

**361st**: Lt. Robert G. Adams (375th Ftr Sqn) KIA
P-51D E2-V 44-14678 "Pat"
Hit by a Me-110 northeast of Mannheim and bailed out too low near Heppenheim.

**January 26, 1945**
Groups Operating: P-51 361st
Missions: Sweep of the battle front area.
Claims: nil
Losses: nil

**January 27, 1945**
KIAc's
357th: Lt. Walter E. Corby (362nd Ftr Sqn)
AT-6 42-84593
Crashed into a hillside near Swingate in bad weather.

**January 28, 1945**
Groups Operating: P-51 20th, 78th, 355th, 359th, 361st, 479th
Missions: Support for bombers to Cologne, Kaisertuhlm and Hohenburdberg.
Claims: nil
Losses: nil

**January 29, 1945**
Groups Operating: P-51 4th, 20th, 55th, 78th, 339th, 353rd, 355th, 356th, 357th, 359th, 361st, 364th, 479th
P-47 56th
Missions: Support of bombers to Kassel and various rail targets in Germany.
Claims: 4-0-1 air
0-3 ground

| *Group* | | *Claims* | *Location* |
|---|---|---|---|
| **55th** | | | |
| 338th: | Maj. D.S. Cramer | Me-109 dest(air) | Ulzen |
| | Lt. T. Kiernan | Me-109 dest(air) | NE Oldenburg |
| | Lt. W.J. Konantz | Me-109 dest(air) | NE Oldenburg |
| | Lt. R.D. Miller | Me-109 dest(air) | NE Oldenburg |
| | Capt. B. McDowell | Me-109 dam(air) | Ulzen |
| **56th** | | | |
| 63rd: | Capt. G.E. Bostwick | Me-410 dam(grd) | Berge A/F |
| **364th** | | | |
| 385th: | Capt. N.L. Box | u/i a/c dam(grd) | Darmstadt |
| | Lt. A.B. McCormick | u/i a/c dam(grd) | Darmstadt |

*Losses-*

**355th**: Lt. Scott P. Prothro (354th Ftr Sqn) POW
P-51D WR-B 44-15279 "Miss Miami"
Hit by flak near Geldern.

**359th**: Lt. Richard H. Daniels (368th Ftr Sqn) KIA
P-51D CV-
Strafed U.S. positions near Ingwiller; ignored warnings and was shot down by anti-aircraft units.

*Remarks*
55th: 2-1 locos, 0-30 railcars, 0-1 building
56th: 4-0 flak positions, 3-0 vehicles, 0-5 railcars, 0-9 buildings
353rd: P-51 c/l; o.k.
P-51D SX-G
357th: 0-1 loco, 0-1 radio installation
359th: 3-1 locos, 0-87 railcars, 6-2 vehicles, 0-3 barges
Lt. John M. Marr (368th Ftr Sqn) b/o St. Genis de Saintogne; inj.
P-51D CV-
Lt. Garland F. Madison (368th Ftr Sqn) b/o Exeter; o.k.
P-5C CV-Y 42-103197
364th: 2-5 locos, 0-34 railcars, 1-2 vehicles, 0-2 switch-houses

**January 31, 1945**
Groups Operating: P-51 78th, 355th, 364th
Missions: Support for bombers but all were recalled.
Claims: nil
Losses: nil

*Remarks*
78th: 4-0 locos, 4-0 vehicles, 0-2 buildings

**February 1, 1945**
Groups Operating: P-51 4th, 20th, 55th, 353rd, 357th, 359th, 479th
Missions: Support of bombers to Mannheim and Wesel (and other targets of opportunity) plus some groups swept.
Claims: nil
Losses: nil

*Remarks*
20th: Lt. Ted P. Hambelton (77th Ftr Sqn) b/o Luxembourg; o.k.
P-51D LC-G 44-13637
359th: 0-6 locos, 0-25 railcars

KIAc's
359th: Lt. Lawrence A. Ziska (370th Ftr Sqn)
P-51K CS-D 44-11355
Died in a crash near East Wretham.

364th: Lt. Edgar A. Knapp (384th Ftr Sqn)
P-51D 5Y-T 44-11233
Suffered mechanical failure at Admiralty Point Bombing Range and bailed out too low.

**February 2, 1945**
Groups Operating: P-51 352nd
Missions: Twenty-two pilots flew a sweep in the Coblenz area.
Claims: nil
Losses: nil

**February 3, 1945**
Groups Operating: P-51 4th, 20th, 55th, 78th, 339th, 352nd, 353rd, 355th, 356th, 357th, 359th, 361st, 364th, 479th
P-47 56th
Missions: Support of bombers to Berlin and Magdeburg, PRU escorts, and the 56th swept the Friedersdorf area.
Claims: 21-1-7 air
21-11 ground

| *Group* | | *Claims* | *Location* |
|---|---|---|---|
| **55th** | | | |
| HdQts: | LtCol. E.G. Righetti | (2)Ju-88 dest(air) | Boizenburg |
| | | FW-190 dest(air) | Boizenburg |
| | | Ju-88 prob(air) | Boizenburg |

| | | | |
|---|---|---|---|
| 38th: | Lt. D.M. Amoss | (1.5)FW-58 dest(air) | Templin A/F |
| | Lt. L.F. Spieker | (.5)FW-58 dest(air) | Templin A/F |
| | Lt. K.R. McGinnis | (4)Fi-156 dest(grd) | Templin A/F |
| 343rd: | Lt. B.H. Howes | (2)FW-190 dest(air) | Boizenburg |
| | | Ju-88 dest(air) | Boizenburg |
| | Lt. R.G. Gibbs | FW-190 dest(air) | Boizenburg |
| | | Ju-88 dest(air) | Boizenburg |
| | Capt. W.H. Lewis | Ju-88 dest(air) | Gartow |
| | Lt. P.L. Moore | Ju-88 dest(air) | Boizenburg |
| | Lt. B.J. Liles | He-111 dest(grd) | Stade A/F |
| | | He-111 dam(grd) | Stade A/F |
| | Lt. V.P. Krambo | He-111 dam(grd) | Stade A/F |
| **56th** | | | |
| 62nd: | Capt. F.D. Williamson | FW-190 dest(air) | Berlin |
| | | Me-109 dest(air) | Berlin |
| | | FW-190 dam(air) | Berlin |
| 63rd: | Maj. P.A. Conger | Me-109 dest(air) | Friedersdorf A/F |
| | | FW-190 dest(air) | Friedersdorf A/F |
| | | Me-109 dam(air) | Friedersdorf A/F |
| | Capt. C.M. Hart | (2)FW-190 dest(air) | Friedersdorf A/F |
| | Capt. J.C. Fahringer | Me-109 dest(air) | SE Berlin |
| | | (2)Me-109 dam(air) | SE Berlin |
| | | FW-190 dam(air) | SE Berlin |
| | Lt. P.G. Kuhn | FW-190 dest(air) | Friedersdorf A/F |
| | Lt. F.M. Ogden | FW-190 dest(air) | SE Berlin |
| | Lt. R.R. Davis | Me-109 dam(air) | SE Berlin |
| **78th** | | | |
| 84th: | Lt. L. DeAnda | (2)FW-200 dest(grd) | Luneburg A/F |
| | | Hs-126 dest(grd) | Luneburg A/F |
| | Lt. L.M. Grisham | (3)FW-190 dest(grd) | Luneburg A/F |
| | Lt. P.S. Ostrander | (2)FW-190 dest(grd) | Luneburg A/F |
| | | FW-190 dam(grd) | Luneburg A/F |
| | Lt. E.L. Stier | FW-190 dest(grd) | Luneburg A/F |
| | | Me-410 dest(grd) | Luneburg A/F |
| | Lt. F.E. Oiler | Me-410 dest(grd) | Luneburg A/F |
| | | Ju-88 dest(grd) | Luneburg A/F |
| | | Me-410 dam(grd) | Luneburg A/F |
| | Lt. J.S. Bond | FW-190 dest(grd) | Luneburg A/F |
| | | Me-410 dam(grd) | Luneburg A/F |
| | Lt. W.S. Blodgett | FW-190 dest(grd) | Luneburg A/F |
| | Lt. A.A. Garback | FW-190 dest(grd) | Luneburg A/F |
| | Lt. J.M. Farmer | Ju-87 dest(grd) | Luneburg A/F |
| | Capt. D. Ledington | (2)Me-410 dam(grd) | Luneburg A/F |
| | Lt. R.K. Corbett | (2)Ju-87 dam(grd) | Luneburg A/F |
| | Lt. J.E. Moores | FW-200 dam(grd) | Luneburg A/F |
| **355th** | | | |
| 357th: | Lt. S.S. Hardee | Ju-88 dam(grd) | Gardelegen |
| **364th** | | | |
| 383rd: | Lt. L.V. Andrew | Me-262 dam(air) | S/Gardelegen |

*Losses-*

**SF**: Lt. John J. Allen (1st) MIA
P-51D 5E-N 44-13686 "Rugged Rebel II"
Suffered mechanical failure near Hengelo.

**56th**: Lt. David M. Magel (63rd Ftr Sqn) KIA
P-47D UN- 44-19777
Hit by a FW-190 southeast of Berlin.

**78th**: Lt. William B. Senarens (83rd Ftr Sqn) POW
P-51D HL-T 44-15729 "Bill's Bus"
Hit by flak and bailed out near Wilhelmshaven.

Lt. Leon M. Grisham (84th Ftr Sqn) POW
P-51D WZ-M 44-63182
Hit by flak near Luneburg.

Lt. Warren J. Sawell (84th Ftr Sqn) POW
P-51D WZ-N 44-15746
Hit by flak near Luneburg.

**352nd**: Lt. Fred H. Powell (486th Ftr Sqn) POW
P-51D PZ-A 44-15124
Suffered mechanical failure near Geldern.

**353rd**: Maj. Leslie W. Seppala (HdQts) POW
P-51D SX-B 44-14303 "Double Trouble"
Hit by flak and bailed out near Hagenow.

**355th**: Lt. William A. Cummins (358th Ftr Sqn) KIA
P-51D YF-
Hit by flak and crashed into trees near Ulzen.

**357th**: Lt. George C. Kouris (364th Ftr Sqn) POW
P-51D C5-Z 44-13586 "Greece Lightning"
Suffered mechanical failure southwest of Brunswick.

*Remarks*
55th: 13-0 locos, 0-6 railcars
339th: 6-0 locos, 0-125 railcars, 20-30 vehicles
353rd: 14-0 locos, 0-6 railcars, 2-1 vehicles, 0-1 barge
F/O Bruce A. Eddy (350th Ftr Sqn) c/l; o.k.
P-51D LH-S
355th: 2-1 locos, 9-10 railcars
356th: 0-4 locos, 0-25 railcars, 1-0 vehicle, 1-1 buildings
Capt. Francis M. Russell (360th Ftr Sqn) c/l France; injured
P-51D PI-

**February 4, 1945**
KIAc's
4th: Lt. Alvin O. Wallace (336th Ftr Sqn)
P-51D VF- 44-15531
Spun-in near Great Sampford.

56th: Lt. Kenneth L. Smith (62nd Ftr Sqn)
P-47M LM-
Died in a crash near Tollesburg.

356th: Lt. Ralph E. Odenwald (359th Ftr Sqn)
P-51D OC- 44-15223
Crashed into Bradwell Bay while on a practice gunnery mission.

**February 5, 1945**
Groups Operating: P-51 20th, 78th
Missions: Seven pilots were to fly a PRU escort but the mission was recalled.
Claims: nil
Losses: nil

KIAc's

479th: Lt. Norbert W. Rock(435th Ftr Sqn)
P-51D J2-H 44-14840 "The Victory Queen"

**February 6, 1945**
Groups Operating: P-51 4th, 20th, 55th, 78th, 339th, 352nd, 353rd, 355th, 356th, 357th, 359th, 361st, 364th, 479th
P-47 56th
Missions: Support of bombers to Magdeburg and Chemnitz, plus PRU escorts.
Claims: 0-0-1 air
2-1 ground

| *Group* | | *Claims* | *Location* |
|---|---|---|---|
| **55th** | | | |
| 338th: | Capt. B. McDowell | Ju-88 dest(grd) | Gerolzhofen A/F |
| | Lt. R. Deloach | (.5)Me-410 dest(grd) | Gerolzhofen A/F |
| | Lt. H.B. Sims | (.5)Me-410 dest(grd) | Gerolzhofen A/F |
| | Lt. H. Bodiford | Me-110 dam(grd) | Gerolzhofen A/F |
| **364th** | | | |
| 384th: | Capt. J.M. Fowle | Ar-234 dam(air) | SE Zuider Zee |

*Losses-*

**4th**: F/O William D. Bates (334th Ftr Sqn) KIA
P-51D QP-V 44-13884
Suffered mechanical failure and bailed out fifty-five miles south of Southold.

Lt. Paul G. Santos (335th Ftr Sqn) KIA
P-51D WD-T 44-15615
Hit by flak near Torgau.

**55th**: Capt. Bert McDowell, Jr. (338th Ftr Sqn) POW
P-51K CL-V 44-11687 "Betty Mac"
Hit by flak at Gerolzhofen Airfield and bellied-in near Wertheim.

**339th**: Capt. Robert W. Bloxham (505th Ftr Sqn) KIA
P-51D 6N- 44-13379 "Miss Idaho"
Crashed into the Channel in bad weather.

Lt. Gerald W. Palmer (505th Ftr Sqn) KIA
P-51D 6N-
Crashed on the Isle of Wight during bad weather.

Lt. Kessler O. Thomas (505th Ftr Sqn) KIA
P-51D 6N-
Crashed at Nuthampstead in bad weather.

*Remarks*
4th: 0-13 locos, 15-0 railcars, 0-11 vehicles
55th: 14-1 locos, 37-17 railcars, 1-0 vehicle, 0-1 flak tower, 0-1 building
Lt. John W. Cunnick (38th Ftr Sqn) c/l France; o.k.
P-51D CG-
Lt. Richard G. Gibbs (343rd Ftr Sqn) c/l NE Toul; o.k.
P-51K CY-I 44-11676
78th: Maj. William H. Julian (83rd Ftr Sqn) b/o Earls Colne; o.k.
P-51D HL-D 44-63271
356th: 4-2 locos, 1-11 railcars, 2-2 vehicles

364th: F/O Curtis L. Smart (385th Ftr Sqn) b/o Ford; o.k.
P-51D 5E- 44-13835

**February 7, 1945**

KIAc's

359th: Lt. Henry L. Thompson (368th Ftr Sqn)
P-51B CV-O 42-106809
Crashed into the North Sea after suffering mechanical failure.

**February 8, 1945**

Groups Operating: P-51 20th, 55th, 78th, 352nd, 361st, 479th

Missions: The 352nd and 361st flew patrols over the battle area while one flight from each of the other four groups flew PRU escorts.

Claims: 1-0-0 air
0-0 ground

| *Group* | | *Claims* | *Location* |
|---|---|---|---|
| **361st** | | | |
| 376th: | Lt. R. Hobbs | (.5)He-111 dest(air) | Erfurt |
| | Lt. R.W. Wood | (.5)He-111 dest(air) | Erfurt |

Losses: nil

*Remarks*

361st: 0-1 loco

**February 9, 1945**

Groups Operating: P-51 4th, 20th, 55th, 78th, 339th, 352nd, 353rd, 355th, 356th, 357th, 359th, 361st, 364th, 479th
P-47 56th

Missions: Support of bombers to Magdeburg, Weimar, Lutzkendorf, Paderborn, Arnsberg, Dulmen, and Bielefeld, plus some PRU escorts.

Claims: 22-5-8 air
43-44 ground

| *Group* | | *Claims* | *Location* |
|---|---|---|---|
| **SF** | | | |
| 2nd: | Lt. W.E. Whalen | (2)Me-109 dest(air) | Dessau |
| | | Me-109 prob(air) | Dessau |
| | LtCol. J.A. Brooks | (2)Me-109 dest(air) | SE Magdeburg |
| **20th** | | | |
| 77th: | Lt. P.L. Schallo | Me-109 dest(air) | Esperstadt A/F |
| | | (2)FW-190 dest(grd) | Esperstadt A/F |
| | | Me-410 dest(grd) | Esperstadt A/F |
| | Lt. G.R. Hall | Me-109 dest(air) | Esperstadt A/F |
| | | FW-190 dest(grd) | Esperstadt A/F |
| | | FW-190 dam(grd) | Esperstadt A/F |
| | | Me-410 dam(grd) | Esperstadt A/F |
| | Lt. F.V. Purse | Me-109 dam(air) | Mulhausen |
| | Capt. L.E. Einhaus | (6)FW-190 dest(grd) | Esperstadt A/F |
| | Capt. C.H. Cole | (6)FW-190 dest(grd) | Esperstadt A/F |
| | | FW-190 dam(grd) | Esperstadt A/F |
| | Lt. R.D. Jones | (4)FW-190 dest(grd) | Esperstadt A/F |
| | | Me-109 dest(grd) | Esperstadt A/F |
| | Lt. G.L. Reynolds | (2)FW-190 dest(grd) | Esperstadt A/F |
| | | (2)Me-410 dest(grd) | Esperstadt A/F |
| | Maj. M.J. Gilbertson | (3)FW-190 dest(grd) | Esperstadt A/F |
| | | Me-110 dam(grd) | Esperstadt A/F |
| | Lt. W.C. Fay | (3)FW-190 dest(grd) | Esperstadt A/F |
| | Lt. F. Larsen | (2)FW-190 dest(grd) | Esperstadt A/F |
| | | u/i a/c dest(grd) | Esperstadt A/F |
| | Lt. D.R. Pitz | (2)FW-190 dest(grd) | Esperstadt A/F |
| | | Me-110 dam(grd) | Esperstadt A/F |
| | Lt. J.P. Starke | FW-190 dest(grd) | Esperstadt A/F |
| | | Me-410 dest(grd) | Esperstadt A/F |
| | Capt. E.C. Jennings | FW-190 dest(grd) | Esperstadt A/F |
| **78th** | | | |
| 82nd: | Lt. W.E. Hydorn | Me-262 prob(air) | Fulda |
| 83rd: | Capt. E.H. Miller | Me-262 prob(air) | Fulda |
| **339th** | | | |
| 504th: | Lt. J.J. Sainlar | Me-262 dam(air) | Meiningen |
| 505th: | Lt. S.C. Ananian | Me-262 dest(air) | Fulda |
| **353rd** | | | |
| 352nd: | Lt. J.E. Davenport | He-111 dest(grd) | Kothen |
| **355th** | | | |
| HdQts: | Col. E.W. Stewart | Ju-188 dest(grd) | Kothen |
| | | (2)Ju-188 dam(grd) | Kothen |
| | Capt. L.D. Minchew | FW-190 dam(grd) | Kothen |
| 354th: | Capt. J.E. Duffy | FW-190 dest(air) | SW Berlin |
| 357th: | Lt. E.P. Ludeke | FW-190 dest(air) | Brandenburg |
| | Lt. W.S. Lyons | Me-109 dest(air) | Brandenburg |
| | Lt. R.W. Delhamer | (.5)Do-217 dam(air) | Lonnewitz A/F |
| | Lt. E.H. Riffle | (.5)Do-217 dam(air) | Lonnewitz A/F |
| | Lt. S.S. Hardee | Ju-88 dest(grd) | Kothen |
| | | Me-109 dam(grd) | Kothen |
| | | Ju-52 dam(grd) | Kothen |
| | Lt. W.F. Forehand | Ju-88 dest(grd) | Kothen |
| | | u/i a/c dam(grd) | Kothen |
| | Lt. G.C. Schmidt | Me-109 dam(grd) | Kothen |
| | Lt. R.F. Misner | u/i a/c dam(grd) | Kothen |
| **357th** | | | |
| HdQts: | Maj. R.W. Foy | Me-262 dam(air) | Fulda |
| 363rd: | Capt. D.H. Bochkay | Me-262 dest(air) | Fulda |
| | Lt. J.L. Carter | Me-262 dest(air) | E/Giessen |
| **359th** | | | |
| 368th: | Capt. C.C. Ettlesen | u/i a/c dam(grd) | Halle |
| **479th** | | | |
| 434th: | Capt. G.W. Gleason | Me-109 dest(air) | SE Magdeburg |
| | | FW-190 dest(air) | SE Magdeburg |
| | Maj. R. Olds | Me-109 dest(air) | SE Magdeburg |
| | Lt. R.D. Creighton | Me-109 dest(air) | SE Magdeburg |
| | | FW-190 prob(air) | SE Magdeburg |
| | Lt. E.H. Wendt | Me-109 dest(air) | SE Magdeburg |
| | | Me-109 dam(air) | SE Magdeburg |
| | Lt. J.C. Donnell | (2)Me-109 dam(air) | SE Magdeburg |
| 435th: | Maj. H.H. Jordan | FW-190 dest(air) | W/Brandenburg |
| | Capt. N.R. Benoit | FW-190 dest(air) | SW Brandenburg |
| | Capt. G.L. Doolittle | Me-109 dest(air) | SE Brandenburg |
| | Lt. D.E. King | Me-109 dest(air) | SE Brandenburg |
| | Lt. J.R. Rogers | Me-109 dest(air) | SE Brandenburg |
| | | Me-109 dam(air) | SE Brandenburg |
| | Lt. F.F. Shriner | Me-109 prob(air) | SE Brandenburg |

*Losses-*

**20th:** Lt. Julio Nunzo (77th Ftr Sqn) KIA
P-51C LC-I 43-25041
Hit by flak at Esperstadt Airfield.

**78th:** Lt. Willard Warren (82nd Ftr Sqn) POW
P-51D MX-Q 44-63185 "Kitty's Kat"
Suffered mechanical failure and bailed out near Frankfurt.]

**355th:** Lt. Thomas J. Taylor (358th Ftr Sqn) KIA
P-51D YF-A 44-14428
Hit by flak and crashed near Liege.

**357th:** Capt. James W. Browning (363rd Ftr Sqn) KIA
P-51D B6-L 44-15630 "Junior Miss"
Hit by either a Me-262 or B-17 fire near Fulda.

**359th:** Capt. Charles C. Ettlesen (368th Ftr Sqn) KIA
P-51K CV-V 44-11651
Last seen strafing a train near Gotha.

**479th:** Lt. Carl B. Jarrell (435th Ftr Sqn) KIA
P-51D J2- 44-14364
Hit by enemy aircraft near Belzig.

*Remarks*

4th: Lt. Thomas H. Elffner (335th Ftr Sqn) c/l; o.k.
P-51 WD-

20th: 1-0 loco, 0-20 railcars, 4-2 hangars, 0-1 gun position

55th: 20-0 locos, 25-10 railcars, 3-17 vehicles

339th: 6-10 railcars

353rd: 0-2 locos, 0-1 railcar

355th: 7-10 locos, 0-38 railcars, 7-25 vehicles
P-51 c/l Birch; o.k.

357th: Lt. Noel V. Breen (364th Ftr Sqn) cr. Leiston; o.k.
P-51D C5- 44-14884

359th: 8-0 locos, 2-0 railcars

364th: 0-1 loco, 0-5 railcars, 1-0 vehicle
Lt. Robert S. Jorgenson (385th Ftr Sqn) b/o Ostend; o.k.
P-51D 5E-

479th: 6-5 locos

**February 10, 1945**

Groups Operating: P-51 20th, 55th, 78th, 352nd, 355th, 356th, 361st

Missions: Support of bombers to Dulmen, strafing sweeps in the Steinhuder Lake area, and a few PRU escorts.

Claims: nil

*Losses-*

**355th:** Lt. Oran Stalcup (354th Ftr Sqn) KIA
P-51D WR-X 44-13571 "Texas Terror IV"
Suffered mechanical failure and ditched in the Channel.

KIAc's

357th: Lt. Holsey C. Johnson (362nd Ftr Sqn)
P-51B G4- 43-6755
Died in a crash off Felixstowe.

**February 11, 1945**
Groups Operating: P-51 4th, 352nd, 357th, 359th, 361st
Missions: Support of bombers to Dulmen, sweeps, and PRU escorts.
Claims: nil

*Losses-*

**4th:** Lt. Henry A. Kaul (336th Ftr Sqn) KIA
P-51D VF-D 44-63233 "Inky's Dinky"
Hit trees while strafing near Lemgo.

*Remarks*
4th: 0-21 locos, 3-45 railcars, 2-6 vehicles, 0-6 barges, 0-1 tug, 0-8 buildings
359th: 24-10 locos, 6-111 railcars, 8-10 vehicles, 0-18 barges, 1-17 buildings

KIAc's
4th: Lt. Morton R. Savage (334th Ftr Sqn)
P-51D QP-W
Hit a radio tower near Nuthampston while flying in heavy fog.

**February 12, 1945**
Groups Operating: P-51 361st
Missions: Patrol of the battle area.
Claims: nil
Losses: nil

KIAc's
339th: Lt. Johnnie M. Allman (505th Ftr Sqn)
P-51 6N-
Crashed six miles west of Duxford.

**February 13, 1945**
Groups Operating: P-51 352nd
Missions: Four aircraft flew a weather recon in the Brunswick-Hanover area.
Claims: nil
Losses: nil

KIAc's
356th: Lt. Walter M. Baskin (361st Ftr Sqn)
P-51D QI-D 44-15642
Spun-in near Trimley while practicing dog-fighting.

**February 14, 1945**
Groups Operating: P-51 4th, 20th, 55th, 78th, 339th, 352nd, 353rd, 355th, 356th, 357th, 359th, 361st, 364th, 479th
P-47 56th
Missions: Support for bombers to Dresden, Chemnitz, and Magdeburg, plus PRU escorts.
Claims: 18-1-10 air
0-0 ground

| *Group* | | *Claims* | *Location* |
|---|---|---|---|
| **20th** | | | |
| 55th: | Capt. J.K. Brown | (.5)Me-262 dam(air) | Stuttgart |
| | Lt. K.D. McNeel | (.5)Me-262 dam(air) | Stuttgart |
| **356th** | | | |
| 359th: | Lt. A.L. Brown | FW-190 dest(air) | Dresden-Chemnitz |
| | | FW-190 dam(air) | Dresden-Chemnitz |
| | Lt. R.C. Miller | FW-190 dam(air) | Dresden-Chemnitz |
| 360th: | Lt. W.O. Hedrick | FW-190 dam(air) | S/Chemnitz |
| 361st: | Maj. D.J. Strait | (2)FW-190 dest(air) | S/Chemnitz |
| | Lt. M.W. Baylor | (2)FW-190 dest(air) | S/Chemnitz |
| | | FW-190 dam(air) | S/Chemnitz |
| | Lt. J.A. Bowers | (2)FW-190 dest(air) | S/Chemnitz |
| | Lt. H.E. Whitmore | (2)FW-190 dam(air) | S/Chemnitz |
| **364th** | | | |
| 383rd: | Capt. C.A. Barnes | FW-190 dest(air) | Chemnitz |
| | Lt. C.E. Hammett | FW-190 prob(air) | Chemnitz |
| **479th** | | | |
| 434th: | Maj. R. Olds | (2)Me-109 dest(air) | SW Berlin |
| | | FW-190 dest(air) | SW Berlin |
| | Lt. E.H. Wendt | (2)Me-109 dest(air) | SW Berlin |
| | LtCol. A.F. Jeffrey | Me-109 dest(air) | SW Berlin |
| | | Me-109 dam(air) | SW Berlin |
| | Capt. R.G. McChrystal | Me-109 dest(air) | SW Berlin |
| | Lt. D.L. Born | Me-109 dest(air) | SW Berlin |
| | Lt. W.H. Daudistel | Me-109 dest(air) | SW Berlin |
| | Lt. J.T. Golden | Me-109 dest(air) | SW Berlin |
| | Capt. D.J. Pierce | (2)Me-109 dam(air) | SW Berlin |

*Losses-*

**20th:** Lt. Jack D. Leon (55th Ftr Sqn) KIA
P-51D KI-M 44-14319
Damaged by an exploding truck while strafing near Dresden.

**55th:** Lt. John L. Rieder (38th Ftr Sqn) MIA
P-51D CG-A 44-13549
Damaged by an exploding ground target near Magdeburg.

**78th:** Lt. Andrew R. Innocenzi (83rd Ftr Sqn) MIA-E
P-51D HL-F 44-14852 "Lottie"
Suffered mechanical failure and landed in Poland.

Lt. James S. Peterson (83rd Ftr Sqn) MIA-E
P-51K HL-N 44-11695 "Prouka"
Escorted Lt. Innocenzi to Poland.

**355th:** Maj. John H. Wilson (357th Ftr Sqn) KIA
P-51D OS-W 44-14260 "Becky"
Damaged by flak and crashed while landing at a strip in Belgium.

**359th:** LtCol. Roy W. Evans (HdQts) POW
P-51D IV- 44-14894 "Lucky"
Hit by flak in the Dresden area.

Lt. Roy C. Garrett (368th Ftr Sqn) KIA
P-51D CV-X 44-14650 "Snookie"
Lost coolant and bailed out near Emmerich.

**361st:** Lt. Thomas A. Kneiffel (375th Ftr Sqn) POW
P-51D E2- 44-14609 "Vixen"
Ran out of fuel near Berkum.

**479th:** Lt. John C. Donnell, Jr. (434th Ftr Sqn) KIA
P-51D L2-V 44-14651 "Pin-Up Girl"
Hit by flak near Dreiskau.

*Remarks*
4th: 0-4 locos, 0-5 barracks, 0-1 gun position
20th: 6-2 locos, 3-1 vehicles
55th: 26-4 locos, 16-72 railcars, 6-4 buildings, 3-2 vehicles, 0-1 flak tower
78th: 6-0 locos, 0-45 railcars
339th: 14-2 locos, 30-43 railcars, 5-2 vehicles
353rd: 23-9 locos, 8-37 railcars, 5-5 vehicles
355th: 2-7 locos, 3-21 railcars, 0-1 barge
359th: 2-0 locos, 0-2 railcars
361st: Lt. William H. Street (375th Ftr Sqn) c/l Belgium; o.k.
P-51D E2-
364th: 2-0 locos, 0-15 railcars
Lt. Ralph W. Queal (383rd Ftr Sqn) c/l Horham; o.k.
P-51D N2-

KIAc's
364th: F/O Thomas W. Kiley (383rd Ftr Sqn)
P-51D N2-
Collided with an RAF bomber northwest of Steeple Morden.

**February 15, 1945**
Groups Operating: P-51 20th, 55th, 353rd, 356th, 357th, 359th, 364th, 479th
P-47 56th
Missions: Support for bombers to Magdeburg, Dresden, Cottbus, and Rheine, plus PRU escorts.
Claims: 2-0-0 air
0-0 ground

| *Group* | | *Claims* | *Location* |
|---|---|---|---|
| **55th** | | | |
| 38th: | Lt. D.M. Amoss | Me-262 dest(air) | Amberg |
| 338th: | Lt. E.H. Duquette | (.5)Hs-129 dest(air) | Scharndau |
| | Lt. C.D. Henry | (.5)Hs-129 dest(air) | Scharndau |

*Losses-*

**364th:** F/O Irvin E. Lang (384th Ftr Sqn) MIA
P-51D 5Y- 44-13764
Ran out of fuel east of Bonn.

*Remarks*
20th: 0-1 loco
55th: 24-6 locos, 1-15 railcars, 3-2 vehicles
353rd: 7-0 locos, 2-43 railcars, 0-1 barge
Lt. John G. Lancaster (351st Ftr Sqn) c/l West Malling; o.k.
P-51D YJ-Z 44-14610
356th: 3-2 locos, 0-28 railcars
359th: Lt. Anthony D. Maiorano (368th Ftr Sqn) b/o Beveland Island; o.k.
P-51D CV-R 44-15618 "Diane"
364th: 2-0 locos, 30-0 railcars

**February 16, 1945**
Groups Operating: P-51 339th, 352nd, 361st
Missions: Support for bombers to Hamm, Nordstern, Osnabruck, and Wesel.
Claims: nil
Losses: nil

*Remarks*
339th: F/O Gilbert G. Cohen (504th Ftr Sqn) c/l Coltishall; o.k.
P-51 5Q-

**February 17, 1945**
Groups Operating: P-51 55th, 353rd, 357th
Missions: Support for bombers to Erfurt plus PRU escorts.
Claims: nil

*Losses-*

**55th**: Lt. Frank D. Bradford, II (338th Ftr Sqn) MIA
P-51D CL-
Crashed twenty miles east of Frankfurt.

**353rd**: Lt. Paul M. McKenney, Jr. (351st Ftr Sqn) KIA
P-51D YJ-S 44-14690
Crashed on take-off from Raydon.

*Remarks*
55th: 12-0 locos, 15-126 railcars, 5-0 vehicles, 0-1 building
353rd: 9-1 locos, 0-11 railcars, 3-0 vehicles
Lt. Lindsay W. Grove(352nd Ftr Sqn) c/l; o.k.
P-51D SX-O

**February 18, 1945**
KIAc's
56th: Lt. Byron J. Fisher (61st Ftr Sqn)
P-47 HV-
Collided with an RAF P-51.

**February 19, 1945**
Groups Operating: P-51 4th, 20th, 55th, 78th, 339th, 353rd, 355th, 356th, 357th, 359th, 364th, 479th
Missions: Support of bombers to Osnabruck, Wesel, Rheine, and Munster, plus sweeps of the Hanover-Magdeburg-Brunswick area.
Claims: 2-0-0 air
1-1 ground

| *Group* | | *Claims* | *Location* |
|---|---|---|---|
| **55th** | | | |
| 38th: | Lt. K.R. McGinnis | FW-190 dest(air) | NW Ingolstadt |
| | F/O W.V. Totten | FW-190 dest(grd) | Deiningen A/F |
| | | FW-190 dam(grd) | Deiningen A/F |
| 343rd: | Lt. B.H. Howes | Me-108 dest(air) | S/Hameln |

*Losses-*

**20th**: Lt. Robert E. Murrell (77th Ftr Sqn) KIA
P-51D LC-K 44-14975
Hit a tree while strafing near Detmold.

**55th**: Lt. Grady Morris (343rd Ftr Sqn) POW
P-51D CY-A 44-14298 "Pink"
Hit by flak near Lippstadt and bailed out west of Hamm.

**359th**: Lt. Anthony D. Maiorano (368th Ftr Sqn) POW
P-51D CV-D 44-15096 "Ice-Cold Katie"
Lost coolant and bailed out north of Trier.

**364th**: Lt. James A. Bussey (383rd Ftr Sqn) KIA
P-51D N2- 44-14653 "Blood and Soda"
Hit by flak near Helmstadt.

Lt. John G. McNamara (383rd Ftr Sqn) POW
P-51D N2-H 44-13813 "Little Dutchess"
Suffered mechanical failure near Wulfen.

Lt. Jack T. Barrie (385th Ftr Sqn) KIA
P-51D 5E- 44-13657
Hit by flak and crashed near Dahre.

Lt. James L. McCubbin (385th Ftr Sqn) POW
P-51D 5E- 44-15672
Hit by flak near Steinhorst.

*Remarks*
20th: 10-3 locos, 1-70 railcars, 5-4 vehicles, 2-0 horse-drawn vehicles, 0-1 building
55th: 81-4 locos, 62-10 railcars, 103-5 vehicles, 4-1 buildings
78th: Lt. Austin S. Miller (82nd Ftr Sqn) b/o Continent; o.k.
P-51D MX-O 44-63256
364th: 25-4 locos, 7-203 railcars, 4-0 vehicles, 1-1 building

**February 20, 1945**
Groups Operating: P-51 4th, 20th, 55th, 78th, 339th, 353rd, 355th, 356th, 357th, 359th, 364th, 479th
P-47 56th
Missions: Support of bombers to Nurnberg, sweeps, and PRU escorts.
Claims: 16-1-1 air
46-32 ground

| *Group* | | *Claims* | *Location* |
|---|---|---|---|
| **4th** | | | |
| 336th: | Capt. J.H. Joiner | (1.5)FW-190 dest(air) | N/Ingolstadt |
| | Capt. K.E. Carlson | (.5)FW-190 dest(air) | N/Ingolstadt |
| **20th** | | | |
| 55th: | Lt. K.D. McNeel | Me-109 dest(air) | Nurnberg |
| | Capt. J.S. Ford | Me-109 prob(air) | S/Nurnberg |
| | | (2)Me-109 dest(grd) | S/Nurnberg |
| 77th: | Lt. W.C. Fay | W-34 dest(air) | Straubing |
| | Lt. L.H. Kerns | Fi-156 dest(air) | N/Straubing |
| | Lt. F.L. Van Sickle | Me-108 dest(air) | Straubing |
| | | Me-108 dest(grd) | Straubing |
| | | Fi-156 dest(grd) | Straubing |
| | | u/i a/c dest(grd) | Straubing |
| | Lt. H.J. Piatkiewicz | FW-44 dest(air) | Straubing |
| | | (2)Me-110 dam(grd) | Straubing |
| | Lt. A.B. North | Me-108 dest(air) | Straubing |
| | | Me-108 dest(grd) | Straubing |
| | | Me-109 dest(grd) | Straubing |
| | | u/i a/c dest(grd) | Straubing |
| | | u/i a/c dam(grd) | Straubing |
| | Lt. G.L. Reynolds | u/i a/c dest(grd) | Straubing |
| | Capt. D.W. Van Sickle | He-111 dam(grd) | Straubing |
| | Lt. T.P. Hambelton | Me-109 dam(grd) | Straubing |
| | Lt. R.D. Jones | u/i a/c dam(grd) | Starubing |
| 79th: | Lt. F.E. Strock | (3)He-111 dest(grd) | Weiden A/F |
| | | (2)He-111 dam(grd) | Weiden A/F |
| | Lt. E.F. Pogue | (2)He-111 dest(grd) | Weiden A/F |
| | Lt. A. Ziegelbauer | (2)He-111 dest(grd) | Weiden A/F |
| | | He-111 dam(grd) | Weiden A/F |
| | Lt. D.A. Beschen | (1.5)He-111 dest(grd)* | Weiden A/F |
| | | He-111 dam(grd) | Weiden A/F |
| | Lt. V.J. Rudnick | (.5)He-111 dest(grd)* | Weiden A/F |
| | | He-111 dam(grd) | Weiden A/F |
| | Lt. J.K. Hollins | He-111 dest(grd) | Weiden A/F |
| | | (2)He-111 dam(grd) | Weiden A/F |
| | Lt. R.H. Pollock | (1.5)He-111 dest(grd)** | Weiden A/F |
| | | Me-410 dam(grd) | Weiden A/F |
| | Lt. J.C. Santee | (.5)He-111 dest(grd)** | Weiden A/F |
| | | He-111 dam(grd) | Weiden A/F |
| | Lt. W.E. Bullers | He-111 dest(grd) | Weiden A/F |
| | | (2)He-111 dam(grd) | Weiden A/F |
| | Lt. D.N. Jones | He-111 dest(grd) | Weiden A/F |
| | | He-111 dam(grd) | Weiden A/F |
| | Lt. C. Kies | He-111 dest(grd) | Weiden A/F |
| | | (3)He-111 dam(grd) | Weiden A/F |
| | Lt. R.M. Scott | He-111 dest(grd) | Weiden A/F |
| | | He-111 dam(grd) | Weiden A/F |
| | Maj. R.J. Meyer | Me-110 dam(grd) | Weiden A/F |
| | Capt. J.K. Taylor | Me-110 dam(grd) | Weiden A/F |
| | F/O A.L. Shaffer | Me-110 dam(grd) | Weiden A/F |
| **55th** | | | |
| 338th: | Lt. K.A. Lashbrook | Me-109 dest(air) | Womding |
| 343rd: | Lt. W. Strauch | (2)Me-109 dest(grd) | Giebelstadt A/F |
| | Capt. R.D. Brown | Ju-88 dest(grd) | Giebelstadt A/F |
| **356th** | | | |
| 361st: | Maj. D.J. Strait | (3)Fi-156 dest(air) | SE Bayreuth |
| | Lt. C.D. Burdick | (2.5)Fi-156 dest(air) | SE Bayreuth |
| | Lt. E.L. Slanker | (.5)Fi-156 dest(air) | SE Bayreuth |
| | | Fi-156 dam(air) | SE Bayreuth |
| | Capt. F.A. Morgan | (3)u/i a/c dest(grd) | Windleschenlaibach |
| | | Me-110 dest(grd) | Windleschenlaibach |
| | | Ju-88 dest(grd) | Windleschenlaibach |
| | Capt. R.F. Schlack | Ju-88 dest(grd) | Furth |
| | | (3)Ju-88 dam(grd) | Furth |
| | F/O J.K. Dupuy | Ju-88 dest(grd) | Windleschenlaibach |
| | | (.5)u/i a/c dest(grd) | Windleschenlaibach |
| | Lt. J.C. Lindsay | FW-190 dest(grd) | Bayreuth-Eindbach |
| | | (.5)u/i a/c dest(grd) | Windleschenlaibach |
| | Lt. R.J. Cox | FW-190 dest(grd) | Windleschenlaibach |
| | | (2)FW-190 dam(grd) | Bayreuth-Eindbach |
| | Lt. W.C. Jarvis | Ju-88 dest(grd) | Furth |
| **479th** | | | |
| 434th: | Maj. R. Olds | FW-190 dest(grd) | Windleschenlaibach |
| | | Do-217 dest(grd) | Windleschenlaibach |
| | Lt. R.B. Kline | (2)Do-217 dest(grd) | Windleschenlaibach |
| | | (.5)He-111 dest(grd)* | Windleschenlaibach |
| | | (.5)FW-190 dam(grd) | Windleschenlaibach |
| | Lt. J.T. Golden | (1.5)He-111 dest(grd)* | Windleschenlaibach |
| | | (.5)FW-190 dam(grd) | Windleschenlaibach |
| | Lt. E.E. Sears | Do-217 dest(grd) | Windleschenlaibach |
| | Capt. D.J. Pierce | (.5)He-111 dest(grd)** | Windleschenlaibach |
| | | (.5)He-111 dam(grd) | Windleschenlaibach |
| | Lt. P.A. Brown | (.5)He-111 dest(grd)** | Windleschenlaibach |
| | | (.5)He-111 dam(grd) | Windleschenlaibach |

*Losses-*

**4th:** Capt. John C. Fitch (335th Ftr Sqn) POW
P-51D WD- 44-15351
Hit by flak and bailed out southwest of Newmarkt.

**20th:** Capt. Joseph S. Ford (55th Ftr Sqn) POW
P-51K KI-E 44-11638 "Lil Easy"
Hit by flak near Nurnberg.

Lt. William J. McGee (55th Ftr Sqn) POW
P-51D KI-Y 44-13905 "Joe"
Landed to pick up Capt. Ford and became stuck in the mud.

Lt. Sidney S. Stitzer (55th Ftr Sqn) KIA
P-51D KI-B 44-13664
Hit by debris from an exploding railcar near Kompendorf.

**55th:** Lt. Alfred E. Carr, Jr. (38th Ftr Sqn) MIA-E
P-51D CG-S 44-14068 "Little Joe"
Hit by flak and bellied-in near Hall.

Lt. John W. Miller (38th Ftr Sqn) ASR
P-51D CG-N 44-13937
Ditched in the Channel after mechanical failure.

Lt. Robert L. Sill (38th Ftr Sqn) KIA
P-51K CG- 44-11370
Hit by flak near Seinhausen.

Lt. Charles R. Michaelson (343rd Ftr Sqn) POW
P-51D CY-E 44-63567
Hit by flak near Crailsheim and bailed out near Hall.

**78th:** Capt. Charles L. Lyle (84th Ftr Sqn) KIA
P-51K WZ-D 44-11694
Hit by flak near Stuttgart.

Lt. Merle V. Brendle (84th Ftr Sqn) KIA
P-51D WZ-G 44-63207
Hit by flak near Stuttgart and crashed near Valenciennes.

**339th:** Lt. William M. Beecher (505th Ftr Sqn) KIA
P-51B 6N- 42-106936
Suffered vertigo and crashed near Valenciennes.

**356th:** Capt. William F. Traupe (359th Ftr Sqn) KIA
P-51D OC- 44-63250
Hit by flak and bailed out near Heilbronn but his chute failed.

Lt. Carlton L. Welch (360th Ftr Sqn) POW
P-51D PI-U 44-11220 "Fourth Apocalypsian"
Hit by flak and bailed out south of Leipzig.

*Remarks*
4th: 1-5 locos, 0-15 railcars
20th: 15-5 locos, 25-115 railcars, 1-0 vehicle, 0-2 buildings
Lt. Baxter M. Phillips (77th Ftr Sqn) c/l Charleroi; o.k.
P-51D LC-C 44-13793
55th: 89-10 locos, 24-64 railcars, 1-0 vehicle, 3-1 buildings, 0-5 radar towers
Lt. Albert M. Koenig (38th Ftr Sqn) b/o NW Luxembourg; o.k.
P-51D CG- 44-13820
78th: 15-5 locos, 1-95 railcars, 4-8 vehicles
Lt. Robert J. Blossom (82nd Ftr Sqn) c/l France; o.k.
P-51D MX-A 44-63198
339th: 16-0 locos, 37-25 railcars, 5-12 vehicles
Lt. Arlen W. Wells (504th Ftr Sqn) c/l; o.k.
P-51D 5Q-A 44-14060
F/O Gilbert G. Cohen (504th Ftr Sqn) c/l Continent; o.k.
P-51 5Q-
353rd: 11-0 locos, 1-0 railcar, 2-13 vehicles
356th: 4-0 locos, 0-40 railcars, 2-0 vehicles, 0-2 flak towers
357th: 1-0 loco, 0-35 railcars

**February 21, 1945**
Groups Operating: P-51 4th, 20th, 55th, 78th, 339th, 352nd, 353rd, 355th, 356th, 357th, 359th, 361st, 364th, 479th
P-47 56th
Missions: Support of bombers to the Nurnberg area including sweeps and strafing afterwards. Several groups provided sections for PRU escorts and the 352nd and 361st supported 9th Air Force operations.
Claims: 1-0-0 air
4-15 ground

| *Group* | | *Claims* | *Location* |
|---|---|---|---|
| **352nd** | | | |
| 487th: | Lt. R.H. Littge | Ju-88 dam(grd) | SW Kassel |
| **356th** | | | |
| 360th: | Lt. A.A. Paquet | FW-190 dam(grd) | NW Crailsheim |
| | | W-34 dam(grd) | NW Crailsheim |
| | Lt. J.W. Crump | FW-190 dam(grd) | NW Crailsheim |
| | Capt. W.G. Thomas | He-111 dam(grd) | S/Nurnberg |
| | Lt. R.S. Ragsdale | (.5)He-111 dam(grd) | S/Nurnberg |
| | Lt. J.P. Weller | (.5)He-111 dam(grd) | S/Nurnberg |
| 361st: | Lt. H.E. Whitmore | Me-262 dest(air) | Stettin |
| **359th** | | | |
| 369th: | Maj. E.F. Pezda | FW-200 dest(grd) | Schweinfurt |
| | Lt. A.B. Morris | Ju-88 dest(grd) | Nordlingen |
| | | Me-410 dam(grd) | Nordlingen |
| | Maj. F.S. Hodges | FW-200 dam(grd) | Deiningen |
| | Capt. R.C. Thomson | FW-190 dam(grd) | Nordlingen |
| | | u/i a/c dam(grd) | Nordlingen |
| | Lt. F.S. McGehee | FW-200 dam(grd) | Deiningen |
| | | Me-410 dam(grd) | Deiningen |
| | Capt. R.M. Francis | Me-410 dam(grd) | Schweinfurt |
| **479th** | | | |
| 434th: | Lt. O.J. Huval | He-111 dest(grd) | Gotha |
| | Lt. G.E. Jacobson | He-111 dest(grd) | Gotha |
| 436th: | Capt. J.C. Malone | Ju-188 dam(grd) | Nordhausen |
| | Lt. G.H. Witzel | Ju-188 dam(grd) | Nordhausen |

*Losses-*

**4th:** Lt. Andrew C. Lacy (334th Ftr Sqn) POW
P-51K QP-P 44-11677 "Lynette Sue"
Bailed out west of Neresheim after a flak hit.

Lt. August W. Rabe (335th Ftr Sqn) POW
P-51D WD-O 44-14435
Bellied-in after hitting a tree while strafing southwest of Coburg.

**55th:** Lt. George E. Eichorn (343rd Ftr Sqn) POW
P-51D CY-H 44-15060 "Jill's Jalopy"
Hit by flak in the Mistelfeld area.

**78th:** Lt. Burton Newmark (84th Ftr Sqn) POW
P-51D WZ-K 44-63171 "Lady Eve"
Bailed out southwest of Coblenz after a flak hit.

**355th:** Lt. James J. Costigan (354th Ftr Sqn) KIA
P-51K WR-C 44-11359 "Lil Lila Lee"
Hit by flak in the Amsbach area.

*Remarks*
4th: 7-5 locos, 12-66 railcars, 6-3 vehicles
20th: 6-0 locos, 24-0 railcars, 0-2 buildings
55th: 23-2 locos, 5-9 railcars, 0-5 vehicles
339th: 1-1 locos, 13-15 railcars, 1-0 vehicle
353rd: 9-0 locos, 2-32 railcars, 3-1 vehicles, 0-3 flak towers, 0-4 buildings
Lt. Raymond Hilgenburg (351st Ftr Sqn) c/l France; o.k.
P-51D YJ-
355th: 1-0 loco, 0-21 railcars
356th: 0-1 railcar, 0-1 barge, 0-1 hangar, 0-1 flak position
357th: 0-2 locos, 0-20 railcars, 2-0 vehicles
359th: 0-1 hangar

**February 22, 1945**
Groups Operating: P-51 4th, 20th, 55th, 78th, 339th, 352nd, 353rd, 355th, 356th, 357th, 359th, 361st, 364th, 479th
P-47 56th
Missions: Support of bombers to numerous rail and communication targets in Germany plus PRU escorts.
Claims: 5-1-16 air
18-26 ground

| *Group* | | *Claims* | *Location* |
|---|---|---|---|
| **SF** | | | |
| 2nd: | Lt. W.E. Whalen | (2)FW-190 dest(grd) | Thale A/F |
| | | (3)FW-190 dam(grd) | Thale A/F |
| **4th** | | | |
| 336th: | Lt. H.R. Crawford | (3)FW-190 dest(grd) | Halberstadt |
| | Maj. F.W. Glover | Do-217 dest(grd) | Halberstadt |
| | | Me-109 dest(grd) | Halberstadt |
| | Capt. C.R. Alfred | Me-410 dest(grd) | Halberstadt |
| | | Do-217 dest(grd) | Halberstadt |
| | Maj. J.D. McFarlane | Do-217 dest(grd) | Halberatadt |
| **20th** | | | |
| 55th: | Capt. R.M. Howard | Me-262 dam(air) | Salzwedel |
| **78th** | | | |
| 84th: | Lt. R.D. Higgins | Ju-86 dam(grd) | Memmingen |
| **352nd** | | | |
| HdQts: | Maj. E.D. Duncan | Me-262 dam(air) | Stendal |
| 328th: | Lt. C.E. Goodman | Me-262 dam(air) | Stendal |
| 486th: | Lt. C.D. Price | Me-262 dest(air) | Wahrenholz |

| | | | |
|---|---|---|---|
| **353rd** | | | |
| 350th: | Maj. W.K. Blickenstaff | Me-262 dest(air) | Berlin |
| 351st: | Capt. G.B. Compton | Me-262 dest(air) | Brandenburg |
| **355th** | | | |
| 354th: | Lt. R.M. White | (2)Me-410 dest(grd) | Halberstadt |
| | | FW-190 dam(grd) | Halberstadt |
| **359th** | | | |
| 369th: | Capt. W.F. Collins | (2)Ju-88 dest(grd) | Parchim |
| | | Ju-88 dam(grd) | Parchim |
| | Lt. F.S. McGehee | (3)Ju-88 dam(grd) | Parchim |
| | Lt. H. Tenenbaum | Ju-88 dam(grd) | Schwerin |
| 370th: | Lt. D.L. Windmiller | Me-410 dam(grd) | Pritzwalk |
| **364th** | | | |
| 383rd: | Lt. E.H. Horman | FW-190 dest(air) | SW Bremen |
| | | (2)FW-190 dam(air) | SW Bremen |
| | Lt. E.W. Kortendick | FW-190 dest(air) | S/Quackenbruck |
| | | FW-190 dam(air) | S/Quackenbruck |
| | Lt. W.V. Pyle | (2)FW-190 dam(air) | SW Bremen |
| | Lt. G.O. Warner | (2)Me-262 dam(air) | W/Berlin |
| | Lt. R.L. Hunt | Mr-262 dam(air) | Wittstock |
| 384th: | Capt. R.W. Stevens | (.5)Me-262 prob(air) | Wittstock |
| | Lt. C.B. Kirby | (.5)Me-262 prob(air) | Wittstock |
| | Capt. S.C. Phillips | Me-262 dam(air) | Stendal |
| | Lt. L.L. Lefforge | Me-262 dam(air) | Stendal |
| | Lt. L.H. Phipps | Me-262 dam(air) | Stendal |
| | Lt. S.J. Price | Me-262 dam(air) | Stendal |
| | Lt. W.E. Randolph | Me-262 dam(air) | Stendal |
| **479th** | | | |
| 436th: | Capt. W.C. Anderson | He-111 dest(grd) | Halberstadt |
| | Lt. R.E. Henry | Ju-88 dest(grd) | Halberstadt |
| | | He-111 dam(grd) | Halberstadt |
| | Lt. A.J. Smigel | He-111 dest(grd) | Halberstadt |
| | | (2)Ju-88 dam(grd) | Halberstadt |
| | Lt. A.J. Soordino | Ju-88 dest(grd) | Halberstadt |
| | | (2)He-111 dam(grd) | Halberstadt |
| | Maj. C.A.P. Duffie | (3)u/i a/c dam(grd) | Halberstadt |
| | | Ju-88 dam(grd) | Halberstadt |
| | Lt. C.H. Darling | (2)Ju-88 dam(grd) | Halberstadt |
| | Maj. C.J. Moore | Ju-52 dam(grd) | Halberstadt |
| | Capt. J.C. Malone | Ju-88 dam(grd) | Halberstadt |
| | Lt. E.J. Hopcroft | He-111 dam(grd) | Halberstadt |
| | Lt. A.R. DiPaola | FW-190 dam(grd) | Halberstadt |

*Losses-*

**78th**: Capt. Wilbur J. Coss (82nd Ftr Sqn) KIA
P-51K MX-D 44-11663
Collided with a P-51 near Valenciennes.

F/O Ralph E. Hamilton (83rd Ftr Sqn) POW
P-51D HL-J 44-15650 "Debra Dell"
Hit by flak at Crailsheim and bailed out northwest of Wurzburg.

**339th**: Capt. Ray F. Herrmann (504th Ftr Sqn) KIA
P-51K 5Q- 44-11745 "Happy III"
Hit by flak in the Coburg area.

Capt. Robert T. Wood (504th Ftr Sqn) KIA
P-51D 5Q-J 44-14153
Hit by flak in the Coburg area.

**353rd**: Lt. John M. Balason (350th Ftr Sqn) POW
P-51D LH-J 44-14793 "Miss Betty D"
Hit by flak near Bielefeld.

**355th**: Lt. George A. Kemper, Jr. (354th Ftr Sqn) POW
P-51D WR-P 44-14275 "Down For Double"
Hit by flak near Quackenbruck and bellied-in near Dummer Lake.

**356th**: Lt. Alden S. Thomas (360th Ftr Sqn) POW
P-51D PI-M 44-15149 "Virgy I"
Hit by flak west of Ulzen.

**359th**: Lt. David P. Dunmire (368th Ftr Sqn) KIA
P-51K CV-F 44-11647 "Freddy Junior"
Hit by flak near Dusseldorf.

Lt. Russell E. Masters (369th Ftr Sqn) KIA
P-51D IV-V 44-13610
Suffered mechanical failure and bailed out off the Dutch coast.

**361st**: Lt. Richard E. Chandler (374th Ftr Sqn) POW
P-51D B7- 44-13340
Hit by flak near Gross Almerode.

**364th**: Lt. Fred A. Ross (383rd Ftr Sqn) POW
P-51D N2-Y 44-14747 "Rough Rider"
Hit by a FW-190 near Delmarhorst.

Lt. Francis X. Radley (385th Ftr Sqn) KIA
P-51D 5E-N 44-13994
Hit by a Me-262 near Stendal.

**479th**: Lt. Albert R. DiPaolo (436th Ftr Sqn) POW
P-51D 9B-T 44-15412
Hit by flak near Halberstadt and crashed near Quedlinburg.

Lt. Peter C. Vassuer (436th Ftr Sqn) MIA
P-51K 9B-P 44-11739
Hit by fire from a P-51 while strafing Halberstadt.

*Remarks*

4th: 0-2 locos, 1-9 railcars, 1-1 vehicle, 0-1 building
20th: 1-1 locos, 0-11 railcars
55th: 4-10 locos, 0-12 railcars
56th: 0-1 loco, 6-10 vehicles, 0-1 building
78th: 10-1 locos
Lt. Robert E. Smith (82nd Ftr Sqn) c/l Valenciennes; o.k.
P-51K MX-X 44-11680
339th: 23-3 locos, 30-65 railcars, 2-0 vehicles
353rd: 17-0 locos, 0-63 railcars, 0-4 vehicles, 0-2 barges, 0-2 gun positions
355th: 2-0 locos, 3-0 vehicles
356th: 5-2 locos, 0-12 railcars
359th: 6-1 locos, 1-12 railcars, 0-3 vehicles, 0-1 barge
364th: 1-1 locos, 0-45 railcars, 1-0 vehicle, 0-1 barge
P-51 c/l; o.k.

KIAc's

55th: Lt. Samuel E. Kershaw (338th Ftr Sqn)
P-51D CL-
Died in a crash near Hornchurch.

**February 23, 1945**

Groups Operating: P-51 4th, 20th, 55th, 78th, 339th, 353rd, 355th, 356th, 357th, 359th, 364th, 479th
P-47 56th

Missions: Support of bombers to numerous marshalling yards and other targets plus a few PRU escorts.

Claims: 7-0-0 air
18-14 ground

| *Group* | | *Claims* | *Location* |
|---|---|---|---|
| **353rd** | | | |
| 352nd: | Lt. D.W. Schoen | He-111 dest(grd) | Kitzingen |
| | | Me-110 dest(grd) | Kitzingen |
| | | Me-110 dam(grd) | Kitzingen |
| | Lt. J.R. Evans | He-177 dest(grd) | Kitzingen |
| | | (.5)Me-110 dest(grd) | Kitzingen |
| | Lt. L.O. Pletz | He-111 dest(grd) | Kitzingen |
| | | (.5)Me-110 dest(grd) | Kitzingen |
| **355th** | | | |
| 354th: | Capt. J.E. Duffy | (2)u/i a/c dest(grd) | Leipheim |
| | | Me-262 dest(grd) | Leipheim |
| | LtCol. G.M. Graham | Me-109 dest(grd) | Naumberg |
| | | FW-190 dam(grd) | Naumberg |
| | Capt. H.R. Mann | Ju-88 dest(grd) | Neuburg |
| | Lt. N.F. Mills | u/i a/c dest(grd) | Neuburg |
| | Lt. R.J. Walsh | Me-109 dest(grd) | Neuburg |
| | Lt. R.A. Goth | Ju-88 dam(grd) | Neuburg |
| | Lt. D.M. Vickery | Ju-88 dam(grd) | Neuburg |
| 357th: | LtCol. J.L. Elder | Me-109 dest(grd) | Neuburg |
| | | Me-109 dam(grd) | Neuburg |
| | Lt. E.H. Riffle | Me-262 dest(grd) | Neuburg |
| | Lt. G.C. Schmidt | Me-110 dest(grd) | Neuburg |
| | Lt. R.L. Garlich | Me-163 dest(grd) | Neuburg |
| | Lt. S.S. Hardee | Me-109 dest(grd) | Neuburg |
| | Lt. E.P. Ludeke | (3)Me-163 dam(grd) | Neuburg |
| | Lt. W.F. Forehand | Me-262 dam(grd) | Neuburg |
| | Lt. H.K. Greenwell | Me-262 dam(grd) | Neuburg |
| | Lt. T.C. Long | Me-163 dam(grd) | Neuburg |
| | Lt. D.P. Watkins | Me-163 dam(grd) | Neuburg |
| | Lt. J.J. Weidemann | Me-163 dam(grd) | Neuburg |
| **356th** | | | |
| 360th: | Capt. M.P. Yannell | He-177 dest(grd) | Giebelstadt |
| | | He-177 dam(grd) | Giebelstadt |
| **364th** | | | |
| 384th: | Capt. D.J. Pick | (2.5)Me-109 dest(air) | Stuttgart |
| | | Me-109 dam(grd) | Stuttgart |
| | Capt. R.W. Stevens | (2)Me-109 dest(air) | Stuttgart |
| | Lt. H.C. Schwartz | (2)Me-109 dest(air) | Stuttgart |
| | F/O J.F. Nelson | (.5)Me-109 dest(air) | Stuttgart |

*Losses-*

**78th:** Lt. John B. Wade (83rd Ftr Sqn) POW
P-51K HL-H 44-11364
Hit by flak at Ingolstadt and bailed out near Donauworth.

**355th:** Lt. Robert M. White (354th Ftr Sqn) POW
P-51C WR-V 42-103795 "Dutchess of Manhattan"
Hit by flak at Neuburg.

**357th:** Lt. Richard W. Taylor (363rd Ftr Sqn) KIA
P-51D B6- 44-14768
Hit by flak and crashed near the Zuider Zee.

**359th:** Lt. Lawrence F. Meyer (369th Ftr Sqn) KIA
P-51D IV-D 44-15394
Hit by flak near Fulda.

Capt. Washington D. Lyon (370th Ftr Sqn) KIA
P-51D CS-C 44-14987 "Patty Whack"
Last seen in the Zwickau area.

Lt. Garland J. McGregor (370th Ftr Sqn) KIA
P-51D CS-
Was radio relay and crashed at East Wretham.

Lt. Malcolm C. Paulette (370th Ftr SQn) KIA
P-51D CS-G 44-14773 "Micky the Twist"
Ran out of fuel in the Zwickau area.

*Remarks*
4th: 0-1 loco
55th: 2-5 railcars
339th: 0-5 railcars, 1-0 vehicle
Lt. Richard E. Krauss (503rd Ftr SQn) c/l Debden; o.k.
P-51D D7-
353rd: 7-4 locos, 0-72 railcars, 4-1 vehicles, 0-3 radar towers, 0-1 building
355th: 3-11 locos, 6-52 railcars, 5-0 vehicles
357th: 1-0 loco, 0-12 railcars
359th: 2-4 locos, 0-28 railcars, 11-9 vehicles

**February 24, 1945**
Groups Operating: P-51 4th, 20th, 55th, 78th, 339th, 352nd, 353rd, 355th, 357th, 359th, 361st
Missions: Support of bombers to Hamburg, Misburg, Bremen, and Wesel with strafing afterwards. Some units also provided escort for PRU aircraft.
Claims: 0-0-0 air
1-2 ground

| *Group* | | *Claims* | *Location* |
|---|---|---|---|
| **55th** | | | |
| 343rd: | Lt. F.C. Lawrence | Ju-88 dest(grd) | Zwischenahn A/F |
| | | u/i a/c dam(grd) | Zwischenahn A/F |
| | Lt. V.P. Gordon | Me-110 dam(grd) | Zwischenahn A/F |

*Losses-*

**4th:** F/O Alvin L. Hand (334th Ftr Sqn) POW
P-51K QP-X 44-11661 "Iron Ass"
Hit by flak while strafing near Emmen.

**20th:** Lt. Leonard M. Wright, Jr. (79th Ftr Sqn) POW
P-51D MC-Z 44-11244 "Nina Merle"
Lost coolant and bailed out near Darfeld.

**55th:** Lt. Kenneth D. Cottrell (338th Ftr Sqn) MIA-E
P-51D CL-V 44-14702 "Miss Donna"
Suffered mechanical failure and bailed out near Emmen.

Lt. Thomas M. Love (343rd Ftr Sqn) POW
P-51D CY-J 44-14296 "Mardy"
Hit by flak near Zwischenahn Airfield.

**78th:** Lt. Edwin B. Anderson (82nd Ftr Sqn) POW
P-51D MX-C 44-63177
Hit by flak near Dummer Lake.

Lt. Lucien J. Bibeau (82nd Ftr Sqn) KIA
P-51K MX-U 44-11688
Hit by flak in the Dummer Lake area.

Lt. Lloyd L. Eadline (83rd Ftr Sqn) KIA
P-51D HL-Y 44-63248
Hit by flak near Quackenbruck and bailed out over the Zuider Zee.

Lt. Louis R. Musgrave (84th Ftr Sqn) KIA
P-51D WZ-F 44-15359
Hit by flak in the Einbeck/Hanover area.

**352nd:** Lt. Sylvester J. Evans (328th Ftr Sqn) POW
P-51K PE-K 44-11750 "Lonesome Polecat"
Hit by flak near Bathmer and bellied-in southeast of Deventer.

Lt. Fred R. Jones (486th Ftr Sqn) KIA
P-51D PZ-F 44-13362 "Sleepy Chicken"
Hit by flak at Almelo.

**353rd:** Lt. Raymond Hilgenburg (351st Ftr Sqn) KIA
P-51D YJ-Q 44-14949 "Mr. Gray"
Hit by flak near Apeldoorn.

**355th:** Lt. Sellers S. Hardee (357th Ftr Sqn) KIA
P-51D OS-H 44-14402
Spun-in after taking-off from Steeple Morden.

*Remarks*
4th: 0-5 locos, 0-5 barges, 0-1 vehicle
55th: 3-0 locos, 2-15 railcars, 1-2 barges, 1-4 vehicles, 0-1 ship
353rd: 0-3 locos, 18-6 railcars, 3-0 vehicles, 0-1 building
357th: 0-1 loco, 2-0 railcars, 9-0 vehicles, 0-5 barges

**February 25, 1945**
Groups Operating: P-51 4th, 20th, 55th, 78th, 339th, 352nd, 353rd, 355th, 356th, 357th, 359th, 361st, 364th, 479th
P-47 56th
Missions: Support of bombers to Munich, Aschaffenburg, and various targets of opportunity, sweeps, and PRU escorts.
Claims: 22-1-3 air
23-17 ground

| *Group* | | *Claims* | *Location* |
|---|---|---|---|
| **7th(P)** | | | |
| 22nd: | Lt. R.S. Quiggins | FW-190 dest(air) | W/Aschaffenburg |
| **4th** | | | |
| 334th: | Lt. C.G. Payne | Me-262 dest(air) | SE Naunberg |
| | | (.5)Me-410 dest(grd) | Rohrensee |
| | Lt. D.M. Malmsten | (.5)FW-190 dest(air) | Dessau |
| | Lt. W.C. O'Bryan | (.5)FW-190 dest(air) | Dessau |
| | Lt. A.R. Bowers | FW-190 dest(grd) | Rohrensee |
| | | Me 410 dest(grd) | Rohrensee |
| | | Me-110 dest(grd) | Rohrensee |
| | Capt. T.R. Bell | FW-190 dest(grd) | Rohrensee |
| | | (.5)Me-410 dest(grd) | Rohrensee |
| | | (.5)Me-110 dest(grd) | Rohrensee |
| | | (.5)Me-110 dest(grd) | Rohrensee |
| | Lt. G.A. Denson | (.5)Me-110 dest(grd) | Rohrensee |
| | | (.5)Me-110 dest(grd) | Rohrensee |
| | Lt. H.E. Clifton | (2)Me-109 dam(grd) | Kothen |
| | Lt. D.G. Lowther | Ju-88 dam(grd) | Kothen |
| 335th: | Maj. P.W. McKennon | (2)u/i a/c dam(grd) | Pretzech A/F |
| | Lt. R.C. Bucholz | Ju-88 dam(grd) | NE Torgau |
| | Lt. G.D. Green | Me-410 dam(grd) | Pretzech A/F |
| 336th: | Lt. B.O. Brooker | (.5)FW-190 prob(air) | Kothen |
| | Lt. P.M. Morgan | (.5)FW-190 prob(air) | Kothen |
| | Capt. K.E. Carlson | u/i a/c dest(grd) | Kothen |
| | Lt. R.J. Corbett | He-111 dest(grd) | Kothen |
| | | He-111 dam(grd) | Kothen |
| | Lt. J.E. Hileman | u/i a/c dest(grd) | Kothen |
| **20th** | | | |
| 55th: | Capt. C.H. Cole | (4)FW-190 dest(air) | Stendal |
| | Lt. E.L. Kier | (2)Me-109 dest(air) | Dummer Lake |
| | Maj. M.A. Cristadoro | FW-190 dest(air) | Stendal |
| | Capt. R.W. Fruechtenicht | Me-109 dest(air) | Dummer Lake |
| | | Me-109 dam(air) | Dummer Lake |
| | Lt. C.R. Nicholson | FW-190 dest(air) | Gardelegen |
| | Lt. K.L. Pettit | Me-109 dest(air) | Dummer Lake |
| **55th** | | | |
| 38th: | Capt. D.M. Cummings | (2)Me-262 dest(air) | Giebelstadt A/F & Leipheim A/F |
| | Capt. D.E. Penn | Me-262 dest(air) | Giebelstadt A/F |
| | Lt. M.O. Anderson | Me-262 dest(air) | W/Giebelstadt A/F |
| | | FW-190 dest(grd) | Giebelstadt A/F |
| | Lt. J.F. O'Neill | Me-262 dest(air) | SE Giebelstadt |
| | | Me-262 dest(grd) | SE Giebelstadt |
| | Lt. B. Clemmons | Me-262 dest(air) | SE Mannheim |
| | Lt. D.T. Menegay | Me-262 dest(air) | W/Giebelstadt A/F |
| 338th: | Lt. L.K. John | FW-190 dest(grd) | Illesheim |
| | | Me-109 dest(grd) | Illesheim |
| | Capt. P. Brooks | Me-109 dest(grd) | Illesheim |
| | | Me-109 dam(grd) | Illesheim |
| | Lt. C.D. Henry | FW-190 dest(grd) | Illesheim |
| | | FW-190 dam(grd) | Illesheim |
| | Lt. J.J. Sullivan | FW-190 dest(grd) | Illesheim |
| | Lt. A.E. Wright | FW-190 dest(grd) | Illesheim |
| | Lt. K.C. Schneider | FW-190 dam(grd) | Illesheim |

| | | | |
|---|---|---|---|
| **353rd** | | | |
| 351st: | Capt. G.E. Markham | FW-200 dam(grd) | Lechfeld |
| **355th** | | | |
| 357th: | Lt. T.C. Long | Ju-188 dest(grd) | Fassberg |
| 358th: | Lt. W.W. Tolby | Me-109 dest(grd) | E/Munster |
| | | Me-109 dam(grd) | E/Munster |
| **356th** | | | |
| 359th: | Lt. J.F. Brown | He-111 dest(grd) | Berndorf |
| | Lt. A.L. Brown | He-111 dam(grd) | Berndorf |
| | Lt. H.R. Gohsler | He-111 dam(grd) | Berndorf |
| **357th** | | | |
| 362nd: | Capt. C.E. Weaver | He-111 dest(grd) | Memmingen |
| | | FW-190 dam(grd) | Memmingen |
| | | Ju-88 dam(grd) | Memmingen |
| | Lt. J.F. Duncan | He-111 dest(grd) | Memmingen |
| **364th** | | | |
| 384th: | Lt. J.E. Soehl | FW-190 dest(air) | SW Ulzen |
| | | FW-190 dam(air) | SW Ulzen |
| | Capt. R.L. Stiefvater | FW-190 dam(air) | N/Gifhorn |
| 385th: | Lt. E. Murphy | (.5)Ar-234 dest(air) | Steinhuder Lake |
| | Lt. R.E. White | (.5)Ar-234 dest(air) | Steinhuder Lake |

*Losses-*

**4th:** Capt. Kendall E. Carlson (336th Ftr Sqn) POW
P-51K VF-Y 44-11356
Hit the ground while strafing Kothen Airfield.

**20th:** Capt. Charles H. Cole, Jr. (55th Ftr Sqn) POW
P-51D KI-K 44-72160
Hit by a FW-190 near Stendal and bellied-in southwest of Magdeburg.

Lt. Horace B. Smith (55th Ftr Sqn) KIA
P-51D KI-K 44-63808
Hit by flak near Arnheim.

Lt. Raymond K. Soleau (55th Ftr Sqn) KIA
P-51D KI-G 44-11197
Hit by enemy aircraft near Stendal.

**78th:** Lt. Charles S. Oldfield (84th Ftr Sqn) MIA-E
P-51D WZ-C 44-63555
Hit by flak near Crailsheim.

Lt. Mark T. Wilson, Jr. (84th Ftr Sqn) MIA-E
P-51D WZ-N 44-15740
Hit by flak near Crailsheim.

**356th:** Maj. Richard A. Rann (359th Ftr Sqn) POW
P-51D OC-E 44-15271 "Starduster"
Hit by flak near Hechingen and bailed out near Schaffshausen.

Lt. Alston L. Brown (359th Ftr Sqn) KIA
P-51D OC- 44-14998
Hit by flak at Berndorf Airfield.

Lt. Kenneth C. Scott (359th Ftr Sqn) KIA
P-51D OC-S 44-15280 "Flying Dutchman"
Hit by flak at Berndorf Airfield and bellied-in near Muehringen; aircraft exploded when hitting the ground.

**364th:** Lt. William E. Randolph (384th Ftr Sqn) POW
P-51D 5Y-R 44-15532
Hit by flak near Unterlisz and bailed out southwest of Fassberg.

*Remarks*

| | |
|---|---|
| 4th: | 0-17 locos, 0-27 vehicles |
| 20th: | 17-3 locos, 2-52 railcars, 21-54 vehicles, 3-0 horse-drawn vehicles |
| 55th: | 8-0 locos, 11-21 railcars, 1-20 vehicles, 0-4 barracks |
| 56th: | 2-0 locos, 0-4 railcars, 9-49 vehicles |
| 339th: | 0-1 loco, 0-8 railcars<br>Lt. Kenneth E. Moreland (503rd Ftr Sqn) c/l Sedan; o.k.<br>P-51D D7- |
| 353rd: | 6-0 locos, 0-42 railcars, 5-0 vehicles |
| 355th: | 8-0 locos, 18-62 railcars, @116-0 vehicles |
| 356th: | 1-0 loco, 1-0 flak tower<br>Lt. Jarvis M. Ter Haar (361st Ftr Sqn) c/l France; injured<br>P-51D QI-Z 44-15082 |
| 357th: | Capt. Chester K. Maxwell (364th Ftr Sqn) c/l; o.k.<br>P-51D C5-H 44-63861 |
| 359th: | 1-0 loco, 0-6 railcars<br>Lt. Henry D. Semple (370th Ftr Sqn) b/o Continent; o.k.<br>P-51D CS-S 44-14129 |
| 364th: | 12-2 locos, 15-45 railcars, 2-0 vehicles |

**February 26, 1945**
Groups Operating: P-51 4th, 20th, 55th, 78th, 339th, 352nd, 353rd, 355th, 356th, 357th, 359th, 361st, 364th, 479th
P-47 56th
Missions: Support of bombers to Berlin.
Claims: 0-0-0 air
7-0 ground

| *Group* | | *Claims* | *Location* |
|---|---|---|---|
| **55th** | | | |
| 343rd: | Lt. V.P. Gordon | FW-190 dest(grd) | S/Varel |
| | Lt. J.C. McVay | Me-110 dest(grd) | S/Varel |
| **364th** | | | |
| 385th: | Lt. K.R. Horner | (2)He-111 dest(grd) | SE Jade Bay |
| | Lt. A.B. McCormick | (1.5)He-111 dest(grd) | SE Jade Bay |
| | Lt. C.R. Roesch | (1.5)He-111 dest(grd) | SE Jade Bay |

*Losses-*

**20th:** Lt. Ralph D. Whitley (79th Ftr Sqn) POW
P-51D MC-C 44-13846 "Lil Bit"
Ran out of fuel and bailed out near Zutphen.

**78th:** F/O Charles R. O'Brien (83rd Ftr Sqn) POW(K)
P-51K HL-J 44-11627 "Green Eyes"
Suffered mechanical failure near Oldebrook; was later shot while trying to escape.

Lt. Leonard S. Olson (83rd Ftr Sqn) POW
P-51K HL-A 44-11655 "Poop Shooter"
Crashed while trying to land and rescue Lt. O'Brien.

**357th:** Lt. Roy Anthony (363rd Ftr Sqn) ASR
P-51D B6-H 44-14356 "Lonesome Polecat"
Bailed out ten miles off Southwold.

*Remarks*

| | |
|---|---|
| 20th: | Capt. John K. Taylor (79th Ftr Sqn) c/l; o.k.<br>P-51D MC-D 44-14844 "Joyce III" |
| 55th: | 2-1 locos, 0-1 railcar, 1-1 vehicles, 0-1 building |
| 353rd: | 9-0 locos, 0-17 railcars, 8-2 vehicles |
| 355th: | 7-12 locos, 19-99 railcars, 5-63 vehicles |
| 357th: | 0-3 vehicles |

**February 27, 1945**
Groups Operating: P-51 4th, 20th, 55th, 78th, 339th, 352nd, 353rd, 355th, 356th, 357th, 359th, 361st, 364th, 479th
P-47 56th
Missions: Support of bombers to Halle and Leipzig plus PRU escorts.
Claims: 2-0-0 air
83-28 ground

| *Group* | | *Claims* | *Location* |
|---|---|---|---|
| **4th** | | | |
| 334th: | Lt. D.M. Malmsten | (3)u/i a/c dest(grd) | Weimar A/F |
| | | (2)Ju-88 dest(grd) | Weimar A/F |
| | | Me-109 dest(grd) | Weimar A/F |
| | Maj. G.E. Montgomery | Do-217 dest(grd) | Weimar A/F |
| | | Me-108 dest(grd) | Weimar A/F |
| | | Ju-87 dest(grd) | Weimar A/F |
| | Lt. J.W. Ayers | (3)u/i a/c dest(grd) | Weimar A/F |
| | | (.5)Ju-52 dest(grd) | Weimar A/F |
| | Capt. T.R. Bell | (3)Me-109 dest(grd) | Weimar A/F |
| | Capt. H.E. Clifton | (3)Me-108 dest(grd) | Weimar A/F |
| | Lt. W.O. Antonides | (2)Ju-88 dest(grd) | Weimar A/F |
| | Lt. J.D. McFadden | Me-108 dest(grd) | Weimar A/F |
| | | Ju-87 dest(grd) | Weimar A/F |
| | Lt. C.G. Payne | (2)Me-108 dest(grd) | Weimar A/F |
| | Lt. L.C. Garvin | Me-108 dest(grd) | Weimar A/F |
| | Lt. C.W. Harre | Me-108 dest(grd) | Weimar A/F |
| | Lt. L.F. Wells | Me-109 dest(grd) | Weimar A/F |
| | Lt. R.S. Voyles | (.5)Ju-52 dest(grd) | Weimar A/F |
| 336th: | Maj. F.W. Glover | (2)Me-109 dest(grd) | Weimar A/F |
| | | FW-190 dest(grd) | Weimar A/F |
| | Lt. G.L. Kesler | (2)Ju-52 dest(grd) | Weimar A/F |
| | | Me-109 dest(grd) | Weimar A/F |
| | Lt. M.N. Dickey | Ju-87 dest(grd) | Weimar A/F |
| | | C-47 dest(grd) | Weimar A/F |
| | Maj. J.D. McFarlane | Me-108 dest(grd) | Weimar A/F |
| | Lt. H.R. Crawford | u/i a/c dest(grd) | Weimar A/F |
| | Lt. H.L. Davis | Me-108 dest(grd) | Weimar A/F |
| | Lt. R.O. Davis | Ju-88 dest(grd) | Weimar A/F |
| | Lt. E.F. Hustwit | Me-410 dest(grd) | Weimar A/F |
| | Lt. D.P. Pederson | u/i a/c dest(grd) | Weimar A/F |
| **55th** | | | |
| 343rd: | Capt. R.L. Buttke | (.5)Ju-88 dest(air) | Nurnburg |
| | Lt. L.D. Boring | (.5)Ju-88 dest(air) | Nurnburg |

| | | | |
|---|---|---|---|
| **56th** | | | |
| HdQts: | LtCol. L.C. Smith | (2)u/i a/c dest(grd) | Weimar A/F |
| | | (3)u/i a/c dam(grd) | Weimar A/F |
| 61st: | Lt. R.A. Baughman | (2)u/i a/c dest(grd) | Weimar A/F |
| **353rd** | | | |
| 350th: | Maj. W.L. Boone | (2)FW-190 dest(grd) | Rohrensee |
| | | (2)He-219 dest(grd) | Rohrensee |
| | | Ar-234 dest(grd) | Rohrensee |
| | | Ju-188 dest(grd) | Rohrensee |
| | | Me-410 dest(grd) | Rohrensee |
| | | (3)u/i a/c dam(grd) | Rohrensee |
| | | He-219 dam(grd) | Rohrensee |
| | | FW-190 dam(grd) | Rohrensee |
| | Lt. R.J. Lanoue | (2)Me-410 dest(grd) | Rohrensee |
| | | (2)u/i a/c dest(grd) | Rohrensee |
| | | FW-190 dest(grd) | Rohrensee |
| | | FW-190 dam(grd) | Rohrensee |
| | Capt. H.G. Kolb | (3)FW-190 dest(grd) | Rohrensee |
| | | (1.5)Me-410 dest(grd) | Rohrensee |
| | | (.5)u/i a/c dest(grd) | Rohrensee |
| | | FW-190 dam(grd) | Rohrensee |
| | Lt. R.C. Gordon | (2)Me-110 dest(grd) | Rohrensee |
| | | Ju-88 dest(grd) | Rohrensee |
| | | (2)Me-110 dam(grd) | Rohrensee |
| | | (2)Ju-88 dam(grd) | Rohrensee |
| | Lt. J.W. Clark | (2)Me-110 dest(grd) | Rohrensee |
| | | Me-109 dest(grd) | Rohrensee |
| | | (2)Me-410 dam(grd) | Rohrensee |
| | Lt. C.A. Larsen | (2)Me-410 dest(grd) | Rohrensee |
| | Lt. A.G. Spriggs | Me-109 dest(grd) | Rohrensee |
| | | u/i a/c dest(grd) | Rohrensee |
| | F/O R.N. Gustke | Me-410 dest(grd) | Rohrensee |
| | | Ju-88 dest(grd) | Rohrensee |
| | | (.5)FW-190 dest(grd) | Rohrensee |
| | | (4)u/i a/c dam(grd) | Rohrensee |
| | Lt. W. Grizzle | (1.5)Me-410 dest(grd) | Rohrensee |
| | | FW-190 dam(grd) | Rohrensee |
| | | u/i a/c dam(grd) | Rohrensee |
| | Lt. H.H. Hakonen | Me-410 dest(grd) | Rohrensee |
| | | (.5)u/i a/c dest(grd) | Rohrensee |
| | | Me-410 dam(grd) | Rohrensee |
| | Lt. J.D. McMullen | (1.5)FW-190 dest(grd) | Rohrensee |
| | | Ju-88 dest(grd) | Rohrensee |
| | | FW-190 dam(grd) | Rohrensee |
| | | Ju-88 dam(grd) | Rohrensee |
| | Lt. H.E. Caton | Ju-88 dest(grd) | Rohrensee |
| | | (2)Me-109 dam(grd) | Rohrensee |
| | Lt. R.S. Liebold | Me-410 dest(grd) | Rohrensee |
| | | Me-410 dam(grd) | Rohrensee |
| **355th** | | | |
| 358th: | Capt. J.N. McElroy | Do-217 dest(air) | SW Plauen |

*Losses-*

**4th**: Lt. Robert S. Voyles (334th Ftr Sqn) POW
P-51D QP-A 44-14537 "Old Witch"
Hit by flak at Weimar Airfield.

Lt. Harold R. Crawford (336th Ftr Sqn) POW
P-51K VF- 44-11665
Hit by flak at Weimar Airfield.

**55th**: Lt. Victor P. Krambo (343rd Ftr Sqn) POW
P-51D CY-U 44-15406
Damaged by a ground explosion near Boattingen.

**357th**: Lt. Daniel N. Myers (363rd Ftr Sqn) ASR
P-51D B6-
Ran out of fuel and bailed out over the North Sea.

*Remarks*
20th: 5-3 vehicles, 1-0 wagon
55th: 22-19 locos, 0-64 railcars, 10-2 vehicles, 2-1 buildings
56th: 1-0 loco, 0-76 railcars, 0-2 vehicles
78th: 1-0 loco, 0-14 railcars
353rd: 21-12 railcars
357th: 0-2 locos, 10-25 railcars, 4-0 vehicles
359th: 1-0 loco, 0-5 railcars, 1-0 vehicle, 0-1 building
364th: 1-3 vehicles, 0-1 motorcycle
479th: P-51 c/l Dettling; o.k.

KIAc's
357th: Lt. Robert R. Hoffman (364th Ftr Sqn)
P-51B B6-P 43-24766(this was a 363rd Ftr Sqn a/c)
Collided with Lt. Eisert near Leiston.

Lt. Ralph E. Eisert (364th Ftr Sqn)
P-51B C5-X 42-106447
Collided with Lt. Hoffman near Leiston.

**February 28, 1945**
Groups Operating: P-51 4th, 20th, 55th, 78th, 339th, 352nd, 353rd, 355th, 356th, 357th, 359th, 361st, 364th, 479th
P-47 56th
Missions: Support of bombers to rail targets in Germany; the 56th carried out fighter-bomber operations in the Ablar-Offenbach-Werdorf area, some P-51 units flew strafing sweeps in the Wurzburg-Munich area, and PRU escorts.
Claims: 0-0-1 air
17-12 ground

| *Group* | | *Claims* | *Location* |
|---|---|---|---|
| **20th** | | | |
| 77th: | Lt. R.A. Rege | Me-109 dam(grd) | Gelsheim |
| **55th** | | | |
| 343rd: | Lt. B.H. Howes | FW-190 dest(grd) | SW Nurnburg |
| **78th** | | | |
| 82nd: | Lt. W.F. Bechtelheimer | (.5)Me-262 dam(air) | Hersfeld-Fulda |
| | Lt. J.E. Parker | (.5)Me-262 dam(air) | Hersfeld-Fulda |
| **353rd** | | | |
| 350th: | Lt. M.W. Hightshoe | (1.5)Me-110 dest(grd) | S/Gotha |
| | | Me-109 dest(grd) | S/Gotha |
| | | Me-410 dest(grd) | S/Gotha |
| | Lt. R.J. Lanoue | (3)Me-110 dest(grd) | S/Gotha |
| | Lt. J.D. McMullen | (1.5)Me-110 dest(grd) | S/Gotha |
| | Lt. J.A. Madson | u/i a/c dest(grd) | S/Gotha |
| | | Ju 88 dam(grd) | S/Gotha |
| | Lt. G.W. Robison | Me-410 dest(grd) | Sonneborn |
| | Lt. G.D. Kammer | He-111 dam(grd) | Sonneborn |
| **357th** | | | |
| HdQts: | Maj. R.W. Foy | Ju-88 dest(grd) | Lubeck-Blankensee |
| | | FW-200 dam(grd) | Lubeck-Blankensee |
| | | Me-109 dam(grd) | Lubeck-Blankensee |
| 363rd: | Capt. J.R. Stern | Ju-88 dam(grd) | Lubeck-Blankensee |
| 364th: | Lt. E.R. Fry | (2)u/i a/c dest(grd) | Lubeck-Blankensee |
| | Lt. S. Wasylyk | u/i a/c dest(grd) | Lubeck-Blankensee |
| | LtCol. J.A. Storch | (2)u/i a/c dam(grd) | Lubeck-Blankensee |
| | Lt. R.R. Lepore | (4)u/i a/c dam(grd) | Lubeck-Blankensee |
| **359th** | | | |
| 368th: | Lt. G.H. Blackburn | Me-109 dest(grd) | Gunzburg |
| | Lt. A.G. Martin | Me-109 dest(grd) | Gunzburg |

*Losses-*

**55th**: Capt. Jerry R. McDonald (338th Ftr Sqn) MIA
P-51D CL-
Hit by flak near Ingolstadt.

**78th**: F/O Harold R. Liebenrood (82nd Ftr Sqn) POW
P-51D MX-G 44-63203
Suffered mechanical failure southeast of Cologne.

**359th**: Maj. Edwin F. Pezda (369th Ftr Sqn) POW
P-51D IV-F 44-14625 "Pauline"
Hit by flak near Kunzelsau.

Capt. Harry L. Matthew (369th Ftr Sqn) POW
P-51D IV-T 44-15081 "Pistol Packin' Mama III"
Hit power lines and bailed out near Neustadt.

**479th**: Lt. Charles T. Schoen, Jr. (436th Ftr Sqn) KIA
P-51D 9B-E 44-14583 "Dearest Mine"
Hit by flak near Reichenaschen.

*Remarks*
20th: 17-2 locos, 0-76 railcars, 1-0 building
55th: 13-3 locos, 18-113 railcars, 19-11 vehicles, 14-18 buildings
56th: 3-2 locos, 4-58 railcars
339th: 2-8 railcars
353rd: 1-1 locos, 3-33 railcars, 0-3 vehicles, 0-4 gun positions
Maj. Wayne K. Blickenstaff (350th Ftr Sqn) c/l Raydon; o.k.
P-51D LH-U
355th: 2-0 locos, 5-32 railcars
357th: 0-2 locos,0-8 railcars, 0-1 hangar
359th: 12-5 locos, 5-58 railcars, 16-4 vehicles

**March 1, 1945**
Groups Operating: P-51 4th, 78th, 339th, 353rd, 355th, 356th, 361st, 364th, 479th
Missions: Support for bombers to Ingolstadt, Ulm, Bruschal, Heilbronn, and other secondary targets, plus some PRU escorts.
Claims: 3-0-3 air
9-7 ground

| *Group* | | *Claims* | *Location* |
|---|---|---|---|
| **SF** | | | |
| 2nd: | Lt. J.K. Wilkins | Me-262 dest(air) | Ingolstadt |
| | Maj. F.B. Elliott | Me-262 dam(air) | Ingolstadt |
| | Capt. C.W. Getz | Me-262 dam(air) | Ingolstadt |
| **78th** | | | |
| 84th: | Lt. R.D. Higgins | Me-109 dam(grd) | Boblingen |
| | | u/i a/c dam(grd) | Boblingen |
| | Lt. C.E. Taylor | u/i a/c dam(grd) | Boblingen |
| **339th** | | | |
| 505th: | Lt. S.C. Ananian | (2)Ju-88 dest(grd) | S/Feldkirchen |
| | LtCol. J.L. Thury | Ju-88 dest(grd) | S/Feldkirchen |
| | Lt. C.H. Bundgaard | Ju-88 dest(grd) | S/Feldkirchen |
| | Lt. T.W. Marvel | Ju-88 dest(grd) | S/Feldkirchen |
| | Lt. J.C. Woolery | Do-217 dest(grd) | S/Feldkirchen |
| | Lt. H.D. Ziegler | Ju-88 dest(grd) | S/Feldkirchen |
| | Lt. R.E. Irion | (.5)Ju-88 dest(grd) | S/Feldkirchen |
| | | (.5)Ju-88 dest(grd) | S/Feldkirchen |
| | Lt. B.B. Booth | (.5)Ju-88 dest(grd) | S/Feldkirchen |
| | Lt. O.K. Biggs | (.5)Ju-88 dest(grd) | S/Feldkirchen |
| **353rd** | | | |
| 352nd: | Capt. W.W. Johnson | Bu-181 dest(air) | Nordlingen |
| | | (4)u/i a/c dam(grd) | Nordlingen |
| **355th** | | | |
| HdQts: | Maj. H.H. Kirby | Me-262 dam(air) | Donauworth |
| 358th: | Lt. W.W. Beaty | Me-262 dest(air) | Ingolstadt |

*Losses-*

**78th**: Lt. Ernest V. Boehner (82nd Ftr Sqn) KIA
P-51K MX-E 44-11652
Hit by flak west of Kassel.

Lt. Roy D. Higgins (84th Ftr Sqn) KIA
P-51D WZ-N 44-72178
Hit by flak at Boblingen and bailed out too low.

Lt. William D. Townsend, Jr. (84th Ftr Sqn) MIA
P-51D WZ-E 44-72190
Wing hit the ground while strafing near Heimsheim.

**355th**: Capt. Jack M. Beckman (358th Ftr Sqn) KIA
P-51D YF-T 44-14230 "Trigger III"
Hit by flak while chasing a Me-262 near Ingolstadt.

**356th**: Lt. Walter O. Hedrick (360th Ftr Sqn) POW
P-51D PI-F 44-11156 "Brenda"
Suffered mechanical failure and bailed out near Strasbourg.

**364th**: F/O Wilson W. Montague (385th Ftr Sqn) KIA
P-51D 5E-B 44-14254 "Majero"
Hit by flak southwest of Ludwigshafen.

**479th**: Maj. Thomas F. Trabucco (435th Ftr Sqn) KIA
P-51D J2-A 44-15374 "Dotty"
Lost for unknown reasons near Haldenwang.

*Remarks*

4th: 0-6 locos, 0-11 railcars, 7-4 vehicles
Capt. Edward L. Gimbel (336th Ftr Sqn) c/l Brussels; o.k.
P-51D VF- 44-14029
78th: 1-0 loco, 0-3 railcars, 3-3 vehicles, 0-2 radio towers
339th: 1-0 loco, 0-12 railcars, 0-1 vehicle, 0-11 buildings
353rd: 25-1 locos, 10-137 railcars, 14-12 vehicles, 0-4 buildings, 0-3 flak towers
355th: 1-1 loco, 4-28 railcars, 0-23 vehicles, 0-4 buildings
Lt. Jack H. Dressler (357th Ftr Sqn) c/l Steeple Morden; o.k.
P-51D OS-S 44-14753
356th: Lt. Lucien O. Sonnier (359th Ftr Sqn) b/o Monewden; o.k.
P-51D OC-D 44-15185 "T-Lou"
364th: 3-2 locos, 0-34 railcars, 2-0 vehicles
479th: P-51 c/l; o.k.
P-51D L2-T 44-14423

KIAc's

55th: Lt. William R. Watkins (338th Ftr Sqn)
P-51D CY- 44-14161
Killed in a crash near Canewdown.

**March 2, 1945**

Groups Operating: P-51 4th, 20th, 55th, 78th, 339th, 352nd, 353rd, 355th, 356th, 357th, 359th, 361st, 364th, 479th
P-47 56th
Missions: Support of bombers to Dresden, Chemnitz, and Magdeburg, plus PRU escorts.
Claims: 67-7-23 air
34-26 ground

| *Group* | | *Claims* | *Location* |
|---|---|---|---|
| **20th** | | | |
| 77th: | Lt. R.D. Jones | FW-190 dam(air) | Chemnitz |
| | Lt. D.F. McAllister | FW-190 dam(air) | Chemnitz |
| **78th** | | | |
| HdQts: | LtCol. J.D. Landers | (2)Me-109 dest(air) | Burg A/F |
| 83rd: | Lt. D.M. McDuffie | (4)Me-109 dest(air) | Burg A/F |
| | Maj. W.H. Julian | (2)Me-109 dest(air) | Burg A/F |
| | | Me-109 dam(air) | Burg A/F |
| | Lt. J.D. Hodge | (2)Me-109 dest(air) | Burg A/F |
| | Capt. F.E. Higginbottom | Me-109 dest(air) | Burg A/F |
| | | Me-109 prob(air) | Burg A/F |
| | Lt. H. Davis | Me-109 dest(air) | Burg A/F |
| | | Me-109 dam(air) | Burg A/F |
| | Lt. R.I. Kuehl | Me-109 dest(air) | Burg A/F |
| | | Me-109 dam(air) | Burg A/F |
| | Capt. R.E. Wise | Me-109 dam(air) | Burg A/F |
| | Lt. R.F. Rohm | Me-109 dam(air) | Burg A/F |
| **339th** | | | |
| 503rd: | Lt. L. Poutre | (2)Me-109 dest(air) | E/Magdeburg |
| | | FW-190 dest(air) | E/Magdeburg |
| | Maj. W.E. Bryan | FW-190 dest(air) | E/Magdeburg |
| | | Me-109 dest(air) | E/Magdeburg |
| | | FW-190 dam(air) | E/Magdeburg |
| | Lt. F.R. Gerard | (2)Me-109 dest(air) | E/Magdeburg |
| | | Me-109 dam(air) | E/Magdeburg |
| | Lt. W.R. Preddy | FW-190 dest(air) | E/Magdeburg |
| | | Me-109 prob(air) | E/Magdeburg |
| | Lt. J.W. Gokey | Me-109 dest(air) | E/Magdeburg |
| | Lt. S.J. Chetneky | Me-109 dest(air) | E/Magdeburg |
| | | Me-109 dam(air) | E/Magdeburg |
| | Lt. F. Butler | FW-190 prob(air) | E/Magdeburg |
| | | Me-109 dam(air) | E/Magdeburg |
| | Capt. W.W. Behrend | Me-109 dam(air) | E/Magdeburg |
| | Lt. C.H. French | Me-109 dam(air) | E/Magdeburg |
| | Lt. R.J. Frisch | Me-109 dam(air) | E/Magdeburg |
| 505th: | Lt. J.F. Marts | (2)Me-109 dest(air) | E/Magdeburg |
| | Capt. J.R. Starnes | Me-109 dest(air) | E/Magdeburg |
| | | u/i a/c dam(grd) | E/Magdeburg |
| | Lt. J.C. Withers | (.5)Me-109 dest(air) | E/Magdeburg |
| | Lt. H.D. Ziegler | (.5)Me-109 dest(air) | E/Magdeburg |
| | Lt. G.W. Jones | Me-109 dam(air) | Osnabruck |
| | Lt. O.K. Biggs | (3)Do-217 dest(grd) | Mockern |
| | | (2)Do-217 dam(grd) | Mockern |
| | Lt. H.W. Burch | (3)Do-217 dest(grd) | Mockern |
| | Lt. H.F. Howard | (3)Do-217 dest(grd) | Mockern |
| | Lt. B.A. Connor | (2)Do-217 dest(grd) | Mockern |
| **352nd** | | | |
| HdQts: | LtCol. W.O. Jackson | FW-189 dest(air) | Prague |
| | | (2)u/i a/c dam(grd) | Prague |
| 486th: | Capt. E.L. Heller | FW-190 dest(air) | SE Leipzig |
| | | FW-190 dam(air) | SE Leipzig |
| | Lt. C.D. Price | FW-190 dest(air) | Zwebau |
| | Lt. E.A. Paulsen | FW-190 dest(air) | Zwickau |
| | | FW-190 prob(air) | Zwickau |
| | Lt. D.M. Reichman | FW-190 dest(air) | Zwebau |
| | Capt. L.E. Kilgo | (.5)FW-190 dest(air) | Prague |
| | Lt. E.L. Mundell | (.5)FW-190 dest(air) | Prague |
| | Lt. M.J. Stover | FW-190 prob(air) | Zwickau |
| | | FW-190 dam(air) | Zwickau |
| | Capt. C.V. Harker | FW-190 dam(grd) | Prague |
| | | Me-410 dam(grd) | Prague |
| | Lt. C.C. Pattillo | (2)u/i a/c dam(grd) | Prague |
| **353rd** | | | |
| HdQts: | LtCol. W.B. Bailey | (2)FW-190 dest(air) | S/Wittenburg |
| 350th: | Lt. L.W. Lee | Me-109 dest(air) | Ruhland |
| | | Me-109 dam(air) | Ruhland |
| | Lt. R.J. Lanoue | Me-109 dest(air) | Ruhland |
| | Lt. G.D. Page | Me-109 dest(air) | Ruhland |
| | Lt. W.M. Agnew | Me-109 prob(air) | Ruhland |
| | Maj. W.L. Boone | Me-109 dam(air) | Ruhland |
| 351st: | Maj. V.L. Byers | FW-190 dest(air) | Wittenburg |
| | | Me-109 prob(air) | Wittenburg |
| 352nd: | Lt. A.C. Cundy | (2)FW-190 dest(air) | Dessau |
| | | Me-109 dest(air) | Dessau |
| | Lt. H.Q. Waggoner | (2)FW-190 dest(air) | Ruhland |
| | | Me-109 dest(air) | Ruhland |
| | Lt. E.J. Sullivan | FW-190 dest(air) | S/Wittenburg |
| | Lt. L.W. Grove | Me-109 dest(air) | S/Berlin |
| | Lt. J. Schreiber | Me-109 dest(air) | Magdeburg |
| **357th** | | | |
| 362nd: | Capt. J.L. Sublett | Me-109 dest(air) | NE Leipzig |
| | | FW-190 dest(air) | NE Leipzig |
| | Lt. M.A. Becraft | Me-109 dest(air) | Kamenz A/F |

| | | | |
|---|---|---|---|
| | | (2)He-111 dest(grd) | Kamenz A/F |
| | | (2)u/i a/c dest(grd) | Kamenz A/F |
| | Lt. J.F. Duncan | Me-109 dest(air) | NE Leipzig |
| | | Me-109 dam(air) | NE Leipzig |
| | Lt. O.T. Ridley | (.5)Me-109 dest(air)* | NE Leipzig |
| | Lt. W.W. Gruber | FW-190 dam(air) | NE Leipzig |
| | Lt. G.A. Robinson | (4)He-111 dest(grd) | Kamenz A/F |
| | | He-111 dam(grd) | Kamenz A/F |
| | | u/i a/c dam(grd) | Kamenz A/F |
| 363rd: | Capt. D.C. McGee | Me-109 dest(air) | NE Magdeburg |
| 364th: | Capt. A.C. Murphy | (2)Me-109 dest(air) | SE Magdeburg |
| | Capt. R.G. Schimanski | (1.5)Me-109 dest(air)** | SE Magdeburg |
| | | (2)He-111 dest(grd) | E/Magdeburg |
| | Lt. D.E. Karger | (.5)Me-109 dest(air)** | SE Magdeburg |
| | | (4)u/i a/c dest(grd) | E/Magdeburg |
| | | (2)Ju-88 dam(grd) | E/Magdeburg |
| | | Ju-188 dam(grd) | E/Magdeburg |
| | | u/i a/c dam(grd) | E/Magdeburg |
| | Lt. R.M. Bank | Me-109 dest(air) | SE Magdeburg |
| | | He-111 dam(grd) | E/Magdeburg |
| | Lt. O. Howes | Me-109 dest(air) | SE Magdeburg |
| | | He-111 dest(grd) | E/Magdeburg |
| | Lt. V.V. Zettler | Me-109 dest(air) | SE Magdeburg |
| | | (4)He-111 dest(grd) | E/Magdeburg |
| | F/O J.A. Steiger | Me-109 dest(air) | SW Magdeburg |
| | Capt. P.R. Hatala | (.5)Me-109 dest(air)* | NE Leipzig |
| | Lt. D.R. Williams | (2)Ju-88 dest(grd) | E/Magdeburg |
| | | (8)He-111 dam(grd) | E/Magdeburg |
| | | u/i a/c dam(grd) | E/Magdeburg |
| | Lt. R.R. Lepore | (2)He-111 dest(grd) | E/Magdeburg |
| | Lt. H. Wesling | He-111 dam(grd) | E/Magdeburg |
| **364th** | | | |
| 384th: | Lt. F.T. O'Connor | Me-262 dam(air) | NE Frankfurt |

*Losses-*

**55th**: Lt. Samuel F. Anderson (38th Ftr Sqn) KIA
P-51D CG-B 44-13818 "Mah Ideel"
Last seen in the overcast near Limburg.

**78th**: Lt. Henry M. Staub (83rd Ftr Sqn) POW
P-51D HL-R 44-63285
Hit by a Me-109 near Magdeburg.

**339th**: Lt. Esteban A. Terrants (503rd Ftr Sqn) KIA
P-51C D7-H 43-25050
Hit by enemy fighters near Schlanau.

Lt. Bertis A. Connor, Jr. (505th Ftr Sqn) POW
P-51K 6N- 44-11363 "Therese"
Hit by flak near Mockern.

Lt. Harry F. Howard (505th Ftr Sqn) POW
P-51D 6N-E 44-14622
Hit trees while strafing near Mockern.

**353rd**: Lt. John W. Rohrs (351st Ftr Sqn) KIA
P-51D YJ-U 44-14781 "Don Helen"
Hit by either flak or bomber fire near Madel.

Lt. Joseph Schreiber (352nd Ftr Sqn) POW
P-51D SX-Z 44-15691 "Lil Shirl"
Hit by enemy fighters near Belzig.

Lt. Edward J. Sullivan (352nd Ftr Sqn) POW
P-51D SX-Q 44-15184 "Truly Trudie"
Hit by enemy fighters near Niebel.

**357th**: F/O Patrick L. Mallion (363rd Ftr Sqn) KIA
P-51D B6-Y 44-14888 "Melody's Answer"
Hit by flak near Haseloff.

Lt. Matthew Crawford (363rd Ftr Sqn) POW
P-51D B6- 44-15161 "Joyce Diane"
Hit by flak near Gruezburg.

Capt. Alva C. Murphy (364th Ftr Sqn) KIA
P-51D C5- 44-63765
Hit by flak southwest of Magdeburg.

Lt. Raymond M. Bank (364th Ftr Sqn) POW
P-51D C5-Y 44-15266 "Fireball"
Hit by enemy fighters southeast of Ruhland.

Lt. Roscoe R. Lepore (364th Ftr Sqn) POW
P-51D C5-C 44-14555 "Pretty Pat"
Hit by flak east of Magdeburg.

*Remarks*

4th: Lt. William H. Hastings (336th Ftr Sqn) c/l; o.k.
P-51D VF-G 44-14492
Lt. Maurice W. Miller (336th Ftr Sqn) c/l; o.k.
P-51D VF-

355th: Lt. Edwin W. Fees (358th Ftr Sqn) c/l; o.k.
P-51D YF-X 44-13708

479th: 436th Ftr Sqn P-51 c/l Wattisham; o.k.
P-51D 9B-

KIAc's

359th: Lt. Merle G. Aunspaugh (368th Ftr Sqn)
P-51D CV-
While on a practice gunnery flight, he dropped too low and crashed into trees near Polebrook.

**March 3, 1945**

Groups Operating: P-51 4th, 20th, 55th, 78th, 339th, 352nd, 353rd, 355th, 356th, 357th, 359th, 361st, 364th, 479th
P-47 56th

Missions: Support of bombers to Misburg, Ruhland, Nienburg, Brunswick, Bielefeld, and Magdeburg.

Claims: 1-0-6 air
13-30 ground

| ***Group*** | | ***Claims*** | ***Location*** |
|---|---|---|---|
| **4th** | | | |
| HdQts: | Col. E.W. Stewart | Me-262 dam(air) | Gardelegen |
| **55th** | | | |
| 343rd: | Lt. V.P. Gordon | Me-109 dest(grd) | Prague/Letnany |
| | | Ju-52 dest(grd) | Prague/Letnany |
| | | (4)Me-109 dam(grd) | Prague/Letnany |
| | Lt. B.J. Liles | Me-109 dest(grd) | Prague/Letnany |
| | | (2)Me-109 dam(grd) | Prague/Letnany |
| | | (2)Ju-52 dam(grd) | Prague/Letnany |
| | | Ju-88 dam(grd) | Prague/Letnany |
| | Lt. B.H. Howes | Me-109 dest(grd) | Prague/Letnany |
| | | Me-109 dam(grd) | Prague/Letnany |
| | | Me-110 dam(grd) | Prague/Letnany |
| | | Ju-52 dam(grd) | Prague/Letnany |
| | | Ju-88 dam(grd) | Prague/Letnany |
| | Lt. W.R. Erickson | Me-110 dest(grd) | Prague/Letnany |
| | | Me-109 dam(grd) | Prague/Letnany |
| | | Ju-88 dam(grd) | Prague/Letnany |
| | Lt. M. Satenstein | (4)Me-109 dam(grd) | Prague/Letnany |
| | Lt. H. Cohen | (2)Me-109 dam(grd) | Prague/Letnany |
| | Lt. W. Mearns | Me-109 dam(grd) | Prague/Letnany |
| | | Ju-88 dam(grd) | Prague/Letnany |
| **339th** | | | |
| 503rd: | Lt. R.G. Johnson | Me-262 dam(air) | Celle |
| 505th: | LtCol. J.L. Thury | (3)Ju-88 dest(grd) | E/Magdeburg |
| | | Do-217 dest(grd) | E/Magdeburg |
| | | Ju-88 dam(grd) | E/Magdeburg |
| | Capt. J.R. Starnes | He-111 dest(grd) | E/Magdeburg |
| | Lt. G.W. Jones | u/i a/c dest(grd) | E/Magdeburg |
| | Lt. R.C. Thieme | Ju-88 dest(grd) | E/Magdeburg |
| | Lt. H.D. Ziegler | Ju-88 dest(grd) | E/Magdeburg |
| | Lt. J.C. Withers | Ju-88 dam(grd) | E/Magdeburg |
| **352nd** | | | |
| 328th: | Lt. W.H. Sanford | Me-109 dest(air) | W/Dresden |
| **353rd** | | | |
| 351st: | Lt. J.E. Frye | Me-262 dam(air) | SE Hamburg |
| **355th** | | | |
| 357th: | Lt. W.S. Lyons | Me-262 dam(air) | Brunswick |
| **357th** | | | |
| 362nd: | Capt. J.L. Sublett | Me-262 dam(air) | NE Magdeburg |
| 364th: | Capt. I.L. McGuire | Me-262 dam(air) | S/Brunswick |
| **359th** | | | |
| 368th: | Lt. A.A. Cowie | u/i a/c dam(grd) | Hanover |
| **479th** | | | |
| 435th: | Lt. R.G. Candelaria | (3)Me-109 dam(grd) | Dummer Lake |
| | Lt. B.C. Means | Me-109 dam(grd) | Dummer Lake |

*Losses-*

**4th**: Capt. George H. Davis (335th Ftr Sqn) POW
P-51D WD- 44-63599
Hit by flak in the Celle-Ulzen area.

Lt. Kenneth Green (335th Ftr Sqn) POW
P-51D WD-U 44-14923 "See Me Later"
Hit by flak and crashed near Rotterdam.

**55th**: Lt. Brooks J. Liles (343rd Ftr Sqn) POW
P-51D CY- 44-14175 "Sweet Marie II"
Hit by flak at Prague/Letnany Airfield.

Lt. Bernard H. Howes (343rd Ftr Sqn) POW
P-51D CY-C 44-63745
Landed at Prague/Letnany to pick-up Lt. Liles but failed to take-off.

**339th**: Lt. Otis A. Kurth (504th Ftr Sqn) KIA
P-51D 5Q-
Died after crashing in England upon return.

Lt. George W. Jones, Jr. (505th Ftr Sqn) KIA
P-51D 6N- 44-11204
Suffered mechanical failure near Mockbern and bailed out too low.

Lt. Harry D. Ziegler (505th Ftr Sqn) POW
P-51D 6N- 44-14023 "Chute! You're Faded"
Hit by flak near Mockbern and bellied-in near Magdeburg.

**359th**: Lt. Albert A. Cowie (368th Ftr Sqn) POW
P-51K CV-G 44-11696
Hit by flak near Hanover and bellied-in near Halberstadt.

**479th**: Lt. Elbert N. Harris (434th Ftr Sqn) MIA
P-51D L2-A 44-63189 "Mary"
Suffered mechanical failure near Magdeburg.

*Remarks*
4th: 0-2 locos, 1-0 vehicle
55th: 21-8 locos, 0-20 railcars, 8-10 vehicles, 0-1 building
339th: 3-0 locos, 20-0 railcars, 1-0 vehicle
352nd: 0-1 loco, 10-5 railcars
353rd: 5-0 locos, 0-18 railcars
359th: 2-1 locos, 13-0 railcars, 2-0 vehicles, 0-2 buildings

**March 4, 1945**
Groups Operating: P-51 4th, 20th, 55th, 78th, 339th, 352nd, 353rd, 355th, 356th, 357th, 359th, 361st, 364th, 479th
P-47 56th
Missions: Support for bombers to Ulm and numerous targets of opportunity due to weather conditions.
Claims: nil

*Losses-*

**78th**: Lt. Louis R. Hereford (84th Ftr Sqn) KIA
P-51D WZ-S 44-63209 "Sherman Was Right!"
Lost in bad weather southeast of Nordlingen.

*Remarks*
55th: Capt. Jessie D. Thompson (38th Ftr Sqn) b/o Troyes; o.k.
P-51D CG-
339th: Lt. Dennis B. Rawls (503rd Ftr Sqn) c/l Fowlmere; o.k.
P-51D D7-D 44-15134
Lt. Henry W. Gauger (503rd Ftr Sqn) c/l Continent; o.k.
P-51D D7-

**March 5, 1945**
Groups Operating: P-51 4th, 20th, 55th, 78th, 339th, 352nd, 353rd355th, 356th, 357th, 359th, 361st, 364th, 479th
P-47 56th
Missions: Support for bombers to Chemnitz and Hamburg, plus some PRU escorts.
Claims: nil

*Losses-*

**78th**: Lt. Robert K. Platt (82nd Ftr Sqn) KIA
P-51D MX-K 44-63238
Crashed on take-off from Duxford.

*Remarks*
339th: Lt. Henry W. Gauger (503rd Ftr Sqn) c/l Continent; o.k.
P-51 D7-
355th: Lt. Harold P. Knutty (358th Ftr Sqn) b/o Bierset; o.k.
P-51D YF-H
361st: Lt. Ray D. Schrup (376th Ftr Sqn) c/l Roermond; o.k.
P-51D E9-
364th: Lt. Fred L. Raffel (384th Ftr Sqn) b/o Tonges; o.k.
P-51D 5Y-Q 44-15538

**March 6, 1945**
Groups Operating: P-51 352nd, 361st
Missions: Patrols of the battle area.
Claims: nil
Losses: nil

KIAc's
20th: Lt. Mark F. Smith (79th Ftr Sqn)
P-51D MC-

**March 7, 1945**
Groups Operating: P-51 55th, 78th, 356th, 357th, 364th, 479th
P-47 56th
Missions: Support for bombers to Soest, Siegen, and various targets of opportunity, plus PRU escorts.
Claims: nil
Losses: nil

KIAc's
78th: Lt. Donald A. Bath (84th Ftr Sqn)
P-51D WZ-G 44-63799
Stalled out while dog-fighting and crashed near Duxford.

**March 8, 1945**
Groups Operating: P-51 4th, 20th, 339th, 353rd, 355th, 359th
Missions: Support for bombers to Siegen, Betzdorf, Langendreer, Dortmund, Frankfurt, Bottrop, Huls, Gelsenkirchen, Essen, and other targets of opportunity.
Claims: nil
Losses: nil

**March 9, 1945**
Groups Operating: P-51 55th, 78th, 352nd, 356th, 357th, 359th, 361st, 364th, 479th
P-47 56th
Missions: Support for bombers to Frankfurt, Kassel, and Munster. Some units carried out sweeps and some PRU escorts.
Claims: 1-0-1 air
0-0 ground

| *Group* | | *Claims* | *Location* |
|---|---|---|---|
| **55th** | | | |
| 38th: | Lt. J.F. O'Neill | Me-262 dam(air) | Giebelstadt A/F |
| **361st** | | | |
| 375th: | Capt. A. Maurice | FW-190 dest(air) | W/Giessen |

Losses: nil

*Remarks*
359th: Lt. Arthur B. Morris (369th Ftr Sqn) b/o East Wretham; o.k.
P-51D IV-E 44-14988
361st: P-51 c/l Continent; o.k.
P-51 c/l Continent; o.k.

**March 10, 1945**
Groups Operating: P-51 4th, 20th, 55th, 339th, 352nd, 353rd, 355th, 356th, 357th, 359th, 361st, 364th, 479th
P-47 56th
Missions: Support for bombers to Arnsberg, Paderborn, Bielefeld, Soest, Dortmund, and Schwerte. Some PRU escorts were flown and the 352nd and 361st supported 9th Air Force operations.
Claims: 1-0-1 air
0-0 ground

| *Group* | | *Claims* | *Location* |
|---|---|---|---|
| **56th** | | | |
| 62nd: | Lt. N.D. Gould | Me-109 dest(air) | Remagen |
| | Lt. D.A. Carroll | (.5)FW-190 dest(air) | Remagen |
| | Lt. D. Henley | (.5)FW-190 dest(air) | Remagen |

*Losses-*

**359th**: Lt. George H. Blackburn (368th Ftr Sqn) KIA
P-51D CV-G 44-15067 "Little Ann"
Hit by flak at Remagen.(Originally believed to have been hit by American gunners, it has been discovered that German anti-aircraft fire was responsible)

Lt. John W. McCormack (368th Ftr Sqn) KIA
P-51D CV-A 44-63740 "Little Audrey"
Hit by flak at Remagen(See remarks above)

*Remarks*
339th: Lt. Jerome J. Sainlar (504th Ftr Sqn) b/o St. Trond; o.k.
P-51D 5Q-
359th: Capt. Ray S. Wetmore (370th Ftr Sqn) c/l France; o.k.
P-51D CS-

**March 11, 1945**
Groups Operating: P-51 4th, 20th, 55th, 78th, 339th, 352nd, 353rd, 355th, 356th, 357th, 359th, 361st, 364th, 479th
P-47 56th
Missions: Support for bombers to Kiel, Hamburg, and Bremen, plus PRU escorts.
Claims: nil

*Losses-*

**78th**: Lt. Jack D. Hodge (83rd Ftr Sqn) KIA
P-51D HL-Q 44-15627 "Windy City Mama"
Lost coolant and bailed out near Vesjle.

**353rd**: Lt. Arthur C. Cundy (352nd Ftr Sqn) KIA
P-51D SX-D
Suffered mechanical failure and bailed out forty miles off Great Yarmouth.

**359th**: LtCol. James V. Wilson (HdQts) POW
P-51D IV- 44-72207
Lost coolant and bailed out north of the Frisian Islands.

**479th**: Lt. Lewis C. Smith (436th Ftr Sqn) KIA
P-51D 9B- 44-14576
Bailed out east of Lowestoft and was dead when reached by ASR personnel.

*Remarks*
353rd: Lt. Leroy O. Pletz (352nd Ftr Sqn) c/l; o.k.
P-51D SX-
356th: Lt. Clarence L. Walters (359th Ftr Sqn) c/l Martlesham Heath; o.k.
P-51D OC-Y
Lt. John C. Lindsay (361st Ftr Sqn) c/l St. Trond; o.k.
P-51D QI-

KIAc's
56th: Lt. Frank R. Aheron (62nd Ftr Sqn)
P-47M LM-
Died in a crash near Cranfield.

**March 12, 1945**
Groups Operating: P-51 4th, 20th, 55th, 78th, 339th, 352nd, 353rd, 355th, 356th, 357th, 359th, 361st, 364th, 479th
P-47 56th
Missions: Support of bombers to Swinemunde and other marshalling yards, plus PRU escorts.
Claims: 4-0-1 air
0-0 ground

| Group | | Claims | Location |
|---|---|---|---|
| **339th** | | | |
| 505th: | Capt. O.P. Farmer | (1.5)Me-109 dest(air) | Hellevad |
| | F/O J.R. Coker | Me-109 dest(air) | Hellevad |
| | | Me-109 dam(air) | Hellevad |
| | F/O J. Pesanka | Me-109 dest(air) | Hellevad |
| | Lt. V.D. Carr | (.5)Me-109 dest(air) | Hellevad |

*Losses-*

**4th**: Maj. John D. McFarlane (336th Ftr Sqn) MIA-E
P-51D VF-L 44-14350
Lost coolant and bailed out near Mon Island.

**78th**: Lt. Dean C. Johnson (83rd Ftr Sqn) MIA-E
P-51D HL-A 44-72214 "Poop Shooter II"
Lost coolant and bailed out near Laaland.

Lt. Anton A. Rosengreen (84th Ftr Sqn) ASR
P-51D WZ-N 44-72200
Was radio relay and bailed out over the Channel after suffering mechanical failure.

**339th**: Lt. Richard C. O'Brien (505th Ftr Sqn) MIA-E
P-51D 6N- 44-14086 "Angel of Mercy"
Suffered mechanical failure and bailed out near Laaland.

*Remarks*
56th: Lt. Alfred M. Bolender (63rd Ftr Sqn) c/l Continent; o.k.
P-47M UN-
356th: LtCol. James N. Wood (360th Ftr Sqn) c/l Martlesham Heath; o.k.
P-51D PI-V 44-15115 "Naughty Nordie"

**March 13, 1945**
Groups Operating: P-51 361st
Missions: Sweep of the Coblenz-Remagen area.
Claims: nil
Losses: nil

KIAc's
56th: Lt. Luther P. Hines (61st Ftr Sqn)
P-47M HV-
Collided with Lt. Tuttle during a cross-over.

Lt. Richard B. Tuttle (61st Ftr Sqn)
P-47M HV-
Collided with Lt. Hines during a cross-over.

**March 14, 1945**
Groups Operating: P-51 4th, 20th, 55th, 78th, 39th, 352nd, 353rd, 355th, 356th, 357th, 359th, 361st, 364th, 479th
P-47 56th
Missions: Support of bombers to oil and rail targets in Germany, patrols of the Remagen area, and PRU escorts.
Claims: 17-0-0 air
0-0 ground

| Group | | Claims | Location |
|---|---|---|---|
| **SF** | | | |
| 2nd: | Lt. C.R. Rodebaugh | Me-262 dest(air) | Coblenz |
| **56th** | | | |
| 62nd: | Lt. N.D. Gould | Ar-234 dest(air) | Coblenz |
| | Lt. S. Pruitt | Me-109 dest(air) | Frankfurt |
| | Lt. S.N. Ball | (.5)Ar-234 dest(air) | Coblenz |
| | Lt. W.S. Lear | (.5)Ar-234 dest(air) | Coblenz |
| **352nd** | | | |
| 328th: | Capt. D.S. Bryan | Ar-234 dest(air) | Elsaffthal |
| **353rd** | | | |
| 351st: | Capt. G.E. Markham | (3)Me-109 dest(air) | Luckenwalde |
| | Capt. W.J. Maguire | (2)Me-109 dest(air) | Luckenwalde |
| | Lt. G.S. Montgomery | (2)Me-109 dest(air) | Luckenwalde |
| | Lt. T.C. Brock | Me-109 dest(air) | Luckenwalde |
| | Lt. J.O. Fulton | Me-109 dest(air) | Luckenwalde |
| | Lt. J.A. Hynes | Me-109 dest(air) | Luckenwalde |
| | Lt. E.J. Risk | Me-109 dest(air) | Luckenwalde |
| **356th** | | | |
| 360th: | Lt. R.E. Barnhart | Ar-234 dest(air) | Bielefeld-Hildesheim |

*Losses-*

**56th**: Lt. Earl L. Townsend (62nd Ftr Sqn) KIA
P-47M LM-
Suffered mechanical failure and crashed off Ostend.

**361st**: Capt. Eugene Cole (375th Ftr Sqn) POW
P-51D E2-G 44-14792 "Margene"
Hit by flak and bellied-in east of Rossbach.

*Remarks*
78th: Lt. Donald R. Montieth (83rd Ftr Sqn) and Lt. Marvin C. Bigelow (83rd Ftr Sqn) collided while landing; both P-51's destroyed and pilots injured.
P-51D HL-K 44-15524 (Montieth)
P-51D HL-J 44-72036 (Bigelow)
361st: Lt. Edward P. Washburn (374th Ftr Sqn) c/l; o.k.
P 51D B7

**March 15, 1945**
Groups Operating: P-51 4th, 20th, 55th, 78th, 339th, 352nd, 353rd, 355th, 356th, 357th, 359th, 361st, 364th, 479th
P-47 56th
Missions: Support of bombers to Oranianberg and Zossen Army Headquarters, plus PRU escorts.
Claims: 1-0-0 air
0-0 ground

| Group | | Claims | Location |
|---|---|---|---|
| **359th** | | | |
| 370th: | Capt. R.S. Wetmore | Me-163 dest(air) | Wittenburg |

*Losses-*

**20th**: F/O Allen L. Shaffer (79th Ftr Sqn) KIA
P-51K MC-H 44-11357
Suffered mechanical failure near Hoorn.

**55th**: Lt. Eugene H. Duquette (338th Ftr Sqn) ASR
P-51D CL-P 44-14730(?)
Suffered mechanical failure and bailed out fifty miles east of Lowestoft.

**56th**: Lt. Willard C. Scherz (63rd Ftr Sqn) KIA
P-47M UN-
Spun-in after taking-off from Boxted.

**355th**: Lt. Jack H. Dressler (357th Ftr Sqn) MIA-E
P-51D OS-
Hit by flak and landed in Russian territory.

Lt. Johnnie W. Long (358th Ftr Sqn) MIA-E
P-51D YF-F 44-13879
Hit by flak near Hanover and bellied-in inside Russian lines.

**356th**: Lt. Roger A. Batie (359th Ftr Sqn) POW
P-51D OC-N 44-15274 "Mojahalka"
Suffered mechanical failure near Winterswijk.

**364th**: Lt. Daniel E. King (384th Ftr Sqn) POW
P-51D 5Y-D 44-14762 "Florence II"
Suffered mechanical failure southwest of Minden.

*Remarks*
20th: Lt. Reginald A. Nauman (55th Ftr Sqn) c/l Peterborough; o.k.
P-51D KI-

339th: Lt. Dennis B. Rawls (503rd Ftr Sqn) c/l Fowlmere; o.k.
P-51D D7-J 44-15074

**March 17, 1945**
Groups Operating: P-51 4th, 20th, 55th, 78th, 339th, 352nd, 353rd, 355th, 356th, 357th, 359th, 361st, 364th, 479th
Missions: Support of bombers to Bohlen, Ruhland, Munster, Hanover, Bitterfeld, and Molbis, plus a few PRU escorts.
Claims: nil

*Losses-*

**78th**: Lt. Paul H. Stearns (82nd Ftr Sqn) MIA-E
P-51D MX-Y 44-63183
Suffered mechanical failure and landed inside Russian lines.

**353rd**: Lt. Edward H. Duke (350th Ftr Sqn) POW
P-51D LH-Z 44-14974
Suffered mechanical failure and bailed out southeast of Koln.

**364th**: Lt. Robert A. Auguste (385th Ftr Sqn) KIA
P-51D 5E- 44-63184
Suffered mechanical failure and crashed near Frieburg.

*Remarks*
361st: Lt. Merne L. Weldusky (374th Ftr Sqn) c/l Belgium; o.k.
P-51D B7-
Lt. Russell E. Kenoyer (376th Ftr Sqn) b/o France; o.k.
P-51D E9-D 44-14217

**March 18, 1945**
Groups Operating: P-51 4th, 20th, 55th, 78th, 339th, 352nd, 353rd, 355th, 356th, 357th, 359th, 361st, 364th, 479th
Missions: Support of bombers to Berlin and a few PRU escorts.
Claims: 15-0-4 air
0-0 ground

| *Group* | | *Claims* | *Location* |
|---|---|---|---|
| **55th** | | | |
| 38th: | F/O W.V. Totten | Me-262 dam(air) | Prenzlau |
| 338th: | Lt. A.S. Dargan | (2)FW-190 dest(air) | N/Giessen |
| | Lt. T. Kiernan | FW-190 dest(air) | N/Giessen |
| | Lt. H.J. Schonenberg | FW-190 dest(air) | N/Giessen |
| **339th** | | | |
| 503rd: | Maj. D.E. Shafer | FW-190 dest(air) | Dummer Lake |
| | | FW-190 dam(air) | Dummer Lake |
| | Capt. F.R. Gerard | FW-190 dest(air) | Dummer Lake |
| | Lt. F.E. McElwee | FW-190 dest(air) | Dummer Lake |
| | Lt. L. Poutre | FW-190 dam(air) | Dummer Lake |
| 504th: | Lt. J.J. Ballard | FW-190 dest(air) | Barnstorf |
| **352nd** | | | |
| 487th: | Maj. W.T. Halton | Me-109 dest(air) | Bad Frienwalde |
| | F/O J.N. White | Me-109 dest(air) | E/Oder |
| | Lt. R.H. Littge | (.5)Me-109 dest(air) | Bad Frienwalde |
| | Lt. J.N. Wood | (.5)Me-109 dest(air) | Bad Frienwalde |
| **359th** | | | |
| 369th: | Capt. R.L. Cox | FW-190 dest(air) | Joachimsthal |
| | Lt. R.S. Gaines | Me-109 dest(air) | Joachimsthal |
| | F/O H.E. Berndt | Me-109 dam(air) | Joachimsthal |
| **364th** | | | |
| 383rd: | Lt. J.C. Hunter | FW-190 dest(air) | Schwerin |
| | Lt. E. Chlevin | He-111 dest(air) | Schwerin |

*Losses-*

**4th**: Maj. Pierce W. McKennon (335th Ftr Sqn) MIA-E
P-51D WD-A 44-63166 "Ridge Runner"
Hit by flak and bailed out near Neubrandenburg. Lt. George Green landed, picked up McKennon, and the two flew back to England.

**55th**: Lt. Robert L. Van Horn (338th Ftr Sqn) KIA
P-51D CL- 44-14598 "Lady Lorene"
Suffered mechanical failure near Trier.

**352nd**: Lt. Albert L. Peterson (487th Ftr Sqn) POW
P-51D HO- 44-15369 "Sweet Fern"
Last seen with Russian aircraft north of Frankfurt.

Lt. Joseph P. Vickery (487th Ftr Sqn) KIA
P-51D HO-R 44-15629 "Ellen-Jerry"
Last seen on the deck near Schwiebus.

**353rd**: Lt. Garnet D. Page (350th Ftr Sqn) MIA-E
P-51D LH-R 44-15137 "Baby Duck"
Hit by a Lagg-3 and bellied-in in Russian territory.

F/O Jerry M. Campbell (351st Ftr Sqn) POW
P-51D YJ-A 44-14732 "Tampa Tramp"
Lost coolant and bailed out southeast of Dummer Lake.

**361st**: Lt. Norman E. Zentz (375th Ftr Sqn) POW
P-51D E2-A 44-14908 "Wisconsin Witch"
Downed by flak over Germany.

**364th**: Lt. William E. Hoppa (383rd Ftr Sqn) POW
P-51D N2-W 44-14243 "Betty"
Suffered mechanical failure and bailed out near Brunswick.

*Remarks*
339th: Capt. Francis R. Gerard (503rd Ftr Sqn) c/l St. Trond; o.k.
P-51D D7-U 44-15003
355th: Lt. Robert F. Misner (357th Ftr Sqn) c/l; o.k.
P-51D OS-X 44-13677 "Miss Steve"
356th: Lt. John W. Meade (359th Ftr Sqn) c/l Martlesham Heath; o.k.
P-51D OC-

**March 19, 1945**
Groups Operating: P-51 4th, 55th, 78th, 339th, 352nd, 353rd, 355th, 356th, 357th, 359th, 361st, 364th, 479th
Missions: Support for bombers to various airfields and marshalling yards, plus a few PRU escorts.
Claims: 40-0-21 air
0-0 ground

| *Group* | | *Claims* | *Location* |
|---|---|---|---|
| **4th** | | | |
| 334th: | Maj. L.H. Norley | Me-109 dest(air) | SE Frankfurt |
| **78th** | | | |
| HdQts: | LtCol. J.D. Landers | Me-109 dest(air) | Osnabruck |
| | Maj. C.M. Christ | Me-109 dest(air) | Osnabruck |
| 82nd: | Capt. R.A. Hewitt | (2)Me-109 dest(air) | Osnabruck |
| | Lt. I.H. Keatley | (2)Me-109 dest(air) | Osnabruck |
| | Lt. A.S. Miller | (2)Me-109 dest(air) | Osnabruck |
| | Lt. J.E. Parker | FW-190 dest(air) | Osnabruck |
| | | Ar-234 dest(air) | Osnabruck |
| | | (3)FW-190 dam(air) | Osnabruck |
| | Capt. W.H. Brown | Me-109 dest(air) | Osnabruck |
| | | (.5)Ar-234 dest(air) | Osnabruck |
| | | (2)Me-109 dam(air) | Osnabruck |
| | Lt. H.H. Lamb | (.5)Ar-234 dest(air) | Osnabruck |
| | | Me-109 dam(air) | Osnabruck |
| | | FW-190 dam(air) | Osnabruck |
| | Lt. W.E. Bourque | Me-109 dest(air) | Osnabruck |
| | Lt. A.A. Rosenblum | FW-190 dest(air) | Osnabruck |
| | | Me-109 dam(air) | Osnabruck |
| | Lt. E.O. Schneider | Me-109 dest(air) | Osnabruck |
| | Lt. G.V. Elsey | Me-109 dam(air) | Osnabruck |
| 83rd: | Lt. H. Davis | (2)Me-109 dest(air) | Osnabruck |
| | Lt. H.L. Sealey | (2)Me-109 dest(air) | Osnabruck |
| | | FW-190 dam(air) | Osnabruck |
| | Lt. A.T. Colletti | FW-190 dest(air) | Osnabruck |
| | | Me-109 dam(air) | Osnabruck |
| | Lt. R.H. Talbot | Me-109 dest(air) | Osnabruck |
| | | Me-109 dam(air) | Osnabruck |
| | Lt. P.W. Klaasen | Me-109 dest(air) | Osnabruck |
| | | Me-109 dam(air) | Osnabruck |
| | Lt. J.A. Kirk | Me-109 dest(air) | Osnabruck |
| | Capt. F.E. Higginbottom | (.5)Me-109 dest(air) | Osnabruck |
| | Lt. R.I. Kuehl | (.5)Me-109 dest(air) | Osnabruck |
| | Lt. W.B. Spangler | (2)Me-109 dam(air) | Osnabruck |
| 84th: | Maj. H.L. Downing | Me-109 dest(air) | Osnabruck |
| | | FW-190 dest(air) | Osnabruck |
| | Lt. W.J. DeGain | FW-190 dest(air) | Osnabruck |
| | Lt. H.R. Slack | Me-109 dest(air) | Osnabruck |
| | Lt. T.V. Thain | Me-109 dest(air) | Osnabruck |
| | Lt. P.S. Ostrander | Me-109 dest(air) | Osnabruck |
| | Lt. J.E. Moores | FW-190 dest(air) | Osnabruck |
| | Lt. A.A. Garback | (.5)Me-109 dest(air) | Osnabruck |
| | Lt. E.F. Smith | (.5)Me-109 dest(air) | Osnabruck |
| | Lt. C.W. Clemons | FW-190 dam(air) | Osnabruck |
| **355th** | | | |
| 354th: | Capt. C.H. Spencer | Me-262 dest(air) | Kitzingen |
| **357th** | | | |
| HdQts: | Maj. R.W. Foy | Me-262 dest(air) | W/Gieesen |
| 363rd: | Capt. R.S. Fifield | Me-262 dest(air) | E/Leipzig |
| | Capt. J.L. Carter | (2)Me-262 dam(air) | N/Chemnitz |
| | Capt. A.G. Manthos | Me-262 dam(air) | E/Leipzig |
| | Lt. J.W. Cannon | Me-262 dam(air) | E/Leipzig |
| **359th** | | | |
| 368th: | Maj. N.K. Cranfill | Me-262 dest(air) | Leipzig |
| | | Me-262 dam(air) | Leipzig |

| | | Claims | Location |
|---|---|---|---|
| **479th** | | | |
| 434th: | Maj. R. Olds | Me-109 dest(air) | Handorf A/F |
| | | FW-190 dest(air) | Handorf A/F |
| | Lt. G.E. Jacobson | (.5)FW-190 dest(air) | Handorf A/F |
| | Lt. F.M. Taylor | (.5)FW-190 dest(air) | Handorf A/F |

*Losses-*

**55th**: Lt. Stanley E. Chapple (38th Ftr Sqn) ASR
P-51D CG-
Bailed out off Walcheren after suffering mechanical failure.

**78th**: Lt. Ralph L. Bush, Jr. (83rd Ftr Sqn) KIA
P-51D HL-T 44-72351 "Frisco Belle"
Hit by a Me-109 near Osnabruck.

Lt. Elmer K. Nieland (83rd Ftr Sqn) POW
P-51D HL-C 44-15721
Hit by a Me-109 near Osnabruck.

Maj. Harry L. Downing (84th Ftr Sqn) POW
P-51D WZ-E 44-72407
Hit by a Me-109 near Osnabruck.

Lt. James A. Bolen, Jr. (84th Ftr Sqn) KIA
P-51D WZ-D 44-72386
Hit by a Me-109 near Osnabruck.

Lt. Thomas M. Reeves (84th Ftr Sqn) POW
P-51D WZ-W 44-15675
Hit by a Me-109 near Osnabruck.

**353rd**: Lt. James E. Frye (351st Ftr Sqn) KIA
P-51D YJ-M 44-14706 "Ginny"
Suffered mechanical failure and bailed out forty miles off Orfordness.

Lt. Richard E. Hahn (352nd Ftr Sqn) POW
P-51D SX-Y 44-14631 "Shirley Dean"
Suffered mechanical failure and bailed out northwest of Zeitz.

**359th**: Lt. Clifton Enoch (368th Ftr Sqn) KIA
P-51D CV-Z 44-15371
Was chasing Me-262's and failed to pull out of a dive near Leipzig.

*Remarks*
356th: Col. Philip E. Tukey (HdQts) c/l Martlesham Heath; o.k.
P-51D PI-T 44-72455

**March 20, 1945**
Groups Operating: P-51 4th, 20th, 55th, 78th, 339th, 355th, 356th, 357th, 359th, 479th
Missions: Support of bombers to Hamburg and Hemmingstadt plus PRU escorts.
Claims: 4-0-6 air
3-5 ground

| *Group* | | *Claims* | *Location* |
|---|---|---|---|
| **20th** | | | |
| 77th: | Lt. J.C. Cowley | Me-262 dam(air) | E/Hamburg |
| **55th** | | | |
| 338th: | Capt. H.B. Sims | u/i a/c dam(grd) | Aurich |
| **339th** | | | |
| 503rd: | Lt. R.S. Hill | (2)Me-262 dam(air) | Hamburg |
| 504th: | Lt. V.N. Barto | Me-262 dest(air) | Hamburg |
| | Lt. K.V. Berguson | Me-262 dam(air) | Hamburg |
| | LtCol. W.C. Clark | u/i a/c dest(grd) | Grossenbrode |
| | | He-111 dam(grd) | Grossenbrode |
| | Lt. R.M. Kuhlman | FW-200 dest(grd) | Grossenbrode |
| | | Ju-52 dam(grd) | Grossenbrode |
| | Lt. L.J. Barrett | He-111 dest(grd) | Grossenbrode |
| | Lt. G.H. Chenez | Ju-52 dam(grd) | Grossenbrode |
| 505th: | Lt. R.E. Irion | Me-262 dest(air) | Schwerin |
| **356th** | | | |
| 359th: | Lt. E.G. Rudd | Me-262 dam(air) | Wesermunde-Hamburg |
| **357th** | | | |
| 362nd: | Capt. J.L. Sublett | Me-109 dest(air) | Quackenbruck |
| 363rd: | Lt. R.L. Thorkelson | FW-190 dest(air) | Dummer Lake |
| | Lt. J.T. Windham | FW-190 dam(air) | Dummer Lake |
| | | Ju-88 dam(grd) | Dummer Lake |

*Losses-*

**55th**: Capt. Robert D. Brown (343rd Ftr Sqn) INT
P-51D CY-V 44-14135
Hit by flak at Flensburg and bailed out; smuggled to Sweden by underground forces.

**339th**: Lt. Jerome J. Ballard (504th Ftr Sqn) POW
P-51D 5Q-Q 44-14647 "Podunk"
Hit by flak near Kaltenkirchen.

*Remarks*
339th: Lt. Lawrence Poutre (503rd Ftr Sqn) c/l Bottisham; o.k.
P-51D D7-
359th: Lt. Robert W. Hopkins (369th Ftr Sqn) c/l East Wretham; o.k.
P-51D IV-

KIAc's
339th: Lt. Kenneth V. Berguson (504th Ftr Sqn)
P-51D 5Q-
Died in a crash near Grimsby.

**March 21, 1945**
Groups Operating: P-51 4th, 20th, 55th, 78th, 339th, 352nd, 353rd, 355th, 356th, 357th, 359th, 361st, 364th, 479th
Missions: Support of bombers to jet airfields and PRU escorts.
Claims: 11-0-0 air
46-37 ground

| *Group* | | *Claims* | *Location* |
|---|---|---|---|
| **4th** | | | |
| 334th: | Lt. D.M. Malmsten | (2)Me-109 dest(grd) | Achmer A/F |
| | Lt. P.M. Burney | Me-109 dest(grd) | Achmer A/F |
| | Lt. W.B. Hoelscher | FW-190 dest(grd) | Achmer A/F |
| 335th: | Lt. S.W. Connors | u/i a/c dam(grd) | Achmer A/F |
| 336th: | Capt. C.R. Alfred | (3)Do-217 dest(grd) | Achmer A/F |
| | | Me-109 dam(grd) | Achmer A/F |
| | | Do-217 dam(grd) | Achmer A/F |
| | Lt. W.W. Collins | Me-410 dam(grd) | Achmer A/F |
| | | Do-217 dam(grd) | Achmer A/F |
| | Lt. W.D. Riedel | (2)u/i a/c dam(grd) | Achmer A/F |
| **55th** | | | |
| HdQts: | LtCol. E.G. Righetti | (2)FW-190 dest(grd) | Hopsten A/F |
| 38th: | Lt. D.M. Amoss | (3)FW-190 dest(air) | SW Munster |
| 343rd: | Capt. R.E. Welch | (2)FW-190 dest(grd) | Hopsten A/F |
| | | Ju-88 dam(grd) | Rheine |
| | Lt. P.A. Erby | FW-190 dest(grd) | Hopsten A/F |
| | Lt. P.L. Moore | FW-190 dest(grd) | Hopsten A/F |
| **78th** | | | |
| 82nd: | Lt. R.H. Anderson | Me-262 dest(air) | Giebelstadt |
| | Lt. W.E. Bourque | Me-262 dest(air) | Giebelstadt |
| | Capt. W.H. Brown | (.5)Me-262 dest(air) | Giebelstadt |
| | Lt. A.A. Rosenbloom | (.5)Me-262 dest(air) | Giebelstadt |
| | Maj. R.E. Conner | Me-262 dest(grd) | Dresden |
| | | (2)Me-262 dam(grd) | Dresden |
| 83rd: | Capt. E.H. Miller | Me-262 dest(air) | Wittenburg |
| | Lt. J.A. Kirk | Me-262 dest(air) | Meiningen |
| **339th** | | | |
| 504th: | Lt. N.C. Greer | (.5)Me-262 dest(air) | Wurzburg |
| | Lt. B.E. Langohr | (.5)Me-262 dest(air) | Wurzburg |
| **353rd** | | | |
| 350th: | Maj. W.L. Boone | (4)Ar-234 dest(grd) | Achmer A/F |
| | | (4)Ar-234 dam(grd) | Achmer A/F |
| | | Me-109 dam(grd) | Achmer A/F |
| | F/O R.N. Gustke | (4)Ar-234 dest(grd) | Achmer A/F |
| | | Me-109 dest(grd) | Achmer A/F |
| | | (4)Ar-234 dam(grd) | Achmer A/F |
| | Lt. R.J. Lanoue | (2)Ar-234 dest(grd) | Achmer A/F |
| | | He-111 dest(grd) | Achmer A/F |
| | Lt. D.A. Howie | (2)FW-190 dest(grd) | Achmer A/F |
| | Lt. F. O'Neill | Ju-88 dest(grd) | Achmer A/F |
| | Lt. J.P. Onkey | Me-109 dest(grd) | Achmer A/F |
| | Lt. W.A.S. Prescott | Ju-88 dest(grd) | Achmer A/F |
| | | Ar-234 dam(grd) | Achmer A/F |
| | Lt. J.D. McMullen | He-111 dest(grd) | Achmer A/F |
| | | Ar-234 dam(grd) | Achmer A/F |
| | Lt. J.L. Guthrie | Me-109 dam(grd) | Achmer A/F |
| 351st: | Capt. F.N. Emory | (2)Me-109 dest(grd) | Achmer A/F |
| | | FW-190 dam(grd) | Achmer A/F |
| | | u/i a/c dam(grd) | Achmer A/F |
| | Lt. G.J. Miller | (2)FW-190 dest(grd) | Achmer A/F |
| | | (2)FW-190 dam(grd) | Achmer A/F |
| | Capt. G.B. Compton | Ar-234 dest(grd) | Achmer A/F |
| | Lt. D.E. Lewis | Me-109 dest(grd) | Achmer A/F |
| | | Me-109 dam(grd) | Achmer A/F |
| | F/O H.A. Morris | He-111 dest(grd) | Achmer A/F |
| 352nd: | Lt. A. Michel | (4)FW-190 dest(grd) | Achmer A/F |
| | Lt. W.K. Bixby | u/i a/c dest(grd) | Achmer A/F |
| **356th** | | | |
| 359th: | Lt. R.J. Stone | FW-190 dam(grd) | Achmer A/F |

| | | | |
|---|---|---|---|
| **361st** | | | |
| 375th: | Lt. R.D. Anderson | Me-262 dest(air) | Belzig |
| 376th: | Lt. H.M. Chapman | Me-262 dest(air) | Dresden |
| **364th** | | | |
| 383rd: | Capt. L.V. Andrew | Me-109 dam(grd) | Achmer A/F |
| | | Ju-88 dam(grd) | Achmer A/F |
| 385th: | Capt. T.P. Farrell | FW-190 dest(grd) | Achmer A/F |
| | | (3)Ju-188 dam(grd) | Achmer A/F |
| | Lt. K.R. Horner | Me-109 dest(grd) | Achmer A/F |
| | | Me-109 dam(grd) | Achmer A/F |
| | Capt. J.E. Hargrove | (2)FW-190 dam(grd) | Achmer A/F |
| | Maj. W.S. Crombie | u/i a/c dam(grd) | Achmer A/F |

*Losses-*

**4th**: Capt. Albert J. Davis (335th Ftr Sqn) KIA
P-51D WD- 44-63676
Hit by flak near Hesepe and bailed out too low.

Lt. Robert A. Cammer (335th Ftr Sqn) POW
P-51D WD-K 44-14361 "Fiesty Sue"
Hit by flak at Achmer Airfield.

**55th**: Lt. Dudley M. Amoss (38th Ftr Sqn) POW
P-51D CG- 44-15123 "Queenie"
Hit by flak near Hopsten Airfield.

Lt. June B. Stallings (38th Ftr Sqn) KIA
P-51D CG-
Hit by flak at Hopsten Airfield.

**78th**: Maj. Richard E. Conner (82nd Ftr Sqn) MIA-E
P-51D MX-D 44-72233
Hit by flak at Lonnewitz and bellied-in within Russian lines.

**352nd**: Lt. Erwin E. Pryor (487th Ftr Sqn) KIA
P-51D HO-W 44-13361
Crashed at Chievres upon returning from the mission.

**353rd**: Lt. Thomas C. Brock (351st Ftr Sqn) MIA
P-51K YJ-B 44-11698
Hit by flak and bellied-in near Achmer Airfield.

F/O Bruce A. Eddy (351st Ftr Sqn) POW
P-51D YJ-M 44-14569 "Lil Boston Bull"
Lost coolant and bailed out near Krefeld.

Lt. Harry U. Gilmore (351st Ftr Sqn) POW
P-51D YJ-R 44-14748 "Kansas City Kitty"
Hit by flak at Achmer Airfield.

Lt. Alvin Michel (352nd Ftr Sqn) MIA-E
P-51D SX-U 44-14039 "Gloria Doll"
Hit by flak at Achmer Airfield and bailed out near Enschede.

**355th**: LtCol. Emil L. Sluga (358th Ftr Sqn) POW
P-51D YF-L 44-13354 "Slugger"
Hit by flak near Horsten and bailed out near Stadlohn.

**364th**: Lt. Chelius C. Howard (385th Ftr Sqn) KIA
P-51D 5E-I 44-13814
Hit by flak at Achmer Airfield.

*Remarks*
4th: Lt. Douglas P. Pederson (336th Ftr Sqn) c/l Belgium; o.k.
P-51D VF-
55th: 0-1 hangar
353rd: 1-0 loco, 0-5 railcars, 2-1 vehicles, 6-2 hangars, 0-5 barges, 0-11 gun positions

**March 22, 1945**
Groups Operating: P-51 4th, 20th, 55th, 78th, 339th, 352nd, 353rd, 355th, 356th, 357th, 359th, 361st, 364th, 479th
Missions: Support of bombers to airfields and marshalling yards in Germany and PRU escorts. The 4th, 355th, and 479th groups supported 15th Air Force bombers while the 352nd and 361st escorted RAF heavies.
Claims: 14-0-3 air
13-11 ground

| ***Group*** | | ***Claims*** | ***Location*** |
|---|---|---|---|
| **4th** | | | |
| HdQts: | LtCol. S.S. Woods | (5)FW-190 dest(air) | Furstenwalde-Eggersdorf |
| 334th: | Lt. F.E. Farington | FW-190 dest(air) | Furstenwalde |
| | Lt. J.E. Jahnke | FW-190 dest(air) | Furstenwalde |
| | Lt. W.O. Antonides | (2)FW-190 dam(air) | Eggersdorf |
| 336th: | Lt. W.D. Riedel | (2)FW-190 dest(air) | NE Ruhland |
| | Lt. R.O. Davis | FW-190 dest(air) | Furstenwalde |
| | Lt. H.N. Hagen | FW-190 dest(air) | SE Berlin |
| **55th** | | | |
| 38th: | Lt. J.W. Cunnick | Me-262 dest(air) | Lechfeld |
| | Lt. J.F. O'Neill | Me-262 dest(grd) | Lechfeld |
| 343rd: | Capt. F.E. Birtciel | Me-262 dam(air) | Schwabisch Hall |
| **78th** | | | |
| 82nd: | Lt. E.L. Peel | (.5)Me-262 dest(air) | Ulm |
| | Lt. M.B. Stutzman | (.5)Me-262 dest(air) | Ulm |
| 83rd: | Capt. H.T. Barnaby | Me-262 dest(air) | Giebelstadt |
| **355th** | | | |
| 354th: | Lt. S.E. Silva | (2)Me-262 dest(grd) | Kitzingen |
| | | Me-109 dest(grd) | Kitzingen |
| | | (3)Me-262 dam(grd) | Kitzingen |
| | F/O H.W. Falvey | Me-262 dest(grd) | Kitzingen |
| | | Me-109 dest(grd) | Wurzburg |
| | | Me-262 dam(grd) | Kitzingen |
| | Lt. J.M. Fletcher | Me-109 dest(grd) | Wurzburg |
| | Lt. J. Jabara | FW-190 dest(grd) | Wurzburg |
| | | FW-190 dam(grd) | Wurzburg |
| | Lt. D.C. Tulhoski | FW-190 dest(grd) | Wurzburg |
| | Lt. W.J. Gadpaille | He-111 dest(grd) | Memmingen |
| | Lt. C.G. Todd | He-111 dest(grd) | Memmingen |
| | Lt. R.M. White | He-111 dest(grd) | Memmingen |
| | | He-111 dam(grd) | Memmingen |
| | Lt. P.W. Vineyard | He-111 dest(grd) | Memmingen |
| | F/O T.R. Hixon | He-111 dam(grd) | Memmingen |
| | Lt. C.E. Decklar | He-111 dam(grd) | Memmingen |
| | Lt. D.B. Langley | FW-190 dam(grd) | Wurzburg |
| | Lt. M.J. McLeod | Me-262 dam(grd) | Kitzingen |
| **356th** | | | |
| 361st: | Lt. R.C. Nystrom | He-111 dam(grd) | Plantlunne |

*Losses-*

**55th**: Lt. John F. O'Neill (38th Ftr Sqn) MIA
P-51D CG-
Hit by flak near Lechfeld.

F/O George Nastanovitch (343rd Ftr Sqn) POW
P-51D CY-G 44-14985 "The Millie G"
Hit by flak and bailed out near Halle.

**355th**: Lt. David C. Tulhoski (354th Ftr Sqn) POW
P-51D WR-Y 44-72186 "Dragon Wagon"
Hit by flak near Wurzburg.

*Remarks*
339th: F/O John J. Rice (505th Ftr Sqn) c/l Fowlmere; o.k.
P-51 6N-
355th: LtCol. Bert W. Marshall (HdQts) c/l Steeple Morden; o.k.
P-51D WR-
359th: Lt. Jack R. Shulte (370th Ftr Sqn) c/l East Wretham; o.k.
P-51D CS-S 44-14192

**March 23, 1945**
Groups Operating: P-51 4th, 20th, 55th, 78th, 339th, 352nd, 353rd, 355th, 356th, 357th, 359th, 361st, 364th, 479th
Missions: Support for bombers to rail targets in Germany, sweeps, and PRU escorts, plus the 352nd and 361st supported 9th Air Force operations.
Claims: 1-0-0 air
0-1 ground

| ***Group*** | | ***Claims*** | ***Location*** |
|---|---|---|---|
| **359th** | | | |
| 368th: | Capt. G.A. Doersch | (.5)Ar-196 dest(air) | Salzwedel |
| | Lt. K.L. Barber | (.5)Ar-196 dest(air) | Salzwedel |
| | Capt. M.F. Boussu | He-111 dam(grd) | Salzwedel |

Losses: nil

*Remarks*
339th: F/O John J. Rice (505th Ftr Sqn) c/l Fowlmere; o.k.
P-51B 6N-G

KIAc's
56th: Lt. Carl J. Bokina (63rd Ftr Sqn)
P-47M UN-X
Killed near Boxted on a training flight.

**March 24, 1945**
Groups Operating: P-51 4th, 20th, 55th, 78th, 339th, 352nd, 353rd, 355th, 356th, 357th, 359th, 361st, 364th, 479th
P-47 56th
Missions: Area support for bombers to various targets in conjunction with the Rhine crossings plus some PRU escorts.
Claims: 59-2-12 air
0-3 ground

| *Group* | | *Claims* | *Location* |
|---|---|---|---|
| **20th** | | | |
| HdQts: | LtCol. R.F. Gustke | Ju-88 dam(grd) | Gutersloh |
| **55th** | | | |
| 38th: | Capt. L.F. Spiecker | Me-109 dest(air) | S/Soest |
| | Capt. D.M. Cummings | (.5)Me-109 dest(air) | S/Soest |
| | Lt. H.B. Mooers | (.5)Me-109 dest(air) | S/Soest |
| **78th** | | | |
| 82nd: | Lt. R.J. Blossom | He-111 dam(grd) | Diepholz |
| **339th** | | | |
| 505th: | Maj. A.A. Tower | FW-190 dam(grd) | Ziegenhall] |
| **353rd** | | | |
| HdQts: | Maj. R.A. Elder | (4)FW-190 dest(air) | NW Kassel |
| | | Me-109 dest(air) | NW Kassel |
| | | Me-109 dam(air) | NW Kassel |
| | Capt. R.E. Hartley | (2)FW-190 dest(air) | NW Kassel |
| | | Me-109 dest(air) | NW Kassel |
| | | Me-109 dam(air) | NW Kassel |
| 350th: | LtCol. W. Blickenstaff | (3)FW-190 dest(air) | NW Kassel |
| | | (2)Me-109 dest(air) | NW Kassel |
| | Lt. J.L. Guthrie | (3)Me-109 dest(air) | NW Kassel |
| | | Me-109 dam(air) | NW Kassel |
| | | FW-190 dam(air) | NW Kassel |
| | Lt. L.W. Lee | (2)FW-190 dest(air) | NW Kassel |
| | | Me-109 dest(air) | NW Kassel |
| | Lt. J.W. Clark | (2)FW-190 dest(air) | NW Kassel |
| | Lt. J.F. May | (2)FW-190 dest(air) | NW Kassel |
| | Lt. W.A.S. Prescott | (2)Me-109 dest(air) | NW Kassel |
| | Lt. G.W. Robison | FW-190 dest(air) | NW Kassel |
| | Lt. W.R. Hubbell | Me-109 dest(air) | NW Kassel |
| | | Me-109 prob(air) | NW Kassel |
| | Lt. F. O'Neill | Me-109 dest(air) | NW Kassel |
| | | Me-109 dam(air) | NW Kassel |
| | Lt. H.H. Hakonen | FW-190 prob(air) | NW Kassel |
| | F/O R.N. Gustke | FW-190 dam(air) | NW Kassel |
| **357th** | | | |
| HdQts: | LtCol. A.J. Evans | Me-109 dest(air) | W/Gutersloh |
| | Maj. R.W. Foy | Me-109 dest(air) | N/Gutersloh |
| 362nd: | Capt. C.E. Weaver | Me-109 dest(air) | W/Gutersloh |
| | Lt. J.F. Duncan | Me-109 dest(air) | W/Gutersloh |
| | Lt. W.W. Gruber | Me-109 dest(air) | W/Gutersloh |
| 364th: | Capt. P.R. Hatala | (2)Me-109 dest(air) | W/Gutersloh |
| | Lt. D.E. Karger | (2)Me-109 dest(air) | W/Gutersloh |
| | LtCol. J.A. Storch | Me-109 dest(air) | W/Gutersloh |
| | Capt. R.G. Schimanski | Me-109 dest(air) | W/Gutersloh |
| | | Me-109 dam(air) | W/Gutersloh |
| | F/O C.F. Schneider | Me-109 dest(air) | W/Gutersloh |
| | | (2)Me-109 dam(air) | W/Gutersloh |
| | Lt. S. Wasylyk | Me-109 dest(air) | W/Gutersloh |
| | Lt. G.L. Weber | Me-109 dest(air) | W/Gutersloh |
| | Lt. L.A. Westphal | Me-109 dest(air) | W/Gutersloh |
| | Lt. R.R. Wright | Me-109 dest(air) | W/Gutersloh |
| | | Me-109 dam(air) | W/Gutersloh |
| **359th** | | | |
| 369th: | Capt. W.F. Collins | (2)Me-109 dest(air) | Eikelon A/F |
| | Capt. R.C. Thomson | (2)Me-109 dest(air) | Eikelon A/F |
| | Lt. R.T. Lnacaster | (2)Me-109 dest(air) | Eikelon A/F |
| | Lt. F.S. McGehee | (2)Me-109 dest(air) | Eikelon A/F |
| | Lt. D.E. Kelly | (1.5)Me-109 dest(air) | Eikelon A/F |
| | Lt. H. Tenenbaum | (1.5)Me-109 dest(air) | Eikelon A/F |
| | Maj. J.W. Parsons | Me-109 dest(air) | Eikelon A/F |
| | Lt. B.H. Thomson | Me-109 dest(air) | Eikelon A/F |
| | Lt. L. Patton | (2)Me-109 dam(air) | Eikelon A/F |

Losses:

**SF**: Lt. Leonard H. Monefelt (2nd) KIA
P-51D WR- 44-14441
Killed in a crash at Steeple Morden.

**20th**: Lt. Chester J. Swierczynski (77th Ftr Sqn) POW
P-51D LC-Q 44-72298
Lost oil near Gutersloh and bailed out near Handorf.

**55th**: Lt. Stanley E. Chapple (38th Ftr Sqn) MIA
P-51D CG- 44-72080
Hit by enemy fighters near Soest.

**353rd**: Lt. Wiley Grizzle (350th Ftr Sqn) KIA
P-51D LH-S 44-63896 "The G-Nat"
Hit by enemy fighters northwest of Kassel.

Lt. James H. Hopkins (350th Ftr Sqn) KIA
P-51B LH-K 42-106619 "Queenie"
Hit by enemy fighters northwest of Kassel.

Lt. Carl A. Larsen (350th Ftr Sqn) POW
P-51D LH-N 44-14687 "Lethal Ethel"
Hit by enemy fighters northwest of Kassel.

Lt. John F. May (350th Ftr Sqn) POW
P-51D LH-A 44-14990 "Doris II"
Hit by enemy fighters northwest of Kassel.

Lt. John P. Onkey (350th Ftr Sqn) POW
P-51D LH-Q 44-14811 "Lady Gwen"
Hit by enemy fighters northwest of Kassel.

**356th**: Lt. William C. Jarvis (361st Ftr Sqn) ASR
P-51D QI-L 44-15139
Lost oil pressure and bailed out east of Lowestoft.

**357th**: Lt. Otto D. Jenkins (362nd Ftr Sqn) KIA
P-51D G4-X 44-63199 "Toolin' Fools Revenge"
Buzzed Leiston upon return from the mission and crashed into trees around the field.(He had just finished his tour).

**361st**: Capt. Russell D. Wade (375th Ftr Sqn) KIA
P-51D E2-T 44-14149 "Talley's Hoosier Hobo"
Hit by flak near Iserlehn.

*Remarks*

20th: 6-5 vehicles, 1-38 railcars, 0-2 gun positions
55th: 3-0 locos, 3-38 railcars, 46-4 vehicles
78th: 29-13 vehicles, 0-1 railcar
339th: 21-8 locos, 0-78 railcars, 53-49 vehicles
Lt. William R. Preddy (503rd Ftr Sqn) c/l Duxford; o.k.
P-51D D7-
352nd: 1-0 loco, 0-13 railcars, 2-1 vehicles
353rd: 1-0 loco, 11-4 vehicles
355th: 0-4 railcars, 1-1 switch-tower
Lt. Edward P. McNeff (357th Ftr Sqn) c/l; o.k.
P-51D OS-Y 44-14858
356th: 2-0 vehicles, 0-5 barges, 1-0 building
357th: 2-1 locos, 3-0 railcars, 16-2 vehicles
359th: 7-4 locos, 0-6 railcars, 14-17 vehicles
361st: Lt. John R. Voss (374th Ftr Sqn) c/l Belgium; o.k.
P-51D B7-J
364th: 10-5 vehicles, 1-0 barge

**March 25, 1945**
Groups Operating: P-51 339th, 352nd, 361st, 479th
P-47 56th
Missions: Support of 2nd Bomb Division to oil targets while the 352nd and 361st flew fightr-bomber sorties.
Claims: 4-0-1 air
0-0 ground

| *Group* | | *Claims* | *Location* |
|---|---|---|---|
| **56th** | | | |
| 63rd: | Maj. G.E. Bostwick | Me-262 dest(air) | Parchim A/F |
| | Lt. E.M. Crosthwait | Me-262 dest(air) | Parchim A/F |
| **352nd** | | | |
| 487th: | Capt. R.H. Littge | Me-262 dest(air) | Rechlin A/F |
| **479th** | | | |
| 434th: | Lt. E.H. Wendt | Me-262 dest(air) | SW Hamburg |
| 435th: | Lt. F.W. Salze | Me-262 dam(air) | SE Hamburg |

*Losses-*

**352nd**: Lt. Wesley N. Roebuck (487th Ftr Sqn) KIA
P-51D HO-J 44-14475 "Peanuts"
Hit by a Me-262 near Ulzen.

*Remarks*

339th: Lt. Leo H. Becker (505th Ftr Sqn) c/l; o.k.
P-51D 6N-R 44-13680 "The Roller"
352nd: 3-10 vehicles

**March 26, 1945**
Groups Operating: P-51 4th, 20th, 55th, 78th, 339th, 352nd, 353rd, 355th, 361st, 364th
Missions: Support of bombers to Plauen, sweeps, and PRU escorts.
Claims: nil

*Losses-*

**4th**: Lt. Harry L. Davis (336th Ftr Sqn) KIA
P-51D VF-B 44-13317
Crashed near Woodbridge after a possible collision.

Lt. Earl F. Hustwit (336th Ftr Sqn) KIA
P-51D VF- 44-72411
Suffered mechanical failure and crashed west of Valkenburg.

**20th**: Lt. Kenneth L. Pettit (55th Ftr Sqn) KIA
P-51D KI-T(?) 44-13860(?)
Suffered mechanical failure and crashed at Ipswich.

*Remarks*
66th(FW): LtCol. Olin E. Gilbert b/o Lille; o.k.
P-51D HL-A 44-72314
339th: Lt. Clarence I. Ferrell (503rd Ftr Sqn) c/l; o.k.
P-51D D7-
353rd: Maj. William F. Tanner (350th Ftr Sqn) b/o Chelmsford; o.k.
P-51D LH-F 44-72302

KIAc's
355th: Capt. Wendell W. Beaty (358th Ftr Sqn)
P-51D YF-
Spun-in over Calais in bad weather.

**March 27, 1945**
Groups Operating: P-51 356th, 357th
P-47 56th
Missions: Support of RAF bombers to Paderborn.
Claims: nil
Losses: nil

**March 28, 1945**
Groups Operating: P-51 4th, 20th, 78th, 339th, 352nd, 355th, 361st, 364th
Missions: Support for bombers to Berlin and Hanover, plus PRU escorts.
Claims: nil
Losses: nil

*Remarks*
339th: Lt. William R. Guyton (505th Ftr Sqn) c/l Colchester; o.k.
P-51D 6N-K 44-14734 "Baby Mine"
F/O Ellis E. Hupp (505th Ftr Sqn) c/l Colchester; o.k.
P-51D 6N-I 44-14554
355th: Lt. Walter B. Lister (358th Ftr Sqn) c/l Steeple Morden; o.k.
P-51D YF-

KIAc's
479th: Lt. Jesse F. Morris (436th Ftr Sqn)
P-51D 9B-

**March 30, 1945**
Groups Operating: P-51 4th, 20th, 55th, 78th, 339th, 352nd, 353rd, 355th, 356th, 357th,359th, 361st, 364th, 479th
P-47 56th
Missions: Support of bombers to Hamburg, Bremen, and Wilhelmshaven, plus PRU escorts.
Claims: 6.5-1-5 air
5-5 ground

| *Group* | | *Claims* | *Location* |
|---|---|---|---|
| **55th** | | | |
| 343rd: | Lt. P.L. Moore | Me-262 dest(air) | Lubeck A/F |
| | Lt. P.A. Erby | Me-262 dam(air) | SW Lubeck A/F |
| **78th** | | | |
| HdQts: | LtCol. J.D. Landers | (.5)Me-262 dest(air) | Rendsburg |
| 84th: | Lt. T.V. Thain | (.5)Me-262 dest(air) | Rendsburg |
| | Lt. P.S. Ostrander | Me-262 dest(grd) | Kaltenkirchen |
| | | Me-262 dam(grd) | Kaltenkirchen |
| **339th** | | | |
| HdQts: | Col. J.B. Henry | Me-262 prob(air) | SW Hamburg |
| 504th: | Capt. R.F. Sargent | Me-262 dest(air) | Kaltenkirchen |
| | Lt. C.W. Bennett | Me-262 dest(air) | Hamburg |
| | | Me-262 dam(air) | Hamburg |
| 505th: | Capt. G.T. Rich | Me-262 dam(air) | N/Luneburg |
| | Lt. S.C. Ananian | Me-262 dam(air) | N/Luneburg |
| **355th** | | | |
| HdQts: | Maj. H.H. Kirby | FW-190 dest(grd) | Lowenstadt |
| | | Me-109 dest(grd) | Lowenstadt |
| | | (.5)He-111 dam(grd) | Lowenstadt |
| 354th: | LtCol. G.M. Graham | (.5)Ju-52 dam(grd) | Schleswig |
| | | (.5)Ju-52 dam(grd) | Schleswig |
| | | (.5)Ju-52 dam(grd) | Schleswig |
| | Lt. D.B. Langley | (.5)Ju-52 dam(grd) | Schleswig |
| | | (.5)Ju-52 dam(grd) | Schleswig |
| | | (.5)Ju-52 dam(grd) | Schleswig |
| 357th: | Lt. W.J. Cullerton | He-111 dest(grd) | Lowenstadt |
| | Lt. H.I. Knight | He-111 dest(grd) | Lowenstadt |
| | | (.5)He-111 dam(grd) | Lowenstadt |
| **361st** | | | |
| 376th: | Lt. K.J. Scott | Me-262 dest(air) | W/Rendsburg |
| **364th** | | | |
| 383rd: | Lt. J.B. Guy | (.5)Me-262 dest(air) (shared with an unknown pilot) | Brandenburg |
| | Lt. R.L. Hunt | Me-262 dam(air) | Brandenburg |

*Losses-*

**339th**: Lt. Evergard L. Wager (505th Ftr Sqn) KIA
P-51D 6N-H 44-72065
Hit by a Me-262 northwest of Hamburg.

**352nd**: Lt. Francis J. McCarthy (328th Ftr Sqn) KIA
P-51D PE-F 44-14882 "3rd Baser The Second"
Suffered mechanical failure near Oldenburg.

**353rd**: Lt. Merlin A. Arnold (351st Ftr Sqn) KIA
P-51K YJ-A 44-11333
Suffered mechanical failure and bailed out twelve miles off Great Yarmouth. Hit the tail and died of injuries.

**357th**: Lt. Daniel N. Myers (363rd Ftr Sqn) POW
P-51D B6- 44-72238 "Superwolf"
Suffered mechanical failure and bailed out north of Schiermonnikoog Island.

*Remarks*
361st: Lt. Carl W. Wolfe (376th Ftr Sqn) c/l; o.k.
P-51D E9-

KIAc's
353rd: Lt. John Matula (351st Ftr Sqn)
P-51D YJ-L 44-14771 "Willit Run?"
Died in a crash near Wratting Common.

**March 31, 1945**
Groups Operating: P-51 4th, 20th, 55th, 78th, 339th, 352nd, 353rd, 355th, 356th, 357th, 359th, 361st, 364th, 479th
P-47 56th
Missions: Support of bombers to Zeitz, Brandenburg, Brunswick, and Halle, plus PRU escorts.
Claims: 6-0-7 air
1-0 ground

| *Group* | | *Claims* | *Location* |
|---|---|---|---|
| **SF** | | | |
| 2nd: | Lt. M.H. Castleberry | Me-262 dest(air) | SW Brunswick |
| | Capt. R.W. Nyman | Me-262 dam(air) | SW Brunswick |
| **56th** | | | |
| 61st: | Lt. F.H. Bennett | Me-262 dam(air) | Steinhuder Lake |
| **78th** | | | |
| 82nd: | Lt. W.L. Coleman | Me-262 dest(air) | Stendal |
| **353rd** | | | |
| HdQts: | Maj. W.M. Long | Me-109 dest(air) | Hanover |
| 352nd: | Lt. H.B. Tordoff | Me-262 dest(air) | Dessau |
| **355th** | | | |
| 357th: | Lt. T.C. Long | Ju-88 dest(grd) | Magdeburg |
| **357th** | | | |
| 362nd: | Maj. L.K. Carson | Me-262 dam(air) | N/Juist Island |
| | Lt. M.A. Becraft | Me-262 dam(air) | N/Juist Island |
| **361st** | | | |
| 374th: | Lt. B.R. Hicks | FW-190 dest(air) | N/Frankfurt |
| | Lt. T.J. Moore | FW-190 dest(air) | N/Frankfurt |
| 375th: | Lt. G.R. Stockmeier | Me-262 dam(air) | Brunswick |
| | Lt. E.E. Tinkham | Me-262 dam(air) | Brunswick |
| **479th** | | | |
| 434th: | Lt. R.I. Bromschwig | Me-262 dam(air) | Braunschweig |

*Losses-*

**4th**: F/O Kenneth E. Foster (334th Ftr Sqn) POW
P-51K QP-Z 44-11336 "Buffalo Bertie"
Suffered mechanical failure near Hengelo.

**78th**: Lt. Paul S. Ostrander (84th Ftr Sqn) KIA
P-51D WZ-A 44-63215
Hit by flak near Rheine and bailed out off The Hague.

**339th**: F/O Joseph R. Coker (505th Ftr Sqn) POW
P-51D 6N- 44-15558
Suffered mechanical failure near Plauen.

**361st**: F/O Deane E. Jackson (374th Ftr Sqn) KIA
P-51D B7- 44-15657
Lost for unknown reasons.

**April 1, 1945**
Groups Operating: P-51 355th, 356th, 357th
Missions: Eight aircraft from each group flew ASR patrols.
Claims: nil
Losses: nil

KIAc's
56th: Lt. John F. Frazier (61st Ftr Sqn)
P-47M HV-
Died in a mid-air collision.

**April 2, 1945**
Groups Operating: P-51 4th, 20th, 55th, 78th, 339th, 353rd, 355th, 356th, 359th, 364th, 479th
P-47 56th
Missions: Support of bombers to airfields in Denmark plus PRU escorts.
Claims: nil

*Losses-*

**364th**: Lt. Edward M. Hassel (385th Ftr Sqn) KIA
P-51D 5E-V 44-13814 "Fancy Francis"
Suffered mechanical failure and bailed out forty miles northeast of Great Yarmouth.

*Remarks*
479th: Lt. Carl W. Sherer (436th Ftr Sqn) c/l Sproughton; o.k.
P-51D 9B-S 44-15662

**April 3, 1945**
Groups Operating: P-51 4th, 20th, 55th, 78th, 339th, 352nd, 353rd, 355th, 356th, 357th, 359th, 361st, 364th
Missions: Support of bombers to Kiel and PRU escorts.
Claims: nil

*Losses-*

**SF**: Lt. William E. Cox (1st) MIA
P-51D 9H-F 44-13754
Suffered mechanical failure near Flensburg.

Lt. John Stein, Jr. (3rd) KIA
P-51K CY- 44-12152
Collided with another aircraft near Rendsburg.

**357th**: Lt. Jacob E. Giel (362nd Ftr Sqn) KIA
P-51D G4- 44-14862 "Winnie Gal"
Hit by another plane's drop tank and crashed into the North Sea.

**359th**: Lt. Charles E. Stubblefield (369th Ftr Sqn) KIA
P-51D IV-F 44-72503 "Gravel Gertie"
Suffered oxygen failure and crashed sixty miles off Lowestoft.

*Remarks*
55th: Capt. Frank E. Birtciel (343rd Ftr Sqn) b/o Belgium; o.k.
P-51D CY-G 44-15701 "The Millie G"
Lt. William Mearns (343rd Ftr Sqn) c/l; o.k.
P-51D CY-
339th: Lt. Kenneth E. Moreland (503rd Ftr Sqn) c/l; o.k.
P-51K D7- 44-12160
357th: P-51 c/l Leiston; o.k.
361st: F/O Jared M. Lundin (375th Ftr Sqn) c/l; o.k.
P-51D E2-T 44-13568

**April 4, 1945**
Groups Operating: P-51 4th, 20th, 55th, 78th, 339th, 352nd, 353rd, 355th, 356th, 357th, 359th, 361st, 364th, 479th
P-47 56th
Missions: Support of bombers to Kiel, Fassberg, Hamburg, and airfields in Germany plus PRU escorts.
Claims: 12-1-20 air
10-4 ground

| *Group* | | *Claims* | *Location* |
|---|---|---|---|
| **SF** | | | |
| 2nd: | Lt. W.H. Bancroft | Me-262 dam(air) | S/Ratzeburg |
| **4th** | | | |
| 334th: | Lt. R.A. Dyer | Me-262 dest(air) | SE Parchim |
| | Lt. M.J. Kennedy | (.5)Me-262 dest(air) | S/Ludwigslust |
| | Capt. R.H. Kanaga | Me-262 prob(air) | Schwerin |
| | Lt. C.W. Harre | Me-262 dam(air) | S/Parchim |
| 335th: | Lt. E. Jungling | Me-262 dam(air) | NE Parchim |
| 336th: | Lt. H.H. Fredericks | (.5)Me-262 dest(air) | S/Ludwigslust |
| | | Me-262 dam(air) | S/Ludwigslust |
| **56th** | | | |
| 61st: | Capt. W.D. Clark | Me-262 dam(air) | Salzwedel |
| | F/O J.W. Kassap | Me-262 dam(air) | W/Hamburg |
| **339th** | | | |
| HdQts: | LtCol. W.C. Clark | Me-262 dam(air) | Parchim |
| | | u/i a/c dest(grd) | Weimar |
| | | u/i a/c dam(grd) | Weimar |
| 504th: | Capt. N.C. Greer | Me-262 dest(air) | Parchim |
| | Lt. R.C. Havighurst | Me-262 dest(air) | Parchim |
| | Capt. K.B. Everson | (.5)Me-262 dest(air) | Parchim |
| | Lt. R.C. Croker | (.5)Me-262 dest(air) | Parchim |
| | Lt. L.M. Carter | u/i a/c dam(grd) | Weimar |
| 505th: | Capt. H.R. Corey | Me-262 dest(air) | Rostock |
| | Maj. A.A. Tower | (2)Me-410 dest(grd) | NE Tribsees |
| | Capt. G.T. Rich | Do-217 dest(grd) | NE Tribsees |
| | Lt. S.C. Ananian | Ju-88 dest(grd) | NE Tribsees |
| | Lt. W.R. MacClarence | Me-410 dest(grd) | NE Tribsees |
| **355th** | | | |
| 354th: | Capt. A.S. White | FW-190 dest(grd) | Ludwigslust |
| | Lt. J.E. Molnar | BV-138 dest(grd) | Muritz Lake |
| | F/O T.R. Hixon | u/i a/c dest(grd) | Muritz Lake |
| | | (2)Ju-88 dam(grd) | Muritz Lake |
| | Lt. P.W. Barnhart | (.5)Do-24 dest(grd) | Muritz Lake |
| | Lt. C.E. Decklar | (.5)Do-24 dest(grd) | Muritz Lake |
| 357th: | Lt. T.C. Long | (2)FW-190 dest(air) | Halberstadt |
| | Lt. W.J. Cullerton | FW-190 dest(air) | Halberstadt |
| | Lt. E.H. Riffle | Ar-234 dest(air) | Magdeburg |
| | Lt. R.W. Cooper | Me-262 dam(air) | Ludwigslust |
| **361st** | | | |
| 374th: | Lt. H.S. Dixon | Me-262 dam(air) | W/Berlin |
| | Lt. L.J. Jewell | Me-262 dam(air) | W/Berlin |
| 375th: | Lt. L.F. Gendron | (4)Me-262 dam(air) | S/Hamburg |
| | Lt. W.H. Street | (2)Me-262 dam(air) | S/Hamburg |
| | Lt. H.A. Euler | Me-262 dam(air) | S/Hamburg |
| | Lt. R.J. Farney | Me-262 dam(air) | S/Hamburg |
| **364th**(#1) | | | |
| 383rd: | LtCol. G.F. Ceuleers | Me-262 dest(air) | Hamburg-Dessau |
| 385th: | Lt. J.S. Rogers | Me-262 dam(air) | Fassberg A/F |
| (#2-PRU) | | | |
| 385th: | Lt. J.W. Ruland | FW-190 dest(air) | Potsdam |
| **479th** | | | |
| 435th: | Lt. E.H. Sims | Me-262 dam(air) | W/Luneburg |

*Losses-*

**20th**: Lt. John W. Cudd, Jr. (77th Ftr Sqn) ASR
P-51K LC-Z 44-11673
Lost coolant and bailed out off Great Yarmouth.

**355th**: Lt. Robert A. Goth (354th Ftr Sqn) KIA
P-51D WR-R 44-14704 "Psyche"
Hit by a FW-190 near Ludwigslust.

Lt. Richard A. Gray (354th Ftr Sqn) POW
P-51D WR-O 44-13591 "Chugger II"
Hit by flak near Ludwigslust.

Lt. Thomas F. Truell, Jr. (354th Ftr Sqn) KIA
P-51D WR-P 44-14228 "Lady Barbara II"
Hit by a FW-190 near Ludwigslust.

*Remarks*
20th: 1-0 loco, 0-2 railcars
78th: 83rd Ftr Sqn P-51 c/l; o.k.
P-51D HL-P 44-15575
339th: 0-1 building
355th: 2-3 locos, 9-2 railcars, 0-3 barges, 0-1 steamer, 0-3 flak positions, 0-2 buildings
356th: Lt. John F. Pound(361st Ftr Sqn) b/o Meppel; o.k.
P-51D QI-Z 44-72391

KIAc's
479th: Lt. Thurman E. Sands (434th Ftr Sqn)
P-51B L2- 43-6393
Hit a train while practicing strafing near Haughley Station.

**April 5, 1945**
Groups Operating: P-51 4th, 20th, 55th, 78th, 339th, 352nd, 353rd, 355th, 361st, 364th, 479th
P-47 56th
Missions: Support for bombers to Ingolstadt, Plauen, Nurnberg, and other targets of opportunity plus PRU escorts.
Claims: 1-0-2 air
8-3 ground

| *Group* | | *Claims* | *Location* |
|---|---|---|---|
| **56th** | | | |
| 63rd: | Lt. J.C. Fahringer | Me-262 dest(air) | N/Regensburg |

| | | | |
|---|---|---|---|
| **339th** | | | |
| 505th: | Lt. S.C. Ananian | Me-262 dam(air) | Boblingen |
| **353rd** | | | |
| 351st: | Capt. G.B. Compton | (3)Me-410 dest(grd) | Weiden |
| | | Me-110 dest(grd) | Weiden |
| | Lt. T.P. Pryor | (3)Me-410 dest(grd) | Weiden |
| | | Me-110 dam(grd) | Weiden |
| **364th** | | | |
| 384th: | Lt. G.Z. Schroeder | Me-262 dam(air) | N/Regensburg |
| 385th: | F/O W.K. Masters | Me-109 dest(grd) | SW Nurnberg |
| | Capt. E.N. Farrell | Me-262 dam(grd) | SW Nurnberg |
| | Lt. F.O. Spain | FW-190 dam(grd) | SW Nurnberg |

*Losses-*

**355th**: Lt. Robert G. McDonnell (354th Ftr Sqn) KIA
P-51K WR-J 44-11759
Hit by flak near Buren.

*Remarks*
20th: Lt. John C. Cowley (77th Ftr Sqn) b/o Brussels; injured
P-51D LC-N 44-15379

**April 6, 1945**
Groups Operating: P-51 4th, 20th, 55th, 78th, 339th, 352nd, 353rd, 355th, 356th, 357th, 359th, 361st, 364th, 479th
P-47 56th
Missions: Support of bombers to Halle, Leipzig, and Gera plus some PRU escorts.
Claims: nil

*Losses-*

**356th**: Lt. Raleigh S. Ragsdale (360th Ftr Sqn) KIA
P-51D PI-Q 44-15552 "Big Lefty-Little Ann"
Suffered mechanical failure near Coblenz and crashed while trying to belly-in near Mayenne.

*Remarks*
4th: Lt. Gilbert L. Kesler (336th Ftr Sqn) c/l Aachen; o.k.
P-51D VF- 44-72285
Lt. William B. Meredith (336th Ftr Sqn) c/l Aachen; o.k.
P-51D VF- 44-13375
55th: P-51 c/l Wormingford; o.k.
364th: Capt. Hayden W. Head (385th Ftr Sqn) b/o Cambridge; o.k.
P-51D 5E-P 44-15576

KIAc's
56th: F/O Joseph A. Del Corso (61st Ftr Sqn)
P-47M HV-
Dove into the ground near Boxted.

**April 7, 1945**
Groups Operating: P-51 4th, 20th, 55th, 78th, 339th, 352nd, 353rd, 355th, 356th, 357th, 359th, 361st, 364th, 479th
P-47 56th
Missions: Support of bombers to various airfields and marshalling yards plus PRU escorts.
Claims: 58-5-11 air
0-0 ground

| ***Group*** | | ***Claims*** | ***Location*** |
|---|---|---|---|
| **4th** | | | |
| 334th: | Lt. J.W. Ayers | Me-109 dest(air) | NE Duneburg |
| | Lt. R.H. Buchanan | Me-109 dest(air) | SE Krummel |
| | Lt. W.B. Hoelscher | Me-109 dest(air) | SE Krummel |
| 336th: | Lt. M.L. Davis | Me-109 dest(air) | SW Bremen |
| **55th** | | | |
| HdQts: | Capt. M. Clark | Me-109 dest(air) | Celle |
| 38th: | Capt. D.M. Cummings | (2)Me-109 dest(air) | Celle |
| | Lt. J.W. Cunnick | Me-109 dest(air) | Celle |
| | Lt. R.B. Mooers | Me-109 dest(air) | E/Celle |
| | Lt. D.A. Cavanaugh | (.5)Me-109 dest(air) | Celle |
| | Lt. D.T. Menegay | (.5)Me-109 dest(air) | Celle |
| **56th** | | | |
| 62nd: | Capt. R.E. Winters | Me-109 dest(air) | S/Hamburg |
| 63rd: | Maj. G.E. Bostwick | (2)Me-109 dest(air) | S/Bremen-Hamburg |
| | | Me-262 dam(air) | S/Bremen |
| | Lt. C.T. McBath | Me-109 dest(air) | N/Celle |
| | Lt. F.M. Ogden | Me-109 prob(air) | S/Hamburg |
| **78th** | | | |
| 83rd: | Lt. F.E. Harrington | Me-109 dest(air) | Dummer Lake |
| | | FW-190 dest(air) | Dummer Lake |
| | Capt. R.T. Green | Me-109 dest(air) | Dummer Lake |
| | Lt. R.I. Kuehl | Me-109 dest(air) | Dummer Lake |
| 84th: | Lt. R.K. Corbett | (.5)Me-109 dest(air) | NE Dummer Lake |
| | Lt. H.R. Slack | (.5)Me-109 dest(air) | NE Dummer Lake |
| **339th** | | | |
| 503rd: | Lt. R.G. Johnson | FW-190 dest(air) | Celle |
| | Lt. R.E. Krauss | Me-109 dest(air) | Celle |
| | Lt. P.E. Petitt | FW-190 dest(air) | Celle |
| | | Me-262 dam(air) | Celle |
| | Lt. L. Poutre | Me-109 dest(air) | Celle |
| 504th: | Capt. K.B. Everson | Me-109 dest(air) | Celle |
| | Capt. F.D. Guernsey | FW-190 dest(air) | Celle |
| | | Me-109 dam(air) | Celle |
| | Lt. L.M. Carter | Me-109 dest(air) | Celle |
| | | Me-262 dam(air) | Celle |
| | Lt. R.H. Cresswell | Me-109 dest(air) | Celle |
| | Lt. V.N. Barto | (.5)Me-109 dest(air) | Celle |
| | Lt. L.A. Kunz | (.5)Me-109 dest(air) | Celle |
| | Lt. R.V.E. Blizzard | Me-262 prob(air) | Celle |
| | | Me-262 dam(air) | Celle |
| | Lt. C. Hermanson | Me-109 prob(air) | Celle |
| | Lt. C.M. Mason | Me-262 dam(air) | Ulzen |
| 505th: | Capt. B.J. Bline | FW-190 dest(air) | SW Ulzen |
| | LtCol. J.L. Thury | (.5)Me-109 dest(air) | NE Steinhuder L. |
| | Lt. O.K. Biggs | (.5)Me-109 dest(air) | NE Steinhuder L. |
| | F/O J.J. Rice | Me-262 dam(air) | Ulzen |
| **352nd** | | | |
| HdQts: | Col. J.D. Mayden | Me-109 dest(air) | N/Minden |
| **353rd** | | | |
| 351st: | Capt. C.L. McGraw | (3)Me-109 dest(air) | Steinhuder Lake |
| | Capt. G.E. Markham | Me-109 dest(air) | E/Steinhuder L. |
| | | Me-109 dam(air) | E/Steinhuder L. |
| | Capt. H.W. Chase | Me-109 dest(air) | NE Steinhuder L. |
| | Lt. R.F. Hahn | Me-109 dest(air) | Steinhuder Lake |
| 352nd: | Capt. H.B. Tordoff | Me-109 dest(air) | E/Hamburg |
| **355th** | | | |
| 354th: | Capt. J.E. Mellen | FW-190 dest(air) | S/Bremen |
| | Lt. P.W. Vineyard | Me-109 dest(air) | SE Bremen |
| | Lt. G.D. Beeler | FW-190 dest(air) | S/Bremen |
| 357th: | Lt. W.F. Forehand | Me-109 dest(air) | SE Hamburg |
| | Lt. R.V. Finnesey | Me-262 dam(air) | SE Bremen |
| **356th** | | | |
| 359th: | Capt. J.F. Brown | Me-109 dest(air) | NE Steinhuder L. |
| | Lt. H.R. Gohsler | Me-109 dest(air) | E/Steinhuder L. |
| | | Me-109 prob(air) | E/Steinhuder L. |
| | Lt. J.B. Cornett | FW-190 dest(air) | NE Steinhuder L. |
| | Lt. P.C. O'Quinn | Me-262 dam(air) | NE Steinhuder L. |
| **357th** | | | |
| 363rd: | Capt. J.T. Windham | Me-109 dest(air) | Salzwedel |
| 364th: | Capt. I.L. McGuire | Me-109 dest(air) | NW Magdeburg |
| **479th** | | | |
| 434th: | Maj. R. Olds | Me-109 dest(air) | Dummer L.-Bremen |
| | | Me-262 dam(air) | Dummer L.-Bremen |
| | Lt. G.E. Jacobson | Me-109 dest(air) | Celle |
| | Lt. R.L. Munson | Me-109 dest(air) | Celle |
| | Lt. J.K. Nagel | Me-109 dest(air) | Soltau |
| | Lt. H.O. Thompson | Me-262 dest(air) | Luneburg |
| 435th: | Lt. R.G. Candelaria | (4)Me-109 dest(air) | SW Luneburg |
| | | Me-262 prob(air) | SW Luneburg |
| | Capt. V.E. Hooker | Me-109 dest(air) | SE Bremen |
| | | Me-262 dest(air) | SE Bremen |

*Losses-*

**55th**: Lt. Harold J. Konantz (338th Ftr Sqn) POW
P-51D CL-P 44-72296 "Saturday Night"
Hit by B-17 fire near Pritzwalk.

**78th**: Lt. Robert H. Talbot (83rd Ftr Sqn) POW
P-51D HL-H 44-72217
Hit by fire from a P-51 and bailed out near Dummer Lake.

**339th**: Lt. David A. MacKenzie (503rd Ftr Sqn) KIA
P-51K D7-K 44-11325
Hit by B-17 fire near Ahrensburg.

**355th**: Lt. Newell F. Mills, Jr. (354th Ftr Sqn) KIA
P-51D WR- 44-72306
Lost in bad weather near Bremen; possible collision.

Lt. Gilbert M. Plowman (354th Ftr Sqn) KIA
P-51D WR-Z 44-15346 "Bobbie Socks"
Lost in bad weather near Bremen; possible collision.

*Remarks*
4th: Lt. Jerome E. Jahnke (334th Ftr Sqn) c/l Debden; o.k.
P-51D QP-Q 44-14142
339th: Lt. Robert S. Paul (505th Ftr Sqn) c/l Fowlmere; o.k.
P-51 6N-

356th: Lt. Edgar J. Garneau (361st Ftr Sqn) c/l Martlesham Heath; o.k.
P-51D QI-

**April 8, 1945**
Groups Operating: P-51 4th, 20th, 55th, 78th, 339th, 352nd, 353rd, 355th, 356th, 359th, 361st, 364th, 479th
P-47 56th
Missions: Support of bombers to Halberstadt, Grafenwohr, Derben, and various other airfields and marshalling yards plus PRU escorts.
Claims: 3-0-0 air
1-1 ground

| *Group* | | *Claims* | *Location* |
|---|---|---|---|
| **355th** | | | |
| 354th: | LtCol. G.M. Graham | (2)Me-109 dest(air) | Oberpfaffenhofen |
| | Lt. C.E. Decklar | Me-109 dest(air) | Oberpfaffenhofen |
| 357th: | Lt. J.J. Weidemann | Me-109 dest(grd) | Ansbach |
| | | Me-109 dam(grd) | Ansbach |

*Losses-*

**5th**: Lt. Russell P. Judd (ERS) KIA
P-47D 5F-O 42-74705 "Lady Loralie"
Collided with F/O Davis over Fritton Lake.

F/O Louis S. Davis, III (ERS) KIA
P-47D 5F-D 42-76175 "Big Dick II"
Collided with Lt. Judd over Fritton Lake.

**355th**: Lt. William J. Cullerton (357th Ftr Sqn) POW(E)
P-51D OS- 44-64011
Hit by flak near Ansbach and bailed out; was shot on the ground by SS troops and rescued by German civilians.

<u>KIAc's</u>
4th: Lt. Homer C. Smith (336th Ftr Sqn)
P-51C VF-T 42-103603
Died in a crash northwest of Cambridge.

**April 9, 1945**
Groups Operating: P-51 4th, 20th, 55th, 78th, 339th, 352nd, 353rd, 355th, 356th, 357th, 359th, 361st, 364th, 479th
P-47 56th
Missions: Support of bombers to Neuburg and various jet airfields plus PRU escorts.
Claims: 1-0-5 air
88-61 ground

| *Group* | | *Claims* | *Location* |
|---|---|---|---|
| **4th** | | | |
| 335th: | Maj. P.W. McKennon | (2)Ju-52 dest(grd) | Munich-Brunnthal |
| | | Me-410 dest(grd) | Munich-Brunnthal |
| | | Ju-52 dam(grd) | Munich-Brunnthal |
| | Lt. R.C. Bucholz | (3)u/i a/c dest(grd) | Munich-Brunnthal |
| | Lt. T.H. Elffner | (2)Me-410 dest(grd) | Munich-Brunnthal |
| | Lt. L.I. Burgess | Ju-88 dest(grd) | Munich-Brunnthal |
| | | Ju-88 dam(grd) | Munich-Brunnthal |
| | | u/i a/c dam(grd) | Munich-Brunnthal |
| | Lt. M.D. Heaton | Fi-156 dest(grd) | Munich-Brunnthal |
| | | u/i a/c dest(grd) | Munich-Brunnthal |
| | Lt. R.C. Hunter | u/i a/c dest(grd) | Munich-Brunnthal |
| | | (2)u/i a/c dam(grd) | Munich-Brunnthal |
| | Lt. L.D. Jennings | Ju-88 dest(grd) | Munich-Brunnthal |
| | Lt. H.A. Lee | Me-410 dest(grd) | Munich-Brunnthal |
| | Lt. R.L. Couse | Ju-88 dam(grd) | Munich-Brunnthal |
| | | u/i a/c dam(grd) | Munich-Brunnthal |
| | Lt. W.H. George | (2)Me-410 dam(grd) | Munich-Brunnthal |
| | Lt. R.C. Hawley | (2)u/i a/c dam(grd) | Munich-Brunnthal |
| | Lt. R.A. Moe | Do-217 dam(grd) | Munich-Brunnthal |
| | | u/i a/c dam(grd) | Munich-Brunnthal |
| | Lt. S.W. Connors | Me-410 dam(grd) | Munich-Brunnthal |
| | Lt. E.J. McLoughlin | u/i a/c dam(grd) | Munich-Brunnthal |
| **20th** | | | |
| 55th: | Capt. R.M. Tracy | Ju-88 dam(grd) | Munich |
| 79th: | Maj. W.R. Yarbrough | Ju-88 dest(grd) | E/Munich |
| **55th** | | | |
| HdQts: | LtCol. E.G. Righetti | (3)Me-262 dest(grd) | MBLG |
| | | (2)u/i a/c dest(grd) | MBLG |
| | | FW-190 dest(grd) | MBLG |
| | | (2)u/i a/c dam(grd) | MBLG |
| 38th: | Lt. D.J. Best | (3)He-280 dest(grd) | MBLG |
| | Lt. J.W. Cunnick | FW-190 dest(grd) | MBLG |
| | | Me-262 dest(grd) | MBLG |
| | | Ju-88 dest(grd) | MBLG |
| | | FW-190 dam(grd) | MBLG |
| | | Me-262 dam(grd) | MBLG |
| | Lt. K.R. McGinnis | (2)He-111 dest(grd) | MBLG |
| | | He-111 dam(grd) | MBLG |
| | Lt. J.E. Mirando | (2)FW-190 dest(grd) | MBLG |
| | | (2)FW-190 dam(grd) | MBLG |
| | Lt. W.B. Staggs | (2)FW-190 dest(grd) | MBLG |
| | Lt. C.T. Williams | (2)FW-190 dest(grd) | MBLG |
| | | (2)FW-190 dam(grd) | MBLG |
| | Lt. J.T. Maloney | Me-262 dest(grd) | MBLG |
| | | (2)u/i a/c dam(grd) | MBLG |
| | Lt. D.D. Bachman | Me-262 dest(grd) | MBLG |
| | | He-111 dam(grd) | MBLG |
| | Lt. C.R. Schendel | (2)u/i a/c dam(grd) | MBLG |
| | Lt. W.T. Achramowicz | FW-190 dam(grd) | MBLG |
| | Lt. M.O. Anderson | u/i a/c dam(grd) | MBLG |
| 343rd: | Maj. E.B. Giller | Me-262 dest(air) | Munich |
| | | Me-410 dest(grd) | MBLG |
| | | He-111 dest(grd) | MBLG |
| | | Me-262 dest(grd) | MBLG |
| | | Me-410 dam(grd) | MBLG |
| | Capt. R.E. Welch | (2)Me-109 dest(grd) | Furtenfeldbruck |
| | | (2)Me-410 dest(grd) | MBLG |
| | | Me-262 dest(grd) | MBLG |
| | | He-177 dest(grd) | Furtenfeldbruck |
| | | Me-262 dam(grd) | MBLG |
| | Capt. F.E. Birtciel | (2)He-111 dest(grd) | MBLG |
| | | (2)Ju-88 dest(grd) | MBLG |
| | | Me-109 dest(grd) | MBLG |
| | | Ju-88 dam(grd) | MBLG |
| | Lt. D.E. Adams | Me-109 dest(grd) | Furtenfeldbruck |
| | | Me-410 dest(grd) | MBLG |
| | | Me-109 dam(grd) | Furtenfeldbruck |
| | Lt. G.E. Arnold | Me-262 dest(grd) | MBLG |
| | | Me-410 dest(grd) | MBLG |
| | Lt. L.D. Boring | Me-109 dest(grd) | MBLG |
| | | Me-410 dest(grd) | MBLG |
| | | Me-109 dam(grd) | MBLG |
| | Lt. H. Mahany | He-111 dest(grd) | MBLG |
| | | Me-262 dest(grd) | MBLG |
| | | He-111 dam(grd) | MBLG |
| | Lt. R.G. Allen | Me-410 dest(grd) | MBLG |
| | Lt. G.A. Apple | Me-109 dest(grd) | MBLG |
| | | Me-410 dam(grd) | MBLG |
| | Lt. R.K. Abel | u/i a/c dest(grd) | MBLG |
| | Lt. E.E. Leon | Ju-52 dest(grd) | MBLG |
| | | Me-262 dam(grd) | MBLG |
| | Lt. E.H. Geary | Me-109 dest(grd) | MBLG |
| | | Me-109 dam(grd) | MBLG |
| | Lt. D.R. Gifford | Me-410 dest(grd) | MBLG |
| | | (2)Me-410 dam(grd) | MBLG |
| | Lt. V.P. Gordon | Do-217 dest(grd) | Furtenfeldbruck |
| | Lt. W. Mearns | Me-410 dam(grd) | MBLG |
| **339th** | | | |
| 504th: | Lt. H.F. Hunt | Me-262 dam(air) | Leipzig |
| | Lt. L.M. Orcutt | Me-262 dam(air) | Leipzig |
| **353rd** | | | |
| 351st: | Capt. F.N. Emory | (2)Me-262 dest(grd) | S/Neubiberg |
| | | Me-410 dest(grd) | S/Neubiberg |
| | | u/i a/c dest(grd) | S/Neubiberg |
| | F/O H.A. Morris | Me-210 dest(grd) | S/Neubiberg |
| | | Me-262 dam(grd) | S/Neubiberg |
| | Lt. J.A. Hynes | Me-262 dam(grd) | S/Neubiberg |
| **355th** | | | |
| 354th: | LtCol. G.M. Graham | (2.5)He-111 dest(grd) | Memmingen |
| | Lt. P.W. Barnhart | He-111 dest(grd) | Memmingen |
| | Lt. D.B. Langley | He-111 dest(grd) | Memmingen |
| | Capt. A.S. White | (.5)He-111 dest(grd) | Memmingen |
| | Lt. J. Jabara | (.5)Ju-88 dest(grd) | Memmingen |
| | F/O H.W. Falvey | (.5)Ju-88 dest(grd) | Memmingen |
| | Lt. R.P. Pearson | He-111 dam(grd) | Memmingen |
| 358th: | Lt. W.J. Lynch | Me-110 dest(grd) | Heilfingen |
| | | He-111 dest(grd) | Heilfingen |
| | | u/i a/c dam(grd) | Heilfingen |
| | Lt. E.W. Fees | Me-110 dest(grd) | Heilfingen |
| | Lt. J.H. Lanius | Me-110 dest(grd) | Heilfingen |
| | Lt. F.N. McCollom | Me-110 dest(grd) | Heilfingen |
| | | He-111 dam(grd) | Heilfingen |
| | Lt. C.C. Patrinely | He-111 dest(grd) | Heilfingen |
| | | (.5)Me-110 dest(grd) | Heilfingen |
| | Lt. H.P. Knutty | (.5)Me-110 dest(grd) | Heilfingen |
| | Lt. C.E. Plemons | He-111 dam(grd) | Heilfingen |
| **356th** | | | |
| 360th: | Maj. M.P. Yannell | FW-190 dest(grd) | Biberach |
| | | u/i a/c dest(grd) | Biberach |
| | | Me-410 dam(grd) | Biberach |
| | Lt. R.J. Rensch | u/i a/c dest(grd) | Biberach |
| | | (3)u/i a/c dam(grd) | Biberach |
| | | Me-109 dam(grd) | Biberach |
| | Lt. E.W. Schrull | FW-190 dam(grd) | Biberach |
| | | u/i a/c dam(grd) | Biberach |
| | Lt. T.N. Mauldin | u/i a/c dam(grd) | Biberach |

**359th**

| | | | |
|---|---|---|---|
| 368th: | F/O R.G. Muzzy | (1.5)Me-262 dam(air) | Augsburg |
| | Capt. M.F. Boussu | Me-262 dam(air) | Augsburg |
| | Lt. F. Rea | (.5)Me-262 dam(air) | Augsburg |
| | Capt. G.A. Doersch | FW-190 dest(grd) | Gernering A/F |
| | | He-111 dam(grd) | Gernering A/F |
| | Lt. R.H. Elliott | (2)Ju-88 dam(grd) | Munich |

*Losses-*

**SF**: Lt. James H. Reed (3rd) KIA
P-51D 9H-
Lost over the Channel for unknown reasons.

**4th**: Lt. Robert C. Bucholz (335th Ftr Sqn) KIA
P-51D WD-T 44-14389 "Suzy"
Hit by flak at Munich-Brunnthal.

Lt. Herman S. Rasmussen (335th Ftr Sqn) KIA
P-51D WD- 44-13788
Hit by flak at Munich-Brunnthal and bailed out too low south of Neubiberg.

**55th**: Lt. Richard K. Abel (343rd Ftr Sqn) KIA
P-51D CY-H 44-64159 "Jill's Jalopy IV"
Hit by flak at Munich-Brunnthal Landing Ground.

**357th**: Lt. William B. Haack (363rd Ftr Sqn) KIA
P-51D B6- 44-13570
Suffered mechanical failure near Augsburg.

*Remarks*

20th: 0-1 radio station
Lt. Richard P. Iehle ((55th Ftr Sqn) c/l; o.k.
P-51D KI-

355th: Lt. Raymond Shewfelt (358th Ftr Sqn) c/l Tantonville; o.k.
P-51D YF-M 44-14524

356th: Lt. Edgar J. Garneau (361st Ftr Sqn) c/l Martlesham Heath; o.k.
P-51D QI-K 44-15345

357th: P-51 c/l Leiston; o.k.

359th: Capt. George A. Doersch (368th Ftr Sqn) c/l W/Mannheim; o.k.
P-51D CV-H 44-63179

**April 10, 1945**

Groups Operating: P-51 4th, 20th, 55th, 78th, 339th, 352nd, 353rd, 355th, 356th, 357th, 359th, 364th, 479th
P-47 56th

Missions: Support of bombers to Oranienburg, Neuruppin, Rechlin, and Brandenburg plus PRU escorts.

Claims: 21-1-12 air
328-222 ground

| *Group* | | *Claims* | *Location* |
|---|---|---|---|
| **4th** | | | |
| 334th: | Maj. G.E. Montgomery | Me-410 dest(grd) | Wittstock |
| | Lt. D.G. Lowther | Ju-52 dest(grd) | Wittstock |
| | Lt. J.D. McFadden | Ju-88 dest(grd) | Wittstock |
| | Lt. R.J. Miller | u/o a/c dest(grd) | Wittstock |
| 336th: | Lt. W.W. Collins | Me-262 dest(air) | Lubeck |
| **20th** | | | |
| HdQts: | Col. R.P. Montgomery | Ar-196 dest(grd) | Werder A/F |
| | | Si-204 dest(grd) | Werder A/F |
| | | Ju-52 dest(grd) | Werder A/F |
| | | Do-217 dam(grd) | Werder A/F |
| | | Si-204 dam(grd) | Werder A/F |
| 55th: | Capt. J.K. Brown | Me-262 dest(air) | Neuruppin |
| | Capt. D. Michel | Me-262 dam(air) | Neuruppin |
| | Lt. R.W. Meinzen | Me-262 dam(air) | Neuruppin |
| | Lt. E.L. Kier | (5)Ju-88 dest(grd) | Berlin |
| | | (4)Ju-88 dam(grd) | Berlin |
| | Lt. J.A. Peterburs | (5)u/i a/c dest(grd) | Berlin |
| | Capt. R.M. Tracy | Me-110 dest(grd) | Berlin |
| | | Me-109 dest(grd) | Berlin |
| | | Ju-52 dest(grd) | Berlin |
| | | u/i a/c dest(grd) | Berlin |
| | Lt. G.L. Williams | (4)Ju-88 dest(grd) | Berlin |
| | | (4)Ju-88 dam(grd) | Berlin |
| | Lt. P.F. Seifert | Me-110 dam(grd) | Werder A/F |
| | | He-111 dam(grd) | Werder A/F |
| 77th: | Lt. W.T. Drozd | Me-262 dest(air) | Oranienburg |
| | Lt. A.B. North | Me-262 dest(air) | Oranienburg |
| | Lt. J.W. Cudd | (.5)Me-262 dest(air) | Berlin |
| | F/O J. Rosenblum | (.5)Me-262 dest(air) | Berlin |
| | Lt. G.R. Hall | Me-262 dam(air) | Werder A/F |
| | | He-111 dest(grd) | Werder A/F |
| | | Me-109 dest(grd) | Werder A/F |
| | | Ju-290 dam(grd) | Werder A/F |
| | | He-111 dam(grd) | Werder A/F |
| | Lt. R.S. Morris | Me-410 dest(grd) | Fassberg A/F |
| | | u/i a/c dest(grd) | Fassberg A/F |
| | Lt. L.H. Kerns | Me-410 dest(grd) | Fassberg A/F |
| | Lt. J.E. Simanonok | Ju-88 dest(grd) | Oranienburg |
| | Lt. W.E. Umla | Ju-52 dest(grd) | Schonwalde A/F |
| | | (2)Ju-52 dam(grd) | Schonwalde A/F |
| 79th: | Capt. J.K. Hollins | Me-262 dest(air) | Neustadt |
| | F/O F.H. Jurgens | (3)He-111 dest(grd) | Werder A/F |
| | | (2)Si-204 dest(grd) | Werder A/F |
| | | (2)Caudron dest(grd) | Werder A/F |
| | | u/i a/c dest(grd) | Werder A/F |
| | Lt. D. Stewart | (3)Me-110 dest(grd) | Werder A/F |
| | | (2)FW-190 dest(grd) | Werder A/F |
| | | Me-109 dest(grd) | Werder A/F |
| | | He-111 dest(grd) | Werder A/F |
| | Lt. E.F. Pogue | (3)He-111 dest(grd) | Werder A/F |
| | | Me-109 dest(grd) | Werder A/F |
| | | He-111 dam(grd) | Werder A/F |
| | | Me-109 dam(grd) | Werder A/F |
| | Lt. L.J. Degenhardt | (2)u/i a/c dest(grd) | Werder A/F |
| | | u/i a/c dam(grd) | Werder A/F |
| | Lt. J.L. Gubana | Me-109 dest(grd) | Werder A/F |
| | | Ju-88 dest(grd) | Werder A/F |
| | | (2)u/i a/c dam(grd) | Werder A/F |
| | Lt. J.B. Lee | Ju-52 dest(grd) | Werder A/F |
| | | Me-109 dam(grd) | Werder A/F |
| | | Si-204 dam(grd) | Werder A/F |
| **55th** | | | |
| HdQts: | Maj. P.E. Hoeper | Me-262 dest(grd) | Burg |
| 38th: | Lt. K.R. McGinnis | Me-262 dest(air) | Galworde |
| | Lt. D.D. Bachman | Me-262 dam(air) | Galworde |
| | Lt. C.C. Gould | (2)Me-109 dest(grd) | Wesendorf |
| | | u/i a/c dest(grd) | Wesendorf |
| | | Me-109 dam(grd) | Wesendorf |
| | Lt. J.T. Maloney | (2)Me-109 dest(grd) | Wesendorf |
| | | FW-190 dest(grd) | Wesendorf |
| | Lt. D.J. Best | (2)He-111 dest(grd) | Wesendorf |
| | | Me-109 dam(grd) | Wesendorf |
| | Lt. J.W. Cunnick | He-111 dest(grd) | Wesendorf |
| | | Me-109 dest(grd) | Wesendorf |
| | | He-111 dam(grd) | Wesendorf |
| | Lt. M.O. Anderson | u/i a/c dest(grd) | Wesendorf |
| 338th: | Lt. K.A. Lashbrook | Me-262 dest(air) | Burg |
| | Lt. H. Bodiford | Fi-156 dest(air) | SE Luneburg |
| | Lt. C.S. Chioles | Me-262 dam(air) | SE Hanover |
| | Capt. S.D. Gevorkian | (2)Ju-88 dest(grd) | Burg |
| | | FW-190 dest(grd) | Burg |
| | Lt. R.E. Darling | (2)Me-410 dest(grd) | Burg |
| | Lt. V.B. Tally | (2)Me-410 dest(grd) | Burg |
| | Lt. W.H. Barnes | FW-190 dest(grd) | Burg |
| | | (2)FW-190 dam(grd) | Burg |
| | Lt. A.F. Connors | FW-190 dest(grd) | Burg |
| | Lt. A.S. Dargan | Me-410 dest(grd) | Burg |
| | | Me-410 dam(grd) | Burg |
| | Lt. R.C. Herbst | Me-262 dest(grd) | Burg |
| | Lt. J.C. White | Ar-234 dest(grd) | Burg |
| 343rd: | Capt. R.E. Welch | (2)He-111 dest(grd) | Burg |
| | Lt. R.G. Gibbs | He-111 dest(grd) | Burg |
| | | Ju-87 dam(grd) | Burg |
| **56th** | | | |
| 61st: | Capt. C.R. Bond | Ju-88 dest(grd) | Rechlin |
| | | Do-24 dest(grd) | Muritz Lake |
| | | Do-217 dam(grd) | Muritz Lake |
| | | Ju-88 dam(grd) | Rechlin |
| | Lt. E.E. Ellis | Do-217 dest(grd) | Oranienburg |
| | | He-177 dest(grd) | Oranienburg |
| | | u/i a/c dest(grd) | Oranienburg |
| | | (4)u/i a/c dam(grd) | Oranienburg |
| | Lt. J.E. Jones | (2)Do-24 dest(grd) | Muritz Lake |
| | | u/i a/c dest(grd) | Muritz Lake |
| | Lt. F.H. Barrett | (2)Ju-88 dest(grd) | Oranienburg |
| | | (3)Ju-88 dam(grd) | Oranienburg |
| | Lt. R.S. Kyler | Me-109 dest(grd) | Muritz Lake |
| | | u/i a/c dest(grd) | Muritz Lake |
| | Capt. C.B. Cole | u/i a/c dest(grd) | Oranienburg |
| | | (5)u/i a/c dam(grd) | Oranienburg |
| | Lt. B.O. Blodgett | Do-24 dest(grd) | Muritz Lake |
| | Lt. P.J. Clinton | Do-24 dest(grd) | Muritz Lake |
| | | u/i a/c dam(grd) | Muritz Lake |
| | Lt. R.W. Higgins | u/i a/c dest(grd) | Muritz Lake |
| | | u/i a/c dam(grd) | Muritz Lake |
| | Lt. E.B. Lightfoot | u/i a/c dest(grd) | Muritz Lake |
| | Lt. C.J. Raymond | Do-217 dest(grd) | Oranienburg |
| | Lt. L.M. Winski | He-115 dest(grd) | Muritz Lake |
| | | (2)u/i a/c dam(grd) | Muritz Lake |
| 62nd: | Lt. W.J. Sharbo | Me-262 dest(air) | Muritz Lake |
| | | (2)He-111 dest(grd) | Neuruppin |
| | | He-177 dam(grd) | Neuruppin |
| | | Ju-88 dam(grd) | Neuruppin |
| | Capt. W.F. Wilkerson | Me-262 dam(air) | Muritz Lake |
| | | (2)He-111 dest(grd) | Rechlin |
| | | He-111 dam(grd) | Rechlin |

| | | | |
|---|---|---|---|
| | Lt. F.G. Koch | (2)u/i a/c dest(grd) | Neuruppin |
| | | (4)u/i a/c dam(grd) | Neuruppin |
| | Lt. D.A. Carroll | Me-109 dest(grd) | Rechlin |
| | | Ju-88 dest(grd) | Rechlin |
| | Lt. C.A. Tingen | Ju-88 dest(grd) | Rechlin |
| | | He-111 dam(grd) | Rechlin |
| | | Ju-88 dam(grd) | Rechlin |
| | Lt. L.F. Butiste | He-111 dest(grd) | Neuruppin |
| | | u/i a/c dest(grd) | Neuruppin |
| | Lt. R.B. Jones | He-111 dest(grd) | Neuruppin |
| | | He-111 dam(grd) | Neuruppin |
| | Lt. D. Henley | Ju-88 dest(grd) | Neuruppin |
| | | Ju-88 dam(grd) | Neuruppin |
| | Lt. W.J. Stevenson | Ju-88 dest(grd) | Neuruppin |
| | | Ju-88 dam(grd) | Neuruppin |
| | Lt. D.M. Gunner | He-111 dest(grd) | Muritz Lake |
| | Lt. H.O. Womack | He-111 dest(grd) | Neuruppin |
| | F/O C.R. Albright | (.5)u/i a/c dest(grd)[*] | Muritz Lake |
| | | Ju-88 dam(grd) | Muritz Lake |
| | Capt. R.E. Winter | u/i a/c dam(grd) | Rechlin |
| 63rd: | Lt. E.W. Andermatt | Me-262 dam(air) | Damm A/F |
| | Maj. G.E. Bosteick | (2)Ju-88 dest(grd) | Werder A/F |
| | | (2)u/i a/c dest(grd) | Werder A/F |
| | Capt. W.L. Flagg | (2)Do-217 dest(grd) | Werder A/F |
| | | Me-109 dest(grd) | Werder A/F |
| | | u/i a/c dest(grd) | Werder A/F |
| | | Me-109 dam(grd) | Werder A/F |
| | Lt. E.S. Barrentine | (2)Ju-88 dest(grd) | Neuruppin |
| | | He-177 dam(grd) | Neuruppin |
| | | Ju-88 dam(grd) | Neuruppin |
| | Lt. J.C. Naylor | Me-109 dest(grd) | Werder A/F |
| | | FW-190 dest(grd) | Werder A/F |
| | | Do-217 dam(grd) | Werder A/F |
| | | u/i a/c dam(grd) | Werder A/F |
| | Lt. W.R. Hoffman | (2)u/i a/c dest(grd) | Werder A/F |
| | Lt. J.A. Arnold | FW-190 dest(grd) | Stendal |
| | Lt. A.T. Shupe | FW-190 dest(grd) | Stendal |
| | | (2)FW-190 dam(grd) | Stendal |
| | Lt. T.W. Smith | Ju-88 dest(grd) | Werder A/F |
| | | Ju-88 dam(grd) | Werder A/F |
| | Lt. V.A. Smith | Ju-88 dest(grd) | Werder A/F |
| | | u/i a/c dam(grd) | Werder A/F |
| | Lt. B.E. Vest | Ju-88 dest(grd) | Stendal |
| | | Me-109 dam(grd) | Stendal |
| | Capt. J.C. Fahringer | (4)FW-190 dam(grd) | Stendal |
| | Lt. C.T. McBath | Ju-88 dam(grd) | Werder A/F |
| **78th** | | | |
| HdQts: | LtCol. J.D. Landers | (2)Me-109 dest(grd) | Werder A/F |
| | | FW-190 dest(grd) | Werder A/F |
| | | He-111 dest(grd) | Werder A/F |
| | | Ju-188 dest(grd) | Werder A/F |
| | | Ju-88 dest(grd) | Werder A/F |
| 82nd: | Lt. L.R. Campi | (2)Me-109 dest(grd) | Werder A/F |
| | | FW-190 dest(grd) | Werder A/F |
| | | (2)u/i a/c dam(grd) | Werder A/F |
| | Lt. E.J. Carroll | FW-190 dest(grd) | Werder A/F |
| | | Ju-52 dest(grd) | Werder A/F |
| | | u/i a/c dest(grd) | Werder A/F |
| | | (5)u/i a/c dam(grd) | Werder A/F |
| | Lt. H.H. Lamb | Me-410 dest(grd) | Werder A/F |
| | | Ju-52 dest(grd) | Werder A/F |
| | | Ju-88 dest(grd) | Werder A/F |
| | | Ju-52 dam(grd) | Werder A/F |
| | Lt. M.B. Stutzman | FW-190 dest(grd) | Werder A/F |
| | | He-111 dest(grd) | Werder A/F |
| | | (2)u/i a/c dam(grd) | Werder A/F |
| | Lt. R.B. Abernathy | Me-109 dest(grd) | Werder A/F |
| | | Me-109 dam(grd) | Werder A/F |
| | | u/i a/c dam(grd) | Werder A/F |
| | Lt. W.F. Bechtelheimer | u/i a/c dest(grd) | Werder A/F |
| | Lt. R.J. Blossom | He-111 dest(grd) | Werder A/F |
| | | Me-109 dam(grd) | Werder A/F |
| | Lt. W.E. Bourque | Me-109 dest(grd) | Werder A/F |
| | | Ju-52 dam(grd) | Werder A/F |
| | | u/i a/c dam(grd) | Werder A/F |
| | Lt. G.V. Elsey | FW-190 dest(grd) | Werder A/F |
| | Lt. A.S. Miller | He-111 dest(grd) | Werder A/F |
| | | FW-190 dam(grd) | Werder A/F |
| | Lt. E.L. Peel | u/i a/c dest(grd) | Werder A/F |
| | | (2)u/i a/c dam(grd) | Werder A/F |
| | Lt. G.W. Stilwell | Me-410 dest(grd) | Werder A/F |
| | | Me-410 dam(grd) | Werder A/F |
| | Lt. D.C. Hart | FW-190 dam(grd) | Werder A/F |
| | Lt. H.L. Roe | Do-217 dam(grd) | Werder A/F |
| 83rd: | Lt. F.E. Harrington | (2)FW-190 dest(grd) | Werder A/F |
| | | Ju-87 dest(grd) | Werder A/F |
| | | u/i a/c dest(grd) | Werder A/F |
| | | FW-190 dam(grd) | Werder A/F |
| | | Ju-87 dam(grd) | Werder A/F |
| | | u/i a/c dam(grd) | Werder A/F |

| | | | |
|---|---|---|---|
| | Lt. J.A. Kirk | He-111 dest(grd) | Werder A/F |
| | | Bu-133 dest(grd) | Werder A/F |
| | Lt. R.I. Kuehl | Me-410 dest(grd) | Brandenburg-Briest |
| | | u/i a/c dam(grd) | Brandenburg-Briest |
| | Lt. E.W. Strobel | FW-190 dest(grd) | Werder A/F |
| | | u/i a/c dam(grd) | Werder A/F |
| | Lt. J.S. Peterson | FW-190 dest(grd) | Hustedt A/F |
| | Lt. R.E. Phaneuf | He-111 dest(grd) | Gardelegen |
| | Capt. F.E. Higginbottom | Me-262 dam(grd) | Burg-Magdeburg |
| | Lt. D.R. Monteith | FW-190 dam(grd) | Brandenburg-Briest |
| 84th: | Lt. H.R. Slack | FW-190 dest(grd) | Werder A/F |
| | | Ju-87 dest(grd) | Werder A/F |
| | | Ju-52 dest(grd) | Werder A/F |
| | Capt. P.T. Keiller | Ar-196 dest(grd) | Werder A/F |
| | | Me-323 dest(grd) | Werder A/F |
| | | Ar-196 dam(grd) | Werder A/F |
| | Lt. J.R. Sole | u/i a/c dest(grd) | Ulzen |
| | | u/i a/c dam(grd) | Ulzen |
| | Lt. R.A. Spaulding | u/i a/c dest(grd) | Werder A/F |
| | Lt. J.D. Calvin | u/i a/c dam(grd) | Ulzen |
| **339th** | | | |
| 503rd: | Lt. R.J. French | (4)Ju-88 dest(grd) | N/Neuruppin |
| | | Ju-88 dam(grd) | N/Neuruppin |
| | | u/i a/c dam(grd) | N/Neuruppin |
| | LtCol. D.E. Shafer | Me-109 dest(grd) | N/Neuruppin |
| | | Ju-88 dest(grd) | N/Neuruppin |
| | | (4)Ju-88 dam(grd) | N/Neuruppin |
| 504th: | Capt. K.B. Everson | (3)Me-410 dest(grd) | N/Neuruppin |
| | | (3)Me-410 dam(grd) | N/Neuruppin |
| | | (2)Me-110 dam(grd) | N/Neuruppin |
| | Capt. R.F. Sargent | (3)Me-410 dest(grd) | N/Neuruppin |
| | | (2)Me-410 dam(grd) | N/Neuruppin |
| | Lt. C. Hermanson | (3)Me-410 dest(grd) | N/Neuruppin |
| | | (2)Me-410 dam(grd) | N/Neuruppin |
| | Maj. W.H. Julian | (2)Me-410 dest(grd) | N/Neuruppin |
| | | (2)Me-410 dam(grd) | N/Neuruppin |
| | Lt. L.W. Allers | (2)Me-410 dest(grd) | N/Neuruppin |
| | | Me-410 dam(grd) | N/Neuruppin |
| | Lt. V.N. Barto | (2)Ju-88 dest(grd) | N/Neuruppin |
| | | Ju-88 dam(grd) | N/Neuruppin |
| | Lt. L.J. Barrett | (2)Ju-88 dest(grd) | N/Neuruppin |
| | | (2)Me-410 dam(grd) | N/Neuruppin |
| | Lt. C.W. Bennett | (2)Me-410 dest(grd) | N/Neuruppin |
| | | (2)Me-410 dam(grd) | N/Neuruppin |
| | Lt. R.V.E. Blizzard | (2)Me-410 dest(grd) | N/Neuruppin |
| | | (2)Me-410 dam(grd) | N/Neuruppin |
| | Lt. G.H. Chenez | (2)Me-410 dest(grd) | N/Neuruppin |
| | | (2)Me-410 dam(grd) | N/Neuruppin |
| | Lt. R.C. Croker | (2)Me-410 dest(grd) | N/Neuruppin |
| | | (4)Me-410 dam(grd) | N/Neuruppin |
| | Lt. L.A. Kunz | (2)Me-410 dest(grd) | N/Neuruppin |
| | | (3)Me-410 dam(grd) | N/Neuruppin |
| | Lt. C.M. Mason | (2)Me-410 dest(grd) | N/Neuruppin |
| | | Me-410 dam(grd) | N/Neuruppin |
| | F/O R.W. Smith | Me-410 dest(grd) | N/Neuruppin |
| | | Ju-88 dam(grd) | N/Neuruppin |
| | Lt. D.F. Krueger | (2)Me-410 dam(grd) | N/Neuruppin |
| 505th: | Maj. A.A. Tower | (2)Do-217 dest(grd) | Wittstock |
| | | (2)Me-410 dest(grd) | Wittstock |
| | | (2)Hs-129 dest(grd) | Wittstock |
| | | (2)Ju-88 dest(grd) | Wittstock |
| | | Do-217 dam(grd) | Wittstock |
| | | Me-410 dam(grd) | Wittstock |
| | Lt. J.T. Murphy | (3)Do-217 dest(grd) | Wittstock |
| | | (2)Ju-88 dest(grd) | Wittstock |
| | | (3)u/i a/c dam(grd) | Wittstock |
| | Lt. R.H. Paul | (3)Do-217 dest(grd) | Wittstock |
| | | (2)Ju-88 dest(grd) | Wittstock |
| | | (2)Ju-52 dam(grd) | Wittstock |
| | Capt. H.R. Corey | (4)Ju-88 dest(grd) | Wittstock |
| | | FW-189 dam(grd) | Wittstock |
| | | Ju-88 dam(grd) | Wittstock |
| | | Ju-52 dam(grd) | Wittstock |
| | Lt. O.K. Biggs | (4)Ju-88 dest(grd) | Wittstock |
| | | (2)Ju-88 dam(grd) | Wittstock |
| | Lt. H.W. Burch | (3)Me-410 dest(grd) | Wittstock |
| | | He-111 dest(grd) | Wittstock |
| | | Me-410 dam(grd) | Wittstock |
| | | u/i a/c dam(grd) | Wittstock |
| | LtCol. J.L. Thury | (2)u/i a/c dest(grd) | N/Neuruppin |
| | | Ju-88 dest(grd) | N/Neuruppin |
| | | He-111 dam(grd) | N/Neuruppin |
| | | u/i a/c dam(grd) | N/Neuruppin |
| | Lt. H.L. Caywood | (3)Ju-88 dest(grd) | N/Neuruppin |
| | | (2)Ju-88 dam(grd) | N/Neuruppin |
| | Lt. W.R. Guyton | (2)Ju-88 dest(grd) | Wittstock |
| | | Do-217 dest(grd) | Wittstock |
| | Lt. R.E. Irion | (2)Ju-188 dest(grd) | Wittstock |
| | | Do-217 dest(grd) | Wittstock |
| | | Me-110 dam(grd) | Wittstock |

| | | | |
|---|---|---|---|
| | Lt. W.R. MacClarence | (3)Ju-88 dest(grd) | N/Neuruppin |
| | Lt. T.W. Marvel | (3)Me-410 dest(grd) | N/Neuruppin |
| | | Me-410 dam(grd) | N/Neuruppin |
| | Capt. O.P. Farmer | (2)Ju-88 dest(grd) | N/Neuruppin |
| | Lt. V.D. Carr | Do-217 dest(grd) | N/Neuruppin |
| | | Ju-88 dest(grd) | N/Neuruppin |
| | | (2)Me-410 dam(grd) | N/Neuruppin |
| | F/O J.J. Rice | (2)Do-217 dest(grd) | N/Neuruppin |
| | | Do-217 dam(grd) | N/Neuruppin |
| | Lt. W.R. Phillippi | (2)Ju-88 dest(grd) | N/Neuruppin |
| | Capt. J.R. Starnes | Do-217 dest(grd) | N/Neuruppin |
| | | (3)Do-217 dam(grd) | N/Neuruppin |
| | Lt. J.C. Withers | Ju-88 dest(grd) | N/Neuruppin |
| | | (2)Ju-88 dam(grd) | N/Neuruppin |
| | F/O E.E. Hupp | Do-217 dest(grd) | N/Neuruppin |
| | | Do-217 dam(grd) | N/Neuruppin |

**352nd**

| | | | |
|---|---|---|---|
| 328th: | LtCol. E.D. Duncan | (.5)Me-262 dest(air) | Berlin-Wittenburg |
| | Maj. R.G. McAuliffe | (.5)Me-262 dest(air) | Berlin-Wittenburg |
| 487th: | Lt. C.A. Pattillo | Me-262 dest(air) | E/Ulzen |
| | Lt. J.W. Prichard | (.5)Me-262 dest(air) | Neuruppin |
| | Lt. C.A. Ricci | (.5)Me-262 dest(air) | Neuruppin |
| | Lt. K.M. Walron | Me-262 dam(air) | Salzwedel |

**353rd**

| | | | |
|---|---|---|---|
| 350th: | Capt. R.W. Abernathy | Me-262 dest(air) | Dessau |
| | Lt. J.W. Clark | (.5)Me-262 dest(air) | Dessau |
| | Lt. B.D. McMahan | (.5)Me-262 dest(air) | Dessau |
| 351st: | Capt. G.B. Compton | Me-262 dest(air) | Dessau-Kothen |

**355th**

| | | | |
|---|---|---|---|
| HdQts: | Maj. H.H. Kirby | Ju-88 dest(grd) | Rechlin/Larz |
| | | (3)Ju-88 dam(grd) | Rechlin/Larz |
| 354th: | LtCol. G.M. Graham | Me-109 dest(grd) | Rechlin/Larz |
| | | B-24 dest(grd) | Rechlin/Larz |
| | | (3)Me-109 dam(grd) | Rechlin/Larz |
| | Lt. J.M. Fletcher | (2)u/i a/c dest(grd) | Rechlin/Larz |
| | Lt. J. Jabara | (2)Me-410 dest(grd) | Rechlin/Larz |
| | | (3)u/i a/c dam(grd) | Rechlin/Larz |
| | F/O H.W. Falvey | Ju-52 dest(grd) | Rechlin/Larz |
| | | (.5)He-111 dest(grd) | Rechlin/Larz |
| | | (4)u/i a/c dam(grd) | Rechlin/Larz |
| | Lt. D.V. Galer | u/i a/c dest(grd) | Memmingen |
| | Lt. O.N. Stanton | u/i a/c dest(grd) | Wesendorf |
| | F/O T.R. Hixon | (.5)He-111 dest(grd) | Rechlin/Larz |
| | | (4)u/i a/c dam(grd) | Rechlin/Larz |
| | Lt. P.W. Barnhart | u/i a/c dest(grd) | Husum |
| | | (2)FW-190 dam(grd) | Husum |
| | | u/i a/c dam(grd) | Husum |
| | | u/i a/c dam(grd) | Rechlin/Larz |
| 357th: | Lt. R.L. Garlich | He-111 dest(grd) | Rechlin/Larz |
| | | Do-24 dest(grd) | Rechlin/Larz |
| | | (.5)u/i a/c dest(grd)* | Muritz Lake |
| | Lt. R.F. Misner | Ju-88 dest(grd) | Rechlin/Larz |
| | | Ju-88 dam(grd) | Rechlin/Larz |
| | Lt. D.P. Watkins | He-111 dest(grd) | Rechlin/Larz |
| | Lt. R.W. Cooper | (.5)B-24 dest(grd) | Rechlin/Larz |
| | Lt. W.T. Burnett | (.5)B-24 dest(grd) | Rechlin/Larz |
| | | Me-109 dam(grd) | Rechlin/Larz |
| 358th: | Capt. W.V. Gresham | Me-262 dam(air) | W/Kubeck |

**356th**

| | | | |
|---|---|---|---|
| 360th: | Lt. W.C. Gatlin | Me-262 dest(air) | Oranienburg |
| | Lt. T.N. Mauldin | Me-262 prob(air) | Oranienburg |
| | Lt. E.W. Schrull | Me-262 dam(air) | Oranienburg |

**357th**

| | | | |
|---|---|---|---|
| HdQts: | Col. I.H. Dregne | (2)Me-262 dest(grd) | Neuruppin |
| | | FW-190 dest(grd) | Neuruppin |
| | | Ju-88 dam(grd) | Neuruppin |
| | LtCol. A.J. Evans | He-111 dest(grd) | Neuruppin |
| | | Me-210 dest(grd) | Neuruppin |
| | | He-111 dam(grd) | Neuruppin |
| | | Me-210 dam(grd) | Neuruppin |
| | | Do-217 dam(grd) | Neuruppin |
| | | He-177 dam(grd) | Neuruppin |
| 362nd: | Lt. J.F. Duncan | (2)Me-210 dest(grd) | Neuruppin |
| | | Me-110 dest(grd) | Neuruppin |
| | | Me-262 dam(grd) | Neuruppin |
| | Lt. J.W. Dunn | He-111 dest(grd) | Neuruppin |
| | | Do-217 dest(grd) | Neuruppin |
| | | (2)He-111 dam(grd) | Neuruppin |
| | | FW-190 dam(grd) | Neuruppin |
| | Lt. E.A. Gordon | (2)He-111 dest(grd) | Neuruppin |
| | Lt. N.M. Hewit | (2)He-111 dest(grd) | Neuruppin |
| | Lt. E.C. Danner | Ju-88 dest(grd) | Neuruppin |
| 363rd: | Maj. D.C. McGee | Me-410 dest(grd) | Neuruppin |
| | | He-111 dest(grd) | Neuruppin |
| | | (2)u/i a/c dam(grd) | Neuruppin |
| | Lt. R.R. Kalessa | u/i a/c dest(grd) | Neuruppin |
| | | u/i a/c dam(grd) | Neuruppin |
| 364th: | Lt. V.V. Zettler | (3)Ju-88 dest(grd) | Neuruppin |
| | Capt. R.W. Moore | He-111 dest(grd) | Neuruppin |
| | F/O J.A. Steiger | Ju-88 dest(grd) | Neuruppin |
| | Lt. L.E. Zacharie | (2)He-111 dam(grd) | Neuruppin |
| | Lt. H.E. Arrendale | Ju-88 dam(grd) | Neuruppin |

**359th**

| | | | |
|---|---|---|---|
| 368th: | Lt. J.T. Marron | Me-262 dam(air) | NW Gustrow |
| 369th: | Lt. R.J. Guggemos | Me-262 dest(air) | Gardelegen A/F |
| | | (2)Me-109 dest(grd) | Dennefeld |
| | Lt. H. Tenenbaum | Me-262 dest(air) | Gardelegen A/F |
| | Lt. R.R. Klaver | Me-262 dam(air) | Wittenburg |

**364th**

| | | | |
|---|---|---|---|
| 384th: | Capt. D.J. Pick | (.5)Me-262 dest(air) | Staaken A/F |
| | Lt. H.C. Schwartz | (.5)Me-262 dest(air) | Staaken A/F |
| | | FW-200 dest(grd) | W/Berlin |
| | LtCol. R.E. Lacy | Me-410 dest(grd) | Oranienburg |
| | | He-177 dam(grd) | Oranienburg |
| | Lt. J.L. Hughes | He-111 dest(grd) | Oranienburg |
| | | Me-109 dam(grd) | Oranienburg |
| | Lt. S.R. Honaker | Do-217 dam(grd) | W/Berlin |
| | | He-111 dam(grd) | W/Berlin |
| | Lt. D.L. Leftwich | He-111 dam(grd) | Oranienburg |
| 385th: | Maj. W.S. Crombie | Me-262 dest(grd) | Stendal |
| | | Ju-88 dest(grd) | Stendal |
| | | u/i a/c dest(grd) | Stendal |
| | | (2)FW-190 dam(grd) | Stendal |
| | | Ju-88 dam(grd) | Stendal |
| | Lt. W.W. Helmholz | (2)Me-262 dest(grd) | Stendal |
| | | FW-190 dest(grd) | Stendal |
| | | FW-190 dam(grd) | Stendal |
| | F/O T.F. Lasch | Ju-88 dest(grd) | Stendal |
| | Lt. J.W. Munn | FW-190 dest(grd) | Stendal |

*Losses-*

**SF**: Lt. William L. Rogers (1st) POW
P-51D 9H-H 44-63748 "Little Dutchess"
Suffered mechanical failure near Berlin.

**20th**: Capt. Richard M. Tracy (55th Ftr Sqn) POW
P-51D KI-G 44-13527
Hit by flak near Berlin.

Lt. Joseph A. Peterburs (55th Ftr Sqn) POW
P-51D KI-B 44-15078 "Josephine"
Hit by flak and bellied-in before reaching Russian lines.

Lt. David Stewart (79th Ftr Sqn) POW
P-51D MC-F 44-13751 "Wanda's Worry"
Hit by flak at Werder Airfield.

**55th**: Lt. Joseph M. Holland (338th Ftr Sqn) KIA
P-51D CL- 44-72274
Hit by flak near Burg.

**56th**: Lt. Paul W. Stitt (62nd Ftr Sqn) KIA
P-47M LM-
Damaged by flak and crashed in Belgium.

**78th**: Lt. Herbert A. Stinson (82nd Ftr Sqn) POW
P-51D MX-Z 44-15556 "Doug"
Hit by flak at Werder Airfield.

Lt. Richard I. Kuehl (83rd Ftr Sqn) MIA-E
P-51D HL-X 44-15702
Hit by flak at Brandenburg-Briest and bailed out near Helmstadt.

Lt. Roger A. Spaulding (84th Ftr Sqn) POW
P-51D WZ-O 44-64156 "The Virgin Ann IV"
Hit by flak at Werder Airfield and bailed out near Brandenburg.

**364th**: F/O Ted F. Lasch (385th Ftr Sqn) KIA
P-51D 5E-B 44-15019 "Lucky Lady VI"
Hit by flak near Margraten.

*Remarks*

56th: Lt. Clarence A. Tingen (62nd Ftr Sqn) c/l; o.k.
P-47M LM-
Lt. Richard W. Higgins (61st Ftr Sqn) c/l; o.k.
P-47M HV-

78th: 1-29 railcars, 2-0 hangars
P-51 c/l; o.k.

364th: 0-2 hangars

**April 11, 1945**

Groups Operating: P-51 4th, 20th, 55th, 78th, 339th, 352nd, 353rd, 355th, 357th, 359th, 364th, 479th
P-47 56th

Missions: Support of bombers to various marshalling yards and airfields in Germany plus PRU escorts.
Claims: nil
Losses: nil

**April 12, 1945**
Groups Operating: P-51 352nd, 361st
Missions: Support of 9th Air Force operations.
Claims: nil
Losses: nil

KIAc's
56th: Lt. Edward B. Lightfoot (61st Ftr Sqn)
P-47M HV-
Collided with Lt. Slanker and crashed near Raydon.

356th: Lt. Eldon L. Slanker (361st Ftr Sqn)
P-51D QI-M 44-15073
Collided with Lt. Lightfoot and crashed near Raydon.

**April 13, 1945**
Groups Operating: P-51 4th, 20th, 355th, 356th, 359th, 364th, 479th
P-47 56th
Missions: Support of bombers to Neumunster and a few PRU escorts.
Claims: 0-0-0 air
265-204 ground

| *Group* | | *Claims* | *Location* |
|---|---|---|---|
| **4th** | | | |
| 335th: | Capt. W.J. O'Donnell | Ar-196 dest(grd) | Ratzeburger Lake |
| | Lt. L.D. Jennings | He-115 dest(grd) | Ratzeburger Lake |
| | | u/i a/c dam(grd) | Ratzeburger Lake |
| | Lt. J.J. Scanlon | (2)Ar-196 dam(grd) | Ratzeburger Lake |
| **20th** | | | |
| 77th: | Lt. B.M. Phillips | (.5)Me-110 dam(grd) | E/Hamburg |
| | Lt. H.J. Piatkiewicz | (.5)Me-110 dam(grd) | E/Hamburg |
| 79th: | Maj. W.R. Yarbrough | (2)FW-190 dam(grd) | Jagel-Hutzfeld |
| | | Ju-88 dam(grd) | Jagel-Hutzfeld |
| | Lt. L.P. Bishop | (2)u/i a/c dam(grd) | Jagel-Hutzfeld |
| | Lt. E.F. Pogue | Me-109 dam(grd) | Jagel-Hutzfeld |
| | | He-177 dam(grd) | Jagel-Hutzfeld |
| **56th** | | | |
| HdQts: | LtCol. L.A. Dade | (2)Me-110 dest(grd) | Eggebeck A/F |
| | | u/i a/c dest(grd) | Eggebeck A/F |
| | | Me-110 dam(grd) | Eggebeck A/F |
| | LtCol. D.D. Renwick | He-111 dest(grd) | Eggebeck A/F |
| 61st: | Lt. R.S. Kyler | (4)Ju-88 dest(grd) | Eggebeck A/F |
| | | Me-410 dest(grd) | Eggebeck A/F |
| | Lt. B.O. Blodgett | (3)Ju-88 dest(grd) | Eggebeck A/F |
| | | u/i a/c dest(grd) | Eggebeck A/F |
| | | (2)Ju-88 dam(grd) | Eggebeck A/F |
| | Capt. V.E. Bast | (3)Ju-88 dest(grd) | Eggebeck A/F |
| | | (2)Ju-88 dam(grd) | Eggebeck A/F |
| | Lt. E.H. Treff | (3)Ju-88 dest(grd) | Eggebeck A/F |
| | | (5)Ju-88 dam(grd) | Eggebeck A/F |
| | Lt. W.G. Bartle | (2)Ju-88 dest(grd) | Eggebeck A/F |
| | | Me-109 dam(grd) | Eggebeck A/F |
| | Capt. C.B. Cole | Ju-88 dest(grd) | Eggebeck A/F |
| | | u/i a/c dam(grd) | Eggebeck A/F |
| | Lt. F.S. Rader | He-111 dest(grd) | Eggebeck A/F |
| | | (2)He-111 dam(grd) | Eggebeck A/F |
| | Lt. W.N. Winski | Ju-88 dest(grd) | Eggebeck A/F |
| | | (2)Ju-88 dam(grd) | Eggebeck A/F |
| | | Me-110 dam(grd) | Eggebeck A/F |
| | Lt. R.W. Hoeflein | Me-109 dest(grd) | Eggebeck A/F |
| | | (2)Ju-88 dam(grd) | Eggebeck A/F |
| | | u/i a/c dam(grd) | Eggebeck A/F |
| | Lt. C.J. Raymond | u/i a/c dest(grd) | Eggebeck A/F |
| | | (5)u/i a/c dam(grd) | Eggebeck A/F |
| | Lt. W.F. Smith | Me-110 dest(grd) | Eggebeck A/F |
| | | (2)u/i a/c dam(grd) | Eggebeck A/F |
| | Lt. R.W. Higgins | (2)Ju-88 dam(grd) | Eggebeck A/F |
| | Lt. J.T. Allen | u/i a/c dam(grd) | Eggebeck A/F |
| | Lt. D.L. Mauldin | Ju-88 dam(grd) | Eggebeck A/F |
| 62nd: | Capt. P.F. Fleming | (3)Do-217 dest(grd) | Eggebeck A/F |
| | | He-111 dest(grd) | Eggebeck A/F |
| | Lt. L.F. Geren | (4)He-111 dest(grd) | Eggebeck A/F |
| | | (3)He-111 dam(grd) | Eggebeck A/F |
| | Lt. S.N. Ball | (2)Do-217 dest(grd) | Eggebeck A/F |
| | | He-111 dest(grd) | Eggebeck A/F |
| | Lt. D. Henley | (2)He-111 dest(grd) | Eggebeck A/F |
| | | Ju-87 dest(grd) | Eggebeck A/F |
| | | (2)He-111 dam(grd) | Eggebeck A/F |
| | Lt. D.A. Westover | (2)Do-217 dest(grd) | Eggebeck A/F |
| | | FW-190 dest(grd) | Eggebeck A/F |
| | | (2)Me-109 dam(grd) | Eggebeck A/F |
| | Lt. V.L. Elliott | (2)Do-217 dest(grd) | Eggebeck A/F |
| | | Ju-88 dam(grd) | Eggebeck A/F |
| | Lt. R.B. Jones | FW-190 dest(grd) | Eggebeck A/F |
| | | He-111 dest(grd) | Eggebeck A/F |
| | | (2)He-111 dam(grd) | Eggebeck A/F |
| | | FW-190 dam(grd) | Eggebeck A/F |
| | | Ju-88 dam(grd) | Eggebeck A/F |
| | Lt. W.J. Stevenson | (2)Ju-88 dest(grd) | Eggebeck A/F |
| | | (3)Ju-88 dam(grd) | Eggebeck A/F |
| | Lt. H.F. Beeler | FW-190 dest(grd) | Eggebeck A/F |
| | | He-111 dam(grd) | Eggebeck A/F |
| | F/O W.H. Carrington | Ju-87 dest(grd) | Eggebeck A/F |
| | | (2)Do-217 dam(grd) | Eggebeck A/F |
| | Lt. D.M. Gunner | He-111 dest(grd) | Eggebeck A/F |
| | | (2)He-111 dam(grd) | Eggebeck A/F |
| | Lt. I.W. Rich | (2)Me-109 dam(grd) | Eggebeck A/F |
| | Lt. D.A. Carroll | He-111 dam(grd) | Eggebeck A/F |
| | Lt. S. Pruitt | He-111 dam(grd) | Eggebeck A/F |
| 63rd: | Lt. R.L. Murphy | (5)u/i a/c dest(grd) | Eggebeck A/F |
| | | (3)He-111 dest(grd) | Eggebeck A/F |
| | | FW-200 dest(grd) | Eggebeck A/F |
| | | Me-210 dest(grd) | Eggebeck A/F |
| | | u/i a/c dam(grd) | Eggebeck A/F |
| | Lt. P.G. Kuhn | (2)Me-410 dest(grd) | Eggebeck A/F |
| | | FW-190 dest(grd) | Eggebeck A/F |
| | | u/i a/c dest(grd) | Eggebeck A/F |
| | | u/i a/c dam(grd) | Eggebeck A/F |
| | Lt. T.W. Queen | (3)u/i a/c dest(grd) | Eggebeck A/F |
| | | Me-410 dest(grd) | Eggebeck A/F |
| | Lt. V.A. Smith | (2)He-111 dest(grd) | Eggebeck A/F |
| | | (2)Ju-88 dest(grd) | Eggebeck A/F |
| | | (2)Ju-88 dam(grd) | Eggebeck A/F |
| | | (2)u/i a/c dam(grd) | Eggebeck A/F |
| | Lt. T.B. Hennessy | (2)Me-110 dest(grd) | Eggebeck A/F |
| | | Me-110 dam(grd) | Eggebeck A/F |
| | Capt. W.L. Flagg | FW-190 dest(grd) | Eggebeck A/F |
| | | Ju-88 dest(grd) | Eggebeck A/F |
| | | FW-190 dam(grd) | Eggebeck A/F |
| | Lt. R.E. Bailey | (2)Me-110 dest(grd) | Eggebeck A/F |
| | | (2)Me-110 dam(grd) | Eggebeck A/F |
| | Lt. C.R. Clark | Me-110 dest(grd) | Eggebeck A/F |
| | | Ju-88 dest(grd) | Eggebeck A/F |
| | | (2)Me-110 dam(grd) | Eggebeck A/F |
| | Lt. J.W. Keeler | Me-110 dest(grd) | Eggebeck A/F |
| | | u/i a/c dest(grd) | Eggebeck A/F |
| | | Me-410 dam(grd) | Eggebeck A/F |
| | Capt. S.F. Stebelton | u/i a/c dest(grd) | Eggebeck A/F |
| | | (3)u/i a/c dam(grd) | Eggebeck A/F |
| | Lt. J.A. Arnold | u/i a/c dest(grd) | Eggebeck A/F |
| | | He-111 dam(grd) | Eggebeck A/F |
| | | u/i a/c dam(grd) | Eggebeck A/F |
| | Lt. E.S. Barrentine | Me-110 dest(grd) | Eggebeck A/F |
| | | (2)u/i a/c dam(grd) | Eggebeck A/F |
| | Lt. C.T. McBath | Me-109 dest(grd) | Eggebeck A/F |
| | | Me-109 dam(grd) | Eggebeck A/F |
| | | He-111 dam(grd) | Eggebeck A/F |
| | Lt. E.J. Huff | u/i a/c dest(grd) | Eggebeck A/F |
| | | Me-410 dam(grd) | Eggebeck A/F |
| | | He-177 dam(grd) | Eggebeck A/F |
| | Lt. C. Taylor | Me-110 dest(grd) | Eggebeck A/F |
| | | (2)Me-110 dam(grd) | Eggebeck A/F |
| | | Me-109 dam(grd) | Eggebeck A/F |
| **355th** | | | |
| HdQts: | LtCol. B.W. Marshall | (2)u/i a/c dest(grd) | Husum |
| | | Me-109 dest(grd) | Husum |
| | | (2)u/i a/c dam(grd) | Husum |
| | | FW-190 dam(grd) | Husum |
| | LtCol. C.H. Kinnard | (2.5)He-111 dest(grd)* | Schleswig |
| 354th: | Capt. S.E. Silva | (2)Me-109 dest(grd) | Husum |
| | | He-111 dest(grd) | Husum |
| | | Me-109 dam(grd) | Husum |
| | Lt. J.E. Mellen | (3)u/i a/c dest(grd) | Husum |
| | | (2)He-111 dam(grd) | Husum |
| | Lt. D.M. Vickery | (3)He-111 dest(grd) | Husum |
| | | (2)He-111 dam(grd) | Husum |
| | Lt. D.V. Galer | He-111 dest(grd) | Husum |
| | | Ju-88 dest(grd) | Husum |
| | | u/i a/c dam(grd) | Husum |
| | Capt. J.E. Duffy | Ju-88 dest(grd) | Husum |
| | | u/i a/c dam(grd) | Husum |
| | Lt. J. Jabara | He-111 dest(grd) | Husum |
| | | Me-109 dest(grd) | Husum |
| | | Me-109 dam(grd) | Husum |
| | Lt. D.B. Langley | (2)He-111 dest(grd) | Husum |
| | | Me-109 dest(grd) | Husum |
| | | (2)FW-190 dam(grd) | Husum |
| | F/O H.W. Falvey | FW-190 dest(grd) | Husum |
| | | Ju-88 dest(grd) | Husum |
| | | Ju-88 dam(grd) | Husum |
| | Lt. F.A. Sarver | FW-190 dest(grd) | Husum |
| | | FW-190 dam(grd) | Husum |

| | | | |
|---|---|---|---|
| | Lt. A.B. Kaplan | He-111 dest(grd) | Husum |
| | | FW-190 dam(grd) | Husum |
| | Lt. A.J. Mincemeyer | He-111 dest(grd) | Husum |
| | Lt. R.P. Pearson | Me-109 dest(grd) | Husum |
| | Lt. G.D. Beeler | He-111 dest(grd) | Husum |
| | Lt. R. Westerveld | Me-109 dest(grd) | Husum |
| | Lt. A.G. Kozacka | FW-190 dest(grd) | Husum |
| | | (2)u/i a/c dam(grd) | Husum |
| | Lt. M.J. McLeod | u/i a/c dest(grd) | Husum |
| | | He-111 dam(grd) | Husum |
| | Lt. A.J. Scheid | He-111 dam(grd) | Husum |
| | | FW-190 dam(grd) | Husum |
| 357th: | Lt. R.W. Cooper | (1.5)He-111 dest(grd)[@@] | Schleswig |
| | | FW-200 dest(grd) | Schleswig |
| | Lt. R.L. Garlich | (2)He-111 dest(grd) | Schleswig |
| | Lt. V.D. Iglesias | (2)He-111 dest(grd) | Schleswig |
| | Lt. R.F. Misner | (1.5)He-111 dest(grd)[@@] | Schleswig |
| | | He-111 dam(grd) | Schleswig |
| | Lt. M.E. Beise | He-111 dam(grd) | Schleswig |
| | F/O J.D. Hober | He-111 dam(grd) | Schleswig |
| | Lt. J.E. Lake | He-111 dam(grd) | Schleswig |
| | Lt. F.H. Rodgers | He-111 dam(grd) | Schleswig |
| 358th: | Capt. J.F. Tulloch | (4)He-111 dest(grd) | Schleswig |
| | Lt. R.F. Parks | (2)FW-190 dest(grd) | Flensburg |
| | | (2)He-111 dest(grd) | Flensburg |
| | Lt. A.R. Curran | FW-190 dest(grd) | Flensburg |
| | | Ju-88 dest(grd) | Flensburg |
| | Lt. R.J. Nicodemus | (.5)He-111 dest(grd)[&] | Schleswig |
| | | (.5)He-111 dest(grd)[@] | Schleswig |
| | Lt. H.P. Knutty | Me-109 dest(grd) | Schleswig |
| | | (.5)He-111 dest(grd)[&] | Schleswig |
| | Lt. L.J. Rouleau | He-111 dest(grd) | Schleswig |
| | Lt. L.R. Leaf | (.5)He-111 dest(grd)[@] | Schleswig |
| | Lt. M. Lacazette | (.5)He-111 dest(grd)[&&] | Schleswig |
| | Lt. W.B. Lister | (.5)He-111 dest(grd)[&&] | Schleswig |
| | Lt. V.E. Gore | (.5)He-111 dest(grd)[*] | Schleswig |
| | Lt. W.J. Schlecht | Me-109 dest(grd) | Schleswig |
| | | (.5)He-111 dest(grd)[**] | Schleswig |
| | Lt. R.V. Finnessey | (.5)He-111 dest(grd)[**] | Schleswig |
| | Lt. E.W. Fees | (.5)He-111 dest(grd)[#] | Schleswig |
| | | He-111 dam(grd) | Schleswig |
| | Lt. C.C. Patrinely | (.5)He-111 dest(grd)[#] | Schleswig |
| **356th** | | | |
| 360th: | Maj. M.P. Yannell | FW-190 dest(grd) | Schwerin |
| | Lt. B.D. McNary | (2)FW-190 dam(grd) | Schwerin |
| | | He-111 dam(grd) | Schwerin |
| | Lt. N.B. Ceraolo | FW-190 dam(grd) | Schwerin |
| | Lt. G.W. Seanor | Do-217 dam(grd) | Schwerin |
| **359th** | | | |
| 368th: | Capt. J.A. Denman | (4)Me-110 dest(grd) | Neumunster |
| | Lt. K.E. Barber | (3)Me-110 dest(grd) | Neumunster |
| | | u/i a/c dest(grd) | Neumunster |
| | Lt. J.W. Herb | (2)Me-110 dest(grd) | Neumunster |
| | | (2)Do-217 dest(grd) | Neumunster |
| | Lt. G.E. Madison | Me-110 dest(grd) | Luneburg |
| | | u/i a/c dest(grd) | Luneburg |
| | Capt. J.B. Hunter | He-111 dest(grd) | Luneburg |
| 370th: | LtCol. D.D. McKee | (2)Ar-196 dest(grd) | Schwerin Lake |
| | Lt. M.H. Newton | (2)Ar-196 dest(grd) | Schwerin Lake |
| **364th** | | | |
| 383rd: | Capt. J.L. Truett | (4)Ju-52 dest(grd) | Flensburg |
| | | Do-217 dest(grd) | Flensburg |
| | | Me-109 dam(grd) | Flensburg |
| | | FW-190 dam(grd) | Flensburg |
| | Capt. J.C. Hunter | (3)FW-190 dest(grd) | Flensburg |
| | | (2)Ju-52 dest(grd) | Flensburg |
| | | Me-110 dest(grd) | Flensburg |
| | | (3)Ju-52 dam(grd) | Flensburg |
| | | Me-109 dam(grd) | Flensburg |
| | Capt. R.W. Orndorff | (2)Ju-52 dest(grd) | Flensburg |
| | | Me-109 dest(grd) | Flensburg |
| | | FW-190 dest(grd) | Flensburg |
| | | Fi-156 dam(grd) | Flensburg |
| | Lt. W.F. Kissel | (4)Ju-52 dest(grd) | Flensburg |
| | | (2)Me-109 dam(grd) | Flensburg |
| | | Me-110 dam(grd) | Flensburg |
| | | Ju-52 dam(grd) | Flensburg |
| | Lt. R.M. Baughn | (2)Ju-52 dest(grd) | Flensburg |
| | | FW-190 dest(grd) | Flensburg |
| | | Me-109 dam(grd) | Flensburg |
| | | FW-190 dam(grd) | Flensburg |
| | Lt. G.E. Smith | (2)FW-190 dest(grd) | Flensburg |
| | | Ju-52 dest(grd) | Flensburg |
| | | (2)FW-190 dam(grd) | Flensburg |
| | | Ju-52 dam(grd) | Flensburg |
| | Lt. J.B. Guy | Me-109 dest(grd) | Flensburg |
| | | Ju-52 dest(grd) | Flensburg |
| | | FW-190 dam(grd) | Flensburg |
| | | Ju-52 dam(grd) | Flensburg |
| | Lt. C.E. Jackson | (2)FW-190 dest(grd) | Flensburg |
| | | FW-190 dam(grd) | Flensburg |
| | Lt. E.W. Kortendick | Me-109 dest(grd) | Flensburg |
| | | Fi-156 dest(grd) | Flensburg |
| | | (2)FW-190 dam(grd) | Flensburg |
| | | Ju-52 dam(grd) | Flensburg |
| | Lt. E.H. Horman | (2)Ju-52 dest(grd) | Flensburg |
| | | Ju-52 dam(grd) | Flensburg |
| | Lt. H.D. Sandkaut | (2)Ju-52 dest(grd) | Flensburg |
| | | Do-217 dam(grd) | Flensburg |
| | | FW-190 dam(grd) | Flensburg |
| | Lt. J.A. Seth | Me-109 dest(grd) | Flensburg |
| | | FW-190 dest(grd) | Flensburg |
| | | Me-109 dam(grd) | Flensburg |
| | Lt. E. Holmes | Me-109 dest(grd) | Flensburg |
| | | (3)Me-109 dam(grd) | Flensburg |
| | Lt. C.W. Hornick | Me-109 dest(grd) | Flensburg |
| | | Me-109 dam(grd) | Flensburg |
| | | Ju-52 dam(grd) | Flensburg |
| | Lt. L. Leon | FW-190 dest(grd) | Flensburg |
| | | Me-109 dam(grd) | Flensburg |
| | | Ju-52 dam(grd) | Flensburg |
| | Lt. V.A. O'Brien | Ju-52 dest(grd) | Flensburg |
| | | (2)FW-190 dam(grd) | Flensburg |
| 384th: | Capt. R.K. Allen | (2)u/i a/c dest(grd) | Kaltenkirchen |
| | Lt. R.V. Herndon | Ju-88 dest(grd) | Kaltenkirchen |
| | Capt. R.S. Faulkner | u/i a/c dam(grd) | Kaltenkirchen |
| | Lt. P.J. Hahn | FW-190 dam(grd) | Kaltenkirchen |
| 385th: | Capt. A.B. McCormick | Do-217 dest(grd) | E/Luneburg |
| | | Ju-188 dest(grd) | E/Luneburg |
| | | (.5)FW-190 dest(grd) | E/Luneburg |
| | | Do-217 dam(grd) | E/Luneburg |
| | | FW-190 dam(grd) | E/Luneburg |
| | Lt. J.G. Johnson | Ju-188 dest(grd) | E/Luneburg |
| | | (.5)FW-190 dest(grd) | E/Luneburg |
| | | FW-190 dam(grd) | E/Luneburg |
| | Capt. H.W. Head | Ju-88 dest(grd) | Tarnewitz |
| **479th** | | | |
| 434th: | Maj. R. Olds | Ar-234 dest(grd) | Lubeck |
| | | Me-410 dam(grd) | Tarnewitz |
| | Capt. D.J. Pierce | Ar-234 dest(grd) | Lubeck |
| | | Ju-88 dam(grd) | Kaltenkirchen |
| | Lt. R.M. Rossell | Ar-234 dest(grd) | Lubeck |
| | Lt. J.K. Nagel | Ju-88 dest(grd) | Kaltenkirchen |
| | Lt. L.H. Hendrickson | FW-190 dest(grd) | Kaltenkirchen |
| | Lt. J.T. Golden | u/i a/c dest(grd) | Ratzeburger Lake |
| | | (2)u/i a/c dam(grd) | Ratzeburger Lake |
| | Lt. P.A. Brown | (.5)u/i a/c dest(grd)[*] | Ratzeburger Lake |
| | | u/i a/c dam(grd) | Ratzeburger Lake |
| | Lt. R.G. Simpson | (.5)u/i a/c dest(grd)[*] | Ratzeburger Lake |
| | Lt. R.B. Kline | (.5)u/i a/c dest(grd)[**] | Ratzeburger Lake |
| | | u/i a/c dam(grd) | Ratzeburger Lake |
| | Lt. F.M. Taylor | (.5)u/i a/c dest(grd)[**] | Ratzeburger Lake |
| | | u/i a/c dam(grd) | Ratzeburger Lake |
| | Lt. O.J. Huvall | (.5)u/i a/c dest(grd)[@] | Ratzeburger Lake |
| | | u/i a/c dam(grd) | Ratzeburger Lake |
| | Lt. C.W. Bowers | (.5)u/i a/c dest(grd)[@] | Ratzeburger Lake |
| | | u/i a/c dam(grd) | Ratzeburger Lake |
| | Lt. R.D. Creighton | (2)u/i a/c dam(grd) | Ratzeburger Lake |
| 435th: | Capt. V.E. Hooker | (2)Ju-88 dest(grd) | Tarnewitz |
| | | Ju-88 dam(grd) | Tarnewitz |
| | Capt. T.J. Sowerby | Ju-88 dest(grd) | Tarnewitz |
| | | (4)Ju-88 dam(grd) | Tarnewitz |
| | Lt. W.B. Rourke | Ju-88 dest(grd) | Tarnewitz |
| | | (2)Ju-88 dam(grd) | Tarnewitz |
| 436th: | Capt. J.C. Malone | (2)FW-190 dest(grd) | Salzwedel |
| | | Me-110 dest(grd) | Salzwedel |
| | | (2)FW-190 dam(grd) | Salzwedel |
| | | Me-410 dam(grd) | Salzwedel |
| | Lt. K.J. Hanson | (3)FW-190 dest(grd) | Salzwedel |
| | | Me-110 dest(grd) | Salzwedel |
| | Lt. E.J. Hopcroft | (2)Me-410 dest(grd) | Salzwedel |
| | | Me-109 dest(grd) | Salzwedel |
| | Capt. P.S. Shane | Me-410 dest(grd) | Salzwedel |
| | | u/i a/c dest(grd) | Salzwedel |
| | | Me-109 dam(grd) | Salzwedel |
| | Lt. C.H. Darling | (2)FW-190 dest(grd) | Salzwedel |
| | | Me-110 dam(grd) | Salzwedel |
| | | u/i a/c dam(grd) | Salzwedel |
| | Lt. C.H. Philbrick | Me-109 dest(grd) | Salzwedel |
| | | FW-190 dest(grd) | Salzwedel |
| | | (3)Me-109 dam(grd) | Salzwedel |
| | | u/i a/c dam(grd) | Salzwedel |
| | Lt. R.C.J. Palson | (2)He-111 dest(grd) | Salzwedel |
| | | He-111 dam(grd) | Salzwedel |
| | | FW-190 dam(grd) | Salzwedel |
| | Lt. B.R. Kleineman | FW-190 dest(grd) | Salzwedel |
| | | Me-110 dest(grd) | Salzwedel |

| | | | |
|---|---|---|---|
| | Lt. J.H. Early | FW-190 dest(grd) | Salzwedel |
| | | Me-110 dest(grd) | Salzwedel |
| | | Me-410 dam(grd) | Salzwedel |
| | Lt. S.F. Long | (2)FW-190 dest(grd) | Salzwedel |
| | Lt. G.H. Witzel | (2)FW-190 dest(grd) | Salzwedel |
| | | FW-190 dam(grd) | Salzwedel |
| | | Me-110 dam(grd) | Salzwedel |
| | Lt. E. Zellman | Me-109 dest(grd) | Salzwedel |
| | | Me-410 dest(grd) | Salzwedel |
| | | Me-109 dam(grd) | Salzwedel |
| | Lt. J.M. Archibald | FW-190 dest(grd) | Salzwedel |
| | | Me-110 dam(grd) | Salzwedel |
| | Lt. W.B. Steph | FW-190 dest(grd) | Salzwedel |
| | | Me-109 dam(grd) | Salzwedel |

*Losses-*

**56th**: Lt. William R. Hoffman (63rd Ftr Sqn) KIA
P-47M UN-P 44-21134 "Teacher's Pet"
Hit by flak at Eggebeck Airfield.

**355th**: Lt. Warner J. Schlecht (358th Ftr Sqn) POW
P-51D YF-B 44-64068
Bellied-in after a flak hit near Rendsburg.

**359th**: Lt. John W. Herb (368th Ftr Sqn) KIA
P-51D CV-E 44-72260 "Mary Lou"
Hit a tree which caused a coolant leak; tried to belly-in northwest of Hamburg but crashed into a woods.

**364th**: Capt. Hayden W. Head (385th Ftr Sqn) POW
P-51D 5E-M 44-14667 "Little Sport"
Hit by flak at Tarnewitz and bellied-in near Gadesbusch.

F/O Newton R. Cobb (385th Ftr Sqn) POW
P-51D 5E-A 44-14035 "Etta Jane"
Hit by flak and bellied-in west of Klutz.

Lt. Frank W. Glasso (385th Ftr Sqn) POW
P-51D 5E- 44-72376
Hit by flak and bailed out near Schaal Lake.

**479th**: Lt. Ossie J. Huval (434th Ftr Sqn) MIA
P-51K L2-A 44-12156 "The Flying Frenchman"
Lost for unknown reasons near Bremen.

Lt. Richard G. Candelaria (435th Ftr Sqn) POW
P-51K J2-K 44-11755 "My Pride and Joy"
Hit by flak and bellied-in near Tarnewitz.

*Remarks*
20th: 1-1 locos, 0-1 railcar
56th: 1-0 loco, 1-0 hangar, 4-0 gun positions
359th: 18-3 locos, 5-5 railcars, 1-8 barges, 1-1 tugs
364th: 2-1 locos, 1-0 vehicle, 0-2 flak positions, 0-1 control tower
479th: 5-0 locos

**April 15, 1945**
Groups Operating: P-51 4th, 339th
Missions: Support for 9th Air Force bombers to the Ulm area plus a few PRU escort sorties.
Claims: nil

*Losses-*

**339th**: Lt. Roland L. Gousie (505th Ftr Sqn) POW
P-51D 6N-C 44-14656 "Dottie"
Hit by flak south of Stuttgart and bailed out west of Blauberen.

*Remarks*
4th: Lt. Edward J. Wozniak (334th Ftr Sqn) c/l N/Wattan; o.k.
P-51D QP-T

KIAc's
353rd: Lt. William O. Fitch (350th Ftr Sqn)
P-51D LH-L 44-63197 "Mascara Maggie"
Collided with a P-51 and crashed near Thaxted.

**April 16, 1945**
Groups Operating: P-51 4th, 20th, 55th, 78th, 339th, 352nd, 353rd, 355th, 356th, 357th, 359th, 361st, 364th, 479th
P-47 56th
Missions: Support of bombers to Regensburg and Landshut plus PRU escorts.
Claims: 3-0-0 air
743-406 ground

| ***Group*** | | ***Claims*** | ***Location*** |
|---|---|---|---|
| **SF**: | LtCol. F.B. Elliott | (2)u/i a/c dest(grd) | SE Germany |
| | | FW-190 dest(grd) | SE Germany |
| | | FW-190 dam(grd) | SE Germany |
| **4th** | | | |
| HdQts: | LtCol. S.S. Woods | (2)Ju-88 dest(grd) | Praha |
| | | (5)Ju-88 dam(grd) | Praha |
| 334th: | Lt. W.O. Antonides | (2)Me-109 dest(grd) | Gablingen |
| | | FW-190 dest(grd) | Gablingen |
| | | Me-410 dest(grd) | Gablingen |
| | | u/i a/c dest(grd) | Gablingen |
| | | u/i a/c dam(grd) | Gablingen |
| | Maj. L.H. Norley | (2)FW-190 dest(grd) | Gablingen |
| | | Ju-52 dest(grd) | Gablingen |
| | | u/i a/c dest(grd) | Gablingen |
| | Lt. W.C. O'Bryan | (3)u/i a/c dest(grd) | Gablingen |
| | Lt. J.W. Ayers | Me-109 dest(grd) | Gablingen |
| | | FW-190 dest(grd) | Gablingen |
| | | u/i a/c dest(grd) | Gablingen |
| | Lt. A.R. Bowers | (2)Me-109 dest(grd) | Gablingen |
| | | Ju-88 dest(grd) | Gablingen |
| | | (3)Me-109 dam(grd) | Gablingen |
| | Lt. R.H. Buchanan | FW-190 dest(grd) | Gablingen |
| | | Me-410 dest(grd) | Gablingen |
| | | (2)FW-190 dam(grd) | Gablingen |
| | | Me-109 dam(grd) | Gablingen |
| | Lt. W.G. Spencer | FW-190 dest(grd) | Gablingen |
| | | Me-109 dest(grd) | Gablingen |
| | | u/i a/c dest(grd) | Gablingen |
| | Lt. R.A. Dyer | FW-190 dest(grd) | Gablingen |
| | | Me-109 dest(grd) | Gablingen |
| | | u/i a/c dest(grd) | Gablingen |
| | | FW-190 dam(grd) | Gablingen |
| | | Me-109 dam(grd) | Gablingen |
| | | Me-410 dam(grd) | Gablingen |
| | Lt. G.A. Denson | (2)FW-190 dest(grd) | Gablingen |
| | | Me-410 dest(grd) | Gablingen |
| | | He-177 dest(grd) | Gablingen |
| | | FW-190 dam(grd) | Gablingen |
| | | Me-410 dam(grd) | Gablingen |
| | | u/i a/c dam(grd) | Gablingen |
| | Lt. M.W. Arthur | Me-109 dest(grd) | Gablingen |
| | | (.5)FW-190 dest(grd) | Gablingen |
| | Lt. M.L. Spencer | (.5)FW-190 dest(grd) | Gablingen |
| | Lt. P.E. Burnett | u/i a/c dest(grd) | Gablingen |
| | Lt. W.J. Dvorak | u/i a/c dest(grd) | Gablingen |
| | | (2)u/i a/c dam(grd) | Gablingen |
| | Lt. C.W. Harre | Me-109 dest(grd) | Gablingen |
| | | (3)u/i a/c dam(grd) | Gablingen |
| | | Me-109 dam(grd) | Gablingen |
| | Lt. M.J. Kennedy | u/i a/c dest(grd) | Gablingen |
| | | Ju-88 dam(grd) | Gablingen |
| | | Ju-87 dam(grd) | Gablingen |
| | Lt. D.G. Lowther | u/i a/c dest(grd) | Gablingen |
| 335th: | Lt. K.G. Helfrecht | (2)Me-410 dest(grd) | Gablingen |
| | | (2)FW-190 dest(grd) | Gablingen |
| | | He-177 dest(grd) | Gablingen |
| | | (2)Ju-87 dam(grd) | Gablingen |
| | Lt. G.D. Green | (2)Ju-88 dest(grd) | Praha/Letnany |
| | | Do-217 dest(grd) | Praha/Letnany |
| | | u/i a/c dest(grd) | Praha/Letnany |
| | Lt. L.D. Jennings | (2)Do-217 dest(grd) | Praha |
| | | (2)Me-210 dest(grd) | Praha |
| | Maj. P.W. McKennon | (2)Do-217 dest(grd) | Praha/Letnany |
| | | u/i a/c dest(grd) | Praha/Letnany |
| | | Me-410 dam(grd) | Praha/Letnany |
| | Lt. W.F. Underwood | FW-190 dest(grd) | Praha |
| | | Me-410 dest(grd) | Praha |
| | | u/i a/c dest(grd) | Praha |
| | Lt. O.B. Bucher | (2)Ju-52 dest(grd) | Praha/Letnany |
| | | Me-410 dest(grd) | Praha |
| | | Me-410 dam(grd) | Praha |
| | Lt. R.L. Couse | (2)Do-217 dest(grd) | Praha/Letnany |
| | | Ju-88 dam(grd) | Praha/Letnany |
| | Capt. W.J. O'Donnell | (2)u/i a/c dest(grd) | Praha/Letnany |
| | | (2)u/i a/c dam(grd) | Praha/Letnany |
| | Lt. J.E. Halligan | Me-110 dest(grd) | Praha |
| | | FW-190 dest(grd) | Praha |
| | | u/i a/c dest(grd) | Praha |
| | | Ju-88 dest(grd) | Praha |
| | | Me-110 dam(grd) | Praha |
| | | (4)u/i a/c dam(grd) | Praha |
| | Lt. R.C. Hunter | (2)Do-217 dest(grd) | Praha/Letnany |
| | | Ju-88 dest(grd) | Praha/Letnany |
| | Lt. H.B. Miller | Do-217 dest(grd) | Praha/Letnany |
| | | Ju-52 dest(grd) | Praha/Letnany |
| | | Do-217 dam(grd) | Praha/Letnany |
| | | Ju-52 dam(grd) | Praha/Letnany |
| | Lt. C.B. Greenlese | u/i a/c dest(grd) | Praha |
| | | (5)u/i a/c dam(grd) | Praha |
| | Lt. W.D. Henderson | (3)Me-109 dam(grd) | Praha |
| | | u/i a/c dam(grd) | Praha |
| | Lt. P.J. Lucas | (2)u/i a/c dam(grd) | Praha/Letnany |
| | F/O L.W. Freeman | He-177 dam(grd) | Praha/Letnany |

| | | | |
|---|---|---|---|
| 336th: | Lt. D.P. Pederson | (5)Ju-52 dest(grd) | Praha |
| | | (3)Ju-52 dam(grd) | Praha |
| | F/O D.P. Baugh | (5)Ju-88 dest(grd) | Praha |
| | Lt. B.L. Griffin | (4)u/i a/c dest(grd) | Praha |
| | Lt. H.H. Fredericks | (2)Ju-88 dest(grd) | Praha/Letnany |
| | | Me-110 dest(grd) | Praha/Letnany |
| | | Me-110 dam(grd) | Praha/Letnany |
| | Lt. W.H. Ayer | (2)u/i a/c dest(grd) | Praha |
| | Lt. J.P. Murchake | (2)Ju-88 dest(grd) | Praha |
| | | Ju-88 dam(grd) | Praha |
| | Lt. M.C. Franklin | (2)Ju-52 dest(grd) | Praha |
| | | u/i a/c dam(grd) | Praha |
| | Capt. C.R. Alfred | u/i a/c dest(grd) | Praha |
| | | u/i a/c dam(grd) | Praha |
| | Lt. B.O. Brooker | (2)Me-410 dest(grd) | Praha |
| | | (3)Me-110 dam(grd) | Praha |
| | | Ju-52 dam(grd) | Praha |
| | Capt. L.A. Carpenter | Me-410 dest(grd) | Praha |
| | | u/i a/c dam(grd) | Praha |
| | Lt. M.L. Davis | Me-110 dest(grd) | Praha |
| | | (2)Me-110 dam(grd) | Praha |
| | Capt. E.L. Gimbel | Me-110 dest(grd) | Praha |
| | | (2)Me-110 dam(grd) | Praha |
| | Capt. H.N. Hagen | Me-109 dest(grd) | SW Pilzen |
| | Lt. W.H. Hastings | Me-110 dest(grd) | Praha |
| | | Me-110 dam(grd) | Praha |
| | Lt. W.B. Meredith | Me-109 dest(grd) | Praha |
| | Lt. M.W. Miller | u/i a/c dest(grd) | Praha |
| | Lt. W.W. Collins | Do-217 dam(grd) | Praha |
| | | Me-109 dam(grd) | Praha |
| **20th** | | | |
| 77th: | Maj. M.J. Gilbertson | u/i a/c dest(grd) | Cham A/F |
| **55th** | | | |
| HdQts: | LtCol. E.G. Righetti | (3)He-111 dest(grd) | Bad Aibling |
| | | (2)Ju-88 dest(grd) | Munich-Brunnthal |
| | | Si-204 dest(grd) | Munich-Brunnthal |
| | | (5)Si-204 dam(grd) | Munich-Brunnthal |
| 38th: | Capt. J.W. Kavanaugh | Me-262 dest(grd) | Munich-Brunnthal |
| | | u/i a/c dest(grd) | Munich-Brunnthal |
| | | u/i a/c dam(grd) | Munich-Brunnthal |
| | Lt. J.W. Cunnick | (2)Me-109 dest(grd) | N/Landshut |
| | | Me-109 dam(grd) | N/Landshut |
| | Lt. C.C. Gould | (2)He-111 dest(grd) | N/Ansbach |
| | | Me-109 dam(grd) | N/Ansbach |
| | Lt. J.E. Anderson | Do-217 dest(grd) | Munich-Brunnthal |
| | Lt. L.J. Fleming | Do-217 dest(grd) | Munich-Brunnthal |
| | Lt. J.T. Maloney | Ju-52 dest(grd) | Bad Aibling |
| | | u/i a/c dam(grd) | Bad Aibling |
| | Lt. D.T. Menegay | Ju-88 dest(grd) | Munich-Brunnthal |
| | Capt. C.T. Williams | Me-109 dam(grd) | Bad Aibling |
| | | u/i a/c dam(grd) | Bad Aibling |
| | Maj. C.L. Peterson | u/i a/c dam(grd) | Munich-Brunnthal |
| | Lt. R.F. Quinn | u/i a/c dam(grd) | Bad Aibling |
| 338th: | Maj. E.E. Ryan | Me-262 dest(air) | Horsching A/F |
| | | He-111 dest(grd) | N/Landshut |
| | Capt. S.D. Gevorkian | (3)FW-190 dest(grd) | N/Landshut |
| | | (3)FW-190 dam(grd) | N/Landshut |
| | Lt. L.K. John | (3)FW-200 dest(grd) | N/Landshut |
| | Lt. H. Bodiford | (2)u/i a/c dest(grd) | N/Landshut |
| | | He-111 dest(grd) | N/Landshut |
| | Lt. C.D. Henry | (2)FW-190 dest(grd) | N/Landshut |
| | F/O J.E. Brady | Me-109 dest(grd) | N/Landshut |
| | Lt. R.E. Cooper | FW-190 dest(grd) | N/Landshut |
| | Lt. R.E. Darling | Me-109 dest(grd) | Erding |
| | | (2)Me-109 dam(grd) | Erding |
| | Lt. R. Deloach | He-111 dest(grd) | N/Landshut |
| | Lt. R.C. Herbst | Me-109 dest(grd) | Erding |
| | Lt. J.C. White | Me-109 dest(grd) | N/Landshut |
| | Lt. J.H. Wiley | He-111 dest(grd) | N/Landshut |
| 343rd: | Maj. E.B. Giller | He-111 dest(grd) | Munich-Brunnthal |
| | | Me-109 dest(grd) | Munich-Brunnthal |
| | | Ju-52 dest(grd) | Munich-Brunnthal |
| | | Ju-88 dam(grd) | Munich-Brunnthal |
| | Capt. R.E. Welch | Me-110 dest(grd) | Munich-Brunnthal |
| | | Me-410 dest(grd) | Munich-Brunnthal |
| | Capt. C.E. Coggeshall | FW-190 dest(grd) | Ainring A/F |
| | Capt. W. Strauch | FW-189 dest(grd) | Ainring A/F |
| | Lt. G.A. Apple | FW-190 dest(grd) | Ainring A/F |
| | Lt. J.H. Bevington | FW-190 dest(grd) | Ainring A/F |
| | Lt. R.G. Allen | (.5)BV-140 dest(grd) | Lake Chiem |
| | Lt. L.D. Boring | (.5)BV-140 dest(grd) | Lake Chiem |
| | Lt. G.E. Arnold | Me-410 dam(grd) | Munich-Brunnthal |
| **56th** | | | |
| 61st: | Lt. D.L. Mauldin | (2)Me-109 dam(grd) | Muhldorf |
| | | u/i a/c dam(grd) | Muhldorf |
| | Lt. J.R. Stish | u/i a/c dam(grd) | Muhldorf |
| 62nd: | Lt. C.A. Tingen | He-177 dest(grd) | Muhldorf |
| 63rd: | Lt. B.E. Vest | Ju-88 dest(grd) | Ingolstadt |
| | Capt. J.C. Fahringer | Ju-88 dam(grd) | Ingolstadt |
| **66th(FW)** | | | |
| HdQts: | LtCol. O.E. Gilbert | (3)FW-190 dest(grd) | Pilzen/Prague |
| | | (1.5)Ju-87 dest(grd)* | Pilzen/Prague |
| | | He-111 dest(grd) | Pilzen/Prague |
| | | Ju-52 dest(grd) | Pilzen/Prague |
| | | (2)u/i a/c dam(grd) | Pilzen/Prague |
| | | FW-190 dam(grd) | Pilzen/Prague |
| | (He flew with the 78th Ftr Grp on the mission) | | |
| **78th** | | | |
| HdQts: | LtCol. J.D. Landers | (9)He-177 dest(grd) | Praha/Kakewice |
| | Maj. G. Bryan | (2)u/i a/c dest(grd) | Praha/Kakewice |
| | | Me-109 dest(grd) | Praha/Kakewice |
| | | Ju-52 dest(grd) | Praha/Kakewice |
| | | (3)u/i a/c dam(grd) | Praha/Kakewice |
| 82nd: | Lt. D.J. Henahan | (2.5)Ju-87 dest(grd)* | Pilzen/Prague |
| | | FW-190 dest(grd) | Pilzen/Prague |
| | | Ju-52 dest(grd) | Pilzen/Prague |
| | | FW-190 dam(grd) | Pilzen/Prague |
| | | Ju-52 dam(grd) | Pilzen/Prague |
| | | u/i a/c dam(grd) | Pilzen/Prague |
| | Capt. M.O. Croy | FW-190 dest(grd) | Pilzen/Prague |
| | Capt. J.I. Brown | Ju-52 dest(grd) | Pilzen/Prague |
| | | Ju-86 dam(grd) | Pilzen/Prague |
| | | u/i a/c dam(grd) | Pilzen/Prague |
| | Lt. R.J. Blossom | Do-217 dest(grd) | Pilzen/Prague |
| | Lt. G.V. Elsey | Me-109 dest(grd) | Pilzen/Prague |
| | | Me-109 dam(grd) | Pilzen/Prague |
| | Lt. E.L. Peel | u/i a/c dest(grd) | Pilzen/Prague |
| | | FW-190 dam(grd) | Pilzen/Prague |
| | | u/i a/c dam(grd) | Pilzen/Prague |
| | Lt. G.W. Stilwell | FW-190 dest(grd) | Pilzen/Prague |
| | | (4)Me-109 dam(grd) | Pilzen/Prague |
| | | u/i a/c dam(grd) | Pilzen/Prague |
| | Lt. F.R. Swauger | Me-109 dest(grd) | Pilzen/Prague |
| | Capt. R.B. Holmes | (5)u/i a/c dam(grd) | Pilzen/Prague |
| | Capt. D.C. Hart | (2)u/i a/c dam(grd) | Pilzen/Prague |
| | Lt. A.M. Rosenberg | (2)FW-190 dam(grd) | Pilzen/Prague |
| | | u/i a/c dam(grd) | Pilzen/Prague |
| | Lt. J.E. Parker | FW-190 dam(grd) | Pilzen/Prague |
| | Lt. H.L. Roe | He-111 dam(grd) | Pilzen/Prague |
| | Lt. M.B. Stutzman | Me-109 dam(grd) | Pilzen/Prague |
| 83rd: | Capt. E.R. Kulik | (4)FW-190 dest(grd) | N/Prague |
| | | Me-109 dest(grd) | N/Prague |
| | | Ju-87 dest(grd) | N/Prague |
| | | u/i a/c dest(grd) | N/Prague |
| | Lt. A.T. Colletti | (4)Ju-87 dest(grd) | N/Prague |
| | | FW-190 dest(grd) | N/Prague |
| | | (2)FW-190 dam(grd) | N/Prague |
| | | FW-200 dam(grd) | N/Prague |
| | | u/i a/c dam(grd) | N/Prague |
| | Lt. G.C. Doss | (5)Ju-87 dest(grd) | N/Prague |
| | | Me-109 dam(grd) | N/Prague |
| | Lt. D.M. McDuffie | (2)Me-109 dest(grd) | N/Prague |
| | | (2)FW-190 dest(grd) | N/Prague |
| | | Ju-87 dest(grd) | N/Prague |
| | Lt. F.E. Harrington | (2)u/i a/c dest(grd) | N/Prague |
| | | Me-109 dest(grd) | N/Prague |
| | | Me-262 dest(grd) | N/Prague |
| | | (3)u/i a/c dam(grd) | N/Prague |
| | Lt. J.A. Kirk | FW-190 dest(grd) | N/Prague |
| | | Ju-88 dest(grd) | N/Prague |
| | | Ju-87 dest(grd) | N/Prague |
| | | u/i a/c dest(grd) | N/Prague |
| | | (3)Ju-87 dam(grd) | N/Prague |
| | Lt. D.J. DeVillers | (2)Me-109 dest(grd) | N/Prague |
| | | (2)Ju-87 dest(grd) | N/Prague |
| | | He-111 dest(grd) | N/Prague |
| | | (2)Me-109 dam(grd) | N/Prague |
| | | (2)Ju-87 dam(grd) | N/Prague |
| | Lt. D.S. Sweat | (2)FW-190 dest(grd) | N/Prague |
| | | (2)Ju-87 dest(grd) | N/Prague |
| | | u/i a/c dest(grd) | N/Prague |
| | | (2)FW-190 dam(grd) | N/Prague |
| | | Ju-87 dam(grd) | N/Prague |
| | Lt. R.E. Phaneuf | (2)Ju-87 dest(grd) | N/Prague |
| | | FW-190 dest(grd) | N/Prague |
| | | Ju-52 dest(grd) | N/Prague |
| | | (2)Ju-87 dam(grd) | N/Prague |
| | | Me-109 dam(grd) | N/Prague |
| | | He-111 dam(grd) | N/Prague |
| | Lt. E.W. Strobel | (3)Ju-87 dest(grd) | N/Prague |
| | | Me-109 dam(grd) | N/Prague |
| | Lt. R.A. Messinger | (3)Ju-52 dest(grd) | N/Prague |
| | | FW-190 dest(grd) | N/Prague |
| | | (3)Ju-87 dam(grd) | N/Prague |
| | Lt. A.A. Palopoli | (3)Ju-87 dest(grd) | N/Prague |

| | | | |
|---|---|---|---|
| | Lt. W.B. Spengler | FW-190 dest(grd) | N/Prague |
| | | (3)Ju-87 dam(grd) | N/Prague |
| 84th: | Lt. C.E. Taylor | (4)Ju-52 dest(grd) | Praha/Kakewice |
| | | (3)Me-110 dest(grd) | Praha/Kakewice |
| | | FW-190 dest(grd) | Praha/Kakewice |
| | | He-111 dest(grd) | Praha/Kakewice |
| | | FW-190 dam(grd) | Praha/Kakewice |
| | Lt. H.R. Slack | (4)Ju-52 dest(grd) | Praha/Kakewice |
| | | Ju-52 dam(grd) | Praha/Kakewice |
| | | u/i a/c dam(grd) | Praha/Kakewice |
| | Lt. D.E. Josey | (2)FW-190 dest(grd) | Praha/Kakewice |
| | | Me-109 dest(grd) | Praha/Kakewice |
| | | He-111 dest(grd) | Praha/Kakewice |
| | | u/i a/c dest(grd) | Praha/Kakewice |
| | | (2)FW-190 dam(grd) | Praha/Kakewice |
| | | Ju-52 dam(grd) | Praha/Kakewice |
| | | u/i a/c dam(grd) | Praha/Kakewice |
| | Lt. N. Hepner | (2)Me-109 dest(grd) | Praha/Kakewice |
| | | He-111 dest(grd) | Praha/Kakewice |
| | | Ju-52 dest(grd) | Praha/Kakewice |
| | | u/i a/c dest(grd) | Praha/Kakewice |
| | | (2)Ju-52 dam(grd) | Praha/Kakewice |
| | | Me-109 dam(grd) | Praha/Kakewice |
| | | Ju-88 dam(grd) | Praha/Kakewice |
| | Capt. D. Ledington | (2)Ju-52 dest(grd) | Praha/Kakewice |
| | | u/i a/c dest(grd) | Praha/Kakewice |
| | | Ju-52 dam(grd) | Praha/Kakewice |
| | Lt. L. DeAnda | (3)Ju-52 dest(grd) | Praha/Kakewice |
| | Lt. W.S. Blodgett | (2)Me-110 dest(grd) | Praha/Kakewice |
| | | Ju-52 dest(grd) | Praha/Kakewice |
| | | Me-110 dam(grd) | Praha/Kakewice |
| | Lt. J.E. Moores | (2)Ju-52 dest(grd) | Praha/Kakewice |
| | | Ju-88 dest(grd) | Praha/Kakewice |
| | | (3)Ju-52 dam(grd) | Praha/Kakewice |
| | | u/i a/c dam(grd) | Praha/Kakewice |
| | Lt. W.J. DeGain | u/i a/c dest(grd) | Praha/Kakewice |
| | | (2)u/i a/c dam(grd) | Praha/Kakewice |
| | | Ju-87 dam(grd) | Praha/Kakewice |
| | Lt. W.H. Lutz | He-111 dest(grd) | Praha/Kakewice |
| | | (2)u/i a/c dam(grd) | Praha/Kakewice |
| | Lt. H.V. Wingfield | u/i a/c dest(grd) | Praha/Kakewice |
| | Lt. J.A. Nunley | Me-110 dam(grd) | Praha/Kakewice |
| | | Me-109 dam(grd) | Praha/Kakewice |
| | Lt. G.E. Gallant | Ju-52 dam(grd) | Praha/Kakewice |
| | Lt. P.R. Henderson | Ju-52 dam(grd) | Praha/Kakewice |
| **339th** | | | |
| HdQts: | Capt. R.H. Ammon | (4)Me-109 dest(grd) | NE Prague |
| | | (3)Ju-88 dest(grd) | NE Prague |
| | | FW-190 dest(grd) | NE Prague |
| | | He-111 dest(grd) | NE Prague |
| | LtCol. W.C. Clark | (3)FW-190 dest(grd) | Klatovy |
| | | (2)Me-109 dest(grd) | Klatovy |
| | | Ju-52 dest(grd) | Klatovy |
| | | FW-190 dam(grd) | Klatovy |
| | | Me-109 dam(grd) | Klatovy |
| | Maj. V.B. Hathorn | (2)FW-190 dest(grd) | Klatovy |
| | | Me-109 dest(grd) | Klatovy |
| 503rd: | Lt. S.J. Chetneky | (3)Me-109 dest(grd) | NE Prague |
| | | (2)Ju-88 dest(grd) | NE Prague |
| | | He-111 dest(grd) | NE Prague |
| | | (2)Ju-88 dam(grd) | NE Prague |
| | | Me-109 dam(grd) | NE Prague |
| | Lt. J.R. Byers | (3)Ju-88 dest(grd) | NE Prague |
| | | Me-109 dest(grd) | NE Prague |
| | | FW-190 dest(grd) | NE Prague |
| | Lt. C.I. Ferrell | (4)Ju-88 dest(grd) | NE Prague |
| | | (2)FW-190 dam(grd) | NE Prague |
| | Lt. E.E. Haidle | (2)FW-190 dest(grd) | Kralupy |
| | | FW-190 dam(grd) | Kralupy |
| | | Me-109 dam(grd) | Kralupy |
| | Lt. J.W. Gokey | Do-217 dest(grd) | Kralupy |
| | | (3)u/i a/c dam(grd) | Kralupy |
| | Lt. R.S. Hill | u/i a/c dest(grd) | Kralupy |
| | | u/i a/c dam(grd) | Kralupy |
| | Lt. W.H. Boyd | Me-109 dam(grd) | Kralupy |
| | Lt. R.J. Frisch | Me-109 dam(grd) | Kralupy |
| | Lt. W.R. Preddy | u/i a/c dam(grd) | Kralupy |
| 504th: | Lt. R.V.E. Blizzard | (4)Me-109 dest(grd) | Klatovy |
| | Lt. W.M. Hudson | (3)FW-190 dest(grd) | Klatovy |
| | | Me-109 dest(grd) | Klatovy |
| | Capt. K.B. Everson | (3)FW-190 dest(grd) | Klatovy |
| | Lt. G.H. Chenez | (3)Me-109 dest(grd) | Klatovy |
| | Lt. F.A. Clifton | (2)Me-109 dest(grd) | Klatovy |
| | | FW-190 dest(grd) | Klatovy |
| | Lt. R.T. Aldrich | (2)Me-109 dest(grd) | Klatovy |
| | | (2)Me-109 dam(grd) | Klatovy |
| | Lt. L.M. Carter | (2)Me-109 dest(grd) | Klatovy |
| | | (2)Me-109 dam(grd) | Klatovy |
| | Lt. C. Hermanson | (2)Me-109 dest(grd) | Klatovy |
| | Lt. D.F. Krueger | FW-190 dest(grd) | Klatovy |
| | | Me-109 dest(grd) | Klatovy |
| | | FW-190 dam(grd) | Klatovy |
| | Lt. R.H. Cresswell | Me-109 dest(grd) | Klatovy |
| | | u/i a/c dest(grd) | Klatovy |
| | | FW-190 dam(grd) | Klatovy |
| | | u/i a/c dam(grd) | Klatovy |
| | F/O R.W. Smith | Me-109 dest(grd) | Klatovy |
| | | FW-190 dest(grd) | Klatovy |
| | Maj. W.H. Julian | u/i a/c dest(grd) | Klatovy |
| | | Me-109 dam(grd) | Klatovy |
| | | FW-190 dam(grd) | Klatovy |
| | Lt. H.F. Hunt | FW-190 dest(grd) | Klatovy |
| | | FW-190 dam(grd) | Klatovy |
| | Lt. L.W. Allers | Me-109 dest(grd) | Klatovy |
| | | (2)Me-109 dam(grd) | Klatovy |
| | Lt. V.N. Barto | Me-109 dest(grd) | Klatovy |
| | Lt. L.A. Kunz | (2)FW-190 dam(grd) | Klatovy |
| 505th: | Capt. H.R. Corey | (4)u/i a/c dest(grd) | NE Prague |
| | Lt. H.L. Caywood | (3)Me-109 dest(grd) | NE Prague |
| | | u/i a/c dest(grd) | NE Prague |
| | | (2)Ju-88 dam(grd) | NE Prague |
| | | Me-109 dam(grd) | NE Prague |
| | Lt. O.K. Biggs | Me-109 dest(grd) | NE Prague |
| | | Ju-88 dest(grd) | NE Prague |
| | | u/i a/c dest(grd) | NE Prague |
| | F/O L.A. Steiger | (3)FW-190 dest(grd) | NE Prague |
| | F/O J.J. Rice | (2)Me-109 dest(grd) | NE Prague |
| | | Ju-88 dest(grd) | NE Prague |
| | | Me-109 dam(grd) | NE Prague |
| | | Ju-88 dam(grd) | NE Prague |
| | Lt. J.C. Woolery | (2)u/i a/c dest(grd) | NE Prague |
| | | FW-190 dest(grd) | NE Prague |
| | LtCol. J.L. Thury | Me-109 dest(grd) | NE Prague |
| | | Me-262 dest(grd) | NE Prague |
| | Capt. O.P. Farmer | Me-109 dest(grd) | NE Prague |
| | | u/i a/c dest(grd) | NE Prague |
| | Lt. H.W. Burch | Ju-52 dest(grd) | NE Prague |
| | | Ju-88 dest(grd) | NE Prague |
| | Lt. W.R. Guyton | Me-109 dest(grd) | NE Prague |
| | | Ju-88 dest(grd) | NE Prague |
| | Lt. W.R. MacClarence | (2)u/i a/c dest(grd) | NE Prague |
| | Lt. T.W. Marvel | Me-109 dest(grd) | NE Prague |
| | | Ju-88 dest(grd) | NE Prague |
| | Capt. P.M. Loveless | FW-190 dest(grd) | NE Prague |
| | | Ju-87 dam(grd) | NE Prague |
| | Lt. V.D. Carr | Do-217 dest(grd) | NE Prague |
| | Lt. J. Pesanka | u/i a/c dest(grd) | NE Prague |
| | Lt. F.W. Smith | FW-190 dest(grd) | NE Prague |
| | | u/i a/c dam(grd) | NE Prague |
| **352nd** | | | |
| HdQts: | LtCol. W.O. Jackson | (2)Me-109 dest(grd) | Ganacker |
| | | (2)FW-190 dest(grd) | Ganacker |
| | | Me-109 dam(grd) | Ganacker |
| | | u/i a/c dam(grd) | Ganacker |
| 328th: | Lt. C.E. Goodman | (2)Me-109 dest(grd) | Landau |
| | | (4)Me-109 dam(grd) | Landau |
| | Lt. W.H. Sanford | (2)FW-190 dest(grd) | Landau |
| | F/O D.A. Webb | FW-190 dest(grd) | Landau |
| | Maj. R.G. McAuliffe | (2)FW-190 dam(grd) | Landau |
| | Lt. J.G. Cartee | (2)FW-190 dam(grd) | Landau |
| | LtCol. E.D. Duncan | Me-109 dam(grd) | Landau |
| 486th: | Capt. E.L. Heller | (3)FW-190 dest(grd) | Ganacker |
| | | (2)Ju-87 dest(grd) | Ganacker |
| | | Me-109 dest(grd) | Ganacker |
| | | u/i a/c dest(grd) | Ganacker |
| | Lt. C.C. Pattillo | (3)FW-190 dest(grd) | Ganacker |
| | | (2)Me-109 dest(grd) | Ganacker |
| | | Ju-88 dest(grd) | Ganacker |
| | | (2)Me-109 dam(grd) | Ganacker |
| | | FW-190 dam(grd) | Ganacker |
| | Lt. G.W. Wensch | (2)FW-190 dest(grd) | Ganacker |
| | F/O M.D. Johnson | FW-190 dest(grd) | Ganacker |
| | | Me-109 dest(grd) | Ganacker |
| | | (2)u/i a/c dam(grd) | Ganacker |
| | Lt. C.D. Price | He-111 dest(grd) | Ganacker |
| | | Me-109 dest(grd) | Ganacker |
| | | (3)u/i a/c dam(grd) | Ganacker |
| | Lt. R.O. Swinson | FW-190 dam(grd) | Ganacker |
| 487th: | Capt. R.H. Littge | (2)Me-109 dest(grd) | Ganacker |
| | | Me-210 dest(grd) | Ganacker |
| | | (3)Me-109 dam(grd) | Ganacker |
| | | FW-190 dam(grd) | Ganacker |
| | Lt. H.S. Sykes | (3)u/i a/c dest(grd) | Ganacker |
| | | Me-109 dest(grd) | Ganacker |
| | | Fi-156 dest(grd) | Ganacker |
| | | Me-109 dam(grd) | Ganacker |
| | | u/i a/c dam(grd) | Ganacker |
| | Lt. C.A. Pattillo | FW-190 dest(grd) | Ganacker |

| Unit | Pilot | Claim | Location |
|---|---|---|---|
| | | Me-109 dest(grd) | Ganacker |
| | | (2)FW-190 dam(grd) | Ganacker |
| | | Me-109 dam(grd) | Ganacker |
| | Lt. W. Padden | (2)u/i a/c dest(grd) | Ganacker |
| | Lt. K.M. Waldron | Me-109 dest(grd) | Ganacker |
| | | FW-190 dest(grd) | Ganacker |
| | Lt. R.W. Creamer | Me-109 dest(grd) | Ganacker |
| | | (2)FW-190 dam(grd) | Ganacker |
| | | u/i a/c dam(grd) | Ganacker |
| **353rd** | | | |
| HdQts: | Col. B. Rimerman | (3)FW-190 dest(grd) | Reichersberg |
| | | Me-109 dest(grd) | Reichersberg |
| | | Me-108 dest(grd) | Reichersberg |
| | | Ju-87 dest(grd) | Reichersberg |
| | Capt. W.J. Lane | FW-190 dest(grd) | Pocking |
| 350th: | Capt. H.G. Kolb | (5)FW-190 dest(grd) | Pocking |
| | | (2)Me-109 dest(grd) | Pocking |
| | | (1.5)Fi-156 dest(grd) | Pocking |
| | | (.5)Fi-156 dest(grd) | Pocking |
| | | (.5)Hs-126 dest(grd) | Pocking |
| | | (2)Ju-87 dam(grd) | Pocking |
| | Lt. B.D. McMahan | (4)FW-190 dest(grd) | Pocking |
| | | (.5)Fi-156 dest(grd) | Pocking |
| | | (.5)Fi-156 dest(grd) | Pocking |
| | | (.5)Hs-126 dest(grd) | Pocking |
| | Capt. M.W. Hightshoe | (4)FW-190 dest(grd) | Pocking |
| | | Me-109 dest(grd) | Pocking |
| | Lt. J.H. McClure | (2)Me-109 dest(grd) | Pocking |
| | | FW-190 dest(grd) | Pocking |
| | | FW-200 dest(grd) | Pocking |
| | | Ju-88 dest(grd) | Pocking |
| | F/O R.N. Gustke | (3)FW-190 dest(grd) | Pocking |
| | | (2)Ju-87 dest(grd) | Pocking |
| | Lt. J.D. McMullen | (5)FW-190 dest(grd) | Pocking |
| | Lt. R.C. Gordon | (3)FW-190 dest(grd) | Pocking |
| | Lt. W.A.S. Prescott | (2)FW-190 dest(grd) | Pocking |
| | | Me-109 dest(grd) | Pocking |
| | Lt. B. Greenfield | FW-190 dest(grd) | Pocking |
| | | Me-109 dest(grd) | Pocking |
| | | Ju-87 dest(grd) | Pocking |
| | | Me-109 dam(grd) | Pocking |
| | | Ju-87 dam(grd) | Pocking |
| | | u/i a/c dam(grd) | Pocking |
| | Maj. R.A. Elder | FW-190 dest(grd) | Pocking |
| | | Ju-87 dest(grd) | Pocking |
| | | (3)Ju-87 dam(grd) | Pocking |
| | | Me-109 dam(grd) | Pocking |
| | Lt. L.W. Lee | (2)FW-190 dest(grd) | Pocking |
| 351st: | Lt. G.J. Miller | (6)FW-190 dest(grd) | Reichersberg |
| | | (2)Me-109 dest(grd) | Reichersberg |
| | | Do-217 dest(grd) | Reichersberg |
| | Capt. G.B. Compton | (3)Ju-188 dest(grd) | Reichersberg |
| | | (2)Ju-88 dest(grd) | Reichersberg |
| | | (3)u/i a/c dam(grd) | Reichersberg |
| | Capt. H.W. Chase | (4)FW-190 dest(grd) | Reichersberg |
| | | FW-190 dam(grd) | Reichersberg |
| | Capt. F.N. Emory | (2)FW-190 dest(grd) | Reichersberg |
| | | Ju-87 dest(grd) | Reichersberg |
| | | u/i a/c dest(grd) | Reichersberg |
| | | Me-110 dam(grd) | Reichersberg |
| | | FW-190 dam(grd) | Reichersberg |
| | Capt. R.E. Hartley | (2)FW-200 dest(grd) | Reichersberg |
| | | FW-190 dest(grd) | Reichersberg |
| | | Ju-87 dest(grd) | Reichersberg |
| | Lt. R.F. Hahn | (4)Ju-88 dest(grd) | Reichersberg |
| | | Ju-88 dam(grd) | Reichersberg |
| | Lt. D.G. Larson | (3)FW-190 dest(grd) | Reichersberg |
| | | (4)FW-190 dam(grd) | Reichersberg |
| | Lt. J.M. Nicklebur | (3)Ju-88 dest(grd) | Reichersberg |
| | | (2)Ju-88 dam(grd) | Reichersberg |
| | Lt. R.K. Wiehe | He-111 dest(grd) | Reichersberg |
| | | FW-190 dest(grd) | Reichersberg |
| | | Me-109 dest(grd) | Reichersberg |
| | | He-111 dam(grd) | Reichersberg |
| | Maj. V.L. Byers | Fi-156 dest(grd) | Reichersberg |
| | | FW-190 dest(grd) | Reichersberg |
| | | Me-262 dam(grd) | Reichersberg |
| | Capt. L.B. Highfield | Me-110 dest(grd) | Reichersberg |
| | | Ju-88 dest(grd) | Reichersberg |
| | | He-111 dam(grd) | Reichersberg |
| | Lt. T.R. Drybrough | (2)FW-190 dest(grd) | Reichersberg |
| | | u/i a/c dam(grd) | Reichersberg |
| | Lt. J.O. Fulton | FW-190 dest(grd) | Reichersberg |
| | | Ju-88 dest(grd) | Reichersberg |
| | | Ju-88 dam(grd) | Reichersberg |
| | Lt. C.W. Geiger | (2)u/i a/c dest(grd) | Reichersberg |
| | F/O H.S. Murray | (2)FW-190 dest(grd) | Reichersberg |
| | Lt. T.P. Pryor | FW-190 dest(grd) | Reichersberg |
| | | Do-217 dest(grd) | Reichersberg |
| | Capt. C.L. McGraw | He-111 dest(grd) | Reichersberg |
| | | (2)He-111 dam(grd) | Reichersberg |
| | F/O H.A. Morris | Me-110 dest(grd) | Reichersberg |
| | | (2)Me-109 dam(grd) | Reichersberg |
| | | FW-190 dam(grd) | Reichersberg |
| | Lt. S.S. Petticrew | Ju-88 dest(grd) | Reichersberg |
| | | Me-109 dam(grd) | Reichersberg |
| | Lt. E.J. Risk | FW-190 dest(grd) | Reichersberg |
| 352nd: | Lt. E.A. Knickelbein | FW-190 dest(grd) | Bad Aibling |
| | | Me-110 dest(grd) | Bad Aibling |
| | | Fi-156 dest(grd) | Bad Aibling |
| | Capt. H.B. Tordoff | Me-109 dest(grd) | Bad Aibling |
| | | Do-217 dest(grd) | Bad Aibling |
| | | (.5)Ju-88 dest(grd) | Bad Aibling |
| | | u/i a/c dam(grd) | Bad Aibling |
| | Lt. J.G. Bartley | (.5)Ju-88 dest(grd) | Bad Aibling |
| | Lt. L.W. Grove | (2)He-111 dest(grd) | Pocking |
| | | He-111 dam(grd) | Pocking |
| | Lt. J.W. Lamb | Me-109 dest(grd) | Pocking |
| | | Me-109 dam(grd) | Pocking |
| | | u/i a/c dam(grd) | Pocking |
| | Lt. F.W. Leitner | Me-109 dest(grd) | Bad Aibling |
| | | Me-109 dam(grd) | Bad Aibling |
| | | Me-110 dam(grd) | Bad Aibling |
| | Lt. L.O. Pletz | He-111 dest(grd) | Bad Aibling |
| | | (2)He-111 dam(grd) | Bad Aibling |
| | Lt. R.T. Rose | He-111 dest(grd) | Bad Aibling |
| | | Ju-88 dam(grd) | Bad Aibling |
| | Lt. W.K. Bixby | Ar-196 dam(grd) | Pocking |
| | | u/i a/c dam(grd) | Pocking |
| | Lt. W.R. Harbin | Ju-88 dam(grd) | Pocking |
| | Lt. J.A. McIntosh | He-111 dam(grd) | Pocking |
| **355th** | | | |
| 354th: | LtCol. G.M. Graham | (3)Ju-88 dest(grd) | Eger A/F |
| | Capt. J.E. Mellen | He-111 dest(grd) | Eger A/F |
| | | He-177 dest(grd) | Eger A/F |
| | | Ju-88 dest(grd) | Eger A/F |
| | Lt. C.G. Todd | He-111 dest(grd) | Eger A/F |
| | | Ju-88 dest(grd) | Eger A/F |
| | | He-111 dam(grd) | Eger A/F |
| | Lt. J.M. Fletcher | (2)u/i a/c dest(grd) | Eger A/F |
| | | u/i a/c dam(grd) | Eger A/F |
| | Lt. R.L. Heaton | He-111 dest(grd) | Eger A/F |
| | | Ju-88 dest(grd) | Eger A/F |
| | Lt. D.V. Galer | Ju-88 dest(grd) | Eger A/F |
| | | u/i a/c dest(grd) | Eger A/F |
| | | (2)u/i a/c dam(grd) | Autobahn |
| | | Me-109 dam(grd) | Autobahn |
| | | Me-410 dam(grd) | Autobahn |
| | Lt. R.M. McLear | (2)u/i a/c dest(grd) | Autobahn |
| | Lt. J.E. Molnar | (2)Me-110 dest(grd) | Autobahn |
| | | u/i a/c dam(grd) | Autobahn |
| | Maj. N.J. Fortier | u/i a/c dest(grd) | Eger A/F |
| | Capt. J.E. Duffy | u/i a/c dest(grd) | Landstedt |
| | Lt. M.J. McLeod | u/i a/c dest(grd) | Eger A/F |
| | | (3)u/i a/c dam(grd) | Eger A/F |
| | Lt. D.J. Sanders | u/i a/c dest(grd) | Eger A/F |
| | Lt. A.J. Scheid | Ju-88 dest(grd) | Autobahn |
| 357th: | LtCol. J.L. Elder | (2)FW-190 dest(grd) | SE Germany |
| | | (2)u/i a/c dest(grd) | SE Germany |
| | | (3)u/i a/c dam(grd) | SE Germany |
| | Maj. H.S. Bille | (2)u/i a/c dest(grd) | Eger A/F |
| | | He-177 dest(grd) | Eger A/F |
| | | Ju-87 dest(grd) | Eger A/F |
| | | (2)u/i a/c dam(grd) | Eger A/F |
| | Capt. C.C. Colson | Me-110 dest(grd) | Bad Aibling |
| | | Ju-88 dest(grd) | Bad Aibling |
| | Lt. R.W. Cooper | He-177 dest(grd) | SE Germany |
| | | FW-190 dest(grd) | SE Germany |
| | Lt. D.P. Watkins | Me-110 dest(grd) | Bad Aibling |
| | | He-111 dest(grd) | Bad Aibling |
| | Lt. H.I. Knight | (2)FW-190 dest(grd) | SE Germany |
| | | He-177 dam(grd) | SE Germany |
| | | u/i a/c dam(grd) | SE Germany |
| | Lt. R.F. Misner | (2)FW-190 dest(grd) | SE Germany |
| | | (3)FW-190 dam(grd) | SE Germany |
| | Lt. E.H. Whitney | (1.5)Me-109 dest(grd) | SE Germany |
| | Lt. F.E. Gelsone | FW-190 dest(grd) | SE Germany |
| | | (.5)Me-109 dest(grd) | SE Germany |
| | | (2)Me-109 dam(grd) | SE Germany |
| | Lt. M.E. Beise | FW-190 dest(grd) | SE Germany |
| | | (2)FW-190 dam(grd) | SE Germany |
| | Lt. R.L. Garlich | Ju-87 dest(grd) | Eger A/F |
| | Lt. W.T. Kubatin | Me-109 dest(grd) | SE Germany |
| | Lt. J.E. Lake | FW-190 dest(grd) | Erferding A/F |
| | Lt. R.B. Owens | u/i a/c dest(grd) | SE Germany |
| | Lt. R.J. Kirk | Me-109 dest(grd) | SE Germany |
| | | Me-109 dam(grd) | SE Germany |
| | Lt. R.J. Patelunes | u/i a/c dest(grd) | SE Germany |

| Unit | Pilot | Claim | Location |
|---|---|---|---|
| | Lt. J.J. Weidemann | FW-190 dest(grd) | SE Germany |
| | | (3)FW-190 dam(grd) | SE Germany |
| | Lt. R.C. Keuhl | (.5)He-111 dest(grd) | Bad Aibling |
| | | He-111 dam(grd) | Bad Aibling |
| | | Me-109 dam(grd) | Bad Aibling |
| | Lt. W.L. Griswold | (.5)He-111 dest(grd) | Bad Aibling |
| | | He-111 dam(grd) | Bad Aibling |
| | | Me-110 dam(grd) | Bad Aibling |
| 358th: | Lt. H.G. Marsh | (5)FW-190 dest(grd) | Straubing |
| | | (2)FW-190 dam(grd) | Starubing |
| | Lt. F.N. McCollom | (2)FW-190 dest(grd) | Straubing |
| | | Ju-88 dest(grd) | Straubing |
| | | u/i a/c dest(grd) | Straubing |
| | Lt. W.J. Lynch | (2)FW-190 dest(grd) | Straubing |
| | | Ju-88 dest(grd) | Straubing |
| | Lt. R.C. Rowbatham | (3)FW-190 dest(grd) | Straubing |
| | | (2)FW-190 dam(grd) | Straubing |
| | Capt. L.J. Dissette | (2)FW-190 dest(grd) | Straubing |
| | | (2)FW-190 dam(grd) | Straubing |
| | Capt. G.A. Seely | (2)FW-190 dest(grd) | Straubing |
| | | Me-110 dam(grd) | Straubing |
| | | u/i a/c dam(grd) | Straubing |
| | Lt. C.E. Plemmons | Me-110 dest(grd) | Straubing |
| | | FW-190 dest(grd) | Straubing |
| | Lt. E.C. Nelson | FW-190 dest(grd) | Straubing |
| | | Ju-88 dam(grd) | Straubing |
| | Lt. L.J. Rouleau | (2)FW-190 dam(grd) | Straubing |
| **357th** | | | |
| 364th: | Lt. B.K. Braley | Me-109 dest(grd) | Muhldorf |
| | | Me-109 dam(grd) | Muhldorf |
| | Lt. M.F. Cedoz | (2)u/i a/c dam(grd) | Muhldorf |
| **359th** | | | |
| 368th: | Lt. J.T. Marron | (2)Me-109 dest(grd) | E/Plattling |
| | Capt. J.B. Hunter | Me-109 dest(grd) | E/Plattling |
| | | (2)Me-109 dam(grd) | E/Plattling |
| | Lt. J.H. McDonald | Me-109 dest(grd) | E/Plattling |
| | | (2)Me-109 dam(grd) | E/Plattling |
| **361st** | | | |
| HdQts: | LtCol. R.B. Caviness | Me-109 dest(grd) | Halndorf |
| 376th: | Lt. L.P. Chadwick | (3)Ju-52 dest(grd) | Reichersberg |
| | Lt. H.G. Spencer | (3)Ju-52 dest(grd) | Reichersberg |
| | Lt. G.R. Vanden Heuval | (2)FW-190 dest(grd) | Reichersberg |
| | | Me-410 dest(grd) | Kircheim |
| | | Ju-52 dam(grd) | Reichersberg |
| | Lt. H.M. Chapman | (2)u/i a/c dest(grd) | Reichersberg |
| | Maj. W.W. Patton | Me-109 dest(grd) | Halndorf |
| | | Me-109 dam(grd) | Halndorf |
| | | u/i a/c dam(grd) | Halndorf |
| | Lt. A.J. Chalmers | FW-190 dest(grd) | Reichersberg |
| | Lt. V.C. Eisenhut | FW-190 dest(grd) | Reichersberg |
| | | Fi-156 dam(grd) | Halndorf |
| | Lt. M.C. Kelly | Fi-156 dest(grd) | Reichersberg |
| | Lt. D.W. Jones | u/i a/c dest(grd) | Reichersberg |
| | Lt. D. Grounds | Ju-52 dam(grd) | Reichersberg |
| **364th** | | | |
| HdQts: | Capt. E.E. Bankey | (2)Me-109 dest(air) | N/Nordingen |
| | | (2)Ju-188 dest(grd) | Pocking |
| | | FW-190 dest(grd) | Pocking |
| | | Do-217 dest(grd) | Pocking |
| | | (2)FW-190 dam(grd) | Pocking |
| | | (2)Ju-188 dam(grd) | Pocking |
| | LtCol. E.P. Roberts | (3)Fi-156 dam(grd) | Marienbad |
| 383rd: | Lt. J.A. Seth | (2)Me-109 dest(grd) | Marienbad |
| | F/O D.F. Healey | FW-190 dest(grd) | Marienbad |
| | | Fi-156 dest(grd) | Marienbad |
| | | Do-217 dam(grd) | Marienbad |
| | | u/i a/c dam(grd) | Marienbad |
| | Capt. L.V. Andrew | Me-410 dest(grd) | Marienbad |
| | Capt. C.E. Hammett | Ju-52 dest(grd) | Marienbad |
| | Capt. J.L. Truett | Fi-156 dest(grd) | Marienbad |
| | | (.5)FW-190 dest(grd) | Marienbad |
| | | Do-217 dam(grd) | Marienbad |
| | | Fi-156 dam(grd) | Marienbad |
| | Lt. G.F. Hill | (.5)FW-190 dest(grd) | Marienbad |
| | | FW-190 dam(grd) | Marienbad |
| | Lt. E. Chlevin | FW-190 dest(grd) | Marienbad |
| | | (.5)Do-217 dest(grd) | Marienbad |
| | | Do-217 dam(grd) | Marienbad |
| | | Ju-52 dam(grd) | Marienbad |
| | F/O J.J. Jacaruso | (.5)Do-217 dest(grd) | Marienbad |
| | | u/i a/c dam(grd) | Marienbad |
| | Lt. D.C. Fisher | FW-190 dest(grd) | Marienbad |
| | Lt. W.K. Hood | Me-109 dest(grd) | Marienbad |
| | | FW-190 dam(grd) | Marienbad |
| | | Do-217 dam(grd) | Marienbad |
| | Lt. R.L. Hunt | u/i a/c dest(grd) | Marienbad |
| | | FW-190 dam(grd) | Marienbad |
| | Capt. C.A. Barnes | FW-190 dam(grd) | Marienbad |
| | | Ju-52 dam(grd) | Marienbad |
| | Lt. R.M. Baughn | (2)u/i a/c dam(grd) | Marienbad |
| | Lt. E.P. Hausenbauer | Ju-52 dam(grd) | Marienbad |
| | Lt. R.W. Queal | Do-217 dam(grd) | Marienbad |
| 384th: | Lt. J.E. Soehl | (3)u/i a/c dest(grd) | Pocking |
| | LtCol. R.E. Lacy | FW-190 dest(grd) | Pocking |
| | Lt. H.C. Schwartz | Ju-87 dest(grd) | Pocking |
| | | (3)Me-109 dam(grd) | Pocking |
| | Lt. J.E. Taylor | FW-190 dest(grd) | Pocking |
| | Lt. D.L. Leftwich | FW-190 dest(grd) | Pocking |
| 385th: | Lt. K.R. Horner | Ju-188 dest(grd) | Pocking |
| | | FW-190 dest(grd) | Pocking |
| | | Ju-87 dest(grd) | Pocking |
| | | FW-190 dam(grd) | Pocking |
| | Capt. J.E. Hargrove | Me-109 dest(grd) | Pocking |
| | | Ju-87 dest(grd) | Pocking |
| | Lt. D.L. Bloodgood | (2)FW-190 dest(grd) | Pocking |
| | Lt. J.W. Kiernan | (2)Me-109 dest(grd) | Pocking |
| | | Me-109 dam(grd) | Pocking |
| | Lt. C.R. Roesch | (2)FW-190 dest(grd) | Pocking |
| | | FW-190 dam(grd) | Pocking |
| | Lt. F.O. Spain | FW-190 dest(grd) | Pocking |
| | | Fi-156 dest(grd) | Pocking |
| | | (3)Ju-87 dam(grd) | Pocking |
| | Lt. J.W. Munn | FW-190 dest(grd) | Pocking |
| | | (4)FW-190 dam(grd) | Pocking |
| | Lt. E.M. Jones | (3)FW-190 dam(grd) | Pocking |
| | Lt. J.G. Johnson | (2)FW-190 dam(grd) | Pocking |
| **479th** | | | |
| 434th: | Maj. R. Olds | (2)Ju-87 dest(grd) | Reichersberg |
| | | Me-109 dest(grd) | Reichersberg |
| | | Me-110 dest(grd) | Reichersberg |
| | | He-177 dest(grd) | Reichersberg |
| | Capt. D.J. Pierce | Me-109 dest(grd) | Kirchem |
| | | Me-109 dest(grd) | Reichersberg |
| | | FW-190 dest(grd) | Reichersberg |
| | | Ju-88 dest(grd) | Reichersberg |
| | | (2)Me-109 dam(grd) | Reichersberg |
| | Lt. J.T. Golden | (3)u/i a/c dest(grd) | Reichersberg |
| | Lt. G.E. Jacobson | (2)FW-190 dest(grd) | Reichersberg |
| | | FW-190 dam(grd) | Reichersberg |
| | | Ju-88 dam(grd) | Reichersberg |
| | Lt. R.L. Munson | (2)FW-190 dest(grd) | Reichersberg |
| | | FW-190 dam(grd) | Reichersberg |
| | Lt. P.A. Brown | u/i a/c dest(grd) | Erferding A/F |
| | Lt. D.H. Scott | u/i a/c dest(grd) | Erferding A/F |
| | Lt. H.L. Stott | Ju-88 dest(grd) | Reichersberg |
| | | Ju-88 dam(grd) | Reichersberg |
| | Lt. J.A. Plezibat | FW-190 dest(grd) | Reichersberg |
| | Lt. D.F. Tommie | Me-109 dest(grd) | Reichersberg |
| | | FW-190 dam(grd) | Reichersberg |
| 435th: | Capt. V.E. Hooker | u/i a/c dest(grd) | S/Pocking |
| | | Me-109 dam(grd) | S/Pocking |
| | Lt. R.B. Frost | (2)u/i a/c dam(grd) | S/Pocking |
| 436th: | Maj. C.A.P. Duffie | (4)FW-190 dest(grd) | Landstedt |
| | Lt. C.B. Elmgren | (4)FW-190 dest(grd) | Landstedt |
| | Lt. R.E. Henry | (3)FW-190 dest(grd) | Landstedt |
| | Lt. A.J. Smigel | (2)FW-190 dest(grd) | Landstedt |
| | | Me-109 dest(grd) | Landstedt |
| | Lt. G.H. Witzel | (3)FW-190 dest(grd) | Landstedt |
| | Capt. P.S. Shane | (2)FW-190 dest(grd) | Landstedt |
| | Lt. G.G. McLaurin | (2)FW-190 dest(grd) | Landstedt |
| | Lt. R.C.J. Palson | (2)FW-190 dest(grd) | Landstedt |
| | Capt. C.V. Ernst | He-111 dest(grd) | Landstedt |
| | Capt. J.C. Malone | FW-190 dest(grd) | Landstedt |
| | Lt. C.H. Darling | He-111 dest(grd) | Landstedt |
| | Lt. E.J. Hopcroft | He-111 dest(grd) | Landstedt |
| | Lt. C.H. Philbrick | Me-109 dest(grd) | Landstedt |
| | Lt. W.N. Rawley | FW-190 dest(grd) | Landstedt |
| | Lt. W.B. Steph | Me-109 dest(grd) | Landstedt |
| | Lt. T.H. Thompson | He-111 dest(grd) | Landstedt |

*Losses-*

**4th**: LtCol. Sidney S. Woods (HdQts) POW
P-51D QP-A 44-72251
Hit by flak at Praha.

Lt. Edward J. McLoughlin (335th Ftr Sqn) POW
P-51D WD-P 44-13389
Hit by flak at Praha and crashed near Kbely.

Capt. Carl R. Alfred (336th Ftr Sqn) KIA
P-51D VF- 44-72523
Hit by flak at Praha and crashed near Prague.

Capt. Leroy A. Carpenter, Jr. (336th Ftr Sqn) KIA
P-51D VF- 44-63831
Hit by flak at Praha and crashed near Kbely.

Capt. Edward L. Gimbel (336th Ftr Sqn) POW
P-51D VF- 44-72769
Hit by flak at Praha.

Lt. William H. Ayer (336th Ftr Sqn) POW
P-51D VF- 44-13375
Hit by flak at Praha.

Lt. Benjamin L. Griffin (336th Ftr Sqn) POW
P-51D VF-H 44-14277 "Jersey Bounce II"
Hit by flak at Praha and crashed near Kbely.

Lt. Maurice W. Miller, Jr. (336th Ftr Sqn) POW
P-51D VF-S 44-14527 "Mary"
Hit by flak at Praha and crashed near Kbely.

**55th**: Lt. Donald J. Best (38th Ftr Sqn) KIA
P-51D CG- 44-72409 "Little Lulu"
Hit by flak at Munich-Brunnthal and crashed near Augsburg.

Lt. Vernon B. Tally (338th Ftr Sqn) POW
P-51D CL-W 44-63287 "My Jane"
Hit by flak at Munich-Brunnthal and bellied-in near Bonn.

Capt. Chester E. Coggeshall, Jr. (343rd Ftr Sqn) KIA
P-51D CY-T 44-15608
Hit by flak at Munich-Brunnthal.

Lt. Patrick L. Moore (343rd Ftr Sqn) KIA
P-51D CY-Y 44-14235 "Little Jan"
Hit by flak and spun-in south of Munich.

**56th**: Capt. Edward W. Appel (62nd Ftr Sqn) MIA-E
P-47M LM- 44-21230
Hit by flak and bellied-in near Muhldorf.

**78th**: Capt. Manfred O. Croy (82nd Ftr Sqn) KIA
P-51D MX-G 44-72165
Hit by flak at Straubing and bailed out too low.

Capt. Robert B. Holmes (82nd Ftr Sqn) KIA
P-51D MX-R 44-63214
Hit by flak at Ganacker.

Lt. Robert Swauger (82nd Ftr Sqn) POW
P-51D MX-E 44-15495
Hit by flak at Marienbad.

**352nd**: Lt. Cuthbert A. Pattillo (487th Ftr Sqn) POW
P-51K HO-Y 44-11556 "Sweet & Lovely"
Hit by flak at Ganacker and bailed out near Ingolstadt.

Lt. Walter Padden (487th Ftr Sqn) KIA
P-51D HO-N 44-13321 "Sexhunate"
Hit by flak at Ganacker and crashed near Ingolstadt.

**353rd**: Lt. Donald E. Howie (350th Ftr Sqn) KIA
P-51D LH- 44-15594 "Miss Kay"
Hit by flak at Pocking.

Lt. Walter A.S. Prescott (350th Ftr Sqn) KIA
P-51D LH- 44-72175 "Little Red II"
Hit by flak at Pocking.

Lt. Edward J. Risk (351st Ftr Sqn) KIA
P-51D YJ-G 44-14796 "Lady Margaret"
Hit by flak at Obernburg Airfield.

**355th**: Lt. Joseph E. Lake (357th Ftr Sqn) KIA
P-51D OS-
Hit by flak at Erferding Airfield and spun-in.

Lt. Thurman C. Long (357th Ftr Sqn) POW
P-51D OS- 44-72987
Hit by flak near Linz.

Capt. Lawrence J. Dissette (358th Ftr Sqn) MIA-E
P-51D YF-Q 44-14644 "Damn Yank III"
Hit by flak at Straubing and bailed out northwest of the field.

Lt. William J. Lynch (358th Ftr Sqn) POW
P-51K YF-R 44-11642
Hit by flak at Straubing and bellied-in south of the field.

Lt. Francis N. McCollom (358th Ftr Sqn) POW
P-51D YF-N 44-14385 "Wooly Lamb"
Hit by flak at Straubing and bellied-in east of Regensburg.

Lt. John A. Rogers (358th Ftr Sqn) MIA-E
P-51K YF-F 44-12122 "Lady Dana"
Hit by flak at Straubing and bellied-in.

**361st**: Lt. Delmar A. Ford (376th Ftr Sqn) POW
P-51D E9-S 44-15663 "Baby Doll"
Hit by flak at Pocking.

Lt. Russell E. Kenoyer (376th Ftr Sqn) MIA
P-51D E9-L 44-13894 "Francis"
Hit by flak at Pocking.

**364th**: F/O Sidney S. Stern (385th Ftr Sqn) POW
P-51D 5E-W 44-13890 "Green Eyes"
Hit by flak and bellied-in near Pocking.

**479th**: Lt. John T. Golden (434th Ftr Sqn) POW
P-51D L2-G 44-14856 "Junior"
Hit by flak and crashed near Regensburg.

Lt. Harold F. Krauss, Jr. (434th Ftr Sqn) KIA
P-51D L2-F 44-14929 "Little Droppy"
Hit by flak and crashed while landing at an Allied field.

Lt. Donald H. Stott (434th Ftr Sqn) KIA
P-51D L2-S 44-14629 "Shoo Shoo Baby"
Hit by flak at Erferding Airfield.

Lt. Frank M. Taylor (434th Ftr Sqn) POW
P-51D L2-H 44-14740 "Hot Toddy"
Hit by flak at Erferding Airfield.

*Remarks*
4th: Lt. Paul E. Burnett (334th Ftr Sqn) c/l Otterburg; o.k.
P-51D QP-H 44-72377
78th: Lt. Eugene L. Peel (82nd Ftr Sqn) c/l Frankfurt; o.k.
P-51D MX-Q 44-72119
339th: 1-0 house
353rd: 1-0 flak position
Lt. William K. Bixby (352nd Ftr Sqn) c/l; o.k.
P-51D SX-
355th: Lt. Ben F. Donathan (358th Ftr Sqn) b/o France; o.k.
P-51D YF-
357th: Capt. John A. Kirla (362nd Ftr Sqn) c/l Leiston; o.k.
P-51D G4-H 44-72180
364th: 1-0 hangar, 1-0 vehicle, 5-0 gun positions
Capt. Jasper E. Hargrove (385th Ftr Sqn) c/l Frankfurt; o.k.
P-51D 5E-H 44-13583
479th: Lt. Dalton F. Tommie (434th Ftr Sqn) c/l; o.k.
P-51D L2-C

KIAc's
**SF**: Lt. Joseph D. Nelson (1st)
P-51D
Died in a crash near Ridgewell.

**April 17, 1945**
Groups Operating: P-51 4th, 20th, 55th, 78th, 339th, 352nd, 353rd, 355th, 356th, 357th, 359th, 361st, 364th, 479th
P-47 56th
Missions: Support of bombers to rail targets in southwestern Germany and Czechoslovakia plus PRU escorts.
Claims: 12-0-5 air
269-128 ground

| *Group* | | *Claims* | *Location* |
|---|---|---|---|
| **4th** | | | |
| 336th: | Maj. F.W. Glover | Ju-87 dest(grd) | Pilzen |
| | Lt. W.W. Collins | Me-110 dest(grd) | Pilzen |
| | Lt. D.N. Groshong | Me-110 dest(grd) | Pilzen |
| | | Ju-87 dam(grd) | Pilzen |
| | Lt. W.B. Meredith | u/i a/c dest(grd) | Pilzen |
| | | (2)Me-109 dam(grd) | Pilzen |
| | Lt. H.H. Fredericks | Ju-87 dam(grd) | Pilzen |
| **20th** | | | |
| 77th: | F/O J. Rosenblum | Me-262 dam(air) | S/Dresden |
| 79th: | Lt. R.M. Scott | Me-262 dam(air) | SE Dresden |
| **55th** | | | |
| HdQts: | LtCol. E.G. Righetti | (6)u/i a/c dest(grd) | Riess/Canitz |
| | | (3)Me-109 dest(grd) | Riess/Canitz |
| 338th: | Lt. H. Bodiford | FW-190 dest(air) | SE Dresden |
| | Lt. R.E. Cooper | FW-190 dest(air) | SE Dresden |
| | Lt. T. Kiernan | FW-190 dest(air) | S/Dresden |
| | Lt. J.H. Wiley | FW-190 dam(air) | S/Dresden |
| | Capt. C.D. Henry | FW-190 dest(grd) | Riess/Canitz |
| | | u/i a/c dest(grd) | Riess/Canitz |
| | Maj. E.E. Ryan | (.5)u/i a/c dest(grd) | Leipzig |

| Unit | Pilot | Claim | Location |
|---|---|---|---|
| | Lt. J.R. Ethridge | (.5)u/i a/c dest(grd) | Leipzig |
| | Lt. R. Deloach | Fi-156 dam(grd) | Riess/Canitz |
| 343rd: | Lt. R.G. Gibbs | (2)FW-190 dest(air) | Kamenz A/F |
| | Capt. R. Strauch | FW-190 dest(air) | Kamenz A/F |
| | Capt. R.E. Welch | FW-190 dest(air) | Kamenz A/F |
| | Lt. P.A. Erby | FW-190 dest(air) | Kamenz A/F |
| | Lt. L.D. Boring | (2)Fi-156 dest(grd) | Bautzen/Litten |
| | | FW-190 dest(grd) | Bautzen/Litten |
| | | u/i a/c dest(grd) | Bautzen/Litten |
| | F/O G.W. Bernardo | (3)FW-190 dest(grd) | Dresden |
| | | Ju-88 dest(grd) | Dresden |
| | | (2)FW-190 dam(grd) | Dresden |
| | Lt. W.A. Fisher | (2)FW-190 dest(grd) | Dresden |
| | | (2)Me-410 dest(grd) | Dresden |
| | Lt. H. Mahany | (3)Me-410 dest(grd) | Dresden |
| | | (2)FW-190 dest(grd) | Dresden |
| | | (2)FW-190 dam(grd) | Dresden |
| | Lt. G.A. Apple | FW-190 dest(grd) | Dresden |
| | | Ju-88 dest(grd) | Dresden |
| | Lt. G.E. Arnold | (2)Fi-156 dest(grd) | Bautzen/Litten |
| | Lt. H. Cohen | Me-109 dest(grd) | Bautzen/Litten |
| | Lt. E.H. Geary | Me-410 dest(grd) | Bautzen/Litten |
| | | Me-410 dam(grd) | Bautzen/Litten |
| | Lt. D.E. Adams | Me-109 dam(grd) | Bautzen/Litten |
| **78th** | | | |
| HdQts: | Maj. G. Bryan | (2)u/i a/c dest(grd) | W/Dresden |
| | | (3)u/i a/c dam(grd) | W/Dresden |
| 82nd: | Capt. R.A. Hewitt | Me-262 dest(grd) | Prague |
| | Lt. A.A. Rosenblum | u/i a/c dest(grd) | Kralupy |
| 84th: | Lt. J.R. Sole | (3)u/i a/c dest(grd) | W/Dresden |
| | | (4)u/i a/c dam(grd) | W/Dresden |
| | Lt. D.R. Josey | FW-190 dest(grd) | W/Dresden |
| | | Ju-88 dest(grd) | W/Dresden |
| | | u/i a/c dest(grd) | W/Dresden |
| | | FW-190 dam(grd) | W/Dresden |
| | | Ju-88 dam(grd) | W/Dresden |
| | Lt. W.M. McClellan | Me-410 dest(grd) | W/Dresden |
| | | Ju-88 dest(grd) | W/Dresden |
| | | u/i a/c dest(grd) | W/Dresden |
| | | (3)u/i a/c dam(grd) | W/Dresden |
| | | Me-410 dam(grd) | W/Dresden |
| **339th** | | | |
| 503rd: | Lt. J.C. Campbell | Me-262 dest(air) | Pokycany |
| | Lt. R.J. Frisch | Me-262 dest(grd) | Klatovy |
| | | Ju-88 dest(grd) | Klatovy |
| | Lt. C.H. French | Me-109 dest(grd) | Kleesdorf |
| | Lt. J.R. Potthoff | Ju-88 dam(grd) | Klatovy |
| 504th: | Capt. K.B. Everson | (2)Me-109 dest(grd) | Klatovy-Anberg |
| | | (2)Fi-156 dest(grd) | Klatovy-Anberg |
| | | (2)Ju-88 dest(grd) | Klatovy-Anberg |
| | | Me-210 dest(grd) | Klatovy-Anberg |
| | Lt. L.M. Orcutt | (6)Me-109 dest(grd) | Klatovy-Anberg |
| | | (2)Ju-88 dest(grd) | Klatovy-Anberg |
| | Lt. F.A. Clifton | Me-109 dest(grd) | Klatovy-Anberg |
| | | Fi-156 dest(grd) | Klatovy-Anberg |
| | | Ju-88 dest(grd) | Klatovy-Anberg |
| | Lt. H.F. Hunt | Me-109 dest(grd) | Klatovy-Anberg |
| | | FW-190 dest(grd) | Klatovy-Anberg |
| | | Fi-156 dest(grd) | Klatovy-Anberg |
| | | Ju-88 dest(grd) | Klatovy-Anberg |
| | Lt. L.J. Barrett | Ju-52 dest(grd) | Mauching |
| 505th: | LtCol. J.L. Thury | (2)FW-190 dest(grd) | SE Pocking |
| | | (2)Me-109 dest(grd) | SE Pocking |
| | | Ju-88 dest(grd) | SE Pocking |
| | Capt. B.J. Bline | (2)Me-109 dest(grd) | SE Pocking |
| | | (2)Ju-88 dest(grd) | SE Pocking |
| | Capt. P.M. Loveless | (3)Do-217 dest(grd) | SE Pocking |
| | | Me-109 dest(grd) | SE Pocking |
| | | Do-217 dam(grd) | SE Pocking |
| | | Ju-88 dam(grd) | SE Pocking |
| | Capt. H.R. Corey | (2)Ju-188 dest(grd) | SE Pocking |
| | | Me-109 dest(grd) | SE Pocking |
| | Lt. T.W. Marvel | Me-109 dest(grd) | SE Pocking |
| | | He-111 dest(grd) | SE Pocking |
| | | u/i a/c dest(grd) | SE Pocking |
| | Capt. J.A. Diefenback | Do-217 dest(grd) | SE Pocking |
| | | u/i a/c dest(grd) | SE Pocking |
| | Lt. H.W. Burch | (2)Do-217 dest(grd) | SE Pocking |
| | Lt. W.R. MacClarence | Ju-188 dest(grd) | SE Pocking |
| | | He-111 dest(grd) | SE Pocking |
| | Lt. J.T. Murphy | Me-109 dest(grd) | SE Pocking |
| | | He-111 dest(grd) | SE Pocking |
| | | (2)Me-109 dam(grd) | SE Pocking |
| | | Ju-88 dam(grd) | SE Pocking |
| | Lt. J. Pesanka | Me-109 dest(grd) | SE Pocking |
| | | He-111 dest(grd) | SE Pocking |
| | Lt. F.W. Smith | Me-109 dest(grd) | SE Pocking |
| | | Ju-88 dest(grd) | SE Pocking |
| | Lt. J.C. Woolery | Me-109 dest(grd) | SE Pocking |
| | | Ju-88 dest(grd) | SE Pocking |
| | | Me-109 dam(grd) | SE Pocking |
| | Lt. O.K. Biggs | Ju-88 dest(grd) | SE Pocking |
| | Lt. V.D. Carr | Ju-88 dest(grd) | SE Pocking |
| | | Me-109 dam(grd) | SE Pocking |
| | Lt. R.E. Irion | Me-110 dest(grd) | SE Pocking |
| | F/O E.E. Hupp | Do-217 dest(grd) | SE Pocking |
| | Lt. R.H. Paul | Ju-88 dest(grd) | SE Pocking |
| **352nd** | | | |
| HdQts: | Col. J.D. Mayden | (2)Me-109 dest(grd) | Plattling |
| | | FW-190 dest(grd) | Plattling |
| | | u/i a/c dest(grd) | Plattling |
| | | (2)Me-109 dam(grd) | Plattling |
| 328th: | Lt. C.W. Weber | (3)Me-109 dest(grd) | Plattling |
| | | u/i a/c dest(grd) | Plattling |
| | | (2)FW-190 dam(grd) | Plattling |
| | LtCol. E.D. Duncan | (2)Me-109 dest(grd) | Plattling |
| | Lt. F.A. Cast | (2)Me-109 dest(grd) | Plattling |
| | | Me-109 dam(grd) | Plattling |
| | F/O C. Vander Vean | FW-190 dest(grd) | Plattling |
| | | u/i a/c dest(grd) | Plattling |
| | | (2)FW-190 dam(grd) | Plattling |
| | Maj. R.G. McAuliffe | FW-190 dest(grd) | Plattling |
| | | u/i a/c dam(grd) | Plattling |
| | Lt. J.C. Hurley | Me-109 dest(grd) | Plattling |
| | | (2)Me-109 dam(grd) | Plattling |
| | Lt. S.R. Price | Me-109 dest(grd) | Plattling |
| | | Me-109 dam(grd) | Plattling |
| 486th: | Lt. J.D. Carter | (5)FW-190 dest(grd) | Plattling |
| | | FW-190 dam(grd) | Plattling |
| | Maj. D.H. Higgins | (2)Ju-52 dest(grd) | Plattling |
| | | Me-109 dest(grd) | Plattling |
| | | Me-109 dam(grd) | Plattling |
| | F/O R.A. Wanda | (2)FW-190 dest(grd) | Plattling |
| | | Me-109 dest(grd) | Plattling |
| | | (2)FW-190 dam(grd) | Plattling |
| | | u/i a/c dam(grd) | Plattling |
| | Lt. G.A. Rushman | (2)FW-190 dest(grd) | Plattling |
| | | (2)FW-190 dam(grd) | Plattling |
| | Lt. G.W. Wensch | u/i a/c dest(grd) | Plattling |
| | | FW-190 dam(grd) | Plattling |
| | | u/i a/c dam(grd) | Plattling |
| | F/O J.P. McKenna | FW-190 dest(grd) | Plattling |
| | | Me-109 dest(grd) | Plattling |
| | | FW-190 dam(grd) | Plattling |
| | | Me-109 dam(grd) | Plattling |
| | | u/i a/c dam(grd) | Plattling |
| | Lt. J.B. Whitney | Me-109 dest(grd) | Plattling |
| | | Fi-156 dest(grd) | Plattling |
| | | Me-109 dam(grd) | Plattling |
| 487th: | Capt. R.H. Littge | (4)Me-109 dest(grd) | Plattling |
| | | (2)Me-262 dest(grd) | Plattling |
| | Lt. K.M. Waldron | (2)FW-190 dest(grd) | Plattling |
| | | (2)Me-109 dest(grd) | Plattling |
| | | Fi-156 dest(grd) | Plattling |
| | | (2)FW-190 dam(grd) | Plattling |
| | F/O R.W. Frum | (3)FW-190 dest(grd) | Plattling |
| | | (2)FW-190 dam(grd) | Plattling |
| | LtCol. W.T. Halton | FW-190 dest(grd) | Plattling |
| | | Me-109 dest(grd) | Plattling |
| | | (2)FW-190 dam(grd) | Plattling |
| | Lt. J.N. White | (2)Me-109 dest(grd) | Plattling |
| | | FW-190 dest(grd) | Plattling |
| | | Me-109 dam(grd) | Plattling |
| | | FW-190 dam(grd) | Plattling |
| | Lt. R.G. Reed | (2)Me-109 dest(grd) | Plattling |
| | | (3)Me-109 dam(grd) | Plattling |
| | Lt. M.C. Reynolds | FW-190 dest(grd) | Plattling |
| | | Me-109 dest(grd) | Plattling |
| | F/O J.F. Graves | u/i a/c dest(grd) | Plattling |
| **353rd** | | | |
| 352nd: | Maj. W.W. Johnson | (2)FW-190 dest(grd) | Muhldorf |
| | | (3)FW-190 dam(grd) | Muhldorf |
| | | Me-109 dam(grd) | Ganacker |
| | Capt. W.C. Davis | (4)FW-190 dest(grd) | Ganacker |
| | | FW-190 dam(grd) | Ganacker |
| | Capt. H.Q. Waggoner | (3)Me-109 dest(grd) | Ganacker |
| | | Ju-88 dest(grd) | Ganacker |
| | Lt. B.J. Lancaster | Me-109 dest(grd) | Ganacker |
| | | FW-190 dest(grd) | Ganacker |
| | | (.5)He-111 dest(grd) | Ganacker |
| | | Me-109 dam(grd) | Ganacker |
| | Lt. W.E. Beach | Me-109 dest(grd) | Ganacker |
| | | (.5)He-111 dest(grd) | Ganacker |
| | Lt. L.W. Grove | FW-190 dest(grd) | Ganacker |
| | | u/i a/c dam(grd) | Ganacker |
| | Lt. R.T. Rose | Ju-88 dest(grd) | Ganacker |
| | | Me-109 dam(grd) | Ganacker |
| | | Ju-88 dam(grd) | Ganacker |

| Unit | Pilot | Claim | Location |
|---|---|---|---|
| | Lt. J.W. Lamb | u/i a/c dest(grd) | Ganacker |
| | F/O R.C. Hassell | Me-109 dest(grd) | Ganacker |
| | | Me-109 dam(grd) | Ganacker |
| | Lt. E.A. Knickelbein | (2)Me-109 dam(grd) | Ganacker |
| | | FW-190 dam(grd) | Ganacker |
| | | Fi-156 dam(grd) | Ganacker |
| | Lt. R.R. Anderson | Me-109 dam(grd) | Ganacker |
| | Lt. H.R. Lammie | FW-190 dam(grd) | Ganacker |
| | Lt. F.W. Leitner | FW-190 dam(grd) | Ganacker |
| | Lt. L.C. McAdory | Me-109 dam(grd) | Ganacker |
| | Lt. J.A. McIntosh | Me-109 dam(grd) | Ganacker |
| | Lt. L.O. Pletz | Me-109 dam(grd) | Ganacker |
| | Lt. R.B. Snyder | Me-109 dam(grd) | Ganacker |
| **355th** | | | |
| 358th: | Capt. W.V. Gresham | He-177 dest(grd) | Cheb A/F |
| | | (3)u/i a/c dam(grd) | Eger A/F |
| | Lt. R.F. Parks | u/i a/c dam(grd) | Eger A/F |
| **357th** | | | |
| HdQts: | LtCol. J.W. Hayes | Me-262 dam(air) | SE Brux |
| | Col. I.H. Dregne | Ju-88 dest(grd) | Prague/Ruzny |
| | | (2)Ju-88 dam(grd) | Prague/Ruzny |
| 362nd: | Maj. L.K. Carson | FW-200 dest(grd) | Prague/Ruzny |
| | Lt. J.F. Duncan | Me-262 dest(grd) | Prague/Ruzny |
| | | Me-109 dest(grd) | Prague/Ruzny |
| | Lt. E.C. Danner | u/i a/c dest(grd) | Prague/Ruzny |
| 364th: | F/O J.A. Steiger | Me-262 dest(air) | NE Prague |
| | Lt. O. Howes | Ju-88 dest(grd) | Prague/Ruzny |
| **359th** | | | |
| HdQts: | LtCol. D.A. Baccus | u/i a/c dest(grd) | Ganacker-Plattling |
| | | Me-109 dam(grd) | Ganacker-Plattling |
| 369th: | Capt. W.F. Collins | FW-190 dest(grd) | W/Dresden |
| 370th: | LtCol. D.D. McKee | FW-190 dest(grd) | Ganacker-Plattling |
| **361st** | | | |
| 375th: | Lt. W.R. Stevens | Ju-188 dest(grd) | Eger A/F |
| | Lt. S.C. Kovach | (2)u/i a/c dam(grd) | Pilzen |
| | | Ju-52 dam(grd) | Pilzen |
| | Lt. P.A. Dougherty | u/i a/c dam(grd) | Eger A/F |
| | F/O A.L. Segert | Ju-52 dam(grd) | Eger A/F |
| 376th: | Maj. W.W. Patton | (2)FW-190 dest(grd) | Pilzen |
| | LtCol. R. Freedman | u/i a/c dest(grd) | Pilzen |
| | Lt. A.J. Chalmers | FW-190 dest(grd) | Pilzen |
| | Lt. M.C. Kelly | u/i a/c dest(grd) | Pilzen |
| | Lt. H.M. Chapman | (2)FW-190 dam(grd) | Pilzen |
| **364th** | | | |
| HdQts: | Capt. W.L. Goff | Me-262 dest(air) | Pilzen |
| | LtCol. J.H. Lowell | He-111 dest(grd) | Karlsbad |
| | | Me-262 dest(grd) | Karlsbad |
| | | FW-200 dest(grd) | Karlsbad |
| | Capt. E.E. Bankey | (2)He-111 dest(grd) | Karlsbad |
| | | (2)He-111 dam(grd) | Karlsbad |
| 383rd: | Capt. R.W. Orndorff | Me-262 dest(air) | Praha |
| | Lt. R.M. Baughn | Me-262 dest(grd) | SE Pilzen |
| | Lt. W.F. Kissel | Me-262 dest(grd) | Falkenst |
| | Capt. G.O. Warner | (3)Me-262 dam(grd) | SE Pilzen |
| | Lt. G.F. Hill | Me-262 dam(grd) | SE Pilzen |
| 384th: | Lt. S.J. Price | Me-262 dam(air) | Dresden |
| | Lt. J.E. Taylor | He-111 dest(grd) | Karlsbad |
| | | FW-200 dest(grd) | Karlsbad |
| | Lt. W.A. Leavell | He-111 dest(grd) | Karlsbad |
| | | He-111 dam(grd) | Karlsbad |
| | Lt. J.L. Hughes | He-111 dest(grd) | Karlsbad |
| | | He-111 dam(grd) | Karlsbad |
| 385th: | Lt. J.S. Rogers | He-111 dest(grd) | Karlsbad |
| | | Ju-52 dest(grd) | Karlsbad |
| | | Ar-66 dest(grd) | Karlsbad |
| | | (2)He-111 dam(grd) | Karlsbad |
| | F/O W.K. Masters | He-111 dest(grd) | Karlsbad |
| | | Ar-66 dest(grd) | Karlsbad |
| | Capt. E. Murphy | FW-190 dest(grd) | Karlsbad |
| | Lt. E.E. Anderson | He-111 dest(grd) | Karlsbad |
| | | He-111 dam(grd) | Karlsbad |
| | Lt. E.H. Jones | (2)He-111 dam(grd) | Karlsbad |
| | Capt. R.E. White | FW-200 dam(grd) | Karlsbad |
| | Lt. J.W. Ruland | He-111 dam(grd) | Karlsbad |
| **479th** | | | |
| 434th: | Capt. D.J. Pierce | (2)FW-190 dest(grd) | Puchhoff |
| | | Me-109 dest(grd) | Landau |
| | | Me-109 dam(grd) | Landau |
| | | u/i a/c dam(grd) | Landau |
| | Lt. D.L. Born | (2)u/i a/c dest(grd) | Puchhoff |
| | | Me-109 dest(grd) | Puchhoff |
| | Lt. C.M. Peacock | (2)FW-190 dest(grd) | Puchhoff |
| | F/O A.J. Valluzzi | (2)Me-109 dest(grd) | Puchhoff |
| | Lt. D.W. Mastin | u/i a/c dest(grd) | Puchhoff |
| 435th: | Capt. T.J. Sowerby | (2)Me-262 dest(grd) | Puchhoff |
| | Lt. R.H. Hoffman | (2)Me-262 dest(grd) | Puchhoff |
| | | Fi-156 dest(grd) | Puchhoff |
| | | Me-262 dam(grd) | Puchhoff |
| | Lt. R.J. Baird | Me-262 dest(grd) | Puchhoff |
| | Lt. S.R. Routh | Me-262 dest(grd) | Puchhoff |
| | Lt. E.H. Sims | Me-262 dest(grd) | Puchhoff |
| | Lt. F.W. Salze | Me-262 dest(grd) | Puchhoff |
| | Lt. D.W. Thorn | Me-262 dam(grd) | Puchhoff |
| | | u/i a/c dam(grd) | Puchhoff |
| | Capt. V.E. Hooker | u/i a/c dam(grd) | Puchhoff |
| | Lt. C.R. Mathews | Me-262 dam(grd) | Puchhoff |
| | Lt. G.M. Salter | u/i a/c dam(grd) | Puchhoff |
| 436th: | Maj. C.A.P. Duffie | (2)Ju-87 dest(grd) | Karlsbad |
| | | FW-190 dest(grd) | Karlsbad |
| | Lt. R.C.J. Palson | (2)FW-190 dest(grd) | Puchhoff |
| | | (2)FW-190 dest(grd) | Puchhoff |
| | Lt. E.J. Hopcroft | Fi-156 dest(grd) | Landau |
| | | FW-190 dest(grd) | Puchhoff |
| | | Me-109 dest(grd) | Puchhoff |
| | | u/i a/c dam(grd) | Puchhoff |
| | Lt. C.B. Elmgren | (2)Fi-156 dest(grd) | Karlsbad |
| | | u/i a/c dest(grd) | Karlsbad |
| | Lt. G.H. Witzel | FW-190 dest(grd) | Karlsbad |
| | | u/i a/c dest(grd) | Karlsbad |
| | Lt. P.J. Romano | Ju-87 dest(grd) | Karlsbad |
| | | u/i a/c dest(grd) | Karlsbad |
| | LtCol. G.E. Falkner | u/i a/c dest(grd) | Karlsbad |
| | Capt. P.S. Shane | Me-109 dest(grd) | Karlsbad |
| | Lt. K.J. Hansen | FW-189 dest(grd) | Karlsbad |
| | Lt. C.H. Darling | u/i a/c dest(grd) | Karlsbad |
| | Lt. A.J. Smigel | u/i a/c dest(grd) | Karlsbad |
| | | u/i a/c dam(grd) | Karlsbad |
| | Lt. C.S. Kreger | FW-190 dam(grd) | Puchhoff |

*Losses-*

**4th:** Lt. Robert O. Davis (336th Ftr Sqn) KIA
P-51D VF- 44-14387
Hit by flak near Pilzen.

**55th:** LtCol. Elwyn G. Righetti (HdQts) KIA
P-51D CL-M 44-72227 "KatyDid"
Hit by flak in the Dresden area; bellied-in and was later killed on the ground by civilians.

Lt. Robert K. Thacker (338th Ftr Sqn) POW
P-51D CL- 44-15639
Hit by flak and bailed out west of Dresden.

Lt. George A. Apple (343rd Ftr Sqn) KIA
P-51D CY-D 44-15735
Hit by flak near Dresden.

Lt. Philip A. Erby (343rd Ftr Sqn) KIA
P-51D CY-F 44-15025
Hit by flak while chasing a FW-190 near Kamenz Airfield.

Lt. Daniel A. Langelier (343rd Ftr Sqn) MIA
P-51D CY- 44-72349
Hit by flak near Dresden.

**78th:** Lt. Allen A. Rosenblum (82nd Ftr Sqn) POW
P-51D MX-C 44-72367
Hit by flak near Kralupy.

Lt. Alvin M. Rosenberg (82nd Ftr Sqn) POW
P-51D MX-D 44-72357
Hit by flak west of Adorf.

**339th:** Capt. Raymond F. Reuter (503rd Ftr Sqn) KIA
P-51D D7-J 44-72485
Last seen chasing enemy fighters near Prague.

Lt. William R. Preddy (503rd Ftr Sqn) KIA
P-51K D7-A 44-11623 "Rusty"
Last seen chasing enemy fighters near Prague.

**352nd:** Lt. Miron C. Reynolds (487th Ftr Sqn) KIA
P-51D HO-L 44-14801 "The Hawk-eye-owan"
Hit by flak near Plattling.

**353rd:** Lt. James W. Lamb (352nd Ftr Sqn) KIA
P-51D SX-N 44-14712 "Little Chum"
Hit by flak near Ganacker.

Lt. Billy J. Lancaster (352nd Ftr Sqn) POW
P-51K SX-K 44-11559 "Princess Marie"
Hit by flak at Ganacker and bailed out near Regensburg.

**357th**: Lt. James C. Monahan (364th Ftr Sqn) POW
P-51D C5-B 44-14900 "Nellie Jean"
Suffered mechanical failure northwest of Prague.

Lt. Robert W. Muller (364th Ftr Sqn) POW
P-51D C5-D 44-14648 "Princess Pat"
Hit by flak at Prague/Ruzny Airfield.

Lt. Irving E. Snedeker (364th Ftr Sqn) POW
P-51D C5-M 44-13783 "Roving Rhoda"
Hit by flak at Prague/Ruzny Airfield.

**361st**: Lt. Joseph B. Wolfe (375th Ftr Sqn) KIA
P-51D E2-L 44-14411 "Miss Marge"
Hit by flak at Eger Airfield.

**364th**: Lt. Duane C. Hague (383rd Ftr Sqn) POW
P-51D N2-P 44-72358
Hit by flak near Prague.

*Remarks*
4th: Maj. Pierce W. McKennon (335th Ftr Sqn) c/l; o.k.
P-51D WD-A 44-14221 "Ridge Runner"
339th: 3-2 flak positions, 1-0 vehicle, 2-0 hangars
352nd: F/O Rollin W. Frum (487th Ftr Sqn) c/l; o.k.
P-51D HO-D 44-72335
357th: 0-1 vehicle
364th: Lt. Gordon F. Hill (383rd Ftr Sqn) c/l; o.k.
P-51D N2-F 44-14133
385th Ftr Sqn P-51 c/l Beccles; o.k.
P-51D 5E-

**April 18, 1945**
Groups Operating: P-51 4th, 20th, 55th, 78th, 339th, 352nd, 353rd, 355th, 356th, 357th, 359th, 361st, 364th, 479th
P-47 56th
Missions: Support of bombers to marshalling yards in Germany, some support for 9th Air Force bombers, and PRU escorts.
Claims: 4-0-6 air
12-7 ground

| *Group* | | *Claims* | *Location* |
|---|---|---|---|
| **339th** | | | |
| 503rd: | LtCol. D.E. Shafer | Ar-234 dest(air) | Regensburg |
| 505th: | LtCol. J.L. Thury | Me-262 dam(air) | Tabor |
| **356th** | | | |
| 359th: | Lt. L. Oliver | Ar-234 dest(air) | Wertingen |
| 360th: | Capt. O.L. Burwell | Me-262 dam(air) | Ingolstadt |
| | Lt. W.C. Gatlin | (.33)Me-262 dam(air) | Ingolstadt |
| | Lt. L.B. Proctor | (.33)Me-262 dam(air) | Ingolstadt |
| | Lt. G.W. Seanor | (.33)Me-262 dam(air) | Ingolstadt |
| **357th** | | | |
| 362nd: | Capt. C.E. Weaver | Me-262 dest(air) | Prague/Ruzny |
| | Maj. L.K. Carson | (2)Me-262 dam(air) | Prague/Ruzny |
| | Lt. R.H. Bradner | (.5)Me-262 dam(air) | SW Prague/Ruzny |
| | Lt. F.A. Dellorto | (.5)Me-262 dam(air) | SW Prague/Ruzny |
| 363rd: | Maj. D.H. Bochkay | Me-262 dest(air) | SW Prague |
| **479th** | | | |
| 434th: | Lt. G.E. Jacobson | (2)Ju-88 dest(grd) | Ingolstadt |
| | | FW-190 dest(grd) | Ottingen |
| | Lt. J.K. Nagel | Me-109 dest(grd) | Deiningen |
| | | FW-190 dest(grd) | Deiningen |
| | | Ju-88 dest(grd) | Ottingen |
| | Lt. C.W. Bowers | Me-109 dest(grd) | Ottingen |
| | | Me-110 dest(grd) | Ottingen |
| | | u/i a/c dest(grd) | Deiningen |
| | | u/i a/c dam(grd) | Deiningen |
| | Lt. G.H. Leeney | FW-190 dest(grd) | Ottingen |
| | Lt. E.E. Honance | Me-109 dest(grd) | Deiningen |
| | | Me-109 dam(grd) | Deiningen |
| 435th: | Lt. J.H. Kerber | u/i a/c dest(grd) | Mettenheim |
| | Capt. V.E. Hooker | (2)u/i a/c dam(grd) | Mettenheim |
| | Lt. W.M. Barkey | u/i a/c dam(grd) | Mettenheim |
| | Lt. E.H. Sims | u/i a/c dam(grd) | Mettenheim |
| | Lt. E.A. Splittsteesar | u/i a/c dam(grd) | Mettenheim |

*Losses-*

**357th**: Lt. Oscar T. Ridley (362nd Ftr Sqn) MIA-E
P-51D G4-E 44-14789 "Sad Sack"
Hit by flak west of Prague.

**479th**: Capt. Jay C. Malone (436th Ftr Sqn) KIA
P-51D 9B- 44-14601 "Queenie-El Diablo"
Hit by flak near Neuburg.

*Remarks*
339th: Lt. Ralph S. Hill (503rd Ftr Sqn) c/l Fowlmere; o.k.
P-51D D7-W 44-15510
355th: Lt. Robert W. Delhamer (357th Ftr Sqn) c/l; o.k.
P-51D OS-
361st: Maj. Robert E. Douglas (374th Ftr Sqn) b/o; o.k.
P-51D B7-

**April 19, 1945**
Groups Operating: P-51 20th, 55th, 78th, 339th, 352nd, 353rd, 356th, 357th, 359th, 364th, 479th
Missions: Support for bombers to rail targets in Germany plus PRU escorts.
Claims: 12-0-5 air
0-0 ground

| *Group* | | *Claims* | *Location* |
|---|---|---|---|
| **55th** | | | |
| 338th: | Lt. R. Deloach | Me-262 dest(air) | W/Prague |
| **357th** | | | |
| HdQts: | LtCol. J.W. Hayes | Me-262 dest(air) | W/Prague |
| 363rd: | Capt. R.S. Fifield | Me-262 dest(air) | Prague |
| | Lt. P.N. Bowles | Me-262 dest(air) | Prague |
| | Lt. C.W. Ofsthun | Me-262 dest(air) | SW Prague/Ruzny |
| | Lt. W.J. Currie | Me-262 dam(air) | Prague |
| | Lt. F.A. Kyle | Me-262 dam(air) | Prague |
| | Lt. G.A. Zarnke | Me-262 dam(air) | Prague |
| 364th: | Lt. J.P. McMullen | Me-262 dest(air) | Prague/Ruzny |
| | Capt. I.L. McGuire | (.5)Me-262 dest(air) | S/Dresden |
| | Lt. G.L. Weber | (.5)Me-262 dest(air) | S/Dresden |
| | Lt. D.C. Kocher | Me-262 dam(air) | Dresden |
| **364th** | | | |
| 383rd: | Capt. C.E. Hammett | FW-190 dest(air) | Lubben |
| | | (.5)Do-217 dest(air) | Lubben |
| | F/O D.F. Healey | FW-190 dest(air) | Lubben |
| | | (.5)Do-217 dest(air) | Lubben |
| | Lt. D.C. Fisher | FW-190 dest(air) | Lubben |
| | Lt. R.W. Queal | FW-190 dest(air) | Lubben |
| | | FW-190 dam(air) | Lubben |

*Losses-*

**352nd**: Lt. John F. Reiners (328th Ftr Sqn) KIA
P-51D PE- 44-11229
Crashed on take-off from Bodney.

*Remarks*
357th: Lt. Harlan Q. Van Roy (363rd Ftr Sqn) c/l Leiston; o.k.
P-51D B6-V 44-13753
359th: Lt. John J. Murray (370th Ftr Sqn) c/l Croxton; o.k.
P-51D CS-
364th: Lt. Kenneth R. Horner (385th Ftr Sqn) b/o Frankfurt; WIA
P-51D 5E- 44-73035
Lt. Sim L. Lett (385th Ftr Sqn) c/l; o.k.
P-51D 5E-

**April 20, 1945**
Groups Operating: P-51 4th, 20th, 55th, 78th, 339th, 352nd, 353rd, 355th, 356th, 357th, 359th, 361st, 364th, 479th
P-47 56th
Missions: Support for bombers hitting rail targets near Berlin and in Czechoslovakia plus a few PRU escorts.
Claims: 6-1-4 air
0-0 ground

| *Group* | | *Claims* | *Location* |
|---|---|---|---|
| **355th** | | | |
| HdQts: | LtCol. C.H. Kinnard | (2)Me-109 dest(air) | Letnany A/F |
| | | Me-109 dam(air) | Letnany A/F |
| 357th: | Maj. H.S. Bille | (2)Me-109 dest(air) | Letnany A/F |
| | | (2)Me-109 dam(air) | Letnany A/F |
| | Lt. V.D. Iglesias | Me-109 dest(air) | Letnany A/F |
| 358th: | Lt. H.P. Knutty | (.5)Me-109 dest(air) | Kbely A/F |
| | Lt. K.L. Snook | (.5)Me-109 dest(air) | Kbely A/F |
| | Capt. G.A. Seely | Me-109 prob(air) | Kbely A/F |
| | Lt. R.F. Parks | Me-109 dam(air) | Kbely A/F |

*Losses-*

**SF**: Capt. Thomas L. Fitzsimmons (3rd) KIA
P-51D CL-
Hit by flak east of Rotterdam.

*Remarks*
357th: Lt. Donald Kocher (364th Ftr Sqn) c/l Luxembourg; o.k.
P-51D C5- 44-13861

**April 21, 1945**
Groups Operating: P-51 4th, 20th, 55th, 78th, 355th, 357th
P-47 56th
Missions: Support of bombers to Munich, Ingolstadt, and Salzburg.
Claims: nil

*Losses-*

**78th**: LtCol. Leonard P. Marshall (HdQts) KIA
P-51D WZ-Z 44-63212 "The Face VI"
Suffered mechanical failure near Mannheim and crashed north of Strasbourg.

Capt. Dorian Ledington (84th Ftr Sqn) KIA
P-51D WZ-A 44-72772
Crashed west of Coblenz in bad weather.

Lt. John R. Sole (84th Ftr Sqn) KIA
P-51D WZ-B 44-63712 "Flyin' Time Bomb"
Lost in bad weather; bailed out too low west of Coblenz.

*Remarks*
78th: Lt. Gene C. Doss (83rd Ftr Sqn) c/l Valenciennes; o.k.
P-51D HL-T 44-72360

**April 22, 1945**
KIAc's
479th: Lt. Robert C. Young (436th Ftr Sqn)
P-51D 9B-

**April 25, 1945**
Groups Operating: P-51 4th, 20th, 78th, 352nd, 353rd, 355th, 356th, 357th, 359th, 361st, 364th, 479th
Missions: Support of bombers to airfields and marshalling yards in southern Germany and Czechoslovakia.
Claims: 1-1-0 air
0-0 ground

| *Group* | | *Claims* | *Location* |
|---|---|---|---|
| **4th** | | | |
| 334th: | Lt. W.B. Hoelscher | Me-262 prob(air) | Prague/Ruzny |
| **479th** | | | |
| 434th: | Lt. H.O. Thompson | Ar-234 dest(air) | Traunstein-Berchtesgaden |

*Losses-*

**4th**: Lt. William B. Hoelscher (334th Ftr Sqn) MIA-E
P-51D QP-V 44-15347
Hit by flak at Prague/Ruzny Airfield.

**78th**: Lt. Edward J. Carroll (82nd Ftr Sqn) KIA
P-51D MX-W 44-15382
Crashed near Sawston in heavy fog.

**359th**: F/O Jack D. Highfield (368th Ftr Sqn) MIA-E
P-51D CV-
Suffered mechanical failure and bellied-in south of Dortmund.

*Remarks*
20th: Lt. Lynn P. Bishop (79th Ftr Sqn) b/o Dusseldorf; o.k.
P-51D MC-M 44-72402

**May 1, 1945**
KIAc's
56th: Lt. Albin P. Zychowski (61st Ftr Sqn)
P-47M HV-
Mushed into the ground near Tiverton.

**May 3, 1945**
Groups Operating: P-51 352nd
Missions: Support of bombers dropping leaflets over Germany.
Claims: nil
Losses: nil

KIAc's
55th: Capt. William F. McGill (338th Ftr Sqn)
P-51D CL-
Died when a P-51 collided with his plane while taxi-ing

357th: Capt. Robert S. Fifield (363rd Ftr Sqn)
P-51D B6- 44-63710
Died in a crash near Westleton.

**May 4, 1945**
KIAc's
479th: Lt. Anthony J. Scordino (436th Ftr Sqn)
P-51K 9B- 44-11749

**May 6, 1945**
Groups Operating: P-51 364th
Missions: Support for bombers dropping leaflets over France and Germany.
Claims: nil
Losses: nil

**May 7, 1945**
Groups Operating: P-51 356th
Missions: Support for bombers dropping leaflets over Germany.
Claims: nil
Losses: nil

**May 17, 1945**
KIAc's:
4th: Capt. Richard L. Tannehill (335th Ftr Sqn)
P-51D WD- 44-72340
Spun-in near Llanbedr, Wales.

**May 19, 1945**
KIAc's
359th: Lt. James J. Ferris (368th Ftr Sqn)
P-51B CV-G 42-106929
Turned too sharp and crashed near Stoke Ferry.

**May 21, 1945**
KIAc's
357th: Lt. Alfred W. Bierweiler (362nd Ftr Sqn)
P-51D G4-Q 44-11190 "Lady Ovella"
Crashed southwest of Ipswich.

**May 22, 1945**
KIAc's
56th: Lt. Franklin S. Rader (61st Ftr Sqn)
Typhoon(on D.S. to RAF)
Crashed near Greatham Farm on a test flight.

**May 29, 1945**
KIAc's
4th: Lt. Harold H. Fredericks (336th Ftr Sqn)
P-51D VF-S 44-72181
Crashed near Manchester on a ferry flight.

Lt. Barnaby M. Wilhoit (336th Ftr Sqn)
P-51D VF-
Crashed into a mountain near Burtonwood while on a ferry flight.

357th: Lt. Manuel K. Soo (364th Ftr Sqn)
P-51D C5-Z 44-13578
Crashed near Brussels.

**May 31, 1945**
KIAc's
355th: Lt. Robert L. Crabb (354th Ftr Sqn)
P-51D WR-
Stalled and spun-in fifteen miles from Steeple Morden.

**May ???, 1945**
KIAc's
55th: Lt. John R. Duxbury (343rd Ftr Sqn)
P-51B CY- 43-6928

**June & July 1945 KIAc's**

**June 1945**
4th: Lt. Sterling J. Price (384th Ftr Sqn/364th Ftr Grp)
P-51D 5Y-
Collided with a P-51 while taking-off from Honington.

9th: Lt. Thomas C. Creevy (361st Ftr Sqn/356th Ftr Grp)
P-51D QI-Z 44-15401 "Moonshine"
Crashed while doing aerobatics near Podington.

11th: Lt. Randolph W. Cooper (357th Ftr Sqn/355th Ftr Grp)
P-51D OS- 44-13512

14th: Lt. George F. Barrett (363rd Ftr Sqn/357th Ftr Grp)
P-51D B6-
Collided with a P-51 and crashed off Felixstowe.

15th: Lt. George W. Porter (503rd Ftr Sqn/339th Ftr Grp)
P-51D D7-T 44-15509

18th: Lt. Preston W. McKeon (361st Ftr Sqn/356th Ftr Grp)
P-51D QI-
Collided with a B-17 and spun-in.

20th: Lt. Richard J. Rensch (360th Ftr Sqn/356th Ftr Grp)
P-51D PI- 44-15577
Buzzed Valley Airdrome, Wales; did a slow roll into the overcast and disappeared.

21st: Lt. William T. Burnett (357th Ftr Sqn/355th Ftr Grp)
P-51D OS-Y 44-14858

30th: Lt. Thomas N. Jessup (503rd Ftr Sqn/339th Ftr Grp)
P-51D D7-L 44-15168

Lt. William C. Boucek (360th Ftr Sqn/356th Ftr Grp)
P-51D PI- 44-15164
Lost a wing near Bentwaters; bailed out but his chute failed.

Lt. Edward W. Kortendick (383rd Ftr Sqn/364th Ftr Grp)
P-51B N2- 43-6731
Hit power lines while descending with engine trouble near Crosthwaite.

**July 1945**

3rd: Lt. Edward A. Knickelbein (352nd Ftr Sqn/353rd Ftr Grp)
P-51D SX-F 44-14644
Collided with a P-51 near Wattisham.

7th: Lt. Glen W. St. John (328th Ftr Sqn/352nd Ftr Grp)
P-51K PE-Q 44-11644 "Juliet"

8th: Lt. Shelby N. Jett (361st Ftr Sqn/356th Ftr Grp)
A-35
Died of injuries suffered in a crash on the 7th.

10th: Capt. James M. Farmer (84th Ftr Sqn/78th Ftr Grp)
P-51D WZ-Y 44-63187 "Bum Steer"

12th: Lt. Donald F. Blaicher (352nd Ftr Sqn/353rd Ftr Grp)
P-51D SX-Z 44-14805
Died in a crash near Eye.

17th: Capt. Kenneth C. Gilbert (505th Ftr Sqn/339th Ftr Grp)
P-51B 6N-Q 42-106657

19th: Lt. Hilton O. Thompson (434th Ftr Sqn/479th Ftr Grp)
P-51D L2- 44-14523

20th: Lt. Richard J. Stone (359th Ftr Sqn/356th Ftr Grp)
P-51D OC-H 44-15181
Lost control and crashed near Wickham Market.

23rd: F/O John H. Klug (368th Ftr Sqn/359th Ftr Grp)
P-51D CV-D 44-13762

Lt. J. Warren Geron (375th Ftr Sqn/361st Ftr Grp)
P-51D E2-M 44-15038 "Tony"

Lt. John E. Havey (375th Ftr Sqn/361st Ftr Grp)
P-51D E2-I 44-14556 "Libby"

# PART TWO:
# Fighter Group Histories

## THE 4TH FIGHTER GROUP
## 334TH, 335TH, 336TH FIGHTER SQUADRONS

The 4th Fighter Group was activated on September 12, 1942, at Bushey Hall, England. The unit was formed from the three RAF "Eagle" Squadrons, Nos. 71, 121, and 133. Under British control from September 21, the first official USAAF mission was on October 2, 1942. The group's 576th mission came on April 25, 1945, and during this time pilots claimed 550 aerial and 461.25 ground victories while 242 Spitfires, P-47's, and P-51's were lost on operations and 18 pilots died in accidents.

Stations for the 4th were Debden, from September of 1942, until July of 1945, then Steeple Morden until November. Aircraft flown were Spitfires, until April of 1943; P-47C and D from March of 1943 until the end of February of 1944; and the P-51B, C, D, and K from late February of 1944 until war's end. The 4th was awarded a Distinguished Unit Citation for missions flown between March 5 and April 24, 1944, in which it destroyed over 300 German aircraft.

### Claims

| | Air | | | Grd | |
|---|---|---|---|---|---|
| | Destroyed | Probable | Damaged | Destroyed | Damaged |
| HdQts | 23.5 | 1 | 5 | 7.5 | 15.5 |
| 334th | 201.17 | 15 | 60 | 178 | 105.75 |
| 335th | 159.67 | 24 | 48 | 94.84 | 85 |
| 336th | 165.67 | 20 | 41 | 180.92 | 80.25 |
| | 550 | 60 | 154 | 461.25 | 286.5 |

### Commanders

| | |
|---|---|
| Col. Edward W. Anderson | September 27, 1942-August 20, 1943 |
| LtCol. Chesley G. Peterson | August 20, 1943-January 1, 1944 |
| Col. Donald J.M. Blakeslee | January 1, 1944-September 15, 1944 |
| LtCol. Claiborne H. Kinnard | September 15, 1944-October 24, 1944 |
| Col. Donald J.M. Blakeslee | October 25, 1944-November 3, 1944 |
| LtCol. Claiborne H. Kinnard | November 3, 1944-November 29, 1944 |
| LtCol. William A. Trippett | November 29, 1944-December 5, 1944 |
| LtCol. Jack J. Oberhansly | December 5, 1944-December 7, 1944 |
| LtCol. Harry J. Dayhuff | December 7, 1944-February 21, 1945 |
| Col. Everett W. Stewart | February 21, 1945-September 1945 |

### Wing and Command Assignments

| | |
|---|---|
| Assigned to VIII Fighter Command | September 12, 1942 |
| VIII Fighter Command, 4th Air Defense Wing | June 30, 1943 |
| VIII Fighter Command, 65th Fighter Wing | August 7, 1943 |
| 2nd Bomb Division, 65th Fighter Wing | September 15, 1944 |
| 2nd Air Division, 65th Fighter Wing | January 1, 1945 |

### Aircraft Markings

Spitfires were in the standard RAF scheme of Ocean Gray and Dark Green upper surfaces and Medium Sea Gray on the lower. All P-47's operated were in the standard USAAF scheme of olive drab upper and neutral gray lower surfaces with white theater bands on the tails and around the cowl. Early P-51's were in this scheme as well until the Spring of 1944 when NMF aircraft were obtained. A few later models received dark green on their upper surfaces with at least one P-51D being entirely olive drab with NMF under surfaces. Col. Kinnard's P-51D was also decked out with green zebra stripes on the upper wings and tail surfaces but this was short-lived. Beginning in March of 1944, aircraft carried a red spinner and twelve inch cowl band and in December of 1944, this was extended to 24 inches. In January of 1945, the red was swept back and down to the wing root. Squadron colors were introduced in October of 1944, and were: red for the 334th, white with a red outline for the 335th, and blue for the 336th.

Squadron codes were:

334th Ftr Sqn: XR (Spitfire)
QP (P-47 & P-51)
335th Ftr Sqn: AV (Spitfire)
WD (P-47 & P-51)
336th Ftr Sqn: MD (Spitfire)
VF (P-47 & P-51)

### 4th Fighter Group Statistical Report

| Month | Missions | Air | Grd | Losses | KIAc |
|---|---|---|---|---|---|
| September 1942 | 2 | 1-0-0 | 0-0 | 12 | 0 |
| October | 14 | 4-0-2 | 0-0 | 1 | 0 |
| November | 15 | 2-0-0 | 0-0 | 1 | 1 |
| December | 17 | 0-2-0 | 0-0 | 0 | 0 |
| January 1943 | 25 | 6-0-1 | 0-0 | 2 | 0 |
| February | 28 | 0-0-0 | 0-0 | 2 | 1 |
| March | 40 | 0-0-1 | 0-0 | 1 | 1 |
| April | 11 | 3-0-1 | 0-0 | 3 | 1 |
| May | 19 | 3-3-9 | 0-0 | 5 | 0 |
| June | 16 | 6-0-1 | 0-0 | 1 | 2 |
| July | 18 | 14-2-9 | 0-0 | 3 | 0 |
| August | 13 | 22-2-10 | 0-0 | 1 | 0 |
| September | 12 | 2-1-2 | 0-0 | 4 | 0 |
| October | 7 | 8-1-4 | 0-0 | 2 | 0 |
| November | 10 | 3-4-1 | 0-0 | 2 | 0 |
| December | 10 | 8-0-4 | 0-0 | 0 | 1 |
| January 1944 | 10 | 32-2-4 | 0-0 | 2 | 0 |
| February | 18 | 26-3-11 | 1-0 | 4 | 1 |
| March | 18 | 118.5-14-33 | 41.5-23 | 29 | 1 |
| April | 19 | 92.5-4-17 | 117.75-89 | 24 | 1 |
| May | 22 | 53.5-6-7 | 20-18 | 21 | 1 |
| June | 27 | 17-0-5 | 4-1 | 24 | 2 |
| July | 25 | 16.5-3-9 | 0-0 | 11 | 0 |
| August | 30 | 15-1-4 | 16-6 | 25 | 0 |
| September | 22 | 32-4-5 | 21-5 | 12 | 0 |
| October | 17 | 5-0-1 | 0-0 | 3 | 0 |
| November | 19 | 13-2-3 | 12-34 | 9 | 1 |
| December | 18 | 17-3-4 | 0-0 | 3 | 0 |
| January 1945 | 15 | 7-0-0 | 31-0 | 4 | 0 |
| February | 17 | 4-1-0 | 60-8 | 10 | 2 |
| March | 24 | 12-0-3 | 7-7 | 9 | 0 |
| April | 18 | 7-2-3 | 130-95 | 12 | 1 |
| May | 0 | 0-0-0 | 0-0 | 0 | 3 |
| | 576 | 550-60-154 | 461.25-286.5 | 242 | 18 |

### Losses by Squadron

| | MIA | | | KIAc | | |
|---|---|---|---|---|---|---|
| | Spitfire | P-47 | P-51 | Spitfire | P-47 | P-51 |
| HdQts | 0 | 1 | 4 | 0 | 0 | 0 |
| 334th | 2 | 14 | 63 | 1 | 3 | 3 |
| 335th | 4 | 10 | 75 | 0 | 1 | 2 |
| 336th | 13 | 2 | 54 | 0 | 1 | 7 |
| | 19 | 27 | 196 | 1 | 5 | 12 |

### Claims by Type

| | Air | | | Grd | |
|---|---|---|---|---|---|
| | Destroyed | Probable | Damaged | Destroyed | Damaged |
| Spitfire | 13 | 2 | 4 | 0 | 0 |
| P-47 | 127 | 18 | 56 | 0 | 0 |
| P-51 | 410 | 40 | 84 | 461.25 | 286.5 |

### Claims by Enemy Aircraft Type

| | Air | | | Grd | |
|---|---|---|---|---|---|
| | Destroyed | Probable | Damaged | Destroyed | Damaged |
| Me-109 | 263.5 | 28 | 56 | 27 | 23 |
| FW-190 | 214 | 24 | 77 | 60 | 17 |
| Me-110 | 32 | 1 | 10 | 17 | 16 |
| Me-262 | 6 | 2 | 4 | 12 | 34 |
| Ju-88 | 6 | 0 | 4 | 73.75 | 53 |
| He-111 | 5 | 1 | 0 | 9 | 5 |
| Me-410 | 5 | 0 | 1 | 26 | 9 |
| Fi-156 | 4 | 1 | 0 | 1 | 0 |
| Do-217 | 3.5 | 1 | 1 | 26 | 8 |
| Me-210 | 3 | 1 | 1 | 4 | 2 |
| FW-200 | 3 | 0 | 0 | 1.5 | 2 |
| Me-163 | 2 | 0 | 0 | 0 | 0 |
| Ju-52 | 1 | 1 | 0 | 57 | 26 |
| u/i a/c | 1 | 0 | 0 | 70 | 65.5 |
| Bu-131 | 1 | 0 | 0 | 10 | 0 |
| He-177 | 0 | 0 | 0 | 25 | 5 |
| Me-108 | 0 | 0 | 0 | 11 | 0 |
| Ju-87 | 0 | 0 | 0 | 9 | 5 |
| Hs-123 | 0 | 0 | 0 | 9 | 0 |
| Do-24 | 0 | 0 | 0 | 3 | 1 |
| Hs-126 | 0 | 0 | 0 | 3 | 0 |
| Ar-196 | 0 | 0 | 0 | 2 | 2 |
| Si-204 | 0 | 0 | 0 | 2 | 0 |
| Do-18 | 0 | 0 | 0 | 1 | 11 |
| He-115 | 0 | 0 | 0 | 1 | 0 |
| C-47 | 0 | 0 | 0 | 1 | 0 |
| Me-323 | 0 | 0 | 0 | 0 | 1 |
| Ju-188 | 0 | 0 | 0 | 0 | 1 |

### 4th Fighter Group Squadron Commanders

**334th Ftr Sqn**

| | |
|---|---|
| Maj. Gregory A. Daymond | September 29, 1942-March 3, 1943 |
| Maj. Oscar H. Coen | March 3, 1943-April 13, 1943 |
| Maj. Thomas J. Andrews | April 13, 1943-May 19, 1943 |
| LtCol. John F. Malone | May 19, 1943-August 4, 1943 |

| | |
|---|---|
| LtCol. Oscar H. Coen | August 4, 1943-October 26, 1943 |
| LtCol. James A. Clark | October 26, 1943-March 15, 1944 |
| Capt. Duane W. Beeson | March 15, 1944-April 5, 1944 |
| Capt. Raymond C. Care | April 5, 1944-April 15, 1944 |
| Maj. Winslow M. Sobanski | April 15, 1944-June 6, 1944 |
| Maj. Howard D. Hively | June 6, 1944-July 29, 1944 |
| Maj. Gerald Brown | July 29, 1944-November 1, 1944 |
| Maj. Howard D. Hively | November 1, 1944-January 25, 1945 |
| Maj. Louis H. Norley | January 25, 1945-September 21, 1945 |

**335th Ftr Sqn**

| | |
|---|---|
| Maj. William J. Daley | September 29, 1942-November 22, 1942 |
| Maj. Donald J.M. Blakeslee | November 22, 1942-May 19, 1943 |
| Maj. Gilbert O. Halsey | May 19, 1943-August 13, 1943 |
| Maj. Roy W. Evans | August 13, 1943-February 5, 1944 |
| Maj. George Carpenter | February 5, 1944-April 18, 1944 |
| Maj. James R. Happel | April 18, 1944-June 21, 1944 |
| Maj. Leon M. Blanding | June 21, 1944-July 29, 1944 |
| Capt. Robert C. Church | July 29, 1944-August 18, 1944 |
| Capt. Pierce W. McKennon | August 18, 1944-August 28, 1944 |
| Maj. Louis H. Norley | August 28, 1944-September 22, 1944 |
| Maj. Pierce W. McKennon | September 22, 1944-September 21, 1945 |

**336th Ftr Sqn**

| | |
|---|---|
| Maj. Carroll W. McColpin | September 29, 1942-November 28, 1942 |
| Maj. Oscar H. Coen | November 28, 1942-March 3, 1943 |
| Maj. John G. DuFour | March 4, 1943-September 1, 1943 |
| Maj. Carl H. Miley | September 1, 1943-October 10, 1943 |
| Maj. Leroy Gover | October 10, 1943-November 29, 1943 |
| LtCol. Seldon R. Edner | November 29, 1943-January 1, 1944 |
| Maj. Gilbert O. Halsey | January 1, 1944-March 8, 1944 |
| Maj. James A. Goodson | March 8, 1944-April 13, 1944 |
| Capt. Willard W. Millikan | April 13, 1944-May 10, 1944 |
| Maj. James A. Goodson | May 10, 1944-June 20, 1944 |
| Maj. Wilson V. Edwards | June 21, 1944-July 5, 1944 |
| Maj. John D. McFarlane | July 5, 1944-August 24, 1944 |
| Maj. Fred W. Glover | August 24, 1944-June 2, 1945 |

**4th Fighter Group Aces**

| Name | Air | Grd | Total | Sqn |
|---|---|---|---|---|
| Maj. John T. Godfrey | 16.33 | 13.67 | 30 | 336th |
| Maj. James A. Goodson | 14 | 15 | 29 | 336th |
| Lt. Ralph K. Hofer | 15 | 13.4 | 28.5 | 334th |
| Capt. Don S. Gentile | 21.83 | 6 | 27.83[*] | 336th |
| Maj. Fred W. Glover | 10.33 | 14.5 | 24.83 | 336th |
| Capt. Duane W. Beeson | 17.33 | 4.75 | 22.08 | 334th |
| Maj. Pierce W. McKennon | 11 | 6.67 | 17.67 | 335th |
| Maj. Gerald E. Montgomery | 3 | 14.5 | 17.5 | 334th |
| Col. Donald J.M. Blakeslee | 14.5 | 1.5 | 16[**] | 335th |
| | | | | HdQts |
| Maj. George Carpenter | 13.83 | 2 | 15.83 | 335th |
| Capt. Nicholas Megura | 11.83 | 3.75 | 15.58 | 334th |
| Capt. Charles F. Anderson | 10 | 5.5 | 15.5 | 335th |
| Maj. Louis H. Norley | 10.33 | 5 | 15.33 | 334th |
| | | | | 335th |
| | | | | 336th |
| LtCol. James A. Clark, Jr. | 10.5 | 4.5 | 15 | 334th |
| | | | | HdQts |
| Capt. Willard W. Millikan | 13 | 2 | 15 | 336th |
| Maj. Howard D. Hively | 12 | 2.5 | 14.5 | 334th |
| Capt. Albert L. Schlegel | 8.5 | 5 | 13.5 | 335th |
| Capt. Joseph L. Lang | 7.83 | 4 | 11.83 | 334th |
| Lt. Hipolitus T. Biel | 5.33 | 6 | 11.33 | 334th |
| Capt. Frank C. Jones | 5 | 5.5 | 10.5 | 335th |
| Capt. Donald M. Malmsten | 1.5 | 9 | 10.5 | 334th |
| Capt. Kendall E. Carlson | 6 | 4 | 10 | 336th |
| Capt. Ted E. Lines | 10 | 0 | 10 | 335th |
| LtCol. Sidney S. Woods | 7 | 3 | 10[***] | HdQts |
| Lt. Paul S. Riley | 6.5 | 3 | 9.5 | 335th |
| Lt. Van E. Chandler | 5 | 4 | 9 | 336th |
| Maj. Shelton W. Monroe | 4.33 | 4.5 | 8.83 | 334th |
| | | | | 335th |
| | | | | HdQts |
| Maj. James R. Happel | 4 | 4.67 | 8.67 | 335th |
| Capt. Victor J. France | 4.33 | 4.33 | 8.66 | 334th |
| Capt. Joseph H. Bennett | 8.5 | 0 | 8.5[@] | 336th |
| Capt. David W. Howe | 6 | 2.5 | 8.5 | 334th |
| Capt. Bernard L. McGrattan | 8.5 | 0 | 8.5 | 335th |
| Capt. Carl R. Alfred | 0 | 8 | 8 | 336th |
| Lt. James W. Ayers | 1 | 7 | 8 | 334th |
| Lt. Grover C. Siems, Jr. | 4.33 | 3.5 | 7.83 | 334th |
| Lt. Vermont Garrison | 7.33 | 0.25 | 7.58 | 336th |
| Capt. Joseph H. Joiner | 3.5 | 4 | 7.5 | 336th |
| Capt. William B. Smith | 3 | 4.25 | 7.25 | 334th |
| Lt. William O. Antonides | 0 | 7 | 7 | 334th |
| Capt. Donald R. Emerson | 4.5 | 2.5 | 7 | 336th |
| LtCol. Chesley G. Peterson | 7 | 0 | 7[@@] | HdQts |
| Capt. Raymond C. Care | 6 | 0.5 | 6.5 | 334th |
| Lt. Arthur R. Bowers | 0 | 6 | 6 | 334th |
| LtCol. Roy W. Evans | 6 | 0 | 6[@@@] | 335th |
| Lt. Loton D. Jennings | 0 | 6 | 6 | 335th |
| Maj. Henry L. Mills | 6 | 0 | 6 | 334th |
| Lt. Robert F. Nelson | 1 | 5 | 6 | 336th |
| F/O Douglas P. Pederson | 0 | 6 | 6 | 336th |
| Lt. Frank E. Speer | 1 | 5 | 6 | 334th |
| Capt. Thomas R. Bell | 0 | 5.5 | 5.5 | 334th |
| Capt. Archie W. Chatterly | 4.5 | 1 | 5.5 | 334th |
| Lt. Gilbert L. Kesler | 0.5 | 5 | 5.5 | 336th |
| Capt. Carl G. Payne | 2 | 3.5 | 5.5 | 334th |
| Lt. Clemmons A. Fiedler | 4.33 | 1 | 5.33 | 335th |
| F/O Donald P. Baugh | 0 | 5 | 5 | 336th |
| Lt. Gordon A. Denson | 0 | 5 | 5 | 334th |
| Capt. Melvin N. Dickey | 0 | 5 | 5 | 336th |
| Capt. Harry N. Hagen | 2 | 3 | 5 | 336th |
| Lt. Kenneth G. Helfrecht | 0 | 5 | 5 | 334th |
| Capt. Robert D. Hobert | 2 | 3 | 5 | 336th |
| Capt. Jack D. McFadden | 0 | 5 | 5 | 334th |
| Capt. Spiros N. Pissanos | 5 | 0 | 5 | 334th |
| Capt. Kenneth G. Smith | 5 | 0 | 5 | 335th |
| Col. Claiborne H. Kinnard | 8 | 17 | 25[#] | HdQts |
| Col. Everett W. Stewart | 7.83 | 1.5 | 9.33[##] | HdQts |
| Lt. William E. Whalen | 6 | 2 | 8[###] | 334th |
| LtCol. Jack J. Oberhansly | 6 | 1.6 | 7.6[&] | HdQts |
| Maj. Gerald Brown | 5 | 0 | 5[&&] | 334th |

[*] - includes 2 air victories with the RAF
[**] - includes 3 air victories with the RAF
[***] - includes 2 air victories with the 49th Ftr Grp, PTO, and 1 ground victory with the 479th Ftr Grp, ETO
[@] - includes 5 air victories with the 56th Ftr Grp, ETO
[@@] - includes 6 air victories with the RAF
[@@@] - includes 1 air victory with the 359th Ftr Grp, ETO
[#] - includes 7 air and 14 ground victories with the 355th Ftr Grp, ETO
[##] - all victories with the 352nd & 355th Ftr Grps, ETO
[###] - in cludes 5 air and 2 ground victries with the 2nd Scout Force, ETO
[&] - all victories with the 78th Ftr Grp, ETO
[&&] - all victories with the 55th Ftr Grp, ETO

**4th Fighter Group Scorers**

**HdQts**

| | Air | Grd | |
|---|---|---|---|
| R.A. Ackerly | 0-0-0 | 1-0 | |
| E.W. Anderson | 2-0-0 | 0-0 | |
| D.J.M. Blakeslee | 9.5-0-3 | 1.5-6 | plus 335th Ftr Sqn & 3-3-7 air w/RAF |
| J.A. Clark, Jr. | 5-0-0 | 4.5-0 | plus 334th Ftr Sqn |
| C.H. Kinnard, Jr. | 1-0-0 | 3-0 | plus 7-0-1 air & 14-4 grd w/355th Ftr Grp |
| C.G. Peterson | 1-1-1 | 0-0 | plus 6-3-6 air w/RAF |
| E.W. Stewart | 0-0-1 | 0-0 | plus 7.83-1-3 air & 1.5-6 grd w/352nd and 355th Ftr Grps |
| S.S. Woods | 5-0-0 | 2-5 | plus 2 air w/49th Ftr Grp, PTO & 1-0 grd w/479th Ftr Grp |

**334th Ftr Sqn**

| | | | |
|---|---|---|---|
| S.M. Anderson | 3-0.5-0 | 0-0 | |
| T.J. Andrews | 1-0-0 | 0-0 | |
| W.O. Antonides | 0-0-2 | 7-1 | |
| M.W. Arthur | 0-0-0 | 1.5-0 | |
| J.W. Ayers | 1-0-0 | 7-0 | |
| J.L. Barden | 0-0-0 | 0.5-0 | |
| D.W. Beeson | 17.33-1-3 | 4.75-5.25 | |
| T.R. Bell | 0-0-0 | 5.5-0 | |
| H.T. Biel | 5.33-0-2 | 6-5.25 | |
| H.J. Blanchfield | 0-0-0 | 4.33-2 | |
| R.A. Boock | 3-0.5-0 | 0-0 | |
| A.R. Bowers | 0-0-0 | 6-3 | |
| C.F. Brown | 1-0-0 | 2.5-1 | |
| R.H. Buchanan | 1-0-0 | 2-3 | |
| A.F. Bunte | 3-0-2 | 0-0 | |
| P.E. Burnett | 0-0-0 | 1-0 | |
| P.M. Burney | 0-0-0 | 1-0 | |
| R.C. Care | 6-1-0 | 0.5-0 | |
| C.D. Carr | 0-0-0 | 1-3.25 | |
| A.W. Chatterly | 4.5-1-0 | 1-3 | |
| J.A. Clark, Jr. | 5.5-0-2 | 0-0 | plus HdQts |
| R.P. Claus | 0-0-0 | 0-1 | |
| H.E. Clifton, Jr. | 1-0-1 | 3-2 | |
| T.J. Cronin | 1.5-0-0 | 0-0 | |
| A.C. Cwiklinski | 2.5-0-2 | 0-0 | |
| G.A. Denson | 0-0-0 | 5-3 | |
| R.A. Dickmeyer | 2.5-0-1 | 0-0 | |
| W.J. Dvorak | 0-0-0 | 1-3 | |
| R.A. Dyer | 1-0-0 | 3-7 | |
| F.E. Farington | 1-0-0 | 0-0 | |
| J.P. Fernandez | 0.5-0-0 | 0-1 | |
| K.E. Foster | 0-0-0 | 0-1 | |

| | | | |
|---|---|---|---|
| V.J. France | 4.33-0-1 | 4.33-3 | |
| T.E. Fraser | 1-0-0 | 0-3 | |
| R.B. Frazer | 0-1-1 | 0-0 | |
| L.C. Garvin | 0-0-0 | 1-0 | |
| W.G. Gillette | 3-1-2 | 1.5-1 | |
| P.B. Hardy | 2-1-3 | 0-0 | |
| C.W. Harre | 0-0-1 | 4-6 | |
| W.F. Hedrick | 1-0-1 | 0-0 | |
| A.C. Hewatt | 0.5-0-0 | 0-0 | |
| R.L. Hills | 1-0-0 | 2-1 | |
| H.D. Hively | 12-1-1 | 2.5-2 | |
| W.B. Hoelscher | 2.5-1-1 | 1-1 | |
| R.K. Hofer | 15-0-2 | 13.5-0 | |
| D.W. Howe | 6-0-0 | 2.5-1.5 | |
| J.E. Jahnke | 1-0-0 | 0.5-0 | |
| T.E. Joyce | 2.5-0-0 | 0-0.5 | |
| R.H. Kanaga | 0-1-0 | 0-0 | |
| M.J. Kennedy | 0.5-0-0 | 1.5-2 | |
| R.P. Kenyon | 2-0-0 | 1-2 | |
| M.H. Kolter | 1-1-0 | 1-2.5 | |
| A.C. Lacy | 0-0-1 | 0-0 | |
| J.L. Lang | 7.83-0-1 | 4-4.5 | |
| D.B. Leaf | 0-0-1 | 0-0 | |
| D.G. Lowther | 0-0-0 | 2-1 | |
| D.M. Malmsten | 1.5-0-0 | 9-2.5 | |
| A.H. Markel | 1-0-1 | 0.5-2 | |
| J.D. McFadden | 2-0-1 | 3-2 | |
| N. Megura | 11.83-0-6 | 3.75-3 | |
| R.J. Miller | 0-0-0 | 1-0 | |
| H.L. Mills | 6-2-1 | 0-0 | |
| S.W. Monroe | 4.33-0-1 | 4.5-1.5 | |
| G.E. Montgomery | 3-0-0 | 14.5-5 | |
| W.B. Morgan | 0-0-1 | 0-0 | |
| H.N. Moulton | 2-0-1 | 0-0 | |
| L.H. Norley | 1-0-0 | 4-0 | plus 335th & 336th Ftr Sqns |
| W.C. O'Bryan | 0.5-0-0 | 3-0 | |
| W.T. O'Regan | 1-1-0 | 0-0 | |
| C.G. Payne | 2-0-0 | 3.5-1 | |
| L.R. Pierce | 1.5-0-1 | 1.33-1 | |
| S.N. Pissanos | 5-0-1 | 0-0 | |
| A. Rafalovich | 2.5-0-1 | 0.5-0 | |
| V.R.T. Rentschler | 2-0-1 | 0-0 | |
| M.R. Savage | 0-0-1 | 0-0 | |
| J.J. Scally | 1-0-0 | 0-0 | |
| J.F. Scott | 2.5-0-0 | 0-1 | |
| A.J. Senecal | 1.5-0-0 | 0-2 | |
| T.S. Sharp | 0-0-1 | 2-1 | |
| G.C. Siems, Jr. | 4.33-0-0 | 3.5-3 | |
| J.T. Simon | 0.5-0-0 | 0-0 | |
| C.D. Smith | 2-0-0 | 0-0 | |
| W.B. Smith | 3-0-2 | 4.5-0 | |
| O.C. Snell | 1-0-0 | 0-0 | |
| W.M. Sobanski | 2.83-1-4 | 1-3 | |
| F.E. Speer | 1-0-0 | 5-0 | |
| M.L. Spencer | 0-0-0 | 0.5-0 | |
| W.G. Spencer | 0-0-0 | 3-0 | |
| E.J. Steppe | 0-0-0 | 0-1 | |
| D.A. Van Epps | 0.5-0-3 | 0.5-1 | |
| R.S. Voyles | 0-0-0 | 0.5-0 | |
| E.C. Walsh | 0-1-2 | 0-0 | |
| L.F. Wells | 0-0-0 | 1-0 | |
| L.R. Werner | 2-0-2 | 0-0 | |
| E.D. Whalen | 3.5-0-0 | 0-0 | |
| W.E. Whalen | 1-0-0 | 0-0 | plus 5-1-0 air & 2-3 grd w/2nd SF |
| V.H. Wynn | 2.5-0-0 | 2-0 | |

**335th Ftr Sqn**

| | | | |
|---|---|---|---|
| C.F. Anderson | 10-0.5-2 | 5.5-2 | |
| R.J. Anderson | 0-0-1 | 0-0 | |
| W.C. Anderson | 0-0-0 | 1-1 | plus 1-0 grd w/479th Ftr Grp |
| G.W. Barnes | 0-0-1 | 0-0 | |
| E.D. Beatie | 2-1-0 | 0-0 | |
| D.J.M. Blakeslee | 2-0-0 | 0-0 | |
| L.M. Blanding | 1-0-3 | 0-0 | |
| F.R. Boyles | 2-0-0 | 0-0 | |
| J.H. Brandenburg | 0.5-0-0 | 0-0 | |
| C.L. Brock | 1-0-0 | 0-0 | |
| O.B. Bucher, Jr. | 0-0-0 | 3-1 | |
| R.C. Bucholz | 0-0-0 | 3-1 | |
| L.I. Burgess | 0-0-0 | 1-2 | |
| G. Carpenter | 13.83-1-8 | 2-3 | |
| G.W. Ceglarski | 0-0-0 | 2-1 | plus 1-0-0 air w/2nd SF |
| R.C. Church | 2-0-0 | 0-1 | |
| R.P. Clotfelter | 2-0-1 | 0-0 | |
| S.W. Connors | 0-0-0 | 0-2 | |
| G.W. Cooley | 3-0-1 | 0-0 | |
| R.L. Couse | 0-0-0 | 2-3 | |
| J.N. Creamer | 0.5-0-0 | 0-0 | |
| W.J. Daley | 0-0-1 | 0-0 | plus 8 air w/RAF |
| A.J. Davis | 3-0-0 | 0-0 | |
| B. Diamond, Jr. | 1-0-0 | 3-0 | |
| J.D. Dye | 3-1-0 | 0-0 | |
| W.B. Eaton | 0-0-0 | 2-1 | |
| T.H. Elffner | 0-0-0 | 2-0 | |
| P.M. Ellington | 2-0-0 | 0-0 | |
| R.W. Evans | 5-0-1 | 0-0 | plus 1-0-1 air w/359th Ftr Grp |
| G.B. Fetrow | 1-1-1 | 0-0 | |
| C.A. Fiedler | 4.33-0-2 | 1-3 | |
| F.M. Fink | 1-0-0 | 0-0 | |
| J.C. Fitch | 0.5-0-0 | 1-0 | |
| E.P. Freeburger | 0.5-0-0 | 0-0 | |
| L.W. Freeman | 0-0-0 | 0-1 | |
| W.H. George | 0-0-0 | 0-2 | |
| J. Goetz | 0.5-0-0.5 | 0-0 | |
| J.W. Goodwyn | 1.5-1-1 | 0.5-2 | |
| G.D. Green | 0-1-0 | 4-1 | |
| C.B. Greenlease | 0-0-0 | 1-5 | |
| J.E. Halligan, Jr. | 0-0-0 | 4-5 | |
| G.O. Halsey | 0-0-1 | 0-0 | |
| J.R. Happel | 4-1-1.5 | 4.67-0 | |
| W.C. Hawkins | 1-0-0 | 0-0 | |
| R.C. Hawley | 0-0-0 | 0-2 | |
| M.D. Heaton | 0-0-0 | 2-0 | |
| K.G. Helfrecht | 0-0-0 | 5-2 | |
| W.D. Henderson | 0-0-0 | 0-4 | |
| R.H. Homuth | 1-0-0 | 0-0 | |
| R.C. Hunter, Jr. | 0-0-0 | 4-2 | |
| F.E. Hupe | 0-0-1 | 0-0 | |
| P.S. Iden | 1-0-0 | 0-0 | |
| L.D. Jennings, Jr. | 0-0-0 | 6-1 | |
| F.C. Jones | 5-1-3 | 5.5-3 | |
| E. Jungling | 0-0-1 | 0-1 | |
| J.E. Kolbe | 2-0-0 | 1-0 | |
| H.A. Lee | 0-0-0 | 1-0 | |
| R.E. Lewis | 0.5-0-0 | 0-0 | |
| T.E. Lines | 10-0-0 | 0-0 | |
| P.J. Lucas, Jr. | 0-0-0 | 0-2 | |
| C.E. Manning | 2-1-1 | 0-0 | |
| E.N. McCall | 0.5-0-0 | 0-2 | |
| B.L. McGrattan | 8.5-0-0 | 0-0 | |
| P.W. McKennon | 11-0-2.5 | 6.67-6 | |
| E.J. McLoughlin | 0-0-0 | 0-1 | |
| E.R. Mead | 0-1-0 | 0-0 | |
| H.B. Miller | 0-0-0 | 2-2 | |
| R.A. Moe | 0-0-0 | 0-2 | |
| W.E. Newell | 0-1-0 | 0-0 | |
| L.H. Norley | 2-0-0 | 0-0 | plus 334th & 336th Ftr Sqns |
| W.J. O'Donnell | 1-0-0 | 3-2 | |
| C.V. Padgett | 2-0-0 | 0-0 | |
| D.D. Perkins | 1-0-0 | 0-0 | |
| J.N. Peters | 0-1-0 | 0-0 | |
| C.E. Poage, Jr. | 0-2-0 | 3-0 | |
| L.M. Read | 1-0-0 | 1-0 | |
| R.I. Reed | 0.5-0-0 | 0-0 | |
| P.S. Riley | 6.5-2-2 | 3-0 | |
| R.J. Rinebolt | 1-0-0 | 0-0 | |
| D.H. Ross | 1-0-0 | 0-0 | plus 1-0-0 air w/357th Ftr Grp |
| J.W. Russell, Jr. | 2-2-0 | 1-1 | |
| R.W. Saunders | 1-0-0 | 1-2 | |
| J.J. Scanlon | 0-0-0 | 0-2 | |
| M.G. Scarbrough | 0-1-0 | 0-2 | |
| A.L. Schlegel | 8.5-2.5-1.5 | 5-3 | |
| Z.S. Sensibaugh | 0-0-0 | 0-1 | |
| E.H. Shapleigh | 1.5-0-0 | 0-0 | |
| F.D. Smith | 3-1-0 | 0-0 | |
| K.G. Smith | 5-0-1 | 0-0 | |
| F.J. Smolinsky | 1-0-0 | 0-0 | |
| R.L. Stallings | 1-0-0 | 0-1 | |
| G.I. Stanford, Jr. | 3-0-0 | 1-4 | |
| A.C. Stanhope | 3-0-3 | 0-0 | |
| J.F. Steele | 1-0-0 | 0-0 | |
| W.F. Underwood | 0-0-0 | 3-0 | |
| H.A. Ward | 0-1-0 | 0-0 | |
| L.W. Waterman | 1-0-1 | 0-0 | |
| C.W. Willruth | 1-0-0 | 0-0 | |
| B.C. Wyman | 0-0-1 | 0-0 | |
| D.A. Young | 2-0-4 | 0-0 | |

**336th Ftr Sqn**

| | | | |
|---|---|---|---|
| C.R. Alfred | 0-0-0 | 8-3 | |
| W.H. Ayer | 0-0-0 | 2-0 | |
| D.P. Baugh | 0-0-0 | 5-0 | |
| J.H. Bennett | 3-3-1 | 0-0 | plus 5.5-2-1 air w/56th & 356th Ftr Grps |
| B.O. Brooker | 0-0.5-0 | 2-5 | |
| K.E. Carlson | 6-0-3 | 4-2 | |
| L.A. Carpenter | 0-0-0 | 2-1 | |
| V.E. Chandler | 5-0-1 | 4-0 | |
| G.C. Chapman | 1-0-0 | 0-0 | |
| O.H. Coen | 2-0-0 | 0-0 | plus 2-1.5-3 air & 0-0.5 grd w/RAF & 356th Ftr Grp |

| | | | |
|---|---|---|---|
| W.W. Collins | 1-0-0 | 1-4 | |
| R.J. Corbett | 0-0-0 | 4-1 | |
| H.R. Crawford | 0-0-0 | 4-0 | |
| H.L. Davis | 0-0-0 | 1-0 | |
| M.L. Davis | 1-0-0 | 1-2 | |
| R.O. Davis | 1-0-0 | 1-0 | |
| M.N. Dickey | 0-0-0 | 5-0 | |
| J.G. DuFour | 1-0-1 | 0-0 | |
| H.E. Dugan, Jr. | 1-0-0 | 0-0 | |
| P.H. Dunn | 0-1-1 | 0-0 | |
| C.W. Dupree | 1-0-0 | 2-0 | |
| D.R. Emerson | 4.5-1-0 | 2.5-3 | |
| M.C. Franklin | 0-0-0 | 2-1 | |
| H.H. Fredericks | 0.5-1-1 | 3.5-2 | |
| V. Garrison | 7.33-1-3 | 0.25-0 | |
| D.S. Gentile | 19.83-0-3 | 6-0 | plus 2 air w/RAF |
| E.L. Gimbel | 0-0-0 | 1-2 | |
| O.M. Glass, Jr. | 1-0-0 | 2-2 | |
| F.W. Glover | 10.33-1-0 | 14.5-3 | |
| J.T. Godfrey | 16.33-2-4 | 13.67-10 | |
| J.A. Goodson | 14-1-1 | 15-0 | |
| L. Gover | 1-1-2 | 0-0 | |
| B.L. Griffin | 0-0-0 | 4-0 | |
| D.L. Groshong | 2-0-0 | 2-1 | |
| F.M. Grove | 1-0-0 | 1-5 | |
| H.N. Hagen | 2-0-0 | 3-0 | |
| F.S. Harris | 0-0-0 | 1.5-1 | |
| W.H. Hastings | 0-0-0 | 1-1 | |
| G.A. Herter | 2-0-1 | 0-0 | |
| J.A. Hileman | 0-1-1 | 1-0 | |
| R.D. Hobert | 2-0-0 | 3-2 | |
| R.E. Hughes | 0-1-1 | 0-1 | |
| G.W. Hunt | 1-0-0 | 0-0 | |
| E.F. Hustwit | 1.5-0-0 | 1-0 | |
| H.A. Ingalls | 0-0-0 | 1-0 | |
| M.E. Jackson | 1-0-0 | 0-0 | |
| W.E. Johnson | 0-0-0 | 2-1 | |
| J.H. Joiner | 3.5-0-0 | 4-1 | |
| H.A. Kaul | 0-0-0 | 1-1 | |
| G.L. Kesler | 0.5-0-0 | 5-0 | |
| O.F. LaJeunesse | 1-0-1 | 1-1 | |
| J.C. Lane | 1-0-1 | 0-0 | |
| G.H. Logan, Jr. | 1-0-0 | 0.5-0 | |
| J.A. Matthews | 2-0-0 | 0-0 | |
| T.A. McCord | 0-0-0 | 2-0 | |
| T.K. McDill | 2-0-1 | 0.5-0 | |
| J.D. McFarlane | 1-0-0 | 2-0 | |
| W.B. Meredith | 0-0-0 | 2-2 | |
| R.J. Messenger | 1-0-0 | 0-0 | |
| C.H. Miley | 1-1-2 | 0-0 | |
| M.W. Miller, Jr. | 0-0-0 | 1-0 | |
| W.W. Millikan | 13-0-0 | 2-1 | |
| G.E. Mirsch | 0-0-1 | 0-0 | |
| P.M. Morgan | 0-0.5-0 | 0-0 | |
| J.P. Murchake, Jr. | 0-0-0 | 2-1 | |
| R.F. Nelson | 1-0-0 | 5-6 | |
| C.J. Netting | 0.5-0-1 | 0-2 | |
| L.H. Norley | 7.33-0-0 | 1-0 | plus 334th & 335th Ftr Sqns |
| D.J. Patchen | 0-0-0 | 2.5-0 | |
| J.A. Patteeuw | 0-0-0 | 2-0 | |
| D.P. Pederson | 0-0-0 | 6-3 | |
| C.H. Peterson | 0-0-0 | 1-0 | |
| K.D. Peterson | 3-0-1 | 1-0 | |
| D.J. Pierni | 1-0-0 | 2-1 | |
| E.A. Quist | 0-1-0 | 0-0 | |
| J.L. Raphael | 0-0-1 | 0-0 | |
| R.H. Richards | 2-0-1 | 0-0 | |
| W.D. Riedel | 2-0-0 | 1-2 | |
| C.H. Shilke | 0-0-0 | 2.5-0 | |
| R. Simon | 2-0-0 | 2-0 | |
| G.C. Smith | 2-0-0 | 0-0 | |
| W.F. Sooman | 1-0-1 | 0-0 | |
| M.F. Stepp, Jr. | 0-0-1 | 0-0 | |
| R.S. Tussey | 1-1-0 | 1-2.25 | |
| N. Van Wyk | 0-0-0 | 0.5-4 | |
| A.O. Wallace | 0.5-0-0 | 1-0 | |
| P.L. Wiggin | 0-0-0 | 1-0 | |
| W.H. Williams | 0-0-0 | 1-0 | |
| F.W. Young | 2-0-0 | 0-0 | |

### 4th Fighter Group Scoring

**September 26, 1942**

| | | | |
|---|---|---|---|
| 336th: | Capt. M.E. Jackson | FW-190 dest(air) | Brest |

**October 2, 1942**

| | | | |
|---|---|---|---|
| HdQts: | Capt. O.H. Coen | FW-190 dest(air) | SW Dunkirk |
| | W/Cdr.R.Duke-Woolley | (.5)FW-190 dest(air) | SE Calais |
| 334th: | Lt. S.M. Anderson | FW-190 dest(air) | SW Dunkirk |
| | Lt. J.A. Clark | (.5)FW-190 dest(air) | SE Calais |
| | Lt. W.B. Morgan | FW-190 dam(air) | S/Nieuport |
| 335th: | Lt. G.B. Fetrow | FW-190 dest(air) | SW Dunkirk |
| | Maj. W.J. Daley | FW-190 dam(air) | E/Calais |

**November 19, 1942**

| | | | |
|---|---|---|---|
| 335th: | Lt. F.J. Smolinsky | FW-190 dest(air) | SW Flushing |

**November 20, 1942**

| | | | |
|---|---|---|---|
| 335th: | Lt. R.W. Evans | Fi-156 dest(air) | SE Furnes |

**December 6, 1942**

| | | | |
|---|---|---|---|
| 335th: | Lt. G.B. Fetrow | FW-190 prob(air) | NE Gis Nez |

**December 15, 1942**

| | | | |
|---|---|---|---|
| 334th: | Lt. S.M. Anderson | (.5)Ju-52 prob(air) | SW Flushing |
| | Lt. R.A. Boock | (.5)Ju-52 prob(air) | SW Flushing |

**January 14, 1943**

| | | | |
|---|---|---|---|
| 334th: | Lt. S.M. Anderson | FW-190 dest(air) | W/Ostend |
| | Lt. R.A. Boock | FW-190 dest(air) | W/Ostend |

**January 22, 1943**

| | | | |
|---|---|---|---|
| HdQts: | Maj. O.H. Coen | FW-190 dest(air) | W/Dunkirk |
| 334th: | Lt. S.M. Anderson | FW-190 dest(air) | W/Dunkirk |
| | Lt. R.A. Boock | FW-190 dest(air) | W/Dunkirk |
| 335th: | Lt. G.B. Fetrow | FW-190 dam(air) | W/Dunkirk |
| 336th: | Lt. J.A. Matthews | FW-190 dest(air) | Mardyk-Dunkirk |

**March 12, 1943**

| | | | |
|---|---|---|---|
| 336th: | Lt. D.S. Gentile | FW-190 dam(air) | Audruieq |

NOTE: From April 1943 on, claims will be in P-47's

**April 15, 1943**

| | | | |
|---|---|---|---|
| HdQts: | LtCol. C.G. Peterson | FW-190 dest(air) | W/Ostend |
| 334th: | Lt. R.A. Boock | FW-190 dest(air) | Belgian Coast |
| | Lt. J.A. Clark | FW-190 dam(air) | Belgian Coast |
| 335th: | Maj. D.J.M. Blakeslee | FW-190 dest(air) | Knocke |

**May 4, 1943**

| | | | |
|---|---|---|---|
| 335th: | Lt. G. Carpenter | FW-190 dam(air) | Walcheren |

**May 14, 1943**

| | | | |
|---|---|---|---|
| HdQts: | LtCol. C.G. Peterson | FW-190 prob(air) | W/St. Nicholas |
| | | FW-190 dam(air) | W/St. Nicholas |
| 335th: | Maj. D.J.M. Blakeslee | FW-190 dest(air) | N/Knocke |
| | Lt. A.C. Stanhope | FW-190 dam(air) | E/Flushing |
| 336th: | Capt. L. Gover | FW-190 prob(air) | S/St. Nicholas |
| | | (2)FW-190 dam(air) | S/St. Nicholas |
| | Capt. M.L. Stepp | FW-190 dam(air) | W/Antwerp |

**May 16, 1943**

| | | | |
|---|---|---|---|
| 335th: | Lt. E.D. Beatie | FW-190 prob(air) | Walcheren |
| | Capt. G.O. Halsey | FW-190 dam(air) | Flushing |
| | Lt. A.C. Stanhope | FW-190 dam(air) | Walcheren |

**May 18, 1943**

| | | | |
|---|---|---|---|
| 334th: | Capt. T.J. Andrews | Me-109 dest(air) | Blankenberghe-Knocke |
| | Lt. D.W. Beeson | Me-109 dest(air) | Blankenberghe-Knocke |

**May 21, 1943**

| | | | |
|---|---|---|---|
| 334th: | Lt. S.N. Pissanos | FW-190 dam(air) | Ghent |

**June 22, 1943**

| | | | |
|---|---|---|---|
| 335th: | Lt. E.D. Beatie | Me-109 dest(air) | Beveland-Walcheren |
| | | FW-190 dest(air) | Beveland-Walcheren |
| | Lt. F.D. Smith | FW-190 dest(air) | Beveland-Walcheren |
| 336th: | Lt. J.A. Goodson | FW-190 dest(air) | NW Hulst |

**June 26, 1943**

| | | | |
|---|---|---|---|
| 334th: | Lt. D.W. Beeson | Me-109 dest(air) | Dieppe |
| | Lt. R.C. Care | Me-109 dest(air) | Dieppe |
| | Lt. D.B. Leaf | Me-109 dam(air) | Dieppe |

**July 14, 1943**

| | | | |
|---|---|---|---|
| 335th: | Capt. D.A. Young | FW-190 dam(air) | Amiens |

**July 26, 1943**

| | | | |
|---|---|---|---|
| 334th: | Lt. H.L. Mills | FW-190 prob(air) | Brielle-Rotterdam |

**July 28, 1943**

| | | | |
|---|---|---|---|
| HdQts: | Col. E.W. Anderson | (2)Me-109 dest(air) | E/Rotterdam |
| 334th: | Lt. D.W. Beeson | Me-109 dest(air) | SE Utrecht |
| | | FW-190 dam(air) | SE Utrecht |
| | Lt. R.C. Care | FW-190 dest(air) | E/Rotterdam |
| | Lt. H.L. Mills | FW-190 dam(air) | E/Rotterdam |
| 335th: | Capt. R.W. Evans | Me-109 dest(air) | W/Arnheim |
| | | FW-190 dam(air) | W/Arnheim |
| | Lt. L.M. Blanding | FW-190 dest(air) | SE Utrecht |

| | | | |
|---|---|---|---|
| | | FW-190 dam(air) | SE Utrecht |
| | Lt. F.R. Boyles | FW-190 dest(air) | SE Utrecht |
| | Capt. G. Carpenter | FW-190 dam(air) | SE Utrecht |
| 336th: | Capt. L. Gover | FW-190 dest(air) | E/Rotterdam |
| | Capt. C.H. Miley | Me-109 dest(air) | E/Rotterdam |
| | | FW-190 prob(air) | E/Rotterdam |
| | Lt. G.E. Mirsch | FW-190 dam(air) | E/Rotterdam |

**July 30, 1943**

| | | | |
|---|---|---|---|
| 335th: | Capt. D.A. Young | FW-190 dest(air) | SE Rotterdam |
| | | FW-190 dam(air) | SE Rotterdam |
| | Lt. F.R. Boyles | FW-190 dest(air) | Zaltboemel |
| | Lt. P.W. McKennon | FW-190 dest(air) | Zaltboemel |
| | Lt. A.C. Stanhope | FW-190 dest(air) | SE Arnheim |
| | | FW-190 dam(air) | SE Arnheim |
| | Lt. K.G. Smith | FW-190 dest(air) | Schouwen |

**August 12, 1943**

| | | | |
|---|---|---|---|
| 334th: | Capt. J.A. Clark | FW-190 dest(air) | Sittard |
| | Capt. W.T. O'Regan | Me-109 dest(air) | E/Sittard |
| | | Me-109 prob(air) | E/Sittard |
| | Lt. S.N. Pissanos | Me-109 dest(air) | W/Walcheren |
| 335th: | Lt. C.V. Padgett | Me-109 dest(air) | W/Duren |

**August 16, 1943**

| | | | |
|---|---|---|---|
| 334th: | Capt. J.A. Clark | (2)FW-190 dest(air) | N/Paris |
| | Lt. H.L. Mills | (2)FW-190 dest(air) | NW Paris |
| | F/O C.D. Smith | (2)FW-190 dest(air) | SE Paris |
| | Lt. R.C. Care | FW-190 dest(air) | N/Paris |
| | | FW-190 prob(air) | N/Paris |
| | Lt. H.D. Hively | FW-190 dest(air) | NW Paris |
| 335th: | Capt. F.D. Smith | FW-190 dest(air) | SE Paris |
| | Capt. D.A. Young | FW-190 dest(air) | Paris |
| | | (2)FW-190 dam(air) | Paris |
| | Capt. R.W. Evans | Me-109 dest(air) | S/Paris |
| | Lt. F.M. Fink | FW-190 dest(air) | NW Paris |
| | Lt. J.R. Happel | FW-190 dest(air) | Paris |
| | Lt. A.C. Stanhope | Me-109 dest(air) | Melun-Paris |
| 336th: | Lt. J.A. Goodson | (2)FW-190 dest(air) | Paris |
| | | FW-190 dam(air) | Paris |
| | Maj. J.G. DuFour | Me-109 dest(air) | N/Paris |
| | | Me-109 dam(air) | N/Paris |
| | Lt. J.G. Matthews | FW-190 dest(air) | St. Denis-L'Isle Adam |
| | Lt. K.E. Carlson | FW-190 dam(air) | Paris |
| | Lt. D.S. Gentile | Me-109 dam(air) | Paris |

**August 31, 1943**

| | | | |
|---|---|---|---|
| 335th: | Lt. A.C. Stanhope | FW-190 dam(air) | Glisy-Montdidier |
| 336th: | Capt. C.H. Miley | (2)FW-190 dam(air) | N/Paris |

**September 3, 1943**

| | | | |
|---|---|---|---|
| 336th: | Lt. J.A. Goodson | FW-190 prob(air) | Paris |

**September 6, 1943**

| | | | |
|---|---|---|---|
| 335th: | Maj. R.W. Evans | FW-190 dest(air) | N/Chateau Thierry |

**September 9, 1943**

| | | | |
|---|---|---|---|
| 334th: | Capt. J.A. Clark | FW-190 dam(air) | NE Paris |

**September 15, 1943**

| | | | |
|---|---|---|---|
| 334th: | Lt. W.M. Sobanski | FW-190 dam(air) | SW Paris |

**September 27, 1943**

| | | | |
|---|---|---|---|
| 336th: | Lt. W.W. Millikan | FW-190 dest(air) | Potten |

**October 2, 1943**

| | | | |
|---|---|---|---|
| 334th: | Lt. D.W. Beeson | FW-190 dest(air) | E/Wilhelmshaven |
| 335th: | F/O A.L. Schlegel | Me-109 dest(air) | SE Emden |
| | | Me-109 dam(air) | SE Emden |

**October 8, 1943**

| | | | |
|---|---|---|---|
| 334th: | Lt. D.W. Beeson | (2)Me-109 dest(air) | Meppel-Zwolle |
| | | Me-109 dam(air) | Meppel-Zwolle |
| | Maj. J.A. Clark | Me-109 dest(air) | Meppel-Zwolle |
| | F/O R.K. Hofer | Me-109 dest(air) | NE Amsterdam |
| | Lt. H.L. Mills | Me-109 prob(air) | Meppel-Zwolle |
| | Lt. R.B. Fraser | Me-109 dam(air) | Meppel-Zwolle |
| 335th: | Maj. R.W. Evans | Me-109 dest(air) | SW Oldenburg |
| | Lt. D.H. Ross | Me-210 dest(air) | Edewecht |

**October 10, 1943**

| | | | |
|---|---|---|---|
| 334th: | Lt. D.W. Beeson | FW-190 dam(air) | Arnheim |

**November 3, 1943**

| | | | |
|---|---|---|---|
| 334th: | Lt. A. Rafalovich | Me-109 dest(air) | NE Zuider Zee |
| | Lt. R.B. Fraser | Me-109 prob(air) | Lemmer |

**November 5, 1943**

| | | | |
|---|---|---|---|
| 335th: | Capt. F.D. Smith | FW-190 dest(air) | E/Eindhoven |

**November 11, 1943**

| | | | |
|---|---|---|---|
| 336th: | F/O J.L. Raphael | FW-190 dam(air) | W/Hook of Holland |

**November 26, 1943**

| | | | |
|---|---|---|---|
| 335th: | Lt. C.V. Padgett | Me-109 dest(air) | Rude |

**November 29, 1943**

| | | | |
|---|---|---|---|
| 334th: | Lt. D.W. Beeson | Me-109 prob(air) | Bremen |
| 335th: | Capt. F.D. Smith | Me-109 prob(air) | Hude |
| 336th: | Lt. J.T. Godfrey | Me-109 prob(air) | Bremen |

**December 1, 1943**

| | | | |
|---|---|---|---|
| 335th: | Capt. G. Carpenter | Ju-88 dam(air) | E/Cologne |
| 336th: | Lt. J.T. Godfrey | Me-109 dest(air) | Ruhr Valley |
| | | Me-109 dam(air) | Ruhr Valley |

**December 11, 1943**

| | | | |
|---|---|---|---|
| 334th: | Lt. V.J. France | Me-109 dest(air) | Leeuwarden |
| 335th: | Lt. P.W. McKennon | Me-109 dam(air) | Leeuwarden |
| | Lt. B.C. Wyman | Me-109 dam(air) | Leeuwarden |

**December 16, 1943**

| | | | |
|---|---|---|---|
| 336th: | Capt. D.S. Gentile | (.33)Ju-88 dest(air) | E/Zuider Zee |
| | Lt. V. Garrison | (.33)Ju-88 dest(air) | E/Zuider Zee |
| | Lt. L.H. Norley | (.33)Ju-88 dest(air) | E/Zuider Zee |

**December 20, 1943**

| | | | |
|---|---|---|---|
| HdQts: | LtCol. D.J.M. Blakeslee | Me-110 dest(air) | Bremen-Wilhelmshaven |
| | (claimed while "breaking-in" the 354th Ftr Grp, a P-51 unit of the 9th Air Force) | | |
| 336th: | Lt. W.W. Millikan | Me-109 dest(air) | NW Bremen |

**December 22, 1943**

| | | | |
|---|---|---|---|
| 334th: | Lt. V.H. Wynn | (1.5)Me-109 dest(air) | Enschede |
| 336th: | Lt. J.T. Godfrey | (1.5)Me-109 dest(air) | Enschede |

**January 5, 1944**

| | | | |
|---|---|---|---|
| 336th: | Capt. D.S. Gentile | FW-190 dest(air) | W/Tours |
| | Lt. R.J. Messenger | FW-190 dest(air) | Tours |

**January 7, 1944**

| | | | |
|---|---|---|---|
| HdQts: | LtCol. D.J.M. Blakeslee | FW-190 dest(air) | Hosdin |
| 336th: | Capt. J.A. Goodson | (2)FW-190 dest(air) | Bethune |
| | Lt. V. Garrison | FW-190 dam(air) | La Chateau |

**January 14, 1944**

| | | | |
|---|---|---|---|
| 334th: | Lt. E.D. Whalen | (1.5)FW-190 dest(air) | Soissons |
| | Lt. D.W. Beeson | FW-190 dest(air) | Soissons |
| | Lt. H.T. Biel | FW-190 dest(air) | Cambrai |
| | Lt. G.E. Montgomery | FW-190 dest(air) | Soissons |
| | Lt. A. Rafalovich | (.5)FW-190 dest(air) | Soissons |
| 336th: | Capt. D.S. Gentile | (2)FW-190 dest(air) | Compiegne |
| | Lt. V. Garrison | (2)FW-190 dest(air) | Compiegne |
| | F/O R.H. Richards | FW-190 dest(air) | Compiegne |

**January 21, 1944**

| | | | |
|---|---|---|---|
| 336th: | F/O R.H. Richards | FW-190 dest(air) | Valenciennes-Douai |
| | | FW-190 dam(air) | Valenciennes-Douai |
| | Lt. K.D. Peterson | FW-190 dam(air) | Douai |

**January 29, 1944**

| | | | |
|---|---|---|---|
| 334th: | Capt. H.L. Mills | (2)Me-109 dest(air) | Aachen |
| | Lt. D.W. Beeson | Me-109 dest(air) | Aachen |
| | | FW-190 dest(air) | Aachen |
| | Lt. S.N. Pissanos | (2)Me-109 dest(air) | Aachen |
| | Lt. A.W. Chatterly | Me-109 dest(air) | Aachen |
| | Lt. V.J. France | FW-190 dest(air) | Hasselt |
| | Lt. E.D. Whalen | Me-109 dest(air) | Aachen |

**January 30, 1944**

| | | | |
|---|---|---|---|
| 335th: | Lt. C.F. Anderson | Me-109 dest(air) | Lingen |
| | | Me-109 dam(air) | Lingen |
| | Capt. J.R. Happel | Me-109 prob(air) | Lingen |
| | Lt. E.R. Mead | Me-109 prob(air) | Gronau |

**January 31, 1944**

| | | | |
|---|---|---|---|
| 334th: | Lt. D.W. Beeson | Me-109 dest(air) | Gilze-Rijen |
| | Capt. W.M. Sobanski | (.5)Me-109 dest(air) | Gilze-Rijen |
| | Lt. H.N. Moulton | (.5)Me-109 dest(air) | Gilze-Rijen |
| 335th: | Lt. R.P. Clotfelter | Me-109 dest(air) | Zevenbergen |
| | Lt. P.M. Ellington | Me-109 dest(air) | Overflakkee |
| 336th: | Lt. K.E. Carlson | Me-109 dest(air) | Gilze-Rijen |
| | Lt. V. Garrison | Me-109 dest(air) | Gilze-Rijen |

**February 6, 1944**

| | | | |
|---|---|---|---|
| 334th: | F/O R.K. Hofer | Me-109 dest(air) | W/Paris |
| | Lt. V.J. France | Me-109 dam(air) | W/Paris |
| 335th: | Maj. G. Carpenter | FW-190 dam(air) | Versaille |
| 336th: | Lt. V. Garrison | FW-190 dest(air) | Beauvais-Marigny |
| | Lt. R.D. Hobert | FW-190 dest(air) | Beauvais-Marigny |

**February 10, 1944**

| | | | |
|---|---|---|---|
| 334th: | Lt. H.T. Biel | Me-109 dest(air) | Hengele |
| | | Me-109 dam(air) | Hengele |
| | Lt. V.J. France | FW-190 dest(air) | Lingen |
| | Lt. G.E. Montgomery | Me-109 dest(air) | Emmerich |
| 335th: | Lt. C.E. Manning | FW-190 dest(air) | SW Hanover |
| | | FW-190 dam(air) | SW Hanover |
| | Lt. C.F. Anderson | (.5)Me-109 prob(air) | SW Hanover |
| | Lt. A.L. Schlegel | (.5)Me-109 prob(air) | SW Hanover |
| 336th: | Lt. V. Garrison | Me-109 dest(air) | Dummer Lake |
| | Lt. W.W. Millikan | FW-190 dest(air) | N/Dummer Lake |
| | Lt. L.H. Norley | Me-109 dest(air) | Dummer Lake |

**February 20, 1944**

| | | | |
|---|---|---|---|
| 334th: | Capt. D.W. Beeson | FW-190 dest(air) | Aachen |
| | Capt. H.L. Mills | FW-190 dest(air) | Aachen |
| 335th: | Lt. P.M. Ellington | Me-110 dest(air) | Coblenz |
| | Lt. C.A. Fiedler | Me-110 dest(air) | Coblenz |
| | | Me-110 dam(air) | Coblenz |
| | Lt. P.W. McKennon | FW-190 dest(air) | Marburg |
| | Lt. R.I. Reed | (.5)Me-110 dest(air) | Coblenz |
| | Lt. P.S. Riley | (.5)Me-110 dest(air) | Coblenz |
| | Maj. G. Carpenter | Me-110 dam(air) | W/Coblenz |
| 336th: | Lt. V. Garrison | FW-190 dam(air) | Malmedy |

**February 21, 1944**

| | | | |
|---|---|---|---|
| 334th: | Capt. R.C. Care | FW-190 dest(air) | Dummer Lake |
| | Lt. D.W. Howe | FW-190 dest(air) | S/Dummer Lake |
| | Capt. W.M. Sobanski | FW-190 prob(air) | S/Dummer Lake |
| | Lt. A. Rafalovich | FW-190 dam(air) | Dummer Lake |
| 335th: | Lt. G.W. Barnes | Ju-88 dam(air) | Havern |
| | Lt. R.P. Clotfelter | Me-110 dam(air) | Havern |

**February 22, 1944**

| | | | |
|---|---|---|---|
| 335th: | Maj. G. Carpenter | FW-190 dest(air) | Erkelenz |
| | Lt. B.L. McGrattan | FW-190 dest(air) | Erkelenz |
| | Lt. P.W. McKennon | (.5)Me-109 dest(air) | SW Ooltgersplant |
| | | (.5)FW-190 dam(air) | Erkelenz |
| | F/O J. Goetz | (.5)Me-109 dest(air) | SW Ooltgersplant |
| | | (.5)FW-190 dam(air) | Erkelenz |

**February 24, 1944**

| | | | |
|---|---|---|---|
| 335th: | Lt. A.L. Schlegel | FW-190 prob(air) | NE Magdeburg |

**February 25, 1944**

| | | | |
|---|---|---|---|
| 334th: | Capt. D.W. Beeson | FW-190 dest(air) | Beckingen |
| 335th: | Lt. P.W. McKennon | FW-190 dest(air) | SE Luxembourg |
| 336th: | Capt. D.S. Gentile | FW-190 dest(air) | SE Luxembourg |
| | Lt. V. Garrison | FW-190 dest(air) | Luxembourg |
| | Lt. G.A. Herter | FW-190 dest(air) | SE Luxembourg |

NOTE: Starting on February 28, all claims will be with P-51s

**February 28, 1944**

| | | | |
|---|---|---|---|
| 334th: | Capt. D.W. Beeson | (.25)Ju-88 dest(grd) | All claims are |
| | Lt. N. Megura | (.25)Ju-88 dest(grd) | at Soissons |
| | Lt. W.B. Smith | (.25)Ju-88 dest(grd) | |
| 336th: | Lt. V. Garrison | (.25)Ju-88 dest(grd) | |

**March 2, 1944**

| | | | |
|---|---|---|---|
| 334th: | Lt. V.H. Wynn | Me-109 dest(air) | S/Coblenz |
| 336th: | Lt. G.A. Herter | FW-190 dest(air) | SW Coblenz |
| | | FW-190 dam(air) | SW Coblenz |
| | Lt. J.T. Godfrey | FW-190 dam(air) | SW Coblenz |

**March 3, 1944**

| | | | |
|---|---|---|---|
| 336th: | Capt. D.S. Gentile | (2)FW-190 dest(air) | Wittenburg |
| | | Do-217 dam(air) | Wittenburg |
| | Lt. V. Garrison | FW-190 dest(air) | NW Berlin |
| | | Me-110 prob(air) | NW Berlin |
| | | Me-110 dam(air) | NW Berlin |
| | Lt. K.E. Carlson | Me-110 dest(air) | E/Hanover |
| | Lt. W.W. Millikan | Me-110 dest(air) | Wittenburg |
| | Capt. P.H. Dunn | He-111 prob(air) | Bordeaux |
| | | Me-210 dam(air) | Wittenburg |

**March 4, 1944**

| | | | |
|---|---|---|---|
| 334th: | Lt. N. Megura | Me-109 dest(air) | NW Leipzig |
| 335th: | Lt. P.S. Riley | Me-109 prob(air) | NW Berlin |
| | Lt. H.A. Ward | Me-109 prob(air) | Berlin |
| 336th: | Lt. W.F. Sooman | Ju-52 dest(air) | Helmstedt |

**March 5, 1944**

| | | | |
|---|---|---|---|
| 334th: | Lt. H.D. Hively | (2)Me-109 dest(air) | Mont de Marson |
| | Lt. S.N. Pissanos | (2)Me-109 dest(air) | Bordeaux |
| | Capt. D.W. Beeson | Me-109 dest(air) | S/Bordeaux |
| | | (.5)FW-200 dest(grd) | Bordeaux |
| | | (shared with an unknown | P-51 pilot) |
| | | FW-200 dam(grd) | Bordeaux |
| | Lt. C.D. Carr | Ju-88 dam(grd) | Fontenet A/F |
| 335th: | Lt. J.D. Dye | FW-190 dest(air) | Redon |
| | Lt. J.F. Steele | FW-200 dest(air) | Bergerac A/F |
| | Capt. K.G. Smith | (.5)FW-200 dest(air) | Bergerac A/F |
| | Lt. E.P. Freeburger | (.5)FW-200 dest(air) | Bergerac A/F |
| | Capt. J.R. Happel | FW-190 dam(air) | E/Bordeaux |
| | Lt. P.S. Riley | Me-109 dam(air) | S/Bordeaux |
| 336th: | Capt. K.D. Peterson | FW-200 dest(air) | Bordeaux |
| | | FW-200 dest(grd) | Bordeaux |

**March 6, 1944**

| | | | |
|---|---|---|---|
| HdQts: | LtCol. D.J.M. Blakeslee | Me-210 dest(air) | Berlin |
| 334th: | Lt. N. Megura | (2)Me-110 dest(air) | SW Berlin |
| | | Me-110 dam(air) | SW Berlin |
| | Maj. H.L. Mills | FW-190 dest(air) | W/Brandenburg |
| | Lt. A.W. Chatterly | Me-110 dest(air) | W/Brandenburg |
| | | Me-210 prob(air) | W/Brandenburg |
| | | (2)u/i a/c dam(grd) | W/Brandenburg |
| | | Ju-88 dam(grd) | W/Brandenburg |
| | Lt. A. Rafalovich | Me-109 dest(air) | Brandenburg |
| | Lt. E.D. Whalen | Me-110 dest(air) | Nienburg |
| | Capt. D.A. Van Epps | (.5)Me-110 dest(air) | Nienburg |
| | | Me-110 dam(air) | Nienburg |
| | | FW-190 dam(air) | Nienburg |
| | | FW-190 dam(grd) | Nienburg |
| | Lt. H.N. Moulton | (.5)Me-110 dest(air) | Nienburg |
| | | FW-190 dam(air) | Nienburg |
| 335th: | Capt. C.E. Manning | Do-217 dest(air) | SE Brandenburg |
| | | Do-217 prob(air) | SE Brandenburg |
| | Lt. C.F. Anderson | Do-217 dest(air) | SE Brandenburg |
| | Lt. J.D. Dye | Do 217 dest(air) | SW Berlin |
| | Lt. B.L. McGrattan | Me-110 dest(air) | NE Magdeburg |
| | Lt. P.W. McKennon | Me-109 dest(air) | S/Berlin |
| | F/O L.W. Waterman | Me-110 dest(air) | SW Berlin |
| | | Me-110 dam(air) | SW Berlin |
| 336th: | Lt. J.T. Godfrey | Me-109 dest(air) | N/Hanover |
| | | FW-190 dam(air) | N/Hanover |
| | F/O F.W. Glover | FW-190 prob(air) | W/Berlin |

**March 8, 1944**

| | | | |
|---|---|---|---|
| 334th: | Lt. N. Megura | FW-190 dest(air) | W/Berlin |
| | | Me-109 dest(air) | W/Berlin |
| | | FW-190 dam(air) | W/Berlin |
| | | Ju-88 dam(air) | Ruhr |
| | Maj. J.A. Clark | Me-109 dest(air) | S/Berlin |
| | Lt. A.F. Bunte | Fi-156 dest(air) | Brunswick |
| | | Me-109 dam(air) | SW Berlin |
| | Lt. V.J. France | Me-109 dest(air) | Stendal |
| | Lt. D.W. Howe | Me-109 dest(air) | S/Berlin |
| 335th: | Capt. K.G. Smith | Me-110 dest(air) | Magdeburg |
| | | Bu-181 dam(air) | Magdeburg |
| | Lt. R.P. Clotfelter | FW-190 dest(air) | Magdeburg |
| | Lt. J.D. Dye | Me-109 dest(air) | Luckenwalde |
| | | FW-190 prob(air) | Dahme |
| | Lt. A.L. Schlegel | Me-109 prob(air) | NE Magdeburg |
| | Capt. L.M. Blanding | Me-109 dam(air) | Burg-Genthin |
| | Lt. C.A. Fiedler | Me-109 dam9air) | NE Berlin |
| 336th: | Capt. D.S. Gentile | (3.5)Me-109 dest(air) | Berlin |
| | Lt. J.T. Godfrey | (2.5)Me-109 dest(air) | Berlin |
| | Lt. R.S. Tussey | Ju-88 dest(air) | Magdeburg |
| | Lt. W.F. Sooman | Me-109 dam(air) | SW Berlin |

**March 16, 1944**

| | | | |
|---|---|---|---|
| HdQts: | Col. D.J.M. Blakeslee | Me-110 dam(air) | SW Munich |
| 334th: | Lt. A.W. Chatterly | Me-110 dest(air) | Munich |
| | F/O R.K. Hofer | Me-110 dest(air) | Munich |
| 335th: | Maj. G. Carpenter | (2)Me-110 dest(air) | SW Munich |
| | | FW-190 dam(grd) | SW Munich |
| | Capt. K.G. Smith | Me-110 dest(air) | Wurm Lake |
| | Lt. P.S. Riley | Me-110 dest(air) | SW Munich |
| | | Me-110 dam(air) | SW Munich |
| 336th: | Maj. J.A. Goodson | (2)Me-110 dest(air) | Kaufburen |
| | Lt. K.E. Carlson | (2)Me-110 dest(air) | Kaufburen |
| | F/O F.W. Glover | (2)Me-110 dest(air) | Kaufburen |
| | Lt. J.T. Godfrey | Me-110 dest(air) | Kaufburen |

**March 18, 1944**

| | | | |
|---|---|---|---|
| HdQts: | LtCol. D.J.M. Blakeslee | FW-190 dest(air) | S/Augsburg |
| 334th: | F/O R.K. Hofer | (2)Me-109 dest(air) | SE Mannheim |
| | Capt. D.W. Beeson | Me-109 dest(air) | E/Mannheim |
| | Lt. A.W. Chatterly | Me-109 dest(air) | SE Mannheim |
| | Lt. N. Megura | Me-109 dest(air) | SE Mannheim |
| | Lt. H.T. Biel | Me-109 dam(air) | SE Mannheim |
| 335th: | Maj. G. Carpenter | Me-109 dest(air) | SE Saarbrucken |
| | | Me-109 prob(air) | SE Saarbrucken |
| | Capt. K.G. Smith | FW-190 dest(air) | Gunzburg |
| | Lt. B.L. McGrattan | He-111 dest(air) | NE Augsburg |
| 336th: | Capt. D.S. Gentile | FW-190 dest(air) | Augsburg |
| | Maj. J.A. Goodson | (2)He-111 dest(grd) | Mannheim |
| | Lt. K.E. Carlson | (2)He-111 dam(grd) | Ludwigshafen |

**March 21, 1944**

| Unit | Pilot | Claim | Location |
|---|---|---|---|
| HdQts: | Maj. J.A. Clark | FW-190 dest(air) | Bordeaux |
| | | FW-190 dest(grd) | Bordeaux |
| 334th: | Lt. A.W. Chatterly | (.5)FW-190 dest(air) | NE Bordeaux |
| | Lt. N. Megura | (.5)FW-190 dest(air) | NE Bordeaux |
| | | He-177 dest(grd) | NE Bordeaux |
| | Lt. V.J. France | (2)FW-190 dest(grd) | Bordeaux |
| | F/O R.K. Hofer | He-177 dest(grd) | Langen A/F |
| | Capt. H.D. Hively | (.5)Ju-88 dest(grd)* | Langen A/F |
| | Lt. A. Rafalovich | (.5)Do-217 dest(grd) | E/Bordeaux |
| | Capt. D.A. Van Epps | (.5)Do-217 dest(grd) | E/Bordeaux |
| | Lt. L.R. Pierce | Me-110 dam(grd) | Langen A/F |
| 335th: | Maj. G. Carpenter | (1.5)FW-190 dest(air) | NE Bordeaux |
| | | (.5)FW-190 dest(grd) | NE Bordeaux |
| | | (.5)Ju-52 dest(grd) | NE Bordeaux |
| | Lt. C.F. Anderson | (1.5)FW-190 dest(air) | NE Bordeaux |
| | | (.5)FW-190 dest(grd) | NE Bordeaux |
| | | (.5)Ju-52 dest(grd) | NE Bordeaux |
| | Capt. K.G. Smith | (.5)Fi-156 dest(air) | NE Bordeaux |
| | Lt. J.H. Brandenburg | (.5)Fi-156 dest(air) | NE Bordeaux |
| | Lt. W.C. Hawkins | Me-110 dest(air) | Cozes |
| | Lt. A.L. Schlegel | He-111 dest(air) | Saintes |
| | Lt. P.W. McKennon | FW-190 dest(air) | W/Lans de Bussac |
| | Lt. C.A. Fiedler | FW-190 dest(grd) | Lans de Bussac |
| | Lt. J.W. Goodwyn | (.5)Ju-88 dest(grd)* | Langen A/F |
| | Lt. R.C. Church | FW-190 dam(grd) | NE Bordeaux |
| 336th: | Capt. R.D. Hobert | FW-190 dest(air) | SW Evreux |
| | Lt. D.R. Emerson | FW-190 prob(air) | SW Evreux |
| | Maj. J.A. Goodson | Me-410 dest(grd) | Langen A/F |

**March 23, 1944**

| Unit | Pilot | Claim | Location |
|---|---|---|---|
| HdQts: | Col. D.J.M. Blakeslee | FW-190 dam(air) | Osnabruck |
| | Maj. J.A. Clark | Me-109 dest(air) | SE Steinhuder L. |
| | | FW-190 dest(air) | SE Steinhuder L. |
| 334th: | Capt. D.W. Beeson | (2)Me-109 dest(air) | E/Munster |
| | Lt. A.F. Bunte | Me-109 dest(air) | Osnabruck-Herford |
| | | Me-109 dam(air) | Osnabruck-Herford |
| | F/O R.K. Hofer | FW-190 dest(air) | E/Hamm |
| | | Me-109 dam(air) | E/Hamm |
| | Lt. N. Megura | FW-190 dest(air) | Munster |
| | Lt. L.R. Pierce | Me-109 dest(air) | Munster-Hamm |
| | Capt. H.D. Hively | FW-190 dam(air) | Herford |
| 336th: | Maj. J.A. Goodson | (2)Me-109 dest(air) | Munster |
| | Capt. D.S, Gentile | (2)Me-109 dest(air) | Munster |
| | Lt. J.T. Godfrey | Me-109 dest(air) | Munster |

**March 27, 1944**

| Unit | Pilot | Claim | Location |
|---|---|---|---|
| HdQts: | Maj. J.A. Clark | (1.5)Ju-88 dest(grd)* | Cazaux A/F |
| 334th: | Lt. W.B. Smith | Me-109 dest(air) | Lake Biscarosse |
| | | Me-109 dest(grd) | Angouleme |
| | Lt. A.W. Chatterly | Me-109 dest(air) | Angouleme |
| | Lt. N. Megura | Me-109 dam(air) | Angars |
| | | (.5)Ju-88 dest(grd)** | All remaining |
| | | FW-190 dam(grd) | 334th claims are |
| | Lt. E.H. Markel | (.5)Ju-88 dest(grd)** | at Cazaux A/F |
| | Capt. D.W. Beeson | (1.5)Ju-88 dest(grd)# | |
| | | Hs-126 dest(grd) | |
| | Lt. H.T. Biel | (1.5)Ju-88 dest(grd)# | |
| | | Me-410 dest(grd) | |
| | | FW-190 dam(grd) | |
| | Lt. G.E. Montgomery | (2)Ju-88 dest(grd) | |
| | | FW-190 dest(grd) | |
| | | Ju-52 dest(grd) | |
| | | Ju-88 dam(grd) | |
| | Lt. V.H. Wynn | Do-217 dest(grd) | |
| | | Ju-88 dest(grd) | |
| | Lt. V.J. France | Ju-88 dest(grd) | |
| | | Ju-52 dest(grd) | |
| | | Ju-88 dam(grd) | |
| | Capt. H.D. Hively | Ju-88 dest(grd) | |
| | Lt. S.W. Monroe | Me-410 dest(grd) | |
| | Lt. R.P. Kenyon | Do-217 dam(grd) | |
| | | Ju-88 dam(grd) | |
| | Lt. R.P. Claus | Ju-88 dam(grd) | |
| 335th: | Maj. G. Carpenter | FW-190 dest(air) | SW Bordeaux |
| | Lt. C.F. Anderson | FW-190 dest(air) | W/Bordeaux |
| | Capt. J.R. Happel | (.5)FW-190 dam(air) | Libourne |
| | Lt. A.L. Schlegel | (.5)FW-190 dam(air) | Libourne |
| 336th: | Capt. D.S. Gentile | (2)Me-110 dest(grd) | All 336th claims |
| | Lt. W.W. Millikan | He-177 dest(grd) | are at Cazaux |
| | Lt. L.H. Norley | Ju-88 dest(grd) | |
| | Lt. D.R. Emerson | (.5)Ju-88 dest(grd)* | |
| | Capt. R.D. Hobert | Ju-88 dam(grd) | |

**March 28, 1944**

| Unit | Pilot | Claim | Location |
|---|---|---|---|
| 334th: | Lt. A.H. Markel | Me-109 dam(grd) | W/Dreux |
| 335th: | Lt. C.F. Anderson | u/i a/c dest(grd) | S/Dreux |
| | Lt. P.W. McKennon | Ju-88 dam(grd) | S/Dreux |

**March 29, 1944**

| Unit | Pilot | Claim | Location |
|---|---|---|---|
| HdQts: | LtCol. J.A. Clark | FW-190 dest(air) | Gifhorn |
| 334th: | Lt. H.T. Biel | FW-190 dest(air) | Gifhorn |
| | Lt. A.F. Bunte | FW-190 dest(air) | Magdeburg |
| | Lt. D.W. Howe | FW-190 dest(air) | NW Brunswick |
| | Capt. W.M. Sobanski | FW-190 dam(air) | Hanover |
| | | Ju-52 dest(grd) | Steinhuder Lake |
| | Capt. D.A. Van Epps | FW-190 dam(air) | Brunswick |
| 335th: | Maj. G. Carpenter | Me-109 dest(air) | Gifhorn |
| | | (.33)He-111 dest(air) | Brunswick |
| | | Me-109 dam(air) | Gifhorn |
| | Lt. C.F. Anderson | (2.5)FW-190 dest(air) | Gifhorn |
| | | (shared with an unknown P-51 pilot) | |
| | Lt. R.C. Church | Me-109 dest(air) | NE Gifhorn |
| | Lt. C.A. Fiedler | Me-109 dest(air) | N/Brunswick |
| | Lt. P.W. McKennon | Me-109 dest(air) | NE Brunswick |
| | Lt. P.S. Riley | Me-109 dest(air) | E/Ulzen |
| | Lt. R.W. Saunders | Me-109 dest(air) | Lingen |
| | Lt. W.E. Newell | FW-190 prob(air) | Brunswick |
| 336th: | Capt. D.S. Gentile | (2)FW-190 dest(air) | Brunswick |
| | | Me-109 dest(air) | Brunswick |
| | Capt. K.D. Peterson | (2)FW-190 dest(air) | SW Brunswick |
| | Lt. J.T. Godfrey | FW-190 dest(air) | Brunswick |
| | | (.33)He-111 dest(air) | Brunswick |
| | Lt. R.S. Tussey | FW-190 prob(air) | SE Brunswick |
| | Lt. O.F. LaJeunesse | Ju-88 dam(air) | E/Hanover |
| | | Ju-88 dest(grd) | E/Hanover |
| | Maj. J.A. Goodson | Ju-88 dest(grd) | NE Brunswick |
| | | (2)Ju-88 dam(grd) | NE Brunswick |

**April 1, 1944**

| Unit | Pilot | Claim | Location |
|---|---|---|---|
| 334th: | Capt. D.W. Beeson | Me-109 dest(air) | N/Lake Constance |
| | F/O R.K. Hofer | Me-109 dest(air) | NW Lake Constance |
| | Lt. N. Megura | Me-109 dam(air) | NW Lake Constance |
| 335th: | Maj. G. Carpenter | Me-109 dam(air) | Antwerp |
| | Lt. C.F. Anderson | Me-109 dam(air) | Antwerp |
| 336th: | Capt. D.S. Gentile | Me-109 dest(air) | SW Stuttgart |
| | Lt. R.F. Nelson | Ju-88 dam(grd) | Belgium |

**April 5, 1944**

| Unit | Pilot | Claim | Location |
|---|---|---|---|
| HdQts: | Col. D.J.M. Blakeslee | (2)Ju-88 dam(grd) | Brandenburg-Briest |
| | | u/i a/c dam(grd) | Brandenburg-Briest |
| 334th: | Capt. D.W. Beeson | (.33)Ju-88 dest(air)* | Plaue A/F |
| | | (1.5)Ju-88 dest(grd) | Weisserwarte/Busch |
| | | (shared with an unknown pilot) | |
| | | Me-323 dam(grd) | Brandenburg-Briest |
| | | Me-109 dam(grd) | Brandenburg-Briest |
| | | (.25) of (5)Ju-52 dam(grd) | Brandenburg-Briest |
| | Lt. H.T. Biel | (.33)Ju-88 dest(air)* | Plaue A/F |
| | | He-111 dest(grd) | All remaining |
| | | Ju-88 dam(grd) | 334th claims are |
| | | (.25) of (5)Ju-52 dam(grd) | Brandenburg/Briest |
| | Lt. H.J. Blanchfield | (2)Do-217 dest(grd) | |
| | | (.33)He-111 dest(grd) | |
| | | (2)Ju-52 dam(grd) | |
| | Lt. G.E. Montgomery | (2)Ju-88 dest(grd) | |
| | Lt. V.J. France | (.33)He-111 dest(grd) | |
| | | FW-190 dam(grd) | |
| | | Ju-52 dam(grd) | |
| | Lt. L.R. Pierce | Ju-88 dest(grd) | |
| | | (.33)He-111 dest(grd) | |
| | Lt. C.D. Carr | Ju-52 dest(grd) | |
| | | Ju-88 dam(grd) | |
| | | (.25) of (5)Ju-52 dam(grd) | |
| 335th: | Lt. C.A. Fiedler | (.33)Ju-88 dest(air)* | Plaue A/F |
| | | (2)Ju-88 dam(grd) | Plaue A/F |
| | | u/i a/c dam(grd) | Plaue A/F |
| | Lt. C.F. Anderson | (2)Si-204 dest(grd) | Brandenburg |
| | Lt. F.C. Jones | (2)u/i a/c dest(grd) | SE Berlin |
| | Lt. J.W. Goodwyn | (.5)He-111 dest(air) | N/Brandenburg |
| | | (2)Ju-88 dam(grd) | Brandenburg |
| | Lt. P.S. Riley | (.5)He-111 dest(air) | N/Brandenburg |
| | | (2)He-111 dest(grd) | Brandenburg |
| | Lt. A.L. Schlegel | He-111 dest(grd) | Brandenburg |
| | | Ju-88 dest(grd) | Brandenburg |
| | | Ju-52 dam(grd) | Brandenburg |
| | | u/i a/c dam(grd) | Brandenburg |
| | Maj. G. Carpenter | u/i a/c dest(grd) | Berlin |
| | Lt. R.W. Saunders | Ju-52 dest(grd) | W/Brandenburg |
| | | Me-110 dam(grd) | W/Brandenburg |
| | | Ju-88 dam(grd) | W/Brandenburg |
| | Lt. G.I. Stanford | (3)Ju-88 dam(grd) | Brandenburg |
| 336th: | Capt. R.D. Hobert | (3)Ju-88 dest(grd) | All 336th claims |
| | | Ju-88 dam(grd) | are at Stendal |
| | Maj. J.A. Goodson | Ju-88 dest(grd) | unless noted |
| | | FW-190 dest(grd) | |
| | | Ju-52 dest(grd) | |
| | | (.5)Ju-88 dest(grd)** | |
| | | (.5)Ju-88 dest(grd)@ | |
| | | (.5)Ju-88 dest(grd) | |
| | | (shared with an unknown P-51 pilot) | |

| | | | |
|---|---|---|---|
| | Capt. D.S. Gentile | (3)Ju-88 dest(grd) | All claims are |
| | | (.5)Ju-88 dest(grd)[@] | at Stendal |
| | | (.5)Ju-88 dest(grd)[@@] | unless noted |
| | Lt. J.T. Godfrey | (1.5)Ju-88 dest(grd)[@@] | |
| | | Me-110 dest(grd) | |
| | | (2)Me-110 dam(grd) | |
| | | (2)Ju-88 dam(grd) | |
| | | Ju-52 dam(grd) | |
| | Lt. D.R. Emerson | (.5)Ju-88 dest(grd)[**] | |
| | | (.5)Ju-88 dest(grd) | |
| | | (shared with an unknown P-51 pilot) | |
| | | Ju-88 dam(grd) | |
| | Lt. D.J. Patchen | (2.5)Ju-88 dest(grd) | |
| | | (shared with an unknown P-51 pilot) | |
| | F/O F.W. Glover | (2)Ju-52 dest(grd) | |
| | | (2)Ju-88 dam(grd) | |
| | Lt. R. Simon | (2)u/i a/c dest(grd) | W/Brandenburg |
| | Lt. K.E. Carlson | Ju-88 dest(grd) | |
| | Lt. R.S. Tussey | Me-110 dest(grd) | |
| | | Ju-88 dam(grd) | |
| | | (.25) of (5)Ju-52 dam(grd) | Brandenburg-Briest |
| | Lt. R.F. Nelson | Ju-88 dest(grd) | Brandenburg |
| | | He-177 dam(grd) | Brandenburg |
| | | Ju-88 dam(grd) | Brandenburg |
| | Lt. W.E. Johnson | (1.5)Ju-88 dest(grd) | Stendal |
| | | (shared with an unknown P-51 pilot) | |
| | | Ju-88 dam(grd) | Stendal |
| | Lt. R.E. Hughes | u/i a/c dam(grd) | Stendal |

**April 8, 1944**

| | | | |
|---|---|---|---|
| 334th: | Lt. S.W. Monroe | (1.5)FW-190 dest(air)[*] | Celle |
| | | (.5)Me-109 dest(air)[*] | Celle |
| | Capt. R.C. Care | Me-109 dest(air) | Ulzen |
| | Capt. H.N. Moulton | Me-109 dest(air) | Celle |
| | Lt. A.H. Markel | FW-190 dest(air) | Celle |
| | | Me-109 dam(air) | Celle |
| | Lt. W.B. Smith | FW-190 dest(air) | Celle |
| | | FW-190 dam(air) | Celle |
| | F/O R.K. Hofer | Me-109 dest(air) | Celle |
| | Capt. W.M. Sobanski | Me-109 dam(air) | Celle |
| | | FW-190 dam(air) | Celle |
| | Lt. H.T. Biel | Ju-52 dest(grd) | Celle |
| | | Me-109 dam(grd) | Celle |
| | | Ju-88 dam(grd) | Celle |
| | Lt. M.H. Kolter | (2)FW-190 dam(grd) | Celle |
| 335th: | Maj. G. Carpenter | (2)FW-190 dest(air) | Celle |
| | Lt. C.A. Fiedler | (2)Me-109 dest(air) | Wolfenbuttel |
| | Lt. A.L. Schlegel | (1.5)FW-190 dest(air)[*] | Celle |
| | | (.5)Me-109 dest(air)[*] | Celle |
| | | FW-190 dest(grd) | Brunswick |
| | | FW-190 dam(grd) | Brunswick |
| | Capt. J.R. Happel | He-111 dest(air) | S/Ulzen |
| | Lt. C.F. Anderson | FW-190 dest(air) | Gifhorn |
| | Lt. B.L. McGrattan | Me-109 dest(air) | Wolfenbuttel |
| | Lt. P.W. McKennon | FW-190 dest(air) | NW Brunswick |
| | | FW-190 dam(air) | NW Brunswick |
| | Lt. P.S. Riley | FW-190 dest(air) | N/Brunswick |
| | Lt. G.I. Stanford | Me-109 dest(air) | Gifhorn |
| | Lt. F.C. Jones | Me-109 dam(air) | Wolfenbuttel |
| 336th: | Capt. D.S. Gentile | (3)FW-190 dest(air) | Ruhrburg |
| | Lt. W.W. Millikan | (3)Me-109 dest(air) | Ulzen |
| | Lt. L.H. Norley | (3)FW-190 dest(air) | Ulzen |
| | Capt. J.H. Bennett | Me-109 dest(air) | Huden |
| | F/O F.W. Glover | FW-190 dest(air) | Ulzen |
| | Lt. R. Simon | FW-190 dest(air) | Brunswick |
| | Lt. R.E. Hughes | FW-190 prob(air) | Ulzen |
| | | Me-109 dam(air) | Ulzen |

**April 9, 1944**

| | | | |
|---|---|---|---|
| 334th: | Lt. A.H. Markel | u/i a/c dam(grd) | S/Osnabruck |
| 335th: | Capt. J.R. Happel | (.33)Ju-88 dest(grd) | All claims are |
| | | (.33)Ju-88 dest(grd) | at Lingen- |
| | Lt. P.W. McKennon | (.33)Ju-88 dest(grd) | Plantlunne |
| | | (.33)Ju-88 dest(grd) | |
| 336th: | Lt. J.T. Godfrey | Me-410 dest(grd) | |
| | | (.33)Ju-88 dest(grd) | |
| | | (.33)Ju-88 dest(grd) | |

**April 10, 1944**

| | | | |
|---|---|---|---|
| HdQts: | LtCol. J.A. Clark | (2)u/i a/c dest(grd) | All claims are |
| 334th: | Lt. G.E. Montgomery | (1.5)Bu-131 dest(grd)[*] | at Romorantin |
| | Lt. H.T. Biel | u/i a/c dest(grd) | |
| | Lt. H.J. Blanchfield | Hs-126 dest(grd) | |
| | Lt. R.L. Hills | u/i a/c dest(grd) | |
| | Lt. G.C. Siems | (.5)Bu-131 dest(grd)[*] | |
| | Lt. D.W. Howe | (.5)u/i a/c dest(grd) | |
| | | (shared with an unknown P-51 pilot) | |
| | Lt. D.M. Malmsten | u/i a/c dam(grd) | |
| 335th: | Capt. J.R. Happel | (2)Bu-131 dest(grd) | |
| | | (2)u/i a/c dest(grd) | |
| | Lt. P.S. Riley | Bu-131 dest(air) | |
| | | Bu-131 dest(grd) | |
| | Lt. J.W. Russell | u/i a/c dest(grd) | |
| | | u/i a/c dam(grd) | |
| | Lt. A.L. Schlegel | u/i a/c dest(grd) | |
| | Lt. G.I. Stanford | u/i a/c dest(grd) | |
| | | u/i a/c dam(grd) | |
| | Lt. C.F. Anderson | (.5)Bu-131 dest(grd) | |
| | | (shared with an unknown P-51 pilot) | |
| | Lt. F.C. Jones | (2)u/i a/c dam(grd) | |
| | Lt. P.W. McKennon | u/i a/c dam(grd) | |
| | Lt. M.G. Scarbrough | u/i a/c dam(grd) | |
| | Lt. Z.S. Sensibaugh | u/i a/c dam(grd) | |
| 336th: | Maj. J.A. Goodson | (4.5)u/i a/c dest(grd) | All claims are |
| | | Hs-126 dest(grd) | at Romorantin |
| | Lt. R.F. Nelson | u/i a/c dest(grd) | |
| | Lt. C.H. Schilke | (.5)u/i a/c dest(grd) | |
| | Lt. N. Van Wyk | (4)u/i a/c dam(grd) | |

**April 11, 1944**

| | | | |
|---|---|---|---|
| 334th: | Capt. R.C. Care | Me-110 dest(air) | All claims are |
| | F/O R.K. Hofer | Me-110 dest(air) | SE Stettin |
| | Lt. W.B. Smith | (.5)Do-217 dest(air) | |
| | | (shared with an unknwon P-51 pilot) | |
| | | (2)FW-190 dest(grd) | |
| | | Me-410 dam(grd) | |
| | Capt. W.M. Sobanski | Me-110 dam(air) | |
| | Lt. H.T. Biel | Me-410 dest(grd) | |
| | | Me-110 dest(grd) | |
| | Lt. R.L. Hills | FW-190 dest(grd) | |
| | | Ju-88 dest(grd) | |
| | | FW-190 dam(grd) | |

**April 12, 1944**

| | | | |
|---|---|---|---|
| 335th: | Lt. C.F. Anderson | (2)Me-109 dest(air) | NW Brunswick |
| | | Ju-88 dam(grd) | NW Brunswick |
| | Maj. G. Carpenter | Me-109 dest(air) | NW Brunswick |
| | | Ju-88 dam(grd) | NW Brunswick |
| | Lt. F.C. Jones | Me-109 dest(air) | Brunswick |

**April 13, 1944**

| | | | |
|---|---|---|---|
| 334th: | Capt. W.M. Sobanski | FW-190 dest(air) | Ludwigshafen |
| | Lt. N. Megura | FW-190 dest(air) | SE Mannheim |
| 335th: | Maj. G. Carpenter | FW-190 dest(air) | SW Schweinfurt |
| | Lt. P.W. McKennon | FW-190 dest(air) | SW Schweinfurt |
| 336th: | Lt. L.H. Norley | FW-190 dest(air) | Schweinfurt |

**April 15, 1944**

| | | | |
|---|---|---|---|
| 334th: | Lt. G.E. Montgomery | He-177 dest(grd) | Hagenow |
| | | Ju 88 dest(grd) | Hagenow |
| | Lt. H.J. Blanchfield | Ju-88 dest(grd) | Hagenow |
| | Capt. R.C. Care | (.5)Ju-88 dest(grd) | Magdeburg |
| | Lt. H.T. Biel | (.5)Ju-88 dest(grd) | Magdeburg |
| 335th: | Lt. C.F. Anderson | He-177 dest(grd) | Hagenow |
| | | He-177 dam(grd) | Hagenow |
| | Lt. F.C. Jones | He-177 dest(grd) | Hagenow |
| | Lt. A.L. Schlegel | He-177 dest(grd) | Hagenow |
| | Lt. M.G. Scarbrough | He-177 dam(grd) | Hagenow |
| 336th: | Lt. R.F. Nelson | Fi-156 dest(air) | Fassberg |
| | | (2)He-177 dest(grd) | Fassberg |
| | F/O F.W. Glover | Me-110 dest(grd) | Hagenow |
| | | u/i a/c dam(grd) | Hagenow |
| | Lt. W.W. Millikan | He-177 dest(grd) | Hagenow |
| | Lt. O.F. LaJeunesse | He-177 dam(grd) | NE Hanover |

**April 18, 1944**

| | | | |
|---|---|---|---|
| HdQts: | Col. D.J.M. Blakeslee | He-177 dest(grd) | Fassberg |
| | | u/i a/c dam(grd) | Fassberg |
| 334th: | Capt. V.J. France | (.33)Me-109 dest(air) | Fassberg |
| | Lt. N. Megura | (.33)Me-109 dest(air) | Fassberg |
| | | Ju-88 dam(grd) | Brandenburg |
| | | u/i a/c dam(grd) | Brandenburg |
| | Lt. G.C. Siems | (.33)Me-109 dest(air) | Fassberg |
| | | u/i a/c dam(grd) | Fassberg |
| | F/O R.K. Hofer | (2)He-177 dest(grd) | Fassberg |
| | Lt. R.P. Kenyon | He-111 dest(grd) | Fassberg |
| | Lt. D.W. Howe | (2)Ju-52 dest(grd) | All remaining |
| | | (.25) of (6)Ju-52 dam(grd) | claims are at |
| | Lt. J.L. Lang | (3)Ju-52 dest(grd) | Juterbog |
| | | (.25) of (6)Ju-52 dam(grd) | |
| | Lt. S.W. Monroe | (2)Ju-52 dest(grd) | |
| | | (.25) of (6)Ju-52 dam(grd) | |
| | Lt. D.M. Malmsten | Ju-52 dest(grd) | |
| | | (.25) of (6)Ju-52 dam(grd) | |
| 335th: | Maj. G. Carpenter | Me-109 dest(air) | Rathenow-Nauen |
| | | FW-190 dest(air) | Rathenow-Nauen |
| | Lt. P.W. McKennon | FW-190 dest(air) | Rathenow |
| 336th: | Lt. D.R. Emerson | Me-109 dest(air) | Wenzendorf |
| | Lt. R.F. Nelson | Me-109 dest(grd) | Genthin A/F |
| | | Me-109 dam(grd) | Genthin A/F |

| | | | |
|---|---|---|---|
| | | Ju-88 dam(grd) | Genthin A/F |
| | | u/i a/c dam(grd) | Genthin A/F |
| | Lt. G.H. Logan | (.5)FW-190 dest(grd) | Wenzendorf |
| | Lt. N. Van Wyk | (.5)FW-190 dest(grd) | Wenzendorf |

**April 19, 1944**

| | | | |
|---|---|---|---|
| 334th: | Lt. R.P. Kenyon | Me-109 dest(air) | Eschwege |
| | Lt. N. Megura | (.5)FW-190 dest(air) | Eschwege |
| | Lt. M.H. Kolter | Me-109 prob(air) | Eschwege-Kassel |
| 335th: | Lt. B.L. McGrattan | Me-109 dest(air) | Eschwege |
| | | (.5)FW-190 dest(air) | Eschwege |
| | Lt. P.W. McKennon | Me-109 dest(air) | Eschwege |
| 336th: | Lt. W.W. Millikan | Me-109 dest(air) | NE Eschwege |

**April 22, 1944**

| | | | |
|---|---|---|---|
| HdQts: | Col. D.J.M. Blakeslee | (2)Me-109 dest(air) | Kassel |
| 334th: | Lt. W.B. Smith | (.5)Me-109 dest(air)* | SW Kassel |
| 335th: | Capt. A.L. Schlegel | (2)Me-109 dest(air) | SW Kassel |
| | Lt. F.C. Jones | Me-109 dest(air) | Kassel |
| | Lt. P.S. Riley | (.5)Me-109 dest(air)* | SW Kassel |
| 336th: | Lt. W.W. Millikan | (4)Me-109 dest(air) | All remaining |
| | Lt. J.T. Godfrey | (3)Me-109 dest(air) | claims are |
| | Lt. L.H. Norley | (2)Me-109 dest(air) | SW Kassel |
| | Lt. K.E. Carlson | (1.5)Me-109 dest(air)** | |
| | Lt. R. Simon | Me-109 dest(air) | |
| | Lt. D.R. Emerson | (.5)Me-109 dest(air)** | |

**April 23, 1944**

| | | | |
|---|---|---|---|
| 336th: | Maj. J.A. Goodson | (2)Me-109 dest(air) | Wienar Neustadt |

(Claimed while "breaking-in" a P-51 unit in the MTO)

**April 24, 1944**

| | | | |
|---|---|---|---|
| HdQts: | Col. D.J.M. Blakeslee | (1.5)FW-190 dest(air) | N/Worms |
| | | FW-190 dam(air) | N/Worms |
| 334th: | Lt. N. Megura | (2)FW-190 dest(air) | S/Frankfurt |
| | | FW-190 dam(air) | S/Frankfurt |
| | Lt. D.W. Howe | Me-109 dest(air) | Darmstadt |
| | Lt. L.R. Pierce | FW-190 dam(air) | N/Frankfurt |
| 335th: | Capt. A.L. Schlegel | (2.5)FW-190 dest(air) | N/Worms |
| | Capt. J.R. Happel | FW-190 dest(air) | NE Worms |
| | Lt. P.S. Riley | FW-190 dest(air) | N/Mannheim |
| | | FW-190 prob(air) | N/Mannheim |
| | Lt. B.L. McGrattan | FW-190 dest(air) | Knocke |
| | Lt. L. Read | FW-190 dest(air) | N/Worms |
| | Lt. M.G. Scarbrough | FW-190 prob(air) | S/Mannheim |
| 336th: | Lt. J.T. Godfrey | FW-190 dest(air) | NW Ludwigshafen |
| | | FW-190 dam(air) | NW Ludwigshafen |
| | Lt. T.K. McDill | FW-190 dam(air) | NW Ludwigshafen |
| | Lt. C.J. Netting | FW-190 dam(air) | NW Ludwigshafen |

**April 27, 1944**

| | | | |
|---|---|---|---|
| 335th: | Lt. L. Read | u/i a/c dest(grd) | Toul |

**April 29, 1944**

| | | | |
|---|---|---|---|
| 334th: | Lt. N. Megura | Ju-52 dest(grd) | All claims are |
| | | (.5)Ju-52 dest(grd)* | at Nordhausen |
| | | (.5)Ju-52 dest(grd)** | |
| | Lt. S.W. Monroe | (1.5)Ju-52 dest(grd)* | |
| | Lt. J.L. Barden | (.5)Ju-52 dest(grd)** | |
| 336th: | Lt. J.T. Godfrey | Do-217 dest(grd) | |
| | | (.5)Ju-52 dest(grd)@ | |
| | | (.5)Ju-52 dest(grd)@@ | |
| | | Do-217 dam(grd) | |
| | Lt. I.E. Grounds | (.5)Ju-52 dest(grd)@ | |
| | Lt. J.A. Patteeuw | (.5)Ju-52 dest(grd)@@ | |

**April 30, 1944**

| | | | |
|---|---|---|---|
| HdQts: | Col. D.J.M. Blakeslee | (.5)Do-24 dest(grd)* | Lyon Anchorage |
| 334th: | Capt. W.M. Sobanski | (.33)Me-110 dest(air) | N/Lyon |
| | Lt. J.L. Lang | (.33)Me-110 dest(air) | N/Lyon |
| | | Me-110 dest(grd) | Lyon |
| | | (2)Me-110 dam(grd) | Lyon |
| | | He-111 dam(grd) | Lyon |
| | Lt. S.W. Monroe | (.33)Me-110 dest(air) | N/Lyon |
| | | Me-110 dam(grd) | Lyon/Bron |
| 336th: | Lt. F.W. Glover | (1.5)u/i a/c dest(grd) | Valence A/F |
| | Capt. J.T. Godfrey | (.5)Do-24 dest(grd)** | Lyon Anchorage |
| | Lt. T.K. McDill | (.5)Do-24 dest(grd)** | Lyon Anchorage |
| | Lt. H.H. Frederick | (.5)u/i a/c dest(grd) | Valence A/F |
| | Lt. J.A. Patteeuw | (.5)Do-24 dest(grd)* | Lyon Anchorage |
| | Lt. F.S. Harris | (.5)Do-24 dest(grd)@ | Lyon Anchorage |
| | Lt. W.E. Johnson | (.5)Do-24 dest(grd)@ | Lyon Anchorage |
| | Lt. W.W. Millikan | Do-24 dam(grd) | Lyon Anchorage |

**May 1, 1944**

| | | | |
|---|---|---|---|
| 334th: | Lt. R.K. Hofer | Me-109 dest(air) | Koln |
| 335th: | Lt. F.C. Jones | Me-109 dest(air) | Zweibricken |
| | | Me-109 dam(air) | Zweibricken |
| | Lt. B.L. McGrattan | Me-109 dest(air) | Losheim |
| | Lt. J.W. Goodwyn | Me-109 dam(air) | Losheim |
| 336th: | Capt. J.T. Godfrey | Me-109 dest(air) | NW Saarbrucken |

**May 9, 1944**

| | | | |
|---|---|---|---|
| 334th: | Lt. G.C. Siems | Ju-88 dest(grd) | Reims-Champiegne |
| | Capt. H.D. Hively | (2)Ju-88 dam(grd) | Reims-Champiegne |

**May 12, 1944**

| | | | |
|---|---|---|---|
| 334th: | Capt. H.D. Hively | Me-109 dest(air) | Plauen |
| | Lt. G.C. Siems | Me-109 dest(air) | Coburg |
| | Lt. R.K. Hofer | (.5)Me-109 dest(air) | N/Coburg |
| | Lt. L.R. Pierce | (.5)Me-109 dest(air) | N/Coburg |
| 335th: | Capt. J.R. Happel | Me-109 dest(air) | Giessen |
| | Lt. E.H. Shapleigh | (1.5)Me-109 dest(air) | Giessen-Marburg |
| | Lt. R.H. Homuth | Me-109 dest(air) | E/Giessen |
| | Lt. T.E. Lines | Me-109 dest(air) | E/Frankfurt |
| | Lt. G.I. Stanford | (.5)Me-109 dest(air) | Giessen-Marburg |
| 336th: | Maj. J.A. Goodson | Me-109 dest(air) | Kassel |
| | Lt. T.K. McDill | Me-109 dest(air) | Kassel |

**May 13, 1944**

| | | | |
|---|---|---|---|
| 336th: | Lt. H.H. Frederick | Me-109 prob(air) | SE Canabruck |

**May 19, 1944**

| | | | |
|---|---|---|---|
| 334th: | Capt. H.D. Hively | (3)Me-109 dest(air) | Lubeck-Schwerin |
| | Lt. J.L. Lang | Me-109 dest(air) | Weismar |
| | | u/i a/c dest(air) | Weismar |
| | | Me-109 dam(air) | Weismar |
| | Lt. D.W. Howe | Me-109 dest(air) | Neustadt Bay |
| | Lt. J.F. Scott | (.5)Me-109 dest(air) | Lubeck-Schwerin |
| | | (shared with a 339th Ftr Grp P-51) | |

**May 21, 1944**

| | | | |
|---|---|---|---|
| 334th: | Lt. R.K. Hofer | (.5)Bu-131 dest(air) | Rathenow |
| | | Bu-131 dest(grd) | Rathenow |
| | Lt. A.C. Hewatt | (.5)Bu-131 dest(air) | Rathenow |
| | Lt. G.C. Siems | (2)Me-210 dest(grd) | Rathenow |
| | | (2)Me-210 dam(grd) | Rathenow |
| | Lt. F.E. Speer | Ju-52 dest(grd) | Rathenow |
| | | Ju-88 dest(grd) | Rathenow |
| | Lt. T.E. Fraser | (2)Ju-88 dam(grd) | Buch A/F |
| | | u/i a/c dam(grd) | Buch A/F |

**May 22, 1944**

| | | | |
|---|---|---|---|
| 334th: | Lt. R.K. Hofer | Me-109 dest(air) | Hamburg |
| | Capt. N. Megura | (.5)Me-109 dest(air) | SW Kiel |
| | | (shared with an unknown P-38 pilot) | |
| 336th: | Capt. W.W. Millikan | Me-109 dest(air) | NW Kiel |
| | Capt. J.H. Bennett | Me-109 prob(air) | Lubeck |

**May 24, 1944**

| | | | |
|---|---|---|---|
| 334th: | Lt. R.K. Hofer | (2)Me-109 dest(air) | E/Hamburg |
| | Capt. H.D. Hively | Me-109 dest(air) | Hamburg |
| | Lt. T.E. Fraser | FW-190 dest(air) | E/Hamburg |
| | Lt. W.G. Gillette | Me-109 dest(air) | NE Hamburg |
| | Lt. J.L. Lang | Me-109 dest(air) | N/Hamburg |
| | Lt. F.E. Speer | Me-109 dest(air) | E/Hamburg |
| 335th: | Lt. J.W. Russell | Me-109 dest(air) | Hamburg-Lubeck |
| | Lt. J.W. Goodwyn | Me-109 prob(air) | N/Hamburg |
| | Lt. F.C. Jones | Me-109 prob(air) | Hamburg |

**May 25, 1944**

| | | | |
|---|---|---|---|
| 336th: | Capt. J.H. Bennett | (2)Me-109 dest(air) | All claims are |
| | | (2)FW-190 prob(air) | at Strasbourg |
| | | FW-190 dam(air) | |
| | Maj. J.A. Goodson | FW-190 dest(air) | |
| | Lt. T.K. McDill | Me-109 dest(air) | |
| | Lt. I.E. Grounds | FW-190 dam(air) | |

**May 28, 1944**

| | | | |
|---|---|---|---|
| 334th: | Lt. J.L. Lang | (1.5)Me-109 dest(air) | Magdeburg |
| | | (shared with a 352nd Ftr Grp P-51) | |
| | Capt. W.M. Sobanski | Me-109 dest(air) | Wittenburg-Magdeburg |
| | Lt. R.K. Hofer | Me-109 dest(air) | Magdeburg |
| | Lt. R.P. Kenyon | Me-109 dest(air) | Magdeburg |
| | Lt. M.H. Kolter | Me-109 dest(air) | Magdeburg |
| | Lt. G.C. Siems | FW-190 dest(air) | Magdeburg |

**May 29, 1944**

| | | | |
|---|---|---|---|
| HdQts: | Col. D.J.M. Blakeslee | Me-410 dest(air) | N/Falkenburg |
| | | (2)Do-18 dam(grd) | Dievenow |
| 334th: | Lt. O.C. Snell | Me-109 dest(air) | Cammin |
| | Lt. R.K. Hofer | (4)He-177 dest(grd) | Mackfitz A/F |
| | Lt. F.E. Speer | (3)He-177 dest(grd) | Mackfitz A/F |
| | Lt. M.H. Kolter | Ar-196 dest(grd) | All remaining |
| | | (.5)Do-18 dam(grd)* | 334th claims are |
| | Capt. T.E. Joyce | (.5)Do-18 dam(grd)* | at Dievenow |
| | Lt. J.F. Scott | Do-18 dam(grd) | |
| | Lt. E.J. Steppe | Do-18 dam(grd) | |
| | Capt. W.M. Sobanski | (.5)Do-18 dam(grd)** | |
| | | (.5)Do-18 dam(grd)@ | |
| | Lt. J.P. Fernandez | (.5)Do-18 dam(grd)** | |
| | | (.5)Do-18 dam(grd)@ | |
| | Lt. T.S. Sharp | Do-18 dam(grd) | |

| | | | |
|---|---|---|---|
| 335th: | Capt. B.L. McGrattan | FW-190 dest(air) | Laaland Island |
| | Lt. R.C. Church | Me-109 dest(air) | Elmarn Belt |
| 336th: | Lt. D.R. Emerson | (.5)Me-110 dest(air) | N/Falkenburg |
| | | Do-18 dam(grd) | N/Falkenburg |
| | Lt. C.J. Netting | (.5)Me-110 dest(air) | N/Falkenburg |
| | | (2)Do-18 dam(grd) | N/Falkenburg |

**May 30, 1944**

| | | | |
|---|---|---|---|
| 334th: | Lt. R.K. Hofer | (2.5)FW-190 dest(air) | Oschersleben |
| | Lt. J.F. Scott | Me-109 dest(air) | Dessau-Bernburg |
| | Lt. T.S. Sharp | FW-190 dam(air) | W/Brandenburg |
| | | (2)FW-190 dest(grd) | Oschersleben |
| 335th: | Lt. F.C. Jones | (1.5)FW-190 dest(air) | Oschersleben |
| | | FW-190 dam(air) | Oschersleben |
| 336th: | Lt. O.F. Lajeunesse | Me-109 dest(air) | Magdeburg |

**May 31, 1944**

| | | | |
|---|---|---|---|
| 334th: | Lt. R.K. Hofer | (3)Bu-131 dest(grd) | Luxeuil A/F |

**June 6, 1944**

| | | | |
|---|---|---|---|
| 334th: | Lt. S.W. Monroe | FW-190 dest(air) | All claims are |
| | Lt. J.F. Scott | FW-190 dest(air) | at Evreux |
| | Lt. G.C. Siems | FW-190 dest(air) | |
| | Lt. J.P. Fernandez | (.5)FW-190 dest(air) | |
| | Lt. J.T. Simon | (.5)FW-190 dest(air) | |

**June 20, 1944**

| | | | |
|---|---|---|---|
| HdQts: | LtCol. J.A. Clark | Me-410 dest(air) | SW Anklam |
| 334th: | Lt. W.G. Gillette | Ju-88 dest(air) | E/Pasewalk |
| | | Do 217 dest(grd) | Neubrandenburg |
| | | (.5)Ju-88 dest(grd)* | Neubrandenburg |
| | Lt. R.A. Dickmeyer | Me-109 dest(air) | E/Pasewalk |
| | Lt. D.M. Malmsten | Ju-88 dest(air) | Pasewalk |
| | Lt. S.W. Monroe | Me-109 dest(air) | E/Pasewalk |
| | Capt. T.E. Joyce | (.5)Me-109 dest(air) | E/Pasewalk |
| | Lt. A.C. Cwiklinski | (.5)Me-109 dest(air) | E/Pasewalk |
| | | Me-109 dam(air) | E/Pasewalk |
| 335th: | Capt. F.C. Jones | Me-109 dest(air) | Stettin |
| | Lt. G.W. Cooley | Me-109 dest(air) | Politz |
| | | Me-109 dam(air) | Politz |
| | Lt. G.I. Stanford | (.5)Me-210 dest(air) | Ratzeburger Lake |
| | F/O L.B. Godwin | (.5)Me-210 dest(air) | Ratzeburger Lake |
| 336th: | Capt. O.M. Glass | Me-109 dest(air) | S/Anklam |
| | Lt. D.R. Emerson | FW-190 dest(air) | S/Anklam |
| | Lt. C.H. Shilke | Do-217 dest(grd) | Neubrandenburg |
| | | (.5)Ju-88 dest(grd)* | Neubrandenburg |
| | Lt. F.S. Harris | Do-217 dest(grd) | Neubrandenburg |
| | | Do-217 dam(grd) | Neubrandenburg |

**June 21, 1944**

| | | | |
|---|---|---|---|
| 334th: | Lt. J.L. Lang | Me-109 dest(air) | SE Warsaw |
| | Lt. R.K. Hofer | Me-109 dam(air) | Siedlce |
| 335th: | Capt. F.C. Jones | Me-109 dest(air) | Kobryn |
| | | Me-109 dam(air) | Kobryn |

**July 2, 1944**

| | | | |
|---|---|---|---|
| HdQts: | Col. D.J.M. Blakeslee | Me-109 dest(air) | Budapest |
| 334th: | Capt. H.D. Hively | (3)Me-109 dest(air) | Budapest |
| | Capt. W.F. Hedrick | Me-109 dest(air) | Budapest |
| | | Me-109 dam(air) | Budapest |
| | Lt. G.C. Siems | Me-109 dest(air) | Budapest |
| 336th: | Lt. D.R. Emerson | (.5)Me-109 dest(air) | W/Budapest |
| | | (shared with a 352nd Ftr Grp P-51) | |

**July 7, 1944**

| | | | |
|---|---|---|---|
| 334th: | Capt. T.E. Joyce | (2)Me-109 dest(air) | Aschersleben |
| | Lt. W.G. Gillette | Me-109 dest(air) | Sangerhausen |
| | | Me-109 prob(air) | Sangerhausen |
| | | (2)Me-109 dam(air) | Sangerhausen |
| | Lt. P.B. Hardy | Me-109 dest(air) | Blankenberg |
| | | Me-109 prob(air) | Blankenberg |
| | | (2)Me-109 dam(air) | Blankenberg |
| | Lt. J.J. Scally | Me-410 dest(air) | Sangerhausen |
| | Lt. J.D. McFadden | Me-109 dam(air) | Aschersleben |
| | Lt. S.W. Monroe | FW-190 dam(air) | E/Pasewalk |
| | Lt. E.C. Walsh | Me-109 dam(air) | Eisleben |
| 335th: | Lt. J.W. Goodwyn | Me-109 dest(air) | Bad Frankenhausen |
| 336th: | Lt. G.C. Chapman | FW-190 dest(air) | Bernburg |

**July 17, 1944**

| | | | |
|---|---|---|---|
| 335th: | Maj. L.M. Blanding | Me-109 dam(air) | NE Munich |

**July 19, 1944**

| | | | |
|---|---|---|---|
| 336th: | Lt. I.E. Grounds | (2)Me-109 dest(air) | E/Munchen |
| | Lt. F.M. Grove | Me-109 dest(air) | E/Munchen |

**July 28, 1944**

| | | | |
|---|---|---|---|
| 334th: | Capt. H.D. Hively | Me-109 prob(air) | Nordhausen |

**August 5, 1944**

| | | | |
|---|---|---|---|
| 336th: | Capt. J.T. Godfrey | Me-109 dest(air) | N/Osnabruck |
| | | (3)Ju-52 dest(grd) | SE Munden |
| | | (3)Ju-52 dam(grd) | SE Munden |
| | Lt. F.W. Glover | Me-109 dest(air) | Gardelegen |

**August 6, 1944**

| | | | |
|---|---|---|---|
| 336th: | Capt. J.T. Godfrey | Me-410 dest(air) | NE Berlin |
| | | Me-109 dam(air) | SE Berlin |
| | Capt. O.M. Glass | (2)Ju-52 dest(grd) | SE Berlin |
| | | Me-109 dam(grd) | SE Berlin |
| | | Ju-52 dam(grd) | SE Berlin |
| | Lt. F.W. Glover | Me-109 dest(grd) | SE Berlin |
| | Lt. J.A. Patteeuw | Me-410 dest(grd) | SE Berlin |

**August 8, 1944**

| | | | |
|---|---|---|---|
| 335th: | Capt. F.C. Jones | Ju-88 dest(grd) | Stravanger/Sola |

**August 16, 1944**

| | | | |
|---|---|---|---|
| 336th: | Lt. I.E. Grounds | Me-109 dest(air) | Magdeburg |

**August 18, 1944**

| | | | |
|---|---|---|---|
| 334th: | Lt. A.C. Cwiklinski | (2)Me-109 dest(air) | SW Beauvais |
| | | Me-109 dam(air) | SW Beauvais |
| | Lt. P.B. Hardy | Me-109 dest(air) | SW Beauvais |
| | | Me-109 dam(air) | SW Beauvais |
| | Lt. W.E. Whalen | Me-109 dest(air) | Beauvais |
| 335th: | Lt. B. Diamond | Me-109 dest(air) | NE Paris |
| | Lt. P.S. Iden | Me-109 dest(air) | NE Paris |
| | Lt. D.D. Perkins | Me-109 dest(air) | Beaumont-Sur-Oise |

**August 24, 1944**

| | | | |
|---|---|---|---|
| 335th: | Lt. T.E. Lines | (2)Me-109 dest(air) | SE Emden |
| 336th: | Capt. J.T. Godfrey | (4)Ju-52 dest(grd) | Nordhausen |
| | Lt. M.N. Dickey | (3)Ju-52 dest(grd) | Nordhausen |
| | Capt. P.L. Wiggin | Ju-52 dest(grd) | Nordhausen |

**August 25, 1944**

| | | | |
|---|---|---|---|
| 336th: | Lt. H.N. Hagan | Me-109 dest(air) | SW Rostock |
| | Lt. G.H. Logan | Me-109 dest(air) | E/Schwerin |
| | Lt. I.E. Grounds | Me-109 prob(air) | SW Rostock |
| | | (2)Me-109 dam(air) | SW Rostock |

**September 10, 1944**

| | | | |
|---|---|---|---|
| 335th: | Lt. T.E. Lines | (3)Me-109 dest(air) | Strasbourg |
| | | Ju-88 dest(air) | S/Kaiserlautern |

**September 11, 1944**

| | | | |
|---|---|---|---|
| HdQts: | LtCol. C.H. Kinnard | Me-109 dest(air) | Halle |
| | | Me-410 dest(grd) | Halle |
| 334th: | Capt. G.E. Montgomery | Me-109 dest(air) | Aschersleben |
| | Lt. L.R. Werner | Me-109 dest(air) | Eisenach-Gotha |
| | | FW-190 dam(air) | Eisenach-Gotha |
| | Lt. H.E. Clifton | FW-190 dam(air) | Aschersleben |
| 335th: | Lt. G.W. Cooley | (2)FW-190 dest(air) | NW Naumburg |
| | Lt. R.J. Rinebolt | FW-190 dest(air) | NW Naumburg |
| | Lt. J.W. Russell | Me-109 dest(air) | Erfurt |
| | | Me-109 prob(air) | Erfurt |
| | | FW-190 prob(air) | Erfurt |
| | Lt. J.N. Peters | Me-109 prob(air) | NW Naumburg |
| 336th: | Lt. H.E. Dugan | Me-109 dest(air) | Korbach |
| | Lt. J.H. Joiner | Me-109 dest(air) | Korbach |
| | Lt. C.W. Dupree | (2)FW-190 dest(grd) | All remaining |
| | F/O D.J. Pierni | (2)FW-190 dest(grd) | claims are at |
| | Lt. F.M. Grove | FW-190 dest(grd) | Langensalza |
| | | (2)FW-190 dam(grd) | |
| | | Ju-188 dam(grd) | |
| | Lt. H.A. Ingalls | FW-190 dest(grd) | |
| | Lt. C.H. Patterson | FW-190 dest(grd) | |

**September 12, 1944**

| | | | |
|---|---|---|---|
| 334th: | Lt. R.A. Dickmeyer | (1.5)FW-190 dest(air) | Wiesbaden |
| 335th: | Lt. A.J. Davis | Me-109 dest(air) | NE Frankfurt |
| 336th: | Lt. E.F. Hustwit | (1.5)FW-190 dest(air) | Wiesbaden |
| | Lt. V.E. Chandler | FW-190 dest(air) | Wiesbaden |
| | | FW-190 dam(air) | Wiesbaden |
| | Lt. G.W. Hunt | Me-109 dest(air) | NW Frankfurt |
| | Lt. J.C. Lane | Me-109 dest(air) | Trier |
| | | Me-109 dam(air) | Trier |
| | Lt. E.A. Quist | Me-109 prob(air) | NW Frankfurt |

**September 13, 1944**

| | | | |
|---|---|---|---|
| HdQts: | LtCol. C.H. Kinnard | (2)Hs-123 dest(grd) | Gelcheim |
| 334th: | Capt. W.B. Smith | u/i a/c dest(grd) | Schwabisch Hall |
| | Lt. W.G. Gillette | FW-200 dam(grd) | Halle |
| 335th: | Lt. B. Diamond | (3)Hs-123 dest(grd) | Gelcheim |
| | F/O C.E. Poage | (3)Hs-123 dest(grd) | Gelcheim |
| | Lt. G.W. Ceglarski | (2)u/i a/c dest(grd) | Gelcheim |
| | | u/i a/c dam(grd) | Gelcheim |
| | Lt. W.B. Eaton | Hs-123 dest(grd) | Gelcheim |

**September 17, 1944**

| | | | |
|---|---|---|---|
| 335th: | Lt. T.E. Lines | (3)FW-190 dest(air) | Bocholt |
| | Lt. A.J. Davis | (2)FW-190 dest(air) | Bocholt |
| | Capt. L.H. Norley | FW-190 dest(air) | Bocholt |

**September 25, 1944**

| | | | |
|---|---|---|---|
| 336th: | Lt. W.H. Williams | Ju-88 dest(grd) | Lippsringe |

**September 27, 1944**

| | | | |
|---|---|---|---|
| 334th: | Lt. A.J. Senecal | Me-109 dest(air) | Giessen |
| 335th: | Lt. R.J. Anderson | FW-190 dam(air) | S/Kassel |
| 336th: | Lt. G.C. Smith | Me-109 dest(air) | S/Kassel |
| | | FW-190 dest(air) | S/Kassel |
| | Capt. J.D. McFarlane | FW-190 dest(air) | SE Kassel |
| | Lt. C.W. Dupree | FW-190 dest(air) | SW Kassel |

**September 28, 1944**

| | | | |
|---|---|---|---|
| 334th: | Lt. D.W. Howe | FW-190 dest(air) | NE Kassel |

**October 6, 1944**

| | | | |
|---|---|---|---|
| 334th: | Lt. L.R. Werner | Me-109 dest(air) | Neven |
| | | FW-190 dam(air) | Neven |
| 335th: | Lt. R.E. Lewis | (.5)Me-410 dest(air) | NW Heligoland |
| | Lt. E.N. McCall | (.5)Me-410 dest(air) | NW Heligoland |
| 336th: | Lt. J.H. Joiner | Me-109 dest(air) | Korbach |

**October 14, 1944**

| | | | |
|---|---|---|---|
| 334th: | Capt. J.L. Lang | (2)Me-109 dest(air) | Nancy/St. Dizier |

**November 2, 1944**

| | | | |
|---|---|---|---|
| 335th: | Capt. L.H. Norley | Me-163 dest(air) | SE Leipzig |
| | Lt. C.L. Brock | Me-109 dest(air) | Merseburg |
| | Lt. J.E. Kolbe | Me-109 dest(air) | Leipzig |
| 336th: | Capt. F.W. Glover | Me-163 dest(air) | E/Leipzig |

**November 6, 1944**

| | | | |
|---|---|---|---|
| 334th: | Lt. J.D. McFadden | Me-109 dest(air) | Rheine |
| | Lt. E.C. Walsh | Me-109 prob(air) | Rheine |
| | | Me-109 dam(air) | Rheine |
| | Lt. R.A. Dickmeyer | Me-109 dam(air) | Rheine |
| 336th: | Lt. V.E. Chandler | FW-190 dest(air) | Minden |

**November 18, 1944**

| | | | |
|---|---|---|---|
| HdQts: | Maj. R.A. Ackerly | Me-262 dest(grd) | Unless noted, |
| 334th: | Lt. C.F. Brown | (2)Me-262 dest(grd) | all claims are |
| | | Me-262 dam(grd) | at Leipheim |
| | F/O C.W. Harre | (2)Me-262 dest(grd) | |
| | | (2)Me-262 dam(grd) | |
| | Maj. H.D. Hively | Me-262 dest(grd) | |
| | Capt. G.E. Montgomery | Me-262 dest(grd) | |
| | | (4)Me-262 dam(grd) | |
| | Lt. C.G. Payne | Me-262 dest(grd) | |
| | | Me-262 dam(grd) | |
| | Lt. R.A. Dyer | (4)Me-262 dam(grd) | |
| | Lt. J.D. McFadden | (2)Me-262 dam(grd) | |
| | Lt. A.J. Senecal | (2)Me-262 dam(grd) | |
| | Lt. W.J. Dvorak | Me-262 dam(grd) | |
| | F/O K.E. Foster | Me-262 dam(grd) | |
| | Lt. W.B. Hoelscher | Me-262 dam(grd) | |
| 335th: | Capt. J.C. Fitch | (.5)Me-262 dest(air) | S/Leipheim |
| | | Me-109 dest(grd) | |
| | Lt. J.N. Creamer | (.5)Me-262 dest(air) | S/Leipheim |
| | Capt. W.C. Anderson | Me-262 dest(grd) | |
| | | Me-262 dam(grd) | |
| | Lt. W.B. Eaton | Me-262 dest(grd) | |
| | | Me-262 dam(grd) | |
| | Lt. J.E. Kolbe | Me-262 dest(grd) | |
| | Lt. R.J. Mabie | (2)Me-262 dam(grd) | |
| | Lt. E.N. McCall | Me-262 dam(grd) | |
| | | Me-109 dam(grd) | |
| | Lt. E. Jungling | Me-262 dam(grd) | |
| | Lt. R.L. Stallings | Me-109 dam(grd) | |
| 336th: | Lt. F.M. Grove | (2)Me-262 dam(grd) | |
| | Capt. D.R. Emerson | Me-262 dam(grd) | |
| | Lt. D.J. Pierni | Me-262 dam(grd) | |
| | Lt. J.H. Joiner | (.5)Me-262 dam(grd) | |
| | | (.5)Me-262 dam(grd) | |
| | | (.5)Me-262 dam(grd) | |
| | Lt. H.A. Kaul | (.5)Me-262 dam(grd) | |
| | | (.5)Me-262 dam(grd) | |
| | | (.5)Me-262 dam(grd) | |

**November 21, 1944**

| | | | |
|---|---|---|---|
| 335th: | Lt. J.E. Kolbe | Me-109 dest(air) | NW Merseburg |
| 336th: | Capt. F.W. Glover | (3)Me-109 dest(air) | W/Merseburg |
| | Lt. D.N. Groshong | (2)Me-109 dest(air) | W/Merseburg |
| | Lt. J.E. Hileman | Me-109 prob(air) | W/Merseburg |
| | | Me-109 dam(air) | W/Merseburg |

**December 2, 1944**

| | | | |
|---|---|---|---|
| 334th: | Lt. C.F. Brown | FW-190 dest(air) | Hottenbach |
| | Lt. J.D. McFadden | FW-190 dest(air) | Hottenbach |
| | Lt. A.C. Lacy | FW-190 dam(air) | Hottenbach |
| | Lt. M.R. Savage | Me-109 dam(air) | SE Bingen |

**December 5, 1944**

| | | | |
|---|---|---|---|
| 334th: | Maj. H.D. Hively | FW-190 dest(air) | NW Nordhorn |

**December 18, 1944**

| | | | |
|---|---|---|---|
| 334th: | Lt. H.E. Clifton | Me-109 dest(air) | E/Dortmund |
| 335th: | Capt. W.J. O'Donnell | Me-109 dest(air) | NE Frankfurt |
| | Lt. R.L. Stallings | FW-190 dest(air) | NE Frankfurt |

**December 24, 1944**

| | | | |
|---|---|---|---|
| 335th: | Lt. C.W. Willruth | Me-109 dest(air) | W/Giessen |
| | Lt. G.D. Green | Me-109 prob(air) | W/Giessen |

**December 25, 1944**

| | | | |
|---|---|---|---|
| 334th: | Lt. T.J. Cronin | (1.5)FW-190 dest(air)* | S/Bonn |
| | Lt. W.B. Hoelscher | FW-190 dest(air) | NE Trier |
| | | (.5)Me-109 dest(air) | NE Trier |
| | | FW-190 dam(air) | NE Trier |
| | Lt. V.R.T. Rentschler | FW-190 dest(air) | NE Trier |
| | | (.5)Me-109 dest(air) | NE Trier |
| | | FW-190 dam(air) | NE Trier |
| 335th: | Maj. P.W. McKennon | (.5)FW-190 dest(air)* | S/Bonn |
| | Lt. C.E. Poage | (2)FW-190 prob(air) | SE Duren |
| 336th: | Capt. D.R. Emerson | (2)FW-190 dest(air) | SW Coblenz |
| | Lt. V.E. Chandler | Me-109 dest(air) | SW Coblenz |
| | | FW-190 dest(air) | SW Coblenz |
| | Maj. F.W. Glover | FW-190 dest(air) | SW Coblenz |

**January 1, 1945**

| | | | |
|---|---|---|---|
| 336th: | Lt. F.W. Young | Me-262 dest(air) | Ulzen |
| | | Me-109 dest(air) | Ulzen |
| | Lt. V.E. Chandler | Me-109 dest(air) | Ulzen |
| | Lt. D.J. pierni | Me-109 dest(air) | Ulzen |
| | Lt. G.L. Kesler | (.5)Me-109 dest(air) | Ulzen |
| | Lt. A.O. Wallace | (.5)Me-109 dest(air) | Ulzen |

**January 2, 1945**

| | | | |
|---|---|---|---|
| 334th: | Lt. C.G. Payne | (.5)Me-109 dest(air) | Westerburg |
| | | (.5)Me-109 dest(air) | Westerburg |
| | Lt. V.R.T. Rentschler | (.5)Me-109 dest(air) | Westerburg |
| | Lt. A.J. Senecal | (.5)Me-109 dest(air) | Westerburg |

**January 16, 1945**

| | | | |
|---|---|---|---|
| 334th: | Lt. J.W. Ayers | (.5)He-177 dest(grd) | Neuburg |
| | Lt. M.J. Kennedy | (.5)He-177 dest(grd) | Neuburg |
| | Lt. C.F. Brown | (.5)Me-262 dest(grd) | Neuburg |
| | Lt. J.E. Jahnke | (.5)Me-262 dest(grd) | Neuburg |
| 336th: | Capt. J.H. Joiner | (4)FW-190 dest(grd) | All claims are |
| | Lt. V.E. Chandler | (2)FW-190 dest(grd) | At Neuhausen |
| | | (2)Ju-52 dest(grd) | |
| | Maj. F.W. Glover | (2)Ju-87 dest(grd) | |
| | | FW-190 dest(grd) | |
| | Lt. R.J. Corbett | (2)Ju-87 dest(grd) | |
| | | FW-190 dest(grd) | |
| | Capt. C.R. Alfred | (2)FW-190 dest(grd) | |
| | Lt. H.N. Hagan | FW-190 dest(grd) | |
| | | He-177 dest(grd) | |
| | Lt. G.L. Kesler | FW-190 dest(grd) | |
| | | He-177 dest(grd) | |
| | Lt. T.A. McCord | FW-190 dest(grd) | |
| | | Ju-87 dest(grd) | |
| | Capt. L.A. Carpenter | FW-190 dest(grd) | |
| | Lt. D.N. Groshong | FW-190 dest(grd) | |
| | Lt. H.A. Kaul | FW-190 dest(grd) | |
| | Lt. W.D. Riedel | FW-190 dest(grd) | |
| | Lt. A.O. Wallace | FW-190 dest(grd) | |

**February 20, 1945**

| | | | |
|---|---|---|---|
| 336th: | Capt. J.H. Joiner | (1.5)FW-190 dest(air) | N/Ingolstadt |
| | Capt. K.E. Carlson | (.5)FW-190 dest(air) | N/Ingolstadt |

**February 22, 1945**

| | | | |
|---|---|---|---|
| 336th: | Lt. H.R. Crawford | (3)FW-190 dest(grd) | All claims are |
| | Maj. F.W. Glover | Do-217 dest(grd) | at Halberstadt |
| | | Me-109 dest(grd) | |
| | Capt. C.R. Alfred | Me-410 dest(grd) | |
| | | Do-217 dest(grd) | |
| | Maj. J.D. McFarlane | Do-217 dest(grd) | |

**February 25, 1945**

| | | | |
|---|---|---|---|
| 334th: | Lt. C.G. Payne | Me-262 dest(air) | SE Naunberg |
| | | (.5)Me-410 dest(grd) | Rohrensee |
| | Lt. D.M. Malmsten | (.5)FW-190 dest(air) | Dessau |
| | Lt. W.C. O'Bryan | (.5)FW-190 dest(air) | Dessau |
| | Lt. A.R. Bowers | FW-190 dest(grd) | Rohrensee |

| | | | |
|---|---|---|---|
| | | Me-410 dest(grd) | Rohrensee |
| | | Me-110 dest(grd) | Rohrensee |
| | Capt. T.R. Bell | FW-190 dest(grd) | Rohrensee |
| | | (.5)Me-410 dest(grd) | Rohrensee |
| | | (.5)Me-110 dest(grd) | Rohrensee |
| | | (.5)Me-110 dest(grd) | Rohrensee |
| | Lt. G.A. Denson | (.5)Me-110 dest(grd) | Rohrensee |
| | | (.5)Me-110 dest(grd) | Rohrensee |
| | Lt. H.E. Clifton | (2)Me-109 dam(grd) | Kothen |
| | Lt. D.G. Lowther | Ju-88 dam(grd) | Kothen |
| 335th: | Maj. P.W. McKennon | (2)u/i a/c dam(grd) | Pretzech A/F |
| | Lt. R.C. Bucholz | Ju-88 dam(grd) | NE Torgau |
| | Lt. G.D. Green | Me-410 dam(grd) | Pretzech A/F |
| 336th: | Lt. B.O. Brooker | (.5)FW-190 prob(air) | Kothen |
| | Lt. P.M. Morgan | (.5)FW-190 prob(air) | Kothen |
| | Capt. K.E. Carlson | u/i a/c dest(grd) | Kothen |
| | Lt. R.J. Corbett | He-111 dest(grd) | Kothen |
| | | He-111 dam(grd) | Kothen |
| | Lt. J.E. Hileman | u/i a/c dest(grd) | Kothen |

**February 27, 1945**

| | | | |
|---|---|---|---|
| 334th: | Lt. D.M. Malmsten | (3)u/i a/c dest(grd) | All claims are |
| | | (2)Ju-88 dest(grd) | at Weimar A/F |
| | | Me-109 dest(grd) | |
| | Maj. G.E. Montgomery | Do-217 dest(grd) | |
| | | Me-108 dest(grd) | |
| | | Ju-87 dest(grd) | |
| | Lt. J.W. Ayers | (3)u/i a/c dest(grd) | |
| | | (.5)Ju-52 dest(grd) | |
| | Capt. T.R. Bell | (3)Me-109 dest(grd) | |
| | Capt. H.E. Clifton | (3)Me-108 dest(grd) | |
| | Lt. W.O. Antonides | (2)Ju-88 dest(grd) | |
| | Lt. J.D. McFadden | Me-108 dest(grd) | |
| | | Ju-87 dest(grd) | |
| | Lt. C.G. Payne | (2)Me-108 dest(grd) | |
| | Lt. L.C. Garvin | Me-108 dest(grd) | |
| | Lt. C.W. Harre | Me-108 dest(grd) | |
| | Lt. L.F. Wells | Me-109 dest(grd) | |
| | Lt. R.S. Voyles | (.5)Ju-52 dest(grd) | |
| 336th: | Maj. F.W. Glover | (2)Me-109 dest(grd) | All claims are |
| | | FW-190 dest(grd) | at Weimar A/F |
| | Lt. G.L. Kesler | (2)Ju-52 dest(grd) | |
| | | Me-109 dest(grd) | |
| | Lt. M.N. Dickey | Ju-87 dest(grd) | |
| | | C-47 dest(grd) | |
| | Maj. J.D. McFarlane | Me-108 dest(grd) | |
| | Lt. H.R. Crawford | u/i a/c dest(grd) | |
| | Lt. H.L. Davis | Me-108 dest(grd) | |
| | Lt. R.O. Davis | Ju-88 dest(grd) | |
| | Lt. E.F. Hustwit | Me-410 dest(grd) | |
| | Lt. D.P. Pederson | u/i a/c dest(grd) | |

**March 3, 1945**

| | | | |
|---|---|---|---|
| HdQts: | Col. E.W. Stewart | Me-262 dam(air) | Gardelegen |

**March 19, 1945**

| | | | |
|---|---|---|---|
| 334th: | Maj. L.H. Norley | Me-109 dest(air) | SE Frankfurt |

**March 21, 1945**

| | | | |
|---|---|---|---|
| 334th: | Lt. D.M. Malmsten | (2)Me-109 dest(grd) | All claims are |
| | Lt. P.M. Burney | Me-109 dest(grd) | at Achmer A/F |
| | Lt. W.B. Hoelscher | FW-190 dest(grd) | |
| 335th: | Lt. S.W. Connors | u/i a/c dam(grd) | |
| 336th: | Capt. C.R. Alfred | (3)Do-217 dest(grd) | |
| | | Me-109 dam(grd) | |
| | | Do-217 dam(grd) | |
| | Lt. W.W. Collins | Me-410 dam(grd) | |
| | | Do-217 dam(grd) | |
| | Lt. W.D. Riedel | (2)u/i a/c dam(grd) | |

**March 22, 1945**

| | | | |
|---|---|---|---|
| HdQts: | LtCol. S.S. Woods | (5)FW-190 dest(air) | Furstenwalde-Eggersdorf |
| 334th: | Lt. F.E. Farington | FW-190 dest(air) | Furstenwalde |
| | Lt. J.E. Jahnke | FW-190 dest(air) | Furstenwalde |
| | Lt. W.O. Antonides | (2)FW-190 dam(air) | Eggersdorf |
| 336th: | Lt. W.D. Reidel | (2)FW-190 dest(air) | NE Ruhland |
| | Lt. R.O. Davis | FW-190 dest(air) | Furstenwalde |
| | Lt. H.N. Hagan | FW-190 dest(air) | SE Berlin |

**April 4, 1945**

| | | | |
|---|---|---|---|
| 334th: | Lt. R.A. Dyer | Me-262 dest(air) | SE Parchim |
| | Lt. M.J. Kennedy | (.5)Me-262 dest(air) | S/Ludwigslust |
| | Capt. R.H. Kanaga | Me-262 prob(air) | Schwerin |
| | Lt. C.W. Harre | Me-262 dam(air) | S/Parchim |
| 335th: | Lt. E. Jungling | Me-262 dam(air) | NE Parchim |
| 336th: | Lt. H.H. Frederick | (.5)Me-262 dest(air) | S/Ludwigslust |
| | | Me-262 dam(air) | S/Ludwigslust |

**April 7, 1945**

| | | | |
|---|---|---|---|
| 334th: | Lt. J.W. Ayers | Me-109 dest(air) | NE Duneburg |
| | Lt. R.H. Buchanan | Me-109 dest(air) | SE Krummel |
| | Lt. W.B. Hoelscher | Me-109 dest(air) | SE Krummel |
| 336th: | Lt. M.L. Davis | Me-109 dest(air) | SW Bremen |

**April 9, 1945**

| | | | |
|---|---|---|---|
| 335th: | Maj. P.W. McKennon | (2)Ju-52 dest(grd) | All claims are |
| | | Me-410 dest(grd) | at Munich- |
| | | Ju-52 dam(grd) | Brunnthal |
| | Lt. R.C. Bucholz | (3)u/i a/c dest(grd) | |
| | Lt. T.H. Elffner | (2)Me-410 dest(grd) | |
| | Lt. L.I. Burgess | Ju-88 dest(grd) | |
| | | Ju-88 dam(grd) | |
| | | u/i a/c dam(grd) | |
| | Lt. M.D. Heaton | Fi-156 dest(grd) | |
| | | u/i a/c dest(grd) | |
| | Lt. R.C. Hunter | u/i a/c dest(grd) | |
| | | (2)u/i a/c dam(grd) | |
| | Lt. L.D. Jennings | Ju-88 dest(grd) | |
| | Lt. H.A. Lee | Me-410 dest(grd) | |
| | Lt. R.L. Couse | Ju-88 dam(grd) | |
| | | u/i a/c dam(grd) | |
| | Lt. W.H. George | (2)Me-410 dam(grd) | |
| | Lt. R.C. Hawley | (2)u/i a/c dam(grd) | |
| | Lt. R.A. Moe | Do-217 dam(grd) | |
| | | u/i a/c dam(grd) | |
| | Lt. S.W. Connors | Me-410 dam(grd) | |
| | Lt. E.J. McLoughlin | u/i a/c dam(grd) | |

**April 10, 1945**

| | | | |
|---|---|---|---|
| 334th: | Maj. G.E. Montgomery | Me-410 dest(grd) | Wittstock |
| | Lt. D.G. Lowther | Ju-52 dest(grd) | Wittstock |
| | Lt. J.D. McFadden | Ju-88 dest(grd) | Wittstock |
| | Lt. R.J. Miller | u/i a/c dest(grd) | Wittstock |
| 336th: | Lt. W.W. Collins | Me-262 dest(air) | Lubeck |

**April 13, 1945**

| | | | |
|---|---|---|---|
| 335th: | Capt. W.J. O'Donnell | Ar-196 dest(grd) | Ratzeburger Lake |
| | Lt. L.D. Jennings | He-115 dest(grd) | Ratzeburger Lake |
| | | u/i a/c dam(grd) | Ratzeburger Lake |
| | Lt. J.J. Scanlon | (2)Ar-196 dam(grd) | Ratzeburger Lake |

**April 16, 1945**

| | | | |
|---|---|---|---|
| HdQts. | LtCol. S.S. Woods | (2)Ju-88 dest(grd) | Praha |
| | | (5)Ju-88 dam(grd) | Praha |
| 334th: | Lt. W.O. Antonides | (2)Me-109 dest(grd) | All 334th claims |
| | | FW-190 dest(grd) | are at Gablingen |
| | | Me-410 dest(grd) | |
| | | u/i a/c dest(grd) | |
| | | u/i a/c dam(grd) | |
| | Maj. L.H. Norley | (2)FW-190 dest(grd) | |
| | | Ju-52 dest(grd) | |
| | | u/i a/c dest(grd) | |
| | Lt. W.C. O'Bryan | (3)u/i a/c dest(grd) | |
| | Lt. J.W. Ayers | Me-109 dest(grd) | |
| | | FW-190 dest(grd) | |
| | | u/i a/c dest(grd) | |
| | Lt. A.R. Bowers | (2)Me-109 dest(grd) | |
| | | Ju-88 dest(grd) | |
| | | (3)Me-109 dam(grd) | |
| | Lt. R.H. Buchanan | FW-190 dest(grd) | |
| | | Me-410 dest(grd) | |
| | | (2)FW-190 dam(grd) | |
| | | Me-109 dam(grd) | |
| | Lt. W.G. Spencer | FW-190 dest(grd) | |
| | | Me-109 dest(grd) | |
| | | u/i a/c dest(grd) | |
| | Lt. R.A. Dyer | FW-190 dest(grd) | |
| | | Me-109 dest(grd) | |
| | | u/i a/c dest(grd) | |
| | | FW-190 dam(grd) | |
| | | Me-109 dam(grd) | |
| | | Me-410 dam(grd) | |
| | Lt. G.A. Denson | (2)FW-190 dest(grd) | |
| | | Me-410 dest(grd) | |
| | | He-177 dest(grd) | |
| | | FW-190 dam(grd) | |
| | | Me-410 dam(grd) | |
| | | u/i a/c dam(grd) | |
| | Lt. M.W. Arthur | Me-109 dest(grd) | |
| | | (.5)FW-190 dest(grd) | |
| | Lt. P.E. Burnett | u/i a/c dest(grd) | |
| | Lt. W.J. Dvorak | u/i a/c dest(grd) | |
| | | (2)u/i a/c dam(grd) | |
| | Lt. C.W. Harre | Me-109 dest(grd) | |
| | | (3)u/i a/c dam(grd) | |
| | Lt. M.J. Kennedy | u/i a/c dest(grd) | |
| | | Ju-88 dam(grd) | |
| | | Ju-87 dam(grd) | |
| | Lt. D.G. Lowther | u/i a/c dest(grd) | |
| | Lt. M.L. Spencer | (.5)FW-190 dest(grd) | |

| | | | |
|---|---|---|---|
| 335th: | Lt. K.G. Helfrecht | (2)Me-410 dest(grd) | Gablingen |
| | | (2)FW-190 dest(grd) | Gablingen |
| | | He-177 dest(grd) | Gablingen |
| | | (2)Ju-87 dam(grd) | Gablingen |
| | Lt. G.D. Green | (2)Ju-88 dest(grd) | Praha/Letnany |
| | | Do-217 dest(grd) | Praha/Letnany |
| | | u/i a/c dest(grd) | Praha/Letnany |
| | Lt. L.D. Jennings | (2)Do-217 dest(grd) | Praha |
| | | (2)Me-110 dest(grd) | Praha |
| | Maj. P.W. McKennon | (2)Do-217 dest(grd) | Praha/Letnany |
| | | u/i a/c dest(grd) | Praha/Letnany |
| | | Me-410 dam(grd) | Praha/Letnany |
| | Lt. W.F. Underwood | FW-190 dest(grd) | Praha |
| | | Me-410 dest(grd) | Praha |
| | | u/i a/c dest(grd) | Praha |
| | Lt. O.B. Bucher | (2)Ju-52 dest(grd) | Praha/Letnany |
| | | Me-410 dest(grd) | Praha |
| | | Me-410 dam(grd) | Praha |
| | Lt. R.L. Couse | (2)Do-217 dest(grd) | Praha/Letnany |
| | | Ju-88 dam(grd) | Praha/Letnany |
| | Capt. W.J. O'Donnell | (2)u/i a/c dest(grd) | Praha/Letnany |
| | | (2)u/i a/c dam(grd) | Praha/Letnany |
| | Lt. J.E. Halligan | Me-110 dest(grd) | Praha |
| | | FW-190 dest(grd) | Praha |
| | | u/i a/c dest(grd) | Praha |
| | | (4)u/i a/c dam(grd) | Praha |
| | | Me-110 dam(grd) | Praha |
| | Lt. R.C. Hunter | (2)Do-217 dest(grd) | Praha/Letnany |
| | | Ju-88 dest(grd) | Praha/Letnany |
| | Lt. H.B. Miller | Do-217 dest(grd) | Praha/Letnany |
| | | Ju-52 dest(grd) | Praha/Letnany |
| | | Do-217 dam(grd) | Praha/Letnany |
| | | Ju-52 dam(grd) | Praha/Letnany |
| | Lt. C.B. Greenlese | u/i a/c dest(grd) | Praha |
| | | (5)u/i a/c dam(grd) | Praha |
| | Lt. W.D. Henderson | (3)Me-109 dam(grd) | Praha |
| | | u/i a/c dam(grd) | Praha |
| | Lt. P.J. Lucas | (2)u/i a/c dam(grd) | Praha/Letnany |
| | F/O L.W. Freeman | He-177 dam(grd) | Praha/Letnany |
| 336th: | Lt. D.P. Pederson | (5)Ju-52 dest(grd) | All 336th claims |
| | | (3)Ju-52 dam(grd) | are at Praha |
| | F/O D.P. Baugh | (5)Ju-88 dest(grd) | unless noted |
| | Lt. B.L. Griffin | (4)u/i a/c dest(grd) | |
| | Lt. H.H. Frederick | (2)Ju-88 dest(grd) | Praha/Letnany |
| | | Me-110 dest(grd) | Praha/Letnany |
| | | Me-110 dam(grd) | Praha/Letnany |
| | Lt. W.H. Ayer | (2)u/i a/c dest(grd) | |
| | Lt. J.P. Murchake | (2)Ju-88 dest(grd) | |
| | | Ju-88 dam(grd) | |
| | Lt. M.C. Franklin | (2)Ju-52 dest(grd) | |
| | | u/i a/c dam(grd) | |
| | Capt. C.R. Alfred | u/i a/c dest(grd) | |
| | | u/i a/c dam(grd) | |
| | Lt. B.O. Brooker | (2)Me-410 dest(grd) | |
| | | (3)Me-110 dam(grd) | |
| | | Ju-52 dam(grd) | |
| | Capt. L.A. Carpenter | Me-410 dest(grd) | |
| | | u/i a/c dam(grd) | |
| | Lt. M.L. Davis | Me-110 dest(grd) | |
| | | (2)Me-110 dam(grd) | |
| | Capt. E.L. Gimbel | Me-110 dest(grd) | |
| | | (2)Me-110 dam(grd) | |
| | Capt. H.N. Hagan | Me-109 dest(grd) | SW Pilzen |
| | Lt. W.H. Hastings | Me-110 dest(grd) | |
| | | Me-110 dam(grd) | |
| | Lt. W.B. Meredith | Me-109 dest(grd) | |
| | Lt. M.W. Miller | u/i a/c dest(grd) | |
| | Lt. W.W. Collins | Do-217 dam(grd) | |
| | | Me-109 dam(grd) | |

**April 17, 1945**

| | | | |
|---|---|---|---|
| 336th: | Maj. F.W. Glover | Ju-87 dest(grd) | All claims are |
| | Lt. W.W. Collins | Me-110 dest(grd) | at Pilzen |
| | Lt. D.N. Groshong | Me-110 dest(grd) | |
| | | Ju-87 dam(grd) | |
| | Lt. W.B. Meredith | u/i a/c dest(grd) | |
| | | (2)Me-109 dam(grd) | |
| | Lt. H.H. Frederick | Ju-87 dam(grd) | |

**April 25, 1945**

| | | | |
|---|---|---|---|
| 334th: | Lt. W.B. Hoelscher | Me-262 prob(air) | Prague/Ruzny |

### 4th Fighter Group Losses

**September 21, 1942**
Lt. John T. Slater (335th) KIA; Hit by flak near Flushing.
Spitfire AV-

**September 26, 1942**
F/Lt. Edward G. Brettell (336th) POW (K); Hit by flak near Brest.
Was later executed March 24, 1944.
Spitfire MD- BS313
Capt. Marion E. Jackson (336th) POW; Hit by flak and a FW-190 near Brest.
Spitfire MD- BS279
P/O William H. Baker (336th) KIA; Last heard from reporting he was ditching.
Spitfire MD- BS446
Lt. Charles A. Cook (336th) POW; Ran low on fuel then hit by a FW-190 near Brest.
Spitfire MD- BR640
Lt. George H. Middleton (336th) POW; Ran out of fuel near Brest.
Spitfire MD- BS301
Lt. Gene P. Neville (336th) KIA; Hit by flak near Guingamp.
Spitfire MD- BS140
Lt. Leonard T. Ryerson (336th) KIA; Hit by flak near Brest.
Spitfire MD- BS275
Lt. Dennis D. Smith (336th) KIA; Hit by flak near Brest.
Spitfire MD- BS137
Lt. Robert E. Smith (336th) MIA-E; Hit by flak near Brest.
Spitfire MD- BS447
Lt. George B. Sperry (336th) POW; Hit by flak near Brest.
Spitfire MD- BR638
Lt. Gil P. Wright (336th) POW; Hit by flak near Brest.
Spitfire MD- BS138

**October 20, 1942**
Lt. Anthony J. Seaman (334th) KIA; Plane exploded and crashed east of Harwich.
Spitfire XR-

**November 20, 1942**
Lt. Roy W. Evans (335th) ASR; Bailed out over the North Sea after mechanical trouble.
Spitfire AV-

**November 26, 1942**
Capt. Robert S. Sprague (334th) KIAc; Crashed near Debden on a test flight.
Spitfire XR-

**January 22, 1943**
Lt. Chester P. Grimm (335th) KIA; Hit by flak in the Dunkirk-St. Omer area.
Spitfire AV-

**January 26, 1943**
Lt. Robert A. Boock (334th) ASR; Suffered mechanical failure and ditched 6 miles off the coast.
Spitfire XR-

**February 1, 1943**
Lt. John Mitchellweis, Jr. (336th) KIAc; Plane caught fire and he bailed out northwest of Debden but his parachute failed.
P-47C OO 41-6200

**February 5, 1943**
Capt. William P. Kelly (335th) KIA; Hit by flak and crashed off Walcheren.
Spitfire AV-

**February 13, 1943**
Lt. Jap A. Powell (336th) KIA; Suffered mechanical failure and bailed out too low off the English coast.
Spitfire MD- AR341

**March 12, 1943**
Lt. Hazen S. Anderson (336th) POW; Hit by a FW-190 northwest of St. Omer.
Spitfire MD- BL240

**April 3, 1943**
Lt. Frank J. Smolinsky (335th) KIAc; Crashed near Sawbridgeworth after take-off.
P-47C WD-D 41-6181

**April 15, 1943**
LtCol. Chesley G. Peterson (HdQts) ASR; Bailed out 30 miles off the English coast.
P-47C QP-K 41-6414
Capt. Stanley M. Anderson (334th) KIA; Hit by a FW-190 and crashed off Ostend.
P-47C QP-E 41-6407
Capt. Richard D. McMinn (334th) KIA; Hit by a FW-190 and crashed off Ostend.
P-47C QP-M 41-6204

**May 4, 1943**
Lt. John F. Lutz (334th) KIA; Suffered mechanical failure and bailed out off Flushing.
P-47C QP-P 41-6196

**May 18, 1943**
Lt. Robert A. Boock (334th) KIA; Hit by fighters and crashed in the Blankenberghe-Ostend area.
P-47C QP-S

**May 21, 1943**
Lt. Leland L. MacFarlane (334th) KIA; Last seen chasing a fighter near Ghent.
P-47D QP-N 42-7920
Lt. William B. Morgan (334th) POW; Hit by fighters and ditched off Ostend.
P-47D QP-U 42-8644

**June 14, 1943**
Lt. Garrett C. King (334th) KIAc; Hit by lightning and crashed near Swaffam.
P-47C QP-T

**June 15, 1943**
Lt. Howard D. Hively (334th) ASR; Bailed out over the Channel after mechanical trouble.
P-47C QP-J 41-6576

**June 19, 1943**
Lt. Vincent R. Castle (334th) KIAc; Pulled up, stalled, then crashed near Debden.
P-47D QP-E 42-7881

**July 14, 1943**
Lt. Ward K. Wortman (335th) KIA; Hit by fighters near Amiens.
P-47D WD-Z 42-7939

**July 28, 1943**
Lt. Henry L. Ayres (336th) POW; Hit by fighters near Zevenhausen.
P-47C VF- 41-6238

**July 30, 1943**
Lt. Fred D. Merritt (335th) KIA; Hit by a Me-109 southeast of Rotterdam.
P-47C WD- 41-6248

**August 16, 1943**
Lt. Joseph G. Matthews (336th) MIA-E; Hit by fighters near St. Denis.
P-47D VF- 42-7949

**September 2, 1943**
Lt. Dale B. Leaf (334th) KIA; Last seen with FW-190's near Formerie.
P-47C QP-I

**September 7, 1943**
Lt. Aubrey C. Stanhope (335th) POW; Chased a FW-190 then hit by flak near Hulst.
P-47C WD-X 41-6207

**September 9, 1943**
Lt. Vernon Boehle (334th) ASR; Damaged by fighters and bailed out 45 miles south of Beachy Head.
P-47C QP-O 41-6400 "Indianapolis"
Lt. Frank M. Fink (335th) POW; Bailed out near Paris after mechanical trouble.
P-47C WD- 41-6328

**October 8, 1943**
F/O Clyde D. Smith (334th) POW; Hit by fighters near Meppel.
P-47D QP-U 42-7915
Lt. Robert G. Patterson (335th) POW; Hit by fighters near Stadskannel.
P-47D WD- 42-7911

**November 3, 1943**
F/O Frank D. Gallion (334th) KIA; Hit by fighters near the Zuider Zee and crashed at Ijesselmeer.
P-47D QP-F 42-7924
Lt. Ivan R. Moon (334th) KIA; Hit by fighters near Oosterland.
P-47C QP-M 41-6587

**December 2, 1943**
F/O John P. McNabb (334th) KIAc; Plane burst into flames and crashed near Kenton.
P-47C QP-L 41-6484

**January 29, 1944**
Lt. Burton C. Wyman (335th) KIA; Hit by fighters near Fumay.
P-47D WD-N 42-75119

**January 30, 1944**
Lt. Edwin R. Mead (334th) POW; Hit by fighters east of Lingen.
P-47D WD-B 42-8506

**February 3, 1944**
F/O William A. Cox (334th) KIA; Hit by fighters near Emden.
P-47D QP-X 42-75254

**February 6, 1944**
Lt. Hubert N. Ballew (335th) POW; Hit by a FW-190 near Paris.
P-47D WD-W 42-8495

**February 20, 1944**
Lt. Richard I. Reed (335th) KIA; Hit by fighters northeast of Coblenz.
P-47D WD-R 42-75051

**February 24, 1944**
Lt. Joseph W. Sullivan (335th) KIA; Hit by fighters northwest of Coblenz.
P-47C WD-Y 41-6369

**February 28, 1944**
Lt. Robert B. Frazer (334th) KIAc; Plane stalled and flipped into the ground near Debden.
P-51B QP-N 43-6656

**March 2, 1944**
Lt. George K. Villinger (336th) KIA; Hit by fighters near Linburg.
P-51B VF-C 43-6985

**March 3, 1944**
Lt. George W. Barnes (335th) KIA; Suffered mechanical trouble and crashed into the Channel.
P-51B WD-L 43-6643
Capt. Philip H. Dunn (336th) POW; Became lost then ran out of fuel near the Spanish border.
P-51B VF-Y 43-6903
Lt. Vermont Garrison (336th) POW; Hit by flak near Boulogne.
P-51B VF-H 43-6871
Lt. Glenn A. Herter (336th) KIA; Hit by fighters near Wittenberg.
P-51B VF-R 43-6740

**March 4, 1944**
Capt. Paul M. Ellington (335th) POW; Bailed out over Holland after mechanical trouble.
P-51B WD-U 43-7004
Lt. Hugh A. Ward (335th) POW; Suffered mechanical failure near Berlin.
P-51B WD-R 43-6810
Lt. Robert H. Richards (336th) KIA; Crashed at Framlingham upon return.
P-51B VF- 43-6786

**March 5, 1944**
Lt. Spiros N. Pissanos (334th) MIA-E; Suffered mechanical trouble south of Le Havre.
P-51B QP-D 43-6798

**March 6, 1944**
Maj. Henry L. Mills (334th) POW; Bailed out west of Brandenburg after mechanical trouble.
P-51B QP-Q 43-6690
Lt. Edmund D. Whalen (334th) KIA; Damaged by debris from a Me-110 near Nienburg.
P-51B QP-O 43-6899
Capt. Cecil E. Manning (335th) POW; Hit by fire from a Do-217 near Sogel.
P-51B WD-H 43-6887
Lt. Robert J. Messenger (336th) POW; Hit by fighters near Dessau.
P-51B VF-U 43-6630 "Missouri Mauler"

**March 8, 1944**
Maj. Seldon R. Edner (HdQts) POW; Hit by fighters near Hegensburg.
P-51B VF- 43-6442

**March 16, 1944**
Lt. Ernest R. Skilton (336th) KIA; Hit by flak near Gussenstadt.
P-51B VF- 43-6652

**March 18, 1944**
Lt. Edward P. Freeburger (335th) KIA; Hit by fighters near Ulm and crashed near Nancy.
P-51B WD F 43 6460
Lt. Woodrow F. Sooman (336th) POW; Suffered mechanical trouble near Frankfurt.
P-51B VF-D 43-6936

**March 21, 1944**
Lt. Alex Rafalovich (334th) POW; Hit by flak and bailed out north of Bordeaux.
P-51B QP-N 43-6839
Lt. Robert G. Williams (334th) POW; Hit by flak near Angars.
P-51B QP-U 43-6869
Capt. Earle W. Carlowe (335th) POW (E); Hit by flak and bailed out north of Bordeaux.
P-51B WD-P 43-6639
Capt. Kenneth G. Smith (335th) POW; Hit by flak near Bordeaux and crashed near Caen.
P-51B WD-K 43-6803
Lt. James H. Brandenburg (335th) KIA; Hit by flak north of Bordeaux and bailed out too low.
P-51B WD-E 43-6641
F/O Joseph Goetz (335th) KIA; Hit by flak north of Bordeaux.
P-51B WD-L 43-12469
Lt. William C. Hawkins (335th) MIA-E; Hit by flak north of Bordeaux.
P-51B WD-H 43-6316

**March 27, 1944**
Capt. Archie W. Chatterly (334th) POW; Hit by flak near Lake Biscarosse.
P-51B QP-G 43-6860

**March 28, 1944**
Lt. Ray P. Clotfelter (335th) POW; Suffered mechanical failure near Dreux.
P-51B WD-B 43-6843

**March 29, 1944**
Lt. William E. Newell (335th) POW; Hit by fighters near Lingen.
P-51B WD-P 43-6759
Lt. Glenn J. Smart (335th) ASR; Bailed out over the Channel after being damaged by fighters.
P-51B WD-W 43-6973
Capt. Kenneth D. Peterson (336th) POW; Hit by fighters near Braunschwig.
P-51B VF-F 43-6696

**March 31, 1944**
Lt. Peter G. Lehman (336th) KIAc; Crashed near Duxford after spinning-out during practice dog-fighting.
P-51B VF-S 43-6844

**April 5, 1944**
Capt. Duane W. Beeson (334th) POW; Hit by flak at Brandenburg and bailed out near Stendal.
P-51B QP-B 43-6819 "Bee"
Lt. Allan F. Bunte (334th) POW; Hit wires near Gardelegen and crashed into a lake near Potsdam.
P-51B QP-L 43-6946
Lt. Charles D. Carr (334th) POW; Hit by flak at Brandenburg.
P-51B QP-I 43-6837

Capt. Robert D. Hobert (336th) KIA; Bailed out over the Channel and died of exposure.
P-51B VF- 43-6836

**April 8, 1944**
Capt. Howard N. Moulton, Jr. (334th) POW; Hit by a FW-190 near Celle and bailed out near Wittengen.
P-51B QP-D 43-6967
Lt. Robert P. Claus (334th) KIA; Hit by fighters near Celle.
P-51B QP-U 43-7029
Lt. Robert E. Hughes (336th) POW; Hit by fighters near Celle.
P-51B VF- 43-6866

**April 9, 1944**
Capt. David A. Van Epps (334th) POW; Hit by flak near Tutrow.
P-51B QP-T 43-6941

**April 10, 1944**
Lt. Clemens A. Fiedler (335th) KIA; Hit by flak at Romorantin A/F.
P-51B WD-W 43-7190

**April 13, 1944**
Capt. Vasseure F. Wynn (334th) POW; Hit by a FW-190 near Aschaffenberg.
P-51B QP-X 43-7035
Lt. Ralph W. Saunders (335th) KIUA; Hit by fighters near Schweinfurt.
P-51B WD-Z 43-6325

**April 15, 1944**
Capt. Ray C. Care (334th) POW; Hit by flak near Celle.
P-51B QP-R 43-7183
Lt. Robert H. Seifert (336th) KIA; Suffered mechanical trouble and bailed out over the Channel.
P-51B VF- 43-6818

**April 18, 1944**
Capt. Victor J. France (334th) KIA; Hit the ground while chasing a Me-109 near Stendal.
P-51B QP-K 43-6832 "Miss Dallas"
Maj. George Carpenter (335th) POW; Hit by a FW-190 near Rathenow.
P-51B WD-I 42-106675
Lt. Lloyd F. Henry (335th) KIA; Hit by fighters near Berlin.
P-51B WD-S 43-6579 "Snafu"

**April 19, 1944**
Capt. Charles F. Anderson (335th) KIA; Disappeared over Belgium after reporting engine trouble.
P-51B WD-L 43-7181

**April 22, 1944**
Lt. Robert F. Nelson (336th) POW; Suffered mechanical trouble southeast of Kassel.
P-51B VF-Y 43-6802

**April 24, 1944**
Capt. Hipolitus T. Biel (334th) KIA; Hit by fighters near Darmstadt.
P-51B QP-X 42-106636
Lt. Paul S. Riley (335th) POW; Collided with a FW-190 near Worms.
P-51B WD-Y 43-6922
Lt. Milton G. Scarbrough (335th) POW; Hit by fighters near Worms.
P-51B WD-F 43-6767

**April 29, 1944**
Lt. John L. Barden (334th) POW; Downed by fire from another P-51 while strafing near Nordhausen.
P-51B QP-B 42-106682
Lt. Peter R. Kennedy (334th) POW; Hit by flak near Fuechtof.
P-51B QP-L 43-6646

**April 30, 1944**
Lt. Fred W. Glover (336th) MIA-E; Hit by flak at Valence A/F and bailed out north of Tain.
P-51B VF- 42-106856

**May 6, 1944**
Lt. Ralph G. Boyce (335th) KIAc; Crashed while trying to land at Ridgewell.
P-51B WD-

**May 9, 1944**
Capt. Herbert J. Blanchfield (334th) POW; Hit by flak and bailed out southeast of St. Dizier.
P-51B QP-E 42-106767
Lt. Vernon A. Burroughs (334th) POW; Hit by fighters southwest of St. Dizier.
P-51B QP-N 43-6636 "Ill Wind?"
Lt. Robert S. Sherman (334th) POW; Hit the ground near Thrablemont.
P-51B QP-D 43-7002
Lt. Lloyd W. Waterman (335th) POW; Suffered mechanical trouble near Pont a Binson.
P-51B WD-A 42-106911 "Yippee Joe!!"

**May 11, 1944**
Lt. Robert S. Tussey (336th) KIA; Bailed out over the North Sea after mechanical trouble.
P-51B VF- 43-24771

**May 13, 1944**
Lt. Leonard R. Pierce (334th) KIA; Bailed out east of Southwold after mechanical failure.
P-51B QP-G 42-106441

**May 19, 1944**
Lt. Donald J. Patchen (336th) POW; Hit by flak near Hanover.
P-51B VF-A 43-6584

**May 21, 1944**
Lt. William W. Hunt (335th) KIA; Hit by flak near Zossen.
P-51B WD-F 43-6901

**May 22, 1944**
Capt. Nicholas Megura (334th) INT; Shot-up by a P-38 and landed in Sweden.
P-51B QP-F 43-7158

**May 24, 1944**
Lt. Harry E. Jennings (335th) KIA; Hit by fighters near Hamburg.
P-51B WD-W 42-106429 "Judy IV"

**May 25, 1944**
Capt. Joseph H. Bennett (336th) POW; Hit by fighters near Strasbourg
P-51B VF-N 43-6572
Lt. Thomas K. McDill (336th) POW; Hit by fighters near Strasbourg.
P-51B VF-Q 43-6633

**May 27, 1944**
Lt. Elliot H. Shapleigh (335th) MIA-E; Bailed out near Laon after mechanical failure.
P-51B WD-O 42-106464

**May 28, 1944**
Lt. Richard L. Bopp (334th) POW; Ran out of fuel near Ruhland.
P-51B QP-H 42-106846
Lt. Aubrey E. Hewatt (334th) POW; Hit by a Me-109 east of Magdeburg.
P-51B QP-Y 43-6933

**May 29, 1944**
Lt. Frank E. Speer (334th) POW; Hit by flak at Mackfitz A/F and bellied-in near Stargard.
P-51B QP-W 43-6560

**May 30, 1944**
Lt. Mark H. Kolter (334th) KIA; Hit by flak southwest of Brandenburg
P-51B QP-Q 43-7178
Capt. Willard W. Millikan (336th) POW; Collided with Lt. Young near Wittenberg.
P-51B VF-U 43-24769 "Missouri Mauler"
Lt. Samuel H. Young (336th) POW; Collided with Capt. Millikan near Wittenberg.
P-51B VF- 43-24787

**May 31, 1944**
Capt. Carroll B. McElroy (335th) POW; Lost in bad weather near Sandbergen.
P-51C WD-G 42-103609
Lt. Robert H. Homuth (335th) KIA; Lost in bad weather near Onkerzde.
P-51B WD-S 43-7032

**June 4, 1944**
Lt. Robert L. Kackerback (336th) KIAc; Crashed near Steeple Bumpstead.
P-51B VF- 43-7059

**June 6, 1944**
Maj. Winslow M. Sobanski (334th) KIA; Hit by fighters near Dreux.
P-51B QP-J 43-6898 "Deacon"
Lt. Thomas E. Fraser (334th) POW; Hit by fighters near Rouen.
P-51B QP-G 43-24825 "Jerry"
Lt. Edward J. Steppe (334th) KIA; Hit by fighters near Dreux.
P-51D QP-M 43-6957 "Turnip Termite"
Capt. Bernard L. McGrattan (335th) KIA; Hit by fighters near Rouen.
P-51B WD-D 42-106576
Lt. Cecil E. Garbey (335th) KIA; Hit by fighters near Rouen.
P-51B WD-E 43-6575
Lt. Harold L. Ross, Jr. (335th) KIA; Hit by fighters near Rouen.
P-51B WD-K 42-106786
F/O Walter Smith (335th) KIA; Hit by fighters near Rouen.
P-51B WD-H 43-7172 "Three Jokers"
Lt. Harold H. Frederick (336th) MIA-E; Bellied-in near Evreux after suffering flak damage.
P-51C VF- 42-103287
Lt. Oscar F. LeJeunesse (336th) POW; Hit by flak and bailed out near Lyon.
P-51C VF- 42-103332

**June 7, 1944**
Lt. Osce R. Jones (335th) POW; Hit by flak in the Dol-Deb area.
P-51B WD-J 43-7042
Lt. Kenneth D. Smith (336th) KIA; Collided with a P-51 on take-off from Debden.
P-51B VF- 43-6613

**June 8, 1944**
Lt. Eacott G. Allen (334th) MIA-E; Collided with Lt. Scott near Le Mans.
P-51B QP-K 42-106823
Lt. James F. Scott (334th) KIA; Collided with Lt. Allen near Le Mans.
P-51B QP-P 43-7150
Lt. James T. Byrd, Jr. (334th) KIAc; Dove into the ground near Leiston.
P-51B QP-D 43-6433

**June 10, 1944**
Lt. Frank D. Caple (336th) POW; Hit by flak near Dieppe.
P-51B VF- 43-6889
Lt. Conrad J. Netting (336th) KIA; Hit by flak near St. Michel.
P-51B VF- 42-106669 "Coujon IV"

**June 11, 1944**
Lt. Leon J. Cole, Jr. (334th) KIA; Hit the ground while strafing near Villedieu.
P-51C QP-B 42-103292
Lt. Harry B. Noon (334th) KIA; Hit trees while dive-bombing near Villidieu.
P-51B QP-U 43-6586

**June 18, 1944**
Lt. James H. Glynn, Jr. (334th) MIA-E; Hit by flak and bailed out near Avranches.
P-51B WD-B 43-7187
Lt. Robert W. Little (335th) POW; Hit by flak in the Dol-Deb area.
P-51B WD-G 43-6770
Lt. Harvie J. Arnold (336th) KIA; Hit by flak near Combourg.
P-51D VF-J 44-13307

**June 19, 1944**
Lt. Dean J. Hill (335th) KIA; Crashed into the Channel in bad weather.
P-51B WD-F 43-6896

**June 20, 1944**
Lt. Vol R. Harris, Jr. (335th) POW; Hit by fighters near Stettin.
P-51B WD-R 42-106706
Maj. James A. Goodson (336th) POW; Hit by flak near Neubrandenburg.
P-51D VF-B 44-13303

**June 21, 1944**
Lt. Frank T. Sibbett (335th) KIA; Hit by a Me-109 near Siedlce.
P-51B WD-X 43-6784

**July 2, 1944**
Lt. Ralph K. Hofer (334th) KIA; Hit by a Me 109 near Budapest and crashed near Mostar.
P-51B QP-X 43-6746
Lt. Thomas S. Sharp (334th) KIA; Hit by a fighter near Budapest.
P-51B QP-D 42-106650
Lt. George I. Stanford, Jr. (335th) POW; Hit by fighters near Budapest.
P-51D WD-K 44-13402
Lt. J.C. Norris (336th) POW; Hit by fighters near Budapest.
P-51B VF- 43-6650

**July 7, 1944**
Lt. John J. Scally (334th) POW; Collided with a Me-410 near Nordhausen.
P-51B QP-E 43-6567

**July 11, 1944**
Lt. James S. Hanrahan (335th) POW (E); Suffered mechanical trouble near Bonniques.
P-51B WD-N 43-6562

**July 13, 1944**
Maj. Wilson V. Edwards (HdQts) POW; Hit by flak near Mannheim and bailed out near Metz.
P-51D VF- 44-13608

**July 19, 1944**
Lt. Curtis Simpson (335th) INT; Landed in Switzerland after mechanical trouble.
P-51B WD-U 42-106438
Lt. Kermit O. Dahlen (335th) KIA; Hit by a Me-109 near Munich.
P-51B WD- 43-6463

**July 20, 1944**
Lt. Lester B. Godwin (335th) MIA-E; Hit by flak near Aachen and bailed out near Antwerp.
P-51C WD-H 42-103561

**July 22, 1944**
Lt. Lloyd G. Kingham (335th) KIA; Spun-in near Audley End after take-off.
P-51D WD-R 44-13641

**August 2, 1944**
Lt. Gerald C. Chapman (336th) KIA; Hit by flak near Beauvais.
P-51B VF- 43-6846

**August 3, 1944**
Maj. Fonzo D. Smith (HdQts) POW; Suffered mechanical trouble near Athis.
P-51D VF- 44-13934

**August 7, 1944**
Lt. Donald M. Malmsten (334th) MIA-E; Hit by flak near Dijon.
P-51B QP-U 43-24979
Lt. Sidney V. Wadsworth (335th) POW; Hit by flak near Pont de Pany.
P-51B WD-V 43-6437

**August 8, 1944**
Lt. Thomas A. Underwood (334th) POW; Hit by flak and bailed out near Varnaug.
P-51B QP-C 43-24793
Capt. Frank C. Jones (335th) KIA; Hit by flak over Norway and crashed into the North Sea.
P-51D WD-P 44-14027
Lt. Robert G. Fischer (335th) KIA; Hit by flak at Stravanger/Sola A/F.
P-51B WD-N 42-106940

**August 13, 1944**
Lt. Stephen Boren (335th) KIA; Hit trees while strafing near Troesnes.
P-51D WD-W 44-13997

**August 15, 1944**
Lt. Norman W. Aachen (334th) POW; Hit by flak near Bad Zwischenachmer.
P-51B QP-A 43-6882

**August 18, 1944**
Lt. Arthur C. Cwiklinski (334th) MIA-E; Hit by a Me-109 south of Beauvais.
P-51D QP-X 44-13314
Lt. C.G. Howard (334th) KIA; Hit by a Me-109 near Beauvais.
P-51B QP-D 43-24841
Lt. Dean E. Lange (334th) POW; Hit by a Me-109 southwest of Beauvais
P-51C QP-N 42-103791
Lt. John T. Conley (335th) KIA; Hit by a Me-109 near Les Andelys.
P-51B WD-N 43-24813
Lt. Robert J. Cooper (335th) KIA; Hit by a Me-109 near Les Andelys.
P-51B WD-Z 42-106855
Lt. Leo Dailey (335th) KIA; Hit by a Me-109 near La Ferte.
P-51B WD-M 42-106555
Lt. Bernard J. Rosenson (335th) KIA; Hit by a Me-109 near Les Andelys.
P-51D WD-O 44-13567
Lt. Donald E. Smith (335th) KIA; Hit by a Me-109 near Les Andelys.
P-51D WD-R 44-13563
Capt. Otey M. Glass, Jr. (336th) MIA-E; Hit by fighters near Gisor.
P-51B VF-G 42-106797

**August 24, 1944**
Capt. John T. Godfrey (336th) POW; Hit by fire from another P-51 while strafing at Nordhausen.
P-51D VF-F 44-13412

**August 25, 1944**
Lt. Kenneth J. Rudkin (334th) POW; Hit by flak near Lubeck.
P-51D QP-R 44-13732

**August 28, 1944**
Lt. Herbert Vander Vate, Jr. (334th) KIA; Hit by flak near Strasbourg.
P-51D QP-K 44-14310
Maj. Archibald M. Thomson (335th) MIA-E; Hit by flak near Strasbourg
P-51D WD-F 44-13534
Capt. Pierce W. McKennon (335th) MIA-E; Hit by flak near Niederbronn
P-51D WD-A 44-13883
Capt. Albert L. Schlegel (335th) KIA; Hit by flak near Strasbourg.
P-51D WD-O 44-14066
Lt. Ferris S. Harris (336th) KIA; Hit by flak near Strasbourg.
P-51C VF- 42-103796

**September 9, 1944**
Lt. Earl C. Walsh (334th) ASR; Bailed out 30 miles off Schouwen.
P-51D QP-V 44-13352

**September 10, 1944**
Lt. Robert W. White (336th) KIA; Crashed near Boxted upon return.
P-51B VF- 43-6891

**September 11, 1944**
Lt. William R. Groseclose (335th) POW; Hit by a Me-109 near Naumberg.
P-51D WD-Q 44-13431
Lt. Paul S. Iden (335th) KIA; Hit by a Me-109 near Naumberg.
P-51B WD-Z 43-6959
Lt. James W. Russell (335th) POW; Hit by fighters near Fulda.
P-51D WD-R 44-14158
Lt. Henry A. Ingalls (336th) POW; Hit by flak at Langensalza.
P-51B VF- 43-6573
Lt. Roy L. Patterson (336th) KIA; Hit by flak near Lursendorf.
P-51D VF- 44-14266

**September 12, 1944**
Capt. Thomas E. Joyce (334th) POW; Hit by flak and bellied-in near Darmstadt.
P-51D QP-K 44-14271
Lt. James C. Lane (336th) POW; Bailed out northeast of Trier after mechanical trouble.
P-51D VF- 44-13260

**September 13, 1944**
Capt. William B. Smith (334th) KIA; Hit by flak at Schwabisch Hall.
P-51D QP-Y 44-14281

**September 17, 1944**
Lt. Clifford F. Holske (335th) POW; Hit by fighters near Bocholt.
P-51D WD-I 44-14054
Lt. Nicholas W. Vozzy (335th) KIA; Hit by fighters near Bocholt.
P-51B WD-J 43-6841

**October 2, 1944**
Lt. George H. Logan, Jr. (336th) KIA; Suffered mechanical failure and bailed out northeast of Apeldoorn.
P-51D VF- 44-14172

**October 7, 1944**
F/O Kenneth E. Foster (334th) ASR; Bailed out over the Channel after mechanical trouble.
P-51B QP-T 43-6719

**October 14, 1944**
Capt. Joseph L. Lang (334th) KIA; Hit by a Me-109 near Kaiserlautern and crashed near Eurville.
P-51D QP-Z 44-14123

**November 5, 1944**
Lt. Russell J. Anderson (335th) POW; Hit by flak near Baden Baden.
P-51D WD-U 44-14339

**November 6, 1944**
Lt. John L. Childs (334th) KIA; Hit by a FW-190 near Rheine.
P-51D QP-Z 44-14772
Lt. Earl C. Walsh (334th) POW; Hit by a Me-109 near Rheine.
P-51D QP-N 44-14229
Lt. Charles Y. Mead (336th) KIAc; Bailed out too low near Little Walden after mechanical trouble.
P-51C VF- 42-103794

**November 8, 1944**
Lt. Earl A. Quist (336th) POW; Last heard from near the German border.
P-51D VF-L 44-13961

**November 18, 1944**
Lt. Ralph E. Lewis (335th) KIA; Hit by flak near Gunzburg.
P-51D WD-X 44-14529

**November 20, 1944**
Lt. Donald L. Bennett (334th) POW; Suffered mechanical failure east of the Zuider Zee.
P-51D QP-R 44-13615
Lt. Leonard R. Werner (334th) KIA; Suffered mechanical trouble east of the Zuider Zee.
P-51D QP-Q 44-13411

**November 21, 1944**
Lt. Carmen J. Delnero (334th) KIA; Hit by a Me-109 near Meerane.
P-51D QP-H 44-14119 "Sizzlin' Liz"
Lt. George L. Klaus (336th) POW; Hit by flak northeast of Halle.
P-51B VF-D 43-6942 "Meiner Kleiner"

**December 18, 1944**
Capt. Charles D. Hewes (335th) KIA; Hit by flak near Giessen.
P-51D WD- 44-15455

**December 25, 1944**
Lt. Charles E. Poage (335th) POW; Hit by a FW-190 near Laacher See.
P-51D WD- 44-14540 "Ascend Charlie"
Capt. Donald R. Emerson (336th) KIA; Downed by allied ground fire and crashed in Belgium.
P-51D VF-D 44-15054

**January 2, 1945**
Lt. Arthur J. Senecal (334th) KIA; Hit by flak near Konigsfeld and bailed out too low.
P-51B QP-Z 43-6587

**January 16, 1945**
Capt. Victor R.T. Rentschler (334th) POW; Hit by flak at Neuburg and bailed out near Reutlingen.
P-51D QP-M 44-15324
Lt. Fred D. Hall (336th) KIA; Crashed near Folkstone upon return.
P-51D VF- 44-14533

**January 17, 1945**
Lt. Robert L. Stallings (335th) KIA; Suffered mechanical failure near Den Helder and crashed off Lowestoft.
P-51K WD-J 44-11339

**February 4, 1945**
Lt. Alvin O. Wallace (336th) KIAc; Spun-in near Great Sampford.
P-51D VF- 44-15531

**February 6, 1945**
F/O William D. Bates (334th) KIA; Bailed out south of Southold after mechanical trouble.
P-51D QP-V 44-13884
Lt. Paul G. Santos (335th) KIA; Hit by flak near Torgau.
P-51D WD-T 44-15615

**February 11, 1945**
Lt. Henry A. Kaul (336th) KIA; Hit trees strafing near Lemgo.
P-51D VF-D 44-63233 "Inky's Dinky"
Lt. Morton R. Savage (334th) KIAc; Hit a radio tower near Nuthampstead.
P-51D QP-W

**February 20, 1945**
Capt. John C. Fitch (335th) POW; Hit by flak and bailed out southwest of Newmarkt.
P-51D WD- 44-15351

**February 21, 1945**
Lt. Andrew C. Lacy (334th) POW; Hit by flak and bailed out near Neresheim.
P-51K QP-P 44-11677 "Lynette Sue"
Lt. August W. Rabe (335th) POW; Hit trees while strafing and bellied-in near Coburg.
P-51D WD-O 44-14435

**February 24, 1945**
F/O Alvin L. Hand (334th) POW; Hit by flak near Emmen.
P-51K QP-X 44-11661 "Iron Ass"

**February 25, 1945**
Capt. Kendall E. Carlson (336th) POW; Hit the ground while strafing Kothen A/F.
P-51K VF-Y 44-11356

**February 27, 1945**
Lt. Robert S. Voyles (334th) POW; Hit by flak at Weimar A/F.
P-51D QP-A 44-14537 "Old Witch"
Lt. Harold R. Crawford, Jr. (336th) POW; Hit by flak at Weimar A/F.
P-51K VF- 44-11665

**March 3, 1945**
Capt. George H. Davis (335th) POW; Hit by flak in the Celle- Ulzen area.
P-51D WD- 44-63599
Lt. Kenneth Green (335th) POW; Hit by flak and crashed near Rotterdam.
P-51D WD-U 44-14923 "See Me Later"

**March 12, 1945**
Maj. John D. McFarlane (336th) MIA-E; Lost coolant and bailed out near Mon Island.
P-51D VF-L 44-14350

**March 18, 1945**
Maj. Pierce W. McKennon (335th) MIA-E; Downed by flak near Neubrandenburg. Rescued by Lt. George Green who flew them both back to England.
P-51D WD-A 44-63166 "Ridge Runner"

**March 21, 1945**
Capt. Albert J. Davis (335th) KIA; Hit by flak near Hesepe and bailed out too low.
P-51D WD- 44-63670
Lt. Robert A. Cammer (335th) POW; Hit by flak at Achmer.
P-51D WD-K 44-14361 "Fiesty Sue"

**March 26, 1945**
Lt. Harry L. Davis (336th) KIA; Crashed near Woodbridge after a possible collision.
P-51D VF-B 44-13317
Lt. Earl F. Hustwit (336th) KIA; Crashed west of Valkenburg after mechanical trouble.
P-51D VF- 44-72411

**March 31, 1945**
F/O Kenneth E. Foster (334th) POW; Suffered mechanical trouble near Hengelo.
P-51K QP-Z 44-11336 "Buffalo Bertie"

**April 8, 1945**
Lt. Homer C. Smith (336th) KIAc; Crashed northwest of Cambridge.
P-51C VF-T 42-103603

**April 9, 1945**
Lt. Robert C. Bucholz (335th) KIA; Hit by flak at Munich-Brunnthal.
P-51D WD-T 44-14389 "Suzy"
Lt. Herman S. Rasmussen (335th) KIA; Hit by flak at Munich-Brunnthal and bailed out to low south of Neubiberg.
P-51D WD- 44-13788

**April 16, 1945**
LtCol. Sidney S. Woods (HdQts) POW; Hit by flak at Praha.
P-51D QP-A 44-72251
Lt. Edward J. McLoughlin (335th) POW; Hit by flak at Praha and crashed near Kbely.
P-51D WD-P 44-13389
Capt. Carl R. Alfred (336th) KIA; Hit by flak at Praha and crashed near Prague.
P-51D VF- 44-72523
Capt. Leroy A. Carpenter, Jr. (336th) KIA; Hit by flak at Praha and crashed near Kbely.
P-51D VF- 44-63831
Capt. Edward L. Gimbel (336th) POW; Hit by flak at Praha.
P-51D VF- 44-72769
Lt. William H. Ayer (336th) POW; Hit by flak at Praha.
P-51D VF- 44-13375
Lt. Ben L. Griffin (336th) POW; Hit by flak at Praha and crashed near Kbely.
P-51D VF-H 44-14277 "Jersey Bounce II"
Lt. Maurice W. Miller (336th) POW; Hit by flak at Praha and crashed near Kbely.
P-51D VF-S 44-14527 "Mary"

**April 17, 1945**
Lt. Robert O. Davis (336th) KIA; Hit by flak near Pilzen.
P-51D VF- 44-14387

**April 25, 1945**
Lt. William B. Hoelscher (334th) MIA-E; Hit by flak at Prague/Ruzny A/F.
P-51D QP-V 44-15347

**May 17, 1945**
Capt. Richard L. Tannehill (335th) KIAc; Crashed near Llanbedr.
P-51D WD- 44-72340

**May 29, 1945**
Lt. Harold H. Frederick (336th) KIAc; Crashed near Crewe.
P-51D VF S 44-72181 "Sunny VIII"
Lt. Barnaby M. Wilhoit (336th) KIAc; Crashed near Burtonwood.
P-51D VF-

**Headquarters**
Ackerly, Robert A., Maj.; November 1944-January 1945; to 335th Ftr Sqn; ex-334th Ftr Sqn
Anderson, Edward W., Col.; September 1942-August 1943; to 67th Ftr Wing
P-47C VF-E 41-6575

Blakeslee, Donald J.M., Col.; May 1943-November 1944; ex-RAF and 335th and 336th Ftr Sqns
P-47D WD-C 42-7863
P-51B WD-C 43-6437
P-51B WD-C 42-106726
P-51D WD-C 44-13779
Carlson, Donald R., Maj.; January 1944-June 1944; to 334th Ftr Sqn; August 1944-March 1945; to 356th Ftr Grp
153:20 hours
Clark, James A., Jr., LtCol.; March 1944-September 1944; ex-334th Ftr Sqn
P-51B QP-W 43-6560
P-51B QP-W 42-106650
P-51D QP-W 44-13372
Dayhuff, Harry J., LtCol.; December 1944-February 1945; ex-78th Ftr Grp
P-51D VF-I 44-15647
Edner, Seldon R., Maj.; January 1944-March 8, 1944(POW) ex-RAF and 335th and 336th Ftr Sqns
Edwards, Wilson V., Maj.; July 1944-July 13, 1944(POW) ex-336th Ftr Sqn
P-51D VF-B 44-13608
Gover, Leroy, Maj.; January 1944-March 1944; ex-RAF and 336th Ftr Sqn
257 total missions
P-47D VF-G 42-74688 "Miss San Carlos"
Halsey, Gilbert O., Maj.; August 1943-January 1944; ex-RAF and 336th Ftr Sqn
Hively, Howard D., Maj.; January 1945-January 1945; ex-RAF and 334th Ftr Sqn
P-51D QP-J 44-15347
Kinnard, Claiborne H., LtCol.; September 1944-December 1944; to 355th Ftr Grp; ex-355th Ftr Grp
P-51D QP-A 44-14292 "Man O'War"
Markel, Alfred H., Capt.; August 1944-November 1944; ex-334th Ftr Sqn
Monroe, Shelton W., Maj.; April 1945-September 1945; ex-334th and 335th Ftr Sqns
Oberhansly, Jack J., LtCol.; December 1944-February 1945; ex-78th Ftr Grp
150 total missions
P-51K QP-X 44-11661 "Iron Ass"
O'Donnell, William J., Maj.; April 1945-June 1945; ex-335th Ftr Sqn
P-51D WD-B 44-14557 "The Dutchess"
Peterson, Chesley G., Col.; September 1942-January 1944; ex-RAF
200 missions total
Stepp, Malta L., Jr., Capt.; May 1943-July 1943; ex-RAF and 336th Ftr Sqn
P-47C VF-A 41-6541
Stewart, Everett W., Col.; February 1945-September 1945; ex-352nd and 355th Ftr Grps
P-51D VF-S 44-72181 "Sunny VIII"
Trippet, William A., LtCol.; November 1944-June 1945
P-51K VF- 44-11665
Woods, Sidney S., LtCol.; February 1945-April 16, 1945(POW) ex-49th Ftr Grp, PTO and 479th Ftr Grp
68 missions total
P-51D QP-A 44-72251

**334th Fighter Squadron**
Achen, Norman W., Lt.; June 1944-August 15, 1944(POW)
Ackerly, Robert A., Maj.; October 1944-November 1944; to HdQts
Adams, George W., Lt.; October 1943-November 1943; to 336th Ftr Sqn
Adams, Eacott G., Lt.; April 1944-June 8, 1944(MIA E)
Anderson, Stanley M., Capt.; September 1942-April 15, 1943(KIA) ex-71 Sqn, RAF
Spit. XR- BL376
Andreu, Andre J., F/O; May 1943-May 1943; to 336th Ftr Sqn
Andrew, Thomas J., Maj.; September 1942-September 1943, ex-71 Sqn, RAF
Spit. XR-S AB 929
P-47C QP-V 41-6413
Antonides, William O., Lt.; January 1945-September 1945
19 missions
P-51D QP-J
Arthur, Marvin W., Lt.; November 1944-EOW
35 missions, 165 hours
P-51D QP-U 44-13984 "Davy Lee"
P-51D QP-U 44-73304 "Blondie"
Ayers, James W., Lt.; June 1944-EOW
P-51B QP-K 43-6518
Barden, John L., Lt.; April 1944-April 29, 1944(POW)
9 missions
P-51B QP-B 42-106682
Bates, William D., F/O; November 1944-February 6, 1945(KIA)
Beason, Calvin H., Lt.; November 1944-EOW
P-51D QP-P 44-14518 "Nad"
Beeson, Duane W., Capt.; October 1942-April 5, 1944(POW); ex-71 Sqn, RAF
Spit. XR-J BL422
P-47D QP-B 42-7890 "Boise Bee"
P-51B QP-B 43-6819 "Bee"
Bell, Thomas R., Capt.; September 1944-EOW
P-51D QP-G
Bennett, Donald L., Lt.; September 1944-November 20, 1944(POW)
P-51D QP-R 44-13615
Biel, Hipolitus T., Lt.; September 1943-April 24, 1944(KIA)
P-47D QP-T
P-51B QP-T
Blanchfield, Herbert J., Capt.; August 1943-May 9, 1944(POW)
P-47C QP-E 41-6187
P-51B QP-E 43-6746
P-51B QP-E 42-106767
Boehle, Vernon A., Capt.; October 1942-November 1943; to 9th Air Force; ex-71 Sqn, RAF
Spit. XR- EN783
P-47C QP-O 41-6400 "Indianapolis"
Boock, Robert A., Lt.; October 1942-May 18, 1943(KIA); ex-71 Sqn, RAF
Spit. XR- AB941
P-47C QP-S 41-6405
Booth, Douglas E., Lt.; May 1943-September 1943; ex-RAF
Bopp, Richard L., Lt.; May 1944-May 28, 1944(POW)
Boretsky, Clarence L., Lt.; June 1944-March 1945
P-51D QP-B 44-13984 "Meg"
Bowers, Arthur R., Lt.; November 1944-EOW
30 missions
P-51D QP-S "Sweet Arlene"
Brite, W.C., Lt.
Brown, Carl F., Capt.; June 1944-EOW
72 missions
Brown, Gerald, Maj.; June 1944-October 1944; ex-55th Ftr Grp
P-51D QP-L
Buchanan, Ralph H., Lt.; July 1944-EOW
P-51D QP-W 44-72155 "The Count"
Bunte, Allan F., Lt.; May 1943-April 5, 1944(POW)
Burnett, Paul E., Lt.; November 1944-September 1945
P-51D QP- 44-72327 "Marjorie"
Burney, Philo M., Lt.; January 1945-September 1945
Burroughs, Vernon A., Lt.; May 1944-May 9, 1944(POW); ex-355th Ftr Grp
Byrd, James T., Jr., Lt.; June 1944-June 8, 1944(KIAc)
0 missions
Callahan, James F., Lt.; May 1944-September 1944
Care, Raymond C., Capt.; October 1942-February 1944; to 65th Ftr Wg; April 1944-April 15, 1944 (POW); ex-71 Sqn, RAF
104 missions
Spit. XR- "Calamity Jane"
P-47C QP-R 41-6404
P-47D QP-R 42-7981
P-51B QP-R 43-7183
Carlson, Donald R., Maj.; June 1944-August 1944; to HdQts
Carr, Charles D., Lt.; October 1943-April 5, 1944(POW)
Castle, Vincent R., Lt.; February 1943-June 19, 1943(KIAc)
17 missions
P-47C QP-E 41-6407
P-47D QP-E 42-7881
Chatterly, Archie W., Lt.; January 1943-March 27, 1944(POW)
P-47C QP-G 41-6358 "Cal or Bust"
P-51B QP-G 43-6860
Childs, John L., Lt.; October 1944-November 6, 1944(KIA)
Clark, James A., LtCol.; September 1942-May 1944; to HdQts, ex-71 Sqn, RAF
Spit. XR-W BM293
P-47C QP-W 41-6195
P-47D QP-W 42-75252
P-51B QP-W 43-6560
Claus, Robert P., Lt.; February 1944-April 8, 1944(KIA)
Clifton, Henry E., Jr., Capt.; July 1944-March 1945
Coen, Oscar H., Maj.; March 1943-October 1943; ex-336th Ftr Sqn
104 missions, 295 hours total
P-47C QP-V 41-6413
Cole, Leon J., Jr., Lt.; June 1944-June 11, 1944(KIA)
Cox, Lynd J., Lt.; June 1944-January 1945
Cox, William A., F/O; December 1943-February 3, 1944(KIA)
P-47D QP-S 42-75254
Cronin, Timothy J., Lt.; May 1944-March 1945
Cwiklinski, Arthur C., Lt.; June 1944-August 18, 1944(MIA-E)
P-51D QP-X 44-13314
Daymond, Gregory A., Maj.; September 1942-March 1943; ex-71 Sqn, RAF
P-47C QP-M 41-6204
Delnero, Carmen J., Lt.; September 1944-November 21, 1944(KIA)
Denson, Gordon A., Lt.; January 1945-September 1945
24 missions, 126 hours
P-51D QP-E "Priscilla"
Dickmeyer, Robert A., Lt.; June 1944-December 1944
P-51D QP-D 44-13596 "Jan"
Douglas, Richard V., Lt.; January 1943-September 1943
P-47C QP-Y 41-6410
Dvorak, William J., Capt.; August 1944-EOW
P-51D QP-I "Zoomin' Zombie"
Dyer, Raymond A., Lt.; September 1944-September 1945
P-51D QP-V 44-14323 "Dyer-Ria"
Farington, Fred E., Jr., Lt.; September 1944-EOW
P-51D QP-N "Skippy"
Fernandez, Joseph P., Lt.; May 1944-
Ford, Gervais W., Capt.; January 1945-EOW; ex-453rd Bomb Grp(35 missions)
18 missions
Foster, Kenneth E., F/O; September 1944-March 31, 1945(POW)
P-51K QP-Z 44-11336 "Buffalo Bertie"
France, Victor J., Capt.; October 1942-April 18, 1944(KIA); ex-71 Sqn, RAF
Spit. XR-Q AD196 "Miss North Dallas"
P-47C QP-K 41-6414
P-47D QP-K 42-7876 "Miss Dallas"
P-51B QP-K 43-6832 "Miss Dallas"
Fraser, Thomas E., Lt.; May 1944-June 6, 1944(POW)
P-51B QP-G 43-24825 "Jerry"
Frazer, Robert B., Lt.; August 1943-February 28, 1944(KIAc)
P-51B QP-N 43-6656
Gallant, Joseph E., Lt.

Gallion, Frank D., F/O; October 1943-November 3, 1943(KIA)
Garvin, Leo C., Lt.; -September 1945
Gillette, Willard G., Lt.; May 1944-October 1944
Grey, Lawrence O., F/O; August 1943-November 1943; to 311th Ferry Sqn
Griffin, Ben L., Lt.; October 1944-December 1944; to 336th Ftr Sqn
Halligan, James E., Lt.; March 1945-September 1945
Hand, Alvin L., F/O; January 1945-February 24, 1945(POW)
Hardy, Preston B., Lt.; April 1944-October 1944
Harre, Charles W., Lt.; September 1944-April 1945
Harrington, James C., Lt.; September 1942- ex-71 Sqn, RAF
Spit. XR- BL370
Hedrick, William F., Capt.; May 1944-February 1945
Helfrecht, Kenneth G., Lt.; October 1944-September 1945
47 missions
P-51D QP-K "Georgie"
P-51D QP-R 44-14110 "Georgie"
Henwick, Roy A., Capt.; July 1944-October 1944; D.S. pilot from SAAF
P-51D QP-M
Hewatt, Aubrey E., Lt.; April 1944-May 28, 1944(POW)
Hills, Robert L., Capt.; October 1943-September 1944
P-51B QP-S 43-6717
Hively, Howard D., Maj.; September 1942-January 1945; ex-71 Sqn, RAF
P-47C QP-J 41-6576
P-51B QP-J 43-6898 "Deacon"
P-51D QP-J 44-13306
P-51D QP-J 44-15347
Hoelscher, William B., Lt.; August 1944-April 25, 1945(MIA-E)
Hofer, Ralph L., Lt.; September 1943-July 2, 1944(KIA)
72 missions, 286 hours
P-47C QP-L 41-6484 "Missouri Kid"
P-51B QP-L 42-106924 "Salem Representative"
Hollander, William J., Capt.; September 1942-May 1943; ex-71 Sqn, RAF
P-47C QP-B 41-6538 "Welakahoo"
Hopson, Alfred H., Capt.; September 1942-December 1943(Inj.); ex-71 Sqn, RAF
Spit. XR- EN915
P-47C QP-I 41-6202
P-47C QP-I 41-6212
Howard, C.G., Lt.; June 1944-August 18, 1944(KIA)
Howe, David W., Capt.; September 1943-March 1945; ex-RCAF
502:05 hours
P-51B QP-S 43-6717
P-51D QP-G 44-13884
Hughes, Walter R., Lt.; October 1944-January 1945; to 2nd Scouting Force
Jahnke, Jerome, Lt.; July 1944-EOW
P-51D QP-O 44-14142
James, Daniel L., Lt.; January 1945-EOW
25 missions
P-51D QP- "Lil Nell"
Jones, J.E., Lt.
Joyce, Thomas E., Capt.; May 1944-September 12, 1944(POW)
Kanaga, Robert H., Capt.; August 1944-April 1945
Kennedy, Michael J., Lt.; October 1944-September 1945
Kennedy, Peter R., Lt.; April 1944-April 29, 1944(POW)
Kenyon, Robert P., Capt.; March 1944-October 1944
King, Garrett C., Lt.; January 1943-June 14, 1943(KIAc)
13 missions
Kolter, Mark H., Lt.; April 1944-May 30, 1944(KIA)
Lacy, Andrew C., Lt.; September 1944-February 21, 1945(POW)
P-51K QP-P 44-11667 "Lynette Sue"
Lang, Joseph L., Capt.; December 1943-October 14, 1944(KIA)
P-51B QP-Z 43-24841
P-51D QP-Z 44-13352
P-51D QP-Z 44-14123
Lange, Dean E., Lt.; June 1944-August 18, 1944(POW)
Leaf, Dale B., Lt.; May 1943-September 2, 1943(KIA)
Lowther, Donald G., Lt.; January 1945-EOW
Lutz, John F., Lt.; September 1942-May 4, 1943(KIA); ex-71 Sqn, RAF
P-47C QP-P 41-6196
MacFarlane, Leland L., Lt.; January 1943-May 21, 1943(KIA)
P-47C QP-H 41-6406
Malmsten, Donald M., Capt.; April 1944-August 7, 1944(MIA-E)
September 1944-EOW
P-51B QP-M 43-6957 "Turnip Termite"
P-51D QP-V 44-14560 "Crotch Rot"
Markel, Alfred H., Capt.; May 1943-August 1944; to HdQts
McFadden, Jack D., Capt.; June 1944-EOW
P-51D QP-Q 44-14202
McMinn, Richard D., Capt.; September 1942-April 15, 1943(KIA); ex-71 Sqn, RAF
Spit. XR- AD464
P-47C QP-M 41-6204
McNabb, John P., F/O; September 1943-December 2, 1943(KIAc)
Megura, Nicholas, Capt.; July 1943-May 22, 1944(INT)
P-47D QP-N "Ill Wind?"
P-51B QP-N 43-6636 "Ill Wind?"
Miller, Robert J., Lt.; -April 1945
Mills, Henry L., Maj.; October 1942-March 6, 1944(POW); ex-71 Sqn, RAF
P-47C QP-Q 41-6191
P-47D QP-Q 42-74751
P-51B QP-Q 43-6690
Monroe, Shelton W., Maj.; January 1944-January 1945; to 335th Ftr Sqn
P-51D QP-O 44-13411

Montgomery, Gerald E., Maj.; May 1943-EOW
P-47D QP-H 42-7980 "Texas"
P-51B QP-H 42-106846
P-51D QP-H 44-14119 "Sizzlin Liz"
P-51D QP-H 44-15326 "Sizzlin Liz"
P-51D QP-H 44-72382 "Sizzlin Liz"
Moon, Ivan R., Lt.; September 1943-November 3, 1943(KIA)
Morgan, William B., Lt.; September 1942-May 21, 1943(POW); ex-71 Sqn, RAF
Spit. XR- BL550
Moulton, Howard N., Jr., Capt.; January 1944-April 8, 1944(POW)
Needham, David K., Lt.; May 1944-September 1944
P-51B QP-V
Noon, Harry B., Lt. ;June 1944-June 11, 1944(KIA)
Norley, Louis H., Maj.; January 1945-September 1945; ex-335th & 336th Ftr Sqns
160 missions, 554 hours total
P-51D QP-O 44-72196
P-51D QP-O 44-73108 "Red Dog XII"
O'Bryan, William C., Lt; January 1945-
O'Regan, William T., Capt.; September 1942-September 1943; ex-71 Sqn, RAF
Spit. XR- AD564
P-47C QP-X 41-6392
Payne, Carl G., Capt.; September 1944-September 1945
P-51D QP-J 44-72381
Pierce, Leonard R., Lt.; March 1944-May 13, 1944(KIA)
Pissanos, Spiros N., Capt.; October 1942-March 5, 1944(MIA-E); ex-71 Sqn, RAF
106 missions
P-47D QP-D 42-7945 "Miss Plainfield
P-51B QP-D 43-6798
Priser, Robert L., Capt.; September 1942-November 1943; to 9th Air Force (later POW January 1944); ex-71 Sqn, RAF
88 missions total
P-47C QP-E 41-6187
Rafalovich, Alex, Capt.; February 1943-March 21, 1944(POW)
P-47C QP-W 41-6195
Rentschler, Victor R.T., Capt.; June 1944-January 16, 1945(POW)
Ross, Gilbert G., Lt.; September 1942-October 1943; ex-; 71 Sqn, RAF
31 missions
P-47C QP-Y 41-6410
Rudkin, Kenneth J., Lt.; June 1944-August 25, 1944(POW)
Savage, Morton R., Lt.; September 1944-February 11, 1945(KIA)
Scally, John J., Lt.; June 1944-July 7, 1944(POW)
Schnell, John M., Jr., Lt.; March 1945-EOW
Scotts, James F., Lt.; April 1944-June 8, 1944(KIA)
Seaman, Anthony J., Lt.; September 1942-October 20, 1942(KIA); ex-71 Sqn, RAF
Senecal, Arthur J., Lt.; August 1944-January 2, 1945(KIA)
Sharp, Thomas S., Lt.; May 1944-July 2, 1944(KIA)
Sherman, Robert S., Lt.; April 1944-May 9, 1944(POW)
Siehl, Thomas J., Lt.; March 1945-September 1945
Siems, Grover C., Jr., Lt.; April 1944-July 1944(WIA July 2)
P-51D QP-O 44-13322 "Gloria III"
Simon, Jack T., Lt.; May 1944-September 1944
Skinner, Billy F., Lt.; March 1945-September 1945
Skirball, Alan, Lt.; January 1945-EOW
Slone, Orville W., Lt.; March 1945-September 1945
Smith, Clyde D., Lt.; May 1943-October 8, 1943(POW)
Smith, William B., Capt.; May 1943-September 13, 1944(KIA)
P-47C QP-Y 41-6410 "Little Butch"
P-51C QP-Y 42-103781
P-51D QP-Y 44-14281
Snell, Orrin C., Lt.; May 1944-May 1944(Inj. May 15); ex-RAF
Sobanski, Winslow M., Maj.; May 1943-June 6, 1944(KIA); ex-336th Ftr Sqn
P-47D QP-F 42-75126 "Mike IV"
P-51B QP-F
Speer, Frank E., Lt.; April 1944-May 29, 1944(POW)
P-51B QP-M 43-6957
Spencer, Milton L., Lt.; March 1945-
Spencer, William G., Lt.; January 1945-September 1945
Sprague, Robert S., Capt.; September 1942-November 26, 1942(KIA); ex-71 Sqn, RAF
Steppe, Edward J., Lt.; May 1944-June 6, 1944(KIA)
Stewart, H.L., Lt.; September 1942-January 1943; ex-71 & 121 Sqns, RAF
Sylvester, Ray L., Lt.; March 1945-September 1945
Underwood, Thomas A., Lt.; July 1944-August 8, 1944(POW)
Vander Vate, Herbert, Jr., Lt.; June 1944-August 28, 1944(KIA)
Van Epps, David A., Capt.; September 1943-April 9, 1944(POW)
P-47D QP-I 42-8641 "Great Dane II"
Voyles, Robert S., Lt.; September 1944-February 27, 1945(POW)
P-51D QP-A 44-14292 "Old Witch"
P-51D QP-A 44-14537 "Old Witch"
Walsh, Earl C., Lt.; June 1944-November 6, 1944(POW)
Wells, Lewis F., Lt.; July 1944-April 1945
Werner, Leonard R., Lt.; June 1944-November 20, 1944(KIA)
Whalen, Edmund D., Lt.; November 1943-March 6, 1944(KIA)
Whalen, William E., Lt.; July 1944-September 1944; to 2nd Scouting Force
P-51B QP-O 43-6899
Whitlow, Gordon H., Lt.; September 1942-May 21, 1943(KIA); ex-71 Sqn, RAF
Spit. XR- AB929
Wilkinson, James W., Lt.; January 1943-April 1943(Injured)
P-47C QP-S 41-6405
Later to 78th Ftr Grp, ETO
Williams, Robert G., Capt.; May 1943-March 21, 1944(POW); ex-RAF
103 missions

Wozniak, Edward J., Lt.; July 1944-April 1945
P-51D QP-T 44-63583 "Helen"
Wynn, Vasseure F., Capt.; September 1943-April 13, 1944(POW); ex-RAF

**335th Fighter Squadron**

Ackerly, Robert A., Maj.; January 1945-June 1945; to HdQts; ex-334th Ftr Sqn & HdQts
P-51D WD-P 44-72416 "Man-I-Ack"
Allen, David R., Capt.; November 1944-March 1945; to 355th Ftr Grp
Anderson, Charles F., Capt.; August 1943-April 19, 1944(KIA)
P-47D WD-L "Hell's Belle"
P-51B WD-L 43-7181
Anderson, Russell J., Lt.; August 1944-November 15, 1944(POW)
Anderson, William C., Capt.; September 1944-February 1945; to 479th Ftr Grp
Ballew, Hubert N., Lt.; September 1943-February 6, 1944(POW)
Bancroft, William H., Lt.; September 1944-January 1945; to 2nd Scouting Force
Barnes, George W., Lt.; October 1943-March 3, 1944(KIA)
Beatie, Ernest D., Lt.; October 1942-November 1943; ex-121 Sqn, RAF
Berry, Darwin L., Lt.; June 1944-December 1944
270 hours
P-51D WD-K 44-14361 "Fiesty Sue"
Blakeslee, Donald J.M., Maj.; November 1942-May 1943; to HdQts; ex-336th Ftr Sqn
P-47D WD-C 42-7863
Blanding, Leon M., Maj.; October 1942-March 1944; to 495th Ftr Trg Grp; ex-121 Sqn, RAF
June 1944-July 1944; to HdQts
Boren, Stephen R., Lt.; July 1944-August 13, 1944(KIA)
Bowyer, George W., Lt.; June 1944-June 1944 (WIA)
Boyce, Ralph G., Lt.; May 1944-May 6, 1944(KIAc)
0 missions
Boyles, Frank R., Capt.; September 1942-October 1943; to 65th Ftr Wg; ex-121 Sqn, RAF
Brandenburg, James H., Lt.; September 1943-March 21, 1944(KIA)
Brock, Charles L., Lt.; May 1944-March 1945
Bucholz, Robert C., Lt.; November 1944-April 9, 1945(KIA)
Bucher, Oliver B., Jr., Capt.; November 1944-September 1945
Burgess, Leslie I., Lt.; January 1945-September 1945
Cammer, Robert A., Lt.; November 1944-March 21, 1945(POW)
Carlow, Earle W., Capt.; January 1943-March 21, 1944(POW-E)
Carpenter, George, Maj.; September 1942-April 18, 1944(POW); ex-121 Sqn, RAF
257 hours
Spit. AV-X EN918
P-47C WD-I 41-6226
P-51B WD-I 43-6576 "Virginia"
P-51B WD-I 42-106675
Ceglarski, George W., Lt.; June 1944-September 1944; to 2nd Scouting Force
P-51D WD- "Sweet Stuff"
Church, Robert C., Capt.; September 1943-September 1944
P-51B WD-A 43-24813
Clotfelter, Ray P., Lt.; October 1943-March 28, 1944(POW)
Conley, John T., Lt.; July 1944-August 18, 1944(KIA)
Connors, Stanley W., Lt.; September 1944-May 1945
Cooley, George W., Lt.; June 1944-November 1944
P-51C WD- 42-103291
Cooper, Robert J., Lt.; July 1944-August 18, 1944(KIA)
Couse, Robert L., Lt.; January 1945-September 1945
P-51D WD-D 44-14570
Creamer, John N., Capt.; August 1944-March 1945
300 hours
Crine, James D., Lt.; April 1945-EOW
0 missions
Dahlen, Kermit O., Lt.; July 1944-July 19, 1944(KIA)
1 mission
Dailey, Leo, Lt.; June 1944-August 18, 1944(KIA)
Daley, William J., Maj.; September 1942-November 1942; ex-121 Sqn, RAF
Spit. AV-D EN853
Davis, Albert J., Capt.; June 1944-March 21, 1945(KIA)
Davis, George H., Capt.; January 1945-March 3, 1945(POW); ex-336th Ftr Sqn
Diamond, Brack, Capt.; June 1944-January 1945
Dimpfl, Helmut R., Lt.; April 1945-September 1945
0 missions
Draugh, Carl S., Lt.; April 1945-September 1945
0 missions
Dye, James D., Lt.; February 1943-March 1944(WIA March 21
Eaton, Wilbur B., Lt.; June 1944-February 1945; ex-RAF and PRG pilot
P-51B WD-U 43-6897 "See Me Later"
P-51D WD-U 44-14923 "See Me Later"
Edner, Seldon R., LtCol.; September 1942-January 1943; to 495th Ftr Trg Grp; ex-121 Sqn, RAF
August 1943-October 1943; to 336th Ftr Sqn
Elffner, Thomas H., Lt.; September 1944-May 1945
Ellington, Paul M., Capt.; October 1942-March 4, 1944(POW); ex-121 Sqn, RAF
P-47C WD-F 41-6214
P-47D WD-U 42-7968
Evans, Charles H., Capt.; May 1944-January 1945
Evans, Roy W., Maj.; October 1942-February 1944; ex-71 Sqn, RAF
P-47C WD-H 41-6206
P-47D WD-E 42-74686
Farmer, Robert V., Lt.; April 1945-September 1945
0 missions
Fetrow, Gene B., Capt.; September 1942-June 1943; ex-121 Sqn, RAF
Fiedler, Clemens A., Lt.; August 1943-April 10, 1944(KIA)
P-47C WD-S 41-6185
P-51B WD-S 43-6579 "Snafu"
Fink, Frank M., Lt.; October 1942-September 9, 1943(POW); ex-121 Sqn, RAF
Fischer, Robert G., Lt.; June 1944-October 8, 1944(KIA)
Fitch, John C., Capt.; September 1944-February 20, 1945(POW); ex-MTO pilot
Fowler, Bigelow, Capt.; May 1944-December 1944
Fowler, Duane, Lt.; April 1945-September 1945
0 missions
Fox, Philip J., Lt.; October 1942-December 1942; ex-121 Sqn, RAF
Freeburger, Edward P., Lt.; February 1944-March 18, 1944(KIA)
Freeman, Lucian W., F/O; January 1945-EOW
Garbey, Cecil E., Lt.; May 1944-June 6, 1944(KIA)
George, William H., Capt.; September 1944-May 1945
62 missions, 300 hours
Glynn, James H., Lt.; June 1944-June 18, 1944(MIA-E)
Godwin, Lester B., Lt.; May 1944-July 20, 1944(MIA-E)
Goetz, Joseph, F/O; February 1944-March 21, 1944(KIA); ex-56th Ftr Grp
Goodwyn, John W., Capt.; February 1944-September 1944
P-51B WD-R 43-6718
Green, George D., Lt.; July 1944-July 1945
P-51D WD-M 44-63736 "Suzon"
P-51D WD-KK 44-14137 "Suzanne"
Green, Kenneth, Lt.; February 1945-March 3, 1945(POW)
Green, Benson K., Lt.; October 1942-December 1942; ex-133 Sqn, RAF
Greenlease, Charles B., Lt.; January 1945-EOW
Grimm, Chester P., Lt.; October 1942-January 22, 1943(KIA)
Groseclose, William R., Lt.; July 1944-September 11, 1944(POW)
Guernsey, Frank D., Lt.; August 1944-August 1944; to 339th Ftr Grp
Halligan, James E., Jr., Lt.; January 1945-EOW
Halsey, Gilbert O., Maj.; September 1942-August 1943; to HdQts; ex-121 Sqn, RAF
Hanrahan, James S., Lt.; June 1944-July 11, 1944(POW-E)
Happel, James R., Maj.; October 1942-June 1944; ex-121 Sqn RAF
P-47C WD-X 41-6182
P-51B WD-X 43-6784
Hardin, Charles A., Lt.; October 1942-February 1943; ex-121 & 133 Sqns, RAF
Harris, Vol R., Jr., Lt.; June 1944-June 20, 1944(POW)
Hawkins, William C., Lt.; March 1944-March 21, 1944(MIA-E)
2 missions
Hawley, Robert C., Lt.; January 1945-September 1945
Heaton, Mack D., Lt.; January 1945-EOW
Henderson, William D., Capt.; September 1944-EOW
Henry, Lloyd F., Lt.; March 1944-April 18, 1944(KIA)
Hewes, Charles D., Capt; October 1944-December 18, 1944(KIA)
Hill, Dean J., Lt.; April 1944-June 19, 1944(KIA)
Holske, Clifford F., Lt.; June 1944-September 17, 1944(POW)
Homuth, Robert H., Lt.; April 1944-May 31, 1944(KIA)
Hunt, William W., Lt.; April 1944-May 21, 1944(KIA)
Hunter, Robert C., Jr., Lt.; February 1945-September 1945
Hupe, Franklin E., Lt.; May 1943-June 1944; ex-78th Ftr Grp
Iden, Paul S., Lt.; June 1944-September 11, 1944(KIA)
Jennings, Harry E., Lt.; May 1944-May 24, 1944(KIA)
Jennings, Loton D., Jr., Lt.; October 1944-EOW
Jones, Frank C., Capt.; March 1944-August 8, 1944(KIA)
62 missions
P-51B WD-P 43-6897
P-51D WD-P 44-13389
Jones, Osce R., Lt.; April 1944-June 7, 1944(POW)
Jungling, Enoch, Lt.; September 1944-EOW
Kelly, William P., Capt.; October 1942-February 5, 1943(KIA); ex-121 Sqn, RAF
Kingham, Lloyd G., Lt.; June 1944-July 22, 1944(KIA)
Kiser, Olin A., Lt.; September 1944-May 1945
Kolbe, John E., Lt.; June 1944-December 1944
Konsler, Charles E., Lt.; September 1944-May 1945
P-51D WD-D 44-13555
Lee, Henry A., Lt.; January 1945-September 1945
Lewis, Ralph E., Lt.; September 1944-November 18, 1944(KIA)
Lindsay, Hugh W., Lt.; July 1944-March 1945
Lines, Ted E., Capt.; April 1944-November 1944
P-51B WD-H 43-7172 "Three Jokers"
P-51D WD-O 44-13555 "Thunderbird"
P-51D WD-O 44-14570
Little, Robert W., Lt.; June 1944-June 18, 1944(POW)
Looney, James H., Lt.; April 1945-EOW
0 missions
Lucas, Paul J., Jr., Lt.; January 1945-September 1945
P-51D WD-F 44-11200
Mabie, Robert J., Capt.; July 1944-May 1945
P-51D WD-I 44-13564
P-51D WD-I 44-14221
P-51D WD-I 44-72478
MacDonald, James S., Lt.; October 1942-November 1942; to 12th Air Force(31st Ftr Grp); ex-133 Sqn, RAF
Manning, Cecil E., Capt.; July 1943-March 6, 1944(POW)
McCall, Elmer N., Lt.; June 1944-December 1944
McElroy, Carroll B., Capt.; May 1944-May 31, 1944(POW)
McGrattan, Bernard L., Capt.; September 1943-June 6, 1944(KIA)
P-47D WD-D 42-7936
P-51B WD-D 43-6767
P-51B WD-D 42-106576

McKennon, Pierce W., Maj.; February 1943-August 28, 1944(MIA-E)
September 1944-September 1945
560 hours
P-47C WD-A 41-6582
P-47D WD-A 42-8696
P-51B WD-A 42-106911 "Yippee Joe!!"
P-51D WD-A 44-13883
P-51D WD-A 44-14570 "Ridge Runner"
P-51D WD-A 44-14221 "Ridge Runner"
P-51D WD-A 44-72398 "Ridge Runner"
P-51D WD-A 44-63166 "Ridge Runner"
McLoughlin, Edward J., Lt.; February 1945-April 16, 1945(POW)
Mead, Edwin R., Lt.; May 1943-January 30, 1944(POW)
Merritt, Fred D., Lt.; January 1943-July 30, 1943(KIA)
Miles, Orval C., Lt.; May 1944-March 1945
Miller, Howard B., Lt.; February 1945-September 1945
Moe, Robert A., Lt.; February 1945-September 1945
25 missions
P-51D WD- "Umbreago"
Monroe, Shelton W., Maj.; January 1945-April 1945; to HdQts; ex-334th Ftr Sqn
Newell, William E., Lt.; March 1944-March 29, 1944(POW)
Norley, Louis H., Maj.; August 1944-January 1945; to 334th Ftr Sqn; ex-336th Ftr Sqn
160 missions, 554 hours total
P-51D WD-O 44-15028
O'Donnell, William J., Maj.; October 1944-April 1945; to HdQts
P-51D WD-B 44-14557 "The Duchess"
Osborne, Julian M., Lt.; September 1942-November 1942; ex-121 Sqn, RAF
Otto, Leonard F., Lt.; January 1945-EOW
Padgett, Cadman V., Capt.; September 1942-January 1944; ex-121 Sqn, RAF
Palmer, Richard W., Lt.; April 1945-September 1945
0 missions
Patterson, Robert G., Lt.; October 1942-October 8, 1943(POW); ex-121 Sqn, RAF
Perkins, Donald D., Capt.; April 1944-November 1944
P-51D WD- 44-13564
Peters, John N., Lt.; June 1944-January 1945
Peterson, Donald J., Lt.; July 1944-April 1945
P-51D WD-H 44-13977 "Cookie"
Poage, Charles E., Jr., Lt.; July 1944-December 25, 1944(POW)
Rabe, August W., Lt.; August 1944-February 21, 1945(POW); ex-RAF
Rasmussen, Herman S., Lt.; December 1944-April 9, 1945(KIA)
Read, Leighton M., Capt.; May 1943-February 1945
Reed, Richard I., Lt.; October 1943-February 20, 1944(KIA)
Riley, Paul S., Lt.; September 1943-April 24, 1944(POW)
P-47C WD-Y 41-6369
P-51B WD-Y 43-6922
Rinebolt, Richard J., Lt.; July 1944-March 1945
P-51D WD-L 44-13903
Rosenson, Bernard J., Lt.; July 1944-August 18, 1944(KIA)
Ross, Donald H., Lt.; October 1942-November 1943; to 357th Ftr Grp; ex-133 Sqn, RAF
Ross, Harold L., Jr., Lt.; April 1944-June 6, 1944(KIA)
Rowles, William P., Lt.; January 1944-June 1944
Russell, James W., Jr., Capt.; April 1944-September 11, 1944(POW)
P-51D WD-P 44-14098
Sanders, James M., Lt.; October 1942-May 1943
Santos, Paul G., Lt.; August 1944-February 6, 1945(KIA); ex-RAF
Saunders, Ralph W., Lt.; March 1944-April 13, 1944(KIA)
Scanlon, James J., Lt.; March 1945-EOW; ex-453rd Bomb Grp
(35 missions)
Scarbrough, Milton G., Lt.; April 1944-April 24, 1944(POW)
Schlegel, Albert J., Capt.; July 1943-August 28, 1944(KIA)
P-47D WD-O 42-7879
P-51B WD-O 43-6725
P-51B WD-O 42-106464
P-51D WD-O 44-14066
Sensibaugh, Zack S., Lt.; April 1944-September 1944
P-51D WD-L 44-13903
Seymour, Almond W., Lt.; March 1945-September 1945
Shapleigh, Eliot H., Lt.; April 1944-May 27, 1944(MIA-E)
Sibbett, Frank T., Lt.; May 1944-June 21, 1944(KIA)
Simpson, Curtis, Lt.; May 1944-July 19, 1944(MIA-E)
P-51B WD-U 42-106438
Skerritt, Richard A., Lt.; March 1945-September 1945
Skogstad, Paul H., Lt.; March 1945-September 1945
Slater, John T., Lt.; September 1942-September 24, 1942(KIA); ex-121 Sqn, RAF
Smart, Glenn J., Lt.; February 1944-May 1944; ex-336th Ftr Sqn
Smith, Donald E., Lt.; June 1944-August 18, 1944(KIA)
Smith, Fonzo D., Maj.; September 1942-August 3, 1944(POW); ex-121 Sqn, RAF
P-47D WD-W 42-7936 "Pistol Packin Mama"
Smith, John H., Lt.; March 1945-September 1945
Smith, Kenneth G., Capt.; October 1942-March 21, 1944(POW); ex-121 Sqn, RAF
P-47C WD-X 41-6207 "Mark II"
P-51B WD-X 43-6803
Smith, Walter, F/O; May 1944-June 6, 1944(KIA)
Smolinsky, Frank J., Lt.; October 1942-April 3, 1943(KIAc)
P-47C WD-D 41-6181 "Stinky"
Sparkman, William S., Lt.; March 1945-September 1945
Stafford, Alston W., Lt.; March 1945-September 1945
Stallings, Robert L., Lt.; September 1944-January 17, 1945(KIA)
Stanford, George I., Jr., Lt.; March 1944-July 2, 1944(POW)
P-51B WD-F 43-6896
Stanhope, Aubrey C., Lt.; October 1942-September 7, 1943(POW); ex-121 Sqn, RAF
P-47C WD-O 41-6233
Steele, James F., Lt.; May 1943-June 1944
Sullivan, Joseph W., Lt.; February 1944-February 24, 1944(KIA)
Talbott, William H., Lt.; August 1943-December 1943; to hospital; ex-RAF
Tannehill, Richard L., Capt.; April 1945-May 17, 1945(KIAc)
0 missions
Taylor, Ben A., Lt.; September 1942-November 1942; ex-121 Sqn, RAF
Thacker, Charles A., Lt.; March 1945-September 1945
Thomson, Archibald M., Maj.; June 1944-August 28, 1944(MIA-E)
Throop, Montgomery H., Lt.; February 1943-November 1943; to 357th Ftr Grp
Trietsch, Ralph G., Lt.; March 1945-EOW
Tyler, Robert N., Lt.; September 1944-July 1945
Underwood, Wade F., Lt.; January 1945-September 1945
Van Wyk, Neil, Capt.; November 1944-February 1945; ex-336th Ftr Sqn
Vozzy, Nicholas W., Lt.; July 1944-September 17, 1944(KIA)
Wadsworth, Sidney V., Lt.; June 1944-August 7, 1944(POW)
Ward, Hugh A., Lt.; October 1943-March 4, 1944(POW)
Waterman, Lloyd W., Lt.; September 1943-May 9, 1944(POW)
Williams, Robert G., Lt.; January 1943-May 1943; to 334th Ftr Sqn
Willis, Donald K., Lt.; October 1942-April 1943; ex-121 Sqn, RAF
Willruth, Calvin W., Capt.; September 1944-EOW
65 missions
P-51D WD-Y 44-15028 "Dotty"
Wortman, Ward K., Lt.; February 1943-July 14, 1943(KIA)
P-47D WD-Z 42-7939
Wyman, Burton C., Lt.; August 1943-January 29, 1944(KIA)
Young, Donald A., Maj.; September 1942-October 1943; ex-121 Sqn, RAF

**336th Fighter Squadron**

Adams, George W., Lt.; November 1943- ex-334th Ftr Sqn
Alexander, Richard L., Capt.; October 1942-January 1943; ex-133 Sqn, RAF; later 52nd Ftr Grp, MTO
Alfred, Carl R., Capt.; July 1944-April 16, 1945(KIA)
P-51D VF- 44-14552
P-51D VF- 44-72523
Anderson, Hazen S., Lt.; October 1942-March 12, 1943(POW); ex-133 Sqn, RAF
Andreu, Andre J., F/O; May 1943-June 1943; to 495th Ftr Trg Grp; ex-334th Ftr Sqn
Arnold, Harvie J., Lt.; June 1944-June 18, 1944(KIA)
Awalt, Robert W., F/O; April 1945-September 1945
0 missions
Axe, Harold, Jr., F/O; April 1945-September 1945
0 missions
Ayer, William H., Lt.; November 1944-April 16, 1945(POW)
Ayon, Henry R., F/O; April 1945-July 1945
0 missions
Ayres, Henry L., Jr., Lt.; October 1942-July 28, 1943(POW); ex-133 Sqn, RAF
Baker, William H., Jr., Lt.; September 1942-September 26, 1942(KIA); ex-133 Sqn, RAF
Baugh, Donald P., F/O; November 1944-July 1945
38 missions
P-51D VF-U 44-14388
Bennett, Joseph H., Capt.; April 1944-May 25, 1944(POW); ex-56th & 356th Ftr Grps
62 missions total
P-51B VF-T 42-106686 "Ann III"
Bennett, Joseph L., Lt.; October 1942-February 1944; ex-133 Sqn, RAF
Bishop, Leicester B., Capt.; October 1942-January 1944; ex-133 Sqn, RAF
Blakeslee, Donald J.M., Capt.; September 1942-November 1942; to 335th Ftr Sqn; ex-401, 411, 121, and 133 Sqns, RAF
Boguseuic, Ray D., F/O; April 1945-September 1945
0 missions
Bond, Oscar R., Jr., F/O; April 1945-September 1945
0 missions
Bonds, Frank C., Lt.; October 1943-November 1944
P-51B VF- 43-6891
Booth, Douglas E., Lt.; September 1942-May 1943; to 334th Ftr Sqn; ex-121 Sqn, RAF
Bousfield, Clarence H., F/O; April 1945-September 1945
0 missions
Bradley, Robert T., Lt.; May 1944-May 1944; to 355th Ftr Grp
Braley, Richard G., Capt.; January 1943-September 1944
Brooker, Beachem O., Jr., Lt.; November 1944-September 1945
Cameron, Donald K., Lt.; October 1942-
Caple, Frank D., Lt.; June 1944-June 10, 1944(POW)
1 mission
Carlson, Kendall E., Capt.; July 1943-February 25, 1945(POW)
P-47C VF-E 41-6575
P-51B VF-E 43-6507
P-51K VF-E 44-11356
Carpenter, Leroy A., Jr., Capt.; September 1944-April 16, 1945(KIA)
Cavallo, Robert J., Lt.; November 1944-September 1945
Chandler, Van E., Lt.; June 1944-January 1945
P-51B VF-U 43-24877
P-51D VF-U 44-14388 "Wheezy"
Chapman, Gerald C., Lt.; June 1944-August 2, 1944(KIA)
Chick, Lewis W., Maj.; January 1943-April 1943; to 8th Air Force HdQts
Coen, Oscar H., Maj.; October 1942-March 1943; to 334th Ftr Sqn; ex-71 Sqn, RAF
Collins, Wilmer W., Lt.; November 1944-July 1945
Cook, Charles A., Jr., Capt.; September 1942-September 26, 1942(POW); ex-133 Sqn, RAF
Corbett, Richard J., Lt.; May 1944-March 1945
Crawford, Harold R., Jr., Lt.; November 1944-February 27, 1945(POW)

Davis, George H., Capt.; September 1944-January 1945; to 335th Ftr Sqn
P-51D VF-D 44-63233 "Inky's Dinky"
Davis, Harry L., Lt.; November 1944-March 26, 1945(KIA)
Davis, Marvin L., Lt.; November 1944-EOW
Davis, Robert O., Lt.; January 1945-April 17, 1945(KIA)
Dettling, Fred C., Lt.; April 1945-September 1945
0 missions
Dickey, Melvin N., Capt.; July 1944-June 1945
P-51D VF-R "Betty Jane"
P-51D VF-R 44-13630 "Betty Jane II"
Drage, Donald D., Lt.; April 1945-September 1945
0 missions
DuFour, John G., Maj.; October 1942-September 1943
Spit. MD-E AB271
P-47C VF-E 41-6575 "Doreen II"
Dugan, Harry E., Jr., Lt.; May 1944-December 1944
P-51B VF- "Penny"
P-51D VF- "Penny II"
Dunn, Philip H., Capt.; Summer 1943-March 3, 1944(POW)
P-47C VF-Y 41-6903
P-51B VF-Y 43-7933 "Miss Skippy"
Dupree, Charles W., Lt.; June 1944-January 1945
Edge, Joseph M., Lt.; April 1945-September 1945
0 missions
Edner, Seldon R., LtCol.; October 1943-January 1944; to HdQts; ex-121 Sqn, RAF
Emerson, Donald R., Capt.; March 1944-December 25, 1944(KIA)
89 missions
P-51B VF-L 43-6889
P-51D VF-L 44-13317
Fleming, Claude R., Lt.; April 1945-August 1945
0 missions
Foster, Lucius F., Lt.; October 1942-August 1943; ex-121 Sqn, RAF
Spit. MD-L EN793
Franklin, Melvin C., Lt.; February 1945-September 1945
21 missions
P-51D VF-N "The Ring"
Frederick, Harold H., Lt.; February 1944-June 6, 1944(MIA-E)
September 1944-May 29, 1945(KIAc)
P-51B VF-H 43-6362 "Jersey Bounce"
P-51D VF-H 44-14277 "Jersey Bounce III"
Fuchs, Ray G., Lt.; October 1942-November 1943; to 9th
Air Force; ex-133 Sqn, RAF
Spit. MD- BM537
Garrison, Vermont, Lt.; September 1943-March 3, 1944(POW)
P-47D VF-H 42-74663
P-51B VF-H 43-6871
Gentile, Donald S., Capt.; September 1942-April 1944; ex-133 Sqn RAF
185 missions, 387 hours total
Spit. MD-T BL255 "Buckeye Don"
P-47D VF-T 42-8659 "Donnie Boy"
P-51B VF-T 43-6913 "Shangri-La"
Gibson, Robert W., Capt.; April 1945-July 1945
0 missions
Gimbel, Edward L., Capt.; June 1944-April 16, 1945(POW)
Glass, Otey M., Jr., Capt.; June 1944-August 18, 1944(MIA-E)
Glover, Fred W., Maj.; February 1944-April 30, 1944(MIA-E)
June 1944-June 1945
P-51B VF-C 43-12214 "Rebel Queen"
P-51D VF-B 44-14787
P-51D VF-B 44-63153
Godfrey, John T., Maj.; September 1943-August 24, 1944(POW)
P-47D VF-P 42-7884 "Reggie's Reply"
P-51B VF-P 43-6765
P-51B VF-P 42-106730 "Reggie's Reply"
Goodson, James A., Maj.; October 1942-June 20, 1944(POW); ex-133 Sqn, RAF
P-47D VF-W 42-7959
P-51B VF-B 43-24848
P-51D VF-B 44-13300
P-51D VF-B 44-13303
Gover, Leroy, Maj.; September 1942-January 1944; ex-133 Sqn, RAF
159 missions, 233:55 hours
Spit. MD-B BL722
P-47C VF-G 41-6256
P-47C VF-G 41-6574 "Miss San Carlos
P-47D VF-G 42-74688 "Miss San Carlos"
Griffin, Ben L., Lt.; December 1944-April 16, 1945(POW); ex-334th Ftr Sqn
Groshong, Douglas N., Lt.; September 1944-July 1945
P-51D VF-F 44-73021 "Clarine"
Grounds, Ira E., Capt.; April 1944-November 1944
Grove, Francis M., Capt.; May 1944-November 1945
P-51C VF-T 42-103603
P-51D VF-T 44-72767
Hagan, Harry N., Capt.; June 1944-May 1945
P-51D VF-Y 44-14317 "Duke"
P-51D VF-Y 44-72053
Hall, Fred D., Lt.; October 1944-January 16, 1945(KIA)
Halsey, Gilbert O., Maj.; January 1944-March 1944; ex-335th Ftr Sqn & HdQts
P-47D VF- 42-7884
Harris, Ferris S., Lt.; April 1944-August 28, 1944(KIA)
P-51C VF- 42-103796

Hastings, William H., Lt.; February 1945-September 1945
Hernandez, Edwin, Lt.; June 1944-March 1945
Herter, Glenn A., Lt.; May 1943-March 3, 1944(KIA)
P-47C VF-R 41-6354
Hessey, Francis D., Capt.; April 1945-September 1945
0 missions
Higgins, Joseph W., Capt.; April 1944-September 1944
P-51B VF-D 43-6942 "Meiner Kleiner"
Hileman, James E., Lt.; October 1944-April 1945
P-51D VF-C 44-15191 "Mary Belle"
Hobert, Robert D., Capt.; May 1943-April 5, 1944(KIA)
P-47C VF-I 41-6256 "Blue Goofis"
P-47D VF-I 42-75274
P-51B VF-I 43-6836
Hornickel, William E., Lt.; June 1944-September 1944; to 2nd Scouting Force
Hughes, Robert E., Lt.; September 1943-April 8, 1944(POW)
P-51B VF- 43-6768
Hunt, Gilbert W., Lt.; April 1944-November 1944
P-51B VF-F "Judy"
P-51D VF-F "Judy"
Hustwit, Earl F., Lt.; July 1944-March 26, 1945(KIA)
Ingalls, Henry A., Lt.; June 1944-September 11, 1944(POW)
Ingold, Conrad C., Lt.; May 1943-February 1944; to 56th Ftr Grp
Izant, John W., Lt.; February 1945-September 1945
19 missions
Jackson, Marion E., Capt.; September 1942-September 26, 1942(POW); ex-133 Sqn, RAF
Johnson, Warren E., Lt.; March 1944-September 1944
P-51B VF-W 43-6705
Joiner, Joseph H., Capt.; May 1944-June 1945
P 51B VF- 43-6573
P-51D VF- 44-13630
P-51D VF- 44-14548
Kackerback, Robert L., Lt.; June 1944-June 4, 1944(KIAc)
0 missions
Kallner, Richard F., Lt.; September 1944-May 1945
Kaul, Henry A., Lt.; October 1944-February 11, 1945(KIA)
Kesler, Gilbert L., Lt.; September 1944-May 1945
57 missions
P-51C VF-C 42-103602
P-51D VF-Y 44-72285 "Becky"
Klaus, George L., Lt.; October 1944-November 21, 1944(POW)
Knight, Jack A., Lt.; April 1945-July 1945
0 missions
Lambert, Donald E., Lt.; October 1942-January 1943; ex-133 Sqn, RAF
Spit. MD-L EN793
Lane, James C., Lt.; April 1944-September 12, 1944(POW)
P-51D VF-J 44-13260
P-51D VF-J 44-13307 "Butch"
Leaf, Dale B., Lt.; November 1942-May 1943; to 334th Ftr Sqn
Spit. MD- AR372
Lehman, Peter G., Lt.; August 1943-March 31, 1944(KIAc)
P-47C VF-S 41-6573 "Bevoapabm"
P-51B VF-S
Lejeunesse, Oscar F., Lt.; March 1944-June 6, 1944(POW-E)
Logan, George H., Jr., Lt.; April 1944-October 2, 1944(KIA)
Mable, William P., Lt.; April 1945-July 1945
0 missions
Matthews, Joseph G., Lt.; October 1942-August 16, 1943(MIA-E); ex-133 Sqn, RAF
Spit. MD- AB988
McColpin, Carroll W., Maj.; September 1942-November 1942; ex-71, 133, & 607 Sqns, RAF
Spit. MD-L EN793
McCord, Thomas A., Lt.; September 1944-May 1945
P-51D VF- "Doris II"
McDill, Thomas K., Lt.; April 1944-May 25, 1944(POW)
McFarlane, John D., Maj.; June 1944-March 12, 1945(MIA-E)
P-51D VF-L 44-13961
McMahan, James R., Lt.; February 1945-September 1945
12 missions
P-51D VF-A 44-14276 "Marcy"
Mead, Charles Y., Lt.; September 1944-November 6, 1944(KIAc)
Meredith, William B., Lt.; February 1945-July 1945
12 missions
Messenger, Robert J., Lt.; October 1942-March 6, 1944(POW); ex-133 Sqn, RAF
Spit. MD- BL582
P-47D VF- 42-75392
Middleton, George H., Lt.; September 1942-September 26, 1942(POW); ex-133 Sqn, RAF
Miley, Carl H., Maj.; October 1942-November 1943; ex-133 Sqn, RAF
Spit. MD- BL240
P-47C VF-L 41-6579
Miller, Ervin L., Capt.; September 1942-August 1943; ex-130 and 133 Sqns, RAF
P-47C VF-M 41-6529
Miller, Maurice W., Jr., Lt.; January 1945-April 16, 1945(POW)
20 missions
P-51D VF-S 44-14527 "Mary"
Millikan, Willard W., Capt.; June 1943-May 30, 1944(POW)
P-47C VF-U 41-6180 "Missouri Mauler
P-51B VF-U 43-6997 "Missouri Mauler
P-51B VF-U 43-6630 "Missouri Mauler
P-51B VF-U 43-24769 "Missouri Mauler"

Mirsch, George E., Lt.; October 1942-April 1944; ex-133 Sqn, RAF
P-47C VF-B 41-6571 "The Earl"
P-47C VF-B 41-6533
Mitchellweis, John, Lt.; October 1942-February 1, 1943(KIAc); ex-133 Sqn, RAF
Moore, Richard E., Lt.; January 1945-September 1945
Morgan, Paul M., Lt.; June 1944-April 1945
Murchake, John P., Jr., Lt.; January 1945-September 1945
27 missions
P-51D VF-G 44-64142 "Tiger Baby"
Nee, Donald D., Lt.; October 1942-November 1943; to 354th Ftr Grp, 9th Air Force; ex-133 Sqn, RAF
Spit. MD- AR372
P-47C VF-N 41-6197 "Cisco"
P-47C VF-N 41-6536 "Cisco"
Nelson, Robert F., Lt.; August 1943-April 22, 1944(POW)
P-51B VF-Q 43-6633
Netting, Conrad J., Lt.; April 1944-June 10, 1944(KIA)
Neville, Gene P., Lt.; September 1942-September 26, 1942(KIA); ex-133 Sqn, RAF
Norley, Louis H., Maj.; July 1943-August 1944; to 335th Ftr Sqn
160 missions, 554 hours total
P-47C VF-O 41-6183 "Red Dog"
P-51B VF-O 43-12416
P-51B VF-O 43-6802
Norris, J.C., Lt.; June 1944-July 2, 1944(KIA)
Patchen, Donald J., Lt.; March 1944-May 19, 1944(POW)
Patteeuw, Joseph A., Capt.; April 1944-November 1944
P-51B VF-Z 43-6846
P-51D VF-Z 44-13325
Patterson, C.H., Lt.
Patterson, Rufus L., Lt.; July 1944-September 11, 1944(KIA)
Pederson, Douglas P., Lt.; November 1944-July 1945
32 missions
P-51D VF-D 44-72789
Peterson, Kenneth D., Capt.; October 1942-March 29, 1944(POW); ex-133 Sqn, RAF
Spit. MD- BL773
P-47C VF-F 41-6539 "Arizona Pete"
P-51B VF-F 43-6696
Pierce, Donald J., Capt.; September 1944-February 1945; to 479th Ftr Grp
P-51D VF- 44-13375
Pierni, Donald J., Capt.; May 1944-March 1945
72 missions, 318 hours
Powell, Jap A., Lt.; October 1942-February 13, 1943(KIA); ex-133 Sqn, RAF
Quist, Earl A., Lt.; July 1944-November 8, 1944(POW)
P-51D VF-D 44-15054
Raphael, Jack L., Lt.; August 1943-June 1944; ex-RCAF
53 missions
P-47C VF-M 41-6529 "Eager Beaver"
Richards, Robert L., Lt.; September 1943-March 4, 1944(KIA)
Ridler, George E., Lt.; March 1945-September 1945
20 missions
P-51D VF-C 44-15191 "Peg O'My Heart"
Riedel, William D., Capt.; September 1944-September 1945
Robertson, Chesley H., Lt.; October 1942-; ex-133 Sqn, RAF
Ryerson, Leonard T., Lt.; September 1942-September 26, 1942(KIA); ex-133 Sqn, RAF
Schaefer, Woodrow W., Lt.; September 1944-April 1945
Seifert, Robert H., Lt.; April 1944-April 15, 1944(KIA)
Shilke, Charles H., Lt.; April 1944-November 1944
Simon, Reuben, Capt.; June 1943-May 1944
P-47D VF-K 42-7895
P-51B VF-K 43-6838
Skilton, Ernest R., Lt.; January 1944-March 16, 1944(KIA)
Slade, William C., Lt.; October 1942-May 1943; ex-133 Sqn, RAF
Smart, Glenn J., Lt.; October 1942-November 1943; ex-133 Sqn, RAF
Spit. MD- AA924
P-47D VF-K 42-7895
Smith, Dennis D., Lt.; September 1942-September 26, 1942(KIA); ex-133 Sqn, RAF
Smith, George C., Lt.; May 1944-December 1944
P-51C VF-C 42-103602 "Connie"
Smith, Homer C., Lt.; March 1945-April 8, 1945(KIAc)
Smith, Kenneth D., Lt.; April 1944-June 7, 1944(KIA)
Smith, Robert E., Lt.; September 1942-September 26, 1942(MIA-E); ex-133 Sqn, RAF
Sneed, David L., Lt.; March 1945-September 1945
1 mission
Sobanski, Winslow M., Lt.; October 1942-May 1943; to 334th Ftr Sqn
Sooman, Woodrow F., Lt.; February 1943-March 18, 1944(POW)
P-47C VF-D 41-6192 "Lollapoluza"
P-51B VF-D 43-6936
Sperry, George B., Lt.; September 1942-September 26, 1942(POW); ex-133 Sqn, RAF
Stephenson, Andrew J., Lt.; October 1942-December 1943; ex-133 Sqn, RAF
P-47C VF-S 41-6573
Stepp, Malta L., Jr., Capt.; October 1942-May 1943; to HdQts; ex-133 Sqn, RAF
P-47C VF-A 41-6541
Stumpf, John J., Lt.; March 1945-September 1945
2 missions
Swan, John B., Jr., Lt.; March 1945-September 1945
0 missions
Thompson, William P., Lt.; March 1945-September 1945
1 mission
Tussey, Robert S., Lt.; February 1944-May 11, 1944(KIA)
Van Wyk, Neil, Capt.; October 1943-November 1944; to 335th Ftr Sqn
P-47C VF-X 41-6194
P-51B VF-X 43-6772
Vigmonstad, Torgeir F., Lt.; February 1945-July 1945
12 missions
Villinger, George K., Lt.; August 1943-March 2, 1944(KIA)
P-51B VF-C 43-6985
Wallace, Alvin O., Lt.; September 1944-February 4, 1945(KIAc)
Wehrman, Robert H., Capt.; September 1943-October 1944
P-47C VF-N 41-6536
P-51B VF-N 43-7005
White, Robert W., Lt.; June 1944-September 10, 1944(KIA)
Wiggin, Pierce L., Lt.; May 1943-September 1944
P-47C VF-A 41-6541
P-51B VF-A
Wilhoit, Barnaby M., F/O; March 1945-May 29, 1945(KIAc)
2 missions
Williams, Warren H., Lt.; June 1944-November 1944
Wright, Gil G., Lt.; September 1942-September 26, 1942(POW); ex-133 Sqn, RAF
Young, Franklin W., Capt.; June 1944-May 1945
P-51D VF-A 44-14276 "Martha Jane"
Young, Samuel H., Jr., Lt.; April 1944-May 30, 1944(POW)

**Aircraft of the 334th Fighter Squadron**

P-47C-2-RE

| Aircraft | Pilot |
|---|---|
| 41-6187 QP-E "Uncle Den" | H.J. Blanchfield |
| 41-6187 QP-L "Quack" | R.L. Priser |
| 41-6191 QP-Q | H.L. Mills |
| 41-6195 QP-W | J.A. Clark |
| 41-6204 QP-M | |
| 41-6212 QP-I | A.H. Hopson |

P-47C-5-RE

| Aircraft | Pilot |
|---|---|
| 41-6358 QP-G "Cal Or Bust" | A.W. Chatterly |
| 41-6369 QP-Y | P.S. Riley |
| 41-6392 QP-X | W.T. O'Regan |
| 41-6400 QP-O "Indianapolis" | V.A. Boehle |
| 41-6404 QP-R | R.C. Care |
| 41-6405 QP-S | R.A. Boock |
| 41-6406 QP-H | |
| 41-6407 QP-E | |
| 41-6410 QP-Y "Little Butch" | W.B. Smith |
| 41-6413 QP-V | O.H. Coen/T.J. Andrews |
| 41-6414 QP-K | V.J. France |
| 41-6484 QP-L "The Missouri Kid" | R.K. Hofer |
| 41-6538 QP-B "Welakahao" | W.J. Hollander |
| 41-6576 QP-J | H.D. Hively |
| 41-6598 QP-M | |

P-47D-1-RE

| Aircraft | Pilot |
|---|---|
| 42-7876 QP-K "Miss Dallas" | V.J. France |
| 42-7881 QP-E | V.R. Castle |
| 42-7890 QP-B "Boise Bee" | D.W. Beeson |
| 42-7915 QP-U | |
| 42-7920 QP-N | |
| 42-7924 QP-F | |
| 42-7928 QP-Z | |
| 42-7945 QP-D "Miss Plainfield" | S.N. Pissanos |

P-47D-2-RE

| Aircraft | Pilot |
|---|---|
| 42-7980 QP-H "Texas" | G.E. Montgomery |
| 42-7981 QP-R | R.C. Care |

P-47D-5-RE

| Aircraft | Pilot |
|---|---|
| 42-8619 QP-O "Man-Made Monster" | HACK |
| 42-8641 QP-I "Great Dane II" | D.A. Van Epps |
| 42-8644 QP-N "Lilliput" | |
| 42-8644 QP-U | |

P-47D-6-RE

| Aircraft | Pilot |
|---|---|
| 42-74751 QP-Q | H.L. Mills |

P-47D-10-RE

| Aircraft | Pilot |
|---|---|
| 42-75126 QP-F "Mike" | W.J. Sobanski |

P-47D-11-RE

| Aircraft | Pilot |
|---|---|
| 42-75250 QP-P | |
| 42-75252 QP-W | J.A. Clark |
| 42-75254 QP-X | |

Unknown Serials

| Aircraft | Pilot |
|---|---|
| QP-P "Ill Wind?" | N. Megura |

P-51C-1-NT

42-103292 QP-B

P-51C-10-NT

42-103781 QP-Y
42-103791 QP-N

P-51C-10-NT

| | |
|---|---|
| 43-24979 QP-U | |

P-51B-1-NA

| | |
|---|---|
| 43-12412 QP- | |
| 43-12428 QP- | |

P-51B-5-NA

| | |
|---|---|
| 43-6433 QP-D | |
| 43-6489 QP- | |
| 43-6510 QP- | |
| 43-6518 QP-K | J.W. Ayers |
| 43-6542 QP- | |
| 43-6560 QP-W | J.A. Clark |
| 43-6567 QP-E | |
| 43-6586 QP-U | |
| 43-6587 QP-Z | |
| 43-6587 QP-O | |
| 43-6591 QP-V | H.B. Noon |
| 43-6636 QP-N "Ill Wind?" | N. Megura |
| 43-6646 QP-L | |
| 43-6656 QP-N | R.B. Frazer |
| 43-6690 QP-Q | H.L. Mills |
| 43-6717 QP-S | D.W. Howe |
| 43-6719 QP-T | |
| 43-6726 QP-W | J.A. Clark |
| 43-6746 QP-E | H.J. Blanchfield |
| 43-6798 QP-D | S.N. Pissanos |
| 43-6819 QP-B "Bee" | D.W. Beeson |
| 43-6832 QP-K "Miss Dallas" | V.J. France |
| 43-6837 QP-I | |
| 43-6839 QP-N | |
| 43-6860 QP-G | A.W. Chatterly |
| 43-6869 QP-U | |
| 43-6882 QP-A | |
| 43-6898 QP-J "The Deacon" | H.D. Hively |
| 43-6899 QP-O | |
| 43-6933 QP-Y | |
| 43-6941 QP-T | |
| 43-6946 QP-L | |
| 43-6957 QP-M "Turnip Termite" | D.M. Malmsten |
| 43-6967 QP-D | |
| 43-7002 QP-D | |
| 43-7029 QP-U | |
| 43-7035 QP-X | |

P-51B-10-NA

| | |
|---|---|
| 43-7150 QP-P | |
| 43-7158 QP-F | |
| 43-7178 QP-Q | |
| 43-7183 QP-R | R.C. Care |
| 42-106441 QP-G | |
| 42-106636 QP-X | |
| 42-106650 QP-W | J.A. Clark |
| 42-106682 QP-B | J.L. Barden |

P-51B-15-NA

| | |
|---|---|
| 42-106767 QP-E | H.J. Blanchfield |
| 42-106823 QP-K | |
| 42-106846 QP-H | |
| 42-106924 QP-L "Salem Representative" | R.K. Hofer |
| 43-24762 QP- | |
| 43-24793 QP-C | |
| 43-24825 QP-G "Jerry" | T.E. Fraser |
| 43-24841 QP-Z | J.L. Lang |

P-51D-5-NT

| | |
|---|---|
| 44-11225 QP-D | |
| 44-11336 QP-Z "Buffalo Bertie" | K.E. Foster |

P-51K-5-NT

| | |
|---|---|
| 44-11661 QP-X "Iron Ass" | J.J. Oberhansly |
| 44-11677 QP-P "Lynette Sue" | A.C. Lacy |

P-51D-5-NA

| | |
|---|---|
| 44-13306 QP-J | H.D. Hively |
| 44-13306 QP-F | |
| 44-13314 QP-X | A.C. Cwiklinski |
| 44-13322 QP-O "Gloria III" | G.C. Siems |
| 44-13352 QP-Z | J.L. Lang |
| 44-13372 QP-W | J.A. Clark |
| 44-13411 QP-Q | S.W. Monroe |
| 44-13615 QP-R | D.R. Bennett |
| 44-13372 QP-R | |
| 44-13884 QP-G | D.W. Howe |
| 44-13884 QP-B | |
| 44-13956 QP-D "Jan" | R.A. Dickmeyer |
| 44-13984 QP-B "Meg" | C.L. Boretsky |
| 44-13984 QP-U "Davy Lee" | M.W. Arthur |

P-51D-10-NA

| | |
|---|---|
| 44-14110 QP-R "Georgie" | K.G. Helfrecht |
| 44-14119 QP-H "Sizzlin Liz" | G.E. Montgomery |
| 44-14123 QP-Z | J.L. Lang |
| 44-14142 QP-O | J.E. Jahnke |
| 44-14202 QP-Q | J.D. McFadden |
| 44-14229 QP-N | |
| 44-14271 QP-K | |
| 44-14281 QP-Y | W.B. Smith |
| 44-14292 QP-A "Man O'War" | C.H. Kinnard |
| 44-14292 QP-A "Old Witch" | R.S. Voyles |
| 44-14310 QP-K | |
| 44-14323 QP-VV "Dyer-Ria" | R.A. Dyer |
| 44-14518 QP-P "Nad" | C.H. Beason |
| 44-14537 QP-A "Old Witch" | R.S. Voyles |
| 44-14560 QP-V "Crotch Rot" | D.M. Malmsten |
| 44-14606 QP-D "Jan" | |
| 44-14772 QP-Z | |

P-51D-15-NA

| | |
|---|---|
| 44-15216 QP-F | |
| 44-15312 QP-N | |
| 44-15324 QP-M | |
| 44-15326 QP-H "Sizzlin Liz" | G.E. Montgomery |
| 44-15347 QP-J | H.D. Hively |
| 44-15347 QP-O | L.H. Norley |
| 44-15381 QP-X | |

P-51D-20-NA

| | |
|---|---|
| 44-63223 QP-K "Georgie" | K.G. Helfrecht |
| 44-63233 QP-S "Sweet Arlene" | A.R. Bowers |
| 44-63583 QP-T "Helen" | E.J. Wozniak |
| 44-72063 QP-K | |
| 44-72155 QP-W "The Count" | R.H. Buchanan |
| 44-72196 QP-O | L.H. Norley |
| 44-72251 QP-A | S.S. Woods |
| 44-72327 QP- "Marjorie" | P.E. Burnett |
| 44-72346 QP-K "Lil Aggie" | |
| 44-72377 QP-H | |
| 44-72381 QP-J | C.G. Payne |
| 44-72382 QP-H "Sizzlin Liz" | G.E. Montgomery |

P-51D-25-NA

| | |
|---|---|
| 44-73108 QP-O "Red Dog XII" | L.H. Norley |
| 44-73141 QP- "Anne II" | |
| 44-73155 QP- "My Achin' Back" | |
| 44-73304 QP-U "Blondie" | M.W. Arthur |

Unknown Serials

| | | |
|---|---|---|
| P-51B | QP-O "Gloria" | G.C. Siems |
| P-51B | QP-O "Gloria II" | G.C. Siems |
| P-51D | QP-N "Skippy" | F.E. Farington |
| P-51D | QP-I "Zoomin' Zombie" | W.J. Dvorak |
| P-51D | QP- "Lil Nell" | D.L. James |
| P-51D | QP- "Lazy Daisy" | |
| P-51D | QP-Q "Frankie" | |

**Aircraft of the 335th Fighter Squadron**

P-47C-1-RE

| | |
|---|---|
| 41-6162 WD-B | |

P-47C-2-RE

| | |
|---|---|
| 41-6178 WD-E | |
| 41-6181 WD-D "Stinky" | F.J. Smolinsky |
| 41-6182 WD-X | J.R. Happel |
| 41-6185 WD-S | D.A. Young/C.A. Fiedler |
| 41-6190 WD- | |
| 41-6206 WD-H | R.W. Evans |
| 41-6207 WD-X "Mark II" | K.G. Smith |
| 41-6214 WD-F | P.M. Ellington |
| 41-6225 WD- | |
| 41-6226 WD-I | G. Carpenter |
| 41-6233 WD-O | A.C. Stanhope |
| 41-6248 WD- | |
| 41-6260 WD- | |

P-47C-5-RE

| | |
|---|---|
| 41-6328 WD- | |
| 41-6359 WD-K | |
| 41-6368 WD- | |
| 41-6369 WD-Y | |
| 41-6578 WD- | |
| 41-6582 WD-A | P.W. McKennon |
| 41-6621 WD-R | |

P-47D-2-RE

| | |
|---|---|
| 42-7863 WD-C | D.J.M. Blakeslee |
| 42-7879 WD-M | |

42-7901 WD-G
42-7911 WD-
42-7936 WD-W "Pistol Packin' Mama" F.D. Smith
42-7936 WD-D B.L. McGrattan
42-7939 WD-Z W.K. Wortman
42-7968 WD-U P.M. Ellington

P-47D-5-RE
42-8495 WD-W
42-8506 WD-B
42-8675 WD-E

P-47D-6-RE
42-74621 WD-L
42-74686 WD-E R.W. Evans
42-74717 WD-T
42-74718 WD-H
42-74726 WD-

P-47D-10-RE
42-75051 WD-R
42-75112 WD-Z
42-75119 WD-N

Unknown Serials
WD-L "Hell's Belle" C.F. Anderson

P-51C-1-NT
42-102999 WD-
42-103036 WD-
42-103291 WD-X

P-51C-5-NT
42-103561 WD-H
42-103609 WD-G

P-51C-10-NT
42-103781 WD-G
42-103784 WD-
43-25061 WD-E

P-51B-1-NA
43-12177 WD-
43-12193 WD-2 HACK
43-12194 WD-
43-12195 WD-Z
43-12407 WD-
43-12427 WD-
43-12469 WD-L

P-51B-5-NA
43-6316 WD-H
43-6325 WD-Z
43-6437 WD-C D.J.M. Blakeslee
43-6437 WD-V
43-6460 WD-F
43-6463 WD-
43-6489 WD-
43-6557 WD-
43-6562 WD-N
43-6570 WD-3 "Joe's Junk" HACK
43-6575 WD-I "Virginia" G. Carpenter
43-6575 WD-E
43-6579 WD-S "Snafu" C.A. Fiedler
43-6639 WD-P
43-6641 WD-E
43-6643 WD-L
43-6718 WD-R J.W. Goodwyn
43-6725 WD-U
43-6753 WD-M
43-6759 WD-P
43-6767 WD-D B.L. McGrattan
43-6767 WD-F
43-6770 WD-O A.L. Schlegel
43-6770 WD-G
43-6784 WD-X J.R. Happel
43-6803 WD-K K.G. Smith
43-6810 WD-R
43-6841 WD-J
43-6843 WD-B
43-6863 WD-V
43-6887 WD-H
43-6896 WD-A P.W. McKennon
43-6896 WD-F G.I. Stanford
43-6897 WD-P F.C. Jones
43-6897 WD-U "See Me Later" W.B. Eaton
43-6901 WD-G
43-6922 WD-V P.S. Riley
43-6959 WD-T
43-6959 WD-Z
43-6973 WD-W
43-7004 WD-U
43-7032 WD-K
43-7032 WD-S
43-7042 WD-J
43-7098 WD-F

P-51B-10-NA
43-7149 WD-
43-7164 WD-
43-7172 WD-H "Three Jokers" T.E. Lines
43-7181 WD-L C.F. Anderson
43-7187 WD-B
43-7190 WD-W
42-106429 WD-W "Judy IV"
42-106438 WD-U
42-106464 WD-O A.L. Schlegel
42-106555 WD-M
42-106576 WD-D B.L. McGrattan
42-106675 WD-I G. Carpenter
42-106706 WD-R
42-106726 WD-C D.J.M. Blakeslee
42-106726 WD-W
42-106726 WD-S

P-51B-15-NA
42-106786 WD-K
42-106855 WD-Z
42-106911 WD-A "Yippee Joe!!" P.W. McKennon
42-106940 WD-N
43-24794 WD-
43-24813 WD-A R.C. Church
43-24813 WD-N

P-51D-5-NT
44-11200 WD-F P.J. Lucas
44-11339 WD-J

P-51D-5-NA
44-13319 WD-G
44-13389 WD-P F.C. Jones
44-13399 WD-
44-13402 WD-K
44-13534 WD-F
44-13555 WD-O "Thunderbird" T.E. Lines
44-13555 WD-D C.E. Konsler
44-13563 WD-H
44-13563 WD-R
44-13564 WD-I R.J. Mabie
44-13567 WD-O
44-13641 WD-R
44-13727 WD-Z
44-13777 WD-
44-13779 WD-C D.J.M. Blakeslee
44-13788 WD-
44-13883 WD-A P.W. McKennon
44-13903 WD-L R.J. Rinebolt/Z.S. Sensibaugh
44-13977 WD-T
44-13977 WD-H "Cookie" D.J. Peterson
44-13982 WD-V
44-13997 WD-W
44-14027 WD-P
44-14041 WD-W "Wava"

P-51D-10-NA
44-14054 WD-I
44-14066 WD-O A.L. Schlegel
44-14098 WD-P J.W. Russell
44-14102 WD-
44-14125 WD-
44-14137 WD-KK "Suzonne" G.D. Green
44-14158 WD-R
44-14221 WD-A "Ridge Runner" P.W. McKennon
44-14221 WD-I R.J. Mabie
44-14339 WD-U
44-14339 WD-T
44-14361 WD-K "Fiesty Sue" D.L. Berry
44-14389 WD-T "Suzy"
44-14418 WD-
44-14431 WD-Q
44-14435 WD-O
44-14438 WD-U "Little Nan"
44-14529 WD-X
44-14540 WD- "Ascend Charlie"
44-14557 WD-B "The Duchess" W.J. O'Donnell
44-14570 WD-A "Ridge Runner" P.W. McKennon
44-14570 WD-D R.L. Couse

P-51D-15-NA
44-14923 WD-U "See Me Later" W.B. Eaton

| Aircraft | Pilot |
|---|---|
| 44-15028 WD-Y "Dotty" | C.W. Willruth |
| 44-15028 WD-O | L.H. Norley |
| 44-15330 WD- | |
| 44-15351 WD- | |
| 44-15455 WD- | |
| 44-15551 WD- | |
| 44-15615 WD-T | |

P-51D-20-NA

| Aircraft | Pilot |
|---|---|
| 44-63166 WD-A "Ridge Runner" | P.W. McKennon |
| 44-63599 WD- | |
| 44-63670 WD- | |
| 44-63737 WD-M "Suzon" | G.D. Green |
| 44-72061 WD-N | |
| 44-72241 WD-W | |
| 44-72265 WD- | |
| 44-72308 WD-A "Ridge Runner" | P.W. McKennon |
| 44-72340 WD- | |
| 44-72369 WD- | |
| 44-72416 WD-P "Man-I-Ack" | R.A. Ackerly |
| 44-72416 WD-P "Rita Marie" | |
| 44-72478 WD-I | |

P-51D-25-NA

| Aircraft | Pilot |
|---|---|
| 44-73029 WD- | |
| 44-73097 WD- | |
| 44-73100 WD-B | |
| 44-73112 WD- | |

Unknown Serials

| Aircraft | Pilot |
|---|---|
| P-51D WD- "Sweet Stuff" | G.W. Ceglarski |
| P-51D WD- "Umbreago" | R.A. Moe |

### Aircraft of the 336th Fighter Squadron

P-47C-2-RE

| Aircraft | Pilot |
|---|---|
| 41-6180 VF-U "Missouri Mauler" | W.W. Millikan |
| 41-6183 VF-O "Red Dog" | L.H. Norley |
| 41-6192 VF-D "Lollapoluza" | W.F. Sooman |
| 41-6194 VF-X | |
| 41-6197 VF-N "Cisco" | D.D. Nee |
| 41-6256 VF-I "Blue Goofis" | R.D. Hobert |

P-47C-5-RE

| Aircraft | Pilot |
|---|---|
| 41-6354 VF-R | G.R. Herter |
| 41-6529 VF-M "Eager Beaver" | J.L. Raphael |
| 41-6533 VF-B | G.E. Mirsch |
| 41-6536 VF-N "Cisco" | D.D. Nee |
| 41-6539 VF-F "Arizona Pete" | K.D. Peterson |
| 41-6541 VF-A | M.L. Stepp |
| 41-6571 VF-B "The Earl" | G.E. Mirsch |
| 41-6572 VF-N | |
| 41-6573 VF-S "Bcvoapabm" | P.G. Lehman |
| 41-6574 VF-G "Miss San Carlos" | L. Gover |
| 41-6575 VF-E "Doreen II" | J.G. DuFour/K.E. Carlson |
| 41-6579 VF-L | C.H. Miley |

P-47D-1-RE

| Aircraft | Pilot |
|---|---|
| 42-7873 VF-J | |
| 42-7884 VF-P "Reggie's Reply" | J.T. Godfrey |
| 42-7895 VF-K | G.J. Smart |
| 42-7933 VF-Y "Miss Skippy" | P.H. Dunn |

P-47D-2-RE

| Aircraft | Pilot |
|---|---|
| 42-7959 VF-W | J.A. Goodson |

P-47D-5-RE

| Aircraft | Pilot |
|---|---|
| 42-8659 VF-T "Donnie Boy" | D.S. Gentile |

P-47D-6-RE

| Aircraft | Pilot |
|---|---|
| 42-74663 VF-H | V. Garrison |
| 42-74688 VF-G "Miss San Carlos" | L. Gover |

P-47D-11-RE

| Aircraft | Pilot |
|---|---|
| 42-75274 VF-I | R.D. Hobert |

P-47D-22-RE

| Aircraft | Pilot |
|---|---|
| 42-25804 VF-G | |

P-51C-1-NT

| Aircraft | Pilot |
|---|---|
| 42-103009 VF- | |
| 42-103287 VF- | |
| 42-103322 VF- | |

P-51C-5-NT

| Aircraft | Pilot |
|---|---|
| 42-103332 VF- | |
| 42-103602 VF-C "Connie" | G.C. Smith |
| 42-103603 VF-T | F.M. Grove |

P-51C-10-NT

| Aircraft | Pilot |
|---|---|
| 42-103786 VF-O | I. Grounds |
| 42-103794 VF- | |
| 42-103796 VF- | |

P-51B-1-NA

| Aircraft | Pilot |
|---|---|
| 43-12214 VF-C "Rebel Queen" | F.W. Glover |
| 43-12416 VF-O | L.H. Norley |

P-51B-5-NA

| Aircraft | Pilot |
|---|---|
| 43-6362 VF-H "Jersey Bounce" | H.H. Fredericks |
| 43-6442 VF- | |
| 43-6507 VF- | |
| 43-6512 VF- | |
| 43-6572 VF-N | |
| 43-6573 VF-P | J.H. Joiner |
| 43-6584 VF- | |
| 43-6630 VF-U "Missouri Mauler" | W.W. Millikan |
| 43-6633 VF-Q | R.F. Nelson |
| 43-6650 VF- | |
| 43-6652 VF- | |
| 43-6686 VF-E "Lois" | |
| 43-6696 VF-F | |
| 43-6705 VF-W | W.E. Johnson |
| 43-6714 VF- | |
| 43-6730 VF- | |
| 43-6740 VF-R | |
| 43-6765 VF-P | J.T. Godfrey |
| 43-6768 VF- | R.E. Hughes |
| 43-6772 VF-X "Flying Dutchman" | N. Van Wyk |
| 43-6786 VF- | |
| 43-6802 VF-O | L.H. Norley |
| 43-6818 VF- | |
| 43-6836 VF- | |
| 43-6838 VF-T | |
| 43-6840 VF-Z | J.A. Patteeuw |
| 43-6846 VF- | |
| 43-6856 VF- | |
| 43-6866 VF- | |
| 43-6871 VF-H | V. Garrison |
| 43-6876 VF- | |
| 43-6889 VF-L | D.R. Emerson |
| 43-6891 VF- | |
| 43-6903 VF-Y | P.H. Dunn |
| 43-6913 VF-T "Shangri La" | D.S. Gentile |
| 43-6936 VF-D | W.F. Sooman |
| 43-6942 VF-D "Meiner Kleiner" | J.W. Higgins |
| 43-6963 VF- | |
| 43-6972 VF-N "Paul" | |
| 43-6975 VF-S | |
| 43-6985 VF-C | G.K. Villinger |
| 43-6997 VF-U "Missouri Mauler" | W.W. Millikan |
| 43-7005 VF-N | G.A. Herter |
| 43-7059 VF- | |

P-51B-10-NA

| Aircraft | Pilot |
|---|---|
| 42-106669 VF- | |
| 42-106673 VF-K "Hey Rube!" | R. Simon |
| 42-106688 VF-T "Ann III" | J.H. Bennett |
| 42-106730 VF-P "Reggie's Reply" | J.T. Godfrey |

P-51B-15-NA

| Aircraft | Pilot |
|---|---|
| 42-106797 VF-G | |
| 42-106856 VF- | |
| 42-106975 VF-N | |
| 43-24769 VF-U "Missouri Mauler" | W.W. Millikan |
| 43-24771 VF- | |
| 43-24787 VF- | |
| 43-24848 VF-B | J.A. Goodson |
| 43-24877 VF-U | V.E. Chandler |

P-51K-1-NT

| Aircraft | Pilot |
|---|---|
| 44-11356 VF-E | K.E. Carlson |

P-51K-5-NT

| Aircraft | Pilot |
|---|---|
| 44-11665 VF- | |

P-51D-5-NA

| Aircraft | Pilot |
|---|---|
| 44-13260 VF- | |
| 44-13300 VF-B | J.A. Goodson |
| 44-13303 VF-B | J.A. Goodson |
| 44-13307 VF-J "Butch" | J.C. Lane |
| 44-13315 VF- | |
| 44-13317 VF-B | D.R. Emerson |
| 44-13317 VF-L | |
| 44-13325 VF-Z | J.A. Patteeuw |
| 44-13325 VF-ZZ "Roasie's Beau" | |
| 44-13375 VF- | D.J. Pierce |
| 44-13412 VF-F | |
| 44-13519 VF-I | |

| | |
|---|---|
| 44-13602 VF- | |
| 44-13608 VF- | |
| 44-13630 VF-R "Betty Jane II" | M.N. Dickey |
| 44-13649 VF-F | |
| 44-13691 VF- | |
| 44-13848 VF-B | |
| 44-13862 VF- | |
| 44-13893 VF- | |
| 44-13934 VF- | |
| 44-13961 VF-L | J.D. McFarlane |
| 44-14029 VF- | |

P-51D-10-NA

| | |
|---|---|
| 44-14172 VF- | |
| 44-14266 VF- | |
| 44-14276 VF-A "Martha Jane" | F.W. Young |
| 44-14276 VF-A "Marcy" | J.R. McMahan |
| 44-14277 VF-H "Jersey Bounce III" | H.H. Fredericks |
| 44-14317 VF-Y "Duke" | H.N. Hagan |
| 44-14350 VF-L | |
| 44-14387 VF-E | |
| 44-14388 VF-U "Wheezy" | V.E. Chandler |
| 44-14432 VF- | |
| 44-14492 VF-G | |
| 44-14527 VF-S "Mary" | M.W. Miller |
| 44-14533 VF- | |
| 44-14548 VF-H | J.H. Joiner |
| 44-14552 VF- | C.R. Alfred |
| 44-14590 VF- | |
| 44-14787 VF-B | F.W. Glover |

P-51D-15-NA

| | |
|---|---|
| 44-15054 VF-D | E.A. Quist |
| 44-15191 VF-C "Mary Belle" | J.E. Hileman |
| 44-15191 VF-C "Peg O'My Heart" | G.E. Rodler |
| 44-15291 VF- | |
| 44-15350 VF- | |
| 44-15375 VF-T | F.M. Grove |
| 44-15395 VF- | |
| 44-15531 VF- | |
| 44-15575 VF- | |
| 44-15613 VF-M "Peaches" | C.H. Bousefield |
| 44-15647 VF-I "Johnetta IV" | |

P-51D-20-NA

| | |
|---|---|
| 44-63233 VF-D "Inky's Dinky" | G.H. Davis |
| 44-63831 VF- | |
| 44-64054 VF- | |
| 44-64142 VF-G "Tiger Baby" | J.P. Murchake |
| 44-64153 VF-B | F.W. Glover |
| 44-72053 VF-Y | H.N. Hagan |
| 44-72151 VF- | |
| 44-72181 VF-S "Sunny VIII" | E.W. Stewart |
| 44-72215 VF-N | |
| 44-72285 VF-Y "Becky" | G.L. Kesler |
| 44-72411 VF- | |
| 44-72523 VF- | C.R. Alfred |

P-51D-25-NA

| | |
|---|---|
| 44-72767 VF-T | F.M. Grove |
| 44-72769 VF- | |
| 44-72789 VF-D | D.P. Pederson |
| 44-72816 VF-J "The Duchess" | |
| 44-73021 VF-F "Clarine" | D.N. Groshong |
| 44-73049 VF-E | |
| 44-73061 VF-X "Blood and Guts" | |
| 44-73218 VF-C | |

Unknown Serials

| | | |
|---|---|---|
| P-51D | VF-N "The Ring" | M.C. Franklin |
| P-51D | VF-R "Betty Jane" | M.N. Dickey |
| P-51B | VF- "Penny" | H.E. Dugan |
| P-51D | VF- "Penny II" | H.E. Dugan |
| P-51D | VF- "Doris II" | T.A. McCord |

• • •

## THE 20TH FIGHTER GROUP
## 55TH, 77TH, 79TH FIGHTER SQUADRONS

The 20th Fighter Group was activated on November 15, 1930, at Mather Field, California. Training at various locations during the 1930s and early 1940s, the 20th headed overseas on August 20, 1943, aboard the "Queen Elizabeth". The first of 312 missions came on December 28, 1943, (although the individual squadrons flew several prior to this with the 55th Fighter Group) with the last coming on April 25, 1945. While in England, the group claimed 210.6 aerial and 226.5 ground victories while 145 P-38's and P-51's were lost on operations and 9 pilots died in accidents.

While overseas, he group was based at Kingscliffe from August 26, 1943, until October of 1945. The 20th was equipped with the P-38H and J from August of 1943 until July of 1944, and the P-51C, D, and K, from July of 1944 until the end of the war. The 20th was awarded a Distinguished Unit Citation for a sweep flown on April 8, 1944, in which over 25 German planes and numerous ground targets were destroyed.

### Claims

| | Air Destroyed | Air Probable | Air Damaged | Grd Destroyed | Grd Damaged |
|---|---|---|---|---|---|
| HdQts | 11.83 | 1 | 3.5 | 11 | 5 |
| 55th | 67.5 | 4 | 16.5 | 70 | 41 |
| 77th | 75.67 | 4 | 29 | 85 | 49 |
| 79th | 55.6 | 3 | 28 | 60.5 | 36 |
| | 210.6 | 12 | 77 | 226.5 | 131 |

### Commanders

| | |
|---|---|
| Col. Barton M. Russell | August 20, 1943-March 2, 1944 |
| LtCol. Mark E. Hubbard | March 2, 1944-March 18, 1944 |
| Maj. Herbert E. Johnson, Jr. | March 19, 1944-March 20, 1944 |
| LtCol. Harold J. Rau | March 20, 1944-June 25, 1944 |
| LtCol. Cy Wilson | June 25, 1944-August 27, 1944 |
| Col. Harold J. Rau | August 28, 1944-December 18, 1944 |
| Col. Robert P. Montgomery | December 18, 1944-October 1945 |

### Wing and Command Assignments

| | |
|---|---|
| Assigned to VIII Fighter Command | August 25, 1943 |
| VIII Fighter Command, 67th Fighter Wing | October 6, 1943 |
| 1st Bomb Division, 67th Fighter Wing | September 15, 1944 |
| 1st Air Division, 67th Fighter Wing | January 1, 1945 |

### Aircraft Markings

Original P-38's were in the olive drab/neutral gray scheme with NMF planes being received in March of 1944. Starting in December of 1943, squadron symbols were placed on the outer vertical tails, a triangle for the 55th, a circle for the 77th, and a square for the 79th. These symbols were white on camouflaged ships and black on NMF planes. From March of 1944, group markings consisted of yellow spinners and cowl bands on each nacelle.

All P-51's received were in NMF but a number of these later had dark green applied to portions of the upper surfaces. The squadron symbols were still carried on the vertical tail with the individual aircraft letter placed inside in either black or NMF depending on the finish. Starting in July of 1944, the P-51's had the front twelve inches of the spinner painted white with the aft portion black. The first eleven inches of the cowling aft of the spinner was then painted black, backed by a 5 inch white band. In November of 1944, additional stripes, seven black and six white, were added to extend the markings. In some cases the white was not painted on but left NMF. Also, the new stripes did not cover the olive drab anti-glare panel.

Squadron codes were:

55th Ftr Sqn: KI
77th Ftr Sqn: LC
79th Ftr Sqn: MC

### 20th Fighter Group Statistical Report

| Month | Missions* | Air | Grd | Losses | KIAc |
|---|---|---|---|---|---|
| November 1943 | 0 | 1-0-0 | 0-0 | 5 | 0 |
| December | 3 | 1-0-1 | 0-0 | 2 | 0 |
| January 1944 | 9 | 19-3-16 | 0-0 | 15 | 2 |
| February | 16 | 24-2-13 | 0-0 | 20 | 0 |
| March | 13 | 10-1-0 | 0-0 | 9 | 1 |
| April | 23 | 12.6-0-2 | 25.5-25 | 11 | 0 |
| May | 21 | 4-0-3 | 2-0 | 10 | 0 |
| June | 35 | 5-0-0 | 0-0 | 14 | 0 |
| July | 23 | 14-0-5 | 1-0 | 7 | 0 |
| August | 26 | 35-1-12 | 31-23 | 15 | 0 |
| September | 16 | 7-0-4 | 6-1 | 1 | 3 |
| October | 16 | 0-0-0 | 44-16 | 5 | 1 |
| November | 20 | 28.5-3-3 | 0-2 | 8 | 1 |
| December | 16 | 6-0-0 | 0-0 | 3 | 0 |
| January 1945 | 15 | 19.5-1-6 | 0-0 | 2 | 0 |
| February | 19 | 19-1-4 | 63-31 | 11 | 0 |
| March | 23 | 0-0-3 | 0-1 | 3 | 1 |
| April | 18 | 5-0-5 | 54-32 | 4 | 0 |
| | 312 | 210.6-12-77 | 226.5-131 | 145 | 9 |

* - Does not include 10 missions flown by individual squadrons with the 55th Fighter Group in November and December of 1943.

### Losses by Squadron

| | MIA | | KIAc | |
|---|---|---|---|---|
| | P-38 | P-51 | P-38 | P-51 |
| HdQts | 4 | 2 | 0 | 0 |
| 55th | 28 | 23 | 1 | 4 |
| 77th | 30 | 20 | 1 | 1 |
| 79th | 30 | 8 | 1 | 1 |
| | 92 | 53 | 3 | 6 |

### Claims by Aircraft Type

| | Air | | | Grd | |
|---|---|---|---|---|---|
| | Destroyed | Probable | Damaged | Destroyed | Damaged |
| P-38 | 87.6 | 6 | 39 | 28.5 | 25 |
| P-51 | 123 | 6 | 38 | 198 | 106 |

### Claims by Enemy Aircraft Type

| | Air | | | Grd | |
|---|---|---|---|---|---|
| | Destroyed | Probable | Damaged | Destroyed | Damaged |
| Me-109 | 96 | 7 | 30 | 10 | 5 |
| FW-190 | 71.5 | 4 | 28 | 36 | 5 |
| Me-110 | 13 | 0 | 4 | 8 | 12 |
| Me-262 | 5.5 | 0 | 10 | 0 | 0 |
| Me-210 | 4 | 0 | 2 | 1 | 0 |
| Do-217 | 4 | 0 | 2 | 1 | 1 |
| Me-410 | 3 | 1 | 1 | 9 | 2 |
| He-177 | 2.6 | 0 | 0 | 3 | 2 |
| Me-108 | 2 | 0 | 0 | 2 | 0 |
| FW-200 | 2 | 0 | 0 | 0 | 0 |
| He-111 | 1 | 0 | 0 | 29.5 | 19 |
| u/i a/c | 1 | 0 | 0 | 28 | 15 |
| Fi-156 | 1 | 0 | 0 | 1 | 0 |
| W-34 | 1 | 0 | 0 | 1 | 0 |
| FW-44 | 1 | 0 | 0 | 0 | 0 |
| Ju-290 | 1 | 0 | 0 | 0 | 0 |
| Z.506 | 1 | 0 | 0 | 0 | 0 |
| Ju-88 | 0 | 0 | 0 | 39 | 47 |
| Do-24 | 0 | 0 | 0 | 16 | 5 |
| Do-18 | 0 | 0 | 0 | 12 | 5 |
| He-115 | 0 | 0 | 0 | 8 | 0 |
| BV-140 | 0 | 0 | 0 | 7 | 5 |
| Ju 52 | 0 | 0 | 0 | 7 | 4 |
| Si-204 | 0 | 0 | 0 | 3 | 2 |
| Ar-196 | 0 | 0 | 0 | 3 | 0 |
| Caudron | 0 | 0 | 0 | 2 | 0 |
| Hs-126 | 0 | 0 | 0 | 1 | 0 |
| Ju-87 | 0 | 0 | 0 | 0 | 1 |

### 20th Fighter Group Squadron Commanders

**55th Ftr Sqn**

| | |
|---|---|
| LtCol. David R. McGovern | January 12, 1943-December 4, 1943 |
| Maj. Frank C. Clark | December 29, 1943-March 18, 1944 |
| Maj. Donald H. McAuley | March 18, 1944-April 23, 1944 |
| Maj. Maurice R. McLary | April 23, 1944-April 24, 1944 |
| LtCol. Cy Wilson | April 24, 1944-June 25, 1944 |
| unknown | June 25, 1944-July 18, 1944 |
| LtCol. Martin L. Low | July 18, 1944-December 6, 1944 |
| Maj. Richard P. Gatterdam | December 6, 1944-March 23, 1945 |
| Maj. Jack C. Price | March 23, 1945-April 18, 1945 |
| Maj. Maurice A. Cristadoro | April 18, 1945-July 22, 1945 |

**77th Ftr Sqn**

| | |
|---|---|
| LtCol. Robert P. Montgomery | August 1, 1942-November 11, 1943 |
| Maj. Herbert E. Johnson, Jr. | November 13, 1943-March 9, 1944 |
| Maj. Russell F. Gustke | March 9, 1944-June 18, 1944 |
| Capt. Donald A. Reihmer | June 18, 1944-August 4, 1944 |
| Maj. Maurice R. McLary | August 4, 1944-September 11, 1944 |
| Maj. Russell F. Gustke | September 11, 1944-December 18, 1944 |
| Maj. Merle B. Nichols | December 18, 1944-May 1945 |

**79th Ftr Sqn**

| | |
|---|---|
| Maj. Nathaniel H. Blanton | December 7, 1942-November 14, 1943 |
| Maj. Richard L. Ott | November 14, 1943-January 30, 1944 |
| Maj. Carl E. Jackson | January 31, 1944-February 20, 1944 |
| Maj. R.C. Franklin | February 23, 1944-May 10, 1944 |
| Maj. Delynn E. Anderson | May 10, 1944-September 27, 1944 |
| Maj. Jack M. Ilfrey | September 27, 1944-December 9, 1944 |
| LtCol. Robert J. Meyer | December 9, 1944-April 4, 1945 |
| Maj. Walter R. Yarbrough | April 4, 1944-Summer 1945 |

### 20th Fighter Group Aces

| Name | Air | Grd | Total | Sqn |
|---|---|---|---|---|
| Capt. Charles H. Cole | 5 | 6 | 11 | 55th<br>77th |
| Capt. Ernest C. Fiebelkorn | 9 | 2 | 11 | 77th |
| Capt. James M. Morris | 7.33 | 2.83 | 10.16 | 77th |
| Capt. Joseph L. Mansker | 3 | 7 | 10 | 55th |
| Lt. Fred H. Alexander | 2 | 6 | 8 | 77th |
| Maj. Jack M. Ilfrey | 8 | 0 | 8[*] | 79th |
| Lt. Fred H. Jurgens | 0 | 8 | 8 | 79th |
| Capt. Joseph T. McKeon | 6 | 2 | 8[**] | 55th<br>77th |
| Capt. Reps D. Jones | 2 | 5 | 7 | 77th |
| Capt. Edward L. Kier | 2 | 5 | 7 | 55th |
| Lt. David Stewart | 0 | 7 | 7 | 55th |
| Maj. Merle J. Gilbertson | 2.83 | 4 | 6.83 | 77th |
| LtCol. Mark E. Hubbard | 6.5 | 0 | 6.5[***] | HdQts |
| Col. Robert P. Montgomery | 3.33 | 3 | 6.33 | HdQts |
| Maj. Richard P. Gatterdam | 3.7 | 2.5 | 6.2 | 55th<br>79th |
| Lt. Louis W. Adams, Jr. | 4 | 2 | 6 | 77th |
| Capt. Harley L. Brown | 6 | 0 | 6 | 55th |
| Capt. Lowell E. Einhaus | 0 | 6 | 6 | 77th |
| Lt. Edward F. Pogue | 0 | 6 | 6 | 79th |
| Capt. Garth L. Reynolds | 2 | 4 | 6 | 77th |
| Capt. Lindol F. Graham | 5.5 | 0 | 5.5 | 79th |
| Lt. Albert B. North | 2 | 3 | 5 | 77th |
| Lt. Joseph A. Peterburs | 0 | 5 | 5 | 55th |
| LtCol. John P. Randolph | 1 | 4 | 5 | HdQts |
| Col. Harold J. Rau | 1 | 4 | 5 | HdQts |
| Lt. Kenneth C. Smeltz | 1 | 4 | 5 | 55th |
| Capt. Willis B. Taylor | 3 | 2 | 5 | 55th |
| Maj. Jack C. Price | 5 | 0 | 5[@] | 55th<br>HdQts |

[*] - includes 6 air victories with the 1st Ftr Grp, MTO
[**] - includes 5 air victories with the 475th Ftr Grp, PTO
[***] - includes 4 air victories with the 33rd Ftr Grp, MTO
[@] - all victories with the 78th Ftr Grp, ETO

### 20th Fighter Group Scorers

**HdQts**

| | Air | Grd | |
|---|---|---|---|
| R.F. Gustke | 0-0-0 | 0-1 | plus 77th Ftr Sqn & 1 air w/14th Ftr Grp, MTO |
| M.E. Hubbard | 2.5-1-0 | 0-0 | plus 4 air w/33rd Ftr Grp, MTO |
| C.E. Jackson | 0-0-0.5 | 0-0 | plus 79th Ftr Sqn |
| H.E. Johnson, Jr. | 0.5-0-0 | 0-0 | plus 77th Ftr Sqn |
| R.P. Montgomery | 3.3-0-2 | 3-2 | |
| J.P. Randolph | 1-0-0 | 4-2 | |
| H.J. Rau | 1-0-0 | 4-0 | |
| B.M. Russell | 0.5-0-0 | 0-0 | |
| C. Wilson | 3-0-1 | 0-0 | |

**55th Ftr Sqn**

| | | | |
|---|---|---|---|
| H.M. Anderson | 0-0-0 | 1-0 | |
| C.F. Bain | 0-0-0 | 1-1 | |
| H.B. Baker | 1-0-1 | 0-0 | |
| S.A. Baker | 1.5-0-0 | 0-0 | |
| T.C. Barnes | 0-0-0 | 1-1 | |
| D.B. Benedict | 0-0-0 | 1-0 | |
| R.I. Bowman | 1-0-0 | 1-1 | |
| H.L. Brown | 6-0-1 | 0-1 | |
| J.K. Brown | 3-0-0.5 | 0-0 | |
| J.E. Burford | 0-0-0 | 2-3 | |
| H.B. Bynum | 0-0-0 | 2-0 | |
| E.W. Cavell | 0-0-0 | 1-1 | |
| D.E. Chrissinger | 1-0-0 | 0-0 | |
| M.A. Cristadoro | 1-0-0 | 0-0 | |
| C.E. Cole, Jr. | 4-0-0 | 0-0 | plus 77th Ftr Sqn |
| J.S. Ford | 0-1-0 | 4-1 | |
| D.R. Franklin | 0-0-1 | 0-0 | |
| D.I. Freedman | 1-0-1 | 0-0 | |
| R.D. Frey | 2-0-0 | 0-0 | |
| R.W. Fruechtenicht | 1-0-2 | 0-0 | |
| R.P. Gatterdam | 2-0-0 | 0-0 | plus 79th Ftr Sqn |
| E.E. Geiger | 1-0-0 | 0-0 | |
| C.A. Hallberg | 2.5-0-1 | 0-0 | |
| R.M. Howard | 0-0-1 | 3-4 | |
| E.W. Hower | 0-0-0 | 1-1 | |
| W.M. Hurst | 1-0-1 | 2-0 | |
| E.L. Kier | 2-0-0 | 5-4 | |
| J.E. Klink | 1-0-0 | 0-0 | |
| D.E. Larrabee | 1-0-0 | 0-0 | |
| J.D. Leon | 3-1-0 | 1-1 | |

| | | | |
|---|---|---|---|
| R.O. Loehnert | 2-0-0 | 0-0 | |
| M. Maldanado | 0-0-0 | 1-1 | |
| J.L. Mansker | 3-1-0 | 7-3 | |
| D.H. McAuley | 2-1-0 | 0-0 | |
| J.T. McKeon | 0-0-0 | 2-0 | plus 77th Ftr Sqn & 5 air w/8th & 475th Ftr Grp, PTO |
| M.R. McLary | 3-0-3 | 0-0 | |
| K.D. McNeel | 1-0-1.5 | 1.5-0 | |
| R.W. Meinzen | 0-0-1 | 0-0 | |
| D. Michel | 0-0-1 | 0-0 | |
| R.E. Miles | 1-0-0 | 0-0 | |
| W.H. Mullins | 1-0-0 | 0-0 | |
| C.R. Nicholson | 1-0-0 | 0-0 | |
| D.D. Oxley | 0-0-0 | 3-1 | |
| J.A. Peterburs | 0-0-0 | 5-0 | |
| K.L. Pettit | 1-0-0 | 0-0 | |
| E. Planchak, Jr. | 2-0-0 | 0-0 | |
| J.S. Reynolds | 0.5-0-0 | 0-0 | |
| R.H. Riemensnider | 0-0-0 | 2.5-1 | |
| R.M. Scrutchfield | 0-0-0 | 2-3 | |
| R.F. Seifert | 0-0-0 | 0-2 | |
| J.C. Serros | 0.5-0-0 | 0-0 | |
| W.G. Schultz | 1.5-0-0 | 0-0 | |
| K.C. Smeltz | 1-0-0 | 4-3 | |
| S.G. Stitzer | 1-0-0 | 0-0 | |
| V.R. Stockton | 0-0-0.5 | 0-0 | |
| W.B. Taylor | 3-0-0 | 2-0 | |
| J.H. Tennant | 3-0-0 | 0-0 | |
| R.M. Tracy | 0-0-0 | 4-1 | |
| E.E. Wasil | 0-0-0 | 2-0 | |
| R.P. Watson | 1-0-0 | 0-0 | |
| W.W. Wells | 0-0-0 | 2-3 | |
| G.L. Williams | 0-0-0 | 4-4 | |
| J.J. Yelton | 3-0-0 | 0-0 | |

**77th Ftr Sqn**

| | | | |
|---|---|---|---|
| L.W. Adams | 4-0-1 | 2-0 | |
| F.H. Alexander | 2-0-0 | 6-2 | |
| C.C. Arthaud | 2-0-0 | 0-0 | |
| I.C. Baker | 1-0-0 | 0-0 | |
| R.T. Bond | 0.5-0-0 | 0-0 | |
| G.R. Brucks | 0-0-0 | 0-1 | |
| P. Chubin | 0-0-1 | 0-3 | |
| A.F. Clark | 2.5-0-0 | 0-0 | |
| C.H. Cole, Jr. | 1-0-0 | 6-1 | plus 55th Ftr Sqn |
| J.C. Cowley | 0-0-1 | 0-0 | |
| J.W. Cudd, Jr. | 0.5-0-0 | 0-0 | |
| J.E. Davis | 0.33-0-0 | 0-0 | |
| W.T. Drozd | 1-0-0 | 0-0 | |
| C.W. Dungan | 0-0-0 | 1-0 | |
| L.E. Einhaus | 0-0-0 | 6-0 | |
| J.W. Fagg | 0-0-0 | 0-1 | |
| W.C. Fay | 1-0-0 | 3-0 | |
| I.W. Fernandes | 1-0-1 | 1.33-0.5 | |
| E.C. Fiebelkorn | 9-0-1 | 2-2 | |
| R.R. Flowers | 0-0-0 | 2.5-0 | |
| R.S. Flynn | 0.5-0-0 | 0-0 | |
| R.L. Frakes | 0.33-0-0 | 0-0 | |
| J.L. Gard | 1-0-0 | 0-0 | |
| J.M. Garner | 3-0-0 | 1.5-1 | |
| R.C. Garrett | 0-0-1 | 0-0 | |
| A.L. Gese | 0-0-2 | 0-0 | |
| M.J. Gilbertson | 2.83-0-1 | 4-1 | |
| R.F. Gustke | 2-0-0 | 0-1 | plus HdQts |
| G.R. Hall | 1-0-1 | 3-4 | |
| B.C. Halpin | 1-0-0 | 0-0 | |
| T.P. Hambelton | 0-0-0 | 0-2 | |
| H.F. Hendricks | 0-0-0 | 0-2 | |
| J.H. Herbert | 0-0-0 | 1-0 | |
| C.G. Horne | 1-0-0 | 0-4 | |
| E.C. Jennings | 0-0-0 | 1-0 | |
| H.E. Johnson, Jr. | 3-1-1 | 1-2 | plus HdQts |
| R.D. Jones | 2-1-1 | 5-1 | |
| L.H. Kerns | 1-0-0 | 1-0 | |
| W.F. Kuemmerle | 0-0-0 | 1.33-0 | |
| F. Larsen | 0-0-0 | 3-0 | |
| J.D. McArthur | 0-0-0 | 1-0 | |
| E.J. Machen | 1-0-0 | 2-2 | |
| D.F. McAllister | 0-0-1 | 0-0 | |
| P.J. McCully, Jr. | 0-0-1 | 0-0 | |
| J.T. McKeon | 1-0-1 | 0-0 | plus 55th Ftr Sqn |
| R.E. Moncrieff | 1-0-1 | 1-0 | |
| J.M. Morris | 7.33-0-0 | 2.83-0 | |
| R.A. Morris | 0-0-0 | 2-0 | |
| R.E. Murrell | 1-0-0 | 0-0 | |
| A.B. North | 2-0-0 | 3-1 | |
| A.D. Payne | 0-0-1 | 0-0 | |
| B.M. Phillips | 0-0-0 | 0-0.5 | |
| H.J. Piatkiewicz | 1-0-0 | 0-2.5 | |
| E.R. Pitz | 0-0-0 | 2-1 | |
| F.V. Purse | 0-0-1 | 0-0 | |
| R.G. Quinn | 0-0-1 | 0-0 | |
| B.H. Rader | 2-0-0 | 0.5-1 | |
| R.A. Rege | 0-0-0 | 0-1 | |
| D.A. Reihmer | 0.5-0-2 | 1-0 | |
| G.L. Reynolds | 2-0-0 | 4-0 | |
| L.J. Robertson | 2-1-0 | 0-0 | |
| J. Rosenblum | 0.5-0-1 | 0-0 | |
| L.E. Rowlett | 3-0-1 | 0-0 | |
| P.J. Sabo | 0.33-0-2 | 0-0 | plus 1-1-1 w/370th Ftr Grp, ETO |
| P.L. Schallo | 1-0-1 | 3-0 | |
| J.E. Simanonok | 0-0-0 | 1-0 | |
| T.E. Slanker | 1-0-1 | 1-1 | |
| F.E. Snodgrass | 0-0-0 | 0.5-1 | |
| J.P. Starke | 0.5-0-0 | 2-0 | |
| R.T. Stovall | 0-0-0 | 1-0 | |
| W.E. Umla | 0-0-0 | 1-2 | |
| D.W. Van Sickle | 0-1-0 | 0.5-3 | |
| F.L. Van Sickle | 1-0-0 | 3-0 | |
| R.L. Van Woert | 0-0-1 | 0-0 | |
| W.L. Whiteside | 1.5-0-0 | 0-4 | |
| T.M. Williams | 1.5-0-1 | 0-0 | |

**79th Ftr Sqn**

| | | | |
|---|---|---|---|
| D.E. Anderson | 0.2-0-1 | 2-0 | |
| J.L. Armstrong | 0-0-1 | 0-0 | |
| R.W. Bebout | 3-0-0 | 0-0 | |
| D.A. Beschen | 1-0-0 | 1.5-1 | |
| H.O. Binkley | 2-0-1 | 2-0 | |
| L.P. Bishop | 0-0-0 | 0-2 | |
| R.H. Black | 1-0-1 | 2-0 | |
| W.E. Bullers | 0-0-0 | 2-2 | |
| M.L. Byrd | 0.5-0-0 | 0-0 | |
| R.E. Campbell | 2-0-1 | 0-0 | |
| J.E. Carpenter, Jr. | 2-0-0 | 1-0 | |
| D.C. Cooper | 0-0-1 | 0-0 | |
| E.H. Coughran | 0-0-0 | 3-0 | |
| L.J. Degenhardt | 0-0-0 | 2-1 | |
| C.J. Dixon | 0-0-0 | 0-1 | |
| M.D. Fall | 0.5-0-0 | 0-0 | |
| R.C. Franklin, Jr. | 2.2-0-0 | 1-0 | |
| R.P. Gatterdam | 1.7-1-0 | 2.5-0 | plus 55th Ftr Sqn |
| L.F. Graham | 5.5-0-2 | 0-0 | |
| J.L. Gubana | 0-0-0 | 2-2 | |
| T.A. Hanzo | 0-0-2 | 0-0 | |
| A.W. Heiden | 0.5-0-0 | 0.5-1 | |
| J.K. Hollins | 1-0-0 | 1-2 | |
| J.M. Ilfrey | 2-0-0 | 0-0 | plus 6 air w/1st Ftr Grp, MTO |
| M.G. Ingebrigsten | 0-0-0 | 1.5-0 | |
| C.E. Jackson | 3-0-0 | 0-0 | plus HdQts |
| D.W. Jones | 1-0-0 | 1-1 | |
| F.H. Jurgens | 0-0-0 | 8-0 | |
| D.F. Kelso | 1-0-1 | 0-0 | |
| C. Kies | 0-0-0 | 1-3 | |
| Q. Klatt | 2.5-0-0 | 0-0 | |
| J.B. Lee | 0-0-0 | 1-2 | |
| F.E. LeFevre | 2-0-1 | 2-0 | |
| W.H. Lewis, Jr. | 1-0-1 | 0-0 | |
| J.T. Martin | 0.5-0-0 | 0-0 | |
| H. Mednick | 0-0.5-1 | 0-0 | |
| R.J. Meyer | 3-1-3 | 0.5-1 | |
| M.B. Nichols | 3-0-2 | 0-0 | |
| R.L. Ott | 3.5-0.5-1 | 0-0 | |
| E.F. Pogue | 0-0-0 | 6-4 | |
| R.H. Pollock | 0-0-0 | 1.5-2 | |
| K.C. Price | 1-0-1 | 0-0 | |
| R.L. Pubentz | 1-0-0 | 0-0 | |
| J.M. Reichard | 0.5-0-0 | 0-0 | |
| F.H. Roark, Jr. | 1.5-0-0 | 0-0 | |
| V.J. Rudnick | 0-0-0 | 0.5-1 | |
| J.C. Santee | 0-0-0 | 0.5-1 | |
| R.M. Scott | 0-0-2 | 1-1 | |
| A.L. Shaffer | 1-0-0 | 0-1 | |
| W.W. Smith | 2-0-1 | 0-0 | |
| L.S. Smutko | 0-0-1 | 0-0 | |
| M.P. Snow | 1-0-0 | 0-0 | |
| K.H. Stevens | 0-0-1 | 0-0 | |
| D. Stewart | 0-0-0 | 7-0 | |
| F.E. Strock | 0-0-0 | 3-2 | |
| J.K. Taylor | 0-0-0 | 0-1 | |
| H.J. Watson, Jr. | 0-0-1 | 0-0 | |
| G.M. Webb | 1-0-1 | 0-0 | |
| Z.M. Wyman | 0-0-0 | 1.5-0 | |
| W.R. Yarbrough | 0-0-0 | 1-3 | |
| J.C. Yaryan | 1-0-0 | 0-0 | |
| A. Ziegelbauer | 0-0-0 | 2-1 | |

## 20th Fighter Group Scoring

| | | | |
|---|---|---|---|
| **November 26, 1943** | | | |
| 77th: | Maj. H.E. Johnson | Do-217 dest(air) | S/Lemwerder A/F |
| **December 1, 1943** | | | |
| 77th: | Lt. J.L. Gard | FW-190 dest(air) | Coblenz |
| **December 31, 1943** | | | |
| 79th: | Lt. L.F. Graham | FW-190 dam(air) | Bordeuax |
| **January 4, 1944** | | | |
| 79th: | Lt. M.B. Nichols | Do-217 dam(air) | Kiel |
| **January 5, 1944** | | | |
| HdQts: | Maj. R.P. Montgomery | FW-190 dam(air) | W/Neumunster |
| **January 7, 1944** | | | |
| HdQts: | Capt. C.E. Jackson | (.5)Me-109 dam(air) | Ludwigshafen |
| 55th: | Lt. W.B. Taylor | Me-109 dest(air) | Worms |
| | Lt. V.R. Stockton | (.5)Me-109 dam(air) | Ludwigshafen |
| **January 14, 1944** | | | |
| HdQts: | Col. B.M. Russell | (.5)FW-190 dest(air) | Rouen |
| 79th: | Lt. M.B. Nichols | FW-190 dest(air) | Rouen |
| | F/O M.L. Byrd | (.5)FW-190 dest(air) | Rouen |
| | Maj. R.L. Ott | (.5)FW-190 prob(air) | S/Fecamp |
| | | FW-190 dam(air) | S/Fecamp |
| | Lt. H. Mednick | (.5)FW-190 prob(air) | S/Fecamp |
| | | FW-190 dam(air) | S/Fecamp |
| | Capt. R.J. Meyer | (2)Me-109 dam(air) | Rouen |
| | Lt. T.A. Hanzo | (2)FW-190 dam(air) | S/Fecamp |
| | Capt. L.F. Graham | Me-109 dam(air) | Rouen |
| | Lt. F.E. LeFevre | Me-109 dam(air) | S/Rouen |
| | Lt. L.S. Smutko | Me-109 dam(air) | Rouen |
| **January 24, 1944** | | | |
| 55th: | Capt. D.H. McAuley | FW-190 dest(air) | Courtrai |
| | | FW-190 prob(air) | Courtrai |
| | Capt. M.R. McLary | FW-190 dest(air) | Courtrai |
| | | FW-190 dam(air) | Courtrai |
| | Lt. H.B. Baker | FW-190 dam(air) | Courtrai |
| **January 29, 1944** | | | |
| 55th: | Lt. R.D. Frey | Me-110 dest(air) | Undenheim |
| | Lt. C.A. Hallberg | Me-110 dest(air) | Undenheim |
| 77th: | Lt. W.L. Whiteside | Me-109 dest(air) | SW Frankfurt |
| | | (.5)Me-210 dest(air)* | SW Frankfurt |
| | Lt. E.J. Machen | Me-110 dest(air) | SW Frankfurt |
| | Lt. R.T. Bond | (.5)Me-210 dest(air)** | S/Coblenz |
| | Lt. R.S. Flynn | (.5)Me-210 dest(air)** | S/Coblenz |
| | Lt. R.C. Garrett | Me-110 dam(air) | W/Frankfurt |
| 79th: | Capt. L.F. Graham | (2)FW-190 dest(air) | E/Lille |
| | | FW-190 dest(air) | Coblenz |
| | Maj. R.L. Ott | Me-110 dest(air) | Mainz |
| | | (.5)Me-210 dest(air)* | SW Frankfurt |
| | Capt. R.P. Gatterdam | FW-190 prob(air) | Coblenz |
| **January 30, 1944** | | | |
| 77th: | Lt. M.J. Gilbertson | Do-217 dam(air) | Osnabruck |
| 79th: | Maj. R.L. Ott | FW-190 dest(air) | Minden |
| | | Do-217 dest(air) | Minden |
| | Capt. R.P. Gatterdam | (.5)Me-210 dest(air) | Brunswick |
| | Lt. J.T. Martin | (.5)Me-210 dest(air) | Brunswick |
| | Lt. M.D. Fall | (.5)Do-217 dest(air) | Minden |
| | Lt. F.H. Roark | (.5)Do-217 dest(air) | Minden |
| **February 5, 1944** | | | |
| HdQts: | LtCol. R.P. Montgomery | (.33)FW-200 dest(air) | Bourges A/F |
| 77th: | Capt. P.J. Sabo | (.33)FW-200 dest(air) | Bourges A/F |
| | Lt. J.E. Davis | (.33)FW-200 dest(air) | Bourges A/F |
| | Lt. R.L. Frakes | (.33)He-111 dest(air) | Bourges A/F |
| | Lt. M.J. Gilbertson | (.33)He-111 dest(air) | Bourges A/F |
| | Lt. J.M. Morris | (.33)He-111 dest(air) | Bourges A/F |
| **February 8, 1944** | | | |
| 77th: | Lt. J.M. Morris | (2)FW-190 dest(air) | Sedan |
| | | Me-109 dest(air) | Losheim |
| | | Me-109 dest(air) | Denain |
| **February 10, 1944** | | | |
| HdQts: | LtCol. R.P. Montgomery | FW-190 dam(air) | Nienburg |
| 55th: | Capt. M.R. McLary | Me-110 dest(air) | Gifhorn |
| | | Me-410 dest(air) | Gifhorn |
| | | FW-190 dam(air) | Gifhorn |
| | | Me-110 dam(air) | Gifhorn |
| | Lt. R.D. Frey | Me-110 dest(air) | Celle |
| | Lt. W.B. Taylor | Me-109 dest(air) | NW Hanover |
| 77th: | Capt. P.J. Sabo | Me-110 dam(air) | Hanover |
| | | Me-210 dam(air) | Hanover |
| | Lt. A.L. Gese | Me-210 dam(air) | Brunswick |
| 79th: | Capt. C.E. Jackson | FW-190 dest(air) | N/Hanover |
| | Capt. R.J. Meyer | FW-190 dest(air) | N/Hanover |
| | Lt. F.E. LeFevre | Me-210 dest(air) | Lingen |
| | Lt. D.C. Cooper | FW-190 dam(air) | N/Hanover |
| **February 11, 1944** | | | |
| 77th: | Lt. J.M. Morris | Me-109 dest(air) | Giessen |
| | Lt. B.N. Rader | Me-109 dest(air) | Giessen |
| | Maj. H.E. Johnson | Me-109 dam(air) | Chateau d'Ardenne |
| | Lt. R.G. Quinn | Me-109 dam(air) | Chateau d'Ardenne |
| 79th: | Capt. R.J. Meyer | Me-410 prob(air) | SW Frankfurt |
| | Lt. M.B. Nichols | Me-410 dam(air) | W/Frankfurt |
| **February 20, 1944** | | | |
| 55th: | Lt. C.A. Hallberg | Me-110 dam(air) | NE Coblenz |
| 77th: | Maj. H.E. Johnson | FW-190 dest(air) | Wernigerode |
| | | FW-190 prob(air) | Wernigerode |
| | Lt. T.M. Williams | FW-190 dest(air) | Brunswick |
| | | (.5)Me-109 dest(air) | Brunswick |
| | | FW-190 dam(air) | Brunswick |
| | Lt. C.C. Arthaud | (.5)Me-109 dest(air) | Brunswick |
| | Lt. A.L. Gese | FW-190 dam(air) | Brunswick-Gotha |
| 79th: | Capt. L.F. Graham | (2)Me-110 dest(air) | SW Brunswick |
| | Capt. C.E. Jackson | (2)FW-190 dest(air) | SW Brunswick |
| **February 22, 1944** | | | |
| 55th: | Lt. E.E. Geiger | Z.506 dest(air) | Cleve |
| **February 24, 1944** | | | |
| 77th: | Lt. J.M. Morris | Me-110 dest(air) | Schweinfurt |
| **March 6, 1944** | | | |
| 55th: | Lt. J.J. Yelton | FW-190 dest(air) | Oldenburg |
| **March 18, 1944** | | | |
| HdQts: | LtCol. M.E. Hubbard | (2.5)Me-109 dest(air) | Memmingen |
| | | Me-109 prob(air) | Memmingen |
| 55th: | Maj. D.H. McAuley | Me-109 dest(air) | Erding |
| | Capt. J.C. Serros | (.5)Me-110 dest(air) | Memmingen |
| | Lt. C.A. Hallberg | (.5)Me-110 dest(air) | Memmingen |
| 77th: | Lt. A.F. Clark | (1.5)Me-109 dest(air) | Memmingen |
| 79th: | Maj. R.C. Franklin | Me 110 dest(air) | Ulm |
| | Capt. M.B. Nichols | Me-110 dest(air) | Ulm |
| | Capt. L.F. Graham | (.5)Me-110 dest(air) | Ulm |
| | Lt. A.W. Heiden | (.5)Me-110 dest(air) | Ulm |
| **April 5, 1944** | | | |
| 55th: | Lt. J.J. Yelton | FW-190 dest(air) | SW Hanover |
| | | FW-200 dest(air) | SW Hanover |
| **April 8, 1944** | | | |
| HdQts: | LtCol. H.J. Rau | Me-109 dest(air) | All claims are at Salzwedel |
| | | (3)Ju-88 dest(grd) | |
| | | Ju-52 dest(grd) | |
| 77th: | Maj. H.E. Johnson | He-177 dest(air) | |
| | | u/i a/c dest(grd) | |
| | | Me-110 dam(grd) | |
| | | u/i a/c dam(grd) | |
| | Capt. E.J. Machen | (2)Ju-88 dest(grd) | |
| | | (2)Ju-88 dam(grd) | |
| | Lt. C.G. Horne | FW-190 dest(grd) | |
| | | (3)u/i a/c dam(grd) | |
| | | Ju-88 dam(grd) | |
| | Capt. J.M. Morris | Me-410 dest(grd) | |
| | | (.5)Ju-88 dest(grd) | |
| | | (.33)u/i a/c dest(grd) | |
| | Lt. I.W. Fernandes | Do-217 dest(grd) | |
| | | (.33)u/i a/c dest(grd) | |
| | | (.5)Ju-52 dam(grd) | |
| | Lt. E.C. Fiebelkorn | u/i a/c dest(grd) | |
| | | (2)Ju-88 dam(grd) | |
| | Lt. B.N. Rader | (.5)Ju-88 dest(grd) | |
| | | (.5)Ju-52 dam(grd) | |
| | Lt. W.F. Kuemmerle | (.33)u/i a/c dest(grd) | |
| | Lt. W.L. Whiteside | (4)Ju-88 dam(grd) | |
| | Lt. P. Chubin | (3)Ju-88 dam(grd) | |
| | Lt. H.F. Hendricks | (2)Ju-88 dam(grd) | |
| | Lt. J.W. Fagg | Ju-88 dam(grd) | |
| 79th: | Maj. R.C. Franklin | Me-109 dest(air) | |
| | | (.2)He-177 dest(air) | |
| | Capt. D.E. Anderson | (.2)He-177 dest(air) | |
| | | (2)He-177 dest(grd) | |
| | Capt. R.P. Gatterdam | (.2)He-177 dest(air) | |
| | | (these three shared the He-177 w/Capt. E.C. Hedlund and Lt. R.H. Dettre of the 474th Ftr Grp) | |
| | Lt. M.P. Snow | Me-109 dest(air) | Hermannsburg |
| | Lt. F.E. LeFevre | Me-109 dest(air) | All remaining claims are at Salzwedel |
| | | (2)Ju-88 dest(grd) | |
| | Lt. R.H. Black | Ju-88 dest(grd) | |
| | | u/i a/c dest(grd) | |

| | | | |
|---|---|---|---|
| | Lt. A.W. Heiden | (.5)He-111 dest(grd) (shared with Capt. Hedlund) | |
| | | Ju-88 dam(grd) | |

**April 23, 1944**

| | | | |
|---|---|---|---|
| 55th: | Capt. R.M. Scrutchfield | He-111 dest(grd) | Chateaudun |
| | | (2)u/i a/c dam(grd) | Chateaudun |
| | | Ju-87 dam(grd) | Chateaudun |
| 79th: | Maj. R.C. Franklin | He-111 dest(grd) | Chateaudun |

**April 24, 1944**

| | | | |
|---|---|---|---|
| 55th: | Lt. W.G. Schultz | (1.5)Me-109 dest(air) | Worms |
| | Capt. W.B. Taylor | Me-109 dest(air) | W/Worms |
| | Lt. R.P. Watson | Me-109 dest(air) | W/Worms |
| 77th: | Capt. D.A. Reihmer | (.5)Me-109 dest(air) | Worms |

**April 29, 1944**

| | | | |
|---|---|---|---|
| 77th: | Capt. D.A. Reihmer | (2)Me-109 dam(air) | Wittenburg |

**April 30, 1944**

| | | | |
|---|---|---|---|
| 77th: | Capt. J.M. Morris | He-177 dest(grd) | Bricy A/F |
| | Lt. E.C. Fiebelkorn | Me-410 dest(grd) | Bricy A/F |
| | Lt. W.F. Kuemmerle | Me-410 dest(grd) | Bricy A/F |

**May 11, 1944**

| | | | |
|---|---|---|---|
| 77th: | Capt. D.A. Reihmer | Ju-88 dest(grd) | Bretigny A/F |
| | Lt. J.D. McArthur | Ju-88 dest(grd) | Bretigny A/F |

**May 12, 1944**

| | | | |
|---|---|---|---|
| 77th: | Lt. I.C. Baker | Me-109 dest(air) | SW Kassel |

**May 22, 1944**

| | | | |
|---|---|---|---|
| 77th: | Maj. R.F. Gustke | FW-190 dest(air) | NW Kiel |

**May 24, 1944**

| | | | |
|---|---|---|---|
| 79th: | Capt. J.M. Ilfrey | (2)Me-109 dest(air) | Eberswalde |
| | Maj. D.E. Anderson | Me-109 dam(air) | Eberswalde |
| | Lt. K.H. Stevens | Me-109 dam(air) | Eberswalde |
| | Lt. H.J. Watson | Me-109 dam(air) | Eberswalde |

**June 25, 1944**

| | | | |
|---|---|---|---|
| HdQts: | LtCol. C. Wilson | Me-109 dest(air) | S/Paris |

**June 28, 1944**

| | | | |
|---|---|---|---|
| 55th: | Lt. R.E. Miles | Me-109 dest(air) | Nivelles |
| 79th: | Lt. R.W. Bebout | FW-190 dest(air) | Beaumont |

**June 30, 1944**

| | | | |
|---|---|---|---|
| 55th: | Capt. H.B. Baker | Me-109 dest(air) | Dreux |
| | Lt. D.H. Larrabee | Me-109 dest(air) | Dreux |

**July 4, 1944**

| | | | |
|---|---|---|---|
| 77th: | Lt. R.E. Moncrieff | Me-109 dest(grd) | Tours |

**July 5, 1944**

| | | | |
|---|---|---|---|
| HdQts: | LtCol. H.E. Johnson | (.5)He-177 dest(air) | Cognac |
| 55th: | Lt. J.S. Reynolds | (.5)He-177 dest(air) | Cognac |

**July 7, 1944**

| | | | |
|---|---|---|---|
| 55th: | Lt. R.O. Loehnert | (2)Me-109 dest(air) | Halle |
| | Lt. C.A. Hallberg | Me-109 dest(air) | Halle |
| 77th: | Capt. J.M. Morris | Me-410 dest(air) | Leipzig-Halle |
| | Lt. I.W. Fernandes | FW-190 dest(air) | Halle |
| | | FW-190 dam(air) | Halle |
| | Lt. A.F. Clark | FW-190 dest(air) | Halle |
| | Lt. L.W. Adams | Me-410 dest(air) | Oschersleben |
| | | FW-190 dam(air) | Halle |
| | Lt. A.D. Payne | FW-190 dam(air) | Halle |
| | Lt. P. Chubin | FW-190 dam(air) | Halle |

**July 9, 1944**

| | | | |
|---|---|---|---|
| 79th: | Lt. J.E. Carpenter | Ju-290 dest(air) | Moulins |

**July 14, 1944**

| | | | |
|---|---|---|---|
| 55th: | Lt. W. Mullins | FW-190 dest(air) | S/Nogent |
| 77th: | Lt. C.C. Arthaud | (.5)FW-190 dest(air) | SW Reims |
| | Lt. E.C. Fiebelkorn | (.5)FW-190 dest(air) | SW Reims |

NOTE: From July 29 on, all claims are in P-51's

**July 29, 1944**

| | | | |
|---|---|---|---|
| 77th: | Lt. L.W. Adams | (2)Me-109 dest(air) | Gutersloh |
| | Lt. R.E. Moncrieff | Me-109 dest(air) | Gutersloh |
| | | Me-109 dam(air) | Gutersloh |

**August 4, 1944**

| | | | |
|---|---|---|---|
| 77th: | Lt. F.H. Alexander | He-111 dest(grd) | Putnitz |
| | Lt. G.R. Brucks | Ju-88 dam(grd) | Barth |
| | Lt. B.N. Rader | Ju-88 dam(grd) | Barth |

**August 5, 1944**

| | | | |
|---|---|---|---|
| 77th: | Capt. M.J. Gilbertson | Me-109 dest(air) | NW Hamburg |
| | Lt. E.C. Fiebelkorn | Me-109 dest(air) | S/Hamburg |
| | Lt. L.E. Rowlett | Me-109 dam(air) | S/Hamburg |
| 79th: | Lt. H.O. Binkley | Me-109 dest(air) | Hamburg-Bremen |
| | Lt. R.E. Campbell | Me-109 dest(air) | Hamburg-Bremen |
| | | Me-109 dam(air) | Hamburg-Bremen |
| | Lt. G.M. Webb | Me-109 dam(air) | Hamburg-Bremen |

**August 6, 1944**

| | | | |
|---|---|---|---|
| HdQts: | LtCol. C. Wilson | FW-190 dam(air) | Potsdam |
| 55th: | Lt. J.E. Klink | Do-217 dest(air) | Strausberg A/F |
| | Lt. J.L. Mansker | FW-190 dest(air) | S/Brandenburg |
| | Lt. K.C. Smeltz | FW-190 dest(air) | Schonfeld A/F |
| 77th: | Lt. F.H. Alexander | (2)Me-109 dest(air) | Belzig |
| | Lt. B.N. Rader | Me-109 dest(air) | Potsdam |
| 79th: | Lt. W.H. Lewis | Me-109 dest(air) | SW Berlin |
| | | Me-109 dam(air) | SW Berlin |

**August 9, 1944**

| | | | |
|---|---|---|---|
| HdQts: | LtCol. J.P. Randolph | Me-109 dest(air) | S/Augsburg |
| 55th: | Lt. R.I. Bowman | Me-109 dest(air) | S/Augsburg |
| | Lt. D.R. Franklin | Me-109 dam(air) | S/Augsburg |
| 79th: | Lt. Q. Klatt | (2.5)FW-190 dest(air) | SW Ulm |
| | Capt. R.J. Meyer | (2)FW-190 dest(air) | SW Ulm |
| | | FW-190 dam(air) | SW Ulm |
| | Capt. W.W. Smith | (2)FW-190 dest(air) | SW Ulm |
| | | FW-190 dam(air) | SW Ulm |
| | Lt. R.W. Bebout | (2)FW-190 dest(air) | SW Ulm |
| | Capt. J.O. Yaryan | FW-190 dest(air) | SW Ulm |
| | Lt. H.O. Binkley | FW-190 dest(air) | SW Ulm |
| | | FW-190 dam(air) | SW Ulm |
| | Lt. J.E. Carpenter | FW-190 dest(air) | SW Ulm |
| | Lt. K.C. Price | FW-190 dest(air) | SW Ulm |
| | | FW-190 dam(air) | SW Ulm |
| | Lt. F.H. Roark | FW-190 dest(air) | SW Ulm |
| | Lt. J.N. Reichard | (.5)FW-190 dest(air) | SW Ulm |
| | Lt. J.L. Armstrong | FW-190 dam(air) | SW Ulm |

**August 16, 1944**

| | | | |
|---|---|---|---|
| HdQts: | LtCol. C. Wilson | Me-109 dest(air) | Eisenach |
| | | FW-190 dest(air) | Eisenach |
| 77th: | Capt. M.J. Gilbertson | Me-109 dest(air) | Mulhausen |
| | Capt. J.T. McKeon | Me-109 dest(air) | Mulhausen |
| | | FW-190 dam(air) | Mulhausen |
| | Lt. L.W. Adams | Me-109 dest(air) | Northeim |
| | Lt. C.C. Arthaud | FW-190 dest(air) | Eisenach |
| | Lt. L.E. Rowlett | Me-109 dest(air) | Mulhausen |
| | Lt. L.J. Robertson | Me-109 prob(air) | Altenburg |
| 79th: | Lt. R.E. Campbell | Me-109 dest(air) | S/Hanover |

**August 25, 1944**

| | | | |
|---|---|---|---|
| HdQts: | LtCol. J.P. Randolph | BV-140 dest(grd) | All claims are at Parow A/F |
| | | Ju-88 dest(grd) | |
| | | (2)Ju-88 dam(grd) | |
| 55th: | Lt. J.L. Mansker | (5)Ju-88 dest(grd) | |
| | | BV-140 dest(grd) | |
| | | (3)Ju-88 dam(grd) | |
| | Lt. K.C. Smeltz | (3)Ju-88 dest(grd) | |
| | | (2)Ju-88 dam(grd) | |
| | | BV-140 dam(grd) | |
| | Lt. J.E. Burford | BV-140 dest(grd) | |
| | | Hs-126 dest(grd) | |
| | | (2)Ju-88 dam(grd) | |
| | | Ju-52 dam(grd) | |
| | Lt. H.B. Bynum | Ju-88 dest(grd) | |
| | | Ju-52 dest(grd) | |
| | Lt. J.S. Ford | Ju-88 dest(grd) | |
| | | Ju-52 dest(grd) | |
| | | Ju-88 dam(grd) | |
| | Lt. R.H. Riemensnider | (1.5)Do-18 dest(grd) | |
| | | u/i a/c dest(grd) | |
| | | Do-18 dam(grd) | |
| | Lt. E.E. Wasil | (2)Do-18 dest(grd) | |
| | Lt. W.W. Wells | Me-410 dest(grd) | |
| | | u/i a/c dest(grd) | |
| | | u/i a/c dam(grd) | |
| | | (2)Ju-88 dam(grd) | |
| | Capt. E.W. Hower | BV-140 dest(grd) | |
| | | Ju-88 dam(grd) | |
| | Lt. H.M. Anderson | Ju-88 dest(grd) | |
| | Lt. C.F. Bain | Ju-88 dest(grd) | |
| | | Ju-88 dam(grd) | |
| | Lt. R.M. Howard | BV-140 dest(grd) | |
| | | BV-140 dam(grd) | |
| | Lt. D.D. Oxley | FW-190 dest(grd) | |
| | | Ju-88 dam(grd) | |
| | Lt. K.D. McNeel | (.5)Do-18 dest(grd) | |
| | Lt. H.L. Brown | Ju-88 dam(grd) | |

**August 27, 1944**

| | | | |
|---|---|---|---|
| 55th: | Lt. K.C. Smeltz | Ju-88 dest(grd) | Habjeerg A/F |

**September 10, 1944**

| | | | |
|---|---|---|---|
| 79th: | Lt. E.H. Coughran | (3)u/i a/c dest(grd) | SW Stuttgart |
| | Lt. H.O. Binkley | Me-110 dest(grd) | SW Stuttgart |
| | | u/i a/c dest(grd) | SW Stuttgart |
| | Lt. C.J. Dixon | u/i a/c dam(grd) | SW Stuttgart |

**September 28, 1944**

| | | | |
|---|---|---|---|
| 77th: | Lt. E.C. Fiebelkorn | (3)Me-109 dest(air) | S/Magdeburg |
| | | Me-109 dam(air) | S/Magdeburg |
| | Lt. L.J. Robertson | (2)FW-190 dest(air) | Aschersleben |
| | Lt. T.E. Slanker | FW-190 dest(air) | S/Magdeburg |
| | | FW-190 dam(air) | S/Magdeburg |
| | | Me-210 dest(grd) | S/Magdeburg |
| | Lt. P.J. McCully | Me-109 dam(air) | S/Magdeburg |
| | Lt. R.L. Van Woert | Me-109 dam(air) | S/Magdeburg |

**October 6, 1944**

| | | | |
|---|---|---|---|
| HdQts: | LtCol. J.P. Randolph | (2)Do-24 dest(grd) | Kubitzer Bay |
| 55th: | Capt. J.T. McKeon | (2)Do-24 dest(grd) | All claims are |
| | Capt. W.B. Taylor | Do-24 dest(grd) | at Kubitzer Bay |
| | | u/i a/c dest(grd) | |
| | Lt. W.M. Hurst | (2)Do-24 dest(grd) | |
| | Lt. R.M. Howard | BV-140 dest(grd) | |
| | | Do-24 dest(grd) | |
| | | (3)BV-140 dam(grd) | |
| | Lt. D.D. Oxley | (2)Do-24 dest(grd) | |
| | Lt. R.I. Bowman | Do-24 dest(grd) | |
| | | Do-24 dam(grd) | |
| | Lt. T.C. Barnes | Do-24 dest(grd) | |
| | | Do-24 dam(grd) | |
| | Lt. D.B. Benedict | Do-24 dest(grd) | |
| | Lt. E.W. Cavell | Do-24 dest(grd) | |
| | | Do-24 dam(grd) | |
| | F/O J.D. Leon | Do-24 dest(grd) | |
| | | Do-24 dam(grd) | |
| | Lt. M. Maldanado | Do-24 dest(grd) | |
| | | Do-24 dam(grd) | |
| | Lt. J.L. Mansker | u/i a/c dest(grd) | |
| | Lt. K.D. McNeel | u/i a/c dest(grd) | |
| 77th: | Lt. F.H. Alexander | (3)He-111 dest(grd) | All 77th & 79th |
| | | He-115 dest(grd) | claims are at |
| | | Do-18 dest(grd) | Bad Berg-Dievenow |
| | | (2)He-111 dam(grd) | |
| | Lt. R.R. Flowers | (2.5)Do-18 dest(grd)* | |
| | Lt. L.W. Adams | Ar-196 dest(grd) | |
| | | Do-18 dest(grd) | |
| | Lt. J.M. Garner | (1.5)Do-18 dest(grd)* | |
| | | Do-18 dam(grd) | |
| | Capt. J.H. Herbert | Ar-196 dest(grd) | |
| | Lt. F.E. Snodgrass | (.5)Do-18 dest(grd)** | |
| | | Do-18 dam(grd) | |
| | Lt. D.W. Van Sickle | (.5)Do-18 dest(grd)** | |
| | | Do-18 dam(grd) | |
| 79th: | Capt. R.P. Gatterdam | (2.5)He-115 dest(grd) | |
| | Lt. M.G. Ingebrigsten | (1.5)He-115 dest(grd) | |
| | Lt. W.E. Bullers | He-115 dest(grd) | |
| | Lt. J.E. Carpenter | He-115 dest(grd) | |
| | Lt. Z.M. Wyman | u/i a/c dest(grd) | |
| | Lt. R.H. Pollock | u/i a/c dam(grd) | |

**October 7, 1944**

| | | | |
|---|---|---|---|
| 55th: | Capt. R.M. Scrutchfield | Do-18 dest(grd) | Ribnitz A/F |
| 77th: | Capt. R.T. Stovall | Ju-88 dest(grd) | Peenemunde |
| | Lt. C.W. Dungan | Ju-88 dest(grd) | Peenemunde |
| | Lt. T.P. Hambelton | Ju-88 dam(grd) | Peenemunde |
| | Lt. D.W. Van Sickle | u/i a/c dam(grd) | Peenemunde |
| 79th: | Capt. R.J. Meyer | (.5)He-115 dest(grd) | Bad Berg-Dievenow |
| | Lt. Z.M. Wyman | (.5)He-115 dest(grd) | Bad Berg-Dievenow |

**November 2, 1944**

| | | | |
|---|---|---|---|
| HdQts: | LtCol. R.P. Montgomery | (2)Me-109 dest(air) | Halle-Merseburg |
| | | FW-190 dest(air) | Halle-Merseburg |
| 55th: | Capt. J.H. Tennant | (2)FW-190 dest(air) | Halle-Merseburg |
| | | Me-109 dest(air) | Halle-Merseburg |
| | Lt. H.L. Brown | (2)FW-190 dest(air) | Halle-Merseburg |
| | | Me-109 dest(air) | Halle-Merseburg |
| | | Me-109 dam(air) | Halle-Merseburg |
| | Lt. J.L. Mansker | (2)Me-109 dest(air) | Halle-Merseburg |
| | | Me-109 prob(air) | Halle-Merseburg |
| | Lt. D.E. Chrissinger | Me-109 dest(air) | Halle |
| | Lt. D.I. Freedman | Me-109 dest(air) | Halle |
| | | Me-109 dam(air) | Halle |
| | Lt. W.M. Hurst | Me-109 dest(air) | Halle |
| | F/O J.D. Leon | Me-109 dest(air) | SW Merseburg |
| | | Me-109 prob(air) | SW Merseburg |
| 77th: | Lt. E.C. Fiebelkorn | (3)Me-109 dest(air) | N/Leipzig |
| | Lt. J.M. Garner | (2)Me-109 dest(air) | N/Leipzig |
| | Lt. L.E. Rowlett | (2)Me-109 dest(air) | Merseburg |
| | Lt. R.D. Jones | Me-109 dest(air) | Merseburg |
| | | Me-109 prob(air) | Merseburg |
| | Lt. G.L. Reynolds | Me-109 dest(air) | Merseburg |
| | Lt. P.L. Schallo | Me-109 dam(air) | N/Leipzig |
| 79th: | Capt. R.P. Gatterdam | Me-109 dest(air) | SW Merseburg |
| | Capt. G.M. Webb | Me-109 dest(air) | SW Merseburg |
| | Lt. R.L. Pubentz | Me-109 dest(air) | SW Merseburg |

**November 4, 1944**

| | | | |
|---|---|---|---|
| 77th: | Maj. R.F. Gustke | He-177 dam(grd) | SW Dummer Lake |
| | Lt. T.E. Slanker | FW-190 dam(grd) | W/Munster |

**November 8, 1944**

| | | | |
|---|---|---|---|
| 77th: | Lt. E.C. Fiebelkorn | (.5)Me-262 dest(air) | Dummer Lake |
| | | (shared with a 357th Ftr Grp P-51) | |

**November 21, 1944**

| | | | |
|---|---|---|---|
| 77th: | Lt. B.C. Halpin | Me-109 dest(air) | Munster |

**December 2, 1944**

| | | | |
|---|---|---|---|
| 55th: | Lt. E. Planchak | (2)Me-109 dest(air) | Coblenz-St. Goar |
| | Lt. H.L. Brown | FW-190 dest(air) | Coblenz-St. Goar |
| 77th: | LtCol. R.F. Gustke | Me-109 dest(air) | Coblenz |
| | Lt. J.M. Garner | FW-190 dest(air) | Coblenz |
| | Lt. R.E. Murrell | FW-190 dest(air) | Coblenz |

**January 1, 1945**

| | | | |
|---|---|---|---|
| 55th: | Capt. W.M. Hurst | Me-262 dam(air) | Magdeburg |

**January 14, 1945**

| | | | |
|---|---|---|---|
| 55th: | Maj. R.P. Gatterdam | (2)FW-190 dest(air) | All claims are |
| | Lt. H.L. Brown | (2)Me-109 dest(air) | at Perleberg |
| | Lt. J.K. Brwon | (2)FW-190 dest(air) | |
| | Lt. J.D. Leon | (2)FW-190 dest(air) | |
| | Lt. S.A. Baker | (1.5)FW-190 dest(air) | |
| | | (shared with an unknown pilot) | |
| | Lt. S.G. Stitzer | FW-190 dest(air) | |
| | Lt. R.W. Fruechtenicht | FW-190 dam(air) | |
| | Lt. K.D. McNeel | Me-262 dam(air) | |
| 77th: | Capt. C.H. Cole | Me-109 dest(air) | All claims are |
| | Lt. R.D. Jones | FW-190 dest(air) | at Perleberg |
| | Capt. M.J. Gilbertson | (.5)Me-109 dest(air) | |
| | Lt. J.P. Starke | (.5)Me-109 dest(air) | |
| | Lt. D.W. Van Sickle | Me-109 prob(air) | |
| 79th: | Maj. M.B. Nichols | Me-109 dest(air) | Perleberg |
| | Lt. D.A. Beschen | Me-109 dest(air) | E/Wittenburg |
| | Lt. R.H. Black | Me-109 dest(air) | E/Wittenburg |
| | | Me-109 dam(air) | E/Wittenburg |
| | Lt. D.N. Jones | Me-109 dest(air) | E/Wittenburg |
| | Lt. D.F. Kelso | Me-109 dest(air) | E/Wittenburg |
| | | Me-109 dam(air) | E/Wittenburg |
| | F/O A.L. Shaffer | Me-109 dest(air) | NW Berlin |
| | Lt. R.M. Scott | Me-109 dam(air) | E/Wittenburg |

**February 9, 1945**

| | | | |
|---|---|---|---|
| 77th: | Lt. P.L. Scahllo | Me-109 dest(air) | All claims are |
| | | (2)FW-190 dest(grd) | at Esperstadt A/F |
| | | Me-410 dest(grd) | |
| | Lt. G.R. Hall | Me-109 dest(air) | |
| | | FW-190 dest(grd) | |
| | | FW-190 dam(grd) | |
| | | Me-410 dam(grd) | |
| | Lt. F.V. Purse | Me-109 dam(air) | Mulhausen |
| | Capt. L.E. Einhaus | (6)FW-190 dest(grd) | All remaining |
| | Capt. C.H. Cole | (6)FW-190 dest(grd) | claims are at |
| | | FW-190 dam(grd) | Esperstadt A/F |
| | Lt. R.D. Jones | (4)FW-190 dest(grd) | |
| | | Me-109 dest(grd) | |
| | Lt. G.L. Reynolds | (2)FW-190 dest(grd) | |
| | | (2)Me-410 dest(grd) | |
| | Maj. M.J. Gilbertson | (3)FW-190 dest(grd) | |
| | | Me-110 dam(grd) | |
| | Lt. W.C. Fay | (3)FW-190 dest(grd) | |
| | Lt. F. Larsen | (2)FW-190 dest(grd) | |
| | | u/i a/c dest(grd) | |
| | Lt. D.R. Pitz | (2)FW-190 dest(grd) | |
| | | Me-110 dam(grd) | |
| | Lt. J.P. Starke | FW-190 dest(grd) | |
| | | Me-410 dest(grd) | |
| | Capt. E.C. Jennings | FW-190 dest(grd) | |

**February 14, 1945**

| | | | |
|---|---|---|---|
| 55th: | Capt. J.K. Brown | (.5)Me-262 dam(air) | Stuttgart |
| | Lt. K.D. McNeel | (.5)Me-262 dam(air) | Stuttgart |

**February 20, 1945**

| | | | |
|---|---|---|---|
| 55th: | Lt. K.D. McNeel | Me-109 dest(air) | Nurnburg |
| | Capt. J.S. Ford | Me-109 prob(air) | S/Nurnburg |
| | | (2)Me-109 dest(grd) | S/Nurnburg |

| | | | |
|---|---|---|---|
| 77th: | Lt. A.B. North | Me-108 dest(air) | Straubing |
| | | Me-108 dest(grd) | Straubing |
| | | Me-109 dest(grd) | Straubing |
| | | u/i a/c dest(grd) | Straubing |
| | | u/i a/c dam(grd) | Straubing |
| | Lt. F.L. Van Sickle | Me-108 dest(air) | Straubing |
| | | Me-108 dest(grd) | Straubing |
| | | Fi-156 dest(grd) | Straubing |
| | | u/i a/c dest(grd) | Straubing |
| | Lt. H.J. Piatkiewicz | FW-44 dest(air) | Straubing |
| | | (2)Me-110 dam(grd) | Straubing |
| | Lt. W.C. Fay | W-34 dest(air) | Straubing |
| | Lt. L.H. Kerns | Fi-156 dest(air) | N/Straubing |
| | Lt. G.L. Reynolds | u/i a/c dest(air) | Straubing |
| | Capt. D.W. Van Sickle | He-111 dam(grd) | Straubing |
| | Lt. T.P. Hambelton | Me-109 dam(grd) | Straubing |
| | Lt. R.D. Jones | u/i a/c dam(grd) | Straubing |
| 79th: | Lt. F.E. Strock | (3)He-111 dest(grd) | All claims are |
| | | (2)He-111 dam(grd) | at Weiden A/F |
| | Lt. E.F. Pogue | (2)He-111 dest(grd) | |
| | Lt. A. Ziegelbauer | (2)He-111 dest(grd) | |
| | | He-111 dam(grd) | |
| | Lt. D.A. Beschen | (1.5)He-111 dest(grd)* | |
| | | He-111 dam(grd) | |
| | Lt. R.H. Pollock | (1.5)He-111 dest(grd)** | |
| | | Me-410 dam(grd) | |
| | Lt. W.E. Bullers | He-111 dest(grd) | |
| | | (2)He-111 dam(grd) | |
| | Lt. J.K. Hollins | He-111 dest(grd) | |
| | | (2)He-111 dam(grd) | |
| | Lt. D.N. Jones | He-111 dest(grd) | |
| | | He-111 dam(grd) | |
| | Lt. C. Kies | He-111 dest(grd) | |
| | | (3)He-111 dam(grd) | |
| | Lt. R.M. Scott | He-111 dest(grd) | |
| | | He-111 dam(grd) | |
| | Lt. V.J. Rudnick | (.5)He-111 dest(grd)* | |
| | | He-111 dam(grd) | |
| | Lt. J.C. Santee | (.5)He-111 dest(grd) | |
| | | He-111 dam(grd) | |
| | Maj. R.J. Meyer | Me-110 dam(grd) | |
| | Capt. J.K. Taylor | Me-110 dam(grd) | |
| | F/O A.L. Shaffer | Me-110 dam(grd) | |

**February 22, 1945**

| | | | |
|---|---|---|---|
| 55th: | Capt. R.M. Howard | Me-262 dam(air) | Salzwedel |

**February 25, 1945**

| | | | |
|---|---|---|---|
| 55th: | Capt. C.H. Cole | (4)FW-190 dest(air) | Stendal |
| | Lt. E.L. Kier | (2)Me-109 dest(air) | Dummer Lake |
| | Maj. M.A. Cristadoro | FW-190 dest(air) | Stendal |
| | Capt. R.W. Fruechtenicht | Me-109 dest(air) | Dummer Lake |
| | | Me-109 dam(air) | Dummer Lake |
| | Lt. C.R. Nicholson | FW-190 dest(air) | Gardelegen |
| | Lt. K.L. Pettit | Me-109 dest(air) | Dummer Lake |

**February 28, 1945**

| | | | |
|---|---|---|---|
| 77th: | Lt. R.A. Rege | Me-109 dam(grd) | Gelsheim |

**March 2, 1945**

| | | | |
|---|---|---|---|
| 77th: | Lt. R.D. Jones | FW-190 dam(air) | Chemnitz |
| | Lt. D.F. McAllister | FW-190 dam(air) | Chemnitz |

**March 20, 1945**

| | | | |
|---|---|---|---|
| 77th: | Lt. J.C. Cowley | Me-262 dam(air) | E/Hamburg |

**March 24, 1945**

| | | | |
|---|---|---|---|
| HdQts: | LtCol. R.F. Gustke | Ju-88 dam(grd) | Gutersloh |

**April 9, 1945**

| | | | |
|---|---|---|---|
| 55th: | Capt. R.M. Tracy | Ju-88 dam(grd) | Munich |
| 79th: | Maj. W.R. Yarbrough | Ju-88 dest(grd) | E/Munich |

**April 10, 1945**

| | | | |
|---|---|---|---|
| HdQts: | Col. R.P. Montgomery | Ar-196 dest(grd) | Werder A/F |
| | | Si-204 dest(grd) | Werder A/F |
| | | Ju-52 dest(grd) | Werder A/F |
| | | Si-204 dam(grd) | Werder A/F |
| | | Do-217 dam(grd) | Werder A/F |
| 55th: | Capt. J.K. Brown | Me-262 dest(air) | Neuruppin |
| | Capt. D. Michel | Me-262 dam(air) | Neuruppin |
| | Lt. R.W. Meinzen | Me-262 dam(air) | Neuruppin |
| | Lt. E.L. Kier | (5)Ju-88 dest(grd) | Berlin |
| | | (4)Ju-88 dam(grd) | Berlin |
| | Lt. J.A. Peterburs | (5)u/i a/c dest(grd) | Berlin |
| | Capt. R.M. Tracy | Me-109 dest(grd) | Berlin |
| | | Me-110 dest(grd) | Berlin |
| | | Ju-52 dest(grd) | Berlin |
| | | u/i a/c dest(grd) | Berlin |
| | Lt. G.L. Williams | (4)Ju-88 dest(grd) | Berlin |
| | | (4)Ju-88 dam(grd) | Berlin |
| | Lt. P.F. Seifert | Me-110 dam(grd) | Werder A/F |
| | | He-111 dam(grd) | Werder A/F |
| 77th: | Lt. W.T. Drozd | Me-262 dest(air) | Oranienburg |
| | Lt. A.B. North | Me-262 dest(air) | Oranienburg |
| | Lt. J.W. Cudd | (.5)Me-262 dest(air) | Berlin |
| | F/O J. Rosenblum | (.5)Me-262 dest(air) | Berlin |
| | Lt. G.R. Hall | Me-262 dam(air) | Werder A/F |
| | | He-111 dest(grd) | Werder A/F |
| | | Me-109 dest(grd) | Werder A/F |
| | | Ju-290 dam(grd) | Werder A/F |
| | | He-111 dam(grd) | Werder A/F |
| | Lt. R.A. Morris | Me-410 dest(grd) | Fassberg A/F |
| | | u/i a/c dest(grd) | Fassberg A/F |
| | Lt. L.H. Kerns | Me-410 dest(grd) | Fassberg A/F |
| | Lt. J.E. Simanonok | Ju-88 dest(grd) | Oranienburg |
| | Lt. W.E. Umla | Ju-52 dest(grd) | Schonwalde A/F |
| | | (2)Ju-52 dam(grd) | Schonwalde A/F |
| 79th: | Capt. J.K. Hollins | Me-262 dest(air) | Neustadt |
| | F/O F.H. Jurgens | (3)He-111 dest(grd) | All claims are |
| | | (2)Si-204 dest(grd) | at Werder A/F |
| | | (2)Caudron dest(grd) | |
| | | u/i a/c dest(grd) | |
| | Lt. D. Stewart | (3)Me-110 dest(grd) | |
| | | (2)FW-190 dest(grd) | |
| | | Me-109 dest(grd) | |
| | | He-111 dest(grd) | |
| | Lt. E.F. Pogue | (3)He-111 dest(grd) | |
| | | Me-109 dest(grd) | |
| | | He-111 dam(grd) | |
| | | Me-109 dam(grd) | |
| | Lt. L.J. Degenhardt | (2)u/i a/c dest(grd) | |
| | | u/i a/c dam(grd) | |
| | Lt. J.L. Gubana | Me-109 dest(grd) | |
| | | Ju-88 dest(grd) | |
| | | (2)u/i a/c dam(grd) | |
| | Lt. J.B. Lee | Ju-52 dest(grd) | |
| | | Me-109 dam(grd) | |
| | | Si-204 dam(grd) | |

**April 13, 1945**

| | | | |
|---|---|---|---|
| 77th: | Lt. H.J. Piatkiewicz | (.5)Me-110 dam(grd) | E/Hamburg |
| | Lt. B.M. Phillips | (.5)Me-110 dam(grd) | E/Hamburg |
| 79th: | Maj. W.R. Yarbrough | (2)FW-190 dam(grd) | All claims are |
| | | Ju-88 dam(grd) | at Jagel- |
| | Lt. L.P. Bishop | (2)u/i a/c dam(grd) | Hutzfeld |
| | Lt. E.F. Pogue | Me-109 dam(grd) | |
| | | He-177 dam(grd) | |

**April 16, 1945**

| | | | |
|---|---|---|---|
| 77th: | Maj. M.J. Gilbertson | u/i a/c dest(grd) | Cham A/F |

**April 17, 1945**

| | | | |
|---|---|---|---|
| 77th: | F/O J. Rosenblum | Me-262 dam(air) | S/Dresden |
| 79th: | Lt. R.M. Scott | Me-262 dam(air) | SE Dresden |

### 20th Fighter Group Losses

**November 7, 1943**

Maj. John C. Wilkins (HdQts) KIA; Took off late and disappeared.
P-38H LC- 42-67022

Capt. Herbert W. Cumming (79th) KIA; Hit by a FW-190 and crashed into the Channel.
P-38H MC-F 42-67039

**November 25, 1943**

Lt. Bill Lane (77th) KIA; Hit by flak near St. Omer then lost his other engine 10 miles from Nuthampstead.
P-38H LC- 42-67032

**November 29, 1943**

Lt. John S. Hascall (77th) POW; Hit by fighters near Aschendorf.
P-38H LC- 42-67016

**November 30, 1943**

Lt. Robert L. Thomas, Jr. (77th) POW; Hit by a Me-109 over the Dutch Islands and bailed out over the Channel.
P-38H LC- 42-67038

**December 1, 1943**

Lt. Jack L. Gard (77th) POW; Hit by a Me-109 near Coblenz.
P-38H LC- 42-66723

**December 31, 1943**

Lt. John W. Crago (55th) KIA; Crashed near Woodnewton shortly after take-off.
P-38J KI-L 42-67489

**January 4, 1944**

F/O Henry M. Higginbotham (77th) KIA; Last seen near Neumunster.
P-38J LC- 42-67191

F/O Joseph L. Hamilton (79th) POW; Ran out of fuel near Cherbourg.
P-38J MC- 42-67187

**January 5, 1944**
Lt. Arthur T. Altman, Jr. (55th) KIA; Hit by flak at Wangerooge Island.
P-38J KI- 42-67194
Lt. Robert H. French (55th) POW; Suffered mechanical failure then was hit by a FW-190 near Neumunster.
P-38J KI- 42-67198
Lt. Bennie R. Carbajal (77th) KIA; Last seen near Neumunster.
P-38J LC- 42-67186

**January 8, 1944**
F/O Martin F. Kane (77th) KIAc; Crashed near Drinkstone.
P-38J MC- 42-67809

**January 14, 1944**
Lt. Neal J. Archer, Jr. (79th) KIA; Hit by a Me-109 south of Rouen.
P-38J MC- 42-67760

**January 24, 1944**
Lt. John R. Frazier (55th) KIA; Last seen with FW-190's near Ghent.
P-38J KI- 42-67661
Lt. James C. Hart (77th) POW; Hit by flak near Coblenz and crashed near Liege.
P-38J LC- 42-67818
Lt. Fred M. Hartig (79th) KIA; Suffered mechanical failure and crashed into the North Sea.
P-38J MC-

**January 26, 1944**
Lt. Esborn D. Otis (79th) KIAc; Crashed in The Wash on a training flight.
P-38J MC-E 42-67492

**January 29, 1944**
Lt. Richard T. Bond (77th) KIA; Collided with Lt. Flynn south of Coblenz.
P-38J LC-B 42-67228
Lt. Robert S. Flynn (77th) KIA; Collided with Lt. Bond south of Coblenz.
P-38J LC-I 42-67735
F/O William M. Harper (79th) KIA; Hit by a FW-190 near Coblenz.
P-38J MC- 42-67665
Lt. Robert B. Moss (79th) POW; Hit by a Me-210 southwest of Frankfurt.
P-38J MC-D 42-67680 "Bee Pee"

**January 30, 1944**
Maj. Richard L. Ott (79th) KIA; Lost an engine near Minden then was hit by a FW-190 near Osnabruck.
P-38J MC-L 42-67516
Lt. Mack D. Fall (79th) KIA; Hit by a FW-190 near Minden and bailed out near Hengelo.
P-38J MC-A 42-67646

**February 4, 1944**
Lt. Donald L. Durand (77th) KIA; Hit by fighters near Frankfurt and crashed near Liege.
P-38J LC- 42-67407

**February 6, 1944**
F/O Markrel L. Byrd (79th) POW; Hit by flak and bailed out near Bernay.
P-38J MC-K 42-67854

**February 8, 1944**
Lt. Robert L. Frakes (77th) POW; Hit by flak near Corry le Chateau.
P-38J LC-A 42-67234
Lt. William H. Rierson (79th) POW; Suffered mechanical trouble and bailed out over France.
P-38J MC- 42-67306

**February 10, 1944**
Lt. Royal D. Frey (55th) POW; Suffered mechanical failure then was hit by flak near Ludenhausen.
P-38J KI-W 42-67855
Lt. John W. Lundin (55th) KIA; Hit by a FW-190 near Hazelunne.
P-38J KI- 42-67887
Lt. Jack W. Taylor (55th) KIA; Spun-in near Sutton Bridge upon return from the mission.
P-38J KI-
Capt. Robert W. Holmes (77th) POW; Suffered mechanical failure near Achmer.
P-38J LC-D 42-67759

**February 11, 1944**
LtCol. Robert P. Montgomery (HdQts) MIA-E; Hit by fighters near Valenciennes.
P-38J LC-M 42-68036
Lt. Miles N. Keatherly (77th) POW; Hit by fighters near Chateau d'Ardenne.
P-38J LC- 42-67726
Lt. Joseph O. Minton (77th) KIA; Hit by fighters near Chateau d'Ardenne.
P-38J LC-C 42-67728
Lt. Donald C. Cooper (79th) KIA; Hit by fighters near St. Aignon.
P-38J MC-C 42-67718
Lt. Thomas A. Hanzo (79th) POW; Hit by fighters near Chateau d'Ardenne.
P-38J MC-G 42-67981
Lt. Melvin Orr (79th) MIA; Hit by fighters near Birkenfeld.
P-38J MC- 42-67848
Lt. Myron R. Sands (79th) POW; Hit by fighters near Epioux.
P-38J MC-S 42-67850
Lt. Leonard S. Smutko (79th) POW; Hit by a Me-410 near Birkenfeld.
P-38J MC- 42-67821

**February 20, 1944**
Capt. Carl E. Jackson (79th) POW; Suffered mechanical trouble and bellied-in near Sassenheim.
P-38J MC-J 42-67988 "Jack"

**February 24, 1944**
Lt. Everett E. Geiger (55th) POW; Suffered mechanical failure near Hillgrom.
P-38J KI-V 42-67860
Lt. Otto A. Quiring (55th) KIA; Ran out of fuel near Schluctern.
P-38J KI-Y 42-67878

**February 29, 1944**
Lt. Robert P. Johnson (77th) POW; Suffered mechanical failure and bailed out near Amsterdam.
P-38J LC- 42-67831

**March 3, 1944**
Lt. Donald D. Goble (55th) KIA; Suffered mechanical failure and crashed into the North Sea.
P-38J KI- 42-67705

**March 4, 1944**
Lt. Harry E. Bisher (55th) MIA-E; Lost an engine over the Channel, turned back toward the Continent then was hit by a FW-190 near St. Leger.
P-38J KI- 42-67923
Lt. Edward C. Pfeiffer (55th) POW; Suffered mechanical failure near Sonneberg.
P-38J KI-O 42-68097
Lt. James C. Scott (55th) KIA; Suffered oxygen failure northwest of Amsterdam.
P-38J KI- 42-67864

**March 16, 1944**
Lt. Robert A. Matyasz (55th) KIA; Hit by flak near Liege.
P-38J KI-U 42-67907

**March 18, 1944**
LtCol. Mark E. Hubbard (HdQts) POW; Hit by flak near Augsburg.
P-38J LC-T 42-67708
Lt. Allen D. Singleton, Jr. (55th) ASR; Bailed out over the Channel after mechanical trouble.
P-38J KI- 42-67883
Lt. Ival E. Butler (77th) KIA; Suffered mechanical failure and bailed out off Texel Island.
P-38J LC- 42-67525
Capt. Lindol F. Graham (79th) KIA; Hit the ground after strafing a Me-110 he had just shot down near Ulm.
P-38J MC-L 42-67926 "Susie"

**March 24, 1944**
Lt. Lauren J. Taylor (55th) KIAc.
P-38J KI-

**April 5, 1944**
Lt. Jack J. Yelton (55th) POW; Hit by flak near Lippstadt.
P-38J KI-T 42-67753 "Cactus Jack"

**April 8, 1944**
Lt. Allen D. Singleton, Jr. (55th) POW; Hit by flak near Ulzen.
P-38J KI- 42-67719
Capt. Evan J. Machen (77th) KIA; Hit by flak near Salzwedel.
P-38J LC-J 42-68181
Lt. John F. Esau (79th) POW; Hit by a Me-109 near Salzwedel and bailed out north of Celle.
P-38J MC- 42-68084
Lt. Mitchell P. Snow (79th) KIA; Collided with a Me-109 which had just been shot down near Salzwedel.
P-38J MC-D 42-68012

**April 12, 1944**
Lt. James H. Corbet (79th) KIA; Lost over Holland for unknown reasons. Possibly on D.S. to 9th Air Force.
P-38J MC- 42-67862

**April 18, 1944**
Lt. Leland K. Henslee (55th) KIA; Engine blew up and bailed out 25 miles off the Belgian coast.
P-38J KI-U 42-68126

**April 23, 1944**
Maj. Donald H. McAuley (55th) KIA; Hit by flak near Chateaudun.
P-38J KI-A 42-67949 "Lil Henry"
Lt. Robert W. Ahern (55th) KIA; Hit by flak near Valmeray.
P-38J KI-L 42-67885

**April 28, 1944**
Lt. Ferdinand E. LeFevre (79th) KIA; Hit by flak over Calais and bailed out over the Channel.
P-38J MC-U 42-68035

**April 30, 1944**
Lt. Albert R. Fogg (79th) POW; Hit by flak near Tours.
P-38J MC-G 42-68140 "Puddin"

**May 1, 1944**
Lt. Philip E. Pearson (55th) KIA; Hit by flak south of Liege.
P-38J KI-I 42-67763
Lt. William G. Schultz (55th) KIA; Hit by flak south of Liege.
P-38J KI-P 42-104314

**May 8, 1944**
Lt. John J. Connor, Jr. (55th) MIA; Suffered mechanical trouble near Ostenholz.
P-38J KI-C 42-67901

**May 9, 1944**
Lt. Ben E. McCarty (79th) POW; Hit by fighters near Nancy.
P-38J MC- 42-104289

**May 13, 1944**
Lt. Hal W. Everett (77th) POW; Hit by flak at Leck A/F.
P-38J LC-K 42-68026

**May 22, 1944**
Capt. William K. Coon (77th) POW; Hit by a FW-190 northwest of Kiel.
P-38J LC- 43-28270

**May 24, 1944**
Lt. Raymond E. Huarte (79th) POW; Hit by fighters north of Hamburg.
P-38J MC- 42-67858

**May 25, 1944**
Lt. Peter A. Boele (55th) KIA; Hit by flak near Flushing and crashed into the North Sea.
P-38J KI-T 42-104395
Lt. Marvin F. Bench, Jr. (79th) KIA; Hit by flak near the Dutch Islands.
P-38J MC- 42-68094
Lt. Harry J. Watson, Jr. (79th) POW; Hit by flak near Nuiewlande.
P-38J MC-M 42-67929 "Bob Cat II"

**June 12, 1944**
Lt. Albert L. Gese (77th) KIA; Hit by flak north of Flens.
P-38J LC-X 42-67462
Lt. Hugh L. Jacobson (77th) KIA; Last seen strafing near Brest.
P-38J LC- 42-68111
Lt. Dixon V. Kendrick (77th) POW; Hit by flak near Caen.
P-38J LC-M 42-67478
Lt. Benjamin N. Rader (77th) ASR; Bailed out 12 miles off the Normandy coast after mechanical problems.
P-38J LC-Z 42-68045

**June 13, 1944**
Lt. Russell G. Quinn (77th) KIA; Hit by flak near Domfort.
P-38J LC- 44-23174
Capt. Jack M. Ilfrey (79th) MIA-E; Hit by flak north of Angars.
P-38J MC-O 43-28431 "Happy Jack's Go Buggy"

**June 14, 1944**
Lt. Stanley P. Spencer (55th) KIA; Hit by flak near Hengelo.
P-38J KI-M 42-68170
Capt. Terrence M. Williams (77th) POW; Hit by flak near Zwolle.
P-38J LC-K 42-68066

**June 15, 1944**
Lt. Walter F. Perra (77th) KIA; Hit by flak near Dreux.
P-38J LC-V 42-104067 "Little Bug"

**June 16, 1944**
Maj. Paul A. Lobinger (HdQts) KIA; Crashed near Purleigh on return.
P-38J LC- 43-28430

**June 17, 1944**
Lt. Richard M. Hairston (77th) POW; Hit by flak near Amiens.
P-38J LC- 43-28684
Lt. Earl O. Smith, Jr. (79th) KIA; Hit by flak and bailed out near Le Treport.
P-38J MC-W 42-67905
Lt. Emery K. Ryan (79th) KIA; Hit by flak near Amiens. Bailed out but his chute failed.
P-38J MC-R 42-104308

**June 22, 1944**
Lt. John A. Pierson (55th) KIA; Hit by flak near Jussy.
P-38J KI-V 42-68131 "Murph III"

**July 4, 1944**
Lt. Ernest G. Riddle (77th) KIA; Crashed near Peteworth upon return.
P-38J LC-

**July 7, 1944**
Capt. James M. Morris (77th) POW; Hit by a Me-410 in the Leipzig-Halle area.
P-38J LC-O 43-28397

**July 13, 1944**
Lt. Charles W. Dungan (77th) ASR; Bailed out over the ThamesEstuary after mechanical trouble.
P-38J LC-M 42-68156

**July 14, 1944**
Lt. Adam L. Hunt, Jr. (55th) MIA; Hit by flak near Menehould.
P-38J KI-L 43-28354

**July 16, 1944**
Lt. John E. Klink (55th) ASR; Hit by flak and bailed out off Margate.
P-38J KI-N 42-104207

**July 19, 1944**
Lt. Owen T. Hillyard (79th) KIA; Crashed into the North Sea after mecahnical trouble.
P-38J MC-X 42-67251

**July 31, 1944**
Lt. Leonard L. Richter (79th) KIA; Crashed upon return from the mission.
P-51 MC-

**August 2, 1944**
Lt. Stephen J. Nelson (55th) KIA; Crashed near Werrington upon return.
P-51B KI-

**August 4, 1944**
Capt. Donald A. Reihmer (HdQts) MIA-E; Hit by flak west of Peenemunde.
P-51D LC-R 44-13696
Capt. Harry B. Baker (55th) KIA; Crashed on take-off from Kingscliffe.
P-51D KI-

**August 5, 1944**
Lt. Irwin W. Fernandes (77th) KIA; Hit by fighters near Zoven.
P-51D LC-Y 44-13713

**August 6, 1944**
Lt. Walker L. Whiteside (77th) KIA; Hit by fighters near Hennickendorf.
P-51D LC-J 44-13792

**August 10, 1944**
Lt. Lee W. Anderson (55th) MIA; Hit by flak near Epioux.
P-51D KI- 44-13679
Lt. William D. Rollins (77th) KIA; Hit by flak near Heispelt.
P-51D LC-J 44-13811

**August 12, 1944**
Lt. Alvin F. Clark (77th) MIA-E; Hit by debris from an exploding tarin and bailed out near Reims.
P-51D LC-B 44-13775
Lt. Paul Denbo (79th) KIA; Hit by flak near Peche.
P-51D MC- 44-13620

**August 25, 1944**
Lt. Charles F. Bain (55th) KIA; Hit by flak at Parow A/F and bailed out over the Baltic Sea.
P-51C KI-D 43-25033

**August 27, 1944**
LtCol. Cy Wilson (HdQts) POW; Hit by flak over Denmark and bailed out off the coast.
P-51D KI-W 44-13951 "Wrangler Jr."
Lt. Harry M. Anderson (55th) KIA; Hit by flak near Kallingen.
P-51D KI-F 44-13733
Lt. Alphonso H. Kent, Jr. (55th) POW; Hit by flak over Denmark and bailed out off the coast.
P-51C KI- 43-25049 "Shorty"
Lt. Edward W. Doering (77th) POW; Hit by flak over Denmark and bailed out off the coast.
P-51D LC-A 44-13991

**August 28, 1944**
Lt. John L. Armstrong (79th) POW; Suffered mechanical failure near Bad Kreuznach.
P-51D MC-S 44-13791 "Guardian Angel"

**September 17, 1944**
Lt. David E. Cruickshank (55th) KIAc;
P-51 KI-
Lt. William R. Taylor (55th) KIAc;
P-51 KI-

**September 27, 1944**
Lt. Harry L. Knapp (77th) KIAc; Crashed southeast of Yaxley.
P-51D LC-C 44-13992

**September 28, 1944**
Lt. Kenneth M. Geiger (77th) POW; Hit by fighters near Magdeburg.
P-51D LC-Y 44-14269 "Flamme de Pouseuite"

**October 7, 1944**
Capt. Joseph T. McKeon (55th) POW; Collided with Lt. Brown near Stettin.
P-51D KI-N 44-13541 "Olivia de"
Lt. Robert C. Brown (55th) POW; Collided with Capt. McKeon near Stettin.
P-51D KI-A 44-14331
Lt. Charles W. Dungan (77th) MIA-E; Hit by flak near Peenemunde and bailed out over Denmark.
P-51C LC-Q 43-25046

**October 18, 1944**
Lt. Walter H. Mullins (55th) KIAc;
P-51D KI-S 44-13859

**October 19, 1944**
Capt. Willis B. Taylor (55th) POW; Suffered mechanical failure and bailed out near Boppard.
P-51D KI-K 44-13892 "Idiot's Delight"

**October 26, 1944**
Lt. Kenneth Kautz, Jr. (79th) POW; Suffered mechanical failure and bailed out east of the Zuider Zee.
P-51D MC-K 44-13580 "Little Ronnie"

**November 1, 1944**
Lt. Denis J. Allison (77th) KIA; Hit by a Me-262 near Hengelo.
P-51D LC-A 44-14378 "Hookin' Bull"

**November 2, 1944**
Capt. Jerome C. Serros (55th) KIA; Suffered mechanical failure and bailed out east of the Zuider Zee.
P-51D KI-G 44-13838 "Okie Bloke"
Lt. Jack W. Kennedy (77th) KIA; Suffered mechanical failure and bailed out off Ostend.
P-51D LC-M 44-13746 "Little Sister"

Lt. Richard L. Van Woert (77th) KIA; Hit by fighters near Merseburg.
P-51D LC-U 44-13840 "Van's Can"

**November 8, 1944**
Lt. Elmer H. Coughran (77th) KIA; Suffered mechanical failure and crashed inside Allied lines.
P-51D LC-

**November 9, 1944**
Lt. Edward A. Loetscher (55th) KIA; Crashed while strafing near Saarbrucken.
P-51D KI-K 44-13715
Lt. John R. Wilson (77th) KIA; Wing came off while dive-bombing near Saarbrucken.
P-51D LC-S 44-13670

**November 18, 1944**
Lt. Donald E. Chrissinger (55th) KIAc; Crashed while landing at Kingscliffe after a test flight.
P-51D KI-E 44-13702

**November 21, 1944**
Lt. Bernard C. Halpin (77th) POW; Hit by a Me-109 near Munster.
P-51D LC-L 44-14063

**December 2, 1944**
Lt. Merle P. Joseph (77th) KIA; Last seen in overcast near Brussels.
P-51D LC-Z 44-13824

**December 6, 1944**
Lt. Calvin Katz (77th) KIA; Aborted and crashed near Ipswich.
P-51D LC-

**December 10, 1944**
Lt. Everett T. Urbanski (55th) KIA; Suffered mechanical failure near Frankfurt.
P-51D KI-N 44-14870

**January 3, 1945**
F/O Charles E. Sheffield (77th) KIA; Lost coolant and bailed out 18 miles northwest of Ostend.
P-51D LC-K 44-13748

**January 17, 1945**
Lt. Eugene L. Planchak (55th) POW; Hit by flak north of Munster and bailed out north of Dusseldorf.
P-51D KI-K 44-15591 "Dragon Wagon IV"

**February 9, 1945**
Lt. Julio Nunzo (77th) KIA; Hit by flak at Esperstadt A/F.
P-51C LC-I 43-25041

**February 14, 1945**
Lt. Jack D. Leon (55th) KIA; Damaged by an exploding truck near Dresden.
P-51D KI-M 44-14319

**February 19, 1945**
Lt. Robert E. Murrell (77th) KIA; Hit trees while strafing near Detmold.
P-51D LC-K 44-14975

**February 20, 1945**
Capt. Joseph S. Ford (55th) POW; Hit by flak near Nurnberg.
P-51K KI-E 44-11638 "Lil Easy"
Lt. William J. McGee (55th) POW; Landed to rescue Capt. Ford and got stuck in mud.
P-51D KI-Y 44-13905 "Joe"
Lt. Sidney S. Stitzer (55th) KIA; Damaged by debris from an exploding railcar near Kampendorf.
P-51D KI-B 44-13664

**February 24, 1945**
Lt. Leonard M. Wright, Jr. (79th) POW; Lost coolant and bailed out near Darfeld.
P-51D MC-Z 44-11244 "Nina Merle"

**February 25, 1945**
Capt. Charles H. Cole, Jr. (55th) POW; Hit by a FW-190 near Stendal and bellied-in southwest of Magdeburg.
P-51D KI-K 44-72160
Lt. Horace B. Smith (55th) KIA; Hit by flak near Arnheim.
P-51D KI-K 44-63808
Lt. Raymond K. Soleau (55th) KIA; Hit by fighters near Stendal.
P-51D KI-G 44-11197

**February 26, 1945**
Lt. Edgar D. Whitley (79th) POW; Ran out of fuel and bailed out near Zutphen.
P-51D MC-C 44-13846 "Lil Bit"

**March 6, 1945**
Lt. Mark F. Smith (79th) KIAc;
P-51D MC-

**March 15, 1945**
F/O Allen L. Shaffer (79th) KIA; Suffered mechanical failure near Hoorn.
P-51K MC-H 44-11357

**March 24, 1945**
Lt. Chester J. Swierczynski (77th) POW; Lost oil pressure near Gutersloh and bailed out near Handorf.
P-51D LC-Q 44-72298

**March 26, 1945**
Lt. Kenneth L. Pettit (55th) KIA; Suffered mechanical failure and crashed near Ipswich.
P-51D KI-T 44-13860

**April 4, 1945**
Lt. John W. Cudd, Jr. (77th) ASR; Lost coolant and bailed out off Great Yarmouth.
P-51K LC-Z 44-11673

**April 10, 1945**
Capt. Richard M. Tracy (55th) POW; Hit by flak near Berlin.
P-51D KI-G 44-13527
Lt. Joseph A. Peterburs (55th) POW; Hit by flak near Berlin and bellied-in before reaching Russian lines.
P-51D KI-B 44-15078 "Josephine"
Lt. David Stewart (79th) POW; Hit by flak at Werder A/F.
P-51D MC-F 44-13751 "Wanda's Worry"

**Headquarters**
Baker, Schuyler A., Lt.; April 1945-EOW; ex-55th Ftr Sqn
Gustke, Russell F., LtCol.; December 1944-April 1945; ex-14th Ftr Grp, MTO & 55th & 77th Ftr Sqns
636:25 total hours
P-51D LC-E 44-14744
Hetherington, Thomas F., Jr., Lt.; June 1943-January 1944 (injured on December 30, 1943)
1 mission, 3:20 hours
Hubbard, Mark E., LtCol.; February 1944-March 18, 1944(POW); ex-33rd Ftr Grp, MTO
12 missions, 59:20 hours
Jackson, Carl E., Capt.; August 1943-January 1944; to 79th Ftr Sqn
P-38J MC-J 42-67988 "Jack"
Johnson, Herbert E., Jr., LtCol.; March 1944-August 1944; ex-77th Ftr Sqn
72 missions, 303:45 hours
P-38J MC-V 42-68019
Kermes, William J., Capt.; February 1944-May 1944; ex-77th Ftr Sqn
2 missions, 7:15 hours
Lobinger, Paul A., Maj.; January 1943-June 16, 1944(KIA)
21:55 hours
Mansker, Joseph L., Capt.; January 1945-April 1945; ex-55th Ftr Sqn (see for details)
Montgomery, Robert P., LtCol.; November 1943-February 11, 1944 (MIA-E); September 1944-October 1945; ex-77th Ftr Sqn
56 missions, 274:55 hours
P-38J LC-M 42-67478
P-38J LC-M 42-68036
P-51D LC-D 44-14843 "Gumpy"
P-51D LC-D 44-72519 "Gumpy"
Nichols, Merle B., Maj.; August 1944-September 1944; to 77th Ftr Sqn; ex-79th Ftr Sqn
Price, Jack C., Maj.; February 1945-March 1945; to 55th Ftr Sqn; April 1945-EOW; ex-78th Ftr Grp, ETO
99 missions, 281:15 hours total
P-51D LC-G 44-14693 "Feather Merchant IV"
Randolph, John P., LtCol.; July 1944-November 1944; to 359th Ftr Grp, ex-20th Pur Sqn, PTO
26 missions, 146:25 hours
P-51D MC-N 44-13541 "Nancy"
Rau, Harold J., Col.; March 1944-June 1944; August 1944-December 1944 ex-356th Ftr Grp, ETO
73 missions, 275 hours total
P-38J MC-R 42-68165 "Gentle Annie"
P-38J MC-R 42-67722 "Gentle Annie"
P-51D MC-R 44-14337 "Gentle Annie"
Reichard, James N., Capt.; March 1945-EOW; ex-79th Ftr Sqn
337:10 hours
Russell, Barton M., Col.; August 1942-March 1944
11 missions
P-38J LC-B 42-67888 "Black Barney"
Schallo, Philip L., Capt.; March 1945-June 1945; ex-77th Ftr Sqn
277:05 hours
Slanker, Ted E., Capt.; April 1945-EOW; ex-77th Ftr Sqn
Stockton, Vincent R., Lt.; April 1944-February 1945; to 67th Ftr Wg. Ex-55th Ftr Sqn
Wemyss, George S., Maj.; February 1944-EOW; ex-77th Ftr Sqn
77:10 hours
P-38J LC-B "Seven Eleven"
Wilkins, John C., Maj.; June 1943-November 7, 1943(KIA)
1 mission
Wilson, Cy, LtCol.; June 1944-August 27, 1944(POW); ex-55th Ftr Sqn
78 missions, 318:40 hours
P-38J KI-W 43-28393 "Wrangler"
P-51D KI-W 44-13951 "Wrangler Jr."

**55th Fighter Squadron**
Ahern, Robert W., Lt.; August 1943-April 23, 1944(KIA)
29 missions, 128:25 hours
Altman, Arthur T., Jr., Lt.; August 1943-January 5, 1944(KIA)
2 missions, 6 hours
Ames, Francis P., Lt.; April 1945-EOW
0 missions
Anderson, Harry M., Lt.; March 1944-August 27, 1944(MIA)
63 missions, 259:20 hours
P-51D KI-F 44-13733
Anderson, Lee W., Lt.; May 1944-August 10, 1944(MIA-E)
37 missions, 160:55 hours
Anderson, Robert J., Lt.; April 1945-EOW
0 missions

Anderson, Simon K., Lt.; April 1945-EOW
0 missions
Anthony, Shelton J., Jr., Lt.; March 1945-EOW
2 missions, 13:05 hours
Arnold, Charles W., Jr., Lt.; April 1945-EOW
0 missions
Bain, Charles F., Lt.; April 1944-August 25, 1944(POW)
47 missions, 172:25 hours
Baker, Harry B., Capt.; January 1943-August 4, 1944(KIA)
45 missions, 192:30 hours
Baker, Schuyler A., Lt.; September 1944-April 1945 to HdQts
58 missions, 292:30 hours
Barber, Charles O., Lt.; April 1945-EOW
0 missions
Barnes, Thomas C., Lt.; June 1944-December 1944
53 missions, 270 hours
Benedict, Douglas B., Capt.; September 1944-April 1945
57 missions, 286 hours
Bisher, Harry E., Lt.; September 1942-March 4, 1944(MIA-E)
17 missions, 62:20 hours
P-38J KI-N 42-67823 "Kitty"
Boele, Peter A., Lt.; March 1944-May 25, 1944(KIA)
17 missions, 74:40 hours
Bowman, Ralph I., Capt.; July 1944-January 1945
62 missions, 296 hours
P-51D KI-F 44-14330
Brown, Harley L., Capt.; August 1944-March 1945
56 missions, 280:10 hours
P-51D KI-A 44-11205 "Be Good/
Brownie's Ballroom"
Brown, John K., Capt.; September 1944-EOW
59 missions, 311:20 hours
P-51D KI-G 44-11197
Brown, Robert C., Lt.; September 1944-October 7, 1944(POW)
1 mission
Buie, Joseph N., Lt.; December 1943-August 1944
68 missions, 300 hours
Burford, James E., Lt.; March 1944-September 1944
67 missions, 285:05 hours
P-51D KI-L 44-13790 "Lil Jughaid"
Bynum, Horace B., Lt.; April 1944-October 1944
63 missions, 270 hours
P-51D KI-K 44-13715
Cardy, William G., Lt.; April 1945-EOW
0 missions
Cavell, Everett W., Capt.; May 1944-October 1944
52 missions, 244:30 hours
P-51D KI-W 44-14198
Chase, Robert E., Lt.; January 1945-EOW
25 missions, 159:40 hours
Chrissinger, Donald E., Lt.; August 1944-November 18, 1944(KIAc)
26 missions, 135:35 hours
Clark, Frank C., Maj.; December 1943-March 1944; ex-14th Ftr Grp, MTO
4 missions
Cole, Charles H., Capt.; February 1945-February 25, 1945(POW); ex-77th Ftr Sqn (see for details)
Collins, Bradford J., Lt.; March 1945-EOW
2 missions, 6:20 hours
Connor, John J., Lt.; January 1944-May 8, 1944(KIA)
30 missions, 128:30 hours
Conyer, Wilford R., Lt.; March 1945-EOW
5 missions, 24:25 hours
Cosgriff, Edward H., Jr., Capt.; September 1944-EOW
56 missions, 273:10 hours
P-51D KI-H 44-14880 "Frisco Belle"
Cox, Russell J., Lt.; March 1945-EOW
4 missions, 24:30 hours
Crago, John W., Lt.; August 1943-December 31, 1943(KIA)
0 missions
Cree, Ronald R., Lt.; March 1945-EOW
5 missions, 24:05 hours
Cristadoro, Maurice A., Jr., Maj.; February 1945-July 1945; ex-356th Ftr Grp, ETO
17 missions, 111:10 hours
Cruikshank, David E., Lt.; February 1944-September 17, 1944(KIAc)
68 missions, 282:35 hours
Deardorff, Philip C., F/O; March 1945-EOW
2 missions, 6:10 hours
Decker, Vern L., Lt.; February 1945-EOW
19 missions, 108:15 hours
P-51D KI- "Candy Baby"
Doody, Thomas J., Lt.; November 1944-EOW
49 missions, 268:20 hours
Douthit, Carl D., Lt.; February 1945-EOW
17 missions, 94:20 hours
Drost, John E., Lt.; April 1945-EOW
0 missions
Dyer, John F., Lt.; February 1944-April 1944(injured on April 18)
5 missions, 27:15 hours
Ferriola, Jack, F/O; March 1945-EOW
3 missions, 18:20 hours
Ford, Joseph S., Capt.; December 1943-February 20, 1945(POW)
89 missions, 336:10 hours
P-38J KI-E
P-51D KI-E 44-13702 "Joe"
P-51K KI-E 44-11638 "Lil Easy"
Franklin, Dewey R., Lt.; July 1944-November 1944
53 missions, 271:55 hours
P-51D KI-U 44-14157
Frazier, John R., Lt.; August 1943-January 24, 1944(KIA)
5 missions, 12:35 hours
Freedman, David I., Lt.; September 1944-March 1945
54 missions, 285:10 hours
P-51D KI- "Supermouse"
French, Robert H., Lt.; August 1943-January 5, 1944(POW)
1 mission
Frey, Royal D., Lt.; August 1943-February 10, 1944(POW)
11 missions, 35:25 hours
P-38J KI-W 42-67855
Fruechtenicht, Richard W., Capt.; September 1944-EOW
61 missions, 315:45 hours
P-51D KI-D 44-14120
Fuller, Ralph R., Lt.; January 1945-EOW
30 missions, 179:10 hours
Gatterdam, Richard P., Maj.; November 1944-March 1945; ex-79th Ftr Sqn
91 missions, 430:10 hours total
P-51D KI-G 44-15327 "Puddin"
Gee, Richard A., Capt.; October 1942-March 1944; to 496th Ftr Trg Grp
16 missions
Geiger, Everett E., Lt.; August 1943-February 24, 1944(POW)
12 missions, 59 hours
P-38J KI-V 42-67034
P-38J KI-V 42-67860
Goble, Donald D., Lt.; August 1943-March 3, 1944(KIA)
12 missions, 43:30 hours
Hallberg, Chester A., Capt.; August 1943-August 1944
74 missions, 300:05 hours
P-38J KI-G 42-67743
P-38J KI-G 42-104210
P-51D KI-G 44-13838 "Little Louise"
Henslee, Leland K., Lt.; March 1944-April 18, 1944(KIA)
3 missions, 10:50 hours
Howard, Ronald M., Capt.; August 1944-March 1945
55 missions, 280:10 hours
P-51D KI-R 44-13827 "Rondelle"
Hower, Earl W., Capt.; August 1943-October 1944
72 missions, 273:30 hours
P-38J KI- "Flying Dutchman"
P-51D KI-N 44-13799 "Flying
Dutchman"
Hunt, Adam L., Lt.; July 1944-July 14, 1944(MIA-E)
2 missions, 8:15 hours
Hurst, William M., Capt.; July 1944-January 1945
61 missions, 297:35 hours
P-51D KI-T 44-13860
Iehle, Richard P., Lt.; February 1945-EOW
19 missions, 99:30 hours
P-51D KI-B "Ginny/Green Eyes"
Kelly, Anthony C., Lt.; April 1944-November 1944
52 missions, 226:10 hours
P-51D KI-B 44-13664
Kent, Alphonso H., Jr., Lt.; August 1944-August 27, 1944(POW)
4 missions, 13 hours
Kensick, Raymond J., Lt.; October 1944-January 1945 (injured January 15)
17 missions, 89:35 hours
Kier, Edward L., Capt.; October 1944-EOW
46 missions, 261 hours
P-51D KI-F 44-14330
King, George A., Jr., Lt.; March 1945-EOW: ex-bomber pilot
(35 missions, 265:30 hours)
0 missions
Klink, John E., Lt.; February 1944-August 1944
74 missions, 300:40 hours
Korn, John J., Jr., F/O; April 1945-EOW
0 missions
Larrabee, Dale L., Lt.; April 1944-September 1944
58 missions, 270:30 hours
P-51D KI-I "Claudine I"
Leon, Jack D., Lt.; September 1944-February 14, 1945(KIA)
41 missions, 183:30 hours
P-51D KI-M 44-14319 "Mary Joe"
Loehnert, Richard O., Lt.; November 1943-November 1944
70 missions, 300:05 hours
P-38J KI-S 42-67916 "California Cutie"
P-51D KI-S
Loetscher, Edward A., Lt.; October 1944-November 9, 1944(KIA)
2 missions, 9:30 hours
Low, Martin L., LtCol.; April 1944-December 1944; ex-475th Ftr Grp, PTO
65 missions, 270:55 hours
P-38J KI-P
P-51D KI-P 44-14253 "Mighty Low"

Lowman, Wallace E., Capt.; October 1944-EOW
50 missions, 271:50 hours
Lundin, John W., Lt.; August 1943-February 10, 1944(KIA)
12 missions, 39:25 hours
Malchow, Edgar G., Lt.; February 1944-August 1944
72 missions, 301:25 hours
Maldanado, Mario, Lt.; August 1944-February 1945
55 missions, 273:35 hours
Mansker, Joseph L., Capt.; July 1944-January 1945; to HdQts
50 missions, 265:55 hours
P-51D KI-X 44-13892
P-51D KI-X 44-14749
Martin, William E., Lt.; February 1944-September 1944
67 missions, 287:20 hours
P-51D KI- "Lil Daddy"
Matayasz, Robert W., Lt.; February 1944-March 16, 1944(KIA)
6 missions, 29 hours
McAuley, Donald H., Maj.; January 1943-April 23, 1944(KIA)
28 missions, 118:45 hours
P-38J KI-H 42-67949 "Lil Henry"
McAvoy, Walter J., F/O; March 1945-EOW
2 missions, 8 hours
McConnell, James A., F/O; March 1945-EOW
4 missions
McGee, William J., Lt.; October 1944-February 20, 1945(POW)
30 missions, 158:35 hours
McGovern, David R., LtCol.; January 1943-December 1943; ex-35th Pur Sqn, PTO (2 kills)
0 missions
McKeon, Joseph T., Capt.; September 1944-October 7, 1944(POW); ex-8th & 475th Ftr Grps, PTO, and 77th Ftr Sqn
37 missions, 190:55 hours total
P-51D KI-M 44-14319 "Olivia de"
McLary, Maurice R., Maj.; August 1943-August 1944
63 missions, 288:35 hours
P-38J KI-Y "Murph"
P-38J KI-Y "Murph II"
P-38J KI-Y 42-67484 "Murph III"
McNeel, Kenneth D., Lt.; August 1944-April 1945
56 missions, 287:35 hours
P-51D KI-V 44-13776
Meinzen, Robert W., Lt.; October 1944-EOW
56 missions, 289:30 hours
P-51D KI-W 44-15249
Michel, Douglas, Capt.; August 1944-May 1945
45 missions, 292:30 hours (plus 48 hours w/5th ERS)
P-51D KI-P 44-14253 "Lil Eva"
Miles, Robert E., Lt.; November 1943-November 1944
70 missions, 300:25 hours
P-38J KI- "Posse"
Milian, Paul J., Lt.; October 1944-EOW
50 missions, 243:15 hours
P-51D KI-N "Hoodinky"
Mullins, Walter H., Lt.; June 1944-October 18, 1944(KIAc)
44 missions, 207:35 hours
P-51D KI-S 44-13859
Nauman, Reginald A., Lt.; November 1944-EOW
19 missions, 111:20 hours
Neidy, Dewey L., Lt.; September 1944-April 1945
59 missions, 290:30 hours
Nelson, Stephen J., Lt.; June 1944-August 1, 1944(KIA)
11 missions, 65:20 hours
Nicholson, Charles R., Lt.; November 1944-EOW
37 missions, 197:50 hours
Oxley, Daniel D., Capt.; June 1944-December 1944
55 missions, 270 hours
P-51C KI-H 43-25065 "Ambrose II"
Pannell, Melvin C., Capt.; May 1943-August 1944
78 missions, 301 hours
P-51C KI- "Jeannie"
Pearson, Philip, Jr., Lt.; February 1944-May 1, 1944(KIA)
11 missions, 48:35 hours
Peel, William J., Lt.; November 1944-EOW
41 missions, 220:10 hours
Peterburs, Joseph A., Lt.; November 1944-April 10, 1945(POW)
46 missions, 255 hours
P-51D KI-B 44-15078 "Josephine"
Pettit, Kenneth L., Lt.; January 1945-March 26, 1945(KIA)
17 missions, 94:20 hours
Pfeiffer, Edward G., Lt.; January 1944-March 4, 1944(POW)
8 missions, 29:35 hours
Pierson, John A., Lt.; February 1944-June 22, 1944(KIA)
36 missions, 72 hours
Planchak, Eugene, Jr., Lt.; September 1944-January 17, 1945(POW)
46 missions, 204 hours
P-51D KI-K 44-15591 "Dragon Wagon"
Price, Jack C., Maj.; March 1945-April 1945; to HdQts; ex-78th Ftr Grp, ETO
(see HdQts for details)
Prow, Emmett M., Lt.; January 1945-EOW
33 missions, 193:40 hours
Quiring, Otto A., Lt.; January 1944-February 24, 1944(KIA)
6 missions, 27:10 hours
Rackley, David H., Lt.; January 1945-EOW
34 missions, 199:35 hours
P-51C KI-Z 43-25028
Reynolds, James S., Lt.; June 1944-November 1944
51 missions, 254 hours
P-51C KI-D 43-25033
Riemensnider, Robert H., Maj.; January 1944-July 1945
80 missions, 371:05 hours
P-38J KI-Y 42-68108 "Bobby"
P-51D KI-Y 44-13903 "Bobby"
Rawley, Arthur N., Lt.; August 1943-August 1944
24 missions, 105:55 hours
Ryan, Mont J., Capt.; September 1944-EOW
54 missions, 276:40 hours
Scott, James C., Lt.; October 1942-March 4, 1944(KIA)
18 missions
Scrutchfield, Roy M., Capt.; September 1942-December 1944
66 missions, 221:10 hours
P-38J KI-N 42-67823 "Jeanne"
P-38J KI-N 43-28430 "Jeanne"
P-51D KI-N
Seifert, Paul F., Capt.; October 1944-EOW
57 missions, 278 hours
Serros, Jerome C., Capt.; August 1943-November 2, 1944(KIA)
65 missions, 274 hours
P-38J KI-B 42-67756 "Stubborn Virgin"
Schultz, William G., Lt.; February 1944-May 1, 1944(KIA)
15 missions, 54 hours
Singleton, Allen D., Jr., Lt.; February 1944-April 8, 1944(POW)
5 missions, 19:15 hours
Skroback, Walter H., Lt.; December 1944-EOW
46 missions, 252:35 hours
P-51D KI-C 44-13794 "Piccilo Pete"
Smeltz, Kenneth C., Lt.; April 1944-September 1944
53 missions, 272:10 hours
P-51D KI-V 44-13776 "Nancy Gay"
Smith, Horace B., Lt.; November 1944-February 25, 1945(KIA)
17 missions, 80:45 hours
Smith, William W., Maj.; August 1944-October 1944; ex-79th Ftr Sqn
P-51D KI-G 44-13838 "Okie Bloke"
Soleau, Raymond H., Lt.; November 1944-February 25, 1945(KIA)
22 missions, 125:40 hours
Solomon, Leonard, Lt.; September 1944-March 1945
55 missions, 282:35 hours
P-51C KI-Z 43-25028
Spencer, Stanley P., Lt.; April 1944-June 14, 1944(KIA)
20 missions, 84:10 hours
Stevens, Kent H., Lt.; July 1944-October 1944; ex-79th Ftr Sqn
59 missions, 270:05 hours total
Stitzer, Sidney G., Lt.; November 1944-February 20, 1945(KIA)
20 missions, 99:50 hours
Stockton, Vincent R., Lt.; May 1943-April 1944; to HdQts
37 missions, 174.40 hours
Stovall, Richard T., Capt.; Mid 1943-May 1944; to 77th Ftr Sqn
July 1944-August 1944
33 missions total
Swirski, Walter E., Lt.; March 1945-EOW; ex-bomber pilot
(33 missions, 260 hours)
0 missions
Taylor, Jack, Lt.; May 1943-February 10, 1944(KIA)
8 missions, 36:30 hours
Taylor, William R., Lt.; August 1944-September 17, 1944(KIAc)
5 missions, 28:05 hours
Taylor, Willis B., Capt.; October 1942-October 19, 1944(POW)
57 missions, 263:30 hours
P-38J KI-U 42-67482
P-38J KI-U 42-67907
Tenant, John H., Capt.; May 1944-December 1944
62 missions, 270:05 hours
P-51D KI-Z 44-13695
Tracy, Richard M., Capt.; November 1944-April 10, 1945(POW)
36 missions, 195:10 hours
Urbanski, Everett T., Lt.; October 1944-December 10, 1944(KIA)
9 missions, 43:25 hours
Wasil, Edwin E., Lt.; April 1944-September 1944
59 missions, 271:05 hours
P-38J KI-O 43-28301 "Mama's Boy"
P-51C KI-O 43-25031 "Mama's Boy"
Watson, Rodney P., Lt.; February 1944-September 1944
68 missions, 286:50 hours
P-38J KI- "Dotty"
Wells, William W., Lt.; April 1944-September 1944
57 missions, 270 hours
P-38J KI-R
P-51D KI-R 44-13827 "Little Wheel"
Williams, Dale M., Capt.; June 1944-December 1944
58 missions, 270 hours
Williams, Gene L., Lt.; January 1945-EOW
27 missions, 178:25 hours

Wilson, Cy, LtCol.; April 1944-June 1944; to HdQts
78 missions, 318:40 hours total
P-38J KI-W 43-28393 "Wrangler"
Yelton, Jack J., Lt.; August 1943-April 5, 1944(POW)
14 missions, 82 hours
P-38J KI-T 42-67753 "Cactus Jack"

**77th Fighter Squadron**
Adams, Louis W., Lt.; March 1944-November 1944
58 missions, 275:50 hours
P-51D LC-L 44-13655
P-51D LC-L 44-14063 "Robb"
Alexander, Fred H., Lt.; March 1944-October 1944
63 missions, 270:20 hours
P-51D LC-H 44-13836 "It's The Kid!
P-51D LC-M 44-13746 "It's The Kid!
Alison, Denis J., Lt.; August 1944-November 1, 1944(KIA)
16 missions, 82:10 hours
Arthaud, Charles C., Lt.; January 1944-September 1944
68 missions, 285:45 hours
Babbitt, Raymond G., Jr., Lt.; March 1945-EOW
2 missions, 12:30 hours
Baird, Harry D., Jr., Lt.; March 1945-EOW
3 missions, 11:05 hours
Baker, Irvin C., Capt.; November 1943-January 1945
81 missions, 400:50 hours
P-38J LC-Z "The Haycock Belle"
Baker, Kemper W., Lt.; March 1945-EOW
2 missions, 11:10 hours
Baldock, David N., Lt.; April 1945-August 23, 1945(KIAc)
0 missions
Bond, Richard T., Lt.; October 1942-January 29, 1944(KIA)
11 missions, 37:10 hours
Brucks, George R., Lt.; March 1944-November 1944
58 missions, 250:15 hours
Butler, Ival E., Lt.; February 1944-March 18, 1944(KIA)
6 missions, 16:40 hours
Carbajal, Bennie R., F/O; May 1943-January 5, 1944(KIA)
3 missions, 11:37 hours
Chambers, Robert O., Lt.; January 1945-February 1945; (injured February 3)
0 missions
Chubin, Peter, Lt.; February 1944-September 1944
68 missions, 274:10 hours
Clark, Alvin F., Lt.; December 1943-August 12, 1944(MIA-E)
65 missions, 285:50 hours
Clough, Carl W., Lt.; February 1944-September 1944
67 missions, 261:20 hours
Coe, Richard A., Lt.; April 1945-EOW
0 missions
Cole, Charles H., Capt.; September 1944-February 1945; to 55th Ftr Sqn
43 missions, 227:25 hours total
Colquitt, Earl M., Lt.; April 1945-EOW
0 missions
Coon, William K., Capt.; January 1943-May 22, 1944(POW)
36 missions, 157:25 hours
Cowley, John C., Lt.; October 1944-April 1945(WIA April 5)
42 missions, 209:30 hours
Croker, Howard J., Lt.; March 1945-EOW
2 missions, 11:30 hours
Cudd, John W., Lt.; February 1945-EOW
17 missions, 92:15 hours
Cunliffe, Charles S., Lt.; March 1945-EOW
3 missions, 11:30 hours
Davis, Jack E., Lt.; December 1943-September 1944
71 missions, 326:40 hours
Dempsey, Richard J., Capt.; July 1944-December 1944
41 missions, 205:45 hours
Derrenbacker, James S., Lt.; February 1945-EOW
15 missions, 89:20 hours
Doering, Edward W., Lt.; July 1944-August 27, 1944(POW)
18 missions
Donnelly, John L., F/O; March 1945-EOW
2 missions, 11:35 hours
Dorey, Richard E., Lt.; February 1945-EOW
15 missions, 88:35 hours
Douthitt, Augustus R., Lt.; March 1945-EOW
3 missions, 12:15 hours
Drozd, Walter T., Lt.; January 1945-EOW
29 missions, 160 hours
P-51D LC-E 44-14744 "Skinny"
Dungan, Charles W., Lt.; July 1944-October 7, 1944(MIA-E)
25 missions, 107:15 hours
P-51C LC-Q 43-25046 "Kathleen"
Durand, Donald L., Lt.; December 1943-February 4, 1944(KIA)
4 missions, 11 hours
Einhaus, Lowell E., Capt.; August 1944-February 1945
49 missions, 275:15 hours
P-51D LC-V 44-13918
Enos, Leroy F., F/O; April 1945-EOW
0 missions

Everett, Hal W., Lt.; February 1944-May 13, 1944(POW)
23 missions, 91:45 hours
Fagg, James W., Lt.; February 1944-September 1944
68 missions, 286:15 hours
P-51D LC-W 44-13798
Fay, William C., Capt.; October 1944-EOW
52 missions, 275:10 hours
P-51K LC-Q 44-11566
Fernandes, Irwin W., Lt.; February 1944-August 5, 1944(KIA)
57 missions, 217:35 hours
Fiebelkorn, Ernest C., Capt.; January 1944-December 1944
70 missions, 320:10 hours
P-38J LC-N 42-68068
P-51D LC-N 44-11161 "June Nite"
Fleming, Eugene J., Capt.; August 1943-August 1944
78 missions, 300 hours
Flowers, Ray R., Capt.; July 1944-January 1945
53 missions, 270:15 hours
P-51D LC-E 44-11154 "Mary Ellen"
Flynn, Robert S., Lt.; August 1943-January 29, 1944(KIA)
5 missions, 16:15 hours
Frakes, Robert L., Lt.; August 1943-February 8, 1944(POW)
12 missions, 39:40 hours
Gard, Jack L., Lt.; August 1943-December 1, 1943(POW)
2 missions, 6:35 hours
Garner, James M., Capt.; August 1944-February 1945
55 missions, 278:30 hours
P-51D LC-J 44-14136
Garrett, Richard C., Capt.; August 1943-August 1944
69 missions, 303:25 hours
Geiger, Kenneth M., Lt.; August 1944-September 28, 1944(POW)
11 missions, 61:35 hours
Gese, Albert L., Lt.; August 1943-June 12, 1944(MIA-E)
29 missions, 144:40 hours
Gilbertson, Merle J., Maj.; February 1943-EOW
100 missions, 434:35 hours
P-38J LC-P 42-67819
P-38J LC-P 42-68155 "Diamond Lil"
P-51D LC-A 44-14822 "Sad Sack"
Gjolme, Harold H., Capt.; March 1944-EOW
67 missions, 276:10 hours
P-51D LC-B 44-13687 "Duration Plus 6"
Gustke, Russell F., LtCol.; February 1944-December 1944; to HdQt
636:25 total hours; ex-14th Ftr Grp
MTO and 55th Ftr Grp, ETO
Hairston, Richard M., Lt.; May 1944-June 17, 1944(POW)
14 missions, 52:25 hours
Hall, Glenn R., Capt.; October 1944-EOW
42 missions
P-51D LC-K 44-14996 "Nancy"
Halpin, Bernard C., Lt.; September 1944-November 21, 1944(POW)
14 missions, 60:55 hours
Hambelton, Ted P., Capt.; September 1944-April 1945
65 missions, 326:45 hours
Hart, James C., Lt.; August 1943-January 24, 1944(POW)
5 missions, 25 hours
Hascall, John S., Lt.; August 1943-November 29, 1943(KIA)
2 missions
Hendricks, Howard F., Lt.; February 1944-September 1944
69 missions, 287:35 hours
Herbert, James H., Capt.; June 1944-December 1944
272:40 hours
P-51D LC-B 44-13587 "Paper Doll"
Higginbotham, Henry M., F/O; August 1943-January 4, 1944(KIA)
2 missions, 8 hours
Holmes, Robert W., Capt.; December 1943-February 10, 1944(POW)
6 missions, 20:50 hours
Horne, Claude G., Capt.; January 1944-September 1944
76 missions, 327:50 hours
P-38J LC-R
P-51D LC-R 44-13902
Huey, Cartheledge J., Jr., Capt.; October 1944-EOW
46 missions, 254:45 hours
P-51D LC-X 44-13692 "Maggie"
Jacobson, Hugh H., Lt.; March 1944-June 12, 1944(KIA)
22 missions, 87:25 hours
Jennings, Edwin C., Capt.; August 1944-March 1945
55 missions, 280:30 hours
P-51D LC-W 44-13798 "Jean"
Jones, Reps D., Capt.; September 1944-EOW
60 missions, 315:15 hours
P-51D LC-F 44-13823 "Miss Miami"
Johnson, Herbert E., Jr., LtCol.; November 1943-March 1944; to HdQts; ex-14th Ftr Grp, MTO
72 missions, 303:45 hours total
P-38J LC-V 42-67708
P-38J LC-V 42-68019
Johnson, Robert P., Lt.; February 1944-February 29, 1944(POW)
2 missions, 2:20 hours
Joseph, Merle P., Lt.; October 1944-December 2, 1944(KIA)
7 missions, 26 hours

Kane, Martin F., F/O; December 1943-January 8, 1944(KIAc)
0 missions
Katz, Calvin, Lt.; October 1944-December 6, 1944(KIA)
7 missions, 32:20 hours
Keathley, Miles N., Lt.; August 1943-February 11, 1944(POW)
13 missions, 51:25 hours
Kendrick, Dixon V., Lt.; February 1944-June 12, 1944(POW)
15 missions, 87 hours
Kennedy, Jack W., Lt.; September 1944-November 2, 1944(KIA)
8 missions, 41 hours
Kermes, William J., Capt.; October 1942-February 1944; to HdQts
3 missions, 7:15 hours
Kerns, Leo H., Capt.; October 1944-EOW
49 missions, 257:20 hours
P-51D LC-X 44-15328 "Hoya Boy"
King, Robert H., Lt.; October 1944-EOW
48 missions, 248:20 hours
P-51D LC-B 44-13587 "Dizzy Rebel"
Knapp, Harry L., Lt.; September 1944-September 27, 1944 (KIAc)
0 missions
Kuemmerle, Walter F., Lt.; February 1944-September 1944
62 missions, 274:05 hours
P-51D LC-D 44-13852
Lane, Bill, Lt.; August 1943-November 25, 1943(KIA)
1 mission
Larsen, Fred, Capt.; September 1944-April 1945
61 missions, 315:50 hours
MacArthur, John D., Lt.; April 1944-October 1944
61 missions, 270:05 hours
P-51C LC-D 43-25042 "Pat's Pony"
Machen, Evan J., Capt.; September 1943-April 8, 1944(KIA)
20 missions, 101:10 hours
McAllister, David F., Lt.; January 1945-EOW
25 missions, 131:25 hours
P-51D LC-I 44-13760 "Cindee Lind"
McCully, Paul J., Capt.; April 1944-December 1944
72 missions, 321:45 hours
McKeon, Joseph T., Capt.; July 1944-September 1944; to 55th Ftr Sqn; ex-8th & 475th Ftr Grps, PTO
37 missions, 197:55 hours total
P-51D LC-C 44-13992 "Regina Coeli"
McLary, Maurice R., Maj.; August 1944-September 1944; ex-55th Ftr Sqn
70 missions, 288:35 hours total
P-51D LC-V 44-13918 "Murph IV"
Minton, Joseph O., Lt.; August 1943-February 11, 1944(KIA)
6 missions, 35:57 hours
Moncrieff, Rex E., Lt.; January 1944-September 1944
69 missions, 285:30 hours
P-51D LC-B 44-13775 "That's All Brother"
Montgomery, Robert P., Maj.; August 1940-November 1943; to HdQts
Morris, James M., Capt.; October 1942-July 7, 1944(POW)
65 missions, 287:10 hours
P-38J LC-E 42-67717 "My Dad"
Morris, Richard A., Lt.; January 1945-EOW
24 missions, 149:45 hours
P-51D LC-M 44-15605 "Mart's Cart"
Murrell, Robert E., Lt.; September 1944-February 19, 1945(KIA)
201:40 hours
Nichols, Merle B., Maj.; September 1944-May 1945; ex-79th Ftr Sqn & HdQts
482:35 hours
P-51D LC-O 44-14891 "Wilda"
North, Albert B., Lt.; November 1944-EOW
38 missions, 190:05 hours
P-51D LC-W 44-13798 "Kitty B"
Nuno, Julio, Lt.; November 1944-February 9, 1945(KIA)
17 missions, 92:45 hours
Papuzynski, Leonard W., Lt.; January 1945-EOW
20 missions, 152:40 hours
Payne, Arlon D., Capt.; May 1943-September 1944
68 missions, 295:25 hours
Perra, Walter F., Lt.; April 1944-June 15, 1944(KIA)
20 missions, 81:20 hours
Phillips, Baxter M., Lt.; November 1944-EOW
40 missions, 215:05 hours
P-51D LC-V 44-13918 "Gloria"
Piatkiewicz, Henry J., Lt.; December 1944-EOW
42 missions, 229:25 hours
Pierce, Pier W., Lt.; January 1945-EOW
23 missions
P-51D LC-J 44-14136 "Subtle Annie"
Pitz, Edwin R., Lt.; November 1944-EOW
44 missions, 233:25 hours
P-51D LC-L 44-14598 "Lil Erp"
Podkowa, Paul, Lt.; January 1945-EOW
22 missions, 133:50 hours
Purse, Frank W., Capt.; August 1944-April 1945
60 missions, 307:45 hours
Quinn, Russell G., Lt.; March 1943-June 13, 1944(KIA)
40 missions, 150:15 hours
Radcliffe, Lester G., Lt.; April 1945-EOW; ex-bomber pilot
(35 missions)
0 missions
Rader, Benjamin N., Lt.; January 1944-September 1944
81 missions, 351 hours
Rea, Parks M., Lt.; April 1945-EOW; ex-bomber pilot
(35 missions)
0 missions
Rege, Robert A., Lt.; January 1945-EOW
28 missions, 168:45 hours
Reid, John W., Lt.; January 1944-October 1944
66 missions, 271:55 hours
P-51D LC-N 44-13848
Reihmer, Donald A., Capt.; February 1944-August 4, 1944(MIA-E)
66 missions, 261:30 hours total
P-38J LC- "Filly From Philly"
Reynolds, Garth L., Capt.; September 1944-May 1945
59 missions, 310 hours
P-51D LC-S 44-15321
Richter, Frank K., Lt.; March 1945-EOW
4 missions, 23;55 hours
Riddle, Ernest S., Lt.; June 1944-July 4, 1944(KIA)
5 missions
Robb, William E., Lt.; June 1944-December 1944
53 missions, 270:10 hours
P-51D LC-E 44-13889
Robbins, Richard, Jr., Lt.; June 1944-July 1944(injured July 12)
11 missions, 44:30 hours
Roberts, Frank W., Lt.; June 1944-December 1944
55 missions, 270:05 hours
P-51D LC-C 44-13793
Robertson, Lawrence J., Lt.; June 1944-December 1944
53 missions, 270:05 hours
Rollins, William D., Lt.; June 1944-August 10, 1944(KIA)
17 missions, 85 hours
Rosenblum, Jerome, Lt.; January 1945-EOW
26 missions, 142;05 hours
P-51D LC-C 44-11335 "Gloria"
Rowlett, Lloyd E., Lt.; June 1944-December 1944
56 missions, 270:20 hours
P-51C LC-I 43-25041
P-51D LC-I 44-13760
Sabo, Paul J., Capt.; October 1944-February 1944; to 9th Air Force
15 missions, 57:45 hours
Schallo, Philip L., Capt.; September 1944-March 1945; to HdQts
57 missions, 277:05 hours
Senesac, Guy W., Lt.; August 1943-November 1943; to Ferry Command
0 missions
Seymour, James E., Lt.; January 1945-EOW
30 missions, 160:30 hours
Sheffield, Charles E., Jr., F/O; November 1944-January 3, 1945(KIA)
8 missions, 45:40 hours
Simanonok, Joseph E., Lt.; November 1944-EOW
45 missions, 235:45 hours
Slanker, Ted E., Capt.; July 1944-April 19451 to HdQts
58 missions, 295:50 hours
P-51D LC-P 44-14824 "The Butcher Boy"
Snodgrass, Fred E., Capt.; September 1944-EOW
53 missions, 294:45 hours
Starke, John P., Lt.; November 1944-EOW
45 missions, 243:10 hours
P-51D LC-P 44-13803
Stovall, Richard T., Capt.; September 1944-November 1944; ex-55th Ftr Sqn
33 missions total
Swierczynski, Chester J., Lt.; January 1945-March 24, 1945(POW)
11 missions, 54:55 hours
Taylor, Lauren J., Lt.; May 1943-March 25, 1944(KIAc)
21 missions, 95:55 hours
Thomas, Robert L., Jr., Lt.; October 1943-November 30, 1943(POW)
2 missions, 4:30 hours
Umla, Walter E., Jr., Lt.; January 1945-EOW
29 missions, 155:05 hours
Van Sickle, Dick W., Capt.; September 1944-April 1945
53 missions, 288 hours
P-51D LC- "Windsor Wonder"
Van Sickle, Frank L., Capt.; September 1944-April 1945
56 missions, 307:45 hours
Van Woert, Richard L., Lt.; August 1944-November 2, 1944(KIA)
23 missions, 135:25 hours
P-51D LC-U 44-13840 "Van's Can"
Whiteside, Walker L., Lt.; November 1943-August 6, 1944(KIA)
56 missions, 236 hours
P-38J LC-I 42-68176 "Sky Cowboy"
Williams, Terrence M., Capt.; January 1943-June 14, 1944(POW)
54 missions, 200:30 hours
Wilson, John R., Lt.; September 1944-November 9, 1944(KIA)
15 missions, 86 hours

**79th Fighter Squadron**

Allen, Brooks, Lt.; March 1945-EOW
3 missions, 18:35 hours
Anderson, Delynn E., Maj.; March 1943-September 1944
57 missions, 285 hours
P-38J MC-A 42-67646 "Kentucky Kernal

P-38J MC-A 42-67750 "Kentucky Kernal
P-38J MC-A 43-28404 "Kentucky Kernal
P-51D MC-A 44-14003 "Kentucky Kernal
Anderson, Earl M., Jr., Lt.; March 1945-EOW
2 missions, 12 hours
Archer, Neal J., Jr., Lt.; August 1943-January 14, 1944(KIA)
2 mission, 10:45 hours
Armstrong, John L., Lt.; March 1944-August 28, 1944(POW)
61 missions, 249 hours
P-38J MC-S "The Guardian Angel"
Baldwin, James H., Lt.; February 1944-August 1944
73 missions, 301:10 hours
P-38J MC- "Baby Baby"
Ballou, David B., Lt.; April 1945-EOW
0 missions
Barnard, Donald M., Lt.; January 1945-EOW
25 missions, 164:50 hours
Bates, Robert C., Lt.; April 1945-EOW
0 missions
Bebout, Russell W., Lt.; February 1944-September 1944
66 missions, 285 hours
P-38J MC-Y 43-28689 "Betsy"
P-51D MC-Y 44-13753 "Betsy IV"
Beesley, Vernon M., Lt.; April 1944-October 1944; to 67th Ftr Wg
5 missions, 20:45 hours
Beiter, Bert H., F/O; March 1945-EOW
2 missions, 11:35 hours
Bench, Marion F., Jr., Lt.; August 1943-May 25, 1944(KIA)
44 missions, 174:05 hours
Berkshire, Ronald R., F/O; March 1945-EOW
2 missions, 14:50 hours
Beschen, Darrell S., Capt.; September 1944-EOW
58 missions, 332:55 hours
P-51D MC-R 44-14337 "Bridget's Bunnion"
Binkley, Harold O., Capt.; May 1944-December 1944
81 missions, 360 hours
P-38J MC-J "Osage Chief"
P-51D MC-J 44-13855 "Osage Chief"
Bishop, Lynn P., Lt.; January 1945-EOW
20 missions, 129:10 hours
P-51D MC- "Little Jo"
Black, Richard H., Lt.; February 1944-February 1945
65 missions, 271:25 hours
P-51D MC-R "Black's Bird"
Blanton, Nathaniel H., Maj.; December 1942-November 1943; to 496th Ftr Trg Grp; ex-17th Pur Sqn, PTO (4 kills)
0 missions
Bradford, Irving T., Lt.; September 1944-November 1944; to 67th Ftr Wg
16 missions, 83:15 hours
Bradshaw, James D., Lt.; August 1943-August 1944
72 missions, 300:05 hours
P-38J MC-B "Gator Bait"
P-51D MC-B 44-13660 "Jeanie"
Bray, Robert E., Lt.; April 1945-EOW
0 missions
Bullers, Walter E., Lt.; September 1944-April 1945
58 missions, 309:30 hours
Byrd, Markrel L., F/P; November 1943-February 6, 1944(POW)
7 missions, 33:05 hours
Cameron, William A., Capt.; March 1944-November 1944
86 missions, 360:15 hours
P-51D MC-C 44-13846 "Soar Lassie"
Campbell, Robert E., Lt.; May 1944-October 1944
62 missions, 275 hours
P-51D MC-F 44-13751 "Wanda's Worry"
Carpenter, Jesse E., Jr., Capt.; May 1944-November 1944
53 missions, 266:30 hours
Chapman, Donald A., Jr., Lt.; April 1945-EOW
0 missions
Cooper, Donald W., Lt.; August 1943-February 11, 1944(KIA)
9 missions, 38:50 hours
Corbet, James H., Lt.; August 1943-April 13, 1944(KIA)
18 missions, 90:45 hours
Coughran, Elmer H., Lt.; July 1944-January 1945
56 missions, 275:50 hours
Crawford, Richard W., Lt.; March 1945-EOW
2 missions, 11:30 hours
Crites, Drexel E., Lt.; March 1944-September 1944
65 missions, 278:55 hours
Crutchley, Edward W., Lt.; February 1945-EOW
21 missions, 117:45 hours
Cumming, Herbert W., Capt.; January 1943-November 7, 1943(KIA)
1 mission, 4:40 hours
Dailey, Howard W., F/O; March 1945-EOW
2 missions, 11:40 hours
Daniel, Thomas J., Capt.; June 1944-January 1945
60 missions, 300 hours
P-51D MC-E 44-14365 "Corky"
Daye, Merlin M., F/O; April 1945-EOW
0 missions
Degenhardt, Louis J., Lt.; February 1945-EOW
19 missions, 104:45 hours
Denbo, Paul, Lt.; May 1944-August 12, 1944(KIA)
46 missions, 184:10 hours
P-38J MC- 42-67892 "Talent Scout"
Diehl, Ramon A., Lt.; February 1945-EOW
17 missions, 99:50 hours
Dixon, Clyde G., Capt.; August 1944-February 1945
51 missions, 270:20 hours
P-51D MC- "Peggy Jo"
Donnellan, Andrew B., Lt.; February 1945-EOW
13 missions, 74:05 hours
Dufresne, Robert R., Lt.; September 1944-April 1945
53 missions, 297:35 hours
Esau, John F., Lt.; February 1944-April 8, 1944(KIA)
6 missions, 24:55 hours
Fall, Mack D., Lt.; October 1942-January 30, 1944(POW)
9 missions, 29:35 hours
Festersen, John C., Lt.; May 1945-EOW; ex-bomber pilot
(45 mission, 367:15 hours)
0 missions
Fogg, Albert R., Lt.; February 1944-April 30, 1944(POW)
18 missions, 73:30 hours
Franklin, R.C., Maj.; February 1944-May 1944; ex-55th Ftr Grp
200:05 hours
P-38J MC-F 42-68037 "Strictly Stella's Baby"
P-38J MC-F 42-104086 "Strictly Stella's Baby"
Gall, William, Lt.; June 1943-August 1944
34 missions, 131 hours
Gatterdam, Richard P., Maj.; October 1942-November 1944; to 55th Ftr Sqn
430:10 hours total
P-38J MC-G 42-67491
P-38J MC-G 42-68140 "Puddin"
P-51D MC-G 44-14003
Gardner, Philip D., Lt.; January 1945-EOW
34 mission, 190 hours
P-51D MC-U 44-13873 "Georgia Boy"
Gardner, Thomas M., Lt.; July 1944-January 1945
57 missions, 270 hours
Gilpin, Calvin F., F/O; March 1945-EOW
1 mission, 5:40 hours
Graham, Lindol F., Capt.; October 1942-March 18, 1944(KIA)
29 missions, 130:10 hours
P-38J MC-L 42-67497 "Susie"
P-38J MC-L 42-67926 "Susie"
Gubana, Joseph L., Lt.; January 1945-EOW
23 missions, 152:20 hours
Hahn, James W., Lt.; January 1945-EOW
29 missions, 166:30 hours
Halloran, William J., F/O March 1945-EOW
1 mission, 5:20 hours
Hamilton, Joseph L., F/O; November 1943-January 4, 1944(POW)
1 mission, 4:30 hours
Hamme, Charles R., Capt.; July 1944-January 1945
59 missions, 296:30 hours
P-51D MC-Y 44-13753
Hanzo, Thomas A., Lt.; September 1942-February 11, 1944(POW)
15 missions, 62:05 hours
Harper, William M., F/O; November 1943-January 29, 1944(KIA)
4 missions, 14 hours
Hartig, Fred M., Jr., Lt.; December 1943-January 24, 1944(KIA)
4 missions, 15:45 hours
P-38J MC- "Thelma"
Heiden, Arthur W., Lt.; February 1944-August 1944
63 missions, 300 hours
P-38J MC-H 42-67427
P-51D MC-H 42-104086 "Lucky Lady"
P-51D MC-H 44-13620
Hennessey, Joseph P., Lt.; January 1945-EOW
27 missions, 162:05 hours
Hillyard, Owen T., Lt.; July 1944-July 19, 1944(KIA)
3 mission, 12;20 hours
Hollins, John K., Capt.; September 1944-EOW
50 missions, 273:40 hours
Horst, Harold, Lt.; June 1944-December 1944
58 missions, 270 hours
P-51C MC-D 43-25029
Huarte, Raymond E., Lt.; March 1944-May 24, 1944(POW)
15 missions, 66 hours
Ilfrey, Jack M., Maj.; April 1944-June 13, 1944(MIA-E)
June 1944-December 1944; ex-1st Ftr Grp, MTO (72 missions, 208 hours)
70 missions, 320 hours
P-38J MC-O 43-28431 "Happy Jack's Go Buggy"
P-51D MC-I 44-13761 "Happy Jack's Go Buggy"
Ingebrigsten, Melbourne G., Capt.; September 1944-May 1945
64 missions, 309:05 hours
P-51D MC-A 44-15049 "Miss U Louise"
P-51D MC-A 44-15752 "Miss U Louise"
Jackson, Carl E., Maj.; January 1944-February 20, 1944(POW); ex-HdQts
13 missions
P-38J MC-J 42-67988 "Jack"

Jones, Dale N., Capt.; September 1944-EOW
49 missions, 273:40 hours
P-51D MC-Z 44-11244 "Nina Merle"
P-51D MC-J 44-72266 "Nina Merle II"

Jurgens, Fred H., Lt.; January 1945-EOW
27 missions, 166:05 hours
P-51D MC-K 44-15341 "Brown Eyes"

Kautz, Kenneth, Jr., Lt.; August 1944-October 26, 1944(KIA)
22 missions, 117:25 hours

Kelso, Duane F., Lt.; September 1944-February 1945
35 missions, 163:10 hours

Kemp, Arthur R., Lt.; February 1944-September 1944
66 missions, 275:30 hours
P-38J MC- "Janey K"
P-38J MC- "Janey K II"
P-38J MC- "Janey K III"

Kies, Clifford, Capt.; August 1944-February 1945 (WIA February 20)
59 missions, 282:55 hours
P-51D MC-N 44-11195 "Little Roue"

Kirby, James C., Jr., Capt.; August 1944-EOW
66 missions, 348:15 hours

Klatt, Quintus, Lt.; February 1944-September 1944
66 missions, 258 hours

Learned, Albert S., Lt.; February 1944-September 1944
72 missions, 290:05 hours

Lee, John B., Lt.; October 1944-EOW
52 missions, 275:20 hours
P-51D MC-L 44-15198 "EK & Jay Bee"

Lefevre, Ferdinand E., Lt.; August 1943-April 28, 1944(KIA)
36 missions, 149 hours
P-38J MC-U 42-67725
P-38J MC-U 42-68035

Lewis, Willard H., Jr., Lt.; February 1944-September 1944
69 missions, 287 hours
P-38J MC-L 42-67928 "Hells Belle"
P-51C MC-L 43-25054 "Hells Belle"

Martin, Jack T., Lt.; May 1943-January 1944(WIA January 30)
5 missions, 19:30 hours

McCarty, Benjamin F., Lt.; February 1944-May 9, 1944(POW)
22 missions, 68:20 hours
P-38J MC- 42-104289 "Nan's Honey"

Mednick, Harvey, Lt.; May 1943-April 1944; to 67th Ftr Wg
6 missions, 27:35 hours
P-38J MC- "Little Eve"

Merriman, George W., Capt.; February 1944-September 1944
66 missions, 288 hours
P-38J MC-M "Almy"
P-51D MC-M "Almy Too"

Meyer, Robert J., LtCol.; July 1943-May 1945
107 missions, 484 hours
P-38J MC-M 42-67652 "Bob Cat"
P-38J MC-M 42-67929 "Bob Cat II"
P-38J MC-M 42-104308 "Bob Cat III"
P-51D MC-M 44-13876 "Bob Cat IV"
P-51D MC-M 44-72402 "Bob Cat V"

Moss, Robert B., Lt.; August 1943-January 29, 1944(POW)
4 missions, 16:05 hours

Nichols, Merle B., Maj.; August 1943-May 1944; to HdQts
482:35 hours total
P-38J MC-N 42-67515 "Wilda"
P-38J MC-N 42-67868 "Wilda"

Orr, Melvin H., Lt.; March 1943-February 11, 1944(POW)
9 missions, 32:40 hours

Otis, Esburn D., Lt.; August 1943-January 26, 1944(KIAc)
4 missions, 16 hours

Ott, Richard L., Maj.; October 1942-January 30, 1944(KIA)
14 missions, 51:05 hours

Pardoe, Thomas E., Jr., Lt.; May 1943-May 1944; to 67th Ftr Wg
5 missions, 14:90 hours

Peres, Robert G., Lt.; May 1943-November 1943; to 310th Ferry Sqn
0 missions

Peterson, Roger S., Capt.; June 1944-January 1945
57 missions, 295 hours

Phipps, Robert R., Jr., Capt.; June 1944-December 1944
55 missions, 270:25 hours
P-51D MC-B 44-13660 "My Kath"

Pogue, Edward F., Lt.; November 1944-EOW
42 missions, 228:10 hours
P-51D MC-R 44-13535 "Chattanooga Choo-Choo"

Pollock, Robert H., Capt.; September 1944-April 1945
62 missions, 314:15 hours

Price, Keith C., Lt.; June 1944-January 1945
55 missions, 270:10 hours
P-51C MC-L 43-25054 "Beaverhead Filly"

Pubentz, Robert L., Capt.; June 1944-January 1945
50 missions, 270 hours
P-51D MC-H 44-14349

Reckeweg, Robert M., Jr., Lt.; June 1944-November 1944
52 missions, 250 hours
P-51D MC-S 44-14238

Reichard, James N., Capt.; June 1944-March 1945; to HdQts
69 missions, 337:10 hours
P-51C MC-V 43-25064 "Pretty Baby"

Reihmer, Donald A., Capt.; August 1943-February 1944; to 77th Ftr Sqn
14 missions (79th only)

Richter, Leonard L., Lt.; June 1944-July 31, 1944(KIA)
15 missions, 83:20 hours

Rierson, William H., Lt.; January 1944-February 8, 1944(POW)
5 missions, 20:20 hours

Roark, Frank H., Jr., Capt.; January 1944-September 1944
71 missions, 310:05 hours

Rudnick, Vincent J., Lt.; October 1944-EOW
50 missions, 258 hours
P-51D MC-X 44-13720 "Mine 3 Express"

Ryan, Emery K., Lt.; May 1944-June 17, 1944(KIA)
9 missions, 58:55 hours

Rye, Robert E., Lt.; February 1944-July 1944; to 67th Ftr Wg
16 missions, 78:55 hours

Saltzman, Stephen G., Lt.; April 1944-May 1944 (WIA May 25)
9 missions, 36:45 hours

Sands, Myron R., Lt.; January 1944-February 11, 1944(POW)
6 missions, 29 hours

Santee, John C., Lt.; November 1944-EOW
38 missions, 224 hours

Sass, Donald A., Capt.; September 1944-EOW
52 missions, 255:30 hours
P-51D MC-T "Sneebo"

Schwarz, Albert P., Lt.; November 1944-EOW
41 missions, 229:40 hours

Schons, Kenneth H., Lt.; November 1944-EOW
43 missions, 250:15 hours
P-51D MC-A 44-11219 "The Virgin"

Scott, Robert M., Lt.; November 1944-EOW
243 missions, 47 hours
P-51C MC-L 43-25054 "Shoot, You're Faded"

Shaffer, Allen L., F/O; November 1944-March 15, 1945(KIA)
25 missions, 127:05 hours

Shelton, Joseph E., Lt.; November 1944-EOW
43 missions, 225:05 hours

Skinner, Kenneth A., Lt.; November 1944-EOW
42 missions, 228:15 hours

Smith, Donald E., Lt.; November 1944-EOW
30 missions, 166 hours

Smith, Earl O., Lt.; April 1944-June 17, 1944(MIA-E)
25 missions, 102:35 hours
P-38J MC-R 42-104308

Smith, Mark F., Lt.; November 1944-March 6, 1945(KIAc)
25 missions, 141:10 hours

Smith, William W., Maj.; May 1944-August 1944; to 55th Ftr Sq
271:15 hours total
P-38J MC- "Okie Bloke"
P-51D MC- "Okie Bloke"

Smutko, Leonard S., Lt.; August 1943-February 11, 1944(POW)
12 missions, 53:55 hours

Snow, Mitchell P., Lt.; August 1943-April 8, 1944(KIA)
26 missions, 98:25 hours

Stevens, Kent H., Lt.; February 1944-July 1944; to 55th Ftr Sqn
59 missions, 270:05 hours total

Stewart, David, Lt.; November 1944-April 10, 1945(POW)
38 missions, 206:15 hours
P-51D MC-F 44-13751 "Wanda's Worry"

Strock, Frank E., Lt.; November 1944-EOW
43 missions, 226 hours

Stultz, Robert P., Capt.; May 1944-December 1944
65 missions, 270 hours

Taylor, John K., Capt.; January 1945-EOW
27 missions, 150:05 hours

Taylor, Wesley H., Lt.; June 1944-December 1944
55 missions, 271 hours
P-51D MC-T 44-13667

Ticktin, Boyd L., Lt.; August 1944-October 1944; to 67th Ftr Wg
4 missions, 17:15 hours

Watson, Harry J., Jr., Lt.; April 1944-May 25, 1944(POW)
9 missions, 38:30 hours

Webb, Glenn M., Capt.; April 1944-November 1944
78 missions, 362 hours
P-51D MC-Z 44-13760 "Glen Gary Guy"

Wells, Robert L., Lt.; December 1943-March 1944 (injured March 16); ex-MTO pilot (177:15 hrs)
5 missions, 22:45 hours

Whitley, Ralph D., Lt.; September 1944-February 26, 1945(POW
44 missions, 217:45 hours
P-51D MC-C 44-13846 "Lil Bit"

Williams, Woodrow W., Lt.; March 1944-July 1944 (injured July 27)
45 missions, 169:40 hours

Wolf, George P., Lt.; April 1945-EOW; ex-bomber pilot
(36 missions, 266:55 hours)
0 missions

Wright, Leonard M., Jr., Lt.; January 1945-February 24, 1945(POW)
1 mission, 3:30 hours

Wyman, Zell, Capt.; May 1943-October 1944
60 missions, 270:15 hours
P-38J MC- "Coon Dog"
P-38J MC- "Coon Dog II"
P-38J MC- "Coon Dog III"
P-51D MC- "Coon Dog IV"
Yarbrough, Walter R., Maj.; September 1944-May 1945
50 missions, 271:50 hours
P-51D MC-Y 44-72383 "Janey Girl II From Texas"
Yaryan, Jess O., Capt.; October 1942-December 1944
63 missions, 270:05 hours
P-38J MC-Q
P-51D MC-Q 44-13653 "Carrie Bee"
Ziegelbauer, Andrew M., Lt.; September 1944-August 1945
53 missions, 282:30 hours

**Aircraft of the 55th Fighter Squadron**

P-38H-5-LO
42-67019 KI-X
42-67034 KI-V — E.E. Geiger
42-67052 KI-Z
42-67081 KI-K "Pistol Packin' Mama"

P-38J-5-LO
42-67194 KI-
42-67198 KI-
42-67204 KI-J
42-67256 KI-F

P-38J-10-LO
42-67451 KI-R
42-67482 KI-U — W.B. Taylor
42-67484 KI-V "Murph III" — M.R. McLary
42-67486 KI-J
42-67489 KI-L
42-67505 KI-R "Jeanne" — R.M. Scrutchfield
42-67649 KI-M
42-67656 KI-I
42-67657 KI-A — D.A. McAuley
42-67661 KI-
42-67705 KI-
42-67719 KI-
42-67742 KI-E
42-67743 KI-G — C.A. Hallberg
42-67753 KI-T "Cactus Jack" — J.J. Yelton
42-67756 KI-B "Stubborn Virgin" — J.C. Serros
42-67763 KI-I
42-67823 KI-N "Kitty" — H.E. Bisher
42-67855 KI-W — R.D. Frey
42-67860 KI-V — E.E. Geiger
42-67864 KI-
42-67878 KI-Y
42-67883 KI-
42-67885 KI-L

P-38J-10-LO(cont.)
42-67887 KI-
42-67891 KI-Z
42-67907 KI-U — W.B. Taylor
42-67916 KI-S "California Cutie" — R.O. Loehnert
42-67923 KI-
42-67949 KI-A "Lil Henry" — D.H. McAuley
42-68010 KI-K
42-68051 KI-D
42-68077 KI-X
42-68097 KI-O
42-68108 KI-Y "Bobby" — R.H. Riemensnider
42-68126 KI-U
42-68131 KI-V
42-68153 KI-J
42-68160 KI-H
42-68170 KI-M

P-38J-15-LO
43-28301 KI-O "Mama's Boy" — E.E. Wasil
43-28354 KI-L
43-28358 KI-I
43-28393 KI-W "Wrangler" — C. Wilson
43-28362 KI-Q
43-28430 KI-N "Jeanne" — R.M. Scrutchfield
43-28634 KI-M
43-28700 KI-D
42-104207 KI-N
42-104210 KI-G — C.A. Hallberg
42-104239 KI-P
42-104314 KI-P

Unknown Serials
KI-N "Flying Dutchman" — E.W. Hower
KI-Y "Murph" — M.R. McLary
KI-Y "Murph II" — M.R. McLary
KI- "Posse" — R.E. Miles
KI- "Dotty" — R.P. Watson

P-51B-5-NA
43-6865 KI-Q — HACK

P-51C-10-NT
43-25028 KI-Z — L. Solomon/D.H. Rackley
43-25031 KI-O "Mama's Boy II" — E.E. Wasil
43-25033 KI-D — J.S. Reynolds
43-25049 KI- "Shorty"
43-25065 KI-H "Ambrose II" — D.D. Oxley

P-51D-5-NT
44-11196 KI-G — J.K. Brown
44-11205 KI-A "Be Good" — H.L. Brown

P-51K-5-NT
44-11638 KI-E "Lil Easy" — J.S. Ford

P-51K-10-NT
44-12159 KI-C

P-51D-5-NA
44-13331 KI-A
44-13541 KI-N
44-13664 KI-B — A.C. Kelly
44-13679 KI-
44-13695 KI-Z
44-13702 KI-E "Joe" — J.S. Ford
44-13715 KI-K — H.B. Bynum
44-13733 KI-F — H.M. Anderson
44-13768 KI-L
44-13776 KI-V "Nancy Gay" — K.D. McNeel/K.C. Smeltz
44-13778 KI-J
44-13790 KI-L "Lil Jughaid" — J.E. Burford
44-13794 KI-C "Piccilo Pete" — W.H. Skroback
44-13799 KI-N "Flying Dutchman" — E.W. Hower
44-13827 KI-R "Little Wheel" — W.W. Wells
44-13827 KI-R "Rondelle" — R.M. Howard
44-13838 KI-G "Little Louise" — C.A. Hallberg
44-13838 KI-G "Okie Blokie IV" — W.W. Smith
44-13859 KI-S — W.H. Mullins
44-13860 KI-T — W.M. Hurst
44-13892 KI-X "Idiot's Delite"
44-13903 KI-Y "Bobby" — R.H. Riemensnider
44-13951 KI-W "Wrangler Jr." — C. Wilson
44-13965 KI-Z — J.H. Tennant

P-51D-10-NA
44-14120 KI-D — R.W. Fruechtenicht
44-14157 KI-U — D.R. Franklin
44-14198 KI-W — E.W. Cavell
44-14253 KI-P "Mighty Low" — M.L. Low
44-14253 KI-P "Lil Eva" — D. Michel
44-14319 KI-M "Mary Jo" — J.D. Leon
44-14319 KI-M "Olivia de" — J.T. McKeon
44-14430 KI-F — R.I. Bowman/E.L. Kier
44-14749 KI-X — J.L. Mansker

P-51D-15-NA
44-14870 KI-N
44-14880 KI-H "Frisco Belle" — E.H. Cosgriff
44-15018 KI-G
44-15065 KI-W
44-15078 KI-B "Josephine" — J.A. Peterburs
44-15249 KI-W — R.W. Meinzen
44-15311 KI-K "Little Lady"
44-15327 KI-G "Puddin" — R.P. Gatterdam
44-15591 KI-K "Dragon Wagon IV" — E.W. Planchak

P-51D-20-NA
44-63210 KI-S
44-63808 KI-K
44-72160 KI-K
44-72388 KI-Y "Bobby" — R.H. Riemensnider

Unknown Serials
P-51D KI-B "Ginny" — R.P. Iehle
P-51D KI- "Lil Daddy" — W.E. Martin
P-51C KI- "Jeannie" — M.C. Pannell
P-51D KI- "Candy Baby" — V.L. Decker
P-51D KI-I "Claudine I" — D.L. Larrabee
P-51D KI- "Supermouse" — D.I. Freedman
P-51D KI-M "Mary Jane" — E.M. Prow

P-51D KI-O "Rum"
P-51D KI- "Missmanooky"
P-51D KI- "Portland Rose"
P-51D KI- "Slapsimaxi"
P-51D KI- "Susie III"

**Aircraft of the 77th Fighter Squadron**

P-38H-1-LO
42-66723 LC-

P-38H-5-LO
42-66770 LC-L
42-67016 LC-
42-67022 LC-
42-67038 LC-
42-67048 LC-A

P-38J-5-LO
42-67186 LC-
42-67191 LC-
42-67202 LC-D
42-67202 LC-Y
42-67213 LC-T
42-67228 LC-B
42-67229 LC-D
42-67234 LC-A
42-67262 LC-G
42-67281 LC-N
42-67306 LC-

P-38J-10-LO
42-67407 LC-
42-67442 LC-A
42-67443 LC-O
42-67450 LC-E "Eze Does It" Droop-Snoot
42-67462 LC-X
42-67471 LC-S
42-67472 LC-K
42-67478 LC-M R.P. Montgomery
42-67509 LC-F
42-67523 LC-S P.J. Sabo
42-67525 LC-
42-67707 LC-B
42-67708 LC-V H.E. Johnson
42-67714 LC-Z
42-67717 LC-E "My Dad" J.M. Morris
42-67725 LC- "Old Baldy"
42 67726 LC
42-67728 LC-C
42-67735 LC-I
42-67758 LC-Q
42-67759 LC-D
42-67767 LC-H
42-67770 LC-L
42-67779 LC-Y
42-67809 LC-H
42-67818 LC-
42-67819 LC-P
42-67828 LC-B
42-67831 LC-
42-67871 LC-G
42-67888 LC-B "Black Barney" B.M. Russell
42-67901 LC-X
42-67915 LC-J
42-68016 LC-R
42-68019 LC-V H.E. Johnson
42-68026 LC-K
42-68036 LC-M R.P. Montgomery
42-68045 LC-Z
42-68066 LC-K
42-68068 LC-N E.C. Fiebelkorn
42-68106 LC-R
42-68111 LC-
42-68155 LC-P "Diamond Lil" M.J. Gilbertson
42-68156 LC-V H.E. Johnson
44-68159 LC-C
42-68171 LC-C
42-68176 LC-I "Sky Cowboy" W.L. Whiteside
42-68177 LC-C
42-68181 LC-J

P-38J-15-LO
43-28270 LC-
43-28379 LC-B
43-28380 LC-G
43-28397 LC-Q
43-28539 LC-Z
43-28684 LC-
43-28686 LC-X
42-104067 LC-V "Little Bug"
42-104069 LC-A

P-38J-15-LO
44-23174 LC-

Unknown Serials
LC-Z "The Haycock Belle" I.C. Baker
LC- "Hell's Bells"
LC- "Filly From Philly IV" D.A. Reihmer
LC- "Wilma"
LC- "Wilma II"
LC- "Duffie"
LC- "Bucket of Bolts"

P-51B-1-NA
43-12417 LC-B HACK

P-51B-10-NA
42-106476 LC-Z HACK
42-106662 LC-A HACK

P-51C-10-NT
43-25041 LC-I L.E. Rowlett
43-25042 LC-D "Pat's Pony" J.D. McArthur
43-25046 LC-Q "Kathleen" C.W. Dungan

P-51D-5-NT
44-11154 LC E "Mary Ellen" R.R. Flowers
44-11161 LC-N "June Nite" E.C. Fiebelkorn
44-11217 LC-J "Balls O'Fire"
44-11324 LC-U
44-11335 LC-C "Gloria" J. Rosenblum

P-51K-1-NT
44-11354 LC-H

P-51K-5-NT
44-11566 LC-Q W.C. Fay
44-11673 LC-Z

P-51D-5-NA
44-13378 LC-A
44-13587 LC-B "Paper Doll" J.H. Herbert
44-13587 LC-B "Dizzy Rebel" R.H. King
44-13637 LC-G
44-13655 LC-L L.W. Adams
44-13670 LC-S
44-13687 LC-B "Duration Plus 6" H.H. Gjolme
44-13692 LC-X "Maggie" C.L. Huey
44-13696 LC-R
44-13713 LC-Y
44-13746 LC-M "It's The Kid!" F.H. Alexander
44-13748 LC-K
44-13760 LC-I R.E. Rowlett
44-13760 LC-I "Cindee Lind" D.F. McAllister
44-13775 LC-B "That's All Brother" R.E. Moncrieff
44-13792 LC-J
44-13793 LC-C F.W. Roberts
44-13798 LC-W J.W. Fagg
44-13798 LC-W "Jean" E.C. Jennings
44-13798 LC-W "Kitty B" A.B. North
44-13803 LC-P J.P. Starke
44-13811 LC-J
44-13819 LC-F
44-13824 LC-Z
44-13836 LC-H "It's The Kid!" F.H. Alexander
44-13840 LC-U "Van's Can" R.L. Van Woert
44-13848 LC-N J.W. Reid
44-13852 LC-D W.F. Kuemmerle
44-13889 LC-E W.E. Robb
44-13902 LC-R C.G. Horne
44-13918 LC-V "Murph IV" M.R. McLary
44-13918 LC-V "Gloria" B.M. Phillips
44-13968 LC-V
44-13991 LC-A
44-13992 LC-C "Regina Coeli" J.T. McKeon

P-51D-10-NA
44-14063 LC-L "Robb" L.W. Adams
44-14136 LC-J "Subtle Annie" P.W. Pierce
44-14269 LC-Y "Flamme De Pursuit"
44-14598 LC-L "Li'l Erp" E.R. Pitz
44-14692 LC-Y "My Rosie"
44-14692 LC-I
44-14693 LC-G "Feather Merchant IV" J.C. Price
44-14744 LC-E "Skinny" W.T. Drozd
44-14822 LC-A "Sad Sack" M.J. Gilbertson
44-14823 LC-F "Miss Miami" R.D. Jones

44-14824 LC-P "The Butcher Boy" T.E. Slanker
44-14843 LC-D "Gumpy" R.P. Montgomery

P-51D-15-NA
44-14891 LC-O "Wilda" M.B. Nichols
44-14975 LC-K
44-14996 LC-K "Nancy" G.R. Hall
44-15321 LC-S G.L. Reynolds
44-15328 LC-X "Hoya Boy" L.H. Kerns
44-15379 LC-N
44-15605 LC-M "Mart's Cart" R.A. Morris

P-51D-20-NA
44-72107 LC-N "BJ Belle of the West"
44-72298 LC-Q
44-72519 LC-D "Gumpy" R.P. Montgomery

Unknown Serials
P-51D LC-S "Snowball's Gesrium"
P-51D LC-G "Trudy"
P-51D LC- "Windsor Wonder" D.W. Van Sickle
P-51D LC- "Idiot's Deelite"
P-51D LC- "Miss D-Meaner"
P-51D LC- "Little Sister"
P-51D LC- "Little Freddie"
P-51D LC- "Lil Sandra"
P-51D LC- "Lil Aleta"
P-51D LC- "Gabriel's Horn"
P-51D LC- "Doodle Darling"
P-51D LC- "Dick, Jr."
P-51D LC- "Blue Streak"
P-51D LC- "Connecticut Yankee"

**Aircraft of the 79th Fighter Squadron**

P-38H-5-LO
42-67039 MC-F

P-38J-5-LO
42-67187 MC-
42-67200 MC-K
42-67206 MC-X
42-67251 MC-X
42-67285 MC-J
42-67298 MC-Q J.O. Yaryan
42-67306 MC-

P-38J-10-LO
42-67427 MC-H A.W. Heiden
42-67448 MC-V
42-67471 MC-S
42-67474 MC-U
42-67491 MC-G R.P. Gatterdam
42-67492 MC-E
42-67497 MC-L "Susie" L.F. Graham
42-67498 MC-
42-67502 MC-H
42-67511 MC-R
42-67514 MC-Q J.O. Yaryan
42-67515 MC-N "Wilda" M.B. Nichols
42-67516 MC-L
42-67646 MC-A "Kentucky Kernal" D.E. Anderson
42-67651 MC-Z
42-67652 MC-M "Bobcat" R.J. Meyer
42-67665 MC-
42-67672 MC-Y
42-67680 MC-D "Bee Pee"
42-67681 MC-M
42-67708 MC-P
42-68718 MC-C
42-68722 MC-R "Gentle Annie" H.J. Rau
42-67723 MC-I
42-67715 MC-U F.E. LeFevre
42-67727 MC-L
42-67736 MC-J
42-67750 MC-A
42-67760 MC-
42-67821 MC-
42-67848 MC-
42-67850 MC-S
42-67854 MC-K
42-67858 MC-
42-67862 MC-
42-67868 MC-N M.B. Nichols
42-67892 MC- "Talent Scout" P. Denbo
42-67905 MC-W
42-67926 MC-L "Susie" L.F. Graham
42-67928 MC-L "Hells Belle" W.H. Lewis
42-67929 MC-M "Bobcat II" R.J. Meyer
42-67931 MC-K
42-67962 MC-L
42-67963 MC-H
42-67981 MC-G
42-67988 MC-J "Jack" C.E. Jackson
42-68012 MC-D
42-68015 MC-I
42-68019 MC-
42-68035 MC-U F.E. LeFevre
42-68037 MC-F "Strictly Stella's Baby" R.C. Franklin
42-68073 MC-C
42-68084 MC-
42-68094 MC-
42-68140 MC-G "Puddin"
42-68150 MC-K
42-68165 MC-R "Gentle Annie" H.J. Rau
42-68168 MC-W

P-38J-15-LO
43-28404 MC-A "Kentucky Kernal" D.E. Anderson
43-28408 MC-R
43-28412 MC-N
43-28431 MC-O "Happy Jacks' Go Buggy" J.M. Ilfrey
43-28433 MC-B
43-28689 MC-Y "Betsy" R.W. Bebout
43-28718 MC-A
42-104086 MC-F "Strictly Stella's Baby" R.C. Franklin
42-104086 MC-H "Lucky Lady" A.W. Heiden
42-104095 MC-G
42-104289 MC- "Nan's Honey" B.F. McCarty
42-104308 MC-M "Bobcat III" R.J. Meyer
42-104308 MC-R E.O. Smith

Unknown Serials
MC-N "Okie Blokie" W.W. Smith
MC-S "The Guardian Angel" J.L. Armstrong
MC-J "Osage Chief" H.O. Binkley
MC-B "Gator Bait" J.D. Bradshaw
MC- "Thelma" F.M. Hartig
MC- "Baby Baby" J.H. Baldwin
MC- "Baby Baby II" J.H. Baldwin
MC- "Baby Baby III" J.H. Baldwin
MC- "Janey K" A.R. Kemp
MC- "Janey K II" A.R. Kemp
MC- "Janey K III" A.R. Kemp
MC- "Coon Dog" Z. Wyman
MC- "Coon Dog II" Z. Wyman
MC- "Coon Dog III" Z. Wyman
MC- "Little Eve" H. Mednick
MC- "Blowtorch"
MC- "Chief Cockeye"

P-51B-1-NA
43-12185 MC-W HACK

P-51C-10-NT
43-25025 MC-C "Sissey"
43-25029 MC-D H. Horst
43-25043 MC-O
43-25054 MC-L "Hell's Belle" W.H. Lewis
43-25054 MC-L "Beaverhead Filly" K.C. Price
43-25054 MC-L "Shoot You're Faded" R.M. Scott
43-25064 MC-V "Pretty Baby" J.N. Reichard

P-51D-5-NT
44-11195 MC-N "Little Roue" C. Kies
44-11219 MC-A "The Virgin" K.H. Schons
44-11244 MC-J "Nina Merle" D.N. Jones
44-11347 MC-S

P-51K-1-NT
44-11357 MC-H

P-51D-5-NA
44-13535 MC-R "Chattanooga Choo Choo" E.F. Pogue
44-13541 MC-N "Nancy" J.P. Randolph
44-13580 MC-K
44-13620 MC-H A.W. Heiden
44-13653 MC-Q "Carrie Bee" J.O. Yaryan
44-13653 MC-Q "Polly"
44-13660 MC-B "My Kath" R.R. Phipps
44-13660 MC-B "Jeanie" J.D. Bradshaw
44-13661 MC-W
44-13667 MC-T
44-13720 MC-X "Mine 3 Express" V.J. Rudnick
44-13751 MC-F "Wanda's Worry" R.E. Campbell/D. Stewart
44-13752 MC-G
44-13753 MC-Y "Kitty & Bunny" C.R. Hamme
44-13760 MC-Z "Glengary Guy" G.M. Webb
44-13760 MC-Z "Jackie"

44-13761 MC-I "Happy Jack's Go Buggy" J.M. Ilfrey
44-13791 MC-S "Guardian Angel"
44-13846 MC-C "Soar Lassie II" W.A. Cameron
44-13846 MC-C "Lil Bit" R.D. Whitley
44-13855 MC-J "Osage Chief" H.O. Binkley
44-13873 MC-U "Georgia Boy" P.D. Gardner
44-13876 MC-M "Bobcat IV" R.J. Meyer
44-14003 MC-A "Kentucky Kernal" D.E. Anderson
44-14003 MC-G R.P. Gatterdam

P-51D-10-NA
44-14238 MC-S R.M. Reckweig
44-14337 MC-R "Gentle Annie" H.J. Rau
44-14337 MC-R "Bridget's Bunnion" D.A. Beschen
44-14337 MC-R "Wildarcliff III"
44-14349 MC-H "Jeanie Marie" D. Andra
44-14365 MC-E "Danny Boy"
44-14365 MC-E "Corky" T.J. Daniel
44-14844 MC-D "Joyce" J.K. Taylor

P-51D-15-NA
44-15049 MC-A "Miss U Louise" M.G. Ingebrigsten
44-15198 MC-L "EK & Jay Bee" J.B. Lee
44-15341 MC-K "Brown Eyes" F.H. Jurgens
44-15484 MC-V
44-15752 MC-A "Miss U Louise" M.G. Ingebrigsten

P-51D-20-NA
44-72266 MC-J "Nina Merle III" D.N. Jones
44-72316 MC-S "Miss Martha"
44-72383 MC-Y "Janey Girl II From Texas" W.R. Yarbrough
44-72402 MC-M "Bobcat V" R.J. Meyer

Unknown Serials
P-51B MC-X "Bond Baby" HACK
P-51D MC-M "Almy Too" G.W. Merriman
P-51D MC-R "Black's Bird" R.H. Black
P-51D MC-C "Soar Lassie" W.A. Cameron
P-51D MC-D "Joyce II" J.K. Taylor
P-51D MC-D "Joyce III" J.K. Taylor
P-51D MC-J "Nina Merle II" D.N. Jones
P-51D MC-T "Sneebo" D.A. Sass
P-51D MC- "Coon Dog IV" Z. Wyman
P-51D MC- "Peggy Jo" C.G. Dixon
P-51D MC-A "Butch"
P-51D MC-B "Snuggle Bunny"
P-51D MC-B "Panty Waste"
P-51D MC- "Full Boost"
P-51D MC "Lola Ruth"

• • •

## THE 55TH FIGHTER GROUP
## 38TH, 338TH, 343RD FIGHTER SQUADRONS

The 55th Fighter Group was activated on January 15, 1941, at Hamilton Field, California. Training in the western United States, the group headed overseas on September 5, 1943, aboard the "Orion" The first of 360 missions came on October 15, 1943, with the final one coming on April 21, 1945. During the 55th's combat tour, pilots claimed 302.5 aerial and 266 ground victories while 185 P-38's and P-51's were lost on operations and 13 fliers died in accidents.

Stations for the group were Nuthampstead, from September 14, 1943, until April 16, 1944, and Wormingford, from April 16 until July of 1945. Aircraft flown were the P-38H and J, from September of 1943, until July of 1944, and the P-51C, D, and K, from July of 1944 onward. The 55th was awarded two Distinguished Unit Citations, the first for a series of missions flown between September 3 and 13, 1944, in which over 100 enemy planes were destroyed; and the second for a mission on February 19, 1945, in which over 80 locomotives were destroyed.

### Claims

| | Air | | | Grd | |
|---|---|---|---|---|---|
| | Destroyed | Probable | Damaged | Destroyed | Damaged |
| HdQts | 9 | 0 | 4 | 24 | 8 |
| 38th | 111 | 9 | 29 | 68 | 45 |
| 338th | 108 | 6 | 32 | 71 | 28 |
| 343rd | 74.5 | 5 | 18 | 103 | 68 |
| | 302.5 | 23 | 83 | 266 | 149 |

### Commanders

| | |
|---|---|
| Col. Frank B. James | May 15, 1943-February 3, 1944 |
| Col. Jack S. Jenkins | February 6, 1944-April 10, 1944 |
| Col. George T. Crowell | April 10, 1944-February 22, 1945 |
| LtCol. Elwyn G. Righetti | February 22, 1945-April 17, 1945 |
| Col. Ben Rimerman | April 22, 1945-May 20, 1945 |

### Wing and Command Assignments

| | |
|---|---|
| Assigned to VIII Fighter Command | September 16, 1943 |
| VIII Fighter Command, 66th Fighter Wing | October 5, 1943 |
| 3rd Bomb Division, 66th Fighter Wing | September 15, 1944 |
| 3rd Air Division, 66th Fighter Wing | January 1, 1945 |

### Aircraft Markings

Original P-38's were in olive drab/neutral gray schemes with NMF planes being received in early March of 1944. From December of 1943, squadron symbols were applied to the outer vertical tails; a triangle for the 38th, a circle for the 338th, and a square for the 343rd. These symbols were either white or black depending on the aircraft's finish.

All P-51's were in NMF with a few planes receiving a coat of dark green on the upper surfaces. The squadron symbols were used initially on the P-51's tails, but after only a few days, they were eliminated. As a group marking, the spinner was banded green-yellow-green with a 12 inch cowl band of green and yellow checkerboards. From October of 1944, rudder colors were used: none for the 38th, green for the 338th, and yellow for the 343rd. In March of 1945, the 38th began painting rudders red. Also, many P-51's had a 2 inch band in the squadron color framing the rear of the cowl band. The 343rd was unique in that many planes had dark green upper surfaces on the wings and tailplanes, plus green on the fuselage swept forward and up to the anti-glare panel. This was used for several months in late 1944-early 1945 before being discontinued. In addition, many 343rd planes carried the squadron's rearing stallion figure on the rudder.

Squadron codes were:

38th Ftr Sqn: CG
338th Ftr Sqn: CL
343rd Ftr Sqn: CY

### 55th Fighter Group Statistical Report

| Month | Air | Grd | Losses | KIAc |
|---|---|---|---|---|
| October 1943 | 0-0-0 | 0-0 | 1 | 0 |
| November | 23-11-18 | 0-0 | 14 | 0 |
| December | 4-0-1 | 0-0 | 7 | 1 |
| January 1944 | 13-4-6 | 0-0 | 13 | 1 |
| February | 8-1-7 | 0-0 | 5 | 0 |
| March | 3-2-4 | 0-0 | 8 | 0 |
| April | 7-0-3 | 1-0 | 11 | 0 |
| May | 7-0-1 | 6-5 | 9 | 2 |
| June | 15-1-5 | 0-0 | 16 | 1 |
| July | 27-1-8 | 0-0 | 8 | 1 |
| August | 7-0-0 | 6-0 | 17 | 1 |
| September | 72-2-12 | 31-34 | 12 | 0 |
| October | 2-0-0 | 0-0 | 5 | 1 |
| November | 18.5-0-2 | 5-8 | 10 | 0 |
| December | 26-0-5 | 0-1 | 6 | 1 |
| January 1945 | 14-0-4 | 24-4 | 6 | 0 |
| February | 25-1-0 | 23-9 | 11 | 1 |
| March | 11-0-4 | 12-25 | 12 | 1 |
| April | 20-0-3 | 158-63 | 12 | 0 |
| May | 0-0-0 | 0-0 | 0 | 0 |
| | 302.5-23-83 | 266-149 | 186 | 13 |

### Losses by Squadron

| | MIA | | KIAc | |
|---|---|---|---|---|
| | P-38 | P-51 | P-38 | P-51 |
| HdQts | 2 | 1 | 0 | 0 |
| 38th | 29 | 30 | 3 | 0 |
| 338th | 32 | 33 | 0 | 6 |
| 343rd | 24 | 34 | 2 | 2 |
| | 87 | 98 | 5 | 8 |

### Claims by Type

| | Air | | | Grd | |
|---|---|---|---|---|---|
| | Destroyed | Probable | Damaged | Destroyed | Damaged |
| P-38 | 102 | 19 | 49 | 6 | 6 |
| P-51 | 200.5 | 4 | 34 | 260 | 143 |

### Claims by Enemy Aircraft Type

| | Air | | | Grd | |
|---|---|---|---|---|---|
| | Destroyed | Probable | Damaged | Destroyed | Damaged |
| Me-109 | 146.5 | 16 | 48 | 34 | 31 |
| FW-190 | 85 | 2 | 19 | 52 | 29 |
| Me-262 | 16 | 0 | 7 | 17 | 3 |
| Trainer | 15 | 0 | 0 | 0 | 0 |
| Ju-88 | 11 | 2 | 1 | 40 | 14 |
| Me-410 | 7 | 1 | 3 | 21 | 11 |

| | | | | | |
|---|---|---|---|---|---|
| Me-210 | 4 | 1 | 2 | 2 | 4 |
| Ar-196 | 4 | 0 | 0 | 0 | 0 |
| Me-110 | 2 | 0 | 2 | 5 | 5 |
| He-111 | 2 | 0 | 0 | 34 | 12 |
| Hs-129 | 2 | 0 | 0 | 1 | 0 |
| FW-58 | 2 | 0 | 0 | 0 | 0 |
| Do-217 | 1 | 1 | 1 | 6 | 1 |
| Fi-156 | 1 | 0 | 0 | 8 | 2 |
| Ju-188 | 1 | 0 | 0 | 0 | 0 |
| Hs-126 | 1 | 0 | 0 | 0 | 0 |
| Me-108 | 1 | 0 | 0 | 0 | 0 |
| DFS-230 | 1 | 0 | 0 | 0 | 0 |
| u/i a/c | 0 | 0 | 0 | 27 | 19 |
| Ju-52 | 0 | 0 | 0 | 6 | 4 |
| He-280 | 0 | 0 | 0 | 3 | 0 |
| FW-200 | 0 | 0 | 0 | 3 | 0 |
| He-177 | 0 | 0 | 0 | 2 | 3 |
| Si-204 | 0 | 0 | 0 | 1 | 5 |
| Ju-87 | 0 | 0 | 0 | 1 | 4 |
| BV-140 | 0 | 0 | 0 | 1 | 1 |
| FW-189 | 0 | 0 | 0 | 1 | 0 |
| Ar-234 | 0 | 0 | 0 | 1 | 0 |
| Glider | 0 | 0 | 0 | 0 | 1 |

### 55th Fighter Group Aces

| Name | Air | Grd | Total | Sqn |
|---|---|---|---|---|
| LtCol. John D. Landers | 14.5 | 20 | 34.5[*] | 38th |
| LtCol. Elwyn G. Righetti | 7.5 | 27.5 | 34.5 | 338th HdQts |
| Capt. Robert E. Welch | 6 | 12 | 18 | 343rd |
| Maj. Darrell S. Cramer | 7 | 2 | 9[**] | 338th |
| Lt. John W. Cunnick, III | 2 | 7 | 9 | 38th |
| Capt. Samuel D. Gevorkian | 2 | 7 | 9 | 338th |
| Maj. Edward B. Giller | 3 | 6 | 9 | 343rd |
| Lt. Bernard H. Howes | 6 | 2 | 8 | 343rd |
| Lt. Keith R. McGinnis | 2 | 6 | 8 | 38th |
| LtCol. Joseph Myers, Jr. | 4.5 | 3 | 7.5[***] | 38th HdQts |
| Lt. Dudley M. Amoss | 5.5 | 1.5 | 7 | 38th |
| Lt. Lloyd D. Boring | 0.5 | 6.5 | 7 | 343rd |
| Capt. William H. Lewis | 7 | 0 | 7 | 343rd |
| Lt. Howard Mahany, Jr. | 0 | 7 | 7 | 343rd |
| Capt. Donald M. Cummings | 6.5 | 0 | 6.5[@] | 38th |
| Capt. Carroll D. Henry | 1.5 | 5 | 6.5 | 338th |
| Lt. Clifford C. Gould | 1 | 5 | 6 | 38th |
| Capt. Robert L. Buttke | 5.5 | 0 | 5.5 | 343rd |
| Capt. Albert J. Ramm | 0.5 | 5 | 5.5 | 338th |
| Lt. William H. Allen | 5 | 0 | 5 | 343rd |
| Lt. Donald J. Best | 0 | 5 | 5 | 38th |
| Capt. Frank E. Birtciel | 0 | 5 | 5 | 343rd |
| Lt. Hugh Bodiford | 2 | 3 | 5 | 338th |
| Maj. Gerald Brown | 5 | 0 | 5 | 38th |
| Capt. Merle M. Coons | 5 | 0 | 5 | 38th |
| Capt. Earl R. Fryer | 4 | 1 | 5 | 38th |
| Lt. Richard G. Gibbs | 4 | 1 | 5 | 343rd |
| Lt. Russell C. Haworth | 5 | 0 | 5 | 338th |
| Lt. Leedom K. John | 0 | 5 | 5 | 338th |
| Lt. John T. Maloney | 0 | 5 | 5 | 38th |
| LtCol. John L. McGinn | 5 | 0 | 5[@@] | 338th |
| Lt. Thomas D. Schank | 5 | 0 | 5 | 338th |
| Col. Ben Rimerman | 4.5 | 8 | 12.5[@@@] | HdQts |

[*] - includes 6 air victories with the 49th Ftr Grp, PTO, and 4.5 air and 16 ground victories with the 78th and 357th Ftr Grps, ETO
[**] - includes 0.5 air victories with the 347th Ftr Grp, PTO
[***] - includes 1.5 air and 3 ground victories with the 78th Ftr Grp, ETO
[@] - includes 1 air victory with the 27th Ftr Grp, MTO
[@@] - includes 3 air victories with the 347th Ftr Grp, PTO
[@@@] - all victories with the 353rd Ftr Grp, ETO

### 55th Fighter Group Scorers

**HdQts**

| | Air | Grd | |
|---|---|---|---|
| T.E. Beaird | 1-1-1 | 0-0 | |
| M. Clark | 1-0-0 | 0-0 | plus 38th Ftr Sqn |
| P.E. Hoeper | 0-0-0 | 1-0 | plus 343rd Ftr Sqn |
| F.B. James | 1-0-0 | 0-0 | |
| J.S. Jenkins | 2-1-1 | 0-0 | |
| W.J. Kelly | 1-0-0 | 0-0 | |
| E.G. Righetti | 3-1-0 | 23-8 | plus 338th Ftr Sqn |
| M.K. Shipman | 0-0-1 | 0-0 | plus 1 air w/14th Ftr Grp & 38th Ftr Sqn |
| D.W. Webb | 0-0-1 | 0-0 | plus 343rd Ftr Sqn |

**38th Ftr Sqn**

| | | | |
|---|---|---|---|
| W.T. Achramowicz | 0-0-0 | 0-1 | |
| D.M. Amoss | 5.5-0-0 | 1.5-0 | |
| J.E. Anderson | 0-0-0 | 1-0 | |
| M.O. Anderson | 2-0-0 | 2.5-1 | |
| J.H. Ayers | 1-1-0 | 0-0 | |
| D.D. Bachman | 0-0-1 | 1-1 | |
| D.J. Best | 0-0-0 | 5-1 | |
| W.K. Birch | 0-1-0 | 0-0 | |
| C.E. Breathwit | 1-0-0 | 0-0 | |
| G. Brown | 5-0-1 | 0-0 | |
| R.E. Callaghan | 1-0-0 | 0-1 | |
| A.E. Carr | 0-0-0 | 1.5-1 | |
| D.L. Castle | 1-0-1 | 0-0 | |
| D.A. Cavanaugh | 0.5-0-0 | 0-0 | |
| M. Clark | 3.5-0-1 | 0-3 | plus HdQts |
| B. Clemmons | 3.5-0-1 | 0.5-1 | |
| O.B. Clifton | 0-0-0 | 1-0 | |
| J.F. Coonan | 2.5-0-0 | 0-0 | plus 1 air w/51st Ftr Grp, CBI |
| M.F. Coons | 5-1-0 | 0-0 | |
| D.H. Courtney | 1.5-0-0 | 0-1 | |
| K.I. Crawford | 1-0-0 | 1-0 | |
| D.M. Cummings | 5.5-0-0 | 0-0 | plus 1 air w/27th Ftr Grp, MTO |
| J.W. Cunnick, III | 2-0-0 | 7-4 | |
| C.W. Des Voignes | 1.5-0.5-0 | 0-0 | |
| R.E. Erickson | 0-0-2 | 0-0 | |
| L.J. Fleming | 0-0-0 | 1-0 | |
| R.W. Forsblad | 1-0-1 | 0-0 | |
| E.R. Fryer | 4-0-0 | 1-0 | |
| C.C. Gould | 1-0-0 | 5-2 | |
| J.H. Hancock | 2-1-0 | 0-0 | |
| L.V. Hokinson, Jr. | 2-0-0 | 0-0 | |
| E.M. Holderman | 3-0-1 | 0-2 | |
| T.H. Holleman | 2-0-0 | 0-0 | |
| D.G. Jackson | 1-0-0 | 0-0 | |
| D.F. Jewell, Jr. | 1.5-0-0 | 0.5-0 | |
| M. Joel | 2.5-2-3 | 0-0 | |
| R. Jones | 1-0-0 | 0-0 | |
| J.W. Kavanaugh | 2.5-0-0 | 2-1 | |
| A.M. Koenig | 0-0-0 | 0-1 | |
| W.L. Kreft | 0.5-0-0 | 0-0 | |
| J.D. Landers | 4-0-1 | 4-1 | plus 6 air w/49th Ftr Grp, PTO, & 4.5-0-0 air & 16-0 grd w/78th & 357th Ftr Grps |
| R.L. Lapham | 1-0-0 | 0-0 | |
| N.L. Larson | 1-0-0 | 0-0 | |
| G.F. Leinweber | 1-0-0 | 0-0 | |
| T.B. Luckett | 0-0-0 | 1-0 | |
| J.T. Maloney | 0-0-0 | 5-3 | |
| R.F. Maloney | 2.5-1-1 | 2-0 | |
| F.M. Matney | 3.5-0-0 | 1-0 | |
| K.R. McGinnis | 2-0-0 | 6-1 | |
| D.T. Menegay | 1.5-0-0 | 1-0 | |
| J.E. Mirando | 0-0-0 | 2-2 | |
| H.B. Mooers | 0.5-0-1 | 0-0 | |
| R.B. Mooers | 1-0-0 | 0-0 | |
| J. Myers | 3-0-2 | 0-0 | plus 1.5-0-0 air & 3-1 grd w/78th Ftr Grp |
| J.F. O'Neil | 1-0-1 | 2-0 | |
| A.B. Parsons | 0-0-0 | 1.5-2 | |
| D.E. Penn | 2-0-3 | 1-0 | |
| C.L. Peterson | 0-0-0 | 0-1.5 | |
| R.F. Quinn | 0-0-0 | 0-1 | |
| W.J. Reilly | 2-0-0 | 0.5-0 | |
| H.W. Rhodes | 1-0-0 | 0-0 | |
| C.R. Schendel | 0-0-0 | 0-2 | |
| C.C. Sherman | 4.5-0-0 | 0-0 | |
| M.K. Shipman | 1.5-1.5-1 | 0-0 | plus HdQts |
| J.W. Silk | 1-0-0 | 0-0.5 | |
| D.H. Snell | 1-0-0 | 0-0 | |
| V.H. Soule | 0-0-0 | 0-2 | |
| L.F. Spiecker | 1.5-0-0 | 0-0 | |
| W.B. Staggs | 0.5-0-0 | 2-0 | |
| D.L. Steiner | 2-0-1 | 0-0 | |
| R.S. Thompson | 0-0-1 | 0-0 | |
| A.L. Thorsen | 1-0-1 | 0-0 | |
| R.P. Tibor | 1-0-0 | 0-0 | |
| N.R. Tipton | 1-0-1 | 1-0 | |
| W.V. Totten | 0-0-1 | 3.5-1 | |
| F.J. Waice | 0-0-0 | 0-2 | |
| C.R. Watts | 1-0-1 | 1-0 | |
| G.V. Wegner | 0-0-0 | 0-1 | |
| C.T. Williams | 0-0-0 | 2-4 | |
| W. Wyche | 0-0-1 | 0-0 | |

**338th Ftr Sqn**

| | | |
|---|---|---|
| M. Alba | 2-0-1 | 1-0 |
| L.D. Anderson | 3-0-0 | 0-0 |
| W.H. Barnes | 0-0-0 | 1-2 |
| R.I. Barrett | 1-0-0 | 1-0 |
| C.E. Beall | 1-0-0 | 0-0 |
| L.J. Berry | 1-0-0 | 0-0 |

| | | | |
|---|---|---|---|
| C.A. Biedul | 1-0-0 | 0-0 | |
| M.E. Blanchard | 2-0-2 | 0-0 | |
| D.F. Blount | 2-0-1 | 0-0 | |
| H. Bodiford | 2-0-0 | 3-2 | |
| V.W. Bollwerk | 2-1-3 | 1-0 | |
| J.E. Brady | 0-0-0 | 1-0 | |
| F.D. Bradford | 1-0-1 | 0-0 | |
| P. Brooks | 0-0-0 | 2.5-2 | |
| W.H. Burns | 0.5-1-0 | 0-0 | |
| C.E. Buskirk | 1-0-0 | 1-0.5 | |
| C.S. Chioles | 0-0-1 | 0-0 | |
| A.F. Conners | 0-0-0 | 1-0 | |
| R.E. Cooper | 1-0-0 | 1-0 | |
| D.S. Cramer | 6.5-0-1 | 2-2 | plus 0.5 air w/347th Ftr Grp, PTO |
| A.S. Dargan, Jr. | 2-0-0 | 1-1 | |
| R.E. Darling | 0-0-0 | 3-2 | |
| R. Deloach | 1-0-0 | 1-1 | |
| P. Dempsey | 1-0-0 | 2-3 | |
| E.H. Duquette | 0.5-0-0 | 0-0 | |
| W.H. Earnest | 1-0-0 | 0-0 | |
| J.R. Ethridge | 0-0-0 | 0.5-0 | |
| J.R. Eskridge | 1-0-0 | 0-0 | |
| R.K. Fruh | 3-2-0 | 0-0 | |
| G.E. Funk, Jr. | 0.5-0-1 | 0-0 | |
| K.H. Garlock | 0-0-1 | 0-0 | |
| J.K. Garrett | 3-0-0 | 0-0 | |
| W.P. Gebhardt | 1-0-0 | 0-0 | |
| J.L. Gerry | 2-0-0 | 0-1 | |
| S.D. Gevorkian | 2-0-0 | 6-3 | |
| K.M. Glasser | 1-0-0 | 0-0 | |
| O.E. Goodman | 2.5-0-0 | 0-0 | |
| E.S. Gregg | 0.5-0-0 | 0-0 | |
| D.R. Haily | 1-0-1 | 0-0 | |
| S.E. Hansard | 1-0-0 | 1-0 | |
| R.C. Haworth | 5-0-1 | 0-0 | |
| C.D. Henry | 1.5-0-0 | 5-2 | |
| R.C. Herbst | 0-0-0 | 2-0.5 | |
| W.J. Ingram | 3.5-0-1 | 0-0 | |
| L.K. John | 0-0-0 | 5-0 | |
| C.O. Jones | 1-0-1 | 0-0 | |
| J.E. Kester | 1-0-0 | 0-0 | |
| T. Kiernan, Jr. | 3-0-0 | 0-0 | |
| W.J. Konantz | 3-0-0 | 1-0 | |
| G. Korinek | 1-0-1 | 0-0 | |
| W.J. Lanham | 1-0-0 | 0-0 | |
| H.E. Larsen | 2-0-0 | 0-0 | |
| K.A. Lashbrook | 3-0-0 | 0-0 | |
| W.J. Leonard | 1-0-1 | 0-0 | |
| J.P. Marsiglia | 0-1-1 | 0-0 | |
| J.R. McDonald | 1-0-0 | 1-0 | |
| B. McDowell | 0-0-1 | 2-0 | |
| J.L. McGinn | 2-0-2 | 0-0 | plus 3 air w/347th Ftr Grp, PTO |
| J.E. McKee | 1-1-0 | 0-0 | |
| D.J. Meade | 0-0-0 | 2-0 | |
| R.D. Miller | 2-0-0 | 2-1 | |
| J.L. Odegard | 0-0-1 | 0-0 | |
| T.A. Parker | 2-0-1 | 0-0 | |
| C.A. Patterson | 4-0-0 | 0-0 | |
| A.J. Ramm | 0.5-0-0 | 5-0 | |
| S.P. Richardson | 1-0-0 | 0-0 | |
| E.G. Righetti | 4.5-0-2 | 4-0 | plus HdQts |
| E.E. Ryan | 1-0-0 | 1.5-0 | plus 343rd Ftr Sqn |
| T.D. Schank | 5-0-3 | 0-0 | |
| K.C. Schneider | 0-0-0 | 0-1 | |
| H.J. Schonenberg | 2-0-0 | 0-0 | |
| F.R. Sharp | 0-0-0 | 1.5-0 | |
| H.B. Sims | 0-0-0 | 0.5-1 | |
| J.J. Sullivan | 0-0-0 | 1-0 | |
| V.B. Tally | 0-0-0 | 2-0 | |
| A.J. Tinto | 2-0-0 | 0-0 | |
| J.M. Wakeland | 3-0-2 | 0-0 | |
| J.C. White | 0-0-0 | 2-0 | |
| M.J. Wiens | 0-0-0 | 1-2 | |
| J.H. Wiley | 0-0-1 | 1-0 | |
| A.E. Wright | 0-0-0 | 1-1 | |

**343rd Ftr Sqn**

| | | | |
|---|---|---|---|
| R.K. Abel | 0-0-0 | 1-0 | |
| D.E. Adams | 0-0-0 | 2-2 | |
| R.G. Allen | 0-0-0 | 1.5-0 | |
| W.H. Allen | 5-0-0 | 0-0 | |
| G.A. Apple | 0-0-0 | 4-1 | |
| G.E. Arnold | 0-0-0 | 4-1 | |
| R.D. Bartlett | 0.5-0-0 | 3-1.5 | |
| H.M. Bauer | 1-0-0 | 0-0 | |
| N.P. Bebaeff | 1-0-0 | 0-0 | |
| G.W. Bernardo | 0-0-0 | 4-2 | |
| J.H. Bevington | 0-0-0 | 1-0 | |
| F.E. Birtciel | 0-0-1 | 5-1 | |
| R.D. Bishop | 1-0-1 | 1-0 | |
| F.A. Blair | 0-0-0 | 2-1.5 | |
| L.D. Boring | 0.5-0-0 | 6.5-1 | |
| R.D. Brown | 1-0-0 | 2-0 | |
| R.L. Buttke | 5.5-0-2 | 0-0 | |
| C.E. Coggeshall | 0-0-0 | 1-0 | |
| H. Cohen | 0-0-0 | 1-2 | |
| G.H. Cole | 1-0-0 | 1-0 | |
| A.A. DeYoung | 0-0-1 | 0-0 | |
| P.S. Dripps | 0-0-1 | 1-2 | |
| E.J. Dvorak | 0.5-0-0 | 0-0 | |
| J. Eliades | 0.5-0-0 | 0-0 | |
| R.W. Erb, Jr. | 1-0-0 | 0-0 | |
| P.A. Erby | 1-0-1 | 1-0 | |
| W.R. Erickson | 0-0-0 | 1-2 | |
| G.R. Fair | 1-0-0 | 0-0 | |
| W.A. Fisher | 0-0-0 | 4-0 | |
| D.M. Fry | 0-0-0 | 1-1 | |
| E.H. Geary | 0-0-0 | 2-2 | |
| R.G. Gibbs | 4-0-0 | 1-1 | |
| D.R. Gifford | 0-0-0 | 1-2 | |
| E.B. Giller | 3-0-0 | 6-2 | |
| V.P. Gordon | 0-0-0 | 4-5 | |
| J.W. Hiner | 1-0-0 | 0-0 | |
| R.P. Hjelm | 2-0-0 | 0-0 | |
| P.E. Hoeper | 1-0-0 | 0-0 | plus HdQts |
| T.E. Hoffman | 4-0-0 | 0-0 | |
| B.H. Howes | 6-0-0 | 2-4 | |
| M.R. King | 0-0-0 | 1-1 | |
| V.P. Krambo | 0-0-0 | 0-1 | |
| F.C. Lawrence, Jr. | 0-0-0 | 4-5 | |
| E.E. Leon | 0-0-0 | 1-1 | |
| F.J. Leone | 0-1-1 | 0-0 | |
| G.D. Leslie | 0.5-0-1 | 1-0 | |
| W.H. Lewis | 7-0-1 | 0-0 | |
| B.J. Liles | 1-0-0 | 2-6 | |
| H. Mahany, Jr. | 0-0-0 | 7-3 | |
| R.M. Malmstedt | 1-1-1 | 0-0 | |
| R.A. Maxwell | 1-0-0 | 0-0 | |
| J.C. McVay | 1-0-0 | 1-0 | |
| W. Mearns | 0-0-0 | 0-3 | |
| D.L. Mercier | 1.5-0-0 | 1-0 | |
| P.L. Moore | 2-0-0 | 1-0 | |
| G. Morris | 1-0-0 | 0-0 | |
| D.A. Parker | 1-0-0 | 2-2 | |
| W.R. Perez, Jr. | 1-0-0 | 0-0 | |
| W.K. Pope | 0-0-0 | 0-2 | |
| C.D. Porter | 2-0-1 | 0-0 | |
| P.R. Porter | 0-0-0 | 0-2 | |
| W.E. Rosenhoff | 0-0-0 | 1-2 | |
| E.E. Ryan | 2-2-4 | 0-0 | plus 338th Ftr Sqn |
| M. Satenstein | 0-0-0 | 0-4 | |
| R.S. Seely | 1-0-0 | 0-0 | |
| K.J. Sorace | 0-0-1 | 0-0 | |
| W. Strauch | 1-0-0 | 3-0 | |
| F.L. Tischer | 0-1-0 | 0-0 | |
| D.W. Webb | 2-0-0 | 0-0 | plus HdQts |
| R.E. Welch | 6-0-1 | 12-2 | |
| K.T. Williams | 0-0-0 | 2-0 | |
| R.H. Yee Litt | 1-0-0 | 0-0 | |

**55th Fighter Group Scoring**

**November 3, 1943**

| | | | |
|---|---|---|---|
| HdQts: | LtCol. J.S. Jenkins | Me-109 dest(air) | Spiekeroog Isle |
| | | FW-190 prob(air) | Wilhelmshaven |
| 38th: | Maj. M. Joel | (.5)FW-190 dest(air) | Westerholt-Wittmund |
| | | (2)FW-190 dam(air) | N/Wilhelmshaven |
| | Lt. W.L. Kreft | (.5)FW-190 dest(air) | Westerholt-Wittmund |
| | Capt. J. Myers | FW-190 dam(air) | N/Wilhelmshaven |
| 343rd: | Lt. R.L. Buttke | (2)Me-109 dest(air) | E/Wilhelmshaven |
| | Capt. R.M. Malmstedt | Me-109 dam(air) | Wilhelmshaven |
| | Lt. E.E. Ryan | Me-109 dam(air) | Wilhelmshaven |

**November 5, 1943**

| | | | |
|---|---|---|---|
| 38th: | Capt. M.K. Shipman | (1.5)Me-109 dest(air) | Doetinchem & (.5) Nijmegen |
| | | (.5)Me-109 prob(air) | Winterswijk |
| | Maj. M. Joel | Me-109 dest(air) | W/Arnheim |
| | Capt. J. Myers | Me-109 dest(air) | Arnheim |
| | Lt. G.F. Leinweber | Me-109 dest(air) | Rotterdam |
| | Lt. C.W. Des Voignes | (.5)Me-109 dest(air) | Nijmegen |
| | | (.5)Me-109 prob(air) | Winterswijk |
| | Lt. R.W. Forsblad | FW-190 dam(air) | E/Rotterdam |
| | Lt. D.L. Steiner | Do-217 dam(air) | Munster |

**November 13, 1943**

| | | | |
|---|---|---|---|
| HdQts: | Capt. T.E. Beaird | FW-190 dam(air) | W/Bremen |
| 38th: | Maj. M. Joel | Ju-88 dest(air) | Bremen |
| | | Ju-88 prob(air) | Bremen |

| | | | |
|---|---|---|---|
| | | Me-109 prob(air) | Bremen |
| | | Me-109 dam(air) | Bremen |
| | Capt. J. Myers | Me-109 dest(air) | Bremen |
| | | Ju-88 dam(air) | Bremen |
| | Lt. R.F. Maloney | FW-190 dest(air) | Bremen |
| | | FW-190 dam(air) | Bremen |
| | Lt. G. Brown | Me-109 dam(air) | Bremen |
| 338th: | Lt. C.E. Beall | FW-190 dest(air) | Bremen |
| | Capt. J.P. Marsiglia | Me-210 prob(air) | Hagen |
| | Lt. K.H. Garlock | Me-210 dam(air) | Hagen |
| 343rd: | Capt. E.E. Ryan | Me-109 dest(air) | W/Bremen |
| | | FW-190 prob(air) | W/Bremen |
| | Capt. E.B. Giller | Ju-88 dest(air) | W/Bremen |

**November 25, 1943**

| | | | |
|---|---|---|---|
| HdQts: | LtCol. J.S. Jenkins | FW-190 dest(air) | La Bassee |
| 38th: | Lt. R.F. Maloney | Me-109 dest(air) | Lille |
| | | Me-109 prob(air) | Hazebrouck |
| | Lt. D.L. Steiner | Me-109 dest(air) | Lille |
| | Lt. W.K. Birch | Me-109 prob(air) | NW Arras |
| 338th: | Capt. C.A. Patterson | FW-190 dest(air) | Lens |
| 343rd: | Capt. R.M. Malmstedt | Me-109 prob(air) | Lille |
| | Capt. E.E. Ryan | (2)Me-109 dam(air) | Lille |

**November 26, 1943**

| | | | |
|---|---|---|---|
| 38th: | Lt. R.E. Erickson | FW-190 dam(air) | W/Bremen |
| 343rd: | Maj. D.W. Webb | Me-210 dest(air) | NE Bremen |
| | Capt. R.M. Malmstedt | Ju-88 dest(air) | NE Bremen |

**November 29, 1943**

| | | | |
|---|---|---|---|
| HdQts: | Capt. T.E. Beaird | Me-109 prob(air) | W/Bremen |
| 38th: | Capt. J.H. Ayers | Me-109 dest(air) | W/Bremen |
| | Lt. R.E. Erickson | Me-109 dam(air) | W/Bremen |
| 338th: | Capt. C.A. Patterson | Me-109 dest(air) | N/Emmen |
| | Capt. J.P. Marsiglia | Me-109 dam(air) | E/Emmen |

**December 13, 1943**

| | | | |
|---|---|---|---|
| 338th: | Capt. C.O. Jones | Me-109 dam(air) | N/Oldenburg |
| 343rd: | Lt. J.W. Hiner | Ju-88 dest(air) | NW Hamburg |

**December 31, 1943**

| | | | |
|---|---|---|---|
| HdQts: | Col. F.B. James | FW-190 dest(air) | Niort |
| 38th: | Capt. J. Myers | Me-109 dest(air) | N/Blaye et St. Luce |
| 343rd: | Lt. H.M. Bauer | FW-190 dest(air) | Niort |

**January 5, 1944**

| | | | |
|---|---|---|---|
| 38th: | Capt. J.H. Hancock | FW-190 dest(air) | SW Kiel |
| | | Me-109 prob(air) | SW Kiel |
| | Lt. D.L. Steiner | FW-190 dest(air) | SW Kiel |
| | Maj. M.K. Shipman | Me-109 dam(air) | E/Meldorf |
| | Lt. R.S. Thompson | Me-109 dam(air) | SW Kiel |
| | Lt. W. Wyche | Me-109 dam(air) | SW Kiel |
| 338th: | Maj. C.O. Jones | Me-109 dest(air) | Neumunster |
| | F/O C.E. Buskirk | Me-109 dest(air) | Neumunster |
| | Lt. P. Dempsey | Me-109 dest(air) | Neumunster |

**January 7, 1944**

| | | | |
|---|---|---|---|
| 343rd: | Lt. K.J. Sorace | Me-109 dam(air) | Ludwigshafen |

**January 11, 1944**

| | | | |
|---|---|---|---|
| HdQts: | LtCol. J.S. Jenkins | Me-210 dam(air) | Dummer Lake |

**January 29, 1944**

| | | | |
|---|---|---|---|
| 338th: | Lt. H.E. Larsen | FW-190 dest(air) | Frankfurt |

**January 31, 1944**

| | | | |
|---|---|---|---|
| 38th: | Lt. L.V. Hokinson | (2)FW-190 dest(air) | Eindhoven |
| | Lt. G. Brown | Me-109 dest(air) | Venlo |
| | Maj. M.K. Shipman | Me-109 prob(air) | N/Venlo |
| 338th: | Capt. C.A. Patterson | (2)Me-109 dest(air) | Goch & Kessel |
| | Lt. M.E. Blanchard | Me-109 dest(air) | Goch |
| | Capt. V.W. Bollwerk | Me-109 prob(air) | Geldern |
| | Lt. W.H. Burns | Me-109 prob(air) | N/Venlo |
| | Lt. G. Korinek | Me-109 dam(air) | N/Venlo |
| 343rd: | Maj. D.W. Webb | Me-109 dest(air) | NW Venlo |

**February 5, 1944**

| | | | |
|---|---|---|---|
| HdQts: | Capt. T.E. Beaird | Me-109 dest(air) | Chartres |
| 38th: | Lt. C.R. Watts | Me-109 dam(air) | Chartres |

**February 10, 1944**

| | | | |
|---|---|---|---|
| 338th: | Capt. V.W. Bollwerk | Me-110 dest(air) | Brunswick |
| | Lt. R.K. Fruh | Me-110 dest(air) | Brunswick |
| | Lt. J.L. Odegard | Me-110 dam(air) | Brunswick |
| 343rd: | Capt. R.L. Buttke | (2)Me-210 dest(air) | NW Brunswick |
| | | Me-110 dam(air) | NW Brunswick |
| | Capt. P.E. Hoeper | Me-210 dest(air) | Brunswick |

**February 21, 1944**

| | | | |
|---|---|---|---|
| 343rd: | Lt. P.S. Dripps | Me-109 dam(air) | Ruhr Valley |

**February 24, 1944**

| | | | |
|---|---|---|---|
| 338th: | Lt. A.J. Tinto | Me-109 dest(air) | W/Gotha |
| 343rd: | Capt. E.E. Ryan | FW-190 dam(air) | E/Gotha |

**February 25, 1944**

| | | | |
|---|---|---|---|
| HdQts: | Maj. M.K. Shipman | Me-410 dam(air) | Augsburg |
| 38th: | Lt. N.R. Tipton | Me-410 dam(air) | Augsburg |
| 343rd: | Capt. E.B. Giller | Me-410 dest(air) | SE Augsburg |
| | Capt. E.E. Ryan | Me-410 prob(air) | Augsburg |

**March 18, 1944**

| | | | |
|---|---|---|---|
| 38th: | Lt. G. Brown | FW-190 dest(air) | Nancy |
| 338th: | Lt. R.K. Fruh | Me-109 dest(air) | E/French Border |
| | | (2)Me-109 prob(air) | E/French Border |
| | Lt. G. Korinek | Me-109 dest(air) | E/Frieburg |
| | Capt. V.W. Bollwerk | (3)Me-109 dam(air) | SE Strasbourg |
| 343rd: | Lt. F.J. Leone | FW-190 dam(air) | SE Strasbourg |

**April 8, 1944**

| | | | |
|---|---|---|---|
| 38th: | Capt. G. Brown | Me-109 dest(air) | Lingen |

**April 13, 1944**

| | | | |
|---|---|---|---|
| HdQts: | Maj. D.W. Webb | Me-109 dam(air) | Donauworth |

**April 15, 1944**

| | | | |
|---|---|---|---|
| 38th: | Capt. G. Brown | FW-190 dest(air) | Munster |
| | | He-111 dest(air) | Munster |
| | Lt. D.E. Penn | Ju-88 dest(grd) | Osnabruck |

**April 22, 1944**

| | | | |
|---|---|---|---|
| 343rd: | Capt. R.L. Buttke | Me-109 dest(air) | W/Hamm |
| | | Me-109 dam(air) | W/Hamm |
| | Capt. E.E. Ryan | FW-190 dest(air) | W/Hamm |
| | Lt. G.R. Fair | Me-109 dest(air) | W/Hamm |

**April 24, 1944**

| | | | |
|---|---|---|---|
| 343rd: | Lt. C.D. Porter | Me-109 dest(air) | NW Lake Constance |
| | Lt. A.A. DeYoung | Me-109 dam(air) | NW Lake Constance |

**May 12, 1944**

| | | | |
|---|---|---|---|
| 38th: | Lt. N.R. Tipton | FW-190 dest(air) | Wiesbaden |

**May 20, 1944**

| | | | |
|---|---|---|---|
| 38th: | Lt. A.L. Thorsen | FW-190 dam(air) | Troyes |
| 338th: | Lt. J.K. Garnett | FW-190 dest(air) | Sens |
| | Lt. H.E. Larsen | FW-190 dest(air) | Sens |

**May 21, 1944**

| | | | |
|---|---|---|---|
| 38th: | Lt. D.E. Penn | Hs-129 dest(air) | Brunswick |
| | Capt. J.D. Landers | (.5)u/i a/c dest(grd) | E/Helmstedt |
| | | (.5)u/i a/c dest(grd) | E/Helmstedt |
| | Lt. N.R. Tipton | (.5)u/i a/c dest(grd) | E/Helmstedt |
| | | (.5)u/i a/c dest(grd) | E/Helmstedt |
| | Lt. V.H. Soule | (2)u/i a/c dam(grd) | E/Helmstedt |
| 338th: | Lt. P. Dempsey | (2)Me-109 dest(grd) | Helmstedt |
| | | (3)FW-190 dam(grd) | Helmstedt |
| | Maj. V.W. Bollwerk | Hs-129 dest(grd) | Helmstedt |
| | Lt. S.E. Hansard | Ju-88 dest(grd) | Magdeburg |

**May 22, 1944**

| | | | |
|---|---|---|---|
| 38th: | Maj. J.H. Hancock | FW-190 dest(air) | SW Kiel |
| | Lt. C.W. Des Voignes | FW-190 dest(air) | SW Neumunster |
| 338th: | Lt. M.E. Blanchard | FW-190 dest(air) | Neumunster |

**June 11, 1944**

| | | | |
|---|---|---|---|
| 338th: | Maj. V.W. Bollwerk | Me-109 dest(air) | Beauvais |
| | Lt. S.P. Richardson | Me-109 dest(air) | Beauvais |
| | Lt. T.D. Schank | Me-109 dest(air) | Beauvais |
| | Lt. A.J. Tinto | Me-109 dest(air) | Beauvais |
| | Capt. M.E. Blanchard | Me-109 dam(air) | Beauvais |
| 343rd: | Lt. R.P. Hjelm | (2)FW-190 dest(air) | Clermont |
| | Lt. C.D. Porter | FW-190 dest(air) | Clermont |
| | | Me-109 dam(air) | Clermont |
| | Lt. R.S. Seely | Me-109 dest(air) | W/Beauvais |
| | Lt. F.J. Leone | Me-109 prob(air) | Clermont |

**June 14, 1944**

| | | | |
|---|---|---|---|
| 38th: | Lt. D.H. Snell | FW-190 dest(air) | Paris |
| | Lt. C.R. Watts | Me-109 dest(air) | Paris |
| | Capt. D.E. Penn | Me-109 dam(air) | S/Paris |
| 338th: | Lt. L.J. Berry | Me-109 dest(air) | Paris |
| | Lt. T.A. Parker | Me-109 dam(air) | Paris |

**June 25, 1944**

| | | | |
|---|---|---|---|
| 38th: | Maj. J.D. Landers | FW-190 dest(air) | SW Paris |
| | | Me-109 dam(air) | SW Paris |
| | Lt. W.J. Reilly | FW-190 dest(air) | SW Paris |
| | Lt. H.W. Rhodes | Me-109 dest(air) | SW Paris |
| | Lt. R.P. Tibor | Me-109 dest(air) | SW Paris |

**July 6, 1944**

| | | | |
|---|---|---|---|
| 338th: | Capt. O.E. Goodman | Me-109 dest(air) | Laon |
| | Lt. J.K. Garnett | Me-109 dest(air) | Laon |
| | Lt. K.M. Glaser | Me-109 dest(air) | Laon |
| | Capt. M.E. Blanchard | Me-109 dam(air) | Laon |

**July 7, 1944**

| | | | |
|---|---|---|---|
| 38th: | Maj. J.D. Landers | (3)Me-410 dest(air) | Bernburg |
| | Lt. E.M. Holderman | (2)Me-410 dest(air) | Bernburg |
| | | Me-410 dam(air) | Bernburg |
| | Lt. R.E. Callaghan | Me-410 dest(air) | Bernburg |
| | Lt. W.J. Reilly | FW-190 dest(air) | Bernburg |
| 338th: | Capt. L.D. Anderson | (2)Me-109 dest(air) | Bernburg |
| | Lt. T.A. Parker | Me-109 dest(air) | SW Magdeburg |
| | | FW-190 dest(air) | SW Magdeburg |
| | Capt. O.E. Goodman | FW-190 dest(air) | W/Bernburg |
| | | (.5)Me-109 dest(air) | W/Bernburg |
| | Lt. G.E. Funk | (.5)Me-109 dest(air) | W/Bernburg |
| | Lt. C.A. Biedul | FW-190 dest(air) | W/Bernburg |
| | Lt. W.H. Earnest | FW-190 dest(air) | W/Bernburg |
| 338th: | Lt. J.K. Garnett | FW-190 dest(air) | W/Bernburg |
| | Lt. J.L. Gerry | FW-190 dest(air) | W/Bernburg |
| | Lt. D.R. Hailey | FW-190 dest(air) | W/Bernburg |
| | | Me-109 dam(air) | W/Bernburg |
| | Lt. J.E. McKee | FW-190 dest(air) | W/Bernburg |
| | | Me-109 prob(air) | W/Bernburg |
| | Lt. J.M. Wakeland | FW-190 dam(air) | W/Bernburg |

NOTE: From July 21 on, all claims are in P-51's

**July 21, 1944**

| | | | |
|---|---|---|---|
| 38th: | Capt. R.W. Forsblad | Me-109 dest(air) | Munich |
| 338th: | Lt. D.F. Blount | (2)Me-109 dest(air) | NE Kempton |
| | | Me-109 dam(air) | NE Kempton |

**July 25, 1944**

| | | | |
|---|---|---|---|
| 338th: | Lt. T.D. Schank | (2)Me-109 dest(air) | Dreux |
| | | (3)Me-109 dam(air) | Dreux |

**August 10, 1944**

| | | | |
|---|---|---|---|
| 338th: | Capt. L.D. Anderson | Me-109 dest(air) | Damville |
| | Lt. J.R. Eskridge | Me-109 dest(air) | Damville |
| | Lt. S.E. Hansard | Me-109 dest(air) | Damville |
| | Lt. W.J. Ingram | Me-109 dest(air) | Damville |

**August 24, 1944**

| | | | |
|---|---|---|---|
| 38th: | Maj. J.D. Landers | (2)Ju-88 dest(grd) | Burg A/F |
| | Lt. K.I. Crawford | Ju-88 dest(grd) | Burg A/F |
| | Lt. E.R. Fryer | Ju-88 dest(grd) | Burg A/F |
| | Lt. T.B. Luckett | Ju-88 dest(grd) | Burg A/F |
| | Lt. C.R. Watts | Ju-88 dest(grd) | Burg A/F |

**August 28, 1944**

| | | | |
|---|---|---|---|
| 338th: | Lt. W.J. Lanham | Do-217 dest(air) | Dromersheim |
| | Lt. R.C. Haworth | (.5)DFS-230 dest(air) | Dromersheim |
| | Lt. A.J. Ramm | (.5)DFS-230 dest(air) | Dromersheim |
| 343rd: | Lt. D.L. Mercier | He-111 dest(air) | SW Coblenz |

**September 3, 1944**

| | | | |
|---|---|---|---|
| HdQts: | LtCol. W.J. Kelley | FW-190 dest(air) | Antwerp |
| 38th: | Capt. M. Clark | FW-190 dest(air) | Antwerp |
| | Lt. B.C. Clemmons | FW-190 dest(air) | Antwerp |
| | | FW-190 dam(air) | Antwerp |
| | | Me-109 dam(grd) | Antwerp |
| | Lt. C.C. Sherman | FW-190 dest(air) | Antwerp |
| 338th: | Maj. J.L. McGinn | FW-190 dest(air) | Brussels |
| | Lt. D.S. Cramer | FW-190 dest(air) | Brussels |
| | Lt. H.J. Schonenberg | FW-190 dest(air) | Brussels |

**September 5, 1944**

| | | | |
|---|---|---|---|
| 38th: | Maj. J.D. Landers | Ju-88 dest(grd) | All 38th claims |
| | | u/i a/c dam(grd) | are at Stuttgart/ |
| | Maj. A.B. Parsons | He-111 dest(grd) | Boblingen |
| | Lt. R.F. Maloney | Ju-88 dest(grd) | |
| | Lt. F.M. Matney | FW-190 dest(grd) | |
| | Capt. M. Clark | Me-109 dam(grd) | |
| | | Ju-87 dam(grd) | |
| | Lt. D.H. Courtney | Ju-87 dam(grd) | |
| | Lt. A.M. Koenig | u/i a/c dam(grd) | |
| | Lt. F.J. Waice | FW-190 dam(grd) | |
| 343rd: | Lt. W.H. Allen | (5)Trainer dest(air) | N/Goppingen |
| | Lt. W.H. Lewis | (5)Trianer dest(air) | N/Goppingen |
| | Lt. T.E. Hoffman | (4)Trainer dest(air) | N/Goppingen |
| | Lt. W.R. Perez | Trainer dest(air) | N/Goppingen |
| | Lt. R.D. Bartlett | (2)He-111 dest(grd) | Unless noted, |
| | | Me-110 dest(grd) | all 343rd claims |
| | | Me-109 dam(grd) | are at Stuttgart/ |
| | | (.5)Glider dam(grd) | Echterdingen |
| | Lt. F.A. Blair | He-177 dest(grd) | |
| | | u/i a/c dam(grd) | |
| | | (.5)Ju-52 dam(grd) | |
| | Lt. P.S. Dripps | He-111 dest(grd) | |
| | | (2)He-111 dam(grd) | |
| | Lt. F. Lawrence | He-111 dest(grd) | |
| | Lt. G.D. Leslie | Ju-52 dest(grd) | |
| | Lt. W.E. Rosenhoff | He-111 dest(grd) | |
| | | He-111 dam(grd) | |
| | | Me-410 dam(grd) | |
| | Lt. M.R. King | Ju-87 dest(grd) | Goppingen |
| | | Me-110 dam(grd) | Goppingen |
| | Capt. D.A. Parker | (.5)Ju-52 dam(grd) | Stutt/Echter. |
| | | (.5)Glider dam(grd) | Stutt/Echter. |
| | Lt. P.R. Porter | (2)He-111 dam(grd) | Stutt/Echter. |
| | Lt. W.K. Pope | (2)He-177 dam(grd) | Goppingen |

**September 10, 1944**

| | | | |
|---|---|---|---|
| 38th: | Lt. O.B. Clifton | Ju-88 dest(grd) | Kitzingen |
| | Lt. R.F. Maloney | Ju-88 dest(grd) | Kitzingen |
| | Lt. G.V. Wegner | Ju-88 dam(grd) | Kitzingen |
| 343rd: | Lt. E.J. Dvorak | (.5)Hs-126 dest(air) | Schwabmunchen |
| | Lt. G.D. Leslie | (.5)Hs-126 dest(air) | Schwabmunchen |
| | Capt. D.A. Parker | He-111 dest(grd) | Illesheim |
| | | Ju-88 dest(grd) | Illesheim |
| | Lt. F.C. Lawrence | (2)Me-210 dest(grd) | Illesheim |
| | | (4)Me-210 dam(grd) | Illesheim |
| | Lt. K.T. Williams | He-111 dest(grd) | NE Augsburg |
| | | Ju-88 dest(grd) | NE Augsburg |
| | Capt. R.D. Brown | He-111 dest(grd) | NE Augsburg |
| | Lt. F.A. Blair | u/i a/c dest(grd) | Illesheim |
| | Lt. D.M. Fry | He-111 dest(grd) | NE Augsburg |
| | | He-111 dam(grd) | NE Augsburg |
| | Lt. G.H. Cole | Me-109 dest(grd) | S/Augsburg |
| | Lt. D.L. Mercier | Me-109 dest(grd) | NE Augsburg |

**September 11, 1944**

| | | | |
|---|---|---|---|
| 38th: | Lt. E.R. Fryer | (3)Me-109 dest(air) | S/Erfurt |
| | Lt. F.M. Matney | (2)Me-109 dest(air) | Erfurt |
| | Lt. M.M. Coons | Me-109 dest(air) | Erfurt |
| | | Me-109 prob(air) | Erfurt |
| | Lt. K.I. Crawford | Me-109 dest(air) | S/Erfurt |
| | Lt. T.H. Holleman | Me-109 dest(air) | E/Meiningen |
| | Lt. C.C. Sherman | Me-109 dest(air) | Erfurt |
| | Lt. A.L. Thorsen | Me-109 dest(air) | SE Erfurt |
| 338th: | Lt. W.J. Ingram | (2.5)Me-109 dest(air) | All 338th claims |
| | | Me-109 dam(air) | are S/Meiningen |
| | | (shared with an unknown pilot) | |
| | Lt. R.C. Haworth | (2)Me-109 dest(air) | |
| | | Me-109 dam(air) | |
| | Lt. J.M. Wakeland | (2)Me-109 dest(air) | |
| | | Me-109 dam(air) | |
| | Lt. D.S. Cramer | (1.5)Me-109 dest(air) | |
| | | (shared with an unknown pilot) | |
| | LtCol. J.L. McGinn | Me-109 dest(air) | |
| | | (2)Me-109 dam(air) | |
| | Lt. R.I. Barrett | Me-109 dest(air) | |
| | Lt. R.K. Fruh | Me-109 dest(air) | |
| | Lt. W.J. Konantz | Me-109 dest(air) | |
| | Lt. W.J. Leonard | Me-109 dest(air) | |
| | | Me-109 dam(air) | |
| 343rd: | Lt. R.D. Bishop | FW-190 dest(air) | Saalfeld |
| | | FW-190 dam(air) | Saalfeld |
| | | FW-190 dest(grd) | Saalfeld |
| | Lt. R.H. Yee Litt | FW-190 dest(air) | Sonneburg |
| | Lt. F.L. Tischer | Me-109 prob(air) | Sonneburg |

**September 12, 1944**

| | | | |
|---|---|---|---|
| 38th: | Lt. C.C. Sherman | (1.5)Me-109 dest(air)* | Frankfurt |
| | Lt. E.B. Lawrence | Me-109 dest(air) | Frankfurt |
| | Lt. J.W. Silk | Me-109 dest(air) | Frankfurt |
| | | (.5)He-177 dam(grd) | Herzogenaurach |
| | Capt. M. Clark | (.5)Me-109 dest(air)** | N/Frankfurt |
| | | Me-410 dam(grd) | All 38th ground |
| | F/O D.M. Amoss | u/i a/c dest(grd) | claims are at |
| | | (.5)Ju-52 dest(grd) | Herzogenaurach |
| | Maj. A.B. Parsons | (.5)u/i a/c dest(grd) | |
| | | Me-410 dam(grd) | |
| | | Ju-87 dam(grd) | |
| | Lt. W.J. Reilly | (.5)Ju-52 dest(grd) | |
| | Lt. D.F. Jewell | (.5)u/i a/c dest(grd) | |
| | Capt. E.M. Holderman | (2)Ju-88 dam(grd) | |
| | Lt. R.E. Callaghan | Ju-88 dam(grd) | |
| | Lt. F.J. Waice | Ju-88 dam(grd) | |
| | Capt. C.L. Peterson | (.5)He-177 dam(grd) | |
| 338th: | Capt. W.H. Burns | (.5)Me-109 dest(air)** | N/Frankfurt |
| | Lt. R.C. Haworth | (.5)Me-109 dest(air)* | Frankfurt |
| | Lt. M. Alba | He-111 dest(grd) | Giessen |

**September 13, 1944**

| | | | |
|---|---|---|---|
| 38th: | Capt. M. Calrk | Me-109 dest(air) | All 38th claims |
| | Capt. E.M. Holderman | Me-109 dest(air) | are at Erfurt |
| | Lt. D.L. Castle | Me-109 dest(air) | |
| | | Me-109 dam(air) | |

| | | | |
|---|---|---|---|
| | Lt. B. Clemmons | Me-109 dest(air) | |
| | Lt. J.F. Coonan | Me-109 dest(air) | |
| | Lt. M.M. Coons | Me-109 dest(air) | |
| | Lt. R.L. Lapham | Me-109 dest(air) | |
| 338th: | Lt. D.S. Cramer | (1.5)Me-109 dest(air) | All 338th claims |
| | Lt. M. Alba | Me-109 dest(air) | are Eisenach-Gotha |
| | Lt. R.D. Miller | Me-109 dest(air) | |
| | Lt. T.D. Schank | Me-109 dest(air) | |
| | Lt. J.M. Wakeland | Me-109 dest(air) | |
| | Capt. E.S. Gregg | (.5)Me-109 dest(air) | |
| 343rd: | Lt. G.H. Cole | Me-109 dest(air) | All 343rd claims |
| | Lt. W.H. Lewis | Me-109 dest(air) | are Eisenach-Gotha |
| | | Me-109 dam(air) | |
| | Lt. R.E. Welch | Me-109 dest(air) | |
| | | Me-109 dam(air) | |

**September 19, 1944**

| | | | |
|---|---|---|---|
| 338th: | Lt. W.P. Gebhardt | Me-109 dest(air) | S/Dusseldorf |
| | Lt. J.L. Gerry | Me-109 dest(air) | Cologne |
| | Lt. T.D. Schank | Me-109 dest(air) | Cologne |
| | Lt. G.E. Funk | Me-109 dam(air) | S/Dusseldorf |

**October 7, 1944**

| | | | |
|---|---|---|---|
| 38th: | Lt. C.C. Sherman | Me-109 dest(air) | Leipzig |
| 338th: | Lt. D.S. Cramer | Me-109 dest(air) | Leipzig |

**November 2, 1944**

| | | | |
|---|---|---|---|
| 38th: | Capt. M.M. Coons | FW-190 dest(air) | W/Merseburg |
| | Capt. E.R. Fryer | FW-190 dest(air) | Merseburg |
| | Lt. C.C. Gould | Me-109 dest(air) | S/Merseburg |
| | Lt. T.H. Holleman | FW-190 dest(air) | Merseburg |
| | Lt. N.L. Larson | Me-109 dest(air) | W/Merseburg |
| | Capt. J.F. Coonan | (.5)FW-190 dest(air) | W/Merseburg |
| | Lt. D.H. Courtney | (.5)FW-190 dest(air) | W/Merseburg |
| | Lt. D.F. Jewell | (.5)Me-109 dest(air) | W/Merseburg |
| | Lt. F.M. Matney | (.5)Me-109 dest(air) | W/Merseburg |
| 338th: | Lt. M. Alba | Me-109 dest(air) | Merseburg |
| | | Me-109 dam(air) | Merseburg |
| | Lt. S.D. Gevorkian | Me-109 dest(air) | NW Leipzig |
| | Lt. R.C. Haworth | Me-109 dest(air) | Merseburg |
| | Lt. J.E. Kester | FW-190 dest(air) | W/Leipzig |
| | LtCol. E.G. Righetti | (.5)Me-109 dest(air) | SW Leipzig |
| | Capt. D.S. Cramer | (.5)Me-109 dest(air) | SW Leipzig |
| 343rd: | Capt. R.D. Brown | Me-109 dest(air) | SE Leipzig |
| | Capt. D.A. Parker | Me-109 dest(air) | Weimar |
| | Lt. N.P. Bebaeff | Me-109 dest(air) | Naumberg |
| | Lt. R.W. Erb | Me-109 dest(air) | W/Merseburg |
| | Lt. R.E. Welch | Me-109 dest(air) | Naumberg |
| | Lt. R.D. Bartlett | (.5)Me-109 dest(air)* | SW Leipzig |
| | Lt. J. Eliades | (.5)Me-109 dest(air)* | SW Leipzig |
| | Lt. D.L. Mercier | (.5)Me-109 dest(air) | Erfurt-Weimar |
| | | (shared with a 359th Ftr Grp P-51) | |
| | Lt. G.D. Leslie | Me-109 dam(air) | Naumberg |

**November 26, 1944**

| | | | |
|---|---|---|---|
| 338th: | Capt. D.S. Cramer | (2)FW-190 dest(grd) | All claims are |
| | | Me-109 dam(grd) | at Vorden A/F |
| | Lt. R.I. Barrett | FW-190 dest(grd) | |
| | Lt. A.J. Ramm | FW-190 dest(grd) | |
| | Lt. M.J. Wiens | FW-190 dest(grd) | |
| | | (2)FW-190 dam(grd) | |
| | Lt. P. Brooks | FW-190 dam(grd) | |
| | Lt. C.D. Henry | FW-190 dam(grd) | |
| | Lt. J.L. Gerry | FW-190 dam(grd) | |
| | Lt. A.E. Wright | FW-190 dam(grd) | |
| | Capt. C.E. Buskirk | (.5)FW-190 dam(grd) | |
| | Lt. R.C. Herbst | (.5)FW-190 dam(grd) | |

**December 5, 1944**

| | | | |
|---|---|---|---|
| 38th: | Capt. M.M. Coons | Me-109 dest(air) | N/Berlin |
| | | FW-190 dest(air) | N/Berlin |
| | Capt. M. Clark | FW-190 dest(air) | NE Berlin |
| | Lt. D.F. Jewell | FW-190 dest(air) | NE Berlin |
| | Lt. J.W. Kavanaugh | FW-190 dest(air) | NE Berlin |
| | Lt. F.M. Matney | FW-190 dest(air) | NE Berlin |

**December 11, 1994**

| | | | |
|---|---|---|---|
| 343rd: | Capt. D.A. Parker | Me-410 dam(grd) | SE Kassel |

**December 24, 1944**

| | | | |
|---|---|---|---|
| 38th: | Lt. M.O. Anderson | Me-109 dest(air) | W/St. Vith |
| | Lt. C.E. Breathwit | Me-109 dest(air) | W/St. Vith |
| | Lt. D.G. Jackson | FW-190 dest(air) | Coblenz |
| | Lt. R.F. Maloney | (.5)FW-190 dest(air) | S/Coblenz |
| | Lt. W.B. Staggs | (.5)FW-190 dest(air) | S/Coblenz |
| | Capt. D.E. Penn | (2)Me-109 dam(air) | W/St. Vith |
| 338th: | LtCol. E.G. Righetti | (3)FW-190 dest(air) | SE Munster |
| | | (2)FW-190 dam(air) | SE Munster |
| | Lt. F.D. Bradford | FW-190 dest(air) | E/Frankfurt |
| | | FW-190 dam(air) | E/Frankfurt |
| | Lt. R.C. Haworth | Me-109 dest(air) | Vogelsburg |
| | Lt. J.R. McDonald | Me-109 dest(air) | S/Coblenz |
| | Lt. S.D. Gevorkian | (.5)Me-109 dest(air) | Friedburg |
| | | (.5)FW-190 dest(air) | Friedburg |
| | Lt. K.A. Lashbrook | (.5)Me-109 dest(air) | Friedburg |
| | | (.5)FW-190 dest(air) | Friedburg |
| 343rd: | Lt. J.C. McVay | FW-190 dest(air) | S/Frankfurt |
| | Lt. G. Morris | FW-190 dest(air) | S/Frankfurt |
| | Lt. R.E. Welch | Me-109 dest(air) | S/Duren |

**December 25, 1944**

| | | | |
|---|---|---|---|
| 343rd: | Lt. B.H. Howes | (2)Me-109 dest(air) | SW Frankfurt |
| | Lt. R.E. Welch | (2)Me-109 dest(air) | W/Coblenz |
| | Lt. R.A. Maxwell | Me-109 dest(air) | W/Coblenz |

**January 3, 1945**

| | | | |
|---|---|---|---|
| 38th: | Capt. J.F. Coonan | Ar-196 dest(air) | SE Ulm |
| | Lt. R. Jones | Ar-196 dest(air) | SE Ulm |
| | Lt. J.W. Kavanaugh | (1.5)Ar-196 dest(air) | SE Ulm |
| | Lt. D.H. Courtney | (.5)Ar-196 dest(air) | SE Ulm |

**January 6, 1945**

| | | | |
|---|---|---|---|
| 338th: | Lt. A.J. Ramm | (2)Ju-88 dest(grd) | All claims are |
| | | (2)u/i a/c dest(grd) | at Giebelstadt |
| | LtCol. E.G. Righetti | (3)Ju-88 dest(grd) | |
| | Lt. D.J. Meade | Ju-88 dest(grd) | |
| | | u/i a/c dest(grd) | |
| | Capt. C.E. Buskirk | Ju-88 dest(grd) | |
| | Capt. B. McDowell | Ju-88 dest(grd) | |
| | Lt. P. Brooks | Do-217 dest(grd) | |
| | Lt. W.J. Konantz | Ju-88 dest(grd) | |
| | Lt. R.D. Miller | Do-217 dest(grd) | |

**January 13, 1945**

| | | | |
|---|---|---|---|
| 338th: | LtCol. E.G. Righetti | Me-109 dest(air) | W/Wurzburg |
| | | Ju-88 dest(grd) | Giebelstadt |
| | Lt. C.D. Henry | Me-109 dest(air) | W/Giebelstadt |
| | Lt. W.J. Konantz | Me-262 dest(air) | Giebelstadt |
| | Lt. R.D. Miller | Me-262 dest(grd) | Giebelstadt |
| | | Ju-88 dam(grd) | Giebelstadt |
| | Lt. P. Brooks | (.5)Do-217 dest(grd) | Giebelstadt |
| | Lt. F.R. Sharp | (.5)Do-217 dest(grd) | Giebelstadt |

**January 14, 1945**

| | | | |
|---|---|---|---|
| 38th: | Capt. D.M. Cummings | Me-109 dest(air) | E/Wittenburg |
| | Capt. M. Clark | FW-190 dam(air) | NW Osnabruck |
| | Lt. H.B. Mooers | FW-190 dam(air) | NW Osnabruck |
| 338th: | Capt. D.S. Cramer | Me-262 dam(air) | Parchim A/F |
| | | Me-110 dam(grd) | SE Salzwedel |
| | Lt. J.R. McDonald | Me-262 dest(grd) | Parchim |
| | Lt. F.R. Sharp | Me-110 dest(grd) | SE Salzwedel |
| | Lt. H. Bodiford | Do-217 dam(grd) | SE SAlzwedel |
| 343rd: | Lt. B.J. Liles | FW-190 dest(air) | W/Salzwedel |

**January 15, 1945**

| | | | |
|---|---|---|---|
| 38th: | Lt. B. Clemmons | (.5)Ju-188 dest(air) | SW Stuttgart |
| | Lt. D.H. Courtney | (.5)Ju-188 dest(air) | SW Stuttgart |

**January 21, 1945**

| | | | |
|---|---|---|---|
| 38th: | Lt. M.O. Anderson | (.5)u/i a/c dest(grd)* | All claims are |
| | Lt. A.E. Carr | (.5)u/i a/c dest(grd)* | at Stuttgart/ |
| | Lt. B. Clemmons | (.5)u/i a/c dest(grd)** | Boblingen |
| | F/O W.V. Totten | (.5)u/i a/c dest(grd)** | |

**January 22, 1945**

| | | | |
|---|---|---|---|
| 38th: | F/O W.V. Totten | (2)Ju-88 dest(grd) | Hanover/Langenhagen |
| | Lt. A.E. Carr | Ju-88 dest(grd) | Hanover-Langenhagen |
| | | Ju-88 dam(grd) | same as above |

**January 29, 1945**

| | | | |
|---|---|---|---|
| 338th: | Maj. D.S. Cramer | Me-109 dest(air) | Ulzen |
| | Lt. T. Kiernan | Me-109 dest(air) | NE Oldenburg |
| | Lt. W.J. Konantz | Me-109 dest(air) | NE Oldenburg |
| | Lt. R.D. Miller | Me-109 dest(air) | NE Oldenburg |
| | Capt. B. McDowell | Me-109 dam(air) | Ulzen |

**February 3, 1945**

| | | | |
|---|---|---|---|
| HdQts: | LtCol. E.G. Righetti | (2)Ju-88 dest(air) | Boizenburg |
| | | FW-190 dest(air) | Boizenburg |
| | | Ju-88 prob(air) | Boizenburg |
| 38th: | Lt. D.M. Amoss | (1.5)FW-58 dest(air) | Templin A/F |
| | Lt. L.F. Spiecker | (.5)FW-58 dest(air) | Templin A/F |
| | Lt. K.R. McGinnis | (4)Fi-156 dest(grd) | Templin A/F |
| 343rd: | Lt. B.R. Howes | (2)FW-190 dest(air) | Boizenburg |
| | | Ju-88 dest(air) | Boizenburg |
| | Lt. R.G. Gibbs | FW-190 dest(air) | Boizenburg |
| | | Ju-88 dest(air) | Boizenburg |
| | Capt. W.H. Lewis | Ju-88 dest(air) | Gartow |
| | Lt. P.L. Moore | Ju-88 dest(air) | Boizenburg |
| | Lt. B.J. Liles | He-111 dest(grd) | Stade A/F |
| | | He-111 dam(grd) | Stade A/F |

| | | | |
|---|---|---|---|
| | Lt. V.P. Krambo | He-111 dam(grd) | Stade A/F |
| **February 6, 1945** | | | |
| 338th: | Capt. B. McDowell | Ju-88 dest(grd) | All claims at |
| | Lt. R. Deloach | (.5)Me-410 dest(grd) | Gerolzhofen A/F |
| | Lt. H.B. Sims | (.5)Me-410 dest(grd) | |
| | Lt. H. Bodiford | Me-110 dam(grd) | |
| **February 15, 1945** | | | |
| 38th: | Lt. D.M. Amoss | Me-262 dest(air) | Amberg |
| 338th: | Lt. E.H. Duquette | (.5)Hs-129 dest(air) | Scharndau |
| | Lt. C.D. Henry | (.5)Hs-129 dest(air) | Scharndau |
| **February 19, 1945** | | | |
| 38th: | Lt. K.R. McGinnis | FW-190 dest(air) | NW Ingolstadt |
| | F/O W.V. Totten | FW-190 dest(grd) | Deiningen |
| | | FW-190 dam(grd) | Deiningen |
| 343rd: | Lt. B.H. Howes | Me-108 dest(air) | S/Hameln |
| **February 20, 1945** | | | |
| 338th: | Lt. K.A. Lashbrook | Me-109 dest(air) | Womding |
| 343rd: | Lt. W. Strauch | (2)Me-109 dest(grd) | Giebelstadt |
| | Capt. R.D. Brown | Ju-88 dest(grd) | Giebelstadt |
| **February 24, 1945** | | | |
| 343rd: | Lt. F.C. Lawrence | Ju-88 dest(grd) | All claims at |
| | | u/i a/c dam(grd) | Zwischenahn |
| | Lt. V.P. Gordon | Me-110 dam(grd) | |
| **February 25, 1945** | | | |
| 38th: | Capt. D.M. Cummings | Me-262 dest(air) | Giebelstadt |
| | | Me-262 dest(air) | Leipheim |
| | Capt. D. Penn | Me-262 dest(air) | Giebelstadt |
| | Lt. M.O. Anderson | Me-262 dest(air) | W/Giebelstadt |
| | | FW-190 dest(grd) | Giebelstadt |
| | Lt. J.F. O'Neil | Me-262 dest(air) | SE Giebelstadt |
| | | Me-262 dam(grd) | SE Giebelstadt |
| | Lt. B. Clemmons | Me-262 dest(air) | SE Mannheim |
| | Lt. D.T. Menegay | Me-262 dest(air) | W/Giebelstadt |
| 338th: | Lt. L.K. John | Me-109 dest(grd) | All claims are |
| | | FW-190 dest(grd) | at Illesheim |
| | Capt. P. Brooks | Me-109 dest(grd) | |
| | | Me-109 dam(grd) | |
| | Lt. C.D. Henry | FW-190 dest(grd) | |
| | | FW-190 dam(grd) | |
| | Lt. J.J. Sullivan | FW-190 dest(grd) | |
| | Lt. A.E. Wright | FW-190 dest(grd) | |
| | Lt. K.C. Schneider | FW-190 dam(grd) | |
| **February 26, 1945** | | | |
| 343rd: | Lt. V.P. Gordon | FW-190 dest(grd) | S/Varel |
| | Lt. J.C. McVay | Me-110 dest(grd) | S/Varel |
| **February 27, 1945** | | | |
| 343rd: | Capt. R.L. Buttke | (.5)Ju-88 dest(air) | Nurnburg |
| | Lt. L.D. Boring | (.5)Ju-88 dest(air) | Nurnburg |
| **February 28, 1945** | | | |
| 343rd: | Lt. B.H. Howes | FW-190 dest(grd) | SW Nurnburg |
| **March 3, 1945** | | | |
| 343rd: | Lt. V.P. Gordon | Me-109 dest(grd) | All claims are |
| | | Ju-52 dest(grd) | at Prague/Letnany |
| | | (4)Me-109 dam(grd) | |
| | Lt. B.J. Liles | Me-109 dest(grd) | |
| | | (2)Ju-52 dam(grd) | |
| | | Ju-88 dam(grd) | |
| | Lt. B.H. Howes | Me-109 dest(grd) | |
| | | Me-109 dam(grd) | |
| | | Me-110 dam(grd) | |
| | | Ju-52 dam(grd) | |
| | | Ju-88 dam(grd) | |
| | Lt. W.R. Erickson | Me-110 dest(grd) | |
| | | Me-109 dam(grd) | |
| | | Ju-88 dam(grd) | |
| | Lt. M. Satenstein | (4)Me-109 dam(grd) | |
| | Lt. H. Cohen | (2)Me-109 dam(grd) | |
| | Lt. W. Mearns | Me-109 dam(grd) | |
| | | Ju-88 dam(grd) | |
| **March 9, 1945** | | | |
| 38th: | Lt. J.F. O'Neil | Me-262 dam(air) | Giebelstadt |
| **March 18, 1945** | | | |
| 38th: | F/O W.V. Totten | Me-262 dam(air) | Prenzlau |
| 338th: | Lt. A.S. Dargan | (2)FW-190 dest(air) | N/Giessen |
| | Lt. T. Kiernan | FW-190 dest(air) | N/Giessen |
| | Lt. H.J. Schonenberg | FW-190 dest(air) | N/Giessen |
| **March 20, 1945** | | | |
| 338th: | Capt. H.B. Sims | u/i a/c dam(grd) | Aurich |
| **March 21, 1945** | | | |
| HdQts: | LtCol. E.G. Righetti | (2)FW-190 dest(grd) | Hopsten A/F |
| 38th: | Lt. D.M. Amoss | (3)FW-190 dest(air) | SW Munster |
| 343rd: | Capt. R.E. Welch | (2)FW-190 dest(grd) | Hopsten A/F |
| | | Ju-88 dam(grd) | Rheine |
| | Lt. P.A. Erby | FW-190 dest(grd) | Hopsten A/F |
| | Lt. P.L. Moore | FW-190 dest(grd) | Hopsten A/F |
| **March 22, 1945** | | | |
| 38th: | Lt. J.W. Cunnick | Me-262 dest(air) | Lechfeld |
| | Lt. J.F. O'Neil | Me-262 dest(grd) | Lechfeld |
| 343rd: | Capt. F.E. Birtciel | Me-262 dam(air) | Schwabisch-Hall |
| **March 24, 1945** | | | |
| 38th: | Capt. L.F. Spiecker | Me-109 dest(air) | S/Soest |
| | Capt. D.M. Cummings | (.5)Me-109 dest(air) | S/Soest |
| | Lt. H.B. Mooers | (.5)Me-109 dest(air) | S/Soest |
| **March 30, 1945** | | | |
| 343rd: | Lt. P.L. Moore | Me-262 dest(air) | Lubeck A/F |
| | Lt. P.A. Erby | Me-262 dam(air) | SW Lubeck A/F |
| **April 7, 1945** | | | |
| HdQts: | Capt. M. Clark | Me-109 dest(air) | Celle |
| 38th: | Capt. D.M. Cummings | (2)Me-109 dest(air) | Celle |
| | Lt. J.W. Cunnick | Me-109 dest(air) | Celle |
| | Lt. R.B. Mooers | Me-109 dest(air) | E/Celle |
| | Lt. D.A. Cavanaugh | (.5)Me-109 dest(air) | Celle |
| | Lt. D.T. Menegay | (.5)Me-109 dest(air) | Celle |
| **April 9, 1945** | | | |
| HdQts: | LtCol. E.G. Righetti | (3)Me-262 dest(grd) | All HdQts & |
| | | (2)u/i a/c dest(grd) | 38th claims are |
| | | FW-190 dest(grd) | at Munich- |
| | | (2)u/i a/c dam(grd) | Brunnthal Landing |
| 38th: | Lt. D.J. Best | (3)He-280 dest(grd) | Ground (MBLG) |
| | Lt. J.W. Cunnick | FW-190 dest(grd) | |
| | | Me-262 dest(grd) | |
| | | Ju-88 dest(grd) | |
| | | FW-190 dam(grd) | |
| | | Me-262 dam(grd) | |
| | Lt. K.R. McGinnis | (2)He-111 dest(grd) | |
| | | He-111 dam(grd) | |
| | Lt. J.E, Mirando | (2)FW-190 dest(grd) | |
| | | (2)FW-190 dam(grd) | |
| | Lt. W.B. Staggs | (2)FW-190 dest(grd) | |
| | Lt. C.T. Williams | (2)FW-190 dest(grd) | |
| | | (2)FW-190 dam(grd) | |
| | Lt. D.D. Bachman | Me-262 dest(grd) | |
| | | He-111 dam(grd) | |
| | Lt. J.T. Maloney | Me-262 dest(grd) | |
| | | (2)u/i a/c dam(grd) | |
| | Lt. C.R. Schendel | (2)u/i a/c dam(grd) | |
| | Lt. W.T. Achramowicz | FW-190 dam(grd) | |
| | Lt. M.O. Anderson | u/i a/c dam(grd) | |
| 343rd: | Maj. E.B. Giller | Me-262 dest(air) | Munich |
| | | Me-410 dest(grd) | MBLG |
| | | Me-262 dest(grd) | MBLG |
| | | Me-410 dam(grd) | MBLG |
| | Capt. R.E. Welch | (2)Me-109 dest(grd) | Furtenfeldbruck |
| | | (2)Me-410 dest(grd) | MBLG |
| | | Me-262 dest(grd) | MBLG |
| | | He-177 dest(grd) | Furtenfeldbruck |
| | | Me-262 dam(grd) | MBLG |
| | Capt. F.E. Birtciel | (2)He-111 dest(grd) | MBLG |
| | | (2)Ju-88 dest(grd) | MBLG |
| | | Me-109 dest(grd) | MBLG |
| | | Ju-88 dam(grd) | MBLG |
| | Lt. D.E. Adams | Me-109 dest(grd) | Furtenfeldbruck |
| | | Me-410 dest(grd) | MBLG |
| | | Me-109 dam(grd) | Furtenfeldbruck |
| | Lt. G.E. Arnold | Me-262 dest(grd) | MBLG |
| | | Me-410 dest(grd) | MBLG |
| | Lt. L.D. Boring | Me-109 dest(grd) | MBLG |
| | | Me-410 dest(grd) | MBLG |
| | | Me-109 dam(grd) | MBLG |
| | Lt. H. Mahany | He-111 dest(grd) | MBLG |
| | | Me-262 dest(grd) | MBLG |
| | | He-111 dam(grd) | MBLG |
| | Lt. R.G. Allen | Me-410 dest(grd) | MBLG |
| | Lt. G.A. Apple | Me-109 dest(grd) | MBLG |
| | | Me-410 dam(grd) | MBLG |
| | Lt. R.K. Abel | u/i a/c dest(grd) | MBLG |
| | Lt. E.E. Leon | Ju-52 dest(grd) | MBLG |
| | | Me-262 dam(grd) | MBLG |
| | Lt. E.H. Geary | Me-109 dest(grd) | MBLG |
| | | Me-109 dam(grd) | MBLG |

| | | | |
|---|---|---|---|
| | Lt. D.R. Gifford | Me-410 dest(grd) | MBLG |
| | | (2)Me-410 dam(grd) | MBLG |
| | Lt. V.P. Gordon | Do-217 dest(grd) | Furtenfeldbruck |
| | Lt. W. Mearns | Me-410 dam(grd) | MBLG |

**April 10, 1945**

| | | | |
|---|---|---|---|
| HdQts: | Maj. P.E. Hoeper | Me-262 dest(grd) | Burg |
| 38th: | Lt. K.R. McGinnis | Me-262 dest(air) | Galworde |
| | Lt. D.D. Bachman | Me-262 dam(air) | Galworde |
| | Lt. C.C. Gould | (2)Me-109 dest(grd) | Remaining 38th |
| | | u/i a/c dest(grd) | claims are at |
| | | Me-109 dam(grd) | Wesendorf |
| | Lt. J.T. Maloney | (2)Me-109 dest(grd) | |
| | | FW-190 dest(grd) | |
| | Lt. D.J. Best | (2)He-111 dest(grd) | |
| | | Me-109 dam(grd) | |
| | Lt. J.W. Cunnick | He-111 dest(grd) | |
| | | Me-109 dest(grd) | |
| | | He-111 dam(grd) | |
| | Lt. M.O. Anderson | u/i a/c dest(grd) | |
| 338th: | Lt. H. Bodiford | Fi-156 dest(air) | SE Luneburg |
| | Lt. K.A. Lashbrook | Me-262 dest(air) | Burg |
| | Lt. C.S. Chioles | Me-262 dam(air) | SE Hanover |
| | Capt. S.D. Gevorkian | (2)Ju-88 dest(grd) | Burg |
| | | FW-190 dest(grd) | All remaining |
| | Lt. R.E. Darling | (2)Me-410 dest(grd) | claims are at |
| | Lt. V.B. Tally | (2)Me-410 dest(grd) | Burg |
| | Lt. W.H. Barnes | FW-190 dest(grd) | |
| | | (2)FW-190 dam(grd) | |
| | Lt. A.F. Connors | FW-190 dest(grd) | |
| | Lt. A.S. Dargan | Me-410 dest(grd) | |
| | | Me-410 dam(grd) | |
| | Lt. R.C. Herbst | Me-262 dest(grd) | |
| | Lt. J.C. White | Ar-234 dest(grd) | |
| 343rd: | Capt. R.E. Welch | (2)He-111 dest(grd) | Burg |
| | Lt. R.G. Gibbs | He-111 dest(grd) | Burg |
| | | Ju-87 dam(grd) | Burg |

**April 16, 1945**

| | | | |
|---|---|---|---|
| HdQts: | LtCol. E.G. Righetti | (3)He-111 dest(grd) | Bad Aibling |
| | | (2)Ju-88 dest(grd) | MBLG |
| | | Si-204 dest(grd) | MBLG |
| | | (5)Si-204 dam(grd) | MBLG |
| 38th: | Capt. J.W. Kavanaugh | Me-262 dest(grd) | MBLG |
| | | u/i a/c dest(grd) | MBLG |
| | | u/i a/c dam(grd) | MBLG |
| | Lt. J.W. Cunnick | (2)Me-109 dest(grd) | N/Landshut |
| | | Me-109 dam(grd) | N/Landshut |
| | Lt. C.C. Gould | (2)He-111 dest(grd) | N/Ansbach |
| | | Me-109 dam(grd) | N/Ansbach |
| | Lt. J.E. Anderson | Do-217 dest(grd) | MBLG |
| | Lt. L.J. Fleming | Do-217 dest(grd) | MBLG |
| | Lt. J.T. Maloney | Ju-52 dest(grd) | Bad Aibling |
| | | u/i a/c dam(grd) | Bad Aibling |
| | Lt. D.T. Menegay | Ju-88 dest(grd) | MBLG |
| | Capt. C.T. Williams | Me-109 dam(grd) | Bad Aibling |
| | | u/i a/c dam(grd) | Bad Aibling |
| | Maj. C.L. Peterson | u/i a/c dam(grd) | MBLG |
| | Lt. R.F. Quinn | u/i a/c dam(grd) | Bad Aibling |
| 338th: | Maj. E.E. Ryan | Me-262 dest(air) | Horsching A/F |
| | | He-111 dest(grd) | N/Landshut |
| | Capt. S.D. Gevorkian | (3)FW-190 dest(grd) | Landshut |
| | | (3)FW-190 dam(grd) | Landshut |
| | Lt. L.K. John | (3)FW-200 dest(grd) | N/Landshut |
| | Lt. H. Bodiford | (2)u/i a/c dest(grd) | N/Landshut |
| | | He-111 dest(grd) | N/Landshut |
| | Lt. C.D. Henry | (2)FW-190 dest(grd) | N/Landshut |
| | Lt. R.E. Cooper | FW-190 dest(grd) | N/Landshut |
| | Lt. R.E. Darling | Me-109 dest(grd) | Erding |
| | | (2)Me-109 dam(grd) | Erding |
| | F/O J.E. Brady | Me-109 dest(grd) | N/Landshut |
| 338th: | Lt. R. Deloach | He-111 dest(grd) | N/Landshut |
| | Lt. J.C. White | Me-109 dest(grd) | N/Landshut |
| | Lt. R.C. Herbst | Me-109 dest(grd) | Erding |
| | Lt. J.H. Wiley | He-111 dest(grd) | N/Landshut |
| 343rd: | Maj. E.B. Giller | He-111 dest(grd) | MBLG |
| | | Me-109 dest(grd) | MBLG |
| | | Ju-52 dest(grd) | MBLG |
| | | Ju-88 dam(grd) | MBLG |
| | Capt. R.E. Welch | Me-110 dest(grd) | MBLG |
| | | Me-410 dest(grd) | MBLG |
| | Capt. C.E. Coggeshall | FW-190 dest(grd) | Ainring A/F |
| | Capt. W. Strauch | FW-189 dest(grd) | Ainring A/F |
| | Lt. G.A. Apple | FW-190 dest(grd) | Ainring A/F |
| | Lt. J.H. Bevington | FW-190 dest(grd) | Ainring A/F |
| | Lt. R.G. Allen | (.5)BV-140 dest(grd) | Lake Chiem |
| | Lt. L.D. Boring | (.5)BV-140 dest(grd) | Lake Chiem |
| | Lt. G.E. Arnold | Me-410 dam(grd) | MBLG |

**April 17, 1945**

| | | | |
|---|---|---|---|
| HdQts: | LtCol. E.G. Righetti | (6)u/i a/c dest(grd) | Riess/Canitz |
| | | (3)Me-109 dest(grd) | Riess/Canitz |
| 338th: | Lt. H. Bodiford | FW-190 dest(air) | SE Dresden |
| | Lt. R.E. Cooper | FW-190 dest(air) | SE Dreden |
| | Lt. T. Kiernan | FW-190 dest(air) | S/Dresden |
| | Lt. J.H. Wiley | FW-190 dam(air) | S/Dresden |
| | Capt. C.D. Henry | FW-190 dest(grd) | Riess/Canitz |
| | | u/i a/c dest(grd) | Riess/Canitz |
| | Maj. E.E. Ryan | (.5)u/i a/c dest(grd) | Leipzig |
| | Lt. J.R. Ethridge | (.5)u/i a/c dest(grd) | Leipzig |
| | Lt. R. Deloach | Fi-156 dam(grd) | Riess/Canitz |
| 343rd: | Lt. R.G. Gibbs | (2)FW-190 dest(air) | Kamenz A/F |
| | Capt. W. Strauch | FW-190 dest(air) | Kamenz A/F |
| | Capt. R.E. Welch | FW-190 dest(air) | Kamenz A/F |
| | Lt. P.A. Erby | FW-190 dest(air) | Kamenz A/F |
| | Lt. H. Mahany | (3)Me-410 dest(grd) | Dresden |
| | | (2)FW-190 dest(grd) | Dresden |
| | | (2)FW-190 dam(grd) | Dresden |
| | Lt. L.D. Boring | (2)Fi-156 dest(grd) | Bautzen/Litten |
| | | FW-190 dest(grd) | Bautzen/Litten |
| | | u/i a/c dest(grd) | Bautzen/Litten |
| | F/O G.W. Bernardo | (3)FW-190 dest(grd) | Dresden |
| | | Ju-88 dest(grd) | Dresden |
| | | (2)FW-190 dam(grd) | Dresden |
| | Lt. W.A. Fisher | (2)FW-190 dest(grd) | Dresden |
| | | (2)Me-410 dest(grd) | Dresden |
| | Lt. G.A. Apple | FW-190 dest(grd) | Dresden |
| | | Ju-88 dest(grd) | Dresden |
| | Lt. G.E. Arnold | (2)Fi-156 dest(grd) | Bautzen/Litten |
| 343rd: | Lt. H. Cohen | Me-109 dest(grd) | Bautzen/Litten |
| | Lt. E.H. Geary | Me-410 dest(grd) | Bautzen/Litten |
| | | Me-410 dam(grd) | Bautzen/Litten |
| | Lt. D.E. Adams | Me-109 dam(grd) | Bautzen/Litten |

**April 19, 1945**

| | | | |
|---|---|---|---|
| 338th: | Lt. R. Delaoch | Me-262 dest(air) | W/Prague |

### 55th Fighter Group Losses

**October 18, 1943**
Lt. Hugh R. Gillette (38th) KIA; Suffered mechanical failure and crashed into the North Sea.
P-38H CG-I 42-66719

**November 13, 1943**
Lt. John A. Stacker (38th) KIA; Hit by fighters near Oldenburg.
P-38H CG- 42-67059
Lt. Charles F. Beall (338th) KIA; Hit by fighters near Bremen.
P-38H CL- 42-67049
Lt. Lynn R. Goetzman (338th) POW; Hit by fighters near Bremen.
P-38H CL- 42-67073
Lt. William C. Florentine, Jr. (338th) POW; Hit by fighters near Bremen.
P-38H CL- 42-66732
Lt. Robert N. Jensen (338th) POW; Hit by fighters and bailed out near Hahlemer Moor.
P-38H CL- 42-66724
Lt. William W. Shank (338th) KIA; Hit by fighters near Bremen.
P-38H CL- 42-66727
Lt. Gene C. Stephens (338th) KIA; Hit by fighters near Bremen.
P-38H CL- 42-67078

**November 25, 1943**
Lt. Manuel J. Aldecoa (343rd) KIA; Collided with a FW-190 near La Bassee. He bailed out but his parachute failed.
P-38H CY- 42-67061

**November 29, 1943**
Maj. Milton Joel (38th) KIA; Hit by fighters near Ijsselmeer.
P-38H CG- 42-67020
Lt. Albert A. Albino (38th) KIA; Hit by fighters near Hoogeveen.
P-38H CG- 42-67051
Lt. John J. Carroll (38th) POW; Hit by fighters near Zwartsluis.
P-38H CG- 42-67090
Lt. James M. Garvin (38th) KIA; Hit by fighters near Oldenburg.
P-38H CG- 42-67046
Lt. Fleming W. Suiter (338th) KIA; Hit by fighters near Meppel.
P-38H CL- 42-67069
Lt. James W. Gilbride (343rd) KIA; Hit by fighters near Avereest.
P-38H CY- 42-67097

**December 1, 1943**
Lt. Wilton G. Erickson (38th) KIA; Suffered mechanical failure near Siegburg.
P-38H CG- 42-67033
Lt. William C. Turner (338th) KIA; Spun-in near Gillingham.
P-38H CL-

**December 2, 1943**
Capt. Roland L. Malmstedt (343rd) KIAc; Suffered mechanical trouble while taking-off on a test hop.
P-38H CY-

*Nicholas Megura's 334th Mustang QP-N 43-6636 "Ill Wind?"*

*Alwin Juchheim of the 83rd Fighter Squadron with his crewchief Robert McCord. The P-47 is HL-J 42-74690.*

*Roy Scrutchfield's 55th Fighter Squadron P-38, KI-N 43-28430 "Jeanne."*

*CV-S 42-22468 "Geronimo" of the 368th Fighter Squadron.*

*368th Fighter Squadron Mustang of Emer Cater, CV-E 43-6491.*

*361st Fighter Squadron ace Sidney Hewett with his crew and personal P-47. Left to right: Elwin D. Phillips (armorer), Hewett, Ben Giardinere (crewchief), and Mike Yahwak (assistant) The Thunderbolt is QI-F 42-74702 "Clarkie II."*

343rd Fighter Squadron P-38 of William Allen, CY-V 42-67966 "Pretty Patty."

P-51B of Thomas Fraser, 334th Fighter Squadron. QP-G 43-24825 "Jerry."

P-51C of the 374th Fighter Squadron after belly-landing in late May of 1944. B7-V 42-103362.

Another bellied-in Mustang, this time from the 503rd Fighter Squadron. D7-V 42-106882.

Edwin Heller's 486th Fighter Squadron P-51B in May of 1944 PZ-H 43-6704 "Hell-Er-Bust."

*357th Fighter Squadron P-47 of Chester Butcher, OS-F 42-22538.*

*Flak damaged 505th Fighter Squadron P-51B, 6N-T 42-106720.*

*364th Fighter Squadron P-51B, C5-O 42-106923.*

*Lucian Dade's P-47D of the 62nd Fighter Squadron in early June 1944, LM-P 42-26417.*

503rd Fighter Squadron P-51B, D7-A 42-106812.

376th P-51's ready to go on June 6, 1944. E9-S 42-106707 "Sleepytime Gal" was the mount of Clarence Sullivan.

Mustangs of the 374th Fighter Squadron also on D-Day. In front is Robert Eckfeldt's B7-E 42-106839 "Bald Eagle III."

*Right: "The Duchess V", 328th Fighter Squadron P-51B of Richard Brookins.*

*Below: Francis Grabreski's last P-47 with the 61st Fighter Squadron, HV-A 42-26418.*

*P-51's of the 486th Fighter Squadron prior to the first Russian Shuttle in late June of 1944. Front four planes are PZ-J 44-13398 of Willie Jackson, PZ-B 43-6436 "Bayou Baby" of Don Higgins, PZ-B 42-106613 "Ellie" of Warren Brashear, and PZ-V 42-106857 "Texas Knight" of Lester Howell.*

*Henry Brown's 354th Fighter Squadron P-51B in June of 1944, WR-Z 42-106448 "The Hun Hunter From Texas."*

*Above: Unidentified pilot with D7-S 42-106570 of the 503rd Fighter Squadron.*

*Right: Bruce Rowlett in a 375th Fighter Squadron P-51B on July 2, 1944.*

*6N-O 43-24796 "Blackie II" of the 505th Fighter Squadron.*

*Above: Marvin Bledsoe's 350th Fighter Squadron P-47D LH-J 42-26581 "Little Princess."*

*Left: 363rd Fighter Squadron ace William O'Brien.*

Carl Luksic, 487th Fighter Squadron ace.

Daniel D. McKee of the 370th Fighter Squadron.

Top 63rd Fighter Squadron scorer Walker Mahurin.

374th Fighter Squadron CO and ace Roy Webb with his P-47 "Sweet Thing III."

*Robert Booth, an early ace of the 369th Fighter Squadron.*

*First ace for the 20th Fighter Group Lindol Graham.*

*Leading 8th Air Force ace for a period in early 1944 was Don Gentile of the 336th Fighter Squadron.*

*Aleutian Theater vet and 370th Fighter Squadron CO, John Murphy.*

*Robert Lamb who flew with the 61st and 63rd Fighter Squadrons.*

*328th and 487th Fighter Squadron ace William Halton.*

*William Hodges of the 370th Fighter Squadron.*

*Einar Malmstrom, CO of the 356th Fighter Group, with his groundcrew. Left to right; Henry Yoder (crewchief), Malmstrom, Willis Youtsey (assistant).*

*Right: 486th Fighter Squadron ace Henry Miklajcyk.*

Pacific vet and long-serving member of the 361st Fighter Group, Joe Kruzel.

Renowned 328th and 487th Fighter Squadron ace George Preddy.

Don Bochkay on his 363rd Fighter Squadron P-51 "Speedball Alice."

*First 361st Fighter Squadron air ace David Thwaites with his crew. Left to right: Lionel Ratte (crewchief), Victor Foytho (armorer), Thwaites, and Frank Strozzi (assistant)*

*Alton Wallace of the 486th Fighter Squadron.*

*77th Fighter Squadron ace James Morris with his crewchief, Joe McFarland.*

*Quince Brown in his 84th Fighter Squadron P-47 "Okie."*

*Former MTO ace Jack Ilfrey, now with the 79th Fighter Squadron.*

*328th Fighter Squadron CO and ace, Earl Abbott.*

*Popular CO of the 375th Fighter Squadron, George Merritt.*

*John Vogt who made ace while flying with the 56th and 356th Fighter Groups.*

*Little publicized 487th Fighter Squadron ace Glennon Moran.*

*Hub Zemke in the cockpit of one of his 56th Fighter Group P-47s.*

*Robert Landry, CO 0f the 56th Fighter Group (left) with Dave Schilling.*

*352nd Fighter Squadron ace Clifford Armstrong and crew. Front left to right: Earl Dunn (armorer) and Robert Weinzgacz (assistant) Back: Joe Brandon (crewchief) and Armstrong.*

**December 16, 1943**
Lt. William K. Burch (38th) KIA; Spun-in near Waverly.
P-38H CG-

**December 22, 1943**
Lt. Robert W. Brown (338th) POW; Hit by fighters near Kropswolde.
P-38H CY-F 42-67047 (a 343rd a/c)
Lt. John R. Pruitt (338th) KIA; Hit by fighters near Lotte.
P-38H CL- 42-67021

**December 31, 1943**
Lt. Harold M. Bauer (343rd) ASR; Ran out of fuel and ditched 15 miles off Lizard Point.
P-38H CY-
Lt. Frank A. Larson (343rd) POW; Hit by fighters and crashed into the Bay of Biscay.
P-38H CY- 42-67056

**January 5, 1944**
Lt. Edward F. Peters (38th) POW; Hiy by fighters near Neumunster.
P-38J CG- 42-67650
Lt. Herbert T. Winters (38th) KIA; Hit by fighters near Neumunster.
P-38H CY-T 42-67060 (a 343rd a/c)
Lt. John Barnett (343rd) KIA; Suffered mechanical failure over the Baltic Sea.
P-38H CY- 42-67045
Lt. Robert J. Kenning (343rd) KIA; Hit by flak near Rendsburg.
P-38H CY-R 42-67084

**January 7, 1944**
Capt. Joseph P. Marsiglia (338th) POW; Hit by fighters near Krattnick.
P-38H CL- 42-67048

**January 11, 1944**
Lt. William E. Harbert (338th) KIA; Lost for unknown reasons.
P-38H CL- 42-67100

**January 23, 1944**
Lt. Henry J. Tiedemann, Jr. (38th) KIAc;
P-38H CG-

**January 24, 1944**
Lt. Robert S. Thompson (38th) POW; Hit by fighters near Zeebruggee.
P-38J CG- 42-67520

**January 31, 1944**
Lt. David D. Fisher (38th) KIA; Hit by fighters near Venlo.
P-38J CG-C 42-67757
Lt. Leroy V. Hokinson (38th) MIA-E; Hit by fighters near Venlo.
P-38J CG- 42-67813
Lt. Morris Leve (38th) KIA; Hit by fighters near Venlo.
P-38J CG- 42-67768
Lt. Martin B. Miller (38th) KIA, Hit by fighters near Venlo.
P-38J CG- 42-67221
Lt. Leon M. Patterson (38th) KIA; Hit by fighters near Venlo and crashed into the North Sea.
P-38J CG- 42-67301
Lt. Delorn A. Steiner (38th) KIA; Hit by fighters near Venlo.
P-38J CG- 42-67711

**February 6, 1944**
Lt. William J. Ashton (343rd) KIA; Hit by a FW-190 near Evreux.
P-38J CY- 42-67893
Lt. Ray L. Sumpter (343rd) KIA; Collided with a P-38 and spun into the Channel.
P-38J CY-I 42-67479

**February 10, 1944**
Lt. Jack R. Foster (338th) POW; Hit by fighters near Ettenbestal.
P-38J CL-P 42-67816 "Princess Pat"

**February 24, 1944**
Lt. William Turner (38th) KIA; Hit by flak near Watten.
P-38J CG- 42-67939
Capt. Wesley M. Tibbetts (338th) KIA; Hit by fighters near Gotha.
P-38J CL- 42-67752

**March 4, 1944**
Lt. Howard J. Bone (338th) KIA; Crashed near Mesden after take-off.
P-38J CL-
Lt. Robert V. Lloyd (343rd) MIA; Suffered mechanical failure near Ijsselmeer.
P-38J CY- 42-68162

**March 8, 1944**
Lt. Joseph M. Fluty (343rd) KIA; Crashed near Dovercourt.
P-38J CY-

**March 15, 1944**
Lt. Ben H. Gourley (343rd) KIA; Hit by flak and ditched 60 miles east of Lowestoft.
P-38J CY- 42-67228

**March 18, 1944**
Lt. Bradford R. Wikholm (338th) KIA; Hit by fighters near Ettenheim.
P-38J CL- 42-67989

**March 22, 1944**
Lt. Victor J. LaBella (338th) POW; Suffered mechanical trouble near Langenhorst.
P-38J CL- 42-67919

**March 24, 1944**
Lt. Ernest W. George (338th) POW; Collided with Lt. West near Delouze.
P-38J CL- 42-67467
Lt. Fred W. West (338th) MIA-E; Collided with Lt. George near Delouze.
P-38J CL- 42-67738

**April 8, 1944**
Lt. Thomas F. Knudson (338th) MIA; Hit by a Me-109 east of Minden.
P-38J CL- 42-67721

**April 9, 1944**
Lt. Newell Anderson (338th) KIA; Crashed on take-off from Nuthampstead.
P-38J CL-

**April 10, 1944**
LtCol. Jack S. Jenkins (HdQts) POW; Hit by flak at Coulommiers.
P-38J CG-J 42-67825 "Texas Ranger IV"
Lt. Anthony Piscitelli (343rd) KIA; Hit by flak at Coulommiers.
P-38J CY- 42-67866

**April 12, 1944**
Lt. Elton S. Walters (38th) KIA; Hit by flak and crashed off Ostend.
P-38J CG- 42-67730

**April 13, 1944**
Lt. Melvin A. Hawes (38th) ASR; Ditched in the Channel after mechanical trouble.
P-38J CG-

**April 15, 1944**
Lt. Julius M. Hummel (38th) POW; Hit by flak near Osnabruck.
P-38J CG- 42-68157
Lt. William Laubner (38th) KIA; Hit by flak near Osnabruck.
P-38J CG- 42-68079
Lt. Tunis J. Lyon (338th) KIA; Hit by flak near Herford.
P-38J CL- 42-67413

**April 22, 1944**
Capt. Bernie V. Guthrie (HdQts) KIA; Hit by a Me-109 near Waldbrol.
P-38J CY-J 42-68048
Lt. Clair A. Penners (343rd) POW; Hit by fighters near Kirchunden.
P-38J CY-Q 42-67966 "Little Man"

**May 7, 1944**
Lt. Russell W. Erb (343rd) ASR; Ditched in the Channel after mechanical failure.
P-38J CY-

**May 18, 1944**
Lt. Kenneth H. Underwood (38th) KIAc; Crashed near Bury St. Edmunds.
P-38J CG-K 42-104334

**May 20, 1944**
Lt. John W. Thomas (338th) KIA; Last seen near Sens.
P-38J CL- 42-67715

**May 21, 1944**
Lt. Noah R. Tipton (38th) POW; Hit by flak and bellied-in near Kempton.
P-38J CG- 42-68076
Lt. Burt R. Shepard (38th) POW; Hit by flak and bellied-in near Helmstedt.
P-38J CG- 42-67713
Capt. Karl H. Garlock (338th) POW; Hit by flak near Brunswick.
P-38J CL- 42-67771
Lt. Horace K. Walter (338th) KIA; Last seen near Flensburg with an engine out.
P-38J CL- 42-104280
Lt. James H. Weisel (343rd) POW; Hit by flak and bellied-in near Celle.
P-38J CY- 42-68086
Lt. Henry K. Warwick (343rd) MIA; Hit by flak and disappeared near Celle.
P-38J CY- 42-104250

**May 27, 1944**
Lt. Clifford O. Williams (343rd) MIA-E; Hit by flak near Legers.
P-38J CY- 42-67875
Lt. Victor T. McConnell (343rd) KIAc; Crashed 4 miles from Nuthampstead.
P-38J CY-

**June 11, 1944**
Maj. Val W. Bollwerk (338th) POW; Hit by a FW-190 near Amiens.
P-38J CL- 42-104396
Lt. Karl J. Goethel (343rd) MIA-E; Hit by a FW-190 near Estrees.
P-38J CY- 43-28388
Lt. Rex P. Hjelm (343rd) MIA-E; Hit by a FW-190 near Clermont.
P-38J CY- 42-68102

**June 14, 1944**
Lt. Arthur Baranick (338th) MIA; Hit by a Me-109 north of Paris.
P-38J CL- 42-68130

Capt. Kenneth J. Sorace (343rd) MIA-E; Hit by a Me-109 north of Paris.
P-38J CY-S 43-28666
Lt. Louis J. Sturdivan (343rd) MIA; Hit by a Me-109 north of Paris.
P-38J CY- 42-67964

**June 15, 1944**
Lt. Edwin C. Wheeler (338th) POW; Collided with a P-38 northwest of Hanover.
P-38J CL- 42-67867

**June 16, 1944**
Lt. Vernie B. Greenamyre (38th) POW; Hit by flak near Amiens.
P-38J CG- 43-28423
Lt. George W. Patterson (338th) POW; Hit by flak near Abbeville.
P-38J CL- 43-28273
Lt. Clair D. Porter (343rd) KIA; Hit by flak near Oisemont.
P-38J CY- 43-28713

**June 17, 1944**
Lt. William C. DuRose (38th) MIA-E; Hit by flak near Chaulnes.
P-38J CG- 43-28724

**June 21, 1944**
Lt. Malcolm G. Armstrong (338th) MIA; Hit by flak and bailed out west of Borkum.
P-38J CL- 42-68127

**June 23, 1944**
Lt. Grant H. Corey (38th) MIA; Hit by a Me-109 near Dreux.
P-38J CG- 42-104284
Lt. Robert B. Hoffman (38th) MIA; Hit by a Me-109 near Dreux.
P-38J CG- 42-67578

**June 24, 1944**
Lt. George Korinek (338th) POW; Hit by flak near Aquigny.
P-38J CL- 42-68083

**June 28, 1944**
Lt. Arthur Carmel (38th) KIAc;
P-38J CG-

**June 30, 1944**
Lt. Warren E. Loring (343rd) MIA-E; Hit by flak and bailed out west of Nevers.
P-38J CY- 42-67876

**July 5, 1944**
Lt. Lawrence J. Berry (338th) KIA; Hit by flak near Houdon.
P-38J CL- 43-28461

**July 9, 1944**
Lt. John E. Walker (343rd) POW; Hit by flak near Angars.
P-38J CY-Q 42-68014

**July 13, 1944**
Capt. Clair W. Des Voignes (38th) KIA; Collided with a P-47 near St. Denis.
P-38J CG- 43-28279

**July 20, 1944**
Lt. Wallace H. Earnest (338th) KIA; Suffered mechanical failure and crashed into the Channel.
P-51C CL- 43-25069

**July 21, 1944**
Lt. Delbert F. Blount (338th) POW; Suffered mechanical trouble near Kempton.
P-51D CL-H 44-13807

**July 25, 1944**
Lt. Stoddard B. Gerald (338th) POW; Hit by flak near Lisieux.
P-51D CL- 44-13703

**July 28, 1944**
Lt. Howard W. Rhodes (38th) MIA; Suffered mechanical failure near Naumberg and bailed out west of Merseburg.
P-51D CG-L 44-13609
Lt. Joseph K. Garnett (338th) KIAc; Crashed south of Boxted.
P-51D CL-

**July 30, 1944**
Lt. James D. Brokaw (343rd) KIA; Suffered mechanical failure near Brumetz.
P-51D CY- 44-13665

**August 10, 1944**
Lt. David G. Elliott (38th) POW (E); Damaged by ground explosion near Sommesous.
P-51D CG-K 44-13623
Lt. William H. Lewis (38th) MIA; Hit by flak near Montmirail.
P-51D CG-O 44-13973
Lt. Lester E. Jaklish (38th) MIA; Hit by flak near Fere-Champenoise.
P-51D CG-W 44-13888
Lt. Arthur M. McFarland (338th) KIA; Hit trees while strafing near Chalons.
P-51D CL-J 44-14007

**August 12, 1944**
Lt. Richard J. Keough (338th) POW; Caught in a ground explosion near Boult.
P-51D CL- 44-14028
Lt. James R. McCutcheon (338th) KIA; Hit by flak near Revigny.
P-51D CL-A 44-13744
Lt. William E. McMillan (338th) KIA; Hit the ground while strafing near Prunay.
P-51D CL-S 44-13739

**August 13, 1944**
Lt. Robert M. Littlefield (38th) MIA-E; Hit by flak near Rouen.
P-51D CG-V 44-13577
Lt. Donald D. Gilmore (338th) KIA; Hit by flak near Serans.
P-51D CL-B 44-13360

**August 16, 1944**
Lt. Joseph B. Jiorles (343rd) POW; Suffered mechanical failure near Borringhausen.
P-51D CY- 44-14051

**August 17, 1944**
Lt. James W. Roberts (343rd) KIA; Hit by flak near Virelles.
P-51D CY- 44-13612 "Oh Murder!"

**August 23, 1944**
Lt. Bill Chambliss (338th) KIAc; Crashed near Little Horkesley.
P-51B CL-

**August 24, 1944**
Lt. Thomas B. Luckett (38th) KIA; Hit by flak near Burg A/F.
P-51D CG-X 44-13749 "Jeanne"

**August 26, 1944**
Lt. John R. Eskridge (338th) POW; Suffered mechanical failure near Soerten.
P-51D CL- 44-14014
Lt. Samuel D. Gevorkian (338th) MIA-E; Ran out of fuel and bellied-in near Truc Vert.
P-51D CL-P 44-13954 "DaQuake"
Lt. Samuel E. Hansard (338th) KIA; Ran out of fuel and crashed into the Channel.
P-51D CL- 44-14094
Lt. John E. Kester (338th) MIA-E; Ran out of fuel and bellied-in near Truc Vert.
P-51D CL- 44-13663
Lt. James W. Hiner (343rd) KIA; Damaged by a ground explosion near St. Michel and bailed out west of Nancy.

**September 1, 1944**
Lt. John E. Bauer (338th) POW; Last seen west of Paris.
P-51D CL- 44-13625 "Georgetta"

**September 5, 1944**
Lt. William C. Cole (343rd) KIA; Hit by flak and crashed into the North Sea.
P-51C CY- 42-103507 "Gremlin Leader"

**September 9, 1944**
Lt. Ray E. Mull (343rd) MIA-E; Suffered mechanical failure and bailed out northeast of Turnhout.
P-51D CY- 44-11158

**September 10, 1944**
Lt. Maynard R. King (343rd) KIA; Hit by flak at Herzogenaurach A/F.
P-51D CY- 44-13843

**September 11, 1944**
Lt. Kenneth I. Crawford (38th) KIA; Hit by fighters near Oberof.
P-51D CG-T 44-13723 "One Mustang"
Lt. William M. Lewis, Jr. (38th) KIA; Hit by fighters near Gera.
P-51D CG- 44-14176
Lt. Wayne E. Rosenhoff (343rd) POW; Damaged by an exploding plane near Sonneburg.
P-51D CY- 44-13724
Lt. Kenneth T. Williams (343rd) KIA; Suffered mechanical failure near Chemnitz.
P-51D CY- 44-13850

**September 12, 1944**
Lt. Douglas E. Mayer (38th) KIA; Hit by flak near Rheine.
P-51D CG-Y 44-13909 "Mom's Pride"

**September 13, 1944**
Lt. Durward D. Carson (338th) POW; Suffered mechanical failure near Oberof.
P-51D CL-H 44-13607 "Marybelle III"
Lt. David M. Fry (343rd) POW; Suffered mechanical failure near Homburg.
P-51D CY- 44-13374 "Julia"

**September 17, 1944**
Lt. Paul R. Porter (343rd) ASR; Suffered mechanical failure and bailed out over the Channel.
P-51D CY-S 44-13907

**October 3, 1944**
Lt. Alfred E. Carr, Jr. (38th) ASR; Suffered mechanical failure and bailed out over the North Sea.
P-51D CG- 44-14097

**October 6, 1944**
Lt. Warren E. Lewis (343rd) POW; Ran out of fuel near Rheurt.
P-51D CY-N 44-14442

**October 7, 1944**
Capt. Peter Dempsey (338th) POW; Hit by flak near Almenhausen.
P-51D CL-P 44-14291 "DaQuake"

**October 9, 1944**
Lt. Francis R. Sharp (338th) KIAc
P-51D CL-I 44-13668

**October 14, 1944**
Lt. Edwin D. Lawrence (38th) KIA; Crashed in England on return.
P-51D CG-D 44-13701

**October 15, 1944**
Lt. John T. Kibler, Jr. (343rd) MIA; Suffered mechanical trouble near St. Nicholas.
P-51D CY-X 44-14632

**November 2, 1944**
Lt. Fred L. Sturgess (38th) POW; Hit by fighters near Leipzig.
P-51D CG-I 44-13747 "Six-Gun Pete"

**November 5, 1944**
Lt. Gus D. Leslie (343rd) MIA; Hit by flak near Eberach.
P-51D CY-A 44-13363 "Bama Blitz"

**November 6, 1944**
Lt. Paul R. Porter (343rd) KIA; Suffered mechanical failure and bailed out over the Channel.
P-51D CY-K 44-13874 "Junie Bug II"

**November 8, 1944**
Capt. Earl R. Fryer (38th) KIA; Hit by flak near Hilversum.
P-51D CG-Z 44-13804 "Spunktown"
Capt. Eugene S. Gregg, Jr. (38th) POW; Hit by flak near Boenninghardt.
P-51D CG- 44-14026

**November 20, 1944**
Lt. Richard L. Lapham (38th) MIA; Hit by flak near Werkenden.
P-51D CG- 44-14586 "Phyllis Jean"
Lt. Jordan Eliades (343rd) POW; Hit by flak near Haaten.
P-51D CY-C 44-14535

**November 26, 1944**
Lt. Huey R. Coward (38th) KIA; Hit by fighters near Emlichheim.
P-51D CG- 44-15022
Lt. Richard I. Barrett (338th) POW; Hit by flak at both Achmer and Vorden Airfields and crashed near Soesterburg.

**November 27, 1944**
Lt. Robert K. Harbeck (338th) KIA; Suffered mechanical failure and crashed into the North Sea.
P-51D CL- 44-14204 "Skylark"

**December 11, 1944**
Capt. Harry E. Larsen (338th) KIA; Hit by flak near Padberg.
P-51D CL- 44-14211 "Harvest Moon"

**December 23, 1944**
Lt. John E. McDonnell (343rd) KIA; Hit by flak near Ober-Raden.
P-51D CY-L 44-13643 "Sweet Pootie"

**December 24, 1944**
Lt. Kenneth W. Griffith (338th) KIA; Hit by fighters near Lippstadt.
P-51D CL- 44-13767
Lt. Kenneth J. Mix (343rd) KIA; Collided with a 357th Ftr Grp P-51 near Daun.
P-51D CY-M 44-13837 "Miss Marilyn"

**December 25, 1944**
Lt. Robert A. Maxwell (343rd) POW; Hit by fighters near Mayenne.
P-51D CY-B 44-14384 "Lil Pearl"

**December 30, 1944**
Lt. Harold B. Metcalf (338th) KIA; Suffered mechanical failure near Fellen.
P-51D CL- 44-13867

**December 31, 1944**
Lt. Richard L. Engel (343rd) KIAc; Crashed into the Channel on a training flight.
P-51D CY- 44-14171 "Daisy Jr."

**January 3, 1945**
Capt. John F. Coonan (38th) POW; Hit by flak near Gutenzell.
P-51D CG-P 44-14358

**January 6, 1945**
Capt. Clair E. Buskirk (338th) POW; Hit by flak near Giebelstadt and bailed out near Schluctern.
P-51D CL- 44-14901

**January 7, 1945**
F/O Frank R. Russell (38th) MIA; Reported he was low on fuel and was last seen over Holland.
P-51D CG- 44-14274

**January 13, 1945**
Lt. Philip Eastman, Jr. (338th) POW; Hit by flak near Stettin.
P-51D CL- 44-63245

**January 14, 1945**
Lt. John E. Kester (338th) KIA; Hit by flak near Parchim.
P-51D CL-N 44-15045 "Sunday Morning"

**January 18, 1945**
Lt. John E. Finlayson (38th) MIA; Crashed into the Channel in bad weather.
P-51D CG-A 44-14580 "Ellie, My Little Six"

**February 6, 1945**
Capt. Bert McDowell, Jr. (338th) POW; Hit by flak at Gerolzhofen A/F and bellied-in near Wertheim.
P-51K CL-V 44-11687 "Betty Mac"

**February 14, 1945**
Lt. John L. Rieder (38th) MIA; Damaged by a ground explosion near Magdeburg.
P-51D CG-A 44-13549

**February 17, 1945**
Lt. Frank D. Bradford, II (338th) MIA; Crashed 20 miles east of Frankfurt.
P-51D CL-

**February 19, 1945**
Lt. Grady Morris (343rd) POW; Hit by flak at Lippstadt and bailed out west of Hamm.
P-51D CY-A 44-14298 "Pink"

**February 20, 1945**
Lt. Alfred E. Carr, Jr. (38th) MIA-E; Hit by flak and bellied-in near Hall.
P-51D CG-S 44-14068 "Little Joe"
Lt. John W. Miller (38th) ASR; Ditched in the Channel after mechanical trouble.
P-51D CG-N 44-13937
Lt. Robert L. Sill (38th) KIA; Hit by flak near Seinhausen.
P-51K CG-R 44-11370
Lt. Charles R. Michaelson (343rd) POW; Hit by flak near Crailsheim.
P-51D CY-E 44-63567

**February 21, 1945**
Lt. George E. Eichhorn (343rd) POW; Hit by flak near Mistelfeld.
P-51D CY-H 44-15060 "Jill's Jalopy"

**February 22, 1945**
Lt. Samuel E. Kershaw (338th) KIAc; Crashed near Hornchurch.
P-51D CL-

**February 24, 1945**
Lt. Kenneth D. Cottrell (338th) MIA-E; Hit by flak near Emmen.
P-51D CL-V 44-14702 "Miss Donna"
Lt. Thomas M. Love (343rd) POW; Hit by flak at Zwischenahn A/F.
P-51D CY-J 44-14296 "Mardy"

**February 27, 1945**
Lt. Victor P. Krambo (343rd) POW; Damaged by a ground explosion near Boattingen.
P-51D CY-U 44-15406

**February 28, 1945**
Capt. Jerry R. McDonald (338th) MIA; Hit by flak near Ingolstadt.
P-51D CL-

**March 1, 1945**
Lt. William R. Watkins (338th) KIAc; Crashed near Canedown.
P-51D CY- 44-14161 (343rd a/c)

**March 2, 1945**
Lt. Sam F. Anderson (38th) KIA; Last seen in overcast near Limburg.
P-51D CG-B 44-13818 "Mah Ideel"

**March 3, 1945**
Lt. Brooks J. Liles (343rd) POW; Hit by flak at Prague/Letnany A/F.
P-51D CY- 44-14175 "Sweet Marie II"
Lt. Bernard H. Howes (343rd) POW; Landed to pick-up Lt. Liles but could not take-off.
P-51D CY-C 44-63745

**March 15, 1945**
Lt. Eugene H. Duquette (338th) ASR; Bailed out 50 miles east of Lowestoft after mechanical trouble.
P-51D CL-P 44-14730

**March 18, 1945**
Lt. Robert L. Van Horn (338th) KIA; Suffered mechanical failure and crashed near Trier.
P-51D CL- 44-14598 "Lady Lorene"

**March 19, 1945**
Lt. Stanley E. Chapple (38th) ASR; Bailed out off Walcheren after mechanical failure.
P-51D CG-

**March 20, 1945**
Capt. Robert D. Brown (343rd) INT; Hit by flak near Flensburg and bailed out; smuggled by underground to Sweden.
P-51D CY-V 44-14135

**March 21, 1945**
Lt. Dudley M. Amoss (38th) POW; Hit by flak at Hopsten A/F.
P-51D CG- 44-15123 "Queenie"
Lt. June B. Stallings (38th) KIA; Hit by flak at Hopsten A/F.
P-51D CG-

**March 22, 1945**
Lt. John F. O'Neil (38th) MIA; Hit by flak at Lechfeld.
P-51D CG-
F/O George Nostanovitch (343rd) POW; Hit by flak near Halle.
P-51D CY-G 44-14985 "The Millie G"

**March 24, 1945**
Lt. Stanley E. Chapple (38th) MIA; Hit by fighters near Soest.
P-51D CG- 44-72080

**April 7, 1945**
Lt. Harold J. Konantz (338th) POW; Hit by B-17 fire near Pritzwalk.
P-51D CL-P 44-72296 "Saturday Night"

**April 9, 1945**
Lt. Richard K. Abel (343rd) KIA; Hit by flak at Munich-Brunnthal.
P-51D CY-H 44-64159 "Jill's Jalopy"

**April 10, 1945**
Lt. Joseph M. Holland (338th) KIA; Hit by flak near Burg.
P-51D CL- 44-72274

**April 16, 1945**
Lt. Donald J. Best (38th) KIA; Hit by flak at Munich-Brunnthal and crashed near Augsburg.
P-51D CG- 44-72409 "Little Lulu"
Lt. Vernon B. Tally (338th) POW; Hit by flak at Munich-Brunnthal and bellied-in near Bonn.
P-51D CL-W 44-63287 "My Jane"
Capt. Chester E. Coggeshall (343rd) KIA; Hit by flak at Munich-Brunnthal.
P-51D CY-T 44-15608 "Cape Cod Express"
Lt. Patrick L. Moore (343rd) KIA; Hit by flak and spun-in south of Munich.
P-51D CY-Y 44-14235 "Little Jan"

**April 17, 1945**
LtCol. Elwyn G. Righetti (HdQts) KIA; Hit by flak near Dresden. Bellied-in and was killed by civilians.
P-51D CL-M 44-72227 "Katy Did"
Lt. Robert K. Thacker (338th) POW; Hit by flak and bailed out west of Dresden.
P-51D CL- 44-15639
Lt. George A. Apple (343rd) KIA; Hit by flak near Dresden.
P-51D CY-D 44-15735
Lt. Philip A. Erby (343rd) KIA; Hit by flak while chasing a FW-190 near Kamenz A/F.
P-51D CY-F 44-15025
Lt. Daniel A. Langelier (343rd) MIA; Hit by flak near Dresden.
P-51D CY- 44-72349

**May 3, 1945**
Capt. William F. McGill (338th) KIAc;
P-51D CL-

**May ???, 1945**
Lt. John R. Duxbury (343rd) KIAc;
P-51B CY- 43-6928

**Headquarters**
Beaird, Thomas E., Jr., Capt.; States-April 1944
Brooks, Philip, Maj.; April 1945-EOW; ex-338th Ftr Sqn
Busching, Richard W., Maj.; March 1944-July 1944; ex-338th Ftr Sqn
Clark, McCauley, Capt.; January 1945-EOW; ex-38th Ftr Sqn
Cramer, Darrell S., Maj.; February 1945-June 1945; ex-338th Ftr Sqn(see for details)
Crowell, George T., Col.; States-February 1945
P-38H CY-C
P-38J CY-C
P-51D CY-C
Guthrie, Bernie V., Capt.; February 1944-April 22, 1944(KIA)
Gustke, Rusell F., Maj.; States-February 1944; to 20th Ftr Grp; ex-14th Ftr Grp, MTO
Hayes, Jack W., Jr., LtCol.; May 1945-July 1946; ex-357th Ftr Grp & bomber pilot
Hoeper, Paul E., Maj.; June 1944-EOW; ex-343rd Ftr Sqn
P-51D CY-H 44-64159 "Jill's Jalopy VII"
James, Frank B., Col.; States-February 1944
Jenkins, Jack S., LtCol.; States-April 10, 1944(POW)
P-38H CG-J 42-67074 "Texas Ranger"
P-38J CG-J "Texas Ranger II"
P-38J CG-J "Texas Ranger III"
P-38J CG-J 42-67825 "Texas Ranger IV"
Jones, Charles O., LtCol.; April 1944-January 1945; ex-338th Ftr Sqn
Kelly, Wendell J., LtCol.; June 1944-November 1944; ex-367th Ftr Grp, 9th Air Force
Myers, Joseph, Jr., LtCol.; February 1945-June 1945; ex-38th Ftr Sqn & 78th Ftr Grp
130 missions, 430 hours total
P-51K CG-V
Parker, Douglas A., Capt.; July 1944-September 1944; to 343rd Ftr Sqn
Parsons, Albert B., Maj.; July 1944-September 1944; to 38th Ftr Sqn; ex-479th Ftr Grp
Patterson, Chet A., Maj.; April 1944-November 1944; ex-38th Ftr Sqn
Righetti, Elwyn G., LtCol.; February 1945-April 17, 1945(KIA); ex-338th Ftr Sqn
P-51D CL-M 44-72227 "KatyDid"
Rimerman, Ben, Col.; April 1945-May 1945; ex-353rd Ftr Grp
P-51D CY-V 44-72469
Shipman, Mark K., Maj.; February 1944-April 1944; ex-38th Ftr Sqn
P-38J CG- "Skylark V"
Tally, Vernon B., Lt.; March 1945-April 1945; to 338th Ftr Sqn
Thompson, Jesse D., Capt.; September 1944-February 1945
Webb, Dallas W., Maj.; April 1944- ex-343rd Ftr Sqn
P-38J CY-W "Spider"

**38th Fighter Squadron**
Achramowicz, Walter T., Lt.; August 1944-July 1945
56 missions
Albino, Albert A., Lt.; May 1943-November 29, 1943(KIA)
P-38H CG- "Spirit of Aberdeen"
Amoss, Dudley M., Lt.; August 1944-March 21, 1945(POW)
59 missions
P-51D CG-B 44-13818 "Mah Ideel"
Anderson, John E., Lt.; March 1945-EOW
13 missions
Anderson, Millard O., Capt.; October 1944-August 1945
53 missions
Anderson, Sam F., Lt.; February 1945-March 2, 1945(MIA)
1 mission
Ayers, Jerry H., Capt.; May 1942-May 1944
P-38H CG-Q 42-67077 "Mountain Ayers"
Bachman, Darrell D., Lt.; March 1945-EOW
12 missions
Beckett, Lawrence E., Lt.; March 1945-EOW
15 missions
Bender, Robert V., Lt.; February 1945-September 1945
11 missions
Best, Donald J., Lt.; February 1945-April 16, 1945(KIA)
11 missions
Birch, William K., Lt.; April 1943-December 16, 1943(KIA)
Breathwit, Carl E., Capt.; September 1944-March 1945
55 missions
Brown, Gerald, Capt.; March 1943-May 1944
P-38H CG-G 42-67028
P-38J CG-G
Caldwell, William R., Lt.; June 1944-July 1944(Injured July 5)
Callaghan, Robert E., Lt.; June 1944-January 1945
Carmel, Arthur, Lt.; June 1944-June 28, 1944(KIAc)
Carr, Alfred E., Jr., Lt.; September 1944-February 20, 1945(POW)
32 missions
Carroll, John J., Lt.; June 1943-November 29, 1943(POW)
Castle, Dorman L., Lt.; April 1944-December 1944
Cavanaugh, Dennis A., Lt.; March 1945-April 1945(Injured)
10 missions
Chamberlain, Claude, Lt.; May 1944-November 1944
Chapman, Charles W., Lt.; December 1943-March 1944 (Injured March 17)
Chapple, Stanley E., Lt.; January 1945-March 24, 1945(KIA)
16 missions
Clark, McCauley, Capt.; August 1944-January 1945; to HdQts
P-51D CG-S "Tennessee Belle"
Clemmons, Billy, Lt.; August 1944-April 1945
62 missions
Clifton, Oscar B., Capt.; April 1944-October 1944
Conners, Robert M., Lt.; March 1945-July 1945
12 missions
Coonan, John F., Capt.; September 1944-January 3, 1945(POW); ex-51st Ftr Grp, CBI
Coons, Merle M., Capt.; June 1944-December 1944
P-51D CG-C 44-14068 "The Worry Bird"
Cory, Grant, Lt.; June 1944-June 23, 1944(KIA)
Courtney, David H., Lt.; August 1944-March 1945
60 missions
Coward, Huey R., Lt.; August 1944-November 26, 1944(KIA)
24 missions
Cox, Robert M., Capt.; August 1944-April 1945
63 missions
Cox, Robert W., Lt.; May 1945-July 1945
0 missions
Crawford, Kenneth I., Lt.; May 1944-September 11, 1944(KIA)
P-51D CG-Z 44-13804 "Arabel"
Cummings, Donald M., Capt.; December 1944-EOW; ex-27th Ftr Grp, MTO
33 missions
P-51D CG-U 44-15192
Cunnick, John W., III, Lt.; January 1945-July 1945
37 missions
Daley, Joseph F., Lt.; April 1945-EOW
4 missions
Des Voignes, Clair W., Capt.; May 1943-July 13, 1944(KIA)
Dunning, George R., Lt.; April 1945-EOW
4 missions
Dupuy, John C., Lt.; April 1945-September 1945
2 missions
DuRose, William C., Lt.; May 1944-June 17, 1944(MIA-E)
Earls, Lester, Capt.; December 1943-September 1944
P-51D CG-N 44-13927 "Miss Boomerang"
Elliott, David G., Lt.; May 1944-August 10, 1944(POW-E)
Erickson, Robert E., Lt.; May 1943-May 1944
Erickson, Wilton G., Lt.; November 1943-December 1, 1943(KIA)
1 mission
Fisher, David D., Lt.; May 1943-January 31, 1944(KIA)
Fisher, Paul, Lt.; April 1943-August 1944
Fleming, Lawrence J., Lt.; January 1945-EOW
38 missions, 197 hours

Forsblad, Richard W., Capt.; April 1943-August 1944
Fryer, Earl R., Capt.; May 1944-November 8, 1944(KIA)
P-51D CG-Z 44-13804 "Spunktown"
Garvin, James M., Lt.; April 1943-November 29, 1943(KIA)
Gillette, Hugh R., Lt.; April 1943-May 1943; to 343rd Ftr Sqn
Gould, Clifford C., Lt.; May 1944-December 1944
Greenmyre, Vernie B., Lt.; February 1944-June 16, 1944(POW)
P-38J CG- "Man??? Dwaine"
Griswold, Oliver W., Capt.; June 1944-July 1945
Hancock, James H., Maj.; June 1942-July 1944
P-38H CG- "Repulsive"
Hawes, Melvin A., Lt.; February 1944-May 1944 (Injured May 13)
Hoffman, Robert M., Lt.; April 1944-June 23, 1944(KIA)
Hokinson, Leroy V., Jr., Lt.; December 1943-January 31, 1944(MIA-E)
6 missions
Holderman, Eugene M., Capt.; June 1944-December 1944
Holleman, Tunis H., Lt.; June 1944-December 1944
Hummel, Julius M., Lt.; February 1944-April 15, 1944(POW)
Jackson, Donald G., Lt.; September 1944-May 1945
Jaklich, Lester E., Lt.; February 1944-August 10, 1944(KIA)
P-38J CG-W "Angel Puss"
P-51D CG-W 44-13888 "Angel Puss"
Jewell, David F., Jr., Lt.; July 1944-March 1945
P-51D CG- "Miss Boomerang Margie"
Joel, Milton, Maj.; October 1942-November 29, 1943(KIA)
Jones, Robert, Lt.; August 1944-March 1945
40 missions
Kavanaugh, John W., Capt.; September 1944-April 1945
55 missions
P-51D CG-I "Missouri Banshee"
Klank, Walter C., Lt.; August 1944-October 1944; to 3rd Scouting Force
13 missions
Koenig, Albert M., Lt.; August 1944-April 1945
63 missions
Kreft, Willard L., Lt.; April 1943-May 1944
Landers, John D., Maj.; March 1944-September 1944; ex-49th Ftr Grp, PTO
P-38J CG-O "Big Beautiful Doll"
P-51D CG-O 44-13823 "Big Beautiful Doll"
Lapham, Richard L., Lt.; August 1944-November 20, 1944(MIA)
36 missions
Larson, Norman L., Lt.; July 1944-December 1944
Laubner, William, Lt.; February 1944-April 15, 1944(MIA)
Lawrence, Edwin B., Lt.; July 1944-October 14, 1944(KIA)
Leinweber, Gerald F., Lt.; May 1943-May 1944
P-38J CG-U "Texas Rebel"
Leve, Morris, Lt.; August 1942-January 31, 1944(KIA)
Lewis, William H., Lt.; July 1944-August 10, 1944(KIA)
Lewis, William M., Jr., Lt.; July 1944-September 11, 1944(KIA)
Littlefield, Robert M., Lt.; April 1944-August 10, 1944(MIA-E)
Luckett, Thomas B., Lt.; June 1944-August 24, 1944(KIA)
Maloney, John T., Lt.; February 1945-November 1945
23 missions
P-51D CG-U
Maloney, Robert F., Capt.; May 1943-March 1945
P-51D CG-Z 44-15421
Matney, Francis M., Lt.; July 1944-January 1945
P-51D CG- "Nina"
Mayer, Douglas E., Lt.; August 1944-September 12, 1944(KIA)
11 missions
McGinnis, Keith R., Lt.; December 1944-November 1945
47 missions
P-51D CG-N
Menegay, Donald T., Lt.; December 1944-September 1945
44 missions
Miller, John W., Lt.; December 1944-August 1945
36 missions
Miller, Martin B., Lt.; December 1943-January 31, 1944(KIA)
Mirando, Joseph F., Lt.; December 1944-September 1945
46 missions
Monty, William, Lt.; February 1944-June 1944 (Injured June 17)
Mooers, Harold B., Lt.; December 1944-September 1945
42 missions
Mooers, Roger B., Lt.; November 1944-September 1945
22 missions
Morrow, Ralph E., Lt.; December 1944-July 1945
51 missions
Myers, Joseph, Jr., Maj.; June 1942-April 1944; later 78th Ftr Grp & HdQts
130 missions, 430 hours total
P-38H CG-O
P-38J CG-O "Journey's End"
Odiorne, John M., F/O; April 1945-EOW
4 missions
O'Neil, John F., Lt.; December 1944-March 22, 1945(KIA)
31 missions
Parsons, Albert B., Maj.; September 1944-December 1944; ex-HdQts
Patterson, Leon M., Lt.; December 1943-January 31, 1944(KIA)
Penn, Donald E., Maj.; August 1943-March 1945
P-51D CG-Q 44-14451 "Big Bitch"
Peters, Allen R., Lt.; May 1943-May 1944
Peters, Edward F., Lt.; August 1943-January 5, 1944(POW)
Peterson, Clayton L., Maj.; September 1944-September 1945; ex-49th Ftr Grp, PTO
P-51D CG- "Hell's Angel"
Quinn, Richard F., Lt.; December 1944-EOW
34 missions
Rauh, Richard J., F/O; April 1945-August 1945
3 missions
Rieder, John L., Lt.; September 1944-February 14, 1945(MIA)
39 missions
Reilly, William J., Lt.; April 1944-October 1944
Rhodes, Harold W., Lt.; April 1944-July 28, 1944(MIA)
Rosenburgh, Robert A., Capt.; December 1943-September 1944
Russell, Frank R., F/O; December 1944-January 7, 1945(MIA)
15 missions
Ryan, Andrew J., Lt.; May 1945-July 1945
0 missions
Schendel, Charles R., Lt.; March 1945-September 1945
14 missions
Sharp, Robert L., F/O; May 1945-July 1945
0 missions
Shepard, Bert R., Lt.; February 1944-May 21, 1944(POW)
Sherman, Clifford C., Lt.; May 1944-October 1944
P-51D CG- "New Arrival"
Shipman, Mark K., Maj.; April 1943-February 1944; to HdQts; ex-14th Ftr Grp, MTO
P-38H CG-S 42-67080 "Skylark IV"
Silk, John W., Lt.; May 1944-October 1944
Sill, Robert L., Lt.; September 1944-February 20, 1945(KIA)
46 missions
Simpson, Richard S., Capt.; December 1943-August 1944
Snell, Donald H., Capt.; February 1944-September 1944
P-51D CG-A 44-13549 "My Ready Steady"
Soule, Van Halen, Capt.; February 1944-September 1944
Spiecker, Lester F., Capt.; September 1944-April 1945
58 missions
St. Germain, Roger C., Lt.; May 1945-July 1945
0 missions
Stacker, John A., Lt.; August 1943-November 13, 1943(KIA)
4 missions
Staggs, William B., Capt.; September 1944-September 1945
56 missions
Stallings, June B., Lt.; February 1945-March 21, 1945(MIA)
11 missions
Steiner, Delorn L., Lt.; April 1943-January 31, 1944(KIA)
Sturgess, Fred L., Lt.; September 1944-November 2, 1944(POW)
10 missions
Taylor, Edward S., Lt.; May 1945-EOW
0 missions
Thompson, Robert S., Lt.; November 1943-January 24, 1944(POW)
Thorsen, Arthur L., Lt.; February 1944-October 1944
P-51D CG-I 44-13747 "Six Gun Pete"
Tibor, Robert P., Lt.; February 1944-September 1944
Tiedemann, Henry J., Jr., Lt.; December 1943-January 23, 1944(KIAc)
Tipton, Noah R., Lt.; December 1943-May 21, 1944(POW)
P-38J CG-X 42-67971 "Noah's Ark"
Totten, Wesley V., F/O; September 1944-March 1945
52 missions
Tracey, Dean E., Lt.; January 1945-July 1945
30 missions
Turner, William, Lt.; November 1943-February 24, 1944(KIA)
Underwood, Kenneth H., Lt.; February 1944-May 18, 1944(KIAc)
23 missions
Waice, Francis J., Lt.; August 1944-February 1945
54 missions
Walters, Elton S., Lt.; February 1944-April 12, 1944(KIA)
Watts, Cecil R., Capt.; January 1944-August 1944
P-51C CG-M 43-25044 "East Side Rat"
Wegner, Gordon V., Lt.; April 1944-October 1944
Williams, Clarence T., Capt.; September 1944-May 1945
57 missions
Winter, Herbert T., Lt.; November 1943-January 5, 1944(KIA)
Woods, Albert M., Capt.; December 1943-August 1944
P-38J CG-O 42-67904
P-51D CG-O 44-13973 "Sweet Ellouise"
Wyche, Wilton E., Capt.; September 1942-May 1944

**338th Fighter Squadron**
Alba, Michael, Capt.; June 1944-December 1944
Anderson, Lanoy D., Maj.; June 1944-November 1944
Anderson, Newell, F/O; April 1943-April 9, 1944(KIA)
Armstrong, Malcolm G., Lt.; June 1944-June 21, 1944(MIA)
Atckison, Richard G., Lt.; January 1944-March 1944; ex-14th Ftr Grp, MTO (1 victory)
Baranick, Arthur, Lt.; November 1943-June 14, 1944(MIA)
Barnes, William H., Lt.; March 1945-EOW
Barrett, Richard I., Lt.; September 1944-November 26, 1944(POW)
Bauer, John E., Lt.; August 1944-September 1, 1944(MIA)
Beall, Charles E., Lt.; September 1942-November 13, 1943(KIA
Berry, Lawrence J., Lt.; April 1944-July 5, 1944(KIA)
Biedul, Chester A., Lt.; November 1943-August 1944
P-38J CL- "Miss Ann"
Black, Robert E., Lt.; March 1945-July 1945
Blanchard, Merle E., Capt.; States-August 1944

Blount, Delbert F., Lt.; March 1944-July 21, 1944(POW)
Bodiford, Hugh, Lt.; October 1944-July 1945
P-51D CL-U
Bollwerk, Val W., Maj.; December 1943-June 11, 1944(POW)
Bone, Howard J., Lt.; November 1943-March 4, 1944(KIA)
Brady, James E., F/O; January 1945-November 1945
Bradford, Frank E., Lt.; September 1944-February 17, 1945(MIA)
Brooks, Philip, Maj.; August 1944-April 1945; to HdQts
Brown, Robert W., Lt.; States-December 22, 1943(POW)
Busching, Richard W., Maj.; September 1942-March 1944; to HdQts
Burns, William H., Capt.; States-December 1944
P-38J CL- "Miss Lightning Baby"
Buskirk, Clait E., Capt.; November 1943-January 6, 1945(POW)
Carson, Durwood D., Lt.; August 1944-September 13, 1944(POW)
Chambliss, Bill, Lt.; August 1944-August 23, 1944(KIAc)
0 missions
Chioles, Constantin S., Capt.; October 1944-July 1945
Conners, Arthur F., Lt.; January 1945-July 1945
Cooper, Roy E., Lt.; January 1945-October 1945
Cottrell, Kenneth D., Lt.; January 1945-February 24, 1945(MIA-E)
Cramer, Darrell S., Maj.; July 1944-February 1945; to HdQts; ex-347th Ftr Grp, PTO
60 missions, 300 hours
P-51D CL-Z 44-14121 "Mick #5"
Dargan, Archie S., Jr., Lt.; January 1945-September 1945
Darling, Richard E., Lt.; February 1945-EOW
Deloach, Robert, Lt.; January 1945-December 1945
Dempsey, Peter, Capt.; April 1943-October 7, 1944(POW)
Deatherage, Glenn K., Lt.; May 1945-July 1945
0 missions
Ditlevson, Dean W., Lt.; April 1945-July 1945
Doolan, John H., Lt.; April 1945-EOW
Duquette, Eugene H., Lt.; January 1945-EOW
Earnest, Wallace H., Lt.; May 1944-July 20, 1944(KIA)
Eastman, Philip, Jr., Lt.; October 1944-January 3, 1945(POW)
Eder, Charles J., Lt.; April 1945-EOW
Egre, Burdette V., Lt.; April 1945-EOW
Eiselt, Frank W., Lt.; April 1945-EOW
Elson, Norm, Lt.; February 1945-June 1945
Eskridge, John R., Lt.; June 1944-August 26, 1944(POW)
Ethridge, Jack R., Lt.; October 1944-April 1945
Florentine, William C., Jr., Lt.; States-November 13, 1943(POW)
Foster, Jack R., Lt.; January 1944-February 10, 1944(POW)
Freeman, Ray W., Lt.; March 1944-October 1944
Frescari, Aldo, F/O; December 1944-April 1945
Fruh, Robert K., Lt.; November 1943-October 1944
Funk, George E., Jr., Lt.; June 1944-December 1944
Garlock, Karl H., Capt.; March 1944-May 21, 1944(POW); ex-343rd Ftr Sqn
Garnett, Joseph E., Lt.; March 1944-July 28, 1944(KIAc)
Gebhardt, William P., Lt.; July 1944-December 1944
George, Ernest W., Lt.; States-March 24, 1944(POW)
Gerald, Stoddard B., Lt.; June 1944-July 25, 1944(POW)
Gerry, James L., Lt.; June 1944-December 1944
Gevorkian, Sam D., Capt.; June 1944-August 26, 1944(MIA-E); October 1944-August 8, 1945(KIAc)
P-51D CL-F 44-14156
Gilmore, Donald D., Lt.; March 1944-August 13, 1944(KIA)
Glaser, Kenneth M., Lt.; March 1944-September 5, 1944(MIA-E)
Goetzman, Lynn R., Lt.; States-November 13, 1943(POW)
Goodman, Orville E., Capt.; States-August 1944
Gregg, Eugene S., Jr., Capt.; October 1944-November 8, 1944(POW)
Griffith, Kenneth W., Lt.; October 1944-December 24, 1944(KIA)
Haily, David R., Lt.; March 1944-September 1944
Hansard, Samuel E., Lt.; March 1944-August 26, 1944(KIA)
Harbeck, Robert K., Lt.; September 1944-November 27, 1944(KIA)
1 mission
Harbert, William E., Lt.; April 1943-January 11, 1944(KIA)
Haworth, Russell C., Lt.; July 1944-December 1944
64 missions
P-51D CL-K 44-13642 "Krazy Kid"
Henry, Carroll D., Capt.; September 1944-June 1945
58 missions, 287 hours
P-51D CL-G 44-63227 "Little Trixie"
Herbst, Richard C., Lt.; September 1944-July 1945
Holland, Joseph M., Lt.; March 1945-April 10, 1945(KIA)
Ingram, William J., Lt.; February 1944-October 1944
Jensen, Robert N., Lt.; April 1943-November 13, 1943(POW)
12 missions
P-38H CL- 42-66724 "Miss Margaret"
Jonoski, Ted S., Lt.; December 1943-September 1944
John, Leedom K., Lt.; December 1944-September 1945
47 missions, 233 hours
P-51D CL-K 44-13642 "Ornery"
Jones, Charles O., Maj.; September 1942-April 1944; to HdQts
Keough, Richard J., Lt.; June 1944-August 12, 1944(POW)
Kershaw, Sam E., Lt.; February 1945-February 22, 1945(KIAc)
0 missions
Kester, John E., Lt.; August 1944-August 26, 1944(MIA-E); October 1944-January 14, 1945(KIA)
Kiernan, Thomas, Jr., Capt.; January 1945-July 1945
Knudson, Thomas K., Lt.; November 1943-April 8, 1944(KIA)
Konantz, Harold J., Lt.; March 1945-April 7, 1945(POW)
7 missions
Konantz, Walter J., Lt.; July 1944-April 1945
64 missions, 294:40 hours
P-51D CL-P 44-14278 "Saturday Night"
P-51D CL-P 44-72296
Korinek, George, Lt.; November 1943-June 24, 1944(POW)
LaBella, Victor, Lt.; November 1943-March 22, 1944(POW)
Lanham, Wayne J., Lt.; February 1944-September 1944
Larsen, Harry E., Capt.; April 1943-December 11, 1944(KIA)
Lashbrook, Kenneth A., Lt.; September 1944-April 1945
63 missions
P-51D CL-T "Li'l Doll"
Leonard, William J., Lt.; May 1944-December 1944
Lyin, Tunis J., Lt.; February 1944-April 15, 1944(MIA)
Mandeville, Harry C., Lt.; February 1945-EOW
Marsiglia, Joseph P., Capt.; September 1942-January 7, 1944(POW)
McCutcheon, James R., Lt.; August 1944-August 12, 1944(KIA)
McDonald, Jerry R., Capt.; July 1944-February 28, 1945(KIA)
McDowell, Bert, Jr., Capt.; August 1944-February 6, 1945(POW)
55 missions
P-51K CL-V 44-11687 "Betty-Mac"
McFarland, Arthur H., Lt.; July 1944-August 10, 1944(KIA)
McGill, William F., Capt.; January 1945-May 3, 1945(KIAc); ex-MTO pilot
P-51D CL- 44-13743 "Skippy"
McGinn, John L., LtCol.; April 1944-October 1944; ex-18th & 347th Ftr Grps, PTO
64 missions, 271:40 hours
P-38J CL-P 43-28833 "DaQuake"
P-51D CL-P 44-14291 "DaQuake"
P-51D CL-P 44-14730 "DaQuake"
McKee, John E., Lt.; May 1944-November 1944
McMillan, William E., Lt.; July 1944-August 12, 1944(KIA)
Meade, Donald J., Lt.; December 1944-March 1945
Mercurio, Elmer L., Lt.; May 1944-November 1944
P-51D CL-X 44-13743 "Skippy"
Metcalf, Harold B., Lt.; December 1944-December 30, 1944(KIA)
Miller, Roy D., Lt.; August 1944-June 1945
Oates, Ettry J., Capt.; October 1944-July 1945
Odegard, John L., Capt.; April 1943-May 1944
P-38J CL- 42-67962 "Bambi"
Parker, Thomas A., Capt.; December 1943-August 1944
Patterson, Chet A., Maj.; September 1942-February 1944; later to HdQts
P-38J CL-P 42-67816 "Princess Pat"
Peterson, George W., Lt.; April 1944-June 16, 1944(POW)
7 missions
Pierce, Thomas E., F/O; April 1945-EOW
Presari, Aldo, F/O; December 1944-April 1945
Pruitt, John R., Lt.; April 1943-December 22, 1943(KIA)
Ramm, Albert J., Capt.; August 1944-April 1945
P-51D CL-F "Ginny"
Reeves, Paul R., Lt.; September 1944-April 1945
Richardson, Stanley P., Capt.; December 1943-August 1944
P-38H CL-X 42-67057
P-38J CL-X 42-67305
Righetti, Elwyn G., LtCol.; October 1944-February 1945; to HdQts
P-51D CL-M 44-14223 "KatyDid"
Ryan, Eugene E., Maj.; April 1945-December 1945; ex-343rd Ftr Sqn
Saken, Lawrence A., F/O; May 1945-July 1945
0 missions
Schank, Thomas D., Lt.; April 1944-October 1944
P-38J CL-T 42-104106 "Stinger"
P-51D CL-I 44-13668 "Rocky Mtn. Canary"
Schneider, Kenneth C., Lt.; September 1944-April 1945
Schranz, William, Lt.; May 1945-July 1945
0 missions
Schonenberg, Herman J., Lt.; August 1944-April 1945
Shank, William W., Lt.; States-November 13, 1943(KIA)
Sharp, Francis R., Lt.; September 1944-October 9, 1944(KIAc)
Sheppard, Lawrence B., F/O; May 1945-July 1945
0 missions
Sims, Hal B., Capt.; October 1944-April 1945
Skoglund, Bruce C., F/O; May 1945-July 1945
0 missions
Snow, Ted R., F/O; May 1945-July 1945
0 missions
Stephens, Gene C., Lt.; States-November 13, 1943(POW)
Stephens, John E., Lt.; May 1945-EOW
0 missions
Suiter, Fleming C., Lt.; April 1943-November 29, 1943(POW)
Sullivan, Jeremiah J., Lt.; September 1944-April 1945
Tally, Vernon B., Lt.; April 1945-April 16, 1945(POW); ex-HdQts
Thacker, Robert L., Lt.; September 1944-April 17, 1945(POW)
Thomas, John W., Lt.; April 1944-May 20, 1944(KIA)
Tibbetts, Wesley M., Capt.; September 1942-February 24, 1944(KIA)
Tinto, Anthony J., Capt.; November 1943-September 1944
Turner, Lloyd P., Lt.; States-September 1944
Turner, William G., Lt.; April 1943-December 1, 1943(KIA)
Van Horn, Robert L., Lt.; January 1945-March 18, 1945(KIA)
Wakeland, John M., Lt.; April 1944-October 1944
Walser, Ray F., Lt.; February 1945-EOW
Walter, Horace K., Lt.; April 1944-May 21, 1944(KIA)
Watkins, William R., Lt.; January 1945-EOW

West, Fred W., Lt.; December 1943-March 24, 1944(MIA-E)
Wheeler, Edwin C., Lt.; April 1944-June 15, 1944(POW)
White, John C., Lt.; February 1945-August 5, 1945(KIAc)
White, Thomas A., Maj.; States-July 1944; ex-82nd Ftr Grp, MTO (6 kills)
P-38J CL-V "Janet"
Wiens, Maynard J., Capt.; May 1944-February 1945
Wikholm, Bradford K., Lt.; February 1944-March 18, 1944(KIA)
Wiley, James H., Jr., Lt.; January 1945-EOW
Wirth, Fred C., Jr., Lt.; January 1945-EOW
Wright, Albert E., Capt.; September 1944-March 1945

**343rd Fighter Squadron**

Abel, Richard K., Lt.; March 1945-April 9, 1945(KIA)
Adams, Donald E., Lt.; March 1945-EOW
P-51D CY-R
Aldecoa, Manuel J., Lt.; States-November 25, 1943(KIA)
Allen, Ray G., Lt.; March 1945-EOW
P-51D CY-A 44-13350 "Merrimack"
Allen, William H., Lt.; May 1944-October 1944
89 missions, 270 hours
P-38J CY-V 42-67966 "Pretty Patty"
P-51D CY-J 44-14049 "Pretty Patty II"
Apple, George A., Lt.; March 1945-April 17, 1945(KIA)
Arnold, Guy E., Lt.; March 1945-EOW
P-51D CY-V
Ashton, William J., Lt.; December 1943-February 6, 1944(KIA)
Baribault, Richard F., Lt.; March 1945-July 1945
P-51D CY-Y
Barnett, John, Lt.; States-January 5, 1944(KIA)
Bartlett, Richard D., Lt.; May 1944-November 1944
P-51D CY-O
Bartz, Norman J., Capt.; -September 1944
Bauer, Harold M., Lt.; States-May 1944
Bebaeff, Nick P., Lt.; June 1944-January 1945
P-51D CY-Y 44-15246 "Miss Mayna"
Bernardo, George W., F/O; March 1945-September 1945
P-51D CY-X 44-14632
Bevington, Jack L., Lt.; March 1945-EOW
P-51D CY-L
Birtciel, Frank E., Capt.; August 1943-April 1945
121 missions
P-38J CY-D 42-67872
P-51D CY-D 44-14561 "Miss Velma"
P-51D CY-A 44-13350 "Miss Velma"
Bishop, Richard D., Lt.; May 1944-October 1944
P-51D CY-M
Blair, Floyd A., Lt.; June 1944-December 1944
P-51D CY-E
Boring, Lloyd D., Lt.; October 1944-April 1945
P-51D CY-D 44-15735 "Dizzy Jess"
Brokaw, James D., Lt.; June 1944-July 30, 1944(MIA)
Brown, Robert D., Capt.; States-March 20, 1945(INT)
P-38J CY-V
P-51D CY-V 44-14135
Buttke, Robert L., Capt.; March 1943-April 1945
P-38H CY-F 42-67047 "Lavenia"
P-38J CY-F "Lavenia"
P-51D CY-F 44-15025 "Beautiful Lavenia"
Coggeshall, Chester E., Capt.; April 16, 1945(KIA)
P-51D CY-T 44-15608 "Cape Cod Express"
Cohen, Henry E., Lt.; January 1945-July 1945
P-51D CY-O
Cole, Gene H., Lt.; May 1944-November 1944
P-51D CY-F
Cooter, Alvin B., Lt.; May 1945-July 1945
0 missions
Courtney, John, Lt.; September 1944-March 1945
P-51D CY-C
Dey, Russell C., Jr., Lt.; April 1945-July 1945
DeYoung, Arthur A., Capt.; States-September 1944
Dixon, Donald F., Lt.; April 1945-EOW
Dripps, Paul S., Capt.; States-January 1945
P-51D CY-P
Duxbury, John R., Lt.; April 1945-May 1945(KIAc)
Dvorak, Edward J., Lt.; February 1944-September 1944
Eichorn, George E., Lt.; January 1945-February 21, 1945(POW)
Eliades, Jordan, Lt.; September 1944-November 20, 1944(POW)
Engle, Richard L., Lt.; December 1944-December 31, 1944(KIAc)
Erb, Russell W., Jr., Lt.; -November 1944; to 354th Ftr Grp
P-38J CY-H 42-68095 "Drippy Lil"
Erby, Philip A., Lt.; March 1945-April 17, 1945(KIA)
Erickson, Wayne R., Lt.; January 1945-July 1945
Fair, Gene R., Lt.; States-June 1944
Finlayson, John E., Lt.; October 1944-January 18, 1945(KIA)
Fischer, Frank L., Lt.; June 1944-December 1944
Fisher, Walter R., Lt.; January 1945-July 1945
P-51D CY-J
Fluty, Joseph M., Lt.; States-March 8, 1944(KIA)
Franklin, R.C., Maj.; February 1943-February 1944; to 20th Ftr Grp
Fry, David M., Lt.; June 1944-September 13, 1944(POW)
Gangemi, Philip, Lt.; August 1944-March 1945
P-51D CY-X 44-14632
Garlock, Karl H., Capt.; February 1944-March 1944; to 338th Ftr Sqn
Geary, Edward H., Lt.; February 1945-July 1945
P-51D CY-K "Princess Pat"
Gehrig, John, Lt.; January 1945-September 1945
P-51D CY-W 44-14379 "Hiya Mert"
Geibel, Richard M., Lt.; June 1944-September 1944
Gibbs, Richard G., Lt.; January 1945-EOW
42 missions, 192 hours
P-51D CY-Q 44-15314
Gifford, Donald R., Lt.; January 1945-September 1945
P-51D CY-I
Gilbride, James W., Lt.; States-November 29, 1943(KIA)
P-38H CY-L 42-67053 "Vivacious Vera"
Gillette, Hugh R., Lt.; May 1943-October 18, 1943(KIA); ex-38th Ftr Sqn
Giller, Edward B., Maj.; February 1943-June 1945
115 missions, 420 hours
P-38J CY-G "The Millie G"
P-51D CY-G 44-14985 "The Millie G"
P-51D CY-G 44-15701 "The Millie G"
P-51D CY-G 44-63204 "The Millie G"
P-51D CY-G 44-72123 "The Millie G"
Goethel, Carl J., Lt.; February 1944-June 11, 1944(MIA-E)
Gordon, Vincent P., Capt.; October 1944-July 1945
P-51D CY-P 44-14348 "Lady Val"
Goudelock, Hugh J., Lt.; November 1943-May 1944
Gourley, Ben H., Lt.; February 1944-March 15, 1944(KIA)
Hiner, James W., Lt.; States-August 26, 1944(MIA)
P-38J CY- "The Brat"
Hjelm, Rex P., Lt.; February 1944-June 11, 1944(MIA-E)
Hodge, Charles H., Lt.; February 1944-
Hoeper, Paul E., Maj.; February 1943-June 1944; September 1944-November 1944; to HdQt
P-38J CY-H "Jill's Jalopy"
P-51D CY-H 44-15060 "Jill's Jalopy VI"
Hoffman, Ted E., Lt.; July 1944-March 1945
P-51D CY-T 44-15608 "Sonny Boy"
Howes, Bernard H., Lt.; September 1944-March 3, 1945(POW)
P-51D CY-C
Jiorle, Joseph B., Lt.; -August 16, 1944(POW)
Kelley, Robert E., Capt.; States-July 1944
Kenning, Robert J., Lt.; December 1943-January 5, 1944(KIA)
Kibler, John T., Jr., Lt.; September 1944-October 15, 1944(MIA)
King, Maynard R., Lt.; August 1944-September 10, 1944(KIA)
Krambo, Victor P., Lt.; September 1944-February 27, 1945(POW)
P-51D CY-U 44-15406
Langelier, Daniel A., Lt.; March 1945-April 17, 1945(KIA)
Larson, Frank A., Lt.; December 1943-December 31, 1943(POW)
Lawrence, Floyd C., Jr., Capt.; July 1944-April 1945
P-51D CY-L 44-14149 "Sweet Pootie"
P-51D CY-L 44-13643 "Sweet Pootie"
Leon, Ernest E., Lt.; March 1945-EOW
P-51D CY-L 44-14149
Leone, Frank J., Capt.; December 1943-September 1944
Leslie, Gus D., Lt.; July 1944-November 5, 1944(POW)
P-51D CY-A 44-13363 "Bama Blitz"
Lewis, Warren E., Lt.; September 1944-October 6, 1944(POW)
Lewis, William H., Capt.; June 1944-February 1945
325 hours
P-51D CY-S 44-13907
Light, Clyde W., Lt.; March 1945-EOW
P-51D CY-T
Liles, Brooks J., Lt.; October 1944-March 3, 1945(POW)
17 missions
Lloyd, Robert V., Lt.; December 1943-March 4, 1944(MIA)
Loring, Warren E., Lt.; June 1944-June 30, 1944(MIA-E)
Love, Thomas M., Lt.; September 1944-February 24, 1945(POW)
P-51D CY-I 44-14296 "Mardy"
Mahany, Howard, Jr., Lt.; March 1945-July 1945
P-51D CY-M
Malmstedt, Roland M., Capt.; February 1943-December 2, 1943(KIAc)
P-38J CY-M
Marshall, Roy T., Lt.; December 1943-February 1944
Maxwell, Robert A., Lt.; September 1944-December 25, 1944(KIA)
May, James, Lt.; States-August 1944
P-38J CY-J 43-28285 "The Black Hawk IV"
McCabe, John, Lt.; September 1944-April 1945
P-51D CY-K
McConnell, Victor T., Lt.; April 1944-May 27, 1944(KIA)
McDonnell, John E., Lt.; September 1944-December 23, 1944(KIA)
McHargh, Sterling W., Lt.; September 1944-February 1945
P-51D CY-Y
McKelvey, Harry C., F/O; April 1945-EOW
McVay, James C., Lt.; September 1944-March 1945
P-51D CY-J
Mearns, William, Lt.; December 1944-September 1945
P-51D CY-S
Mercier, Donald L., Lt.; June 1944-December 1944
62 missions
P-51D CY-B 44-14384 "Lil Pearl"

Michaelson, Charles R., Lt.; December 1944-February 20, 1945(POW)
Milner, Robert A., Lt.; December 1944-September 1945
P-51D CY-U
Mix, Kenneth J., Lt.; December 1944-December 24, 1944(KIA)
Moore, Patrick L., Lt.; December 1944-April 16, 1945(KIA)
P-51D CY-Y
Morris, Grady, Lt.; December 1944-February 19, 1945(POW)
P-51D CY-Y 44-14235 "Little Jan"
Moss, William R., Lt.; February 1945-April 1945
Mull, Ray L., Lt.; August 1944-September 9, 1944(MIA-E)
Murray, John S., Lt.; States-June 1944
Nastanovich, George, F/O; February 1945-March 22, 1945(POW)
Nease, Robert F., Lt.; April 1945-September 1945
P-51D CY-C
Ozinga, Richard, Lt.; August 1944-March 1945
P-51D CY-M 44-13837 "Miss Marilyn II"
Parker, Douglas A., Capt.; September 1944-EOW; ex-HdQts
P-51D CY-D 44-14885 "Nervous Nell"
Penners, Clair A., Lt.; States-April 22, 1944(POW)
Perez, William R., Jr., Lt.; April 1944-January 1945
P-51D CY-W
Piscitelli, Anthony L., Lt.; -April 10, 1944(KIA)
Pope, William K., Lt.; April 1944-January 1945
P-51D CY-Q
Porter, Clair D., Lt.; States-June 16, 1944(POW)
Porter, Paul R., Lt.; June 1944-November 2, 1944(KIA)
P-51D CY-K 44-13874 "June Bug II"
Raducha, Ben J., F/O; April 1945-EOW
Roberts, James W., Lt.; -August 17, 1944(KIA)
Rosenhoff, Wayne E., Lt.; June 1944-September 11, 1944(POW)
Ryan, Eugene E., Maj.; February 1943-April 1945; to 338th Ftr Sqn
P-38H CY-R 42-67084
P-38J CY-R
P-51D CY-R 44-63231
Satenstein, Marvin, Lt.; September 1944-March 1945
P-51D CY-W 44-14379 "Pudgy"
Seely, Ralph A., Lt.; February 1944-August 1944
Sorace, Kenneth J., Capt.; States-June 14, 1944(MIA-E)
P-38H CY-S 42-67066 "Pitter Pat"
P-38J CY-S 42-67900
Spanlan, Stephen, F/O; May 1945-EOW
0 missions
Stanton, Richard C., Lt.; States-August 1944
Steele, George H., Lt.; May 1945-EOW
0 missions
Stepanlan, Stephen, F/O; May 1945-EOW
0 missions
Stephenson, Franklin A., Capt.; February 1944-September 1944
Stevens, Richard C., Lt.; April 1945-July 1945
P-51D CY-N
Strauch, Walter, Capt.; October 1944-September 1945
P-51D CY-B 44-72362
Sturdivan, William H., Lt.; April 1944-June 14, 1944(MIA)
Sumpter, Ray L., Lt.; -February 6, 1944(KIA)
Thompson, Clifford O., Lt.; May 1945-EOW
0 missions
Tischer, Frank L., Lt.; June 1944-January 1945
P-51D CY-Z 44-14580 "Ellie-My Little Six"
Van Abel, Richard K., Lt.; March 1945-April 9, 1945(KIA)
Vieck, Louis L., Lt.; December 1943-February 1944
Walker, John E., Lt.; April 1944-July 9, 1944(POW)
Warwick, Henry K., Lt.; December 1943-May 21, 1944(KIA)
Webb, Dallas W., Maj.; February 1943-April 1944; to HdQts
P-38J CY-W "Spider"
Weisel, James H., Lt.; February 1944-May 21, 1944(POW)
Welch, Robert E., Capt.; September 1944-September 1945
P-51D CY-O
P-51D CY-Z 44-72138
Wickenden, Henry R., Lt.; May 1944-November 1944
P-51D CY-U
Williams, Clifford O., Lt.; April 1944-May 27, 1944(MIA-E)
Williams, Kenneth T., Lt.; June 1944-September 11, 1944(KIA)
Willis, William H., Lt.; May 1944-November 1944
P-5!D CY-X
Wright, Whitelaw, Jr., Lt.; May 1944-November 1944
P-51D CY-S
Yee Litt, Robert H., Lt.; June 1944-January 1945
P-51D CY-I

**Aircraft of the 38th Fighter Squadron**

P-38H-1-LO
42-66719 CG-I

P-38H-5-LO
42-67015 CG-
42-67020 CG-
42-67028 CG-G G. Brown
42-67033 CG-
42-67046 CG-
42-67051 CG-
42-67057 CG-C
42-67059 CG-
42-67064 CG-C
42-67074 CG-J "Texas Ranger" J.S. Jenkins
42-67077 CG-Q "Mountain Ayers" J.H. Ayers
42-67080 CG-S "Skylark IV" M.K. Shipman
42-67083 CG-
42-67090 CG-
42-67095 CG-
42-67199 CG-Y

P-38J-5-LO
42-67221 CG-
42-67301 CG-

P-38J-10-LO
42-67494 CG-W
42-67520 CG-
42-67578 CG-
42-67650 CG-
42-67711 CG-
42-67713 CG-
42-67730 CG-
42-67757 CG-C
42-67768 CG-
42-67813 CG-
42-67825 CG-J "Texas Ranger IV" J.S. Jenkins
42-67904 CG-O A.M. Woods
42-67939
42-67971 CG-X "Noah's Ark" N.R. Tipton
42-68076 CG-
42-68079 CG-
42-68132 CG-I
42-68157 CG-

P-38J-15-LO
42-104284 CG-
42-104287 CG-I
42-104306 CG-
42-104334 CG-K
43-28279 CG-
43-28423 CG-
43-28724 CG-

Unknown Serials
CG-O "Journey's End" J. Myers
CG-J "Texas Ranger II" J.S. Jenkins
CG-J "Texas Ranger III" J.S. Jenkins
CG-O "Big Beautiful Doll" J.D. Landers
CG-W "Angel Puss" L.E. Jaklich
CG-U "Texas Rebel" G.F. Leinweber
CG- "Repul-s-ive" J.H. Hancock
CG- "Spirit of Aberdeen" A.A. Albino
CG- "Man??? Dwaine" V.B. Greenmyre
CG- "Maxine"
CG- "Fuba!" DROOPSNOOT

P-51B-1-NA
43-12195 CG-1 HACK

P-51B-10-NA
42-106851 CG-I HACK

P-51C-10-NT
43-25044 CG-M "East Side Rat" C.R. Watts
43-25071 CG-Q

P-51K-1-NT
44-11361 CG- "Abdul"
44-11370 CG-R

P-51D-5-NA
44-13260 CG-
44-13343 CG-G
44-13549 CG-A "My Ready Steady" D.H. Snell
44-13573 CG-V
44-13577 CG-U
44-13600 CG-P
44-13609 CG-L
44-13623 CG-K
44-13650 CG-R
44-13663 CG- "Pink"
44-13701 CG-D
44-13723 CG-T "One Mustang"
44-13743 CG-H
44-13747 CG-I "Six Gun Pete" A.L. Thorsen
44-13749 CG-X "Jeanne"
44-13789 CG-S

44-13804 CG-Z "Spunktown" E.R. Fryer
44-13804 CG-Z "Arabel" K.I. Crawford
44-13813 CG-C
44-13818 CG-B "Mah Ideel" D.M. Amoss
44-13819 CG-A
44-13823 CG-O "Big Beautiful Doll" J.D. Landers
44-13886 CG- "Miss Jane"
44-13887 CG-E
44-13888 CG-W "Angel Puss" L.E. Jaklich
44-13909 CG-Y "Mom's Pride"
44-13913 CG-F
44-13927 CG-N "Miss Boomerang" L. Earls
44-13973 CG-O "Sweet Ellouise" A.M. Woods

P-51D-10-NA
44-14026 CG-
44-14068 CG-C "The Worry Bird" M.M. Coons
44-14068 CG-S "Little Joe"
44-14097 CG-
44-14154 CG-
44-14167 CG-
44-14176 CG-
44-14274 CG-
44-14296 CG-S "Tennessee Belle" M. Clark
44-14358 CG-P
44-14451 CG-Q "Big Bitch" D.E. Penn
44-14586 CG-

P-51D-15-NA
44-15022 CG-
44-15123 CG-Z "Queenie"
44-15192 CG-U D.M. Cummings
44-15213 CG-
44-15421 CG-Z R.F. Maloney

P-51D-20-NA
44-63225 CG-C
44-72080 CG-
44-72409 CG-

P-51D-25-NA
44-72784 CG-N

Unknown Serials
CG-U "New Arrival" C. Sherman
CG-I "Missouri Banshee" J.W. Kavanaugh
CG- "Nina" F.M. Matney
CG- "Hell's Angel" C.L. Peterson
CG- "Miss Boomerang Margie" D.F. Jewell
CG- "My Kitten"
CG- "Annette"
CG- "Eve"

### Aircraft of the 338th Fighter Squadron

P-38H-1-LO
42-66724 CL- "Miss Margaret" R.N. Jensen
42-66727 CL-

P-38H-5-LO
42-66732 CL-
42-67021 CL-
42-67042 CL-L
42-67048 CL-
42-67049 CL-
42-67057 CL-X S.P. Richardson
42-67069 CL-
42-67073 CL-
42-67078 CL-

P-38J-10-LO
42-67305 CL-X S.P. Richardson
42-67413 CL-
42-67440 CL-J
42-67467 CL-
42-67715 CL-
42-67721 CL-
42-67738 CL-
42-67752 CL-
42-67771 CL-
42-67816 CL-P "Princess Pat" C.A. Patterson
42-67867 CL-
42-67874 CL-T
42-67919 CL-
42-67962 CL- "Bambi" J.L. Odegard
42-67989 CL-
42-68083 CL-
42-68127 CL-
42-68130 CL-

P-38J-15-LO
42-104106 CL-T "Stinger" T.D. Schank
42-104280 CL-
42-104396 CL-
43-28273 CL-
43-28471 CL-
43-28833 CL-P "DaQuake" J.L. McGinn

Unknown Serials
CL-V "Janet" T.A. White
CL- "Miss Ann" C.A. Biedul
CL- "Hell's Angel" L.P. Turner
CL- "Miss Lightning Baby" W.H. Burns
CL- "Miss Judy"

P-51C-10-NT
43-25069 CL-

P-51K-5-NT
44-11639 CL-L
44-11687 CL-V "Betty-Mac" B. McDowell

P-51K-10-NT
44-12136 CL-Q

P-51D-5-NA
44-13360 CL-B
44-13368 CL-
44-13607 CL-H "Mary Belle III"
44-13642 CL-K "Krazy Kid" R.C. Haworth
44-13642 CL-K "Ornery" L.K. John
44-13668 CL-I "Rocky Mountain Canary" T.D. Schank
44-13703 CL-
44-13725 CL- "Georgette"
44-13739 CL-S
44-13743 CL-X "Skippy" E.L. Mercurio/W.F. McGill
44-13744 CL-A
44-13767 CL-
44-13807 CL-H
44-13867 CL-
44-13954 CL-
44-14007 CL-J
44-14014 CL-
44-14026 CL-
44-14028 CL-S

P-51D-10-NA
44-14067 CL-
44-14094 CL-
44-14112 CL-A "Dottie"
44-14121 CL-Z "Mick #5" D.S. Cramer
44-14156 CL-F S.D. Gevorkian
44-14204 CL- "Skylark"
44-14211 CL- "Harvest Moon"
44-14223 CL-M "Katy Did" E.G. Righetti
44-14278 CL-P "Saturday Night" W.J. Konantz
44-14291 CL-P "DaQuake" J.L. McGinn
44-14598 CL- "Lady Lorene"
44-14702 CL-V "Miss Donna"
44-14730 CL-V "DaQuake" J.L. McGinn

P-51D-15-NA
44-14901 CL-
44-15022 CL- "Purple Shaft"
44-15405 CL- "Sunday Morning"
44-15602 CL-
44-15639 CL-

P-51D-20-NA
44-63227 CL-G "Little Trixie" C.D. Henry
44-63242 CL-
44-63245 CL-
44-63287 CL-W "My Jane"
44-63619 CL-D
44-63727 CL-
44-63818 CL-P
44-72227 CL-M "Katy Did" E.G. Righetti
44-72296 CL-P "Saturday Night" W.J. Konantz

P-51D-25-NA
44-72945 CL-
44-73165 CL-

Unknown Serials
CL-T "Li'l Doll" K.A. Lashbrook
CL-F "Ginny" A.J. Ramm
CL- "Bama Girl"

**Aircraft of the 343rd Fighter Squadron**

P-38H-1-LO
42-66718 CY-T
42-66719 CY-

P-38H-5-LO
42-66966 CY-Q "Little Man"
42-67045 CY-
42-67047 CY-F "Lavenia" R.L. Buttke
42-67053 CY-L "Vivacious Vera" J.W. Gilbride
42-67056 CY-
42-67060 CY-E
42-67061 CY-
42-67066 CY-S "Pitter Pat" K.J. Sorace
42-67084 CY-R E.E. Ryan
42-67097 CY-

P-38J-5-LO
42-67228 CY-

P-38J-10-LO
42-67479 CY-I
42-67866 CY-
42-67872 CY-D F.E. Birtciel
42-67875 CY-
42-67876 CY-
42-67893 CY-
42-67900 CY-S K.J. Sorace
42-67964 CY-
42-67966 CY-J "Pretty Patty" W.H. Allen
42-68014 CY-Q
42-68048 CY-J
42-67086 CY-
42-68095 CY-H "Drippy Lil" R.W. Erb
42-68102 CY-
42-68182 CY-

P-38J-15-LO
42-104250 CY-
43-28285 CY-J "The Blackhawk IV" J. May
43-28388 CY-
43-28666 CY-S K.J. Sorace
43-28713 CY-

Unknown Serials
CY-G "The Millie G" E.B. Giller
CY-H "Jill's Jalopy" P.E. Hoeper
CY-W "Spider" D.W. Webb
CY- "The Brat" J.W. Hiner

P-51B-5-NA
43-6928 CY-9 HACK

P-51D-5-NT
44-11158 CY-M

P-51K-5-NT
44-11676 CY-I

P-51D-5-NA
44-13350 CY-A "Miss Velma" F.E. Birtciel
44-13350 CY-A "Merrimack" R.G. Allen
44-13363 CY-A "Bama Blitz" G.D. Leslie
44-13374 CY-D "Julia"
44-13612 CY- "Oh Murder"
44-13643 CY-L "Sweet Pootie" F.C. Lawrence
44-13665 CY-
44-13724 CY-
44-13837 CY-M "Miss Marilyn II" R. Ozinga
44-13843 CY-
44-13850 CY-
44-13874 CY-K "Junie Bug II" P.R. Porter
44-13904 CY-Y
44-13907 CY-S W.H. Lewis
44-14049 CY-J "Pretty Patty II" W.H. Allen

P-51D-10-NA
44-14135 CY-V R.D. Brown
44-14140 CY-O "Wing Of The Morning"
44-14149 CY-L "Sweet Pootie" F.C. Lawrence
44-14175 CY-Q "Cherry" B.J. Liles
44-14175 CY-Q "Sweet Marie II"
44-14235 CY-Y "Lil Jan" G. Morris
44-14295 CY-J
44-14296 CY-I "Mardy" T.M. Love
44-14298 CY-A
44-14348 CY-P "Lady Val" V.P. Gordon
44-14379 CY-W "Pudgy" M. Satenstein
44-14379 CY-W "Hiya Mert" J. Gehrig
44-14384 CY-B "Lil Pearl" D.L. Mercier
44-14442 CY-N
44-14475 CY-Q
44-14535 CY-C J. Courtney
44-14561 CY-D "Miss Velma" F.E. Birtciel
44-14580 CY-Z "Ellie, My Little Six" F.L. Tischer
44-14632 CY-X P. Gangemi/G.W. Bernardo

P-51D-15-NA
44-14885 CY-D "Nervous Nell" D.A. Parker
44-14985 CY-G "The Mille G" E.B. Giller
44-15025 CY-F "Beautiful Lavenia" R.L. Buttke
44-15060 CY-H "Jill's Jalopy VI" P.E. Hoeper
44-15246 CY-Y "Miss Manya" N.P. Bebaeff
44-15314 CY-Q R.G. Gibbs
44-15406 CY-U V.P. Krambo
44-15608 CY-T "Cape Cod Express" C.E. Coggeshall
44-15608 CY-T "Sonny Boy" T.E. Hoffman
44-15701 CY-G "The Millie G" E.B. Giller
44-15375 CY-D "Dizzy Jess" L.D. Boring

P-51D-20-NA
44-73204 CY-G "The Mille G" E.B. Giller
44-63231 CY-R E.E. Ryan
44-63567 CY-E "My Little Honey"
44-63745 CY-C
44-64159 CY-H "Jill's Jalopy VII" P.E. Hoeper
44-72123 CY-G "The Millie G" E.B. Giller
44-72138 CY-Z R.E. Welch
44-72242 CY-R
44-72349 CY-
44-72362 CY-B W. Strauch
44-72469 CY-V B. Rimerman

Unknown Serials
CY-K "Princess Pat" E.H. Geary
CY-U "Lucky Wabbit II"
CY- "Miss Jane"
CY- "Blonde Bomber"
P-51B CY-10 "Old Smooth Mouth" HACK

• • •

## THE 56TH FIGHTER GROUP
## 61ST, 62ND, 63RD FIGHTER SQUADRONS

The 56th Fighter Group was activated on January 15, 1941, at Savannah, Georgia. Training in the eastern United States, the group headed overseas aboard the "Queen Elizabeth" on January 6, 1943. The first of 462 missions came on April 13, 1943, with the final one coming on April 21, 1945. While in England, the group claimed 665.5 aerial and 320.5 ground victories while 139 P-47's were lost on operations and 27 pilots died in accidents.

Stations for the 56th included Kingscliffe, from January 12, 1943, Horsham St. Faith, from April 5, 1943; Halesworth, from July 8, 1943; and Boxted, from April 18, 1944 until October of 1945. Aircraft flown were the P-47C, D, and M, from February of 1943 thru September of 1945. The group was awarded two Distinguished Unit Citations: the first for the period of February 20 to March 9, 1944, in which the unit destroyed almost 100 German aircraft; and the second for support of the airborne invasion of Holland on September 18, 1944.

**Claims**

| | Air | | | Grd | |
|---|---|---|---|---|---|
| | Destroyed | Probable | Damaged | Destroyed | Damaged |
| HdQts | 48.75 | 2 | 15 | 31 | 22 |
| 61st | 220 | 24 | 82 | 75 | 97 |
| 62nd | 222.5 | 15 | 81 | 114 | 96 |
| 63rd | 174.25 | 18 | 64 | 100.5 | 73 |
| | 665.5 | 59 | 242 | 320.5 | 288 |

**Commanders**

| | |
|---|---|
| Col. Hubert Zemke | September 1, 1942-October 30, 1943 |
| Col. Robert B. Landry | October 30, 1943-January 11, 1944 |
| LtCol. David C. Schilling | January 11, 1944-January 18, 1944 |
| Col. Hubert Zemke | January 19, 1944-August 12, 1944 |
| Col. David C. Schilling | August 12, 1944-January 27, 1945 |
| LtCol. Lucian A. Dade, Jr. | January 27, 1945-August 1945 |

**Wing and Command Assignments**

| | |
|---|---|
| Assigned to VIII Fighter Command | January 12, 1943 |
| VIII Fighter Command, 4th Air Defense Wing | June 30, 1943 |
| VIII Fighter Command, 65th Fighter Wing | August 7, 1943 |
| 2nd Bomb Division, 65th Fighter Wing | September 15, 1944 |
| 2nd Air Division, 65th Fighter Wing | January 1, 1945 |

### Aircraft Markings

All original P-47's were in olive drab/neutral gray schemes with white theater bands on the wings and tail surfaces and a white cowl band. NMF planes were received in March of 1944 and many of these were painted over. In February of 1944, the cowl bands were painted in the squadron color: red for the 61st, yellow for the 62nd, and white for the 63rd (although a few did have blue applied). From March of 1944, the group marking consisted of a red cowl band with the squadron colors moving to the rudder. Again, the 63rd had none until September of 1944, when blue was officially adopted. From May of 1944, many planes had a green and gray shadow shading on the upper surfaces with some having green and gray mottle, light and dark gray shading, or full olive drab. For the most part, under surfaces remained in NMF, although a few did have light gray or sky.

With the arrival of P-47M's in January of 1945, each squadron developed a particular paint scheme for it's planes. All retained the group's red cowl band, however. In the 61st, all upper surfaces were matt black with red rudders, serial numbers, and code letters, which were usually outlined with white; the 62nd had dark green and light gray shadow shading with yellow rudders, serials, and code letters; the 63rd had dark and light blue shadow shading with medium blue rudders and serial numbers. Code letters were in NMF outlined in white. The under surfaces of all planes were NMF, as were cockpit frames and the leading edges of the wings and horizontal tails.

Squadron codes were:

61st Ftr Sqn: HV
62nd Ftr Sqn: LM
63rd Ftr Sqn: UN

### 56th Fighter Group Statistical Report

| Month | Missions | Air | Grd | Losses | KIAc |
|---|---|---|---|---|---|
| April 1943 | 5 | 0-0-0 | 0-0 | 2 | 0 |
| May | 19 | 0-2-5 | 0-0 | 1 | 0 |
| June | 14 | 6-1-3 | 0-0 | 5 | 1 |
| July | 19 | 3-1-2 | 0-0 | 3 | 0 |
| August | 14 | 28-1-15 | 0-0 | 5 | 2 |
| September | 18 | 14-1-0 | 0-0 | 4 | 0 |
| October | 9 | 40-5-8 | 0-0 | 1 | 0 |
| November | 10 | 44-5-16 | 0-0 | 6 | 1 |
| December | 11 | 32-1-10 | 0-0 | 8 | 0 |
| January 1944 | 10 | 38-4-15 | 0-0 | 2 | 0 |
| February | 14 | 70-6-35 | 3-14 | 3 | 2 |
| March | 16 | 83-10-30 | 5-11 | 17 | 1 |
| April | 24 | 18-0-17 | 36-34 | 5 | 3 |
| May | 28 | 55-5-11 | 0-0 | 9 | 1 |
| June | 52 | 35-2-16 | 1-0 | 10 | 0 |
| July | 25 | 46-0-16 | 10-9 | 7 | 0 |
| August | 37 | 10-0-0 | 8-10 | 6 | 0 |
| September | 23 | 26-1-4 | 74-46 | 16 | 1 |
| October | 18 | 1-1-1 | 14-8 | 3 | 1 |
| November | 18 | 14.5-3-5 | 5-1 | 8 | 0 |
| December | 17 | 60-7-21 | 11-14 | 9 | 2 |
| January 1945 | 15 | 19-2-1 | 2-1 | 3 | 1 |
| February | 14 | 9-0-6 | 4-3 | 1 | 2 |
| March | 17 | 7-0-1 | 0-0 | 2 | 4 |
| April | 15 | 6-1-5 | 147.5-137 | 3 | 3 |
| May | 0 | 0-0-0 | 0-0 | 0 | 2 |
| | 462 | 665.5-59-242 | 320.5-288 | 139 | 27 |

### Losses by Squadron

| | MIA | KIAc |
|---|---|---|
| HdQts | 2 | 0 |
| 61st | 34 | 11 |
| 62nd | 52 | 11 |
| 63rd | 51 | 5 |

### Claims by Enemy Aircraft Type

| | Air | | | Grd | |
|---|---|---|---|---|---|
| | Destroyed | Probable | Damaged | Destroyed | Damaged |
| FW-190 | 278 | 29 | 110 | 44 | 34 |
| Me-109 | 264 | 19 | 85 | 30 | 30 |
| Me-110 | 71 | 6 | 28 | 19 | 21 |
| Me-210 | 13 | 2 | 7 | 15 | 11 |
| Ju-88 | 12 | 3 | 2 | 55 | 50 |
| Ju-52 | 11 | 0 | 0 | 3 | 0 |
| Me-262 | 4.5 | 0 | 6 | 4 | 9 |
| He-111 | 4 | 0 | 0 | 55 | 47 |
| Do-217 | 4 | 0 | 0 | 16 | 10 |
| Ar-234 | 2 | 0 | 0 | 0 | 0 |
| Me-410 | 1 | 0 | 2 | 6 | 5 |
| FW-44 | 1 | 0 | 0 | 0 | 0 |
| W-34 | 0 | 0 | 1 | 0 | 0 |
| u/i a/c | 0 | 0 | 1 | 47.5 | 63 |
| He-177 | 0 | 0 | 0 | 6 | 3 |
| Do-24 | 0 | 0 | 0 | 5 | 0 |
| Ju-87 | 0 | 0 | 0 | 4 | 2 |
| He-115 | 0 | 0 | 0 | 3 | 1 |
| FW-200 | 0 | 0 | 0 | 2 | 2 |
| Ar-196 | 0 | 0 | 0 | 2 | 0 |
| Fi-156 | 0 | 0 | 0 | 2 | 0 |
| Bu-131 | 0 | 0 | 0 | 2 | 0 |

### 56th Fighter Group Squadron Commanders

**61st Ftr Sqn**

| | |
|---|---|
| Maj. Loren G. McCollom | Mid 1942-June 8, 1943 |
| LtCol. Francis S. Gabreski | June 9, 1943-January 13, 1944 |
| Maj. James C. Stewart | January 13, 1944-April 13, 1944 |
| LtCol. Francis S. Gabreski | April 13, 1944-July 20, 1944 |
| Maj. Gordon E. Baker | July 20, 1944-September 26, 1944 |
| Maj. Donovan F. Smith | September 26, 1944-January 10, 1945 |
| Maj. James R. Carter | January 10, 1945-EOW |

**62nd Ftr Sqn**

| | |
|---|---|
| Maj. David C. Schilling | January 17, 1943-August 21, 1943 |
| Maj. Horace C. Craig | August 21, 1943-February 8, 1944 |
| Maj. Leroy A. Schreiber | February 8, 1944-April 15, 1944 |
| LtCol. Lucian A. Dade, Jr. | April 16, 1944-August 13, 1944 |
| Capt. Michael J. Quirk | August 13, 1944-September 10, 1944 |
| LtCol. Leslie C. Smith | September 11, 1944-January 26, 1945 |
| Maj. Felix D. Williamson | January 26, 1945-EOW |

**63rd Ftr Sqn**

| | |
|---|---|
| Maj. Philip E. Tukey, Jr. | Mid 1942-September 30, 1943 |
| Maj. Sylvester V. Burke | September 30, 1943-February 19, 1944 |
| Maj. Gerald W. Johnson | February 19, 1944-March 27, 1944 |
| Maj. Robert A., Lamb | March 27, 1944-May 23, 1944 |
| Capt. Donald M. Goodfleisch | May 23, 1944-July 17, 1944 |
| Capt. Joseph L. Egan, Jr. | July 17, 1944-July 19, 1944 |
| Maj. Harold E. Comstock | July 19, 1944-January 20, 1945 |
| Maj. Paul A. Conger | January 20, 1945-March 22, 1945 |
| Maj. George E. Bostwick | March 22, 1945-EOW |

### 56th Fighter Group Aces

| Name | Air | Grd | Total | Sqn |
|---|---|---|---|---|
| Col. David C. Schilling | 22.5 | 10.5 | 33 | 62nd<br>HdQts |
| LtCol. Francis S. Gabreski | 28 | 3.5 | 31.5 | 61st<br>HdQts |
| Maj. Robert S. Johnson | 27 | 0 | 27 | 61st<br>62nd |
| Col. Hubert Zemke | 17.75 | 8.5 | 26.25* | HdQts |
| Capt. Fred J. Christensen | 21.5 | 0 | 21.5 | 62nd |
| Maj. Walker M. Mahurin | 19.75 | 0 | 19.75 | 63rd |
| Maj. Gerald W. Johnson | 16.5 | 0 | 16.5** | 61st<br>63rd |
| Capt. Michael J. Quirk | 11 | 5 | 16 | 62nd |
| Maj. George E. Bostwick | 8 | 7 | 15 | 62nd<br>63rd |
| Capt. Joseph H. Powers | 14.5 | 0 | 14.5 | 61st<br>62nd |
| Maj. Leroy A. Schreiber | 12 | 2 | 14 | 61st<br>62nd |
| Maj. Michael J. Jackson | 8 | 5.5 | 13.5 | 62nd |
| Lt. Randel L. Murphy | 2 | 11 | 13 | 63rd |
| Maj. Felix D. Williamson | 13 | 0 | 13 | 62nd |
| LtCol. James C. Stewart | 11.5 | 1 | 12.5 | 61st<br>HdQts |
| Maj. Paul A. Conger | 11.5 | 0 | 11.5 | 61st<br>63rd |
| LtCol. Leslie C. Smith | 7 | 4.5 | 11.5 | 61st<br>62nd<br>HdQts |
| Maj. Bolek M. Gladych | 10 | 1 | 11 | 61st |
| Lt. Billy G. Edens | 7 | 3 | 10 | 62nd |
| Capt. Robert J. Keen | 6 | 4 | 10 | 61st<br>62nd |
| Lt. Russell S. Kyler | 3 | 7 | 10 | 61st |
| Capt. Robert J. Rankin | 10 | 0 | 10 | 61st |
| LtCol. Lucian A. Dade, Jr. | 3 | 6 | 9 | 62nd<br>63rd<br>HdQts |
| Capt. Stanley B. Morrill | 9 | 0 | 9 | 62nd |
| Capt. Joseph H. Bennett | 8.5 | 0 | 8.5*** | 61st |
| Capt. Walter L. Flagg | 2 | 6 | 8 | 63rd |
| Capt. Glen D. Schiltz, Jr. | 8 | 0 | 8 | 63rd |
| Capt. John H. Truluck | 7 | 1 | 8 | 63rd |
| Maj. John W. Vogt, Jr. | 8 | 0 | 8@ | 63rd |
| Lt. Donald Henley, Jr. | 3 | 4.5 | 7.5 | 62nd |
| Maj. Donovan F. Smith | 5.5 | 2 | 7.5 | 61st |
| Maj. Harold E. Comstock | 5 | 2 | 7 | 63rd |

| | | | | |
|---|---|---|---|---|
| Capt. Steven Gerick | 5 | 2 | 7 | 61st |
| Lt. Frank W. Klibbe | 7 | 0 | 7 | 61st |
| Maj. Robert A. Lamb | 7 | 0 | 7 | 61st<br>63rd |
| Lt. Evan D. McMinn | 5 | 2 | 7 | 61st |
| Capt. Mark L. Moseley | 6.5 | 0 | 6.5 | 62nd |
| Lt. George H. Butler | 3 | 3 | 6 | 62nd |
| Maj. James R. Carter | 6 | 0 | 6 | 61st |
| Lt. Claude A. Chinn | 0 | 6 | 6 | 63rd |
| Capt. Walter V. Cook | 6 | 0 | 6 | 62nd |
| Capt. George F. Hall | 6 | 0 | 6 | 63rd |
| Capt. Cameron M. Hart | 6 | 0 | 6 | 63rd |
| Lt. Norman D. Gould | 4 | 1.5 | 5.5 | 62nd |
| Lt. Frank E. McCauley | 5.5 | 0 | 5.5 | 61st |
| Lt. Darrell E. McMahan | 1.5 | 4 | 5.5 | 62nd |
| Lt. Sanborn N. Ball, Jr. | 1.5 | 3.5 | 5 | 62nd |
| Lt. Eugene M. Beason | 1 | 4 | 5 | 62nd |
| Lt. Burton O. Blodgett | 0 | 5 | 5 | 61st |
| Capt. Joseph L. Egan, Jr. | 5 | 0 | 5 | 63rd |
| Lt. Joseph W. Icard | 5 | 0 | 5 | 62nd |
| Lt. James M. Jure | 3.5 | 1.5 | 5 | 61st |
| Capt. Warren E. Kerr | 0 | 5 | 5 | 63rd |
| Lt. Philip G. Kuhn, Jr. | 1 | 4 | 5 | 63rd |
| Lt. Roy L. Patterson | 1 | 4 | 5 | 62nd |
| Lt. Thomas W. Queen, Jr. | 0 | 5 | 5 | 63rd |
| Lt. Walter J. Sharbo | 3 | 2 | 5 | 62nd |
| Lt. Vernon A. Smith | 0 | 5 | 5 | 63rd |
| Lt. Eugene J. Timony | 1 | 4 | 5 | 63rd |
| Capt. William F. Wilkerson | 1 | 4 | 5 | 62nd |

* - includes 2.5 air victories with the 479th Ftr Grp, ETO
** - includes 1 air victory with the 356th Ftr Grp, ETO
*** - includes 3 air victories with the 4th Ftr Grp, ETO
@ - includes 3 air victories with the 356th Ftr Grp, ETO

### 56th Fighter Group Scorers

**HdQts**

| | Air | Grd | |
|---|---|---|---|
| L.A. Dade, Jr. | 0-0-0 | 6-1 | plus 62nd Ftr Sqn |
| F.S. Gabreski | 10-0-1 | 2.5-4 | plus 61st Ftr Sqn |
| R.B. Landry | 1-0-0 | 0-0 | |
| D.D. Renwick | 0-0-0 | 1-0 | plus 61st Ftr Sqn |
| D.C. Schilling | 22.5-0-6 | 10.5-4.5 | |
| L.C. Smith | 0-0-0 | 2-3 | plus 61st & 62nd Ftr Sqns |
| J.C. Stewart | 0-0-1 | 1-2 | plus 61st Ftr Sqn |
| H. Zemke | 15.25-2-7 | 8.5-7 | plus 2.5-0-1 air w/479th Ftr Grp |

**61st Ftr Sqn**

| | | | |
|---|---|---|---|
| W.R. Aggers | 0.5-0-0 | 0-0 | |
| J.T. Allen | 0-0-1 | 0-1 | |
| R.L. Altschuler | 0-0-1 | 0-1 | |
| M.A. Anderson | 0-0-1 | 0-0 | |
| T. Anderz | 1-0-0 | 0-0 | |
| G.E. Baker | 0-0-0 | 2.5-1 | plus 62nd Ftr Sqn |
| W.H. Barnes | 0-0-0 | 3-1 | |
| E.E. Barnum | 2-0-2 | 0-0 | |
| W.G. Bartle | 0-0-0 | 2-1 | |
| F.H. Barrett | 0-0-1 | 2-4.5 | |
| V.E. Bast | 1-0-0 | 3-4 | |
| R.A. Baughman | 1-0-0 | 2-0 | |
| O.M. Belk | 1-0-0 | 0-0 | |
| J.H. Bennett | 5.5-0-2 | 0-0 | plus 3-4-1 air w/4th & 356th Ftr Grps |
| H.O. Bevins | 0-1-0 | 0-0 | |
| A.T. Biales | 0-1-0 | 0-0 | |
| G.J. Blake | 2-0-0 | 0-0 | |
| B.O. Blodgett | 0-0-0 | 5-2 | |
| C.R. Bond | 0-0-0 | 2-4 | |
| W.E. Bour | 0-0-0 | 0-1 | |
| N.E. Brooks | 1-0-1 | 0-0 | |
| A.J. Bux, Jr. | 0-0-0 | 0.5-0.5 | |
| J.R. Carter | 6-3-3 | 0-0 | |
| B.E. Cathers | 0-1-0 | 1-1 | |
| J.J. Clark | 2-0-1 | 0.5-1 | |
| W.D. Clark | 1-1-2 | 2-1 | |
| P.J. Clinton, Jr. | 0-0-0 | 1-1 | |
| C.B. Cole | 0-0-0 | 2-6 | |
| P.A. Conger | 6.5-0-2 | 0-1.5 | plus 63rd Ftr Sqn |
| J.R. Curtis | 0-0-1 | 0-0 | plus 63rd Ftr Sqn |
| C.A. Dudley | 0-0-1 | 0-0 | |
| E.E. Ellis | 0-0-0 | 3-4 | |
| J.D. Foster | 2-1-2 | 0-0 | |
| J.F. Frazier | 2-0-0 | 0-0 | |
| D.M. Funcheon | 3-1-2 | 0-1 | |
| F.S. Gabreski | 18-1-2 | 1-1 | plus HdQts |
| S. Gerick | 5-0-9 | 2-0 | |
| A.H. Gerow | 1-1-0 | 0-0 | |
| S.H. Getz | 0.5-0-1 | 2.5-2 | |
| B.M. Gladych | 10-0-0 | 1-6 | |
| S.D. Hamilton, Jr. | 2-1-7 | 0-0 | |
| W.M. Hartshorn | 0-0-0 | 0-1 | |
| R.M. Heineman | 3-0-0 | 0-1 | |
| R.A. Herin | 1-0-0 | 0-0 | |
| R.W. Higgins | 0-0-0 | 1-3 | |
| L.P. Hines, Jr. | 0-0-1 | 0-0 | |
| R.W. Hoeflein | 0-0-0 | 1-3 | |
| H.R. Holtmeier | 0-0-0 | 0-1 | |
| Z. Janicki | 0-1-1 | 0-0 | |
| G.W. Johnson | 7.5-0-3 | 0-0 | plus 63rd Ftr Sqn & 1-0-0.5 air w/356th Ftr Grp |
| R.S. Johnson | 25-0-3 | 0-0 | plus 62nd Ftr Sqn |
| J.E. Jones | 0-0-0 | 3-0 | |
| J.M. Jure | 3.5-1-0 | 1.5-2 | |
| J.W. Kassap | 0-0-1 | 0-0 | |
| R.J. Keen | 6-1-1 | 4-3 | |
| F.W. Klibbe | 7-0-0 | 0-0 | |
| R.S. Kyler | 3-0-0 | 7-0 | |
| R.A. Lamb | 7-1-1 | 0-0 | |
| W.A. Lanowski | 4-0-0 | 0-0 | |
| E.B. Lightfoot, Jr. | 0-0-0 | 1-0 | |
| W.A. Marangello | 1-0-0 | 0-0 | |
| A.C. Maul | 2-0-1 | 0-0 | |
| D.L. Mauldin | 0-0-0 | 0-4 | |
| F.E. McCauley | 5.5-1-1 | 0-0 | |
| L.G. McCollom | 0-1-1 | 0-0 | plus 1-1-0 air w/353rd Ftr Grp |
| E.D. McMinn | 5-0-2 | 2-4 | |
| D.H. Mudge, Jr. | 1-0-2 | 0-0 | |
| C.E. Mussey | 2-1-1 | 0-0 | |
| P. Neyland | 1.5-0-1 | 0-1 | |
| W.J. Osborne | 0.5-0-0 | 0-0 | |
| W.S. Patterson | 1-0-1 | 1-1 | |
| J.H. Perry | 2-1-0 | 0-0 | |
| J.I. Popplewell | 1-0-0 | 0-0 | |
| J.H. Powers | 12-0-4 | 0-0 | plus 62nd Ftr Sqn |
| F.S. Rader | 0-0-0 | 1-2 | |
| R.J. Rankin | 10-1-2 | 0-0 | |
| C.J. Raymond | 1-0-0 | 2-5 | |
| D.D. Renwick | 1-0-1 | 0-0 | plus HdQts |
| R.W. Roberts | 2-0-1 | 0-0 | |
| L.A. Schreiber | 2-0-0 | 0-0 | plus 62nd Ftr Sqn |
| E.A. Sisson, Jr. | 1-0-0 | 1-2 | |
| D.F. Smith | 5.5-1-2 | 2-1 | |
| L.C. Smith | 6-0-3 | 1-2 | plus HdQts & 62nd Ftr Sqn |
| W.F. Smith | 0-0-0 | 1-2 | |
| J.C. Stewart | 11.5-1-2 | 0-0 | plus HdQts |
| J.R. Stish | 0-0-0 | 0-1 | |
| D.E. Stream | 1-0-0 | 1-0 | |
| C.C. Thornton | 1-0-0 | 0.5-2 | |
| E.H. Treff | 0-0-0 | 3-5 | |
| R.E. Walker | 1-0-1 | 0-0 | |
| C.E. Westman | 0-0-0 | 0.5-1 | |
| L.M. Winski | 0-0-0 | 2-5 | |
| C.R. Woock | 0-1-2 | 1-0 | |
| M.C. Wood | 1.5-0-1 | 0-0 | |

**62nd Ftr Sqn**

| | | | |
|---|---|---|---|
| F.R. Aheron | 0-1-0 | 0-0 | |
| C.R. Albright | 0-0-0 | 0.5-2 | |
| G.E. Baker | 1-0-1 | 0-0 | plus 61st Ftr Sqn |
| S.N. Ball, Jr. | 1.5-0-0 | 3.5-0 | |
| E.M. Beason | 1-0-0 | 4-1 | |
| H.F. Beeler | 0-0-0 | 1-1 | |
| E.E. Bennett | 0.5-0-0 | 0-0 | |
| R.B. Bluhm, Jr. | 1-0-1 | 0-1 | |
| G.E. Bostwick | 5-0-1 | 3-0 | plus 63rd Ftr Sqn |
| M.K. Boyle | 1.5-1-1 | 1-0 | |
| W.A. Brainerd | 0-0-1 | 0-0 | |
| L.R. Brown | 1-3-1 | 1-1 | |
| J.P. Bryant | 2-0-1 | 0-0 | |
| T.S. Buszko | 1-0-1 | 0-0 | |
| L.F. Butiste | 1-0-2 | 2-0 | |
| G.H. Butler | 3-0-0 | 3-1 | |
| A.W. Canizares | 1-0-1 | 1-0 | |
| A.R. Carcione | 3.5-0-0 | 1-0 | |
| C.E. Carlson | 1-0-0 | 0-0 | |
| W.H. Carrington | 0-0-0 | 1-2 | |
| J.L. Carwell | 0-0-0 | 1-0 | |
| D.A. Carroll | 0.5-0-0 | 2-1 | |
| A. Chasko | 1-0-1 | 0.5-4 | |
| W.P. Chattaway | 1-0-2 | 0-0 | |
| R.C. Cherry | 4.5-1-1 | 0-0 | |
| G.R. Choate, Jr. | 0-0-0 | 1-0 | |
| F.J. Christensen, Jr. | 21.5-0-2 | 0-2 | |
| W.V. Cook | 6-0-0 | 0-0 | |
| H. Coronios | 1-0-1 | 0-0 | |
| H.C. Craig | 1-2-1 | 0-0 | |
| L.A. Dade, Jr. | 3-0-2 | 0-0 | plus HdQts |
| W.C. Daley | 4-0-0 | 0.5-1 | |
| R. Dauphin | 0-1-2 | 0-0 | |

| | | | |
|---|---|---|---|
| R.W. Davis | 2-0-0 | 2-1 | |
| V.H. Day | 0-0-2 | 0-0 | |
| J.B. Eaves | 3.5-0-0 | 1-0 | |
| B.G. Edens | 7-0-0 | 3-2 | |
| T.A. Edwards | 0-0-0 | 1-1 | |
| V.L. Elliott | 0-0-0 | 2-1 | |
| J.W. Ferguson, Jr. | 1-0-0 | 0.5-0 | |
| J.E. Fields | 4-0-1 | 0-0 | |
| P.E. Fleming | 0-0-0 | 4-0 | |
| H.E. Gallagher | 0-0-1 | 0-0 | |
| L.F. Geren | 0.5-0-0 | 4-3 | |
| C.L. Ginn | 0-0-0 | 0-2 | |
| G.G. Goldstein | 2-0-0 | 0-0 | |
| W.P. Gordon, Jr. | 1-0-0 | 0-0 | |
| N.D. Gould | 4-0-0 | 1.5-1 | |
| J.E. Greene | 1-0-3 | 0-0 | |
| D.M. Gunner | 0-0-0 | 2-2 | |
| C.R. Harrison | 3-0-1 | 0-0 | |
| H.F. Hartney, Jr. | 0-0-1 | 0-0 | |
| D. Henley, Jr. | 3-0-0 | 4.5-3 | |
| J.W. Icard | 5-0-1 | 0-0 | |
| M.J. Jackson | 8-0-2 | 5.5-4 | |
| R.A. Johnson | 3-0-1 | 0-0 | |
| R.S. Johnson | 2-0-0 | 0-0 | plus 61st Ftr Sqn |
| J.M. Jones | 3-0-4 | 1-0 | |
| R.B. Jones, Jr. | 0-0-0 | 3-5 | |
| H.E. King | 1-0-1 | 3-0 | |
| A.P. Knafelz | 1-0-1 | 0-0 | |
| B.M. Knox | 1-0-1 | 0-1 | |
| F.G. Koch | 0-0-0 | 2-4 | |
| W.S. Lear | 1.5-0-0 | 0-0 | |
| G.H. Lewis | 1-0-0 | 0-0 | |
| W.A. McClure | 1.5-0-3 | 0-0 | |
| W.W. McElhare | 2-0-4 | 0-0 | |
| F.B. McIntosh | 0-0-0 | 3-6 | |
| D.E. McMahan | 1.5-0-0 | 4-0 | |
| W.H. Merrill, Jr. | 2-0-2 | 0-0 | |
| S.B. Morrill | 9-0-4 | 0-6 | |
| M.L. Moseley | 6.5-0-2 | 0-0 | |
| S.T. Murray | 0-0-0 | 4.5-1 | |
| F.C. Newell | 0.5-0-0 | 0-0 | |
| F.A. Nolan | 2-0-0 | 2-2 | |
| D.A. Nordquist | 0-0-1 | 0-0 | |
| E.W. O'Neill, Jr. | 4.5-0-0 | 0-0 | |
| R.L. Patterson | 1-0-0 | 4-1 | |
| A.O. Perry | 4-0-1 | 0-0 | |
| J.W. Pierce | 1.5-0-0 | 2-1 | |
| J.H. Powers, Jr. | 2.5-0-1 | 0-0 | plus 61st Ftr Sqn |
| H.M. Pruden, Jr. | 0.5-0-0 | 0-0 | |
| S. Pruitt, Jr. | 1-0-0 | 0-1 | |
| M.J. Quirk | 11-1-1 | 5-7 | |
| C.L. Reeder | 1-2-2 | 0-0 | |
| I.W. Rich | 0-0-0 | 0-2 | |
| F.L. Roy | 1-0-0 | 0-0 | |
| L.A. Schreiber | 10-1-4 | 2-4 | plus 61st Ftr Sqn |
| W.J. Sharbo | 3-0-0 | 2-2 | |
| D.C. Sheridan | 1-0-0 | 0-0 | |
| K.L. Smith | 1-0-0 | 0-0 | |
| L.C. Smith | 1-0-0 | 1.5-0 | plus HdQts & 61st Ftr Sqn |
| W.J. Stevenson | 0-0-0 | 3-4 | |
| W.H. Stovall, Jr. | 2-0-1 | 0-0 | |
| R.B. Taylor | 2-1-0 | 0-0 | |
| C.A. Tingen | 0-0-0 | 2-2 | |
| C.E. Tucker | 1-0-1 | 0-0 | |
| I.E. Valenta | 2-0-4 | 0-0 | |
| G.H. Van Noy, Jr. | 1-0-0 | 0-1 | |
| J. Vitale | 0.5-0-0 | 0-0 | |
| D.A. Westover, Jr. | 0.5-0-2 | 3-2 | |
| W.F. Wilkerson | 1-0-1 | 4-4 | |
| F.D. Williamson | 13-0-1 | 0-0 | |
| R.E. Winters | 2-1-1 | 2-1 | |
| H.O. Womack | 0.5-0-0 | 2-2 | |

**63rd Ftr Sqn**

| | | | |
|---|---|---|---|
| L.A. Adrianse | 2-0-1 | 0-0 | |
| E.M. Albright, Jr. | 1-0-0 | 2-1 | |
| E.M. Andermatt | 0-1-1 | 0-0 | |
| R.B. Anderson | 4-0-0 | 0-0 | |
| J.A. Aranyos | 0-0-0 | 2-2 | |
| J.A. Arnold | 0-0-0 | 2-2 | |
| R.E. Bailey | 0-0-0 | 2-2 | |
| E.S. Barrentine | 0-0-0 | 3-4 | |
| S.K. Batson | 2-0-1 | 0-0 | |
| M.H. Becker | 2.75-0-1 | 1-0 | |
| G.E. Bostwick | 3-0-1 | 4-1 | plus 62nd Ftr Sqn |
| J.D. Brown | 1-0-1 | 0-0 | |
| S.V. Burke | 3-0-2 | 0-0 | |
| R.D. Campbell | 0-0-1 | 1-0 | |
| B.P. Casteel | 1-0-1 | 0-0 | |
| A.S. Cavallo | 3-1-0 | 0-0 | |
| C.A. Chinn | 0-0-0 | 6-1 | |
| C.C. Clamp, Jr. | 0-1-0 | 0-0 | |
| C.R. Clark | 1-0-0 | 2-2 | |
| J.E. Coenen | 2-0-0 | 0-0 | |
| H.E. Comstock | 5-1-6 | 2-0 | |
| P.A. Conger | 5-0-2 | 0-0 | plus 61st Ftr Sqn |
| E.M. Crosthwaite, Jr. | 1-0-0 | 0-0 | |
| J.R. Curtis | 3.5-0-0 | 0-0 | plus 61st Ftr Sqn |
| S.D. Dale | 0.5-0-0 | 2-0.25 | |
| R.J. Daniel | 2-0-0 | 1-0.5 | |
| R.R. Davis | 2-0-1 | 0-0 | |
| J.L. Egan, Jr. | 5-0-1 | 0-0 | |
| J.C. Fahringer | 4-0-3 | 0-5 | |
| W.L. Flagg | 2-0-1 | 6-2 | |
| R.T. Fling | 1-0-0 | 0-0 | |
| W.R. Frederick | 0.5-0-4 | 1-1 | |
| R. Frederickson | 3-1-0 | 0-1.5 | |
| D.M. Goodfleisch | 2-2-2 | 0-0 | |
| W.R. Groce | 3.5-0-1 | 0-2 | |
| T. Guerrero, Jr. | 1-0-0 | 0-0 | |
| G.F. Hall | 6-1-2 | 0-0 | |
| C.M. Hart | 6-1-2 | 0-0 | |
| E.A. Henderson | 0-0-0 | 1-0 | |
| T.B. Hennessey | 0-0-0 | 2-1 | |
| W.R. Hoffman | 1-0-0 | 2-0 | |
| E.J. Huff | 0-0-0 | 1-2 | |
| M.J. Hughes | 1-0-1 | 0-0 | |
| W.H. Janson | 0-1-0 | 0-0 | |
| G.W. Johnson | 8-1-1 | 0-0 | plus 61st Ftr Sqn |
| W.D. Johnson | 0.75-0-0 | 0-1 | |
| J.W. Keeler | 0-0-0 | 2-1 | |
| W.E. Kerr, Jr. | 0-0-0 | 5-1 | |
| P.G. Kuhn | 1-0-0 | 4-1 | |
| J.A. Kyle | 1-0-1 | 0.5-0 | |
| L.M. Langdon | 2-0-1 | 0-0 | |
| J.E. Lister | 2-0-1 | 0-0 | |
| S.J. Lowman, Jr. | 0.25-0-0 | 1-0 | |
| V.P. Ludwig | 3-0-0 | 0-0 | |
| D.W. Magel | 0-0-1 | 0-0 | |
| R.W. Magel | 1-0-0 | 0-0 | |
| W.M. Mahurin | 19.75-3-1 | 0-0 | |
| J.C. Marcotte | 0-1-0 | 0-0 | |
| D.W. Marshall | 0-0-0 | 0.5-2.25 | |
| H.L. Matthew | 0-0-0 | 1.5-0 | |
| C.T. McBath | 3-0-0 | 1-3 | |
| R.L. Murphy | 2-0-0 | 11-2 | |
| J.C. Naylor | 0-0-0 | 2-2 | |
| W.J. O'Connor | 1.5-0-0 | 0-0 | |
| F.M. Ogden, III | 1-1-0 | 0-0 | |
| D.V. Peters | 2.25-0-0 | 2-2 | |
| R.D. Petty | 0-0-1 | 0-0 | |
| W.H. Pitts | 2-0-0 | 0-0 | |
| I.T. Porowski | 0.25-0-0 | 0-0 | |
| T.W. Queen, Jr. | 0-0-1 | 5-2 | |
| C.W. Reed | 2.25-0-0 | 1-0 | |
| A.H. Robey | 4-0-3 | 0-0 | |
| C.M. Rotzler | 1-0-0 | 2-4 | |
| T.W. Saling, III | 0-0-0 | 0.5-0 | |
| W.C. Scherz | 1-1-2 | 0-0 | |
| G.D. Schiltz, Jr. | 8-0-3 | 0-0 | |
| A.T. Shupe | 0-0-0 | 1-2 | |
| B.R. Smith | 3-0-1 | 0-0 | |
| T.W. Smith, Jr. | 0-0-0 | 1-1 | |
| V.A. Smith | 0-0-0 | 5-5 | |
| S.O. Stamps | 0.5-0-1 | 0-1 | |
| S.F. Stebelton | 0-0-0 | 1-3 | |
| C. Taylor | 0-0-0 | 1-3 | |
| E.J. Timony | 1-0-0 | 4-0 | |
| J.H. Truluck | 7-0-3 | 1-3 | |
| P.B. Tremble | 2-1-1 | 0-0 | |
| B.E. Vest | 0-0-0 | 2-1 | |
| J.W. Vogt, Jr. | 5-0-0 | 0-0 | plus 3-0-0 air w/356th Ftr Grp |
| J.C. Wakefield | 3-0-0 | 0-0 | |
| H.F. Warner, Jr. | 0-0-0 | 1-0.25 | |
| R.T. Warboys | 1-0-0 | 1-0 | |
| R.B. Westfall | 0-0-1 | 0-0 | |
| E.D. Whitley | 2-0-1 | 0-0 | |
| J.D. Wilson | 2-0-0 | 0-0 | |
| A.J. Wisniewski | 0-0-1 | 0.5-1.25 | |

**56th Fighter Group Scoring**

**May 14, 1943**

| | | | |
|---|---|---|---|
| HdQts: | Col. H. Zemke | FW-190 dam(air) | NE Antwerp |
| 61st: | Lt. A.T. Biales | FW-190 prob(air) | NW Antwerp |
| | Lt. M.A. Anderson | FW-190 dam(air) | NE Antwerp |
| | Lt. G.W. Johnson | FW-190 dam(air) | NE Antwerp |

| Unit | Pilot | Claim | Location |
|---|---|---|---|
| **May 15, 1943** | | | |
| 61st: | Capt. F.S. Gabreski | FW-190 dam(air) | NE Rotterdam |
| | Lt. D.H. Mudge | FW-190 dam(air) | NE Rotterdam |
| **May 29, 1943** | | | |
| 61st: | Maj. L.G. McCollom | Me-109 prob(air) | SE St. Moen |
| **June 12, 1943** | | | |
| 62nd: | Capt. W.V. Cook | FW-190 dest(air) | Ypres |
| **June 13, 1943** | | | |
| HdQts: | Col. H. Zemke | (2)FW-190 dest(air) | Cassel |
| | | FW-190 dam(air) | Cassel |
| 61st: | Lt. R.S. Johnson | FW-190 dest(air) | SE Bergues |
| | Lt. J.R. Curtis | FW-190 dam(air) | S/Furnes |
| **June 26, 1943** | | | |
| 61st: | Lt. G.W. Johnson | FW-190 dest(air) | N/Dieppe |
| 62nd: | Lt. C.R. Harrison | FW-190 dest(air) | NE Rouen |
| | Capt. R. Dauphin | FW-190 dam(air) | Dieppe |
| 63rd: | Lt. D.M. Goodfleisch | FW-190 prob(air) | E/Rouen |
| **July 30, 1943** | | | |
| 61st: | Capt. L.A. Schreiber | (2)Me-109 dest(air) | Arnheim |
| | Lt. J.H. Powers | Me-109 dest(air) | Arnheim |
| | Lt. D.F. Smith | Me-109 prob(air) | Nijmegen |
| | Maj. L.G. McCollom | Me-109 dam(air) | Arnheim |
| | Lt. L.C. Smith | FW-190 dam(air) | Arnheim |
| **August 12, 1943** | | | |
| 62nd: | Lt. J.M. Jones | FW-190 dam(air) | W/Maastricht |
| **August 17, 1943** | | | |
| HdQts: | Col. H. Zemke | Me-110 dest(air) | St. Trond |
| 61st: | Capt. G.W. Johnson | (2)Me-109 dest(air) | Hasselt/Diest |
| | | (.5)Me-110 dest(air) | N/Liege |
| | | Me-109 dam(air) | Hasselt/Diest |
| | Lt. F.E. McCauley | FW-190 dest(air) | Hasselt |
| | | (.5)Me-110 dest(air) | N/Liege |
| | | FW-190 dam(air) | Hasselt |
| | Capt. D.D. Renwick | Me-109 dest(air) | Liege |
| 62nd: | Lt. C.R. Harrison | Me-110 dest(air) | Ans |
| | Lt. C.L. Reeder | Me-110 dest(air) | Ans |
| | | Me-210 dam(air) | Ans |
| | Lt. V.H. Day | (2)Me-210 dam(air) | Ans |
| 63rd: | Lt. G.D. Schiltz | (3)FW-190 dest(air) | Ans-St. Nicholas |
| | | Me-210 dam(air) | Ans-St. Nicholas |
| | Capt. W.M. Mahurin | (2)FW-190 dest(air) | Eupen-St. Nicholas |
| | Lt. H.E. Comstock | Me-109 dest(air) | Ans |
| | Lt. J.H. Truluck | FW-190 dest(air) | Ans-St. Nicholas |
| | | Me-210 dam(air) | Ans-St. Nicholas |
| | Lt. E.D. Whitley | Me-110 dest(air) | Ans |
| | | Me-110 dam(air) | Ans |
| | Lt. G.F. Hall | Me-109 prob(air) | Eupen-St. Nicholas |
| | Lt. D.M. Goodfleisch | Me-110 dam(air) | Ans |
| **August 19, 1943** | | | |
| HdQts: | Col. H. Zemke | FW-190 dam(air) | Numensdorp |
| 61st: | Lt. F.E. McCauley | (2)Me-109 dest(air) | Oosterhout & Schoonhoven |
| | Capt. R.A. Lamb | FW-190 dest(air) | Breda |
| | Capt. G.W. Johnson | Me-109 dest(air) | Gilze-Rijen |
| | | Me-109 dam(air) | Gilze-Rijen |
| | Lt. R.S. Johnson | Me-109 dest(air) | NE Woensdrecht |
| | Lt. J.R. Carter | Me-109 dam(air) | W/Gilze-Rijen |
| 62nd: | Lt. M.J. Quirk | FW-190 dest(air) | Gilze-Rijen |
| 63rd: | Lt. J.L. Egan | FW-190 dest(air) | Tholen Island |
| | Lt. J.W. Vogt | Me-109 dest(air) | Walcheren Island |
| | Lt. E.D. Whitley | Me-109 dest(air) | Walcheren Island |
| **August 24, 1943** | | | |
| 61st: | Capt. F.S. Gabreski | FW-190 dest(air) | Dreux |
| | Lt. R.S. Johnson | FW-190 dam(air) | Evreux |
| 62nd: | Capt. L.A. Schreiber | FW-190 dest(air) | S/Paris |
| | Lt. J.M. Jones | FW-190 dest(air) | S/Paris |
| | Capt. H.C. Craig | FW-190 dam(air) | S/Paris |
| **September 3, 1943** | | | |
| HdQts: | Col. H. Zemke | FW-190 dest(air) | NW Romilly-Sur-Seine |
| 61st: | Maj. F.S. Gabreski | FW-190 dest(air) | St. Germain |
| | Lt. H.O. Bevins | Ju-88 prob(air) | Paris |
| 63rd: | Capt. L.A. Adrianse | FW-190 dest(air) | Romilly |
| | Capt. D.M. Goodfleisch | FW-190 dest(air) | SE Paris |
| **September 7, 1943** | | | |
| 62nd: | Lt. A.R. Carcione | Me-109 dest(air) | Tessel Island |
| | Lt. R.A. Johnson | Me-109 dest(air) | Tessel Island |
| **September 9, 1943** | | | |
| 63rd: | Capt. W.M. Mahurin | FW-190 dest(air) | S/Beauvais |
| **September 16, 1943** | | | |
| 62nd: | Lt. G.G. Goldstein | Me-109 dest(air) | Vitre |
| | Lt. R.B. Taylor | FW-190 dest(air) | Fourgeres |
| **September 27, 1943** | | | |
| 63rd: | Lt. J.H. Truluck | Me-109 dest(air) | Borkum Island |
| | | FW-190 dest(air) | Borkum Island |
| | Lt. J.E. Coenen | (2)FW-190 dest(air) | S/Juist Island |
| | Lt. W.J. O'Connor | Me-109 dest(air) | Borkum Island |
| **October 2, 1943** | | | |
| HdQts: | Maj. D.C. Schilling | Me-109 dest(air) | SE Groningen |
| | | FW-190 dest(air) | NE Emden |
| | Col. H. Zemke | FW-190 dest(air) | Groningen |
| **October 4, 1943** | | | |
| HdQts: | Maj. D.C. Schilling | Me-110 dest(air) | E/Duren |
| 61st: | Lt. F.E. McCauley | Me-110 dest(air) | E/Aachen |
| | | Me-110 prob(air) | E/Aachen |
| | Lt. W.A. Marangello | Me-110 dest(air) | W/Aachen |
| | Lt. J.R. Carter | Me-110 prob(air) | E/Aachen |
| 63rd: | Capt. W.M. Mahurin | (3)Me-110 dest(air) | E/Duren |
| | Lt. V.P. Ludwig | (3)Me-110 dest(air) | E/Duren |
| | Capt. D.M. Goodfleisch | Me-110 dest(air) | E/Duren |
| | Lt. J.D. Brown | Me-110 dest(air) | E/Duren |
| | Lt. H.E. Comstock | Me-110 dest(air) | Bruhl |
| | Lt. B.R. Smith | Me-110 dest(air) | Bruhl |
| | Lt. G.D. Schiltz | Me-110 dest(air) | E/Duren |
| | Lt. J.W. Vogt | Me-110 dest(air) | E/Duren |
| | Lt. J.D. Wilson | Me-110 dest(air) | E/Duren |
| **October 8, 1943** | | | |
| HdQts: | Maj. D.C. Schilling | FW-190 dest(air) | Quackenbruck |
| 61st: | Lt. R.S. Johnson | FW-190 dest(air) | Lingen |
| | Capt. D.D. Renwick | FW-190 dam(air) | Lingen |
| 62nd: | Capt. L.A. Schreiber | FW-190 dest(air) | Quackenbruck |
| | Lt. H. Coronios | FW-190 dest(air) | Quackenbruck |
| | | FW-190 dam(air) | Quackenbruck |
| | Lt. M.J. Quirk | FW-190 dest(air) | Quackenbruck |
| | Capt. R. Dauphin | FW-190 prob(air) | Quackenbruck |
| | Lt. C.L. Reeder | FW-190 dam(air) | Quackenbruck |
| **October 10, 1943** | | | |
| HdQts: | Maj. D.C. Schilling | FW-190 dest(air) | Altenberge |
| 61st: | Capt. G.W. Johnson | Me-110 dest(air) | N/Munster |
| | | Me-210 dest(air) | N/Munster |
| | Lt. R.S. Johnson | FW-190 dest(air) | N/Munster |
| | | Me-110 dest(air) | N/Munster |
| 62nd: | Capt. W.V. Cook | Me-210 dest(air) | Altenberge |
| | Lt. A.R. Carcione | Me-109 dest(air) | Nienburg |
| | Lt. J.B. Eaves | Me-109 dest(air) | Altenberge |
| | Lt. J.M. Jones | FW-190 dest(air) | Altenberge |
| | Lt. R.B. Taylor | FW-190 dest(air) | Altenberge |
| | | FW-190 prob(air) | Altenberge |
| | Lt. W.A. Brainard | Me-210 dam(air) | Altenberge |
| 63rd: | Lt. G.D. Schiltz | FW-190 dam(air) | W/Munster |
| **October 14, 1943** | | | |
| HdQts: | Maj. J.C. Stewart | Me-110 dam(air) | W/Aachen |
| 61st: | Capt. G.W. Johnson | FW-190 dest(air) | Eupen |
| | Lt. N.E. Brooks | Me-110 dest(air) | W/Aachen |
| | Lt. F.E. McCauley | Me-110 dest(air) | W/Aachen |
| **October 18, 1943** | | | |
| HdQts: | Maj. J.C. Stewart | (.5)Me-210 dest(air) | NE Maastricht |
| 61st: | Lt. M.C. Wood | (.5)Me-210 dest(air) | NE Maastricht |
| **October 20, 1943** | | | |
| HdQts: | Col. H. Zemke | FW-190 dest(air) | Eindhoven |
| 63rd: | Lt. J.W. Vogt | FW-190 dest(air) | N/Ans |
| | Capt. D.M. Goodfleisch | FW-190 prob(air) | Dison |
| | FW-190 dam(air) | Chateau d' Ardenne | |
| | F/O A.H. Robey | FW-190 dam(air) | S/Aachen |
| **November 3, 1943** | | | |
| 61st: | Lt. R.S. Johnson | Me-109 dest(air) | N/Ameland Isle |
| 63rd: | Capt. W.M. Mahurin | Me-110 dest(air) | N/Juist |
| | | (.5)Me-109 dest(air) | N/Essens |
| | Lt. W.J. O'Connor | (.5)Me-109 dest(air) | N/Essens |
| | Lt. A.J. Wisniewski | Me-110 dam(air) | N/Juist |
| **November 5, 1943** | | | |
| HdQts: | Col. H. Zemke | FW-190 dest(air) | Enschede-Rheine |
| 61st: | Maj. F.S. Gabreski | FW-190 dest(air) | S/Rheine |
| | | FW-190 dam(air) | S/Rheine |
| | Lt. E.E. Barnum | FW-190 dest(air) | S/Rheine |
| 63rd: | Lt. G.F. Hall | Me-210 dest(air) | Enschede |
| | Lt. C.W. Reed | FW-190 dest(air) | Rheine-Munster |
| | Lt. J.D. Wilson | FW-190 dest(air) | Rheine-Munster |
| | Capt. L.A. Adrianse | FW-190 dam(air) | Rheine-Munster |
| | F/O A.H. Robey | FW-190 dam(air) | Rheine-Munster |

**November 11, 1943**

| | | | |
|---|---|---|---|
| 62nd: | Capt. W.V. Cook | (2)FW-190 dest(air) | Bocholt |
| | Capt. E.W. O'Neill | FW-190 dest(air) | Munster |
| | Lt. G.G. Goldstein | FW-190 dest(air) | Munster |
| | F/O J.W. Icard | FW-190 dest(air) | Munster |
| | Capt. L.A. Schreiber | FW-190 dam(air) | Munster |
| 63rd: | Capt. S.V. Burke | Me-109 dest(air) | NW Munster |

**November 26, 1943**

| | | | |
|---|---|---|---|
| HdQts: | LtCol. D.C. Schilling | (2)FW-190 dest(air) | SE Oldenburg |
| | | Me-210 dam(air) | SE Oldenburg |
| | Maj. J.C. Stewart | Do-217 dest(air) | SE Oldenburg |
| 61st: | Maj. F.S. Gabreski | (2)Me-110 dest(air) | SE Oldenburg |
| | F/O F.W. Klibbe | Me-109 dest(air) | SE Oldenburg |
| 62nd: | Capt. W.V. Cook | (2)Me-110 dest(air) | Papenburg |
| | Capt. R.A. Johnson | (2)Me-110 dest(air) | Papenburg |
| | F/O I.E. Valenta | (2)Me-110 dest(air) | Papenburg |
| | | (2)Me-110 dam(air) | Papenburg |
| | Capt. E.W. O'Neill | FW-190 dest(air) | Papenburg |
| | | (.5)Me-110 dest(air) | Papenburg |
| | Lt. M.K. Boyle | (.5)Me-110 dest(air) | Papenburg |
| | Lt. J.P. Bryant | Me-110 dest(air) | Papenburg |
| | Lt. A.R. Carcione | Me-210 dest(air) | Papenburg |
| | Lt. F.J. Christensen | Me-110 dest(air) | Papenburg |
| | Lt. S.B. Morrill | Me-109 dest(air) | Papenburg |
| | | Me-109 dam(air) | Papenburg |
| | Maj. H.C. Craig | Me-110 prob(air) | Papenburg |
| 63rd: | Capt. W.M. Mahurin | (3)Me-110 dest(air) | S/Oldenburg-Zuider Zee |
| | | Me-110 prob(air) | S/Oldenburg-Zuider Zee |
| | Lt. H.E. Comstock | Me-110 dest(air) | Friesoythe |
| | | Me-110 dam(air) | Friesoythe |
| | | FW-190 dam(air) | Friesoythe |
| | Lt. J.H. Truluck | FW-190 dest(air) | Friesoythe |
| | | Me-110 dam(air) | Friesoythe |
| | Lt. J.D. Brown | FW-190 dam(air) | Friesoythe |
| | Lt. R.D. Petty | Me-110 dam(air) | Friesoythe |

**November 29, 1943**

| | | | |
|---|---|---|---|
| HdQts: | LtCol. D.C. Schilling | (.5)FW-190 dest(air) | S/Oldenburg |
| 61st: | Maj. F.S. Gabreski | (2)Me-109 dest(air) | NE Bremen |
| | Lt. J.H. Powers | Me-109 dest(air) | NE Bremen |
| | Capt. R.A. Lamb | Me-109 prob(air) | Bremen |
| 62nd: | Lt. F.D. Williamson | (.5)FW-190 dest(air) | S/Oldenburg |
| | Capt. L.A. Schreiber | (.5)Me-210 dest(air) | S/Oldenburg |
| | Lt. H.M. Pruden | (.5)Me-210 dest(air) | S/Oldenburg |
| 63rd: | Capt. W.M. Mahurin | Me-109 dest(air) | Leer-Papenburg |
| | | Me-109 dam(air) | Leer-Papenburg |
| | Lt. H.E. Comstock | Me-109 prob(air) | Papenburg |
| | Lt. B.R. Smith | Me-109 dam(air) | Lathen |

**December 1, 1943**

| | | | |
|---|---|---|---|
| 61st: | Lt. J.D. Foster | FW-190 dest(air) | Beverloo |
| | Lt. D.H. Mudge | Me-109 dest(air) | Ruhr Valley |
| 62nd: | Lt. F.J. Christensen | Me-109 dest(air) | SE Roermond |
| | Capt. R.A. Johnson | Me-109 dam(air) | SE Roermond |

**December 11, 1943**

| | | | |
|---|---|---|---|
| HdQts: | Col. R.B. Landry | Me-109 dest(air) | NE Emden |
| 61st: | Capt. R.A. Lamb | (3)Me-110 dest(air) | N/Langeroog Isle |
| | Lt. P.A. Conger | (2)Me-110 dest(air) | Langeroog Island |
| | | Ju-88 dest(air) | Langeroog Island |
| | | Me-110 dam(air) | Langeroog Island |
| | Lt. R.W. Roberts | Me-110 dest(air) | Langeroog Island |
| | | Ju-88 dest(air) | Langeroog Island |
| | | Ju-88 dam(air) | Langeroog Island |
| | Lt. D.F. Smith | (2)Me-110 dest(air) | Emden |
| | | (.5)FW 190 dest(air) | Emden |
| | | Me-110 dam(air) | Emden |
| | F/O W.R. Aggers | (.5)FW-190 dest(air) | Emden |
| | Lt. J.H. Powers | Me-110 dest(air) | N/Nordeerney Isle |
| | | Me-109 dest(air) | N/Aurich |
| | | Me-110 dam(air) | N/Aurich |
| | Maj. F.S. Gabreski | Me-110 dest(air) | Essens |
| | Lt. S.D. Hamilton | (2)Me-110 dam(air) | NW Emden |
| 62nd: | Lt. S.B. Morrill | Me-109 dest(air) | Eelde |
| 63rd: | Lt. G.D. Schiltz | Me-210 dest(air) | Emden |

**December 20, 1943**

| | | | |
|---|---|---|---|
| 61st: | Capt. J.H. Bennett | Me-110 dest(air) | Falkenburg |
| | Lt. J.H. Powers | Me-109 dest(air) | NE Bremen |
| | | (.5)Me-109 dam(air) | NE Bremen |
| | | (.5)Me-210 dam(air) | NE Bremen |
| | Lt. M.C. Wood | (.5)Me-109 dam(air) | NE Bremen |
| | | (.5)Me-210 dam(air) | NE Bremen |
| 62nd: | Maj. H.C. Craig | Do-217 dest(air) | SE Bremen |
| | Capt. E.W. O'Neill | Me-109 dest(air) | Vegesack |
| | Lt. M.J. Quirk | Me-109 dest(air) | S/Bremen |
| 63rd: | Lt. C.C. Clamp | FW-190 prob(air) | Bremen |

**December 22, 1943**

| | | | |
|---|---|---|---|
| 61st: | Lt. R.S. Johnson | Me-109 dest(air) | N/Almelo |
| 62nd: | Lt. F.D. Williamson | Me-109 dest(air) | W/Rheims |
| 63rd: | Capt. W.M. Mahurin | (2)Me-109 dest(air) | Hesepe |

**December 30, 1943**

| | | | |
|---|---|---|---|
| 61st: | Lt. R.S. Johnson | FW-190 dest(air) | Soissons |
| | Capt. R.A. Lamb | FW-190 dam(air) | S/Soissons |

**December 31, 1943**

| | | | |
|---|---|---|---|
| 61st: | Lt. R.S. Johnson | (2)FW-190 dest(air) | N/St. Gilles |

**January 4, 1944**

| | | | |
|---|---|---|---|
| 62nd: | Lt. M.J. Quirk | FW-190 dest(air) | Stadlohn |

**January 5, 1944**

| | | | |
|---|---|---|---|
| HdQts: | Maj. J.C. Stewart | FW-190 dest(air) | SW Bonn |
| 61st: | Lt. R.S. Johnson | FW-190 dest(air) | N/Liege |
| 62nd: | Lt. F.J. Christensen | FW-190 dest(air) | Ans |
| | Lt. S.B. Morrill | Me-109 dest(air) | Duren |

**January 11, 1944**

| | | | |
|---|---|---|---|
| HdQts: | LtCol. D.C. Schilling | FW-190 dest(air) | Osnabruck |
| | | FW-190 dam(air) | Osnabruck |
| 61st: | Capt. J.R. Carter | Me-109 dest(air) | N/Osnabruck |
| | | Me-109 prob(air) | N/Osnabruck |
| | | Me-109 dam(air) | N/Osnabruck |
| | Lt. J.D. Foster | Me-109 dest(air) | NE Osnabruck |
| | | Me-109 dam(air) | NE Osnabruck |
| | Capt. J.H. Bennett | (2)Me-109 dam(air) | Schwastorf |
| 62nd: | Lt. S.B. Morrill | Me-109 dest(air) | Bramsche |
| | Lt. M.J. Quirk | Me-109 prob(air) | Lingen |
| 63rd: | Lt. G.D. Schiltz | (3)Me-109 dest(air) | N/Osnabruck |
| | Maj. S.V. Burke | Me-109 dest(air) | N/Osnabruck |
| | | Me-109 dam(air) | N/Osnabruck |
| | Lt. A.H. Robey | Me-109 dest(air) | N/Osnabruck |
| | | Me-109 dam(air) | N/Osnabruck |
| | Lt. B.R. Smith | FW-190 dest(air) | Osnabruck |

**January 21, 1944**

| | | | |
|---|---|---|---|
| 61st: | Lt. R.S. Johnson | FW-190 dest(air) | N/Rouen |
| | Capt. L.C. Smith | FW-190 dam(air) | NE Rouen |

**January 29, 1944**

| | | | |
|---|---|---|---|
| HdQts: | LtCol. F.S. Gabreski | Me-110 dest(air) | S/Coblenz |
| | LtCol. D.C. Schilling | Me-109 dest(air) | Bonn |
| 61st: | Capt. J.H. Bennett | (1.5)Me-110 dest(air) | Simmern |
| | Lt. M.C. Wood | Me-210 dest(air) | Simmern |
| | Lt. P. Neyland | (.5)Me-110 dest(air) | Simmern |
| 63rd: | Lt. A.S. Cavallo | Me-210 dest(air) | SW Coblenz |
| | | Me-210 prob(air) | SW Coblenz |
| | Lt. H.E. Comstock | FW-190 dam(air) | W/Ostend |

**January 30, 1944**

| | | | |
|---|---|---|---|
| HdQts: | LtCol. F.S. Gabreski | Me-109 dest(air) | Lingen |
| | | Me-210 dest(air) | Lingen |
| 61st: | Lt. R.S. Johnson | Me-109 dest(air) | E/Lingen |
| | | Me-210 dest(air) | E/Lingen |
| | Capt. J.R. Carter | FW-190 dest(air) | Leeuwen |
| | Lt. E.E. Barnum | Me-210 dest(air) | Lingen |
| | Lt. F.W. Klibbe | Me-109 dest(air) | Lingen |
| | Lt. J.H. Powers | FW-190 dest(air) | Meppen |
| 62nd: | Lt. M.J. Quirk | Me-109 dest(air) | Almelo |
| | | Me-109 dam(air) | Almelo |
| | Lt. A.R. Carcione | (.5)Ju-88 dest(air) | Twente |
| | Lt. S.B. Morrill | (.5)Ju-88 dest(air) | Twente |
| | | Ju-88 dam(air) | Twente |
| | Lt. M.L. Moseley | Me-210 dam(air) | Hanskamp |
| 63rd: | Lt. G.F. Hall | (2)Me-109 dest(air) | S/Quackenbruck |
| | | (2)Me-109 dam(air) | S/Quackenbruck |
| | Lt. L.M. Langdon | (2)Me-109 dest(air) | S/Quackenbruck |
| | | Me-109 dam(air) | S/Quackenbruck |
| | Capt. W.M. Mahurin | Ju-88 dest(air) | S/Quackenbruck |
| | | Ju-88 prob(air) | S/Quackenbruck |
| | Lt. J.L. Egan | Me-210 dest(air) | S/Quackenbruck |

**February 3, 1944**

| | | | |
|---|---|---|---|
| 63rd: | Capt. W.M. Mahurin | Me-109 dest(air) | SE Ruhlertwist |
| | Lt. C.W. Reed | Me-109 dest(air) | SE Ruhlertwist |
| | Lt. W.H. Janson | Me-109 prob(air) | SE Ruhlertwist |
| | Lt. R.B. Westfall | Me-109 dam(air) | SE Ruhlertwist |

**February 4, 1944**

| | | | |
|---|---|---|---|
| 62nd: | Capt. M.J. Quirk | FW-190 dest(air) | Charleroi |
| | | Me-110 dest(air) | St. Omer |
| | Lt. F.J. Christensen | FW-190 dest(air) | Charleroi |
| | Lt. J.E. Fields | FW-190 dest(air) | Charleroi |
| | Lt. S.B. Morrill | (2)FW-190 dam(air) | Charleroi |
| | Lt. J.M. Jones | FW-190 dam(air) | Charleroi |
| | Lt. I.E. Valenta | FW-190 dam(air) | Charleroi |

**February 6, 1944**

| | | | |
|---|---|---|---|
| 61st: | Capt. R.A. Lamb | Me-109 dest(air) | Beauvais |
| | Lt. S.D. Hamilton | Me-109 dest(air) | Paris |
| | Lt. J.H. Powers | Me-109 dest(air) | Beauvais |
| | Lt. R.J. Rankin | Me-109 dest(air) | Paris |
| 62nd: | Capt. E.W. O'Neill | FW-190 dest(air) | Paris |
| | Lt. J.W. Icard | FW-190 dam(air) | Albert |

**February 8, 1944**

| | | | |
|---|---|---|---|
| 62nd: | Lt. J.W. Icard | Me-109 dest(air) | Cambrai |
| | Capt. L.A. Schreiber | Me-109 prob(air) | Cambrai |
| 63rd: | Maj. S.V. Burke | Me-109 dam(air) | Quesnoy |

**February 11, 1944**

| | | | |
|---|---|---|---|
| HdQts: | Col. H. Zemke | Me-109 dest(grd) | Rheims |
| | | (2)Me-109 dam(grd) | Rheims |
| 61st: | Maj. J.C. Stewart | FW-190 dest(air) | Duren |
| | Lt. R.L. Altschuler | Me-110 dam(grd) | Rheims |
| | Lt. D.M. Funcheon | Me-110 dam(grd) | Rheims |
| 62nd: | Lt. F.J. Christensen | Me-109 dest(air) | Bierset |
| | Lt. J.W. Icard | Me-109 dest(air) | Bierset |
| | Lt. S.B. Morrill | Me-109 dest(air) | Dison |
| | Capt. L.A. Schreiber | Me-109 dam(air) | Namur |
| 63rd: | Maj. S.V. Burke | Me-109 dest(air) | Hody-Spa |

**February 20, 1944**

| | | | |
|---|---|---|---|
| HdQts: | LtCol. F.S. Gabreski | (2)Me-110 dest(air) | W/Hanover |
| | | Me-110 dam(air) | W/Hanover |
| 61st: | Lt. R.S. Johnson | (2)Me-110 dest(air) | W/Hanover |
| | | (2)Me-110 dam(air) | W/Hanover |
| | Lt. D.F. Smith | (2)Me-110 dest(air) | Steinhuder Lake |
| | | Me-110 dam(air) | Steinhuder Lake |
| | Capt. J.R. Carter | Me-110 dest(air) | Steinhuder Lake |
| | Capt. R.A. Lamb | Ju-88 dest(air) | E/Minden |
| | Lt. J.D. Foster | Me-110 prob(air) | Steinhuder Lake |
| | | Me-110 dam(air) | Steinhuder Lake |
| | Lt. S.D. Hamilton | Me-110 prob(air) | Steinhuder Lake |
| | | Me-109 dam(air) | Steinhuder Lake |
| | Lt. D.M. Funcheon | (2)Me-110 dam(air) | Steinhuder Lake |
| | Lt. R.L. Altschuler | Me-110 dam(air) | Steinhuder Lake |
| | Lt. C.E. Mussey | Me-110 dam(air) | Steinhuder Lake |
| 62nd: | Capt. L.A. Schreiber | (3)Me-109 dest(air) | Steinhuder Lake |
| | | Me-109 dam(air) | Steinhuder Lake |
| | | Do-217 dam(grd) | Steinhuder Lake |
| | Lt. F.J. Christensen | Ju-88 dest(air) | Steinhuder Lake |
| | | (.5)Do-217 dest(air) | Steinhuder Lake |
| | Lt. S.B. Morrill | Me-110 dest(air) | Steinhuder Lake |
| | | (.5)Do-217 dest(air) | Steinhuder Lake |
| | | (6)Me-110 dam(grd) | Steinhuder Lake |

**February 21, 1944**

| | | | |
|---|---|---|---|
| 61st: | Capt. B.M. Gladych | (2)Me-109 dest(air) | Zuider Zee |
| | Lt. D.M. Funcheon | Me-109 dest(air) | Zuider Zee |
| | Lt. F.W. Klibbe | Me-109 dest(air) | Zuider Zee |
| | F/O E.D. McMinn | Me-109 dest(air) | Zuider Zee |
| | Lt. C.E. Mussey | Me-109 dest(air) | Zuider Zee |
| 62nd: | Lt. R.B. Bluhm | Me-109 dest(air) | Zwolle |
| | Lt. C.R. Harrison | Me-109 dest(air) | Soesterberg |
| | Lt. J.W. Icard | FW-190 dest(air) | Soesterberg |
| | Capt. L.A. Schreiber | FW-190 dam(air) | Osnabruck |
| 63rd: | Maj. G.W. Johnson | FW-190 dest(air) | NW Zwolle |
| | Capt. J.W. Vogt | Me-110 dest(air) | N/Munster |
| | Lt. J.L. Egan | Me-109 dest(air) | Elburg |
| | Capt. G.D. Schiltz | Me-109 dam(air) | Zuider Zee |

**February 22, 1944**

| | | | |
|---|---|---|---|
| HdQts: | LtCol. F.S. Gabreski | FW-190 dest(air) | N/Lippstadt |
| | | Do-217 dest(grd) | Eindhoven |
| 61st: | Capt. L.C. Smith | (2)FW-190 dest(air) | Lippstadt |
| | Maj. J.C. Stewart | Me-109 dest(air) | SW Munster |
| | F/O E.D. McMinn | FW-190 dest(air) | Lippstadt |
| | Lt. D.F. Smith | FW-190 dest(air) | Lippstadt |
| | F/O S. Gerick | Me-110 dam(air) | E/Paderborn |
| 62nd: | Capt. M.J. Quirk | (1.5)FW-190 dest(air) | Breda |
| | Lt. J.E. Fields | (.5)FW-190 dest(air) | Breda |
| | | (.5)FW-190 dest(air) | Breda |
| | Capt. L.A. Schreiber | (.5)FW-190 dest(air) | Breda |
| | Lt. F.L. Roy | FW-190 dest(air) | Breda |
| | Capt. R. Dauphin | Me-110 dam(air) | Paderborn |
| | Lt. J.P. Bryant | FW-190 dam(air) | Breda |
| | Lt. A.R. Carcione | Me-109 dest(grd) | Eindhoven |
| | Lt. C.L. Ginn | Do-217 dam(grd) | Eindhoven |
| 63rd: | Lt. G.F. Hall | (2)Me-110 dest(air) | Raderborn |
| | Capt. L.A. Adrianse | Me-110 dest(air) | Raderborn |
| | Capt. J.W. Vogt | Me-110 dest(air) | Raderborn |
| | Lt. J.L. Egan | Me-109 dest(air) | Munster |
| | | FW-190 dam(air) | Munster |
| | Maj. G.W. Johnson | FW-190 prob(air) | SW Gutersloh |

**February 24, 1944**

| | | | |
|---|---|---|---|
| 61st: | Maj. J.C. Stewart | FW-190 dest(air) | Kassel |
| | Lt. G.J. Blake | FW-190 dest(air) | N/Minden |
| | Lt. D.M. Funcheon | FW-190 dest(air) | Holzminden |
| | | FW-190 prob(air) | Holzminden |
| | Lt. J.H. Powers | FW-190 dest(air) | Minden |
| | Lt. E.E. Barnum | FW-190 dam(air) | Kassel |
| 62nd: | Lt. W.P. Gordon | FW-190 dest(air) | SW Hanover |
| | Lt. S.B. Morrill | Me-109 dest(air) | E/Asnabruck |
| | Lt. I.E. Valenta | FW-190 dam(air) | SW Hanover |
| | Lt. F.J. Christensen | FW-190 dam(grd) | Quackenbruck |
| | | Me-110 dam(grd) | Quackenbruck |
| 63rd: | Maj. G.W. Johnson | FW-190 dest(air) | Minden |
| | Lt. J.H. Truluck | FW-190 dest(air) | Herford |
| | Lt. A.S. Cavallo | FW-190 dam(air) | Minden |
| | Lt. H.E. Comstock | FW-190 dam(air) | Peterhagen |

**February 25, 1944**

| | | | |
|---|---|---|---|
| 61st: | Capt. R.A. Lamb | Me-109 dest(air) | Landau |
| | Lt. D.M. Funcheon | Me-109 dest(air) | Landau |
| | Lt. E.E. Barnum | Me-109 dam(air) | Landau |
| 62nd: | Capt. M.J. Quirk | FW-190 dest(air) | Homburg |
| | Lt. T.S. Buszko | FW-190 dam(air) | Homburg |

**February 29, 1944**

| | | | |
|---|---|---|---|
| 63rd: | Maj. G.W. Johnson | Ju-52 dest(air) | Horderwijk |

**March 2, 1944**

| | | | |
|---|---|---|---|
| 63rd: | Maj. G.W. Johnson | Me-109 dest(air) | SE Aachen |

**March 6, 1944**

| | | | |
|---|---|---|---|
| HdQts: | Col. H. Zemke | (1.25)Me-109 dest(air) | Minden-Osnabruck |
| | | FW-190 dest(air) | Minden-Osnabruck |
| | | FW-190 prob(air) | Minden-Osnabruck |
| 61st: | Maj. J.C. Stewart | (2)FW-190 dest(air) | N/Dummer Lake |
| | Lt. R.S. Johnson | FW-190 dest(air) | N/Dummer Lake |
| | Lt. S.D. Hamilton | Me-109 dam(air) | NE Dummer Lake |
| | Capt. B.M. Gladych | Me-109 dest(grd) | Vechta |
| | F/O E.D. McMinn | (2)Me-109 dam(grd) | Vechta |
| 62nd: | Lt. F.J. Christensen | FW-190 dest(air) | N/Dummer Lake |
| | Lt. J.W. Icard | FW-190 dest(air) | Dummer Lake |
| | Lt. D.A. Nordquist | FW-190 dam(air) | N/Dummer Lake |
| 63rd: | Capt. W.M. Mahurin | FW-190 dest(air) | Wenzendorf A/F |
| | | FW-190 prob(air) | Wenzendorf A/F |
| | Lt. G.F. Hall | FW-190 dest(air) | Ulzen |
| | Lt. M.H. Becker | (.25)Me-109 dest(air) | Minden-Osnabruck |
| | Lt. D.V. Peters | (.25)Me-109 dest(air) | Minden-Osnabruck |
| | Lt. C.W. Reed | (.25)Me-109 dest(air) | Minden-Osnabruck |
| | Maj. G.W. Johnson | FW-190 dam(air) | Wenzendorf A/F |
| | Lt. B.P. Casteel | Me-109 dam(air) | Steinhuder Lake |

**March 8, 1944**

| | | | |
|---|---|---|---|
| HdQts: | LtCol. D.C. Schilling | FW-190 dam(air) | Dummer Lake |
| | | Me-210 dest(grd) | Dummer Lake |
| | LtCol. F.S. Gabreski | FW-190 dest(grd) | Weinstorf A/F |
| | | (4)FW-190 dam(grd) | Weinstorf A/F |
| 61st: | Capt. J.H. Bennett | (2)Me-109 dest(air) | E/Steinhuder L. |
| | | FW-190 dest(air) | Munstorf A/F |
| | Maj. J.C. Stewart | FW-190 dest(air) | S/Steinuder Lake |
| | Me-110 dest(air) | S/Steinhuder Lake | |
| | Lt. R.S. Johnson | (2)Me-109 dest(air) | NE Steinhuder L. |
| | Capt. B.M. Gladych | FW-190 dest(air) | Dummer Lake |
| | | (3)FW-190 dam(grd) | Dummer Lake |
| | Lt. G.J. Blake | FW-190 dest(air) | NE Steinhuder L. |
| | Lt. F.W. Klibbe | FW-190 dest(air) | Steinhuder Lake |
| | Lt. C.E. Mussey | Me-109 dest(air) | E/Steinhuder Lake |
| | | Ju-88 prob(air) | E/Steinhuder Lake |
| | Capt. L.C. Smith | FW-190 dam(air) | Steinhuder Lake |
| | Lt. N.E. Brooks | FW-190 dam(air) | Dummer Lake |
| | Lt. D.H. Mudge | FW-190 dam(air) | S/Steinhuder Lake |
| 62nd: | Capt. L.A. Schreiber | Me-109 dest(air) | Steinhuder Lake |
| | | FW-190 dest(air) | Steinhuder Lake |
| | Lt. R.C. Cherry | FW-190 dest(air) | Steinhuder Lake |
| | | FW-190 prob(air) | Steinhuder Lake |
| | | FW-190 dam(air) | Steinhuder Lake |
| | Lt. J.E. Fields | FW-190 dest(air) | Steinhuder Lake |
| | | FW-190 dam(air) | Steinhuder Lake |
| | Lt. M.L. Moseley | FW-190 dest(air) | Dummer Lake-Steinhuder Lake |
| | | FW-190 dam(air) | Dummer Lake-Steinhuder Lake |
| | Lt. F.D. Williamson | FW-190 dest(air) | Minden |
| | Capt. M.J. Quirk | (.5)FW-190 dest(air) | Celle |
| | Lt. J.B. Eaves | (.5)FW-190 dest(air) | Celle |
| | Lt. C.L. Reeder | (2)FW-190 prob(air) | Hanover |
| | Lt. W.A. McClure | FW-190 dam(air) | Minden |
| 63rd: | Capt. W.M. Mahurin | (2)FW-190 dest(air) | Wesendorf A/F |
| | | Ju-88 dest(air) | Wesendorf A/F |
| | Maj. G.W. Johnson | (2)Me-109 dest(air) | Dummer L.-Celle |
| | Lt. M.H. Becker | Me-109 dest(air) | E/Dummer Lake |
| | Lt. A.H. Robey | Me-109 dest(air) | Dummer Lake |
| | Lt. B.R. Smith | Me-110 dest(air) | NW Steinhuder L. |

| | | | |
|---|---|---|---|
| | Lt. J.H. Truluck | Me-109 dest(air) | Dummer Lake |
| | Lt. J.C. Marcotte | FW-190 prob(air) | Dummer Lake |
| | Lt. S.O. Stamps | Me-109 dam(air) | S/Dummer Lake |

**March 15, 1944**

| | | | |
|---|---|---|---|
| 61st: | Lt. R.S. Johnson | (2)FW-190 dest(air) | Dummer Lake |
| | | Me-109 dest(air) | Dummer Lake |
| | Lt. R.J. Rankin | (2)Me-109 dest(air) | Dummer Lake |
| | | Me-109 prob(air) | Dummer Lake |
| | | FW-190 dam(air) | Dummer Lake |
| | Lt. J.H. Powers | FW-190 dest(air) | Dummer Lake |
| | | Me-109 dest(air) | Dummer Lake |
| | | FW-190 dam(air) | Dummer Lake |
| | Capt. L.C. Smith | Me-109 dest(air) | Solingen-Dummer Lake |
| | Lt. F.W. Klibbe | FW-190 dest(air) | S/Barenburg |
| | F/O S. Gerick | Me-109 dest(air) | Dummer Lake |
| | | Me-109 dam(air) | Dummer Lake |
| | Maj. J.C. Stewart | Me-109 dam(air) | Dummer Lake |
| | F/O E.D. McMinn | Me-109 dam(air) | NE Dummer Lake |
| 62nd: | Lt. F.J. Christensen | (2)FW-190 dest(air) | Dummer Lake |
| | | (2)FW-190 dam(air) | Dummer Lake |
| | Capt. M.J. Quirk | FW-190 dest(air) | Dummer Lake |
| | Lt. J.P. Bryant | FW-190 dest(air) | Dummer Lake |
| | Lt. J.E. Fields | FW-190 dest(air) | Dummer Lake |
| | Lt. J.M. Jones | FW-190 dest(air) | Dummer Lake |
| | | FW-190 dam(air) | Dummer Lake |
| | Lt. M.L. Moseley | FW-190 dest(air) | Dummer Lake |
| 63rd: | Maj. G.W. Johnson | (2)Me-109 dest(air) | Nienburg |
| | Lt. A.H. Robey | (2)FW-190 dest(air) | Vechta |
| | Lt. J.L. Egan | FW-190 dest(air) | Nienburg |
| | Lt. D.V. Peters | Me-109 dest(air) | Hanover |
| | Lt. J.H. Truluck | FW-190 dest(air) | Hanover |
| | | Me-109 dam(air) | Hanover |
| | Lt. M.H. Becker | FW-190 dam(air) | Hanover |

**March 16, 1944**

| | | | |
|---|---|---|---|
| HdQts: | LtCol. F.S. Gabreski | (2)FW-190 dest(air) | Nancy |
| | Col. H. Zemke | Me-109 dam(air) | Chalons |
| 61st: | Lt. J.H. Powers | Me-109 dest(air) | St. Dizier |
| | | FW-190 dam(air) | St. Dizier |
| | F/O E.D. McMinn | FW-190 dest(air) | St. Dizier |
| 62nd: | Lt. F.J. Christensen | (2)FW-190 dest(air) | St. Dizier |
| | Capt. L.A. Schreiber | Me-109 dest(air) | St. Dizier |
| | | (.5)FW-190 dest(air) | St. Dizier |
| | Lt. T.S. Buszko | FW-190 dest(air) | St. Dizier |
| | Lt. S.B. Morrill | FW-190 dest(air) | St. Dizier |
| | Lt. F.D. Williamson | FW-190 dest(air) | St. Dizier |
| | Lt. A.W. Canizares | (.5)FW-190 dest(air) | St. Dizier |
| | | Me-109 dam(air) | St. Dizier |
| | Lt. M.K. Boyle | FW-190 prob(air) | St. Dizier |
| | Lt. J.M. Jones | FW-190 dam(air) | St. Dizier |
| | Lt. C.L. Ginn | FW-190 dam(grd) | Burvinnes A/F |
| 63rd: | Lt. A.S. Cavallo | Me-109 dam(air) | Vitry |

**March 18, 1944**

| | | | |
|---|---|---|---|
| 61st: | Lt. J.H. Powers | FW-190 dest(air) | Cambrai-Givet |
| | Lt. D.E. Stream | FW-190 dest(air) | Cambrai-Givet |
| | Lt. S.D. Hamilton | FW-190 dam(air) | Cambrai-Givet |

**March 20, 1944**

| | | | |
|---|---|---|---|
| 61st: | Maj. J.C. Stewart | (2)Me-109 dest(air) | S/Charleville |
| | | Me-109 prob(air) | S/Charleville |
| | Lt. D.E. Stream | u/i a/c dest(grd) | Charleville |

**March 27, 1944**

| | | | |
|---|---|---|---|
| HdQts: | LtCol. F.S. Gabreski | (2)Me-109 dest(air) | NE Nantes |
| | LtCol. D.C. Schilling | Ju-52 dest(grd) | Chateaudun |
| 61st: | Capt. B.M. Gladych | Me-109 dest(air) | S/Angars |
| | Capt. L.C. Smith | u/i a/c dam(grd) | Gael A/F |
| 63rd: | Maj. W.M. Mahurin | (.25)Do-217 dest(air) | S/Chartres |
| | Lt. W.D. Johnson | (.25)Do-217 dest(air) | S/Chartres |
| | F/O S.J. Lowman | (.25)Do-217 dest(air) | S/Chartres |
| | Lt. I.T. Porowski | (.25)Do-217 dest(air) | S/Chartres |

**March 29, 1944**

| | | | |
|---|---|---|---|
| HdQts: | LtCol. D.C. Schilling | Me-109 dest(air) | NE Dummer Lake |
| | | Me-109 dam(air) | NE Dummer Lake |
| 61st: | Lt. R.J. Rankin | Me-109 dest(air) | NE Nienburg |

**April 8, 1944**

| | | | |
|---|---|---|---|
| 62nd: | Capt. J.M. Jones | Ju-88 dest(grd) | Quackenbruck |
| | Maj. L.A. Schreiber | (.5)Me-410 dest(grd) | Quackenbruck |
| | | (.5)Me-109 dest(grd) | Quackenbruck |
| | Lt. A.W. Canizares | (.5)Me-410 dest(grd) | Quackenbruck |
| | | (.5)Me-109 dest(grd) | Quackenbruck |

**April 9, 1944**

| | | | |
|---|---|---|---|
| HdQts: | LtCol. D.C. Schilling | (2)FW-190 dest(air) | NE Schleswig |
| | | FW-190 dam(air) | NE Schleswig |
| | | W-34 dam(air) | Schleswig |
| | | Ar-196 dest(grd) | Schleswig |
| | LtCol. F.S. Gabreski | (.5)u/i a/c dest(grd)* | Schleswig |
| 61st: | Capt. T. Anderz | Me-109 dest(air) | SE Kiel |
| | Capt. R.S. Johnson | FW-190 dest(air) | NW Kiel |
| | Capt. L.C. Smith | Me-109 dest(air) | E/Neumunster |
| | Lt. S.D. Hamilton | FW-190 dest(air) | NW Kiel |
| | | (2)FW-190 dam(air) | NW Kiel |
| 62nd: | Capt. J.H. Powers | Me-109 dest(air) | S/Kiel |
| | Maj. L.A. Schreiber | (.5)Me-109 dest(air) | Lubeck |
| | | (3)Me-109 dam(grd) | Lubeck |
| | Lt. A.W. Canizares | (.5)Me-109 dest(air) | Lubeck |
| | Lt. W.A. McClure | (2)FW-190 dam(air) | Lubeck |
| | Capt. C.R. Harrison | Me-109 dam(air) | Lubeck |
| 63rd: | Lt. H.L. Matthew | Me-109 dest(grd) | Jagel A/F |
| | | (.5)u/i a/c dest(grd)* | Schleswig |
| | F/O W.R. Frederick | He-115 dest(grd) | Schleswig |
| | | He-115 dam(grd) | Schleswig |
| | Lt. W.E. Kerr | Ar-196 dest(grd) | Schleswig |

**April 11, 1944**

| | | | |
|---|---|---|---|
| 62nd: | Lt. M.K. Boyle | u/i a/c dam(air) | Schleswig |
| | | He-115 dest(grd) | Schleswig |
| | Lt. R.B. Bluhm | u/i a/c dam(grd) | Schleswig |

**April 13, 1944**

| | | | |
|---|---|---|---|
| HdQts: | LtCol. D.C. Schilling | Me-109 dest(air) | Ludwigshafen |
| 61st: | Capt. R.S. Johnson | (2)FW-190 dest(air) | Kaiserlautern |
| 62nd: | Lt. M.K. Boyle | Me-109 dest(air) | Ludwigshafen |
| | Capt. J.H. Powers | Me-109 dam(air) | Ludwigshafen |

**April 15, 1944**

| | | | |
|---|---|---|---|
| HdQts: | Col. H. Zemke | (3)He-111 dest(grd) | Flensburg |
| | | (3)He-111 dam(grd) | Flensburg |
| 61st: | Capt. P.A. Conger | FW-190 dest(air) | Elmshorn |
| | F/O E.D. McMinn | He-111 dest(grd) | Flensburg |
| | | Me-210 dest(grd) | Flensburg |
| | | He-111 dam(grd) | Flensburg |
| | | Me-210 dam(grd) | Flensburg |
| | Capt. L.C. Smith | He-111 dest(grd) | Flensburg |
| | | He-111 dam(grd) | Flensburg |
| | Lt. E.A. Sisson | He-111 dest(grd) | Flensburg |
| | | (2)Me-410 dam(grd) | Flensburg |
| | Lt. H.R. Holtmeier | Ju-88 dam(grd) | Flensburg |
| 62nd: | Capt. F.J. Christensen | (2)Me-109 dest(air) | Altona |
| | Lt. W.P. Chattaway | FW-190 dest(air) | Altona |
| | | (2)FW-190 dam(air) | Altona |
| | Lt. J.E. Greene | (3)FW-190 dam(air) | N/Hamburg |
| | Lt. H.E. Gallagher | FW-190 dam(air) | Altona |
| | Lt. W.H. Merrill | FW-190 dam(air) | Altona |
| | Maj. L.A. Schreiber | He-111 dest(grd) | Schleswig |
| 63rd: | Lt. W.D. Johnson | (.5)FW-190 dest(air) | Flensburg-Husum |
| | | He-111 dam(grd) | Flensburg |
| | Lt. S.O. Stamps | (.5)FW-190 dest(air) | Flensburg-Husum |
| | | He-111 dam(grd) | Flensburg |
| | Lt. M.H. Becker | He-111 dest(grd) | Flensburg |
| | F/O S.J. Lowman | He-111 dest(grd) | Flensburg |
| | Lt. C.W. Reed | He-111 dest(grd) | Flensburg |

**April 20, 1944**

| | | | |
|---|---|---|---|
| 62nd: | Capt. F.D. Williamson | (.5)Ju-88 dest(air) | NE Paris |
| | Lt. W.A. McClure | (.5)Ju-88 dest(air) | NE Paris |

**April 24, 1944**

| | | | |
|---|---|---|---|
| HdQts: | Maj. J.C. Stewart | Ju-87 dest(grd) | Thronville A/F |
| | | Ju-87 dam(grd) | Thronville A/F |
| | | u/i a/c dam(grd) | Thronville A/F |
| 61st: | LtCol. F.S. Gabreski | He-111 dam(grd) | Frieburg A/F |
| 63rd: | Lt. W.E. Kerr | (2)Me-109 dest(grd) | Thalheim A/F |
| | | Me-110 dest(grd) | Thalheim A/F |
| | | Me-110 dam(grd) | Thalheim A/F |
| | Lt. J.A. Aranyos | Do-217 dest(grd) | Thalheim A/F |
| | | Me-109 dest(grd) | Thalheim A/F |
| | | Do-217 dam(grd) | Thalheim A/F |
| | | Me-210 dam(grd) | Thalheim A/F |
| | Lt. S.B. Dale | Me-109 dest(grd) | Thalheim A/F |
| | | FW-190 dest(grd) | Thalheim A/F |
| | | (.25)u/i a/c dam(grd) | Thalheim A/F |
| | Lt. D.V. Peters | Me-109 dest(grd) | Thalheim A/F |
| | | Me-210 dest(grd) | Thalheim A/F |
| | | (2)Me-109 dam(grd) | Thalheim A/F |
| | Capt. J.H. Truluck | Do-217 dest(grd) | Thalheim A/F |
| | | (3)Do-217 dam(grd) | Thalheim A/F |
| | Lt. H.F. Warner | Ju-87 dest(grd) | Thalheim A/F |
| | | (.25)u/i a/c dam(grd) | Thalheim A/F |
| | Lt. D.W. Marshall | (.5)Me-210 dest(grd) | Thalheim A/F |
| | | (1.25)u/i a/c dam(grd) | Thalheim A/F |
| | | Me-109 dam(grd) | Thalheim A/F |
| | Lt. A.J. Wisniewski | (.5)Me-210 dest(grd) | Thalheim A/F |
| | | Ju-87 dam(grd) | Thalheim A/F |
| | | (.25)u/i a/c dam(grd) | Thalheim A/F |

**April 25, 1944**

| Unit | Pilot | Claim | Location |
|---|---|---|---|
| HdQts: | Col. H. Zemke | (2)Ju-88 dest(grd) | Metz |
| 61st: | F/O S. Gerick | Me-109 dest(grd) | Metz |
| | Capt. B.M. Gladych | FW-190 dam(grd) | Metz |
| | | Ju-88 dam(grd) | Metz |
| | | u/i a/c dam(grd) | Metz |
| | Lt. R.M. Heineman | Me-109 dam(grd) | Metz |

**April 29, 1944**

| Unit | Pilot | Claim | Location |
|---|---|---|---|
| HdQts: | Maj. J.C. Stewart | Me-109 dam(air) | W/Steinhuder L. |

**May 4, 1944**

| Unit | Pilot | Claim | Location |
|---|---|---|---|
| 62nd: | Lt. R.C. Cherry | Me-410 dest(air) | Nordhausen |
| | | (.5)FW-190 dest(air) | Nordhausen |
| | Capt. J.H. Powers | Me-109 dest(air) | Quackenbruck |
| | Lt. E.E. Bennett | (.5)FW-190 dest(air) | Nordhausen |
| | Lt. R.B. Bluhm | Me-109 dam(air) | Dummer Lake |

**May 8, 1944**

| Unit | Pilot | Claim | Location |
|---|---|---|---|
| 61st: | Lt. F.W. Klibbe | Me-109 dest(air) | W/Celle |
| | | FW-190 dest(air) | W/Celle |
| | LtCol. F.S. Gabreski | Me-109 dest(air) | Celle |
| | Lt. J.H. Perry | FW-190 prob(air) | W/Celle |
| 62nd: | Capt. R.S. Johnson | Me-109 dest(air) | Brunswick-Hanover |
| | | FW-190 dest(air) | Brunswick-Hanover |
| | Lt. G.H. Lewis | FW-190 dest(air) | Oschersleben |
| | Lt. H.E. Hartney | FW-190 dam(air) | Celle |

**May 12, 1944**

| Unit | Pilot | Claim | Location |
|---|---|---|---|
| HdQts: | Col. H. Zemke | Me-109 dest(air) | SW Coblenz |
| 61st: | Lt. R.J. Rankin | (5)Me-109 dest(air) | NW Marburg |
| | Capt. P.A. Conger | (2)FW-190 dest(air) | N/Marburg |
| | | FW-190 dam(air) | N/Marburg |
| | F/O S. Gerick | FW-190 dest(air) | NW Marburg |
| | | Me-109 dam(air) | NW Marburg |
| | Lt. A.C. Maul | Me-109 dest(air) | N/Marburg |
| | Lt. C.C. Thomton | Me-109 dest(air) | Marburg |
| | Lt. P. Neyland | Me-109 dam(air) | N/Marburg |
| 62nd: | Lt. J.E. Greene | Me-109 dest(air) | Frankfurt |
| | Lt. H.E. King | Me-109 dest(air) | Frankfurt |
| | Capt. J.H. Powers | (.5)Me-109 dest(air) | Frankfurt |
| | F/O J. Vitale | (.5)Me-109 dest(air) | Frankfurt |
| 63rd: | Lt. J.C. Wakefield | (3)Me-109 dest(air) | NW Frankfurt |
| | Lt. A.S. Cavallo | (2)FW-190 dest(air) | Coblenz |

**May 13, 1944**

| Unit | Pilot | Claim | Location |
|---|---|---|---|
| 61st: | Lt. R.J. Keen | (3)FW-190 dest(air) | W/Hagenow |
| | | FW-190 prob(air) | W/Hagenow |
| | Lt. J.M. Jure | FW-190 dest(air) | NE Hamburg |
| 62nd: | Maj. L.A. Dade | FW-190 dest(air) | Lubeck |

**May 19, 1944**

| Unit | Pilot | Claim | Location |
|---|---|---|---|
| 61st: | Maj. L.C. Smith | (2)FW-190 dest(air) | N/Wernigerode |
| | Lt. R.M. Heineman | FW-190 dest(air) | Halberstadt |
| 62nd: | Capt. J.B. Eaves | (2)FW-190 dest(air) | N/Hanover |

**May 22, 1944**

| Unit | Pilot | Claim | Location |
|---|---|---|---|
| 61st: | LtCol. F.S. Gabreski | (3)FW-190 dest(air) | Hoperhofen A/F |
| | | FW-190 prob(air) | Hoperhofen A/F |
| | Lt. R.M. Heineman | (2)FW-190 dest(air) | Hoperhofen A/F |
| | F/O E.D. McMinn | (2)FW-190 dest(air) | Rotenburg |
| | | FW-190 dam(air) | Rotenburg |
| | Capt. J.R. Carter | FW-190 dest(air) | Hoperhofen A/F |
| | | FW-190 prob(air) | Hoperhofen A/F |
| | | FW-190 dam(air) | Hoperhofen A/F |
| | Lt. J.J. Clark | FW-190 dest(air) | Hoperhofen A/F |
| | | FW-190 dam(air) | Hoperhofen A/F |
| | Lt. R.A. Herin | FW-190 dest(air) | Hoperhofen A/F |
| | Lt. P. Neyland | FW-190 dest(air) | Hoperhofen A/F |
| | P/O W.A. Lanowski | FW-190 dest(air) | Hoperhofen A/F |

**May 31, 1944**

| Unit | Pilot | Claim | Location |
|---|---|---|---|
| HdQts: | Col. H. Zemke | (2)FW-190 dest(air) | Gutersloh-Detmold |
| | | FW-190 prob(air) | Gutersloh-Detmold |
| | | FW-190 dam(air) | Gutersloh-Detmold |
| 62nd: | Capt. C.E. Tucker | FW-190 dest(air) | Meldorf |
| | | FW-190 dam(air) | Meldorf |
| | Lt. W.A. McClure | FW-190 dest(air) | Meldorf |
| 63rd: | Lt. D.V. Peters | FW-190 dest(air) | NW Kassel |
| | Lt. R.D. Campbell | FW-190 dam(air) | NW Kassel |

**June 6, 1944**

| Unit | Pilot | Claim | Location |
|---|---|---|---|
| (#5) | | | |
| 62nd: | Lt. W.W. McElhare | FW-190 dest(air) | Rambouillet |
| (#7) | | | |
| HdQts: | Col. H. Zemke | FW-190 dest(air) | NE Bernay |
| 61st: | Capt. B.M. Gladych | Me-109 dest(air) | Croisy |

**June 7, 1944**

| Unit | Pilot | Claim | Location |
|---|---|---|---|
| (#3) | | | |
| 63rd: | Lt. J.R. Curtis | FW-190 dest(air) | Lyons la Foret |
| (#4) | | | |
| 61st: | LtCol. F.S. Gabreski | Me-109 dest(air) | E/Dreux |
| | | FW-190 dest(air) | E/Dreux |
| | Capt. B.M. Gladych | Me-109 dest(air) | SE Houdan |
| | F/O S. Gerick | Me-109 dest(air) | SE Houdan |
| | | Me-109 dam(air) | SE Houdan |
| | Lt. J.I. Popplewell | Me-109 dest(air) | SE Houdan |
| (#5) | | | |
| 62nd: | Lt. G.E. Bostwick | Me-109 dest(air) | Grandviller A/F |
| | Lt. M.L. Moseley | (.5)Ju-88 dest(air) | St. Andre de L'Eure |
| | Lt. J.W. Pierce | (.5)Ju-88 dest(air) | St. Andre de L'Eure |
| (#7) | | | |
| HdQts: | Col. H. Zemke | (2)FW-190 dest(air) | Chartres/Etampes |
| | | FW-190 dam(air) | Chartres/Etampes |
| 61st: | Lt. R.J. Rankin | Me-109 dest(air) | SE Senlis |
| | | Me-109 dam(air) | SE Senlis |
| | F/Lt. Z. Janicki | FW-190 prob(air) | S/Rouen |
| | | FW-190 dam(air) | S/Rouen |
| (#8) | | | |
| 63rd: | Lt. M.H. Becker | (.5)FW-190 dest(air) | Les Andelys-Craches |
| | Lt. S.B. Dale | (.5)FW-190 dest(air) | Les Andelys-Craches |

**June 8, 1944**

| Unit | Pilot | Claim | Location |
|---|---|---|---|
| 62nd: | Lt. B.G. Edens | (2)Me-109 dest(air) | All claims |
| | | FW-190 dest(air) | were made |
| | Lt. M.L. Moseley | (2)FW-190 dest(air) | at St. Andre |
| | Lt. G.H. Butler | Me-109 dest(air) | de L'Eure |
| | Lt. G.H. Van Noy | Me-109 dest(air) | |

**June 12, 1944**

| Unit | Pilot | Claim | Location |
|---|---|---|---|
| 61st: | LtCol. F.S. Gabreski | (2)Me-109 dest(air) | Evreux |
| | F/O S. Gerick | (2)Me-109 dest(air) | Evreux |
| | | (4)Me-109 dam(air) | Evreux |
| | Lt. O.M. Belk | Me-109 dest(air) | Quittebeuf |
| | Lt. C.A. Dudley | Me-109 dam(air) | Evreux |
| | Lt. A.C. Maul | Me-109 dam(air) | Evreux |
| | Lt. W.S. Patterson | Me-109 dam(air) | Evreux |

**June 14, 1944**

| Unit | Pilot | Claim | Location |
|---|---|---|---|
| 63rd: | Lt. W.R. Frederick | (3)Me-109 dam(air) | S/Soissons |

**June 16, 1944**

| Unit | Pilot | Claim | Location |
|---|---|---|---|
| 61st: | Lt. E.A. Sisson | Me-109 dest(air) | Rouen |

**June 24, 1944**

| Unit | Pilot | Claim | Location |
|---|---|---|---|
| HdQts: | Col. H. Zemke | Ju-88 dest(grd) | Sailly-Laurette |

**June 27, 1944**

| Unit | Pilot | Claim | Location |
|---|---|---|---|
| 61st: | LtCol. F.S. Gabreski | Me-109 dest(air) | La Perth A/F |
| | Lt. J.M. Jure | Me-109 dest(air) | Esternay |
| | | Me-109 prob(air) | Esternay |
| | Lt. W.S. Patterson | Me-109 dest(air) | Connentre |
| | F/Lt. W.A. Lanowski | Me-109 dest(air) | La Perth A/F |
| | Lt. S. Gerick | Me-109 dam(air) | Esternay |
| 62nd: | Capt. F.J. Christensen | Me-109 dest(air) | Cambrai-Lens |
| | Lt. R.C. Cherry | Me-109 dest(air) | La Perth |
| | Lt. W.W. McElhare | Me-109 dam(air) | La Perth |

**June 30, 1944**

| Unit | Pilot | Claim | Location |
|---|---|---|---|
| 63rd: | Lt. M.H. Becker | Ju-88 dest(air) | S/Noyon |

**July 4, 1944**

| Unit | Pilot | Claim | Location |
|---|---|---|---|
| HdQts: | Col. H. Zemke | Me-109 dam(air) | N/Conches |
| 61st: | Capt. J.R. Carter | Me-109 dest(air) | W/Louviers |
| 62nd: | Lt. G.E. Bostwick | (3)Me-109 dest(air) | Conches |
| | | Me-109 dam(air) | Conches |
| | Maj. L.A. Dade | (2)Me-109 dest(air) | Conches |
| | | (2)Me-109 dam(air) | Conches |
| | Lt. W.H. Merrill | (2)Me-109 dest(air) | Conches |
| | | Me-109 dam(air) | Conches |
| | Maj. G.E. Baker | Me-109 dest(air) | Conches |
| | | Me-109 dam(air) | Conches |
| | Capt. M.J. Jackson | Me-109 dest(air) | Conches |
| | Capt. M.L. Moseley | Me-109 dest(air) | Conches |
| | Lt. A.P. Knafelz | Me-109 dest(air) | Conches |
| | | Me-109 dam(air) | Conches |
| | Lt. B.M. Knox | Me-109 dest(air) | Conches |
| | | Me-109 dam(air) | Conches |
| | Lt. W.W. McElhare | Me-109 dest(air) | Conches |
| | | (3)Me-109 dam(air) | Conches |
| | Lt. D.C. Sheridan | Me-109 dest(air) | Conches |
| | Lt. F.C. Newell | (.5)Me-109 dest(air) | Conches |
| | Lt. D.E. McMahan | (.5)Me-109 dest(air) | Conches |
| 63rd: | Lt. J.R. Curtis | (1.5)Me-109 dest(air) | Bernay-Evreux & (.5) at Conches |
| | Lt. W.R. Frederick | (.5)Me-109 dest(air) | Conches |
| | | FW-190 dam(air) | N/Chateaudun |
| | F/O R.W. Magel | Me-109 dest(air) | SW Evreux |

**July 5, 1944**

| | | | |
|---|---|---|---|
| 61st: | Lt. R.J. Keen | (3)Me-109 dest(air) | Evreux |
| | | Me-109 dam(air) | Evreux |
| | LtCol. F.S. Gabreski | Me-109 dest(air) | Evreux |
| | Maj. B.M. Gladych | Me-109 dest(air) | Evreux |
| | F/Lt. W.A. Lanowski | Me-109 dest(air) | Evreux |
| 62nd: | Capt. F.J. Christensen | FW-190 dest(air) | N/Evreux |
| | Lt. G.H. Butler | FW-190 dest(air) | N/Evreux |
| | Lt. R.C. Cherry | FW-190 dest(air) | W/Paris |
| | Lt. B.G. Edens | FW-190 dest(air) | N/Evreux |
| | Lt. J.W. Pierce | FW-190 dest(air) | N/Evreux |
| | Capt. M.J. Jackson | FW-190 dam(air) | N/Evreux |
| | Lt. H.E. King | FW-190 dam(air) | N/Evreux |
| 63rd: | Lt. W.L. Flagg | Me-109 dest(air) | Evreux |
| | | Me-109 dam(air) | Evreux |

**July 6, 1944**

| | | | |
|---|---|---|---|
| 62nd: | Capt. M.L. Moseley | Me-109 dest(air) | Beaumont |
| | Lt. G.E. Bostwick | Me-109 dest(air) | Beaumont |
| 63rd: | Lt. B.P. Casteel | FW-190 dest(air) | E/Chartres |
| | Lt. J.R. Curtis | Me-109 dest(air) | N/Evreux |
| | Lt. T. Guerrero | FW-190 dest(air) | E/Chartres |

**July 7, 1944**

| | | | |
|---|---|---|---|
| 61st: | Lt. S. Gerick | u/i a/c dest(grd) | Peine A/F |
| 62nd: | Capt. F.J. Christensen | (6)Ju-52 dest(air) | Gardelegen A/F |
| | Lt. B.G. Edens | (3)Ju-52 dest(air) | Gardelegen A/F |
| | Capt. M.J. Jackson | Ju-52 dest(air) | Gardelegen A/F |

**July 20, 1944**

| | | | |
|---|---|---|---|
| 61st: | Lt. W.H. Barnes | (3)He-111 dest(grd) | Bassenheim A/F |
| | | He-111 dam(grd) | Bassenheim A/F |
| | Lt. S.H. Getz | (2)He-111 dest(grd) | Bassenheim A/F |
| | | (2)He-111 dam(grd) | Bassenheim A/F |
| | LtCol. F.S. Gabreski | He-111 dest(grd) | Bassenheim A/F |
| | Capt. D.F. Smith | He-111 dest(grd) | Bassenheim A/F |
| | | He-111 dam(grd) | Bassenheim A/F |
| | Lt. W.S. Patterson | He-111 dest(grd) | Bassenheim A/F |
| | | He-111 dam(grd) | Bassenheim A/F |
| | Lt. P. Neyland | He-111 dam(grd) | Bassenheim A/F |
| | Lt. C.C. Thomton | He-111 dam(grd) | Bassenheim A/F |
| | Lt. C.E. Westman | He-111 dam(grd) | Bassenheim A/F |

**July 24, 1944**

| | | | |
|---|---|---|---|
| HdQts: | LtCol. D.C. Schilling | (.5)Me-210 dest(grd) | Villaroche |
| | | (.5)Me-210 dam(grd) | Villaroche |
| 61st: | Lt. A.J. Bux | (.5)Me-210 dest(grd) | Villaroche |
| | | (.5)Me-210 dam(grd) | Villaroche |

**August 3, 1944**

| | | | |
|---|---|---|---|
| 63rd: | Lt. R.B. Anderson | FW-190 dest(air) | SW Sarrebourg |

**August 4, 1944**

| | | | |
|---|---|---|---|
| HdQts. | Col. H. Zemke | (1.5)He-111 dest(grd) | Plantlunne |
| | | (2)He-111 dam(grd) | Plantlunne |
| 61st: | Lt. A.C. Maul | Me-109 dest(air) | S/Hamburg |
| | Maj. G.E. Baker | (.5)u/i a/c dest(grd)* | Salenter Lake |
| | Lt. C.E. Westman | (.5)u/i a/c dest(grd)* | Salenter Lake |
| | Lt. J.M. Jure | (.5)u/i a/c dest(grd)** | Salenter Lake |
| | Lt. S.H. Getz | (.5)u/i a/c dest(grd)** | Salenter Lake |
| 62nd: | Lt. B.G. Edens | (2)He-111 dest(grd) | Plantlunne |
| | | (2)He-111 dam(grd) | Plantlunne |
| | Lt. J.W. Ferguson | (.5)He-111 dest(grd) | Plantlunne |
| | Capt. M.J. Quirk | (3)He-111 dam(grd) | Plantlunne |

**August 12, 1944**

| | | | |
|---|---|---|---|
| (#1) | | | |
| 61st: | Maj. B.M. Gladych | Ju-88 dest(air) | Cambrai |
| (#2) | | | |
| 63rd: | Capt. R.T. Fling | Me-109 dest(air) | Mauberge |

**August 15, 1944**

| | | | |
|---|---|---|---|
| 63rd: | Capt. R.D. Campbell | Me-109 dest(grd) | St. Trond |
| | Lt. C.M. Rotzler | Me-109 dam(grd) | St. Trond |

**August 28, 1944**

| | | | |
|---|---|---|---|
| HdQts: | LtCol. D.C. Schilling | He-111 dest(air) | S/Trier |
| 61st: | Capt. P.A. Conger | (.5)He-111 dest(air) | S/Saarbrucken |
| | Lt. J.M. Jure | (.5)He-111 dest(air) | S/Saarbrucken |
| | Maj. G.E. Baker | Ju-88 dest(grd) | Wach |
| 62nd: | Capt. M.J. Jackson | Ju-88 dest(air) | Irsch |
| | Lt. B.M. Knox | He-111 dam(grd) | Jerny |
| 63rd: | Lt. E.M. Albright | He-111 dest(air) | N/Saarbrucken |
| | Lt. W.L. Flagg | Me-109 dest(air) | Charleroi |
| | Lt. W.R. Groce | He-111 dest(air) | N/Kaiserlautern |
| | Lt. T.W. Queen | Ju-88 dam(grd) | Bad Brommach |

**September 5, 1944** (#1)

| | | | |
|---|---|---|---|
| HdQts: | Maj. L.A. Dade | (2)Me-210 dest(grd) | Gelnhausen |
| | | He-111 dest(grd) | Gelnhausen |
| 61st: | Lt. W.D. Clark | Me-110 dest(grd) | Merzhausen |
| | | Me-410 dest(grd) | Merzhausen |
| | | u/i a/c dam(grd) | Merzhausen |
| | Capt. B.E. Cathers | Ju-88 dest(grd) | Merzhausen |
| | | u/i a/c dam(grd) | Merzhausen |
| | Lt. J.M. Jure | He-111 dest(grd) | Merzhausen |
| | | Ju-88 dam(grd) | Merzhausen |
| | | u/i a/c dam(grd) | Merzhausen |
| | Lt. C.C. Thomton | (.5)Me-110 dest(grd) | Merzhausen |
| | | u/i a/c dam(grd) | Merzhausen |
| | Lt. J.J. Clark | (.5)Me-110 dest(grd) | Merzhausen |
| | | FW-190 dam(grd) | Merzhausen |
| | Lt. W.E. Bour | He-111 dam(grd) | Merzhausen |
| 62nd: | Capt. M.J. Jackson | (2)Ju-88 dest(grd) | Limburg |
| | | (1.5)Me-210 dest(grd) | Limburg |
| | | Me-109 dest(grd) | Limburg |
| | | (2)Ju-88 dam(grd) | Limburg |
| | Lt. S.T. Murray | (2)Fi-156 dest(grd) | Limburg |
| | | (2)Ju-88 dest(grd) | Limburg |
| | | (.5)Me-210 dest(grd) | Limburg |
| | | Me-109 dam(grd) | Limburg |
| | Capt. H.E. King | He-111 dest(grd) | Merzhausen |
| | | Me-110 dest(grd) | Merzhausen |
| | | Ju-88 dest(grd) | Merzhausen |
| | Lt. F.B. McIntosh | Me-110 dest(grd) | Limburg |
| | | Me-210 dest(grd) | Limburg |
| | | (2)Me-210 dam(grd) | Limburg |
| | | (2)Ju-88 dam(grd) | Limburg |
| | | Me-110 dam(grd) | Limburg |
| | Capt. W.F. Wilkerson | He-111 dest(grd) | Limburg |
| | Lt. H.O. Womack | Me-210 dest(grd) | Merzhausen |
| | | Me-109 dam(grd) | Limburg |
| | | Ju-88 dam(grd) | Limburg |
| 63rd: | Lt. R.B. Anderson | (2)Me-109 dest(air) | NE Coblenz |
| | Lt. C.M. Hart | Me-109 dest(air) | NE Coblenz |
| | | Me-109 prob(air) | NE Coblenz |
| | | Me-109 dam(air) | NE Coblenz |
| | Lt. R.J. Daniel | Me-109 dest(air) | NE Coblenz |
| | Lt. J.A. Kyle | Me-109 dest(air) | NE Coblenz |
| | Lt. R.T. Warboys | Me-109 dest(air) | NE Coblenz |
| | Lt. T.W. Queen | Me-109 dam(air) | NE Coblenz |

| | | | |
|---|---|---|---|
| (#2) | | | |
| HdQts: | LtCol. D.C. Schilling | (2)FW-190 dest(grd) | Gelnhausen |
| | | (2)u/i a/c dest(grd) | Gelnhausen |
| | | FW-190 dam(grd) | Gelnhausen |
| 61st: | Capt. R.J. Keen | (3)FW-190 dest(grd) | Gelnhausen |
| | | (3)FW-190 dam(grd) | Gelnhausen |
| | Capt. P.A. Conger | (1.5)Me-210 dam(grd) | Gelnhausen |
| | Lt. F.H. Barrett | (1.5)Me-210 dam(grd) | Gelnhausen |
| | Lt. W.M. Hartshorn | FW-190 dam(grd) | Gelnhausen |
| 62nd: | Lt. G.H. Butler | FW-44 dest(air) | NE Gelnhausen |
| | | (2)Me-109 dest(grd) | Gelnhausen |
| | | FW-190 dest(grd) | Gelnhausen |
| | Capt. M.J. Quirk | (4)FW-190 dest(grd) | Gelnhausen |
| | | (4)FW-190 dam(grd) | Gelnhausen |
| | Lt. D.E. McMahan | (4)FW-190 dest(grd) | Gelnhausen |
| | Lt. R.L. Patterson | (2)FW-190 dest(grd) | Gelnhausen |
| | | u/i a/c dam(grd) | Gelnhausen |
| | Lt. E.M. Beason | FW-190 dest(grd) | Gelnhausen |
| | | u/i a/c dam(grd) | Gelnhausen |
| | Lt. T.A. Edwards | FW-190 dest(grd) | Gelnhausen |
| | | FW-190 dam(grd) | Gelnhausen |
| | Lt. F.B. McIntosh | FW-190 dest(grd) | Gelnhausen |
| | | FW-190 dam(grd) | Gelnhausen |
| | Lt. J.W. Pierce | FW-190 dest(grd) | Gelnhausen |
| | | FW-190 dam(grd) | Gelnhausen |
| | Lt. R.E. Winters | FW 190 dest(grd) | Gelnhausen |
| 63rd: | Lt. E.J. Timony | FW-190 dest(air) | S/Coblenz |
| | | (2)Bu-131 dest(grd) | Gelnhausen |
| | | FW-190 dest(grd) | Gelnhausen |
| | Lt. E.M. Albright | FW-190 dest(grd) | Gelnhausen |
| | | Ju-52 dest(grd) | Gelnhausen |
| | Lt. C.M. Rotzler | (2)FW-190 dest(grd) | Gelnhausen |
| | | (2)FW-190 dam(grd) | Gelnhausen |
| | | Me-109 dam(grd) | Gelnhausen |
| | Lt. C.A. Chinn | u/i a/c dest(grd) | Gelnhausen |
| | Lt. R.J. Daniel | FW-190 dest(grd) | Gelnhausen |
| | Lt. E.A. Henderson | FW-190 dest(grd) | Gelnhausen |
| | Lt. T.W. Queen | FW-190 dest(grd) | Gelnhausen |
| | | FW-190 dam(grd) | Gelnhausen |
| | Lt. R.T. Warboys | Me-109 dest(grd) | Gelnhausen |

**September 8, 1944**

| | | | |
|---|---|---|---|
| 61st: | Maj. G.E. Baker | u/i a/c dest(grd) | Euskirchen |
| 62nd: | Lt. G.E. Bostwick | (3)FW-190 dest(grd) | Coblenz |
| | Lt. L.R. Brown | u/i a/c dest(grd) | Coblenz |
| | Lt. J.L. Carwell | Me-109 dest(grd) | Coblenz |
| | Lt. B.G. Edens | u/i a/c dest(grd) | Coblenz |
| 63rd: | Lt. E.J. Timony | Ju-88 dest(grd) | Euskirchen |

| | | | |
|---|---|---|---|
| | Lt. J.E. Lister | (3)Ju-88 dam(grd) | Euskirchen |
| | Lt. E.M. Albright | u/i a/c dam(grd) | Euskirchen |
| | Lt. R. Frederickson | Me-110 dam(grd) | Euskirchen |
| | Lt. W.R. Groce | Me-109 dam(grd) | Euskirchen |

**September 10, 1944**

| | | | |
|---|---|---|---|
| 62nd: | Capt. M.J. Quirk | He-111 dest(grd) | Seligenstadt A/F |
| | Lt. J.W. Pierce | He-111 dest(grd) | Seligenstadt A/F |
| | Lt. G.H. Butler | u/i a/c dam(grd) | Seligenstadt A/F |
| | Lt. G.H. Van Noy | Ju-88 dam(grd) | Seligenstadt A/F |

**September 12, 1944**

| | | | |
|---|---|---|---|
| 61st: | Lt. J.J. Clark | Me-109 dest(air) | N/Brandenburg |
| | Lt. J.M. Jure | Me-109 dest(air) | N/Brandenburg |
| | Lt. S.H. Getz | Me-109 dam(air) | N/Brandenburg |
| 62nd: | Lt. D.E. McMahan | Me-109 dest(air) | Sachau A/F |

**September 16, 1944**

| | | | |
|---|---|---|---|
| 61st: | Capt. R.J. Keen | Ju-88 dest(grd) | Dummer Lake |
| | Capt. D.F. Smith | He-177 dest(grd) | Alhorn A/F |
| 62nd: | Lt. F.A. Nolan | He-111 dam(grd) | Dummer Lake |
| 63rd: | Capt. H.E. Comstock | He-177 dest(grd) | Alhorn A/F |

**September 21, 1944**

| | | | |
|---|---|---|---|
| HdQts: | LtCol. D.C. Schilling | (3)FW-190 dest(air) | Lochem |
| 61st: | Maj. B.M. Gladych | (2)FW-190 dest(air) | E/Arnheim |
| | Lt. R.S. Kyler | FW-190 dest(air) | Deventer |
| | Lt. S.H. Getz | (.5)FW-190 dest(air) | Deventer |
| | Lt. W.J. Osborne | (.5)FW-190 dest(air) | Deventer |
| 62nd: | Capt. M.J. Jackson | FW-190 dest(air) | NE Arnheim |
| | Lt. L.R. Brown | FW-190 dest(air) | Arnheim |
| | Lt. D. Henley | FW-190 dest(air) | Arnheim |
| | Lt. R.L. Patterson | FW-190 dest(air) | Arnheim |
| | Lt. R.E. Winter | FW-190 dest(air) | NE Arnheim |
| 63rd: | Lt. W.H. Pitts | (2)FW-190 dest(air) | NE Arnheim |
| | Lt. W.R. Groce | FW-190 dest(air) | NE Arnheim |
| | Lt. J.A. Kyle | FW-190 dam(air) | NE Arnheim |

**October 5, 1944**

| | | | |
|---|---|---|---|
| HdQts: | LtCol. D.C. Schilling | (3)Me-210 dest(grd) | S/Geseke |
| | | (3)Me-210 dam(grd) | S/Geseke |
| 62nd: | Lt. R.W. Davis | Me-109 dest(grd) | S/Geseke |
| | | Ju-88 dest(grd) | S/Geseke |
| | | Me-109 dam(grd) | S/Geseke |
| | Lt. R.L. Patterson | Me-109 dest(grd) | S/Geseke |
| | | Ju-88 dest(grd) | S/Geseke |
| | Capt. J.B. Eaves | FW-190 dest(grd) | S/Geseke |
| | Lt. E.M. Beason | Me-110 dest(grd) | S/Geseke |
| | Lt. G.R. Choate | Me-110 dest(grd) | S/Geseke |
| | Lt. F.A. Nolan | Ju-88 dest(grd) | S/Geseke |
| | Lt. R.E. Winters | Me-109 dest(grd) | S/Geseke |
| | Capt. W.F. Wilkerson | (2)He-111 dam(grd) | S/Geseke |
| | | Me-109 dam(grd) | S/Geseke |
| 63rd: | Lt. J.E. Lister | Me-109 dam(air) | S/Geseke |
| | Lt. W.E. Kerr | Me-110 dest(grd) | S/Geseke |

**October 12, 1944**

| | | | |
|---|---|---|---|
| 63rd: | Lt. J.E. Lister | FW-190 dest(air) | Dummer Lake |
| | F/O E.W. Andermatt | Me-109 prob(air) | Dummer Lake |

**October 15, 1944**

| | | | |
|---|---|---|---|
| 62nd: | Lt. L.R. Brown | Me-109 dam(grd) | Rheine A/F |
| 63rd: | Lt. J.A. Kyle | (.5)Me-109 dest(grd) | Rheine A/F |
| | Lt. T.W. Saling | (.5)Me-109 dest(grd) | Rheine A/F |

**November 1, 1944**

| | | | |
|---|---|---|---|
| 63rd: | Lt. W.R. Groce | (.5)Me-262 dest(air) | E/Arnheim-Hengelo |
| | | (shared with a 352nd Ftr Grp P-51) | |

**November 6, 1944**

| | | | |
|---|---|---|---|
| 62nd: | Capt. M.J. Jackson | Me-410 dam(air) | Deventer |

**November 18, 1944**

| | | | |
|---|---|---|---|
| 61st: | Capt. J.R. Carter | Me-109 dest(air) | E/Hanau |
| | Capt. W.A. Lanowski | FW-190 dest(air) | E/Hanau |
| | Lt. R.A. Baughman | FW-190 dest(air) | E/Hanau |
| | Lt. A.H. Gerow | FW-190 dest(air) | E/Hanau |
| | | FW-190 prob(air) | E/Hanau |
| | Lt. R.S. Kyler | FW-190 dest(air) | E/Hanau |
| | Lt. C.J. Raymond | FW-190 dest(air) | E/Hanau |
| | Capt. B.E. Cathers | FW-190 prob(air) | E/Hanau |
| | Lt. W.D. Clark | FW-190 prob(air) | E/Hanau |
| | | FW-190 dam(air) | E/Hanau |
| | Lt. L.P. Hines | FW-190 dam(air) | E/Hanau |
| | Lt. R.E. Walker | FW-190 dam(air) | E/Hanau |
| 62nd: | Capt. M.J. Jackson | FW-190 dest(air) | E/Hanau |
| | Capt. W.F. Wilkerson | FW-190 dest(air) | E/Hanau |
| | Lt. J.W. Ferguson | FW-190 dest(air) | E/Hanau |
| | Lt. N.D. Gould | Me-109 dest(air) | E/Hanau |
| 63rd: | Lt. R.R. Davis | FW-190 dest(air) | E/Hanau |
| | Lt. W.C. Scherz | FW-190 dam(air) | E/Hanau |
| | Lt. C.A. Chinn | (3)Me-109 dest(grd) | Gross Ostheim |
| | Maj. H.E. Comstock | He-111 dest(grd) | Gross Ostheim |
| | Lt. R.L. Murphy | FW-190 dest(grd) | Gross Ostheim |
| | Lt. R.J. Daniel | (.5)u/i a/c dam(grd) | Gross Ostheim |
| | Lt. R. Frederickson | (.5)u/i a/c dam(grd) | Gross Ostheim |

**November 27, 1944**

| | | | |
|---|---|---|---|
| 63rd: | Lt. R. Frederickson | (2)Me-109 dest(air) | SE Dummer Lake |
| | Lt. J.E. Lister | Me-109 dest(air) | SE Dummer Lake |

**December 2, 1944**

| | | | |
|---|---|---|---|
| 62nd: | Capt. R.W. Davis | (2)Me-109 dest(air) | E/Coblenz |
| 63rd: | Maj, P.A. Conger | (2)Me-109 dest(air) | S/Marburg |
| | Capt. J.C. Fahringer | (2)Me-109 dest(air) | S/Marburg |
| | Lt. R.B. Anderson | Me-109 dest(air) | S/Marburg |
| | Lt. S.K. Batson | Me-109 dest(air) | S/Marburg |
| | Lt. R. Frederickson | Me-109 dest(air) | S/Marburg |
| | | Me-109 prob(air) | S/Marburg |
| | Lt. W.R. Groce | Me-109 dest(air) | S/Marburg |
| | | Me-109 dam(air) | S/Marburg |
| | Lt. P.B. Trumble | Me-109 dest(air) | S/Marburg |
| | Lt. D.M. Magel | Me-109 dam(air) | S/Marburg |

**December 4, 1944**

| | | | |
|---|---|---|---|
| 61st: | Lt. C.R. Woock | u/i a/c dest(grd) | Neuburg |
| | Lt. C.R. Bond | (2)u/i a/c dam(grd) | Ingolstadt |
| 62nd: | Capt. M.J. Jackson | Me-262 dest(grd) | Neuburg |
| | | Me-262 dam(grd) | Neuburg |
| | | FW-200 dam(grd) | Neuburg |
| | Capt. F.A. Nolan | FW-200 dest(grd) | Neuburg |
| | | Me-262 dam(grd) | Neuburg |
| | Capt. W.F. Wilkerson | He-111 dest(grd) | Neuburg |
| | Lt. E.M. Beason | He-177 dest(grd) | Neuburg |
| | | FW-190 dest(grd) | Neuburg |
| | Lt. N.D. Gould | Me-262 dest(grd) | Neuburg |
| | | Me-262 dam(grd) | Neuburg |
| | Lt. S.N. Ball | (.5)u/i a/c dest(grd) | Neuburg |
| | Lt. D. Henely | (.5)u/i a/c dest(grd) | Neuburg |
| | Lt. A. Chasko | (.5)He-177 dest(grd) | Neuburg |
| | | (4)Me-262 dam(grd) | Neuburg |
| | Lt. W.C. Daley | (.5)He-177 dest(grd) | Neuburg |
| | | Me-262 dam(grd) | Neuburg |
| 63rd: | Lt. C.A. Chinn | (2)Me-262 dest(grd) | Neuburg |
| | | Me-262 dam(grd) | Neuburg |
| | Lt. W.R. Groce | u/i a/c dam(grd) | Neuburg |
| | Lt. R.L. Murphy | FW-200 dam(grd) | Neuburg |

**December 23, 1944**

| | | | |
|---|---|---|---|
| HdQts: | Col. D.C. Schilling | (3)Me-109 dest(air) | Euskirchen-Bonn |
| | | (2)FW-190 dest(air) | Euskirchen-Bonn |
| 61st: | Capt. J.H. Perry | (2)FW-190 dest(air) | Coblenz |
| | Lt. J.F. Frazier | (2)FW-190 dest(air) | Coblenz |
| | Lt. V.E. Bast | FW-190 dest(air) | Coblenz |
| | Lt. C.R. Woock | FW-190 prob(air) | E/Bonn |
| | | (2)FW-190 dam(air) | E/Bonn |
| | Lt. J.T. Allen | FW-190 dam(air) | E/Bonn |
| 62nd: | Capt. F.D. Williamson | Me-109 dest(air) | Euskirchen |
| | | FW-190 dest(air) | Euskirchen |
| | Lt. A.O. Perry | (2)FW-190 dest(air) | Bonn-Coblenz |
| | Lt. S.N. Ball | FW-190 dest(air) | Euskirchen |
| | Lt. E.M. Beason | Me-109 dest(air) | Euskirchen-Bonn |
| | Lt. C.E. Carlson | FW-190 dest(air) | Euskirchen-Bonn |
| | Lt. A. Chasko | Me-109 dest(air) | Euskirchen-Bonn |
| | | FW-190 dam(air) | Euskirchen-Bonn |
| | Lt. W.C. Daley | Me-109 dest(air) | Bonn-Coblenz |
| | Lt. N.D. Gould | FW-190 dest(air) | Euskirchen |
| | Lt. W.S. Lear | FW-190 dest(air) | Euskirchen |
| | Lt. L.F. Geren | (.5)FW-190 dest(air) | Euskirchen-Bonn |
| | Lt. D.A. Westover | (.5)FW-190 dest(air) | Euskirchen-Bonn |
| | Lt. L.R. Brown | (3)FW-190 prob(air) | Coblenz |
| | | FW-190 dam(air) | Coblenz |
| | Lt. R.E. Winter | Me-109 prob(air) | Euskirchen-Bonn |
| | | FW-190 dam(air) | Euskirchen-Bonn |
| | Lt. W.H. Stovall | FW-190 dam(air) | Euskirchen-Bonn |
| 63rd: | Maj. H.E. Comstock | (2)FW-190 dest(air) | SW Bonn |
| | | (2)FW-190 dam(air) | SW Bonn |
| | Capt. C.M. Hart | (2)FW-190 dest(air) | NW Coblenz |
| | | FW-190 dam(air) | NW Coblenz |
| | Lt. R.L. Murphy | (2)FW-190 dest(air) | NW Coblenz |
| | Lt. S.K. Batson | FW-190 dest(air) | NW Coblenz |
| | Lt. C.R. Clark | FW-190 dest(air) | NW Coblenz |
| | Lt. R.J. Daniel | FW-190 dest(air) | NW Coblenz |
| | Lt. W.R. Hoffman | FW-190 dest(air) | NW Coblenz |
| | F/O M.J. Hughes | FW-190 dest(air) | NW Coblenz |
| | | FW-190 dam(air) | NW Coblenz |
| | Lt. W.C. Scherz | FW-190 dest(air) | NW Coblenz |
| | | FW-190 prob(air) | NW Coblenz |
| | | FW-190 dam(air) | NW Coblenz |
| | Lt. P.B. Trumble | FW-190 dam(air) | NW Coblenz |

**December 25, 1944**

| 61st: | Lt. W.D. Clark | FW-190 dest(air) | Cologne |
|---|---|---|---|
| 62nd: | Lt. W.C. Daley | (2)Me-109 dest(air) | Bonn-Coblenz |
| | F/O W.J. Sharbo | (2)Me-109 dest(air) | Bonn-Coblenz |
| | Capt. M.J. Jackson | Me-109 dest(air) | Bonn-Coblenz |
| 63rd: | Capt. C.M. Hart | Me-109 dest(air) | SE Cologne |
| | Lt. S.K. Batson | Me-109 dam(air) | SW Cologne |

**December 26, 1944**

| 62nd: | Lt. A.O. Perry | (2)FW-190 dest(air) | Coblenz |
|---|---|---|---|
| | | FW-190 dam(air) | Coblenz |
| | Maj. L.C. Smith | FW-190 dest(air) | Coblenz |

**December 31, 1944**

| 62nd: | Capt. F.A. Nolan | (2)FW-190 dest(air) | Quackenbruck |
|---|---|---|---|
| | Lt. W.H. Stovall | (2)FW-190 dest(air) | Burgsteinfort |
| | F/O L.F. Butiste | FW-190 dest(air) | Quackenbruck |
| | | FW-190 dam(air) | Quackenbruck |
| | | Me-109 dam(air) | Quackenbruck |

**January 14, 1945**

| 61st: | Lt. R.S. Kyler | Me-109 dest(air) | E/Rheine |
|---|---|---|---|
| | Lt. R.E. Walker | Me-109 dest(air) | Rheine |
| 62nd: | Capt. F.D. Williamson | (4)Me-109 dest(air) | N/Burg |
| | | FW-190 dest(air) | N/Burg |
| | Maj.. M.J. Jackson | Me-109 dest(air) | Rheine |
| | | FW-190 dest(air) | Rheine |
| | Lt. D. Henely | (1.5)Me-109 dest(air) | Magdeburg |
| | Lt. H.O. Womack | (.5)Me-109 dest(air) | Magdeburg |
| | Lt. K.L. Smith | Me-109 dest(air) | Rheine |
| | Lt. W.C. Daley | Me-109 dest(air) | Rheine |
| | Lt. F.R. Aheron | Me-109 prob(air) | Magdeburg |
| 63rd: | Lt. C.T. McBath | (2)Me-109 dest(air) | Munster |
| | Maj. P.A. Conger | Me-109 dest(air) | Stendal |
| | | Me-109 dam(air) | Stendal |
| | Lt. R.R. Davis | Me-109 dest(air) | Munster |
| | Lt. C.M. Rotzler | Me-109 dest(air) | Munster |
| | Lt. P.B. Trumble | Me-109 dest(air) | Stendal |
| | | Me-109 prob(air) | Stendal |

**January 21, 1945**

| 62nd: | LtCol. L.C. Smith | Ju-88 dest(grd) | Thalheim |
|---|---|---|---|
| | | (.5)Ju-52 dest(grd) | Huntingen |
| | Lt. N.D. Gould | (.5)Ju-52 dest(grd) | Huntingen |

**January 29, 1945**

| 63rd: | Capt. G.E. Bostwick | Me-410 dam(grd) | Berge A/F |
|---|---|---|---|

**February 3, 1945**

| 62nd. | Capt. F.D. Williamson | FW-190 dest(air) | Berlin |
|---|---|---|---|
| | | Me-109 dest(air) | Berlin |
| | | FW-190 dam(air) | Berlin |
| 63rd: | Maj. P.A. Conger | Me-109 dest(air) | Friedersdorf A/F |
| | | FW-190 dest(air) | Friedersdorf A/F |
| | | Me-109 dam(air) | Friedersdorf A/F |
| | Capt. C.M. Hart | (2)FW-190 dest(air) | Friedersdorf A/F |
| | Capt. J.C. Fahringer | Me-109 dest(air) | SE Berlin |
| | | (2)Me-109 dam(air) | SE Berlin |
| | | FW-190 dam(air) | SE Berlin |
| | Lt. P.G. Kuhn | FW-190 dest(air) | Friedersdorf A/F |
| | Lt. F.M. Ogden | FW-190 dest(air) | SE Berlin |
| | Lt. R.R. Davis | Me-109 dam(air) | SE Berlin |

**February 27, 1945**

| HdQts: | LtCol. L.C. Smith | (2)u/i a/c dest(grd) | Weimar A/F |
|---|---|---|---|
| | | (3)u/i a/c dam(grd) | Weimar A/F |
| 61st: | Lt. R.A. Baughman | (2)u/i a/c dest(grd) | Weimar A/F |

**March 10, 1945**

| 62nd: | Lt. N.D. Gould | Me-109 dest(air) | Remagen |
|---|---|---|---|
| | Lt. D.A. Carroll | (.5)FW-190 dest(air) | Remagen |
| | Lt. D. Henely | (.5)FW-190 dest(air) | Remagen |

**March 14, 1945**

| 62nd: | Lt. N.D. Gould | Ar-234 dest(air) | Coblenz |
|---|---|---|---|
| | Lt. S. Pruitt | Me-109 dest(air) | Frankfurt |
| | Lt. S.N. Ball | (.5)Ar-234 dest(air) | Coblenz |
| | Lt. W.S. Lear | (.5)Ar-234 dest(air) | Coblenz |

**March 25, 1945**

| 63rd: | Maj. G.E. Bostwick | Me-262 dest(air) | Parchim A/F |
|---|---|---|---|
| | Lt. E.M. Crosthwait | Me-262 dest(air) | Parchim A/F |

**March 31, 1945**

| 61st: | Lt. F.H. Barrett | Me-262 dam(air) | Steinhuder Lake |
|---|---|---|---|

**April 4, 1945**

| 61st: | Capt. W.D. Clark | Me-262 dam(air) | Salzwedel |
|---|---|---|---|
| | F/O J.W. Kassap | Me-262 dam(air) | W/Hamburg |

**April 5, 1945**

| 63rd: | Capt. J.C. Fahringer | Me-262 dest(air) | N/Regensburg |
|---|---|---|---|

**April 7, 1945**

| 62nd: | Capt. R.E. Winter | Me-109 dest(air) | S/Hamburg |
|---|---|---|---|
| 63rd: | Maj. G.E. Bostwick | (2)Me-109 dest(air) | S/Bremen-Hamburg |
| | | Me-262 dam(air) | S/Bremen-Hamburg |
| | Lt. C.T. McBath | Me-109 dest(air) | N/Celle |
| | Lt. F.M. Ogden | Me-109 prob(air) | S/Hamburg |

**April 10, 1945**

| 61st: | Capt. C.R. Bond | Ju-88 dest(grd) | Rechlin |
|---|---|---|---|
| | | Do-24 dest(grd) | Muritz Lake |
| | | Do-217 dam(grd) | Muritz Lake |
| | | Ju-88 dam(grd) | Rechlin |
| | Lt. E.E. Ellis | Do-217 dest(grd) | Oranienburg |
| | | He-177 dest(grd) | Oranienburg |
| | | u/i a/c dest(grd) | Oranienburg |
| | | (4)u/i a/c dam(grd) | Oranienburg |
| | Lt. J.E. Jones | (2)Do-24 dest(grd) | Muritz Lake |
| | | u/i a/c dest(grd) | Muritz Lake |
| | Lt. F.H. Barrett | (2)Ju-88 dest(grd) | Oranienburg |
| | | (3)Ju-88 dam(grd) | Oranienburg |
| | Lt. R.S. Kyler | Me-109 dest(grd) | Muritz Lake |
| | | u/i a/c dest(grd) | Muritz Lake |
| | Capt. C.B. Cole | u/i a/c dest(grd) | Oranienburg |
| | | (5)u/i a/c dam(grd) | Oranienburg |
| | Lt. B.O. Blodgett | Do-24 dest(grd) | Muritz Lake |
| | Lt. P.J. Clinton | Do-24 dest(grd) | Muritz Lake |
| | | u/i a/c dam(grd) | Muritz Lake |
| | Lt. R.W. Higgins | u/i a/c dest(grd) | Muritz Lake |
| | | u/i a/c dam(grd) | Muritz Lake |
| | Lt. E.B. Lightfoot | u/i a/c dest(grd) | Muritz Lake |
| | Lt. C.J. Raymond | Do-217 dest(grd) | Oranienburg |
| | Lt. L.M. Winski | He-115 dest(grd) | Muritz Lake |
| | | (2)u/i a/c dam(grd) | Muritz Lake |
| 62nd: | Lt. W.J. Sharbo | Me-262 dest(air) | Muritz Lake |
| | | (2)He-111 dest(grd) | Neuruppin |
| | | He-177 dam(grd) | Neuruppin |
| | | Ju-88 dam(grd) | Neuruppin |
| | Capt. W.F. Wilkerson | Me-262 dam(air) | Muritz Lake |
| | | (2)He-111 dest(grd) | Rechlin |
| | | He-111 dam(grd) | Rechlin |
| | Lt. F.G. Koch | (2)u/i a/c dest(grd) | Neuruppin |
| | | (4)u/i a/c dam(grd) | Neuruppin |
| | Lt. D.A. Carroll | Me-109 dest(grd) | Rechlin |
| | | Ju-88 dest(grd) | Rechlin |
| | Lt. D.M. Gunner | He-111 dest(grd) | Muritz Lake |
| | Lt. C.A. Tingen | Ju-88 dest(grd) | Rechlin |
| | | He-111 dam(grd) | Rechlin |
| | | Ju-88 dam(grd) | Rechlin |
| | Lt. L.F. Butiste | He-111 dest(grd) | Neuruppin |
| | | u/i a/c dest(grd) | Neuruppin |
| | Lt. R.B. Jones | He-111 dest(grd) | Neuruppin |
| | | He-111 dam(grd) | Neuruppin |
| | Lt. D. Henley | Ju-88 dest(grd) | Neuruppin |
| | | Ju-88 dam(grd) | Neuruppin |
| | Lt. W.J. Stevenson | Ju-88 dest(grd) | Neuruppin |
| | | Ju-88 dam(grd) | Neuruppin |
| | Lt. H.O. Womack | He-111 dest(grd) | Neuruppin |
| | F/O C.R. Albright | (.5)u/i a/c dest(grd) | Muritz Lake |
| | | (shared with a 355th Ftr Grp P-51) | |
| | | Ju-88 dam(grd) | Muritz Lake |
| | Capt. R.E. Winter | u/i a/c dam(grd) | Rechlin |
| 63rd: | Lt. E.W. Andermatt | Me-262 dam(air) | Damm A/F |
| | Maj. G.E. Bostwick | (2)Ju-88 dest(grd) | Werder |
| | | (2)u/i a/c dest(grd) | Werder |
| | Capt. W.L. Flagg | (2)Do-217 dest(grd) | Werder |
| | | Me-109 dest(grd) | Werder |
| | | u/i a/c dest(grd) | Werder |
| | | Me-109 dam(grd) | Werder |
| | Lt. E.S. Barrentine | (2)Ju-88 dest(grd) | Neuruppin |
| | | He-177 dam(grd) | Neuruppin |
| | | Ju-88 dam(grd) | Neuruppin |
| | Lt. J.C. Naylor | Me-109 dest(grd) | Werder |
| | | FW-190 dest(grd) | Werder |
| | | Do-217 dam(grd) | Werder |
| | | u/i a/c dam(grd) | Werder |
| | Lt. W.R. Hoffman | (2)u/i a/c dest(grd) | Werder |
| | Lt. J.A. Arnold | FW-190 dest(grd) | Stendal |
| | Lt. A.T. Shupe | FW-190 dest(grd) | Stendal |
| | | (2)FW-190 dam(grd) | Stendal |
| | Lt. T.W. Smith | Ju-88 dest(grd) | Werder |
| | | Ju-88 dam(grd) | Werder |
| | Lt. V.A. Smith | Ju-88 dest(grd) | Werder |
| | | u/i a/c dam(grd) | Werder |
| | Lt. B.E. Vest | Ju-88 dest(grd) | Stendal |
| | | Me-109 dam(grd) | Stendal |
| | Capt. J.C. Fahringer | (4)FW-190 dam(grd) | Stendal |
| | Lt. C.T. McBath | Ju-88 dam(grd) | Werder |

**April 13, 1945**

| | | | |
|---|---|---|---|
| HdQts: | LtCol. L.A. Dade | (2)Me-110 dest(grd) | All claims |
| | | u/i a/c dest(grd) | on this date |
| | | Me-110 dam(grd) | were made at |
| | LtCol. D.D. Renwick | He-111 dest(grd) | Eggebeck A/F |
| 61st: | Lt. R.S. Kyler | (4)Ju-88 dest(grd) | |
| | | Me-410 dest(grd) | |
| | Lt. B.O. Blodgett | (3)Ju-88 dest(grd) | |
| | | u/i a/c dest(grd) | |
| | | (2)Ju-88 dam(grd) | |
| | Capt. V.E. Bast | (3)Ju-88 dest(grd) | |
| | | (2)u/i a/c dam(grd) | |
| | | (2)Ju-88 dam(grd) | |
| | Lt. E.H. Treff | (3)Ju-88 dest(grd) | |
| | | (5)Ju-88 dam(grd) | |
| | Lt. W.G. Bartle | (2)Ju-88 dest(grd) | |
| | | Me-109 dam(grd) | |
| | Capt. C.B. Cole | Ju-88 dest(grd) | |
| | | u/i a/c dam(grd) | |
| | Lt. F.S. Rader | He-111 dest(grd) | |
| | | (2)He-111 dam(grd) | |
| | Lt. L.M. Winski | Ju-88 dest(grd) | |
| | | (2)Ju-88 dam(grd) | |
| | | Me-110 dam(grd) | |
| | Lt. R.W. Hoeflein | Me-109 dest(grd) | |
| | | (2)Ju-88 dam(grd) | |
| | | u/i a/c dam(grd) | |
| | Lt. C.J. Raymond | u/i a/c dest(grd) | |
| | | (5)u/i a/c dam(grd) | |
| | Lt. W.F. Smith | Me-110 dest(grd) | |
| | | (2)u/i a/c dam(grd) | |
| | Lt. R.W. Higgins | (2)Ju-88 dam(grd) | |
| | Lt. J.T. Allen | u/i a/c dam(grd) | |
| | Lt. D.L. Mauldin | Ju-88 dam(grd) | |
| 62nd: | Capt. P.F. Fleming | (3)Do-217 dest(grd) | |
| | | He-111 dest(grd) | |
| | Lt. L.F. Geren | (4)He-111 dest(grd) | |
| | | (3)He-111 dest(grd) | |
| | Lt. S.N. Ball | (2)Do-217 dest(grd) | |
| | | He-111 dest(grd) | |
| | Lt. D. Henley | (2)He-111 dest(grd) | |
| | | Ju-87 dest(grd) | |
| | | (2)He-111 dam(grd) | |
| | Lt. D.A. Westover | (2)Do-217 dest(grd) | |
| | | FW-190 dest(grd) | |
| | | (2)Me-109 dam(grd) | |
| | Lt. V.L. Elliott | (2)Do-217 dest(grd) | |
| | | Ju-88 dam(grd) | |
| | Lt. R.B. Jones | FW-190 dest(grd) | |
| | | He-111 dest(grd) | |
| | | (2)He-111 dam(grd) | |
| | | FW-190 dam(grd) | |
| | | Ju-88 dam(grd) | |
| | Lt. W.J. Stevenson | (2)Ju-88 dest(grd) | |
| | | (3)Ju-88 dam(grd) | |
| | Lt. H.F. Beeler | FW-190 dest(grd) | |
| | | He-111 dam(grd) | |
| | F/O W.H. Carrington | Ju-87 dest(grd) | |
| | | (2)Do-217 dam(grd) | |
| | Lt. D.M. Gunner | He-111 dest(grd) | |
| | | (2)He-111 dam(grd) | |
| | Lt. I.W. Rich | (2)Me-109 dam(grd) | |
| | Lt. D.A. Carroll | He-111 dam(grd) | |
| | Lt. S. Pruitt | He-111 dam(grd) | |
| 63rd: | Lt. R.L. Murphy | (5)u/i a/c dest(grd) | |
| | | (3)He-111 dest(grd) | |
| | | FW-200 dest(grd) | |
| | | Me-210 dest(grd) | |
| | | u/i a/c dam(grd) | |
| | Lt. P.G. Kuhn | (2)Me-410 dest(grd) | |
| | | FW-190 dest(grd) | |
| | | u/i a/c dest(grd) | |
| | | u/i a/c dam(grd) | |
| | Lt. T.W. Queen | (3)u/i a/c dest(grd) | |
| | | Me-410 dest(grd) | |
| | Lt. V.A. Smith | (2)Ju-88 dest(grd) | |
| | | (2)He-111 dest(grd) | |
| | | (2)Ju-88 dam(grd) | |
| | | (2)u/i a/c dam(grd) | |
| | Capt. W.L. Flagg | FW-190 dest(grd) | |
| | | Ju-88 dest(grd) | |
| | | FW-190 dam(grd) | |
| | Lt. T.B. Hennessy | (2)Me-110 dest(grd) | |
| | | Me-110 dam(grd) | |
| | Lt. R.E. Bailey | (2)Me-110 dest(grd) | |
| | | (2)Me-110 dam(grd) | |
| | Lt. C.R. Clark | Me-110 dest(grd) | |
| | | Ju-88 dest(grd) | |
| | | (2)Me-110 dam(grd) | |
| | Lt. J.W. Keeler | Me-110 dest(grd) | |
| | | u/i a/c dest(grd) | |
| | | Me-410 dam(grd) | |
| | Capt. S.F. Stebelton | u/i a/c dest(grd) | |
| | | (3)u/i a/c dam(grd) | |
| | Lt. J.A. Arnold | u/i a/c dest(grd) | |
| | | He-111 dam(grd) | |
| | | u/i a/c dam(grd) | |
| | Lt. E.S. Barrentine | Me-110 dest(grd) | |
| | | (2)u/i a/c dam(grd) | |
| | Lt. C.T. McBath | Me-109 dest(grd) | |
| | | Me-109 dam(grd) | |
| | | He-111 dam(grd) | |
| | Lt. E.J. Huff | u/i a/c dest(grd) | |
| | | Me-410 dam(grd) | |
| | | He-177 dam(grd) | |
| | Lt. C. Taylor | Me-110 dest(grd) | |
| | | (2)Me-110 dam(grd) | |
| | | Me-109 dam(grd) | |

**April 16, 1945**

| | | | |
|---|---|---|---|
| 61st: | Lt. D.L. Mauldin | (2)Me-109 dam(grd) | Muhldorf |
| | | u/i a/c dam(grd) | Muhldorf |
| | Lt. J.R. Stish | u/i a/c dam(grd) | Muhldorf |
| 62nd: | Lt. C.A. Tingen | He-177 dest(grd) | Muhldorf |
| 63rd: | Lt. B.E. Vest | Ju-88 dest(grd) | Ingolstadt |
| | Capt. J.C. Fahringer | Ju-88 dam(grd) | Ingolstadt |

## 56th Fighter Group Losses

**April 29, 1943**
Capt. John C. McClure (62nd) POW; Hit by fighters near Breskens.
P-47C LM- 41-6394
Lt. Winston S. Garth, Jr. (62nd) POW; Hit by fighters and bailed out off the Dutch coast.
P-47C LM-

**May 31, 1943**
Lt. Patrick M. Williams (63rd) KIA; Crashed near Courtrai after suffering an oxygen failure.
P-47D UN-I 42-7946

**June 5, 1943**
Lt. Richard H. Allison (61st) KIAc; Crashed on a cross-country flight.
P-47C HV- 41-6550

**June 26, 1943**
Capt. Robert H. Wetherbee (HdQts) KIA; Hit by fighters in the Dieppe-Rouen area.
P-47C HV-
Capt. Merle C. Eby (61st) KIA; Hit by fighters in the Dieppe-Rouen area.
P-47C HV-
Lt. Louis T. Barron (61st) KIA; Hit by fighters in the Dieppe-Rouen area.
P-47C HV-
Lt. Ralph A. Johnson (62nd) ASR; Damaged by a Me-109 and bailed out off the English coast.
P-47C LM-
Capt. Roger B. Dyar (63rd) KIA; Hit by fighters in the Dieppe-Rouen area.
P-47C UN-D 41-6534

**July 29, 1943**
Lt. Robert J. Steele (62nd) POW; Hit by a Me-109 in the Nordwijk-Katwijk area.
P-47D LM- 42-7887

**July 30, 1943**
Lt. Jack W. Horton (61st) KIA; Hit by fighters near Hank.
P-47C HV-E 41-6265 "Francy Ann"
Lt. Robert E. Stover (62nd) KIA; Hit by fighters and bailed out 20 miles east of Felixstowe.
P-47C LM- 41-6209

**August 16, 1943**
Lt. George R. Spaleny (62nd) POW; Suffered mechanical failure and bailed out near Gournay.
P-47C LM-

**August 17, 1943**
Lt. Voorhis H. Day (62nd) KIA; Last seen chasing Me-110's near Ans.
P-47D LM-M 42-7891
Lt. Robert M. Stultz (62nd) KIA; Last seen with Lt. Day near Ans.
P-47C LM- 41-6398
Lt. Arthur Sugas (63rd) KIA; Hit by fighters near Ans.
P-47C UN-S 41-6372

**August 19, 1943**
Lt. Glenn E. Hodges (63rd) POW; Suffered mechanical failure and ditched in the North Sea.
P-47C UN-O 41-6216

**August 22, 1943**
Lt. Conway C. Saux (62nd) KIAc; Collided with Lt. Tettemer and crashed near Valley Farm.
P-47C LM-X 41-6224
Lt. Donald Tettemer (62nd) KIAc; Collided with Lt. Saux and crashed near Sotherton Hall Farm.
P-47C LM-P 41-6189

**September 2, 1943**
Lt. Walter T. Hannigan (63rd) KIA; Hit by fighters near Ghent.
P-47D UN-U 42-7934
Lt. Wilfred A. Van Abel (63rd) POW; Hit by fighters near Hazebrouck.
P-47C UN-Q 41-6537

**September 3, 1943**
Lt. Hiram O. Bevins (61st) POW; Hit by a FW-190 and bellied-in near Paris.
P-47C HV-B 41-6232

**September 27, 1943**
Capt. Harry P. Dugas (63rd) KIA; Hit by fighters near Juist Island.
P-47C UN-W 41-6199

**October 8, 1943**
Lt. Dover C. Fleming, Jr. (63rd) KIA; Hit by fighters near Amsterdam.
P-47C UN-P 41-6268

**November 7, 1943**
F/O Robert E. Sheehan (63rd) MIA-E; Suffered mechanical failure near Doesburg.
P-47D UN-C 42-7985

**November 11, 1943**
Lt. Malcolm C. Van Meter (62nd) KIA; Suffered mechanical trouble and crashed into the North Sea.
P-47D LM-Z 42-74626
Lt. Wayne J. O'Connor (63rd) KIA; Hit by a FW-190 near Goesfeld.
P-47D UN-O 42-74722

**November 17, 1943**
Lt. Harry Coronios (62nd) KIAc; Crashed east of Happisburgh.
P-47D LM-D 42-8614

**November 26, 1943**
Lt. Byron L. Morrill (62nd) POW; Ran out of fuel and bailed out near the Zuider Zee.
P-47D LM-C 42-7979

**November 29, 1943**
Lt. Fred C. Windmayer (63rd) KIA; Suffered mechanical failure and crashed into the North Sea.
P-47D UN-F 42-7893

**November 30, 1943**
Lt. William B. Grosvenor (61st) MIA-E; Suffered mechanical failure and bailed out off the Belgian coast.
P-47D HV- 42-75216

**December 1, 1943**
Lt. Cleve M. Brown, Jr. (61st) POW; Hit by fighters near Ghent.
P-47C HV-L 41-6211 "Jackie"
Lt. Harry M. Pruden, Jr. (62nd) KIA; Hit by fighters near Cologne.
P-47D LM- 42-74631
Lt. Vance P. Ludwig (63rd) KIA; Hit by fighters near St. Trond.
P-47D UN-K 42-8607

**December 5, 1943**
Lt. George G. Goldstein (62nd) POW; Suffered mechanical failure near St. Sauflieu.
P-47C LM-L 41-6242

**December 11, 1943**
Lt. Edward J. Kruer (61st) KIA; Collided with Lt. Strand near Spiekeroog.
P-47D HV- 42-8606
Lt. Larry H. Strand (61st) KIA; Collided with Lt. Kruer near Spiekeroog.
P-47D HV-I 42-7967

**December 20, 1943**
Lt. Robert B. Taylor (62nd) KIA; Ran out of fuel and crashed into the North Sea.
P-47D LM-H 42-22527 "Taylor Maid II"

**December 31, 1943**
Lt. William A. Marangello (61st) KIA; Suffered an oxygen failure and crashed into the North Sea.
P-47C HV-S 41-6337

**January 21, 1944**
Lt. Allen E. Dimmick (61st) KIA; Hit by a FW-190 near Rouen.
P-47D HV-S 42-75658

**January 29, 1944**
Lt. Kenneth K. Lewis (63rd) KIA; Hit by a FW-190 near Knocke.
P-47D UN-V 42-22748

**February 3, 1944**
Lt. Lloyd M. Langdon (63rd) KIA; Ran out of fuel and bailed out 40 miles off the English coast.
P-47D UN-T 42-8463

**February 5, 1944**
Lt. John A. Patton (61st) KIA; Hit by a FW-190 near Forges.
P-47D HV- 42-75063
Lt. Roger A. Phillips (61st) KIAc; Collided with Lt. Albert northeast of Wangford.
P-47C HV-M 41-6319
Lt. Richard A. Albert (63rd) KIAc; Collided with Lt. Phillips northeast of Wangford.
P-47D UN-K 42-7943

**February 24, 1944**
Lt. Wilbur N. Kelley (62nd) KIA; Hit by flak near Quackenbruck.
P-47D LM-K 42-75037 "Onny's Angel"

**March 2, 1944**
Lt. Edward N. Rougeau (62nd) POW; Suffered mechanical trouble near Beverloo.
P-47D LM-V 42-8676

**March 4, 1944**
Lt. Irvin E. Valenta (62nd) KIA; Last seen spinning down near The Hague.
P-47D LM-U 42-7942 "Pokey"

**March 6, 1944**
Lt. Andrew B. Stauss (61st) KIA; Hit by fighters near Diepholz.
P-47D HV- 42-75397

**March 8, 1944**
Lt. Anthony R. Carcione (62nd) KIA; Hit by fighters near Minden.
P-47D LM- 42-74697
Lt. Joseph W. Icard (62nd) KIA; Hit by fighters near Diepholz.
P-47D LM-I 42-75040
Lt. Caleb L. Reeder (62nd) POW; Hit by flak near Fockinghausen.
P-47D LM-O 42-74623
Lt. Fred L. Roy (62nd) KIA; Hit by fighters near Diepholz.
P-47D LM- 42-75697
Lt. John C. Marcotte (63rd) POW; Hit by flak and bailed out near Schmalge.
P-47D UN-N 42-7885

**March 15, 1944**
Lt. John Kozcy, Jr. (61st) KIA; Hit by fighters near Quackenbruck.
P-47D HV-N 42-22456

**March 22, 1944**
Lt. Donald M. Funcheon (61st) KIA; Crashed into the Channel in bad weather.
P-47D HV-F 42-75126
Lt. Claude E. Mussey (61st) KIA; Crashed into the Channel in bad weather.
P-47D HV-Y 42-8579
Lt. Dale E. Stream (61st) KIA; Crashed into the Channel in bad weather.
P-47D HV-P 42-8461 "Lucky"
Lt. Melvin C. Wood (61st) POW; Hit by flak near Egmond.
P-47D HV- 42-75446

**March 27, 1944**
Lt. James E. Fields (62nd) POW; Hit by flak near Chartres.
P-47D LM-L 42-75213
Maj. Gerald W. Johnson (63rd) POW; Hit by flak near Cheux.
P-47D UN-V 42-76249
Maj. Walker M. Mahurin (63rd) MIA-E; Downed by a Do-217 south of Chartres.
P-47D UN-M 42-8487
Lt. Evert G. Everett (63rd) KIA; Hit by flak and crashed into the Channel.
P-47D UN- 42-75234

**March 29, 1944**
Capt. Stanley B. Morrill (62nd) KIAc; Died in a B-24 explosion near Halesworth.

**April 1, 1944**
Lt. Thomas P. Owens, Jr. (61st) KIA; Hit by flak near Lille and crashed in the Neuville/St. Vaast area.
P-47D HV- 42-75839

**April 9, 1944**
Lt. Arlington W. Canizares (62nd) KIA; Ran out of fuel and bailed out over the North Sea. Rescued but died.
P-47D LM-D

**April 15, 1944**
Capt. Dick H. Mudge (61st) POW; Hit by flak south of Eggebeck.
P-47D HV-X 42-8691
Maj. LeRoy A. Schreiber (62nd) [illegible] at Flensburg
P-47D LM-T 42-25577
Capt. Charles R. Harrison (62nd) KIA; Hit by a FW-190 west of Hamburg.
P-47D LM-H 42-75388

**April 22, 1944**
Lt. George M. Bracken (61st) KIAc;
P-47D HV- 42-75540
Lt. Archie H. Robey (63rd) KIAc; Crashed 20 miles off Orfordness.
P-47D UN-P 42-8426

**April 30, 1944**
Lt. George H. Lovett (63rd) KIAc; Spun-in near Stansted.
P-47D UN-T 42-75137

**May 8, 1944**
Lt. Gordon H. Lewis (62nd) POW; Hit by flak near Versbeck and bailed out near Oschersleben.
P-47D LM-N 42-76503

**May 12, 1944**
LtCol. Preston Piper (HdQts) POW; Hit by a Me-109 near Coblenz.
P-47D UN-L 42-74750 "Lady Jane"
Lt. Jack E. Greene (62nd) POW; Hit by fighters near Frankfort.
P-47D LM-H 42-75162

Lt. Willard D. Johnson (63rd) POW; Hit by a Me-109 near Coblenz.
P-47D UN-W 42-75109 "Louisiana Pirate"

**May 13, 1944**
Lt. Harold E. Hartney, Jr. (62nd) KIA; Hit by fighters near Brockenlomde.
P-47D LM-Z 42-75444

**May 17, 1944**
Lt. James E. Elliott (62nd) KIAc; Collided with an A-20.
P-47D UN-B (a 63rd a/c used for training)

**May 19, 1944**
Lt. Anthony S. Cavallo (63rd) ASR; Suffered mechanical failure and bailed out over the North Sea.
P-47D UN-G 42-22772 "El Diablo II"

**May 22, 1944**
Lt. Cletus B. Nale (61st) KIA; Hit by a FW-190 near Suederwalsede.
P-47D HV- 42-74752
Lt. Richard M. Heineman (61st) KIA; Hit by a FW-190 near Hoperhofen.
P-47D HV-W 42-76509
Lt. Eugene E. Bennett (62nd) ASR; Bailed out over the Channel.
P-47D LM-

**June 6, 1944**
Lt. Evan D. McMinn (61st) KIA; Hit by flak near Bernay.
P-47D HV- 42-25963

**June 7, 1944**
Lt. Eugene E. Bennett (62nd) MIA-E; Hit by flak near Orbec.
P-47D LM- 42-76254
Lt. Alfred D. Evans, Jr. (62nd) KIA; Hit by flak near Angeuil.
P-47D LM- 42-76118
Lt. Donald J. Funcheon (62nd) KIA; Hit by flak near Angeuil.
P-47D LM- 42-26274
Lt. Wendel A. McClure (62nd) MIA-E; Hit by fighters near Beauvais.
P-47D LM-S 42-26342
Lt. Harry F. Warner (63rd) KIA; Damaged by a bomb blast near Liancourt.
P-47D UN- 43-25286

**June 10, 1944**
Lt. Joseph Vitale (62nd) MIA-E; Hit by flak near Mayenne.
P-47D LM- 43-25523

**June 13, 1944**
Capt. Zbigniew Janicki (61st) KIA; Last heard from near Saumur saying he was landing.
P-47D HV-

**June 21, 1944**
Lt. Harold L. Matthew (63rd) KIA; Crashed while strafing near Paderborn.
P-47D UN- 42-26305

**June 22, 1944**
Capt. Charles E. Tucker (62nd) KIA; Collided with a P-47 while landing.
P-47D LM-J 42-75282 "Eradicator"

**July 4, 1944**
Lt. Sam B. Dale, Jr. (63rd) KIA; Hit by fighters near Evreux.
P-47D UN-C 42-75859

**July 5, 1944**
Lt. Timothy J. Sullivan (61st) KIA; Hit by fighters near St. Martin.
P-47D HV- 42-75578

**July 6, 1944**
Lt. Sam P. Lowman, Jr. (63rd) KIA; Hit by fighters near Bernay.
P-47D UN-P 42-25701

**July 13, 1944**
Lt. James A. Palmer (62nd) KIA; Collided with a P-38 near St. Denis.
P-47D LM-M 42-25713

**July 15, 1944**
Lt. Robert E. Jenkins (63rd) KIA; Hit by flak near Molineuf.
P-47D UN-O 42-76578

**July 19, 1944**
Capt. Joseph L. Egan, Jr. (63rd) KIA; Hit by flak near St. Avolt.
P-47D UN-G 42-26524 "Lil Goody"

**July 20, 1944**
LtCol. Francis S. Gabreski (61st) POW; Hit the ground while strafing Bassenheim Airfield.
P-47D HV-A 42-26418

**August 3, 1944**
Lt. Roach S. Stewart (63rd) KIA; Hit by flak southwest of Sarreburg.
P-47D UN-S 42-25969

**August 7, 1944**
Lt. Arthur C. Maul (61st) KIA; Collided with a P-47 near Marles.
P-47D HV-M 42-25836 "Pengie III"

F/O Robert W. Magel (63rd) POW; Hit by flak near Peronne.
P-47D UN-G 42-75206

**August 12, 1944**
Lt. William H. Barnes (61st) MIA-E; Suffered mechanical failure near Landries.
P-47D HV- 42-75704

**August 15, 1944**
Capt. Robert D. Campbell (63rd) KIA; Hit by flak near St. Trond.
P-47D UN- 42-75870

**August 27, 1944**
Lt. Thomas J. Price (62nd) KIA; Hit the ground while strafing near Heerstert.
P-47D LM-F 42-75093

**September 1, 1944**
Lt. John R. Allen (62nd) KIAc;
P-47D LM-

**September 5, 1944**
Lt. William M. Heaton (61st) KIA; Hit by flak near Altenkirchen and crashed near Limburg.
P-47D HV- 42-26468
Lt. Earl Hertel (61st) POW; Hit by flak near Koln.
P-47D HV-S 42-75237
Lt. Chester E. Frye (63rd) POW; Hit by flak near Eupen.
P-47D UN-T 42-26258 "Moptop's Pride"

**September 9, 1944**
Capt. Roy T. Fling (63rd) KIA; Hit by flak near Etten.
P-47D UN-V 42-28543
Lt. Everett E. Henderson (63rd) KIA; Hit the ground while strafing near Etten.
P-47D UN- 42-8575

**September 10, 1944**
Capt. Michael J. Quirk (62nd) POW; Hit by flak near Seligenstadt.
P-47D LM-K 42-27382
Lt. Billy G. Edens (62nd) POW; Hit by flak near Trier.
P-47D LM-H 42-25522

**September 17, 1944**
Lt. Edward M. Albright, Jr. (63rd) KIA; Hit by flak near Zoelen.
P-47D UN-A 44-19786

**September 18, 1944**
Lt. Trevor A. Edwards (62nd) POW; Hit by flak near Eindhoven.
P-47D LM-G 42-26337
Lt. William W. McElhare (62nd) POW; Hit by flak near Effern.
P-47D LM-X 42-26636
Capt. Gordon S. Stevens (63rd) KIA; Hit by flak near Thuernich.
P-47D UN- 44-19730
Lt. Robert G. Kelly (63rd) POW; Hit by flak near Erkelenz.
P-47D UN-A 42-25531
Lt. Elwood D. Raymond (63rd) KIA; Hit by flak and crashed into the North Sea.
P-47D UN-F 42-26057

**September 21, 1944**
Lt. Oscar L. Cagle, Jr. (63rd) KIA; Hit by fighters near Lochem.
P-47D UN-C 42-26316
Lt. Harold E. Spicer (63rd) KIA; Last seen chasing a FW-190 near Devekamp.
P-47D UN-T 42-25515 "Ann K"

**September 28, 1944**
Lt. Walter H. Pitts (63rd) KIA; Flew into the ground while strafing southwest of Coblenz.
P-47D UN-

**October 10, 1944**
Capt. John B. Eaves (62nd) KIAc; Suffered mechanical failure and hit an embankment while trying to land.
P-47D LM-

**October 11, 1944**
Lt. Julius DeMayo (63rd) KIA; Hit by flak near Euskirchen.
P-47D UN-L 42-27322

**October 24, 1944**
Lt. William J. Osborne (61st) KIA; Hit by flak near Marken Island.
P-47D HV-U 42-26646 "Pockey Doc"
Lt. George R. Choate, Jr. (62nd) KIA; Hit by flak southeast of Elburg.
P-47D LM- 44-19929

**November 5, 1944**
Lt. Robert F. Healey (63rd) KIA; Ran out of fuel and bailed out over the Channel.
P-47D UN-R 42-76530
Lt. Albert L. Henry (63rd) KIA; Hit by flak near Neuhuetten.
P-47D UN-X 42-76471

**November 10, 1944**
Lt. Thomas W. Saling, III (63rd) KIA; Hit by flak near Ulzen.
P-47D UN- 44-19887

**November 18, 1944**
Capt. Gordon J. Blake (61st) POW; Hit by a FW-190 east of Hanau.
P-47D HV-N 42-28623
Lt. Jack D. DeMars (61st) KIA; Hit by a FW-190 east of Hanau.
P-47D HV- 42-26831

**November 20, 1944**
Capt. Robert J. Bradford (63rd) KIA; Hit by flak east of Aachen.
P-47D UN- 42-75670

**November 27, 1944**
Lt. Leo J. Czarnota (63rd) POW; Suffered mechanical failure near Engden.
P-47D UN- 42-25957

**November 30, 1944**
F/O Alben G. Calmes (62nd) KIA; Hit by flak near Westerburg.
P-47D LM-C 42-28806

**December 2, 1944**
Capt. Eugene E. Barnum (61st) KIA; Collided with Lt. Baker near Guell.
P-47D HV- 44-19739
Lt. Donald Allayaud (62nd) KIA; Hit by fighters near Valenciennes.
P-47D LM- 42-28683
Lt. Wyman A. Baker (63rd) KIA; Collided with Capt. Barnum near Guell.
P-47D UN-C 42-28741

**December 14, 1944**
Lt. Lowell C. Buchmiller (62nd) KIAc; Crashed into the North Sea on a practice hop.
P-47D LM-

**December 18, 1944**
Lt. Wilburn A. Haggard (62nd) POW; Hit by flak near Neuschierholz.
P-47D LM-A 42-28688

**December 23, 1944**
Lt. Lewis R. Brown (62nd) POW; Hit by fighters in the Euskirchen-Bonn area.
P-47D LM-B 44-20615
Lt. Charles E. Carlson (62nd) KIA; Hit by fighters in the Euskirchen-Bonn area.
P-47D LM-M 44-19767
F/O John E. Lewis (63rd) KIA; Hit by fighters near Queekenburg.
P-47D UN- 44-19911

**December 30, 1944**
Lt. Samuel K. Batson (63rd) KIAc; Suffered engine failure on take-off.
P-47D UN-

**December 31, 1944**
Lt. Andrew Chasko (62nd) POW; Hit by flak near Mesum.
P-47D LM- 44-19930
Lt. William H. Stovall, Jr. (62nd) KIA; Collided with a P-47 near Burgsteinfurt.

**January 14, 1945**
Lt. Jack D. Hedke (61st) KIA; Damaged by a FW-190 and crashed 25 miles off Clacton.
P-47D HV-
Lt. James S. Wither (62nd) KIA; Hit by a FW-190 near Burg.
P-47D LM- 44-19964

**January 21, 1945**
Lt. Robert S. Hall (63rd) KIA; Rammed by a P-47 on take-off.
P-47D UN-
Lt. Max H. Dahl (62nd) KIAc; Collided with a P-47 near Romford.
P-47D LM-

**February 3, 1945**
Lt. David M. Magel (63rd) KIA; Hit by a FW-190 southeast of Berlin.
P-47D UN- 44-19777

**February 4, 1945**
Lt. Kenneth L. Smith (62nd) KIAc; Crashed near Tollesburg.
P-47M LM-

**February 18, 1945**
Lt. Byron J. Fisher (61st) KIAc; Collided with an RAF P-51.
P-47M HV-

**March 11, 1945**
Lt. Frank R. Aheron (62nd) KIAc; Crashed near Cranfeld.
P-47M LM-

**March 13, 1945**
Lt. Luther P. Hines (61st) KIAc; Collided with Lt. Tuttle.
P-47M HV-
Lt. Richard B. Tuttle (61st) KIAc; Collided with Lt. Hines.
P-47M HV-

**March 14, 1945**
Lt. Earl L. Townsend (62nd) KIA; Suffered mechanical failure and crashed off Ostend.
P-47M LM-

**March 15, 1945**
Lt. Willard C. Scherz (63rd) KIA; Spun-in after taking-off from Boxted.
P-47M UN-

**March 23, 1945**
Lt. Carl J. Bokina (63rd) KIAc; Crashed near Boxted.
P-47M UN-X

**April 1, 1945**
Lt. John F. Frazier (61st) KIAc; Collided with a P-47.
P-47M HV-

**April 6, 1945**
F/O Joseph A. Del Corso (61st) KIAc; Dove into the ground near Boxted.
P-47M HV-

**April 10, 1945**
Lt. Paul W. Stitt (62nd) KIA; Damaged by flak and crashed in Belgium.
P-47M LM-

**April 12, 1945**
Lt. Edward B. Lightfoot (61st) KIAc; Collided with a 356th Fighter Group P-51 near Raydon.
P-47M HV-

**April 13, 1945**
Lt. William R. Hoffman (63rd) KIA; Hit by flak at Eggebeck A/F.
P-47M UN-P 44-21134 "Teacher's Pet"

**April 16, 1945**
Capt. Edward W. Appel (62nd) MIA-F; Hit by flak and bellied-in near Muhldorf.
P-47M LM-

**May 1, 1945**
Lt. Albin P. Zychowski (61st) KIAc; Mushed into the ground near Tiverton.
P-47M HV-

**May 22, 1945**
Lt. Franklin S. Rader (61st) KIAc; Crashed near Greatham Farm while on D.S. to the RAF.
Typhoon

**Headquarters**
Baker, Gordon E., Maj.; September 1944; ex-61st & 62nd Ftr Sqns
Dade, Lucian A., Jr., LtCol.; June 1943-April 1944; to 62nd Ftr Sqn,; August 1944-August 1945; ex-63rd Ftr Sqn
P-47D LM-P 42-75583
P-47D LM-P 42-25959
P-47D LM-P 42-26417
P-47M LM-P 44-21114
Gabreski, Francis S., LtCol.; January 1944-April 1944; to 61st Ftr Sqn, ex-61st Ftr Sqn
166 missions total
P-47D HV-A 42-75510
P-47D HV-A 42-25864
Landry, Robert B., Col.; October 1943-January 1944
P-47D UN-W 42-75109 "Louisiana Pirate"
McCollom, Loren G., Maj.; June 1943-August 1943; to 353rd Ftr Grp, ex-61st Ftr Sqn
P-47C HV-M 41-6319 "Butch"
Piper, Preston, LtCol.; April 1944-May 12, 1944(POW); former bomber pilot
7 missions
Renwick, Donald D., LtCol.; March 1945-October 1945; ex-61st Ftr Sqn
Schilling, David C., Col.; August 1943-January 1945; ex-62nd Ftr Sqn
132 missions, 360 hours
P-47D LM-S 42-7938
P-47D LM-S 42-75388
P-47D LM-S 42-75237 "Whack!"
P-47D LM-S 42-26641
P-47M LM-S 44-21125
Smith, Leslie C., LtCol.; January 1945-March 1945; ex-61st and 62nd Ftr Sqns
138 missions, 435:05 hours total
P-47D LM-L 44-19745
P-47M LM-L
Stewart, James C., LtCol.; July 1943-January 1944; to 61st Ftr Sqn; April 1944-April 1944; to VIII FC
200 hours
P-47D HV-S 42-75658
Thompson, Dick W., Capt.; February 1944-; ex-61st Ftr Sqn
Wetherbee, Robert H., Capt.; May 1943-June 26, 1943(KIA); ex-61st Ftr Sqn
Wright, Vic B., Maj.; States-July 1945
Zemke, Hubert, Col.; September 1942-August 1944; to 479th Ftr Grp
155 missions total
P-47C LM-Z 41-6330 "Mon Tavarish"
P-47D UN-Z 42-75864
P-47D UN-Z 42-76471
P-47D UN-Z 42-26413 "Happy Warrior"

**61st Fighter Squadron**
Adcock, Thomas D., Lt.; April 1945-July 1945
0 missions
Aggers, William R., Lt.; September 1943-August 1944
P-47D HV-A 42-75154 "Sad Sam"

Allen, John T., Lt.; November 1944-EOW
29 missions
P-47M HV-N 44-21195 "Dee"
Allison, Richard H., Lt.; States-June 5, 1943(KIAc)
13 missions
Allsip, John W., Lt.; February 1945-July 1945
4 missions
Altschuler, Richard L., Capt.; October 1943-April 1944; ex-62nd Ftr Sqn
Anderson, Milton A., Lt.; States-November 1943; to 310th Ferry Sqn
P-47C HV- "Idaho Spud"
Anderz, Tadeusz, Capt.; February 1944-@June 1944; ex-RAF
Atchison, Roy C., Lt.; February 1945-February 1945; to 5th ERS
Bachand, Robert E., Lt.; April 1944-September 1944
Baker, Gordon E., Maj.; July 1944-September 1944; to HdQts; ex-62nd Ftr Sqn
Barnes, William H., Lt.; June 1944-August 12, 1944(MIA-E)
Barnum, Eugene E., Capt.; States-December 2, 1944(KIA)
Barrett, Fred H., Lt.; August 1944-EOW
42 missions
Barron, Louis T., Lt.; States-June 26, 1943(KIA)
16 missions
Bartle, William G., Lt.; August 1944-July 1945
48 missions
Bast, Victor E., Capt.; August 1944-EOW
54 missions
Baughman, Robert A., Capt.; June 1944-April 1945
Belk, Oscar M., Jr., Lt.; December 1943-August 1944
Bennett, Joseph H., Capt.; November 1943-March 1944; to 4th Ftr Grp, ex-356th Ftr Grp
P-47D HV-L 42-751?? "Ann II"
Benton, Bruce T., Lt.; October 1944-EOW; ex-62nd Ftr Sqn
Bevins, Hiram O., Lt.; States-September 3, 1943(POW)
31 missions
P-47C HV-B 41-6232
Biales, Albert, Lt.; States-November 1943; to 310th Ferry Sqn
Bigley, William A., Lt.; April 1945-EOW
0 missions
Blake, Gordon J., Capt.; August 1943-November 18, 1944(POW)
Blodgett, Burton O., Lt.; August 1944-EOW
31 missions
Bond, Charles R., Capt.; August 1944-July 1945
52 missions
Bour, William E., Capt.; June 1944-March 1945
Bracken, George M., Jr., Lt.; April 1944-April 22, 1944(KIAc)
Bradley, George P., Lt.; November 1944-EOW
25 missions; ex-bomber pilot
Brooks, Norman E., Capt.; States-April 1944
P-47D HV-R 42-7941 "Slugger"
Brown, Cleve M., Jr., Lt.; States-December 1, 1943(POW)
Bux, Arthur J., Jr., Capt.; June 1944-January 1945
P-47D HV-T 44-19770
Carmichael, Thomas L., Lt.; October 1944-January 1945; ex-62nd Ftr Sqn
Carter, James R., Maj.; July 1942-May 1945
137 missions, 435 hours
P-47C HV-J
P-47D HV-J 42-7960
P-47M HV-C 44-21129
Cathers, Benjamin E., Capt.; June 1944-January 1945
Chamberlain, Earl A., Lt.; March 1945-EOW
0 missions
Clancy, Harry W., F/O; May 1945-July 1945
0 missions
Clark, James J., Lt.; April 1944-September 1944
Clark, William D., Jr., Capt.; August 1944-April 1945
65 missions
Clinton, Philip J., Jr., Lt.; September 1944-EOW
44 missions
Cole, Charles B., Capt.; March 1945-June 1945
8 missions
Conger, Paul A., Maj.; States-October 1944; to 63rd Ftr Sqn
168 missions, 560 hours total
P-47D HV-N 42-7880
P-47D HV-N 42-75435 "Hollywood High Hatter"
Curtis, Joseph R., Lt.; States-October 1943; to 496th Ftr Trg Grp
Del Corso, Joseph A., Lt.; February 1945-April 6, 1945(KIAc)
0 missions
DeMars, Jack D., Lt.; September 1944-November 18, 1944(KIA)
20 missions
Dimmick, Allen E., Lt.; January 1944-January 21, 1944(KIA)
1 mission
Dudley, Charles A., Lt.; April 1944-October 1944
Eby, Merle C., Capt.; States-June 26, 1943(KIA)
24 missions
Edwards, Herbert J., Lt.; October 1944-EOW; ex-62nd Ftr Sqn
Ellis, Edmund E., Lt.; November 1944-EOW
28 missions
Fisher, Byron J., Lt.; November 1944-February 18, 1945(KIAc)
16 missions, 59:30 hours
Foster, Justus D., Capt.; States-March 1944
P-47D HV-O 42-75244
Fox, Giles V., Lt.; April 1945-EOW
0 missions
Frazier, John F., Lt.; October 1944-April 1, 1945(KIAc)
36 missions
Funcheon, Donald M., Lt.; August 1943-March 22, 1944(KIA)
P-47D HV-F 42-75126
Gabreski, Francis S., LtCol.; February 1943-January 1944; to HdQts; April 1944-July 20, 1944(POW)
166 missions total
P-47D HV-A 42-7871
P-47D HV-A 42-75510
P-47D HV-A 42-25864
P-47D HV-A 42-26418
Gerick, Steven, Capt.; December 1943-August 1944
P-47D HV-O 42-26024 "Tally Ho Chaps!"
Gerow, Arthur H., Lt.; October 1944-July 1945
Getz, Stuart H., Capt.; June 1944-December 1944
Gillies, Merton J., Lt.; June 1944-January 1945
Gladych, Bolek M., Maj.; February 1944-May 1945; ex-RAF
P-47D HV-M "Pengie"
P-47D HV-M 42-75224 "Pengie II"
P-47D HV-M 42-25836 "Pengie III"
P-47M HV-M 44-21127
Godbout, Alex, Jr., Lt.; January 1945-EOW
11 missions
Green, Earl W., F/O; April 1944-May 1944; to 353rd Ftr Grp
Grosvenor, William D., Lt.; May 1943-November 30, 1943(MIA-E)
Haeck, Jack J., Capt.; June 1944-December 1944
Hamilton, Samuel D., Jr., Capt.; August 1943-August 1944
P-47D HV-N 42-22456 "Liberty Belle"
Hard, Walter J., F/O; April 1945-July 1945
0 missions
Hartshorn, William M., Lt.; August 1944-September 1944
21 missions
Hayes, Carl E., Lt.; December 1943-
Heaton, William M., Lt.; April 1944-September 5, 1944(KIA)
Hedke, Jack D., Lt.; October 1944-January 14, 1945(KIA)
Heineman, Richard M., Lt.; January 1944-May 22, 1944(KIA)
Herin, Reginald A., Jr., Lt.; February 1944-May 1944; to 356th Ftr Grp
Hertel, Earl, Lt.; April 1944-September 5, 1944(POW)
Hines, Luther P., Jr., Lt.; October 1944-March 13, 1945(KIAc)
31 missions
Higgins, Richard W., Lt.; November 1944-EOW
27 missions
Hillgrove, Arthur A., Lt.; April 1945-EOW
0 missions
Hoeflein, Robert W., Lt.; November 1944-EOW
P-47M HV-W 44-21187 "Lil Snorkey"
Holtmeier, Herbert R., Lt.; February 1944-August 1944
Horton, Jack W., Lt.; May 1943-July 30, 1943(KIA)
13 missions
Howard, Robert L., Lt.; April 1945-July 1945
0 missions
Hudson, William R., Lt.; April 1944-September 1944
Israel, James R., F/O; April 1945-July 1945
0 missions
Janson, William H., Capt.; July 1944-September 1944; to 63rd Ftr Sqn, ex-63rd Ftr Sqn
Janicki, Zbigniew, F/Lt.; February 1944-June 13, 1944(KIA); ex-RAF
Johnson, Gerald W., Maj.; May 1942-November 1943; to 356th Ftr Grp, later 63rd Ftr Sqn
88 missions, 196 hours total
P-47D HV-D 42-7877 "In The Mood"
Johnson, Robert S., Capt.; July 1942-April 1944; to 62nd Ftr Sqn
91 missions total
P-47C HV-P 41-6235 "All Hell"
P-47D HV-P 42-8461 "Lucky"
P-47D HV-P 42-76234
Jones, John E., Capt.; January 1945-July 1945; ex-362nd Ftr Grp, 9th Air Force
9 missions
Jure, James M., Lt.; April 1944-September 1944
Kassap, John W., F/O; November 1944-EOW
24 missions
Keen, Robert J., Capt.; January 1944-August 1944; to 62nd Ftr Sqn
Kelley, Solon C., III, Capt.; February 1945-October 1945; ex-51st Ftr Grp, CBI (1 victory)
9 missions
Kish, Ernest, Capt.; April 1944-December 1944
Klibbe, Frank W., Lt.; September 1943-May 1944
61 missions
P-47D HV-V 42-76179 "Little Chief"
Kozey, John, Jr., Lt.; February 1944-March 15, 1944(POW)
Kruer, Edward J., Lt.; July 1943-December 11, 1943(KIA)
Kuhn, Raymond R., F/O; April 1945-July 1945
0 missions
Kyler, Russell S., Lt.; August 1944-July 1945
58 missions
P-47D HV-J "Lorene"
P-47M HV-J 44-21116 "Lorene"
Lamb, Robert A., Maj.; States-March 1944; to 63rd Ftr Sqn
275 hours total
P-47C HV-L 41-6211 "Jackie"
P-47D HV-L 42-7877
Lamb, Robert E., F/O; April 1945-July 1945
0 missions

Lanowski, Witold A., Capt.; May 1944-EOW; ex-RAF
78 missions, 313:50 hours
P-47D HV-Z 42-26044 "Silver Lady"
P-47M HV-Z 44-21108
Levkulich, George E., Lt.; April 1944-September 1944
Lightfoot, Edward B., Jr., Lt.; October 1944-April 12, 1945(KIAc)
Lundburg, Lawrence, Lt.; December 1943-@February 1944
Marangello, William A., Lt.; July 1943-December 31, 1943(KIA)
Maul, Arthur C., Lt.; April 1944-August 7, 1944(KIA)
Mauldin, David L., Lt.; October 1944-EOW
26 missions
McCollom, Loren G., Maj.; States-June 1943; to HdQts
P-47C HV-M 41-6319 "Butch"
McCauley, Frank E., Lt.; July 1942-November 1943; to 495th Ftr Trg Grp
46 missions, 84:23 hours
P-47C HV-Z 41-6271 "Rat Racer"
McMinn, Evan D., Lt.; December 1943-June 6, 1944(KIA)
P-47D HV-F 42-8458
Miller, Bernard S., Lt.; November 1944-EOW
Mudge, Dick H., Jr., Capt.; States-April 15, 1944(POW)
P-47C HV-X "Poison Dick"
P-47D HV-X 42-8691
Murayda, Michael J., Lt.; November 194-July 1945
Mussey, Claude E., Lt.; December 1943-March 22, 1944(KIA)
P-47D HV-Y 42-8579
Nale, Cletus B., Lt.; April 1944-May 22, 1944(KIA)
Neyland, Praeger, Capt.; December 1943-August 1944
P-47D HV-B 42-75508 "Pistol Packin' Mama"
Osborne, William J., Lt.; August 1944-October 24, 1944(KIA)
Owens, Thomas P., Jr., Lt.; December 1943-April 1, 1944(KIA)
Panagiote, John E., Lt.; January 1945-July 1945
10 missions
Patterson, Warren S., Capt.; May 1944-October 1944
Patton, John A., Lt.; States-February 5, 1944(KIA)
P-47C HV- "Sleepy"
Perry, Joseph H., Maj.; September 1943-May 1945
Phillips, Roger A., Lt.; January 1944-February 5, 1944(KIAc)
Popplewell, Joel I., Lt.; April 1944-September 1944
P-47D HV-C 42-75565 "Slugger"
Powers, Joseph H., Jr., Capt.; July 1942-April 1944; to 62nd Ftr Sqn
P-47C HV-V 41-6267
P-47D HV-P 42-75163 "Power's Girl"
Rader, Franklin S., Lt.; October 1944-May 22, 1945(KIAc)
Rankin, Robert J., Capt.; September 1943-August 1944
P-47D HV-H "Wicked Wacker Weegie"
Raymond, Charles J., Lt.; August 1944-EOW
53 missions
Renwick, Donald D., Capt.; States-December 1943; to 495th Ftr Trg Grp, later with HdQts
P-47C HV-T 41-6352 "Doc"
Roberts, Robill W., Capt.; States-April 1944
Schreiber, Leroy A., Capt.; July 1943-August 1943; to 62nd Ftr Sqn
Sisson, Edward A., Jr., Lt.; February 1944-August 1944
Smith, Donovan F., Maj.; States-January 1945
123 missions, 385 hours
P-47C HV-M 41-6319 "Hun Hunter"
P-47D HV-S 42-75393 "Ole Cock"
P-47D HV-S "Ole Cock II"
P-47D HV-S 42-28382 "Ole Cock III"
Smith, Howard W., Lt.; January 1945-EOW
9 missions
Smith, Judson S., Lt.; May 1945-July 1945
0 missions
Smith, Leslie C., LtCol.; July 1942-September 1944; to 62nd Ftr Sqn and later HdQts
138 misions, 435:05 hours total
P-47C HV-S 41-6337
P-47D HV-U 42-26254
Smith, William F., Lt.; March 1945-July 1945
5 missions
Stauss, Andrew B., Lt.; December 1943-March 6, 1944(KIA)
Stewart, James C., LtCol.; January 1944-April 1944; to HdQts; ex-HdQts
200 hours
P-47D HV-Q 42-74650
P-47D HV-S 42-75658
Stish, Jerome R., Lt.; October 1944-EOW
Stollfus, Gordon A., Lt.; January 1945-February 1945; to 5th ERS, ex-362nd Ftr Grp, 9th Air Force
Strand, Lawrence R., Lt.; States-December 11, 1943(KIA)
Stream, Dale E., Lt.; February 1944-March 22, 1944(KIA)
Sullivan, Timothy J., Lt.; June 1944-July 5, 1944(MIA)
Theyken, Richard, Lt.; November 1944-EOW
Thompson, Dick W., Capt.; October 1943-February 1944; to HdQts
Thomton, Cleon C., Lt.; April 1944-September 1944
Tracy, Kirby N., Lt.; States-July 1943; to 6th Ftr Wg
17 missions (later KIAc)
Treff, Ernest H., Lt.; January 1945-EOW
8 missions
Tuttle, Richard B., Lt.; January 1945-March 13, 1945(KIAc)
0 missions
Ulfers, Leo W., Lt.; October 1944-EOW
Walker, Robert E., Lt.; September 1944-July 1945
42 missions
Weeks, J.W. Marshall, Lt.; January 1945-February 1945; to 5th ERS
Westman, Carl E., Lt.; April 1944-September 17, 1944(MIA)
Wetherbee, Robert H., Capt.; States-May 1943; to HdQts
Wilson, George W., Lt.; November 1944-EOW
Winski, Longfin M., Lt.; November 1944-July 1945
20 missions
Woock, Charles R., Capt.; October 1944-EOW
53 missions
Wood, Melvin C., Lt.; August 1943-March 22, 1944(POW)
185 hours
Zychowski, Albin P., Lt.; November 1944-May 1, 1945(KIAc)
32 missions

**62nd Fighter Squadron**
Abell, Sidney B., Lt.; February 1945-March 1945; to 5th ERS
Aberth, Ralph M., Lt.; April 1945-July 1945
Abram, Andrew W., Lt.; February 1945-July 1945
Aheron, Frank R., Lt.; October 1944-March 11, 1945(KIAc)
Albright, Clinton R., Lt.; January 1945-EOW
Allayaud, Donald, Lt.; October 1944-December 2, 1944(KIA)
Allen, John R., Lt.; August 1944-September 1, 1944(KIAc)
Altschuler, Richard L., Capt.; States-October 1943; to 61st Ftr Sqn
Appel, Edward W., Capt.; January 1945-April 16, 1945(MIA-E); ex-bomber pilot
16 missions
Armstrong, Donald C., Jr., Lt.; October 1944-March 1945; to 5th ERS
Atkinson, Herbert B., Lt.; May 1945-EOW
0 missions
Baker, Gordon E., Maj.; June 1944-July 1944; to 61st Ftr Sqn
Ball, Sanborn N., Lt.; November 1944-July 1945
P-47M LM-R 44-21200
Barnwell, Archibald S., Jr., F/O; May 1945-EOW
0 missions
Bass, Hampton B., Jr., F/O; February 1945-March 1945; to 5th ERS
Beason, Eugene M., Lt.; July 1944-January 1945
P-47D LM-P 42-26417
Beeler, Hugh F., Lt.; October 1944-July 1945
Benjamin, Swift T., Lt.; April 1944-May 1944; to 353rd Ftr Grp
Benton, Bruce T., Lt.; September 1944-October 1944; to 61st Ftr Sqn
Bennett, Eugene E., Lt.; April 1944-June 7, 1944(MIA-E)
Blaisdell, Harold E., Jr., Lt.; April 1944-September 1944
Bliss, Whitney C., Jr., Lt.; March 1945-EOW
Bluhm, Roy B., Lt.; January 1944-May 1944; to 356th Ftr Grp
Bostwick, George E., Capt.; April 1944-September 1944; later to 63rd Ftr Sqn
92 missions, 390:55 hours total
P-47D LM-G 42-26042 "Ugly Duckling"
Boyle, Mark K., Capt.; September 1943-May 1944
P-47D LM-Z 42-75444 "The Magnet"
Brainard, Wayne A., Capt.; States-July 1944
Brennan, James A., F/O; April 1945-EOW
Brown, Lewis R., Lt.; July 1944-December 23, 1944(POW)
Bryant, John P., Lt.; States-March 1944
78 missions
P-47C LM-A 41-6234
P-47D LM-A 42-75178
Buchmiller, Lowell C., Lt.; September 1944-December 14, 1944(KIAc)
Buckwalter, John L., Jr., Lt.; March 1945-EOW
Buszko, Thaddeus S., Capt.; December 1943-August 1944
78 missions
P-47D LM-E 42-75125 "Hawkeye"
P-47D LM-E "Flak Shack"
Butiste, Leo F., Lt.; September 1944-July 1945
P-47M LM-X 44-21199
Butler, George H., Lt.; April 1944-December 1944
76 missions, 286 hours
P-47D LM-B 44-20615 "West O'The Rockies"
Calmes, Alben G., F/O; September 1944-November 30, 1944(KIA)
Canizares, Arlington W., Lt.; January 1944-April 9, 1944(KIA)
P-47D LM-D
Carcione, Anthony R., Lt.; States-March 8, 1944(KIA)
P-47D LM-Q 42-7937 "Terrible Tony"
Carlson, Charles E., Lt.; November 1944-December 23, 1944(KIA)
Carmichael, Thomas L., Lt.; September 1944-October 1944; to 61st Ftr Sqn
Carrington, William H., F/O; January 1945-July 1945
Carroll, Dennis A., Lt.; January 1945-EOW
Carwell, Jackie L., Lt.; April 1944-September 1944
Chapman, Warren M., Lt.August 1943-
Chasko, Andrew, Lt.; September 1944-December 31, 1944(POW)
Chattaway, William P., Lt.; March 1944-August 1944; ex-78th Ftr Grp
Chenednik, Peter D., Lt.; September 1944-February 1945; to 65th Ftr Wg
Cherry, Robert C., Lt.; December 1943-August 1944
83 missions, 303 hours
P-47D LM-J 42-75282 "Eradicator"
P-47D LM-I 42-75074 "Eradicator"
Christensen, Fred J., Jr., Capt.; August 1943-September 1944
107 missions
P-47D LM-C 42-75207 "Rozzie Geth"
P-47D LM-C 42-26628 "Rozzie Geth II
Choate, George R., Jr., Lt.; August 1944-October 24, 1944(KIA)
Cline, Raymond S., Lt.; December 1944-July 1945
Coleman, Harry A., Lt.; August 1943-September 1943; to VIII Service Command

Cook, Walter V., Capt.; June 1942-February 1944
66 missions
P-47C LM-W 41-6343 "Cookie"
Coronios, Harry, Lt.; States-November 17, 1943(KIAc)
Craig, Horace C., Maj.; States-February 1944
200 hours
P-47D LM-R 42-7870 "Pappy"
Dade, Lucian A., Jr., LtCol.; April 1944-August 1944; to HdQts; ex-63rd Ftr Sqn & HdQts
P-47D LM-P 42-25959
P-47D LM-P 42-26417
Dahl, Max H., Lt.; December 1944-January 21, 1945(KIAc)
Daley, William C., Capt.; October 1944-July 1945
Daupin, Ray, Capt.; States-@August 1944
P-47C LM-D 41-6342 "Saucy Shirley"
P-47D LM-D 42-8614 "Saucy Shirley II"
P-47D LM-D 42-75160 "Saucy Shirley III"
Davenport, William J., Lt.; April 1944-September 1944
Davis, Lewis S., III, F/O; February 1945-March 1945; to 5th ERS
Davis, Reigel W., Capt.; June 1944-December 1944
Day, Voorhis H., Lt.; States-August 17, 1943(KIA)
30 missions
P-47C LM-M 41-6237
P-47D LM-M 42-7891
DeSantos, John H., Lt.; October 1944-EOW
Dewey, Ernest E., Lt.; December 1044-July 1945
Ducey, David F., Lt.; November 1944-EOW
Eaves, John B., Capt.; States-October 10, 1944(KIAc)
Edens, Billy G., Lt.; April 1944-September 10, 1944(POW)
83 missions, 300 hours
P-47D LM-F 42-75093
P-47D LM-F 42-76363
Edwards, Herbert J., F/O; September 1944-October 1944; to 61st Ftr Sqn
Edwards, Trevor A., Lt.; August 1944-September 18, 1944(POW)
Elliott, Virgil L., Lt.; November 1944-EOW
Evans, Alfred D., Jr., Lt.; April 1944-June 7, 1944(KIA)
Ferguson, John W., Jr., Capt.; June 1944-February 1945; April 1945-May 1945; to HdQts
Fields, James E., Lt.; December 1943-March 27, 1944(POW)
P-47D LM-L 42-75213
Fleming, Philip E., Capt.; August 1944-April 1945
Furlong, Donald J., Lt.; May 1944-June 7, 1944(KIA); ex-bomber pilot (93rd Bomb Group)
Gallagher, Harold E., Lt.; September 1943-May 1944
Garth, Winston S., Lt.; States-April 29, 1943(POW)
4 missions
Gerber, John A., Lt.; November 1944-March 1945; to 2nd SF
Geren, Lloyd F., Lt.; October 1944-July 1945
Ginn, Charles L., Lt.; States-April 1944
Godfrey, Hillyard C., Lt.; August 1943-
P-47D LM- "Devil Baby"
Goetz, Joseph, F/O; December 1943-February 1944; to 4th Ftr Grp
Goldstein, George G., Lt.; States-December 5, 1943(POW)
P-47C LM-L 41-6242
Gordon, William P., Lt.; January 1944-July 1944
P-47D LM-G 42-75599 "Maximum Goose"
Gorman, William, Lt.; December 1943-
Gould, Norman D., Lt.; October 1944-EOW
P-47M LM-O 44-21210
Greene, Jack E., Lt.; December 1943-May 12, 1944(POW)
P-47D LM-H 42-75162
Gunner, Donald M., Lt.; October 1944-EOW
Haggard, William A., Lt.; October 1944-December 18, 1944(POW)
Hail, Albert W., Jr., F/O; April 1945-July 1945
Hale, Richard B., Lt.; October 1944-EOW
Hall, Robert W., Lt.; October 1944-EOW
Harrison, Charles R., Jr., Capt.; States-April 15, 1944(KIA)
P-47D LM-H 42-75388
Hartney, Harold E., Jr., Lt.; April 1944-May 13, 1944(KIA)
Henley, Donald, Jr., Lt.; August 1944-April 1945
69 missions, 301:30 hours
P-47D LM-H 42-75631
P-47M LM-H 44-21233
Hitchcock, Robert L., Lt.; March 1945-July 1945
Hodges, James P., Lt.; July 1944-December 1944
Icard, Joseph W., Lt.; August 1943-March 8, 1944(KIA)
P-47D LM-I 42-75040
P-47D LM-I 42-75241
Jackson, Michael J., Maj.; June 1944-March 1945
86 missions
P-47D LM-J 44-19790 "Teddy"
P-47D LM-J 44-21117 "Teddy"
Johnson, Ralph A., Maj.; States-April 1944
P-47C LM-J 41-6239 "Kentucky Pud"
P-47D LM-J 42-22481
Johnson, Robert S., Maj.; April 1944-May 1944; ex-61st Ftr Sqn
91 missions total
P-47D LM-Q 42-25512 "Penrod & Sam"
Johnson, Walter L., Lt.; March 1945-EOW
Jones, James M., Capt.; States-May 1944
P-47D LM-Y 42-7947 "Ah'm Available
P-47D LM-Y 42-75143
Jones, Robert B., Jr., Lt.; January 1945-EOW
Keen, Robert J., Capt.; August 1944-September 1944; ex-61st Ftr Sqn
Kelley, Wilbur N., Lt.; September 1943-February 24, 1944(KIA)
P-47D LM-K 42-75037 "Onny's Angel"
King, Herman E., Capt.; April 1944-September 1944; ex-359th Ftr Grp
P-47D LM-X 42-25517
Klein, John J., Lt.; December 1943-
Knafelz, Albert P., Lt.; December 1943-August 1944
P-47D LM-A 42-26298 "I Wanted Wings"
Knox, Baird M., Lt.; April 1944-October 1944
Koch, Frank G., Lt.; January 1945-EOW
Kopas, Andrew G., Lt.; December 1944-July 1945
Lear, Warren S., Lt.; November 1944-EOW
Lewis, Gordon H., Lt.; April 1944-May 8, 1944(POW)
McClure, James E., Capt.; December 1943-August 1944
McClure, John C., Capt.; December 1941-April 29, 1943(POW)
3 missions
McClure, Wendell A., Lt.; December 1943-June 7, 1944(MIA-E)
P-47D LM-S 42-26342
McElhare, William W., Lt.; May 1944-September 18, 1944(POW); ex-bomber pilot
P-47D LM-K 42-25905
McIntosh, Fred B., Capt.; June 1944-December 1944
McMahan, Darrell E., Lt.; June 1944-November 1944
P-47D LM-A 42-26298
Merrill, Wiley H., Jr., Capt.; February 1944-September 1944
P-47D LM-K 42-25295
Millar, Monroe S., Lt.; March 1945-July 1945
Morrill, Byron L., Lt.; States-November 26, 1943(POW)
P-47D LM-C 42-7979
Morrill, Stanley B., Capt.; August 1943-March 29, 1944(KIAc)
P-47C LM-F 41-6387 "Fats"
Moseley, Mark L., Capt.; August 1943-August 1944
P-47D LM-H 42-25522
Murray, Steven T., Lt.; April 1944-September 1944
Newell, Frank C., Lt.; February 1944-September 1944
Nolan, Francis A., Capt.; June 1944-January 1945
Nordquist, Dean A., Lt.; December 1943-May 1944; to 5th ERS
O'Neill, Eugene W., Capt.; December 1941-February 1944
200 hours
P-47C LM-O 41-6347 "Lil Abner"
Palmer, James A., Lt.; June 1944-July 13, 1944(KIA)
Parsons, Townsend A., Capt.; June 1944-October 1944
Patterson, Roy L., Lt.; July 1944-December 1944
P-47D LM-Y 44-19883
Perkins, William R., Capt.; June 1944-October 1944
Perry, Alfred O., Lt.; September 1944-EOW
P-47D LM-Q 44-20721
Peterson, Wayne B., Lt.; States-August 1943
6 missions
Pierce, Jack W., Lt.; April 1944-September 1944
Polansky, Fred A., Lt.; August 1944-July 1945
Powers, Joseph H., Capt.; April 1944-May 1944; ex-61st Ftr Sqn
P-47D LM-P 42-76363
Price, Thomas J., Lt.; August 1944-August 27, 1944(KIA)
Pruden, Harry M., Jr., Lt.; September 1943-December 1, 1943(KIA)
Pruitt, Sherman, Jr., Lt.; December 1944-EOW
Quirk, Michael J., Capt.; States-September 10, 1944(POW)
P-47C LM-K 41-6215
P-47D LM-K 42-75242
P-47D LM-K 42-27382
Reeder, Caleb L., Jr., Lt.; May 1943-March 8, 1944(POW)
Rich, Irving W., Lt.; January 1945-EOW
Rougeau, Edward N., Lt.; January 1944-March 2, 1944(POW)
Roy, Fred L., Lt.; January 1944-March 8, 1944(KIA)
Saux, Conway C., Lt.; States-August 22, 1943(KIAc)
29 missions
Schilling, David C., Maj.; June 1941-August 1943; to HdQts
P-47D LM-S 42-7938
Schreiber, Leroy A., Maj.; August 1943-April 15, 1944(KIA); ex-61st Ftr Sqn
P-47D LM-T 42-74660
P-47D LM-T 42-22537
Sharbo, Walter J., Lt.; November 1944-EOW
P-47D LM-C "Marion"
P-47M LM-C 44-21237 "North Dakota Kid"
Shaw, John S., Lt.; March 1945-July 1945
Sheridan, Dayton C., Lt.; January 1944-August 1944
P-47D LM-M "Nigger Haid"
Smith, Kenneth L., Lt.; September 1944-February 4, 1945(KIAc)
Smith, Leslie C., LtCol.; September 1944-January 1945; to HdQt; ex-61st Ftr Sqn
138 missions, 435:05 hours total
P-47D LM-L 44-19925
P-47D LM-L 44-19745
Spaleny, George R., Lt.; States-August 16, 1943(POW)
24 missions
Steele, Robert J., Lt.; States-July 29, 1943(POW)
23 missions
Stevenson, William J., Lt.; January 1945-EOW
Stitt, Paul W., Lt.; January 1945-April 10, 1945(KIA)
Stultz, Robert M., Lt.; States-August 17, 1943(KIA)
25 missions
Stovall, William H., Jr., Lt.; October 1944-December 31, 1944(KIA)

Stover, Robert E., Lt.; States-July 30, 1943(KIA)
19 missions
Taylor, Robert B., Lt.; States-December 20, 1943(KIA)
P-47C LM-H "Taylor Maid"
P-47D LM-H 42-22527 "Taylor Maid II"
Tettemer, Donald B., Lt.; May 1943-August 22, 1943(KIAc)
15 missions
Tevels, Albert R., Lt.; January 1945-EOW
Tingen, Clarence A., Lt.; January 1945-EOW
Townsend, Earl L., Lt.; January 1945-March 14, 1945(KIA)
Tucker, Charles E., Capt.; May 1944-June 22, 1944(KIA)
Ulch, Shirley D., F/O; April 1945-July 1945
Valenta, Irvin E., Lt.; August 1943-March 4, 1944(KIA)
P-47D LM-U 42-7942 "Pokey"
Van Meter, Malcolm, Lt.; September 1943-November 11, 1943(KIA)
Van Noy, George H., Capt.; April 1944-October 1944
Vitale, Joseph, Lt.; April 1944-June 10, 1944(MIA-E)
Walker, Robert D., Lt.; April 1945-EOW
Walker, Joseph P., Lt.; May 1943-June 1944
P-47D LM- "Miss Box"
Walker, Julian L., Lt.; January 1945-July 1945
Weigle, Donald B., Lt.; January 1944-March 1944 (INJ.)
Westover, Donald A., Lt.; October 1944-EOW
Wilkerson, William F., Capt.; August 1944-EOW
65 missions, 300 hours
P-47D LM-Y
P-47M LM-Y 44-21214
Williamson, Felix D., Maj.; May 1943-EOW
P-47D LM-M 42-22541 "Willie"
P-47D LM-M 42-25713
P-47D LM-M 44-20555
P-47M LM-M 44-21219
Winters, Robert E., Capt.; August 1944-EOW
P-47D LM-K 44-19879
P-47M LM-K
Wither, James S., Lt.; November 1944-January 14, 1945(KIA)
Womack, Herschel O., Lt.; August 1944-April 1945
Woodward, John A., Lt.; May 1945-July 1945
0 missions
Yancho, John W., F/O; April 1945-July 1945

**63rd Fighter Squadron**
Abbotts, John, Lt.; March 1945-EOW
0 missions
Adrianse, Lyle A., Capt.; States-February 1944
P-47C UN-A 41-6362 "The Michigan Mauler"
P-47D UN-A 42-8488 "Lofty"
Albers, Paul R., Lt.; April 1945-July 1945
0 missions
Albert, Francis L., F/O; April 1945-July 1945
0 missions
Albert, Richard A., Lt.; January 1944-February 5, 1944(KIAc)
Albright, Edward M., Jr., Lt.; June 1944-September 17, 1944(KIA)
P-47D UN- "George"
Alvis, Richard J., Lt.; February 1945-March 1945; to 5th ERS
Andermatt, Eugene W., Lt.; September 1944-July 1945
59 missions, 281:35 hours
P-47D UN-A 42-28824
P-47M UN-A 44-21203 "Miss June"
Anderson, Richard B., Capt.; July 1944-February 1945
Aranyos, John A., Lt.; January 1944-August 1944
81 missions, 302 hours
P-47D UN-R 42-76468 "Ol Steel Butt"
Armstrong, Ben F., F/O; February 1945-July 1945
3 missions, 18 hours
Armstrong, Tobin, Lt.; February 1945-July 1945
5 missions, 29:30 hours
Arnold, John A., Lt.; October 1944-July 1945
38 missions, 180:05 hours
Bailey, Robert E., Lt.; October 1944-EOW
28 missions, 139:25 hours
P-47M UN-X 44-21131
Baker, Wyman A., Lt.; October 1944-December 2, 1944(KIA)
1 mission
Ball, Cecil G., Lt.; April 1945-July 1945
0 missions
Bannerman, Edward S., Jr., Lt.; March 1945-EOW
0 missions
Barrentine, Emmett S., Lt.; January 1945-July 1945
10 missions, 51:15 hours
Batdorf, Gordon E., Lt.; States-January 1944; to 9th AF
P-47C UN-B 41-6261
Batson, Samuel K., Lt.; October 1944-December 30, 1944(KIAc)
21 missions, 92:20 hours
Baylard, Robert L., Lt.; February 1945-July 1945
Becker, Marvin H., Lt.; February 1944-August 1944
80 missions, 300:55 hours
P-47D UN-B 42-26299
Bedford, Morgan R., Lt.; April 1945-July 1945
0 missions
Bode, Charles A., Lt.; April 1945-EOW
0 missions
Bokina, Carl J., Lt.; December 1944-March 23, 1945(KIAc)
Bolender, Alfred M., Lt.; December 1944-EOW
21 missions, 103:15 hours
Bostwick, George E., Maj.; January 1945-EOW; ex-62nd Ftr Sqn
92 missions, 390:55 hours total
P-47M UN-Z 44-21112
Bradford, Robert J., Capt.; September 1944-November 20, 1944(KIA)
Bradshaw, John T., F/O; November 1944-July 1945
13 missions, 64 hours
P-47M UN-A 44-21135
Brown, Jack D., Lt.; States-March 1944
P-47C UN-J 41-6203 "Windy"/"The Flying Ute"
P-47D UN-J 42-8525
Burke, Sylvester V., Maj.; January 1941-February 1944
P-47D UN-R 42-7853
P-47D UN-R 42-75394
Cagle, Oscar L., Jr., Lt.; August 1944-September 21, 1944(KIA)
Calderone, Robert M., Lt.; April 1944-September 1944
Campbell, Robert D., Capt.; January 1944-August 15, 1944(KIA)
82 missions, 313:55 hours
Campbell, Russell W., Lt.; November 1944-EOW
35 missions, 173:10 hours
Casteel, Barney P., Lt.; January 1944-August 1944
79 missions, 301 hours
P-47D UN-A 43-25531
Cavallo, Anthony S., Lt.; September 1943-May 1944
P-47D UN-G 42-22772 "El Diablo II"
P-47D UN-G 42-25861
Charlton, Wade B., Lt.; October 1944-EOW
45 missions, 213:05 hours
P-47M UN-C 44-21121
Chinn, Claude A., Lt.; June 1944-December 1944
66 missions, 272:15 hours
P-47D UN-R 42-76468 "Ol Steel Butt"
P-47D UN-C 42-28741
Christensen, William J., Lt.; April 1944-May 1944; to 353rd Ftr Grp
Clamp, Charles C., Lt.; States-May 1944
200 hours
P-47C UN-L 41-6329
P-47D UN-D 42-74635
Clark, Charles R., Lt.; November 1944-EOW
38 missions, 184 hours
P-47M UN-S 44-21163
Coenen, John E., Lt.; States-November 1943; to hospital
P-47C UN-F 41-6227
P-47D UN-U 42-8410
Compton, George A., Lt.; July 1942-September 1943; to VIII FC
37 missions
P-47C UN-X 41-6367
Comstock, Harold E., Maj.; July 1942-January 1945
138 missions, 385 hours
P-47C UN-Y 41-6326
P-47D UN-Y 42-75870
P-47D UN-Z 42-26413
P-47D UN-Y 44-19757
Conger, Paul A., Maj.; October 1944-March 1945; ex-61st Sqn
168 missions, 560 hours total
P-47M UN-P 44-21134 "Bernyce"
Crosthwaite, Edwin M., Jr., Lt.; December 1944-EOW
14 missions, 70 hours
P-47M UN-E 44-21137
Crouch, Worth B., Jr., F/O; February 1945-EOW
2 missions, 11:35 hours
Curtis, Joseph R., Capt.; May 1944-September 1944; ex-61st Sqn
P-47D UN-C 42-26316
Czarnota, Leo J., Lt.; October 1944-November 27, 1944(POW)
Dade, Lucian A., Maj.; States-July 1943; to HdQts
P-47C UN-P 41-6268
Dale, Samuel B., Jr., Lt.; January 1944-July 4, 1944(KIA)
50 missions, 200:05 hours
Daniel, Robert J., Lt.; July 1944-February 1945
Davis, James T., Lt.; November 1944-EOW
26 missions, 134:45 hours
Davis, Ramon R., Lt.; July 1944-March 1945
P-47D UN-V 42-28796
P-47D UN-V 44-19804
Dawson, Paul C., Lt.; October 1944-EOW
49 missions, 232:40 hours
P-47M UN-Z 44-21175
Decker, Melvin E., Lt.; March 1945-EOW
3 missions, 17:35 hours
DeMayo, Julius, Lt.; August 1944-October 11, 1944(KIA)
Douglas, Norwood C., Lt.; April 1944-May 1944; to 356th Ftr Grp
Dugas, Harry P., Capt.; States-September 27, 1943(KIA)
P-47C UN-W 41-6199
Dyar, Roger B., Capt.; States-June 26, 1943(KIA)
P-47C UN-D 41-6395
P-47C UN-D 41-6539

Egan, Joseph L., Jr., Capt.; States-July 19, 1944(KIA)
P-47C UN-E 41-6230 "Holy Joe"
P-47C UN-E 41-6584 "Holy Joe"
P-47D UN-E 42-75855
Epstein, Solomon S., F/O; March 1945-July 1945
0 missions
Everett, Evert G., Lt.; December 1943-March 27, 1944(KIA)
P-47D UN-Q 42-75234
Fahringer, John C., Capt.; October 1944-EOW
46 missions, 213;50 hours
P-47D UN-F 44-20594
P-47M UN-F 44-21160 "Devastatin' Deb"
Ferber, Alex B., Lt.; April 1944-August 1944
75 missions, 300:15 hours
Flagg, Walter L., Capt.; April 1944-June 1945
95 missions, 387 hours
P-47D UN-H 42-25317
P-47M UN-F 44-21140 "Shoot! You're Faded"
Fleming, Dover C., Jr., Lt.; August 1943-October 8, 1943(KIAc)
9 missions
Fling, Roy T., Capt.; June 1944-September 9, 1944(KIA)
Frederick, Walter R., Lt.; October 1943-July 1944; Later flew in the PTO with the 507th Ftr Grp and was KIA
85 missions, 300 hours
P-47D UN-I 42-8693
P-47D UN-I 42-26059 "Quaker Schielmeil"
Frederickson, Russell, Lt.; July 1944-January 1945
P-47D UN-R 42-28438
Frye, Chester B., Lt.; June 1944-September 5, 1944(POW)
Glasscock, Truman G., F/O; April 1945-EOW
0 missions
Goodfleisch, Donald M., Capt.; States-July 1944
107 missions, 300:25 hours
P-47D UN-G 42-7878 "Lil Goody"
P-47D UN-G 42-8554
P-47D UN-G 42-75206
P-47D UN-G 42-26524 "Lil Goody"
Green, Jay P., Lt.; December 1944-March 1945; to 5th ERS
Groce, Walter R., Lt.; July 1944-April 1945
P-47D UN-D 42-26243
P-47M UN-G 44-21226
Guerrero, Thomas, Jr., Lt.; June 1944-September 18, 1944(INJ)
Hall, George F., Capt.; States-October 1944
299 hours
P-47D UN-H 42-7896
P-47D UN-F 42-75266
Hall, Robert S., Lt.; November 1944-January 21, 1945(KIA)
Hannigan, WAlter T., Lt.; States-September 2, 1943(KIA)
P-47D UN-U 42-7934
Hart, Cameron M., Capt.; June 1944-April 1945
60 missions
P-47D UN-B 42-26299
P-47D UN-B 44-19937
P-47M UN-B
Healey, Robert F., Lt.; October 1944-November 5, 1944(KIA)
Henderson, Everett A., Lt.; August 1944-September 9, 1944(KIA)
Hennessey, Thomas B., Lt.; December 1944-EOW
21 missions, 103:40 hours
P-47M UN-H 44-21181
Henry, Albert L., Lt.; October 1944-November 5, 1944(KIA)
Henry, Donald E., Lt.; May 1945-EOW
0 missions
Hodges, Glenn L., Lt.; May 1943-August 19, 1943(POW)
10 missions
Hoffman, William R., Lt.; October 1944-April 13, 1945(KIA)
P-47M UN-P 44-21134 "Teacher's Pet"
Hopson, Alfred H., Capt.; August 1944-September 1944; to 4th Ftr Grp; ex-RAF & 4th Ftr Grp
Huff, Edgar J., Lt.; January 1945-July 1945
9 missions, 48:45 hours
P-47M UN-B "Ole Miss Lib"
Hughes, Melvin J., F/O; November 1944-EOW
17 missions, 85:50 hours
P-47M UN- "The Mighty Myth"
Hutchens, John C., Lt.; March 1945-EOW
0 missions
Ingold, Conrad C., Lt.; January 1944-February 1944; to 4th Ftr Grp
Janson, William H., Capt.; April 1943-April 1944; to 61st Sqn; September 1944-December 1944
390:05 hours
P-47C UN-P 41-6268
P-47D UN-U 42-8410
Jenkins, Robert E., Lt.; June 1944-July 15, 1944(KIA)
Jocelyn, Rodney F., Lt.; May 1945-July 1945
0 missions
Johnson, Gerald W., Maj.; February 1944-March 27, 1944(POW); ex-61st Ftr Sqn & 356th Ftr Grp
P-47D UN-V 42-76249
Johnson, Willard D., Lt.; February 1944-May 12, 1944(POW)
P-47D UN- 42-8525
Kariva, George C., Lt.; April 1944-May 1944; to 356th Ftr Grp
Kelley, Robert G., Lt.; August 1944-September 18, 1944(POW)
Keeler, John W., Lt.; January 1945-July 1945
12 missions, 63:35 hours
P-47M UN-K 44-21132 "Mrs. K"
Kerr, Warren E., Jr., Capt.; February 1944-December 1944
68 missions, 270 hours
Kling, David P., Lt.; April 1944-December 1944
70 missions, 272:20 hours
Knief, Wallace N., Lt.; October 1944-July 1945
22 missions, 98:35 hours
Koon, Nelson F., F/O; April 1945-July 1945
0 missions
Kuhn, Philip G., Jr., Lt.; November 1944-EOW
36 missions
P-47M UN-K 44-21225 "Fireball"
Kyle, James A., Capt.; June 1944-December 1944
69 missions, 272:15 hours
Laflam, Arnold A., Lt.; February 1944-August 1944
78 missions, 300:55 hours
Lamb, Robert A., Maj.; March 1944-May 1944; ex-61st Ftr Sqn
275 total hours
Langdon, Lloyd M., Lt.; December 1943-February 3, 1944(KIA)
P-47D UN-T 42-8463
Lewis, John E., Lt.; November 1944-December 23, 1944(KIA)
5 missions
Lewis, Kenneth K., Lt.; December 1943-January 29, 1944(KIA)
P-47D UN-V 42-22748
Lister, James E., Lt.; April 1944-December 1944
46 missions, 274:05 hours
Lovett, George H., Jr., Lt.; January 1944-April 30, 1944(KIAc)
Lowman, Samuel J., Jr., Lt.; February 1944-July 6, 1944(KIA)
63 missions, 243:10 hours
Ludwig, Vance P., Lt.; States-December 1, 1943(KIA)
P-47D UN-K 42-8465
P-47D UN-K 42-8607
McBath, Charles T., Lt.; November 1944-July 1945
36 missions, 169:40 hours
P-47M UN-M 44-21150 "Dottie Dee II"
McDonnell, John T., Lt.; February 1944-August 1944; to 65th FW
Magel, David M., Lt.; August 1944-February 3, 1945(KIA)
Magel, Robert W., F/O; April 1944-August 7, 1944(POW)
Mahurin, Walker M., Maj.; May 1942-March 27, 1944(MIA-E)
85 missions, 192 hours
P-47C UN-M 41-6334
P-47D UN-M 42-8487
Maloney, Kenneth A., F/O; December 1943-January 1944; to 9th AF
Marcotte, John C., Lt.; February 1944-March 8, 1944(POW)
Marshall, Donald W., Lt.; February 1944-November 1944
83 missions, 324:40 hours
Martin, Arthur J., Lt.; August 1944-May 1945
300 hours
P-47M UN-M 44-21185
Matthews, Harold L., Lt.; December 1943-June 21, 1944(KIA)
P-47D UN-P 42-8554
Murphy, Randel L., Lt.; September 1944-April 1945
62 missions, 225:45 hours
P-47D UN-N 42-29364
P-47M UN-N 44-21141 "The Brat"
Naylor, James C., Lt.; January 1945-July 1945
12 missions, 64 hours
P-47M UN-D 44-21157
O'Connell, Joseph J., Lt.; September 1944-October 1944; became a ground officer
O'Connor, Wayne J., Lt.; States-November 11, 1943(KIA)
P-47C UN-O 41-6216
P-47D UN-O 42-22534
P-47D UN-O 42-74722
Oczkowski, Henry, Lt.; April 1944-August 1944; to 65th FW
Ogden, Frank M., III, Lt.; August 1944-EOW
51 missions, 239:05 hours
P-47M UN-O 44-21217
Peppers, Frank H., Lt.; States-January 1944; to 9th AF
P-47D UN-F 42-7893
Peters, Donald V., Lt.; August 1943-July 1944
85 missions, 300 hours
P-47D UN-O 42-74676
P-47D UN-O 42-76578
Petty, Raymond D., Lt.; States-January 1944; to 9th AF
P-47D UN-I 42-7975
P-47D UN-I 42-8693 "Liquidator"
Pitts, Walter H., Lt.; August 1944-September 28, 1944(KIA)
Porowski, Isadore T., Lt.; September 1943-July 1944; to 3rd GTTF
86 missions, 300 hours
P-47D UN-P 42-8609
P-47D UN-P 42-75180
Poulos, Edward J., Lt.; November 1944-June 1945
Queen, Thomas W., Jr., Lt.; July 1944-EOW
60 missions, 264;30 hours
P-47D UN-H 42-25317
P-47M UN-H 44-21181
Raymond, Elwood D., Lt.; August 1944-September 18, 1944(KIA)

Reed, Charles W., Lt.; September 1943-May 1944
P-47C UN-X 41-6367
P-47D UN-X 42-75185 "Princess Pat"
Later flew in the PTO with the 507th Ftr Grp
Robey, Archie H., Lt.; September 1943-April 22, 1944(KIAc)
P-47D UN-A 42-75071
Rohan, Clifford P., F/O April 1945-EOW
0 missions
Ross, John E., Lt.; October 1943-July 1944
86 missions, 300 hours
P-47D UN-K 42-75217
Rotzler, Charles M., Lt.; July 1944-April 1945
Saling, Thomas W., III, Lt.; September 1944-November 10, 1944(KIA)
Scherz, Willard C., Lt.; September 1944-March 15, 1945(KIA)
P-47M UN- 44-21222
Schiltz, Glen D., Capt.; July 1942-February 1944
200 hours
P-47C UN-Z 41-6259
P-47D UN-Z 42-8269
P-47D UN-Z 42-75232
Schreiber, Charles H., F/O; October 1943-January 1944; to 27th ASG
Sheehan, Robert E., F/O; September 1943-November 7, 1943(MIA-E)
9 missions
Shupe, Arthur T., Lt.; January 1945-EOW
13 missions, 69:05 hours
P-47M UN-S 44-21118
Smith, Bernard R., Lt.; September 1943-May 1944
P-47C UN-S 41-6330 "Sunshine"
P-47D UN-S 42-75412
Smith, Thomas W., Jr., Lt.; January 1945-EOW
12 missions, 65:50 hours
Smith, Vernon A., Lt.; January 1945-EOW
12 missions, 61:40 hours
P-47M UN-V 44-21198
Spicer, Harold E., Lt.; August 1944-September 21, 1944(KIA)
Stamps, Samuel O., Lt.; December 1943-June 1944
P-47D UN-S 42-22762 "Tinkle"
P-47D UN-S 42-75863
Stebelton, Samuel F., Capt.; November 1944-July 1945
26 missions, 124:05 hours
P-47M UN-S 44-21126
Stevens, Gordon S., Capt.; May 1944-September 18, 1944(KIA); former bomber pilot
Stewart, Roach S., Lt.; April 1944-August 3, 1944(KIA)
61 missions, 238:45 hours
Sugas, Arthur, Lt.; States-August 17, 1943(KIA)
P-47C UN-S 41-6372
Tate, William K., Lt.; May 1945-July 1945
0 missions
Taylor, Carter, Lt.; January 1945-July 1945
12 missions, 60:50 hours
Timony, Eugene J., Lt.; April 1944-September 1944
70 missions, 270 hours
P-47D UN-T 42-26258 "Moptop's Pride
Truluck, John H., Capt.; May 1943-April 1944
71 missions, 201:30 hours
P-47D UN-L 42-74750 "Lady Jane"
Trumble, Pershing B., Lt.; August 1944-April 1945
P-47D UN-T 42-26676
P-47M UN-T
Tukey, Philip E., Jr., Maj.; States-September 1943; to VIII FC
P-47C UN-T 41-6375
P-47D UN-T 42-8463
Van Abel, Wilfred A., Lt.; States-September 2, 1943(POW)
P-47C UN-Q 41-6537
Vest, Boss E., Lt.; January 1945-July 1945
14 missions, 76:35 hours
P-47M UN-J 44-21154
Vogt, John W., Jr., Capt.; States-February 1944
P-47C UN-V 41-6325 "Lucky Little Devil"
P-47D UN-V 42-22748
Wakefield, J. Carroll, Capt.; December 1943-July 1944
86 missions, 303 hours
P-47D UN-H 42-74643
Wallace, Maynard B., Lt.; March 1945-July 1945
0 missions
Warboys, Richard T., Lt.; April 1944-September 1944
Warner, Harry F., Jr., Lt.; December 1943-June 7, 1944(KIA)
P-47D UN-Q 42-8673
Westfall, Russell B., Capt.; August 1943-August 1944
89 missions, 302:75 hours
P-47D UN-B 42-75278 "Anamosa"
P-47D UN-B 42-26466 "Anamosa II"
Whitley, Edgar D., Lt.; States-September 1943; to VIII FC
P-47D UN-N 42-7895
Windmayer, Fred C., Lt.; September 1943-November 29, 1943(KIA)
17 missions
P-47D UN-T 42-8463
Williams, Patrick M., Lt.; States-May 31, 1943(KIA)
P-47C UN-W 41-6199
Wilson, John D., Lt.; April 1943-December 1943
28 missions
P-47D UN-I 42-7946
P-47D UN-Q 42-8673
Wisniewski, Adam J., Lt.; August 1943-May 1944
202 hours
P-47D UN-N 42-7885
P-47D UN-N 42-75575

**Aircraft of the 61st Fighter Squadron**

P-47C-2-RE
41-6211 HV-L "Jackie" R.A. Lamb
41-6221 HV-W
41-6232 HV-B H.O. Bevins
41-6235 HV-P "All Hell" R.S. Johnson
41-6251 HV-O "Joker"
41-6254 HV-Y
41-6265 HV-E "Francy Ann"
41-6267 HV-V J.H. Powers
41-6271 HV-Z "Rat Racer" F.E. McCauley

P-47C-5-RE
41-6319 HV-M "Butch" L.G. McCollom
41-6319 HV-M "Hun Hunter" D.F. Smith
41-6322 HV-W "Little Butch"
41-6337 HV-S L.C. Smith
41-6352 HV-T "Doc" D.D. Renwick
41-6357 HV-
41-6385 HV-Y
41-6401 HV-G
41-6550 HV-
41-6620 HV-
41-6635 HV-

P-47D-1-RE
42-7871 HV-A F.S. Gabreski
42-7877 HV-D "In the Mood" G.W. Johnson
42-7877 HV-L R.A. Lamb
42-7880 HV-N P.A. Conger
42-7938 HV-
42-7941 HV-R "Slugger" N.E. Brooks

P-47D-2-RA
42-22456 HV-N "Liberty Belle" S.D. Hamilton
42-22478 HV-

P-47D-2-RE
42-7960 HV-J J.R. Carter
42-7967 HV-I
42-8369 HV-E "Francy Ann II"

P-47D-4-RA
42-22744 HV-I "El Shaf-Toe"
42-22790 HV-L

P-47D-5-RE
42-8458 HV-F E.D. McMinn
42-8461 HV-P "Lucky" R.S. Johnson
42-8579 HV-Y C.E. Mussey
42-8606 HV-
42-8691 HV-X D.H. Mudge

P-47D-6-RE
42-74620 HV-B
42-74622 HV-J
42-74650 HV-Q J.C. Stewart
42-74724 HV-Y
42-74728 HV-C
42-74752 HV-

P-47D-10-RE
42-75053 HV-L
42-75063 HV-
42-75070 HV-D
42-75121 HV-Z
42-75126 HV-F D.M. Funcheon
42-75140 HV-U
42-75154 HV-A "Sad Sam" W.R. Aggers
42-75163 HV-P "Power's Girl" J.H. Powers

P-47D-11-RE
42-75216 HV-
42-75218 HV-K
42-75224 HV-M "Pengie" B.M. Gladych
42-75231 HV-R
42-75234 HV-R
42-75244 HV-O J.D. Foster
42-75269 HV-O

42-75282 HV-J
42-75345 HV-T
42-75393 HV-S "Ole Cock II" D.F. Smith
42-75397 HV-
42-75432 HV-T
42-75435 HV-N "Hollywood High Hatter" P.A. Conger
42-75446 HV-
42-75508 HV-B "Pistol Packin' Mama" P. Neyland
42-75508 HV-B "The Cotton Chopper"
42-75509 HV-W
42-75510 HV-A F.S. Gabreski
42-75540 HV-
42-75565 HV-C "Slugger" J.I. Popplewell
42-75604 HV-T

P-47D-15-RE
42-76179 HV-V "Little Chief" F.W. Klibbe
42-76234 HV-P R.S. Johnson
42-76254 HV-Y
42-76330 HV-L

P-47D-16-RE
42-75658 HV-S J.C. Stewart
42-75694 HV-K
42-75704 HV-
42-75839 HV-

P-47D-20-RE
42-76432 HV-T
42-76458 HV-Q "Pat"
42-76509 HV-W
42-76534 HV-

P-47D-21-RA
43-25555 HV-U

P-47D-22-RE
42-25836 HV-M "Pengie III" B.M. Gladych
42-25864 HV-A F.S. Gabreski
42-25963 HV-
42-26024 HV-O "Tally Ho Chaps!" S. Gerick
42-26044 HV-Z "Silver Lady"
42-26254 HV-U L.C. Smith
42-26274 HV-
42-26291 HV-I

P-47D-25-RE
42-26404 HV-H
42-26418 HV-A F.S. Gabreski
42-26240 HV-B
42-26468 HV-
42-26538 HV-E
42-26626 HV-X
42-26634 HV-H
42-26646 HV-U "Pockey Doc"

P-47D-26-RA
42-28383 HV-S "Ole Cock III" D.F. Smith

P-47D-27-RE
42-26831 HV-

P-47D-28-RA
42-28520 HV-P
42-28623 HV-N
42-28668 HV-K
42-28834 HV-H

P-47D-28-RE
44-19714 HV-
44-19718 HV-M
44-19739 HV-
44-19770 HV-T A.J. Bux
44-19777 HV-
44-19955 HV-C

P-47M-1-RE
44-21108 HV-Z W.A. Lanowski
44-21115 HV-Q
44-21116 HV-J "Lorene" R.S. Kyler
44-21127 HV-M B.M. Gladych
44-21129 HV-C J.R. Carter
44-21182 HV-S
44-21187 HV-W "Lil Snorkey" R.W. Hoeflein
44-21195 HV-N "Dee" J.T. Allen
44-21212 HV-U

Unknown Serials
P-47C HV-X "Poison Dick" D.H. Mudge
P-47C HV- "Sleepy" J.A. Patton
P-47C HV- "Idaho Spud" M.A. Anderson
P-47D HV-H "Wicked Wacker Weegie" R.J. Rankin
P-47D HV-J "Lorene" R.S. Kyler
P-47D HV- "Bonnie"
42-751?? HV-L "Ann II" J.H. Bennett
P-47D HV-C "Dream Baby"
P-47C HV- "War Passion"
P-47D HV- "Screamin' Mimi"
P-47M HV-O "Joy Boy"
P-47D ??582 HV-S
P-47D ??742 HV-I
P-47D ??795 HV-Y

**Aircraft of the 62nd Fighter Squadron**

P-47C-2-RE
41-6189 LM-P
41-6193 LM-B "Ginger"
41-6209 LM-
41-6215 LM-K M.J. Quirk
41-6224 LM-X "Two Roll Charlie"
41-6231 LM-E
41-6234 LM-A J.P. Bryant
41-6237 LM-M V.H. Day
41-6239 LM-J "Kentucky Pud" R.A. Johnson
41-6242 LM-L G.G. Goldstein
41-6253 LM-P
41-6253 LM-X
41-6295 LM-K

P-47C-5-RE
41-6330 LM-Z "Mon Tobniii" H. Zemke
41-6342 LM-D "Saucy Shirley" R. Dauphin
41-6343 LM-W "Little Cookie" W.V. Cook
41-6347 LM-O "Lil Abner" E.W. O'Neill
41-6387 LM-F "Fats" S.B. Morrill
41-6394 LM-M
41-6398 LM-

P-47D-1-RE
42-7866 LM-G "The Greek"
42-7870 LM-R "Pappy" H.C. Craig
42-7887 LM-J
42-7891 LM-M V.H. Day
42-7937 LM-Q "Terrible Tony" A.R. Carcione
42-7938 LM-S D.C. Schilling
42-7942 LM-U "Pokey" I.E. Valenta
42-7947 LM-Y "Ah'm Available" J.M. Jones
42-7975 LM-I

P-47D-2-RA
42-22481 LM-J R.A. Johnson
42-22527 LM-H "Taylor Maid II" R.B. Taylor
42-22537 LM-T L.A. Schreiber
42-22541 LM-M "Willie" F.D. Williamson

P-47D-2-RE
42-7979 LM-C B.L. Morrill
42-7983 LM-S
42-7992 LM-K

P-47D-4-RA
42-22754 LM-C
42-22763 LM-W "Virginia"
42-22764 LM-B

P-47D-5-RE
42-8614 LM-D "Saucy Shirley II" R. Dauphin
42-8676 LM-V

P-47D-6-RE
42-74623 LM-O
42-74626 LM-Z
42-74660 LM-T L.A. Schreiber
42-74664 LM-N
42-74697 LM-

P-47D-10-RE
42-75037 LM-K "Onny's Angel" W.N. Kelley
42-75040 LM-I J.W. Icard
42-75074 LM-I "Eradicator" R.C. Cherry
42-75093 LM-F B.G. Edens
42-75125 LM-E "Hawkeye" T.S. Buszko
42-75143 LM-Y J.M. Jones
42-75160 LM-D "Saucy Shirley III" R. Dauphin
42-75162 LM-H
42-75178 LM-A J.P. Bryant
42-75207 LM-C "Rozzie Geth" F.J. Christensen
42-75213 LM-L J.E. Fields

P-47D-11-RE
42-75237 LM-S "Whack!" D.C. Schilling
42-75241 LM-I J.W. Icard
42-75242 LM-K M.J. Quirk
42-75246 LM-F
42-75276 LM-M
42-75282 LM-J "Eradicator" R.C. Cherry
42-75388 LM-S D.C. Schilling
42-75388 LM-H C.R. Harrison
42-75444 LM-Z "The Magnet" M.K. Boyle
42-75583 LM-P L.A. Dade
42-75599 LM-G "Maximum Goose" W.P. Gordon
42-75599 LM-G "Barbara Ann"

P-47D-15-RE
42-76250 LM-S "Sneaky McGee"
42-76254 LM-P
42-76363 LM-F B.G. Edens
42-76364 LM-O

P-47D-16-RE
42-75631 LM-H D. Henley
42-75697 LM-
42-76093 LM-Y
42-76096 LM-E

P-47D-20-RE
42-76503 LM-N
42-25559 LM-R
42-25295 LM-K W.H. Merrill

P-47D-21-RA
43-25523 LM-
43-25566 LM-J
43-25577 LM-T

P-47D-21-RE
42-25512 LM-Q "Penrod & Sam" R.S. Johnson
42-25517 LM-X H.E. King
42-25522 LM-H M.L. Moseley

P-47D-22-RE
42-25959 LM-P L.A. Dade
42-25713 LM-M F.D. Williamson
42-25905 LM-K W.W. McElhare
42-26042 LM-G "Ugly Duckling" G.E. Bostwick
42-26060 LM-C
42-26280 LM-Z
42-26295 LM-X
42-26298 LM-A "I Wanted Wings" A.P. Knafelz
42-26337 LM-G

P-47D-25-RE
42-26417 LM-P L.A. Dade/E.M. Beason
42-26542 LM-N
42-26562 LM-N
42-26628 LM-C "Rozzie Geth II" F.J. Christensen
42-26636 LM-X
42-26641 LM-S D.C. Schilling

P-47D-27-RE
42-26986 LM-I "Miss Wolf"
42-27380 LM-D
42-27382 LM-K M.J. Quirk
42-27383 LM-

P-47D-28-RA
42-28675 LM-R
42-28683 LM-
42-28688 LM-A
42-28806 LM-C "Barbara Bee"
42-28812 LM-T
42-28878 LM-S
42-29337 LM-W

P-47D-28-RE
44-19745 LM-L L.C. Smith
44-19767 LM-M
44-19776 LM-O
44-19780 LM-R
44-19790 LM-J "Teddy" M.J. Jackson
44-19792 LM-K
44-19870 LM-P
44-19879 LM-K R.E. Winters
44-19883 LM-Y R.L. Patterson
44-19925 LM-L L.C. Smith
44-19928 LM-X
44-19929 LM-
44-19930 LM-
44-19960 LM-P
44-19964 LM-

P-47D-30-RE
44-20555 LM-I
44-20578 LM-H
44-20615 LM-B "West O'The Rockies" G.H. Butler
44-20617 LM-R
44-20721 LM-Q A.O. Perry

P-47M-1-RE
44-21114 LM-P L.A. Dade
44-21117 LM-J "Teddy" M.J. Jackson
44-21125 LM-S D.C. Schilling
44-21128 LM-K
44-21169 LM-
44-21176 LM-D
44-21177 LM-B
44-21199 LM-X L.F. Butiste
44-21200 LM-R S.N. Ball
44-21210 LM-O N.D. Gould
44-21211 LM-Z
44-21214 LM-Y W.F. Wilkerson
44-21219 LM-I F.D. Williamson
44-21226 LM-K
44-21228 LM-R
44-21230 LM-
44-21233 LM-H D. Henley
44-21237 LM-C "North Dakota Kid" W.J. Sharbo
44-21242 LM-S

Unknown Serials
P-47C LM-H "Taylor Maid" R.B. Taylor
P-47D LM-C "Marion" W.J. Sharbo
P-47D LM-M "Nigger Haid" D.C. Sheridan
P-47D LM-E "Flak Shack" T.S. Buszko
P-47D LM- "Doris"
P-47D LM- "Eileen"
P-47D LM- "Princess Peggy"
P-47D LM- "Devil Baby" H.C. Godfrey
P-47D LM- "Miss Box" J.P. Walker

**Aircraft of the 63rd Fighter Squadron**

P-47C-2-RE
41-6182 UN-
41-6199 UN-W H.P. Dugas
41-6199 UN-W P.M. Williams
41-6201 UN-
41-6203 UN-J "Windy"/"The Flying Ute" J.D. Brown
41-6214 UN-
41-6216 UN-O W.J. O'Connor
41-6227 UN-F J.E. Coenen
41-6230 UN-E "Holy Joe" J.L. Egan
41-6249 UN-
41-6250 UN-
41-6259 UN-Z G.D. Schiltz
41-6260 UN-
41-6261 UN-B G.E. Batdorf
41-6262 UN-
41-6263 UN-
41-6268 UN-P L.A. Dade
41-6268 UN-P W.H. Janson

P-47C-5-RE
41-6320 UN-Y
41-6325 UN-V "Lucky Little Devil" J.W. Vogt
41-6326 UN-Y H.E. Comstock
41-6329 UN-L C.C. Clamp
41-6330 UN-S "Sunshine" B.R. Smith
41-6334 UN-M W.M. Mahurin
41-6362 UN-A "The Michigan Mauler" L.A. Adrianse
41-6367 UN-X G.A. Compton/C.W. Reed
41-6372 UN-S A. Sugas
41-6375 UN-T P.E. Tukey
41-6395 UN-D R.B. Dyar
41-6534 UN-D R.B. Dyar
41-6537 UN-Q W.A. Van Abel
41-6584 UN-E J.L. Egan
41-6622 UN-K V.P. Ludwig

P-47D-1-RE
42-7853 UN-R S.V. Burke
42-7878 UN-G "Lil Goody" D.M. Goodfleisch
42-7885 UN-N A.J. Wisniewski
42-7885 UN-N
42-7893 UN-F F.H. Peppers
42-7895 UN-N E.D. Whitley
42-7896 UN-H G.F. Hall
42-7934 UN-U W.T. Hannigan

42-7943 UN-K
42-7946 UN-I J.D. Wilson

P-47D-2-RA
42-22534 UN-O W.J. O'Connor

P-47D-2-RE
42-7975 UN-I R.D. Petty
42-8269 UN-Z G.D. Schiltz

P-47D-4-RA
42-22748 UN-V J.W. Vogt/K.K. Lewis
42-22762 UN-S "Tinkle" S.O. Stamps
42-22772 UN-G "El Diablo II" A.S. Cavallo
42-22834 UN-T

P-47D-5-RE
42-8410 UN-U J.E. Coenen/W.H. Janson
42-8426 UN-P
42-8463 UN-T P.E. Tukey/L.M. Langdon/
42-8463 UN-T F.C. Windmayer
42-8465 UN-K V.P. Ludwig
42-8487 UN-M W.M. Mahurin
42-8488 UN-A "Lofty" L.A. Adrianse
42-8525 UN-J J.D. Brown
42-8554 UN-G "Lil Goody" D.M. Goodfleisch
42-8554 UN-P H.L. Matthews
42-8575 UN-
42-8607 UN-K V.P. Ludwig
42-8609 UN-P I.T. Porowski
42-8673 UN-Q J.D. Wilson/H.F. Warner
42-8693 UN-I "Liquidator" R.D. Petty
42-8693 UN-I W.R. Frederick

P-47D-6-RE
42-74635 UN-D C.C. Clamp
42-74643 UN-H J.C. Wakefield
42-74676 UN-O D.V. Peters
42-74722 UN-O W.J. O'Connor
42-74750 UN-L "Lady Jane" J.H. Truluck

P-47D-10-RE
42-75063 UN-J
42-75069 UN-E
42-75071 UN-A A.H. Robey
42-75109 UN-W "Louisiana Pirate" R.B. Landry
42-75109 UN-W J.W. Vogt
42-75137 UN-T
42-75180 UN-F I.T. Porowski
42-75185 UN-X "Princess Pat" C.W. Reed
42-75206 UN-G "Lil Goody" D.M. Goodfleisch

P-47D-11-RE
42-75217 UN-V J.W. Vogt
42-75217 UN-K J.E. Ross
42-75232 UN-Z G.D. Schiltz
42-75234 UN-Q E.G. Evert
42-75266 UN-F G.F. Hall
42-75276 UN-Q "Category E" 2-seat radar plane
42-75278 UN-B "Anamosa" R.B. Westfall
42-75394 UN-R S.V. Burke
42-75395 UN-A
42-75412 UN-S B.R. Smith
42-75461 UN-
42-75575 UN-N A.J. Wisniewski

P-47D-15-RE
42-76249 UN-V G.W. Johnson

P-47D-16-RE
42-75670 UN-
42-75683 UN-S S.O. Stamps
42-75855 UN-E J.L. Egan
42-75859 UN-C
42-75864 UN-Z H. Zemke
42-75870 UN-Y H.E. Comstock

P-47D-20-RE
42-76468 UN-R "Ole Steel Butt" J.A. Aranyos
42-76471 UN-Z H. Zemke
42-76578 UN-O D.V. Peters
42-25286 UN-
42-25317 UN-H T.W. Queen

P-47D-21-RA
43-25515 UN-T "Ann K"
43-25531 UN-A B.P. Casteel
43-25585 UN-V "Pat"

P-47D-21-RE
42-25531 UN-

P-47D-22-RE
42-25721 UN-P
42-25861 UN-G A.S. Cavallo
42-25957 UN-
42-25969 UN-S
42-26057 UN-W
42-26057 UN-F
42-26059 UN-I "Quaker Schiemiel" W.R. Frederick
42-26243 UN-D W.R. Groce
42-26258 UN-T "Moptop's Pride" E.J. Timony
42-26291 UN-I
42-26293 UN-L "Belle of Bellmont"
42-26299 UN-B M.H. Becker/C.M. Hart
42-26305 UN-
42-26316 UN-C J.R. Curtis

P-47D-25-RE
42-26413 UN-Z "Happy Warrior" H.E. Comstock
42-26466 UN-B "Anamosa II" R.B. Westfall
42-26475 UN-J
42-26524 UN-G "Lil Goody" D.M. Goodfleisch
42-26530 UN-R
42-26629 UN-
42-26658 UN-N
42-26676 UN-T P.B. Trumble

P-47D-26-RA
42-28438 UN-R R. Frederickson

P-47D-27-RE
42-26824 UN-A
42-27322 UN-L

P-47D-28-RA
42-28543 UN-V "Pat"
42-28548 UN-
42-28566 UN-E
42-28627 UN-M "Shack Rat"
42-28689 UN-U
42-28741 UN-C C.A. Chinn
42-28796 UN-V R.R. Davis
42-28810 UN-O F.A. Ogden
42-28824 UN-A E.W. Andermatt
42-28853 UN-X
42-28910 UN-I
42-29364 UN-N R.L. Murphy

P-47D-28-RE
44-19730 UN-
44-19752 UN-
44-19757 UN-Y
44-19768 UN-
44-19786 UN-A
44-19804 UN-V R.R. Davis
44-19805 UN-S
44-19868 UN-H "Scarsdale Scout"
44-19887 UN-
44-19909 UN-T "Suzie"
44-19911 UN-
44-19937 UN-B C.M. Hart
44-19951 UN-K

P-47D-30-RE
44-20455 UN-X
44-20543 UN-F
44-20594 UN-F J.C. Fahringer
44-20597 UN-W
44-20711 UN-W
44-20722 UN-C

P-47M-1-RE
44-21112 UN-Z G.E. Bostwick
44-21118 UN-S A.T. Shupe
44-21120 UN-L
44-21121 UN-C W.B. Charlton
44-21126 UN-S S.F. Stebelton
44-21131 UN-X R.E. Bailey
44-21132 UN-K "Mrs. K" J.W. Keeler
44-21134 UN-P "Bernyce" P.A. Conger
44-21134 UN-P "Teacher's Pet" W.R. Hoffman
44-21135 UN-A J.T. Bradshaw
44-21137 UN-E E.E. Crosthwait
44-21140 UN-F "Shoot! You're Faded"
44-21141 UN-N "The Brat" R.L. Murphy
44-21150 UN-M "Dottie Dee II" C.T. McBath
44-21153 UN-W
44-21154 UN-J B.E. Vest

| | |
|---|---|
| 44-21157 UN-D | J.C. Naylor |
| 44-21159 UN- | |
| 44-21160 UN-F "Devastatin' Deb" | J.C. Fahringer |
| 44-21163 UN-S | C.R. Clark |
| 44-21175 UN-Z "Zemke's Wolfpack" | P.C. Dawson |
| 44-21181 UN-H | T.B. Hennessey |
| 44-21185 UN-M | A.J. Martin |
| 44-21186 UN-H | |
| 44-21189 UN-I | |
| 44-21198 UN-V | V.A. Smith |
| 44-21201 UN-C | |
| 44-21203 UN-A "Miss June" | E.W. Andermatt |
| 44-21215 UN- | |
| 44-21217 UN-O | F.M. Ogden |
| 44-21221 UN-C | |
| 44-21222 UN- | W.C. Scherz |
| 44-21225 UN-K "Fireball" | P.G. Kuhn |
| 44-21226 UN-G | W.R. Groce |
| 44-21234 UN-R | |

| Unknown Serials | |
|---|---|
| P-47D UN- "George" | E.M. Albright |
| P-47M UN-B "Ole Miss Lib" | E.J. Huff |
| P-47M UN- "The Mighty Myth" | M.J. Hughes |
| P-47M UN- "Lookin' Fer Trouble" | |

• • •

## THE 78TH FIGHTER GROUP
## 82ND, 83RD, 84TH FIGHTER SQUADRONS

The 78th Fighter Group was activated on February 3, 1942, at Baer Field, Indiana. Training in the west, the group headed overseas on November 24, 1942, aboard the "Queen Elizabeth". Equipped with P-38's when it reached England, the 78th lost all it's planes and almost all it's pilots in early 1943. Re-equipping with P-47's, the first of 450 missions came on April 13, 1943, with the last coming on April 25, 1945. While overseas, the group claimed 326 aerial and 342.5 ground victories while 188 P-47's and P-51's were lost on operations and 17 pilots died in accidents.

Stations for the 78th were Goxhill, from December 1, 1942, and Duxford, from April 13, 1943, until October of 1945. Aircraft flown in combat were the P-47C and D, from January of 1943 until January of 1945, and the P-51D and K, from December of 1944 onwards. The group was awarded two Distinguished Unit Citations, the first for support of the airborne invasion of Holland from September 17-23, 1944,; and the second for strafing accomplishments on April 16, 1945, in which over 100 German planes were destroyed.

### Claims

| | Air | | | Grd | |
|---|---|---|---|---|---|
| | Destroyed | Probable | Damaged | Destroyed | Damaged |
| HdQts | 11.5 | 0 | 4 | 23 | 6 |
| 82nd | 102.5 | 10 | 39.5 | 91.5 | 117 |
| 83rd | 118.5 | 11 | 54 | 112 | 65 |
| 84th | 93.5 | 4 | 25.5 | 113 | 105 |
| | 326 | 25 | 123 | 342.5 | 293 |

### Commanders

| | |
|---|---|
| Col. Arman Peterson | May 1942-July 1, 1943 |
| Maj. James J. Stone, Jr. | July 1, 1943-July 12, 1943 |
| LtCol. Melvin F. McNickle | July 12, 1943-July 30, 1943 |
| Col. James J. Stone, Jr. | July 31, 1943-May 22, 1944 |
| Col. Frederic C. Gray, Jr. | May 22, 1944-February 21, 1945 |
| LtCol. John D. Landers | February 22, 1945-July 1, 1945 |

### Wing and Command Assignments

| | |
|---|---|
| Assigned to VIII Fighter Command | November 29, 1942 |
| VIII Fighter Command, 4th Air Defense Wing | June 30, 1943 |
| VIII Fighter Command, 65th Fighter Wing | August 7, 1943 |
| VIII Fighter Command, 66th Fighter Wing | August 18, 1943 |
| 3rd Bomb Division, 66th Fighter Wing | September 15, 1944 |
| 3rd Air Division, 66th Fighter Wing | January 1, 1945 |

### Aircraft Markings

Original P-47's were in olive drab/neutral gray schemes with the standard white cowl and theater bands. NMF planes were received in the spring of 1944 with many having dark green applied to the upper surfaces. Most retained NMF under surfaces but a few did have a light blue-gray apllied. In April of 1944, group markings were applied: a square set pattern of black and white checkerboards on the cowl, extending back to the shutters, with six squares per longitudinal row. In November of 1944, rudder colors were brought into use: red for the 82nd, white for the 83rd, and black for the 84th.

All P-51's were in NMF. Group markings consisted of half black and half white spinners, divided longitudinally. The cowling was divided into a black and white square set checkerboard, with eight squares per longitudinal row, except under the nose where the checkerboard extended to the wing root. Most planes also carried a 2 inch red stripe which framed the rear of the checkerboard. Rudder colors remained the same, the only change being that the 83rd now outlined the white rudder with red.

Squadron codes were:

82nd Ftr Sqn: MX
83rd Ftr Sqn: HL
84th Ftr Sqn: WZ

### 78th Fighter Group Statistical Report

| Month | Air | Grd | Losses | KIAc |
|---|---|---|---|---|
| January 1943 | 0-0-0 | 0-0 | 0 | 3 |
| Febraury | 0-0-0 | 0-0 | 0 | 0 |
| March | 0-0-0 | 0-0 | 0 | 1 |
| April | 0-0-0 | 0-0 | 1 | 1 |
| May | 6-2-4 | 0-0 | 6 | 0 |
| June | 7-2-0 | 0-0 | 2 | 0 |
| July | 21-3-10 | 0-0 | 7 | 0 |
| August | 5-0-4 | 0-0 | 2 | 0 |
| September | 9-2-0 | 0-0 | 1 | 0 |
| October | 7-0-1 | 0-0 | 1 | 1 |
| November | 6-1-3 | 0-0 | 3 | 0 |
| December | 11-3-5 | 0-0 | 1 | 1 |
| January 1944 | 12-1-5 | 0-0 | 8 | 0 |
| February | 34-2-11 | 3-18 | 7 | 0 |
| March | 12-0-6 | 9-23 | 8 | 1 |
| April | 17-2-9 | 32-43 | 6 | 1 |
| May | 25-0-10 | 8-14 | 8 | 0 |
| June | 20-0-6 | 1-0 | 18 | 1 |
| July | 9-2-7 | 23-10 | 11 | 2 |
| August | 5-0-2 | 24-8 | 11 | 0 |
| September | 13-0-5 | 46-25 | 21 | 0 |
| October | 12-0-3 | 1-1 | 2 | 1 |
| November | 13-2-3 | 5-5 | 4 | 1 |
| December | 8-0-1 | 0-0 | 1 | 0 |
| January 1945 | 14-0-6 | 0-0 | 8 | 1 |
| February | 0-2-1 | 16-9 | 21 | 0 |
| March | 54-1-21 | 2-7 | 17 | 1 |
| April | 5-0-0 | 172.5-130 | 13 | 0 |
| May | 0-0-0 | 0-0 | 0 | 0 |
| June | 0-0-0 | 0-0 | 0 | 0 |
| July | 0-0-0 | 0-0 | 0 | 1 |
| | 326-25-123 | 342.5-293 | 188 | 17 |

### Losses by Squadron

| | | MIA | | | KIAc | | |
|---|---|---|---|---|---|---|---|
| | P-38 | P-47 | P-51 | P-38 | P-47 | P-51 | Other |
| HdQts | 0 | 5 | 1 | 0 | 0 | 0 | 0 |
| 82nd | 0 | 46 | 19 | 1 | 2 | 0 | 0 |
| 83rd | 0 | 43 | 16 | 2 | 3 | 1 | 0 |
| 84th | 0 | 34 | 24 | 0 | 4 | 2 | 2 |
| | 0 | 128 | 60 | 3 | 9 | 3 | 2 |

### Claims by Type

| | Air | | | Grd | |
|---|---|---|---|---|---|
| | Destroyed | Probable | Damaged | Destroyed | Damaged |
| P-47 | 253 | 22 | 95 | 152 | 147 |
| P-51 | 73 | 3 | 28 | 190.5 | 146 |

### Claims by Enemy Aircraft Type

| | Air | | | Grd | |
|---|---|---|---|---|---|
| | Destroyed | Probable | Damaged | Destroyed | Damaged |
| Me-109 | 160 | 7 | 55 | 31 | 22 |
| FW-190 | 132 | 15 | 61 | 49 | 23 |
| Me-262 | 12 | 2 | 2 | 4 | 4 |
| Me-110 | 10 | 1 | 4 | 16 | 4 |
| Ju-87 | 4 | 0 | 1 | 30.5 | 24 |
| Me-210 | 3 | 0 | 0 | 0 | 1 |
| Ar-234 | 2 | 0 | 0 | 0 | 0 |
| Ju-88 | 1 | 0 | 0 | 25 | 21 |
| Ju-188 | 1 | 0 | 0 | 9 | 8 |
| Do-217 | 1 | 0 | 0 | 9 | 8 |
| He-111 | 0 | 0 | 0 | 52 | 88 |
| u/i a/c | 0 | 0 | 0 | 43 | 77 |
| Ju-52 | 0 | 0 | 0 | 37 | 23 |
| He-177 | 0 | 0 | 0 | 10 | 0 |

| | | | | | |
|---|---|---|---|---|---|
| Me-410 | 0 | 0 | 0 | 9 | 12 |
| Bu-133 | 0 | 0 | 0 | 4 | 5 |
| FW-200 | 0 | 0 | 0 | 2 | 2 |
| Ar-196 | 0 | 0 | 0 | 2 | 1 |
| Fi-156 | 0 | 0 | 0 | 2 | 0 |
| Hs-126 | 0 | 0 | 0 | 2 | 0 |
| Go-242 | 0 | 0 | 0 | 1 | 7 |
| DFS-230 | 0 | 0 | 0 | 1 | 1 |
| Me-323 | 0 | 0 | 0 | 1 | 1 |
| Trainer | 0 | 0 | 0 | 1 | 1 |
| Hs-129 | 0 | 0 | 0 | 1 | 0 |
| Hs-123 | 0 | 0 | 0 | 1 | 0 |
| Glider | 0 | 0 | 0 | 0 | 8 |
| Ju-86 | 0 | 0 | 0 | 0 | 2 |

### 78th Fighter Group Squadron Commanders

**82nd Ftr Sqn**

| | |
|---|---|
| LtCol. Harry J. Dayhuff | May 11, 1942-August 17, 1943 |
| LtCol. Jack J. Oberhansly | August 17, 1943-May 18, 1944 |
| Maj. Norman D. Munson | May 18, 1944-May 23, 1944 |
| Capt. James W. Wilkinson | May 23, 1944-June 4, 1944 |
| Capt. William A. Guilfoyle | June 4, 1944-June 8, 1944 |
| LtCol. Ben I. Mayo | June 8, 1944-July 14, 1944 |
| Maj. Norman D. Munson | July 14, 1944-July 19, 1944 |
| Capt. Charles R. Clark | July 20, 1944-August 2, 1944 |
| LtCol. Joseph Myers, Jr. | August 2, 1944-August 22, 1944 |
| LtCol. Jack J. Oberhansly | August 22, 1944-August 28, 1944 |
| Maj. Richard E. Conner | August 28, 1944-December 2, 1944 |
| LtCol. Joseph Myers, Jr. | December 2, 1944-December 3, 1944 |
| Maj. Harry L. Downing | December 3, 1944-February 17, 1945 |
| LtCol. Richard E. Conner | February 17, 1945-March 4, 1945 |
| Maj. Harry L. Downing | March 4, 1945-March 14, 1945 |
| LtCol. Richard E. Conner | March 14, 1945-March 19, 1945 |
| LtCol. Richard A. Hewitt | March 20, 1945-May 10, 1945 |

**83rd Ftr Sqn**

| | |
|---|---|
| Maj. James J. Stone | May 7, 1942-July 1, 1943 |
| Maj. Jesse C. Davis, Jr. | July 1, 1943-January 18, 1944 |
| LtCol. Olin E. Gilbert | January 18, 1944-July 13, 1944 |
| Maj. William H. Julian | July 13, 1944-October 9, 1944 |
| LtCol. Samuel R. Beckley | October 9, 1944-December 31, 1944 |
| Maj. William H. Julian | December 31, 1944-January 6, 1945 |
| LtCol. Samuel R. Beckley | January 6, 1945-January 12, 1945 |
| Maj. William H. Julian | January 12, 1945-March 20, 1945 |
| LtCol. Samuel R. Beckley | March 20, 1945-October 1945 |

**84th Ftr Sqn**

| | |
|---|---|
| LtCol. Eugene P. Roberts | August 1942-September 28, 1943 |
| Maj. Jack C. Price | September 28, 1943-February 25, 1944 |
| Maj. Harold E. Stump | February 25, 1944-June 10, 1944 |
| Capt. Richard M. Holly | June 11, 1944-July 13, 1944 |
| LtCol. Ben I. Mayo | July 13, 1944-September 25, 1944 |
| LtCol. Leonard P. Marshall | September 25, 1944-March 14, 1945 |
| Maj. Harry L. Downing | March 14, 1945-March 19, 1945 |
| LtCol. Richard E. Conner | March 19, 1945-March 21, 1945 |
| Capt. Dorian Ledington | March 21, 1945-April 21, 1945 |
| Maj. William E. May | April 21, 1945-April 24, 1945 |
| Maj. Bruce B. Hunt | April 24, 1945-May 21, 1945 |

### 78th Fighter Group Aces

| Name | Air | Grd | Total | Sqn |
|---|---|---|---|---|
| LtCol. John D. Landers | 14.5 | 20 | 34.5* | HdQts |
| Capt. Alwin M. Juchheim | 9 | 6 | 15 | 83rd |
| Maj. Quince L. Brown | 12.33 | 1 | 13.33 | 84th |
| Lt. Francis E. Harrington | 4 | 8 | 12 | 83rd |
| LtCol. Olin E. Gilbert | 2 | 8.5 | 10.5** | 83rd<br>HdQts |
| Lt. John A. Kirk, III | 4 | 6 | 10 | 83rd |
| Capt. Charles M. Peal | 2 | 8 | 10 | 83rd |
| Lt. Duncan M. McDuffie | 4 | 5 | 9 | 83rd |
| LtCol. Eugene P. Roberts | 9 | 0 | 9 | 84th<br>HdQts |
| Lt. Clyde E. Taylor | 0 | 9 | 9 | 84th |
| Lt. Henry R. Slack | 1.5 | 7 | 8.5 | 84th |
| Maj. Richard A. Hewitt | 4 | 4.33 | 8.33 | 82nd |
| LtCol. Richard E. Conner | 4.5 | 3.5 | 8 | 82nd |
| Lt. Danford E. Josey | 0 | 8 | 8 | 84th |
| LtCol. William H. Julian | 5 | 3 | 8*** | 83rd |
| Capt. James W. Wilkinson | 6 | 2 | 8 | 82nd |
| Capt. John J. Hockery | 7 | 0.8 | 7.8 | 82nd |
| LtCol. Jack J. Oberhansly | 6 | 1.6 | 7.6 | 82nd<br>HdQts |
| LtCol. Joseph Myers, Jr. | 4.5 | 3 | 7.5@ | 82nd |
| Capt. Edward R. Kulik | 0 | 7 | 7 | 83rd |
| Lt. Peter E. Pompetti | 5 | 2 | 7 | 84th |
| Capt. Robert T. Green | 4.5 | 2 | 6.5 | 83rd |
| LtCol. Ben I. Mayo, Jr. | 4 | 2.5 | 6.5 | 82nd<br>84th |
| Capt. Robert R. Bonebrake | 3 | 3 | 6 | 83rd |
| Lt. Robert R. Bosworth | 1 | 5 | 6 | 82nd |
| Maj. Gillespie Bryan | 0 | 6 | 6 | HdQts |
| Lt. Anthony T. Colletti | 1 | 5 | 6 | 83rd |
| Lt. Louis DeAnda | 0 | 6 | 6 | 84th |
| Lt. Donald J. DeVilliers | 0 | 6 | 6 | 83rd |
| Maj. Raymond E. Smith | 1 | 5 | 6 | 84th |
| Lt. Grant M. Turley | 6 | 0 | 6 | 82nd |
| Capt. Warren M. Wesson | 4 | 2 | 6 | 82nd |
| Lt. Merle R. Capp | 2 | 3.5 | 5.5 | 82nd<br>84th |
| Lt. Huie H. Lamb, Jr. | 2.5 | 3 | 5.5 | 82nd |
| Capt. Harold T. Barnaby | 4 | 1 | 5 | 83rd |
| Lt. Gene C. Doss | 0 | 5 | 5 | 83rd |
| Lt. Neal Hepner | 0 | 5 | 5 | 84th |
| Capt. Dorian Ledington | 2 | 3 | 5 | 84th |
| Capt. Charles P. London | 5 | 0 | 5 | 83rd |
| Lt. Charles E. Parmelee | 3 | 2 | 5 | 84th |
| Lt. Richard E. Phaneuf | 0 | 5 | 5 | 83rd |
| Maj. Jack C. Price | 5 | 0 | 5 | 84th |
| Lt. Dale S. Sweat | 0 | 5 | 5 | 83rd |

* - includes 6 air victories with the 49th Ftr Grp, PTO, and 5 air and 5 ground victories with the 55th and 357th Ftr Grps, ETO

** - includes 6.5 ground victories with 66th Ftr Wing

*** - includes 3 ground victories with the 339th Ftr Grp, ETO

@ - includes 3 air victories with the 55th Ftr Grp, ETO

### 78th Fighter Group Scorers

**HdQts**

| | Air | Grd | |
|---|---|---|---|
| G. Bryan | 0-0-0 | 6-6 | |
| C.M. Christ | 1-0-0 | 0-0 | |
| H.J. Dayhuff | 0.5-0-0 | 0-0 | plus 82nd Ftr Sqn |
| O.E. Gilbert | 0-0-0 | 2-0 | plus 83rd Ftr Sqn & 66th Ftr Wg |
| F.C. Gray, Jr. | 0.5-0-0 | 0-0 | |
| R.T. Himes | 0-0-1 | 0-0 | |
| R.B. Holmes | 1-0-0 | 0-0 | plus 82nd Ftr Sqn |
| J.D. Landers | 3.5-0-0 | 15-0 | plus 6 air w/49th Ftr Grp, PTO & 5-0-1 air & 5-1 grd w/55th & 357th Ftr Grps |
| J.J. Oberhansly | 1-0-0 | 0-0 | plus 82nd Ftr Sqn |
| A. Peterson | 1-0-2 | 0-0 | |
| E.P. Roberts | 3-0-0 | 0-0 | plus 84th Ftr Sqn & 0-3 grd w/364th Ftr Grp |
| J.J. Stone, Jr. | 0-0-1 | 0-0 | plus 83rd Ftr Sqn |

**82nd Ftr Sqn**

| | | | |
|---|---|---|---|
| R.B. Abernathy | 0-0-0 | 1-2 | |
| R.E. Adamina | 1-0-0 | 0-0 | |
| R.H. Anderson | 1-0-0 | 0-0 | |
| R.L. Baker | 1.33-0-1 | 2-0 | |
| W.F. Bechtelheimer | 0-0-0.5 | 1-0 | |
| J.J. Bernhard | 0-0-0 | 0-3 | |
| R.J. Blossom | 0-0-1 | 2-2 | |
| R.C. Boeckman | 0-0-0 | 1-0 | |
| W.L. Boone | 0-0-0 | 0.79-3 | plus 2-1-1 air & 11-10 grd w/353rd Ftr Grp |
| R.R. Bosworth | 1-0-0 | 5-0 | |
| W.E. Bourque | 2-0-0 | 1-2 | |
| J.E. Brasher | 1-0-0 | 1.93-5 | |
| J.I. Brown, III | 0-0-1 | 1-2 | |
| W.H. Brown | 2-0-2 | 0-0 | |
| L.R. Campi | 0-0-0 | 3-2 | |
| M.R. Capp | 2-0-0 | 0-0 | plus 84th Ftr Sqn |
| E.J. Carroll | 0-0-0 | 3-5 | |
| C.R. Clark | 0-0-1 | 0.12-0 | |
| W.L. Coleman | 4-0-0 | 0-0 | |
| R.E. Conner | 4.5-0-0 | 3.5-2 | |
| M.O. Croy, Jr. | 2.5-0-0 | 1-0 | |
| H.J. Dayhuff | 1-0-0 | 0-0 | plus HdQts |
| A.V. DeGenaro | 1-1-1 | 0-0 | |
| C.W. DeWitt | 0-0-1 | 2.4-5 | |
| R.W. Dunham | 0-0-0.5 | 0-1 | |
| H.L. Eakes | 0-0-0 | 0.79-0 | |
| T.L. Eggleston | 0-0-0 | 3.5-0 | |
| G.V. Elsey | 0-0-1 | 2-1 | |
| C.G. Godard | 0-1-0 | 0-1 | |
| W.A. Guilfoyle | 0-0-0 | 0-0.5 | |
| D.D. Hagarty | 3-0-1 | 0-2 | |
| C.B. Hahn | 1-0-0 | 0-0 | |
| D.C. Hart | 1-0-1 | 1-3 | |
| P.H. Hazelett | 0-0-0 | 3-2 | |
| R.V. Hearn | 0-0-0 | 0.12-0 | |

| | | | |
|---|---|---|---|
| W.T. Hegman | 1-1-0 | 0-0 | |
| D.J. Henahan | 0-0-0 | 4.5-3 | |
| R.A. Hewitt | 4-0-1 | 4.33-1 | |
| A.W. Hill | 0.5-0-1 | 0-0 | |
| J.J. Hockery | 7-1-0 | 0.8-0 | |
| R.B. Holmes | 0-0-0 | 0-5 | plus HdQts |
| L.H. Hosford | 0-0-0 | 0-0.5 | |
| W.E. Hydorn, Jr. | 0-1-1 | 0-0 | |
| V.Y. Jones | 1.5-1-0 | 0-0 | |
| I.H. Keatley | 2-0-1 | 0-1 | |
| P. Keller | 0-0-0 | 0-1 | |
| J.E. Kinsolving | 0-0-0 | 1.5-0 | |
| W.O. Lacy | 0-0-0 | 2-2 | |
| H.H. Lamb, Jr. | 2.5-0-2 | 3-1 | |
| J.T. Lamb, Jr. | 1-0-0 | 0-1 | |
| H.R. Liebenrood | 1-0-0 | 0.5-0 | |
| D.E. Ludwig | 0-0-0 | 0-1 | |
| G.J. Lundigan | 0.33-0-0 | 0-0 | |
| L.P. Marshall | 0.33-0-0 | 0-0 | plus 84th Ftr Sqn |
| M.S. Martinez | 4-0-1 | 0-0 | |
| J.L. Mattern, Jr. | 0-0-1 | 0-0 | |
| W.E. May | 1.5-0-0 | 0.12-1 | |
| B.I. Mayo, Jr. | 1-0-1 | 0-0 | plus 84th Ftr Sqn |
| A.S. Miller | 2-0-1 | 1-2 | |
| R.I. Miller | 0-0-1 | 0-0 | |
| N.D. Munson | 0-0-1 | 4-4.43 | |
| J. Myers, Jr. | 1.5-0-0 | 3-1 | plus 3-0-2 air w/55th Ftr Grp |
| J.J. Oberhansly | 5-2-1 | 1.6-1 | plus HdQts |
| J.E. Parker | 2-0-3.5 | 0-1 | |
| E.L. Peel | 0.5-0-0 | 2-4 | |
| A.B. Richie | 1-0-0 | 0-0 | |
| H.C. Roe | 0-0-0 | 0-2 | |
| A.M. Rosenberg | 0-0-0 | 0-3 | |
| A.A. Rosenblum | 2.5-0-1 | 1-0 | |
| E.O. Schneider | 1-0-0 | 0-0 | |
| H.F. Scholz | 3-0-1 | 1-0 | |
| H.K. Shope | 0-0-1 | 6-0 | |
| H.B. Slater | 0-0-1 | 2-1 | |
| R.E. Smith | 1-0-0 | 0-0 | |
| R.P. Spaulding | 1-0-0 | 0-0 | |
| J.B. Stallings | 0.5-0-0 | 0-0 | |
| G.W. Stillwell | 0-0-0 | 2-6 | |
| M.B. Stutzman | 0.5-0-0 | 2-3 | |
| W.S. Swanson | 1-0-1 | 0-0 | |
| F.R. Swauger | 0-0-0 | 1-0 | |
| G.M. Turley | 6-0-0 | 0-0 | |
| W.V. Van Dyk | 0-0-0 | 1-0 | |
| K.R. Wagner | 1-0-1 | 1-0 | |
| W.I. Warren | 2-0-0 | 1-0 | |
| B.M. Watkins | 2-0-0 | 1.33-9 | |
| C. Webb | 0-0-1 | 0.67-2 | |
| W.M. Wesson | 4-0-0 | 2-3 | |
| G.L. Weston | 0-1-0 | 0-0 | |
| J.W. Wilkinson | 6-0-1 | 2-13 | |
| R.E. Wilkinson | 0-0-0 | 0.5-0 | |
| R.L. Wolfe | 0-0-1 | 0.5-1 | |
| M.K. Woller | 2-0-0 | 0.5-3 | |
| W.D. Wren | 0-1-0 | 0-0 | |
| M.R. Wright | 0-0-2 | 0-0 | |
| D.C. Zboinski | 0-0-0 | 0-1 | |

**83rd Ftr Sqn**

| | | | |
|---|---|---|---|
| K.C. Allstaedt | 1.5-0-0 | 2-1 | |
| H.S. Askelson | 2-0-0 | 0-0 | |
| H.T. Barnaby | 4-0-1 | 1-0 | |
| S.R. Beckley | 0-0-1 | 0-0 | |
| W.E. Bennett | 0-0-0 | 1.5-0 | |
| P. Bingham | 0.5-0-0 | 0-0 | |
| H.L. Blystone | 0-0-1 | 2-0 | |
| D. Bodenhamer, Jr. | 0-0-1 | 0-0 | |
| R.R. Bonebrake | 3-0-1 | 3-0 | |
| G.G. Boteler | 1.5-0-0 | 0-0 | |
| R.L. Burgher | 0-0-0 | 1.5-0 | |
| L.R. Casey | 0-0-1 | 0.5-0 | |
| P.A. Caulfield | 2-0-1 | 0-0 | |
| A.T. Colletti | 1-0-1 | 5-4 | |
| J.M. Cooper | 0-0-2 | 0-0 | |
| H.I. Davis | 3-0-1 | 0-0 | |
| J.C. Davis, Jr. | 2-0-0 | 0-0 | |
| D.J. DeVilliers | 0-0-0 | 6-4 | |
| G.C. Doss | 0-0-0 | 5-1 | |
| K.W. Dougherty | 3-1-0 | 0-0 | |
| E.J. Downey | 1-0-0 | 0-0 | |
| K.P. Dunaway | 0-0-0 | 0-2 | |
| L.L. Eadline | 1-0-0 | 0-0 | |
| R.E. Ealey | 2-0-0 | 0-0 | |
| F.A. Fish | 1-0-0 | 0-0 | |
| H.O. Foster | 0-0-1 | 0-0 | |
| O.E. Gilbert | 2-0-0 | 0-0 | plus HdQts |
| R.T. Green | 4.5-0-0 | 2-0 | |
| F.E. Harrington | 4-0-1 | 8-8 | |
| D.D. Hartley | 0-0-0 | 0.5-0 | |
| R.B. Hathway | 1-0-1 | 0-1 | |
| F.E. Higginbottom | 2.5-1-0 | 0-4 | |
| J.D. Hodge | 2-0-0 | 0-0 | |
| P.C. Holden | 2.5-0-1 | 2-1 | |
| C.W. Hotchkiss | 1-0-0 | 0-0 | |
| C.P. Hurst | 0-0-0 | 0-2 | |
| J.H. Johnson | 1-0-1 | 0-0 | |
| A.M. Juchheim | 9-2-2 | 6-1 | |
| W.H. Julian | 5-0-2 | 0-0 | plus 3-4 grd w/339th Ftr Grp |
| J.A. Kirk, III | 4-0-0 | 6-3 | |
| E.T. Kitley | 1-0-2 | 0-0 | |
| P.W. Klaasen | 1-0-1 | 0-0 | |
| R.H. Knapp | 1-0-0 | 0-0 | |
| W.J. Korsmeyer | 0-0-0 | 1-0 | |
| R.I. Kuehl | 2.5-0-1 | 1-1 | |
| E.R. Kulik | 0-0-0 | 7-1 | |
| C.E. Kuykendall | 1-0-1 | 0-0 | |
| J. LaGrange, Jr. | 1-0-0 | 0-0 | |
| D.A. Lawhead | 0-1-2 | 0-0 | |
| C.P. London | 5-1-2 | 0-0 | |
| W.H. Madole | 2-0-3 | 0-0 | |
| V.J. Massa | 0.5-0-1 | 0.5-0 | |
| W.M. McDermott | 3-0-1 | 0-0 | |
| D.M. McDuffie | 4-0-0 | 5-0 | |
| D.W. McLeod | 2-0-2 | 0-0 | |
| E.E. McTaggart | 1-0-0 | 0-0 | |
| R.A. Messinger | 0-0-0 | 4-3 | |
| E.H. Miller | 1-1-0 | 2-0 | |
| J.B. Miller | 0-0-0 | 1-1 | |
| D.R. Monteith | 0-0-0 | 0-1 | |
| J.A. Moothart | 0.5-0-1 | 0.5-0 | |
| H.J. Morris | 0.5-0-0 | 0-0 | plus 0-0-2 air w/353rd Ftr Grp |
| R.E. Mullins | 0-0-1 | 0-0 | |
| R.W. Oxley | 0.5-0-0 | 0-1 | |
| A.A. Palopoli | 0-0-0 | 3-0 | |
| C.M. Peal | 2-0-0 | 8-2 | |
| J.S. Peterson | 0-0-0 | 1-0 | |
| R.E. Phaneuf | 0-0-0 | 5-4 | |
| E.W. Powell | 1-0-0 | 0-0 | |
| F.R. Pursell | 3-0-1 | 0-0 | |
| M.D. Putnam | 1-0-1 | 0-0 | |
| J.S. Reems | 1.5-0-0 | 2.5-0 | |
| G. Riccardo | 0-1-1 | 1.5-2 | |
| H.C. Roff, Jr. | 3-2-2 | 0-0 | |
| R.F. Rohm | 0-0-1 | 0-0 | |
| H.L. Sealey | 2-0-1 | 0-0 | |
| T.W. Shepard, Jr. | 1-0-0 | 0-0 | |
| R.W. Smith | 0-0-0 | 1-2 | |
| W.B. Sommer | 0-0-0 | 3-0 | |
| B.W. Sorenson | 0.5-0-0 | 2.5-1 | |
| W.B. Spenglerf | 0-0-2 | 1-3 | |
| J.E. Stokes, Jr. | 1-0-0 | 0-0 | |
| J.J. Stone, Jr. | 2-1-0 | 0-0 | plus HdQts |
| E.W. Strobel | 0-0-0 | 4-2 | |
| D.S. Sweat | 0-0-0 | 5-3 | |
| R.T. Talbot | 1-0-1 | 0-0 | |
| W. Tonkin | 1-0-1 | 0-0 | |
| W.H. Waldheim | 1-0-0 | 0.5-5 | |
| A.B. Werder | 0-0-1 | 0-0 | |
| F. White | 2-0-0 | 0-0 | |
| R.E. Wise | 1-0-2 | 0-1 | |
| H.R. Zumwalt | 0-0-2 | 0-0 | |

**84th Ftr Sqn**

| | | | |
|---|---|---|---|
| L.J. Abel | 1.33-0-1 | 1-3 | |
| R.L. Baron | 0-0-0 | 1.5-2 | |
| H.F. Beck | 0-0-0 | 1.5-2 | |
| R.E. Belliveau | 0-0-1 | 0-1 | |
| J.R. Bertrand | 1-0-0 | 0-0 | |
| W.S. Blodgett | 0-0-0 | 4-1 | |
| J.S. Bond | 0-0-0 | 1-1 | |
| H.L. Boyle | 1-0-0 | 0-0 | |
| C.R. Brown | 2-0-0 | 0-0 | |
| Q.L. Brown | 12.33-0-0 | 1-2 | |
| J.F. Byers | 1-0-0 | 0-0 | |
| S.B. Calderon | 0-0-0 | 0-4 | |
| J.D. Calvin | 0-0-0 | 0-1 | |
| M.R. Capp | 0-0-0 | 3.5-1 | plus 82nd Ftr Sqn |
| J.F. Casey | 0-0-1 | 1-0 | |
| R.E. Clague | 0-0-0 | 0.5-0 | |
| C.W. Clemmons | 0-0-1 | 0-0 | |
| R.K. Corbett | 0.5-0-0 | 0-2 | |
| L.K. Covelle, Jr. | 2-0-0 | 0-0 | |
| W.K. Dacci | 1-0-0 | 0-0 | |
| L. DeAnda | 0-0-0 | 6-0 | |
| W.J. DeGain | 2-0-0 | 1-3 | |
| W.W. Dougherty | 0-1-0 | 0-0 | |
| A.H. Downing | 0-0-1 | 0-0 | |

| | | | |
|---|---|---|---|
| H.L. Downing | 2-0-0 | 0-0 | |
| G.H. Doyle | 0-2-1 | 1-2 | |
| A.F. Eaton | 0-0-1 | 2.5-0 | |
| H.W. Elin | 0-0-0 | 0-1 | |
| J.M. Farmer | 0-0-0 | 2-0 | |
| E.F. Fleming | 0-0-1 | 0-0 | |
| G.E. Gallant | 0-0-0 | 0-1 | |
| A.A. Garback | 0.5-0-0 | 2-1 | |
| W.K. Grimes | 1-0-0.5 | 1.5-0 | |
| L.M. Grisham | 0-0-0 | 3-0 | |
| A.P. Haning | 0-0-0 | 2.5-1 | |
| W.J. Hardin | 0-0-1 | 0-0 | |
| P.R. Henderson | 0-0-0 | 0-1 | |
| N. Hepner | 0-0-0 | 5-4 | |
| L.R. Hereford | 1-0-0 | 0-0 | |
| R.D. Higgins | 0-0-0 | 0-3 | |
| R.M. Holly | 1-0-0 | 0-0 | plus 0.5 v 50th Ftr Sqn, Iceland |
| W.F. Hunt | 1-0-0 | 0-3 | |
| J.D. Irvin | 4-0-1 | 0-0 | |
| D.E. Josey | 0-0-0 | 8-6 | |
| H.H. Just | 0-0-0 | 0-1 | |
| P.T. Keillor | 0-0-0 | 2-1 | |
| C.N. Keppler | 1-0-0 | 0-0 | plus 2-0-4 air & 0-2.83 grd w/361st Ftr Grp |
| G.W. Koontz | 2-0-0 | 0-0 | |
| H.W. Kramer | 0-0-0 | 0-1 | |
| R.O. Laho | 0-0-0 | 0-1 | |
| E.S. Lang | 0.33-0-0.5 | 1-3 | |
| P.L. Larson | 3-0-0 | 0-0 | |
| H.T. Lay | 2-0-0 | 0-0 | |
| D. Ledington | 2-0-0 | 3-3 | |
| D.T. Loyd | 1-0-0 | 0-0 | |
| W.J. Luckey, Jr. | 2-0-0 | 0-0 | |
| W.H. Lutz | 2-0-2 | 2-2 | |
| L.P. Marshall | 1-0-0 | 0-2 | plus 82nd Ftr Sqn |
| J.P. Maxwell | 2-0-1 | 0-0 | |
| B.I. Mayo, Jr. | 3-0-0 | 2.5-0 | plus 82nd Ftr Sqn |
| W.M. McClellan | 0-0-0 | 3-4 | |
| A.G. McGuire | 0-0-0 | 3-5 | |
| R.J. McIntosh | 2-0-1 | 0-0 | |
| P.H. McKenney | 0-0-0 | 0-1.5 | |
| J.E. Moores | 1-0-0 | 3-5 | |
| J.W. Mundy | 0-0-1 | 0-1 | |
| J.A. Nunley | 0-0-0 | 0-2 | |
| F.E. Oiler | 1-0-1 | 2-1 | |
| P.S. Ostrander | 1-0-0 | 3-2 | |
| J.O. Patton | 0-0-0 | 0-1 | |
| C.E. Parmelee | 3-0-0 | 2-0 | |
| P.E. Pompetti | 5-0-3.5 | 2-3 | |
| J.C. Price | 5-0-1 | 0-0 | |
| J.B. Putnam, Jr. | 2-0-0 | 1-0 | |
| E.P. Roberts | 6-1-0 | 0-0 | plus HdQts |
| E.E. Russell | 0-0-1 | 1-0 | |
| E.H. Schneider | 0-0-0 | 0.5-0 | |
| C.W. Silsby | 2-0-1 | 0-0 | |
| H.R. Slack, IV | 1.5-0-0 | 7-2 | |
| E.F. Smith | 0.5-0-0 | 0-0 | |
| M.H. Smith | 0-0-0 | 0-2 | |
| R.E. Smith, Jr. | 1-0-1 | 5-3.5 | |
| J.R. Sole | 0-0-0 | 4-5 | |
| R.A. Spaulding | 0-0-0 | 1-0 | |
| R.H. Spooner | 2-0-0 | 0-1 | |
| E.L. Stier | 1-0-1 | 2-0 | |
| H.E. Stump | 1-0-0 | 0-0 | |
| C.E. Taylor | 0-0-0 | 9-2 | |
| T.V. Thain, Jr. | 1.5-0-0 | 0-0 | |
| M.T. Wilson, Jr. | 1-0-0 | 0.5-4 | |
| H.V. Wingfield | 0-0-0 | 1-0 | |
| E.W. Wood | 0-0-0 | 3-2 | |

**78th Fighter Group Scoring**

**May 14, 1943**

| | | | |
|---|---|---|---|
| HdQts: | Col. A. Peterson | FW-190 dam(air) | E/Flushing |
| 82nd: | Capt. R.E. Adamina | FW-190 dest(air) | Antwerp |
| | Capt. J.J. Oberhansly | FW-190 prob(air) | Antwerp |
| 83rd: | Maj. J.J. Stone | FW-190 dest(air) | NE St. Nicholas |
| | Capt. E.E. McTaggart | FW-190 dest(air) | SW Antwerp |
| | Capt. C.P. London | FW-190 prob(air) | NW Antwerp |
| | Lt. W.H. Julian | FW-190 dam(air) | St. Nicholas |

**May 16, 1943**

| | | | |
|---|---|---|---|
| HdQts: | Col. A. Peterson | FW-190 dam(air) | E/Flushing |
| 84th: | F/O C.R. Brown | (2)FW-190 dest(air) | Flushing |
| | Capt. J.D. Irvin | FW-190 dest(air) | E/Sluis |
| | Lt. A.H. Downing | FW-190 dam(air) | E/Sluis |

**June 13, 1943**

| | | | |
|---|---|---|---|
| 82nd: | Lt. W.T. Hegman | FW-190 prob(air) | Armentiers |
| | Lt. W.D. Wren | FW-190 prob(air) | Armentiers |

**June 22, 1943**

| | | | |
|---|---|---|---|
| HdQts: | Col. A. Peterson | FW-190 dest(air) | N/Walcheren |
| 83rd: | Capt. C.P. London | FW-190 dest(air) | W/Walcheren |
| | F/O H.S. Askelson | FW-190 dest(air) | Walcheren |

**June 24, 1943**

| | | | |
|---|---|---|---|
| 83rd: | Lt. T.W. Shepard | FW-190 dest(air) | Ostend |

**June 29, 1943**

| | | | |
|---|---|---|---|
| 83rd: | Capt. C.P. London | (2)Me-109 dest(air) | Gournay |

**July 1, 1943**

| | | | |
|---|---|---|---|
| 83rd: | Capt. J.C. Davis | FW-190 dest(air) | Schouwen |
| | Lt. W.H. Madole | FW-190 dest(air) | Schouwen |
| | Maj. J.J. Stone | FW-190 prob(air) | W/Schouwen |
| | Capt. J.M. Cooper | FW-190 dam(air) | Schouwen |
| 84th: | Lt. J.F. Byers | FW-190 dest(air) | Brielle |
| | Maj. E.P. Roberts | FW-190 prob(air) | Goederoode |
| | Capt. R.T. Himes | FW-190 dam(air) | Goederoode |

**July 14, 1943**

| | | | |
|---|---|---|---|
| 82nd: | Lt. A.V. DeGenaro | FW-190 dest(air) | Amiens |
| | | FW-190 prob(air) | Amiens |
| | | FW-190 dam(air) | Amiens |
| 83rd: | Capt. C.P. London | Me-109 dam(air) | Le Touquet |
| | | FW-190 dam(air) | Le Touquet |
| 84th: | Capt. J.C. Price | FW-190 dest(air) | N/Abbeville |

**July 29, 1943**

| | | | |
|---|---|---|---|
| 83rd: | Capt. J.M. Cooper | FW-190 dam(air) | Ghent |

**July 30, 1943**

| | | | |
|---|---|---|---|
| 82nd: | Maj. H.J. Dayhuff | Me-109 dest(air) | Haldern |
| | Lt. A.B. Richie | FW-190 dest(air) | Haldern |
| | Lt. A.W. Hill | FW-190 dam(air) | Haldern |
| | Lt. M.R. Wright | FW-190 dam(air) | Haldern |
| 83rd: | Capt. C.P. London | Me-109 dest(air) | Haldern |
| | | FW-190 dest(air) | Haldern |
| | LtCol. J.J. Stone | Me-109 dest(air) | Borkelo |
| | Lt. W.H. Madole | FW-190 dest(air) | Raesfeld |
| 84th: | Maj. E.P. Roberts | (2)FW-190 dest(air) | Winterswijk |
| | | Me-109 dest(air) | Rhenon |
| | Capt. J.D. Irvin | FW-190 dest(air) | Winterswijk |
| | | Me-109 dest(air) | Winterswijk |
| | | FW-190 dam(air) | Winterswijk |
| | Capt. J.C. Price | (2)FW-190 dest(air) | Winterswijk |
| | Lt. J.R. Bertrand | FW-190 dest(air) | Winterswijk |
| | F/O G.W. Koontz | FW-190 dest(air) | Winterswijk |
| | F/O P.E. Pompetti | Me-109 dest(air) | Didam |
| | Lt. C.W. Silsby | Me-109 dam(air) | Winterswijk |

**August 17, 1943**

| | | | |
|---|---|---|---|
| 84th: | Maj. E.P. Roberts | Me-110 dest(air) | SE Aachen |
| | F/O P.E. Pompetti | Me-210 dest(air) | SE Aachen |

**August 19, 1943**

| | | | |
|---|---|---|---|
| 83rd: | Lt. K.W. Dougherty | Me-109 dest(air) | Woensdrecht |
| | Lt. D. Bodenhamer | Me-109 dam(air) | Woensdrecht |

**August 24, 1943**

| | | | |
|---|---|---|---|
| 83rd: | Lt. W.H. Madole | (3)FW-190 dam(air) | Evreux |
| 84th: | Maj. E.P. Roberts | Me-109 dest(air) | Rouen-Evreux |
| | | FW-190 dest(air) | Rouen-Evreux |

**September 27, 1943**

| | | | |
|---|---|---|---|
| 82nd: | Maj. J.J. Oberhansly | Me-109 dest(air) | Emden |
| | | Me-109 prob(air) | Emden |
| | F/O M.S. Martinez | Me-109 dest(air) | Emden |
| 83rd: | Maj. J.C. Davis | Me-109 dest(air) | Emden |
| | Lt. E.W. Powell | Me-109 dest(air) | Emden |
| 84th: | Lt. P.E. Pompetti | Me-109 dest(air) | NW Emden |
| | | Me-110 dest(air) | NW Emden |
| | Capt. J.D. Irvin | Me-109 dest(air) | NW Emden |
| | Capt. H.E. Stump | Me-109 dest(air) | NW Emden |
| | Lt. Q.L. Brown | Me-109 dest(air) | NW Emden |
| | Lt. W.W. Dougherty | Me-109 prob(air) | NW Emden |

**October 10, 1943**

| | | | |
|---|---|---|---|
| HdQts: | Maj. E.P. Roberts | Me-110 dest(air) | W/Enschede |
| | | Me-210 dest(air) | W/Enschede |
| 84th: | Lt. C.W. Silsby | Me-110 dest(air) | Ochtrup |
| | | Me-210 dest(air) | Ochtrup |
| | Lt. P.L. Larson | Me-110 dest(air) | Ochtrup |

**October 20, 1943**

| | | | |
|---|---|---|---|
| HdQts: | LtCol. E.P. Roberts | Me-109 dest(air) | Dinant |
| 84th: | Capt. J.C. Price | Me-109 dam(air) | Dinant |

**October 24, 1943**

| | | | |
|---|---|---|---|
| 82nd: | Capt. W.E. May | (.5)Me-109 dest(air) | St. Gaillon |
| | Lt. A.W. Hill | (.5)Me-109 dest(air) | St. Gallion |

**November 3, 1943**

| | | | |
|---|---|---|---|
| 82nd: | Lt. C.B. Hahn | Me-109 dest(air) | Barzal |
| | Lt. N.D. Munson | Me-109 dam(air) | Barzal |
| | Lt. W.S. Swanson | Me-109 dam(air) | Barzal |

**November 26, 1943**

| | | | |
|---|---|---|---|
| 82nd: | Lt. W.M. Wesson | FW-190 dest(air) | Beauvais |
| 83rd: | Lt. H.S. Askelson | Me-109 dest(air) | Paris |
| 84th: | Maj. J.C. Price | FW-190 dest(air) | Paris |
| | | Me-109 dest(air) | Paris |

**November 30, 1943**

| | | | |
|---|---|---|---|
| 82nd: | Maj. J.J. Oberhansly | FW-190 dest(air) | Eupen |
| | Lt. C.G. Godard | Me-109 prob(air) | Eupen |
| | Lt. M.R. Wright | Me-109 dam(air) | Eupen |

**December 1, 1943**

| | | | |
|---|---|---|---|
| 82nd: | Lt. J.W. Wilkinson | Me-109 dest(air) | Eupen |
| 83rd: | Lt. H.C. Roff | Me-110 prob(air) | Duren |
| 84th: | Lt. C.N. Keppler | FW-190 dest(air) | Liege-Aachen |
| | Lt. G.H. Doyle | (2)FW-190 prob(air) | Liege-Aachen |
| | Lt. P.E. Pompetti | FW-190 dam(air) | Liege-Aachen |
| | Lt. E.E. Russell | FW-190 dam(air) | SE Aachen |

**December 11, 1943**

| | | | |
|---|---|---|---|
| 84th: | Lt. G.W. Koontz | Me-109 dest(air) | SW Groningen |
| | Lt. E.F. Fleming | Me-109 dam(air) | SW Groningen |

**December 20, 1943**

| | | | |
|---|---|---|---|
| 83rd: | Lt. H.T. Barnaby | Me-109 dest(air) | SW Bremen |

**December 22, 1943**

| | | | |
|---|---|---|---|
| 83rd: | Lt. M.D. Putnam | Me-109 dest(air) | W/Munster |
| | | Me-109 dam(air) | W/Munster |

**December 30, 1943**

| | | | |
|---|---|---|---|
| 82nd: | Lt. W.T. Hegman | Me-109 dest(air) | Reims |
| | Lt. M.S. Martinez | Me-109 dest(air) | Reims |
| | Lt. W.M. Wesson | Me-109 dest(air) | Reims |
| 83rd: | Lt. W.H. Julian | Me-109 dest(air) | Reims |

**December 31, 1943**

| | | | |
|---|---|---|---|
| 83rd: | Lt. W.H. Julian | FW-190 dest(air) | NE Lorient |
| | Lt. H.C. Roff | FW-190 dest(air) | NE Lorient |
| | | FW-190 dam(air) | NE Lorient |

**January 4, 1944**

| | | | |
|---|---|---|---|
| 82nd: | Lt. M.S. Martinez | Me-109 dest(air) | Antwerp |
| | | Me-110 dam(air) | Antwerp |
| 83rd: | Lt. H.C. Roff | FW-190 dest(air) | Munster |
| | Lt. J.E. Stokes | FW-190 dest(air) | Munster |
| 84th: | Lt. Q.L. Brown | (2)FW-190 dest(air) | Coesfeld |
| | Lt. P.E. Pompetti | Me-109 dest(air) | Coesfeld |
| | | FW-190 dam(air) | Coesfeld |

**January 5, 1944**

| | | | |
|---|---|---|---|
| 84th: | Lt. Q.L. Brown | Me-109 dest(air) | La Rochelle |
| | Lt. P.L. Larson | Me-109 dest(air) | La Rochelle |
| | Lt. R.E. Smith | Me-109 dam(air) | La Rochelle |

**January 14, 1944**

| | | | |
|---|---|---|---|
| 84th: | Lt. P.E. Pompetti | Me-109 dam(air) | NE Lille |

**January 24, 1944**

| | | | |
|---|---|---|---|
| 82nd: | Lt. J.J. Hockery | Me-110 dest(air) | Engheim |
| | Lt. C.R. Clark | Me-110 dam(air) | Engheim |
| 83rd: | Lt. R.H. Knapp | FW-190 dest(air) | Liege |

**January 29, 1944**

| | | | |
|---|---|---|---|
| HdQts: | LtCol. H.J. Dayhuff | (.5)FW-190 dest(air) | Coblenz |
| 82nd: | Lt. M.S. Martinez | FW-190 dest(air) | Coblenz |
| | Lt. W.S. Swanson | FW-190 dest(air) | Coblenz |
| | Lt. V.Y. Jones | (.5)FW-190 dest(air) | Coblenz |
| | | FW-190 prob(air) | Coblenz |

**January 30, 1944**

| | | | |
|---|---|---|---|
| 84th: | Lt. Q.L. Brown | Me-109 dest(air) | Rheine |

**February 5, 1944**

| | | | |
|---|---|---|---|
| 84th: | Lt. L.J. Abel | FW-190 dam(air) | Bernay |
| | Lt. E.S. Lang | (.5)FW-190 dam(air) | Bernay |
| | Lt. P.E. Pompetti | (.5)FW-190 dam(air) | Bernay |

**February 6, 1944**

| | | | |
|---|---|---|---|
| 82nd: | Lt. W.M. Wesson | FW-190 dest(air) | All claims are |
| | | (2)He-111 dam(grd) | at Orleans |
| | Lt. J.W. Wilkinson | FW-190 dest(air) | |
| | | (.5)He-111 dam(grd) | |
| | | (.5)Ju-52 dam(grd) | |
| | F/O J.E. Brasher | (2)He-111 dam(grd) | |
| | Lt. D.E. Ludwig | (.5)He-111 dam(grd) | |
| | | (.5)Ju-52 dam(grd) | |
| 84th: | Lt. P.E. Pompetti | Hs-129 dest(grd) | Orleans/Bricy |
| | | Ju-88 dam(grd) | Orleans/Bricy |

**February 8, 1944**

| | | | |
|---|---|---|---|
| 82nd: | Lt. W.M. Wesson | He-177 dest(grd) | All claims are |
| | | He-111 dest(grd) | at Paris |
| | Lt. J.W. Wilkinson | (2)He-111 dam(grd) | |
| | Lt. C. Webb | (2)He-111 dam(grd) | |
| | Lt. P. Keller | He-111 dam(grd) | |

**February 10, 1944**

| | | | |
|---|---|---|---|
| 82nd: | Lt. G.M. Turley | (2)Me-109 dest(air) | Osnabruck |
| | Lt. V.Y. Jones | Me-109 dest(air) | Rheine |
| | Lt. W.M. Wesson | FW-190 dest(air) | Osnabruck |
| 83rd: | Lt. H.T. Barnaby | FW-190 dest(air) | Lingen |
| | | Me-109 dest(air) | Lingen |
| | | Me-109 dam(air) | Lingen |
| | F/O E.J. Downey | FW-190 dest(air) | Lingen |
| | Lt. H.C. Roff | Me-109 dest(air) | Lingen |
| | Lt. W.H. Waldheim | Me-109 dest(air) | Lingen |
| 84th: | Lt. G.H. Doyle | Ju-88 dam(grd) | Soesterberg |
| | Lt. R.E. Smith | Ju-88 dam(grd) | Soesterberg |

**February 11, 1944**

| | | | |
|---|---|---|---|
| 82nd: | Lt. G.M. Turley | Me-109 dest(air) | Verdun |
| | | FW-190 dest(air) | Verdun |
| | Lt. J.E. Brasher | Me-109 dest(air) | NE Luxembourg |
| | Lt. J.J. Hockery | Me-109 dest(air) | NW Luxembourg |
| | Lt. C. Webb | FW-190 dam(air) | Rouen |

**February 13, 1944**

| | | | |
|---|---|---|---|
| 82nd: | Capt. W.L. Boone | Ju-88 dam(grd) | Bryes-Sud A/F |
| | Lt. J.E. Brasher | Ju-88 dam(grd) | Bryes-Sud A/F |
| | Lt. W.M. Wesson | Ju-88 dam(grd) | Bryes-Sud A/F |

**February 20, 1944**

| | | | |
|---|---|---|---|
| HdQts: | Col. J.J. Stone | FW-190 dam(air) | Coblenz |
| 82nd: | Lt. J.J. Hockery | FW-190 dest(air) | Coblenz |
| | Lt. G.M. Turley | FW-190 dest(air) | Coblenz |
| | Lt. J.W. Wilkinson | Me-109 dest(air) | Coblenz |

**February 22, 1944**

| | | | |
|---|---|---|---|
| 82nd: | Maj. J.J. Oberhansly | FW-190 dest(air) | Gilze-Rijen |
| | | FW-190 dest(air) | Walcheren |
| | | Me-109 dest(air) | Cologne |
| | | Me-109 dam(air) | Cologne |
| 83rd: | Capt. K.W. Dougherty | Me-109 dest(air) | Nijmegen |
| | | Me-109 prob(air) | Nijmegen |
| | Lt. J.H. Johnson | FW-190 dest(air) | Dusseldorf |
| | | FW-190 dam(air) | Dusseldorf |
| | Lt. A.M. Juchheim | Me-109 dest(air) | E/Eindhoven |
| | | FW-190 dam(air) | E/Eindhoven |
| | Lt. C.W. Hotchkiss | FW-190 dest(air) | Walcheren |
| | Lt. W.M. McDermott | FW-190 dest(air) | Nijmegen |
| | Lt. V.J. Massa | Me-109 dam(air) | Aachen |
| | Lt. H.C. Roff | FW-190 dam(air) | Nijmegen |
| | Lt. H.R. Zumwalt | Me-109 dam(air) | Aachen |

**February 24, 1944**

| | | | |
|---|---|---|---|
| 82nd: | Lt. G.M. Turley | Me-109 dest(air) | Dummer Lake |
| 83rd: | Lt. A.M. Juchheim | (2)Me-109 dest(air) | Furstenau |
| | Lt. R.E. Wise | FW-190 dest(air) | Furstenau |
| | | u/i a/c dam(grd) | Furstenau |
| | Lt. R.B. Hathway | Me-109 dest(air) | Furstenau |
| | Lt. C.M. Peal | Me-109 dest(air) | Furstenau |
| | Lt. W. Tonkin | FW-190 dest(air) | Furstenau |
| | Lt. H.C. Roff | Me-109 prob(air) | Furstenau |

**February 25, 1944**

| | | | |
|---|---|---|---|
| 83rd: | Capt. K.W. Dougherty | Me-109 dest(air) | Boekingen |

**March 2, 1944**

| | | | |
|---|---|---|---|
| 84th: | Lt. E.S. Lang | (.5)Hs-126 dest(grd) | Chartres |
| | | (.5)Ju-52 dest(grd) | Chartres |
| | Lt. P.E. Pompetti | (.5)Hs-126 dest(grd) | Chartres |
| | | (.5)Ju-52 dest(grd) | Chartres |

**March 6, 1944**

| | | | |
|---|---|---|---|
| 82nd: | Capt. J.W. Wilkinson | FW-190 dest(air) | Barenburg |
| | Lt. R.P. Spalding | FW-190 dest(air) | Barenburg |
| | Lt. R.L. Wolfe | FW-190 dam(air) | Barenburg |
| 83rd: | Lt. W. Tonkin | Me-109 dam(air) | NE Dummer Lake |
| | Lt. R.E. Wise | Me-109 dam(air) | NE Dummer Lake |

**March 8, 1944**

| | | | |
|---|---|---|---|
| 84th: | Lt. E.S. Lang | (.5)FW-190 dam(grd) | Bohmte |
| | Lt. P.E. Pompetti | (.5)FW-190 dam(grd) | Bohmte |

**March 15, 1944**

| | | | |
|---|---|---|---|
| 84th: | Lt. Q.L. Brown | Me-109 dest(air) | W/Munster |
| | Lt. R.E. Smith | Me-109 dest(air) | W/Munster |

**March 16, 1944**

| | | | |
|---|---|---|---|
| 82nd: | Lt. R.A. Hewitt | Me-109 dest(air) | Strasbourg |
| | | Me-109 dam(air) | Strasbourg |
| 83rd: | Lt. A.B. Werder | FW-190 dam(air) | Chievres |
| 84th: | Lt. Q.L. Brown | (2)Me-109 dest(air) | St. Dizier |
| | | FW-190 dest(air) | St. Dizier |
| | | Ju-88 dest(grd) | St. Dizier |
| | | (2)u/i a/c dam(grd) | St. Dizier |
| | Lt. J.P. Maxwell | Me-109 dest(air) | St. Dizier |
| | | Me-109 dam(air) | St. Dizier |
| | Lt. E.E. Russell | Me-110 dest(grd) | St. Dizier |
| | Lt. E.S. Lang | Me-210 dam(grd) | S/Nancy |
| | | Me-110 dam(grd) | S/Nancy |
| | Lt. P.E. Pompetti | Me-109 dam(grd) | S/Nancy |

**March 17, 1944**

| | | | |
|---|---|---|---|
| 83rd: | Lt. B.W. Sorenson | (.5)Do-217 dest(grd) | N/Reims |
| | Lt. W.H. Waldheim | (.5)Do-217 dest(grd) | N/Reims |
| | | (4)Bu-133 dam(grd) | N/Reims |
| | | Do-217 dam(grd) | N/Reims |
| | Lt. R.B. Hathway | u/i a/c dam(grd) | N/Reims |
| 84th: | Lt. E.S. Lang | (.5)He-111 dam(grd) | Beauvais |
| | Lt. P.E. Pompetti | (.5)He-111 dam(grd) | Beauvais |

**March 23, 1944**

| | | | |
|---|---|---|---|
| 84th: | Lt. Q.L. Brown | FW-190 dest(air) | Goch |
| | Lt. L.J. Abel | Me-410 dest(grd) | Brussels |
| | | (3)Me-410 dam(grd) | Brussels |

**March 24, 1944**

| | | | |
|---|---|---|---|
| 82nd: | Lt. J.J. Hockery | Ju-188 dest(air) | Paris |
| 84th: | Capt. G.H. Doyle | Ju-52 dest(grd) | Beaumont Sur Oise |
| | | Ju-52 dam(grd) | Beaumont Sur Oise |
| | Lt. J.F. Casey | u/i a/c dest(grd) | St. Dizier |
| | Lt. R.E. Belliveau | Ju-52 dam(grd) | Beaumont Sur Oise |
| | F/O J.W. Mundy | Ju-52 dam(grd) | Beaumont Sur Oise |

**March 30, 1944**

| | | | |
|---|---|---|---|
| 82nd: | Lt. J.J. Bernhard | Glider dam(grd) | Wesel |
| | Lt. J.W. Wilkinson | Glider dam(grd) | Wesel |
| 83rd: | Lt. P.C. Holden | Me-109 dest(grd) | N/Venlo |
| | Lt. C.M. Peal | Me-410 dam(grd) | N/Venlo |
| 84th: | Lt. L.J. Abel | (.33)Do-217 dest(air) | Twente/Enschede |
| | Lt. Q.L. Brown | (.33)Do-217 dest(air) | Twente/Enschede |
| | Lt. E.S. Lang | (.33)Do-217 dest(air) | Twente/Enschede |
| | Lt. H.H. Just | Me-323 dam(grd) | Deelan |

**April 1, 1944**

| | | | |
|---|---|---|---|
| 82nd: | Lt. P.H. Hazelett | Ju-87 dest(grd) | All claims are |
| | | u/i a/c dest(grd) | at Verdun |
| | Lt. K.R. Wagner | He-111 dest(grd) | |
| | Capt. W.L. Boone | (.67)u/i a/c dest(grd) | |
| | | (.12)Do-217 dest(grd) | |
| | | Me-410 dam(grd) | |
| | | Ju-52 dam(grd) | |
| | Lt. B.M. Watkins | (.67)u/i a/c dest(grd) | |
| | | (.12)Do-217 dest(grd) | |
| | | (2)u/i a/c dam(grd) | |
| | Capt. W.E. May | (.12)Do-217 dest(grd) | |
| | Lt. C.R. Clark | (.12)Do-217 dest(grd) | |
| | Lt. H.L. Eakes | (.12)Do-217 dest(grd) | |
| | Lt. J.J. Hockery | (.12)Do-217 dest(grd) | |
| | Lt. R.V. Hearn | (.12)Do-217 dest(grd) | |
| | Lt. C. Webb | (.67)u/i a/c dest(grd) | |
| | F/O C.W. DeWitt | (.12)Do-217 dest(grd) | |
| | | He-111 dam(grd) | |
| | Lt. D.D. Hagarty | (2)Do-217 dam(grd) | |
| | Lt. C.G. Godard | Ju-88 dam(grd) | |

**April 5, 1944**

| | | | |
|---|---|---|---|
| 82nd: | Lt. H.L. Eakes | (.33)Go-242 dest(grd) | All claims are |
| | | (.33)DFS-230 dest(grd) | at Ruwer |
| | Lt. J.J. Hockery | (.33)Go-242 dest(grd) | |
| | | (.33)DFS-230 dest(grd) | |
| | F/O C.W. DeWitt | (.33)Go-242 dest(grd) | |
| | | (.33)DFS-230 dest(grd) | |
| | Lt. M.K. Woller | Go-242 dam(grd) | |
| | | DFS-230 dam(grd) | |
| | Capt. W.E. May | Go-242 dam(grd) | |
| | Lt. J.E. Brasher | Go-242 dam(grd) | |
| | Lt. P.H. Hazelett | Go-242 dam(grd) | |
| | Lt. R.A. Hewitt | Go-242 dam(grd) | |
| | Lt. J.W. Wilkinson | Ju-188 dam(grd) | Cambrai |

**April 8, 1944**

| | | | |
|---|---|---|---|
| 82nd: | Maj. J.J. Oberhansly | Me-109 dest(grd) | All claims are |
| | | (.6)Me-110 dest(grd) | at Trier |
| | | Ju-52 dam(grd) | |
| | Capt. N.D. Munson | (1.6)Me-110 dest(grd) | |
| | | (.33)Ar-196 dest(grd) | |
| | Lt. J.E. Brasher | (.6)Me-110 dest(grd) | |
| | | (.33)Ar-196 dest(grd) | |
| | | Ju-52 dam(grd) | |
| | Lt. R.A. Hewitt | Ju-52 dest(grd) | |
| | | (.33)Ar-196 dest(grd) | |
| | Lt. M.K. Woller | (.6)Me-110 dest(grd) | |
| | | Ju-52 dam(grd) | |
| | F/O C.W. DeWitt | (.6)Me-110 dest(grd) | |
| 84th: | F/O J.W. Mundy | FW-190 dam(air) | Antwerp |
| | Lt. W.F. Hunt | (3)Glider dam(grd) | NE Frankfurt |
| | Lt. M.H. Smith | (2)Glider dam(grd) | NE Frankfurt |
| | Lt. J.O. Patton | u/i a/c dam(grd) | NE Frankfurt |
| | Lt. R.E. Smith | Glider dam(grd) | NE Franlfurt |

**April 9, 1944**

| | | | |
|---|---|---|---|
| 82nd: | Capt. W.E. May | FW-190 dest(air) | Dummer Lake |

**April 10, 1944**

| | | | |
|---|---|---|---|
| 83rd: | Lt. A.M. Juchheim | (3)FW-190 dest(grd) | All claims are |
| | | Hs-123 dest(grd) | at Romorantin |
| | Lt. C.M. Peal | (3)Bu-133 dest(grd) | |
| | | Me-109 dest(grd) | |
| | | Bu-133 dam(grd) | |
| | Lt. H.L. Blystone | (2)u/i a/c dest(grd) | |
| | Lt. K.C. Allstaedt | FW-190 dest(grd) | |
| | | Trainer dest(grd) | |
| | | Trainer dam(grd) | |
| | Lt. P.C. Holden | FW-190 dest(grd) | |
| | | u/i a/c dam(grd) | |

**April 11, 1944**

| | | | |
|---|---|---|---|
| 82nd: | Lt. J.W. Wilkinson | Ju-88 dest(grd) | Rheine |
| | | (2)Ju-88 dam(grd) | Rheine |
| | Lt. B.M. Watkins | u/i a/c dam(grd) | Osnabruck |
| 83rd: | Lt. A.M. Juchheim | FW-190 dest(air) | Luneburg |
| | | FW-190 prob(air) | Luneburg |
| 84th: | Capt. G.H. Doyle | Me-109 dam(air) | Hanover |

**April 12, 1944**

| | | | |
|---|---|---|---|
| 82nd: | Capt. J.J. Hockery | Ju-87 dest(air) | Sedan |
| | Lt. D.D. Hagarty | Ju-87 dest(air) | Sedan |
| | | Ju-87 dam(air) | Sedan |
| | Lt. J.T. Lamb | Ju-87 dest(air) | Sedan |
| | | Ju-87 dam(grd) | Sedan |
| | Lt. K.R. Wagner | FW-190 dest(air) | Malmedy |
| | Lt. B.M. Watkins | Ju-87 dest(air) | Sedan |
| | | (3)Ju-87 dam(grd) | Sedan |
| | Maj. L.P. Marshall | (.33)FW-190 dest(air) | Malmedy |
| | Lt. R.L. Baker | (.33)FW-190 dest(air) | Malmedy |
| | Lt. G.J. Lundigan | (.33)FW-190 dest(air) | Malmedy |
| | Lt. J.W. Wilkinson | (2)Me-109 dam(grd) | Florennes |
| 84th: | Capt. Q.L. Brown | FW-190 dest(air) | Duren |

**April 13, 1944**

| | | | |
|---|---|---|---|
| 83rd: | Lt. A.M. Juchheim | FW-190 dest(air) | Beuchenbeuren |
| | | FW-190 dest(grd) | Beuchenbeuren |
| | Lt. C.M. Peal | FW-190 dest(air) | Beuchenbeuren |
| | Lt. G. Riccardo | FW-190 dam(air) | Korbach |
| | Lt. H.R. Zumwalt | FW-190 dam(air) | NE Trier |

**April 24, 1944**

| | | | |
|---|---|---|---|
| 82nd: | Lt. J.E. Brasher | Do-217 dest(grd) | Diest |
| 83rd: | Lt. V.J. Massa | (.5)Me-110 dest(grd) | Trier |
| | Lt. A.M. Juchheim | (.5)Me-110 dest(grd) | Trier |
| | Lt. C.P. Hurst | Do-217 dam(grd) | Diest |
| | | u/i a/c dam(grd) | Diest |

**April 25, 1944**

| | | | |
|---|---|---|---|
| 83rd: | Lt. K.C. Allstaedt | FW-190 dest(air) | S/Verdun |
| | Lt. H.J. Morris | (.5)FW-190 dest(air) | S/Verdun |
| | Lt. B.W. Sorenson | (.5)FW-190 dest(air) | S/Verdun |

**April 28, 1944**

| | | | |
|---|---|---|---|
| 82nd: | Lt. J.J. Bernhard | (2)He-111 dam(grd) | Chateaudun |
| | Lt. R.L. Wolfe | He-111 dam(grd) | Chateaudun |

**April 30, 1944**

| | | | |
|---|---|---|---|
| 83rd: | Lt. A.M. Juchheim | (2)FW-190 dest(air) | Dreux |
| | | FW-190 prob(air) | Dreux |
| | | FW-190 dam(air) | Dreux |
| | Maj. O.E. Gilbert | FW-190 dest(air) | SW Paris |
| | Lt. W.M. McDermott | (.5)FW-190 dest(air) | Dreux |
| | Lt. F. White | (.5)FW-190 dest(air) | Dreux |
| | Lt. E.T. Kitley | (2)FW-190 dam(air) | Dreux |
| | Lt. L.R. Casey | FW-190 dam(air) | Dreux |

**May 8, 1944**

| 83rd: | Lt. P.A. Caulfield | Me-109 dam(air) | Verdun |
|---|---|---|---|
| | Lt. P.C. Holden | Me-109 dam(air) | Verdun |

**May 11, 1944**

| 82nd: | Lt. C.W. DeWitt | u/i a/c dest(grd) | All 82nd claims |
|---|---|---|---|
| | | (3)u/i a/c dam(grd) | are at Dijon |
| | Capt. J.W. Wilkinson | (.5)He-111 dest(grd) | |
| | | (2)u/i a/c dam(grd) | |
| | | Go-242 dam(grd) | |
| | Lt. W.V. Van Dyk | (.5)He-111 dest(grd) | |
| | | (.5)Ju-52 dest(grd) | |
| | Lt. B.M. Watkins | (.5)Ju-52 dest(grd) | |
| | | (3)u/i a/c dam(grd) | |
| | Lt. P.H. Hazelett | Go-242 dam(grd) | |
| 83rd: | Lt. F.R. Pursell | FW-190 dest(air) | Montargis |
| | Lt. W.M. McDermott | FW-190 dam(air) | Montgaris |
| 84th: | Lt. R.J. McIntosh | FW-190 dest(air) | W/Orleans |
| | | FW-190 dam(air) | W/Orleans |
| | Lt. J.B. Putnam | FW-190 dest(air) | Orleans |

**May 12, 1944**

| 82nd: | Lt. D.D. Hagarty | (2)FW-190 dest(air) | Trier |
|---|---|---|---|
| | Capt. J.W. Wilkinson | FW-190 dest(air) | Coblenz |
| | Lt. M.R. Capp | FW-190 dest(air) | Coblenz |
| | Lt. R.L. Baker | FW-190 dest(air) | Coblenz |
| | Lt. B.M. Watkins | FW-190 dest(air) | Coblenz |

**May 19, 1944**

| 82nd: | Lt. M.K. Woller | (2)Me-109 dest(air) | Dummer Lake |
|---|---|---|---|
| | Capt. J.W. Wilkinson | FW-190 dest(air) | Dummer Lake |
| | | FW-190 dam(air) | Dummer Lake |
| | Lt. M.R. Capp | Me-109 dest(air) | Dummer Lake |
| | Lt. H.B. Slater | Me-109 dam(air) | Dummer Lake |
| | Lt. C.W. DeWitt | FW-190 dam(air) | Dummer Lake |
| | Lt. R.L. Baker | Me-109 dam(air) | Dummer Lake |
| | | Me-110 dest(grd) | Dummer Lake |
| | | Me-110 dest(grd) | Plantlunne |
| | Lt. K.R. Wagner | Me-109 dam(air) | Dummer Lake |
| 82nd: | Lt. P.H. Hazelett | Me-110 dest(grd) | Plantlunne |
| | Capt. W.A. Guilfoyle | (.5)He-111 dam(grd) | Plantlunne |
| | Lt. L.H. Hosford | (.5)He-111 dam(grd) | Plantlunne |
| 83rd: | Capt. R.E. Ealey | Me-109 dest(air) | Lingen |
| | Lt. P.C. Holden | Me-109 dest(air) | Lingen |
| | Lt. F. White | Me-109 dest(air) | Lingen |
| 84th: | Capt. W.F. Hunt | Me-109 dest(air) | E/Nienburg |
| | Lt. H.L. Boyle | FW-190 dest(air) | Quackenbruck |
| | Lt. L.K. Covelle | Me-109 dest(air) | Nienburg |
| | Lt. R.M. Holly | Me-109 dest(air) | Nienburg |
| | Lt. W.J. Luckey | Me-109 dest(air) | Nienburg |

**May 25, 1944**

| 82nd: | Capt. J.W. Wilkinson | (.5)FW-190 dest(grd) | Metz |
|---|---|---|---|
| | Lt. R.E. Wilkinson | (.5)FW-190 dest(grd) | Metz |
| 83rd: | Capt. A.M. Juchheim | Me-109 dest(air) | SE St. Dizier |
| | | (.5)He-111 dest(grd) | St. Dizier |
| | Lt. W.M. McDermott | Me-109 dest(air) | St. Dizier |
| | Lt. L.R. Casey | (.5)He-111 dest(grd) | St. Dizier |
| 84th: | Lt. R.E. Belliveau | Me-109 dam(air) | Chaumont |
| | F/O H.W. Kramer | FW-190 dam(grd) | Paris |

**May 27, 1944**

| 83rd: | Capt. A.M. Juchheim | Me-109 dest(air) | Frieburg |
|---|---|---|---|

**May 28, 1944**

| 82nd: | Lt. C.W. DeWitt | Ju-52 dam(grd) | Hanover |
|---|---|---|---|
| 83rd: | Lt. W.M. McDermott | (.5)Me-109 dest(air) | Gardelegen |
| | Lt. F. White | (.5)Me-109 dest(air) | Gardelegen |

**May 29, 1944**

| 82nd: | Capt. J.W. Wilkinson | FW-190 dam(grd) | Twente-Enschede |
|---|---|---|---|

**June 6, 1944**

| HdQts: | Col. F.C. Gray | (.5)FW-190 dest(air) | Mayenne |
|---|---|---|---|
| 83rd: | Lt. P.A. Caulfield | FW-190 dest(air) | Mayenne |
| | Lt. V.J. Massa | (.5)FW-190 dest(air) | Mayenne |

**June 7, 1944**

| 84th: | Capt. B.I. Mayo | Me-109 dest(air) | S/Montdidier |
|---|---|---|---|
| | Lt. L.K. Covelle | Me-109 dest(air) | Montdidier |
| | Lt. D. Ledington | Me-109 dest(air) | Montdidier |
| | Lt. D.T. Loyd | Me-109 dest(air) | Montdidier |
| | Lt. W.J. Hardin | Me-109 dam(air) | Montdidier |

**June 8, 1944**

| 84th: | Lt. J.F. Casey | Me-109 dam(air) | W/Gourey |
|---|---|---|---|

**June 10, 1944**

| 83rd: | Maj. D.W. McLeod | (2)Me-109 dest(air) | S/Lisieux |
|---|---|---|---|
| | | (2)Me-109 dam(air) | S/Lisieux |
| | Capt. R.E. Ealey | Me-109 dest(air) | Argentan |
| | Lt. F.R. Pursell | FW-190 dest(air) | Argentan |
| | | FW-190 dam(air) | Argentan |
| | Lt. R.B. Hathway | FW-190 dam(air) | Argentan |
| 84th: | Lt. L.J. Abel | Me-109 dest(air) | La Ferte Mace |
| | Lt. D. Ledington | Me-109 dest(air) | La Ferte Mace |
| | Lt. R.J. McIntosh | FW-190 dest(air) | La Ferte Mace |

**June 13, 1944**

| 83rd: | Maj. O.E. Gilbert | FW-190 dest(air) | Orleans |
|---|---|---|---|
| | Lt. P.C. Holden | Me-109 dest(air) | Orleans |

**June 17, 1944**

| 83rd: | Lt. E.T. Kitley | FW-190 dest(air) | S/Laigle |
|---|---|---|---|
| | Lt. K.C. Allstaedt | (.5)FW-190 dest(air) | Laigle |
| | Lt. R.W. Oxley | (.5)FW-190 dest(air) | Laigle |

**June 20, 1944**

| 82nd: | Capt. B.I. Mayo | Me-109 dest(air) | Montdidier |
|---|---|---|---|
| 83rd: | Lt. G.G. Boteler | (.5)Me-109 dest(air) | Amiens |
| | Lt. P.C. Holden | (.5)Me-109 dest(air) | Amiens |
| 84th: | Lt. W.K. Dacci | Me-109 dest(air) | Montdidier |

**June 30, 1944**

| 82nd: | Lt. H.K. Shope | Me-109 dest(grd) | Meilleray |
|---|---|---|---|

**July 1, 1944**

| 82nd: | Lt. H.F. Scholz | FW-190 dest(air) | Reims |
|---|---|---|---|
| | Capt. B.I. Mayo | FW-190 dam(air) | St. Quentin |
| 83rd: | Lt. R.E. Mullins | Me-109 dam(air) | Cambrai |
| 84th: | Capt. H.T. Lay | Me-109 dest(air) | St. Quentin |
| | Lt. W.J. Luckey | Me-109 dest(air) | St. Quentin |
| | Capt. A.F. Eaton | Me-109 dam(air) | St. Quentin |

**July 5, 1944**

| 83rd: | Maj. W.H. Julian | FW-190 dest(air) | Evreux |
|---|---|---|---|
| | Lt. G. Riccardo | FW-190 prob(air) | Evreux |
| | Capt. D.A. Lawhead | (2)FW-190 dam(air) | Evreux |
| | Lt. R.R. Bonebrake | FW-190 dam(air) | Evreux |

**July 6, 1944**

| 83rd: | Lt. F.E. Higginbottom | FW-190 dest(air) | Rambouillet |
|---|---|---|---|
| | Lt. F.R. Pursell | FW-190 dest(air) | Rambouillet |
| | Capt. D.A. Lawhead | FW-190 prob(air) | Rambouillet |
| | Lt. H.L. Blystone | FW-190 dam(air) | Rambouillet |
| 84th: | Capt. H.T. Lay | FW-190 dest(air) | NW Paris |
| | Lt. C.E. Parmelee | FW-190 dest(air) | NW Paris |
| | Lt. J.B. Putnam | FW-190 dest(air) | NW Paris |

**July 19, 1944**

| 82nd: | Maj. N.D. Munson | (2.5)u/i a/c dest(grd) | Stuttgart |
|---|---|---|---|
| | Lt. J.R. Kinsolving | Ju-52 dest(grd) | Stuttgart |
| | | (.5)u/i a/c dest(grd) | Stuttgart |
| 83rd: | Lt. E.H. Miller | (2)Ju-188 dest(grd) | All 83rd claims |
| | Lt. B.W. Sorenson | (2)Ju 188 dest(grd) | are at Linburg- |
| | | Ju-188 dam(grd) | Coblenz |
| | Capt. R.W. Smith | Ju-188 dest(grd) | |
| | | (2)Ju-188 dam(grd) | |
| | Capt. R.R. Bonebrake | Do-217 dest(grd) | |
| | Lt. J.B. Miller | Ju-188 dest(grd) | |
| | Lt. G. Riccardo | Ju-188 dest(grd) | |
| | | Ju-188 dam(grd) | |
| | Lt. F.E. Higginbottom | (2)Ju-188 dam(grd) | |
| | Lt. R.W. Oxley | Ju-188 dam(grd) | |
| 84th: | Maj. B.I. Mayo | (1.5)Do-217 dest(grd) | All 84th claims |
| | | u/i a/c dest(grd) | are at Eutingen |
| | Capt. A.F. Eaton | (1.5)Do-217 dest(grd) | |
| | | Me-410 dest(grd) | |
| | F/O A.G. McGuire | Me-110 dest(grd) | |
| | | Do-217 dam(grd) | |
| | Lt. C.E. Parmelee | Do-217 dest(grd) | |
| | Lt. J.B. Putnam | Ju-188 dest(grd) | |
| | Lt. S.B. Calderon | Do-217 dam(grd) | |
| | | Ju-87 dam(grd) | |

**July 31, 1944**

| 83rd: | Lt. W.E. Bennett | u/i a/c dest(grd) | Neustadt |
|---|---|---|---|
| | Lt. W.J. Korsmeyer | u/i a/c dest(grd) | Neustadt |
| | Lt. J.S. Reems | u/i a/c dest(grd) | Neustadt |

**August 6, 1944**

| 82nd: | Capt. R.E. Conner | (.5)Me-109 dest(air) | Hamburg |
|---|---|---|---|
| | Lt. J.B. Stallings | (.5)Me-109 dest(air) | Hamburg |
| | F/O R.I. Miller | Me-109 dam(air) | Hamburg |
| | Lt. H.K. Shope | Me-109 dam(air) | Hamburg |

**August 10, 1944**

| HdQts: | LtCol. O.E. Gilbert | He-111 dest(grd) | Chateau Salines |
|---|---|---|---|
| | | u/i a/c dest(grd) | Chateau Salines |
| 82nd: | Lt. R.R. Bosworth | Ju-88 dest(grd) | Verdun |
| | Lt. R.W. Dunham | Ju-88 dam(grd) | Verdun |

| Unit | Pilot | Claim | Location |
|---|---|---|---|
| 83rd: | Capt. C.M. Peal | (2.5)Ju-52 dest(grd)[*] | All 83rd claims |
| | | (1.5)He-111 dest(grd)[**] | are at Chateau |
| | Lt. R.T. Green | (1.5)He-111 dest(grd)[**] | Salines |
| | | (.5)Ju-52 dest(grd)[*] | |
| | Capt. R.R. Bonebrake | He-111 dest(grd) | |
| | | Ju-52 dest(grd) | |
| | Lt. R.L. Burgher | He-111 dest(grd) | |
| | | (.5)Ju-52 dest(grd)[@] | |
| | Lt. J.S. Reems | He-111 dest(grd) | |
| | | (.5)Ju-52 dest(grd)[@] | |
| | Lt. D.J. DeVillers | He-111 dest(grd) | |
| | Lt. G. Riccardo | (.5)He-111 dest(grd)[@@] | |
| | | u/i a/c dam(grd) | |
| | F/O J.A. Moothart | (.5)He-111 dest(grd)[@@] | |
| | Lt. K.P. Dunaway | He-111 dam(grd) | |
| | | Ju-52 dam(grd) | |
| | Lt. J.B. Miller | u/i a/c dam(grd) | |
| 84th: | Lt. H.F. Beck | (1.5)Ju-88 dest(grd) | Conflans |
| | Lt. W.K. Grimes | Me-109 dest(grd) | Conflans |
| | | (.5)Ju-88 dest(grd) | Conflans |

**August 11, 1944**

| Unit | Pilot | Claim | Location |
|---|---|---|---|
| 84th: | Lt. C.E. Parmelee | (2)Me-109 dest(air) | NW Paris |

**August 17, 1944**

| Unit | Pilot | Claim | Location |
|---|---|---|---|
| 84th: | Lt. R.L. Baron | (.5)Me-109 dest(grd) | W/Chaudun |
| | | Me-109 dam(grd) | W/Chaudun |
| | Capt. R.E. Smith | (.5)Me-109 dest(grd) | W/Chaudun |
| | | (.5)Me-109 dam(grd) | W/Chaudun |
| | Lt. M.R. Capp | (.5)Me-109 dest(grd) | S/Hamm |
| | Lt. E.H. Schneider | (.5)Me-109 dest(grd) | S/Hamm |
| | Lt. P.H. McKenney | (1.5)Me-109 dam(grd) | W/Chaudun |

**August 27, 1944**

| Unit | Pilot | Claim | Location |
|---|---|---|---|
| 82nd: | Capt. R.E. Conner | Me-110 dest(grd) | Thionville |
| | Lt. R.C. Boeckman | He-111 dest(grd) | Chatel Cherary |
| | Lt. T.L. Eggleston | (.5)He-111 dest(grd) | Chatel Cherary |
| | Lt. R.L. Wolfe | (.5)He-111 dest(grd) | Chatel Cherary |

**August 28, 1944**

| Unit | Pilot | Claim | Location |
|---|---|---|---|
| HdQts: | LtCol. J.J. Oberhansly | Ju-88 dest(air) | Charleroi |
| 82nd: | Maj. J. Myers | (.5)Me-262 dest(air) | Termonde |
| | Lt. M.O. Croy | (.5)Me-262 dest(air) | Termonde |

**September 1, 1944**

| Unit | Pilot | Claim | Location |
|---|---|---|---|
| 83rd: | Lt. G.G. Boteler | Me-110 dest(air) | All 83rd claims |
| | Lt. C.E. Kuykendall | Me-110 dest(air) | are at Gilze- |
| | | Me-110 dam(air) | Rijen |
| | Lt. J. LaGrange | (.5)Me-110 dest(air) | |
| | | (.5)Me-110 dest(air) | |
| | Lt. P. Bingham | (.5)Me-110 dest(air) | |
| | F/O J.A. Moothart | (.5)Me-110 dest(air) | |
| | | Me-110 dam(air) | |
| 84th: | Maj. Q.L. Brown | Me-109 dest(air) | Liege-Trier |
| | Lt. C.E. Parmelee | FW-190 dest(grd) | SW Antwerp |
| | Lt. H.W. Elin | FW-190 dam(grd) | SW Antwerp |

**September 9, 1944**

| Unit | Pilot | Claim | Location |
|---|---|---|---|
| 82nd: | Lt. W.L. Coleman | (3)FW-190 dest(air) | Hersfeld |
| | Lt. H.F. Scholz | (2)FW-190 dest(air) | Giessen |
| | | FW-190 dam(air) | Giessen |
| | | Ju-88 dest(grd) | Munster |
| | Lt. J.L. Mattern | FW-190 dam(air) | Coblenz |
| | Lt. R.W. Dunham | (.5)FW-190 dam(air) | Giessen |
| | Lt. H.K. Shope | Ju-88 dest(grd) | Giessen |
| | Capt. R.E. Conner | (.5)Me-109 dest(grd) | Giessen |
| | Lt. D.C. Hart | (.5)Me-109 dest(grd) | Giessen |
| 84th: | Maj. B.I. Mayo | (2)FW-190 dest(air) | Giessen |
| | Lt. W.K. Grimes | FW-190 dest(air) | Giessen |
| | | (.5)FW-190 dam(air) | Giessen |

**September 10, 1944**

| Unit | Pilot | Claim | Location |
|---|---|---|---|
| 82nd: | Lt. R.R. Bonebrake | (4)Ju-88 dest(grd) | All 82nd claims |
| | Maj. J. Myers | (3)He-111 dest(grd) | are at Meinbullen |
| | | He-111 dam(grd) | |
| | Lt. T.L. Eggleston | (3)He-111 dest(grd) | |
| | Capt. R.A. Hewitt | (2)Ju-88 dest(grd) | |
| | Lt. W.O. Lacy | (2)Ju-88 dest(grd) | |
| | | (2)Ju-88 dam(grd) | |
| | Lt. H.B. Slater | (2)He-111 dest(grd) | |
| | | He-111 dam(grd) | |
| | F/O W.I. Warren | Ju-88 dest(grd) | |
| | Lt. I.H. Keatley | He-111 dam(grd) | |
| 83rd: | Lt. W.B. Sommer | Me-410 dest(grd) | All 83rd claims |
| | | FW-190 dest(grd) | are at Gersheim |
| | Lt. W.E. Bennett | (.5)He-111 dest(grd) | |
| | Lt. D.D. Hartley | (.5)He-111 dest(grd) | |
| | Lt. F.E. Harrington | Me-410 dam(grd) | |
| | | Ju-87 dam(grd) | |
| 84th: | Capt. R.E. Smith | (4.5)He-111 dest(grd)[*] | All 84th claims |
| | | He-111 dam(grd) | are at Meinbullen |
| | Lt. M.R. Capp | (3)He-111 dest(grd) | |
| | | He-111 dam(grd) | |
| | Lt. E.W. Wood | (2)He-111 dest(grd) | |
| | | Fi-156 dest(grd) | |
| | | (2)He-111 dam(grd) | |
| | Lt. A.P. Hanning | (2.5)He-111 dest(grd)[*] | |
| | | He-111 dam(grd) | |
| | Lt. A.G. McGuire | (2)He-111 dest(grd) | |
| | | (4)He-111 dam(grd) | |
| | Lt. R.L. Baron | He-111 dest(grd) | |
| | | He-111 dam(grd) | |
| | Lt. A.A. Garback | He-111 dest(grd) | |
| | | He-111 dam(grd) | |
| | Lt. R.E. Clague | (.5)He-111 dest(grd)[**] | |
| | Lt. M.T. Wilson | (.5)He-111 dest(grd)[**] | |
| | | (4)Ju-88 dam(grd) | |
| | Lt. S.B. Calderon | (2)He-111 dam(grd) | |

**September 17, 1944**

| Unit | Pilot | Claim | Location |
|---|---|---|---|
| 82nd: | Lt. H.K. Shope | Me-109 dest(grd) | Gilze-Rijen |

**October 7, 1944**

| Unit | Pilot | Claim | Location |
|---|---|---|---|
| 82nd: | Maj. R.E. Conner | Me-262 dest(air) | Osnabruck |
| | Maj. J. Myers | Me-109 dest(air) | Leipzig |
| | Lt. R.R. Bosworth | Me-109 dest(air) | Leipzig |
| | Lt. A.S. Miller | Me-109 dam(air) | Leipzig |

**October 12, 1944**

| Unit | Pilot | Claim | Location |
|---|---|---|---|
| 82nd: | Maj. R.E. Conner | FW-190 dest(air) | Hamburg |
| | Lt. H.H. Lamb | Me-109 dest(air) | Hamburg |

**October 15, 1944**

| Unit | Pilot | Claim | Location |
|---|---|---|---|
| 82nd: | Lt. H.H. Lamb | Me-262 dest(air) | Bohmte |
| 83rd: | Lt. R.T. Green | (3.5)FW-190 dest(air) | Bohmte |
| | Lt. J.S. Reems | (1.5)FW-190 dest(air) | Bohmte |
| | F/O L.L. Eadline | FW-190 dest(air) | Bohmte |
| | Lt. H.O. Foster | Me-262 dam(air) | Bohmte |
| | Lt. F.E. Harrington | FW-190 dam(air) | Bohmte |
| | Lt. W.B. Sommer | Me-109 dest(grd) | Fassberg |
| | Lt. F.E. Higginbottom | Do-217 dam(grd) | Munster |

**November 9, 1944**

| Unit | Pilot | Claim | Location |
|---|---|---|---|
| 84th: | Lt. J.M. Farmer | Fi-156 dest(grd) | Hanover |
| | Capt. L.P. Marshall | (2)He-111 dam(grd) | Schenfheim |
| | Lt. R.O. Laho | Ju-88 dam(grd) | Schenfheim |
| | Lt. R.H. Spooner | Ju-88 dam(grd) | Schenfheim |

**November 21, 1944**

| Unit | Pilot | Claim | Location |
|---|---|---|---|
| HdQts: | Capt. R.B. Holmes | Me-109 dest(air) | Hanover |
| 82nd: | Maj. R.E. Conner | (2)Me-109 dest(air) | Hanover |
| | | Ju-88 dest(grd) | Gutersloh |
| | Capt. R.A. Hewitt | Me-109 dest(air) | Hanover |
| | Lt. A.A. Rosenblum | Me-109 dest(air) | Hanover |
| | F/O G.L. Weston | Me-109 prob(air) | Hanover |
| | Lt. W.E. Hydorn | FW-190 dam(air) | Hanover |
| | Lt. D.C. Hart | Me-109 dam(air) | Hanover |
| | | (.5)Ju-88 dest(grd) | Gutersloh |
| | F/O H.R. Liebenrood | (.5)Ju-88 dest(grd) | Gutersloh |
| | Lt. D.C. Zboinski | Ju-88 dam(grd) | Gutersloh |

**November 26, 1944**

| Unit | Pilot | Claim | Location |
|---|---|---|---|
| 82nd: | Capt. J.J. Hockery | (2)Me-109 dest(air) | All 82nd claims |
| | | FW-190 prob(air) | are at Rheine |
| | Lt. M.O. Croy | (2)Me-109 dest(air) | |
| | Lt. D.C. Hart | Me-109 dest(air) | |
| | F/O H.R. Liebenrood | Me-109 dest(air) | |
| | Lt. I.H. Keatley | Me-109 dam(air) | |
| 83rd: | Capt. R.R. Bonebrake | Me-109 dest(air) | S/Dummer Lake |
| | Capt. H.T. Barnaby | u/i a/c dest(grd) | Weisswarte A/F |
| 84th: | Capt. P.L. Larson | FW-190 dest(air) | Vorden A/F |
| | Lt. W.H. Lutz | FW-190 dest(grd) | Vorden A/F |

**December 19, 1944**

| Unit | Pilot | Claim | Location |
|---|---|---|---|
| 83rd: | Capt. R.R. Bonebrake | Me-109 dest(air) | All claims are |
| | | FW-190 dest(air) | S/Coblenz |
| | Lt. F.E. Harrington | Me-109 dest(air) | |
| | | FW-190 dest(air) | |
| | Lt. J.A. Kirk | Me-109 dest(air) | |
| | | FW-190 dest(air) | |
| | Lt. F.A. Fish | Me-109 dest(air) | |
| | Maj. S.R. Beckley | Me-109 dam(air) | |

**December 31, 1944**

| Unit | Pilot | Claim | Location |
|---|---|---|---|
| 84th: | Capt. J.P. Maxwell | FW-190 dest(air) | Solingen |

NOTE: From January 1, 1945, all claims are in P-51's

**January 14, 1945**

| Unit | Pilot | Claim | Location |
|---|---|---|---|
| 82nd: | Lt. W. Warren | (2)FW-190 dest(air) | Cologne |
| | Lt. R.E. Smith | FW-190 dest(air) | Cologne |
| | Capt. J.I. Brown | Me-109 dam(air) | Cologne |

| | | | |
|---|---|---|---|
| | Lt. R.J. Blossom | FW-190 dam(air) | Cologne |
| 83rd: | Capt. P.A. Caulfield | FW-190 dest(air) | N/Diepholz |
| 84th: | Lt. W.H. Lutz | FW-190 dest(air) | SW Cologne |
| | | Me-109 dest(air) | SW Cologne |
| | | (2)FW-190 dam(air) | SW Cologne |
| | Lt. R.H. Spooner | Me-109 dest(air) | SW Cologne |
| | | FW-190 dest(air) | SW Cologne |
| | Maj. L.P. Marshall | Me-109 dest(air) | S/Cologne |
| | Lt. W.J. DeGain | Me-109 dest(air) | E/Cologne |
| | Lt. L.R. Herford | Me-109 dest(air) | SW Cologne |
| | Lt. F.E. Oiler | FW-190 dest(air) | Cologne |
| | | Me-109 dam(air) | Cologne |
| | Lt. E.L. Stier | Me-109 dest(air) | SW Cologne |
| | | Me-109 dam(air) | SW Cologne |
| | Lt. M.T. Wilson | Me-109 dest(air) | SE Cologne |

**February 3, 1945**

| | | | |
|---|---|---|---|
| 84th: | Lt. L. DeAnda | (2)FW-200 dest(grd) | All claims are |
| | | Hs-126 dest(grd) | at Luneburg |
| | Lt. L.M. Grisham | (3)FW-190 dest(grd) | |
| | Lt. P.S. Ostrander | (2)FW-190 dest(grd) | |
| | | FW-190 dam(grd) | |
| | Lt. E.L. Stier | FW-190 dest(grd) | |
| | | Me-410 dest(grd) | |
| | Lt. F.E. Oiler | Me-410 dest(grd) | |
| | | Ju-88 dest(grd) | |
| | | Me-410 dam(grd) | |
| 84th: | Lt. A.A. Garback | FW-190 dest(grd) | |
| | Lt. J.M. Farmer | Ju-87 dest(grd) | |
| | Lt. J.S. Bond | FW-190 dest(grd) | |
| | | Me-410 dam(grd) | |
| | Lt. W.S. Blodgett | FW-190 dest(grd) | |
| | Capt. D. Ledington | (2)Me-410 dam(grd) | |
| | Lt. R.K. Corbett | (2)Ju-87 dam(grd) | |
| | Lt. J.E. Moores | FW-200 dam(grd) | |

**February 9, 1945**

| | | | |
|---|---|---|---|
| 82nd: | Lt. W.E. Hydorn | Me-262 prob(air) | Fulda |
| 83rd: | Capt. E.H. Miller | Me-262 prob(air) | Fulda |

**February 22, 1945**

| | | | |
|---|---|---|---|
| 84th: | Lt. R.D. Higgins | Ju-86 dam(grd) | Memmingen |

**February 28, 1945**

| | | | |
|---|---|---|---|
| 82nd: | Lt. W.F. Bechtelheimer | (.5)Me-262 dam(air) | Hersfeld-Fulda |
| | Lt. J.E. Parker | (.5)Me-262 dam(air) | Hersfeld-Fulda |

**March 1, 1945**

| | | | |
|---|---|---|---|
| 84th: | Lt. R.D. Higgins | Me-109 dam(grd) | Boblingen |
| | | u/i a/c dam(grd) | Boblingen |
| | Lt. C.E. Taylor | u/i a/c dam(grd) | Boblingen |

**March 2, 1945**

| | | | |
|---|---|---|---|
| HdQts. | LtCol. J.D. Landers | (2)Me-109 dest(air) | All claims are |
| 83rd: | Lt. D.M. McDuffie | (4)Me-109 dest(air) | at Burg A/F |
| | Maj. W.H. Julian | (2)Me-109 dest(air) | |
| | | Me-109 dam(air) | |
| | Lt. J.D. Hodge | (2)Me-109 dest(air) | |
| | Capt. F.E. Higginbottom | Me-109 dest(air) | |
| | | Me-109 prob(air) | |
| | Lt. H. Davis | Me-109 dest(air) | |
| | | Me-109 dam(air) | |
| | Lt. R.I. Kuehl | Me-109 dest(air) | |
| | | Me-109 dam(air) | |
| | Capt. R.E. Wise | Me-109 dam(air) | |
| | Lt. R.F. Rohm | Me-109 dam(air) | |

**March 19, 1945**

| | | | |
|---|---|---|---|
| HdQts: | LtCol. J.D. Landers | Me-109 dest(air) | All claims are |
| | Maj. C.M. Christ | Me-109 dest(air) | at Osnabruck |
| 82nd: | Capt. R.A. Hewitt | (2)Me-109 dest(air) | |
| | Lt. I.H. Keatley | (2)Me-109 dest(air) | |
| | Lt. A.S. Miller | (2)Me-109 dest(air) | |
| | Lt. J.E. Parker | Me-109 dest(air) | |
| | | Ar-234 dest(air) | |
| | | (3)Me-109 dam(air) | |
| | Capt. W.H. Brown | Me-109 dest(air) | |
| | | (.5)Ar-234 dest(air) | |
| | | (2)Me-109 dam(air) | |
| | Lt. H.H. Lamb | (.5)Ar-234 dest(air) | |
| | | Me-109 dam(air) | |
| | | FW-190 dam(air) | |
| | Lt. W.E. Bourque | Me-109 dest(air) | |
| | Lt. A.A. Rosenblum | FW-190 dest(air) | |
| | | Me-109 dam(air) | |
| | Lt. E.O. Schneider | Me-109 dest(air) | |
| | Lt. G.V. Elsey | Me-109 dam(air) | |
| 83rd: | Lt. H. Davis | (2)Me-109 dest(air) | |
| | Lt. H.L. Sealey | (2)Me-109 dest(air) | |
| | | FW-190 dam(air) | |
| | Lt. A.T. Colletti | FW-190 dest(air) | |
| | | Me-109 dam(air) | |
| | Lt. P.W. Klaasen | Me-109 dest(air) | |
| | | Me-109 dam(air) | |
| | Lt. J.A. Kirk | Me-109 dest(air) | |
| | Lt. R.H. Talbot | Me-109 dest(air) | |
| | | Me-109 dam(air) | |
| | Capt. F.E. Higginbottom | (.5)Me-109 dest(air) | |
| | Lt. R.I. Kuehl | (.5)Me-109 dest(air) | |
| | Lt. W.B. Spengler | (2)Me-109 dam(air) | |
| 84th: | Maj. H.L. Downing | Me-109 dest(air) | |
| | | FW-190 dest(air) | |
| | Lt. W.J. DeGain | FW-190 dest(air) | |
| | Lt. J.E. Moores | FW-190 dest(air) | |
| | Lt. P.S. Ostrander | Me-109 dest(air) | |
| | Lt. H.R. Slack | Me-109 dest(air) | |
| | Lt. T.V. Thain | Me-109 dest(air) | |
| | Lt. A.A. Garback | (.5)Me-109 dest(air) | |
| | Lt. E.F. Smith | (.5)Me-109 dest(air) | |
| | Lt. C.W. Clemons | FW-190 dam(air) | |

**March 21, 1945**

| | | | |
|---|---|---|---|
| 82nd: | Lt. R.H. Anderson | Me-262 dest(air) | Giebelstadt |
| | Lt. W.E. Bourque | Me-262 dest(air) | Giebelstadt |
| | Capt. W.H. Brown | (.5)Me-262 dest(air) | Giebelstadt |
| | Lt. A.A. Rosenblum | (.5)Me-262 dest(air) | Giebelstadt |
| | Maj. R.E. Conner | Me-262 dest(grd) | Dresden |
| | | (2)Me-262 dam(grd) | Dresden |
| 83rd: | Capt. E.H. Miller | Me-262 dest(air) | Wittenburg |
| | Lt. J.A. Kirk | Me-262 dest(air) | Meiningen |

**March 22, 1945**

| | | | |
|---|---|---|---|
| 82nd; | Lt. E.L. Peel | (.5)Me-262 dest(air) | Ulm |
| | Lt. M.B. Stutzman | (.5)Me-262 dest(air) | Ulm |
| 83rd: | Capt. H.T. Barnaby | Me-262 dest(air) | Giebelstadt |

**March 24, 1945**

| | | | |
|---|---|---|---|
| 82nd: | Lt. R.J. Blossom | He-111 dam(grd) | Diepholz |

**March 30, 1945**

| | | | |
|---|---|---|---|
| HdQts: | LtCol. J.D. Landers | (.5)Me-262 dest(air) | Rendsburg |
| 84th: | Lt. T.V. Thain | (.5)Me-262 dest(air) | Rendsburg |
| | Lt. P.S. Ostrander | Me-262 dest(grd) | Kaltenkirchen |
| | | Me-262 dam(grd) | Kaltenkirchen |

**March 31, 1945**

| | | | |
|---|---|---|---|
| 82nd: | Lt. W.L. Coleman | Me-262 dest(air) | Stendal |

**April 7, 1945**

| | | | |
|---|---|---|---|
| 83rd: | Lt. F.E. Harrington | Me-109 dest(air) | Dummer Lake |
| | | FW-190 dest(air) | Dummer Lake |
| | Capt. R.T. Green | Me-109 dest(air) | Dummer Lake |
| | Lt. R.I. Kuehl | Me-109 dest(air) | Dummer Lake |
| 84th: | Lt. R.K. Corbett | (.5)Me-109 dest(air) | NE Dummer Lake |
| | Lt. H.R. Slack | (.5)Me-109 dest(air) | NE Dummer Lake |

**April 10, 1945**

| | | | |
|---|---|---|---|
| HdQts: | LtCol. J.D. Landers | (2)Me-109 dest(grd) | All HdQts & |
| | | FW-190 dest(grd) | 82nd claims are |
| | | He-111 dest(grd) | at Werder A/F |
| | | Ju-188 dest(grd) | |
| | | Ju-88 dest(grd) | |
| 82nd: | Lt. L.R. Campi | (2)Me-109 dest(grd) | |
| | | FW-190 dest(grd) | |
| | | (2)u/i a/c dam(grd) | |
| | Lt. E.J. Carroll | FW-190 dest(grd) | |
| | | Ju-52 dest(grd) | |
| | | u/i a/c dest(grd) | |
| | | (5)u/i a/c dam(grd) | |
| | Lt. H.H. Lamb | Me-410 dest(grd) | |
| | | Ju-88 dest(grd) | |
| | | Ju-52 dest(grd) | |
| | | Ju-52 dam(grd) | |
| | Lt. M.B. Stutzman | FW-190 dest(grd) | |
| | | He-111 dest(grd) | |
| | | (2)u/i a/c dam(grd) | |
| | Lt. R.B. Abernathy | Me-109 dest(grd) | |
| | | Me-109 dam(grd) | |
| | | u/i a/c dam(grd) | |
| | Lt. W.F. Bechtelheimer | u/i a/c dest(grd) | |
| | Lt. R.J. Blossom | He-111 dest(grd) | |
| | | Me-109 dam(grd) | |
| | Lt. W.E. Bourque | Me-109 dest(grd) | |
| | | Ju-52 dam(grd) | |
| | | u/i a/c dam(grd) | |
| | Lt. G.V. Elsey | FW-190 dest(grd) | |
| | Lt. A.S. Miller | He-111 dest(grd) | |
| | | FW-190 dam(grd) | |
| | | u/i a/c dam(grd) | |
| | Lt. E.L. Peel | u/i a/c dest(grd) | |
| | | (2)u/i a/c dam(grd) | |

| | | | |
|---|---|---|---|
| | Lt. G.W. Stillwell | Me-410 dest(grd) | |
| | | Me-410 dam(grd) | |
| | Lt. D.C. Hart | FW-190 dam(grd) | |
| | Lt. H.L. Roe | Do-217 dam(grd) | |
| 83rd: | Lt. F.E. Harrington | (2)FW-190 dest(grd) | Werder |
| | | Ju-87 dest(grd) | Werder |
| | | u/i a/c dest(grd) | Werder |
| | | FW-190 dam(grd) | Werder |
| | | Ju-87 dam(grd) | Werder |
| | | u/i a/c dam(grd) | Werder |
| | Lt. J.A. Kirk | He-111 dest(grd) | Werder |
| | | Bu-133 dest(grd) | Werder |
| | Lt. R.I. Kuehl | Me-410 dest(grd) | Brandenburg-Briest |
| | | u/i a/c dam(grd) | Brandenburg-Briest |
| | Lt. J.S. Peterson | FW-190 dest(grd) | Hustedt A/F |
| | Lt. R.E. Phaneuf | He-111 dest(grd) | Gardelegen |
| | Lt. E.W. Strobel | FW-190 dest(grd) | Werder |
| | | u/i a/c dam(grd) | Werder |
| | Capt. F.E. Higginbottom | Me-262 dam(grd) | Burg Bai Magdeburg |
| | Lt. D.R. Monteith | FW-190 dam(grd) | Brandenburg-Briest |
| 84th: | Lt. H.R. Slack | FW-190 dest(grd) | Werder |
| | | Ju-87 dest(grd) | Werder |
| | | Ju-52 dest(grd) | Werder |
| | Capt. P.T. Keiller | Ar-196 dest(grd) | Werder |
| | | Me-323 dest(grd) | Werder |
| | | Ar-196 dam(grd) | Werder |
| | Lt. R.A. Spaulding | u/i a/c dest(grd) | Werder |
| | Lt. J.R. Sole | u/i a/c dest(grd) | Ulzen |
| | | u/i a/c dam(grd) | Ulzen |
| | Lt. J.D. Calvin | u/i a/c dam(grd) | Ulzen |

**April 16, 1945**

| | | | |
|---|---|---|---|
| HdQts: | LtCol. J.D. Landers | (9)He-177 dest(grd) | Praha/Kakewice |
| | Maj. G. Bryan | (2)u/i a/c dest(grd) | Praha/Kakewice |
| | | Me-109 dest(grd) | Praha/Kakewice |
| | | Ju-52 dest(grd) | Praha/Kakewice |
| | | (3)u/i a/c dam(grd) | Praha/Kakewice |
| 82nd: | Lt. D.J. Henehan | (2.5)Ju-87 dest(grd) | All 82nd claims are at Pilzen/Prague |
| | | FW-190 dest(grd) | |
| | | Ju-52 dest(grd) | |
| | | FW-190 dam(grd) | |
| | | Ju-52 dam(grd) | |
| | | u/i a/c dam(grd) | |
| | | (shared with LtCol. O.E. Gilbert of the 66th Ftr Wg) | |
| | Capt. M.O. Croy | FW-190 dest(grd) | |
| | Capt. J.I. Brown | Ju-52 dest(grd) | |
| | | Ju-86 dam(grd) | |
| | | u/i a/c dam(grd) | |
| | Lt. R.J. Blossom | Do-217 dest(grd) | |
| | Lt. G.V. Elsey | Me-109 dest(grd) | |
| | | Me-109 dam(grd) | |
| | Lt. E.L. Peel | u/i a/c dest(grd) | |
| | | FW-190 dam(grd) | |
| | | u/i a/c dam(grd) | |
| | Lt. G.W. Stillwell | FW-190 dest(grd) | |
| | | (4)Me-109 dam(grd) | |
| | | u/i a/c dam(grd) | |
| | Lt. F.R. Swauger | Me-109 dest(grd) | |
| | Capt. R.B. Holmes | (5)u/i a/c dam(grd) | |
| | Capt. D.C. Hart | (2)u/i a/c dam(grd) | |
| | Lt. A.M. Rosenburg | (2)FW-190 dam(grd) | |
| | | u/i a/c dam(grd) | |
| | Lt. J.E. Parker | FW-190 dam(grd) | |
| | Lt. M.B. Stutzman | Me-109 dam(grd) | |
| | Lt. H.L. Roe | He-111 dam(grd) | |
| 83rd: | Capt. E.R. Kulik | (4)FW-190 dest(grd) | All 83rd claims are N/Prague |
| | | Me-109 dest(grd) | |
| | | Ju-87 dest(grd) | |
| | | u/i a/c dest(grd) | |
| | | FW-190 dam(grd) | |
| | Lt. A.T. Colletti | (4)Ju-87 dest(grd) | |
| | | FW-190 dest(grd) | |
| | | (2)FW-190 dam(grd) | |
| | | FW-200 dam(grd) | |
| | | u/i a/c dam(grd) | |
| | Lt. D.J. DeVillers | (2)Me-109 dest(grd) | |
| | | (2)Ju-87 dest(grd) | |
| | | He-111 dest(grd) | |
| | | (2)Me-109 dam(grd) | |
| | | (2)Ju-87 dam(grd) | |
| | Lt. G.C. Doss | (5)Ju-87 dest(grd) | |
| | | Me-109 dam(grd) | |
| | Lt. D.M. McDuffie | (2)Me-109 dest(grd) | |
| | | (2)FW-190 dest(grd) | |
| | | Ju-87 dest(grd) | |
| | Lt. D.S. Sweat | (2)FW-190 dest(grd) | |
| | | (2)Ju-87 dest(grd) | |
| | | u/i a/c dest(grd) | |
| | | (2)FW-190 dam(grd) | |
| | | Ju-87 dam(grd) | |
| | Lt. F.E. Harrington | (2)u/i a/c dest(grd) | |
| | | Me-109 dest(grd) | |
| | | Me-262 dest(grd) | |
| | | (3)u/i a/c dam(grd) | |
| | Lt. J.A. Kirk | FW-190 dest(grd) | |
| | | Ju-87 dest(grd) | |
| | | Ju-88 dest(grd) | |
| | | u/i a/c dest(grd) | |
| | | (3)Ju-87 dam(grd) | |
| | Lt. R.A. Messinger | (3)Ju-52 dest(grd) | |
| | | FW-190 dest(grd) | |
| | | (3)Ju-87 dam(grd) | |
| | Lt. R.E. Phaneuf | (2)Ju-87 dest(grd) | |
| | | FW-190 dest(grd) | |
| | | Ju-52 dest(grd) | |
| | | (2)Ju-87 dam(grd) | |
| | | Me-109 dam(grd) | |
| | | He-111 dam(grd) | |
| | Lt. A.A. Palopoli | (3)Ju-87 dest(grd) | |
| | Lt. E.W. Strobel | (3)Ju-87 dest(grd) | |
| | | Me-109 dam(grd) | |
| | Lt. W.B. Spengler | FW-190 dest(grd) | |
| | | (3)Ju-87 dam(grd) | |
| 84th: | Lt. C.E. Taylor | (4)Ju-52 dest(grd) | All 84th claims are at Praha/Kakewice |
| | | (3)Me-110 dest(grd) | |
| | | FW-190 dest(grd) | |
| | | He-111 dest(grd) | |
| | | FW-190 dam(grd) | |
| | Lt. D.E. Josey | (2)FW-190 dest(grd) | |
| | | Me-109 dest(grd) | |
| | | He-111 dest(grd) | |
| | | u/i a/c dest(grd) | |
| | | (2)FW-190 dam(grd) | |
| | | Ju-52 dam(grd) | |
| | | u/i a/c dam(grd) | |
| | Lt. N. Hepner | (2)Me-109 dest(grd) | |
| | | He-111 dest(grd) | |
| | | Ju-52 dest(grd) | |
| | | u/i a/c dest(grd) | |
| | | (2)Ju-52 dam(grd) | |
| | | Me-109 dam(grd) | |
| | | Ju-88 dam(grd) | |
| | Lt. H.R. Slack | (4)Ju-52 dest(grd) | |
| | | Ju-52 dam(grd) | |
| | | u/i a/c dam(grd) | |
| | Capt. D. Ledington | (2)Ju-52 dest(grd) | |
| | | u/i a/c dest(grd) | |
| | | Ju-52 dam(grd) | |
| | Lt. L. DeAnda | (3)Ju-52 dest(grd) | |
| | Lt. W.S. Blodgett | (2)Me-110 dest(grd) | |
| | | Ju-52 dest(grd) | |
| | | Me-110 dam(grd) | |
| | Lt. J.E. Moores | (2)Ju-52 dest(grd) | |
| | | Ju-88 dest(grd) | |
| | | (3)Ju-52 dam(grd) | |
| | | u/i a/c dam(grd) | |
| | Lt. W.J. DeGain | u/i a/c dest(grd) | |
| | | (2)u/i a/c dam(grd) | |
| | | Ju-87 dam(grd) | |
| | Lt. W.H. Lutz | He-111 dest(grd) | |
| | | (2)u/i a/c dam(grd) | |
| | Lt. H.V. Wingfield | u/i a/c dest(grd) | |
| | Lt. J.A. Nunley | Me-109 dam(grd) | |
| | | Me-110 dam(grd) | |
| | Lt. G.E. Gallant | Ju-52 dam(grd) | |
| | Lt. P.R. Henderson | Ju-52 dam(grd) | |

**April 17, 1945**

| | | | |
|---|---|---|---|
| HdQts: | Maj. G. Bryan | (2)u/i a/c dest(grd) | W/Dresden |
| | | (3)u/i a/c dam(grd) | W/Dresden |
| 82nd: | Capt. R.A. Hewitt | Me-262 dest(grd) | Prague |
| | Lt. A.A. Rosenblum | u/i a/c dest(grd) | Kralupy |
| 84th: | Lt. D.R. Josey | FW-190 dest(grd) | All 84th claims are W/Dresden |
| | | Ju-88 dest(grd) | |
| | | u/i a/c dest(grd) | |
| | | FW-190 dam(grd) | |
| | | Ju-88 dam(grd) | |
| | Lt. W.M. McClellan | Me-410 dest(grd) | |
| | | Ju-88 dest(grd) | |
| | | u/i a/c dest(grd) | |
| | | (3)u/i a/c dam(grd) | |
| | | Me-410 dam(grd) | |
| | Lt. J.R. Sole | (3)u/i a/c dest(grd) | |
| | | (4)u/i a/c dam(grd) | |

### 78th Fighter Group Losses

**January 26, 1943**

Lt. Stephen L. White (82nd) KIAc; Collided with Lt. Perry on a ferry flight.
P-38F 42-12928

Lt. Donald S. Beals (83rd) KIAc; Disappeared on a ferry flight.
P-38H 41-7576
Lt. Henry L. Perry (83rd) KIAc; Collided with Lt. White on a ferry flight.
P-38F 42-12905

**March 1, 1943**
F/O Robert I. Ronning (83rd) KIAc; Collided with a P-47 and crashed near Goxhill.
P-47C

**April 13, 1943**
LtCol. Joseph E. Dickman (HdQts) ASR; Suffered mechanical trouble and bailed out off Calais.
P-47C WZ-M 41-6399

**April 15, 1943**
Lt. Leroy V. Dodd (83rd) KIAc; Crashed near Bedford on a test hop.
P-47C HL-W 41-6241

**May 14, 1943**
Capt. Robert E. Adamina (82nd) POW; Hit by fighters and ditched off the Belgian coast.
P-47C MX-D 41-6198
Capt. Elmer E. McTaggart (83rd) MIA-E; Hit by fighters and bailed out near Knocke.
P-47C HL-C 41-6382
F/O Samuel R. Martinek (83rd) POW; Hit by fighters and bailed out northwest of Knocke.
P-47C HL-T 41-6208

**May 15, 1943**
Lt. Jack S. Sandmeier (82nd) KIA; Suffered mechanical failure and bailed out over the North Sea.
P-47C MX-

**May 16, 1943**
F/O Charles R. Brown (84th) POW; Hit by a FW-190 near Eecloo and bailed out near Walcheren.
P-47C WZ- 41-6318

**May 20, 1943**
Lt. Richard A. Murray (84th) KIA; Suffered mechanical failure and bailed out 40 miles off the English coast.
P-47C WZ-S 41-6383

**June 13, 1943**
Lt. Ora R. Brown (82nd) KIA; Lost for unknown reasons.
P-47C MX-
Lt. Donald M. Marshall (84th) POW; Hit by fighters near Lumbres.
P-47C WZ-D 41-6353

**July 1, 1943**
Col. Arman Peterson (HdQts) KIA; Hit by fighters near Ouddorp.
P-47D MX-P 42-7948 "Flagari"

**July 14, 1943**
Lt. August V. DeGenaro (82nd) ASR; Hit by a FW-190 and bailed out over the Channel.
P-47C MX-S 41-6218
Lt. Donald G. Jackson (82nd) KIA; Hit by fire from a B-17 and crashed near Amiens.
P-47C MX-J 41-6222

**July 30, 1943**
LtCol. Melvin F. McNickle (HdQts) POW; Suffered oxygen failure then collided with Lt. Byers near Winterswijk.
P-47D WZ-M 42-7961
Lt. Paul H. Lehman (82nd) ASR; Damaged by flak and bailed out over the Channel.
P-47C MX-W 41-6542
Lt. Warren E. Graff (82nd) MIA-E; Hit by fighters and bailed out near Bakelo.
P-47C MX-Y 41-6391
Lt. James F. Byers (84th) KIA; Collided with LtCol. McNickle near Winterswijk.
P-47D WZ-I 42-7935

**August 15, 1943**
Lt. [illegible] M. Smith (83rd) KIA; Spun-in west of Duxford while returning as a spare.
P-47D HL-Y 42-7952

**August 27, 1943**
Lt. Robert F. Brower (82nd) KIA; Spun-in near Henlow while taking-off.
P-47C MX-

**September 22, 1943**
Lt. Quentin Charlton (83rd) KIA; Suffered a fuel leak and bailed out over the North Sea.
P-47C HL-N 41-6411

**October 18, 1943**
Lt. Franklin B. Resseguie (84th) POW; Suffered mechanical trouble in the Lens-St. Omer area.
P-47C WZ-E 41-6240

**October 24, 1943**
Lt. Carl E. Cross (84th) KIAc;
P-47C WZ-

**November 26, 1943**
Lt. John Herrick (82nd) POW; Hit by fighters near Beauvais and bailed out near Chantilly.
P-47C MX-U 41-6188
F/O Ralph E. Cormier (83rd) KIA; Hit by fighters near Paris.
P-47D HL-E 42-8681

Lt. Wayne M. Dougherty (84th) POW; Hit by a Me-109 near Paris and bailed out near Morselles.
P-47D WZ-L 42-8573

**December 10, 1943**
Lt. Melvin R. Wright (82nd) KIAc; Split-essed into the ground near Duxford.
P-47D MX-

**December 30, 1943**
F/O James C.P. Eastwood (83rd) KIA; Suffered mechanical failure and bailed out 50 miles off Beachy Head.
P-47C HL-A 41-6540

**January 5, 1944**
Lt. Arthur S. Granger (83rd) KIA; Hit by fighters near Rennes.
P-47D HL-N 42-8622
Lt. Kenneth Hindersinn (83rd) POW; Hit by a FW-190 near Caen.
P-47D HL-K 42-74652
Lt. Major C. Leach (83rd) KIA; Hit by a FW-190 near Rennes.
P-47C HL-L 41-6331
Lt. Melvin D. Putnam (83rd) KIA; Hit by a FW-190 near Rennes.
P-47C HL-Q 41-6581
Lt. George T. Hartman (84th) KIA; Hit by a FW-190 north of La Rochelle.
P-47D WZ-E 42-8538

**January 24, 1944**
Lt. Clifford B. Hahn (82nd) KIA; Ran out of fuel and crashed into the Channel.
P-47D MX-J 42-7923
Lt. William F. Neel (82nd) KIA; Ran out of fuel and crashed into the Channel.
P-47D MX-Y 42-22467

**January 29, 1944**
F/O Milton H. Ramsey (82nd) MIA-E; Hit by fighters near Coblenz.
P-47D MX-J 42-22463

**February 10, 1944**
Lt. Vernon Y. Jones (82nd) KIA; Hit by fighters near Tongeren.
P-47D MX-X 42-7883
Lt. Donald E. Ludwig (82nd) KIA; Hit by flak and crashed into the North Sea.
P-47C MX-H 41-6249

**February 11, 1944**
Lt. William S. Swanson (82nd) KIA; Hit by a Me-109 southwest of Arras.
P-47D MX-P 42-74733
Lt. Donald R. Morsch (82nd) KIA; Hit by a Me-109 southwest of Arras.
P-47D MX-D 42-22755
F/O Archie F. Daniels (83rd) KIA; Crashed near Nuthampstead after take-off due to mechanical trouble.
P-47D HL-T 42-7963

**February 22, 1944**
Lt. John H. Johnson (83rd) POW; Hit by a FW-190 near Eindhoven.
P-47C HL-A 41-6335

**February 29, 1944**
Lt. Robert C. Orr (82nd) POW; Bailed out in the Amiens-Lille area after mechanical trouble.
P-47D MX-O 42-7916

**March 4, 1944**
Lt. Everett W. Powell (83rd) POW; Suffered mechanical failure near Malines.
P-47C HL-U 41-6374

**March 6, 1944**
Lt. Grant M. Turley (82nd) KIA; Hit by a FW-190 near Barenburg.
P-47D MX-N 42-7998 "Kitty"
F/O Edward J. Downey (83rd) KIA; Hit by a FW-190 near Hasselunne.
P-47D HL-W 42-7983

**March 8, 1944**
Lt. George C. [illegible] (83rd) KIA; [illegible] Needham Market upon return
P-47C HL-J 41-6229

**March 13, 1944**
Lt. Roy E. Wendell (84th) KIAc; Shot down by another P-47 on a gunnery flight.
P-47C WZ-L 41-6223 "Isabel"

**March 16, 1944**
Lt. Walter Tonkin (83rd) KIA; Hit the ground while chasing an enemy plane near Chievres.
P-47D HL-U 42-8543

**March 17, 1944**
Lt. Courtlyn W. Hotchkiss (83rd) POW; Hit by flak near Reims.
P-47D HL-B 42-8688
Lt. Peter E. Pompetti (84th) POW; Hit by flak at Beauvais and bailed out near Villeteneuse.
P-47D WZ-Z 42-74641

**March 30, 1944**
Lt. Albert B. Werder (83rd) KIA; Hit by flak and bailed out near Venlo.
P-47D HL-R 42-7906

**April 1, 1944**
Lt. Calvin Webb (82nd) KIA; Hit by flak at Verdun and crashed near Armentieres.
P-47C MX-I 41-6535

**April 5, 1944**
Lt. Harry L. Eakes (82nd) KIA; Hit by flak near St. Valery.
P-47D MX-E 42-75602

**April 11, 1944**
Lt. William H. Reese (83rd) KIA; Hit by flak near Lingen.
P-47C HL-A 41-6210

**April 13, 1944**
Lt. Donald R. Roberts (82nd) POW; Hit by a FW-190 north of Saarbrucken.
P-47D MX-H 42-76074

**April 15, 1944**
Capt. Charles W. Silsby (84th) KIA; Last seen over the North Sea in bad weather.
P-47D WZ-A 42-25537
F/O Joseph W. Mundy (84th) KIA; Last seen with Capt. Silsby.
P-47D WZ-V 42-76412
Lt. Martin G. O'Connell (83rd) KIAc; Crashed near Duxford.
P-47D HL-O 42-76474

**May 8, 1944**
Lt. John D. Motsenbocker (83rd) POW; Hit by a Me-109 near Verdun.
P-47D HL-P 42-76227

**May 11, 1944**
Lt. Anthony L. Kosinski (82nd) MIA-E; Hit by flak at Dijon A/F.
P-47D MX-O 42-25994
Lt. James F. Steele (83rd) INT; Hit by flak at Dijon A/F and landed in Switzerland.
P-47D MX-Q 42-76131

**May 12, 1944**
Lt. Daniel D. Hagarty (82nd) POW; Hit by fighters near Trier.
P-47D MX-R 42-26025

**May 24, 1944**
Lt. William H. Genge (82nd) POW; Suffered mechanical failure south of Alkmaar.
P-47D MX-F 42-76585

**May 28, 1944**
Lt. Philip H. Hazelett (82nd) KIA; Hit by flak near Osnabruck.
P-47D MX-Y 42-26064
Lt. William S. Orvis, Jr. (82nd) KIA; Hit by flak near Erlberben.
P-47D MX-W 42-76318
Capt. Alwin M. Juchheim (83rd) POW; Collided with a 9th Air Force
P-51 near Gardelegen.
P-47D HL-A 42-26016

**June 4, 1944**
Capt. James W. Wilkinson (82nd) KIAc; Crashed into a mountain near Llandovery, Wales.
P-47D MX-G 42-26526

**June 5, 1944**
Lt. John C.E. Steinwedel (82nd) KIA; Crashed near Amiens after icing up.
P-47D MX-Y 42-76473

**June 6, 1944**
Lt. Wallace R. Haily (84th) ASR; Hit by flak and bailed out over the Channel.
P-47D WZ-F 43-25578

**June 7, 1944**
Lt. Harry H. Just, Jr. (84th) KIA; Hit by a Me-109 near Montdidier.
P-47D WZ-T 42-25712
Lt. Harold H. Rice (84th) POW; Hit by a Me-109 near Montdidier.
P-47D WZ-K 42-76184

**June 10, 1944**
Lt. Robert L. Baker (82nd) KIA; Hit by flak near Beaumont.
P-47D MX-X 42-76547
Lt. Richard S. Kuehner (82nd) KIA; Hit trees while strafing near Beaumont.
P-47D MX-U 42-26317
Maj. Donald W. McLeod (83rd) MIA-E; Hit by a Me-109 near Argentan.
P-47D HL-V 42-76505
Lt. Vincent J. Massa (83rd) KIA; Hit by a Me-109 near Argentan.
P-47D HL-S 43-25319
Lt. William M. McDermott (83rd) KIA; Collided with a P-47 and crashed near Southminster.
P-47D HL-E 42-26053
Maj. Harold E. Stump (84th) KIA; Hit by a Me-109 near Argentan.
P-47D WZ-X 42-25736
Capt. William F. Hunt (84th) KIA; Hit by a Me-109 near Argentan.
P-47D WZ-W 42-26031
Lt. James F. Casey (84th) POW; Hit by fighters near Argentan.
P-47D WZ-M 42-26149
Lt. Daniel T. Loyd (84th) KIA; Hit by a Me-109 near Argentan.
P-47D WZ-Z 42-25981
Lt. Robert J. McIntosh (84th) MIA-E; Hit by a FW-190 near Argentan.
P-47D WZ-Q 42-76506

**June 11, 1944**
Lt. Lawrence R. Casey (83rd) POW; Suffered mechanical trouble near Bernay.
P-47D HL-N 42-75610

**June 12, 1944**
Capt. John C. Ramsey (82nd) KIA; Hit by flak near Chartrettes.
P-47D MX-C 42-75591

**June 20, 1944**
Lt. Ben H. Hodges (82nd) KIA; Hit by a Me-109 near Montdidier.
P-47D MX-I 42-26446

**June 22, 1944**
Lt. Ollie E. Gibbs (83rd) KIA; Suffered mechanical and crashed on take-off.
P-47D HL-E 42-26623

**July 1, 1944**
Lt. Edward T. Kitley (83rd) KIA; Collided with Lt. Raese on take-off
P-47D HL-R 43-25513
Lt. Cleon W. Raese, Jr. (83rd) KIA; Collided with Lt. Kitley on take-off.
P-47D HL-F 43-25588
Lt. Ross Orr (84th) KIA; Hit by a Me-109 near St. Quentin.
P-47D WZ-X 42-26640

**July 4, 1944**
Lt. Lonnie L. Moseley (84th) POW; Lost oil pressure and bailed out near Routot.
P-47D WZ-L 42-25529

**July 5, 1944**
Lt. William Newton, III (84th) KIA; Downed by a Spitfire near Breteuil.
P-47D WZ-T 42-26583

**July 6, 1944**
Lt. Robert E. Mullins (83rd) KIA; Hit by a FW-190 near Rambouillet.
P-47D HL-M 42-26536

**July 9, 1944**
Lt. Jack B. Miller (83rd) ASR; Lost oil pressure then was bounced by a Spitfire and bailed out over the Channel.
P-47D HL-P 42-76232

**July 11, 1944**
Lt. Lester E. Ford (84th) POW; Hit by a Me-109 near Etables.
P-47D WZ-N 43-25313

**July 17, 1944**
Capt. Harry T. Lay (84th) KIA; Hit by flak in the Liffel-Le Grand area.
P-47D WZ-Z 42-26652

**July 19, 1944**
Lt. John B. Putnam (84th) KIAc; Was a passenger on a B-17 which crashed at Duxford.
Lt. Martin H. Smith, Jr. (84th) KIAc; Was a passenger on a B-17 which crashed at Duxford.

**July 26, 1944**
Lt. Harold J. Morris (82nd) KIA; Hit trees while strafing west of Laval.
P-47D MX-V 42-26461

**July 31, 1944**
Lt. Willard J. Lorsmeyer (83rd) POW; Hit by flak near Neustadt.
P-47D HL-V 42-26672

**August 2, 1944**
Capt. Charles R. Clark (82nd) POW; Hit by flak and bailed out near Euverman.
P-47D MX-F 42-26314

**August 5, 1944**
Lt. John J. Myler (84th) KIA; Hit by flak east of Bremen.
P-47D WZ-P 42-74723

**August 6, 1944**
F/O Gene T. Cummings (84th) POW; Suffered mechanical failure and bailed out near Bissel.
P-47D WZ-H 42-76584

**August 8, 1944**
Lt. James T. Fitzgerald (82nd) POW; Hit by flak east of Brias.
P-47D MX-J 43-25536

**August 10, 1944**
Lt. Louis A. Dicks (82nd) KIA; Hit by flak north of Epernay.
P-47D MX-Q 42-26333

**August 13, 1944**
Lt. Billy V. Smith (82nd) KIA; Crashed near Duxford after suffering mechanical trouble.
P-47D MX- 42-26512

**August 14, 1944**
Capt. Charles M. Peal (83rd) KIA; Hit by flak near Noyon.
P-47D HL-X 42-26449

**August 18, 1944**
Lt. Jack B. Miller (83rd) KIA; Collided with a P-51 near Bottisham.
P-47D HL-S 42-26458

**August 26, 1944**
Capt. Wilbur J. Coss (82nd) MIA-E; Hit by flak and bailed out near Peruwels.
P-47D MX-K 42-26585

**August 28, 1944**
LtCol. Olin E. Gilbert (HdQts) MIA-E; Hit by flak and bellied-in near Charleroi.
P-47D HL-X 42-28408
Lt. John F. Lacy (84th) POW; Caught in a ground explosion near Beaumont.
P-47D WZ-O 42-8650

**September 1, 1944**
Lt. Kenneth P. Dunaway (83rd) POW; Hit by flak near Gilze-Rijen and bailed out near Brussels.
P-47D HL-U 42-22776
Lt. Robert N. Jones (83rd) KIA; Caught in an explosion of a train and bailed out near Mahres.
P-47D HL-K 42-26543

**September 3, 1944**
Lt. Richard D. Stark (82nd) POW; Hit by flak near Maastricht and bellied-in near Roermond.
P-47D MX-G 42-27607

**September 5, 1944**
Capt. Gray H. Doyle (HdQts) KIA; Hit by flak near Metelen.
P-47D HL-P 44-19573
Lt. Charles E. Kuykendall (83rd) MIA-E; Hit by flak near Hooksbergen.
P-47D HL-B 42-26563 "Jeri"

**September 6, 1944**
Lt. Percy Bingham (83rd) POW; Hit by flak near Namur.
P-47D HL-T 42-76512
Lt. George Rich, III (83rd) POW; Hit by flak near Heuzer.
P-47D HL-J 42-76486
Maj. Quince L. Brown (84th) KIA; Hit by flak at Vogelsand, bailed out near Schleiden, and killed on the ground by civilians.
P-47D WZ-Z 44-19569 "Okie II"

**September 9, 1944**
Lt. Kenneth L. Moore (82nd) KIA; Hit by a FW-190 near Dellhofer.
P-47D MX-O 42-76351

**September 10, 1944**
Lt. William O. Lacy (82nd) KIA; Hit by flak near Meinbullen.
P-47D MX-B 42-75243
Lt. Robert E. Clague (84th) POW; Hit by flak near Graefenhausen.
P-47D WZ-F 42-25698
Lt. Lawton Clark (84th) KIA; Flew into trees while strafing near Heilbronn.
P-47D WZ-E 42-26590 "Thoroughbred"
Lt. Paul H. McKenny (84th) POW; Hit by flak near Aschaffenberg.
P-47D WZ-J 43-25303
Lt. Charles E. Parmelee (84th) KIA; Hit by flak and bellied-in near Wiesbaden where his plane ran into a wall.
P-47D WZ-L 43-25593

**September 17, 1944**
Lt. Donald C. Hart (82nd) ASR; Hit by flak and bailed out over the Channel.
P-47D MX-H 42-26330

**September 18, 1944**
Lt. Richard C. Snyder (82nd) POW; Hit by flak and bellied-in near Rotterdam.
P-47D MX-M 42-75551
Lt. John R. Loegering (83rd) POW; Hit by flak and bellied-in near Goch.
P-47D HL-Q 42-76587 "Thrunny Bit"
Lt. Russell C. MacDuffie (83rd) POW; Hit by flak near Turnhout.
P-47D HL-M 42-26020 "Duffie's Special"
Lt. John R. Fee (84th) POW; Hit by flak near Nijmegen.
P-47D WZ-C 42-25985
Lt. Eugene W. Wood (84th) KIA; Hit by flak near Nijmegen.
P-47D WZ-D 43-25297

**September 23, 1944**
Lt. Dunstan D. Hertley (83rd) KIA; Hit by flak near Heteren.
P-47D HL-X 42-26365

**October 1, 1944**
Lt. Dwight G. Belt (84th) KIAc; Collided with a B-17 and crashed near Greenstead Green.
P-47D WZ-U 42-25690

**October 7, 1944**
Lt. Robert D. Smith (84th) KIA; Hit trees while strafing near Neustadt.
P-47D WZ-I 43-25305

**October 15, 1944**
Lt. Jack LaGrange, Jr. (83rd) POW; Hit by flak near Heber.
P-47D HL-K 42-28544 "Fast Action Jackson"

**November 9, 1944**
Lt. Alan R. Jacobson (83rd) KIA; Hit by flak near Eisenberg and bailed out too low.
P-47D HL-B 44-19932
Lt. William G. Kelly (84th) KIAc;
P-47D WZ-

**November 21, 1944**
Lt. Harry A. Thompson (82nd) POW; Hit by flak and bellied-in southeast of Munster.
P-47D MX-B 44-19908

**November 26, 1944**
Capt. John J. Hockery (82nd) POW; Hit by flak near Rheine.
P-47D MX-L 44-19950
Lt. Troy L. Eggleston (82nd) KIA; Hit by fighters near Rheine.
P-47D MX-V 42-27297

**December 29, 1944**
Lt. Huie H. Lamb (82nd) ASR; Lost coolant and ditched in the North Sea.
P-51D MX-V 44-63286 "Etta Jeanne"

**January 2, 1945**
F/O George W. Morrison (82nd) POW; Suffered mechanical failure north of Saarbrucken.
P-51K MX-D 44-11657

**January 6, 1945**
F/O Gordon L. Weston (82nd) KIA; Hit a smokestack while in fog on the way back to Duxford.
P-51K MX-L 44-11672
Capt. Wilbur K. Grimes (84th) MIA-E; Hit by flak near Speyer and bailed out near Marche.
P-51K WZ-F 44-11691

**January 13, 1945**
Lt. Herbert W. Elin (84th) KIA; Spun-in near Bassingbourbe in bad weather.
P-51D WZ-C 44-63181

**January 15, 1945**
Lt. Richard H. Spooner (84th) POW; Hit by flak east of Bruchstadt.
P-51D WZ-I 44-15720

**January 17, 1945**
Lt. Gerald F. Boner (83rd) KIA; Suffered mechanical failure and bailed out east of Great Yarmouth.
P-51D HL-G 44-15506 "Miss Debbie"
Lt. Allen R. Packer (84th) POW; Hit by flak and bailed out northwest of Hamburg.
P-51D WZ-J 44-63188

**January 20, 1945**
Lt. Kenneth J. DeMaagd (84th) POW; Hit by flak and bellied-in near Wesel.
P-51K WZ-J 44-11682
F/O William C. Bradley (83rd) KIAc; Spun-in over the Isle of Grange.
P-51K HL- 44-11679

**February 3, 1945**
Lt. William B. Senarens (83rd) POW; Hit by flak and bailed out near Wilhelmshaven.
P-51D HL-T 44-15729 "Bill's Bus"
Lt. Leon M. Grisham (84th) POW; Hit by flak near Luneburg.
P-51D WZ-M 44-63182
Lt. Warren J. Sawell (84th) POW; Hit by flak near Luneburg.
P-51D WZ-N 44-15746

**February 9, 1945**
Lt. Willard E. Warren (82nd) POW; Suffered mechanical trouble and bailed out near Frankfurt.
P-51D MX-Q 44-63185 "Kitty's Kat"

**February 14, 1945**
Lt. Andrew R. Innocenzi (83rd) MIA-E; Suffered mechanical trouble and landed in Russia.
P-51D HL-F 44-14852 "Lottie"
Lt. James S. Peterson (83rd) MIA-E; Escorted Lt. Innocenzi.
P-51K HL-N 44-11695 "Prouka"

**February 20, 1945**
Capt. Charles L. Lyle (84th) KIA; Hit by flak near Stuttgart.
P-51K WZ-D 44-11694
Lt. Merle V. Brendle (84th) KIA; Hit by flak near Stuttgart and crashed near Valenciennes.
P-51D WZ-G 44-63207

**February 21, 1945**
Lt. Burton J. Newmark (84th) POW; Hit by flak and bailed out southwest of Coblenz.
P-51D WZ-K 44-63171 "Lady Eve"

**February 22, 1945**
Capt. Wilbur J. Coss (82nd) KIA; Collided with a P-51 near Valenciennes.
P-51K MX-D 44-11663
Lt. Ralph E. Hamilton (83rd) POW; Hit by flak near Crailsheim and bailed out northwest of Wurzburg.
P-51D HL-J 44-15650 "Debra Dell"

**February 23, 1945**
Lt. John B. Wade (83rd) POW; Hit by flak near Ingolstadt and bailed out near Donauworth.
P-51K HL-H 44-11364

**February 24, 1945**
Lt. Edwin B. Anderson (82nd) POW; Hit by flak near Dummer Lake.
P-51D MX-C 44-63177
Lt. Lucian J. Bibeau (82nd) KIA; Hit by flak near Dummer Lake.
P-51K MX-U 44-11688
Lt. Lloyd L. Eadline (83rd) KIA; Hit by flak near Quackenbruck and bailed out near the Zuider Zee.
P-51D HL-Y 44-63248
Lt. Louis R. Musgrave (84th) KIA; Hit by flak in the Einbeck-Hanover area.
P-51D WZ-F 44-15359

**February 25, 1945**
Lt. Charles S. Oldfield (84th) MIA-E; Hit by flak near Crailsheim.
P-51D WZ-C 44-63555
Lt. Mark T. Wilson, Jr. (84th) MIA-E; Hit by flak near Crailsheim.
P-51D WZ-N 44-15740

**February 26, 1945**
F/O Charles R. O'Brien (83rd) POW (K); Suffered mechanical trouble near Oldebrook. Was later shot while escaping.
P-51K HL-J 44-11627 "Green Eyes"
Lt. Leonard S. Olson (83rd) POW; Crashed while trying to land to rescue F/O O'Brien.
P-51K HL-A 44-11655 "Poop Shooter"

**February 28, 1945**
F/O Harold R. Liebenrood (82nd) POW; Suffered mechanical failure southeast of Cologne.
P-51D MX-G 44-63203

**March 1, 1945**
Lt. Ernest V. Boehner (82nd) KIA; Hit by flak west of Kassel.
P-51K MX-F 44-11652
Lt. Roy D. Higgins (84th) KIA; Hit by flak at Boblingen and bailed out too low.
P-51D WZ-N 44-72178
Lt. William D. Townsend (84th) KIA; Hit the ground while strafing near Heimsheim.
P-51D WZ-E 44-72190

**March 2, 1945**
Lt. Henry M. Staub (83rd) POW; Hit by a Me-109 near Magdeburg.
P-51D HL-R 44-63285

**March 4, 1945**
Lt. Louis R. Hereford (84th) KIA; Lost in bad weather southeast of Nordlingen.
P-51D WZ-S 44-63209 "Sherman Was Right!"

**March 5, 1945**
Lt. Robert K. Platt (82nd) KIA; Crashed on take-off from Duxford.
P-51D MX-K 44-63238

**March 7, 1945**
Lt. Donald A. Bath (84th) KIAc; Stalled out while dog-fighting and crashed near Duxford.
P-51D WZ-G 44-63799

**March 11, 1945**
Lt. Jack D. Hodge (83rd) KIA; Lost coolant and bailed out near Vesjle.
P-51D HL-Q 44-15627 "Windy City Mama"

**March 12, 1945**
Lt. Dean C. Johnson (83rd) MIA-E; Lost coolant and bailed out near Laaland.
P-51D HL-A 44-72214 "Poop Shooter II"
Lt. Anton A. Rosengreen (84th) ASR; Suffered mechanical failure and bailed out over the Channel. He was acting as relay.
P-51D WZ-N 44-72200

**March 17, 1945**
Lt. Paul H. Stearns (82nd) MIA-E; Suffered mechanical trouble and landed inside Russian lines.
P-51D MX-Y 44-63183

**March 19, 1945**
Lt. Ralph L. Bush, Jr. (83rd) KIA; Hit by a Me-109 near Osnabruck.
P-51D HL-T 44-72351 "Frisco Belle"
Lt. Elmer K. Nieland (83rd) POW; Hit by a Me-109 near Osnabruck.
P-51D HL-C 44-15721
Maj. Harry L. Downing (84th) POW; Hit by a Me-109 near Osnabruck.
P-51D WZ-E 44-72407
Lt. James A. Bolen, Jr. (84th) KIA; Hit by a Me-109 near Osnabruck.
P-51D WZ-D 44-72386
Lt. Thomas N. Reeves (84th) POW; Hit by a Me-109 near Osnabruck.
P-51D WZ-W 44-15675

**March 21, 1945**
LtCol. Richard E. Conner (82nd) MIA-E; Hit by flak at Lonnewitz and bellied-in near Russian lines.
P-51D MX-D 44-72233

**March 31, 1945**
Lt. Paul S. Ostrander (84th) KIA; Hit by flak near Rheine and bailed out off the Dutch coast.
P-51D WZ-A 44-63215

**April 7, 1945**
Lt. Robert H. Talbot (83rd) POW; Shot down by a P-51 near Dummer Lake.
P-51D HL-H 44-72217

**April 10, 1945**
Lt. Herbert A. Stinson (82nd) KIA; Hit by flak at Werder A/F.
P-51D MX-Z 44-15556 "Doug"
Lt. Richard I. Kuehl (83rd) POW; Hit by flak at Brandenburg-Briest and bailed out near Helmstadt.
P-51D HL-X 44-15702
Lt. Roger A. Spaulding (84th) POW; Hit by flak at Werder A/F and bailed out near Brandenburg.
P-51D WZ-O 44-64156 "The Virgin Ann IV"

**April 16, 1945**
Capt. Manford O. Croy (82nd) KIA; Hit by flak at Straubing and bailed out too low.
P-51D MX-G 44-72165
Capt. Robert B. Holmes (82nd) KIA; Hit by flak at Ganacker.
P-51D MX-R 44-63214
Lt. Fred R. Swauger (82nd) POW; Hit by flak near Marienbad.
P-51D MX-E 44-15495

**April 17, 1945**
Lt. Alvin M. Rosenberg (82nd) POW; Hit by flak west of Adorf.
P-51D MX-D 44-72357
Lt. Allen A. Rosenblum (82nd) POW; Hit by flak near Kralupy.
P-51D MX-C 44-72367

**April 21, 1945**
LtCol. Leonard P. Marshall (HdQts) KIA; Crashed north of Strasbourg after developing mechanical trouble.
P-51D WZ-Z 44-63212 "The Face VI"
Capt. Dorain Ledington (84th) KIA; Crashed west of Coblenz in bad weather.
P-51D WZ-A 44-72772
Lt. John R. Sole (84th) KIA; Bailed out too low in bad weather west of Coblenz.
P-51D WZ-B 44-63712

**April 25, 1945**
Lt. Edward J. Carroll (82nd) KIA; Crashed near Sawston in heavy fog.
P-51D MX-W 44-15382

**July 10, 1945**
Capt. James M. Farmer (84th) KIAc;
P-51D WZ-Y 44-63187 "Bum Steer"

**Headquarters**
Bryan, Gillespie, Maj.; March 1945-May 1945; to 84th Ftr Sqn
8 missions
Caulfield, Peter A., Maj.; April 1945-EOW; ex-83rd Ftr Sqn
Christ, Charles M., LtCol.; September 1944-EOW; ex-84th Ftr Sqn
Dayhuff, Harry J., LtCol.; August 1943-April 1944; ex-83rd Ftr Sqn
P-47C MX-Z 41-6618 "Mackie"
Dickman, Joseph L., LtCol.; September 1942-April 13, 1943(Inj.)
1 mission
P-47C WZ-M 41-6399
Doyle, Gray H., Capt.; August 1944-September 5, 1944(KIA); ex-84th Ftr Sqn
Eby, Robert E., LtCol.; May 1942-September 1944
P-47C MX-H 41-6249 "Vee Gaile"
P-47D MX-H
Gilbert, Olin E., LtCol.; July 1944-August 28, 1944(MIA-E); December 1944-March 1945; to 66th Ftr Wg; ex-83rd Ftr Sqn
P-47D HL-X 42-26449
P-51D HL-A 44-63216 "Anne-Nihilator
Gray, Frederic C., Jr., Col.; May 1944-January 1945
P-47D HL-Z 42-25996 "Mr. Ted"
P-47D HL-Z 42-26391 "Mr. Ted II"
P-51D HL-Z 44-63279 "Mr. Ted III"
Himes, Ralph F., Maj.; May 1942-March 1944
P-47C WZ-M 41-6532 "Cali Kid"
Hunt, Bruce B., Maj.; April 1945-April 1945; to 83rd Ftr Sqn
Landers, John D., LtCol.; February 1945-June 1945; ex-49th Ftr Grp, PTO and 55th and 357th Ftr Grps
17 missions w/78th Ftr Grp
P-51D WZ-I 44-72218 "Big Beautiful Doll"
Lee, Morris K., Capt.; May 1942-August 1942; to ground duty due to illness
Lyle, Charles L., Capt.; October 1944-December 1944; to 84th Ftr Sqn
Marshall, Leonard P., LtCol.; March 1945-April 21, 1945(KIA); ex-82nd and 84th Ftr Sqns
P-51D WZ-Z 44-63212 "The Face VI"
May, William E., LtCol.; September 1944-EOW; ex-82nd Ftr Sqn
143 missions total
McNickle, Melvin F., LtCol.; July 1943-July 30, 1943(POW)
P-47D WZ-M 42-7961
Myers, Joseph, Jr., LtCol.; December 1944-February 1945; to 55th Ftr Grp; ex-55th Ftr Grp and 82nd Ftr Sqn
130 missions, 430 hours total
P-51D MX-S
Oberhansly, Jack J., LtCol.; August 1944-December 1944; to 4th Ftr Grp; ex-82nd Ftr Sqn
150 missions total
P-47D MX-X 44-19566 "Iron Ass"
Peterson, Arman, Col.; May 1942-July 1, 1943(KIA)
P-47D MX-P 42-7948 "Flagari"
Roberts, Eugene P., LtCol.; September 1943-December 1943; ex-84th Ftr Sqn; later 364th Ftr Grp
116 missions total
P-47C WZ-Z 41-6630 "Spokane Chief"
Smith, Robert W., Maj.; October 1944-EOW; ex-83rd Ftr Sqn
Stone, James J., Jr., Col.; July 1943-May 1944; ex-83rd Ftr Sqn
P-47C HL-Z 41-6373
P-47D HL-Z
Watkins, Benjamin M., Capt.; June 1944-July 1944; ex-82nd Ftr Sqn

**82nd Fighter Squadron**
Abernathy, Robert B., Lt.; November 1944-EOW
53 missions
Adamina, Robert E., Capt.; May 1942-May 14, 1943(POW)
Allison, James B., Lt.; August 1944-September 1944; to 83rd Ftr Sqn
Anderson, Bryant Y., Lt.; February 1943-October 1943; to 66th Ftr Wg

Anderson, Edwin B., Lt.; December 1944-February 24, 1945(POW)
9 missions
Anderson, Robert H., Lt.; September 1944-July 1945
Baker, Robert L., Lt.; February 1944-June 10, 1944(POW)
P-47D MX-C 42-8471 "Squint"
Beatty, Homer J., Lt.; February 1943-July 1943
Bechtelheimer, Wayne F., Lt.; September 1944-EOW
Beck, Harold F., Lt.; April 1944-July 1944; to 84th Ftr Sqn
P-47D MX-Q 42-26333 "Hun Buster"
Belovich, Robert F., Lt.; August 1943-December 1943
Bertrand, John R., Maj.; February 1943-March 1943; to 84th Ftr Sqn
Bernhard, Jack J., Lt.; February 1943-June 1944
Bibeau, Lucien J., Lt.; December 1944-February 24, 1945(KIA)
11 missions
Blossom, Robert J., Lt.; October 1944-EOW
49 missions
P-51D MX-A 44-63198 "Keep Kickin"
P-51D MX-A 44-72237 "Keep Kickin II
Boeckman, Rex C., Capt.; June 1944-February 1945
Boehner, Ernest V., Lt.; December 1944-March 1, 1945(KIA)
13 missions
Bolgert, E. Fred., Lt.; June 1944-December 1944
69 missions
Boone, Walker L., Capt.; July 1943-April 1944; later to 353rd Ftr Grp
P-47D MX- "Margaret"
Bosworth, Robert R., Lt.; June 1944-November 1944
Bourque, Walter E., Lt.; December 1944-EOW
44 missions
P-51D MX-T 44-15745
Brasher, J.E., Lt.; December 1943-May 1944
65 missions
P-47D MX- "Dude"
Bridges, William D., Lt.; April 1945-EOW
0 missions
Broberg, Melvin E., Lt.; April 1945-EOW
0 missions
Brower, Robert F., Lt.; February 1943-August 27, 1943(KIAc)
P-47C MX-F 41-6179
Brown, John I., III, Capt.; October 1944-July 1945
Brown, Ora R., Lt.; February 1943-June 13, 1943(KIA)
Brown, Winfield H., Maj.; June 1944-EOW
P-47D MX-F "Lady Helen"
P-51D MX-F 44-72191 "Lady Helen II"
Bruss, Elroy A., Lt.; April 1945-EOW
0 missions
Campi, Louis R., Lt.; February 1945-July 1945
20 missions
P-51D MX-R 44-72911
Capp, Merle R., Lt.; April 1944-July 1944; to 84th Ftr Sqn
59 missions total
P-47D MX-F
Carroll, Edward J., Lt.; February 1945-April 25, 1945(KIA)
17 missions
Casey, Lawrence R., Lt.; April 1944-September 1944
later 414th Ftr Grp, PTO
Cedergren, John H., Lt.; April 1945-EOW
0 missions
Chattaway, William P., Lt.; February 1943-March 1944; to 56th Ftr Grp
Childs, John C., Lt.; August 1944-July 1945
P-47D MX-W 42-26387 "Miss Behave"
P-51D MX-S 44-63246 "Little Rebel"
Clark, Charles R., Capt.; February 1943-August 2, 1944(POW)
Clark, Guy R., Lt.; April 1945-EOW
0 missions
Coleman, Wayne L., Capt.; July 1944-July 1945
P-51D MX-U 44-73042
Conner, Richard E., LtCol.; May 1944-March 21, 1945(MIA-E) May 1945-May 1945
P-47D MX-Y 42-26475
P-51D MX-D 44-72233
Coss, Wilbur J., Jr., Cpt.; July 1944-August 26, 1944(MIA-E); September 1944-February 22, 1945(KIA)
Cross, Louis D., Lt.; February 1943-March 1944
Croy, Manford O., Jr., Capt.; July 1944-April 16, 1945(KIA)
Dayhuff, Harry J., LtCol.; May 1942-August 1943; to HdQts
P-47C MX-Z 41-6618 "Mackie"
DeGenaro, August V., Lt.; May 1943-July 1943(WIA July 14)
DeWitt, Charles W., Capt.; February 1944-September 1944
Dicks, Louis A., Lt.; April 1944-August 10, 1944(KIA)
Downing, Harry L., Maj.; December 1944-March 1945; ex-84th Ftr Sqn
Dunham, Richard N., Lt.; September 1944-July 1945
Dunken, Allen G., Lt.; February 1943-March 1944
P-47D MX-U 42-8671 "Hun Hopper"
Dunlap, Richard C., F/O July 1944-September 1944
Eakes, Harvey L., Lt.; February 1944-April 5, 1944(KIA)
15 missions
Eggleston, Troy L., Lt.; September 1944-November 26, 1944(KIA)
Elsey, George V., Lt.; November 1944-July 1945
47 missions
P-51D MX-U 44-73042 "Sooner Hot Shot"
Evans, Herman L., Lt.; November 1943-May 1944
Evans, Ronald S., Lt.; October 1943-August 1944
Fisher, Gordon, Lt.; March 1945-EOW
4 missions
Fitzgerald, James T., Lt.; June 1944-August 8, 1944(POW)
Florenz, Andrew L., Lt.; April 1945-EOW
0 missions
Genge, William H., Lt.; May 1944-May 24, 1944(POW)
1 mission
Godard, Claude B., Jr., Lt.; September 1943-May 1944
Graff, Warren E., F/O; January 1943-July 30, 1943(MIA-E)
Guilfoyle, William A., Capt.; February 1944-August 1944
Hagarty, Daniel D., Lt.; March 1944-May 12, 1944(POW); ex-bomber pilot
32 missions
Hahn, Clifford B., Lt.; August 1943-January 24, 1944(KIA)
Hart, Donald C., Capt.; July 1944-July 1945
P-47D MX-Q 44-19777
P-51D MX-X 44-72205 "Sweet Hart"
Hazelett, Philip H., Lt.; January 1944-May 28, 1944(KIA)
Hearn, Roger V., Lt.; November 1943-May 1944
Hegman, William T., Lt.; February 1943-February 1944
200 hours
P-47C MX-N 41-6252 "Bee Ware"
Heil, Frank L., Lt.; March 1945-EOW
5 missions
Henahan, Donald J., Lt.; March 1945-EOW
6 missions
Herrick, John, Lt.; October 1943-November 26, 1943(POW)
6 missions
Hewitt, Richard A., Maj.; August 1943-June 1945
127 missions, 426 hours
P-47C MX-R 41-6345 "Miss Tibbie"
P-51D MX-U 44-64147 "Big Dick"
Hill, Archie W., Capt.; February 1943-November 1943; to 325th Ftr Grp, MTO
Hockery, John J., Capt.; July 1943-November 26, 1944(POW)
P-47D MX-L
P-47D MX-L 44-19950
Hodges, Ben F., Lt.; June 1944-June 20, 1944(KIA)
7 missions
Hoffman, Melvin F., F/O; November 1944-EOW
Holmes, Robert B., Capt.; December 1944-April 16, 1945(KIA)
Hosford, Lynn H., Jr., Lt.; April 1944-September 1944
285 hours
P-47D MX-O 42-76351 "Margaret's Mace"
Hydorn, William E., Lt.; November 1944-July 1945
46 missions
Jackson, Donald G., Lt.; February 1943-July 14, 1943(KIA)
P-47C MX-J 41-6222 "Mudcreeker"
Jones, Vernon Y., Lt.; November 1943-February 10, 1944(KIA)
27 missions
Keatley, Ivan H., Capt.; August 1944-July 1945
P-51D MX-Y 44-72352 "Cutie II"
Keller, Paul, Lt.; September 1943-May 1944
Kinsolving, James E., Lt.; April 1944-October 1944
74 missions, 274 hours
P-47D MX-K 42-26585
Kohlman, Bertrand L., Lt.; February 1943-March 1943; to 83rd Ftr Sqn
Kosinski, Anthony I., Lt.; January 1944-May 11, 1944(MIA-E)
Kuehner, Richard S., Lt.; April 1944-June 10, 1944(KIA)
Lacy, William O., Lt.; August 1944-September 10, 1944(KIA)
Lamb, Huie H., Jr., Lt.; August 1944-July 1945
60 missions, 275:30 hours
P-47D MX-O 42-28422
P-51D MX-V 44-63286 "Etta Jeanne"
P-51K MX-V 44-11631 "Etta Jeanne II
Lamb, John T., Lt.; January 1944-@August 1944
Lehman, Paul H., Lt.; February 1943-February 1944
Liebenrood, Harold R., F/O; November 1944-February 28, 1945(POW)
26 missions
Ludwig, Donald E., Lt.; January 1944-February 10, 1944(KIA)
1 mission
Lundigan, George J., Capt.; May 1944-August 1944
Marshall, Leonard P., Maj.; May 1942-September 1944; to 84th Ftr Sqn
Martinez, Manuel S., Capt.; May 1943-May 1944; Later with 1st Air Commando Group, 10th Air Force, CBI
P-47D MX-F 42-8620
Mattern, James L., Lt.; June 1944-December 1944
P-47D MX-P 42-28740
May, William E., Capt.; February 1943-April 1944; to HdQts later
143 missions total
Mayo, Ben I., Maj.; June 1944-July 1944; to 84th Ftr Sqn, ex-84th Ftr Sqn
62 missions total
P-47D MX-X 42-26671 "No Guts, No Glory!"
Miller, Austin S., Lt.; September 1944-July 1945
Miller, Richard I., Lt.; July 1944-September 1944
Moore, Kenneth L., Lt.; August 1944-September 9, 1944(KIA)
Morrison, George W., F/O; October 1944-January 2, 1945(POW)
Morris, Harold J., Lt.; January 1944-July 26, 1944(KIA); ex-353rd Ftr Grp
Morsch, Donald R., Lt.; January 1944-February 11, 1944(KIA)
5 missions
Munson, Norman D., Maj.; February 1943-July 19, 1944(KIA)
P-47D MX-C 42-8575 "Lady Yvonne"
Myers, Joseph, Jr., LtCol.; August 1944-December 1944; to HdQts; ex-55th Ftr Grp
130 missions, 430 hours total
P-47D MX-S 42-27339

Neel, William F., Lt.; February 1943-January 24, 1944(KIA)
Nelson, Lawrence W., Jr., Lt.; August 1944-April 1945
Oberhansly, Jack J., LtCol.; May 1942-May 1944; to HdQts
150 missions total
P-47C MX-X 41-6542 "Iron Ass"
P-47D MX-X 42-7883 "Iron Ass"
Orr, Ronald C., Lt.; February 1944-February 29, 1944(POW)
2 missions
Orvis, William S., Lt.; May 1944-May 28, 1944(KIA)
2 missions
Parker, James E., Lt.; December 1944-EOW
47 missions
Peel, Eugene L., Lt.; December 1944-EOW
42 missions
Platt, Robert K., Lt.; February 1945-March 5, 1945(KIA)
7 missions
Ramsey, John C., Capt.; June 1944-June 12, 1944(KIA)
2 missions
Ramsey, Milton H., Lt.; December 1943-January 29, 1944(MIA-E)
9 missions
Richards, Hayden E., Lt.; May 1944-September 1944
P-47D MX-T 42-76557 "Judy"
Richie, Arthur B., Capt.; February 1943-February 1944
Roberts, Donald R., Lt.; April 1944-April 13, 1944(POW)
2 missions
Roe, Harry L., Lt.; February 1945-EOW
23 missions
P-51D MX-Z 44-72938 "Miss Pam"
Rosenberg, Alvin M., Lt.; December 1944-April 17, 1945(POW)
41 missions
Rosenblum, Allen A., Lt.; September 1944-April 17, 1945(POW)
Ryan, Maurice J., Lt.; March 1945-EOW
5 missions
Sandmeier, Jack S., Lt.; February 1943-May 15, 1943(KIA)
Scheibler, Joseph A., Lt.; November 1943-May 1944
Schneider, Edwin O., Lt.; October 1944-July 1945
Scholz, Howard S., Lt.; May 1944-September 1944
Sharp, Fred I., Lt.; May 1944-September 1944
285 hours
P-47D MX- "Rough Edge"
Shope, Herbert K., Capt.; June 1944-January 1945
Slater, Henry B., Lt.; April 1944-September 1944
Smith, Billy V., Lt.; July 1944-August 13, 1944(KIA)
Smith, Robert E., Lt.; October 1944-July 1945
Snyder, Richard C., Lt.; August 1944-September 18, 1944(POW)
Spaulding, Robert P., Lt.; February 1943-March 1944
Stallings, James B., Lt.; April 1944-September 1944
Stark, Richard D., Lt.; August 1944-September 3, 1944(POW)
Stearns, Paul H., Lt.; October 1944-March 17, 1945(MIA-E)
Steele, James F., Lt.; February 1943-May 11, 1944(INT)
Steele, Richard D., Lt.; April 1944-September 1944
Steinwedel, John C.E., Lt.; April 1944-June 5, 1944(KIA)
Stillwell, George W., Lt.; January 1945-EOW
28 missions
Stinson, Herbert A., Lt.; October 1944-April 10, 1945(KIA)
P-51D MX-Z 44-15556 "Doug"
Stutzman, Milton B., Lt.; January 1945-EOW
25 missions
Swankowski, Donald H., Lt.; April 1944-September 1944
Swanson, William S., Lt.; November 1943-February 11, 1944(KIA)
29 missions
Swauger, Fred R., Lt.; January 1945-April 16, 1945(POW)
17 missions
Thompson, Harry A., Lt.; October 1944-November 21, 1944(POW)
Turley, Grant M., Lt.; September 1943-March 6, 1944(KIA)
47 missions, 113 hours
P-47D MX-N 42-7998 "Kitty"
Ulerick, Estel E., Lt.; February 1944-March 1944 (Injured March 17)
Van Dyk, Warren V., Lt.; April 1944-September 1944
Wagner, Karl R., Lt.; June 1943-May 1944
Warren, Willard E., Lt.; August 1944-February 9, 1945(POW)
Watkins, Benjamin M., Capt.; January 1944-June 1944; to HdQts
Webb, Calvin, Lt.; December 1943-April 1, 1944(KIA)
Wesson, Warren M., Lt.; February 1943-May 1944
P-47D MX-E 42-8530 "Jeanie V.O.S."
Weston, Gordon L., F/O; October 1944-January 6, 1945(KIA)
White, Stephen L., Lt.; States-January 26, 1943(KIAc)
White, Zane W., F/O; May-July 1945
0 missions
Wilkinson, James W., Capt.; November 1943-June 4, 1944(KIAc); ex-4th Ftr Grp
87 missions total
P-47D MX-L 42-7954 "Pin-Up Girl"
Wilkinson, Ruben E., Lt.; April 1944-September 1944
Wolfe, Roland L., Capt.; March 1944-September 1944
Woller, Myron K., Capt.; January 1944-August 1944
Wren, William D., Lt.; September 1943-March 1944
Wright, Melvin R., Lt.; February 1943-December 10, 1943(KIAc)
Young, Wilson G., Capt.; April 1944-September 1944
Zboinski, Dolphe C., Lt.; November 1944-March 1945
16 missions

**83rd Fighter Squadron**
Abernathy, Ishmael W., Lt.; April 1943-November 1943
Allison, James B., Jr., Lt.; September 1944-March 1945; to 5th ERS; ex-82nd Ftr Sqn
Allstaedt, Kenneth C., Lt.; April 1944-September 1944
P-47D HL-W 42-25552
Andrews, Merrill, F/O; April 1945-July 1945
0 missions
Askelson, Howard S., Capt.; February 1943-March 1944
Barnaby, Harold T., Capt.; February 1943-April 1945
106 missions
P-47D HL-I 42-7889
Beals, Donald S., Lt.; States-January 26, 1943(KIAc)
Beckley, Samuel R., LtCol.; August 1944-October 1945
P-51D HL-B 44-63178 "Beck-Dor"
Bennett, Wallace R., Capt.; July 1944-December 1944
P-47D HL-O
Bigelow, Marvin C., Lt.; November 1944-EOW
23 missions, 108:20 hours
Bingham, Percy, Lt.; August 1944-September 1944 (injured September 6)
Blystone, Harry L., Lt.; March 1944-September 1944
Bodenhamer, Donald, Maj.; February 1943-March 1944; later to CBI
Bonebrake, Robert R., Capt.; June 1944-January 1945
P-47D HL-E 42-25724
P-47D HL-E 44-19750
Boner, Gerald F., Lt.; January 1945-January 17, 1945(KIA)
2 missions
Boteler, George G., Lt.; April 1944-September 1944
Bradley, William E., F/O January 1945-January 20, 1945(KIAc)
0 missions
Burgher, Russell L., Lt.; July 1944-March 1945
Burman, Charles L., Lt.; April 1944-November 1944
Bush, Ralph L., Lt.; March 1945-March 19, 1945(KIA)
2 missions
Bzdelik, Joseph, F/O; August 1944-November 1944
Carey, William J., Lt.; April 1945-EOW
0 missions
Casey, Lawrence R., Lt.; April 1944-October 1944 later 414th Ftr Grp, PTO
Caulfield, Peter A., Capt.; January 1944-April 1945
Chapman, William T., Lt.; June 1943-March 1944
86 missions
P-47C HL-N 41-6411 "Muscle Bound"
P-47D HL-N 42-75610 "Muscle Bound"
Charlton, Quentin, Lt.; September 1943-September 22, 1943(KIA
7 missions
Chetwood, Kenneth, Lt.; April 1943-October 1943; later 353rd Ftr Grp
Chippendale, Henry, Lt.; April 1945-EOW
0 missions
Colletti, Anthony T., Lt.; February 1945-July 1945
21 missions
Cooper, James M., Maj.; May 1942-June 1944; to 356th Ftr Grp
P-47C HL-A 41-6361 "Hellza Poppin"
Cormier, Ralph E., Lt.; October 1943-November 26, 1943(KIA)
Daniels, Archie F., F/O; December 1943-February 11, 1944(KIA)
Davis, Hubert, Lt.; January 1945-July 1945
35 missions
P-51D HL-W 44-63864 "Twilight Tear"
Davis, Jesse C., Jr., Maj.; May 1942-January 1944
P-47C HL-X 41-6402 "Owley & Tobe"
Decker, Richard E., Capt.; November 1942-February 1943; to 14th Ftr Grp, MTO
DeVilliers, Donald J., Lt.; July 1944-July 1945
Dodd, Leroy V., Lt.; February 1943-April 15, 1943(KIAc)
0 missions
Doherty, Pat H., Lt.; April 1945-EOW
0 missions
Doss, Gene C., Lt.; July 1944-EOW
Dougherty, Kenneth W., Capt.; February 1943-April 1944
P-47C HL-D 41-6364 "Jacquelyn"
P-47D HL-D 42-74634
Downey, Edward J., F/O; December 1943-March 6, 1944(KIA)
Dunaway, Kenneth P., Lt.; July 1944-September 1, 1944(POW)
Eadline, Lloyd L., Lt.; October 1944-February 24, 1945(KIA)
Ealey, Robert E., Capt.; May 1943-June 1944
Eastwood, James C.P., F/O; December 1943-December 30, 1943(KIA)
1 mission
Eckert, Ray H., Lt.; March 1945-EOW
0 missions
Eggleston, Richfield, Lt.; August 1944-November 1944
Eierman, Robert F., Lt.; April 1945-EOW
0 missions
Euler, John E., Lt.; March 1945-EOW
6 missions
Fish, Frank A., Lt.; July 1944-January 1945
P-47D HL-V 42-28636 "Flying Fish"
Fisher, James E., Lt.; March 1945-EOW
5 missions
Follen, John E., Lt.; April 1945-July 1945; ex-447th Bomb Grp
Foster, Hugh O., Lt.; September 1944-February 1945 injured and off ops December 1944
Gabriel, Watson R., Lt.; March 1945-EOW
5 missions
Galston, Robert H., Lt.; March 1945-July 1945
4 missions

Gibbs, Ollie E., Lt.; June 1944-June 22, 1944(KIA)
Gilbert, Olin E., LtCol.; November 1943-July 1944; to HdQts
P-47D HL-X 42-25837
P-47D HL-X 42-26449
Gordon, William P., Lt.; April 1943-July 1943; to 495th Ftr Trg Grp
Granger, Arthur S., Lt.; November 1943-January 5, 1944(KIA)
Green, Robert T., Capt.; July 1944-April 1945
86 missions, 372 hours
P-47D HL-C 42-28518 "Green Hornet"
P-51K HL-K 44-11573 "Green Hornet"
Hamilton, Ralph E., Lt.; September 1944-February 22, 1945(POW)
Hamilton, Willard D., Lt.; April 1943-May 1944
Harrington, Francis E., Lt.; May 1944-April 1945
73 missions, 350 hours
P-47D HL-I "Boston Bean"
P-51D HL-I 44-15586 "Boston Bean"
Hartley, Dunstan D., Lt.; July 1944-September 23, 1944(KIA)
Hathway, Randall B., Lt.; April 1944-September 1944
Higginbottom, Foy E., Capt.; April 1944-EOW
545 hours
P-51K HL-M 44-11625
Hilbert, Marquis D., F/O; October 1944-March 1945
Hindersinn, Kenneth, Lt.; November 1943-January 5, 1944(POW)
Hobbie, Eldridge M., Lt.; October 1944-EOW
Hodge, Jack D., Lt.; November 1944-March 11, 1945(KIA)
35 missions
Holden, Paul C., Lt.; April 1944-August 1944
Holloway, Richard L., Lt.; March 1945-October 1945
6 missions
Hopton, Walter J., Lt.; March 1945-EOW
16 missions
Hotchkiss, Courtlyn W., Lt.; January 1944-March 17, 1944(POW)
Hunt, Bruce B., LtCol.; April 1945-July 1945; ex-HdQts
Hurst, Carl P., Capt.; November 1943-June 1944
Innocenzi, Andrew R., Lt.; October 1944-February 14, 1945(MIA-E
Jackson, Joseph W., Lt.; July 1944-November 1944
P-47D HL-K 42-28544 "Fast Action Jackson"
Jacobson, Alan R., Lt.; July 1944-November 9, 1944(KIA)
Johnson, Dean C., Lt.; November 1944-March 12, 1945(MIA-E)
39 missions
Johnson, John H., Lt.; January 1944-February 22, 1944(POW)
Jones, Robert N., Lt.; July 1944-September 1, 1944(KIA)
Juchheim, Alwin M., Capt.; September 1943-May 28, 1944(POW)
76 missions, 237 hours
P-47D HL-J 42-74690
P-47D HL-J 42-26020 "Lady Jane"
Julian, William H., Maj.; February 1943-March 1945; to 339th Ftr Grp
P-47C HL-R 41-6628
P-51K HL-D 44-12126
Junod, F/O; February 1943-March 1943
Kirk, John A., Lt.; October 1944-July 1945
49 missions, 248 hours
P-51D HL-C 44-63620 "Small Boy Here"
Kitley, Edward T., Lt.; March 1944-July 1, 1944(KIA)
Klassen, Peter W., Lt.; September 1944-EOW
Klein, F/O; February 1943-March 1943
Knapp, Robert H., Lt.; February 1943-February 1944
119 missions
P-47C HL-J 41-6229 "Percy"
Kochanek, Francis J., Lt.; May 1944-June 1944(WIA June 10)
16 missions
Kohlman, Bertrand L., Lt.; March 1943-June 1944; ex-82nd Ftr Sqn
Kolb, John J., Lt.; November 1943-May 1944
200 hours
Korsmeyer, Willard J., Lt.; July 1944-July 31, 1944(POW)
4 missions
Kuehl, Richard I., Lt.; March 1945-April 10, 1945(POW)
25 missions
Kulik, Edward R., Capt.; July 1944-May 1945
68 missions, 340 hours
P-47D HL-X 42-26449
P-51D HL-X 44-72964
Kuykendall, Charles E., Lt.; August 1944-September 5, 1944(MIA-E)
LaGrange, Jack, Jr., Lt.; July 1944-October 15, 1944(POW)
Lawhead, Douglas A., Capt.; February 1944-August 1944
P-47D HL-G 42-25719
Leach, Major C., Lt.; @November 1943-January 5, 1944(KIA)
Leatherman, Vernon A., Capt.; August 1944-September 1944; ex-353rd Ftr Grp
Loegering, John R., Lt.; August 1944-September 18, 1944(POW)
London, Charles P., Capt.; May 1942-November 1943
65 missions
P-47C HL-B 41-6335 "El Jeepo"
MacDuffie, Russell C., Lt.; August 1944-September 18, 1944(POW)
Madole, William H., Lt.; May 1943-November 1943; to 325th Ftr Grp, MTO
P-47C HL-S 41-6540 "Skonk Hunter"
Maitland, George C., Lt.; February 1944-March 8, 1944(KIA)
Martinek, Sam R., F/O; February 1943-May 14, 1943(POW)
4 missions
Massa, Vincent J., Lt.; March 1944-June 10, 1944(KIA)
McDermott, William M., Lt.; March 1944-June 10, 1944(KIA)
P-47D HL-E 42-26053
McDuffie, Duncan M., Capt.; November 1944-EOW
45 missions
McLeod, Donald W., Maj.; June 1944-June 10, 1944(MIA-E); ex-RAF
1 mission
McTaggart, Elmer E., Capt.; States-May 14, 1943(MIA-E); later 367th Ftr Grp, 9th Air Force
7 missions
Messinger, Richard A., Lt.; March 1945-August 1945
23 missions
Miller, Edwin H., Capt.; July 1944-March 1945
P-51K HL-N 44-11563 "The Brat"
Miller, Jack B., Lt.; July 1944-August 18, 1944(KIA)
Milliron, Edwin, Lt.; October 1944-January 1945
Monteith, Donald R., Lt.; December 1944-July 1945
44 missions
Montfort, James M., Lt.; April 1943-June 1944
Moothart, James A., Lt.; July 1944-February 1945
Motsenbocker, John D., Lt.; January 1944-May 8, 1944(POW)
Mullins, Robert E., Lt.; May 1944-July 6, 1944(KIA)
Nieland, Elmer K., Lt.; October 1944-March 19, 1945(POW)
O'Brien, Charles R., F/O; December 1944-February 26, 1945(POW-D)
21 missions
O'Connell, Martin G., Jr., Lt.; April 1944-April 15, 1944(KIAc)
Olson, Leonard S., Lt.; December 1944-February 26, 1945(POW)
25 missions
Oxley, Richard W., Lt.; April 1944-September 1944
Palopoli, Anthony A., Lt.; October 1944-EOW
300 hours
Peal, Charles M., Capt.; April 1943-August 10, 1944(KIA)
P-47D HL-P 42-7914 "Miss Norma"
P-47D HL-P 42-76232 "Miss Norma II"
P-47D HL-P "Miss Norma III"
Perry, Henry L., Lt.; States-January 26, 1943(KIAc)
Peterson, James S., Lt.; December 1944-February 14, 1945(MIA-E) March 1945-EOW
28 missions
P-51D HL-U 44-63208 "Wanderin' Boy"
Phaneuf, Richard E., Lt.; November 1944-EOW
49 missions
Poole, Robert E., F/O; April 1943-December 1943
Powell, Everett W., Lt.; June 1943-March 4, 1944(POW)
Pursell, Franklin R., Lt.; April 1944-September 1944
P-47D HL-H 42-25528
Putnam, Melvin D., Lt.; May 1943-January 5, 1944(KIA)
Raese, Cleon W., Jr., Lt.; June 1944-July 1, 1944(KIA)
Reems, Julian, Capt.; May 1944-November 1944
Reese, William H., Lt.; January 1944-April 11, 1944(KIA)
Regner, Fred J., Lt.; March 1945-EOW
5 missions
P-51D HL-P 44-72046
Riccardo, Gennaro, Lt.; February 1944-September 1944
Rich, George, III, Lt.; August 1944-September 6, 1944(POW)
Roff, Harry C., Lt.; May 1943-March 1944
P-47D HL-G 42-7951 "Spirit of Sycamore Hill"
Rohm, Robert F., Lt.; February 1945-July 1945
36 missions
P-51D HL-J 44-72036 "Normie"
Ronning, Robert I., F/O; February 1943-March 1, 1943(KIAc)
0 missions
Seeley, Howard L., Lt.; August 1944-April 1945
Senarens, William B., Lt.; August 1944-February 3, 1945(POW)
P-51D HL-T 44-15729 "Bill's Bus"
Shepard, Thomas W., Lt.; April 1943-April 1944
Smith, Jayson M., Lt.; April 1943-August 15, 1943(KIA)
20 missions
Smith, Robert W., Maj.; April 1944-December 1944
Sommer, Warren B., Lt.; June 1944-November 1944
Sorenson, Boyd W., Lt.; April 1944-September 1944
89 missions
Spengler, William B., Lt.; January 1945-September 1945
32 missions
Staub, Henry M., Lt.; October 1944-March 2, 1945(POW)
Stokes, James E., Lt.; June 1943-February 1944
P-47C HL-M 41-6210 "Upstairs Cat"
Stones, James J., Jr., LtCol.; May 1942-July 1943; to HdQts
P-47C HL-Z 41-6373
Strobel, Earle W., Lt.; January 1945-EOW
28 missions
Sweat, Dale S., Lt.; March 1945-EOW
7 missions
Talbot, Robert H., Lt.; January 1945-April 7, 1945(POW)
23 missions
Tonkin, Walter, Lt.; November 1943-March 16, 1944(KIA)
P-47D HL-U 42-8543
Tucker, John D., F/O; April 1945-EOW
0 missions
Wade, John B., Lt.; December 1944-February 23, 1945(POW)
16 missions
Waldheim, William H., Lt.; April 1943-January 1944
Werder, Albert B., Lt.; February 1944-March 30, 1944(KIA)
White, Fred, Lt.; April 1944-September 1944
P-47D HL-N 42-25312

Wilkes, Dwight E., Capt.; June 1943-May 1944
300 hours
P-47C HL-F 41-6246
Wise, Robert E., Capt.; January 1944-March 1945
P-51D HL-U 44-63208 "The Horrible Hoosier III"
Zumwalt, Harding R., Lt.; February 1943-April 1944
71 missions, 200 hours
P-47D HL-Y 42-8524

**84th Fighter Squadron**
Abel, Luther J., Lt.; March 1944-July 1944
Ankeny, Paul, F/O; April 1945-EOW
0 missions
Arpin, Arthur N., Lt.; May 1942-February 1943; to MTO
Barba, Andrew M., Lt.; February 1943-May 1944
P-47D WZ-E 42-74694 "Joker"
Baron, Richard L., Lt.; June 1944-November 1944
Bath, Donald A., Lt.; October 1944-March 7, 1945(KIAc)
27 missions
Beck, Harold F., Lt.; July 1944-September 1944; ex-82nd Ftr Sqn
Behm, Willard P., Lt.; April 1945-EOW
8 missions
Belliveau, Robert E., Capt.; April 1943-April 1944
Belt, Dwight G., Lt.; July 1944-October 1, 1944(KIAc)
Bendorf, Cyril T., Lt.; November 1944-July 1945
46 missions
P-51D WZ-F 44-72325
Bertrand, John R., Maj.; March 1943-May 1944; ex-82nd Ftr Sqn
Blodgett, Warren S., Lt.; November 1944-EOW
45 missions
P-51D WZ-X 44-72099 "Little Chic"
Bolen, James A., Lt.; February 1945-March 19, 1945(KIA)
3 missions
Bond, John S., Lt.; December 1944-July 1945
Bowman, Lonnie E., Lt.; April 1945-July 1945
0 missions
Boyle, Herbert L., Capt.; January 1944-July 1944
86 missions
P-47D WZ-J 42-26624 "Old Smoothy"
Brendle, Merle V., Lt.; December 1944-February 20, 1945(KIA)
9 missions
Bretherton, Richard, Lt.; December 1944-July 1945
29 missions
Brown, Charles R., F/O; February 1943-May 16, 1943(POW)
2 missions
Brown, Quince L., Maj.; June 1943-September 6, 1944(KIA)
136 missions
P-47D WZ-J 42-74753 "Okie"
P-47D WZ-J 42-25698 "Okie II"
Byers, James F., Lt.; April 1943-July 30, 1943(KIA)
27 missions
Calderon, Severino B., Lt.; June 1944-January 1945
Calloway, Carl E., Capt.; July 1944-March 1945
Calvin, John D., Lt.; February 1945-September 1945
19 missions
P-51D WZ-D 44-73119 "Merry Bee"
Capp, Merle R., Lt.; July 1944-September 1944; ex-82nd Ftr Sqn
59 missions total
Casey, James F., Lt.; September 1943-June 10, 1944(POW)
Christ, Charles M., LtCol.; July 1944-September 1944; to HdQts
Clague, Robert E., Lt.; November 1943-September 10, 1944(POW)
Clark, Lawton E., Lt.; June 1944-September 10, 1944(KIA)
P-47D WZ-E 42-26590 "Thoroughbred"
Clemons, Clark W., Lt.; February 1945-EOW
19 missions
P-51D WZ-W 44-72927 "Frances Dell"
Coffey, Charles F., Lt.; February 1945-July 1945
8 missions
P-51D WZ-N 44-15707 "Kitten Jean"
Coit, John H., Lt.; April 1945-EOW
0 missions
Connelly, Rueben S., Lt.; April 1945-EOW
0 missions
Cooper, James M., Maj.; June 1944-July 1944; to 356th Ftr Grp; ex-83rd Ftr Sqn
Corbett, Richard K., Lt.; December 1944-July 1945
26 missions
Covelle, Lloyd K., Capt.; August 1943-June 1944
P-47D WZ-M 42-26149
Cross, Carl E., Lt.; September 1943-October 1943
Cummings, Gene T., F/O; July 1944-August 6, 1944(POW)
5 missions
Dacci, William K., Lt.; January 1944-June 1944
DeAnda, Louis, Lt.; October 1944-July 1945
41 missions
P-51D WZ-K 44-15692
DeGain, William J., Lt.; November 1944-EOW
47 missions
P-51D WZ-H 44-63632 "Lee D"
DeMaagd, Kenneth J., Lt.; December 1944-January 20, 1945(POW)
2 missions
Dion, Louis C., F/O; February 1943-April 1943; to hospital
0 missions
Dougherty, Wayne M., Lt.; April 1943-November 26, 1943(POW)
Downing, Andrew H., Lt.; April 1943-December 1943
Downing, Harry L., Maj.; October 1944-December 1944; to 82nd Ftr Sqn
Doyle, Gray H., Capt.; April 1943-February 1944; to HdQts
Eaton, Alfred F., Capt.; June 1944-November 1944
P-47D WZ-U 42-26682 "Ozark Queen"
Elin, Herbert W., Lt.; July 1944-January 13, 1945(KIA)
Farmer, James M., Capt.; September 1944-July 10, 1945(KIAc)
P-51D WZ-H 44-15731 "Mischievious Nell"
Fee, John R., Lt.; December 1943-September 18, 1944(POW)
Fleming, Edward F., Capt.; February 1943-April 1944
P-47C WZ-H 41-6409
Ford, Lester E., Lt.; June 1944-July 11, 1944(POW)
7 missions
Gallant, George E., Lt.; March 1945-EOW
2 missions
Garback, Alfred A., Lt.; September 1944-EOW
P-51D WZ-G 44-63779 "Screamin' Demon"
Giles, Lake, Lt.; April 1944-September 1944
Goldsworthy, Robert G., Lt.; January 1945-April 1945; ex-357th Ftr Grp
14 missions
Gore, Robert N., Lt.; February 1943-November 1943; to 310th Ferry Sqn
Grimes, Wilbur K., Capt.; June 1944-January 1945
Grisham, Leon M., Lt.; September 1944-February 3, 1945(POW)
Hailey, Wallace R., Lt.; May 1944-June 1944
Haning, Allen P., Lt.; June 1944-November 1944
Hardin, William J., Lt.; December 1943-June 1944
Hartman, George T., Lt.; February 1943-January 5, 1944(KIA)
P-47D WZ-E 42-22459 "Joker"
Haskins, D.D., Lt.; March 1945-EOW
5 missions
Hays, George J., Capt.; April 1943-May 1944
P-47C WZ-K 41-6243 "Pappy"
Hemphill, John S., Lt.; March 1945-EOW
1 mission
Henderson, Paul R., Lt.; March 1945-July 1945
4 missions
Hepner, Neal, Lt.; March 1945-September 1945
4 missions
Hereford, Louis R., Lt.; December 1944-March 4, 1945(KIA)
9 missions
Higgins, Roy D., Lt.; July 1944-March 1, 1945(KIA)
P-47D WZ-G 44-19934 "Ginny"
P-51D WZ-G 44-63799 "Ginny"
Holly, Richard M., Capt.; February 1944-August 1944; Earlier served w/50th Ftr Sqn, Iceland (0.5 victories)
P-47D WZ-Y 42-25871 "Nigger II"
Hunt, Bruce B., Maj.; April 1945-May 1945; ex-HdQts
Hunt, William F., Capt.; April 1943-June 10, 1944(KIA)
Hupe, Franklin E., F/O; February 1943-April 1943; to 4th Ftr Grp
Irvin, John D., Maj.; May 1942-March 1944
P-47C WZ-B 41-6367 "Geronimo"
Josey, Danford E., Lt.; March 1945-July 1945
4 missions
Just, Harry H., Jr., Lt.; February 1944-June 7, 1944(KIA)
Keillor, Peter T., Capt.; September 1944-July 1945; ex-13th Air Force, PTO
P-51K WZ-L 44-11747
Kelly, William G., Lt.; October 1944-November 9, 1944(KIAc)
Keppler, Charles N., Lt.; April 1943-February 1944; to 361st Ftr Grp
P-47C WZ-L 41-6223 "Isabel"
Koontz, Glenn H., Capt.; April 1943-June 1944
Kramer, Harold W., Lt.; April 1944-September 1944
Lacey, John F., Lt.; April 1944-August 28, 1944(POW)
Laho, Robert O., Lt.; June 1944-November 1944
P-47D WZ-X 42-28615 "My Baby"
Lang, Ernest S., Lt.; October 1943-April 1944
Larson, Philip R., Capt.; April 1943-January 1945
Lay, Harry T., Capt.; June 1944-July 17, 1944(KIA); ex-91st Bomb Group
Ledington, Dorian, Capt.; January 1944-April 21, 1945(KIA)
P-51D WZ-A 44-72772
Lentz, Norbert G., Lt.; February 1943-June 1944
P-47C WZ-F 41-6333
Loyd, Daniel T., Lt.; May 1944-June 10, 1944(KIA)
16 missions
Luckey, William J., Capt.; April 1944-September 1944
Lutz, Willis H., Lt.; October 1944-EOW
Lyle, Charles L., Capt.; December 1944-February 20, 1945(KIA); ex-HdQts
Marlow, Macie V., Lt.; October 1943-April 1944
Marshall, Donald M., Lt.; April 1943-June 13, 1943(POW)
8 missions
Marshall, Leonard P., LtCol.; September 1944-March 1945; to HdQts
P-47D WZ-Z 44-19762 "The Face V"
P-51D WZ-Z 44-63212 "The Face VI"
Marshall, Lloyd Q., Lt.; June 1944-November 1944
Maxwell, Julius P., Capt.; April 1944-January 1945
133 missions, 432 hours
P-47D WZ-O 42-74742 "War Eagle"

Mayo, Ben I., LtCol.; April 1944-June 1944; to 82nd Ftr Sqn; July 1944-September 1944
62 missions total
P-47D WZ-P 42-26551
P-47D WZ-V 42-26567 "No Guts, No Glory!"
McClellan, William M., Lt.; October 1944-EOW
P-51D WZ-U 44-63191 "Lucky Baby"
McGuire, Allen G., Lt.; June 1944-November 1944
McIntosh, Robert J., Lt.; April 1944-June 10, 1944(MIA-E)
31 missions
McKenney, Paul H., Lt.; June 1944-September 10, 1944(POW)
Miller, William H., Lt.; June 1944-September 1944
Moores, James E., Lt.; November 1944-July 1945
53 missions
Mosely, Lonnie L., Lt.; June 1944-July 4, 1944(POW)
Mundy, Joseph W., F/O; January 1944-April 15, 1944(KIA)
Murphy, John L., Lt.; December 1944-EOW
26 missions
P-51D WZ-G 44-15577 "Just Hangen' Around"
Murray, Richard A., Lt.; April 1943-May 20, 1943(KIA)
9 missions
Musgrave, Louis R., Lt.; October 1944-February 24, 1945(KIA)
Myler, John J., Lt.; July 1944-August 5, 1944(KIA)
Newmark, Burton J., Lt.; October 1944-February 21, 1945(POW)
25 missions
P-51D WZ-K 44-63171 "Lady Eve"
Newton, William, III, Lt.; May 1944-July 5, 1944(KIA)
Nunley, James A., Lt.; March 1945-July 1945
3 missions
Oiler, Frank E., Lt.; June 1944-March 1945
P-47D WZ-S 42-28878 "Eileen"
P-51D WZ-S 44-63209 "Sherman Was Right!"
Oldfield, Charles S., Lt.; November 1944-February 25, 1945(MIA-E)
21 missions
Ostrander, Paul S., Lt.; September 1944-March 31, 1945(KIA)
P-51K WZ-J 44-11743 "The Porcelain Pillbox"
Orr, Ross, Lt.; January 1944-July 1, 1944(POW)
Packer, Allen R., Lt.; September 1944-January 17, 1945(POW)
Parmelee, Charles E., Lt.; June 1944-September 10, 1944(KIA)
41 missions
P-47D WZ-I 43-25305
Patton, James O., Lt.; January 1944-September 1944
Pearson, Donald K., Lt.; April 1943-April 1944
Peterson, Earl M., Lt.; November 1943-April 1944
P-47D WZ-D 42-74657 "Vicky"
Pompetti, Peter E., Lt.; February 1943-March 17, 1944(POW)
95 missions, 226:33 hours
P-47C WZ-R 41-6393 "Axe The Axis"
Price, Jack C., Maj.; July 1942-February 1944; later 20th Ftr Grp
99 missions, 281:15 hours total
P-47C WZ-A 41-6270 "Feather Merchant"
P-47D WZ-A 42-74641 "Feather Merchant II"
Putnam, John B., Jr., Lt.; April 1944-July 19, 1944(KIAc)
Reeves, Thomas N., Lt.; November 1944-March 19, 1945(POW)
28 missions
Resseguie, Franklin D., Lt.; October 1943-October 18, 1943(POW)
1 mission
Rice, Hamilton H., Lt.; January 1944-June 7, 1944(POW)
Rickett, George G., Lt.; May 1944-June 1944; to 5th ERS
Roberts, Eugene P., LtCol.; July 1942-September 1943; to HdQts; later 364th Ftr Grp
116 missions total
P-47C WZ-Z 41-6630 "Spokane Chief"
Rosengreen, Anton A., Lt.; January 1945-September 1945
23 missions
Russell, Ernest E., Lt.; October 1943-May 1944
Ryan, Frank A., F/O; January 1945-July 1945
11 missions
Saffold, Paul W., Jr., Capt.; February 1943-May 1944
96 missions
P-47D WZ-Q 42-7894 "Rebel"
Sawall, Warren J., Lt.; November 1944-February 3, 1945(POW)
15 missions
Schneider, Carl H., Lt.; April 1944-September 1944
Schneider, Edwin H., Lt.
Schoenfeldt, George R., Lt.; March 1945-EOW
3 missions
Sheppard, Lawrence B., F/O; Post VE-Day??
Silsby, Charles W., Capt.; May 1943-April 15, 1944(KIA)
Slack, Henry R., Lt.; November 1944-July 1945
49 missions
P-51K WZ-K 44-11763
Smith, Eugene F., Lt.; January 1945-EOW
21 missions
Smith, Martin H., Jr., Lt.; January 1944-July 19, 1944(KIAc)
Smith, Ray E., Maj.; October 1943-April 1945
P-47D WZ-N 42-8537
P-51D WZ-B 44-63712 "Fly'n Time Bomb"
Smith, Robert D., Lt.; October 1944-EOW
Sole, John R., Lt.; January 1945-April 21, 1945(KIA)
26 missions
Spaulding, Roger A., Lt.; January 1945-April 10, 1945(POW)
19 missions
Spooner, Richard H., Lt.; September 1944-January 15, 1945(POW)
Stier, Earl L., Capt.; September 1944-EOW
P-51D WZ-Y 44-63187 "Bum Steer"
Straley, Warren G., Capt.; March 1943-March 1944; later to CBI
Stump, Harold E., Maj.; May 1942-June 10, 1944(KIA)
P-47C WZ-C 41-6259 "Bad Medicine"
Taylor, Clyde E., Lt.; January 1945-July 1945
25 missions, 137:30 hours
P-51D WZ-C 44-63842
Taylor, Richard W., Lt.; January 1945-January 1945; to 357th Ftr Grp
1 mission
Thain, Thomas V., Lt.; January 1945-July 1945 24 missions
P-51D WZ-S 44-72203 "Sweet and Lovely"
Townsend, William D., Lt.; November 1944-March 1, 1945(KIA)
31 missions
Vallee, William H., F/O Post VE-Day??
Wendell, Roy E., Lt.; January 1944-March 13, 1944(KIAc)
11 missions
Whitefield, Charles D., Lt.; July 1944-November 1944
66 missions, 273 hours
P-47D WZ-Y 42-25871 "Roger the Lodger"
Wilson, Donald R., Lt.; January 1944-July 1944
Wilson, Mark T., Lt.; September 1944-February 25, 1945 (MIA-E)
Wingfield, Hugh V., Lt.; March 1945-EOW
4 missions
Wood, Eugene W., Lt.; September 1944-September 18, 1944(KIA

**Aircraft of the 82nd Fighter Squadron**

P-47C-2-RE

| | |
|---|---|
| 41-6179 MX-E | R.F. Brower |
| 41-6188 MX-U | |
| 41-6198 MX-D | |
| 41-6218 MX-S "Ranny" | |
| 41-6219 MX-A "Rocket Jo" | |
| 41-6222 MX-J "Mud Creeker" | D.G. Jackson |
| 41-6249 MX-H "Vee Gaile" | R.E. Eby |
| 41-6252 MX-N "Bee Ware" | W.T. Hegman |
| 41-6255 MX-Q | |
| 41-6266 MX-T "Buzz" | |

P-47C-5-RE

| | |
|---|---|
| 41-6318 MX-K | |
| 41-6345 MX-R "Miss Tibbie" | R.A. Hewitt |
| 41-6365 MX-F | |
| 41-6379 MX-M "Queen Mu" | |
| 41-6380 MX-G | |
| 41-6391 MX-Y | |
| 41-6396 MX-U | |
| 41-6418 MX-Z | |
| 41-6535 MX-I | |
| 41-6542 MX-X "Iron Ass" | J.J. Oberhansly |
| 42-6618 MX-Z "Hun Ram-er" | H.J. Dayhuff |
| 42-6630 MX-O | |

P-47D-1-RE

| | |
|---|---|
| 42-7883 MX-X "Iron Ass" | J.J. Oberhansly |
| 41-7916 MX-O | |
| 41-7923 MX-I | |
| 42-7948 MX-P "Flagari" | A. Peterson |

P-47D-2-RE

| | |
|---|---|
| 42-7954 MX-L "Pin-Up Girl" | J.W. Wilkinson |
| 42-7998 MX-N "Kitty" | G.M. Turley |

P-47D-2-RA

| | |
|---|---|
| 42-22463 MX-J | |
| 42-22467 MX-Y | |
| 42-22476 MX-S "Fortune's Fool" | |
| 42-22518 MX- | |

P-47D-4-RA

| | |
|---|---|
| 42-22755 MX-D | |

P-47D-5-RE

| | |
|---|---|
| 42-8471 MX-C "Squint" | R.L. Baker |
| 42-8476 MX-X | |
| 42-8502 MX-K | |
| 42-8505 MX-K "Smilin' Jack" | |
| 42-8530 MX-E "Jeanie-V.O.S." | W.M. Wesson |
| 42-8560 MX-I | |
| 42-8572 MX-A | |
| 42-8575 MX-C "Lady Yvonne" | N.D. Munson |
| 42-8586 MX- | |
| 42-8620 MX-F | M.S. Martinez |
| 42-8671 MX-U "Hun Hopper" | A.G. Dunken |

P-47D-6-RE

| | |
|---|---|
| 42-74733 MX-N | |

| | |
|---|---|
| 42-74733 MX-P | |
| 42-74783 MX-B | |

P-47D-10-RE

| | |
|---|---|
| 42-75128 MX- | |
| 42-75204 MX- | |

P-47D-11-RE

| | |
|---|---|
| 42-75243 MX-B | |
| 42-75406 MX-Z | |
| 42-75551 MX-M | |
| 42-75561 MX- | |
| 42-75571 MX- | |
| 42-75591 MX-C | |
| 42-75602 MX-E | |

P-47D-15-RE

| | |
|---|---|
| 42-76131 MX-O | |
| 42-76318 MX-W | |
| 42-76351 MX-O "Margaret's Mace" | L.H. Hosford |

P-47D-16-RE

| | |
|---|---|
| 42-76074 MX-H | |

P-47D-20-RE

| | |
|---|---|
| 42-76473 MX-Y | |
| 42-76547 MX-X | |
| 42-76557 MX-T "Judy" | H.E. Richards |
| 42-76585 MX-F | |
| 43-25318 MX-P | |

P-47D-21-RA

| | |
|---|---|
| 43-25536 MX-J | |
| 43-25593 MX-N | |

P-47D-21-RE

| | |
|---|---|
| 42-25406 MX-Z | |
| 42-25524 MX- | |

P-47D-22-RE

| | |
|---|---|
| 42-25742 MX-O | |
| 42-25994 MX-O | |
| 42-26005 MX-N | |
| 42-26025 MX-R "Duffie's Special" | |
| 42-26064 MX-Y | |
| 42-26241 MX-V | |
| 42-26312 MX- | |
| 42-26314 MX-F | |
| 42-26317 MX-U | |
| 42-26333 MX-Q "Hun Buster" | H.F. Beck |
| 42-26353 MX- "Lady Katherine" | |
| 42-26387 MX-W "Miss Behave" | |

P-47D-23-RA

| | |
|---|---|
| 42-27605 MX-R | |
| 42-27606 MX-A | HACK |

P-47D-25-RE

| | |
|---|---|
| 42-26446 MX-I | |
| 42-26461 MX-V | |
| 42-26475 MX-Y | R.E. Conner |
| 42-26585 MX-K | J.E. Kinsolving |
| 42-26633 MX-E | |
| 42-26638 MX- | |
| 42-26671 MX-X "No Guts, No Glory" | B.I. Mayo |
| 42-26676 MX-C | |

P-47D-26-RA

| | |
|---|---|
| 42-28422 MX-O | H.H. Lamb |

P-47D-27-RE

| | |
|---|---|
| 42-27297 MX-V | |
| 42-27339 MX-S | J. Myers |
| 42-27378 MX-K | |
| 42-27380 MX-D | |
| 42-27380 MX-V | |
| 42-27605 MX- | |
| 42-27607 MX-G | |

P-47D-28-RA

| | |
|---|---|
| 42-28455 MX-L | |
| 42-28566 MX-X | |
| 42-28740 MX-P | J.L. Mattern |
| 42-28798 MX-M "Cutie" | |
| 42-28805 MX- | |

P-47D-28-RE

| | |
|---|---|
| 44-19566 MX-X "Iron Ass" | J.J. Oberhansly |
| 44-19717 MX- | |
| 44-19777 MX-Q | D.C. Hart |
| 44-19792 MX-K | |
| 44-19798 MX- | |
| 44-19908 MX-B | |
| 44-19930 MX- | |
| 44-19950 MX-L | J.J. Hockery |
| 44-19963 MX-H | |

Unknown Serials

| | |
|---|---|
| MX- "Rough Edge" | F.I. Sharp |
| MX- "Dude" | J.E. Brasher |
| MX- "Judye-T" | |
| MX- "Kali-Kid" | |
| MX- "Katy" | |

P-51B-1-NA

| | |
|---|---|
| 43-12213 MX-F | HACK |

P-51B-15-NA

| | |
|---|---|
| 42-106826 MX- | HACK |

P-51K-5-NT

| | |
|---|---|
| 44-11620 MX-H | |
| 44-11631 MX-V "Etta Jeanne II" | H.H. Lamb |
| 44-11649 MX-A | |
| 44-11650 MX-N | |
| 44-11652 MX-F | |
| 44-11653 MX-M | |
| 44-11657 MX-D | |
| 44-11663 MX-D | |
| 44-11672 MX-L | |
| 44-11675 MX-N | |
| 44-11680 MX-X | |
| 44-11688 MX-U | |

P-51K-10-NT

| | |
|---|---|
| 44-12125 MX-V | |

P-51D-15-NA

| | |
|---|---|
| 44-15077 MX-B | |
| 44-15382 MX-W | |
| 44-15469 MX-J | |
| 44-15495 MX-E | |
| 44-15505 MX-S | |
| 44-15556 MX-Z "Doug" | H.A. Stinson |
| 44-15574 MX-I | W.F. Bechtelheimer |
| 44-15693 MX-L | |
| 44-15716 MX-P | |
| 44-15722 MX- | |
| 44-15745 MX-T | W.E. Bourque |

P-51D-20-NA

| | |
|---|---|
| 44-63170 MX-U | |
| 44-63177 MX-C | |
| 44-63183 MX-Y "Cutie" | I.H. Keatley |
| 44-63185 MX-Q "Kitty's Kid" | |
| 44-63198 MX-A "Keep Kickin'" | R.J. Blossom |
| 44-63203 MX-X "Let's Make Mary" | |
| 44-63214 MX-R | |
| 44-63238 MX-K | |
| 44-63246 MX-S "Little Rebel" | J.C. Childs |
| 44-63256 MX-O | |
| 44-63286 MX-V "Etta Jeanne" | H.H. Lamb |
| 44-64147 MX-U "Big Dick" | R.A. Hewitt |
| 44-72034 MX- | |
| 44-72119 MX-Q | |
| 44-72165 MX-G | |
| 44-72191 MX-F "Lady Helen II" | W.H. Brown |
| 44-72205 MX-X "Sweet Hart" | D.C. Hart |
| 44-72233 MX-D | R.E. Conner |
| 44-72237 MX-A "Keep Kickin' II" | R.J. Blossom |
| 44-72352 MX-Y "Cutie II" | I.H. Keatley |
| 44-72357 MX-D | |
| 44-72365 MX-O | |
| 44-72367 MX-C | |

P-51D-25-NA

| | |
|---|---|
| 44-72740 MX-C | |
| 44-72835 MX-I | |
| 44-72911 MX-R | L.R. Campi |
| 44-72938 MX-Z "Miss Pam" | H.L. Roe |
| 44-73041 MX-Q | |
| 44-73042 MX-U "Sooner Hot Shot" | G.V. Elsey |

Unknown Serials

| | |
|---|---|
| MX-F "Lady Helen" | W.H. Brown |

**Aircraft of the 83rd Fighter Squadron**

P-47C-2-RE
41-6208 HL-T
41-6210 HL-M "Upstairs Cat" J.E. Stokes
42-6229 HL-J "Percy" R.H. Knapp
41-6241 HL-W
41-6246 HL-F D.E. Wilkes

P-47C-5-RE
41-6331 HL-L
41-6335 HL-B "El Jeepo" C.P. London
41-6361 HL-A "Hellza Poppin'" J.M. Cooper
41-6363 HL-K
41-6364 HL-D "Jacquelyn" K.W. Dougherty
41-6373 HL-Z J.J. Stone
41-6374 HL-V
41-6382 HL-C
41-6402 HL-X "Owley and Tobe" J.C. Davis
41-6411 HL-N "Muscle Bound" W.T. Chapman
41-6540 HL-S "Skonk Hunter" W.H. Madole
41-6581 HL-Q
41-6628 HL-R W.H. Julian

P-47D-1-RE
42-7882 HL-H "Sabatoge, Jr."
42-7889 HL-I H.T. Barnaby
42-7906 HL-R
42-7914 HL-P "Miss Norma" C.M. Peal
42-7944 HL-V

P-47D-2-RE
42-7951 HL-G "Spirit of Sycamore Hill" H.C. Roff
42-7952 HL-Y
42-7963 HL-T
42-7983 HL-W

P-47D-2-RA
42-22482 HL- "5 PO"

P-47D-4-RA
42-22776 HL-U
42-22781 HL-L

P-47D-5-RE
42-8524 HL-Y H.R. Zumwalt
42-8543 HL-U W. Tonkin
42-8564 HL-D
42-8608 HL-W
42-8608 HL-B
42-8622 HL-N
42-8658 HL-P
42-8681 HL-E
42-8688 HL-B

P-47D-6-RE
42-74634 HL-D K.W. Dougherty
42-74652 HL-K
42-74686 HL-
42-74690 HL-J A.M. Juchheim
42-74693 HL-Z J.J. Stone
42-74705 HL-B

P-47D-10-RE
42-75147 HL-X
42-75182 HL-
42-75196 HL-O "Lil Eva"

P-47D-11-RE
42-75402 HL-A
42-75403 HL-A
42-75610 HL-N "Muscle Bound" W.T. Chapman

P-47D-15-RE
42-76165 HL-C
42-76221 HL-Y
42-76227 HL-P
42-76232 HL-P "Miss Norma II" C.M. Peal

P-47D-20-RE
42-76474 HL-O
42-76479 HL-V
42-76486 HL-J
42-76505 HL-V
42-76512 HL-T
42-76563 HL-B "Jerri"
42-76587 HL-D "Thrun' My Bit"
42-25312 HL-N F. White

P-47D-20-RA
43-25319 HL-S

P-47D-21-RE
42-25528 HL-H F.R. Pursell

P-47D-21-RA
43-25552 HL-W K.C. Allstaedt
43-25588 HL-K
43-25558 HL-F

P-47D-22-RE
42-25719 HL-G D.A. Lawhead
42-25724 HL-E R.R. Bonebrake
42-25742 HL-V "Zombie"
42-25758 HL-L
42-25837 HL-X O.E. Gilbert
42-25889 HL-
42-25996 HL-Z "Mr. Ted" F.C. Gray
42-26016 HL-A
42-26020 HL-J "Lady Jane" A.M. Juchheim
42-26020 HL-J "Duffie's Special"
42-26053 HL-E W.M. McDermott

P-47D-23-RA
42-27781 HL-L

P-47D-25-RE
42-26391 HL-Z "Mr. Ted" F.C. Gray
42-26449 HL-X O.E. Gilbert
42-26458 HL-S
42-26536 HL-M
42-26543 HL-K
42-26563 HL-B
42-26584 HL-D "Gelene"
42-26591 HL-J
42-26623 HL-E
42-26672 HL-V
42-26676 HL-

P-47D-26-RA
42-28408 HL-X

P-47D-27-RE
42-27370 HL-R

P-47D-28-RA
42-28518 HL-C "Green Hornet" R.T. Green
42-28544 HL-K "Fast Action Jackson" J.W. Jackson
42-28635 HL-X
42-28636 HL-V "Flying Fish" F.A. Fish
42-28651 HL-S
42-28689 HL-

P-47D-28-RE
44-19562 HL-G
44-19654 HL-
44-19573 HL-P
44-19590 HL-
44-19750 HL-E R.R. Bonebrake
44-19765 HL-
44-19785 HL-J
44-19854 HL-L
44-19895 HL-S
44-19932 HL-B
44-19964 HL-

Unknown Serials
HL-I "Boston Bean" F.E. Harrington
HL-P "Miss Norma III" C.M. Peal
HL-U "The Horrible Hoosier" R.E. Wise

P-51B-5-NA
43-6736 HL-BK HACK

P-51B-15-NA
42-106789 HL-T
42-106876 HL-

P-51K-1-NT
44-11364 HL-H

P-51K-5-NT
44-11557 HL-L
44-11563 HL-N "The Brat" E.H. Miller
44-11573 HL-K "Green Hornet" R.T. Green
44-11625 HL-M F.E. Higginbottom
44-11627 HL-J "Green Eyes"
44-11655 HL-A "Poop Shooter"

44-11679 HL-
44-11695 HL-N "Prouka"

P-51K-10-NT
44-12136 HL-D W.H. Julian
44-12158 HL-

P-51D-10-NA
44-14417 HL-A
44-14852 HL-F "Lottie"

P-51D-15-NA
44-15187 HL-T
44-15497 HL-O
44-15499 HL-
44-15506 HL-G "Miss Debbie"
44-15524 HL-D
44-15524 HL-K
44-15575 HL-P
44-15586 HL-I "Boston Bean" F.E. Harrington
44-15627 HL-Q "Windy City Mama"
44-15650 HL-J "Debra Dell"
44-15702 HL-X
44-15721 HL-C
44-15729 HL-T "Bill's Bus" W.B. Senarens

P-51D-20-NA
44-63178 HL-Z "Beck-Dor" S.R. Beckley
44-63208 HL-U "The Horrible Hoosier III" R.E. Wise
44-63208 HL-U "Wanderin' Boy" J.S. Peterson
44-63216 HL-A "Anne Nihilator" O.E. Gilbert
44-63248 HL-Y
44-63271 HL-D
44-63279 HL-Z "Mr. Ted III" F.C. Gray
44-63285 HL-R
44-63620 HL-C "Small Boy Here" J.A. Kirk
44-63683 HL-G
44-63864 HL-W "Twilight Tear" H. Davis
44-72027 HL-H "Kitten"
42-72036 HL-J "Normie" R.F. Rohm
44-72046 HL-P
44-72146 HL-P
44-72214 HL-A "Poop Shooter II"
44-72217 HL-H
44-72338 HL-J
44-72351 HL-T "Frisco Belle"
44-72381 HL-R
44-72481 HL-

P-51D-25-NA
44-72830 HL-Z "Quinine"
44-72964 HL-X E.R. Kulik

**Aircraft of the 84th Fighter Squadron**

P-47C-2-RE
41-6201 WZ-U "Pappy" G.J. Hays
41-6223 WZ-L "Isabel"
41-6228 WZ-N
41-6240 WZ-E
41-6243 WZ-K "Cover Girl"
41-6245 WZ-M
41-6259 WZ-C "Bad Medicine" H.E. Stump
41-6269 WZ-X
41-6270 WZ-A "Feather Merchant" J.C. Price

P-47C-5-RE
41-6333 WZ-F N.G. Lentz
41-6353 WZ-D
41-6357 WZ-B "Geronimo" J.D. Irvin
41-6383 WZ-S
41-6386 WZ-T R.N. Gore
41-6393 WZ-R "Axe The Axis" P.E. Pompetti
41-6409 WZ-W E.F. Fleming
41-6415 WZ-V "Wild Hare"
41-6532 WZ-M "Cali Kid" R.F. Himes
41-6580 WZ-G
41-6630 WZ-Z "Spokane Chief" E.P. Roberts

P-47D-1-RE
42-7886 WZ-P
42-7894 WZ-Q "Rebel" P.W. Saffold
42-7899 WZ-H "El Bango"
42-7918 WZ-Y
42-7935 WZ-I

P-47D-2-RE
42-7961 WZ-M
42-7986 WZ-S

P-47D-2-RA
42-22459 WZ-E "Joker" G.T. Hartman
42-22518 WZ-U
42-22539 WZ-R

P-47D-5-RE
42-8537 WZ-J
42-8537 WZ-N R.E. Smith
42-8538 WZ-E
42-8551 WZ-C
42-8573 WZ-L
42-8574 WZ-D
42-8602 WZ-K
42-8630 WZ-S
42-8650 WZ-O J.P. Maxwell

P-47D-6-RE
42-74641 WZ-A "Feather Merchant II" J.C. Price
42-74641 WZ-Z
42-74657 WZ-D "Vicky" E.M. Peterson
42-74694 WZ-G "Joker" A.M. Barba
42-74716 WZ-B
42-74723 WZ-X
42-74742 WZ-O "War Eagle/Snafu" J.P. Maxwell
42-74753 WZ-J "Okie" Q.L. Brown
42-74753 WZ-V

P-47D-11-RE
42-75429 WZ-S
42-75462 WZ-K
42-75526 WZ-
42-75540 WZ-

P-47D-15-RE
42-76184 WZ-K
42-76329 WZ-A

P-47D-16-RE
42-75871 WZ-

P-47D-20-RA
43-25297 WZ-D
43-25303 WZ-J "Tessie's Tot"
43-25305 WZ-I
43-25313 WZ-N

P-47D-20-RE
42-76412 WZ-V
42-76506 WZ-O
42-76584 WZ-H

P-47D-21-RA
43-25539 WZ-R
43-25584 WZ-Q
43-25593 WZ-L

P-47D-21-RE
42-25529 WZ-L
42-25537 WZ-A

P-47D-22-RE
42-25690 WZ-U
42-25698 WZ-I "Jeanie"
42-25698 WZ-J "Okie II" Q.L. Brown
42-25712 WZ-T
42-25736 WZ-X
42-25871 WZ-Y "Nigger II" R.M. Holly
42-25871 WZ-Y "Roger The Lodger" C.D. Whitefield
42-25981 WZ-Z
42-25985 WZ-C
42-26031 WZ-W
42-26149 WZ-M

P-47D-25-RE
42-26540 WZ-W
42-26551 WZ-P B.I. Mayo
42-26567 WZ-V "No Guts, No Glory" B.I. Mayo
42-26581 WZ-
42-26583 WZ-T
42-26590 WZ-E "Thoroughbred" L.E. Clark
42-26624 WZ-J "Old Smoothy" H.L. Boyle
42-26629 WZ-M "Serenade in Blue"
42-26640 WZ-X
42-26652 WZ-Z
42-26682 WZ-U "Ozark Queen" A.F. Eaton

P-47D-28-RA
42-28615 WZ-X "My Baby" R.O. Laho
42-28648 WZ-
42-28660 WZ-F "Butch"
42-28878 WZ-S "Eileen" F.E. Oiler

P-47D-28-RE
44-19569 WZ-Z
44-19729 WZ-
44-19732 WZ-
44-19762 WZ-Z "The Face V" L.P. Marshall
44-19912 WZ-E
44-19934 WZ-G "Ginny" R.D. Higgins
44-19966 WZ-

P-51B-5-NA
43-6533 WZ-S HACK

P-51B-15-NA
42-106826 WZ-S HACK
42-106886 WZ-P

P-51K-5-NT
44-11578 WZ-
44-11629 WZ-
44-11666 WZ-O
44-11669 WZ-
44-11682 WZ-I
44-11691 WZ-F
44-11693 WZ-B
44-11694 WZ-D
44-11743 WZ-J "Porcelain Pillbox" P.S. Ostrander
44-11747 WZ-L P.T. Keillor
44-11763 WZ-K H.R. Slack

P-51D-10-NA
44-14251 WZ-I "Contrary Mary" R.B. Caviness

P-51D-15-NA
44-15359 WZ-W
44-15577 WZ-G "Just Hang'en Around" J.L. Murphy
44-15675 WZ-W T.N. Reeves
44-15683 WZ-V
44-15692 WZ-K L. DeAnda
44-15707 WZ-N "Kitten Jean" C.F. Coffee
44-15720 WZ-I
44-15731 WZ-H "Mischievious Nell" J.M. Farmer
44-15740 WZ-N
44-15746 WZ-N

P-51D-20-NA
44-63163 WZ-
44-63171 WZ-K "Lady Eve" B.R. Newmark
44-63174 WZ-T
44-63181 WZ-C
44-63182 WZ-M
44-63187 WZ-Y "Bum Steer" E.L. Stier
44-63188 WZ-J
44-63191 WZ-U "Lucky Baby" W.M. McClellan
44-63206 WZ-
44-63207 WZ-G

P-51D-20-NA
44-63209 WZ-S "Sherman Was Right!" F.E. Oiler
44-63212 WZ-Z "The Face VI" L.P. Marshall
44-63215 WZ-A
44-63250 WZ-A
44-63555 WZ-C
44-63632 WZ-H "Lee D" W.J. DeGain
44-63635 WZ-D
44-63712 WZ-B "Fly'n Time Bomb" R.E. Smith
44-63755 WZ-T
44-63779 WZ-G "Scream'n Demon" A.A. Garback
44-63799 WZ-G R.D. Higgins
44-63840 WZ-O
44-63842 WZ-C C.E. Taylor
44-64091 WZ-J
44-64156 WZ-O "The Virgin Ann IV"
44-72099 WZ-X "Little Chic" W.S. Blodgett
44-72163 WZ-J
44-72167 WZ-M
44-72178 WZ-N
44-72187 WZ-
44-72190 WZ-E
44-72203 WZ-S "Sweet & Lovely" T.V. Thain
44-72218 WZ-I "Big Beautiful Doll" J.D. Landers
44-72325 WZ-F C.T. Bendorf
44-72386 WZ-D
44-72407 WZ-E

P-51D-25-NA
44-72772 WZ-A D. Ledington
44-72927 WZ-W "Frances Dell" C.W. Clemons
44-73119 WZ-O "Merry Bee" J.D. Calvin

• • •

## THE 339TH FIGHTER GROUP
## 503RD, 504TH, 505TH FIGHTER SQUADRONS

The 339th Fighter Group was activated on August 10, 1943, at Hunter Field, Georgia. Training in the southern and western United States, the group headed overseas on March 22, 1944, aboard the "Stirling Castle." The first of 264 missions came on April 30, 1944, with the last on April 20, 1945. During the 339th's time overseas, the group claimed 236.5 aerial and 431 ground victories, while 105 P-51's were lost on operations and 10 pilots died in accidents.

The 339th was based at Fowlmere from April 4, 1944, to October of 1945, and flew the P-51B, C, D, and K during that same time. The group was awarded a Distinguished Unit Citation for missions flown on September 10 and 11, 1944, in which pilots destroyed over 60 German planes.

### Claims

| | Air | | | Ground | |
|---|---|---|---|---|---|
| | Destroyed | Probable | Damaged | Destroyed | Damaged |
| HdQts | 5 | 1 | 6 | 20.5 | 3 |
| 503rd | 96 | 7 | 30 | 42 | 42 |
| 504th | 51 | 8 | 18 | 97 | 51 |
| 505th | 84.5 | 1 | 14 | 271.5 | 129 |
| | 236.5 | 17 | 68 | 431 | 225 |

### Commanders

| | |
|---|---|
| Col. John B. Henry, Jr. | August 17, 1943-October 1, 1944 |
| LtCol. Harold W. Scruggs | October 1, 1944-December 27, 1944 |
| Col. John B. Henry, Jr. | December 27, 1944-February 15, 1945 |
| LtCol. Carl T. Goldenburg | February 15, 1945-February 22, 1945 |
| Col. John B. Henry, Jr. | February 22, 1945-April 13, 1945 |
| LtCol. William C. Clark, Jr. | April 13, 1945-October 1945 |

### Wing and Command Assignments

| | |
|---|---|
| Assigned to VIII Fighter Command | April 4, 1944 |
| VIII Fighter Command, 66th Fighter Wing | April 4, 1944 |
| 3rd Bomb Division, 66th Fighter Wing | September 15, 1944 |
| 3rd Air Division, 66th Fighter Wing | January 1, 1945 |

### Aircraft Markings

All P-51's were operated in NMF although a few planes did have dark green applied to portions of the wings or upper fuselage. Group markings consisted of white-red-white banded spinners with a twelve inch red and white checkerboard cowl band. From November of 1944, rudder colors were used: red for the 503rd, green for the 504th, and none for the 505th. Beginning in early 1945, many planes also carried a thin band in the squadron color as a backing to the cowl band.

Squadron codes were:

503rd Ftr Sqn: D7
504th Ftr Sqn: 5Q
505th Ftr Sqn: 6N

### 339th Fighter Group Statistical Report

| Month | Missions | Air | Grd | Losses | KIAc |
|---|---|---|---|---|---|
| April 1944 | 1 | 0-0-0 | 0-0 | 0 | 1 |
| May | 28 | 41.5-3-13 | 21-23 | 14 | 1 |
| June | 43 | 35-2-8 | 5-2 | 14 | 1 |
| July | 25 | 17-2-3 | 30-12 | 6 | 1 |
| August | 28 | 24-0-2 | 13-3 | 17 | 0 |
| September | 19 | 28-3-4 | 59-62 | 11 | 0 |
| October | 17 | 0-0-0 | 0-0 | 3 | 0 |
| November | 17 | 40-2-5 | 1-0 | 10 | 1 |
| December | 14 | 6-0-3 | 0-0 | 7 | 0 |
| January 1945 | 15 | 0-0-0 | 0-0 | 3 | 0 |
| February | 17 | 1-0-1 | 0-0 | 6 | 1 |
| March | 24 | 27-3-18 | 31-9 | 10 | 1 |
| April | 16 | 17-2-11 | 271-114 | 4 | 0 |
| May | 0 | 0-0-0 | 0-0 | 0 | 0 |
| June | 0 | 0-0-0 | 0-0 | 0 | 2 |
| July | 0 | 0-0-0 | 0-0 | 0 | 1 |
| | 264 | 236.5-17-68 | 431-225 | 105 | 10 |

**Losses by Squadron**

| | MIA | KIAc |
|---|---|---|
| HdQts | 3 | 0 |
| 503rd | 31 | 6 |
| 504th | 21 | 2 |
| 505th | 50 | 2 |
| | 105 | 10 |

**Claims by Enemy Aircraft Type**

| | Air Destroyed | Air Probable | Air Damaged | Grd Destroyed | Grd Damaged |
|---|---|---|---|---|---|
| FW-190 | 107 | 7 | 17 | 42 | 13 |
| Me-109 | 95.5 | 7 | 29 | 71 | 22 |
| Me-262 | 11 | 2 | 19 | 2 | 0 |
| Trainer | 6 | 0 | 0 | 1 | 1 |
| Me-410 | 4 | 1 | 1 | 52 | 44 |
| Ju-88 | 3 | 0 | 0 | 115 | 48 |
| Do-217 | 3 | 0 | 0 | 42 | 10 |
| Ju-87 | 3 | 0 | 0 | 3 | 2 |
| Ju-52 | 2 | 0 | 0 | 10 | 8 |
| He-111 | 1 | 0 | 0 | 11 | 14 |
| Ar-234 | 1 | 0 | 0 | 0 | 0 |
| u/i a/c | 0 | 0 | 1 | 52 | 57 |
| Me-110 | 0 | 0 | 1 | 4 | 4 |
| Ju-188 | 0 | 0 | 0 | 13 | 0 |
| Fi-156 | 0 | 0 | 0 | 8 | 1 |
| Hs-129 | 0 | 0 | 0 | 2 | 0 |
| Do-18 | 0 | 0 | 0 | 1 | 0 |
| FW-200 | 0 | 0 | 0 | 1 | 0 |
| Me-210 | 0 | 0 | 0 | 1 | 0 |
| FW-189 | 0 | 0 | 0 | 0 | 1 |

**339th Fighter Group Squadron Commanders**

**503rd Ftr Sqn**

| | |
|---|---|
| LtCol. Harold W. Scruggs | States-June 8, 1944 |
| Maj. John Aitken | June 8, 1944-October 2, 1944 |
| LtCol. Harvey E. Henderson | October 2, 1944-December 5, 1944 |
| LtCol. Dale E. Shafer | December 6, 1944-September 1945 |

**504th Ftr Sqn**

| | |
|---|---|
| LtCol. Edgar B. Gravette | States-January 1945 |
| Maj. Lewis S. Peter | January 1945-January 20, 1945 |
| LtCol. William C. Clark, Jr. | January 20, 1945-March 8, 1945 |
| LtCol. William H. Julian | March 9, 1945-September 1945 |

**505th Ftr Sqn**

| | |
|---|---|
| Maj. Donald A. Larson | States-August 4, 1944 |
| Maj. Joseph L. Thury | August 5, 1944-October 1944 |
| Maj. Langhorne Reid | October 1944-December 4, 1944 |
| LtCol. Joseph L. Thury | December 4, 1944-July 1945 |

**339th Fighter Group Aces**

| Name | Air | Grd | Total | Sqn |
|---|---|---|---|---|
| LtCol. Joseph L. Thury | 2.5 | 25.5 | 28 | 505th |
| Maj. Archie A. Tower | 1.5 | 18 | 19.5 | 505th |
| Capt. Kirke B. Everson | 1.5 | 13 | 14.5 | 504th |
| Capt. Robert H. Ammon | 5 | 9 | 14 | 503rd<br>504th<br>HdQts |
| Lt. Oscar K. Biggs | 0.5 | 11.5 | 12 | 505th |
| Capt. Harry R. Corey | 1 | 11 | 12 | 505th |
| Capt. James R. Starnes | 6 | 6 | 12 | 505th |
| Lt. Harold W. Burch | 0 | 11 | 11 | 505th |
| Maj. William E. Bryan, Jr. | 7.5 | 2 | 9.5 | 503rd<br>HdQts |
| LtCol. William C. Clark | 1 | 8 | 9* | 504th<br>HdQts |
| Maj. Donald A. Larson | 6 | 3 | 9 | 505th |
| Lt. Thomas W. Marvel | 0 | 9 | 9 | 505th |
| LtCol. Dale E. Shafer, Jr. | 7 | 2 | 9** | 503rd |
| Capt. Francis R. Gerard | 8 | 0 | 8 | 503rd |
| LtCol. William H. Julian | 5 | 3 | 8*** | 504th |
| Lt. William R. MacClarence | 0 | 8 | 8 | 505th |
| Lt. William F. Mudge, Jr. | 2 | 6 | 8 | 505th |
| Lt. Leon M. Orcutt, Jr. | 0 | 8 | 8 | 504th |
| Lt. Herbert L. Caywood | 0 | 7 | 7 | 505th |
| Lt. Steve J. Chetneky | 1 | 6 | 7 | 503rd |
| Capt. Owen P. Farmer | 2 | 5 | 7 | 505th |
| Lt. Christopher J. Hanseman | 5 | 2 | 7 | 505th |
| Lt. William A. Jones | 2 | 5 | 7 | 505th |
| Lt. Jerome T. Murphy | 0 | 7 | 7 | 505th |
| Capt. Richard B. Olander | 1.5 | 5 | 6.5 | 505th |
| Capt. George T. Rich | 1.5 | 5 | 6.5 | 505th |
| Lt. Robert V.E. Blizzard | 0 | 6 | 6 | 504th |
| Lt. Frank A. Clifton | 0 | 6 | 6 | 504th |
| Lt. Robert J. Frisch | 0 | 6 | 6 | 503rd |
| Lt. Robert E. Irion | 1 | 5 | 6 | 505th |
| Lt. Robert H. Paul | 0 | 6 | 6 | 505th |
| Lt. Lawrence J. Powell, Jr. | 2.5 | 3.5 | 6 | 505th |
| Lt. James C. Woolery | 0 | 6 | 6 | 505th |
| Maj. John Aitken, Jr. | 4.5 | 1 | 5.5@ | 503rd<br>504th |
| Capt. Philip M. Loveless, Jr. | 0.5 | 5 | 5.5 | 505th |
| Capt. Edward H. Beavers, Jr. | 5 | 0 | 5 | 503rd |
| Capt. Brooks J. Bline | 1 | 4 | 5 | 505th |
| Lt. Carl H. Bundgaard | 2 | 3 | 5 | 505th |
| Lt. John R. Byers | 0 | 5 | 5 | 503rd |
| Lt. Merle F. Caldwell | 2 | 3 | 5 | 504th |
| Lt. Gordon H. Chenez | 0 | 5 | 5 | 504th |
| Lt. Jack S. Daniell | 5 | 0 | 5 | 505th |
| Lt. William R. Guyton | 0 | 5 | 5 | 505th |
| Lt. Cephas Hermanson | 0 | 5 | 5 | 504th |
| Lt. Harlan F. Hunt | 0 | 5 | 5 | 504th |
| Lt. Boyd O. Jackson | 0 | 5 | 5 | 505th |
| Capt. Evan M. Johnson, V | 5 | 0 | 5 | 505th |
| Capt. William H. Krauss | 0.5 | 4.5 | 5 | 505th |
| Lt. Lester C. Marsh | 5 | 0 | 5 | 503rd |
| Lt. Jay F. Marts | 2 | 3 | 5 | 505th |
| F/O John J. Rice | 0 | 5 | 5 | 505th |

* - includes 1 air victory with 66th Ftr Wing
** - includes 4 air victories with the 31st Ftr Grp, MTO
*** - includes 5 air victories with the 78th Ftr Grp, ETO
@ - includes 1.5 air victories with the 52nd Ftr Grp, MTO

**339th Fighter Group Scorers**

**HdQts**

| | Air | Grd | |
|---|---|---|---|
| R.H. Ammon | 0-0-0 | 9-0 | plus 503rd Ftr Sqn |
| W.C. Clark | 0-0-1 | 7-3 | plus 1-0-0 air w/66th Ftr Wg & 1-1 grd w/504th Ftr Sqn |
| C.W. Dowell | 0.5-0-0 | 0-0 | |
| V.B. Hathorn | 0-0-0 | 3-0 | |
| J.B. Henry, Jr. | 0-1-0 | 0-0 | |
| M.G.H. McPharlin | 1.5-0-3 | 1-0 | plus 1.5 air w/RAF |
| J.R. Reynolds | 1-0-0 | 0.5-0 | |
| H.W. Scruggs | 2-0-2 | 0-0 | plus 503rd Ftr Sqn |

**503rd Ftr Sqn**

| | Air | Grd | |
|---|---|---|---|
| J. Aitken, Jr. | 3-0-1 | 1-0 | plus 1.5 air w/52nd Ftr Grp, MTO |
| B.A. Allen | 1-0-1 | 0-0 | |
| R.H. Ammon | 5-0-2 | 0-0 | plus HdQts |
| E.H. Beavers, Jr. | 5-0-0 | 0-0 | |
| W.W. Behrend | 1-0-1 | 0-0 | |
| W.H. Boyd | 0-0-0 | 0-1 | |
| R.B. Brown | 0.5-0-2 | 0-0 | |
| W.E. Bryan, Jr. | 7.5-0.5-1 | 2-0 | |
| J.P. Bush | 0.5-0-0 | 1-0 | |
| F. Butler, Jr. | 0-1-1 | 0-0 | |
| J.R. Byers | 0-0-0 | 5-0 | |
| J.C. Campbell, Jr. | 1-0-0 | 0-0 | |
| W.T. Carter | 0-0-0 | 0-3 | |
| S.J. Chetneky | 1-0-1 | 6-3 | |
| C.E. Cloud | 1-0-0 | 0-0 | |
| C.S. Coe | 2.5-0-0 | 0-0 | |
| J.R. Crockett | 0-0-0 | 2-0 | |
| R.H. Deary | 0-0-0 | 1-2 | |
| M.B. Edens | 2-0-0 | 0-0 | |
| E.E. Erickson | 1.5-1-0 | 1-0 | |
| C.I. Ferrell | 0-0-0 | 4-2 | |
| P.D. Fickel | 1-0-0 | 0-0 | |
| L.J. Fiorito | 2-0-0 | 1-1 | |
| N.T. Folwell | 0-0-0 | 0-4 | |
| C.H. French | 0-0-1 | 1-0 | |
| L.J. French | 1-0-0 | 0-0 | |
| F.R. Gerard | 8-0-2 | 0-0 | |
| J.W. Gokey | 1-0-1 | 1-3 | |
| E.H. Graham, Jr. | 1.5-0-1 | 0-0 | |
| E.E. Haidle | 0-0-0 | 2-2 | |
| A.S. Harte, Jr. | 1-0-0 | 0-2 | |
| A.G. Hawkins | 1-0-1 | 0-0 | |
| H.E. Henderson | 2-0-0 | 0-0 | |
| R.S. Hill, Jr. | 0-0-2 | 1-1 | |
| D.W. Johnson | 3-0-0 | 0-0 | |
| R.G. Johnson | 1-0-1 | 0-0 | |
| C.W. Knott | 1.5-0-0 | 0.5-0 | |

| | | | |
|---|---|---|---|
| R.E. Krauss | 1-0-0 | 0-0 | |
| A.L. Lowery | 0-0-0 | 1-0 | |
| L.C. Marsh | 5-1-1 | 0-0 | |
| R.D. Mayer | 3-0-0 | 0-0 | |
| D.E. McClish | 1-1-0 | 0-0 | |
| F.E. McElwee | 1-0-0 | 0-0 | |
| V.W. Meyer | 2.5-0-1 | 0-0 | |
| N. Ostrow | 1.5-0-0 | 0-0 | |
| P.E. Petitt | 2-0-1 | 0-0 | |
| J.R. Potthoff | 0-0-0 | 0-1 | |
| L. Poutre | 4-0-1 | 0-0 | |
| W.R. Preddy | 1-1-0 | 0-1 | |
| J.B. Price | 1-0-0 | 0-2 | |
| G.H. Reynolds | 0-0-0 | 1-0 | |
| J.G. Robinson | 0.5-0-0 | 0-0 | |
| H.W. Scruggs | 0.5-0-0 | 0-0 | plus HdQts |
| D.E. Shafer, Jr. | 3-0-2 | 2-4 | plus 4 air w/31st Ftr Grp, MTO |
| C.E. Shake | 0.5-0-0 | 0.5-0 | |
| E.B. Stephenson, Jr. | 2-0-1 | 0-1 | |
| F.M. Stillwell | 1-1-0 | 0-0 | |
| W.D. Stockton | 0-0-1 | 1-0 | |
| F.D. Talcott | 0-0.5-0 | 0-0 | |
| R.C. West | 1-0-0 | 0-0 | |
| R.S. Whitelaw | 1.5-0-0 | 0-4 | |
| J.P. Wilson | 2-0-0 | 0-0 | |
| J. Wolfort | 0.5-0-1 | 1-0 | |
| L.M. Wright | 1-0-1 | 0-2 | |
| V. Wyatt | 2.5-0-0 | 0-0 | |
| unknown pilot | 0.5-0-0 | 0-0 | |

**504th Ftr Sqn**

| | | | |
|---|---|---|---|
| R.T. Aldrich | 0-0-0 | 2-2 | |
| L.W. Allers | 1-0-0 | 3-3 | |
| R.N. Attebury | 2-0-0 | 1-0 | |
| M.R. Ball | 1-0-2 | 0-0 | |
| J.J. Ballard | 1-0-0 | 0-0 | |
| L.J. Barrett, Jr. | 0-0-0 | 4-2 | |
| V.N. Barto | 1.5-0-1 | 3-1 | |
| A.W. Bates, Jr. | 1-0-0 | 0-0 | |
| C.W. Bennett | 1-0-1 | 2-2 | |
| K.V. Berguson | 0-0-1 | 0-0 | |
| R.V.E. Blizzard | 0-1-1 | 6-2 | |
| M.F. Caldwell | 2-0-0 | 3-0 | |
| L.M. Carter | 1-0-1 | 2-3 | |
| M.L. Cernicky | 0-1-0 | 0-0 | |
| G.H. Chenez | 0-0-0 | 5-3 | |
| W.C. Clark | 0-0-0 | 1-1 | plus HdQts |
| F.A. Clifton | 0-0-0 | 6-0 | |
| L.L. Corbin | 0-0-0 | 1-0 | |
| R.H. Cresswell | 1-0-0 | 2-2 | |
| R.C. Croker | 0.5-0-0 | 2-4 | |
| L.D. Eisenhart | 1-0-0 | 1-0 | |
| K.B. Everson | 1.5-0-0 | 13-5 | |
| E.B. Gravette | 1-0-1 | 0-0 | |
| N.C. Greer | 1.5-0-0 | 0-0 | |
| W.B. Griffith | 1-0-0 | 0-0 | |
| F.D. Guernsey, Jr. | 1-0-1 | 0-0 | |
| G.P. Harry | 0-0-1 | 0-1 | |
| R.C. Havighurst | 1-0-0 | 0-0 | |
| C. Hermanson | 0-1-0 | 5-2 | |
| R.F. Herrmann | 3-0-0 | 0-0 | |
| W.M. Hudson | 0-0-0 | 4-0 | |
| H.F. Hunt | 0-0-1 | 5-1 | |
| C.M. Hunter | 1-0-0 | 0-0 | |
| W.H. Julian | 0-0-0 | 3-4 | plus 5-0-2 air w/78th Ftr Grp |
| R.R. Kuhlman | 0-0-0 | 1-1 | |
| D.F. Krueger | 0-0-0 | 2-3 | |
| L.A. Kunz | 0.5-0-0 | 2-5 | |
| B.E. Langohr | 0.5-0-0 | 0-0 | |
| C.M. Mason | 0-0-1 | 2-1 | |
| C.M. Mead | 1-0-0 | 0-0 | |
| L.M. Orcutt, Jr. | 0-0-1 | 8-0 | |
| W.R. O'Sullivan | 1-0-0 | 0-0 | |
| D.E. Penny | 2-0-0 | 0-0 | |
| R.C. Penrose | 1-0-0 | 0-0 | |
| L.S. Peter, Jr. | 1-1-0 | 0-0 | |
| B.C. Routt | 4-0-1 | 0-0 | |
| F.S. Rutan, Jr. | 2-0-0 | 0-0 | |
| J.J. Sainlar | 0-0-1 | 0-0 | |
| R.F. Sargent | 1-0-0 | 3-2 | |
| R.W. Smith | 0-0-0 | 3-1 | |
| B.V. Stevens | 3-1-2 | 1-0 | |
| H.S. Stockman | 2-2-1 | 0-0 | |
| H.G. Thibert | 1-0-0 | 0-0 | |
| J.R. Trester | 0-1-0 | 0-0 | |
| F.T. Waters, Jr. | 0-0-0 | 1-0 | |
| H.R. Waymire | 1-0-0 | 0-0 | |
| R.H. Wilcox | 2-0-0 | 0-0 | |
| M.R. Winkelman | 1-0-0 | 0-0 | |
| R.T. Wood | 1-0-0 | 0-0 | |
| D.A. Zeine | 1-0-0 | 0-0 | |

**505th Ftr Sqn**

| | | |
|---|---|---|
| S.C. Ananian | 1-0-2 | 3-0 |
| E.C. Ball | 0-0-1 | 0-0 |
| O.K. Biggs | 0.5-0-0 | 11.5-4 |
| B.J. Bline | 1-0-0 | 4-0 |
| B.B. Booth | 0-0-0 | 0.5-0 |
| C.H. Bundgaard | 2-0-1 | 3-4 |
| H.W. Burch | 0-0-0 | 11-2 |
| V.D. Carr | 0.5-0-0 | 4-3 |
| H.L. Caywood | 0-0-0 | 7-5 |
| J.R. Coker | 1-0-1 | 0-0 |
| B.A. Conner, Jr. | 0-0-0 | 2-0 |
| H.R. Corey | 1-0-0 | 11-3 |
| J.S. Daniell | 5-0-0 | 0-0 |
| J.A. Diefenback | 0-0-0 | 2-0 |
| H.M. Everett | 3.5-0-1 | 0-0 |
| P.H. Ewing | 0-0-0 | 2-0 |
| O.P. Farmer, Jr. | 2-0-1 | 5-3 |
| W.G. Fish | 0.5-0-0 | 0-0 |
| H.E. Girzi, Jr. | 1-0-0 | 0-0 |
| G.E. Graham | 0.5-0-0 | 2.5-5 |
| W.R. Guyton | 0-0-0 | 5-0 |
| C.J. Hanseman | 5-0-0 | 2-1 |
| J.R. Hanson | 1.5-0-0 | 1-0 |
| J.G. Holloway | 2-0-0 | 0-0 |
| H.F. Howard | 0-0-0 | 3-0 |
| G.J. Hrico | 0.5-0-0 | 0.5-2 |
| E.E. Hupp, Jr. | 0-0-0 | 2-1 |
| R.E. Irion | 1-0-0 | 5-1 |
| W. Jaaskelainen | 1-0-0 | 1-1 |
| B.O. Jackson | 0-0-0 | 5 4 |
| E.M. Johnson, V | 5-0-1 | 0-1 |
| G.W. Jones, Jr. | 0-0-1 | 1-0 |
| W.A. Jones | 2-0-0 | 5-3 |
| G. Knight | 0-0-0 | 0.5-0 |
| W.H. Krauss | 0.5-0-0 | 4.5-4 |
| D.A. Larson | 6-1-1 | 3-0 |
| P.M. Loveless, Jr. | 0.5-0-0 | 5-3 |
| J.L. Lynch | 2.5-0-0 | 1-0 |
| W.R. MacClarence | 0-0-0 | 8-0 |
| C. Malarz | 0.5-0-0 | 3-4 |
| J.F. Marts | 2-0-0 | 3-4 |
| T.W. Marvel | 0-0-0 | 9-1 |
| P.J. McMahan | 3.5-0-0 | 0-0 |
| R.M. Mitchell, Jr. | 0-0-0 | 1-1 |
| W.R. Moore | 0-0-0 | 1.5-0 |
| W.F. Mudge | 2-0-0 | 6-2 |
| J.B. Muller | 0.5-0-0 | 2-0 |
| J.T. Murphy | 0-0-0 | 7-6 |
| M.N. Nay | 0-0-0 | 0-1 |
| R.B. Olander | 1.5-0-0 | 5-3 |
| W.R. Opitz | 0.5-0-0 | 0-0 |
| G.W. Palmer | 0.5-0-0 | 0-0 |
| R.H. Paul, Jr. | 0-0-0 | 6-2 |
| G.F. Perry | 0.5-0-0 | 0-0 |
| J. Pesanka | 1-0-0 | 3-0 |
| W.R. Phillippi | 1.5-0-0 | 2-0 |
| L.J. Powell, Jr. | 2.5-0-0 | 3.5-5 |
| L. Reid, Jr. | 2-0-0 | 0-0 |
| J.J. Rice | 0-0-1 | 5-3 |
| G.T. Rich | 1.5-0-1 | 5-1 |
| R.A. Rohm | 0-0-0 | 2-0 |
| J.F. Sawicki | 0-0-0 | 1-0 |
| B.V. Shaw | 0-0-0 | 1-1 |
| A. Sirochman | 1-0-0 | 2.5-1 |
| W.R. Slovak | 0-0-0 | 2-3 |
| F.W. Smith | 0-0-0 | 3-1 |
| T.B. Staggers | 0-0-0 | 4-3 |
| J.R. Starnes | 6-0-0 | 6-5 |
| L.A. Steiger | 0-0-0 | 3-0 |
| C.R. Stewart | 0-0-0 | 3.5-4 |
| B. Stiles | 1-0-0 | 0-0 |
| R.W. Strong | 1-0-0 | 1-0 |
| R.A. Tannous | 1-0-1 | 2.5-6 |
| R.C. Thieme | 0-0-0 | 1-0 |
| J.L. Thury, Jr. | 2.5-0-1 | 25.5-10 |
| A.E. Tongue, Jr. | 2-0-0 | 0-0 |
| A.A. Tower | 1.5-0-0 | 18-8 |
| J.C. Withers | 0.5-0-0 | 1-3 |
| J.C. Woolery | 0-0-0 | 6-1 |
| A.D. Young | 0-0-0 | 3.5-0 |
| H.D. Ziegler | 0.5-0-0 | 2-0 |
| unknown pilot | 0.5-0-0 | 0-0 |

## 339th Fighter Group Scoring

**May 9, 1944**

| | | | |
|---|---|---|---|
| 505th: | Lt. H.E. Everett | Me-109 dest(air) | Vouziers |
| | | Me-109 dam(air) | Vouziers |
| | Lt. W.A. Jones | Me-109 dest(air) | Vouziers |

**May 13, 1944**

| | | | |
|---|---|---|---|
| 505th: | Capt. D.A. Larson | FW-190 prob(air) | SE Lubeck |

**May 19, 1944**

| | | | |
|---|---|---|---|
| HdQts: | Maj. M.G.H. McPharlin | (.5)Me-109 dest(air) | Lubeck-Schwerin |
| | | (shared with a 4th Ftr Grp P-51) | |
| | | Me-109 dam(air) | Lubeck-Schwerin |
| 503rd: | Lt. J.R. Crockett | (2)Ju-52 dest(grd) | Ludwigslust |
| | Lt. J. Wolfort | u/i a/c dest(grd) | Ludwigslust |
| | Capt. W.T. Carter | (3)u/i a/c dam(grd) | Steinhuder Lake |
| | Lt. N.T. Folwell | (3)Me-109 dam(grd) | Pritzwalk |
| | | Trainer dam(grd) | Pritzwalk |
| | Lt. R.S. Whitelaw | (3)u/i a/c dam(grd) | Steinhuder Lake |
| 504th: | Lt. W.R. O'Sullivan | FW-190 dest(air) | Berlin |
| 505th: | Lt. E.M. Johnson | (1.5)FW-190 dest(air) | Gustrow |
| | Lt. J.R. Stearns | (.5)FW-190 dest(air) | Gustrow |

**May 21, 1944**

| | | | |
|---|---|---|---|
| 503rd: | Lt. L.M. Wright | He-111 dest(air) | Riesa A/F |
| | | Ju-88 dam(grd) | Riesa A/F |
| | Lt. W.E. Bryan | (2)u/i a/c dest(grd) | Pelenz-Meckau |
| | Lt. R.H. Deary | u/i a/c dest(grd) | Pelenz-Meckau |
| | | (2)u/i a/c dam(grd) | Pelenz-Meckau |
| | Lt. E.E. Erickson | u/i a/c dest(grd) | Pelenz-Meckau |
| | Lt. L.J. Fiorito | Me-109 dest(grd) | Pelenz-Meckau |
| | | Ju-88 dam(grd) | Pelenz-Meckau |
| | Lt. A.L. Lowery | u/i a/c dest(grd) | Pelenz-Meckau |
| | Lt. G.H. Reynolds | u/i a/c dest(grd) | Pelenz-Meckau |
| | Lt. A.S. Harte | (2)Ju-88 dam(grd) | Riesa A/F |
| | Lt. J.B. Price | (2)Ju-88 dam(grd) | Pelenz |
| | Lt. E.B. Stephenson | Ju-88 dam(grd) | Riesa A/F |
| | Lt. R.S. Whitelaw | u/i a/c dam(grd) | Pelenz |
| 504th: | Capt. B.C. Rout | (2)Me-109 dest(air) | Dobeln |
| | Lt. G.P. Harry | Me-109 dam(air) | Leipzig |
| | | Ju-87 dam(grd) | Leipzig |
| | Lt. L.D. Eisenhart | FW-190 dest(grd) | W/Leipzig |
| 505th: | Lt. J.L. Lynch | (1.5)Do-217 dest(air) | Riesa |
| | | Trainer dest(air) | Riesa |
| | Lt. C.J. Hanseman | (2)Trainer dest(air) | W/Dresden |
| | | (.5)Ju-88 dest(air)* | W/Dresden |
| | Capt. L. Reid | (1.5)Ju-88 dest(air)* | W/Dresden |
| | Lt. J.R. Hanson | (1.5)Trainer dest(air)** | Leipzig-Dresden |
| | Lt. R.W. Strong | Trainer dest(air) | Dresden |
| | Lt. H.M. Everett | (.5)Ju-88 dest(air)@ | Schwepnitz |
| | Lt. G.F. Perry | (.5)Do-217 dest(air) | Riesa |
| | Lt. J.R. Starnes | (.5)Trainer dest(air)** | Leipzig-Dresden |
| | Lt. W.F. Mudge | (.5)Ju-88 dest(air)@ | Schwepnitz |
| | Lt. O.P. Farmer | u/i a/c dam(air) | Oschatz |

**May 24, 1944**

| | | | |
|---|---|---|---|
| (#1) | | | |
| 503rd: | Maj. H.W. Scruggs | (.5)FW-190 dest(air)* | NW Berlin |
| | Lt. R.S. Whitelaw | (.5)FW-190 dest(air)* | NW Berlin |
| | Lt. W.E. Bryan | (.5)FW-190 dest(air)** | Dannenberg |
| | Lt. E.H. Graham | (.5)FW-190 dest(air)** | Dannenberg |
| | Lt. R.B. Brown | (.5)Me-109 dest(air)@@ | SW Berlin |
| | | (2)Me-109 dam(air) | SW Berlin |
| | Lt. J. Wolfort | (.5)Me-109 dest(air)@@ | SW Berlin |
| | | Me-109 dam(air) | SW Berlin |
| 504th: | Lt. W.B. Griffith | Me-109 dest(air) | Berlin |
| | Lt. B.V. Stevens | Me-109 prob(air) | Berlin |
| | | (2)Me-109 dam(air) | Berlin |
| | Lt. M.R. Ball | Me-109 dam(air) | Berlin |
| 505th: | Maj. D.A. Larson | (2)Me-109 dest(air) | Berlin |
| | | FW-190 dest(air) | Berlin |
| | | FW-190 dam(air) | Berlin |
| | Lt. E.M. Johnson | FW-190 dest(air) | Berlin |
| | Lt. J.L. Lynch | Me-109 dest(grd) | Gifhorn |
| (#2) | | | |
| 503rd: | Lt. C.W. Knott | (.5)Me-109 dest(air) | SW Soissons |
| | | (.5)Me-109 dest(grd) | SW Soissons |
| | Lt. C.E. Shake | (.5)Me-109 dest(air) | SW Soissons |
| | | (.5)Me-109 dest(grd) | SW Soissons |
| 505th: | Lt. H.M. Everett | (2)FW-190 dest(air) | St. Quentin |
| | Lt. C.J. Hanseman | (1.5)Me-109 dest(air) | St. Gobain-Laon |
| | | (shared with an unknown pilot) | |

**May 25, 1944**

| | | | |
|---|---|---|---|
| 505th: | Lt. G.J. Hrico | (.5)FW-190 dest(air) | Paris |
| | Lt. W.F. Mudge | (.5)FW-190 dest(air) | Paris |

**May 27, 1944**

| | | | |
|---|---|---|---|
| 505th: | Capt. J.L. Thury | Fi-156 dest(grd) | Frankfurt |
| | | He-111 dest(grd) | Frankfurt |
| | | Fi-156 dam(grd) | Frankfurt |
| | | u/i a/c dam(grd) | Frankfurt |
| | Lt. P.H. Ewing | Fi-156 dest(grd) | Frankfurt |
| | | u/i a/c dest(grd) | Frankfurt |
| | Lt. R.B. Olander | Me-109 dest(grd) | Reims |
| | Lt. R.A. Rohm | Fi-156 dest(grd) | Frankfurt |
| | Lt. J.F. Sawicki | Fi-156 dest(grd) | Frankfurt |

**May 28, 1944**

| | | | |
|---|---|---|---|
| HdQts: | Maj. M.G.H. McPharlin | Me-109 dest(air) | Magdeburg |
| | | Me-109 dam(air) | Magdeburg |

**May 29, 1944**

| | | | |
|---|---|---|---|
| HdQts: | Maj. M.G.H. McPharlin | Do-18 dest(grd) | Dievenow |
| 505th: | Capt. J.L. Thury | FW-190 dest(air) | NE Stettin |
| | Lt. J.R. Starnes | FW-190 dest(air) | NE Stettin |

**May 30, 1944**

| | | | |
|---|---|---|---|
| 503rd: | Lt. W.E. Bryan | (2)FW-190 dest(air) | Magdeburg |
| 504th: | Lt. B.V. Stevens | (2)FW-190 dest(air) | SE Brunswick |
| | Maj. E.B. Gravette | FW-190 dest(air) | Magdeburg |
| | | FW-190 dam(air) | Magdeburg |
| | Capt. L.S. Peter | FW-190 prob(air) | Magdeburg |

**June 6, 1944**

| | | | |
|---|---|---|---|
| HdQts: | Maj. M.G.H. McPharlin | FW-190 dam(air) | Evreux |
| 505th: | Lt. P.J. McMahan | (2)Ju-87 dest(air) | Orleans |
| | Lt. W.F. Mudge | Ju-87 dest(air) | Orleans |

**June 7, 1944**

| | | | |
|---|---|---|---|
| 504th: | Capt. L.S. Peter | FW-190 dest(air) | Laval |
| | Lt. R.N. Attebury | FW-190 dest(air) | Laval |
| | | FW-190 dest(grd) | Laval |
| | Lt. M.F. Caldwell | FW-190 dest(grd) | Laval |
| | Lt. L.L. Corbin | FW-190 dest(grd) | Laval |
| | Lt. B.V. Stevens | FW-190 dest(grd) | Laval |
| | Lt. F.T. Waters | FW-190 dest(grd) | Laval |

**June 8, 1944**

| | | | |
|---|---|---|---|
| 503rd: | Lt. R.H. Ammon | FW-190 dest(air) | Fougeres |
| | | Me-109 dam(air) | Rennes |
| | Lt. R.S. Whitelaw | FW-190 dest(air) | Rennes |
| 504th: | Lt. M.R. Ball | FW-190 dest(air) | Rennes |
| 505th: | Lt. A.A. Tower | FW-190 dest(air) | Laigle |
| | | (.5)Do-217 dest(air) | Laigle |
| | Lt. W.R. Opitz | (.5)Do-217 dest(air) | Laigle |
| | Lt. J.R. Starnes | Me-109 dest(air) | Fougeres |
| | | (.5)FW-190 dest(air)* | Rennes |
| | Lt. P.J. McMahon | (.5)FW-190 dest(air)* | Rennes |
| | Lt. W. Jaaskelainen | FW-190 dest(air) | Rennes |
| | Lt. W.A. Jones | FW-190 dest(air) | Rennes |
| | Lt. R.B. Olander | (.5)FW-190 dest(air)** | Rennes |
| | Lt. A. Sirochman | (.5)FW-190 dest(air)** | Rennes |

**June 10, 1944**

| | | | |
|---|---|---|---|
| 504th: | Lt. H.S. Stockman | Me-109 prob(air) | SE Le Havre |
| | Lt. M.R. Ball | Me-109 dam(air) | SE Le Havre |
| 505th: | Lt. C.J. Hanseman | Me-109 dest(air) | Laigle |
| | | Ju-88 dam(grd) | Laigle |
| | Capt. L. Reid | (.5)Ju-52 dest(air) | Laigle |
| | Lt. E.M. Johnson | (.5)Ju-52 dest(air) | Laigle |

**June 15, 1944**

| | | | |
|---|---|---|---|
| 503rd: | Capt. V. Wyatt | FW-190 dest(air) | Montiers |
| | Lt. L.J. Fiorito | Me-109 dest(air) | Montiers |
| | Lt. V.W. Meyer | FW-190 dest(air) | Montiers |
| 504th: | Lt. H.R. Waymire | Me-109 dest(air) | Chateaudun |

**June 21, 1944**

| | | | |
|---|---|---|---|
| 503rd: | Capt. W.E. Bryan | Me-410 dest(air) | Stettin |
| | | (.5)Me-410 prob(air) | Stettin |
| | Lt. R.C. West | Me-410 dest(air) | Stettin |
| | Lt. F.D. Talcott | (.5)Me-410 prob(air) | Stettin |
| 504th: | Lt. H.G. Thibert | Me-109 dest(air) | Soldin |
| 505th: | Lt. E.C. Ball | Me-410 dam(air) | N/Berlin |

**June 27, 1944**

| | | | |
|---|---|---|---|
| 505th: | Capt. J.L. Thury | FW-190 dest(air) | SE Paris |
| | Lt. O.P. Farmer | (.5)FW-190 dest(air) | Paris |
| | Lt. W.G. Fish | (.5)FW-190 dest(air) | Paris |

**June 29, 1944**

| | | | |
|---|---|---|---|
| HdQts: | LtCol. H.W. Scruggs | (2)FW-190 dest(air) | Eisleben |
| | | (2)FW-190 dam(air) | Eisleben |
| 503rd: | Lt. V.W. Meyer | FW-190 dest(air) | Eisleben |
| | | (.5)Me-410 dest(air)* | Eisleben |
| | | Me-109 dam(air) | Eisleben |
| | Lt. C.W. Knott | FW-190 dest(air) | Eisleben |
| | Lt. L.M. Wright | Me-109 dam(air) | Leipzig |
| | | Ju-88 dam(grd) | Leipzig |
| 504th: | Lt. L.D. Eisenhart | FW-190 dest(air) | Nordhausen |
| 505th: | Lt. E.M. Johnson | (.5)Me-109 dest(air) | All claims are |
| | | (.5)Me-410 dest(air)** | Halle-S/Magdeburg |
| | Lt. G.E. Graham | (.5)Me-410 dest(air)** | |
| | Lt. A. Sirochman | (.5)Me-109 dest(air) | |
| | Unknown 505th pilot | (.5)Me-410 dest(air)* | |

| **July 7, 1944** | | | |
|---|---|---|---|
| 503rd: | Capt. V. Wyatt | (.5)Me-109 dest(air) | Leipzig |
| | Lt. J.P. Bush | (.5)Me-109 dest(air) | Leipzig |
| | Lt. R.H. Ammon | Me-109 dam(air) | Leipzig |
| 504th: | Lt. M.F. Caldwell | (2)Me-109 dest(air) | Eisleben |
| | Lt. R.H. Wilcox | (2)Me-109 dest(air) | Eisleben |
| | Maj. B.C. Routt | Me-109 dest(air) | Eisleben |

| **July 11, 1944** | | | |
|---|---|---|---|
| 503rd: | Capt. E.B. Stephenson | Me-110 dam(air) | Landsberg |
| 505th: | Lt. J.R. Starnes | Trainer dest(grd) | NE Lake Constance |

| **July 19, 1944** | | | |
|---|---|---|---|
| 505th: | Maj. J.L. Thury | Me-109 dest(grd) | All claims are |
| | | u/i a/c dest(grd) | SW Augsburg |
| | Lt. W.F. Mudge | FW-190 dest(grd) | |
| | | Ju-188 dest(grd) | |
| | Lt. C.J. Hanseman | Ju-188 dest(grd) | |
| | | u/i a/c dest(grd) | |
| | Lt. J.R. Hanson | Ju-188 dest(grd) | |
| | Lt. R.B. Olander | Ju-188 dest(grd) | |
| | Lt. J.R. Starnes | Ju-188 dest(grd) | |
| | Lt. A.A. Tower | Ju-188 dest(grd) | |
| | Lt. G. Knight | (.5)Ju-188 dest(grd)[*] | |
| | Lt. W.H. Krauss | (.5)Ju-188 dest(grd)[*] | |
| | Lt. A. Sirochman | (.5)Ju-188 dest(grd)[**] | |
| | Lt. R.H. Tannous | (.5)Ju-188 dest(grd)[**] | |

| **July 25, 1944** | | | |
|---|---|---|---|
| HdQts: | Maj. J.R. Reynolds | FW-190 dest(air) | Etrepagny |
| 503rd: | Capt. E.B. Stephenson | Me-109 dest(air) | Etrepagny |
| | Capt. V. Wyatt | Me-109 dest(air) | Etrepagny |
| | Lt. E.H. Beavers | FW-190 dest(air) | Etrepagny |
| 505th: | Lt. J.G. Holloway | Me-109 dest(air) | Beauvais |

| **July 28, 1944** | | | |
|---|---|---|---|
| 505th: | Maj. D.A. Larson | Ju-52 dest(air) | Ansbach |

| **July 29, 1944** | | | |
|---|---|---|---|
| 504th: | Lt. F.S. Rutan | (2)Me-109 dest(air) | Naumburg |
| | Lt. H.S. Stockman | Me-109 dest(air) | Merseburg-Naumburg |
| | | Me-109 prob(air) | Merseburg-Naumburg |
| | | Me-109 dam(air) | Merseburg-Naumburg |
| | Lt. R.N. Attebury | FW-190 dest(air) | Naumburg |
| | Lt. J.R. Trester | Me-109 prob(air) | Merseburg-Naumburg |
| 505th: | Lt. W.H. Krauss | (.5)Me-109 dest(air) | All claims are |
| | Lt. J.R. Starnes | (.5)Me-109 dest(air) | NW Naumburg |
| | Lt. W.F. Mudge | Ju-52 dest(grd) | |
| | Lt. G.J. Hrico | (.5)Ju-52 dest(grd) | |
| | Lt. W.A. Jones | (.5)Ju-52 dest(grd) | |

| **July 31, 1944** | | | |
|---|---|---|---|
| 505th: | Maj. J.L. Thury | (2)u/i a/c dest(grd) | All claims are |
| | | (.5)Me-410 dest(grd) | at Holzkirchen |
| | | u/i a/c dam(grd) | |
| | Lt. W.F. Mudge | FW-190 dest(grd) | |
| | | Me-110 dest(grd) | |
| | | Ju-88 dest(grd) | |
| | | (2)u/i a/c dam(grd) | |
| | Lt. R.B. Olander | u/i a/c dest(grd) | |
| | | Ju-87 dest(grd) | |
| | | u/i a/c dam(grd) | |
| | Lt. J.R. Starnes | FW-190 dest(grd) | |
| | | u/i a/c dest(grd) | |
| | | FW-190 dam(grd) | |
| | Lt. T.B. Staggers | FW-190 dest(grd) | |
| | | u/i a/c dest(grd) | |
| | Lt. B.O. Jackson | FW-190 dest(grd) | |
| | Lt. L.J. Powell | Me-410 dest(grd) | |
| | | u/i a/c dam(grd) | |
| | Lt. C.R. Stewart | u/i a/c dest(grd) | |
| | | u/i a/c dam(grd) | |
| | Lt. G.E. Graham | (.5)Me-410 dest(grd) | |
| | | u/i a/c dam(grd) | |
| | Lt. O.P. Farmer | (3)u/i a/c dam(grd) | |
| | Lt. M.N. Nay | u/i a/c dam(grd) | |

| **August 3, 1944** | | | |
|---|---|---|---|
| 505th: | Maj. D.A. Larson | Do-217 dest(grd) | All claims are |
| | | FW-190 dest(grd) | at Benestroff |
| | Lt. G.E. Graham | Do-217 dest(grd) | |
| | Lt. A. Sirochman | u/i a/c dest(grd) | |
| | | u/i a/c dam(grd) | |
| | Lt. B.V. Shaw | FW-190 dam(grd) | |

| **August 4, 1944** | | | |
|---|---|---|---|
| 503rd: | Lt. L.J. Fiorito | FW-190 dest(air) | SW Hamburg |
| 505th: | Maj. D.A. Larson | (2)Me-109 dest(air) | Ulzen-Celle |
| | | Me-410 dest(grd) | E/Celle |
| | Lt. J.G. Holloway | Me-109 dest(air) | S/Hamburg |
| | Lt. J.R. Starnes | Me-109 dest(air) | S/Hamburg |
| | Lt. J.B. Muller | (.5)Me-109 dest(air)[*] | Ulzen |
| | | Me-410 dest(grd) | E/Celle |
| | Lt. A.E. Tongue | Me-109 dest(air) | Ulzen-Celle |
| | | (.5)Me-109 dest(air)[*] | Ulzen |
| | | (.5)Me-109 dest(air)[**] | S/Hamburg |
| | Lt. L.J. Powell | FW-190 dest(air) | S/Hamburg |
| | | (.5)Me-109 dest(air)[**] | S/Hamburg |
| | Lt. R.A. Rohm | Ju-88 dest(grd) | E/Celle |
| | Lt. B.V. Shaw | Ju-88 dest(grd) | E/Celle |
| | Lt. A. Sirochman | Ju-88 dest(grd) | E/Celle |
| | Lt. R.W. Strong | Ju-88 dest(grd) | E/Celle |
| | Lt. W.R. Slovak | Ju-88 dam(grd) | E/Celle |

| **August 5, 1944** | | | |
|---|---|---|---|
| 503rd: | Maj. J. Aitken | (2)FW-190 dest(air) | S/Hameln |
| | Capt. W.E. Bryan | FW-190 dest(air) | S/Hameln |
| | Lt. E.H. Graham | Me-109 dam(air) | S/Hameln |

| **August 6, 1944** | | | |
|---|---|---|---|
| 503rd: | Capt. E.B. Stephenson | Me-109 dest(air) | S/Schwerinner L. |
| | Lt. W.W. Behrend | Me-109 dest(air) | S/Schwerinner L. |
| | Lt. P.D. Fickel | Me-109 dest(air) | S/Schwerinner L. |
| 504th: | Lt. D.E. Penny | Me-109 dest(air) | Havelburg |
| | Lt. M.R. Winkelman | Me-109 dest(air) | Havelburg |
| | Lt. R.T. Wood | Me-109 dest(air) | Havelburg-Pritzwalk |
| | Lt. D.A. Zeine | Me-109 dest(air) | Havelburg |

| **August 16, 1944** | | | |
|---|---|---|---|
| 503rd: | Lt. F.R. Gerard | Me-109 dest(air) | Gotha |
| 504th: | Maj. B.C. Routt | Me-109 dest(air) | All claims are |
| | | Me-109 dam(air) | at Mulhausen |
| | Lt. C.M. Hunter | Me-109 dest(air) | |
| | Lt. R.C. Penrose | Me-109 dest(air) | |
| | Lt. H.S. Stockman | Me-109 dest(air) | |

| **August 28, 1944** | | | |
|---|---|---|---|
| HdQts: | Maj. J.R. Reynolds | (.5)Ju-88 dest(grd) | All claims are |
| 503rd: | Lt. J.P. Bush | Ju-88 dest(grd) | at Savernne |
| 505th: | Lt. J.F. Marts | Ju-88 dest(grd) | |
| | Lt. A.D. Young | (.5)Ju-88 dest(grd) | |

| **September 5, 1944** | | | |
|---|---|---|---|
| 503rd: | Lt. N. Ostrow | (1.5)Me-109 dest(air) | Schaffhausen |
| | Lt. E.E. Erickson | (.5)Me-109 dest(air) | Schaffhausen |
| 505th: | Capt. E.M. Johnson | Me-410 dam(grd) | Sinsheim |
| | Lt. C.H. Bundgaard | Me-410 dam(grd) | Sinsheim |
| | Lt. G.E. Graham | Me-410 dam(grd) | Sinsheim |

| **September 10, 1944** | | | |
|---|---|---|---|
| 505th: | Lt. C. Malarz | (2)Ju 88 dest(grd) | Unless noted, all |
| | | Me-410 dest(grd) | claims are at |
| | | (3)He-111 dam(grd) | Weizenburg |
| | | Ju-88 dam(grd) | |
| | Lt. B.O. Jackson | (2)u/i a/c dest(grd) | |
| | | Ju-88 dest(grd) | |
| | | (4)u/i a/c dam(grd) | |
| | Lt. A.D. Young | (3)u/i a/c dest(grd) | |
| | Lt. W.A. Jones | u/i a/c dest(grd) | |
| | | Ju-87 dest(grd) | |
| | | (.5)Me-109 dest(grd) | |
| | | (2)He-111 dam(grd) | |
| | Lt. C.R. Stewart | (2)Ju-88 dest(grd) | Munich |
| | | (.5)Me-109 dest(grd) | |
| | | (3)Ju-88 dam(grd) | Munich |
| | Maj. J.L. Thury | Ju-52 dest(grd) | |
| | | Ju-88 dest(grd) | |
| | Capt. A.A. Tower | Ju-88 dest(grd) | Munich |
| | | Ju-52 dest(grd) | Munich |
| | | (2)He-111 dam(grd) | Munich |
| | | Ju-88 dam(grd) | Munich |
| | Lt. J.F. Marts | (2)Me-410 dest(grd) | |
| | | (2)He-111 dam(grd) | |
| | | Ju-88 dam(grd) | |
| | | u/i a/c dam(grd) | |
| | Lt. L.J. Powell | Me-410 dest(grd) | |
| | | Do-217 dest(grd) | |
| | | (4)u/i a/c dam(grd) | |
| | Lt. R.H. Tannous | Me-410 dest(grd) | |
| | | u/i a/c dest(grd) | |
| | | (6)u/i a/c dam(grd) | |
| | Lt. O.P. Farmer | u/i a/c dest(grd) | |
| | Lt. W.R. Moore | Ju-88 dest(grd) | Munich |
| | Lt. J.B. Muller | Ju-88 dest(grd) | |
| | Lt. G.T. Rich | FW-190 dest(grd) | |
| | Capt. R.M. Mitchell | Ju-88 dam(grd) | |
| | Lt. W.H. Krauss | Ju-88 dam(grd) | |

| **September 11, 1944** | | | |
|---|---|---|---|
| 503rd: | Lt. F.R. Gerard | (3)Me-109 dest(air) | All 503rd claims |
| | | FW-190 dest(air) | are at Annaberg |
| | | Me-109 dam(air) | |

| | | | |
|---|---|---|---|
| | Lt. R.D. Mayer | (2)Me-109 dest(air) | |
| | Lt. C.S. Coe | (1.5)FW-190 dest(air)* | |
| | Maj. J. Aitken | Me-109 dest(air) | |
| | | FW-190 dam(air) | |
| | Capt. C.E. Cloud | Me-109 dest(air) | |
| | Lt. E.E. Erickson | FW-190 dest(air) | |
| | | FW-190 prob(air) | |
| | Lt. J.B. Price | FW-190 dest(air) | |
| | Lt. E.H. Graham | (.5)FW-190 dest(air)* | |
| | | (.5)Me-109 dest(air) | |
| | Lt. D.E. McClish | (.5)FW-190 dest(air)** | |
| | | (.5)Me-109 dest(air) | |
| | | FW-190 prob(air) | |
| | Capt. J.G. Robinson | (.5)FW-190 dest(air)** | |
| | Lt. W.D. Stockton | FW-190 dam(air) | |
| 505th: | Capt. A.A. Tower | (2)Ju-88 dest(grd) | All 505th claims |
| | | He-111 dest(grd) | are at Munich |
| | | Me-410 dest(grd) | |
| | | Ju-87 dest(grd) | |
| | | (2)Ju-88 dam(grd) | |
| | Lt. W.H. Krauss | (2)Me-410 dest(grd) | |
| | | Me-110 dest(grd) | |
| | | Ju-88 dest(grd) | |
| | | (3)Me-410 dam(grd) | |
| | Maj. J.L. Thury | (2)Ju-88 dest(grd) | |
| | | Me-109 dam(grd) | |
| | | Me-410 dam(grd) | |
| | | He-111 dam(grd) | |
| | | Ju-88 dam(grd) | |
| | Lt. C.H. Bundgaard | (2)Ju-88 dest(grd) | |
| | | (3)Ju-52 dam(grd) | |
| | Lt. G.T. Rich | (2)u/i a/c dest(grd) | |
| | | Me-410 dest(grd) | |
| | | Me-410 dam(grd) | |
| | Lt. W.R. Slovak | Me-410 dest(grd) | |
| | | u/i a/c dest(grd) | |
| | | (2)Me-410 dam(grd) | |
| | Lt. T.B. Staggers | Me-110 dest(grd) | |
| | | Ju-88 dest(grd) | |
| | | Me-110 dam(grd) | |
| | | He-111 dam(grd) | |
| | | Ju-88 dam(grd) | |
| | Lt. W.A. Jones | Ju-88 dest(grd) | |
| | | Ju-52 dest(grd) | |
| | | Ju-88 dam(grd) | |
| | Capt. R.B. Olander | u/i a/c dest(grd) | |
| | | (2)u/i a/c dam(grd) | |
| | Lt. G.E. Graham | Me-410 dest(grd) | |
| | | Me-410 dam(grd) | |
| | | Do-217 dam(grd) | |
| | | Ju-88 dam(grd) | |
| | Lt. W. Jaaskelainen | Ju-88 dest(grd) | |
| | | He-111 dam(grd) | |

**September 12, 1944**

| | | | |
|---|---|---|---|
| 503rd: | Capt. A.S. Harte | Me-109 dest(air) | Magdeburg |
| 504th: | Capt. B.V. Stevens | Me-109 dest(air) | Halberstadt |
| 505th: | Capt. R.B. Olander | Me-109 dest(air) | Goslar |

**September 13, 1944**

| | | | |
|---|---|---|---|
| 503rd: | Maj. J. Aitken | Ju-88 dest(grd) | Holzkirchen |
| | Lt. W.D. Stockton | Ju-88 dest(grd) | Holzkirchen |
| 504th: | Lt. M.F. Caldwell | FW-190 dest(grd) | Munich |
| | | u/i a/c dest(grd) | Munich |
| 505th: | Capt. R.M. Mitchell | Do-217 dest(grd) | SE Munich |
| | Lt. W.R. Moore | (.5)Ju-88 dest(grd) | SE Munich |
| | Lt. L.J. Powell | (.5)Ju-88 dest(grd) | SE Munich |
| | Lt. G.J. Hrico | (2)u/i a/c dam(grd) | SE Munich |

**September 23, 1944**

| | | | |
|---|---|---|---|
| 503rd: | Lt. R.H. Ammon | (2)FW-190 dest(air) | SW Wesel |
| | Lt. E.H. Beavers | FW-190 dest(air) | SW Wesel |
| | Lt. L.C. Marsh | FW-190 dest(air) | SW Wesel |
| | Lt. R.D. Mayer | FW-190 dest(air) | SW Wesel |
| 504th: | Lt. M.L. Cernicky | FW-190 prob(air) | Venlo |
| 505th: | Lt. L.J. Powell | FW-190 dest(air) | Geldern-Weeze |
| | Lt. R.H. Tannous | FW-190 dest(air) | Geldern-Weeze |
| | | FW-190 dam(air) | Geldern-Weeze |

**September 28, 1944**

| | | | |
|---|---|---|---|
| 503rd: | Lt. R.H. Ammon | (2)FW-190 dest(air) | SE Brunswick |

**November 2, 1944**

| | | | |
|---|---|---|---|
| 504th: | Lt. R.F. Herrmann | FW-190 dest(air) | Mulhausen |
| | Lt. D.E. Penny | Me-109 dest(air) | Naumburg |

**November 18, 1944**

| | | | |
|---|---|---|---|
| 503rd: | Capt. E.H. Beavers | Me-109 dest(air) | Mannheim |
| | Capt. D.E. Shafer | Me-109 dest(air) | Mannheim |
| | Lt. L.C. Marsh | Me-109 dest(air) | Mannheim |
| | Lt. F.M. Stillwell | Me-109 prob(air) | Mannheim |
| 504th: | Lt. C.M. Mead | Me-109 dest(air) | Dauchau |
| 505th: | Capt. E.M. Johnson | Me-109 dest(air) | Heilbronn |
| | | Me-109 dam(air) | Heilbronn |
| | Lt. C.H. Bundgaard | Me-109 dest(air) | Neustadt |
| | Lt. C. Malarz | (.5)Me-109 dest(air) | Neustadt |
| | Lt. G.T. Rich | (.5)Me-109 dest(air) | Neustadt |

**November 21, 1944**

| | | | |
|---|---|---|---|
| HdQts: | Capt. C.W. Dowell | (.5)Me-109 dest(air) | Munster |
| 505th: | Lt. G.T. Rich | Me-109 dest(air) | Warburg |
| | F/O G.W. Palmer | (.5)Me-109 dest(air) | Munster |
| | Lt. B.O. Jackson | Ju-88 dest(grd) | NE Munster |

**November 26, 1944**

| | | | |
|---|---|---|---|
| 503rd: | Capt. D.W. Johnson | (3)FW-190 dest(air) | All 503rd claims |
| | Lt. L.C. Marsh | (3)FW-190 dest(air) | are SE Dummer |
| | | FW-190 prob(air) | Lake |
| | | FW-190 dam(air) | |
| | LtCol. H.E. Henderson | (2)FW-190 dest(air) | |
| | Capt. E.H. Beavers | (2)FW-190 dest(air) | |
| | Capt. M.B. Edens | (2)FW-190 dest(air) | |
| | Lt. J.P. Wilson | (2)FW-190 dest(air) | |
| | Lt. C.S. Coe | FW-190 dest(air) | |
| | Lt. L.J. French | FW-190 dest(air) | |
| | Lt. P.E. Petitt | FW-190 dest(air) | |
| | Lt. F.M. Stillwell | FW-190 dest(air) | |
| | Lt. B.A. Allen | FW-190 dam(air) | |
| | Lt. J.W. Gokey | FW-190 dam(air) | |
| 504th: | Lt. A.W. Bates | FW-190 dest(air) | S/Dummer Lake |
| 505th: | Lt. J.S. Daniell | (5)FW-190 dest(air) | All 505th claims |
| | Lt. W.R. Phillippi | (1.5)FW-190 dest(air) | are S/Hanover |
| | Lt. C.H. Bundgaard | FW-190 dest(air) | |
| | | FW-190 dam(air) | |
| | Lt. H.E. Girzi | FW-190 dest(air) | |
| | Lt. B. Stiles | FW-190 dest(air) | |
| | Lt. P.M. Loveless | (.5)FW-190 dest(air) | |

**December 5, 1944**

| | | | |
|---|---|---|---|
| 503rd: | Capt. D.E. Shafer | FW-190 dam(air) | S/Wittstock |

**December 31, 1944**

| | | | |
|---|---|---|---|
| 503rd: | Capt. W.E. Bryan | FW-190 dest(air) | S/Hamburg |
| | Capt. A.G. Hawkins | FW-190 dest(air) | S/Hamburg |
| | | Me-262 dam(air) | S/Hamburg |
| | Lt. B.A. Allen | FW-190 dest(air) | S/Hamburg |
| 504th: | Lt. R.F. Herrmann | (2)FW-190 dest(air) | Hamburg |
| | Lt. L.W. Allers | FW-190 dest(air) | Hamburg |
| | Lt. V.N. Barto | FW-190 dam(air) | Hamburg |

**February 9, 1945**

| | | | |
|---|---|---|---|
| 504th: | Lt. J.J. Sainlar | Me-262 dam(air) | Meiningen |
| 505th: | Lt. S.C. Ananian | Me-262 dest(air) | Fulda |

**March 1, 1945**

| | | | |
|---|---|---|---|
| 505th: | Lt. S.C. Ananian | (2)Ju-88 dest(grd) | All claims are |
| | LtCol. J.L. Thury | Ju-88 dest(grd) | S/Feldkirchen |
| | Lt. C.H. Bundgaard | Ju-88 dest(grd) | |
| | Lt. T.W. Marvel | Ju-88 dest(grd) | |
| | Lt. J.C. Woolery | Do-217 dest(grd) | |
| | Lt. H.D. Ziegler | Ju-88 dest(grd) | |
| | Lt. R.E. Irion | (.5)Ju-88 dest(grd) | |
| | | (.5)Ju-88 dest(grd) | |
| | Lt. O.K. Biggs | (.5)Ju-88 dest(grd) | |
| | Lt. B.B. Booth | (.5)Ju-88 dest(grd) | |

**March 2, 1945**

| | | | |
|---|---|---|---|
| 503rd: | Lt. L. Poutre | (2)Me-109 dest(air) | All 503rd claims |
| | | FW-190 dest(air) | are E/Magdeburg |
| | Maj. W.E. Bryan | FW-190 dest(air) | |
| | | Me-109 dest(air) | |
| | | FW-190 dam(air) | |
| | Lt. F.R. Gerard | (2)Me-109 dest(air) | |
| | | Me-109 dam(air) | |
| | Lt. S.J. Chetneky | Me-109 dest(air) | |
| | | Me-109 dam(air) | |
| | Lt. J.W. Gokey | Me-109 dest(air) | |
| | Lt. W.R. Preddy | FW-190 dest(air) | |
| | | Me-109 prob(air) | |
| | Lt. F. Butler | FW-190 prob(air) | |
| | | Me-109 dam(air) | |
| | Capt. W.W. Behrend | Me-109 dam(air) | |
| | Lt. C.H. French | Me-109 dam(air) | |
| | Lt. R.J. Frisch | Me-109 dam(air) | |
| 505th: | Lt. J.F. Marts | (2)Me-109 dest(air) | E/Magdeburg |
| | Capt. J.R. Starnes | Me-109 dest(air) | E/Magdeburg |
| | | u/i a/c dam(grd) | E/Magdeburg |
| | Lt. J.C. Withers | (.5)Me-109 dest(air) | E/Magdeburg |
| | Lt. H.D. Ziegler | (.5)Me-109 dest(air) | E/Magdeburg |
| | Lt. G.W. Jones | Me-109 dam(air) | Osnabruck |

| | | | |
|---|---|---|---|
| | Lt. O.K. Biggs | (3)Do-217 dest(grd) | All claims are |
| | | (2)Do-217 dam(grd) | at Mockern |
| | Lt. H.W. Burch | (3)Do-217 dest(grd) | |
| | Lt. B.A. Connor | (2)Do-217 dest(grd) | |
| | Lt. H.F. Howard | (2)Do-217 dest(grd) | |

**March 3, 1945**

| | | | |
|---|---|---|---|
| 503rd: | Lt. R.G. Johnson | Me-262 dam(air) | Celle |
| 505th: | LtCol. J.L. Thury | (3)Ju-88 dest(grd) | All 505th claims |
| | | Do-217 dest(grd) | are E/Magdeburg |
| | | Ju-88 dam(grd) | |
| | Capt. J.R. Starnes | He-111 dest(grd) | |
| | Lt. G.W. Jones | u/i a/c dest(grd) | |
| | Lt. R.C. Thieme | Ju-88 dest(grd) | |
| | Lt. H.D. Ziegler | Ju-88 dest(grd) | |
| | Lt. J.C. Withers | Ju-88 dam(grd) | |

**March 12, 1945**

| | | | |
|---|---|---|---|
| 505th: | Capt. O.P. Farmer | (1.5)Me-109 dest(air) | All claims are |
| | F/O J.R. Coker | Me-109 dest(air) | at Hellevad |
| | | Me-109 dam(air) | |
| | F/O J. Pesanka | Me-109 dest(air) | |
| | Lt. V.D. Carr | (.5)Me-109 dest(air) | |

**March 18, 1945**

| | | | |
|---|---|---|---|
| 503rd: | Maj. D.E. Shafer | FW-190 dest(air) | Dummer Lake |
| | | FW-190 dam(air) | Dummer Lake |
| | Capt. F.R. Gerard | FW-190 dest(air) | Dummer Lake |
| | Lt. F.E. McElwee | FW-190 dest(air) | Dummer Lake |
| | Lt. L. Poutre | FW-190 dam(air) | Dummer Lake |
| 504th: | Lt. J.J. Ballard | FW-190 dest(air) | Barnstorf |

**March 20, 1945**

| | | | |
|---|---|---|---|
| 503rd: | Lt. R.S. Hill | (2)Me-262 dam(air) | Hamburg |
| 504th: | Lt. V.N. Barto | Me-262 dest(air) | Hamburg |
| | Lt. K.V. Berguson | Me-262 dam(air) | Hamburg |
| | LtCol. W.C. Clark | u/i a/c dest(grd) | Grossenbrode |
| | | He-111 dam(grd) | Grossenbrode |
| | Lt. R.R. Kuhlman | FW-200 dest(grd) | Grossenbrode |
| | | Ju-52 dam(grd) | Grossenbrode |
| | Lt. L.J. Barrett | He-111 dest(grd) | Grossenbrode |
| | Lt. G.H. Chenez | Ju-52 dam(grd) | Grossenbrode |
| 505th: | Lt. R.E. Irion | Me-262 dest(air) | Schwerin |

**March 21, 1945**

| | | | |
|---|---|---|---|
| 504th: | Lt. N.C. Greer | (.5)Me-262 dest(air) | Wurzburg |
| | Lt. B.E. Langohr | (.5)Me-262 dest(air) | Wurzburg |

**March 24, 1945**

| | | | |
|---|---|---|---|
| 505th: | Maj. A.A. Tower | FW-190 dam(grd) | Ziegenhall |

**March 30, 1945**

| | | | |
|---|---|---|---|
| HdQts: | Col. J.B. Henry | Me-262 prob(air) | SW Hamburg |
| 504th: | Capt. R.F. Sargent | Me-262 dest(air) | Kaltenkirchen |
| | Lt. C.W. Bennett | Me-262 dest(air) | Hamburg |
| | | Me-262 dam(air) | Hamburg |
| 505th: | Capt. G.T. Rich | Me-262 dam(air) | N/Luneburg |
| | Lt. S.C. Ananian | Me-262 dam(air) | N/Luneburg |

**April 4, 1945**

| | | | |
|---|---|---|---|
| HdQts: | LtCol. W.C. Clark | Me-262 dam(air) | Parchim A/F |
| | | u/i a/c dest(grd) | Wiemar |
| | | u/i a/c dam(grd) | Wiemar |
| 504th: | Capt. N.C. Greer | Me-262 dest(air) | Parchim |
| | Lt. R.C. Havighurst | Me-262 dest(air) | Parchim |
| | Capt. K.B. Everson | (.5)Me-262 dest(air) | Parchim |
| | Lt. R.C. Croker | (.5)Me-262 dest(air) | Parchim |
| | Lt. L.M. Carter | u/i a/c dam(grd) | Wiemar |
| 505th: | Capt. H.R. Corey | Me-262 dest(air) | Rostock |
| | Maj. A.A. Tower | (2)Me-410 dest(grd) | All claims are |
| | Capt. G.T. Rich | Do-217 dest(grd) | NE Tribsees |
| | Lt. S.C. Ananian | Ju-88 dest(grd) | |
| | Lt. W.R. MacClarence | Me-410 dest(grd) | |

**April 5, 1945**

| | | | |
|---|---|---|---|
| 505th: | Lt. S.C. Ananian | Me-262 dam(air) | Boblingen |

**April 7, 1945**

| | | | |
|---|---|---|---|
| 503rd: | Lt. R.G. Johnson | FW-190 dest(air) | All 503rd claims |
| | Lt. R.E. Krauss | Me-109 dest(air) | at Celle |
| | Lt. P.E. Petitt | FW-190 dest(air) | |
| | | Me-262 dam(air) | |
| | Lt. L.Poutre | Me-109 dest(air) | |
| 504th: | Capt. K.B. Everson | Me-109 dest(air) | Unless noted, |
| | Capt. F.D. Guernsey | FW-190 dest(air) | all claims are |
| | | Me-109 dam(air) | at Celle |
| | Lt. L.M. Carter | Me-109 dest(air) | |
| | | Me-262 dam(air) | |
| | Lt. R.H. Cresswell | Me-109 dest(air) | |
| | Lt. V.N. Barto | (.5)Me-109 dest(air) | |
| | Lt. L.A. Kunz | (.5)Me-109 dest(air) | |
| | Lt. R.V.E. Blizzard | Me-262 prob(air) | |
| | | Me-262 dam(air) | |
| | Lt. C. Hermanson | Me-109 prob(air) | |
| | Lt. C.M. Mason | Me-262 dam(air) | Ulzen |
| 505th: | Capt. B.J. Bline | FW-190 dest(air) | SW Ulzen |
| | LtCol. J.L. Thury | (.5)Me-109 dest(air) | NE Steinhuder L. |
| | Lt. O.K. Biggs | (.5)Me-109 dest(air) | NE Steinhuder L. |
| | F/O J.J. Rice | Me-262 dam(air) | Ulzen |

**April 9, 1945**

| | | | |
|---|---|---|---|
| 504th: | Lt. H.F. Hunt | Me-262 dam(air) | Leipzig |
| | Lt. L.M. Orcutt | Me-262 dam(air) | Leipzig |

**April 10, 1945**

| | | | |
|---|---|---|---|
| 503rd: | Lt. R.J. Frisch | (4)Ju-88 dest(grd) | All 503rd & |
| | | Ju-88 dam(grd) | 504th claims |
| | | u/i a/c dam(grd) | are N/Neuruppin |
| | LtCol. D.E. Shafer | Me-109 dest(grd) | |
| | | Ju-88 dest(grd) | |
| | | (4)Ju-88 dam(grd) | |
| 504th: | Capt. K.B. Everson | (3)Me-410 dest(grd) | |
| | | (3)Me-410 dam(grd) | |
| | | (2)Me-110 dam(grd) | |
| | Capt. R.F. Sargent | (3)Me-410 dest(grd) | |
| | | (2)Me-410 dam(grd) | |
| | Lt. C. Hermanson | (4)Me-410 dest(grd) | |
| | | (2)Me-410 dam(grd) | |
| | Maj. W.H. Julian | (2)Me-410 dest(grd) | |
| | | (2)Me-410 dam(grd) | |
| | Lt. L.W. Allers | (2)Me-410 dest(grd) | |
| | | Me-410 dam(grd) | |
| | Lt. C.W. Bennett | (2)Me-410 dest(grd) | |
| | | (2)Me-410 dam(grd) | |
| | Lt. R.V.E. Blizzard | (2)Me-410 dest(grd) | |
| | | (2)Me-410 dam(grd) | |
| | Lt. V.N. Barto | (2)Ju-88 dest(grd) | |
| | | Ju-88 dam(grd) | |
| | Lt. L.J. Barrett | (2)Ju-88 dest(grd) | |
| | | (2)Me-410 dam(grd) | |
| | Lt. G.H. Chenez | (2)Me-410 dest(grd) | |
| | | (2)Me-410 dam(grd) | |
| | Lt. R.C. Croker | (2)Me-410 dest(grd) | |
| | | (4)Me-410 dam(grd) | |
| | Lt. L.A. Kunz | (2)Me-410 dest(grd) | |
| | | (3)Me-410 dam(grd) | |
| | Lt. C.M. Mason | (2)Me-410 dest(grd) | |
| | | Me-410 dam(grd) | |
| | F/O R.W. Smith | Me-410 dest(grd) | |
| | | Ju-88 dam(grd) | |
| | Lt. D.F. Krueger | (2)Me-410 dam(grd) | |
| 505th: | Maj. A.A. Tower | (2)Do-217 dest(grd) | Claims are at |
| | | (2)Me-410 dest(grd) | Wittstock |
| | | (2)Hs-129 dest(grd) | |
| | | (2)Ju-88 dest(grd) | |
| | | Do-217 dam(grd) | |
| | | Me-410 dam(grd) | |
| | Lt. R.H. Paul | (3)Do-217 dest(grd) | |
| | | (2)Ju-88 dest(grd) | |
| | | (2)Ju-52 dam(grd) | |
| | Lt. J.T. Murphy | (3)Do-217 dest(grd) | |
| | | (2)Ju-88 dest(grd) | |
| | | (3)u/i a/c dam(grd) | |
| | Capt. H.R. Corey | (4)Ju-88 dest(grd) | |
| | | FW-189 dam(grd) | |
| | | Ju-88 dam(grd) | |
| | | Ju-52 dam(grd) | |
| | Lt. O.K. Biggs | (4)Ju-88 dest(grd) | |
| | | (2)Ju-88 dam(grd) | |
| | Lt. H.W. Burch | (3)Me-410 dest(grd) | |
| | | He-111 dest(grd) | |
| | | Me-410 dam(grd) | |
| | | u/i a/c dam(grd) | |
| | Lt. W.R. Guyton | (2)Ju-88 dest(grd) | |
| | | Do-217 dest(grd) | |
| | Lt. R.E. Irion | (2)Ju-188 dest(grd) | |
| | | Do-217 dest(grd) | |
| | | Me-110 dam(grd) | |
| | LtCol. J.L. Thury | (2)u/i a/c dest(grd) | Claims are all |
| | | Ju-88 dest(grd) | N/Neuruppin |
| | | He-111 dam(grd) | |
| | | u/i a/c dam(grd) | |
| | Lt. H.L. Caywood | (3)Ju-88 dest(grd) | |
| | | (2)Ju-88 dam(grd) | |
| | Lt. W.R. MacClarence | (3)Ju-88 dest(grd) | |
| | Lt. T.W. Marvel | (3)Me-410 dest(grd) | |
| | | Me-410 dam(grd) | |
| | Capt. O.P. Farmer | (2)Ju-88 dest(grd) | |
| | Lt. V.D. Carr | Do-217 dest(grd) | |
| | | Ju-88 dest(grd) | |
| | | (2)Me-410 dam(grd) | |

| | | | |
|---|---|---|---|
| | F/O J.J. Rice | (2)Do-217 dest(grd) | |
| | | Do-217 dam(grd) | |
| | Lt. W.R. Phillippi | (2)Ju-88 dest(grd) | |
| | Capt. J.R. Starnes | Do-217 dest(grd) | |
| | | (3)Do-217 dam(grd) | |
| | Lt. J.C. Withers | Ju-88 dest(grd) | |
| | | (2)Ju-88 dam(grd) | |
| | F/O E.E. Hupp | Do-217 dest(grd) | |
| | | Do-217 dam(grd) | |

**April 16, 1945**

| | | | |
|---|---|---|---|
| HdQts: | Capt. R.H. Ammon | (4)Me-109 dest(grd) | NE Prague |
| | | (3)Ju-88 dest(grd) | NE Prague |
| | | FW-190 dest(grd) | NE Prague |
| | | He-111 dest(grd) | NE Prague |
| | LtCol. W.C. Clark | (3)FW-190 dest(grd) | Klatovy |
| | | (2)Me-109 dest(grd) | Klatovy |
| | | Ju-52 dest(grd) | Klatovy |
| | | FW-190 dam(grd) | Klatovy |
| | | Me-109 dam(grd) | Klatovy |
| | Maj. V.B. Hathorn | (2)FW-190 dest(grd) | Klatovy |
| | | Me-109 dest(grd) | Klatovy |
| 503rd: | Lt. S.J. Chetneky | (3)Me-109 dest(grd) | NE Prague |
| | | (2)Ju-88 dest(grd) | NE Prague |
| | | He-111 dest(grd) | NE Prague |
| | | (2)Ju-88 dam(grd) | NE Prague |
| | | Me-109 dam(grd) | NE Prague |
| | Lt. J.R. Byers | (3)Ju-88 dest(grd) | NE Prague |
| | | Me-109 dest(grd) | NE Prague |
| | | FW-190 dest(grd) | NE Prague |
| | Lt. C.I. Ferrell | (4)Ju-88 dest(grd) | NE Prague |
| | | (2)FW-190 dam(grd) | NE Prague |
| | Lt. E.E. Haidle | (2)FW-190 dest(grd) | Remaining 503rd |
| | | FW-190 dam(grd) | claims are at |
| | | Me-109 dam(grd) | Kralupy |
| | Lt. J.W. Gokey | Do-217 dest(grd) | |
| | | (3)u/i a/c damgrd) | |
| | Lt. R.S. Hill | u/i a/c dest(grd) | |
| | | u/i a/c dam(grd) | |
| | Lt. W.H. Boyd | Me-109 dam(grd) | |
| | Lt. R.J. Frisch | Me-109 dam(grd) | |
| | Lt. W.R. Preddy | u/i a/c dam(grd) | |
| 504th: | Lt. R.V.E. Blizzard | (4)Me-109 dest(grd) | All 504th claims |
| | Lt. W.M. Hudson | (3)FW-190 dest(grd) | are at Klatovy |
| | | Me-109 dest(grd) | |
| | Capt. K.B. Everson | (3)FW-190 dest(grd) | |
| | Lt. G.H. Chenez | (3)Me-109 dest(grd) | |
| | Lt. F.A. Clifton | (2)Me-109 dest(grd) | |
| | | FW-190 dest(grd) | |
| | Lt. R.T. Aldrich | (2)Me-109 dest(grd) | |
| | | (2)Me-109 dam(grd) | |
| | Lt. L.M. Carter | (2)Me-109 dest(grd) | |
| | | (2)Me-109 dam(grd) | |
| | Lt. D.F. Krueger | FW-190 dest(grd) | |
| | | Me-109 dest(grd) | |
| | | FW-190 dam(grd) | |
| | Lt. C. Hermanson | (2)Me-109 dest(grd) | |
| | Lt. R.H. Cresswell | Me-109 dest(grd) | |
| | | u/i a/c dest(grd) | |
| | | FW-190 dam(grd) | |
| | | u/i a/c dam(grd) | |
| | F/O R.W. Smith | Me-109 dest(grd) | |
| | | FW-190 dest(grd) | |
| | Maj. W.H. Julian | u/i a/c dest(grd) | |
| | | Me-109 dam(grd) | |
| | | FW-190 dam(grd) | |
| | Lt. H.F. Hunt | FW-190 dest(grd) | |
| | | FW-190 dam(grd) | |
| | Lt. L.W. Allers | Me-109 dest(grd) | |
| | | (2)Me-109 dam(grd) | |
| | Lt. V.N. Barto | Me-109 dest(grd) | |
| | Lt. L.A. Kunz | (2)FW-190 dam(grd) | |
| 505th: | Capt. H.R. Corey | (4)u/i a/c dest(grd) | All claims are |
| | Lt. H.L. Caywood | (3)Me-109 dest(grd) | NE Prague |
| | | u/i a/c dest(grd) | |
| | | (2)Ju-88 dam(grd) | |
| | | Me-109 dam(grd) | |
| | Lt. O.K. Biggs | Me-109 dest(grd) | |
| | | Ju-88 dest(grd) | |
| | | u/i a/c dest(grd) | |
| | Lt. J.C. Woolery | (2)u/i a/c dest(grd) | |
| | | FW-190 dest(grd) | |
| | F/O L.A. Steiger | (3)FW-190 dest(grd) | |
| | F/O J.J. Rice | (2)Me-109 dest(grd) | |
| | | Ju-88 dest(grd) | |
| | | Me-109 dam(grd) | |
| | | Ju-88 dam(grd) | |
| | LtCol. J.L. Thury | Me-262 dest(grd) | |
| | | Me-109 dest(grd) | |
| | Capt. O.P. Farmer | Me-109 dest(grd) | |
| | | u/i a/c dest(grd) | |
| | Lt. W.R. Guyton | Me-109 dest(grd) | |
| | | Ju-88 dest(grd) | |
| | Lt. W.R. MacClarence | (2)u/i a/c dest(grd) | |
| | Lt. T.W. Marvel | Me-109 dest(grd) | |
| | | Ju-88 dest(grd) | |
| | Lt. H.W. Burch | Ju-52 dest(grd) | |
| | | Ju-88 dest(grd) | |
| | Capt. P.M. Loveless | FW-190 dest(grd) | |
| | | Ju-87 dam(grd) | |
| | Lt. V.D. Carr | Do-217 dest(grd) | |
| | Lt. J. Pesanka | u/i a/c dest(grd) | |
| | Lt. F.W. Smith | FW-190 dest(grd) | |
| | | u/i a/c dam(grd) | |

**April 17, 1945**

| | | | |
|---|---|---|---|
| 503rd: | Lt. J.C. Campbell | Me-262 dest(air) | Pokycany |
| | Lt. R.J. Frisch | Me-262 dest(grd) | Klatovy |
| | | Ju-88 dest(grd) | Klatovy |
| | Lt. C.H. French | Me-109 dest(grd) | Kleesdorf |
| | Lt. J.R. Potthoff | Ju-88 dam(grd) | Klatovy |
| 504th: | Capt. K.B. Everson | (2)Me-109 dest(grd) | All 504th claims |
| | | (2)Fi-156 dest(grd) | are at Klatovy- |
| | | (2)Ju-88 dest(grd) | Anberg |
| | | Me-210 dest(grd) | |
| | Lt. L.M. Orcutt | (6)Me-109 dest(grd) | |
| | | (2)Ju-88 dest(grd) | |
| | Lt. F.A. Clifton | Me-109 dest(grd) | |
| | | Fi-156 dest(grd) | |
| | | Ju-88 dest(grd) | |
| | Lt. H.F. Hunt | Me-109 dest(grd) | |
| | | FW-190 dest(grd) | |
| | | Fi-156 dest(grd) | |
| | | Ju-88 dest(grd) | |
| | Lt. L.J. Barrett | Ju-52 dest(grd) | Mauching |
| 505th: | LtCol. J.L. Thury | (2)Me-109 dest(grd) | All 505th claims |
| | | (2)FW-190 dest(grd) | are SE Pocking |
| | | Ju-88 dest(grd) | |
| | Capt. B.J. Bline | (2)Me-109 dest(grd) | |
| | | (2)Ju-88 dest(grd) | |
| | Capt. P.M. Loveless | (3)Do-217 dest(grd) | |
| | | Me-109 dest(grd) | |
| | | Do-217 dam(grd) | |
| | | Ju-88 dam(grd) | |
| | Capt. H.R. Corey | (2)Ju-188 dest(grd) | |
| | | Me-109 dest(grd) | |
| | Lt. T.W. Marvel | Me-109 dest(grd) | |
| | | He-111 dest(grd) | |
| | | u/i a/c dest(grd) | |
| | Capt. J.A. Diefenback | Do-217 dest(grd) | |
| | | u/i a/c dest(grd) | |
| | Lt. H.W. Burch | (2)Do-217 dest(grd) | |
| | Lt. W.R. MacClarence | Ju-188 dest(grd) | |
| | | He-111 dest(grd) | |
| | Lt. J.T. Murphy | Me-109 dest(grd) | |
| | | He-111 dest(grd) | |
| | | (2)Me-109 dam(grd) | |
| | | Ju-88 dam(grd) | |
| | Lt. J. Pesanka | Me-109 dest(grd) | |
| | | He-111 dest(grd) | |
| | Lt. F.W. Smith | Me-109 dest(grd) | |
| | | Ju-88 dest(grd) | |
| | Lt. J.C. Woolery | Me-109 dest(grd) | |
| | | Ju-88 dest(grd) | |
| | | Me-109 dam(grd) | |
| | Lt. O.K. Biggs | Ju-88 dest(grd) | |
| | Lt. V.D. Carr | Ju-88 dest(grd) | |
| | | Me-109 dam(grd) | |
| | Lt. R.E. Irion | Me-110 dest(grd) | |
| | Lt. R.H. Paul | Ju-88 dest(grd) | |
| | F/O E.E. Hupp | Do-217 dest(grd) | |

**April 18, 1945**

| | | | |
|---|---|---|---|
| 503rd: | LtCol. D.E. Shafer | Ar-234 dest(air) | Regensburg |
| 505th: | LtCol. J.L. Thury | Me-262 dam(air) | Tabor |

**339th Fighter Group Losses**

**April 29, 1944**
Lt. Ralph M. Degner (504th) KIAc;
P-51B 5Q-

**May 7, 1944**
Lt. Arch B. Luper (505th) KIA; Hit by flak near Gees and bailed out near Solingen.
P-51B 6N- 42-106807

**May 15, 1944**
Lt. Albert L. Wyer (503rd) POW; Lost coolant and bailed out near St. Pol.
P-51C D7- 42-103393

**May 19, 1944**
Lt. James R. Crockett (503rd) KIA; Caught in an explosion of a loco near Messdorf.
P-51B D7-Q 42-106785
Lt. Walter R. O'Sullivan (504th) POW; Hit by a Me-109 near Lubeck.
P-51C 5Q- 42-103342

**May 21, 1944**
Capt. Walter T. Carter (503rd) POW; Hit by flak near Leipzig.
P-51B D7-B 42-106863 "Mon Petite"
Lt. Robert F. Mulvey (503rd) KIA; Ran out of fuel near Willesbord.
P-51C D7- 42-103295
Lt. Arthur R. Steier (503rd) KIA; Hit by flak near Eilenberg.
P-51B D7- 42-106674
Lt. Floyd P. Heneghan (505th) KIA; Hit by flak at Riesa Airfield.
P-51B 6N- 42-106678

**May 24, 1944**
Lt. Joseph Wolfort (503rd) KIA; Hit by flak near Roxel.
P-51B D7-T 42-106755
Lt. Harold M. Everett (505th) POW (E); Hit by fighters near Grougis.
P-51B 6N- 42-106646

**May 27, 1944**
Lt. Robert L. Dickens, Jr. (503rd) KIAc; Collided with an A-20 at Little Walden.
P-51B D7-U 42-106907

**May 29, 1944**
Lt. James L. Lynch (505th) KIA; Last heard from south of the Isle of Wight saying he was low on fuel.
P-51B 6N-C 42-106626 "Butch"
Lt. Gordon F. Perry (505th) KIA; Crashed into the Channel after running out of fuel.
P-51B 6N- 42-106745

**May 30, 1944**
Lt. Paul M. Meyer (504th) KIA; Hit by a FW-190 near Eggersdorf.
P-51B 5Q-A 42-106601
Lt. Edward A. Thistlethwaite (504th) POW; Hit by a FW-190 near Kleinmuehlingen.
P-51B 5Q-T 42-106908 "Cajun"

**June 6, 1944**
Maj. Michael G.H. McPharlin (HdQts) KIA; Suffered mechanical failure near Evreux.
P-51B 6N-Z 42-106909 "Wee Ginny"
Lt. Elton J. Brownshadel (504th) KIA; Died in a crash after taking-off from Fowlmere.
P-51B 5Q-

**June 8, 1944**
Lt. Robert C. Smith (503rd) KIA; Hit by FW-190's near Fourgeres
P-51C D7- 42-103299
Lt. Philip H. Ewing (505th) MIA-E; Damaged by a bomb blast near Lisieux.
P-51B 6N- 42-106699
Lt. Joseph F. Sawicki, Jr. (505th) KIA; Hit by FW-190's near Rennes.
P-51B 6N-F 42-106653

**June 10, 1944**
Lt. Hetzel K. Boden (504th) POW; Hit by flak and bailed out over the Channel.
P-51B 5Q- 42-106700

**June 13, 1944**
Lt. Jack E. Shively (504th) KIA; Hit by flak near Saumur.
P-51B 5Q- 42-106847

**June 15, 1944**
Lt. Richard W. Montell, Jr. (504th) KIA; Hit by enemy fighters near Quillebeuf.
P-51B 5Q- 43-24772

**June 17, 1944**
Lt. Walter M. Armistead (505th) POW; Suffered mechanical failure near Chateaudun.
P-51B 6N-T 42-106720

**June 19, 1944**
Capt. Nathan T. Folwell (503rd) KIA; Crashed near Le Mans in bad weather.
P-51B D7- 42-106905
Lt. Robert B. Brown (503rd) KIA; Crashed near Le Mans in bad weather.
P-51B D7-P 42-106889
Lt. Ralph H. Dearey (503rd) KIA; Crashed near Le Mans in bad weather.
P-51B D7-R 42-106615

**June 22, 1944**
Lt. Arthur L. Lowery (503rd) KIA; Hit the ground while strafing near Denain.
P-51C D7-W 42-103346

**June 24, 1944**
Lt. Rodney C. West (503rd) KIAc; Died in a jeep accident.

**June 29, 1944**
Capt. Richard S. Whitelaw (503rd) KIA; Hit by enemy fighters near Kalsbrieth.
P-51B D7-C 42-106821

**July 4, 1944**
Lt. Carl H. Bundgaard (505th) MIA-E; Suffered mechanical failure and bailed out near Buzancais.
P-51C 6N- 42-103314

**July 11, 1944**
Lt. Peter J. McMahan (505th) KIA; Hit the ground while strafing near Busigny.
P-51C 6N- 42-103559

**July 16, 1944**
Lt. Wesley G. Fish (505th) POW; Hit by flak near Nancy and bailed out near Verdun.
P-51D 6N- 44-13413

**July 25, 1944**
Lt. John W. Cozad (503rd) KIAc;
P-51D D7-B 44-13622

**July 29, 1944**
Lt. Ray N. Attebury (504th) POW; Hit by enemy fighters near Rosslaben.
P-51B 5Q- 42-106642
Lt. Fred S. Rutan, Jr. (504th) POW; Hit by FW-190's near Naumberg and bailed out near Bad Frankenhausen.
P-51C 5Q- 42-103394 "Whistler's Wings"
Lt. Chris J. Hanseman (505th) KIA; Hit the ground while strafing northwest of Naumberg.
P-51D 6N-H 44-13556 "Eleanor IV"

**August 2, 1944**
Lt. Lewis H. Schneider (504th) KIA; Hit by flak near Lassigny.
P-51B 5Q-U 42-106641

**August 4, 1944**
Maj. Donald A. Larson (505th) KIA; Collided with Lt. Burns northwest of Ulzen.
P-51D 6N-B 44-13881
Lt. Robert F. Burns (505th) POW; Collided with Maj. Larson northwest of Ulzen.
P-51D 6N- 44-13897
Lt. Roland W. Strong (505th) POW; Suffered mechanical failure near Wilhelmshaven.
P-51B 6N- 43-24773

**August 5, 1944**
Lt. Edward C. Flaherty (503rd) KIA; Collided with a P-51 on take-off and crashed near Thriplow.
P-51B D7-

**August 6, 1944**
Lt. Victor W. Meyer (503rd) KIA; Hit by a Me-109 and bailed out north of Hamburg.
P-51D D7-J 44-13601
Lt. Franklin D. Talcott (503rd) INT; Lost coolant and landed in Sweden.
P-51D D7-L 44-13917 "You've Had It"
Lt. Arthur E. Tongue, Jr. (505th) KIA; Spun-in 5 miles east of Cambridge.
P-51B 6N- 42-106842

**August 8, 1944**
Lt. Edwin C. Ball (505th) KIA; Hit by flak near Roulers.
P-51B 6N- 42-106937

**August 13, 1944**
Lt. Myer R. Winkelman (504th) KIA; Caught in a bomb blast near St. Just.
P-51D 5Q-B 44-13521
Lt. Andrew Sirochman (505th) MIA-E; Caught in a bomb blast near St. Omer.
P-51B 6N-Q 42-106918

**August 16, 1944**
Lt. Charles M. Hunter (504th) KIA; Last seen chasing a Me-109 near Mulhausen.
P-51D 5Q-T 44-13584

**August 17, 1944**
Lt. William J. Pastor (504th) KIA; Hit by flak near Ghent.
P-51B 5Q-I 42-106649

**August 24, 1944**
Lt. Bernell V. Shaw (505th) POW; Hit by flak near Gerville.
P-51D 6N- 44-13385

**August 26, 1944**
Lt. Ely N. Van Cleave (504th) ASR; Suffered mechanical failure and bailed out northwest of Guernsey Island.
P-51 5Q-

**August 27, 1944**
Lt. John M. Carothers (503rd) KIA; Suffered mechanical failure and crashed into the North Sea.
P-51C D7-N 42-103325 "Reddy Teddy"

**August 28, 1944**
Lt. Russell W. Wilcox (505th) KIA; Bailed out off Margate.
P-51 6N-

**September 5, 1944**
Lt. Martin N. Nay (505th) MIA-E; Hit by flak near Rastadt and bellied-in near Kemplich.
P-51D 6N- 44-13828

**September 10, 1944**
Maj. John R. Reynolds (HdQts) KIA; Hit by flak near Weizenburg.
P-51D D7- 44-14069
Lt. Raymond F. Reuter (503rd) MIA-E; Suffered mechanical failure near Saarburg.
P-51B D7-G 42-106614

**September 11, 1944**
Lt. William A. Jones (505th) POW; Suffered mechanical trouble then was hit by a Me-262 near Eberach.
P-51C 6N- 42-103742 "Man O'War"
Lt. Ted B. Staggers (505th) POW; Hit by flak southeast of Munich.
P-51D 6N-U 44-13616 "Baggy Pants"

**September 13, 1944**
Lt. William R. Moore (505th) POW; Hit by flak near Katzenburg.
P-51C 6N-F 42-103756
Lt. William R. Slovak (505th) KIA; Hit by flak near Saverlach.
P-51D 6N- 44-13847

**September 23, 1944**
Lt. Alfred O. Manke (503rd) POW; Hit by a FW-190 near Wesel.
P-51D D7- 44-14247
Capt. Raymond M. Mitchell, Jr. (505th) POW; Hit by flak near Jagen.
P-51D 6N- 44-14542
Lt. James B. Muller (505th) POW; Hit by a FW-190 near Haltern.
P-51D 6N-A 44-13624 "Sniffles"

**September 26, 1944**
Lt. Paul D. Fickel (503rd) POW; Lost coolant and bailed out near Altgoedens.
P-51D D7-Z 44-13980 "Shy Ann"

**October 5, 1944**
Lt. Stephen C. Ananian (505th) ASR; Hit by flak near the Zuider Zee and bailed out off Aldeburgh.
P-51B 6N-M 42-106946 "Bison Bull"

**October 18, 1944**
Lt. Raymond D. Mayer (503rd) KIA; Hit wires and crashed near Rotenkirchen.
P-51D D7-X 44-13955
Lt. William D. Stockton (503rd) KIA; Crashed near Ghent.
P-51D D7-

**November 18, 1944**
Lt. Vincent J. Spaziano (503rd) KIA; Hit by Allied flak and crashed near Ghent.
P-51D D7- 44-14829
Lt. Laird D. Travis (505th) KIA; Hit by flak near Kaiserlautern.
P-51D 6N- 44-15368 "Nornie"
Lt. Allen D. Young (505th) POW; Hit by flak near Trier.
P-51D 6N- 44-14729 "Betty Lou"
Lt. Alan F. Crump (503rd) KIAc; Crashed near Fowlmere.
P-51D D7-A 44-14004

**November 21, 1944**
Capt. Charles W. Dowell (505th) KIA; Hit by flak near Meckenheim.
P-51D 6N- 44-14092
Lt. Leland M. Stoudt (505th) KIA; Hit by flak near Handorf.
P-51D 6N- 44-14115
Lt. Boyd O. Jackson (505th) KIA; Hit by flak near Handorf.
P-51D 6N- 44-15306

**November 26, 1944**
Lt. Ely N. Van Cleave (504th) KIA; Hit by a FW-190 near Hassell.
P-51D 5Q-S 44-13938
Lt. Bert Stiles (505th) KIA; Followed a FW-190 into the ground south of Hanover.
P-51D 6N-X 44-14113 "Tarheel"

**November 27, 1944**
Capt. Edward H. Beavers, Jr. (503rd) KIA; Hit by flak at an airfield near Cologne.
P-51D D7-Z 44-14525 "Joanie"
Lt. Felix J. Girone (503rd) KIA; Hit by enemy fighters near Rengershausen.
P-51D D7-A 44-14587 "PeeWee Peckerwood"

**December 4, 1944**
Lt. Richard C. Cain (505th) POW; Suffered mechanical failure near Trier.
P-51D 6N- 44-14072

**December 5, 1944**
LtCol. Harvey E. Henderson (503rd) POW; Hit by a FW-190 near Rechlin.
P-51D D7- 44-15520
Lt. James A. Baker (505th) KIA; Suffered mechanical failure near Giessen.
P-51D 6N- 44-13370

**December 12, 1944**
Lt. Harry G. Loskill (504th) POW; Suffered mechanical failure near Kuels.
P-51D 5Q-F 44-13378 "Ollie"

**December 29, 1944**
Lt. Charles M. Meade (504th) KIA; Suffered mechanical failure near Coblenz.
P-51D 5Q- 44-14287 "Pin-Up Girl"

**December 31, 1944**
Capt. Anthony G. Hawkins (503rd) KIA; Last seen chasing a Me-262 near Soltau.
P-51D D7-Q 44-14626
Lt. James A. Mankie (503rd) POW; Hit by a Me-262 near Westertimke.
P-51D D7-Q 44-15700 "Sweet Jeanne"

**January 14, 1945**
Lt. Lawrence J. Powell, Jr. (505th) POW; Hit wires while strafing and bailed out near Ibbenburen.
P-51D 6N- 44-14731 "St. Louis Blues"

**January 17, 1945**
Capt. Richard B. Olander (505th) KIA; Hit by flak near Gladbeck.
P-51D 6N-C 44-15616 "Pauline"
Lt. Walden E. Howard (505th) KIA; Hit by flak and crashed near Stadthagen.
P-51B 6N-A 42-106676 "Princess Marie"

**February 6, 1945**
Capt. Robert W. Bloxham (505th) KIA; Crashed into the Channel in bad weather.
P-51D 6N- 44-13379 "Miss Idaho
Lt. Gerald W. Palmer (505th) KIA; Crashed on the Isle of Wight in bad weather.
P-51D 6N-
Lt. Kessler O. Thomas (505th) KIA; Crashed at Nuthampstead in bad weather.
P-51D 6N-

**February 12, 1945**
Lt. Johnnie M. Allman (505th) KIAc; Crashed 6 miles west of Duxford.
P-51D 6N-

**February 20, 1945**
Lt. William M. Beecher (505th) KIA; Suffered vertigo near Valenciennes.
P-51B 6N- 42-106936

**February 22, 1945**
Capt. Ray F. Herrmann (504th) KIA; Hit by flak near Coburg.
P-51K 5Q- 44-11745 "Happy III"
Capt. Robert T. Wood (504th) KIA; Hit by flak near Coburg.
P-51D 5Q-J 44-14153

**March 2, 1945**
Lt. Esteban A. Terrants (503rd) KIA; Hit by enemy fighters near Schlanau.
P-51C D7-H 43-25050
Lt. Bertis A. Connor, Jr. (505th) POW; Hit by flak near Mockern.
P-51K 6N-S 44-11363 "Therese"
Lt. Harry F. Howard (505th) POW; Hit trees while strafing near Mockern.
P-51D 6N-E 44-14622

**March 3, 1945**
Lt. Otis A. Kurth (504th) KIA; Crashed in England upon return.
P-51D 5Q-
Lt. George W. Jones, Jr. (505th) KIA; Suffered mechanical failure near Mockern and bailed out too low.
P-51D 6N- 44-11204
Lt. Harry D. Ziegler (505th) POW; Hit by flak near Mockern and bellied-in near Magdeburg.
P-51D 6N- 44-14023 "Chute! You're Faded"

**March 12, 1945**
Lt. Richard C. O'Brien (505th) MIA-E; Suffered mechanical failure and bailed out near Laaland.
P-51D 6N- 44-14086 "Angel of Mercy"

**March 20, 1945**
Lt. Jerome J. Ballard (504th) POW; Hit by flak near Kaltenkirchen.
P-51D 5Q-Q 44-14647 "Podunk"
Lt. Kenneth V. Berguson (504th) KIAc; Crashed near Grimsby.
P-51D 5Q-

**March 30, 1945**
Lt. Evergard L. Wager (505th) KIA; Hit by a Me-262 northwest of Hamburg.
P-51D 6N-H 44-72065 "Dibbo"

**March 31, 1945**
F/O Joseph R. Coker (505th) POW; Suffered mechanical trouble near Plauen.
P-51D 6N- 44-15558

**April 7, 1945**
Lt. David A. MacKenzie (503rd) KIA; Hit by fire from a B-17 near Ahrensburg.
P-51K D7-K 44-11325

**April 15, 1945**
Lt. Roland L. Gousie (505th) POW; Hit by flak south of Stuttgart and bailed out west of Blauberen.
P-51D 6N-C 44-14656 "Dottie"

**April 17, 1945**
Capt. Ray F. Reuter (503rd) KIA; Last seen chasing enemy fighters near Prague.
P-51D D7-J 44-72485
Lt. William R. Preddy (503rd) KIA; Last seen chasing enemy fighters near Prague.
P-51K D7-A 44-11623 "Rusty"

**June 15, 1945**
Lt. George W. Porter (503rd) KIAc;
P-51D D7-T 44-15509

**June 30, 1945**
Lt. Thomas N. Jessup (503rd) KIAc;
P-51D D7-L 44-15168

**July 17, 1945**
Capt. Kenneth C. Gilbert (505th) KIAc;
P-51B 6N-Q 42-106657

**Headquarters**

Ammon, Robert H., Capt.; March 1945-September 1945; ex-503rd and 504th Ftr Sqns
Bryan, William E., Jr., Maj.; March 1945-September 1945; ex-503rd Ftr Sqn
Caler, Rollin C., Lt.; States-June 1944
Clark, William C., LtCol.; March 1945-September 1945; ex-504th Ftr Sqn
  P-51D 5Q-C 44-64148 "Happy IV"
Dowell, Charles W., Capt.; October 1944-November 21, 1944(KIA)
Goldenburg, Carl T., LtCol.; December 1944-April 1945
  P-51D "Honey Child"
Hathorn, Vernon B., Jr., Maj.; States-July 1945; ex-54th Ftr Grp Aleutians
Henry, John B., Jr., Col.; August 1943-April 1945
  94 missions
  P-51B 6N-A 42-106676 "San Antone Rose"
  P-51D 6N-A 44-72255 "San Antone Rose"
Long, Robert D., LtCol.; December 1944-September 1945
McPharlin, Michael G.H., Maj.; States-June 6, 1944(KIA); ex-71 Sqn, RAF
  P-51B 6N-Z 42-106909 "Wee Ginny"
Propst, John R., LtCol.; June 1944-April 1945
Reynolds, John R., Maj.; July 1944-September 10, 1944(KIA)
Scruggs, Harold W., LtCol.; June 1944-December 1944; ex-503rd Ftr Sqn
Wight, Carroll H., Maj.; States-August 1944

**503rd Fighter Squadron**

Aitken, John, Maj.; May 1944-October 1944; ex-504th Ftr Sqn; 270 hours
  P-51B D7-A
  P-51D D7-A 44-14004
Allen, Bernice A., Lt.; July 1944-January 1945
Ammon, Robert H., Lt.; May 1944-October 1944; later with 504th Ftr Sqn and HdQts
  P-51D D7- "Annie Mae"
Beavers, Edward H., Capt.; July 1944-November 27, 1944(KIA)
  43 missions
  P-51D D7-Z 44-13980 "Shy Ann"
  P-51D D7-Z 44-14525
Behrend, William W., Capt.; June 1944-March 1945; former bomber pilot
Boychuck, Alec, Capt.; August 1944-March 1945
Boyd, William H., Lt.; February 1945-August 1945
  29 missions
Brown, Robert B., Lt.; States-June 19, 1944(KIA)
Bryan, William E., Jr., Maj.; States-March 1945; to HdQts
  106 missions
  P-51B D7-J 42-106798
  P-51D D7-J 44-13601
  P-51D D7-J 44-15074 "Big Noise"
Bush, Jerry P., Lt.; States-September 1944
  P-51B D7-Z 42-106934
  P-51D D7-Z 44-13980
Butler, Frederick, Jr., Capt.; October 1944-June 1945
Byers, John R., Lt.; March 1945-July 1945
  20 missions
Campbell, John C., Lt.; February 1945-July 1945
  31 missions
Carothers, John M., Lt.; August 1944-August 27, 1944(KIA)
Carter, Walter T., Capt.; States-May 21, 1944(POW)
  P-51B D7-B 42-106863 "Mon Petite"
Chetneky, Steve J., Lt.; December 1944-June 1945; former bomber pilot
  26 missions
  P-51D D7- "Hard Luck, Jr."
Clark, Jack W., Lt.; July 1944-October 1944; to 353rd Ftr Grp
Cloud, Carl E., Capt.; States-October 1944
Coe, Charles S., Lt.; July 1944-January 1945
  P-51D D7- "Night-Mare"
Cozad, John W., Lt.; June 1944-July 25, 1944(KIAc)
Crockett, James R., Lt.; States-May 19, 1944(KIA)
Crump, Alan F., Lt.; September 1944-November 18, 1944(KIAc)
Dearey, Ralph H., Lt.; May 1944-June 19, 1944(POW)
Dickens, Robert L., Jr., Lt.; May 1944-May 27, 1944(KIAc)
Edens, Malcolm B., Capt.; November 1944-April 1945
Erickson, Earl E., Lt.; May 1944-October 1944
  P-51B D7-Y 42-106614
  P-51D D7-S 44-14390 "Janie Girl"
Farrell, Joseph G., Capt.; September 1944-June 1945
Ferrell, Clarence I., Lt.; October 1944-July 1945
Fickel, Paul D., Lt.; July 1944-September 26, 1944(POW)
Fiorito, Leonard J., Capt.; January 1944-October 1944
  P-51C D7-M 42-103600 "Sally"
  P-51D D7-M 44-14065 "Sally II"
Flaherty, Edward C., Lt.; July 1944-August 5, 1944(KIA)
Folwell, Nathan T., Capt.; States-June 19, 1944(KIA)
France, James L., F/O; April 1945-September 1945
  0 missions
Francis, Luther B., Lt.; October 1944-July 1945
Fratello, Thomas C., F/O; April 1945-September 1945
  0 missions
French, Bernard J., Lt.; September 1944-October 1944; to 353rd Ftr Grp
French, Carl H., Lt.; October 1944-April 1945
French, Lloyd J., Capt.; September 1944-April 1945
  P-51K D7-A 44-11623 "Rusty"
Frisch, Robert J., Lt.; October 1944-April 1945
  53 missions
  P-51D D7-J 44-14118 "Worry Bird"
  P-51D D7-J 44-73287 "Worry Bird"
Ganer, Seymour, Lt.; April 1945-July 1945
  0 missions
Gaugher, Henry W., Lt.; March 1945-July 1945
  3 missions
Gerard, Francis R., Capt.; States-April 1945
  80 missions, 420 hours
  P-51B D7-U 42-106907
  P-51B D7-U 42-106798
  P-51D D7-U 44-13808
  P-51D D7-U 44-15003
Girone, Felix J., Lt.; September 1944-November 27, 1944(KIA)
Gokey, John W., Capt.; September 1944-July 1945
  P-51D D7-V 44-15560
Gordon, William R., Lt.; March 1945-July 1945
  12 missions
Grad, Carl E., F/O; April 1945-September 1945
  0 missions
Graham, Ethelbert H., Jr., Lt.; States-September 1944
  P-51B D7-O 43-24800 "Miss Max"
Grothendieck, Carl W., F/O; April 1945-September 1945
  0 missions
Haidle, Elmer E., Lt.; October 1944-July 1945
Harte, Allan S., Jr., Capt.; States-October 1944
  P-51B D7-X
  P-51D D7-X 44-13955
Hauff, John J., Lt.; States-October 1944
Hawkins, Anthony G., Capt.; June 1944-December 31, 1944(KIA)
Henderson, Harvey E., LtCol.; September 1944-December 5, 1944(POW)
Hill, Ralph S., Jr., Lt.; October 1944-April 1945
Hull, James F., Lt.; March 1945-July 1945
  0 missions
Hutton, John E., Jr., Lt.; March 1945-July 1945
  1 mission
Johnson, Allen D., Lt.; March 1945-July 1945
  1 mission
Johnson, Donald W., Capt.; July 1945-January 1945
Johnson, Raymond G., Lt.; October 1944-July 1945
Johnson, William G., Lt.; March 1945-July 1945
  1 mission
Johnstone, George J., Lt.; March 1945-July 1945
  0 missions
Keim, Paul T., Lt.; June 1944-October 1944
Kelly, George P., III, Lt.; States-October 1944
Kernesky, George, Lt.; April 1945-September 1945
  0 missions
King, John B., Lt.; March 1945-July 1945
  0 missions
Knott, Clarence W., Capt.; States-October 1944
  P-51D D7-F 44-13629 "Dee"
Krauss, Richard E., Lt.; November 1944-July 1945
Linger, Claude D., Lt.; September 1944-October 1944; to 353rd Ftr Grp
Lowery, Arthur L., Lt.; States-June 22, 1944(KIA)
MacKenzie, Davie A., Lt.; October 1944-April 7, 1945(KIA)
Manke, Alfred O., Lt.; July 1944-September 23, 1944(POW)
Mankie, James A., Lt.; October 1944-December 31, 1944(POW)
  P-51D D7-Q 44-15700 "Sweet Jeanne"
Marsh, Lester C., Lt.; June 1944-December 1944
  51 missions
  P-51D D7-P 44-14947
Mayer, Raymond D., Lt.; August 1944-October 18, 1944(KIA)
McClish, Donald E., Capt.; June 1944-January 1945
McElwee, Francis E., Lt.; February 1945-July 1945
  31 missions
Meyer, Victor W., Lt.; June 1944-August 5, 1944(KIA)
Moreland, Kenneth E., Lt.; February 1945-August 1945
  31 missions
Mulvey, Robert F., Lt.; States-May 21, 1944(KIA)
Ostrow, Nathan, Capt.; June 1944-February 1945
Perry, William W., Capt.; October 1944-March 1945
Petitt, Philip E., Capt.; September 1944-April 1945
  P-51K D7-K 44-11325 "Princess Pat"
Porter, George W., Lt.; December 1944-June 15, 1945(KIAc) former bomber pilot
Potthoff, John P., Lt.; March 1945-EOW
  22 missions
Poutre, Rex L., Capt.; October 1944-April 1945
  P-51D D7-L 44-15482
Preddy, William R., Lt.; February 1945-April 17, 1945(KIA)
  26 missions
Price, Jack B., Lt.; States-October 1944
Rawls, Dennis B., Lt.; December 1944-June 1945; former bomber pilot
Reuter, Ray F., Capt.; July 1944-September 10, 1944(MIA-E); October 1944-April 17, 1945(KIA)
  P-51D D7-S 44-15430
Reynolds, Gardner H., Capt.; States-October 1944
Robinson, James G., Capt.; August 1944-February 1945
Sams, Thomas G., Capt.; November 1944-July 1945
Scruggs, Harold W., LtCol.; August 1943-June 1944; to HdQts
Shafer, Dale E., LtCol.; September 1944-September 1945; ex-31st Ftr Grp, MTO
  52 missions
  P-51D D7-C 44-14671
  P-51D D7-C 44-72147

Shake, Charles E., Lt.; May 1944-June 1944; to ???
Smith, Linwood P., Lt.; March 1945-July 1945
    6 missions
Smith, Robert C., Lt.; May 1944-June 8, 1944(KIA); ex-357th Ftr Grp
Spaziano, Vincent J., Lt.; September 1944-November 18, 1944(KIA)
Steier, Arthur H., Lt.; January 1944-May 21, 1944(KIA)
Stephenson, Enoch B., Jr., Maj.; States-October 1944
    P-51D D7-A 44-13377
Stillwell, Frank M., Capt.; June 1944-February 1945
    P-51D D7-D 44-15314 "The Bengal Lancer"
Stockton, William D., Lt.; July 1944-October 18, 1944(KIA)
Talcott, Franklin D., Lt.; May 1944-August 5, 1944(INT)
Terrats, Esteban A., Lt.; February 1945-March 2, 1945(MIA)
    5 missions
Titus, Robert D., Lt.; June 1944-September 1944
Warren, Donald W., Lt.; July 1944-October 1944; to 353rd Ftr Grp
Wells, Richard G., F/O; April 1945-September 1945
    0 missions
West, Rodney C., Lt.; States-June 24, 1944(KIAc)
Whitelaw, Richard S., Capt.; States-June 29, 1944(KIA)
    P-51B D7-C 42-106821
Wilson, John P., Capt.; September 1944-July 1945
Wolfort, Joseph, Lt.; January 1944-May 24, 1944(KIA)
    P-51B D7-T 42-106755
Wright, Lyle M., Lt.; States-December 1944
    P-51C D7-H 42-103567
    P-51B D7-H 42-106658
Wyatt, Valdee, Capt.; States-October 1944
    P-51B D7-P 42-106889
    P-51D D7-P 44-13324
Wyer, Albert L., Lt.; States-May 15, 1944(POW)

**504th Fighter Squadron**
Aitken, John, Maj.; States-May 1944; to 503rd Ftr Sqn; ex-52nd Ftr Grp, MTO
Aldrich, Richard T., Lt.; October 1944-September 1945
    P-51K 5Q-E 44-11640 "Hell's Fable"
Allers, Lorne W., Lt.; October 1944-July 1945
Ammon, Robert H., Capt.; January 1945-March 1945; to HdQts; ex-503rd Ftr Sqn
Arnold, Merlin A., Lt.; September 1944-October 1944; to 353rd Ftr Grp
Atteberry, Raymond N., Lt.; May 1944-July 29, 1944(POW)
    P-51B 5Q-V 42-106773 "Dinny"
Ball, Melville R., Capt.; States-January 1945
Ballard, Jerome J., Lt.; July 1944-March 20, 1945(POW)
Barrett, Lawrence J., Lt.; October 1944-April 1945
    P-51D 5Q-M 44-72282 "Watonga State Bank, Safe and Dependable"
Barto, Vernon N., Lt.; October 1944-April 1945
    P-51D 5Q-D "Lou'n Sue"
Bates, Arthur W., Jr., Lt.; July 1944-March 1945
Beadle, Ermy L., Lt.; August 1944-October 7, 1944(Inj.)
Bennett, Carroll W., Capt.; December 1944-October 1945
Berguson, Kenneth V., Lt.; October 1944-March 20, 1945(KIAc)
Blizzard, Robert V.E., Lt.; October 1944-July 1945
    P-51B 5Q-O 42-106886 "Punkie"
    P-51D 5Q-O 44-15499 "Punkie II"
Borden, Hetzel K., Lt.; May 1944-June 10, 1944(POW)
Brownshadel, Elton J., Lt.; January 1944-June 6, 1944(KIA)
Caldwell, Merle F., Lt.; States-October 1944
    P-51C 5Q-J 42-103737 "The Yankee Kid"
Carter, Lyle M., Lt.; October 1944-April 1945
    P-51D 5Q-B "Hillbilly"
Cernicky, Melvin L., Lt.; June 1944-November 1944
Chenez, Gordon H., Lt.; October 1944-July 1945
Clark, William C., LtCol.; January 1945-April 1945; to HdQts
    P-51D 5Q-C 44-64148 "Happy IV"
Clifton, Frank A., Lt.; March 1945-July 1945
Cohen, Gilbert G., Lt.; October 1944-July 1945
    P-51D 5Q- "Hebe's Heap"
Cole, Douglas P., Lt.; March 1945-July 1945
    P-51D 5Q- "Mary"
Corbin, Luther L., Lt.; May 1944-November 1944
    P-51B 5Q-Q 42-106672 "Problem"
Craigo, Cecil E., Jr., Capt.; States-December 1944
    P-51B 5Q-E 42-106690
Creswell, Raymond H., Lt.; October 1944-July 1945
Croker, Robert C., Lt.; October 1944-July 1945
    P-51D 5Q-G 44-72354 "Madame Queen"
Degner, Ralph M., Lt.; States-April 29, 1944(KIAc)
Eisenhart, Lee D., Capt.; States-September 1944
    P-51B 5Q-G 42-106933 "Bonny Bea"
Everson, Kirke B., Capt.; February 1945-July 1945
    P-51D 5Q-E 44-14372 "Mary Beth"
Fulton, Joseph O., Jr., Lt.; September 1944-October 1944; to 353rd Ftr Grp
Garland, Edgar L., F/O; April 1945-September 1945
Gooch, William D., F/O; April 1945-September 1945
Gravette, Edgar B., LtCol.; States-December 1944; ex-54th Ftr Grp, Aleutians
    P-51B 5Q-F "Ollie"
    P-51D 5Q-F 44-13378 "Ollie"
Green, Claude W., F/O; April 1945-September 1945
Greer, Nile C., Capt.; August 1944-April 1945
Griffith, Walter B., Lt.; May 1944-October 1944
    P-51B 5Q- "Tamsin Lee"
Guernsey, Frank D., Jr., Maj.; October 1944-July 1945; ex-54th Ftr Grp, Aleutians and 4th Ftr Grp
Harry, G.P., Lt.; May 1944-July 28, 1944(Inj.)
Haslam, Fred C., Lt.; June 1944-April 1945
Havighurst, Robert C., Lt.; January 1945-July 1945
Hendricks, Charles J., Lt.; February 1945-EOW
Hermansen, Cephas, Lt.; January 1945-October 1945
    P-51D 5Q- "Diane"
Herrmann, Ray F., Capt.; July 1944-February 22, 1945(KIA)
Hoffman, William R., Lt.; May 1944-December 1944
Hudson, Will M., Lt.; January 1945-October 1945
    P-51K 5Q-T 44-11684 "White Lightnin'"
Hunerwadel, Hugh P., Lt.; March 1945-July 1945
Hunt, Harlan F., Lt.; January 1945-October 1945
Hunter, Charles M., Lt.; June 1944-August 16, 1944(KIA)
Hurley, William T., Capt.; June 1944-April 1945
    P-51D 5Q-W "Dopey Lou"
Julian, William H., LtCol.; March 1945-September 1945; ex-78th Ftr Grp
Kerrigan, John S., Lt.; April 1945-September 1945
King, James C., Lt.; March 1945-July 1945
Klein, Fred, Jr., Lt.; April 1945-September 1945
Knapp, Frank J., Lt.; April 1945-September 1945
Knipper, Robert R., Lt.; April 1945-September 1945
Krueger, Donald F., Lt.; November 1944-July 1945
    P-51D 5Q-F 44-72495
Kuhlman, Robert M., Capt.; September 1944-July 1945
    P-51D 5Q-W 44-15021 "Anabel"
Kunz, Leonard A., Lt.; November 1944-July 1945
Kurth, Otis A., Lt.; November 1944-March 3, 1945(KIA)
Langohr, Billy E., Lt.; October 1944-July 1945
Larson, Duane S., Lt.; States-November 1944
    P-51B 5Q-O 42-106886 "Swede"
Loskill, Harry G., Lt.; October 1944-December 12, 1944(POW)
Mason, Clair M., Capt.; October 1944-July 1945
    P-51D 5Q-Z 44-72188 "Pedunk II"
McClure, James M., Capt.; January 1944-November 1944
    P-51B 5Q-P 43-24804 "Miss Priss"
Mead, Charles M., Lt.; June 1944-December 29, 1944(KIA)
Montell, Richard W., Lt.; June 1944-June 15, 1944(KIA)
Myer, Paul M., Lt.; States-May 30, 1944(KIA)
Orcutt, Leon M., Jr., Lt.; October 1944-July 1945
    P-51D 5Q-S 44-14672 "Lil Injun"
O'Sullivan, Walter R., Lt.; January 1944-May 19, 1944(POW)
Pastor, William J., Lt.; July 1944-August 17, 1944(KIA)
Penny, Donald E., Lt.; June 1944-November 1944
Penrose, Richard C., Capt.; July 1944-March 1945
    71 missions, 320 hours
    P-51D 5Q-E 44-14372 "Beaver Chant"
Peter, Lewis S., Jr., Maj.; August 1943-March 1945; ex-54th Ftr Grp, Aleutians
    P-51D 5Q-B 44-13330 "Picilo Pete"
Rosen, George J., Lt.; September 1944-October 1944; to 353rd Ftr Grp
Routt, Bill C., Maj.; States-November 1944; ex-54th Ftr Grp, Aleutians
    P-51B 5Q-A 42-106838 "Fabasca IV"
    P-51D 5Q-A 44-14060 "Fabasca V"
Rutan, Fred S., Jr., Lt.; January 1944-July 29, 1944(POW)
    P-51C 5Q- 42-103394 "Whistler's Wings"
Sainlar, Jerome J., Lt.; November 1944-July 1945
Saleem, Albert, Lt.; States-June 1944
Sargent, Robert F., Capt.; March 1945-May 1945
Schneider, Lewis H., Lt.; July 1944-August 2, 1944(KIA)
Shively, Jack E., Lt.; June 1944-June 13, 1944(KIA)
    1 mission
Showker, Fred S., Capt.; States-October 1944
Smith, Lee W., Lt.; March 1945-July 1945
Smith, Roland W., Lt.; March 1945-July 1945
Stevens, Bradford V., Capt.; States-July 1945
    P-51D 5Q- "Marinell"
Stockman, Hervey S., Lt.; States-September 1944
    68 missions
    P-51B 5Q-X 42-106789 "Fuxum"
Sutton, John L., Lt.; June 1944-December 1944
Thibert, Henry G., Capt.; States-September 1944
Thistlethwaite, Edward A., Lt.; States-May 30, 1944(POW)
Thompson, Ralph P., Lt.; States-November 1944
Trester, John R., Lt.; July 1944-January 1945
    P-51D 5Q-H
Van Cleave, Ely N., Lt.; July 1944-November 26, 1944(KIA)
Waters, Frank T., Jr., Lt.; January 1944-October 1944
    65 missions, 270 hours
    P-51B 5Q-Z 43-24781 "Brother Bill"
Waymire, Harvey R., Lt.; January 1944-November 1944
Weller, Richard E., Capt.; States-September 1944
Wells, Arlen W., Capt.; July 1944-March 1945
Wilcox, Richard H., Lt.; States-October 1944
    P-51B 5Q- "G'Bye Now"
Winkelman, Myer R., Lt.; July 1944-August 13, 1944(KIA)
Wood, Robert T., Capt.; July 1944-February 22, 1945(KIA)
Zeine, Donald A., Lt.; States-October 1944

**505th Fighter Squadron**
Allman, Johnnie M., Lt.; February 1945-February 12, 1945(KIAc)
Ammerman, Roy W., Lt.; May 1944-October 1944

Ananian, Stephen C., Lt.; September 1944-April 1945
64 missions
P-51D 6N-K 44-14734 "Baby Mine"
Armistead, Walter M., Lt.; June 1944-June 17, 1944(POW)
3 missions
Baker, James A., Lt.; July 1944-December 5, 1944(KIA)
Ball, Edwin C., Lt.; States-August 8, 1944(KIA)
Becker, Leo H., Lt.; September 1944-April 1945
Beecher, William M., Lt.; February 1945-February 20, 1945(KIA)
Biggs, Oscar K., Lt.; February 1945-July 1945
P-51D 6N-E 44-72449 "Imogene"
Bline, Brooks J., Capt.; January 1945-July 1945
Bloxham, Richard W., Capt.; July 1944-February 6, 1945(KIA)
Booth, Billy B., Lt.; September 1944-April 1945
Brock, Thomas C., F/O; September 1944-October 1944; to 353rd Ftr Grp
Bundgaard, Carl H., Lt.; June 1944-July 4, 1944(MIA-E) August 1944-March 1945
Burch, Harold W., Lt.; February 1945-July 1945
P-51D 6N-D 44-72098
Burns, Robert F., Lt.; July 1944-August 4, 1944(POW)
Byrd, Cecil L., Lt.; July 1944-May 1945
P-51D 6N-S 44-15168 "Elizabeth Jane"
Cain, Richard C., Lt.; August 1944-December 4, 1944(POW)
35 missions
Carr, Vernon D., Lt.; September 1944-July 1945
P-51D 6N- "Angel of Mercy"
Caywood, Herbert L., Lt.; October 1944-April 1945
Coker, Joseph R., F/O; February 1945-March 31, 1945(POW)
Conner, Bertis A., Jr., Lt.; September 1944-March 2, 1945(POW)
P-51D 6N-A 44-15498 "Lone Star Lady
Corey, Harry R., Capt., September 1944-July 1945
64 missions, 326 hours
P-51D 6N-K 44-15467 "Maureen Ann"
Daniell, Jack S., Lt.; July 1944-March 1945
P-51D 6N-K 44-14745 "Sweet'n Low Down"
Diefenbeck, James A., Capt.; February 1945-April 1945
Evans, Frank T., Lt.; January 1944-September 1944
Everett, Harold M., Lt.; January 1944-May 24, 1944(POW-E)
Ewing, Philip H., Lt.; January 1944-June 8, 1944(MIA-E)
Farmer, Owen P., Capt.; States-June 1945
P-51D 6N-H 44-13987 "Dibbo"
P-51D 6N-H 44-14946 "Dibbo"
P-51D 6N-H 44-72084 "Dibbo"
P-51D 6N-H 44-72065 "Dibbo"
Fish, Wesley G., Lt.; May 1944-July 16, 1944(POW)
Frink, James P., Lt.; April 1945-September 1945
Gelpke, Robert E., F/O; April 1945-September 1945
Gilbert, Kenneth C., Capt.; States-July 17, 1945(KIAc)
Gilmore, Harry U., Lt.; September 1944-October 1944; to 353rd Ftr Grp
Girzi, Henry E., Jr., Lt.; September 1944-April 1945
Gousie, Roland E., Lt.; September 1944-April 15, 1945(POW)
55 missions
P-51D 6N-C 44-14656 "Dottie"
Graham, Gerald E., Lt.; May 1944-November 1944
P-51B 6N-I 42-106946 "Mary Lee"
P-51D 6N-I 44-14433 "Mary Lee"
Gregory, Vincent L., Lt.; April 1945-September 1945
Guyton, William R., Lt.; March 1945-September 1945
P-51D 6N-I "Eileen"
Hanseman, Chris J., Lt.; States-July 29, 1944(KIA)
P-51B 6N-H "Eleanor"
P-51B 6N-H "Eleanor II"
P-51B 6N-H "Eleanor III"
P-51D 6N-H 44-13556 "Eleanor IV"
Hanson, James R., Lt.; January 1944-September 1944
Heneghan, Floyd P., Lt.; States-May 21, 1944(KIA)
Hill, Joseph S., Lt.; April 1945-September 1945
Holloway, John G., Capt.; States-September 1944
P-51B 6N-A
P-51D 6N-A 44-13624 "Sniffles"
Howard, Harry F., Lt.; January 1945-March 2, 1945(POW)
Howard, Waldron E., Lt.; October 1944-January 17, 1945(KIA)
Hrico, George J., Capt.; January 1944-November 1944
Hupp, Ellis E., Jr., Lt.; March 1945-July 1945
Irion, Robert E., Capt.; September 1944-July 1945
P-51D 6N-N 44-15001 "Silver Streak"
Jaaskelainen, William, Lt.; States-September 1944
P-51B 6N-T 42-106721 "Lil Sack"
Jackson, Boyd O., Lt.; July 1944-November 21, 1944(KIA)
38 missions
Jessup, Thomas N., Lt.; March 1945-June 30, 1945(KIAc)
Johnson, Evan M., V, Capt.; States-November 1944
P-51B 6N-J
P-51D 6N-J 44-13741 "The Comet"
P-51D 6N-J 44-15039 "Pistol Packin' Mama"
Jones, George W., Jr., Lt.; September 1944-March 3, 1945(KIA)
P-51D 6N-Y 44-15318 "Miss E.T.O."
Jones, William A., Lt.; States-September 11, 1944(POW)
297 hours
P-51C 6N-E 43-25038 "Impatient Virgin"
Jorgenson, Loyd N., Lt.; April 1945-September 1945
Karkuma, Karl O., Lt.; April 1945-September 1945
Knight, George, Lt.; States-September 1944
Knighton, Ralph M., Lt.; March 1945-July 1945
Kotora, Harold J., Lt.; March 1945-July 1945
Kovar, Robert J., Lt.; March 1945-July 1945
Krauss, William H., Capt.; June 1944-December 1944
P-51D 6N- 44-14383 "Umbriago"
Lanfer, William A., Lt.; March 1945-July 1945
Laverick, John H., Lt.; March 1945-July 1945
Larson, Donald A., Maj.; August 1943-August 4, 1944(KIA)
P-51B 6N-B
P-51D 6N-B 44-13609 "Mary, Queen of Scots"
P-51D 6N-B 44-13881
Lawes, Bayard F., Lt.; March 1945-July 1945
Loveless, Philip M., Jr., Capt.; October 1944-April 1945
Luper, Arch B., Lt.; States-May 7, 1944(KIA)
Lynch, James L., Lt.; States-May 29, 1944(KIA)
P-51B 6N-O 43-24796 "Blackie II"
MacClarence, William R., Lt.; February 1945-July 1945
Malarz, Chester, Capt.; July 1944-February 1945
P-51B 6N-M 42-106946 "Bison Bull"
P-51D 6N-M
Marts, Jay F., Lt.; August 1944-March 1945
P-51D 6N-J 44-14239 "Junior"
Marvel, Thomas W., Lt.; September 1944-April 1945
McMahan, Peter J., Lt.; States-July 11, 1944(KIA)
Mitchell, Raymond M., Jr., Capt.; August 1944-September 23, 1944(POW)
Moore, William R., Lt.; July 1944-September 13, 1944(POW)
Mudge, William F., Lt.; States-September 1944
270 hours
Muller, James B., Lt.; July 1944-September 23, 1944(POW)
Murphy, Jerome T., Lt.; February 1945-July 1945
P-51D 6N-S 44-72384
Nay, Martin N., Lt.; June 1944-September 5, 1944(MIA-E)
40 missions
O'Brien, Richard C., Lt.; November 1944-March 12, 1945(INT)
Olander, Richard B., Capt.; States-January 17, 1945(KIA)
85 missions, 354 hours
P-51B 6N-S "Therese"
P-51D 6N-S 44-14170 "Therese"
P-51K 6N-S 44-11363 "Therese"
Opitz, William R., Lt.; May 1944-June 13, 1944(Inj.)
Ott, Maurice, Lt.; April 1945-September 1945
Palmer, Gerald W., Lt.; October 1944-February 6, 1945(KIA)
Paul, Robert H., Jr., Lt.; February 1945-July 1945
Perry, Gordon F., Lt.; States-May 29, 1944(KIA)
Pesanka, John, Lt.; February 1945-July 1945
Petticrew, Stanley S., Lt.; September 1944-October 1944; to 353rd Ftr Grp
Phillippi, William R., Lt.; September 1944-April 1945
Powell, Lawrence J., Jr., Lt.; June 1944-January 14, 1945(POW)
68 missions
P-51C 6N- "Happy"
P-51D 6N- "Happy Jr."
Reid, Langhorne, Jr., Maj.; States-December 1944
Rice, John J., F/O; March 1945-July 1945
Rich, George T., Capt.; August 1944-April 1945
63 missions
P-51D 6N- 44-14023 "Chute! You're Faded"
Rohm, Richard A., Lt.; States-September 1944
Sawicki, Joseph F., Lt.; May 1944-June 9, 1944(KIA)
Shaw, Bernell V., Lt.; July 1944-August 25, 1944(POW)
Shepherd, George W., Jr., F/O; March 1945-July 1945
Sirochman, Andrew, Lt.; States-August 13, 1944(MIA-E)
Slovak, William R., Lt.; July 1944-September 13, 1944(KIA)
Smith, Floyd W., Lt.; March 1945-August 1945
Smith, Shirley K., Capt.; April 1945-July 1945
Staggers, Theodore B., Lt.; July 1944-September 11, 1944(POW)
Starnes, James R., Capt.; States-September 1945
113 missions, 520 hours
P-51B 6N-X 42-106936 "Tarheel"
P-51D 6N-X 44-14113 "Tarheel"
P-51D 6N-X 44-14387 "Tarheel"
P-51D 6N-X 44-72152 "Tarheel"
Steiger, Leroy A., F/O; March 1945-July 1945
Stewart, Carl R., Lt.; May 1944-September 1944
Stiles, Bert, Lt.; September 1944-November 26, 1944(KIA) former bomber pilot
Stoudt, Leland M., Lt.; September 1944-November 21, 1944(KIA)
Strong, Roland W., Lt.; May 1944-August 4, 1944(POW)
Tannous, Richard H., Lt.; June 1944-October 1944
Thieme, Richard G., Lt.; September 1944-March 1945
70 missions, 302 hours
P-51D 6N-W 44-14705 "Boomerang"
Thomas, Kessler O., Lt.; October 1944-February 6, 1945(KIA)
Thury, Joseph L., LtCol.; August 1943-July 1945
P-51B 6N-C "Pauline"
P-51D 6N-C 44-14656 "Pauline"
P-51D 6N-C 44-15616 "Pauline"
P-51D 6N-C 44-72437 "Pauline"
Tongue, Arthur E., Lt.; July 1944-August 6, 1944(KIA)
Tower, Archie A., Maj.; January 1944-September 1945
P-51B 6N-D
P-51D 6N-D 44-73074 "Lucky Boy"

Travis, Laird D., Lt.; September 1944-November 18, 1944(KIA)
Wager, Evergard L., Lt.; February 1945-March 30, 1945(KIA)
Wark, Raymond D., Lt.; March 1945-July 1945
Wilcox, Russell W., Lt.; August 1944-August 28, 1944(KIA)
Withers, John C., Lt.; October 1944-April 1945
Woolery, James C., Lt.; October 1944-July 1945
P-51D 6N-I 44-14433 "Pepper"
P-51D 6N-I 44-72512 "Pepper"
Young, Allen D., Lt.; August 1944-November 18, 1944(POW)
Ziegler, Harry D., Lt.; October 1944-March 3, 1945(POW)

**Aircraft of the 503rd Fighter Squadron**

P-51C-1-NT
42-103295 D7-
42-103299 D7-
42-103325 D7-N "Reddy Teddy"
42-103327 D7-I

P-51C-5-NT
42-103346 D7-W
42-103393 D7-
42-103567 D7-H L.M. Wright
42-103600 D7-M "Sally" L.J. Fiorito

P-51C-10-NT
43-25050 D7-H

P-51B-10-NA
42-106570 D7-S
42-106579 D7-Q
42-106601 D7-A
42-106610 D7-X
42-106610 D7-Q
42-106614 D7-G
42-106614 D7-Y E.E. Erickson
42-106615 D7-R
42-106658 D7-H L.M. Wright
42-106674 D7-
42-106678 D7-B
42-106683 D7-
42-106700 D7-
42-106710 D7-Y

P-51B-15-NA
42-106755 D7-T J. Wolfort
42-106756 D7-S
42-106761 D7-L
42-106781 D7-D
42-106785 D7-Q
42-106791 D7-V
42-106798 D7-J W.E. Bryan
42-106803 D7-A
42-106812 D7-A
42-106821 D7-C R.S. Whitelaw
42-106840 D7-K
42-106863 D7-B "Mon Petite" W.T. Carter
42-106869 D7-E
42-106882 D7-V
42-106889 D7-P V. Wyatt
42-106905 D7-
42-106934 D7-Z J.P. Bush
43-24773 D7-
43-24800 D7-O "Miss Max" E.H. Graham

P-51K-1-NT
44-11373 D7-R

P-51D-5-NT
44-11199 D7-B
44-11325 D7-K "Princess Pat" P.E. Petitt

P-51K-5-NT
44-11623 D7-A "Rusty" L.J. French

P-51D-5-NA
44-13324 D7-P V. Wyatt
44-13329 D7-W
44-13377 D7-A E.B. Stephenson
44-13527 D7-R
44-13601 D7-J W.E. Bryan
44-13614 D7-Y
44-13627 D7-E
44-13629 D7-F "Dee" C.W. Knott
44-13662 D7-B
44-13808 D7-U "Yi Yi" F.R. Gerard
44-13890 D7-Z J.P. Bush
44-13917 D7-L "You've Had It"
44-13955 D7-X A.S. Harte
44-13965 D7-Z "Gruesome Twosome" 2-seat conversion
44-13980 D7-Z "Shy Ann" E.H. Beavers
44-13987 D7-
44-13995 D7-X
44-14004 D7-A J. Aitken
44-14012 D7-B

P-51D-10-NA
44-14065 D7-M "Sally II" L.J. Fiorito
44-14069 D7-
44-14118 D7-J "Worry Bird" R.J. Frisch
44-14247 D7-
44-14327 D7-I
44-14390 D7-S "Janie Girl" E.E. Erickson
44-13390 D7-N
44-14525 D7-Z E.H. Beavers
44-14587 D7-A "PeeWee Peckerwood"
44-14620 D7-O
44-14626 D7-H "Sweet Sue"
44-14671 D7-C D.E. Shafer
44-14829 D7-
44-14849 D7-C "Whoa! To Joe's Woes"

P-51D-15-NA
44-14904 D7-F
44-14947 D7-P L.C. Marsh
44-15003 D7-U F.R. Gerard
44-15074 D7-J "Big Noise" W.E. Bryan
44-15134 D7-D "The Bengal Lancer" F.M. Stillwell
44-15291 D7-N
44-15426 D7-A
44-15430 D7-S R.F. Reuter
44-15482 D7-L R.L. Poutre
44-15509 D7-T
44-15510 D7-W "China Girl"
44-15512 D7-B
44-15520 D7-
44-15560 D7-V J.W. Gokey
44-15700 D7-Q "Sweet Jeanne" J.A. Mankie

P-51D-20-NA
44-64012 D7-H
44-72075 D7-P
44-72147 D7-C D.E. Shafer
44-72211 D7-L
44-72307 D7-P
44-72310 D7-D
44-72333 D7-U
44-72485 D7-J W.E. Bryan

P-51D-25-NA
44-73287 D7-J "Worry Bird" R.J. Frisch

Unknown Serials
D7- "Night-Mare" C.S. Coe
D7- "Hard Luck, Jr." S.J. Chetneky
D7-Z "The Yellow Peril"

**Aircraft of the 504th Fighter Squadron**

P-51C-5-NT
42-103342 5Q-
42-103394 5Q- "Whistler's Wings" F.S. Rutan
42-103737 5Q-J "The Yankee Kid III" M.F. Caldwell

P-51B-10-NA
42-106601 5Q-
42-106641 5Q-U
42-106642 5Q-
42-106649 5Q-I
42-106662 5Q-Y
42-106672 5Q-Q "Problem" L.L. Corbin
42-106676 5Q-Z "Little Princess"
42-106690 5Q-E C.E. Craigo
42-106773 5Q-V "Dinny" R.N. Atteberry

P-51B-15-NA
42-106789 5Q-X "Fuxum" H.S. Stockman
42-106838 5Q-A "Fabasca IV" B.C. Routt
42-106847 5Q-
42-106886 5Q-O "Swede" D.S. Larson
42-106886 5Q-O "Punkie" R.V.E. Blizzard
42-106908 5Q-T "Cajun"
42-106933 5Q-G "Bonny Bea" L.G. Eisenhart
43-24772 5Q-
43-24781 5Q-Z "Brother Bill" F.T. Waters
43-24804 5Q-P "Miss Priss" J.M. McClure

P-51D-5-NT
44-11189 5Q-

P-51K-5-NT
44-11640 5Q-F "Hell's Fable" R.T. Aldrich
44-11684 5Q-T "White Lightnin'" W.M. Hudson
44-11745 5Q- "Happy III"

P-51D-5-NA
44-13330 5Q-B "Picilo Pete" L.S. Peter
44-13378 5Q-F "Ollie" E.B. Gravette
44-13521 5Q-B
44-13569 5Q-B
44-13584 5Q-T
44-13868 5Q-
44-13938 5Q-S

P-51D-10-NA
44-14060 5Q-A "Fabasca V" B.C. Routt
44-14070 5Q-
44-14153 5Q-J
44-14169 5Q-
44-14208 5Q-L "Patty III"
44-14287 5Q- "Pin-Up Girl"
44-14321 5Q-I
44-14372 5Q-E "Beaver Chant" R.C. Penrose
44-14372 5Q-E "Mary Beth" K.B. Everson
44-14647 5Q-Q "Podunk"
44-14672 5Q-S "Lil Injun" L.C. Orcutt

P-51D-15-NA
44-15021 5Q-W "Anabel" R.M. Kuhlman
44-15499 5Q-O "Punkie II" R.V.E. Blizzard
44-15562 5Q-

P-51D-20-NA
44-64148 5Q-C "Happy IV" W.C. Clark
44-72161 5Q-I
44-72188 5Q-Z "Pedunk II" C.M. Mason
44-72282 5Q-M "Watonga State Bank, Safe and Dependable" L.J. Barrett
44-72495 5Q-F D.F. Krueger
44-72534 5Q-G "Madame Queen" R.C. Croker

Unknown Serials
P-51B 5Q-F "Ollie" E.B. Gravette
P-51B 5Q- "Tamsin Lee" W.B. Griffith
P-51B 5Q- "Aphrodite"
P-51B 5Q- "Sassy Six"
P-51D 5Q-W "Dopey Lou" W.T. Hurley
P-51D 5Q- "Hebe's Heap" G.G. Cohen
P-51D 5Q- "Diane" C. Hermanson
P-51D 5Q-B "Hillbilly"
P-51D 5Q "Mary" D.P. Cole
P-51D 5Q- "Marinell" B.V. Stevens
P-51D 5Q-D "Lou'n Sue" V.N. Barto
P-51B 5Q- "G'Bye Now" R.H. Wilcox
P-51D 5Q-L "Patty"
P-51D 5Q-L "Patty II"
P-51D 5Q- "Virginia Lee"

**Aircraft of the 505th Fighter Squadron**

P-51C-1-NT
42-103305 6N-U
42-103314 6N-

P-51C-5-NT
42-103359 6N-
42-103559 6N-
42-103742 6N- "Man O'War"
42-103756 6N-F

P-51C-10-NT
43-25038 6N-E "Impatient Virgin" W.A. Jones
42-103955 6N-G

P-51B-10-NA
42-106626 6N-C "Butch"
42-106646 6N-
42-106653 6N-F
42-106657 6N-Q
42-106664 6N-M
42-106676 6N-A "San Antone Rose" J.B. Henry
42-106676 6N-A "Princess Marie"
42-106678 6N-
42-106699 6N-
42-106720 6N-T "Lil Sack" W. Jaaskelainen

P-51B-15-NA
42-106645 6N-
42-106807 6N-
42-106842 6N-
42-106909 6N-Z "Wee Ginny" M.G.H. McPharlin
42-106918 6N-Q
42-106936 6N-X "Tarheel" J.R. Starnes
42-106937 6N-
42-106946 6N-I "Mary Lee" G.H. Graham
42-106946 6N-M "Bison Bull" C. Malarz
43-24773 6N-
43-24796 6N-O "Blackie II"

P-51D-5-NT
44-11204 6N-

P-51K-1-NT
44-11363 6N-S "Therese" R.B. Olander

P-51D-5-NA
44-13370 6N-
44-13379 6N- "Miss Idaho"
44-13385 6N-
44-13413 6N-
44-13471 6N-J "The Comet" E.M. Johnson
44-13556 6N-H "Eleanor IV" C.J. Hanseman
44-13609 6N-B "Mary, Queen of Scots" D.A. Larson
44-13616 6N-U "Baggy Pants"
44-13624 6N-A "Sniffles II" J.G. Holloway
44-13680 6N-R "The Roller"
44-13828 6N-
44-13847 6N-
44-13881 6N-B D.A. Larson
44-13946 6N-H "Dibbo" O.P. Farmer
44-14023 6N- "Chute! You're Faded" G.T. Rich

P-51D-10-NA
44-14052 6N-P "Mariam"
44-14072 6N-
44-14086 6N- "Angel of Mercy"
44-14092 6N-
44-14113 6N-X "Tarheel" J.R. Starnes
44-14115 6N-
44-14170 6N-S "Therese" R.B. Olander
44-14239 6N-J "Junior" J.F. Marts
44-14383 6N- "Umbriago" W.H. Krauss
44-14387 6N-X "Tarheel" J.R. Starnes
44-14433 6N-I "Mary Lee" G.H. Graham
44-14433 6N-I "Pepper" J.C. Woolery
44-14542 6N-
44-14554 6N-I
44-14622 6N-E "Little One II"
44-14656 6N-C "Pauline" J.L. Thury
44-14656 6N-C "Dotty" R.E. Gousie
44-14705 6N-W "Boomerang!" R.G. Thieme
44-14729 6N- "Betty Lou"
44-14731 6N- "St. Louis Blues"
44-14734 6N-K "Baby Mine" S.C. Ananian
44-14738 6N-O "Arrowhead"
44-14745 6N-K "Sweet'n Low Down" J.S. Daniell

P-51D-15-NA
44-14886 6N-D
44-15001 6N-N "Silver Streak" R.E. Irion
44-15039 6N-J "Pistol Packin' Mama" E.M. Johnson
44-15168 6N-S "Elizabeth Jane" C.L. Byrd
44-15306 6N-
44-15318 6N-F "Esther"
44-15318 6N-Y "Miss E.T.O." G.W. Jones
44-15368 6N- "Nornie"
44-15427 6N-B
44-15467 6N-K "Maureen Ann" H.R. Corey
44-15498 6N-A "Lone Star Lady" B.A. Conner
44-15558 6N-
44-15616 6N-C "Pauline" J.L. Thury

P-51D-20-NA
44-72065 6N-H "Dibbo" O.P. Farmer
44-72084 6N-H "Dibbo" O.P. Farmer
44-72098 6N-D H.W. Burch
44-72152 6N-X "Tarheel" J.R. Starnes
44-72255 6N-A "San Antone Rose" J.B. Henry
44-72384 6N-S J.T. Murphy
44-72437 6N-C "Pauline" J.L. Thury
44-72449 6N-E "Imogene" O.K. Biggs
44-72512 6N-I "Pepper" J.C. Woolery

P-51D-25-NA
44-72679 6N-N "B Ware"
44-72713 6N-K "Little Betty Anne"
44-73074 6N-D "Lucky Boy" A.A. Tower

Unknown Serials

| | |
|---|---|
| P-51B 6N-C "Pauline" | J.L. Thury |
| P-51B 6N-H "Eleanor" | C.J. Hanseman |
| P-51B 6N-H "Eleanor II" | C.J. Hanseman |
| P-51B 6N-H "Eleanor III" | C.J. Hanseman |
| P-51B 6N-D "Lucky Boy" | A.A. Tower |
| P-51B 6N-A "Sniffles" | J.G. Holloway |
| P-51D 6N-I "Eileen" | W.R. Guyton |
| P-51B 6N-S "Therese" | R.B. Olander |
| P-51B 6N- "Happy" | L.J. Powell |
| P-51D 6N- "Angel of Mercy" | V.D. Carr |
| P-51D 6N-D "Marge" | |

• • •

## THE 352ND FIGHTER GROUP
## 328TH, 486TH, 487TH FIGHTER SQUADRONS

The 352nd Fighter Group was activated on October 1, 1942, at Mitchel Field, New York. Training in the east, the group headed overseas on July 1, 1943, aboard the "Queen Elizabeth". The first of 420 missions came on September 9, 1943, with the last coming on May 3, 1945. While overseas, the group claimed 502.67 aerial and 275 ground victories while 115 P-47's and P-51's were lost on operations and 11 pilots died in accidents. From mid December of 1944, the 352nd was temporarily attached to the 9th Air Force and moved to the Continent to assist that organization's operations.

Stations for the group were Bodney, from July 7, 1943; Asche, Belgium, from December 23, 1944; Chievres, Belgium, from January 27, 1945; and Bodney, from April 13, 1945, to November of 1945. Aircraft flown were the P-47D, from July of 1943 until April 20, 1944, and the P-51B, C, D, and K, from April 8, 1944 onwards. The 352nd was awarded a Distinguished Unit Citation for an escort on May 8, 1944, when the group destroyed over 20 enemy planes. The 487th Fighter Squadron was also awarded a DUC for actions on January 1, 1945, when pilots destroyed over 20 German fighters.

### Claims

| | Air | | | Grd | |
|---|---|---|---|---|---|
| | Destroyed | Probable | Damaged | Destroyed | Damaged |
| HdQts | 23.5 | 2.33 | 7 | 10 | 6 |
| 328th | 139.17 | 11.67 | 34 | 55 | 39 |
| 486th | 113 | 5 | 21 | 98 | 64 |
| 487th | 227 | 10 | 32 | 112 | 79 |
| | 502.67 | 29 | 94 | 275 | 188 |

### Commanders

| | |
|---|---|
| Col. Joseph L. Mason | May 18, 1943-July 24, 1944 |
| LtCol. James D. Mayden | July 24, 1944-September 1, 1944 |
| Col. Joseph L. Mason | September 1, 1944-November 15, 1944 |
| Col. James D. Mayden | November 15, 1944-September 1945 |

### Wing and Command Assignments

| | |
|---|---|
| Assigned to VIII Fighter Command | July 6, 1943 |
| VIII Fighter Command, 67th Fighter Wing | October 6, 1943 |
| 1st Bomb Division, 67th Fighter Wing | September 15, 1944 |
| IX TAC, 9th Air Force (D.S.) | December 23, 1944 |
| VIII Fighter Command | February 1, 1945 |
| 1st Air Division, 67th Fighter Wing | April 13, 1945 |

### Aircraft Markings

All P-47's were in olive drab/neutral gray schemes with the standard white cowl and theater bands. The first P-51's assigned were in the same scheme with NMF planes arriving in April of 1944. In April, the spinner and 12 inch cowl band were painted medium blue as a group marking, and later in the month, the blue was extended and swept up to the cockpit. When invasion stripes were applied in early June of 1944, the aircraft letter was moved from the aft fuselage to the vertical tail (except in the 486th which placed it on the nose just behind the exhaust stacks). The practice of applying the letter on the tail continued for all squadrons even after the stripes were removed in the summer of 1944. From November of 1944, rudder colors were used: red for the 328th, yellow for the 486th, and blue for the 487th.

Squadron codes were:

328th Ftr Sqn: PE
486th Ftr Sqn: PZ
487th Ftr Sqn: HO

### 352nd Fighter Group Statistical Report

| Month | Air | Grd | Losses | KIAc |
|---|---|---|---|---|
| September 1943 | 0-0-0 | 0-0 | 1 | 1 |
| October | 0-0-0 | 0-0 | 1 | 0 |
| November | 3-1-0 | 0-0 | 3 | 0 |
| December | 19-2-3 | 0-0 | 4 | 0 |
| January 1944 | 15-2-4 | 0-0 | 2 | 1 |
| February | 19.67-0-14 | 0-0 | 5 | 0 |
| March | 10-1-1 | 0-0 | 3 | 0 |
| April | 33-1-2 | 107-73 | 10 | 0 |
| May | 101-8-10 | 26-19 | 8 | 2 |
| June | 25-1-10 | 8-3 | 17 | 4 |
| July | 41.5-3-20 | 1-4 | 14 | 0 |
| August | 21-2-2 | 6-8 | 12 | 1 |
| September | 31-0-5 | 25-4 | 10 | 0 |
| October | 0-0-0 | 0-0 | 3 | 1 |
| November | 82-6-11 | 0-3 | 6 | 0 |
| December | 51-0-6 | 0-0 | 3 | 0 |
| January 1945 | 32.5-0-1 | 0-0 | 1 | 0 |
| February | 1-0-2 | 0-1 | 3 | 0 |
| March | 13-2-2 | 0-6 | 5 | 0 |
| April | 4-0-1 | 102-67 | 4 | 0 |
| May | 0-0-0 | 0-0 | 0 | 0 |
| June | 0-0-0 | 0-0 | 0 | 1 |
| | 502.67-29-94 | 275-188 | 115 | 11 |

### Losses by Squadron

| | MIA | | KIAc | |
|---|---|---|---|---|
| | P-47 | P-51 | P-47 | P-51 |
| HdQts | 1 | 2 | 0 | 0 |
| 328th | 7 | 34 | 1 | 4 |
| 486th | 5 | 23 | 0 | 1 |
| 487th | 8 | 35 | 1 | 4 |
| | 21 | 94 | 2 | 9 |

### Claims by Type

| | Air | | | Grd | |
|---|---|---|---|---|---|
| | Destroyed | Probable | Damaged | Destroyed | Damaged |
| P-47 | 71.67 | 7 | 22 | 14 | 4 |
| P-51 | 431 | 22 | 72 | 261 | 184 |

### Claims by Enemy Aircraft Type

| | Air | | | Grd | |
|---|---|---|---|---|---|
| | Destroyed | Probable | Damaged | Destroyed | Damaged |
| Me-109 | 320.5 | 15 | 45 | 44 | 31 |
| FW-190 | 138 | 12 | 25 | 42 | 34 |
| Ju-88 | 11 | 1 | 7 | 46 | 27 |
| Me-110 | 10.67 | 1 | 3 | 15 | 9 |
| Me-262 | 7.5 | 0 | 4 | 2 | 0 |
| Me-410 | 5 | 0 | 8 | 2 | 1 |
| Me-210 | 2 | 0 | 1 | 13 | 3 |
| Ar-234 | 2 | 0 | 1 | 0 | 0 |
| Ju-52 | 2 | 0 | 0 | 30 | 4 |
| He-177 | 1 | 0 | 0 | 5 | 2 |
| FW-200 | 1 | 0 | 0 | 2 | 1 |
| FW-189 | 1 | 0 | 0 | 1 | 0 |
| Trainer | 1 | 0 | 0 | 0 | 0 |
| u/i a/c | 0 | 0 | 0 | 30 | 45 |
| He-111 | 0 | 0 | 0 | 25 | 20 |
| Ju-86 | 0 | 0 | 0 | 5 | 2 |
| Hs-129 | 0 | 0 | 0 | 3 | 1 |
| Do-217 | 0 | 0 | 0 | 3 | 1 |
| Fi-156 | 0 | 0 | 0 | 3 | 0 |
| Ju-87 | 0 | 0 | 0 | 2 | 0 |
| Hs-123 | 0 | 0 | 0 | 1 | 0 |
| Bu-133 | 0 | 0 | 0 | 1 | 0 |
| Caudron | 0 | 0 | 0 | 0 | 2 |
| Ju-290 | 0 | 0 | 0 | 0 | 2 |
| Ju-188 | 0 | 0 | 0 | 0 | 1 |
| Ar-196 | 0 | 0 | 0 | 0 | 1 |
| Glider | 0 | 0 | 0 | 0 | 1 |

### 352nd Fighter Group Squadron Commanders

**328th Ftr Sqn**

| | |
|---|---|
| Maj. Everett W. Stewart | December 1942-January 23, 1944 |
| Maj. Harold G. Lund | January 23, 1944-March 11, 1944 |
| Maj. I.B. Jack Donaldson | March 11, 1944-March 21, 1944 |
| Maj. Willie O. Jackson | March 21, 1944-April 15, 1944 |
| Maj. Harold G. Lund | April 15, 1944-July 22, 1944 |
| LtCol. John C. Edwards | July 22, 1944-October 28, 1944 |
| Maj. George E. Preddy | October 28, 1944-December 25, 1944 |
| Maj. Earl L. Abbott | December 26, 1944-January 24, 1945 |

| | |
|---|---|
| Capt. Donald S. Bryan | January 25, 1945-January 31, 1945 |
| LtCol. Earl D. Duncan | January 31, 1945-September 1945 |

**486th Ftr Sqn**

| | |
|---|---|
| LtCol. Luther H. Richmond | February 1943-April 15, 1944 |
| Maj. Willie O. Jackson | April 15, 1944-August 1944 |
| Maj. Franklyn N. Greene | August 1944-October 16, 1944 |
| LtCol. Willie O. Jackson | October 16, 1944-February 22, 1945 |
| LtCol. Franklin N. Greene | February 22, 1945-March 1945 |
| Maj. Donald H. Higgins | March 1945-EOW |

**487th Ftr Sqn**

| | |
|---|---|
| Maj. John C. Meyer | December 5, 1942-May 15, 1944 |
| Maj. George E. Preddy | May 15, 1944-August 2, 1944 |
| LtCol. John C. Meyer | August 2, 1944-November 20, 1944 |
| LtCol. William T. Halton | November 20, 1944-EOW |

**352nd Fighter Group Aces**

| Name | Air | Grd | Total | Sqn |
|---|---|---|---|---|
| LtCol. John C. Meyer | 24 | 13 | 37 | 487th<br>HdQts |
| Maj. George E. Preddy | 26.83 | 5 | 31.83 | 328th<br>487th |
| Capt. Raymond H. Littge | 10.5 | 13 | 23.5 | 487th |
| Capt. Edwin L. Heller | 5.5 | 14.5 | 20 | 486th |
| Capt. John F. Thornell, Jr. | 17.25 | 2 | 19.25 | 328th |
| Capt. William T. Whisner | 15.5 | 3 | 18.5 | 487th |
| Lt. Glennon T. Moran | 13 | 3 | 16 | 487th |
| Maj. Stephen W. Andrew | 9 | 6.5 | 15.5* | 486th |
| Lt. Carl J. Luksic | 8.5 | 7 | 15.5 | 487th |
| Capt. Woodrow W. Anderson | 4.5 | 9 | 13.5 | 486th |
| Maj. Donald S. Bryan | 13.33 | 0 | 13.33 | 328th |
| Capt. Clarence O. Johnson | 7 | 6 | 13** | 487th |
| Capt. Henry J. Miklajcyk | 7.5 | 5.5 | 13 | 486th |
| LtCol. William T. Halton | 10.5 | 2 | 12.5 | 328th<br>487th |
| LtCol. Willie O. Jackson, Jr. | 7 | 4 | 11 | 328th<br>486th<br>HdQts |
| Capt. Frank A. Cutler | 7.5 | 3 | 10.5 | 486th |
| Lt. Karl M. Waldron, Jr. | 3 | 7 | 10 | 487th |
| Col. Everett W. Stewart | 7.83 | 1.5 | 9.33*** | 328th |
| Capt. Clayton E. Davis | 5 | 4 | 9 | 487th |
| Capt. Virgil K. Meroney | 9 | 0 | 9 | 487th |
| Capt. Charles J. Cesky | 8.5 | 0 | 8.5 | 328th |
| Capt. Sanford K. Moats | 8.5 | 0 | 8.5 | 487th |
| Lt. Malcolm C. Pickering | 4 | 4 | 8 | 487th |
| Capt. Walter E. Starck | 7 | 0 | 7 | 487th |
| Capt. John B. Coleman, Jr. | 4.33 | 2.5 | 6.83 | 328th |
| Lt. William W. Furr | 3.5 | 3 | 6.5 | 328th |
| Lt. Charles E. Goodman | 4.5 | 2 | 6.5 | 328th |
| Capt. Francis W. Horne | 5.5 | 1 | 6.5 | 328th |
| Col. James D. Mayden | 2 | 4 | 6 | HdQts |
| Lt. Charles C. Pattillo | 0 | 6 | 6 | 486th |
| Capt. Alex F. Sears | 5 | 1 | 6 | 487th |
| Capt. Alton J. Wallace | 3 | 3 | 6 | 486th |
| Lt. Donald Y. Whinnem | 1 | 5 | 6 | 486th |
| Maj. Earl L. Abbott | 4.75 | 1 | 5.75 | 328th |
| Lt. Charles J. Bennette | 2 | 3.5 | 5.5 | 328th |
| Lt. Robert H. Berkshire | 4.5 | 1 | 5.5 | 487th |
| Lt. Joseph D. Carter | 0.5 | 5 | 5.5 | 486th |
| Maj. Donald H. Higgins | 2.5 | 3 | 5.5 | 486th |
| Lt. Richard C. Brookins | 4.25 | 1 | 5.25 | 328th |
| Lt. Edmond Zellner | 3.25 | 2 | 5.25 | 328th |
| Capt. Ernest O. Bostrom | 5 | 0 | 5 | 486th |
| Capt. Ralph W. Hamilton | 4 | 1 | 5 | 487th |
| Capt. Earl R. Lazear | 5 | 0 | 5 | 486th |
| Capt. Robert G. MacKean | 0 | 5 | 5 | 486th |
| Col. Joseph L. Mason | 5 | 0 | 5 | HdQts |
| Lt. Raymond G. Phillips | 2 | 3 | 5 | 328th |
| Lt. Alden P. Rigby | 4 | 1 | 5 | 487th |
| Capt. Duerr H. Schuh | 5 | 0 | 5 | 487th |
| Capt. William J. Stangel | 5 | 0 | 5 | 328th |
| Capt. Henry M. Stewart, II | 4 | 1 | 5 | 487th |
| Lt. Henry S. Sykes | 0 | 5 | 5 | 487th |

* - includes 1 air victory with the 49th Ftr Grp, PTO
** - includes 4 air victories with the 82nd Ftr Grp, MTO, and 1 air victory with the 479th Ftr Grp, ETO
*** - includes 7 air and 1.5 ground victories with the 355th Ftr Grp, ETO

**352nd Fighter Group Scorers**

**HdQts**

| | Air | Grd | |
|---|---|---|---|
| E.L. Clark | 2-2.33-1 | 2-0 | |
| E.D. Duncan | 0-0-1 | 0-0 | plus 328th & 487th Ftr Sqns |
| J.C. Edwards | 2-0-1 | 0-0 | |
| W.O. Jackson, Jr. | 1-0-0 | 4-4 | plus 328th & 486th Ftr Sqns |
| J.L. Mason | 5-0-2 | 0-0 | |
| J.D. Mayden | 2-0-0 | 4-2 | |
| J.C. Meyer | 11.5-0-2 | 0-0 | plus 487th Ftr Sqn |

**328th Ftr Sqn**

| | | | |
|---|---|---|---|
| E.L. Abbott | 4.75-0-1 | 1-3 | |
| L.J. Allain, Jr. | 0.5-0-0 | 0-0 | |
| C.J. Bennette | 2-0-2 | 3.5-0 | |
| E.W. Briggs | 0-2-1 | 0-0 | |
| R.C. Brookins | 4.25-0-1 | 1-0 | |
| D.S. Bryan | 13.33-0-4 | 0-0 | |
| J. Campbell | 0-0-0 | 1-1 | |
| M.M. Carlone | 0.5-0-0 | 0-0 | |
| J.G. Cartee | 0-0-0 | 0-2 | |
| F.A. Cast | 0-0-0 | 2-1 | |
| C.J. Cesky | 8.5-0-0 | 0-0 | |
| A.J. Chesser | 1-0-0 | 0-0 | |
| G.R. Clark | 3-0-0 | 0-0 | |
| J.B. Coleman | 4.33-0-0 | 2.5-1 | |
| R.L. Cornick | 1-0-0 | 0-0 | |
| E.B. Dubay | 1.5-0-0 | 0-0 | |
| E.D. Duncan | 0.5-0-0 | 2-1 | plus HdQts & 487th Ftr Sqn |
| S.E. Dyke | 1-0-0 | 2-0 | |
| L. Fieg | 0-1-0 | 0-4 | |
| W.W. Furr | 3.5-0-1 | 3-0 | |
| J.W. Galiga | 1-1-2 | 0-0 | |
| C.E. Goodman | 4.5-0-1 | 2-4 | |
| W.T. Halton | 1-0-0 | 0-1 | plus 487th Ftr Sqn |
| W.E. Hendrian | 2-0.33-0 | 2-1 | |
| F.R. Hill | 1-0-0 | 0-0 | |
| F.W. Horne | 5.5-1-0 | 1-1 | |
| A.E. Hudson | 4-0-0 | 0-0 | |
| J.C. Hurley | 1-0-0 | 1-2 | |
| L.V. Intravartola | 1-0-1 | 0-0 | |
| W.O. Jackson, Jr. | 0-1-0 | 0-0 | plus HdQts & 486th Ftr Sqn |
| E.W. James | 1-0-0 | 0-0 | |
| F.L. Kebelman, Jr. | 3-0-0 | 0-0 | |
| J.L. Laing | 0.5-0-0 | 0-0 | |
| J.F. Lambright | 1.5-0-2 | 0-0 | |
| M.V. Long | 1-0-1 | 0.5-1 | |
| D.J. Maxwell | 2-0-2 | 0-0 | |
| R.G. McAuliffe | 0.5-0-0 | 1-3 | plus 3 air w/82nd Ftr Grp, MTO |
| L.E. McCarthy | 2.5-0-2 | 0-0 | |
| G.A. Middleton | 0-0-1 | 0-0 | |
| F.W. Miller | 3-0-0 | 1-0 | |
| H.L. Miller, Jr. | 1-0-1 | 0-0 | |
| R.R. Mitchell | 1-0-0 | 0-0 | |
| W.E. Montgomery | 1-0-1 | 0-0 | |
| W.F. Parlee | 1-0-0 | 0-0 | |
| R.G. Phillips | 2-0-3 | 3-0 | |
| R.H. Powell | 0.83-0-2 | 4-3.5 | |
| G.E. Preddy | 4-1-1 | 0-0 | plus 487th Ftr Sqn |
| S.R. Price | 0-0-0 | 1-1 | |
| Q.L. Quinn | 2-1-0 | 0.5-0 | |
| G. Rayborn | 0-0-0 | 2-0 | |
| C.E. Rogers | 2-0-0 | 0-0 | |
| W.H. Sanford | 2-0-0 | 2-0 | |
| W.D. Schwenke | 1-0-0 | 0-0 | |
| R.F. Semon | 1-0-0 | 0-0 | |
| R.H. Sharp | 0.5-0-1 | 2-2.5 | |
| E.L. Smith | 1.5-0-0 | 1-1 | |
| W.J. Stangel | 5-0-0 | 0-0 | |
| E.W. Stewart | 0.83-0-1 | 0-0 | plus 7-1-3 air & 1.5-6 grd w/4th & 355th Ftr Grps |
| J.W. Stott | 1-0-0 | 0-0 | |
| J.F. Thornell, Jr. | 17.25-0-2 | 2-1 | |
| C. Vander Vean | 0-0-0 | 2-2 | |
| J.H. Walker, Jr. | 2-0-0 | 0-0 | |
| D.A. Webb, Jr. | 0-0-0 | 1-0 | |
| C.W. Weber | 0-0-0 | 4-2 | |
| H.W. White, Jr. | 2-0-0 | 0-0 | |
| E.J. Whiting | 0-1-0 | 0-0 | |
| W.D. Wilson | 0-0-1 | 0-0 | |
| F.A. Yochim | 1-1-1 | 1-0 | |
| E. Zellner | 3.25-1-0 | 2-0 | |
| D.T. Zimms | 1.33-0.33-0 | 1-0 | |

**486th Ftr Sqn**

| | | | |
|---|---|---|---|
| W.W. Anderson | 4.5-0-0 | 9-1 | |
| S.W. Andrew | 8-0-0 | 6.5-2 | plus 1 air w/49th Ftr Grp, PTO |
| E.O. Bostrom | 5-0-0 | 0-0 | |
| W.H. Brashear | 0-0-0 | 1-0 | |
| J.D. Carter | 0.5-0-0 | 5-1 | |
| T.W. Colby | 1-0-0 | 3-3 | |
| G.G. Contos | 1.5-0-0 | 0-0 | |
| M.E. Corcoran | 2-0-0 | 1-2 | |
| M.R. Cunningham | 1-0-0 | 1.5-0 | |
| F.A. Cutler | 7.5-0-0 | 3-1 | |
| H.L. Edwards | 2-0-0 | 0-0 | |

| | | | |
|---|---|---|---|
| R.C. Frascotti | 0-0-0 | 2-0 | |
| C.M. Freeman | 1-0-0 | 0-0 | |
| D.J. French | 3-0-4 | 0-0 | |
| W.T. Gerbe, Jr. | 2.5-0-0 | 0-0 | |
| J.L. Gerst | 1-0-0 | 0-0 | |
| E.J. Gignac | 1.5-0-0 | 0-0 | |
| B.J. Grabovski | 0-0-1 | 0-3 | |
| F.N. Greene | 3-0-1 | 0-0 | |
| C.E. Griffiths | 1-0-0 | 0-0 | |
| C.V. Harker | 0-0-1 | 3-3 | |
| E.L. Heller | 5.5-0-1 | 14.5-5 | |
| R.L. Henderson | 2-0-0 | 0-0 | |
| D.H. Higgins | 2.5-0-0 | 3-1 | |
| L.L. Howell | 2-0-0 | 0-1 | |
| W.O. Jackson, Jr. | 6-0-3 | 0-0 | plus HdQts & 328th Ftr Sqn |
| M.D. Johnson | 0-0-0 | 2-0 | |
| L.E. Kilgo | 0.5-0-0 | 0-0 | |
| T.R. Kyle | 0-0-1 | 0-0 | |
| E.R. Lazear, Jr. | 5-1-0 | 0-0 | |
| G.E. Lundquist | 2-0-0 | 0-0 | |
| R.G. MacKean | 0-0-0 | 5-0 | |
| A.L. Marshall | 0.5-0-0 | 0-2 | |
| J.P. McKenna | 0-0-0 | 2-3 | |
| D.W. McKibben | 1-1-0 | 1-0 | |
| E.J. Meyer | 0-0-0 | 1-2 | |
| H.J. Miklajacyk | 7.5-0-0 | 5.5-0 | |
| S.G. Miles | 1-0-0 | 3-3 | |
| R.J. Miller | 1-0-1 | 0-0 | |
| E.L. Mundell, Jr. | 3.5-0-0 | 0-0 | |
| L.W. Northrop | 2-0-0 | 0-0 | |
| C.C. Pattillo | 0-0-0 | 6-5 | |
| E.A. Paulsen | 1-1-0 | 0-0 | |
| C.D. Price | 2-0-0 | 2-3 | |
| W.C. Raub | 1-0-0 | 0-0 | |
| L.A. Rauk | 2-0-0 | 0-0 | |
| W.H. Reese | 4-0-0 | 0-0 | |
| D.M. Reichman | 2-0-0 | 0-0 | |
| L.H. Richmond | 1-0-0 | 0-0 | |
| G.A. Rushman | 0-0-0 | 2-2 | |
| J.D. Stearns | 1.5-0-0 | 0-0 | |
| M.B. Stoll | 1-0-1 | 0-0 | |
| M.J. Stover | 0-1-2 | 0-0 | |
| R.O. Swinson | 0-0-0 | 0-1 | |
| L.J. Vitek | 3.5-0-1 | 0-0 | |
| A.J. Wallace | 3-0-0 | 3-5 | |
| R.A. Wanda | 0-0-0 | 3-3 | |
| G.W. Wensch | 1-0-0 | 3-2 | |
| D.Y. Whinnem | 1-1-1 | 5-6 | |
| J.B. Whitney | 0-0-0 | 0-2 | |
| K.S. Williams | 1-0-0 | 0-1 | |

**487th Ftr Sqn**

| | | | |
|---|---|---|---|
| F.M. Allison | 1.5-0-0 | 2-3 | |
| J.B. Ayers | 0-0-0 | 2-0 | |
| H.H. Barnes | 2.5-0-2 | 0-0 | |
| J.A. Bateman | 2-0-0 | 0-0 | |
| J.R. Bennett | 2-0-3 | 1-1 | |
| R.H. Berkshire | 4.5-0-2 | 1-0 | |
| A. Bielok | 0.5-0-0 | 0-0 | |
| G.L. Bowers | 0-0-0 | 1-0 | |
| D.T. Britt | 1-0-0 | 0-0 | |
| R.K. Butler | 0.5-0-1 | 0-0 | |
| J.V. Conard | 2.5-0-0 | 0-0 | |
| C.O. Corson | 1-0-0 | 0-0 | |
| R.W. Creamer | 0-0-0 | 1-3 | |
| C.E. Davis | 5-0-0 | 4-4 | |
| W.G. Diamond | 2-0-1 | 0-0 | |
| D.K. Dilling | 3-0-0 | 0-0 | |
| K.K. Dittmer | 1-0-0 | 0-0 | |
| C.B. Doleac | 1-0-0 | 0-0 | |
| D.R. Donahue | 0.33-0-1 | 0-0 | |
| R.C. Draftz | 1-0-0 | 0-0 | |
| E.D. Duncan | 0-0-0 | 1-0 | plus HdQts & 328th Ftr Sqn |
| C.E. Ellison | 3-0-0 | 0-1 | |
| J.H. Forga, Jr. | 3-0-0 | 1-0 | |
| W.E. Fowler | 2.5-0-0 | 1-1 | |
| R.W. Frumm | 0-0-0 | 3-2 | |
| A.H. Goebel | 1-0-0 | 0-0 | |
| R.W. Graham | 0-0-0 | 0-1 | |
| J.F. Graves | 0-0-0 | 1-0 | |
| C.M. Greer | 0-0-3 | 0-2 | |
| R.L. Grow | 0.5-0-0 | 0-0 | |
| R.L. Hall | 0-0-0 | 0-2 | |
| W.T. Halton | 9.5-0-0 | 2-2 | plus 328th Ftr Sqn |
| R.W. Hamilton | 4-1-1 | 1-6 | |
| S.L. Heyer | 1-0-0 | 0-0 | |
| D.M. Huston | 2-0-0 | 1-0 | |
| N.R. Jesup | 4-0-0 | 0-0 | |
| C.O. Johnson | 2-0-0 | 6-1 | plus 5 air w/82nd Ftr Grp, MTO & 479th Ftr Grp |
| J.P. Kessler | 1.33-2-2 | 1-1 | |
| E.H. King | 0-0-0 | 0-1 | RAF pilot |
| J.C. Landrum | 0-0-0 | 1-0 | |
| R.H. Littge | 10.5-0-0 | 13-8 | |
| C.J. Luksic | 8.5-0-0 | 7-3 | |
| D.W. McIntire | 1-0-0 | 0-1 | |
| W.E. McIntyre | 1-0-0 | 0-0 | |
| E.B. McMahan | 1-0-1 | 2-0 | |
| V.K. Meroney | 9-0-1 | 0-0 | |
| J.C. Meyer | 12.5-1-0 | 13-6 | plus HdQts |
| W.C. Miller, Jr. | 1-0-2 | 0-0 | |
| S.K. Moats | 8.5-0-1 | 0-0 | |
| G.T. Moran | 13-0-3 | 3-6 | |
| M.J. Nutter | 4-0-0 | 0-0 | |
| R.G. O'Nan | 2-0-0 | 0-0 | |
| W. Padden | 0-0-0 | 2-0 | |
| C.J. Palmer | 2-0-0 | 1-0 | |
| C.A. Pattillo | 1-0-0 | 2-3 | |
| M.C. Pickering | 4-0-0 | 4-2 | |
| G.E. Preddy | 22.83-2-3 | 5-6 | plus 328th Ftr Sqn |
| J.W. Prichard | 0.5-0-0 | 0-0 | |
| R.G. Reed | 0-0-0 | 2-3 | |
| M.C. Reynolds | 0-0-0 | 2-0 | |
| C.A. Ricci | 0.5-0-0 | 0-0 | |
| A.P. Rigby | 4-0-0 | 1-0 | |
| H.S. Riley, Jr. | 1-1-0 | 0-0 | |
| R.I. Ross | 1-0-0 | 2-2 | |
| R.H. Ross | 1-0-0 | 0-0 | |
| A.F. Sears | 5-0-0 | 1-0 | |
| D.H. Schuh | 5-0-0 | 0-0 | |
| W.S. Smith | 1-0-0 | 0-0 | |
| W.E. Starck | 7-1-2 | 0-0 | |
| H.M. Stewart, II | 4-0-0 | 1-2 | |
| J.L. Sweeney | 0.5-0-0 | 0-0 | |
| H.S. Sykes | 0-0-0 | 5-2 | |
| G.P. Taylor | 1-0-0 | 0-0 | |
| J.P. Vickery | 2-0-2 | 0-0 | |
| K.M. Waldron | 3-0-1 | 7-2 | |
| P.B. Waters | 1-0-0 | 2-0 | |
| W.T. Whisner | 15.5-2-0 | 3-0 | |
| J.N. White | 1-0-0 | 3-2 | |
| J.N. Wood, Jr. | 3-0-0 | 1-0 | |

**352nd Fighter Group Scoring**

| | | | |
|---|---|---|---|
| **November 26, 1943** | | | |
| 487th: | Maj. J.C. Meyer | Me-109 dest(air) | E/Groningen |
| | | Me-109 prob(air) | E/Groningen |
| | Capt. D.K. Dilling | Me-109 dest(air) | E/Groningen |
| | Lt. J.R. Bennett | (.5)Me-109 dest(air) | E/Groningen |
| | Lt. R.H. Berkshire | (.5)Me-109 dest(air) | E/Groningen |
| **December 1, 1943** | | | |
| 487th: | Lt. V.K. Meroney | Me-109 dest(air) | S/Rheydt |
| | | (.5)Me-210 dest(air) | S/Rheydt |
| | Capt. G.E. Preddy | Me-109 dest(air) | S/Rheydt |
| | Lt. R.L. Grow | (.5)Me-210 dest(air) | S/Rheydt |
| **December 4, 1943** | | | |
| 487th: | Lt. V.K. Meroney | Me-109 dest(air) | Rotterdam-Utrecht |
| | | (.5)FW-190 dest(air) | Rotterdam-Utrecht |
| | Maj. J.C. Meyer | Me-109 dest(air) | W/Utrecht |
| | F/O J.L. Sweeney | (.5)FW-190 dest(air) | Rotterdam-Utrecht |
| **December 11, 1943** | | | |
| 328th: | Lt. R.L. Cornick | Me-110 dest(air) | Drachten |
| 487th: | Capt. D.K. Dilling | Me-110 dest(air) | Leeuwarden |
| **December 20, 1943** | | | |
| 486th: | Capt. F.N. Greene | Me-109 dest(air) | SW Emden |
| 487th: | Capt. D.K. Dilling | Me-109 dest(air) | NW Oosterwolde |
| | Capt. W.E. McIntyre | Me-109 dest(air) | NW Oosterwolde |
| | Lt. D.T. Britt | Me-109 dest(air) | NW Oosterwolde |
| | Lt. H.S. Riley | FW-190 dest(air) | NW Oosterwolde |
| **December 22, 1943** | | | |
| 328th: | Lt. J.B. Coleman | Me-110 dest(air) | Zwolle |
| | Lt. F.W. Horne | Me-110 dest(air) | Zwolle |
| | Maj. E.W. Stewart | (.5)Me-110 dest(air) | Zwolle |
| | | Me-210 dam(air) | Zwolle |
| | Lt. R.H. Powell | (.5)Me-110 dest(air) | Zwolle |
| 487th: | Maj. J.C. Meyer | Me-109 dest(air) | N/Lingen |
| | Capt. G.E. Preddy | Me-210 dest(air) | E/Zuider Zee |
| | Lt. J.R. Bennett | (.5)Me-109 dest(air) | E/Zwolle |
| | | FW-190 dam(air) | E/Zwolle |
| | Lt. E.B. McMahan | (.5)Me-109 dest(air) | E/Zwolle |
| | | FW-190 dam(air) | Lingen |
| | Lt. H.S. Riley | Me-109 prob(air) | E/Meppen |

**December 30, 1943**

| | | | |
|---|---|---|---|
| HdQts: | LtCol. E.L. Clark | (.33)Me-110 prob(air) | Chalons |
| 328th: | Lt. W.F. Hendrian | (.33)Me-110 prob(air) | Chalons |
| | Lt. D.T. Zimms | (.33)Me-110 prob(air) | Chalons |

**January 5, 1944**

| | | | |
|---|---|---|---|
| 328th: | Maj. E.W. Stewart | (.33)He-177 dest(air) | La Ferte Bernard |
| | Lt. J.B. Coleman | (.33)He-177 dest(air) | La Ferte Bernard |
| | Lt. R.H. Powell | (.33)He-177 dest(air) | La Ferte Bernard |

**January 29, 1944**

| | | | |
|---|---|---|---|
| 328th: | Lt. J.B. Coleman | Me-109 dest(air) | Pelm |
| | Lt. D.S. Bryan | (.5)FW-190 dest(air) | Namur |
| | Lt. Q.L. Quinn | (.5)FW-190 dest(air) | Namur |
| | Capt. E.L. Abbott | FW-190 dam(air) | Pelm |
| 487th: | Capt. G.E. Preddy | FW-190 dest(air) | Malmedy |
| | Lt. C.E. Davis | FW-190 dest(air) | Malmedy |
| | Lt. V.K. Meroney | FW-190 dest(air) | Malmedy |
| | Lt. W.T. Whisner | FW-190 dest(air) | Malmedy |

**January 30, 1944**

| | | | |
|---|---|---|---|
| HdQts: | LtCol. E.L. Clark | (2)Me-109 prob(air) | W/Zuider Zee |
| | | Me-109 dam(air) | W/Zuider Zee |
| 328th: | Lt. D.S. Bryan | FW-190 dest(air) | Emmen |
| | Lt. W.D. Schwenke | Me-109 dest(air) | Ruhlertwist |
| | Lt. J.F. Thornell | Me-109 dest(air) | Ruhlertwist |
| | | Me-109 dam(air) | Ruhlertwist |
| | Lt. F.W. Horne | (.5)FW-190 dest(air) | Emmen |
| | Lt. Q.L. Quinn | (.5)FW-190 dest(air) | Emmen |
| 486th: | Capt. E.J. Gignac | (.5)Me-110 dest(air) | Nordhorn |
| | Lt. A.L. Marshall | (.5)Me-110 dest(air) | Nordhorn |
| 487th: | Lt. V.K. Meroney | Me-109 dest(air) | Zwolle |
| | | Me-109 dam(air) | Zwolle |
| | Lt. R.I. Ross | Me-109 dest(air) | Zwolle |

**February 3, 1944**

| | | | |
|---|---|---|---|
| 487th: | Lt. V.K. Meroney | FW-190 dest(air) | Groningen |

**February 4, 1944**

| | | | |
|---|---|---|---|
| HdQts: | LtCol. E.L. Clark | FW-190 dest(air) | Hasselt |
| 328th: | Lt. F.W. Horne | FW-190 dest(air) | Brussels |
| | Lt. F.W. Miller | FW-190 dest(air) | Brussels |
| | Lt. J.H. Walker | FW-190 dest(air) | Hasselt |
| | Lt. F.A. Yochim | FW-190 dam(air) | Hasselt |

**February 10, 1944**

| | | | |
|---|---|---|---|
| 486th: | Capt. F.N. Greene | Me-109 dam(air) | Enschede |
| | Lt. C.V. Harker | Me-109 dam(air) | Enschede |
| | Lt. D.Y. Whinnem | Me-109 dam(air) | Enschede |
| 487th: | Lt. V.K. Meroney | Me-109 dest(air) | Hengelo |
| | Lt. W.E. Starck | Me-109 dest(air) | Arnheim |

**February 20, 1944**

| | | | |
|---|---|---|---|
| 328th: | Lt. L.E. McCarthy | (2)Me-110 dest(air) | Blankenheim |
| | | (2)Me-110 dam(air) | Blankenheim |
| | Capt. W.T. Halton | Me-109 dest(air) | Louvain |
| | Lt. H.L. Miller | Me-110 dest(air) | Blankenheim |
| | Lt. R.G. Phillips | Me-110 dest(air) | Blankenheim |
| | | Me-110 dam(air) | Blankenheim |
| | | FW-190 dam(air) | Blankenheim |
| | Capt. D.S. Bryan | (.33)Me-110 dest(air) | Vogelsand |
| | Lt. D.T. Zimms | (.33)Me-110 dest(air) | Vogelsand |
| | | (shared with Col. R.W. Osborn of the 66th Ftr Wg) | |
| | Lt. M.V. Long | FW-190 dam(air) | Vogelsand |
| 486th: | Lt. F.A. Cutler | (2)Me-109 dest(air) | Nivelles |
| | Maj. W.O. Jackson | Me-109 dest(air) | Charleroi |
| | | Me-109 dam(air) | Charleroi |
| | Lt. K.S. Williams | Me-109 dest(air) | Charleroi |

**February 21, 1944**

| | | | |
|---|---|---|---|
| 487th: | Lt. R.H. Berkshire | Me-109 dam(air) | N/Osnabruck |

**February 24, 1944**

| | | | |
|---|---|---|---|
| HdQts: | Col. J.L. Mason | Me-109 dest(air) | Schwagstorf |
| 328th: | Capt. D.S. Bryan | Me-109 dest(air) | Dummer Lake |
| | Lt. R.H. Sharp | Me-109 dam(air) | Dummer Lake |
| 487th: | Lt. G.T. Moran | Me-109 dest(air) | Enschede |
| | | Me-109 dam(air) | Enschede |
| | Lt. R.W. Hamilton | Me-109 dam(air) | Enschede |

**March 8, 1944**

| | | | |
|---|---|---|---|
| 486th: | Capt. E.J. Gignac | Me-109 dest(air) | Minden |
| 487th: | Capt. V.K. Meroney | Me-109 dest(air) | Meppen |
| | Lt. D.R. Donohue | Me-109 dam(air) | Meppen |

NOTE - Gignac flew a P-51, 487th flew P-47's

**March 15, 1944**

| | | | |
|---|---|---|---|
| 328th: | Lt. J.F. Thornell | (2)Me-109 dest(air) | Heusden |
| | Capt. D.S. Bryan | Me-109 dest(air) | Heusden |
| | Lt. F.W. Miller | Me-109 dest(air) | Heusden |
| | Lt. F.A. Yochim | Me-109 prob(air) | Heusden |
| 486th: | Capt. S.W. Andrew | Me-109 dest(air) | Aldensaal |

NOTE - all claims with P-47's

**March 16, 1944**

| | | | |
|---|---|---|---|
| 328th: | Capt. W.F. Parlee | Me-109 dest(air) | Saulx |
| 487th: | Capt. V.K. Meroney | Me-109 dest(air) | S/Bar de Luc |

**March 22, 1944**

| | | | |
|---|---|---|---|
| 328th: | Capt. E.L. Abbott | (.25)FW-200 dest(air) | Hesepe |
| | Lt. R.C. Brookins | (.25)FW-200 dest(air) | Hesepe |
| | Lt. J.F. Thornell | (.25)FW-200 dest(air) | Hesepe |
| | Lt. E. Zellner | (.25)FW-200 dest(air) | Hesepe |

**April 8, 1944**

| | | | |
|---|---|---|---|
| HdQts: | LtCol. E.L. Clark | (2)Me-210 dest(grd) | All claims were |
| 328th: | Capt. J.B. Coleman | (2)Me-110 dest(grd) | at Quackenbruck |
| | | u/i a/c dam(grd) | |
| | Capt. W.E. Hendrian | (2)Me-210 dest(grd) | |
| | | Me-210 dam(grd) | |
| | Lt. C.J. Bennette | u/i a/c dest(grd) | |
| | | (.5)Me-110 dest(grd) | |
| | Lt. W.W. Furr | Me-210 dest(grd) | |
| | Lt. F.W. Miller | Me-210 dest(grd) | |
| | Lt. R.H. Powell | Me-210 dest(grd) | |
| | | Me-210 dam(grd) | |
| | Lt. D.T. Zimms | Me-110 dest(grd) | |
| | Lt. M.V. Long | (.5)Me-110 dest(grd) | |
| | | Me-110 dam(grd) | |
| | Lt. R.C. Brookins | (.5)Me-210 dest(grd) | |
| | | (.5)u/i a/c dest(grd) | |
| | Lt. F.A. Yochim | (.5)Me-210 dest(grd) | |
| | | (.5)u/i a/c dest(grd) | |

**April 9, 1944**

| | | | |
|---|---|---|---|
| 328th: | Lt. M.V. Long | FW-190 dest(air) | Osnabruck |
| | Lt. F.A. Yochim | FW-190 dest(air) | Dummer Lake |
| | Maj. W.O. Jackson | FW-190 prob(air) | Dummer Lake |
| 487th: | Lt. C.J. Luksic | (3)Ju-88 dest(grd) | W/Dummer Lake |
| | Capt. C.E. Davis | (2)Ju-88 dest(grd) | Vechta |
| | Lt. W.T. Whisner | (2)Ju-88 dest(grd) | Vechta |
| | Lt. R.H. Berkshire | Ju-88 dest(grd) | Vechta |
| | Lt. E.B. McMahan | Ju-88 dest(grd) | Vechta |
| | Lt. C.J. Palmer | Ju-88 dest(grd) | Vechta |

NOTE: 328th flew P-47's; 487th flew P-51's

**April 10, 1944**

| | | | |
|---|---|---|---|
| 328th: | Lt. F.W. Miller | FW-190 dest(air) | Dormans |
| | Lt. J.F. Thornell | FW-190 dest(air) | Dormans |
| | Capt. D.S. Bryan | (.5)FW-190 dest(air) | Dormans |
| | Lt. J.L. Laing | (.5)FW-190 dest(air) | Dormans |
| 487th: | Maj. J.C. Meyer | Me-109 dest(air) | SW Rheims |
| | | (.5)FW-190 dest(air) | SW Rheims |
| | Lt. R.G. O'Nan | FW-190 dest(air) | SW Rheims |
| | Capt. C.E. Davis | (.5)Me-109 dest(air) | SW Rheims |
| | Lt. C.J. Luksic | (.5)FW-190 dest(air) | SW Rheims |
| | Lt. E.B. McMahan | (.5)Me-109 dest(air) | SW Rheims |

NOTE: 328th flew P-47's; 487th flew P-51's. From this date on, all claims were in Mustangs.

**April 11, 1944**

| | | | |
|---|---|---|---|
| 486th: | Lt. F.A. Cutler | (2)FW-190 dest(air) | W/Torgau |
| | | (.5)Ju-52 dest(air) | W/Torgau |
| | | Ju-88 dest(grd) | Lonnewitz |
| | | Ju-52 dam(grd) | Lonnewitz |
| | Lt. W.W. Anderson | (.5)Ju-52 dest(air) | W/Torgau |
| | | Ju-88 dest(grd) | Lonnewitz |
| | | Ju-88 dam(grd) | Lonnewitz |
| | Capt. S.W. Andrew | (2)Ju-86 dest(grd) | Finsterwalde |
| | Lt. M.E. Corcoran | Ju-88 dest(grd) | Lonnewitz |
| | | Me-109 dam(grd) | Lonnewitz |
| | | u/i a/c dam(grd) | Lonnewitz |
| | Lt. T.W. Colby | Ju-86 dest(grd) | SE Berlin |
| | | (2)Ju-86 dam(grd) | SE Berlin |
| | Lt. S.G. Miles | Ju-88 dest(grd) | SE Berlin |
| | Lt. A.L. Marshall | Ju-88 dam(grd) | Nehesdorf |
| | | u/i a/c dam(grd) | Nehesdorf |
| 487th: | Lt. C.J. Luksic | (2)Ju-88 dest(grd) | W/Berlin |
| | | Me-110 dest(grd) | W/Berlin |
| | | He-111 dest(grd) | W/Berlin |
| | | (3)Ju-88 dam(grd) | W/Berlin |
| | Maj. J.C. Meyer | (2)u/i a/c dest(grd) | SE Berlin |
| | | FW-200 dam(grd) | SE Berlin |
| | | Ju-290 dam(grd) | SE Berlin |
| | Maj. G.E. Preddy | He-111 dest(grd) | SE Berlin |
| | | He-111 dam(grd) | SE Berlin |
| | Capt. C.E. Davis | Ju-52 dest(grd) | W/Berlin |

| | | | |
|---|---|---|---|
| | Lt. F.M. Allison | Ju-88 dest(grd) | SW Berlin |
| | | Ju-88 dam(grd) | SW Berlin |
| | Lt. J.P. Kessler | FW-200 dest(grd) | SW Berlin |
| | | Ju-52 dam(grd) | SW Berlin |
| | Lt. G.T. Moran | Ju-88 dest(grd) | SE Berlin |
| | | Ar-196 dam(grd) | SE Berlin |
| | | u/i a/c dam(grd) | SE Berlin |
| | | Caudron dam(grd) | SE Berlin |
| | Lt. R.I. Ross | FW-189 dest(grd) | SW Berlin |
| | | Ju-88 dam(grd) | SW Berlin |
| | | Ju-52 dam(grd) | SW Berlin |
| | Lt. W.E. Fowler | Me-110 dam(grd) | Stendal |
| | Lt. D.W. McIntire | Ju-290 dam(grd) | SE Berlin |

**April 13, 1944**

| | | | |
|---|---|---|---|
| 486th: | Lt. R.C. Frascotti | Me-110 dest(grd) | All claims |
| | | FW-190 dest(grd) | were S/Stuttgart |
| | Lt. W.W. Anderson | Hs-123 dest(grd) | |
| | Lt. F.A. Cutler | Me-109 dest(grd) | |
| | Lt. D.Y. Whinnem | He-111 dest(grd) | |
| | Capt. S.W. Andrew | (.5)He-111 dest(grd) | |
| | Lt. M.R. Cunningham | (.5)He-111 dest(grd) | |
| | Lt. K.S. Williams | He-111 dam(grd) | |
| 487th: | Lt. R.I. Ross | Trainer dest(air) | All claims were |
| | | u/i a/c dest(grd) | SE Stuttgart |
| | Maj. J.C. Meyer | (2)He-111 dest(grd) | |
| | | Ju-52 dest(grd) | |
| | Maj. G.E. Preddy | Bu-133 dest(grd) | |
| | Lt. G.T. Moran | Ju-88 dest(grd) | |
| | | FW-190 dam(grd) | |
| | Capt. J.R. Bennett | u/i a/c dam(grd) | |

**April 15, 1944**

| | | | |
|---|---|---|---|
| 328th: | Lt. W.W. Furr | Me-110 dest(grd) | Diepholz |
| 486th: | Lt. M.E. Corcoran | (2)FW-190 dest(air) | NE Vechta |
| | Lt. A.J. Wallace | (2)FW-190 dest(air) | NE Vechta |
| | LtCol. R.H. Richmond | FW-190 dest(air) | E/Vechta |
| | Lt. M.R. Cunningham | FW-190 dest(air) | NE Vechta |
| | Lt. H.J. Miklajcyk | FW-190 dest(air) | SE Vechta |

**April 19, 1944**

| | | | |
|---|---|---|---|
| 328th: | Lt. J.F. Thornell | (2)FW-190 dest(air) | SW Kassel |
| | | FW-190 dam(air) | SW Kassel |
| 486th: | Lt. D.W. McKibben | Me-109 dest(air) | SE Kassel |

**April 20, 1944**

| | | | |
|---|---|---|---|
| 486th: | Capt. S.W. Andrew | Me-109 dest(air) | E/Paris |
| 487th: | Lt. C.J. Luksic | (1.5)Me-109 dest(air) | SE Paris |
| | Lt. A. Bielok | (.5)Me-109 dest(air) | SE Paris |
| | Maj. G.E. Preddy | Me-109 dam(air) | Beauvais-Chartres |

**April 22, 1944**

| | | | |
|---|---|---|---|
| 328th: | Capt. J.B. Coleman | (.5)Me-210 dest(grd) | Dummer Lake |
| | Lt. Q.L. Quinn | (.5)Me-210 dest(grd) | Dummer Lake |
| | Capt. W.T. Halton | Ju-188 dam(grd) | Dummer Lake |
| 487th: | Maj. G.E. Preddy | (.33)Ju-88 dest(air) | Stade A/F |
| | | Ju-52 dest(grd) | Salzwedel |
| | Lt. D.R. Donohue | (.33)Ju-88 dest(air) | Stade A/F |
| | Lt. J.P. Kessler | (.33)Ju-88 dest(air) | Stade A/F |
| | LtCol. J.C. Meyer | Me-210 dest(grd) | Stade A/F |
| | | (2)He-111 dam(grd) | Stade A/F |
| | Capt. E.B. McMahan | Ju-88 dest(grd) | Stade A/F |
| | Capt. C.E. Davis | Ju-88 dest(grd) | N/Hanover |
| | | Ju-88 dam(grd) | N/Hanover |
| | Lt. W.E. Fowler | Me-110 dest(grd) | N/Hannover |
| | Capt. R.W. Hamilton | (3)He-111 dam(grd) | Salzwedel |

**April 23, 1944**

| | | | |
|---|---|---|---|
| 486th: | Lt. D.W. McKibben | Ju-88 dest(grd) | SE Paris |
| | Lt. E.J. Meyer | Ju-88 dest(grd) | SE Paris |
| | | Me-110 dam(grd) | SE Paris |
| | Lt. E.L. Heller | (.5)Ju-52 dest(grd) | SE Paris |
| | Lt. H.J. Miklajcyk | (.5)Ju-52 dest(grd) | SE Paris |

**April 24, 1944**

| | | | |
|---|---|---|---|
| 486th: | Lt. H.J. Miklajcyk | Ju-52 dest(air) | E/Neuburg |
| | | (3)Ju-88 dest(grd) | E/Neuburg |
| | Lt. E.L. Heller | (3)Me-110 dest(grd) | Crailsheim-Bokingen |
| | | (2)Ju-88 dest(grd) | Crailsheim-Bokingen |
| | | Ju-52 dest(grd) | Crailsheim-Bokingen |
| | | u/i a/c dest(grd) | Crailsheim-Bokingen |
| | | (4)Me-110 dam(grd) | Crailsheim-Bokingen |
| | | Ju-52 dam(grd) | Crailsheim-Bokingen |
| | Capt. R.G. MacKean | (3)He-111 dest(grd) | Ingolstadt |
| | | (2)Ju-88 dest(grd) | Ingolstadt |
| | Lt. W.W. Anderson | (2)Ju-88 dest(grd) | Ingolstadt |
| | | Do-217 dest(grd) | Ingolstadt |
| | | He-111 dest(grd) | Neuburg |
| | Lt. C.V. Harker | Do-217 dest(grd) | Ingolstadt |
| | | Me-410 dest(grd) | Neuburg |
| | | Ju-88 dam(grd) | Neuburg |
| | Lt. A.J. Wallace | Do-217 dest(grd) | Neuburg |
| | | Ju-88 dest(grd) | Ingolstadt |
| | | (4)Ju-88 dam(grd) | Ingolstadt |
| | | Me-109 dam(grd) | Neuburg |
| | Lt. T.W. Colby | (2)He-177 dest(grd) | Ingolstadt |
| | | u/i a/c dam(grd) | Ingolstadt |
| | Lt. D.Y. Whinnem | (2)Ju-88 dest(grd) | Ingolstadt |
| | | (6)Ju-88 dam(grd) | Ingolstadt |
| | Capt. S.W. Andrew | u/i a/c dest(grd) | Neuburg |
| | | Ju-88 dam(grd) | Ingolstadt |
| | Lt. S.G. Miles | Me-110 dest(grd) | Ingolstadt |
| | | (3)u/i a/c dam(grd) | Ingolstadt |

**April 25, 1944**

| | | | |
|---|---|---|---|
| 486th: | Capt. S.W. Andrew | Ju-88 dest(grd) | Metz |
| | Lt. M.R. Cunningham | Hs-129 dest(grd) | Metz |
| | Lt. C.V. Harker | Me-110 dest(grd) | Metz |
| | Lt. H.J. Miklajcyk | Hs-129 dest(grd) | Metz |
| | Lt. S.G. Miles | FW-190 dest(grd) | Metz |
| | Lt. A.J. Wallace | Hs-129 dest(grd) | Metz |

**April 28, 1944**

| | | | |
|---|---|---|---|
| 328th: | Lt. R.H. Powell | Ju-88 dest(grd) | Herbeuville |
| | | (.5)Ju-88 dam(grd) | Avord A/F |
| | Capt. R.H. Sharp | (.5)Ju-88 dam(grd) | Avord A/F |
| 486th: | Capt. S.W. Andrew | FW-200 dest(grd) | Chateaudun |
| | Lt. E.J. Miller | Ju-88 dam(grd) | Orleans-Bricy |
| 487th: | Capt. R.W. Hamilton | Ju-88 dest(grd) | Bourges |
| | | He-111 dam(grd) | Bourges |
| | Lt. F.M. Allison | He-111 dest(grd) | Bourges |
| | | u/i a/c dam(grd) | Bourges |
| | Lt. M.C. Pickering | Ju-88 dest(grd) | Bourges |
| | | He-111 dam(grd) | Bourges |
| | Maj. G.E. Preddy | He-111 dam(grd) | Bourges |

**April 29, 1944**

| | | | |
|---|---|---|---|
| 328th: | Capt. E.L. Abbott | Me-109 dest(air) | Neuhaldensleben |
| | | Glider dam(grd) | Burg |
| | Lt. S.E. Dyke | (.5)FW-190 dest(air) | Calvorde |
| | Lt. F.W. Horne | (.5)FW-190 dest(air) | Calvorde |
| | Lt. L. Fieg | u/i a/c dam(grd) | Burg |

**April 30, 1944**

| | | | |
|---|---|---|---|
| 486th: | Lt. W.W. Anderson | FW-190 dest(air) | All claims were |
| | | (2)Me-110 dest(grd) | at Clermont- |
| | Capt. S.W. Andrew | FW-190 dest(air) | Berrand A/F |
| 487th: | Lt. W.T. Whisner | FW-190 dest(air) | |
| | Capt. C.E. Davis | (3)u/i a/c dam(grd) | |
| | Lt. R.L. Hall | (2)u/i a/c dam(grd) | |

**May 8, 1944**

| | | | |
|---|---|---|---|
| HdQts: | Col. J.L. Mason | FW-190 dest(air) | N/Nienburg |
| | | FW-190 dam(air) | N/Nienburg |
| | LtCol. J.C. Edwards | FW-190 dam(air) | Nienburg |
| 328th: | Lt. J.F. Thornell | (3)Me-109 dest(air) | Nienburg |
| | Lt. R.G. Phillips | Me-109 dest(air) | SE Nienburg |
| | Lt. Q.L. Quinn | Me-109 dest(air) | NW Bremen |
| | | FW-190 prob(air) | E/Bremen |
| | Lt. J.W. Galiga | FW-190 prob(air) | Nienburg |
| | Lt. F.W. Horne | FW-190 prob(air) | E/Bremen |
| | Lt. E.J. Whiting | Me-109 prob(air) | Unter Lusz |
| | Lt. H.L. Miller | Me-109 dam(air) | NE Bremen |
| 486th: | Capt. F.A. Cutler | (2)Me-109 dest(air) | Gifhorn |
| | | u/i a/c dest(grd) | Gifhorn |
| | Lt. E.L. Heller | (2)Me-109 dest(air) | Gifhorn |
| | Maj. S.W. Andrew | FW-190 dest(air) | NE Hanover |
| 487th: | Lt. C.J. Luksic | (3)FW-190 dest(air) | Brunswick |
| | | (2)Me-109 dest(air) | Brunswick |
| | Capt. C.E. Davis | (3)Me-109 dest(air) | Brunswick |
| | | (.5)FW-190 dest(air) | Brunswick |
| | LtCol. J.C. Meyer | (3)Me-109 dest(air) | Hanover-Brunswick Bremen |
| | Lt. R.G. O'Nan | Me-109 dest(air) | NE Brunswick |
| | Lt. M.C. Pickering | FW-190 dest(air) | Nienburg |
| | Lt. W.E. Fowler | (.5)FW-190 dest(air) | Brunswick |

**May 12, 1944**

| | | | |
|---|---|---|---|
| 328th: | Lt. G.R. Clark | Me-109 dest(air) | Coburg |
| | Lt. J.W. Galiga | (.5)Me-109 dest(air)* | Coburg |
| 486th: | Maj. S.W. Andrew | FW-190 dest(air) | Gotha |
| 487th: | Capt. F.M. Allison | (1.5)Me-109 dest(air)** | SE Coblenz |
| | | Me-109 dam(grd) | SE Coblenz |
| | LtCol. J.C. Meyer | Me-109 dest(air) | SW Frankfurt |
| | | He-177 dest(grd) | SW Frankfurt |
| | Lt. D.W. McEntire | Me-109 dest(air) | SE Coblenz |
| | Lt. R.K. Butler | (.5)Me-109 dest(air)** | SE Coblenz |
| | Lt. H.H. Barnes | (.5)Me-109 dest(air)* | Coburg |
| | Lt. W.T. Whisner | Ju-52 dest(grd) | Frankenhausen |
| | Maj. G.E. Preddy | (3)u/i a/c dam(grd) | Frankenhausen |

**May 13, 1944**

| Unit | Pilot | Claim | Location |
|---|---|---|---|
| HdQts: | Col. J.L. Mason | (2)Me-109 dest(air) | Demmin-Friedland |
| | | FW-190 dest(air) | Demmin-Friedland |
| | | Me-109 dam(air) | Demmin-Friedland |
| 328th: | Capt. J.B. Coleman | (2)Me-109 dest(air) | Demmin |
| | Lt. F.W. Horne | (2)FW-190 dest(air) | Demmin |
| 486th: | Capt. W.W. Anderson | Me-109 dest(air) | Tribsees |
| | | u/i a/c dest(grd) | Wangerooge |
| | Capt. F.A. Cutler | Me-109 dest(air) | Neubrandenburg |
| | Capt. F.N. Greene | Me-109 dest(air) | Tribsees |
| | Capt. D.H. Higgins | Me-109 dest(air) | Tribsees |
| | Lt. S.G. Miles | Me-109 dest(air) | Tribsees |
| 487th: | Maj. G.E. Preddy | (2)Me-109 dest(air) | Neubrandenburg |
| | Lt. M.J. Nutter | Me-109 dest(air) | Neubrandenburg |
| | Lt. C.J. Luksic | (.5)Ju-88 dest(air) | E/Neubrandenburg |
| | Lt. G.T. Moran | (.5)Ju-88 dest(air) | E/Neubrandenburg |

**May 19, 1944**

| Unit | Pilot | Claim | Location |
|---|---|---|---|
| HdQts: | LtCol. E.L. Clark | Me-109 dest(air) | NW Wittenburg |
| 328th: | Lt. R.C. Brookins | Me-109 dest(air) | Wittenburg-Havelburg |
| | Capt. R.H. Sharp | (.5)Me-109 dest(air)[*] | Wittenburg |
| | Lt. M.M. Carlone | (.5)Me-109 dest(air)[*] | Wittenburg |
| | Lt. E. Zellner | (.5)Me-109 dest(air) | Wittenburg |
| | | (shared with a 359th Ftr Grp P-51) | |
| | | Me-109 prob(air) | Wittenburg |
| 486th: | Maj. S.W. Andrew | Me-109 dest(air) | Rathenow |
| | Lt. T.W. Colby | Me-109 dest(air) | Rathenow |
| 487th: | Lt. C.J. Luksic | Me-109 dest(air) | Ludwigslust |
| | Lt. G.T. Moran | Me-109 dest(air) | Ludwigslust |
| | Lt. J.P. Kessler | Me-109 prob(air) | Ludwigslust |
| | | Me-109 dam(air) | Ludwigslust |

**May 21, 1944**

| Unit | Pilot | Claim | Location |
|---|---|---|---|
| 328th: | Lt. R.G. Phillips | FW-190 dest(grd) | All claims |
| | | Ju-52 dest(grd) | were at Alt |
| | | u/i a/c dest(grd) | Ruppin |
| | Capt. R.H. Sharp | (2)Ju-88 dest(grd) | |
| | | He-111 dam(grd) | |
| | | u/i a/c dam(grd) | |
| | Lt. C.J. Bennette | He-111 dest(grd) | |
| | | u/i a/c dest(grd) | |
| | Lt. S.E. Dyke | (2)He-111 dest(grd) | |
| | Lt. R.H. Powell | (2)He-111 dest(grd) | |
| | | (2)He-111 dam(grd) | |
| | Lt. G. Rayborn | (2)He-111 dest(grd) | |
| | Lt. J.F. Thornell | (2)He-111 dest(grd) | |
| | | He-177 dam(grd) | |
| | Lt. E. Zellner | (2)Ju-86 dest(grd) | |
| | Capt. E.L. Abbott | u/i a/c dest(grd) | |
| | | (2)u/i a/c dam(grd) | |
| | Lt. J. Campbell | He-111 dest(grd) | |
| | | Do-217 dam(grd) | |
| | Lt. W.W. Furr | Ju-52 dest(grd) | |
| | Lt. F.W. Horne | u/i a/c dest(grd) | |
| | | He-111 dam(grd) | |
| | Lt. E.L. Smith | He-111 dest(grd) | |
| | | u/i a/c dam(grd) | |
| | Lt. L. Fieg | (3)u/i a/c dam(grd) | |

**May 24, 1944**

| Unit | Pilot | Claim | Location |
|---|---|---|---|
| 328th: | Lt. W.W. Furr | Me-109 dest(air) | W/Perleberg |
| | Lt. E. Zellner | Me-109 dest(air) | W/Perleberg |
| 486th: | Capt. W.W. Anderson | Me-109 dest(air) | NW Berlin |
| | Lt. J.L. Gerst | Me-109 dest(air) | NW Berlin |

**May 27, 1944**

| Unit | Pilot | Claim | Location |
|---|---|---|---|
| HdQts: | LtCol. J.C. Edwards | Me-109 dest(air) | Karlsruhe |
| 328th: | Lt. J.F. Thornell | (2)Me-109 dest(air) | S/Strasbourg |
| | Lt. E. Zellner | Me-109 dest(air) | S/Strasbourg |
| | | (.5)FW-190 dest(air) | S/Strasbourg |
| | | (shared with a 357th Ftr Grp P-51) | |
| | Lt. W.W. Furr | Me-109 dest(air) | S/Strasbourg |
| | | Me-109 dam(air) | S/Strasbourg |
| | Lt. D.T. Zimms | Me-109 dest(air) | S/Strasbourg |
| 487th: | Lt. R.H. Berkshire | (2)Me-109 dest(air) | Strasbourg |
| | Lt. G.T. Moran | (2)Me-109 dest(air) | Strasbourg |
| | Capt. R.W. Hamilton | FW-190 dest(air) | Strasbourg |
| | | FW-190 prob(air) | Strasbourg |
| | Capt. W.E. Starck | Me-109 dest(air) | Strasbourg |

**May 28, 1944**

| Unit | Pilot | Claim | Location |
|---|---|---|---|
| 328th: | Capt. H.W. White | FW-190 dest(air) | W/Magdeburg |
| | Lt. J.F. Thornell | Me-109 dest(air) | W/Magdeburg |
| | Lt. R.G. Phillips | Me-109 dam(air) | W/Magdeburg |
| 486th: | Lt. E.L. Heller | (1.5)Me-109 dest(air) | Dessau & Magdeburg |
| | | (.5) (shared with a 4th Ftr Grp P-51) | |
| | Maj. S.W. Andrew | Me-109 dest(air) | NE Dessau |
| | Capt. W.W. Anderson | Me-109 dest(air) | Dessau |
| | Lt. L.L. Howell | Me-109 dest(air) | Dessau |
| 487th: | Lt. H.H. Barnes | Me-109 dest(air) | W/Leipzig |
| | | Me-109 dam(air) | W/Leipzig |

**May 29, 1944**

| Unit | Pilot | Claim | Location |
|---|---|---|---|
| 328th: | Lt. J.F. Thornell | (2)Me-109 dest(air) | N/Neubrandenburg |
| | Capt. E.L. Abbott | Me-109 dest(air) | N/Neubrandenburg |
| 487th: | Lt. G.T. Moran | (1.5)Me-109 dest(air) | Gustrow & (.5) Wolgast |
| | | FW-190 dest(air) | Gustrow |
| | Lt. W.T. Whisner | FW-190 dest(air) | Gustrow |
| | Lt. J.V. Conard | (.5)Me-109 dest(air) | Wolgast |
| | Lt. R.K. Butler | Me-109 dam(air) | Gustrow |
| | Capt. R.W. Hamilton | (2)u/i a/c dam(grd) | Jasmunder Bay |

**May 30, 1944**

| Unit | Pilot | Claim | Location |
|---|---|---|---|
| 328th: | Lt. W.W. Furr | (1.5)FW-190 dest(air) | Schoningen |
| | | (shared with an unknown P-51 pilot) | |
| | Lt. R.C. Brookins | Me-109 dest(air) | Halberstadt |
| 486th: | Maj. S.W. Andrew | FW-190 dest(air) | Magdeburg |
| 487th: | Maj. G.E. Preddy | (2.5)Me-109 dest(air) | Magdeburg |
| | Lt. R.H. Berkshire | Me-109 dest(air) | Magdeburg |
| | | FW-190 dest(air) | Ulzen |
| | Lt. G.T. Moran | Me-109 dest(air) | Ulzen |
| | | FW-190 dest(air) | Ulzen |
| | | FW-190 dam(air) | Ulzen |
| | Capt. J.P. Kessler | Me-109 dest(air) | Halberstadt |
| | | Me-109 prob(air) | Halberstadt |
| | Capt. C.J. Palmer | FW-190 dest(air) | Halberstadt |
| | Lt. H.H. Barnes | Me-109 dest(air) | N/Halberstadt |
| | Lt. M.C. Pickering | FW-190 dest(air) | Halberstadt |
| | Lt. W.T. Whisner | (.5)Me-109 dest(air) | Magdeburg |

**June 6, 1944**

| Unit | Pilot | Claim | Location |
|---|---|---|---|
| 328th: | Lt. R.C. Brookins | FW-190 dest(air) | SE Rouen |
| | | FW-190 dam(air) | SE Rouen |
| | Lt. L.J. Allain | (.5)FW-190 dest(air) | SE Rouen |
| | Lt. F.W. Horne | (.5)FW-190 dest(air) | SE Rouen |

**June 8, 1944**

| Unit | Pilot | Claim | Location |
|---|---|---|---|
| 486th: | Lt. D.Y. Whinnem | (2)FW-190 dest(grd) | Le Mans |
| | Maj. S.W. Andrew | FW-190 dam(grd) | Le Mans |

**June 10, 1944**

| Unit | Pilot | Claim | Location |
|---|---|---|---|
| 328th: | Lt. J.F. Thornell | (2)Me-109 dest(air) | Bayeaux |
| | Lt. C.J. Bennette | Me-109 dest(air) | Bayeaux |
| | | Me-109 dam(air) | Bayeaux |
| 487th: | Lt. H.H. Barnes | Me-109 dam(air) | NW Mortain |

**June 12, 1944**

| Unit | Pilot | Claim | Location |
|---|---|---|---|
| 328th: | Lt. L.E. McCarthy | (.5)Me-109 dest(air) | S/St. Malo |
| | Lt. J.F. Thornell | (.5)Me-109 dest(air) | S/St. Malo |
| 487th: | Maj. G.E. Preddy | Me-109 dest(air) | SW Rennes |
| | Lt. G.T. Moran | Me-109 dest(air) | SW Rennes |

**June 15, 1944**

| Unit | Pilot | Claim | Location |
|---|---|---|---|
| 328th: | Lt. G.A. Middleton | FW-190 dam(air) | Laigle |

**June 20, 1944**

| Unit | Pilot | Claim | Location |
|---|---|---|---|
| 486th: | Lt. L.L. Howell | Me-109 dest(air) | Magdeburg |
| | | He-177 dam(grd) | N/Burg |
| | Lt. W.C. Raub | Me-109 dest(air) | Magdeburg |
| | Maj. S.W. Andrew | Ju-52 dest(grd) | N/Burg |
| | Lt. W.H. Brashear | Ju-88 dest(grd) | N/Burg |
| 487th: | Maj. G.E. Preddy | FW-190 dest(air) | E/Bernburg |
| | | (.5)Me-410 dest(air) | E/Bernburg |
| | Lt. J.N. Wood | (.5)Me-410 dest(air) | E/Bernburg |
| | Capt. W.E. Starck | FW-190 prob(air) | NW Magdeburg |
| | Lt. R.H. Berkshire | Me-410 dam(air) | Magdeburg |

**June 21, 1944**

| Unit | Pilot | Claim | Location |
|---|---|---|---|
| 328th: | Lt. S.E. Dyke | (.5)Me-410 dest(air)[*] | Dahmsdorf |
| | Lt. J.F. Thornell | (.5)Me-410 dest(air)[*] | Dahmsdorf |
| | Lt. J.W. Galiga | (.5)Me-410 dest(air)[**] | Dahmsdorf |
| | Lt. E.L. Smith | (.5)Me-410 dest(air)[**] | Dahmsdorf |
| | Lt. E.W. Briggs | Me-410 dam(air) | Dahmsdorf |
| | Lt. D.J. Maxwell | Me-410 dam(air) | Dahmsdorf |
| | Lt. R.H. Powell | Me-410 dam(air) | Dahmsdorf |
| 486th: | Lt. L.W. Northrop | (2)Me-109 dest(air) | E/Warsaw |
| | Lt. E.L. Heller | Me-109 dest(air) | Brest-Litovsk |
| | Lt. D.Y. Whinnem | Me-109 dest(air) | E/Warsaw |
| 487th: | Maj. G.E. Preddy | Me-109 dest(air) | E/Magdeburg |
| | Lt. G.T. Moran | Me-109 dest(air) | E/Magdeburg |
| | Lt. C.M. Greer | Me-109 dam(air) | E/Magdeburg |

**June 25, 1944**

| Unit | Pilot | Claim | Location |
|---|---|---|---|
| 487th: | Lt. G.T. Moran | Me-109 dest(air) | Soissons |
| | | Me-109 dam(air) | Soissons |

**June 27, 1944**

| Unit | Pilot | Claim | Location |
|---|---|---|---|
| 487th: | Lt. J.V. Conard | (2)FW-190 dest(air) | N/Noyon |
| | Lt. C.O. Corson | FW-190 dest(air) | N/Noyon |
| | Lt. A.F. Sears | FW-190 dest(air) | N/Noyon |

**June 29, 1944**

| | | | |
|---|---|---|---|
| 487th: | Maj. G.E. Preddy | Ju-52 dest(grd) | Burg A/F |
| | Lt. G.T. Moran | Ju-52 dest(grd) | Burg A/F |
| | Lt. M.C. Pickering | He-111 dest(grd) | Burg A/F |
| | | Me-110 dam(grd) | Burg A/F |
| | Lt. J.N. Wood | He-111 dest(grd) | Burg A/F |

**July 1, 1944**

| | | | |
|---|---|---|---|
| 328th: | Lt. R.H. Powell | Me-109 dam(air) | Bethune |
| 487th: | Capt. W.E. Starck | Me-109 dest(air) | St. Quentin |
| | | Me-109 dam(air) | St. Quentin |
| | Lt. C.M. Greer | Me-109 dam(air) | St. Quentin |

**July 2, 1944**

| | | | |
|---|---|---|---|
| 486th: | Capt. D.H. Higgins | FW-190 dest(air) | Budapest |
| | | (.5)Me-109 dest(air) | W/Budapest |
| | | (shared with a 4th Ftr Grp P-51) | |

**July 13, 1944**

| | | | |
|---|---|---|---|
| HdQts: | LtCol. J.C. Edwards | Me-109 dest(air) | SE Strasbourg |
| 487th: | Lt. C.M. Greer | Me-109 dam(air) | E/Schweighausen |

**July 18, 1944**

| | | | |
|---|---|---|---|
| 328th: | Capt. H.W. White | Me-109 dest(air) | Wismar |
| | Lt. F.L. Kebelman | Me-109 dest(air) | Wismar |
| | Lt. E.L. Smith | Me-109 dest(air) | Wismar |
| | Lt. J.W. Galiga | (2)Ju-88 dam(air) | Wismar |
| | Lt. W.D. Wilson | Me-109 dam(air) | Wismar |
| | F/O W.E. Montgomery | Ju-88 dam(air) | Wismar |
| 486th: | Maj. W.O. Jackson | Me-109 dest(air) | N/Warnemunde |
| | | Ju-88 dest(air) | N/Warnemunde |
| | Lt. E.O. Bostrom | Ju-88 dest(air) | SE Warnemunde |
| | Lt. D.J. French | Me-410 dest(air) | NE Berlin |
| | | (3)Me-410 dam(air) | NE Berlin |
| | Lt. R.J. Miller | Me-410 dest(air) | S/Rostock |
| | | Me-410 dam(air) | S/Rostock |
| | Lt. D.M. Reichman | Ju-88 dest(air) | S/Rostock |
| | Lt. M.B. Stoll | Ju-88 dest(air) | N/Warnemunde |
| | Lt. D.W. McKibben | Me-109 prob(air) | N/Warnemunde |
| | Lt. M.J. Stover | Me-109 dam(air) | NE Berlin |
| 487th: | Maj. G.E. Preddy | (2)Ju-88 dest(air) | NE Rostock |
| | | Me-109 dest(air) | NE Rostock |
| | | Ju-88 prob(air) | NE Rostock |
| | | (2)Ju-88 dam(air) | NE Rostock |
| | Lt. C.E. Ellison | (3)Ju-88 dest(air) | SE Rostock |
| | Lt. W.E. Fowler | (2)Me-109 dest(air) | Demmin |
| | Lt. S.K. Moats | Me-109 dest(air) | SE Rostock |
| | Lt. J.P. Vickery | (2)Ju-88 dam(air) | NE Rostock |
| | Capt. J.P. Kessler | Me-109 dam(air) | NE Rostock |

**July 19, 1944**

| | | | |
|---|---|---|---|
| 486th: | Capt. L.A. Rauk | (2)Me-109 dest(air) | E/Munich |
| | Lt. E.L. Mundell | (2)Me-109 dest(air) | E/Munich |
| | Lt. L.J. Vitek | (2)Me-109 dest(air) | Munich |
| | | Me-109 dam(air) | Munich |
| | Maj. W.O. Jackson | Me-109 dest(air) | E/Munich |
| | Lt. E.R. Lazear | Me-109 prob(air) | NE Munich |
| 487th: | Lt. R.C. Draftz | Me-109 dest(air) | Wolfratshausen |

**July 20, 1944**

| | | | |
|---|---|---|---|
| 487th: | Maj. G.E. Preddy | Me-410 dest(grd) | Nordhausen |
| | | He-111 dam(grd) | Nordhausen |
| | Lt. C.M. Greer | (2)He-111 dam(grd) | Nordhausen |
| | Lt. R.W. Graham | He-111 dam(grd) | Nordhausen |

**July 21, 1944**

| | | | |
|---|---|---|---|
| 487th: | Capt. W.E. Starck | Me-109 dest(air) | E/Munich |
| | Lt. M.C. Pickering | Me-109 dest(air) | E/Munich |
| | Maj. G.E. Preddy | (.5)Me-109 dest(air) | E/Munich |
| | Lt. S.K. Moats | (.5)Me-109 dest(air) | E/Munich |

**July 29, 1944**

| | | | |
|---|---|---|---|
| 328th: | Lt. C.J. Bennette | Me-109 dest(air) | Merseburg |
| | | Me-109 dam(air) | Merseburg |
| | Lt. C.J. Cesky | FW-190 dest(air) | Merseburg |
| 486th: | Maj. G.E. Lundquist | (2)Me-109 dest(air) | Magdeburg |
| 487th: | Maj. G.E. Preddy | Me-109 dest(air) | Naumburg |
| | Capt. C.J. Palmer | Me-109 dest(air) | Merseburg |
| | Lt. S.K. Moats | Me-109 dest(air) | Merseburg |
| | Lt. A.F. Sears | Me-109 dest(air) | W/Naumburg |

**August 5, 1944**

| | | | |
|---|---|---|---|
| 486th: | Lt. D.J. French | (2)Me-109 dest(air) | Wilhelmshaven |
| | | Me-109 dam(air) | Wilhelmshaven |
| | Lt. D.Y. Whinnem | Me-109 prob(air) | S/Hamburg |
| | | Me-109 dam(air) | S/Hamburg |
| 487th: | Maj. G.E. Preddy | Me-109 dest(air) | S/Hamburg |
| | | Me-109 prob(air) | S/Hamburg |
| | Lt. G.T. Moran | Me-109 dest(air) | S/Hamburg |
| | Lt. A.F. Sears | Me-109 dest(air) | S/Hamburg |
| | Lt. G.P. Taylor | Me-109 dest(air) | S/Hamburg |

**August 6, 1944**

| | | | |
|---|---|---|---|
| 328th: | Lt. C.J. Cesky | (2)Me-109 dest(air) | E/Luneburg |
| 486th: | Capt. H.J. Miklajcyk | (2)Me-109 dest(air) | SE Hamburg |
| 487th: | Maj. G.E. Preddy | (6)Me-109 dest(air) | Luneburg-Havelburg |
| | F/O C.B. Doleac | Me-109 dest(air) | Hamburg |
| | Lt. S.L. Heyer | Me-109 dest(air) | Hamburg |

**August 16, 1944**

| | | | |
|---|---|---|---|
| 328th: | Capt. W.E. Hendrian | (.5)Me-109 dest(air) | W/Mehlis |
| | Lt. C.J. Cesky | (.5)Me-109 dest(air) | W/Mehlis |
| 486th: | Capt. A.J. Wallace | Me-109 dest(air) | Eisenach |
| 487th: | Lt. M.C. Pickering | FW-190 dest(air) | Plauen |

**August 25, 1944**

| | | | |
|---|---|---|---|
| 487th: | LtCol. J.C. Meyer | He-177 dest(grd) | All claims are |
| | | Ju-52 dest(grd) | at Neubrandenburg |
| | | (2)u/i a/c dam(grd) | |
| | Lt. R.H. Littge | (2)Me-210 dest(grd) | |
| | | Me-109 dam(grd) | |
| | Capt. C.O. Johnson | He-177 dest(grd) | |
| | | Hs-129 dam(grd) | |
| | Lt. J.H. Forga | Me-109 dest(grd) | |
| | Lt. C.E. Ellison | Me-110 dam(grd) | |
| | Lt. G.T. Moran | Me-210 dam(grd) | |
| | | Caudron dam(grd) | |
| | F/Lt. E.H. King | Me-109 dam(grd) | |

**September 10, 1944**

| | | | |
|---|---|---|---|
| 487th: | Capt. C.O. Johnson | (5)Ju-52 dest(grd) | All claims are |
| | LtCol. J.C. Meyer | (3)Ju-52 dest(grd) | at Wertheim |
| | | u/i a/c dest(grd) | |
| | Lt. J.B. Ayers | Ju-52 dest(grd) | |
| | | u/i a/c dest(grd) | |
| | Lt. M.C. Pickering | (2)u/i a/c dest(grd) | |
| | Lt. P.B. Waters | (2)Ju-52 dest(grd) | |
| | Capt. J.R. Bennett | Ju-52 dest(grd) | |
| | Lt. G.L. Bowers | Ju-52 dest(grd) | |
| | Lt. D.M. Huston | Ju-52 dest(grd) | |
| | Lt. J.C. Landrum | Ju-52 dest(grd) | |
| | Lt. A.P. Rigby | u/i a/c dest(grd) | |

**September 11, 1944**

| | | | |
|---|---|---|---|
| 328th: | Capt. W.E. Hendrian | FW-190 dest(air) | E/Meiningen |
| | Lt. R.F. Semon | FW-190 dest(air) | E/Meiningen |
| 487th: | LtCol. J.C. Meyer | (3)Me-109 dest(air) | Gottingen-Nordhausen-Muhlhausen |
| | | FW-190 dest(air) | same as above |
| | Lt. J.H. Forga | (2)FW-190 dest(air) | Gottingen |
| | | Me-109 dest(air) | Gottingen |
| | Capt. C.O. Johnson | (2)Me-109 dest(air) | Gottingen |
| | Capt. J.R. Bennett | FW-190 dest(air) | Gottingen-Nordhausen-Muhlhausen |
| | | (2)Me-109 dam(air) | same as above |
| | Lt. D.H. Schuh | Me-109 dest(air) | Einbeck-Gottingen |
| | Lt. P.B. Waters | FW-190 dest(air) | Gottingen |
| | Lt. R.H. Littge | (2)Ju-88 dest(grd) | Gotha |
| | | (2)Ju-88 dam(grd) | Gotha |
| | Lt. A.F. Sears | u/i a/c dest(grd) | Langensalza |
| | Lt. H.M. Stewart | Ju-88 dest(grd) | Gotha |
| | | (2)Ju-88 dam(grd) | Gotha |

**September 12, 1944**

| | | | |
|---|---|---|---|
| 328th: | Lt. C.J. Cesky | FW-190 dest(air) | N/Pritzwalk |
| | Lt. J.W. Stott | FW-190 dest(air) | N/Pritzwalk |
| 486th: | Lt. E.R. Lazear | (3)Me-109 dest(air) | Kyritz |
| | Lt. W.T. Gerbe | (2)Me-109 dest(air) | Kyritz |
| | Capt. H.J. Miklajcyk | (1.5)FW-190 dest(air) | Kustrin |
| | | Ju-52 dest(grd) | Kustrin |
| | Lt. J.D. Carter | (.5)FW-190 dest(air) | Kustrin |
| | Lt. E.O. Bostrom | FW-190 dest(air) | Berlin |
| | Lt. C.M. Freeman | Me-109 dest(air) | Kyritz |
| | Lt. J.D. Stearns | FW-190 dest(air) | S/Havelburg |
| | Lt. G.W. Wensch | Me-109 dest(air) | Kyritz |
| | Lt. T.R. Kyle | Me-109 dam(air) | NW Berlin |
| | Lt. M.B. Stoll | Me-109 dam(air) | Havelburg |

**September 27, 1944**

| | | | |
|---|---|---|---|
| 328th: | Capt. D.S. Bryan | (2)Me-109 dest(air) | NW Frankfurt |
| | | Me-109 dam(air) | NW Frankfurt |
| | Lt. R.C. Brookins | FW-190 dest(air) | NW Frankfurt |
| | F/O W.E. Montgomery | Me-109 dest(air) | NW Frankfurt |

**November 1, 1944**

| | | | |
|---|---|---|---|
| 486th: | Lt. W.T. Gerbe | (.5)Me-262 dest(air) | Arnheim-Hengelo |
| | | (shared with a 56th Ftr Grp P-47) | |

**November 2, 1944**

| | | | |
|---|---|---|---|
| HdQts: | LtCol. J.D. Mayden | Me-109 dest(air) | Merseburg |
| 328th: | Capt. D.S. Bryan | (5)Me-109 dest(air) | All claims are |
| | | (2)Me-109 dam(air) | at Merseburg |
| | Lt. A.E. Hudson | (4)Me-109 dest(air) | |
| | Lt. C.E. Goodman | (3)Me-109 dest(air) | |

| | | | |
|---|---|---|---|
| | Capt. W.J. Stangel | (2)Me-109 dest(air) | |
| | | (.5)Me-109 dest(air) | |
| | | (.5)Me-109 dest(air) | |
| | Maj. E.L. Abbott | (2)Me-109 dest(air) | |
| | Lt. G.R. Clark | (2)Me-109 dest(air) | |
| | Lt. C.E. Rogers | (2)Me-109 dest(air) | |
| | Maj. G.E. Preddy | Me-109 dest(air) | |
| | Lt. F.R. Hill | Me-109 dest(air) | |
| | Lt. E.W. James | (.5)Me-109 dest(air) | |
| | | (.5)Me-109 dest(air) | |
| | Lt. D.J. Maxwell | Me-109 dest(air) | |
| | Lt. E.W. Briggs | Me-109 prob(air) | |
| 486th: | Capt. H.J. Miklajcyk | Me-109 dest(air) | Merseburg |
| | | FW-190 dest(air) | Merseburg |
| | Lt. E.O. Bostrom | (2)Me-109 dest(air) | W/Halle |
| | Lt. H.L. Edwards | Me-109 dest(air) | Merseburg |
| | Lt. L.J. Vitek | Me-109 dest(air) | SW Merseburg |
| | LtCol. W.O. Jackson | Me-109 dam(air) | N/Merseburg |
| | | FW-190 dam(air) | N/Merseburg |
| 487th: | Lt. J.P. Vickery | (2)Me-109 dest(air) | Merseburg |
| | Capt. W.T. Halton | Me-109 dest(air) | E/Merseburg |
| | Capt. W.T. Whisner | Me-109 dest(air) | Merseburg |
| | Lt. N.R. Jesup | FW-190 dest(air) | Merseburg |
| | Lt. D.H. Schuh | Me-109 dest(air) | Merseburg |
| | Lt. K.M. Waldron | Me-109 dest(air) | Merseburg |
| | Lt. J.N. Wood | Me-109 dest(air) | E/Merseburg |

**November 21, 1944**

| | | | |
|---|---|---|---|
| HdQts: | LtCol. J.C. Meyer | (3)FW-190 dest(air) | SW Merseburg |
| 328th: | Lt. F.L. Kebelman | (2)Me-109 dest(air) | Merseburg |
| | Maj. G.E. Preddy | FW-190 dest(air) | Merseburg |
| | | FW-190 prob(air) | Merseburg |
| | | FW-190 dam(air) | Merseburg |
| | Lt. L.V. Intravartola | Me-109 dest(air) | W/Merseburg |
| | | FW-190 dam(air) | W/Merseburg |
| | Lt. D.J. Maxwell | FW-190 dest(air) | Merseburg |
| | | FW-190 dam(air) | Merseburg |
| | Maj. E.L. Abbott | (.5)FW-190 dest(air) | Merseburg |
| | | (shared with an unknown P-51) | |
| | Capt. W.E. Hendrian | (.5)FW-190 dest(air) | Merseburg |
| | Lt. J.F. Lambright | (.5)FW-190 dest(air) | Merseburg |
| | | FW-190 dam(air) | Merseburg |
| | Lt. E.W. Briggs | FW-190 prob(air) | W/Merseburg |
| | Lt. L. Fieg | Me-109 prob(air) | W/Merseburg |
| 487th: | Capt. W.T. Whisner | (5)FW-190 dest(air) | SW Merseburg |
| | | (2)FW-190 prob(air) | SW Merseburg |
| | Lt. N.R. Jesup | (2)FW-190 dest(air) | SW Merseburg |
| | Lt. K.M. Waldron | (2)FW-190 dest(air) | SW Merseburg |
| | Capt. W.E. Starck | FW-190 dam(air) | SW Merseburg |
| | Lt. W.C. Miller | FW-190 dam(air) | SW Merseburg |

**November 27, 1944**

| | | | |
|---|---|---|---|
| HdQts: | LtCol. J.C. Meyer | Me-109 dest(air) | E/Munster |
| 328th: | Lt. C.J. Cesky | Me-109 dest(air) | Hanover |
| | Lt. E.B. Dubay | Me-109 dest(air) | Hanover |
| 487th: | Capt. W.E. Starck | (3)Me-109 dest(air) | (2)Hameln & (1)Osnabruck |
| | Capt. R.W. Hamilton | (2)Me-109 dest(air) | Hameln |
| | Capt. W.T. Whisner | (2)Me-109 dest(air) | Hameln |
| | Lt. R.H. Littge | (2)Me-109 dest(air) | Hameln |
| | Maj. E.D. Duncan | Me-109 dest(air) | Hameln |
| | Capt. W.T. Halton | Me-109 dest(air) | Hameln |
| | Capt. W.S. Smith | Me-109 dest(air) | Munster |
| | Lt. K.K. Dittmer | Me-109 dest(air) | N/Hanover |
| | Lt. D.M. Huston | Me-109 dest(air) | Munster |
| | Lt. S.K. Moats | Me-109 dest(air) | Munster |
| | | Me-109 dam(air) | Munster |
| | Lt. A.P. Rigby | Me-109 dest(air) | Minden |
| | Lt. H.M. Stewart | Me-109 dest(air) | Hameln |

**November 30, 1944**

| | | | |
|---|---|---|---|
| 486th: | LtCol. W.O. Jackson | Me-109 dest(air) | W/Chemnitz |
| | Capt. C.E. Griffiths | Me-109 dest(air) | Glauchau |
| | Lt. E.R. Lazear | Me-109 dest(air) | S/Merseburg |
| | Lt. B.J. Grabovski | (2)FW-190 dam(grd) | W/Leipzig |
| | | He-111 dam(grd) | W/Leipzig |

**December 5, 1944**

| | | | |
|---|---|---|---|
| 486th: | Lt. B.J. Grabovski | Me-262 dam(air) | Osnabruck |

**December 9, 1944**

| | | | |
|---|---|---|---|
| 486th: | Lt. H.L. Edwards | Me-262 dest(air) | Kircheim |

**December 23, 1944**

| | | | |
|---|---|---|---|
| 328th: | Capt. D.S. Bryan | FW-190 dest(air) | S/Liege |
| | Lt. W.H. Sanford | FW-190 dest(air) | S/Liege |

**December 25, 1944**

| | | | |
|---|---|---|---|
| 328th: | Capt. C.J. Cesky | (3)FW-190 dest(air) | Maastricht |
| | Maj. G.E. Preddy | (2)Me-109 dest(air) | SW Coblenz |
| | Capt. W.J. Stangel | (2)Me-109 dest(air) | SW Coblenz |
| | Lt. A.J. Chesser | FW-190 dest(air) | Maastricht |
| | Lt. C.E. Goodman | Me-109 dest(air) | SW Coblenz |
| | Lt. J.F. Lambright | Me-109 dest(air) | SW Coblenz |
| | | Me-109 dam(air) | SW Coblenz |
| | Lt. R.R. Mitchell | Me-109 dest(air) | SW Coblenz |

**December 26, 1944**

(#1)

| | | | |
|---|---|---|---|
| HdQts: | LtCol. J.C. Meyer | (1.5)Me-109 dest(air) | Ollheim |
| | | (shared with an unknown P-51 pilot) | |
| 487th: | Maj. W.T. Halton | Me-109 dest(air) | SW Bonn |
| | Capt. R.W. Hamilton | Me-109 dest(air) | SW Bonn |
| | Capt. M.J. Nutter | Me-109 dest(air) | SW Bonn |
| | Lt. W.G. Diamond | Me-109 dest(air) | Ollheim |
| | Lt. R.H. Littge | Me-109 dest(air) | Ollheim |
| | Lt. A.F. Sears | Me-109 dest(air) | Ollheim |

(#2)

| | | | |
|---|---|---|---|
| HdQts: | LtCol. J.C. Meyer | Me-109 dest(air) | Uxheim |
| 487th: | Lt. D.H. Schuh | (3)Me-109 dest(air) | Veldenbor |
| | Lt. J.A. Bateman | Me-109 dest(air) | SE St. Vith |
| | Lt. W.C. Miller | Me-109 dest(air) | Veldenbor |
| | | Me-109 dam(air) | Veldenbor |

**December 27, 1944**

| | | | |
|---|---|---|---|
| HdQts: | LtCol. J.C. Meyer | (2)FW-190 dest(air) | SW Bonn |
| | | (2)FW-190 dam(air) | SW Bonn |
| 486th: | Lt. R.L. Henderson | (2)Me-109 dest(air) | W/Bonn |
| | Lt. W.H. Reese | (2)Me-109 dest(air) | SW Bonn |
| | LtCol. W.O. Jackson | Me-109 dest(air) | SW Bonn |
| | Maj. F.N. Greene | Me-109 dest(air) | SE Liege |
| | Lt. E.R. Lazear | Me-109 dest(air) | SW Bonn |
| 487th: | Maj. W.T. Halton | (3.5)Me-109 dest(air)* | SW Bonn |
| | Lt. R.H. Littge | (3)FW-190 dest(air) | Mauen |
| | Capt. M.J. Nutter | (2)Me-109 dest(air) | SW Bonn |
| | Lt. J.A. Bateman | Me-109 dest(air) | SW Bonn |
| | Lt. S.K. Moats | FW-190 dest(air) | SW Bonn |
| | Lt. R.H. Ross | FW-190 dest(air) | Mauen |
| | Lt. J.N. Wood | FW-190 dest(air) | W/Mauen |
| | F/O E.H. Goebel | (.5)Me-109 dest(air)* | SW Bonn |
| | | (.5)Me-109 dest(air) | Bonn |
| | | (shared with a 364th Ftr Grp P-51) | |

**December 31, 1944**

| | | | |
|---|---|---|---|
| HdQts: | LtCol. J.C. Meyer | Ar-234 dest(air) | Euskirchen |
| 328th: | Capt. D.S. Bryan | Ar-234 dam(air) | S/Verviers |

**January 1, 1945**

| | | | |
|---|---|---|---|
| HdQts: | LtCol. J.C. Meyer | (2)FW-190 dest(air) | All claims are |
| 487th: | Capt. W.T. Whisner | (2)Me-109 dest(air) | N/Liege |
| | | (2)FW-190 dest(air) | |
| | Lt. S.K. Moats | (4)FW-190 dest(air) | |
| | Capt. H.M. Stewart | (3)Me-109 dest(air) | |
| | Lt. A.P. Rigby | (2)FW-190 dest(air) | |
| | | (.5)Me-109 dest(air) | |
| | | (.5)Me-109 dest(air) | |
| | | (both shared with an unknown pilot) | |
| | Lt. R.H. Littge | (2)FW-190 dest(air) | |
| | Maj. W.T. Halton | FW-190 dest(air) | |
| | Lt. W.G. Diamond | FW-190 dest(air) | |
| | | FW-190 dam(air) | |
| | Lt. D.M. Huston | FW-190 dest(air) | |
| | Lt. N.R. Jesup | FW-190 dest(air) | |
| | Lt. A.F. Sears | Me-109 dest(air) | |

**January 14, 1945**

| | | | |
|---|---|---|---|
| 486th: | Lt. W.H. Reese | (2)FW-190 dest(air) | All claims are |
| | Lt. E.O. Bostrom | FW-190 dest(air) | at Almelo |
| | Lt. E.L. Mundell | FW-190 dest(air) | |
| | Lt. G.G. Contos | (.5)FW-190 dest(air)* | |
| | | (.5)FW-190 dest(air) | |
| | | (shared with an unknown pilot) | |
| | Lt. J.D. Stearns | (.5)FW-190 dest(air)* | |

**January 23, 1945**

| | | | |
|---|---|---|---|
| 486th: | Capt. L.J. Vitek | (.5)Me-109 dest(air) | SW Dusseldorf |
| | Lt. G.G. Contos | (.5)Me-109 dest(air) | SW Dusseldorf |

**January 24, 1945**

| | | | |
|---|---|---|---|
| 328th: | Lt. E.B. Dubay | (.5)Me-109 dest(air) | Duren |
| | Lt. C.E. Goodman | (.5)Me-109 dest(air) | Duren |
| 487th: | Maj. W.T. Halton | Me-109 dest(air) | Cologne |
| | Lt. R.H. Littge | Me-109 dest(air) | Bonn |

**February 21, 1945**

| | | | |
|---|---|---|---|
| 487th: | Lt. R.H. Littge | Ju-88 dam(grd) | SW Kassel |

**February 22, 1945**

| | | | |
|---|---|---|---|
| 328th: | Maj. E.D. Duncan | Me-262 dam(air) | Stendal |
| | Lt. C.E. Goodman | Me-262 dam(air) | Stendal |
| 486th: | Lt. C.D. Price | Me-262 dest(air) | Wahrenholz |

**March 2, 1945**

| | | | |
|---|---|---|---|
| HdQts: | LtCol. W.O. Jackson | FW-189 dest(air) | Prague |
| | | (2)u/i a/c dam(grd) | Prague |
| 486th: | Capt. E.L. Heller | FW-190 dest(air) | SE Leipzig |
| | | FW-190 dam(air) | SE Leipzig |
| | Lt. E.A. Paulsen | FW-190 dest(air) | Zwickau |
| | | FW-190 prob(air) | Zwickau |
| | Lt. C.D. Price | FW-190 dest(air) | Zwickau |
| | Lt. D.M. Reichman | FW-190 dest(air) | Zwickau |
| | Capt. L.E. Kilgo | (.5)FW-190 dest(air) | Prague |
| | Lt. E.L. Mundell | (.5)FW-190 dest(air) | Prague |
| | Lt. M.J. Stover | FW-190 prob(air) | Zwickau |
| | | FW-190 dam(air) | Zwickau |
| | Capt. C.V. Harker | FW-190 dam(grd) | Prague |
| | | Me-410 dam(grd) | Prague |
| | Lt. C.C. Pattillo | (2)u/i a/c dam(grd) | Prague |

**March 3, 1945**

| | | | |
|---|---|---|---|
| 328th: | Lt. W.H. Sanford | Me-109 dest(air) | W/Dresden |

**March 14, 1945**

| | | | |
|---|---|---|---|
| 328th: | Capt. D.S. Bryan | Ar-234 dest(air) | Elsaffthal |

**March 18, 1945**

| | | | |
|---|---|---|---|
| 487th: | Maj. W.T. Halton | Me-109 dest(air) | Bad Frienwalde |
| | F/O J.N. White | Me-109 dest(air) | E/Oder |
| | Lt. R.H. Littge | (.5)Me-109 dest(air) | Bad Frienwalde |
| | Lt. J.N. Wood | (.5)Me-109 dest(air) | Bad Frienwalde |

**March 25, 1945**

| | | | |
|---|---|---|---|
| 487th: | Capt. R.H. Littge | Me-262 dest(air) | Rechlin A/F |

**March 30, 1945**

| | | | |
|---|---|---|---|
| 328th: | Lt. J.C. Hurley | Me-262 dest(air) | N/Magdeburg |

**April 7, 1945**

| | | | |
|---|---|---|---|
| HdQts: | Col. J.D. Mayden | Me-109 dest(air) | N/Minden |

**April 10, 1945**

| | | | |
|---|---|---|---|
| 328th: | LtCol. E.D. Duncan | (.5)Me-262 dest(air) | Berlin-Wittenburg |
| | Maj. R.G. McAuliffe | (.5)Me-262 dest(air) | Berlin-Wittenburg |
| 487th: | Lt. C.A. Pattillo | Me-262 dest(air) | E/Ulzen |
| | Lt. J.W. Prichard | (.5)Me-262 dest(air) | Neuruppin |
| | Lt. C.A. Ricci | (.5)Me-262 dest(air) | Neuruppin |
| | Lt. K.M. Waldron | Me-262 dam(air) | Salzwedel |

**April 16, 1945**

| | | | |
|---|---|---|---|
| HdQts: | LtCol. W.O. Jackson | (2)Me-109 dest(grd) | Ganacker |
| | | (2)FW-190 dest(grd) | Ganacker |
| | | Me-109 dam(grd) | Ganacker |
| | | u/i a/c dam(grd) | Ganacker |
| 328th: | Lt. C.E. Goodman | (2)Me-109 dest(grd) | All 328th claims |
| | | (4)Me-109 dam(grd) | are at Landau |
| | Lt. W.H. Sanford | (2)FW-190 dest(grd) | |
| | F/O D.A. Webb | FW-190 dest(grd) | |
| | Maj. R.G. McAuliffe | (2)FW-190 dam(grd) | |
| | Lt. J.G. Cartee | (2)FW-190 dam(grd) | |
| | LtCol. E.D. Duncan | Me-109 dam(grd) | |
| 486th: | Capt. E.L. Heller | (3)FW-190 dest(grd) | All 486th claims |
| | | (2)Ju-87 dest(grd) | are at Ganacker |
| | | Me-109 dest(grd) | |
| | | u/i a/c dest(grd) | |
| | Lt. C.C. Pattillo | (3)FW-190 dest(grd) | |
| | | (2)Me-109 dest(grd) | |
| | | Ju-88 dest(grd) | |
| | | (2)Me-109 dam(grd) | |
| | | FW-190 dam(grd) | |
| | F/O M.D. Johnson | FW-190 dest(grd) | |
| | | Me-109 dest(grd) | |
| | | (2)u/i a/c dam(grd) | |
| | Lt. C.D. Price | He-111 dest(grd) | |
| | | Me-109 dest(grd) | |
| | | (3)u/i a/c dam(grd) | |
| | Lt. G.W. Wensch | (2)FW-190 dest(grd) | |
| | Lt. R.O. Swinson | FW-190 dam(grd) | |
| 487th: | Lt. H.S. Sykes | (3)u/i a/c dest(grd) | All 487th claims |
| | | Me-109 dest(grd) | are at Ganacker |
| | | Fi-156 dest(grd) | |
| | | Me-109 dam(grd) | |
| | | u/i a/c dam(grd) | |
| | Capt. R.H. Littge | (2)Me-109 dest(grd) | |
| | | Me-210 dest(grd) | |
| | | (3)Me-109 dam(grd) | |
| | | FW-190 dam(grd) | |
| | Lt. W. Padden | (2)u/i a/c dest(grd) | |
| | Lt. C.A. Pattillo | FW-190 dest(grd) | |
| | | Me-109 dest(grd) | |
| | | (2)FW-190 dam(grd) | |
| | | Me-109 dam(grd) | |
| | Lt. K.M. Waldron | Me-109 dest(grd) | |
| | | FW-190 dest(grd) | |
| | Lt. R.W. Creamer | Me-109 dest(grd) | |
| | | (2)FW-190 dam(grd) | |
| | | u/i a/c dam(grd) | |

**April 17, 1945**

| | | | |
|---|---|---|---|
| HdQts: | Col. J.D. Mayden | (2)Me-109 dest(grd) | All claims are |
| | | FW-190 dest(grd) | at Plattling |
| | | u/i a/c dest(grd) | |
| | | (2)Me-109 dam(grd) | |
| 328th: | Lt. C.W. Weber | (3)Me-109 dest(grd) | |
| | | u/i a/c dest(grd) | |
| | | (2)FW-190 dam(grd) | |
| | LtCol. E.D. Duncan | (2)Me-109 dest(grd) | |
| | Lt. F.A. Cast | (2)Me-109 dest(grd) | |
| | | Me-109 dam(grd) | |
| | F/O C. Vander Vear | FW-190 dest(grd) | |
| | | u/i a/c dest(grd) | |
| | | (2)FW-190 dam(grd) | |
| | Maj. R.G. McAuliffe | FW-190 dest(grd) | |
| | | u/i a/c dam(grd) | |
| | Lt. J.C. Hurley | Me-109 dest(grd) | |
| | | (2)Me-109 dam(grd) | |
| | Lt. S.R. Price | Me-109 dest(grd) | |
| | | Me-109 dam(grd) | |
| 486th: | Lt. J.D. Carter | (5)FW-190 dest(grd) | |
| | | FW-190 dam(grd) | |
| | Maj. D.H. Higgins | (2)Ju-52 dest(grd) | |
| | | Me-109 dest(grd) | |
| | | Me-109 dam(grd) | |
| | F/O R.A. Wanda | (2)FW-190 dest(grd) | |
| | | Me-109 dest(grd) | |
| | | (2)FW-190 dam(grd) | |
| | | u/i a/c dam(grd) | |
| | F/O J.P. McKenna | FW-190 dest(grd) | |
| | | Me-109 dest(grd) | |
| | | FW-190 dam(grd) | |
| | | Me-109 dam(grd) | |
| | | u/i a/c dam(grd) | |
| | Lt. G.A. Rushman | (2)FW-190 dest(grd) | |
| | | (2)FW-190 dam(grd) | |
| | Lt. J.B. Whitney | Me-109 dest(grd) | |
| | | Fi-156 dest(grd) | |
| | | Me-109 dam(grd) | |
| | Lt. G.W. Wensch | u/i a/c dest(grd) | |
| | | FW-190 dam(grd) | |
| | | u/i a/c dam(grd) | |
| 487th: | Capt. R.H. Littge | (4)Me-109 dest(grd) | |
| | | (2)Me-262 dest(grd) | |
| | Lt. K.M. Waldron | (2)FW-190 dest(grd) | |
| | | (2)Me-109 dest(grd) | |
| | | Fi-156 dest(grd) | |
| | | (2)FW-190 dam(grd) | |
| | F/O R.W. Frum | (3)FW-190 dest(grd) | |
| | | (2)FW-190 dam(grd) | |
| | Lt. J.N. White | (2)Me-109 dest(grd) | |
| | | FW-190 dest(grd) | |
| | | Me-109 dam(grd) | |
| | | FW-190 dam(grd) | |
| | LtCol. W.T. Halton | FW-190 dest(grd) | |
| | | Me-109 dest(grd) | |
| | | (2)FW-190 dam(grd) | |
| | Lt. R.G. Reed | (2)Me-109 dest(grd) | |
| | | (3)Me-109 dam(grd) | |
| | Lt. M.C. Reynolds | FW-190 dest(grd) | |
| | | Me-109 dest(grd) | |
| | F/O J.F. Graves | u/i a/c dest(grd) | |

### 352nd Fighter Group Losses

**September 13, 1943**
Lt. Arthur C. Eaker (328th) KIAc;
P-47D PE-

**September 14, 1943**
Lt. William H. Alm (486th) KIA; Crashed off Knocke after suffering mechanical trouble.
P-47D PZ- 42-22531

**October 10, 1943**
Lt. Fred D. Olson (328th) KIA; Damaged by fighters and crashed northeast of Lowestoft.
P-47D PE- 42-8635

**November 30, 1943**
Lt. Robert L. Babbitt (486th) KIA; Hit by fighters near Oir Schut.
P-47D PZ- 42-22516
Lt. Robert M. Brown (486th) KIA; Hit by fighters near Goirle.
P-47D PZ- 42-8411
Lt. David C. Kramer (486th) MIA-E; Hit by fighters near Neerpelt.
P-47D PZ- 42-8514

**December 22, 1943**
Lt. Richard L. Grow (487th) KIA; Hit by fighters near Haule.
P-47D HO-G 42-22487

**December 30, 1943**
Capt. Hayes L. Button (487th) POW; Hit by flak near Dunkirk.
P-47D HO-B 42-8483
Capt. Donald K. Dilling (487th) MIA-E; Ran out of fuel and bailed out off the enemy coast.
P-47D HO-S 42-8447 "Queen City Mama"
Capt. Winfield E. McIntyre (487th) POW; Hit by flak and crashed near Desvres.
P-47D HO- 42-22551

**January 26, 1944**
Lt. Lester L. Lowry (487th) KIAc; His plane dove into the ground near Bodney while on a local flight.
P-47D HO-Z 42-8516

**January 29, 1944**
Lt. Joel W. McPherson (HdQts) MIA-E; Ran out of fuel and bailed out near Rouillac.
Capt. George E. Preddy (487th) ASR; Damaged by flak and bailed out over the Channel.
P-47D HO-Y 42-8421

**February 3, 1944**
Lt. Ray L. Cornick (328th) KIA; Ran out of fuel and crashed into the North Sea.
P-47D PE-R 42-8563 "Ilene"
F/O Joseph L. Sweeney (487th) KIA; Ran out of fuel and crashed into the North Sea.
P-47D HO- 42-75405

**February 8, 1944**
Lt. James Meagher (328th) KIA; Hit by fighters near St. Gobert.
P-47D PE-M 42-8556 "Patricia Lee"
Lt. Harold C. Nussman (328th) KIA; Hit by fighters near Chaug.
P-47D PE-X 42-8419 "Blondie"
Lt. John H. Walker, Jr. (328th) KIA; Hit by fighters near Burelles.
P-47D PE-V 42-8527 "Ramblin' Rebel"

**March 8, 1944**
Lt. Earl H. Bond (486th) KIA; Collided with a P-47 after take-off and crashed near Bracon Ash.
P-47D PZ-O 42-8652 "The Bid"

**March 11, 1944**
Lt. William D. Schwenke (328th) KIA; Damaged by flak and bailed out west of the Somme Estuary.
P-47D PE-S 42-8424 "Kathie"
Lt. Harold S. Riley, Jr. (487th) KIA; Hit by flak near Oisemont.
P-47D HO-R 42-22530 "The Kid"

**April 8, 1944**
Capt. Virgil K. Meroney (487th) POW; Hit by flak at Bramsche A/F.
P-51B HO-V 43-7166

**April 9, 1944**
Lt. Fred A. Yochim (328th) POW; Hit by fighters near Osnabruck.
P-47D PE-V 42-8434 "Desiree Y"
Lt. Ralph I. Williamson (487th) KIA; Was relay and aircraft exploded near Harwick for unknown reasons.
P-47D HO-

**April 11, 1944**
Lt. Alfred L. Marshall (486th) KIA; Hit by flak and bailed out south of Hanover.
P-51B PZ-Q 43-7031 "Sweet Chariot"

**April 15, 1944**
Lt. Fremont W. Miller (328th) ASR; Damaged by flak and bailed out over the Channel. Was rescued on April 18.
P-47D PE-W 42-8511 "Red Raider"
LtCol. Luther H. Richmond (486th) POW; Hit by flak near Vechta.
P-51B PZ-R 43-7196 "Sweetie II"
Lt. Robert I. Ross (487th) KIA; Hit by flak in the Diepholz-Vechta area and crashed into the North Sea.
P-51B HO-R 43-7192

**April 22, 1944**
Lt. Marion V. Long (328th) POW; Hit by flak west of Lingen.
P-51B PE-Y 42-106624 "Helen"

**April 24, 1944**
Capt. Robert G. MacKean (486th) KIA; Hit by flak near Lenting.
P-51B PZ-Z 43-7198

**April 28, 1944**
Lt. James L. Laing (328th) POW; Hit by flak near Herbeuville and bailed out near Chateaudun.
P-51C PE- 42-103290

**May 8, 1944**
Lt. George Kopecky (487th) POW; Hit by fighters near Nienburg.
P-51B HO-G 43-7105
Lt. John B. Worchester (486th) KIAc;
P-51B PZ-F 43-6850 "The Joker"

**May 9, 1944**
Capt. Ernest B. McMahan (487th) KIAc; Crashed while practicing dive-bombing at Mersa Flats.
P-51C HO-B 42-103310

**May 12, 1944**
Lt. Alfred P. Howard, Jr. (487th) KIA; Hit by fighters near Rainrod.
P-51B HO-Y 43-6929

**May 13, 1944**
Capt. Frank A. Cutler (486th) KIA; Collided with a Me-109 near Zarneka.
P-51B PZ-Y 42-106483 "Miss Lace"

**May 19, 1944**
Lt. Michele M. Carlone (328th) KIA; Hit by fighters near Wittenberg.
P-51B PE-N 42-106668

**May 21, 1944**
LtCol. Eugene L. Clark (HdQts) POW; Hit by flak near Diepholz.
P-51C PE-L 42-103316 "Panama Mamita"

**May 24, 1944**
Lt. James D. Hannon (487th) POW; Hit by flak near Stendal and bellied-in near Celle.
P-51B HO-C 43-6805 "Marjorie II"
Lt. Carl J. Luksic (487th) POW; Hit by flak near Stendal and bailed out near Celle.
P-51B HO-Z 42-106788

**May 28, 1944**
Capt. Woodrow W. Anderson (486th) KIA; Hit by fighters near Quedlinburg.
P-51B PZ-A 42-106635 "Texas Blue Bonnet"

**June 5, 1944**
Lt. William W. Furr (328th) POW; Suffered mechanical failure near Merville.
P-51B PE-T 42-106717

**June 6, 1944**
Lt. Robert C. Frascotti (486th) KIA; Crashed on take-off from Bodney.
P-51B PZ-F 43-6685 "Umbriago"
Lt. Robert K. Butler (487th) POW; Hit by flak near Epaignes.
P-51B HO-W 42-106449 "Princess Elizabeth"
Lt. Robert G. O'Nan (487th) POW; Hit by flak near Evreux.
P-51B HO-E 43-7096 "Barbara M"

**June 7, 1944**
Maj. Edward J. Gignac (HdQts) KIA; Hit by flak near Le Merterault.
P-51B PZ-J 42-106661 "Hot Stuff"
Lt. Robert L. Hall (487th) KIA; Hit by flak near Argentan.
P-51B HO-R 43-24845
Lt. Clifford P. Garney (487th) KIA; Spun-in over England while returning from a mission.
P-51B HO-M 42-106471 "Lambie II"
Lt. William C. Mulvey (487th) KIAc; Crashed after take-off.
P-51

**June 8, 1944**
Lt. John Campbell (328th) KIA; Hit by flak near Chartres.
P-51B PE-J 43-24801
Lt. Harry L. Miller, Jr. (328th) KIA; Last seen over France in heavy overcast.
P-51B PE-Q 43-6988 "Denali"
Lt. Ted P. Fahrenwald (486th) MIA-E; Hit by flak near Elbeuf.
P-51C PZ-F 42-103336

**June 9, 1944**
Lt. Robert H. Sharp (328th) KIAc;
P-51B PE-I 43-7174
Lt. Richard A. Pratt (328th) KIAc;
P-51B PE-P 42-106868 "Hildegarde"

**June 10, 1944**
Lt. Raymond G. Phillips (328th) KIA; Hit by flak and crashed into the Channel.
P-51B PE-W 42-106756
Lt. Lincoln C. Bundy (486th) KIA; Hit by flak near La Mailleraue.
P-51B PZ-R 43-7153 "Rustler"
Lt. Donald J. Markle (486th) KIA; Hit trees while strafing near St. Malo.
P-51B PZ-M 43-6776

**June 18, 1944**
Lt. Robert S. Daugherty (487th) KIAc; Collided with a P-51 while on a training flight near Bodney.
P-51B HO-N 43-7160

**June 20, 1944**
Lt. Waldo C. Raub (486th) KIA; Collided with an enemy plane near Burg.
P-51B PZ-R 42-106609

**June 25, 1944**
F/O William W. Drisko (487th) POW; Hit by a Me-109 near Soissons.
P-51B HO-A 43-6902

**June 26, 1944**
Lt. Robert H. Berkshire (487th) MIA-E; Hit by flak near Noyon.
P-51B HO-G 43-7167 "Brutal Lulu"

**June 28, 1944**
Lt. Adolph Bielok (487th) KIA; Hit by flak near St. Omer.
P-51B HO-L 43-6868

**July 2, 1944**
Maj. Stephen W. Andrew (486th) POW; Suffered mechanical trouble near Adony.
P-51B PZ-A 42-106467
Lt. Lester L. Howell (486th) KIA; Hit by fighters near Budapest.
P-51B PZ-V 42-106857 "Texas Knight"

**July 16, 1944**
Lt. Jule V. Conard (487th) POW; Suffered mechanical failure near Munich and was last seen near Aalen.
P-51B HO-P 42-106451 "Cripes A'Mighty"

**July 18, 1944**
Lt. James A. Burr (328th) KIA; Last seen chasing enemy fighters near Warmemunde.
P-51D PE- 44-13320
Lt. John W. Galiga (328th) KIA; Last seen chasing fighters near Parchim.
P-51B PE-K 43-7165

**July 19, 1944**
Lt. William D. Wilson (328th) POW; Ran out of fuel and bailed out near Lille.
P-51B PE-V 43-7165

**July 21, 1944**
Lt. Richard H. Casper (328th) KIA; Ran out of fuel and crashed into the North Sea.
P-51B PE-M 43-6906 "Patty III"
Lt. Elmo B. Dubay (328th) ASR; Ran out of fuel and bailed out northeast of Cromer.
P-51D PE-H 44-13582
Lt. Robert R. Lampman (328th) KIA; Ran out of fuel and crashed into the North Sea.
P-51B PE-Z 42-106459 "La Riena Peg"
Lt. James C. Lanter (328th) KIA; Ran out of fuel and crashed into the North Sea.
P-51B PE-I 43-24788
Lt. David T. Zimms (328th) ASR; Ran out of fuel and bailed out northeast of Cromer.
P-51B PE-C 42-106694 "Stinky"

**July 29, 1944**
Maj. Gustav E. Lundquist (486th) POW; Hit by a FW-190 near Sanderhausen.
P-51D PZ-M 44-13395

**July 31, 1944**
Lt. McDonald Godfrey (328th) POW; Spun-out in overcast near Brussels.
P-51B PE-G 42-106827 "Candy Lamb"
Lt. Edmond Zellner (328th) MIA-E; Hit by flak near Charleroi and bailed out southwest of Brussels.
P-51D PE- 44-13910

**August 5, 1944**
Lt. David J. French (486th) POW; Hit by fighters near Appeln.
P-51B PZ-F 43-6864
Lt. Clifford R. Wilcox (487th) POW; Hit by fighters near Ziesar.
P-51C HO-C 42-103312 "Channel Belle"

**August 6, 1944**
Lt. Walter Gehrke (328th) KIA; Lost a wing east of Luneburg.
P-51C PE-J 42-103787
Capt. Quentin L. Quinn (328th) KIAc; Crashed near Thetford.
P-51D PE-

**August 12, 1944**
Lt. Gerald D. Thurman (486th) KIA; Suffered mechanical trouble over the Channel.
P-51D PZ-I 44-13736 "Dotty"
Lt. Robert W. Graham (487th) POW; Hit by flak near Marest.
P-51D HO-B 44-13619 "William's Villian"

**August 13, 1944**
Lt. Leroy J. Allain, Jr. (328th) POW; Hit by flak near Royville.
P-51B PE-R 42-106460 "Lois"
Lt. Harry H. Barnes (487th) POW; Hit by flak near Fauville.
P-51D HO-V 44-13588

**August 17, 1944**
Lt. William H. Reese (486th) MIA-E; Hit by flak near Chalons.
P-51D PZ-R 44-13398
Capt. Clayton E. Davis (487th) MIA-E; Hit by flak near Noyon.
P-51D HO-C 44-13651

**August 25, 1944**
Lt. Richard F. Semon (328th) ASR; Bailed out northeast of Great Yarmouth after mechanical trouble.
P-51C PE-X 42-103789

**August 27, 1944**
Lt. Charles E. Ferris (486th) KIA; Suffered mechanical failure and bailed out near Heligoland.
P-51D PZ-N 44-13688 "Donna Dae VI"
Lt. Carl J. Fuenpstueck (486th) POW; Hit by fighters near Kiel.
P-51B PZ-A 42-106480

**September 8, 1944**
Capt. Duncan R. Donahue (487th) KIA; Caught in a ground explosion near Keilbach.
P-51D HO-L 44-14109

**September 11, 1944**
Lt. Garland Rayborn (328th) KIA; Hit by fighters south of Gotha.
P-51D PE-Z 44-13785 "La Riena Peg II"
Lt. Howard R. Combs, Jr. (486th) KIA; Hit by flak near Herzberg.
P-51D PZ-T 44-14043 "Lil Evey"

**September 12, 1944**
Lt. Joseph A. Broadwater (328th) KIA; Hit by fighters near Muncheberg.
P-51B PE-T 42-106872

**September 23, 1944**
Maj. Jack D. Blanchard (328th) MIA-E; Hit by flak near Bergharen.
P-51D PE-T 44-13996 "Slender, Tender, and Tall"
Capt. Clarence O. Johnson (487th) KIA; Hit by a Me-109 near Lusiendorf.
P-51D HO- 44-14078
Lt. Joseph B. Ayers (487th) KIA; Hit by a Me-109 near Lusiendorf.
P-51B HO-J 42-106901 "Helen of Troy III"
Lt. John F. Clark (487th) POW; Hit by a Me-109 near Heidkamp.
P-51B HO-O 42-106454 "Louisiana Lady"
Lt. Phanor B. Waters (487th) KIA; Hit by a Me-109 near Almelo.
P-51B HO-S 43-7094 "Gracie"

**September 25, 1944**
Lt. Evan J. Evans (487th) POW; Hit by flak near Biblis.
P-51B HO-I 43-6707 "Peanuts"

**October 5, 1944**
Capt. John B. Coleman, Jr. (328th) MIA-E; Bellied-in northwest of Tilburg after mechanical trouble.
P-51D PE-M 44-13983 "Patty IV"

**October 6, 1944**
Lt. James H. Forga, Jr. (487th) KIA; Lost coolant and bailed out west of Wangerooge.
P-51B HO-G 43-7139 "Lili Marlene"

**October 24, 1944**
Lt. Thompson R. Kyle (486th) POW; Hit by flak near Engelhern.
P-51B PZ-B 42-106613 "Ellie"
Lt. Jack C. Landrum (487th) KIAc;
P-51D HO-F 44-13597 "Stardust"

**November 2, 1944**
Lt. Glenn R. Clark (328th) POW; Hit by fighters near Halberstadt.
P-51D PE-D 44-11153 "Mom & Dad"
Capt. Henry J. Miklajcyk (486th) KIA; Hit by fighters near Halle.
P-51D PZ-K 44-13690 "The Syracusan 3rd"

**November 9, 1944**
Lt. Charles E. Rogers (328th) KIA; Suffered mechanical failure northeast of Lille.
P-51D PE-S 44-14273 "Georgia Peach II"

**November 27, 1944**
Lt. Arthur E. Hudson (328th) KIA; Hit by fighters near Aulendorf.
P-51D PE-Z 44-15012 "Jeanie Boy"
Capt. Walter E. Starck (487th) POW; Hit by fighters near Hameln.
P-51D HO-F 44-14794 "Buzz Boy"
Capt. Walter S. Smith (487th) POW; Hit by fighters near Munster.
P-51D HO- 44-14638 "Sweet Sue"

**December 25, 1944**
Maj. George E. Preddy (328th) KIA; Downed by Allied ground fire while chasing a FW-190 near Liege.
P-51D PE-P 44-14906 "Cripes A'Mighty"

**December 26, 1944**
Lt. Carl G. Tafel, Jr. (487th) KIA; Hit by fighters near Heimerzheim.
P-51D HO-C 44-13953 "Nancy M"

**December 31, 1944**
F/O Hugh A. Howard, Jr. (328th) KIA; Crashed into the Channel in bad weather.
P-51D PE-K 44-13759 "Lonesome Polecat"

**January 24, 1945**
Maj. Earl L. Abbott (328th) KIA; Hit by fighters near Aachen.
P-51D PE-A 44-14710 "Flossie"

**February 3, 1945**
Lt. Fred H. Powell (486th) POW; Suffered mechanical failure near Geldern.
P-51D PZ-A 44-15124

**February 24, 1945**
Lt. Sylvester J. Evans (328th) POW; Hit by flak near Bathmer and bellied-in southeast of Deventer.
P-51K PE-K 44-11750 "Lonesome Polecat"
Lt. Fred R. Jones (486th) KIA; Hit by flak near Almelo.
P-51D PZ-F 44-13362 "Sleepy Chicken"

**March 18, 1945**
Lt. Albert L. Peterson (487th) POW; Last seen north of Frankfurt.
P-51D HO- 44-15369 "Sweet Fern"
Lt. Joseph P. Vickery (497th) KIA; Last seen near Schwiebus.
P-51D HO-R 44-15629 "Ellen-Jerry"

**March 21, 1945**
Lt. Ervin E. Pryor (487th) KIA; Crashed at Chievres upon return.
P-51D HO-W 44-13361

**March 25, 1945**
Lt. Wesley N. Roebuck (487th) KIA; Hit by a Me-262 near Ulzen.
P-51D HO-J 44-14475 "Peanuts"

**March 30, 1945**
Lt. Francis J. McCarthy (328th) KIA; Suffered mechanical trouble near Oldenburg.
P-51D PE-F 44-14882 "The Second Baser 3rd"

**April 16, 1945**
Lt. Cuthbert A. Pattillo (487th) POW; Hit by flak at Ganacker A/F and bailed out near Ingolstadt.
P-51K HO-Y 44-11556 "Sweet & Lovely"
Lt. Walter Padden (487th) KIA; Hit by flak at Ganacker A/F and crashed near Ingolstadt.
P-51D HO-N 44-13321 "Sexshunate"

**April 17, 1945**
Lt. Miron C. Reynolds (487th) KIA; Hit by flak at Plattling.
P-51D HO-L 44-14801 "The Hawk-eye-owan"

**April 19, 1945**
Lt. John F. Reiners (328th) KIA; Crashed on take-off from Bodney.
P-51D PE- 44-11229

**July 7, 1945**
Lt. Glen W. St. John (328th) KIAc;
P-51K PE-Q 44-11644 "Juliet"

**Headquarters**
Clark, Eugene L., LtCol.; States-May 21, 1944(POW)
P-47D PE-Z 42-8508 "Panama Papacito"
P-51B PE-Z 42-106459
Edwards, John C., LtCol.; States-July 1944; to 328th Ftr Sqn
P-47D HO-E 42-8474 "Barbara M"
P-51B HO-E 43-7096 "Barbara M"
P-51D HO-E 44-13406 "Barbara M 4th"
Gates, Richard J., Maj.; June 1944-EOW; ex-486th Ftr Sqn
Gignac, Edward J., Maj.; April 1944-June 7, 1944(KIA); ex-486th Ftr Sqn
P-51B PZ-G 43-7165 "Gigs-Up II"
Jackson, Willie O., Jr., LtCol.; February 1945-July 1945; ex-486th Ftr Sqn
104 missions total
P-51D PZ-J 44-14709
Mason, Joseph L., Col.; May 1943-November 1944
P-47D PZ-M 42-8466 "This Is It!"
P-47D PZ-M 42-22486 "This Is It!"
P-51B PZ-M 43-6776 "This Is It!"
P-51B PZ-M 42-106609 "This Is It!"
P-51D PZ-M 44-13395 "This Is It!"
P-51D PZ-M 44-14911 "This Is It!"
Mayden, James D., Col.; July 1944-September 1945
P-51C PE-X 42-103789 "Straw Boss"
P-51D PE-X 44-14111 "Straw Boss 2nd
McPherson, Joel W., Lt.; States-January 29, 1944(POW)
Meyer, John C., LtCol.; November 1944-January 1945; ex-487th Ftr Sqn
135 missions, 462 hours total
P-51D HO-M 44-15041 "Petie 3rd"

**328th Fighter Squadron**
Abbott, Earl L., Maj.; States-January 24, 1945(KIA)
91 missions
P-47D PE-A 42-8435 "Sandra Lee"
P-47D PE-A 42-8653 "Flossie"
P-51B PE-A 42-106844 "Flossie II"
P-51D PE-A 44-14710 "Flossie III"
Allain, Leroy J., Jr., Lt.; June 1944-August 13, 1944(POW)
Alm, William H., Lt.; States-September 14, 1943(KIA)
Altenpohl, William F., F/O; February 1945-EOW
Bennette, Charles J., Lt.; States-August 1944
P-47D PE-O 42-75057
P-51B PE-O "Archie the Operator 2"
Blanchard, Jack D., Maj.; August 1944-September 23, 1944(MIA-E)
Briggs, Earle W., Lt.; States-July 1944
P-51D PE-I 44-13865 "Claire G II"
Broadwater, Joseph D., Lt.; July 1944-September 12, 1944(KIA)
Brocklehurst, James A., F/O; March 1945-EOW
Brookins, Richard C., Lt.; March 1944-October 1944
P-51B PE-D 43-7174 "The Duchess V"
Bryan, Donald S., Maj.; March 1943-May 1945
P-47D PE-B 42-8381 "Little One"
P-51B PE-B 43-6894 "Little One II"
P-51D PE-B 44-14061 "Little One III
Burr, James A., Lt.; May 1944-July 18, 1944(KIA)
Campbell, John, Lt.; May 1944-June 8, 1944(KIA)
Camerer, Milton G., Lt.; June 1944-
P-51D PE-O 44-14646 "Oklahoma Kid"
Carlone, Michele M., Lt.; February 1944-May 19, 1944(KIA)
P-51B PE- "Lady Connie"
Cartee, James G., Lt.; September 1944-EOW
P-51K PE-C̲ 44-11560 "Steph'n Jane"
Casper, Richard H., Lt.; June 1944-July 21, 1944(KIA)
Cast, Fred A., Lt.; September 1944-EOW
P-51D PE-U 44-13533 "Eileen I"
Cesky, Charles J., Capt.; June 1944-January 1945
P-51D PE-L 44-13927 "Diann Ruth"
P-51D PE-L 44-13401 "Diann Ruth II"
Chesser, Alvin J., Lt.; August 1944-EOW
78 missions
P-51D PE-E 44-13406 "Bama Rebel"
Clark, Glenn R., Lt.; May 1944-November 2, 1944(POW)
P-51D PE-D 44-11153 "Mom & Dad"
Coleman, John B., Capt.; November 1942-October 5, 1944(MIA-E)
P-47D PE-J 42-22529 "Mavourneen"
P-51B PE-J 43-7200
P-51B PE-J 43-24801
P-51C PE-J 42-103787
Cornick, Ray L., Lt.; November 1942-February 3, 1944(KIA)
P-47D PE-R 42-22513 "Ilene"
P-47D PE-R 42-8563 "Ilene II"
Dodd, Richard V., Lt.; July 1944-EOW
Donaldson, I.B. Jack, Maj.; March 1944-March 1944; ex-487th Ftr Sqn
61 missions total
Dubay, Elmo B., Capt.; @July 1944-May 1945
P-51D PE-V 44-13849 "Buster 2nd"
Duncan, Earl D., LtCol.; January 1945-September 1945; ex-HdQts
P-51K PE-Q 44-11644 "Juliet"
Dyke, Samuel E., Lt.; February 1944-September 1944
P-51B PE-W 42-106756
Edwards, John C., LtCol.; July 1944-October 1944; ex-HdQts
Eacker, Arthur C., Lt.; August 1944-September 13, 1944(KIAc)
Edelon, George J., Capt.; June 1944-May 1945
P-51D PE-T 44-14968 "Momita"
Evans, Sylvester J., Lt.; August 1944-February 24, 1945(POW)
Fieg, Lothar, Capt.; States-@March 1945
66 missions
P-47D PE-F 42-8456 "Denali"
P-51B PE-F 43-6988 "Denali"
P-51D PE-F 44-13801
P-51D PE-F 44-14882 "Katy Did"
Furr, William W., Lt.; February 1944-June 5, 1944(POW)
P-47D PE-R 42-8563
P-51B PE-R 42-106640 "Lois"
Galiga, John W., Lt.; February 1944-July 18, 1944(KIA)
P-51B PE-K 43-7165 "Lady Lynn"
Gehrke, Walter, Lt.; June 1944-August 6, 1944(KIA)
Godfrey, McDonald, Lt.; May 1944-July 31, 1944(POW)
Goodman, Charles E., Lt.; August 1944-EOW
P-51D PE-N 44-15530 "Family Ties"
Halton, William T., LtCol.; States-October 1944; to 487th Ftr Sqn
186 missions, 561 hours total
P-47D PE-T 42-8439 "Slender, Tender & Tall"
P-51B PE-T 42-106717 "Slender, Tender, & Tall"
P-51D PE-T 44-13996 "Slender, Tender, & Tall"
Hendrian, William E., Capt.; States-March 1945
132 missions, 470 hours
P-51B PE-P "Blondie"
P-51D PE-P 44-13806 "Kentucky Babe"
Hill, Francis R., Lt.; July 1944-; ex-452nd Bomb Grp(35 missions)
P-51D PE-Q 44-15273 "Mary Lu"
Hoffman, Lt.; September 1943-
Horne, Francis W., Capt.; September 1943-September 1944
P-47D PE-C 42-8580 "Hiyo Silver"
P-51B PE-S 42-106703 "Snoot's Sniper"
Howard, Hugh A., Jr., F/O; October 1944-December 31, 1944(KIA)
Hudson, Arthur E., Lt.; July 1944-November 27, 1944(KIA)
Hurley, James C., Lt.; July 1944-EOW
Hylan, Nathan W., Maj.; (KIAc)
Intravartola, Leonard V., Lt.; June 1944-January 1945
P-51D PE-H 44-13921 "Helena"
Jackson, Willie O., Jr., Maj.; March 1944-April 1944; to 486th Ftr Sqn, ex-486th Ftr Sqn
James, Eugene W., Lt.; July 1944-EOW
P-51D PE-E̲ 44-14207 "Rose Marie"
Kebelman, Frank L., Jr., Capt.; June 1944-March 1945
64 missions
P-51D PE-K 44-13759 "Lonesome Polecat"
P-51K PE-K 44-11750 "Lonesome Polecat"
Laing, James L., Lt.; December 1942-April 28, 1944(POW)
P-47D PE-K 42-8657 "Jamie Mi Boy"
Lambright, James F., Lt.; July 1944-August 1945
Lampman, Robert P., Lt.; June 1944-July 21, 1944(KIA)
Lanter, James C., Lt.; June 1944-July 21, 1944(KIA)
Lund, Harold G., Maj.; States-July 1944; ex-PTO pilot
P-47D PE-L 42-8481 "Muriel"
P-51B PE-L "Muriel"
Long, Marion V., Lt.; December 1942-April 22, 1944(POW)
P-47D PE-Y 42-8486
P-51B PE-Y "Helen"
Maxwell, DeWayne J., Capt.; June 1944-January 1945
P-51D PE-M 44-14764 "Mr. Lucky"
P-51D PE-M 44-14964 "Mr. Lucky"
McAuliffe, Richard G., Maj.; March 1945-EOW; ex-82nd Ftr Grp, MTO (3 kills)
P-51K PE-J 44-11628 "Vivienne III"
McCarthy, Francis J., Lt.; January 1945-March 30, 1945(KIA)

McCarthy, Lawrence E., Lt.; States-@April 1945
P-47D PE-M 42-76320 "Patty"
P-51B PE-M 43-6906 "Patty II"
P-51B PE-M "Patty III"
P-51D PE-M 44-13983 "Patty IV"
Meagher, James, Lt.; States-February 8, 1944(KIA)
Middleton, George A., Capt.; June 1944-April 1945
P-51C PE-F 42-103801 "The Worra Bird"
Miller, Fremont W., Lt.; December 1942-April 1944(Injured April 15)
58 missions, 158 hours
P-47D PE-W 42-8511 "Red Raider"
P-47D PE-W 42-22519 "Red Raider"
Miller, Harry L., Jr., Lt.; States-June 8, 1944(KIA)
P-47D PE-D 42-8660 "Stinky"
P-51B PE-D 42-106859
Mitchell, Ray R., Lt.; July 1944-May 1945
69 missions
Montgomery, William E., F/O; July 1944-March 1945
P-51D PE-W 44-13685 "One & Only"
Nussman, Howard C., Lt.; States-February 8, 1944(KIA)
P-47D PE-N 42-8515 "Dixie Boy"
Olson, Fred D., Lt.; States-October 10, 1943(KIA)
Owen, Charles D., Lt.; October 1944-EOW
P-51D PE-G 44-14684 "Tesseroo"
Parlee, Wendell F., Capt.; December 1942-August 1944
P-47D PE-E 42-8680 "Betty"
P-51B PE-E
Petty, James P., F/O; March 1945-EOW
Phillips, Ray G., Lt.; September 1943-June 10, 1944(KIA)
P-47D PE-P 42-7997 "Hildegarde"
P-51B PE-P 42-106868 "Hildegarde"
Powell, Robert H., Lt.; September 1943-August 1944
93 missions
P-47D PE-K 42-8657 "The West, By Gawd, Virginian"
P-51B PE-P 42-106757 (same name)
P-51B PE-P 42-106914 (same name)
P-51D PE-P 44-13930 (same name)
Pratt, Richard A., Lt.; June 1944-June 9, 1944(KIAc)
0 missions
Preddy, George E., Maj.; October 1944-December 25, 1944(KIA); ex-487th Ftr Sqn
143 missions, 532 hours total
P-51D PE-P 44-14906 "Cripes A' Mighty"
Price, Steve R., Lt.; -EOW
Provost, Lt.; December 1944-
Quinn, Quentin L., Capt.; December 1942-August 6, 1944(KIA)
P-47D PE-Q J2-8517 "INB/Eleanor"
P-51B PE-Q 42-106663 "That's A-Crock"
Quittmeyer, Robert H., Lt.; December 1944-EOW
P-51D PE-Q
Rayborn, Garland, Lt.; April 1944-September 11, 1944(KIA)
P-51B PE-Z 42-106459 "La Riena Peg"
P-51D PE-Z 44-13785 "La Riena Peg"
Redman, Thomas M., Lt.; December 1944-EOW
P-51D PE-K "Peg"
Reiners, John F., Lt.; December 1944-April 19, 1945(KIA)
Ridge, R.W., Lt.; December 1944-EOW
Robinson, Victor J., Lt.; December 1944-EOW
Rogers, Charles E., Lt.; June 1944-November 9, 1944(KIA)
Rutherford, Joseph R., Lt.; October 1944-EOW
Sanford, William H., Lt.; August 1944-EOW
Schwenke, William D., Jr., Lt.; States-March 11, 1944(KIA)
P-47D PE-S 42-8424 "Kathie"
Semon, Richard F., Lt.; June 1944-
P-51D PE-S 44-14343 "Dingbat"
Sharp, Robert H., Capt.; States-June 9, 1944(KIAc)
P-47D PE-V 42-8587 "Ramblin Rebel"
P-51B PE-V "Ramblin Rebel"
Smith, Elmer L., Lt.; April 1944-September 1944
Spicer, George W., Lt.; February 1945-March 1945; to 361st Ftr Grp
Stangel, William J., Capt.; August 1944-March 1945
P-51D PE-C "Stinky"
P-51D PE-C 44-14015 "Stinky 2"
Stefanik, Joseph P., Lt.; February 1945-EOW
St. John, Glen W., Lt.; February 1945-May 3, 1945(KIAc)
Stewart, Everett W., Maj.; States-January 1944; to 355th Ftr Grp; ex-18th Ftr Grp, PTO
P-47D PE-G 42-8437 "Sunny IV"
Stott, John W., Lt.; April 1944-September 1944
P-51B PE-Y 42-106852 "Sugarfoot"
Taylor, Emery L., Lt.; October 1944-EOW
Thornell, John F., Jr., Capt.; February 1943-July 1944
90 missions, 290:55 hours
P-47D PE-I 42-22474 "Patty Ann"
P-51B PE-T 42-106872 "Patty Ann"
Vander Vean, Cornelius, F/O; December 1944-EOW
Walker, John H., Jr., Lt.; September 1943-February 8, 1944(KIA)
Walters, Jesse W., Lt.; February 1945-March 1945; to 361st Ftr Grp
Webb, Dana A., Jr., F/O; January 1945-EOW
Weber, Carl W., Lt.; February 1945-EOW
Welch, William B., Lt.; June 1944-December 1944
P-51D PE- "Edwina"
White, Henry W., Jr., Capt.; States-EOW
89 missions
P-47D PE-H 42-8627 "Dallas Darling"
P-47D PE-H 42-74627 "Dallas Darling
P-51D PE-H 44-13582 "Dallas Darling
Whiting, Edmund J., Lt.; May 1944-January 1945
Wilson, William D., Lt.; July 1944-July 19, 1944(POW)
Winter, Frank, Lt.; February 1945-EOW
Yochim, Fred A., Lt.; September 1943-April 9, 1944(POW)
P-47D PE-V 42-8434 "Desiree Y"
Zellner, Edmond, Lt.; September 1943-July 31, 1944(MIA-E)
89 missions
P-47D PE-U 42-22547 "We Three"
P-51B PE-U 42-106832 "We Three"
P-51D PE-U 44-13533 "We Three"
Zimms, David T., Lt.; September 1943-August 1944

**486th Fighter Squadron**

Anderson, Woodrow W., Capt.; September 1943-May 28, 1944(KIA)
P-47D PZ-A
P-51B PZ-A 43-7000
P-51B PZ-A 42-106635 "Texas Bluebonnet"
Andrew, Stephen W., Maj.; December 1942-July 2, 1944(POW); ex-49th Ftr Grp, PTO
91 missions
P-47D PZ-A 42-8699 "Prairie Farmer"
P-51B PZ-A 42-106467
Babbitt, Robert E., Lt.; States-November 30, 1943(KIA)
Barket, Thomas B., Lt.; November 1944-February 1945; to 5th ERS
Bond, Earl H., Lt.; States-March 8, 1944(KIA)
P-47D PZ-O 42-8652 "The Bid"
Bostrom, Ernest O., Capt.; May 1944-April 1945
P-51D PZ-O 44-13929 "Little Marjorie"
Brashear, Warren H., Lt.; September 1943-December 1944
P-51B PZ-B 42-106613
P-51D PZ-B 44-14075
Brown, Robert M., Lt.; States-November 30, 1943(KIA)
Bundy, Lincoln D., Lt.; June 1944-June 10, 1944(KIA)
Cameron, Clarence W., Lt.; August 1944-EOW
Carter, Joseph D., Lt.; August 1944-EOW
Colby, Thomas W., Capt.; November 1942-EOW
P-47D PZ-T 42-8682 "Lil Evey"
P-51B PZ-T 43-6864 "Lil Evey"
P-51D PZ-T 44-13736 "Lil Evey II"
P-51D PZ-T 44-13603 "Lil Evey III"
P-51K PZ-T 44-11654 "Lil Evey IV"
Combs, Howard R., Jr., Lt.; July 1944-September 11, 1944(KIA)
P-51D PZ-W 44-13737
Contos, George G., Lt.; June 1944-February 1945
P-51D PZ-C 44-15701 "Lillian"
Corcoran, Martin E., Lt.; November 1942-August 1944
P-47D PZ-L 42-22491
P-51B PZ-L 42-106439 "Button Nose"
Cunningham, Murdoch R., Lt.; States-June 1944
P-47D PZ-D 42-8460
P-51B PZ-D 42-106472 "The Flying Scot"
Cutler, Frank A., Capt.; December 1942-May 13, 1944(KIA)
P-47D PZ-P
P-51B PZ-P 43-6578 "Soldiers Vote"
Edwards, Harry L., Lt.; June 1944-March 1945
P-51D PZ-I 44-13944 "Miss Cherokee"
Fahrenwald, Ted P., Lt.; States-June 8, 1944(MIA-E)
P-47D PZ-F 42-75138
P-51B PZ-F 43-6850 "The Joker"
P-51C PZ-F 42-103336
Ferris, Charles E., Lt.; June 1944-August 27, 1944(KIA)
P-51B PZ- "Tommyhawk"
Frascotti, Robert C., Lt.; September 1943-June 6, 1944(KIA)
88 missions
P-51B PZ-F 43-6685 "Umbriago"
Freeman, Cecil M., Lt.; June 1944-April 1945
P-51D PZ-F 44-13362 "Sleepy Chicken"
French, David J., Lt.; June 1944-August 5, 1944(POW)
P-51B PZ-F 43-6864
Fuenpstueck, Carl J., Lt.; August 1944-August 27, 1944(POW)
Fuhrman, Carlton L., Lt.; May 1944-October 1944
P-51D PZ-D 44-14091
Gates, Richard J., Capt.; January 1944-June 1944; to HdQts
Gerbe, William T., Jr., Lt.; August 1944-April 1945
76 missions
P-51D PZ-Z 44-14087 "Little Gyp"
Gerst, Joseph L., Lt.; April 1944-September 1944
P-51B PZ-X 43-6865 "Smoky Joe"
Gignac, Edward J., Maj.; December 1942-April 1944; to HdQts
ex-49th & 35th Ftr Grps, PTO
P-47D PZ-G 42-22548 "Gigs-Up"
P-51B PZ-G 43-7185 "Gigs-Up II"
Grabovski, Bruno J., Lt.; June 1944-March 1945
P-51B PZ-Q 42-106439 "Duchess"
P-51K PZ-Q 44-11633 "Duchess"
Green, Jack A., Lt.; June 1944-April 1945

Greene, Franklyn N., Maj.; States-March 1945
P-47D PZ-I 42-22509 "Snow White"
P-51B PZ-I 42-106480 "Geronimo"
P-51D PZ-I 44-13944 "Geronimo"
P-51D PZ-I 44-14911 "Geronimo"
Gremaux, Leonard A., Lt.; April 1944-December 1944
P-51D PZ-G 44-14150 "Little Stinker"
Griffiths, Charles E., Jr., Capt.; April 1944-December 1944
63 missions, 270 hours
P-51B PZ-G 43-7000 "Marj"
P-51D PZ-G 44-14187 "Marj"
Harker, Chester V., Capt.; States-September 1945
P-47D PZ-H 42-22486 "Cile"
P-51B PZ-H 43-6509 "Cile II"
P-51D PZ-H 44-13979 "Cile III"
P-51D PZ-H 44-15611 "Cile VI"
Hein, Ralph L., F/O; March 1945-EOW; ex-361st Ftr Grp
Heller, Edwin L., Capt.; March 1943-May 1945
520 hours
P-47D PZ-H 42-75183 "Happy"
P-51B PZ-H 43-6704 "Hell-er-Bust"
P-51D PZ-H 44-14696 "Hell-er-Bust"
Henderson, Richard L., Lt.; June 1944-January 1945; ex-448th Bomb Group
68 missions
P-51D PZ-R 44-14401 "Miss Suzie-Q"
Higgins, Donald H., Maj.; States-September 1945
84 missions
P-47D PZ-B 42-75076
P-51B PZ-B 43-6436 "Bayou Baby"
P-51K PZ-B 44-11365
Howell, Lester L., Lt.; April 1944-July 2, 1944(KIA)
P-51B PZ-V 42-106857 "Texas Knight
Jackson, Willie O., Jr., LtCol.; May 1943-March 1944; to 328th Ftr Sqn; April 1944-February 1945; to HdQts
104 missions
P-47D PZ-J 42-8452
P-51B PZ-J 42-106661 "Hot Stuff"
P-51D PZ-J 44-13398
P-51D PZ-J 44-14709
Johnson, Marion D., F/O March 1945-EOW; ex-361st Ftr Grp
Jones, Fred R., Lt.; September 1944-February 24, 1945(KIA)
Karan, Alex A., Lt.; September 1944-September 1945
P-51D PZ-K 44-14877 "Beautiful Betty"
Karl, Bernard H., Lt.; May 1944-December 1944
P-51B PZ-K 43-7185 "Joe & Bill"
Kilgo, Lee E., Capt.; August 1944-EOW
P-51D PZ-K 44-15390 "Alabama"
Kivela, Eino R., F/O April 1945-EOW
Kramer, David C., Lt.; States-November 30, 1943(MIA-E)
Kyle, Thompson R., Lt.; June 1944-October 24, 1944(POW)
35 missions
Lazear, Earl R., Jr., Capt.; June 1944-March 1945
P-51D PZ-L 44-14877 "Pennie's Earl"
Leibfarth, Russell J., Capt.; June 1944-May 1945
P-51B PZ-L 42-106439
Lind, Arthur L., Lt.; June 1944-April 1945
P-51D PZ-W 44-13737
Lundquist, Gustav E., Maj.; July 1944-July 29, 1944(POW)
1 mission
MacKean, Robert G., Capt.; States-April 24, 1944(KIA)
P-47D PZ-Z 42-8548
P-51B PZ-Z 43-7198
Markle, Donald J., Lt.; April 1944-June 10, 1944(KIA)
P-51B PZ-M 43-6776
Marshall, Alfred L., Lt.; States-April 11, 1944(KIA)
P-47D PZ-Q 42-74644 "Sweet Chariot"
P-51B PZ-Q 43-7031 "Sweet Chariot"
Martin, Harry W., F/O; April 1945-EOW
McClung, Franklin B., F/O; April 1945-EOW
McKenna, James P., F/O; March 1945-EOW; ex-361st Ftr Grp
McKibben, Donald W., Lt.; December 1942-September 1944
P-47D PZ-Y 42-76323 "Sneezy"
P-51B PZ-Y 42-106483 "Miss Lace"
P-51C PZ-Y 42-103283
Meyer, Earl J., Lt.; States-June 1944
P-47D PZ-E 42-8459 "Bonnie Lee"
P-51B PZ-E 43-6731 "Bonnie Lee"
Miklajcyk, Henry J., Capt.; States-November 2, 1944(KIA)
P-47C PZ-K 41-6531 "The Syracusan"
P-51B PZ-K 42-106430 "The Syracusan II"
P-51D PZ-K 44-13690 "The Syracusan 3rd"
Miles, Stanley G., Capt.; States-June 1944
P-47D PZ-S 42-8490 "Bundle of Joy"
P-51B PZ-S 43-6500
Miller, Robert J., Lt.; June 1944-April 1945
P-51D PZ- "Larry D"
Mundell, Earl L., Jr., Lt.; June 1944-March 1945
P-51B PZ-M 43-6865
P-51D PZ-M 44-14091

Northrup, Leo W., Lt.; States-August 1944
P-47D PZ-N "Donna Dae"
P-51B PZ-N 43-6736 "Donna Dae"
P-51D PZ-N 44-13688 "Donna Dae"
O'Brien, Louis V., F/O; April 1945-EOW
0 missions
Pattillo, Charles C., Lt.; December 1944-EOW
P-51D PZ-W 44-13737 "Little Rebel"
Paulsen, Eugene A., Lt.; December 1944-EOW
P-51D PZ-F 44-13362 "My Bet"
P-51D PZ-F 44-63202 "My Bet"
Peter, Robert E., Lt.; July 1944-EOW
P-51D PZ-P 44-14187
Powell, Fred H., Lt.; September 1944-February 3, 1945(POW)
Price, Charles D., Lt.; December 1944-September 1945
P-51D PZ-X 44-13671 "Little Skunk"
Raub, Waldo C., Lt.; June 1944-June 20, 1944(KIA)
Rauk, Lloyd A., Capt.; States-August 1944
P-47D PZ-R "Dopey Rauk-et"
P-51D PZ-R 44-13398 "Rauk-et"
Reese, William H., Capt.; @June 1944-August 17, 1944(MIA-E); September 1944-EOW
P-51D PZ-R 44-15068 "Rascal"
Reichman, David M., Lt.; June 1944-EOW
P-51D PZ-N 44-13979 "Miss Anne"
Richmond, Luther H., LtCol.; February 1943-April 15, 1944(POW)
67 missions
P-47D PZ-R 42-8412 "Sweetie"
P-51B PZ-R 43-7196
Rushman, Glenn A., Lt.; September 1944-EOW
57 missions, 237 hours
P-51D PZ-P 44-15142 "Miss Ginny"
Salvesan, Kenneth L., Lt.; September 1944-September 1945
Schmidley, Herbert L., Lt.; February 1945-EOW
Shaw, Joseph E., Lt.; September 1944-EOW
Sloan, James T., Lt.; February 1945-EOW
Smigelski, Frank P., Lt.; July 1944-April 1945
P-51D PZ-A 44-14224 "Hellgate Express"
Soutiere, Leonard O., Lt.; February 1945-EOW
Stearns, John D., Lt.; July 1944-September 1945
P-51D PZ-C 44-15701 "Delivery Boy"
Stoll, Marvin B., Lt.; June 1944-April 1945
Stover, Merton J., Lt.; June 1944-
P-51B PZ-S 42-106613 "Ellie"
P-51D PZ-S 44-14220 "Ellie"
Swinson, Ronald O., Lt.; February 1945-EOW
Thurman, Gerald D., Lt.; June 1944-August 12, 1944(KIA)
Turner, John L., Lt.; February 1945-EOW
Vitek, Lumir J., Capt.; June 1944-May 1945
P-51B PZ-V 43-6736 "Little Ogre"
P-51B PZ-V 42-106751 "Little Ogre"
P-51D PZ-V 44-14215 "Little Ogre"
Wallace, Alton J., Capt.; States-EOW
64 missions
P-47D PZ-W 42-8377 "Little Rebel"
P-51B PZ-W 43-7022 "Little Rebel"
P-51D PZ-W 44-13737 "Little Rebel"
Wanda, Roy A., F/O; December 1944-EOW
31 missions
P-51D PZ-Z 44-14087 "Denny Boy"
Washburn, Edward F., Lt.; February 1945-EOW
Wensch, Glenn W., Lt.; August 1944-EOW
P-51D PZ-H 44-15611 "Diablo"
Whinnem, Donald Y., Lt.; September 1943-September 1944
P-51B PZ-W 42-106752 "HMS Hellion"
Whitney, James B., Lt.; February 1945-EOW
Wilkerson, Donald A., Lt.; December 1944-EOW
P-51K PZ-W "Jeannie"
Williams, Edward R., Lt.; February 1945-September 1945
P-51D PZ-T 44-13736 "Dotty"
Williams, Kenneth S., Lt.; March 1944-September 1944
P-47D PZ-P 42-75399
P-51B PZ-P "Izzy"
Worcester, John B., Lt.; April 1944-May 8, 1944(KIAc)

**487th Fighter Squadron**
Allison, Fred M., Jr., Capt.; December 1942-June 1944
70 missions, 202 hours
P-47D HO-A 42-75072 "Opal Lee"
P-51B HO-A 42-106502 "Opal Lee"
Andrews, Jimmie B., F/O; September 1943-November 1943; to 310th Ferry Sqn
Arnold, Guy C., Lt.; States-September 1944
P-47D HO-A 42-8432 "Babylon Panther"
P-51D HO-A 44-13530 "Babylon Panther"
Ayers, Joseph B., Lt.; June 1944-September 23, 1944(KIA)
Barnes, Harry H., Lt.; February 1944-August 13, 1944(MIA-E)
P-51B HO-B 42-106751
P-51D HO-B 44-13619 "William's Villian"
Bateman, James A., Lt.; July 1944-April 1945
P-51D HO-F 44-14794 "Buzz Boy"
P-51D HO-F 44-15712 "Buzz Boy II"

Bennett, John R., Maj.; November 1942-April 1945
134 missions, 500 hours
P-47D HO-Y 42-8421
P-51B HO-Y 43-6506
P-51D HO-Y 44-13876 "Pistol Packin' Mama"
P-51K HO-Y 44-11556 "Pistol Packin' Mama"
Berkshire, Robert H., Lt.; December 1942-June 27, 1944(MIA-E)
P-47D HO-U 42-22515 "Brutal Lulu"
P-51B HO-U 43-6593 "Brutal Lulu"
Bielok, Adolph., Lt.; March 1944-June 28, 1944(KIA)
Bowers, Glenn L., Lt.; May 1944-February 1945
Britt, Daniel T., Jr., Lt.; States-January 1944
Butler, Robert K., Lt.; February 1944-June 6, 1944(MIA-E); August 1944-April 1945
P-51C HO-V 42-103312 "Channel Belle"
Button, Hayes D., Capt.; September 1943-December 30, 1943(POW)
P-47D HO-B 42-8488
Castle, Henry G., Lt.; November 1944-January 1945; to 361st Ftr Grp
Chapman, J., Lt.; September 1943-November 1943; to 310th Ferry Sqn
Cheney, William B., F/O; May 1945-July 1945
0 missions
Clark, John F., Lt.; June 1944-September 23, 1944(KIA)
35 missions
Cole, Charles E., F/O; March 1945-EOW; ex-361st Ftr Grp
Collard, Royal E., Lt.; June 1944-October 1944
P-51B HO- "Tepee"
Collins, Robert J., Lt.; November 1944; ex-356th Ftr Grp
Conard, Jule V., Lt.; May 1944-July 16, 1944(POW)
P-51C HO-C 42-103341 "Spirit of Lufberry"
Corson, Charles O., Lt.; June 1944-July 1945
Crawford, James L., Lt.; October 1944-September 1945
50 missions
P-51D HO-P 44-14487 "Mary Lou"
Creamer, Richard W., Lt.; October 1944-September 1945
P-51D HO-C 44-13384
Daugherty, Robert S., Lt.; June 1944-June 18, 1944(KIAc)
0 missions
Davis, Clayton E., Capt.; States-August 17, 1944(MIA-E)
P-47D HO-C "Marjorie"
P-51B HO-C 43-6805 "Marjorie II"
P-51D HO-C 44-13651
Diamond, Walker G., Lt.; October 1944-September 1945
P-51D HO-D 44-11335
Dilling, Donald K., Capt.; States-December 30,1943(MIA-E)
P-47D HO-S 42-8447
Dittmer, Karl K., Lt.; October 1944-January 1945; ex-385th Bomb Grp
P-51D HO-I 44-14955 "Dopey Okie"
Dodson, Lt.; February 1944-
Doleac, Cyril B., Lt.; July 1944-August 1945
P-51D HO-E 44-14397 "Ex-Lax... Shht'n Git!"
P-51D HO-X 44-15383 "Maid of Orleans"
Donahue, Duncan R., Capt.; States-September 8, 1944(KIA)
P-51B HO-D 43-7167 "Gusiller III"
Donaldson, I.B. Jack, Maj.; January 1943-March 1944; to 328th Ftr Sqn; ex-21st Pur Sqn & 49th Ftr Grp, PTO
61 missions, 171 hours total
P-47D HO-D 42-8454 "Maureen"
Draftz, Robert C., Lt.; June 1944-EOW
P-51D HO-D 44-14285 "Tillie"
Drisko, William W., Lt.; June 1944-June 25, 1944(MIA-E); September 1944-
Duncan, Earl D., LtCol.; September 1944-January 1945; to HdQts
Ellison, Charles E., Capt.; September 1943-August 1944
P-47D HO-E 42-76088
P-51B HO-E 43-7139
P-51D HO-E 44-13547
Evans, Evan J., Lt.; July 1944-September 25, 1944(POW)
Forga, James H., Jr., Lt.; June 1944-October 6, 1944(KIA)
Fowler, William E., Lt.; February 1944-September 1944
P-51B HO-F 43-6658 "Sweet'n Hot"
P-51D HO-F 44-13597 "Stardust"
Frum, Rollin W., F/O; March 1945-EOW; ex-361st Ftr Grp
Garney, Clifford P., Lt.; April 1944-June 7, 1944(KIA)
Gaylor, James F., Lt.; January 1944-
Gee, Langhorne S., Lt.; States-November 1943; to 310th Ferry Sqn
Goebel, Anthony H., Lt.; October 1944-July 1945
Goodwin, Donald C., Lt.; June 1944-February 1945
P-51D HO-W 44-13361
Graham, Robert W., Lt.; July 1944-August 12, 1944(KIA)
Graves, James F., F/O; March 1945-EOW; ex-361st Ftr Grp
P-51D HO-F 44-15712 "Lady Gue"
Greer, Cyrus M., Lt.; May 1944-January 1945
72 missions
P-51B HO-G 43-7139 "Lili Marlene"
P-51D HO-G 44-14819 "Lili Marlene II"
Grow, Richard L., Lt.; November 1942-December 22, 1943(KIA)
Hall, Robert L., Lt.; March 1944-June 7, 1944(KIA)
Halton, William T., LtCol.; October 1944-EOW; ex-328th Ftr Sqn
186 missions, 561 hours total
P-51D HO-T 44-13557 "Slender, Tender, & Tall"
P-51D HO-T 44-14812 "Slender, Tender, & Tall"
Hamilton, Ralph W., Capt.; January 1943-March 1945
130 missions, 461:25 hours
P-47D HO-H 42-22457 "Frances B"
P-51B HO-H 43-6754 "Frances B Too"
P-51D HO-H 44-14668 "Jeanne H"
Hannon, James D., Lt.; April 1944-May 24, 1944(POW)
Heyer, Sheldon, Lt.; June 1944-July 1945
P-51B HO-N 43-6958 "Sweetie Face"
P-51D HO-N 44-14151 "Sweetie Face"
Howard, Alfred P., Jr., Lt.; April 1944-May 12, 1944(KIA)
P-51B HO- "Legal Eagle"
Huston, Dean M., Lt.; July 1944-April 1945
P-51D HO-L 44-14801 "The Hawk-Eye-Owan"
Jesup, Nelson R., Lt.; May 1944-March 1945
P-51B HO-I 43-6707 "Peanuts"
P-51D HO-J 44-14475 "Peanuts"
Johnson, Clarence O., Capt.; August 1944-September 23, 1944(KIA); ex-82nd Ftr Grp, MTO & 479th Ftr Grp
P-51D HO-C 44-13953 "Bula B IV"
Kegg, Thomas V., Lt.; January 1945-EOW
Kessler, John P., Capt.; States-August 1944
P-47D HO-K
P-51B HO-K 43-7094
P-51B HO-K 42-106836
Kopecky, George, Lt.; February 1944-May 8, 1944(POW)
Landrum, Jack C., Lt.; July 1944-October 24, 1944(KIAc)
Lauderdale, Thomas, Lt.; October 1944-March 1945(injured)
Littge, Raymond H., Capt.; June 1944-May 1945
91 missions, 391 hours
P-51C HO-M 42-103320 "Silver Dollar"
P-51D HO-M 44-11330 "E Pluribus Unum"
P-51D HO-M 44-72216 "Miss Helen"
Lowry, Lester L., Lt.; January 1944-January 26, 1944(KIAc)
Luksic, Carl J., Lt.; December 1942-May 24, 1944(POW)
P-47D HO-Z 42-75860 "Lucky Boy"
P-51B HO-Z 43-7145 "Elly's Lucky Boy"
P-51B HO-Z 42-106788 "Elly's Lucky Boy"
McBride, Leo, Lt.; April 1944-
McEntire, David W., Lt.; States-June 1944
P-47D HO-I 42-8431 "Amelia Christine"
P-51B HO-I 43-6707
McIntyre, Winfield E., Capt.; States-December 30, 1943(POW)
P-47D HO- "Ida Marian"
McMahan, Ernest B., Capt.; December 1942-May 9, 1944(KIAc)
P-47D HO-T 42-74720
P-51B HO-T 43-6503 "Honey Baby"
Meroney, Virgil K., Capt.; October 1942-April 8, 1944(POW)
P-47D HO-V 42-8473 "Sweet Louise"
P-51B HO-V 43-7166
Meyer, John C., LtCol.; December 1942-November 1944; to HdQts
135 missions, 462 hours total
P-47D HO-M 42-8529 "Lambie"
P-51B HO-M 42-106471 "Lambie/Petie"
P-51D HO-M 44-14151 "Petie 2nd"
P-51D HO-M 44-15041 "Petie 3rd"
Miller, William C., Jr., Lt.; July 1944-March 1945
P-51D HO-S 44-14812 "Sweet Fern"
Moats, Sanford K., Capt.; June 1944-June 1945
89 missions, 367 hours
P-51B HO-K 42-106751 "Kay"
P-51D HO-K 44-14848 "Kay III"
Moran, Glennon T., Lt.; September 1943-August 1944
90 missions
P-47D HO-M 42-22785
P-51B HO-M 43-6912
P-51C HO-M 42-103320 "Miss Ann"
Mulvey, William C., Lt.; June 1944-June 7, 1944(KIAc)
0 missions
Neumann, Robert F., Lt.; April 1945-EOW
Nutter, Marion J., Capt.; States-March 1945
81 missions
P-47D HO-N
P-51B HO-N 43-7160 "Margie"
P-51B HO-N
P-51D HO-N 44-13321 "Sexshunate"
O'Nan, Robert G., Lt.; January 1944-June 6, 1944(POW)
Oefinger, Richard W., Lt.; April 1945-EOW
Padden, Walter, Lt.; December 1944-April 16, 1945(KIA)
Palmer, Clarence J., Capt.; States-August 1944
85 missions, 301 hours
P-47D HO-J 42-8382 "Helen of Troy"
P-51B HO-J 43-6439 "Helen of Troy 2nd"
P-51B HO-J 42-106901 "Helen of Troy 3rd"
Palmquist, James D., Lt.; April 1945-EOW
Pattillo, Cuthbert A., Lt.; December 1944-April 16, 1945(POW)
35 missions
P-51K HO-Y 44-11556 "Sweet & Lovely"
Peterson, Albert L., Lt.; December 1944-March 18, 1945(POW)
Pickering, Malcolm C., Lt.; April 1944-September 1944
P-51B HO-S 43-7094 "Gracie"

Preddy, George E., Maj.; January 1943-August 1944; later 328th Ftr Sqn; ex-49th Ftr Grp, PTO
143 missions, 532 hours
P-47D HO-P 42-8500 "Cripes A' Mighty"
P-51B HO-P 42-106451 "Cripes A' Mighty 2nd"
P-51D HO-P 44-13321 "Cripes A' Mighty 3rd"
Prichard, Joseph W., Lt.; December 1944-EOW
P-51D HO-V 44-14668
Pryer, Edwin E., Lt.; September 1944-March 21, 1945(KIAc)
Reading, Francis C., Jr., Lt.; January 1945-EOW
Reed, Robert G., Lt.; December 1944-EOW
Reed, Robert L., Lt.; May 1944-
Reynolds, Miron C., Lt.; February 1945-April 17, 1945(KIA)
Ricci, Carlo A., Lt.; February 1945-EOW
P-51D HO-Z 44-72389 "Ron-Marie"
Rigby, Alden P., Lt.; July 1944-March 1945
70 missions
P-51D HO-R 44-15629 "Eleen & Jerry"
Riley, Harold S., Jr., Lt.; December 1942-March 11, 1944(KIA)
P-47D HO-R 42-22530
Roebuck, Wesley N., Lt.; December 1944-March 25, 1945(KIA)
Ross, Robert I., Lt.; September 1943-April 15, 1944(KIA)
P-47D HO-O 42-8678 "Skip"
Ross, Russell H., Lt.; September 1944-EOW
65 missions
P-51D HO-Q 44-14790 "Miss Nita"
Sandor, Andrew E., F/O; February 1945-March 1945; to 361st Ftr Grp
Schuh, Duerr H., Capt.; July 1944-March 1945
67 missions, 272 hours
P-51D HO-A 44-13530 "Dutchess"
Sears, Alex F., Capt.; June 1944-June 1945
P-51D HO-E 44-14778 "Sheepherder"
Seesland, William H., Lt.; February 1945-EOW
Smith, Walter S., Capt.; June 1944-November 27, 1944(POW)
Starck, Walter E., Capt.; November 1942-November 27, 1944(POW)
106 missions, 361 hours
P-47D HO-X 42-8694
P-51B HO-X 43-6929 "Starck Mad"
P-51B HO-X 43-24807 "Starck Mad"
Stewart, Henry M., II, Lt.; June 1944-February 1945
P-51D HO-N 44-13321 "The Margarets"
P-51D HO-N 44-14716 "The Margarets"
Sykes, Henry S., Lt.; August 1944-July 1945
Tafel, Carl G., Jr., Lt.; June 1944-December 26, 1944(KIA)
P-51D HO-C 44-13953 "Nancy M"
Taylor, Guy P., Lt.; May 1944-November 1944
P-51B HO-T 43-6697
Vickery, Joseph P., Lt.; June 1944-March 18, 1945(KIA)
P-51D HO-C 44-15031 "Rattop IV"
Vinay, Daniel, Jr., Lt.; October 1944-EOW
Waldron, Karl M., Jr., Lt.; August 1944-EOW
P-51B HO-U 42-106836
P-51D HO-U 44-15513 "Goliath"
Walker, Horace N., Lt.; February 1945-March 1945; to 361st Ftr Grp
Waters, Phanor B., Lt.; August 1944-September 23, 1944(KIA)
Whisner, William T., Capt.; September 1943-February 1945
137 missions
P-47D HO-W 42-8400 "Beverly"
P-51B HO-W 42-106449 "Princess Elizabeth"
P-51D HO-W 44-14237 "Moonbeam McSwine"
White, James N., Lt.; December 1944-EOW
P-51D HO-S 44-14812 "Socky"
Wickenheiser, Cletus, Lt.; February 1945-March 1945; to 361st Ftr Grp
Wilcox, Clifford R., Lt.; May 1944-August 5, 1944(POW)
Williamson, Ralph I., Lt.; March 1944-April 8, 1944(KIA)
Wittekiend, Kenneth F., Lt.; February 1945-July 1945
Wood, James N., Lt.; May 1944-EOW
89 missions
P-51C HO-Z 42-103758 "The Fox"
P-51D HO-Z 44-15041 "The Fox"
Woodhall, James E., Lt.; March 1945-EOW
Wright, Madison C., Lt.; March 1945-July 1945

**Aircraft of the 328th Fighter Squadron**

P-47D-2-RE
42-7997 PE-P "Hildegarde" R.G. Phillips
42-8380 PE-C
42-8381 PE-B "Little One" D.S. Bryan

P-47D-5-RE
42-8419 PE-X "Blondie"
42-8424 PE-S "Kathie" W.S. Schwenke
42-8434 PE-V "Desiree Y" F.A. Yochim
42-8435 PE-A "Sandra Lee" E.L. Abbott
42-8436 PE-Y
42-8437 PE-G "Sunny IV" E.W. Stewart
42-8439 PE-T "Slender, Tender, & Tall" W.T. Halton
42-8454 PE-D
42-8456 PE-F "Denali" L. Fieg
42-8481 PE-L "Muriel" H.G. Lund
42-8486 PE-Y M.V. Long
42-8493 PE-F
42-8508 PE-Z "Panama Papacito" E.L. Clark
42-8509 PE-I
42-8511 PE-W "Red Raider" F.W. Miller
42-8515 PE-N "Dixie Boy" H.C. Nussman
42-8517 PE-Q "INB/Eleanor" Q.L. Quinn
42-8520 PE-M
42-8527 PE-V "Ramblin' Rebel" R.H. Sharp
42-8556 PE-M "Patricia Lee"
42-8563 PE-R "Ilene II" R.L. Cornick
42-8580 PE-C "HiYo Silver" F.W. Horne
42-8627 PE-H "Dallas Darling" H.W. White
42-8653 PE-A "Flossie" E.L. Abbott
42-8657 PE-K "Jamie Mi Boy" J.L. Laing
42-8657 PE-K "The West, By Gawd, Virginian" R.H. Powell
42-8660 PE-D "Stinky" H.L. Miller
42-8680 PE-E "Betty" W.F. Parlee

P-47D-2-RA
42-22474 PE-I "Patti Ann" J.F. Thornell
42-22513 PE-R "Ilene" R.L. Cornick
42-22519 PE-W "Red Raider" F.W. Miller
42-22529 PE-J "Mavourneen" J.B. Coleman
42-22547 PE-U E. Zellner

P-47D-6-RE
42-74627 PE-H "Dallas Darling" H.W. White

P-47D-10-RE
42-75057 PE-O C.J. Bennette

P-47D-15-RE
42-76320 PE-M "Patty" L.E. McCarthy

P-51C-1-NT
42-103290 PE-
42-103316 PE-L

P-51C-5-NT
42-103747 PE-W

P-51C-10-NT
42-103787 PE-J
42-103789 PE-X "Strawboss" J.D. Mayden
42-103801 PE-F "The Worra Bird" G.A. Middleton

P-51B-5-NA
43-6894 PE-B "Little One II" D.S. Bryan
43-6906 PE-M "Patty III" L.E. McCarthy
43-6934 PE-H "Dallas Darling" H.W. White
43-6988 PE-F "Denali" L. Fieg

P-51B-10-NA
43-7146 PE-V "Buster" E.B. Dubay
43-7165 PE-K "Lady Lynn" J.W. Galiga
43-7174 PE-D "The Duchess V" R.C. Brookins
43-7200 PE-J J.B. Coleman
42-106459 PE-Z E.L. Clark
42-106459 PE-Z "La Riena Peg" G. Rayborn
42-106460 PE-R "Lois" W.W. Furr
42-106624 PE-
42-106663 PE-Q "That's A-Crock" Q.L. Quinn
42-106668 PE-N
42-106681 PE-O "The Maine-iacs" C.J. Bennette
42-106686 PE-P
42-106703 PE-S "Snoot's Sniper" F.W. Horne
42-106710 PE-T "Slender, Tender, & Tall" W.T. Halton
42-106744 PE-E "Pinky"

P-51B-15-NA
42-106756 PE-W S.E. Dyke
42-106757 PE-P "The West, By Gawd, Virginian" R.H. Powell
42-106801 PE-J
42-106827 PE-E "Candy Lamb"
42-106832 PE-U "We Three" E. Zellner
42-106844 PE-A "Flossie II" E.L. Abbott
42-106852 PE-Y "Sugarfoot" J.W. Stott
42-106859 PE-D H.L. Miller
42-106868 PE-P "Hildegarde" R.G. Phillips
42-106872 PE-I "Patti Ann II" J.F. Thornell
42-106914 PE-P "The West, By Gawd, Virginian" R.H. Powell
43-24788 PE-I E.W. Briggs
43-24801 PE-J J.B. Coleman

P-51D-5-NT
44-11153 PE-D "Mom + Dad" G.R. Clark
44-11226 PE-Y
44-11229 PE-M

P-51K-5-NT
44-11560 PE-C "Steph'n Jane" J.G. Cartee
44-11626 PE-Z "It's Supermouse" R.V. Dodd
44-11628 PE-J "The Worra Bird 3rd" G.A. Middleton
44-11628 PE-J "Vivienne III" R.G. McAuliffe
44-11644 PE-Q "Juliet" E.D. Duncan
44-11664 PE-T "Adriene III"
44-11750 PE-K "Lonesome Polecat Jr." F.L. Kebelman

P-51D-5-NA
44-13401 PE-L "Diann Ruth II" C.J. Cesky
44-13406 PE-E "Bama Rebel" A.J. Chesser
44-13533 PE-U "We Three" E. Zellner
44-13533 PE-U "Eileen" F.A. Cast
44-13582 PE-H "Dallas Darling" H.W. White
44-13685 PE-W "One & Only" W.E. Montgomery
44-13759 PE-K "Lonesome Polecat" F.L. Kebelman
44-13785 PE-Z "La Riena Peg II" G. Rayborn
44-13801 PE-F L. Fieg
44-13806 PE-P "Kentucky Babe" W.E. Hendrian
44-13849 PE-V "Buster 2nd" E.B. Dubay
44-13849 PE-V "Little Hunter"
44-13865 PE-I "Claire G II" E.W. Briggs
44-13871 PE-S
44-13910 PE-
44-13921 PE-H "Helena" L.V. Intravartola
44-13927 PE-L "Diann Ruth" C.J. Cesky
44-13930 PE-P "The West, By Gawd, Virginian" R.H. Powell
44-13996 PE-T "Slender, Tender, & Tall" W.T. Halton
44-13983 PE-M "Patty IV" L.E. McCarthy
44-14015 PE-C "Stinky II" W.J. Stangel

P-51D-10-NA
44-14061 PE-B "Little One III" D.S. Bryan
44-14084 PE-G "Tesseroo" C.D. Owen
44-14084 PE-G "Helen"
44-14105 PE-C
44-14111 PE-X "Strawboss 2" J.D. Mayden
44-14207 PE-E "Rose Marie" E.W. James
44-14250 PE-R "Geraldine"
44-14273 PE-S "Georgia Rebel II"
44-14343 PE-S "Dingbat" R.F. Semon
44-14646 PE-O "Oklahoma Kid" M.G. Camerer
44-14710 PE-A "Flossie III" E.L. Abbott
44-14764 PE-M "Mr. Lucky" D.J. Maxwell
44-14828 PE-J

P-51D-15-NA
44-14882 PE-F "Katy Did" L. Fieg
44-14896 PE-H
44-14906 PE-P "Cripes A'Mighty" G.E. Preddy
44-14964 PE-M D.J. Maxwell
44-14968 PE-T "Momita" G.J. Edelen
44-15012 PE- "Genie Boy"
44-15037 PE-I
44-15111 PE-D
44-15273 PE-Q "Mary Lu" F.R. Hill
44-15530 PE-N C.E. Goodman

P-51D-20-NA
44-63179 PE-B "Chub A'Luk" F.J. McCarthy
44-63179 PE-R

Unknown Serials
P-51B PE- "Archie the Operator" C.J. Bennette
P-51B PE- "Lady Connie" M.M. Carlone
P-51B PE-X "Blondie" W.E. Hendrian
P-51B PE- "Marion" M.V. Long
P-51B PE-L "Muriel" H.G. Lund
P-51B PE-V "Ramblin' Rebel" R.H. Sharp
P-51D PE- "Edwina" W.B. Welch
P-51K PE-K "Peg" T.M. Redmond
P-51D PE- "Sparky II"
P-51D PE- "Flying Ginny"
P-51D PE- "Buckeye"
P-51D PE- "Capt. Marvel"
P-51D PE- "Dreamgirl"

**Aircraft of the 486th Fighter Squadron**

P-47C-5-RE
41-6531 PZ-K "The Syracusan" H.J. Miklajcyk

P-47D-2-RE
42-7993 PZ-X "Bromo Baby"
42-8377 PZ-W "Little Rebel" A.J. Wallace

P-47D-5-RE
42-8411 PZ-
42-8412 PZ-R "Sweetie" L.H. Richmond
42-8452 PZ-J W.O. Jackson
42-8459 PZ-E "Bonnie Lee" E.J. Meyer
42-8466 PZ-M "This Is It!" J.L. Mason
42-8460 PZ-D "The Flying Scot" M.R. Cunningham
42-8490 PZ-S "Bundle of Joy" S.G. Miles
42-8514 PZ-
42-8548 PZ-Z R.G. MacKean
42-8652 PZ-O "The Bid" E.H. Bond
42-8682 PZ-T "Lil Evey" T.W. Colby
42-8699 PZ-A "Prairie Farmer" S.W. Andrew

P-47D-2-RA
42-22486 PZ-H "Cile" C.V. Harker
42-22491 PZ-L M.E. Corcoran
42-22509 PZ-I "Snow White" F.N. Greene
42-22516 PZ-
42-22531 PZ-
42-22548 PZ-G "Gigs-Up" E.J. Gignac

P-47D-6-RE
42-74644 PZ-Q "Sweet Chariot" A.L. Marshall

P-47D-10-RE
42-75076 PZ-B D.H. Higgins
42-75138 PZ-F T.P. Fahrenwald
42-75183 PZ-H "Hell-er-Bust" E.L. Heller

P-47D-11-RE
42-75399 PZ-P K.S. Williams

P-47D-15-RE
42-76323 PZ-Y "Sneezy" D.W. McKibben

Unknown Serials
PZ-N "Donna Dae" L.W. Northrup
PZ-U "Dopey Rauk-et" L.A. Rauk

P-51C-1-NT
42-103283 PZ-Y D.W. McKibben

P-51C-5-NT
42-103336 PZ-F T.P. Fahrenwald

P-51B-5-NA
43-6436 PZ-B "Bayou Baby" D.H. Higgins
43-6500 PZ-S S.G. Miles
43-6509 PZ-H "Cile II" C.V. Harker
43-6578 PZ-P "Soldier's Vote" F.A. Cutler
43-6685 PZ-F "Umbriago" R.C. Frascotti
43-6704 PZ-H "Hell-er-Bust" E.L. Heller
43-6731 PZ-E "Bonnie Lee" E.J. Meyer
43-6736 PZ-N "Donna Dee IV" L.W. Northrup
43-6736 PZ-V "The Little Ogre" L.J. Vitek
43-6776 PZ-M "This Is It!" J.L. Mason
43-6776 PZ-M D.J. Markle
43-6850 PZ-F "The Joker" T.P. Fahrenwald
43-6864 PZ-T "Li'l Evey" T.W. Colby
43-6865 PZ-X "Smoky Joe" J.L. Gerst
43-7000 PZ-A W.W. Anderson
43-7000 PZ-G "Marj" C.E. Griffiths
43-7022 PZ-W "Little Rebel" A.J. Wallace
44-7031 PZ-Q "Sweet Chariot" A.L. Marshall

P-51B-10-NA
43-7153 PZ-R
43-7165 PZ-G "Gigs-Up II" E.J. Gignac
43-7185 PZ-K "Joe & Bell" B.H. Karl
43-7196 PZ-R L.H. Richmond
43-7198 PZ-Z R.G. MacKean
42-106430 PZ-K "The Syracusan II" H.J. Miklajcyk
42-106430 PZ-K "Bonnie Lee"
42-106439 PZ-L "Button Nose" M.E. Corcoran
42-106439 PZ-Q "Duchess" B.J. Grabovski
42-106450 PZ-E
42-106467 PZ-A S.W. Andrew
42-106472 PZ-D "The Flying Scot II" M.R. Cunningham/C.L.Fuhrman
42-106480 PZ-I "Geronimo" F.N. Greene
42-106480 PZ-T
42-106483 PZ-Y "Miss Lace" D.W. McKibben
42-106609 PZ-M "This Is It!" J.L. Mason
42-106613 PZ-B "Ellie" W.H. Brashear
42-106635 PZ-A "Texas Bluebonnet" W.W. Anderson
42-106661 PZ-J "Hot Stuff" W.O. Jackson
42-106736 PZ-V

P-51B-15-NA
42-106752 PZ-W "H.M.S. Hellion" D.Y. Whinnem
42-106752 PZ-V "The Little Ogre" L.J. Vitek
42-106753 PZ-3 HACK

42-106857 PZ-V "Texas Knight" L.L. Howell
42-106864 PZ-F

P-51K-1-NT
44-11365 PZ-B

P-51K-5-NT
44-11633 PZ-Q "Duchess" B.J. Grabovski
44-11654 PZ-T "Li'l Evey V" T.W. Colby

P-51D-5-NA
44-13338 PZ-H
44-13362 PZ-F "Sweet Bet" E.A. Paulsen
44-13362 PZ-F "Sleepy Chicken" C.M. Freeman
44-13395 PZ-M "This Is It!" J.L. Mason
44-13398 PZ-J W.O. Jackson
44-13398 PZ-R "Rauk-et" L.A. Rauk
44-13603 PZ-T "Li'l Evey III" T.W. Colby
44-13656 PZ-B "Bayou Baby II" D.H. Higgins
44-13671 PZ-X "Little Skunk" C.M. Price
44-13688 PZ-N "Donna Dee VI" L.W. Northrup
44-13690 PZ-K "The Syracusan 3rd" H.J. Miklajcyk
44-13736 PZ-T "Li'l Evey II" T.W. Colby
44-13736 PZ-T "Dotty" E.R. Williams
44-13737 PZ-W "Little Rebel" A.J. Wallace/C.C. Pattillo
44-13737 PZ-W "H.M.S. Hellion" D.Y. Whinnem
44-13871 PZ-S
44-13929 PZ-O "Little Margie" E.O. Bostrom
44-13944 PZ-I "Geronimo" F.N. Greene
44-13944 PZ-E "Miss Cherokee" H.L. Edwards
44-13979 PZ-H "Miss Anne" D.M. Reichman
44-14043 PZ-T "Li'l Evey IV" T.W. Colby

P-51D-10-NA
44-14057 PZ-J
44-14075 PZ-B "Ellie" W.H. Brashear
44-14087 PZ-Z "Little Gyp" W.T. Gerbe
44-14087 PZ-T "Denny Boy" R.A. Wanda
44-14091 PZ-D C.L. Fuhrman
44-14091 PZ-M E.L. Mundell
44-14150 PZ-G "Little Stinker" L.A. Gremaux
44-14187 PZ-G "Margie" C.E. Griffiths
44-14187 PZ-P
44-14215 PZ-V "Little Ogre" L.J. Vitek
44-14220 PZ-S M.J. Stover
44-14224 PZ-A "Hellgate Express" F.P. Smigelski
44-14225 PZ-V
44-14401 PZ-R "Miss Susie-Q" R.L. Henderson
44-14696 PZ-H "Hell-er-Bust" E.L. Heller
44-14709 PZ-J W.O. Jackson

P-51D-15-NA
44-14877 PZ-L "Pennie's Earl" E.R. Lazear
44-14877 PZ-K "Beautiful Betty" A.A. Karan
44-14911 PZ-I "Geronimo" F.N. Greene
44-14911 PZ-M "This Is It!" J.L. Mason
44-14979 PZ-H "Cile III" C.V. Harker
44-15068 PZ-R "Rascal" W.H. Reese
44-15124 PZ-A
44-15142 PZ-P "Miss Ginny" G.A. Rushman
44-15172 PZ-T
44-15390 PZ-K "Alabama" L.E. Kilgo
44-15515 PZ-R
44-15611 PZ-H "Diablo" G.W. Wensch
44-15611 PZ-H "Cile VI" C.V. Harker
44-15701 PZ-C "Delivery Boy" J.D. Stearns
44-15701 PZ-C "Lillian" G.G. Contos

P-51D-20-NA
44-63202 PZ-F "Sweet Bet" E.A. Paulsen

Unknown Serials
P-51B PZ-P "Izzy" K.S. Williams
P-51B PZ- "Tommyhawk" C.E. Ferris
P-51D PZ- "Larry D" R.J. Miller
P-51K PZ-W "Jeannie" D.A. Wilkerson
P-51D PZ- "Edna"
P-51D PZ- "Lady Connie"

**Aircraft of the 487th Fighter Squadron**

P-47D-2-RE
42-8004 HO-W
42-8382 HO-J "Helen of Troy" C.J. Palmer
42-8400 HO-W "Beverly" W.T. Whisner

P-47D-5-RE
42-8421 HO-Y J.R. Bennett
42-8431 HO-I "Amelia Christine" D.W. McEntire
42-8432 HO-A "Babylon Panther" G.C. Arnold
42-8447 HO-S D.K. Dilling
42-8454 HO-D "Maureen" I.B.J. Donaldson
42-8457 HO-H
42-8473 HO-V "Sweet Louise" V.K. Meroney
42-8474 HO-E "Barbara M" J.C. Edwards
42-8481 HO-U
42-8483 HO-B H.D. Button
42-8500 HO-P "Cripes A'Mighty" G.E. Preddy
42-8516 HO-Z
42-8529 HO-M "Lambie" J.C. Meyer
42-8633 HO-Q
42-8651 HO-
42-8678 HO-O "Skip" R.I. Ross
42-8684 HO-X "Lucia" W.E. Starck

P-47D-2-RA
42-22457 HO-H "Frances B" R.W. Hamilton
42-22487 HO-G
42-22492 HO-F
42-22511 HO-
42-22515 HO-U "Brutal Lulu" R.H. Berkshire
42-22530 HO-R H.S. Riley

P-47D-4-RA
42-22785 HO-M G.T. Moran

P-47D-6-RE
42-74720 HO-T E.B. McMahan

P-47D-10-RE
42-75072 HO-A "Opal Lee" F.M. Allison

P-47D-11-RE
42-75223 HO-
42-75405 HO-
42-75532 HO-

P-47D-15-RE
42-75860 HO-Z "Lucky Boy" C.J. Luksic

P-47D-16-RE
42-76088 HO-E C.E. Ellison

Unknown Serials
HO-C "Marjorie" C.E. Davis
HO- "Ida Marian" W.E. McIntyre

P-51C-1-NT
42-103310 HO-B "William's Villian" H.H. Barnes
42-103312 HO-V "Channel Belle" R.K. Butler
42-103320 HO-M "Miss Ann" G.T. Moran
42-103320 HO-M "Silver Dollar" R.H. Littge

P-51C-5-NT
42-103341 HO-C "Spirit of Lufbery" J.V. Conard
42-103758 HO-Z "The Fox" J.N. Wood

P-51B-5-NA
43-6439 HO-J "Helen of Troy 2nd" C.J. Palmer
43-6503 HO-T "Honey Baby" E.B. McMahan
43-6506 HO-Y J.R. Bennett
43-6593 HO-U "Brutal Lulu" R.H. Berkshire
43-6658 HO-F "Sweet'n Hot" W.E. Fowler
43-6697 HO-T G.P. Taylor
43-6707 HO-I D.W. McEntire
43-6707 HO-I "Peanuts" N.R. Jesup
43-6754 HO-H "Frances B, Too" R.W. Hamilton
43-6805 HO-C "Marjorie II" C.E. Davis
43-6868 HO-L
43-6902 HO-A
43-6912 HO-M G.T. Moran
43-6929 HO-X "Starck Mad!" W.E. Starck
43-6958 HO-N "Sweetie Face" S.N. Heyer
43-7094 HO-K J.P. Kessler
43-7094 HO-S "Gracie" M.C. Pickering
43-7096 HO-E "Barbara M" J.C. Edwards
43-7105 HO-G

P-51B-10-NA
43-7139 HO-E C.E. Ellison
43-7139 HO-G "Lilli Marlene" C.M. Greer
43-7145 HO-Z "Elly's Lucky Boy" C.J. Luksic
43-7160 HO-N "Margie" M.J. Nutter
43-7166 HO-V V.K. Meroney
43-7167 HO-D "Gusillier III" D.R. Donahue
43-7188 HO-Z
43-7192 HO-R
42-106449 HO-W "Princess Elizabeth" W.T. Whisner
42-106451 HO-P "Cripes A'Mighty 2nd" G.E. Preddy

42-106454 HO-O "Louisiana Lady"
42-106471 HO-M "Lambie II/Petie" J.C. Meyer
42-106502 HO-A "Opal Lee" F.M. Allison
42-106654 HO-H "Frances B., Too" R.W. Hamilton
42-106697 HO-T

P-51B-15-NA
42-106751 HO-U "Kay" S.K. Moats
42-106788 HO-Z "Elly's Lucky Boy" C.J. Luksic
42-106831 HO-R
42-106836 HO-K J.P. Kessler
42-106901 HO-J "Helen of Troy 3" C.J. Palmer
43-24807 HO-X "Stark Mad!" W.E. Starck
43-24845 HO-R

P-51D-5-NT
44-11330 HO-M "E Pluribus Unum" R.H. Littge
44-11335 HO-D "Twila Sue" W.G. Diamond

P-51K-5-NT
44-11556 HO-Y "Pistol Packin' Mama" J.R. Bennett
44-11556 HO-Y "Sweet & Lovely" C.A. Pattillo

P-51D-5-NA
44-13320 HO-L
44-13321 HO-P "Cripes A'Mighty 3rd" G.E. Preddy
44-13321 HO-N "Sexshunate" M.J. Nutter
44-13361 HO-W D.C. Goodwin
44-13384 HO-C R.W. Creamer
44-13406 HO-E "Barbara M 4th" J.C. Edwards
44-13530 HO-A "Babylon Panther" G.C. Arnold
44-13530 HO-A "Dutchess" D.N. Schuh
44-13547 HO-E C.E. Ellison
44-13557 HO-T "Slender, Tender, & Tall" W.T. Halton
44-13588 HO-H
44-13597 HO-F "Stardust" W.E. Fowler
44-13619 HO-B "William's Villian" H.H. Barnes
44-13651 HO-C C.E. Davis
44-13758 HO-Z
44-13782 HO-Z
44-13878 HO-Y "Pistol Packin' Mama" J.R. Bennett
44-13953 HO-C "Nancy M" C.G. Tafel

P-51D-10-NA
44-14078 HO-
44-14109 HO-L
44-14151 HO-M "Petie 2nd" J.C. Meyer
44-14151 HO-N "Sweetie Face" S.N. Heyer
44-14160 HO-V "Nancy M 2nd"
44-14161 HO-N
44-14206 HO-Y
44-14237 HO-W "Moonbeam McSwine" W.T. Whisner
44-14285 HO-D "Tillie" R.C. Draftz
44-14397 HO-E "Ex-Lax...Shht'n' Git" C.B. Doleac
44-14475 HO-J "Peanuts" N.R. Jesup
44-14487 HO-P "Mary Lou" J.L. Crawford
44-14668 HO-H "Jeanne M" R.W. Hamilton
44-14668 HO-V "My Coleen" J.W. Prichard
44-14716 HO-P "The Margarettes" H.M. Stewart
44-14778 HO-E "Sheepherder" A.F. Sears
44-14785 HO-B "Channel Belle 2nd"
44-14790 HO-Q "Miss Nita" R.H. Ross
44-14794 HO-F "Buzz Boy" J.A. Bateman
44-14801 HO-L "The Hawk-Eye-Owan" D.M. Huston
44-14812 HO-S "Sweet Fern" W.C. Miller
44-14812 HO-S "Socky" J.N. White
44-14812 HO-T "Slender, Tender, & Tall" W.T. Halton
44-14819 HO-G "Lilli Marlene II" C.M. Greer
44-14845 HO-R
44-14848 HO-K "Kay III" S.K. Moats

P-51D-15-NA
44-14955 HO-I "Dopey Okie" K.K. Dittmer
44-15031 HO-C "Rattop IV" J.P. Vickery
44-15041 HO-M "Petie 3rd" J.C. Meyer
44-15041 HO-Z "The Fox" J.N. Wood
44-15383 HO-X "Maid of Orleans" C.B. Doleac
44-15513 HO-U "Goliath" K.M. Waldron
44-15613 HO-J
44-15629 HO-R "Eleen & Jerry" A.P. Rigby
44-15712 HO-F "Buzz Boy II" J.A. Bateman
44-15712 HO-F "Lady Gue" J.F. Graves

P-51D-20-NA
44-72216 HO-M "Miss Helen" R.H. Littge
44-72389 HO-Z "Ron-Marie" C.A. Ricci

Unknown Serials
P-51B HO- "Tepee" R.E. Collard
P-51B HO- "Legal Eagle" A.P. Howard

• • •

## THE 353RD FIGHTER GROUP
## 350TH, 351ST, 352ND FIGHTER SQUADRONS

The 353rd Fighter Group was activated on October 1, 1942, at Mitchel Field, New York. Training in the eastern United States, the group headed overseas on June 1, 1943, aboard the "Queen Mary". The first of 447 missions came on August 12, 1943, with the final flight coming on April 25, 1945. While in England, the 353rd claimed 328 aerial and 404.5 ground victories while 141 P-47's and P-51's were lost on operations and 15 pilots died in accidents.

Bases for the 353rd were Goxhill, from June 7, 1943; Metfield, from August 3, 1943; and Raydon, from April 12, 1944, until October of 1945. Aircraft flown were the P-47D (with a few C-models), from July of 1943 until November of 1944, and the P-51D and K (with a few B-models) from October of 1944. The 353rd was awarded a Distinguished Unit Citation for it's support of the airborne invasion of Holland from September 17-23, 1944.

### Claims

| | Air | | | Grd | |
|---|---|---|---|---|---|
| | Destroyed | Probable | Damaged | Destroyed | Damaged |
| HdQts | 40 | 2 | 12 | 18.83 | 17.33 |
| 350th | 106 | 16 | 37 | 165.5 | 81 |
| 351st | 99 | 10 | 43 | 102 | 50.84 |
| 352nd | 83 | 10 | 25 | 118.17 | 75.5 |
| | 328 | 38 | 117 | 404.5 | 224.67 |

### Commanders

| | |
|---|---|
| LtCol. Joseph A. Morris | October 15, 1942-August 16, 1943 |
| LtCol. Loren G. McCollom | August 16, 1943-November 25, 1943 |
| Col. Glenn E. Duncan | November 26, 1943-July 7, 1944 |
| Col. Ben Rimerman | July 7, 1944-April 21, 1945 |
| Col. Glenn E. Duncan | April 21, 1945-September 1945 |

### Wing and Command Assignments

| | |
|---|---|
| Assigned to VIII Fighter Command | June 7, 1943 |
| VIII Fighter Command, 66th Fighter Wing | August 18,, 1943 |
| 3rd Bomb Division, 66th Fighter Wing | September 15, 1944 |
| 3rd Air Division, 66th Fighter Wing | January 1, 1945 |

### Aircraft Markings

Original P-47's were in the olive drab/neutral gray scheme with white cowl and theater bands. In early 1944, NMF planes arrived and a large number of these were then painted. In April of 1944, a group marking was applied: a diamond set pattern of black and yellow checkerboards on the cowling extending back to the shutters. Col. Duncan's P-47's were the only ones to carry a checkerboard pattern instead of the diamond set design.

All P-51's arrived in NMF with a few receiving dark green applications on the upper surfaces. Group markings consisted of black-yellow-black-yellow banded spinners, plus a yellow and black checkerboard cowl band, square set and composed of three rows. In late November of 1944, the checkerboard was extended back past the exhaust stacks, with eight squares per longitudinal row. Also in November, squadron rudder colors were applied: yellow for the 350th, none for the 351st, and black for the 352nd.

Squadron codes were:

350th Ftr Sqn: LH
351st Ftr Sqn: YJ
352nd Ftr Sqn: SX

### 353rd Fighter Group Statistical Report

| Month | Missions | Air | Grd | Losses | KIAc |
|---|---|---|---|---|---|
| July 1943 | 0 | 0-0-0 | 0-0 | 0 | 2 |
| August | 15 | 2-0-5 | 0-0 | 3 | 0 |
| September | 13 | 14-0-6 | 0-0 | 3 | 3 |
| October | 11 | 18-5-22 | 0-0 | 4 | 0 |
| November | 10 | 13-0-10 | 0-0 | 4 | 0 |
| December | 11 | 7-4-4 | 0-0 | 3 | 0 |
| January 1944 | 11 | 17-1-2 | 1-1.67 | 1 | 0 |
| February | 14 | 21-3-3 | 3.5-5 | 8 | 0 |
| March | 19 | 13-1-3 | 2-17 | 6 | 0 |
| April | 29 | 1-2-1 | 2-6 | 7 | 0 |
| May | 24 | 5-0-5 | 3-4 | 10 | 0 |
| June | 58 | 36-5-22 | 37-25 | 16 | 2 |
| July | 29 | 8-0-3 | 12-0 | 3 | 0 |
| August | 39 | 29-3-3 | 77-21 | 17 | 2 |
| September | 23 | 22-3-4 | 2-4 | 8 | 1 |
| October | 23 | 0-0-0 | 4-3 | 5 | 1 |
| November | 22 | 25-5-9 | 22-13 | 9 | 0 |
| December | 22 | 19-2-4 | 0-0 | 3 | 0 |

| | | | | | |
|---|---|---|---|---|---|
| January 1945 | 16 | 9-0-1 | 2-5 | 3 | 0 |
| February | 17 | 2-0-0 | 53-29 | 4 | 0 |
| March | 23 | 57-4-9 | 30-21 | 19 | 1 |
| April | 18 | 10-0-1 | 154-70 | 5 | 1 |
| May | 0 | 0-0-0 | 0-0 | 0 | 0 |
| June | 0 | 0-0-0 | 0-0 | 0 | 0 |
| July | 0 | 0-0-0 | 0-0 | 0 | 2 |
| | 447 | 328-38-117 | 404.5-224.67 | 141 | 15 |

**Losses by Squadron**

| | MIA | | KIAc | |
|---|---|---|---|---|
| | P-47 | P-51 | P-47 | P-51 |
| HdQts | 3 | 1 | 0 | 0 |
| 350th | 32 | 19 | 5 | 2 |
| 351st | 28 | 14 | 1 | 1 |
| 352nd | 30 | 14 | 3 | 3 |
| | 93 | 48 | 9 | 6 |

**Claims by Type**

| | Air | | | Grd | |
|---|---|---|---|---|---|
| | Destroyed | Probable | Damaged | Destroyed | Damaged |
| P-47 | 206 | 27 | 93 | 139.5 | 83.67 |
| P-51 | 122 | 11 | 24 | 265 | 141 |

**Claims by Enemy Aircraft Type**

| | Air | | | Grd | |
|---|---|---|---|---|---|
| | Destroyed | Probable | Damaged | Destroyed | Damaged |
| Me-109 | 163 | 18 | 70 | 51 | 51 |
| FW-190 | 122 | 17 | 34 | 106 | 37.67 |
| Me-110 | 16 | 2 | 4 | 28 | 11 |
| Me-262 | 8 | 0 | 5 | 2 | 3 |
| Me-210 | 5 | 1 | 3 | 1 | 1 |
| Ju-88 | 4 | 0 | 1 | 36.5 | 22 |
| He-111 | 2 | 0 | 0 | 53 | 19 |
| Do-217 | 2 | 0 | 0 | 6 | 2 |
| Fi-156 | 2 | 0 | 0 | 5 | 1 |
| Me-410 | 1 | 0 | 0 | 36 | 9 |
| u/i a/c | 1 | 0 | 0 | 34 | 43 |
| Bu-181 | 1 | 0 | 0 | 0 | 0 |
| Ju-52 | 1 | 0 | 0 | 1 | 0 |
| Ar-234 | 0 | 0 | 0 | 13 | 10 |
| Ju-87 | 0 | 0 | 0 | 7 | 6 |
| He-177 | 0 | 0 | 0 | 5 | 2 |
| FW-200 | 0 | 0 | 0 | 4 | 1 |
| Ju-188 | 0 | 0 | 0 | 4 | 0 |
| Bu-133 | 0 | 0 | 0 | 4 | 0 |
| He-219 | 0 | 0 | 0 | 2 | 1 |
| Me-163 | 0 | 0 | 0 | 2 | 1 |
| Me-108 | 0 | 0 | 0 | 1 | 0 |
| Hs-126 | 0 | 0 | 0 | 1 | 0 |
| B-17 | 0 | 0 | 0 | 1 | 0 |
| Hs-129 | 0 | 0 | 0 | 0 | 2 |
| He-115 | 0 | 0 | 0 | 0 | 1 |
| Ar-196 | 0 | 0 | 0 | 0 | 1 |

**353rd Fighter Group Squadron Commanders**

**350th Ftr Sqn**

| | |
|---|---|
| LtCol. Ben Rimerman | December 1942-November 25, 1943 |
| Maj. Stanley R. Pidduck, Jr. | November 25, 1943-May 1, 1944 |
| Maj. Dewey E. Newhart | May 1, 1944-June 12, 1944 |
| LtCol. Kenneth W. Gallup | June 12, 1944-November 9, 1944 |
| LtCol. Wayne K. Blickenstaff | November 9, 1944-April 2, 1945 |
| LtCol. Robert A. Elder | April 2, 1945-September 24, 1945 |

**351st Ftr Sqn**

| | |
|---|---|
| LtCol. Shannon Christian | October 1942-November 10, 1943 |
| Maj. Walter C. Beckham | November 10, 1943-February 22, 1944 |
| Capt. Fred H. LeFebre | February 23, 1944-March 2, 1944 |
| LtCol. Shannon Christian | March 2, 1944-July 21, 1944 |
| Capt. Vic L. Byers, Jr. | July 21, 1944-August 2, 1944 |
| LtCol. Fred H. LeFebre | August 2, 1944-January 27, 1945 |
| Maj. Vic L. Byers, Jr. | January 28, 1945-November 1945 |

**352nd Ftr Sqn**

| | |
|---|---|
| LtCol. William B. Bailey | October 1942-July 7, 1944 |
| Maj. James N. Poindexter | July 7, 1944-August 5, 1944 |
| Capt. Victor N. Curtis | August 5, 1944-August 13, 1944 |
| Capt. Thomas J. Forkin | August 13, 1944-August 17, 1944 |
| LtCol. Wilbert H. Junttila | August 17, 1944-July 20, 1945 |

**Aces of the 353rd Fighter Group**

| Name | Air | Grd | Total | Sqn |
|---|---|---|---|---|
| Col. Glenn E. Duncan | 19.5 | 6.83 | 26.33 | HdQts |
| Capt. Gordon B. Compton | 5.5 | 15 | 20.5 | 351st |
| Maj. Walter C. Beckham | 18 | 0 | 18 | 351st |
| Capt. Melville W. Hightshoe | 0 | 14.5 | 14.5 | 350th |
| Capt. Herbert G. Kolb | 0 | 14.5 | 14.5 | 350th |
| Maj. Walker L. Boone | 2 | 11.79 | 13.79* | 350th |
| F/O Richard N. Gustke | 0 | 12.5 | 12.5 | 350th |
| Col. Ben Rimerman | 4.5 | 8 | 12.5 | 350th HdQts |
| Capt. Horace Q. Waggoner | 5 | 7.5 | 12.5 | 352nd |
| Capt. Frank N. Emory | 2 | 10 | 12 | 351st |
| Lt. Roland J. Lanoue | 1 | 11 | 12 | 350th |
| LtCol. Kenneth W. Gallup | 9 | 2 | 11 | 350th HdQts |
| Lt. Gerald J. Miller | 0 | 11 | 11 | 351st |
| Maj. James N. Poindexter | 7 | 4 | 11 | 352nd |
| LtCol. Wayne K. Blickenstaff | 10 | 0 | 10 | 350th HdQts |
| Lt. Joseph D. McMullen | 0 | 10 | 10 | 350th |
| Capt. Harrison B. Tordoff | 5 | 4.5 | 9.5 | 352nd |
| Capt. Raymond E. Hartley, Jr. | 5 | 4 | 9** | 351st HdQts |
| Lt. Raymond P. Greenwood | 0 | 8 | 8 | 352nd |
| Capt. William J. Maguire | 7 | 1 | 8 | 351st |
| Lt. Swift T. Benjamin | 1 | 6.5 | 7.5 | 350th |
| LtCol. Robert A. Elder | 5 | 2 | 7 | 350th HdQts |
| Maj. William J. Price | 3 | 4 | 7 | 350th |
| Capt. Leslie P. Cles | 0 | 6.5 | 6.5 | 352nd |
| Lt. Thomas W. Jones | 0.5 | 6 | 6.5 | 352nd |
| Maj. William F. Tanner | 5.5 | 1 | 6.5 | 350th |
| LtCol. William B. Bailey | 3 | 3 | 6 | 352nd HdQts |
| Capt. Harold W. Chase | 2 | 4 | 6 | 351st |
| Lt. Arthur C. Cundy | 6 | 0 | 6 | 352nd |
| Capt. William C. Davis | 0 | 6 | 6 | 352nd |
| Lt. Ray C. Gordon | 0 | 6 | 6 | 350th |
| Lt. Louis W. Lee | 4 | 2 | 6 | 350th |
| Lt. Bruce D. McMahan | 0.5 | 5.5 | 6 | 350th |
| Capt. Fred L. Uttwenweiler | 0 | 6 | 6 | 352nd |
| Lt. Walter A.S. Prescott | 2 | 4 | 6 | 350th |
| Capt. Vernon G. Rafferty | 2.5 | 3.5 | 6 | 350th |
| Capt. Marvin V. Bledsoe | 0 | 5.5 | 5.5 | 350th |
| Maj. Vic L. Byers, Jr. | 2.5 | 3 | 5.5 | 351st |
| Lt. Jack W. Clark | 2.5 | 3 | 5.5 | 350th |
| Capt. William J. Jordan | 1 | 4.5 | 5.5 | 352nd |
| Lt. Harold O. Miller | 2 | 3.5 | 5.5 | 352nd |
| Maj. Wilton W. Johnson | 3 | 2.33 | 5.33 | 352nd |
| Capt. Robert W. Abernathy | 5 | 0 | 5 | 350th |
| Lt. Clifford F. Armstrong | 3 | 2 | 5 | 352nd |
| Lt. Lindsay W. Grove | 1 | 4 | 5 | 352nd |
| Lt. Robert F. Hahn | 1 | 4 | 5 | 351st |
| Capt. Gene E. Markham | 5 | 0 | 5 | 351st |
| Lt. James H. McClure | 0 | 5 | 5 | 350th |
| Capt. Charles L. McGraw | 3 | 2 | 5 | 351st |
| Lt. Robert A. Newman | 4 | 1 | 5 | 352nd |
| Lt. Thomas P. Pryor, Jr. | 0 | 5 | 5 | 351st |
| Lt. Edwin D. Reinhardt | 0 | 5 | 5 | 352nd |

* - includes 0.79 ground victories with the 78th Ftr Grp, ETO
** - includes 2 air victories with the 325th Ftr Grp, MTO

**353rd Fighter Group Scorers**

**HdQts**

| | Air | Grd | |
|---|---|---|---|
| W.B. Bailey | 2-0-0 | 3-0 | plus 352nd Ftr Sqn |
| G.E. Duncan | 19.5-1-7 | 6.83-10.5 | |
| J.W. Eanes | 1-0-0 | 0-0 | |
| R.A. Elder | 5-0-1 | 0-0 | plus 350th Ftr Sqn |
| K.W. Gallup | 3-0-0 | 1-1 | plus 350th Ftr Sqn |
| R.E. Hartley | 3-0-1 | 0-0 | plus 2 air w/325th Ftr Grp, MTO & 351st Ftr Sqn |
| W.M. Long | 1-0-0 | 0-0 | |
| L.G. McCollom | 1-1-0 | 0-0 | plus 0-1-1 air w/ 56th Ftr Grp |
| J.A. Morris | 0-0-1 | 0-0 | |
| B. Rimerman | 2.5-0-0 | 8-2.5 | plus 350th Ftr Sqn |
| C.L. Stafford | 1-0-1 | 0-3.33 | |
| W.T. Thistlethwaite | 1-0-1 | 0-0 | |

**350th Ftr Sqn**

| Pilot | | | |
|---|---|---|---|
| O.I. Aal | 1-0-0 | 2-0 | |
| R.W. Abernathy | 5-0-1 | 0-0.5 | |
| W.M. Agnew | 0-1-0 | 0-0 | |
| R.T. Allison | 0-1-0 | 1-0 | |
| J.M. Ard | 0-0-0 | 1-0 | |
| H.E. Asper | 2-0-0 | 0-0 | |
| B.C. Auchincloss | 3-1-2 | 1.5-1 | |
| S.T. Benjamin | 1-0-1 | 6.5-4 | |
| M.V. Bledsoe | 0-0-0 | 5.5-4 | |
| W.K. Blickenstaff | 10-1-2 | 0-0 | |
| W.L. Boone | 2-1-1 | 11-10 | plus 0.79-3 grd w/ 78th Ftr Grp |
| J.B. Brooks | 0.5-0-0 | 1-0 | |
| H.E. Caton | 0-0-0 | 2-2 | |
| K. Chetwood | 0.5-1-0 | 0-0 | |
| J.W. Clark | 2.5-0-0 | 3-2 | |
| N.N. Cowen | 1-0-0 | 0-0 | |
| T.C. Creekmur | 1-0-0 | 0-0 | |
| L.M. Davis | 0-0-1 | 2-1 | |
| M.P. Dawson | 0-0-1 | 0-0 | |
| A.L. Deeds | 1-0-0 | 1-1 | |
| G.P. Devine | 1-0-1 | 0-0 | |
| C.W. Dinse | 1.5-0-1 | 0-0 | |
| C.O. Durant | 0-0-1 | 1-1 | |
| R.A. Elder | 0-0-0 | 2-4 | plus HdQts |
| A.K. Ferrell | 0-0-0 | 1-1 | |
| D.A. Fry | 2-0-0 | 0-0 | |
| J.F. Furness | 3-0-0 | 0-0 | |
| K.W. Gallup | 6-1-0 | 1-0 | plus HdQts |
| R.C. Gordon | 0-0-0 | 6-4 | |
| L.M. Grainger | 2-0-1 | 0-0 | |
| B. Greenfield | 0-0-0 | 3-3 | |
| W. Grizzle | 0-0-0 | 1.5-2 | |
| R.N. Gustke | 0-0-1 | 12.5-8 | |
| J.L. Guthrie | 3-0-2 | 0-1 | |
| H.H. Hakonen | 0-1-0 | 1.5-1 | |
| R.S. Hart | 1-0-0 | 0-1 | |
| H.E. Haynes | 1-0-0 | 1-0 | |
| R.W. Hedler | 2.5-0-0 | 0-0 | |
| M.W. Hightshoe | 0-0-0 | 14.5-5 | |
| D.E. Howie | 0-0-0 | 2-0 | |
| W.R. Hubbell | 1-1-0 | 0-0 | |
| W.F. Hurst | 2-0-1 | 0-0 | |
| R.N. Ireland | 0-2-1 | 0-0 | |
| J.E. Jessup | 1-1-0 | 1-0 | |
| G.D. Kammer | 0-0-0 | 0-1 | |
| W.P. Knowling | 0-1-0 | 1-0 | |
| H.G. Kolb | 0-0-1 | 14.5-3 | |
| W.J. Lane | 0-0-0 | 1-0 | |
| R.J. Lanoue | 1-0-0 | 11-1 | |
| C.A. Larsen | 0-0-0 | 3-1 | |
| G.S.H. Lee | 1-0-0 | 0-0 | |
| L.W. Lee | 4-0-1 | 2-0 | |
| R.S. Liebold | 0-0-0 | 1-1 | |
| T. Lorance | 0-0-0 | 0-1 | |
| J.A. Madson | 0-0-0 | 1-1 | |
| J.F. May | 2-0-0 | 0-0 | |
| J.H. McClure | 0-0-0 | 5-0 | |
| B.D. McMahan | 0.5-0-0 | 5.5-0 | |
| J.D. McMullen | 0-0-0 | 10-3 | |
| E.S. Middleton | 2-0-1 | 0-0 | |
| C.W. Mueller | 0-0-0 | 0-1 | |
| D.E. Newhart | 2.5-1-4 | 0-0 | |
| W.W. Odom | 1.5-0-0 | 0-0 | |
| F. O'Neill | 1-0-1 | 1-0 | |
| J.P. Onkey | 0-0-0 | 1-0 | |
| F.J. Orzelek | 1-0-0 | 0-0 | |
| G.D. Page | 1-0-0 | 0-0 | |
| S.R. Pidduck | 0-0-0 | 0-1 | |
| W.A.S. Prescott | 2-0-0 | 4-1 | |
| W.J. Price | 3-0-0 | 4-3.5 | |
| G.F. Province | 1-0-0 | 0-0 | |
| V.G. Rafferty | 2.5-0-0 | 3.5-1 | |
| B. Rimerman | 2-1-2 | 0-0 | plus Hdqts |
| G.W. Robison | 1-0-0 | 1-0 | |
| J. Rosenberg | 0-0-1 | 0-0 | |
| C. Rowan | 1-0-0 | 0-0 | |
| J.O. Ruscitto | 3-1-2 | 1-0 | |
| J.L. Schilt | 1.5-0-0 | 1.5-1 | |
| W.D. Smith | 0-0-0 | 2-0 | |
| A.C. Spriggs | 0-0-0 | 2-0 | |
| J.F. Starr | 0-0-1 | 1-2 | |
| R.A. Stearns | 3.5-0-1 | 0-0 | |
| W.F. Tanner | 5.5-0-1 | 1-1 | |
| R.F. Unangst | 1-0-0 | 1-0 | |
| I.E. Venell | 0-0-1 | 0-0 | |
| F.T. Walsh | 2-0-0 | 0-0 | |
| J.H. Winder | 4-0-0 | 0-0 | |
| D.L. Yocum | 0-0-2 | 1-1 | |
| J. Zolner | 1-0-0 | 0-0 | |

**351st Ftr Sqn**

| Pilot | | | |
|---|---|---|---|
| G.N. Ahles | 0-0-1 | 0-0 | |
| E.J. Albert | 1-0-0 | 0-0 | |
| M.A. Arnold | 0-0-0.5 | 0-0 | |
| A.W. Barlow | 1-0-0 | 0-0 | |
| W.C. Beckham | 18-2-4 | 0-0.83 | |
| T.C. Brock | 1-0-0 | 0-1 | |
| W.R. Burkett | 0-0-0.5 | 0-0 | |
| V.L. Byers | 2.5-1-1 | 3-2.5 | |
| H.J. Carbonneau | 1-0-0 | 0-0 | |
| A.C. Carroll | 1-0-1 | 1-1 | |
| H.W. Chase | 2-0-1 | 4-1 | |
| D.L. Claiville | 0-0-0 | 0.5-0 | |
| W.G. Cobb | 1-0-0 | 0-0 | |
| G.B. Compton | 5.5-0-1 | 15-5 | |
| C.W. Craft | 0-2-0 | 0-0.5 | |
| T.R. Drybrough | 1-1-0 | 3-1 | |
| J.L. Dwyer | 0-0-0 | 0-0.5 | |
| F.N. Emory | 2-0-1 | 10-4.5 | |
| H.K. Field | 2-0-0 | 0-0 | |
| W.J. Frank | 0.5-0-0 | 0-0 | |
| G.W. Franklin | 1-0-2 | 2-0 | |
| J.E. Frye | 1-0-1 | 0-0 | |
| J.O. Fulton | 1-0-0 | 2-1 | |
| J.W. Furneaux | 1-0-0 | 1-0 | |
| C.W. Geiger | 0-0-0 | 2-0 | |
| R.F. Hahn | 1-0-0 | 4-1 | |
| L.G. Hally | 0-0-0 | 4.5-0 | |
| A.S. Hartley | 4-0-2 | 0-0 | |
| R.E. Hartley | 0-0-0 | 4-0 | plus HdQts |
| J.J. Hatch | 4-0-0 | 0-0 | |
| L.B. Highfield | 0-0-0 | 2-1 | |
| R. Hilgenburg | 0.5-0-0 | 0-0 | |
| J.F. Hinchey | 3-0-1 | 1-0 | |
| M.B. Hungate | 2-0-1 | 0-0 | |
| H.F. Hunter | 1-1-0 | 0-0 | |
| D.M. Hurlburt | 0.5-0-0 | 0-0 | |
| J.A. Hynes | 1-0-0 | 0-1 | |
| O.A. Kinkade | 3-0-2 | 0-0 | |
| D.F. Kohler | 0-0-0 | 1-0 | |
| B.E. Kraft | 0-0-1 | 0-0 | |
| W.K. Lahke | 1-0-0 | 1-0 | |
| D.G. Larson | 0-0-0 | 3-4 | |
| V.A, Leatherman | 0-1-0 | 0-0 | |
| F.H. LeFebre | 2.5-0-1 | 0-0 | |
| D.E. Lewis | 0-0-0 | 1-1 | |
| W.J. Maguire | 7-0-2 | 1-0 | |
| H.P. Maree | 2-0-0 | 0.5-0 | |
| G.E. Markham | 5-0-2.5 | 0-1 | |
| C.L. McGraw | 3-0-0 | 2-2 | |
| G.H. McLaughlin | 2-1-1 | 1-3 | |
| G.J. Miller | 0-0-0 | 11-2 | |
| H.D. Milligan | 0-0-0 | 0.5-0.5 | |
| F.J. Mincik | 0-0-1 | 0-0 | |
| J.R. Mitchell | 0-0-1 | 1-1 | |
| G.S. Montgomery | 2.5-0-0 | 0-0 | |
| H. Moretz | 1-0-0 | 0-0.5 | |
| H.A. Morris | 0-0-0 | 3-4 | |
| H.J. Morris | 0-0-2 | 0-0 | plus 0.5-0-0 air w/78th Ftr Grp |
| B.J. Murray | 1-0-0 | 0-0 | |
| H.S. Murray | 0-0-0 | 2-0 | |
| J.M. Nickelbur | 1-0-1 | 3-2 | |
| N.T. Ott | 0-0-1 | 0-1 | |
| G.F. Perpente | 0-0-1 | 0-0.5 | |
| S.S. Petticrew, Jr. | 0-0-0 | 1-1 | |
| T.P. Pryor | 0-0-0 | 5-1 | |
| E.J. Risk | 1-0-0 | 1-0 | |
| J.W. Rohrs | 0.5-0-0 | 0-0 | |
| G.J. Rosen | 0.5-0-0 | 0-0 | |
| R.C. Strobell | 1-1-0 | 0-0 | |
| H.D. Stump | 0-0-2 | 0-0 | |
| J.A. Sullivan | 0-0-0 | 0-1 | |
| J. Terzian | 0.5-0-0 | 0-2.5 | |
| R.M. Tumlin | 1-0-2 | 1-0 | |
| V.L. Vogel | 0-0-1 | 0-0 | |
| R.F. Vomaske | 1-0-0 | 0-0 | |
| J.R. Walsh | 0-0-1.5 | 0-0 | |
| W.J. Weaver | 1-0-1 | 0-0 | |
| R.K. Wiehe | 1-0-0 | 3-1 | |
| M.Q. Williams | 0-0-0 | 1-0 | |
| J.E. Woods | 0-0-1 | 0-0 | |

**352nd Ftr Sqn**

| Pilot | | | |
|---|---|---|---|
| R.R. Akard | 0-0-0 | 1-0 | |
| K. Ames | 0-0-0 | 1-0 | |
| R.R. Anderson | 0-0-0 | 0-1 | |
| C.F. Armstrong | 3-0-0 | 2-0 | |
| W.B. Bailey | 1-0-0 | 0-0 | plus HdQts |
| D.L. Barber | 2-0-0 | 0-0 | |
| J.G. Bartley | 0-0-0 | 0.5-0 | |

| | | |
|---|---|---|
| W.E. Beach | 0-0-0 | 1.5-0 |
| W.K. Bixby | 0-0-0 | 1-2 |
| F.H. Bouldin | 3-0-0 | 0-0 |
| G.S. Burlingame | 1-0-0 | 0-0 |
| G.G. Callans | 2-0-0 | 1-1 |
| L.P. Cles | 0-1-0 | 6.5-1.5 |
| D.J. Corrigan | 1-0-0 | 0-0 |
| J.F. Cross | 1-0-0 | 0-0 |
| A.C. Cundy | 6-0-0 | 0-0 |
| V.N. Curtis | 0-0-0 | 2-0.5 |
| J.E. Davenport | 0-0-2 | 1-0 |
| W.C. Davis | 0-0-0 | 6-1 |
| H.H. Dustin | 1-0-0 | 0-0 |
| R. Eluhow | 0-0-0 | 2.5-0 |
| J.R. Evans | 3-1-0 | 1.5-1.5 |
| E.M. Fogarty | 0-1-0.33 | 0-0 |
| T.J. Forkin | 2-0-1 | 0.5-1.5 |
| J.W. Gonnam | 4.5-1-1 | 0-1.5 |
| R.P. Greenwood | 0-0-0 | 8-1 |
| L.W. Grove | 1-0-0 | 4-3 |
| W.R. Harbin | 0-0-0 | 0-1 |
| D.E. Harris | 0-0-0 | 0-1 |
| R.C. Hassell | 0-0-0 | 1-2 |
| H. Herfurth | 0-0-0 | 0-2.5 |
| V.N. Hernandez | 0-0-0 | 1-0 |
| J.R. Hicks | 0-0-1 | 3-0 |
| C.J. Hoey | 1-0-2 | 0-0 |
| L. Hunt | 0-0-0 | 0-0.5 |
| L.W. Ista | 1-0-0 | 0-0 |
| W.W. Johnson | 3-0-1 | 2.33 8 |
| T.W. Jones | 0.5-0-0 | 6-0 |
| W.J. Jordan | 1-1-0 | 4.5-0 |
| W.H. Junttila | 2-0-2.33 | 0-0 |
| R.V. Keywan | 1-0-3.33 | 0-1.5 |
| E.A. Knicklebein | 0-0-0 | 3-4 |
| J.L. Knoble | 3-0-1 | 0-0 |
| S.J. Kritz | 0-0-0 | 0-1 |
| J.W. Lamb | 0-0-0 | 2-2 |
| H.R. Lammie | 0-0-0 | 0-2 |
| B.J. Lancaster | 0-0-0 | 2.5-1 |
| J.W. Leitner | 0-0-0 | 1-3 |
| W.S. Marchant | 0-0-1 | 1.5-4 |
| B.B. Mayhew | 0-0-0 | 0-1 |
| L.M. McAdory | 0-0-0 | 0-1 |
| W.T. McGarry | 0-0-0 | 0-1 |
| J.A. McIntosh | 0-0-0 | 0-2 |
| A. Michel | 0-0-0 | 4-0 |
| H.O. Miller | 2-0-2 | 3.5-0 |
| M. Morrison | 1-0-0 | 1-1 |
| J.L. Motley | 0-0-0 | 1-0 |
| R.A. Newman | 4-0-1 | 1-0 |
| B. Parker | 0.5-0-0 | 0-0 |
| L.O. Pletz | 0-0-0 | 2.5-3 |
| J.N. Poindexter | 7-0-1 | 4-2.5 |
| G.N. Porterfield | 2-0-0 | 0.5-0 |
| E.D. Reinhardt | 0-0-0 | 5-0 |
| R.E. Robertson | 2-0-2 | 0-0 |
| R.T. Rose | 0-0-0 | 2-3 |
| D.W. Schoen | 0-0-0 | 2-1 |
| J. Schreiber | 1-0-0 | 0-0 |
| C.E. Sladek | 1-0-0 | 0-0 |
| R.B. Snyder | 0-0-0 | 0-1 |
| C.H. Sperry | 0-2-0 | 0.33-0 |
| S.E. Stephenson | 0-0-1 | 0-0 |
| E.G. Stiff | 0-1-0 | 0-0 |
| W.F. Streit | 3-0-2 | 0.5-1 |
| E.J. Sullivan | 1-0-0 | 0-0 |
| J.J. Swanezy | 0-0-0 | 2-0 |
| E.D. Thomas | 0-0-0 | 1-2 |
| H.E. Tear | 0-1-0 | 0-0 |
| H.B. Tordoff | 5-0-0 | 4.5-1 |
| J.M. Tuttle | 0-0-0 | 2-0 |
| F.L. Uttwenweiler | 0-0-0 | 6-3 |
| H.Q. Waggoner | 5-0-0 | 7.5-4 |
| G.L. Willits | 0.5-0-0 | 0-0 |

## 353rd Fighter Group Scoring

**August 16, 1943**

| | | | |
|---|---|---|---|
| HdQts: | LtCol. J.A. Morris | FW-190 dam(air) | NW Paris |
| | Maj. G.E. Duncan | FW-190 dam(air) | NW Paris |

**August 17, 1943**

| | | | |
|---|---|---|---|
| HdQts: | Maj. L.G. McCollom | Me-109 dest(air) | Diest |

**August 19, 1943**

| | | | |
|---|---|---|---|
| 351st: | Lt. H.J. Morris | Me-109 dam(air) | Gilze-Rijen |

**August 24, 1943**

| | | | |
|---|---|---|---|
| 350th: | Lt. W.F. Hurst | FW-190 dest(air) | Rouen |
| | Lt. I.E. Venell | FW-190 dam(air) | Rouen |
| 351st: | Capt. W.C. Beckham | FW-190 dam(air) | N/Paris |

**September 22, 1943**

| | | | |
|---|---|---|---|
| 352nd: | Capt. C.J. Hoey | Me-109 dest(air) | SW Utrecht |
| | Lt. J.W. Gonnam | Me-109 dest(air) | Schoonhaven |

**September 23, 1943**

| | | | |
|---|---|---|---|
| HdQts: | Maj. G.E. Duncan | FW-190 dest(air) | Nantes |
| 351st: | Capt. W.C. Beckham | FW-190 dest(air) | S/Nantes |
| | Lt. E.J. Albert | FW-190 dest(air) | S/Nantes |
| | Lt. V.L. Vogel | Me-109 dam(air) | S/Rennes |
| 352nd: | Lt. J.N. Poindexter | FW-190 dest(air) | Chateaubriant |
| | Lt. W.F. Streit | Me-109 dam(air) | Chateaubriant |

**September 27, 1943**

| | | | |
|---|---|---|---|
| 350th: | Lt. W.W. Odom | (1.5)Me-109 dest(air) | Emden |
| | Maj. B. Rimerman | Me-109 dest(air) | S/Emden |
| | Lt. D.A. Fry | Me-109 dest(air) | W/Emden |
| | Capt. D.E. Newhart | (.5)Me-109 dest(air) | Emden |
| | | Me-109 dam(air) | Emden |
| | Lt. J. Rosenberg | Me-109 dam(air) | Emden |
| 351st: | Capt. O.A. Kinkade | Me-109 dest(air) | SW Emden |
| | | Me-109 dam(air) | SW Emden |
| | Lt. W.J. Maguire | Me-109 dest(air) | W/Emden |
| | | Me-109 dam(air) | W/Emden |
| | Lt. H.F. Hunter | Me-109 dest(air) | SW Emden |

**October 2, 1943**

| | | | |
|---|---|---|---|
| HdQts: | Maj. G.E. Duncan | Me-109 dest(air) | All claims are |
| | | Me-109 prob(air) | at Emden |
| 350th: | Lt. M.P. Dawson | Me-109 dam(air) | |
| | Lt. R.N. Ireland | Me-109 dam(air) | |
| 351st: | Capt. W.C. Beckham | FW-190 prob(air) | |
| | | Me-109 prob(air) | |

**October 4, 1943**

| | | | |
|---|---|---|---|
| HdQts: | Maj. G.E. Duncan | Me-109 dam(air) | Malines |
| 351st: | Capt. W.C. Beckham | Me-109 dest(air) | Malines |
| | Lt. G.B. Compton | Me-109 dam(air) | Malines |

**October 8, 1943**

| | | | |
|---|---|---|---|
| HdQts: | Lt. W.T. Thistlethwaite | FW-190 dam(air) | Rhede |
| 350th: | Capt. D.E. Newhart | Me-210 dam(air) | Aschendorf |
| 351st: | Capt. F.H. LeFebre | (.5)Me-110 dest(air) | Friesoythe |
| | Lt. D.M. Hurlburt | (.5)Me-110 dest(air) | Friesoythe |
| | Capt. W.C. Beckham | FW-190 dam(air) | Rhede |
| | Capt. J.R. Walsh | FW-190 dam(air) | Wildeshausen |
| | Capt. O.A. Kinkade | FW-190 dam(air) | SW Emden |
| 352nd: | Capt. C.J. Hoey | Me-109 dam(air) | Garrel |

**October 10, 1943**

| | | | |
|---|---|---|---|
| HdQts: | LtCol. L.G. McCollom | Me-110 prob(air) | Rheine |
| 350th: | Lt. W.F. Hurst | FW-190 dest(air) | Zutphen |
| | Lt. W.F. Tanner | FW-190 dest(air) | Hengelo |
| 351st: | Capt. W.C. Beckham | Me-110 dest(air) | Munster |
| | | Me-110 dest(air) | Gransbergen |
| | | Me-210 dest(air) | Munster |
| | Lt. F.J. Mincik | Me-110 dam(air) | W/Munster |
| | F/O J.E. Wood | Me-110 dam(air) | Metelen |
| | Capt. J.R. Walsh | (.5)Me-210 dam(air) | NW Munster |
| | Lt. W.R. Burkett | (.5)Me-210 dam(air) | NW Munster |
| 352nd: | Lt. E.M. Fogarty | (.33)Me-110 dam(air) | Amersfoort |
| | Lt. W.H. Junttila | (.33)Me-110 dam(air) | Amersfoort |
| | Lt. R.V. Keywan | (.33)Me-110 dam(air) | Amersfoort |

**October 14, 1943**

| | | | |
|---|---|---|---|
| 350th: | Maj. B. Rimerman | FW-190 dest(air) | Duren |
| | Lt. D.A. Fry | FW-190 dest(air) | Duren |
| | Capt. D.E. Newhart | FW-190 dam(air) | Duren |
| 351st: | Capt. W.C. Beckham | (2)FW-190 dest(air) | Aachen |
| | Capt. O.A. Kinkade | Me-109 dest(air) | Turnhout |
| | Lt. W.J. Maguire | FW-190 dest(air) | Flacher |
| | Lt. G.F. Perpente | Me-109 dam(air) | Turnhout |
| | Lt. B.E. Kraft | FW-190 dam(air) | Turnhout |
| 352nd: | Maj. W.B. Bailey | Me-109 dest(air) | Eecloo |
| | Lt. W.H. Junttila | Me-109 dest(air) | All remaining |
| | | Me-109 dam(air) | claims are at |
| | Lt. R.A. Newman | Me-109 dest(air) | Turnhout |
| | | Me-109 dest(air) | |
| | Lt. W.F. Streit | Me-109 dest(air) | |
| | Lt. R.V. Keywan | Me-109 dam(air) | |

**October 20, 1943**

| | | | |
|---|---|---|---|
| 351st: | Lt. H.J. Morris | Me-109 dam(air) | Duren |
| 352nd: | Lt. E.M. Fogarty | Me-109 prob(air) | Sittard |
| | Capt. C.J. Hoey | Me-109 dam(air) | Sittard |

**November 3, 1943**

| | | | |
|---|---|---|---|
| 351st: | Lt. H.D. Stump | Me-109 dam(air) | SW Wilhelmshaven |
| 352nd: | Lt. J.N. Poindexter | Me-110 dest(air) | All claims are |
| | | Me-210 dest(air) | at Wilhelmshaven |
| | Lt. W.H. Junttila | Me-110 dest(air) | |
| | Lt. R.A. Newman | Me-110 dest(air) | |
| | Lt. M. Morrison | Me-110 dest(air) | |

**November 5, 1943**

| | | | |
|---|---|---|---|
| HdQts: | Maj. G.E. Duncan | Me-109 dam(air) | Gelsenkirchen |
| 350th: | Lt. W.J. Price | Me-210 dest(air) | Ruhr Valley |
| | Lt. R.A. Stearns | Me-210 dest(air) | Venlo |
| | Maj. B. Rimerman | (2)FW-190 dam(air) | Dusseldorf & Munchen-Gladbach |
| | Lt. W.F. Hurst | Me-109 dam(air) | W/Gelsenkirchen |
| 351st: | Capt. W.C. Beckham | Me-410 dest(air) | SW Gelsenkirchen |
| | | FW-190 dam(air) | SW Gelsenkirchen |
| | Capt. O.A. Kinkade | Me-109 dest(air) | W/Mors |
| | Lt. F.N. Emory | Me-210 dam(air) | Rheinburg |
| 352nd: | Lt. L.W. Ista | Me-109 dest(air) | Gelsenkirchen |
| | Capt. R.E. Robertson | FW-190 dam(air) | Dinslaken |

**November 11, 1943**

| | | | |
|---|---|---|---|
| HdQts: | Maj. G.E. Duncan | Me-109 dest(air) | Numansdorp |
| | | FW-190 dest(air) | Munster |
| | | Me-109 dam(air) | Numansdorp |
| 351st: | Capt. W.C. Beckham | FW-190 dest(air) | Dulman |

**November 13, 1943**

| | | | |
|---|---|---|---|
| 350th: | Lt. C.W. Dinse | FW-190 dam(air) | Meppen |

**December 1, 1943**

| | | | |
|---|---|---|---|
| 350th: | Lt. R.N. Ireland | FW-190 prob(air) | Solingen |
| | Lt. W.K. Blickenstaff | Me-109 dam(air) | Solingen |
| | Lt. C.O. Durant | Me-110 dam(air) | Solingen |
| 351st: | Capt. W.C. Beckham | (2)FW-190 dest(air) | Koln |
| 352nd: | Lt. R.A. Newman | Me-210 dest(air) | Solingen |

**December 20, 1943**

| | | | |
|---|---|---|---|
| HdQts: | LtCol. G.E. Duncan | FW-190 dest(air) | Rastede |
| 352nd: | Lt. E.G. Stiff | FW-190 prob(air) | Varel |

**December 22, 1943**

| | | | |
|---|---|---|---|
| 351st: | Capt. F.H. LeFebre | Me-109 dest(air) | Heerds |
| 352nd: | Lt. C.H. Sperry | Me-109 prob(air) | Canabruck |

**December 30, 1943**

| | | | |
|---|---|---|---|
| 350th: | Lt. R.A. Stearns | Me-109 dam(air) | All claims are |
| 352nd: | Lt. W.W. Johnson | FW-190 dest(air) | at Charleville |
| | Lt. J.W. Gonnam | (.5)Me-109 dest(air) | |
| | | Me-109 prob(air) | |
| | | Me-109 dam(air) | |
| | Lt. G.L. Willits | (.5)Me-109 dest(air) | |

**January 4, 1944**

| | | | |
|---|---|---|---|
| HdQts: | LtCol. G.E. Duncan | FW-190 dam(air) | Sendenhorst |

**January 5, 1944**

| | | | |
|---|---|---|---|
| HdQts: | LtCol. G.E. Duncan | Me-109 dest(air) | Eindhoven-Gilze-Rijen |

**January 7, 1944**

| | | | |
|---|---|---|---|
| 352nd: | Lt. J.W. Gonnam | (3)Me-109 dest(air) | Orleans |

**January 14, 1944**

| | | | |
|---|---|---|---|
| HdQts: | Lt. C.L. Stafford | (.33)FW-190 dam(grd) | All claims are |
| 351st: | Maj. W.C. Beckham | (.33)FW-190 dam(grd) | at Rosieres-en-Santerre |
| | | (shared with a 361st Ftr Grp P-47) | |
| | Capt. V.L. Byers | (.5)FW-190 dam(grd) | |
| | Lt. H.D. Milligan | (.5)FW-190 dam(grd) | |

**January 21, 1944**

| | | | |
|---|---|---|---|
| HdQts: | Lt. W.T. Thistlethwaite | Me-109 dest(air) | St. Quentin |
| | LtCol. G.E. Duncan | (.33)Do-217 dest(grd) | Albert |
| 351st: | Maj. W.C. Beckham | (2)Me-109 dest(air) | St. Quentin |
| | Lt. W.W. Johnson | (.33)Do-217 dest(grd) | Albert |
| | Lt. C.H. Sperry | (.33)Do-217 dest(grd) | Albert |

**January 24, 1944**

| | | | |
|---|---|---|---|
| HdQts: | LtCol. G.E. Duncan | (2)Me-110 dest(air) | Tirlemont |
| 350th: | Capt. D.E. Newhart | Me-110 dest(air) | Termonde |
| | | Me-109 dest(air) | Louvain-Beauvechan A/F |
| | Lt. J.F. Furness | Me-110 dest(air) | Tirlemont |
| | Capt. C.W. Dinse | (.5)Me-110 dest(air) | Termonde |
| | Lt. R.A. Stearns | (.5)Me-110 dest(air) | Termonde |

**January 30, 1944**

| | | | |
|---|---|---|---|
| 350th: | Lt. W.F. Tanner | FW-190 dest(air) | Zuider Zee |
| | Lt. F.T. Walsh | Me-110 dest(air) | Vechta |
| | Lt. K. Chetwood | Me-110 prob(air) | Vechta |
| 351st: | Maj. W.C. Beckham | Me-109 dest(air) | N/Deventer |
| 352nd: | Lt. R.A. Newman | Ju-88 dest(air) | Quackenbruck |
| | Lt. W.F. Streit | Ju-88 dam(air) | Quackenbruck |

**February 3, 1944**

| | | | |
|---|---|---|---|
| 350th: | Capt. D.E. Newhart | Me-109 prob(air) | S/Oldenburg |
| | | Me-109 dam(air) | S/Oldenburg |
| | Lt. R.N. Ireland | Me-109 prob(air) | Wilhelmshaven |
| 351st: | Maj. W.C. Beckham | Me-109 dest(air) | S/Oldenburg |
| | | FW-190 dest(air) | S/Oldenburg |

**February 5, 1944**

| | | | |
|---|---|---|---|
| HdQts: | LtCol. G.E. Duncan | FW-190 dest(air) | Sancerre |

**February 8, 1944**

| | | | |
|---|---|---|---|
| 350th: | Capt. C.W. Dinse | FW-190 dest(air) | Luxembourg |
| 351st: | Maj. W.C. Beckham | Me-109 dest(air) | E/St. Hubert |
| | | FW-190 dest(air) | St. Hubert |
| 352nd: | Capt. R.E. Robertson | FW-190 dest(air) | St. Hubert |
| | Lt. C.F. Armstrong | FW-190 dest(air) | St. Hubert |
| | Lt. G.G. Callans | FW-190 dest(air) | St. Hubert |
| | Lt. D.J. Corrigan | FW-190 dest(air) | Libramont |

**February 10, 1944**

| | | | |
|---|---|---|---|
| 351st: | Capt. F.N. Emory | FW-190 dest(air) | Lingen |
| 352nd: | Lt. C.F. Armstrong | Me-109 dest(air) | Lingen |
| | Lt. W.J. Jordan | Me-210 prob(air) | Lingen |

**February 13, 1944**

| | | | |
|---|---|---|---|
| 351st: | Maj. W.C. Beckham | FW-190 dam(air) | Cambrai |

**February 22, 1944**

| | | | |
|---|---|---|---|
| HdQts: | LtCol. G.E. Duncan | FW-190 dest(air) | Turnhout |
| | | (.5)Ju-88 dest(grd) | Bonn |
| | | (shared with a 366th Ftr Grp P-47 pilot) | |
| 351st: | Lt. G.B. Compton | Ju-88 dest(air) | W/Diest |
| | | FW-190 dest(grd) | All 351st claims |
| | | (.25)FW-190 dam(grd) | are NE Bonn |
| | | (.25)FW-190 dam(grd) | |
| | Maj. W.C. Beckham | (.25)FW-190 dam(grd) | |
| | | (.25)FW-190 dam(grd) | |
| | Capt. F.N. Emory | (.25)FW-190 dam(grd) | |
| | | (.25)FW-190 dam(grd) | |
| | Lt. G.F. Perpente | (.25)FW-190 dam(grd) | |
| | | (.25)FW-190 dam(grd) | |
| 352nd: | Capt. J.N. Poindexter | (2)Me-109 dest(air) | NW Koln |
| | Lt. R.A. Newman | FW-190 dest(grd) | Antwerp |

**February 24, 1944**

| | | | |
|---|---|---|---|
| HdQts: | LtCol. G.E. Duncan | FW-190 dest(air) | Steinhuder L. |
| | | Ju-88 dam(grd) | Steinhuder L. |
| 350th: | Lt. R.A. Stearns | (2)FW-190 dest(air) | Obernkirchen |
| | Lt. C. Rowan | FW-190 dest(air) | Steinhuder L. |
| | Lt. F.T. Walsh | FW-190 dest(air) | Steinhuder L. |
| 352nd: | Capt. J.N. Poindexter | FW-190 dam(air) | Steinhuder L. |

**February 25, 1944**

| | | | |
|---|---|---|---|
| 352nd: | Lt. W.F. Streit | (.5)Me-110 dest(grd) | Luxembourg |
| | | Ju-88 dam(grd) | Charleroi |
| | Lt. W.S. Marchant | (.5)Me-110 dest(grd) | Luxembourg |
| | | Do-217 dam(grd) | Charleroi |

**March 6, 1944**

| | | | |
|---|---|---|---|
| HdQts: | LtCol. G.E. Duncan | (2)FW-190 dest(air) | Steinhuder L. |
| 351st: | Capt. V.L. Byers | (.5)FW-190 dest(air) | SW Nienburg |
| | Lt. J. Terzian | (.5)FW-190 dest(air) | SW Nienburg |

**March 8, 1944**

| | | | |
|---|---|---|---|
| HdQts: | LtCol. B. Rimerman | FW-190 prob(air) | Hanover |
| 350th: | Lt. R.S. Hart | FW-190 dest(air) | Dummer Lake-Steinhuder Lake |
| | Lt. J. Zolner | FW-190 dest(air) | Hanover |
| 352nd: | Capt. R.E. Robertson | FW-190 dest(air) | All claims are |
| | | FW-190 dam(air) | N/Dummer Lake |
| | Lt. J.L. Knoble | FW-190 dest(air) | |
| | | FW-190 dam(air) | |
| | Lt. H.H. Dustin | FW-190 dest(air) | |

**March 16, 1944**

| | | | |
|---|---|---|---|
| HdQts: | Col. G.E. Duncan | (1.5)u/i a/c dam(grd) | All claims are |
| 351st: | Lt. J. Terzian | (1.5)u/i a/c dam(grd) | at Laon |
| 352nd: | Lt. J.W. Gonnam | (.5)Me-110 dam(grd) | |
| | | (.5)Me-110 dam(grd) | |
| | | (.5)He-111 dam(grd) | |
| | Lt. H. Herfurth | (.5)Me-110 dam(grd) | |
| | | (.5)Me-110 dam(grd) | |
| | | (.5)He-111 dam(grd) | |

**March 26, 1944**

| | | | |
|---|---|---|---|
| 350th: | Lt. C.O. Durant | FW-190 dam(grd) | Chartres |
| 351st: | Lt. J.A. Sullivan | Me-109 dam(grd) | Chartres |

**March 29, 1944**

| | | | |
|---|---|---|---|
| HdQts: | Col. G.E. Duncan | Me-110 dest(grd) | All claims are |
| | | B-17 dest(grd) | at Dummer Lake |
| | | (6)u/i a/c dam(grd) | |
| | | Me-210 dam(grd) | |

**March 29, 1944**

| | | | |
|---|---|---|---|
| 351st: | Capt. V.L. Byers | Ju-88 dam(grd) | SE Steinhuder L. |
| | Lt. J. Terzian | u/i a/c dam(grd) | SE Steinhuder L. |
| 352nd: | Capt. T.J. Forkin | (2)Me-109 dest(air) | All claims are |
| | | Me-109 dam(air) | SW Bremen |
| | Lt. G.G. Callans | Me-109 dest(air) | |
| | Lt. W.J. Jordan | Me-109 dest(air) | |
| | Lt. W.F. Streit | Me-109 dest(air) | |

**April 8, 1944**

| | | | |
|---|---|---|---|
| 350th: | Maj. S.R. Pidduck | Me-109 dam(grd) | All claims are |
| | Lt. R.S. Hart | u/i a/c dam(grd) | at Hoperhofen |
| | Lt. T. Lorance | FW-190 dam(grd) | |
| | Lt. C.W. Mueller | u/i a/c dam(grd) | |

**April 9, 1944**

| | | | |
|---|---|---|---|
| 350th: | Lt. W.F. Tanner | He-115 dam(grd) | Eckenforder Bay |

**April 10, 1944**

| | | | |
|---|---|---|---|
| 350th: | Lt. C.O. Durant | Me-110 dest(grd) | Villaroche |

**April 22, 1944**

| | | | |
|---|---|---|---|
| 351st: | Lt. H.K. Field | FW-190 dest(air) | N/Hamm |
| | Lt. H.F. Hunter | FW-190 prob(air) | N/Hamm |

**April 24, 1944**

| | | | |
|---|---|---|---|
| 351st: | Capt. V.A. Leatherman | FW-190 prob(air) | Mannheim |
| | F/O R.M. Tumlin | FW-190 dam(air) | Mannheim |

**April 28, 1944**

| | | | |
|---|---|---|---|
| HdQts: | Col. G.E. Duncan | u/i a/c dest(grd) | Chateaudun |
| | | u/i a/c dam(grd) | Chateaudun |

**May 12, 1944**

| | | | |
|---|---|---|---|
| HdQts: | Col. G.E. Duncan | FW-190 dest(air) | Wiesbaden |
| | | (2)FW-190 dam(air) | Wiesbaden |
| 350th: | Lt. K. Chetwood | (.5)Me-109 dest(air) | Selters |
| | Lt. W.F. Tanner | (.5)Me-109 dest(air) | Selters |

**May 19, 1944**

| | | | |
|---|---|---|---|
| 352nd: | Lt. W.W. Johnson | Me-109 dam(air) | SW Brunswick |
| | Lt. W.S. Marchant | Me-109 dam(air) | SW Brunswick |

**May 25, 1944**

| | | | |
|---|---|---|---|
| 352nd: | Lt. W.S. Marchant | u/i a/c dest(grd) | N/Reims |
| | | (3)Me-109 dam(grd) | N/Reims |

**May 27, 1944**

| | | | |
|---|---|---|---|
| 352nd: | F/O J.R. Hicks | Me-109 dam(air) | Saverne |
| | Lt. L.P. Cles | Me-109 dest(grd) | Saverne |
| | Lt. H.Q. Waggoner | Do-217 dest(grd) | Saverne |

**May 28, 1944**

| | | | |
|---|---|---|---|
| HdQts. | Maj. K.W. Gallup | Me-109 dest(air) | Gutersloh |

**May 30, 1944**

| | | | |
|---|---|---|---|
| 352nd: | Capt. J.N. Poindexter | (2)FW-190 dest(air) | Peine |

**May 31, 1944**

| | | | |
|---|---|---|---|
| 352nd: | Lt. H. Herfurth | Me-410 dam(grd) | Gutersloh |

**June 7, 1944**

(#4)

| | | | |
|---|---|---|---|
| 352nd: | Capt. J.N. Poindexter | Me-109 dest(grd) | All claims are |
| | | (1.5)Me-109 dam(grd) | at Compiegne |
| | Lt. R.P. Greenwood | Me-109 dest(grd) | |
| | Lt. E.D. Reinhardt | Me-109 dest(grd) | |
| | Lt. R.V. Keywan | (1.5)Me-109 dam(grd) | |

(#6)

| | | | |
|---|---|---|---|
| 351st: | Lt. G.H. McLaughlin | (2)Me-109 dest(air) | All claims are |
| | | Me-109 dest(grd) | at Beauvais/Tille |
| | | (3)Me-109 dam(grd) | |
| | Lt. W.J. Maguire | (2)Me-109 dest(air) | |
| | | Me-109 dam(air) | |
| | Lt. W.G. Cobb | Me-109 dest(air) | |
| | Lt. H.K. Field | Me-109 dest(air) | |
| | Lt. G.W. Franklin | Me-109 dest(air) | |
| | | (2)Me-109 dam(air) | |
| | Lt. A.S. Hartley | Me-109 dest(air) | |
| | | (2)Me-109 dam(air) | |
| | Lt. M.B. Hungate | Me-109 dest(air) | |
| | Lt. J.R. Mitchell | Me-109 dam(air) | |

(#7)

| | | | |
|---|---|---|---|
| 352nd: | F/O J.R. Hicks | (2)FW-190 dest(grd) | Angars |
| | | Ju-88 dest(grd) | Angars |
| | Lt. L.P. Cles | Me-109 dest(grd) | All remaining |
| | | Me-110 dest(grd) | claims are at |
| | Lt. H.Q. Waggoner | FW-190 dest(grd) | Cormeilles-en- |
| | | (2)FW-190 dam(grd) | Vixen |
| | Lt. B.B. Mayhew | FW-190 dam(grd) | |
| | Lt. W.T. McGarry | FW-190 dam(grd) | |

(#9)

| | | | |
|---|---|---|---|
| HdQts: | Col. G.E. Duncan | Ju-52 dest(air) | E/Ribecourt |
| | | (.5)Me-109 dest(air) | E/Ribecourt |
| 351st: | Capt. G.B. Compton | (.5)Me-109 dest(air) | E/Ribecourt |

**June 8, 1944**

(#1)

| | | | |
|---|---|---|---|
| HdQts: | Maj. K.W. Gallup | FW-190 dest(grd) | Le Mans |
| | | FW-190 dam(grd) | Le Mans |
| 350th: | Lt. J.F. Starr | He-111 dest(grd) | Breteuil |
| | | (2)Me-109 dam(grd) | Breteuil |
| | F/O D.L. Yocum | Me-110 dest(grd) | Breteuil |
| | | Me-110 dam(grd) | Breteuil |
| 351st: | Capt. G.B. Compton | FW-190 dest(air) | SW Angars |
| | Capt. F.N. Emory | FW-190 dest(air) | SW Angars |
| | Lt. J.J. Hatch | FW-190 dest(air) | SW Angars |
| | Lt. W.J. Weaver | FW-190 dest(air) | SW Angars |
| | | FW-190 dam(air) | SW Angars |
| | Lt. J.R. Mitchell | Me-109 dest(grd) | Angars |
| | | He-111 dam(grd) | Breteuil |
| 352nd: | Lt. C.F. Armstrong | (1.5)FW-190 dest(grd) | Angars |
| | | (.5)Ju-88 dest(grd) | Angars |
| | Lt. H.O. Miller | FW-190 dest(grd) | Angars |
| | | (.5)Ju-88 dest(grd) | Angars |
| | Lt. H.Q. Waggoner | (1.5)FW-190 dest(grd) | Angars |

(#2)

| | | | |
|---|---|---|---|
| 351st: | Lt. H.J. Carboneau | Me-109 dest(air) | Domfort |
| | Lt. G.H. McLaughlin | FW-190 prob(air) | Domfort |
| | Lt. R.C. Strobell | FW-190 prob(air) | Domfort |
| | Lt. G.N. Ahles | FW-190 dam(air) | Domfort |

**June 10, 1944**

| | | | |
|---|---|---|---|
| 352nd: | Lt. C.F. Armstrong | FW-190 dest(air) | SW Nantes-Gassicourt |

**June 12, 1944**

(#1)

| | | | |
|---|---|---|---|
| HdQts: | Col. G.E. Duncan | (3)Me-109 dest(air) | Evreux-Dreux |
| 350th: | Lt. J.O. Ruscitto | Me-109 dest(air) | Dreux |
| | | Me-109 dam(air) | Dreux |
| | Lt. S.T. Benjamin | Me-109 dam(air) | Dreux |
| 352nd: | Lt. H.O. Miller | Me-109 dest(air) | Dreux |
| | Lt. R.V. Keywan | Me-109 dest(air) | Evreux-Dreux |
| | | (2)Me-109 dam(air) | Evreux-Dreux |
| | Lt. C.H. Sperry | Me-109 prob(air) | Dreux |

(#2)

| | | | |
|---|---|---|---|
| HdQts: | Maj. K.W. Gallup | (2)Me-109 dest(air) | SW Paris |
| | LtCol. B. Rimerman | (1.5)Me-109 dest(air) | S/Paris |
| 350th: | Lt. J.F. Furness | (2)Me-109 dest(air) | SW Paris |
| | Lt. W.F. Tanner | (2)Me-109 dest(air) | SW Paris |
| | Lt. J.F. Starr | Me-109 dam(air) | SW Paris |
| 351st: | Lt. R.M. Tumlin | Me-109 dest(air) | SW Paris |
| | | Me-109 dam(air) | SW Paris |
| | Lt. W.J. Frank | (.5)Me-109 dest(air) | S/Paris |
| | Lt. N.T. Ott | Me-109 dam(air) | SW Paris |

**June 17, 1944**

| | | | |
|---|---|---|---|
| 351st: | Lt. J.J. Hatch | FW-190 dest(air) | Falaise |

**June 20, 1944**

(#1)

| | | | |
|---|---|---|---|
| HdQts: | Col. G.E. Duncan | (2)He-111 dest(grd) | All claims are |
| 352nd: | Capt. V.N. Curtis | He-111 dest(grd) | at Plantlunne |
| | Capt. J.N. Poindexter | He-111 dest(grd) | |
| | Lt. R.P. Greenwood | He-111 dest(grd) | |
| | Lt. D.E. Harris | u/i a/c dam(grd) | |
| | Lt. H.Q. Waggoner | Ju-88 dam(grd) | |

(#2)

| | | | |
|---|---|---|---|
| HdQts: | LtCol. B. Rimerman | (.5)He-111 dest(grd) | HdQts, 350th, & |
| | | (2)u/i a/c dam(grd) | 351st claims are |
| 350th: | Lt. J.B. Brooks | Me-110 dest(grd) | at Plantlunne |
| | Lt. R.F. Unangst | Ju-88 dest(grd) | |
| | Lt. V.G. Rafferty | (.5)He-111 dest(grd) | |
| 351st: | Capt. G.B. Compton | Ju-88 dest(grd) | |
| | | (.5)He-111 dam(grd) | |
| | Lt. J.L. Dwyer | (.5)He-111 dam(grd) | |
| 352nd: | Capt. L.P. Cles | Me-110 dest(grd) | All claims are at |
| | | Hs-129 dam(grd) | Twente/Enschede |
| | Lt. E.D. Reinhardt | He-111 dest(grd) | |
| | Lt. H.Q. Waggoner | Hs-129 dam(grd) | |

**June 22, 1944**

| | | | |
|---|---|---|---|
| 352nd: | Lt. H.O. Miller | Me-109 dest(air) | S/Rouen |

**June 24, 1944**

| | | | |
|---|---|---|---|
| 351st: | Capt. L.G. Hally | He-111 dest(grd) | Deelan |
| | | (.5)Me-109 dest(grd) | Deelan |
| | Capt. G.B. Compton | Ju-52 dest(grd) | Deelan |
| | Lt. D.L. Claiville | (.5)Me-109 dest(grd) | Deelan |

**June 25, 1944**

| | | | |
|---|---|---|---|
| 351st: | Capt. W.J. Maguire | Me-410 dest(grd) | Bourges |
| | Lt. G.W. Franklin | Me-410 dest(grd) | Bourges |
| | Lt. J.W. Furneaux | Me-410 dest(grd) | Bourges |
| | Lt. N.T. Ott | Me-410 dam(grd) | Bourges |

**June 27, 1944**

| | | | |
|---|---|---|---|
| 350th: | Maj. K.W. Gallup | Me-109 dest(air) | Epernay |
| | Lt. S.T. Benjamin | (.5)Me-109 dest(grd) | Chalons |
| | Lt. M.V. Bledsoe | (.5)Me-109 dest(grd) | Chalons |
| | Lt. V.G. Rafferty | Me-109 dam(grd) | Chalons |
| 351st: | Lt. A.S. Hartley | Me-109 dest(air) | S/Chalons |
| | Lt. M.B. Hungate | Me-109 dam(air) | SE Epernay |
| | Lt. G.H. McLaughlin | Me-109 dam(air) | S/Chalons |
| 352nd: | Lt. H.O. Miller | (2)Me-109 dam(air) | N/Troyes |

**June 29, 1944**

| | | | |
|---|---|---|---|
| 352nd: | Capt. V.N. Curtis | (.5)He-111 dam(grd) | Plantlunne |
| | Lt. L. Hunt | (.5)He-111 dam(grd) | Plantlunne |

**June 30, 1944**

| | | | |
|---|---|---|---|
| 350th: | Capt. W.K. Blickenstaff | Me-109 prob(air) | W/Chalons |
| | | Me-109 dam(air) | W/Chalons |
| | Lt. J.O. Ruscitto | Me-109 prob(air) | W/Chalons |
| | F/O D.L. Yocum | (2)Me-109 dam(air) | W/Chalons |

**July 5, 1944**

| | | | |
|---|---|---|---|
| HdQts: | Col. G.E. Duncan | Me-109 dest(air) | Pont Audemer |

**July 6, 1944**

| | | | |
|---|---|---|---|
| 350th: | Maj. K.W. Gallup | Me-109 dest(air) | SW Limay |
| 352nd: | Lt. D.L. Barber | FW-190 dest(air) | Evreux-Paris |

**July 7, 1944**

| | | | |
|---|---|---|---|
| HdQts: | Col. G.E. Duncan | He-111 dest(grd) | Wesendorf |
| 351st: | Lt. G.W. Franklin | FW-190 dest(grd) | Wesendorf |
| | Lt. R.M. Tumlin | He-111 dest(grd) | Wesendorf |

**July 9, 1944**

| | | | |
|---|---|---|---|
| 350th: | Capt. E.S. Middleton | Me-109 dam(air) | Argentan |
| | Lt. B.C. Auchincloss | Me-109 dam(air) | E/Evreux |
| 351st: | Lt. J.J. Hatch | (2)Me-109 dest(air) | All claims are |
| | Capt. W.J. Maguire | Me-109 dest(air) | at Argentan |
| | Lt. J.W. Furneaux | Me-109 dest(air) | |
| | Lt. R.C. Strobell | Me-109 dest(air) | |
| | Capt. V.L. Byers | Me-109 dam(air) | |

**July 30, 1944**

| | | | |
|---|---|---|---|
| 352nd: | Capt. L.P. Cles | (2.5)u/i a/c dest(grd) | All claims are |
| | Lt. W.J. Jordan | (2.5)u/i a/c dest(grd) | at Orleans/Bricy |
| | Lt. R. Eluhow | (2)u/i a/c dest(grd) | |
| | Capt. V.N. Curtis | u/i a/c dest(grd) | |
| | Lt. T.W. Jones | u/i a/c dest(grd) | |

**August 1, 1944**

| | | | |
|---|---|---|---|
| 352nd: | Capt. J.N. Poindexter | Me-410 dest(grd) | Laon/Couvron |
| | Lt. R.P. Greenwood | Me-410 dest(grd) | Laon/Couvron |
| | F/O K. Ames | Me-410 dest(grd) | Laon/Couvron |

**August 2, 1944**

| | | | |
|---|---|---|---|
| HdQts: | LtCol. B. Rimerman | Me-109 dest(air) | S/Compiegne |

**August 4, 1944**

(#1)

| | | | |
|---|---|---|---|
| HdQts: | Capt. C.L. Stafford | Me-109 dest(air) | SE Bremen |
| | | Me-109 dam(air) | SE Bremen |
| 350th: | Maj. K.W. Gallup | Me-109 dest(air) | Neunkirchen |
| | | Me-109 prob(air) | Neunkirchen |
| | Capt. E.S. Middleton | Me-109 dest(air) | NE Soltau |
| | Lt. O.I. Aal | Me-109 dest(air) | NE Hanover |
| | Lt. T.C. Creekmur | Me-109 dest(air) | E/Verdun |
| | Lt. J.O. Ruscitto | Me-109 dam(air) | Wenzendorf |
| 351st: | Lt. A.S. Hartley | (2)Me-109 dest(air) | Steinhuder Lake-Dummer Lake |
| | Lt. A.W. Barlow | Me-109 dest(air) | S/Bremen |
| | Lt. H. Moretz | Me-109 dest(air) | S/Bremen |
| | Lt. C.W. Craft | (2)Me-109 prob(air) | NE Bremen |
| | Lt. J.F. Hinchey | Me-109 dam(air) | S/Bremen |
| 352nd: | Lt. H.B. Tordoff | (2)Me-109 dest(air) | E/Bremen |
| | Lt. D.L. Barber | Me-109 dest(air) | E/Bremen |
| | Lt. H.O. Miller | (2)He-111 dest(grd) | Plantlunne |
| | Lt. R.P. Greenwood | He-111 dest(grd) | Plantlunne |

(#2)

| | | | |
|---|---|---|---|
| HdQts: | LtCol. W.B. Bailey | (2)He-111 dest(grd) | All claims are |
| | | Ju-88 dest(grd) | at Plantlunne |
| 350th: | Lt. V.G. Rafferty | (3)He-111 dest(grd) | |
| 351st: | Capt. L.G. Hally | He-111 dest(grd) | |
| | | Ju-88 dest(grd) | |
| | Capt. V.L. Byers | Ju-88 dest(grd) | |
| 352nd: | Lt. T.W. Jones | (2)He-111 dest(grd) | |
| | | u/i a/c dest(grd) | |
| | Capt. F.L. Uttwenweiler | (2)He-111 dest(grd) | |
| | Lt. J.M. Tuttle | (2)u/i a/c dest(grd) | |
| | Lt. H.B. Tordoff | He-111 dest(grd) | |
| | | u/i a/c dest(grd) | |
| | Lt. E.D. Reinhardt | He-111 dest(grd) | |
| | | Me-410 dest(grd) | |
| | F/O J.J. Swanezy | He-111 dest(grd) | |
| | | Me-410 dest(grd) | |
| | Lt. R.P. Greenwood | He-111 dest(grd) | |
| | Lt. W.J. Jordan | (.5)u/i a/c dest(grd) | |
| | Lt. G.N. Porterfield | (.5)u/i a/c dest(grd) | |

**August 5, 1944**

| | | | |
|---|---|---|---|
| 350th: | Maj. K.W. Gallup | Me-109 dest(air) | Rheine |

**August 7, 1944**

| | | | |
|---|---|---|---|
| 350th: | Lt. S.T. Benjamin | Me-410 dest(grd) | All claims are |
| | Lt. M.V. Bledsoe | Me-410 dest(grd) | SE Amiens |
| | Lt. W.P. Knowling | Me-410 dest(grd) | |
| | Lt. M.W. Hightshoe | Me-410 dam(grd) | |
| | | Me-109 dam(grd) | |

**August 11, 1944**

(#1)

| | | | |
|---|---|---|---|
| 350th: | LtCol. K.W. Gallup | u/i a/c dest(grd) | Maraville |
| | Lt. J.O. Ruscitto | Me-109 dest(grd) | Maraville |

(#2)

| | | | |
|---|---|---|---|
| 351st: | Capt. V.L. Byers | Me-109 dest(air) | S/Paris |
| | Lt. M.B. Hungate | Me-109 dest(air) | S/Paris |

**August 12, 1944**

(#1)

| | | | |
|---|---|---|---|
| HdQts: | LtCol. B. Rimerman | Ju-88 dest(grd) | SW Coulommiers |
| 351st: | Lt. J.F. Hinchey | Ju-88 dest(grd) | SW Coulommiers |
| | Lt. W.K. Lahke | Me-109 dest(grd) | SW Coulommiers |
| | Lt. C.W. Craft | (.5)Ju-88 dam(grd) | SW Coulommiers |
| | Lt. H. Moretz | (.5)Ju-88 dam(grd) | SW Coulommiers |
| 352nd: | Lt. T.W. Jones | (2)He-111 dest(grd) | E/Paris |
| | Lt. W.J. Jordan | (.5)u/i a/c dest(grd) | E/Paris |
| | Lt. R. Eluhow | (.5)u/i a/c dest(grd) | E/Paris |

(#3)

| | | | |
|---|---|---|---|
| 352nd: | Lt. R.R. Akard | FW-190 dest(grd) | S/Tournan |
| | Lt. E.D. Reinhardt | FW-190 dest(grd) | S/Tournan |

(#4)

| | | | |
|---|---|---|---|
| 352nd: | Lt. R.P. Greenwood | (2)u/i a/c dest(grd) | E/Paris |
| | | FW-190 dest(grd) | E/Paris |

**August 14, 1944**

| | | | |
|---|---|---|---|
| 350th: | Lt. R.F. Unangst | Ju-88 dest(air) | Chateau Thierry |

**August 24, 1944**

| | | | |
|---|---|---|---|
| 350th: | Lt. H.E. Asper | Me-109 dest(air) | S/Hanover |
| | Lt. B.C. Auchincloss | Me-109 dest(air) | S/Hanover |

**August 26, 1944**

| | | | |
|---|---|---|---|
| 352nd: | Lt. W.M. Newton | FW-190 dest(air) | S/Charleroi |

**August 27, 1944**

| | | | |
|---|---|---|---|
| HdQts: | LtCol. B. Rimerman | (.5)FW-190 dest(grd)* | Metz |
| | | (.5)Me-109 dam(grd) | Metz |
| 350th: | Lt. B.C. Auchincloss | (1.5)FW-190 dest(grd)** | Verdun |
| | | FW-190 dam(grd) | Verdun |
| | Lt. L.M. Davis | (2)FW-190 dest(grd) | Verdun |
| | | FW-190 dam(grd) | Verdun |
| | Lt. J.L. Schilt | (1.5)FW-190 dest(grd)** | Verdun |
| | | FW-190 dam(grd) | Verdun |
| 351st: | Capt. L.G. Hally | Ju-88 dest(grd) | NE Metz |
| | Lt. M.Q. Williams | Me-109 dest(grd) | W/Metz |
| 352nd: | Lt. J.L. Motley | Me-109 dest(grd) | Metz |
| | Lt. T.J. Forkin | (.5)FW-190 dest(grd)* | Metz |
| | | (.5)Me-109 dam(grd) | Metz |
| | | Ju-88 dam(grd) | Metz |

**August 28, 1944**

(#1)

| | | | |
|---|---|---|---|
| 350th: | LtCol. K.W. Gallup | (1.5)Fi-156 dest(air) | Verdun |
| | | (.5)He-111 dest(air) | SE Arlon |
| | Lt. R.W. Hedler | He-111 dest(air) | SE Arlon |
| | Lt. J.B. Brooks | (.5)Fi-156 dest(air) | Verdun |
| | Lt. J.L. Schilt | (.5)He-111 dest(air) | SE Arlon |
| | Capt. W.D. Smith | He-111 dest(grd) | Verdun |
| 352nd: | Lt. T.W. Jones | (.5)Ju-88 dest(air) | SE Luxembourg |
| | Lt. B. Parker | (.5)Ju-88 dest(air) | SE Luxembourg |

(#2)

| | | | |
|---|---|---|---|
| 350th: | Capt. J.O. Ruscitto | (2)Me-110 dest(air) | Wavre |
| | Capt. W.J. Price | Me-410 dest(grd) | Wavre |
| | | (2)Me-410 dam(grd) | Wavre |

| Unit | Pilot | Claim | Location |
|---|---|---|---|
| | Lt. R.T. Allison | Me-410 dest(grd) | Wavre |
| 351st: | Lt. W.K. Lahke | Me-109 dest(air) | Dinan |
| 352nd: | Lt. F.H. Bouldin | Me-110 dest(air) | SE Brussels |

**August 29, 1944**

| Unit | Pilot | Claim | Location |
|---|---|---|---|
| 350th: | Lt. S.T. Benjamin | (3)Me-109 dest(grd) | Unless noted, |
| | | (2)Me-410 dest(grd) | all claims are |
| | | (4)Me-109 dam(grd) | at Diest |
| | Lt. M.V. Bledsoe | (2)Me-110 dest(grd) | |
| | | (2)Me-109 dest(grd) | |
| | | (2)Me-110 dam(grd) | |
| | | (2)Me-109 dam(grd) | |
| | Capt. W.J. Price | (3)Me-109 dest(grd) | |
| | | Me-109 dam(grd) | |
| | Lt. M.W. Hightshoe | (2)Me-109 dest(grd) | |
| | | Me-410 dest(grd) | |
| | | (2)Me-109 dam(grd) | |
| | Lt. O.I. Aal | (2)Me-110 dest(grd) | |
| | Capt. W.D. Smith | u/i a/c dest(grd) | Wavre |
| 351st: | Lt. D.F. Kohler | u/i a/c dest(grd) | Chievres |

**September 5, 1944**

| Unit | Pilot | Claim | Location |
|---|---|---|---|
| 352nd: | Capt. G.S. Burlingame | Do-217 dest(air) | Apeldoorn |

**September 8, 1944**

| Unit | Pilot | Claim | Location |
|---|---|---|---|
| 350th: | Lt. S.T. Benjamin | Do-217 dest(air) | Hesepe |
| | Lt. M.W. Hightshoe | Do-217 dam(grd) | Hesepe |

**September 13, 1944**

| Unit | Pilot | Claim | Location |
|---|---|---|---|
| HdQts: | Capt. C.L. Stafford | (3)Me-109 dam(grd) | SW Stuttgart |
| 351st: | Lt. C.L. McGraw | Do-217 dest(grd) | NW Stuttgart |
| | Lt. H.P. Maree | (.5)FW-200 dest(grd) | Hellingen |
| | Lt. H.D. Milligan | (.5)FW-200 dest(grd) | Hellingen |

**September 21, 1944**

| Unit | Pilot | Claim | Location |
|---|---|---|---|
| 350th: | Lt. R.W. Hedler | (1.5)FW-190 dest(air) | SE Arnheim |
| | Lt. J.L. Schilt | FW-190 dest(air) | S/Arnheim |
| | Lt. V.G. Rafferty | (.5)FW-190 dest(air) | SE Arnheim |
| | Lt. R.T. Allison | FW-190 prob(air) | SW Nijmegen |
| | Lt. B.C. Auchincloss | FW-190 dam(air) | SE Arnheim |
| 351st: | Lt. R.F. Vomaske | Me-109 dest(air) | Arnheim-Nijmegen |

**September 23, 1944**

| Unit | Pilot | Claim | Location |
|---|---|---|---|
| HdQts: | Capt. J.W. Eanes | FW-190 dest(air) | All claims are |
| 350th: | Lt. B.C. Auchincloss | FW-190 dest(air) | SE Arnheim |
| | | Me-109 dest(air) | |
| | | FW-190 prob(air) | |
| | Lt. V.G. Rafferty | FW-190 dest(air) | |
| | | Me-109 dest(air) | |
| | Capt. E.S. Middleton | FW-190 dest(air) | |
| | Capt. W.J. Price | FW-190 dest(air) | |
| | Lt. R.W. Abernathy | Me-109 dest(air) | |
| | Lt. H.E. Asper | FW-190 dest(air) | |
| | Lt. G.P. Devine | FW-190 dest(air) | |
| | | FW-190 dam(air) | |
| | Lt. H.E. Haynes | Me-109 dest(air) | |
| | Lt. G.P. Province | FW-190 dest(air) | |
| | Lt. W.P. Knowling | Me-109 prob(air) | |
| | Lt. L.M. Grainger | FW-190 dam(air) | |
| | Lt. L.M. Davis | Me-109 dam(air) | |
| 352nd: | Lt. J.F. Cross | FW-190 dest(air) | |
| | Lt. G.N. Porterfield | FW-190 dest(air) | |
| | Lt. C.N. Sladek | FW-190 dest(air) | |

**September 27, 1944**

| Unit | Pilot | Claim | Location |
|---|---|---|---|
| 352nd: | Lt. H.B. Tordoff | Me-109 dest(air) | Hanau |

NOTE: From this point on, all claims will be in P-51's

**October 24, 1944**

| Unit | Pilot | Claim | Location |
|---|---|---|---|
| 352nd: | Capt. F.L. Uttwenweiler | (4)He-111 dest(grd) | N/Luxembourg |
| | | (3)He-111 dam(grd) | N/Luxembourg |

**November 2, 1944**

| Unit | Pilot | Claim | Location |
|---|---|---|---|
| 350th: | Lt. L.M. Grainger | (2)Me-109 dest(air) | Merseburg |
| | Lt. R.W. Abernathy | Me-109 dest(air) | Merseburg |
| | Capt. H.G. Kolb | FW-190 dam(air) | NW Merseburg |
| 352nd: | Capt. L.P. Cles | FW-190 prob(air) | Naumburg |
| | Lt. H.E. Tear | Me-109 prob(air) | Naumburg |

**November 8, 1944**

| Unit | Pilot | Claim | Location |
|---|---|---|---|
| 352nd: | Capt. L.P. Cles | (.5)Ju-88 dam(grd) | Plantlunne |
| | Lt. J.R. Evans | (.5)Ju-88 dam(grd) | Plantlunne |

**November 10, 1944**

| Unit | Pilot | Claim | Location |
|---|---|---|---|
| 350th: | Lt. J.M. Ard | Bu-133 dest(grd) | Fulda |
| | Lt. H.E. Caton | Bu-133 dest(grd) | Fulda |
| | Lt. A.L. Deeds | Bu-133 dest(grd) | Fulda |
| | Lt. H.E. Haynes | Bu-133 dest(grd) | Fulda |

**November 18, 1944**

| Unit | Pilot | Claim | Location |
|---|---|---|---|
| 350th: | Capt. W.J. Price | u/i a/c dest(grd) | Unless noted, all |
| | | (.5)u/i a/c dam(grd) | claims are at |
| | Lt. M.W. Hightshoe | (2)He-177 dest(grd) | Lechfeld |
| | | u/i a/c dest(grd) | |
| | Capt. W.F. Tanner | He-177 dest(grd) | |
| | Lt. J.E. Jessup | Me-110 dest(grd) | |
| | Lt. C.A. Larsen | He-111 dest(grd) | |
| | | He-111 dam(grd) | |
| | Lt. A.K. Ferrell | He-111 dest(grd) | |
| | | He-111 dam(grd) | |
| | Lt. A.L. Deeds | FW-190 dam(grd) | |
| | Lt. R.W. Abernathy | (.5)u/i a/c dam(grd) | |
| 351st: | Lt. G.E. Markham | Me-262 dam(air) | S/Augsburg |
| | Capt. G.B. Compton | (2)Ju-88 dest(grd) | |
| | | u/i a/c dam(grd) | |
| | Capt. A.C. Carroll | He-111 dest(grd) | |
| | | He-111 dam(grd) | |
| | Lt. T.R. Drybrough | FW-190 dest(grd) | |
| | F/O T.C. Brock | Ju-88 dam(grd) | Prittrishing |
| 352nd: | Lt. W.C. Davis | (2)He-111 dest(grd) | |
| | Capt. W.J. Jordan | FW-190 dest(grd) | |
| | Capt. J.N. Poindexter | He-177 dest(grd) | |
| | | He-177 dam(grd) | |
| | Lt. V.M. Hernandez | Ju-88 dest(grd) | |
| | Lt. M. Morrison | Me-163 dest(grd) | |
| | | He-177 dam(grd) | |
| | Lt. E.D. Thomas | Ju-88 dest(grd) | |
| | | Me-163 dam(grd) | |
| | | u/i a/c dam(grd) | |
| | Lt. S.J. Kritz | FW-190 dam(grd) | |

**November 26, 1944**

| Unit | Pilot | Claim | Location |
|---|---|---|---|
| 350th: | Capt. W.L. Boone | FW-190 dest(air) | Minden |
| | Capt. J.H. Winder | FW-190 dest(air) | Dummer Lake |
| | F/O F.J. Orzelek | FW-190 dest(air) | SE Dummer Lake |

**November 27, 1944**

| Unit | Pilot | Claim | Location |
|---|---|---|---|
| 350th: | Maj. W.K. Blickenstaff | (4)FW-190 dest(air) | Steinhuder Lake-Brunswick |
| | Capt. W.L. Boone | FW-190 dest(air) | Brunswick |
| | | FW-190 prob(air) | Brunswick |
| | Capt. J.H. Winder | FW-190 dest(air) | Brunswick |
| | Lt. J.E. Jessup | FW-190 prob(air) | Brunswick |
| | Lt. R.W. Abernathy | FW-190 dam(air) | Brunswick |
| 351st: | Capt. A.C. Carroll | FW-190 dest(air) | Unless noted, all |
| | | FW-190 dam(air) | claims are NE |
| | Capt. G.B. Compton | FW-190 dest(air) | Steinhuder Lake |
| | Lt. H.W. Chase | Me-109 dest(air) | |
| | | Me-109 dam(air) | |
| | Lt. T.R. Drybrough | FW-190 dest(air) | |
| | | FW-190 prob(air) | |
| | Lt. G.E. Markham | FW-190 dest(air) | |
| | Lt. J.M. Nicklebur | FW-190 dest(air) | |
| | | Me-109 dam(air) | |
| | Lt. R.K. Wiehe | Me-109 dest(air) | |
| | Lt. R. Hilgenburg | (.5)Me-109 dest(air) | N/Dummer Lake |
| | Lt. G.S. Montgomery | (.5)Me-109 dest(air) | N/Dummer Lake |
| 352nd: | Capt. J.L. Knoble | Me-109 dest(air) | All claims are |
| | Lt. A.C. Cundy | Me-109 dest(air) | at Magdeburg |
| | Lt. F.H. Bouldin | Me-109 dest(air) | |
| | Lt. J.R. Evans | Me-109 dest(air) | |
| | Lt. J.E. Davenport | (2)Me-109 dam(air) | |
| | Maj. W.H. Junttila | Me-109 dam(air) | |

**December 5, 1944**

| Unit | Pilot | Claim | Location |
|---|---|---|---|
| 350th: | Capt. W.F. Tanner | FW-190 dest(air) | S/Steinhuder L. |
| | | FW-190 dam(air) | S/Steinhuder L. |
| | Lt. N.N. Cowen | FW-190 dest(air) | S/Steinhuder L. |
| | Lt. A.L. Deeds | FW-190 dest(air) | S/Steinhuder L. |
| 351st: | Maj. F.H. LeFebre | FW-190 dest(air) | N/Berlin |
| | | Me-109 dam(air) | N/Berlin |
| 352nd: | Lt. J.R. Evans | (2)FW-190 dest(air) | All claims are |
| | | FW-190 prob(air) | NE Berlin |
| | Capt. W.W. Johnson | FW-190 dest(air) | |
| | Capt. J.L. Knoble | FW-190 dest(air) | |
| | Lt. F.H. Bouldin | FW-190 dest(air) | |
| | Lt. W.R. Curry | FW-190 prob(air) | |

**December 23, 1944**

| Unit | Pilot | Claim | Location |
|---|---|---|---|
| 351st: | Capt. H.D. Stump | Me-262 dam(air) | Magdeburg-SE Hanover |
| 352nd: | Lt. S.E. Stephenson | Me-262 dam(air) | W/Magdeburg |

**December 24, 1944**

| Unit | Pilot | Claim | Location |
|---|---|---|---|
| 350th: | Capt. J.H. Winder | (2)Me-109 dest(air) | Coblenz-Limburg |
| | Lt. R.W. Abernathy | (2)Me-109 dest(air) | Coblenz-Limburg |
| | Lt. G.S.H. Lee | Me-109 dest(air) | Coblenz |
| 352nd: | Lt. A.C. Cundy | Me-109 dest(air) | Leacher Lake |
| | Lt. H.Q. Waggoner | Me-109 dest(air) | SW Euskirchen |
| (PRU) | | | |
| 350th: | Lt. J.E. Jessup | Me-109 dest(air) | Leipzig |

**December 25, 1944**

| | | | |
|---|---|---|---|
| 352nd: | Lt. H.Q. Waggoner | Me-109 dest(air) | NE St. Vith |

**December 31, 1944**

| | | | |
|---|---|---|---|
| 352nd: | Lt. G.N. Porterfield | FW-190 dest(air) | W/Coblenz |

**January 14, 1945**

| | | | |
|---|---|---|---|
| 351st: | Lt. J.F. Hinchey | (2)FW-190 dest(air) | NE Hanover |
| | | Me-109 dest(air) | NE Hanover |
| | Lt. H.P. Maree | FW-190 dest(air) | SE Hamburg |
| | | Me-109 dest(air) | SE Hamburg |
| | Lt. J.E. Frye | Me-109 dest(air) | NE Hanover |
| | Lt. B.J. Murray | Me-262 dest(air) | Wittenburg |
| | Lt. J.W. Rohrs | (.5)Me-262 dest(air) | E/Wittenburg |
| | Lt. G.J. Rosen | (.5)Me-262 dest(air) | E/Wittenburg |
| | Lt. M.A. Arnold | (.5)Me-262 dam(air) | E/Hanover |
| | Lt. G.E. Markham | (.5)Me-262 dam(air) | E/Hanover |
| 352nd: | Lt. A.C. Cundy | FW-190 dest(air) | SW Dummer Lake |
| | Lt. J.R. Evans | (.5)u/i a/c dam(grd) | Remaining claims |
| | | (.5)u/i a/c dam(grd) | are at Branden- |
| | F/O R.C. Hassel | (.5)u/i a/c dam(grd) | burg/Briest |
| | | (.5)u/i a/c dam(grd) | |

**January 16, 1945**

| | | | |
|---|---|---|---|
| 352nd: | Capt. G.G. Callans | Me-163 dest(grd) | All claims are |
| | | Ju-88 dam(grd) | at Deiningen |
| | Lt. L.W. Grove | FW-190 dest(grd) | |
| | | Ju-88 dam(grd) | |
| | Lt. H.R. Lammie | Ju-88 dam(grd) | |

**February 9, 1945**

| | | | |
|---|---|---|---|
| 352nd: | Lt. J.E. Davenport | He-111 dest(grd) | Kothen |

**February 22, 1945**

| | | | |
|---|---|---|---|
| 350th: | Maj. W.K. Blickenstaff | Me-262 dest(air) | Berlin |
| 351st: | Capt. G.B. Compton | Me-262 dest(air) | Brandenburg |

**February 23, 1945**

| | | | |
|---|---|---|---|
| 352nd: | Lt. D.W. Schoen | He-111 dest(grd) | All claims are |
| | | Me-110 dest(grd) | at Kitzingen |
| | | Me-110 dam(grd) | |
| | Lt. J.R. Evans | He-177 dest(grd) | |
| | | (.5)Me-110 dest(grd) | |
| | Lt. L.O. Pletz | He-111 dest(grd) | |
| | | (.5)Me-110 dest(grd) | |

**February 25, 1945**

| | | | |
|---|---|---|---|
| 351st: | Capt. G.E. Markham | FW-200 dam(grd) | Lechfeld |

**February 27, 1945**

| | | | |
|---|---|---|---|
| 350th: | Maj. W.L. Boone | (2)FW-190 dest(grd) | All claims are |
| | | (2)He-219 dest(grd) | at Rohrensee |
| | | Ar-234 dest(grd) | |
| | | Ju-188 dest(grd) | |
| | | Me-410 dest(grd) | |
| | | (3)u/i a/c dam(grd) | |
| | | FW-190 dam(grd) | |
| | | He-219 dam(grd) | |
| | Capt. H.G. Kolb | (3)FW-190 dest(grd) | |
| | | (1.5)Me-410 dest(grd) | |
| | | (.5)u/i a/c dest(grd) | |
| | | FW-190 dam(grd) | |
| | Lt. R.J. Lanoue | (2)Me-410 dest(grd) | |
| | | (2)u/i a/c dest(grd) | |
| | | FW-190 dest(grd) | |
| | | FW-190 dam(grd) | |
| | Lt. R.C. Gordon | (2)Me-110 dest(grd) | |
| | | Ju-88 dest(grd) | |
| | | (2)Me-110 dam(grd) | |
| | | (2)Ju-88 dam(grd) | |
| | Lt. J.W. Clark | (2)Me-110 dest(grd) | |
| | | Me-109 dest(grd) | |
| | | (2)Me-410 dam(grd) | |
| | F/O R.N. Gustke | Me-410 dest(grd) | |
| | | Ju-88 dest(grd) | |
| | | (.5)FW-190 dest(grd) | |
| | | (4)u/i a/c dam(grd) | |
| | Lt. J.D. McMullen | (1.5)FW-190 dest(grd) | |
| | | Ju-88 dest(grd) | |
| | | FW-190 dam(grd) | |
| | | Ju-88 dam(grd) | |
| | Lt. C.A. Larsen | (2)Me-410 dest(grd) | |
| | Lt. A.G. Spriggs | Me-109 dest(grd) | |
| | | u/i a/c dest(grd) | |
| | Lt. W. Grizzle | (1.5)Me-410 dest(grd) | |
| | | FW-190 dam(grd) | |
| | | u/i a/c dam(grd) | |
| | Lt. H.H. Hakonen | Me-410 dest(grd) | |
| | | (.5)u/i a/c dest(grd) | |
| | | Me-410 dam(grd) | |
| | Lt. H.E. Caton | Ju-88 dest(grd) | |
| | | (2)Me-109 dam(grd) | |
| | Lt. R.S. Liebold | Me-410 dest(grd) | |
| | | Me-410 dam(grd) | |

**February 28, 1945**

| | | | |
|---|---|---|---|
| 350th: | Lt. M.W. Hightshoe | (1.5)Me-110 dest(grd) | S/Gotha |
| | | Me-109 dest(grd) | S/Gotha |
| | | Me-410 dest(grd) | S/Gotha |
| | Lt. R.J. Lanoue | (3)Me-110 dest(grd) | S/Gotha |
| | Lt. J.D. McMullen | (1.5)Me-110 dest(grd) | S/Gotha |
| | Lt. J.A. Madson | u/i a/c dest(grd) | S/Gotha |
| | | Ju-88 dam(grd) | S/Gotha |
| | Lt. G.W. Robison | Me-410 dest(grd) | Sonneborn |
| | Lt. G.D. Kammer | He-111 dam(grd) | Rohrensee |

**March 1, 1945**

| | | | |
|---|---|---|---|
| 352nd: | Maj. W.W. Johnson | Bu-181 dest(air) | Nordlingen |
| | | (4)u/i a/c dam(grd) | Nordlingen |

**March 2, 1945**

| | | | |
|---|---|---|---|
| HdQts: | LtCol. W.B. Bailey | (2)FW-190 dest(air) | S/Wittenburg |
| 350th: | Lt. L.W. Lee | Me-109 dest(air) | Ruhland |
| | | Me-109 dam(air) | Ruhland |
| | Lt. R.J. Lanoue | Me-109 dest(air) | Ruhland |
| | Lt. G.D. Page | Me-109 dest(air) | Ruhland |
| | Lt. W.M. Agnew | Me-109 prob(air) | Ruhland |
| | Maj. W.L. Boone | Me-109 dam(air) | Ruhland |
| 351st: | Maj. V.L. Byers | FW-190 dest(air) | Wittenburg |
| | | Me-109 prob(air) | Wittenburg |
| 352nd: | Lt. A.C. Cundy | (2)FW-190 dest(air) | Dessau |
| | | Me-109 dest(air) | Dessau |
| | Lt. H.Q. Waggoner | (2)FW-190 dest(air) | Ruhland |
| | | Me-109 dest(air) | Ruhland |
| | Lt. L.W. Grove | Me-109 dest(air) | S/Berlin |
| | Lt. E.J. Sullivan | FW-190 dest(air) | S/Wittenburg |
| | Lt. L. Schreiber | Me-109 dest(air) | Magdeburg |

**March 3, 1945**

| | | | |
|---|---|---|---|
| 351st: | Lt. J.E. Frye | Me-262 dam(air) | SE Hamburg |

**March 14, 1945**

| | | | |
|---|---|---|---|
| 351st: | Capt. G.E. Markham | (3)Me-109 dest(air) | All claims are |
| | Capt. W.J. Maguire | (2)Me-109 dest(air) | at Luckenwalde |
| | Lt. G.S. Montgomery | (2)Me-109 dest(air) | |
| | Lt. T.C. Brock | Me-109 dest(air) | |
| | Lt. J.O. Fulton | Me-109 dest(air) | |
| | Lt. J.A. Hynes | Me-109 dest(air) | |
| | Lt. E.J. Risk | Me-109 dest(air) | |

**March 21, 1945**

| | | | |
|---|---|---|---|
| 350th: | Maj. W.L. Boone | (4)Ar-234 dest(grd) | All claims are |
| | | (4)Ar-234 dam(grd) | at Achmer |
| | | Me-109 dam(grd) | |
| | F/O R.N. Gustke | (4)Ar-234 dest(grd) | |
| | | Me-109 dest(grd) | |
| | | (4)Ar-234 dam(grd) | |
| | Lt. R.J. Lanoue | (2)Ar-234 dest(grd) | |
| | | He-111 dest(grd) | |
| | Lt. D.A. Howie | (2)FW-190 dest(grd) | |
| | Lt. F. O'Neill | Ju-88 dest(grd) | |
| | Lt. J.P. Onkey | Me-109 dest(grd) | |
| | Lt. W.A.S. Prescott | Ju-88 dest(grd) | |
| | | Ar-234 dam(grd) | |
| | Lt. J.D. McMullen | He-111 dest(grd) | |
| | | Ar-234 dam(grd) | |
| | Lt. J.L. Guthrie | Me-109 dam(grd) | |
| 351st: | Capt. F.N. Emory | (2)Me-109 dest(grd) | |
| | | FW-190 dam(grd) | |
| | | u/i a/c dam(grd) | |
| | Lt. G.J. Miller | (2)FW-190 dest(grd) | |
| | | (2)FW-190 dam(grd) | |
| | Capt. G.B. Compton | Ar-234 dest(grd) | |
| | Lt. D.E. Lewis | Me-109 dest(grd) | |
| | | Me-109 dam(grd) | |
| | F/O H.A. Morris | He-111 dest(grd) | |
| 352nd: | Lt. A. Michel | (4)FW-190 dest(grd) | |
| | Lt. W.K. Bixby | u/i a/c dest(grd) | |

**March 24, 1945**

| | | | |
|---|---|---|---|
| HdQts: | Maj. R.A. Elder | (4)FW-190 dest(air) | All claims are |
| | | Me-109 dest(air) | NW Kassel |
| | | Me-109 dam(air) | |
| | Capt. R.E. Hartley | (2)FW-190 dest(air) | |
| | | Me-109 dest(air) | |
| | | Me-109 dam(air) | |
| 350th: | LtCol. W.K. Blickenstaff | (3)FW-190 dest(air) | |
| | | (2)Me-109 dest(air) | |
| | Lt. J.L. Guthrie | (3)Me-109 dest(air) | |
| | | Me-109 dam(air) | |
| | | FW-190 dam(air) | |

| | | | |
|---|---|---|---|
| | Lt. L.W. Lee | (2)FW-190 dest(air) | |
| | | Me-109 dest(air) | |
| | Lt. J.W. Clark | (2)FW-190 dest(air) | |
| | Lt. J.F. May | (2)FW-190 dest(air) | |
| | Lt. W.A.S. Prescott | (2)Me-109 dest(air) | |
| | Lt. G.W. Robison | FW-190 dest(air) | |
| | Lt. W.R. Hubbell | Me-109 dest(air) | |
| | | Me-109 prob(air) | |
| | Lt. F. O'Neill | Me-109 dest(air) | |
| | | Me-109 dam(air) | |
| | Lt. H.H. Hakonen | FW-190 prob(air) | |
| | F/O R.N. Gustke | FW-190 dam(air) | |

**March 31, 1945**

| | | | |
|---|---|---|---|
| HdQts: | Maj. W.M. Long | Me-109 dest(air) | Hanover |
| 352nd: | Lt. H.B. Tordoff | Me-262 dest(air) | Dessau |

**April 5, 1945**

| | | | |
|---|---|---|---|
| 351st: | Capt. G.B. Compton | (3)Me-410 dest(grd) | Weiden |
| | | Me-110 dest(grd) | Weiden |
| | Lt. T.P. Pryor | (3)Me-410 dest(grd) | Weiden |
| | | Me-110 dam(grd) | Weiden |

**April 7, 1945**

| | | | |
|---|---|---|---|
| 351st: | Capt. C.L. McGraw | (3)Me-109 dest(air) | Steinhuder Lake |
| | Capt. G.E. Markham | Me-109 dest(air) | E/Steinhuder L. |
| | | Me-109 dam(air) | E/Steinhuder L. |
| | Capt. H.W. Chase | Me-109 dest(air) | NE Steinhuder L. |
| | Lt. R.F. Hahn | Me-109 dest(air) | Steinhuder Lake |
| 352nd: | Capt. H.B. Tordoff | Me-109 dest(air) | E/Hamburg |

**April 9, 1945**

| | | | |
|---|---|---|---|
| 351st: | Capt. F.N. Emory | (2)Me-262 dest(grd) | All claims are |
| | | Me-410 dest(grd) | S/Neubiberg |
| | | u/i a/c dest(grd) | |
| | F/O H.A. Morris | Me-210 dest(grd) | |
| | | Me-262 dam(grd) | |
| | Lt. J.A. Hynes | Me-262 dam(grd) | |

**April 10, 1945**

| | | | |
|---|---|---|---|
| 350th: | Capt. R.W. Abernathy | Me-262 dest(air) | Dessau |
| | Lt. J.W. Clark | (.5)Me-262 dest(air) | Dessau |
| | Lt. B.D. McMahan | (.5)Me-262 dest(air) | Dessau |
| 351st: | Capt. G.B. Compton | Me-262 dest(air) | Dessau-Kothen |

**April 16, 1945**

| | | | |
|---|---|---|---|
| HdQts: | Col. B. Rimerman | (3)FW-190 dest(grd) | Reichersberg |
| | | Me-109 dest(grd) | Reichersberg |
| | | Me-108 dest(grd) | Reichersberg |
| | | Ju-87 dest(grd) | Reichersberg |
| | Capt. W.J. Lane | FW-190 dest(grd) | Pocking |
| 350th: | Capt. H.G. Kolb | (5)FW-190 dest(grd) | All 350th claims |
| | | (2)Me-109 dest(grd) | are at Pocking |
| | | (1.5)Fi-156 dest(grd) | |
| | | (.5)Fi-156 dest(grd) | |
| | | (.5)Hs-126 dest(grd) | |
| | | (2)Ju-87 dam(grd) | |
| | Lt. B.D. McMahan | (4)FW-190 dest(grd) | |
| | | (.5)Fi-156 dest(grd) | |
| | | (.5)Fi-156 dest(grd) | |
| | | (.5)Hs-126 dest(grd) | |
| | Capt. M.W. Hightshoe | (4)FW-190 dest(grd) | |
| | | Me-109 dest(grd) | |
| | F/O R.N. Gustke | (3)FW-190 dest(grd) | |
| | | (2)Ju-87 dest(grd) | |
| | Lt. J.H. McClure | (2)Me-109 dest(grd) | |
| | | FW-190 dest(grd) | |
| | | FW-200 dest(grd) | |
| | | Ju-88 dest(grd) | |
| | Lt. J.D. McMullen | (5)FW-190 dest(grd) | |
| | Lt. R.C. Gordon | (3)FW-190 dest(grd) | |
| | Lt. W.A.S. Prescott | (2)FW-190 dest(grd) | |
| | | Me-109 dest(grd) | |
| | Lt. B. Greenfield | FW-190 dest(grd) | |
| | | Me-109 dest(grd) | |
| | | Ju-87 dest(grd) | |
| | | Me-109 dam(grd) | |
| | | Ju-87 dam(grd) | |
| | | u/i a/c dam(grd) | |
| | Maj. R.A. Elder | FW-190 dest(grd) | |
| | | Ju-87 dest(grd) | |
| | | (3)Ju-87 dam(grd) | |
| | | Me-109 dam(grd) | |
| | Lt. L.W. Lee | (2)FW-190 dest(grd) | |
| 351st: | Lt. G.J. Miller | (6)FW-190 dest(grd) | All 351st claims |
| | | (2)Me-109 dest(grd) | at Reichersberg |
| | | Do-217 dest(grd) | |
| | Capt. G.B. Compton | (3)Ju-188 dest(grd) | |
| | | (2)Ju-88 dest(grd) | |
| | | (3)u/i a/c dam(grd) | |
| | Capt. H.W. Chase | (4)FW-190 dest(grd) | |
| | | FW-190 dam(grd) | |
| | Capt. F.N. Emory | (2)FW-190 dest(grd) | |
| | | Ju-87 dest(grd) | |
| | | u/i a/c dest(grd) | |
| | | Me-110 dam(grd) | |
| | | FW-190 dam(grd) | |
| | Capt. R.E. Hartley | (2)FW-200 dest(grd) | |
| | | FW-190 dest(grd) | |
| | | Ju-87 dest(grd) | |
| | Lt. R.F. Hahn | (4)Ju-88 dest(grd) | |
| | | Ju-88 dam(grd) | |
| | Maj. V.L. Byers | Fi-156 dest(grd) | |
| | | FW-190 dest(grd) | |
| | | Me-262 dam(grd) | |
| | Lt. T.P. Pryor | FW-190 dest(grd) | |
| | | Do-217 dest(grd) | |
| | F/O H.S. Murray | (2)FW-190 dest(grd) | |
| | Lt. J.O. Fulton | FW-190 dest(grd) | |
| | | Ju-88 dest(grd) | |
| | | Ju-88 dam(grd) | |
| | Lt. T.R. Drybrough | (2)FW-190 dest(grd) | |
| | | u/i a/c dam(grd) | |
| | Lt. D.G. Larson | (3)FW-190 dest(grd) | |
| | | (4)FW-190 dam(grd) | |
| | Lt. J.M. Nicklebur | (3)Ju-88 dest(grd) | |
| | | (2)Ju-88 dam(grd) | |
| | Lt. R.K. Wiehe | He-111 dest(grd) | |
| | | FW-190 dest(grd) | |
| | | Me-109 dest(grd) | |
| | | He-111 dam(grd) | |
| | Capt. L.B. Highfield | Me-110 dest(grd) | |
| | | Ju-88 dest(grd) | |
| | | He-111 dam(grd) | |
| | Lt. C.W. Geiger | (2)u/i a/c dest(grd) | |
| | Capt. C.L. McGraw | He-111 dest(grd) | |
| | | (2)He-111 dam(grd) | |
| | Lt. S.S. Petticrew | Ju-88 dest(grd) | |
| | | Me-109 dam(grd) | |
| | Lt. E.J. Risk | FW-190 dest(grd) | |
| | F/O H.A. Morris | Me-110 dest(grd) | |
| | | (2)Me-109 dam(grd) | |
| | | FW-190 dam(grd) | |
| 352nd: | Capt. H.B. Tordoff | Me-109 dest(grd) | All claims at |
| | | Do-217 dest(grd) | Bad Aibling |
| | | (.5)Ju-88 dest(grd) | |
| | | u/i a/c dam(grd) | |
| | Lt. J.G. Bartley | (.5)Ju-88 dest(grd) | |
| | Lt. E.A. Knickelbein | FW-190 dest(grd) | |
| | | Me-110 dest(grd) | |
| | | Fi-156 dest(grd) | |
| | Lt. L.O. Pletz | He-111 dest(grd) | |
| | | (2)He-111 dam(grd) | |
| | Lt. F.W. Leitner | Me-109 dest(grd) | |
| | | Me-109 dam(grd) | |
| | | Me-110 dam(grd) | |
| | Lt. R.T. Rose | He-111 dest(grd) | |
| | | Ju-88 dam(grd) | |
| | Lt. L.W. Grove | (2)He-111 dest(grd) | All claims are |
| | | He-111 dam(grd) | at Pocking |
| | Lt. J.W. Lamb | Me-109 dest(grd) | |
| | | Me-109 dam(grd) | |
| | | u/i a/c dam(grd) | |
| | Lt. W.K. Bixby | Ar-196 dam(grd) | |
| | | u/i a/c dam(grd) | |
| | Lt. J.A. McIntosh | He-111 dam(grd) | |
| | Lt. W.R. Harbin | Ju-88 dam(grd) | |

**April 17, 1945**

| | | | |
|---|---|---|---|
| 352nd: | Capt. W.C. Davis | (4)FW-190 dest(grd) | Unless noted, |
| | | FW-190 dam(grd) | claims are at |
| | Capt. H.Q. Waggoner | (3)Me-109 dest(grd) | Ganacker |
| | | Ju-88 dest(grd) | |
| | Maj. W.W. Johnson | (2)FW-190 dest(grd) | Muldorf |
| | | (3)FW-190 dam(grd) | Muldorf |
| | | Me-109 dam(grd) | |
| | Lt. B.J. Lancaster | Me-109 dest(grd) | |
| | | FW-190 dest(grd) | |
| | | (.5)He-111 dest(grd) | |
| | | Me-109 dam(grd) | |
| | Lt. W.E. Beach | Me-109 dest(grd) | |
| | | (.5)He-111 dest(grd) | |
| | Lt. L.W. Grove | FW-190 dest(grd) | |
| | | u/i a/c dam(grd) | |
| | Lt. R.T. Rose | Ju-88 dest(grd) | |
| | | Me-109 dam(grd) | |
| | | Ju-88 dam(grd) | |
| | Lt. J.W. Lamb | u/i a/c dest(grd) | |
| | F/O R.C. Hassel | Me-109 dest(grd) | |
| | | Me-109 dam(grd) | |

| | |
|---|---|
| Lt. E.A. Knickelbein | (2)Me-109 dam(grd)<br>FW-190 dam(grd)<br>Fi-156 dam(grd) |
| Lt. R.R. Anderson | Me-109 dam(grd) |
| Lt. H.R. Lammie | FW-190 dam(grd) |
| Lt. F.W. Leitner | FW-190 dam(grd) |
| Lt. L.O. Pletz | Me-109 dam(grd) |
| Lt. R.B. Snyder | Me-109 dam(grd) |
| Lt. J.A. McIntosh | Me-109 dam(grd) |
| Lt. L.M. McAdory | Me-109 dam(grd) |

**353rd Fighter Group Losses**

**July 24, 1943**
Lt. Jack D. Lepird (352nd) KIAc; Crashed while on a high altitude test flight.
P-47D SX-
Lt. Harry H. McPherson (352nd) KIAc; Crashed while on a high altitude test flight.
P-47D SX-

**August 16, 1943**
LtCol. Joseph A. Morris (HdQts) KIA; Last seen chasing a FW-190 northwest of Paris.
P-47D YJ-

**August 31, 1943**
Lt. Lester L. Dansky (352nd) KIA; Collided with Lt. Murden north of Amiens.
P-47D SX- 42-7999
Lt. Robert T. Murden (352nd) KIA; Collided with Lt. Dansky north of Amiens.
P-47D SX- 42-8383

**September 5, 1943**
Capt. Irvin E. Venell (350th) KIAc; Crashed in bad weather enroute to Biggin Hill.
P-47D LH-K 42-7956
Lt. Harold W. Long (350th) KIAc; Crashed in bad weather enroute to Biggin Hill.
P-47D LH-Y 42-8475

**September 6, 1943**
F/O Earl W. Perry, Jr. (352nd) KIA; Hit by a FW-190 near La Chatelet
P-47D SX- 42-7901

**September 15, 1943**
Lt. Walter J. Donovan (352nd) KIA; Ran out of fuel and crashed into the Channel.
P-47D SX- 42-8494

**September 18, 1943**
Lt. Francis J. Hajosy (352nd) KIAc; Engine failed while landing at Metfield.
P-47D SX-

**September 23, 1943**
Lt. George S. Dietz (352nd) KIA; Hit by fighters near Nantes.
P-47D SX- 42-7995

**October 14, 1943**
Lt. Dwight A. Fry (350th) MIA-E; Hit by a FW-190 near Budel.
P-47D LH-H 42-8513
Lt. Robert C. Peters (350th) KIA; Crashed at Herongate upon returning.
P-47D LH-T

**October 22, 1943**
Lt. Alan W. Lowe (350th) KIA; Spun-in near St. Omer in overcast.
P-47D LH- 42-8683
Lt. Walter B. Stone (350th) KIA; Spun-in near St. Omer in overcast.
P-47D LH- 42-7989

**November 5, 1943**
Lt. Robert L. Newman (350th) KIA; Hit by fighters and crashed into the North Sea.
P-47D LH- 42-7907
Capt. Orville A. Kinkade (351st) POW; Hit by fighters and bailed out near Volkerals.
P-47C YJ-K 41-6583 "Alyce"
Lt. Benedict E. Kraft (351st) POW; Hit by fighters and bailed out near Mulheim.
P-47D YJ-Q 42-8428

**November 25, 1943**
LtCol. Loren G. McCollom (HdQts) POW; Hit by flak at St. Omer.
P-47D YJ-S 42-8395 "Cookie"

**December 22, 1943**
Lt. Leroy W. Ista (352nd) KIA; Ran out of fuel and crashed off Lowestoft.
P-47D SX- 42-22458

**December 30, 1943**
Lt. William W. Odom (350th) KIA; Hit by a FW-190 near Charleville.
P-47D LH- 42-8398
Lt. Russell E. Moriarity (352nd) POW; Hit by fighters near Charleville.
P-47D SX- 42-74636

**January 11, 1944**
Lt. Victor L. Vogel (352nd) KIA; Suffered mechanical trouble and spun-into the North Sea.
P-47D SX-F 42-7904

**February 3, 1944**
Capt. Wilfred E. Hurst (350th) KIA; Rammed by a P-47 near Deintrop.
P-47D LH-M 42-7940
Lt. David C. Kenney (351st) KIA; Hit by fighters near Wedeborn.
P-47D YJ- 42-75191
Lt. Lloyd A. Thornell (351st) KIA; Suffered mechanical failure and ditched in the Channel.
P-47D YJ- 42-75135

**February 5, 1944**
Lt. Edgar J. Albert (351st) KIA; Hit by a FW-190 northwest of Orleans.
P-47D YJ- 42-75161

**February 22, 1944**
Maj. Walter C. Beckham (351st) POW; Hit by flak near Bonn and bailed out near Neukirchen.
P-47D YJ-X 42-75226
Lt. Donald M. Hurlburt (351st) KIA; Hit by flak and crashed into the North Sea.
P-47D YJ- 42-75653
Lt. Joseph E. Wood (351st) KIA; Hit by flak and crashed into the North Sea.
P-47D YJ- 42-75647
Lt. Edison G. Stiff (352nd) KIA; Hit by flak near Eckern.
P-47D SX-L 42-75065

**March 4, 1944**
Lt. William R. Burkett (351st) KIA; Hit by flak and last seen near Liege.
P-47D YJ- 42-75850

**March 6, 1944**
Lt. Robert N. Ireland (350th) KIA; Crashed while landing with battle-damage at Metfield.
P-47D LH- 42-22771

**March 8, 1944**
Lt. John Zolner (350th) MIA-E; Hit by flak near Hanover and bailed out near Almelo.
P-47D LH- 42-8557

**March 16, 1944**
Lt. Harry H. Dustin (352nd) KIA; Hit by flak near Clastres.
P-47D SX-Q 42-75544
Lt. Robert A. Newman (352nd) KIA; Hit by flak near Laon.
P-47D SX-N 42-75530 "Wham Bam"

**March 29, 1944**
Lt. Francis L. Edwards (351st) ASR; Hit by flak at Twente/Enschede and bailed out over the Channel.
P-47D YJ-

**April 8, 1944**
Lt. Gordon L. Willits (352nd) KIA; Hit a tree at Zwischenachmer and crashed near Ijsseleer.
P-47D SX-X 42-22768

**April 9, 1944**
Lt. Richard A. Stearns (350th) POW; Hit by flak at Wittensee A/F.
P-47D LH- 42-8499
Lt. Jack Terzian (351st) ASR; Bailed out 70 miles off Great Yarmouth.
P-47D YJ-

**April 22, 1944**
Lt. Paul J. Trudeau (351st) ASR; Bailed out over the North Sea and was rescued on April 23.
P-47D YJ-M 42-75114 "Boston Bull"

**April 23, 1944**
Lt. Cletus W. Peterson (351st) POW; Hit by flak and bailed out southeast of Lingen.
P-47D YJ-P 42-75149 "Double S"
Capt. Jesse W. Gonnam (352nd) POW; Hit by flak at Achmer/Bramsche.
P-47D SX-U 42-76394

**April 24, 1944**
Lt. William C. Crampton (351st) POW; Hit by fighters at Neustadt.
P-47D YJ- 42-75804

**May 12, 1944**
Lt. William T. Thistlethwaite (351st) KIA; Hit by flak and bailed out 20 miles off the enemy coast.
P-47D YJ-Q 42-76352

**May 21, 1944**
Lt. Chauncey Rowan (350th) POW; Hit by flak near Bremen.
P-47D LH-D 42-76280
Lt. Raymond Eluhow (352nd) ASR; Bailed out east of Woodbridge after flak damage.
P-47D SX-P

**May 22, 1944**
Lt. Jack Terzian (351st) POW; Hit by flak near Letterhouten.
P-47D YJ- 42-25730

**May 28, 1944**
Lt. Joseph R. Farley (351st) KIA; Hit by flak near Loddenherde.
P-47D YJ- 42-75457

**May 29, 1944**
Lt. Arthur C. Bergeron (350th) KIA; Hit by flak near Quackenbruck.
P-47D LH- 42-26109
Lt. Joseph C. McDonald (350th) KIA; Hit by flak and bellied-in near Meppel.
P-47D LH-U 42-76320

Lt. Albert W. Barlow (351st) ASR; Bailed out 16 miles east of Orfordness.
P-47D YJ-

**May 30, 1944**
Lt. Francis L. Edwards (352nd) KIA; Hit by fighters near Peine.
P-47D SX-Z 42-75683 "Big Totsy"
Lt. Harry F. Hunter (351st) POW; Hit by flak near Montdidier.
P-47D YJ- 42-75688

**June 6, 1944**
F/O Earl W. Green (352nd) MIA-E; Hit by flak near Mortain.
P-47D SX-R 42-75552 "Highlander"

**June 7, 1944**
Capt. Francis T. Walsh (350th) KIA; Crashed into the Channel after flak damage.
P-47D LH- 42-8515
Lt. Herbert K. Field (351st) KIA; Hit by a Me-109 and bailed out over the Channel.
P-47D YJ-F 42-75570
Lt. Luther Avakian (352nd) KIA; Hit by flak near Meulers.
P-47D SX-Y 42-76195 "The Mole"

**June 10, 1944**
Lt. Martin D. Coffey (350th) KIA; Hit by flak near Gace.
P-47D LH- 43-25581
F/O James R. Hicks (352nd) KIA; Hit by flak in the Pas de Calais area.
P-47D SX-W 42-8630 "Bobbie Baby"
Lt. Virgil C. Johnston (352nd) KIA; Hit by flak near Rennes.
P-47D SX-I 42-25771
Lt. William S. Marchant (352nd) KIA; Hit by flak near Rennes.
P-47D SX-O 42-76501

**June 12, 1944**
Capt. Dewey E. Newhart (350th) KIA; Hit by a Me-109 near Dreux.
P-47D LH-U 42-26402
Lt. Richard L. Bedford (350th) POW; Hit by a Me-109 near Dreux.
P-47D LH- 42-25768
Lt. Earl C. Main (350th) POW; Hit by a Me-109 near Dreux.
P-47D LH- 42-26313
Lt. Goffred R. Moretto (350th) MIA-E; Hit by a Me-109 near Dreux.
P-47D LH- 43-25541
Lt. Edwin H. Peters (350th) ASR; Hit by a Me-109 and bailed out over the Channel.
P-47D LH-
F/O John J. Phelan (350th) KIA; Hit by a Me-109 near Evreux.
P-47D LH- 42-22779
Lt. John R. Gabriel, Jr. (352nd) MIA-E; Hit by a Me-109 near Evreux.
P-47D SX-D 42-26011
Lt. Richard V. Keywan (352nd) KIA; Hit by a Me-109 near St. Andre de'Lure.
P-47D SX-A 42-75707 "Little Hotsy"

**June 28, 1944**
Lt. John F. Starr (350th) KIAc; Crashed near Raydon while on a test hop with new pilots.
P-47D LH-

**June 30, 1944**
Lt. Robert W. Larson (351st) KIAc; Collided with a P-47 and crashed near Tibenham.
P-47D YJ-K 42-8511

**July 4, 1944**
Lt. Lloyd Hunt (352nd) MIA-E; Hit by flak and bellied-in southwest of Troyes.
P-47D SX-W 42-26667

**July 5, 1944**
Lt. Daniel L. Claiville (351st) KIA; Hit by a Me-109 near Pont Audemer.
P-47D YJ-B 42-26047

**July 7, 1944**
Col. Glenn E. Duncan (HdQts) MIA-E; Hit by flak near Wesendorf and bellied-in near Nienburg.
P-47D LH-Z 42-25971 "Dove of Peace"

**August 1, 1944**
Lt. Delbert E. Harris (352nd) POW; Hit by flak south of Bourgtheroude.
P-47D SX-P 42-26036
F/O Kenneth Ames (352nd) KIA; Hit by flak near Laon/Couvron A/F.
P-47D SX-D 42-26533

**August 4, 1944**
Lt. Harry Y. Aldridge (350th) KIA; Hit by flak near Oldenzaal.
P-47D LH- 42-76268
Lt. Denny L. Yocum (350th) KIA; Hit by a Me-109 near Bremen.
P-47D LH-Z 42-26663

**August 5, 1944**
Lt. John J. Hatch (351st) KIA; Suffered mechanical failure and bailed out east of Felixstowe.
P-47D YJ-D 42-26027 "Georgie Fay"

**August 6, 1944**
Lt. Thomas C. Creekmur (350th) KIAc; Crashed near Weeping Hill.
P-47D LH-R

**August 7, 1944**
Lt. Richard Daines (352nd) KIA; Hit by flak near Dernancourt.
P-47D SX-I 42-26631

**August 8, 1944**
Lt. Robert S. Hart (350th) KIA; Caught in a bomb blast near Gaudechard.
P-47D LH- 42-26454

**August 11, 1944**
Lt. Robert A. Metz (350th) KIAc; Crashed near Raydon on a test flight.
P-47D LH-R

**August 12, 1944**
Lt. Ray P. Greenwood (352nd) MIA-E; Hit by flak near Paris.
P-47D SX-O 42-26570
Lt. James M. Tuttle (352nd) MIA-E; Damaged by a bomb blast near Melun.
P-47D SX-J 42-22466

**August 13, 1944**
Lt. Max K. Graham (350th) KIA; Hit by flak near Gambais.
P-47D LH- 42-26269
Lt. George W. McInis (350th) KIA; Hit by flak near Gambois.
P-47D LH- 42-8404
Capt. Victor N. Curtis (352nd) MIA-E; Hit by flak and bellied-in.
P-47D SX-Y

**August 18, 1944**
Lt. Dwight W. Johnson (351st) POW; Hit by flak near Bethunne.
P-47D YJ-U 42-75863
F/O John J. Swanezy, Jr. (352nd) MIA E; Hit the ground while strafing near Paris.
P-47D SX-F 42-75622 "Hun Buster"

**August 26, 1944**
Lt. Alex S. Hartley (351st) ASR; Hit by flak and bailed out southeast of Manston.
P-47D YJ-M 42-26126 "Lil Boston Bull"

**August 29, 1944**
Capt. William D. Smith (350th) KIA; Hit by flak at Chievres.
P-47D LH-H 42-26668 "Skipper"
Lt. Olger I. Aal (350th) KIA; Caught in an explosion at Diest.
P-47D LH-O 44-19580

**September 5, 1944**
Lt. John W. Furneaux (351st) POW; Hit by flak near Nijverdal.
P-47D YJ-T 42-8678 "Jose"

**September 8, 1944**
Lt. Albert W. Barlow, Jr. (351st) MIA-E; Hit by flak and bailed out near Aachen.
P-47D YJ-J 42-22579 "Jeannie"

**September 17, 1944**
Lt. Robert N. Greene (351st) MIA-E; Caught in a bomb blast near Wekeron.
P-47D YJ-E 42-75815 "Patricia Baby"

**September 18, 1944**
Capt. James O. Ruscitto (350th) MIA-E; Hit by flak and bellied-in near Tilburg.
P-47D LH-R 42-28357 "Natalie Ann II"

**September 21, 1944**
Capt. Lloyd G. Hally (351st) KIA; Chased a FW-190 and was hit by flak near Nijmegen.
P-47D YJ-D 42-22523 "Angel of Mercy"

**September 23, 1944**
Capt. Ellis S. Middleton (350th) KIA; Hit by fighters southeast of Arnheim.
P-47D LH-V 42-26525
Lt. John G. Edwards (350th) KIA; Hit by fighters southeast of Arnheim.
P-47D LH-S 42-26642
Lt. Gerald F. Province (350th) KIA; Hit by fighters southeast of Arnheim.
P-47D LH-Z 44-19577

**September 28, 1944**
Lt. Charles E. Sladek (352nd) KIAc; Spun-in near Woolpit while on a test flight.
P-51D SX-P

**October 3, 1944**
Capt. Harold E. Daniel (351st) POW; Suffered mechanical failure and bailed out somewhere over France.
P-51D YJ- 44-14505

**October 18, 1944**
Lt. Robert D. Corgan (352nd) POW; Lost coolant and bailed out near Coblenz.
P-51D SX-D 44-11188

**October 24, 1944**
Capt. Carl F. Mueller (350th) POW; Suffered mechanical trouble and bellied-in southeast of Hamburg.
P-51D LH-M 44-14770 "Fern Marie III"
Lt. Robert W. Hedler (350th) KIA; Hit by flak near Bremen.
P-51D LH-S 44-14654 "Molly M"

**October 25, 1944**
Lt. Bernard J. French (351st) KIA; Hit by fire from a B-24 off Terschelling Island.
P-51D YJ-K 44-14558 "Jean III"

**October 27, 1944**
Lt. Marvin E. Albertson (350th) KIAc; Collided with a P-51 and crashed near Little Staughton.
P-51D LH-

**November 2, 1944**
Lt. Lester M. Grainger (350th) ASR; Ran out of fuel and bailed out over the Channel.
P-51D LH-G

**November 8, 1944**
Capt. Leslie P. Cles (352nd) POW; Hit by flak at Plantlunne and bellied-in near Hohenkoerber.
P-51D SX-U 44-14831 "Pregnant Patty"

**November 25, 1944**
Lt. Frank Elkins (350th) POW; Hit by flak near Hanau.
P-51D LH-X 44-11167 "Danny Boy"
Lt. William L. Miller (350th) POW; Ran out of fuel and bailed out near Texel Island.
P-51D LH-G 44-14969 "Lady Grace"
Lt. Clarence G. Bevington (351st) KIA; Lost a wing while strafing near Zell.
P-51D YJ-B 44-11216
Lt. James W. Jeter (351st) KIA; Suffered mechanical failure and crashed in Belgium.
P-51D YJ-G 44-14972

**November 26, 1944**
Lt. Stephen J. Kritz (352nd) KIA; Crashed on take-off from Raydon.
P-51D SX-Z 44-14259

**November 27, 1944**
Lt. George C. Moran (350th) KIA; Hit by fighters near Winzenburg.
P-51D LH-L 44-14666 "Zelma"
Lt. James F. Cross (352nd) KIA; Hit by fighters near Altenau.
P-51D SX-U 44-15388 "Stasia"

**December 4, 1944**
Lt. Victor N. Hernandez (352nd) MIA; Suffered mechanical failure northwest of Wiesbaden.
P-51D SX-Q

**December 5, 1944**
Lt. Noah N. Cowen (350th) KIA; Hit by a FW-190 near Wunstorf.
P-51D LH-E 44-14538 "Margaret Too"
Lt. Alvin L. Deeds (350th) KIA; Hit by a FW-190 near Hohnhorst.
P-51D LH-P 44-14727 "Bee-Jay"

**January 3, 1945**
Maj. James N. Poindexter (352nd) KIA; Aborted due to mechanical trouble and crashed near St. Capel.
P-51D SX-G 44-14589 "Honey IV"

**January 13, 1945**
Lt. George S.H. Lee (350th) KIA; Crashed near Sudbury after take-off.
P-51D LH-

**January 18, 1945**
Lt. Anthony R. Rosatone (352nd) KIA; Suffered mechanical failure and last last seen south of Brussels.
P-51D SX-U 44-15587 "Stasia II"

**February 3, 1945**
Maj. Leslie W. Seppala (HdQts) POW; Hit by flak and bailed out near Hagenau.
P-51D SX-B 44-14303 "Double Trouble"

**February 17, 1945**
Lt. Paul M. McKenney (351st) KIA; Crashed on take-off from Raydon.
P-51D YJ-S 44-14690

**February 22, 1945**
Lt. John M. Balason (350th) POW; Hit by flak near Bielefeld.
P-51D LH-J 44-14793 "Miss Betty D"

**February 24, 1945**
Lt. Ray Hilgenburg (351st) KIA; Hit by flak near Apeldoorn.
P-51D YJ-Q 44-14949 "Mr. Gray"

**March 2, 1945**
Lt. John W. Rohrs (351st) KIA; Hit by flak near Madel.
P-51D YJ-U 44-14781 "Don Helen"
Lt. Joseph Schreiber (352nd) POW; Hit by fighters near Belzig.
P-51D SX-Z 44-15691 "Lil Shirl"
Lt. Edward J. Sullivan (352nd) POW; Hit by fighters near Niebel.
P-51D SX-Q 44-15184 "Truly Trudie"

**March 11, 1945**
Lt. Arthur C. Cundy (352nd) KIA; Suffered mechanical failure and bailed out 40 miles off Great Yarmouth.
P-51D SX-D

**March 17, 1945**
Lt. Edward H. Duke (350th) POW; Suffered mechanical failure and bailed out southeast of Koln.
P-51D LH-Z 44-14974

**March 18, 1945**
Lt. Garnet D. Page (350th) MIA-E; Hit by a Lagg-3 and bellied-in near Russian lines.
P-51D LH-R 44-15137 "Baby Duck"
F/O Jerry M. Campbell (351st) POW Lost coolant and bailed out southeast of Dummer Lake.

**March 19, 1945**
Lt. James E. Frye (351st) KIA; Suffered mechanical failure and bailed out 40 miles off Orfordness.
P-51D YJ-M 44-14706 "Ginny"
Lt. Richard E. Hahn (352nd) POW; Suffered mechanical failure and bailed out northwest of Zeitz.
P-51D SX-Y 44-14631 "Shirley Dean"

**March 21, 1945**
Lt. Thomas C. Brock (351st) MIA; Hit by flak and bellied-in near Achmer.
P-51K YJ-B 44-11698
F/O Bruce A. Eddy (351st) POW; Lost coolant and bailed out near Krefeld.
P-51D YJ-M 44-14569 "Lil Boston Bull"
Lt. Harry U. Gilmore (351st) POW; Hit by flak at Achmer.
P-51D YJ-R 44-14748 "Kansas City Kitty"
Lt. Alvin Michel (352nd) MIA-E; Hit by flak at Achmer and bailed out near Enschede.
P-51D SX-U 44-14039 "Gloria Doll"

**March 24, 1945**
Lt. Wiley Grizzle (350th) KIA; Hit by fighters northwest of Kassel.
P-51D LH-S 44-63896 "The G-Nat"
Lt. James H. Hopkins (350th) KIA; Hit by fighters northwest of Kassel.
P-51B LH-K 42-106619 "Queenie"
Lt. Carl A. Larsen (350th) POW; Hit by fighters northwest of Kassel.
P-51D LH-N 44-14687 "Lethal Ethel"
Lt. John F. May (350th) POW; Hit by fighters northwest of Kassel.
P-51D LH-A 44-14990 "Doris II"
Lt. John P. Onkey (350th) POW; Hit by fighters northwest of Kassel.
P-51D LH-Q 44-14811 "Lady Gwen"

**March 30, 1945**
Lt. Merlin A. Arnold (351st) KIA; Suffered mechanical failure and bailed out 12 miles off Great Yarmouth but hit the tail.
P-51K YJ-A 44-11333
Lt. John Matula (351st) KIAc; Crashed near Wratting Common.
P-51D YJ-L 44-14771 "Willit Run?"

**April 15, 1945**
Lt. William O. Fitch (350th) KIAc; Crashed near Thaxted.
P-51D LH-L 44-63197 "Mascara Maggie"

**April 16, 1945**
Lt. Donald E. Howie (350th) KIA; Hit by flak at Pocking.
P-51D LH- 44-15594 "Miss Kay"
Lt. Walter A.S. Prescott (350th) KIA; Hit by flak at Pocking.
P-51D LH- 44-72175 "Little Red III"
Lt. Edward J. Risk (351st) KIA; Hit by flak at Obernburg A/F.
P-51D YJ-G 44-14796 "Lady Margaret"

**April 17, 1945**
Lt. James W. Lamb (352nd) KIA; Hit by flak at Ganacker.
P-51D SX-N 44-14712 "Little Chum"
Lt. Billy J. Lancaster (352nd) POW; Hit by flak at Ganacker and bailed out near Regensburg.
P-51K SX-K 44-11559 "Princess Marie"

**July 3, 1945**
Lt. Edward A. Knickelbein (352nd) KIAc; Collided with a P-51 and crashed near Wattisham.
P-51D SX-F 44-14644

**July 12, 1945**
Lt. Donald F. Blaicher (352nd) KIAc; Crashed near Eye.
P-51D SX-Z 44-14805

**Headquarters**
Bailey, William B., LtCol.; July 1944-September 1945; ex-352nd Ftr Sqn
186 missions, 454:05 hours
P-47D SX-B 42-26459 "Butch II"
P-51D SX-B 44-14303 "Double Trouble"
P-51D SX-B 44-63864 "Double Trouble Two"
Blickenstaff, Wayne K., LtCol.; April 1945-July 1945; ex-350th Ftr Sqn
133 missions
P-51D LH-U 44-72374 "Betty-E"
Carroll, Arthur C., Capt.; October 1944-December 1944; to 351st Ftr Sqn and ex-351st Ftr Sqn
Duncan, Glenn E., Col.; March 1943-July 7, 1944 (MIA-E); April 1945-September 1945
78 missions
P-47D LH-X 42-7988 "Dove of Peace"
P-47D LH-X 42-8634 "Dove of Peace"
P-47D LH-X 42-25506 "Dove of Peace"
P-47D LH-X 42-25971 "Dove of Peace"
P-51D LH-X 44-73060 "Dove of Peace"
Eames, John W., Capt., August 1944-EOW
41 missions
Elder, Robert A., LtCol.; February 1945-April 1945; to 350th Ftr Sqn; (see 350th for details)
Gallup, Kenneth W., LtCol.; May 1944-June 1944; to 350th Ftr Sqn; September 1944-November 1944; (see 350th for details)

Hartley, Raymond E., Jr., Capt.; March 1945-April 1945; to 351st Ftr Sqn; ex-325th Ftr Grp, MTO
2 victories
12 missions
Herfurth, Herman, Lt.; December 1942-March 1944; to 352nd Ftr Sqn (see 352st for details)
Hoey, Charles J., Maj.; February 1944-September 1944; ex-352nd Ftr Sqn
76 missions
P-47D SX-A 42-75707
P-47D YJ-S
Lane, Warren J., Capt.; March 1945-April 1945; to 350th Ftr Sqn; ex-Iceland
5 missions
Long, William M., Maj.; March 1945-July 1945
8 missions
Maguire, William J., Capt.; May 1945-August 11, 1945(KIAc); ex-351st Ftr Sqn (see 351st for details)
McCollom, Loren G., LtCol.; August 1943-November 25, 1943(POW); ex-56th Ftr Grp
17 missions
Miller, Robert C., Capt.; April 1945-April 1945; to 352nd Ftr Sqn
3 missions
Morris, Joseph A., LtCol.; October 1942-August 16, 1943(KIA)
5 missions
Rimerman, Ben, Col.; November 1943-April 1945; to 55th Ftr Grp; ex-350th Ftr Sqn
124 missions
P-47D LH-V 42-8001
P-47D LH-V
P-51K LH-V 44-11646
Rose, John B., Jr., Maj.; December 1942-May 1945
86 missions
Seppela, Leslie W., Maj.; September 1944-February 3, 1945(POW)
28 missions
Stafford, Charles L., Capt.; October 1942-September 1944
80 missions
P-47D YJ-
Thistlethwaite, William T., Lt.; December 1942-March 1944; to 351st Ftr Sqn (see 351st for details)

**350th Fighter Squadron**
Aal, Olger I., Lt.; June 1944-August 29, 1944(KIA)
38 missions
Abernathy, Robert W., Capt.; August 1944-April 1945
71 missions, 321:20 hours
P-51D LH-G 44-14811 "Lady Gwen"
P-51D LH-G 44-14969 "Lady Gwen II"
Agnew, William M., Lt.; October 1944-July 1945
53 missions
Albertson, Marvin E., Lt.; June 1944-October 27, 1944(KIAc)
60 missions
Aldridge, Harry Y., Lt.; June 1944-August 4, 1944(KIA)
21 missions
Allison, Ralph T., Capt.; June 1944-March 1945
77 missions
P-51D LH-S 44-14654 "Molly M"
P 51D LH-S 44-63896 "Molly M"
Angelo, Walter I., Lt.; States-December 1943 to 8th AF Service Command
24 missions
Ard, John M., Lt.; June 1944-November 1944
61 missions
Asper, Harold E., Lt.; June 1944-November 1944
61 missions
Auchincloss, Bayard C., Lt.; April 1944-October 1944
73 missions, 270 hours
Balason, John M., Lt.; October 1944-February 22, 1945(POW); ex-18th Ftr Sqn, 11th AF, Alaska
36 missions
P-51D LH-J 44-14783 "Miss Betsy D"
Bedford, Richard L., Lt.; January 1944-June 12, 1944(POW)
59 missions
Bengston, Lawrence O., F/O; April 1945-EOW
2 missions
Benjamin, Swift T., Lt.; May 1944-October 1944; ex-56th Ftr Grp, ETO
73 missions, 270 hours
Bergeron, Arthur C., Lt.; January 1944-May 29, 1944(KIA)
48 missions
Bledsoe, Marvin V., Capt.; June 1944-October 1944
70 missions, 270 hours
P-47D LH-J 42-26581 "Little Princess"
Blickenstaff, Wayne K., LtCol.; October 1942-April 1945; to HdQts
133 missions
P-47D LH-U 42-74647
P-47D LH-U 42-76320
P-47D LH-U 42-26402 "Soubrette"
P-51D LH-U "The Betty E"
P-51D LH-U 44-72374 "Betty-E"
Boone, Walker L., Maj.; September 1944-March 1945; ex-78th Ftr Grp, ETO
35 missions
P-51D LH-E 44-14538 "Margaret Too"
P-51D LH-E "Margaret 3"
Bowron, Everett B., F/O April 1945-EOW
0 missions
Bramm, Howard E., F/O April 1945-EOW
0 missions
Brimer, Albert B., Lt.; August 1944-July 1945
40 missions
Brown, Harold C., Lt.; May 1944-September 1944
65 missions, 270 hours
Brooks, Joseph B., Lt.; April 1944-September 1944
70 missions, 270 hours
Caton, Horace E., Lt.; October 1944-April 1945
64 missions, 301:30 hours
Chetwood, Kenneth, Capt.; December 1943-August 1944; ex-78th Ftr Grp, ETO
75 missions
P-47D LH-L "Maggie III"
P-47D LH-L 42-26619 "Maggie IV"
P-47D LH-L 42-26455 "Maggie V"
Clark, Jack W., Lt.; October 1944-April 1945; ex-339th Ftr Grp, ETO
56 missions, 300:55 hours
Coffey, Martin D., Lt.; May 1944-June 10, 1944(MIA)
19 missions
Cowen, Noah N., Lt.; October 1944-December 5, 1944(KIA)
7 missions
Creekmur, Thomas C., Lt.; June 1944-August 6, 1944(KIAc)
23 missions
Davis, Lonnie M., Capt.; July 1944-April 1945
72 missions, 301:10 hours
P-47D LH-Q 42-76141 "Arkansas Traveler"
P-51D LH-D 44-14945 "Arkansas Traveler II"
Dawson, Melvin P., Lt.; November 1942-April 1944
65 missions, 200 hours
Deeds, Alvin L., Lt.; August 1944-December 5, 1944(KIA)
38 missions
Devane, John L., Capt.; November 1942-April 1944
63 missions, 200 hours
P-47D LH-Z
Devine, Gerald P., Lt.; April 1944-November 1944
52 missions
P-51D LH- "The Mad Irishman"
Dinse, Charles W., Capt.; States-June 1944
66 missions
Dugar, Eugene B., Lt.; April 1945-EOW
2 missions
Duke, Edward H., Jr., Lt.; November 1944-March 17, 1945(POW)
34 missions
P-51D LH-Y "My Frans"
Durant, Charles O., Lt.; States-May 1944
64 missions, 200 hours
Dyer, Joseph E., Capt.; October 1944-July 1945
35 missions
P-51D LH-L 44-63197 "Mascara Maggie"
Edwards, John G., Lt.; August 1944-September 23, 1944(KIA)
12 missions
Elder, Robert A., LtCol.; April 1945-EOW; ex-HdQts
24 missions
P-51D LH-S 44-72736 "Miss Gamble"
Elkins, Frank E., Lt.; October 1944-November 25, 1944(POW)
4 missions
Ferrell, Arthur E., Lt.; June 1944-March 1945
68 missions
P-47D LH- "Vicki Jane"
P-47D LH- "Vicki Jane 2nd"
P-51D LH- "Vicki Jane 3rd"
Fitch, William O., Lt.; April 1945-April 15, 1945(KIAc)
0 missions
Fortier, Robert E., Capt.; States-May 1944
61 missions, 200 hours
P-47D LH-A
Fry, Dwight A., Lt.; States-October 14, 1943(MIA-E)
21 missions
P-47D LH-H 42-8513
Furness, Joseph F., Capt.; States-June 1944
75 missions
P-47D LH-J 42-7907 "Lonesome Polecat"
Gallup, Kenneth W., LtCol.; June 1944-September 1944; to HdQts, ex-HdQts
70 missions
P-47D LH-N 42-22275 "Rat-A-Dat"
P-47D LH-N 42-26649 "Rat-A-Dat"
P-47D LH-N 44-19562 "Rat-A-Dat 3rd
Garey, Abel H., Lt.; January 1944-July 1944
88 missions
Glorioso, John, Lt.; April 1945-EOW
0 missions
Gordon, Ray C., Lt.; December 1944-August 1945
27 missions
P-51D LH-N 44-72292 "Miss Florida"
Graham, Max K., Lt.; July 1944-August 13, 1944(KIA)
1 mission
Graham, Milton H., Lt.; June 1944-October 1944; to 50th Ftr Control Sqn
12 missions
Grainger, Lester M., Lt.; August 1944-April 1945
64 missions, 302:25 hours
P-51D LH-G 44-14969 "Lady Grace II"
P-51D LH-G "Lady Grace 3rd"
Greenfield, Bernard, Lt.; December 1944-EOW
19 missions
P-51D LH-P 44-72845 "Lil Miss Boomerang"

Grizzle, Wiley H., Jr., Lt.; December 1944-March 24, 1945(KIA)
11 missions
P-51D LH-S 44-63896 "The G-Nat"
Gross, Richard H., Lt.; April 1945-EOW
3 missions
Gustke, Richard N., F/O; December 1944-June 1945
26 missions
Guthrie, John L., Lt.; December 1944-EOW
23 missions
Hakonen, Howard H., Lt.; December 1944-EOW
21 missions
P-51D LH-Y 44-11193 "Beautiful Dope"
Hargus, William W., Lt.; January 1944-July 1944
83 missions
Hart, Robert S., Lt.; September 1943-August 8, 1944(KIA)
53 missions
Haynes, Harry E., Capt.; August 1944-June 1945; ex-bomber pilot
56 missions
P-51D LH-M 44-11204 "Hey Bolo!"
P-51D LH-M 44-72399 "Hey Bolo! II"
Hedler, Robert W., Lt.; April 1944-October 24, 1944(KIA)
30 missions
Hightshoe, Melville W., Capt.; July 1944-April 1945
72 missions, 320:20 hours
P-47D LH-X
P-51D LH-X 44-11167 "Danny Boy"
P-51D LH-X 44-15516 "Danny Boy 2nd"
Hilton, Chandler P., Lt.; April 1945-EOW
0 missions
Hopkins, James H., Lt.; February 1945-March 24, 1945(KIA)
2 missions
Hubbell, William R., Lt.; February 1945-July 1945
12 missions
Hurst, Wilfred F., Capt.; States-February 3, 1944(KIA)
43 missions
Ireland, Robert N., Lt.; States-March 6, 1944(KIA)
48 missions
Jessup, John E., Lt.; August 1944-March 1945
59 missions
Jung, Harold F., Jr., Lt.; October 1944-EOW
41 missions
P-51D LH-P 44-15671 "Miss Ellen"
Kammer, George D., Lt.; October 1944-EOW
31 missions
Knowling, William P., Lt.; June 1944-January 1945
70 missions
Kolb, Herbert G., Capt.; August 1944-EOW
48 missions
P-51D LH-R 44-15137 "Baby Duck"
P-51D LH-R 44-72259 "Baby Duck"
Lane, Warren J., Capt.; April 1945-EOW; ex-HdQts
5 missions
Lanoue, Roland J., Lt.; November 1944-July 1945
44 missions
P-51D LH-H 44-15519 "Fran 2nd"
Larsen, Carl A., Lt.; August 1944-March 24, 1945(POW)
52 missions
Lausen, John F., Lt.; May 1944-June 1944; to 3rd GTTF
1 mission
Lee, George S.H., Lt.; October 1944-January 13, 1945(KIA)
13 missions
P-51D LH- "Potchy"
Lee, Louis W., Lt.; November 1944-EOW
33 missions
P-51D LH-Q 44-14698
Leibold, Robert S., Lt.; November 1944-EOW
27 missions
Levine, Morton I., Lt.; March 1945-EOW
7 missions
Linger, Claude D., Lt.; October 1944-November 1944; to 50th Ftr Control Sqn; ex-339th Ftr Grp
4 missions
Long, Harold W., Lt.; States-September 5, 1943(KIAc)
9 missions
Lorance, Thomas, Lt.; States-April 1944
60 missions, 200 hours
P-47D LH- "The Goon"
Lowe, Alan W., Lt.; States-October 22, 1943(KIA)
10 missions
Madsen, John A., Lt.; November 1944-March 1945
28 missions
Main, Earl C., Lt.; February 1944-June 12, 1944(POW)
54 missions
Manahan, William A., Lt.; March 1945-July 1945
6 missions
May, John F., Lt.; January 1945-March 24, 1945(POW)
10 missions
McAfee, William C., Lt.; March 1945-EOW
7 missions
McClure, James H., Lt.; November 1944-July 1945
31 missions
McDonald, Joseph C., Lt.; April 1944-May 29, 1944(POW)
13 missions
McInnis, George W., Lt.; July 1944-August 13, 1944(KIA)
6 missions
McIntosh, Robert L., Lt.; March 1945-June 1945
7 missions
McKean, Roland N., Lt.; States-April 1944
61 missions, 200 hours
McMahan, Bruce D., Lt.; February 1945-June 1945
14 missions
McMullen, Joseph D., Lt.; November 1944-EOW
40 missions
Mele, Raymond R., F/O; April 1945-June 1945
2 missions
Metz, Robert A., Lt.; June 1944-August 11, 1944(KIAc)
24 missions
Middleton, Ellis S., Capt.; June 1944-September 23, 1944(POW)
59 missions
Miller, William L., Lt.; October 1944-November 25, 1944(POW)
5 missions
Moran, George C., Lt.; July 1944-November 27, 1944(MIA)
50 missions
Moretto, Goffred F., Lt.; April 1944-June 12, 1944(MIA-E)
40 missions
Mueller, Carl W., Capt.; September 1943-October 24, 1944(POW)
76 missions
Murray, James E., Lt.; April 1944-August 1944
4 missions
New, Almon W., Lt.; May 1944-October 1944
73 missions
Newhart, Dewey E., Maj.; October 1942-June 12, 1944(KIA)
70 missions
P-47D LH-D 42-76141 "Mud'n Mules"
Newman, Robert L., Lt.; States-November 5, 1943(KIA)
16 missions
Odom, William W., Lt.; States-December 30, 1943(KIA)
36 missions
O'Neill, Francis, Lt.; February 1945-EOW
15 missions
Onkey, John P., Lt.; January 1945-March 24, 1945(MIA)
6 missions
Orzelek, Frank J., F/O; October 1944-March 1945
32 missions
Page, Garnett D., Lt.; January 1945-March 18, 1945(MIA-E)
5 missions
Pasley, Harold P., Lt.; March 1944-September 1944
81 missions
Peters, Edwin H., Lt.; May 1944-June 12, 1944(WIA)
24 missions
Peters, Robert C., Lt.; August 1943-October 14, 1943(KIA)
10 missions
Phelan, John J., F/O; May 1944-June 12, 1944(KIA)
23 missions
Pidduck, Stanley R., Jr., Maj.; States-May 1944
67 missions
Prescott, Walter A.S., Lt.; October 1944-April 16, 1945(MIA)
47 missions
Price, William J., Maj.; November 1942-December 1944
108 missions
P-47D LH-F 42-8623 "Janie"
P-47D LH-F 42-26477 "Janie"
P-51D LH-F 44-14419 "Janie"
Province, Gerald F., Lt.; August 1944-September 23, 1944(MIA)
9 missions
Rafferty, Vernon G., Capt.; June 1944-November 1944
68 missions, 270 hours
P-47D LH-M 42-26659 "Fern Marie"
P-47D LH-M "Fern Marie II"
P-51D LH-M 44-14770 "Fern Marie III"
Rimerman, Ben, LtCol.; October 1942-November 1943; to HdQts (see for details)
Robison, George W., Lt.; October 1944-July 1945
45 missions
Rosenberg, Joseph, Lt.; States-December 1943; to 8th AF Service Command
15 missions
Rowan, Chauncy, Lt.; September 1943-May 21, 1944(POW)
63 missions
P-47D LH-D 42-76280 "Jenny"
Ruscitto, James O., Capt.; June 1944-September 18, 1944(MIA-E)
54 missions
P-47D LH-R "Natalie Ann"
P-47D LH-R 42-28357 "Natalie Ann II"
Schilt, John L., Lt.; June 1944-December 1944
66 missions
P-51D LH- 44-11155 "Minnehaha"
Smith, William D., Capt.; June 1944-August 29, 1944(KIA)
43 missions
Spriggs, Alfred G., Lt.; January 1945-June 1945
13 missions
Starr, John F., Jr., Lt.; March 1944-June 28, 1944(KIAc)
55 missions

Stearns, Richard A., Lt.; September 1943-April 9, 1944(POW)
52 missions
P-47D LH- 42-8499 "The Georgia Peach"
Stone, Walter B., Lt.; September 1943-October 22, 1943(KIA)
5 missions
Sullivan, John A., Capt.; States-May 1944
71 missions, 200 hours
Tanner, William F., Maj.; States-July 1945
135 hours
P-47D LH-O "Prudence"
P-47D LH-O 42-74669 "Prudence II"
P-47D LH-O "Prudence III"
P-47D LH-O "Prudence IV"
P-47D LH-O 42-26472 "Prudence V"
P-51D LH-O "Prudence VI"
P-51D LH-O 44-72212 "Prudence 7th"
Tuttle, Robert S., Lt.; March 1944-September 1944
78 missions
Unangst, Robert F., Lt.; May 1944-October 1944
68 missions
P-47D LH-D 42-26656 "Ernestyne"
Venell, Irvin E., Capt.; States-September 5, 1943(KIAc)
12 missions
P-47D LH-K 42-7956
Walsh, Francis T., Capt.; States-June 7, 1944(KIA)
73 missions
Warren, Donald W., Lt.; October 1944-March 1945; ex-339th Ftr Grp
30 missions
Winder, John H., III, Capt.; September 1943-January 1945
P-47D LH-T "Carol"
P-51D LH-T "Carol"
Yocum, Denny L., Lt.; May 1944-August 4, 1944(KIA)
58 missions
Zolner, John, Lt.; States-March 8, 1944(MIA-E)
53 missions

**351st Fighter Squadron**

Ahles, George N., Capt.; December 1942-August 1944
88 missions, 300 hours
P-47D YJ-A 42-8619 "Lonesome Polecat"
P-47D YJ-A 42-26246 "Lonesome Polecat"
Albert, Edgar J., Lt.; December 1942-February 5, 1944(KIA)
35 missions
P-47D YJ-U 42-74738 "Doris"
Arnold, Merlin A., Lt.; October 1944-March 30, 1945(KIA); ex-339th Ftr Grp
53 missions
P-51D YJ-A 44-14732 "Tampa Tramp"
P-51D YJ-A 44-14887
Bachand, Robert E., Lt.; May 1944-October 1944
63 missions
Barlow, Albert W., Jr., Lt.; May 1944-September 8, 1944(MIA-E)
69 missions
P-47D YJ-B "Flak Bait"
Beckham, Walter C., Maj.; October 1942-February 22, 1944(POW)
57 missions, 123 hours
P-47D YJ-X 42-8476 "Little Demon"
P-47D YJ-X 42-75226
Bevington, Clarence G., Lt.; August 1944-November 25, 1944(KIA); ex-5th ERS
1 mission
Biddy, Hardy L., Lt.; April 1944-September 1944
76 missions
P-47D YJ-H 42-75189
Bishop, John W., Lt.; June 1944-October 1944
68 missions
P-47D YJ-E 42-75815 "Patricia Baby
Brock, Thomas C., Lt.; October 1944-March 21, 1945(MIA); ex-339th Ftr Grp
48 missions
P-51K YJ-B 44-11698
Brown, Jack G., F/O; April 1945-EOW
0 missions
Burkett, William R., Lt.; December 1942-March 4, 1944(KIA)
44 missions
P-47D YJ-B 42-8401 "Scatterbolts"
Butler, R.K., Lt.; States only
Byers, Vic L., Jr., Maj.; December 1942-July 1945
113 missions, 406:25 hours
P-47D YJ-V 42-7958 "Hawkeye"
P-47D YJ-V 42-75863
P-47D YJ-V 43-25557
P-51D YJ-V 44-14593
P-51D YJ-V 44-15160
Campbell, Jerry M., F/O; January 1945-March 18, 1945(MIA-E)
7 missions
Carbonneau, Henry J., Lt.; May 1944-November 1944
71 missions
Carroll, Arthur C., Capt.; September 1944-October 1944; to HdQts
December 1944-July 1945
62 missions
P-51D YJ-L 44-72231

Chase, Harold W., Capt.; October 1944-July 1945
48 missions
P-51D YJ-Z 44-14610
Christian, Shannon, LtCol.; October 1942-November 1943; to 8th AF HdQts February 1944-July 1944
71 missions
P-47D YJ-S 42-8395 "Cookie"
P-47D YJ-S 42-76103 "Cookie II"
Christensen, William J., Lt.; May 1944-November 1944
71 missions
P-47D YJ-Y 42-75856 "Betts"
P-51D YJ-Y 44-11191
Claiville, Daniel L., Lt.; June 1944-July 5, 1944(MIA)
20 missions
Cobb, William G., Lt.; May 1944-October 1944
55 missions
P-47D YJ-P 42-22781
Compton, Gordon B., Capt.; October 1942-EOW
114 missions, 420 hours
P-47D YJ-O 42-25702 "Big Bouncer"
P-51D YJ-O 44-14806 "Little Bouncer"
P-51D YJ-O 44-72299 "Little Bouncer"
Craft, Charles W., Lt.; June 1944-December 1944
66 missions
Crampton, William C., Lt.; March 1944-April 24, 1944(POW)
22 missions
Daniel, Harold E., Capt.; August 1944-October 3, 1944(POW)
23 missions
P-47D YJ-M 42-28566 "Ticket Home"
Drybrough, Thomas R., Lt.; October 1944-EOW
44 missions, 224 hours
P-51D YJ-D 44-14628 "The Uninvited"
Dustin, Harry H., Lt.; September 1943-September 1943; to 352nd Ftr Sqn
Dwyer, John L., Lt.; May 1944-September 1944
72 missions
Eccles, Robert L., Lt.; October 1942-January 7, 1943(KIAc)
Eddy. Bruce A., F/O; January 1945-March 21, 1945(KIA)
7 missions
Edwards, Francis L., Lt.; December 1942-May 1944; to 352nd Ftr Sqn
65 missions
Emory, Frank N., Capt.; December 1942-April 1945
118 missions, 450:25 hours
P-47D YJ-E 42-8602 "Sis"
P-47D YJ-E 42-75815 "Sis II"
P-47D YJ-E "Sis III"
P-51D YJ-E 44-14573 "Sis IV"
Farley, Joseph R., Lt.; April 1944-May 28, 1944(POW)
8 missions
Fenwick, Richard W., Lt.; April 1945-EOW
4 missions
Field, Herbert K., Lt.; December 1942-June 7, 1944(KIA)
67 missions
P-47D YJ-F
P-47D YJ-F 42-75570 "Devil's Thumb"
Frank, William J., Jr., Lt.; April 1944-October 1944
68 missions
Franklin, George W., Lt.; April 1944-September 1944
66 missions
P-47D YJ-I 42-26050
French, Bernard J., Lt.; October 1944-October 25, 1944(KIA); ex-339th Ftr Grp
6 missions
Frye, James E., Lt.; November 1944-March 19, 1945(KIA)
28 missions
P-51D YJ-M 44-14706 "Ginny"
Fulton, Joseph O., Jr., Lt.; October 1944-April 1945; ex-339th Ftr Grp
63 missions, 300 hours
P-51D YJ-B 44-14816 "Lois W"
Furneaux, John W., Lt.; May 1944-September 5, 1944(POW)
70 missions
P-47D YJ-T 42-8628 "Jose"
Galgan, John C., Jr., Lt.; April 1945-EOW
0 missions
Geiger, Clarence W., Lt.; October 1944-EOW
52 missions
P-51D YJ-G 44-15624
Gerrick, William M., Lt.; April 1945-EOW
0 missions
Gilmer, Harry U., Lt.; October 1944-March 21, 1945(POW); ex-339th Ftr Grp
52 missions
P-51D YJ-V
Greene, Robert N., Lt.; September 1944-September 17, 1944 (MIA-E)
2 missions
Hahn, Robert H., Lt.; October 1944-July 1945
50 missions
P-51D YJ-H 44-14658
Hally, Lloyd G., Capt.; June 1944-September 21, 1944(KIA)
54 missions
P-47D YJ-D 42-22523 "Angel of Mercy"
Hartley, Alex S., Capt.; May 1944-October 1944
68 missions
Hartley, Raymond E., Jr., Capt.; April 1945-EOW; ex-HdQts & 325th Ftr Grp, MTO
12 missions

Hatch, John J., Lt.; May 1944-August 5, 1944(KIA)
42 missions
P-47D YJ-N 43-25572 "Smoocher"
Highfield, Leroy B., Capt.; July 1944-EOW
67 missions
P-47D YJ-H
P-51D YJ-H 44-14658
Hilgenburg, Raymond, Lt.; October 1944-February 24, 1945(KIA)
33 missions
P-51K YJ-X 44-11565
Hinchey, James F., Lt.; July 1944-April 1945
64 missions, 301 hours
P-47D YJ-I
P-51D YJ-I 44-14728
Hungate, Max B., Lt.; March 1944-September 1944
71 missions
P-47D YJ-J
Hunter, Harry F., Lt.; States-May 30, 1944(POW)
51 missions
Hurlburt, Donald M., Lt.; August 1943-February 22, 1944(KIA)
34 missions
Hynes, John A., Lt.; February 1945-EOW
20 missions
P-51D YJ-E 44-14573
Jeter, James W., Lt.; October 1944-November 25, 1944(MIA)
5 missions
Johnson, Dwight W., Lt.; July 1944-August 18, 1944(POW)
22 missions
Kenney, David C., Lt.; States-February 3, 1944(KIA)
23 missions
P-47D YJ-D "Woolverine"
King, Francis N., Lt.; States-May 1944
66 missions
Kinkade, Orville A., Capt.; States-November 5, 1943(POW)
23 missions
P-47C YJ-K 41-6583 "Alyce"
Knickelbein, Leslie H., Lt.; May 1944-October 1944
71 missions
Kohler, Donald F., Lt.; July 1944-February 1945
64 missions
P-47D YJ-B
P-51D YJ-B 44-14816
Kraft, Benedict E., Lt.; States-November 5, 1943(POW)
18 missions
P-47D YJ-Q 42-8428 "Pat"
Lahke, William K., Lt.; June 1944-December 1944
69 missions
P-47D YJ-K 42-75676 "Janny M"
P-51D YJ-U 44-14781 "Janny M"
Lancaster, John G., Lt.; November 1944-EOW
39 missions
P-51D YJ-G 44-73048
Larson, Delvin G., Lt.; February 1945-June 1945
20 missions
Larson, Robert W., Lt.; June 1944-June 30, 1944(KIAc)
0 missions
Law, James G., Lt.; April 1945-EOW
0 missions
Leatherman, Vernon G., Capt.; States-May 1944
68 missions
LeFebre, Fred H., LtCol.; October 1942-February 1945
119 missions
P-47D YJ-L 42-7906 "Chief Yahoo"
P-51D YJ-L 44-14771 "Willit Run?"
Lewis, Donald E., Lt.; November 1944-EOW
42 missions
P-51D YJ-P 44-14430
P-51D YJ-P 44-72267
Magaro, Francis S., Lt.; February 1945-March 1945; ex-bomber pilot; 0 missions
Maguire, William J., Capt.; December 1942-May 1945; to HdQts
124 missions
P-47D YJ-M 42-75114 "Boston Bull"
P-47D YJ-M 42-26126 "Boston Bull"
P-51D YJ-M 44-14893 "Lil Boston Bull"
P-51D YJ-M 44-14569 "Lil Boston Bull"
Marchant, William S., Lt.; September 1943-September 1943; to 352nd Ftr Sqn
Maree, Howard P., Lt.; August 1944-March 1945
56 missions
Markham, Gene E., Capt.; October 1944-July 1945
48 missions
P-51D YJ-Q 44-14929 "Mr. Gray"
P-51D YJ-Q 44-72171 "Mr. Gray II"
Matula, John, Lt.; January 1945-March 30, 1945(KIAc)
10 missions
McComas, John L., Lt.; March 1945-EOW
6 missions
McCutchan, Francis G., Lt.; March 1945-EOW
9 missions
McDermott, James L., Lt.; March 1945-November 1945
8 missions
McGraw, Charles L., Capt.; August 1944-August 1945
55 missions
P-47D YJ-R 42-75740 "Liberty Queen"
P-51D YJ-R 44-14748 "Kansas City Kitty"
McKenney, Paul M., Jr., Lt.; November 1944-February 17, 1945(KIA)
11 missions
McLaughlin, Grover H., Lt.; May 1944-September 1944
72 missions
Meadors, Fletcher E., Lt.; October 1944-December 10, 1944(Inj.)
10 missions
Miller, Gerald J., Lt.; January 1945-EOW
22 missions, 118 hours
P-51D YJ-V 44-14595
Milligan, Harry D., Capt.; September 1943-January 1945
119 missions
Mincik, Frank J., Lt.; September 1943-June 1944
64 missions
P-47D YJ-U "Minnie"
Mitchell, John L., Lt.; May 1944-July 1944(court martial)
26 missions
Montgomery, George S., Lt.; August 1944-April 1945
64 missions, 300:15 hours
P-51D YJ-G 44-14796 "Lady Margaret"
Moretz, Hazel, Lt.; June 1944-November 1944
70 missions
Morris, Harold J., Lt.; December 1944-January 1944; to 78th Ftr Grp and later KIA
23 missions
P-47D YJ-Y 42-8478 "Barbara"
Morris, Harry A., Jr., F/O; November 1944-EOW
40 missions
P-51D YJ-W
Murphey, Walter E., Lt.; August 1944-April 1945
63 missions, 302:15 hours
Murray, Billy J., Lt.; August 1944-April 1945
67 missions, 300:35 hours
Murray, Harold S., F/O; November 1944-EOW
32 missions
P-51D YJ-S 44-72174
Nicklebur, John M., Lt.; August 1944-April 1945
67 missions, 300:10 hours
P-51D YJ-N 44-14688
Ott, Nelson T., Lt.; June 1944-August 1944
41 missions
Pennington, Walter H., Jr., Lt.; February 1945-EOW
20 missions
Perpente, George F., Lt.; December 1942-April 1944
62 missions
P-47D YJ-G "Super Rabbit"
Peterson, Cletus W., Lt.; September 1943-April 23, 1944(POW)
39 missions
Petticrew, Stan S., Jr., Lt.; October 1944-April 1945; ex-339th Ftr Grp
61 missions, 303 hours
P-51D YJ-Y 44-11191 "Birmingham Anne"
Pryor, Thomas P., Jr., Lt.; January 1945-EOW
24 missions
Risk, Edward J., Lt.; February 1945-April 16, 1945(MIA)
16 missions
Rohrs, John W., Lt.; October 1944-March 2, 1945(KIA)
31 missions
P-51D YJ-U 44-14781 "Don-Helen"
Rosen, George J., Lt.; October 1944-April 1945; ex-339th Ftr Grp
62 missions, 300 hours
P-51D YJ-J 44-14756
Sheck, Robert L., Jr., F/O; April 1945-EOW
2 missions
Shillinger, Robert P., Lt.; February 1945-EOW
21 missions
Stachura, Robert M., F/O; April- 1945-EOW
4 missions
Stanley, Richard D., Lt.; December 1942-May 1944
72 missions
Stapp, Glenn E., F/O; March 1945-EOW
5 missions
Strobell, Robert C., Lt.; February 1944-August 1944
80 missions
P-47D YJ-K 42-8511
Stump, Hassel D., Capt.; July 1943-January 1945
108 missions
P-47D YJ-G "Squirt"
P-51D YJ-S 44-14690 "Squirt"
Terzian, Jack, Lt.; April 1943-May 22, 1944(POW)65 missions, 189 hours
P-47D YJ-Z 42-22469 "Marty"
Thistlethwaite, William T., Lt.; March 1944-May 12, 1944(KIA); ex-HdQts
48 missions
P-47D YJ-Q 42-76352
Thompson, Horace B., Jr., Lt.; October 1944-July 1945
20 missions
Thornell, Lloyd A., Lt.; December 1942-February 3, 1944(KIA)
34 missions
P-47D YJ-Q "Mid's Bid"

Toppell, Irving, Lt.; States-April 1944
67 missions
Trietz, John G., Lt.; States-April 1944
60 missions, 200 hours
P-47D YJ-J 42-7987 "Jeannie"
P-47D YJ-J 42-22759 "Jeannie"
Trudeau, Paul J., Lt.; February 1944-May 1944; to 5th ERS
27 missions
Tumlin, Rupert M., Lt.; February 1944-July 1944
84 missions, 300 hours
P-47D YJ-D 42-26027 "Georgie Fay"
Vieck, Louis L., Lt.; February 1944-March 1944; to 352nd Ftr Sqn; ex-55th Ftr Grp, ETO
0 missions
Vomaske, Richard F., Lt.; July 1944-December 1944
63 missions
Walsh, Jack R., Capt.; States-January 1944
24 missions
Weaver, William J., Lt.; January 1944-August 1944
81 missions
P-47D YJ-B "My Best Bett"
P-47D YJ-B 42-74615 "My Best Bett II"
Wiehe, Robert K., Lt.; October 1944-August 1945
44 missions
P-51D YJ-F 44-14689
Williams, Monroe Q., Lt.; August 1944-March 1945
67 missions
P-51D YJ-W 44-13978
Wood, Joseph E., Lt.; August 1943-February 22, 1944(KIA)
34 missions

**352nd Fighter Squadron**

Akard, Richard R., Lt.; April 1944-November 1944
55 missions
P-47D SX-U 42-25957
P-51D SX-G 44-14729
Ames, Kenneth, F/O; June 1944-August 1, 1944(KIA)
15 missions
P-47D SX-G
Anderson, Roy R., Lt.; January 1945-EOW
18 missions
P-51D SX-W
Andrews, Edward C., Lt.; April 1944-September 1944
77 missions
P-47D SX-Q 42-25959
P-47D SX-Z 42-26549 "Eager Eddie"
Armstrong, Clifford F., Lt.; December 1942-June 1944
91 missions, 301 hours
P-47D SX-F 42-7904 "8 Gun Melody"
P-47D SX-F 42-756?? "Hun Buster"
Avakian, Luther, Lt.; April 1944-June 7, 1944(KIA)
29 missions
P-47D SX-Y 42-76195 "The Mole"
Bailey, William B., LtCol.; October 1942-July 1944; to HdQts
186 missions, 454:05 hours
P-47D SX-B 42-746?? "Butch"
P-47D SX-B 42-26459 "Butch II"
Barber, Donald L., Capt.; June 1944-July 1945
72 missions
P-47D SX-M "Gloria Ann"
P-51D SX-M 44-14742 "Gloria Ann II"
Bartley, James G., Lt.; January 1945-EOW
22 missions
P-51D SX-B 44-14095 "Little Midget"
P-51D SX-G 44-73107 "Little Midget"
Barton, Lt.; States-April 18, 1943(KIAc)
Beach, William E., Lt.; January 1945-EOW
21 missions
P-51D SX-O
Bixby, William K., III, Lt.; January 1945-EOW
24 missions
P-51D SX-Y
Blaicher, Donald F., Lt.; April 1945-July 12, 1945(KIAc); ex-bomber pilot
0 missions
Bouldin, Frank H., Jr., Lt.; August 1944-March 1945
64 missions
P-51D SX-I 44-14495 "Dallas Doll"
Bowker, William R., Lt.; April 1945-EOW
0 missions
Briggs, Charles W., Lt.; January 1945-EOW
20 missions
P-51D SX-U 44-15315 "Don Helen"
Burlingame, Gordon S., Capt.; December 1942-January 1945
94 missions
P-47D SX-M 42-22482 "Stinky Poo"
P-47D SX-M "Davy Don Chariot"
P-51D SX-M 44-14620 "Davy Don Chariot"
Cabanne, William C., Lt.; January 1945-June 1945
20 missions
P-51D SX-S "Cat's Caboose"
Callans, Glenn G., Capt.; April 1943-March 1945
113 missions
P-47D SX-V
P-51D SX-V 44-14791
Christopher, Richard S., Lt.; August 1944-March 1945
68 missions
P-51D SX-J
Cles, Leslie P., Capt.; December 1942-November 8, 1944(POW)
101 missions
P-47D SX-U 42-8522 "Betsy"
P-47D SX-U 42-25957 "Betsy"
P-51D SX-U 44-14831 "Pregnant Patty"
Corgan, Robert D., Lt.; July 1944-October 18, 1944(MIA)
40 missions
P-51D SX-D 44-11188
Corrigan, Donald J., Lt.; October 1942-May 1944
66 missions
P-47D SX-P
Cross, James F., Lt.; August 1944-November 27, 1944(MIA)
33 missions
P-51D SX-D
Cundy, Arthur C., Lt.; August 1944-March 11, 1945(KIA)
69 missions
P-51D SX-B 44-15092 "Alabama Rammer Jammer"
Curry, William R., Lt.; September 1944-March 1945
63 missions
P-51D SX-D 44-14963
Curtis, Victor N., Capt.; June 1944-August 13, 1944(MIA-E)
56 missions
P-47D SX-X "Puritan Maid"
Daines, Richard, Lt.; July 1944-August 7, 1944(KIA)
8 missions
Dansky, Lester L., Lt.; December 1942-August 31, 1943(KIA)
8 missions
Davenport, John E., Lt.; September 1944-July 1945
56 missions
P-51C SX-M 42-103363 "Lucky Leaky II"
Davis, William C., Capt.; July 1944-EOW
60 missions
P-47D SX-A
P-51D SX-A 44-14642
P-51D SX-V 44-72392 "Aurora Houn' Dog"
Dietz, George S., Lt.; September 1943-September 23, 1943 (KIA)
4 missions
Donovan, Walter J., Lt.; September 1943-September 15, 1943 (KIA)
1 mission
Dubois, Allen C., Lt.; August 1944-March 1945
67 missions
P-51D SX-G 44-14720
Durlin, Robert C., Capt.; October 1942-September 15, 1943(Inj.)
12 missions
Dustin, Harry H., Lt.; September 1943-March 16, 1944(MIA); ex-350th Ftr Sqn
33 missions
P-47D SX-Z 42-75683 "Big Totsy"
Edwards, Edmund B., Capt.; August 1944-July 1945
52 missions
P-51D SX-S "Dirt Dauber"
Edwards, Francis L., Lt.; May 1944-May 30, 1944(KIA); ex-351st Ftr Sqn (65 missions)
1 missions
Eluhow, Raymond, Lt.; April 1944-August 1944
81 missions
P-47D SX-V 42-26455 "The Flying Russian"
Evans, James R., Lt.; August 1944-May 1945
62 missions
P-51D SX-Y 44-14631 "Shirley Dean"
Fogarty, Edward M., Lt.; October 1942-May 1944
64 missions
P-47D SX-O 42-76501
Forkin, Thomas J., Capt.; October 1942-January 1945
93 missions
P-47D SX-W
P-51D SX-W 44-14486
Gabriel, John R., Lt.; June 1944-June 12, 1944(MIA-E)
4 missions
Geurtz, Robert P., Lt.; October 1942-June 1944
62 missions
P-47D SX-I 42-8930
Gonnam, Jesse W., Capt.; October 1942-April 23, 1944(POW)
64 missions
P-47D SX-U 42-76394
Green, Earl W., F/O; May 1944-June 6, 1944(MIA-E); ex-56th Ftr Grp
7 missions
Greenwood, Raymond P., Lt.; May 1944-August 12, 1944(MIA-E)
65 missions, 245 hours
P-47D SX-O 42-26570
Grove, Lindsay W., Lt.; December 1944-EOW
32 missions, 180 hours
P-51D SX-D "Miss Jackie"
P-51D SX-D 44-14693 "Miss Jackie II"
Hahn, Richard E., Lt.; December 1944-March 18, 1945(MIA)
21 missions

Hajosy, Francis J., Lt.; September 1943-September 18, 1943 (KIAc)
 0 missions
Harbin, William R., Lt.; December 1944-EOW
 24 missions
 P-51D SX-G 44-72408 "Little Jo"
Harris, Delbert E., Jr., Lt.; June 1944-August 1, 1944(POW)
 29 missions
 P-47D SX-P 42-26036
Hassell, Robert C., Jr., Lt.; December 1944-EOW
 36 missions
 P-51D SX-E "Johnny"
Herfurth, Herman, Lt.; March 1944-June 1944; ex-HdQts
 70 missions
 P-47D SX-X "Puritan Maid"
Hernandez, Victor M., Lt.; August 1944-December 4, 1944(POW)
 31 missions
 P-51D SX-Q
Hicks, James R., F/O; April 1944-June 10, 1944(KIA)
 24 missions
 P-47D SX-W 42-8630
Hoey, Charles J., Maj.; August 1943-February 1944; to HdQts
 P-47D SX-A 42-75707
Huff, Charles A., Jr., Lt.; April 1945-EOW
 0 missions
Hunt, Lloyd, Lt.; May 1944-July 4, 1944(MIA-E)
 39 missions
 P-47D SX-L
 P-47D SX-W 42-26667 "Bobbie Baby"
Ista, Leroy W., Lt.; December 1942-December 22, 1943(KIA)
 29 missions
Johnson, Wilton W., Maj.; February 1943-EOW
 114 missions, 365:35 hours
 P-47D SX-D
 P-47D SX-D 42-26011
 P-51D SX-D
Johnston, Virgil C., Jr., Lt.; May 1944-June 10, 1944(MIA)
 14 missions
 P-47D SX-I 42-25771
Jones, Thomas W., Lt.; May 1944-November 1944
 66 missions
 P-47D SX-L
 P-47D SX-R 42-26665
 P-51D SX-Y
Jordan, William J., Capt.; December 1942-December 1944
 106 missions, 380 hours
 P-47D SX-T 42-8396 "Lucky"
 P-51D SX-T 44-14631 "Lucky Too"
Junttila, Wilbert H., LtCol.; October 1942-July 1945
 113 missions
 P-47D SX-K 42-8414
 P-47D SX-K 42-75608 "Ginny"
 P-51K SX-K 44-11559 "The Flying Finn"
 P-51D SX-K 44-14693 "The Flying Finn"
Keywan, Richard V., Lt.; September 1943-June 12, 1944(KIA)
 68 missions
 P-47D SX-A 42-75707 "Little Hotsy"
Kipfer, Charles W., Lt.; October 1942-May 1944
 62 missions
 P-47D SX-Q 42-75544
 P-47D SX-Q 42-25959
Knickelbein, Edward A., Lt.; February 1945-July 3, 1945(KIAc)
 15 missions
Knoble, Joseph F., Capt.; February 1944-September 1945
 117 missions
 P-47D SX-N 42-25568 "Little Chum"
 P-51D SX-N 44-14712 "Little Chum II"
Kritz, Stephen J., Lt.; October 1944-November 26, 1944(KIA)
 5 missions
Lamb, James W., Lt.; November 1944-April 17, 1945(MIA)
 39 missions
Lammie, Harold R., Lt.; November 1944-EOW
 37 missions
 P-51D SX-P 44-11196 "Bunny"
Lancaster, Billy J., Lt.; February 1945-April 17, 1945(MIA)
 18 missions
 P-51K SX-K 44-11559 "Princess Marie"
Lang, Albert P., Lt.; November 1944-EOW
 49 missions
 P-51D SX-F 44-14694 "Eleanor"
Leitner, Frank W., Lt.; March 1945-June 1945
 10 missions
Lepird, Jack D., Lt.; April 1943-July 24, 1943(KIAc)
 0 missions
Lettas, Andrew N., F/O; April 1945-June 1945
 3 missions
MacIntosh, John A., Jr., Lt.; March 1945-EOW
 7 missions
Makikuhna, Douglas A., Lt.; November 1944-EOW
 39 missions
 P-51D SX-A 44-14642 "Miss Ethel"
Marchant, William S., Lt.; September 1943-June 10, 1944(KIA); ex-351st Ftr Sqn
 63 missions
 P-47D SX-Z 42-75683
Martorella, Michael J., Lt.; November 1944-EOW
 39 missions
 P-51D SX-I 44-14495 "Jeanne"
Mathias, W.M., Lt.; October 1942-early 1943
Mayhew, Buren B., Lt.; May 1944-August 1944
 75 missions, 300 hours
 P-47D SX-J
McAdory, Louis M., Lt.; February 1945-EOW
 18 missions
McGarry, William T., Lt.; May 1944-September 1944
 75 missions, 300 hours
 P-47D SX-I 42-26631
McGough, Francis P., Lt.; March 1945-EOW
 0 missions
McNally, Richard M., Lt.; April 1945-June 1945
 3 missions
McPherson, Harry H., Lt.; October 1942-July 24, 1943(KIAc)
 0 missions
Michel, Alvin, Lt.; November 1944-March 21, 1945(POW)
 29 missions
 P-51D SX-U 44-14039
Miller, Harold, Lt.; January 1945-June 1945
 20 missions
 P-51D SX-R 44-14804 "Honey Bee II"
Miller, Harold O., Lt.; April 1944-August 1944
 77 missions, 300 hours
 P-47D SX-S "Sniffles"
Miller, Robert C., Capt.; April 1945-June 1945; ex-HdQts
 3 missions
Moriarity, Russell E., Lt.; September 1943-December 30, 1943(POW)
 9 missions
Morrison, Maurice, Capt.; April 1943-May 1945
 120 missions
 P-47D SX-R 42-8687 "Highlander"
 P-47D SX-R 42-75552
 P-51D SX-R 44-14804 "El Gato"
Motley, James L., Lt.; June 1944-January 1945
 69 missions
 P-47D SX-H
 P-51D SX-H 44-14674
Murden, Robert T., Lt.; July 1943-August 31, 1943(POW)
 7 missions
Nance, Harold E., Lt.; June 1944-January 1945
 69 missions
 P-51D SX-Z 44-14259 "Poopdeck Pappy"
Nelson, Henry B., Lt.; February 1945-EOW
 15 missions
Newman, Robert A., Lt.; October 1942-March 16, 1944(KIA)
 37 missions
 P-47D SX-N 42-75530 "Wham Bam"
Newton, William M., Jr., Lt.; May 1944-October 1944
 77 missions
 P-47D SX-A
Niklaus, Herbert F., Lt.; June 1944-February 1945
 68 missions
 P-51D SX-F 44-14694 "Eleanor"
Owens, Hildreth R., Lt.; September 1943-May 1944
 59 missions
 P-47D SX-L
Parker, Bill, Lt.; June 1944-November 1944
 67 missions
 P-47D SX-Q 42-25959
Perry, Earl W., Jr., F/O; January 1943-September 6, 1943(KIA)
 6 missions
Pletz, Leroy O., Lt.; October 1944-July 1945
 57 missions
 P-51K SX-M 44-11624 "Donna Mite"
Poindexter, James N., Maj.; October 1942-January 3, 1945(KIA)
 111 missions
 P-47D SX-H "Honey"
 P-47D SX-G 42-26586 "Honey II"
 P-51D SX-G 44-14720 "Honey III"
 P-51D SX-G 44-14589 "Honey IV"
Porterfield, George N., Lt.; June 1944-February 1945
 70 missions
 P-47D SX-N 42-25568 "Elsie"
 P-51D SX-N 44-11196
Reinhardt, Edwin D., Lt.; May 1944-November 1944
 70 missions, 255 hours
 P-47D SX-Y "O.U. Kid-Rack'em Ohio"
Robertson, Raynor E., Maj.; October 1942-May 1944
 78 missions, 250 hours
 P-47D SX-S
Rosatone, Anthony R., Lt.; August 1944-January 18, 1945(KIA)
 51 missions
 P-51D SX-U 44-15388 "Stasia"
 P-51D SX-U 44-15587 "Stasia II"

Rose, Robert T., Lt.; February 1945-EOW
17 missions
P-51D SX-K 44-72754 "Snuggle Bunny"

Schillinger, Joseph A., Lt.; September 1943-May 1944
61 missions
P-47D SX-J

Schoen, Donald W., Lt.; October 1944-July 1945
56 missions
P-51D SX-H 44-14674 "Little Witch"

Schreiber, Joseph, Lt.; October 1944-March 2, 1945(POW)
33 missions
P-51D SX-Z 44-14805 "Brad's Dad"
P-51D SX-Z 44-15691 "Brad's Dad"

Sladek, Charles E., Lt.; August 1944-September 28, 1944(KIAc)
9 missions

Snyder, Ralph B., Lt.; October 1944-EOW
48 missions
P-51D SX-Z 44-14805 "Shirley Dean"

Sperry, Clint H., Lt.; December 1942-July 1944
97 missions
P-47D SX-E "Mary Jane"

Stephenson, Stewart E., Lt.; August 1944-March 1945
65 missions
P-51D SX-E 44-14726

Stiff, Edison G., Lt.; September 1943-February 22, 1944(KIA)
26 missions
P-47D SX-L 42-75065

Streit, William F., Lt.; October 1942-June 1944
100 missions
P-47D SX-Y 42-76195 "Scottie Bill"

Sullivan, Edward J., Lt.; October 1944-March 2, 1945(POW)
38 missions
P-51D SX-Q 44-15184 "Truly Trudie"

Swanezy, John J., F/O; June 1944-August 18, 1944(MIA)
31 missions
P-47D SX-F 42-75622

Tear, Harry E., Jr., Lt.; June 1944-February 1945
75 missions
P-47D SX-O
P-51D SX-O

Thomas, Edward D., Lt.; October 1944-EOW
49 missions
P-51D SX-U 44-14610 "Shirley Dean"

Tordoff, Harrison B., Capt.; June 1944-July 1945
85 missions
P-47D SX-L "Anne"
P-51D SX-L 44-14805 "Upupa E Pops!"
P-51D SX-L 44-72364 "Upupa E Pops!"

Tuttle, James M., Lt.; June 1944-August 12, 1944(MIA-E)
25 missions, 101 hours

Uttwenweiler, Fred L., Capt.; June 1944-January 1945
61 missions
P-47D SX-E
P-51D SX-E 44-14726

Vieck, Louis L., Lt.; March 1944-March 1944; ex-351st Ftr Sqn & 55th Ftr Grp

Vogel, Victor L., Lt.; January 1943-January 11, 1944(KIA)
27 missions

Waggoner, Horace Q., Capt.; March 1944-July 1945
104 missions, 492 hours
P-47D SX-M "Miss Illini"
P-47D SX-M 42-26661 "Miss Illini II
P-51D SX-M 44-14892 "Miss Illini III"
P-51K SX-M 44-11565 "Miss Illini III"

Willits, Gordon L., Lt.; July 1943-April 8, 1944(KIA)
53 missions
P-47D SX-X 42-22768

**Aircraft of the 350th Fighter Squadron**

P-47D-1-RE
42-7905 LH-
42-7907 LH-J "Lonesome Polecat" J.F. Furness
42-7940 LH-M
42-7956 LH-K
42-7988 LH-X "Dove of Peace" G.E. Duncan
42-7989 LH-
42-8001 LH-V B. Rimerman
42-8003 LH-
42-8005 LH-
42-8373 LH-Y
42-8393 LH-Q
42-8398 LH-

P-47D-2-RA
42-22475 LH-N "Kat"
42-22505 LH-X "Dove of Peace" G.E. Duncan

P-47D-4-RA
42-22275 LH-N "Rat-A-Dat" K.W. Gallup
42-22771 LH-
42-22779 LH-

P-47D-5-RE
42-8404 LH-
42-8475 LH-Y
42-8480 LH-Z
42-8499 LH- "The Georgia Peach" R.A. Stearns
42-8503 LH-
42-8513 LH-H D.A. Fry
42-8515 LH-
42-8557 LH-
42-8608 LH-D
42-8623 LH-F "Janie" W.J. Price
42-8634 LH-X "Dove of Peace" G.E. Duncan
42-8683 LH-
42-8697 LH-Y

P-47D-6-RE
42-74647 LH-U W.K. Blickenstaff
42-74665 LH-T "Fatty's Patty"
42-74669 LH-O "Prudence II" W.F. Tanner
42-74672 LH-L "El Shafto"
42-74753 LH-G "Texas Ranger"

P-47D-10-RE
42-75074 LH-N

P-47D-11-RE
42-75220 LH-P "Maid Marion"

P-47D-15-RE
42-76141 LH-D "Mud'n Mules" D.E. Newhart
42-76141 LH-Q "Arkansas Traveler" L.M. Davis
42-75157 LH-Y
42-76189 LH-L
42-76268 LH-
42-76280 LH-D "Jenny" C. Rowan
42-76294 LH-
42-76320 LH-U W.K. Blickenstaff

P-47D-20-RE
42-76543 LH-

P-47D-21-RE
42-25506 LH-X "Dove of Peace" G.E. Duncan

P-47D-21-RA
43-25541 LH-
43-25581 LH-

P-47D-22-RE
42-25768 LH-
42-25971 LH-X "Dove of Peace" G.E. Duncan
42-26109 LH-
42-26269 LH-
42-26280 LH-
42-26313 LH-
42-26357 LH-Y

P-47D-25-RE
42-26402 LH-U W.K. Blickenstaff
42-26422 LH-E
42-26454 LH-
42-26455 LH-L "Maggie V" K. Chetwood
42-26472 LH-O "Prudence V" W.F. Tanner
42-26477 LH-F "Janie" W.J. Price
42-26525 LH-V
42-26581 LH-J "Little Princess" M.V. Bledsoe
42-26581 LH-H
42-26619 LH-L "Maggie IV" K. Chetwood
42-26634 LH-Q "Rat-A-Dat" K.W. Gallup
42-26642 LH-
42-26649 LH-N "Elizabeth"
42-26656 LH-D "Ernestyne" R.F. Unangst
42-26659 LH-M "Fern Marie" V.G. Rafferty
42-26663 LH-Z
42-26668 LH-H "Skipper"
42-26692 LH-S

P-47D-26-RA
42-28357 LH-R "Natalie Ann II" J.O. Ruscitto

P-47D-28-RE
44-19562 LH-N "Rat-A-Dat III" K.W. Gallup
44-19577 LH-Z
44-19580 LH-

Unknown Serials
LH-T "Carol" J.T. Winder

LH-K "The Goon" T. Lorance
LH-M "Fern Marie II" V.G. Rafferty
LH- "Vicki Jane" A. Ferrell
LH-W "Cutie"
LH- "Rum Hound"

P-51C-5-NT
42-103302 LH-

P-51B-5-NA
43-6377 LH- HACK
43-6448 LH- HACK

P-51B-15-NA
42-106619 LH-K "Queenie"
42-106704 LH-
42-106751 LH-L HACK
42-106902 LH-
43-24781 LH- HACK

P-51D-5-NT
44-11155 LH-
44-11160 LH-J "Star Dust"
44-11167 LH-X "Danny Boy" M.W. Hightshoe
44-11193 LH-Y "Beautiful Dope" H.H. Hakonen
44-11204 LH-M "Hey Bolo!" H.E. Haynes

P-51K-1-NT
44-11353 LH-

P-51K-5-NT
44-11646 LH-V B. Rimerman

P-51D-5-NA
44-13842 LH-

P-51D-10-NA
44-14180 LH-B
44-14249 LH-
44-14416 LH-M
44-14419 LH-F "Janie" W.J. Price
44-14538 LH-E "Margaret Too" W.L. Boone
44-14572 LH-
44-14654 LH-S "Molly M" R.T. Allison
44-14666 LH-L "Zelma"
44-14673 LH-I "Galloping Ghost"
44-14676 LH-
44-14686 LH-
44-14687 LH-N "Lethal Ethel"
44-14698 LH-Q L.W. Lee
44-14700 LH-
44-14707 LH-
44-14727 LH-P "Bee-Jay"
44-14770 LH-M "Fern Marie III" V.G. Rafferty
44-14780 LH-B
44-14793 LH-J "Miss Betty D" J.M. Balason
44-14810 LH-
44-14811 LH-Q "Lady Gwen" R.W. Abernathy

P-51D-15-NA
44-14945 LH-D "Arkansas Traveler II" L.M. Davis
44-14969 LH-G "Lady Grace II" L.M. Grainger
44-14974 LH-Z
44-14990 LH-A
44-15021 LH-W "Anabel"
44-15137 LH-R "Baby Duck" H.G. Kolb
44-15516 LH-X "Danny Boy 2nd" M.W. Hightshoe
44-15519 LH-H "Fran 2nd" R.J. Lanoue
44-15521 LH-G "Mary Ag"
44-15529 LH-
44-15584 LH-
44-15671 LH-P "Miss Ellen" H.F. Jung

P-51D-20-NA
44-63197 LH-L "Mascara Maggie" J.E. Dyer
44-63879 LH-
44-63896 LH-S "Molly M" R.T. Allison
44-63896 LH-S "The G-Nat" W.H. Grizzle
44-63897 LH-
44-72096 LH-F "Miss Betsy"
44-72136 LH-
42-72168 LH-A "Lady Doris II"
44-72175 LH- "Little Red II"
44-72212 LH-O "Prudence 7th" W.F. Tanner
44-72259 LH-R "Baby Duck II" H.G. Kolb
44-72263 LH-Q "Cozy Rosie"
44-72292 LH-N "Miss Florida" R.C. Gordon
44-72302 LH-F
44-72374 LH-U "Betty-E" W.K. Blickenstaff
44-72399 LH-M "Hey Bolo! II" H.E. Haynes

P-51D-25-NA
44-72736 LH-S "Miss Gamble" R.A. Elder
44-72737 LH-
44-72845 LH-P "Lil' Miss Boomerang" B. Greenfield
44-72958 LH-
44-73046 LH-W
44-73060 LH-X "Dove of Peace" G.E. Duncan
44-73166 LH-

Unknown Serials
44-14??? LH-U "The Betty E" W.K. Blickenstaff
LH-T "Carol" J.T. Winder
LH-G "Lady Grace 3rd" L.M. Grainger
LH-Y "My Frans" E.H. Duke
LH- "Mad Irishman" G.P. Devine
LH- "Vicki Jane 3rd" A.E. Ferrell
LH-E "Margaret 3" W.L. Boone
LH- "Wichita Warrior II"
LH- "Potchy" G.S.H. Lee
LH- "The Little Witch"

**Aircraft of the 351st Fighter Squadron**

P-47C-5-RE
41-6528 YJ-
41-6583 YJ-K "Alyce" O.A. Kinkade
41-6585 YJ-

P-47D-1-RE
42-7906 YJ-L "Chief Yahoo" F.H. LeFebre
42-7926 YJ-
42-7958 YJ-V "Hawkeye" V.L. Byers
42-7972 YJ-
42-7987 YJ-J "Jeannie" J.G. Trietz
42-8002 YJ-
42-8372 YJ-
42-8375 YJ-
42-8379 YJ- "Big Nose"
42-8380 YJ-
42-8385 YJ-
42-8395 YJ-S "Cookie" S. Christian

P-47D-2-RA
42-22469 YJ-Z "Marty" J. Terzian
42-22523 YJ-D "Angel of Mercy" L.G. Hally

P-47D-4-RA
42-22759 YJ-J "Jeannie" J.G. Trietz
42-22781 YJ-P W.G. Cobb

P-47D-5-RE
42-8401 YJ-B "Scatterbolts" W.R. Burkett
42-8428 YJ-Q "Pat" B.E. Kraft
42-8476 YJ-X "Little Demon" W.C. Beckham
42-8478 YJ-Y "Barbara" H.J. Morris
42-8479 YJ-
42-8487 YJ-
42-8511 YJ-K R.C. Strobell
42-8602 YJ-E "Sis" F.N. Emory
42-8619 YJ-A "Lonesome Polecat" G.N. Ahles
42-8628 YJ-T "Jose" J.W. Furneaux
42-8675 YJ-

P-47D-6-RE
42-74615 YJ-B "My Best Bett" W.J. Weaver
42-74615 YJ-H "My Best Bett"
42-74671 YJ-
42-74706 YJ-N "Babe"
42-74736 YJ-
42-74738 YJ-U "Doris" E.J. Albert

P-47D-10-RE
42-75114 YJ-M "Boston Bull" W.J. Maguire
42-75135 YJ-
42-75149 YJ-P "Double S"
42-75161 YJ-
42-75189 YJ-H H.L. Biddy
42-75191 YJ-

P-47D-11-RE
42-75226 YJ-X W.C. Beckham
42-75315 YJ-
42-75457 YJ-
42-75507 YJ-R "Dottie"
42-75563 YJ-V
42-75570 YJ-F "Devil's Thumb" H.K. Field

P-47D-15-RE
42-75647 YJ-

| | |
|---|---|
| 42-75653 YJ- | |
| 42-75670 YJ-W | |
| 42-75676 YJ-K "Janny M" | W.K. Lahke |
| 42-75688 YJ- | |
| 42-75702 YJ- | |
| 42-75740 YJ-R "Liberty Queen" | C.L. McGraw |
| 42-75804 YJ- | |
| 42-75807 YJ- | |
| 42-75815 YJ-E "Sis II" | F.N. Emory |
| 42-75815 YJ-E "Patricia Baby" | J.W. Bishop |
| 42-75850 YJ- | |
| 42-75856 YJ-Y "Betts" | W.J. Christensen |
| 42-75863 YJ-U | |
| 42-75874 YJ-F | |
| 42-76103 YJ-S "Cookie II" | S. Christian |
| 42-76352 YJ-Q "Mid's Bid" | L.A. Thornell |
| 42-76352 YJ-Q | W.A. Thistlethwaite |

| P-47D-21-RA | |
|---|---|
| 43-25557 YJ-V | V.L. Byers |
| 43-25572 YJ-N "Smoocher" | J.J. Hatch |

| P-47D-22-RE | |
|---|---|
| 42-25702 YJ-O "Big Bouncer" | G.B. Compton |
| 42-25710 YJ-F | |
| 42-25730 YJ- | |
| 42-25840 YJ-H | |
| 42-26027 YJ-D "Georgie Fay" | R.M. Tumlin |
| 42-26047 YJ-B | |
| 42-26050 YJ-I | G.W. Franklin |
| 42-26126 YJ-M "Lil Boston Bull" | W.J. Maguire |
| 42-26246 YJ-A "Lonesome Polecat" | G.N. Ahles |
| 42-26332 YJ-Z | |

| P-47D-23-RA | |
|---|---|
| 42-27906 YJ-L | |

| P-47D-25-RE | |
|---|---|
| 42-26428 YJ-L | |

| P-47D-28-RA | |
|---|---|
| 42-28566 YJ-M "Ticket Home" | H.E. Daniel |
| 42-28798 YJ- | |
| 42-28878 YJ- | |

| P-47D-28-RE | |
|---|---|
| 44-19792 YJ- | |
| 44-19934 YJ- | |
| 44-19950 YJ- | |

| Unknown Serials | |
|---|---|
| YJ-D "Woolverine" | D.C. Kenney |
| YJ-G "Super Rabbit" | G.F. Perpente |
| YJ-U "Minnie" | F.J. Mincik |
| YJ-B "Flak Bait" | A.W. Barlow |
| - 857 YJ-P | |
| - 745 YJ-G | |
| - 884 YJ-N | |
| - 720 YJ-B | |
| - 314 YJ-H | |

| P-51B-1-NA | |
|---|---|
| 43-12433 YJ-4 | HACK |
| 43-12339 YJ- | HACK |
| 43-12439 YJ- | HACK |
| 43-12454 YJ- | HACK |

| P-51B-15-NA | |
|---|---|
| 42-106744 YJ- | HACK |
| 43-24781 YJ- | HACK |

| P-51D-5-NT | |
|---|---|
| 44-11160 YJ-V | V.L. Byers |
| 44-11191 YJ-Y | W.J. Christensen |
| 44-11191 YJ-Y "Birmingham Anne" | S.S. Petticrew |
| 44-11216 YJ-B | |

| P-51K-1-NT | |
|---|---|
| 44-11333 YJ-K | |

| P-51K-5-NT | |
|---|---|
| 44-11565 YJ-X | R. Hilgenburg |
| 44-11698 YJ-B | |

| P-51D-5-NA | |
|---|---|
| 44-13710 YJ- | |
| 44-13972 YJ- | |
| 44-13978 YJ-W | M.Q. Williams |

| P-51D-10-NA | |
|---|---|
| 44-14430 YJ-P | D.E. Lewis |
| 44-14505 YJ- | |
| 44-14558 YJ-K "Jean III" | |
| 44-14569 YJ-M "Lil Boston Bull" | W.J. Maguire |
| 44-14573 YJ-E "Sis IV" | F.N. Emory |
| 44-14595 YJ-V | G.J. Miller |
| 44-14610 YJ-Z | H.W. Chase |
| 44-14628 YJ-D "The Uninvited" | T.R. Drybrough |
| 44-14658 YJ-H | L.B. Highfield |
| 44-14688 YJ-N | J.M. Nicklebur |
| 44-14689 YJ-F | R.K. Wiehe |
| 44-14690 YJ-S "Squirt" | H.D. Stump |
| 44-14706 YJ-M "Ginny" | J.E. Frye |
| 44-14728 YJ-I | J.F. Hinchey |
| 44-14732 YJ-A "Tampa Tramp" | M.A. Arnold |
| 44-14748 YJ-R "Kansas City Kitty" | C.L. McGraw |

| P-51D-10-NA | |
|---|---|
| 44-14756 YJ-J | G.J. Rosen |
| 44-14771 YJ-L "Willit Run?" | F.H. LeFebre |
| 44-14774 YJ-T "Butch 3rd" | |
| 44-14781 YJ-U "Don-Helen" | J.W. Rohrs |
| 44-14781 YJ-U "Janny M" | W.K. Lahke |
| 44-14796 YJ-G "Lady Margaret" | G.S. Montgomery |
| 44-14808 YJ-O "Little Bouncer" | G.B. Compton |
| 44-14816 YJ-B "Lois W" | J.O. Fulton |

| P-51D-15-NA | |
|---|---|
| 44-14887 YJ-A | M.A. Arnold |
| 44-14893 YJ-M "Lil Boston Bull" | W.J. Maguire |
| 44-14893 YJ-O | |
| 44-14949 YJ-Q "Mr. Gray" | G.E. Markham |
| 44-14969 YJ- "Lady Grace II" | |
| 44-14972 YJ- | |
| 44-15533 YJ- | |
| 44-15624 YJ-G | C.W. Geiger |

| P-51D-20-NA | |
|---|---|
| 44-72171 YJ-Q "Mr. Gray II" | G.E. Markham |
| 44-72174 YJ-S | H.S. Murray |
| 44-72231 YJ-L | A.C. Carroll |
| 44-72267 YJ-P | D.E. Lewis |
| 44-72277 YJ- | |
| 44-72299 YJ-O "Little Bouncer" | G.B. Compton |
| 44-72330 YJ-K | |

| P-51D-25-NA | |
|---|---|
| 44-73048 YJ-G | J.G. Lancaster |

**Aircraft of the 352nd Fighter Squadron**

| P-47D-1-RE | |
|---|---|
| 42-7901 SX- | |
| 42-7904 SX-F "8 Gun Melody" | C.F. Armstrong |
| 42-7985 SX-R | |
| 42-7995 SX- | |
| 42-7999 SX- | |
| 42-8383 SX- | |
| 42-8390 SX-I | |
| 42-8392 SX- | |
| 42-8396 SX-T "Lucky" | W.J. Jordan |

| P-47D-2-RA | |
|---|---|
| 42-22458 SX- | |
| 42-22466 SX-J | |
| 42-22482 SX-M "Junky Too" | G.S. Burlingame |

| P-47D-4-RA | |
|---|---|
| 42-22769 SX- | |
| 42-22768 SX-X | G.L. Willits |

| P-47D-5-RE | |
|---|---|
| 42-8414 SX-K | W.H. Junttila |
| 42-8494 SX- | |
| 42-8522 SX-U "Betsy" | L.P. Cles |
| 42-8531 SX- | |
| 42-8630 SX-W | J.R. Hicks |
| 42-8687 SX-R "Highlander" | M. Morrison |

| P-47D-6-RE | |
|---|---|
| 42-74636 SX- | |
| 42-74680 SX-I | |

| P-47D-10-RE | |
|---|---|
| 42-75065 SX-Z | H.R. Owens |
| 42-75065 SX-L | E.G. Stif |

P-47D-11-RE

| Aircraft | Pilot |
|---|---|
| 42-75530 SX-N "Wham Bam" | R.A. Newman |
| 42-75544 SX-Q | C.W. Kipfer |
| 42-75552 SX-R "Highlander" | M. Morrison |
| 42-75608 SX-K "Ginny" | W.H. Junttila |

P-47D-15-RE

| Aircraft | Pilot |
|---|---|
| 42-75622 SX-F "Hun Buster" | C.F. Armstrong |
| 42-75683 SX-Z "Big Totsy" | H.H. Dustin/W.S. Marchant |
| 42-75707 SX-A | C.J. Hoey |
| 42-75707 SX-A "Little Hotsy" | R.V. Keywan |
| 42-76195 SX-Y "Scottie Bill" | W.F. Streit |
| 42-76195 SX-Y "The Mole" | L. Avakian |

P-47D-20-RE

| Aircraft | Pilot |
|---|---|
| 42-76394 SX-U | J.W. Gonnam |
| 42-76501 SX-O | E.M. Fogarty |

P-47D-21-RA

| Aircraft | Pilot |
|---|---|
| 43-25568 SX-N "Little Chum" | J.L. Knoble |
| 43-25568 SX-N "Elsie" | G.N. Porterfield |

P-47D-22-RE

| Aircraft | Pilot |
|---|---|
| 42-25571 SX-I | V.C. Johnston |
| 42-25957 SX-U "Betsy" | L.P. Cles |
| 42-25959 SX-Q | B. Parker |
| 42-26011 SX-D | W.W. Johnson |
| 42-26036 SX-P | D.E. Harris |

P-47D-25-RE

| Aircraft | Pilot |
|---|---|
| 42-26455 SX-V "The Flying Russian" | R. Eluhow |
| 42-26459 SX-B "Butch II" | W.B. Bailey |
| 42-26533 SX-D | |
| 42-26549 SX-Z "Eager Eddie" | E.C. Andrews |
| 42-26570 SX-O | R.P. Greenwood |
| 42-26586 SX-G "Honey II" | J.N. Poindexter |
| 42-26631 SX-I | W.T. McGarry |
| 42-26661 SX-M "Miss Illini" | H.Q. Waggoner |
| 42-26665 SX-R "Buzz Bunny" | T.W. Jones |
| 42-26667 SX-W "Bobbie Baby" | L. Hunt |

Unknown Serials

| Aircraft | Pilot |
|---|---|
| SX-H "Honey" | J.N. Poindexter |
| SX-B "Butch" | W.B. Bailey |
| SX-X "Puritan Maid" | V.N. Curtis |
| SX-M "Gloria Ann" | D.L. Barber |
| SX-L "Anne" | H.B. Tordoff |
| SX-M "Davy Don Chariot" | G.S. Burlingame |
| SX-E "Mary Jane" | C.H. Sperry |
| SX-Y "O.U. Kid-Rack'em Ohio" | E.D. Reinhardt |
| SX-S "Sniffles" | H.O. Miller |
| SX- "Rainie II" | |
| SX-G "Squirt" | |
| SX- "The Bruiser" | |

P-51C-5-NT

| Aircraft | Pilot |
|---|---|
| 42-103363 SX-M "Lucky Leaky II" | J.E. Davenport |

P-51B-5-NA

| Aircraft | Pilot |
|---|---|
| 43-6800 SX-2 | HACK |

P-51D-5-NT

| Aircraft | Pilot |
|---|---|
| 44-11188 SX-D | R.D. Corgan |
| 44-11196 SX-P "Bunny" | H.R. Lammie |

P-51K-5-NT

| Aircraft | Pilot |
|---|---|
| 44-11559 SX-K "The Flying Finn" | W.H. Junttila |
| 44-11559 SX-K "Princess Marie" | B.J. Lancasyer |
| 44-11565 SX-X "Miss Illini III" | H.Q. Waggoner |
| 44-11624 SX-M "Donna Mite" | L.O. Pletz |

P-51D-5-NA

| Aircraft | Pilot |
|---|---|
| 44-14039 SX-U "Gloria Doll II" | A. Michel |

P-51D-10-NA

| Aircraft | Pilot |
|---|---|
| 44-14095 SX-B "Little Midget/Missy" | M.Q. Williams |
| 44-14259 SX-Z "Poopdeck Pappy" | H.E. Nance |
| 44-14270 SX-G | |
| 44-14303 SX-B "Double Trouble" | W.B. Bailey |
| 44-14486 SX-W | T.J. Forkin |
| 44-14495 SX-I "Dallas Doll" | F.H. Bouldin |
| 44-14495 SX-I "Jeanne" | M.J. Martorella |
| 44-14589 SX-G "Honey IV" | J.N. Poindexter |
| 44-14610 SX-U "Shirley Dean" | E.D. Thomas |
| 44-14620 SX-M "Davy Don Chariot" | G.S. Burlingame |
| 44-14631 SX-T "Lucky Too" | T.J. Jordan |
| 44-14631 SX-T "Shirley Dean" | |
| 44-14631 SX-U | |
| 44-14642 SX-A "Miss Ethel" | W.C. Davis |
| 44-14674 SX-H "Little Witch" | D.W. Schoen |
| 44-14693 SX-K "The Flying Finn" | W.H. Junttila |
| 44-14694 SX-F "Eleanor" | H.F. Niklaus |
| 44-14712 SX-N "Little Chum II" | J.F. Knoble |
| 44-14713 SX- | |
| 44-14720 SX-G "Honey II" | J.N. Poindexter |
| 44-14720 SX-G | A.C. Dubois |
| 44-14726 SX-E | F.L. Uttwenweiler |
| 44-14742 SX-M "Gloria Ann II" | D.L. Barber |
| 44-14791 SX-V | G.G. Callans |
| 44-14804 SX-R "El Gato" | M. Morrison |
| 44-14804 SX-R "Honey Bee II" | H. Miller |
| 44-14805 SX-L "Upupa E Pops!" | H.B. Tordoff |
| 44-14805 SX-Z "Brad's Dad" | J. Schreiber |
| 44-14805 SX-Z "Shirley Dean" | R.B. Snyder |
| 44-14831 SX-U "Pregnant Patty" | L.P. Cles |

P-51D-15-NA

| Aircraft | Pilot |
|---|---|
| 44-14892 SX-X "Miss Illini III" | H.Q. Waggoner |
| 44-14693 SX-D "Miss Jackie" | W.A. Curry/L.W. Grove |
| 44-15092 SX-B "Alabama Rammer Jammer" | A.C. Cundy |
| 44-15092 SX-B "Lulu Belle II" | |
| 44-15184 SX-Q "Truly Trudie" | E.J. Sullivan |
| 44-15315 SX-U "Don Helen" | C.W. Briggs |
| 44-15388 SX-U "Stasia" | A.R. Rosatone |
| 44-15587 SX-U "Stasia II" | A.R. Rosatone |
| 44-15691 SX-Z "Brad's Dad" | J. Schreiber |

P-51D-20-NA

| Aircraft | Pilot |
|---|---|
| 44-63684 SX-B "Double Trouble Two" | W.B. Bailey |
| 44-72106 SX-U | |
| 44-72219 SX- | |
| 44-72254 SX- | |
| 44-72364 SX-L "Upupa E Pops!" | H.B. Tordoff |
| 44-72392 SX-V "Aurora Hawn Dog, Feed It, It's Hungry" | W.C. Davis |
| 44-72408 SX-G "Little Jo" | W.R. Harbin |

P-51D-25-NA

| Aircraft | Pilot |
|---|---|
| 44-72754 SX-K "Snuggle Bunny" | R.T. Rose |
| 44-73107 SX-G "Little Midget" | J.G. Bartley |

Unknown Serials

| Aircraft | Pilot |
|---|---|
| SX-E "Johnny" | R.C. Hassell |
| SX-S "Dirt Dauber" | |
| SX-S "Cat's Caboose" | |
| SX- "Carolyn" | |
| SX- "Fiffinella" | |

• • •

## THE 353RD "C" FIGHTER GROUP

On March 15, 1944, pilots from four fighter groups assembled at Metfield, home of the 353rd Fighter Group, to form a special training organization. Known as "Bill's Buzz Boys", after General William Kepner, their purpose was to develop tactics on ground strafing and pass this knowledge on to their home units once the organization was disbanded. In addition to Col. Glenn E. Duncan, who headed the unit, the following pilots were put on detached service to the 353rd "C":

| **353rd Ftr Grp** | **359th Ftr Grp** |
|---|---|
| Lt. Kenneth Chetwood | Capt. Charles C. Ettlesen |
| Lt. Charles O. Durant, Jr. | Lt. Clifford E. Carter |
| Lt. Francis L. Edwards | Lt. John H. Oliphint |
| Lt. John A. Sullivan | Lt. Robert L. Thacker |
| **355th Ftr Grp** | **361st Ftr Grp** |
| Capt. Albert B. Starr | Lt. Eugene W. Kinnaird |
| Lt. Norman J. Fortier, Jr. | Lt. Martin H. Johnson, Jr. |
| Lt. Kenneth R. Williams | Lt. Joseph D. Kelly |
| Lt. Gilbert S. Wright | Lt. Johnny C. Wright |

This unit flew 8 missions (83 effective sorties) and claimed 0-0-1 in the air and 16-18 on the ground in addition to numerous locomotives, railcars, etc. destroyed or damaged. Three P-47's were lost with two pilots MIA (the third was picked up by ASR personnel). Claims for aircraft destroyed/damaged and the losses have been attached to the pilot's assigned group.

### Claims and Losses for "Bill's Buzz Boys"

**March 26, 1944**

|  |  |  |
|---|---|---|
| Capt. Starr | u/i a/c dest(grd) | Chateaudun |
| Lt. Oliphint | Me-110 dest(grd) | same |
| | He-177 dam(grd) | same |
| Lt. Carter | He-111 dam(grd) | same |
| Lt. Durant | FW-190 dam(grd) | Chartres |
| Lt. Sullivan | Me-109 dam(grd) | same |

**March 29, 1944**

|  |  |  |
|---|---|---|
| Col. Duncan | Me-110 dest(grd) | Dummer Lake |
| | B-17 dest(grd) | same |

| | | |
|---|---|---|
| | (6)u/i a/c dam(grd) | same |
| | Me-210 dam(grd) | same |
| Lt. Carter | (2)Me-410 dest(grd) | same |
| Lt. Johnson | FW-190 dest(grd) | Rheine |
| | Ju-88 dest(grd) | Rheine |
| Lt. Fortier | u/i a/c dest(grd) | Dummer Lake |
| Lt. J. Wright | Ju-188 dest(grd) | same |
| | (2)u/i a/c dam(grd) | same |
| Lt. Kinnaird | (2)FW-190 dam(grd) | same |
| Capt. Ettlesen | u/i a/c dam(grd) | same |
| Lt. Kelly | Ju-88 dam(grd) | same |

**April 1, 1944**

| | | |
|---|---|---|
| Lt. Carter | Me-109 dam(air) | Dummer Lake |
| Lt. Kelly | (2)Ju-88 dest(grd) | Gutersloh |
| Lt. Kinnaird | Ju-88 dest(grd) | same |
| Lt. J. Wright | Ju-88 dest(grd) | same |

**April 10, 1944**

| | | |
|---|---|---|
| Lt. J. Wright | Me-110 dest(grd) | Villaroche |
| | Me-110 dam(grd) | same |
| Lt. Durant | Me-110 dest(grd) | same |

**Losses**

Lt. Williams (POW) March 26, 1944
Lt. Edwards (ASR) March 29
Lt. Carter (KIA) April 8

• • •

## THE 355TH FIGHTER GROUP
## 354TH, 357TH, 358TH FIGHTER SQUADRONS

The 355th Fighter Group was activated on November 12, 1942, at Orlando, Florida. Training in the south and east, the group headed overseas aboard the "Queen Elizabeth" on July 1, 1943. The first of 362 missions was flown on September 14, 1943, with the final one coming on April 25, 1945. While in England, the group claimed 340 aerial and 494.5 ground victories while 179 P-47's and P-51's were lost on operations and 6 pilots died in accidents.

The only wartime base for the 355th was Steeple Morden, from July 9, 1943, until July 18, 1945. Aircraft flown were the P-47D, from July of 1943 until March of 1944, and the P-51B, C, D, and K, from March of 1944 onwards. The 355th was awarded a Distinguished Unit Citation for a mission on April 5, 1944, in which attacks against German airfields produced over 50 victories.

### Claims

| | Air | | | Grd | |
|---|---|---|---|---|---|
| | Destroyed | Probable | Damaged | Destroyed | Damaged |
| HdQts | 17 | 2 | 6 | 14 | 14.5 |
| 354th | 133 | 4 | 29 | 209.5 | 152 |
| 357th | 109.5 | 10 | 48 | 168.5 | 163.5 |
| 358th | 80.5 | 7 | 41 | 102.5 | 82 |
| | 340 | 23 | 124 | 494.5 | 412 |

### Commanders

| | |
|---|---|
| Col. William J. Cummings | January 16, 1943-November 4, 1944 |
| Col. Everett W. Stewart | November 4, 1944-February 21, 1945 |
| LtCol. Claiborne H. Kinnard, Jr. | February 21, 1945-June 7, 1945 |

### Wing and Command Assignments

| | |
|---|---|
| Assigned to VIII Fighter Command | July 6, 1943 |
| VIII Fighter Command, 65th Fighter Wing | August 1943 |
| 2nd Bomb Division, 65th Fighter Wing | September 15, 1944 |
| 2nd Air Division, 65th Fighter Wing | January 1, 1945 |

### Aircraft Markings

All P-47's and early P-51's were in olive drab/neutral gray schemes with white cowl bands, spinners, and theater bands. In April of 1944, NMF P-51's arrived any many had dark green applied to the upper surfaces in various ways. The white spinner and 12 inch cowl band was used as a group marking until late 1944, when in November, the cowl band and spinners were painted in squadron colors: red for the 354th, blue for the 357th, and yellow for the 358th. Spinners remained white on all planes, but at least one P-51K in the 354th had a red-white-red striped spinner.

Squadron codes were:

354th Ftr Sqn: WR
357th Ftr Sqn: OS
358th Ftr Sqn: YF

### 355th Fighter Group Statistical Report

| Month | Missions | Air | Grd | Losses | KIAc |
|---|---|---|---|---|---|
| September 1943 | 6 | 0-0-0 | 0-0 | 0 | 1 |
| October | 8 | 2-0-1 | 0-0 | 2 | 0 |
| November | 10 | 7-0-5 | 0-0 | 13 | 0 |
| December | 11 | 1-3-5 | 0-0 | 6 | 1 |
| January 1944 | 11 | 4-0-3 | 0-0 | 4 | 0 |
| February | 15 | 12-0-8 | 0-0 | 1 | 0 |
| March | 16 | 51-5-23 | 34-47 | 12 | 0 |
| April | 18 | 55-3-15 | 100-126 | 19 | 0 |
| May | 22 | 20.5-4-11 | 5-9 | 9 | 0 |
| June | 51 | 26-1-9 | 31-8 | 17 | 0 |
| July | 24 | 28.5-4-9 | 37-31 | 11 | 0 |
| August | 28 | 22-0-1 | 6-1 | 29 | 0 |
| September | 17 | 23-0-8 | 26-18 | 9 | 0 |
| October | 16 | 3-0-1 | 3-1 | 5 | 0 |
| November | 18 | 29-1-8 | 34-20 | 8 | 0 |
| December | 17 | 20-1-5 | 1-0 | 4 | 0 |
| January 1945 | 16 | 11-0-1 | 11-13 | 3 | 0 |
| February | 16 | 5-0-1 | 18-22 | 8 | 0 |
| March | 25 | 2-0-2 | 17-14 | 5 | 1 |
| April | 17 | 18-1-7 | 171.5-102 | 14 | 0 |
| May | 0 | 0-0-0 | 0-0 | 0 | 1 |
| June | 0 | 0-0-0 | 0-0 | 0 | 2 |
| | 362 | 340-23-124 | 494.5-412 | 179 | 6 |

### Losses by Squadron

| | MIA | | KIAc | |
|---|---|---|---|---|
| | P-47 | P-51 | P-47 | P-51 |
| HdQts | 1 | 1 | 0 | 0 |
| 354th | 4 | 49 | 2 | 1 |
| 357th | 10 | 55 | 0 | 2 |
| 358th | 14 | 45 | 0 | 1 |
| | 29 | 150 | 2 | 4 |

### Claims by Type

| | Air | | | Grd | |
|---|---|---|---|---|---|
| | Destroyed | Probable | Damaged | Destroyed | Damaged |
| P-47 | 40 | 3 | 22 | 12 | 2 |
| P-51 | 300 | 20 | 102 | 482.5 | 410 |

### Claims by Enemy Aircraft Type

| | Air | | | Grd | |
|---|---|---|---|---|---|
| | Destroyed | Probable | Damaged | Destroyed | Damaged |
| Me-109 | 173 | 15 | 65 | 65 | 38 |
| FW-190 | 106.5 | 6 | 37 | 52 | 38 |
| Me-410 | 25.5 | 0 | 7 | 11 | 9 |
| Ju-87 | 9 | 1 | 6 | 5 | 2 |
| Me-108 | 5 | 0 | 1 | 1 | 2 |
| Ju-88 | 4 | 0 | 0 | 87 | 58 |
| Do-217 | 3 | 0 | 1 | 44 | 73 |
| Me-210 | 3 | 0 | 1 | 3 | 4 |
| FW-44 | 3 | 0 | 1 | 0 | 3 |
| Me-262 | 2 | 0 | 5 | 13 | 27 |
| W-34 | 2 | 0 | 0 | 0 | 1 |
| Ju-188 | 1 | 1 | 0 | 3 | 2 |
| Ar-234 | 1 | 0 | 0 | 0 | 0 |
| Hs-129 | 1 | 0 | 0 | 0 | 0 |
| He-177 | 1 | 0 | 0 | 5 | 1 |
| u/i a/c | 0 | 0 | 0 | 71.5 | 68 |
| He-111 | 0 | 0 | 0 | 70 | 30 |
| Me-110 | 0 | 0 | 0 | 33 | 33 |
| Ju-52 | 0 | 0 | 0 | 8 | 6 |
| He-60 | 0 | 0 | 0 | 6 | 4 |
| FW-200 | 0 | 0 | 0 | 3 | 1 |
| Do-24 | 0 | 0 | 0 | 2 | 0 |
| Me-323 | 0 | 0 | 0 | 2 | 2 |
| B-24 | 0 | 0 | 0 | 2 | 0 |
| He-280 | 0 | 0 | 0 | 2 | 0 |
| Me-163 | 0 | 0 | 0 | 1 | 5 |
| BV-138 | 0 | 0 | 0 | 1 | 0 |
| DFS-230 | 0 | 0 | 0 | 1 | 1 |
| Fi-156 | 0 | 0 | 0 | 1 | 1 |
| Glider | 0 | 0 | 0 | 1 | 0 |
| Trainer | 0 | 0 | 0 | 1 | 0 |
| Ar-196 | 0 | 0 | 0 | 0 | 2 |
| Go-242 | 0 | 0 | 0 | 0 | 1 |

### 355th Fighter Group Squadron Commanders

**354th Ftr Sqn**

| | |
|---|---|
| Maj. Joseph R. Williams | February 3, 1943-November 26, 1943 |
| Maj. Claiborne H. Kinnard, Jr. | November 27, 1943-June 12, 1944 |
| Maj. Henry B. Kucheman, Jr. | June 12, 1944-July 31, 1944 |
| Maj. Bert W. Marshall, Jr. | July 31, 1944-October 23, 1944 |
| Maj. Gordon M. Graham | October 23, 1944-June 17, 1945 |

**357th Ftr Sqn**

| | |
|---|---|
| LtCol. Edward W. Szaniawski | February 2, 1943-May 19, 1944 |
| Maj. Fred L. Ramsdell, Jr. | May 20, 1944-July 26, 1944 |
| LtCol. John L. Elder | July 26, 1944-September 1945 |

**358th Ftr Sqn**

| | |
|---|---|
| LtCol. Raymond B. Myers | February 8, 1943-June 29, 1944 |
| Maj. Charles J. Rosenblatt | June 29, 1944-July 10, 1944 |
| Capt. William J. Hovde | July 10, 1944-August 1, 1944 |
| Maj. Emil L. Sluga | August 2, 1944-September 8, 1944 |
| Capt. Lawrence J. Dissette | September 9, 1944-September 21, 1944 |
| Maj. William J. Hovde | September 22, 1944-September 29, 1944 |
| LtCol. Emil L. Sluga | September 30, 1944-March 21, 1945 |
| Maj. Walter V. Gresham | March 22, 1945-May 8, 1945 |
| LtCol. William J. Hovde | May 8, 1945-October 8, 1945 |

### 355th Fighter Group Aces

| Name | Air | Grd | Total | Sqn |
|---|---|---|---|---|
| Capt. Henry W. Brown | 14.2 | 14.5 | 28.7 | 354th |
| Col. Claiborne H. Kinnard | 8 | 17 | 25* | 354th<br>HdQts |
| LtCol. John L. Elder | 8 | 13 | 21 | 357th |
| Lt. William J. Cullerton | 5 | 15 | 20 | 357th |
| LtCol. Gordon M. Graham | 7 | 9.5 | 16.5 | 354th |
| Capt. James E. Duffy, Jr. | 5.2 | 9 | 14.2 | 354th |
| Lt. Ray S. Morris | 3.5 | 10 | 13.5 | 354th |
| Maj. William J. Hovde | 10.5 | 2 | 12.5 | 358th |
| Capt. Fred R. Haviland | 6 | 6 | 12 | 357th |
| Maj. Norman J. Fortier | 5.83 | 5.5 | 11.33 | 354th |
| Capt. James N. McElroy | 5 | 6 | 11 | 358th |
| Maj. Henry S. Bille | 6 | 4 | 10 | 357th |
| LtCol. Bert W. Marshall, Jr. | 7 | 3 | 10 | 354th<br>HdQts |
| Capt. Joseph E. Mellen | 2 | 8 | 10 | 354th |
| Col. Everett W. Stewart | 7.83 | 1.5 | 9.33** | HdQts |
| Capt. Robert E. Woody | 7 | 2 | 9 | 354th |
| LtCol. Edward W. Szaniawski | 4 | 4.66 | 8.66 | 357th |
| LtCol. Raymond B. Myers | 4.5 | 4 | 8.5 | 358th |
| F/O Harold W. Falvey | 0 | 8 | 8 | 354th |
| Capt. Norman E. Olson | 6 | 2 | 8 | 357th |
| Maj. Charles W. Lenfest | 5.5 | 2 | 7.5 | 354th |
| Maj. Walter V. Gresham, Jr. | 4 | 3 | 7 | 358th |
| Lt. James Jabara | 1.5 | 5.5 | 7*** | 354th |
| Lt. Ben D. Johnston, Jr. | 4 | 3 | 7 | 357th |
| Lt. William D. Martin | 4 | 3 | 7 | 354th |
| Capt. Stanley E. Silva | 1 | 6 | 7 | 354th |
| Maj. John H. Wilson | 3.5 | 3.5 | 7 | 357th |
| Lt. Robert L. Garlich | 0 | 6.5 | 6.5 | 357th |
| Lt. William P. Boulet | 3 | 3 | 6 | 354th |
| Capt. Lawrence J. Dissette | 1 | 5 | 6 | 358th |
| Maj. Henry H. Kirby, Jr. | 1 | 5 | 6 | 357th<br>HdQts |
| Maj. Henry B. Kucheman, Jr. | 4 | 2 | 6 | 354th |
| Lt. Thurman C. Long | 2 | 4 | 6 | 357th |
| Capt. Leslie D. Minchew | 5.5 | 0.5 | 6 | 354th<br>357th<br>HdQts |
| Capt. Brady C. Williamson | 1.7 | 4 | 5.7 | 354th |
| Capt. Walter J. Koraleski | 5.53 | 0 | 5.53 | 354th |
| LtCol. Gerald J. Dix | 4 | 1.5 | 5.5 | HdQts |
| Capt. Robert G. Kurtz | 0.5 | 5 | 5.5 | 354th |
| Lt. Clarence R. Barger | 0.33 | 5 | 5.33 | 354th |
| Lt. Randolph W. Cooper | 0 | 5 | 5 | 357th |
| Lt. Jack M. Fletcher | 0 | 5 | 5 | 354th |
| Lt. Donald Galer | 0 | 5 | 5 | 354th |
| Capt. Charles D. Hauver | 5 | 0 | 5 | 354th |
| Lt. William J. Lynch | 0 | 5 | 5 | 358th |
| Lt. Halbert G. Marsh | 0 | 5 | 5 | 358th |
| Lt. Darwin D. McCasland | 2 | 3 | 5 | 357th |
| Lt. Francis N. McCollom | 0 | 5 | 5 | 358th |
| Lt. Philip M.N. McHugh | 2 | 3 | 5 | 357th |
| Lt. Edward J. Moroney | 2 | 3 | 5 | 357th |
| Capt. Thomas F. Neal, Jr. | 4.5 | 0.5 | 5 | 354th |
| Lt. Emil F. Perry | 2 | 3 | 5 | 354th |
| Lt. Robert O. Peters | 3 | 2 | 5 | 358th |
| Lt. Royce W. Priest | 5 | 0 | 5 | 354th |

* - includes 1 air and 3 ground victories with the 4th Ftr Grp, ETO
** - includes 0.83 air victories with the 352nd Ftr Grp, ETO
*** - includes 1.5 air victories with the 363rd Ftr Grp, ETO

### 355th Fighter Group Scorers

**HdQts**

| | Air | Grd | |
|---|---|---|---|
| W.J. Cummings, Jr. | 0-0-0 | 2-1 | |
| G.J. Dix | 4-1-2 | 1.5-0 | |
| C.H. Kinnard, Jr. | 5-0-1 | 3-0 | plus 354th Ftr Sqn & 1-0-0 air & 3-0 grd w/4th Ftr Grp |
| H.H. Kirby, Jr. | 1-0-1 | 3-3.5 | plus 357th Ftr Sqn |
| B.W. Marshall, Jr. | 0-0-0 | 3-3 | plus 354th Ftr Sqn |
| L.D. Minchew | 0-0-0 | 0-1 | plus 354th & 357th Ftr Sqns |
| E.W. Stewart | 7-1-2 | 1.5-6 | plus 0.83-0-2 air w/4th & 352nd Ftr Grps |

**354th Ftr Sqn**

| | Air | Grd | |
|---|---|---|---|
| J.P. Austin | 0-0-0 | 1-2 | |
| C.R. Barger | 0.33-0-0 | 5-2 | |
| P.W. Barnhart | 0-0-0 | 2.5-4 | |
| P.W. Bauman, Jr. | 0-0-1 | 0-0 | |
| G.D. Beeler | 1-0-0 | 1-0 | |
| S.G. Betounes | 0.5-0-0 | 0-4 | |
| R.T. Bradley | 0-0-0 | 1-0 | |
| W.P. Boulet | 3-0-1 | 3-5 | |
| H.W. Brown | 14.5-0-3 | 14.5-4 | |
| R.C. Brown | 0-0-0 | 3-1 | |
| R.A. Browning | 0-0-0 | 2-2 | |
| R.G. Cross | 2-0-0 | 1.5-1 | |
| H.F. Culp | 0-0-0 | 0.5-0 | |
| C.E. Decklar | 3-0-0 | 0.5-1 | |
| J.E. Duffy, Jr. | 5.2-0-0 | 9-12 | |
| J.C. Ellison | 0-0-0 | 2-0 | |
| H.W. Falvey | 0-0-1 | 8-7 | |
| J.M. Fletcher | 0-0-0 | 5-1 | |
| J.M. Folger | 1-0-1 | 0-0 | |
| N.J. Fortier | 5.83-0-2 | 5.5-3 | |
| W.J. Gadpaille | 0-0-0 | 1-0 | |
| D.V. Galer | 0-0-0 | 5-5 | |
| R.A. Goth | 0-0-0 | 0-1 | |
| C.H. Graham | 1-0-0 | 2-1 | |
| G.M. Graham | 7-1-1 | 9.5-7.5 | |
| C.D. Hauver | 5-0-1 | 0-0 | |
| R.L. Heaton | 0-0-0 | 2-0 | |
| T.R. Hixon, Jr. | 0-0-0 | 1.5-7 | |
| G.C. Hoffman | 1-0-0 | 1-0 | |
| B.G. Houston, Jr. | 0-0-2 | 1-5 | |
| H.M. Husih | 0.5-0-0 | 0-0 | |
| R.E. Hulderman | 0-0-1 | 1.5-0 | |
| J. Jabara | 0-0-0 | 5.5-5 | plus 1.5-1-1 air w/363rd Ftr Grp, ETO |
| N.P. Jackson | 0-0-1 | 1-0 | |
| D.J. Jacobson | 0-0-1 | 2-2 | |
| C.G. Johnston | 0.2-0-0 | 4.5-0 | |
| A.B. Kaplan | 0-0-0 | 1-1 | |
| G.A. Kemper, Jr. | 2-0-0 | 0-0 | |
| C.H. Kinnard, Jr. | 2-0-0 | 11-4 | plus HdQts |
| W.J. Koraleski, Jr. | 5.53-0-0 | 0-2 | |
| A.G. Kozacka | 0-0-0 | 1-2 | |
| H.B. Kucheman, Jr. | 4-0-1 | 2-3 | |
| R.G. Kurtz | 0.5-0-0 | 5-3 | |
| D.B. Langley | 0-0-0 | 4-4.5 | |
| C.W. Lenfest | 5.5-0-1 | 2-4 | |
| H.R. Mann | 0-0-0 | 1.5-0 | |
| B.W. Marshall, Jr. | 7-0-1 | 0-0 | plus HdQts |
| W.D. Martin | 4-0-0 | 3-2 | |
| C.R. McCurry | 0-0-0 | 1-0 | |
| R.M. McLear | 2-0-0 | 2-0 | |
| M.J. McLeod | 0-0-0 | 2-5 | |
| J.E. Mellen | 2-0-0 | 8-0 | |
| L.G. Mendenhall | 0.5-0-1 | 3-3 | |
| N.F. Mills, Jr. | 3-0-0 | 1-0 | |
| A.J. Mincemeyer | 0-0-0 | 1-0 | |
| L.D. Minchew | 0-0-0 | 0.5-0 | plus HdQts & 357th Ftr Sqn |
| J.E. Molnar | 1-0-1 | 3-1 | |
| R.S. Morris | 3.5-0-0 | 10-2 | |
| R.F. Murdoch | 0-1-1 | 0-0 | |
| T.F. Neal, Jr. | 4.5-0-0 | 0.5-1 | |
| G.T. Patterson | 0-0-0 | 1-0 | |
| R.P. Pearson | 0-0-0 | 1-1 | |
| W.B. Peglar | 4-0-0 | 1-0 | RAF pilot |
| E.F. Perry | 2-1-1 | 3-1 | |
| R.W. Priest | 5-0-0 | 0-0 | |
| D.J. Sanders | 0-0-0 | 1-0 | |
| F.A. Sarver | 0-0-0 | 1-1 | |
| A.J. Scheid | 0-0-0 | 1-2 | |
| W.A. Schwab | 1-0-0 | 0-0 | |
| F.W. Schultz | 1-0-2 | 0.5-0 | |
| R.C. Schutt | 0-0-0 | 1-3 | |
| S.E. Silva | 1-0-0 | 6-4 | |
| C.H. Spencer | 1-0-0 | 0-0 | |
| O.N. Stanton | 0-0-0 | 1-0 | |
| A.B. Starr | 0-0-0 | 1-0 | |
| C.H. Sweat | 1-0-0 | 0-0 | |

| | | | |
|---|---|---|---|
| F.K. Taylor | 0.5-0-0 | 0-0 | |
| R.G. Taylor | 1.5-0-0 | 0-0 | |
| C.G. Todd | 0-0-0 | 3-1 | |
| T.P. Todd, Jr. | 0-0-0 | 0-1 | |
| F.W. Trembarth | 0-0-0 | 1-0 | |
| D.C. Tulhoski | 0-0-0 | 1-0 | |
| D.M. Vickery, Jr. | 0-0-0 | 3-3 | |
| R.L. Vincent | 1-0-1 | 0-0 | |
| P.W. Vineyard, Jr. | 1-0-0 | 1-0 | |
| R.J. Walsh | 0-0-0 | 1-0 | |
| R. Westerveld | 0-0-0 | 1-0 | |
| A.S. White | 1-0-1 | 0.5-0 | |
| Ric M. White | 0-0-0 | 1-2 | |
| Rob M. White | 0-0-0 | 3.5-1 | |
| S.C. Williams | 0.5-0-0 | 2-1 | |
| B.C. Williamson | 1.7-0-1 | 4-5 | |
| T.L. Wood | 1-0-0 | 1-0 | |
| R.E. Woody | 7-1-1 | 2-5 | |
| M.L. Woolard | 1-0-0 | 0-0 | |
| G.S. Wright | 2-0-0 | 0-1 | |

**357th Ftr Sqn**

| | | | |
|---|---|---|---|
| B.R. Barab | 1-0-0 | 0-0 | |
| M.E. Beise | 0-0-0 | 1-3 | |
| A.E. Benson | 0-0-1 | 0-2 | |
| R. Bernoske | 1-1-0 | 0-0 | |
| H.S. Bille | 6-1-4 | 4-3 | |
| C.R. Buckles | 0.5-0-0 | 0-0 | |
| W.T. Burnett | 0-0-0 | 0.5-1 | |
| V.A. Burroughs | 3-1-4 | 1-1 | |
| C.J. Butcher | 0-0-1 | 0-2 | |
| R.B. Butler | 0.5-0-0 | 3-3 | |
| J.V. Cavender, Jr. | 0-0-0 | 1-2 | |
| J.M. Chapman | 1-0-0 | 0-3 | |
| C.C. Colson | 1-0-1 | 2-5 | |
| R.W. Cooper | 0-0-1 | 5-0 | |
| W.O. Costello | 0-1-0 | 0-0 | |
| J.A. Cotter | 3-0-0 | 1-1 | |
| W.A. Cox | 0-0-0 | 0-1 | |
| J.L. Crandell | 1-0-0 | 2-3 | |
| W.J. Cullerton | 5-0-0 | 15-2 | |
| R.W. Delhamer | 0-0-0.5 | 3-1 | |
| R.F. DeMers | 2-0-0 | 1.33-3 | |
| R.J. DuFresne | 0-0-2 | 2-0 | |
| W.S. Easterly | 1-0-1 | 1-0 | |
| J.L. Elder, Jr. | 8-0-1 | 13-5 | |
| J.C. Engelbreit | 0.5-0-0 | 2-2 | |
| J.E. Erickson | 0-0-1 | 4-0 | |
| F.L. Eshelman | 1-0-1 | 0-0 | |
| W.F. Forehand | 1-0-0 | 1-2 | |
| G.W. Forker | 0-0-0 | 3-0 | |
| T.J. Foster | 1-0-0 | 0-0 | |
| L.B. Fuller | 2.5-1-1 | 0-0 | |
| R.L. Garlich | 0-0-0 | 6.5-1 | |
| F.E. Gelsone | 0-0-0 | 1.5-2 | |
| A.G. Gilleland | 0-0-0 | 1-2 | |
| H.K. Greenwell | 0-0-0 | 0-1 | |
| W.L. Griswold, Jr. | 0-0-0 | 0.5-2 | |
| J. Guerrant | 0-0-1 | 0-0 | |
| S.S. Hardee | 0-0-0 | 2-3 | |
| F.R. Haviland, Jr. | 6-0-2 | 6-6 | |
| E.M. Hendrickson | 1-1-0 | 0-0 | |
| B.L. Hill | 1-0-0 | 2-5 | |
| H.K. Hillman | 1-0-1 | 1-3 | |
| J.D. Hober | 0-0-0 | 0-1 | |
| V.D. Iglesias | 2-0-0 | 2-0 | |
| W.W. James | 1-0-2 | 1-0 | |
| L.D. Johnson | 0-0-0 | 0-1 | |
| B.D. Johnston | 4-0-3 | 3-3 | |
| J.O. Juntilla | 0-0-0 | 4-4 | |
| R.B. Kaminski | 1-0-0 | 1-4 | |
| F.W. Kelley | 2-0-1 | 0-0 | |
| J.F. Kerch | 0-1-0 | 0.33-2 | |
| R.C. Keuhl | 0-0-0 | 0.5-2 | |
| M.A. King | 0-0-1 | 2-1 | |
| R.J. Kirk | 0-0-0 | 1-1 | |
| H.H. Kirby, Jr. | 0-0-1 | 2-0 | plus HdQts |
| H.I. Knight | 0-0-0 | 3-2.5 | |
| W.T. Kubetin | 0-0-0 | 1-0 | |
| J.E. Lake | 0-0-0 | 1-2 | |
| C.W. Lamer | 3-0-0 | 0-0 | |
| C.M. Lee | 0-1-0 | 0-4 | |
| T.C. Long | 2-0-0 | 4-3 | |
| E.P. Ludeke | 1-0-0 | 0-2 | |
| W.S. Lyons | 2-0-1 | 0-0 | |
| W.E. MacFarlane | 1.5-0-1 | 2-5 | |
| J.H. Max | 2-0-0 | 0.5-2 | |
| D.D. McCasland | 2-1-0 | 3-1 | |
| P.M.N. McHugh | 2-0-1 | 3-3 | |
| E.P. McNeff | 1.5-0-1 | 1-0 | |
| K.M. Michels | 1-0-0 | 0-0 | |
| K.J. Miller | 0-0-0 | 2-0 | |
| L.D. Minchew | 5.5-0-4 | 0-0 | plus HdQts & 354th Ftr Sqn |
| R.F. Misner | 0-0-0 | 4.5-6 | |
| H.L. Monahan | 2-0-0 | 1-1 | |
| E.J. Moroney | 2-0-0 | 2-3 | |
| J.E. Nelson | 0-0-0 | 0-1 | |
| R.L. Norman | 1-0-1 | 0.67-2 | |
| N.E. Olson | 6-0-2 | 2-1 | |
| R.B. Owens | 0-0-0 | 1-0 | |
| H.F. Packard | 0-0-0 | 2-4 | |
| R.J. Patelunas | 0-0-0 | 1-0 | |
| F.L. Ramsdell, Jr. | 1-0-0 | 0-0 | |
| I. Reedy | 0.5-0-0 | 1-2 | |
| W.L. Reiff | 0-0-0 | 0-1 | |
| E.H. Riffle | 1-0.0.5 | 2-0 | |
| F.H. Rodgers | 0-0-0 | 0-1 | |
| C.J. Salinsky | 1-0-0 | 3-4 | |
| G.C. Schmidt | 0-0-0 | 1-1 | |
| D.E. Schoenfeldt | 0-0-1 | 2-4 | |
| W.A. Shade | 0-0-0 | 1.5-0 | |
| H.W. Spencer | 2-0-0 | 2-0 | |
| R.W. Strachan | 0-0-0 | 1-0 | |
| J.D. Sturm | 1-0-0 | 2.5-7 | |
| E.W. Szaniawski | 4-1-2 | 3.67-4 | |
| D.P. Watkins | 0-0-0 | 3-1 | |
| J.J. Weidemann | 0-0-0 | 2-5 | |
| E.H. Whitney | 0-0-0 | 1.5-0 | |
| H.O. Wilkes | 1-0-0 | 0-0 | |
| B.G. Williams | 0-0-0 | 2-0 | |
| J.H. Wilson | 3.5-0-2 | 3.5-2 | |

**358th Ftr Sqn**

| | | | |
|---|---|---|---|
| A.K. Alexander | 1.5-0-0 | 0-0 | |
| R.R. Allen | 0-0-0 | 1-0 | |
| R.G. Baker | 2-0-1 | 0-0 | |
| W.W. Beaty | 1-0-0 | 1-0 | |
| J.M. Beckman | 1-0-2 | 3-6 | |
| C.W. Blair, Jr. | 1-0-1 | 0-0 | |
| D.C. Blaylock | 0-0-0 | 1-3 | |
| C.J. Brien, Jr. | 0.5-0-0 | 0-0 | |
| R.H. Brown | 1-0-0 | 0-0 | |
| R.L. Coleman | 0-0-1 | 0-0 | |
| V.W. Covault | 0-1-0 | 1-1 | |
| A.R. Curran | 0-0-0 | 3-0 | |
| J.J. DeGeorge, Jr. | 1-0-2.25 | 0-0 | |
| J.B. Dickson | 3-1-0 | 0-0 | |
| R.M. Dillon | 1-0-0 | 1-1 | |
| L.J. Dissette | 1-0-0 | 5-5 | |
| D.A. Donovan | 1.5-0-0 | 0-0 | |
| W.H. Douglas | 0-0-0 | 1-0 | |
| L.M. Dudley, Jr. | 3-0-0 | 1-0 | |
| A.G. Duppstadt | 0-0-0 | 2-1 | |
| C.F. Ekstrom | 1-0-1 | 0-0 | |
| E.W. Fees | 0-0-0 | 1.5-1 | |
| R.V. Finnessey | 0-0-1 | 0.5-0 | |
| L.S. Frost | 1-0-1 | 0-2 | RAF pilot |
| R.J. Fussell | 2.5-0-0 | 1-2 | |
| V.E. Gore | 0-0-0 | 2.5-2 | |
| W.V. Gresham, Jr. | 4-1-2 | 3-3 | |
| J.C. Harrington | 0.5-0-0 | 2-6 | |
| H.J. Hoffman | 1-0-0.25 | 2-4 | |
| W.J. Hovde | 10.5-0-1 | 2-1 | |
| J.C. Hull | 0-0-1 | 0-0 | |
| P.H. Kenney | 2-0-3 | 1-0 | |
| H.P. Knutty | 0.5-0-0 | 2-0 | |
| M. Lacazette | 0-0-0 | 0.5-0 | |
| J.H. Lanius | 0-0-0 | 1-0 | |
| L.R. Leaf, Jr. | 0-0-0 | 0.5-0 | |
| W.B. Lister | 0-0-0 | 0.5-0 | |
| W.J. Lynch | 0-0-0 | 5-1 | |
| J.S. MacConkey | 0-0-0 | 3-5 | |
| H.H. Macurdy | 2-1-0 | 0-0 | |
| J.J. Maisch, Jr. | 2-0-0 | 1-0 | |
| H.G. Marsh | 0-0-0 | 5-2 | |
| D.M. Martyn | 1.5-0-1 | 0-0 | |
| F.R. Masters | 3-0-0 | 0-0 | |
| F.N. McCollom | 0-0-0 | 5-1 | |
| J.H. McConnell | 0-0-0.25 | 0-0 | |
| J.N. McElroy | 5-0-6 | 6-1 | |
| W.J. McGinty | 1-0-0 | 1-2 | |
| R.I. McNally | 0-0-0 | 2-0 | |
| T.O. Meteyer | 1-0-0 | 0-0 | |
| R.L. Michelena | 1-0-1 | 1-1 | |
| K.E. Mikalauskas | 1-0-0 | 0-0 | |
| R.B. Myers | 4.5-0-2 | 4-6 | |
| E.C. Nelson, Jr. | 0-0-0 | 1-1 | |
| R.J. Nicodemus | 0-0-0 | 1-0 | |
| H.W. Pardee, Jr. | 0-0-0 | 1-4 | |
| C.C. Patrinely | 0-0-0 | 2-0 | |

| | | |
|---|---|---|
| R.F. Parks | 0-0-1 | 4-1 |
| R.O. Peters | 3-0-0 | 2-0 |
| N.E. Peterson | 1-0-1 | 2-3 |
| C.E. Plemons | 0-0-0 | 2-1 |
| C.H. Rankin | 0-0-1 | 0-0 |
| J.E. Reed | 1-0-2 | 2-0 |
| A.T. Robinson | 1-1-2 | 0-2 |
| C.J. Rosenblatt | 1-0-0 | 1-4 |
| L.J. Rouleau, Jr. | 0-0-0 | 1-2 |
| R.C. Rowbotham | 0-0-0 | 3-2 |
| A.R. Santos | 2-0-0 | 0-0 |
| W.J. Schlecht | 0-0-0 | 1.5-0 |
| G.A. Seely | 0-1-0 | 2-2 |
| E.L. Sluga | 3.5-0-2 | 0-0 |
| K.L. Snook | 0.5-0-0 | 0-0 |
| R.M. Thompson | 2-1-0 | 0-0 |
| W.W. Tolby, Jr. | 1-0-0 | 0-1 |
| J.F. Tulloch, Jr. | 0-0-0 | 4-0 |
| J.H. Upchurch | 0-0-0.25 | 0-0 |
| J.J. Vigna | 0-0-1 | 0-0 |
| R.N. Watkins | 0-0-1 | 0-0 |
| M.E. Webb | 0-0-1 | 0-0 |
| W. Winn, Jr. | 0-0-0 | 0-1 |
| J.J. Woertz | 1-0-0 | 0-0 |
| T.W. Worth | 0-0-0 | 0-1 |
| N.B. Woodson | 0-0-1 | 0-0 |

### 355th Fighter Group Scoring

**October 4, 1943**

| | | | |
|---|---|---|---|
| 358th: | Capt. C.F. Ekstrom | Me-109 dest(air) | Liege-Maastricht |

**October 20, 1943**

| | | | |
|---|---|---|---|
| 358th: | Maj. R.B. Myers | FW-190 dest(air) | Ath |
| | | FW-190 dam(air) | Ath |

**November 5, 1943**

| | | | |
|---|---|---|---|
| 354th: | Lt. C.H. Sweat | FW-190 dest(air) | NW Gelsenkirchen |
| | Lt. P.W. Bauman | Me-109 dam(air) | NW Gelsenkirchen |
| | Lt. R.L. Vincent | Me-109 dam(air) | NW Gelsenkirchen |
| 357th: | Lt. E.L. Sluga | Me-210 dest(air) | Alben |
| | Lt. F.W. Kelley | Me-109 dam(air) | Uden |
| | Lt. C.H. Rankin | Me-210 dam(air) | Alben |

**November 7, 1943**

| | | | |
|---|---|---|---|
| 357th: | Capt. N.E. Olson | Me-210 dest(air) | Amiens |

**November 13, 1943**

| | | | |
|---|---|---|---|
| 354th: | Lt. T.F. Neal | Me-109 dest(air) | W/Bremen |
| | Lt. R.L. Vincent | Me-109 dest(air) | W/Meppen |
| 357th: | Capt. N.E. Olson | Me-109 dest(air) | Zwolle |

**November 29, 1943**

| | | | |
|---|---|---|---|
| 358th: | Lt. J.J. Woertz | Me-109 dest(air) | W/Bremen |
| | Lt. J.C. Hull | Me-109 dam(air) | Bremen |

**December 1, 1943**

| | | | |
|---|---|---|---|
| 357th: | Lt. B.D. Johnston | Me-109 dest(air) | All 357th claims |
| | | Me-109 dam(air) | are W/Cologne |
| | Lt. R. Bernoske | Me-109 prob(air) | |
| | Capt. N.E. Olson | Me-109 dam(air) | |
| | Lt. W.S. Easterly | Me-109 dam(air) | |
| 358th: | Lt. H.H. Macurdy | Me-109 prob(air) | NW Aachen |
| | Capt. C.F. Ekstrom | Me-109 dam(air) | Duren |

**December 30, 1943**

| | | | |
|---|---|---|---|
| 354th: | Lt. R.F. Murdoch | Me-109 prob(air) | Soissons |
| | | Me-109 dam(air) | Soissons |

**January 21, 1944**

| | | | |
|---|---|---|---|
| 354th: | Lt. J.E. Duffy | FW-190 dest(air) | NW Dourdan |
| 357th: | Lt. A.E. Benson | FW-190 dam(air) | NW Dourdan |

**January 29, 1944**

| | | | |
|---|---|---|---|
| 357th: | Capt. J.H. Wilson | FW-190 dest(air) | W/Frankfurt |
| | Lt. R.J. Dufresne | (2)FW-190 dam(air) | W/Frankfurt |
| 358th: | Lt. H.H. Macurdy | FW-190 dest(air) | Liege |
| | | Me-109 dest(air) | Coblenz |

**February 5, 1944**

| | | | |
|---|---|---|---|
| 357th: | Capt. N.E. Olson | (2)Me-109 dest(air) | W/Vendome |
| 358th: | Lt. J.J. DeGeorge | (.25)Me-109 dam(air) | S/Tours |
| | Lt. H.J. Hoffman | (.25)Me-109 dam(air) | S/Tours |
| | Lt. J.H. McConnell | (.25)Me-109 dam(air) | S/Tours |
| | Lt. J. Upchurch | (.25)Me-109 dam(air) | S/Tours |

**February 11, 1944**

| | | | |
|---|---|---|---|
| 357th: | Maj. E.W. Szaniawski | (2)Me-109 dest(air) | S/Koln |
| | Lt. V.A. Burroughs | FW-190 dest(air) | S/Koln |
| | | Me-109 dam(air) | S/Koln |

**February 20, 1944**

| | | | |
|---|---|---|---|
| 354th: | Lt. L.G. Mendenhall | Me-109 dam(air) | NE Bonn |
| 357th: | Capt. N.E. Olson | Me-109 dest(air) | Siegen |
| | Lt. B.D. Johnston | Me-109 dest(air) | Siegen |
| 358th: | Lt. J.B. Dickson | Me-109 dest(air) | Marienburg |

**February 21, 1944**

| | | | |
|---|---|---|---|
| 357th: | Capt. J.L. Elder | FW-190 dest(air) | All claims are |
| | Capt. N.E. Olson | FW-190 dest(air) | Dummer Lake |
| | | FW-190 dam(air) | |
| | Lt. V.A. Burroughs | FW-190 dam(air) | |
| | Lt. C.J. Butcher | FW-190 dam(air) | |
| | Lt. B.D. Johnston | FW-190 dam(air) | |
| | Lt. R.L. Norman | FW-190 dam(air) | |

**February 22, 1944**

| | | | |
|---|---|---|---|
| 358th: | Lt. W.J. Hovde | FW-190 dest(air) | SE Munster |
| | Lt. P.H. Kenney | FW-190 dest(air) | SE Munster |

**March 2, 1944**

| | | | |
|---|---|---|---|
| 358th: | Lt. C.W. Blair | Me-109 dest(air) | NE Liege |
| | Lt. W.V. Gresham | FW-190 dest(air) | SE Charleroi |
| | Lt. H.J. Hoffman | Me-109 dest(air) | NE Liege |
| | Maj. R.B. Myers | (.5)Me-109 dest(air) | NE Liege |
| | F/O W.J. McGinty | (.5)Me-109 dest(air) | NE Liege |
| | F/O L.M. Dudley | (.5)FW-190 dest(air) | SE Charleroi |
| | Lt. R.J. Fussell | (.5)FW-190 dest(air) | SE Charleroi |

**March 6, 1944**

| | | | |
|---|---|---|---|
| HdQts: | LtCol. E.W. Stewart | Me-109 dest(air) | NW Hanover |
| 354th: | Capt. W.J. Koraleski | (2.33)Me-109 dest(air) | Dummer Lake |
| | F/O C.R. Barger | (.33)Me-109 dest(air) | Dummer Lake |
| | Lt. N.J. Fortier | (.33)Me-109 dest(air) | Dummer Lake |
| 357th: | Lt. W.S. Easterly | FW-190 dest(air) | E/Dummer Lake |
| | Lt. B.L. Hill | FW-190 dest(air) | W/Lingen |
| | Lt. D.D. McCasland | Me-109 dest(air) | E/Dummer Lake |
| 358th: | Lt. J.B. Dickson | Me-109 dest(air) | N/Enschede |

**March 8, 1944**

| | | | |
|---|---|---|---|
| HdQts: | Maj. G.J. Dix | FW-190 dest(air) | NE Brunswick |
| 354th: | Lt. H.W. Brown | (3.5)Ju-88 dest(grd) | Hesepe |
| | | Me-110 dest(grd) | Hesepe |
| | | (2)Ju-88 dam(grd) | Hesepe |
| | F/O C.R. Barger | (3)Ju-88 dest(grd) | Hesepe |
| | Capt. C.G. Johnston | (.5)Ju-88 dest(grd) | Hesepe |
| 357th: | Lt. R.L. Norman | FW-190 dest(air) | Dummer Lake |

NOTE: HdQts & 354th flew P-47's while 357th flew P-51's. From March 16 on, all claims will be in P-51's.

**March 16, 1944**

| | | | |
|---|---|---|---|
| HdQts: | LtCol. E.W. Stewart | Me-109 dest(air) | Augsburg-Luneville |
| | | Me-109 prob(air) | Augsburg-Luneville |
| | | Me-109 dam(air) | Augsburg-Luneville |
| 354th: | Lt. T.F. Neal | (2.5)Me-109 dest(air) | NW Ulm |
| | Lt. C.W. Lenfest | (1.5)Me-109 dest(air) | NW Ulm |
| | Capt. W.J. Koraleski | Me-109 dest(air) | Ulm |
| | Lt. J.E. Duffy | Me-109 dest(air) | W/Ulm |
| | Lt. R.S. Morris | Me-109 dest(air) | NW Ulm |
| 357th: | Lt. V.A. Burroughs | Me-109 dest(air) | S/Reutlingen |
| | Lt. C.C. Colson | Me-109 dest(air) | S/Reutlingen |
| | Lt. H.S. Bille | Me-109 dam(air) | S/Reutlingen |
| | Lt. H.H. Kirby | Me-109 dam(air) | W/Augsburg |
| | Lt. W.E. MacFarlane | Me-109 dam(air) | W/Augsburg |
| | Lt. D.E. Schoenfeldt | Me-109 dam(air) | S/Reutlingen |
| 358th: | Maj. C.J. Rosenblatt | Me-109 dest(air) | NW Augsburg |
| | Lt. J.J. DeGeorge | Me-109 dest(air) | W/Augsburg |
| | | (2)Me-109 dam(air) | W/Augsburg |
| | Lt. J.B. Dickson | Me-109 dest(air) | W/Augsburg |
| | | Me-109 prob(air) | W/Augsburg |
| | Lt. W.V. Gresham | Me-109 dest(air) | W/Augsburg |
| | Lt. P.H. Kenney | Me-109 dest(air) | W/Augsburg |
| | | (3)Me-109 dam(air) | W/Augsburg |
| | Lt. J.E. Reed | (2)Me-109 dam(air) | W/Augsburg |

**March 18, 1944**

| | | | |
|---|---|---|---|
| HdQts: | LtCol. E.W. Stewart | Me-109 dest(air) | SW Munich |
| 354th: | Lt. H.W. Brown | Me-109 dest(air) | Nancy |
| | | Me-110 dam(air) | W/Munich |
| | Lt. T.F. Neal | Me-109 dest(air) | NE Munich |
| | Lt. C.W. Lenfest | (.5)Me-109 dest(air) | NE Munich |
| | | Me-109 dam(air) | NE Munich |
| | Lt. L.G. Mendenhall | (.5)Me-109 dest(air) | NE Munich |
| 358th: | Lt. W.J. Hovde | (2)FW-190 dest(air) | Gunzburg-Augsburg |
| | | FW-190 dam(air) | Gunzburg-Augsburg |

**March 20, 1944**

| | | | |
|---|---|---|---|
| 354th: | Lt. H.W. Brown | FW-190 dam(air) | Coxyde |
| | Lt. B.C. Williamson | FW-190 dam(air) | Coxyde |

**March 26, 1944**

| | | | |
|---|---|---|---|
| 354th: | Capt. A.B. Starr | u/i a/c dest(grd) | Chateaudun |
| | | (flying a P-47 w/"Bill's Buzz Boys") | |

**March 27, 1944**

| | | | |
|---|---|---|---|
| 357th: | Capt. J.H. Wilson | (.5)Me-109 dest(air) | All claims are |
| | Lt. I. Reedy | (.5)Me-109 dest(air) | at Biscarosse A/F |
| | Lt. C.J. Butcher | (2)Ju-88 dam(grd) | |
| | Capt. J.L. Elder | Ju-88 dam(grd) | |
| | Lt. C.C. Colson | Ju-88 dam(grd) | |
| | Lt. C.M. Lee | Ju-88 dam(grd) | |

**March 28, 1944**

| | | | |
|---|---|---|---|
| HdQts: | LtCol. G.J. Dix | (.5)Ju-88 dest(grd)* | Unless notes, |
| 354th: | Capt. C.G. Johnston | Me-110 dest(grd) | all claims are |
| | Lt. R.S. Morris | He-111 dest(grd) | at Dijon |
| | Lt. T.F. Neal | (.5)He-111 dest(grd)** | |
| | Lt. H.F. Culp | (.5)Ju-88 dest(grd)* | |
| | Lt. B.C. Williamson | u/i a/c dam(grd) | |
| 357th: | Maj. E.W. Szaniawski | Me-110 dest(grd) | |
| | | Me-410 dest(grd) | |
| | | Ju-88 dest(grd) | |
| | | (3)Ju-88 dam(grd) | |
| | | Me-210 dam(grd) | |
| | Lt. R.B. Butler | (2)Ju-88 dest(grd) | |
| | | (2)Ju-88 dam(grd) | |
| | | Go-242 dam(grd) | |
| | Lt. B.L. Hill | He-111 dest(grd) | |
| | | Do-217 dest(grd) | |
| | | (2)Ju-88 dam(grd) | |
| | | He-111 dam(grd) | |
| | | Me-110 dam(grd) | |
| | | u/i a/c dam(grd) | |
| | Lt. B.D. Johnston | (2)Me-210 dest(grd) | |
| | | Ju-88 dest(grd) | |
| | | Me-210 dam(grd) | |
| | | Me-109 dam(grd) | |
| | | Ju-88 dam(grd) | |
| | F/O J.D. Sturm | He-111 dest(grd) | |
| | | Ju-88 dest(grd) | |
| | | (2)Ju-88 dam(grd) | |
| | | He-111 dam(grd) | |
| | Capt. N.E. Olson | He-111 dest(grd) | |
| | | FW-190 dam(grd) | |
| | Lt. R.F. DeMers | He-111 dest(grd) | |
| | | (2)He-111 dam(grd) | |
| | | Ju-88 dam(grd) | |
| | Lt. V.A. Burroughs | Fi-156 dest(grd) | |
| | | Ju-88 dam(grd) | |
| | Lt. H.K. Hillman | Ju-88 dest(grd) | |
| | | Me-109 dam(grd) | |
| | | Me-210 dam(grd) | |
| | | Ju-88 dam(grd) | |
| | Lt. H.F. Packard | Ju-88 dest(grd) | |
| | | (3)Ju-88 dam(grd) | |
| | Lt. D.E. Schoenfeldt | Ju-88 dest(grd) | |
| | | (2)Ju-88 dam(grd) | |
| | Lt. L.D. Minchew | (.5)He-111 dest(grd)** | |
| | Lt. R.B. Kaminski | Ju-88 dam(grd) | |
| 358th: | Lt. W.J. Hovde | He-111 dam(grd) | Marigny |

**March 29, 1944**

| | | | |
|---|---|---|---|
| HdQts: | LtCol. E.W. Stewart | (2)Me-108 dest(air) | E/Goslar A/F |
| | | FW-190 dam(air) | S/Brunswick |
| | | (2)Me-108 dam(grd) | Goslar A/F |
| 354th: | Maj. C.H. Kinnard | FW-190 dest(air) | SW Brunswick |
| | Capt. W.J. Koraleski | FW-190 dest(air) | Brunswick |
| | Lt. H.W. Brown | FW-190 dest(air) | Brunswick |
| | Lt. C.W. Lenfest | Me-108 dest(air) | Goslar A/F |
| | | Trainer dest(grd) | Goslar A/F |
| | Lt. N.J. Fortier | u/i a/c dest(grd) | Dummer Lake |
| | | (flying a P-47 w/"Bill's Buzz Boys") | |
| | Lt. R.A. Browning | (.5)u/i a/c dam(grd)* | Brunswick |
| | | (.5)u/i a/c dam(grd)* | Brunswick |
| 357th: | Lt. B.D. Johnston | (2)FW-190 dest(air) | Brunswick |
| | | FW-190 dam(air) | Brunswick |
| | Capt. J.L. Elder | FW-190 dest(air) | NE Brunswick |
| | | FW-190 dam(air) | NE Brunswick |
| | Capt. F.L. Ramsdell | FW-190 dest(air) | NE Brunswick |
| | Lt. V.A. Burroughs | FW-190 dest(air) | NE Brunswick |
| | | FW-190 prob(air) | NE Brunswick |
| | | (2)FW-190 dam(air) | NE Brunswick |
| | Lt. D.D. McCasland | FW-190 dest(air) | Brunswick |
| | | FW-190 prob(air) | Brunswick |
| | Lt. R.B. Kaminski | FW-190 dest(air) | NE Brunswick |
| | | (2)u/i a/c dam(grd) | NE Brunswick |
| | | (.5)u/i a/c dam(grd)* | NE Brunswick |
| | | (.5)u/i a/c dam(grd)* | NE Brunswick |
| | Lt. C.M. Lee | FW-190 prob(air) | NE Brunswick |
| | Lt. H.K. Hillman | FW-190 dam(air) | NE Brunswick |

**April 5, 1944**

| | | | |
|---|---|---|---|
| HdQts: | Col. W.J. Cummings | (2)Do-217 dest(grd) | Munich |
| | | Do-217 dam(grd) | Munich |
| 354th: | Maj. C.H. Kinnard | W-34 dest(air) | All 354th claims |
| | | (2)Do-217 dest(grd) | are at Landsberg |
| | | Me-110 dest(grd) | |
| | | (2)Do-217 dam(grd) | |
| | Lt. B.C. Williamson | W-34 dest(air) | |
| | | (.5)FW-44 dest(air)** | |
| | | (.2)Do-217 dest(air) | |
| | | Do-217 dam(grd) | |
| | | FW-44 dam(grd) | |
| | Capt. W.J. Koraleski | (.5)Me-109 dest(air) | |
| | | (.5)FW-44 dest(air)* | |
| | | (.2)Do-217 dest(air) | |
| | | Do-217 dam(grd) | |
| | | Me-110 dam(grd) | |
| | Lt. R.E. Woody | (.5)Me-109 dest(air) | |
| | | (.5)FW-44 dest(air)* | |
| | | (.5)FW-44 dest(air)** | |
| | | Do-217 dam(grd) | |
| | | Me-110 dam(grd) | |
| | Lt. H.W. Brown | (.5)Me-108 dest(air) | |
| | | (.2)Do-217 dest(air) | |
| | Lt. C.W. Lenfest | (.5)Me-108 dest(air) | |
| | | (4)Do-217 dam(grd) | |
| | Lt. J.E. Duffy | (.2)Do-217 dest(air) | |
| | | (5)Do-217 dam(grd) | |
| | | FW-44 dam(grd) | |
| | Capt. C.G. Johnston | (.2)Do-217 dest(air) | |
| | Lt. B.G. Houston | Me-108 dam(air) | |
| | | (4)Do-217 dam(grd) | |
| | | Me-110 dam(grd) | |
| | Lt. L.G. Mendenhall | (3)Ju-88 dest(grd) | |
| | | (3)Ju-88 dam(grd) | |
| | Lt. W.P. Boulet | FW-200 dest(grd) | |
| | | Do-217 dest(grd) | |
| | | (2)Do-217 dam(grd) | |
| | Lt. R.S. Morris | Me-110 dest(grd) | |
| | | He-111 dest(grd) | |
| | | He-111 dam(grd) | |
| | Lt. R.G. Kurtz | Do-217 dest(grd) | |
| | | (2)Do-217 dam(grd) | |
| 357th: | Lt. R.B. Butler | Ju-88 dest(grd) | Ottingen |
| | Lt. R.B. Kaminski | Me-110 dest(grd) | Deiningen |
| | Lt. H.L. Packard | Me-110 dest(grd) | Deiningen |
| | | Me-110 dam(grd) | Deiningen |
| | Lt. I. Reedy | Ju-88 dest(grd) | Ottingen |
| | | Me-109 dam(grd) | Ottingen |
| | | Ju-88 dam(grd) | Ottingen |
| | Lt. J.D. Sturm | FW-200 dam(grd) | Ottingen |
| | | Me-110 dam(grd) | Ottingen |
| | | Ju-88 dam(grd) | Ottingen |
| | | Ju-52 dam(grd) | Ottingen |
| | Lt. C.M. Lee | (3)Me-110 dam(grd) | Ottingen |
| | Lt. J.F. Kerch | (2)Me-110 dam(grd) | Ottingen |
| | Lt. A.E. Benson | (2)Do-217 dam(grd) | Landsberg |
| 358th: | F/O L.M. Dudley | FW-44 dest(air) | Oberpfaffenhofen |
| | | Me-110 dest(grd) | Landsberg |
| | F/O J.M. Beckman | Me-109 dam(air) | Landsberg |
| | | Do-217 dest(grd) | Landsberg |
| | | Ju-88 dest(grd) | Landsberg |
| | | (5)Do-217 dam(grd) | Landsberg |
| | Maj. R.B. Myers | (2)Do-217 dest(grd) | Munich |
| | | DFS-230 dest(grd) | Munich |
| | | (6)Do-217 dam(grd) | Munich |
| | Lt. L.J. Dissette | (2)Me-110 dest(grd) | Munich |
| | | Me-110 dam(grd) | Landsberg |
| | | DFS-230 dam(grd) | Landsberg |
| | Lt. W.V. Gresham | (2)He-111 dest(grd) | Munich |
| | Lt. J.C. Harrington | (2)Me-110 dest(grd) | Munich |
| | | (6)Me-110 dam(grd) | Munich |
| | Lt. H.J. Hoffman | Me-110 dest(grd) | Munich |
| | | u/i a/c dest(grd) | Munich |
| | | (2)Do-217 dam(grd) | Munich |
| | | (2)u/i a/c dam(grd) | Munich |
| | F/O J.S. MacConkey | (2)Do-217 dest(grd) | Munich |
| | | (3)Do-217 dam(grd) | Munich |
| | | Me-110 dam(grd) | Munich |
| | Lt. J.E. Reed | Me-109 dest(grd) | Munich |
| | | Do-217 dest(grd) | Munich |
| | Maj. C.J. Rosenblatt | Do-217 dest(grd) | Landsberg |
| | | (4)Do-217 dam(grd) | Landsberg |
| | Lt. J.N. McElroy | Me-110 dest(grd) | Munich |
| | | Me-110 dam(grd) | Munich |
| | Lt. N.E. Peterson | Ju-88 dest(grd) | Munich |
| | | (3)Ju-88 dam(grd) | Munich |
| | Lt. A.T. Robinson | (2)Do-217 dam(grd) | E/Schwerin |

**April 8, 1944**

| | | | |
|---|---|---|---|
| 354th: | Capt. R.G. Kurtz | (.5)Me-109 dest(air) | Sachau A/F |
| | Lt. H.W. Brown | (.5)Me-109 dest(air) | Sachau A/F |
| | Lt. B.G. Houston | Me-109 dam(air) | Brunswick |
| 357th: | Maj. E.W. Szaniawski | Me-109 dest(air) | Meppen |
| | | Me-109 dam(air) | Meppen |
| | Lt. L.D. Minchew | Me-109 dest(air) | W/Brunswick |
| | Lt. E.P. McNeff | Me-109 dam(air) | Gifhorn |
| | Capt. J.L. Elder | (2)Ju-88 dest(grd) | Gifhorn |
| | Lt. H.H. Kirby | Do-217 dest(grd) | Gifhorn |
| | | Ju-88 dest(grd) | Gifhorn |
| | Capt. N.E. Olson | Ju-88 dest(grd) | Gifhorn |
| | Capt. J.H. Wilson | Me-210 dest(grd) | Gifhorn |
| | Lt. D.D. McCasland | Ju-88 dest(grd) | Gifhorn |
| 358th: | Capt. E.L. Sluga | (1.5)Me-109 dest(air) | E/Brunswick |
| | Capt. W.J. Hovde | Me-109 dest(air) | E/Brunswick |
| | Lt. J.C. Harrington | (.5)Me-109 dest(air) | E/Brunswick |

**April 10, 1944**

| | | | |
|---|---|---|---|
| 354th: | Capt. R.G. Kurtz | Do-217 dest(grd) | All claims are |
| | | FW-190 dest(grd) | at Bourges A/F |
| | Maj. C.H. Kinnard | Ju-88 dest(grd) | |
| | | u/i a/c dam(grd) | |
| | Capt. R.E. Woody | He-111 dest(grd) | |
| | | He-111 dam(grd) | |
| | Lt. J.P. Austin | Me-109 dest(grd) | |
| | | u/i a/c dam(grd) | |
| | Lt. J.E. Duffy | He-111 dest(grd) | |
| | | W-34 dam(grd) | |
| | Lt. R.C. Schutt | (2)Do-217 dam(grd) | |
| | | u/i a/c dam(grd) | |
| | Lt. W.P. Boulet | He-111 dam(grd) | |
| | Lt. T.F. Neal | u/i a/c dam(grd) | |

**April 11, 1944**

| | | | |
|---|---|---|---|
| HdQts: | LtCol. E.W. Stewart | Me-410 dest(air) | NW Pyritz |
| | | Ju-188 dest(air) | Schau |
| | | (2)Ar-196 dam(grd) | Sorau |
| 354th: | Lt. H.W. Brown | FW-190 dest(air) | E/Berlin |
| | | Ju-52 dest(grd) | Strasbourg |
| | | Ju-88 dam(grd) | Strasbourg |
| | Capt. R.E. Woody | Ju-188 prob(air) | S/Madu Lake |
| | | Ju-87 dam(grd) | S/Madu Lake |
| | Capt. C.G. Johnston | (2)Ju-88 dest(grd) | Strasbourg |
| | | He-111 dest(grd) | Strasbourg |
| | Lt. D.J. Jacobson | (2)Ju-88 dest(grd) | Strasbourg |
| | | FW-190 dam(grd) | Strasbourg |
| | | Ju-88 dam(grd) | Strasbourg |
| | Lt. R.C. Brown | Ju-52 dest(grd) | Strasbourg |
| | | He-111 dam(grd) | Strasbourg |
| | Lt. R.C. Schutt | Me-108 dest(grd) | S/Madu Lake |
| | Capt. R.G. Kurtz | Ju-88 dam(grd) | Madu Lake |
| | Lt. J.P. Austin | u/i a/c dam(grd) | Pyritz |
| | Lt. W.P. Boulet | FW-44 dam(grd) | S/Madu Lake |
| 357th: | Lt. D.D. McCasland | (2)Ju-88 dest(grd) | Wensdorf |
| | | FW-190 dam(grd) | Wensdorf |
| | Capt. W.S. Easterly | Ju-88 dest(grd) | Wensdorf |
| | Lt. D.E. Schoenfeldt | Ju-88 dest(grd) | Wensdorf |
| | | (2)Ju-88 dam(grd) | Wensdorf |
| 358th: | Maj. R.B. Myers | Me-410 dest(air) | W/Berlin |
| | Capt. E.L. Sluga | Me-109 dest(air) | NE Berlin |
| | | Me-109 dam(air) | NE Berlin |
| | Lt. J.E. Reed | Me-109 dest(air) | N/Berlin |
| | F/O L.M. Dudley | (1.25)Me-410 dest(air) | Remaining claims |
| | | (.25)Ju-88 dest(air) | are all NE Berlin |
| | Lt. R.J. Fussell | (.5)Me-410 dest(air) | |
| | | (.25)Me-410 dest(air) | |
| | | (.25)Ju-88 dest(air) | |
| | Lt. W.V. Gresham | (.5)Me-410 dest(air) | |
| | | (.25)Me-410 dest(air) | |
| | | (.25)Ju-88 dest(air) | |
| | Lt. D.M. Martyn | (.25)Me-410 dest(air) | |
| | | (.25)Ju-88 dest(air) | |

**April 13, 1944**

| | | | |
|---|---|---|---|
| 354th: | Maj. C.H. Kinnard | (3)Ju-88 dest(grd) | All 354th claims |
| | | Do-217 dest(grd) | are at |
| | | Do-217 dam(grd) | Oberpfaffenhofen |
| | F/O C.R. Barger | Do-217 dest(grd) | |
| | | Ju-88 dest(grd) | |
| | | Do-217 dam(grd) | |
| | | Ju-88 dam(grd) | |
| | Lt. H.W. Brown | (2)Ju-88 dest(grd) | |
| | Lt. R.C. Brown | (2)Ju-88 dest(grd) | |
| | Lt. R.A. Browning | (2)Do-217 dest(grd) | |
| | Lt. J.E. Duffy | Me-110 dest(grd) | |
| | | Do-217 dest(grd) | |
| | | (2)Me-210 dam(grd) | |
| | | He-111 dam(grd) | |
| | | Do-217 dam(grd) | |
| | Lt. R.S. Morris | (2)Do-217 dest(grd) | |
| | | Do-217 dam(grd) | |
| | Lt. B.C. Williamson | (2)Do-217 dest(grd) | |
| | | Do-217 dam(grd) | |
| | | u/i a/c dam(grd) | |
| | Capt. R.E. Woody | Ju-88 dest(grd) | |
| | | Me-110 dam(grd) | |
| | Lt. W.P. Boulet | He-177 dest(grd) | |
| | | Me-110 dam(grd) | |
| 357th: | Maj. E.W. Szaniawski | Me-109 dest(air) | Augsburg |
| | | Me-109 prob(air) | Augsburg |
| | | Me-109 dam(air) | Augsburg |
| | | (.33)Me-110 dest(grd) | Crailsheim |
| | | (.33)Me-323 dest(grd) | Crailsheim |
| | Capt. H.S. Bille | Me-109 dest(air) | Augsburg |
| | | Me-323 dam(grd) | Crailsheim |
| | Capt. J.H. Wilson | Me-109 dest(air) | Augsburg |
| | | (.5)Me-323 dest(grd) | Crailsheim |
| | | Me-323 dam(grd) | Crailsheim |
| | Lt. H.K. Hillman | Me-109 dest(air) | Augsburg |
| | Lt. J.D. Sturm | Me-109 dest(air) | Augsburg |
| | | (.5)Me-323 dest(grd) | Crailsheim |
| | Capt. J.F. Kerch | Me-109 prob(air) | Augsburg |
| | | (.33)Me-323 dest(grd) | Crailsheim |
| | Lt. R.L. Norman | (.33)Me-110 dest(grd) | Crailsheim |
| | | (.33)Me-323 dest(grd) | Crailsheim |
| | Lt. R.F. DeMers | (.33)Me-110 dest(grd) | Crailsheim |
| 358th: | Maj. R.B. Myers | FW-190 dest(air) | Nordlingen |

**April 15, 1944**

| | | | |
|---|---|---|---|
| 357th: | Capt. J.L. Elder | Me-109 dest(air) | E/Celle |
| | Lt. W.E. MacFarlane | u/i a/c dest(grd) | E/Celle |
| 358th: | Lt. J.N. McElroy | (5)Do-217 dest(grd) | All 358th claims |
| | Maj. R.B. Myers | Do-217 dest(grd) | are at Glienicke |
| | Capt. L.J. Dissette | Do-217 dest(grd) | |
| | | u/i a/c dam(grd) | |
| | F/O J.M. Beckman | Do-217 dest(grd) | |
| | | Do-217 dam(grd) | |
| | Lt. P.H. Kenney | Do-217 dest(grd) | |
| | F/O J.S. MacConkey | Do-217 dest(grd) | |
| | | Do-217 dam(grd) | |
| | Lt. T.H. Worth | Me-110 dam(grd) | |

**April 19, 1944**

| | | | |
|---|---|---|---|
| 354th: | Capt. R.E. Woody | Me-109 dest(air) | Nordhausen |
| 358th: | Lt. R.J. Fussell | FW-190 dest(air) | SW Brunswick |
| | Lt. T.O. Meteyer | Me-109 dest(air) | SW Brunswick |
| | Lt. J.N. McElroy | Me-109 dam(air) | SW Brunswick |

**April 20, 1944**

| | | | |
|---|---|---|---|
| 354th: | Capt. R.G. Kurtz | He-111 dest(grd) | Blois A/F |
| | | Ju-52 dest(grd) | Blois A/F |
| | Lt. B.G. Houston | FW-190 dest(grd) | Blois A/F |
| | Lt. R.A. Browning | Ju-88 dam(grd) | Blois A/F |

**April 24, 1944**

| | | | |
|---|---|---|---|
| HdQts: | LtCol. G.J. Dix | FW-190 dest(air) | NE Augsburg |
| | | Me-109 dam(air) | NE Augsburg |
| 354th: | Capt. R.E. Woody | (4.5)Me-109 dest(air)* | SE Munich |
| | | Me-109 dam(air) | SE Munich |
| | Capt. H.B. Kucheman | (3)Me-109 dest(air) | NW Munich |
| | Lt. W.P. Boulet | (2.5)Me-109 dest(air)* | SE Munich |
| | | (.5)Me-109 dest(air)** | SE Munich |
| | | Me-109 dam(air) | SE Munich |
| | Lt. H.W. Brown | (2)Me-109 dest(air) | S/Munich |
| | Lt. N.J. Fortier | (1.5)Me-109 dest(air)** | SE Munich |
| | | Me-109 dam(air) | Munich |
| 357th: | Lt. R.F. DeMers | (2)Me-109 dest(air) | NE Munich |
| | Capt. H.S. Bille | FW-190 dest(air) | NW Munich |
| | Capt. J.H. Wilson | Me-109 dest(air) | NW Munich |
| | | Me-109 dam(air) | NW Munich |
| | Lt. R.B. Butler | (.5)Me-109 dest(air) | NE Munich |
| | Lt. E.P. McNeff | (.5)Me-109 dest(air) | NE Munich |
| | Lt. L.D. Minchew | Me-109 dam(air) | SW Munich |
| | F/O M.A. King | Me-109 dam(air) | NW Munich |

**April 29, 1944**

| | | | |
|---|---|---|---|
| 354th: | Lt. H.W. Brown | Me-109 dest(air) | Brunswick |

**May 1, 1944**

| | | | |
|---|---|---|---|
| 354th: | Lt. N.J. Fortier | FW-190 dam(air) | Trier |
| 358th: | Capt. L.J. Dissette | Me-109 dest(air) | Traben-Trarbach |

**May 4, 1944**

| | | | |
|---|---|---|---|
| 358th: | Lt. D.M. Martyn | Me-109 dest(air) | All claims are |
| | | Me-109 dam(air) | SW Hanover |
| | Capt. W.V. Gresham | Me-109 prob(air) | |
| | | Me-109 dam(air) | |
| | Lt. A.T. Robinson | Me-109 prob(air) | |
| | | Me-109 dam(air) | |
| | Lt. C.W. Blair | Me-109 dam(air) | |
| | Lt. R.L. Coleman | Me-109 dam(air) | |

**May 13, 1944**

| Unit | Pilot | Claim | Location |
|---|---|---|---|
| HdQts: | LtCol. G.J. Dix | (2)Me-410 dest(air) | SE Landsberg |
| 354th: | Lt. N.J. Fortier | FW-190 dest(air) | NE Bremen |
| | | Ju-88 dest(air) | N/Landsberg |
| | Lt. R.S. Morris | (2)Me-410 dest(air) | E/Berlin |
| | Lt. H.W. Brown | Me-210 dest(air) | Landsberg |
| | Lt. W.D. Martin | Hs-129 dest(air) | Landsberg |
| | Lt. E.F. Perry | FW-190 dest(air) | NE Bremen |
| | | FW-190 prob(air) | NE Bremen |
| | | FW-190 dam(air) | NE Bremen |
| | Lt. D.J. Jacobson | Me-410 dam(air) | Landsberg |

**May 21, 1944**

| Unit | Pilot | Claim | Location |
|---|---|---|---|
| 357th: | Lt. J.C. Engelbreit | (.5)Me-108 dest(air) | W/Schwerin |
| | | Do-217 dest(grd) | SE Schwerin |
| | | (2)Do-217 dam(grd) | SE Schwerin |
| | Lt. W.E. MacFarlane | (.5)Me-108 dest(air) | W/Schwerin |
| | | Do-217 dest(grd) | Schwerin |
| | | (5)Do-217 dam(grd) | Schwerin |
| | Lt. M.A. King | (2)Do-217 dest(grd) | SE Schwerin |
| | | Do-217 dam(grd) | SE Schwerin |

**May 22, 1944**

| Unit | Pilot | Claim | Location |
|---|---|---|---|
| HdQts: | LtCol. G.J. Dix | Me-109 prob(air) | SW Kiel |
| 357th: | Lt. J. Guerrant | Me-109 dam(air) | Kiel |

**May 24, 1944**

| Unit | Pilot | Claim | Location |
|---|---|---|---|
| 354th: | Lt. E.F. Perry | FW-190 dest(grd) | Cormeilles-en-Vixen |
| | | FW-190 dam(grd) | Cormeilles-en-Vixen |
| 357th: | Lt. T.J. Foster | Me-109 dest(air) | Kyritz |
| 358th: | LtCol. R.B. Myers | Me-109 dest(air) | Berlin |
| | | Me-109 dam(air) | Berlin |

**May 28, 1944**

| Unit | Pilot | Claim | Location |
|---|---|---|---|
| 357th: | Lt. F.L. Eshelman | Me-109 dest(air) | N/Limburg |
| | Lt. W.E. MacFarlane | Me-109 dest(air) | N/Limburg |

**May 30, 1944**

| Unit | Pilot | Claim | Location |
|---|---|---|---|
| 358th: | Lt. A.R. Santos | (2)FW-190 dest(air) | SE Brunswick |
| | Lt. D.A. Donovan | Me-109 dest(air) | SE Brunswick |
| | | (.5)FW-190 dest(air) | SE Brunswick |
| | | (shared with an unknown pilot) | |
| | Lt. A.T. Robinson | FW-190 dest(air) | SE Hanover |
| | | FW-190 dam(air) | SE Hanover |

**June 6, 1944**

| Unit | Pilot | Claim | Location |
|---|---|---|---|
| HdQts: | LtCol. G.J. Dix | Ju-87 dam(air) | Chartres |
| | | Ju-87 dest(grd) | Chartres |
| 354th: | Capt. B.W. Marshall | Ju-87 dest(air) | Chartres-Dire |
| | Lt. N.J. Fortier | Ju-87 dest(air) | Chartres |
| | Lt. R.S. Morris | (.5)Ju-87 dest(air) | Chartres-Dire |
| | Lt. F.K. Taylor | (.5)Ju-87 dest(air) | Chartres-Dire |
| | Lt. C.H. Graham | Ju-87 dest(grd) | Chartres |
| 357th: | Capt. F.W. Kelley | (2)Ju-87 dest(air) | All 357th claims |
| | Lt. R. Bernoske | Ju-87 dest(air) | are NE Janville |
| | Lt. J.A. Cotter | Ju-87 dest(air) | |
| | Lt. L.B. Fuller | Ju-87 dest(air) | |
| | | Ju-87 prob(air) | |
| | | Ju-87 dam(air) | |
| | Lt. W.W. James | Ju-87 dest(air) | |
| | | (2)Ju-87 dam(air) | |
| | | Ju-87 dest(grd) | |
| | Capt. J.H. Wilson | Ju-87 dam(air) | |
| | Lt. L.D. Minchew | Ju-87 dam(air) | |

**June 8, 1944**

| Unit | Pilot | Claim | Location |
|---|---|---|---|
| 358th: | Lt. C.J. Brien | (.5)He-177 dest(air) | N/Angoulieme |
| | Lt. W.J. McGinty | (.5)He-177 dest(air) | N/Angoulieme |

**June 20, 1944**

| Unit | Pilot | Claim | Location |
|---|---|---|---|
| 354th: | Capt. B.W. Marshall | (2)Me-109 dest(air) | Bergen |
| | Lt. W.D. Martin | (2)Me-109 dest(air) | Rugen |
| | Lt. G.S. Wright | (2)Me-109 dest(air) | Bergen |
| | Maj. H.B. Kucheman | Me-410 dest(air) | NW Stettin |
| | | Me-410 dam(air) | NW Stettin |
| | Lt. C.H. Graham | Me-410 dest(air) | NW Stettin |
| | Lt. G.C. Hoffman | Me-109 dest(air) | Rugen |
| | Lt. R.G. Taylor | Me-410 dest(air) | Rugen |
| | Lt. H.M. Huish | (.5)Me-410 dest(air) | Rugen |
| | Lt. S.C. Williams | (.5)Me-410 dest(air) | Rugen |
| | Lt. R.E. Hulderman | Me-410 dam(air) | Bergen |
| | Lt. A.S. White | Me-410 dam(air) | Bergen |
| 357th: | Capt. L.D. Minchew | Me-109 dest(air) | Pomeranian Bay |
| | Lt. C.R. Buckles | (.5)Me-410 dest(air) | Pomeranian Bay |
| | Lt. L.B. Fuller | (.5)Me-410 dest(air) | Pomeranian Bay |

**June 21, 1944**

| Unit | Pilot | Claim | Location |
|---|---|---|---|
| 357th: | Capt. F.R. Haviland | Me-109 dest(air) | N/Magdeburg |
| | Lt. J.M. Chapman | Me-109 dest(air) | Juterbog |
| | Lt. C.J. Salinsky | Me-109 dest(air) | N/Magdeburg |

**June 24, 1944**

| Unit | Pilot | Claim | Location |
|---|---|---|---|
| 354th: | LtCol. C.H. Kinnard | (3)Me-109 dest(grd) | All 354th claims |
| | Lt. R.S. Morris | (3)Me-109 dest(grd) | are at Seiches |
| | Lt. J.C. Ellison | (2)Me-109 dest(grd) | |
| | Lt. W.D. Martin | (2)Me-109 dest(grd) | |
| | Lt. E.F. Perry | (2)Me-109 dest(grd) | |
| | Lt. R.G. Cross | Me-109 dest(grd) | |
| | Lt. R.E. Hulderman | Me-109 dest(grd) | |
| | Lt. F.W. Trembarth | Me-109 dest(grd) | |
| | Maj. H.B. Kucheman | (2)Me-109 dam(grd) | |
| | Lt. G.S. Wright | Me-109 dam(grd) | |
| 357th: | Capt. F.R. Haviland | (3)Me-109 dest(grd) | E/Angars |
| | Lt. C.J. Salinsky | (3)Me-109 dest(grd) | NE Angars |
| | | (2)Me-109 dam(grd) | NE Angars |
| | Lt. J.L. Crandell | (2)Me-109 dest(grd) | E/Angars |
| | | (3)Me-109 dam(grd) | E/Angars |
| | Lt. H.W. Spencer | (2)Me-109 dest(grd) | E/Angars |
| | Lt. G.W. Forker | Me-109 dest(grd) | NE Angars |
| | Lt. E.P. McNeff | Me-109 dest(grd) | E/Angars |
| | Lt. P.M.N. McHugh | Me-109 dest(grd) | E/Angars |

**July 5, 1944**

| Unit | Pilot | Claim | Location |
|---|---|---|---|
| HdQts: | LtCol. C.H. Kinnard | (.5)Ju-88 dest(grd) | Chateauroux |
| 354th: | Lt. W.A. Schwab | Ju-88 dest(air) | Chateauroux |
| | Lt. R.E. Hulderman | (.5)Ju-88 dest(grd) | Chateauroux |

**July 7, 1944**

| Unit | Pilot | Claim | Location |
|---|---|---|---|
| HdQts: | LtCol. C.H. Kinnard | (2)Me-410 dest(air) | Lingen |
| | | Me-109 dest(air) | Lingen |
| 354th: | Lt. R.G. Cross | (2)Me-410 dest(air) | Lingen |
| | Lt. E.F. Perry | Me-410 dest(air) | Lingen |
| | Lt. S.G. Betounes | (.5)Ju-88 dest(air) | Lingen |
| | Lt. R.G. Taylor | (.5)Ju-88 dest(air) | Lingen |
| 357th: | Capt. L.D. Minchew | (2.5)Me-410 dest(air) | Nordhausen |
| | | (shared with an unknown P-38 pilot) | |
| | | (2)Me-410 dam(air) | Nordhausen |
| | Capt. F.R. Haviland | (2)Me-410 dest(air) | Halle |
| | | Me-410 dam(air) | Halle |
| | Lt. J.A. Cotter | Me-410 dest(air) | S/Halle |
| | Lt. L.B. Fuller | Me-410 dest(air) | Halle-Nordhausen |
| | Lt. E.P. McNeff | Me-109 dest(air) | Nordhausen |
| | Lt. F.L. Eshelman | Me-109 dam(air) | Nordhausen |

**July 8, 1944**

| Unit | Pilot | Claim | Location |
|---|---|---|---|
| 354th: | Maj. H.B. Kucheman | (2)Me-410 dest(grd) | All claims are |
| | | Me-109 dam(grd) | SW Chalons |
| | Lt. R.S. Morris | Me-109 dest(grd) | |
| | | Me-410 dest(grd) | |
| | Lt. S.C. Williams | Me-109 dest(grd) | |
| | | Me-410 dest(grd) | |
| | | Me-410 dam(grd) | |
| | Lt. R.T. Bradley | Me-109 dest(grd) | |
| | Lt. W.D. Martin | Me-109 dest(grd) | |
| | | (2)Me-109 dam(grd) | |
| | Lt. C.H. Graham | Me-109 dest(grd) | |
| | | Me-109 dam(grd) | |
| | Lt. N.P. Jackson | Me-109 dest(grd) | |
| | Capt. N.J. Fortier | (.5)Me-109 dest(grd) | |
| | Lt. R.G. Cross | (.5)Me-109 dest(grd) | |
| | | Me-410 dam(grd) | |
| 357th: | Lt. P.M.N. McHugh | (2)Me-410 dest(grd) | |
| | | (3)Me-410 dam(grd) | |
| | Lt. G.W. Forker | Me-109 dest(grd) | |
| | Lt. R.W. Strachan | Me-109 dest(grd) | |
| | Lt. W.A. Cox | Me-410 dam(grd) | |
| | Lt. W.L. Reiff | Me-109 dam(grd) | |
| 358th: | Lt. V.W. Covault | FW-190 dest(grd) | |
| | | FW-190 dam(grd) | |
| | Lt. W.J. McGinty | FW-190 dest(grd) | |
| | | (2)FW-190 dam(grd) | |
| | Lt. R.I. McNally | FW-190 dest(grd) | |
| | Lt. R.L. Michelena | FW-190 dest(grd) | |
| | | FW-190 dam(grd) | |
| | Lt. H.W. Pardee | FW-190 dest(grd) | |
| | | (3)Me-109 dam(grd) | |
| | Lt. W. Winn | Me-109 dam(grd) | |

**July 13, 1944**

| Unit | Pilot | Claim | Location |
|---|---|---|---|
| 357th: | Lt. E.M. Hendrickson | Me-109 dest(air) | Sarreburg |
| | | Me-109 prob(air) | Sarreburg |
| | Lt. P.M.N. McHugh | Me-109 dam(air) | Sarreburg |

**July 19, 1944**

| Unit | Pilot | Claim | Location |
|---|---|---|---|
| 354th: | Lt. J.M. Folger | FW-190 dest(air) | Biberach |
| 358th: | Capt. W.J. Hovde | Me-109 dest(air) | Augsburg |
| | Lt. J.N. McElroy | FW-190 dest(air) | Augsburg |
| | | FW-190 dam(air) | Augsburg |
| | Lt. R.M. Thompson | Me-109 dest(air) | Augsburg |
| | Lt. V.W. Covault | FW-190 prob(air) | Augsburg |
| | F/O A.G. Duppstadt | Ju-88 dest(grd) | Munich |
| | | Glider dest(grd) | Munich |
| | | Ju-88 dam(grd) | Munich |

**July 20, 1944**

| Group | Pilot | Claim | Location |
|---|---|---|---|
| 354th: | Capt. N.J. Fortier | Me-109 dest(air) | W/Oschatz |
| | Lt. J.M. Folger | Me-109 dam(air) | W/Oschatz |
| 357th: | Lt. W.O. Costello | Me-109 prob(air) | W/Leipzig |
| 358th: | Lt. R.O. Peters | (2)FW-190 dest(air) | E/Leipzig |
| | | Do-217 dest(air) | E/Leipzig |
| | | He-111 dest(grd) | E/Leipzig |
| | | Ju-88 dest(grd) | E/Leipzig |
| | Lt. N.E. Peterson | Me-109 dest(air) | Dresden |
| | | Me-109 dam(air) | Dresden |

**July 21, 1944**

| Group | Pilot | Claim | Location |
|---|---|---|---|
| 358th: | Lt. R.M. Thompson | Me-109 prob(air) | Munich |

**July 24, 1944**

| Group | Pilot | Claim | Location |
|---|---|---|---|
| 354th: | Lt. G.C. Hoffman | He-280 dest(grd) | Lechfeld |
| | Lt. G.T. Patterson | He-280 dest(grd) | Lechfeld |
| | Capt. N.J. Fortier | Me-262 dam(grd) | Lechfeld |
| 357th: | Lt. J.A. Cotter | u/i a/c dest(grd) | Lechfeld |
| | | Me-109 dam(grd) | Lechfeld |
| | Lt. A.G. Gilleland | Do-217 dest(grd) | Lechfeld |
| | | Do-217 dam(grd) | Lechfeld |
| | | FW-190 dam(grd) | Lechfeld |
| | Lt. C.J. Salinsky | Me-109 dam(grd) | Lechfeld |
| | | u/i a/c dam(grd) | Lechfeld |
| 358th: | Capt. W.J. Hovde | Do-217 dest(grd) | All claims are |
| | | Ju-88 dest(grd) | at Augsburg |
| | Lt. D.C. Blaylock | Do-217 dest(grd) | |
| | | (3)Do-217 dam(grd) | |
| | Lt. R.M. Dillon | Ju-88 dest(grd) | |
| | | u/i a/c dam(grd) | |
| | Lt. W.H. Douglas | FW-190 dest(grd) | |
| | Lt. J.J. Maisch | Do-217 dest(grd) | |
| | Lt. N.E. Peterson | Ju-88 dest(grd) | |
| | Lt. H.W. Pardee | Do-217 dam(grd) | |

**July 28, 1944**

| Group | Pilot | Claim | Location |
|---|---|---|---|
| 354th: | Capt. B.W. Marshall | Me-109 dest(air) | Mulhausen |
| 358th: | Lt. J.N. McElroy | Me-109 dest(air) | S/Merseburg |
| | | FW-190 dest(air) | S/Merseburg |
| | Lt. R.N. Watkins | Me-109 dam(air) | S/Merseburg |

**August 1, 1944**

| Group | Pilot | Claim | Location |
|---|---|---|---|
| 358th: | Lt. R.M. Dillon | Me-109 dest(air) | Chateaudun |

**August 3, 1944**

| Group | Pilot | Claim | Location |
|---|---|---|---|
| 354th: | F/Lt. W.B. Peglar | Me-109 dest(air) | E/Mannheim |
| | | FW-190 dest(air) | E/Mannheim |
| | Capt. C.W. Lenfest | Me-109 dest(air) | E/Mannheim |
| 357th: | Capt. F.R. Haviland | FW-190 dest(air) | Saareburg |
| | | Me-109 dam(air) | Saareburg |
| | Capt. L.D. Minchew | Me-109 dest(air) | Baden Baden |
| | Lt. J.A. Cotter | Me-109 dest(air) | Baden Baden |

**August 6, 1944**

| Group | Pilot | Claim | Location |
|---|---|---|---|
| 354th: | Capt. C.W. Lenfest | Me-109 dest(air) | S/Hamburg |
| | Capt. B.W. Marshall | Me-109 dest(air) | S/Hamburg |
| | Lt. W.D. Martin | Me-109 dest(air) | S/Hamburg |

**August 11, 1944**

| Group | Pilot | Claim | Location |
|---|---|---|---|
| 354th: | F/Lt. W.B. Peglar | Ju-52 dest(grd) | Saarbrucken |

**August 14, 1944**

| Group | Pilot | Claim | Location |
|---|---|---|---|
| 357th: | Lt. W.A. Shade | Ju-88 dest(grd) | Vitry |
| | | (.5)Ju-88 dest(grd) | Saareburg |
| | Maj. J.L. Elder | Ju-88 dest(grd) | Saareburg |
| | Lt. G.W. Forker | Ju-88 dest(grd) | Saareburg |
| | Lt. J.H. Max | (.5)Ju-88 dest(grd) | Saareburg |
| | Lt. L.D. Johnson | Ju-88 dam(grd) | Saareburg |

**August 15, 1944**

| Group | Pilot | Claim | Location |
|---|---|---|---|
| 358th: | Capt. W.V. Gresham | Me-109 dest(air) | NW Zwolle |

**August 16, 1944**

| Group | Pilot | Claim | Location |
|---|---|---|---|
| 357th: | Maj. J.L. Elder | (2)Me-109 dest(air) | All claims are |
| | Capt. H.S. Bille | (2)Me-109 dest(air) | SE Hildeshiem |
| | Lt. W.J. Cullerton | (2)Me-109 dest(air) | unless noted |
| | Lt. H.W. Spencer | (2)Me-109 dest(air) | |
| | Capt. C.W. Lamer | Me-109 dest(air) | |
| | Lt. J.L. Crandell | Me-109 dest(air) | |
| | Lt. K.M. Michels | Me-109 dest(air) | S/Hildesheim |

**August 26, 1944**

| Group | Pilot | Claim | Location |
|---|---|---|---|
| 357th: | Lt. W.J. Cullerton | FW-200 dest(grd) | Speyer |

**September 10, 1944**

| Group | Pilot | Claim | Location |
|---|---|---|---|
| 354th: | Lt. H.W. Brown | (6)He-60 dest(grd) | Frankfurt |
| | Lt. S.G. Betounes | (4)He-60 dam(grd) | Frankfurt |

**September 11, 1944**

| Group | Pilot | Claim | Location |
|---|---|---|---|
| 354th: | Lt. H.W. Brown | (3)Me-109 dest(air) | S/Kassel |
| | Capt. B.W. Marshall | (2)Me-109 dest(air) | S/Kassel |
| | | Me-109 dam(air) | S/Kassel |
| | F/Lt. W.B. Peglar | (2)Me-109 dest(air) | S/Kassel |
| | Lt. R.W. Priest | Me-109 dest(air) | S/Kassel |
| | Lt. F.W. Schultz | Me-109 dest(air) | S/Kassel |
| | | (.5)Me-109 dest(grd) | Marburg |
| | Lt. R.M. White | (1.5)Me-109 dest(grd) | Marburg |
| | Capt. B.C. Williamson | FW-190 dest(grd) | S/Kassel |
| | Lt. C.R. McCurry | Ju-52 dest(grd) | S/Kassel |
| 358th: | Lt. J.J. Maisch | (2)Me-109 dest(air) | Marburg |
| | F/Lt. L.S. Frost | Me-109 dest(air) | S/Kassel |
| | | Me-109 dam(air) | S/Kassel |
| | | (2)Do-217 dam(grd) | S/Kassel |

**September 12, 1944**

| Group | Pilot | Claim | Location |
|---|---|---|---|
| 357th: | Lt. P.M.N. McHugh | (2)FW-190 dest(air) | E/Muritz Lake |
| | Lt. H.L. Monahan | FW-190 dest(air) | E/Muritz Lake |
| | Capt. H.S. Bille | FW-190 dam(air) | NE Berlin |
| | Lt. J.E. Erickson | FW-190 dam(air) | E/Muritz Lake |
| | Lt. W.J. Cullerton | (3)u/i a/c dest(grd) | Schwartz A/F |
| | | (2)Me-110 dest(grd) | Schwartz A/F |
| | | (2)Ju-88 dest(grd) | Schwartz A/F |
| | | Me-110 dam(grd) | Schwartz A/F |
| | | Ju-88 dam(grd) | Schwartz A/F |
| | Lt. J.O. Juntilla | (2)Ju-88 dest(grd) | Schwartz A/F |
| | | Ju-52 dest(grd) | Schwartz A/F |
| | | u/i a/c dest(grd) | Schwartz A/F |
| | | (2)Ju-88 dam(grd) | Schwartz A/F |
| | | (2)u/i a/c dam(grd) | Schwartz A/F |
| | Capt. F.R. Haviland | (3)Ju-88 dest(grd) | Schwartz A/F |
| | | Me-110 dam(grd) | Schwartz A/F |
| | | Do-217 dam(grd) | Schwartz A/F |
| | Lt. J.M. Chapman | (2)Me-410 dam(grd) | Wittstock |
| | | Do-217 dam(grd) | Wittstock |
| 358th: | Lt. R.M. Thompson | Me-109 dest(air) | Hanover |
| | Lt. J.J. Vigna | FW-190 dam(air) | E/Berlin |

**September 18, 1944**

| Group | Pilot | Claim | Location |
|---|---|---|---|
| HdQts: | Capt. H.H. Kirby | Me-109 dest(air) | NW Warsaw |
| 354th: | Capt. H.W. Brown | Me-109 dest(air) | Warsaw |
| | | Me-109 dam(air) | Warsaw |
| | | Ju-87 dam(grd) | Warsaw |
| 357th: | Maj. J.L. Elder | Me-109 dest(air) | NW Warsaw |
| 358th: | Lt. R.L. Michelena | Me-109 dest(air) | Warsaw |
| | | Me-109 dam(air) | Warsaw |
| | Lt. M.E. Webb | Me-109 dam(air) | Warsaw |

**September 27, 1944**

| Group | Pilot | Claim | Location |
|---|---|---|---|
| HdQts: | LtCol. E.W. Stewart | (.5)Ju-88 dest(grd) | All claims are |
| 354th: | Capt. H.W. Brown | (2)FW-190 dest(air) | at Eschwege |
| | Lt. R.W. Priest | FW-190 dest(air) | |
| | Capt. B.C. Williamson | FW-190 dest(grd) | |
| | Lt. H.R. Mann | (.5)Ju-88 dest(grd) | |

**October 3, 1944**

| Group | Pilot | Claim | Location |
|---|---|---|---|
| 354th: | Maj. C.W. Lenfest | FW-190 dest(grd) | Nordlingen |
| | Capt. H.W. Brown | Me-110 dest(grd) | Nordlingen |

**October 6, 1944**

| Group | Pilot | Claim | Location |
|---|---|---|---|
| 357th: | Capt. C.W. Lamer | (2)FW-190 dest(air) | W/Berlin |
| | Capt. C.C. Colson | Me-109 dam(air) | W/Berlin |

**October 7, 1944**

| Group | Pilot | Claim | Location |
|---|---|---|---|
| 357th: | Lt. H.L. Monahan | FW-190 dest(air) | SW Leipzig |
| | | Me-109 dest(grd) | SW Leipzig |

**November 2, 1944**

| Group | Pilot | Claim | Location |
|---|---|---|---|
| 354th: | Lt. R.W. Priest | Me-109 dest(air) | W/Naumberg |
| | Lt. M.L. Woolard | Me-109 dest(air) | W/Naumberg |
| 357th: | Lt. W.J. Cullerton | Me-109 dest(air) | Unless noted, |
| | | FW-190 dest(air) | all claims are |
| | | (6)u/i a/c dest(grd) | at Wernigerode |
| | Maj. J.L. Elder | Me-109 dest(air) | |
| | | (5)u/i a/c dest(grd) | |
| | Lt. E.J. Moroney | Me-109 dest(air) | |
| | | (2)u/i a/c dest(grd) | |
| | Lt. H.O. Wilkes | FW-190 dest(air) | S/Wernigerode |
| | Lt. J.E. Erickson | (4)u/i a/c dest(grd) | |
| | Capt. R.J. DuFresne | (2)u/i a/c dest(grd) | |
| | Lt. K.J. Miller | (2)u/i a/c dest(grd) | |
| | Lt. B.G. Williams | (2)u/i a/c dest(grd) | |
| | Capt. J.C. Engelbreit | u/i a/c dest(grd) | |
| | Lt. J.V. Cavender | u/i a/c dest(grd) | |
| | F/O E.H. Riffle | u/i a/c dest(grd) | |
| 358th: | Lt. K.E. Mikalauskas | FW-190 dest(air) | Merseburg |
| | Lt. J.N. McElroy | Me-109 dam(air) | Merseburg |

**November 18, 1944**

| Unit | Pilot | Claim | Location |
|---|---|---|---|
| 354th: | Capt. N.J. Fortier | (2)Me-262 dest(grd) | All claims are |
| | | u/i a/c dam(grd) | at Leipheim |
| | Capt. J.E. Duffy | Me-262 dest(grd) | |
| | Lt. T.L. Wood | Me-262 dest(grd) | |
| | Lt. T.P. Todd | Me-262 dam(grd) | |
| | Lt. R.M. White | Me-262 dam(grd) | |
| 357th: | Lt. T.C. Long | (2)Me-262 dest(grd) | |
| | | (2)Me-262 dam(grd) | |
| | Maj. J.H. Wilson | Me-262 dest(grd) | |
| | | Me-262 dam(grd) | |
| | Capt. F.R. Haviland | (4)Me-262 dam(grd) | |
| | Capt. C.C. Colson | (4)Me-262 dam(grd) | |
| | Lt. E.J. Moroney | (3)Me-262 dam(grd) | |
| | Lt. J.H. Max | (2)Me-262 dam(grd) | |
| | Lt. J.E. Nelson | Me-262 dam(grd) | |
| 358th: | Lt. W.W. Beaty | Me-262 dest(grd) | |

**November 26, 1944**

| Unit | Pilot | Claim | Location |
|---|---|---|---|
| 354th: | Lt. R.W. Priest | (2)FW-190 dest(air) | Misburg |
| | Lt. C.D. Hauver | (2)FW-190 dest(air) | W/Hanover |
| | Lt. R.M. McLear | (2)Me-109 dest(air) | Gifhorn-W/Hanover |
| | Capt. J.E. Duffy | FW-190 dest(air) | Gifhorn-Hanover |
| | Lt. J.E. Mellen | FW-190 dest(air) | S/Misburg |
| | F/O J.E. Molnar | FW-190 dest(air) | S/Misburg |
| | | FW-190 dam(air) | S/Misburg |
| | Lt. F.W. Schultz | Me-109 dam(air) | Gifhorn-W/Hanover |
| | | FW-190 dam(air) | Gifhorn-W/Hanover |
| | F/O H.W. Falvey | FW-190 dam(air) | Gifhorn |
| | Lt. N.P. Jackson | FW-190 dam(air) | S/Misburg |
| 357th: | Capt. F.R. Haviland | Me-109 dest(air) | W/Gardelegen |
| | | FW-190 dest(air) | W/Gardelegen |
| | Lt. E.J. Moroney | (2)FW-190 dest(air) | W/Gardelegen |
| | Lt. J.H. Max | (2)FW-190 dest(air) | W/Gardelegen |
| | Lt. B.R. Barab | Me-109 dest(air) | W/Gardelegen |
| | Lt. W.S. Lyons | Me-109 dest(air) | W/Gardelegen |
| | Capt. H.S. Bille | Me-109 prob(air) | W/Gardelegen |
| 358th: | F/O F.R. Masters | (3)FW-190 dest(air) | Hanover |
| | Lt. J.M. Beckman | FW-190 dest(air) | Hanover-Berlin |
| | Maj. E.L. Sluga | FW-190 dam(air) | Hanover |
| | Lt. N.B. Woodson | FW-190 dam(air) | W/Hanover |

**December 5, 1944**

| Unit | Pilot | Claim | Location |
|---|---|---|---|
| 354th: | Capt. J.E. Duffy | FW-190 dest(air) | N/Berlin |
| | Lt. S.E. Silva | FW-190 dest(air) | N/Berlin |
| 358th: | Maj. W.J. Hovde | (4.5)FW-190 dest(air) | All claims are |
| | | Me-109 dest(air) | at Berlin |
| | Lt. R.G. Baker | (2)FW-190 dest(air) | |
| | | FW-190 dam(air) | |
| | Lt. A.K. Alexander | (1.5)FW-190 dest(air) | |
| | Lt. R.H. Brown | FW-190 dest(air) | |
| | Lt. J.N. McElroy | FW-190 dest(air) | |
| | | (3)FW-190 dam(air) | |

**December 12, 1944**

| Unit | Pilot | Claim | Location |
|---|---|---|---|
| 358th: | Lt. A.R. Curran | u/i a/c dest(grd) | Gotha |

**December 25, 1944**

| Unit | Pilot | Claim | Location |
|---|---|---|---|
| 354th: | Lt. C.D. Hauver | Me-109 dest(air) | NW Trier |
| | | FW-190 dest(air) | NW Trier |
| | Maj. G.M. Graham | FW-190 dest(air) | NW Trier |
| | | FW-190 prob(air) | NW Trier |
| 357th: | Lt. V.D. Iglesias | FW-190 dest(air) | W/Coblenz |

**December 31, 1944**

| Unit | Pilot | Claim | Location |
|---|---|---|---|
| 354th: | Maj. G.M. Graham | (2)FW-190 dest(air) | SW Hamburg |
| | Lt. C.D. Hauver | FW-190 dest(air) | SW Hamburg |
| | | FW-190 dam(air) | SW Hamburg |

**January 14, 1945**

| Unit | Pilot | Claim | Location |
|---|---|---|---|
| 354th: | Lt. N.F. Mills | (2)Me-109 dest(air) | E/Meppen |
| | | FW-190 dest(air) | E/Meppen |
| | Maj. G.M. Graham | (2)FW-190 dest(air) | E/Meppen |
| | | FW-190 dam(air) | E/Meppen |
| | Lt. G.A. Kemper | FW-190 dest(air) | E/Meppen |
| | | FW-190 dest(air) | SW Dummer Lake |
| | Lt. C.E. Decklar | Me-109 dest(air) | E/Meppen |
| | | FW-190 dest(air) | E/Meppen |
| | Lt. T.L. Wood | Me-109 dest(air) | E/Meppen |
| 357th: | Maj. J.L. Elder | Me-109 dest(air) | Munster |

**January 15, 1945**

| Unit | Pilot | Claim | Location |
|---|---|---|---|
| 354th: | F/O H.W. Falvey | FW-190 dest(grd) | Landsberg |
| | | u/i a/c dest(grd) | Landsberg |
| | | u/i a/c dam(grd) | Landsberg |
| | Maj. G.M. Graham | Ju-188 dest(grd) | Kotha |
| | | (2)u/i a/c dam(grd) | Oberpfaffenhofen |
| | Capt. N.J. Fortier | Ju-52 dest(grd) | Oberpfaffenhofen |
| | | Ju-52 dam(grd) | Oberpfaffenhofen |
| 357th: | Lt. R.W. Delhamer | (2)Me-110 dest(grd) | All claims are |
| | | u/i a/c dest(grd) | at Landsberg |
| | | Fi-156 dam(grd) | |
| | Maj. J.H. Wilson | u/i a/c dest(grd) | |
| | Lt. J.V. Cavender | (2)Me-110 dam(grd) | |
| | Lt. R.L. Garlich | u/i a/c dam(grd) | |
| | Lt. J.E. Lake | u/i a/c dam(grd) | |
| 358th: | Lt. R. Allen | Me-110 dest(grd) | |
| | Lt. R.J. Fussell | u/i a/c dest(grd) | |
| | | (2)u/i a/c dam(grd) | |
| | Lt. V.E. Gore | u/i a/c dest(grd) | |
| | | (2)u/i a/c dam(grd) | |

**February 3, 1945**

| Unit | Pilot | Claim | Location |
|---|---|---|---|
| 357th: | Lt. S.S. Hardee | Ju-88 dam(grd) | Gardelegen |

**February 9, 1945**

| Unit | Pilot | Claim | Location |
|---|---|---|---|
| HdQts: | Col. E.W. Stewart | Ju-188 dest(grd) | Kothen |
| | | (2)Ju-188 dam(grd) | Kothen |
| | Capt. L.D. Minchew | FW-190 dam(grd) | Kothen |
| 354th: | Capt. J.E. Duffy | FW-190 dest(air) | SW Berlin |
| 357th: | Lt. E.P. Ludeke | FW-190 dest(air) | Brandenburg |
| | Lt. W.S. Lyons | Me-109 dest(air) | Brandenburg |
| | Lt. R.W. Delhamer | (.5)Do-217 dam(air) | Lonnewitz |
| | Lt. E.H. Riffle | (.5)Do-217 dam(air) | Lonnewitz |
| | Lt. W.F. Forehand | Ju-88 dest(grd) | Kothen |
| | | u/i a/c dam(grd) | Kothen |
| | Lt. S.S. Hardee | Ju-88 dest(grd) | Kothen |
| | | Me-109 dam(grd) | Kothen |
| | | Ju-52 dam(grd) | Kothen |
| | Lt. R.F. Misner | u/i a/c dam(grd) | Kothen |
| | Lt. G.C. Schmidt | Me-109 dam(grd) | Kothen |

**February 22, 1945**

| Unit | Pilot | Claim | Location |
|---|---|---|---|
| 354th: | Lt. R.M. White | (2)Me-410 dest(grd) | Halberstadt |
| | | FW-190 dam(grd) | Halberstadt |

**February 23, 1945**

| Unit | Pilot | Claim | Location |
|---|---|---|---|
| 354th: | Capt. J.E. Duffy | (2)u/i a/c dest(grd) | Leipheim |
| | | Me-262 dest(grd) | Leipheim |
| | LtCol. G.M. Graham | Me-109 dest(grd) | Naumberg |
| | | FW-190 dam(grd) | Landsberg |
| | Capt. H.R. Mann | Ju-88 dest(grd) | Neuburg |
| | Lt. N.F. Mills | u/i a/c dest(grd) | Neuburg |
| | Lt. R.J. Walsh | Me-109 dest(grd) | Neuburg |
| | Lt. R.A. Goth | Ju-88 dam(grd) | Neuburg |
| | Lt. D.M. Vickery | Ju-88 dam(grd) | Neuburg |
| 357th: | LtCol. J.L. Elder | Me-109 dest(grd) | All 357th claims |
| | | Me-109 dam(grd) | are at Neuburg |
| | Lt. S.S. Hardee | Me-109 dest(grd) | |
| | Lt. G.C. Schmidt | Me-110 dest(grd) | |
| | Lt. E.H. Riffle | Me-262 dest(grd) | |
| | Lt. E.P. Ludeke | (2)Me-163 dam(grd) | |
| | Lt. W.F. Forehand | Me-262 dam(grd) | |
| | Lt. R.L. Garlich | Me-163 dam(grd) | |
| | Lt. H.K. Greenwell | Me-262 dam(grd) | |
| | Lt. T.C. Long | Me-163 dam(grd) | |
| | Lt. D.P. Watkins | Me-163 dam(grd) | |
| | Lt. J.J. Weidemann | Me-163 dam(grd) | |

**February 25, 1945**

| Unit | Pilot | Claim | Location |
|---|---|---|---|
| 357th: | Lt. T.C. Long | Ju-188 dam(grd) | Fassberg |
| 358th: | Lt. W.W. Tolby | Me-109 dest(air) | E/Munster |
| | | Me-109 dam(grd) | E/Munster |

**February 27, 1945**

| Unit | Pilot | Claim | Location |
|---|---|---|---|
| 358th: | Capt. J.N. McElroy | Do-217 dest(air) | SW Plauen |

**March 1, 1945**

| Unit | Pilot | Claim | Location |
|---|---|---|---|
| HdQts: | Maj. H.H. Kirby | Me-262 dam(air) | Donauworth |
| 358th: | Lt. W.W. Beaty | Me-262 dest(air) | Ingolstadt |

**March 3, 1945**

| Unit | Pilot | Claim | Location |
|---|---|---|---|
| 357th: | Lt. W.S. Lyons | Me-262 dam(air) | Brunswick |

**March 19, 1945**

| Unit | Pilot | Claim | Location |
|---|---|---|---|
| 354th: | Capt. C.H. Spencer | Me-262 dest(air) | Kitzingen |

**March 22, 1945**

| Unit | Pilot | Claim | Location |
|---|---|---|---|
| 354th: | Lt. S.E. Silva | (2)Me-262 dest(grd) | Kitzingen |
| | | Me-109 dest(grd) | Kitzingen |
| | | (3)Me-262 dam(grd) | Kitzingen |
| | F/O H.W. Falvey | Me-262 dest(grd) | Kitzingen |
| | | Me-109 dest(grd) | Wurzburg |
| | | Me-262 dam(grd) | Kitzingen |
| | Lt. J.M. Fletcher | Me-109 dest(grd) | Wurzburg |
| | Lt. W.J. Gadpaille | He-111 dest(grd) | Memmingen |
| | Lt. J. Jabara | FW-190 dest(grd) | Wurzburg |
| | | FW-190 dam(grd) | Wurzburg |
| | Lt. D.C. Tulhoski | FW-190 dest(grd) | Wurzburg |

| Unit | Pilot | Claim | Location |
|---|---|---|---|
| | Lt. C.G. Todd | He-111 dest(grd) | Memmingen |
| | Lt. P.W. Vineyard | He-111 dest(grd) | Memmingen |
| | Lt. R.M. White | He-111 dest(grd) | Memmingen |
| | | He-111 dam(grd) | Memmingen |
| | Lt. C.E. Decklar | He-111 dam(grd) | Memmingen |
| | F/O T.R. Hixon | He-111 dam(grd) | Memmingen |
| | Lt. D.B. Langley | FW-190 dam(grd) | Wurzburg |
| | Lt. M.J. McLeod | Me-262 dam(grd) | Kitzingen |

**March 30, 1945**

| Unit | Pilot | Claim | Location |
|---|---|---|---|
| HdQts: | Maj. H.H. Kirby | Me-109 dest(grd) | Lowenstadt |
| | | FW-190 dest(grd) | Lowenstadt |
| | | (.5)He-111 dam(grd) | Lowenstadt |
| 354th: | LtCol. G.M. Graham | (.5)Ju-52 dam(grd) | Schleswig |
| | | (.5)Ju-52 dam(grd) | Schleswig |
| | | (.5)JU-52 dam(grd) | Schleswig |
| | Lt. D.B. Langley | (.5)Ju-52 dam(grd) | Schleswig |
| | | (.5)Ju-52 dam(grd) | Schleswig |
| | | (.5)Ju-52 dam(grd) | Schleswig |
| 357th: | Lt. W.J. Cullerton | He-111 dest(grd) | Lowenstadt |
| | Lt. H.I. Knight | He-111 dest(grd) | Lowenstadt |
| | | (.5)He-111 dam(grd) | Lowenstadt |

**March 31, 1945**

| Unit | Pilot | Claim | Location |
|---|---|---|---|
| 357th: | Lt. T.C. Long | Ju-88 dest(grd) | Magdeburg |

**April 4, 1945**

| Unit | Pilot | Claim | Location |
|---|---|---|---|
| 354th: | Capt. A.S. White | FW-190 dest(air) | Ludwigslust |
| | F/O T.R. Hixon | u/i a/c dest(grd) | Muritz Lake |
| | | (2)Ju-88 dam(grd) | Muritz Lake |
| | Lt. J.E. Molnar | BV-138 dest(grd) | Muritz Lake |
| | Lt. P.W. Barnhart | (.5)Do-24 dest(grd) | Muritz Lake |
| | Lt. C.E. Decklar | (.5)Do-24 dest(grd) | Muritz Lake |
| 357th: | Lt. T.C. Long | (2)FW-190 dest(air) | Halberstadt |
| | Lt. W.J. Cullerton | FW-190 dest(air) | Halberstadt |
| | Lt. E.H. Riffle | Ar-234 dest(air) | Magdeburg |
| | Lt. R.W. Cooper | Me-262 dam(air) | Ludwigslust |

**April 7, 1945**

| Unit | Pilot | Claim | Location |
|---|---|---|---|
| 354th: | Capt. J.E. Mellen | FW-190 dest(air) | S/Bremen |
| | Lt. G.D. Beeler | FW-190 dest(air) | S/Bremen |
| | Lt. P.W. Vineyard | Me-109 dest(air) | SE Bremen |
| 357th: | Lt. W.F. Forehand | Me-109 dest(air) | SE Hamburg |
| 358th: | Lt. R.V. Finnesey | Me-262 dam(air) | SE Bremen |

**April 8, 1945**

| Unit | Pilot | Claim | Location |
|---|---|---|---|
| 354th: | LtCol. G.M. Graham | (2)Me-109 dest(air) | Oberpfaffenhofen |
| | Lt. C.E. Decklar | Me-109 dest(air) | Oberpfaffenhofen |
| 357th: | Lt. J.J. Weidemann | Me-109 dest(grd) | Ansbach |
| | | Me-109 dam(grd) | Ansbach |

**April 9, 1945**

| Unit | Pilot | Claim | Location |
|---|---|---|---|
| 354th: | LtCol. G.M. Graham | (2.5)He-111 dest(grd) | All 354th claims |
| | Lt. P.W. Barnhart | He-111 dest(grd) | are at Memmingen |
| | Capt. A.S. White | (.5)He-111 dest(grd) | |
| | F/O H.W. Falvey | (.5)Ju-88 dest(grd) | |
| | Lt. J. Jabara | (.5)Ju-88 dest(grd) | |
| | Lt. R.P. Pearson | He-111 dam(grd) | |
| 358th: | Lt. W.J. Lynch | Me-110 dest(grd) | All 358th claims |
| | | He-111 dest(grd) | are at Heilfingen |
| | | u/i a/c dam(grd) | |
| | Lt. C.C. Patrinely | He-111 dest(grd) | |
| | | (.5)Me-110 dest(grd) | |
| | Lt. E.W. Fees | Me-110 dest(grd) | |
| | Lt. J.H. Lanius | Me-110 dest(grd) | |
| | Lt. F.N. McCollom | Me-110 dest(grd) | |
| | | He-111 dam(grd) | |
| | Lt. H.P. Knutty | (.5)Me-110 dest(grd) | |
| | Lt. C.E. Plemons | He-111 dam(grd) | |

**April 10, 1945**

| Unit | Pilot | Claim | Location |
|---|---|---|---|
| HdQts: | Maj. H.H. Kirby | Ju-88 dest(grd) | Rechlin/Larz |
| | | (3)Ju-88 dam(grd) | Rechlin/Larz |
| 354th: | LtCol. G.M. Graham | Me-109 dest(grd) | Rechlin/Larz |
| | | B-24 dest(grd) | Rechlin/Larz |
| | | (3)Me-109 dam(grd) | Rechlin/Larz |
| | Lt. J.M. Fletcher | (2)u/i a/c dest(grd) | Rechlin/Larz |
| | Lt. J. Jabara | (2)Me-410 dest(grd) | Rechlin/Larz |
| | | (3)u/i a/c dam(grd) | Rechlin/Larz |
| | F/O H.W. Falvey | Ju-52 dest(grd) | Rechlin/Larz |
| | | (.5)He-111 dest(grd) | Rechlin/Larz |
| | | (4)u/i a/c dam(grd) | Rechlin/Larz |
| | Lt. P.W. Barnhart | u/i a/c dest(grd) | Husum |
| | | (2)FW-190 dam(grd) | Husum |
| | | u/i a/c dam(grd) | Husum |
| | | u/i a/c dam(grd) | Rechlin/Larz |
| | Lt. D.V. Galer | u/i a/c dest(grd) | Memmingen |
| | Lt. O.N. Stanton | u/i a/c dest(grd) | Wesendorf |
| | F/O T.R. Hixon | (.5)He-111 dest(grd) | Rechlin/Larz |
| | | (4)u/i a/c dam(grd) | Rechlin/Larz |
| 357th: | Lt. R.L. Garlich | He-111 dest(grd) | All 357th claims |
| | | Do-24 dest(grd) | are at Rechlin/ |
| | | (.5)u/i a/c dest(grd) | Larz |
| | | (shared with a 56th Ftr Grp P-47) | |
| | Lt. R.F. Misner | Ju-88 dest(grd) | |
| | | Ju-88 dam(grd) | |
| | Lt. D.P. Watkins | He-111 dest(grd) | |
| | Lt. W.T. Burnett | (.5)B-24 dest(grd) | |
| | | Me-109 dam(grd) | |
| | Lt. R.W. Cooper | (.5)B-24 dest(grd) | |
| 358th: | Capt. W.V. Gresham | Me-262 dam(air) | W/Lubeck |

**April 13, 1945**

| Unit | Pilot | Claim | Location |
|---|---|---|---|
| HdQts: | LtCol. B.W. Marshall | (2)u/i a/c dest(grd) | Husum |
| | | Me-109 dest(grd) | Husum |
| | | (2)u/i a/c dam(grd) | Husum |
| | | FW-190 dam(grd) | Husum |
| | LtCol. C.H. Kinnard | (2.5)He-111 dest(grd)* | Schleswig |
| 354th: | Capt. J.E. Mellen | (3)u/i a/c dest(grd) | All 354th claims |
| | | (2)He-111 dest(grd) | are at Husum |
| | Capt. S.E. Silva | (2)Me-109 dest(grd) | |
| | | He-111 dest(grd) | |
| | | Me-109 dam(grd) | |
| | Lt. D.B. Langley | (2)He-111 dest(grd) | |
| | | Me-109 dest(grd) | |
| | | (2)FW-190 dam(grd) | |
| | Lt. D.M. Vickery | (3)He-111 dest(grd) | |
| | | (2)He-111 dam(grd) | |
| | F/O H.W. Falvey | FW-190 dest(grd) | |
| | | Ju-88 dest(grd) | |
| | | Ju-88 dam(grd) | |
| | Lt. D.V. Galer | He-111 dest(grd) | |
| | | Ju-88 dest(grd) | |
| | | u/i a/c dam(grd) | |
| | Lt. J. Jabara | He-111 dest(grd) | |
| | | Me-109 dest(grd) | |
| | | Me-109 dam(grd) | |
| | Capt. J.E. Duffy | Ju-88 dest(grd) | |
| | | u/i a/c dam(grd) | |
| | Lt. G.D. Beeler | He-111 dest(grd) | |
| | Lt. A.B. Kaplan | He-111 dest(grd) | |
| | | FW-190 dam(grd) | |
| | Lt. A.G. Kozacka | FW-190 dest(grd) | |
| | | (2)u/i a/c dam(grd) | |
| | Lt. M.J. McLeod | u/i a/c dest(grd) | |
| | | He-111 dam(grd) | |
| | Lt. A.J. Mincemeyer | He-111 dest(grd) | |
| | Lt. R.P. Pearson | Me-109 dest(grd) | |
| | Lt. F.A. Sarver | FW-190 dest(grd) | |
| | | FW-190 dam(grd) | |
| | Lt. R. Westerveld | Me-109 dest(grd) | |
| | Lt. A.J. Scheid | He-111 dam(grd) | |
| | | FW-190 dam(grd) | |
| 357th: | Lt. R.W. Cooper | (1.5)He-111 dest(grd)@@ | All 357th claims |
| | | FW-200 dest(grd) | are at Schleswig |
| | Lt. R.L. Garlich | (2)He-111 dest(grd) | |
| | Lt. V.D. Iglesias | (2)He-111 dest(grd) | |
| | Lt. R.F. Misner | (1.5)He-111 dest(grd)@@ | |
| | Lt. M.E. Beise | He-111 dam(grd) | |
| | F/O J.D. Hober | He-111 dam(grd) | |
| | Lt. J.E. Lake | He-111 dam(grd) | |
| | Lt. F.H. Rodgers | He-111 dam(grd) | |
| 358th: | Capt. J.F. Tulloch | (4)He-111 dest(grd) | Schleswig |
| | Lt. R.F. Parks | (2)FW-190 dest(grd) | Flensburg |
| | | (2)He-111 dest(grd) | Flensburg |
| | Lt. A.R. Curran | FW-190 dest(grd) | Flensburg |
| | | Ju-88 dest(grd) | Flensburg |
| | Lt. V.E. Gore | (1.5)He-111 dest(grd)* | All remaining |
| | Lt. H.P. Knutty | Me-109 dest(grd) | claims are at |
| | | (.5)He-111 dest(grd)## | Schleswig |
| | Lt. W.J. Schlecht | Me-109 dest(grd) | |
| | | (.5)He-111 dest(grd)** | |
| | Lt. R.J. Nicodemus | (.5)He-111 dest(grd)## | |
| | | (.5)He-111 dest(grd)@ | |
| | Lt. L.J. Rouleau | He-111 dest(grd) | |
| | Lt. E.W. Fees | (.5)He-111 dest(grd)# | |
| | | He-111 dam(grd) | |
| | Lt. R.V. Finnessey | (.5)He-111 dest(grd)** | |
| | Lt. M. Lacazette | (.5)He-111 dest(grd)& | |
| | Lt. L.R. Leaf | (.5)He-111 dest(grd)@ | |
| | Lt. W.B. Lister | (.5)He-111 dest(grd)& | |
| | Lt. C.C. Patrinely | (.5)He-111 dest(grd)# | |

**April 16, 1945**

| Unit | Pilot | Claim | Location |
|---|---|---|---|
| 354th: | LtCol. G.M. Graham | (3)Ju-88 dest(grd) | Eger A/F |
| | Capt. J.E. Mellen | He-111 dest(grd) | Eger A/F |
| | | He-177 dest(grd) | Eger A/F |
| | | Ju-88 dest(grd) | Eger A/F |
| | Lt. J.M. Fletcher | (2)u/i a/c dest(grd) | Eger A/F |
| | | u/i a/c dam(grd) | Eger A/F |

| | | | |
|---|---|---|---|
| | Lt. D.V. Galer | Ju-88 dest(grd) | Eger A/F |
| | | u/i a/c dest(grd) | Eger A/F |
| | | (2)u/i a/c dam(grd) | Autobahn |
| | | Me-109 dam(grd) | Autobahn |
| | | Me-410 dam(grd) | Autobahn |
| | Lt. R.L. Heaton | He-111 dest(grd) | Eger A/F |
| | | Ju-88 dest(grd) | Eger A/F |
| | Lt. R.M. McLear | (2)u/i a/c dest(grd) | Autobahn |
| | Lt. J.E. Molnar | (2)Me-110 dest(grd) | Autobahn |
| | | u/i a/c dam(grd) | Autobahn |
| | Lt. C.G. Todd | He-111 dest(grd) | Eger A/F |
| | | Ju-88 dest(grd) | Eger A/F |
| | | He-111 dam(grd) | Eger A/F |
| | Maj. N.J. Fortier | u/i a/c dest(grd) | Eger A/F |
| | Capt. J.E. Duffy | u/i a/c dest(grd) | Landstadt |
| | Lt. M.J. McLeod | u/i a/c dest(grd) | Eger A/F |
| | | (3)u/i a/c dam(grd) | Eger A/F |
| | Lt. D.J. Sanders | u/i a/c dest(grd) | Eger A/F |
| | Lt. A.J. Scheid | Ju-88 dest(grd) | Autobahn |
| 357th: | LtCol. J.L. Elder | (2)FW-190 dest(grd) | SE Germany |
| | | (2)u/i a/c dest(grd) | SE Germany |
| | | (3)u/i a/c dam(grd) | SE Germany |
| | Capt. C.C. Colson | Me-110 dest(grd) | Bad Aibling |
| | | Ju-88 dest(grd) | Bad Aibling |
| | Lt. R.W. Cooper | He-177 dest(grd) | SE Germany |
| | | FW-190 dest(grd) | SE Germany |
| | Lt. H.I. Knight | (2)FW-190 dest(grd) | SE Germany |
| | | He-177 dam(grd) | SE Germany |
| | | u/i a/c dam(grd) | SE Germany |
| | Lt. R.F. Misner | (2)FW-190 dest(grd) | SE Germany |
| | | (3)FW-190 dam(grd) | SE Germany |
| | Lt. D.P. Watkins | Me-110 dest(grd) | Bad Aibling |
| | | He-111 dest(grd) | Bad Aibling |
| | Lt. E.H. Whitney | (1.5)Me-109 dest(grd)* | SE Germany |
| | Lt. F.E. Gelsone | FW-190 dest(grd) | SE Germany |
| | | (.5)Me-109 dest(grd)* | SE Germany |
| | | (2)Me-109 dam(grd) | SE Germany |
| | Lt. J.E. Lake | FW-190 dest(grd) | Erferding |
| | Lt. M.E. Beise | FW-190 dest(grd) | SE Germany |
| | | (2)FW-190 dam(grd) | SE Germany |
| | Lt. R.L. Garlich | Ju-87 dest(grd) | Eger A/F |
| | Lt. W.T. Kubatin | Me-109 dest(grd) | SE Germany |
| | Lt. R.J. Kirk | Me-109 dest(grd) | SE Germany |
| | | Me-109 dam(grd) | SE Germany |
| | Lt. R.B. Owens | u/i a/c dest(grd) | SE Germany |
| | Lt. R.J. Patelunas | u/i a/c dest(grd) | SE Germany |
| | Lt. J.J. Weidemann | FW-190 dest(grd) | SE Germany |
| | | (3)FW-190 dam(grd) | SE Germany |
| | Lt. W.L. Griswold | (.5)He-111 dest(grd) | Bad Aibling |
| | | He-111 dam(grd) | Bad Aibling |
| | | Me-110 dam(grd) | Bad Aibling |
| | Lt. R.C. Keuhl | (.5)He-111 dest(grd) | Bad Aibling |
| | | He-111 dam(grd) | Bad Aibling |
| | | Me-109 dam(grd) | Bad Aibling |
| 358th: | Lt. H.G. Marsh | (5)FW-190 dest(grd) | All claims are |
| | | (2)FW-190 dam(grd) | at Straubing |
| | Lt. F.N. McCollom | (2)FW-190 dest(grd) | |
| | | Ju-88 dest(grd) | |
| | | u/i a/c dest(grd) | |
| | Lt. W.J. Lynch | (2)FW-190 dest(grd) | |
| | | Ju-88 dest(grd) | |
| | Lt. R.C. Rowbatham | (3)FW-190 dest(grd) | |
| | | (2)FW-190 dam(grd) | |
| | Capt. L.J. Dissette | (2)FW-190 dest(grd) | |
| | | (2)FW-190 dam(grd) | |
| | Capt. G.A. Seeley | (2)FW-190 dest(grd) | |
| | | Me-110 dam(grd) | |
| | | u/i a/c dam(grd) | |
| | Lt. C.E. Plemons | Me-110 dest(grd) | |
| | | FW-190 dest(grd) | |
| | Lt. E.C. Nelson | FW-190 dest(grd) | |
| | | Ju-88 dam(grd) | |
| | Lt. L.J. Rouleau | (2)FW-190 dam(grd) | |

**April 17, 1945**

| | | | |
|---|---|---|---|
| 358th: | Capt. W.V. Gresham | He-177 dest(grd) | Cheb A/F |
| | | (3)u/i a/c dam(grd) | Eger A/F |
| | Lt. R.F. Parks | u/i a/c dam(grd) | Eger A/F |

**April 20, 1945**

| | | | |
|---|---|---|---|
| HdQts: | LtCol. C.H. Kinnard | (2)Me-109 dest(air) | Letnany A/F |
| | | Me-109 dam(air) | Letnany A/F |
| 357th: | Maj. H.S. Bille | (2)Me-109 dest(air) | Letnany A/F |
| | | (2)Me-109 dam(air) | Letnany A/F |
| | Lt. V.D. Iglesias | Me-109 dest(air) | Letnany A/F |
| 358th: | Lt. H.P. Knutty | (.5)Me-109 dest(air) | Kbely A/F |
| | Lt. K.L. Snook | (.5)Me-109 dest(air) | Kbely A/F |
| | Capt. G.A. Seeley | Me-109 prob(air) | Kbely A/F |
| | Lt. R.F. Parks | Me-109 dam(air) | Kbely A/F |

### 355th Fighter Group Losses

**September 25, 1943**
Lt. James Donovan (354th) KIAc; Spun-in between Ossington and Wigsley.
P-47D WR-

**October 4, 1943**
Lt. Ralph Dean (358th) KIA; Damaged by a FW-190, he crashed on the English coast on return.
P-47D YF-Z 42-74667

**October 18, 1943**
Lt. Eugene W. Maben, Jr. (358th) KIA; Last seen spinning down east of Cambrai.
P-47D YF-N 42-22532

**November 5, 1943**
Lt. Clark Collins (357th) KIA; Hit by a Me-109 west of Schouwen.
P-47D OS-T 42-8406 "Eager Eve"

**November 7, 1943**
Lt. Edwin O. Carlson (357th) KIA; Collided with Lt. Westphal near Montdidier.
P-47D OS-Q 42-7984 "On The Ball"
Lt. James S. Westphal (357th) POW; Collided with Lt. Carlson near Montdidier.
P-47D OS-L 42-8370 "Alabama Bound"
Capt. Walter H. Kossack (358th) POW; Bellied-in near the French coast after running low on fuel.
P-47D YF-X 42-8477
Lt. William E. Roach (358th) POW; Landed near Caen after running low on fuel.
P-47D YF-U 42-22490 "Beetle"
F/O Chester W. Watson (358th) KIA; Ran out of fuel and bailed out over the Channel.
P-47D YF-Z 42-8629

**November 13, 1943**
LtCol. Thomas H. Hubbard (HdQts) MIA-E; Hit by flak near Bergentheim.
P-47D WR- 42-7944
Lt. John Lanphier (358th) KIA; Last seen being chased by Me-109's near Dalfsen.
P-47D YF-W 42-8626

**November 15, 1943**
Lt. Lawrence E. McGraw (357th) KIA; Lost on weather recon, possible collision with Lt. McNally.
P-47D OS-U 42-8408 "Jean's Little Moe"
Lt. Donald B. McNally (357th) KIA; Lost on weather recon, possible collision with Lt. McGraw.
P-47D OS-P 42-8413 "Ma Fran"

**November 29, 1943**
Lt. Alfred J. Delnegro (354th) KIA; Disappeared for unknown reasons.
P-47D WR-D 42-7996
Lt. Charles K. Hecht, Jr. (358th) KIA; Low on fuel and landed at Gasselternijveen.
P-47D YF-U 42-8631
Lt. Richard A. Peery (358th) POW; Hit by enemy fighters near Bremen.
P-47D YF-L 42-22484 "Slugger"

**December 1, 1943**
Lt. Jesse M. Williamson (357th) POW; Hit by flak near Coblenz.
P-47D OS-Z 42-22545
Capt. James C. Hull (358th) KIA; Last seen in clouds near Lierre.
P-47D YF-A 42-8006

**December 4, 1943**
Lt. Roland L. Vincent (354th) KIAc; Crashed near Colerne after losing tail in a dive.
P-47D WR-S 42-8433

**December 11, 1943**
Lt. Jack J. Woertz (358th) KIA; Stalled and crashed while landing at Hastings.
P-47D YF-Y 42-75045

**December 30, 1943**
Lt. Ray F. Murdoch, Jr. (354th) POW; Hit by a Me-109 near Soissons.
P-47D WR-K 42-8453
Capt. Carl F. Ekstrom (358th) KIA; Hit by flak at St. Inglevert.
P-47D YF-M 42-8526
F/O Charles E. Wambier (358th) KIA; Hit by a Me-109 near Reims.
P-47D YF-U 42-75425

**January 24, 1944**
Lt. Frank L. Pipher, Jr. (357th) KIA; Hit by flak and crashed into the Channel.
P-47D OS-L 42-75184

**January 29, 1944**
Capt. Ben T. Martin (357th) MIA-E; Hit by a FW-190 near Limburg and bailed out near Coblenz.
P-47D OS-Q 42-8610
Lt. Harold H. Macurdy (358th) MIA-E; Hit by a Me-109 near Coblenz.
P-47D YF-H 42-75455
Lt. Chauncy H. Rankin (358th) KIA; Hit by a Me-109 near Coblenz.
P-47D YF-G 42-8504

**February 11, 1944**
Lt. Roland J. DuFresne (357th) MIA-E; Suffered mechanical failure and bailed out near Cologne.
P-47D OS-S 42-8550

**March 8, 1944**
Lt. Charles H. Sweat (354th) KIA; Hit by flak at Hesepe Airfield.
P-47D WR-R 42-8441

Lt. Daniel S. Rothenberg (357th) KIA; Hit by a FW-190 near Osnabruck.
P-51B OS- 43-6989

**March 9, 1944**
Lt. William Momberger (357th) KIA; Crashed near Bassingbourne while forming-up.
P-47D OS-E 42-22549 "Kay"

**March 11, 1944**
Lt. Lawrence F. Allard (354th) POW; Hit by flak near Munster.
P-51B WR-K 43-6849
F/O John A. Chalot (358th) POW; Suffered mechanical failure near Gladbeck.
P-51B YF-R 43-6554

**March 16, 1944**
Capt. Donald H. Wright (358th) POW; Last seen chasing a Me-109 east of Augsburg.
P-51B YF-S 43-6842 "Mona Lou"
Lt. Harold I. Carver (358th) POW; Hit by a Me-109 near Gunzburg.
P-51B YF-J 43-6527 "Indiana Clipper"

**March 26, 1944**
Lt. Kenneth D. Williams (354th) POW; Hit by flak near Chateaudun. He was flying with "Bill's Buzz Boys" at the time.
P-47D YF-K 42-8443

**March 27, 1944**
Lt. Chester J. Butcher (357th) POW; Hit by flak near Biscarosse.
P-51B OS-F 43-6777 "The Butcher"

**March 29, 1944**
Capt. Ben D. Johnston, Jr. (357th) POW; Suffered mechanical failure near Brussels.
P-51B OS-I 43-12452
Capt. Howard L. Lambert, Jr. (357th) KIA; Ditched in the Channel after running low on fuel.
P-51B OS-O 43-6508
Capt. James H. McConnell (358th) POW; Hit by flak near Arnheim and bailed out near Rotterdam.
P-51B YF-C 43-6317 "Duel Purpose"

**April 5, 1944**
Lt. Harold F. Culp (354th) KIA; Hit power lines near Landsberg.
P-51B WR-P 43-7076
Lt. Byron L. Hill (357th) KIA; Hit by flak at Deininegn Airfield.
P-51B OS-C 43-6980
Lt. Edward Ondris (358th) KIA; Downed by a Me-109 near Landsberg.
P-51B YF-M 43-6937.

**April 8, 1944**
Capt. Norman E. Olson (357th) KIA; Hit by flak near Celle and crashed near Hoefen.
P-51B OS-X 43-6589
Lt. Irving Reedy (357th) POW; Hit by fighters near Brunswick.
P-51B OS-U 42-106463
Lt. James B. Dickson (358th) KIA; Hit by fighters near Emden.
P-51B YF-X 43-7147

**April 11, 1944**
Capt. Curtis G. Johnston (354th) POW; Hit by flak near Sorau.
P-51B WR-O 43-6944
Capt. William S. Easterly (357th) POW; Hit by flak at Wesendorf.
P-51B OS-J 43-6627 "Brenda"

**April 15, 1944**
Capt. Walter J. Koraleski, Jr. (354th) POW; Lost coolant and bailed out near Utrecht.
P-51B WR-L 43-6968 "Miss Thunder"
Capt. Joseph F. Kerch (357th) POW; Hit by flak at Wagonhof Airfield.
P-51B OS-U 42-106698 "Bea"
Lt. Darwin D. McCasland (357th) POW; Hit by flak at Wagonhof A/F.
P-51B OS-M 43-6525
Lt. Paul H. Kenney (358th) POW; Hit by flak near Wittstock.
P-51B YF-P 43-6925

**April 19, 1944**
F/O Jack S. MacConkey (358th) KIA; Hit by a Me-109 near Gottingen.
P-51B YF-L 43-7156 "Slugger"

**April 24, 1944**
Lt. Ray F. DeMers (357th) KIA; Hit by flak near Bingen.
P-51B OS-G 42-106723
Lt. Howard K. Hillman (357th) KIA; Hit by fighters near Munich.
P-51B OS-O 43-7103 "Miss Doris"
Lt. Robert L. Norman (357th) KIA; Hit by fighters near Munich.
P-51B OS-R 42-106433
Lt. Jack D. Sturm (357th) POW; Hit by fighters near Knocke.
P-51B OS-N 43-7140

**April 26, 1944**
Lt. William P. Boulet (354th) POW; Hit by fire from a B-17 near Clausthal.
P-51B WR-F 43-6948 "Lorie II"

**April 29, 1944**
Capt. Thomas F. Neal, Jr. (354th) KIA; Hit by a FW-190 near Rathenow.
P-51B WR-J 43-6577

**May 1, 1944**
Lt. Rudolph B. Kaminski (357th) KIA; Hit by a Me-109 near Metz.
P-51B OS-B 43-6648

**May 4, 1944**
Lt. Donald M. Martyn (358th) KIA; Hit by a Me-109 near Hanover.
P-51B YF-V 43-6873

**May 19, 1944**
LtCol. Edward W. Szaniawski (357th) POW; Hit by flak near Diepholz.
P-51B OS-A 43-7142 "Available Jones 5th"
Lt. Hudson F. Packard (357th) KIA; Collided with a Do-217 near Kolonie Breiteich.
P-51B OS-I 42-106762

**May 20, 1944**
Lt. Clarence Donaldson (354th) KIA; Hit by a Me-109 near Erkelenz.
P-51B WR-B 43-6574
Lt. Donald J. Jacobson (354th) KIA; Hit by a Me-109 near Erkelenz.
P-51B WR-D 43-6857

**May 24, 1944**
Lt. Herbert F. Fritts (354th) KIA; Crashed into a train while strafing near Hamburgen.
P-51B WR-F 42-106874 "Lorie III"

**May 28, 1944**
Lt. Clarence R. Barger (354th) POW; Hit by a Me-109 near Zerbst.
P-51B WR-T 43-6631
Lt. Walter M. Christensen (354th) KIA; Hit by a Me-109 near Buhlendorf.
P-51B WR-O 43-6983

**June 3, 1944**
Lt. Robert A. Browning (354th) POW; Lost coolant west of Paris and bellied-in near Abbeville.
P-51B WR-K 42-106708

**June 4, 1944**
F/O Henry W. Davis (354th) KIA; Lost coolant then hit by flak near St. Quentin.
P-51B WR-W 43-6520

**June 6, 1944**
Lt. Walter A. Douglas (357th) POW; Hit by flak near Calais.
P-51B OS- 42-106862
Lt. George W. Phillips (357th) KIA; Hit by flak near La Mailerage and hit the tail while bailing out.
P-51B OS-H 43-6640

**June 7, 1944**
Lt. Robert D. Coutre (354th) MIA-E; Hit by flak near Nogent.
P-51B WR-P 43-6895
Lt. Thomas J. Foster (357th) KIA; Damaged by a bomb blast near Aunay Sous Anueau.
P-51B OS-G 42-106742
Lt. John Guerrant, Jr. (357th) KIA; Hit by a Me-109 near Aquiny.
P-51B OS-N 42-106810
Lt. Harwood H. Harrell (357th) MIA-E; Hit by flak near Chateaudun.
P-51B OS-E 43-6886 "Kay"
Lt. Nils E. Holman, Jr. (357th) KIA; Hit by a Me-109 near Aquiny.
P-51B OS-E 43-6916
Lt. Walter E. MacFarlane (357th) POW; Hit by a Me-109 near Aquiny.
P-51B OS-S 43-7039 "Red Eye"

**June 8, 1944**
LtCol. Gerald J. Dix (HdQts) POW; Hit by flak near Niort.
P-51B YF-D 43-7164
Lt. David A. Donovan (358th) MIA-E; Hit by flak near Montboyen.
P-51B YF-K 43-6879 "Mary Joyce"
F/O Edward R. Williams (358th) KIA; Damaged by flak and crashed at Eyeworth upon return.
P-51B YF-N

**June 19, 1944**
Lt. Ralph L. Coleman (358th) KIA; Spun-in near Bordeaux.
P-51B YF-Q 42-106858
Lt. Willis W. Reeves, Jr. (358th) KIA; Spun-in near Bordeaux.
P-51B YF-E 43-6523 "Leakin' Liz"

**June 22, 1944**
Lt. Myles A. King (357th) POW; Lost coolant near Albert.
P-51C OS-U 42-103282

**June 27, 1944**
Lt. Thomas W. Ruark (354th) MIA-E; Hit by a Me-109 near Chateau Thierry.
P-51C WR-K 42-103802

**July 5, 1944**
Lt. Victor E. Denti (354th) KIA; Hit by flak near Chateauroux.
P-51B WR-N 42-106870

**July 6, 1944**
Lt. Norman E. Dixson (357th) POW; Hit by flak near Schwerin.
P-51B OS-K 42-106634

**July 7, 1944**
Lt. Heber M. Huish (354th) KIA; Damaged by debris from a Me-410 near Halle.
P-51B WR-T 43-6915

Lt. Leonard B. Fuller (357th) KIA; Hit by flak near Naumburg.
P-51D OS-E 44-13526

**July 8, 1944**
Lt. James P. Lowder, Jr. (358th) KIA; Hit by flak at Montmiral.
P-51B YF-R 43-6945 "Wizard Kite"

**July 18, 1944**
Lt. Fred W. Johnson (354th) ASR; Bailed out 30 miles off Great Yarmouth.
P-51B WR-

**July 19, 1944**
Lt. Warren A. Schwab (354th) POW; Suffered mechanical failure near Biberach.
P-51B WR-V 43-6938

**July 20, 1944**
Lt. Walter O. Costello (357th) MIA-E; Hit by flak near Oschatz and bailed out near Avranches.
P-51B OS-N 43-24795
Lt. Robert W. Strachan (357th) ASR; Bailed out northeast of Margate.
P-51B OS-

**July 24, 1944**
Lt. Peter N. Sawchuck (354th) KIA; Hit by flak near Lechfeld.
P-51C WR-J 42-103334 "Martin's Gloria"
Lt. Albert H. Debacker (357th) ASR; Suffered mechanical failure and bailed out over the Channel.
P-51C OS- 42-103009
Lt. Wayne E. Walburn (358th) POW; Hit by flak near Lechfeld and bellied-in near Mindelheim.
P-51B YF-C 42-106780

**August 2, 1944**
Maj. John L. Elder (357th) ASR; Damaged by flak near Albert and ditched in the Channel.
P-51D OS-
Lt. Franklin R. Gowing (357th) MIA-E; Hit by flak near St. Pol and bailed out near Concour.
P-51B OS-R 42-106733
Lt. Ben F. Orr, Jr. (358th) KIA; Hit by flak near Londimiernes.
P-51B YF-C 43-6820

**August 3, 1944**
Capt. Robert G. Kurtz (354th) POW; Hit by a Me-109 near Gompelscheuer.
P-51D WR-A 44-14001
Lt. Garlyn O. Hoffman (354th) POW; Collided with Lt. Patterson near Neuweiler.
P-51B WR-H 43-24824
Lt. Gilbert T. Patterson (354th) KIA; Collided with Lt. Hoffman near Neuweiler.
P-51B WR-X 43-6885 "Texas Terror III"
Lt. Floyd K. Taylor (354th) MIA-E; Suffered mechanical failure and bellied-in near Switz.
P-51D WR-K 44-13912
Lt. John A. Cotter (357th) POW; Hit by flak while chasing a Me-109 near Mannheim.
P-51D OS- 44-13654

**August 6, 1944**
Lt. John M. Folger (354th) KIA; Hit by a Me-109 near Bremervorde.
P-51B WR-Q 43-7137

**August 8, 1944**
Lt. Robert Bernoske (357th) MIA-E; Hit by flak northeast of Vitry.
P-51B OS-Z 42-106815
Lt. Charles M. Lee (357th) KIA; Hit by flak near St. Dizier.
P-51B OS-V 43-6835

**August 11, 1944**
Lt. Frank Michela (358th) KIA; Hit by flak near Metz.
P-51B YF-H 43-6649

**August 12, 1944**
Lt. Francis L. Eshelman (357th) MIA-E; Lost coolant and bailed out near Meaux.
P-51B OS-I 43-6626 "Terry Fran"

**August 14, 1944**
Lt. William A. Shade (357th) MIA-E; Hit by flak near Saarebourg.
P-51D OS-S 44-13734

**August 15, 1944**
Lt. Michael E. Graczyk (358th) POW; Hit by flak near Fulda.
P-51B YF-C 43-6834

**August 16, 1944**
Lt. John D. Riggs, Jr. (357th) KIA; Hit by a Me-109 near Hildesheim.
P-51B OS-W 43-7101

**August 18, 1944**
Capt. Bert W. Marshall, Jr. (354th) MIA-E; Downed by flak east of Paris and rescued by Lt. Royce W. Priest.
P-51D WR-F
Capt. Emil L. Sluga (358th) ASR; Damaged by flak and bailed out over the Channel.
P-51D YF-R 44-13625
Lt. Cleveland J. Brien, Jr. (358th) MIA-E; Hit by flak near Soissons
P-51B YF-A 42-106860

**August 26, 1944**
Lt. Richard G. Daves (358th) KIA; Crashed into the Channel for unknown reasons.
P-51B YF-Z 43-7036 "Jackie II"

**August 28, 1944**
Lt. Bert Smith (354th) MIA-E; Hit by flak near Metz.
P-51B WR-O 43-6431
Lt. John T. Hurley (357th) MIA-E; Hit by flak near Metz.
P-51D OS-M 44-14201 "Mustang"
Lt. Lawrence A. Phillips (358th) MIA-E; Hit by flak near Metz.
P-51D OS-K 44-13945
Lt. Arthur C. Duppstadt (358th) MIA-E; Hit by flak near Metz.
P-51D YF-E 44-13302 "Raunchy Runt"
Lt. John J. Gilmore, Jr. (358th) KIA; Hit by flak near Metz.
P-51B YF-B 43-6385 "Shanghai Lil"
Lt. Kenneth Hughes (358th) MIA-E; Hit by flak near Metz.
P-51B YF-C 42-106932 "Jo-Jo"
Lt. William W. Tolby (358th) MIA-E; Landed to pick up Lt. Duppstadt near Metz but failed to take-off.
P-51B YF-W 42-106452 "Buzz Boy"
Lt. Wilson B. Weber (358th) KIA; Hit by flak near Metz and bailed out but his chute failed.
P-51D YF-N 44-13565 "Baltimore Jo-Jo"

**September 3, 1944**
Lt. Sumner C. Williams (354th) MIA-E; Suffered mechanical trouble and bellied-in near Nantes.
P-51D WR-W 44-13349

**September 11, 1944**
Capt. Kenneth G. Rafferty (354th) KIA; Hit by flak near Marburg.
P-51B WR-P 42-106950 "The Iowa Beaut"
Lt. Charles R. McCurry (354th) KIA; Hit by flak near Marburg and bailed out but his chute failed.
P-51B WR-R 43-6943 "Patricia"
Capt. Walter L. Morgan (358th) KIA; Hit by flak near Kirchain.
P-51B YF-S 43-7023 "Big Stoop"

**September 12, 1944**
Lt. James C. Ellison (354th) KIA; Hit by a FW-190 near Eberswalde.
P-51B WR-Y 43-7182
Lt. John M. Chapman (357th) POW; Hit by flak at Schwartz Airfield.
P-51D OS-N 44-13796
Lt. Roddy W. Reed (358th) KIA; Last seen flying on the deck after after flak damage.
P-51D YF-E 44-14077 "Raunchy Runt II"

**September 18, 1944**
Lt. Robert O. Peters (358th) KIA; Downed by a P-51 near Warsaw.
P-51D YF-X 44-13675
Lt. Joseph J. Vigna (358th) KIA; Hit by a Me-109 near Warsaw.
P-51C YF-M 42-103317 "Dakota Kid"

**October 3, 1944**
Maj. Charles W. Lenfest (354th) POW; Landed near Deiningen to try and rescue Capt. Brown but got stuck in mud.
P-51D WR-B 44-14409 "Jane III"
Capt. Henry W. Brown (354th) POW; Hit by flak near Nordlingen and bellied-in near Deiningen.
P-51D WR-Z 44-13305 "Hun Hunter From Texas"

**October 5, 1944**
Lt. James O. Juntilla (357th) POW; Suffered mechanical near Aartwood.
P-51C OS-F 42-103735 "Gooch's Revenge"

**October 18, 1944**
Lt. William Lonkausky (357th) KIA; Hit by flak near Cologne.
P-51D OS-E 44-14186

**October 22, 1944**
Capt. Norman B. McDonald (354th) KIA; A P-51 rammed his ship while taxi-ing at Steeple Morden.
P-51D WR-T 44-14760

**November 2, 1944**
Lt. Albert A. Zimmerman (354th) KIA; Suffered mechanical trouble near Voorthoszen.
P-51D WR-M 44-13630
Capt. Joseph C. Englebreit (357th) POW; Hit by flak near Wernigerode.
P-51D OS-C 44-14203 "Spook III"

**November 9, 1944**
Lt. Carl V. Hull, Jr. (354th) POW; Hit by flak near Miltenberg.
P-51D WR-V 44-14536

**November 16, 1944**
Lt. Marion L. Woolard (354th) POW-D; Hit by flak near Barleburg. Was later killed in April of 1945 by an artillery barrage.
P-51B WR-W 42-106896

**November 20, 1944**
Lt. Robert White (357th) KIA; Ditched in the North Sea after suffering mechanical trouble.
P-51D OS-
Lt. Edward F. Baraburda (358th) KIA; Hit by flak near Zulpich.
P-51D YF-C 44-13564 "Little Nobody"

**November 26, 1944**
Lt. Bernard R. Barab (357th) KIA; Collided with Lt. Kelley west of Dummer Lake.
P-51D OS- 44-13574
Lt. Charles W. Kelley (357th) KIA; Collided with Lt. Barab west of Dummer Lake.
P-51B OS- 42-106910

**December 5, 1944**
Lt. Ben C. Williams (357th) POW; Suffered mechanical failure and bailed out north of Berlin.
P-51D OS-D 44-15013

**December 10, 1944**
Lt. Maury H. Ivey (354th) POW; Suffered mechanical failure west of Bingen.
P-51D WR-B 44-14293 "Lackin' Shackin"

**December 15, 1944**
Lt. Arthur K. Alexander (358th) POW; Suffered mechanical failure and bailed out north of Munster.
P-51D YF-J 44-15014

**December 25, 1944**
Lt. Harold L. Monahan (357th) KIA; Hit by a FW-190 south of Coblenz.
P-51D OS- 44-15304

**January 13, 1945**
Lt. Thomas A. Ksanzak (358th) KIA; Spun-in near Melbourne after take-off.
P-51D YF-O 44-13319

**January 20, 1945**
Lt. Frank R. Masters (358th) POW; Hit by flak near Minden.
P-51D YF-V 44-63162

**January 29, 1945**
Lt. Scott P. Prothro (354th) POW; Hit by flak near Geldern.
P-51D WR-B 44-15279 "Miss Miami"

**February 3, 1945**
Lt. William A. Cummins (358th) KIA; Hit by flak near Ulzen.
P-51D YF-

**February 9, 1945**
Lt. Thomas J. Taylor (358th) KIA; Hit by flak and crashed near Liege.
P-51D YF-A 44-14428

**February 10, 1945**
Lt. Oran Stalcup (354th) KIA; Ditched in the Channel after suffering mechanical failure.
P-51D WR-X 44-13571 "Texas Terror IV"

**February 14, 1945**
Maj. John H. Wilson (357th) KIA; Damaged by flak and crashed while landing at an Allied field on the Continent.
P-51D OS-W 44-14260 "Becky"

**February 21, 1945**
Lt. James J. Costigan (354th) KIA; Hit by flak near Amsbach.
P-51K WR-C 44-11359 "Lil Lila Lee"

**February 22, 1945**
Lt. George A. Kemper, Jr. (354th) POW; Hit by flak near Quackenbruck and bellied-in near Dummer Lake.
P-51D WR-P 44-14275 "Down For Double"

**February 23, 1945**
Lt. Robert M. White (354th) POW; Hit by flak near Neuburg.
P-51C WR-V 42-103795 "Dutchess of Manhattan"

**February 24, 1945**
Lt. Sellers S. Hardee (357th) KIA; Spun-in after take-off.
P-51D OS-H 44-14402

**March 1, 1945**
Capt. Jack M. Beckman (358th) KIA; Hit by flak while chasing a Me-262 near Ingolstadt.
P-51D YF-T 44-14230 "Trigger III"

**March 15, 1945**
Lt. Jack H. Dressler (357th) MIA-E; Hit by flak and bellied-in near Russian lines.
P-51D OS-
Lt. Johnnie W. Long (358th) MIA-E; Hit by flak near Hanover and bellied-in near Russian lines.
P-51D YF-F 44-13879

**March 21, 1945**
LtCol. Emil L. Sluga (358th) POW; Hit by flak near Horsten and bailed out near Stadlohn.
P-51D YF-L 44-13354 "Slugger"

**March 22, 1945**
Lt. David C. Tuholski (354th) POW; Hit by flak near Wurzburg.
P-51D WR-Y 44-72186 "Dragon Wagon"

**March 26, 1945**
Capt. Wendell W. Beaty (358th) KIAc; Crashed near Calais in bad weather while on a practice hop.
P-51D YF-

**April 4, 1945**
Lt. Robert A. Goth (354th) KIA; Hit by a FW-190 near Ludwigslust.
P-51D WR-R 44-14704 "Psyche"
Lt. Richard A. Gray (354th) POW; Hit by flak near Ludwigslust.
P-51D WR-O 44-13591 "Chugger II"
Lt. Thomas F. Truell, Jr. (354th) KIA; Hit by a FW-190 near Ludwigslust.
P-51D WR-P 44-14228 "Lady Barbara II"

**April 5, 1945**
Lt. Robert G. McDonnell (354th) KIA; Hit by flak near Buren.
P-51K WR-J 44-11759

**April 7, 1945**
Lt. Newell F. Mills, Jr. (354th) KIA; Lost in bad weather near Bremen.
P-51D WR- 44-72306
Lt. Gilbert M. Plowman (354th) KIA; Lost in bad weather near Bremen.
P-51D WR-Z 44-15346 "Bobbie Socks"

**April 8, 1945**
Lt. William J. Cullerton (357th) POW-E; Hit by flak near Ansbach. Shot by SS troops but rescued by civilians.
P-51D OS- 44-64011

**April 13, 1945**
Lt. Werner J. Schlecht (358th) POW; Hit by flak near Rendsburg.
P-51D YF-B 44-62068

**April 16, 1945**
Lt. Joseph E. Lake (357th) KIA; Hit by flak at Erferding.
P-51D OS-
Lt. Thurman C. Long (357th) POW; Hit by flak near Linz.
P-51D OS- 44-72987
Capt. Lawrence J. Dissette (358th) MIA-E; Hit by flak at Straubing and bellied-in northwest of the field.
P-51D YF-Q 44-14644 "Damn Yank III"
Lt. William J. Lynch (358th) POW; Hit by flak at Straubing.
P-51K YF-R 44-11642
Lt. Francis N. McCollom (358th) POW; Hit by flak at Straubing and bellied-in east of Regensburg.
P-51D YF-N 44-14385 "Wooly Lamb"
Lt. John A. Rogers (358th) MIA-E; Hit by flak at Straubing.
P-51K YF-F 44-12122 "Lady Dana"

**May 31, 1945**
Lt. Robert L. Crabb (354th) KIAc; Stalled out and crashed 15 miles from Steeple Morden.
P-51D WR-

**June 11, 1945**
Lt. Randolph W. Cooper (357th) KIAc;
P-51D OS- 44-13512

**June 21, 1945**
Lt. William T. Burnett (357th) KIAc;
P-51D OS-Y 44-14858

**Headquarters**
Butler, Reed B., Capt.; June 1944; ex-357th Ftr Sqn
P-51B OS-H
Chick, Lewis W., Maj.; October 1943-November 1943; to 325th Ftr Grp, MTO; ex-4th Ftr Grp
Cummings, William J., Col.; January 1943-November 1944; ex-24th Pur Grp, PTO
P-47D OS-V 42-8518 "Wild Bill"
P-51B OS-V "Wild Bill"
P-51D OS-V "Wild Bill"
DeMont, Russell D., Maj.; November 1944-EOW; ex-93rd Bomb Group
Dillon, Richard M., Capt.; March 1945-EOW; ex-358th Ftr Sqn
Dix, Gerald J., LtCol.; February 1943-June 8, 1944(POW); ex-17th Pur Sqn, PTO
P-47D YF-D
P-51B YF-D 43-7164
Gilchrist, William D., LtCol.
Haviland, Fred R., Jr., Capt.; November 1944-January 1945; ex-357th Ftr Sqn
P-51D OS-H 44-14402 "Barbara"
Hubbard, Thomas H., LtCol.; February 1943-November 13, 1943(MIA-E); ex-24th Pur Grp & 347th Ftr Grp, PTO
P-47D WR-P 42-8404 "Lil Jo"
Kinnard, Claiborne H., LtCol.; June 1944-September 1944; to 4th Ftr Grp; ex-354th Ftr Sqn
February 1945-June 1945
P-51B WR-A 42-106950 "Man O'War"
P-51D WR-A 44-15625 "Man O'War"
P-51D WR-A 44-72144 "Man O'War"
Kirby, Henry H., Jr., Maj.; July 1944-EOW; ex-357th Ftr Sqn
P-51B OS-N 43-24795 "Arkansas Traveler"
P-51D OS-N 44-13771 "Arkansas Traveler"
Marshall, Bert W., Jr., LtCol.; October 1944-September 1945; ex-354th Ftr Sqn
P-51D WR-B 44-15279 "Jane V"
P-51D WR-B 44-72253 "Jane VI"
P-51D WR-B 44-72953 "Jane VII"
Minchew, Leslie D., Capt.; October 1944-July 1945; ex-357th Ftr Sqn
P-51D OS-Q 44-14753
Rosenblatt, Charles J., Maj.; July 1943-June 1944; to 358th Ftr Sqn
P-47D YF-F
Stewart, Everett W., Col.; January 1944-February 1945; to 4th Ftr Grp; ex-352nd Ftr Grp
180 missions, 510 hours total
P-51B WR-S "Sunny V"
P-51D WR-S 44-13540 "Sunny VI"
P-51D WR-S 44-15255 "Sunny VII"

**354th Fighter Squadron**
Allard, Lawrence F., Lt.; States-March 11, 1944(POW)
P-47D WR-K
P-51B WR-K 43-6849

Austin, James P., Capt.; January 1943-August 1944
77 missions, 300:15 hours
P-47D WR-V
P-51B WR-V 43-6938
Barger, Clarence R., Lt.; January 1944-May 28, 1944(KIA)
45 missions, 160 hours
P-47D WR-C 42-75275 "Hellen"
P-51B WR-C 43-6631 "Hellen 2nd"
Barnhart, Philip W., Lt.; January 1945-November 1945
Barnes, Robert L., Lt.; March 1944-September 1944
77 missions, 300:15 hours
Bauman, Peter W., Jr., Lt.; States-May 1944
24missions, 74:45 hours
Beeler, Glenn D., Lt.; October 1944-June 1945
P-51K WR-J 44-11759 "My Baby Doll"
Benson, Arvid E., Lt.; States-August 1944
60 missions, 206:20 hours
P-51B WR-G 43-6457
Betounes, Samuel G., Lt.; June 1944-December 1943
Bradley, Robert T., Lt.; May 1944-December 1944; ex-4th Ftr Grp
Boulet, William P., Lt.; States-April 26, 1944(POW)
47 missions, 165:10 hours
P-47D WR-E
P-51B WR-E 43-7153
Brown, Henry W., Capt.; September 1943-October 3, 1944(POW)
72 missions
P-47D WR-Z 42-74703 "Baby"
P-51B WR-Z 42-106448 "Hun Hunter From Texas"
P-51D WR-Z 44-13305 "Hun Hunter From Texas"
Brown, Richard C., Lt.; March 1943-May 1944
54 missions, 200 hours
P-47D WR-T
P-51B WR-T 43-6915
Browning, Robert A., Lt.; February 1944-June 3, 1944(POW)
P-51B WR-K 42-106708
Burns, Charles R., Lt.; May 1945-EOW
0 missions
Christensen, Walter M., Lt.; April 1944-May 28, 1944(KIA)
14 missions, 61:30 hours
Costigan, James J., Lt.; January 1945-February 21, 1945(KIA)
Coulter, Bennett C., Lt.; May 1945-EOW
0 missions
Coutre, Robert D., Lt.; May 1944-June 7, 1944(MIA-E)
7 missions, 22:30 hours
Crabb, Robert L., Lt.; May 1945-May 31, 1945(KIAc); ex-B-24 pilot
0 missions
Cross, Richard G., Lt.; February 1944-September 1944
77 missions, 300:15 hours
P-51B WR-L 42-106450 "Dottie"
Culp, Harold F., Lt.; @December 1943-April 5, 1944(KIA)
31 missions, 101:55 hours
P-51B WR-P 43-7076
Davis, Henry W., Lt.; April 1944-June 4, 1944(KIA)
11 missions, 45 hours
Decklar, Carl E., Lt.; November 1944-September 1945
P-51K WR-H 44-11360 "Dot Darlin"
Delnegro, Alfred J., Lt.; States-November 29, 1943(KIA)
12 missions, 28:55 hours
P-47D WR-D 42-7996
Denti, Victor E., Lt.; June 1944-July 5, 1944(KIA)
17 missions, 67:05 hours
DeSieno, Carl D., Lt.; August 1944-September 1944
4 missions, 9:40 hours
Donaldson, Clarence, Lt.; April 1944-May 20, 1944(KIA)
7 missions, 28:40 hours
Donovan, James, Lt.; September 1943-September 25, 1943(KIAc)
0 missions
Duffy, James E., Jr., Capt.; January 1943-EOW
P-47D WR-Y 42-74681
P-51B WR-Y 43-7182 "Dragon Wagon"
P-51D WR-Y 44-14603 "Dragon Wagon"
P-51D WR-Y 44-63764 "Dragon Wagon"
Ellison, James E., Lt.; June 1944-September 12, 1944(KIA)
31 missions, 131:35 hours
Falvey, Harold W., F/O; September 1944-June 1945
P-51D WR-E 44-15652
P-51D WR-E 44-63222
Fletcher, Jack M., Lt.; November 1944-September 1945
P-51D WR-T
Folger, John M., Lt.; April 1944-August 6, 1944(KIA)
52 missions, 228:20 hours
P-51B WR-Q 43-7137
Fortier, Norman J., Maj.; January 1943-September 1945
112 missions, 457 hours
P-47D WR-N
P-51C WR-N 42-103802 "Bud"
P-51B WR-N 42-106870 "Bud"
P-51D WR-N 44-15373
P-51D WR-N 44-72361
Fritts, Herbert E., Lt.; April 1944-May 24, 1944(KIA)
16 missions, 67 hours
Gadpaille, Warren J., Lt.; November 1944-June 1945
P-51D WR-Z 44-15346 "Bobbie Socks"
Galer, Donald V., Lt.; November 1944-EOW
P-51D WR-Q "Cherraine"
Goth, Robert A., Lt.; November 1944-April 4, 1945(KIA)
Graham, Clarence H., Lt.; May 1944-October 1944
P-51B WR-M 42-106437 "Darlin Doris"
P-51D WR-M 44-13630 "Darlin Doris"
Graham, Gordon M., LtCol.; September 1944-June 1945
73 missions, 368:05 hours
P-51D WR-F 44-15255 "Down For Double"
Gray, Richard A., Lt.; January 1945-April 4, 1945(POW); ex-466th Bomb Grp(37 missions)
1 mission
Harness, Robert L., Lt.; March 1944-September 1944
77 missions, 300:15 hours
P-51B WR-R
Hauver, Charles D., Lt.; July 1944-December 1944
P-51B WR-R 43-6943 "Patricia"
P-51D WR-R 44-14090 "Princess Pat"
P-51D WR-R 44-14704 "Princess Pat II"
Heaton, Robert L., Lt.; September 1944-June 1945
P-51D WR-O 44-13591 "Chugger"
P-51D WR-O 44-15621 "Chugger II"
Hixon, Thomas R., Jr., F/O; January 1945-EOW
Hoffman, Garlyn O., Lt.; May 1944-August 3, 1944(POW)
34 missions, 154:35 hours
Horvath, Joseph F., Lt.; July 1944-September 1944
21 missions, 91:05 hours
Houston, Byron G., Jr., Lt.; States-May 1944
55 missions, 203:25 hours
P-51B WR-S 43-7157 "Marjorie II"
Huish, Heber M., Lt.; June 1944-July 7, 1944(KIA)
12 missions, 56:55 hours
Hulderman, Robert E., Lt.; May 1944-October 1944
58 missions, 264:25 hours
P-51B WR-P 42-106950 "The Iowa Beaut"
P-51D WR-P 44-14079 "The Iowa Beaut II"
Hull, Carl V., Jr., Lt.; June 1944-November 9, 1944(POW)
P-51D WR-I 44-14536
Ivey, Maury H., Lt.; September 1944-December 10, 1944(POW)
P-51D WR-B 44-14293 "Lackin Shackin
Jabara, James, Lt.; February 1945-November 1945; ex-363rd Ftr Grp
108 missions total
P-51D WR-K 44-14346 "Ceegar Kid"
Jackson, Norbert P., Lt.; June 1944-December 1944
P-51D WR-C 44-13963
Jacobson, Donald J., Lt.; March 1944-May 20, 1944(KIA)
17 missions, 72:50 hours
Johnson, Fred M., Lt.; June 1944-December 1944
P-51D WR-J 44-14089 "Sweet Dorsey"
Johnston, Curtis G., Capt.; May 1943-April 11, 1944(POW)
53 missions, 135 hours
P-47D WR-O 42-8444
P-51B WR-O 43-6944
Kaplan, Alfred B., Lt.; January 1945-November 1945
P-51D WR-M 44-72427 "Daphne"
Kemper, George A., Jr., Lt.; September 1944-February 22, 1945(POW)
P-51D WR-P 44-13540 "Betsy K"
Kilmer, James L., Lt.; June 1944-December 1944
P-51D WR-L 44-13611
Kinnard, Claiborne H., LtCol.; November 1943-June 1944; to HdQts; ex-356th Ftr Grp
P-47D WR-A
P-51B WR-A 43-6431 "Man O'War"
P-51B WR-A 42-106950 "Man O'War"
Koraleski, Walter J., Capt.; February 1943-April 15, 1944(POW)
60 missions, 189:10 hours
P-47D WR-L "Miss Thunder"
P-51B WR-L 43-6968
Kozacka, Arthur G., Lt.; February 1945-EOW
Kucheman, Henry B., Jr., Maj.; February 1943-July 1944
82 missions, 302 hours
P-47D WR-U 42-8434 "Lil Lo"
P-51B WR-U 42-106450 "Lil Lo"
P-51D WR-U 44-13571 "Lil Lo"
Kurtz, Robert G., Capt.; April 1943-August 3, 1944(POW)
56 missions, 202:05 hours
P-47D WR-A
P-51B WR-A 43-6895 "Hat Jane"
P-51D WR-A 44-14001
Langley, Donald B., Lt.; February 1945-EOW
Lenfest, Charles W., Maj.; April 1943-October 3, 1944(POW)
P-47D WR-F 42-22464 "Lorie"
P-51B WR-F 43-6948 "Lorie II"
P-51B WR-F 42-106874 "Lorie III"
P-51B WR-F 43-6870 "Lorie IV"
P-51D WR-F 44-14275 "Lorie V"
Mann, Herbert R., Capt.; July 1944-March 1945

Marshall, Bert W., Jr., Maj.; May 1944-October 1944; to HdQts
P-51B WR-B 43-6457 "Jane"
P-51D WR-B 44-14293 "Jane II"
P-51D WR-B 44-14409 "Jane III"
P-51D WR-B 44-14799 "Jane IV"
Martin, William D., Lt.; April 1944-September 1944
79 missions, 300 hours
P-51C WR-J 42-103334 "Martin's Gloria"
P-51D WR-J 44-13756 "Martin's Gloria"
McCurry, Charles R., Lt.; July 1944-September 11, 1944(KIA)
McDonald, Norman B., Capt.; July 1944-October 22, 1944(KIA)
P-51D WR-T 44-14760
McDonnell, Robert G., Lt.; February 1945-April 5, 1945(KIA)
McLear, Robert M., Lt.; August 1944-March 1945; to 2nd Scouting Force
P-51B WR-G "Little Shorty"
McLeod, Michael J., Lt.; February 1945-September 1945
Mellen, Joseph E., Capt.; October 1944-May 1945
P-51K WR-C 44-11359 "Lil Lila Lee"
Mendenhall, Lee G., Maj.; March 1943-March 1945
P-47D WR-X "Texas Terror"
P-47D WR-X 42-74615 "Texas Terror II"
P-51B WR-X 43-6885 "Texas Terror III
P-51D WR-X 44-13571 "Texas Terror IV"
Mills, Newell F., Jr., Lt.; September 1944-April 7, 1945(KIA)
Milner, James L., Lt.; June 1944-September 1944
42 missions, 177:05 hours
Mincemeyer, Allen J., Lt.; January 1945-EOW
Minchew, Leslie D., Lt.; States-December 1943; to 357th Ftr Sqn
P-47D WR-M
Molnar, John E., Lt.; September 1944-EOW
Morris, Ray S., Lt.; States-July 1944
74 missions, 300:35 hours
P-47D WR-M
P-51B WR-M 42-106437 "Darlin Doris"
Murdoch, Ray F., Jr., Lt.; States-December 30, 1943(POW)
7 missions, 20:35 hours
P-47D WR-K 42-8453
Neal, Thomas F., Jr., Capt.; States-April 29, 1944(KIA)
50 missions, 159:55 hours
P-47D WR-J 42-8557
P-51B WR-J 43-6577
O'Neill, James J., Lt.; February 1945-EOW
Page, Howard R., Lt.; April 1945-June 1945
Patrick, Robert J., F/O; April 1945-June 1945
Patterson, Gilbert T., Lt.; June 1944-August 3, 1944(KIA)
23 missions, 99:35 hours
Pearson, Richard P., Lt.; September 1944-September 1945
P-51K WR-W 44-11362 "Bub's Boy"
Peglar, Warren B., F/Lt.; July 1944-September 1944; RAF D.S.
Perry, Emil F., Capt.; February 1944-August 1944
78 missions, 300:25 hours
P-51B WR-I
Plowman, Gilbert M., Lt.; March 1945-April 7, 1945(KIA)
Pool, Oliver K., F/O; April 1945-EOW
Priest, Royce W., Lt.; May 1944-December 1944
67 missions, 310 hours
P-51B WR-E "Weepin' Deacon"
P-51D WR-E 44-13764 "Weepin' Deacon II"
P-51D WR-E 44-15279 "Weepin' Deacon III"
Protho, Scott P., Lt.; September 1944-January 29, 1945(POW)
P-51D WR-B 44-15279 "Miss Miami"
Quarles, Lee S., Lt.; April 1945-EOW
Rafferty, Kenneth G., Capt.; September 1944-September 11, 1944(KIA)
2 missions, 10:30 hours
Roberts, Frederick, F/O; April 1945-EOW
Rotchford, Howard E., Lt.; April 1945-EOW
Ruark, Thomas W., Lt.; June 1944-June 27, 1944(MIA-E)
3 missions, 8:35 hours
Rood, Thomas M., Lt.; March 1945-EOW
P-51D WR-I "Miss Janice"
Ross, Donald F., Lt.; April 1945-June 1945
Sanders, Donald J., Lt.; February 1945-June 1945
Sarver, Frank A., Lt.; March 1945-EOW
Sawchuck, Peter N., Lt.; July 1944-July 24, 1944(KIA)
2 missions, 10 hours
Scheid, Adolph J., Lt.; March 1945-EOW
Schwab, Warren A., Lt.; June 1944-July 19, 1944(POW)
24 missions, 107:45 hours
Schultz, Floyd W., Lt.; June 1944-December 1944
Schutt, Ralph C., Jr., Lt.; March 1944-September 1944
65 missions, 300 hours
Shannon, Joseph M., F/O; August 1944-September 1944
8 missions, 40 hours
Silva, Stanley E., Capt.; October 1944-June 1945
P-51K WR-B 44-11667 "My Catherine S"
P-51D WR-B 44-72186 "My Catherine S"
Smith, Bert I., Lt.; August 1944-August 28, 1944(MIA-E)
Smith, Kirby D.E., Lt.; October 1944-January 1945; to 2nd Scouting Force
Spencer, Charles H., Capt.; August 1944-April 1945
Spitler, Garth, Lt.; July 1944-January 1945
Stalcup, Oran, Lt.; August 1944-February 10, 1945(KIA)
P-51D WR-X 44-13571 "Jolly Roger"
Stanton, O.N., Lt.; July 1944-May 1945
Starr, Albert B., Capt.; States-May 1944
61 missions, 200:10 hours
P-47D WR-Q
P-51B WR-Q 43-7137
Sweat, Charles H., Lt.; States-March 8, 1944(KIA)
40 missions, 113:55 hours
P-47D WR-R 42-8441
Taylor, Floyd K., Lt.; May 1944-August 3, 1944(MIA-E)
Taylor, Robert G., Lt.; April 1944-August 1944
68 missions, 300 hours
Todd, Charles G., Lt.; July 1944-January 1945
P-51D WR-A 44-72996
Todd, Theodore P., Jr., Lt.; November 1944-September 1945
Trembarth, Floyd W., Lt.; June 1944-December 1944
Truell, Thomas F., Jr., Lt.; March 1945-April 4, 1945(KIA)
P-51D WR-P 44-14228 "Lady Barbara II"
Tulhoski, David C., Lt.; December 1944-March 22, 1945(POW)
Vickery, Durran M., Jr., Lt.; December 1944-September 1945
P-51B WR-M 42-106437 "Alabama Bound"
P-51D WR-L 44-14910 "Ann Anita/Alabama Bound"
Vincent, Roland L., Lt.; States-December 4, 1943(KIAc)
16 missions, 41:55 hours
Vineyard, Paul W., Jr., Lt.; December 1944-EOW
P-51B WR-U 42-106450
Walsh, Robert J., Lt.; December 1944-EOW
P-51D WR-G 44-13756 "Stubborn Stella"
Westerveld, Robert, Lt.; December 1944-EOW
White, Alvin S., Capt.; June 1944-May 1945
P-51D WR-S 44-14228 "Mary Lou"
White, Richard M., Lt.; August 1944-June 1945
White, Robert M., Lt.; August 1944-February 23, 1945(POW)
P-51C WR-V 42-103795 "Duchess of Manhattan"
Williams, Joseph R., Capt.; States-November 1943; to 356th Ftr Grp
17 missions, 36:50 hours
Williams, Kenneth D., Lt.; States-March 26, 1944(MIA-E)
33 missions, 99:25 hours
Williams, Sumner C., Lt.; May 1944-September 3, 1944(MIA-E)
49 missions, 206:50 hours
P-51D WR-W 44-13359
Williamson, Brady C., Capt.; March 1943-January 1945
98 missions
P-47D WR-H
P-51B WR-H
P-51D WR-H 44-14252 "Palma"
P-51D WR-A 44-14374 "Palma II"
Wood, Thomas L., Capt.; July 1944-February 1945
Woody, Robert E., Capt.; States-May 1944
55 missions, 201:30 hours
P-47D WR-W 42-8493
P-51B WR-W 43-6520 "Woody's Maytag"
Woolard, Marion L., Lt.; August 1944-November 16, 1944(POW-D)
P-51B WR-L 42-106896
Wright, Gilbert S., Lt.; September 1943-July 1944
76 missions, 300:10 hours
P-47D WR-H
P-51B WR-H 43-24824 "Sophia S"
Zimmerman, Albert A., Lt.; August 1944-November 2, 1944(KIA)

**357th Fighter Squadron**

Badavas, Charles, Lt.; June 1944-March 1945
Barab, Bernard R., Lt.; September 1944-November 26, 1944(KIA)
Beise, Melvin E., Lt.; January 1945-EOW
Bernoske, Robert., Lt.; April 1944-August 8, 1944(MIA-E)
Bille, Henry S., Maj.; February 1943-September 1945
P-47D OS-K 42-8397
P-51B OS-K
P-51D OS-K 44-14314 "Prune Face"
Bowen, James E., Lt.; June 1944-January 1945
Buckles, Clifford R., Lt.; June 1944-September 1944; to 1st Scouting Force
Burnett, William T., Lt.; January 1945-June 21, 1945(KIAc)
Burroughs, Vernon A., Lt.; States-May 1944; to 4th Ftr Grp
P-47D OS-B 42-8438 "Dizzy Miss"
P-51B OS-B 43-6722 "Dizzy Miss"
Butcher, Chester J., Lt.; States-March 27, 1944(POW)
P-47D OS-F 42-22538 "The Butcher"
P-51B OS-F 43-6777 "The Butcher"
Butler, Reed B., Capt.; States-June 1944; to HdQts
P-47D OS-H 42-8000
P-51B OS-H
Carlson, Edwin O., Lt.; States-November 7, 1943(KIA)
Cavender, James V., Jr., Lt.; August 1944-EOW
Chapman, John M., Lt.; June 1944-September 12, 1944(POW)
Chesler, Bernard, F/O; December 1944-April 1945
Collins, Clark, Lt.; States-November 5, 1943(KIA)
Colson, Charles C., Capt.; States-EOW
Cooper, Randolph W., Lt.; January 1945-June 11, 1945(KIAc)

*Joseph Shupe of the 370th Fighter Squadron.*

*83rd Fighter Squadron ace Charles Peal.*

*Another Pacific vet who became an ace in Europe was Thomas Hayes of the 357th Fighter Group.*

*Long serving 335th Fighter Squadron ace Pierce McKennon.*

*Top strafer in the 375th Fighter Squadron, Martin Johnson.*

*James Clark who served with the 334th Fighter Squadron and later as Deputy CO of the 4th Fighter Group.*

*Top scorer in the 328th Fighter Squadron, John Thornell.*

*Robert Hatter of the 368th Fighter Squadron who burned six German planes on May 21, 1944.*

*Former Pacific flyer Stephen Andrew of the 486th Fighter Squadron.*

*Olin Gilbert of the 83rd Fighter Squadron and Headquarters, 78th Fighter Group.*

*Edwin Heller, top strafer in the 486th Fighter Squadron.*

*Leading 351st Fighter Squadron scorer Gordon Compton.*

Four aces of the 56th Fighter Group in mid-1944; left to right Hub Zemke, Dave Schilling, Francis Gabreski, Fred Christensen.

Wilton Johnson of the 352nd Fighter Squadron receiving an award from Murray Woodbury, CO of the 66th Fighter Wing.

362nd Fighter Squadron pilots in early 1944; on left is Konstantin Vogel (KIA March 18) with Harvey Mace.

James Poindexter of the 352nd Fighter Squadron.

Nine victory ace Stanley Morrill of the 62nd Fighter Squadron.

*Robert Stultz, 79th Fighter Squadron, with his crewchief Clarence Green.*

*62nd Fighter Squadron replacement pilot Harold Blaisdell.*

*Left: Willard Lewis of the 79th Fighter Squadron.*

*Another Pacific vet and CO of the 361st Fighter Group, Thomas Christian.*

*Left: 351st Fighter Squadron member George Perpente and crew.*

*P-38J of the 434th Fighter Squadron (serial was 42-67424).*

*Members of the 4th Fighter Group after returning from the Russia Shuttle in early July 1944. In the background are two 334th Fighter Squadron Mustangs, QP-W 44-13372 of James Clark and QP-L 42-106924 "Salem Representative" of Ralph Hofer.*

*Above: William Smith's KI-G 44-13838 "Okie Bloke IV" of the 55th Fighter Squadron.*

*Right: 328th Fighter Squadron P-51B of John Thornell, PE-T 42-106872 "Pattie Ann II."*

*Wilford Drake's 361st Fighter Squadron P-47, QI-J 42-26275 "Joy Ann."*

*Above: Mustangs of the 375th (left) and 376th (lower) Fighter Squadrons in flight.*

*Right: 486th Fighter Squadron P-51 of Thomas Colby, PZ-T 44-13603 "Lil Evey III."*

*Below: John Landers' 38th Fighter Squadron P-51, CG-O 44-13823 "Big Beautiful Doll."*

354th Fighter Squadron Mustang of Bert Marshall, WR-B 44-14409 "Jane III."

P-51B flown by Joe Higgins of the 336th Fighter Squadron, VF-D 43-6942 "Meiner Kleiner."

B7-R 44-13357 "Tika IV" of Vernon Richards, 374th Fighter Squadron.

Harvey Maces' last plane, G4-B 44-13558 "Sweet Helen II."

*384th Fighter Squadron P-51 of David Williams, 5Y-W 44-14076 "Dot."*

*79th Fighter Squadron P-51 of Harold Rau, MC-R 44-14337 "Gentle Annie."*

A pair of 62nd Fighter Squadron Thunderbolts prior to take-off. In front is Dave Schilling's LM-S 42-26641 while behind is LM-Z 42-26280.

Jack Ilfrey on his 79th Fighter Squadron P-51, MC-I 44-13761 "Happy Jack's Go Buggy."

Crash-landed 358th Fighter Squadron P-51B in August of 1944, YF-X 43-6845.

Oscar Fladmark's 368th Fighter Squadron P-51 after a landing gear collapse before take-off on September 5, 1944. CV-R 42-106879.

*Right: Everett Stewart's 354th Fighter Squadron Mustang WR-S 44-13540 "Sunny VI."*

*Below: James Meholic with his crewchief Pat Cavuto with OC-E 42-26129 of the 359th Fighter Squadron.*

*Meholic's later OC-E 42-26851.*

*Formation of 383rd Fighter Squadron P-51's. In front is N2-W 44-13936 "Carolina Moon."*

*Donovan Smith's 61st Fighter Squadron P-47, HV-S 42-28382 "Ole Cock III."*

*354th Fighter Squadron P-51 of Robert McLear, WR-G "Little Shorty."*

*Walt Mullins' 55th Fighter Squadron P-51, KI-S 44-13859.*

*503rd Fighter Squadron P-51's in flight. Front to back are D7-F 44-13629 "Dee" of Clarence Knott, D7-Z 44-13980 "Shy Ann" of Ed Beavers, D7-M 44-14065 "Sally II" of Leonard Fiorito, and D7-O.*

*Frank Birtciel's first 343rd Fighter Squadron P-51, CY-D 44-14561 "Miss Velma."*

*P-51 of Don Graham, CO of the 357th Fighter Group, B6-W 44-13388 "Bodacious."*

*Line-up of 82nd Fighter Squadron P-47's. In front is MX-S 42-27339 of Joe Myers while second is MX-W 42-26387 "Miss Behave."*

*Another 343rd Fighter Squadron P-51, this time CY-M 44-13837 "Miss Marilyn II" of Richard Ozinga.*

505th Fighter Squadron mount of James Starnes, 6N-X 44-14113 "Tar Heel."

350th Fighter Squadron P-47 flown by William Tanner, LH-O 42-26472 "Prudence V."

Above: Hershel Pascoe's 363rd Fighter Squadron P-51, B6-D 44-13714 "Desert Rat."

Right: Henry Brown (left) with other 354th Fighter Squadron personnel in front of Brown's WR-Z 44-13305 "Hun Hunter From Texas."

*Frank Oiler's 84th Fighter Squadron P-47, WZ-S 42-28878 "Eileen."*

*A pair of 339th Fighter Group Mustangs above thick clouds.*

*Richard Andrino (left) and Orvil Burwell in front of 360th Fighter Squadron P-47 PI-C 42-26683 "Mugsy."*

*KI-P of the 55th Fighter Squadron along with a 446th Bomb Group B-24.*

*Charles Servocky flew this 360th Fighter Squadron P-47, PI-F 42-76204 "Bright Eyes."*

*George Rich in his 505th Fighter Squadron P-51 "Chute! You're Faded."*

*William Bailey's first 352nd Fighter Squadron P-51, SX-B 44-14303 "Double Trouble."*

375th Fighter Squadron ace Robert Wright with his crew. Left to right are Tidwell (radio), Walt Johnson (armorer), Wright, and Charles Upright (crewchief).

Another shot of Wright and crew with E2-K 42-106631 "Toby" Left to right: Tidwell, Upright, Wright, Fred Carpenter (assistant), and Johnson.

Willie Jackson who made ace flying with the 328th and 486th Fighter Squadrons and Headquarters, 352nd Fighter Group.

343rd Fighter Squadron "ace-in-a-day" William Allen with his crew of CY-V 44-14049 "Pretty Patty II". Left to right are Unk, Gus Hoglund (assistant), Allen, and Joe Ruzika (crewchief).

77th Fighter Squadron ace Fred Alexander and crew. Left to right are Fred Frame (crewchief), Milton McAtee (assistant), Alexander, and unk.

Ben Mayo who served with the 82nd and 84th Fighter Squadrons.

Costello, Walter O., Lt.; July 1944-July 20, 1944(MIA-E)
    2 missions
Cotter, John A., Lt.; May 1944-August 3, 1944(POW)
Cox, William A., Lt.; @May 1944-September 1944; to 1st Scouting Force
Crandell, Jack L., Lt.; States-October 1944
Cullerton, William J., Lt.; June 1944-April 8, 1945(POW-E)
    P-51D OS-X 44-13677 "Miss Steve"
Delhamer, Robert W., Lt.; September 1944-August 1945
    P-51D OS-B 44-11194 "Super Gal-II"
DeMers, Ray F., Lt.; January 1944-April 24, 1944(KIA)
Dixon, Norman E., Lt.; June 1944-July 6, 1944(POW)
    13 missions
Douglas, Walter A., Lt.; April 1944-June 6, 1944(POW)
Dressler, Jack H., Lt.; December 1944-March 15, 1945(MIA-E)
    P-51D OS-L 44-14314 "Sexless Stella One More Time"
DuFresne, Roland J., Capt.; States-February 11, 1944(MIA-E)
Easterly, William S., Capt.; @January 1944-April 11, 1944(POW)
    P-47D OS-J 43-8389 "Sheaf's Jug"
    P-51B OS-J
Elder, John L., Jr., LtCol.; February 1943-September 1945
    P-47D OS-R 42-8544 "Moon"
    P-47D OS-R 42-22784 "Moon"
    P-51B OS-R 43-6776 "Moon"
    P-51B OS-R 42-106443 "Moon"
    P-51B OS-R 42-106723
    P-51D OS-R 44-63633
    P-51D OS-R 44-73065
Engelbreit, Joseph C., Capt.; April 1944-November 2, 1944(POW)
Erickson, Juel E., Lt.; August 1944-February 1945
Eshelman, Francis L., Lt.; April 1944-August 12, 1944(MIA-E)
    P-51B OS-I 43-6626
Forehand, Willard F., Lt.; September 1944-April 1945
Forker, George W., Lt.; February 1944-August 1944
    300 hours
Foster, Thomas J., Lt.; May 1944-June 7, 1944(KIA)
Fuller, Leonard B., Lt.; -July 7, 1944(KIA)
    P-47D OS-E 42-22549 "Kay"
    P-51B OS-E 43-6886 "Kay"
Garlich, Robert L., Lt.; November 1944-September 1945
    P-51D OS-D 44-13734 "Luscious Lu"
    P-51D OS-D 44-14966 "Luscious Lu II
Gelsone, Frank E., Lt.; January 1945-August 1945
Gilleland, Alvah G., Lt.; June 1944-December 1944
Gowing, Franklin R., Lt.; July 1944-August 2, 1944(MIA-E)
    6 missions
Greenwell, Howard K., Lt.; December 1944-March 1945; to 2nd Scouting Force
Griswold, Walter L., Jr., Lt.; October 1944-July 1945
    P-51D OS-U 44-14786 "Joereine II"
Guerrant, John, Lt.; April 1944-June 7, 1944(KIA)
Hardee, Sellers S., Lt.; October 1944-February 26, 1945(KIA)
Harrell, Harwood H., Lt.; May 1944-June 7, 1944(MIA-E)
Hartzog, James F., F/O; January 1945-EOW
Haviland, Fred R., Jr., Capt.; May 1944-November 1944; to HdQts
    P-51C OS-H 42-103753 "Barbara"
    P-51D OS-H 44-14402 "Barbara"
Hendrickson, Edwin M., Lt.; March 1944-August 1944
    300 hours
    P-51D OS-U 44-13353 "Gin Rummy"
Hill, Byron L., Lt.; States-April 5, 1944(KIA)
Hillman, Howard K., Lt.; February 1944-April 24, 1944(KIA)
Hober, Joseph D., F/O; December 1944-August 1945
Hollman, Nils B., Jr., Lt.; May 1944-June 7, 1944(KIA)
Hurley, John T., Lt.; June 1944-August 28, 1944(MIA-E)
Iglesias, Victor D., Lt.; October 1944-EOW
    P-51D OS-A 44-15595 "Jersey Bounce"
James, Wayne W., Lt.; April 1944-September 1944
Johnson, Leonard D., Lt.; July 1944-December 1944
Johnston, Ben D., Capt.; February 1943-March 29, 1944(POW)
    P-47D OS-I 42-22471
    P-51B OS-I
Juntilla, James O., Lt.; July 1944-October 5, 1944(POW)
Kaminski, Rudolph B., Lt.; February 1944-May 1, 1944(KIA)
Kelley, Charles W., Lt.; September 1944-November 26, 1944(KIA)
Kelley, Fred W., Capt.; States-September 1944
Kerch, Joseph F., Capt.; States-April 15, 1944(POW)
    P-51B OS-U 42-106463 "Bea"
    P-51B OS-U 42-106698 "Bea"
Keuhl, Robert C., Lt.; February 1945-EOW
Kincheloe, James L., Lt.; February 1945-July 1945
King, Myles A., Lt.; January 1944-June 22, 1944(POW)
Kirk, Robert J., Lt.; February 1945-EOW
Kirby, Henry H., Jr., Maj.; States-June 1944; to HdQts
    P-47D OS-N 42-8399 "Arkansas Traveler"
    P-51B OS-N 43-7140 "Arkansas Traveler"
Knight, Harold I., Lt.; Febraury 1945-EOW
    P-51D OS-M 44-14173 "Sue Sue"
Kubetin, William T., Lt.; February 1945-EOW
Laing, Donald J., Lt.; States-December 1943
    P-47D OS-X 42-8416
Lake, Joseph E., Lt.; September 1944-April 16, 1945(KIA)
Lambert, Howard L., Jr., Capt.; States-March 29, 1944(KIA)
Lamer, Charles W., Capt.; June 1944-October 1944
Lawrence, Hubert L., Lt.; February 1945-EOW
Lee, Charles M., Lt.; February 1944-August 8, 1944(KIA)
Long, Thurman C., Lt.; August 1944-April 16, 1945(POW)
    P-51B OS-L 42-106444 "Baby Bet"
    P-51D OS-L
Lonkausky, William, Lt.; September 1944-October 18, 1944(KIA)
Ludeke, Edward P., Capt.; June 1944-April 1945
Lyons, William S., Lt.; August 1944-April 1945
MacFarlane, Walter E., Lt.; -June 7, 1944(POW)
Martin, Ben D., Capt.; States-January 29, 1944(MIA-E)
Max, Joseph H., Lt.; July 1944-December 1944
    P-51D OS-G 44-14262 "Patty"
McCasland, Darwin D., Lt.; February 1944-April 15, 1944(POW)
McGinty, William J., Lt.; States-March 1944; to 358th Ftr Sqn
McGraw, Lawrence E., Lt.; States-November 15, 1943(KIA)
McHugh, Philip M.N., Lt.; April 1944-September 1944
McNally, Donald B., Lt.; States-November 15, 1943(KIA)
McNeff, Edward P., Capt.; January 1944-May 1945
    102 missions
McNeil, Ray J., Lt.; August 1944-EOW
Michels, Kenneth M., Lt.; June 1944-December 1944
Miller, Kenneth J., Lt.; July 1944-February 1945
    P-51D OS- "Melba J"
Minchew, Leslie D., Capt.; December 1943-October 1944; to HdQts; ex-354th Ftr Sqn
    P-51B OS-Q
    P-51D OS-Q 44-14753
Misner, Richard F., Lt.; October 1944-August 1945
Momberger, William, Lt.; States-March 9, 1944(KIA)
    P-47D OS-U 42-8498 "Jean's Little Moe"
Monahan, Howard L., Lt.; August 1944-December 25, 1944(KIA)
Moroney, Edward J., Lt.; May 1944-December 1944
    P-51D OS-I 44-15595 "Mary Jane"
Morrow, Harry P., Lt.; September 1943-@November 1943
Nelson, James E., Lt.; October 1944-August 1945
Norman, Robert L., Lt.; January 1944-April 24, 1944(KIA)
Olson, Norman E., Capt.; February 1943-April 8, 1944(KIA)
    P-47D OS-P 42-8413 "Ma Fran"
    P-47D OS-P "Ma Fran 2nd"
    P-47D OS-P "Ma Fran 3rd"
    P-51B OS-X 43-7176 "Ma Fran 4th"
Owens, Robert B., Lt.; March 1945-EOW
Packard, Hudson F., Lt.; February 1944-May 19, 1944(KIA)
Patelunas, Robert J., Lt.; March 1945-July 1945
Patterson, Robert C., Lt.; April 1945-July 1945
Paul, Theodore J., F/O; April 1945-EOW
Phillips, George W., Lt.; June 1944-June 6, 1944(KIA)
    1 mission
Phillips, Lawrence A., Lt.; July 1944-August 28, 1944(POW)
Pipher, Frank L., Jr., Lt.; States-January 24, 1944(KIA)
Prescotti, Ralph S., Lt.; April 1945-EOW
Ramsdell, Fred L., Jr., Maj.; February 1943-August 1944
    P-47D OS-T 42-8406 "Eager Eve"
    P-51B OS-T "Eager Eve"
Radle, Fred M., Jr., F/O; April 1945-July 1945
Reedy, Irving, Lt.; February 1944-April 8, 1944(POW)
Reiff, W.L., Lt.; June 1944-May 1945
Riffle, Elmer H., Lt.; September 1944-August 1945
Riggs, John D., Jr., Lt.; June 1944-August 16, 1944(KIA)
Rodgers, Francis H., Lt.; March 1945-July 1945
Rodgers, Johnathon, Lt.; March 1945-EOW
Rogers, Gilbert S., F/O; April 1945-July 1945
Rothenberg, Daniel S., Lt.; January 1944-March 8, 1944(KIA)
Ruecker, Ralph S., F/O; April 1945-July 1945
Ryan, John F., F/O; April 1945-EOW
Salinsky, John J., Lt.; February 1944-August 1944
    300 hours
Schmidt, George C., Lt.; September 1944-April 1945
Schoenfeldt, Dean E., Lt.; February 1944-August 1944
    300 hours
Shade, William A., Lt.; June 1944-August 14, 1944(MIA-E)
Sitton, Samuel, Jr., Lt.; October 1944-EOW
Spencer, Harold W., Lt.; June 1944-December 1944
Strachan, Robert W., Lt.; June 1944-March 1945
Sturm, Jack D., Lt.; January 1944-April 24, 1944(POW)
Szaniawski, Edward W., LtCol.; February 1943-May 19, 1944(POW)
    P-47D OS-A 42-8415 "Available Jones"
    P-47D OS-A "Available Jones 2nd"
    P-51B OS-A "Available Jones 3rd"
    P-51B OS-A "Available Jones 4th"
    P-51B OS-A 43-7142 "Available Jones 5th"
Thach, Robert G., Jr., Lt.; April 1945-July 1945
Watkins, David P., Lt.; December 1944-September 1945
    P-51D OS-N 44-13677 "Fickle Fanny"
Weidemann, John J., Lt.; December 1944-August 1945
    P-51D OS-H 44-14674 "Ginny J"
    P-51D OS-H 44-72373 "Ginny J"
Westphal, James S., Lt.; States-November 7, 1943(POW)
    P-47D OS-L 43-8370 "Alabama Bound"

White, Robert G., Lt.; September 1944-November 20, 1944(KIA)
Whitney, Emerson H., Lt.; December 1944-EOW
P-51D OS-U 44-14999 "Dapper Dan"
Wilkes, Henry O., Lt.; August 1944-July 1945
Williams, Benjamin G., Lt.; August 1944-December 5, 1944(POW)
Williamson, Jesse M., Lt.; States-December 1, 1943(POW)
Wilson, John H., Maj.; January 1943-February 14, 1945(KIA)
P-47D OS-W 42-8423 "Becky"
P-51B OS-W 43-7101 "Becky"
P-51D OS-W 44-14260 "Becky"

**358th Fighter Squadron**
Alexander, Arthur K., Lt.; September 1944-December 15, 1944(POW)
Allen, David R., Capt.; March 1945-April 1945; ex-4th Ftr Grp
Allen, Roscoe R., Lt.; September 1944-April 1945
Baker, Ray G., Lt.; July 1944-May 1945
Bannowsky, Alton M., Lt.; October 1944-March 1945
Baraburda, Edward F., Lt.; August 1944-November 20, 1944(KIA)
Beaty, Wendell W., Capt.; October 1944-March 26, 1945(KIAc)
47 missions, 230 hours
Beckman, Jack M., Capt.; January 1944-March 1, 1945(KIA); ex-RAF
P-51B YF-R 43-6945 "Judy/Wizard Kite"
P-51D YF-R 44-14126 "Hot Shot"
Blair, Charles W., Jr., Capt.; March 1943-March 1945
P-47D YF-E 42-8570
P-51B YF-E 43-6523 "Leakin' Liz"
P-51D YF-E 44-13302
P-51D YF-E 44-14564
Blaylock, Donald C., Lt.; May 1944-October 1944
Bonner, John, Jr., Lt.; October 1944-April 1945
Bowdler, William D., Lt.; January 1945-June 1945
Brien, Cleveland J., Jr., Lt.; May 1944-August 18, 1944(MIA-E)
P-51B YF-A 42-106860
Brown, Robert H., Lt.; August 1944-March 1945
P-51D YF-V 44-63162
Burlingame, William G., Lt.; January 1944-September 1944
P-51B YF-W 42-106452 "Miss Heck"
Carver, Harold I., Lt.; April 1943-March 16, 1944(POW)
P-47D YF-J 42-22461
P-51B YF-J 43-6527 "Indiana Clipper"
Chalot, John A., F/O; February 1944-March 11, 1944(POW)
Coleman, Ralph L., Lt.; April 1944-June 19, 1944(KIA)
Covault, Vern W., Lt.; April 1944-August 1944
Cummins, William, Lt.; October 1944-February 3, 1945(KIA)
Curran, Arthur R., Lt.; October 1944-May 1945
P-51D YF-P
Daves, Richard G., Lt.; August 1944-August 26, 1944(KIA)
Dean, Ralph, Lt.; February 1943-October 4, 1943(KIA)
4 missions
P-47D YF-Z 42-74667
DeGeorge, John J., Jr., Lt.; States-August 1944
Dickson, James B., Lt.; January 1943-April 8, 1944(KIA)
P-51B YF-X 43-7147 "Big Dogs/Ellen Jean"
Dillon, Richard M., Capt.; June 1944-September 1944; to 2nd Scouting Force
P-51B YF-N 43-7036 "Rugged Rebel"
Dissette, Lawrence J., Capt.; May 1943-April 16, 1945(POW)
95 missions
P-47D YF-Q 42-22518 "Damn Yank"
P-51B YF-Q 42-106858 "Damn Yank II"
P-51B YF-Q "Damn Yank III"
P-51D YF-Q 44-14644 "Damn Yank IV"
Donathan, Ben F., Lt.; December 1944-May 1945
P-51D YF-X 44-13708
Donovan, David A., Lt.; April 1944-June 8, 1944(KIA)
Douglas, Ward H., Lt.; June 1944-October 1944
P-51D YF-K 44-13366 "Baby Buggy"
Dudley, Lawrence M., Jr., Capt.; September 1943-February 1945
Dumas, William P., Lt.; February 1944-March 1944
Duppstadt, Arthur G., Lt.; June 1944-August 28, 1944(MIA-E)
Ekstrom, Karl F., Capt.; February 1943-December 30, 1943(KIA)
P-47D YF-M 42-8526
Fees, Edwin W., Lt.; December 1944-September 1945
Finnessey, Robert V., Lt.; December 1944-September 1945
P-51K YF-R 44-11642
Frost, Lionel S., F/Lt.; RAF on D.S.
Fussell, Roscoe J., Capt.; July 1943-March 1945
Gilmore, John J., Jr., Lt.; May 1944-August 28, 1944(KIA)
Gore, Victor E., Lt.; December 1944-EOW
Graczyk, Michael E., Lt.; June 1944-August 15, 1944(POW)
Gresham, Walter V., Jr., Maj.; January 1943-May 1945
113 missions
P-47D YF-T 42-8498 "Trigger"
P-51B YF-T 43-6592 "Trigger II"
P-51D YF-T 44-14230 "Trigger III"
Harrington, James C., Lt.; States-July 1944
Hecht, Charles K., Jr., Lt.; January 1943-November 29, 1943(KIA)
Hoffman, Harold J., Capt.; February 1943-April 1945
P-47D YF-B 42-22480
P-51D YF-B 44-64068
Hovde, William J., Maj.; April 1943-October 1945
113 missions
P-47D YF-I 42-8368 "Ole"
P-51B YF-I 43-6928 "Ole II"
P-51D YF-I 44-13531 "Ole III"
Hughes, Kenneth L., Lt.; June 1944-August 28, 1944(MIA-E)
P-51B YF-C 42-106932 "Jo-Jo"
Hull, James C., Capt.; January 1943-December 1, 1943(KIA)
P-47D YF-A 42-8006
Humphrey, William L., Lt.; May 1944-September 1944
Kelley, Edward F., III, Capt.; June 1944-September 1944
Kenney, Paul H., Lt.; January 1943-April 15, 1944(POW)
P-47C YF-P 41-6230
P-51B YF-P 43-6925
Knutty, Harold P., Lt.; February 1945-October 1945
23 missions
Kossack, Walter H., Capt.; States-November 7, 1943(POW)
P-47D YF-X 42-8455
P-47D YF-X 42-8477
Kouche, Clarence H., Lt.; September 1944-September 1945
P-51D YF-H 44-14342 "Susan B II"
Kowalski, Daniel A., Lt.; February 1944-August 1944
P-51B YF-C 42-106780
Ksanznak, Thomas A., Lt.; July 1944-January 13, 1945(KIA)
Lacazette, Mario, Lt.; January 1945-June 1945
Lanius, John H., Lt.; September 1944-September 1945
P-51D YF-B
Lanphier, John, Lt.; March 1943-November 13, 1943(KIA)
P-47D YF-W 42-8626
Leaf, Leroy R., Jr., Lt.; January 1945-October 1945
P-51D YF-C
Ledbetter, Charles R., Lt.; February 1945-EOW
22 missions
Lister, Walter B., Lt.; February 1945-June 1945
17 missions
Long, Johnnie W., Lt.; February 1945-March 15, 1945(MIA-E)
3 missions
Lowder, James P., Jr., Lt.; June 1944-July 8, 1944(KIA)
Lynch, William J., Lt.; February 1945-April 16, 1945(POW)
8 missions
Maben, Eugene W., Jr., Lt.; States-October 18, 1943(KIA)
2 missions
P-47D YF-N 42-22532
MacConkey, Jack S., F/O; February 1944-April 19, 1944(KIA)
Macurdy, Harold H., Lt.; March 1943-January 29, 1944(MIA-E)
P-47D YF-H 42-8689
P-47D YF-H 42-75455
Maisch, Joseph J., Jr., Lt.; June 1944-November 1944
P-51D YF-N 44-13565 "Baltimore Jo-Jo"
P-51D YF-N 44-14385 "Baltimore Jo-Jo II"
Mankin, John A., Lt.; February 1943-September 1944
P-47D YF-V 42-22468
Manning, Clarence G., Lt.; February 1945-September 1945
17 missions
Marsh, Halbert G., Lt.; January 1945-September 1945
30 missions
P-51D YF-U 44-63869 "Passion's Playground"
Martin, Edward B., Lt.; January 1945-September 1945
Martyn, Donald M., Lt.; @January 1944-May 4, 1944(KIA)
Masters, Frank R., Lt.; September 1944-January 20, 1945(POW)
Mathes, Edward G., Lt.; February 1945-EOW
22 missions
McCollom, Francis N., Lt.; September 1944-April 16, 1945(POW)
52 missions
P-51D YF-N 44-14385 "Wooly Lamb"
McConnell, James H., Capt.; September 1943-March 29, 1944(POW)
P-47D YF-C "Duel Purpose"
P-51B YF-C 43-6317 "Duel Purpose"
McElroy, James N., Capt.; March 1944-March 1945
99 missions
P-51B YF-S 43-7023 "Big Stoop"
P-51D YF-S 44-14498 "Big Stoop II"
P-51D YF-S "Big Stoop III"
McGinty, William J., Lt.; March 1944-August 1944; ex-357th Ftr Sqn
P-51B YF-G 43-6834 "The Great McGinty"
McNally, Russell I., Lt.; April 1944-September 1944
77 missions
P-51B YF-O 43-6815 "Morphine Sue"
P-51D YF-J 44-13659 "Morphine Sue II"
Mesier, Bernard, F/O; -March 1945
Meteyer, Thomas O., Lt.; February 1944-July 1944
P-51B YF-J 42-106736 "Joyce"
Michela, Frank, Lt.; July 1944-August 11, 1944(KIA)
Michelena, Ralph L., Lt.; June 1944-October 1944
Mikalauskas, Kenneth E., Lt.; July 1944-December 1945
Morgan, Walter L., Capt.; August 1944-September 11, 1944(KIA); ex-52nd Ftr Grp, MTO (2 victories)
Myers, Raymond B., LtCol.; February 1943-June 1944
72 missions
P-47D YF-U 42-7991 "Miss Pam"

P-47D YF-U 42-75425 "Miss Pam"
P-51B YF-U 43-6991 "Miss Pam"
Nelson, Ervin C., Jr., Lt.; March 1945-EOW
Nicodemus, Ralph J., Lt.; February 1945-June 1945
19 missions
Ondris, Edward, Lt.; September 1943-April 5, 1944(KIA)
P-51B YF-M 43-6937
Orr, Ben F., Jr., Lt.; May 1944-August 2, 1944(KIA)
Pardee, Harry W., Jr., Lt.; May 1944-September 1944
Patrinely, Costa C., Lt.; March 1945-EOW
7 missions
Parks, Robert F., Lt.; March 1945-EOW
Pearson, Peter J., Lt.; June 1944-November 1944
P-51B YF-H 43-6649
Peery, Richard A., Lt.; September 1943-November 29, 1943(POW)
Peters, Robert O., Lt.; June 1944-September 18, 1944(KIA)
P-51D YF-X 44-13675
Peterson, Noble E., Capt.; March 1944-April 1945
106 missions
P-51C YF-M 42-103317 "Dakota Kid"
P-51D YF-M 44-14711 "Dakota Kid"
Phinizy, Charles W., III, Lt.; March 1945-EOW
Plemons, Charles E., Lt.; March 1945-EOW
9 missions
Price, Harrison T., Lt.; March 1945-EOW
P-51D YF- "Bingo"
Prouse, Earl L., Lt.; March 1945-EOW
Rankin, Chauncy H., Lt.; March 1943-January 29, 1944(KIA)
P-47D YF-G 42-8504
Reed, Joseph E., Lt.; States-April 1944
Reed, Roddy W., Lt.; September 1944-September 12, 1944(KIA)
Reeves, Willis W., Jr., Lt.; June 1944-June 19, 1944(KIA)
Roach, William E., Lt.; February 1943-November 7, 1943(POW)
3 missions
P-47D YF-E 42-22490 "Beetle"
Roberts, Spencer, Lt.; September 1944-April 1945
P-51D YF-J 44-14898
Robinson, Allan T., Lt.; April 1944-September 1944
Rogers, John A., Lt.; March 1945-April 16, 1945(MIA-E)
Rosenblatt, Charles J., Maj.; June 1944-August 1944; ex-HdQts
P-51B YF-F
P-51D YF-F 44-13879 "Clare 2"
Rouleau, Louis J., Jr., Lt.; March 1945-EOW
4 missions
Rowbotham, Robert C., Lt.; March 1945-EOW
7 missions
Santos, Albert R., Lt.; April 1944-August 1944
Schlecht, Warner J., Lt.; October 1944-April 13, 1945(POW)
Seeley, Grant A., Capt.; -June 1945
Sluga, Emil F., LtCol.; -March 21, 1945(POW)
P-47D YF-L 42-22484 "Slugger"
P-51B YF-L 43-7156 "Slugger"
P-51D YF-L 44-13354 "Slugger"
P-51D YF-L 44-13623 "Slugger"
Smith, Kirby D.E., Capt.; April 1945-May 1945; ex-2nd Scouting Force
0 missions w/358th
Snook, Keo L., Lt.; August 1944-EOW
P-51D YF-F 44-13879 "Lady Dana"
P-51K YF-F 44-12122 "Lady Dana"
Taylor, Thomas J., Lt.; August 1944-February 9, 1945(KIA)
Thompson, Robert M., Lt.; May 1944-October 1944
Tolby, William W., Jr., Lt.; July 1944-August 28, 1944(MIA-E); September 1944-March 1945
Tulloch, John F., Jr., Capt.; October 1944-EOW
P-51D YF-Y 44-14163 "Jake the Snake"
Unterkircher, James O., F/O; March 1945-EOW
Upchurch, James H., Capt.; January 1943-May 1944
P-47D YF-K 42-8443 "Miss Clean Sweep"
P-51B YF-K 43-6879 "Uppie's Hazel"
Vigna, Joseph J., Lt.; July 1944-September 18, 1944(KIA)
Wagner, Robert B., Lt.; August 1944-March 1945
P-51D YF-G 44-15517 "Ginny Lynn"
Walburn, Wayne E., Lt.; July 1944-July 24, 1944(POW)
Wambier, Charles A., Lt.; September 1943-December 30, 1943(KIA
Watkins, Robert N., Lt.; July 1944-February 1945
Watson, Chester W., F/O; September 1943-November 7, 1943(KIA)
Wayne, Robert B., Lt.; -April 1945
Weber, Wilson B., Lt.; July 1944-August 28, 1944(KIA)
Webb, Marcell E., Lt.; June 1944-November 1944
Williams, Edward R., F/O; May 1944-June 8, 1944(KIA)
Winn, William, Jr., Lt.; May 1944-September 1944
Woertz, Jack J., Lt.; January 1943-December 11, 1943(KIA)
P-47D YF-Y 42-8418
P-47D YF-Y 42-75045
Worth, Thomas W., Lt.; September 1943-July 1944
Woodson, Nelson B., Lt.; September 1944-April 1945
P-51D YF-C 44-15294
Wright, Donald H., Capt.; February 1943-March 16, 1944(POW)
P-47D YF-S 42-8427 "Mona Lou"
P-51B YF-S 43-6342 "Mona Lou"

**Aircraft of the 354th Fighter Squadron**

P-47D-1-RE
42-7944 WR-

P-47D-2-RA
42-22464 WR-F "Lorie" — C.W. Lenfest

P-47D-2-RE
42-7996 WR-D — A.J. Del Negro
42-8400 WR-E

P-47D-5-RE
42-8404 WR-P "Lil Jo" — T.H. Hubbard
42-8433 WR-S
42-8434 WR-U "Miss Behave" — H.B. Kucheman
42-8441 WR-R — C.H. Sweat
42-8444 WR-O — C.G. Johnston
42-8445 WR-
42-8453 WR-K — R.F. Murdoch
42-8493 WR-W — R.E. Woody
42-8495 WR-
42-8557 WR-J — T.F. Neal
42-8643 WR-

P-47D-6-RE
42-74615 WR-X "Texas Terror II" — L.G. Mendenhall
42-74681 WR-Y — J.E. Duffy
42-74703 WR-Z "Baby" — H.W. Brown

P-47D-11-RE
42-75275 WR-C "Hellen" — C.R. Barger

P-47D-15-RE
42-76360 WR-

Unknown Serials
WR-X "Texas Terror" — L.G. Mendenhall
WR-L "Miss Thunder" — W.J. Koraleski

P-51C-5-NT
42-103334 WR-J — W.D. Martin
42-103795 WR-S "Papoose"
42-103795 WR-V "Duchess of Manhattan" Ro. M. White
42-103802 WR-N — N.J. Fortier

P-51B-1-NA
43-12177 WR-
43-12188 WR-

P-51B-5-NA
43-6431 WR-A "Man O'War" — C.H. Kinnard
43-6457 WR-G — A.E. Benson
43-6457 WR-B "Jane" — B.W. Marshall
43-6520 WR-W "Woody's Maytag" — R.E. Woody
43-6574 WR-B
43-6577 WR-J — T.F. Neal
43-6580 WR-C
43-6631 WR-C "Hellen 2nd" — C.R. Barger
43-6849 WR-K — L.F. Allard
43-6870 WR-F "Lorie III" — C.W. Lenfest
43-6870 WR-D
43-6885 WR-X "Texas Terror III" — L.G. Mendenhall
43-6895 WR-A "Hat Jane" — R.G. Kurtz
43-6915 WR-T — R.C. Brown
43-6938 WR-V — J.P. Austin
43-6943 WR-R "Patricia" — C.D. Hauver
43-6944 WR-O — C.G. Johnston
43-6948 WR-F "Lorie II" — C.W. Lenfest
43-6968 WR-L "Miss Thunder" — W.J. Koraleski
43-6983 WR-O
43-7053 WR-E — W.P. Boulet
43-7076 WR-P — H.F. Culp

P-51B-10-NA
43-7137 WR-Q — A.B. Starr/J.M. Folger
43-7157 WR-S "Marjorie II" — B.G. Houston
43-7182 WR-Y "Dragon Wagon" — J.E. Duffy
42-106437 WR-M — R.S. Morris
42-106437 WR-M "Darlin' Doris" — C.H. Graham
42-106437 WR-M "Alabama Bound" D.M. Vickery
42-106448 WR-Z "Hun Hunter From Texas" H.W. Brown
42-106450 WR-U "Lil Jo" — H.B. Kucheman
42-106450 WR-L "Dottie" — R.G. Cross
42-106580 WR-
42-106708 WR-K — R.A. Browning

P-51B-15-NA
42-103818 WR-T
42-106870 WR-N — N.J. Fortier

42-106874 WR-F "Lorie IV" C.W. Lenfest
42-106896 WR-L M.L. Woolard
42-106950 WR-A "Man O'War" C.H. Kinnard
42-106950 WR-P "The Iowa Beaut" R.E. Hulderman
43-24824 WR-H "Sophia S" G.S. Wright

P-51D-5-NT
44-11352 WR-M

P-51K-1-NT
44-11359 WR-C "Lil Lila Lee" J.E. Mellen
44-11360 WR-H "Dot Darlin'" C.E. Decklar
44-11362 WR-W "Bub's Boy" R.P. Pearson

P-51K-5-NT
44-11667 WR-B "My Catherine S" S.E. Silva
44-11759 WR-J "My Baby Doll" G.D. Beeler

P-51D-5-NA
44-13305 WR-Z "Hun Hunter From Texas" H.W. Brown
44-13349 WR-W S.C. Williams
44-13540 WR-S "Sunny VI" E.W. Stewart
44-13540 WR-P "Betsy K" G.A. Kemper
44-13571 WR-U "Lil Jo" H.B. Kucheman
44-13571 WR-X "Texas Terror IV" L.G. Mendenhall
44-13571 WR-X "Jolly Roger" O. Stalcup
44-13591 WR-O "Chugger" R.L. Heaton
44-13611 WR-L
44-13630 WR-M "Darlin' Doris" C.H. Graham
44-13756 WR-J "Martin's Gloria" W.D. Martin
44-13756 WR-G "Stubborn Stella" R.J. Walsh
44-13764 WR-E "Weepin' Deacon II" R.W. Priest
44-13764 WR-E "Eaglebeak"
44-13912 WR-K
44-13963 WR-C N.P. Jackson
44-14001 WR-A R.G. Kurtz

P-51D-10-NA
44-14079 WR-P "The Iowa Beaut II" R.E. Hulderman
44-14089 WR-J "Sweet Dorsey" F.M. Johnson
44-14090 WR-R "Princess Pat" C.D. Hauver
44-14173 WR-
44-14228 WR-S "Mary Lou" A.S. White
44-14228 WR-P "Lady Barbara II" T.F. Truell
44-14252 WR-H "Palma" B.C. Williamson
44-14275 WR-F "Lorie V" C.W. Lenfest
44-14293 WR-B "Jane II" B.W. Marshall
44-14293 WR-B "Lackin' Shackin" M.H. Ivey
44-14346 WR-K "Ceegar Kid" J. Jabara
44-14374 WR-A "Palma II" B.C. Williamson
44-14409 WR-B "Jane III" B.W. Marshall
44-14536 WR-I C.V. Hull
44-14563 WR-Q "Sparky"
44-14603 WR-Y "Dragon Wagon" J.E. Duffy
44-14625 WR-A "Man O'War" C.H. Kinnard
44-14704 WR-R "Princess Pat II" C.D. Hauver
44-14704 WR-R "Psyche"
44-14760 WR-T
44-14799 WR-B "Jane IV" B.W. Marshall

P-51D-15-NA
44-14910 WR-L "Ann Anita" D.M. Vickery
44-15255 WR-S "Sunny VII" E.W. Stewart
44-15255 WR-F "Down For Double" G.M. Graham
44-15279 WR-B "Jane V" B.W. Marshall
44-15279 WR-B "Miss Miami" S.P. Protho
44-15346 WR-Z "Bobbie Socks" W.J. Gadpaille
44-15373 WR-N N.J. Fortier
44-15621 WR-M "Chugger II" R.L. Heaton
44-15652 WR-E "Weepin' Deacon III" R.W. Priest
44-15652 WR-E H.W. Falvey

P-51D-20-NA
44-63222 WR-E H.W. Falvey
44-63259 WR-A
44-63677 WR-O "Ruthie R"
44-63764 WR-Y "Dragon Wagon" J.E. Duffy
44-72186 WR-B "My Catherine S" S.E. Silva
44-72253 WR-B "Jane VI" B.W. Marshall
44-72253 WR-L "Big Gas Bird"
44-72329 WR-O
44-72361 WR-N N.J. Fortier
44-72396 WR-I "Mary Lou" Ri. M. White
44-72427 WR-M "Daphne" A.B. Kaplan
44-72446 WR-P
44-72462 WR-V

P-51D-25-NA
44-72953 WR-B "Jane VII" B.W. Marshall
44-72996 WR-A C.G. Todd
44-73144 WR-A "Man O'War" C.H. Kinnard

Unknown Serials
P-51B WR-S "Sunny V" E.W. Stewart
P-51B WR-E "Weepin' Deacon" R.W. Priest
P-51B WR- "Hell's Belle"
P-51D WR-Q "Cherraine" D.V. Galer
P-51B WR-G "Little Shorty" R.M. McLear
P-51D WR-I "Miss Janice" T.M. Rood
P-51D WR-R "Ike II"
P-51K WR-D "Faithful Fernie II"
P-51D WR- "Ma Bonno"

**Aircraft of the 357th Fighter Squadron**

P-47C-2-RE
41-6205 OS-O

P-47D-2-RA
42-22471 OS-I B.D. Johnston
42-22473 OS-N
42-22489 OS-Y
42-22533 OS-
42-22538 OS-F "The Butcher" C.J. Butcher
42-22545 OS-Z
42-22546 OS-G
42-22547 OS-
42-22549 OS-E "Kay" L.B. Fuller

P-47D-2-RE
42-7984 OS-Q "On The Ball" E.O. Carlson
42-8000 OS-H R.B. Butler
42-8370 OS-L "Alabama Bound" J.S. Westphal
42-8389 OS-J "Sheaf's Jug" W.S. Easterly
42-8397 OS-K "Prune Face" H.S. Bille
42-8399 OS-M "Arkansas Traveler" H.H. Kirby

P-47D-4-RA
42-22784 OS-R "Moon" J.L. Elder

P-47D-5-RE
42-8406 OS-T "Eager Eve" F.L. Ramsdell
42-8408 OS-U "Jean's Little Moe" W. Momberger
42-8413 OS-P "Ma Fran" N.E. Olson
42-8415 OS-A "Available Jones" E.W. Szaniawski
42-8416 OS-X D.J. Laing
42-8423 OS-W "Becky" J.H. Wilson
42-8438 OS-B "Dizzy Miss" V.A. Burroughs
42-8518 OS-V "Wild Bill" W.J. Cummings
42-8544 OS-R "Moon" J.L. Elder
42-8550 OS-S
42-8610 OS-G
42-8653 OS-

P-47D-6-RE
42-74653 OS-
42-74672 OS-D
42-74720 OS-T
42-74729 OS-

P-47D-10-RE
42-75184 OS-L

P-47D-15-RE
42-76233 OS-
42-76283 OS-

Unknown Serials
OS-P "Ma Fran 2nd" N.E. Olson
OS-P "Ma Fran 3rd" N.E. Olson
OS-A "Available Jones 2nd" E.W. Szaniawski
OS-A "Available Jones 3rd" E.W. Szaniawski

P-51C-1-NT
42-103009 OS-
42-103282 OS-U

P-51C-5-NT
42-103735 OS-F "Gooch's Revenge"
42-103753 OS-H F.R. Haviland

P-51B-1-NA
43-12184 OS-
43-12193 OS-
43-12194 OS-S
43-12422 OS-N
43-12452 OS-D
43-12456 OS-

P-51B-5-NA
43-6508 OS-O
43-6525 OS-M

43-6561 OS-
43-6589 OS-X
43-6626 OS-I "Terry Fran"
43-6627 OS-Z "Brenda II"
43-6640 OS-H
43-6648 OS-B
43-6722 OS-B "Dizzy Miss" V.A. Burroughs
43-6776 OS-R "Moon" J.L. Elder
43-6777 OS-F "The Butcher" C.J. Butcher
43-6806 OS-
43-6835 OS-V
43-6886 OS-E "Kay" L.B. Fuller
43-6916 OS-E
43-6980 OS-C
43-6989 OS-
43-7027 OS-Q "Georgia Peach"
43-7039 OS-S "Red Eye"
43-7101 OS-W "Becky" J.H. Wilson
43-7103 OS-O "Miss Doris"

P-51B-10-NA
43-7140 OS-N "Arkansas Traveler" H.H. Kirby
43-7142 OS-A "Available Jones 5th" E.W. Szaniawski
43-7170 OS-X "Ma Fran 4th" N.E. Olson
43-7173 OS-
43-7186 OS-
42-106433 OS-R "Moon" J.L. Elder
42-106444 OS-L "Baby Bet" T.C. Long
42-106463 OS-U J.F. Kerch
42-106634 OS-K
42-106698 OS-U J.F. Kerch
42-106723 OS-R "Moon" J.L. Elder

P-51B-15-NA
42-106742 OS-G
42-106762 OS-I
42-106810 OS-N
42-106815 OS-Z
42-106862 OS-
42-106910 OS-
43-24795 OS-M

P-51D-5-NT
44-11194 OS-B "Super Gal-II" R.W. Delhamer
44-11215 OS-Q

P-51K-5-NT
44-11674 OS-H

P 51D-5-NA
44-13353 OS-U "Gin Rummy" E.M. Hendrickson
44-13397 OS-
44-13526 OS-E
44-13557 OS-E
44-13574 OS-
44-13654 OS-G "Georgia Peach"
44-13677 OS-X "Miss Steve" W.J. Cullerton
44-13677 OS-N "Fickle Fanny" D.P. Watkins
44-13726 OS-U
44-13728 OS-G
44-13734 OS-S "Lucious Lu" R.L. Garlich
44-13777 OS-N
44-13796 OS-N
44-13945 OS-K

P-51D-10-NA
44-14173 OS-M "Sue Sue" H.I. Knight
44-14186 OS-E
44-14201 OS-M "Mustang"
44-14203 OS-C "Spook III"
44-14222 OS-S
44-14260 OS-W "Becky" J.H. Wilson
44-14262 OS-G "Patty"
44-14282 OS-G "Fate-That's Life"
44-14314 OS-K "Prune Face" H.S. Bille
44-14314 OS-L "Sexless Stella/One More Time" J.H. Dressler
44-14367 OS-Z
44-14402 OS-H "Barbara" F.R. Haviland
44-14413 OS-P "The Little Rebel"
44-14434 OS-Z "Maria"
44-14497 OS-U
44-14674 OS-H "Ginny J" J.J. Weidemann
44-14753 OS-O L.D. Minchew
44-14786 OS-U "Joereine II" W.L. Griswold
44-14793 OS-U

P-51D-15-NA
44-14858 OS-M "Debbie Lee"
44-14858 OS-Y "Kay"
44-14966 OS-S "Lucious Lu II" R.L. Garlich
44-14999 OS-U "Dapper Dan" E.H. Whitney
44-15013 OS-D
44-15291 OS-T
44-15334 OS-
44-15335 OS-P
44-15349 OS-J
44-15518 OS-S
44-15595 OS-I "Mary Jane" E.J. Moroney
44-15595 OS-A "Jersey Bounce" V.D. Iglesias
44-15684 OS-
44-15749 OS-D "Don Kelly"

P-51D-20-NA
44-63252 OS-V
44-63633 OS-R "Moon" J.L. Elder
44-64011 OS-
44-72373 OS-H "Ginny J" J.J. Weidemann
44-72458 OS-N "Miss Donna Lee"
44-72458 OS-N "Bingo's Baby"

P-51D-25-NA
44-72987 OS-
44-73065 OS-R J.L. Elder

Unknown Serials
P-51B OS-A "Available Jones 4th" E.W. Szaniawski
P-51D OS- "Melba J" K.J. Miller
P-51D OS-N "Rough and Ready"
P-51D OS- "My Butch"

**Aircraft of the 358th Fighter Squadron**

P-47C-2-RE
41-6230 YF-P P.H. Kenney

P-47D-2-RA
42-22461 YF-J H.I. Carver
42-22468 YF-V J.A. Mankin
42-22480 YF-B H.J. Hoffman
42-22484 YF-L "Slugger" E.L. Sluga
42-22485 YF-O
42-22490 YF-U "Beetle" W.E. Roach
42-22518 YF-Q "Damn Yank" L.J. Dissette
42-22532 YF-N E.W. Mabin

P-47D-2-RE
42-7991 YF-U "Miss Pam" R.B. Myers
42-7992 YF-D G.J. Dix
42-8006 YF-A J.C. Hull
42-8368 YF-I "Ole" W.J. Hovde

P-47D-4-RA
42-22746 YF-
42-22779 YF-

P-47D-5-RE
42-8418 YF-Y J.J. Woertz
42-8426 YF-F
42-8427 YF-S "Mona Lou" D.H. Wright
42-8443 YF-K "Miss Clean Sweep" J.H. Upchurch
42-8455 YF-X W.H. Kossack
42-8477 YF-X W.H. Kossack
42-8498 YF-T "Trigger" W.V. Gresham
42-8504 YF-G C.H. Rankin
42-8526 YF-M K.F. Ekstrom
42-8570 YF-E C.W. Blair
42-8626 YF-W J. Lanphier
42-8629 YF-Z
42-8631 YF-U
42-8689 YF-H H.H. Macurdy

P-47D-6-RE
42-74667 YF-Z R. Dean

P-47D-10-RE
42-75045 YF-Y J.J. Woertz
42-75046 YF-

P-47D-11-RE
42-75425 YF-U R.B. Myers
42-75455 YF-H H.H. Macurdy

P-47D-15-RE
42-76294 YF-
42-76360 YF-

Unknown Serials
YF-C "Duel Purpose" J.H. McConnell

P-51C-1-NT
42-103317 YF-M "Dakota Kid" N.E. Peterson

P-51C-10-NT
43-25062 YF-

P-51B-1-NA
43-12162 YF-
43-12190 YF-
43-12407 YF-
43-12475 YF-A

P-51B-5-NA
43-6317 YF-C "Duel Purpose" J.H. McConnell
43-6325 YF-P P.H. Kenney
43-6342 YF-S "Mona Lou" D.H. Wright
43-6385 YF-B "Shanghai Lil"
43-6523 YF-E "Leakin' Liz" C.W. Blair
43-6527 YF-J "Indiana Clipper" H.I. Carver
43-6554 YF-R
43-6592 YF-T "Trigger II" W.V. Gresham
43-6649 YF-H P.J. Pearson
43-6815 YF-O "Morphune Sue" R.I. McNally
43-6820 YF-C
43-6834 YF-G "The Great McGinty" W.J. McGinty
43-6845 YF-X
43-6873 YF-V
43-6875 YF-A "Snookie Too"
43-6879 YF-K "Helen II"
43-6879 YF-K "Uppie's Hazel" J.H. Upchurch
43-6879 YF-K "Mary Joyce"
43-6928 YF-I "Ole II" W.J. Hovde
43-6930 YF-P
43-6937 YF-M E. Ondris
43-6945 YF-R "Wizard Kite" J.M. Beckman
43-6991 YF-U "Miss Pam" R.B. Myers
43-7023 YF-S "Big Stoop" J.N. McElroy
43-7036 YF-N "Rugged Rebel" R.M. Dillon
43-7036 YF-Z

P-51B-10-NA
43-7147 YF-X "Big Dogs/Ellen Jean" J.B. Dickson
43-7156 YF-L "Slugger" E.L. Sluga
43-7164 YF-D G.J. Dix
42-106452 YF-W "Miss Beck/Buzz Boy" W.G. Burlingame
42-106492 YF-
42-106736 YF-J "Joyce" T.O. Meteyer

P-51B-15-NA
42-106780 YF-C D.A. Kowalski
42-106858 YF-Q
42-106860 YF-A C.J. Brien
42-106932 YF-C "Jo-Jo" K.L. Hughes
43-24844 YF-O

P-51K-5-NT
44-11642 YF-R R.V. Finnessey

P-51K-10-NT
44-12122 YF-F "Lady Dana" K.L. Snook

P-51D-5-NA
44-13302 YF-E "Raunchy Runt"
44-13302 YF-E C.W. Blair
44-13319 YF-O
44-13354 YF-L "Slugger" E.L. Sluga
44-13366 YF-K "Baby Buggy" W.H. Douglas
44-13531 YF-I "Ole III" W.J. Hovde
44-13564 YF-C "Little Nobody"
44-13565 YF-N "Baltimore Jo Jo" J.J. Maisch
44-13625 YF-L "Slugger" E.L. Sluga
44-13659 YF-J "Morphine Sue II" R.I. McNally
44-13675 YF-X R.O. Peters
44-13686 YF-N "Rugged Rebel III" R.M. Dillon
44-13708 YF-X B.F. Donathon
44-13879 YF-F "Clare 2" C.J. Rosenblatt
44-13879 YF-F "Lady Dana" K.L. Snook

P-51D-10-NA
44-14077 YF-E "Raunchy Runt II"
44-14126 YF-R "Hot Shot" J.M. Beckman
44-14163 YF-Y "Jake the Snake" J.F. Tulloch
44-14214 YF-V
44-14230 YF-T "Trigger III" W.V. Gresham
44-14252 YF-B
44-14342 YF-H "Susan B II" C.H. Kouche
44-14385 YF-N "Baltimore Jo Jo II" J.J. Maisch
44-14428 YF-A
44-14498 YF-S "Big Stoop II" J.N. McElroy
44-14564 YF-E C.W. Blair
44-14644 YF-Q "Damn Yank IV" L.J. Dissette
44-14711 YF-M "Dakota Kid" N.E. Peterson
44-14799 YF-H "Susan B III" C.H. Kouche

P-51D-15-NA
44-15014 YF-J "Joyce"
44-15294 YF-C N.B. Woodson
44-15517 YF-G "Ginny Lynn" R.B. Wagner

P-51D-20-NA
44-63162 YF-V R.H. Brown
44-63739 YF-Q
44-63869 YF-U "Passion's Playground" H.G. Marsh
44-64068 YF-B H.J. Hoffman
44-64081 YF-Q "The Body's Bastard"
44-72420 YF-W

P-51D-25-NA
44-73165 YF-L

Unknown Serials
P-51B YF-N "Rugged Rebel II" R.M. Dillon
P-51D YF-Q "Damn Yank III" L.J. Dissette
P-51D YF-S "Big Stoop III" J.N. McElroy
P-51D YF-I "Ole IV" W.J. Hovde
44-11??? YF-I "Ole V" W.J. Hovde
P-51D YF-I "Ole VI" W.J. Hovde
P-51D YF- "Bingo" H.T. Price

• • •

## THE 356TH FIGHTER GROUP
## 359TH, 360TH, 361ST FIGHTER SQUADRONS

The 356th Fighter Group was activated on December 12, 1942, at Westover Field, Massachusetts. Training in the eastern United States, the group headed overseas on September 5, 1943, aboard the "HMS Orion". The first of 407 missions came on October 15, 1943, with the final one coming on May 7, 1945. During the time the 356th was overseas, the group claimed 200 aerial and 77 ground victories while 115 P-47's and P-51's were lost on operations and 13 pilots died in accidents.

The 356th was based at Goxhill, from August 25, 1943 (the ground echelon sailed and arrived earlier), and Martlesham Heath, from October 5, 1943 until November of 1945. Aircraft flown were the P-47D, from October of 1943 until November of 1944, and the P-51D and K, from November of 1944 until war's end. The group was awarded a Distinguished Unit Citation for its support of the airborne invasion of Holland on September 17, 18, and 23, 1944.

### Claims

| | Air | | | Ground | |
|---|---|---|---|---|---|
| | Destroyed | Probable | Damaged | Destroyed | Damaged |
| HdQts | 6.5 | 0 | 4 | 10.5 | 3.5 |
| 359th | 48.5 | 12 | 19 | 11 | 25.5 |
| 360th | 49 | 5 | 25 | 16 | 32 |
| 361st | 96 | 6 | 31 | 39.5 | 52 |
| | 200 | 23 | 79 | 77 | 113 |

### Commanders

| | |
|---|---|
| LtCol. Harold J. Rau | February 9, 1943-November 28, 1943 |
| Col. Einar A. Malmstrom | November 29, 1943-April 23, 1944 |
| Col. Philip E. Tukey, Jr. | April 24, 1944-November 3, 1944 |
| LtCol. Donald A. Baccus | November 3, 1944-January 10, 1945 |
| Col. Philip E. Tukey, Jr. | January 10, 1945-November 1945 |

### Wing and Command Assignments

| | |
|---|---|
| Assigned to VIII Fighter Command | August 25, 1943 |
| VIII Fighter Command, 65th Fighter Wing | August 26, 1943 |
| VIII Fighter Command, 67th Fighter Wing | August 8, 1944 |
| 1st Bomb Division, 67th Fighter Wing | September 15, 1944 |
| 1st Air Division, 67th Fighter Wing | January 1, 1945 |

### Aircraft Markings

All P-47's were in olive drab/neutral gray schemes with white cowl and theater bands. In the spring of 1944, NMF planes arrived, but nearly all were given olive drab upper surfaces with the lower surfaces remaining in NMF. As the only form of group marking, the white cowl band was painted over with olive drab.

All P-51's were operated in NMF with many planes having the black theater bands and black spinners. Beginning in early December of 1944, a group marking was introduced: the forward part of the spinner was painted red with thin blue bands and the rearmost portion of the spinner was painted blue. Longitudinal rows of blue diamonds were superimposed on a 12 inch red cowl band and extension, running over the exhaust stacks back to the cockpit. Also from December, squadron colors were applied to the rudder: yellow for the 359th, red for the 360th, and blue for the 361st. In addition, beginning in February of 1945, the entire spinner was painted in the squadron color.

Squadron codes were:

359th Ftr Sqn: OC
360th Ftr Sqn: PI
361st Ftr Sqn: QI

**356th Fighter Group Statistical Report**

| Month | Missions | Air | Grd | Losses | KIAc |
|---|---|---|---|---|---|
| October 1943 | 7 | 0-0-0 | 0-0 | 0 | 0 |
| November | 11 | 5-2-3 | 0-0 | 6 | 0 |
| December | 11 | 1-1-1 | 0-0 | 4 | 0 |
| January 1944 | 13 | 15-3-5 | 0-1 | 3 | 1 |
| February | 19 | 21-2-13 | 0-0 | 3 | 1 |
| March | 19 | 13-2-2 | 4-8 | 9 | 0 |
| April | 24 | 6-0-1 | 25-36 | 12 | 0 |
| May | 26 | 26-4-10 | 0-0 | 13 | 1 |
| June | 44 | 7-0-2 | 8-2 | 11 | 0 |
| July | 35 | 1-0-1 | 1-3 | 2 | 1 |
| August | 40 | 22-1-5 | 0-0 | 9 | 0 |
| September | 22 | 1-0-1 | 8-5 | 9 | 0 |
| October | 18 | 0-0-0 | 9-20 | 1 | 0 |
| November | 15 | 26-2-13 | 5-9 | 6 | 0 |
| December | 16 | 23-3-6 | 0-0 | 12 | 0 |
| January 1945 | 18 | 13-1-4 | 0-1 | 5 | 0 |
| February | 18 | 14-0-7 | 13-13 | 6 | 2 |
| March | 29 | 1-0-1 | 0-2 | 3 | 0 |
| April | 20 | 5-2-4 | 4-13 | 1 | 1 |
| May | 2 | 0-0-0 | 0-0 | 0 | 0 |
| June | 0 | 0-0-0 | 0-0 | 0 | 4 |
| July | 0 | 0-0-0 | 0-0 | 0 | 2 |
| | 407 | 200-23-79 | 77-113 | 115 | 13 |

**Losses by Squadron and Type**

| | MIA | | KIAc | | |
|---|---|---|---|---|---|
| | P-47 | P-51 | P-47 | P-51 | Other |
| HdQts | 1 | 0 | 0 | 0 | 0 |
| 359th | 21 | 14 | 2 | 2 | 0 |
| 360th | 33 | 10 | 2 | 2 | 0 |
| 361st | 30 | 6 | 0 | 4 | 1 |
| | 85 | 30 | 4 | 8 | 1 |

**Claims by Type**

| | Air | | | Grd | |
|---|---|---|---|---|---|
| | Destroyed | Probable | Damaged | Destroyed | Damaged |
| P-47 | 118 | 15 | 45 | 55 | 75 |
| P-51 | 82 | 8 | 34 | 22 | 38 |

**Claims by Enemy Aircraft Type**

| | Air | | | Grd | |
|---|---|---|---|---|---|
| | Destroyed | Probable | Damaged | Destroyed | Damaged |
| FW-190 | 101 | 13 | 44 | 13 | 19 |
| Me-109 | 81 | 8 | 28 | 5 | 4 |
| Fi-156 | 0 | 0 | 1 | 0 | 0 |
| Ju-88 | 4 | 1 | 0 | 14 | 16 |
| Me-262 | 2 | 1 | 6 | 0 | 1 |
| Ar-234 | 2 | 0 | 0 | 0 | 0 |
| Me-110 | 2 | 0 | 0 | 13 | 13 |
| He-177 | 1 | 0 | 0 | 1 | 1 |
| He-111 | 1 | 0 | 0 | 8 | 20 |
| Me-410 | 0 | 0 | 0 | 8 | 9 |
| Ju-52 | 0 | 0 | 0 | 7 | 2 |
| u/i a/c | 0 | 0 | 0 | 7 | 8 |
| Me-323 | 0 | 0 | 0 | 1 | 0 |
| Go-242 | 0 | 0 | 0 | 0 | 14 |
| Do-217 | 0 | 0 | 0 | 0 | 3 |
| Hs-123 | 0 | 0 | 0 | 0 | 1 |
| W-34 | 0 | 0 | 0 | 0 | 1 |
| Glider | 0 | 0 | 0 | 0 | 1 |

**356th Fighter Group Squadron Commanders**

**359th Ftr Sqn**

| | |
|---|---|
| LtCol. Donald A. Baccus | June 9, 1943-April 26, 1944 |
| Maj. Ernest J. White, Jr. | April 26, 1944-August 9, 1944 |
| Maj. Mark J. Burke | August 9, 1944-September 14, 1944 |
| Capt. Richard A. Rann | September 14, 1944-October 22, 1944 |
| LtCol. Ernest J. White, Jr. | October 22, 1944-November 24, 1944 |
| Maj. Richard A. Rann | November 24, 1944-February 25, 1945 |
| LtCol. Wayne E. Rhynard | February 26, 1945-July 22, 1945 |

**360th Ftr Sqn**

| | |
|---|---|
| Maj. Claiborne H. Kinnard, Jr. | May 28, 1943-November 18, 1943 |
| Capt. Joseph H. Bennett | November 18, 1943-November 28, 1943 |
| Maj. Joseph R. Williams | November 29, 1943-March 17, 1944 |
| Maj. Andrew E. Krieger, Jr. | March 17, 1944-May 1, 1944 |
| Maj. John W. Vogt, Jr. | May 1, 1944-October 3, 1944 |
| LtCol. James N. Wood | October 3, 1944-April 4, 1945 |
| Maj. Michael P. Yannell | April 4, 1945-November 1945 |

**361st Ftr Sqn**

| | |
|---|---|
| Maj. Fred C. Roberts, Jr. | January 30, 1943-November 23, 1943 |
| Capt. Emery H. Montgomery | November 23, 1943-November 26, 1943 |
| LtCol. William Waller, III | November 26, 1943-July 16, 1944 |
| LtCol. James M. Cooper | July 16, 1944-January 4, 1945 |
| Maj. Donald J. Strait | January 4, 1945-March 28, 1945 |
| Maj. Donald R. Carlson | March 28, 1945-November 1945 |

**356th Fighter Group Aces**

| Name | Air | Grd | Total | Sqn |
|---|---|---|---|---|
| Maj. Donald J. Strait | 13.5 | 0 | 13.5 | 361st |
| LtCol. Donald A. Baccus | 5 | 4 | 9* | 359th<br>HdQts |
| Maj. Wilbur R. Scheible | 6 | 3 | 9 | 361st<br>HdQts |
| Maj. Michael P. Yannell | 4 | 4 | 8** | 360th |
| Capt. David F. Thwaites | 6 | 1 | 7 | 361st |
| Lt. Clinton D. Burdick | 5.5 | 1 | 6.5 | 361st |
| Capt. Raymond H. Gansberg | 2.5 | 4 | 6.5 | 361st |
| Col. Einar A. Malmstrom | 1 | 5.5 | 6.5 | HdQts |
| Capt. Howard E. Wiggins | 4.5 | 1.5 | 6 | 361st |
| Lt. Clifford T. Ashby | 3.5 | 2 | 5.5 | 361st |
| Capt. Frank A. Morgan | 0.5 | 5 | 5.5 | 361st |
| Capt. Sidney H. Hewett | 2.5 | 2.5 | 5 | 361st |
| LtCol. Gerald W. Johnson | 16.5 | 0 | 16.5@ | 360th |
| Maj. John W. Vogt, Jr. | 8 | 0 | 8@@ | 360th |

* - includes 1 ground victory with the 359th Ftr Grp, ETO
** - includes 2 air victories with the 86th Ftr Grp, MTO
@ - incudes 15.5 air victories with the 56th Ftr Grp, ETO
@@ - includes 5 air victories with the 56th Ftr Grp, ETO

**356th Fighter Group Scorers**

**HdQts**

| | Air | Grd | |
|---|---|---|---|
| D.A. Baccus | 3.5-0-1 | 2-0 | plus 359th Ftr Sqn & 1-1 grd w/359th Ftr Grp |
| O.H. Coen | 0.5-0-1 | 0-0 | plus 3.5-1.5-2 w/RAF & 4th Ftr Grp |
| E.A. Malmstrom | 1-0-0 | 5.5-0 | |
| H.A. Ogden | 0.5-0-2 | 3-2.5 | |
| J.H. Thorne | 1-0-0 | 0-0.5 | plus 359th Ftr Sqn |

**359th Ftr Sqn**

| | | | |
|---|---|---|---|
| L.G. Alphonse | 1-0-0 | 0-0 | |
| D.A. Baccus | 1.5-0-1 | 1-0.25 | plus HdQts |
| A.E. Bergstrom | 0-0-0 | 1-0 | |
| J.E. Blewett | 0-1-0 | 0-0 | |
| R.B. Bradshaw | 0.33-0-0 | 0-1 | |
| W.C. Brearley | 0-0-0 | 0-1 | |
| A.L. Brown | 1-0-2 | 0-1 | |
| J.F. Brown | 1-0-0 | 1-0 | |
| R.E. Carr | 0-1-0 | 0-0 | |
| M.M. Clayborne | 2-0-0 | 0-1 | |
| R.J. Collins | 0.5-0-0 | 0-0.5 | |
| W.C. Cooley | 4-0-0 | 0-0 | |
| J.B. Cornett | 1-0-0 | 0-1 | |
| W.W. Cotter | 1-0-0 | 0-0 | |
| G. Crum | 0-0-1 | 0-0 | |
| R.A. Coughenour, Jr. | 0.5-0-0 | 0-0 | |
| G.W. Engel | 0.33-1-0 | 1-0 | |
| W.L. Farmer | 2-0-0 | 0-0.5 | |
| F.A. Forsyth | 2-1-0 | 0-0.5 | |
| H.R. Gohsler | 2-1-0 | 0-1 | |
| C.J. Hackney, Jr. | 2-0-0 | 0-0 | |
| A.R. Hale | 1-0-1 | 0-0 | |
| J.D. Henry | 0-0-1 | 1-1.5 | |
| W.A. Holm | 0-1-1 | 0-0 | |
| R.K. Holtz | 1-0-0 | 0-0.25 | |
| C.F. Krowiak | 0-0-0 | 0-1.5 | |
| H.F. LeMoyne | 0-0-0 | 0-1 | |

| | | | |
|---|---|---|---|
| J.W. Meade | 1-0-0 | 0-0 | |
| J.J. Meholic | 1.5-0-0 | 0-1 | |
| R.C. Miller | 0-0-1 | 0-0 | |
| W.C. O'Barr | 0.5-0-1 | 0-1.25 | |
| L. Oliver | 2-0-0 | 0-0 | |
| P.C. O'Quinn | 0-0-1 | 0-0 | |
| G.B. Peet | 1.5-0-1 | 0-1.25 | |
| R.A. Rann | 2-0-1 | 0-0 | |
| L.F. Richason | 0-0-1.5 | 3-2 | |
| L.L. Robertson | 0-1-0 | 0-0 | |
| C.H. Rubner, Jr. | 2-0-0 | 0-0 | |
| E.G. Rudd | 0-0-1 | 0-0 | |
| R.C. Scharnberg | 0-0-0 | 0-1 | |
| J.B. Smith | 2-2-0 | 0-2 | |
| R.J. Stone | 0-0-0 | 0-1 | |
| J.D. Tarbutton | 2-0-0.5 | 0-0 | |
| J.H. Thorne | 1-0-0 | 0-0 | plus HdQts |
| E.F. Troge | 1-0-0 | 0-0 | |
| D.F. Tucker | 2-0-1 | 1-0 | |
| R.G. Vossler | 1-1-1 | 0-0 | |
| J.H. Wadlow, Jr. | 0.5-0-0 | 0-1 | |
| R.B. Warren | 0.5-0-0 | 2-1 | |
| H. Weber | 1.5-0-0 | 0-2 | |
| E.J. White, Jr. | 1.33-1-1 | 0-0 | |
| R.R. Withers | 1-0-0 | 0-0 | plus 360th Ftr Sqn |
| J.A. Wyatt | 0-1-1 | 0-0 | |

**360th Ftr Sqn**

| | | | |
|---|---|---|---|
| C.W. Adams | 0-1-0 | 0-0.5 | |
| R.E. Barnhart | 2-0-1 | 0-0 | |
| J.H. Bennett | 0-1-0 | 0-0 | plus 8.5-3-3 air w/4th & 56th Ftr Grps |
| B. Borelli | 1-0-1 | 0-1 | |
| O.L. Burwell | 0-0-1 | 1-1 | |
| N.B. Ceraolo | 0-0-1 | 0-1 | |
| J.R. Cook | 0-0-1 | 0-0 | |
| N.D. Cota, Jr. | 1-0-0.5 | 0-0 | |
| J.W. Crump | 0-0-0 | 0-1 | |
| C.W. Dunn | 0.5-0-0 | 0-0 | |
| W.K. Dunn | 0-0-1 | 0-0 | |
| B.E. Ellingson | 3-0-0 | 0-0 | |
| W.H. Fletcher | 2-0-1 | 1.5-1 | |
| C.J. Garvey | 1-0-0 | 0-0 | |
| W.C. Gatlin | 1-0-0.33 | 0-0 | |
| R.S. Gleason | 1-0-0 | 0-0 | |
| W.O. Hedrick | 0-0-1 | 0-0 | |
| V. Hockmeyer | 0-0-0 | 0-1.5 | |
| G.W. Johnson | 1-0-0.5 | 0-0 | plus 15.5-1-4 air w/56th Ftr Grp |
| W.E. Johnson, Jr. | 2-0-0 | 2-0 | |
| D.F. Jones | 0-0-1 | 0-0 | |
| L.H. Knapp | 0-0-0 | 1-1.5 | |
| A.S. Koczak | 1-0-0 | 0-0 | |
| L.F. Kress | 1.5-0-0 | 0-1.5 | |
| W.E. Leathers | 1-0-0 | 0-0 | |
| R.C. L'Heureux | 1-0-1 | 0-0.5 | |
| R.M. Leidy | 1-0-0 | 1-1 | |
| T.N. Mauldin | 0-1-0 | 0-1 | |
| W.G. Maxwell | 3-0-0.5 | 0-0 | |
| P.E. McCullough | 1-1-1 | 0-0 | |
| H.B. McLaughlin | 0-1-0 | 1-0 | |
| B.D. McNary | 0-0-0 | 0-3 | |
| D.B. Mercer | 1-0-1 | 0-0 | |
| E.M. Nebinger | 0-0-0 | 0.5-0.5 | |
| A.V. Niemi | 1-0-1 | 0-0 | |
| H.S. Olive | 0-0-0 | 0.5-0 | |
| A.A. Paquet | 0-0-0 | 0-2 | |
| H.D. Parker | 1-0-0 | 0-0 | |
| F.W. Peacock | 0-0-0 | 0.5-0 | |
| A.A. Perryman, Jr. | 1-0-1 | 0-0 | |
| E.W. Pleasant | 1-0-1 | 1-1 | |
| L.B. Proctor, Jr. | 0-0-0.33 | 0-0 | |
| R.S. Ragsdale | 0-0-0 | 0-0.5 | |
| R.J. Rensch | 0-0-0 | 1-4 | |
| J.T. Romine | 0-0-1 | 0.5-0.5 | |
| F.M. Russell | 1-0-0 | 0-0 | |
| E.W. Schrull | 0-0-1 | 0-2 | |
| G.W. Seanor | 0-0-0.33 | 0-1 | |
| J.B. Stratford, Jr. | 1-0-0 | 0-0 | |
| C.M. Taylor | 0-0-0.5 | 0.5-0 | |
| T.D. Teel | 1-0-0 | 0-0 | |
| W.G. Thomas | 0-0-0 | 0-1 | |
| T.J. Urban | 2-0-1 | 0-0 | |
| C.A. Vitali | 4-0-1 | 0-0 | |
| J.W. Vogt, Jr. | 3-0-0 | 0-0 | plus 5-0-0 air w/56th Ftr Grp |
| J.P. Weller | 0-0-0 | 0-0.5 | |
| J.H. Williams | 1-0-0 | 0-0 | |
| J.R. Williams | 1-0-0 | 0-0 | |
| R.R. Withers | 3-0-1 | 0-1.5 | plus 359th Ftr Sqn |
| M.P. Yannell | 2-0-2 | 4-2 | plus 2 air w/86th Ftr Grp, MTO |

**361st Ftr Sqn**

| | | |
|---|---|---|
| C.T. Ashby | 3.5-0-1 | 2-1 |
| T.F. Bailey | 1-1-0 | 0-0 |
| B.B. Barnes | 0-0-1 | 0-0 |
| W.M. Baskin | 1.5-0-0 | 0-0 |
| M.W. Baylor | 3-1-1 | 0-0 |
| C.E. Beck | 1-0-0 | 0-0 |
| J.A. Bowers | 3-0-1 | 0-0 |
| J.L. Bruce | 0-0-0 | 0-1 |
| R.R. Burden | 1-0-0 | 0-0 |
| C.D. Burdick | 5.5-0-3 | 1-0 |
| W.W. Burns | 0-0-0 | 1-1 |
| R.H. Campbell | 2-0-0 | 0-0 |
| R.L. Campbell | 0-0-0 | 0-1 |
| D.B. Clayton | 0.5-0-0 | 0.5-0 |
| R.J. Cox | 0-0-0 | 1-2 |
| J.H. Culp | 2-0-0 | 1-0 |
| E.L. Decker | 1-0-0 | 1.5-0 |
| M.W. DeMerit | 0.5-0-0 | 0-0 |
| J.K. Dupuy | 0-0-0 | 1.5-0 |
| H.M. Engelhorn | 1-0-0 | 0-0 |
| M.F. Erickson | 0.5-0-0 | 0-0 |
| E.L. Faison | 1-1-0 | 0-0 |
| E.C. Fremaux | 1-0-0 | 0-1 |
| R.H. Gansberg | 2.5-0-0 | 4-1 |
| R. Gibson | 0-0-0 | 0.5-0 |
| R.W. Gillette | 0.5-0-0 | 0-0 |
| J.M. Hallmark | 0-0-0 | 0-3 |
| J.A. Hargreaves | 1-1-0 | 0-0 |
| S.H. Hewett | 2.5-0-3 | 2.5-1 |
| F.F. Hooker | 2-0-0 | 1-3 |
| W.S. Hurley, Jr. | 1.5-0-0 | 1-2 |
| P.H. Hyde, Jr. | 0-0-1 | 0-0 |
| J.V. Jack | 1-0-0 | 0.5-0 |
| W.C. Jarvis | 2-0-1 | 1-0 |
| S.N. Jett | 0.5-0-0 | 0-1 |
| J.K. Johnson | 0-0-1 | 0-0 |
| H.J. Kaczynski | 0-0-0 | 0-2 |
| D. Kahle | 1-0-1 | 1-2 |
| E. Korhorn | 0-0-1 | 0-0 |
| E.A. Kovacs | 1-0-0 | 0-0 |
| E.P. Lee | 0-0-0 | 0-4 |
| H.C. Leyser | 0.5-0-0.5 | 0-1 |
| J.C. Lindsay | 0-0-0 | 1.5-0 |
| R.C. McDowell | 1-0-0 | 0-0 |
| A.M. Metzger | 1-0-0 | 0-0 |
| E.H. Montgomery | 2-0-1 | 0-0 |
| F.A. Morgan | 0.5-0-0 | 5-0 |
| R.C. Nystrom | 0-0-0 | 0-1 |
| E.M. Parham | 0-0-0 | 1.5-0 |
| J.P. Perrin | 2-0-2 | 0-1 |
| F.S. Porter, Jr. | 1-0-0 | 0-1 |
| J.T. Price | 1-1-0 | 0-0 |
| R.W. Racine | 1-0-0 | 0-0 |
| P.J. Roberts | 0-0-0 | 1-0 |
| R.E. Rodgers | 0-0-1 | 0-0 |
| W.R. Scheible | 6-0-2 | 3-4 |
| R.F. Schlack | 0-0-0 | 1-3 |
| E.L. Slanker | 0.5-0-1 | 0-0 |
| D.J. Strait | 13.5-0-0 | 0-0 |
| B.A. Swift | 1-0-0 | 0-0 |
| E.L. Thompson | 2-0-2 | 2-3 |
| D.F. Thwaites | 6-0-3 | 1-0 |
| R.J. Upp | 0-0-0 | 0-3.5 |
| W. Waller, III | 0.5-0-1.5 | 0-0 |
| H.E. Whitmore | 2-0-2 | 1-2.5 |
| R.N. Whitson | 0-0-1 | 0-0 |
| H.E. Wiggins | 4.5-0-0 | 1.5-3 |
| J.N. Wood | 4.5-0-0 | 0-0 |
| G.L. Yoakum | 1-0-0 | 0-3 |

### 356th Fighter Group Scoring

**November 5, 1943**

| | | | |
|---|---|---|---|
| 361st: | Capt. P.H. Hyde | Me-109 dam(air) | Roermond |

**November 29, 1943**

| | | | |
|---|---|---|---|
| 359th: | Maj. D.A. Baccus | Me-109 dest(air) | NE Meppel |
| | Capt. E.J. White | Me-109 dest(air) | NE Meppel |
| | Lt. J.B. Smith | Me-109 dest(air) | NE Meppel |
| | | Me-109 prob(air) | NE Meppel |
| | Lt. G.B. Peet | Me-109 dam(air) | NE Meppel |
| | Lt. L.F. Richason | Me-109 dam(air) | NE Meppel |
| 360th: | Lt. R.R. Withers | Me-109 dest(air) | Meppel |
| | Capt. J.H. Bennett | Me-109 prob(air) | Meppel |
| 361st: | Lt. A.M. Metzger | Me-109 dest(air) | Meppel |

**December 1, 1943**

| | | | |
|---|---|---|---|
| 361st: | Lt. J.T. Price | FW-190 dest(air) | Brussels-Louvain |
| | | FW-190 prob(air) | Brussels-Louvain |

| | | | |
|---|---|---|---|
| **December 30, 1943** | | | |
| 359th: | Maj. D.A. Baccus | FW-190 dam(air) | NE St. Menahould |
| **January 5, 1944** | | | |
| 361st: | Lt. T.F. Bailey | FW-190 prob(air) | S/Liege |
| **January 11, 1944** | | | |
| (#1) | | | |
| 359th: | Capt. E.J. White | Me-109 prob(air) | Lingen |
| (#2) | | | |
| 359th: | Maj. D.A. Baccus | (.5)Me-110 dest(air) | Steinhuder Lake |
| | Lt. J.H. Wadlow | (.5)Me-110 dest(air) | Steinhuder Lake |
| | Lt. J.B. Smith | Ju-88 dest(air) | Steinhuder Lake |
| 361st: | Lt. R.W. Racine | Me-110 dest(air) | NW Hanover |
| **January 21, 1944** | | | |
| HdQts: | LtCol. O.H. Coen | (.5)FW-190 dam(grd) | St. Leger |
| 359th: | F/O R.G. Vossler | Ju-88 prob(air) | St. Leger |
| | Lt. J.D. Henry | (.5)FW-190 dam(grd) | St. Leger |
| 361st: | Lt. S.H. Hewett | (.5)Ju-88 dest(air) | Cambrai |
| | Lt. D.F. Thwaites | (.5)Ju-88 dest(air) | Cambrai |
| | Maj. E.H. Montgomery | Me-109 dam(air) | NE Dunkirk |
| **January 24, 1944** | | | |
| 360th: | Lt. C.A. Vitali | (3)FW-190 dest(air) | NW Lille |
| | | FW-190 dam(air) | NW Lille |
| | Maj. G.W. Johnson | FW-190 dest(air) | NE Ypres |
| | | (.5)FW-190 dam(air) | NE Ypres |
| | Capt. J.B. Stratford | FW-190 dest(air) | SW Antwerp |
| | Lt. W.E. Johnson | Me-109 dest(air) | W/Bruges |
| | Lt. L.F. Kress | Me-109 dest(air) | NE Lille |
| | Lt. W.G. Maxwell | FW-190 dest(air) | N/Lille |
| | | (.5)FW-190 dam(air) | NE Ypres |
| | Lt. A.V. Niemi | FW-190 dest(air) | N/Lille |
| | | FW-190 dam(air) | N/Lille |
| 361st: | Lt. M.F. Erickson | (.5)FW-190 dest(air) | Ghent-Bruges |
| | Lt. R.H. Gansberg | (.5)FW-190 dest(air) | Ghent-Bruges |
| | Lt. S.H. Hewett | FW-190 dam(air) | Bruges-Ostend |
| **January 29, 1944** | | | |
| 360th: | Lt. R.C. L'Heureux | FW-190 dest(air) | Louvain |
| **February 6, 1944** | | | |
| 361st: | Lt. D.J. Strait | FW-190 dest(air) | Paris-Soissons |
| **February 10, 1944** | | | |
| HdQts: | LtCol. O.H. Coen | FW-190 dam(air) | NE Lingen |
| 359th: | Maj. J.H. Thorne | FW-190 dest(air) | Meppen |
| | Capt. E.J. White | (.33)FW-190 dest(air) | Meppen |
| | Lt. R.D. Bradshaw | (.33)FW-190 dest(air) | Meppen |
| | Lt. G.W. Engel | (.33)FW-190 dest(air) | Meppen |
| | Lt. W.C. O'Barr | FW-190 dam(air) | Meppen |
| 360th: | Lt. W.E. Johnson | FW-190 dest(air) | Ruhlwertwist |
| | F/O C.W. Dunn | (.5)FW-190 dest(air) | Ruhlwertwist |
| | Lt. L.F. Kress | (.5)FW-190 dest(air) | Ruhlwertwist |
| 361st: | Capt. J.N. Wood | (1.5)FW-190 dest(air) | NE Lingen |
| | F/O J.V. Jack | FW-190 dest(air) | NE Lingen |
| | Lt. R.C. McDowell | FW-190 dest(air) | NE Lingen |
| | Lt. J.P. Perrin | FW-190 dest(air) | NE Lingen |
| | | FW-190 dam(air) | NE Lingen |
| | Lt. D.J. Strait | Me-109 dest(air) | NE Lingen |
| | Lt. M.W. DeMerit | (.5)FW-190 dest(air) | NE Lingen |
| **February 11, 1944** | | | |
| HdQts: | LtCol. O.H. Coen | (.5)Me-109 dest(air) | NW Charleville |
| 359th: | Lt. G.B. Peet | (.5)Me-109 dest(air) | NW Charleville |
| 360th: | Lt. C.J. Garvey | FW-190 dest(air) | S/Albert |
| | Lt. P.E. McCullough | FW-190 dest(air) | Marle |
| | | FW-190 prob(air) | S/Albert |
| 361st: | Lt. J.P. Perrin | FW-190 dam(air) | Charleville |
| **February 13, 1944** | | | |
| 360th: | Lt. B.E. Ellingson | Me-109 dest(air) | Chartres |
| | Lt. A.S. Koczak | FW-190 dest(air) | Dieppe |
| | Lt. W.G. Maxwell | FW-190 dest(air) | Chartres |
| | Lt. H.D. Parker | FW-190 dest(air) | Chartres |
| | Lt. P.E. McCullough | FW-190 dam(air) | Chartres |
| 361st: | Lt. S.H. Hewett | Me-109 dest(air) | SE Paris |
| | | (2)FW-190 dam(air) | SE Paris |
| | Lt. D.F. Thwaites | Me-109 dest(air) | SW Paris |
| **February 21, 1944** | | | |
| 359th: | Lt. W.W. Cotter | Me-109 dest(air) | Hanover |
| | Lt. W.A. Holm | Me-109 dam(air) | Hanover |
| | Capt. E.J. White | Me-109 dam(air) | Hanover |
| 360th: | Lt. H.B. McLaughlin | Me-109 prob(air) | Celle |
| | Lt. J.R. Cook | Me-109 dam(air) | Celle |
| **February 24, 1944** | | | |
| 360th: | Lt. W.H. Fletcher | Me-109 dam(air) | SW Aachen |
| **February 25, 1944** | | | |
| HdQts: | Capt. H.A. Ogden | (2)Me-109 dam(air) | Metz |
| **March 6, 1944** | | | |
| 359th: | Lt. W.L. Farmer | Me-109 dest(air) | Nienburg |
| | Lt. J.J. Meholic | Me-109 dest(air) | Nienburg |
| | Lt. C.H. Rubner | Me-109 dest(air) | Nienburg |
| | Lt. G.H. Engel | Me-109 prob(air) | Nienburg |
| | Lt. J.D. Henry | FW-190 dam(air) | Nienburg |
| 361st: | Capt. F.S. Porter | Me-109 dest(air) | N/Steinhuder L. |
| | Lt. S.H. Hewett | Me-109 dest(air) | NW Steinhuder L. |
| | Maj. W. Waller | (.5)Me-109 dest(air) | N/Steinhuder L. |
| | | (.5)Me-109 dam(air) | N/Steinhuder L. |
| | Lt. H.C. Leyser | (.5)Me-109 dest(air) | N/Steinhuder L. |
| | | (.5)Me-109 dam(air) | N/Steinhuder L. |
| **March 8, 1944** | | | |
| 359th: | Lt. J.D. Henry | Me-110 dest(grd) | Hesepe |
| | | Me-110 dam(grd) | Hesepe |
| | Lt. J.H. Wadlow | Me-110 dam(grd) | Hesepe |
| 360th: | Maj. J.R. Williams | Me-109 dest(air) | NW Lingen |
| | Lt. B. Borelli | Me-109 dest(air) | NW Lingen |
| **March 15, 1944** | | | |
| 359th: | Lt. J.J. Meholic | (.5)Me-109 dest(air) | SE Nijmegen |
| | Lt. H. Weber | (.5)Me-109 dest(air) | SE Nijmegen |
| **March 16, 1944** | | | |
| 359th: | Lt. W.C. O'Barr | (.5)Me-109 dest(air) | SE St. Dizier |
| | Lt. R.B. Warren | (.5)Me-109 dest(air) | SE St. Dizier |
| | Lt. R.D. Bradshaw | u/i a/c dam(grd) | S/Dummer Lake |
| **March 18, 1944** | | | |
| 359th: | Lt. W.C. O'Barr | Glider dam(grd) | W/Nancy |
| | | (.25)Do-217 dam(grd) | W/Nancy |
| | Maj. D.A. Baccus | (.25)Do-217 dam(grd) | W/Nancy |
| | Lt. R.K. Holtz | (.25)Do-217 dam(grd) | W/Nancy |
| | Lt. G.B. Peet | (.25)Do-217 dam(grd) | W/Nancy |
| **March 20, 1944** | | | |
| HdQts: | Col. E.A. Malmstrom | Me-109 dest(air) | Charleville |
| 361st: | Capt. F.S. Porter | Me-110 dam(grd) | N/Brussels |
| **March 23, 1944** | | | |
| 359th: | Lt. J.B. Smith | Me-110 dam(grd) | W/Duren |
| **March 29, 1944** | | | |
| HdQts: | Maj. J.H. Thorne | Me-109 dest(air) | Steinhuder Lake |
| 359th: | Lt. C.H. Rubner | Me-109 dest(air) | Steinhuder Lake |
| | Lt. J.B. Smith | Me-109 prob(air) | Steinhuder Lake |
| 360th: | Lt. W.E. Johnson | (2)Me-410 dest(grd) | Cloppenburg A/F |
| | Lt. H.B. McLaughlin | Me-410 dest(grd) | Cloppenburg A/F |
| | Lt. B. Borelli | Me-410 dam(grd) | Cloppenburg A/F |
| **April 1, 1944** | | | |
| HdQts: | Capt. H.A. Ogden | Me-410 dest(grd) | All claims are |
| 359th: | Lt. R.B. Warren | (2)Me-410 dest(grd) | at Dummer Lake |
| | LtCol. D.A. Baccus | Me-410 dest(grd) | |
| | Lt. J.J. Meholic | (.5)Me-410 dam(grd) | |
| | | (.5)Me-410 dam(grd) | |
| | Lt. H. Weber | (.5)Me-410 dam(grd) | |
| | | (.5)Me-410 dam(grd) | |
| **April 8, 1944** | | | |
| 359th: | Lt. J.B. Smith | Do-217 dam(grd) | Salzbergen A/F |
| **April 11, 1944** | | | |
| HdQts: | Col. E.A. Malmstrom | (2)Me-110 dest(grd) | All claims are |
| | | (.25)Me-109 dest(grd) | at Gifhorn |
| | | (.25)Ju-88 dest(grd) | |
| 361st: | Lt. R.H. Gansberg | (2)Me-110 dest(grd) | |
| | | (2)Ju-88 dest(grd) | |
| | Lt. S.H. Hewett | (2)Ju-88 dest(grd) | |
| | | (.5)FW-190 dest(grd) | |
| | | Ju-52 dam(grd) | |
| | Lt. E.M. Parham | Ju-88 dest(grd) | |
| | | (.5)FW-190 dest(grd) | |
| | Lt. W.W. Burns | Ju-88 dest(grd) | |
| | | u/i a/c dam(grd) | |
| | Lt. R. Gibson | (.25)Me-109 dest(grd) | |
| | | (.25)Ju-88 dest(grd) | |
| | Lt. J.V. Jack | (.25)Me-109 dest(grd) | |
| | | (.25)Ju-88 dest(grd) | |
| | F/O E.L. Decker | (.25)Me-109 dest(grd) | |
| | | (.25)Ju-88 dest(grd) | |
| | Lt. H.C. Leyser | u/i a/c dam(grd) | |
| **April 13, 1944** | | | |
| HdQts: | Capt. H.A. Ogden | Me-110 dest(grd) | Bischwiller A/F |
| | | (2)Me-110 dam(grd) | Bischwiller A/F |

| 361st: | Maj. E.H. Montgomery | (2)FW-190 dest(air) | Huy |
|---|---|---|---|
| | F/O E.L. Decker | Me-110 dest(grd) | Bischwiller A/F |
| | Lt. E.P. Lee | (4)He-111 dam(grd) | Hagenow |

**April 23, 1944**

| HdQts: | Col. E.A. Malmstrom | (3)He-111 dest(grd) | All claims are |
|---|---|---|---|
| | Capt. H.A. Ogden | He-111 dest(grd) | at Hagenau |
| | | (.5)Go-242 dam(grd)[*] | |
| | Maj. J.H. Thorne | (.5)He-111 dam(grd)[**] | |
| 359th: | Lt. W.C. Brearley | Go-242 dam(grd) | |
| | Lt. M.M. Clayborne | (.5)Go-242 dam(grd)[***] | |
| | | (.5)He-111 dam(grd)[@] | |
| | F/O F.A. Forsyth | (.5)Go-242 dam(grd)[*] | |
| | Lt. C.F. Krowiak | He-111 dam(grd) | |
| | | (.5)Go-242 dam(grd)[@@] | |
| | Lt. R.B. Warren | (.5)He-111 dam(grd)[@] | |
| | | (.5)Go-242 dam(grd)[***] | |
| | Lt. R.J. Collins | (.5)He-111 dam(grd)[**] | |
| | Lt. W.L. Farmer | (.5)Go-242 dam(grd)[@@] | |
| 360th: | Lt. L.H. Knapp | He-111 dest(grd) | |
| | | (1.5)Go-242 dam(grd)[#] | |
| | Capt. L.F. Kress | (1.5)Go-242 dam(grd)[#] | |
| | Lt. C.W. Adams | (.5)Go-242 dam(grd)[##] | |
| | Lt. R.C. L'Heureux | (.5)Go-242 dam(grd)[##] | |
| | Lt. V. Hockmeyer | (1.5)Go-242 dam(grd)& | |
| | Lt. R.R. Withers | (1.5)Go-242 dam(grd)& | |
| 361st: | F/O J.H. Culp | Me-109 dest(grd) | |
| | Lt. G.L. Yoakum | (2)Go-242 dam(grd) | |
| | | Me-109 dam(grd) | |
| | Lt. H.J. Kaczynski | (2)He-111 dam(grd) | |
| | Capt. J.P. Perrin | He-111 dam(grd) | |
| | Lt. J.L. Bruce | Go-242 dam(grd) | |
| | Lt. R.L. Campbell | He-111 dam(grd) | |
| | Lt. E.C. Fremaux | He-111 dam(grd) | |
| | Lt. R.H. Gansberg | He-111 dam(grd) | |

**April 27, 1944**

| HdQts: | Capt. H.A. Ogden | (.5)FW-190 dest(air) | Reims-Chateau-Thierry |
|---|---|---|---|
| 359th: | Lt. R.K. Holtz | FW-190 dest(air) | Reims-Chateau-Thierry |
| | Lt. R.J. Collins | (.5)FW-190 dest(air) | Reims-Chateau-Thierry |
| 360th: | Lt. W.E. Leathers | FW-190 dest(air) | Laon |
| | Lt. D.B. Mercer | FW-190 dest(air) | Laon |
| | | FW-190 dam(air) | Laon |

**May 4, 1944**

| 361st: | Capt. J.N. Wood | (3)FW-190 dest(air) | N/Steinhuder L. |
|---|---|---|---|
| | Lt. J.H. Culp | (2)FW-190 dest(air) | N/Steinhuder L. |
| | Capt. J.P. Perrin | FW-190 dest(air) | N/Steinhuder L. |
| | Lt. J.K. Johnson | FW-190 dam(air) | N/Steinhuder L. |

**May 13, 1944**

| HdQts: | LtCol. D.A. Baccus | (.5)FW-190 dest(air) | Kiel-Lubeck |
|---|---|---|---|
| | | FW-190 dam(air) | Kiel-Lubeck |
| 359th: | Lt. W.L. Farmer | FW-190 dest(air) | Kiel-Lubeck |
| | Lt. R.L. Coughenour | (.5)FW-190 dest(air) | Kiel-Lubeck |
| | Capt. W.A. Holm | FW-190 prob(air) | Kiel-Lubeck |
| | Lt. J.A. Wyatt | FW-190 prob(air) | Kiel-Lubeck |
| | | FW-190 dam(air) | Kiel-Lubeck |
| 360th: | Lt. R.R. Withers | FW-190 dest(air) | Kiel |
| | Lt. C.W. Adams | FW-190 prob(air) | Kiel |
| | Lt. A.A. Perryman | FW-190 dam(air) | Kiel |
| 361st: | Capt. T.F. Bailey | FW-190 dest(air) | SE Lubeck |
| | Lt. B.A. Swift | FW-190 dest(air) | S/Kiel |
| | Lt. D.F. Thwaites | FW-190 dest(air) | Hamburg |
| | Lt. E.L. Faison | FW-190 prob(air) | SE Lubeck |

**May 19, 1944**

| 359th: | Lt. H. Weber | Me-109 dest(air) | Steinhuder Lake |
|---|---|---|---|
| 360th: | Capt. J.W. Vogt | FW-190 dest(air) | SW Celle |
| | Lt. W.G. Maxwell | Me-109 dest(air) | Nienburg |
| | Lt. A.A. Perryman | FW-190 dest(air) | SW Celle |
| | Lt. F.M. Russell | FW-190 dest(air) | Hanover |
| | Lt. C.A. Vitali | Me-109 dest(air) | Steinhuder Lake |
| | Lt. R.R. Withers | Me-109 dest(air) | Hanover |
| | | Me-109 dam(air) | Hanover |
| | Lt. R.C. L'Heureux | Me-109 dam(air) | Hanover |
| 361st: | Capt. D.J. Strait | Me-109 dest(air) | Quackenbruck |
| | Lt. H.M. Engelhorn | Me-109 dest(air) | Quackenbruck |
| | Lt. R.H. Gansberg | Me-109 dest(air) | Quackenbruck |
| | Lt. D.F. Thwaites | FW-190 dest(air) | Quackenbruck |
| | | (3)FW-190 dam(air) | Quackenbruck |
| | LtCol. W. Waller | Me-109 dam(air) | NE Dummer Lake-E/Minden |

**May 21, 1944**

| 360th: | Capt. N.D. Cota | He-177 dest(air) | Stade |
|---|---|---|---|

**May 25, 1944**

| 360th: | Lt. R.M. Leidy | Me-109 dest(air) | W/Neufchateau |
|---|---|---|---|
| 361st: | Lt. D.F. Thwaites | Me-109 dest(air) | Neufchateau |

**June 7, 1944**

| HdQts: | LtCol. D.A. Baccus | Me-323 dest(grd) | Laval |
|---|---|---|---|
| 359th: | Lt. L.F. Richason | Me-109 dest(grd) | Laval |
| | | Ju-52 dest(grd) | Laval |
| | | Me-109 dam(grd) | Laval |
| | Capt. G.W. Engel | Ju-52 dest(grd) | Laval |
| | Lt. A.E. Bergstrom | Me-109 dest(grd) | Laval |
| 361st: | F/O E.L. Decker | FW-190 dest(air) | SE Laval |
| | Lt. D.F. Thwaites | Ju-52 dest(grd) | Laval |

**June 8, 1944**

| 359th: | Lt. M.M. Clayborne | FW-190 dest(air) | All claims are |
|---|---|---|---|
| 361st: | Lt. H.E. Wiggins | (.5)FW-190 dest(air) | at Beauvais- |
| | | (.5)FW-190 dest(grd) | Nivillers |
| | Lt. G.L. Yoakum | (.5)FW-190 dest(air) | |
| | Capt. D.B. Clayton | (.5)FW-190 dest(grd) | |

**June 10, 1944**

| 359th: | Lt. L.F. Richason | FW-190 dest(grd) | SE Dreux |
|---|---|---|---|
| | | FW-190 dam(grd) | SE Dreux |

**June 11, 1944**

| 361st: | Lt. R.H. Gansberg | Me-109 dest(air) | SW Bernay |
|---|---|---|---|
| | Lt. D. Kahle | Me-109 dest(air) | SW Bernay |

**June 15, 1944**

| 361st: | Capt. W.R. Scheible | Me-109 dest(air) | SE Rouen |
|---|---|---|---|
| | Capt. E. Korhorn | Me-109 dam(air) | SE Rouen |
| | Lt. D. Kahle | Me-109 dam(air) | SE Rouen |

**June 22, 1944**

| 361st: | Lt. W.S. Hurley | (.5)Me-109 dest(air) | Evreux |
|---|---|---|---|
| | Lt. G.L. Yoakum | (.5)Me-109 dest(air) | Evreux |

**July 6, 1944**

| 361st: | Lt. E.L. Thompson | Me-109 dest(air) | S/Fontainbleau |
|---|---|---|---|

**July 19, 1944**

| 359th: | Capt. H. Weber | Me-410 dam(grd) | Le Culot |
|---|---|---|---|
| | Lt. H.F. LeMoyne | Me-410 dam(grd) | Le Culot |

**July 25, 1944**

| 360th: | Capt. N.D. Cota | (.5)Me-109 dam(air) | NW Paris |
|---|---|---|---|
| | Lt. C.M. Taylor | (.5)Me-109 dam(air) | NW Paris |

**July 26, 1944**

| HdQts: | LtCol. D.A. Baccus | He-111 dest(grd) | Cormeilles-en-Vixen |
|---|---|---|---|

**July 29, 1944**

| 359th: | Capt. G.B. Peet | He-111 dam(grd) | St. Andre de L'Eure |
|---|---|---|---|

**August 4, 1944**

| 359th: | Capt. G.B. Peet | Me-109 dest(air) | NE Bremen |
|---|---|---|---|
| | Lt. L.G. Alphonse | Me-109 dest(air) | Selseingen-Ottersberg |
| | Lt. M.M. Clayborne | Me-109 dest(air) | Selseingen-Ottersberg |
| 360th: | Maj. J.W. Vogt | (2)Me-109 dest(air) | SW Hamburg |
| | Lt. W.H. Fletcher | (2)Me-109 dest(air) | SW Hamburg |
| | Lt. R.S. Gleason | Me-109 dest(air) | SW Hamburg |
| | Lt. T.D. Teel | Me-109 dest(air) | SW Hamburg |
| | Lt. J.H. Williams | Me-109 dest(air) | SW Hamburg |
| 361st: | Lt. H.E. Wiggins | (2)Me-109 dest(air) | All claims are |
| | Lt. E.L. Faison | Me-109 dest(air) | at Bremen-Hamburg |
| | Lt. W.S. Hurley | Me-109 dest(air) | |
| | Lt. D.F. Thwaites | Me-109 dest(air) | |
| | Lt. R.E. Rodgers | Me-109 dam(air) | |

**August 12, 1944**

| 361st: | Lt. E.C. Fremaux | (.5)Ju-88 dest(air) | Claims are at |
|---|---|---|---|
| | | (.5)Ju-88 dest(air) | Guise-Avesnes |
| | Capt. D.B. Clayton | (.5)Ju-88 dest(air) | |
| | Lt. R.W. Gillette | (.5)Ju-88 dest(air) | |

**August 18, 1944**

| 359th: | Lt. F.A. Forsyth | FW-190 dest(air) | All claims are |
|---|---|---|---|
| | Lt. R.G. Vossler | FW-190 dest(air) | at Beauvais |
| | | FW-190 dam(air) | |
| | Capt. J.D. Tarbutton | (.5)FW-190 dam(air) | |
| | Lt. L.F. Richason | (.5)FW-190 dam(air) | |
| 361st: | Lt. J.A. Hargreaves | FW-190 dest(air) | |
| | | FW-190 prob(air) | |
| | Lt. E.L. Thompson | FW-190 dest(air) | |
| | | (2)FW-190 dam(air) | |
| | Lt. E.A. Kovacs | FW-190 dest(air) | |

**September 1, 1944**

(#1)

| 360th: | Lt. R.M. Leidy | Me-109 dest(grd) | Le Culot |
|---|---|---|---|
| | | Me-109 dam(grd) | Le Culot |

(#2)

| 360th: | Lt. E.W. Plaesant | Ju-52 dest(grd) | All claims are |
|---|---|---|---|
| | Capt. W.H. Fletcher | (.5)Ju-52 dest(grd)[*] | SE Nancy |

| | | | |
|---|---|---|---|
| | Lt. J.T. Romine | (.5)Ju-52 dest(grd)* | |
| | | (.5)Ju-52 dam(grd) | |
| | Lt. E.M. Nebinger | (.5)Ju-52 dest(grd)** | |
| | | (.5)Ju-52 dam(grd) | |
| | Lt. H.S. Olive | (.5)Ju-52 dest(grd)** | |
| | Lt. F.W. Peacock | (.5)Ju-52 dest(grd)@ | |
| | Lt. C.M. Taylor | (.5)Ju-52 dest(grd)@ | |

**September 5, 1944**

| | | | |
|---|---|---|---|
| 361st: | Capt. D.F. Thwaites | (.5)He-111 dest(air) | Twente/Enschede |
| | Lt. F.A. Morgan | (.5)He-111 dest(air) | Twente/Enschede |

**September 9, 1944**

| | | | |
|---|---|---|---|
| 359th: | Lt. D.F. Tucker | He-111 dest(grd) | W/Bad Nauheim |
| 360th: | Lt. J.T. Romine | FW-190 dam(air) | W/Giessen |

**September 13, 1944**

| | | | |
|---|---|---|---|
| 360th: | Capt. W.H. Fletcher | FW-190 dest(grd) | All claims are |
| | | Me-410 dam(grd) | NW Stuttgart |
| | Lt. O.L. Burwell | Me-410 dest(grd) | |
| | | FW-190 dam(grd) | |
| | Lt. E.W. Pleasant | Me-410 dam(grd) | |

**October 7, 1944**

| | | | |
|---|---|---|---|
| 361st: | Capt. W.R. Scheible | (2)Me-110 dest(grd) | All claims are |
| | | Ju-88 dest(grd) | at Fritzlar |
| | | (4)Ju-88 dam(grd) | |
| | Lt. E.L. Thompson | Ju-88 dest(grd) | |
| | | u/i a/c dest(grd) | |
| | | Me-110 dam(grd) | |
| | | Hs-123 dam(grd) | |
| | | Ju-88 dam(grd) | |
| | Lt. H.E. Whitmore | Ju-88 dest(grd) | |
| | | (2.5)Ju-88 dam(grd) | |
| | Lt. F.F. Hooker | Me-110 dest(grd) | |
| | | Me-110 dam(grd) | |
| | | Me-410 dam(grd) | |
| | Lt. D. Kahle | Me-110 dest(grd) | |
| | | (2)Me-110 dam(grd) | |
| | Lt. P.J. Roberts | Me-110 dest(grd) | |
| | Capt. R.J. Upp | (3.5)Ju-88 dam(grd) | |
| | Capt. J.M. Hallmark | (3)Me-110 dam(grd) | |

**November 4, 1944**

| | | | |
|---|---|---|---|
| 359th: | Capt. R.A. Rann | Me-262 dam(air) | Lingen-Enschede |

**November 25, 1944**

| | | | |
|---|---|---|---|
| 359th: | Lt. J.B. Cornett | Ju-88 dam(grd) | Ettinghausen |
| | Lt. R.C. Scharnberg | Ju-88 dam(grd) | Ettinghausen |
| 361st: | Lt. C.T. Ashby | (2)FW-190 dest(grd) | All claims are |
| | | FW-190 dam(grd) | at Zwickau |
| | Lt. C.D. Burdick | FW-190 dest(grd) | |
| | Lt. W.S. Hurley | FW-190 dest(grd) | |
| | | (2)FW-190 dam(grd) | |
| | Lt. H.E. Wiggins | FW-190 dest(grd) | |
| | | (3)FW-190 dam(grd) | |
| | Lt. S.N. Jett | FW-190 dam(grd) | |

**November 26, 1944**

| | | | |
|---|---|---|---|
| HdQts: | LtCol. D.A. Baccus | (2)Me-109 dest(air) | Dummer Lake |
| 359th: | Capt. R.A. Rann | (2)Me-109 dest(air) | All 359th claims |
| | Lt. W.C. Cooley | (2)Me-109 dest(air) | are NW Dummer L. |
| | Capt. D.F. Tucker | Me-109 dest(air) | |
| | | Me-109 dam(air) | |
| | Lt. H.R. Gohsler | Me-109 dest(air) | |
| | Lt. A.R. Hale | FW-190 dest(air) | |
| 360th: | Capt. M.P. Yannell | (2)Me-109 dest(air) | All 360th claims |
| | | (2)Me-109 dam(air) | are at Dummer L. |
| | Lt. T.J. Urban | Me-109 dest(air) | |
| | Capt. B. Borelli | Me-109 dam(air) | |
| | Lt. R.E. Barnhart | Me-109 dam(air) | |
| | Lt. N.B. Ceraolo | Me-109 dam(air) | |
| | Lt. W.K. Dunn | Me-109 dam(air) | |
| 361st: | Capt. W.R. Scheible | (3)Me-109 dest(air) | All 361st claims |
| | | (2)Me-109 dam(air) | are at Osnabruck- |
| | Lt. H.E. Wiggins | (2)FW-190 dest(air) | Dummer Lake |
| | Capt. D.J. Strait | (1.5)Me-109 dest(air) | |
| | Lt. C.E. Beck | Me-109 dest(air) | |
| | Lt. J.A. Bowers | Me-109 dest(air) | |
| | Lt. R.R. Burden | FW-190 dest(air) | |
| | Lt. W.C. Jarvis | Me-109 dest(air) | |
| | | FW-190 dam(air) | |
| | Lt. H.E. Whitmore | Me-109 dest(air) | |
| | Lt. S.N. Jett | (.5)Me-109 dest(air) | |
| | Lt. B.B. Barnes | FW-190 dam(air) | |

**November 27, 1944**

| | | | |
|---|---|---|---|
| 359th: | Capt. D.F. Tucker | FW-190 dest(air) | All claims are |
| | Capt. R.R. Withers | Me-109 dest(air) | N/Munster |
| | Lt. R.E. Carr | FW-190 prob(air) | |
| | Lt. J.E. Blewett | Me-109 prob(air) | |
| | Lt. G. Crum | Me-109 dam(air) | |

**December 5, 1944**

| | | | |
|---|---|---|---|
| 359th: | Capt. J.D. Tarbutton | (2)FW-190 dest(air) | NW Berlin |
| | Capt. C.J. Hackney | FW-190 dest(air) | Muritz Lake-Berlin |
| | Lt. F.A. Forsyth | FW-190 dest(air) | Muritz Lake-Berlin |
| | | FW-190 prob(air) | Muritz Lake-Berlin |
| | Lt. L. Oliver | FW-190 dest(air) | Muritz Lake-Berlin |
| | Capt. L.L. Robertson | FW-190 prob(air) | N/Berlin |
| | Lt. A.R. Hale | FW-190 dam(air) | Muritz Lake-Berlin |
| 361st: | Capt. W.R. Scheible | (2)FW-190 dest(air) | All claims are |
| | Capt. D.J. Strait | (2)FW-190 dest(air) | at Eberswalde |
| | Lt. R.H. Campbell | (2)FW-190 dest(air) | |
| | Lt. C.T. Ashby | FW-190 dest(air) | |
| | | FW-190 prob(air) | |
| | Lt. C.D. Burdick | FW-190 dest(air) | |
| | | FW-190 dam(air) | |

**December 25, 1944**

| | | | |
|---|---|---|---|
| HdQts: | LtCol. D.A. Baccus | Me-109 dest(air) | Bonn |
| 359th: | Lt. E.F. Troge | FW-190 dest(air) | Bonn |
| | Lt. A.L. Brown | FW-190 dam(air) | Bonn |
| 360th: | Capt. B.E. Ellingson | FW-190 dest(air) | S/Bonn |
| | | Me-109 dest(air) | S/Bonn |
| | Capt. E.W. Plaesant | FW-190 dest(air) | Bonn |
| | | FW-190 dam(air) | Bonn |
| | Lt. D.F. Jones | FW-190 dam(air) | S/Bonn |
| | Lt. T.J. Urban | FW-190 dam(air) | Bonn |
| 361st: | Capt. D.J. Strait | Me-109 dest(air) | SW Coblenz |

**December 26, 1944**

| | | | |
|---|---|---|---|
| 359th: | Lt. W.C. Cooley | (2)FW-190 dest(air) | NE Bonn |
| | Capt. C.J. Hackney | FW-190 dest(air) | NE Bonn |
| | Lt. J.W. Meade | FW-190 dest(air) | NE Bonn |

**January 14, 1945**

| | | | |
|---|---|---|---|
| 360th: | Lt. R.E. Barnhart | FW-190 dest(air) | S/Osnabruck |
| | Lt. T.J. Urban | FW-190 dest(air) | S/Osnabruck |
| 361st: | Lt. C.T. Ashby | (2.5)FW-190 dest(air) | Unless noted, |
| | Lt. W.M. Baskin | (1.5)FW-190 dest(air) | all claims are |
| | Lt. C.D. Burdick | (2)FW-190 dest(air) | SW Dummer Lake |
| | | (2)FW-190 dam(air) | |
| | Lt. F.F. Hooker | (2)FW-190 dest(air) | |
| | | Me-262 dam(grd) | Hesepe A/F |
| | Maj. D.J. Strait | FW-190 dest(air) | |
| | Lt. M.W. Baylor | FW-190 dest(air) | |
| | | FW-190 prob(air) | |
| | Lt. W.C. Jarvis | FW-190 dest(air) | |
| | Lt. J.A. Bowers | FW-190 dam(air) | |
| | Lt. R.N. Whitson | FW-190 dam(air) | |

**February 14, 1945**

| | | | |
|---|---|---|---|
| 359th: | Lt. A.L. Brown | FW-190 dest(air) | Dresden-Chemnitz |
| | | FW-190 dam(air) | Dresden-Chemnitz |
| | Lt. R.C. Miller | FW-190 dam(air) | Dresden-Chemnitz |
| 360th: | Lt. W.O. Hedrick | FW-190 dam(air) | S/Chemnitz |
| 361st: | Maj. D.J. Strait | (2)FW-190 dest(air) | All claims are |
| | Lt. M.W. Baylor | (2)FW-190 dest(air) | S/Chemnitz |
| | | FW-190 dam(air) | |
| | Lt. J.A. Bowers | (2)FW-190 dest(air) | |
| | Lt. H.E. Whitmore | (2)FW-190 dam(air) | |

**February 20, 1945**

| | | | |
|---|---|---|---|
| 361st: | Maj. D.J. Strait | (3)Fi-156 dest(air) | SE Bayreuth |
| | Lt. C.D. Burdick | (2.5)Fi-156 dest(air) | SE Bayreuth |
| | Lt. E.L. Slanker | (.5)Fi-156 dest(air) | SE Bayreuth |
| | | Fi-156 dam(air) | SE Bayreuth |
| | Capt. F.A. Morgan | (3)u/i a/c dest(grd) | Unless noted, |
| | | Me-110 dest(grd) | claims are at |
| | | Ju-88 dest(grd) | Windleschenlaibach |
| | F/O J.K. Dupuy | Ju-88 dest(grd) | |
| | | (.5)u/i a/c dest(grd) | |
| | Lt. J.C. Lindsay | FW-190 dest(grd) | Bayreuth-Eindbach |
| | | (.5)u/i a/c dest(grd) | |
| | Lt. R.J. Cox | FW-190 dest(grd) | |
| | | (2)FW-190 dam(grd) | Bayreuth-Eindbach |
| | Capt. R.F. Schlack | Ju-88 dest(grd) | Furth |
| | | (3)Ju-88 dam(grd) | Furth |
| | Lt. W.C. Jarvis | Ju-88 dest(grd) | Furth |

**February 21, 1945**

| | | | |
|---|---|---|---|
| 360th: | Lt. A.A. Paquet | FW-190 dam(grd) | NW Crailsheim |
| | | W-34 dam(grd) | NW Crailsheim |
| | Lt. J.W. Crump | FW-190 dam(grd) | NW Crailsheim |
| | Capt. W.G. Thomas | He-111 dam(grd) | S/Nurnberg |
| | Lt. R.S. Ragsdale | (.5)He-111 dam(grd) | S/Nurnberg |
| | Lt. J.P. Weller | (.5)He-111 dam(grd) | S/Nurnberg |
| (PRU) | | | |
| 361st: | Lt. H.E. Whitmore | Me-262 dest(air) | Stettin |

**February 23, 1945**

| | | | |
|---|---|---|---|
| 360th: | Capt. M.P. Yannell | He-177 dest(grd) | Giebelstadt |
| | | He-177 dam(grd) | Giebelstadt |

**February 25, 1945**

| | | | |
|---|---|---|---|
| 359th: | Lt. J.F. Brown | He-111 dest(grd) | Bendorf A/F |
| | Lt. A.L. Brown | He-111 dam(grd) | Bendorf A/F |
| | Lt. H.R. Gohsler | He-111 dam(grd) | Bendorf A/F |

**March 14, 1945**

| | | | |
|---|---|---|---|
| 360th: | Lt. R.E. Barnhart | Ar-234 dest(air) | Bielefeld-Hildesheim |

**March 20, 1945**

| | | | |
|---|---|---|---|
| 359th: | Lt. E.G. Rudd | Me-262 dam(air) | Wesermunde-Hamburg |

**March 21, 1945**

| | | | |
|---|---|---|---|
| 359th: | Lt. R.J. Stone | FW-190 dam(grd) | Achmer |

**March 22, 1945**

| | | | |
|---|---|---|---|
| 361st: | Lt. R.C. Nystrom | He-111 dam(grd) | Plantlunne |

**April 7, 1945**

| | | | |
|---|---|---|---|
| 359th: | Capt. J.F. Brown | Me-109 dest(air) | NE Steinhuder L. |
| | Lt. H.R. Gohsler | Me-109 dest(air) | E/Steinhuder L. |
| | | Me-109 prob(air) | E/Steinhuder L. |
| | Lt. J.B. Cornett | FW-190 dest(air) | NE Steinhuder L. |
| | Lt. P.C. O'Quinn | Me-262 dam(air) | NE Steinhuder L. |

**April 9, 1945**

| | | | |
|---|---|---|---|
| 360th: | Maj. M.P. Yannell | FW-190 dest(grd) | All claims are |
| | | u/i a/c dest(grd) | at Biberach |
| | | Me-410 dam(grd) | |
| | Lt. R.J. Rensch | u/i a/c dest(grd) | |
| | | (3)u/i a/c dam(grd) | |
| | | Me-109 dam(grd) | |
| | Lt. E.W. Schrull | FW-190 dam(grd) | |
| | | u/i a/c dam(grd) | |
| | Lt. T.N. Mauldin | u/i a/c dam(grd) | |

**April 10, 1945**

| | | | |
|---|---|---|---|
| 360th: | Lt. W.C. Gatlin | Me-262 dest(air) | Oranienburg |
| | Lt. T.N. Mauldin | Me-262 prob(air) | Oranienburg |
| | Lt. E.W. Schrull | Me-262 dam(air) | Oranienburg |

**April 13, 1945**

| | | | |
|---|---|---|---|
| 360th: | Maj. M.P. Yannell | FW-190 dest(grd) | All claims are |
| | Lt. B.D. McNary | (2)FW-190 dam(grd) | at Schwerin |
| | | He-111 dam(grd) | |
| | Lt. N.B. Ceraolo | FW-190 dam(grd) | |
| | Lt. G.W. Seanor | Do-217 dam(grd) | |

**April 18, 1945**

| | | | |
|---|---|---|---|
| 359th: | Lt. L. Oliver | Ar-234 dest(air) | Wertingen |
| 360th: | Capt. O.L. Burwell | Me-262 dam(air) | Ingolstadt |
| | Lt. W.C. Gatlin | (.33)Me-262 dam(air) | Ingolstadt |
| | Lt. L.B. Proctor | (.33)Me-262 dam(air) | Ingolstadt |
| | Lt. G.W. Seanor | (.33)Me-262 dam(air) | Ingolstadt |

### 356th Fighter Group Losses

**November 11, 1943**
Lt. Dolor A. Martin (360th) KIA; Last seen near Arnhem, possible oxygen failure.
P-47D PI- 42-8668

**November 29, 1943**
Lt. John D. Hull (359th) POW; Ran out of fuel and crashed near Vreeland.
P-47D OC- 42-8598
Lt. Warren A. Beach (359th) POW; Hit by fire from a B-17 while making R/V southwest of Aschendorf.
P-47D OC- 42-8601
Lt. Julius B. Asbridge (360th) POW; Ran out of fuel and crashed near Scheveningen.
P-47D PI-W 42-8502 "Hell's Angel"
Lt. Allen M. Metzger (361st) KIA; Last seen doing a left turn in heavy overcast near Holdorf.
P-47D QI-O 42-8509
Lt. Johnnie F. Martin (361st) KIA; Last seen doing turns in heavy overcast near Hellendoorn.
P-47D QI-Q 42-8692

**December 16, 1943**
Lt. James T. Price (361st) KIA; Spun-in northeast of Felixstowe shortly after take-off.
P-47D QI-K 42-74709

**December 20, 1943**
Capt. Paul H. Hyde (361st) KIA; Collided with a B-24 near Den Helder.
P-47D QI-L 42-8677

**December 30, 1943**
F/O Everett L. Brock (360th) KIA; Collided with Lt. Hayden near Montdidier.
P-47D PI- 42-22542
Lt. William R. Hayden (361st) KIA; Collided with F/O Brock near Montdidier.
P-47D QI-X 42-8662

**January 7, 1944**
Lt. William F. Brown (359th) KIA; Hit by flak near Cologne, he bailed out near Aachen and was killed on the ground.
P-47D OC- 42-8639

**January 11, 1944**
Lt. Rolland W. Racine (361st) KIA; He destroyed a Me-110 near Steinhuder Lake and turned for home. Shortly after, he heard a distress call, reversed his course, and was last seen heading back towards enemy aircraft.
P-47D QI-V 42-22525

**January 14, 1944**
Lt. Robert B. Conroy (359th) POW; Shot-up by a Me-109 near Arras.
P-47D OC-R 42-8694 "Little Texan"
Lt. Raymond C. Fortner (359th) KIAc; Killed on a practice flight near Martlesham Heath.
P-47D OC-S 42-22524

**February 10, 1944**
Lt. Merrill W. DeMerit, Jr. (361st) POW; Shot down by a FW-190 near Lingen.
P-47D QI-N 42-22520

**February 11, 1944**
Capt. Byron A. Evans (360th) KIA; Last seen chasing a Me-109 near St. Quentin.
P-47D PI- 42-8507

**February 21, 1944**
Lt. Thomas Von Holzhausen (361st) KIA; Lost in a fight with Me-109's near Hanover.
P-47D QI-Z 42-74679 "China Doll"

**February 26, 1944**
Lt. William W. Cotter (359th) KIAc; Hit the ground while buzzing Martlesham Heath.
P-47D OC-C 42-8492

**March 6, 1944**
Lt. Milton F. Erickson (361st) POW; Downed by a Me-109 near Lingen.
P-47D QI-N 42-75255

**March 8, 1944**
Lt. Justus D. Henry (359th) KIA; Crashed into a hangar while strafing Hesepe Airfield.
P-47D OC-L 42-8467

**March 18, 1944**
Lt. Bleftherios A. Vangos (361st) POW; Hit by flak near Lille, he bellied-in southeast of Cambrai.
P-47D QI-Y 42-74715 "The Vangoose"

**March 20, 1944**
Lt. Charles J. Garvey, Jr. (360th) POW; Lost in bad weather and came down near Loxbergen.
P-47D PI-D 42-74638 "Nashville Belle"
Lt. Philip E. McCullough (360th) POW; Hit by flak near Beauvechin.
P-47D PI- 42-74622
F/O Howard P. Maupin (360th) MIA-E; Lost in bad weather and came down near Neerwinden.
P-47D PI-N 42-22535 "Kathleen Ann"
Capt. Fred S. Porter, Jr. (361st) POW; Hit by flak while strafing north of Brussels.
P-47D QI-I 42-74646
Lt. DeWitt T. Bell (361st) KIA; Hit by flak while strafing north of Brussels.
P-47D QI-Z 42-75553
Lt. Bernard A. Tuckey (361st) KIA; Spun-out in bad weather off Orfordness.
P-47D QI-P 42-8440

**April 9, 1944**
Lt. Carl W. Dunn (360th) KIA; Acting as spotter, he crashed in bad weather near Gissing.
P-47D PI- 42-76147

**April 10, 1944**
Lt. William E. Johnson, Jr. (360th) KIA; Last seen chasing enemy aircraft through the bomber formation near Argentan.
P-47D PI- 42-74639

**April 11, 1944**
Capt. Hunter D. Parker (360th) POW; Hit by flak and bailed out southeast of Dummer Lake.
P-47D PI-G 42-76449
Lt. Ernest M. Parham (361st) KIA; Hit by flak while strafing Gifhorn Airfield. He reported he was going to bail out but was not seen to do so.
P-47D QI-O 42-76126

**April 23, 1944**
Col. Einar A. Malmstrom (HdQts) POW; Hit by flak at Hagenau Airfield.
P-47D QI-R 42-25513 "Kay-J"
Lt. Daughtry L. Hall (360th) POW; Hit by flak at Hagenau Airfield.
P-47D PI- 42-75134
Lt. Henry J. Kaczynski (361st) POW; Hit by flak at Hagenau Airfield.
P-47D QI-Z 42-76570

**April 24, 1944**
Lt. William B. Ingram (361st) POW; Ran out of fuel northwest of Lille.
P-47D QI-H 43-25271

**April 26, 1944**
Lt. Richard B. Warren (359th) KIA; Returning from the mission, he collided with Lt. Rann and crashed near Bromeswell.
P-47D OC-S 42-75159

**April 27, 1944**
Lt. Raymond K. Holtz (359th) MIA-E; He was shot down by the same FW-190 he destroyed near Laon.
P-47D OC-B 43-25557
Lt. Casimir F. Krowiak (359th) KIA; Downed by a FW-190 northwest of Rheims.
P-47D OC- 42-76220
Capt. John B. Stratford, Jr. (360th) KIA; Shot down by a FW-190 northwest of Rheims.
P-47D PI- 42-76135

**May 4, 1944**
Capt. Sidney H. Hewett (361st) POW; Downed by a FW-190 in the Steinhuder Lake area.
P-47D QI-F 42-76397 "Clarkie"
Lt. Jack H. Culp (361st) POW; Downed by a FW-190 in the Steinhuder Lake area.
P-47D QI-N 42-22766
Lt. John L. Bruce (361st) KIA; Flew as radio-relay. He turned too tight while landing and crashed at Martlesham Heath.
P-47D QI-B 43-25516

**May 7, 1944**
Lt. William H. Wood (359th) POW; Lost oil pressure and bailed out north of Lingen.
P-47D OC-A 42-8417 "Ich Brauche Du"

**May 13, 1944**
Capt. Willis A. Holm (359th) KIA; Shot down by a FW-190 near Hamburg.
P-47D OC-M 42-74689 "Lady Jane"

**May 19, 1944**
Lt. Allen A. Perryman, Jr. (360th) POW; Hit by a Me-109 near Celle.
P-47D PI- 43-25302
Lt. Edwin D. Cook (360th) POW; Hit by enemy fighters near Hanover.
P-47D PI- 42-25294
Lt. James K. Johnson (361st) POW; Hit by enemy aircraft near Quackenbruck.
P-47D QI-Y 42-75505

**May 20, 1944**
Lt. Alex S. Koczak (360th) POW; Bailed out near Valenciennes after engine trouble.
P-47D PI- 42-8533

**May 21, 1944**
Lt. Edwin E. Anderson (360th) POW; Hit by flak near Oldenburg.
P-47D PI- 42-76396
Lt. Wallace G. Maxwell (360th) KIA; Bailed out over the North Sea off Wilhelmshaven after flak damage.
P-47D PI-Q 42-76499

**May 23, 1944**
Lt. Grant F. Moyer (360th) KIAc; Crashed into Bradwell Bay on a practice flight.
P-47D QI-V 42-22479

**May 29, 1944**
Lt. William C. O'Barr (359th) POW; Bailed out southwest of the Northeast Polder after mechanical trouble.
P-47D OC-E 42-76372

**May 31, 1944**
Lt. Lawrence L. Goldwasser (360th) POW; Lost oil pressure and bailed out near Zevenburgen.
P-47D PI- 43-25590

**June 6, 1944**
Lt. George C. Kariva (360th) POW; Suffered mechanical trouble and bailed out over the Channel off Dunkirk.
P-47D PI- 42-75625
F/O Emil L. Sova (360th) POW; Hit by flak and bailed out in the Angars area.
P-47D PI- 43-25997

**June 8, 1944**
Lt. John D. Smith (359th) MIA-E; Hit by a Me-109 east of Amiens and bailed out along the Somme River.
P-47D OC-R 42-76168
Lt. Robert A. Coughenour, Jr. (359th) KIA; Lost oil pressure and crashed off Orfordness.
P-47D OC- 42-26253
Lt. Joseph Obosla (360th) KIA; Caught in a bomb blast near Rouen.
P-47D PI- 42-76431
Lt. Edward P. Lee, Jr. (361st) KIA; Hit by flak near Montdidier.
P-47D QI-S 42-76422
F/O Edmund L. Decker (361st) KIA; Hit the ground while strafing near Bouconvillers.
P-47D QI-K 42-75556
Lt. Raymond F. Engle (361st) KIA; Reported he was low on fuel near Abbeville.
P-47D QI-O 42-8427

**June 10, 1944**
Lt. Elijah P. Harris, Jr. (361st) KIA; Hit by flak near Gassicourt.
P-47D QI-Z 42-7886

**June 14, 1944**
Lt. Fred C. Phillips, Jr. (360th) POW; Suffered engine failure and bailed out near Hertogenbosch.
P-47D PI-P 42-75273 "Hard Luck"

**June 28, 1944**
Lt. Charles B. Earnhart (359th) MIA-E; Hit a tree or pole while strafing in the Ghent-Brussels area.
P-47D OC-O 42-25508

**July 18, 1944**
Lt. Shirley J. Green (360th) KIAc; Collided with another P-47 on a practice hop and crashed near Woodbridge.
P-47D PI-

**July 20, 1944**
Capt. Carman F. Rhoades (360th) POW; Collided with Lt. Robinson near Hisenden.
P-47D PI-M 42-25751 "Joker"
Lt. Robert A. Robinson (360th) POW; Collided with Capt. Rhoades near Hisenden.
P-47D PI- 42-76493

**August 4, 1944**
Lt. Joseph W. Mills (361st) KIA; Lost in a fight with Me-109's near Hamburg.
P-47D QI-S 42-25842

**August 9, 1944**
Lt. Robert E. Rodgers (361st) POW; Hit by flak in the Trier-Liege area.
P-47D QI-M 42-26272 "Angel Eyes"

**August 12, 1944**
Lt. Lester H. Knapp (360th) KIA; Hit by flak near Montcornet.
P-47D PI- 42-26563
Lt. Herbert P. Causer (360th) MIA-E; Hit by flak in the Paris area.
P-47D PI-Y 42-26271

**August 13, 1944**
Lt. Henry L. Lewis (361st) KIA; Hit by British anti-aircraft fire over England.
P-47D QI-X 42-75230

**August 14, 1944**
Lt. Louis G. Alphonse (359th) KIA; Was chasing a Me-109 near Laval when American gunners shot him down.
P-47D OC-C 42-8491

**August 18, 1944**
Lt. John R. Tillman (361st) KIA; Downed by a FW-190 near Beauvais.
P-47D QI-D 42-75549

**August 28, 1944**
Lt. James H. Perry (359th) ASR; Suffered mechanical failure and bailed out over the Channel.
P-47D OC-

**August 29, 1944**
Lt. Thomas D. Teel (360th) KIA; Hit by flak in the Lille area and bailed out; never turned up on any prisoner list.
P-47D PI- 42-25524 "Grace"

**September 1, 1944**
Lt. Frank A. Forsyth (359th) MIA-E; Plane was damaged by debris from an exploding loco and he bellied-in southwest of Brussels.
P-47D OC-I 42-26141 "Fearless Fosdick"

**September 9, 1944**
Lt. John H. Garlent (360th) KIA; Was strafing a loco near Wetzlar when bounced by FW-190's.
P-47D PI- 42-22469 "Old Master"
Lt. Harry F. Rideout (360th) KIA; Last seen being chased by two FW-190's in the Wetzlar-Illerach area.
P-47D PI- 42-25861
Lt. Robert M. Leidy (360th) KIA; Chased a pair of FW-190's then reported he was in trouble in the Coblenz-Eichelhardt area.
P-47D PI-C 42-26683 "Mugsy"

**September 17, 1944**
Lt. Howell L. Broxton (359th) MIA-E; Hit by flak and cart-wheeled in near Groesbeek without injury.
P-47D OC-Y 42-74658 "Little Fi-Fi"
Capt. Westwood H. Fletcher, Jr. (360th) MIA-E; Hit by flak in the Nijmegen area.
P-47D PI-D 42-28472 "Podunk III"
F/O John P. Tucker (360th) KIA; Hit by flak in the Nijmegen area.
P-47D PI- 42-76353 "Naughty Patricia"

**September 18, 1944**
Lt. James H. Perry (359th) KIA; Crashed into an orchard after a flak hit near Nijmegen.
P-47D OC-W 43-25530 "We Four II"
Capt. Reginald C. McDowell (361st) MIA-E; Bellied-in near Groesbeek after flak damage.
P-47D QI-M 42-26534

**October 7, 1944**
Lt. Paul J. Roberts, Jr. (361st) KIA; Hit by flak while strafing Fritzlar Airfield. Bailed out northwest of Marburg but was killed by civilians.
P-47D QI-P 42-76177 "Mad Wolves"

**November 4, 1944**
F/O Willard W. Royer (360th) KIA; Downed by a Me-262 near Enschede.
P-47D PI-N 42-26289 "Georgia's Best"

**November 8, 1944**
Lt. William L. Hoffert (359th) POW; Downed by a Me-262 near Osnabruck.
P-47D OC- 42-28845
Lt. Charles C. McKelvy (359th) POW; Damaged near Osnabruck by a Me-262 then downed by Me-109's near Brussels.
P-47D OC-J 42-76208 "Dodie Darlin"

**November 20, 1944**
Lt. Louis B. Runyan (361st) KIA; Took-off late and was last seen heading southwest from base to join the group.
P-51D QI-V 44-15098

**November 21, 1944**
Lt. Walter O. Hedrick (360th) MIA-E; Became separated from the group and bellied-in near Haro, Spain.
P-51D PI-

**November 25, 1944**
Lt. James A. Des Jardins (360th) KIA; Hit by flak while strafing a marshalling yard near Fulda.
P-51D PI- 44-15133

**December 5, 1944**
Capt. Jean D. Tarbutton (359th) POW; Hit by a FW-190 northwest of Berlin.
P-51D OC-B 44-15219
Lt. Russell C. Scharnberg (359th) KIA; Last seen chasing a FW-190 near Eberswalde.
P-51D OC- 44-11326
Capt. Raymond H. Gansberg (361st) KIA; Last seen in a fight with FW-190's near Eberswalde.
P-51D QI-D 44-15118
Lt. Ben B. Barnes (361st) KIA; Last seen in a fight with FW-190's near Eberswalde.
P-51D QI-R 44-15169
Lt. Jack T. Smith (361st) KIA; Last seen in a fight with FW-190's near Eberswalde.
P-51D QI-N 44-15079

**December 12, 1944**
Lt. Percy C. O'Quinn (359th) ASR; Suffered mechanical failure and bailed out off Margate.
P-51D OC-

**December 18, 1944**
Lt. Donald L. Turnidge (360th) POW; Bailed out near Dusseldorf after mechanical trouble.
P-51D PI- 44-15033

**December 24, 1944**
Lt. Arthur Wong, Jr. (359th) POW; Bailed out near Laacher See after mechanical trouble.
P-51D OC- 44-15193

**December 25, 1944**
Lt. Richard J. Andrino (360th) KIA; Killed in a fight near Bonn.
P-51D PI- 44-15307
Lt. Milton H. Huebner (360th) KIA; Killed in a fight near Bonn.
P-51D PI- 44-15364

**December 26, 1944**
Capt. Claude J. Hackney, Jr. (359th) KIA; Last seen chasing a FW-190 into the overcast east of Bonn.
P-51D OC- 44-15609
Lt. Warren C. Cooley (359th) POW; Hit by flak after a dog-fight northeast of Bonn.
P-51D OC- 44-15029 "Pottsville Express"

**January 13, 1945**
Lt. Wendel J.A. Nelson (360th) KIA; Spun-out in bad weather while forming up and crashed near Grundisburgh.
P-51D PI-N 44-15305

**January 14, 1945**
Lt. Freeman F. Hooker (361st) POW; Hit by flak while strafing Hesepe Airfield.
P-51D QI-Y 44-11329

**January 16, 1945**
Lt. Vance C. Harney (359th) KIA; Aborted with mechanical trouble and crashed near Biggleswade.
P-51D OC- 44-15528

**January 17, 1945**
Lt. Robert E. Carr (359th) KIA; Crashed while taking-off from Beauvais/Tille Airfield.
P-51D OC-M 44-15331 "Junie"

**January 18, 1945**
Lt. Chester W. Lawrence (359th) KIA; Took off from Laon/Couvron to return home and spun-in off Felixstowe.
P-51D OC- 44-63268 "Little Mary"

**February 4, 1945**
Lt. Ralph E. Odenwald (359th) KIAc; Crashed into Bradwell Bay while on a practice gunnery mission.
P-51D OC- 44-15223 "Rene"

**February 13, 1945**
Lt. Walter M. Baskin (361st) KIAc; Spun-in and crashed near Trimley while on a practice flight.
P-51D QI-D 44-15642

**February 20, 1945**
Capt. William F. Traupe (359th) KIA; Damaged by flak, he bailed out near Heilbronn but his chute failed to open.
P-51D OC- 44-63250
Lt. Carlton L. Welch (360th) POW; Hit by flak, he bailed out south of Leipzig.
P-51D PI-U 44-11220 "Fourth Apocalypsian"

**February 22, 1945**
Lt. Alden S. Thomas (360th) POW; Hit by flak west of Ulzen.
P-51D PI-M 44-15149 "Virgy I"

**February 25, 1945**
Maj. Richard A. Rann (359th) POW; Hit by flak near Hechingen, he bailed out near Schaffshausen.
P-51D OC-E 44-15271 "Starduster"
Lt. Alston L. Brown (359th) KIA; Hit by flak at Bendorf Airfield.
P-51D OC- 44-14998
Lt. Henry C. Scott (359th) KIA; Lost oil pressure after a flak hit at Bendorf Airfield. He tried to belly-in but the plane exploded.
P-51D OC-S 44-15280 "Flying Dutchman"

**March 1, 1945**
Lt. Walter O. Hedrick (360th) POW; Bailed out near Strasbourg after mechanical trouble.
P-51D PI-F 44-11156 "Brenda"

**March 15, 1945**
Lt. Roger A. Batie (359th) POW; Lost oil pressure and bailed out near Winterswijk.
P-51D OC-N 44-15274 "Mojahalka"

**March 24, 1945**
Lt. William C. Jarvis (361st) ASR; Lost oil pressure and bailed out east of Lowestoft.
P-51D QI-L 44-15139

**April 6, 1945**
Lt. Raleigh S. Ragsdale (360th) KIA; Suffered engine trouble near Coblenz; he was too low to jump so he bellied-into a field and the plane flipped on impact.
P-51D PI-Q 44-15552 "Big Lefty-Little Ann"

**April 12, 1945**
Lt. Eldon L. Slanker (361st) KIAc; Collided with a 56th Fighter Group P-47 near Raydon.
P-51D QI-M 44-15073

**June 9, 1945**
Lt. Thomas C. Creevy (361st) KIAc; Was doing aerobatics when he lost control and crashed near Podington.
P-51D QI-Z 44-15401

**June 18, 1945**
Lt. Preston W. McKeon (361st) KIAc; Collided with a B-17 while on a test flight.
P-51D QI-

**June 20, 1945**
Lt. Richard J. Rensch (360th) KIAc; Buzzed Valley Airdrome, Wales, (where his brother, a B-17 pilot, was heading home to the U.S.), did a slow roll into the overcast, and disappeared.
P-51D PI-M 44-15577

**June 30, 1945**
Lt. William C. Boucek (360th) KIAc; Lost a wing near Bentwaters, bailed out, but his chute failed.
P-51D PI- 44-15164

**July 8, 1945**
Lt. Shelby N. Jett (361st) KIAc; Died from burns received in an A-35 crash the day before.

**July 20, 1945**
Lt. Richard J. Stone (359th) KIAc; Lost control and crashed near Wickham Market.
P-51D OC-H 44-15181

**Headquarters**
Baccus, Donald A., LtCol.; April 1944-April 1945; to 359th Ftr Grp; ex-359th Ftr Sqn
116 missions
P-47D OC-G 42-76583
P-47D OC-G
P-51D OC-G 44-14993
Coen, Oscar H., LtCol.; October 1943-March 1944; to 9th Air Force; ex-71 Sqn, RAF and 4th Ftr Grp
32 missions
P-47D OC-R 42-75389
Cristadoro, Maurice A., Maj.; October 1944-January 1945; to 20th Ftr Grp
3 missions
Ellis, Richard N., LtCol.; April 1945-EOW
10 missions
P-51D OC- "Telie's Terror"
Herin, Reginald A., Jr., Lt.; March 1945-EOW; ex-360th Ftr Sqn
Kennedy, William J., LtCol.; August 1944-EOW
22 missions
P-47D OC-E 42-26851
P-51D OC-E 44-15271 "Starduster"
Krieger, Andrew E., Jr., Maj.; September 1943-March 1944; to 360th Ftr Sqn; ex-3rd Pur Sqn, PTO
39 missions
P-47D PI-K "Fancy Nancy"
Malmstrom, Einar A., Col.; November 1943-April 23, 1944(POW)
49 missions
P-47D QI-R 42-22550 "Kay-J"
P-47D QI-R 42-25513 "Kay-J"
Nystrom, Richard C., Capt.; April 1945-EOW; ex-361st Ftr Sqn
Ogden, Harold A., Capt.; October 1943-August 1944; ex-359th Ftr Sqn
85 missions
P-47D OC-U 42-22517 "Eager Eagle"
Rau, Harold J., LtCol.; February 1943-November 1943; to VIII HdQts
13 missions
P-47D QI-R 42-8425 "Gentle Annie"
P-47D QI-R 42-22550 "Gentle Annie"

Scheible, Wilbur R., Maj.; March 1945-EOW; ex-361st Ftr Sqn
Schlack, Robert F., Capt.; February 1945-September 1945; ex-361st Ftr Sqn
Thorne, James H., Maj.; March 1944-September 1944; ex-359th Ftr Sqn
99 missions
P-47D OC-K 42-75228
P-47D QI-R 42-26534
P-47D QI-R 42-28792
Tukey, Philip E., Jr., Col.; March 1944-November 1945; ex-56th Ftr Grp
77 missions, 301 hours
P-47D PI-T 42-25531
P-47D PI-T 42-26415
P-51D PI-T 44-72435
P-51D PI-T 44-72455
P-51K PI-T 44-11579

**359th Fighter Squadron**
Alphonse, Louis G., Lt.; May 1944-August 14, 1944(KIA)
40 missions
Baccus, Donald A., LtCol.; June 1943-April 1944; to HdQts
116 missions
P-47D OC-I 42-8568 "The Bloody Shaft"
P-47D OC-G 42-76583
Baker, James B., Jr., Lt.; October 1944-September 1945
42 missions
P-47D OC-V 44-15183 "Bama Baby"
Batie, Roger A., Lt.; August 1944-March 15, 1945(POW)
43 missions
Beach, Warren A., Lt.; February 1943-November 29, 1943(POW)
9 missions
P-47D OC- 42-8601
Bender, Thomas L., Jr., F/O; January 1945-July 1945
1 mission
Bennett, Luther E., Jr., Lt.; October 1944-September 1945
34 missions
P-51K OC-V "Spirit of Aggieland"
Bergstrom, Airus E., Capt.; May 1944-October 1944
72 missions
P-47D OC-P 42-74673 "Carmen"
Blewett, John E., Jr., Lt.; October 1944-September 1945
49 missions
P-51D OC-U 44-15658 "Eager Eagle"
Bradshaw, Robert D., Jr., Lt.; March 1943-May 1944
66 missions, 200 hours
P-47D OC-X 42-74699
Brearley, William C., Capt.; February 1943-May 1945
P-47D OC-C 42-8491
P-51D OC- "Princess Jocelyn"
Brown, Alston L., Lt.; November 1944-February 25, 1945(KIA)
25 missions
P-51D OC- 44-14998
Brown, Jack F., Capt.; August 1944-June 1945; ex-389th & 25th Bomb Grps
57 missions
P-51D OC-A
P-51K OC-A 44-11366 "Bobby Socks"
Brown, William F., Lt.; March 1943-January 7, 1944(KIA)
Broxton, Howell L., Lt.; May 1944-September 17, 1944(MIA-E)
54 missions
P-47D OC-R 42-8549 "Elsie"
Bruner, Fred W., Capt.; May 1944-February 1945
72 missions
P-47D OC-O
P-51D OC-O 44-15403
Burke, Mark J., Maj.; February 1943-October 1944
P-47D OC- 42-76146
Carr, Robert E., Lt.; August 1944-January 17, 1945(KIA)
35 missions
Carroll, Arthur C., Capt.; February 1943-June 1943
Chickering, Rolfe L., Lt.; May 1944-October 1944
75 missions
P-47D OC-K 42-8588 "Gracie"
Childers, Bobby, Maj.; February 1945-November 1945; ex-360th Ftr Sqn
53 missions (17 w/359th)
Clayborne, Millard M., Capt.; January 1944-August 1944
78 missions
P-47D OC-D 42-75171 "Ramblin Rebel"
Cline, John H., Lt.; April 1944-October 1944
64 missions, 257:25 hours
P-47D OC-A 42-8471
Collett, Charles E., Capt.; January 1945-September 1945
20 missions
P-51D OC-K 44-15201
Collins, Robert J., Lt.; March 1943-May 1944; to 5th ERS August 1944-September 1944
Conroy, Robert B., Lt.; March 1943-January 14, 1944(POW)
P-47D OC-X 42-8574
Cooley, Warren C., Lt.; August 1944-December 26, 1944(POW)
26 missions
P-47D OC-H "Lonesome Polecat"
P-51D OC-H 44-15181
Cornett, Jack B., Lt.; August 1944-September 1945
52 missions
Cotter, William W., Lt.; March 1943-February 26, 1944(KIAc)
P-47D OC-C 42-8492
Coughenour, Robert A., Jr., Lt.; April 1944-June 8, 1944(KIA)
10 missions
Craig, William C., Lt.; March 1943-August 1944
69 missions
P-47D OC-N 42-8002 "Wilmarene"
Crum, Glenn, Lt.; September 1944-September 1945
40 missions
P-51D OC-L 44-15177 "Koyli Renee"
Earnhart, Charles B., Lt.; November 1943-June 28, 1944(MIA-E); ex-RCAF
P-47D OC- 42-8617
Easley, Preston W., Lt.; August 1944-February 1945; to 360th Ftr Sqn
60 missions (42 w/359th)
P-47D OC- "The Virginia Squire"
Edinborough, Warren T., Lt.; January 1945-September 1945; ex-405th Ftr Grp, 9th Air Force
18 missions
Engel, Gardner W., Capt.; February 1943-July 1944
300 hours
P-47D OC-P
P-47D OC-P 42-76405 "Mad Marion"
Erschen, Harold E., Lt.; March 1943-August 1943; to 370th Ftr Grp (to ETO w/9th Air Force)
Farmer, William L., Lt.; March 1943-May 1944
200 hours
P-47D OC-H 42-74711
Fortner, Raymond C., Lt.; January 1944-January 14, 1944(KIAc)
0 missions
Forsyth, Frank A., Lt.; March 1943-September 1, 1944(MIA-E) October 1944-December 1944
86 missions
P-47D OC-I 42-26141 "Fearless Fosdick"
P-51K OC-I 44-11351
Gohsler, Harry R., Lt.; September 1944-July 1945
63 missions, 282 hours
P-51D OC-M 44-15331 "Junie"
P-51D OC-Y 44-15138 "Hair-Breath Harry"
Griswold, James B., Capt.; July 1944-January 1945
73 missions, 270 hours
P-47D OC-N 42-8002 "Lonesome Lee"
P-47D OC-N 42-26557"Lonesome Lee II
P-51D OC-N 44-15274
Hackney, Claude J., Jr., Capt.; October 1944-December 26, 1944(KIA)
17 missions
Hale, Alfred R., Capt.; August 1944-September 1945
51 missions
P-51D OC-V 44-72288 "Marge"
Harney, Vance C., Jr., Lt.; November 1944-January 16, 1945(KIA)
21 missions
Henry, Justus D., Lt.; March 1943-March 8, 1944(KIA)
P-47D OC-L 42-8467
Hildebrand, Leonard J., Lt.; October 1944-September 1945
45 missions
Hoffert, William L., Lt.; April 1944-November 8, 1944(POW)
80 missions
P-47D OC-S
Holm, Willis A., Capt.; March 1943-May 13, 1944(KIA)
P-47D OC-M 42-74689 "Lady Jane"
Holtz, Raymond K., Capt.; March 1943-April 27, 1944(MIA-E)
P-47D OC-W 42-8567 "We Four"
P-47D OC-W 43-25530 "We Four II"
Hull, John D., Lt.; March 1943-November 29, 1943(POW)
P-47D OC- 42-8598
Judd, Russell P., Lt.; November 1944-February 1945; to 5th ERS; ex-RCAF
0 missions (later KIA w/5th ERS)
Kirschner, Charles M., Lt.; August 1944-September 1945
52 missions
Knudsen, Howard R., Capt.; March 1943-August 1944
Krowiak, Casimir F., Lt.; April 1944-April 27, 1944(KIA)
3 missions
Lawrence, Chester W., Lt.; November 1944-January 18, 1945(KIA)
22 missions
LeMoyne, Harry F., Capt.; May 1944-November 1944
67 missions
P-47D OC-P "Lazy Mazie"
Lubbers, Robert P., Capt.; April 1944-October 1944
79 missions
Male, Kenneth J., Lt.; February 1945-September 1945
29 missions, 146 hours
Malo, Edward J., Lt.; May 1944-October 1944
71 missions
Marsh, Otto L., Lt.; February 1945-September 1945
22 missions
McCloskey, Brice O., Lt.; March 1945-April 1945
4 missions
McKelvy, Charles C., Jr., Lt.; October 1944-November 8, 1944(POW)
7 missions
P-47D OC-J 42-76208 "Dodie Darlin"
Meade, John W., Lt.; October 1944-September 1945
48 missions
Meholic, James J., Capt.; March 1943-August 1944
300 hours

P-47D OC-E
P-47D OC-E 42-26129
P-47D OC-E 42-26851
Mellinger, Paul R., Lt.; May 1944-October 1944
68 missions, 259 hours
P-47D OC-V 42-8478
Miller, Richard C., Lt.; October 1944-September 1945
48 missions
P-51D OC-P 44-15268 "The Gremlin"
Mueller, Carl F., Lt.; May 1944-August 1944
0 missions (Was on D.S. to Station 101 for entire time)
Murtishaw, George C., Lt.; October 1944-September 1945
37 missions
Nielsen, Howard W., Lt.; October 1944-September 1945
45 missions
P-51D OC-A
O'Barr, William C., Lt.; March 1943-May 29, 1944(POW)
67 missions, 195 hours
P-47D OC-E 42-8654
P-47D OC-E 42-76372
Odenwald, Ralph E., Lt.; October 1944-February 4, 1945(KIAc)
25 missions
P-51D OC-A 44-14864
Ogden, Harold E., Capt.; March 1943-October 1943; to HdQts
Oliver, Leon, Lt.; October 1944-June 1945
45 missions
P-51D OC-S
O'Quinn, Percy C., Lt.; August 1944-September 1945
36 missions
Peet, George B., Capt.; November 1943-September 1944; ex-RCAF
P-47D OC-T 42-8645
Pelletier, George S., Lt.; April 1944-November 1944
69 missions
P-47D OC-X 42-28808 "Mary B"
Perry, James H., Lt.; July 1944-September 18, 1944(KIA)
37 missions
Pietruszka, John F., Lt.; May 1944-December 1944
69 missions
Rann, Richard A., Maj.; November 1943-February 25, 1945(POW); ex-RCAF
120 missions, 395 hours
P-47D OC-S 42-22524
P-47D OC-R 42-75389
P-47D OC-R 42-28675
P-51D OC-R 44-15258
Rhynard, Wayne E., LtCol.; February 1945-July 1945; ex-79th Ftr Grp, MTO
(84 missions & 1 victory)
21 missions, 121 hours
P-51D OC-E 44-72284 "Micharee I"
Richason, Lee F., Capt.; March 1943-October 1944
P-47D OC-G 42-26331 "Slightly Dangerous"
Robertson, Louis L., Capt.; August 1944-April 1945; ex-MTO pilot
33 missions
P-51D OC-T 44-15677
Rubner, Chester H., Jr., Capt.; February 1943-August 1944
Rudd, Edward G., Capt.; September 1944-EOW
61 missions, 255:15 hours
P-51D OC-K 44-15201 "Eunie"
Sanders, R.D., Lt.; January 1945-March 1945; to 1st SF
3 missions
Sargent, Lawton G., Jr., Lt.; January 1945-September 1945
23 missions, 112 hours
Scharnberg, Russell C., Lt.; August 1944-December 5, 1944(KIA)
44 missions
Scott, Henry C., Lt.; January 1945-February 25, 1945(KIA)
3 missions
Sellers, Lorin B., Jr., Lt.; February 1945-July 1945
17 missions
Shelton, Toney, Lt.; May 1944-November 1944
69 missions
Siegel, John A., Lt.; January 1945-September 1945
19 missions
Simmerman, Vernon J., Lt.; January 1945-September 1945
19 missions
Smith, Elmer E., Jr., Lt.; January 1945-September 1945
19 missions
Smith, James B., Capt.; March 1943-June 8, 1944(MIA-E)
P-47D OC-R 42-8694 "Little Texan"
P-47D OC-R 42-76168
Smith, Ned L., F/O; January 1945-March 1945; to 1st SF
7 missions
Sonnier, Lucien O., Lt.; November 1944-September 1945
41 missions
P-51D OC-D 44-15185 "T-Lou"
P-51D OC-D 44-72148 "T-Lou-II"
Stipes, Reuben B., Lt.; February 1945-September 1945
21 missions
Stoenner, Erwin F., Lt.; January 1945-September 1945
19 missions
Stone, Richard J., Lt.; November 1944-July 20, 1945(KIAc)
37 missions
P-51D OC-H 44-15181
Tarbutton, Jean D., Capt.; April 1944-December 5, 1944(POW); ex-11th AF, Aleutians
65 missions
P-47D OC-B 42-26576 "Vee-T"
P-51D OC-B 44-15219
Taylor, George A., Lt.; January 1945-September 1945
16 missions
Thorne, James H., Maj.; March 1943-March 1944; to HdQts
P-47D OC-K 42-75228
Traupe, William F., Capt.; November 1944-February 20, 1945(KIA); ex-360th Ftr Sqn (0 missions)
23 missions
P-51D OC-S 44-15280 "Flying Dutchman"
Troge, Eldon F., Capt.; August 1944-September 1945
52 missions
Tucker, Dick F., Capt.; May 1944-December 1944
76 missions
P-47D OC-T 42-28819 "Jodie Darlin"
Vossler, Richard G., Lt.; November 1943-August 1944; ex-RCAF; Later to PTO w/414th Ftr Grp, 7th Air Force w/P-47N's.
P-47D OC-J 42-8646
P-47D OC-J 42-76208 "Lady Luck"
Wadlow, James H., Jr., Capt.; March 1943-October 1944
P-47D OC-P 42-74673 "Ich Brauche Du"
Walters, Clarence L., Lt.; January 1945-September 1945
28 missions
Warner, Ralph N., Jr., Lt.; March 1945-September 1945
15 missions
Warren, Richard B., Lt.; January 1944-April 26, 1944(KIA)
29 missions
Weber, Herbert, Capt.; March 1943-July 1944
300 hours
P-47D OC-V 42-8478 "Fifinella"
Whitaker, William R., Lt.; January 1945-July 1945
4 missions
White, Ernest J., Jr., LtCol.; February 1943-November 1944
P-47D OC-B
P-47D OC-B 42-74745
P-47D OC-B 43-25557
Wieland, Nelson E., Lt.; November 1944-September 1945
40 missions
P-51D OC-Q 44-15308 "Jean-Tom"
Wilmot, Allen E., Lt.; May 1944-August 1944
18 missions
Withers, Raymond R., Capt.; November 1944-January 1945; ex-360th Ftr Sqn (see for details)
P-51D OC-B 44-15195 "Kathleen"
Wong, Arthur, Jr., Lt.; November 1944-December 24, 1944(POW)
2 missions
Wood, William H., Lt.; March 1944-May 7, 1944(POW)
22 missions
P-47D OC-A 42-8417 "Ich Brauche Du"
Wyatt, James A., Lt.; January 1944-May 1944 (WIA May 13)
26 missions
P-47D OC-A 42-8471

**360th Fighter Squadron**
Adams, Charles W., Lt.; March 1943-May 1944
59 missions
P-47D PI- "Francis' Favorite"
Andrino, Richard J., Lt.; August 1944-December 25, 1944(KIA)
32 missions
Anderson, Edwin E., Lt.; April 1944-May 21, 1944(POW)
4 missions
Asbridge, Julius B., Lt.; February 1943-November 29, 1943(POW)
5 missions
P-47D PI-W 42-8502 "Hell's Angel"
Baker, Arthur M., Lt.; January 1945-September 1945
19 missions
P-51D PI-I
Barnhart, Robert E., Capt.; August 1944-April 1945
75 missions, 303:05 hours
P-47D PI-B 42-28664 "Squirt"
P-51D PI-B 44-15189 "Margie Darling"
Bennett, Joseph H., Capt.; March 1943-November 1943; to 56th Ftr Grp. Later to 4th Ftr Grp and POW May 25, 1944
15 missions
Bluhm, Roy B., Jr., Capt.; May 1944-November 1944; ex-56th Ftr Grp with 1 victory.
49 missions, 341 total hours
P-47D PI-L "Texas Lady"
Boucek, William C., Lt.; March 1945-June 30, 1945(KIAc); ex-bomber pilot
2 missions
Borelli, Bernard, Capt.; February 1943-January 1945
99 missions, 335:25 hours
P-47D PI-Y "Jersey Panic"
P-47D PI-C 44-19894
P-51D PI-C 44-15341
Brewer, Paul M., Jr., Capt.; February 1943-May 1943; to 369th Ftr Grp
Brock, Everett L., F/O; November 1943-December 30, 1943(KIA); ex-RCAF
6 missions
Burwell, Orvil L., Capt.; August 1944-September 1945
66 missions
P-47D PI-D
P-51D PI-D 44-14973 "Lady Doris"

Carlson, Donald D., Capt.; August 1944-April 1945
66 missions, 320 hours
P-47D PI-M "The Thundering Three"
P-51D PI-M 44-15149 "Virgy"
P-51D PI-M "Ginny II"
P-51K PI-M 44-11577 "Ginny III"
Causer, Herbert P., Lt.; July 1944-August 12, 1944(MIA-E); ex-RCAF
3 missions
Ceraolo, Nunzio B., Lt.; September 1944-September 1945
53 missions
P-51D PI-L 44-63251 "Louise"
Charlton, James G., Lt.; January 1945-EOW
26 missions
P-51D PI-B 44-15189
Childers, Bobby, Maj.; September 1944-February 1945; to 359th Ftr Sqn
53 missions (36 w/360th)
Ciocchi, Dante G., Lt.; August 1944-April 1945
65 missions
P-51D PI- 44-15218 "Miss Mary Nel"
Cook, Edwin D., Lt.; February 1944-May 19, 1944(POW)
27 missions
Cook, James R., Capt.; February 1943-July 1944
87 missions
P-47D PI-B "Quirk's Dark Horse"
P-47D PI-B "Quirk's Dark Horse II"
Cook, Thomas A., Lt.; October 1944-September 1945
18 missions (Injured November 27,
1944 and back on ops in April 1945)
P-51D PI-G "Akron Angel"
Corner, Ernest W., Lt.; November 1944-September 1945
49 missions
P-51D PI-X 44-63283 "Paper Doll"
Cota, Norman D., Jr., Maj.; February 1943-October 1944
103 missions
P-47D PI-B 42-74714 "Gremlin Express"
P-47D PI-C 42-25534
Crump, John W., Capt.; August 1944-May 1945
77 missions, 311 hours
P-47D PI-W 42-26322 "Jackie"
P-51D PI-W 44-15056 "Jackie"
Des Jardins, James A., Lt.; October 1944-November 25, 1944(KIA)
4 missions
Douglas, Norwood C., Lt.; April 1944-November 1944; ex-56th Ftr Grp
63 missions
P-47D PI-Z 44-19861 "Chesapeake Beach"
Dunn, Carl W., Lt.; November 1943-April 9, 1944(KIA)
34 missions
Dunn, William K., Capt.; October 1944-September 1945
53 missions, 242:30 hours
P-51D PI-D 44-15289 "Patty"
Easley, Preston W., Capt.; February 1945-September 1945; ex-359th Ftr Sqn
60 missions (18 w/360th)
P-51D PI-E 44-15333 "The Virginia Squire"
Ellingson, Bertram E., Capt.; February 1943-March 1945
108 missions
P-47D PI-E
P-51D PI-E 44-15333
Evans, Byron A., Capt.; March 1943-February 11, 1944(KIA)
31 missions
Fletcher, Westwood H., Capt.; March 1943-September 17, 1944(MIA-E)
93 missions
P-47D PI-D "Podunk"
P-47D PI-D "Podunk II"
P-47D PI-D 42-28472 "Podunk III"
Garlent, John H., Lt.; June 1944-September 9, 1944(KIA)
44 missions
Garvey, Charles J., Lt.; March 1943-March 20, 1944(POW)
32 missions
P-47D PI-D 42-74638 "Nashville Belle"
Gatlin, Wayne C., Lt.; October 1944-September 1945
56 missions, 264 hours
P-51D PI-L 44-14574 "Sweet'n Low Down"
Gleason, Robert S., Lt.; May 1944-February 1945
70 missions
P-47D PI-G 42-25534 "Vicious Virgin
P-51D PI-G 44-15114 "Arasa & Jeff"
Goldwasser, Lawrence L., Lt.; May 1944-May 31, 1944(POW)
10 missions
Green, Shirley J., Lt.; December 1943-July 18, 1944(KIAc)
63 missions
P-47D PI- "Lone Star Lady"
Hall, Daughtry L., Lt.; November 1943-April 23, 1944(POW); ex-RCAF
38 missions
Halverson, Roland J., Capt.; February 1943-June 1944
53 missions
P-47D PI-M "Joker"
P-47D PI-M 42-25751 "Joker"
Hedrick, Walter O., Lt.; October 1944-March 1, 1945(POW)
15 missions
Hepfer, Joseph B., Lt.; April 1944-August 1944
4 missions (WIA in May 1944)
Herin, Reginald A., Jr., Lt.; May 1944-August 1944; ex-56th Ftr Grp with 1 victory; February 1945-March 1945; to HdQts
49 missions
Hickey, James A., Lt.; January 1945-July 1945; ex-bomber pilot
14 missions
P-51D PI-J 44-15052
Hockmeyer, Vincent, Capt.; February 1943-February 1945
99 missions
P-47D PI-H
P-51D PI-H 44-15250 "Raggedy Ann"
Huebner, Milton H., Lt.; August 1944-December 25, 1944(KIA)
37 missions
Johnson, Gerald W., Maj.; November 1943-February 1944; ex-56th Ftr Grp
10 missions
Johnson, William E., Jr., Lt.; March 1943-April 10, 1944(KIA)
47 missions
P-47D PI- "Kitten"
Jones, Donald F., Lt.; November 1944-September 1945
51 missions
P-51D PI-O 44-15300 "Milly"
Kariva, George C., Lt.; May 1944-June 6, 1944(POW); ex-RCAF
3 missions
Kinnard, Claiborne H., Jr., Maj.; March 1943-November 1943; to 355th Ftr Grp
9 missions
P-47D PI-A
Knapp, Lester H., Lt.; March 1944-August 12, 1944(KIA)
78 missions
P-47D PI-W "Knapp's Sack"
Koczak, Alex S., Lt.; February 1943-May 20, 1944(POW)
40 missions
P-47D PI- 42-8469 "Jersey Bounce"
Kress, Lester F., Capt.; February 1943-July 1944
79 missions
P-47D PI-F "Dear Alean"
Krieger, Andrew E., Jr., Maj.; March 1944-May 1944; ex-HdQts
39 missions
P-47D PI-K "Fancy Nancy"
Laviolette, Henry P., Lt.; June 1944-February 1945
74 missions
Lawson, Stuart D., Lt.; March 1943-August 1943
Leathers, Wayne E., Capt.; April 1944-November 1944
80 missions
Leidy, Robert M., Lt.; May 1944-September 9, 1944(KIA)
67 missions
P-47D PI-J "Jeanie Janet"
L'Heureux, Robert C., Capt.; March 1943-August 1944
99 missions
P-47D PI-O
Loffredo, Ralph A., Lt.; March 1943-August 1943; to 370th Ftr Grp and to ETO; KIAc March 4, 1944.
Lundquist, Donald M., Lt.; March 1943-August 1943; to 370th Ftr Grp and to ETO.
Martin, Dolar A., Lt.; March 1943-November 11, 1943(KIA)
6 missions
Mauldin, Thurman N., Lt.; February 1945-September 1945
16 missions, 81:30 hours
P-51D PI-K 44-15211 "Sweet Peay"
Maupin, Howard P., F/O; February 1944-March 20, 1944(MIA-E)
4 missions
Maxwell, Wallace G., Lt.; March 1943-May 21, 1944(KIA)
65 missions
P-47D PI- "Adolph's Horror"
McCullough, Philip E., Lt.; March 1943-March 20, 1944(POW)
40 missions
P-47D PI- "Big Dick"
McHale, Joseph M., Capt.; February 1943-September 1944
89 missions
McLaughlin, Harry B., Capt.; February 1943-May 1944
62 missions
P-47D PI-J "Red Dog"
McNary, Billy D., Lt.; January 1945-September 1945
28 missions
P-51D PI-P
Mercer, Durward B., Lt.; April 1944-October 1944
74 missions, 249:55 hours
P-47D PI-N 42-26289 "Georgia's Best"
Moyer, Grant F., Lt.; May 1944-May 23, 1944(KIAc)
0 missions
Nebinger, Edward M., Lt.; June 1944-January 1945
75 missions
P-47D PI-A
P-51D PI-A 44-15194
Nelson, Howard E., Lt.; January 1945-March 1945; to 1st SF
9 missions
Nelson, Wendel J.A., Lt.; November 1944-January 13, 1945(KIA); ex-RCAF
10 missions
Niemi, Albert V., Capt.; February 1943-September 1944
100 missions
P-47D PI- "The Cape Codder"
Obosla, Joseph, Lt.; April 1944-June 8, 1944(KIA)
30 missions
Olive, Homer S., Lt.; May 1944-November 1944
69 missions

Paquet, Adolph A., Lt.; November 1944-September 1945
45 missions
P-51K PI-Y 44-11570 "Virgie"
Parker, Hunter D., Capt.; February 1943-April 11, 1944(POW)
52 missions
P-47D PI-G 42-8474
P-47D PI-G 42-76449
Pascal, Irvin M., Lt.; March 1943-August 1943
Peacock, Fred W., Lt.; May 1944-December 1944
68 missions
Perryman, Allen A., Jr., Lt.; March 1944-May 19, 1944(POW)
23 missions
Phillips, Fred C., Jr., Lt.; May 1944-June 14, 1944(POW)
2 missions
Pidwell, John C., Lt.; October 1944-September 1945
56 missions, 248:40 hours
P-51D PI-P 44-14295 "Mary Jane"
Pleasant, Edward W., Capt.; May 1944-March 1945
84 missions
Poppell, Clifford S., Lt.; October 1944-September 1945
47 missions
P-51D PI-M 44-15590 "Barbara"
Proctor, Lawrence B., Lt.; October 1944-September 1945
21 missions
P-51D PI-W
Quigley, Dale T., Lt.; August 1944-April 1945
71 missions
Ragsdale, Raleigh S., Lt.; October 1944-April 6, 1945(KIA)
49 missions
P-51D PI-Q 44-15552 "Big Lefty-Little Ann"
Remenicky, Joseph, Lt.; January 1945-July 1945
8 missions
Rensch, Richard J., Lt.; November 1944-June 20, 1944(KIAc)
44 missions
P-51D PI-C 44-15341
Rhoades, Carmen F., Capt.; May 1944-July 20, 1944(POW)
20 missions
P-47D PI-A
Rideout, Harry F., Lt.; May 1944-September 9, 1944(KIA)
51 missions
Robinson, Robert A., Lt.; May 1944-July 20, 1944(POW)
18 missions
Romine, Jack T., Capt.; May 1944-March 1945
78 missions
P-47D PI- "Black Jack"
Royer, Willard W., F/O; August 1944-November 4, 1944(KIA)
21 missions
Russell, Francis M., Capt.; April 1944-March 1945
82 missions
P-47D PI-S "Buckeye Bullet"
P-51D PI-S 44-15601 "Buckeye Bullet"
Rutland, Herbert R., Jr., Lt.; January 1945-September 1945
20 missions, 101:30 hours
P-51D PI-R 44-72931
Schalck, George H., Lt.; January 1945-July 1945
22 missions
P-51D PI-D 44-14973
Schmalz, Robert D., Lt.; January 1945-September 1945
30 missions
P-51K PI-M 44-11577
Schmidt, Robert P., Lt.; January 1945-September 1945
28 missions
P-51D PI-W 44-15056 "Tarbaby"
Schrull, Edward W., Lt.; January 1945-September 1945
22 missions
P-51D PI-V 44-72377
Seanor, George W., Lt.; January 1945-September 1945
33 missions
P-51D PI-H 44-15250 "Ringy Dingy"
Servocky, Charles J., Lt.; May 1944-November 1944
63 missions
P-47D PI-F 42-76204
Shea, Richard J., Lt.; January 1945-September 1945
15 missions
P-51D PI-S 44-15601
Simpson, John W., Lt.; January 1945-March 1945; to 1st SF
8 missions
Sova, Emil F., F/O; April 1944-June 6, 1944(POW)
7 missions
Stanick, John E., Lt.; April 1945-July 1945
0 missions
Stevenson, John F., Lt.; January 1945-September 1945
22 missions
P-51D PI-F 44-15361
Stratford, John B., Jr., Capt.; November 1943-April 27, 1944(KIA)
39 missions
Switzer, Louis R., Lt.; August 1944-April 1945
69 missions
P-51D PI-F 44-11156 "Brenda"
P-51D PI-F 44-15361 "Brenda"

Tauroni, Dominic T., Lt.; May 1945-July 1945; ex-bomber pilot. 0 missions
Taylor, Clyde M., Lt.; May 1944-November 1944
62 missions
P-47D PI- "Florida Gator"
Teel, Thomas D., Lt.; May 1944-August 29, 1944(KIA)
43 missions
Thomas, Alden S., Lt.; January 1945-February 22, 1945(POW)
3 missions
Thomas, William G., Capt.; October 1944-September 1945
38 missions, 180 hours
P-51D PI-K 44-11334 "Lois"
Traupe, William F., Capt.; October 1944-November 1944; to 359th Ftr Sqn
0 missions
Tucker, John P., F/O; April 1944-September 17, 1944(KIA)
31 missions
Turner, Eugene C., Lt.; November 1944-September 1945
43 missions, 201:15 hours
P-51D PI-A 44-15194 "Dotty"
Turnidge, Donald L., Lt.; November 1944-December 18, 1944(POW)
3 missions
Urban, Theodore J., Capt.; August 1944-April 1945
63 missions
P-47D PI-J
P-51D PI-J 44-15052
Vitali, Chester A., Lt.; February 1943-May 1944
63 missions
P-47D PI-L "Dedham Dreadnought"
Vogt, John W., Jr., Maj.; May 1944-October 1944; ex-56th Ftr Grp
64 missions
P-47D PI-V 42-26553 "Jersey Mosquito"
Walters, Clifford D., Lt.; March 1943-June 1944
62 missions
Welch, Carlton L., Lt.; August 1944-February 20, 1945(POW); ex-RCAF
33 missions
P-51D PI-U 44-11220 "Fourth Apocalypsian"
Weller, Joel P., Lt.; January 1945-September 1945
32 missions
P-51D PI-N
Williams, James H., Lt.; May 1944-November 1944
68 missions
Williams, Joseph R., Maj.; November 1943-March 1944; ex-355th Ftr Grp
47 missions
P-47D PI-A
Withers, Raymond R., Capt.; March 1943-November 1944; to 359th Ftr Sqn
105 missions, 372:10 hours total
P-47D PI-N 42-22535 "Kathleen Ann"
P-47D PI-Q 42-28823 "Kathleen Ann"
P-51D PI-Q 44-14936 "Kathleen Ann"
Wood, James N., LtCol.; October 1944-March 1945; ex-361st Ftr Sqn
112 missions (29 w/360th)
P-47D PI-V
P-51D PI-V 44-15115 "Naughty Nordie"
P-51D PI-V 44-72377 "Naughty Nordie"
Wood, Robert H., Lt.; May 1945-July 1945; ex-bomber pilot.
0 missions
Yannell, Michael P., Maj.; October 1944-September 1945; ex-86 Ftr Grp, MTO
48 missions
P-51D PI-Z 44-15069 "Audrey 3rd"
P-51D PI-Z 44-73??? "Audrey 4th"

**361st Fighter Squadron**

Alexander, Robert S., F/O; November 1943-February 1944; to 3rd GTTF, 8th AF
11 missions, 25:35 hours
P-47D QI-X 42-75522
Ashby, Clifford T., Lt.; June 1944-March 1945
77 missions, 313:30 hours
P-47D QI-M 42-76536 "Mary III"
P-51D QI-M 44-15073
Bailey, Thomas F., Capt.; February 1943-August 1944
88 missions, 301:25 hours
P-47D QI-C 42-8650 "Zombie"
P-47D QI-C 42-76594 "Zombie"
Barnes, Benjamin B., Lt.; August 1944-December 5, 1944(KIA)
23 missions, 90:40 hours
P-47D QI-W 42-76231
Baskin, Walter M., Lt.; November 1944-February 13, 1945(KIAc); ex-34th Bomb Grp, (41 missions)
27 missions, 116:15 hours
P-51D QI-D 44-15642
Baylor, Melvin W., Capt.; August 1944-May 1945; ex-RCAF
66 missions, 285:20 hours
P-47D QI-J 42-26275
P-51D QI-J 44-15097 "La Belle Mus Prang"
Beck, Charles E., Capt.; August 1944-August 1945
63 missions, 285:10 hours
P-51D QI-S 44-15343 "Pat"
Bell, DeWitt T., Jr., Lt.; January 1944-March 20, 1944(KIA)
20 missions, 56:42 hours

Bomberger, Amos H., II, Capt.; August 1944-August 1945
66 missions, 284 hours
P-47D QI-B 42-26649 "Miss Carriage"
P-51D QI-B 44-15080 "Carolyn's Vergeltungswaffe"
Bowers, James A., Lt.; October 1944-September 1945
59 missions
P-51D QI-V 44-15098
P-51D QI-V 44-15290
Bruce, John L., Lt.; April 1944-May 4, 1944(KIA)
11 missions, 32:35 hours
P-47D QI-B 43-25516
Burden, Rex R., Lt.; November 1944-September 1945
52 missions
P-51D QI-A 44-15094
Burdick, Clinton R., Lt.; October 1944-September 1945
54 missions
P-51D QI-B 44-15310 "Do Do"
Burns, William W., Lt.; March 1944-July 1944; to 5th ERS
53 missions, 158:20 hours
P-47D QI-Z 42-25850
Camosy, Arturo E., Lt.; March 1943-July 1943
Campbell, Raymond H., Capt.; October 1944-September 1945
55 missions
P-51D QI-Y 44-15354 "Tim-Mit-El"
Campbell, Robert L., Lt.; March 1943-August 1944
81 missions, 223 hours
P-47D QI-J 42-74661
P-47D QI-J 42-75253 "Fat Ass Bird"
Carlson, Donald R., Maj.; March 1945-November 1945; ex-4th Ftr Grp (153:20 hours)
7 missions
P-51D QI-I 44-72436
P-51D QI-I 44-73172
Caron, Donald F., Lt.; January 1945-August 1945; ex-bomber pilot (30 missions, 208 hours)
20 missions
Carwile, Jacob T., Lt.; October 1944-December 1944; to 67th Ftr Wg HdQts
3 missions, 7:35 hours
Clayton, Donald B., Capt.; May 1944-December 1944
72 missions, 270 hours
P-47D QI-E 43-25561
P-51D QI-E 44-15063
Cochran, Paul R., Lt.; October 1944-September 1945
45 missions
P-51D QI-R 44-15570 "Lily Belle"
Cooper, James M., LtCol.; July 1944-January 1945; ex-78th Ftr Grp
46 missions, 177:50 hours
P-47D QI-R 42-28792
P-51D QI-R 44-15169
Cope, Robert E., Lt.; November 1944-September 1945
52 missions
P-51D QI-I 44-15101
P-51D QI-Y 44-72982
Cotton, John W., F/O; March 1945-September 1945; ex-RCAF
5 missions
Cox, Raymond J., Lt.; October 1944-September 1945
56 missions
P-51D QI-Q 44-15089 "Lil Joe"
Creevy, Thomas E., Lt.; May 1945-June 9, 1945(KIAc); ex-bomber pilot
0 missions
Culp, Jack H., Sr., Lt.; January 1944-May 4, 1944(POW)
32 missions, 102 hours
P-47D QI-V 42-75507
Decker, Edmund L., F/O; March 1944-June 8, 1944(KIA)
30 missions, 127:20 hours
P-47D QI-K 42-75556
DeMerit, Merrill W., Lt.; January 1944-February 10, 1944(POW)
3 missions, 9:40 hours
Dendle, Elmer G., Lt.; March 1943-May 1944; to 5th ERS
41 missions, 134:20 hours
P-47D QI-K 42-75438 "Katie"
P-47D QI-K 42-74709
Drake, Wilford D., Lt.; June 1944-November 1944
68 missions, 250:10 hours
P-47D QI-J 42-26275 "Joy Ann"
Dupuy, John K., Lt.; January 1945-September 1945
37 missions
P-51D QI-Z 44-15401 "Moonshine"
Engle, Raymond F., Lt.; April 1944-June 8, 1944(KIA)
27 missions, 95:25 hours
Engelhorn, Homer M., Capt.; February 1944-February 1945
81 missions, 294:45 hours
Epley, Thomas K., Capt.; August 1944-September 1945
61 missions
P-51D QI-E 44-15063
Erickson, Milton F., Lt.; February 1943-March 6, 1944(POW)
36 missions, 89:30 hours
P-47D QI-N 42-22520
P-47D QI-N 42-75255
Faison, Edward L., Capt.; April 1944-December 1944
90 missions, 345 hours
P-47D QI-I 42-76497 "Skipper"
P-47D QI-I 42-28827
P-51D QI-I 44-15101
Fremaux, Edward C., Capt.; December 1943-September 1944
89 missions, 291:55 hours
P-47D QI-V 42-75426 "Swamp Fox"
Gansberg, Raymond H., Capt.; March 1943-December 5, 1944(KIA)
90 missions, 297:50 hours
P-47D QI-P 42-8440
P-47D QI-P 42-76177
P-51D QI-P 44-15109
Garneau, Edgar H., Lt.; February 1945-April 1945; ex-bomber pilot (215:10 hours)
6 missions, 25:50 hours
Gearon, Stanford J., Lt.; April 1945-August 1945
0 missions
Gibson, Robert, Lt.; March 1943-May 1944
65 missions, 200 hours
P-47D QI-H 42-8536
P-47D QI-H 42-75419
Gillette, Richard W., Lt.; June 1944-November 1944
71 missions, 251:15 hours
P-47D QI-Y 42-8510 "Shoo Shoo Baby"
Hall, Herbert B., Jr., Lt.; June 1944-November 1944
76 missions, 270 hours
P-47D QI-H 42-26120 "Ace of Spades"
Hallmark, John M., Maj.; September 1944-September 1945
62 missions
P-51D QI-H 44-15045 "Look Jessie"
Hargreaves, Jack A., Capt.; May 1944-January 1945
79 missions, 270 hours
Harris, Elijah P., Lt.; May 1944-June 10, 1944(KIA)
5 missions, 15:43 hours
Harrop, John O., Lt.; January 1945-September 1945
29 missions
P-51D QI-X 44-15170
P-51D QI-X 44-72951
Hayden, William R., Lt.; March 1943-December 30, 1943(KIA)
16 missions, 37 hours
P-47D QI-X 42-8662
Hewett, Sidney H., Capt.; February 1943-May 4, 1944(POW)
56 missions, 166 hours
P-47D QI-F 42-76397 "Clarkie"
P-47D QI-F 42-74702 "Clarkie"
Higginbotham, Merrion G., Lt.; August 1944-April 1945
33 missions, 102:45 hours
P-51D QI-Y 44-15354
Hooker, Freeman F., Lt.; August 1944-January 14, 1945(POW)
36 missions, 138:40 hours
P-51D QI-Y 44-11329
Hotchkiss, Renna S., Lt.; March 1943-January 1944; to 5th General Hospital
2 missions, 3:48 hours
Humphrey, Robert F., Lt.; January 1945-September 1945
35 missions
P-51D QI-G 44-72257
Hurley, William S., Jr., Capt.; May 1944-February 1945
86 missions, 321 hours
P-47D QI-T 42-76564 "Eerie Eagle"
P-51D QI-C 44-15055
Hyde, Paul H., Jr., Capt.; March 1943-December 20, 1943(KIA)
19 missions, 48:40 hours
P-47D QI-L 42-8677
Ingram, William B., Lt.; April 1944-April 24, 1944(KIA)
4 missions, 8 hours
Jack, Joseph V., Lt.; November 1943-April 1944 (WIA)
35 missions, 111:10 hours
P-47D QI-X 42-75522
James, Richard C., Lt.; January 1945-August 1945
15 missions
Jarvis, William C., Lt.; November 1944-September 1945
50 missions
P-51D QI-L 44-15139
P-51D QI-L 44-63511
Jett, Shelby N., Lt.; November 1944-July 8, 1945(KIAc)
56 missions
P-51D QI-E 44-15666 "Jett Job"
Johnson, James K., Lt.; March 1943-May 19, 1944(POW)
60 missions, 124:15 hours
P-47D QI-G 42-8436
Kaczynski, Henry J., Lt.; April 1944-April 23, 1944(POW)
3 missions, 5:30 hours
Kahle, Dayne, Lt.; April 1944-October 1944
76 missions, 273:10 hours
P-47D QI-A 42-25505 "Rosemary"
P-47D QI-A 42-26630
Kinsey, Samuel P.M., Capt.; March 1945-September 1945; ex-23rd Ftr Grp, CBI (4 victories)
11 missions
Korhorn, Evert, Capt.; March 1943-July 1944
94 missions, 300 hours
P-47D QI-U 42-8394
P-47D QI-U 42-22551
P-47D QI-U 42-26241
P-47D QI-U 42-26651

Kovacs, Elmer A., Lt.; May 1944-October 1944
75 missions, 252:10 hours
P-47D QI-Y 42-75827 "Dottie K"
P-47D QI-Y 42-26451
Lee, Edward P., Lt.; February 1944-June 8, 1944(KIA)
48 missions, 172:25 hours
Lewis, Henry L., Lt.; June 1944-August 13, 1944(KIA)
22 missions, 74:30 hours
Leyser, Harry C., III, Lt.; February 1943-June 1944
63 missions, 200 hours
P-47D QI-W 42-74649 "Betty"
P-47D QI-W 42-74727
Lindsay, John C., Lt.; September 1944-September 1945
62 missions
P-51D QI-T 44-15152 "Dixie Rambler II"
Loffler, Leonard L., Lt.; January 1945-September 1945
33 missions
P-51D QI-C 44-73115
Martin, Johnnie F., Lt.; March 1943-November 29, 1943(KIA)
10 missions
P-47D QI-Q 42-8692
McDowell, Reginald C., Capt.; February 1943-September 18, 1944(Evd)
74 missions, 228:25 hours
P-47D QI-I 42-74646
P-47D QI-I 42-76497 "Irene"
McKeon, Preston W., Lt.; May 1945-June 18, 1945(KIAc); ex-bomber pilot. 0 missions
Metzger, Allen M., Lt.; March 1943-November 29, 1943(KIA)
10 missions, 22:30 hours
P-47D QI-O 42-8509
Mills, Joseph W., Lt.; May 1944-August 4, 1944(KIA)
34 missions, 123:25 hours
P-47D QI-S 42-25842
Montgomery, Emery H., Maj.; March 1943-May 1944
50 missions, 118:20 hours
P-47D QI-B 42-76128
Morel, Paul F., Lt.; May 1944-October 1944
74 missions, 250 hours
P-47D QI-K 42-25505
Morgan, Frank A., Capt.; March 1944-May 1944; to 5th ERS
July 1944-March 1945, ex-RCAF
60 missions, 321 hours
P-47D QI-N 42-26459 "Portland Rose"
P-51D QI-N 44-15079
P-51D QI-N 44-15585 "Donna"
Nystrom, Richard C., Capt.; February 1944-March 1944; to 5th General Hospital
July 1944-April 1945; to HdQts
80 missions, 275:05 hours
Parham, Ernest M., Lt.; December 1943-April 11, 1944(KIA)
32 missions, 87:30 hours
P-47D QI-O 42-75572
P-47D QI-O 42-76126
Perrin, John P., Capt.; March 1943-May 1944
65 missions, 200 hours
P-47D QI-E 42-22533
Porter, Fred S., Jr., Capt.; March 1943-March 20, 1944(POW)
51 missions, 137:30 hours
P-47D QI-M 42-8510 "Fireball"
Pound, John E., Lt.; February 1945-September 1945
22 missions
Price, James T., Lt.; March 1943-December 16, 1943(KIA)
9 missions, 18 hours
P-47D QI-D 42-74724
Racine, Rolland W., Lt.; March 1943-January 11, 1944(KIA)
19 missions, 48:50 hours
P-47D QI-V 42-22525
Ray, Vincent S., Capt.; October 1944-September 1945
57 missions
P-51D QI-P 44-15109 "Shirley Vee"
P-51D QI-P 44-72269
Richardson, Harold P., Lt.; March 1943-August 1943
Riley, Eldon S., Lt.; January 1945-September 1945
32 missions
P-51D QI-W 44-15070
Roberts, Fred C., Jr., Maj.; February 1943-November 1943
9 missions, 21 hours
P-47D QI-A 42-8482
Roberts, Paul J., Jr., Lt.; June 1944-October 7, 1944(KIA)
58 missions, 173:50 hours
P-47D QI-P 42-76177 "Mad Wolves"
Rodgers, Robert E., Lt.; June 1944-August 9, 1944(POW)
18 missions, 65:35 hours
Rosenbauer, Elwood J., Lt.; January 1945-March 1945; to 1st SF
8 missions, 41:40 hours
Runyan, Louis B., Lt.; September 1944-November 20, 1944(KIA)
19 missions, 74:40 hours
Scheible, Wilbur R., Maj.; June 1944-March 1945; to HdQts
70 missions, 245:05 hours
P-47D QI-Z 42-75426
P-51D QI-F 44-15083
Schlack, Robert F., Capt.; June 1944-February 1945; to HdQts
88 missions, 322;40 hours
Shepard, Alan C., Lt.; January 1945-September 1945
35 missions
P-51D QI-N 44-15585 "Jackie"
Skjelbostad, Odmor, Lt.; January 1945-September 1945
32 missions
Slanker, Eldon L., Lt.; January 1945-April 12, 1945(KIAc)
31 missions, 138:25 hours
P-51D QI-M 44-15073
Smith, Jack T., Lt.; November 1944-December 5, 1944(KIA)
2 missions, 4:20 hours
Solomon, Richard F., Lt.; January 1945-September 1945
28 missions
Stoddard, Smith C., Lt.; January 1945-September 1945
28 missions
P-51D QI-S 44-72149
Strait, Donald J., Maj.; February 1943-March 1945
120 missions, 429:15 hours
P-47D QI-T 42-8640 "Jersey Jerk"
P-47D QI-T 42-25844 "Jersey Jerk"
P-47D QI-T 42-76564 "Jersey Jerk"
P-47D QI-T 42-28827 "Jersey Jerk"
P-51D QI-T 44-15152 "Jersey Jerk"
Swift, Blayne A., Lt.; April 1944-October 1944
77 missions, 266:30 hours
P-47D QI-B 42-8608 "Butch"
P-47D QI-B 42-26649
Ter Haar, Jarvis M., Lt.; January 1945-February 25, 1945(WIA)
5 missions
Thompson, Edward L., Lt.; April 1944-October 1944
71 missions, 261:55 hours
P-47D QI-F 42-74736 "Little Nig"
Thorough, Jerome S., Lt.; February 1945-September 1945
27 missions
P-51D QI-O 44-15071
Thwaites, David F., Capt.; December 1943-September 1944
90 missions, 293:50 hours
P-47D QI-L 42-75214 "Polly"
P-47D QI-L 42-26457 "Polly"
Tillman, John R., Lt.; June 1944-August 18, 1944(KIA)
24 missions, 85 hours
Tobiassen, Arthur J., Lt.; September 1944-September 1945
50 missions
P-47D QI-K 42-72976
P-51D QI-K 44-15345
Tomlinson, Robert M., Lt.; September 1944-January 1945
9 missions, 45:45 hours
Tuckey, Bernard A., Lt.; March 1943-March 20, 1944(KIA)
37 missions, 96 hours
Upp, Ronald J., Capt.; June 1944-December 1944
73 missions, 270 hours
P-47D QI-U 42-76594 "Zombie"
P-47D QI-U 42-26651
P-51D QI-U 44-15066
Vangos, Bleftherios A., Lt.; March 1943-March 18, 1944(POW)
39 missions, 110:10 hours
P-47D QI-Y 42-74715 "The Vangoose"
Von Holzhausen, Thomas, Lt.; March 1943-February 21, 1944(KIA)
33 missions, 84 hours
P-47D QI-Z 42-74679 "China Doll"
Wallace, Robert L., Lt.; November 1944-August 1945
50 missions
P-51D QI-U 44-15066 "Ava Honey"
Waller, William, III, LtCol.; November 1943-July 1944
76 missions, 247:35 hours
P-47D QI-A 42-8482 "Skeeter"
P-47D QI-A 42-8630 "Skeeter"
Webb, Russell H., Lt.; January 1945-September 1945
31 missions
P-51D QI-Z 44-72391
Whitmore, Harold E., Lt.; June 1944-March 1945
68 missions, 280:20 hours
P-47D QI-G 42-76379
P-51D QI-G 44-15011 "The Lord Is My Shepherd"
Whitson, Richard N., Lt.; September 1944-September 1945
65 missions
P-51D QI-Z 44-15401 "Moonshine"
Wiggins, Howard E., Capt.; May 1944-January 1945
75 missions, 277:55 hours
P-47D QI-M 42-26272 "Angel Eyes"
P-47D QI-M 42-26534
P-51D QI-X 44-15170
Wood, James N., LtCol.; February 1943-October 1944; to
360th Ftr Sqn
112 missions (83 w/361st)
P-47D QI-S 42-74744 "Blind Date"
P-47D QI-S 42-76422 "Blind Date"
P-47D QI-S 44-19764 "Blind Date"
Yoakum, George L., Lt.; January 1944-September 1944
83 misions, 285:05 hours
P-47D QI-G 42-76379

### Aircraft of the 359th Fighter Squadron

| P-47D-2-RE | |
|---|---|
| 42-8002 OC-N "Wilmarene" | W.G. Craig |
| 42-8002 OC-N "Lonesome Lee" | J.B. Griswold |
| 42-8401 OC- | |
| 42-8407 OC- | |

| P-47D-2-RA | |
|---|---|
| 42-22488 OC-F | |
| 42-22517 OC-U "Eager Eagle" | H.A. Ogden |
| 42-22524 OC-S | R.A. Rann |
| 42-22528 OC- | |

| P-47D-5-RE | |
|---|---|
| 42-8417 OC-A "Ich Brauche Du" | W.H. Wood |
| 42-8467 OC-L | J.D. Henry |
| 42-8471 OC-A | J.H. Cline/J.D. Wyatt |
| 42-8478 OC-V "Fifinelle" | H. Weber |
| 42-8478 OC-V | P.R. Mellinger |
| 42-8491 OC-C | W.C. Brearley |
| 42-8492 OC-C | W.W. Cotter |
| 42-8512 OC-O | |
| 42-8546 OC- | |
| 42-8549 OC-R "Elsie" | H.L. Broxton |
| 42-8567 OC-W "We Four" | R.K. Holtz |
| 42-8559 OC- | |
| 42-8568 OC-I "The Bloody Shaft" | D.A. Baccus |
| 42-8574 OC-X "Princess Pat" | R.B. Conroy |
| 42-8588 OC-K "4-F" | |
| 42-8588 OC-K "Gracie" | R.L. Chickering |
| 42-8598 OC- | J.D. Hull |
| 42-8599 OC- | |
| 42-8601 OC-Z | W.A. Beach |
| 42-8617 OC- | C.B. Earnhart |
| 42-8639 OC- | |
| 42-8645 OC-T | G.B. Peet |
| 42-8646 OC-J | R.G. Vossler |
| 42-8654 OC-E | W.C. O'Barr |
| 42-8694 OC-R "Little Texan" | J.B. Smith |

| P 47D 6 RE | |
|---|---|
| 42-74658 OC-Y "Little Fi-Fi" | |
| 42-74671 OC- | |
| 42-74673 OC-P "Ich Brauche Du" | J.H. Wadlow |
| 42-74673 OC-P "Carmen" | A.E. Bergstrom |
| 42-74684 OC-G | |
| 42-74689 OC-M "Lady Jane" | W.A. Holm |
| 42-74699 OC-X | R.D. Bradshaw |
| 42-74711 OC-II | W.L. Farmer |
| 42-74745 OC-B | E.J. White |

| P-47D-10-RE | |
|---|---|
| 42-75159 OC-S | |
| 42-75171 OC-D "Ramblin' Rebel" | M.M. Clayborne |

| P-47D-11-RE | |
|---|---|
| 42-75288 OC-K | J.H. Thorne |
| 42-75389 OC-R | R.A. Rann |

| P-47D-15-RE | |
|---|---|
| 42-76112 OC- | |
| 42-76146 OC- | M.J. Burke |
| 42-76168 OC-R | J.B. Smith |
| 42-76201 OC-C | |
| 42-76206 OC- | |
| 42-76208 OC-J "Lady Luck" | R.G. Vossler |
| 42-76208 OC-J "Dodie Darlin" | C.C. McKelvy |
| 42-76220 OC- | |

| P-47D-20-RE | |
|---|---|
| 42-76372 OC-E | W.C. O'Barr |
| 42-76405 OC-P "Mad Marion" | G.W. Engel |
| 42-76405 OC-P "Lil Abner" | |
| 42-76416 OC-Q | |
| 42-76491 OC- | |
| 42-76583 OC-G | D.A. Baccus |

| P-47D-21-RA | |
|---|---|
| 43-25530 OC-W "We Four II" | R.K. Holtz |
| 43-25557 OC-B | E.J. White |

| P-47D-21-RE | |
|---|---|
| 42-25508 OC-K | |

| P-47D-22-RE | |
|---|---|
| 42-26129 OC-E | J.J. Meholic |
| 42-26141 OC-I "Fearless Fosdick" | F.A. Forsyth |
| 42-26253 OC- | |
| 42-26283 OC- | |
| 42-26309 OC- | |
| 42-26331 OC-G "Slightly Dangerous" | L.F. Richason |

| P-47D-25-RE | |
|---|---|
| 42-26532 OC-Q | |
| 42-26557 OC-N "Lonesome Lee II" | J.B. Griswold |
| 42-26576 OC-B "Vee-T" | J.D. Tarbutton |

| P-47D-27-RE | |
|---|---|
| 42-26851 OC-E | J.J. Meholic/W.J. Kennedy |

| P-47D-28-RA | |
|---|---|
| 42-28675 OC-R | R.A. Rann |
| 42-28808 OC-X "Mary B" | G.S. Pelletier |
| 42-28819 OC-T "Jodie Darlin" | D.F. Tucker |
| 42-28845 OC- | |

| P-47D-28-RE | |
|---|---|
| 44-19802 OC-S | |

| Unknown Serials | |
|---|---|
| OC-H "Lonesome Polecat" | W.C. Cooley |
| OC-P "Lazy Mazie" | H.F. LeMoyne |
| OC- "The Virginia Squire" | P.W. Easley |
| OC- "Spoiled Brat" | |

| P-51D-5-NT | |
|---|---|
| 44-11212 OC- | |
| 44-11326 OC- | |
| 44-11332 OC-J | |
| 44-11351 OC-I | F.A. Forsyth |

| P-51K-1-NT | |
|---|---|
| 44-11366 OC-A "Bobby Socks" | J.F. Brown |
| 44-11382 OC- | |

| P-51K-5-NT | |
|---|---|
| 44-11564 OC-W | |
| 44-11637 OC- | |

| P-51K-10-NT | |
|---|---|
| 44-12155 OC- | |

| P-51D-10-NA | |
|---|---|
| 44-14864 OC-A | R.A. Odenwald |
| 44-14993 OC-G | D.A. Baccus |
| 44-14998 OC- | A.L. Brown |
| 44-15029 OC- "Pottsville Express" | |
| 44-15138 OC-Y "Hair-Breath Harry" | H.R. Gohsler |
| 44-15177 OC-L "Koyli Renee" | G. Crum |
| 44-15181 OC-H | W.C. Cooley |
| 44-15183 OC-V "Bama Baby" | J.B. Baker |
| 44-15185 OC-D "T-Lou" | L.O. Sonnier |
| 44-15193 OC- | |
| 44-15195 OC-B "Kathleen" | R.R. Withers |
| 44-15199 OC- | |
| 44-15201 OC-K "Eunie" | E.G. Rudd |
| 44-15203 OC-X "Nazi Hot Foot" | |
| 44-15208 OC- | |
| 44-15219 OC-B | J.D. Tarbutton |
| 44-15223 OC- "Renee" | |
| 44-15230 OC- | |
| 44-15231 OC-F | |
| 44-15258 OC-R | R.A. Rann |
| 44-15268 OC-P "The Gremlin" | R.C. Miller |
| 44-15271 OC-E "Starduster" | W.J. Kennedy |
| 44-15274 OC-N | J.B. Griswold |
| 44-15274 OC-N "Mojahalka" | |
| 44-15280 OC-S "Flying Dutchman" | W.F. Traupe |
| 44-15288 OC-W | |
| 44-15308 OC-Q "Jean-Tom" | N.E. Wieland |
| 44-15331 OC-M "Junie" | H.R. Gohsler |
| 44-15403 OC-O | F.W. Bruner |
| 44-15528 OC- | |
| 44-15609 OC- | |
| 44-15658 OC-U "Eager Eagle" | J.E. Blewett |
| 44-15677 OC-T | L.L. Robertson |

| P-51D-20-NA | |
|---|---|
| 44-63250 OC- | |
| 44-63268 OC- "Little Mary" | |
| 44-72078 OC-S | L. Oliver |
| 44-72148 OC-D "T-Lou-II" | L.O. Sonnier |
| 44-72284 OC-E "Micharee I" | W.E. Rhynard |
| 44-72288 OC-V "Marge" | A.R. Hale |
| 44-73432 OC- | |
| 44-72542 OC- | |

| Unknown Serials | |
|---|---|
| OC-V "Spirit of Aggieland" | L.E. Bennett |
| OC-C "Princess Jocelyn" | W.C. Brearley |

OC- "Telie's Terror" R.N. Ellis
OC-Z "Ruth Jane"
OC- "Josephine"
OC- "Toots"
OC- "My Gals"

**Aircraft of the 360th Fighter Squadron**

P-47D-2-RA
42-22469 PI- "Old Master"
42-22534 PI-
42-22535 PI-N "Kathleen Ann" R.R. Withers
42-22542 PI-

P-47D-4-RA
42-22780 PI-H
42-22786 PI-
42-22789 PI-

P-47D-5-RE
42-8469 PI- "Jersey Bounce" A.S. Koczak
42-8474 PI-G H.D. Parker
42-8502 PI-W "Hell's Angel" J.B. Asbridge
42-8507 PI-
42-8533 PI-
42-8668 PI-

P-47D-6-RE
42-74638 PI-D "Nashville Belle" C.J. Garvey
42-74639 PI-
42-74662 PI-
42-74714 PI-B "Gremlin Express" N.D. Cota

P-47D-10-RE
42-75134 PI-

P-47D-11-RE
42-75273 PI-P "Hard Luck"

P-47D-15-RE
42-75625 PI-
42-76066 PI-
42-76135 PI-
42-76147 PI-
42-76171 PI-
42-76204 PI-F "Bright Eyes" C.J. Servocky
42-76353 PI- "Naughty Patricia"

P-47D-20-RE
42-76396 PI-
42-76431 PI-
42-76449 PI-G H.D. Parker
42-76493 PI-
42-76499 PI-Q
42-25294 PI-

P-47D-20-RA
43-25302 PI-

P-47D-21-RA
43-25590 PI-

P-47D-21-RE
42-25524 PI- "Grace"
42-25531 PI-T P.E. Tukey
42-25534 PI-C N.D. Cota
42-25534 PI-G "Vicious Virgin" R.S. Gleason
42-25535 PI-

P-47D-22-RE
42-25751 PI-M "Joker" R.J. Halverson
42-25861 PI-
42-25997 PI-
42-26030 PI-S
42-26147 PI-
42-26240 PI-
42-26254 PI-
42-26271 PI-Y
42-26289 PI-N "Georgia's Best" D.B. Mercer
42-26322 PI-W "Jackie" J.W. Crump

P-47D-25-RE
42-26415 PI-T P.E. Tukey
42-26553 PI-V "Jersey Mosquito" J.W. Vogt
42-26563 PI-
42-26565 PI-
42-26683 PI-C "Mugsy"

P-47D-26-RA
42-28283 PI-Q "Kathleen Ann" R.R. Withers

P-47D-28-RA
42-28472 PI-D "Podunk III" W.H. Fletcher
42-28664 PI-B "Squirt" R.E. Barnhart

P-47D-28-RE
44-19861 PI-Z "Chesapeake Beach" N.C. Douglas
44-19894 PI-C B. Borelli

Unknown Serials
PI-L "Texas Lady" R.B. Bluhm
PI-K "Fancy Nancy" A.E. Krieger
PI-J "Red Dog" H.B. McLaughlin
PI-J "Jeanie-Janet" R.M. Leidy
PI-F "Dear Alean" L.F. Kress
PI-M "Joker" R.J. Halverson
PI-S "Buckeye Bullet" F.M. Russell
PI-Y "Jersey Panic" B. Borelli
PI-M "The Thundering Three" D.D. Carlson
PI-B "Quirk's Dark Horse" J.R. Cook
PI-B "Quirk's Dark Horse II" J.R. Cook
PI-D "Podunk" W.H. Fletcher
PI-D "Podunk II" W.H. Fletcher
PI-L "Dedham Dreadnought" C.A. Vitali
PI- "Adolph's Horror" W.G. Maxwell
PI- "Francis' Favorite" C.W. Adams
PI- "Lone Star Lady" S.J. Green
PI- "Kitten" W.E. Johnson
PI- "Florida Gator" C.M. Taylor
PI- "Black Jack" J.T. Romine
PI- "The Cape Codder" A.V. Niemi
PI- "Big Dick" P.E. McCullough

P-51D-5-NT
44-11156 PI-F "Brenda" L.R. Switzer
44-11220 PI-U "Fourth Apocalypsian" C.L. Welch
44-11334 PI-K "Lois" W.G. Thomas

P-51K-5-NT
44-11570 PI-Y "Virgie" A.A. Paquet
44-11577 PI-M "Ginny III" D.D. Carlson
44-11577 PI-M R.D. Schmalz
44-11579 PI-T P.E. Tukey

P-51D-10-NA
44-14354 PI-
44-14754 PI-L "Sweet'n Low Down" W.C. Gatlin
44-14766 PI-

P-51D-15-NA
44-14925 PI-P "Mary Jane" J.C. Pidwell
44-14936 PI-Q "Kathleen Ann" R.R. Withers
44-14965 PI-
44-14973 PI-D "Lady Doris" O.L. Burwell/G.H. Schalck
44-15009 PI-
44-15033 PI-
44-15052 PI-J T.J. Urban/J.A. Hickey
44-15056 PI-W "Jackie" J.W. Crump
44-15056 PI-W "Tarbaby" R.P. Schmidt
44-15069 PI-Z "Audrey 3rd" M.P. Yannell
44-15114 PI-G "Arasa & Jeff" R.S. Gleason
44-15115 PI-V "Naughty Nordie" J.N. Wood
44-15133 PI-
44-15149 PI-M "Virgy I" D.D. Carlson
44-15164 PI-
44-15189 PI-B "Margie Darling" R.E. Barnhart
44-15189 PI-B J.G. Charlton
44-15194 PI-A E.M. Nebinger
44-15194 PI-A "Dotty" E.C. Turner
44-15210 PI-
44-15211 PI-K "Sweet Peay" T.N. Mauldin
44-15218 PI- "Miss Mary Nel" D.G. Ciocchi
44-15250 PI-H "Raggedy Ann" V. Hockmeyer
44-15250 PI-H "Ringy Dingy" G.W. Seanor
44-15289 PI-D "Patty" W.K. Dunn
44-15300 PI-O "Milly" D.F. Jones
44-15305 PI-N
44-15307 PI-
44-15333 PI-E B.E. Ellingson
44-15333 PI-E "The Virginia Squire" P.W. Easley
44-15341 PI-C B. Borelli/R.J. Rensch
44-15361 PI-F "Brenda" L.R. Switzer
44-15361 PI-F J.F. Stevenson
44-15364 PI-
44-15552 PI-Q "Big Lefty-Little Ann" R.S. Ragsdale
44-15590 PI-M "Barbara" C.S. Poppell
44-15600 PI-
44-15601 PI-S "Buckeye Bullet" F.M. Russell

P-51D-20-NA
44-63251 PI-L "Louise" N.B. Ceraolo
44-63283 PI-X "Paper Doll" E.W. Corner
44-63637 PI-
44-72377 PI-V "Naughty Nordie" J.N. Wood/E.W. Schrull
44-72379 PI-
44-72435 PI-T P.E. Tukey
44-72455 PI-T P.E. Tukey

P-51D-25-NA
44-72931 PI-R H.R. Rutland

Unknown Serials
PI-Z "Audrey 4th" M.P. Yannell
PI-G "Akron Angel" T.A. Cook
PI-M "Ginny II" D.D. Carlson

**Aircraft of the 361st Fighter Squadron**

P-47C-5-RE
41-6580 QI-P HACK

P-47D-1-RE
42-7886 QI-Z

P-47D-2-RE
42-8394 QI-U E. Korhorn

P-47D-2-RA
42-22461 QI-N
42-22468 QI-Z
42-22479 QI-V
42-22520 QI-N M.F. Erickson
42-22525 QI-V R.W. Racine
42-22533 QI-E J.P. Perrin
42-22550 QI-R "Gentle Annie" H.J. Rau
42-22550 QI-R "Kay-J" E.A. Malmstrom
42-22551 QI-U E. Korhorn

P-47D-4-RA
42-22766 QI-N

P-47D-5-RE
42-8417 QI-W
42-8425 QI-R "Gentle Annie" H.J. Rau
42-8425 QI-W
42-8427 QI-O
42-8436 QI-G J.K. Johnson
42-8440 QI-P R.H. Gansberg
42-8482 QI-A "Skeeter" W. Waller
42-8482 QI-P
42-8509 QI-O A.M. Metzger
42-8510 QI-M "Fireball" E.S. Porter
42-8510 QI-Y "Shoo Shoo Baby" R.W. Gillette
42-8536 QI-H R. Gibson
42-8608 QI-B "Butch" B.A. Swift
42-8630 QI-A "Skeeter" W. Waller
42-8640 QI-T "Jersey Jerk" D.J. Strait
42-8650 QI-C "Zombie" T.F. Bailey
42-8662 QI-X W.R. Hayden
42-8677 QI-L P.H. Hyde
42-8685 QI-N
42-8692 QI-Q J.F. Martin

P-47D-6-RE
42-74646 QI-I R.C. McDowell
42-74649 QI-W "Betty" H.C. Leyser
42-74661 QI-J R.L. Campbell
42-74679 QI-Z "China Doll" T. Von Holzhausen
42-74702 QI-F "Clarkie" S.H. Hewett
42-74709 QI-K E.G. Dendle
42-74715 QI-Y "The Vangoose" B.A. Vangos
42-74724 QI-D J.T. Price
42-74725 QI-P
42-74727 QI-W H.C. Leyser
42-74736 QI-F "Little Nig" E.L. Thomspon
42-74744 QI-S "Blind Date" J.N. Wood

P-47D-10-RE
42-75190 QI-O
42-75214 QI-L "Polly" D.F. Thwaites

P-47D-11-RE
42-75230 QI-X
42-75253 QI-J "Fat Ass Bird" R.L. Campbell
42-75255 QI-N M.F. Erickson
42-75419 QI-H R. Gibson
42-75426 QI-V "Swamp Fox" E.C. Fremaux
42-75426 QI-Z W.R. Scheible
42-75438 QI-K "Katie" E.G. Dendle
42-75505 QI-Y
42-75507 QI-V J.H. Culp
42-75522 QI-X R.S. Alexander/J.V. Jack
42-75549 QI-D
42-75553 QI-Z
42-75556 QI-K E.L. Decker
42-75572 QI-O E.M. Parham
42-75586 QI-Y

P-47D-15-RE
42-75827 QI-Y "Dottie K" E.A. Kovacs
42-76126 QI-O E.M. Parham
42-76128 QI-B E.H. Montgonery
42-76177 QI-P R.H. Gansberg
42-76177 QI-P "Mad Wolves" P.J. Roberts
42-76231 QI-W

P-47D-20-RE
42-76379 QI-G G.L. Yoakum/H.E. Whitmore
42-76397 QI-F "Clarkie" S.H. Hewett
42-76422 QI-S "Blind Date" J.N. Wood
42-76497 QI-I "Irene" R.C. McDowell
42-76497 QI-I "Skipper" E.L. Faison
42-76536 QI-N "Mary III" C.T. Ashby
42-76564 QI-T "Jersey Jerk" D.J. Strait
42-76564 QI-T "Eerie Eagle" W.S. Hurley
42-76570 QI-Z
42-76580 QI-D
42-76594 QI-C "Zombie" T.F. Bailey
42-76594 QI-U R.J. Upp

P-47D-20-RA
43-25271 QI-H

P-47D-21-RA
43-25516 QI-B J.L. Bruce
43-25551 QI-Q
43-25561 QI-E D.B. Clayton

P-47D-21-RE
42-25505 QI-A "Rosemary" D. Kahle
42-25505 QI-K P.F. Morel
42-25513 QI-R "Kay-J" E.A. Malmstrom
42-25527 QI-F

P-47D-22-RE
42-25842 QI-S J.W. Mills
42-25844 QI-T "Jersey Jerk" D.J. Strait
42-25850 QI-Z W.W. Burns
42-26120 QI-H "Ace of Spades" H.B. Hall
42-26241 QI-U E. Korhorn
42-26272 QI-M "Angel Eyes" H.E. Wiggins
42-26275 QI-J "Joy Ann" W.D. Drake

P-47D-25-RE
42-26428 QI-Y
42-26451 QI-Y
42-26457 QI-L "Polly" D.F. Thwaites
42-26459 QI-N "Portland Rose" F.A. Morgan
42-26534 QI-R J.H. Thorne
42-26534 QI-M H.E. Wiggins
42-26630 QI-A D. Kahle
42-26649 QI-B B.A. Swift
42-26649 QI-B "Miss Carriage" A.H. Bomberger
42-26651 QI-U E. Korhorn/R.J. Upp

P-47D-26-RA
42-28404 QI-F

P-47D-28-RA
42-28792 QI-R J.H. Thorne/J.M. Cooper
42-28816 QI-D
42-28827 QI-T "Jersey Jerk" D.J. Strait
42-28827 QI-I E.L. Faison

P-47D-28-RE
44-19764 QI-S "Blind Date" J.N. Wood

Unknown Serials
QI- "Flak Happy"

P-51D-5-NT
44-11329 QI-Y F.F. Hooker

P-51D-15-NA
44-15011 QI-G "The Lord Is My Shepherd" H.E. Whitmore
44-15045 QI-H "Look Jessie!" J.M. Hallmark
44-15055 QI-C W.S. Hurley
44-15063 QI-E D.B. Clayton/T.K. Epley
44-15066 QI-U R.J. Upp
44-15066 QI-U "Ava Honey" R.L. Wallace

44-15070 QI-W E.S. Riley
44-15071 QI-O J.S. Thorough
44-15073 QI-M C.T. Ashby/E.L. Slanker
44-15079 QI-N F.A. Morgan
44-15080 QI-B "Carolyn's Vergeltungswaffe" A.H. Bomberger
44-15082 QI-Z
44-15083 QI-F W.R. Scheible
44-15089 QI-Q "Lil Joe" R.J. Cox
44-15094 QI-A R.R. Burden
44-15097 QI-J "La Belle Mus Prang" M.W. Baylor
44-15098 QI-V J.A. Bowers
44-15101 QI-I E.L. Faison/R.E. Cope
44-15109 QI-P R.H. Gansberg
44-15109 QI-P "Shirley Vee" V.S. Ray
44-15118 QI-D
44-15139 QI-L W.C. Jarvis
44-15152 QI-T "Jersey Jerk" D.J. Strait
44-15152 QI-T "Dixie Rambler II" J.C. Lindsay
44-15169 QI-R J.M. Cooper
44-15170 QI-X H.E. Wiggins/J.O. Harrop
44-15290 QI-V J.A. Bowers
44-15310 QI-B "Do Do" C.D. Burdick
44-15343 QI-S "Pat" C.E. Beck
44-15345 QI-K A.J. Tobiassen
44-15354 QI-Y M.G. Higginbotham
44-15354 QI-Y "Tim-Mit-El" R.H. Campbell
44-15401 QI-Z "Moonshine" R.N. Whitson/J.K. Dupuy
44-15570 QI-R "Lily Belle" P.R. Cochran
44-15585 QI-N "Donna" F.A. Morgan
44-15585 QI-N "Jackie" A.C. Shepard
44-15642 QI-D W.M. Baskin
44-15666 QI-E "Jett Job" S.N. Jett

P-51D-20-NA
44-63511 QI-L W.C. Jarvis
44-72149 QI-S S.C. Stoddard
44-72257 QI-G R.F. Humphrey
44-72391 QI-Z R.H. Webb
44-72436 QI-I D.R. Carlson

P-51D-25-NA
44-72951 QI-X J.O. Harrop
44-72876 QI-K A.J. Tobiassen
44-72982 QI-V R.E. Cope
44-73115 QI-C L.L. Loffler
44-73172 QI-I D.R. Carlson

Unknown Serials
QI- "Swamp Angel"
QI- "Patricia"

• • •

## THE 357TH FIGHTER GROUP
## 362ND, 363RD, 364TH FIGHTER SQUADRONS

The 357th Fighter Group was activated on December 1, 1942, at Hamilton Field, California. Training in the western United States, the group headed overseas on November 29, 1943, aboard the "Queen Elizabeth". Initially assigned to the 9th Air Force, the 357th was "traded" to the 8th for the P-47 equipped 358th Fighter Group in late January of 1944. The first of 318 missions came on February 11, 1944, with the final one coming on April 25, 1945. During it's combat time, the group claimed 595.5 aerial and 107 ground victories while 139 P-51's were lost on operations and 13 pilots died in accidents.

Bases for the 357th were Raydon, from November 30, 1943, to January 31, 1944, and Leiston, from January 31, 1944, until July of 1945. Aircraft flown were the P-51B, C, D, and K, from December of 1943 onwards. The 357th was awarded two Distinguished Unit Citations, the first for missions flown on March 6 and June 29, 1944, in which pilots destroyed a large number of enemy planes, and the second for an escort on January 14, 1945, in which the group destroyed over 50 German fighters.

### Claims

| | Air | | | Grd | |
|---|---|---|---|---|---|
| | Destroyed | Probable | Damaged | Destroyed | Damaged |
| HdQts | 30.5 | 0 | 8 | 10.5 | 9 |
| 362nd | 198 | 5 | 36 | 44 | 18 |
| 363rd | 154 | 11 | 35 | 8 | 11 |
| 364th | 213 | 5 | 28 | 44.5 | 31 |
| | 595.5 | 21 | 107 | 107 | 69 |

### Commanders

| | |
|---|---|
| Col. Edward S. Chickering | July 7, 1943-February 17, 1944 |
| Col. Henry R. Spicer | February 17, 1944-March 5, 1944 |
| Col. Donald W. Graham | March 7, 1944-October 10, 1944 |
| LtCol. John D. Landers | October 10, 1944-December 2, 1944 |
| Col. Irwin H. Dregne | December 2, 1944-July 12, 1945 |

### Wing and Command Assignments

| | |
|---|---|
| Assigned to VIII Fighter Command | January 31, 1944 |
| VIII Fighter Command, 66th Fighter Wing | January 31, 1944 |
| 3rd Bomb Division, 66th Fighter Wing | September 15, 1944 |
| 3rd Air Division, 66th Fighter Wing | January 1, 1945 |

### Aircraft Markings

Original P-51's were in olive drab/neutral gray schemes with white spinners and theater bands. NMF planes arrived in the spring of 1944 and many of these received dark green paint on the upper surfaces in various locations. A few also had a light or medium gray paint applied to the lower surfaces. In March of 1944, a group marking was introduced: the spinner was banded red-yellow-red and the 12 inch cowl band was made up of red and yellow checkerboards. From November of 1944, squadron colors were applied to the rudders: none for the 362nd, red for the 363rd, and yellow for the 364th.

Squadron codes were:

362nd Ftr Sqn: G4
363rd Ftr Sqn: B6
364th Ftr Sqn: C5

### 357th Fighter Group Statistical Report

| Month | Missions | Air | Grd | Losses | KIAc |
|---|---|---|---|---|---|
| January 1944 | 0 | 0-0-0 | 0-0 | 1 | 0 |
| February | 9 | 22-2-5 | 0-0 | 10 | 0 |
| March | 16 | 55-4-14 | 5-3 | 17 | 0 |
| April | 20 | 73-3-18 | 0-0 | 15 | 0 |
| May | 24 | 79.5-4-14 | 17-3 | 18 | 0 |
| June | 50 | 28-0-5 | 0-2 | 10 | 0 |
| July | 27 | 29-0-6 | 1-2 | 5 | 0 |
| August | 26* | 10-0-2 | 2-3 | 6 | 1 |
| September | 23 | 66-1-3 | 0-1 | 15 | 1 |
| October | 18 | 19-1-3 | 0-0 | 3 | 0 |
| November | 18 | 41.5-2-8 | 16-4 | 6 | 0 |
| December | 18 | 64-2-1 | 0-1 | 7 | 0 |
| January 1945 | 15 | 60.5-2-4 | 7-0 | 8 | 4 |
| February | 18 | 2-0-1 | 6-11 | 5 | 3 |
| March | 22 | 34-0-15 | 23-19 | 7 | 0 |
| April | 14 | 11-0-8 | 30-20 | 6 | 0 |
| May | 0 | 0-0-0 | 0-0 | 0 | 3 |
| June | 0 | 0-0-0 | 0-0 | 0 | 1 |
| | 318 | 595.5-21-107 | 107-69 | 139 | 13 |

* - includes 5 on the Shuttle to Russia-Italy

### Losses by Squadron

| | MIA | KIAc |
|---|---|---|
| HdQts | 3 | 0 |
| 362nd | 40 | 5 |
| 363rd | 47 | 3 |
| 364th | 49 | 5 |

### Claims by Enemy Aircraft Type

| | Air | | | Grd | |
|---|---|---|---|---|---|
| | Destroyed | Probable | Damaged | Destroyed | Damaged |
| Me-109 | 325.5 | 12 | 40 | 29 | 7 |
| FW-190 | 193.5 | 8 | 35 | 5 | 5 |
| Me-110 | 32 | 1 | 7 | 1 | 3 |
| Me-262 | 18.5 | 0 | 19 | 3 | 1 |
| Me-410 | 12 | 0 | 4 | 1 | 1 |
| Ju-88 | 6 | 0 | 1 | 15 | 9 |
| FW-200 | 3 | 0 | 0 | 1 | 1 |
| He-111 | 1 | 0 | 1 | 30 | 19 |
| Fi-156 | 1 | 0 | 0 | 0 | 0 |
| Me-210 | 1 | 0 | 0 | 3 | 1 |
| Do-217 | 1 | 0 | 0 | 1 | 2 |
| FW-44 | 1 | 0 | 0 | 3 | 0 |
| u/i a/c | 0 | 0 | 0 | 12 | 14 |
| Ju-52 | 0 | 0 | 0 | 3 | 2 |
| He-177 | 0 | 0 | 0 | 0 | 2 |
| Ju-188 | 0 | 0 | 0 | 0 | 1 |
| Do-24 | 0 | 0 | 0 | 0 | 1 |

### 357th Fighter Group Aces

| Name | Air | Grd | Total | Sqn |
|---|---|---|---|---|
| Maj. Leonard K. Carson | 18.5 | 3.5 | 22 | 362nd |
| Maj. Richard A. Peterson | 15.5 | 3.5 | 19 | 364th |
| Maj. John B. England | 17.5 | 1 | 18.5 | 362nd |
| Maj. Robert W. Foy | 15 | 3 | 18 | 363rd<br>HdQts |
| Maj. Clarence E. Anderson | 16.25 | 1 | 17.25 | 363rd |
| Maj. Donald H. Bochkay | 13.83 | 0 | 13.83 | 363rd |
| Capt. John A. Kirla | 11.5 | 0.5 | 12 | 362nd |
| LtCol. John A. Storch | 10.5 | 1.5 | 12 | 364th |
| Lt. Dale E. Karger | 7.5 | 4 | 11.5 | 364th |
| Capt. Charles E. Yeager | 11.5 | 0 | 11.5 | 363rd |
| Capt. Charles E. Weaver | 8 | 3 | 11 | 362nd |
| Col. Irwin H. Dregne | 5 | 5.5 | 10.5 | HdQts |
| Lt. Otto D. Jenkins | 8.5 | 2 | 10.5 | 362nd |
| Lt. John F. Duncan | 4 | 6 | 10 | 362nd |
| Capt. Fletcher E. Adams | 9 | 0 | 9 | 362nd |
| Capt. John L. Sublett | 8 | 1 | 9 | 362nd |
| LtCol. Thomas L. Hayes, Jr. | 8.5 | 0 | 8.5 | 364th<br>HdQts |
| LtCol. Joseph E. Broadhead | 8 | 0 | 8 | 362nd<br>HdQts |
| LtCol. Andrew J. Evans, Jr. | 6 | 2 | 8 | HdQts |
| Maj. Donald C. McGee | 6 | 2 | 8* | 363rd<br>364th |
| Capt. Alva C. Murphy | 6 | 2 | 8 | 362nd<br>364th |
| Lt. Joseph F. Pierce | 7 | 1 | 8 | 363rd |
| Capt. Robert G. Schimanski | 6 | 2 | 8 | 364th |
| Capt. Robert M. Shaw | 8 | 0 | 8 | 364th |
| Lt. Vincent V. Zettler | 1 | 7 | 8 | 364th |
| Capt. Glendon V. Davis | 7.5 | 0 | 7.5 | 364th |
| Capt. Robert H. Becker | 7 | 0 | 7 | 362nd |
| Capt. James W. Browning | 7 | 0 | 7 | 363rd |
| Capt. John B. Carder | 7 | 0 | 7 | 364th |
| Capt. Gilbert M. O'Brien | 7 | 0 | 7 | 362nd |
| Lt. Arval J. Roberson | 6 | 1 | 7 | 362nd |
| Capt. Gerald E. Tyler | 7 | 0 | 7 | 364th |
| Lt. Frank L. Gailer, Jr. | 5.5 | 1 | 6.5 | 363rd |
| Capt. Morris A. Stanley | 5 | 1.5 | 6.5 | 364th |
| Capt. John F. Pugh | 6 | 0 | 6 | 362nd |
| Capt. Thomas H. Adams | 4.5 | 1 | 5.5 | 364th |
| Capt. Paul R. Hatala | 5.5 | 0 | 5.5 | 364th |
| Capt. William R. O'Brien | 5.5 | 0 | 5.5 | 363rd |
| Capt. Leroy A. Ruder | 5.5 | 0 | 5.5 | 364th |
| Lt. Robert C. Smith | 2.5 | 3 | 5.5 | 364th |
| Capt. Robert P. Winks | 5.5 | 0 | 5.5 | 364th |
| Lt. Raymond M. Bank | 5 | 0 | 5 | 364th |
| Lt. Myron A. Becraft | 1 | 4 | 5 | 362nd |
| Lt. Byron K. Braley | 3 | 2 | 5 | 364th |
| Capt. Thomas L. Harris | 5 | 0 | 5 | 364th |
| Maj. Edwin W. Hiro | 5 | 0 | 5 | 363rd |
| Capt. Chester K. Maxwell | 5 | 0 | 5 | 364th |
| Lt. William C. Reese | 5 | 0 | 5 | 364th |
| Capt. Jack R. Warren | 5 | 0 | 5 | 364th |
| LtCol. John D. Landers | 14.5 | 20 | 34.5** | HdQts |

* - includes 5 victories with the 8th Ftr Grp, PTO
** - includes 6 air victories with the 49th Ftr Grp, PTO, and 7.5 air and 19 ground victories with the 55th and 78th Ftr Grps, ETO

### 357th Fighter Group Scorers

**HdQts**

| | Air | Grd | |
|---|---|---|---|
| I.H. Dregne | 5-0-3 | 5.5-3 | |
| H.I. Egenes | 2-0-1 | 0-0 | plus 362nd Ftr Sqn |
| A.J. Evans, Jr. | 6-0-0 | 2-4 | |
| R.W. Foy | 7-0-1 | 2-2 | plus 363rd Ftr Sqn |
| D.W. Graham | 1-0-2 | 0-0 | |
| J.W. Hayes, Jr. | 1-0-1 | 0-0 | |
| T.L. Hayes | 4.5-0-0 | 0-0 | plus 364th Ftr Sqn |
| J.D. Landers | 1-0-0 | 1-0 | plus 6 air w/49th Ftr Grp, PTO & 7.5-0-1 air & 19-0 grd w/55th & 78th Ftr Grps |
| H.R. Spicer | 3-0-0 | 0-0 | |

**362nd Ftr Sqn**

| | | | |
|---|---|---|---|
| F.E. Adams | 9-0-0 | 0-0 | |
| C. Anderson | 2-0-0 | 0-0 | |
| H.R. Ankeny | 1.5-0-0 | 0-1 | |
| J.B. Badger | 0-0-1 | 0-0 | |
| M.F. Baker | 1-0-0 | 0-0 | |
| H.E. Beal, Jr. | 2-0-2 | 0.5-0 | |
| R.H. Becker | 7-0-0 | 0-0 | |
| M.A. Becraft | 1-0-1 | 4-0 | |
| G.A. Behling | 1-0-0 | 0-0 | |
| J.L. Blanchard | 1-0-0 | 0-0 | |
| R.H. Bradner | 0-0-0.5 | 0-0 | |
| J.E. Broadhead | 8-0-2 | 0-0 | |
| R.D. Brown | 2-0-1 | 0-0 | |
| L.K. Carson | 18.5-0-3 | 3.5-0.5 | |
| H.D. Chandler | 0-0-0 | 0-1 | |
| D.W. Cheever | 1-0-0 | 1-0 | |
| F.J. Connaghan | 1-0-0 | 0-0 | |
| J.S. Coon | 0.5-0-1 | 0-0 | |
| E.C. Danner | 0-0-0 | 2-0 | |
| H.H. Delager | 2-0-0 | 0-0 | |
| F.A. Dellorto | 0-0-0.5 | 0-0 | |
| J.F. Duncan | 4-0-1 | 6-1 | |
| J.W. Dunn | 0-0-0 | 2-3 | |
| H.B. Egeland | 1-0-0 | 0-0 | |
| H.I. Egenes | 0-0-1 | 0-0 | plus HdQts |
| J.B. England | 17.5-0-1 | 1-0 | |
| J.R. Frey | 2-0-0 | 0-0 | |
| S.G. Fuller | 0.5-0-0 | 0-0 | |
| J.A. Gasser | 1-0-0 | 0-0 | |
| T.L. Gates | 2-0-1 | 0-0 | |
| W.T. Gilbert | 4-0-0 | 0.5-1.5 | |
| E.A. Gordon | 0-0-0 | 2-0 | |
| W.W. Gruber | 1-0-1 | 0-0 | |
| K.E. Hagan | 1-0-1 | 0-0 | |
| O.E. Harris | 1-0-1 | 0-0 | |
| N.M. Hewitt | 0-0-0 | 2-0 | |
| H.L. Hill | 1-0-0 | 0-0 | |
| P.E. Holmberg | 1-0-0 | 0-0 | |
| A.O. Hood | 0.5-0-0 | 0-0 | |
| E.D. Hyman | 2-0-0 | 0-0 | |
| O.D. Jenkins | 8.5-0-0 | 2-0 | |
| M.R. Kehrer | 1-0-0 | 0-0 | |
| J.W. Kenney | 1-0-1 | 0-0 | |
| J.A. Kirla | 11.5-0-0 | 0.5-0 | |
| A.M. Lingo | 1.5-0-0 | 0-0 | |
| H.F. Mace | 2-0-0 | 0-0 | |
| T.W. Martinek | 3.5-1-0 | 0-0.5 | |
| L.W. Mitchell | 1-0-0 | 0-0 | |
| W.H. Mooney | 0-0-1 | 0-0 | |
| A.C. Murphy | 4-0-0 | 2-0 | plus 364th Ftr Sqn |
| T.E. Norris | 2.5-0-2 | 0-0 | |
| G.M. O'Brien | 7-0-2.5 | 0-0 | |
| P.A. Pelon, Jr. | 2-0-0 | 0-0 | |
| D.T. Perron | 3-0-0 | 0-0 | |
| W.N. Perry, Jr. | 2.5-0-1 | 0-0 | |
| J.F. Pugh | 6-0-0 | 0-0 | |
| A.F. Pyeatt, III | 2-0-0 | 0-0 | |
| D.R. Rice | 1-0-0 | 0-0 | |
| O.T. Ridley | 0.5-0-0 | 0-0 | |
| A.J. Roberson | 6-1-0 | 1-0 | |
| G.A. Robinson | 0-0-0 | 4-2 | |
| J.E. Roughgarden | 0-0-3 | 0-0 | |
| R.L. Schlieker | 1-0-0 | 0-0 | |
| J.H. Sehl | 1-0-0 | 0.5-0 | |
| A.E. Smith | 2-1-2.5 | 2.5-2 | |
| F.C. Smith | 3-0-0 | 0-0 | |
| R.M. Starkey | 1-0-0 | 1-2 | |
| J.L. Sublett | 8-0-1 | 1-0 | |
| E.A. Taylor | 1-0-0 | 0-0 | |
| J.S. Templin | 2-0-0 | 0-0 | |
| D.W. Vogel | 1-0-0 | 0-0 | |
| R.D. Wallen | 1-0-0 | 1-0 | |
| C.E. Weaver | 8-1-1 | 3-2 | |
| C.L. Williams | 3.5-1-2 | 1-0 | |
| H.A. Wyatt | 1-0-0 | 0-0 | |
| E.H. Duke-Woolley | 0-0-0 | 0-0.5 | RAF pilot |

**363rd Ftr Sqn**

| | | | |
|---|---|---|---|
| C.E. Anderson, Jr. | 16.25-2-2 | 1-0 | |
| D.H. Bochkay | 13.83-0-1 | 0-0 | |
| P.N. Bowles | 1-0-0 | 0-0 | |
| A.R. Boyle | 1-0-0 | 0-0 | |
| J.W. Browning | 7-2-1 | 0-0 | |
| J.W. Cannon | 0-0-1 | 0-0 | |
| G.I. Carlisle | 1-0-0 | 0-0 | |
| J.L. Carter | 4-0-2 | 0-0 | |
| J.T. Crump | 1-1-0 | 0-0 | |
| W.J. Currie | 0-0-1 | 0-0 | |
| P.K. DeVries | 2-0-0 | 0-0 | |
| W.R. Dunlop | 4-0-0 | 0-1 | |
| W.S. Fennell | 2-0-0 | 0-0 | |
| R.S. Fifield | 2.5-0-0 | 0-0 | |
| R.W. Foy | 8-0-1 | 1-3 | plus HdQts |
| F.L. Gailer, Jr. | 5.5-0-0 | 1-0 | |
| R.C. Gangwish | 0-1-0 | 0-0 | |
| H.O. Hand | 2.5-0-1 | 0-0 | |
| H.S. Hinman | 0-0-1 | 0-0 | |
| E.W. Hiro | 5-2-2 | 0-0 | |
| T.E. Hughes | 1.5-0-2 | 0-0 | |

| | | | |
|---|---|---|---|
| C.L. Jones | 1-0-1 | 0-0 | |
| R.R. Kalessa | 0-0-0 | 1-1 | |
| H.R. Kayser | 1.25-0-0 | 0-0 | |
| H.M. Kenney | 1-0-1 | 0-0 | |
| F.A. Kyle | 0-0-1 | 0-0 | |
| K. Landis | 1-0-0 | 0-0 | |
| A.G. Manthos | 0-0-2 | 0-0 | |
| D.C. McGee | 1-0-0 | 2-2 | plus 5 air w/8th Ftr Grp, PTO |
| W.R. McGinley | 0-1-0 | 0-0 | |
| W.D. Michaely | 1-0-0 | 0-0 | |
| R.N. Moore | 3-0-1 | 0-0 | |
| W.R. O'Brien | 5.5-2-1 | 0-0 | |
| C.W. Ofsthun | 1-0-0 | 0-0 | |
| W.B. Overstreet | 2.25-0-3 | 2-2 | |
| R.E. Pagels | 1-0-0 | 0-0 | |
| D.J. Pasaka | 2-0-0 | 0-0 | |
| H.T. Pascoe | 1-0-0 | 0-0 | |
| C.K. Peters | 3.33-0-1 | 0-0 | |
| J.F. Pierce | 7-0-1 | 0-0 | |
| F.W. Reust | 0-0-1 | 0-0 | |
| G.J. Rice | 2-0-0 | 0-0 | |
| W.P. Roberts | 1-0-0 | 0-0 | |
| E.A. Rogers | 2.33-0-0 | 0-0 | |
| R.C. Roper | 4-0-0 | 0-0 | |
| D.H. Ross | 1-0-0 | 0-0 | plus 1-0-0 air w/4th Ftr Grp |
| E.K. Simpson | 4.25-0-0 | 0-0 | |
| S. Sitzer | 1-0-0 | 0-0 | |
| J.R. Sloan | 3-0-0 | 0-0 | |
| R.W. Staudte | 0.5-0-0 | 0-0 | |
| J.R. Stern | 4-0-0 | 0-1 | |
| J.E. Taylor | 1-0-0 | 0-0 | |
| R.L. Thorkelson | 1-0-0 | 0-0 | |
| M.H. Throop, Jr. | 3-0-1 | 0-0 | |
| J.T. Windham | 1.5-0-1 | 0-1 | |
| R.E. Wolf | 2-0-1 | 0-0 | |
| L.D. Wood | 1-0-0 | 0-0 | |
| C.E. Yeager | 11.5-0-3 | 0-0 | |
| G.A. Zarnke | 0.5-0-1 | 0-0 | |

**364th Ftr Sqn**

| | | | |
|---|---|---|---|
| T.H. Adams | 4.5-0-0 | 1-0 | |
| M.F. Allen | 2-0-1 | 0-0 | |
| H.E. Arrendale | 0-0-0 | 0-1 | |
| R.M. Bank | 5-0-0 | 0-1 | |
| B.K. Braley | 3-0-0 | 2-1 | |
| K.M. Brown | 0.5-0-0 | 0-0 | |
| J.B. Carder | 7-0-1 | 0-1 | |
| M.F. Cedoz | 0-0-0 | 0-2 | |
| J.E. Colburn | 1-0-0 | 0-0 | |
| C.D. Conklin | 2-0-0 | 1.5-0 | |
| G.V. Davis | 7.5-0-0 | 0-0 | |
| C.H. Dooley | 0.5-0-0 | 1.5-0 | |
| P.D. Fairweather | 1.5-0-0 | 0-0 | |
| L.A. Fecher | 0.5-0-0 | 0-0 | |
| D.L. Finley | 1-0-1 | 0-0 | |
| N.J. Frederick | 3-0-0 | 0.5-0 | |
| E.R. Fry | 0-0-0 | 2-0 | |
| M.E. Gallant | 1-0-0 | 0-0 | |
| T.L. Harris | 5-1-0 | 0-0 | |
| P.R. Hatala | 5.5-0-0 | 0-0 | |
| E.R. Haydon | 0.5-0-0 | 1-0 | |
| T.L. Hayes, Jr. | 4-1-0 | 0-0 | plus HdQts |
| H.H. Hermanson | 1-0-1 | 0-0 | |
| H.P. Howell | 2-0-0 | 0-0 | |
| J.C. Howell | 2.5-0-1 | 0-0 | |
| O. Howes | 1-0-0 | 2-0 | |
| G.A. Hubbard | 0-0-1 | 0-0 | |
| J. Jacobs | 3-0-0 | 0-0 | |
| E.W. Johnson | 1-0-0 | 0-0 | |
| E.J. Juszczyk | 1-0-0 | 0-0 | |
| D.E. Karger | 7.5-0-0 | 4-4 | |
| D.C. Kocher | 0-0-1 | 0-0 | |
| R.W. Lepore | 0-0-0 | 2-4 | |
| C.K. Maxwell | 5-0-0 | 0-0 | |
| F.C. McCall | 3-0-0 | 1-0 | |
| I.L. McGuire | 3.5-0-1 | 0-0 | |
| B.W. McIntyre | 2-0-0 | 0-1 | |
| T.M. McKinney | 3.5-0-0 | 0-0 | |
| J.P. McMullen | 1-0-0 | 0-0 | |
| J.L. Medeiros | 2-0-0 | 0-0 | |
| H. Moebius | 3-0-0 | 0-0 | |
| R.W. Moore | 0-0-0 | 1-0 | |
| H.J. Moorhouse | 1-0-0 | 0-0 | |
| G.W. Morris | 1-0-0 | 0-0 | |
| A.C. Murphy | 2-0-0 | 0-0 | plus 362nd Ftr Sqn |
| H.R. Nowlin | 2.5-0-2 | 1.5-0 | |
| R.A. Peterson | 15.5-1-2 | 3.5-0 | |
| M.A. Postle | 1.5-0-0 | 0-0 | |
| H.E. Redd | 0-0-1 | 0-0 | |
| W.C. Reese | 5-0-0 | 0-0 | |
| L.A. Ruder | 5.5-0-0 | 0-0 | |
| J.J. Salsman | 2-0-1 | 0-0 | |
| D.A. Sandborn | 1-0-0 | 0-0 | |
| R.G. Schimanski | 6-0-1 | 2-0 | |
| C.F. Schneider | 1-0-2 | 0-0 | |
| B.K. Seitzinger | 1-0-1 | 0-0 | |
| R.M. Shaw | 8-1-3 | 0-0 | |
| Ric C. Smith | 3-0-0 | 0-2 | |
| Rob C. Smith | 2.5-1-1 | 3-0 | |
| R.L. Smith | 2-0-0 | 0-0 | |
| I.E. Snedeker | 1.5-0-0 | 0-0 | |
| M.A. Stanley | 5-0-0 | 1.5-0 | |
| J.A. Steiger | 2-0-0 | 1-0 | |
| M.H. Stepelton | 3.5-0-0 | 1-0 | |
| J.A. Storch | 10.5-0-1 | 1.5-2 | |
| J.G. Sullivan | 1.5-0-1 | 0-0 | |
| C.D. Sumner | 4.5-0-1 | 0-0 | |
| G.E. Tyler | 7-0-0 | 0-0 | |
| J.R. Warren | 5-0-0 | 0-0 | |
| S. Wasylyk | 1-0-0 | 1-0 | |
| G.L. Weber | 1.5-0-1 | 0-0 | |
| H. Wesling | 0-0-0 | 0-1 | |
| L.A. Westphal | 1-0-0 | 0-0 | |
| D.R. Williams | 1-0-0 | 2-9 | |
| R.P. Winks | 5.5-0-0 | 0-0 | |
| R.R. Wright 2-0-1 | 0-0 | | |
| L.F. Zacharie | 0-0-0 | 0-2 | |
| H.R. Zetterquist | 1-0-0 | 0-0 | |
| V.V. Zettler, Jr. | 1-0-1 | 7-0 | |

**357th Fighter Group Scoring**

**January 24, 1944**

| | | | |
|---|---|---|---|
| 363rd: | Capt. J.H. Giltner | FW-190 dest(air) | Brussels |
| | | (scored while TDY w/354th Ftr Grp, 9th Air Force) | |

**February 5, 1944**

| | | | |
|---|---|---|---|
| HdQts: | Maj. D.W. Graham | FW-190 dam(air) | Romilly-Sur-Seine |

**February 20, 1944**

| | | | |
|---|---|---|---|
| 362nd: | Lt. C.L. Williams | Me-109 dest(air) | Leipzig |
| 363rd: | Lt. D.H. Ross | Me-109 dest(air) | Duben |
| | Capt. C.E. Anderson | Me-109 dam(air) | N/Dessau |

**February 21, 1944**

| | | | |
|---|---|---|---|
| 363rd: | Lt. A.R. Boyle | Me-109 dest(air) | E/Zwolle |
| | Capt. W.R. O'Brien | Me-109 prob(air) | Bussum |

**February 22, 1944**

| | | | |
|---|---|---|---|
| HdQts: | Col. H.R. Spicer | Me-109 dest(air) | Bernburg |
| 362nd: | Lt. F.E. Adams | Me-109 dest(air) | NW Bernburg |
| | Lt. A.F. Pyeatt | Me-109 dest(air) | NW Bernburg |
| | LtCol. H.I. Egenes | FW-190 dam(air) | E/Magdeburg |
| 363rd: | Lt. E.A. Rogers | Me-109 dest(air) | NW Schoningen |
| | Lt. E.W. Hiro | Me-109 dam(air) | Leopolds Hall |
| 364th: | Capt. J.L. Medeiros | Me-109 dest(air) | Bernburg |
| | Capt. J.R. Warren | Me-109 dest(air) | Bernburg |
| | Lt. J.B. Carder | Me-109 dest(air) | Bernburg |
| | | FW-190 dam(air) | The Hague |

**February 24, 1944**

| | | | |
|---|---|---|---|
| HdQts: | Col. H.R. Spicer | Me-110 dest(air) | Erfurt |
| | | Ju-88 dest(air) | Erfurt |
| 362nd: | Lt. D.R. Rice | FW-190 dest(air) | E/Linz |
| 363rd: | Lt. W.D. Michaely | FW-190 dest(air) | Gotha |
| 364th: | Capt. J.L. Medeiros | FW-190 dest(air) | Gotha |
| | Lt. Rich. C. Smith | Me-109 dest(air) | NW Gotha |
| | Maj. T.L. Hayes | Me-109 prob(air) | NW Gotha |

**February 25, 1944**

| | | | |
|---|---|---|---|
| 362nd: | Lt. R.H. Becker | (1.5)Me-110 dest(air) | Regensburg |
| | Capt. J.E. Broadhead | Me-109 dest(air) | Regensburg |
| | Lt. R.D. Brown | FW-190 dest(air) | Regensburg |
| | Lt. M.R. Kehrer | Ju-88 dest(air) | W/Schweinfurt |
| | Lt. A.F. Pyeatt | FW-190 dest(air) | Regensburg |
| | Capt. A.M. Lingo | (.5)Me-110 dest(air) | Regensburg |

**March 2, 1944**

| | | | |
|---|---|---|---|
| 364th: | Maj. T.L. Hayes | Me-109 dest(air) | N/Frankfurt |
| | Lt. J.B. Carder | Me-109 dest(air) | N/Frankfurt |

**March 4, 1944**

| | | | |
|---|---|---|---|
| 362nd: | Lt. R.D. Wallen | Me-109 dest(air) | Berlin |
| 363rd: | F/O C.E. Yeager | Me-109 dest(air) | SE Kassel |
| | | He-111 dam(air) | Wittenburg |

**March 5, 1944**

| | | | |
|---|---|---|---|
| HdQts: | Capt. I.H. Dregne | FW-190 dam(air) | SE Bordeaux |
| 362nd: | Lt. G.M. O'Brien | FW-190 dest(air) | Bordeaux |
| | | (.5)FW-190 dam(air) | Bordeaux |

| | | | |
|---|---|---|---|
| | Lt. A.E. Smith | (.5)FW-190 dam(air) | Bordeaux |
| 363rd: | Lt. E.A. Rogers | Me-109 dest(air) | E/Bordeaux |
| | | (.33)FW-190 dest(air) | S/Bordeaux |
| | Lt. D.H. Bochkay | (.33)FW-190 dest(air) | S/Bordeaux |
| | Lt. C.K. Peters | (.33)FW-190 dest(air) | S/Bordeaux |
| | Capt. W.R. O'Brien | FW-190 prob(air) | N/Bordeaux |
| | | FW-190 dam(air) | N/Bordeaux |
| 364th: | Capt. G.V. Davis | (2)FW-200 dest(air) | Parthenay A/F |
| | Lt. M.A. Stanley | FW-200 dest(air) | Parthenay A/F |
| | Lt. R.A. Peterson | FW-190 dest(air) | Bordeaux |

**March 6, 1944**

| | | | |
|---|---|---|---|
| HdQts: | LtCol. H.I. Egenes | Me-110 dam(air) | W/Berlin |
| 362nd: | Capt. D.T. Perron | (2)FW-190 dest(air) | SW Berlin |
| | | Me-210 dest(air) | SW Berlin |
| | Capt. J.E. Broadhead | Me-110 dest(air) | E/Berlin |
| | Lt. R.M. Starkey | Me-109 dest(air) | Berlin |
| | Lt. K.E. Hagan | (.5)Me-110 dest(air)[*] | SW Berlin |
| | | (.5)Me-110 dest(air)[**] | Berlin |
| | Lt. A.J. Roberson | (.5)Me-110 dest(air)[**] | Berlin |
| | Lt. C.L. Williams | (.5)Me-110 dest(air)[*] | SW Berlin |
| | Lt. T.E. Norris | Me-109 dam(air) | NE Berlin |
| 363rd: | Lt. D.H. Bochkay | (2)Me-110 dest(air) | W/Berlin |
| | Lt. R.E. Pagels | Me-110 dest(air) | W/Berlin |
| | Lt. J.F. Pierce | Me-110 dest(air) | W/Berlin |
| | Capt. W.R. O'Brien | (.5)Me-110 dest(air)[@] | Berlin |
| | Lt. C.L. Jones | Me-410 dam(air) | W/Berlin |
| 364th: | Capt. G.V. Davis | Me-110 dest(air) | E/Berlin |
| | | (.5)FW-190 dest(air) | NW Berlin |
| | Lt. T.L. Harris | Me-110 dest(air) | E/Berlin |
| | | (.5)FW-190 dest(air) | NW Berlin |
| | Lt. L.A. Ruder | (1.5)Me-110 dest(air)[@] | W/Berlin |
| | Maj. T.L. Hayes | Me-109 dest(air) | E/Ulzen |
| | Lt. J.B. Carder | Me-109 dest(air) | E/Bremen |
| | | Me-109 dam(grd) | Berlin |
| | F/O T.M. McKinney | Me-110 dest(air) | Brandenburg |
| | Lt. M.A. Stanley | Me-110 dest(air) | Brandenburg |
| | Lt. R.C. Smith | (2)He-111 dam(grd) | Ulzen |

**March 8, 1944**

| | | | |
|---|---|---|---|
| HdQts: | LtCol. D.W. Graham | FW-190 dest(air) | Berlin |
| | | Me-109 dam(air) | Berlin |
| 362nd: | Lt. J.B. England | Me-109 dest(air) | Steinhuder Lake |
| 363rd: | Capt. C.E. Anderson | Me-109 dest(air) | NW Hanover |
| | Lt. F.W. Reust | FW-190 dam(air) | SW Berlin |
| 364th: | Maj. T.L. Hayes | Me-410 dest(air) | W/Berlin |
| | Capt. J.R. Warren | FW-190 dest(air) | SE Berlin |
| | Lt. J.B. Carder | FW-190 dest(air) | S/Berlin |
| | Capt. G.V. Davis | (.5)FW-190 dest(air) | Dummer Lake |
| | Lt. T.L. Harris | (.5)FW-190 dest(air) | Dummer Lake |
| | Lt. H.R. Nowlin | FW-190 dam(air) | Berlin |
| | Lt. R.A. Peterson | FW-190 dam(air) | Berlin |

**March 16, 1944**

| | | | |
|---|---|---|---|
| HdQts: | LtCol. H.I. Egenes | (2)Me-109 dest(air) | SW Stuttgart |
| | Maj. I.H. Dregne | Me-109 dest(air) | SW Munich |
| 362nd: | Lt. J.B. England | Me-110 dest(air) | S/Stuttgart |
| | Lt. A.J. Roberson | FW-190 prob(air) | SE Stuttgart |
| | Capt. J.E. Broadhead | Me-410 dam(air) | S/Stuttgart |
| 363rd: | Capt. M.H. Throop | Me-110 dest(air) | N/Lake Constance |
| | Lt. W.R. McGinley | Me-109 prob(air) | S/Stuttgart |
| | Lt. H.S. Hinman | Ju-88 dam(air) | Ludwigshafen |
| 364th: | Capt. J.R. Warren | (2)Me-110 dest(air) | Augsburg |
| | | FW-190 dest(air) | Augsburg |
| | Lt. W.C. Reese | Me-110 dest(air) | Augsburg |
| | | Do-217 dest(air) | Augsburg |
| | Capt. G.V. Davis | Me-109 dest(air) | Ulm |
| | | (.5)Me-110 dest(air) | Ulm |
| | Maj. T.L. Hayes | Me-110 dest(air) | SE Stuttgart |
| | Lt. R.A. Peterson | (.5)Me-110 dest(air) | Ulm |
| | Lt. G.A. Hubbard | Me-109 dam(air) | S/Stuttgart |

**March 18, 1944**

| | | | |
|---|---|---|---|
| 362nd: | Lt. F.E. Adams | Me-109 dest(air) | NW Paris |
| 364th: | Lt. R.A. Peterson | Me-109 dest(air) | Augsburg |

**March 22, 1944**

| | | | |
|---|---|---|---|
| 363rd: | Lt. C.L. Jones | Me-109 dest(air) | Munster |

**March 23, 1944**

| | | | |
|---|---|---|---|
| 364th: | Lt. R.A. Peterson | Me-109 prob(air) | E/Brunswick |

**March 28, 1944**

| | | | |
|---|---|---|---|
| 362nd: | Lt. A.E. Smith | (2.5)Ju-88 dest(grd) | S/Paris |
| | Lt. A.J. Roberson | Ju-88 dest(grd) | S/Paris |
| | Lt. R.M. Starkey | Ju-88 dest(grd) | S/Paris |
| | Lt. L.K. Carson | (.5)Ju-88 dest(grd) | S/Paris |

**March 29, 1944**

| | | | |
|---|---|---|---|
| 362nd: | Capt. J.E. Broadhead | Me-109 dest(air) | Brunswick |

**April 8, 1944**

| | | | |
|---|---|---|---|
| 362nd: | Capt. A.M. Lingo | Me-109 dest(air) | W/Brunswick |
| | Lt. H.R. Ankeny | Me-109 dest(air) | W/Brunswick |
| | Lt. J.F. Pugh | Me-109 dest(air) | S/Brunswick |
| | Lt. L.K. Carson | (.5)Me-109 dest(air) | SW Brunswick |
| | Lt. J.S. Coon | (.5)Me-109 dest(air) | SW Brunswick |
| 363rd: | Lt. D.H. Bochkay | Me-109 dest(air) | NW Braunschweig |

**April 11, 1944**

| | | | |
|---|---|---|---|
| 362nd: | Lt. F.E. Adams | (2)Me-109 dest(air) | N/Magdeburg |
| | Lt. G.M. O'Brien | Me-109 dest(air) | Magdeburg |
| | | (2)Me-109 dam(air) | Magdeburg |
| | Lt. J.F. Pugh | Me-109 dest(air) | Magdeburg |
| | Lt. A.J. Roberson | Me-109 dest(air) | E/Magdeburg |
| | Lt. H.R. Ankeny | (.5)Me-109 dest(air) | NE Magdeburg |
| | Lt. J.B. England | (.5)Me-109 dest(air) | NE Magdeburg |
| | Capt. C.L. Williams | FW-190 dam(air) | N/Magdeburg |
| | Lt. J.E. Roughgarden | FW-190 dam(air) | NE Magdeburg |
| 363rd: | Capt. C.E. Anderson | Me-109 dest(air) | W/Hanover |
| | | (.25)He-111 dest(air) | W/Hanover |
| | | Me-109 dam(air) | W/Hanover |
| | Lt. H.R. Kayser | Me-109 dest(air) | W/Hanover |
| | | (.25)He-111 dest(air) | W/Hanover |
| | Lt. E.K. Simpson | Me-109 dest(air) | W/Hanover |
| | | (.25)He-111 dest(air) | W/Hanover |
| | Capt. P.K. DeVries | Me-109 dest(air) | W/Magdeburg |
| | Capt. M.H. Throop | FW-190 dest(air) | N/Hanover |
| | Lt. H.M. Kenney | FW-190 dest(air) | Steinhuder Lake |
| | | FW-190 dam(air) | Steinhuder Lake |
| | Lt. C.K. Peters | Me-109 dest(air) | Magdeburg |
| | Lt. W.B. Overstreet | (.25)He-111 dest(air) | W/Hanover |
| | | (3)Me-109 dam(air) | W/Hanover |
| | Lt. D.H. Bochkay | (.5)Me-109 dest(air)[*] | Magdeburg |
| 364th: | Lt. J.B. Carder | Me-109 dest(air) | NE Leipzig |
| | Lt. H.R. Nowlin | Me-109 dest(air) | Hanover |
| | Lt. R.A. Peterson | Me-109 dest(air) | Magdeburg |
| | Lt. W.C. Reese | Me-109 dest(air) | E/Hanover |
| | Lt. R.M. Shaw | Me-109 dest(air) | NE Brunswick |
| | Lt. Rob C. Smith | Me-109 dest(air) | NE Magdeburg |
| | Lt. L.A. Ruder | FW-190 dest(air) | NE Magdeburg |
| | Lt. M.A. Postle | (.5)Me-109 dest(air)[*] | Magdeburg |
| | Lt. M.H. Stepelton | (.5)FW-190 dest(air) | Leipzig |
| | Lt. C.D. Sumner | (.5)FW-190 dest(air) | Leipzig |
| | Lt. H.H. Hermanson | Me-109 dam(air) | NW Hanover |

**April 13, 1944**

| | | | |
|---|---|---|---|
| 362nd: | Lt. R.H. Becker | FW-190 dest(air) | S/Mannheim |
| | Lt. L.K. Carson | FW-190 dest(air) | NW Mannheim |
| | Lt. J.B. England | FW-190 dest(air) | W/Mannheim |
| 364th: | Capt. G.V. Davis | Me-109 dest(air) | Frankfurt |
| | Lt. M.A. Postle | Me-109 dest(air) | Luxembourg |
| | Lt. R.M. Shaw | Me-109 dest(air) | Frankfurt |
| | Lt. P.D. Fairweather | (.5)Me-109 dest(air) | Donauworth |
| | Lt. Rob C. Smith | (.5)Me-109 dest(air) | Donauworth |
| | | Me-109 prob(air) | Frankfurt |

**April 19, 1944**

| | | | |
|---|---|---|---|
| HdQts: | Maj. T.L. Hayes | Me-109 dest(air) | S/Kassel |
| 364th: | Capt. G.V. Davis | FW-190 dest(air) | S/Bliecherode |
| | Lt. J.B. Carder | Me-109 dest(air) | SE Kassel |
| | Lt. T.L. Harris | FW-190 dest(air) | S/Bliecherode |
| | Lt. M.A. Stanley | FW-190 dest(air) | S/Bliecherode |

**April 22, 1944**

| | | | |
|---|---|---|---|
| 362nd: | Capt. J.E. Broadhead | FW-190 dest(air) | N/Dummer Lake |
| | | FW-190 dam(air) | N/Dummer Lake |
| | Lt. G.M. O'Brien | FW-190 dest(air) | N/Dummer Lake |

**April 24, 1944**

| | | | |
|---|---|---|---|
| 362nd: | Lt. F.E. Adams | (3)Me-110 dest(air) | Munich |
| | Lt. J.B. England | (3)Me-110 dest(air) | S/Munich |
| | Lt. H.E. Beal | (2)Me-110 dest(air) | E/Munich |
| | | Me-110 dam(air) | E/Munich |
| | Capt. F.C. Smith | Me-109 dest(air) | S/Munich |
| | Capt. C.L. Williams | Me-109 dest(air) | NW Munich |
| | Lt. F.E. Connaghan | Me-110 dest(air) | Munich |
| | Lt. A.E. Smith | Me-110 prob(air) | Munich |
| | | Me-110 dam(air) | Munich |
| | Lt. J.E. Roughgarden | (2)Me-110 dam(air) | E/Munich |
| | Lt. J.S. Coon | Me-110 dam(air) | E/Munich |
| | Lt. O.E. Harris | Me-110 dam(air) | E/Munich |
| 363rd: | Lt. J.F. Pierce | Me-109 dest(air) | W/Munich |
| | | Ju-88 dest(air) | W/Munich |
| | Capt. E.W. Hiro | Me-109 dest(air) | SE Munich |
| | Capt. M.H. Throop | Me-109 dest(air) | N/Munich |
| | Lt. D.H. Bochkay | Me-109 dest(air) | NE Munich |
| | Lt. J.W. Browning | Me-109 dest(air) | N/Augsburg |
| 364th: | Lt. J.B. Carder | Me-109 dest(air) | S/Munich |
| | Lt. T.M. McKinney | Me-109 dest(air) | N/Augsburg |
| | Lt. R.A. Peterson | Me-109 dest(air) | Munich |

| | | | |
|---|---|---|---|
| | Lt. W.C. Reese | Me-109 dest(air) | Munich |
| | Lt. C.D. Sumner | Me-109 dest(air) | Munich |
| | Lt. R.M. Shaw | Me-109 prob(air) | SE Munich |

| **April 29, 1944** | | | |
|---|---|---|---|
| 363rd: | Lt. J.F. Pierce | Me-109 dam(air) | Berlin |

| **April 30, 1944** | | | |
|---|---|---|---|
| 362nd: | Capt. J.E. Broadhead | Me-109 dest(air) | S/Paris |
| | Lt. R.H. Becker | Me-109 dest(air) | S/Paris |
| | Lt. R.D. Brown | Me-109 dest(air) | S/Paris |
| | Lt. G.M. O'Brien | (.5)Me-109 dest(air) | S/Paris |
| 363rd: | Lt. J.F. Pierce | (2)FW-190 dest(air) | NE Orleans |
| | Capt. C.E. Anderson | FW-190 dest(air) | SE Orleans |
| 364th: | Lt. R.A. Peterson | (2)FW-190 dest(air) | Auxerre |
| | Lt. T.M. McKinney | (.5)Me-109 dest(air) | S/Paris |

| **May 8, 1944** | | | |
|---|---|---|---|
| HdQts: | Maj. I.H. Dregne | FW-190 dam(air) | N/Hanover |
| 363rd: | Capt. C.E. Anderson | FW-190 dest(air) | Soltau |
| | Lt. J.F. Pierce | FW-190 dest(air) | Soltau |
| 364th: | Lt. Rob. C. Smith | FW-190 dam(air) | S/Hanover |

| **May 9, 1944** | | | |
|---|---|---|---|
| 363rd: | Lt. L.D. Wood | FW-190 dest(air) | Herenthals |

| **May 12, 1944** | | | |
|---|---|---|---|
| HdQts: | Maj. I.H. Dregne | Me-109 dest(air) | NE Frankfurt |
| 362nd: | Lt. T.E. Norris | (1.5)Me-109 dest(air) | SE Frankfurt |
| | Capt. M.F. Baker | Me-109 dest(air) | N/Wurzburg |
| | Lt. A.O. Hood | (.5)Me-109 dest(air) | SE Frankfurt |
| 363rd: | Capt. C.E. Anderson | Me-109 dest(air) | NE Frankfurt |
| | | Me-109 dest(grd) | NE Frankfurt |
| | Capt. P.K. DeVries | FW-190 dest(air) | NE Frankfurt |
| | Capt. W.R. O'Brien | Me-109 dest(air) | N/Frankfurt |
| | Lt. J.F. Pierce | Me-109 dest(air) | NE Frankfurt |
| | Maj. M.H. Throop | FW-190 dam(air) | NE Frankfurt |
| | Lt. W.B. Overstreet | Ju-52 dest(grd) | NE Frankfurt |
| 364th: | Lt. T.M. McKinney | Me-109 dest(air) | NE Frankfurt |
| | Lt. W.C. Reese | Me-109 dest(air) | N/Schweinfurt |
| | Lt. Ric. C. Smith | FW-190 dest(air) | N/Frankfurt |
| | Lt. Rob. C. Smith | FW-190 dest(air) | N/Frankfurt |
| | Lt. C.D. Sumner | Me-109 dest(air) | NE Frankfurt |
| | Capt. R.A. Peterson | (.5)FW-190 dest(air) | NE Frankfurt |
| | | FW-190 dam(air) | NE Frankfurt |
| | Capt. J.A. Storch | (.5)FW-190 dest(air) | NE Frankfurt |

| **May 13, 1944** | | | |
|---|---|---|---|
| 363rd: | Lt. R.N. Moore | Me-109 dest(air) | W/Hamburg |
| | | Me-109 dam(air) | W/Hamburg |
| 364th: | Capt. R.A. Peterson | (1.5)Me-410 dest(air)[*] | E/Grunberg |
| | Lt. J.G. Sullivan | FW-44 dest(air) | E/Grunberg |
| | | (.5)Me-410 dest(air)[*] | E/Grunberg |
| | | Me-410 dam(air) | E/Grunberg |
| | Lt. C.H. Dooley | (.5)Me-410 dest(air)[**] | E/Grunberg |
| | Lt. R.M. Shaw | (.5)Me-410 dest(air)[**] | E/Grunberg |

| **May 19, 1944** | | | |
|---|---|---|---|
| HdQts: | Maj. I.H. Dregne | Me-109 dest(air) | Wittenburg |
| 362nd: | Capt. F.E. Adams | (.5)Me-109 dest(air) | Hagenow |
| | Lt. A.J. Roberson | (.5)Me-109 dest(air) | Hagenow |
| 363rd: | Lt. R.W. Foy | (3)Me-109 dest(air) | NW Brandenburg |
| | Capt. E.W. Hiro | (2)Me-109 dest(air) | NW Brandenburg |
| | | Me-109 dam(air) | NW Brandenburg |
| | Lt. C.K. Peters | Me-109 dest(air) | NW Brandenburg |
| | | Me-109 dam(air) | NW Brandenburg |
| 364th: | Capt. J.A. Storch | Me-109 dest(air) | NE Salzwedel |
| | Lt. L.A. Ruder | FW-190 dest(air) | N/Berlin |

| **May 21, 1944** | | | |
|---|---|---|---|
| HdQts: | Maj. I.H. Dregne | (1.5)Me-109 dest(grd)[*] | S/Eichhof |
| 362nd: | Lt. R.M. Starkey | Me-110 dam(grd) | Tarnewitz |
| | | Ju-52 dam(grd) | Tarnewitz |
| | Lt. H.R. Ankeny | Me-110 dam(grd) | Tarnewitz |
| 364th: | Lt. Ric. C. Smith | (3)Me-109 dest(grd) | S/Eichhof |
| | Capt. J.A. Storch | Me-109 dest(grd) | S/Eichhof |
| | | (.5)FW-44 dest(grd) | S/Eichhof |
| | Lt. C.H. Dooley | Me-109 dest(grd) | S/Eichhof |
| | | (.5)FW-44 dest(grd) | S/Eichhof |
| | Lt. C.D. Conklin | (1.5)Me-109 dest(grd)[**] | S/Eichhof |
| | Lt. H.R. Nowlin | (1.5)Me-109 dest(grd)[**] | S/Eichhof |
| | Lt. M.A. Stanley | (1.5)Me-109 dest(grd)[*] | S/Eichhof |
| | Lt. M.H. Stepelton | Me-109 dest(grd) | S/Eichhof |

| **May 24, 1944** | | | |
|---|---|---|---|
| 363rd: | Capt. W.R. O'Brien | Me-109 dest(air) | E/Berlin |
| | Capt. E.W. Hiro | FW-190 prob(air) | SE Berlin |
| 364th: | Capt. R.A. Peterson | (.5)u/i a/c dest(grd) | St. Lagar |
| | Lt. N.J. Frederick | (.5)u/i a/c dest(grd) | St. Lagar |

| **May 27, 1944** | | | |
|---|---|---|---|
| 362nd: | Capt. F.E. Adams | FW-190 dest(air) | N/Starsbourg |
| | Capt. J.B. England | Me-109 dest(air) | N/Strasbourg |
| | Lt. H.L. Hill | Me-109 dest(air) | N/Strasbourg |
| | Lt. G.M. O'Brien | FW-190 dest(air) | N/Strasbourg |
| | Lt. J.F. Pugh | FW-190 dest(air) | N/Strasbourg |
| | Lt. A.E. Smith | Me-109 dest(air) | N/Strasbourg |
| | Capt. R.D. Brown | Me-109 dam(air) | Strasbourg |
| | Capt. C.L. Williams | FW-190 dam(air) | N/Strasbourg |
| | Lt. J.B. Badger | Me-109 dam(air) | N/Strasbourg |
| 363rd: | Capt. C.E. Anderson | (2)Me-109 dest(air) | N/Strasbourg |
| | Capt. J.W. Browning | Me-109 dest(air) | Strasbourg |
| | Capt. W.R. O'Brien | Me-109 dest(air) | Strasbourg |
| | Lt. E.K. Simpson | Me-109 dest(air) | Strasbourg |
| | Lt. R.C. Gangwish | Me-109 prob(air) | SE Baden Baden |
| 364th: | Maj. J.A. Storch | (2)Me-109 dest(air) | Strasbourg |
| | | (.5)FW-190 dest(air) | S/Strasbourg |
| | | (shared with a 352nd Ftr Grp P-51) | |
| | Capt. T.L. Harris | (2)Me-109 dest(air) | Colmar |
| | | Me-109 prob(air) | Colmar |
| | Lt. C.D. Conklin | (2)Me-109 dest(air) | Mulhausen |
| | Lt. M.A. Stanley | (2)FW-190 dest(air) | Strasbourg |
| | Lt. P.D. Fairweather | Me-109 dest(air) | Strasbourg |
| | Lt. L.A. Ruder | Me-109 dest(air) | Strasbourg |
| | Lt. R.M. Shaw | Me-109 dest(air) | SW Strasbourg |
| | | Me-109 dam(air) | SW Strasbourg |
| | Lt. M.H. Stepelton | Me-109 dest(air) | Strasbourg |

| **May 28, 1944** | | | |
|---|---|---|---|
| HdQts: | Maj. T.L. Hayes | Me-109 dest(air) | NW Magdeburg |
| 362nd: | Maj. J.E. Broadhead | FW-190 dest(air) | NW Magdeburg |
| | Lt. L.K. Carson | FW-190 dest(air) | N/Magdeburg |
| | Capt. K.E. Hagan | Me-410 dam(air) | N/Magdeburg |
| 363rd: | Lt. C.K. Peters | Me-109 dest(air) | N/Magdeburg |
| | Capt. E.W. Hiro | Me-109 prob(air) | N/Magdeburg |
| 364th: | Capt. R.A. Peterson | Me-109 dest(air) | NW Magdeburg |
| | Lt. J.C. Howell | Me-109 dest(air) | NW Magdeburg |
| | Lt. L.A. Ruder | Me-109 dest(air) | NW Magdeburg |

| **May 30, 1944** | | | |
|---|---|---|---|
| 362nd: | Capt. R.H. Becker | (3)Me-109 dest(air) | Bernburg |
| | Lt. A.J. Roberson | (2)Me-109 dest(air) | NE Bernburg |
| | Lt. L.K. Carson | Me-410 dest(air) | W/Bernburg |
| | Lt. O.E. Harris | Me-410 dest(air) | E/Bernburg |
| | Lt. L.W. Mitchell | Me-109 dest(air) | W/Bernburg |
| | Lt. G.M. O'Brien | Me-109 dest(air) | Celle |
| | | (.5)Me-410 dest(air) | W/Bernburg |
| | Capt. F.E. Adams | (.5)Me-410 dest(air) | W/Bernburg |
| | Lt. D.W. Vogel | FW-190 dest(air) | Magdeburg |
| | Lt. T.E. Norris | Me-109 dam(air) | N/Celle |
| | Lt. R.D. Wallen | FW-190 dest(grd) | W/Bernburg |
| 363rd: | Capt. W.R. O'Brien | (2)Me-109 dest(air) | NE Schonebeck |
| | Capt. C.E. Anderson | Me-109 dest(air) | E/Schonebeck |
| | Capt. J.W. Browning | Me-109 dest(air) | NE Schonebeck |
| | Lt. R.N. Moore | Me-109 dest(air) | NE Schonebeck |
| 364th: | Lt. J.C. Howell | (.5)Me-410 dest(air) | NW Bernburg |
| | Lt. R.M. Shaw | (.5)Me-410 dest(air) | NW Bernburg |

| **June 14, 1944** | | | |
|---|---|---|---|
| 364th: | Lt. J.E. Colburn | FW-190 dest(air) | E/Paris |
| | Lt. R.M. Shaw | FW-190 dest(air) | E/Paris |
| | | FW-190 dam(air) | E/Paris |

| **June 20, 1944** | | | |
|---|---|---|---|
| 362nd: | Lt. L.K. Carson | (.5)Me-110 dam(grd) | Neumunster |
| | Lt. T.W. Martinek | (.5)Me-110 dam(grd) | Neumunster |
| 364th: | Capt. Ric. C. Smith | Me-109 dest(air) | N/Eberswalde |
| | Lt. N.J. Frederick | Me-109 dest(air) | Pasewalk |
| | | (.5)Fi-156 dest(air) | Pasewalk |
| | Lt. J.J. Salsman | Me-109 dest(air) | Pasewalk |
| | Maj. J.A. Storch | (.5)Me-109 dest(air) | Pasewalk |
| | Lt. L.A. Fecher | (.5)Me-109 dest(air) | Pasewalk |
| | Lt. M.F. Allen | (.5)Fi-156 dest(air) | Pasewalk |
| | Lt. D.L. Finley | Me-109 dam(air) | Pasewalk |
| | Lt. H.E. Redd | Me-109 dam(air) | Pasewalk |

| **June 29, 1944** | | | |
|---|---|---|---|
| HdQts: | LtCol. T.L. Hayes | Me-109 dest(air) | W/Leipzig |
| | | (.5)Me-410 dest(air)[*] | NW Leipzig |
| 362nd: | Capt. F.C. Smith | FW-190 dest(air) | Naumberg |
| | Lt. T.E. Norris | Me-410 dest(air) | Naumberg |
| | Lt. J.F. Pugh | Me-109 dest(air) | Naumberg |
| 363rd: | Capt. C.E. Anderson | (3)FW-190 dest(air) | SW Leipzig |
| | Capt. R.W. Foy | (2)Me-109 dest(air) | SW Leipzig |
| | | FW-190 dest(air) | SW Leipzig |
| | Capt. J.W. Browning | (1.5)Me-410 dest(air)[**] | SW Leipzig |
| | | (.5)FW-190 dest(air) | SW Leipzig |
| | Capt. D.H. Bochkay | Me-109 dest(air) | Schoningen |
| | Lt. W.B. Overstreet | FW-190 dest(air) | SW Leipzig |
| | Lt. W.S. Fennell | (.5)Me-410 dest(air)[**] | SW Leipzig |

| | | | |
|---|---|---|---|
| | Lt. R.W. Staudte | (.5)FW-190 dest(air) | SW Leipzig |
| 364th: | Capt. C.D. Sumner | Me-109 dest(air) | SW Leipzig |
| | | FW-190 dest(air) | SW Leipzig |
| | Capt. J.C. Howell | Me-109 dest(air) | SW Leipzig |
| | | FW-190 dam(air) | SW Leipzig |
| | Capt. M.H. Stepelton | FW-190 dest(air) | W/Leipzig |
| | Lt. G.E. Tyler | Me-109 dest(air) | SW Leipzig |
| | Lt. M.F. Allen | (.5)Me-410 dest(air)* | NW Leipzig |
| | | FW-190 dam(air) | SW Leipzig |
| | Capt. B.W. McIntyre | He-177 dam(grd) | Leipzig |

**July 1, 1944**

| | | | |
|---|---|---|---|
| 362nd: | Capt. C.L. Williams | Me-109 dest(air) | E/St. Quentin |
| | Lt. P.E. Holmberg | Me-109 dest(air) | E/St. Quentin |
| | Lt. A.E. Smith | Me-109 dam(air) | E/St. Quentin |
| 364th: | Capt. R.A. Peterson | (2)Me-109 dest(air) | E/St. Quentin |

**July 5, 1944**

| | | | |
|---|---|---|---|
| 363rd: | Capt. D.H. Bochkay | Me-109 dest(air) | SE Rouen |
| | | FW-190 dest(air) | SE Rouen |
| 364th: | Lt. R.M. Shaw | FW-190 dest(air) | SE Rouen |
| | Lt. G.E. Tyler | FW-190 dest(air) | SE Rouen |
| | Capt. C.D. Sumner | FW-190 dam(air) | SE Rouen |

**July 6, 1944**

| | | | |
|---|---|---|---|
| 363rd: | Lt. E.K. Simpson | Ju-88 dest(air) | N/Nordernay Isle |

**July 7, 1944**

| | | | |
|---|---|---|---|
| 363rd: | Capt. C.E. Anderson | Me-109 dest(air) | N/Leipzig |
| | Lt. W.S. Fennell | Me-109 dest(air) | N/Leipzig |
| | Lt. E.K. Simpson | Me-109 dest(air) | N/Leipzig |

**July 14, 1944**

| | | | |
|---|---|---|---|
| HdQts: | LtCol. T.L. Hayes | Me-109 dest(air) | Valence |
| 364th: | Capt. M.H. Stepelton | FW-190 dest(air) | Valence |
| | Lt. D.L. Finley | Me-109 dest(air) | Valence |
| | Lt. N.J. Frederick | Me-109 dest(air) | Valence |

**July 18, 1944**

| | | | |
|---|---|---|---|
| 364th: | Lt. R.M. Shaw | Me-109 dam(air) | NW Rostock |

**July 25, 1944**

| | | | |
|---|---|---|---|
| 362nd: | Capt. L.K. Carson | FW-190 dest(air) | Paris |
| | Capt. J.F. Pugh | Me-109 dest(air) | Versailles |
| 363rd: | Capt. D.H. Bochkay | Me-109 dest(air) | Paris |
| | | Me-109 dam(air) | Paris |
| | Capt. R.W. Foy | FW-190 dest(air) | SE Paris |

**July 29, 1944**

| | | | |
|---|---|---|---|
| 362nd: | Capt. L.K. Carson | Me-109 dest(air) | W/Merseburg |
| | Lt. H.F. Mace | Me-109 dest(air) | W/Merseburg |
| | Lt. G.M. O'Brien | Me-109 dest(air) | W/Merseburg |
| | Capt. R.H. Becker | (.5)Me-109 dest(air) | W/Merseburg |
| | Lt. T.W. Martinek | (.5)Me-109 dest(air) | W/Merseburg |
| 363rd: | Capt. D.H. Bochkay | FW-190 dest(air) | SW Merseburg |
| | Lt. W.B. Overstreet | Me-109 dest(air) | W/Merseburg |
| | | FW-190 dest(grd) | W/Merseburg |
| | | FW-190 dam(grd) | W/Merseburg |
| | | Do-217 dam(grd) | W/Merseburg |
| 364th: | Lt. J.J. Salsman | FW-190 dam(air) | Merseburg |

**July 30, 1944**

| | | | |
|---|---|---|---|
| 362nd: | Maj. T.L. Gates | Me-109 dest(air) | NW Paris |
| | | Me-109 dam(air) | NW Paris |
| | Lt. A.E. Smith | Me-109 dest(air) | NW Paris |
| 363rd: | Maj. E.W. Hiro | Me-109 dest(air) | W/Paris |

**August 6, 1944**

| | | | |
|---|---|---|---|
| 364th: | Lt. R.M. Shaw | Me-109 dest(air) | N/Warsaw |
| | Lt. K.M. Brown | (.5)Ju-88 dest(air) | NE Warsaw |
| | Lt. N.J. Frederick | (.5)Ju-88 dest(air) | NE Warsaw |
| | Maj. J.A. Storch | FW-190 dam(air) | Danzig |
| | Lt. H.R. Nowlin | Me-109 dam(air) | NE Warsaw |

**August 7, 1944**

| | | | |
|---|---|---|---|
| 362nd: | Capt. J.F. Pugh | FW-190 dest(air) | Cracow |
| 364th: | Lt. H.R. Nowlin | (1.5)Me-109 dest(air) | Oswiecim |
| | Maj. J.A. Storch | (.5)Me-109 dest(air) | Oswiecim |

**August 8, 1944**

| | | | |
|---|---|---|---|
| 363rd: | Capt. R.N. Moore | Me-109 dest(air) | Crocil |

**August 18, 1944**

| | | | |
|---|---|---|---|
| 362nd: | Lt. C. Anderson | Me-109 dest(air) | NE Paris |
| | Capt. J.B. England | (.5)Me-109 dest(air) | NE Paris |
| | Lt. W.N. Perry | (.5)Me-109 dest(air) | NE Paris |
| | Lt. W.T. Gilbert | (.5)FW-190 dam(grd) | Rosieres A/F |
| | F/Lt. E.B.H. Woolley | (.5)FW-190 dam(grd) | Rosieres A/F |

**August 24, 1944**

| | | | |
|---|---|---|---|
| 364th: | Lt. H.H. Hermanson | Me-109 dest(air) | S/Brunswick |
| | Lt. G.E. Tyler | Me-109 dest(air) | S/Brunswick |

**August 28, 1944**

| | | | |
|---|---|---|---|
| 362nd: | Capt. C.L. Williams | Ju-52 dest(grd) | Trier |
| | Capt. H.E. Beal | (.5)Ju-52 dest(grd) | Trier |
| | Lt. J.H. Sehl | (.5)Ju-52 dest(grd) | Trier |
| | Lt. A.E. Smith | FW-190 dam(grd) | Trier |
| | | Ju-52 dam(grd) | Trier |

**September 13, 1944**

| | | | |
|---|---|---|---|
| 362nd: | Capt. J.B. England | (2.5)Me-109 dest(air)* | S/Nordhausen |
| | F/O O.D. Jenkins | (1.5)Me-109 dest(air)** | S/Nordhausen |
| | Lt. J.A. Kirla | (1.5)Me-109 dest(air)** | S/Nordhausen |
| | Lt. E.A. Taylor | Me-109 dest(air) | S/Nordhausen |
| | Lt. J.S. Templin | Me-109 dest(air) | S/Nordhausen |
| | Lt. S.G. Fuller | (.5)Me-109 dest(air)* | S/Nordhausen |
| | Lt. J.W. Kenney | Me-109 dam(air) | S/Nordhausen |
| 363rd: | Lt. H.O. Hand | Me-109 dest(air) | E/Kassel |
| | Lt. F.L. Gailer | (.5)Me-109 dest(air) | S/Kassel |
| | Lt. C.E. Yeager | (.5)Me-109 dest(air) | S/Kassel |
| 364th: | Lt. H.P. Howell | (2)Me-109 dest(air) | E/Bad Frankenhausen |
| | Maj. J.A. Storch | (1.5)Me-109 dest(air) | E/Bad Frankenhausen |
| | Lt. R.G. Schimanski | (.5)Me-109 dest(air) | E/Bad Frankenhausen |
| | Lt. M.F. Allen | Me-109 dest(air) | E/Bad Frankenhausen |

**September 15, 1944**

| | | | |
|---|---|---|---|
| 363rd: | Lt. W.R. Dunlop | Do-24 dam(grd) | Cristianmund |

**September 18, 1944**

| | | | |
|---|---|---|---|
| 362nd: | Maj. T.L. Gates | Me-109 dest(air) | Nijmegen |
| | Capt. F.C. Smith | Me-109 dest(air) | Nijmegen |
| | Lt. J.L. Blanchard | Me-109 dest(air) | Nijmegen |
| | Lt. H.B. Egeland | Me-109 dest(air) | Nijmegen |
| | Lt. H.F. Mace | Me-109 dest(air) | Nijmegen |
| | Lt. W.N. Perry | Me-109 dest(air) | Nijmegen |
| | Lt. J.S. Templin | Me-109 dest(air) | Nijmegen |
| 363rd: | Lt. W.R. Dunlop | Me-109 dest(air) | Apeldoorn |
| | Lt. K. Landis | Me-109 dest(air) | W/Arnheim |
| | Lt. H.T. Pascoe | Me-109 dest(air) | Arnheim |
| | Capt. T.E. Hughes | (.5)FW-190 dest(air) | Arnheim |
| | Lt. F.L. Gailer | (.5)FW-190 dest(air) | Arnheim |
| | Lt. W.S. Fennell | (.5)Me-109 dest(air) | W/Arnheim |
| | Lt. R.S. Fifield | (.5)Me-109 dest(air) | W/Arnheim |
| 364th: | Lt. G.E. Tyler | (2)Me-109 dest(air) | N/Maastricht |
| | | FW-190 dest(air) | N/Maastricht |
| | Lt. R.L. Smith | (2)Me-109 dest(air) | N/Maastricht |
| | Lt. J. Jacobs | Me-109 dest(air) | N/Maastricht |
| | | FW-190 dest(air) | N/Maastricht |
| | Capt. B.K. Seitzinger | Me-109 dest(air) | N/Maastricht |
| | | Me-109 dam(air) | N/Maastricht |
| | Lt. B.K. Braley | FW-190 dest(air) | N/Maastricht |
| | Lt. G.W. Morris | FW-190 dest(air) | N/Maastricht |
| | Lt. I.L. McGuire | FW-190 dest(air) | N/Maastricht |
| | Lt. H.E. Moebius | FW-190 dest(air) | N/Maastricht |
| | Lt. H.J. Moorhouse | FW-190 dest(air) | N/Maastricht |
| | Lt. R.M. Shaw | Me-109 dest(air) | N/Maastricht |

**September 19, 1944**

| | | | |
|---|---|---|---|
| 362nd: | F/O O.D. Jenkins | Me-109 dest(air) | SE Ijsselstein |
| | | FW-190 dest(air) | Ijsselstein |
| | Lt. A.J. Roberson | (2)Me-109 dest(air) | Ijsselstein |
| | Lt. J.A. Kirla | Me-109 dest(air) | Ijsselstein |
| | Lt. W.N. Perry | Me-109 dest(air) | Ijsselstein |
| | Lt. J.H. Sehl | Me-109 dest(air) | Ijsselstein |
| | Lt. C.E. Weaver | Me-109 dest(air) | S/Zuider Zee |
| | Capt. C.L. Williams | Me-109 prob(air) | Ijsselstein |
| | Capt. H.E. Beal | Me-109 dam(air) | Ijsselstein |
| 363rd: | Lt. D.J. Pasaka | (2)Me-109 dest(air) | Anklam |
| | Lt. R.C. Roper | (2)Me-109 dest(air) | W/Arnheim |
| | Maj. E.W. Hiro | Me-109 dest(air) | W/Arnheim |
| | Lt. W.R. Dunlop | Me-109 dest(air) | W/Arnheim |
| | Lt. F.L. Gailer | (.5)Me-109 dest(air) | W/Arnheim |
| | Lt. H.O. Hand | (.5)Me-109 dest(air) | W/Arnheim |
| 364th: | Capt. B.W. McIntyre | Me-109 dest(air) | Emmerich |
| | | FW-190 dest(air) | Emmerich |
| | Lt. H.E. Moebius | (2)FW-190 dest(air) | SE Arnheim |
| | Lt. C.K. Maxwell | Me-109 dest(air) | SW Arnheim |
| | | FW-190 dest(air) | SW Arnheim |
| | Lt. B.K. Braley | Me-109 dest(air) | E/Arnheim |
| | Lt. J. Jacobs | Me-109 dest(air) | SE Arnheim |
| | Lt. D.A. Sandborn | Me-109 dest(air) | E/Arnheim |
| | Lt. G.E. Tyler | Me-109 dest(air) | E/Arnheim |

**October 6, 1944**

| | | | |
|---|---|---|---|
| 362nd: | Capt. J.B. England | (2)Me-109 dest(air) | NW Berlin |
| | | Me-109 dam(air) | NW Berlin |
| | Lt. W.T. Gilbert | FW-190 dest(air) | NW Berlin |
| | F/O O.D. Jenkins | FW-190 dest(air) | NW Berlin |

| | | | |
|---|---|---|---|
| | Lt. T.W. Martinek | FW-190 dest(air) | NW Berlin |
| | | FW-190 prob(air) | NW Berlin |
| | Lt. W.H. Mooney | FW-190 dam(air) | NW Berlin |
| | Lt. W.N. Perry | FW-190 dam(air) | NW Berlin |
| 364th: | Capt. R.A. Peterson | FW-190 dest(air) | W/Berlin |

**October 7, 1944**

| | | | |
|---|---|---|---|
| 362nd: | Lt. T.W. Martinek | (2)FW-190 dest(air) | SW Leipzig |
| 363rd: | Lt. F.L. Gailer | FW-190 dest(air) | SW Zeitz |
| 364th: | Capt. R.A. Peterson | Me-109 dest(air) | Jena |
| | Lt. J.J. Salsman | Me-109 dest(air) | SW Leipzig |

**October 12, 1944**

| | | | |
|---|---|---|---|
| 363rd: | Lt. C.E. Yeager | (5)Me-109 dest(air) | Steinhuder Lake-Hanover |
| | Lt. R.C. Roper | (2)Me-109 dest(air) | Hanover |
| | Lt. F.L. Gailer | Me-109 dest(air) | Hanover |

**November 2, 1944**

| | | | |
|---|---|---|---|
| 362nd: | Capt. L.K. Carson | Me-109 dest(air) | Naumberg |
| 363rd: | Capt. T.E. Hughes | FW-190 dest(air) | E/Leipzig |
| | | (2)FW-190 dam(air) | E/Leipzig |
| | Lt. H.O. Hand | Me-109 dest(air) | E/Leipzig |
| | | Me-109 dam(air) | E/Leipzig |
| 364th: | Capt. R.A. Peterson | FW-190 dest(air) | NW Merseburg |
| | Lt. G.L. Weber | FW-190 dam(air) | NW Merseburg |

**November 6, 1944**

| | | | |
|---|---|---|---|
| 363rd: | Capt. C.E. Yeager | Me-262 dest(air) | E/Assen |
| | | (2)Me-262 dam(air) | E/Assen |

**November 8, 1944**

| | | | |
|---|---|---|---|
| 362nd: | Lt. J.W. Kenney | Me-262 dest(air) | Quackenbruck |
| 364th: | Lt. E.R. Haydon | (.5)Me-262 dest(air) | Dummer Lake |
| | | (shared with a 20th Ftr Grp P-51) | |

**November 18, 1944**

| | | | |
|---|---|---|---|
| HdQts: | LtCol. J.D. Landers | Me-109 dest(air) | Villingen A/F |
| | | Me-109 dest(grd) | Villingen A/F |
| 362nd: | Capt. A.C. Murphy | (2)Me-109 dest(grd) | Mengen A/F |
| | Lt. O.D. Jenkins | (2)Me-109 dest(grd) | Mengen A/F |
| | Lt. C.E. Weaver | (2)Me-109 dest(grd) | Mengen A/F |
| | Capt. L.K. Carson | Me-109 dest(grd) | Mengen A/F |
| | Capt. J.B. England | Me-109 dest(grd) | Mengen A/F |
| | F/O D.W. Cheever | Me-109 dest(grd) | Mengen A/F |
| | Lt. W.T. Gilbert | (.5)He-111 dest(grd) | Mengen A/F |
| | Lt. J.A. Kirla | (.5)He-111 dest(grd) | Mengen A/F |
| | Lt. H.D. Chandler | Me-109 dam(grd) | Mengen A/F |
| 363rd: | Capt. R.W. Foy | Me-109 dest(air) | Villingen A/F |
| | | Me-109 dam(air) | Villingen A/F |
| | | Me-109 dest(grd) | Villingen A/F |
| | | (3)Me-109 dam(grd) | Villingen A/F |
| | Lt. F.L. Gailer | Me-109 dest(grd) | Mengen A/F |
| 364th: | Capt. R.A. Peterson | Me-109 dest(air) | Neuhausen A/F |
| | Lt. R.P. Winks | Me-109 dest(air) | Neuhausen A/F |
| | Lt. E.R. Haydon | FW-190 dest(grd) | Neuhausen A/F |

**November 25, 1944**

| | | | |
|---|---|---|---|
| 362nd: | Capt. L.K. Carson | FW-44 dest(grd) | Maraburg |
| | Lt. J.L. Sublett | FW-44 dest(grd) | Maraburg |

**November 27, 1944**

| | | | |
|---|---|---|---|
| HdQts: | Maj. A.J. Evans | FW-190 dest(air) | S/Magdeburg |
| 362nd: | Capt. L.K. Carson | (5)FW-190 dest(air) | S/Magdeburg |
| | Capt. J.B. England | (4)FW-190 dest(air) | S/Magdeburg |
| | Lt. J.L. Sublett | (3)FW-190 dest(air) | S/Magdeburg |
| | Capt. A.C. Murphy | Me-109 dest(air) | S/Magdeburg |
| | | FW-190 dest(air) | S/Magdeburg |
| | Lt. C.E. Weaver | (2)FW-190 dest(air) | S/Magdeburg |
| | | FW-190 prob(air) | S/Magdeburg |
| | | FW-190 dam(air) | S/Magdeburg |
| | Lt. C. Anderson | FW-190 dest(air) | S/Magdeburg |
| | Lt. H.H. Delager | Me-109 dest(air) | S/Magdeburg |
| | Lt. W.T. Gilbert | FW-190 dest(air) | S/Magdeburg |
| 363rd: | Capt. C.E. Yeager | (4)FW-190 dest(air) | SW Magdeburg |
| | Capt. C.E. Anderson | (2)FW-190 dest(air) | Noyehausen & Magdeburg |
| | | FW-190 prob(air) | Magdeburg |
| | Lt. F.L. Gailer | (2)FW-190 dest(air) | SE Magdeburg |
| | Lt. J.R. Sloan | FW-190 dest(air) | SW Magdeburg |
| | Lt. R.E. Wolf | FW-190 dest(air) | Noyehausen A/F |
| 364th: | Lt. R.G. Schimanski | Me-109 dest(air) | S/Brandenburg |

**December 2, 1944**

| | | | |
|---|---|---|---|
| HdQts: | Capt. R.W. Foy | Ju-88 dest(air) | NE Coblenz |
| 362nd: | Capt. L.K. Carson | (2)Me-109 dest(air) | Bingen |
| | Capt. A.C. Murphy | (2)Me-109 dest(air) | Bingen |
| | Lt. H.H. Delager | Me-109 dest(air) | Bingen |
| | Lt. R.L. Schlieker | Me-109 dest(air) | Bingen |

**December 5, 1944**

| | | | |
|---|---|---|---|
| 362nd: | Lt. J.A. Kirla | Me-109 dest(air) | Berlin |
| | | FW-190 dest(air) | Berlin |
| | Maj. J.E. Broadhead | FW-190 dest(air) | Berlin |
| | Capt. L.K. Carson | Me-109 dest(air) | Berlin |
| | Lt. W.T. Gilbert | Me-410 dam(grd) | Berlin |
| 363rd: | Capt. C.E. Anderson | (2)FW-190 dest(air) | W/Berlin |
| | | FW-190 prob(air) | W/Berlin |
| | Capt. D.H. Bochkay | (2)FW-190 dest(air) | NE Berlin |
| | Capt. J.W. Browning | Me-109 dest(air) | N/Berlin |
| | Lt. J.L. Carter | FW-190 dest(air) | N/Berlin |
| | Lt. G.J. Rice | FW-190 dest(air) | N/Berlin |
| | Lt. J.R. Stern | FW-190 dest(air) | N/Berlin |
| | Lt. J.T. Crump | FW-190 prob(air) | N/Berlin |
| | Capt. A.G. Manthos | FW-190 dam(air) | N/Berlin |
| 364th: | Lt. D.E. Karger | (2)FW-190 dest(air) | N/Berlin |
| | Lt. F.C. McCall | (2)FW-190 dest(air) | NW Berlin |
| | Capt. H.R. Zetterquist | FW-190 dest(air) | N/Berlin |
| | Lt. T.H. Adams | FW-190 dest(air) | NW Berlin |
| | Lt. M.E. Gallant | FW-190 dest(air) | NW Berlin |
| | Lt. P.R. Hatala | Me-109 dest(air) | NW Berlin |
| | Lt. E.J. Juszczyk | FW-190 dest(air) | N/Berlin |
| | Lt. R.G. Schimanski | FW-190 dest(air) | N/Berlin |

**December 23, 1944**

| | | | |
|---|---|---|---|
| HdQts: | Capt. R.W. Foy | Me-109 dest(air) | Wetzlar A/F |
| | | Ju-88 dest(air) | Wetzlar A/F |
| 362nd: | Lt. C.E. Weaver | Me-109 dest(air) | N/Donauworth |
| 363rd: | F/O S. Sitzer | Me-109 dest(air) | S/Ludwigshafen |

**December 24, 1944**

| | | | |
|---|---|---|---|
| HdQts: | LtCol. I.H. Dregne | Me-109 dest(air) | Coblenz |
| 362nd: | Lt. O.D. Jenkins | (4)FW-190 dest(air) | Fulda |
| | Lt. J.A. Kirla | (3)FW-190 dest(air) | Fulda |
| | Lt. W.T. Gilbert | (2)FW-190 dest(air) | Fulda |
| | Lt. E.D. Hyman | (2)FW-190 dest(air) | Fulda |
| | Lt. P.A. Pelon | (2)FW-190 dest(air) | Fulda |
| | Capt. L.K. Carson | FW-190 dest(air) | Fulda |
| | Lt. G.A. Behling | FW-190 dest(air) | Fulda |
| | Lt. J.R. Frey | FW-190 dest(air) | Fulda |
| 363rd: | Lt. J.L. Carter | Me-109 dest(air) | W/Coblenz |
| | | FW-190 dest(air) | W/Coblenz |
| | Maj. G.I. Carlisle | Me-109 dest(air) | W/Coblenz |
| | Lt. J.T. Crump | Me-109 dest(air) | W/Coblenz |
| | Lt. W.R. Dunlop | Me-109 dest(air) | W/Coblenz |
| | Lt. W.P. Roberts | Me-109 dest(air) | W/Coblenz |
| | Lt. J.R. Sloan | Me-109 dest(air) | W/Coblenz |
| 364th: | Lt. R.M. Bank | Me-109 dest(air) | S/Kassel |
| | Lt. B.K. Braley | FW-190 dest(air) | S/Kassel |
| | Lt. D.E. Karger | Me-109 dest(air) | S/Kassel |
| | Lt. F.C. McCall | Me-109 dest(air) | E/Fulda |
| | Lt. I.L. McGuire | FW-190 dest(air) | S/Kassel |
| | Lt. R.G. Schimanski | Me-109 dest(air) | Kassel |
| | Lt. R.P. Winks | FW-190 dest(air) | Fulda |

**January 5, 1945**

| | | | |
|---|---|---|---|
| 364th: | Lt. T.H. Adams | (.5)FW-190 dest(air) | N/Hanau |
| | Lt. I.E. Snedeker | (.5)FW-190 dest(air) | N/Hanau |
| | Maj. R.A. Peterson | (2)Ju-88 dest(grd) | Altenstadt A/F |
| | | Me-109 dest(grd) | Altenstadt A/F |
| | Lt. B.K. Braley | Me-109 dest(grd) | Altenstadt A/F |

**January 10, 1945**

| | | | |
|---|---|---|---|
| 364th: | Lt. T.H. Adams | Me-109 dest(air) | Paderborn A/F |
| | | He-111 dest(grd) | Paderborn A/F |
| | Lt. F.C. McCall | He-111 dest(grd) | Paderborn A/F |

**January 14, 1945**

| | | | |
|---|---|---|---|
| HdQts: | LtCol. A.J. Evans | (2)FW-190 dest(air) | NW Brandenburg |
| | | (2)Me-109 dest(air) | NW Brandenburg |
| | Capt. R.W. Foy | (2)FW-190 dest(air) | NW Berlin |
| | | FW-190 dest(grd) | Berlin |
| | LtCol. I.H. Dregne | Me-109 dest(air) | NW Brandenburg |
| | | FW-190 dam(air) | NW Brandenburg |
| 362nd: | Lt. J.A. Kirla | (2)Me-109 dest(air) | All 362nd claims |
| | | (2)FW-190 dest(air) | were NW Berlin |
| | Capt. L.K. Carson | (2)FW-190 dest(air) | |
| | | Me-109 dest(air) | |
| | Lt. J.F. Duncan | (2)FW-190 dest(air) | |
| | Lt. J.L. Sublett | (2)Me-109 dest(air) | |
| | Lt. C.E. Weaver | Me-109 dest(air) | |
| | | FW-190 dest(air) | |
| | Maj. J.E. Broadhead | Me-109 dest(air) | |
| | Maj. J.B. England | Me-109 dest(air) | |
| | Lt. D.W. Cheever | FW-190 dest(air) | |
| | Lt. J.R. Frey | Me-109 dest(air) | |
| | Lt. J.A. Gasser | FW-190 dest(air) | |
| | Lt. H.A. Wyatt | FW-190 dest(air) | |
| 363rd: | Lt. J.R. Stern | (3)Me-109 dest(air) | All 363rd claims |
| | Capt. J.W. Browning | Me-109 dest(air) | were N/Brandenburg |
| | | (2)Me-109 prob(air) | |
| | | Me-109 dam(air) | |
| | Lt. W.R. Dunlop | Me-109 dest(air) | |
| | Lt. G.J. Rice | Me-109 dest(air) | |

| | Lt. J.R. Sloan | Me-109 dest(air) | |
|---|---|---|---|
| | Lt. J.E. Taylor | Me-109 dest(air) | |
| | Lt. R.E. Wolf | Me-109 dest(air) | |
| | | Me-109 dam(air) | |
| | Lt. J.T. Windham | (.5)Me-109 dest(air) | |
| | Lt. G.A. Zarnke | (.5)Me-109 dest(air) | |
| 364th: | Maj. J.A. Storch | (2)FW-190 dest(air) | S/Schwerin |
| | | Me-109 dest(air) | S/Schwerin |
| | Capt. C.K. Maxwell | (3)FW-190 dest(air) | W/Berlin |
| | Lt. R.M. Bank | (3)FW-190 dest(air) | S/Schwerin |
| | Lt. R.P. Winks | (2)FW-190 dest(air) | SW Ludwigslust |
| | | (.5)Me-109 dest(air) | SW Ludwigslust |
| | | (shared with an unknown P-51 pilot) | |
| | Capt. T.H. Adams | (2)FW-190 dest(air) | Ludwigslust |
| | Lt. P.R. Hatala | (2)FW-190 dest(air) | W/Berlin |
| | Lt. E.W. Johnson | FW-190 dest(air) | NE Berlin |
| | Lt. D.E. Karger | Me-109 dest(air) | NW Berlin |
| | Lt. I.E. Snedeker | FW-190 dest(air) | NW Berlin |
| | Lt. D.R. Williams | FW-190 dest(air) | W/Berlin |
| | Lt. V.V. Zettler | FW-190 dam(air) | W/Berlin |

**January 15, 1945**

| 364th: | Lt. R.P. Winks | Me-262 dest(air) | Shongau |
|---|---|---|---|

**January 20, 1945**

| 364th: | Lt. D.E. Karger | Me-262 dest(air) | N/Munich |
|---|---|---|---|
| | Lt. R.R. Wright | Me-262 dest(air) | Lechfeld A/F |

**February 9, 1945**

| HdQts: | Maj. R.W. Foy | Me-262 dam(air) | Fulda |
|---|---|---|---|
| 363rd: | Capt. D.H. Bochkay | Me-262 dest(air) | Fulda |
| | Lt. J.L. Carter | Me-262 dest(air) | E/Giessen |

**February 25, 1945**

| 362nd: | Capt. C.E. Weaver | He-111 dest(grd) | Memmingen |
|---|---|---|---|
| | | FW-190 dam(grd) | Memmingen |
| | | Ju-88 dam(grd) | Memmingen |
| | Lt. J.F. Duncan | He-111 dest(grd) | Memmingen |

**February 28, 1945**

| HdQts: | Maj. R.W. Foy | Ju-88 dest(grd) | All claims are |
|---|---|---|---|
| | | FW-200 dam(grd) | at Lubeck/ |
| | | Me-109 dam(grd) | Blankensee |
| 363rd: | Capt. J.R. Stern | Ju-88 dam(grd) | |
| 364th: | Lt. E.R. Fry | (2)u/i a/c dest(grd) | |
| | Lt. S. Wasylyk | u/i a/c dest(grd) | |
| | Lt. R.W. Lepore | (4)u/i a/c dam(grd) | |
| | LtCol. J.A. Storch | (2)u/i a/c dam(grd) | |

**March 2, 1945**

| 362nd: | Capt. J.L. Sublett | Me-109 dest(air) | NE Leipzig |
|---|---|---|---|
| | | FW-190 dest(air) | NE Leipzig |
| | Lt. M.A. Becraft | Me-109 dest(air) | Kamenz A/F |
| | | (2)He-111 dest(grd) | Kamenz A/F |
| | | (2)u/i a/c dest(grd) | Kamenz A/F |
| | Lt. J.F. Duncan | Me-109 dest(air) | NE Leipzig |
| | | Me-109 dam(air) | NE Leipzig |
| | Lt. O.T. Ridley | (.5)Me-109 dest(air)* | NE Leipzig |
| | Lt. W.W. Gruber | FW-190 dam(air) | NE Leipzig |
| | Lt. G.A. Robinson | (4)He-111 dest(grd) | Kamenz A/F |
| | | He-111 dam(grd) | Kamenz A/F |
| | | u/i a/c dam(grd) | Kamenz A/F |
| 363rd: | Capt. D.C. McGee | Me-109 dest(air) | NE Magdeburg |
| 364th: | Capt. A.C. Murphy | (2)Me-109 dest(air) | SE Magdeburg |
| | Capt. R.G. Schimanski | (1.5)Me-109 dest(air)** | SE Magdeburg |
| | | (2)He-111 dest(grd) | E/Magdeburg |
| | Lt. D.E. Karger | (.5)Me-109 dest(air)** | SE Magdeburg |
| | | (4)u/i a/c dest(grd) | E/Magdeburg |
| | | (2)Ju-88 dam(grd) | E/Magdeburg |
| | | Ju-188 dam(grd) | E/Magdeburg |
| | | u/i a/c dam(grd) | E/Magdeburg |
| | Lt. R.M. Bank | Me-109 dest(air) | SE Magdeburg |
| | | He-111 dam(grd) | E/Magdeburg |
| | Lt. O. Howes | Me-109 dest(air) | SE Magdeburg |
| | | He-111 dest(grd) | E/Magdeburg |
| | Lt. V.V. Zettler | Me-109 dest(air) | SE Magdeburg |
| | | (4)He-111 dest(grd) | E/Magdeburg |
| | F/O J.A. Steiger | Me-109 dest(air) | SW Magdeburg |
| | Capt. P.R. Hatala | (.5)Me-109 dest(air)* | NE Leipzig |
| | Lt. D.R. Williams | (2)He-111 dest(grd) | E/Magdeburg |
| | | (8)He-111 dam(grd) | E/Magdeburg |
| | | u/i a/c dam(grd) | E/Magdeburg |
| | Lt. R.W. Lepore | (2)He-111 dest(grd) | E/Magdeburg |
| | Lt. H. Wesling | He-111 dam(grd) | E/Magdeburg |

**March 3, 1945**

| 362nd: | Capt. J.L. Sublett | Me-262 dam(air) | NE Magdeburg |
|---|---|---|---|
| 364th: | Capt. I.L. McGuire | Me-262 dam(air) | S/Brunswick |

**March 19, 1945**

| HdQts: | Maj. R.W. Foy | Me-262 dest(air) | W/Giessen |
|---|---|---|---|
| 363rd: | Capt. R.S. Fifield | Me-262 dest(air) | E/Leipzig |
| | Capt. J.L. Carter | (2)Me-262 dam(air) | N/Chemnitz |
| | Capt. A.G. Manthos | Me-262 dam(air) | E/Leipzig |
| | Lt. J.W. Cannon | Me-262 dam(air) | E/Leipzig |

**March 20, 1945**

| 362nd: | Capt. J.L. Sublett | Me-109 dest(air) | Quackenbruck |
|---|---|---|---|
| 363rd: | Lt. R.L. Thorkelson | FW-190 dest(air) | Dummer Lake |
| | Lt. J.T. Windham | FW-190 dam(air) | Dummer Lake |
| | | Ju-88 dam(grd) | Dummer Lake |

**March 24, 1945**

| HdQts: | LtCol. A.J. Evans | Me-109 dest(air) | W/Gutersloh |
|---|---|---|---|
| | Maj. R.W. Foy | Me-109 dest(air) | N/Gutersloh |
| 362nd: | Capt. C.E. Weaver | Me-109 dest(air) | W/Gutersloh |
| | Lt. J.F. Duncan | Me-109 dest(air) | W/Gutersloh |
| | Lt. W.W. Gruber | Me-109 dest(air) | W/Gutersloh |
| 364th: | Capt. P.R. Hatala | (2)Me-109 dest(air) | W/Gutersloh |
| | Lt. D.E. Karger | (2)Me-109 dest(air) | W/Gutersloh |
| | LtCol. J.A. Storch | Me-109 dest(air) | W/Gutersloh |
| | Capt. R.G. Schimanski | Me-109 dest(air) | W/Gutersloh |
| | | Me-109 dam(air) | W/Gutersloh |
| | F/O C.F. Schneider | Me-109 dest(air) | W/Gutersloh |
| | | (2)Me-109 dam(air) | W/Gutersloh |
| | Lt. S. Wasylyk | Me-109 dest(air) | W/Gutersloh |
| | Lt. G.L. Weber | Me-109 dest(air) | W/Gutersloh |
| | Lt. L.A. Westphal | Me-109 dest(air) | W/Gutersloh |
| | Lt. R.R. Wright | Me-109 dest(air) | W/Gutersloh |
| | | Me-109 dam(air) | W/Gutersloh |

**March 31, 1945**

| 362nd: | Maj. L.K. Carson | Me-262 dam(air) | N/Juist Island |
|---|---|---|---|
| | Lt. M.A. Becraft | Me-262 dam(air) | N/Juist Island |

**April 7, 1945**

| 363rd: | Capt. J.T. Windham | Me-109 dest(air) | Salzwedel |
|---|---|---|---|
| 364th: | Capt. I.L. McGuire | Me-109 dest(air) | NW Magdeburg |

**April 10, 1945**

| HdQts: | Col. I.H. Dregne | (2)Me-262 dest(grd) | All claims are |
|---|---|---|---|
| | | FW-190 dest(grd) | at Neuruppin |
| | | Ju-88 dam(grd) | |
| | LtCol. A.J. Evans | He-111 dest(grd) | |
| | | Me-210 dest(grd) | |
| | | Do-217 dam(grd) | |
| | | He-111 dam(grd) | |
| | | Me-210 dam(grd) | |
| | | He-177 dam(grd) | |
| 362nd: | Lt. J.F. Duncan | (2)Me-210 dest(grd) | |
| | | Me-110 dest(grd) | |
| | | Me-262 dam(grd) | |
| | Lt. E.A. Gordon | (2)He-111 dest(grd) | |
| | Lt. N.M. Hewit | (2)He-111 dest(grd) | |
| | Lt. J.W. Dunn | He-111 dest(grd) | |
| | | Do-217 dest(grd) | |
| | | (2)He-111 dam(grd) | |
| | | FW-190 dam(grd) | |
| | Lt. E.C. Danner | Ju-88 dest(grd) | |
| 363rd: | Maj. D.C. McGee | Me-410 dest(grd) | |
| | | He-111 dest(grd) | |
| | | (2)u/i a/c dam(grd) | |
| | Lt. R.R. Kalessa | u/i a/c dest(grd) | |
| | | u/i a/c dam(grd) | |
| 364th: | Lt. V.V. Zettler | (3)Ju-88 dest(grd) | |
| | Capt. R.W. Moore | He-111 dest(grd) | |
| | F/O J.A. Steiger | Ju-88 dest(grd) | |
| | Lt. L.E. Zacharie | (2)He-111 dam(grd) | |
| | Lt. H.E. Arrendale | Ju-88 dam(grd) | |

**April 16, 1945**

| 364th: | Lt. B.K. Braley | Me-109 dest(grd) | Muhldorf |
|---|---|---|---|
| | | Me-109 dam(grd) | Muhldorf |
| | Lt. M.F. Cedoz | (2)u/i a/c dam(grd) | Muhldorf |

**April 17, 1945**

| HdQts: | LtCol. J.W. Hayes | Me-262 dam(air) | SE Brux |
|---|---|---|---|
| | Col. I.H. Dregne | Ju-88 dest(grd) | Prague/Ruzny |
| | | (2)Ju-88 dam(grd) | Prague/Ruzny |
| 362nd: | Maj. L.K. Carson | FW-200 dest(grd) | Prague/Ruzny |
| | Lt. J.F. Duncan | Me-262 dest(grd) | Prague/Ruzny |
| | | Me-109 dest(grd) | Prague/Ruzny |
| | Lt. E.C. Danner | u/i a/c dest(grd) | Prague/Ruzny |
| 364th: | F/O J.A. Steiger | Me-262 dest(air) | NE Prague |
| | Lt. O. Howes | Ju-88 dest(grd) | Prague/Ruzny |

**April 18, 1945**

| 362nd: | Capt. C.E. Weaver | Me-262 dest(air) | Prague/Ruzny |
|---|---|---|---|
| | Maj. L.K. Carson | (2)Me-262 dam(air) | Prague/Ruzny |

| | | | |
|---|---|---|---|
| 363rd: | Maj. D.H. Bochkay | Me-262 dest(air) | SW Prague |
| | Lt. R.H. Bradner | (.5)Me-262 dam(air) | SW Prague/Ruzny |
| | Lt. F.A. Dellorto | (.5)Me-262 dam(air) | SW Prague/Ruzny |

**April 19, 1945**

| | | | |
|---|---|---|---|
| HdQts: | LtCol. J.W. Hayes | Me-262 dest(air) | W/Prague |
| 363rd: | Capt. R.S. Fifield | Me-262 dest(air) | Prague |
| | Lt. P.N. Bowles | Me-262 dest(air) | Prague |
| | Lt. C.W. Ofsthun | Me-262 dest(air) | SW Prague/Ruzny |
| | Lt. W.J. Currie | Me-262 dam(air) | Prague |
| | Lt. F.A. Kyle | Me-262 dam(air) | Prague |
| | Lt. G.A. Zarnke | Me-262 dam(air) | Prague |
| 364th: | Lt. J.P. McMullen | Me-262 dest(air) | Prague/Ruzny |
| | Capt. I.L. McGuire | (.5)Me-262 dest(air) | S/Dresden |
| | Lt. G.L. Weber | (.5)Me-262 dest(air) | S/Dresden |
| | Lt. D.C. Kocher | Me-262 dam(air) | Dresden |

**357th Fighter Group Losses**

**January 25, 1944**
Capt. Joseph H. Giltner, Jr. (363rd) POW; Downed by a FW-190 near Antwerp.
P-51B FT- 43-12187 (a 354th Ftr Grp a/c)

**February 9, 1944**
Capt. Lloyd Hubbard (363rd) KIA; Hit by flak at Aresnes Airfield.
P-51B FT- 43-12368 (a 354th Ftr Grp a/c)

**February 13, 1944**
Lt. Robert D. Brown (362nd) ASR; Suffered mechanical failure and bailed out over the Channel.
P-51B G4- 43-6734

**February 20, 1944**
Lt. Donald H. Ross (363rd) POW; Hit by a Me-109 northeast of Leipzig.
P-51B B6- 43-12131

**February 21, 1944**
Lt. Alfred R. Boyle (363rd) POW; Hit by a Me-109 and bailed out near Meppel.
P-51B B6-S 43-6723 "Old Crow"

**February 22, 1944**
Lt. Albert C. Lichter (362nd) POW; Hit by flak and bailed out east of Zwolle.
P-51B G4- 43-6741
Lt. Darwin J. Carroll (364th) KIA; Suffered mechanical failure and bailed out near Kothen.
P-51B C5- 43-6578

**February 24, 1944**
Lt. Donald R. Rice (362nd) POW; Hit by fighters near Coblenz.
P-51B G4- 43-6743
Lt. Charles E. McKee (363rd) POW; Hit by fire from a B-24 and bailed out near Gotha.
P-51B B6- 43-6940

**February 25, 1944**
Lt. Thomas A. Beemer (362nd) KIA; Hit by fire from a B-17 and bailed out near Regensburg.
P-51B G4- 43-6927
Lt. Merlin R. Kehrer (362nd) POW; Hit by fighters near Stuttgart.
P-51B G4-N 43-6625

**March 3, 1944**
Lt. Robert W. Foy (363rd) ASR; Suffered mechanical failure and bailed out east of Manston.
P-51B B6- 43-6998

**March 4, 1944**
Capt. John L. Medeiros (364th) POW; Hit by flak west of Magdeburg.
P-51B C5- 43-6853

**March 5, 1944**
Col. Henry R. Spicer (HdQts) POW; Hit by flak and bailed out southwest of Le Havre.
P-51B B6- 43-6880 "Tony Boy"
F/O Charles E. Yeager (363rd) MIA-E; Hit by enemy fighters and bailed out southeast of Angouleme.
P-51B B6-Y 43-6763 "Glamorous Glenn"

**March 8, 1944**
Lt. William W. Gambill (363rd) POW-D; Hit by a Me-109 west of Hanover. Later killed by an Allied bomb.
P-51C B6-F 42-103041 "Speedball Alice"

**March 16, 1944**
Lt. Robert A. Meyer (362nd) POW; Hit by fighters near Stuttgart and bailed out near Reutlingen.
P-51B G4- 43-6956
Lt. Alvin F. Pyeatt, III (362nd) POW-D; Hit by fighters near Stuttgart and crashed near Reutlingen. Died of wounds.
P-51B G4-S 43-7960 "Scrappy"

**March 18, 1944**
Lt. Konstantin J. Vogel (362nd) KIA; Hit by fighters near Gunzburg.
P-51B G4-H 43-12442
Capt. Jack R. Warren (364th) KIA; Last seen in overcast near Ostend.
P-51B C5-F 43-12124

**March 22, 1944**
Lt. Carter L. Jones (363rd) POW; Hit by flak near Bremen.
P-51B B6- 43-12315

**March 23, 1944**
Lt. Robert P. Humphrey (HdQts) POW; Hit by fighters west of Brunswick.
P-51B B6- 43-7019

**March 27, 1944**
Lt. James E. Strode (364th) KIA; Last seen in overcast and crashed off Clacton.
P-51B C5- 43-6978

**March 28, 1944**
LtCol. Hubert I. Egenes (HdQts) KIA; Hit by flak south of Paris.
P-51B G4- 43-6794
Lt. Lynn H. Drollinger (362nd) MIA-E; Suffered mechanical failure and bailed out northeast of Dijon.
P-51B G4- 43-6729

**March 29, 1944**
Lt. Santiago R. Gutierrez (363rd) KIA; Collided with Lt. McGinley over the North Sea.
P-51B B6- 43-7052
Lt. William R. McGinley (363rd) KIA; Collided with Lt. Gutierrez over the North Sea.
P-51B B6-K 43-6628 "Typhoon McGoon"
Lt. Edward R. Sutton (364th) KIA; Hit by fighters north of Brunswick.
P-51B C5- 43-6454

**April 1, 1944**
Capt. Davis T. Perron (362nd) KIA; Crashed in bad weather near Doullens.
P-51B G4- 43-6782
Lt. Elmer D. Rydberg (362nd) KIA; Crashed in bad weather near Erevent.
P-51B G4- 43-6629

**April 11, 1944**
Capt. Arthur M. Lingo (362nd) KIA; Hit by fighters northeast of Magdeburg.
P-51B G4-M 43-12122
Capt. George D. Currie (364th) POW; Hit by fighters near Brunswick.
P-51B C5- 43-6773
Lt. William A. Gray (364th) POW; Suffered mechanical failure and bailed out north of Hanover.
P-51B C5- 43-6515

**April 12, 1944**
Lt. Fred W. Reust (363rd) POW; Suffered mechanical trouble near Saalfield.
P-51B B6- 43-6720

**April 15, 1944**
Lt. Maurice A. Postle (364th) POW; Suffered mechanical failure near The Hague.
P-51B C5- 43-6413

**April 24, 1944**
Lt. Frank J. Connaghan (362nd) KIA; Collided with a Me-110 near Munich.
P-51B G4-I 43-7176
Lt. Ralph H. Donnell (363rd) POW; Collided with a Me-110 near Munich.
P-51B B6- 43-6986
Lt. Howard S. Hinman (363rd) POW; Hit by fighters near Munich.
P-51B B6- 43-6624
Lt. Joseph F. Stager (364th) POW; Hit by flak near Ludwigshafen and bailed out southeast of Strasbourg.
P-51B C5- 42-106740

**April 27, 1944**
Lt. Ben F. Elliott, Jr. (364th) POW; Suffered mechanical failure and bailed out north of Courtrai.
P-51B C5- 42-106790

**April 28, 1944**
Capt. Glendon V. Davis (364th) MIA-E; Suffered mechanical trouble and bailed out west of Bourges.
P-51B C5-O 43-6867 "Pregnant Polecat"

**April 30, 1944**
Lt. Cordell L. Summers (364th) MIA-E; Hit by flak and bailed out near Auxerre.
P-51B C5- 43-6701
Lt. Charles J. Schreiber (364th) ASR; Damaged by fighters and bailed out ten miles off Clacton.
P-51B C5- 43-6856

**May 8, 1944**
Capt. Ellis A. Rogers (363rd) KIA; Hit by flak near Soltau.
P-51B B6- 106793
Lt. Ray Sparks, Jr. (364th) POW; Hit by flak southwest of Ulzen.
P-51B C5-C 43-6801 "Boiler Maker"

**May 9, 1944**
Lt. Stanley M. Omernik (363rd) POW; Hit by a FW-190 near Herentals.
P-51B B6- 43-7011
Lt. Donovan D. Siverts (363rd) KIA; Hit by a FW-190 nera Herentals.
P-51B B6- 43-6427

**May 12, 1944**
Lt. Roger A. Hilsted (362nd) KIA; Hit by fighters near Wurzburg.
P-51B G4-C 43-6634 "Nooky Booky"
Capt. John B. Carder (364th) POW; Hit by fighters near Bischoffen.
P-51B C5-J 42-106777 "Taxpayer's Delight"

**May 19, 1944**
Lt. Archie F. Bridges (364th) POW; Suffered mechanical failure east of Brandenburg.
P-51B C5- 42-106648

**May 21, 1944**
Lt. William D. Michaely (363rd) POW; Hit by flak near Anklam.
P-51C B6- 42-103286
Lt. Joseph F. Pierce (363rd) KIA; Hit by flak northwest of Anklam.
P-51B B6-Z 43-6429
Lt. William C. Reese (364th) KIA; Hit by flak at Strasbourg.
P-51B C5-F 43-12313 "Bear River Betsy"

**May 24, 1944**
Lt. Joseph M. Jenkins (364th) KIA; Hit by flak near Albert.
P-51C C5- 42-103389
Lt. Joseph G. Sullivan (364th) MIA-E; Hit by flak near Laon.
P-51B C5- 42-106884

**May 27, 1944**
Capt. Robert D. Brown (362nd) INT; Damaged by fighters and landed in Switzerland.
P-51B G4-B 43-6556 "Chicago Gun Moll"
Capt. Thomas L. Harris (364th) POW; Collided with Lt. Post near Strasbourg.
P-51B C5-S 43-6653 "Li'l Red's Rocket"
Lt. Cyril D. Conklin (364th) POW; Hit by fighters near Strasbourg.
P-51B C5- 42-106640
Lt. Dean N. Post, Jr. (364th) KIA; Collided with Capt. Harris near Strasbourg.
P-51B C5- 42-106632

**May 30, 1944**
Capt. Fletcher E. Adams (362nd) KIA; Hit by a Me-109 in the Wesendorf-Celle area.
P-51B G4-L 43-12468 "Southern Belle"
Lt. Robert W. Foy (363rd) ASR; Suffered mechanical failure and bailed out fifty miles off the English coast.
P-51B B6-

**June 6, 1944**
Lt. Roger E. Pagels (363rd) MIA-E; Hit by flak and bailed out over the North Sea.
P-51B B6- 43-6397
Lt. Irving A. Smith (363rd) KIA; Hit by flak near La Fleche.
P-51B B6- 43-6947
Capt. Leroy A. Ruder (364th) KIA; Suffered mechanical failure southeast of Cherbourg.
P-51B C5-X 42-106768 "Linda Lu"

**June 7, 1944**
Lt. John N. Denesha (364th) KIA; Hit by flak near Plancoet.
P-51B C5- 42-106652

**June 8, 1944**
Lt. Ollie E. Harris (362nd) ASR; Bailed out off New Haven.
P-51B G4-

**June 10, 1944**
Lt. John K. Childs (363rd) KIA; Hit by fire from a P-51 while strafing near Mortagne.
P-51B B6-P 43-6563 "Gentleman Jim"

**June 14, 1944**
Lt. James E. Colburn (364th) KIA; Hit by a Me-109 east of Paris.
P-51B C5- 43-24763

**June 17, 1944**
Capt. Kenneth E. Hagan (362nd) MIA-E; Suffered mechanical trouble southwest of Caen.
P-51B G4-G 42-106831

**June 20, 1944**
Lt. Heyward C. Spinks (364th) MIA-E; Hit by flak north of Paris.
P-51B C5-T 43-6935 "Hurry Home Honey"

**June 29, 1944**
Capt. Richard C. Smith (364th) KIA; Hit by fighters near Leipzig.
P-51B C5-K 43-6974 "Mr. Period"

**July 1, 1944**
Lt. Donald W. Vogel (362nd) MIA-E; Hit by fighters near St. Quentin.
P-51B G4-A 43-12455 "Blythe Spirit"

**July 7, 1944**
Lt. Frank Koka (363rd) KIA; Hit by fighters north of Leipzig and bailed out northwest of Bernburg.
P-51B B6- 43-6858

**July 29, 1944**
Lt. Rollin L. Carter (362nd) POW; Suffered mechanical failure near Gelnhausen and bailed out south of Nordhausen.
P-51B G4-Y 43-7143 "Miss Florida"
Lt. Paul E. Holmberg (362nd) KIA; Aircraft exploded west of Merseburg.
P-51B G4-I 43-6727
Lt. Daniel L. Finley (364th) POW-D; Suffered mechanical failure near Bad Oeynhausen. Later died in POW camp.
P-51B C5-A 42-106843 "Round Trip Jr."

**August 4, 1944**
Lt. Wallace J. Reid (364th) POW; Lost coolant and bailed out northeast of Kiel.
P-51B C5- 42-106978

**August 10, 1944**
Capt. Edward K. Simpson, Jr. (363rd) MIA-E (K); Collided with Lt. Ferron west of Sens. Killed on August 14 while with the Maquis.
P-51D B6-V 44-13712 "Reluctant Rebel"
Lt. Donald J. Ferron (363rd) KIA; Collided with Capt. Simpson west of Sens.
P-51B B6- 42-106696

**August 17, 1944**
Lt. Harold M. Kenney (363rd) MIA-E; Hit by flak and bailed out near Charleroi.
P-51D B6-G 44-13522 "Billy's Bitch"
Lt. Charles O. Campbell (363rd) KIAc;
P-51B B6-B 43-6999

**August 25, 1944**
Lt. Walter Baron (364th) INT; Suffered mechanical failure and came down in Sweden.
P-51B C5-B 42-106854 "Peabody's Pet"
Lt. Charles E. Burtner (364th) INT; Escorted Lt. Baron to Sweden.
P-51D C5-I 44-13345 "Mary Ann"

**September 13, 1944**
Lt. Howard L. Johnson (362nd) POW; Suffered mechanical trouble near Gembloux.
P-51B G4-M 42-106654 "Jersey Bounce"
Lt. James A. Valkwitch (362nd) KIA; Suffered mechanical failure near Halle.
P-51B G4-N 42-106473 "Geronimo"
Lt. Marion E. Burnett (363rd) KIA; Hit by fighters east of Kassel.
P-51D B6-C 44-13745 "Hi Phyl"
Lt. Kirby N. Brown (364th) KIA; Hit by flak near Bad Frankenhausen.
P-51D C5-J 44-13698 "Shady Lady"
Lt. Robert C. Goldsworthy (364th) ASR; Bailed out off Clacton.
P-51D C5- 44-13648

**September 15, 1944**
Lt. Louis E. Nowlin (362nd) KIA; Collided with Lt. Graeff over the North Sea.
P-51B G4-O 42-106783 "Flying Panther"
Lt. Kenneth E. Graeff (363rd) KIA; Collided with Lt. Nowlin over the North Sea.
P-51B B6-E 43-24842 "Blackpool Bat"

**September 18, 1944**
Capt. Bernard K. Seitzinger (364th) MIA-E; Hit by a Me-109 northeast of Maastricht.
P-51B C5-S 42-106923 "Almost"
Lt. Robert J. Fandry (364th) KIA; Hit by fighters northeast of Maastricht.
P-51D C5-A 44-13543 "Just Right"

**September 19, 1944**
Lt. James L. Blanchard (362nd) KIA; Hit by a Me-109 in the Arnheim-Deventer area.
P-51D G4-G 44-13741 "Buddy Boy"
Maj. Edwin W. Hiro (363rd) KIA; Hit by a Me-109 near Vreden.
P-51D B6-D 44-13518 "Horse's Itch"
Capt. Bryce W. McIntyre (364th) POW; Downed by a Spitfire near Emmerich.
P-51D C5-E 44-14429 "Tangerine"
Lt. Jerome Jacobs (364th) POW; Hit by a Me-109 southeast of Arnheim.
P-51B C5-E 43-6813 "Evelyn"
Lt. Howard E. Moebius (364th) MIA-E; Hit by fighters near Arnheim.
P-51D C5-M 44-13801

**September 28, 1944**
Lt. John S. Templin (362nd) POW; Suffered mechanical failure southwest of Bad Faulkenhausen.
P-51B G4-S 43-6698 "Bow-Legs"
Lt. James W. Leek (364th) KIAc;
P-51B C5-V 43-6971

**October 12, 1944**
Capt. Herschel T. Pascoe (363rd) POW; Hit by a FW-190 near Wunstorf.
P-51D B6-B 44-13711 "Desert Rat"

**October 18, 1944**
Lt. Horace M. Roycroft (363rd) KIA; Spun-in near Ghent.
P-51D B6-Y 44-13897

**October 19, 1944**
Lt. Charles G. Goss (362nd) MIA-E; Suffered mechanical failure east of Neustadt.
P-51D G4-Z 44-13963 "Morning Star"

**November 2, 1944**
Maj. Lawrence P. Giarrizzo (362nd) KIA; Lost a wing while chasing enemy fighters near Naumberg.
P-51D G4-H 44-13735

**November 8, 1944**
Lt. Warren B. Corwin (362nd) KIA; Damaged by a Me-262 and bellied-in near Termonde.
P-51B G4-V 43-12227
Lt. Warren J. Doransky (363rd) KIA; Suffered mechanical failure and bailed out over the North Sea but his chute failed.
P-51D B6-

**November 16, 1944**
Lt. Robert Wiser (364th) KIA; Hit trees while landing at Leiston.
P-51D C5-Y 44-14549 "Marie"

**November 18, 1944**
Lt. Sam G. Fuller (362nd) KIA; Hit by flak at Mengen Airfield.
P-51D G4-S 44-13596 "Screamin' Demon"

**November 27, 1944**
Lt. Frank L. Gailer, Jr. (363rd) POW; Downed by a P-51 near Groningen.
P-51D B6-A 44-11331 "Expectant"

**December 5, 1944**
Lt. Matthew S. Martin (362nd) POW; Suffered mechanical failure west of Brandenburg.
P-51D G4-N 44-14722 "Temptation"
Capt. Herman R. Zetterquist (364th) POW; Hit by fighters near Eberswalde.
P-51D C5-R 44-13546 "The Shillelagh"

**December 23, 1944**
Capt. Walter N. Perry, Jr. (362nd) KIA; Lost a wing near Fulda.
P-51K G4-X 44-11689 "Toolin' Fool"

**December 24, 1944**
Capt. William H. Mooney (362nd) KIA; Hit by a FW-190 near Fulda.
P-51D G4-X 44-11198 "Libby B"
Lt. William T. Gilbert, Jr. (362nd) KIA; Hit by a FW-190 near Fulda.
P-51D G4-A 44-15620
Lt. Wendell T. Helwig (363rd) KIA; Collided with a 55th Fighter Group P-51 near Daun.
P-51D B6- 44-13923 "Big Beautiful Doll"

**December 30, 1944**
Lt. Harold D. Chandler (362nd) MIA; Hit by flak east of Coblenz.
P-51D G4-G 44-13719 "Pitter Pat"

**January 2, 1945**
F/O Saul Sitzer (363rd) POW; Hit by flak near Cologne.
P-51D B6- 44-14490

**January 10, 1945**
Lt. Fred C. McCall (364th) KIA; Hit by flak near Paderborn.
P-51D C5-U 44-15026 "Cathy Mae"

**January 13, 1945**
Lt. Robert L. Schlieker (362nd) KIA; Crashed east of Woodbridge on return from the mission.
P-51D G4-P 44-14245
Lt. Richard A. Anderson (362nd) KIAc; Crashed near Horsham on a training flight.
P-51B G4-Z 43-6987

**January 14, 1945**
Lt. George A. Behling (362nd) POW; Engine quit while being chasedby a FW-190 northwest of Brandenburg.
P-51D G4-J 44-15527 "Chi-Lassie"
Lt. William R. Dunlop, Jr. (363rd) POW; Hit by fighters northwest of Brandenburg.
P-51D B6- 44-15370
Lt. James R. Sloan (363rd) POW; Hit by a Me-109 northwest of Brandenburg.
P-51D B6-Q 44-14784 "Q-Pee"

**January 16, 1945**
Lt. William B. Thompson (363rd) KIA; Crashed near Framlingham after take-off.
P-51D B6- 44-63220

**January 19, 1945**
Lt. Herman H. Delager (362nd) KIAc; Vanished while on a ferry flight from Stamstead.
P-51D G4-T 44-63658
Lt. Morris E. Gallant (364th) KIAc; Crashed in bad weather on a local test flight.
P-51B C5-G 42-106721 "Seregent"

**January 20, 1945**
Lt. Edward R. Haydon (364th) POW; Hit by flak at Lechfeld and bailed out near Kaufburen.
P-51D C5-J 44-11165 "Lady Nelda"

**January 27, 1945**
Lt. Walter E. Corby (362nd) KIAc; Crashed into a hillside in bad weather. (Also killed was S/Sgt. Melvin Schueneman of the 363rd Ftr Sqn)
AT-6 42-84593

**February 3, 1945**
Lt. George C. Kouris (364th) POW; Suffered mechanical failure southwest of Brunswick.
P-51D C5-Z 44-13586 "Greece Lightning"

**February 9, 1945**
Capt. James W. Browning (363rd) KIA; Last seen in a scrap with Me-262's near Fulda.
P-51D B6-L 44-15630 "Junior Miss"

**February 10, 1945**
Lt. Holsey C. Johnson (362nd) KIAc; Crashed near Felixstowe.
P-51B G4- 43-6755

**February 23, 1945**
Lt. Richard W. Taylor (363rd) KIA; Hit by flak and crashed into the Zuider Zee.
P-51D B6- 44-14768

**February 26, 1945**
Lt. Roy Anthony (363rd) ASR; Bailed out ten miles off Southwold.
P-51D B6-H 44-14356 "Lonesome Polecat"

**February 27, 1945**
Lt. Daniel N. Myers (363rd) ASR; Low on fuel and bailed out over the North Sea.
P-51D B6-
Lt. Robert R. Hoffman (364th) KIAc; Collided with Lt. Eisertnear Leiston.
P-51B B6-P 43-24766 (an ex-363rd a/c used for training)
Lt. Ralph E. Eisert (364th) KIAc; Collided with Lt. Hoffman near Leiston.
P-51B C5-X 42-106447

**March 2, 1945**
F/O Patrick L. Mallion (363rd) KIA; Hit by flak near Haseloff.
P-51D B6-Y 44-14888 "Melody's Answer"
Lt. Matthew Crawford (363rd) POW; Hit by flak near Gruezburg.
P-51D B6- 44-15161 "Joyce Diane"
Capt. Alva C. Murphy (364th) KIA; Hit by flak southwest of Magdeburg.
P-51D C5- 44-63765
Lt. Raymond M. Bank (364th) POW; Hit by fighters southeast of Ruhland.
P-51D C5-Y 44-15266 "Fireball"
Lt. Roscoe R. Lepore (364th) POW; Hit by flak east of Magdeburg.
P-51D C5-C 44-14555 "Pretty Pat"

**March 24, 1945**
Lt. Otto D. Jenkins (362nd) KIA; Crashed into trees while buzzing Leiston after returning from the mission.
P-51D G4-X 44-63199 "Toolin' Fools Revenge"

**March 30, 1945**
Lt. Daniel N. Myers (363rd) POW; Suffered mechanical failure and bailed out north of Schiermonnikoog Island.
P-51D B6- 44-72238 "Superwolf"

**April 3, 1945**
Lt. Jacob E. Giel (362nd) KIA; Hit by a P-51's drop tank and crashed into the North Sea.
P-51D G4- 44-14862 "Winnie Gal"

**April 9, 1945**
Lt. William B. Haack (363rd) KIA; Suffered mechanical failure near Augsburg.
P-51D B6- 44-13570

**April 17, 1945**
Lt. James C. Monahan (364th) POW; Suffered mechanical failure northwest of Prague.
P-51D C5-B 44-14900 "Nellie Jean"
Lt. Robert W. Muller (364th) POW; Hit by flak at Prague/Ruzny.
P-51D C5-D 44-14648 "Princess Pat"
Lt. Irving E. Snedeker (364th) POW; Hit by flak at Prague/Ruzny.
P-51D C5-M 44-13783 "Roving Rhoda"

**April 18, 1945**
Lt. Oscar T. Ridley (362nd) MIA-E; Hit by flak west of Prague.
P-51D G4-E 44-14789 "Sad Sack"

**May 3, 1945**
Capt. Robert S. Fifield (363rd) KIAc; Crashed near Westleton.
P-51D B6- 44-63710

**May 21, 1945**
Lt. Alfred W. Bierweiler (362nd) KIAc; Crashed southwest of Ipswich.
P-51D G4-Q 44-11190 "Lady Ovella"

**May 29, 1945**
Lt. Manuel K. Soo (364th) KIAc; Crashed near Brussels.
P-51D C5-Z 44-13578

**June 14, 1945**
Lt. George F. Barrett (363rd) KIAc; Crashed off Felixstowe after colliding with an RAF plane.
P-51D B6-

**Headquarters**
Carlisle, Guernsey I., Maj.; June 1944-September 1944; to 363rd Ftr Sqn; ex-bomber pilot in MTO
P-51K B6-W 44-11672 "Texan"
Chickering, Edward S., Col.; July 1943-February 1944
0 missions
Dregne, Irwin H., Col.; May 1943-July 1945
P-51B C5-Q "Bobby Jeanne"
P-51D C5-Q 44-13408 "Bobby Jeanne"
P-51K C5-Q 44-11678 "Bobby Jeanne"
Egenes, Hubert I., LtCol.; March 1944-March 28, 1944(KIA); ex-362nd Ftr Sqn
P-51D G4- 43-6794
Evans, Andrew J., Jr., LtCol.; October 1944-EOW
41 missions, 220 hours
P-51D G4-B 44-64051 "Little Sweetie 4"
Foy, Robert W., Maj.; November 1944-April 1945; ex-363rd Ftr Sqn
P-51D B6-V 44-63621 "Little Shrimp"
Graham, Donald W., Col.; November 1943-October 1944; ex-363rd Ftr Sqn
P-51B B6-W 43-6712
P-51D B6-W 44-13388 "Bodacious"
Hayes, Jack W., LtCol.; March 1945-May 1945; to 55th Ftr Grp; ex-bomber pilot
Hayes, Thomas L., Jr., LtCol.; March 1944-August 1944; to HdQts
78 missions, 300 hours total
P-51B C5-N "Frenisi"
P-51D C5-N 44-13318 "Frenisi"

Humphrey, Robert P., Lt.; December 1943-March 23, 1944(POW)
Landers, John D., LtCol.; October 1944-December 1944; to 78th Ftr Grp; ex-49th Ftr Grp, PTO & 55th Ftr Grp, ETO
P-51D B6- 44-13923 "Big Beautiful Doll"
Spicer, Henry R., Col.; February 1944-March 5, 1944(POW)
10 missions
P-51B B6- 43-6880 "Tony Boy"

**362nd Fighter Squadron**
Adams, Fletcher E., Capt.; March 1943-May 30, 1944(KIA)
P-51B G4-L 43-12468 "Southern Belle
Anderson, Clifford, Lt.; July 1944-January 1945
P-51D G4-G 44-13741 "Buddy Boy"
P-51D G4-O 44-14231 "Buddy Boy II"
Anderson, Richard A., Lt.; January 1945-January 13, 1945(KIAc)
Ankeny, Harry R., Capt.; June 1943-August 1944
71 missions, 301:30 hours
P-51B G4-S 43-6825 "Betsy"
P-51D G4-S 44-13596 "Betsy"
Badger, James B., Capt.; States-August 1944
P-51B G4-Y 43-7143 "Miss Florida"
Baker, Maurice F., Capt.; States-@August 1944
P-51B G4-F 43-6824 "Parker 51"
Beal, Harry E., Capt.; March 1943-October 1944
Becker, Robert H., Capt.; April 1943-August 1944
P-51B G4-O 43-6783 "Sebastian"
P-51D G4-O 44-13517 "Sebastian Jr."
Becraft, Myron A., Lt.; October 1944-EOW
51 missions, 237:05 hours
P-51D G4-S 44-63221 "Moose"
Beemer, Thomas, Lt.; States-February 25, 1944(POW)
Behling, George A., Jr., Lt.; August 1944-January 14, 1945(POW)
42 missions
P-51D G4-J 44-15527 "Chi-Lassie"
Bertram, Julian H., Lt.; February 1945-EOW
P-51D G4-V 44-14798 "Butch Baby"
Bierweiler, Alfred W., Lt.; January 1945-May 21, 1945(KIAc)
Black, Joseph, Lt.; January 1945-EOW
P-51D G4-N 44-63880 "Mary's Lil Lamb"
Blanchard, James L., Lt.; June 1944-September 19, 1944(KIA)
Boch, Oliver W., Lt.; January 1945-July 1945; ex-364th Ftr Sqn
Boyne, John J., Lt.; January 1945-July 1945
Bradner, Robert H., Lt.; January 1945-June 1945
Bright, Johnnie L., Lt.; January 1945-EOW
Broadhead, Joseph E., LtCol.; February 1943-April 1945
P-51B G4-V 43-12227 "Baby Mike"
P-51D G4-V 44-14798 "Master Mike"
Brown, Robert D., Capt.; March 1943-May 27, 1944(INT); March 1945-EOW
P-51B G4-B 43-6556 "Chicago Gun Moll"
Brown, Robert W., Lt.; States-February 1944 (injured February 13)
1 mission
Bussard, Jack O., Lt.; January 1945-November 10, 1945(KIAc); ex-364th Ftr Sqn
P-51D G4-S 44-15607 "Lil Mary"
Carson, Leonard K., Maj.; April 1943-November 1945
115 missions, 490:25 hours
P-51B G4-C 43-6634 "Nooky Booky"
P-51D G4-C 44-13316 "Nooky Booky II"
P-51D G4-C 44-14896 "Nooky Booky III"
P-51K G4-C 44-11622 "Nooky Booky IV"
Carter, Rollin L., Lt.; July 1944-July 29, 1944(POW)
Caster, Clarence R., Lt.; August-April 1945
Chandler, Harold D., Lt.; September 1944-December 30, 1944(KIA)
Cheever, Donald W., Lt.; September 1944-June 1945
P-51D G4-Y 44-14640 "Duchess"
Conlin, Raymond T., Lt.; June 1944-October 1944
P-51D G4-C 44-13316 "Olivia de H"
Connaghan, Frank J., Lt.; @January 1944-April 24, 1944(KIA)
Coon, John S., Lt.; States-August 1944
P-51B G4-S 43-6698 "Bow Legs"
P-51D G4-S 44-13596 "Bow Legs"
Corwin, Warren B., Lt.; September 1944-November 8, 1944(KIA)
Danner, Eldrid C., Lt.; January 1945-August 1945
P-51D G4-U 44-13334 "Buffalo Bertie"
Delager, Herman H., Lt.; August 1944-January 19, 1945(KIA)
P-51D G4- "Blind Date"
Dellorto, Francis A., Lt.; February 1945-EOW
Drollinger, Lynn H., Lt.; @January 1944-March 28, 1944(MIA-E)
P-51B G4- "Young Uns"
Duke-Woolley, Eric H., F/Lt.; RAF pilot on D.S.
Duncan, John F., Lt.; November 1944-EOW
P-51D G4-Z 44-14612 "Hot Shot Charlie"
Dunn, John W., Lt.; November 1944-July 1945
Dunn, Robert, Lt.; November 1944-June 1945
Ecker, Richard E., Lt.; November 1944-EOW
Egeland, Howard B., Lt.; @June 1944-
Egenes, Hubert I., LtCol.; December 1942-March 1944; to HdQts; ex-17th Pur Sqn & 40th Ftr Sqn, PTO
England, John B., Maj.; April 1943-February 1945
108 missions, 460 hours
P-51B G4-H
P-51B G4-H 42-106463 "U've Had It!
P-51D G4-H 44-13735 "U've Had It!"
P-51D G4-E 44-14789 "Missouri Armada"
Frey, Jesse R., Capt.; August 1944-April 1945
P-51D G4-M 44-15267 "Ain't Misbehavin"
Fuller, Sam G., Lt.; -November 18, 1944(KIA)
Gasser, James A., Lt.; November 1944-EOW
P-51K G4-K 44-11697 "Muddy"
Gates, Thomas L., Maj.; @May 1944-November 1944
P-51D G4-L "Angel Puss"
Giarrizzo, Lawrence P., Maj.; October 1944-November 2, 1944(KIA)
Giel, Jacob F., Lt.; February 1945-April 3, 1945(KIA)
Gilbert, William T., Lt.; July 1944-December 24, 1944(KIA)
P-51D G4-R 44-15113 "Wanderin Willie Jr."
Gordon, Edwin A., Lt.; January 1945-EOW
P-51D G4-M 44-15267 "Ain't Misbehavin"
Goss, Charles G., Lt.; September 1944-October 19, 1944 (MIA-E)
Gruber, William W., Lt.; September 1944-June 1945
P-51D G4-W 44-14152 "Cooter"
P-51D G4-W 44-14613 "Cooter"
Hagan, Kenneth E., Capt.; March 1943-June 17, 1944(MIA-E); August 1944-
P-51B G4-J "My Bonnie"
P-51K G4-G 44-11683 "Man-O-War"
Harris, Ollie E., Jr., Lt.; March 1944-
Hewit, Norton M., Lt.; February 1945-November 1945
Hill, Hershel L., Lt.; @January 1944-September 1944
Hilsted, Roger A., Lt.; March 1944-May 12, 1944(KIA)
Holmberg, Paul E., Lt.; March 1944-July 29, 1944(KIA)
Hood, Aubrey O., Lt.; March 1944-August 1944
P-51C G4-J 42-103372 "Pop's Firefly"
Hyman, Edward D., Lt.; September 1944-EOW
P-51D G4-P 44-72489 "Rolla-U-Bar"
Jenest, John G., F/O; May 1944-Summer 1944; sent home with medical disability
Jenkins, Otto D., Lt.; August 1944-March 24, 1945(KIA)
P-51B G4-P 42-106829 "Floogie"
P-51D G4-P 44-14245 "Floogie II"
P-51K G4-X 44-11689 "Toolin Fool"
P-51D G4-X 44-63199 "Toolin Fool's Revenge"
Johnson, Holsey C., Lt.; @January 1945-February 10, 1945(KIAc)
Johnson, Howard L., Lt.; -September 13, 1944(POW)
Kehrer, Merlin R., Lt.; December 1943-February 25, 1944(POW)
P-51B G4-B 43-12151
Kenney, James W., Lt.; July 1944-February 1945
P-51B G4-Q 43-6787 "Little Feetie"
Kirla, John A., Capt.; August 1944-EOW
P-51D G4-H 44-14625 "Spook"
P-51D G4-H 44-72180 "Spook"
Leek, James W., Lt.; September 1944-September 28, 1944 (KIAc)
Lichter, Albert C., Lt.; March 1943-February 22, 1944 (POW)
Lingo, Arthur M., Capt.; February 1943-April 11, 1944 (KIA)
P-51B G4-M 43-12122
Mace, Harvey F., Capt.; States-March 1944; to 495th Ftr Trg Grp; June 1944-October 1944
59 missions, 270 hours
P-51B G4-O 43-6923 "Sweet Helen"
P-51D G4-B 44-13558 "Sweet Helen II
Maloney, J., Lt.
Martin, Matthew S., Lt.; September 1944-December 5, 1944(POW)
P-51D G4-N 44-14722 "Temptation"
Martinek, Thomas W., Lt.; May 1944-October 1944
McLane, James C., Lt.; April 1945-EOW
Metcalf, John S., Lt.; April 1945-EOW
Meyer, Robert A., Lt.; @January 1944-March 16, 1944(POW)
Mitchell, Lloyd W., Lt.; @January 1944-September 1944
P-51B G4-D 43-6710 "Miss Marvel"
Mooney, William H., Capt.; August 1944-December 24, 1944(KIA)
P-51D G4-X 44-11198 "Libby-B"
Murphy, Alva C., Capt.; September 1944-January 1945; to 364th Ftr Sqn
P-51D G4-U 44-13334 "Bite Me"
Norris, Thomas E., Lt.; June 1943-August 1944
P-51B G4-Z 43-6987 "Satan"
Nowlin, Louis E., Lt.; August 1944-September 15, 1944(KIA)
O'Brien, Gilbert M., Capt.; June 1943-August 1944
69 missions, 278 hours
P-51B G4-Q 43-6787 "Shanty Irish"
Pelon, Paul A., Jr., Lt.; August 1944-April 1945
P-51D G4-D 44-14849 "Gash Hound"
Perron, Davis T., Capt.; February 1943-April 1, 1944(KIA)
Perry, Walter N., Jr., Capt.; July 1944-December 23, 1944(KIA)
P-51B G4-K 43-6637 "Rubber Check"
Potter, Richard I., Lt.; September 1944-July 1945
P-51D G4-K 44-63195 "Mary Mae"
Pugh, John F., Capt.; June 1943-September 1944
P-51B G4-N 43-6635
P-51B G4-N 42-106473 "Geronimo"
Pyeatt, Alvin F., Jr., Lt.; June 1943-March 16, 1944(POW-D)
4 missions, 13 hours
P-51B G4-S 43-6960 "Scrappy"
Rice, Donald R., Lt.; June 1943-February 24, 1944(POW)
2 missions
Ridley, Oscar T., Lt.; September 1944-April 18, 1945(MIA-E)
P-51D G4-E 44-14789 "Sad Sack"

Roberson, Arval J., Lt.; June 1943-September 1944
P-51B G4-A 43-6688
P-51D G4-A 44-13691 "Passion Wagon"
Robinson, Gilbert A., Lt.; January 1945-EOW
Robinson, Joseph L., Lt.; April 1945-EOW
P-51D G4-B 44-14819 "Big Stud"
Roughgarden, James E., Lt.; States-August 1944
P-51B G4-G
P-51B G4-G 42-106654 "Jersey Bounce"
Rydberg, Elmer D., Lt.; June 1943-April 1, 1944(KIA)
P-51B G4- "Little Lady"
Schreiber, C.J., Lt.; April 1944-September 1944
Schlieker, Robert L., Lt.; November 1944-January 13, 1945(KIA)
Schlossberg, John B., Lt.; May 1944-October 1944
Schoepke, Anton, F/O; January 1945-July 1945
P-51D G4-O 44-64073 "Skin-n-Bones"
Sehl, James H., Lt.
P-51D G4-S 44-13596 "Naughty Aughty"
Shea, Joseph E., Lt.; January 1945-November 1945
P-51D G4-E 44-72819 "My Bonnie"
Shepard, Daniel O., Lt.; June 1944-January 1945
Smith, Alden E., Lt.; States-August 1944
80 missions
P-51B G4-K 43-6637 "American Girl"
Smith, Fred C., Capt.; February 1944-October 1944; ex-361st Ftr Grp
P-51B G4-T 43-7188
P-51D G4-T 44-13552
Starkey, Rodney M., Lt.; @January 1944-September 1944
P-51B G4-X 43-7047 "Remember Me"
Sublett, John L., Capt.; September 1944-April 1945
P-51D G4-Q 44-11190 "Lady Ovella"
Swope, Ira A., Capt.; September 1944-April 1945
Taylor, Erle A., Lt.; June 1944-October 1944
Templin, John S., Lt.; -September 28, 1944(POW)
Trout, Richard E., Lt.; April 1945-EOW
Utz, Fielding A., Lt.; April 1945-July 1945
Valkwitch, James A., Lt.; -September 13, 1944(KIA)
Van Fleet, Amos E., Lt.; April 1945-EOW
Vogel, Donald W., Lt.; @January 1944-July 1, 1944(MIA-E); ex-RAF pilot
Vogel, Konstantin, Lt.; June 1943-March 18, 1944(KIA)
P-51B G4-H 43-12474
Wallen, Robert D., Lt.; March 1943-September 1944
P-51B G4-P "Joan"
P-51B G4-P 42-106829 "Joan"
Weaver, Charles E., Maj.; September 1944-EOW
P-51D G4-A 44-13691 "Passion Wagon"
P-51D G4-A 44-72199
Welch, Roger, Capt.; February 1945-July 1945
White, Robert J., F/O; April 1945-July 1945
Williams, Calvert L., Capt.; States-September 1944
P-51B G4-U 43-6448 "Wee Willie"
P-51D G4-U 44-13334 "Wee Willie II"
Williams, Harry J., Lt.; November 1944-July 1945
Wilson, Keith H., Lt.; April 1945-EOW
Wyatt, Howard A., Capt.; November 1944-EOW
Ziebell, John A., Lt.; November 1944-EOW
P-51K G4-B 44-11571

**363rd Fighter Squadron**
Abner, Allen K., Lt.; January 1945-July 1945
P-51D B6-R 44-14519
Anderson, Clarence E., Jr., Maj.; February 1943-January 1945
116 missions, 480 hours
P-51B B6-S 43-6723 "Old Crow"
P-51B B6-S 43-24823 "Old Crow"
P-51D B6-S 44-14450 "Old Crow"
Anthony, Roy, Lt.; January 1945-July 1945
Atkins, Lloyd J., F/O; February 1945-October 1945
Banks, Ralph E., Lt.; August 1944-EOW
Barrett, George P., Lt.; December 1944-June 14, 1945(KIAc)
30 mission, 146:10 hours
Beeney, Jack, Lt.; February 1945-July 1945
Bender, Guy D., Lt.; February 1945-EOW
Bochkay, Donald H., Maj.; April 1943-October 1945
123 missions, 510 hours
P-51B B6-F 43-6933 "Alice In Wonderland"
P-51C B6-F 42-103041 "Speedball Alice"
P-51D B6-F 44-13681
P-51D B6-F 44-15422
P-51D B6-F 44-72244
P-51D B6-F 44-72147
Bowles, Paul N., Lt.; September 1944-August 1945
P-51D B6-C 44-63168 "Mountaineer"
Boyle, Alfred R., Lt.; March 1943-February 21, 1944(POW)
Browning, James W., Capt.; March 1943-February 9, 1945(KIA)
P-51B B6-P 43-6563 "Gentleman Jim"
P-51D B6-P 44-14937 "Gentleman Jim"
Burnett, Marion E., Lt.; May 1944-September 13, 1944(POW)
Bzdelik, Joseph, F/O; November 1944-EOW
Campbell, Charles O., Lt.; August 1944-August 17, 1944(KIAc)
0 missions
Cannon, Joseph W., Lt.; September 1944-April 1945
72 missions
P-51D B6-B 44-13887 "Little Joe"
P-51D B6-B 44-72258 "Little Joe"
Carlisle, Guernsey I., LtCol.; September 1944-February 1945; ex-HdQts
P-51K B6-W 44-11672 "Texan"
Carr, Edward J., Lt.; August 1944-October 1945
Carter, Johnnie L., Capt.; July 1944-May 1945
Casey, John C., Lt.; February 1945-July 1945
P-51D B6-U "Frisco Kid"
Childs, John K., Lt.; May 1944-June 10, 1944(KIA)
Cleland, Jack, F/Lt.; July 1944-September 1944; RAF pilot on D.S.
P-51D B6-V 44-13573 "Isabel III"
Corby, Walter E., Lt.; September 1944-January 13, 1945(KIAc)
Crawford, Matthew, Lt.; January 1945-March 2, 1945(KIA)
Crump, James T., Lt.; August 1944-EOW
Currie, William J., Lt.; January 1945-July 1945
P-51D B6-X 44-13388 "Super X"
Davis, William S., Lt.; June 1944-July 1945
DeVries, Paul K., Capt.; February 1943-October 1944
Dick, George D., Lt.; April 1945-EOW
Donnell, Ralph H., Lt.; April 24, 1944(POW)
Doranski, Warren J., Lt.; August 1944-November 8, 1944(KIA)
Dunlop, William R., Lt.; July 1944-January 14, 1945(POW)
Emery, Michael R., Lt.; September 1944-October 1945
Fennell, William S., Lt.; June 1944-December 1944
Ferron, Donald J., Lt.; July 1944-August 10, 1944(KIA)
Fifield, Robert S., Capt.; July 1944-May 3, 1945(KIAc)
88 missions, 376:05 hours
Fisher, Norbert G., Lt.; May 1944-December 1944
70 missions, 270:10 hours
P-51B B6-Q 43-6510 "Dam-Phy-No"
Foy, Robert W., Maj.; June 1943-November 1944; to HdQts
P-51B B6-V
P-51D B6-V 44-13712 "Reluctant Rebel"
Franklin, Henry B., Lt.; June 1944-November 1944
Fricker, William H., Lt.; May 1944-November 1944
P-51D B6-O 44-14532 "Ol Flak Joe"
Gailer, Frank L., Jr., Lt.; August 1944-November 27, 1944(POW)
45 missions, 187:30 hours
P-51B B6- "Jeesil Peesil Mommy"
P-51K B6-A 44-11331 "Expectant"
Gambill, William W., Lt.; States-March 8, 1944(POW-D)
Gangwish, Robert C., Lt.; January 1944-September 1944
George, George E., Lt.; April 1944-September 1944
P-51B B6-E 43-24842 "Blackpool Bat"
Giltner, Joseph H., Jr., Capt.; States-January 25, 1944(POW)
Graeff, Kenneth F., Lt.; July 1944-September 15, 1944(KIA)
Graham, Donald W., Maj.; States-November 1943; to HdQts
P-51B B6-W 43-6712
Gutierrez, Santiago R., Lt.; February 1944-March 29, 1944(KIA)
6 missions
Haack, William B., Lt.; February 1945-April 9, 1945(KIA)
Hand, Harold O., Lt.; May 1944-November 1944
Hare, Henry L., Lt.; October 1944-October 1945
Helwig, Wendell D., Lt.; September 1944-December 24, 1944(KIA)
Hinman, Howard S., Lt.; March 1943-April 24, 1944(POW)
Hiro, Edwin W., Maj.; February 1943-September 19, 1944(KIA)
P-51B B6-D "Horse's Itch"
P-51D B6-D 44-13518 "Horse's Itch"
Hubbard, Lloyd M., Capt.; February 1943-February 9, 1944(KIA)
Hughes, Thomas E., Capt.; August 1944-EOW
Jacobs, John T., Lt.; -July 1945
Jones, Carter L., Lt.; -March 22, 1944(POW)
Kalessa, Russell R., Lt.; February 1945-EOW
Kayser, Henry R., Lt.; January 1944-
Kenney, Harold M., Lt.; August 17, 1944(MIA-E)
Koka, Frank, Lt.; June 1944-July 7, 1944(KIA)
Kyle, Frank A., Lt.; February 1945-July 1945
P-51D B6-W 44-14672 "Love of Mine"
Landis, Keehn, Lt.; July 1944-March 1945
P-51D B6-H 44-14356 "Lonesome Polecat"
Lasswell, Gene H., Lt.; February 1945-October 1945
Mallione, Patrick L., Lt.; November 1944-March 2, 1945(KIA)
Mann, Ralph W., Lt.; November 1944-October 1945
Manthos, Atlee G., Capt.; September 1944-EOW
Maynard, Floyd J., Lt.; May 1944-October 1944
McGee, Donald C., Maj.; January 1945-May 1945; ex-364th Ftr Sqn
62 missions, 278 hours total
P-51D B6-J 44-15888 "Whole Hawg"
McGinley, William R., Lt.; States-March 29, 1944(KIA)
11 missions
McKee, Charles E., Lt.; March 1943-February 24, 1944(POW)
McKeown, William T., Lt.; March 1945-EOW
McLane, James, Lt.; March 1945-EOW
4 missions
Michaely, William D., Lt.; June 1943-@August 1944
Miller, Gifford W., Lt.; March 1945-EOW
Miller, John A., Lt.; March 1945-EOW
Moore, Robert N., Capt.; June 1943-October 1945

Myers, Daniel N., Lt.; October 1944-March 30, 1945(POW)
O'Brien, William R., Capt.; March 1943-August 1944
77 missions
P-51B B6-G
P-51D B6-G 44-13522 "Billy's Bitch"
Ofsthun, Carroll W., Lt.; September 1944-April 1945
P-51D B6-Y 44-14977 "The Count"
Omernik, Stanley M., Lt.; April 1944-May 9, 1944(POW)
Overstreet, William B., Lt.; June 1943-September 1944
P-51C B6-O 42-103309 "Berlin Express"
P-51B B6-O 43-24823 "Berlin Express
Pagels, Roger E., Lt.; April 1944-June 6, 1944(MIA-E); September 1944-October 1944
Pasaka, Donald J., Lt.; May 1944-October 1944
Pascoe, Hershel T., Capt.; June 1943-October 12, 1944(POW)
P-51B B6-B 43-6999
P-51D B6-B 44-13714 "Desert Rat"
Pearson, Charles S., Lt.; December 1943-August 1944
P-51B B6-H 43-6755 "Kalamazoo Kid"
Peters, Charles K., Capt.; June 1943-August 1944
P-51B B6-J 43-6564 "Daddy Rabbit"
P-51D B6-J 44-13897 "Daddy Rabbit"
Pielich, Peter, Lt.; October 1944-September 1945
Pierce, Joseph F., Lt.; April 1943-May 21, 1944(KIA)
P-51B B6-N 43-6644
Reust, Fred W., Lt.; States-April 12, 1944(POW)
Reynolds, Harold T., Lt.; -October 1945
Rice, George J., Lt.; October 1944-October 1945(KIAc)
Roberts, Warner P., Lt.; September 1944-April 1945
P-51D B6-K 44-15385 "Mary E"
Rogers, Ellis A., Capt.; States-May 8, 1944(KIA)
32 missions
Roper, Richard C., Lt.; June 1944-October 1944
Ross, Donald H., Lt.; December 1943-February 20, 1944(POW); ex-RAF & 4th Ftr Grp
Roycroft, Horace M., Lt.; October 1944-October 18, 1944(KIA)
Simpson, Edward K., Jr., Capt.; June 1943-August 10, 1944(KIA)
P-51B B6- "All-Away II"
P-51B B6- "The Flying Panther"
Sitzer, Saul, F/O; October 1944-January 2, 1945(POW)
Siverts, Donovan D., Lt.; April 1944-May 9, 1944(KIA)
Skara, John R., Lt.; June 1944-December 1944
P-51B B6-Z 42-106458 "Doodlebug"
Sloan, James R., Lt.; September 1944-January 14, 1945(POW)
43 missions
P-51D B6-Q 44-14784 "Q-Pee"
Smith, Irving A., Lt.; States-June 6, 1944(KIA)
Smith, Robert E., Lt.; April 1944-September 1944
Staudte, Raymond W., Lt.; June 1943-August 1944
Stern, John R., Capt.; August 1944-EOW
P-51D B6-A 44-14736 "Pappy's Answer"
Sullivan, Francis I., Lt., May 1944-November 1944
Taber, Allison Y., F/O; April 1945-EOW
Taylor, James E., Lt.; November 1944-October 1945
Taylor, Richard W., Lt.; January 1945-February 23, 1945(KIA); ex-78th Ftr Grp
Thompson, William B., Lt.; November 1944-January 16, 1945(KIA)
Thorkelson, Robert L., Lt.; November 1944-July 1945
Throop, Montgomery H., Jr., Maj.; January 1944-June 1944; ex-4th Ftr Grp & RAF
P-51B B6- "Shanghai Lil"
Tiede, Ernest C., Jr., Capt.; States-September 1945
P-51B B6-J 43-6564 "7 Up High"
Titus, Robert D., Lt.; May 1944-August 1944
Toups, Denis J., Lt.; November 1944-EOW
Van Drisse, Vernon J., Lt.; April 1945-EOW
Van Pelt, John C., F/O; April 1945-EOW
Van Roy, Harlan Q., Lt.; February 1945-July 1945
West, James H., Lt.; April 1945-July 1945
Windham, James T., Capt.; September 1944-EOW
Wolf, Raymond E., Lt.; September 1944-October 1945(KIAc)
Wood, Lawrence D., Capt.; June 1943-September 1944
Yeager, Charles E., Capt.; March 1943-March 5, 1944(MIA-E) June 1944-January 1945
64 missions
P-51B B6-Y 43-6763 "Glamorous Glen"
P-51D B6-Y 44-13897 "Glamorous Glenn II"
P-51D B6-Y 44-14888 "Glamorous Glen III"
Zarnke, Glenwood A., Lt.; September 1944-EOW
P-51D B6-L 44-15630 "Junior Miss"
P-51D B6-L 44-63680 "Junior Miss II"

**364th Fighter Squadron**

Adams, Thomas H., Capt.; September 1944-June 1945
P-51D C5-L 44-64099 "Arkansas Traveler"
Allen, Merle F., Lt.; May 1944-November 1944
Arrendale, Harold E., Lt.; December 1944-EOW
Baker, Allen P., Lt.; -EOW
Bank, Raymond M., Lt.; September 1944-March 2, 1945(POW)
46 missions, 195 hours
P-51D C5-Y 44-15266 "Fireball"
Baron, Walter, Lt.; -August 25, 1944(INT)
Boch, Oliver W., F/O; December 1944-January 1945; to 362nd Ftr Sqn
Braley, Byron K., Lt.; August 1944-September 1945
P-51D C5- "B.K.'s Battle Buggy"
Bridges, Archie F., Lt.; -May 19, 1944(POW)
Brown, Kirby M., Lt.; May 1944-September 13, 1944(KIA)
Burtner, Charles E., Lt.; May 1944-August 25, 1944(INT)
P-51D C5-I 44-13345 "Mary Ann"
Bussard, Jack O., Lt.; December 1944-January 1945; to 362nd Ftr Sqn
Carder, John B., Capt.; March 1943-May 12, 1944(POW)
P-51B C5-J
P-51B C5-J 42-106777 "Taxpayer's Delight"
Carroll, Darwin J., Lt.; June 1943-February 22, 1944(KIA)
Cedoz, Merle F., Lt.; December 1944-EOW
Chambers, Frank A., Lt.; February 1945-EOW
Colburn, James E., Lt.; -June 14, 1944(KIA)
Conklin, Cyril D., Lt.; -May 27, 1944(POW)
Cosgrove, Arnold F., Lt.; February 1945-EOW
Currie, George D., Capt.; February 1943-April 11, 1944(KIA)
Davis, Glendon V., Capt.; February 1943-April 28, 1944(MIA-E)
P-51B C5-O 43-6867 "Pregnant Polecat"
Denesha, John N., Lt.; May 1944-June 7, 1944(KIA)
Dooley, Chester H., Lt.; @April 1944-October 1944
Eisert, Ralph E., Lt.; February 1945-February 27, 1945(KIAc
0 missions
Elliott, Ben F., Jr., Lt.; December 1943-April 27, 1944(POW)
Fairweather, Paul D., Lt.; March 1943-December 1944
Fandray, Robert J., Lt.; May 1944-September 18, 1944(KIA)
Fecher, Louis A., III, Lt.; May 1944-November 1944
P-51C C5-K 43-25039 "Lil Kitten"
Finley, Daniel L., Lt.; -July 29, 1944(POW-D)
Fitch, Albert W., Lt.; September 1944-EOW
Foard, William W., Lt.; February 1945-June 1945
P-51D C5-A 44-15660 "Swamp Fox"
Frederick, Nicholas J., Lt.; June 1944-November 1944
P-51D C5-Y 44-14549 "Marie"
Fry, Edward R., Lt.; September 1944-September 1945
P-51D C5-D 44-13648 "Princess Pat"
P-51D C5-D 44-73125 "Princess Pat II"
Galbreath, Girard G., Lt.; February 1945-July 1945
Gallant, Morris E., Lt.; September 1944-January 19, 1945(KIA)
Goldsworthy, Robert G., Lt.; June 1944-January 1945; to 7th Photo Grp; later 78th Ftr Grp
Halbrook, Grover T., Lt.; February 1945-EOW
Harris, Thomas L., Capt.; July 1943-May 27, 1944(POW)
P-51B C5-S 43-6653 "Lil Red's Rocket"
Hatala, Paul R., Capt.; August 1944-EOW
66 missions
P-51D C5-B "Jeanne"
Haydon, Edward R., Lt.; September 1944-January 20, 1945(POW)
P-51D C5-J 44-11165 "Lady Nelda"
Hayes, Thomas L., Jr., Maj.; May 1943-March 1944; to HdQts; ex-20th Pur Sqn, PTO
78 missions, 300 hours total
P-51B C5-N "Frenisi"
Henry, James O., Lt.; September 1944-September 1945
Hermanson, Harry H., Lt.; States-September 1944
Hoffman, Robert R., Lt.; February 1945-February 27, 1945(KIAc
0 missions
Holmes, William, III, F/O; February 1945-EOW
Howell, Horace P., Lt.; June 1944-December 1944
P-51D C5-T 44-13586 "Flak Happy"
Howell, John C., Capt.; March 1943-September 1944
P-51B C5-L 43-106447 "Shoo Shoo Baby"
P-51D C5-L 44-13583 "Shoo Shoo Baby"
Howes, Osborn, Lt.; -EOW
Hubbard, Glenn E., Lt.; July 1943-September 1944
P-51B C5-S 42-106923 "Almost"
Jackson, Thomas, Lt.; October 1944-EOW
Jacobs, Jerome, Lt.; July 1944-September 19, 1944(POW)
Jenkins, Joseph M., Lt.; July 1943-May 24, 1944(KIA)
P-51B C5-M "Geechee Gal"
P-51B C5-M "Geechee Girl"
Johnson, Earl W., Lt.; September 1944-July 1945
Juszczyk, Edmond, Lt.; September 1944-EOW
Karger, Dale E., Lt.; September 1944-May 1945
65 missions, 293:45 hours
P-51D C5-U 44-15026 "Cathy Mae"
P-51D C5-U 44-72313 "Cathy Mae II"
Kocher, Donald C., Lt.; October 1944-July 1945
P-51D C5-Z 44-13861 "Lil Poopsie"
Kouris, George C., Lt.; October 1944-February 3, 1945(POW)
P-51D C5-ZZ 44-13587 "Greece Lightning"
Leek, James W., Lt.; September 1944-September 28, 1944 (KIAc)
Lepore, Roscoe R., Lt.; September 1944-March 2, 1945(POW)
P-51D C5-C 44-11224 "Pretty Pat"
P-51D C5-C 44-14555 "Pretty Pat"
Maxwell, Chester K., Capt.; July 1944-May 1945
P-51D C5-H 44-63861 "Lady Esther"
McCall, Fred C., Lt.; September 1944-January 10, 1945(KIA)
McGee, Donald C., Maj.; November 1944-January 1945; to 363rd Ftr Sqn; ex-8th Ftr Grp, PTO
62 missions, 278 hours total
McGuire, Ivan L., Capt.; July 1944-May 1945
P-51D C5-J 44-72056 "Plastered Bastard"
McIntyre, Bryce W., Capt.; June 1944-September 19, 1944(POW)
McKinney, Thomas M., Capt.; March 1943-August 1944
P-51B C5-A 42-106843 "Round Trip Jr."

McMullen, James P., Lt.; -July 1945
Medeiros, John L., Capt.; February 1943-March 4, 1944(POW)
P-51B C5-E 43-6813 "Pappy's Answer"
Moebius, Howard, Lt.; July 1944-September 19, 1944(MIA-E)
Monahan, James C., Lt.; -April 17, 1945(POW)
Moore, Robert W., Capt.; -EOW
Moorhouse, Hugh J., Lt.; August 1944-
P-51D C5- "Baby Jo"
Morris, George W., Lt.; May 1944-November 1944
P-51D C5-I 44-13783 "Baby Marilyn"
Muller, Robert W., Lt.; -April 17, 1945(POW)
Murphy, Alva C., Capt.; January 1945-March 2, 1945(KIA); ex-363nd Ftr Sqn
P-51D C5- 44-63765
Nowlin, Hollis R., Lt.; States-September 1944
P-51C C5-M 42-103348 "Vicious Viv"
P-51D C5-M 44-13801
Peterson, Richard A., Maj.; April 1943-February 1945
118 missions, 500 hours
P-51B C5-T 43-6935 "Hurry Home Honey"
P-51D C5-T 44-13586 "Hurry Home Honey"
P-51D C5-T 44-14868 "Hurry Home Honey"
Pfeiffer, Henry A., Lt.; March 1944-October 1944
P-51B C5-E 43-6813
P-51D C5-E 44-14429 "Tangerine"
P-51D C5-E 44-14507 "Tangerine"
Post, Dean M., Jr., Lt.; -May 27, 1944(KIA)
Postle, Maurice A., Lt.; -April 15, 1944(POW)
Price, Lester L., Lt.; February 1945-July 1945
Redd, Howard E., Lt.; May 1944-November 1944
Reese, William C., Lt.; May 1943-May 21, 1944(KIA)
P-51B C5-F 43-12313 "Bear River Betsy"
Reid, Wallace J., Lt.; July 1944-August 4, 1944(POW)
Ruder, Leroy A., Capt.; June 1943-June 6, 1944(KIA)
P-51B C5-X "Linda Lu"
P-51B C5-X 42-106768 "Linda Lu"
Salsman, John J., Lt.; April 1944-October 1944
P-51C C5-C 42-103601 "Maize-R"
Sandborn, Dwaine A., Lt.; June 1944-November 1944
Schimanski, Robert G., Capt.; July 1944-April 1945
70 missions, 300 hours
P-51D C5-O 44-14334
Schneider, Charles F., F/O; February 1945-October 1945
Seitzinger, Bernard K., Capt.; September 1944-September 18, 1944 (MIA-E)
Shaw, Robert M., Capt.; June 1943-September 1944
P-51B C5-H
P-51D C5-H 44-13815
Smith, Richard C., Capt.; March 1943-June 29, 1944(KIA)
Smith, Robert C., Lt.; March 1943-June 1944; to 339th Ftr Grp
P-51B C5-K 43-6974 "Mr. Period"
Smith, Robert L., Lt.; May 1944-November 1944
Snedeker, Irving E., Lt.; October 1944-April 17, 1945(POW)
P-51D C5-M 44-14783 "Roving Rhoda"
Soo, Manuel K., Lt.; March 1945-May 29, 1945(KIAc); ex-368th Ftr Grp, 9th Air Force
Sparks, Raymond, Jr., Lt.; March 1943-May 8, 1944(POW)
P-51B C5-C 43-6801 "Boilermaker"
Spinks, Heyward C., Lt.; May 1944-June 20, 1944(MIA-E)
Stager, Joseph F., Lt.; April 1944-April 24, 1944(POW)
Stanley, Morris A., Capt.; June 1943-November 1944
P-51B C5-Y
P-51D C5-Y 44-13678 "Linda J"
Steiger, James A., Lt.; February 1945-June 1945
Stepelton, Mark H., Capt.; July 1943-September 1944
P-51B C5- "Lady Julie"
Storch, John A., LtCol.; February 1943-May 1945
P-51B C5-R "The Shillelagh"
P-51D C5-R 44-13546 "The Shillelagh"
P-51D C5-R 44-72164 "The Shillelagh"
Strode, James E., Lt.; June 1943-March 27, 1944(KIA)
Sullivan, Joseph G., Lt.; -May 24, 1944(MIA-E)
Summers, Cordell L., Lt.; June 1943-April 30, 1944(MIA-E)
Sumner, Charles D., Capt.; July 1943-August 1944
P-51B C5-Z "Bat Cave"
P-51C C5-Z 42-103502 "Pride of the Yanks"
Sutton, Edwin R., Lt.; June 1943-March 29, 1944(KIA)
Tyler, Gerald E., Capt.; June 1944-November 1944
P-51B C5-J 43-6376 "Little Duckfoot"
P-51D C5-J 44-14650 "Little Duckfoot"
Warren, Jack R., Capt.; March 1943-March 18, 1944(KIA)
P-51B C5-F 43-12124
Wasylyk, Stephen, Lt.; September 1944-July 1945
P-51D C5-X 44-13621 "Philly Dillies"
Weber, Gilman L., Lt.; September 1944-EOW
P-51D C5-G 44-72372 "Alibabsandi"
Wesling, Howard, Lt.; November 1944-July 1945
Westphal, Lawrence A., Lt.; November 1944-October 1945
Wilhelm, Harold T., Lt.; November 1944-July 1945
Williams, David R., Lt.; November 1944-October 1945
Winks, Robert P., Lt.; July 1944-March 1945
69 missions, 300:45 hours
P-51D C5-W "Trusty Rusty"
Wiser, Robert, Lt.; September 1944-November 16, 1944(KIA)
Wright, Roland R., Lt.; November 1944-EOW
P-51D C5-T 44-14868 "Mormon Mustang"
P-51D C5-T 44-73219 "Mormon Mustang"
Zacharie, Lloyd F., Lt.; November 1944-EOW
P-51D C5-Z 44-13578 "Mom Smith's Lil Angel"
Zetterquist, Herman R., Capt.; October 1944-December 5, 1944(POW)
Zettler, Vincent V., Jr., Lt.; November 1944-June 1945
35 missions, 173 hours
P-51D C5-F 44-72927 "Canton Can"

**Aircraft of the 362nd Fighter Squadron**

P-51C-5-NT
42-103372 G4-J "Pop's Firefly" A.O. Hood

P-51B-1-NA
43-12122 G4-M A.M. Lingo
43-12149 G4-
43-12150 G4-
43-12151 G4-B M.R. Kehrer
43-12171 G4-
43-12188 G4-
43-12227 G4-V "Baby Mike" J.E. Broadhead
43-12412 G4-
43-12416 G4-
43-12433 G4-L
43-12442 G4-
43-12455 G4-A "Blythe Spirit"
43-12456 G4-D
43-12468 G4-L "Southern Belle" F.E. Adams
43-12474 G4-H

P-51B-5-NA
43-6448 G4-U "Wee Willie" C.L. Williams
43-6556 G4-B "Chicago Gun Moll" R.D. Brown
43-6625 G4-N J.F. Pugh
43-6629 G4-
43-6634 G4-C "Nooky Booky" L.K. Carson
43-6637 G4-K "American Girl" A.E. Smith
43-6637 G4-K "Rubber Check" W.N. Perry
43-6688 G4-A A.J. Roberson
43-6698 G4-E "Texas Ranger"
43-6698 G4-S "Bow Legs" J.S. Coon
43-6710 G4-D "Miss Marvel" L.W. Mitchell
43-6721 G4-W
43-6727 G4-I
43-6729 G4-
43-6741 G4-
43-6743 G4-
43-6787 G4-Q "Shanty Irish" G.M. O'Brien
43-6787 G4-Q "Little Feetie" J.W. Kenney
43-6892 G4-
43-6794 G4- H.I. Egenes
43-6824 G4-F "Parker 51" M.F. Baker
43-6825 G4-S "Betsy" H.R. Ankeny
43-6923 G4-O "Sweet Helen" H.F. Mace
43-6927 G4-
43-6956 G4-
43-6960 G4-S "Scrappy" A.F. Pyeatt
43-6987 G4-Z "Satan" T.E. Norris
43-7047 G4-X "Remember Me" R.M. Starkey

P-51B-10-NA
42-106462 G4-H "U've Had It!" J.B. England
42-106473 G4-N "Geronimo" J.F. Pugh
42-106654 G4-G "Jersey Bounce" J.E. Roughgarden

P-51B-15-NA
43-7143 G4-Y "Miss Florida" J.B. Badger
43-7176 G4-I
43-7184 G4-O
43-7188 G4-T F.C. Smith
42-106783 G4-O "Sebastian" R.H. Becker
42-106783 G4-O "Flying Panther"
42-106829 G4-P "Joan" R.D. Wallen
42-106829 G4-P "Floogie" O.D. Jenkins
42-106831 G4-G

P-51D-5-NT
44-11190 G4-Q "Lady Ovella" J.L. Sublett
44-11198 G4-X "Libby-B" W.H. Mooney

P-51K-5-NT
44-11373 G4-
44-11571 G4-B J.A. Zeibell
44-11622 G4-C "Nooky Booky IV" L.K. Carson
44-11683 G4-G "Man-O-War" K.E. Hagan
44-11689 G4-X "Toolin' Fool" O.D. Jenkins
44-11697 G4-K "Muddy" J.A. Gasser

P-51D-5-NA

44-13316 G4-C "Nooky Booky II" L.K. Carson
44-13316 G4-C "Olivia de H" R.T. Conlin
44-13334 G4-U "Wee Willy II" C.L. Williams
44-13334 G4-U "Bite Me" A.C. Murphy
44-13334 G4-U "Buffalo Bertie" E.C. Danner
44-13517 G4-O "Sebastian Jr." R.H. Becker
44-13552 G4-T
44-13558 G4-B "Sweet Helen II" H.F. Mace
44-13570 G4-L "Little Bev"
44-13596 G4-S "Bow Legs" J.S. Coon
44-13596 G4-S "Betsy" H.R. Ankeny
44-13596 G4-S "Naughty Aughty" J.H. Sehl
44-13596 G4-S "Screamin' Demon"
44-13691 G4-A "Passion Wagon" A.J. Roberson/C.E. Weaver
44-13719 G4-G "Pitter Pat"
44-13735 G4-H
44-13738 G4-X
44-13741 G4-G "Buddy Boy" C. Anderson
44-13963 G4-Z "Miss Satan" T.E. Norris
44-13963 G4-Z "Morning Star"

P-51D-10-NA

44-14152 G4-W "Cooter" W.W. Gruber
44-14231 G4-O "Buddy Boy II" C. Anderson
44-14245 G4-P "Floogie II" O.D. Jenkins
44-14390 G4-U
44-14612 G4-Z "Hot Shot Charlie" J.F. Duncan
44-14613 G4-W "Cooter" W.W. Gruber
44-14625 G4-H "Spook" J.A. Kirla
44-14640 G4-Y "Duchess" D.W. Cheever
44-14682 G4- "Winnie Gal"
44-14722 G4-N "Temptation" M.S. Martin
44-14789 G4-E "Missouri Armada" J.B. England
44-14789 G4-E "Sad Sack" O.T. Ridley
44-14798 G4-V "Master Mike" J.E. Broadhead
44-14798 G4-V "Butch Baby" J.H. Bertram
44-14819 G4-B "Big Stud" J.L. Robinson
44-14820 G4-H "Spook" J.A. Kirla
44-14849 G4-D "Gash Hound" P.A. Pelon

P-51D-15-NA

44-14896 G4-C "Nooky Booky III" L.K. Carson
44-14993 G4-
44-15113 G4-R "Wanderin' Willie Jr." W.T. Gilbert
44-15267 G4-M "Ain't Misbehavin'" E.A. Gordon/J.R. Frey
44-15421 G4-Z J.F. Duncan
44-15527 G4-J "Chi-Lassie" G.A. Behling
44-15607 G4-S "Ticket To Loraine"
44-15607 G4-S "Lil Mary" J.O. Bussard
44-15620 G4-A
44-15687 G4-S "The Whistler"

P-51D-20-NA

44-63195 G4-K "Mary Mae" R.I. Potter
44-63199 G4-X "Toolin' Fool's Revenge" O.D. Jenkins
44-63221 G4-S "Moose" M.A. Becraft
44-63222 G4-A "Nevada Skat Cat"
44-63658 G4-T
44-63880 G4-N "Mary's Lil Lamb" J. Black
44-64051 G4-B "Little Sweetie 4" A.J. Evans
44-64973 G4-O "Skin-n-Bones" A. Schoepke
44-72077 G4-L
44-72180 G4-H "Spook" J.A. Kirla
44-72199 G4-A C.E. Weaver
44-72489 G4-P "Rolla-U-" E.D. Hyman

P-51D-25-NA

44-72819 G4-E "My Bonnie" J.E. Shea
44-72821 G4-C "Biggie"

Unknown Serials

P-51B G4-P "Joan" R.D. Wallen
P-51B G4-J "My Bonnie" K.E. Hagen
P-51B G4- "Young Uns" L.H. Drollinger
P-51B G4- "Little Lady" E.D. Rydberg
P-51B G4- "Sweet Eloise"
P-51D G4-L "Angel Puss" T.L. Gates
P-51D G4- "Blind Date" H.H. Delager
P-51D G4- "Destitute Prostitute"

**Aircraft of the 363rd Fighter Squadron**

P-51C-1-NT

42-103002 B6-Y
42-103041 B6-F "Speedball Alice" D.H. Bochkay
42-103286 B6-
42-103309 B6-O "Berlin Express" W.B. Overstreet

P-51B-1-NA

43-12131 B6-
43-12187 B6-
43-12315 B6-
43-12368 B6-

P-51B-5-NA

43-6393 B6-R
43-6397 B6-
43-6413 B6-
43-6427 B6-
43-6429 B6-Z
43-6510 B6-Q "Dam-Phy-No" N.G. Fisher
43-6519 B6-E "Oh Bobby"
43-6563 B6-P "Gentleman Jim" J.W. Browning
43-6564 B6-J "7 Up High" E.C. Tiede
43-6566 B6-K
43-6624 B6-
43-6628 B6-K "Typhoon McGoon"
43-6644 B6-R
43-6712 B6-A "Yardbird"
43-6712 B6-W D.W. Graham
43-6720 B6-
43-6723 B6-S "Old Crow" C.E. Anderson
43-6755 B6-H "Kalamazoo Kid" C.S. Pearson
43-6763 B6-Y "Glamorous Glen" C.E. Yeager
43-6858 B6-
43-6880 B6-"Tony Boy" H.R. Spicer
43-6904 B6-R
43-6940 B6-
43-6947 B6-
43-6963 B6-F "Alice In Wonderland" D.H. Bochkay
43-6986 B6-
43-6999 B6-B H.T. Pascoe
43-7011 B6-
43-7019 B6-
43-7052 B6-

P-51B-10-NA

42-106458 B6-Z "Doodlebug" J.R. Skara
42-106696 B6-

P-51B-15-NA

42-106793 B6-
42-106918 B6-D
43-24766 B6-P
43-24817 B6-N
43-24823 B6-S "Old Crow" C.E. Anderson
43-24823 B6-O "Berlin Express" W.B. Overstreet
43-24842 B6-E "Blackpool Bat" G.G. George

P-51D-5-NT

44-11331 B6-A "Expectant" F.L. Gailer

P-51K-5-NT

44-11672 B6-W "Texan" G.I. Carlisle

P-51D-5-NA

44-13388 B6-W "Bodacious" D.W. Graham
44-13388 B6-W "Super X" W.J. Currie
44-13518 B6-D "Horse's Itch" E.W. Hiro
44-13522 B6-G "Billy's Bitch" W.R. O'Brien
44-13573 B6-V "Isabel III" J. Cleland
44-13681 B6-F D.H. Bochkay
44-13681 B6-M
44-13712 B6-V "Reluctant Rebel" R.W. Foy
44-13714 B6-B "Desert Rat" H.T. Pascoe
44-13716 B6-M
44-13717 B6-P
44-13745 B6-C "Hi Phyl"
44-13887 B6-B "Little Joe" J.W. Cannon
44-13897 B6-J "Daddy Rabbit" C.K. Peters
44-13897 B6-Y "Glamorous Glen II" C.E. Yeager
44-13923 B6- "Big Beautiful Doll" J.D. Landers
44-14009 B6-I

P-51D-10-NA

44-14356 B6-H "Lonesome Polecat" K. Landis
44-14450 B6-S "Old Crow" C.E. Anderson
44-14519 B6-R A.K. Abner
44-14532 B6-O "Ol' Flak Joe" W.H. Fricker
44-14672 B6-W "Love Of Mine" F.A. Kyle
44-14736 B6-A "Pappy's Answer" J.R. Stern
44-14768 B6-
44-14784 B6-Q "Q-Pee" J.R. Sloan

P-51D-15-NA

44-14888 B6-Y "Glamorous Glen III" C.E. Yeager
44-14937 B6-P "Gentleman Jim" J.W. Browning
44-14937 B6-X

44-14977 B6-Y "The Count" C.W. Ofsthun
44-15035 B6-O "Alice Marie II"
44-15161 B6- "Joyce Diane"
44-15370 B6-
44-15385 B6-K "Mary E" W.P. Roberts
44-15422 B6-F D.H. Bochkay
44-15630 B6-L "Junior Miss" G.A. Zarnke

P-51D-20-NA
44-63168 B6-C "Mountaineer" P.N. Bowles
44-63220 B6-
44-63621 B6-V "Little Shrimp" R.W. Foy
44-63680 B6-L "Junior Miss II" G.A. Zarnke
44-63710 B6-
44-63755 B6-W "The Tender Terror"
44-63810 B6-C "Stump Jumper"
44-72147 B6-F D.H. Bochkay
44-72187 B6-O "Alice Marie III"
44-72244 B6-F D.H. Bochkay
44-72258 B6-B "Little Joe" J.W. Cannon
44-72328 B6- "Superwolf"

Unknown Serials
P-51B B6-D "Horse's Itch" E.W. Hiro
P-51B B6-I "Dragon Lady"
P-51B B6- "Jeesil Peesil Mommy" F.L. Gailer
P-51D B6-J "Whole Hawg" D.C. McGee
P-51D B6-U "Frisco Kid" J.C. Casey
P-51B B6- "Shanghai Lil" M.H. Throop
P-51B B6- "All-Away II" E.K. Simpson
P-51B B6- "The Flying Panther" E.K. Simpson
P-51D B6-D "Pony Express"

**Aircraft of the 364th Fighter Squadron**

P-51C-5-NT
42-103348 C5-M "Vicious Viv" H.R. Nowlin
42-103348 C5-O "Daddy's Pet"
42-103389 C5-
42-103502 C5-Z "Pride of the Yanks" C.D. Sumner
42-103601 C5-C "Maize R" J.J. Salsman

P-51C-10-NT
43-25039 C5-K "Li'l Kitten"

P-51B-1-NA
43-12124 C5-F J.R. Warren
43-12313 C5-F "Bear River Betsy" W.C. Reese

P-51B-5-NA
43-6376 C5-J "Little Duckfoot" G.E. Tyler
43-6454 C5-
43-6515 C5-
43-6576 C5-
43-6653 C5-S "Li'l Red's Rocket" T.L. Harris
43-6701 C5-
43-6773 C5-
43-6787 C5-H "Eager Beaver" HACK
43-6799 C5-S
43-6801 C5-C "Boiler Maker" R.D. Sparks
43-6813 C5-E "Pappy's Answer" J.L. Medeiros
43-6813 C5-E H.A. Pfeiffer
43-6813 C5-E "Evelyn"
43-6853 C5-
43-6867 C5-O "Pregnant Polecat" G.V. Davis
43-6935 C5-T "Hurry Home Honey" R.A. Peterson
43-6971 C5-U
43-6974 C5-K "Mr. Period" R.C. Smith
43-6978 C5-

P-51B-10-NA
42-106447 C5-L "Shoo Shoo Baby" J.C. Howell
42-106447 C5-X
42-106470 C5-
42-106632 C5-
42-106640 C5-
42-106648 C5-
42-106652 C5-
42-106721 C5-G "Sergent"

P-51B-15-NA
42-106768 C5-X "Linda Lu" L.A. Ruder
42-106777 C5-J "Taxpayer's Delight" J.B. Carder
42-106790 C5-
42-106826 C5-Y
42-106843 C5-A "Round Trip Jr." T.M. McKinney
42-106854 C5-B "Peabody's Pet"
42-106884 C5-
42-106923 C5-S "Almost" G.A. Hubbard
42-106923 C5-O
42-106978 C5-
43-24763 C5-

P-51D-5-NT
44-11165 C5-J "Lady Nelda" E.R. Haydon
44-11224 C5-C "Pretty Pat" R.R. Lapore

P-51K-5-NT
44-11678 C5-Q "Bobby Jeanne" I.H. Dregne

P-51D-5-NA
44-13318 C5-N "Frenisi" T.L. Hayes
44-13345 C5-I "Mary Ann" C.E. Burtner
44-13406 C5-Q "Bobby Jeanne" I.H. Dregne
44-13543 C5-A "Prune Picker"
44-13543 C5-A "Just Right"
44-13545 C5-I
44-13546 C5-R "The Shillelagh" J.A. Storch
44-13546 C5-R "Pappy's Answer"
44-13552 C5-Y "Pizda"
44-13576 C5-W
44-13578 C5-H
44-13578 C5-Z "Mom Smith's Li'l Angel" L.A. Zacharie
44-13583 C5-L "Shoo Shoo Baby" J.C. Howell
44-13586 C5-T "Hurry Home Honey" R.A. Peterson
44-13586 C5-T "Flak Happy" H.P. Howell
44-13586 C5-ZZ "Greece Lightning" G.C. Kouris
44-13621 C5-X "Philly Dillies" S. Wasylyk
44-13678 C5-V "Linda J" M.A. Stanley
44-13691 C5-V
44-13698 C5-J "Shady Lady"
44-13783 C5-I "Baby Marilyn" G.W. Morris
44-13801 C5-M H.R. Nowlin
44-13861 C5-P
44-13861 C5-Z "Li'l Poopsie" D.C. Kocher
44-13875 C5-H R.M. Shaw
44-13981 C5-P

P-51D-10-NA
44-14334 C5-O R.G. Schimanski
44-14429 C5-E "Tangerine" H.A. Pfeiffer
44-14484 C5-Q
44-14507 C5-E "Tangerine" H.A. Pfeiffer
44-14549 C5-V "Miss Janice"
44-14549 C5-Y "Marie" N.J. Frederick
44-14555 C5-C "Pretty Pat" R.R. Lapore
44-14618 C5-
44-14648 C5-D "Princess Pat" E.R. Fry
44-14660 C5-J "Little Duckfoot" G.E. Tyler
44-14783 C5-M "Roving Rhoda" I.E. Snedeker

P-51D-15-NA
44-14868 C5-T "Hurry Home Honey" R.A. Peterson
44-14868 C5-T "Mormon Mustang" R.R. Wright
44-14884 C5-Q "Baby Jo"
44-14900 C5-B "Nellie Jean"
44-15026 C5-U "Cathy Mae" D.E. Karger
44-15266 C5-Y "Fireball" R.M. Bank
44-15613 C5-Z
44-15660 C5-A "Swamp Fox" W.W. Foard

P-51D-20-NA
44-63687 C5-D "Evelyn"
44-63765 C5-
44-63861 C5-H "Lady Esther" C.K. Maxwell
44-64099 C5-L "Arkansas Traveler" T.H. Adams
44-72056 C5-J "Plastered Bastard" I.L. McGuire
44-72164 C5-R "The Shillelagh" J.A. Storch
44-72231 C5-T
44-72313 C5-U "Cathy Mae II" D.E. Karger
44-72372 C5-G "Alibabsandi" G. Weber
44-72451 C5-V "Campus Queen"

P-51D-25-NA
44-72821 C5-
44-72927 C5-F "Canton Can" V.V. Zettler
44-73125 C5-D "Princess Pat II" E.R. Fry
44-73219 C5-T "Mormon Mustang" R.R. Wright

Unknown Serials
P-51B C5-N "Frenisi" T.L. Hayes
P-51B C5-R "The Shillelagh" J.A. Storch
P-51B C5-M "Geechee Gal" J.M. Jenkins
P-51B C5-M "Geechee Girl" J.M. Jenkins
P-51B C5-Q "Bobby Jeanne" I.H. Dregne
P-51D C5-W "Trusty Rusty" R.P. Winks
P-51B C5- "Lady Julie" M.H. Stepelton
P-51D C5- "B.K.'s Battle Buggy" B.K. Braley
P-51D C5- "Baby Jo" H.J. Moorhouse

P-51D C5- "Mary Al-Mad Papa"
P-51D C5- "Wes' Wicked Wench"
P-51D C5- "Man O'War"
P-51B C5-Z "Bat Cave" C.D. Sumner

• • •

## THE 358TH FIGHTER GROUP
## 365TH, 366TH, 367TH FIGHTER SQUADRONS

The 358th Fighter Group was activated on January 1, 1943, at Richmond, Virginia. Training in the eastern United States, the group headed overseas on October 8, 1943, aboard the "SS Monterey." The first of 16 missions with the 8th Air Force came on December 20, 1943, with the last on January 30, 1944. The 358th was then "traded" to the 9th Air Force in exchange for the P-51 equipped 357th Fighter Group. While with the 8th, pilots claimed 1 aerial victory while 4 P-47's were lost.

The 358th was stationed at Goxhill, from October 21, 1943, and Leiston, from November 29, 1943 until February 1, 1944. Aircraft flown by the 358th was the P-47D, from October 1943 until war's end(including 9th Air Force service).

### Claims

| | Air | | | Grd | |
|---|---|---|---|---|---|
| | Destroyed | Probable | Damaged | Destroyed | Damaged |
| HdQts | 0 | 0 | 1 | 0 | 0 |
| 365th | 0 | 0 | 0 | 0 | 0 |
| 366th | 0 | 0 | 0 | 0 | 0 |
| 367th | 1 | 5 | 3 | 0 | 0 |
| | 1 | 5 | 4 | 0 | 0 |

### Commanders

LtCol. Cecil L. Wells January 1, 1943-September 1944

### Wing and Command Assignments

| | |
|---|---|
| Assigned to VIII Fighter Command | October 21, 1943 |
| VIII Fighter Command, 66th Fighter Wing | November 1943 |

### Aircraft Markings

All group P-47's were operated in olive drab/neutral gray schemes with white theater bands. No special group or squadron markings were applied

Squadron codes were:

365th Ftr Sqn: CH
366th Ftr Sqn: IA
367th Ftr Sqn: CP

### 358th Fighter Group Statistical Report

| Month | Missions | Air | Grd | Losses | KIAc |
|---|---|---|---|---|---|
| October 1943 | 0 | 0-0-0 | 0-0 | 0 | 0 |
| November | 0 | 0-0-0 | 0-0 | 0 | 0 |
| December | 6 | 0-0-0 | 0-0 | 0 | 0 |
| January 1944 | 10 | 1-5-4 | 0-0 | 4 | 0 |
| | 16 | 1-5-4 | 0-0 | 4 | 0 |

### Losses by Squadron

| | MIA | KIAc |
|---|---|---|
| HdQts | 0 | 0 |
| 365th | 1 | 0 |
| 366th | 0 | 0 |
| 367th | 3 | 0 |

### Claims by Enemy Aircraft Type

| | Air | | | Grd | |
|---|---|---|---|---|---|
| | Destroyed | Probable | Damaged | Destroyed | Damaged |
| Me-109 | 1 | 4 | 4 | 0 | 0 |
| FW-190 | 0 | 1 | 0 | 0 | 0 |

### 358th Fighter Group Scorers

**HdQts**

| | Air | Grd |
|---|---|---|
| G.L. Wertenbaker | 0-0-1 | 0-0 |

**365th Ftr Sqn**
none

**366th Ftr Sqn**
none

**367th Ftr Sqn**

| | | |
|---|---|---|
| P.R. Ballinger | 0-0-1 | 0-0 |
| J.H. Pedigo | 0-0-1 | 0-0 |
| L.W. Pool | 0-1-0 | 0-0 |
| J.F. Schilke | 1-0-0 | 0-0 |
| R. Schneider | 0-1-0 | 0-0 |
| G.L. Waters | 0-1-0 | 0-0 |
| L.L. Wilson, Jr. | 0-1-1 | 0-0 |
| D.A. Younglas | 0-1-0 | 0-0 |

### 358th Fighter Group Scoring

**January 5, 1944**

| | | | |
|---|---|---|---|
| 367th: | Maj. D.A. Younglas | FW-190 prob(air) | Belgium |

**January 30, 1944**

| | | | |
|---|---|---|---|
| HdQts: | LtCol. G.L. Wertenbaker | Me-109 dam(air) | Lingen |
| 367th: | Lt. J.F. Schilke | Me-109 dest(air) | all remaining |
| | | Me-109 prob(air) | claims are |
| | Lt. L.L. Wilson | Me-109 prob(air) | E/Zwolle |
| | | Me-109 dam(air) | |
| | Lt. L.W. Pool | Me-109 prob(air) | |
| | Lt. R. Schneider | Me-109 prob(air) | |
| | Lt. G.L. Waters | Me-109 prob(air) | |
| | Lt. P.R. Ballinger | Me-109 dam(air) | |
| | Lt. J.H. Pedigo | Me-109 dam(air) | |

### 358th Fighter Group Losses

**January 7, 1944**

Lt. Mark A. Osborn (365th) KIA; Ran out of fuel and crashed into the North Sea.
P-47D CH- 42-8552
Maj. Donald A. Younglas (367th) KIA; Hit by a FW-190 near Termonde.
P-47D CP- 42-75124
Lt. Corlys A. Bedford (367th) KIA; Hit by a FW-190 near Termonde.
P-47D CP- 42-75064
Lt. Lance A. Pousette (367th) KIA; Hit by a FW-190 near Termonde.
P-47D CP- 42-74678

The following roster of pilots for the 358th Fighter Group is very incomplete. Unit records have not been thoroughly reviewed and the fliers are listed in alphabetical order instead of by squadron as the other groups.

Arnold, Max C., Lt. (367th)
Atkinson, Joseph, Lt. (365th)
Austin, C.A., Capt. (366th)
Ballinger, Philip R., Lt. (367th)
Bedford, Corlys A., Lt. (367th)
Blevins, Edward P., Lt. (366th)
Brockus, Philip D., Lt. (366th)
Buckner, John H., Lt. (366th)
Coldron, Clyde A., Lt. (366th)
Corson, Peter, Lt. (366th)
Coulter, Jack W., Lt. (365th)
DeGruchy, Oliver W., Lt. (366th)
Dian, William, Lt. (366th)
Dickson, John W., Capt. (365th)
Farbstein, Arnold N., Lt. (365th)
Farlow, Allan W., Lt. (366th)
Floyd, Paul D., Lt. (365th)
Hamilton, Augustus, Lt. (366th)
Harber, John R., Lt. (366th)
Hunt, George W., Lt. (365th)
Hylen, Knute N., Lt. (366th)
Idol, Victor E., Lt. (366th)
Johnston, David W., Lt. (365th)
Jones, George E., Lt. (366th)
Kantorski, Edward, Lt. (366th)
Kimball, Charles T., Capt. (366th)
Kropenick, John J., Lt. (366th)
Krug, Robert F., Lt. (366th)
Littlejohn, Erik P., Lt. (366th)
McClellan, Harold L., Lt. (366th)
McClure, Max, Lt. (366th)
McDaniel, Meredith M., Lt. (366th)
Melancon, Alex J., Lt. (366th)
Osborn, Mark A., Lt. (365th)
Pedigo, John H., Lt. (367th)
Pool. Lawrence W., Lt. (367th)
Pousette, Lance A., Lt. (367th)
Ross, Frank M., Maj. (365th)
Rueschoff, Otto M., Lt. (367th)
Schilke, James F., Lt. (367th)

Schneider, Robert, Lt. (367th)
Schuster, Robert C., Lt. (366th)
Seripiglia, Anthony, Lt. (366th)
Shannon, Carl E., Lt. (367th)
Shook, Carmel M., Lt. (366th)
Spreitsma, Edward H., Capt. (367th)
Stewart, James C., Maj. (367th)
Summerlein, Marshall J., Jr., Lt. (367th)
Therriault, Jack A., Maj. (366th)
Tuck, David B., Lt. (366th)
Tusing, Cletus W., Lt. (365th)
Underwood, Joseph D., Capt. (366th)
Van Cott, Clarence E., Lt. (367th)
Voorhees, Alen V., Lt. (367th)
Waters, Glen L., Lt. (367th)
Wells, Cecil L., Col. (HdQts)
Wertenbaker, George L., LtCol. (HdQts)
Wilson, Louis L., Lt. (367th)
Yarian, Burton D., Capt. (365th)
Younglas, Donald A., Maj. (367th)

### Aircraft of the 365th Fighter Squadron

**P-47D-5-RE**
42-8552 CH-

**P-47D-6-RE**
42-74748 CH-

**P-47D-10-RE**
42-75169 CH-
42-75175 CH-H

### Aircraft of the 366th Fighter Squadron

**P-47D-10-RE**
42-75084 IA-
42-75102 IA-O

**P-47D-15-RE**
42-76324 IA-F "Speed Demon"

**Unknown Serials**
IA-V "Lady Luck"

### Aircraft of the 367th Fighter Squadron

**P-47D-6-RE**
42-74678 CP-

**P-47D-10-RE**
42-75039 CP-B
42-75064 CP-
42-75080 CP-X
42-75124 CP-
42-75175 CP-

**Unknown Serials**
CP-W "Martha Ann" C.L. Wells

• • •

## The 359th Fighter Group
## 368th, 369th, 370th Fighter Squadrons

The 359th Fighter Group was activated on January 15, 1943, at Westover Field, Massachusetts. Training in the eastern United States, the group headed overseas on October 8, 1943, aboard three ships; Headquarters and the 368th on the "USAT Argentina", the 369th on the "Thurston", and the 370th on the "Sloterdyk". The first of 346 missions came on December 13, 1943, with the final flight coming on April 25, 1945. While overseas, the group claimed 245 aerial and 117 ground victories while 127 P-47's and P-51's were lost on operations and 10 pilots died in accidents.

The only English home for the 359th was East Wretham, from October 19, 1943, until November of 1945. Aircraft flown were the P-47D, from October pf 1943 to May of 1944, and the P-51B, C, D, and K, from May of 1944 onwards. The 359th was awarded a Distinguished Unit Citation for a mission flown on September 11, 1944, when pilots claimed over 30 German planes destroyed.

### Claims

| | Air | | | Grd | |
|---|---|---|---|---|---|
| | Destroyed | Probable | Damaged | Destroyed | Damaged |
| HdQts | 4.5 | 0 | 1 | 2.33 | 3 |
| 368th | 49.5 | 5.5 | 28 | 48 | 36 |
| 369th | 78.5 | 7.5 | 15 | 23 | 30 |
| 370th | 112.5 | 11 | 28 | 43.67 | 53 |
| | 245 | 24 | 72 | 117 | 122 |

### Commanders

| | |
|---|---|
| Col. Avelin P. Tacon, Jr. | January 1943-July 31, 1944 |
| LtCol. William H. Swanson | July 31, 1944-October 16, 1944 |
| Col. Avelin P. Tacon, Jr. | October 16, 1944-November 12, 1944 |
| Col. John P. Randolph | November 12, 1944-April 7, 1945 |
| LtCol. Donald A. Baccus | April 7, 1945-September 16, 1945 |

### Wing and Command Assignments

| | |
|---|---|
| Assigned to VIII Fighter Command | October 19, 1943 |
| VIII Fighter Command, 66th Fighter Wing | October 20, 1943 |
| VIII Fighter Command, 67th Fighter Wing | November 1943 |
| 1st Bomb Division, 67th Fighter Wing | September 15, 1944 |
| 1st Air Division, 67th Fighter Wing | January 1, 1945 |

### Aircraft Markings

All P-47's were operated in olive drab/neutral gray schemes even after NMF planes were received in March of 1944. Beginning in March, the first 24 inches of the cowl were painted bright green as a group marking. The majority of early P-51's were in NMF but some were flown with the olive drab/neutral gray scheme. The group marking consisted of bright green spinners and twelve inch cowl band. In late 1944, the cowl band was extended and swept downward to the wing root. Rudder colors were introduced in November of 1944; yellow for the 368th, red for the 369th, and dark blue for the 370th. In April and May of 1945, many 368th P-51's also had a yellow spiral on the spinner.

Squadron codes were:

368th Ftr Sqn: CV
369th Ftr Sqn: IV
370th Ftr Sqn: CS

NOTE - when first entering combat the code was CR; this was changed shortly after for unknown reasons.

### 359th Fighter Group Statistical Report

| Month | Missions | Air | Grd | Losses | KIAc |
|---|---|---|---|---|---|
| December 1943 | 10 | 0-0-0 | 0-0 | 0 | 0 |
| January 1944 | 10 | 4-1-5 | 0-0 | 4 | 0 |
| February | 16 | 15-1-2 | 0-0 | 2 | 1 |
| March | 28 | 11-5-12 | 3-3 | 2 | 0 |
| April | 24 | 10-2-5 | 24-18 | 6 | 0 |
| May | 25 | 40-2-4 | 21-30 | 15 | 2 |
| June | 43 | 6-0-1 | 3-3 | 17 | 1 |
| July | 24 | 5-0-2 | 3-19 | 6 | 0 |
| August | 28 | 16-2-8 | 7-5 | 14 | 1 |
| September | 22 | 42-3-8 | 18-19 | 18 | 0 |
| October | 16 | 6-0-2 | 1-1 | 3 | 0 |
| November | 15 | 35.5-6-8 | 1-0 | 8 | 0 |
| December | 16 | 23.5-2-5 | 0-0 | 6 | 0 |
| January 1945 | 13 | 11-0-1 | 0-0 | 6 | 0 |
| February | 17 | 0-0-0 | 6-14 | 12 | 2 |
| March | 25 | 18-0-4 | 0-2 | 5 | 1 |
| April | 17 | 2-0-5 | 29-8 | 3 | 0 |
| May | 0 | 0-0-0 | 0-0 | 0 | 1 |
| June | 0 | 0-0-0 | 0-0 | 0 | 0 |
| July | 0 | 0-0-0 | 0-0 | 0 | 1 |
| | 346 | 245-24-72 | 117-122 | 127 | 10 |

### Losses by Squadron

| | MIA | | KIAc | |
|---|---|---|---|---|
| | P-47 | P-51 | P-47 | P-51 |
| HdQts | 0 | 2 | 0 | 0 |
| 368th | 3 | 41 | 0 | 6 |
| 369th | 2 | 40 | 0 | 1 |
| 370th | 9 | 30 | 1 | 2 |
| | 14 | 113 | 1 | 9 |

### Claims by Type

| | Air | | | Grd | |
|---|---|---|---|---|---|
| | Destroyed | Probable | Damaged | Destroyed | Damaged |
| P-47 | 40 | 9 | 24 | 27 | 21 |
| P-51 | 205 | 15 | 48 | 90 | 101 |

### Claims by Enemy Aircraft Type

| | Air | | | Grd | |
|---|---|---|---|---|---|
| | Destroyed | Probable | Damaged | Destroyed | Damaged |
| Me-109 | 121 | 13 | 31 | 14 | 7 |
| FW-190 | 106 | 10 | 28 | 14 | 10 |
| u/i a/c | 3 | 0 | 1 | 29 | 36 |
| Me-262 | 3 | 0 | 6 | 0 | 0 |
| Me-163 | 3 | 0 | 1 | 0 | 0 |
| Fi-156 | 3 | 0 | 0 | 0 | 0 |
| Me-110 | 2 | 0 | 2 | 12 | 0 |
| Ju-88 | 1 | 1 | 3 | 26 | 46 |
| Ju-52 | 1 | 0 | 0 | 5 | 3 |
| Me-410 | 1 | 0 | 0 | 6 | 7 |
| Ar-196 | 1 | 0 | 0 | 4 | 1 |
| Do-217 | 0 | 0 | 0 | 2 | 0 |
| He-111 | 0 | 0 | 0 | 1 | 7 |
| He-177 | 0 | 0 | 0 | 1 | 2 |
| FW-200 | 0 | 0 | 0 | 1 | 2 |
| BV-140 | 0 | 0 | 0 | 1 | 0 |
| FW-189 | 0 | 0 | 0 | 1 | 0 |
| Go-242 | 0 | 0 | 0 | 0 | 1 |

### 359th Fighter Group Squadron Commanders

**368th Ftr Sqn**

| | |
|---|---|
| LtCol. Albert R. Tyrrell | March 1943-June 21, 1944 |
| Maj. Clifton Shaw | June 22, 1944-August 12, 1944 |
| Maj. Niven K. Cranfill | August 12, 1944-August 27, 1944 |
| Maj. William C. Forehand | August 31, 1944-October 1, 1944 |
| Capt. Charles C. Ettlesen | October 1, 1944-October 9, 1944 |
| Maj. Benjamin H. King | October 9, 1944-November 10, 1944 |
| LtCol. Niven K. Cranfill | November 10, 1944-April 22, 1945 |
| LtCol. James W. Parsons | April 23, 1945-September 22, 1945 |

**369th Ftr Sqn**

| | |
|---|---|
| Maj. Rockford V. Gray | March 1943-November 1943 |
| LtCol. William H. Swanson | November 1943-April 1944 |
| Maj. Chauncey S. Irvine | April 1944-July 26, 1944 |
| Capt. Lester G. Taylor | July 26, 1944-August 3, 1944 |
| Maj. Chauncey S. Irvine | August 3, 1944-October 17, 1944 |
| Maj. James A. Howard | October 17, 1944-November 8, 1944 |
| Maj. Fred S. Hodges | November 9, 1944-January 1, 1945 |
| Maj. Edwin F. Pezda | January 1, 1945-February 28, 1945 |
| Maj. Fred S. Hodges | February 28, 1945-March 2, 1945 |
| Maj. Ralph L. Cox | March 2, 1945-September 1945 |

**370th Ftr Sqn**

| | |
|---|---|
| LtCol. John B. Murphy | March 16, 1943-September 1, 1944 |
| Capt. James K. Lovett | September 1, 1944-September 11, 1944 |
| LtCol. Daniel D. McKee | September 11, 1944-April 21, 1945 |
| Maj. Ray S. Wetmore | April 21, 1945-November 1945 |

### 359th Fighter Group Aces

| Name | Air | Grd | Total | Sqn |
|---|---|---|---|---|
| Maj. Ray S. Wetmore | 21.25 | 3.33 | 24.58 | 370th |
| Maj. George A. Doersch | 10.5 | 1.5 | 12 | 368th<br>370th |
| Lt. Cyril W. Jones | 6 | 5 | 11 | 370th |
| Capt. Claude J. Crenshaw | 7 | 3 | 10 | 369th |
| Capt. Robert B. Hatter | 3 | 6 | 9 | 368th |
| Lt. Robert J. Booth | 8 | 0 | 8 | 369th |
| Capt. William F. Collins | 4 | 3 | 7 | 369th |
| Maj. Ben H. King | 7 | 0 | 7* | 368th |
| Lt. Joseph E. Shupe | 2 | 5 | 7 | 370th |
| LtCol. John B. Murphy | 6.75 | 0 | 6.75** | 370th |
| Capt. George F. Baker | 4.5 | 0.5 | 5 | 368th |
| Maj. Ralph L. Cox | 5 | 0 | 5 | 369th<br>370th |
| LtCol. Niven K. Cranfill | 5 | 0 | 5 | 368th<br>369th<br>HdQts |
| Capt. William R. Hodges | 5 | 0 | 5 | 370th |
| LtCol. Daniel D. McKee | 1 | 4 | 5 | 370th<br>HdQts |
| LtCol. Albert R. Tyrrell | 2 | 3 | 5 | 368th |
| Capt. Robert M. York | 5 | 0 | 5 | 370th |
| LtCol. Donald A. Baccus | 5 | 4 | 9*** | HdQts |
| LtCol. Roy W. Evans | 6 | 0 | 6@ | HdQts |
| Col. John P. Randolph | 1 | 4 | 5@@ | HdQts |

* - includes 3 air victories with the 347th Ftr Grp, PTO
** - includes 0.5 air victories with the 11th Ftr Sqn, Alaska
*** - includes 5 air and 3 ground victories with the 356th Ftr Grp, ETO
@ - includes 5 air victories with the 4th Ftr Grp, ETO
@@ - all victories with 20th Ftr Grp, ETO

### 359th Fighter Group Scorers

**HdQts**

| | Air | Grd | |
|---|---|---|---|
| D.A. Baccus | 0-0-0 | 1-1 | plus 5-0-2 air & 3-0.25 grd w/356th Ftr Grp |
| N.K. Cranfill | 1-0-0 | 0-0 | plus 368th & 369th Ftr Sqns |
| R.W. Evans | 1-0-1 | 0-0 | plus 5-01- air w/4th Ftr Grp |
| R.V. Gray | 1.5-0-0 | 0-0 | |
| J.W. Parsons | 1-0-0 | 0-0 | plus 369th Ftr Sqn |
| S.R. Smith | 0-0-0 | 1.33-0 | plus 370th Ftr Sqn |
| A.P. Tacon, Jr. | 0-0-0 | 0-2 | |

**368th Ftr Sqn**

| | Air | Grd | |
|---|---|---|---|
| B.N. Adkins | 2-0-0 | 0-0 | |
| D.B. Archibald | 0-0-0 | 1-0 | |
| J.M. Ashenmacher | 0-0-0 | 1-1 | |
| G.C. Bach | 0-0-0 | 2-4 | |
| G.F. Baker | 4.5-0-1 | 0.5-0 | |
| K.E. Barber | 0.5-0-0 | 4-0 | |
| L.E. Barnett | 2-1-0 | 0-0 | |
| M.B. Barth | 2-0-0 | 0-0 | |
| E.J. Beal | 3-1-0 | 0-0 | |
| R.E. Benefiel | 1-0-2 | 0.5-0 | |
| G.H. Blackburn | 0-0-0 | 1-0 | |
| W.N. Bolefahr | 2-0-1 | 0-0 | |
| M.F. Boussu | 0-0-1 | 0-1 | |
| R.F. Boyd, Jr. | 0-0-1 | 0-0 | |
| R.E. Burton | 0-0-0 | 0.5-0 | |
| L.D. Carter | 1-0-2 | 0-0 | |
| E.H. Cater | 1-0-1 | 0 0 | |
| A.A. Cowie | 0-0-0 | 0-1 | |
| N.K. Cranfill | 4-0-1 | 0-0 | plus HdQts & 369th Ftr Sqn |
| R.H. Daniels | 0-1-0 | 0-0 | |
| J.A. Denman | 0-0-0 | 4-0 | |
| G.A. Doersch | 0.5-0-0 | 1-1 | plus 370th Ftr Sqn |
| O.P. Drake | 2-0-0 | 0-2 | |
| R.H. Elliott | 0-0-0 | 0-2 | |
| C.C. Ettlesen | 0-0-0 | 0-1 | plus 369th Ftr Sqn |
| J.O. Flack | 0.5-0-0 | 0-0 | |
| O.R. Fladmark | 0.5-0-0 | 1-0 | |
| W.C. Forehand | 1-0-0 | 0-0 | |
| C.R. Gilmore | 1-0-0 | 1-0 | |
| J.H. Haas | 1-0-0 | 0-0 | |
| B.M. Hagan, III | 1-0.5-0 | 1-2 | |
| R.B. Hatter | 3-0-0 | 6-3 | |
| R.W. Hawkinson | 0.5-0-0 | 0-0 | |
| J.W. Herb | 0-0-0 | 4-0 | |
| A.G. Homeyer | 0-0-1 | 1-2 | |
| J.B. Hunter | 1-0-0 | 2-2 | |
| R.B. Janney | 1-0-2 | 1.5-1 | |
| B.D. Kasper | 1-0-0 | 0-0 | |
| J.S. Keesey | 1-1-4 | 0-0 | |
| J.P. Kelsey | 0-0-0 | 0-1 | |
| B.H. King | 4-0-0 | 0-0 | plus 3 air w/347th Ftr Grp, PTO |
| A.F. Kysely | 0-0-1 | 0-0 | |
| C.M. Lambright | 0.5-0-0 | 0-0 | |
| T.S. Lane | 0-0-0 | 2-3 | |
| A.T. Lemmens | 1-0-0 | 0.5-0 | plus 370th Ftr Sqn |
| W.H. Lewis | 0-0-1 | 0-0 | |
| J.J. Lubien | 0-0-0 | 0-2 | |
| G.F. Madison | 0-0-0 | 2-0 | |
| J.T. Marron | 0-0-1 | 2-0 | |
| A.G. Martin | 0-0-0 | 1-0 | |
| J.H. McDonald | 0-0-0 | 1-2 | |
| T.J. McGeever | 2-1-2 | 2-0 | |
| C.E. Mosse | 1-0-1 | 1.5-0 | |
| R.G. Muzzy | 0-0-1.5 | 0-0 | |
| G.M. Randolph | 0-0-0 | 0-3 | |
| F. Rea, Jr. | 0-0-0.5 | 0-0 | |
| C. Shaw | 0-0-1 | 0-0 | |
| A.R. Tyrrell | 2-0-0 | 3-0 | |

**369th Ftr Sqn**

| | Air | Grd | |
|---|---|---|---|
| H.E. Berndt | 0-0-1 | 0-0 | |
| R.J. Booth | 8-0-0 | 0-1 | |
| R.H. Broach | 0.5-1-0 | 0-0 | |
| T.G. Bur | 0.5-0-0 | 0-0 | |
| H.R. Burt | 2-0-0 | 0-0 | |
| R.L. Burtner | 0-0-0 | 3-2 | |
| H.C. Burton | 3.5-0-0 | 0-0 | |
| C.E. Carter | 0-0-2 | 2-1 | |
| W.F. Collins | 4-0-0 | 3-1 | |
| R.L. Cox | 1-0-0 | 0-0 | plus 370th Ftr Sqn |
| N.K. Cranfill | 0-0.5-1 | 0-0 | plus HdQts & 368th Ftr Sqn |
| C.J. Crenshaw | 7-1-0 | 3-1 | |
| G.C. Deen | 2-0-0 | 0-0 | |
| C.C. Ettlesen | 2.5-0-0 | 0.5-2 | plus 368th Ftr Sqn |
| F.S. Fong | 1-0-0 | 0-0 | |
| R.M. Francis | 0-0-0 | 0-1 | |
| R.S. Gaines, Jr. | 1-1-0 | 0-0 | |
| R.J. Guggemos | 1-0-0 | 2-0 | |

| | | | |
|---|---|---|---|
| L.D. Hess | 2-0-0 | 0-0 | |
| K.L. Hobson | 1-0-1 | 0-0 | |
| F.S. Hodges | 0-0-0 | 0-1 | |
| F.W. Holliday | 1-0-1 | 0-0 | |
| C.S. Irvine | 0-0-0 | 0-1 | |
| D.E. Kelly | 1.5-0-0 | 0-0 | |
| J.J. Kelly, III | 1-0-0 | 0-0 | |
| J.E. Keur | 1.5-0-1 | 0-0 | |
| R.R. Klaver | 0-0-1 | 0-0 | |
| T.J. Klem | 0-0-1 | 0-0 | |
| C.H. Kruger | 2-1-0 | 0-0 | |
| D.H. Laing | 0-0-0 | 1-0 | |
| R.T. Lancaster | 2-1-0 | 0-0 | |
| H.A. Linderer | 1-0-0 | 0-0 | |
| H.L. Matthew | 1-0-0 | 0-0 | |
| F.S. McGehee | 2-0-0 | 0-5 | |
| J.J. Majeski | 0-0-0 | 2-3 | |
| A.B. Morris, Jr. | 2-0-0 | 1-1 | |
| J.H. Oliphint | 1.5-0-0 | 1-1 | |
| E.R. Orwig | 0-0-0 | 1-1 | |
| J.R. Parsons, Jr. | 1-0-0 | 2-3 | |
| J.W. Parsons | 1-0-0 | 0-0 | plus HdQts |
| L. Patton | 0-0-2 | 0-0 | |
| G.M. Perrin | 2.5-1-0 | 0-0 | |
| E.F. Pezda | 1-0-0 | 1-2 | |
| R.L. Pherson | 2-0-1 | 0-0 | |
| L.H. Prewitt | 0-0-2 | 0-0 | |
| G.R. Ralston, Jr. | 2-0-0 | 0-0 | |
| R.B. Sander | 0.5-0-0 | 0-0 | |
| V.E. Sansing | 1.5-0-0 | 0-0 | |
| E.L. Sjoblad | 1-0-0 | 0-0 | |
| C.W. Staley | 0-0-0 | 0-10 | |
| L.G. Taylor, Jr. | 1-0-0 | 0-0 | |
| H. Tenenbaum | 3.5-0-0 | 0-1 | |
| R.L. Thacker | 2-1-0 | 0.5-0 | |
| B.H. Thomson | 2-0-0 | 0-0 | |
| R.C. Thomson | 4-0-0 | 0-2 | |

**370th Ftr Sqn**

| | | | |
|---|---|---|---|
| V.W. Ambrose | 0-0-1 | 1-0 | |
| W.K. Baker | 2-0-1 | 0-0 | |
| P.H. Bateman | 1.75-0-0 | 1.33-0 | |
| R.M. Borg | 0-0-0 | 0-2 | |
| C.H. Brown | 1-0-0 | 0-0 | |
| W.E. Buchanan | 1-0-0 | 0-1 | |
| W.D. Burgsteiner | 0-1-0 | 4-1 | |
| V.L. Caid | 2-0-1 | 0-0 | |
| R.M. Callahan | 1-0-0 | 3-6 | |
| D.D. Connelly | 3-0-0 | 0-0 | |
| R.L. Cox | 4-0-0 | 0-0 | plus 369th Ftr Sqn |
| C.V. Cunningham | 0-1-0 | 0-0 | |
| G.A. Doersch | 10-0-3 | 0.5-1 | plus 368th Ftr Sqn |
| E.N. Dunlap | 1-0-1 | 0-0 | |
| H.E. Grimes | 2.5-0-0 | 0-0 | |
| C.W. Hipsher | 0.5-0-1 | 0-0 | |
| W.R. Hodges | 5-2-1 | 0-0 | |
| H.D. Hollis | 1-0-1 | 3-0 | |
| S.J. Huskins | 0.5-0-0 | 0-0 | |
| E.G. Johnson | 2.5-0-2 | 0-0.5 | |
| C.W. Jones | 6-0-1 | 5-4.5 | |
| R.E. Kibler | 3-0-1 | 0-0 | |
| J.W. Lamont | 0-0-1 | 2-0 | |
| R.B. Lancaster | 2-1-1 | 0-0 | |
| A.T. Lemmens | 2-0-0 | 0-0 | plus 368th Ftr Sqn |
| F.O. Lux | 3.5-0-0 | 0-0 | |
| R.O. Major | 1-0-0 | 0-0 | |
| F.R. Marshall, Jr. | 1-0-0 | 0-0 | |
| J.E. McCoskey | 1-0-1 | 0.5-0 | |
| R.L. McInnes | 1-0-1 | 3-4 | |
| D.D. McKee | 1-1-2 | 4-4 | |
| J.B. Murphy | 6.25-1-1 | 0-0 | plus 0.5 air w/11th Ftr Sqn, ATO |
| W.C. Murray | 1-0-0 | 0-2.5 | |
| W.R. Newberg | 1-0-0 | 0-2 | |
| M.H. Newton | 0-0-0 | 2-0 | |
| A.T. Niccolai | 0-0-1 | 0-0 | |
| R.G. Oakley | 1-0-0 | 0-0 | |
| J.H. O'Shea | 1-0-0 | 0-0 | |
| A.C. Porter | 0.25-0-0 | 1-1 | |
| G.E. Ramser | 0-1-0 | 0-0 | |
| L.C. Reese | 0-0-1 | 1-0 | |
| W.J. Rueschenberg | 1-0-0 | 0-0 | |
| J.C. Shoffitt | 0-0-1 | 0-0 | |
| J.E. Shupe | 2-0-0 | 5-4 | |
| R.W. Siltamaki | 1-0-0 | 1-5 | |
| S.R. Smith | 0-1-0 | 2-1 | plus HdQts |
| T.P. Smith | 2-0-2 | 0-0 | |
| H.A. Staup | 2-0-0 | 0-0 | |
| E.W. Tilton | 2-0-0 | 0-0 | |
| R.S. Wetmore | 21.25-0-1 | 3.33-2 | |
| W.W. Wiley | 0-0-0 | 1-10 | |
| J.W. Wilson | 2-1-1 | 0-0 | |
| D.L. Windmiller | 2-0-0 | 0-1 | |
| R.M. York | 5-1-0 | 0-0.5 | |
| L.A. Ziska | 1.5-0-0 | 0-0 | |

**359th Fighter Group Scoring**

**January 29, 1944**

| | | | |
|---|---|---|---|
| HdQts: | Maj. R.V. Gray | (.5)Me-110 dest(air) | Dison |
| 368th: | Capt. C. Shaw | Me-110 dam(air) | Malmedy |
| 369th: | Lt. J.H. Oliphint | (.5)Me-110 dest(air) | Dison |
| | Lt. L.H. Prewitt | Me-110 dam(air) | Dison |

**January 30, 1944**

| | | | |
|---|---|---|---|
| HdQts: | Maj. R.V. Gray | Me-109 dest(air) | Haselunne |
| 369th: | Lt. R.J. Booth | Me-109 dest(air) | Lingen |
| | Lt. R.L. Thacker | Ju-88 dest(air) | Haselunne |
| | | Ju-88 prob(air) | Haselunne |
| | Capt. N.K. Cranfill | Me-109 dam(air) | Lingen |
| | Lt. R.L. Pherson | Ju-88 dam(air) | N/Lingen |
| | Lt. L.H. Prewitt | Ju-88 dam(air) | Haselunne |

**February 3, 1944**

| | | | |
|---|---|---|---|
| 369th: | Lt. R.C. Thomson | FW-190 dest(air) | Zuider Zee |

**February 10, 1944**

| | | | |
|---|---|---|---|
| 369th: | Capt. C.C. Ettlesen | Me-109 dest(air) | Dummer Lake |
| | Lt. C.E. Carter | Me-109 dam(air) | Quackenbruck |
| 370th: | Lt. W.R. Hodges | (2)Me-109 dest(air) | E/Zuider Zee |
| | Capt. C.H. Brown | Me-109 dest(air) | E/Zuider Zee |
| | Lt. R.E. Kibler | Me-109 dest(air) | E/Zuider Zee |
| | Lt. R.O. Major | Me-109 dest(air) | E/Zuider Zee |
| | Lt. R.S. Wetmore | Me-109 dest(air) | E/Zuider Zee |

**February 22, 1944**

| | | | |
|---|---|---|---|
| 368th: | Lt. E.H. Cater | Me-109 dest(air) | Hamm |
| | Lt. A.T. Lemmens | Me-109 dest(air) | Hamm |
| 370th: | Lt. G.A. Doersch | FW-190 dest(air) | Ahlen |
| | Maj. J.B. Murphy | Me-109 prob(air) | Hamm |
| | Lt. A.T. Niccolai | Me-109 dam(air) | Hamm |

**February 24, 1944**

| | | | |
|---|---|---|---|
| 368th: | Maj. A.R. Tyrrell | (2)FW-190 dest(air) | Neuenhaus |
| | Lt. T.J. McGeever | FW-190 dest(air) | Neuenhaus |
| 370th: | Maj. J.B. Murphy | Me-109 dest(air) | Hardenbergh |

**March 2, 1944**

| | | | |
|---|---|---|---|
| 370th: | Capt. D.D. McKee | FW-190 dam(air) | Neufchateau |

**March 4, 1944**

| | | | |
|---|---|---|---|
| 368th: | Capt. C.E. Mosse | Me-109 dam(air) | Bonn |
| 369th: | Lt. R.H. Broach | Me-109 prob(air) | Aachen |
| 370th: | Maj. J.B. Murphy | (.5)FW-190 dest(air) | Bonn |
| | | (.25)Me-109 dest(air) | Bonn |
| | | Me-109 dam(air) | Bonn |
| | Lt. P.H. Bateman | (.5)FW-190 dest(air) | Bonn |
| | | (.25)Me-109 dest(air) | Bonn |
| | Lt. A.C. Porter | (.25)Me-109 dest(air) | Bonn |
| | Lt. R.S. Wetmore | (.25)Me-109 dest(air) | Bonn |
| | Lt. W.R. Hodges | Me-109 prob(air) | Bonn |
| | Lt. H.D. Hollis | Me-109 dam(air) | Bonn |

**March 6, 1944**

| | | | |
|---|---|---|---|
| 368th: | Capt. W.N. Bolefahr | Me-109 dest(air) | Dummer Lake |
| | Lt. E.H. Cater | FW-190 dam(air) | Vechta |
| | Lt. R.B. Janney | FW-190 dam(air) | Dummer Lake-Steinhuder Lake |
| 369th: | Lt. R.J. Booth | FW-190 dest(air) | Quackenbruck |
| | Lt. R.L. Pherson | Me-109 dest(air) | Vechta |

**March 8, 1944**

| | | | |
|---|---|---|---|
| 368th: | Lt. R.B. Janney | Me-109 dam(air) | N/Minden |
| 369th: | Lt. C.W. Staley | FW-190 dam(air) | Nuiden |

**March 15, 1944**

| | | | |
|---|---|---|---|
| 368th: | Lt. T.J. McGeever | Me-109 prob(air) | Steinhuder Lake |
| | | (2)FW-190 dam(air) | Steinhuder Lake |
| 369th: | Lt. C.H. Kruger | Me-109 dest(air) | SW Hanover |
| | | Me-109 prob(air) | SW Hanover |

**March 16, 1944**

| | | | |
|---|---|---|---|
| 369th: | Lt. H.A. Linderer | Me-109 dest(air) | St. Dizier |
| 370th: | Lt. R.S. Wetmore | (2)FW-190 dest(air) | Sommesous |

**March 26, 1944**

| | | | |
|---|---|---|---|
| 369th: | Lt. J.H. Oliphint | Me-110 dest(grd) | Chateaudun |
| | | He-177 dam(grd) | Chateaudun |
| | Lt. C.E. Carter | He-111 dam(grd) | Chateaudun |

**March 27, 1944**

| | | | |
|---|---|---|---|
| 369th: | Lt. F.S. Fong | FW-190 dest(air) | Gallardson |
| | Lt. R.L. Pherson | Me-109 dest(air) | Gallardson |
| 370th: | Capt. D.D. McKee | FW-190 prob(air) | Chartres |
| | | Me-109 dam(air) | Chartres |

**March 29, 1944**

| | | | |
|---|---|---|---|
| 369th: | Lt. C.E. Carter | (2)Me-410 dest(grd) | Dummer Lake |
| | Capt. C.C. Ettlesen | u/i a/c dam(grd) | Dummer Lake |

**April 1, 1944**

| | | | |
|---|---|---|---|
| 369th: | Lt. C.E. Carter | Me-109 dam(air) | Dummer Lake |

**April 11, 1944**

| | | | |
|---|---|---|---|
| 370th: | Lt. G.A. Doersch | FW-190 dest(air) | Brunswick |
| | Lt. E.N. Dunlap | FW-190 dest(air) | Fallersleben |
| | | FW-190 dam(air) | Fallersleben |
| | Capt. S.R. Smith | FW-190 prob(air) | Gutersloh |
| | | (2)FW-190 dest(grd) | Gutersloh |
| | | FW-190 dam(grd) | Gutersloh |
| | Lt. R.E. Kibler | Me-109 dam(air) | Fallersleben |
| | Lt. W.D. Burgsteiner | (4)FW-190 dest(grd) | Gutersloh |
| | | FW-190 dam(grd) | Gutersloh |
| | Lt. R.S. Wetmore | (2)Ju-88 dest(grd) | Volkenrod |
| | | Ju-88 dam(grd) | Volkenrod |
| | Capt. D.D. McKee | Ju-88 dest(grd) | Volkenrod |
| | | (2)Ju-88 dam(grd) | Volkenrod |
| | Lt. V.W. Ambrose | Ju-88 dest(grd) | Gutersloh |
| | Lt. H.D. Hollis | Ju-88 dest(grd) | Vilkenrod |
| | Lt. R.M. Callahan | (5)FW-190 dam(grd) | Gutersloh |
| | Lt. R.M. Borg | (2)u/i a/c dam(grd) | Volkenrod |

**April 15, 1944**

| | | | |
|---|---|---|---|
| 370th: | Lt. G.A. Doersch | Ju-88 dam(air) | Varel |
| | Lt. R.M. Callahan | Ju-88 dest(grd) | Oldenburg |
| | Lt. H.D. Hollis | Ju-88 dest(grd) | Oldenburg |
| | Capt. D.D. McKee | (2)Ju-88 dam(grd) | Oldenburg |

**April 22, 1944**

| | | | |
|---|---|---|---|
| 369th: | Lt. R.J. Booth | FW-190 dest(air) | Hamm |
| | Lt. H.L. Matthew | FW-190 dest(air) | Ostbevern |
| 370th: | Lt. R.E. Kibler | (2)FW-190 dest(air) | Hamm |
| | Lt. H.D. Hollis | FW-190 dest(air) | Hamm |
| | Lt. R.B. Lancaster | FW-190 dest(air) | Hamm |
| | | FW-190 dam(air) | Hamm |
| | Lt. R.S. Wetmore | FW-190 dest(air) | Hamm |

**April 24, 1944**

| | | | |
|---|---|---|---|
| HdQts: | Capt. S.R. Smith | (1.33)u/i a/c dest(grd) | All claims are |
| 368th: | Capt. C.E. Mosse | (.5)u/i a/c dest(grd)* | at St. Dizier |
| | Lt. A.T. Lemmens | (.5)u/i a/c dest(grd)* | |
| | Lt. R.E. Burton | (.5)u/i a/c dest(grd)** | |
| | Lt. R.B. Janney | (.5)u/i a/c dest(grd)** | |
| 370th: | Lt. P.H. Bateman | Me-109 dest(grd) | |
| | | (.33)u/i a/c dest(grd) | |
| | Lt. R.S. Wetmore | Me-109 dest(grd) | |
| | | (.33)u/i a/c dest(grd) | |
| | | Me-109 dam(grd) | |
| | Lt. A.C. Porter | Me-109 dest(grd) | |

**April 25, 1944**

| | | | |
|---|---|---|---|
| 369th: | Lt. R.J. Booth | Me-109 dest(air) | Salmagne |
| 370th: | Lt. R.M. Callahan | FW-190 dest(grd) | Bar le Duc |

**April 29, 1944**

| | | | |
|---|---|---|---|
| 370th: | Lt. C.V. Cunningham | FW-190 prob(air) | Gehrden |

**April 30, 1944**

| | | | |
|---|---|---|---|
| 368th: | Capt. C.E. Mosse | Me-410 dest(grd) | Bricy A/F |
| | Lt. R.B. Janney | Me-410 dest(grd) | Bricy A/F |
| | | Me-410 dam(grd) | Bricy A/F |

NOTE: From May 8 onward, all claims will be in P-51's

**May 8, 1944**

| | | | |
|---|---|---|---|
| 368th: | Capt. W.N. Bolefahr | Me-109 dest(air) | SE Bremen |
| | | Me-109 dam(air) | SE Bremen |
| | Lt. B.M. Hagan | (.5)Me-109 prob(air) | SW Brunswick |
| | Lt. A.G. Homeyer | Me-109 dam(air) | SE Bremen |
| 369th: | Lt. R.J. Booth | (2)Me-109 dest(air) | Mellendorf-Drakenburg |
| | | FW-190 dest(air) | Mellendorf-Drakenburg |
| | Capt. C.C. Ettlesen | Me-109 dest(air) | Hermansburg |
| | Lt. H.C. Burton | Me-109 dest(air) | Hermansburg |
| | Capt. N.K. Cranfill | (.5)Me-109 prob(air) | SW Brunswick |
| 370th: | Lt. G.A. Doersch | FW-190 dest(air) | Eschede |
| | | Me-109 dest(air) | Eschede |
| | | FW-190 dam(air) | Eschede |
| | Lt. J.E. Shupe | (2)FW-190 dest(air) | Eschede |

**May 12, 1944**

| | | | |
|---|---|---|---|
| 369th: | Lt. D.H. Laing | u/i a/c dest(grd) | Thamsbruck |
| | Capt. C.C. Ettlesen | (.5)u/i a/c dest(grd) | Thamsbruck |
| | | u/i a/c dam(grd) | Thamsbruck |
| | Lt. R.L. Thacker | (.5)u/i a/c dest(grd) | Thamsbruck |

**May 19, 1944**

| | | | |
|---|---|---|---|
| 368th: | Capt. C.E. Mosse | Me-109 dest(air) | NW Berlin |
| | Lt. R.B. Janney | Me-109 dest(air) | Neuruppin |
| 369th: | Lt. H.C. Burton | (2)Me-109 dest(air) | Rathenow |
| | Lt. C.H. Kruger | Me-109 dest(air) | Rathenow |
| | Lt. J.H. Oliphint | Me-109 dest(air) | Wittengen |
| | Lt. R.C. Thomson | Me-109 dest(air) | Wittengen |
| | Capt. C.C. Ettlesen | (.5)Me-109 dest(air) | NW Berlin |
| | | (shared with a 352nd Ftr Grp P-51) | |
| 370th: | Lt. R.S. Wetmore | (2)Me-109 dest(air) | Stendal |
| | Lt. P.H. Bateman | FW-190 dest(air) | Stendal |
| | Lt. C.W. Hipsher | Me-109 dam(air) | Stendal |

**May 21, 1944**

| | | | |
|---|---|---|---|
| 368th: | Lt. T.J. McGeever | Ju-52 dest(air) | Gadebusch |
| | | u/i a/c dest(grd) | Gadebusch |
| | Lt. R.B. Hatter | (6)u/i a/c dest(grd) | N/Grevesmuhlen |
| | | (3)u/i a/c dam(grd) | N/Grevesmuhlen |
| | Lt. G.C. Bach | (2)FW-190 dest(grd) | N/Grevesmuhlen |
| | | (4)u/i a/c dam(grd) | N/Grevesmuhlen |
| | Lt. T.S. Lane | (2)u/i a/c dest(grd) | N/Grevesmuhlen |
| | | (3)u/i a/c dam(grd) | N/Grevesmuhlen |
| | Lt. B.M. Hagan | u/i a/c dest(grd) | Carlowe |
| | | (2)u/i a/c dam(grd) | Carlowe |
| | Lt. A.G. Homeyer | FW-190 dest(grd) | N/Grevesmuhlen |
| | | FW-190 dam(grd) | N/Grevesmuhlen |
| | | Ju-52 dam(grd) | N/Grevesmuhlen |
| | Lt. G.M. Randolph | (3)u/i a/c dam(grd) | Gadebusch |
| | Lt. O.P. Drake | He-111 dam(grd) | Wismar-Rostock |
| | | Go-242 dam(grd) | Wismar-Rostock |
| 369th: | Capt. R.H. Broach | (.5)u/i a/c dest(air) | NW Klutz |
| | Lt. R.B. Sander | (.5)u/i a/c dest(air) | NW Klutz |
| | Lt. E.R. Orwig | u/i a/c dest(grd) | Lubeck-Schwerin |
| | | u/i a/c dam(grd) | Lubeck-Schwerin |
| 370th: | Lt. J.E. Shupe | (4)Ju-88 dest(grd) | Schwerin |
| | | (3)Ju-88 dam(grd) | Schwerin |
| | Lt. R.M. Callahan | Ju-88 dest(grd) | Schwerin |
| | | Ju-88 dam(grd) | Schwerin |
| | Lt. W.R. Newburg | (2)Ju-88 dam(grd) | Schwerin |
| | Lt. G.A. Doersch | u/i a/c dam(grd) | Bruel |

**May 24, 1944**

| | | | |
|---|---|---|---|
| 368th: | Lt. J.B. Hunter | (.5)Me-109 dest(air) | NW Berlin |
| 369th: | Lt. V.E. Sansing | (1.5)Me-109 dest(air) | NW Berlin |

**May 29, 1944**

| | | | |
|---|---|---|---|
| 368th: | Lt. B.M. Hagan | Me-109 dest(air) | Ratzburg |
| | Lt. R.B. Hatter | Me-109 dest(air) | Plau |
| 369th: | Lt. R.J. Booth | FW-190 dest(air) | Stettiner-Haven |
| | Lt. R.L. Thacker | FW-190 dest(air) | Malchin |
| 370th: | Lt. H.F. Grimes | (2)FW-190 dest(air) | Stettin |
| | Lt. R.S. Wetmore | (2)FW-190 dest(air) | Stettin |
| | Maj. J.B. Murphy | (1.5)FW-190 dest(air) | Stettin |
| | Capt. R.B. Lancaster | Me-109 dest(air) | Stettin |
| | | Me-109 prob(air) | Stettin |
| | Lt. G.A. Doersch | (.5)FW-190 dest(air) | Stettin |
| | | (.5)FW-190 dest(air) | Stettin |
| | Lt. R.W. Siltamaki | (.5)FW-190 dest(air) | Stettin |

**May 30, 1944**

| | | | |
|---|---|---|---|
| HdQts: | Col. A.P. Tacon | FW-190 dam(grd) | Paderborn |
| 368th: | Capt. W.O. [illegible] | Me-109 dest(air) | Dessau |
| | Lt. R.W. Hawkinson | (.5)Me-109 dest(air) | W/Dessau |
| | Lt. J.B. Hunter | (.5)Me-109 dest(air) | W/Dessau |
| 369th: | Lt. R.J. Booth | Ju-88 dam(grd) | Harsleben |
| 370th: | Lt. H.E. Grimes | (.5)Me-109 dest(air) | Dessau |
| | | (shared with an unknown pilot) | |
| | Lt. C.W. Hipsher | (.5)Me-109 dest(air)* | Dessau |
| | Lt. R.W. Siltamaki | (.5)Me-109 dest(air)* | Dessau |

**June 10, 1944**

| | | | |
|---|---|---|---|
| 368th: | Lt. O.P. Drake | (2)Me-109 dest(air) | Evreux |
| 370th: | Lt. G.A. Doersch | Me-109 dest(air) | Evreux |
| | Lt. V.W. Ambrose | Me-109 dam(air) | Evreux |

**June 12, 1944**

| | | | |
|---|---|---|---|
| 369th: | Lt. L.D. Hess | (2)FW-190 dest(air) | W/Paris |
| | Maj. C.S. Irvine | Me-109 dam(grd) | W/Paris |

**June 20, 1944**

| | | | |
|---|---|---|---|
| 369th: | Lt. H.C. Burton | (.5)Me-410 dest(air) | NW Putbus |
| | Lt. G.M. Perrin | (.5)Me-410 dest(air) | NW Putbus |

**June 21, 1944**

| | | | |
|---|---|---|---|
| 368th: | LtCol. A.R. Tyrrell | Me-410 dest(grd) | Wittstock |
| | | Me-110 dest(grd) | Wittstock |
| | | FW-189 dest(grd) | Wittstock |
| | Lt. J.J. Lubien | (2)u/i a/c dam(grd) | E/Plau |

**July 20, 1944**

| | | | |
|---|---|---|---|
| 370th: | Lt. W.K. Baker | Me-109 dest(air) | Zeitz |
| | | FW-190 dam(air) | Zeitz |
| | F/O L.C. Reese | Me-109 dam(air) | Zeitz |

**July 21, 1944**

| | | | |
|---|---|---|---|
| 370th: | LtCol. J.B. Murphy | Me-109 dest(air) | Ammer Lake |
| | Lt. R.W. Siltamaki | Ju-88 dest(grd) | N/Landsberg |
| | | (3)He-111 dam(grd) | W/Munich |
| | | (2)u/i a/c dam(grd) | W/Munich |
| | F/O L.C. Reese | Ju-88 dest(grd) | N/Landsberg |
| | F/O W.W. Wiley | Ju-88 dest(grd) | N/Landsberg |
| | | (10)Ju-88 dam(grd) | N/Landsberg |

**July 24, 1944**

| | | | |
|---|---|---|---|
| HdQts: | Col. A.P. Tacon | u/i a/c dam(grd) | Ulm |
| 368th: | Lt. D.W. Chatfield | (2)u/i a/c dam(grd) | Ulm |
| | Lt. J.P. Kelsey | u/i a/c dam(grd) | Ulm |
| 370th: | Lt. R.M. Callahan | Fi-156 dest(air) | Neu Ulm |
| | Lt. W.R. Newberg | Fi-156 dest(air) | Neu Ulm |
| | Lt. E.W. Tilton | Fi-156 dest(air) | Neu Ulm |

**August 4, 1944**

| | | | |
|---|---|---|---|
| 370th: | Lt. W.K. Baker | Me-110 dest(air) | Denmark |

**August 5, 1944**

| | | | |
|---|---|---|---|
| 369th: | Capt. E.F. Pezda | Me-109 dest(air) | Tarmstedt |
| | Capt. L.G. Taylor | FW-190 dest(air) | Tarmstedt |
| | Lt. H.R. Burt | Me-109 dest(air) | Tarmstedt |
| | Lt. E.L. Sjoblad | Me-109 dest(air) | Bremen |
| | Lt. F.W. Holliday | Me-109 dam(air) | Bremen-Hamburg |

**August 8, 1944**

| | | | |
|---|---|---|---|
| 368th: | Lt. J.S. Keesey | FW-190 dest(air) | Dreux |
| | | (3)FW-190 dam(air) | Dreux |
| | Lt. C.J. Cavanaugh | FW-190 dam(air) | Dreux |

**August 9, 1944**

| | | | |
|---|---|---|---|
| 368th: | Lt. J.S. Keesey | FW-190 prob(air) | Munich |
| | F/O E.C. Cook | Me-109 dam(air) | Munich |
| 370th: | LtCol. J.B. Murphy | FW-190 dest(air) | Gunzburg |
| | Lt. C.W. Jones | Me-109 dest(air) | Gunzburg |
| | | Me-109 dam(air) | Gunzburg |
| | Lt. F.O. Lux | Me-109 dest(air) | Gunzburg |
| | Lt. E.W. Tilton | Me-109 dest(air) | Gunzburg |
| | Lt. R.M. York | Me-109 dest(air) | Gunzburg |
| | Lt. J.W. Wilson | Me-109 prob(air) | Gunzburg |

**August 16, 1944**

| | | | |
|---|---|---|---|
| HdQts: | Maj. N.K. Cranfill | Me-109 dest(air) | Einbeck |
| 370th: | LtCol. J.B. Murphy | Me-163 dest(air) | SE Leipzig |
| | Lt. C.W. Jones | Me-163 dest(air) | SE Leipzig |
| | Lt. F.O. Lux | Me-109 dest(air) | Erfurt |
| | Lt. J.C. Shoffitt | Me-163 dam(air) | Bohlen |

**August 18, 1944**

| | | | |
|---|---|---|---|
| 369th: | F/O R.L. Burtner | (3)Me-109 dest(grd) | All claims are |
| | | Ju-52 dam(grd) | at St. Dizier |
| | | Ju-88 dam(grd) | |
| | Lt. C.J. Crenshaw | Ju-88 dest(grd) | |
| | | Ju-52 dest(grd) | |
| | | Ju-88 dam(grd) | |
| | Capt. E.F. Pezda | (2)Ju-88 dam(grd) | |

**August 25, 1944**

| | | | |
|---|---|---|---|
| 368th: | Lt. D.B. Archibald | u/i a/c dest(grd) | Gustrow |

**August 27, 1944**

| | | | |
|---|---|---|---|
| 370th: | Lt. L.A. Ziska | u/i a/c dest(air) | Munster |

**August 28, 1944**

| | | | |
|---|---|---|---|
| 368th: | Lt. O.R. Fladmark | Ju-88 dest(grd) | Saarbrucken |

**September 8, 1944**

| | | | |
|---|---|---|---|
| 368th: | Lt. J.M. Ashenmacher | Ju-52 dest(grd) | Cronberg |
| | | Ju-52 dam(grd) | Cronberg |
| | Lt. C.R. Gilmore | Ju-52 dest(grd) | Cronberg |
| | Lt. G.F. Baker | (.5)Ju-52 dest(grd) | Cronberg |
| | Lt. R.E. Benefiel | (.5)Ju-52 dest(grd) | Cronberg |

**September 10, 1944**

| | | | |
|---|---|---|---|
| 369th: | Lt. K.L. Hobson | u/i a/c dest(air) | NW Stuttgart |
| | | u/i a/c dam(air) | NW Stuttgart |

**September 11, 1944**

| | | | |
|---|---|---|---|
| 368th: | Capt. B.H. King | (2)FW-190 dest(air) | Eisleben |
| | | Me-109 dest(air) | Eisleben |
| | Lt. L.E. Barnett | (2)FW-190 dest(air) | Eisleben |
| | | FW-190 prob(air) | Eisleben |
| | Lt. G.F. Baker | (2)FW-190 dest(air) | Halberstadt |
| | Lt. C.R. Gilmore | FW-190 dest(air) | Eisleben |
| | Lt. J.D. Flack | (.5)Me-109 dest(air) | Eisenach |
| | Lt. C.M. Lambright | (.5)Me-109 dest(air) | Eisenach |
| | Lt. R.E. Benefiel | (2)Me-109 dam(air) | Eisenach |
| | Lt. A.F. Kysely | FW-190 dam(air) | Weimar |
| | Lt. W.H. Lewis | Me-109 dam(air) | Eisenach |
| 369th: | Lt. C.J. Crenshaw | (2)Me-109 dest(air) | Kolleda |
| | | u/i a/c dest(grd) | Kolleda |
| | Lt. G.M. Perrin | (2)FW-190 dest(air) | Kolleda |
| | | Me-109 prob(air) | Kolleda |
| | Lt. G.R. Ralston | FW-190 dest(air) | Kolleda |
| | | Me-109 dest(air) | Kolleda |
| | Capt. J.W. Parsons | Me-109 dest(air) | Kolleda |
| | Lt. F.W. Holliday | Me-109 dest(air) | N/Erfurt |
| | Lt. J.E. Keur | Me-109 dest(air) | N/Erfurt |
| | Lt. R.S. Gaines | Me-109 prob(air) | Weimar |
| | Lt. T.J. Klem | Me-109 dam(air) | N/Leipzig |
| | Lt. J.R. Parsons | (2)Ju-88 dest(grd) | S/Merseburg |
| | | (3)Ju-88 dam(grd) | S/Merseburg |
| | Lt. J.J. Mejaski | (2)Ju-88 dest(grd) | S/Merseburg |
| | | (3)Ju-88 dam(grd) | S/Merseburg |
| 370th: | Lt. C.W. Jones | (4)Me-109 dest(air) | Gotha |
| | | He-177 dest(grd) | Gotha |
| | | Ju-88 dest(grd) | Gotha |
| | | (2)Me-410 dam(grd) | Gotha |
| | | (2)Ju-88 dam(grd) | Gotha |
| | | (.5)He-177 dam(grd) | Gotha |
| | Lt. W.E. Buchanan | Me-109 dest(air) | Gotha |
| | | Ju-88 dam(grd) | Gotha |
| | Lt. W.C. Murray | Me-109 dest(air) | Gotha |
| | | (2)Ju-88 dam(grd) | Gotha |
| | | (.5)He-177 dam(grd) | Gotha |
| | Lt. J.H. O'Shea | FW-190 dest(air) | Mulhausen |
| | Lt. J.W. Wilson | Me-109 dest(air) | Mulhausen |
| | | FW-190 dam(air) | Mulhausen |

**September 12, 1944**

| | | | |
|---|---|---|---|
| 368th: | Lt. R.B. Hatter | (2)FW-190 dest(air) | Liebenwalde |
| | Capt. B.H. King | Me-109 dest(air) | Gransee |
| | Lt. M.B. Barth | Me-109 dest(air) | NW Wittenburg |
| | Lt. E.J. Beal | Me-109 dest(air) | Gransee |
| | Lt. L.D. Carter | FW-190 dest(air) | N/Berlin |
| | | FW-190 dam(air) | N/Berlin |
| | Lt. J.H. Haas | FW-190 dest(air) | Pritzwalk |
| 369th: | Lt. H.R. Burt | FW-190 dest(air) | NE Berlin |
| | Lt. G.C. Deen | FW-190 dest(air) | NE Berlin |
| 370th: | Lt. D.D. Connelly | Me-109 dest(air) | S/Berlin |
| | | FW-190 dest(air) | Magdeburg |
| | Lt. C.W. Jones | (3)u/i a/c dest(grd) | S/Memmingen |
| | Lt. R.L. McInnes | (2)u/i a/c dest(grd) | S/Memmingen |
| | | Ju-52 dest(grd) | S/Memmingen |
| | | (4)u/i a/c dam(grd) | S/Memmingen |
| | Lt. J.W. Lamont | (2)u/i a/c dest(grd) | S/Memmingen |

**September 18, 1944**

| | | | |
|---|---|---|---|
| 369th: | Lt. C.J. Crenshaw | Me-109 dest(air) | Dusseldorf |
| | Lt. G.C. Deen | FW-190 dest(air) | Krefeld |
| | Lt. J.R. Parsons | FW-190 dest(air) | Dieren |
| | Lt. J.E. Keur | (.5)Me-109 dest(air) | SE Munster |
| | F/O T.G. Bur | (.5)Me-109 dest(air) | SE Munster |

**October 6, 1944**

| | | | |
|---|---|---|---|
| 370th: | Capt. G.A. Doersch | (2)FW-190 dest(air) | S/Stettin |
| | | FW-190 dam(air) | S/Stettin |
| | Lt. R.L. McInnes | FW-190 dest(air) | S/Stettin |
| | | FW-190 dam(air) | S/Stettin |
| | F/O J.E. McCoskey | FW-190 dest(air) | S/Stettin |

**October 7, 1944**

| | | | |
|---|---|---|---|
| 370th: | Capt. G.A. Doersch | (.5)BV-140 dest(grd) | Dievenow |
| | F/O J.E. McCoskey | (.5)BV-140 dest(grd) | Dievenow |
| | Lt. E.G. Johnson | (.5)Ar-196 dam(grd) | Dievenow |
| | Lt. R.M. York | (.5)Ar-196 dam(grd) | Dievenow |

**October 24, 1944**

| | | | |
|---|---|---|---|
| 368th: | F/O B.N. Adkins | FW-190 dest(air) | Nordhausen |
| | Lt. M.B. Barth | FW-190 dest(air) | Nordhausen |

**November 2, 1944**

| | | | |
|---|---|---|---|
| 368th: | Capt. G.F. Baker | (.5)Me-109 dest(air) | Quedlinburg |
| | | Me-109 dam(air) | Quedlinburg |
| | Lt. O.R. Fladmark | (.5)Me-109 dest(air) | Quedlinburg |
| 370th: | Capt. R.S. Wetmore | (2)Me-109 dest(air) | Erfurt-Weimar |
| | Capt. R.L. Cox | Me-109 dest(air) | Erfurt-Weimar |

| | | | |
|---|---|---|---|
| | Lt. D.D. Connelly | Me-109 dest(air) | Erfurt-Weimar |
| | Capt. S.J. Huskins | (.5)Me-109 dest(air) | Erfurt-Weimar |
| | | (shared with a 55th Ftr Grp P-51) | |
| **November 21, 1944** | | | |
| 368th: | Lt. J.S. Keesey | FW-190 dam(air) | Erfurt |
| | Capt. T.J. McGeever | FW-190 dest(grd) | Gotha |
| 369th: | Lt. C.J. Crenshaw | (4)FW-190 dest(air) | Merseburg |
| | | FW-190 prob(air) | Merseburg |
| | Lt. H. Tenenbaum | FW-190 dest(air) | Merseburg |
| 370th: | Capt. R.L. Cox | (3)FW-190 dest(air) | SW Merseburg |
| | Capt. W.R. Hodges | (2)FW-190 dest(air) | SE Kassel |
| | | FW-190 prob(air) | SE Kassel |
| | | FW-190 dam(air) | SE Kassel |
| | Lt. V.L. Caid | (2)FW-190 dest(air) | SW Merseburg |
| | | FW-190 dam(air) | SW Merseburg |
| | Lt. T.P. Smith | (2)FW-190 dest(air) | SW Merseburg |
| | | (2)FW-190 dam(air) | SW Merseburg |
| | Lt. H.A. Staup | (2)FW-190 dest(air) | SW Merseburg |
| | Maj. D.D. McKee | FW-190 dest(air) | SW Merseburg |
| | Capt. W.D. Burgsteiner | FW-190 prob(air) | SW Merseburg |
| | Lt. J.W. Lamont | FW-190 dam(air) | SW Merseburg |
| **November 26, 1944** | | | |
| HdQts: | Maj. R.W. Evans | Me-109 dest(air) | Kassel |
| | | Me-109 dam(air) | Kassel |
| **November 27, 1944** | | | |
| 368th: | Maj. N.K. Cranfill | (2)Me-109 dest(air) | W/Merseburg |
| | | FW-190 dest(air) | W/Merseburg |
| | Lt. R.H. Daniels | FW-190 prob(air) | SE Hanover |
| 369th: | Lt. R.T. Lancaster | Me-109 prob(air) | S/Hanover |
| 370th: | Capt. R.S. Wetmore | (3)Me-109 dest(air) | SE Hanover |
| | Lt. R.M. York | (3)Me-109 dest(air) | Hanover |
| | | Me-109 prob(air) | Hanover |
| | Lt. D.L. Windmiller | (2)Me-109 dest(air) | Hameln |
| | Lt. F.R. Marshall | Me-109 dest(air) | Hanover |
| **December 23, 1944** | | | |
| 368th: | Lt. R.E. Benefiel | Me-109 dest(air) | Coblenz |
| | Lt. E.C. Cook | Me-109 dest(air) | Coblenz |
| **December 24, 1944** | | | |
| 368th: | Lt. E.J. Beal | (2)FW-190 dest(air) | Cologne |
| | | FW-190 prob(air) | Cologne |
| | Lt. R.A. Boyd | FW-190 dam(air) | Cologne |
| 369th: | Lt. J.J. Kelly | Me-109 dest(air) | Vogelsand |
| | Lt. B.H. Thomson | Me-109 dest(air) | Vogelsand |
| | Lt. J.E. Keur | Me-109 dam(air) | Vogelsand |
| 370th: | Lt. E.G. Johnson | (2)FW-190 dest(air) | Bonn |
| | | (2)FW-190 dam(air) | Bonn |
| | Capt. W.R. Hodges | FW-190 dest(air) | Bonn |
| | Capt. A.T. Lemmens | FW-190 dest(air) | Bonn |
| | Lt. R.G. Oakley | FW-190 dest(air) | Bonn |
| | Lt. J.W. Wilson | FW-190 dam(air) | Bonn |
| **December 31, 1944** | | | |
| 368th: | Capt. G.F. Baker | (2)FW-190 dest(air) | SE Stade |
| 369th: | Lt. W.F. Collins | (1.5)FW-190 dest(air) | SW Hamburg |
| | | (.5)FW-190 dest(air) | SW Hamburg |
| | Lt. A.B. Morris | (1.5)FW-190 dest(air) | SW Hamburg |
| | | (.5)FW-190 dest(air) | SW Hamburg |
| 370th: | Capt. R.S. Wetmore | (1.5)Me-109 dest(air)* | Hanover |
| | Lt. F.O. Lux | (1.5)Me-109 dest(air)** | Hanover |
| | Capt. A.T. Lemmens | Me-109 dest(air) | Hanover |
| | Lt. E.G. Johnson | (.5)Me-109 dest(air) | Hanover |
| | | (shared with an unknown P-51) | |
| | Lt. W.J. Rueschenberg | (.5)Me-109 dest(air)* | Hanover |
| | Lt. L.A. Ziska | (.5)Me-109 dest(air)** | Hanover |
| | Lt. G.E. Ramser | Me-109 prob(air) | Hanover |
| | Lt. J.E. McCoskey | Me-109 dam(air) | Hanover |
| **January 1, 1945** | | | |
| 368th: | F/O B.N. Adkins | FW-190 dest(air) | Havelburg |
| | Lt. B.D. Kasper | Me-109 dest(air) | Stendal |
| | Lt. L.D. Carter | FW-190 dam(air) | Havelburg |
| 370th: | Capt. R.S. Wetmore | Me-109 dest(air) | Luneburg |
| | Lt. R.M. York | FW-190 dest(air) | Luneburg |
| **January 14, 1945** | | | |
| 370th: | Capt. R.S. Wetmore | (4.5)FW-190 dest(air) | Vorden A/F |
| | Capt. G.A. Doersch | (2)FW-190 dest(air) | Vorden A/F |
| | Lt. W.J. Rueschenberg | (.5)FW-190 dest(air) | Vorden A/F |
| **February 9, 1945** | | | |
| 368th: | Capt. C.C. Ettlesen | u/i a/c dam(grd) | Halle |
| **February 21, 1945** | | | |
| 369th: | Maj. E.F. Pezda | FW-200 dest(grd) | Schweinfurt |
| | Lt. A.B. Morris | Ju-88 dest(grd) | Nordlingen |
| | | Me-410 dam(grd) | Nordlingen |
| | Maj. F.S. Hodges | FW-200 dam(grd) | Deiningen |
| | Capt. R.C. Thomson | FW-190 dam(grd) | Nordlingen |
| | | u/i a/c dam(grd) | Nordlingen |
| | Capt. R.M. Francis | Me-410 dam(grd) | Schweinfurt |
| | Lt. F.S. McGehee | FW-200 dam(grd) | Deiningen |
| | | Me-410 dam(grd) | Deiningen |
| **February 22, 1945** | | | |
| 369th: | Capt. W.F. Collins | (2)Ju-88 dest(grd) | Parchim |
| | | Ju-88 dam(grd) | Parchim |
| | Lt. F.S. McGehee | (3)Ju-88 dam(grd) | Parchim |
| | Lt. H. Tenenbaum | Ju-88 dam(grd) | Schwerin |
| 370th: | Lt. D.L. Windmiller | Me-410 dam(grd) | Pritzwalk |
| **February 28, 1945** | | | |
| 368th: | Lt. G.H. Blackburn | Me-109 dest(grd) | Gunzburg |
| | Lt. A.G. Martin | Me-109 dest(grd) | Gunzburg |
| **March 3, 1945** | | | |
| 368th: | Lt. A.A. Cowie | u/i a/c dam(grd) | Hanover |
| **March 15, 1945** | | | |
| 370th: | Capt. R.S. Wetmore | Me-163 dest(air) | Wittenburg |
| **March 18, 1945** | | | |
| 369th: | Capt. R.L. Cox | FW-190 dest(air) | Joachimsthal |
| | Lt. R.S. Gaines | Me-109 dest(air) | Joachimsthal |
| | F/O H.E. Berndt | Me-109 dam(air) | Joachimsthal |
| **March 19, 1945** | | | |
| 368th: | Maj. N.K. Cranfill | Me-262 dest(air) | Leipzig |
| | | Me-262 dam(air) | Leipzig |
| **March 23, 1945** | | | |
| 368th: | Capt. G.A. Doersch | (.5)Ar-196 dest(air) | Salzwedel |
| | Lt. K.E. Barber | (.5)Ar-196 dest(air) | Salzwedel |
| | Capt. M.F. Boussu | He-111 dam(grd) | Salzwedel |
| **March 24, 1945** | | | |
| HdQts: | Maj. J.W. Parsons | Me-109 dest(air) | All claims are |
| 369th: | Capt. W.F. Collins | (2)Me-109 dest(air) | at Eikelon A/F |
| | Capt. R.C. Thomson | (2)Me-109 dest(air) | |
| | Lt. R.T. Lancaster | (2)Me-109 dest(air) | |
| | Lt. F.S. McGehee | (2)Me-109 dest(air) | |
| | Lt. D.E. Kelly | (1.5)Me-109 dest(air) | |
| | Lt. H. Tenenbaum | (1.5)Me-109 dest(air) | |
| | Lt. B.H. Thomson | Me-109 dest(air) | |
| | Lt. L. Patton | (2)Me-109 dam(air) | |
| **April 9, 1945** | | | |
| 368th: | Capt. M.F. Boussu | Me-262 dam(air) | Augsburg |
| | F/O R.G. Muzzy | (1.5)Me-262 dam(air) | Augsburg |
| | Lt. F. Rea | (.5)Me-262 dam(air) | Augsburg |
| | Capt. G.A. Doersch | FW-190 dest(grd) | Gernering A/F |
| | | He-111 dam(grd) | Gernering A/F |
| | Lt. R.H. Elliott | (2)Ju-88 dam(grd) | Munich |
| **April 10, 1945** | | | |
| 368th: | Lt. J.T. Marron | Me-262 dam(air) | NW Gustrow |
| 369th: | Lt. R.J. Guggemos | Me-262 dest(air) | Gardelegen A/F |
| | | (2)Me-109 dest(grd) | Dennefeld |
| | Lt. H. Tenenbaum | Me-262 dest(air) | Gardelegen A/F |
| | Lt. R.R. Klaver | Me-262 dam(air) | Wittenburg |
| **April 13, 1945** | | | |
| 368th: | Capt. J.A. Denman | (4)Me-110 dest(grd) | Neumunster |
| | Lt. K.E. Barber | (3)Me-110 dest(grd) | Neumunster |
| | | u/i a/c dest(grd) | Neumunster |
| | Lt. J.W. Herb | (2)Me-110 dest(grd) | Neumunster |
| | | (2)Do-217 dest(grd) | Neumunster |
| | Lt. G.E. Madison | Me-110 dest(grd) | Luneburg |
| | | u/i a/c dest(grd) | Luneburg |
| | Capt. J.B. Hunter | He-111 dest(grd) | Luneburg |
| 370th: | LtCol. D.D. McKee | (2)Ar-196 dest(grd) | Schwerin |
| | Lt. M.H. Newton | (2)Ar-196 dest(grd) | Schwerin |
| **April 16, 1945** | | | |
| 368th: | Lt. J.T. Marron | (2)Me-109 dest(grd) | E/Plattling |
| | Capt. J.B. Hunter | Me-109 dest(grd) | E/Plattling |
| | | (2)Me-109 dam(grd) | E/Plattling |
| | Lt. J.H. McDonald | Me-109 dest(grd) | E/Plattling |
| | | (2)Me-109 dam(grd) | E/Plattling |
| **April 17, 1945** | | | |
| HdQts: | LtCol. D.A. Baccus | u/i a/c dest(grd) | Ganacker-Plattling |
| | | Me-109 dam(grd) | Ganacker-Plattling |
| 369th: | Capt. W.F. Collins | FW-190 dest(grd) | W/Dresden |
| 370th: | LtCol. D.D. McKee | FW-190 dest(grd) | Ganacker-Plattling |

**359th Fighter Group Losses**

**January 11, 1944**
Lt. Edward J. Hyland (368th) KIA; Hit by a Me-109 near Lingen.
P-47D CV- 42-8542
Capt. James E. Buckley (370th) KIA; Suffered mechanical trouble and crashed into the North Sea.
P-47D CR- 42-75108
Lt. Lynn W. Hair (370th) KIA; Crashed at Chipping Warden upon return.
P-47D CR-
Lt. William N. Tucker, Jr. (370th) KIA; Crashed at Rednal, Wales, upon return.
P-47D CR-

**February 3, 1944**
Lt. Cecil W. Crawford (369th) KIA; Hit by flak near Emden and crashed into the North Sea.
P-47D IV-E 42-22791

**February 10, 1944**
Lt. Alex M. Cosmos (370th) KIAc; Encountered a snowstorm while on a test hop and crashed near Somersham.
P-47D CR-I 42-75091

**February 24, 1944**
Lt. Albert T. Niccolai (370th) KIA; Hit by a Me-109 east of the Zuider Zee.
P-47D CR-F 42-8636

**March 18, 1944**
Capt. Ben H. Albertson (370th) POW; Hit by flak and bailed out near Abbeville.
P-47D CS-N 42-75136

**March 27, 1944**
Lt. John E. Kerns (370th) KIA; Last seen chasing an enemy fighter near Gallardson.
P-47D CS-I 42-7891

**April 8, 1944**
Lt. Clifford E. Carter (369th) KIA; Hit a house and crashed near Herringhausen.
P-47D IV- 42-22464

**April 11, 1944**
Lt. James R. Pino (368th) POW; Suffered mechanical failure and bellied-in near Volkenrod.
P-47D CV-I 42-75141
Lt. Elmer N. Dunlap (370th) POW; Hit by a Me-109 near Fallersleben.
P-47D CS- 42-75079
Lt. Thomas P. Smith (370th) MIA-E; Ran out of fuel and bailed out near Bielefeld.
P-47D CS-P 42-74737

**April 13, 1944**
Lt. Cecil R. Brown (368th) KIA; Suffered mechanical failure and bailed out over the Channel.
P-47D CV- 42-75104

**April 22, 1944**
Lt. Earl W. Thomas, Jr. (370th) KIA; Hit by an enemy fighter near Hamm.
P-47D CS- 42-75262

**May 1, 1944**
Capt. Carey H. Brown (370th) KIAc; Crashed near East Wretham.
P-51C CS-Q 42-103294

**May 2, 1944**
Lt. Raymond L. Botsford (368th) KIAc; Crashed near Thetford.
P-51B CV- 43-6430

**May 8, 1944**
Lt. Stanley E. Sackett (369th) KIA; Hit by enemy fighters near Wunstorf.
P-51B IV-S 42-106904
Lt. Alan C. Porter (370th) KIA; Hit by enemy fighters near Enschede.
P-51B CS-R 43-7179

**May 11, 1944**
Lt. William R. Hodges (370th) MIA-E; Hit by flak at Reims-Champagne Airfield.
P-51B CS-Q 43-24833
Lt. Ralph E. Kibler (370th) KIA; Hit by flak at Reims-Champagne Airfield.
P-51B CS-M 42-106865
Lt. Edward J. Maslow (370th) POW; Hit by flak at Reims-Champagne Airfield.
P-51C CS-D 42-103343

**May 19, 1944**
Capt. Charles E. Mosse (368th) POW; Hit by a Me-109 northwest of Berlin.
P-51B CV-B 42-106890
Lt. James B. Smith (368th) POW; Hit by enemy planes near Krummbeck.
P-51B CV-S 42-106804
Lt. D.H. Laing (369th) POW; Suffered mechanical failure near Klietz.
P-51B IV-E 42-106893

**May 21, 1944**
Lt. Arlen R. Baldridge (368th) POW (D); Hit by flak northwest of Wismar and bellied-in near Barenhorst. After capture, he was shot and killed.
P-51B CV-Y 43-6962
Lt. Clyde M. Huddleston (368th) KIA; Hit by flak near Wismar.
P-51B CV-G 42-106620
Lt. Homer L. Rodeheaver (369th) KIA; Hit by flak in the Reinfeld/Mecklenberg area.
P-51B IV-U 42-106818
Lt. Joseph E. Shupe (370th) KIA; Hit by flak at Schwerin.
P-51B CS-G 42-106921

**May 25, 1944**
Capt. Charles C. Ettlesen (369th) MIA-E; Hit by flak near Saarbrucken and bailed out near Sarrebourg.
P-51C IV-D 42-103354

**May 29, 1944**
Lt. Lowell W. Brundage (369th) KIA; Hit by fighters near Malchin.
P-51B IV-H 42-106691
Lt. Myron C. Morrill (369th) KIA; Hit by fighters near Malchin.
P-51B IV-J 42-106913

**June 4, 1944**
Lt. Emer H. Cater (368th) KIA; Suffered mechanical failure and bailed out twenty miles off Felixstowe.
P-51B CV-E 43-6491 "Wanna Honey"

**June 7, 1944**
Lt. John S. Marcinkiewicz (370th) POW; Damaged by debris from an exploding truck and bailed out near Fecamp.
P-51B CS-L 42-106667 "Sweet Sue"

**June 8, 1944**
Lt. Benjamin M. Hagan, III (368th) POW; Hit by flak near Chartres.
P-51B CV-D 42-106898 "Boots"
Lt. Robert J. Booth (369th) POW; Hit by flak near La Fleche.
P-51B IV-F 43-7199
Lt. John H. Oliphint (369th) POW (E); Hit by flak near La Fleche.
P-51B IV-O 42-106679 "The Mad Rebel"
Lt. Robert B. Sander (369th) KIA; Hit by flak in the Orleans-Tours area.
P-51B IV-L 42-106906 "Mary"

**June 10, 1944**
Capt. Wayne N. Bolefahr (368th) KIA; Hit by flak near Wildert.
P-51B CV- 43-24786
Lt. Olin P. Drake (368th) MIA-E; Hit by a Me-109 near Evreux.
P-51C CV-Z 42-103329

**June 11, 1944**
Lt. William R. Simmons (368th) KIA; Hit by flak near Bretteville.
P-51B CV- 43-6775
Lt. Gilbert R. Ralston (369th) ASR; Damaged by flak and bailed out over the Channel.
P-51B IV-R 43-6620

**June 12, 1944**
Capt. Robert L. Pherson (369th) KIA; Hit by a FW-190 west of Paris.
P-51B IV-N 42-106848 "Deviless 2nd"
Lt. Leroy D. Hess (369th) POW; Hit by a FW-190 west of Paris.
P-51B IV-Q 42-106841
Lt. Howard A. Linderer (369th) POW; Hit by flak and bailed out near Pallseaux.
P-51B IV-G 42-106649

**June 17, 1944**
Maj. Wayne W. Brown (368th) KIAc;
P-51B CV-

**June 20, 1944**
Lt. Virgal E. Sansing (369th) MIA-E; Hit by flak northeast of Paris and bailed out near Compiegne.
P-51B IV-C 42-106670

**June 21, 1944**
LtCol. Albert R. Tyrrell (368th) POW; Hit by flak at Wittstock and bailed out near Parchim.
P-51D CV-A 44-13387

**June 22, 1944**
Lt. Howard E. Grimes (370th) KIA; Hit by flak near Nanteuil-Sur-Marne.
P-51B CS-D 43-24791
Lt. Harold D. Hollis (370th) KIA; Hit by flak near Nanteuil-Sur-Marne.
P-51B CS- 42-106808

**July 11, 1944**
Lt. Bennie F. White (370th) KIA; Last seen over the North Sea.
P-51B CS-J 43-24810

**July 13, 1944**
Lt. Thomas S. Lane (368th) ASR; Suffered mechanical failure and bailed out 20 miles southeast of Bradwell Bay.
P-51B CV-

**July 20, 1944**
Lt. Gordon M. Shortness (370th) KIA; Last seen chasing a Me-109 near Niedermuelsen.
P-51B CS-M 42-106474

**July 21, 1944**
Lt. Luther C. Reese (370th) KIA; Hit by flak and crashed near Aalen.
P-51B CS-E 43-7013
Lt. Robert W. Siltamaki (370th) POW; Hit by flak and crashed near Aalen.
P-51B CS-W 43-12147

**July 28, 1944**
F/O Walter W. Wiley (370th) POW; Ran out of fuel and bailed out south of Rotterdam.
P-51B CS-L 43-6961

**August 2, 1944**
Capt. Robert W. Hawkinson (368th) MIA-E; Hit by flak near Rouen.
P-51D CV-N 44-13386 "Miss Janet"

**August 4, 1944**
Capt. Ray B. Lancaster (370th) INT; Lost oil pressure and landed in Sweden.
P-51D CS-W 44-13939
Lt. Wilson K. Baker, Jr. (370th) INT; Escorted Lancaster to Sweden.
P-51B CS-Q 43-6461 "Hot Pants"
Lt. Richard O. Rabb (370th) INT; Escorted Lancaster to Sweden.
P-51B CS-F 43-12463

**August 8, 1944**
Lt. John C. Allen (368th) KIA; Hit by flak near Dreux.
P-51B CV-I 42-106867
Lt. Willis J. Cherry (368th) KIA; Hit by flak near Poix and bailed out near Sommery.
P-51B CV-X 42-106577

**August 10, 1944**
Lt. Lester W. Hovden (368th) KIA; Lost a wing while dive-bombing near Bishwiller.
P-51B CV-X 42-106702
Lt. Paul E. McCluskey (369th) KIA; Hit by flak near Wingen.
P-51C IV-M 42-103743
Lt. Lawrence A. Bearden (369th) KIAc; Flipped over and spun-in near East Wretham on a training flight.
P-51B IV-

**August 15, 1944**
Lt. Frank A. Westall, Jr. (370th) KIA; Suffered mechanical failure and crashed south of Dunkirk.
P-51B CS-Y 42-106799

**August 17, 1944**
Lt. Theophalus A. Williams (370th) KIA; Hit by a FW-190 near Rouen.
P-51B CS-A 42-106878

**August 18, 1944**
Lt. Rene L. Burtner (369th) MIA-E; Hit by flak at St. Dizier.
P-51B IV-R 43-12186
Lt. Donald S. Melrose (369th) KIA; Hit by flak at St. Dizier.
P-51B IV-D 42-106916 "Loretta"

**August 27, 1944**
Lt. Paul E. Sundheim (370th) POW; Last seen near Munster and crashed near Lochtenberg.
P-51B CS-I 42-106580

**August 28, 1944**
Lt. Ferris C. Suttle (369th) KIA; Last seen near Nancy and crashed near Luneville.
P-51B IV-V 43-24756

**September 1, 1944**
Lt. Edward C. Kasloski (368th) KIA; Lost oil pressure and bailed out over the Channel.
P-51C CV-U 42-103318

**September 10, 1944**
Lt. Benjamin J. Vos, Jr. (370th) KIA; Hit by flak southeast of Wurzburg.
P-51D CS- 44-14240

**September 11, 1944**
F/O Charles R. Bruening (369th) KIA; Hit by fighters near Diemerode.
P-51D IV- 44-14399
Lt. Frank W. Holliday (369th) KIA; Hit by fighters near Meiches.
P-51D IV-P 44-14307
Lt. James F. Hutton (369th) KIA; Hit by fighters near Hemleben.
P-51D IV- 44-14108
Lt. Ivan B. Holloman (369th) MIA-E; Hit by fighters near Kolleda.
P-51D IV-H 44-13689
F/O James J. O'Shea (370th) KIA; Hit by fighters near Mulhausen.
P-51D CS-D 44-13529 "Pandemonium"

**September 12, 1944**
Lt. Louis E. Barnett (368th) KIA; Hit by fighters near Wittenburg.
P-51D CV-Z 44-13404
Lt. James H. Haas (368th) POW; Lost a wing near Pritzwalk.
P-51D CV-E 44-14081 "Tootsie"
Lt. Kenneth L. Hobson (369th) POW; Suffered mechanical failure near Berlin.
P-51D IV-Z 44-14216
Lt. John E. Hughes (369th) KIA; Last seen strafing near Wittenburg.
P-51D IV- 44-14188
Lt. Cyril W. Jones (370th) KIA; Hit by flak and crashed near Coburg.
P-51D CS-W 44-14071 "Dora De"

**September 17, 1944**
Lt. Harold R. Burt (369th) KIA; Suffered mechanical failure northwest of Antwerp.
P-51C IV-K 42-103785

**September 18, 1944**
Lt. Grover C. Deen (369th) POW; Hit by fighters near Hengelo.
P-51C IV-F 42-103799
Lt. Edwin L. Sjoblad (369th) POW; Hit by a FW-190 near Hengelo.
P-51D IV- 44-14545

**September 20, 1944**
Lt. John E. Keur (369th) ASR; Bailed out 3 miles off Lowestoft.
P-51D IV-Q 44-14432

**September 25, 1944**
Lt. John F. Lausen (368th) KIA; Hit by flak near Wiesbaden.
P-51B CV- 43-24100

**September 28, 1944**
Lt. Howard E. Steussey (370th) KIA; Lost in bad weather near Coblenz.
P-51D CS-R 44-13633 "Satan's Lady"

**October 5, 1944**
Lt. Clifford L. Bartlett (368th) KIA; Spun-out near Tirlemont.
P-51D CV-I 44-13669

**October 7, 1944**
Lt. Wallace C. Murray (370th) KIA; Hit by flak near Dievenow.
P-51C CS- 43-25067 "Sandra Lynn"

**October 30, 1944**
Lt. Russell H. Jenner (369th) KIA; Suffered mechanical trouble and crashed near St. Trond.
P-51D IV-Y 44-13336 "Yankee Clipper"

**November 4, 1944**
Lt. Edward J. Thorne (369th) POW; Hit by flak and bailed out near Quackenbruck.
P-51C IV-F 42-103339 "Princess Pat"

**November 5, 1944**
Lt. Maurice N. Haines (369th) POW; Hit by flak and bailed out southwest of Darmstadt.
P-51D IV- 44-14857 "Brooklyn Devil"

**November 8, 1944**
Maj. James A. Howard (369th) KIA; Hit by flak near Meppen.
P-51D IV- 44-14286

**November 20, 1944**
Lt. Merle B. Barth (368th) KIA; Suffered mechanical failure and bailed out near Channel.
P-51D CV-C 44-14062

**November 21, 1944**
Capt. Thomas J. McGeever (368th) KIA; Hit by flak near Gotha.
P-51D CV-F 44-14670
Lt. Carl M. Anderson (368th) KIA; Suffered mechanical failure near Sanderhausen.
P-51D CV-J 44-14444 "Supermouse"
Lt. Stan F. Stegnerski (370th) KIA; Hit by fighters southwest of Merseburg.
P-51D CS-Q 44-14185

**November 27, 1944**
Lt. Dick D. Connelly (370th) KIA; Hit by fighters north of Kassel.
P-51D CS-V 44-14096 "De De III"

**December 18, 1944**
Lt. David B. Archibald (368th) POW; Hit by enemy fighters and flak in the Aachen-Koln area.
P-51D CV-L 44-15555
Lt. Paul E. Olson (368th) POW; Hit by fighters in the Aachen-Koln area.
P-51D CV-T 44-14131

**December 24, 1944**
Lt. Raymond A. Boyd, Jr. (368th) POW; Hit by a FW-190 near Cologne.
P-51D CV-X 44-14329

**December 27, 1944**
Lt. George M. Givan (369th) KIA; Landed at Reims and disappeared over the Thames River flying back later in the day.
P-51D IV- 44-14964
Lt. James R. Parsons, Jr. (369th) KIA; see above
P-51K IV-G 44-11659 "San'Tone Sweetheart"

**December 31, 1944**
Lt. Donald L. Murphy (368th) KIA; Last seen near Stade and crashed near Grossenheim.
P-51D CV-B 44-13786 "Adabelle"

**January 6, 1945**
Capt. Robert V. Beaupre (368th) KIA; Crashed on take-off from East Wretham.
P-51D CV-X 44-14509

**January 13, 1945**
Capt. Karl K. Shearer (369th) KIA; Spun-in near Ashill upon return.
P-51K IV-N 44-11686

**January 14, 1945**
Lt. Jack E. McCoskey (370th) POW; Overshot a FW-190 and crashed near Vorden Airfield.
P-51D CS-X 44-15543 "Lydia May"

**January 16, 1945**
Lt. Graham Lupton (368th) KIA; Suffered mechanical failure near Amersfoort.
P-51B CV-M 42-106693
Lt. Douglas A. Maclean (368th) KIA; Crashed on take-off from East Wretham.
P-51D CV-Y 44-63776

**January 29, 1945**
Lt. Richard H. Daniels (368th) KIA; Shot down by Allied ground gunners near Ingwiller.
P-51D CV-

**February 1, 1945**
Lt. Lawrence A. Ziska (370th) KIAc; Crashed near East Wretham.
P-51K CS-D 44-11355

**February 7, 1945**
Lt. Henry L. Thompson (368th) KIAc; Crashed into the North Sea after mechanical trouble.
P-51B CV-O 42-106809

**February 9, 1945**
Capt. Charles C. Ettlesen (368th) KIA; Last seen strafing a train near Gotha.
P-51K CV-V 44-11651

**February 14, 1945**
LtCol. Roy W. Evans (HdQts) POW; Hit by flak near Dresden.
P-51D IV- 44-14894 "Lucky"
Lt. Roy C. Garrett (368th) KIA; Lost coolant and bailed out near Emmerich.
P-51D CV-X 44-14650 "Snookie"

**February 19, 1945**
Lt. Anthony D. Maiorano (368th) POW; Lost coolant and bailed out north of Trier.
P-51D CV-D 44-15096 "Ice-Cold Katie"

**February 22, 1945**
Lt. David P. Dunmire (368th) KIA; Hit by flak near Dusseldorf.
P-51K CV-F 44-11647 "Freddy Junior"
Lt. Russell E. Masters (369th) KIA; Suffered mechanical failure and bailed out off the Dutch coast.
P-51D IV-V 44-13610

**February 23, 1945**
Lt. Lawrence F. Meyer (369th) KIA; Hit by flak near Fulda.
P-51D IV-D 44-15394
Capt. Washington D. Lyon (370th) KIA; Last seen near Zwickau.
P-51D CS-C 44-14987 "Patty Whack"
Lt. Garland J. McGregor (370th) KIA; Was relay and crashed at East Wretham.
P-51D CS-
Lt. Malcolm C. Paulette (370th) KIA; Ran out of fuel near Zwickau.
P-51D CS-G 44-14773 "Micky the Twist"

**February 28, 1945**
Maj. Edwin F. Pezda (369th) POW; Hit by flak near Kunzelsau.
P-51D IV-F 44-14625 "Pauline"
Capt. Harry L. Matthew (369th) POW; Hit power lines and bailed out near Neustadt.
P-51D IV-T 44-15081 "Pistol Packin' Mama III"

**March 2, 1945**
Lt. Merle G. Aunspaugh (368th) KIAc; On a gunnery flight, he hit trees and crashed near Polebrook.
P-51D CV-

**March 3, 1945**
Lt. Albert A. Cowie (368th) POW; Hit by flak near Hanover and bellied-in near Halberstadt.
P-51K CV-G 44-11696

**March 10, 1945**
Lt. George H. Blackburn (368th) KIA; Hit by flak near Remagen.
P-51D CV-G 44-15067 "Little Ann"
Lt. John W. McCormack (368th) KIA; Hit by flak near Remagen.
P-51D CV-A 44-63740 "Little Audrey"

**March 11, 1945**
LtCol. James V. Wilson (HdQts) POW; Lost coolant and bailed out north of the Frisian Islands.
P-51D IV- 44-72207

**March 19, 1945**
Lt. Clifton Enoch (368th) KIA; Last seen chasing a Me-262 near Leipzig.
P-51D CV-Z 44-15371

**April 3, 1945**
Lt. Charles E. Stubblefield (369th) KIA; Suffered an oxygen failure and crashed off Lowestoft.
P-51D IV-F 44-72503 "Gravel Gertie"

**April 13, 1945**
Lt. John W. Herb (368th) KIA; Hit trees and lost coolant; while trying to belly-in northwest of Hamburg, he crashed into a woods.
P-51D CV-E 44-72260 "Mary Lou"

**April 25, 1945**
F/O Jack D. Highfield (368th) MIA-E; Suffered mechanical trouble and bellied-in south of Dortmund.
P-51D CV-

**May 19, 1945**
Lt. James J. Ferris (368th) KIAc; Crashed near Stoke Ferry.
P-51B CV-G 42-106929

**July 23, 1945**
F/O John H. Klug (368th) KIAc;
P-51D CV-D 44-13762

**Headquarters**
Baccus, Donald A., LtCol.; April 1945-September 1945; ex-356th Ftr Grp
P-51D CV-U 44-72746
Cranfill, Niven K., Capt.; July 1944-August 1944; to 368th Ftr Sqn; ex-369th and 370th Ftr Sqns
Downing, John L., Lt.; October 1943-March 1944; to 370th Ftr Sqn
Evans, Roy W., LtCol.; August 1944-February 14, 1945(POW); ex-RAF and 4th Ftr Grp
P-51D IV-E 44-14988
Gray, Rockford V., Maj.; October 1943-February 1944; to 9th Air Force
Hodges, Fred S., Maj.; March 1945-September 1945; ex-CBI and 369th Ftr Sqn
P-51D IV-L 44-14315 "Jeepers"
Irvine, Chauncey S., Maj.; February 1944-April 1944; to 369th Ftr Sqn; ex-370th Ftr Sqn
Kirk, Karl H., Capt.; July 1944-September 1944; ex-369th Ftr Sqn
Lemmens, Andrew T., Maj.; April 1945-October 1945; ex-368th and 370th Ftr Sqns
P-51D CS-V 44-73102 "Screamin' Demon"
Lovette, James K., Maj.; March 1945-September 1945; ex-370th Ftr Sqn
McKee, Daniel D., LtCol.; Fall 1943-February 1944; to 370th Ftr Sqn April 1945-September 1945; ex-11th AF, Alaska
P-47D CS-Z 42-75118
P-51D CS-A 44-72823 "Rayner Shine"
Minchew, Leslie D., Capt.; May 1945-November 1945; ex-355th Ftr Grp
Parsons, James W., LtCol.; November 1944-April 1945; to 368th Ftr Sqn; ex-369th Ftr Sqn and 54th Ftr Grp, Alaska
P-51D IV-E 44-14127 "Wild Will"
P-51D CV-Q 44-15717 "Wild Will"
Pezda, Edwin F., Maj.; May 1944-November 1944; to 369th Ftr Sqn; ex-369th Ftr Sqn
Randolph, John P., Col.; November 1944-April 1945; ex-20th Ftr Grp
P-51D CV-N 44-14965 "Nancy"
Smith, Samuel R., Capt.; April 1944-August 1944; ex-370th Ftr Sqn
Swanson, William H., LtCol.; April 1944-October 1944; ex-369th Ftr Sqn
P-51B IV-Y 42-106443 "Poison"
P-51D IV-Y 44-13336 "Yankee Clipper"
Tacon, Avelin P., Col.; January 1943-November 1944
P-47D CV-Z 42-8637
P-51C CV-Z 42-103329
P-51D CV-Z 44-13404
Wilson, James V., LtCol.; February 1945-March 11, 1945(POW)

**368th Fighter Squadron**
Addleman, Robert H., Lt.; April 1944-November 1944
270 hours
Adkins, Boyd N., Lt.; September 1944-April 1945
Alexander, Robert S., Lt.; April 1945-September 1945
Allen, John C., Lt.; July 1944-August 8, 1944(KIA)
Anderson, Carl M., Lt.; August 1944-November 21, 1944(KIA)
Archibald, David B., Lt.; August 1944-December 18, 1944(POW)
44 missions
P-51D CV-L 44-14652
P-51D CV-L 44-15555
Ashenmacher, Joseph M., Lt.; January 1944-October 1944
Aunspaugh, Merle G., Lt.; January 1945-March 2, 1945(KIAc)
Bach, Glenn C., Capt.; January 1944-August 1944; ex-369th Ftr Sqn
102 missions, 303 hours
P-51B CV-I 42-106867 "Pegelin"
P-51D CV-I 44-13669 "Pegelin"
Baker, George F., Capt.; August 1944-September 1945
P-51B CV-H 42-106809 "Little Liquidator"
P-51D CV-E 44-14081
P-51D CV-E 44-14500
Baldridge, Arlen R., Lt.; January 1944-May 21, 1944(KIA)
P-51B CV-Y 43-6962
Barber, Kenneth E., Lt.; January 1945-September 1945
Barnett, Louis E., Lt.; August 1944-September 12, 1944(KIA)
Barth, Merle B., Lt.; July 1944-November 20, 1944(KIA)
P-51D CV-C 44-14062
Bartlett, Clifford L., Lt.; July 1944-October 5, 1944(KIA)
Beal, Elby J., Capt.; July 1944-January 1945
270 hours
P-51D CV-R 44-15618 "Diane"
Beaupre, Robert V., Lt.; January 1944-January 6, 1945(KIA)
P-51B CV-X 42-106702
P-51D CV-X 44-14509
Benefiel, Robert E., Capt.; August 1944-February 1945
Blackburn, George H., Lt.; January 1945-March 10, 1945(KIA)
P-51K CV-C 44-11697 "Little Ann"
Bolefahr, Wayne N., Capt.; April 1943-June 10, 1944(KIA)
61 missions
P-47D CV-B 42-22786
P-51B CV-B 43-24764
Botsford, Raymond L., Lt.; January 1944-May 2, 1944(KIAc)
P-47D CV- "Lil Abner"
Boussu, Marvin F., Capt.; September 1944-September 1945
P-51D CV-D 44-15096 "Ice Cold Katie"

Boyd, Ray A., Jr., Lt.; July 1944-December 24, 1944(POW)
P-51D CV-X 44-14329
Britton, Eugene F., Lt.; June 1944-December 1944
61 missions, 270 hours
P-51B CV-K 42-106611
P-51D CV-N 44-14325 "Mass Kid"
Brown, Cecil R., Lt.; January 1944-April 13, 1944(KIA)
P-47D CV- 42-75104
Brown, Ralph L., Maj.; September 1944-February 1945
P-51D CV-Z 44-15371
Brown, Wayne W., Maj.; June 1944-June 17, 1944(KIAc)
Burton, Robert E., Lt.; April 1943-April 1944; to 370th Ftr Sqn
81 missions, 300 hours
Byron, George J., Lt.; March 1945-September 1945
Carter, Leonard D., Lt.; August 1944-April 1945
Cater, Emer H., Lt.; April 1943-June 4, 1944(KIA)
P-47D CV-E 42-74695
P-51B CV-E 43-6491 "Wanna Honey"
Cavanaugh, Cornelius J., Lt.; July 1944-January 1945
67 missions, 272:05 hours
P-51C CV-Y 42-103197 "Sweet Jan Marie"
Chatfield, Donald W., Lt.; July 1944-December 1944
270 hours
Cherry, Willis J., Lt.; July 1944-August 8, 1944(POW)
Cimino, William L., Lt.; March 1945-September 1945
Clark, Buell R., Lt.; March 1945-September 1945
Clark, Edward L., Lt.; March 1945-September 1945
Collins, Cornelius J., Lt.; October 1944-July 1945
Collins, John F., Capt.; October 1944-July 1945
Cook, Emory C., Lt.; June 1944-December 1944
270 hours
P-51B CV-P 43-12478
Cooley, John D., Jr., Lt.; January 1945-September 1945
P-51K CV-V 44-11685 "Janet"
Cosgrove, Capt.; September 1945-October 1945; ex-9th Air Force
Cowie, Albert A., Lt.; January 1945-March 3, 1945(POW)
Crane, Lewis G., Capt.; September 1944-April 1945
Cranfill, Niven K., LtCol.; August 1944-April 1945; ex-HdQts & 369th Ftr Sqn
133 missions total
P-51D CV-Q 44-15100
P-51D CV-Q 44-15717
Daniels, Richard H., Lt.; October 1944-January 29, 1945(KIA)
Dauchert, Eugene F., Lt.; August 1944-April 1945
Denman, John A., Capt.; October 1944-September 1945
P-51K CV-T 44-11758 "Silky"
Doersch, George A., Maj.; February 1945-September 1945; ex-370th Ftr Sqn
P-51D CV-R 44-72067 "Ole Goat"
Drake, Olin P., Lt.; January 1944-June 10, 1944(MIA-E)
P-51B CV- 43-24786
Dunmire, David P., Lt.; October 1944-February 22, 1945(KIA)
Elliott, Robert H., Lt.; February 1945-September 1945
Enoch, Clifton, Jr., Lt.; February 1945-March 18, 1945(KIA)
Ettlesen, Charles C., Capt.; September 1944-February 19, 1945(KIA); ex-369th Ftr Sqn
P-51K CV-V 44-11651
Everhart, Olin C., Lt.; February 1945-July 1945
Ferris, James J., III, Lt.; November 1944-May 19, 1945(KIAc)
Flack, Jack O., Lt.; July 1944-December 1944
270 hours
P-51D CV-B 44-13786 "Adabelle"
Fladmark, Oscar R., Capt.; June 1944-January 1945
P-51B CV-R 42-106879
Fogg, Howard L., Capt.; May 1943-May 1944; to 370th Ftr Sqn June 1944-September 1944
76 missions, 271 hours
P-51D CV-D 44-13762 "Moose Nose"
Forehand, William C., Maj.; April 1943-September 1944
300 hours
P-47D CV-O 42-75113 "Daisy Mae"
P-51B CV-O
P-51D CV-O 44-13539
Foster, William B., Lt.; February 1945-July 1945
Fraser, Lewis L., Lt.; February 1945-July 1945
Garrett, Roy C., Lt.; January 1945-February 14, 1945(KIA)
Gilmore, Chester R., Capt.; May 1944-December 1944
270 hours
Gordon, John T., Lt.; July 1944-July 1945
55 missions, 294 hours
P-51D CV-D 44-13762 "Cookie"
Guggemos, Robert J., Lt.; April 1945-September 1945; ex-369th Ftr Sqn
Haas, James H., Lt.; July 1944-September 12, 1944(POW)
Hagan, Benjamin M., III, Lt.; April 1943-June 8, 1944(POW)
P-47D CV-D 42-22776 "Boots"
P-51B CV-D 42-106898 "Boots"
Hanzalik, Frank, Lt.; October 1944-April 1945; ex-453rd Bomb Group (34 missions)
40 missions
Hatter, Robert B., Capt.; April 1944-October 1944
63 missions, 270 hours
P-51C CV-H 42-103197
Hawkinson, Robert W., Capt.; April 1943-August 2, 1944(MIA-E)
81 missions, 332 hours
P-47D CV- "Lonesome Polecat"
P-51C CV-N 42-103386 "Miss Janet"

Heim, William J., Lt.; April 1945-September 1945
Herb, John W., Lt.; January 1945-April 13, 1945(KIA)
P-51D CV-E 44-72260 "Mary Lou"
Highfield, Jack D., F/O; March 1945-April 25, 1945(MIA-E)
Hill, Joseph M., Jr., F/O; March 1945-September 1945
Homeyer, Albert G., Capt.; January 1944-April 1945; ex-369th Ftr Sqn
Hovden, Lester W., Lt.; July 1944-August 10, 1944(KIA)
Huddleston, Clyde M., Lt.; February 1944-May 21, 1944(KIA)
P-51B CV- 42-106620
Hunter, John B., Capt.; April 1943-April 1945
P-51B CV-C 43-7155
P-51D CV-C 44-14566
P-51D CV-C 44-72331
Hyland, Edward J., Lt.; April 1943-January 11, 1944(KIA)
Janney, Raymond B., II, Capt.; April 1943-July 1944
300 hours
P-47D CV-J
P-51B CV-J 42-106619 "Die Fledermaus"
Kasloski, Edward G., Lt.; June 1944-September 1, 1944(KIA)
Kasper, Billy D., Capt.; July 1944-February 1945
70 missions, 325 hours
P-51B CV-V 42-106949
P-51K CV-V 44-11685
Keesey, John S., Capt.; May 1944-December 1944
68 missions, 270 hours
P-51D CV-E 44-14081 "Tootsie"
Kelsey, Joseph P., Capt.; December 1943-September 1944; ex-369th Ftr Sqn
85 missions, 280 hours
P-51D CV-D 44-13762
Kibler, Ralph E., Lt.; April 1943-January 1944; to 370th Ftr Sqn
King, Ben H., Maj.; August 1944-December 1944; ex-347th Ftr Grp, PTO & 479th Ftr Grp, ETO
122 missions, 470 hours total
P-51D CV-A 44-13898 "Matilda IV"
Klock, Richard E., F/O; March 1945-September 1945
Klug, John H., Jr., F/O; March 1945-July 23, 1945(KIAc)
Kosc, George J., Lt.; May 1944-November 1944
270 hours
Kruezman, Henry B., Lt.; January 1945-September 1945
Kysely, Arvy F., Lt.; June 1944-January 1945
Lambright, Clarence M., Capt.; April 1944-November 1944
270 hours
P-51B CV-T 42-106436
Lane, Thomas S., Capt.; April 1943-August 1944
300 hours
P-47D CV-G 42-75088
P-51C CV- 42-103602
Lanier, John T., F/O; March 1945-September 1945
Lausen, John F., Lt.; August 1944-September 25, 1944(KIA)
Lemmens, Andrew T., Capt.; June 1943-May 1944; to 370th Ftr Sqn
P-47D CV-M 42-8402 "Lucky Pearl"
P-47D CV-M 42-8617 "Lucky Pearl"
Levitt, Leon J., Lt.; January 1945-July 1945
Lewis, Wilbur H., Capt.; May 1944-December 1944
67 missions, 270 hours
P-51B CV-B 43-24764 "The Beachcomber"
Loehr, Emil L., Lt.; February 1945-September 1945
Long, George W., Lt.; December 1944-September 1945
P-51D CV-Y 44-13776 "Kitten"
Lubien, James J., Lt.; June 1944-December 1944
270 hours
P-51D CV- "You've Had It, Chum"
Lupton, Graham, Lt.; December 1944-January 16, 1945(KIA)
Maclean, Douglas A., Lt.; December 1944-January 16, 1945(KIA)
0 missions
Madison, Garland F., Lt.; December 1944-September 1945
Maiorano, Anthony D., Lt.; December 1944-February 19, 1945(POW)
Marcus, Clifford H., Lt.; October 1944-September 1945
Marr, John M., Lt.; December 1944-September 1945
1 mission (injured January 29, 1945)
Marron, John T., Lt.; December 1944-September 1945
P-51D CV-K 44-63689 "Fritzie VI"
Marshall, William J., Lt.; January 1945-September 1945
Marson, Alfred D., Lt.; December 1944-July 1945
33 missions, 145:50 hours
P-51D CV-P 44-15489 "Annie"
Martin, Allen G., Lt.; December 1944-September 1945
Martin, James C., Lt.; May 1945-September 1945; ex-370th Ftr Sqn
Mason, Robert G., F/O; March 1945-September 1945
6 missions, 33:15 hours
P-51B CV-B 42-106876
McCormack, James W., Lt.; December 1944-March 10, 1945(KIA)
P-51D CV-A 44-63740 "Little Audrey"
McDonald, James H., Lt.; January 1945-September 1945
McGeever, Thomas J., Capt.; April 1943-November 21, 1944(KIA)
P-51B CV-F 42-106727
P-51D CV-F 44-14670
Mosse, Charles E., Capt.; October 1943-May 19, 1944(POW); ex-369th Ftr Sqn
P-47D CV-B 42-8485
P-51B CV-B 42-106890
Murphy, Donald L., Lt.; December 1944-December 31, 1944(KIA)

Muzzy, Raymond G., F/O; January 1945-September 1945
Olson, Paul E., Lt.; June 1944-December 18, 1944(POW)
P-51B CV-J 42-106917 "Mari-Helen"
P-51D CV-J 44-14444 "Supermouse"
Parsons, James W., LtCol.; April 1945-September 1945; ex-HdQts & 369th Ftr Sqn
P-51D CV-Q 44-15717 "Wild Will"
Perkins, Earl P., Capt.; April 1943-August 1944
300 hours
P-47D CV-N 42-75095 "Pappy Yokum"
P-51B CV-N
Pino, James R., Lt.; April 1943-April 11, 1944(POW)
P-47D CV-I 42-75141
Randolph, Gaston M., Lt.; April 1943-September 1944
300 hours
Rea, Frank, Jr., Lt.; January 1945-September 1945
Sellers, Wilbur W., Jr., Capt.; May 1945-September 1945
0 missions
Shaw, Clifton, Maj.; April 1943-August 1944
300 hours
Simmons, William R., Lt.; April 1943-June 11, 1944(KIA)
P-47D CV- "Marryin' Sam"
P-51B CV- 43-6775
Smith, James B., Lt.; April 1943-May 19, 1944(POW)
P-47D CV- "Hairless Joe"
Thompson, Henry L., Lt.; January 1945-February 7, 1945(KIAc)
Tyrrell, Albert R., LtCol.; March 1943-June 21, 1944(POW)
62 missions
P-47D CV-A 42-75111
P-51B CV-A
P-51D CV-A 44-13387
Walter, Donald J., Maj.; September 1945-October 1945; ex-9th Air Force
Way, James L., Jr., Capt.; January 1945-September 1945
P-51D CV-Z 44-15371 "Happy"
P-51D CV-Z 44-72281 "Happy 2"
White, Samuel A., Lt.; April 1943-August 1944
300 hours

**369th Fighter Squadron**

Albertson, Benjamin H., Capt.; April 1943-October 1943; to 370th Ftr Sqn
Bach, Glenn C., Lt.; January 1943-January 1944; to 368th Ftr Sqn
Bearden, Lawrence A., Lt.; August 1944-August 10, 1944(KIAc)
Berndt, Harley E., F/O; January 1945-August 1945
16 missions, 76 hours
P-51D IV-S 44-15215 "Torchy"
Bouchard, Lawrence H., Lt.; April 1943-August 1944
300 hours
P-47D IV-L 42-8545 "Mary"
P-51B IV-L 42-106906 "Mary"
Booth, Robert J., Lt.; April 1943-June 8, 1944(POW)
P-47D IV-F 42-8695 "Oily Boid"
P-51B IV-F 43-6757
P-51B IV-F 43-7199
Borg, Robert M., Lt.; April 1943-January 1944; to 370th Ftr Sqn
Broach, Richard H., Capt.; April 1943-May 30, 1944(POW)
P-47D IV-I 42-75210 "Dotty"
P-51B IV-I 42-106771 "Dotty"
Brown, Carey H., Capt.; April 1943-October 1943; to 370th Ftr Sqn
Brown, Clarence R., Lt.; March 1945-September 1945
Brown, Grover W., Lt.; March 1945-September 1945
Bruening, Charles R., F/O; June 1944-September 11, 1944(KIA)
P-51B IV-L 43-12208 "Rose of San Antone"
Brundage, Lowell W., Lt.; April 1943-May 29, 1944(KIA)
P-47D IV-C
P-51B IV-C
Buniowski, John F., Capt.; July 1944-March 1945
Bur, Thomas G., Lt.; July 1944-May 1945
67 missions, 264:30 hours
P-51D IV-N 44-13390 "Big Noise From Winnetka"
Burt, Harold R., Lt.; July 1944-September 17, 1944(KIA)
P-51C IV-K 42-103785
Burtner, Rene L., Capt.; August 1944-August 18, 1944(MIA-E)
September 1944-September 1945
P-51D IV-D 44-14718 "Hubert"
P-51D IV-D 44-15394
Burton, Herbert C., Capt.; April 1944-August 1944; ex-33rd Ftr Sqn, Iceland
49 missions, 200 hours
P-51B IV-C 42-106670
P-51D IV-C 44-13592
Campbell, Robert W., Lt.; December 1943-September 1944
300 hours
P-47D IV-Z 42-75048
P-51B IV-Z 43-12435
P-51D IV-Z 44-14216
Cannon, Donald E., Lt.; June 1944-May 1945
Carroll, Walter J., Lt.; March 1945-September 1945
Carter, Clifford E., Lt.; April 1943-April 8, 1944(KIA)
P-47D IV-W 42-8551 "Green Eyes"
Carter, Richard G., Lt.; March 1945-September 1945
Chaffee, Vernon E., Lt.; March 1945-September 1945
Collins, William F., Capt.; August 1944-September 1945
P-51D IV-V 44-13610
P-51D IV-Y 44-11350
Cox, Ralph L., Maj.; February 1945-September 1945; ex-370th Ftr Sqn
P-51D IV-N 44-72154
Cranfill, Niven K., Maj.; October 1943-July 1944; to HdQts
133 missions
P-47D IV-N 42-74645 "Deviless"
P-51B IV-N 42-106848 "Deviless 2nd"
P-51D IV-N 44-13390 "Deviless 3rd"
Crawford, Cecil W., Lt.; April 1943-February 3, 1944(KIA)
P-47D IV-E
Crenshaw, Claude J., Capt.; May 1944-December 1944
270 hours
P-51B IV-S 42-106689
P-51D IV-I 44-13606 "Louisiana Heat Wave"
P-51D IV-I 44-15016
Cuzner, Harry F., Lt.; December 1943-September 1944
300 hours
P-51C IV-G 42-103793 "San'Tone Sweetheart"
P-51K IV-G 44-11659 "San'Tone Sweetheart"
Davison, Robert W., Capt.; September 1944-June 1945
Dean, Grover C., Lt.; May 1944-September 18, 1944(POW)
P-51C IV-F 42-103799
Ettlesen, Charles C., Capt.; December 1943-May 25, 1944(MIA-E)
P-47D IV-V 42-75054
P-51B IV-V 42-106853
Erwin, Robert D., Lt.; September 1944-September 1945
Fong, Frank S., Lt.; February 1944-February 1945 (D.S. to 5th ERS from May 1944)
Francis, Robert M., Capt.; September 1944-November 1945
Freeman, Albert S., Lt.; February 1945-September 1945
Gaines, Robert S., Jr., Capt.; August 1944-September 1945
71 missions, 331:35 hours
P-51C IV-G 42-103793
P-51K IV-G 44-11664
Garth, Horace E., III, Lt.; February 1945-July 1945
Gates, Harold R., Lt.; February 1945-July 1945
Gray, Rockford V., Maj.; March 1943-October 1943; to HdQts
P-47D IV-A
Givan, George M., Lt.; October 1944-December 27, 1944(KIA)
Guggemos, Robert J., Lt.; October 1944-April 1945; to 368th Ftr Sqn
P-51D IV-O 44-15514
Haines, Maurice N., Lt.; September 1944-November 5, 1944(POW)
Hess, Leroy D., Lt.; May 1944-June 12, 1944(POW)
Hopkins, Robert W., Capt.; October 1944-September 1945
P-51D IV-M 44-72344 "Saucy Sal"
Hobson, Kenneth L., Lt.; August 1944-September 12, 1944(POW)
Hodges, Fred S., Maj.; September 1944-March 1945; to HdQts; ex-AVG pilot, China (1 victory)
P-51D IV-L 44-14315 "Jeepers"
Holliday, Frank W., Lt.; June 1944-September 11, 1944(KIA)
Holloman, Ivan B., Capt.; May 1944-September 11, 1944(MIA-E) December 1944-July 1945
57 missions, 248:40 hours
P-51B IV-V 42-106853 "Traveler"
P-51D IV-V "Traveler II"
Homeyer, Albert G., Capt.; April 1943-January 1944; to 368th Ftr Sqn
Howard, James A., Maj.; September 1944-November 8, 1944(KIA)
Hruby, Conrad Z., F/O; March 1945-September 1945
Hughes, John E., Lt.; August 1944-September 12, 1944(KIA)
Hutton, James F., Lt.; July 1944-September 11, 1944(KIA)
Irvine, Chauncey S., Maj.; April 1944-October 1944; ex-HdQts & 370th Ftr Sqn
P-51B IV-A 42-106803
Jenner, Russell H., Lt.; July 1944-October 30, 1944(KIA)
Jennings, Warner C., Lt.; September 1944-September 1945
48 missions, 225 hours
P-51K IV-I 44-11572 "Michigan Mauler"
Judkins, Vernon T., Lt.; August 1944-September 1945
P-51D IV-W 44-15015 "Babe"
Kelly, Dale E., Lt.; October 1944-September 1945
Kelly, John J., III, Lt.; August 1944-September 1945
Kelsey, Joseph P., Capt.; June 1943-December 1943; to 368th Ftr Sqn
Keur, John E., Lt.; June 1944-January 1945
Kirk, Karl H., Capt.; February 1944-May 1944; to 5th ERS; later HdQts
Klaver, Ralph R., Lt.; September 1944-September 1945
P-51D IV-R 44-15588 "Born to Lose"
Klem, Thomas J., Lt.; August 1944-July 1945
P-51D IV-Z 44-15007
Kruger, Charles H., Capt.; June 1943-August 1944
89 missions, 300:30 hours
P-47D IV-K 42-74642 "Nancy June"
P-51B IV-K 42-106629 "Nancy June 2nd"
P-51C IV-K 42-103785 "Nancy June 3rd"
Laing, D.H., Lt.; January 1944-May 19, 1944(POW)
P-51B IV-E 42-106893
Lancaster, Robert T., Lt.; September 1944-September 1945
P-51D IV- "The Maine Beau"
Linderer, Howard A., Lt.; January 1944-June 12, 1944(POW)
33 missions, 106 hours
P-51B IV-S 42-106689 "Briney Marlin"
Lindsey, Douglas G., Lt.; January 1945-September 1945
23 missions, 113 hours

Lyon, Washington D., Capt.; October 1944-November 1944; to 370th Ftr Sqn
Magee, Raymond E., Capt.; August 1944-March 1945
Masters, Russell E., Lt.; January 1945-February 22, 1945(KIA)
  1 mission
Matthew, Harry L., Capt.; March 1943-February 28, 1945(POW)
  118 missions, 436 hours
  P-47D IV-T "Pistol Packin Mama"
  P-51B IV-T 43-24789 "Pistol Packin Mama"
  P-51D IV-T 44-15081 "Pistol Packin Mama"
McCluskey, Paul E., Lt.; June 1944-August 10, 1944(KIA)
McCormack, Robert E., Lt.; December 1944-September 1945
  23 missions, 123 hours
  P-51D IV- "Gloria Mac"
McGehee, Fred S., Lt.; December 1944-September 1945
McIntosh, Robert W., Lt.; January 1945-September 1945
  21 missions, 97 hours
  P-51D IV-E 44-14127 "Dilbert"
Mejaski, Joseph J., Capt.; June 1944-February 1945
  75 missions, 300 hours
  P-51D IV-M 44-14117 "Stinky"
Melrose, Donald S., Lt.; June 1944-August 18, 1944(KIA)
Mettel, Arnold F., Lt.; July 1944-April 1945
  71 missions
  P-51D IV- "Chicago"
Meyer, Lawrence F., Lt.; December 1944-February 23, 1945(KIA)
Millis, Tracey E., Lt.; December 1944-September 1945
Montague, Bert M., Lt.; December 1944-September 1945
Morrill, Myron C., Jr., Lt.; April 1944-May 29, 1944(KIA)
Morris, Arthur B., Jr., Lt.; October 1944-June 1945
Mosse, Charles E., Capt., April 1943-October 1943, to 368th Ftr Sqn
Nicsic, Stephen, Lt.; States only; later KIA w/370th Ftr Grp, ETO on June 25, 1944
Oliphint, John H., Lt.; April 1943-June 8, 1944(POW-E)
  67 missions, 226 hours
  P-47D IV-O 42-74666 "The Mad Rebel"
  P-51B IV-O 42-106679 "The Mad Rebel
Orwig, Eugene R., Capt.; February 1943-July 1944
  300 hours
  P-47D IV-D
  P-51B IV-D 42-106916 "Loretta"
Painter, Jefferson C., Capt.; June 1943-May 1944; to 5th ERS
  P-47D IV-H
  P-51B IV-H 42-106476
Parsons, James R., Jr., Lt.; July 1944-December 27, 1944(KIA)
Parsons, James W., LtCol.; August 1944-November 1944; to HdQts; ex-54th Ftr Grp, Aleutians
  49 missions, 226:15 hours
  P-51D IV-E 44-14127 "Wild Will"
Patton, Lee, Lt.; January 1945-September 1945
  P-51D IV-Q 44-15242
Perrin, Grant M., Capt.; June 1944-January 1945
  270 hours
  P-51B IV-X 43-12444
  P-51D IV-X 44-14218 "X-Terminator"
Pezda, Edwin F., Maj.; October 1943-May 1944; to HdQts; November 1944-February 28, 1945(POW)
  P-47D IV-B 42-75158
  P-51B IV-B
  P-51D IV-B 44-13301
  P-51K IV-B 44-11635
Pherson, Robert L., Capt.; April 1943-June 12, 1944(KIA)
  P-47D IV-J
  P-51B IV-J 42-106680
Porter, Roger W., Lt.; July 1944-February 1945
  P-51D IV- "Jenny F"
Prewitt, Luster H., Lt.; April 1943-November 1944
  P-47D IV-W
  P-51B IV-W 42-106599
Ralston, Gilbert R., Jr., Capt.; April 1944-December 1944
  61 missions, 371:45 hours
  P-51B IV-R 43-12186
  P-51D IV-R 44-13520
Rodeheaver, Homer L., Lt.; April 1943-May 21, 1944(KIA)
  P-47D IV-U
  P-51B IV-U 42-106818
Sackett, Stanley E., Lt.; April 1943-May 8, 1944(KIA)
  P-47D IV-S
Sander, Robert B., Lt.; April 1944-June 8, 1944(KIA)
  P-51B IV-L 42-106906
Sansing, Virgal E., Lt.; March 1944-June 20, 1944(MIA-E)
Shearer, Karl K., Capt.; November 1944-January 13, 1945(KIA); ex-B-24 pilot(33 missions)
  P-51K IV-N 44-11686
Sjoblad, Edwin L., Lt.; June 1944-September 18, 1944(KIA)
  P-51D IV- 44-14545
Smith, Alma R., Lt.; September 1943-August 1944
  88 missions, 300 hours
  P-47D IV-M
  P-51C IV-M 42-103743
Soderman, Byron N., Lt.; January 1945-September 1945
Staley, Charles W., Lt.; April 1943-August 1944
  74 missions, 300 hours
  P-47D IV-R 42-75270 "Sally"
  P-51B IV-R 43-12434 "Dunquerque"
Stevens, Jack D., Capt.; June 1944-January 1945
Stubblefield, Charles E., Lt.; January 1945-April 3, 1945(KIA)
Suttle, Ferris C., Lt.; June 1944-August 28, 1944(KIA)
  P-51C IV-E 42-103797 "Darling Earline"
Swanson, William H., LtCol.; April 1943-April 1944; to HdQts
  P-47D IV-A
Taylor, Lester G., Capt.; April 1943-September 1944
  P-47D IV-P
  P-51B IV-H
  P-51D IV-H 44-13689
Tenenbaum, Harold, Lt.; October 1944-September 1945
Thacker, Robert L., Capt.; April 1943-September 1944
  75 missions, 301 hours
  P-47D IV-X 42-8698
  P-51B IV-V 43-24756
Thibert, Henry G., Lt.; States only; later to ETO with 339th Ftr Grp
Thomas, Wendel G., Lt.; April 1945-June 1945; ex-bomber pilot
Thomson, Bryce H., Lt.; September 1944-July 1945
Thomson, Robert C., Maj.; March 1943-August 1945
  123 missions, 540 hours
  P-47D IV-Q 42-75085
  P-51B IV-Q 42-106841
  P-51D IV-Q 44-15242
  P-51D IV-Q 44-14432
  P-51D IV-K 44-72780
Thorne, Edward J., Lt.; June 1944-November 4, 1944(POW)
  P-51B IV-Q 43-12439
Webster, Joseph A., Capt.; September 1945-September 1945

**370th Fighter Squadron**

Albertson, Benjamin H., Capt.; October 1943-March 18, 1944(POW); ex-369th Ftr Sqn
Ambrose, Vincent W., Capt.; April 1943-September 1944
  92 missions, 329 hours
  P-47D CS-G 42-8663 "Baltimore Babe"
  P-51B CS-G 42-106921"Baltimore Babe"
  P-51D CS-G 44-14038 "Baltimore Babe"
Baker, Wilson K., Jr., Lt.; May 1944-August 4, 1944(INT)
  P-51B CS-Q 43-6461 "Hot Pants"
Bateman, Jack H., Lt.; April 1943-May 1944; to 5th ERS
  P-47D CS-E "Pee Wee"
  P-47D CS-E 42-8693 "Miss Margaret"
Bateman, Paul H., Lt.; April 1943-July 1944
  301:50 hours
  P-47D CS-O
  P-51B CS-O 42-106926
Becker, Claire A., Lt.; March 1945-September 1945
Bell, Gwyn W., Lt.; March 1945-September 1945
Bell, John E., Lt.; March 1945-September 1945
Bellante, Emildo L., Lt.; March 1945-July 1945
Benneyworth, Albert F., Lt.; March 1945-September 1945
Borg, Robert M., Lt.; January 1944-July 1944; ex-369th Ftr Sqn
  P-47D CS-M 42-8556
  P-51B CS-M 42-106749
Braymen, Kenneth M., Lt.; March 1945-September 1945
Brickner, Albert C., Lt.; March 1945-September 1945
Brinkmeyer, Jack W., Lt.; April 1945-September 1945
Brown, Carey H., Capt.; October 1943-May 1, 1944(KIAc); ex-369th Ftr Sqn
Buchanan, William E., Lt.; June 1944-December 1944
  270 hours
  P-51B CS-P 42-106894
Buckley, James E., Capt.; April 1943-January 11, 1944(KIA)
Burgsteiner, Will D., Capt.; April 1943-December 1944
Burton, Robert E., Lt.; April 1944-July 1944; ex-368th Ftr Sqn
Cadenhead, James W., Lt.; States only
Caid, Vernon L., Lt.; June 1944-November 1944
  70 missions, 270 hours
  P-51C CS- 43-25067 "Sandra Lynn"
Callahan, Robert M., Capt.; October 1943-August 1944
  P-47D CS-L 42-75894
  P-51B CS-L 43-6961
  P-51B CS-L 42-106716
Cheney, David F., Lt.; States only
Connelly, Dick D., Lt.; May 1944-November 27, 1944(KIA)
  P-51D CS-V 44-14076 "De De II"
  P-51D CS-V 44-14096 "De De III"
Cosmos, Alex M., Lt.; April 1943-February 10, 1944(KIAc)
Cox, Ralph L., Maj.; September 1944-February 1945; to 369th Ftr Sqn
  P-51D CS-H 44-14979
Cranfill, Niven K., Capt.; April 1943-October 1943; to 369th Ftr Sqn
Cunningham, Charles V., Capt.; April 1943-August 1944
  P-47D CS-H 42-76416
  P-47D CS-H 42-8671
  P-51B CS-H 42-106704
Doersch, George A., Maj.; April 1943-February 1945; to 368th Ftr Sqn
  147 missions, 526:30 hours
  P-47D CS-J 42-8552
  P-51B CS-J 43-24810
  P-51D CS-J
Downing, John L., Lt.; March 1944-May 1944; to HdQts
  P-47D CS- "Big Dog"

Dunlap, Elmer N., Lt.; January 1944-April 11, 1944(POW)
Fogg, Howard L., Capt.; May 1944-June 1944; to 368th Ftr Sqn
P-51B CS-T 42-106879
Ford, Marlyn C., Lt.; March 1945-September 1945
Giese, Arthur J., Jr., Lt.; February 1945-July 1945
Grimes, Howard E., Lt.; April 1943-June 22, 1944(KIA)
P-51B CS-Y 42-106799
Hagar, Lt.; States-May 14, 1943(KIAc)
Hair, Lynn W., Lt.; April 1943-January 11, 1944(KIA)
Hall, Robert E., Lt.; April 1943-November 1943
Hastings, William H., Lt.; June 1944-November 1944
P-51B CS-X 42-106851
Hipsher, Charles W., Capt.; April 1943-August 1944
P-47D CS-U 42-75413
P-51B CS-U 42-106935
P-51D CS-U 44-13604
Hodges, William R., Capt.; April 1943-May 11, 1944(MIA-E); September 1944-December 1944
P-47D CS-O 42-74719
P-51D CS-O 44-14427
Hollis, Harold D., Lt.; April 1943-June 22, 1944(KIA)
P-47D CS-X 42-75409
P-51B CS-X 42-106851
Huskins, Samuel J., Capt.; April 1943-November 1944
P-51B CS-N 42-106975
Irvine, Chauncey S., Capt.; October 1943-February 1944; to HdQts
Johnson, Emory G., Lt.; August 1944-February 1945
270 hours
P-51D CS-G 44-14773 "Micky The Twist"
Jones, Cyril W., Lt.; August 1944-September 12, 1944(KIA)
16 missions
P-51D CS-W 44-14071 "Dora Dee"
Kerns, John E., Lt.; February 1944-March 27, 1944(KIA)
19 missions
Kibler, Ralph E., Jr., Lt.; January 1944-May 11, 1944(KIA); ex-368th Ftr Sqn
King, Herman E., Lt.; April 1943-April 1944; to 56th Ftr Grp
P-47D CS-K 42-74698
Koenig, Harold E., F/O; March 1945-September 1945
Lamont, John W., Lt.; August 1944-April 1945
Lancaster, Ray B., Capt.; April 1943-August 4, 1944(INT)
P-51B CS-F 42-106805 "Galveston Gal"
Leathley, Eric H., F/O; January 1945-July 1945
Lemmens, Andrew T., Maj.; May 1944-April 1945; to HdQts; ex-368th Ftr Sqn
133 missions, 524:55 hours
P-51B CS-C 43-12294 "Shrimp"
P-51D CS-V 44-15521 "Screamin' Demon"
P-51D CS-V 44-73102 "Screamin' Demon"
Lovette, James K., Maj.; August 1944-March 1945; to HdQts; ex-33rd Ftr Grp, MTO (1 kill)
Lux, Frank O., Capt.; August 1944-April 1945
Lyon, Washington D., Capt.; November 1944-February 23, 1945(KIA); ex-5th ERS & 369th Ftr Sqn
P-51D CS-C 44-14987 "Pattie Whack"
Major, Ross O., Lt.; April 1943-October 1944
P-47D CS-V 42-8578
P-51B CS- "Chicago Lil"
Marcinkiewicz, John S., Lt.; April 1944-June 7, 1944(POW)
P-51B CS-L 42-106667 "Sweet Sue"
Marshall, Frank R., Capt.; September 1944-September 1945
Martin, James C., Lt.; January 1945-May 1945l to 368th Ftr Sqn
Maslow, Edward J., Lt.; April 1944-May 11, 1944(POW); ex-50th Ftr Sqn, Iceland
McAlevey, John F., Lt.; January 1945-September 1945
29 missions, 144 hours
P-51D CS-T 44-73102 "Skeeter's Skooter"
McAllister, John W., Lt.; August 1944-March 1945
McCoskey, Jack E., Lt.; August 1944-January 14, 1945(POW)
47 missions
P-51D CS-X 44-15543 "Lydia May"
McGregor, Garland J., Lt.; January 1945-February 23, 1945(KIA)
McInnes, Robert L., Capt.; July 1944-April 1945
P-51D CS-S 44-14192 "Blondie II"
McKee, Daniel D., LtCol.; April 1943-October 1943; to HdQts; February 1944-April 1945; to HdQts
P-47D CS-Z 42-75118
P-51B CS-A 42-106878
P-51D CS-A 44-14521 "Rayner Shine"
P-51D CS-A 44-72823 "Rayner Shine"
McNeill, John W., Jr., Capt.; April 1944-November 1944
Merry, Milton S., Capt.; July 1944-April 1945
320 hours
Miller, George D., Lt.; February 1945-September 1945
P-51D CS-G 44-14773 "Little Mary"
Morris, Thomas W., Lt.; December 1944-September 1945
Murphy, John B., LtCol.; March 1943-September 1944; ex-11th Ftr Sqn, Aleutians (1/2 kill)
P-47D CS-A 42-8613
P-47D CS-A 42-76024
P-51B CS-A 42-106878
P-51D CS-A 44-13513
Murray, John J., Lt.; December 1944-September 1945
Murray, Wallace C., Lt.; August 1944-October 7, 1944(KIA)
Newberg, Warren R., Lt.; April 1944-November 1944
Newcomer, Earle S., Lt.; December 1944-July 1945
Newton, Madison H., Lt.; December 1944-September 1945
Niccolai, Albert T., Lt.; April 1943-February 24, 1944(KIA)
P-47D CS-F 42-8636
Oakley, Robert G., Lt.; June 1944-February 1945
270 hours
P-51B CS-B "Betty Jane"
P-51D CS-B 44-13394 "Betty Jane II"
O'Shea, James H., Lt.; April 1943-December 1944
O'Shea, James J., F/O; July 1944-September 11, 1944(KIA)
Page, Donald G., Lt.; October 1944-September 1945
40 missions, 230 hours
P-51D CS- "Oh Nurse!"
Paulette, Malcolm C., Lt.; January 1945-February 23, 1945(KIA)
Pezda, Edwin F., Lt.; April 1943-October 1943; to 369th Ftr Sqn
Porter, Alan C., Lt.; January 1944-May 8, 1944(KIA)
P-47D CS-V 42-8578
Rabb, Richard O., Lt.; April 1944-August 4, 1944(INT)
Ramser, Galen E., Capt.; July 1944-March 1945
P-51B CS-H 42-106778 "Zombie"
P-51D CS-U 44-13604
Reese, Luther C., F/O; May 1944-July 21, 1944(KIA)
Rueschenbergm Werner J., Lt.; August 1944-January 1945
Ruggles, James J., Lt.; December 1944-September 1945
P-51D CS- "Rugges Ruthie"
Schector, Harry L., Lt.; December 1944-July 1945
Schulte, Jack R., Lt.; December 1944-July 1945
Schwartz, Ben D., Lt.; December 1944-September 1945
40 missions, 190 hours
Semple, Henry D., Lt.; February 1945-July 1945
Shoffitt, Jimmy C., Capt.; July 1944-April 1945
P-51B CS-T 42-106692 "Josephine"
P-51D CS-T 44-15102 "Josephine II"
Shortness, Gordon M., Lt.; July 1944-July 20, 1944(KIA)
Shouse, Russell E., Lt.; December 1944-September 1945
P-51D CS- "Little Butch"
Shupe, Joseph E., Lt.; January 1944-May 21, 1944(KIA)
P-51C CS-R 42-103319
Siltamaki, Robert W., Lt.; April 1944-July 21, 1944(POW)
Smith, Samuel R., Capt.; October 1943-April 1944; to HdQts
Smith, Seymour, Lt.; December 1944-July 1945
Smith, Thomas P., Capt.; February 1944-April 11, 1944(MIA-E); September 1944-April 1945
76 missions
P-51D CS-E 44-13893 "Caroline"
Stanley, Connie L., Lt.; April 1945-July 1945
Staup, Homer A., Capt.; August 1944-July 1945
P-51D CS-I 44-14168
Steussey, Howard E., Lt.; September 1944-September 28, 1944(KIA)
Stegnerski, Stanley F., Lt.; September 1944-November 21, 1944(KIA)
Stepp, William F., Capt.; September 1944-September 1945
57 missions, 270 hours
P-51K CS-M 44-11574 "Marilyn Beth"
Straub, Richard P., Lt.; September 1944-September 1945
P-51D CS-D 44-14427 "Blue Blazes"
Sundheim, Paul E., Lt.; July 1944-August 27, 1944(POW)
Sutton, Thomas C., Capt.; April 1945-September 1945; ex-MTO pilot
Surowiec, Eugene L., Capt.; October 1944-September 1945
Thomas, Earl W., Jr., Lt.; April 1944-April 22, 1944(KIA)
1 mission
Tilton, Elbert W., Lt.; July 1944-January 1945
P-51D CS-C 44-14987 "Pattie Whack"
Tuchscherer, Daniel R., Lt.; April 1944-September 1944
62 missions, 270 hours
P-51C CS-S 42-102996 "Lovin' Lulu"
Tucker, William N., Jr., Lt.; April 1943-January 11, 1944(KIA)
Turinsky, George, Lt.; April 1945-September 1945; ex-bomber pilot
0 missions
Vos, Benjamin J., Jr., Lt.; August 1944-September 10, 1944(KIA)
Welch, Edward L., Lt.; July 1944-April 1945
Westall, Frank E., Lt.; August 1944-August 15, 1944(KIA)
Wetmore, Ray S., Maj.; April 1943-November 1945
142 missions, 563 hours
P-47D CS-P 42-75068
P-51B CS-P 42-106894
P-51D CS-L 44-14733 "Daddy's Girl"
White, Bennie F., Lt.; June 1944-July 11, 1944(KIA)
Wiley, Walter W., F/O; June 1944-July 28, 1944(POW)
13 missions
Wilson, John W., Lt.; July 1944-February 1945
Williams, Harvey C., Lt.; July 1944-September 1945
Williams, Theophalus A., Lt.; July 1944-August 17, 1944(KIA)
Windmiller, Donald L., Capt.; June 1944-September 1945
P-51D CS-N 44-14179
Wolfe, Albert E., Capt.; August 1944-April 1945
York, Robert M., Capt.; August 1944-February 1945
59 missions, 276:05 hours
P-51D CS-Y 44-14159 "Rudy"
Ziska, Lawrence A., Lt.; August 1944-February 1, 1945(KIAc)

**Aircraft of the 368th Fighter Squadron**

P-47D-2-RE
42-8402 CV-M "Lucky Pearl" A.T. Lemmens

P-47D-2-RA
42-22468 CV-S "Geronimo"
42-22766 CV-S

P-47D-4-RA
42-22776 CV-D "Boots" B.M. Hagan
42-22786 CV-B W.N. Bolefahr

P-47D-5-RE
42-8485 CV-B C.E. Mosse
42-8542 CV-
42-8569 CV-F
42-8592 CV-L
42-8611 CV-H
42-8617 CV-M "Lucky Pearl" A.T. Lemmens
42-8637 CV-Z A.P. Tacon
42-8645 CV-M

P-47D-6-RE
42-74633 CV-W
42-74695 CV-E E.H. Cater
42-74721 CV-K S.A. White

P-47D-10-RE
42-75082 CV-G
42-75088 CV-G T.S. Lane
42-75095 CV-N "Pappy Yokum" E.P. Perkins
42-75104 CV- C.R. Brown
42-75111 CV-A A.R. Tyrrell
42-75113 CV-O "Daisy Mae" W.C. Forehand
42-75128 CV-R
42-75141 CV-I J.R. Pino

P-47D-20-RE
42-76598 CV-V

Unknown Serials
CV- "Lil Abner" R.L. Botsford
CV- "Lonesome Polecat" R.W. Hawkinson
CV- "Marryin' Sam" W.R. Simmons
CV- "Hairless Joe" J.B. Smith

P-51C-1-NT
42-103197 CV-Y "Sweet Jean Marie" C.J. Cavanaugh
42-103197 CV-H R.B. Hatter
42-103318 CV-U

P-51C-5-NT
42-103329 CV-Z A.P. Tacon
42-103332 CV-
42-103602 CV- T.S. Lane

P-51B-1-NA
43-12145 CV-W
43-12478 CV-P E.C. Cook

P-51B-5-NA
43-6491 CV-E "Wanna Honey" E.H. Cater
43-6581 CV-V
43-6775 CV- W.R. Simmons
43-6876 CV-F F. Rea
43-6962 CV-Y A.R. Baldridge
43-6995 CV-Q

P-51B-10-NA
43-7155 CV-C J.B. Hunter
42-106436 CV-T C.M. Lambright
42-106577 CV-X
42-106581 CV-V
42-106611 CV-K E.F. Britton
42-106618 CV-W
42-106619 CV-J "Die Fledermaus" R.B. Janney
42-106620 CV-G C.M. Huddleston
42-106667 CV-Z
42-106673 CV-B
42-106693 CV-M
42-106702 CV-X
42-106727 CV-F

P-51B-15-NA
42-106804 CV-
42-106809 CV-H "Little Liquidator" G.F. Baker
42-106809 CV-O
42-106867 CV-I "Pegelin" G.C. Bach
42-106876 CV-B R.G. Mason
42-106879 CV-R O.R. Fladmark
42-106898 CV-D "Boots" B.M. Hagan
42-106917 CV-J "Mari-Helen" P.E. Olson
42-106929 CV-G "Lola Lee"
42-106949 CV-V B.D. Kasper

43-24764 CV-B "The Beachcomber" W.H. Lewis
43-24764 CV-B W.N. Bolefahr
43-24786 CV-

P-51D-5-NT
44-11222 CV-I "Evelyn"
44-11223 CV-O
44-11236 CV-B

P-51K-5-NT
44-11647 CV-F "Freddy Junior"
44-11651 CV-V C.E. Ettlesen
44-11657 CV-F
44-11671 CV-
44-11685 CV-V B.D. Kasper
44-11685 CV-V "Janet" J.D. Cooley
44-11696 CV-G
44-11697 CV-C "Little Ann" G.H. Blackburn
44-11758 CV-T "Silky" J.A. Denman
44-11761 CV-
44-11797 CV-M

P-51K-10-NT
44-12143 CV-L

P-51D-5-NA
44-13386 CV-N "Miss Janet" R.W. Hawkinson
44-13387 CV-A A.R. Tyrrell
44-13404 CV-Z A.P. Tacon
44-13539 CV-O W.C. Forehand
44-13545 CV-Q
44-13669 CV-I "Pegelin" G.C. Bach
44-13721 CV-W
44-13740 CV-A "Little Audrey"
44-13762 CV-D "Cookie" J.T. Gordon
44-13776 CV-Y "Kitten" G.W. Long
44-13786 CV-B "Adabelle" J.O. Flack
44-13898 CV-A "Matilda IV" B.H. King
44-13943 CV-Q

P-51D-10-NA
44-14062 CV-C M.B. Barth
44-14081 CV-E "Tootsie" J.S. Keesey
44-14100 CV-
44-14131 CV-T
44-14325 CV-N "Mass Kid" E.F. Britton
44-14329 CV-X R.A. Boyd
44-14444 CV-J "Supermouse" P.E. Olson
44-14476 CV-
44-14500 CV-E G.F. Baker
44-14509 CV-X R.V. Beaupre
44-14566 CV-C J.B. Hunter
44-14610 CV-F
44-14650 CV-X "Snooks"
44-14652 CV-L
44-14670 CV-F T.J. McGeever
44-14764 CV-B
44-14769 CV-A

P-51D-15-NA
44-14854 CV-Q
44-14870 CV-E "Peter E., Jr."
44-14965 CV-N "Nancy" J.P. Randolph
44-14965 CV-N "Lady"
44-15067 CV-S "Little Ann" G.H. Blackburn
44-15096 CV-D "Ice Cold Katie" M.F. Boussu
44-15100 CV-Q N.K. Cranfill
44-15371 CV-Z "Happy" J.L. Way
44-15371 CV-Z R.L. Brown
44-15489 CV-P "Anne" A.D. Marson
44-15555 CV-L D.B. Archibald
44-15618 CV-R "Diane" E.J. Beal
44-15711 CV-J J.F. Collins
44-15717 CV-Q N.K. Cranfill
44-15717 CV-Q "Wild Will" J.W. Parsons
44-15870 CV-W

P-51D-20-NA
44-63179 CV-H
44-63689 CV-K "Fritzie VI/Pop, My Boy II" J.T. Marron
44-63721 CV-W
44-63740 CV-A "Little Audrey"
44-63762 CV-D
44-63776 CV-Y
44-64143 CV-L
44-72067 CV-R "Ole Goat" G.A. Doersch
44-72223 CV-O
44-72260 CV-E "Mary Lou" J.W. Herb
44-72281 CV-Z "Happy 2" J.L. Way
44-72331 CV-C J.C. Hunter
44-72406 CV-G

P-51D-25-NA
44-72746 CV-U D.A. Baccus

Unknown Serials
P-51D CV- "You've Had It, Chum" J.J. Lubien
P-51B CV- "Mackie"
P-51B CV- "Mackie 2nd"
P-51D CV-L "Betty Louise"
P-51D CV- "Wee Bonnie"
P-51D CV- "Mackie 3rd"

**Aircraft of the 369th Fighter Squadron**

P-47D-2-RA
42-22464 IV-

P-47D-4-RA
42-22791 IV-E

P-47D-5-RE
42-8545 IV-L "Mary" L.H. Bouchard
42-8557 IV-W "Green Eyes" C.E. Carter
42-8695 IV-F "Oily Boid" R.J. Booth
42-8698 IV-X R.L. Thacker

P-47D-6-RE
42-74642 IV-K "Nancy June" C.H. Kruger
42-74645 IV-N N.K. Cranfill
42-74645 IV-E
42-74666 IV-O "The Mad Rebel" J.H. Oliphint

P-47D-10-RE
42-75048 IV-Z R.W. Campbell
42-75054 IV-V C.C. Ettlesen
42-75085 IV-Q R.C. Thomson
42-75158 IV-B E.F. Pezda
42-75210 IV-I "Dotty" R.H. Broach

P-47D-11-RE
42-75279 IV-R "Sally" C.W. Staley

Unknown Serials
IV-T "Pistol Packin' Mama" H.L. Matthew

P-51C-5-NT
42-103339 IV-F "Princess Pat"
42-103354 IV-D
42-103743 IV-M A.R. Smith

P-51C-10-NT
42-103785 IV-K "Nancy June 3rd" C.H. Kruger
42-103793 IV-G "San'Tone Sweetheart" H.F. Cuzner
42-103797 IV-E "Darlin' Earline" F.C. Suttle
42-103799 IV-F G.C. Deen

P-51B-1-NA
43-12186 IV-R G.R. Ralston
43-12208 IV-L "Rose of San Antone" C.R. Bruening
43-12434 IV-R "Dunquerque" C.W. Staley
43-12435 IV-Z R.W. Campbell
43-12439 IV-Q E.J. Thorne
43-12444 IV-X G.M. Perrin

P-51B-5-NA
43-6620 IV-R
43-6757 IV-F R.J. Booth
43-6757 IV-Z R.W. Campbell

P-51B-10-NA
42-106443 IV-Y "Poison" W.H. Swanson
42-106469 IV-G
42-106476 IV-H J.C. Painter
42-106607 IV-X
42-106599 IV-W L.H. Prewitt
42-106629 IV-K "Nancy June 2nd" C.H. Kruger
42-106670 IV-C
42-106679 IV-O "The Mad Rebel" J.H. Oliphint
42-106680 IV-J R.L. Pherson
42-106689 IV-S C.J. Crenshaw
42-106689 IV-S "Briney Marlin" H.A. Linderer
42-106691 IV-H
42-106730 IV-R

P-51B-15-NA
42-106771 IV-I "Dotty" R.H. Broach
42-106803 IV-A C.S. Irvine
42-106818 IV-U H.L. Rodeheaver
42-106833 IV-V
42-106841 IV-Q R.C. Thomson
42-106848 IV-N "Deviless 2nd" N.K. Cranfill
42-106853 IV-V "Traveler" I.B. Holloman
42-106893 IV-E D.H. Laing
42-106904 IV-
42-106906 IV-L "Mary" L.H. Bouchard
42-106913 IV-J
42-106916 IV-D "Loretta" E.R. Orwig
42-106919 IV-
43-24756 IV-V R.L. Thacker
43-24798 IV-T "Pistol Packin' Mama II" H.L. Matthew

P-51D-5-NT
44-11283 IV-X
44-11350 IV-Y

P-51K-5-NT
44-11572 IV-I "Michigan Mauler" W.C. Jennings
44-11635 IV-B E.F. Pezda
44-11636 IV-A
44-11658 IV-I
44-11659 IV-G "San'Tone Sweetheart" H.F. Cuzner
44-11664 IV-G
44-11675 IV-C
44-11686 IV-N

P-51D-5-NA
44-13301 IV-B E.F. Pezda
44-13336 IV-Y "Yankee Clipper" W.H. Swanson
44-13390 IV-N "Deviless 3rd" N.K. Cranfill
44-13390 IV-N "Big Noise From Winnetka" T.G. Bur
44-13520 IV-R G.R. Ralston
44-13520 IV-U
44-13592 IV-C H.L. Burton
44-13606 IV-I "Louisiana Heat Wave" C.J. Crenshaw
44-13610 IV-V W.F. Collins
44-13688 IV-
44-13689 IV-H L.G. Taylor
44-13689 IV-K
44-13914 IV-I

P-51D-10-NA
44-14108 IV-
44-14117 IV-M "Stinky" J.J. Mejaski
44-14127 IV-E "Wild Will" J.W. Parsons
44-14127 IV-E "Dilbert" R.W. McIntosh
44-14188 IV-
44-14216 IV-Z R.W. Campbell
44-14218 IV-X "X-Terminator" G.M. Perrin
44-14286 IV-
44-14307 IV-P
44-14313 IV-E
44-14315 IV-L "Jeepers" F.S. Hodges
44-14399 IV-
44-14432 IV-Q R.C. Thomson
44-14534 IV-B
44-14543 IV-P "Precious Pat"
44-14545 IV- E.L. Sjoblad
44-14625 IV-F "Pauline"
44-14718 IV-D "Hubert" R.L. Burtner
44-14756 IV-V

P-51D-15-NA
44-14857 IV- "Brooklyn Devil"
44-14894 IV-
44-14964 IV-
44-14988 IV-E R.W. Evans
44-14997 IV-U
44-15007 IV-Z T.J. Klem
44-15015 IV-W "Babe" V.T. Judkins
44-15016 IV-I "Heat Wave" C.J. Crenshaw
44-15081 IV-T "Pistol Packin' Mama III" H.L. Matthew
44-15204 IV-C
44-15215 IV-S "Torchy" H.E. Berndt
44-15242 IV-Q R.C. Thomson
44-15394 IV-D R.L. Burtner
44-15514 IV-O R.J. Guggemos
44-15588 IV-R "Born To Lose" R.R. Klaver
44-15725 IV-V
44-15739 IV-J
44-15741 IV-Y
44-15794 IV-D

P-51D-20-NA
44-72154 IV-N R.L. Cox
44-72207 IV-
44-72330 IV-N
44-72344 IV-M "Saucy Sal" R.W. Hopkins
44-72366 IV-D
44-72380 IV-K
44-72435 IV-J "Gloria Mac" R.E. McCormack
44-72503 IV-F "Gravel Gertie"
44-72603 IV-

P-51D-25-NA
44-72780 IV-K

Unknown Serials
44-14??? IV-G "Delectable Diane"
44-63??? IV-Q "Pard"
P-51D IV-V "Traveler II" I.B. Holloman
P-51D IV- "Jenny F" R.W. Porter
P-51D IV- "The Maine Beau" R.T. Lancaster
P-51D IV- "Chicago" A.E. Mettel
P-51D IV- "Stevie"

**Aircraft of the 370th Fighter Squadron**

P-47D-1-RE
42-7894 CS-L W.D. Burgsteiner

P-47D-2-RA
42-22480 CS-K

P-47D-5-RE
42-8498 CS-Y
42-8498 CS-T
42-8552 CS-J G.A. Doersch
42-8566 CS-M R.M. Borg
42-8571 CS-H C.V. Cunningham
42-8578 CS-V A.C. Porter/R.O. Major
42-8590 CS-L
42-8592 CS-L
42-8611 CS-N
42-8613 CS-A J.B. Murphy
42-8634 CS-Q
42-8636 CS-F A.T. Niccolai
42-8663 CS-G "Baltimore Babe" V.W. Ambrose
42-8693 CS-E "Miss Margaret" J.H. Bateman

P-47D-6-RE
42-74632 CS-D
42-74676 CS-X "Blondie II" HACK
42-74698 CS-K H.E. King
42-74719 CS-O W.R. Hodges
42-74737 CS-P
42-74745 CS-D

P-47D-10-RE
42-75068 CS-P R.S. Wetmore
42-75079 CS-
42-75082 CS-G
42-75091 CS-I
42-75108 CS-
42-75118 CS-Z D.D. McKee
42-75136 CS-N

P-47D-11-RE
42-75253 CS-S
42-75263 CS-
42-75409 CS-X H.D. Hollis
42-75413 CS-U C.W. Hipsher
42-75515 CS-B

P-47D-15-RE
42-76282 CS-O
42-76308 CS-Y

P-47D-16-RE
42-75894 CS-L R.M. Callahan
42-76024 CS-A J.B. Murphy

P-47D-20-RE
42-76416 CS-H C.V. Cunningham

Unknown Serials
CS-E "Pee Wee" J.H. Bateman
CS- "Big Dog" J.L. Downing

P-51C-1-NT
42-102996 CS-S "Lovin' Lulu II" D.R. Tuchscherer
42-103294 CS-Q

P-51C-5-NT
42-103343 CS-D
42-103394 CS-B

P-51C-10-NT
42-103791 CS-Y
43-24948 CS-J
43-25067 CS- "Sandra Lynn" V.L. Caid

P-51B-1-NA
43-12147 CS-W
43-12294 CS-C "Shrimp" A.T. Lemmens
43-12463 CS-F "Some Joke"

P-51B-5-NA
43-6461 CS-Q "Hot Pants" W.K. Baker
43-6826 CS-
43-6879 CS-T A.R. Fogg
43-6961 CS-L R.M. Callahan
43-7013 CS-E

P-51B-10-NA
43-7179 CS-
42-106474 CS-M
42-106580 CS-I
42-106580 CS-J
42-106667 CS-I "Sweet Sue" J.S. Marcinkiewicz
42-106692 CS-T "Josephine" J.C. Shoffitt
42-106704 CS-H C.V. Cunningham
42-106716 CS-L

P-51B-15-NA
42-106749 CS-M R.M. Borg
42-106799 CS-Y H.E. Grimes
42-106805 CS-F "Galveston Gal" R.B. Lancaster
42-106808 CS-
42-106826 CS-U
42-106851 CS-X H.D. Hollis/W.H. Hastings
42 106862 CS-U
42-106865 CS-M
42-106878 CS-A J.B. Murphy/D.D. McKee
42-106894 CS-P R.S. Wetmore
42-106902 CS-C
42-106921 CS-G "Baltimore Babe" V.W. Ambrose
42-106925 CS-N
42-106926 CS-O P.H. Bateman
42-106935 CS-U C.W. Hipsher
42-106941 CS-B
42-106975 CS-N S.J. Huskins
43-24778 CS-H "Zombie" G.E. Ramser
43-24791 CS-D
43-24810 CS-J G.A. Doersch
43-24833 CS-Q

P-51D-5-NT
44-11348 CS-P

P-51K-1-NT
44-11355 CS-D

P-51K-5-NT
44-11574 CS-M "Marilyn Beth" W.F. Stepp
44-11760 CS-O

P-51D-5-NA
44-13394 CS-B "Betty Jane II" R.G. Oakley
44-13513 CS-A J.B. Murphy
44-13529 CS-D "Pandemonium"
44-13604 CS-U C.W. Hipsher
44-13633 CS-R "Satan's Lady"
44-13795 CS-F "Mary" G.D. Miller
44-13893 CS-E "Caroline" T.P. Smith
44-13939 CS-W
44-13966 CS-K
44-14038 CS-G "Baltimore Babe" V.W. Ambrose

P-51D-10-NA
44-14071 CS-W "Dora Dee" C.W. Jones
44-14075 CS-V "De De II" D.D. Connelly
44-14096 CS-V "De De III" D.D. Connelly
44-14122 CS-W
44-14129 CS-S
44-14159 CS-Y "Ruby" R.M. York
44-14168 CS-I H.A. Staup
44-14179 CS-N D.L. Windmiller
44-14185 CS-Q
44-14192 CS-S "Blondie II" R.L. McInnes
44-14240 CS-
44-14265 CS-Q
44-14368 CS-Z
44-14422 CS-
44-14427 CS-D "Blue Blazes" R.P. Straub
44-14518 CS-O
44-14521 CS-A "Rayner Shine" D.D. McKee
44-14618 CS-
44-14630 CS-R
44-14733 CS-L "Daddy's Girl" R.S. Wetmore
44-14773 CS-G "Micky the Twist" E.G. Johnson
44-14778 CS-H G.E. Ramser

P-51D-15-NA
44-14948 CS-J
44-14979 CS-H "Little Dixie"
44-14983 CS-F
44-14987 CS-C "Pattie Whack" E.W. Tilton/W.D. Lyon
44-15067 CS-L
44-15102 CS-T "Josephine II" J.C. Shoffitt
44-15102 CS-T "Skeeter's Skooter" J.F. McAlevey
44-15277 CS-Q "Cisco"
44-15521 CS-V "Screamin' Demon" A.T. Lemmens
44-15543 CS-X "Lydia May" J.E. McCoskey

P-51D-20-NA
44-72208 CS-C "Delectable"

P-51D-25-NA
44-72823 CS-A "Rayner Shine" D.D. McKee
44-73102 CS-V "Screamin' Demon II" A.T. Lemmens

Unknown Serials

| | | |
|---|---|---|
| P-51B | CS- "Chicago Lil" | R.O. Major |
| P-51D | CS- "Oh Nurse!" | D.G. Page |
| P-51D | CS- "Little Butch" | R.E. Shouse |
| P-51D | CS- "Faithful Sally" | |
| P-51D | CS- "Rugges Ruthie" | J.J. Ruggles |

• • •

## THE 361st FIGHTER GROUP
## 374th, 375th, 376th FIGHTER SQUADRONS

The 361st Fighter Group was activated on February 10, 1943, at Richmond, Virginia. Training in the eastern United States, the group headed oveseas on November 23, 1943, aboard the "Queen Elizabeth". The first of 441 missions came on January 21, 1944, with the last being flown on April 21, 1945. While overseas the 361st claimed 221 aerial and 111 ground victories while 91 P-47's and P-51's were lost on operations and 10 pilots died in accidents. Also, from mid December of 1944 through the Spring of 1945, the 361st was temporarily attached to the 9th Air Force and moved to the Continent to assist that command's operations.

Bases for the group included: Bottisham, from December 1, 1943; Little Walden, from September 26, 1944; St. Dizier, France, from December 23, 1944; Chievres, Belgium, from February 1, 1945; and Little Walden, from April 10, 1945 until November of 1945. Aircraft flown were the P-47D, from December of 1943 until early May of 1944, and the P-51B, C, D, and K, from early May of 1944 until war's end. The 361st was also the only 8th Air Force fighter group not to win a Distinguished Unit Citation.

### Claims

| | Air | | | Grd | |
|---|---|---|---|---|---|
| | Destroyed | Probable | Damaged | Destroyed | Damaged |
| HdQts | 8.5 | 0 | 1 | 7 | 3 |
| 374th | 52.5 | 3 | 20 | 22 | 18.5 |
| 375th | 76.5 | 2 | 26 | 41 | 41.33 |
| 376th | 83.5 | 6 | 19.5 | 41 | 17.5 |
| | 221 | 11 | 66.5 | 111 | 80.33 |

### Commanders

| | |
|---|---|
| Col. Thomas J.J. Christian, Jr. | February 10, 1943-August 12, 1944 |
| Col. Ronald F. Fallows | August 14, 1944-August 31, 1944 |
| LtCol. Roy B. Caviness | August 31, 1944-September 20, 1944 |
| LtCol. Joseph J. Kruzel | September 20, 1944-November 3, 1944 |
| LtCol. Roy B. Caviness | November 3, 1944-December 1, 1944 |
| Col. Junius W. Dennison, Jr. | December 1, 1944-April 15, 1945 |
| LtCol. Roy B. Caviness | April 15, 1945-June 29, 1945 |

### Wing and Command Assignments

| | |
|---|---|
| Assigned to VIII Fighter Command | November 30, 1943 |
| VIII Fighter Command, 66th Fighter Wing | December 12, 1943 |
| VIII Fighter Command, 67th Fighter Wing | March 11, 1944 |
| VIII Fighter Command, 65th Fighter Wing | August 8, 1944 |
| 2nd Bomb Division, 65th Fighter Wing | September 15, 1944 |
| XIX TAC, 9th Air Force (D.S.) | December 24, 1944 |
| VIII Fighter Command | February 1, 1945 |
| 2nd Air Division, 65th Fighter Wing | April 10, 1945 |

### Aircraft Markings

Original P-47's were in love drab/neutral gray schemes with standard white cowl and theater bands. NMF planes arrived in the spring of 1944 and both paint schemes were employed. In March of 1944, a group marking was introduced: a 24 inch yellow cowl band replaced the white band.

The majority of early P-51's were in NMF although several planes had olive drab upper surfaces. During the summer of 1944, many planes received applications of dark green on the upper surfaces, most particularly the 375th Fighter Squadron. Initially, the P-51's had a yellow spinner and 12 inch cowl band, and beginning in July of 1944, the yellow was extended and swept to the cockpit. From November of 1944, squadron rudder colors were applied: red for the 374th, medium blue for the 375th, and yellow for the 376th.

Squadron codes were:

374th Ftr Sqn: B7
375th Ftr Sqn: E2
376th Ftr Sqn: E9

### 361st Fighter Group Statistical Report

| Month | Missions | Air | Grd | Losses | KIAc |
|---|---|---|---|---|---|
| January 1944 | 7 | 4-2-2 | 0-0.33 | 2 | 0 |
| February | 16 | 8-0-8 | 0-1 | 3 | 0 |
| March | 21 | 7-0-1 | 5-11 | 2 | 0 |
| April | 25 | 11-2-1 | 20-8 | 6 | 0 |
| May | 27 | 21-1-9 | 8-4 | 10 | 1 |
| June | 42 | 24-0-4.5 | 28-22 | 15 | 0 |
| July | 25 | 18-0-4 | 3-1 | 7 | 0 |
| August | 30 | 12-0-5 | 10-10 | 13 | 2 |
| September | 21 | 37-1-7 | 11-11 | 9 | 0 |
| October | 15 | 9-0-0 | 0-0 | 5 | 2 |
| November | 22 | 39-4-11 | 3-0 | 5 | 1 |
| December | 36 | 16-1-1 | 0-0 | 3 | 0 |
| January 1945 | 35 | 7-0-0 | 0-0 | 2 | 2 |
| February | 24 | 1-0-0 | 0-0 | 2 | 0 |
| March | 70 | 6-0-2 | 0-0 | 4 | 0 |
| April | 25 | 1-0-11 | 23-12 | 3 | 0 |
| May | 0 | 0-0-0 | 0-0 | 0 | 0 |
| June | 0 | 0-0-0 | 0-0 | 0 | 0 |
| July | 0 | 0-0-0 | 0-0 | 0 | 2 |
| | 441 | 221-11-66.5 | 111-80.33 | 91 | 10 |

### Losses by Squadron and Type

| | MIA | | KIAc | | |
|---|---|---|---|---|---|
| | P-47 | P-51 | P-47 | P-51 | Other |
| HdQts | 1 | 2 | 0 | 0 | 0 |
| 374th | 4 | 23 | 0 | 4 | 0 |
| 375th | 7 | 35 | 0 | 3 | 0 |
| 376th | 3 | 16 | 0 | 3 | 1 |
| | 15 | 76 | 0 | 9 | 1 |

### Claims by Type

| | Air | | | Grd | |
|---|---|---|---|---|---|
| | Destroyed | Probable | Damaged | Destroyed | Damaged |
| P-47 | 33 | 4 | 13 | 25 | 21.33 |
| P-51 | 188 | 7 | 53.5 | 86 | 59 |

### Claims by Enemy Aircraft Type

| | Air | | | Grd | |
|---|---|---|---|---|---|
| | Destroyed | Probable | Damaged | Destroyed | Damaged |
| Me-109 | 113 | 5 | 21.5 | 10 | 11 |
| FW-190 | 90 | 6 | 31 | 28 | 14.33 |
| Me-262 | 8 | 0 | 14 | 0 | 0 |
| Me-410 | 5 | 0 | 0 | 6 | 1 |
| He-111 | 2 | 0 | 0 | 6 | 5 |
| Me-110 | 1 | 0 | 0 | 3 | 8 |
| He-177 | 1 | 0 | 0 | 1 | 0 |
| Ju-188 | 1 | 0 | 0 | 1 | 0 |
| Ju-88 | 0 | 0 | 0 | 18 | 11 |
| u/i a/c | 0 | 0 | 0 | 14 | 12 |
| Ju-52 | 0 | 0 | 0 | 17 | 4 |
| BV-138 | 0 | 0 | 0 | 2 | 2 |
| Fi-156 | 0 | 0 | 0 | 2 | 1 |
| Do-217 | 0 | 0 | 0 | 1 | 0 |
| He-115 | 0 | 0 | 0 | 1 | 0 |
| Ar-196 | 0 | 0 | 0 | 1 | 0 |
| Me-163 | 0 | 0 | 0 | 0 | 2 |
| FW-189 | 0 | 0 | 0 | 0 | 1 |
| Me-210 | 0 | 0 | 0 | 0 | 1 |
| Do-24 | 0 | 0 | 0 | 0 | 1 |
| Glider | 0 | 0 | 0 | 0 | 6 |

### 361st Fighter Group Squadron Commanders

**374th Ftr Sqn**

| | |
|---|---|
| LtCol. Roy A. Webb, Jr. | February 1943-July 1944 |
| Maj. Robert E. Sedman | July 1944-September 20, 1944 |
| LtCol. George R. Rew | September 20, 1944-February 25, 1945 |
| Maj. Charles H. Bergmann | February 25, 1945-July 1945 |

**375th Ftr Sqn**

| | |
|---|---|
| Maj. Barry E. Malloan | February 1943-August 27, 1943 |
| Maj. George L. Merritt, Jr. | August 27, 1943-June 7, 1944 |
| Maj. Dayton C. Casto | June 8, 1944-June 20, 1944 |
| LtCol. Roswell Freedman | June 20, 1944-October 11, 1944 |
| Maj. Charles N. Keppler | October 11, 1944-EOW |

**376th Ftr Sqn**

| | |
|---|---|
| LtCol. Roy B. Caviness | February 1943-August 13, 1944 |
| Capt. John F. Duncan | August 13, 1944-September 20, 1944 |
| Maj. James B. Cheney | September 20, 1944-October 15, 1944 |
| LtCol. Roy B. Caviness | October 16, 1944-November 3, 1944 |
| Capt. John F. Duncan | November 3, 1944-January 1945 |
| LtCol. Roswell Freedman | January 1945-June 1945 |

### 361st Fighter Group Aces

| Name | Air | Grd | Total | Sqn |
|---|---|---|---|---|
| Maj. George L. Merritt | 5 | 6 | 11 | 375th |
| Capt. Martin H. Johnson, Jr. | 1 | 9 | 10 | 375th |
| Lt. Dale F. Spencer | 9.5 | 0.5 | 10 | 376th |
| Lt. William J. Sykes | 5 | 5 | 10 | 376th |
| Capt. William R. Beyer | 9 | 0 | 9 | 376th |
| LtCol. Roy A. Webb, Jr. | 4 | 5 | 9 | 374th |
| Lt. George R. Vanden Heuval | 5.5 | 3 | 8.5 | 376th |
| LtCol. Wallace E. Hopkins | 4 | 4 | 8 | HdQts |
| Capt. Robert C. Wright | 3.5 | 4 | 7.5 | 375th |
| Lt. Urban L. Drew | 6 | 1 | 7 | 375th |
| Lt. Robert T. Eckfeldt | 3 | 4 | 7 | 374th |
| LtCol. Joseph J. Kruzel | 6.5 | 0 | 6.5* | HdQts |
| Lt. William T. Kemp | 6 | 0 | 6 | 375th |
| Lt. Sherman Armsby | 4.5 | 1 | 5.5 | 375th |
| Lt. Vernon R. Richards | 2 | 3.5 | 5.5 | 374th |
| Capt. Victor E. Bocquin | 4 | 1 | 5 | 376th |

* - includes 3 air victories with the 17th Pur Sqn, PTO

### 361st Fighter Group Scorers

**HdQts**

| | Air | Grd | |
|---|---|---|---|
| R.B. Caviness | 0-0-0 | 2-0 | plus 376th Ftr Sqn |
| T.J.J. Christian | 0-0-0 | 1 0.5 | |
| W.E. Hopkins | 4-0-0 | 4-1.5 | |
| J.J. Kruzel | 3.5-0-1 | 0-0 | plus 3 air w/17th Pur Sqn, PTO |
| S.L. Naedle | 1-0-0 | 0-0 | |
| J.M. Todd | 0-0-0 | 0-1 | plus 376th Ftr Sqn |

**374th Ftr Sqn**

| | | | |
|---|---|---|---|
| J.O. Adkins | 1-0-1 | 0.5-0 | |
| C.H. Bergmann | 1.5-0-0 | 0-0 | |
| J.R. Bernert | 0-1-0 | 0-0 | |
| M.L. Bryant, Jr. | 1-0-0 | 0.5-0 | |
| D.L. Callaway | 1-0-1 | 0-0 | |
| R.E. Chandler | 1-0-0 | 0-0 | |
| P.B. Collins | 1-0-0 | 0-0 | |
| A.B. Cook | 0-0-0 | 1-1 | |
| A.E. Davis | 1-0-0 | 0-0 | |
| H.S. Dixon | 0-0-1 | 0-0 | |
| L.E. Downey | 2-0-1 | 0-0 | |
| R.T. Eckfeldt | 3-0-0 | 4-2.5 | |
| M.F. Glessner | 1-0-0 | 0-0 | |
| S.J. Harris | 0-0-0 | 1-0 | |
| J.D. Hastin | 0.5-0-0 | 0-0 | |
| B.R. Hicks | 2-0-0 | 0-0 | |
| P.C. Holter, Jr. | 1-0-2 | 0-0 | |
| L.J. Jewell | 0-0-1 | 0-0 | |
| E.W. Keplinger | 1-0-2 | 0-0 | |
| R.P. Lacy, Jr. | 2-0-0 | 0-1 | |
| L.G. LaCroix | 1-0-1 | 0-0 | plus 1 air w/49th Ftr Grp, PTO |
| J.L. Latimer | 1-0-0 | 0-0 | |
| H.B. Lederer | 1.5-0-1 | 0.5-0 | |
| G. Lichter | 2-1-2 | 0-1 | |
| R.E. Locke | 0-0-0 | 0.5-0 | |
| A.B. MaClay | 0-0-0 | 1-4 | |
| J.R. Mau | 3-0-1 | 0-0 | |
| T.J. Moore | 1-0-0 | 0-1 | |
| W.L. Moore | 1-0-1 | 0-0 | |
| E.B. Murdy | 1.5-0-1 | 0-0 | |
| S.M. Popy | 1-0-0 | 0-0 | |
| W.J. Quinn | 2-0-0 | 0-0 | |
| G. Rew | 0-0-0 | 1.5-0 | |
| V.R. Richards | 2-0-0 | 3.5-3 | |
| W.H. Sargent | 0-0-0 | 1-0 | |
| R.E. Sedman | 3-1-0 | 1-2 | |
| J.T. Sloan | 1-0-1 | 0-0 | |
| R.J. Stolzy | 1-0-0 | 1-1 | |
| L.C. Vandiver | 1-0-0 | 0-1 | |
| J.G. Vear | 2-0-1 | 0-0 | |
| J.R. Voss | 0-0-1 | 0-0 | |
| R.A. Webb, Jr. | 4-0-0 | 5-1 | |
| J.C. Wilkinson | 1-0-1 | 0-0 | |
| E.L. Wilsey | 1-0-0 | 0-0 | |
| J.K. Wood | 1.5-0-0 | 0-0 | |

**375th Ftr Sqn**

| | | | |
|---|---|---|---|
| R.G. Adams | 1-0-1 | 0-0 | |
| R.D. Anderson | 1-0-0 | 0-0 | |
| S. Armsby | 4.5-0-0 | 1-3 | |
| T.F. Brubaker | 2-0-0 | 1-0 | |
| D.C. Casto, Jr. | 0-0-1 | 1-0 | |
| E. Cole | 2-1-0 | 1-1 | |
| J.S. Crandell | 2-0-0 | 1.5-0 | |
| C.R. Cummins | 2-0-0 | 0-0 | |
| P.A. Doughtery, Jr. | 0.5-0-0 | 0-1 | |
| U.L. Drew | 6-0-1 | 1-0 | |
| A.C. Duncan | 0-0-0 | 0-0.33 | |
| D.W. Edwards | 1-0-0 | 0-0 | |
| M.E. Elliott | 0-0-0 | 0-0.5 | |
| H.A. Euler | 0-0-1 | 0-0 | |
| R.J. Farney | 3-0-1 | 0-0 | |
| W.B. Farnum | 0-0-1 | 0-0 | |
| D.R. Farrar | 1-0-0 | 0-0 | |
| C.H. Feller | 0-0-0 | 0-1 | |
| L.F. Gendron | 0-0-4 | 0-0 | |
| F.T. Glankler | 0-0-0 | 0-1 | |
| J.W. Guckeyson | 2.5-0-0 | 2.33-2 | |
| W.M. Hart, Jr. | 0.5-0-0 | 0-0 | |
| M.H. Johnson, Jr. | 1-0-0 | 9-0 | |
| W.T. Kemp | 6-0-1 | 0-0.5 | |
| C.N. Keppler | 2-0-4 | 0-3 | plus 1-0-0 air w/78th Ftr Grp |
| E.W. Kinnaird | 0.5-0-0 | 1-2 | |
| P.H. Klees | 2-0-0 | 0-0 | |
| D.F. Knupp | 1-0-0 | 0-0 | |
| S.C. Kovach | 0-0-0 | 0-3 | |
| C.J. Layton | 2-0-0 | 0-0 | |
| E.J. Marevka | 0-0-0 | 1-0 | |
| A. Maurice | 2.5-0-0 | 0-0 | |
| W.E. McCoppin | 1-0-0 | 0-0 | |
| G.L. Merritt, Jr. | 5-0-0 | 6-1 | |
| M.L. Moore | 0-0-0 | 0-1 | |
| D.R. Morehouse | 1-0-1 | 1-4 | |
| D.R. Morgan | 1.5-0-0 | 0-2 | |
| L.H. Mottis | 0-0-0 | 0-1 | |
| C.W. Narvis | 1-0-0 | 1-1 | |
| E.E. Neely | 2-0-2 | 0-2 | |
| S.D. Rames | 1-0-0 | 0.83-0 | |
| W.A. Rautenbush | 0.5-0-0 | 2.33-0 | |
| W.D. Rogers | 0-0-0 | 0.5-2 | |
| B.W. Rowlett | 0-0-0 | 2-2 | |
| W.G. Shackleford | 0-0-1 | 1-2 | |
| A.L. Segert | 0-0-0 | 0-1 | |
| A.B. Snyder, Jr. | 3-0-0 | 0-0 | |
| R.J. Sobieski | 1.5-1-0 | 0-0 | |
| H.A. Spaulding | 0-0-2 | 0-0.5 | |
| W.R. Stevens, Jr. | 1-0-0 | 1-0 | |
| W.H. Street | 2-0-2 | 0-0 | |
| G.R. Stockmeier | 0.5-0-1 | 0-0 | |
| J.J. Sullivan | 2-0-0 | 0-0 | |
| L.H. Sypher | 1-0-1 | 0-0 | |
| J.T. Thomas | 0-0-0 | 1-2 | |
| E.E. Tinkham | 0-0-1 | 0-0 | |
| L.C. Travis | 1-0-0 | 0.5-0 | |
| L.A. Wood | 2-0-0 | 0-0.5 | |
| R.C. Wright | 3.5-0-0 | 4-1 | |

**376th Ftr Sqn**

| | | | |
|---|---|---|---|
| E.C. Alcorn | 1-0-0 | 0-0 | |
| R.J. Bain | 0-0-3 | 0-0 | |
| J.M. Bentley | 1-0-0 | 0-0 | |
| W.R. Beyer | 9-0-0 | 0-0 | |
| V.E. Bocquin | 4-0-0 | 1-1 | |
| J.B. Bricker | 4-0-1 | 0-0 | |
| W.T. Butts | 3-0-0 | 0-0 | |
| R.B. Caviness | 0-0-1 | 1-0 | plus HdQts |
| L.P. Chadwick | 0-1-0 | 3-0 | |
| A.J. Chalmers | 0-0-0 | 2-0 | |
| W.F. Chapin, Jr. | 2-1-0 | 0-0 | |
| H.D. Chapman | 2-0-0.5 | 0-0 | |

| | | | |
|---|---|---|---|
| H.M. Chapman | 1-0-0 | 2-2 | |
| J.B. Cheney | 1.5-0-0 | 0-0 | |
| C.P. Chennault | 2-0-0 | 0-0 | |
| E.L. Czapla | 0-0-0 | 1-0 | |
| B.L. Dennehy | 1-0-1 | 0-0 | |
| J.D. Duncan | 1-0-0 | 0-0 | |
| R.M. Durbin | 1-0-1 | 0-0 | |
| V.C. Eisenhut | 0-0-0 | 1-1 | |
| D.R. Ford | 1-0-0 | 0-0 | |
| W.B. Frank | 0.5-0-2 | 1-0 | |
| R. Freedman | 0-0-0 | 1-0 | |
| D. Grounds | 0-0-0 | 0-1 | |
| C.W. Hanley, Jr. | 2.5-0-0 | 0-0 | |
| R. Hobbs | 0.5-0-0 | 0-0 | |
| D.W. Jones | 0-0-0 | 1-0 | |
| J.D. Kelly | 0-0-0 | 2-1 | |
| M.C. Kelly | 0-0-0 | 2-0 | |
| W.J. Kozicki | 0-1-1 | 0-0 | |
| H.A. Lane | 1-0-0 | 0-0 | |
| C.A. Laxton | 0-0-0 | 0-0.5 | |
| H.D. Mitchell | 3-0-0 | 0-0 | |
| R.W. Myers | 1-0-1 | 0-0 | |
| D.P. Overholt | 2-0-0 | 0-0 | |
| W.W. Patton | 0-0-0 | 3-2 | |
| H.G. Powell | 3-0-0 | 0-0 | |
| J.W. Ruch | 0.5-0-0 | 0-0 | |
| J.J. Sadinski | 1-0-0 | 0-0 | |
| K.J. Scott | 2-1-1 | 0-0 | |
| J.D. Smith | 0-0-0 | 1-0 | |
| D.F. Spencer | 9.5-0-1 | 0.5-0 | |
| H.G. Spencer | 0-0-0 | 3-0 | |
| J.C. Stewart | 0-0-0 | 0-1 | |
| C.E. Sullivan | 1-0-0 | 0-1 | |
| W.J. Sykes | 5-2-0 | 5-0 | |
| J.M. Todd | 0-0-1 | 0-0 | plus HdQts |
| R.G. Van Stryland | 0-0-0 | 0-1 | |
| G.R. Vanden Heuval | 5.5-0-0 | 3-1 | |
| R.R. Volkman | 1-0-0 | 0-1 | |
| D.P. Vulgamore | 2-0-0 | 1-1 | |
| R.W. Ward | 2-0-1 | 0-0 | |
| B.D. Welch | 0-0-0 | 0.5-0 | |
| R.S. White | 2-0-2 | 0-0 | |
| S.C. Wilkerson, Jr. | 1-0-0 | 3-0 | |
| M.C. Williams | 2-0-0 | 0-0 | |
| D.T. Woodward | 0-0-1 | 0-0 | |
| J.C. Wright | 0-0-1 | 3-3 | |
| W.R. Young | 1-0-0 | 0-0 | |

### 361st Fighter Group Scoring

**January 14, 1944**

| | | | |
|---|---|---|---|
| 375th: | Lt. A.C. Duncan | (.33)FW-190 dam(grd) | Rosiers-en-Santerne |
| | | (shared with two 353rd Ftr Grp pilots) | |

**January 30, 1944**

| | | | |
|---|---|---|---|
| 374th: | Maj. R.A. Webb | Me-109 dest(air) | Rheine |
| | Capt. R.E. Sedman | Me-109 dest(air) | Rheine |
| | | Me-109 prob(air) | Rheine |
| | Lt. J.L. Latimer | Me-109 dest(air) | Rheine |
| | Lt. J.D. Hastin | (.5)Me-109 dest(air) | Rheine |
| | Lt. H.B. Lederer | (.5)Me-109 dest(air) | Rheine |
| | Lt. J.R. Bernert | Me-109 prob(air) | Rheine |
| | Lt. G. Lichter | Me-109 dam(air) | Rheine |
| | Lt. W.L. Moore | Me-109 dam(air) | Rheine |

**February 22, 1944**

| | | | |
|---|---|---|---|
| HdQts: | Maj. J.J. Kruzel | FW-190 dam(air) | SW Nijmegen |
| 375th: | Maj. G.L. Merritt | (2)FW-190 dest(air) | NE Tilburg |
| | Lt. C.N. Keppler | FW-190 dest(air) | NE Tilburg |
| 376th: | Lt. R.S. White | (2)FW-190 dam(air) | Cleve |
| | Lt. J.C. Wright | FW-190 dam(air) | S/Nijmegen |

**February 24, 1944**

| | | | |
|---|---|---|---|
| 374th: | Lt. R.J. Stolzy | Me-109 dest(air) | Dummer Lake |
| | | Me-110 dam(grd) | Hesepe A/F |
| 375th: | Capt. J.W. Guckeyson | Me-109 dest(air) | S/Loningen |

**February 25, 1944**

| | | | |
|---|---|---|---|
| 376th: | Lt. E.C. Alcorn | Me-109 dest(air) | Longuyon |
| | Lt. J.D. Duncan | Me-109 dest(air) | Courtrai |
| | Lt. H.A. Lane | FW-190 dest(air) | N/Metz |
| | Maj. R.B. Caviness | FW-190 dam(air) | NE Metz |
| | Capt. J.M. Todd | Me-109 dam(air) | SE St. Quentin |
| | Lt. D.T. Woodward | Me-109 dam(air) | Verdun |

**March 2, 1944**

| | | | |
|---|---|---|---|
| 374th: | Lt. R.P. Lacy | Ju-88 dam(grd) | Chievres |
| | Lt. L.C. Vandiver | Ju-88 dam(grd) | Chievres |

**March 6, 1944**

| | | | |
|---|---|---|---|
| 374th: | Capt. R.E. Sedman | FW-190 dest(air) | Zuider Zee |
| | Lt. W.L. Moore | FW-190 dest(air) | Zuider Zee |
| 375th: | Lt. A.B. Snyder | FW-190 dest(air) | S/Quackenbruck |
| 376th: | Lt. J.M. Bentley | FW-190 dest(air) | Lingen |
| | Lt. M.C. Williams | FW-190 dest(air) | NW Dummer Lake |

**March 8, 1944**

| | | | |
|---|---|---|---|
| HdQts: | LtCol. J.J. Kruzel | (.5)FW-190 dest(air) | W/Dummer Lake |
| 375th: | Capt. J.W. Guckeyson | Me-109 dest(air) | Lemforde |
| | Lt. E.W. Kinnaird | (.5)FW-190 dest(air) | W/Dummer Lake |
| | Lt. C.N. Keppler | Me-109 dam(air) | Lemforde |

**March 17, 1944**

| | | | |
|---|---|---|---|
| HdQts: | Col. T.J.J. Christian | (.5)u/i a/c dam(grd) | Chartres |
| | Capt. J.M. Todd | Me-109 dam(grd) | Chartres |
| 375th: | Maj. G.L. Merritt | Me-109 dest(grd) | Chartres |
| | | Me-109 dam(grd) | Chartres |
| 376th: | Maj. R.B. Caviness | u/i a/c dest(grd) | Chartres |
| | Lt. C.A. Laxton | (.5)u/i a/c dam(grd) | Chartres |
| | Lt. R.G. Van Stryland | Ju-88 dam(grd) | Chartres |

**March 29, 1944**

| | | | |
|---|---|---|---|
| 375th: | Lt. M.H. Johnson | FW-190 dest(grd) | Rheine |
| | | Ju-88 dest(grd) | Rheine |
| | Lt. E.W. Kinnaird | (2)FW-190 dam(grd) | Dummer Lake |
| 376th: | Lt. J.C. Wright | Ju-88 dest(grd) | Dummer Lake |
| | | (2)u/i a/c dam(grd) | Dummer Lake |
| | Lt. J.D. Kelly | Ju-88 dam(grd) | Dummer Lake |

**April 1, 1944**

| | | | |
|---|---|---|---|
| 375th: | Lt. E.W. Kinnaird | Ju-88 dest(grd) | Gutersloh |
| 376th: | Lt. J.D. Kelly | (2)Ju-88 dest(grd) | Gutersloh |
| | Lt. J.C. Wright | Ju-88 dest(grd) | Gutersloh |

**April 8, 1944**

| | | | |
|---|---|---|---|
| HdQts: | Lt. S.L. Naedle | Me-109 dest(air) | W/Dummer Lake |
| 374th: | Capt. R.E. Sedman | Me-109 dest(air) | N/Dummer Lake |
| | Lt. R.T. Eckfeldt | Me-109 dest(air) | N/Dummer Lake |
| | Lt. R.P. Lacy | Me-109 dest(air) | N/Dummer Lake |
| | Lt. L.C. Vandiver | Me-109 dest(air) | N/Dummer Lake |
| 375th: | Lt. A.B. Snyder | Me-109 dest(air) | SW Dummer Lake |
| | | FW-190 dest(air) | N/Zwolle |
| | Lt. E. Cole | Me-109 dest(air) | Diepholz |
| | | FW-190 prob(air) | N/Zwolle |
| | Lt. C.N. Keppler | FW-190 dest(air) | NW Dummer Lake |
| | Lt. R.J. Sobieski | FW-190 prob(air) | N/Zwolle |

**April 9, 1944**

| | | | |
|---|---|---|---|
| 375th: | Lt. D.R. Morehouse | FW-190 dam(air) | NW Dummer Lake |

**April 10, 1944**

| | | | |
|---|---|---|---|
| 376th: | Lt. J.C. Wright | Me-110 dest(grd) | Villaroche |
| | | Me-110 dam(grd) | Villaroche |

**April 15, 1944**

| | | | |
|---|---|---|---|
| 375th: | Lt. W.A. Rautenbush | u/i a/c dest(grd) | Fritzlar |
| | | (.33)Ju-52 dest(grd) | Fritzlar |
| | Capt. J.W. Guckeyson | (.33)Ju-52 dest(grd) | Fritzlar |
| | Lt. S.D. Rames | (.33)Ju-52 dest(grd) | Fritzlar |

**April 18, 1944**

| | | | |
|---|---|---|---|
| 375th: | Maj. G.L. Merritt | Ju-88 dest(grd) | Zwischenaschmer |
| | Lt. M.H. Johnson | Ar-196 dest(grd) | Zwischenaschmer |

**April 24, 1944**

| | | | |
|---|---|---|---|
| 375th: | Lt. M.H. Johnson | Me-109 dest(grd) | Metz |
| | | FW-190 dest(grd) | Metz |
| | | Me-110 dest(grd) | Metz |
| | Capt. D.C. Casto | Me-109 dest(grd) | Metz |
| | Lt. W.A. Rautenbush | Ju-88 dest(grd) | Metz |
| | Lt. D.R. Morehouse | He-111 dam(grd) | Metz |

**April 25, 1944**

| | | | |
|---|---|---|---|
| 375th: | Capt. J.W. Guckeyson | Ju-52 dest(grd) | Nancy |
| | | Fi-156 dest(grd) | Nancy |
| | Lt. E. Cole | FW-190 dest(grd) | Nancy |
| | | u/i a/c dam(grd) | Nancy |

**April 26, 1944**

| | | | |
|---|---|---|---|
| 376th: | Capt. W.B. Frank | Ju-88 dest(grd) | Montdidier |
| | Lt. J.C. Stewart | Ju-88 dam(grd) | Montdidier |

**April 27, 1944**

| | | | |
|---|---|---|---|
| 375th: | Maj. G.L. Merritt | He-111 dest(grd) | Etampes |
| | Lt. J.S. Crandell | (.5)He-111 dest(grd) | Etampes |
| | Lt. S.D. Rames | (.5)He-111 dest(grd) | Etampes |
| | Capt. J.W. Guckeyson | (2)He-111 dam(grd) | Etampes |
| | Capt. C.H. Feller | He-111 dam(grd) | Etampes |
| | Capt. C.N. Keppler | He-111 dam(grd) | Etampes |

| | | | |
|---|---|---|---|
| **April 29, 1944** | | | |
| HdQts: | LtCol. J.J. Kruzel | Me-109 dest(air) | Steinhuder Lake |
| 375th: | Lt. S.D. Rames | Me-109 dest(air) | Steinhuder Lake |
| **May 1, 1944** | | | |
| 375th: | Capt. J.W. Guckeyson | (.5)Ju-188 dest(air) | W/Verdun |
| | Lt. W.A. Rautenbush | (.5)Ju-188 dest(air) | W/Verdun |
| **May 8, 1944** | | | |
| 375th: | Maj. G.L. Merritt | FW-190 dest(air) | N/Nienburg |
| | Lt. L.H. Sypher | Me-109 dest(air) | NE Steinhuder L. |
| | | Me-109 dam(air) | NE Steinhuder L. |
| 376th: | Lt. H.D. Chapman | Me-109 dest(air) | Nienburg |
| | Capt. W.B. Frank | FW-190 dam(air) | Nienburg |

NOTE - Sypher flew a P-51 on this day; all other claims were in P-47's. From this date forward, all will be in P-51's.

| | | | |
|---|---|---|---|
| **May 9, 1944** | | | |
| 375th: | Lt. F.T. Glankler | Me-109 dam(grd) | Juvincourt |
| **May 21, 1944** | | | |
| 374th: | Capt. R.E. Sedman | u/i a/c dest(grd) | Grossenheim |
| | | (2)u/i a/c dam(grd) | Grossenheim |
| **May 24, 1944** | | | |
| 374th: | Lt. P.C. Holter | Me-109 dam(air) | NE Berlin |
| 375th: | Maj. G.L. Merritt | Me-109 dest(air) | NE Berlin |
| | Capt. C.N. Keppler | Me-109 dam(air) | N/Berlin |
| 376th: | Lt. M.C. Williams | Me-109 dest(air) | Berlin |
| **May 27, 1944** | | | |
| 375th: | Maj. G.L. Merritt | FW-190 dest(air) | W/Lille |
| **May 29, 1944** | | | |
| HdQts: | Maj. W.E. Hopkins | (2)FW-190 dest(air) | Pitka |
| 374th: | Maj. R.A. Webb | FW-190 dest(air) | Pitka |
| | Lt. D.L. Callaway | FW-190 dest(air) | Pitka |
| | | FW-190 dam(air) | Pitka |
| | Lt. L.E. Downey | FW-190 dest(air) | Pitka |
| | | FW-190 dam(air) | Pitka |
| | Lt. R.T. Eckfeldt | FW-190 dest(air) | Pitka |
| | Lt. G. Lichter | FW-190 dest(air) | Pitka |
| | | FW-190 prob(air) | Pitka |
| | Lt. E.B. Murdy | (1.5)FW-190 dest(air)* | E/Schwerin |
| 375th: | Maj. G.L. Merritt | (2)He-111 dest(grd) | Lackau-Juterbog |
| | Lt. R.C. Wright | (2)Ju-52 dest(grd) | Lackau-Juterbog |
| | | He-111 dest(grd) | Lackau-Juterbog |
| | | Ju-88 dest(grd) | Lackau-Juterbog |
| | | Ju-88 dam(grd) | Lackau-Juterbog |
| | Lt. D.R. Morehouse | u/i a/c dest(grd) | Lackau-Juterbog |
| 376th: | Lt. D.F. Spencer | (4)Me-410 dest(air) | E/Schwerin |
| | Capt. J.B. Cheney | (.5)FW-190 dest(air)* | E/Schwerin |
| | Capt. W.B. Frank | (.5)FW-190 dest(air)** | Schwerin |
| | | FW-190 dam(air) | Schwerin |
| | Lt. W.T. Butts | (.5)FW-190 dest(air)* | Schwerin |
| | Lt. W.J. Kozicki | FW-190 dam(air) | Schwerin |
| **June 4, 1944** | | | |
| 374th: | Capt. C.H. Bergmann | (.5)Me-109 dest(air) | SE Mulun |
| | Lt. J.K. Wood | (.5)Me-109 dest(air) | SE Mulun |
| | Lt. E.B. Murdy | Me-109 dam(air) | SE Mulun |
| **June 6, 1944** | | | |
| 374th: | Capt. G.R. Rew | (.5)Me-109 dest(grd) | Vendome |
| | Lt. V.R. Richards | (.5)Me-109 dest(grd) | Vendome |
| 375th: | Maj. G.L. Merritt | Ju-88 dest(grd) | Tours |
| **June 7, 1944** | | | |
| 374th: | Lt. W.H. Sargent | Ju-52 dest(grd) | Orleans/Bricy |
| | Lt. R.J. Stolzy | Ju-52 dest(grd) | Orleans/Bricy |
| 375th: | Capt. D.C. Casto | Me-109 dam(air) | Chartres |
| 376th: | Capt. J.B. Cheney | FW-190 dest(air) | N/Chateaudun |
| | Lt. S.C. Wilkerson | He-177 dest(air) | NE Vendome |
| **June 8, 1944** | | | |
| 374th: | Capt. C.H. Bergmann | Me-109 dest(air) | St. Pierre |
| | Lt. J.O. Adkins | Me-109 dest(air) | St. Pierre |
| | Lt. R.T. Eckfeldt | Me-109 dest(air) | St. Pierre |
| | Lt. P.C. Holter | Me-109 dam(air) | St. Pierre |
| **June 12, 1944** | | | |
| 374th: | Capt. G.R. Rew | FW-190 dest(grd) | Chateau Du Loir |
| **June 13, 1944** | | | |
| HdQts: | LtCol. J.J. Kruzel | Me-109 dest(air) | St. Brieuc |
| 374th: | Maj. R.A. Webb | Me-109 dest(air) | St. Brieuc |
| | Lt. L.E. Downey | Me-109 dest(air) | St. Brieuc |
| | Lt. R.P. Lacy | Me-109 dest(air) | St. Brieuc |
| **June 16, 1944** | | | |
| 375th: | Lt. J.S. Crandell | Ju-52 dest(grd) | Toussus/Le Noble |
| | Lt. U.L. Drew | Ju-52 dest(grd) | Toussus/Le Noble |
| | Lt. M.H. Johnson | Ju-52 dest(grd) | Toussus/Le Noble |
| **June 20, 1944** | | | |
| HdQts: | Col. T.J.J. Christian | He-115 dest(grd) | Putnitz |
| 375th: | Capt. C.N. Keppler | (1.5)Glider dam(grd)* | Putnitz |
| | | (.5)Me-110 dam(grd) | Putnitz |
| | Lt. E.E. Neely | (1.5)Glider dam(grd)* | Putnitz |
| | | (.5)Me-110 dam(grd) | Putnitz |
| | Lt. D.R. Morgan | (2)Me-110 dam(grd) | Putnitz |
| | Lt. S. Armsby | (.5)BV-138 dam(grd)@ | Putnitz |
| | | (.5)Glider dam(grd)** | Putnitz |
| | Lt. J.T. Thomas | (.5)BV-138 dam(grd)@ | Putnitz |
| | | (.5)Glider dam(grd)** | Putnitz |
| | Lt. D.R. Morehouse | Me-210 dam(grd) | Putnitz |
| | | (2)Glider dam(grd) | Putnitz |
| | Lt. M.E. Elliott | (.5)BV-138 dam(grd)@@ | Putnitz |
| | Lt. W.D. Rogers | (.5)BV-138 dam(grd)@@ | Putnitz |
| | | (.5)FW-189 dam(grd) | Putnitz |
| | Lt. H.A. Spaulding | (.5)FW-189 dam(grd) | Putnitz |
| 376th: | Lt. S.C. Wilkerson | He-111 dest(grd) | Putnitz |
| | Lt. D.F. Spencer | (.5)BV-138 dest(grd) | Putnitz |
| | Lt. B.D. Welch | (.5)BV-138 dest(grd) | Putnitz |
| | Lt. C.E. Sullivan | Do-24 dam(grd) | Putnitz |
| **June 21, 1944** | | | |
| 375th: | Lt. M.H. Johnson | u/i a/c dest(grd) | Zwischenaschmer |
| **June 25, 1944** | | | |
| HdQts: | LtCol. J.J. Kruzel | FW-190 dest(air) | N/Lisieux |
| 374th: | LtCol. R.A. Webb | FW-190 dest(air) | S/Caen |
| | Lt. V.R. Richards | Me-109 dest(air) | S/Caen |
| | | FW-190 dest(air) | S/Caen |
| 375th: | Lt. J.S. Crandell | (2)Me-109 dest(air) | N/Rouen |
| | Capt. C.R. Cummins | Me-109 dest(air) | N/Lisieux |
| | Lt. U.L. Drew | Me-109 dest(air) | N/Lisieux |
| 376th: | Capt. R.M. Durbin | Me-109 dest(air) | Bernay |
| | Lt. H.D. Chapman | Me-109 dest(air) | Bernay |
| | | (.5)Me-109 dam(air)* | Bernay |
| | | (shared with an unknown P-51 pilot) | |
| **June 29, 1944** | | | |
| HdQts: | LtCol. W.E. Hopkins | (4)FW-190 dest(grd) | Oschersleben |
| | | (1.5)FW-190 dam(grd)* | Oschersleben |
| 374th: | LtCol. R.A. Webb | (5)FW-190 dest(grd) | Oschersleben |
| | | FW-190 dam(grd) | Oschersleben |
| | Lt. R.T. Eckfeldt | (4)FW-190 dest(grd) | Oschersleben |
| | | (2.5)FW-190 dam(grd)** | Oschersleben |
| | Lt. V.R. Richards | (3)FW-190 dest(grd) | Oschersleben |
| | | (2)FW-190 dam(grd) | Oschersleben |
| | | (.5)FW-190 dam(grd)* | Oschersleben |
| | | (.5)FW-190 dam(grd)** | Oschersleben |
| 375th: | Lt. R.C. Wright | (1.5)Me-109 dest(air) | SW Kothen |
| | Capt. E. Cole | Me-109 dest(air) | SE Kothen |
| | Lt. T.F. Brubaker | Me-109 dest(air) | SE Kothen |
| | Lt. S. Armsby | (.5)Me-109 dest(air) | SW Kothen |
| | Lt. E.E. Neely | Me-109 dam(air) | SE Kothen |
| **July 5, 1944** | | | |
| 374th: | Lt. J.R. Mau | Me-109 dest(air) | Amiens |
| | | Me-109 dam(air) | Amiens |
| | Lt. J.K. Wood | Me-109 dest(air) | Amiens |
| | Capt. S.J. Harris | Ju-88 dest(grd) | Chateau Thierry |
| | Lt. G. Lichter | Ju-88 dam(grd) | Chateau Thierry |
| 376th: | Lt. D.F. Spencer | (2)Me-109 dest(air) | Rouen-Evreux |
| | | Me-109 dam(air) | Rouen-Evreux |
| **July 7, 1944** | | | |
| 375th: | Lt. R.C. Wright | (2)Me-109 dest(air) | N/Leipzig |
| | Lt. R.J. Sobieski | Me-410 dest(air) | NW Leipzig |
| | | (.5)Me-109 dest(air) | NW Leipzig |
| | Lt. D.R. Morehouse | Me-109 dest(air) | N/Leipzig |
| | Lt. D.R. Morgan | (.5)Me-109 dest(air) | NW Leipzig |
| 376th: | Lt. D.F. Spencer | (2)Me-109 dest(air) | Wittenburg |
| | Lt. R.S. White | Me-109 dest(air) | Wittenburg |
| | | FW-190 dest(air) | Wittenburg |
| | Capt. R.M. Durbin | FW-190 dam(air) | Halle |
| **July 20, 1944** | | | |
| 375th: | Lt. S. Armsby | (3)Me-109 dest(air) | N/Leipzig |
| | Lt. W.T. Kemp | Me-109 dest(air) | N/Leipzig |
| | | FW-190 dest(air) | N/Leipzig |
| **July 25, 1944** | | | |
| 374th: | Capt. R.E. Locke | (.5)Me-109 dest(grd)* | N/Alencon |
| | Lt. J.O. Adkins | (.5)Me-109 dest(grd)* | N/Alencon |
| | Lt. M.L. Bryant | (.5)Me-109 dest(grd)** | N/Alencon |
| | Lt. H.B. Lederer | (.5)Me-109 dest(grd)** | N/Alencon |

**August 4, 1944**

| | | | |
|---|---|---|---|
| 376th: | Capt. S.C. Wilkerson | (2)Ju-88 dest(grd) | Anklam |
| | Lt. V.E. Bocquin | Ju-88 dest(grd) | Anklam |
| | | Ju-88 dam(grd) | Anklam |
| | Lt. R.R. Volkman | Ju-88 dam(grd) | Anklam |

**August 5, 1944**

| | | | |
|---|---|---|---|
| 374th: | Lt. H.B. Lederer | Me-109 dest(air) | Hoperhofen |
| | | Me-109 dam(air) | Hoperhofen |
| | Lt. P.C. Holter | Me-109 dest(air) | Hoperhofen |
| | Lt. G. Lichter | Me-109 dest(air) | Hoperhofen |
| 375th: | Lt. S. Armsby | Me-109 dest(air) | N/Nienburg |
| | Lt. D.W. Edwards | Me-109 dest(air) | S/Bremen |
| | Capt. W.G. Shackleford | Do-217 dest(grd) | Alhorn |
| | | (2)Me-163 dam(grd) | Alhorn |

**August 7, 1944**

| | | | |
|---|---|---|---|
| 375th: | Lt. W.T. Kemp | FW-190 dest(air) | Chartres |
| | | FW-190 dam(air) | Chartres |
| | | (.5)Me-109 dam(grd) | Chartres |
| | Lt. U.L. Drew | Me-109 dam(air) | Chartres |
| | Lt. L.A. Wood | (.5)Me-109 dam(grd) | Chartres |

**August 8, 1944**

| | | | |
|---|---|---|---|
| HdQts: | LtCol. W.E. Hopkins | (2)FW-190 dest(air) | Evreux |
| 374th: | Lt. E.W. Keplinger | FW-190 dest(air) | Evreux |
| | | FW-190 dam(air) | Evreux |
| | Lt. J.O. Adkins | FW-190 dam(air) | Evreux |

**August 15, 1944**

| | | | |
|---|---|---|---|
| 375th: | Capt. M.H. Johnson | Ju-88 dest(grd) | Wittmunhafen |
| | Lt. J.T. Thomas | Ju-88 dest(grd) | Wittmunhafen |
| | | Ju-88 dam(grd) | Wittmunhafen |
| | Lt. S. Armsby | u/i a/c dest(grd) | Wittmunhafen |
| | | (2)Me-110 dam(grd) | Wittmunhafen |
| | Lt. M.J. Moore | Me-110 dam(grd) | Wittmunhafen |
| | Lt. W.D. Rogers | Ju-88 dam(grd) | Wittmunhafen |

**August 18, 1944**

| | | | |
|---|---|---|---|
| HdQts: | LtCol. R.B. Caviness | Ju-52 dest(grd) | Romilly-Sur-Seine |
| 376th: | Lt. E.L. Czapla | Ju-52 dest(grd) | Romilly-Sur-Seine |
| | Lt. J.D. Smith | Ju-88 dest(grd) | Romilly-Sur-Seine |

**August 25, 1944**

| | | | |
|---|---|---|---|
| 375th: | Lt. M.H. Johnson | Me-109 dest(air) | SW Rostock |
| | Lt. U.L. Drew | Me-109 dest(air) | SW Rostock |
| | Lt. D.R. Morgan | Me-109 dest(air) | E/Wismar |

**September 11, 1944**

| | | | |
|---|---|---|---|
| 375th: | Lt. U.L. Drew | Me-109 dest(air) | S/Gottingen |

**September 12, 1944**

| | | | |
|---|---|---|---|
| 375th: | Lt. W.T. Kemp | (3)Me-109 dest(air) | NE Magdeburg |
| | Maj. C.R. Cummins | Me-109 dest(air) | NE Magdeburg |
| | Lt. D.F. Knupp | Me-109 dest(air) | NE Magdeburg |
| | Lt. C.W. Narvis | Me-109 dest(air) | NE Magdeburg |
| 376th: | Lt. D.F. Spencer | (1.5)Me-109 dest(air) | W/Magdeburg |
| | Lt. R.W. Ward | (.5)Me-109 dest(air) | W/Magdeburg |
| | Lt. V.E. Bocquin | Me-109 dest(air) | NW Magdeburg |
| | Lt. W.T. Butts | Me-109 dest(air) | W/Magdeburg |
| | Lt. C.P. Chennault | Me-109 dest(air) | W/Magdeburg |
| | Lt. D.P. Overholt | Me-109 dest(air) | W/Magdeburg |
| | Lt. D.P. Vulgamore | Me-109 dest(air) | W/Magdeburg |
| | F/O W.F. Chapin | Me-109 prob(air) | W/Magdeburg |

**September 13, 1944**

| | | | |
|---|---|---|---|
| 375th: | Capt. T.F. Brubaker | u/i a/c dest(grd) | Schwabeich Hall |
| | Lt. C.W. Narvis | u/i a/c dest(grd) | Schwabeich Hall |
| | | u/i a/c dam(grd) | Schwabeich Hall |
| | Lt. E.J. Marevka | u/i a/c dest(grd) | Schwabeich Hall |

**September 17, 1944**

| | | | |
|---|---|---|---|
| 376th: | Lt. W.R. Beyer | Me-109 dest(air) | Hasselt-Wesel |

**September 18, 1944**

| | | | |
|---|---|---|---|
| 374th: | Lt. M.L. Bryanr | Me-109 dest(air) | SE Jagel A/F |
| | Lt. A.B. MaClay | Me-109 dest(grd) | Jagel A/F |
| | | (4)Me-109 dam(grd) | Jagel A/F |
| | Lt. A.B. Cook | Me-109 dest(grd) | Jagel A/F |
| | | Me-109 dam(grd) | Jagel A/F |
| | Lt. T.J. Moore | Me-109 dam(grd) | Jagel A/F |
| 375th: | Lt. U.L. Drew | He-111 dest(air) | Fehrman Belt |
| | Lt. W.D. Rogers | (.5)BV-138 dest(grd) | Bug S/P Base |
| | Lt. L.C. Travis | (.5)BV-138 dest(grd) | Bug S/P Base |
| 376th: | Lt. J.B. Bricker | Me-109 dest(air) | N/Schleswig |
| | Lt. W.T. Butts | (.5)Me-109 dest(air) | N/Schleswig |
| | Lt. C.W. Hanley | (.5)Me-109 dest(air) | N/Schleswig |

**September 26, 1944**

| | | | |
|---|---|---|---|
| 375th: | Lt. B.W. Rowlett | FW-190 dest(grd) | Achmer A/F |
| | | He-177 dest(grd) | Achmer A/F |
| | | (2)FW-190 dam(grd) | Achmer A/F |
| | Lt. L.H. Mottis | u/i a/c dam(grd) | Achmer A/F |

**September 27, 1944**

| | | | |
|---|---|---|---|
| 376th: | Lt. W.R. Beyer | (5)FW-190 dest(air) | Eisenach |
| | Lt. V.E. Bocquin | (3)FW-190 dest(air) | Eisenach |
| | Lt. H.G. Powell | (2)FW-190 dest(air) | Eisenach |
| | F/O W.F. Chapin | (2)FW-190 dest(air) | Eisenach |
| | Lt. W.J. Sykes | FW-190 dest(air) | Eisenach |
| | | (2)Me-410 dest(grd) | Eisenach |
| | Lt. D.P. Vulgamore | FW-190 dest(air) | Eisenach |
| | | Me-410 dest(grd) | Eisenach |
| | | Me-410 dam(grd) | Eisenach |
| | Lt. J.B. Bricker | FW-190 dest(air) | Eisenach |
| | | FW-190 dam(air) | Eisenach |
| | Lt. C.W. Hanley | FW-190 dest(air) | Eisenach |
| | Lt. R.W. Myers | FW-190 dest(air) | Eisenach |
| | | FW-190 dam(air) | Eisenach |
| | Lt. R.R. Volkman | FW-190 dest(air) | Eisenach |
| | Lt. R.J. Bain | (2)FW-190 dam(air) | Eisenach |
| | | Me-109 dam(air) | Eisenach |
| | Lt. B.L. Dennehy | FW-190 dam(air) | Eisenach |
| | Lt. R.W. Ward | FW-190 dam(air) | Eisenach |

**October 6, 1944**

| | | | |
|---|---|---|---|
| 375th: | Capt. T.F. Brubaker | Me-109 dest(air) | NW Berlin |

**October 7, 1944**

| | | | |
|---|---|---|---|
| 374th: | Lt. P.B. Collins | Me-109 dest(air) | Naumburg |
| | Lt. A.E. Davis | Me-109 dest(air) | Naumburg |
| | Lt. W.J. Quinn | Me-109 dest(air) | Naumburg |
| 375th: | Lt. U.L. Drew | (2)Me-262 dest(air) | Achmer A/F |
| 376th: | Lt. W.T. Butts | Me-109 dest(air) | Merseburg |
| | Lt. H.D. Mitchell | Me-109 dest(air) | Merseburg |
| | Lt. W.R. Young | Me-109 dest(air) | Merseburg |

**November 2, 1944**

| | | | |
|---|---|---|---|
| 374th: | Lt. J.G. Vear | Me-109 dest(air) | N/Erfurt |
| 375th: | Lt. L.A. Wood | Me-109 dest(air) | S/Weiszenfels |
| 376th: | Lt. W.J. Sykes | Me-109 dest(air) | N/Erfurt |
| | | FW-190 dest(air) | N/Erfurt |
| | Lt. W.R. Beyer | FW-190 dest(air) | N/Erfurt |
| | Lt. J.B. Bricker | FW-190 dest(air) | N/Erfurt |
| | Lt. H.D. Mitchell | FW-190 dest(air) | N/Erfurt |
| | Lt. J.J. Sadinski | FW-190 dest(air) | N/Erfurt |
| | Lt. G.R. Vanden Heuval | FW-190 dest(air) | N/Erfurt |

**November 6, 1944**

| | | | |
|---|---|---|---|
| 374th: | Lt. W.J. Quinn | Me-262 dest(air) | Bessum |
| | F/O J.R. Voss | Me-262 dam(air) | Rehburg |

**November 8, 1944**

| | | | |
|---|---|---|---|
| 375th: | Lt. A. Maurice | Me-262 dest(air) | W/Meppel |

**November 21, 1944**

| | | | |
|---|---|---|---|
| 374th: | Capt. L.G. LaCroix | FW-190 dest(air) | Jena |

**November 26, 1944**

| | | | |
|---|---|---|---|
| 374th: | Maj. M.F. Glessner | FW-190 dest(air) | Wittingen |
| | Lt. R.E. Chandler | FW-190 dest(air) | Wittingen |
| | Lt. B.R. Hicks | FW-190 dest(air) | Wittingen |
| | Lt. J.G. Vear | FW-190 dest(air) | Wittingen |
| | | FW-190 dam(air) | Wittingen |
| | Lt. J.C. Wilkinson | FW-190 dest(air) | Wittingen |
| | | FW-190 dam(air) | Wittingen |
| | Capt. L.G. LaCroix | FW-190 dam(air) | Wittingen |
| 375th: | Capt. E.E. Neely | (2)FW-190 dest(air) | S/Hanover |
| | | FW-190 dam(air) | NE Brunswick |
| | Lt. P.H. Klees | Me-109 dest(air) | Celle-Gifhorn |
| | | FW-190 dest(air) | Celle-Gifhorn |
| | Lt. R.G. Adams | FW-190 dest(air) | Celle-Gifhorn |
| | Lt. R.J. Farney | FW-190 dest(air) | S/Steinhuder Lake |
| | Lt. W.E. McCoppin | Me-109 dest(air) | NE Brunswick |
| | Lt. W.R. Stevens | FW-190 dest(air) | Celle-Gifhorn |
| | Lt. J.J. Sullivan | Me-109 dest(air) | Celle-Gifhorn |
| | Lt. L.C. Travis | FW-190 dest(air) | NE Misburg |
| | Lt. L.A. Wood | FW-190 dest(air) | S/Steinhuder Lake |
| | Lt. H.A. Spaulding | (2)FW-190 dam(air) | Celle-Gifhorn |
| | Lt. W.B. Farnum | FW-190 dam(air) | NE Steinhuder L. |
| 376th: | Capt. W.R. Beyer | Me-109 dest(air) | S/Ulzen |
| | | FW-190 dest(air) | S/Ulzen |
| | Lt. G.R. Vanden Heuval | (2)FW-190 dest(air) | S/Ulzen |
| | Lt. D.R. Ford | FW-190 dest(air) | S/Ulzen |
| | Lt. C.W. Hanley | FW-190 dest(air) | S/Ulzen |
| | Lt. K.J. Scott | FW-190 prob(air) | S/Ulzen |
| | | FW-190 dam(air) | S/Ulzen |
| | Lt. W.J. Kozicki | FW-190 prob(air) | S/Ulzen |
| | Lt. L.P. Chadwick | FW-190 prob(air) | S/Ulzen |

| **November 27, 1944** | | | |
|---|---|---|---|
| 374th: | Lt. S.M. Popy | Me-109 dest(air) | Dummer Lake |
| | Lt. E.L. Wilsey | Me-109 dest(air) | Dummer Lake |
| 375th: | Maj. C.N. Keppler | Me-109 dam(air) | Dummer Lake |
| | Lt. R.G. Adams | Me-109 dam(air) | N/Munster |
| 376th: | Lt. W.J. Sykes | Me-109 dest(air) | S/Munster |
| | | Me-109 prob(air) | S/Munster |
| | | (2)Me-410 dest(grd) | Munster |
| | | Me-110 dest(grd) | Munster |
| | Lt. K.J. Scott | Me-109 dest(air) | S/Munster |
| | Lt. R.W. Ward | Me-109 dest(air) | W/Munster |

| **December 2, 1944** | | | |
|---|---|---|---|
| 374th: | Capt. J.R. Mau | (2)FW-190 dest(air) | Meinsenheim |
| | Lt. E.W. Keplinger | FW-190 dam(air) | Meinsenheim |
| 376th: | Lt. H.D. Mitchell | FW-190 dest(air) | Bingen |

| **December 23, 1944** | | | |
|---|---|---|---|
| 375th: | Lt. C.J. Layton | (2)FW-190 dest(air) | SE Bonn |
| | Lt. W.H. Street | Me-109 dest(air) | SE Bonn |

| **December 24, 1944** | | | |
|---|---|---|---|
| 376th: | Lt. W.J. Sykes | Me-109 dest(air) | Wengerohr |
| | | Me-109 prob(air) | Wengerohr |
| | Lt. J.B. Bricker | Me-109 dest(air) | Wengerohr |
| | Lt. C.E. Sullivan | Me-109 dest(air) | Wengerohr |
| | Lt. G.R. Vanden Heuval | Me-109 dest(air) | Wengerohr |

| **December 26, 1944** | | | |
|---|---|---|---|
| 376th: | Lt. G.R. Vanden Heuval | (1.5)FW 190 dest(air) | Merzig |
| | Lt. C.P. Chennault | FW-190 dest(air) | Merzig |
| | Lt. B.L. Dennehy | FW-190 dest(air) | Merzig |
| | Lt. H.G. Powell | FW-190 dest(air) | N/Merzig |
| | Lt. D.P. Overholt | FW-190 dest(air) | NW Merzig |
| | Capt. J.W. Ruch | (.5)FW-190 dest(air) | Merzig |

| **January 2, 1945** | | | |
|---|---|---|---|
| 375th: | Lt. R.J. Farney | Me-109 dest(air) | W/Stuttgart |
| | Lt. D.L. Farrar | Me-109 dest(air) | W/Stuttgart |
| | Lt. W.H. Street | Me-109 dest(air) | W/Stuttgart |
| | Lt. J.J. Sullivan | Me-109 dest(air) | W/Stuttgart |
| | Lt. A. Maurice | (.5)Me-109 dest(air) | W/Stuttgart |
| | Lt. G.R. Stockmeier | (.5)Me-109 dest(air) | W/Stuttgart |

| **January 25, 1945** | | | |
|---|---|---|---|
| 375th: | Lt. R.J. Farney | Me-109 dest(air) | SE Speyer |
| | Lt. P.A. Dougherty | (.5)Me-110 dest(air) | NE Mannheim |
| | F/O W.M. Hart | (.5)Me-110 dest(air) | NE Mannheim |

| **February 8, 1945** | | | |
|---|---|---|---|
| 376th: | Lt. R. Hobbs | (.5)He-111 dest(air) | Erfurt |
| | Lt. R.W. Ward | (.5)He-111 dest(air) | Erfurt |

| **March 9, 1945** | | | |
|---|---|---|---|
| 375th: | Capt. A. Maurice | FW-190 dest(air) | W/Giessen |

| **March 21, 1945** | | | |
|---|---|---|---|
| 375th: | Lt. R.D. Anderson | Me-262 dest(air) | Belzig |
| 376th: | Lt. H.M. Chapman | Me-262 dest(air) | Dresden |

| **March 30, 1945** | | | |
|---|---|---|---|
| 376th: | Lt. K.J. Scott | Me-262 dest(air) | W/Rendsburg |

| **March 31, 1945** | | | |
|---|---|---|---|
| 374th: | Lt. B.R. Hicks | FW-190 dest(air) | N/Frankfurt |
| | Lt. T.J. Moore | FW-190 dest(air) | N/Frankfurt |
| 375th: | Lt. G.R. Stockmeier | Me-262 dam(air) | Brunswick |
| | Lt. E.E. Tinkham | Me-262 dam(air) | Brunswick |

| **April 4, 1945** | | | |
|---|---|---|---|
| 374th: | Lt. H.S. Dixon | Me-262 dam(air) | W/Berlin |
| | Lt. L.J. Jewell | Me-262 dam(air) | W/Berlin |
| 375th: | Lt. L.F. Gendron | (4)Me-262 dam(air) | S/Hamburg |
| | Lt. W.H. Street | (2)Me-262 dam(air) | S/Hamburg |
| | Lt. H.A. Euler | Me-262 dam(air) | S/Hamburg |
| | Lt. R.J. Farney | Me-262 dam(air) | S/Hamburg |

| **April 9, 1945** | | | |
|---|---|---|---|
| 374th: | Lt. J.T. Sloan | Me-262 dest(air) | W/Berlin |
| | | Me-262 dam(air) | W/Berlin |

| **April 16, 1945** | | | |
|---|---|---|---|
| HdQts: | LtCol. R.B. Caviness | Me-109 dest(grd) | Halndorf |
| 376th: | Lt. G.R. Vanden Heuval | (2)FW-190 dest(grd) | Reichersberg |
| | | Me-410 dest(grd) | Kirchem |
| | | Ju-52 dam(grd) | Reichersberg |
| | Lt. H.G. Spencer | (3)Ju-52 dest(grd) | Reichersberg |
| | Lt. L.P. Chadwick | (3)Ju-52 dest(grd) | Reichersberg |
| | Lt. H.M. Chapman | (2)u/i a/c dest(grd) | Reichersberg |
| | Maj. W.W. Patton | Me-109 dest(grd) | Halndorf |
| | | Me-109 dam(grd) | Halndorf |
| | | u/i a/c dam(grd) | Halndorf |
| | Lt. V.C. Eisenhut | FW-190 dest(grd) | Reichersberg |
| | | Fi-156 dam(grd) | Halndorf |
| | Lt. A.J. Chalmers | FW-190 dest(grd) | Reichersberg |
| | Lt. M.C. Kelly | Fi-156 dest(grd) | Reichersberg |
| | Lt. D.W. Jones | u/i a/c dest(grd) | Reichersberg |
| | Lt. D. Grounds | Ju-52 dam(grd) | Reichersberg |

| **April 17, 1945** | | | |
|---|---|---|---|
| 375th: | Lt. W.R. Stevens | Ju-188 dest(grd) | Eger A/F |
| | Lt. S.C. Kovach | (2)u/i a/c dam(grd) | Pilzen |
| | | Ju-52 dam(grd) | Pilzen |
| | Lt. P.A. Dougherty | u/i a/c dam(grd) | Eger A/F |
| | F/O A.L. Segert | Ju-52 dam(grd) | Eger A/F |
| 376th: | Maj. W.W. Patton | (2)FW-190 dest(grd) | Pilzen |
| | LtCol. R. Freedman | u/i a/c dest(grd) | Pilzen |
| | Lt. A.J. Chalmers | FW-190 dest(grd) | Pilzen |
| | Lt. M.C. Kelly | u/i a/c dest(grd) | Pilzen |
| | Lt. H.M. Chapman | (2)FW-190 dam(grd) | Pilzen |

### 361st Fighter Group Losses

**January 29, 1944**
Lt. Charles B. Screws (374th) MIA-E; Damaged by flak and bailed out off Dunkirk.
P-47D B7- 42-75417

**January 30, 1944**
Lt. Ethelbert F. Amason (374th) KIA; Downed by enemy fighters near Rijssen.
P-47D B7- 42-75567

**February 21, 1944**
Lt. Floyd M. Stegall (375th) MIA-E; Suffered mechanical failure and bailed out near Edam.
P-47D E2- 42-22769

**February 22, 1944**
Lt. Danny B. Nazzarette (376th) KIA; Downed by a FW-190 near Rosemeer.
P-47D E9- 42-75814

**February 24, 1944**
Lt. Dennis B. Weaver (376th) KIA; Hit by fire from an E-boat and crashed east of Southend.
P-47D E9- 42-75401

**March 5, 1944**
Lt. Glenn T. Berge (374th) KIA; Crashed on take-off from Bottisham due to run-away prop.
P-47D B7- 42-75152

**March 22, 1944**
Lt. James A. Rogers (375th) KIA; Hit by flak and ditched 35 miles off Southend.
P-47D E2- 42-8512

**April 8, 1944**
Lt. Albert C. Duncan (375th) KIA; Hit by enemy fighters near Lembauch.
P-47D E2- 42-75424

**April 15, 1944**
Lt. John M. Bentley (376th) POW; Collided with a P-47 near Rhenen.
P-47D E9- 42-22756

**April 18, 1944**
Lt. Scott L. Naedle (HdQts) POW; Hit by flak at Zwischenahn Airfield.
P-47D E2- 42-75122

**April 22, 1944**
Lt. James M. Norman, Jr. (374th) KIA; Hit by flak and crashed off Zeebruggee Mole.
P-47D B7- 42-75521

**April 27, 1944**
Capt. Charles H. Feller (375th) KIA; Hit by flak northwest of Etampes.
P-47D E2-Q 42-75447
Lt. Jack D. Cornett (375th) MIA-E; Hit by flak southeast of Etampes/Montdidier Airfield.
P-47D E2- 42-75219

**May 8, 1944**
Lt. William A. Rautenbush (375th) KIA; Hit by enemy fighters near Brucchausen.
P-47D E2-Y 42-75555
Lt. Collier W. Todd, Jr. (375th) KIA; Hit the ground while flying low near Lohne.
P-47D E2-J 42-75249

**May 16, 1944**
Lt. Eugene W. Kinnaird (375th) KIAc; Crashed near Water Beach.
P-51B E2-X 43-24790

**May 19, 1944**
Lt. Dennis P. Noble (376th) ASR; Suffered mechanical failure and bailed out over the Channel.
P-51B E9-

**May 21, 1944**
Capt. John W. Guckeyson (375th) KIA; Hit by flak south of Stendal.
P-51C E2-W 42-103349 "Contrary Mary"
F/O Cornelius G. Hogelin (375th) KIA; Hit by flak and bailed out off Noordwal.
P-51B E2-B 43-24783

**May 23, 1944**
Lt. Joseph D. Kelly (376th) POW; Hit by flak near Hulsthout, he bailed out east of Lierre.
P-51B E9-L 42-106739

**May 24, 1944**
Lt. Stanley D. Rames (375th) POW; Suffered mechanical trouble near Alts Landberg.
P-51B E2-W 42-106792
Lt. Warren D. Wherry (375th) KIA; Hit by enemy fighters near Alt Lewin.
P-51B E2-B 42-106912
Lt. Morris C. Williams (376th) POW; Hit by enemy aircraft near Alstaette.
P-51B E9-X 42-106660

**May 29, 1944**
Lt. Abe P. Rosenberger (375th) ASR; Suffered mechanical failure and bailed out over the Channel.
P-51B E2-

**June 4, 1944**
Lt. Walter J. Kozicki (376th) MIA-E; Hit by a Me-109 and bailed out northeast of Melun.
P-51B E9-K 43-6498

**June 6, 1944**
Lt. James R. Golden (374th) POW; Oil line broke and bailed out near Forges.
P-51B B7-A 43-6977
Lt. Lawrence B. Perry (375th) KIA; Hit by flak near Dreux.
P-51C E2-A 42-103347
Lt. William D. Willit (376th) POW; Hit by flak near Mondenbleau.
P-51B E9-G 42-106651

**June 7, 1944**
Maj. George L. Merritt, Jr. (375th) KIA; Hit a pole while strafing near Roiffe.
P-51B E2-N 42-106835

**June 8, 1944**
Lt. James D. Hastin (374th) POW; Damaged by a bomb blast near Anet.
P-51B B7- 43-6982

**June 10, 1944**
Capt. Wallace B. Frank (376th) POW; Hit by flak near Gace.
P-51B E9-F 43-24759

**June 19, 1944**
Capt. Joseph L. Latimer (374th) KIA; Lost in bad weather near Vire.
P-51B B7- 42-106735
Lt. David L. Callaway (374th) KIA; Lost in bad weather near Vire.
P-51B B7-C 42-106713
Lt. Lawrence E. Downey (374th) KIA; Lost in bad weather near Vire.
P-51B B7-D 43-24830
Lt. Merrill E. Roberts (374th) MIA-E; Lost in bad weather near Vire
P-51B B7- 43-24785
Lt. Walter H. Sargent (374th) KIA; Lost in bad weather near Vire.
P-51B B7-B 42-106871
Lt. Robert J. Stolzy (374th) KIA; Lost in bad weather near Vire.
P-51C B7- 42-103724

**June 20, 1944**
Lt. Miles E. Elliott (375th) KIA; Hit by flak and bailed out southwest of Ribnitz.
P-51B E2- 42-106861

**June 23, 1944**
F/O George T. Davis (374th) POW; Damaged by a train exploding near Troyes.
P-51B B7- 43-24835

**July 1, 1944**
Lt. John T. Thomas (375th) ASR; Suffered mechanical failure and bailed out over the Channel.
P-51B E2-M 42-106880

**July 5, 1944**
Capt. Shelby J. Harris (374th) POW; Hit by flak south of Beauvais.
P-51D B7-H 44-13333
Lt. John R. Bernert (374th) KIA; Hit by enemy fighters near Amiens.
P-51D B7- 44-13538

**July 9, 1944**
Lt. Leroy H. Sypher (375th) POW; Hit by flak near Louviers.
P-51D E2- 44-13576

**July 21, 1944**
Lt. Warren L. Ewert (375th) POW; Hit by flak near Biblis and bellied-in southwest of Darmstadt.
P-51B E2-P 43-24768

**July 25, 1944**
Lt. Robert O. Comstock (376th) POW; Took off late and last seen trying to catch up with the group.
P-51D E9- 44-13566

**July 31, 1944**
Lt. William V. Staples (374th) KIA; Died in a crash near Cowlinge.
P-51B B7-G 43-24840

**August 4, 1944**
Lt. Pernin G. Potts (374th) POW; Suffered mechanical failure and bailed out near Heligoland.
P-51B B7-M 42-106820
Lt. Joseph V. Kapr (375th) KIA; Hit by flak and bailed out northeast of Stralsund.
P-51B E2-R 42-106741
Capt. Sam C. Wilkerson, Jr. (376th) POW; Hit by flak and bailed out southeast of Griefswald.
P-51D E9-O 44-13673

**August 8, 1944**
Lt. Jacob L. Rawls (374th) POW; Hit by flak near Dreux.
P-51B B7-X 42-106586

**August 9, 1944**
Lt. Donald D. Dellinger (375th) KIAc; Died in a crash 60 miles from Bottisham.
P-51D E2-S 44-13926

**August 12, 1944**
Col. Thomas J.J. Christian, Jr. (HdQts) KIA; Hit by flak nearArras.
P-51D E2-C 44-13410 "Lou IV"
Lt. Clarence E. Zieske (374th) KIA; Hit by flak near Dernancourt.
P-51B B7-A 42-106942
Lt. John E. Engstrom (375th) MIA-E; Hit by flak near Salmagne.
P-51B E2-G 42-106778
Lt. Merle C. Rainey (375th) POW; Hit by flak near Tournai.
P-51B E2-C 42-106787

**August 13, 1944**
Lt. Robert H. Magnuson (374th) POW; Lost northeast of Orleans.
P-51B B7-E 42-106839 "Bald Eagle"
Lt. Loren L. Montgomery (374th) POW; Hit by flak near Orleans.
P-51D B7-O 44-13857

**August 18, 1944**
Lt. Milton A. Dahl (376th) KIA; Collided with a 78th Ftr Grp P-47 near Bottisham.
P-51B E9-A 42-106759

**August 26, 1944**
Lt. Sherman Armsby (375th) KIA; Downed by a ground explosion near Longoyon.
P-51B E2-I 43-24761 "Jacquline"
Lt. Jack S. Crandell (375th) KIA; Hit by flak near Konach.
P-51B E2-K 42-106917 "Nita-Bottom's Up"

**August 29, 1944**
Lt. Henry G. Bosyk (374th) KIAc;
P-51B B7-

**September 11, 1944**
Lt. John H. Lougheed (375th) KIA; Collided with a B-24 near Eerde.
P-51C E2-X 42-103749 "Betty Lou"

**September 12, 1944**
Lt. Robert E. Geck (375th) KIA; Hit by enemy fighters near Ondrup.
P-51B E2-S 42-106677

**September 13, 1944**
Lt. Edward J. Marevka (375th) POW; Hit by flak north of Goppingen and bailed out near Altenhausen.
P-51B E2-M 42-106944

**September 17, 1944**
Lt. Woodrow W. Glover (376th) KIA; Hit by a Me-109 near Geldern.
P-51B E9-A 42-106944 "Mary Jane"

**September 18, 1944**
Lt. Clyde A. Arrants (374th) KIA; Hit by flak near Vioel.
P-51D B7-G 44-13949

**September 19, 1944**
Lt. Robert C. Clement (376th) KIA; Crashed 3 miles east of Newmarket while trying to land.
P-51D E9-J 44-13872

**September 26, 1944**
Lt. Daniel F. Knupp (375th) KIA; Hit by flak near Havenhorst.
P-51B E2- 42-106738

**September 27, 1944**
Lt. Leo H. Lamb (376th) KIA; Collided with a FW-190 near Eisenach.
P-51B E9-W 42-106627

**September 28, 1944**
Lt. John R. Ryan (375th) POW; Hit by flak near Belgershain.
P-51B E2-L 43-24774 "Slick Chick"

**October 3, 1944**
Lt. Charles C. McKivett (374th) KIAc; Crashed after take-off on a practice mission
P-51 B7-

**October 6, 1944**
Capt. Thomas F. Brubaker (375th) POW; Collided with a Me-109 north of Berlin.
P-51D E2-A 44-14132
Lt. David R. Morgan (375th) POW; Suffered mechanical trouble near Erringen.
P-51D E2- 44-14516

**October 7, 1944**
Lt. Robert K. McCandliss (375th) POW; Hit by flak near Wettringen.
P-51B E2-H 42-106830 "Ted's Reply"

**October 14, 1944**
F/O Walter F. Chapin, Jr. (376th) KIAc; Died in a collision over England on a practice hop.
P-51B E9-E 42-106802 "Blue Eyes"

**October 15, 1944**
Maj. James B. Cheney (376th) POW; Suffered mechanical failure near Dorsten.
P-51D E9-H 44-14219 "Scat Cat"

**October 30, 1944**
Lt. Francis Christensen (374th) KIA; Hit by flak near Tarnewitz.
P-51C B7-L 43-25032

**November 1, 1944**
Lt. James A. Eason (375th) KIA; Killed in a crash at Beechamwell upon return from the mission.
P-51B E2- 42-106688

**November 2, 1944**
Lt. Charles E. Moore (375th) KIA; Hit by enemy planes near Naumberg.
P-51B E2-M 42-106900
Lt. Charles W. Narvis (375th) KIA; Suffered mechanical trouble near Roedgen.
P-51D E2-G 44-14226 "Babe Schomarrech"

**November 9, 1944**
Capt. Richard M. Durbin (HdQts) KIA; Crashed while landing at Little Walden.
P-51D B7-H 44-13704

**November 14, 1944**
Lt. John J. Sadinski (376th) KIAc; Died when the C-78 he was flying crashed into a mountain in thick fog.

**November 16, 1944**
Lt. Alfred B. Cook (374th) KIA; Killed in a crash near Baldock.
P-51D B7-R 44-13357

**December 5, 1944**
Lt. Denver J. Wood (374th) POW; Suffered mechanical failure near Leiden.
P-51B B7-V 42-106695

**December 23, 1944**
Lt. Caleb J. Layton (375th) KIA; Hit by enemy fighters near Bonn.
P-51D E2-E 44-14064 "Suzy Anne"

**December 24, 1944**
Lt. William J. Sykes (376th) POW; Hit by a Me-109 near Wengerohr.
P-51D E9-F 44-11203 "Hiya Honey"

**January 4, 1945**
Lt. John R. Wilson (374th) KIAc
P-51
Lt. Robert M. Zelinsky (374th) KIAc
P-51

**January 22, 1945**
Capt. Alton B. Snyder (375th) POW; Hit by flak and bellied-in near Kenn.
P-51D E2-S 44-14803 "Snitz"

**January 25, 1945**
Lt. Robert G. Adams (375th) KIA; Hit by a Me-110 northeast of Mannheim and bailed out too low near Heppenheim.
P-51D E2-V 44-14678 "Pat"

**February 14, 1945**
Lt. Thomas A. Kneifel (375th) POW; Ran out of fuel near Berkum.
P-51D E2- 44-14609 "Vixen"

**February 22, 1945**
Lt. Richard E. Chandler (374th) POW; Hit by flak near Gross Almerode.
P-51D B7- 44-13340

**March 14, 1945**
Capt. Eugene Cole (375th) POW; Hit by flak and bellied-in east of Rossbach.
P-51D E2-G 44-14792 "Margene"

**March 18, 1945**
Lt. Norman E. Jentz (375th) POW; Hit by flak over Germany.
P-51D E2-A 44-14908 "Wisconsin Witch"

**March 24, 1945**
Capt. Russell D. Wade (375th) KIA; Hit by flak near Iserlehn.
P-51D E2-T 44-14149 "Talley's Hoosier Hobo"

**March 31, 1945**
F/O Deane E. Jackson (374th) KIA; Lost for unknown reasons.
P-51D B7- 44-15657

**April 16, 1945**
Lt. Delmar R. Ford (376th) POW; Hit by flak at Pocking.
P-51D E9-S 44-15663
Lt. Russell E. Kenoyer (376th) KIA; Hit by flak at Pocking.
P-51D E9-L 44-13894

**April 17, 1945**
Lt. Joseph B. Wolfe (375th) KIA; Hit by flak at Eger Airfield.
P-51D E2-L 44-14411

**July 23, 1945**
Lt. J. Warren Geron (375th) KIAc; Hit compessibility and crashed near Mitchell's Farm.
P-51D E2-M 44-15038 "Tony"
Lt. John E. Havey (375th) KIAc; Hit compressibility and crashed near Ravenstock Green Farm.
P-51D E2-I 44-14556 "Libby"

**August 5, 1945**
Lt. Curtis Harris (376th) KIAc; Crashed on take-off from Little Walden.
P-51D E9-

**Headquarters**
Casto, Dayton C., Jr., Maj.; July 1944-November 1944; ex-375th Ftr Sqn
Caviness, Roy B., LtCol.; September 1944-October 1944; to 376th Ftr Sqn; ex-376th Ftr Sqn November 1944-EOW
Christian, Thomas J.J., Jr., Col.; February 1943-August 12, 1944(KIA); ex-347th Ftr Grp, PTO
P-47D E2-C 42-75494 "Lou"
P-51B E2-C "Lou II"
P-51B E2-C "Lou III"
P-51D E2-C 44-13410 "Lou IV"
Dennison, Junius W., Col.; December 1944-April 1945
P-51D E2-D 44-15597
Durbin, Richard M., Capt.; October 1944-November 9, 1944(KIA); ex-376th Ftr Sqn
Fallows, Ronald F., Col.; August 1944-September 1944
Freedman, Roswell, Capt.; June 1943-August 1943; to 376th Ftr Sqn
Glessner, Milton F., Maj.; December 1944-January 1945; to 375th Ftr Sqn; ex-376th Ftr Sqn
Hopkins, Wallace E., LtCol.; Spring 1943-September 1944; December 1944-May 1945 (non flying duty)
76 missions
P-47D B7-H
P-51B B7-H 42-106655 "Ferocious Frankie"
P-51D B7-H 44-13704 "Ferocious Frankie"
Hulse, Robert F., Lt.; February 1944-April 1944; to 375th Ftr Sqn; ex-375th Ftr Sqn
Kruzel, Joseph J., LtCol.; March 1943-November 1944; ex-17th Pur Sqn & 49th Ftr Grp, PTO
325 hours (plus 175 hours PTO)
P-47D E9-K 42-25286 "Vi"
P-51B E9-K 43-6498 "Vi"
P-51D E9-K 44-13391 "Vi"
P-51D E9-K 44-14406 "Vi"
Moore, Marvin T., Lt.; November 1944-
Naedle, Scott L., Lt.; May 1943-April 18, 1944(POW)
P-47D E2- 42-75122
O'Dwyer, Thomas, Maj.; -EOW; ex-453rd Bomb Group pilot
75 hours
Petrone, Vic G., Capt.; April 1945-EOW; ex-376th Ftr Sqn
Rosenberger, Abe P., Lt.; April 1944-July 1944; to 375th Ftr Sqn; ex-375th Ftr Sqn
Todd, James M., Maj.; June 1943-October 1944

**374th Fighter Squadron**
Adkins, Jesse O., Lt.; April 1944-November 1944
Amason, Ethelbert F., Lt.; June 1943-January 30, 1944(KIA)
Arrants, Clyde A., Lt.; August 1944-September 18, 1944(KIA)
Aschbrenner, Glenn F., Lt.; August 1944-March 1945
Bacigalup, Hector L., Lt.; August 1944-July 1945
Berge, Glenn T., Lt.; May 1943-March 5, 1944(KIA)
Bergmann, Charles H., Maj.; May 1943-July 1945
P-47D B7-B
P-51B B7-B 42-106871
Bernert, John R., Lt.; States-July 5, 1944(KIA)
Bosyk, Harry G., Lt.; August 1944-August 29, 1944(KIAc)
Brown, Wentworth C., F/O; February 1945-EOW
Bryant, Madison L., Jr., Lt.; April 1944-September 1944
Callaway, David L., Lt.; States-June 19, 1944(KIA)
P-47D B7-C
P-51B B7-C 42-106713
Cearley, John, Jr., Capt.; August 1944-April 1945
P-51D B7-G "Galloping Goose"
Chandler, Richard E., Lt.; September 1944-February 22, 1945(POW)
P-51D B7- 44-14714 "Sweet Adeline"
Christensen, Francis, Lt.; September 1944-October 30, 1944(KIA)
Colet, Frank H., Lt.; @September 1944-July 1945
Collins, Preston B., Lt.; February 1944-October 1944
Cook, Alfred B., Lt.; August 1944-November 1944
Davis, Arnold E., Capt.; July 1944-February 1945
Davis, George T., F/O; June 1944-June 23, 1944(POW)
Dixon, Herbert S., Lt.; August 1944-EOW
P-51D B7-W 44-14305 "Effie Mae II"

Douglas, Robert E., Maj.; April 1945-July 1945
Downey, Lawrence E., Lt.; June 1943-June 19, 1944(KIA)
    P-47D B7-D
    P-51B B7-D 43-24830
Doyle, Kenneth E., F/O; February 1945-EOW
Dunn, Dale E., Lt.; August 1944-April 1945
Eckfeldt, Robert T., Lt.; States-August 1944
    P-47D B7-E 42-75522 "Bald Eagle"
    P-51B B7-E 42-106811 "Bald Eagle II
    P-51B B7-E 42-106839"Bald Eagle III
Fielding, Glenn L., Capt.; February 1944-September 1944
    300 hours
Furbush, Allen E., F/O; February 1945-EOW
Garces, John R., Lt.; November 1944-EOW
    P-51D B7-Z 44-13676 "Kay's Kite"
Garrison, Robert M., F/O February 1945-EOW
Glessner, Milton F., Maj.; September 1944-December 1944; to HdQts; later 375th Ftr Sqn
Golden, James R., Lt.; January 1944-June 6, 1944(POW)
Harris, Shelby J., Capt.; May 1943-July 5, 1944(POW)
Hastin, James D., Lt.; States-June 8, 1944(POW)
    P-47D B7- "Bette of Brooklyn"
Hedges, Walter N., Lt.; October 1944-July 1945
Hicks, Barry R., Lt.; July 1944-EOW
    P-51D B7-H 44-15323
Hill, Alva L., Lt.; November 1944-July 1945
Holbrook, John F., F/O; April 1945-EOW
Holter, Paul C., Jr., Lt.; February 1944-September 1944
Houlette, Robert R., F/O; February 1945-EOW
Jackson, Deane E., Lt.; February 1945-March 31, 1945(KIA)
Jewell, Lyle J., Lt.; November 1944-EOW
    P-51D B7-I 44-14139 "Rusty"
Johnson, Marion D., F/O; February 1945-EOW
Joss, Jack M., Lt.; November 1944-July 1945
    P-51D B7-Q 44-14957 "Darlin Dora"
Kelinske, Felix, Lt.; November 1944-July 1945
Keplinger, Eugene W., Capt.; July 1944-February 1945
Knickman, Edward T., Lt.; August 1944-July 1945
Kolesnikovich, John J., Lt.; November 1944-EOW
Lacy, Roy P., Jr., Capt.; June 1943-September 1944
    P-47D B7-G 42-75441
    P-51B B7-G 43-24840
LaCroix, Lucius G., Capt.; August 1944-April 1945; ex-49th Ftr Grp, PTO
    P-51D B7-V 44-13676
    P-51D B7-V 44-15275
Larenzo, Leroy N., Lt.; April 1945-EOW
Latimer, Joseph L., Capt.; May 1943-June 19, 1944(KIA)
Lederer, Henry B., Capt.; States-August 1944
    P-47D B7-I "Duchess of Manhattan"
    P-51D B7-I 44-13708 "Duchess of Manhattan"
Lee, Bill E., Lt.; April 1945-EOW
Lee, Jack R., F/O; April 1945-EOW
Letimer, Douglas H., Lt.; August 1944-April 1945
Lichter, George, Capt.; States-November 1944
    P-51C B7-V 42-103362
Lind, Lt.; May 1943-September 25, 1943(KIAc)
Locke, Richard E., Maj.; June 1943-September 1944
Maclay, Alfred B., Lt.; August 1944-EOW
Magnuson, Robert H., Lt.; July 1944-August 13, 1944(POW)
Matthews, Ralph E., Lt.; April 1945-July 1945
Mau, Jerome R., Capt.; June 1944-January 1945
Mayeux, Collins J., Lt.; August 1944-July 1945
McKenna, James P., F/O; February 1945-EOW
McKivett, Charles C., Lt.; September 1944-October 3, 1944(KIAc)
Merritt, George L., Jr., Maj.; May 1943-August 1943; to 375th Ftr Sqn
Merritt, Joseph P., Lt.; November 1944-July 1945
Millard, Lt.; May 1943-September 25, 1943(KIAc)
Mitenbuler, Jack C., Capt.; July 1944-March 1945
    P-51D B7-M 44-15606 "Virginia Ann"
Montgomery, Loren L., Lt.; July 1944-August 13, 1944(POW)
Moore, Thomas L., Lt.; June 1944-EOW
    P-51B B7-E 42-106839
    P-51D B7-E 44-15065 "Elusive Eileen"
Moore, Wayne L., Capt.; May 1943-November 1944
    P-47D B7-B "Fascinating Fanny"
Murdy, Edward B., Capt.; States-September 1944
    P-47D B7-M
    P-51B B7-M 42-106820
Norman, James M., Jr., Lt.; States-April 22, 1944(KIA)
Olmstead, John J., Lt.; April 1945-EOW
Onisko, Raymond P., Capt.; September 1944-May 1945; to HdQts
Patton, William W., Maj.; September 1944-April 1945; to 376th Ftr Sqn; ex-376th Ftr Sqn
Petty, James R., F/O; February 1945-EOW
Popy, Stephen M., Lt.; August 1944-EOW
Porter, Ernest J., Capt.; April 1945-EOW
Potts, Pernin G., Lt.; July 1944-August 4, 1944(POW)
Quinn, William J., Capt.; July 1944-April 1945
Rawls, Jacob L., Lt.; July 1944-August 8, 1944(POW)
Rew, George R., LtCol.; May 1943-February 1945
    P-47D B7-R "Scarlet Kate"
    P-51B B7-R 42-106721 "Scarlet Kate"
    P-51B B7-R 42-106763 "Scarlet Kate"
Richards, Vernon R., Lt.; June 1943-September 1944
    79 missions, 280 hours
    P-47D B7-R 42-75452 "Tika"
    P-51D B7-R 44-13357 "Tika IV"
Rizzio, Ernest V., Lt.; September 1944-EOW
    P-51D B7-R 44-15358 "Lil Mil"
Roberts, Merrill E., Lt.; June 1943-June 19, 1944(MIA-E)
Robinson, James J., Lt.; States-September 1944
Sargent, Walter H., Lt.; April 1944-June 19, 1944(KIA)
Schiedly, Howard L., Lt.; March 1945-EOW
Screws, Charles B., Lt.; June 1943-January 29, 1944(MIA-E)
Sedman, Robert E., Maj.; States-September 1944
    P-47D B7-S
    P-51B B7-S 42-106817
Skinner, Harold O., Lt.; March 1944-September 1944
    78 missions, 271 hours
Sloan, James T., Lt.; March 1945-EOW
Smith, Glenn E., Lt.; April 1945-EOW
Staples, William V., Lt.; June 1944-July 31, 1944(KIA)
Stolzy, Robert J., Lt.; States-June 19, 1944(KIA)
Szablewski, Steve, Lt.; @May 1944-September 1944
Vandiver, Loy C., Lt.; States-September 1944
Vear, Judd G., Lt.; August 1944-April 1945
    P-51B B7-V 42-106695
Voss, John R., Lt.; August 1944-April 1945
Washburn, Edward P., Lt.; March 1945-EOW
Webb, Roy A., Jr., LtCol.; February 1943-July 1944
    300 hours
    P-47D B7-W 42-76144 "Sweet Thing"
    P-47D B7-W 42-75512 "Sweet Thing II
    P-51B B7-W 43-24819 "Sweet Thing III"
    P-51D B7-W 44-13537 "Sweet Thing IV
Weldusky, Merne L., Lt.; November 1944-July 1945
Wilkinson, John C., Capt.; July 1944-May 1945
    P-51B B7-N "Pretty One"
    P-51D B7-N 44-11164 "Pretty One II"
    P-51D B7-N 44-15565 "Pretty One III
Wilsey, Edward L., Capt.; States-December 1944
    P-47D B7- "Ruthie Bev"
Wilson, John R., Lt.; June 1944-January 4, 1945(KIAc)
Wood, Denver J., Lt.; July 1944-December 5, 1944(POW)
Wood, Jefferson K., Lt.; States-August 1944
Zelinsky, Robert M., Lt.; December 1944-January 4, 1945(KIAc)
Zieske, Clarence E., Lt.; July 1944-August 12, 1944(KIA)
    8 missions, 39 hours

**375th Fighter Squadron**

Adams, Robert G., Lt.; July 1944-January 25, 1945(KIA)
Allison, Glenn G., Lt.; States-September 2, 1943(KIAc)
Anderson, Richard D., Capt.; November 1944-EOW
Armsby, Sherman, Lt.; April 1944-August 26, 1944(KIA)
    P-51B E2-Y 42-106588
Auth, Herman R., Lt.; October 1944-July 1945
Beder, Seymour J., Lt.; July 1944-March 1945
Bell, Murray C., Lt.; January 1944-September 1944
Brittingham, Buford E., F/O; February 1945-EOW
Brocklehurst, James A., F/O; February 1945-March 1945; to 352nd Ftr Grp
Brubaker, Thomas F., Capt.; States-October 6, 1944(POW)
Carlson, Carl J., Jr., Lt.; September 1944-July 1945
    P-51D E2-A
Casto, Dayton C., Jr., Maj.; September 1943-July 1944; to HdQts
    P-51B E2-C 42-106787 "Maria"
Cockrell, Rayford B., Lt.; October 1944-July 1945
Colburn, Jack A., Lt.; October 1944-EOW
Cole, Charles E., F/O; February 1945-March 1945; to 352nd Ftr Grp
Cole, Eugene, Capt.; States-March 14, 1945(POW)
    P-47D E2-G 42-75560 "Baby Margene"
    P-51B E2-G 42-106778
    P-51D E2-G 44-14792 "Margene"
Cornett, Jack D., Lt.; April 1944-April 27, 1944(MIA-E)
Crandell, Jack S., Lt.; April 1944-August 26, 1944(KIA)
Cummins, Charles R., Maj.; June 1943-October 1944
    P-47D E2- "Geraldine"
Dekle, Thomas A., Jr., Lt.; September 1944-March 1945
Dellinger, Donald D., Lt.; August 1944-August 9, 1944(KIAc)
Dougherty, Paul A., Jr., Lt.; October 1944-EOW
    P-51D E2-N 44-14903 "Dusty"
Drew, Urban L., Lt.; June 1944-November 1944
    73 missions, 319 hours
    P-51D E2-D 44-14164 "Detroit Miss"
Duncan, Albert C., Lt.; States-April 8, 1944(KIA)
Eason, James A., Lt.; July 1944-November 1, 1944(KIA)
Edwards, David V., Lt.; June 1943-September 1944
Elliott, Miles C., Lt.; May 1944-June 20, 1944(KIA)
Engstrom, John E., Lt.; July 1944-August 12, 1944(MIA-E)
    9 missions, 37 hours
Euler, Howard A., Capt.; September 1944-EOW
    P-51D E2-U 44-15725 "Regina"
Ewert, Warren L., Lt.; May 1944-July 21, 1944(POW)
Farney, Robert J., Lt.; October 1944-October 1945
    54 missions
    P-51D E2-V 44-14827 "Croghan Cruiser"

Farnum, Waldo B., Jr., Lt.; October 1944-September 17, 1945(KIAc)
Farrar, Donald L., Capt.; November 1944-EOW
Feller, Charles H., Capt.; May 1943-April 27, 1944(KIA)
Fickes, George W., F/O; States-September 2, 1943(KIAc)
Freedman, Roswell, LtCol.; June 1944-October 1944; to 376th Ftr Sqn
Frum, Rollin W., F/O; February 1945-March 1945; to 352nd Ftr Grp
Geck, Robert E., Lt.; July 1944-September 12, 1944(KIA)
Gendron, Leo F., Lt.; October 1944-EOW
P-51D E2-C 44-14662 "Little Moke"
Geron, J. Warren, Lt.; April 1945-July 23, 1945(KIAc)
Glankler, Francis T., Capt.; January 1944-March 1945
Glessner, Milton F., Jr., Maj.; January 1945-EOW; ex-374th Ftr Sqn & HdQts
P-51D E2-G 44-14085
Guckeyson, John W., Capt.; May 1943-May 21, 1944(KIA)
P-47D E2-W 42-75221
P-51C E2-W 42-103349 "Contrary Mary"
Hall, Lt.; States-June 13, 1943(KIAc)
Hart, Wesley M., Jr., F/O; October 1944-July 1945
Havey, John E., Lt.; October 1944-July 23, 1945(KIAc)
Hofferberth, Gene B., F/O; March 1945-October 1945
Hogelin, Cornelius G., F/O; April 1944-May 21, 1944(KIA)
Hulse, Robert F., Lt.; May 1943-February 1944; to HdQts; April 1944-September 1944
Janus, Bernard V., F/O; March 1945-September 1945
Jentz, Norman E., Lt.; November 1944-March 18, 1945(POW)
Jersey, Vernon D., Lt.; November 1944-July 1945
Johnson, Martin H., Capt.; States-September 1944
75 missions, 268 hours
P-47D E2-H 42-75214
P-51B E2-H 42-106957 "Little Skipper"
P-51D E2-H 44-14103
Johnston, John W., F/O; March 1945-October 1945
3 missions
P-51D E2-Y 44-14460
Jumps, Richard M., Lt.; November 1944-EOW
P-51D E2- "Lassie Come Home"
Kapr, Joseph V., Lt.; July 1944-August 4, 1944(KIA)
Kemp, William T., Lt.; June 1944-February 1945
P-51C E2-X 42-103749 "Betty Lee"
P-51D E2-X 44-14270 "Betty Lee II"
P-51D E2-X 44-15076 "Betty Lee III"
Keppler, Charles N., Maj.; February 1944-EOW; ex-78th Ftr Grp
P-47D E2-L 42-75572 "Isabel"
P-51B E2-L 43-24774
P-51D E2-L 44-14411 "Miss Margie"
P-51D E2-L 44-15366 "Miss Margie"
P-51D E2-L 44-63173 "Miss Margie"
P-51D E2-L 44-72526 "Miss Margie"
Kinnaird, Eugene W., Lt.; States-May 16, 1944(KIAc)
P-47D E2- "The Bruiser"
Kinsman, Granville R., Lt.; November 1944-EOW
Klees, Paul H., Lt.; June 1944-January 1945
P-51D E2-V 44-14827
Kneifel, Thomas A., Lt.; November 1944-February 14, 1945(POW)
Knupp, Daniel F., Lt.; August 1944-September 26, 1944(KIA)
Kovach, Stephen C., Lt.; November 1944-EOW
Lair, Walter C., Lt.; June 1943-@July 1943
Lassberg, Osbert M., Jr., F/O; February 1945-EOW
Layton, Caleb J., Lt.; September 1944-December 23, 1944(KIA)
Lougheed, John H., Lt.; August 1944-September 11, 1944(KIA)
Lundin, Jared C., Lt.; November 1944-EOW
Malloan, Barry E., Maj.; February 1943-August 1943; later to CBI w/23rd Ftr Grp and KIA
Marevka, Edward J., Lt.; July 1944-September 13, 1944(POW)
Marmon, Leon H., Lt.; July 1944-September 1944; to 2nd Scouting Force
Maurice, Anthony, Capt.; August 1944-March 1945
P-51D E2-M 44-15038 "Tony"
McCaffrey, Lt.; States-June 13, 1943(KIAc)
McCandliss, Robert K., Lt.; August 1944-October 7, 1944(POW)
McCopplin, William E., Lt.; July 1944-January 1945
70 missions
Merritt, George L., Jr., Maj.; August 1943-June 7, 1944(KIA)
95 missions
P-47D E2-A 42-75404 "Dr. I.P. Daily
P-51C E2-A 42-103347
Moore, Charles E., Lt.; August 1944-November 2, 1944(KIA)
Moore, Major R., Lt.; June 1944-November 1944
Morehouse, Dean R., Lt.; States-October 1944
P-51B E2-I 43-24761 "Jacqueline"
Morgan, David R., Lt.; May 1944-October 6, 1944(POW)
Mottis, Leonard H., Capt.; August 1944-March 1945
P-51B E2-H "Patsy II"
Murphy, James D., F/O; February 1945-July 1945
Nall, James R., Lt.; May 1943-June 13, 1943(KIAc)
Narvis, Charles W., Lt.; July 1944-November 2, 1944(KIA)
Neely, Elroy D., Capt.; May 1944-January 1945
Perry, Lawrence B., Lt.; States-June 6, 1944(KIA)
Rainey, Merle C., Lt.; States-August 12, 1944(MIA-E)
Rames, Stanley D., Lt.; States-May 24, 1944(POW)
P-47D E2-W 42-75214 "Shiverless"
Rautenbush, William A., Lt.; States-May 8, 1944(KIA)
Rieschel, Robert J., Lt.; June 1943-August 1943
Rogers, James A., Lt.; June 1943-March 22, 1944(KIA)
P-47D E2- "Hayseed Margaret"
Rogers, Will D., Lt.; June 1944-November 1944
P-51D E2-E 44-14064 "Suzy Ann"
Rosenberger, Abe P., Lt.; States-April 1944; to HdQts July 1944-November 1944
P-51B E2-S 42-106677
P-51D E2-S 44-13926
Rowlett, Bruce W., Capt.; States-November 1944
P-51D E2-A 44-13568 "Sky Bouncer"
Ryan, John R., Lt.; @August 1944-September 28, 1944(POW)
Segert, Albert L., F/O; February 1945-EOW
Shackleford, William J., Capt.; June 1943-October 1944
P-47D E2-D 42-8640
P-47D E2-D 42-75096
P-51B E2-D 42-106875 "Queen Jean"
Snyder, Alton B., Jr., Capt.; States-January 22, 1945(POW)
384 hours
P-51D E2-S 44-14803 "Snitz"
Sobieski, Russell J., Lt.; States-October 1944
Soward, Milton E., Lt.; May 1943-States only; later with 365th Ftr Grp, 9th Air Force & KIA April 1944
Spaulding, Howard A., Lt.; May 1944-January 1945
Spicer, George W., F/O; March 1945-EOW
Stegall, Floyd M., F/O; States-February 21, 1944(POW)
Stevens, Walter R., Jr., Capt.; October 1944-July 1945
Stockmeier, Glenn R., Capt.; October 1944-July 1945
P-51D E2-O 44-15314
Street, William H., Lt.; September 1944-EOW
Sullivan, James J., Capt.; October 1944-July 1945
Sypher, Leroy H., Lt.; States-July 9, 1944(POW)
P-47D E2- "P For Pearl"
Thomas, John T., Lt.; April 1944-November 1944
Tinkham, Edwin E., Capt.; September 1944-July 1945
P-51D E2-Q 44-64111 "Second Love"
Todd, Collier W., Jr., Lt.; April 1944-May 8, 1944(KIA)
Travis, Lee C., Capt.; August 1944-April 1945
Wade, Russell D., Capt.; September 1944-March 24, 1945(KIA)
P-51D E2-T 44-13568 "Tally's Hoosier Hobo"
Wagner, George W., Lt.; States-September 1944
Walker, Horace N., F/O; March 1945-July 1945; ex-352nd Ftr Grp
Walters, Jesse W., F/O; March 1945-September 1945
Wherry, Warren D., Lt.; April 1944-May 24, 1944(KIA)
Wilcox, Paul E., F/O; March 1945-EOW
Willis, Charles R., Lt.; January 1945-EOW
P-51D E2-T 44-13579 "Vicky Belle"
Windsor, David W., Lt.; January 1945-EOW
Winn, Howard R., Lt.; January 1945-EOW
Wolfe, Joseph B., Lt.; August 1944-April 17, 1945(KIA)
Wood, Leonard A., Lt.; July 1944-March 1945
75 missions
P-51D E2-G 44-14085 "Yvonne Marie"
Woods, Charles T., Lt.; January 1945-EOW
Wright, Robert C., Capt.; May 1943-September 1944
83 missions, 317 hours
P-47D E2-K
P-51B E2-K 42-106631 "Toby"
Yager, Isadore M., F/O; March 1945-EOW
Zettel, Raymond C., Lt.; June 1943-June 29, 1943(KIAc)

**376th Fighter Squadron**

Alcorn, Estel C., Lt.; States-September 1944
Banks, William H., F/O; February 1945-July 1945
Bain, Robert J., Lt.; June 1944-October 1944
P-51B E9-E 42-106802 "Blue Eyes"
P-51D E9-E 44-14363 "Blue Eyes"
Bell, Bernice E., Lt.; October 1944-EOW
Bender, Arthur L., Lt.; May 1944-
Bentley, John M., Lt.; States-April 15, 1944(POW)
Beyer, William R., Capt.; April 1944-December 1944
87 missions, 301 hours
P-51D E9-N 44-14144
Bocquin, Victor E., Capt.; April 1944-November 1944
P-51B E9-G "Germicide"
P-51D E9-Q 44-14165
Bricker, John B., Lt.; August 1944-April 1945
P-51B E9-B 42-106638 "Impatient Virgin?"
Brock, William R., Lt.; August 1944-January 1945
Butts, Will T., Capt.; April 1944-November 1944
Cable, Howard, Lt.; September 1944-EOW
Castle, Henry G., Lt.; April 1945-EOW
Caviness, Roy B., LtCol.; February 1943-August 1944; to HdQts; October 1944-November 1944; to HdQts
P-47D E9-C 42-22784 "Goona"
P-51B E9-C 42-106688
P-51D E9-C 44-13546 "Goona"
P-51D E9-C 44-14197 "Goona"
P-51D E9-C 44-14251 "Goona"
Chadwick, Lewis P., Lt.; October 1944-EOW
Chalmers, Allen J., Lt.; October 1944-EOW
Chapin, Walter F., Jr., F/O; August 1944-October 14, 1944(KIAc)

Chapman, Harry M., Lt.; October 1944-EOW
P-51D E9-R 44-72940 "Death's Angel"
Chapman, Hugh D., Capt.; March 1944-September 1944
Cheney, James B., Maj.; May 1943-October 15, 1944(POW)
Chennault, Claire P., Lt.; August 1944-April 1945
Clark, Warren A., Lt.; October 1944-EOW
Clement, Robert C., Lt.; July 1944-August 19, 1944(KIA)
Cole, Charles C., Jr., Lt.; October 1944-EOW
Comstock, Harold O., Lt.; March 1944-July 25, 1944(POW)
278:30 hours
Czapla, Eugene L., Lt.; June 1944-October 1944
Dahl, Milton A., Jr., Lt.; July 1944-August 18, 1944(KIA)
Dasinger, Albert, Jr., Lt.; February 1945-EOW
Davison, Francis R., Lt.; July 1944-March 1945
77 missions, 270 hours
Dennehy, Bernard L., Capt.; July 1944-April 1945
P-51D E9-L 44-13894 "Fosha"
Duncan, John D., Capt.; June 1943-March 1945
P-47D E9-D 42-25969
P-51B E9-D 43-24808
P-51D E9-D 44-14217 "Golden Wave"
Durbin, Richard M., Capt.; June 1944-October 1944; to HdQts
Eisenhut, Van C., Lt.; September 1944-EOW
P-51D E9-L 44-15352
Ford, Delmar R., Lt.; October 1944-April 16, 1945(POW)
P-51D E9-S 44-15663 "Baby Doll"
Frank, Wallace B., Capt.; May 1943-June 10, 1944(POW)
P-47D E9-F
P-51B E9-F 43-24759
Freedman, Roswell, LtCol.; August 1943-June 1945; ex-HdQts
P-47D E9-T "Roundtrip"
P-51D E9-T 44-13676
Glover, Woodrow W., Lt.; August 1944-September 17, 1944(KIA)
Graves, James F., F/O; February 1945-March 1945; to 352nd Ftr Grp
Grounds, Duane, Lt.; October 1944-EOW
P-51D E9-G 44-14251
Hanley, Claude W., Jr., Lt.; July 1944-April 1945
Harper, Carlos E., Lt.; January 1944-September 1944
Harris, Curtis S., Lt.; April 1945-August 5, 1945(KIAc)
Harris, Everett E., F/O; April 1945-July 1945
0 missions
Hein, Ralph H., F/O; February 1945-March 1945; to 352nd Ftr Grp
Hobbs, Robert, Lt.; October 1944-EOW
Horman, Roy A., F/O; February 1945-EOW
Jewell, Jackie D., F/O; March 1945-EOW
Johnson, Frank S., Lt.; October 1944-EOW
Johnson, Harold A., F/O; April 1945-EOW
0 missions
Jones, Donald W., Lt.; November 1944-EOW
Kelly, Joseph D., Lt.; June 1943-May 23, 1944(POW)
Kelly, Marion C., Lt.; October 1944-EOW
P-51D E9-M 44-14363
Kenoyer, Russell E., Lt.; October 1944-April 16, 1945(KIA)
Kopp, Andrew J., Lt.; April 1945-July 1945
0 missions
Kozicki, Walter J., Capt.; March 1944-June 4, 1944(MIA-E) September 1944-July 1945
60 missions, 229:35 hours
P-51D E9-P 44-14951 "Pegasis"
Lamb, Leo H., Lt.; August 1944-September 27, 1944(KIA)
Landin, David C., Lt.; June 1943-September 1944
Lane, Howard A., Maj.; States-EOW
Laxton, Cecil A., Lt.; States-September 1944
Ludlow, Lt.; States only
May, Leslie W., Lt.; States-September 1944
P-47D E9-M "Mayday"
P-51B E9-M 42-106754 "Mayday II"
Mitchell, Harold D., Capt.; August 1944-March 1945
Mobley, John W., Lt.; April 1945-EOW
0 missions
Morman, Roy A., Lt.; February 1945-EOW
Musselman, Nelson B., Lt.; April 1945-EOW
0 missions
Myers, Robert W., Lt.; September 1944-EOW
Nazzarette, Daniel B., Lt.; June 1943-February 22, 1944(KIA)
Noble, Dennis P., Capt.; June 1943-June 1944
Overholt, David P., Lt.; July 1944-March 1945
Patton, William W., Maj.; August 1944-September 1944; to 374th Ftr Sqn; ex-PTO April 1945-EOW
Percival, John G., Lt.; July 1944-October 1944; to 2nd Scouting Force
Petrone, Vic G., Capt.; September 1944-April 1945; to HdQts
Powell, Homer G., Lt.; August 1944-April 1945
P-51D E9-P 44-15752 "Gay Crusader"
Reed, Theodore W., Lt.; States-September 1944
Ross, Wade C., F/O; February 1945-July 1945
Ruch, Jay W., Capt.; States-EOW
P-47D E9-A 42-75200
P-51C E9-A 42-103350 "Flying Jeannie II"
P-51B E9-A 42-106944 "Flying Jeannie III"
Sadinski, John J., Lt.; September 1944-November 14, 1944(KIAc)
Sandor, Andrew E., Lt.; March 1945-EOW; ex-352nd Ftr Grp
Schirmer, Robert O., Capt.; States-September 1944
P-47D E9-Y
P-51D E9-Y 44-14042 "Heaven Sent-Hell Bent"
Schrup, Ray L., Lt.; September 1944-EOW
Scott, Kenneth J., Lt.; September 1944-EOW
P-51D E9-J 44-13872
P-51D E9-V 44-14600 "Curiosity Betty"
Smith, Fred C., Capt.; May 1943-February 1944; to 357th Ftr Grp
Smith, James D., Capt.; April 1944-April 1945
87 missions
P-51B E9-Y "Daisy Mae"
P-51D E9-Y 44-14042 "Daisy Mae II"
P-51D E9-Y 44-14514 "Daisy Mae III"
Smith, Norman L., Lt.; August 1944-July 1945
Spencer, Dale F., Lt.; May 1944-September 1944
P-51B E9-S 42-106538 "Little Luke"
Spencer, Herbert F., F/O; September 1944-EOW
Stewart, James C., Lt.; States-August 1944
Sullivan, Charles E., Capt.; States-July 1945
P-51B E9-S 42-106707 "Sleepytime Gal"
Sykes, William J., Lt.; June 1944-December 24, 1944(POW)
68 missions, 272 hours
P-51D E9-S 44-14520 "Hilma Lee"
Van Stryland, Robert G., Capt.; States-July 1944
Vanden Heuval, George R., Lt.; September 1944-October 1945
71 missions, 266:20 hours
P-51D E9-L 44-14685 "Mary Mine"
P-51D E9-Z 44-64005 "Mary Mine"
Volkman, Robert R., Capt.; July 1944-April 1945
P-51D E9-H 44-14197 "Mary Jane"
Vulgamore, Donald P., Lt.; August 1944-July 1945
75 missions
P-51D E9-V
Ward, Robert W., Capt.; July 1944-April 1945
P-51D E9-W 44-14177
Weaver, Dennis B., Lt.; States-February 24, 1944(KIA)
Welch, Billy D., Lt.; June 1943-August 1944
300 hours
White, Raymond S., Capt.; May 1943-October 1944
Wickenheiser, Cletus J., Lt.; March 1945-EOW; ex-352nd Ftr Grp
Wilkerson, Sam C., Jr., Capt.; States-August 4, 1944(POW)
P-47D E9-O 42-75449 "Shopworn Angel
P-51D E9-O 44-14763
Williams, Morris C., Lt.; States-May 24, 1944(POW)
P-47D E9-G 42-75549 "Devil May Care
P-51B E9-G 42-106651
Willet, William D., Lt.; May 1944-June 6, 1944(POW)
Wilson, Albert C., Lt.; July 1944-July 1944 (injured July 8)
Winstanley, Donald R., Lt.; October 1944-August 1945
Wolfe, Carl W., Lt.; October 1944-July 1945
Woodward, Donald T., Capt.; May 1943-January 1945
Wright, Jimmie C., Lt.; States-September 1944
P-47D E9-Q "Small Fry"
P-51B E9-Q 42-106746 "Small Fry II"
P-51B E9-Q "Small Fry III"
P-51D E9-Q 44-14165 "Small Fry IV"
Young, William R., Lt.; August 1944-July 1945
P-51D E9-Y "Sweet Sue"
P-51D E9-Y 44-15024 "Sweet Sue II"

**Aircraft of the 374th Fighter Squadron**

P-47D-10-RE
42-75152 B7-
42-75211 B7-S

P-47D-11-RE

| Aircraft | Pilot |
|---|---|
| 42-75401 B7- | |
| 42-75417 B7- | |
| 42-75441 B7-G | R.P. Lacy |
| 42-75452 B7-R "Tika" | V.R. Richards |
| 42-75512 B7-W "Sweet Thing" | R.A. Webb |
| 42-75521 B7- | |
| 42-75524 B7- | |
| 42-75552 B7-E "Bald Eagle" | R.T. Eckfeldt |
| 42-75567 B7- | |

P-47D-15-RE

| Aircraft | Pilot |
|---|---|
| 42-76140 B7-W "Sweet Thing" | R.A. Webb |

Unknown Serials

| Aircraft | Pilot |
|---|---|
| B7-I "Duchess of Manhattan" | H.B. Lederer |
| B7-R "Scarlet Kate" | G.R. Rew |
| B7-B "Fascinating Fanny" | W.L. Moore |
| B7- "Bette of Brooklyn" | J.D. Hastin |
| B7- "Ruthie Bev" | |
| B7- "Baby Doll" | |

P-51C-1-NT
42-103301 B7-J

P-51C-5-NT
42-103362 B7-V G. Lichter
42-103724 B7-
42-103750 B7-I

P-51C-10-NT
43-25032 B7-L

P-51B-5-NA
43-6977 B7-A
43-6982 B7-

P-51B-10-NA
42-106434 B7-D
42-106586 B7-X
42-106655 B7-H "Ferocious Frankie" W.E. Hopkins
42-106695 B7-V J.G. Vear
42-106713 B7-C D.L. Callaway
42-106721 B7-R "Scarlet Kate" G.R. Rew
42-106735 B7-

P-51B-15-NA
42-106763 B7-R "Scarlet Kate" G.R. Rew
42-106766 B7-
42-106811 B7-E "Bald Eagle II" R.T. Eckfeldt
42-106817 B7-S R.E. Sedman
42-106820 B7-M E.B. Murdy
42-106837 B7-U
42-106839 B7-E "Bald Eagle III" R.T. Eckfeldt
42-106839 B7-E T.L. Moore
42-106866 B7-K
42-106871 B7-B C.H. Bergmann
42-106875 B7-
42-106920 B7-
42-106942 B7-A
43-24763 B7-R "Tika III" V.R. Richards
43-24785 B7-
43-24819 B7-W "Sweet Thing" R.A. Webb
43-24830 B7-D L.E. Downey
43-24835 B7-
43-24840 B7-G R.P. Lacy

P-51D-5-NT
44-11164 B7-C
44-11164 B7-N "Pretty One II" J.C. Wilkinson

P-51K-1-NT
44-11367 B7-K

P-51D-5-NA
44-13333 B7-H
44-13340 B7-
44-13356 B7-D "Mollies +"
44-13357 B7-R "Tika IV" V.R. Richards
44-13392 B7-
44-13515 B7-S
44-13537 B7-W R.A. Webb
44-13538 B7-
44-13626 B7-M
44-13676 B7-V L.G. LaCroix
44-13676 B7-Z "Kay's Kite" J.R. Garces
44-13704 B7-H "Ferocious Frankie" W.E. Hopkins
44-13708 B7-I "Duchess of Manhattan" H.B. Lederer
44-13857 B7-O
44-13877 B7-F
44-13949 B7-G

P-51D-10-NA
44-14055 B7-F HACK
44-14080 B7-D "Miss Menville"
44-14128 B7-K
44-14139 B7-I "Rusty" L.J. Jewell
44-14191 B7-J
44-14261 B7-
44-14275 B7-V
44-14305 B7-W "Effie Mae II" H.S. Dixon
44-14515 B7-P
44-14714 B7- "Sweet Adeline" R.E. Chandler
44-14818 B7-B

P-51D-15-NA
44-14957 B7-Q "Darlin' Dora" J.M. Joss
44-15036 B7-U
44-15059 B7-
44-15065 B7-E "Elusive Eileen" T.J. Moore
44-15275 B7-V "Lil Bunyap" L.G. LaCroix
44-15323 B7-H "Curvacious Irene" B.R. Hicks
44-15358 B7-R "Lil Mil" E.V. Rizzio
44-15365 B7-G
44-15526 B7-P "Miss Mudge"
44-15606 B7-M "Virginia Ann" J.C. Mitenbuler
44-15657 B7-
44-15665 B7-N "Pretty One III" J.C. Wilkinson

P-51D-25-NA
44-73208 B7-E

Unknown Serials
P-51B B7-E "Bald Eagle II" R.T. Eckfeldt
P-51B B7-R "Tika II" V.R. Richards
P-51B B7-N "Pretty One" J.C. Wilkinson
P-51D B7-G "Galloping Goose" J. Cearly
P-51B B7- "Ruthie Bev"
P-51D B7- "The Widdle Wheel"

**Aircraft of the 375th Fighter Squadron**

P-47D-4-RA
42-22769 E2-

P-47D-5-RE
42-8512 E2-
42-8640 E2-D W.G. Shackleford

P-47D-6-RE
42-74714 E2-F

P-47D-10-RE
42-75096 E2-D W.G. Shackleford
42-75122 E2-
42-75198 E2-M
42-75214 E2-H M.H. Johnson
42-75214 E2-W "Shiverless" S.D. Rames

P-47D-11-RE
42-75219 E2-
42-75221 E2-W J.W. Guckeyson
42-75228 E2-L
42-75245 E2-T
42-75249 E2-J
42-75404 E2-A "Dr. I.P. Daily" G.L. Merritt
42-75424 E2-
42-75438 E2-P
42-75447 E2-Q
42-75453 E2-E
42-75454 E2-X
42-75494 E2-C "Lou" T.J.J. Christian
42-75555 E2-Y
42-75558 E2-N
42-75560 E2-G "Baby Margene" E. Cole
42-75572 E2-L "Isabel" C.N. Keppler

P-47D-20-RE
42-76528 E2-I

P-47D-22-RE
42-26109 E2-F

Unknown Serials
E2- "Geraldine" C.R. Cummins
E2- "P For Pearl" L.H. Sypher
E2- "The Bruiser" E.W. Kinnaird
E2- "Hayseed Margaret" J.A. Rogers
E2- "Zombie II"

P-51C-5-NT
42-103347 E2-A G.L. Merritt
42-103349 E2-W "Contrary Mary" J.W. Guckeyson
42-103588 E2-B
42-103749 E2-X "Betty Lee" W.T. Kemp

P-51B-5-NA
43-6570 E2-Q
43-7070 E2-Y

P-51B-10-NA
42-106588 E2-Y S. Armsby
42-106631 E2-K "Toby" R.C. Wright
42-106677 E2-S A.P. Rosenberger
42-106712 E2-T
42-106728 E2-

P-51B-15-NA
42-106741 E2-R
42-106778 E2-G E. Cole
42-106792 E2-W

42-106796 E2-E
42-106810 E2-R "Su Su"
42-106811 E2-H "Suzy G"
42-106830 E2-H "Ted's Reply"
42-106835 E2-N
42-106861 E2-
42-106975 E2-D "Queen Jean" W.G. Shackleford
42-106880 E2-M
42-106900 E2-M
42-106912 E2-B
42-106917 E2-K "Nita"
42-106925 E2-J
42-106948 E2-Z
42-106951 E2-F "Little Skipper" M.H. Johnson
43-24761 E2-I "Jacqueline" D.R. Morehouse
43-24768 E2-P
43-24774 E2-L "Slick Chick"
43-24783 E2-B
43-24790 E2-X

P-51D-5-NA
44-13339 E2-H
44-13410 E2-C "Lou IV" T.J.J. Christian
44-13568 E2-A "Sky Bouncer" B.W. Rowlett
44-13568 E2-T "Tally's Hoosier Hobo" R.J. Wade
44-13576 E2-
44-13579 E2-I "Vicky Belle" C.R. Willis
44-13735 E2-Q
44-13769 E2-N
44-13926 E2-S A.P. Rosenberger
44-14000 E2-H

P-51D-10-NA
44-14064 E2-E "Suzy Ann" W.D. Rogers
44-14085 E2-G M.F. Glessner
44-14085 E2-G "Yvonne Marie" L.A. Wood
44-14103 E2-F
44-14111 E2-L
44-14132 E2-A
44-14149 E2-T
44-14151 E2-
44-14164 E2-D "Detroit Miss" U.L. Drew
44-14164 E2-D "Phyll"
44-14181 E2-B
44-14226 E2- "Babe Schomarrech"
44-14270 E2-X "Betty Lee II" W.T. Kemp
44-14320 E2-B
44-14411 E2-L "Miss Margie" C.N. Keppler
44-14426 E2-G
44-14460 E2-Y J.W. Johnston
44-14516 E2-
44-14556 E2-I "Libby" J.E. Havey
44-14609 E2- "Vixen"
44-14662 E2-C "Little Moke" L.F. Gendron
44-14669 E2-R
44-14678 E2-V "Pat"
44-14792 E2-G "Margene"
44-14803 E2-S "Snitz" A.B. Snyder
44-14827 E2-V P.H. Klees
44-14827 E2-V "Croghan Cruiser" R.J. Farney

P-51D-15-NA
44-14903 E2-N "Dusty" P.A. Dougherty
44-14908 E2-A "Wisconsin Witch"
44-15038 E2-M "Tony" A. Maurice
44-15076 E2-X "Betty Lee III" W.T. Kemp
44-15314 E2-O G.R. Stockmeier
44-15366 E2-L "Miss Margie" C.N. Keppler
44-15597 E2-D J.W. Dennison
44-15604 E2-X
44-15662 E2-C
44-15725 E2-U

P-51D-20-NA
44-63167 E2-W
44-63173 E2-L "Miss Margie" C.N. Keppler
44-64111 E2-Q "Second Love" E.E. Tinkham
44-72526 E2-L "Miss Margie" C.N. Keppler

Unknow Serials
P-51B E2-C "Lou III" T.J.J. Christian
P-51B E2-H "Patsy II" L.H. Mottis
P-51D E2- "Lassie Come Home" R.M. Jumps
P-51D E2- "Blonde Baby II"
P-51D E2- "Lady Luck"

**Aircraft of the 376th Fighter Squadron**

P-47D-4-RA
42-22756 E9-
42-22784 E9-C "Goona" R.B. Caviness

P-47D-1-RE
42-7909 E9-E "Carol"

P-47D-10-RE
42-75105 E9-Z
42-75166 E9-V

P-47D-11-RE
42-75245 E9-
42-75260 E9-A
42-75401 E9-
42-75449 E9-O "Shopworn Angel" S.C. Wilkerson
42-75453 E9-B
42-75478 E9-Z
42-75505 E9-
42-75549 E9-G "Devil May Care" M.C. Williams

P-47D-15-RE
42-75814 E9-
42-76140 E9-W

P-47D-20-RE
42-25286 E9-K "Vi" J.J. Kruzel

P-47D-22-RE
42-25969 E9-D J.D. Duncan

Unknown Serials
E9-Q "Small Fry" J.C. Wright
E9-M "Mayday" L.W. May

P-51C-1-NT
42-103285 E9-X

P-51C-5-NT
42-103330 E9-I
42-103350 E9-A "Flying Jeannie II" J.W. Ruch

P-51C-10-NT
43-25044 E9-B

P-51B-5-NA
43-6498 E9-K "Vi" J.J. Kruzel
43-7040 E9-Y

P-51B-10-NA
42-106476 E9-Q "Small Fry II" J.C. Wright
42-106538 E9-S "Little Luke" D.F. Spencer
42-106560 E9-A
42-106564 E9-B
42-106603 E9-X
42-106627 E9-W
42-106638 E9-B "Impatient Virgin ?" J.B. Bricker
42-106651 E9-G M.C. Williams
42-106660 E9-X
42-106688 E9-C R.B. Caviness
42-106688 E9-T "Lil Larry"
42-106707 E9-S "Sleepytime Gal" C.E. Sullivan

P-51B-15-NA
42-106739 E9-L
42-106754 E9-M "Mayday II" L.W. May
42-106759 E9-A
42-106802 E9-E "Blue Eyes" R.J. Bain
42-106864 E9-B "Jane"
42-106938 E9-P
42-106944 E9-A "Mary Jane" J.B. Cheney
42-106944 E9-A "Flying Jeannie III" J.W. Ruch
42-106945 E9-V
43-24759 E9-F W.B. Frank
43-24799 E9-Z
43-24806 E9-H
43-24808 E9-D J.D. Duncan

P-51K-1-NT
44-11369 E9-H

P-51D-5-NT
44-11203 E9-F "Hiya Honey"

P-51D-5-NA
44-13391 E9-K "Vi" J.J. Kruzel
44-13391 E9-X

44-13546 E9-C "Goona" R.B. Caviness
44-13566 E9-
44-13676 E9-T "Roch" R. Freedman
44-13763 E9-O S.C. Wilkerson
44-13872 E9-J
44-13894 E9-L "Frances"
44-13894 E9-L "Fosha" B.L. Dennehy
44-14042 E9-Y "Heaven Sent-Hell Bent" R.D. Schirmer
44-14042 E9-Y "Daisey Mae II" J.D. Smith
44-14044 E9-B

P-51D-10-NA
44-14144 E9-N W.R. Beyer
44-14165 E9-Q "Small Fry IV" J.C. Wright
44-14165 E9-Q V.E. Bocquin
44-14177 E9-W R.W. Ward
44-14197 E9-C "Goona" R.B. Caviness
44-14197 E9-H "Mary Jane" R.R. Volkman
44-14217 E9-D "Golden Wave" J.D. Duncan
44-14219 E9-H "Scat Cat"
44-14250 E9-S
44-14251 E9-C "Goona" R.B. Caviness
44-14251 E9-G D. Grounds
44-14351 E9-P
44-14363 E9-E "Blue Eyes" R.J. Bain
44-14363 E9-M "Myrt" M.C. Kelly
44-14406 E9-K "Vi" J.J. Kruzel
44-14514 E9-Y "Daisey Mae III" J.D. Smith
44-14520 E9-S "Hilma Lee" W.J. Sykes
44-14526 E9-R
44-14539 E9-R "Princess Geraldine"
44-14600 E9-V "Curiosity Betty II" K.J. Scott
44-14685 E9-L "Mary Mine" G.R. Vanden Heuval
44-14806 E9-U
44-14818 E9-B

P-51D-15-NA
44-14951 E9-P "Pegasis" W.J. Kozicki
44-15024 E9-Y "Sweet Sue II" W.R. Young
44-15040 E9-C
44-15352 E9-L V.C. Eisenhut
44-15372 E9-J
44-15603 E9-F R. Freedman
44-15663 E9-S "Baby Doll" D.A. Ford
44-15752 E9-P "Gay Crusader" H.G. Powell

P-51D-20-NA
44-64005 E9-Z "Mary Mine" G.R. Vanden Heuval
44-72246 E9-D

P-51D-25-NA
44-72762 E9-C R.B. Caviness
44-72940 E9-R "Death's Angel" H.M. Chapman

Unknown Serials
P-51B E9-Q "Small Fry III" J.C. Wright
P-51B E9-G "Germicide" V.E. Bocquin
P-51B E9-A "Little Luke"
P-51B E9- "Toni"
P-51D E9-Y "Sweet Sue" W.R. Young
P-51D E9-F "Rose's Nightmare"
P-51D E9- "Honey"

• • •

## THE 364TH FIGHTER GROUP
### 383RD, 384TH, 385TH FIGHTER SQUADRONS

The 364th Fighter Group was activated on June 1, 1943, at Glendale, California. Training in the western United States, the group headed overseas on February 2, 1944, aboard the "Queen Elizabeth". The first of 345 missions came on March 2, 1944, with the last coming on May 6, 1945. While overseas, the group claimed 262 aerial and 191 ground victories while 138 P-38's and P-51's were lost on operations and 11 pilots died in accidents.

The only station for the 364th was Honington, from February 11, 1944, until November of 1945. Aircraft flown were the P-38J, from February of 1944 to September of 1944, and the P-51C, D, and K, from July of 1944 to November of 1945. The group was awarded a Distinguished Unit Citation for an escort on December 27, 1944, in which pilots destroyed over 25 German fighters.

**Claims**

| | Air | | | Grd | |
|---|---|---|---|---|---|
| | Destroyed | Probable | Damaged | Destroyed | Damaged |
| HdQts | 16 | 1 | 3 | 11 | 9 |
| 383rd | 75 | 9 | 35 | 80 | 82 |
| 384th | 83.5 | 6 | 38 | 28 | 24 |
| 385th | 87.5 | 9 | 24 | 72 | 60 |
| | 262 | 25 | 100 | 191 | 175 |

**Commanders**

| | |
|---|---|
| Col. Fred C. Grambo | July 12, 1943-February 29, 1944 |
| Col. Roy W. Osborn | February 29, 1944-September 9, 1944 |
| LtCol. John B. McManus | September 9, 1944-October 23, 1944 |
| LtCol. John H. Lowell | October 23, 1944-November 2, 1944 |
| Col. Roy W. Osborn | November 3, 1944-January 3, 1945 |
| LtCol. Eugene P. Roberts | January 3, 1945-November 1945 |

**Wing and Command Assignments**

| | |
|---|---|
| Assigned to VIII Fighter Command | February 10, 1944 |
| VIII Fighter Command, 67th Fighter Wing | February 10, 1944 |
| 1st Bomb Division, 67th Fighter Wing | September 15, 1944 |
| 1st Air Division, 67th Fighter Wing | January 1, 1945 |

**Aircraft Markings**

P-38's were operated in both olive drab/neutral gray schemes and NMF. Group markings consisted of white spinners and cowl bands. Squadron markings were geometric symbols placed on the outer vertical tails: a circle for the 383rd, a square for the 384th, and a triangle for the 385th.

All P-51's were in NMF with very few receiving applications of dark green. Squadron codes remained the same as on P-38's but the 364th was unique in that it's aircraft carried the codes aft of the national insignia on the fuselage. The individual letter was placed within the squadron symbol carried on the vertical tail/rudder. This letter was either white or NMF within the black geometric symbol. As a group markings, all planes had a white spinner and cowl band, with the band divided into 6 inch medium blue longitudinal stripes.

Squadron codes were:

383rd Ftr Sqn: N2
384th Ftr Sqn: 5Y
385th Ftr Sqn: 5E

**364th Fighter Group Statistical Report**

| Month | Missions | Air | Grd | Losses | KIAc |
|---|---|---|---|---|---|
| February 1944 | 0 | 0-0-0 | 0-0 | 1 | 0 |
| March | 17 | 13-2-8 | 1-1 | 16 | 1 |
| April | 21 | 2-7-6 | 2-3 | 17 | 1 |
| May | 21 | 15-0-10 | 21-12 | 18 | 1 |
| June | 75 | 7-1-4 | 0-1 | 3 | 0 |
| July | 25 | 0-1-5 | 0-0 | 3 | 2 |
| August | 30 | 28-0-4 | 35-34 | 12 | 0 |
| September | 23 | 26-3-11 | 0-0 | 12 | 0 |
| October | 18 | 9-1-1 | 0-0 | 11 | 0 |
| November | 15 | 40-3-12 | 7-4 | 11 | 0 |
| December | 16 | 87.5-5-15 | 1-0 | 10 | 2 |
| January 1945 | 12 | 8-0-0 | 0-2 | 3 | 0 |
| February | 20 | 12-2-18 | 5-1 | 9 | 2 |
| March | 28 | 2.5-0-2 | 2-9 | 5 | 0 |
| April | 20 | 12-0-4 | 117-108 | 7 | 0 |
| May | 4 | 0-0-0 | 0-0 | 0 | 0 |
| June | 0 | 0-0-0 | 0-0 | 0 | 2 |
| | 345 | 262-25-100 | 191-175 | 138 | 11 |

**Losses by Squadron**

| | MIA | | KIAc | |
|---|---|---|---|---|
| | P-38 | P-51 | P-38 | P-51 |
| HdQts | 3 | 0 | 0 | 0 |
| 383rd | 14 | 24 | 1 | 2 |
| 384th | 22 | 22 | 1 | 5 |
| 385th | 18 | 35 | 2 | 0 |
| | 57 | 81 | 4 | 7 |

**Claims by Type**

| | Air | | | Grd | |
|---|---|---|---|---|---|
| | Destroyed | Probable | Damaged | Destroyed | Damaged |
| P-38 | 37 | 11 | 33 | 24 | 17 |
| P-51 | 225 | 14 | 67 | 167 | 158 |

**Claims by Enemy Aircraft Type**

| | Air | | | Grd | |
|---|---|---|---|---|---|
| | Destroyed | Probable | Damaged | Destroyed | Damaged |
| FW-190 | 147 | 14 | 51 | 34 | 44 |
| Me-109 | 102.5 | 10 | 32 | 19 | 23 |

| | | | | | |
|---|---|---|---|---|---|
| Me-262 | 5.5 | 1 | 16 | 6 | 5 |
| He-111 | 2 | 0 | 0 | 22 | 21 |
| Do-217 | 2 | 0 | 0 | 5 | 11 |
| Ar-234 | 1 | 0 | 1 | 0 | 0 |
| Me-163 | 1 | 0 | 0 | 0 | 0 |
| Trainer | 1 | 0 | 0 | 0 | 0 |
| Ju-52 | 0 | 0 | 0 | 28 | 14 |
| Ju-88 | 0 | 0 | 0 | 29 | 10 |
| u/i a/c | 0 | 0 | 0 | 12 | 12 |
| Me-110 | 0 | 0 | 0 | 6 | 11 |
| Me-210 | 0 | 0 | 0 | 6 | 3 |
| Ju-188 | 0 | 0 | 0 | 5 | 5 |
| Me-410 | 0 | 0 | 0 | 4 | 4 |
| Ju-87 | 0 | 0 | 0 | 4 | 3 |
| Fi-156 | 0 | 0 | 0 | 4 | 5 |
| FW-200 | 0 | 0 | 0 | 3 | 2 |
| Ar-66 | 0 | 0 | 0 | 2 | 0 |
| BV-138 | 0 | 0 | 0 | 1 | 0 |
| Me-323 | 0 | 0 | 0 | 1 | 0 |
| Go-242 | 0 | 0 | 0 | 0 | 1 |
| He-177 | 0 | 0 | 0 | 0 | 1 |

## 364th Fighter Group Squadron Commanders

**383rd Ftr Sqn**

| | |
|---|---|
| Capt. Robert B. Wilson | June 1943-January 29, 1944 |
| LtCol. John B. McManus | January 29, 1944-September 4, 1944 |
| Maj. Samuel J. Wicker | September 4, 1944-October 1944 |
| LtCol. George F. Ceuleers | October 1944-May 30, 1945 |

**384th Ftr Sqn**

| | |
|---|---|
| Maj. John H. Lowell | June 1943-July 29, 1944 |
| Maj. Robert E. Lacy | July 29, 1944-October 1944 |
| LtCol. John H. Lowell | October 1944-January 1945 |
| LtCol. Robert E. Lacy | January 1945-July 21, 1945 |

**385th Ftr Sqn**

| | |
|---|---|
| LtCol. Richard D. Neece | June 1943-October 1944 |
| LtCol. Carl W. Stapleton | October 1944-April 14, 1945 |
| Maj. William S. Crombie | April 14, 1945-November 1945 |

## 364th Fighter Group Aces

| Name | Air | Grd | Total | Sqn |
|---|---|---|---|---|
| LtCol. John H. Lowell | 7.5 | 9 | 16.5 | 384th HdQts |
| Maj. Ernest E. Bankey, Jr. | 9.5 | 6 | 15.5 | 383rd 385th HdQts |
| LtCol. George F. Ceuleers | 10.5 | 0 | 10.5 | 383rd |
| Capt. Arthur B. McCormick | 1 | 9 | 10 | 385th |
| Capt. John C. Hunter | 3 | 6 | 9 | 383rd |
| Capt. Romildo Visconte | 4 | 5 | 9 | 385th |
| Capt. James M. Fowle | 8 | 0 | 8 | 384th |
| Capt. Roy W. Orndorff | 4 | 4 | 8 | 383rd |
| Maj. William S. Crombie | 4 | 3 | 7 | 385th |
| Capt. Gilbert L. Jamison | 7 | 0 | 7 | 385th |
| Maj. Samuel J. Wicker | 7 | 0 | 7 | 383rd |
| Capt. Jesse L. Truett | 0 | 6.5 | 6.5 | 383rd |
| Lt. Kenneth R. Horner | 0 | 6 | 6 | 385th |
| Capt. Edward F. Izor | 4.5 | 1 | 5.5 | 385th |
| Lt. James J. Pascoe | 5.5 | 0 | 5.5 | 385th |
| Lt. Richard M. Baughn | 1 | 4 | 5 | 383rd |
| Lt. Thomas H. Hall | 3 | 2 | 5 | 383rd |
| Capt. William F. Kissel | 0 | 5 | 5 | 383rd |
| Lt. James L. McCubbin | 4 | 1 | 5 | 385th |
| Capt. William F. Wilson | 5 | 0 | 5 | 385th |
| LtCol. Eugene P. Roberts | 9 | 0 | 9* | HdQts |

* - all victories with 78th Ftr Grp, ETO

## 364th Fighter Group Scorers

**HdQts**

| | Air | Grd | |
|---|---|---|---|
| E.E. Bankey, Jr. | 7.5-0-0 | 6-6 | plus 383rd & 385th Ftr Sqns |
| A.L. Chilton | 0-1-0 | 2-0 | |
| J.D. Dale | 1-0-0 | 0-0 | plus 2 air w/17th Pur Sqn, PTO |
| W.L. Goff | 1-0-0 | 0-0 | |
| J.H. Lowell | 4.5-0-2 | 3-0 | plus 384th Ftr Sqn |
| R.W. Osborn | 2-0-1 | 0-0 | plus 1.33 air w/67th Ftr Wg |
| E.P. Roberts | 0-0-0 | 0-3 | plus 9-1-0 air w/78th Ftr Grp |

**383rd Ftr Sqn**

| | | | |
|---|---|---|---|
| A.J. Acosta, Jr. | 1-0-0 | 1-4 | |
| L.V. Andrew | 0-0-1 | 1-2 | |
| L.S. Ayoub | 1.5-0-0 | 0-0 | |
| E.E. Bankey, Jr. | 1-1-0 | 0-0 | plus HdQts & 385th Ftr Sqn |
| J.J. Bannister | 0-0-0 | 0-2 | |
| C.A. Barnes | 1-0-2 | 1-2 | |
| R.M. Baughn | 1-0-0 | 4-4 | |
| E.C. Beaumont | 3-0-2 | 0-0 | |
| N.F. Bettin | 0-1-1 | 0-0 | |
| W.D. Boyd | 1-0-1 | 0.5-0 | |
| M.L. Casagrande | 1-0-0 | 3-2 | |
| G.F. Ceuleers | 10.5-0-3 | 0-0 | |
| H.A. Chesney | 1-0-0 | 0-0.5 | |
| E. Chlevin | 1-0-0 | 1.5-2 | |
| M.E. Coates | 2-0-1 | 2-1.5 | |
| W.T. Dalton | 0-0-0 | 1-1 | |
| R.P. Davis | 1-0-0 | 0-0 | |
| R.H. Dwyer | 1-0-0 | 0-2 | |
| R.H. Farley | 2-0-0 | 0-0 | |
| E.N. Fiery | 2-0-1 | 0-0 | |
| D.C. Fisher | 2-0-0 | 1-0 | |
| J.C. Gaston | 0.5-0-0 | 0-0 | |
| L.A. Gilliland | 2-1-1 | 0-0 | |
| M.W. Glascow | 0-3-1 | 4.5-2 | |
| P.J. Goldberg | 0-0-0 | 1.5-1 | |
| J.B. Guy | 0.5-0-0 | 2-2 | |
| T.H. Hall | 3-0-0 | 2-0 | |
| C.E. Hammett | 2.5-1-0 | 1-0 | |
| C. Hatfield | 0.5-0-0 | 0-0 | |
| E.P. Hausenbauer | 0-0-0 | 0-1 | |
| D.F. Healey, Jr. | 1.5-0-0 | 2-2 | |
| E.P. Heyn | 0-0-1 | 0-0 | |
| G.F. Hill | 0-0-0 | 0.5-2 | |
| E. Holmes | 0-0-0 | 1-3 | |
| W.K. Hood | 0-0-0 | 1-2 | |
| E.H. Horman | 2-0-2 | 2-1 | |
| C.W. Hornick | 0-0-0 | 1-2 | |
| R.L. Hunt | 0-0-2 | 1-1 | |
| J.C. Hunter | 3-0-1 | 6-4 | |
| J.J. Jacaruso | 0-0-0 | 1.5-1 | |
| C.E. Jackson | 0-0-0 | 2-1 | |
| J.A. Kerig | 0-0-1 | 0-0 | |
| J. Kerr | 0-0-1 | 0-0 | |
| W.F. Kissel | 0-0-0 | 5-4 | |
| E.W. Kortendick | 1-0-1 | 2-3 | |
| L. Leon | 0-0-0 | 1-2 | |
| J.B. MacDermott | 1-0-1 | 0-0 | |
| G.A. McCoy | 1-0-0 | 0-0 | |
| J.B. McManus | 0-1-0 | 2-1 | |
| L.J. Miller | 0-0-0 | 0-1 | |
| M.L. Murphy | 0-0-1 | 0-0 | |
| K.F. Nicholson | 2-0-1 | 0.5-0 | |
| V.A. O'Brien | 0-0-0 | 1-2 | |
| R.W. Orndorff | 4-0-0 | 4-1 | |
| J.F. Potochnik | 1-0-0 | 0-0 | |
| W.V. Pyle | 0-0-2 | 0-0 | |
| R.W. Queal, Jr. | 1-0-1 | 0-1 | |
| H.D. Sandkaut | 1-0-0 | 2-2 | |
| H.B. Saylor | 0-1-0 | 0-0 | |
| J.A. Seth | 0-0-0 | 4-1 | |
| G.E. Smith | 0.5-0-1 | 3-3 | |
| F.L. Sorrells | 1-0-1 | 0-0 | |
| N.M. Staranick | 0-0-0 | 0-1 | |
| J.L. Truett | 0-0-0 | 6.5-4 | |
| C.K. Voss | 3-0-0 | 0-0 | |
| G.O. Warner | 0-0-2 | 0-3 | |
| S.J. Wicker | 7-0-0 | 0-0 | |
| B.B. Wilson | 1-0-1 | 2-1 | |
| L.R. Wilson | 0-0-0 | 1-1 | |
| J.D. Woodside | 2-0-1 | 0-0 | |

**384th Ftr Sqn**

| | | |
|---|---|---|
| R.K. Allen | 2.5-0-1 | 2-0 |
| E.O. Bowers | 1.5-0-0 | 0-0 |
| W.E. Bristow | 3-0-2 | 0-0 |
| W.N. Champion | 1-0-0.5 | 0-0 |
| W.P. Derr | 0-0-0 | 0-1 |
| E.H. Duderstadt | 3.5-0-0 | 0-0 |
| E.W. Farnsworth | 2.5-0-0 | 0-0 |
| R.S. Faulkner | 1.5-0-0 | 0-1 |
| W.F. Flynt | 1.5-0-0 | 0-0 |
| J.C. Ford | 2.5-0-0 | 1-0 |
| J.M. Fowle | 8-0-1 | 0-0 |
| J.J. Gawienowski | 2-0-0 | 0-1 |
| J.L. Grimshaw | 1-0-1 | 0-1 |
| P.J. Hahn | 0-0-0 | 0-1 |
| H.V. Herndon | 0-0-0 | 1-0 |
| W.P. Hess | 3-0-0 | 1-0 |
| R.M. Heyman | 1-0-1 | 0-0 |
| F.J. Hoenselaar | 0-0-1 | 0-2 |
| S.R. Honaker | 0-0-0 | 0-2 |

| | | | |
|---|---|---|---|
| J.L. Hughes | 0-0-0 | 2-2 | |
| H.M. James | 1-0-1 | 0-0 | |
| J.V. Johnson | 2-0-0 | 0-0 | |
| V.L. Kercher | 2-0-1 | 0-0 | |
| C.L. Kirby | 0-0.5-1 | 0-0 | |
| J.R. Korecky | 1-0-1 | 0-0 | |
| F.T. Kozloski | 1-0-0 | 0-1 | |
| R.E. Lacy | 0-0-2 | 2.33-2 | |
| W.A. Leavell | 0-0-0 | 1-1 | |
| L.L. Lefforge | 0-1-1 | 0-0 | |
| D.L. Leftwich | 3-0-0 | 1-1 | |
| C.H. Leo | 1-0-1 | 0-0 | |
| M.C. Linn | 0-0-2 | 0-0 | plus 1 air w/1st Ftr Grp, MTO |
| J.H. Lowell | 3-1-0 | 6-3 | plus HdQts |
| E.H. Miller | 3-0-0 | 0-0 | |
| J.F. Nelson | 0.5-0-0 | 0-0 | |
| F.T. O'Connor | 0-0-1 | 0-0 | |
| A.D. Parsley | 1-0-0 | 0-0 | |
| S.C. Phillips | 0-0-2 | 1-1 | |
| L.A. Phipps | 0-0-1 | 0-0 | |
| D.J. Pick | 4-0-1 | 0.33-1 | |
| S.J. Price | 0.5-0-2 | 0-0 | |
| C.J. Pushcar | 0-0-1 | 0-0 | |
| W.E. Randolph | 2.5-0-3 | 0-0 | |
| G.Z. Schroeder | 1-0-1 | 0-0 | |
| H.C. Schwartz | 2.5-0-0 | 2-3 | |
| E.B. Shepard | 1-0-0 | 0-0 | plus 1.5 air w/324th Ftr Grp, MTO |
| J.E. Soehl | 1-0-1 | 3-0 | |
| R.M. Spradlin | 2-1-0 | 0-0 | |
| C.W. Stapleton | 0-0-0 | 0.33-0 | |
| J.R. Steinbacher | 1-0-2 | 0-0 | |
| R.W. Stevens | 3-0.5-1 | 0-0 | |
| R.L. Stiefvater | 1.5-0-1 | 0-0 | |
| J.M. Stuckrath | 2-0-1 | 0-0 | |
| J.E. Taylor | 0-0-0 | 3-0 | |
| L. Visconti | 1-0-0 | 0-0 | |
| J.A. Walker | 0-0-1 | 0-0 | |
| B.C. Ward | 0.5-1-1 | 0-0 | |
| F.S. Welch | 1-0-0 | 0-0 | |
| T.H. Wells, Jr. | 3-0-0 | 0-0 | |
| D.W. Williams | 0-1-0 | 0-0 | |
| J.E. Wilson | 0.5-0-0 | 0-0 | |
| B.P. Yost | 0-0-0 | 1-0 | |

**385th Ftr Sqn**

| | | | |
|---|---|---|---|
| T.L. Allinder | 0.5-1-0 | 0-0 | |
| E.E. Anderson | 0-0-0 | 1-1 | |
| R.A. Auguste | 0-0-0 | 1-0 | |
| E.E. Bankey, Jr. | 1-1-0 | 0-1 | plus 383rd Ftr Sqn & HdQts |
| J.T. Barrie | 1-0-0 | 0-0 | |
| D.L. Bloodgood | 1-0-0 | 2-0 | |
| N.L. Box | 0.5-0-1 | 0-1 | |
| H.D. Burkhard | 0.5-0-0 | 0-1 | |
| W.S. Crombie | 4-0-0 | 3-4 | |
| R.A. Crouch, Jr. | 0-0-0 | 2-0 | |
| R.F. Edwards | 1-0-0 | 0-0 | |
| W.G. Erfkamp | 2.5-0-1 | 1-1 | |
| J.O. Eubanks | 1-0-0 | 1-0 | |
| E.N. Farrell | 4-0-2 | 0-1 | |
| T.P. Farrell | 3.5-0-0 | 1-1 | |
| J.E. Hargrove | 1.5-0-0 | 2-2 | |
| H.W. Head | 3.5-0-1 | 1-1 | |
| W.W. Helmholz, Jr. | 0-0-0 | 3-1 | |
| C.S. Hill | 3-0-0 | 0-0 | |
| C.S. Hogan, Jr. | 1-1-0 | 0-1 | |
| K.R. Horner | 0-0-0 | 6-2 | |
| W.T. Housholder | 2-1-1 | 0-0 | |
| D.J. Hustead | 0-0-1 | 2-3.5 | |
| E.F. Izor | 4.5-0-0 | 1-2 | |
| G.L. Jamison | 7-0-1 | 0-1 | |
| J.G. Johnson | 0-0-0 | 1.5-3 | |
| A.R. Jones | 3-0-1 | 0-0 | |
| E.H. Jones | 0-0-0 | 0-5 | |
| G.L. Jones | 0.5-0-0 | 0-0 | |
| J.W. Kiernan | 0-0-0 | 2-1 | |
| T.F. Lasch | 0-0-0 | 1-0 | |
| S.L. Lett, Jr. | 1.5-0-0 | 0-0 | |
| W.K. Masters | 0-0-0 | 3-0 | |
| F.C. McClanahan | 0-0-2.5 | 2-0 | |
| A.B. McCormick | 1-0-1 | 9-3 | |
| J.L. McCubbin | 4-2-0 | 1-1 | |
| R.M. McKibben | 2-0-0 | 0-0 | |
| J.D. Monahan | 1-0-0 | 0-0 | |
| J.W. Munn | 0-0-0 | 2-4 | |
| E. Murphy | 1.5-0-0 | 1-0 | |
| R.D. Neece | 1-0-0 | 2-0 | |
| W.P. O'Connell | 1-0-0 | 0-0 | |
| J.J. Pascoe | 5.5-1-1 | 0-0 | |
| W.L. Poore | 0-0-1 | 0-0 | |
| F.X. Radley | 0.5-1-0 | 0-0 | |
| E.H. Rivers | 0-0-1 | 0-0 | |
| C.R. Roesch, Jr. | 0-0-1 | 3.5-1 | |
| J.S. Rogers | 0-0-1 | 3-2 | |
| J.W. Ruland | 1-0-0 | 0-1 | |
| W.S. Sagar, Jr. | 1.5-0-1 | 0-0 | |
| R.C. Scott | 0.5-0-0 | 0-0 | |
| R.M. Scott | 1-0-0 | 0-0 | |
| C.L. Smart | 0.5-0-0 | 0-0 | |
| R.O. Smith, Jr. | 0-0-1 | 0-0 | |
| F.O. Spain | 0-0-0 | 2-4 | |
| R.E. Squillaro | 1-0-0 | 0-0 | |
| C.W. Stapleton | 1-0-0 | 1-0 | plus 384th Ftr Sqn |
| H.H. Stubblefield | 0-0-0.5 | 1-4 | |
| W.A. Sullivan | 0-1-0 | 0-0 | |
| J.C. Tallman | 0.5-0-0 | 0-0 | |
| E.A. Taylor | 1-0-1 | 1-0 | |
| E.K. Tazzia | 0-0-1 | 1-0 | |
| A.J. Trybuszewski | 2-0-0 | 0-0 | |
| J.D. Turner | 0.5-0-0 | 0-0 | |
| J.F. Vann | 1-0-0 | 0-0 | |
| R. Visconte | 4-0-1 | 5-1.5 | |
| C.B. Warner | 1-0-0 | 0-0 | |
| S.J. Welsh | 0-0-0 | 1-0 | |
| R.E. White | 0.5-0-0 | 0-1 | |
| E.L. Wilson | 0-0-0 | 2-2 | |
| W.F. Wilson | 5-0-1 | 0-0 | |

**364th Fighter Group Scoring**

| | | | |
|---|---|---|---|
| **March 5, 1944** | | | |
| 384th: | Lt. C.H. Leo | FW-190 dam(air) | N/Angouleme |
| **March 6, 1944** | | | |
| 384th: | Capt. J.H. Lowell | Me-109 dest(air) | W/Hanover |
| | | Me-109 prob(air) | W/Hanover |
| | Lt. S.C. Phillips | Me-109 dam(air) | W/Hanover |
| **March 8, 1944** | | | |
| 383rd: | Capt. L.A. Gilliland | FW-190 dest(air) | N/Magdeburg |
| | | FW-190 dest(air) | N/Rheine |
| | | FW-190 prob(air) | N/Magdeburg |
| | | FW-190 dam(air) | N/Magdeburg |
| | Capt. G.F. Ceuleers | FW-190 dest(air) | Nienburg |
| | | FW-190 dam(air) | Nienburg |
| 384th: | Capt. J.H. Lowell | (2)FW-190 dest(air) | Stendal-Alt Ruppin |
| | Capt. J.C. Ford | FW-190 dest(air) | NE Brunswick |
| | Lt. M.C. Linn | (2)Me-109 dam(air) | E/Steinhuder L. |
| | Lt. R.E. Lacy | FW-190 dam(air) | NE Brunswick |
| 385th: | Lt. W.P. O'Connell | Me-109 dest(air) | Belzig |
| | Lt. R.E. Squillaro | Me-109 dest(air) | W/Berlin |
| | Lt. C.B. Warner | Me-109 dest(air) | Gifhorn |
| | Capt. R.O. Smith | Me-109 dam(air) | Gifhorn |
| **March 15, 1944** | | | |
| 385th: | Capt. R.M. Scott | (.5)FW-190 dest(air) | Dummer Lake |
| | | (.5)Me-109 dest(air) | Dummer Lake |
| | Lt. J.C. Tallman | (.5)FW-190 dest(air) | Dummer Lake |
| | Lt. J.D. Turner | (.5)Me-109 dest(air) | Dummer Lake |
| **March 29, 1944** | | | |
| 384th: | Capt. J.C. Ford | Me-109 dest(air) | Rheine/Enschede |
| | Maj. J.H. Lowell | Ju-52 dest(grd) | Osnabruck |
| | | FW-190 dam(grd) | Osnabruck |
| **April 9, 1944** | | | |
| 384th: | Maj. J.H. Lowell | FW-190 dest(grd) | Bramsche/Rheine |
| | | FW-190 dam(grd) | Bramsche/Rheine |
| **April 11, 1944** | | | |
| 383rd: | Lt. E.E. Bankey | Me-109 dest(air) | Halberstadt |
| | Lt. N.F. Bettin | Me-109 prob(air) | Halberstadt |
| | Lt. B.B. Wilson | Me-109 dam(air) | Halberstadt |
| **April 12, 1944** | | | |
| 383rd: | Lt. M.W. Glascow | FW-190 prob(air) | E/Frankfurt |
| | Lt. C.A. Barnes | Me-109 dam(air) | N/Frankfurt |
| **April 15, 1944** | | | |
| 383rd: | Maj. G.F. Ceuleers | (.5)Me-109 dest(air) | SE Bremen |
| | Lt. L.S. Ayoub | (.5)Me-109 dest(air) | SE Bremen |
| | Lt. H.B. Saylor | Me-109 prob(air) | W/Hamburg |
| 384th: | Capt. R.E. Lacy | (.33)BV-138 dest(grd) | Elbe Estuary |
| | Capt. C.W. Stapleton | (.33)BV-138 dest(grd) | Elbe Estuary |
| | Lt. D.J. Pick | (.33)BV-138 dest(grd) | Elbe Estuary |
| | Lt. F.J. Hoenselaar | Do-217 dam(grd) | Basbeck |
| | | Ju-52 dam(grd) | Basbeck |
| 385th: | Lt. W.L. Poore | Me-109 dam(air) | Vechta |

**April 29, 1944**

| Unit | Pilot | Claim | Location |
|---|---|---|---|
| HdQts: | Maj. A.L. Chilton | Me-109 prob(air) | Stendal |
| 383rd: | Maj. J.B. McManus | FW-190 prob(air) | Stendal |
| | Lt. E.E. Bankey | FW-190 prob(air) | Stendal |
| 384th: | Capt. R.M. Spradlin | Me-109 prob(air) | Brandenburg |
| | Capt. R.E. Lacy | Me-109 dam(air) | N/Brandenburg |
| | Lt. F.J. Hoenselaar | Me-109 dam(air) | Steinhuder Lake-Berlin |
| | Lt. D.J. Pick | FW-190 dam(air) | N/Brunswick |

**May 8, 1944**

| Unit | Pilot | Claim | Location |
|---|---|---|---|
| HdQts: | Col. R.W. Osborn | Me-109 dest(air) | Steinhuder Lake |
| | | Me-109 dam(air) | Steinhuder Lake |
| 383rd: | Lt. M.W. Glascow | Me-109 dam(air) | NE Dummer Lake |
| 384th: | Capt. R.M. Spradlin | (2)Me-109 dest(air) | Steinhuder Lake |
| | Lt. R.M. Heyman | Me-109 dest(air) | Steinhuder Lake |
| | | Me-109 dam(air) | Steinhuder Lake |
| | Lt. A.D. Parsley | Me-109 dest(air) | Steinhuder Lake |

**May 19, 1944**

| Unit | Pilot | Claim | Location |
|---|---|---|---|
| 383rd: | Lt. J. Kerr | FW-190 dam(air) | Trenemunde A/F |
| | Lt. K.F. Nicholson | FW-190 dam(air) | Lubeck Bay |
| 384th: | Capt. R.E. Lacy | He-111 dam(grd) | NW Schleswig |

**May 20, 1944**

| Unit | Pilot | Claim | Location |
|---|---|---|---|
| 385th: | Capt. C.W. Stapleton | Ju-88 dest(grd) | Soissons |
| | Lt. E.E. Bankey | Ju-88 dam(grd) | Soissons |

**May 21, 1944**

| Unit | Pilot | Claim | Location |
|---|---|---|---|
| HdQts: | Maj. A.L. Chilton | Ju-52 dest(grd) | Hagenow |
| | | Ju-88 dest(grd) | Hagenow |
| 383rd: | Lt. M.W. Glascow | FW-190 dest(grd) | Rechlin |
| | | Ju-88 dest(grd) | Rechlin |
| | | (2)Ju-88 dam(grd) | Rechlin |
| | Lt. B.B. Wilson | (2)Ju-88 dest(grd) | Rechlin |
| | | Ju-88 dam(grd) | Rechlin |
| | Maj. J.B. McManus | Me-410 dest(grd) | NW Renow |
| | Lt. C.A. Barnes | Ju-88 dest(grd) | NW Renow |
| | Lt. L.R. Wilson | Me-323 dest(grd) | NW Renow |
| | | Do-217 dam(grd) | NW Renow |
| | Lt. J.J. Bannister | (2)Ju-88 dam(grd) | Rechlin |
| | Lt. L.J. Miller | Me-410 dam(grd) | NW Renow |
| 384th: | Maj. J.H. Lowell | (2)Ju-52 dest(grd) | All 384th claims |
| | | He-111 dest(grd) | are at Parchim- |
| | | Ju-88 dest(grd) | Hagenow- |
| | | FW-190 dam(grd) | Ludwigslust |
| | Capt. J.C. Ford | Ju-88 dest(grd) | |
| | Lt. S.C. Phillips | He-111 dest(grd) | |
| | | Ju-88 dam(grd) | |
| | Lt. B.P. Yost | Ju-52 dest(grd) | |
| 385th: | Lt. C.S. Hill | (.5)He-111 dest(air) | SE Luneburg |
| | Lt. E.F. Izor | (.5)He-111 dest(air) | SE Luneburg |
| | Lt. E.A. Taylor | Me-210 dest(grd) | All claims are |
| | Lt. R. Visconte | Ju-88 dest(grd) | at Schwerin- |
| | Lt. S.J. Welsh | Ju-88 dest(grd) | Luneburg-Ludwigslust |

**May 22, 1944**

| Unit | Pilot | Claim | Location |
|---|---|---|---|
| 383rd: | Capt. S.J. Wicker | (2)FW-190 dest(air) | SW Kiel |
| | Lt. J.B. MacDermott | FW-190 dest(air) | Kiel |
| | | FW-190 dam(air) | Kiel |
| | Lt. K.F. Nicholson | FW-190 dest(air) | SE Kiel |
| | Lt. N.F. Bettin | FW-190 dam(air) | SW Kiel |
| 384th: | Lt. V.L. Kercher | FW-190 dam(air) | SW Kiel |
| 385th: | Lt. H.H. Stubblefield | (.5)FW-190 dam(air) | Neumunster |
| | Lt. F.C. McClanahan | (.5)FW-190 dam(air) | Neumunster |

**May 24, 1944**

| Unit | Pilot | Claim | Location |
|---|---|---|---|
| 383rd: | Lt. W.D. Boyd | (.5)Do-217 dest(grd) | SW Berlin |
| | Lt. K.F. Nicholson | (.5)Do-217 dest(grd) | SW Berlin |
| 385th: | Lt. H.D. Burkhard | (.5)Do-217 dest(air)* | Gifhorn |
| | | Go-242 dam(grd) | Gifhorn |
| | Lt. R.C. Scott | (.5)Do-217 dest(air)* | Gifhorn |
| | Lt. C.S. Hill | (.5)Do-217 dest(air)** | Gifhorn |
| | Lt. J.J. Pascoe | (.5)Do-217 dest(air)** | Gifhorn |

**May 25, 1944**

| Unit | Pilot | Claim | Location |
|---|---|---|---|
| 383rd: | Lt. L.S. Ayoub | FW-190 dest(air) | Paris |
| | Lt. K.F. Nicholson | FW-190 dest(air) | Paris |
| | Lt. J.F. Potochnik | FW-190 dest(air) | SW Paris |
| | Capt. J.A. Kerig | FW-190 dam(air) | Dreux |

**June 25, 1944**
(#1)

| Unit | Pilot | Claim | Location |
|---|---|---|---|
| 383rd: | Lt. C. Hatfield | (.5)Me-109 dest(air) | All claims are |
| 384th: | Lt. V.L. Kercher | (2)Me-109 dest(air) | E/Blois |
| | Lt. W.E. Bristow | Me-109 dest(air) | |
| | | Me-109 dam(air) | |
| | Lt. R.S. Hunt | Me-109 dest(air) | |
| | Lt. J.R. Korecky | Me-109 dest(air) | |
| | | Me-109 dam(air) | |
| | Lt. J.M. Stuckrath | FW-190 dest(air) | |
| | | FW-190 dam(air) | |
| | Capt. J.C. Ford | (.5)Me-109 dest(air) | |
| | Lt. D.W. Williams | Me-109 prob(air) | |
| | Lt. C.J. Pushcar | Me-109 dam(air) | |

(#2)

| Unit | Pilot | Claim | Location |
|---|---|---|---|
| 383rd: | Lt. H.A. Chesney | (.5)Me-109 dam(grd) | Angars |
| | Lt. M.E. Coates | (.5)Me-109 dam(grd) | Angars |

**July 6, 1944**

| Unit | Pilot | Claim | Location |
|---|---|---|---|
| 385th: | Lt. J.J. Pascoe | FW-190 prob(air) | S/Chalons |
| | Capt. F.C. McClanahan | (2)FW-190 dam(air) | Chalons |
| | Lt. W.G. Erfkamp | FW-190 dam(air) | Chalons |
| | Lt. D.J. Hustead | FW-190 dam(air) | Chalons |
| | Lt. E.K. Tazzia | Me-109 dam(air) | Chalons |

NOTE: From here on, claims will be in P-51's

**August 9, 1944**

| Unit | Pilot | Claim | Location |
|---|---|---|---|
| 383rd: | Maj. G.F. Ceuleers | FW-190 dest(air) | Munich |
| | | (2)FW-190 dam(air) | Munich |
| | Lt. E.C. Beaumont | FW-190 dest(air) | Munich |
| | Lt. R.P. Davis | FW-190 dest(air) | Munich |
| | Lt. C.K. Voss | FW-190 dest(air) | Munich |
| | Capt. M.W. Glascow | (2)Ju-88 dest(grd) | Munich |
| | | (.5)u/i a/c dest(grd) | Munich |
| | Lt. T.H. Hall | (2)Ju-88 dest(grd) | W/Munich |
| | Lt. M.E. Coates | FW-190 dest(grd) | W/Munich |
| | | Ju-88 dest(grd) | W/Munich |
| | | Me-109 dam(grd) | W/Munich |
| | Lt. P.J. Goldberg | (1.5)u/i a/c dest(grd) | Munich |
| | | u/i a/c dam(grd) | Munich |
| | Lt. A.J. Acosta | u/i a/c dest(grd) | W/Munich |
| | | u/i a/c dam(grd) | W/Munich |
| | | Ju-88 dam(grd) | W/Munich |
| | Lt. R.H. Dwyer | (2)FW-190 dam(grd) | W/Munich |
| 384th: | Lt. J.J. Gawienowski | (.5)FW-190 dest(air)* | Kaufburen |
| | | (.5)Trainer dest(air) | Kaufburen |
| | | Me-109 dam(grd) | Schongen |
| | Lt. F.T. Kozloski | (.5)FW-190 dest(air)* | Kaufburen |
| | | (.5)Trainer dest(air) | Kaufburen |
| | | FW-190 dam(grd) | Schongen |
| | Capt. C.H. Leo | FW-190 dest(air) | Kaufburen |
| | Capt. J.R. Steinbacher | FW-190 dest(air) | Kaufburen |
| | Capt. J.M. Stuckrath | FW-190 dest(air) | Kaufburen |
| | Lt. W.N. Champion | (.5)FW-190 dest(air)** | Kaufburen |
| | Lt. J.E. Wilson | (.5)FW-190 dest(air)** | Kaufburen |
| | Lt. W.P. Derr | FW-190 dam(grd) | Kaufburen |
| | Lt. J.L. Grimshaw | Me-410 dam(grd) | Schongen |
| 385th: | Lt. R. Visconte | (3)Me-109 dest(grd) | All 385th claims |
| | | Me-110 dest(grd) | are at Gaukonig- |
| | | Me-110 dam(grd) | shafen |
| | | (.5)FW-200 dam(grd) | |
| | Capt. F.C. McClanahan | Me-109 dest(grd) | |
| | | Me-210 dest(grd) | |
| | Lt. R.A. Crouch | Me-109 dest(grd) | |
| | | Me-210 dest(grd) | |
| | Lt. D.J. Hustead | (2)Me-110 dest(grd) | |
| | | (3)Me-110 dam(grd) | |
| | | (.5)FW-200 dam(grd) | |
| | Lt. E.L. Wilson | Me-110 dest(grd) | |
| | | Me-210 dest(grd) | |
| | | (2)Me-110 dam(grd) | |
| | Lt. H.H. Stubblefield | Me-110 dest(grd) | |
| | | (4)Me-110 dam(grd) | |
| | Lt. W.G. Erfkamp | Me-210 dest(grd) | |
| | | Me-210 dam(grd) | |

**August 10, 1944**

| Unit | Pilot | Claim | Location |
|---|---|---|---|
| 383rd: | Maj. G.F. Ceuleers | Me-109 dest(air) | NW Paris |
| | Lt. C.K. Voss | Me-109 dest(air) | W/Paris |
| 384th: | Capt. D.J. Pick | Me-109 dest(air) | SW Paris |
| | Lt. L.A. Johnson | Me-109 dest(air) | SW Paris |

**August 14, 1944**

| Unit | Pilot | Claim | Location |
|---|---|---|---|
| 383rd: | Lt. M.L. Casagrande | (2)He-111 dest(grd) | All claims are |
| | | Ju-88 dest(grd) | at Memmingen |
| | | (2)He-111 dam(grd) | |
| | Lt. E. levin | (2)He-111 dest(grd) | |
| | | (3)He-111 dam(grd) | |
| | LtCol. J.B. McManus | He-111 dest(grd) | |
| | | He-111 dam(grd) | |
| | Lt. W.T. Dalton | Me-410 dest(grd) | |
| | | He-111 dam(grd) | |
| | Lt. A.J. Acosta | (2)Me-410 dam(grd) | |
| | Lt. N.M. Staranick | He-111 dam(grd) | |

**August 15, 1944**

| Unit | Pilot | Claim | Location |
|---|---|---|---|
| HdQts: | LtCol. J.D. Dale | FW-190 dest(air) | W/Frankfurt |
| 383rd: | Lt. T.H. Hall | (2)Me-109 dest(air) | Mannheim |
| | Capt. H.A. Chesney | Me-109 dest(air) | Mannheim |
| | Capt. S.J. Wicker | Me-109 dest(air) | Frankfurt |

| Squadron | Pilot | Claim | Location |
|---|---|---|---|
| | Lt. M.L. Casagrande | Me-109 dest(air) | Mannheim |
| | Lt. R.H. Dwyer | Me-109 dest(air) | Frankfurt |
| | Lt. G.A. McCoy | Me-109 dest(air) | Frankfurt |
| 384th: | Lt. W.N. Champion | (.5)FW-190 dest(air) | W/Weichaden |
| | | (.5)FW-190 dam(air) | W/Weichaden |
| | Lt. L.A. Johnson | (.5)FW-190 dest(air) | W/Weichaden |
| | | (.5)FW-190 dam(air) | W/Weichaden |
| 385th: | Lt. J.O. Eubanks | Me-109 dest(air) | Frankfurt |
| **August 24, 1944** | | | |
| (#1) | | | |
| 384th: | Lt. J.J. Gawienowski | Me-109 dest(air) | E/Hamburg |
| 385th: | Lt. G.L. Jones | (.5)Me-109 dest(air) | Hamburg |
| | Lt. E.A. Taylor | (.5)Me-109 dest(air) | Hamburg |
| (#2) | | | |
| 383rd: | Lt. A.J. Acosta | Me-109 dest(air) | Seyda |
| | Lt. E.C. Beaumont | Me-109 dest(air) | Seyda |
| | | Me-109 dam(air) | Seyda |
| **August 25, 1944** | | | |
| 385th: | LtCol. R.D. Neece | (2)Ju-88 dest(grd) | Anklam |
| | Lt. E.F. Izor | Me-210 dest(grd) | Anklam |
| | | (2)Me-210 dam(grd) | Anklam |
| | Lt. J.O. Eubanks | Ju-88 dest(grd) | Anklam |
| | Lt. E.K. Tazzia | Ju-88 dest(grd) | Anklam |
| **September 11, 1944** | | | |
| 383rd: | Capt. C.A. Barnes | Me-109 dam(air) | Sangerhausen |
| 384th: | Lt. W.E. Bristow | Me-109 dest(air) | Nordhausen |
| | | FW-190 dest(air) | Nordhausen |
| 385th: | Capt. C.S. Hill | Me-109 dest(air) | Sangerhausen |
| | | FW-190 dest(air) | Sangerhausen |
| | Lt. W.F. Wilson | (2)FW-190 dest(air) | W/Leipzig |
| | | Me-109 dest(air) | W/Leipzig |
| | Lt. G.L. Jamison | (2)FW-190 dest(air) | SW Leipzig |
| | Lt. J.J. Pascoe | (2)FW-190 dest(air) | SW Leipzig |
| | Lt. A.J. Trybuszewski | (2)Me-109 dest(air) | W/Leipzig |
| **September 12, 1944** | | | |
| 383rd: | Capt. B.B. Wilson | FW-190 dest(air) | N/Berlin |
| | Lt. C.K. Voss | FW-190 dest(air) | NE Berlin |
| | Capt. M.W. Glascow | (2)FW-190 prob(air) | N/Berlin |
| **September 13, 1944** | | | |
| 385th: | Lt. G.L. Jamison | Me-109 dest(air) | SE Kassel |
| | Lt. J.F. Vann | Me-109 dest(air) | SE Kassel |
| (PRU) | | | |
| 384th: | Lt. J.A. Walker | Me-262 dam(air) | S/Stralsund |
| **September 19, 1944** | | | |
| 384th: | Lt. E.O. Bowers | (1.5)Me-109 dest(air)* | All 384th claims |
| | F/O W.E. Randolph | (.5)Me-109 dest(air)* | are at Duisenberg |
| | | (2)Me-109 dam(air) | |
| | Lt. R.L. Stiefvater | (.5)Me-109 dest(air)** | |
| | Lt. B.W. Ward | (.5)Me-109 dest(air)** | |
| | | Me-109 prob(air) | |
| | | Me-109 dam(air) | |
| 385th: | Lt. J.J. Pascoe | FW-190 dest(air) | Arnheim |
| **September 23, 1944** | | | |
| 385th: | Lt. W.T. Housholder | FW-190 dest(air) | E/Arnheim |
| | | Me-109 dam(air) | E/Arnheim |
| | Lt. R. Visconte | Me-109 dest(air) | Emmerich |
| | | FW-190 dam(air) | Emmerich |
| **September 28, 1944** | | | |
| 383rd: | Lt. W.D. Boyd | FW-190 dest(air) | S/Magdeburg |
| | | FW-190 dam(air) | S/Magdeburg |
| | Lt. F.C. Sorrells | FW-190 dam(air) | S/magdeburg |
| 385th: | LtCol. R.D. Neece | FW-190 dest(air) | W/Magdeburg |
| | Lt. E.F. Izor | FW-190 dest(air) | SW Magdeburg |
| | Capt. E.A. Taylor | FW-190 dam(air) | W/Magdeburg |
| | Lt. J.J. Pascoe | FW-190 dam(air) | W/Magdeburg |
| **October 7, 1944** | | | |
| 385th: | Capt. E.A. Taylor | (.5)Me-163 dest(air) | Brux |
| | Lt. W.G. Erfkamp | (.5)Me-163 dest(air) | Brux |
| **October 12, 1944** | | | |
| 384th: | Capt. E.B. Shepard | Me-109 dest(air) | N/Bremen |
| | Lt. R.L. Stiefvater | FW-190 dest(air) | N/Bremen |
| 385th: | Lt. A.R. Jones | (3)FW-190 dest(air) | N/Bremen |
| | | FW-190 dam(air) | N/Bremen |
| | Capt. W.S. Crombie | Me-109 dest(air) | W/Bremen |
| | Lt. G.L. Jamison | FW-190 dest(air) | NE Bremen |
| | Lt. R. Visconte | FW-190 dest(air) | NE Bremen |
| | Lt. W.A. Sullivan | FW-190 prob(air) | NE Bremen |
| **November 2, 1944** | | | |
| 383rd: | Lt. E.C. Beaumont | Me-109 dest(air) | Merseburg |
| | | FW-190 dam(air) | Merseburg |
| | Lt. T.H. Hall | FW-190 dest(air) | Merseburg |
| 384th: | Lt. J.M. Fowle | Me-109 dest(air) | S/Merseburg |
| 385th: | Capt. E.F. Izor | (3)Me-109 dest(air) | Halle |
| | Lt. J.J. Pascoe | (2)Me-109 dest(air) | Halle |
| | Capt. W.S. Crombie | Me-109 dest(air) | Halle |
| | Lt. E.N. Farrell | Me-109 dest(air) | N/Merseburg |
| | Lt. J.E. Hargrove | Me-109 dest(air) | Halle |
| | Lt. W.T. Housholder | Me-109 dest(air) | Halle |
| | | Me-109 prob(air) | Halle |
| | Lt. A.B. McCormick | Me-109 dest(air) | Halle |
| | | Me-109 dam(air) | Halle |
| | Lt. H.W. Head | Me-109 dam(air) | Merseburg |
| | Lt. E.H. Rivers | FW-190 dam(air) | Merseburg |
| **November 8, 1944** | | | |
| 384th: | Lt. R.W. Stevens | Me-262 dest(air) | Dummer Lake |
| **November 21, 1944** | | | |
| HdQts: | Col. R.W. Osborn | FW-190 dest(air) | S/Merseburg |
| | LtCol. J.H. Lowell | FW-190 dest(air) | E/Leipzig |
| 383rd: | Lt. M.E. Coates | (2)FW-190 dest(air) | S/Nordhausen |
| | | FW-190 dam(air) | S/Nordhausen |
| | Lt. R.H. Farley | (2)FW-190 dest(air) | Meiningen |
| | Lt. J.C. Hunter | (2)FW-190 dest(air) | S/Nordhausen |
| | | FW-190 dam(air) | S/Nordhausen |
| | Lt. E.H. Horman | FW-190 dest(air) | S/Nordhausen |
| | Lt. M.L. Murphy | FW-190 dam(air) | S/Nordhausen |
| 384th: | Lt. J.L. Grimshaw | FW-190 dest(air) | SW Merseburg |
| | | Me-109 dam(air) | SW Merseburg |
| | Lt. E.H. Miller | FW-190 dest(air) | NE Nordhausen |
| | Lt. E.H. Duderstadt | (.5)FW-190 dest(air) | Mulhausen |
| | Lt. E.W. Farnsworth | (.5)FW-190 dest(air) | Mulhausen |
| | Lt. L. Visconti | FW-190 dest(air) | SW Merseburg |
| | Capt. J.R. Steinbacher | (2)FW-190 dam(air) | SW Halle |
| | Capt. W.E. Bristow | FW-190 dam(air) | SW Halle |
| 385th: | Lt. R.F. Edwards | FW-190 dest(air) | Eisleben |
| | Lt. E.N. Farrell | FW-190 dest(air) | SW Merseburg |
| | Lt. R.M. McKibben | FW-190 dest(air) | W/Merseburg |
| | Capt. T.P. Farrell | (.5)FW-190 dest(air)* | Erfurt |
| | Lt. S.L. Lett | (.5)FW-190 dest(air)* | Erfurt |
| | Lt. N.L. Box | (.5)FW-190 dest(air)** | SW Merseburg |
| | | FW-190 dam(air) | SW Merseburg |
| | Lt. H.W. Head | (.5)FW-190 dest(air)** | SW Merseburg |
| | Lt. J.L. McCubbin | u/i a/c dest(grd) | SE Eisleben |
| | | u/i a/c dam(grd) | SE Eisleben |
| | Lt. A.B. McCormick | u/i a/c dest(grd) | SE Eisleben |
| | Lt. C.S. Hogan | u/i a/c dam(grd) | SE Eisleben |
| **November 25, 1944** | | | |
| 385th: | Lt. H.W. Head | FW-190 dam(grd) | Fulda |
| | Lt. G.L. Jamison | Me-109 dam(grd) | Fulda |
| **November 26, 1944** | | | |
| 383rd: | Lt. J.T. Gaston | (.5)Me-109 dest(air) | Dummer Lake |
| | Lt. G.E. Smith | (.5)Me-109 dest(air) | Dummer Lake |
| 384th: | Lt. J.V. Johnson | Me-109 dest(air) | W/Steinhuder L. |
| | | FW-190 dest(air) | W/Steinhuder L. |
| | Lt. J.M. Fowle | FW-190 dest(air) | SE Dummer Lake |
| 385th: | Maj. J.D. Monahan | FW-190 dest(air) | Uchte |
| | Capt. E.E. Bankey | Me-109 dest(air) | NE Dummer Lake |
| | | Me-109 prob(air) | NE Dummer Lake |
| | Capt. R. Visconte | Me-109 dest(air) | Hoyd |
| | Lt. T.L. Allinder | Me-109 prob(air) | Dummer Lake |
| | Lt. A.B. McCormick | (4)Ju-88 dest(grd) | SE Jade Bay |
| | Lt. R.A. Auguste | Ju-88 dest(grd) | SE Jade Bay |
| **November 30, 1944** | | | |
| 384th: | Lt. E.W. Farnsworth | Me-109 dest(air) | SE Zeitz |
| **December 2, 1944** | | | |
| 385th: | Capt. R. Visconte | FW-190 dest(air) | NW Ludwigshafen |
| | Lt. J.L. McCubbin | Me-109 dest(air) | Mannheim |
| **December 5, 1944** | | | |
| HdQts: | LtCol. J.H. Lowell | (3)FW-190 dest(air) | N/Berlin |
| | | FW-190 dam(air) | N/Berlin |
| 384th: | Lt. E.W. Farnworth | FW-190 dest(air) | NW Berlin |
| | Lt. W.E. Flynt | (.5)FW-190 dest(air) | NW Berlin |
| | Lt. D.L. Leftwich | (.5)FW-190 dest(air) | NW Berlin |
| 385th: | Capt. W.F. Wilson | (2)FW-190 dest(air) | All claims are |
| | | FW-190 dam(air) | N/Berlin |
| | Lt. J.L. McCubbin | (2)FW-190 dest(air) | |
| | | (2)FW-190 prob(air) | |
| | Maj. C.W. Stapleton | FW-190 dest(air) | |
| | Capt. T.P. Farrell | FW-190 dest(air) | |
| | Lt. E.N. Farrell | (2)FW-190 dam(air) | |
| **December 23, 1944** | | | |
| 383rd: | Maj. G.F. Ceuleers | (4)Me-109 dest(air) | All 383rd claims |
| | Lt. R.W. Orndorff | (2)FW-190 dest(air) | are NW Trier |
| | Lt. R.M. Baughn | FW-190 dest(air) | |

| | | | |
|---|---|---|---|
| | Lt. C.E. Hammett | FW-190 dest(air) | |
| | Lt. J.D. Woodside | Me-109 dest(air) | |
| | | Me-109 dam(air) | |
| | Lt. E.F. Heyn | Me-109 dam(air) | |
| 384th: | Lt. J.M. Fowle | (4)Me-109 dest(air) | NW Trier |
| | Lt. W.F. Flynt | Me-109 dest(air) | Luxembourg |
| | Lt. T.H. Wells | Me-109 dest(air) | Luxembourg |
| 385th: | Capt. T.P. Farrell | (2)FW-190 dest(air) | NW Trier |
| | Lt. W.G. Erfkamp | (2)Me-109 dest(air) | Luxembourg |
| | Lt. S.L. Lett | FW-190 dest(air) | NW Trier |
| | Lt. C.R. Roesch | FW-190 dam(air) | Luxembourg |

**December 27, 1944**

| | | | |
|---|---|---|---|
| HdQts: | Capt. E.E. Bankey | (4)FW-190 dest(air) | Bonn |
| | | (1.5)Me-109 dest(air) | Bonn |
| | | (shared with a 352nd Ftr Grp P-51) | |
| | LtCol. J.H. Lowell | (.5)Me-109 dest(air)** | W/Coblenz |
| | | Me-109 dam(air) | W/Coblenz |
| 383rd: | Capt. E.N. Fiery | (2)FW-190 dest(air) | Frankfurt |
| | | FW-190 dam(air) | Frankfurt |
| | Lt. H.D. Sandkaut | FW-190 dest(air) | NW Frankfurt |
| | Lt. G.E. Smith | FW-190 dam(air) | SW Frankfurt |
| 384th: | Lt. E.H. Duderstadt | (2)FW-190 dest(air) | W/Coblenz |
| | | Me-109 dest(air) | W/Coblenz |
| | Lt. D.L. Leftwich | (2)FW-190 dest(air) | W/Coblenz |
| | Lt. R.K. Allen | (1.5)Me-109 dest(air)* | SW Coblenz |
| | | FW-190 dam(air) | SW Coblenz |
| | Lt. R.S. Faulkner | FW-190 dest(air) | S/Coblenz |
| | Lt. S.J. Price | (.5)Me-109 dest(air)** | SW Coblenz |
| | Lt. R.W. Stevens | Me-109 dam(air) | Bonn |
| | Lt. H.M. James | Me-109 dam(air) | Bonn |
| 385th: | Capt. G.L. Jamison | (3)FW-190 dest(air) | SW Bonn |
| | | Me-109 dam(air) | E/Liege |
| | Lt. E.N. Farrell | FW-190 dest(air) | SE Bonn |
| | | Me-109 dest(air) | SE Bonn |
| | Lt. J.T. Barrie | Me-109 dest(air) | SW Bonn |
| | Lt. D.L. Bloodgood | FW-190 dest(air) | SE Bonn |
| | Lt. H.W. Head | FW-190 dest(air) | NW Bonn |
| | Lt. C.S. Hogan | FW-190 dest(air) | Laachen Lake |
| | | FW-190 prob(air) | Laachen Lake |
| | Lt. W.S. Sagar | FW-190 dest(air) | W/Coblenz |
| | | (.5)Me-109 dest(air)* | SW Coblenz |
| | | Me-109 dam(air) | W/Coblenz |

**December 31, 1944**

| | | | |
|---|---|---|---|
| 383rd: | Maj. S.J. Wicker | (4)FW-190 dest(air) | SW Hamburg |
| | Lt. D.C. Fisher | FW-190 dest(air) | SW Hamburg |
| | Lt. R.W. Orndorff | FW-190 dest(air) | SW Hamburg |
| 384th: | Lt. W.P. Hess | (3)FW-190 dest(air) | SE Hamburg |
| | | Ju-87 dest(grd) | SE Hamburg |
| | Lt. J.M. Fowle | (2)FW-190 dest(air) | SW Hamburg |
| | Lt. E.H. Miller | (2)FW-190 dest(air) | Hamburg |
| | Lt. W.E. Randolph | (2)FW-190 dest(air) | S/Hamburg |
| | Lt. T.H. Wells | (2)FW-190 dest(air) | Hamburg |
| | Lt. H.M. James | FW-190 dest(air) | SE Hamburg |
| | Lt. G.Z. Schroeder | FW-190 dest(air) | Hamburg |
| | Lt. R.S. Faulkner | (.5)FW-190 dest(air) | SW Hamburg |
| | Lt. D.L. Leftwich | (.5)FW-190 dest(air) | SW Hamburg |
| | Lt. L.L. Lefforge | FW-190 prob(air) | SW Hamburg |
| 385th: | Capt. W.S. Crombie | FW-190 dest(air) | Hamburg |
| | Lt. H.W. Head | FW-190 dest(air) | SE Hamburg |
| | Lt. R.M. McKibben | FW-190 dest(air) | SE Hamburg |
| | Lt. E. Murphy | FW-190 dest(air) | Hamburg |
| | Lt. T.L. Allinder | (.5)FW-190 dest(air) | SW Hamburg |
| | F/O C.L. Smart | (.5)FW-190 dest(air) | SW Hamburg |
| | Lt. F.X. Radley | FW-190 prob(air) | Hamburg |

**January 1, 1945**

| | | | |
|---|---|---|---|
| 383rd: | Maj. G.F. Ceuleers | (2)Me-109 dest(air) | Hamburg |
| | Lt. F.C. Sorrells | Me-109 dest(air) | W/Stendal |
| | Lt. J.D. Woodside | Me-109 dest(air) | Hamburg |
| 385th: | Capt. W.S. Crombie | FW-190 dest(air) | SE Hamburg |
| | Lt. H.W. Head | FW-190 dest(air) | SE Hamburg |
| | Lt. J.L. McCubbin | Me-109 dest(air) | SE Hamburg |
| | Lt. J.E. Hargrove | (.5)FW-190 dest(air) | Hamburg |
| | Lt. F.X. Radley | (.5)FW-190 dest(air) | Hamburg |

**January 29, 1945**

| | | | |
|---|---|---|---|
| 385th: | Capt. N.L. Box | u/i a/c dam(grd) | Darmstadt |
| | Lt. A.B. McCormick | u/i a/c dam(grd) | Darmstadt |

**February 3, 1945**

| | | | |
|---|---|---|---|
| 383rd: | Lt. L.V. Andrew | Me-262 dam(air) | S/Gardelegen |

**February 6, 1945**

| | | | |
|---|---|---|---|
| 384th: | Capt. J.M. Fowle | Ar-234 dam(air) | SE Zuider Zee |

**February 14, 1945**

| | | | |
|---|---|---|---|
| 383rd: | Capt. C.A. Barnes | FW-190 dest(air) | Chemnitz |
| | Lt. C.E. Hammett | FW-190 prob(air) | Chemnitz |

**February 22, 1945**

| | | | |
|---|---|---|---|
| 383rd: | Lt. E.H. Horman | FW-190 dest(air) | SW Bremen |
| | | (2)FW-190 dam(air) | SW Bremen |
| | Lt. E.W. Kortendick | FW-190 dest(air) | S/Quackenbruck |
| | | FW-190 dam(air) | S/Quackenbruck |
| | Lt. W.V. Pyle | (2)FW-190 dam(air) | SW Bremen |
| | Lt. G.O. Warner | (2)Me-262 dam(air) | W/Berlin |
| | Lt. R.L. Hunt | Me-262 dam(air) | Wittstock |
| 384th: | Capt. R.W. Stevens | (.5)Me-262 prob(air) | Wittstock |
| | Lt. C.B. Kirby | (.5)Me-262 prob(air) | Wittstock |
| | | Me-262 dam(air) | Wittstock |
| | Capt. S.C. Phillips | Me-262 dam(air) | Stendal |
| | Lt. L.L. Lefforge | Me-262 dam(air) | Stendal |
| | Lt. L.H. Phipps | Me-262 dam(air) | Stendal |
| | Lt. S.J. Price | Me-262 dam(air) | Stendal |
| | Lt. W.E. Randolph | Me-262 dam(air) | Stendal |

**February 23, 1945**

| | | | |
|---|---|---|---|
| 384th: | Capt. D.J. Pick | (2.5)Me-109 dest(air) | Stuttgart |
| | | Me-109 dam(grd) | Stuttgart |
| | Capt. R.W. Stevens | (2)Me-109 dest(air) | Stuttgart |
| | Lt. H.C. Schwartz | (2)Me-109 dest(air) | Stuttgart |
| | F/O J.F. Nelson | (.5)Me-109 dest(air) | Stuttgart |

**February 25, 1945**

| | | | |
|---|---|---|---|
| 384th: | Lt. J.E. Soehl | FW-190 dest(air) | SW Ulzen |
| | | FW-190 dam(air) | SW Ulzen |
| | Capt. R.L. Stiefvater | FW-190 dam(air) | N/Gifhorn |
| 385th: | Lt. E. Murphy | (.5)Ar-234 dest(air) | Steinhuder Lake |
| | Lt. R.E. White | (.5)Ar-234 dest(air) | Steinhuder Lake |

**February 26, 1945**

| | | | |
|---|---|---|---|
| 385th: | Lt. K.R. Horner | (2)He-111 dest(grd) | SE Jade Bay |
| | Lt. A.B. McCormick | (1.5)He-111 dest(grd) | SE Jade Bay |
| | Lt. C.R. Roesch | (1.5)He-111 dest(grd) | SE Jade Bay |

**March 1, 1945**

| | | | |
|---|---|---|---|
| 384th: | Lt. F.T. O'Connor | Me-262 dam(air) | NE Frankfurt |

**March 18, 1945**

| | | | |
|---|---|---|---|
| 383rd: | Lt. J.C. Hunter | FW-190 dest(air) | Schwerin |
| | Lt. E. Chlevin | He-111 dest(air) | Schwerin |

**March 21, 1945**

| | | | |
|---|---|---|---|
| 383rd: | Capt. L.V. Andrew | Me-109 dam(grd) | All claims are |
| | | Ju-88 dam(grd) | at Achmer |
| 385th: | Capt. T.P. Farrell | FW-190 dest(grd) | |
| | | (3)Ju-188 dam(grd) | |
| | Lt. K.R. Horner | Me-109 dest(grd) | |
| | | Me-109 dam(grd) | |
| | Capt. J.E. Hargrove | (2)FW-190 dam(grd) | |
| | Maj. W.S. Crombie | u/i a/c dam(grd) | |

**March 30, 1945**

| | | | |
|---|---|---|---|
| 383rd: | Lt. J.B. Guy | (.5)Me-262 dest(air) | Brandenburg |
| | | (shared with an unknown P-51 pilot) | |
| | Lt. R.L. Hunt | Me-262 dam(air) | Brandenburg |

**April 4, 1945**

| | | | |
|---|---|---|---|
| 383rd: | LtCol. G.F. Ceuleers | Me-262 dest(air) | Hamburg-Dessau |
| 385th: (PRU) | Lt. J.S. Rogers | Me-262 dam(air) | Fassberg A/F |
| 385th: | Lt. J.W. Ruland | FW-190 dest(air) | Potsdam |

**April 5, 1945**

| | | | |
|---|---|---|---|
| 384th: | Lt. G.Z. Schroeder | Me-262 dam(air) | N/Regensburg |
| 385th: | F/O W.K. Masters | Me-109 dest(grd) | SW Nurnburg |
| | Capt. E.N. Farrell | Me-262 dam(grd) | SW Nurnburg |
| | Lt. F.O. Spain | FW-190 dam(grd) | SW Nurnburg |

**April 10, 1945**

| | | | |
|---|---|---|---|
| 384th: | Capt. D.J. Pick | (.5)Me-262 dest(air) | Staaken A/F |
| | Lt. H.C. Schwartz | (.5)Me-262 dest(air) | Staaken A/F |
| | | FW-200 dest(grd) | W/Berlin |
| | LtCol. R.E. Lacy | Me-410 dest(grd) | Oranienburg |
| | | He-177 dam(grd) | Oranienburg |
| | Lt. J.L. Hughes | He-111 dest(grd) | Oranienburg |
| | | Me-109 dam(grd) | Oranienburg |
| | Lt. D.L. Leftwich | He-111 dam(grd) | Oranienburg |
| | Lt. S.R. Honaker | Do-217 dam(grd) | W/Berlin |
| | | He-111 dam(grd) | W/Berlin |
| 385th: | Maj. W.S. Crombie | Me-262 dest(grd) | All claims are |
| | | Ju-88 dest(grd) | at Stendal |
| | | u/i a/c dest(grd) | |
| | | (2)FW-190 dam(grd) | |
| | | Ju-88 dam(grd) | |
| | Lt. W.W. Helmholz | (2)Me-262 dest(grd) | |
| | | FW-190 dest(grd) | |
| | | FW-190 dam(grd) | |
| | Lt. J.W. Munn | FW-190 dest(grd) | |
| | F/O T.F. lasch | Ju-88 dest(grd) | |

**April 13, 1945**

| | | | |
|---|---|---|---|
| 383rd: | Capt. J.L. Truett | (4)Ju-52 dest(grd) | All 383rd claims |
| | | Do-217 dest(grd) | are at Flensburg |
| | | Me-109 dam(grd) | |
| | | FW-190 dam(grd) | |
| | Capt. J.C. Hunter | (3)FW-190 dest(grd) | |
| | | (2)Ju-52 dest(grd) | |
| | | Me-110 dest(grd) | |
| | | (3)Ju-52 dam(grd) | |
| | | Me-109 dam(grd) | |
| | Capt. R.W. Orndorff | (2)Ju-52 dest(grd) | |
| | | Me-109 dest(grd) | |
| | | FW-190 dest(grd) | |
| | | Fi-156 dam(grd) | |
| | Lt. W.F. Kissel | (4)Ju-52 dest(grd) | |
| | | (2)Me-109 dam(grd) | |
| | | Me-110 dam(grd) | |
| | | Ju-52 dam(grd) | |
| | Lt. G.E. Smith | (2)FW-190 dest(grd) | |
| | | Ju-52 dest(grd) | |
| | | (2)FW-190 dam(grd) | |
| | | Ju-52 dam(grd) | |
| | Lt. R.M. Baughn | (2)Ju-52 dest(grd) | |
| | | FW-190 dest(grd) | |
| | | Me-109 dam(grd) | |
| | | FW-190 dam(grd) | |
| | Lt. J.B. Guy | Me-109 dest(grd) | |
| | | Ju-52 dest(grd) | |
| | | FW-190 dam(grd) | |
| | | Ju-52 dam(grd) | |
| | Lt. J.A. Seth | Me-109 dest(grd) | |
| | | FW-190 dest(grd) | |
| | | Me-109 dam(grd) | |
| | Lt. H.D. Sandkaut | (2)Ju-52 dest(grd) | |
| | | Do-217 dam(grd) | |
| | | FW-190 dam(grd) | |
| | Lt. E.H. Horman | (2)Ju-52 dest(grd) | |
| | | Ju-52 dam(grd) | |
| | Lt. C.E. Jackson | (2)FW-190 dest(grd) | |
| | | FW-190 dam(grd) | |
| | Lt. E.W. Kortendick | Me-109 dest(grd) | |
| | | Fi-156 dest(grd) | |
| | | (2)FW-190 dam(grd) | |
| | | Ju-52 dam(grd) | |
| | Lt. L. Leon | FW-190 dest(grd) | |
| | | Me-109 dam(grd) | |
| | | Ju-52 dam(grd) | |
| | Lt. E. Holmes | Me-109 dest(grd) | |
| | | (3)Me-109 dam(grd) | |
| | Lt. C.W. Hornick | Me-109 dest(grd) | |
| | | Me-109 dam(grd) | |
| | | Ju-52 dam(grd) | |
| | Lt. V.A. O'Brien | Ju-52 dest(grd) | |
| | | (2)FW-190 dam(grd) | |
| 384th: | Capt. R.K. Allen | (2)u/i a/c dest(grd) | 384th claims are |
| | Lt. H.V. Herndon | Ju-88 dest(grd) | at Kaltenkirchen |
| | Capt. R.S. Faulkner | u/i a/c dam(grd) | |
| | Lt. P.J. Hahn | Do-217 dam(grd) | |
| 385th: | Capt. A.B. McCormick | Do-217 dest(grd) | 385th claims are |
| | | Ju-188 dest(grd) | E/Luneburg |
| | | (.5)FW-190 dest(grd) | |
| | | Do-217 dam(grd) | |
| | | FW-190 dam(grd) | |
| | Lt. L.G. Johnson | Ju-188 dest(grd) | |
| | | (.5)FW-190 dest(grd) | |
| | | FW-190 dam(grd) | |
| | Capt. H.W. Head | Ju-88 dest(grd) | |

**April 16, 1945**

| | | | |
|---|---|---|---|
| HdQts: | Capt. E.E. Bankey | (2)Me-109 dest(air) | N/Nordlingen |
| | | (2)Ju-188 dest(grd) | Pocking |
| | | FW-190 dest(grd) | Pocking |
| | | Do-217 dest(grd) | Pocking |
| | | (2)FW-190 dam(grd) | Pocking |
| | | (2)Ju-188 dam(grd) | Pocking |
| | LtCol. E.P. Roberts | (3)Fi-156 dam(grd) | Marienbad |
| 383rd: | Lt. J.A. Seth | (2)Me-109 dest(grd) | 383rd claims are |
| | Capt. C.E. Hammett | Ju-52 dest(grd) | at Marienbad |
| | Capt. L.V. Andrew | Me-410 dest(grd) | |
| | Capt. J.L. Truett | Fi-156 dest(grd) | |
| | | (.5)FW-190 dest(grd) | |
| | | Do-217 dam(grd) | |
| | | Fi-156 dam(grd) | |
| | Lt. G.F. Hill | (.5)FW-190 dest(grd) | |
| | | FW-190 dam(grd) | |
| | Lt. E. Chlevin | FW-190 dest(grd) | |
| | | (.5)Do-217 dest(grd) | |
| | | Do-217 dam(grd) | |
| | | Ju-52 dam(grd) | |
| | F/O J.J. Jacaruso | (.5)Do-217 dest(grd) | |
| | | u/i a/c dam(grd) | |
| | F/O D.F. Healey | FW-190 dest(grd) | |
| | | Fi-156 dest(grd) | |
| | | Do-217 dam(grd) | |
| | | u/i a/c dam(grd) | |
| | Lt. D.C. Fisher | FW-190 dest(grd) | |
| | Lt. W.K. Hood | Me-109 dest(grd) | |
| | | FW-190 dam(grd) | |
| | | Do-217 dam(grd) | |
| | Lt. R.L. Hunt | u/i a/c dest(grd) | |
| | | FW-190 dam(grd) | |
| | Capt. C.A. Barnes | FW-190 dam(grd) | |
| | | Ju-52 dam(grd) | |
| | Lt. R.M. Baughn | (2)u/i a/c dam(grd) | |
| | Lt. E.P. Hausenbauer | Ju-52 dam(grd) | |
| | Lt. R.W. Queal | Do-217 dam(grd) | |
| 384th: | Lt. J.E. Soehl | (3)u/i a/c dest(grd) | All 384th claims |
| | LtCol. R.E. Lacy | FW-190 dest(grd) | are at Pocking |
| | Lt. H.C. Schwartz | Ju-87 dest(grd) | |
| | | (3)Me-109 dam(grd) | |
| | Lt. J.E. Taylor | FW-190 dest(grd) | |
| | Lt. D.L. Leftwich | FW-190 dest(grd) | |
| 385th: | Lt. K.R. Horner | Ju-188 dest(grd) | All claims are |
| | | FW-190 dest(grd) | at Pocking |
| | | Ju-87 dest(grd) | |
| | | FW-190 dam(grd) | |
| | Capt. J.E. Hargrove | Me-109 dest(grd) | |
| | | Ju-87 dest(grd) | |
| | Lt. F.O. Spain | FW-190 dest(grd) | |
| | | Fi-156 dest(grd) | |
| | | (3)Ju-87 dam(grd) | |
| | Lt. J.W. Kiernan | (2)Me-109 dest(grd) | |
| | | Me-109 dam(grd) | |
| | Lt. C.R. Roesch | (2)FW-190 dest(grd) | |
| | | FW-190 dam(grd) | |
| | Lt. D.L. Bloodgood | (2)FW-190 dest(grd) | |
| | Lt. J.W. Munn | FW-190 dest(grd) | |
| | | (4)FW-190 dam(grd) | |
| | Lt. E.H. Jones | (3)FW-190 dam(grd) | |
| | Lt. J.G. Johnson | (2)FW-190 dam(grd) | |

**April 17, 1945**

| | | | |
|---|---|---|---|
| HdQts: | Capt. W.L. Goff | Me-262 dest(air) | Pilzen |
| | LtCol. J.H. Lowell | He-111 dest(grd) | Karlsbad |
| | | FW-200 dest(grd) | Karlsbad |
| | | Me-262 dest(grd) | Karlsbad |
| | Capt. E.E. Bankey | (2)He-111 dest(grd) | Karlsbad |
| | | (2)He-111 dam(grd) | Karlsbad |
| 383rd: | Capt. R.W. Orndorff | Me-262 dest(air) | Praha |
| | Lt. R.M. Baughn | Me-262 dest(grd) | SE Pilzen |
| | Lt. W.F. Kissel | Me-262 dest(grd) | Falkenst |
| | Capt. G.O. Warner | (3)Me-262 dam(grd) | Praha |
| | Lt. G.F. Hill | Me-262 dam(grd) | SE Pilzen |
| 384th: | Lt. S.J. Price | Me-262 dam(air) | Dresden |
| | Lt. J.E. Taylor | He-111 dest(grd) | All remaining |
| | | FW-200 dest(grd) | claims are at |
| | Lt. W.A. Leavell | He-111 dest(grd) | Karlsbad |
| | | He-111 dam(grd) | |
| | Lt. J.L. Hughes | He-111 dest(grd) | |
| | | He-111 dam(grd) | |
| 385th: | Lt. J.S. Rogers | He-111 dest(grd) | |
| | | Ar-66 dest(grd) | |
| | | Ju-52 dest(grd) | |
| | | (2)He-111 dam(grd) | |
| | F/O W.K. Masters | He-111 dest(grd) | |
| | | Ar-66 dest(grd) | |
| | Capt. E. Murphy | FW-190 dest(grd) | |
| | Lt. E.E. Anderson | He-111 dest(grd) | |
| | | He-111 dam(grd) | |
| | Lt. E.H. Jones | (2)He-111 dam(grd) | |
| | Capt. R.E. White | FW-200 dam(grd) | |
| | Lt. J.W. Ruland | He-111 dam(grd) | |

**April 19, 1945**

| | | | |
|---|---|---|---|
| 383rd: | Capt. C.E. Hammett | FW-190 dest(air) | All claims are |
| | | (.5)Do-217 dest(air) | at Lubben |
| | F/O D.F. Healey | FW-190 dest(air) | |
| | | (.5)Do-217 dest(air) | |
| | Lt. R.W. Queal | FW-190 dest(air) | |
| | | FW-190 dam(air) | |
| | Lt. D.C. Fisher | FW-190 dest(air) | |

### 364th Fighter Group Losses

**February 29, 1944**

Col. Fred C. Grambo (HdQts) KIA; Suffered mechanical failure east of the Zuider Zee and crashed at Geithoorn.

P-38J N2- 42-67404

**March 5, 1944**
Capt. Paul F. Miller (HdQts) MIA-E; Ran out of fuel and bailed out near Poiters.
P-38J N2- 42-67745

**March 6, 1944**
Lt. Larry N. Ferguson (384th) MIA; Hit by fighters near Gardelegen and bailed out near Winterfeld.
P-38J 5Y- 42-67461

**March 8, 1944**
Capt. Leown A. Gilliland (383rd) ASR; Ran out of fuel and ditched in the Channel.
P-38J N2-
Lt. Charles E. Brock (383rd) POW; Hit by flak near Berlin and bailed out near Kolbitz.
P-38J N2- 42-67233
Lt. Kenneth F. London (383rd) KIA; Hit by a Me-109 near Nienburg.
P-38J N2- 42-67223

**March 9, 1944**
Lt. Ray D. Kunzler (384th) KIA; Suffered mechanical trouble and hit by flak near Osnabruck.
P-38J 5Y-R 42-67230

**March 15, 1944**
Capt. Richard M. Scott (385th) POW; Hit by fighters near Rheine.
P-38J 5E-S 42-68062
Lt. John C. Tallman (385th) POW; Hit by fighters near Rheine.
P-38J 5E-K 42-68178
Lt. James D. Turner (385th) POW; Hit by fighters near Rheine.
P-38J 5E-Q 42-67205

**March 19, 1944**
Lt. Creyaton Carlson (383rd) KIAc; Spun-in near Honington.
P-38J N2-

**March 22, 1944**
Capt. Roy O. Smith, Jr. (385th) KIA; Hit by flak near Kortgere.
P-38J 5E-G 42-67934
Lt. William R. Jackson (385th) POW; Hit by flak and bailed out over the North Sea.
P-38J 5E- 42-68069

**March 27, 1944**
Lt. William G. Coltman (384th) POW; Collided with Lt. Westmore near Mayenne.
P-38J 5Y- 42-67433
Lt. Harry W. Westmore (384th) POW; Collided with Lt. Coltman near Mayenne.
P-38J 5Y- 42-67428

**March 29, 1944**
Capt. Leown A. Gilliland (383rd) KIA; Suffered mechanical failure and crashed off Lowestoft.
P-38J N2- 42-67416
Lt. Norman D. MacLean (384th) MIA; Hit by flak and bellied-in near Rheine.
P-38J 5Y- 42-67984
Lt. Curtis A. Smith (385th) KIA; Crashed near Tibbenham upon return from the mission.
P-38J 5E-

**April 9, 1944**
Lt. Eugene J. Zakovec (385th) KIA; Hit by flak near Rheine.
P-38J 5E- 42-67957

**April 12, 1944**
Lt. Edmond G. Brennan (383rd) MIA; Hit by fighters east of Frankfurt.
P-38J N2- 42-67445
Lt. Ted G. Bushnell (383rd) POW; Hit by fighters east of Frankfurt.
P-38J N2- 42-104170

**April 13, 1944**
Lt. Walter F. Pogue (384th) MIA; Suffered mecahnical failure near Liege.
P-38J 5Y-F 42-104195

**April 15, 1944**
Capt. Orville E. Myers (384th) KIA; Last seen near Diepholz.
P-38J 5Y-M 42-67737
Lt. Edward L. Henkle (384th) POW; Last seen near Virden.
P-38J 5Y- 42-104214
Lt. Fred F. Kingsbury (384th) MIA; Last seen near Virden.
P-38J 5Y- 42-67240
Lt. Willard E. Moore (384th) POW; Hit by flak at Stade A/F.
P-38J 5Y- 42-68148
Capt. Reed H. Dominy (385th) KIA; Hit by flak north of Dummer Lake and crashed near Vechta.
P-38J 5E- 42-67938
Capt. Robert B. Reynolds (385th) KIA; Hit by flak southeast of Bremen.
P-38J 5E- 42-68041
Lt. William J. Sims (385th) POW; Hit by flak north of Dummer Lake and crashed near Vechta.
P-38J 5E- 42-67851
Lt. Clyde M. Street (385th) MIA; Bailed out 40 miles southeast of Great Yarmouth.
P-38J 5E- 42-67302

**April 24, 1944**
Lt. Walter J. Shea (385th) MIA; Suffered mechanical failure and crashed southeast of Risby.
P-38J 5E-

**April 26, 1944**
Lt. Ira A. Whipple (385th) MIA; Suffered mechanical trouble and crashed 45 miles northeast of Manston.
P-38J 5E- 42-68141

**April 28, 1944**
Lt. William P. O'Connell (385th) KIAc; Crashed near Rushdon.
P-38J 5E-

**April 29, 1944**
Lt. Shornden D. McCloud (384th) POW; Collided with Lt. Smith north of Brunswick.
P-38J 5Y-D 42-67417
Lt. Kenneth M. Shaffer (384th) POW; Hit by a Me-109 near Brandenburg
P-38J 5Y-I 42-67438
Lt. Eugene L. Smith (384th) POW; Collided with Lt. McCloud north of Brunswick.
P-38J 5Y- 42-67447

**May 3, 1944**
Capt. Marcus C. Linn (385th) KIAc; Hit the water while practicing skip-bombing southeast of Clacton.
P-38J 5E- 42-68187

**May 7, 1944**
Lt. Alfred C. Stepman (385th) KIA; Suffered mechanical trouble and ditched 10 miles west of Tessel Island.
P-38J 5E- 42-67248

**May 8, 1944**
Lt. Walter C. Bosworth (383rd) POW; Hit by a Me-109 near Barver.
P-38J N2- 42-104198
Capt. Roy M. Spradlin (384th) POW; Hit by a Me-109 northeast of Hanover.
P-38J 5Y-D 42-68070
Lt. Lynn Steincamp (385th) POW; Suffered mechanical failure and bailed out southeast of Brunswick.
P-38J 5E- 42-104326

**May 19, 1944**
Lt. Nick W. Cruger (383rd) KIA; Damaged by flak and crashed northeast of Cromer.
P-38J N2- 43-28360
Lt. John Kerr (383rd) MIA; Hit by flak and bailed out near Juist.
P-38J N2-A 42-68013
Lt. Marvin H. Brown (384th) POW; Hit by flak at Husum and bellied-in near Nordstrand.
P-38J 5Y-T 42-104402
Lt. Edwin F. Gaines (384th) POW; Hit by flak at Husum and bellied-in near Nordstrand.
P-38J 5Y- 42-67882

**May 21, 1944**
Maj. Andrew L. Chilton (HdQts) KIA; Hit by flak at Hagenow A/F and crashed into a house.
P-38J 5Y-A 43-28734
Lt. LaMarr J. Miller (383rd) POW; Hit by flak at Rechlin/Larz A/F and bellied-in near the field.
P-38J N2-I 43-28272

**May 22, 1944**
Lt. Milton S. Damron (384th) POW; Last seen chasing a FW-190 near Kiel.
P-38J 5Y- 42-68125
Lt. Howard V. Kilpatrick (384th) POW; Last seen in a fight near Kiel with one engine afire.
P-38J 5Y-M 43-28470

**May 25, 1944**
Lt. Vaude V. Ames (383rd) POW; Hit by a FW-190 near Chartres.
P-38J N2- 42-67222
Lt. Leroy Q. Olson (383rd) POW; Hit by a FW-190 near Chartres.
P-38J N2-S 42-68034
Lt. Clarence F. Scrivner (383rd) POW; Hit by a FW-190 near Chartres.
P-38J N2-Z 43-28425
Lt. Donald S. Chaplin (385th) POW; Hit by flak southeast of Paris.
P-38J 5E- 42-68158
Lt. Clarence B. Warner (385th) MIA; Hit by flak southeast of Paris.
P-38J 5E- 43-28760
Lt. John W. Wittgreve (385th) POW; Hit by flak southeast of Paris.
P-38J 5E-N 42-67258

**June 8, 1944**
Lt. Loren R. Wilson (383rd) KIA; Spun-in near Funting upon return.
P-38J N2-K 42-104417

**June 27, 1944**
Lt. Jarrette L. Bowen (384th) POW; Hit by flak northeast of Verdun.
P-38J 5Y- 42-68063
Lt. Max J. Woolley (384th) MIA-E; Hit by flak north of Charleroi.
P-38J 5Y- 42-67979

**July 15, 1944**
Capt. Victor L. Kercher (384th) KIA; Collided with Lt. Yost near La Charite.
P-38J 5Y-K 42-104421 "Daddy's Baby"
Lt. Byron P. Yost (384th) KIA; Collided with Capt. Kercher near La Charite.
P-38J 5Y-F 42-67980

**July 18, 1944**
Capt. John C. Ford (384th) KIAc; Spun-in south of Honington after losing an engine on take-off.
P-38J 5Y-O 42-68101

**July 27, 1944**
Lt. James B. MacDermott (383rd) POW; Suffered mechanical failure and bailed out southeast of Arras.
P-51D N2- 44-13878

**July 30, 1944**
Lt. James R. Korecky (384th) KIAc; Stalled on take-off, clipped a parked B-17 and crashed at the end of the field.
P-51D 5Y-D 44-14034

**August 1, 1944**
Lt. Niel T. Baker (384th) KIA; Collided with a P-51 on take-off and crashed near Tibbenham.
P-51C 5Y-F 43-25040

**August 2, 1944**
Lt. Houston L. Braley (383rd) KIA; Caught in a bomb blast southwest of Compiegne.
P-51D N2- 44-13797

**August 4, 1944**
Lt. Clyde W. Diffenbach (383rd) POW; Suffered mechnical trouble and was last seen near Roeby Haun.
P-51D N2- 44-13922
Lt. John F. Potochnik (383rd) POW; Hit by flak and bailed out north of Zingst.
P-51D N2- 44-13920

**August 8, 1944**
Lt. William P. Dean (385th) KIA; Hit by flak near Fresquienne.
P-51D 5E- 44-14008

**August 9, 1944**
Lt. Ted D. Nielson (384th) MIA; Suffered mechanical failure near Kitzingen and bailed out southeast of Rottenberg.
P-51D 5Y-N 44-13766

**August 10, 1944**
Lt. Paul J. Goldberg (383rd) MIA-E; Hit by a Me-109 near Dreux.
P-51C N2-B 43-25058

**August 17, 1944**
Lt. Harold D. Burkhard (384th) MIA-E; Hit by flak near Erviller and bailed out near Bourbouville.
P-51D 5Y- 44-13700

**August 25, 1944**
Lt. Duane W. Owens (385th) POW; Hit by flak near Anklam.
P-51C 5E-O 42-103593
Lt. Edward K. Tazzia (385th) POW; Hit by flak near Anklam.
P-51C 5E-Y 43-25030 "Lucky II"

**August 27, 1944**
Lt. Argent J. Acosta, Jr. (383rd) KIA; Hit by flak near Kiel.
P-51D N2-W 44-13936 "Carolina Moon"
Lt. Charles A. King (385th) POW; Lost in bad weather near Kiel.
P-51D 5E-I 44-14024

**September 1, 1944**
Lt. Richard P. Davis (383rd) ASR; Suffered mechanical trouble and bailed out over the Channel.
P-51D N2-A 44-13757

**September 5, 1944**
Lt. John R. Vickers (385th) MIA; Suffered mechanical failure southwest of Luxembourg.
P-51D 5E- 44-14236

**September 11, 1944**
Lt. Alfred A. Albrecht (384th) KIA; Hit by fighters near Giessen.
P-51D 5Y- 44-14174
Lt. Daniel W. Davis (385th) POW; Hit by fighters near Sangerhausen.
P-51D 5E-M 44-14033 "Doodlebug"

**September 16, 1944**
Lt. Grant L. Jones (385th) KIA; Hit by flak and bailed out near Nienburg.
P-51D 5E-B 44-13964

**September 17, 1944**
Lt. Harry Johnson, Jr. (383rd) MIA; Hit by flak near Arnheim.
P-51D N2-V 44-13866 "Rosey Doates"
Lt. Douglas R. Drysdale (385th) MIA-E; Hit by flak near Nijmegen and bailed out southwest of Zeeland.
P-51D 5E-T 44-14025 "Lovin' Aline"

**September 19, 1944**
Lt. Elmer O. Bowers (384th) MIA; Hit by a Me-109 in the Wesel-Duisenburg area.
P-51D 5Y-B 44-13822 "Mustang"

**September 23, 1944**
Lt. Norman F. Bettin (383rd) KIA; Hit by flak near Arnheim.
P-51D N2-
Lt. Clyde K. Voss (383rd) MIA-E; Hit by flak near Apeldoorn.
P-51D N2-D 44-13971 "Priss IV"

**September 28, 1944**
Lt. John J. Dupont (383rd) MIA; Hit by fighters west of Magdeburg.
P-51D N2-X 44-13932 "Copperhead"
Lt. Glenn W. Loucks (385th) KIA; Suffered mechanical trouble west of Magdeburg.
P-51D 5E-S 44-13962 "Bloody Rebel"

**October 5, 1944**
Lt. Joseph R. Gonder (385th) MIA; Suffered mechanical trouble and ditched west of Schouwen.
P-51D 5E-K 44-13942 "Pinnochio"

**October 12, 1944**
Lt. Frank T. Kozloski (384th) POW; Hit by flak at Jener A/F.
P-51D 5Y-F 44-14074
Lt. Roy A. Crouch, Jr. (385th) POW; Hit by fighters near Bremen.
P-51D 5E- 44-14708
Lt. Harold J. Joy (385th) KIA; Hit by fighters near Bremen.
P-51D 5E-E 44-13899
Lt. Wilfred A. Pohmer (385th) KIA; Hit by fighters near Bremen.
P-51D 5E- 44-13347

**October 17, 1944**
Lt. Vernon C. Prickett (383rd) POW; Hit by flak near Cologne and bailed out near Duren.
P-51D N2- 44-14242

**October 22, 1944**
Lt. Frank J. Hoder (383rd) POW; Suffered mechanical trouble and bailed out near Haarlem.
P-51D N2- 44-13532 "Betty Joyce"

**October 24, 1944**
Lt. Howard M. Laity (385th) KIA; Hit the ground while strafing near Rengerhausen.
P-51D 5E- 44-13985
Lt. Walter A. Sullivan (385th) POW; Hit by flak near Friedland.
P-51D 5E-D 44-13830

**October 28, 1944**
Lt. Robert F. Brown (385th) MIA-E; Suffered mechanical trouble and bailed out southwest of Munster
P-51D 5E-I 44-14241
Lt. Joseph E. Davis (385th) POW; Suffered mechanical failure and bailed out southeast of Emmerich.
P-51D 5E-H 44-14385

**November 2, 1944**
Lt. William T. Housholder (385th) KIA; Hit by a Me-109 near Merseburg.
P-51D 5E-H 44-14006

**November 6, 1944**
Lt. Stanley M. Pettengill (383rd) POW; Bailed out north of Amsterdam after mechanical trouble.
P-51D N2-B 44-13906 "Doc"

**November 11, 1944**
Lt. James F. Massey (383rd) MIA; Last seen near Dorsten.
P-51D N2- 44-15064

**November 21, 1944**
Lt. Cidney B. Fairrington (384th) POW; Hit by flak near Nordhausen.
P-51D 5Y-V 44-14328
Lt. Henry J. Lysowski (384th) KIA; Hit by flak southeast of Merseburg.
P-51D 5Y- 44-15176
Lt. Rodney E. Simcoke (384th) KIA; Hit by fighters near Merseburg.
P-51D 5Y- 44-13976 "Marcy III"

**November 26, 1944**
Lt. Jack T. Gaston (383rd) POW; Hit by a Me-109 near Groenlo.
P-51D N2-A 44-13707 "Lady Dorothy IV"

**November 27, 1944**
Lt. John L. Bassan (385th) KIA; Suffered mechanical trouble and crashed near St. Dizier.
P-51D 5E-U 44-14336
Lt. Robert F. Edwards (385th) KIA; Hit by flak near Giessen.
P-51D 5E-X 44-14456

**November 30, 1944**
Lt. Richard J. O'Connor (384th) KIA; Bailed out southwest of Giessen after mechanical problems.
P-51D 5Y-B 44-13999
Lt. Erskin H. Rivers (385th) POW; Suffered mechanical failure and bailed out east of Frankfurt
P-51D 5E-J 44-13947

**December 4, 1944**
Lt. Gerald C. Reidenbach (384th) KIAc; His plane exploded on a practice hop and crashed south of Bury St. Edmonds.
P-51B 5Y- 42-106659

**December 5, 1944**
Capt. Romildo Visconte (385th) KIA; Crashed while trying to land at Liege.
P-51D 5E-O 44-14322 "Coffin Wit'Wings"

**December 6, 1944**
Lt. Donald P. Voelker (383rd) MIA; Bailed out near Eisleben after mechanical trouble.
P-51D N2-S 44-14088

**December 9, 1944**
Capt. John R. Steinbacher (384th) KIAc; Turned too tight and spun-in near Honington.
P-51D 5Y- 44-13709

**December 12, 1944**
Capt. Jack V. Johnson (384th) KIA; Hit by flak near Limburg.
P-51D 5Y-L 44-14992 "Penny 3"

Lt. Everett W. Farnsworth (384th) KIA; Hit by flak near Limburg.
P-51D 5Y-Y 44-14018 "Six-Gun Pete"
Lt. George C. Kuhn (384th) KIA; Hit by flak near Ziegenheim.
P-51D 5Y- 44-15580
Lt. Lawrence Visconti (384th) KIA; Hit by fighters near Beienbach.
P-51D 5Y-B 44-14148 "Laurie's Eleanor"

**December 15, 1944**
Lt. Lee R. Russell (384th) MIA; Bailed out 45 miles east of Clacton after mechanical trouble.
P-51D 5Y- 44-15557

**December 27, 1944**
Lt. Ralph L. Hubley (383rd) KIA; Hit by fighters near Roetz.
P-51D N2-F 44-14528

**December 29, 1944**
Lt. William F. Flynt (384th) POW; Suffered mechanical trouble southwest of Giessen.
P-51D 5Y-U 44-63161 "Good Priss"

**December 31, 1944**
Lt. William S. Sagar, Jr. (385th) POW; Hit by fighters southwest of Wenzendorf.
P-51D 5E-K 44-14584

**January 1, 1945**
Lt. John M. Geary (384th) MIA-E; Bailed out north of the Frisian Islands after mechanical trouble.
P-51D 5Y-H 44-15202
Lt. James A. Porter (384th) MIA; Hit by fighters near Oldendorf.
P-51D 5Y- 44-14881

**January 3, 1945**
Lt. Charles E. Keaney (383rd) ASR; Bailed out northeast of Manston.
P-51D N2-N 44-13916

**February 1, 1945**
Lt. Edgar A. Knapp (384th) KIAc; Suffered mechanical trouble at Admiralty Point Bombing Range and bailed out too low.
P-51D 5Y-T 44-11233

**February 14, 1945**
F/O Thomas W. Kiley (383rd) KIAc; Collided with an RAF bomber and crashed northwest of Steeple Morden.
P-51D N2-

**February 15, 1945**
F/O Irvin E. Lang (384th) MIA; Ran out of fuel east of Bonn.
P-51D 5Y- 44-13764

**February 19, 1945**
Lt. James A. Bussey (383rd) KIA; Hit by flak near Helmstadt.
P-51D N2- 44-14653 "Blood & Soda"
Lt. John G. McNamara (383rd) POW; Suffered mechanical trouble near Wulfen.
P-51D N2-H 44-13813
Lt. Jack T. Barrie (385th) KIA; Hit by flak and crashed near Dahre.
P-51D 5E- 44-13657
Lt. James L. McCubbin (385th) POW; Hit by flak near Steinhorst.
P-51D 5E- 44-15672

**February 22, 1945**
Lt. Fred A. Ross (383rd) POW; Hit by a FW-190 near Delmarhorst.
P-51D N2-Y 44-14747
Lt. Francis X. Radley (385th) KIA; Hit by a Me-262 near Stendal.
P-51D 5E-N 44-13994

**February 25, 1945**
Lt. William E. Randolph (384th) POW; Hit by flak near Unterlisz and bailed out southwest of Fassberg.
P-51D 5Y-R 44-15532

**March 1, 1945**
F/O Wilson W. Montague (385th) KIA; Hit by flak southwest of Ludwigshafen.
P-51D 5E-B 44-14254 "Majero"

**March 15, 1945**
Lt. Daniel E. King (384th) POW; Suffered mecahnical failure southwest of Minden.
P-51D 5Y-D 44-14762 "Florence II"

**March 17, 1945**
Lt. Robert A. Auguste (385th) KIA; Suffered mechanical trouble and crashed near Frieburg.
P-51D 5E- 44-63184

**March 18, 1945**
Lt. William E. Hoppa (383rd) POW; Suffered mechanical failure and bailed out near Brunswick.
P-51D N2-W 44-14243 "Betty"

**March 21, 1945**
Lt. Chelius C. Howard (385th) KIA; Hit by flak at Achmer A/F.
P-51D 5E-I 44-15384

**April 2, 1945**
Lt. Edward M. Hassel (385th) KIA; Bailed out 40 miles northeast of Great Yarmouth after mechanical failure.
P-51D 5E-V 44-13814 "Fancy Francis"

**April 10, 1945**
F/O Ted E. Lasch (385th) MIA; Hit by flak near Margraten.
P-51D 5E-B 44-15019 "Lucky Lady VI"

**April 13, 1945**
Capt. Hayden W. Head (385th) POW; Hit by flak at Tarnewitz and bellied-in near Gadebusch.
P-51D 5E-M 44-14667 "Little Sport"
F/O Newton R. Cobb (385th) POW; Hit by flak and bailed out west of Klutz.
P-51D 5E-A 44-14035 "Etta-Jane"
Lt. Frank W. Glasso (385th) POW; Hit by flak and bailed out near Schaal Lake.
P-51D 5E- 44-72376

**April 16, 1945**
F/O Sidney S. Stern (385th) POW; Hit by flak at Pocking.
P-51D 5E-W 44-13890 "Green Eyes"

**April 17, 1945**
Lt. Duane C. Hague (383rd) POW; Hit by flak near Prague.
P-51D N2-P 44-72358

**June 4, 1945**
Lt. Sterling J. Price (384th Ftr Sqn); collided with a P-51 after taking-off from Honington.
P-51D 5Y-

**June 30, 1945**
Lt. Edward W. Kortendick (383rd) KIAc; Hit power lines after mechanical trouble and crashed near Crosthwaite,
P-51B N2- 43-6731

**Headquarters**
Bankey, Ernest E., Jr., Maj.; December 1944-July 1945; ex-383rd and 385th Ftr Sqn
P-51D 5E-B 44-15019 "Lucky Lady VI"
P-51D 5E-B 44-73045 "Lucky Lady VII
Barnes, Chester A., Maj.; April 1945-May 1945; to 383rd Ftr Sqn; ex-383rd Ftr Sqn
Bing, Andrew J., Maj.; July 1943-December 1943; ex-14th Ftr Grp, MTO
Ceuleers, George F., LtCol.; May 1945-July 1945; ex-383rd Ftr Sqn
Cheney, Robert H., Maj.; February 1945-April 1945; to 383rd Ftr Sqn; ex-383rd Ftr Sqn
Chilton, Andrew L., Maj.; December 1943-May 21, 1944(KIA)
P-38J 5Y-A 42-67960
P-38J 5Y-A 43-28734
Dale, Jack D., LtCol.; June 1943-September 1944; ex-17th Pur Sqn, PTO
P-38J 5E-D
P-51D 5E-D 44-14006
Faulkner, Robert S., Capt.; July 1945-November 1945; ex-384th Ftr Sqn
Goff, Walter L., Capt.; August 1944-November 1944; to 383rd Ftr Sqn (see for details)
Grambo, Fred C., Col.; June 1943-February 29, 1944(KIA)
1 mission
Hurlbut, Lucius A., Capt.; September 1943-November 1944
65 missions
Johnson, Neil R., Maj.; October 1944-February 1945; ex-384th Ftr Sqn
Lacy, Robert E., LtCol.; July 1945-July 1945; ex-384th Ftr Sqn
Lowell, John H., LtCol.; January 1945-May 1945; ex-384th Ftr Sqn (see for details)
McManus, John B., LtCol.; September 1944-April 1945; ex-383rd Ftr Sqn (see for details)
Miller, Paul F., Capt.; February 1944-March 5, 1944(MIA-E)
2 missions
Monahan, John D., Maj.; August 1944-October 1944; to 385th Ftr Sqn; ex-11th AF, AL & 479th Ftr Grp, ETO; November 1944-December 1944
P-51D 5Y-D 44-14148 "Laurie's Eleanor"
Osborn, Roy W., Col.; March 1944-January 1945; ex-67th Ftr Wg HdQts
85 missions total
P-38J N2-O 42-68104
P-51D N2-O 44-13923 "Billy Boy"
Petrosky, Michael D., Maj.; May 1944-December 1944; ex-384th Ftr Sqn
Phillips, Sam C., Maj.; April 1945-June 1945; ex-384th Ftr Sqn
Roberts, Eugene P., LtCol.; January 1945-November 1945; ex-78th Ftr Grp, MTO
116 missions total
P-51D 5E-O 44-15061 "Jimmie the First"
Stapleton, Carl W., LtCol.; April 1945-April 1945; ex-384th & (Ops) 385th Ftr Sqns (see for details)

**383rd Fighter Squadron**
Acosta, Argent J., Jr., Lt.; June 1944-August 27, 1944(POW)
Allvin, Eldon, Lt.; August 1943-December 26, 1943(KIAc)
Ames, Vaude V., Lt.; March 1944-May 25, 1944(POW)
15 missions
Andrew, Lowell V., Capt.; September 1944-EOW
P-51D N2-L 44-14290 "Passionate Pat"
Ayoub, Lee S., Capt.; August 1943-September 1944
70 missions
Bankey, Ernest E., Jr., Lt.; August 1943-April 1944; to 385th Ftr Sqn
P-38J N2- "Lucky Lady"
Bannister, John J., Capt.; August 1943-September 1944
72 missions, 272 hours
Barnes, Chester A., Maj.; August 1943-April 1945; to HdQts May 1945-August 1945
Baughn, Richard M., Lt.; October 1944-EOW
49 missions
P-51D N2-B 44-15573 "The Snatch"
Beaumont, Edward C., Lt.; April 1944-November 1944
66 missions, 270 hours
P-51D N2-B 44-14013 "Beau's Baby"

Bechtel, John H., Lt.; August 1943-November 20, 1943(KIAc)
Bettin, Norman F., Lt.; August 1943-September 23, 1944(KIA)
Blaha, Roy C., Lt.; May 1944-November 1944
    270 hours
Bosworth, Walter C., Jr., Lt.; August 1943-May 8, 1944(POW)
Boyd, Warren D., Capt.; August 1943-September 1944
Braggins, Robert E., Lt.; May 1944-November 1944
Braly, Houston L., Lt.; March 1944-August 2, 1944(KIA)
Brendler, Wesley R., Capt.; August 1943-September 1944
    75 missions
Brennan, Edmund, Lt.; August 1943-April 12, 1944(MIA)
    12 missions
Brock, Charles E., Lt.; August 1943-March 8, 1944(POW)
    4 missions
Burdge, Ernest L., Capt.; October 1944-EOW
Bushnell, Theodore G., Lt.; August 1943-April 12, 1944(POW)
    16 missions
Bussey, James A., Lt.; August 1944-February 19, 1945(MIA)
Carillio, Miguel, Lt.; August 1943-December 13, 1943(KIAc)
Carlson, Creyaton, Lt.; February 1944-March 19, 1944(KIAc)
Casagrande, Manuel J., Capt.; August 1943-September 1944
    P-51D N2-J 44-13812 "Cassie's Chassie"
Castellano, Mark J., F/O; April 1945-EOW
Ceuleers, George F., LtCol.; August 1943-May 1945; to HdQts
    103 missions
    P-38J N2-D 42-68043 "Connie & Butch, Inc."
    P-51D N2-D 44-13971
    P-51D N2-D 44-15020
    P-51D N2-D 44-72719 "Constance"
Cheney, Robert H., Maj.; September 1944-February 1945; to HdQt
    April 1945-EOW
    60 missions
    P-51D N2- "Buster"
Chesney, Herbert A., Capt.; March 1944-November 1944
    52 missions
Chlevin, Edward, Lt.; October 1944-EOEW
    37 missions
    P-51D N2-A 44-14073
Clark, Francis L., Lt.; October 1944-EOW
Coates, Mark E., Lt.; May 1944-December 1944
    61 missions, 270 hours
Cochran, Clifford L., Lt.; August 1943-April 1944; to 385th Ftr Sqn
Cruger, Nicholas W., Lt.; August 1943-May 19, 1944(KIA)
Crutchfield, Claude A., F/O; April 1945-EOW
Dalton, William T., Lt.; June 1944-December 1944
Davis, Richard P., Lt.; June 1944-February 1945
    60 missions, 270 hours
Derbes, Donald J., Capt.; June 1944-December 1944
Diffenbach, Clyde W., Lt.; June 1944-August 4, 1944(POW)
Donovan, James F., Lt.; July 1944-January 1945
Dumont, Merrill W., Lt., February 1945-EOW
Dupont, John J., Lt.; June 1944-September 28, 1944(MIA)
Dwyer, Robert H., Lt.; June 1944-December 1944
    62 missions
Farley, Robert H., Lt.; June 1944-December 1944
    P-51D N2-F 44-14528
Fields, James O., Lt.; April 1945-EOW
Fiery, Elmer N., Capt.; June 1944-December 1944
    P-51D N2-Y 44-14747 "Rough Rider"
Fisher, Donald C., Lt.; October 1944-EOW
    45 missions
Gaston, Jack T., Lt.; August 1944-November 26, 1944(KIA)
    36 missions
Gilliette, Sherwood M., Lt.; December 1943-April 1944 (injured)
    16 missions
Gilliland, Leown A., Capt.; August 1943-March 29, 1944(KIA)
    15 missions
Glascow, Marvin W., Capt.; August 1943-September 1944
    P-38J N2-X 42-67412 "The Rebel Kids"
    P-51D N2-X 44-13932 "Copperhead"
Goff, Walter L., Capt.; November 1944-February 1945; to HdQts
    34 missions (plus 29 w/5th ERS)
Goldberg, Paul J., Lt.; May 1944-August 10, 1944(MIA-E)
    40 missions
Goldsberry, Francis R., Lt.; May 1944-December 1944
Guy, John B., Lt.; February 1945-EOW
    23 missions
Hague, Duane C., Lt.; February 1945-April 17, 1945(POW)
    22 missions
Hall, Thomas H., Lt.; April 1944-November 1944
    P-51D N2-Q 44-13854
Hall, William D., Lt.; January 1945-EOW
Hamilton, Donald B., Lt.; April 1945-EOW
    0 missions
Hammett, Charles E., Capt.; September 1944-EOW
    P-51D N2-X 44-15005
Hatfield, Clive, Lt.; May 1944-December 1944
Hausenbauer, Edward P., Lt.; February 1945-EOW
Hawkos, Gordon C., Lt.; April 1945-October 1945
    0 missions

Hazle, Ernest W., Lt.; January 1945-EOW
Healey, Dana F., Jr., F/O; December 1944-July 1945
    48 missions, 194:40 hours
Heyn, Edward F., Lt.; September 1944-EOW
    52 missions
Hill, Gordon F., Lt.; February 1945-EOW
Hoder, Frank J., Lt.; October 1944-October 22, 1944(MIA); ex-bomber pilot(351st Bomb Grp)
Hoffman, Alex F., Lt.; December 1944-May 1945
    34 missions
Holmes, Eldon, Lt.; February 1945-EOW
Hood, William K., Lt.; October 1944-EOW
Hoppa, William E., Lt.; February 1945-March 18, 1945(POW)
Horman, Elmer H., Lt.; October 1944-EOW
    45 missions
Hornick, Carl W., Lt.; February 1945-EOW
Hubley, Ralph L., Lt.; October 1944-December 27, 1944(KIA)
Hunt, Robert L., Lt.; October 1944-EOW
    P-51D N2-T 44-15559
Hunter, John C., Capt.; September 1944-July 1945
    54 missions
    P-51D N2-E 44-15578
Jacaruso, Joseph J., F/O; December 1944-July 1945
Jackson, Cameron E., Lt.; December 1944-EOW
Jessen, Dean L., Lt.; April 1945-EOW
Johnson, Harry, Jr., Lt.; April 1944-September 17, 1944(MIA)
Keany, Charles E., Lt.; September 1944-January 3, 1945(MIA)
Kerig, John A., Capt.; March 1944- (did not complete tour due to eyes)
Kerr, Edwin H., Lt.; February 1945-EOW
Kerr, John, Lt.; August 1943-May 19, 1944(KIA)
Kiley, Thomas W., F/O; February 1945 February 14, 1945(KIAc)
Kissel, William F., Capt.; September 1944-July 1945; ex-MTO
Kortendick, Edward W., Lt.; December 1944-June 30, 1945(KIAc)
Leon, Leonard, Lt.; December 1944-EOW
Levin, Emmanuel, Lt.; April 1944-October 1944
London, Kenneth F., Lt.; August 1943-March 8, 1944(KIA)
    6 missions
MacDermott, James B., Lt.; April 1944-July 27, 1944(POW)
Massey, James S., Lt.; September 1944-November 11, 1944(MIA)
McCoy, Gordon A., Lt.; March 1944-December 1944
    73 missions
McGregor, Roscoe P., Lt.; April 1944-October 1944
McManus, John B., LtCol.; August 1943-September 1944; to HdQts
    85 missions
    P-38J N2-M 42-104171 "Marie"
    P-51D N2-M 44-13941
McNamara, John G., Lt.; December 1944-February 19, 1945(KIA)
Miller, Lamarr J., Lt.; March 1944-May 21, 1944(POW)
Miller, Paul F., Capt.; January 1944-February 1944; to HdQts
Murphy, Michael L., Capt.; April 1944-December 1944
    75 missions
Nelson, Joseph D., Lt.; February 1945-EOW
Nicholson, Kenneth F., Capt.; August 1943-September 1944
    72 missions
    P-38J N2-N 42-68123
    P-51D N2-N 44-13916
O'Brien, Valentine A., Lt.; December 1944-July 1945; ex-bomber pilot
Ogle, Richard A., Lt.; March 1944-December 1944
    71 missions, 270 hours
    P-51D N2- "My-Katy-Car"
Olson, Leroy Q., Lt.; March 1944-May 25, 1944(POW)
    16 missions
Orndorff, Roy W., Capt.; September 1944-July 1945
    P-51D N2-U 44-14315
    P-51D N2-U 44-72423
Pepper, Miles W., Lt.; April 1945-EOW; ex-305th Bomb Grp, (35 missions), 0 missions w/364th
Pettingill, Stanley M., Lt.; August 1944-November 6, 1944(POW)
Potochnik, John F., Lt.; April 1944-August 4, 1944(POW)
Prickett, Vernon C., Lt.; September 1944-October 17, 1944(POW)
Pyle, William V., Lt.; November 1944-EOW
    52 missions, 253 hours
    P-51D N2-X 44-14665 "Phyllis"
Queal, Ralph W., Jr., Lt.; November 1944-EOW
Ross, Fred A., Lt.; November 1944-February 22, 1945(POW)
    26 missions
Sandkaut, Henry D., Lt.; November 1944-July 1945
Saylor, Henry B., Lt.; August 1943-April 1944; to 385th Ftr Sqn
    64 missions, 230 hours total
Scofield, William E., Lt.; October 1944-EOW
Scrivner, Clarence F., Lt.; August 1943-May 25, 1944(POW)
    P-38J N2-Z 43-28425
Seth, Joseph A., Lt.; February 1945-EOW
Sorrells, Fred L., Lt.; September 1944-EOW
    65 missions, 293 hours
Smith, George E., Lt.; September 1944-EOW
    50 missions
    P-51D N2-R 44-15399 "Southern Belle
Smith, Joseph A., Lt.; February 1945-EOW
Staranick, Nicholas M., Capt.; February 1944-November 1944
    350 hours
Steadman, Altus G., Lt.; November 1943-December 13, 1943(KIAc)

Stepman, Alfred, Lt.; February 1944-September 1944
Stinson, Charles T., F/O; November 1944-January 1945
Swift, David F., Lt.; March 1945-July 1945; ex-bomber pilot(398th Bomb Group)
 P-51D N2- "Bomber Jockey"
Truett, Jesse L., Capt.; September 1944-EOW
 60 missions
 P-51D N2-Q
Voelker, Donald P., Lt.; September 1944-December 6, 1944(MIA)
Voss, Clyde K., Lt.; May 1944-September 24, 1944(MIA-E)
 64 missions, 230 hours
 P-51D N2-A 44-13707 "Lady Dorothy IV"
Warner, George O., Capt.; October 1944-EOW
Wennemer, Joseph, Lt.; April 1944-??? (was transferred due to lack of moral fiber)
Wheless, Ellis J., Capt.; September 1944-EOW
 56 missions
 P-51D N2-V "Blue Bonnet Belle II"
Wicker, Samuel J., Maj.; August 1943-January 1945
 P-38J N2-W 42-67415 "Bettye-Jo"
 P-38J N2-W 42-67453 "Bettye-Jo II"
 P-51D N2-W 44-13936 "Bettye-Jo III"
 P-51D N2-W 44-14243 "Bettye-Jo IV"
Wilson, Bruce B., Capt.; August 1943-September 1944
 P-38J N2-A 43-28406 "The Gallant Warrior"
 P-51D N2-A 44-13974 "Bama Queen"
Wilson, Loren R., Lt.; March 1944-June 8, 1944(KIA)
Wilson, Robert B., Capt.; June 1943-January 1944
Woodside, Jackie D., Lt.; September 1944-EOW
 54 missions, 295 hours
 P-51D N2- "Helen"
Yager, Robert H., Capt.; August 1944-EOW
 51 missions

**384th Fighter Squadron**
Adams, George F., Lt.; February 1945-March 1945; ex-bomber pilot
Allbrecht, Alfred A., Lt.; May 1944-September 11, 1944(MIA)
Allen, John J., Lt.; October 1944-February 3, 1945(POW)
Allen, Robert K., Capt.; September 1944-EOW
 P-51D 5Y-A 44-15027
Ammerman, George N., Lt.; April 1944-December 1944
Baker, Niel T., Lt.; April 1944-August 1, 1944(MIA)
Bowen, Jarette L., Lt.; May 1944-June 27, 1944(POW)
Bowers, Elmer O., Lt.; August 1944-September 19, 1944(MIA)
Briscoe, Carroll D., Capt.; February 1945-March 1945; ex-bomber pilot
Bristow, William E., Capt.; April 1944-December 1944
 73 missions, 300 hours
 P-38J 5Y-O 42-68101
 P-51D 5Y-O 44-13825 "Nita"
Brown, Fred, Jr., Capt.; October 1944-December 1944
Brown, Marvin H., Lt.; February 1944-May 19, 1944(POW)
Buckles, Clifford R., Lt.; September 1944-January 1945
Burns, William J., F/O; April 1945-EOW
 0 missions
Callahan, George E., F/O; April 1945-EOW
Callouette, Joseph L., Lt.; April 1944-October 1944
Cecil, Paul K., Lt.; April 1944-September 1944
 61 missions
Champion, William N., Lt.; June 1944-December 1944
 38 missions
Cobb, William I., F/O; April 1945-July 1945
Cochran, Richard C., F/O; April 1945-July 1945
 1 mission
Coltman, William G., Lt.; August 1943-March 27, 1944(POW)
Costin, Edward C., F/O; April 1945-September 1945
 2 missions
Cox, William E., Lt.; November 1944-March 1945
Curtis, Paul H., Lt.; August 1943-October 9, 1943(KIAc)
Damron, Milton S., Lt.; February 1944-May 22, 1944(POW)
Delmaso, Reno F., F/O; April 1945-EOW
Derr, Warner P., Lt.; June 1944-February 1945
 59 missions
Duderstadt, Ernest H., Capt.; June 1944-January 1945
Fairrington, Cidney B., Lt.; June 1944-November 21, 1944(POW)
 36 missions
Farnsworth, Everett W., Lt.; June 1944-December 12, 1944(MIA)
 P-51D 5Y-Y 44-14018 "Six Gun Pete"
Faulker, Robert S., Capt.; September 1944-July 1945; to HdQts
 72 missions
 P-51D 5Y- "Punkin"
 P-51D 5Y- "Punkin II"
Ferguson, Larry N., Lt.; August 1943-March 6, 1944(MIA)
Feist, George M., F/O; April 1945-September 1945
 1 mission
Flynt, William F., Lt.; September 1944-December 29, 1944(POW)
Ford, John C., Capt.; August 1943-July 18, 1944(KIAc)
 P-38J 5Y-F 42-67980
 P-38J 5Y-F 43-28402
Fowle, James M., Capt.; February 1944-April 1945
 P-51D 5Y-J "Terry Claire"
 P-51D 5Y-J 44-13829 "Terry Claire II"
Fox, Wayne O., Lt.; December 1944-January 1945; to 5th ERS; ex-bomber pilot(446th & 482nd Bomb Grps)
Gaines, Edwin F., Lt.; August 1943-May 19, 1944(POW)
Gawienowski, John J., Lt.; August 1943-October 1944
 P-38J 5Y-G
 P-51D 5Y-G 44-13722 "Jersey Bouncer"
Geary, John M., Lt.; December 1944-January 1, 1945(MIA-E); April 1945-July 1945
 24 missions
Goodner, Charles G., Lt.; September 1944-December 1944
Greenig, William F., Lt.; April 1945-EOW
Grimshaw, John L., Lt.; May 1944-December 1944
 62 missions, 269 hours
Hahn, Peter J., Lt.; February 1945-EOW
 27 missions
Harper, William L., Lt.; April 1945-EOW
Hayes, Robert S., Jr., Lt.; February 1945-July 1945
Henderson, Roland A., Lt.; February 1945-EOW
Henkle, Edward L., Lt.; March 1944-April 15, 1944(POW)
Henson, Olen D., Lt.; December 1944-EOW
 36 missions
 P-51D 5Y- "Kitty Blue Eyes"
Herbst, Donald F., Lt.; April 1945-EOW
Herndon, Harvey V., Lt.; February 1945-EOW
 11 missions
Hess, William P., Capt.; May 1944-January 1945
 71 missions
 P-51C 5Y-F 43-25040
Heyman, Richard M., Capt.; August 1943-September 1944
 73 missions
 P-38J 5Y-H
 P-51D 5Y-H 44-13813
Hoenselaar, Floyd J., Capt.; August 1943-October 1944
 P-38J 5Y-Y
 P-51D 5Y-Y 44-13813
Honaker, Stuart R., Lt.; December 1944-EOW
Huarte, Raymond E., Lt.; August 1943-November 1943 (later to ETO w/20th Ftr Grp)
Hughes, John L., Lt.; February 1945-July 1945
 30 missions, 125 hours
Hunt, Robert S., Jr., Lt.; April 1944-October 1944
 P-51D 5Y-H 44-13750
Hurlbut, Lucius A., Lt.; August 1943-September 1943; to HdQts
James, Harold M., Capt.; September 1944-May 1945
 P-51D 5Y-O 44-13825
Johnson, Craig C., Lt.; February 1945-July 1945
Johnson, Jack V., Capt.; April 1944-December 12, 1944(KIA)
Johnson, Louis A., Capt.; March 1944-November 1944
 P-51D 5Y-J 44-13829
Johnson, Neil R., Maj.; July 1944-October 1944; to HdQts
Joseph, Nick M., Lt.; February 1945-EOW
 20 missions
Kemp, Arthur R., Lt.; August 1943-November 1943 (later to ETO w/20th Ftr Grp)
Kercher, Victor L., Capt.; August 1943-July 15, 1944(KIA)
 P-38J 5Y-K 42-67701
 P-38J 5Y-K 42-104421 "Daddy's Baby"
Kilpatrick, Howard V., Lt.; August 1943-May 22, 1944(MIA)
King, Daniel E., Lt.; December 1944-March 15, 1945(POW)
 30 missions
Kingsbury, Fred F., Lt.; August 1943-April 15, 1944(MIA)
Kirby, Clarence B., Lt.; December 1944-EOW
 37 missions
Knapp, Edgar A., Lt.; December 1944-February 1, 1945(KIAc)
Korecky, James R., Lt.; February 1944-July 30, 1944(KIAc)
Kozloski, Frank T., Lt.; April 1944-October 12, 1944(POW)
 58 missions
Kuhn, George C., Lt.; September 1944-December 12, 1944(MIA)
Kunzler, Raymond D., Lt.; August 1944-March 9, 1944(MIA)
Lacy, Robert E., LtCol.; August 1943-July 1945; to HdQts
 96 missions, 386 hours
 P-38J 5Y-D 42-67417
 P-38J 5Y-D 42-68070
 P-38J 5Y-D 42-104405
 P-51D 5Y-D 44-14034
 P-51D 5Y-D 44-14021 "Jackie Jr."
Lang, Irvin E., F/O; December 1944-February 15, 1945(MIA)
Leavell, William A., Lt.; December 1944-EOW
 41 missions, 204 hours
 P-51D 5Y-V "Battle Axe"
Lefforge, Littleton L., Lt.; December 1944-July 1945
 P-51D 5Y-V 44-13988 "Just Plain L"
Leftwich, Daniel L., Capt.; October 1944-July 1945
 68 missions
 P-51D 5Y-M 44-13998 "Silver Streak"
Leo, Carl H., Capt.; August 1943-September 1944
 70 missions, 270 hours
 P-38J 5Y-B "Leo"
 P-38J 5Y-B 43-28372 "Melba Lee"
 P-51D 5Y-B 44-13999
Linn, Marcus C., Lt.; December 1943-April 1944; to 385th Ftr Sqn; ex-1st Ftr Grp, MTO
Lohr, Hugo A., Jr., Lt.; December 1944-EOW
 P-51D 5Y-J 44-13993 "Hugo's Nooky Booky"
Lowell, John H., LtCol.; June 1943-January 1945; to HdQts
 157 missions

P-38J 5Y-L 42-68098 "Penny"
P-38J 5Y-L "Penny 2"
P-51D 5Y-L 44-14992 "Penny 3"
P-51D 5Y-L 44-63263 "Penny 4"
Lysowski, Henry J., Lt.; September 1944-November 21, 1944(MIA)
MacLean, Norman D., Lt.; August 1943-March 29, 1944(MIA)
McCloud, Shornden D., Lt.; February 1944-April 29, 1944(POW)
Miller, Earl H., Lt.; September 1944-April 1945
Moore, Willard E., Lt.; March 1944-April 15, 1944(POW)
Morgan, Harold R., Lt.; April 1945-July 1945
Morrow, Douglas E., Lt.; April 1945-EOW
Muskavitch, Lawrence E., Lt.; September 1944-March 1945
Myers, Orville E., Capt.; August 1943-April 15, 1944(MIA)
P-38J 5Y-M 42-67732
Nelson, James F., F/O; February 1945-EOW
Nielson, Theodore D., Lt.; April 1944-August 9, 1944(MIA)
O'Connor, Fred T., Lt.; September 1944-March 1945
63 missions
P-51D 5Y- "Mary Honey"
O'Connor, Richard J., Lt.; September 1944-November 30, 1944(MIA)
Parsley, Adrian D., Capt.; August 1943-August 1944
P-38J 5Y-Q
P-51D 5Y-Q 44-13952
Pearson, Philip E., Jr., Lt.; August 1943-November 1943 (later to ETO w/20th Ftr Grp & KIA May 1, 1944)
Petrosky, Frank J., Lt.; August 1943-February 1944(injured)
Petrosky, Michael D., Maj.; April 1944-May 1944; to HdQts
Phillips, Sam C., Maj.; August 1943-April 1945; to HdQts July 1945-November 1945
P-38J 5Y-P 42-68101
P-51D 5Y-P 44-14031
P-51D 5Y-P 44-72059
Phipps, Laurel H., Capt.; October 1944-EOW
Piazza, Anthony J., Lt.; February 1945-EOW
30 missions
Pick, Douglas J., Maj.; December 1943-September 1945
P-38J 5Y-U 42-104269
P-51D 5Y-U 44-15356 "Lillamae"
Pochelu, John F., Lt.; August 1943-November 1943
Pogue, Walter W., Lt.; February 1944-April 13, 1944(MIA)
Porter, James A., Lt.; October 1944-January 1, 1945(MIA)
Porter, Theodore S., Lt.; August 1943-October 13, 1943(KIAc)
Post, Edwin A., Lt.; October 1944-February 1945; to 401st Bomb Group
Powers, Russell H., Lt.; October 1944-July 1945
Price, Sterling J., Lt.; November 1944-June 4, 1945(KIAc)
P-51D 5Y-S 44-13915
P-51D 5Y-S 44-14680
Purvis, James W., Capt.; August 1943-September 1944
73 missions, 270 hours
P-38J 5Y-V
P-51D 5Y-V 44-14218 "Mary W"
Pushcar, Carl J., Lt.; April 1944-December 1944
40 missions
P-51C 5Y-M 43-25024
Raffel, Fred L., Lt.; November 1944-March 1945
Randolph, William E., Lt.; September 1944-February 25, 1945(POW)
49 missions
Reidenbach, Gerald C., Lt.; November 1944-December 4, 1944(KIAc)
Roberts, David J., Lt.; November 1944-EOW
P-51D 5Y- "Snorky"
Rogers, William E., Lt.; February 1945-March 1945; ex-bomber pilot
Russell, Lee R., Lt.; November 1944-December 15, 1944(MIA)
Schroeder, George Z., Capt.; October 1944-EOW
55 missions
P-51D 5Y-D 44-11207
Schwartz, Harry C., Lt.; October 1944-EOW
52 missions
P-51D 5Y-H 44-15568 "Little Eva"
Shaffer, Kenneth M., Lt.; February 1944-April 29, 1944(POW)
Shepard, Ernest B., Maj.; February 1944-January 1945; ex-324th Ftr Grp, MTO
Simcoke, Rodney E., Lt.; April 1944-November 21, 1944(KIA)
Smith, Eugene L., Lt.; August 1943-April 29, 1944(POW)
9 missions
Smith, Richard S., Lt.; November 1944-March 1945
Soehl, John E., Lt.; February 1945-EOW
128 hours
Spradlin, Roy M., Capt.; August 1943-May 8, 1944(POW)
19 missions
P-38J 5Y-S 42-68120
Stapleton, Carl W., Capt.; November 1943-April 1944; to 385th Ftr Sqn
113 missions, 485 hours total
P-38J 5Y- "Esie"
Stevens, Richard W., Capt.; August 1944-EOW
P-51D 5Y-W 44-14093 "Puddin II"
Steinbacher, John R., Capt.; July 1944-December 9, 1944(KIAc); ex-bomber pilot
Stiefvater, Richard L., Capt.; August 1944-April 1945
Stover, Charles W., Lt.; April 1944-December 1944
P-51D 5Y-S 44-13915
Stuckrath, John M., Capt.; August 1943-September 1944
P-51D 5Y-S 44-13988
Taylor, John C., Lt.; April 1944-October 1944
63 missions, 270 hours
P-51D 5Y-T 44-13342
Taylor, John E., Lt.; February 1945-July 1945
Virgulac, John J., Lt.; August 1943-November 1943
Visconti, Lawrence, Lt.; September 1944-December 12, 1944(KIA)
Vittitow, Linley G., Lt.; August 1943-November 1943
Walker, John A., Capt.; February 1944-March 1945
P-51D 5Y-Q 44-73090 "Denver Belle"
Ward, Bruce C., Capt.; April 1944-December 1944
71 missions, 316 hours
P-38J 5Y-W "My Norma"
P-51D 5Y-W 44-14032 "My Norma"
Wells, Trent H., Jr., Capt.; September 1944-July 1945
55 missions
P-51D 5Y-T 44-11233
Welsh, Fred C., Lt.; October 1944-July 1945
Westmore, Harry W., Lt.; August 1943-March 27, 1944(POW)
Williams, David W., Lt.; April 1944-November 1944
88 missions
P-38J 5Y-W 42-67232
P-51D 5Y-W 44-13975 "Dot"
P-51D 5Y-W 44-14076 "Dot"
Wilson, John E., Lt.; April 1944-December 1944
333 hours
P-38J 5Y-F "Kay"
P-38J 5Y-F "Kay II"
P-51D 5Y-F 44-14074 "Kay III"
Woolley, Max J., Lt.; August 1943-June 27, 1944(MIA-E)
P-38J 5Y- "The Homesick Angel"
Yost, Byron P., Lt.; April 1944-July 15, 1944(KIA)
P-38J 5Y-Y 43-28429

**385th Fighter Squadron**
Adler, Jerome M., Lt.; August 1943-December 1943; ex-MTO
Allinder, Thomas L., Lt.; July 1944-January 1945
P-51D 5E-Z 44-14724
Anderson, Edward E., Lt.; October 1944-EOW
Auguste, Robert A., Lt.; October 1944-March 17, 1945(MIA)
Bankey, Ernest E., Jr., Maj.; April 1944-December 1944; to HdQts
P-38J 5E- "Lucky Lady"
P-51D 5E-B 44-15019 "Lucky Lady VI
P-51D 5E-B 44-73045"Lucky Lady VII
Barrie, Jack T., Lt.; October 1944-February 19, 1945(MIA)
Basson, John L., Lt.; October 1944-November 27, 1944(MIA)
Bloodgood, Donald L., Lt.; October 1944-April 1945
47 missions
P-51D 5E-B 44-14254 "Majero"
P-51D 5E-B 44-11213 "Majero II"
Box, Norman L., Capt.; March 1944-March 1945
91 missions
Boydston, Robert W., Lt.; October 1944-EOW
43 missions
P-51K 5E-O 44-11619 "The Boilermaker Special"
Brown, Harold E., Capt.; August 1943-???(KIAc)
Brown, Robert F., Lt.; September 1944-October 28, 1944(MIA-E)
Broxom, Alton J., Lt.; April 1944-November 1944
Burkhard, Harold D., Lt.; June 1944-August 17, 1944(MIA-E)
Burkholder, Robert L., Lt.; October 1944-March 1945; to 1st SF
Chaplin, Donald S., Lt.; April 1944-May 25, 1944(POW)
Christiansen, Carl R., Lt.; July 1944-April 1945
Cobb, Newton R., F/O; February 1945-April 13, 1945(POW)
Cochran, Clifford L., Lt.; April 1944-October 1944; ex-383rd Ftr Sqn
Conroy, Calvin W., F/O; April 1945-EOW
Cox, William A., Lt.; September 1944-November 1944; to 1st SF
Crombie, William S., Maj.; September 1944-EOW
62 missions
P-51D 5E-N 44-13994
P-51D 5E-N 44-72343
Crouch, Roy A., Lt.; April 1944-October 12, 1944(POW)
47 missions
Davis, Daniel W., Lt.; August 1944-September 11, 1944(MIA-E)
27 missions
Davis, Joseph F., Lt.; September 1944-October 28, 1944(POW)
Dean, William P., Lt.; July 1944-August 9, 1944(MIA)
DeMille, John L., Lt.; October 1944-December 1944; to 67th Ftr Wg
Dodson, Edmer R., Lt.; April 1945-EOW
Dominy, Reed H., Capt.; August 1943-April 15, 1944(MIA)
Draper, Russell W., Lt.; May 1944-October 1944(WIA Oct. 24)
45 missions
Drysdale, Douglas R., Lt.; August 1944-September 17, 1944(MIA-E); ex-bomber pilot (100th Bomb Group)
Edwards, Robert F., Lt.; September 1944-November 27, 1944(MIA
Erfkamp, Willard G., Lt.; June 1944-December 1944
P-51D 5E-H 44-13835
Eubanks, Jack O., Lt.; May 1944-December 1944
62 missions
Farrell, Everett N., Capt.; September 1944-April 1945
P-51D 5E-P 44-15051 "Sweet Marie"
P-51D 5E-P 44-15576 "Sweet Marie II"

Farrell, Thomas P., Capt.; July 1944-March 1945
P-51D 5E-U 44-14336
P-51D 5E-U 44-15641
Fenner, Franklin A., Lt.; September 1944-EOW
Fine, Gerald W., Lt.; September 1944-EOW
64 missions, 348 hours
P-51D 5E-J "Jeanne"
P-51D 5E-J 44-15493 "Jeanne II"
Finger, William D., F/O; April 1945-EOW
Fisher, Osee W., F/O; April 1945-July 1945
Fosbender, Bentley J., F/O; April 1945-EOW
Foster, S.C., Lt.; August 1943-November 1943
Geary, John M., Lt.; September 1944-December 1944; to 384th Ftr Sqn
Glasso, Frank W., Lt.; February 1945-April 13, 1945(POW)
Gonder, Joseph R., Lt.; September 1944-October 5, 1944(MIA)
Griffin, Donald E., Capt.; October 1944-January 1945; to 1st SF
Hargrove, Jasper E., Capt.; September 1944-July 1945
56 missions, 250 hours
P-51D 5E-H 44-13583 "Dottie Bee II
Hartsfield, Donald R., Lt.; April 1945-EOW
Hassell, Edward M., Lt.; February 1945-April 2, 1945(MIA)
Hausman, Erich A., Lt.; April 1945-EOW
Haynes, Jessie C., Lt.; April 1945-July 1945
Head, Hayden W., Capt.; September 1944-April 13, 1945(POW)
P-51D 5E-M 44-14667 "Little Sport"
Heck, George C., Jr., Lt.; April 1944-November 1944
Hedensburg, Joseph W., Lt.; August 1943-December 1943
Helmholz, Walter W., Jr., Lt.; December 1944-EOW
41 missions, 181 hours
Hendryk, Edward V., Lt.; April 1945-EOW
1 mission
Hill, Cowan S., Capt.; August 1943-October 1944
P-38J 5E-H 42-67272
P-38J 5E-H 43-28422
P-51D 5E-H
Hogan, Clifford S., Jr., Capt.; September 1944-April 1945
61 missions, 293 hours
Horner, Kenneth R., Lt.; December 1944-EOW
35 missions
Houck, Stanley J., Lt.; October 1944-EOW
52 missions
Housholder, William T., Lt.; May 1944-November 2, 1944(MIA)
P-51D 5E-H 44-14006
Howard, Chelius C., Lt.; February 1945-March 21, 1945(KIA)
9 missions
Howland, Donald H., Capt.; August 1943-September 1944
Hustead, Dallas J., Capt.; June 1944-December 1944
Izor, Edward F., Capt.; April 1944-December 1944
P-51D 5E-Q 44-13869
Jackson, Harry H., Lt.; September 1944-EOW
Jackson, Liborn B., Lt.; April 1945-EOW
Jackson, William R., Lt.; August 1943-March 22, 1944(POW)
Jamison, Gilbert L., Capt.; May 1944-December 1944
P-51D 5E-A 44-14035 "Etta Jane"
Janusz, Frank J., Lt.; April 1945-EOW
Johnson, James G., Lt.; February 1945-EOW
19 missions
Johnston, Richard R., Lt.; April 1945-EOW
Jones, Alma R., Lt.; April 1944-November 1944
73 missions
Jones, Edward H., Lt.; February 1945-EOW
26 missions
Jones, Grant L., Lt.; April 1944-September 16, 1944(MIA)
Jorgenson, Robert S., Lt.; December 1944-EOW
35 missions
Joy, Harold J., Lt.; September 1944-October 12, 1944(MIA)
Kelly, Milton T., Lt.; February 1945-EOW
Kenworthy, Charles W., Lt.; December 1944-EOW
38 missions, 180 hours
Kiernan, John W., Lt.; December 1944-EOW
32 missions
King, Charles A., Lt.; May 1944-August 27, 1944(POW)
Kramer, Elmer V., Capt.; May 1945-EOW
Kremer, Warren E., Lt.; December 1944-EOW
37 missions, 175 hours
Laity, Harold M., Lt.; September 1944-October 24, 1944(MIA)
Lasch, Ted F., F/O; February 1945-April 10, 1945(MIA)
Lett, Sim L., Jr., Lt.; October 1944-EOW
P-51D 5E-K 44-14584
Linn, Marcus C., Capt.; April 1944-May 3, 1944(KIAc); ex-384th Ftr Sqn
Loucks, Glenn W., Lt.; September 1944-September 28, 1944(MIA)
Maki, Karlos S., Lt.; December 1944-EOW
Masters, Warren K., F/O; February 1945-EOW
McClanahan, Fred C., Capt.; March 1944-November 1944
68 missions, 270 hours
P-38J 5E-G 42-104092
P-51D 5E-G 44-14254
McCormick, Arthur B., Capt.; September 1944-EOW
68 missions
P-51D 5E-L "Look Homeward Angel"
P-51D 5E-L 44-15179 "Look Homeward Angel II"
McCubbin, James L., Lt.; September 1944-February 19, 1945(POW)
44 missions
P-51D 5E-F 44-11242 "Mary Al"
McKibben, Robert M., Lt.; September 1944-March 1945; to 1st SF
Monahan, John D., Maj.; October 1944-November 1944; to HdQts; ex-11th AF, AL & 479th Ftr Grp
Montague, Wilson W., F/O; January 1945-March 1, 1945(MIA)
Munn, John W., Lt.; February 1945-EOW
31 missions
Murphy, Eugene, Capt.; September 1944-EOW; ex-363rd Ftr Grp, ETO
P-51D 5E-E 44-14862 "Jersey Bouncer"
Neece, Richard D., LtCol.; June 1943-October 1944
P-38J 5E-N 42-67258 "Libbuf Nanny"
P-51D 5E-N 44-13994 "Libbuf Nanny"
O'Connell, William P., Lt.; August 1943-April 28, 1944(KIAc)
Owens, Duane W., Lt.; July 1944-August 25, 1944(POW)
Pascoe, James J., Lt.; April 1944-December 1944
69 missions
P-38J 5E-Z 42-67453
P-51D 5E-W 44-13890 "Green Eyes"
Paul, Russell J., Lt.; January 1945-EOW
Pohmer, Wilfred A., Lt.; September 1944-October 12, 1944(MIA)
Poore, William L., Lt.; August 1943-September 1944
Radley, Francis X., Lt.; November 1944-February 22, 1945(KIA)
P-51D 5E-D 44-15043 "Thelma"
Rauck, William H., Lt.; December 1944-EOW
Reynolds, Robert B., Capt.; February 1944-April 15, 1944(MIA)
Rivers, Erskin H., Lt.; September 1944-November 30, 1944(POW)
P-51D 5E-J 44-13947
Roesch, Clarence R., Jr., Lt.; November 1944-October 1945
40 missions, 176 hours
Rogers, John S., Lt.; November 1944-EOW
Rooney, Gerald W., Capt.; August 1943-September 1944
Ruland, James W., Lt.; November 1944-EOW
Sagar, William S., Jr., Lt.; November 1944-December 31, 1944(POW)
10 missions
Saylor, Henry B., Capt.; April 1944-September 1944; ex-383rd Ftr Sqn
64 missions, 230 hours total
Scott, Richard M., Capt.; August 1943-March 15, 1944(POW)
13 missions
P-38J 5E-S 42-68062
Scott, Roy C., Maj.; August 1943-November 1944
Seely, Ted E., Capt.; August 1943-September 1944
Shea, Walter J., Lt.; April 1944-April 24, 1944(MIA)
Sims, William J., Lt.; February 1944-April 15, 1944(POW)
Smart, Curtis L., Lt.; November 1944-EOW
P-51D 5E-X 44-15726 "Estrellita II"
P-51D 5E-X 44-64077"Estrellita III"
Smith, Curtis A., Lt.; August 1943-March 29, 1944(KIA)
Smith, Roy O., Capt.; August 1943-March 22, 1944(MIA)
P-38J 5E-G 42-67934
Spain, Frank O., Lt.; December 1944-September 1945
40 missions
Squillario, Raymond B., Lt.; August 1943-???(KIAc)
Stapleton, Carl W., LtCol.; April 1944-April 1945; to HdQts; ex-384th Ftr Sqn
113 missions, 485 hours total
P-51D 5E-S 44-14876 "Esie 4"
Steincamp, Lynn A., Lt.; August 1943-May 8, 1944(POW)
Stepman, Alfred C., Lt.; February 1944-May 7, 1944(MIA)
Stern, Sidney S., F/O; February 1945-April 16, 1945(POW)
Stevens, Kent H., Lt.; August 1943-November 1943 (later to ETO w/20th Ftr Grp)
Street, Clyde M., Lt.; February 1944-April 15, 1944(MIA)
Stubblefield, Herman H., Capt.; August 1943-September 1944
77 missions
Sullivan, Walter A., Lt.; September 1944-October 24, 1944(POW)
Sullivan, William F., Lt.; August 1943-November 1943
Tallman, John C., Lt.; August 1943-March 15, 1944(POW)
Taylor, Elmer A., Capt.; August 1943-October 1944
P-51D 5E-E 44-13899
Tazzia, Edward K., Lt.; August 1943-August 25, 1944(POW)
50 missions
Trybuszewski, Alfred J., Capt.; August 1943-September 1944
79 missions, 270 hours
Turner, James D., Lt.; August 1943-March 15, 1944(POW)
Vann, James F., Lt.; August 1943-September 1944
Vickers, John R., Lt.; August 1943-September 5, 1944(MIA)
Visconte, Romildo, Capt.; February 1944-December 5, 1944(KIA)
P-38J 5E-G
P-51D 5E-G 44-14254
Waggoner, Herman A., Lt.; August 1943-@September 1944
Warner, Clarence B., Lt.; August 1943-May 25, 1944(MIA)
Webb, Stephen J., Lt.; August 1943-November 1943
Wegher, Adolph J., Lt.; August 1943-November 1943
Welsh, Stephen J., Lt.; August 1943-September 1944
196:50 hours
Wennemer, John, Lt.; August 1943-April 1944; to 383rd Ftr Sqn
Whipple, Ira A., Lt.; August 1943-April 26, 1944(MIA)
White, Richard E., Capt.; February 1944-January 1945; ex-B-24 co-pilot
P-51D 5E- "Wisconsin Whistler"
Whitehead, Robert L., Lt.; August 1943-November 1943(KIAc)
Wilkins, Edward, Lt.; August 1943-November 1943(KIAc)
Williams, Roy E., Lt.; August 1943-December 13, 1943(KIAc)

Wilson, Ernest E., Lt.; March 1944-August 1944 (injured)
184 hours; ex-RAF
Wilson, Ernest L., Lt.; August 1943-September 1944
Wilson, William F., Capt.; April 1944-December 1944
300:10 hours
P-51D 5E-Y 44-14258
P-51D 5E-Y 44-14838
Wittgreve, John W., Lt.; April 1944-May 25, 1944(POW)
Zakovec, Eugene J., Lt.; August 1943-April 9, 1944(MIA)

### Aircraft of the 383rd Fighter Squadron

P-38J-5-LO
42-67174 N2-F
42-67222 N2-
42-67223 N2-
42-67233 N2-
42-67248 N2-

P-38J-10-LO
42-67412 N2-X "The Rebel Kids" M.W. Glascow
42-67414 N2-Z
42-67415 N2-W "Bettye-Jo" S.J. Wicker
42-67416 N2-
42-67445 N2-
42-67453 N2-W "Bettye-Jo" S.J. Wicker
42-67897 N2-P
42-67898 N2-L
42-67928 N2-E
42-67944 N2-Y
42-67969 N2-B
42-67974 N2-H
42-67978 N2-K "Mim"
42-68013 N2-A
42-68017 N2-D
42-68034 N2-S
42-68043 N2-D "Connie & Butch, Inc." G.F. Ceuleers
42-68104 N2-O R.W. Osborn
42-68123 N2-N
42-68174 N2-F

P-38J-15-LO
43-28262 N2-B
43-28272 N2-I
43-28344 N2-H
43-28360 N2-
43-28406 N2-A "The Gallant Warrior" B.B. Wilson
43-28417 N2-K
43-28418 N2-G
43-28425 N2-Z C.F. Scrivner
43-28452 N2-X
43-28468 N2-
42-104171 N2-M "Marie" J.B. McManus
42-104198 N2-
42-104417 N2-K

Unknown Serials
N2-W "Bettye-Jo II" S.J. Wicker
N2-Q "Sweet Jo"
N2- "Jewel"

P-51B-5-NA
43-6731 N2- HACK

P-51C-10-NT
43-25058 N2-B
43-25066 N2-Y

P-51K-5-NT
44-11558 N2-S
44-11643 N2-H
44-11656 N2-Q "Male Call"
44-11742 N2-V
44-11762 N2-J
44-11762 N2-M

P-51D-5-NA
44-13283 N2- "Caroline Ann"
44-13532 N2- "Betty Joyce"
44-13699 N2-G
44-13707 N2-E J.C. Hunter
44-13707 N2-A "Lady Dorothy IV" C.K. Voss
44-13757 N2-T
44-13795 N2-G
44-13797 N2-
44-13812 N2-J "Cassie's Chassie" M.L. Casagrande
44-13813 N2-H "Little Duchess"
44-13853 N2-L
44-13854 N2-Q T.H. Hall
44-13866 N2-V "Rosey Doates"
44-13878 N2-
44-13891 N2-R
44-13906 N2-B "Doc"
44-13916 N2-N K.F. Nicholson
44-13920 N2-
44-13922 N2-

P-51D-5-NA
44-13923 N2-O "Billy Boy" R.W. Osborn
44-13932 N2-X "Copperhead" M.W. Glascow
44-13936 N2-W "Bettye-Jo III" S.J. Wicker
44-13936 N2-W "Carolina Moon"
44-13941 N2-M J.B. McManus
44-13941 N2-M "Clam Winkle"
44-13971 N2-D G.F. Ceuleers
44-13971 N2-D "Priss IV"
44-13974 N2-A "Bama Queen" B.B. Wilson
44-14005 N2-M
44-14013 N2-B "Beau's Baby" E.C. Beaumont
44-14015 N2-

P-51D-10-NA
44-14073 N2-A
44-14088 N2-S
44-14104 N2-P
44-14133 N2-H
44-14242 N2-
44-14243 N2-W "Bettye-Jo IV" S.J. Wicker
44-14279 N2-
44-14290 N2-L "Passionate Pat" L.V. Andrew
44-14315 N2-U R.W. Orndorff
44-14528 N2-F R.H. Farley
44-14653 N2- "Blood & Soda"
44-14665 N2-X "Phyllis" W.V. Pyle
44-14703 N2- "G.I. Buzz Buggy"
44-14747 N2-Y "Rough Rider" E.N. Fiery

P-51D-15-NA
44-14967 N2-D "Joyce B II"
44-15007 N2-X C.E. Hammett
44-15020 N2-D G.F. Ceuleers
44-15064 N2-
44-15399 N2-R "Southern Belle" G.E. Smith
44-15496 N2-V
44-15542 N2-Z
44-15559 N2-T R.L. Hunt
44-15573 N2-B "The Snatch" R.M. Baughn
44-15578 N2-E J.C. Hunter

P-51D-20-NA
44-63278 N2-W
44-72003 N2-A "Miss McKock"
44-72124 N2-N
44-72353 N2-R
44-72358 N2-P
44-72423 N2-U R.W. Orndorff

P-51D-25-NA
44-72719 N2-D "Constance" G.F. Ceuleers
44-73186 N2-Y "Babs In Arms"

Unknown Serials
N2-O "Shack Lassie"
N2-V "Blue Bonnett Belle II" E.J. Wheless
N2- "Lil Curley"
N2- "Gross Arsch Vogel"
N2- "Bomber Jockey" D.F. Swift
N2- "My-Katy-Car" R.A. Ogle
N2- "Buster" R.H. Cheney
N2- "Helen" J.D. Woodside
N2-D "Where's Elmer ??"
N2- "Little Tex"

### Aircraft of the 384th Fighter Squadron

P-38J-5-LO
42-67230 5Y-R
42-67232 5Y-W D.W. Williams
42-67240 5Y-
42-67260 5Y-V
42-67296 5Y-Z

P-38J-10-LO
42-67417 5Y-D R.E. Lacy
42-67428 5Y-
42-67433 5Y-
42-67438 5Y-I
42-67447 5Y-

| | |
|---|---|
| 42-67452 5Y-B | |
| 42-67461 5Y- | |
| 42-67701 5Y-K | V.L. Kercher |
| 42-67737 5Y-M | O.E. Myers |
| 42-67882 5Y- | |
| 42-67902 5Y-J | |
| 42-67957 5Y- | |
| 42-67960 5Y-A | A.L. Chilton |
| 42-67979 5Y- | |
| 42-67980 5Y-F | J.C. Ford |
| 42-67984 5Y- | |
| 42-68063 5Y- | |
| 42-68070 5Y-D | R.E. Lacy |
| 42-68087 5Y-U | |
| 42-68098 5Y-L "Penny " | J.H. Lowell |
| 42-68101 5Y-O | W.E. Bristow |
| 42-68120 5Y-S | R.M. Spradlin |
| 42-68125 5Y- | |
| 42-68129 5Y-Q | |
| 42-68144 5Y-H | |
| 42-68148 5Y- | |
| 42-68149 5Y-E | |
| 42-68152 5Y-A | |
| 42-68161 5Y-P | S.C. Phillips |

| P-38J-15-LO | |
|---|---|
| 43-28353 5Y-G | |
| 43-28372 5Y-B "Melba Lee" | C.H. Leo |
| 43-28402 5Y-F | J.C. Ford |
| 43-28429 5Y-Y | B.P. Yost |
| 43-28432 5Y-Z | |
| 43-28470 5Y-M | |
| 43-28734 5Y-A | A.L. Chilton |
| 42-104182 5Y-V | |
| 42-104195 5Y-F | |
| 42-104269 5Y-U | D.J. Pick |
| 42-104214 5Y- | |
| 42-104271 5Y-J | |
| 42-104402 5Y-T | |
| 42-104403 5Y-D | |
| 42-104405 5Y-D | R.E. Lacy |
| 42-104421 5Y-K "Daddy's Baby" | V.L. Kercher |
| 44-23161 5Y-Q | |

| Unknown Serials | |
|---|---|
| 5Y-L "Penny 2" | J.H. Lowell |
| 5Y-B "Leo" | C.H. Leo |
| 5Y-W "My Norma" | B.C. Ward |
| 5Y- "The Homesick Angel" | M.J. Woolley |
| 5Y-F "Kay" | J.E. Wilson |
| 5Y-F "Kay II" | J.E. Wilson |
| 5Y- "Mary, The Flying Angel" | |

| P-51B-10-NA | |
|---|---|
| 42-106659 5Y- | HACK |
| 42-106761 5Y-14 | HACK |

| P-51B-15-NA | |
|---|---|
| 43-24806 5Y-11 | HACK |

| P-51C-10-NT | |
|---|---|
| 43-25024 5Y-M | C.J. Pushcar |
| 43-25024 5Y-K | |
| 43-25040 5Y-F | W.P. Hess |

| P-51D-5-NT | |
|---|---|
| 44-11207 5Y-D | G.Z. Schroeder |
| 44-11233 5Y-T | T.H. Wells |

| P-51K-1-NT | |
|---|---|
| 44-11371 5Y-D | |

| P-51K-5-NT | |
|---|---|
| 44-11567 5Y-P "Dana Kay" | |

| P-51D-5-NA | |
|---|---|
| 44-13342 5Y-T | J.C. Taylor |
| 44-13709 5Y- | |
| 44-13722 5Y-G "Jersey Bouncer" | J.J. Gawienowski |
| 44-13750 5Y-H | R.S. Hunt |
| 44-13766 5Y-N | T.D. Nielson |
| 44-13770 5Y-J "Altoona Kid" | |
| 44-13813 5Y-H | R.M. Heyman |
| 44-13822 5Y-B "Mustang" | |
| 44-13825 5Y-O "Nita" | W.E. Bristow |
| 44-13825 5Y-O | H.M. James |
| 44-13829 5Y-J "Terry Claire II" | J.M. Fowle |
| 44-13829 5Y-J | L.A. Johnson |
| 44-13915 5Y-I "Pegasus" | |
| 44-13915 5Y-S | C.W. Stover/S.J. Price |
| 44-13922 5Y-Q | A.D. Parsley |
| 44-13958 5Y-E | |
| 44-13975 5Y-W "Dot" | D.W. Williams |
| 44-13976 5Y- "Mary III" | |
| 44-13986 5Y-B "Mustang" | |
| 44-13988 5Y-S | J.M. Stuckrath |
| 44-13988 5Y-V "Just Plain L" | L.L. Lefforge |
| 44-13993 5Y-J "Hugo's Nooky Booky" | H.A. Lohr |
| 44-13998 5Y-M "Silver Streak" | D.L. Leftwich |
| 44-13998 5Y-P | M.D. Petrosky |
| 44-13999 5Y-B | C.H. Leo |
| 44-14018 5Y-Y | F.A. Hoenselaar |
| 44-14018 5Y-Y "Six Gun Pete" | E.W. Farnsworth |
| 44-14021 5Y-D "Jackie Jr." | R.E. Lacy |
| 44-14031 5Y-P | S.C. Phillips |
| 44-14032 5Y-W "My Norma" | B.C. Ward |
| 44-14034 5Y-D "Jackie" | R.E. Lacy |

| P-51D-10-NA | |
|---|---|
| 44-14074 5Y-F "Kay" | J.E. Wilson |
| 44-14076 5Y-W "Dot" | D.W. Williams |
| 44-14093 5Y-S "Puddin' II" | R.W. Stevens |
| 44-14148 5Y-M "Lauries" | |
| 44-14174 5Y- | |
| 44-14184 5Y-Q | |
| 44-14190 5Y-Q "Boogies Burner" | |
| 44-14218 5Y-W "Mary W" | J.W. Purvis |
| 44-14328 5Y-V | |
| 44-14532 5Y-W | |
| 44-14680 5Y-S | S.J. Price |
| 44-14726 5Y-I | |
| 44-14762 5Y-D "Florence II" | |
| 44-14851 5Y-J "Altoona Kid II" | |

| P-51D-15-NA | |
|---|---|
| 44-14881 5Y- | |
| 44-14992 5Y-L "Penny 3" | J.H. Lowell |
| 44-15027 5Y-A | R.K. Allen |
| 44-15176 5Y- | |
| 44-15202 5Y-H | |
| 44-15261 5Y- | |
| 44-15276 5Y-T | |
| 44-15356 5Y-U "Lillamae" | D.J. Pick |
| 44-15386 5Y-W | |
| 44-15411 5Y-R | |
| 44-15532 5Y-R | |
| 44-15538 5Y-Q | |
| 44-15557 5Y- | |
| 44-15568 5Y-H "Lil Eva" | H.C. Schwartz |
| 44-15580 5Y- | |

| P-51D-20-NA | |
|---|---|
| 44-63161 5Y-U "Good Priss" | |
| 44-63263 5Y-L "Penny 4" | J.H. Lowell |
| 44-63890 5Y-R | |
| 44-72059 5Y-P | S.C. Phillips |

| P-51D-25-NA | |
|---|---|
| 44-73090 5Y-Q "Denver Belle" | J.A. Walker |

| Unknown Serials | |
|---|---|
| 5Y-J "Terry Claire" | J.M. Fowle |
| 5Y-S "Hi Toots" | |
| 5Y- "Punkin" | R.S. Faulkner |
| 5Y- "Punkin II" | R.S. Faulkner |
| 5Y-S "Puddin" | R.W. Stevens |
| 5Y-V "Battle Axe" | W.A. Leavell |
| 5Y- "Mary Honey" | F.T. O'Connor |
| 5Y- "Snorky" | D.J. Roberts |
| 5Y- "Kitty Blue Eyes" | O.D. Henson |

**Aircraft of the 385th Fighter Squadron**

| P-38J-5-LO | |
|---|---|
| 42-67405 5E-Q | |
| 42-67257 5E-F | |
| 42-67258 5E-N "Libbuf Nanny" | R.D. Neece |
| 42-67272 5E-H | |
| 42-67283 5E-T | |

| P-38J-10-LO | |
|---|---|
| 42-67302 5E- | |
| 42-67453 5E-Z | J.J. Pascoe |
| 42-67458 5E-E | |
| 42-67464 5E-M | |
| 42-67851 5E- | |
| 42-67895 5E- | |
| 42-67903 5E-I | |
| 42-67933 5E-K | |

42-67934 5E-G R.O. Smith
42-67947 5E-R
42-68025 5E-S
42-68031 5E-D
42-68041 5E-
42-68050 5E-O
42-68054 5E-U
42-68062 5E-S R.M. Scott
42-68069 5E-
42-68078 5E-V
42-68087 5E-U
42-68141 5E-
42-68178 5E-K
42-68180 5E-J
42-68187 5E-

P-38J-15-LO
43-28361 5E-T
43-28414 5E-X
43-28422 5E-H C.S. Hill
43-28444 5E-B
43-28448 5E-T
43-28550 5E-V
43-28760 5E-
42-104092 5E-G F.C. McClanahan
42-104317 5E-A

Unknown Serials
5E- "Golden Gophers"
5E- "Tiger Lily"
5E- "Jo Ann-Kathy"

P-51B-1-NA
43-12322 5E-21 "Lady Lou" HACK

P-51B-10-NA
43-7194 5E-Y HACK

P-51C-5-NT
42-103593 5E-O

P-51C-10-NT
43-25030 5E-Y "Lucky II"
43-25051 5E-E
43-25058 5E-B

P-51D-5-NT
44-11213 5E-E
44-11213 5E-B "Majero" D.L. Bloodgood
44-11242 5E-F "Mary Al" J.L. McCubbin
44-11340 5E-L

P-51K-1-NT
44-11375 5E-K

P-51K-5-NT
44-11619 5E-O "The Boilermaker Special" R.W. Boydson
44-11648 5E-N
44-11751 5E-H

P-51D-5-NA
44-13347 5E-
44-13657 5E-
44-13686 5E-N "Rugged Rebel"
44-13700 5E-
44-13754 5E-F
44-13793 5E-
44-13814 5E-V "Fancy Frances"
44-13830 5E-D
44-13835 5E-H W.G. Erfkamp
44-13835 5E-Q
44-13845 5E-H
44-13847 5E-J
44-13853 5E-H "Dottie Bee II" J.E. Hargrove
44-13869 5E-Q E.F. Izor
44-13890 5E-W "Green Eyes" J.J. Pascoe
44-13899 5E-E E.A. Taylor
44-13899 5E-H
44-13940 5E-G
44-13942 5E-K "Pinnochio"
44-13947 5E-J E.H. Rivers
44-13962 5E-S "Bloody Rebel"
44-13964 5E-B
44-13985 5E- "Joker III"
44-13994 5E-N "Libbuf Nanny" R.D. Neece
44-13994 5E-N W.S. Crombie
44-14006 5E-D J.D. Dale
44-14006 5E-H W.T. Housholder
44-14008 5E-
44-14024 5E-I
44-14025 5E-T "Lovin' Aline"
44-14030 5E-Y
44-14033 5E-M "Doodlebug"
44-14035 5E-A "Etta Jane" G.L. Jamison

P-51D-10-NA
44-14148 5E-B "Laurie's Eleanor" J.D. Monahan
44-14178 5E-S "Queen Anne"
44-14189 5E-R "Francisco"
44-14236 5E-
44-14241 5E-I
44-14254 5E-G R. Visconte
44-14254 5E-B "Majero II" D.L. Bloodgood
44-14258 5E-Y W.F. Wilson
44-14263 5E-
44-14322 5E-O "Coffin Wit' Wings"
44-14336 5E-U T.P. Farrell
44-14375 5E-K
44-14381 5E-J
44-14456 5E-X
44-14523 5E-
44-14584 5E-K S.L. Lett
44-14667 5E-M "Little Sport" H.W. Head
44-14708 5E-
44-14724 5E-Z T.L. Allinder
44-14835 5E-
44-14838 5E-Y W.F. Wilson
44-14838 5E-I

P-51D-15-NA
44-14862 5E-E "Jersey Bouncer" E. Murphy
44-14876 5E-S "Esie 4" C.W. Stapleton
44-14933 5E-X "Rugged Rebel"
44-14961 5E-T
44-15019 5E-B "Lucky Lady VI" E.E. Bankey
44-15041 5E-O
44-15043 5E-D "Thelma" F.X. Radley
44-15051 5E-P "Sweet Mama" E.N. Farrell
44-15061 5E-O "Jimmie The First" E.P. Roberts
44-15179 5E-L "Look Homeward Angel II" A.B. McCormick
44-15282 5E-R
44-15282 5E-E
44-15384 5E-I
44-15493 5E-J "Jeanne II" G.W. Fine
44-15576 5E-P "Sweet Mama II" E.N. Farrell
44-15641 5E-U T.P. Farrell
44-15643 5E-U
44-15672 5E-
44-15726 5E-X "Estrellita II" C.L. Smart

P-51D-20-NA
44-63184 5E-
44-63194 5E-Y
44-64077 5E-X "Estrellita III" C.L. Smart
44-72179 5E-A
44-72343 5E-N W.S. Crombie
44-72343 5E-K
44-72376 5E-
44-72525 5E-V

P-51D-25-NA
44-73035 5E-
44-73045 5E-B "Lucky Lady VII" E.E. Bankey
44-73348 5E-F

Unknown Serials
P-51D 5E-H "Dottie Bee" J.E. Hargrove
P-51D 5E-J "Jeanne" G.W. Fine
P-51D 5E-L "Look Homeward Angel" A.B. McCormick
P-51D 5E- "Wisconsin Whistler" R.E. White

• • •

## THE 479TH FIGHTER GROUP
## 434TH, 435TH, 436TH FIGHTER SQUADRONS

The 479th Fighter Group was activated on October 15, 1943, at Glendale, California. After training in the western United States, the group sailed aboard the "USS Argentina" on May 2, 1944. The first of 251 missions came on May 26, 1944, with the last being flown on April 25, 1945. While overseas, the 479th claimed 155 aerial and 268 ground victories while 77 P-38's and P-51's were lost on operations and 16 pilots died in accidents.

The 479th was based at Wattisham from May 15, 1944, to November of 1945, and flew the P-38J from May to October of 1944 and the P-51D and K from September 13, 1944, until war's end. The group was awarded a Distinguished Unit Citation for strafing missions on August 18 and September 5, 1944, and for bomber escort performance on September 26, 1944.

### Claims

| | Air | | | Grd | |
|---|---|---|---|---|---|
| | Destroyed | Probable | Damaged | Destroyed | Damaged |
| HdQts | 4 | 0 | 2 | 1 | 0 |
| 434th | 93.5 | 8 | 22 | 126.5 | 56 |
| 435th | 33.5 | 5 | 9 | 35.5 | 46 |
| 436th | 24 | 0 | 6 | 105 | 59 |
| | 155 | 13 | 39 | 268 | 161 |

### Commanders

| | |
|---|---|
| LtCol. Kyle L. Riddle | December 25, 1943-August 10, 1944 |
| Col. Hubert Zemke | August 12, 1944-October 30, 1944 |
| Col. Kyle L. Riddle | October 30, 1944-late 1945 |

### Wing and Command Assignments

| | |
|---|---|
| Assigned to VIII Fighter Command | May 14, 1944 |
| VIII Fighter Command, 65th Fighter Wing | May 15, 1944 |
| 2nd Bomb Division, 65th Fighter Wing | September 15, 1944 |
| 2nd Air Division, 65th Fighter Wing | January 1, 1945 |

### Aircraft Markings

Group P-38's were operated in both olive drab/neutral gray and NMF finish. No specific group markings were applied but many planes removed the paint from the spinners and cowls. Squadron markings consisted of geometric symbols placed on the outer vertical tails, white on olive drab ships and black on NMF planes. The symbols were a triangle(434th), circle(435th), and square(436th). In August of 1944, the symbols were replaced with rudder colors; red, yellow, and no color for the 434th, 435th, and 436th, respectively.

All P-51's were flown on operations in NMF. Group markings consisted only of highly polished spinners. Squadron rudder colors remained as carried on the P-38's, only the 436th now applied black and white checkerboards on it's rudders. From November of 1944, the 436th painted the entire rudder black. The 479th was peculiar in that many Mustangs had the serial number erased from the vertical tails.

Squadron codes were:

434th Ftr Sqn: L2
435th Ftr Sqn: J2
436th Ftr Sqn: 9B

### 479th Fighter Group Statistical Report

| Month | Air | Grd | Losses | KIAc |
|---|---|---|---|---|
| May 1944 | 0-0-0 | 1-0 | 0 | 1 |
| June | 1-0-0 | 0-0 | 12 | 1 |
| July | 4-1-1 | 0-2 | 12 | 1 |
| August | 19-1-2 | 56-40 | 12 | 0 |
| September | 42-0-13 | 45-24 | 6 | 3 |
| October | 4-0-1 | 0-0 | 6 | 1 |
| November | 5-0-1 | 1-1 | 3 | 0 |
| December | 42-8-9 | 0-2 | 10 | 3 |
| January 1945 | 2-0-1 | 2-3 | 1 | 0 |
| February | 20-2-7 | 14-19 | 5 | 1 |
| March | 4-0-2 | 0-4 | 3 | 1 |
| April | 12-1-2 | 149-66 | 7 | 2 |
| June | 0-0-0 | 0-0 | 0 | 0 |
| July | 0-0-0 | 0-0 | 0 | 1 |
| | 155-13-39 | 268-161 | 77 | 16 |

### Losses by Squadron and Type

| | MIA | | KIAc | |
|---|---|---|---|---|
| | P-38 | P-51 | P-38 | P-51 |
| HdQts | 2 | 1 | 0 | 0 |
| 434th | 20 | 18 | 0 | 4 |
| 435th | 10 | 7 | 1 | 5 |
| 436th | 7 | 12 | 3 | 3 |
| | 39 | 38 | 4 | 12 |

### Claims by Type

| | Air | | | Grd | |
|---|---|---|---|---|---|
| | Destroyed | Probable | Damaged | Destroyed | Damaged |
| P-38 | 52 | 2 | 13 | 102 | 66 |
| P-51 | 103 | 11 | 26 | 166 | 95 |

### Claims by Enemy Aircraft Type

| | Air | | | Grd | |
|---|---|---|---|---|---|
| | Destroyed | Probable | Damaged | Destroyed | Damaged |
| Me-109 | 89 | 3 | 22 | 26 | 20 |
| FW-190 | 57 | 9 | 13 | 78 | 24 |
| Me-262 | 3 | 1 | 4 | 8 | 5 |
| Ar-234 | 1 | 0 | 0 | 3 | 0 |
| FW-200 | 1 | 0 | 0 | 2 | 0 |
| Ju-52 | 1 | 0 | 0 | 3 | 3 |
| Me-163 | 1 | 0 | 0 | 0 | 0 |
| Fi-156 | 1 | 0 | 0 | 5 | 0 |
| Ju-88 | 1 | 0 | 0 | 36 | 33 |
| He-111 | 0 | 0 | 0 | 37 | 30 |
| u/i a/c | 0 | 0 | 0 | 24 | 34 |
| Do-217 | 0 | 0 | 0 | 16 | 3 |
| Me-110 | 0 | 0 | 0 | 12 | 3 |
| Me-410 | 0 | 0 | 0 | 9 | 4 |
| Ju-87 | 0 | 0 | 0 | 5 | 0 |
| B-24 | 0 | 0 | 0 | 2 | 0 |
| He-177 | 0 | 0 | 0 | 1 | 0 |
| FW-189 | 0 | 0 | 0 | 1 | 0 |
| Ju-188 | 0 | 0 | 0 | 0 | 2 |

### 479th Fighter Group Squadron Commanders

**434th Ftr Sqn**

| | |
|---|---|
| LtCol. James M. Herren, Jr. | January 1944-October 30, 1944 |
| LtCol. Arthur F. Jeffrey | November 1, 1944-March 1945 |
| Maj. Robin Olds | March 1945-EOW |

**435th Ftr Sqn**

| | |
|---|---|
| Maj. John G. Glover | October 1943-October 1944 |
| Maj. Herbert H. Jordan | October 1944-April 5, 1945 |
| Capt. William C. Anderson | April 5, 1945-EOW |

**436th Ftr Sqn**

| | |
|---|---|
| Capt. William A. Walker | October 1943-May 25, 1944 |
| Maj. John D. Monahan | May 26, 1944-August 1, 1944 |
| Maj. John A. Sullivan | August 1, 1944-December 5, 1944 |
| Maj. Jules D. Biscayart | December 5, 1944-January 1, 1945 |
| Maj. Claire A.P. Duffie | January 1, 1945-November 9, 1945 |

### 479th Fighter Group Aces

| Name | Air | Grd | Total | Sqn |
|---|---|---|---|---|
| Maj. Robin Olds | 13 | 11 | 24 | 434th |
| Capt. George W. Gleason | 12 | 2.5 | 14.5 | 434th |
| LtCol. Arthur F. Jeffrey | 14 | 0 | 14 | 434th |
| Maj. Claire A.P. Duffie | 3 | 8.5 | 11.5 | 434th<br>436th |
| Lt. Gail E. Jacobson | 4.5 | 6 | 10.5 | 434th |
| Lt. Tom C. Olson | 1 | 9.5 | 10.5 | 434th |
| Capt. James M. Hollingsworth | 3 | 7 | 10* | 434th |
| Capt. Donald J. Pierce | 0 | 8.5 | 8.5 | 434th |
| Capt. Theodore J. Spwerby | 2 | 6.5 | 8.5 | 435th |
| Lt. Richard C.J. Palson | 0 | 8 | 8 | 436th |
| Lt. Charles B. Elmgren, Jr. | 0 | 7 | 7 | 436th |
| Lt. Ernest J. Hopcroft | 0 | 7 | 7 | 436th |
| Lt. George H. Witzel | 0 | 7 | 7 | 436th |
| Lt. John T. Golden | 1 | 5.5 | 6.5 | 434th |
| Capt. Hans J. Grasshoff | 2.5 | 4 | 6.5 | 436th |
| Lt. Richard G. Candelaria | 6 | 0 | 6 | 435th |
| Lt. John W. Hansen | 2 | 4 | 6 | 434th |
| LtCol. James M. Herren, Jr. | 4 | 2 | 6 | 434th |
| Capt. Verne E. Hooker | 2 | 4 | 6 | 435th |
| Lt. Tom D. Neely | 2 | 4 | 6 | 434th |
| Lt. Kenneth J. Hansen | 0 | 5 | 5 | 436th |
| Lt. John N. Murr | 2 | 3 | 5 | 434th |
| Lt. Jerome K. Nagel | 1 | 4 | 5 | 434th |
| Capt. Presson S. Shane | 0 | 5 | 5 | 436th |
| Lt. Alfred J. Smigel | 0 | 5 | 5 | 436th |
| Lt. Victor Wolski | 3 | 2 | 5 | 436th |
| Col. Hubert Zemke | 17.75 | 8.5 | 26.25** | HdQts |
| Capt. Clarence O. Johnson | 7 | 6 | 13*** | 436th |
| LtCol. Sidney S. Woods | 7 | 3 | 10@ | HdQts |

* - includes 3 air victories with the 14th Ftr Grp, MTO
** - all but 2.5 air victories with the 56th Ftr Grp, ETO
*** - includes 4 air victories with the 82nd Ftr Grp, MTO, and 2 air and 6 ground victories with the 352nd Ftr Grp, ETO
@ - includes 2 air victories with the 49th Ftr Grp, PTO, and 5 air and 2 ground victories with the 4th Ftr Grp, ETO

### 479th Fighter Group Scorers

**HdQts**

| | Air | Grd | |
|---|---|---|---|
| K.L. Riddle | 1.5-0-1 | 0-0 | |
| S.S. Woods | 0-0-0 | 1-0 | plus 2 air w/49th Ftr Grp, PTO & 5-0-0 air & 2-5 grd w/4th Ftr Grp |
| H. Zemke | 2.5-0-1 | 0-0 | plus 15.5-2-7 air & 8.75-7 grd w/56th Ftr Grp |

**434th Ftr Sqn**

| | Air | Grd | |
|---|---|---|---|
| D.L. Born | 1-0-0 | 3-0 | |
| C.W. Bowers | 0.5-0-0 | 3.5-2 | |
| R.I. Bromschwig | 0-0-2 | 0-0 | |
| P.A. Brown | 1-1-0 | 2-1.5 | |
| R.D. Creighton | 2-1-0 | 0-2 | |
| W.H. Daudistel | 1-0-0 | 0-0 | |
| J.C. Donnell, Jr. | 1-0-2 | 0-0 | |
| W.M. Drake | 1-0-0 | 3-0 | |
| C.A.P. Duffie | 3-0-2 | 1.5-0 | plus 436th Ftr Sqn |
| G.W. Gleason | 12-0-2 | 2.5-1 | |
| J.T. Golden | 1-0-0 | 5.5-2.5 | |
| H.F. Grenning, Jr. | 1-0-0 | 2-2 | |
| J.W. Hansen | 2-0-1 | 4-3 | |
| J.A. Hass | 0-1-0 | 0-0 | |
| W.H. Hehn | 0-0-0 | 2-1 | |
| A.G. Helding | 1-0-0 | 0-0 | |
| R.H. Hendrickson | 0-0-0 | 4-1 | |
| L.A. Hendrickson | 0-0-0 | 1-0 | |
| G.D. Hendrix | 1-0-1 | 2-3 | |
| J.M. Herren, Jr. | 4-0-0 | 2-0 | |
| J.M. Hollingsworth | 0-1-1 | 7-0 | plus 3 air w/14th Ftr Grp, MTO |
| B.E. Hollister | 2-1-0 | 2-0 | |
| E.E. Honace | 0-0-0 | 1-1 | |
| O.J. Huval | 0-0-0 | 1.5-1 | |
| G.E. Jacobson | 4.5-1-0 | 6-2 | |
| A.F. Jeffrey | 14-0-2 | 0-0 | |
| H.M. Jenkins | 1-0-0 | 0-0 | |
| F.J. Keller | 0-0-0 | 2-0.5 | |
| R.B. Kline | 0-0-1 | 3-1.5 | |
| G.H. Leeny | 0-0-0 | 1-0 | |
| H.E. Little | 0-0-0 | 1.5-2 | |
| R.M. Lunstrum | 1-0-0 | 0-0 | |
| R.L. Maley | 1-1-0 | 0-4 | |
| W.H. Marlowe | 0-0-0 | 0.5-0 | |
| D.W. Mastin | 0-0-0 | 1-0 | |
| H.E. Mathews | 1-0-0 | 2-1 | |
| R.G. McChrystal | 3-0-2 | 0-0 | |
| J.W. Morrow | 1-0-0 | 1-0 | |
| R.L. Munson | 1-0-0 | 2-1 | |
| C.J. Murphy | 0-0-0 | 3-2 | |
| J.N. Murr | 2-1-1 | 3-0 | |
| J.K. Nagel | 1-0-0 | 4-0 | |
| T.D. Neely | 2-0-0 | 4-0.5 | |
| R. Olds | 13-0-1 | 11-1 | |
| T.C. Olson | 1-0-0 | 9.5-3 | |
| Q.S. Pavlock | 4-0-0 | 0-0.5 | |
| C.M. Peacock | 0-0-0 | 2-0 | |
| C.L. Peterson | 0-0-0 | 1-0 | |
| D.J. Pierce | 0-0-2 | 8.5-5.5 | |
| J.A. Plezibat | 0-0-0 | 1-0 | |
| W.H. Rodgers | 0-0-0 | 0-4.5 | |
| R.M. Rossell, Jr. | 0-0-0 | 1-0 | |
| E.E. Sears | 1-0-0 | 1-0 | |
| R.G. Simpson | 0-0-0 | 0.5-0 | |
| D.H. Stott | 0-0-0 | 1-0 | |
| H.L. Stott | 0-0-0 | 1-1 | |
| F.M. Taylor | 0.5-0-0 | 0.5-2 | |
| H.O. Thompson | 2-0-0 | 0-0 | |
| J.T. Tipps | 1-0-0 | 1-0 | |
| D.F. Tommie | 0-0-0 | 0-2 | |
| A.J. Valluzzi | 0-0-0 | 2-0 | |
| E.H. Wendt | 4-0-2 | 0-0 | |
| B.A. Williams | 0-0-0 | 2-1 | |

**435th Ftr Sqn**

| | Air | Grd | |
|---|---|---|---|
| R.J. Baird | 0-0-0 | 1-0 | |
| W.M. Barsky | 0-0-0 | 0-1 | |
| N.R. Benoit | 2.5-0-1 | 0-4 | |
| N.W. Butler | 3-0-0 | 1-0 | |
| R.G. Candelaria | 6-1-0 | 0-3 | |
| R.S. Carter | 1-1-0 | 0-0 | |
| R.R. Coursey, Jr. | 1-0-0 | 0-0 | |
| H.W. Detlefson | 0-0-0 | 0.5-1 | |
| G.L. Doolittle | 2-1-1 | 0-0 | |
| R.K. Friend | 1-0-1 | 0.5-3 | |
| R.B. Frost | 0-0-0 | 0-2 | |
| W.N. Gates | 0-0-0 | 1-0 | |
| M.G. Gorian | 1-0-0 | 0-0 | |
| P.D. Gossard | 1-0-0 | 1-0 | |
| C.W. Granville | 0-0-0 | 2-0 | |
| J.W. Harrell, Jr. | 1-0-1 | 0-0 | |
| F.L. Hart | 0-1-0 | 0-0 | |
| R.H. Hoffman | 0-0-0 | 3-1 | |
| V.E. Hooker | 2-0-0 | 4-7 | |
| H.H. Jordan | 2-0-0 | 0-0 | plus 1 air w/475th Ftr Grp, PTO |
| D.E. King | 1-0-0 | 0-0 | |
| J.H. Koerber | 0-0-0 | 1-0 | |
| C.R. Matthews | 0-0-0 | 0-1 | |
| B.C. Means | 1-0-0 | 0-1 | |
| C.F. Monsell, Jr. | 1-0-0 | 1.5-0 | |
| W. Muller | 0-0-0 | 0-2 | |
| D.L. Naule | 0-0-0 | 1-0 | |
| L.P. Petterson | 1-0-0 | 0-0 | |
| W.H. Pickering | 2-0-0 | 0-0 | |
| R.N. Pigg | 0-0-0 | 2-5 | |
| J.R. Rogers | 1-0-1 | 0-0 | |
| W.B. Rourke, Jr. | 0-0-0 | 1-2 | |
| S.R. Routh | 0-0-0 | 1-0 | |
| G.M. Salter | 0-0-0 | 0-1 | |
| F.W. Salze | 0-0-1 | 1-0 | |
| F.H. Shriner | 0-1-0 | 0-0 | |
| E.H. Sims | 0-0-1 | 1-2 | |
| H.C. Smith | 0-0-0 | 4-0 | |
| E.A. Splittsoesser | 0-0-0 | 0-1 | |
| T.J. Sowerby | 2-0-0 | 6.5-7 | |
| J.A. Sullivan | 0-0-1 | 0-0 | plus 436th Ftr Sqn |
| G.K. Sykes | 1-0-1 | 1.5-0 | |
| D.W. Thorn | 0-0-0 | 0-2 | |

**436th Ftr Sqn**

| | Air | Grd | |
|---|---|---|---|
| W.C. Anderson | 0-0-0 | 1-0 | plus 1-1 grd w/4th Ftr Grp |
| J.M. Archibald | 0-0-0 | 1-1 | |
| J.D. Biscayart | 2-0-0 | 0-0 | |
| C.H. Darling | 0-0-0 | 4-4 | |
| A.R. DiPaola | 0-0-0 | 0-1 | |
| C.A.P. Duffie | 0-0-0 | 7-4 | plus 434th Ftr Sqn |
| D.A. Dunn | 3-0-0 | 0-0 | |
| J.R. Earley, III | 0-0-0 | 2-1 | |
| C.B. Elmgren | 0-0-0 | 7-0 | |
| C.V. Ernst | 1-0-0 | 1-0 | |
| G.E. Falkner | 0-0-0 | 1-0 | |
| E.J. Fillipow | 0-0-0 | 0-2 | |
| J.E. Frolking | 0-0-1 | 1-1 | |
| H.J. Grasshoff | 2.5-0-1 | 4-1 | |
| K.J. Hansen | 0-0-0 | 5-0 | |
| V.G. Hartnett | 0-0-0 | 2-1 | |
| J.W. Hedenburg | 0-0-0 | 1-1 | |
| R.E. Henry | 0-0-0 | 4-1 | |
| H.G. Hightower | 0-0-1 | 0-0 | |
| E.J. Hopcroft | 0-0-0 | 7-2 | |
| A.E. Huycke | 1-0-0 | 1-2 | |
| C.O. Johnson | 1-0-0 | 0-0 | plus 4 air w/82nd Ftr Grp, MTO, & 2-0-0 air & 6-1 grd w/352nd Ftr Grp |
| B.R. Kleineman | 0-0-0 | 2-0 | |
| C.S. Kreger | 0-0-0 | 0-1 | |
| E.C. Lewin | 1-0-0 | 3-2 | |
| S.F. Long | 0-0-0 | 2-0 | |
| J.C. Malone | 0-0-0 | 4-5 | |
| G.G. McLaurin | 0-0-0 | 2-0 | |
| M.S. Mickey | 1-0-0 | 0-0 | |
| C.J. Moore, Jr. | 1-0-0 | 1-3 | |
| G.M. Mulvaney | 1-0-0 | 2.5-1 | |
| T.E. Myers | 1.5-0-1 | 0.5-0 | |
| Z. Ogrom | 0-0-0 | 0-3 | |
| R.C.J. Palson | 0-0-0 | 8-2 | |
| C.H. Philbrick, II | 0-0-0 | 3-4 | |
| H.P. Plunk | 0.5-0-0 | 0-0 | |
| W.N. Rawley, Jr. | 0-0-0 | 1-0 | |
| P.J. Romano | 0-0-0 | 2-0 | |
| J.M. Rosness | 0-0-0 | 0-1 | |
| A.J. Scordino | 0-0-0 | 1-2 | |
| P.S. Shane | 0-0-0 | 5-1 | |
| A.J. Smigel | 0-0-0 | 5-3 | |
| R.S. Spencer, Jr. | 2-0-0 | 0-0 | |
| W.B. Steph | 0-0-0 | 2-1 | |
| G. Straub | 1-0-1 | 0-0 | |
| J.R. Struby | 1-0-0 | 0-0 | |
| J.A. Sullivan | 0-0-0 | 0-3 | plus 435th Ftr Sqn |
| T.H. Thompson | 0-0-0 | 1-0 | |
| P.C. Vasseur | 0.5-0-0 | 0-0 | |
| G.H. Witzel | 0-0-0 | 7-3 | |
| V. Wolski | 3-0-1 | 2-1 | |
| F. Zellman | 0-0-0 | 2-1 | |

### 479th Fighter Group Scoring

**May 31, 1944**

| | | | |
|---|---|---|---|
| 434th: | Capt. F.J. Keller | Ju-88 dest(grd) | Humfield |

**June 22, 1944**

| Unit | Pilot | Claim | Location |
|---|---|---|---|
| 436th: | Lt. C.O. Johnson | Fi-156 dest(air) | Reims |

**July 5, 1944**

| Unit | Pilot | Claim | Location |
|---|---|---|---|
| 434th: | Capt. A.F. Jeffrey | FW-200 dest(air) | Cognac/Chateaubernard |
| | Lt. B.A. Williams | Ju-88 dam(grd) | Cognac/Chateaubernard |

**July 6, 1944**

| Unit | Pilot | Claim | Location |
|---|---|---|---|
| 434th: | Lt. J.T. Tipps | Me-109 dest(air) | Valenciennes |
| | Lt. J.A. Hass | FW-190 prob(air) | Cambrai |

**July 24, 1944**

| Unit | Pilot | Claim | Location |
|---|---|---|---|
| 435th: | Capt. J.A. Sullivan | Me-109 dam(air) | SW Evreux |
| 436th: | Lt. H.J. Grasshoff | (.5)Me-109 dest(air) | Evreux |
| | Lt. H.P. Plunk | (.5)Me-109 dest(air) | Evreux |

**July 27, 1944**

| Unit | Pilot | Claim | Location |
|---|---|---|---|
| 434th: | Lt. Q.S. Pavlock | (.5)Ju-88 dam(grd) | Romilly |
| | Lt. W.H. Rodgers | (.5)Ju-88 dam(grd) | Romilly |

**July 29, 1944**

| Unit | Pilot | Claim | Location |
|---|---|---|---|
| 434th: | Capt. A.F. Jeffrey | Me-163 dest(air) | Wilhelmshaven |

**August 3, 1944**

| Unit | Pilot | Claim | Location |
|---|---|---|---|
| 435th: | Capt. W.N. Gates | B-24 dest(grd) | Ensisheim |

**August 5, 1944**

| Unit | Pilot | Claim | Location |
|---|---|---|---|
| 435th: | Capt. R.S. Carter | Me-109 dest(air) | S/Hamburg |
| | | Me-109 prob(air) | S/Hamburg |
| | Capt. G.K. Sykes | Me-109 dest(air) | S/Hamburg |
| | | Me-109 dam(air) | S/Hamburg |
| 436th: | Capt. C.J. Moore | Me-109 dest(air) | NE Stendal |
| | Lt. M.S. Mickey | Me-109 dest(air) | NE Stendal |

**August 8, 1944**

| Unit | Pilot | Claim | Location |
|---|---|---|---|
| 436th: | Lt. H.J. Grasshoff | Me-109 dam(air) | S/Paris |

**August 9, 1944**

| Unit | Pilot | Claim | Location |
|---|---|---|---|
| 434th: | Lt. W.H. Hehn | (2)He-111 dest(grd) | All claims are |
| | | Ju-52 dam(grd) | at Nuneburg |
| | Maj. F.J. Keller | FW-200 dest(grd) | |
| | | (.5)He-111 dam(grd) | |
| | Lt. T.D. Neeley | He-111 dest(grd) | |
| | | (.5)He-111 dam(grd) | |
| | Lt. G.D. Hendrix | Ju-88 dest(grd) | |
| | Lt. H.E. Mathews | FW-200 dest(grd) | |

**August 12, 1944**

| Unit | Pilot | Claim | Location |
|---|---|---|---|
| 434th: | Lt. G.D. Hendrix | Ju-88 dest(air) | Compiegne |

**August 14, 1944**

| Unit | Pilot | Claim | Location |
|---|---|---|---|
| 434th: | Capt. R. Olds | (2)FW-190 dest(air) | Montmirail |

**August 15, 1944**

| Unit | Pilot | Claim | Location |
|---|---|---|---|
| 434th: | Capt. A.F. Jeffrey | Me-109 dest(air) | All 434th claims |
| | Lt. J.W. Hansen | Me-109 dest(air) | are at Steenwijk |
| | | (2)Me-109 dest(grd) A/F | |
| | | Me-109 dam(grd) | |
| | | u/i a/c dam(grd) | |
| | Lt. Q.S. Pavlock | Me-109 dest(air) | |
| | Lt. G.D. Hendrix | Me-109 dest(grd) | |
| | | (2)Me-109 dam(grd) | |
| | Lt. C.J. Murphy | Me-109 dest(grd) | |
| | | Me-109 dam(grd) | |
| 436th: | Lt. G.M. Mulvany | (.5)B-24 dest(grd) | N/Mulhouse |
| | Lt. T.E. Myers | (.5)B-24 dest(grd) | N/Mulhouse |

**August 18, 1944**

| Unit | Pilot | Claim | Location |
|---|---|---|---|
| 434th: | LtCol. J.M. Herren | He-111 dest(grd) | All claims are |
| | | Ju-52 dest(grd) | at Nancy/Essey |
| | Capt. R. Olds | (2)Ju-88 dest(grd) | |
| | | He-111 dest(grd) | |
| | Lt. T.C. Olson | (1.5)He-111 dest(grd) | |
| | | Me-109 dest(grd) | |
| | | Ju-88 dest(grd) | |
| | | (.5)FW-190 dest(grd)[*] | |
| | | He-111 dam(grd) | |
| | Lt. G.W. Gleason | FW-190 dest(grd) | |
| | | (.5)He-111 dest(grd)[***] | |
| | | (.5)He-111 dest(grd)[***] | |
| | | (.5)Ju-88 dest(grd)[@] | |
| | | FW-190 dam(grd) | |
| | Lt. W.M. Drake | (2)Ju-88 dest(grd) | |
| | | FW-190 dest(grd) | |
| | Lt. R.H. Hendrickson | (2)Ju-88 dest(grd) | |
| | | Ju-88 dam(grd) | |
| | Lt. H.F. Grenning | He-111 dest(grd) | |
| | | Ju-88 dest(grd) | |
| | | (2)Ju-88 dam(grd) | |
| | Lt. J.W. Hansen | Ju-88 dest(grd) | |
| | | He-111 dam(grd) | |
| | Capt. C.A.P. Duffie | (1.5)Ju-88 dest(grd)[@@@] | |
| | Lt. H.C. Little | Ju-88 dest(grd) | |
| | | (.5)He-111 dest(grd)[@@] | |
| | | (2)He-111 dam(grd) | |
| | Lt. C.J. Murphy | FW-190 dest(grd) | |
| | | Ju-88 dam(grd) | |
| | Lt. C.L. Peterson | Ju-52 dest(grd) | |
| | Lt. W.H. Rodgers | (4)Ju-88 dam(grd) | |
| | Lt. R.L. Maley | (2)He-111 dam(grd) | |
| | | FW-190 dam(grd) | |
| | Lt. G.D. Hendrix | Ju-88 dam(grd) | |
| 435th: | Lt. H.C. Smith | (4)He-111 dest(grd) | |
| | Capt. G.K. Sykes | (1.5)He-111 dest(grd)[@@] | |
| | Lt. C.W. Granville | He-111 dest(grd) | |
| | | Ju-88 dest(grd) | |
| | Lt. R.N. Pigg | He-111 dest(grd) | |
| | | Ju-88 dest(grd) | |
| | | (4)He-111 dam(grd) | |
| | | Ju-88 dam(grd) | |
| | Lt. P.D. Gossard | He-111 dest(grd) | |
| | Lt. T.J. Sowerby | Ju-88 dest(grd) | |
| | | (.5)FW-190 dest(grd)[**] | |
| | | (2)He-111 dam(grd) | |
| | | Ju-88 dam(grd) | |
| | Lt. V.E. Hooker | (.5)He-111 dest(grd)[#] | |
| | | (.5)He-111 dest(grd)[##] | |
| | | Ju-88 dam(grd) | |
| | Lt. D.L. Naule | He-111 dest(grd) | |
| | Lt. C.F. Monsell | (.5)He-111 dest(grd)[***] | |
| | | (.5)He-111 dest(grd)[***] | |
| | | (.5)He-111 dest(grd)[#] | |
| | Lt. N.W. Butler | (.5)He-111 dest(grd)[*] | |
| | | (.5)He-111 dest(grd)[##] | |
| | Lt. R.K. Friend | (.5)Ju-88 dest(grd)[@@@] | |
| | | (3)He-111 dam(grd) | |
| | Lt. H.W. Detlefson | (.5)Ju-88 dest(grd)[@] | |
| | | He-111 dam(grd) | |
| | Lt. W. Muller | (2)Ju-88 dam(grd) | |

**August 25, 1944**

| Unit | Pilot | Claim | Location |
|---|---|---|---|
| 434th: | Capt. R. Olds | (3)Me-109 dest(air) | Rostock |
| | Capt. C.A.P. Duffie | (2)Me-109 dest(air) | Rostock |
| | Lt. B.E. Hollister | (2)Me-109 dest(air) | Rostock |

**August 28, 1944**

| Unit | Pilot | Claim | Location |
|---|---|---|---|
| 434th: | Capt. A.F. Jeffrey | Ju-52 dest(air) | Sedan/Douzy A/F |
| | Lt. T.C. Olson | FW-190 dest(air) | Sedan/Douzy A/F |
| | | u/i a/c dam(grd) | Sedan/Douzy A/F |
| | Capt. J.M. Hollingsworth | Do-217 dest(grd) | Sedan/Douzy A/F |

**September 5, 1944**

| Unit | Pilot | Claim | Location |
|---|---|---|---|
| HdQts: | LtCol. S.S. Woods | Ju-88 dest(grd) | All HdQts & |
| 434th: | Capt. J.M. Hollingsworth | (4)Me-410 dest(grd) | 434th claims are |
| | | (2)Do-217 dest(grd) | at Ettinghausen |
| | Lt. T.C. Olson | (4)Do-217 dest(grd) | |
| | | Me-110 dest(grd) | |
| | Lt. T.D. Neeley | (2)Me-110 dest(grd) | |
| | | Ju-88 dest(grd) | |
| | Lt. J.N. Murr | (3)Me-110 dest(grd) | |
| | Lt. R.H. Hendrickson | (2)Do-217 dest(grd) | |
| | Lt. B.E. Hollister | (2)Ju-88 dest(grd) | |
| | Lt. B.A. Williams | (2)Do-217 dest(grd) | |
| | Lt. H.E. Mathews | Ju-88 dest(grd) | |
| | Lt. J.W. Morrow | Me-109 dest(grd) | |
| | Lt. C.J. Murphy | Me-410 dest(grd) | |
| | Lt. J.T. Tipps | Do-217 dest(grd) | |
| 435th: | Lt. V.E. Hooker | He-111 dam(grd) | Hoehst Oberau |
| 436th: | Lt. H.J. Grasshoff | (4)FW-190 dest(grd) | Bad Nauheim |
| | | FW-190 dam(grd) | Bad Nauheim |
| | Lt. E.C. Lewin | (2)FW-190 dest(grd) | Bad Nauheim |
| | | Fi-156 dest(grd) | Bad Nauheim |
| | | (2)u/i a/c dam(grd) | Bad Nauheim |
| | Lt. V. Wolski | (2)FW-190 dest(grd) | Bad Nauheim |
| | | FW-190 dam(grd) | Bad Nauheim |
| | Lt. V.G. Hartnett | (2)FW-190 dest(grd) | Bad Nauheim |
| | | FW-190 dam(grd) | Bad Nauheim |
| | Lt. G.M. Mulvaney | (2)FW-190 dest(grd) | Bad Nauheim |
| | | FW-190 dam(grd) | Bad Nauheim |
| | Lt. J.W. Hedenburg | u/i a/c dest(grd) | Hoehst Oberau |
| | | u/i a/c dam(grd) | Hoehst Oberau |
| | Capt. C.J. Moore | u/i a/c dest(grd) | Bad Nauheim |
| | | (2)FW-190 dam(grd) | Bad Nauheim |
| | Lt. A.E. Huycke | He-111 dest(grd) | Marzhausen |
| | | He-111 dam(grd) | Marzhausen |
| | | Do-217 dam(grd) | Marzhausen |
| | Lt. J.E. Frolking | FW-190 dest(grd) | Bad Nauheim |
| | | FW-190 dam(grd) | Bad Nauheim |
| | Maj. J.A. Sullivan | (2)Do-217 dam(grd) | Hoehst Oberau |
| | | He-111 dam(grd) | Bad Nauheim |
| | Lt. Z. Ogrom | (3)FW-190 dam(grd) | Bad Nauheim |

| | | | |
|---|---|---|---|
| | Lt. E.J. Fillipaw | (2)FW-190 dam(grd) | Bad Nauheim |
| | Capt. J.M. Rosness | He-111 dam(grd) | Hoehst Oberau |

**September 10, 1944**

| | | | |
|---|---|---|---|
| 434th: | Lt. R.L. Maley | He-111 dam(grd) | Malmsheim |
| | Lt. H.E. Mathews | He-111 dam(grd) | Malmsheim |

**September 26, 1944**

| | | | |
|---|---|---|---|
| HdQts: | Col. H. Zemke | (2)Me-109 dest(air) | Haltern |
| | | Me-109 dam(air) | Haltern |
| 434th: | LtCol. J.M. Herren | (3)Me-109 dest(air) | All 434th & |
| | Lt. G.W. Gleason | (3)Me-109 dest(air) | 435th claims are |
| | | Me-109 dam(air) | SW Munster |
| | Lt. Q.S. Pavlock | (2)Me-109 dest(air) | |
| | | FW-190 dest(air) | |
| | Capt. C.A.P. Duffie | Me-109 dest(air) | |
| | | (2)Me-109 dam(air) | |
| | Lt. W.M. Drake | Me-109 dest(air) | |
| | Lt. H.F. Grenning | Me-109 dest(air) | |
| | Lt. J.W. Hansen | Me-109 dest(air) | |
| | | Me-109 dam(air) | |
| | Lt. R.L. Maley | Me-109 dest(air) | |
| | Lt. R.G. McChrystal | Me-109 dest(air) | |
| | | Me-109 dam(air) | |
| | Lt. J.W. Morrow | Me-109 dest(air) | |
| | Lt. J.N. Murr | Me-109 dest(air) | |
| 435th: | Lt. N.W. Butler | (2)Me-109 dest(air) | |
| | Lt. W.H. Pickering | (2)Me-109 dest(air) | |
| | Lt. R.K. Friend | Me-109 dest(air) | |
| | | Me-109 dam(air) | |
| | Capt. R.R. Coursey | Me-109 dest(air) | |
| | Lt. M.G. Gorian | Me-109 dest(air) | |
| | Lt. C.F. Monsell | Me-109 dest(air) | |
| 436th: | Lt. H.J. Grasshoff | Me-109 dest(air) | S/Munster |
| | Lt. G.M. Mulvany | Me-109 dest(air) | S/Munster |

NOTE: HdQts & 435th flew P-51's, 434th & 436th flew P-38's

**September 28, 1944**

| | | | |
|---|---|---|---|
| 434th: | Lt. G.W. Gleason | Me-109 dest(air) | W/Halberstadt |
| | | FW-190 dest(air) | W/Halberstadt |
| | LtCol. J.M. Herren | Me-109 dest(air) | W/Halberstadt |
| | Lt. R.M. Lunstrum | FW-190 dest(air) | Halberstadt |
| | Lt. R.B. Kline | Me-109 dam(air) | W/Halberstadt |
| | Lt. E.H. Wendt | FW-190 dam(air) | W/Halberstadt |
| 436th: | Lt. D.A. Dunn | (3)FW-190 dest(air) | All claims are |
| | Lt. V. Wolski | (3)FW-190 dest(air) | W/Magdeburg |
| | | FW-190 dam(air) | |
| | Maj. J.D. Biscayart | (2)FW-190 dest(air) | |
| | Lt. G. Straub | FW-190 dest(air) | |
| | | FW-190 dam(air) | |
| | Lt. J.E. Frolking | FW-190 dam(air) | |
| | Lt. H.G. Hightower | FW-190 dam(air) | |

NOTE: 436th flew P-38's, 434th(except Lt. Wendt) & 435th flew P-51's.

**October 6, 1944**

| | | | |
|---|---|---|---|
| 434th: | Capt. R. Olds | FW-190 dest(air) | W/Berlin |
| | Lt. G.D. Hendrix | FW-190 dam(air) | W/Berlin |
| 436th: | Lt. T.E. Myers | Me-109 dest(air) | E/Berlin |

**October 7, 1944**

| | | | |
|---|---|---|---|
| HdQts: | Col. H. Zemke | (.5)Me-109 dest(air) | W/Chemnitz |
| 434th: | Maj. A.F. Jeffrey | Me-109 dest(air) | S/Leipzig |
| 435th: | Lt. N.R. Benoit | (.5)Me-109 dest(air) | W/Chemnitz |

**November 2, 1944**

| | | | |
|---|---|---|---|
| 434th: | Maj. A.F. Jeffrey | Me-109 dest(air) | Zeitz |
| | Lt. J.C. Donnell | Me-109 dest(air) | SW Leipzig |

**November 6, 1944**

| | | | |
|---|---|---|---|
| 434th: | Lt. W.H. Marlowe | (.5)FW-190 dest(grd) | Hesepe |
| | Lt. T.C. Olson | (.5)FW-190 dest(grd) | Hesepe |

**November 26, 1944**

| | | | |
|---|---|---|---|
| 435th: | Lt. T.J. Sowerby | FW-190 dest(air) | Minden |

**November 27, 1944**

| | | | |
|---|---|---|---|
| 434th: | Lt. T.C. Olson | Me-410 dam(grd) | Vechta |
| 435th: | Lt. L.P. Petterson | FW-190 dest(air) | NE Dummer Lake |
| | Capt. J.W. Harrell | FW-190 dam(air) | NE Dummer Lake |
| 436th: | Lt. H.J. Grasshoff | FW-190 dest(air) | Osnabruck |

**December 5, 1944**

| | | | |
|---|---|---|---|
| HdQts: | LtCol. K.L. Riddle | FW-190 dest(air) | NW Berlin |
| | | FW-190 dam(air) | NW Berlin |
| 434th: | Maj. A.F. Jeffrey | (3)FW-190 dest(air) | Neuruppin |
| | | FW-190 dam(air) | Neuruppin |
| | Lt. G.E. Jacobson | (2)FW-190 dest(air) | Neuruppin |
| | Lt. H.E. Mathews | FW-190 dest(air) | Neuruppin |
| | Lt. R.G. McChrystal | Me-109 dest(air) | Neuruppin |
| | | Me-109 dam(air) | Neuruppin |
| | Lt. B.E. Hollister | FW-190 prob(air) | Neuruppin |
| | Lt. R.L. Maley | FW-190 prob(air) | Neuruppin |
| 435th: | Lt. R.G. Candelaria | (2)FW-190 dest(air) | NW Berlin |
| | Lt. G.L. Doolittle | FW-190 dest(air) | NW Berlin |
| | | FW-190 prob(air) | NW Berlin |
| | | FW-190 dam(air) | NW Berlin |
| | Lt. P.D. Gossard | FW-190 dest(air) | NW Berlin |
| | Lt. B.C. Means | Me-109 dest(air) | NW Berlin |
| | Lt. F.L. Hart | FW-190 prob(air) | NW Berlin |
| | Lt. N.R. Benoit | Me-262 dam(grd) | Bremen |
| 436th: | Lt. T.E. Myers | (.5)FW-190 dest(air) | N/Berlin |
| | | Me-109 dam(air) | N/Berlin |
| | Lt. P.C. Vasseur | (.5)FW-190 dest(air) | N/Berlin |

**December 6, 1944**

| | | | |
|---|---|---|---|
| 435th: | Lt. N.R. Benoit | He-111 dam(grd) | W/Dummer Lake |

**December 23, 1944**

| | | | |
|---|---|---|---|
| 434th: | Maj. A.F. Jeffrey | (3)Me-109 dest(air) | SE Bonn |
| | Lt. G.W. Gleason | (2)FW-190 dest(air) | SE Bonn |
| | | FW-190 dam(air) | SE Bonn |
| | Lt. T.D. Neeley | (2)FW-190 dest(air) | SE Bonn |
| | Lt. G.E. Jacobson | FW-190 dest(air) | SE Bonn |
| 436th: | Capt. C.V. Ernst | Me-109 dest(air) | Cologne |
| | Capt. A.E. Huycke | FW-190 dest(air) | Cologne |
| | Capt. E.C. Lewin | Me-109 dest(air) | NW Cologne |
| | Capt. J.R. Struby | FW-190 dest(air) | E/Cologne |

**December 24, 1944**

| | | | |
|---|---|---|---|
| 435th: | Lt. N.W. Butler | FW-190 dest(air) | SE Liege |

**December 25, 1944**

| | | | |
|---|---|---|---|
| 434th: | Lt. G.W. Gleason | (3)FW-190 dest(air) | SW Bonn |
| | Maj. A.F. Jeffrey | Me-109 dest(air) | SW Bonn |
| | Lt. P.A. Brown | FW-190 dest(air) | SW Bonn |
| | | FW-190 prob(air) | SW Bonn |
| | Lt. R.D. Creighton | FW-190 dest(air) | SW Bonn |
| | Lt. A.G. Helding | FW-190 dest(air) | SW Bonn |
| | Lt. H.M. Jenkins | FW-190 dest(air) | SW Bonn |
| | Lt. J.N. Murr | FW-190 dest(air) | SW Bonn |
| | | FW-190 prob(air) | SW Bonn |
| | | FW-190 dam(air) | SW Bonn |
| | Lt. E.E. Sears | Me-109 dest(air) | SW Bonn |
| | Capt. J.M. Hollingsworth | Me-109 prob(air) | SW Bonn |
| | | Me-109 dam(air) | SW Bonn |
| | Lt. G.E. Jacobson | FW-190 prob(air) | SW Bonn |
| 435th: | Capt. J.W. Harrell | Me-109 dest(air) | SW Aachen |
| | Lt. N.R. Benoit | Me-109 dest(air) | SW Cologne |
| | | Me-109 dam(air) | SW Cologne |
| | Lt. T.J. Sowerby | FW-190 dest(air) | Bonn |
| 436th: | Capt. R.S. Spencer | (2)FW-190 dest(air) | SE Malmedy |

**January 1, 1945**

| | | | |
|---|---|---|---|
| HdQts: | LtCol. K.L. Riddle | (.5)FW-190 dest(air) | Nienburg |
| 434th: | Lt. C.W. Bowers | (.5)FW-190 dest(air) | Nienburg |
| | Lt. R.I. Bromschwig | FW-190 dam(air) | Nienburg |

**January 14, 1945**

| | | | |
|---|---|---|---|
| 435th: | Maj. H.H. Jordan | Me-109 dest(air) | NW Wesel |

**January 21, 1945**

| | | | |
|---|---|---|---|
| 435th: | Lt. T.J. Sowerby | Ju-52 dest(grd) | Leipheim |
| | | Ju-88 dest(grd) | Leipheim |
| | Lt. N.R. Benoit | Me-262 dam(grd) | Leipheim |
| | | Ju-88 dam(grd) | Leipheim |
| | Lt. E.H. Sims | Ju-52 dam(grd) | Leipheim |

**February 9, 1945**

| | | | |
|---|---|---|---|
| 434th: | Capt. G.W. Gleason | Me-109 dest(air) | All 434th claims |
| | | FW-190 dest(air) | are SE Magdeburg |
| | Maj. R. Olds | Me-109 dest(air) | |
| | Lt. R.D. Creighton | Me-109 dest(air) | |
| | | FW-190 prob(air) | |
| | Lt. E.H. Wendt | Me-109 dest(air) | |
| | | Me-109 dam(air) | |
| | Lt. J.C. Donnell | (2)Me-109 dam(air) | |
| 435th: | Maj. H.H. Jordan | FW-190 dest(air) | W/Brandenburg |
| | Capt. N.R. Benoit | FW-190 dest(air) | SW Brandenburg |
| | Capt. G.L. Doolittle | Me-109 dest(air) | SE Magdeburg |
| | Lt. D.E. King | Me-109 dest(air) | SE Magdeburg |
| | Lt. J.R. Rogers | Me-109 dest(air) | SE Magdeburg |
| | | Me-109 dam(air) | SE Magdeburg |
| | Lt. F.F. Shriner | Me-109 prob(air) | SE Magdeburg |

**February 14, 1945**

| | | | |
|---|---|---|---|
| 434th: | Maj. R. Olds | (2)Me-109 dest(air) | All claims are |
| | | FW-190 dest(air) | SW Berlin |
| | Lt. E.H. Wendt | (2)Me-109 dest(air) | |

| | | | |
|---|---|---|---|
| | LtCol. A.F. Jeffrey | Me-109 dest(air) | |
| | | Me-109 dam(air) | |
| | Capt. R.G. McChrystal | Me-109 dest(air) | |
| | Lt. D.L. Born | Me-109 dest(air) | |
| | Lt. W.H. Daudistel | Me-109 dest(air) | |
| | Lt. J.T. Golden | Me-109 dest(air) | |
| | Capt. D.J. Pierce | (2)Me-109 dam(air) | |

**February 20, 1945**

| | | | |
|---|---|---|---|
| 434th: | Maj. R. Olds | Do-217 dest(grd) | All claims are |
| | | FW-190 dest(grd) | Windleschen- |
| | Lt. R.B. Kline | (2)Do-217 dest(grd) | laibach |
| | | (.5)He-111 dest(grd)[*] | |
| | | (.5)FW-190 dam(grd) | |
| | Lt. J.T. Golden | (1.5)He-111 dest(grd)[*] | |
| | | (.5)FW-190 dam(grd) | |
| | Lt. E.E. Sears | Do-217 dest(grd) | |
| | Capt. D.J. Pierce | (.5)He-111 dest(grd)[**] | |
| | | (.5)He-111 dam(grd) | |
| | Lt. P.A. Brown | (.5)He-111 dest(grd)[**] | |
| | | (.5)He-111 dam(grd) | |

**February 21, 1945**

| | | | |
|---|---|---|---|
| 434th: | Lt. O.J. Huval | He-111 dest(grd) | Gotha |
| | Lt. G.E. Jacobson | He-111 dest(grd) | Gotha |
| 436th: | Capt. J.C. Malone | Ju-188 dam(grd) | Nordhausen |
| | Lt. G.H. Witzel | Ju-188 dam(grd) | Nordhausen |

**February 22, 1945**

| | | | |
|---|---|---|---|
| 436th: | Capt. W.C. Anderson | He-111 dest(grd) | All claims are |
| | Lt. R.E. Henry | Ju-88 dest(grd) | at Halberstadt |
| | | He-111 dam(grd) | |
| | Lt. A.J. Smigel | He-111 dest(grd) | |
| | | (2)Ju-88 dam(grd) | |
| | Lt. A.J. Scordino | Ju-88 dest(grd) | |
| | | (2)He-111 dam(grd) | |
| | Maj. C.A.P. Duffie | (3)u/i a/c dam(grd) | |
| | | Ju-88 dam(grd) | |
| | Lt. C.H. Darling | (2)Ju-88 dam(grd) | |
| | Maj. C.J. Moore | Ju-52 dam(grd) | |
| | Capt. J.C. Malone | Ju-88 dam(grd) | |
| | Lt. A.R. DiPaola | FW-190 dam(grd) | |
| | Lt. E.J. Hopcroft | He-111 dam(grd) | |

**March 3, 1945**

| | | | |
|---|---|---|---|
| 435th: | Lt. R.G. Candelaria | (3)Me-109 dam(grd) | Dummer Lake |
| | Lt. B.C. Means | Me-109 dam(grd) | Dummer Lake |

**March 19, 1945**

| | | | |
|---|---|---|---|
| 434th: | Maj. R. Olds | Me-109 dest(air) | Handorf A/F |
| | | FW-190 dest(air) | Handorf A/F |
| | Lt. G.E. Jacobson | (.5)FW-190 dest(air) | Handorf A/F |
| | Lt. F.M. Taylor | (.5)FW-190 dest(air) | Handorf A/F |

**March 25, 1945**

| | | | |
|---|---|---|---|
| 434th: | Lt. E.H. Wendt | Me-262 dest(air) | SW Hamburg |
| 435th: | Lt. F.W. Salze | Me-262 dam(air) | SE Hamburg |

**March 31, 1945**

| | | | |
|---|---|---|---|
| 434th: | Lt. R.I. Bromschwig | Me-262 dam(air) | Braunschweig |

**April 4, 1945**

| | | | |
|---|---|---|---|
| 435th: | Lt. E.H. Sims | Me-262 dam(air) | W/Luneburg |

**April 7, 1945**

| | | | |
|---|---|---|---|
| 434th: | Maj. R. Olds | Me-109 dest(air) | Dummer Lake-Bremen |
| | | Me-262 dam(air) | Dummer Lake-Bremen |
| | Lt. G.E. Jacobson | Me-109 dest(air) | Celle |
| | Lt. R.L. Munson | Me-109 dest(air) | Celle |
| | Lt. J.K. Nagel | Me-109 dest(air) | Soltau |
| | Lt. H.O. Thompson | Me-262 dest(air) | Luneburg |
| 435th: | Lt. R.G. Candelaria | (4)Me-109 dest(air) | SW Luneburg |
| | | Me-262 prob(air) | SW Luneburg |
| | Capt. V.E. Hooker | Me-109 dest(air) | SE Bremen |
| | | Me-262 dest(air) | SE Bremen |

**April 13, 1945**

| | | | |
|---|---|---|---|
| 434th: | Maj. R. Olds | Ar-234 dest(grd) | Lubeck |
| | | Me-410 dam(grd) | Tarnewitz |
| | Capt. D.J. Pierce | Ar-234 dest(grd) | Lubeck |
| | | Ju-88 dam(grd) | Kaltenkirchen |
| | Lt. R.M. Rossel | Ar-234 dest(grd) | Lubeck |
| | Lt. J.K. Nagel | Ju-88 dest(grd) | Kaltenkirchen |
| | Lt. L.A. Hendrickson | FW-190 dest(grd) | Kaltenkirchen |
| | Lt. J.T. Golden | u/i a/c dest(grd) | All remaining |
| | | (2)u/i a/c dam(grd) | 434th claims |
| | Lt. P.A. Brown | (.5)u/i a/c dest(grd)[*] | are at |
| | | u/i a/c dam(grd) | Ratzburger Lake |
| | Lt. R.G. Simpson | (.5)u/i a/c dest(grd)[*] | |
| | Lt. R.B. Kline | (.5)u/i a/c dest(grd)[**] | |
| | | u/i a/c dam(grd) | |
| | Lt. F.M. Taylor | (.5)u/i a/c dest(grd)[**] | |
| | | (2)u/i a/c dam(grd) | |
| | Lt. O.J. Huval | (.5)u/i a/c dest(grd)[@] | |
| | | u/i a/c dam(grd) | |
| | Lt. C.W. Bowers | (.5)u/i a/c dest(grd)[@] | |
| | | u/i a/c dam(grd) | |
| | Lt. R.D. Creighton | (2)u/i a/c dam(grd) | |
| 435th: | Capt. V.E. Hooker | (2)Ju-88 dest(grd) | Tarnewitz |
| | | Ju-88 dam(grd) | Tarnewitz |
| | Lt. T.J. Sowerby | Ju-88 dest(grd) | Tarnewitz |
| | | (4)Ju-88 dam(grd) | Tarnewitz |
| | Lt. W.B. Rourke | Ju-88 dest(grd) | Tarnewitz |
| | | (2)Ju-88 dam(grd) | Tarnewitz |
| 436th: | Capt. J.C. Malone | (2)FW-190 dest(grd) | All claims are |
| | | Me-110 dest(grd) | at Salzwedel |
| | | (2)FW-190 dam(grd) | |
| | | Me-410 dam(grd) | |
| | Capt. P.S. Shane | Me-410 dest(grd) | |
| | | u/i a/c dest(grd) | |
| | | Me-109 dam(grd) | |
| | Lt. G.H. Witzel | (2)FW-190 dest(grd) | |
| | | FW-190 dam(grd) | |
| | | Me-110 dam(grd) | |
| | Lt. K.J. Hansen | (3)FW-190 dest(grd) | |
| | | Me-110 dest(grd) | |
| | Lt. E.J. Hopcroft | (2)Me-410 dest(grd) | |
| | | Me-109 dest(grd) | |
| | Lt. S.F. Long | (2)FW-190 dest(grd) | |
| | Lt. C.H. Darling | (2)FW-190 dest(grd) | |
| | | Me-110 dam(grd) | |
| | | u/i a/c dam(grd) | |
| | Lt. F. Zellman | Me-109 dest(grd) | |
| | | Me-410 dest(grd) | |
| | | Me-109 dam(grd) | |
| | Lt. C.H. Philbrick | FW-190 dest(grd) | |
| | | Me-109 dest(grd) | |
| | | (3)Me-109 dam(grd) | |
| | | u/i a/c dam(grd) | |
| | Lt. R.C.J. Palson | (2)He-111 dest(grd) | |
| | | He-111 dam(grd) | |
| | | FW-190 dam(grd) | |
| | Lt. B.R. Kleineman | FW-190 dest(grd) | |
| | | Me-110 dest(grd) | |
| | Lt. J.R. Early | FW-190 dest(grd) | |
| | | Me-110 dest(grd) | |
| | | Me-410 dam(grd) | |
| | Lt. J.M. Archibald | FW-190 dest(grd) | |
| | | Me-110 dam(grd) | |
| | Lt. W.B. Steph | FW-190 dest(grd) | |
| | | Me-109 dam(grd) | |

**April 16, 1945**

| | | | |
|---|---|---|---|
| 434th: | Maj. R. Olds | (2)Ju-87 dest(grd) | Reichersberg |
| | | Me-109 dest(grd) | Reichersberg |
| | | Me-110 dest(grd) | Reichersberg |
| | | He-177 dest(grd) | Reichersberg |
| | Capt. D.J. Pierce | Me-109 dest(grd) | Kirchen |
| | | Me-109 dest(grd) | Reichersberg |
| | | FW-190 dest(grd) | Reichersberg |
| | | Ju-88 dest(grd) | Reichersberg |
| | | (2)Me-109 dam(grd) | Reichersberg |
| | Lt. J.T. Golden | (3)u/i a/c dest(grd) | Reichersberg |
| | Lt. G.E. Jacobson | (2)FW-190 dest(grd) | Reichersberg |
| | | FW-190 dam(grd) | Reichersberg |
| | | Ju-88 dam(grd) | Reichersberg |
| | Lt. R.L. Munson | (2)FW-190 dest(grd) | Reichersberg |
| | | FW-190 dam(grd) | Reichersberg |
| | Lt. H.L. Stott | Ju-88 dest(grd) | Reichersberg |
| | | Ju-88 dam(grd) | Reichersberg |
| | Lt. J.A. Plezibat | FW-190 dest(grd) | Reichersberg |
| | Lt. P.A. Brown | u/i a/c dest(grd) | Erferding |
| | Lt. D.H. Stott | u/i a/c dest(grd) | Erferding |
| | Lt. D.F. Tommie | Me-109 dam(grd) | Reichersberg |
| | | FW-190 dam(grd) | Reichersberg |
| 435th: | Capt. V.E. Hooker | u/i a/c dest(grd) | S/Pocking |
| | | Me-109 dam(grd) | S/Pocking |
| | Lt. R.B. Frost | (2)u/i a/c dam(grd) | S/Pocking |
| 436th: | Maj. C.A.P. Duffie | (4)FW-190 dest(grd) | All claims are |
| | Lt. C.B. Elmgren | (4)FW-190 dest(grd) | at Landstedt |
| | Lt. G.H. Witzel | (3)FW-190 dest(grd) | |
| | Lt. R.E. Henry | (3)FW-190 dest(grd) | |
| | Lt. A.J. Smigel | (2)FW-190 dest(grd) | |
| | | Me-109 dest(grd) | |
| | Capt. P.S. Shane | (2)FW-190 dest(grd) | |
| | Lt. R.C.J. Palson | (2)FW-190 dest(grd) | |
| | Lt. G.G. McLaurin | (2)FW-190 dest(grd) | |
| | Capt. J.C. Malone | FW-190 dest(grd) | |
| | Capt. C.V. Ernst | He-111 dest(grd) | |
| | Lt. C.H. Darling | He-111 dest(grd) | |
| | Lt. E.J. Hopcroft | He-111 dest(grd) | |

| | | | |
|---|---|---|---|
| | Lt. C.H. Philbrick | Me-109 dest(grd) | |
| | Lt. W.N. Rawley | FW-190 dest(grd) | |
| | Lt. W.B. Steph | Me-109 dest(grd) | |
| | Lt. T.H. Thompson | He-111 dest(grd) | |

**April 17, 1945**

| | | | |
|---|---|---|---|
| 434th: | Capt. D.J. Pierce | (2)FW-190 dest(grd) | Puchhoff |
| | | Me-109 dest(grd) | Landau |
| | | Me-109 dam(grd) | Landau |
| | | u/i a/c dam(grd) | Landau |
| | Lt. D.L. Born | (2)u/i a/c dest(grd) | All 434th & |
| | | Me-109 dest(grd) | 435th claims |
| | Lt. C.M. Peacock | (2)FW-190 dest(grd) | are at Puchhoff |
| | F/O A.J. Valluzzi | (2)Me-109 dest(grd) | |
| | Lt. D.W. Mastin | u/i a/c dest(grd) | |
| 435th: | Lt. C.R. Hoffman | (2)Me-262 dest(grd) | |
| | | Fi-156 dest(grd) | |
| | | Me-262 dam(grd) | |
| | Capt. T.J. Sowerby | (2)Me-262 dest(grd) | |
| | Lt. R.J. Baird | Me-262 dest(grd) | |
| | Lt. S.R. Routh | Me-262 dest(grd) | |
| | Lt. F.W. Salze | Me-262 dest(grd) | |
| | Lt. E.H. Sims | Me-262 dest(grd) | |
| | Lt. D.W. Thorn | Me-262 dam(grd) | |
| | | u/i a/c dam(grd) | |
| | Capt. V.E. Hooker | u/i a/c dam(grd) | |
| | Lt. C.R. Matthews | Me-262 dam(grd) | |
| | Lt. G.M. Salter | u/i a/c dam(grd) | |
| 436th: | Maj. C.A.P. Duffie | (2)Ju-87 dest(grd) | Karlsbad |
| | | FW-190 dest(grd) | Karlsbad |
| | Lt. R.C.J. Palson | (2)FW-190 dest(grd) | Puchhoff |
| | | (2)Me-109 dest(grd) | Puchhoff |
| | Lt. E.J. Hopcroft | Fi-156 dest(grd) | Landau |
| | | FW-190 dest(grd) | Puchhoff |
| | | Me-109 dest(grd) | Puchhoff |
| | | u/i a/c dam(grd) | Puchhoff |
| | Lt. C.B. Elmgren | (2)Fi-156 dest(grd) | Karlsbad |
| | | u/i a/c dest(grd) | Karlsbad |
| | Lt. G.H. Witzel | FW-190 dest(grd) | Karlsbad |
| | | u/i a/c dest(grd) | Karlsbad |
| | Lt. P.J. Romano | Ju-87 dest(grd) | Karlsbad |
| | | u/i a/c dest(grd) | Karlsbad |
| | LtCol. G.E. Falkner | u/i a/c dest(grd) | Karlsbad |
| | Capt. P.S. Shane | Me-109 dest(grd) | Puchhoff |
| | Lt. K.J. Hansen | FW-189 dest(grd) | Karlsbad |
| | Lt. C.H. Darling | u/i a/c dest(grd) | Karlsbad |
| | Lt. A.J. Smigel | u/i a/c dest(grd) | Karlsbad |
| | | u/i a/c dam(grd) | Karlsbad |
| | Lt. C.S. Kreger | FW-190 dam(grd) | Puchhoff |

**April 18, 1945**

| | | | |
|---|---|---|---|
| 434th: | Lt. G.E. Jacobson | (2)Ju-88 dest(grd) | Ingolstadt |
| | | FW-190 dest(grd) | Ottingen |
| | Lt. J.K. Nagel | Me-109 dest(grd) | Deiningen |
| | | FW-190 dest(grd) | Deiningen |
| | | Ju-88 dest(grd) | Ottingen |
| | Lt. C.W. Bowers | Me-109 dest(grd) | Ottingen |
| | | Me-110 dest(grd) | Ottingen |
| | | u/i a/c dest(grd) | Deiningen |
| | | u/i a/c dam(grd) | Deiningen |
| | Lt. C.H. Leeney | FW-190 dest(grd) | Ottingen |
| | Lt. E.E. Honace | Me-109 dest(grd) | Deiningen |
| | | Me-109 dam(grd) | Deiningen |
| 435th: | Lt. J.H. Koerber | u/i a/c dest(grd) | All claims are |
| | Capt. V.E. Hooker | (2)u/i a/c dam(grd) | at Mettenheim |
| | Lt. W.M. Barsky | u/i a/c dam(grd) | |
| | Lt. E.H. Sims | u/i a/c dam(grd) | |
| | Lt. E.A. Splittstoesser | u/i a/c dam(grd) | |

**April 25, 1945**

| | | | |
|---|---|---|---|
| 434th: | Lt. H.O. Thompson | Ar-234 dest(air) | Traunstein-Berchtesgaden |

**479th Fighter Group Losses**

**May 25, 1944**
Capt. William A. Walker (436th) KIAc; Crashed near Wattisham on a local flight.
P-38J 9B-A 42-104318

**June 9, 1944**
Lt. Edward J. Spillane (436th) KIAc;
P-38J 9B-Q

**June 17, 1944**
Lt. James K. Ohligschlager (434th) KIA; Collided with another P-38 near Rennes.
P-38J L2-Q 43-28729
Capt. Calvin J. Butler (435th) KIA; Hit by flak near Paris.
P-38J J2- 44-23168

**June 19, 1944**
Lt. Frank Grdenich (434th) MIA-E; Collided with Lt. Kuentzal near Rennes.
P-38J L2-T 43-28456
Lt. Ward A. Kuentzal (434th) KIA; Collided with Lt. Grdenich near Rennes.
P-38J L2- 42-104427
Lt. Leland K. Horne (435th) MIA; Collided with Lt. McClure near Murau.
P-38J J2- 42-68161
Lt. Donald D. McClure (435th) MIA; Collided with Lt. Horne near Murau.
P-38J J2- 42-68189

**June 20, 1944**
Lt. Lewis K. Nesselbush (436th) POW; Suffered mechanical failure and bailed out near Ottersberg.
P-38J 9B-N 42-67452 "Rabble Rouser"

**June 22, 1944**
Lt. Keith E. Canella (434th) KIA; Hit by flak southeast of Le Fere.
P-38J L2-K 43-28731 "Sweet Mary"
Lt. Dwight F. Ilsley (434th) KIA; Hit by flak near Le Fere.
P-38J L2-G 42-104258
Lt. Leroy Lutz (434th) KIA; Hit by flak near Le Fere.
P-38J L2-L 43-28714 "Lucky Lady"
Lt. Robert S.J. Tucker (434th) MIA; Hit by flak near Cambrai.
P-38J L2-B 43-28439

**June 27, 1944**
Lt. Burton S. Cross (435th) KIA; Hit by flak near Creney.
P-38J J2- 42-104416

**July 4, 1944**
Capt. Robert D. Green (HdQts) KIA; Hit by flak near Laval.
P-38J J2- 43-28467
Lt. Jack S. Denny (434th) MIA; Hit by flak near Cande.
P-38J L2-A 43-28367
Lt. Rayne B. Fairchild (435th) MIA; Hit by flak near Laval.
P-38J J2- 44-23484

**July 5, 1944**
Lt. Clayton F. Proctor (434th) KIA; Hit by flak near Montignac.
P-38J L2-X 42-68029

**July 6, 1944**
Lt. Jene A. Haas (434th) POW; Hit by a FW-190 near Fauril.
P-38J L2-P 42-67732

**July 15, 1944**
Lt. Flamm D. Harper (434th) MIA-E; Hit by debris from an exploding ammo dump near Montmorillion.
P-38J L2-V 42-68147

**July 21, 1944**
Capt. Jack G. Grossenbacher (434th) KIA; Hit by flak northwest of Frankfort and crashed near Kindsbach.
P-38J L2-G 43-28647

**July 24, 1944**
Lt. Alex Evanenko (435th) KIA; Hit by flak and crashed south of Dungeness.
P-38J J2- 43-28716
Capt. Thomas T. Galloway (436th) KIA; Collided with Lt. Kemper southwest of Evreux.
P-38J 9B- 43-28419
Lt. Neil W. Kemper (436th) MIA-E; Collided with Capt. Galloway southwest of Evreux.
P-38J 9B- 44-23172

**July 27, 1944**
Lt. Marden L. McArthur (434th) KIA; Hit by flak near Chartres.
P-38J L2-U 42-67875
Lt. William B. McKay (435th) KIA; Hit by flak near Jaulgonne.
P-38J J2- 44-23160

**July 28, 1944**
Lt. Robert R. Teetor (436th) KIAc;
P-38J 9B-

**August 2, 1944**
Lt. Fred A. Moser, Jr. (436th) POW; Hit by flak near Compenhut and bailed out near Brussels.
P-38J 9B- 42-104397

**August 4, 1944**
Capt. Elmer Hartman (436th) KIA; Crashed on take-off from Wattisham.
P-38J 9B-

**August 5, 1944**
Lt. Carl W. Moore (435th) KIA; Suffered mechanical failure near Ottensen.
P-38J J2- 43-28472

**August 8, 1944**
Capt. John J. Courtney, Jr. (435th) MIA-E; Hit trees while strafing near Rouieres.
P-38J J2- 43-28426

**August 9, 1944**
Maj. Frank J. Keller (434th) POW; Hit by flak and bailed out west of Furth.
P-38J L2-I 43-28377 "Hilo Hattie"

**August 10, 1944**
LtCol. Kyle L. Riddle (HdQts) MIA-E; Hit by flak near Meaux.
P-38J J2-Q 44-23171
Lt. James E. Fleming, Jr. (434th) KIA; Hit by flak near Romery.
P-38J L2-W 43-28341 "Scat"

**August 14, 1944**
Lt. Thomas J. O'Holleran (436th) POW; Hit by flak near Rheims.
P-38J 9B- 43-28432

**August 15, 1944**
Capt. Hiram G. Turner (434th) POW; Hit by flak near Veeingen.
P-38J L2-U 43-28376
Lt. James L. Wallace (434th) KIA; Hit by flak near Uffelte.
P-38J L2-Z 44-23169 "Sleepytime Gal"

**August 18, 1944**
Lt. Philip W. Manning (434th) KIA; Hit by flak at Nancy/Essey Airfield.
P-38J L2-R 42-67296

**August 28, 1944**
Lt. William N. Howard (436th) MIA-E; Hit by flak near Dijon.
P-38J 9B- 42-104407 "Marion"

**September 5, 1944**
Maj. Ray S. Carter (435th) KIA; Hit by flak near Altenstadt.
P-38J J2-N 44-23177

**September 6, 1944**
Lt. Calvin J. Murphy (434th) KIA; Hit by flak near Darmstadt.
P-38J L2-O 42-104425 "Boomerang"

**September 9, 1944**
Lt. Everett P. Ford (435th) KIAc;
P-38J J2-

**September 14, 1944**
Lt. Ivan E. Ervin (435th) KIAc;
P-51B J2-
Lt. Chester W. Granville (435th) KIAc;
P-51D J2- 44-14437

**September 17, 1944**
Capt. George K. Sykes (435th) MIA-E; Hit by flak near Ede.
P-51D J2- 44-14424 "Sugar Kane"

**September 21, 1944**
Lt. Thomas A. Gayrys (434th) KIA; Lost possibly to mechanical trouble.
P-51D L2-G 44-14138 "Miss Fortune"

**September 26, 1944**
Lt. Harry E. Little (434th) POW; Hit by enemy fighters near Munster.
P-38J L2-N 42-67264

**September 27, 1944**
Lt. William H. Rodgers (434th) MIA; Suffered mechanical failure and crashed into the Channel.
P-51D L2-L 44-14324

**October 2, 1944**
Lt. Quentin S. Pavlock (434th) KIA; Crashed on take-off from Wattisham.
P-51D L2-

**October 7, 1944**
Lt. James E. Frolking (436th) MIA-E; Hit by flak near Scheldt and bailed out off the Dutch coast.
P-51D 9B-N 44-14577
Lt. Victor Wolski (436th) ASR; Suffered mechanical failure and bailed out over the Channel.
P-51D 9B- 44-14553

**October 30, 1944**
Col. Hubert Zemke (HdQts) POW; Lost a wing in bad weather southeast of Hamburg and bailed out near Niendorf.
P-51D 9B-Z 44-14351
LtCol. James M. Herren, Jr. (434th) KIA; Collided with a P-51 near Hassel.
P-51D L2-A 44-14396 "Touche'"
Lt. Douglas I. Holmes (434th) POW; Collided with a P-51 near Hassell.
P-51D L2-S 44-14627 "Pauline"
Lt. Douglas T. Thoams (434th) KIAc;
P-51D L2-O 44-14225

**November 6, 1944**
Lt. Marion W. Steele (436th) KIA; Suffered mechanical failure and crashed into the North Sea.
P-51D 9B- 44-11201

**November 8, 1944**
Lt. Heinz W. Detlefson (435th) KIA; Collided with Lt. Smith near Minden.
P-51D J2- 44-14294
Lt. Thomas V. Smith (435th) POW; Collided with Lt. Detlefson near Minden.
P-51D J2- 44-14589

**December 5, 1944**
Lt. Walter A. Neuman (434th) KIA; Hit by fighters near Neuruppin.
P-51D L2-U 44-14592 "Buzzin' Texan"
Lt. Ronald L. Maley (434th) POW; Hit by flak near Scharfenberg.
P-51D L2-T 44-11214 "Tommy Trojan"
Maj. John A. Sullivan (435th) KIA; Suffered mechanical failure and crashed into the North Sea.
P-51D 9B-A 44-14636 "Carol II & III"
Lt. Barrett B. Eskell (436th) POW; Collided with a P-51 near Muenschehagen.
P-51D 9B- 44-14517 "Lil Exterminator"

**December 10, 1944**
Lt. William D. Clark (435th) KIAc;
P-51D J2-

**December 12, 1944**
Lt. Robert N. Pigg (435th) KIA; Suffered mechanical failure and bailed out over Belgium and was then struck by a B-26.
P-51D J2- 44-14344
Lt. Robert B. Hymans (435th) KIAc; Crashed into the North Sea on a practice hop.
P-51B J2-7 43-7157

**December 13, 1944**
Lt. Dewey H. Hollis (434th) KIAc;
P-51B L2-

**December 23, 1944**
Lt. Tom D. Neely (434th) POW; Hit by flak near Ecuwied.
P-51D L2-X 44-14596 "Rumboogie Jr."

**December 25, 1944**
Capt. James M. Hollingsworth (434th) KIA; Hit by enemy fighters near Bonn.
P-51D L2-A 44-14892
Lt. Wendell H. Marlowe (434th) MIA; Hit by fighters near Bonn.
P-51D L2-I 44-15325 "Swanee Jr."
Lt. Edward L. Hurtig (434th) KIA; Hit by enemy planes near Bonn.
P-51D L2-M 44-14416
Lt. Douglas L. Red (436th) KIA; Hit by fighters near Grossenheim.
P-51D 9B- 44-14559 "Daisy Mae"

**January 13, 1945**
Lt. Raymond E. King (436th) KIA; Suffered mechanical failure and ditched off Clacton.
P-51D 9B-J 44-14754

**February 5, 1945**
Lt. Norbert W. Rock (435th) KIAc;
P-51D J2-H 44-14840 "The Victory Queen"

**February 9, 1945**
Lt. Carl B. Jarrell (435th) KIA; Hit by fighters near Belzig.
P-51D J2- 44-14364

**February 14, 1945**
Lt. John C. Donnell, Jr. (434th) KIA; Hit by flak near Dreiskau.
P-51D L2-V 44-14651 "Pin-Up Girl"

**February 22, 1945**
Lt. Albert R. DiPaolo (436th) POW; Hit by flak near Halberstadt and crashed near Quedlinburg.
P-51D 9B-T 44-15412
Lt. Peter C. Vasseur (436th) MIA; Hit by fire from a P-51 while strafing near Halberstadt.
P-51K 9B-P 44-11739

**February 28, 1945**
Lt. Charles T. Schoen, Jr. (436th) KIA; Hit by flak near Reichenaschen.
P-51D 9B-E 44-14583

**March 1, 1945**
Maj. Thomas F. Trabucco (435th) KIA; Lost for unknown reasons near Haldenwang.
P-51D J2-A 44-15374 "Dotty"

**March 3, 1945**
Lt. Elbert N. Harris (434th) MIA; Suffered mechanical failure near Magdeburg.
P-51D L2-A 44-63189 "Mary"

**March 11, 1945**
Lt. Lewis C. Smith (436th) KIA; Bailed out east of Lowestoft, was picked up by ASR but was dead.
P-51D 9B- 44-14576

**March 28, 1945**
Lt. Jesse F. Morris (436th) KIAc;
P-51D 9B-

**April 4, 1945**
Lt. Thurman E. Sands (434th) KIAc; Hit a train while flying low near Haughley Station.
P-51B L2- 43-6393

**April 13, 1945**
Lt. Ossie J. Huval (434th) MIA; Lost for unknown reasons near Bremen.
P-51K L2-A 44-12156 "The Flying Frenchman"
Lt. Richard G. Candelaria (435th) POW; Hit by flak and bellied-in near Tarnewitz.
P-51K J2-K 44-11755 "My Pride and Joy"

**April 16, 1945**
Lt. John T. Golden (434th) POW; Hit by flak near Regensburg.
P-51D L2-G 44-14856 "Junior"
Lt. Harold F. Krauss, Jr. (434th) KIA; Damaged by flak and crashed while landing at an Allied field on the Continent.
P-51D L2-F 44-14929 "Droppy"
Lt. Donald H. Stott (434th) KIA; Hit by flak at Erferding Airfield.
P-51D L2-S 44-14629 "Shoo Shoo Baby"
Lt. Frank M. Taylor (434th) POW; Hit by flak at Erferding Airfield.
P-51D L2-H 44-14740 "Hot Toddy"

**April 18, 1945**
Capt. Jay C. Malone (436th) KIA; Hit by flak at Neuburg.
P-51D 9B- 44-14601 "Queenie-El Diablo"

**April 22, 1945**
Lt. Robert C. Young (436th) KIAc;
P-51D 9B-

**May 4, 1945**
Lt. Anthony J. Scordino (436th) KIAc;
P-51K 9B- 44-11749

**July 19, 1945**
Lt. Hilton O. Thompson (434th) KIAc;
P-51D L2- 44-14523

**Headquarters**
Green, Robert D., Capt.; -July 4, 1944(KIA)
Harrell, John W., Jr., Maj.; ex-435th & 436th Ftr Sqns
82 missions total
Hollingsworth, James M., Capt.; September 1944-November 1944; to 434th Ftr Sqn; ex-434th Ftr Sqn
Parsons, Albert B., Capt.; February 1944-July 1944; to 55th Ftr Grp
Riddle, Kyle L., Col.; December 1943-August 10, 1944(MIA-E); September 1944-November 1945
P-38J J2-R
P-51D J2-R 44-14327
Shriner, Fred F., Lt.; August 1944; ex-435th Ftr Sqn
Stoops, Edward F., Maj.; June 1944; ex-435th Ftr Sqn
Woods, Sidney S., LtCol.; States-September 1944; ex-49th Ftr Grp, PTO; later to 4th Ftr Grp
68 missions (total ETO)
P-38J L2-M 42-67465
Zemke, Hubert, Col.; August 1944-October 30, 1944(POW); ex-56th Ftr Grp
155 missions total
P-38J J2-Z 43-28823
P-51D 9B-Z 44-14351

**434th Fighter Squadron**
Atwater, John S., Lt.; January 1945-EOW
Born, David L., Lt.; October 1944-EOW
P-51D L2-Y 44-14393 "Just Born"
Bouchier, James E., Lt.; October 1944-EOW
Bowers, Clifford W., Lt.; October 1944-EOW
P-51D L2-N 44-14373 "Skunk Chaser"
Bromschwig, Robert L., Lt.; October 1944-EOW
P-51D L2-T 44-11214 "Kraut Knocker"
P-51D L2-T 44-14423 "Kraut Knocker"
Bronaugh, Edward D., Lt.; January 1945-EOW
Brown, Philip A., Lt.; September 1944-
Butler, Calvin J., Lt.; States-May 1944; to 435th Ftr Sqn
Canella, Keith E., Lt.; October 1943-June 22, 1944(KIA)
Creighton, Richard D., Lt.; September 1944-
P-51D L2-T 44-15381 "Super Wabbit"
Daudistel, William H., Lt.; October 1944-EOW
P-51D L2-Z 44-63176 "The Impatient Virgin"
Denny, Jack S., Lt.; May 1944-July 4, 1944(MIA-E); August 1944-
Donnell, John C., Jr., Lt.; September 1944-February 14, 1945(KIA)
Drake, Walter M., Lt.; May 1944-November 1944
P-51D L2-D 44-14425 "Marge"
Duffie, Claire A.P., Maj.; October 1943-October 1944
P-38J L2-A 43-28474 "Give'm Hell For H.L. Jr."
P-51D L2-A 44-14355 "Give'm Hell For H.L. Jr."
Fleming, James E., Lt.; May 1944-August 10, 1944(KIA)
Gates, William H., Capt.; November 1944-; ex-435th Ftr Sqn
Gavrys, Thomas A., Lt.; July 1944-September 21, 1944(MIA)
Gleason, George W., Capt.; May 1944-March 1945
P-51D L2-H 44-14740 "Hot Toddy"
Golden, John T., Lt.; September 1944-April 16, 1945(POW)
P-51D L2-G 44-14856 "Junior"
Grenning, Harold P., Jr., Lt.; January 1944-November 1944
P-51D L2-Y 44-14393 "Flat Top Jr."
Grdenich, Frank, Lt.; January 1944-June 19, 1944(MIA-E)
Grossenbacher, Jack G., Capt.; October 1943-July 21, 1944(KIA)
Hagerman, Harold J., Jr., Lt.; March 1945-EOW
Hansen, John W., Lt.; January 1944-November 1944
P-38J L2-B 43-28349
P-51D L2-B 44-15325 "Swanee Jr."
Harper, Flamm D., Lt.; January 1944-July 15, 1944(MIA-E)
29 missions
Harris, Elbert N., Lt.; November 1944-March 3, 1945(KIA)
Hass, Jene A., Lt.; January 1944-July 6, 1944(POW)
Haynes, Clarence G., Capt.; September 1944-EOW
Hehn, William H., Lt.; January 1944-November 1944
P-38J L2-X 43-28443 "Rumboogie"
P-51D L2-X 44-14596 "Rumboogie Jr."
Helding, Arnold G., Lt.; January 1944-January 1945
P-38J L2-Q 43-28729
P-51D L2-Q 44-13864 "Lil Trouble"
Hendrickson, Laurie A., Lt.; November 1944-EOW
P-51D L2-X 44-14596
Hendrickson, Robert H., Lt.; January 1944-November 1944
Hendrix, George D., Lt.; January 1944-November 1944
Herren, James M., Jr., LtCol.; January 1944-October 30, 1944(KIA)
P-38J L2-A 42-68008 "Touche'"
P-51D L2-A 44-14396 "Touche'"
Hollingsworth, James M., Capt.; July 1944-September 1944; to HdQts; November 1944-December 25, 1944(KIA); ex-14th Ftr Grp, MTO
P-51D L2-A 44-14892 "Miss"
Hollis, Dewey H., Lt.; November 1944-December 13, 1944(KIAc)
Hollister, Berkley E., Lt.; January 1944-December 1944
P-38J L2-V 42-68147
P-51D L2-V 44-14651 "Pin-Up-Girl"
Holmes, Douglas I., Lt.; September 1944-October 30, 1944(POW)
P-51D L2-S 44-14627 "Pauline"
Honance, Eldie E., Lt.; -EOW
Hurtig, Edward L., Lt.; September 1944-December 25, 1944(KIA)
Huval, Ossie J., Lt.; November 1944-April 13, 1945(KIA)
Ilsley, Dwight F., Lt.; June 1944-June 22, 1944(KIA)
Jacobson, Gail E., Lt.; September 1944-EOW
P-51D L2-P 44-15380 "Burn'n Bernie"
Jeffrey, Arthur F., LtCol.; October 1943-April 1945
82 missions, 352 hours
P-38J L2-O 42-104425 "Boomerang"
P-51D L2-O 44-14423 "Boomerang Jr."
P-51K L2-O 44-11674 "Boomerang Jr."
Jenkins, Harold M., Lt.; September 1944-EOW
Keller, Frank J., Maj.; May 1944-August 9, 1944(POW); ex-435th Ftr Sqn
P-38J L2-I 43-28377 "Hilo Hattie"
P-38J L2-I 42-104140
Kines, Walter A., Lt.; January 1944-
Kline, Robert B., Lt.; September 1944-EOW
P-51D L2-M 44-14395 "The Onley Genevieve"
P-51K L2-M 44-11764 "The Onley Genevieve"
Krauss, Harold F., Jr., Lt.; January 1945-April 16, 1945(KIA)
Kuentzal, Ward A., Lt.; States-June 19, 1944(KIA); ex-82nd Ftr Grp, MTO
Leeney, George H., Lt.; -EOW
Lindley, Glenn D., Lt.; July 1944-October 1944; to 2nd Scouting Force
Little, Harry E., Lt.; July 1944-September 26, 1944(POW)
Lulay, Ralph M., F/O; April 1945-EOW
Lunstrum, Richard M., Lt.; June 1944-January 1945
P-51D L2-J 44-14507 "Satan's Angel"
Lutz, Burt W., Lt.; February 1944-; ex-82nd Ftr Grp, MTO
Lutz, Leroy, Lt.; February 1944-June 22, 1944(MIA)
Magill, Robert T., Lt.; April 1945-EOW
Maley, Ronald L., Lt.; July 1944-December 5, 1944(POW)
P-51D L2-T 44-11214 "Tommy Trojan"
Manning, Philip W., Lt.; July 1944-August 18, 1944(KIA)
Marlowe, Wendell H., Lt.; September 1944-December 25, 1944(KIA)
P-51D L2-F 44-14288 "Peregrine Jr."
Mastin, Donald W., Lt.; January 1945-
Mathews, Harold E., Lt.; June 1944-
P-51D L2-C 44-14845 "Tenacious Torchy"
McArthur, Marden L., Lt.; July 1944-July 27, 1944(MIA)
McChrystal, Richard G., Capt.; June 1944-
P-51D L2-L "Pretty Barbara"
McDaniel, Walter R., Lt.; April 1945-EOW
Monaco, Elidio E., Lt.; January 1945-EOW
Morrow, John W., Lt.; July 1944-
P-38J L2-S "Shoo Shoo Baby"
P-51D L2-R 44-15086 "Cactus Jack"
Munson, Robert L., Lt.; January 1945-EOW
Murphy, Calvin J., Jr., Lt.; July 1944-September 6, 1944(KIA)
Murr, John N., Lt.; July 1944-January 1945
Nagel, Jerome K., Lt.; September 1944-EOW
62 missions, 283:50 hours
P-51D L2-L "The Brat"
Neely, Tom D., Lt.; June 1944-December 25, 1944(POW)
P-51D L2-X 44-14596 "Rumboogie Jr."
Neumann, Walter A., Lt.; June 1944-December 5, 1944(KIA)
P-51D L2-U 44-14592 "Buzzin Texan"
Ohligschlager, James K., Lt.; February 1944-June 17, 1944(KIA)
Olds, Robin, Maj.; February 1944-October 1945
107 missions
P-38J L2-W "Scat"
P-38J L2-W 43-28341 "Scat II"
P-51D L2-W 44-14426 "Scat 5"
P-51D L2-W 44-72922 "Scat VII"
Olson, Richard L., Lt.; April 1945-EOW
Olson, Thomas C., Lt.; January 1944-December 1944
P-38J L2-W "Lelah May"
P-51D L2-W "Lelah May"

Pavlock, Quentin S., Lt.; February 1944-October 2, 1944(KIAc)
Peacock, Cecil M., Lt.; January 1945-EOW
Pease, Roscoe I., Jr., Lt.; March 1945-EOW; ex-bomber pilot
Peterson, Carl L., Lt.; February 1944-
Pierce, Donald J., Capt.; February 1945-EOW; ex-4th Ftr Grp
P-51D L2-R 44-72336 "Setonia No.3"
Plezibat, John A., Lt.; January 1945-EOW
Plemens, H., Lt.; -EOW
Proctor, Clayton F., Lt.; June 1944-July 5, 1944(KIA)
Redwood, Robert K., Lt.; January 1945-EOW
Rodgers, William H., Lt.; July 1944-September 27, 1944(KIA)
Rossel, Roy M., Jr., Lt.; December 1944-EOW
Sands, Thurman E., Lt.; December 1944-April 4, 1945(KIAc)
Scheiss, Francis C., Lt.; December 1944-EOW
Sears, Eugene E., Lt.; September 1944-EOW
P-51D L2-U 44-15317 "American Maid"
Simpson, Richard G., Lt.; July 1944-May 1945
Stott, Donald H., Lt.; December 1944-April 16, 1945(KIA)
P-51D L2-S 44-14629 "Shoo Shoo Baby"
Stott, Harold L., Lt.; December 1944-EOW
P-51D L2-K 44-14523 "The Yakima Chief"
Stroop, Joseph E., Capt.; States-
Taylor, Frank M., Lt.; January 1945-April 16, 1945(POW)
Thomas, Douglas T., Lt.; September 1944-October 30, 1944(KIAc)
Thompson, Hilton O., Lt.; December 1944-July 19, 1945(KIAc)
P-51K L2-I 44-11674 "Speedball"
Tipps, John T., Lt.; May 1944-
P-38J L2-R "The Zaniest Wildcat"
P-51D L2-R 44-14311 "The Wildcat"
Tommie, Dalton F., Lt.; December 1944-EOW
P-51D L2-Q 44-13864 "Lil' Trouble"
Tucker, Albert S.J., Jr., Lt.; February 1944-June 22, 1944(KIA)
Turner, Hiram G., Jr., Capt.; October 1943-August 15, 1944(POW)
Valluzzi, Arthur J., F/O; January 1945-EOW
Wallace, James L., Lt.; January 1944-August 15, 1944(KIA)
Walters, Clarence A., Lt.; January 1945-EOW
Weins, Maynard J., Lt.; January 1944-April 1944; later 55th Ftr Grp
Wendt, Eugene H., Lt.; August 1944-; ex-435th Ftr Sqn
P-51D L2-B 44-14391 "Beautiful Jan"
White, J.L., Jr., Lt.
Wickenden, Henry T., Lt.; January 1944-
Williams, Bailey A., Capt.; February 1944-December 1944
P-38J L2-N 42-67264 "Teddie"
P-51D L2-N 44-14373 "Teddie #4"

**435th Fighter Squadron**
Anderson, William C., Capt.; April 1945-EOW; ex-436th Ftr Sqn
Baird, Robert J., Lt.; September 1944-EOW
P-51D J2-H 44-14392 "Apple Knocker"
Barnes, Thomas C., Lt.; January 1944-
Barsky, William M., Lt.; September 1944-EOW
P-51D J2-G 44-14263 "Roarin' Rose"
Benoit, Norman R., Capt.; June 1944-February 1945
P-51D J2-H 44-14840 "The Victory Queen"
Butler, Calvin J., Capt.; May 1944-June 17, 1944(KIA); ex-434th Ftr Sqn
Butler, Nelson W., Lt.; June 1944-March 1945
P-51D J2-H 44-14417
Candelaria, Richard G., Lt.; September 1944-April 13, 1945(POW)
P-51K J2-K 44-11755 "My Pride and Joy"
Carter, Ray S., Maj.; October 1943-September 5, 1944(KIA)
Clarke, William D., Lt.; November 1944-December 10, 1944(KIAc)
Coursey, Richard R., Jr., Capt.; States-November 1944
Courtney, John J., Jr., Capt.; October 1943-August 8, 1944(MIA-E)
Detlefson, Heinz W., Lt.; May 1944-November 8, 1944(KIA)
Dettenmayer, G.R., Lt.; February 1945-EOW; ex-bomber pilot
Doolittle, Gordon L., Capt.; May 1944-February 1945
P-51D J2-P 44-14406 "Mugs"
Ervin, Ivan A., Lt.; June 1944-September 14, 1944(KIAc)
Fairchild, Rayne B., Jr., Lt.; January 1944-July 4, 1944(KIA)
Ford, Everett P., Lt.; May 1944-September 9, 1944(KIAc)
Friend, Raymond K., Capt.; June 1944-March 1945
66 missions, 300 hours
P-38J J2-B "Sweet El"
P-51D J2-B "Sweet El II"
Frost, R.B., Lt.; March 1945-EOW
Gardner, Robert E., Lt.; February 1945-EOW
Gates, William M., Capt.; October 1943-November 1944; to 434th Ftr Sqn
Gilley, William C., Lt.; January 1944-
Glover, John G., Maj.; October 1943-October 1944
P-38J J2-W
P-51D J2-W 44-11162 "Tuscon"
Gorian, Martin G., Lt.; January 1944-November 1944
270 hours
Gossard, Philip D., Capt.; January 1944-December 1944
P-38J J2-O 44-23603 "Ruth"
P-51D J2-O 44-13354 "V For Val"
Granville, Chester W., Lt.; January 1944-September 14, 1944(KIAc)
Gross, Burton S., Lt.; January 1944-June 27, 1944(KIA)
Gunn, William B., Lt.; May 1944-November 1944
Hanlon, B.L., Lt.; November 1944-EOW
Harrell, John W., Jr., Maj.; August 1944- ; to Hdqts; ex-436th Ftr Sqn
82 missions total
Hart, Fred L., Lt.; September 1944-EOW
Heathman, Charles E., Lt.; November 1944-EOW
Hedenberg, John W., Lt.; States-October 1944
Herman, Robert H., Lt.; November 1944-EOW
Hill, Glenn W., Lt.; November 1944-EOW
Hoffman, R.H., Lt.; November 1944-EOW
Hooker, Verne E., Capt.; January 1944-EOW
85 missions
P-38J J2-N
P-51D J2-N 44-14827
P-51D J2-K 44-73138
Horne, Leland K., Lt.; January 1944-June 19, 1944(KIA)
Horst, Harold, Lt.; January 1944-
Hymans, Robert B., Lt.; November 1944-December 12, 1944(KIAc)
Jarrell, Carl B., Lt.; November 1944-February 9, 1945(KIA)
Jordan, Herbert H., Maj.; September 1944-April 1945; ex-475th Ftr Grp, PTO
P-51D J2-Q "Hun-Nee"
Keefe, Lawrence A., Lt.; September 1944-EOW
Keller, Frank J., Capt.; March 1944-May 1944; to 434th Ftr Sqn
King, David E., Lt.; September 1944-EOW
Koerber, James H., Lt.; September 1944-EOW
Maier, William F., Lt.; January 1944-November 1944
Manson, E.L., Lt.; February 1945-EOW
Matthews, A.E., Lt.; March 1945-EOW
Matthews, Cecil R., Lt.; January 1944-EOW
McCann, John P., Lt.; January 1944-December 1944
McClure, Donald D., Lt.; States-June 19, 1944(MIA)
McKay, William B., Lt.; January 1944-July 27, 1944(KIA)
Means, Billy C., Capt.; July 1944-April 1945
Miller, John H., Lt.; July 1944-October 1944; to 2nd Scouting Force
Monsell, Charles F., Jr., Lt.; June 1944-December 1944
Moore, Carl W., Lt.; July 1944-August 5, 1944(KIA)
Morris, Lewis E., Lt.; July 1944-February 1945
Muller, Wilbert, Lt.; January 1944-November 1944
Naule, Donald L., Lt.; January 1944-
Nicholson, T.S., Lt.; February 1945-EOW
Park, D.C., Lt.; February 1945-EOW
Peterson, C.H., Lt.; April 1945-EOW
Petterson, Lewis P., Lt.
Pickering, William H., Lt.; January 1944-December 1944
Pigg, Robert N., Lt.; -December 12, 1944(KIA)
Powers, T.A., Lt.; February 1945-EOW
Prevosti, W.V., F/O; January 1945-EOW
Ralston, R.E., Lt.; February 1945-EOW
Ricker, J.E., Lt.; April 1945-EOW
Rock, Norbert W., Lt.; September 1944-February 5, 1945(KIAc)
P-51D J2-S "Darlin' Fran"
Rogers, John R., Lt.; December 1944-EOW
Rossman, George P., Lt.; December 1944-March 1945; to 2nd Scouting Force
Rourke, W.B., Jr., Lt.; December 1944-EOW
Routh, Sylvan R., Lt.; December 1944-EOW
Rudat, W.A., Lt.; December 1944-EOW
Salter, George M., Jr., Lt.; October 1944-EOW
Salze, Floyd W., Lt.; December 1944-EOW
P-51D J2- "The Birmingham Kid"
Sawyer, D.E., Lt.; April 1945-EOW
Schoonover, G.F., Lt.; December 1944-EOW
P-51D J2-W 44-14366 "Lucky Mark"
Shewfelt, Ray L., Lt.; September 1944-January 1945; to 2nd Scouting Force
25 missions, 110 hours (later
31 missions and 165 hours w/SF)
Shriner, Fred F., Lt.; States-February 1945
Sims, Edward H., Lt.; December 1944-EOW
Smith, Howard C., Capt.; July 1944-February 1945
P-51D J2-W 44-14366
Smith, Thomas V., Lt.; July 1944-November 8, 1944(POW)
Sowerby, Theodore J., Capt.; July 1944-EOW
Splittstoesser, E.A., Lt.; December 1944-EOW
Stage, G., Lt.; January 1945-EOW
Stoops, Edward F., Maj.; States-June 1944; to HdQts
Sullivan, John A., Maj.; States-July 1944; to 436th Ftr Sqn
Sykes, George K., Capt.; October 1943-September 17, 1944(MIA-E)
49 missions
Thompson, R.E., Lt.; December 1944-EOW
Thorn, Donald W., Lt.; September 1944-EOW
Trabucco, Thomas F., Maj.; September 1944-March 1, 1945(KIA)
P-51D J2-A 44-15374 "Dotty"
Trout, Chester E., Lt.; February 1944-March 1944
Waller, Charles S., Lt.
Watkins, D.B., Lt.; April 1945-EOW
Wendt, Eugene H., Lt.; July 1944-August 1944; to 434th Ftr Sqn
Whitmer, L.W., Jr., Lt.; April 1945-EOW
Williams, G.F., Lt.; January 1945-EOW
Zuchowski, Stephen H., Lt.; States-November 1944

**436th Fighter Squadron**
Anderson, William C., Capt.; February 1945-April 1945; to 435th Ftr Sqn; ex-4th Ftr Grp
Archibald, John M., Lt.; January 1945-EOW

Beatty, Frank G., Lt.; -July 1945; ex-492nd & 467th Bomb Grps (35 missions)
Biscayart, Jules D., Maj.; October 1943-December 1944
Darling, Charles H., Lt.; October 1944-July 1945
Darnell, Coleman H., Lt.
Derby, Stanley E., Lt.; October 1944-April 1945
DiPaola, Albert R., Lt.; October 1944-February 22, 1945(POW)
Duffie, Claire A.P., Maj.; January 1945-EOW; ex-434th Ftr Sqn
P-51D 9B-A 44-72516 "Give'm Hell For H.L. Jr."
Dunn, Donald A., Lt.; May 1944-October 1944
Early, John R., III, Lt.; October 1944-July 1945
Elmgren, Charles B., Lt.; October 1944-July 1945
53 missions, 265:20 hours
P-51K 9B-P 44-11739
Ernst, Carl V., Capt.; September 1944-EOW
P-51D 9B- "Akin Assam Dragon"
Eskell, Barrett B., Lt.; October 1944-December 5, 1944(POW)
Falkner, George E., LtCol.; April 1945-EOW; ex-bomber pilot
Fillipow, Edwin J., Lt.; May 1944-November 1944
P-51D 9B- 44-14559 "Daisy Mae"
Frolking, James E., Lt.; May 1944-October 7, 1944(MIA-E)
Galloway, Thomas T., Lt.; October 1943-July 24, 1944(KIA)
Gerrard, Robert C., Lt.; -EOW
P-51D 9B-F "Rosita"
Glenn, John G., Lt.; January 1944-October 1944
P-51D 9B- "Laguna Goona"
Granger, Jesse V., Lt.; May 1944-November 1944
Grasshoff, Hans J., Capt.; January 1944-December 1944
270 hours
P-38J 9B-J "Little Zippie"
P-51D 9B-J 44-14574 "Little Zippie
Greenwood, Travis M., Lt.; January 1944-October 1944
67 missions, 276:30 hours
Hansen, Kenneth J., Lt.; October 1944-EOW
38 missions, 187:20 hours
Harold, Karl F., F/O
Harrell, John W., Maj.; November 1943-August 1944; to 435th Ftr Sqn
82 missions total
P-38J 9B- "Peacemaker"
Hartman, Elmer, Capt.; July 1944-August 4, 1944(KIA)
Hartnett, Vincent G., Capt.; January 1944-
P-38J 9B- 43-28418 "Merrily Ann"
Harynek, Fred, Lt.
Hedenburg, John W., Lt.; States-October 1944
Henry, Price E., Lt.; January 1944-October 1944
Henry, Ray E., Lt.; November 1944-EOW
P-51D 9B- "King's Queen"
Hightower, Howard G., Lt.; January 1944-October 1944
P-38J 9B-T
P-51D 9B-T "Calamity Flo"
Hopcroft, Ernest J., Lt.; October 1944-June 1945
56 missions
P-51D 9B-G "Daisy II"
P-51D 9B-G 44-72431 "Poontang II"
Holverston, Herman F., Lt.; January 1944-November 1944
Howard, William N., Lt.; January 1944-August 28, 1944(MIA-E)
Huycke, Andre E., Capt.; January 1944-December 1944
P-38J 9B-C
P-51D 9B-C "My Best Bett"
Hymans, Robert B., Lt.; November 1944-December 12, 1944(KIAc)
Johnson, Clarence O., Lt.; November 1943-August 1944; to 352nd Ftr Grp; ex-82nd Ftr Grp, MTO
P-38J 9B-R 43-28697 "Bula B III"
Jordan, Herbert H., Maj.; August 1944-September 1944; to 435th Ftr Sqn; ex-475th Ftr Grp, PTO
Joseph, George, F/O; September 1944-March 1945
Kelley, William D., Lt.; November 1944-EOW
Kemper, Niel W., Lt.; July 1944-July 24, 1944(MIA-E)
King, Benjamin H., Maj.; States-August 1944; to 359th Ftr Grp; ex-347th Ftr Grp, PTO
King, Raymond E., F/O; November 1944-January 13, 1945(KIA)
Kleineman, Bernard R., Lt.; September 1944-EOW
P-51D 9B- "Lady Kay"
Kreger, Charles S., Lt.; September 1944-July 1945
P-51D 9B- "Bessie Lee"
Lewin, Edward C., Capt.; May 1944-
P-38J 9B- "Scotty"
P-51D 9B- "Scotty IV"
Long, Sylvester F., Lt.; January 1945-EOW
Malone, Jay C., Capt.; September 1944-April 18, 1945(KIA)
Massey, Alton A., Lt.; January 1945-EOW
McKeown, Arthur J., Lt.; January 1945-July 1945
McLaurin, Grover G., Lt.; October 1944-EOW
P-51D 9B- "Mac's Hack"
Mead, Fred M., Lt.; June 1944-April 1945
P-51D 9B- 44-14578
Melton, Allen B., Lt.; April 1945-EOW
Merritt, W.J., Lt.; February 1945-EOW
Mickey, Melvin S., Lt.; July 1944-February 1945
Monahan, John D., Maj.; October 1943-August 1944; to 364th Ftr Grp
Moore, Clifford J., Jr., Maj.; November 1943-March 1945
P-51D 9B- "The Uninvited"
Morris, Jesse F., Lt.; January 1945-March 29, 1945(KIAc)
Morton, R.C., Lt.; February 1945-EOW
Moser, Fred A., Jr., Capt.; July 1944-August 2, 1944(KIA)
Mosier, Arlett G., Jr., Capt.; June 1944-March 1945
Mulvaney, Gerald M., Lt.; June 1944-March 1945
61 missions, 272 hours
P-51D 9B- "Bottleneck"
Myers, Thomas E., Capt.; July 1944-EOW
P-51D 9B- 44-14613 "As-Cend Charlie
Nesselbush, Lewis K., Lt.; February 1944-June 20, 1944(POW)
Ogrom, Zeymour, Lt.; June 1944-November 1944
O'Holleran, Thomas J., Lt.; June 1944-August 14, 1944(POW)
Olson, Marion A., Lt.; April 1945-EOW
Orrick, Thomas A., Lt.; June 1944-October 1944; to 2nd Scouting Force
Palson, Richard C.J., Lt.; January 1945-EOW
Philbrick, Charles H., II, Lt.; January 1945-EOW
Pleinman, Herbert P., Lt.; April 1945-EOW
Plunk, Henry P., Lt.; June 1944-
P-51D 9B-O "Ambrosia"
Proffatt, V.J., Lt.; May 1945-EOW
0 missions
Pulchinski, E.J., Lt.; February 1945-EOW
Race, Francis E., Lt.; January 1945-EOW
Rawley, Walter N., Jr., Lt.; February 1945-EOW
Red, Douglas L., Lt.; September 1944-December 25, 1944(KIA)
Romano, Pasquale J., Lt.; December 1944-EOW
Rosness, Joseph M., Capt.; February 1944-November 1944
Schoen, Charles F., Jr., Lt.; December 1944-February 28, 1945(KIA)
Schuck, John R., Lt.; September 1944-EOW
Scordino, Anthony J., Lt.; December 1944-May 4, 1945(KIAc)
Shane, Presson S., Capt.; January 1945-July 1945
P-51D 9B- "Jayhawk"
Sherer, Carl W., Lt.; December 1944-EOW
Shonborn, Paul J., Lt.; December 1944-July 1945
P-51D 9B-E 44-14594 "Smoky City Fireball"
Smigel, Alfred J., Lt.; December 1944-EOW
P-51D 9B-U 44-14758 "Chug-A-Lug"
Smith, Lewis C., Lt.; December 1944-March 11, 1945(KIA)
Spencer, Richard S., Jr., Capt.; January 1944-November 1944
P-38J 9B-F "Muz's Mighty Molecule"
P-38J 9B-F "Muz's Mighty Molecule II
P-51D 9B-F "Muz's Mighty Molecule III"
Spillane, Edward J., Lt.; January 1944-June 9, 1944(KIAc)
Steele, Marion W., Lt.; September 1944-November 6, 1944(KIAc)
4 missions
Steph, Walter B., Capt.; September 1944-April 1945
Straub, George, Lt.; States-October 1944
Struby, Joseph R., Capt.; January 1944-November 1944
Sullivan, John A., Maj.; July 1944-December 5, 1944(KIA); ex-435th Ftr Sqn
P-51D 9B-A 44-14636 "Carol II & III"
Teetor, Robert R., Lt.; January 1944-July 28, 1944(KIAc)
Thompson, Tom H., Capt.; September 1944-EOW
P-51D 9B- "Weezy"
Thornton, William E., Lt.
Thrall, Richard P., Lt.; December 1944-EOW
Uhley, Charles P., Lt.; April 1945-EOW
Upsall, Richard H., Jr., Lt.; April 1945-EOW
Vasseur, Peter C., Lt.; September 1944-February 22, 1945(MIA)
Walker, William A., Capt.; October 1943-May 25, 1944(KIAc)
0 missions
P-38J 9B-A 42-104318
Walsh, George W., Lt.; April 1945-EOW
Ward, James W., Lt.; April 1945-EOW
West, Eric P., Lt.; April 1945-July 1945
Wilkins, John K., Capt.; September 1944-January 1945; to 2nd Scouting Force
69 missions (32 later w/2nd SF)
P-51D 9B- 44-14517 "Lil Exterminator"
Witzel, George H., Lt.; October 1944-October 1945
51 missions, 261:50 hours
P-51D 9B-B "Bruiser"
P-51D 9B-N 44-15742 "Bruiser"
Wolski, Victor, Lt.; January 1944-October 1944
P-38J 9B-W
P-51D 9B-W
Young, Robert C., Lt.; February 1945-April 22, 1945(KIAc); ex-bomber pilot
2 missions
Zellner, Fred, Lt.; October 1944-EOW

**Aircraft of the 434th Fighter Squadron**

P-38J-5-LO

| | |
|---|---|
| 42-67264 L2-N "Teddie" | B.A. Williams |
| 42-67296 L2-R | |

P-38J-10-LO

| | |
|---|---|
| 42-67424 L2- | |
| 42-67732 L2-P | |
| 42-67865 L2-U | |
| 42-68008 L2-A "Touche'" | J.M. Herren |
| 42-68029 L2-X | |
| 42-68147 L2-V | B.E. Hollister |

P-38J-15-LO
43-28341 L2-W "Scat II" R. Olds
43-28349 L2-B J.W. Hansen
43-28367 L2-A
43-28376 L2-U
43-28377 L2-I "Hilo Hattie" F.J. Keller
43-28443 L2-X "Rumboogie" W.H. Hehn
43-28456 L2-T
43-28465 L2-M S.S. Woods
43-28474 L2-A "Give'm Hell For H.L. Jr." C.A.P. Duffie
43-28714 L2-L "Lucky Lady"
43-28729 L2-Q A.G. Helding
43-28731 L2-K "Sweet Mary" K.E. Canella
43-28647 L2-G
42-104140 L2-I F.J. Keller
42-104258 L2-G
42-104425 L2-O "Boomerang" A.F. Jeffrey
42-104427 L2-
44-23169 L2-Z "Sleepytime Gal"
44-23171 L2-Q

Unknown Serials
L2-W "Scat" R. Olds
L2-W "Scat III" R. Olds
L2-R "The Zaniest Wildcat" J.T. Tipps
L2-N "Teddie #2" B.A. Williams
L2-N "Teddie #3" B.A. Williams
L2-S "Shoo Shoo Baby" J.W. Morrow
L2-W "Lelah May" T.C. Olson

P-51B-5-NA
43-7040 L2-3 HACK

P-51D-5-NT
44-11214 L2-T "Kraut Knocker" R.I. Bromschwig
44-11214 L2-T "Tommy Trojan" R.L. Maley

P-51K-5-NT
44-11674 L2-O "Boomerang Jr." A.F. Jeffrey
44-11674 L2-I "Speedball" H.O. Thompson
44-11761 L2-X "Miss Georgia Carol" L.A. Hendrickson
44-11764 L2-M "The Onley Genevieve" R.B. Kline

P-51K-10-NT
44-12156 L2-A "The Flying Dutchman"

P-51D-5-NA
44-13864 L2-Q "Lil Trouble" A.G. Helding/D.F. Tommie

P-51D-10-NA
44-14138 L2-G "Miss Fortune"
44-14212 L2-F
44-14225 L2-D "Marge" W.M. Drake
44-14288 L2-F "Peregrine Jr." W.H. Marlow
44-14311 L2-R "The Wildcat" J.T. Tipps
44-14324 L2-L
44-14333 L2-F
44-14355 L2-A "Give'm Hell For H.L. Jr." C.A.P. Duffie
44-14373 L2-N "Teddie #4" B.A. Williams
44-14373 L2-N "Skunkchaser" C.W. Bowers
44-14391 L2-B J.W. Hansen
44-14391 L2-B "Beautiful Jan" E.H. Wendt
44-14393 L2-Y "Just Born" D.L. Born
44-14393 L2-Y "Flat Top Jr." H.P. Grenning
44-14395 L2-M "The Onley Genevieve" R.B. Kline
44-14396 L2-A "Touche'" J.M. Herren
44-14416 L2-M
44-14423 L2-O "Boomerang Jr." A.F. Jeffrey
44-14423 L2-T "Kraut Knocker" R.I. Bromschwig
44-14426 L2-W "Scat 5" R. Olds
44-14507 L2-J "Satan's Angel" R.M. Lunstrum
44-14523 L2-K "The Yakima Chief" H.L. Stott
44-14592 L2-U "Buzzin' Texan" W.A. Neuman
44-14596 L2-X "Rum Boogie Jr." W.H. Hehn/T.D. Neely
44-14627 L2-S "Pauline" D.I. Holmes
44-14629 L2-S "Shoo Shoo Baby" D.H. Stott
44-14645 L2-A "My Janet"
44-14651 L2-V "Pin-Up Girl" B.E. Hollister
44-14740 L2-H "Hot Toddy" G.W. Gleason
44-14845 L2-C "Tenacious Torchy" H.E. Mathews
44-14846 L2-S

P-51D-15-NA
44-14856 L2-G "Junior" J.T. Golden
44-14892 L2-A "Miss" J.M. Hollingsworth
44-14929 L2- "Little Droppy"
44-14931 L2-B
44-14989 L2-D
44-15086 L2-R "Cactus Jack" J.W. Morrow
44-15228 L2-
44-15317 L2-U "American Maid" E.E. Sears
44-15325 L2-B "Swanee Jr." W.H. Gates/J.W. Hansen
44-15380 L2-P "Burn'n Bernie" G.E. Jacobson
44-15381 L2-T "Super Wabbitt" R.D. Creighton

P-51D-20-NA
44-63176 L2-Z "The Impatient Virgin" W.H. Daudistel
44-63189 L2-A "Mary"
44-63236 L2-
44-63843 L2-F "Lauro Jo"
44-72336 L2-R "Setonia No.3" D.J. Pierce

P-51D-25-NA
44-72922 L2-W "Scat VI" R. Olds

Unknown Serials
L2-L "The Brat" J.K. Nagel
L2-L "Pretty Barbara" R.G. McChrystal
L2-W "Lelah May" T.C. Olson

**Aircraft of the 435th Fighter Squadron**

P-38J-10-LO
42-68161 J2-
42-68189 J2-

P-38J-15-LO
43-28426 J2-
43-28467 J2-
43-28472 J2-
43-28716 J2-
43-28823 J2-Z H. Zemke
44-23160 J2-
44-23168 J2-
44-23171 J2-Q
44-23177 J2-N
42-104416 J2-

P-38J-20-LO
44-23484 J2-

P-38J-25-LO
44-23663 J2-O "Ruth" P.D. Gossard

Unknown Serials
J2-B "Sweet El" R.K. Friend
J2- "Bossie"
J2- "Swanee Jr."

P-51B-1-NA
43-12408 J2-X "Tommie" HACK

P-51B-5-NA
43-6865 J2-Q HACK
43-6875 J2-Z HACK

P-51B-10-NA
43-7157 J2-7 HACK

P-51D-5-NT
44-11162 J2-W "Tuscon" J.G. Glover
44-11163 J2-A "Little Jean"
44-11346 J2-T "Squirrel"

P-51K-5-NT
44-11755 J2-K "My Pride and Joy" R.G. Candelaria

P-51D-10-NA
44-14263 J2-G "Roarin' Rose" W.M. Barsky
44-14294 J2-
44-14327 J2-R K.L. Riddle
44-14341 J2-F "Fast Company"
44-14344 J2-
44-14345 J2-B "Little Joan"
44-14354 J2-O "V For Val" P.D. Gossard
44-14366 J2-W "Lucky Mark" G.F. Schoonover
44-14371 J2-Y "Edith"
44-14392 J2-H "Apple Knocker" R.J. Baird
44-14406 J2-P "Mugs" G.L. Doolittle
44-14417 J2-H N.W. Butler
44-14424 J2- "Sugar Kayne"
44-14436 J2-J
44-14437 J2-
44-14509 J2-
44-14827 J2-N V.E. Hooker
44-14840 J2-H "The Victory Queen" N.R. Benoit

P-51D-15-NA
44-15374 J2-A "Dotty" T.F. Trabucco

P-51D-20-NA
44-63236 J2-
44-72395 J2-

P-51D-25-NA
44-72627 J2-N
44-72802 J2-V
44-73137 J2-N
44-73138 J2-K V.E. Hooker

Unknown Serials
J2-B "Sweet El II" R.K. Friend
J2-Q "Hun-Nee" H.H. Jordan
J2-S "Darlin' Fran" N.W. Rock
J2-D "Butch"
J2- "Rebellious Rebel"
J2- "The Birmingham Kid" F.W. Salze

**Aircraft of the 436th Fighter Squadron**

P-38J-5-LO
42-67264 9B-
42-67452 9B-N "Rabble Rouser"

P-38J-15-LO
43-28418 9B- "Merrily Ann" V.G. Hartnett
43-28419 9B-
43-28432 9B-
43-28655 9B-Q
43-28697 9B-R "Bula B III" C.O. Johnson
44-23172 9B-
42-104318 9B-A W.A. Walker
42-104397 9B-
42-104407 9B- "Marion"

Unknown Serials
9B-J "Little Zippie" H.J. Grasshoff
9B-F "Muz's Mighty Molecule" R.S. Spencer
9B- "Peacemaker" J.W. Harrell

P-51B-1-NA
43-12184 9B- HACK
43-12444 9B- HACK
43-12460 9B- HACK

P-51B-15-NA
43-24799 9B- HACK

P-51D-5-NT
44-11201 9B-
44-11228 9B-

P-51K-5-NT
44-11739 9B-P C.B. Elmgren
44-11749 9B-

P-51K-10-NT
44-12117 9B-

P-51D-5-NA
44-13341 9B-Q
44-13902 9B-

P-51D-10-NA
44-14351 9B-Z H. Zemke
44-14517 9B- "Lil Exterminator" J.K. Wilkins
44-14544 9B-
44-14553 9B-
44-14559 9B- "Daisey Mae" E.J. Fillipow
44-14571 9B-
44-14574 9B-J "Little Zippie" H.J. Grasshoff
44-14576 9B-
44-14577 9B-N
44-14578 9B-
44-14583 9B-N "Dearest Mine"
44-14591 9B-
44-14594 9B-E "Smoky City Fireball" P.J. Shonborn
44-14601 9B- "Queenie-El Diablo"
44-14613 9B- "As-Cend Charlie" T.E. Myers
44-14636 9B-A "Carol II + Carol III" J.A. Sullivan
44-14662 9B-S
44-14750 9B-
44-14758 9B-U "Chug-A-Lug" A.J. Smigel
44-14767 9B-
44-14788 9B-
44-14813 9B-

P-51D-15-NA
44-14915 9B-
44-15010 9B-
44-15412 9B-T
44-15533 9B-
44-15553 9B-
44-15662 9B-S
44-15742 9B-N "Bruiser" G.H. Witzel

P-51D-20-NA
44-63192 9B-
44-64069 9B-
44-72431 9B-G "Poontang II" E.J. Hopcroft
44-72516 9B-A "Give'm Hell For H.L. Jr." C.A.P. Duffie

P-51D-25-NA
44-72714 9B-
44-72751 9B-
44-72950 9B-
44-72981 9B-
44-73295 9B-

Unknown Serials
9B-B "Bruiser" G.H. Witzel
9B-C "My Best Bett" A.E. Huycke
9B-C "Akin Assam Dragon" C.V. Ernst
9B-G "Scotty Jr." E.C. Lewin
9B-F "Muz's Mighty Molecule II" R.S. Spencer
9B-O "Ambrosia" H.P. Plunk
9B-T "Calamity Flo" H.G. Hightower
9B-F "Rosita" R.C. Gerrard
9B- "Lady Kay" B.R. Kleinman
9B- "Mac's Hack" G.G. McLaurin
9B- "Jayhawk" P.S. Shane
9B- "Bessie Lee" C.S. Kreger
9B- "Laguna Goona" J.G. Glenn
9B- "King's Queen" R.E. Henry
9B- "Weezy" T.H. Thompson
9B- "The Uninvited" C.J. Moore
9B- "Bottleneck" G.M. Mulvaney
9B- "Lady Ray"

• • •

**65th, 66th, 67th Fighter Wings**

The fighter groups assigned to the 8th Air Force were controlled by three Fighter Wings-the 65th, 66th, and 67th. These were not actual combat units, but individuals assigned to them did occasionally fly with groups under their control. Most times the pilots went along on missions as observers, although in a few instances, pilots flew with their old units to keep in touch with friends and to keep their hand in combat operations.

A fairly large number of men were assigned during the war, but as far as can be determined, only four actually made claims on missions. Since these pilots were officially assigned to Wing Headquarters and not the group with which they flew, their claims are allocated to the Wing. In addition, two pilots were MIA on operations, and again, are listed separate from their host organization.

**The 65th Fighter Wing**

Activated as the 4th Air Defense Wing on March 27, 1943, at Hamilton Field, California, the wing moved overseas in May-June of 1943 and was re-designated as the 65th Fighter Wing in July. Based at Debden from June 14, 1943, and Saffron Walden from June 17, 1943, until September of 1945, the Wing made no claims while one pilot was MIA.

**Commanders**

| | |
|---|---|
| Col. Jesse Auton | April 1943-June 4, 1943 |
| B/Gen. Ross G. Hoyt | June 4, 1943-September 6, 1943 |
| B/Gen. Jesse Auton | September 6, 1943-July 29, 1945 |

**Units Assigned**

| | |
|---|---|
| 4th: June 1943-EOW | 356th: August 1943-August 1944 |
| 56th: June 1943-EOW | 361st: August 1944-EOW |
| 78th: June 1943-August 1943 | 479th: May 1944-EOW |
| 355th: August 1943-EOW | |

**65th Fighter Wing Losses**

**April 8, 1944**
Capt. Frank R. Boyles - KIA; Hit by enemy fighters near Celle. Flew with the 4th Ftr Grp.
P-51B WD-F 43-7098

## The 66th Fighter Wing

Activated as the 5th Air Defense Wing on March 25, 1943, at Norfolk, Virginia, the wing headed overseas in June of 1943. Redesignated as the 66th Fighter Wing in July of 1943, the unit was based at Duxford, from June 3, 1943, and Sawston, from August 20, 1943, until October of 1945. Wing pilots claimed 1 air and 6.5 ground victories without loss.

### Commanders

| | |
|---|---|
| B/Gen. Murray C. Woodbury | April 1, 1943-September 1945 |

### Units Assigned

| | |
|---|---|
| 55th: October 1943-EOW | 357th: January 1944-EOW |
| 78th: August 1943-EOW | 358th: November 1943-February 1944 |
| 339th: April 1944-EOW | 359th: October 1943-November 1943 |
| 353rd: August 1943-EOW | 361st: December 1943-March 1944 |

### 66th Fighter Wing Scorers

| Name | Air | Grd | |
|---|---|---|---|
| W.C. Clark | 1-0-0 | 0-0 | plus 0-0-1 air & 8-4 grd w/339th Ftr Grp |
| O.C. Gilbert | 0-0-0 | 6.5-3 | plus 2-0-0 air & 2-0 grd w/78th Ftr Grp |

### 66th Fighter Wing Scoring

**January 14, 1945**

| | | | |
|---|---|---|---|
| HdQts: | LtCol. W.C. Clark | FW-190 dest(air) | S/Schwerin |

**April 16, 1945**

| | | | |
|---|---|---|---|
| HdQts: | LtCol. O.E. Gilbert | (3)FW-190 dest(grd) | All claims at |
| | | (1.5)Ju-87 dest(grd)* | Pilzen/Prague |
| | | He-111 dest(grd) | |
| | | Ju-52 dest(grd) | |
| | | (2)u/i a/c dam(grd) | |
| | | FW-190 dam(grd) | |

* - shared with Lt. D.J. Henahan of the 78th Ftr Grp

## The 67th Fighter Wing

Activated as the 6th Air Defense Wing on June 15, 1943, at Bedford, Massachusetts, the 6th was re-designated as the 67th Fighter Wing in July of 1943. Heading overseas in August of 1943, the unit was based at Walcott Hall from August 26, 1943, until October of 1945. 67th pilots claimed 2.33 air victories while one flier was MIA.

### Commanders

| | |
|---|---|
| LtCol. Frank K. Johnson | June 15, 1943-August 28, 1943 |
| LtCol. Roy W. Osborn | August 28, 1943-September 6, 1943 |
| B/Gen. Edward W. Anderson | September 6, 1943-July 17, 1945 |

### Units Assigned

| | |
|---|---|
| 20th: August 1943-EOW | 359th: November 1943-EOW |
| 352nd: October 1943-EOW | 361st: March 1944-August 1944 |
| 356th: August 1944-EOW | 364th: February 1944-EOW |

### 67th Fighter Wing Scorers

| Name | Air | Grd | |
|---|---|---|---|
| R.W. Osborn | 1.33-0-0 | 0-0 | plus 2-0-1 air w/364th Ftr Grp |
| D.K. Willis | 1-0-0 | 0-0 | |

### 67th Fighter Wing Scoring

**February 20, 1944**

| | | | |
|---|---|---|---|
| HdQts: | LtCol. R.W. Osborn | (1.33)Me-110 dest(air)* | Vogelsand |

* - shared with Capt. D.S. Bryan and Lt. D.T. Zimms of the 352nd Ftr Grp

**April 10, 1944**

| | | | |
|---|---|---|---|
| HdQts: | Maj. D.K. Willis | u/i a/c dest(air) | Rotterdam |

### 67th Fighter Wing Losses

**April 10, 1944**

Maj. Donald K. Willis - POW; Suffered mechanical failure and bellied-in north of Rotterdam. Was flying with the 20th Ftr Grp.

P-38J KI-X 42-68077

## The Scouting Forces

These special units were formed in the late summer of 1944 to relay weather information to the bombers enroute to their targets. The scouts could advise of weather conditions and suggest course changes and provide other information which normal fighter pilots could not. The original members were ex-bomber pilots who had completed their tours and signed on for a second flying P-51's. They took from 20-25 hours training in an AT-6 plus an additional 15-25 hours in the P-51. Regular fighter pilots were assigned to the scouts to provide escort, enabling the scouts to stay over the target areas longer without fear of being bounced. Originally, the regular fighter pilots were placed on detached service with the scouting forces, but later in the war, pilots were actually assigned to these units.

## The 1st Scouting Force

Formed in July of 1944, as the Experimental Scout Force, the first sorties came on July 16. Redesignated as the 1st Scouting Force in September, the unit later was designated as the 857th Bomb Squadron in March of 1945. Some 131 missions were flown by the unit with the final flights on April 25, 1945. During this time, 5 P-51's were lost on operations and 4 pilots died in accidents. No 1st Scouting Force pilots made claims, but several regular fighter pilots acting as escorts did and these have been credited to the parent unit.

The 1st was based at Steeple Morden from July of 1944; Honington from September of 1944; and Bassingbourn from March of 1945 to July. Aircraft operated were the P-51D and K from July of 1944.

### Commanders

| | |
|---|---|
| Col. Budd J. Peaslee | July 1944-March 1945 |
| LtCol. Allison C. Brooks | March 1945-May 1945 |

### Aircraft Markings

All P-51's were in NMF and originally carried regular 355th Fighter Group markings. The only change was that a black bar was placed below the squadron codes. From the fall of 1944, regular 385th Fighter Squadron, 364th Fighter Group markings were carried, and shortly after the triangle was removed from the tail and all tail surfaces were outlined in red. A red spinner and 12 inch white cowl band finished the markings. Later in the war, the squadron code was changed to 9H.

## The 2nd Scouting Force

Formed in August of 1944, the first sorties came on September 26, 1944, with the last on April 25, 1945. During this time, 136 missions were flown and pilots claimed 12-3-6 air and 5-4 on the ground while 3 P-51's were lost on operations and 1 pilot died in an accident.

The 2nd was based at Steeple Morden from August 1, 1944, until May of 1945, and flew the P-51D and K during this same period.

### Commanders

| | |
|---|---|
| LtCol. John A. Brooks, III | August 1944-May 1945 |

### Aircraft Markings

Original planes carried markings of the 355th Fighter Group with a bar placed above the Squadron codes, i.e, WR. Nose markings consisted of a white spinner and cowl band with natural metal rudders.

### 2nd Scouting Force Scorers

| Name | Air | Grd | |
|---|---|---|---|
| W.H. Bancroft | 0-0-1 | 0-0 | |
| J.A. Brooks, III | 2-0-0 | 0-0 | |
| M.H. Castleberry | 1-0-0 | 0-0 | |
| G.W. Ceglarski | 1-0-0 | 0-0 | plus 2-1 grd w/4th Ftr Grp |
| F.B. Elliott | 0-0-0 | 3-1 | |
| C.W. Getz, II | 0-0-1 | 0-0 | |
| L.H. Marmon | 0-0-1 | 0-0 | |
| J.H. Miller | 0-1-1 | 0-0 | |
| R.W. Nyman | 0-0-1 | 0-0 | |
| C.R. Rodebaugh | 1-0-0 | 0-0 | |
| W.E. Whalen | 5-1-0 | 2-3 | plus 1-0-0 air w/4th Ftr Grp |
| R.V. Whitlow | 1-1-0 | 0-0 | |
| J.K. Wilkins, Jr. | 1-0-0 | 0-0 | |

### The 3rd Scouting Force

Formed in August of 1944, the first sorties came on September 15, 1944, with the last coming on May 7, 1945. During this time, 140 missions were flown and pilots claimed 4-0-0 in the air while 5 P-51's were lost on operations. The unit was redesignated as the 862nd Bomb Squadron in February of 1945 but continued to operate in the same role.

The 3rd was based at Wormingford from August of 1944 until May of 1945, and flew the P-51D and K during this time.

#### Commanders

| | |
|---|---|
| Col. Vincent W. Masters | August 1944-May 1945 |

#### Aircraft Markings

Aircraft flew in regular 55th Fighter Group markings. From late 1944, the rudders were painted in red and white checkerboards to distinguish them from the 55th's planes.

#### 3rd Scouting Force Scorers

| Name | Air | Grd |
|---|---|---|
| H.B. Howard | 3-0-0 | 0-0 |
| W.C. Klank, Jr. | 1-0-0 | 0-0 |

#### Scouting Force Scoring

| | | | |
|---|---|---|---|
| **November 26, 1944** | | | |
| 2nd: | Lt. W.E. Whalen | (3)FW-190 dest(air) | All claims |
| | Capt. R.V. Whitlow | FW-190 dest(air) | are S/Hanover |
| | | FW-190 prob(air) | |
| | Lt. G.W. Ceglarski | FW-190 dest(air) | |
| | Lt. J.H. Miller | FW-190 prob(air) | |
| | | FW-190 dam(air) | |
| | Lt. L.H. Marmon | FW-190 dam(air) | |
| **December 24, 1944** | | | |
| 3rd: | Capt. H.B. Howard | (2)Me-109 dest(air) | Frankfurt-Darmstadt |
| | Lt. W.C. Klank | Me-109 dest(air) | Frankfurt-Darmstadt |
| **December 31, 1944** | | | |
| 3rd: | Capt. H.B. Howard | FW-190 dest(air) | N/Steinhuder L. |
| **February 9, 1945** | | | |
| 2nd: | Lt. W.E. Whalen | (2)Me-109 dest(air) | Dessau |
| | | Me-109 prob(air) | Dessau |
| | LtCol. J.A. Brooks | (2)Me-109 dest(air) | SE Magdeburg |
| **February 22, 1945** | | | |
| 2nd: | Lt. W.E. Whalen | (2)FW-190 dest(grd) | Thale A/F |
| | | (3)FW-190 dam(grd) | Thale A/F |
| **March 1, 1945** | | | |
| 2nd: | Lt. J.K. Wilkins | Me-262 dest(air) | Ingolstadt |
| | Maj. F.B. Elliott | Me-262 dam(air) | Ingolstadt |
| | Capt. C.W. Getz | Me-262 dam(air) | Ingolstadt |
| **March 14, 1945** | | | |
| 2nd: | Lt. C.R. Rodebaugh | Me-262 dest(air) | Coblenz |
| **March 31, 1945** | | | |
| 2nd: | Lt. M.H. Castleberry | Me-262 dest(air) | SW Brunswick |
| | Capt. R.W. Nyman | Me-262 dam(air) | SW Brunswick |
| **April 4, 1945** | | | |
| 2nd: | Lt. W.H. Bancroft | Me-262 dam(air) | S/Ratzburg |
| **April 16, 1945** | | | |
| 2nd: | LtCol. F.B. Elliott | (2)u/i a/c dest(grd) | All claims are |
| | | FW-190 dest(grd) | SE Germany |
| | | FW-190 dam(grd) | |

#### Scouting Force Losses

**August 1, 1944**
Capt. Vincent G. Dressendorfer (1st) KIA; Hit by enemy fighters near La Loupe.
P-51D YF-C 44-13533

**August 23, 1944**
LtCol. Gerald C. Price (1st) KIAc;
P-51D YF-B 44-13636

**September 1, 1944**
Lt. Teleschor Lojewski (1st) KIAc;
Lt. Charles E. Wright (1st) KIAc;
Both died in an AT-6 accident.

**September 11, 1944**
Lt. Robert Bertleson (2nd) KIAc; Crashed near Steeple Morden.
AT-6

**November 26, 1944**
Capt. James B. Stauder (2nd) KIA; Suffered mechanical failureand crashed into the North Sea.
P-51D OS-Z 44-14439

**December 24, 1944**
Lt. Walter C. Klank (3rd) POW; Hit by fighters near Floersheim.
P-51D CL- 44-13886 "Miss Jane I"

**January 10, 1945**
Lt. William J. Doherty (1st) MIA; Last seen near Vielselm.
P-51D 5E- 44-13823 "Caroline Ann"

**January 15, 1945**
Lt. William W. Patton, Jr. (3rd) KIA; Lost for unknown reasons.
P-51D CL- 44-15331

**January 17, 1945**
Lt. William E. Hornickel (2nd) KIA; Suffered mechanical failure and crashed off Wangerooge.
P-51D YF-W 44-14581

**February 3, 1945**
Lt. John J. Allen (1st) KIA; Suffered mechanical failure near Hengelo.
P-51D 5E-N 44-13686 "Rugged Rebel II"

**March 24, 1945**
Lt. Leonard H. Monefelt (2nd) KIA; Crashed near Steeple Morden.
P-51D WR- 44-14441

**April 3, 1945**
Lt. William E. Cox (1st) MIA; Suffered mechanical failure near Flensburg.
P-51D 9H-F 44-13754
Lt. John Stein (3rd) KIA; Collided with a plane near Rendsburg.
P-51K 44-12152

**April 9, 1945**
Lt. James H. Reed (3rd) KIA; Lost for unknown reasons.
P-51D

**April 10, 1945**
Lt. William L. Rogers (1st) POW; Suffered mechanical failure near Berlin.
P-51D 9H-H 44-63748 "Little Dutchess"

**April 16, 1945**
Lt. Joseph D. Nelson (1st) KIAc; Crashed near Ridgewell.
P-51D

**April 20, 1945**
Capt. Thomas L. Fitzsimmons (3rd) POW; Hit by flak east of Rotterdam.
P-51D CL-

The following is a list of pilots assigned to the Scouting Forces. This does not include fighter pilots who were attached for only two or three weeks on temporary duty, and since records for the Scouts are sparce, there may be omissions. Also, the bomb group with which the pilot earlier flew is in parenthesis.

**Experimental and 1st Scouting Force**
Lt. George F. Adams
Maj. Philip M. Algar (384th)
Lt. John J. Allen (306th)
Lt. William S. Bartt
Lt. Robert T. Bennett
Lt. John Bergerson
Capt. Caroll D. Briscoe
LtCol. Allison C. Brooks (401st)
Capt. Fred Brown (401st)
Capt. Fred Burdge (92nd)
Lt. Robert Burkholder
Lt. Francis C. Clark (398th)
Lt. William A. Cox (355th Ftr Grp)
Lt. William E. Cox
Lt. William J. Doherty (381st)
Capt. Vincent G. Dressendorfer (305th)
Lt. Merrill J. DuMont (303rd)
Capt. Paul Ellsworth (305th)
Lt. Maynard Frey (91st)
Capt. Donald E. Griffin (398th)
Lt. William D. Hall (381st)
Capt. Dwight W. Hartman (305th)
Lt. Frank Juns (303rd)
Lt. Teleschor Lojewski
Capt. Dale McCrory (381st)
Lt. Howard E. Nelson
Lt. Joseph D. Nelson
Col. Budd J. Peaslee (389th)
Lt. Edwin Post
LtCol. Gerald C. Price (8th HQ)
Lt. William L. Rogers
Lt. Elwood J. Rosenbauer
Lt. R.D. Sanders
Lt. William E. Schofield (379th)
Lt. John W. Simpson
F/O Ned L. Smith
Lt. Richard L. Smith (303rd)
Lt. Dominic T. Taurone (351st)
Capt. Earl Thomas (303rd)
Lt. Robert H. Wood (306th)
Lt. Charles E. Wright

**2nd Scouting Force**
Lt. David R. Allen
Lt. William H. Bancroft
Lt. Robert Bertleson
Capt. Robert F. Moore (445th)
Capt. Richard W. Nyman (458th)
Lt. Thomas H. Orrick

LtCol. John A. Brooks
Lt. Marvin H. Castleberry
Capt. Roger G. Counselman (453rd)
Capt. Robert A. Edmondson (44th)
LtCol. Frank B. Elliott (466th)
Lt. Holt D. Frierson
Lt. John A. Gerber
Capt. Charles W. Getz, II (491st)
Capt. Henry R. Hays
Lt. William E. Hornickel
Lt. Walter R. Hughes
Capt. Gordon W. Lamers (458th)
Lt. Glenn D. Lindley
Lt. Leon H. Marmon
Lt. John H. Miller
Capt. Leonard H. Monefeldt (448th)
Capt. Ken R. Parten
Lt. John C. Percival
Lt. Charles R. Rodebaugh
Lt. George Rossman
Lt. Ray L. Shewfelt
Lt. Kirby D.E. Smith
Capt. James B. Stauder (392nd)
Lt. Edward J. Torney (446th)
Capt. John L. Weber (458th)
Lt. William E. Whalen
Maj. Robert V. Whitlow (445th)
Capt. John K. Wilkins
Lt. Robert L. Williams
Capt. George T. Ziegler (466th)

**3rd Scouting Force**
Lt. Laverne Abendroth (486th)
Lt. Ed Beaty
Lt. Brian J. Booker
Capt. Ken V. Bope (96th)
Lt. Earl M. DeGeneres (487th)
Lt. David M. Difley (490th)
Lt. Jack Fishman
Capt. Thomas L. Fitzsimmons (486th)
Capt. Andrew W. Fuller (486th)
Capt. Stan E. Gagon (447th)
Capt. Don B. Gutherie (486th)
Lt. Robert F. Hall
Lt. Ray E. Hann
Lt. E. Jack Hitt (96th)
Capt. Herbert B. Howard (100th)
Lt. Richard Jacobson
Lt. Danford E. Josey
Lt. Anthony Kalinski (385th)
Lt. Walter C. Klank
Lt. Richard I. Kuehl
Capt. Orvid V. Lancaster (385th)
Lt. Ben Long
Capt. Wesley G. Lundholm (100th)
Lt. L.S. Malmud
Capt. Clifford J. Manlove (490th)
Col. Vincent W. Masters (385th)
Lt. Don R. McNeely
Lt. Dewey N. Nelson
Capt. William V. Owen (96th)
Lt. William W. Patton
Lt. Robert Q. Phillips (493rd)
Lt. James H. Reed
Lt. William A. Sandbloom (486th)
Lt. William T. Searby
Lt. Charles Seested
Lt. Sharp
Lt. John Stein (390th)
Lt. Ed Unger (486th)
Lt. Peter Voninidi
Lt. Ted H. Williams (91st)
Lt. Friend F. Wilson (94th)

**Aircraft of the Experimental and 1st Scouting Forces**
Note-all WR, OS, and YF coded P-51's had a bar placed below the squadron codes.

42-106727 5E-T "Terrible Tommie"
44-13283 YF-A "Carolyn Anne"
44-13299 OS-M "Lois"
44-13349 WR-W "Margie II"
44-13553 YF-C
44-13557 OS-E
44-13557 5E-E "Easy Does It"
44-13636 YF-B "The Starduster"
44-13659 YF-J "Morphine Sue II" (later 5E-J)
44-13659 9H-J "Chip"
44-13686 5E-N "Rugged Rebel II"
44-13699 OS-D "G.I. Jive"
44-13709 YF-H "Frances Ann" (later 5E-H)
44-13728 OS-G
44-13754 9H-F
44-13764 OS-F
44-13891 5E-G
44-14189 5E-R "Francisco"
44-14375 5E-K
44-14895 9H-
44-14933 5E-X
44-63748 9H-H "Little Dutchess"
44-64149 5E-A
44-72239 9H-Z "Zoom Zoozie"
44-72335 9H-
9H- "Mary Honey"
9H- "Sally"

**Aircraft of the 2nd Scouting Force**
Note-all planes had a bar placed above the squadron codes.

44-11341 YF-D "Sweet Stuff"
44-13374 WR-A
44-13532 YF-P
44-13565 YF-N "Lois Carolyn"
44-13611 WR-L
44-14109 YF-H
44-14309 WR-X "Calamity Jane"
44-14371 WR-Z "Saucy Shirley"
44-14388 WR-A
44-14428 YF-A
44-14439 OS-Z
44-14441 WR-
44-14460 WR-R "Hi Nell"
44-14497 OS-U "Little Speedy"
44-14524 YF-M "Lil Larry II"
44-14581 YF-W "Honeychild 3rd"
44-14898 YF-J "Look"
44-14998 YF-W "Ruthless Ruthie"
44-15013 OS-D
44-15211 WR-A
44-15518 OS-S
44-63162 YF-V
44-63219 OS-Y
44-63739 YF-Q
OS-U "Butch"
WR-B "Madge II"
WR-B "Piggy Eyes"
"Sassi Shari"
"Lil Filly"
"Nonnie"

**Aircraft of the 3rd Scouting Force**

44-12152 CL-
44-13886 CG- "Miss Jane"
44-14053 CG-M "Master's Mistress"
44-14124 "Homer's Roamer"
44-14240 CY-P "June Bug"
44-14676 CL-I
44-14783 CG-C
44-15048 CL-A
44-15331 CL-
44-63204 CY-F
CY- "Mutt"
CY- "And Jeff"
CL-J "My Little Angel"
"Miss Corky"
"Sashay & Sal"
P-51B CL- "Bessie May"